126TH YEAR

WISDEN

CRICKETERS' ALMANACK

1989

EDITED BY GRAEME WRIGHT

PUBLISHED BY JOHN WISDEN & CO LTD

A COMPANY JOINTLY OWNED BY
GRAYS OF CAMBRIDGE (INTERNATIONAL) LIMITED
AND
NORTON OPAX PLC

FT COVER EDITION £14.95 CASED EDITION £16.95

ISBN
Cased edition 0 947766 12 X
Soft cover edition 0 947766 13 8

John Wisden & Co Ltd
Gray-Nicolls
Robertsbridge
East Sussex
TN32 5DH

Computer typeset by SB Datagraphics, Colchester
Printed in Great Britain by William Clowes Limited, Beccles

PREFACE

July 1988 was the wettest July on record since 1939, a statistic which, in another year, would have brought comfort to an editor trying to keep within the extent requested by his publisher. But this edition has never behaved normally. Less cricket was played overseas in 1987-88, a legacy of the World Cup, which appeared in the 1988 *Wisden*, with the result that our printer needed nine more or seven fewer pages to make a "working". Fortunately, Dates in Cricket History was stored in the computer and was called up at late notice. The feature last appeared in *Wisden* in 1985.

A number of factors, the weather among them, contributed to making 1988 a season to forget. Worcestershire supporters would disagree, and who would blame them? Their county was in the running in most of the competitions, and in Graeme Hick they had an outstanding talent. Peter Roebuck, who captained Somerset while Hick scored 405 not out against them, kindly agreed to give his thoughts on the young Zimbabwean. Tony Lewis, former captain of England and Glamorgan, has written a warm appreciation of the "little master", Sunil Gavaskar, who retired after the World Cup, and Mike Selvey, another Glamorgan captain, considers the state of pitches, which gave rise to justifiable concern in 1988. Matthew Engel looks ahead to the arrival of the Australians this summer, and Anthony Bradbury goes back a century to 1889, when the editor of *Wisden* chose the first Cricketers of the Year. This year's selection are Kim Barnett, the Derbyshire captain, Jeffrey Dujon, West Indies' elegant wicket-keeper-batsman, Phil Neale, Worcestershire's captain, the Nottinghamshire all-rounder, Franklyn Stephenson, and Somerset's Australian batsman, Stephen Waugh.

With sadness I have to report the death of R. L. (Bob) Arrowsmith, who for more than ten years wrote most of the obituaries for *Wisden*. His was some of the best writing in the Almanack, and he is greatly missed. I am especially thankful to John Kitchin for his help with the obituary notices in this edition. He came in at comparatively short notice, but he brought with him an immense knowledge of and affection for *Wisden*. Although the Almanack is thought of principally as a book of record, within the obituary notices can be traced the history of cricket.

As in every edition, thanks are due to many people for their time and their contributions. Without Christine Forrest's help, especially in the final stages, this edition might still be waiting to go to press. Gordon Burling, who has again read most of the proofs, has moved up from long-stop to be a stumper of the first order. Little gets past him. Bill Frindall, in addition to updating the records, co-ordinated the checking of the first-class scores with county scorers and statisticians, whose names may be found on page four. To Diane Back and Ted Hirst, who put in many hours preparing the scorecards prior to the checking process, and to Peter Rather and Mike Smith at the typesetters, I am especially grateful.

For their willing assistance, my thanks also go to the secretariats of MCC and TCCB, the county secretaries and their staffs, the secretaries of the minor counties, and the cricket masters at schools. I would also like to correct a statement in the Preface of the 1988 Almanack which said that the England scorer on tour pays his own travel and accommodation expenses. These expenses are met by the TCCB and I apologise for any embarrassment which might have occurred. Finally, I wish to thank those regular contributors from the counties and countries overseas without whom the comprehensiveness of *Wisden* would not be possible.

GRAEME WRIGHT

Eastcote
Middlesex

LIST OF CONTRIBUTORS

The editor acknowledges with gratitude the assistance afforded in the preparation of the Almanack by the following:

Jack Arlidge (Sussex)
John Arlott (Books)
David Armstrong
Chris Aspin (Lancashire Leagues)
Diane Back
Philip Bailey
Jack Bannister (Warwickshire)
Brian Bearshaw (Lancashire)
Sir William Becher
Michael Berry
Scyld Berry
John Billot (Glamorgan)
J. Watson Blair (Scotland)
Anthony Bradbury
Robert Brooke (Births and Deaths)
Kenneth R. Bullock (Canada)
Gordon Burling
C. R. Buttery (New Zealand)
John Callaghan (Yorkshire)
Terry Cooper (Middlesex)
Geoffrey Copinger
Tony Cozier (West Indies)
Norman de Mesquita
Patrick Eagar
Matthew Engel
Paton Fenton (Oxford University)
David Field (Surrey)
Bill Frindall (Records)
Nigel Fuller (Essex)
David Hallett (Cambridge University)
Dave Hardy (The Netherlands)
Peter Hargreaves (Denmark)
Chris Harte
Les Hatton
Eric Hill (Somerset)
Ted Hirst
Grenville Holland (UAU)
Brian Hunt
James Hunt (Leicestershire)
Ken Ingman (ESCA)
Vic Isaacs (Hampshire)
Martin Johnson
Abid Ali Kazi (Pakistan)
John Kitchin
Medha Laud
Stephanie Lawrence
John Lawson (Nottinghamshire)
Alan Lee
Tony Lewis
Andrew Longmore
John MacKinnon (Australia)
John Minshull-Fogg
Chris Moore (Worcestershire)
Dudley Moore (Kent)
Gerald Mortimer (Derbyshire)
David Munden
Adrian Murrell
David Norrie
Lord Orr-Ewing
Graham Otway
A. L. A. Pichanick (Zimbabwe)
William Powell
Qamar Ahmed
Andrew Radd (Northamptonshire)
Peter Roebuck
Dicky Rutnagur
Carol Salmon
Geoffrey Saulez
Derek Scott (Ireland)
Mike Selvey
Peter Sichel (South Africa)
Bill Smith
P. N. Sundaresan (India)
Stephen Thorpe
Sudhir Vaidya
Gerry Vaidyasekera (Sri Lanka)
Mary Vaux
D. R. Walsh (HMC Schools)
Geoffrey Wheeler (Gloucestershire)
Peter Wynne-Thomas

Thanks are accorded also to the following for checking the scorecards of first-class matches S. P. Austin, L. Beaumont, T. Billson, G. R. Blackburn, Mrs C. Byatt, L. V. Chandle B. H. Clarke, W. Davies, B. T. Denning, J. Foley, B. H. Jenkins, D. Kendix, D. A. Oldan J. W. Sewter, H. P. H. Sharp, S. W. Tacey and R. D. Wilkinson.

CONTENTS

Preface 3
Index 6
Notes by the Editor 42
Five Cricketers of the Year 52
The Problem of Pitches by Mike Selvey 61
We Already Knew He Could Bat by Peter Roebuck 65
Wisden's Cricketers of the Year by Anthony Bradbury 70
Sunil Gavaskar – The Little Master by Tony Lewis 76
England v Australia – The Brand Leader? by Matthew Engel 82
Test Cricketers 1877-1988 85
Cricket Records 128
Features of 1988 264
First-Class Averages, 1988 268
Individual Scores of 100 and Over, 1988 275
Ten Wickets in a Match, 1988 278
The Cricket Council, TCCB and NCA 279
The West Indians in England, 1988 280
The Sri Lankans in England, 1988 312
Marylebone Cricket Club 328
Other Matches at Lord's, 1988 332
Britannic Assurance County Championship, 1988 339
The First-Class Counties in 1988 346
Oxford and Cambridge Universities in 1988 621
Other Matches, 1988 649
NatWest Bank Trophy, 1988 658
Benson and Hedges Cup, 1988 682
Refuge Assurance League, 1988 712
Refuge Assurance Cup, 1988 795
The Australian Aboriginal Team in England, 1988 798
Minor Counties Championship, 1988 801
Second Eleven Championship, 1988 820
Bain Clarkson Trophy and Warwick Under-25 Championship, 1988 837
The UAU Championship, 1988 840
The Lancashire Leagues, 1988 842
Irish and Scottish Cricket in 1988 844
Esso/NAYC Under-19 County Festival, 1988 849
Schools Cricket in 1988 851
England in Pakistan, 1987-88 909
England in New Zealand and Australia, 1987-88 924
The West Indians in India, 1987-88 943
The New Zealanders in Australia, 1987-88 962
The Sri Lankans in Australia, 1987-88 972
The Pakistanis in the West Indies, 1987-88 977
Benson and Hedges World Series Cup, 1987-88 992
The Sharjah Cup, 1987-88 1003
McDonald's Bicentennial Youth World Cup, 1987-88 1007
Overseas Domestic Cricket in 1987-88 1012
Women's Cricket, 1988 1104
Births and Deaths of Cricketers 1107
Obituaries 1152
The Laws of Cricket 1181
International Cricket Conference 1210
Qualification and Registration 1213
Rules of Limited-Overs Competitions 1215
Meetings in 1988 1221
Dates in Cricket History 1223
Cricket Books, 1988 by John Arlott 1231
Fixtures, 1989 1255

INDEX

Note: For reasons of space, certain entries which appear in alphabetical order in sections of the Almanack are not included in this index. These include names that appear in Test Cricketers, Births and Deaths of Cricketers, individual batting and bowling performances in the 1988 first-class season, and Oxford and Cambridge Blues.

c. = catches; d. = dismissals; p'ship = partnership; r. = runs; w. = wickets.

** Signifies not out or an unbroken partnership*

A

Aamer Malik (Pak.):– 2 hundreds on début, *135*.

Aamer Wasim (Sialkot):– LBW hat-trick, *157*.

Abdul Azeem (H'bad):– 303* v Tamil Nadu, *133*.

Abdul Kadir (Pak.):– Test p'ship record, *233*.

Abdul Qadir (Pak.):– 205 w. in Tests, *184*; 103 w. in Pakistan season, *157*; 10 w. or more in Test (3), *220, 233*; 9 w. in Test innings, *180*; Test p'ship record, *252*.

Abel, R. (Eng.):– 33,124 r., *141*; 3,309 r. in season, *139*; Highest for Surrey, *134*; 74 hundreds, *137*; 357* v Somerset, *132, 134*; 2 Test hundreds, *196, 205*; Carrying bat in Test, *177*; 379 for 1st wkt, *148*.

Adcock, N. A. T. (SA):– 104 w. in Tests, *183*; 26 w. in series, *208*; Test p'ship record, *234*.

Addresses of representative bodies, *1219-20*.

Adhikari, H. R. (Ind.):– Test captain, *238*; 1 Test hundred, *239*; Test p'ship records, *231, 249*.

Afaq Hussain (Pak.):– Test p'ship record, *233*.

Aftab Baloch (Pak.):– Test début at 16, *192*; 428 v Baluchistan, *132*.

Agha Zahid (HBL):– 2 hundreds in match (2), *136*.

Ahad Khan (Pak. Rlwys):– 9 w. for 7 r., *155*.

Alabaster, J. C. (NZ):– Test p'ship records, *237, 243*.

Alderman, T. M. (Aust.):– 42 w. in series, *182, 203*; 8 w. in innings, *265*; Test p'ship record, *233*.

Alexander, F. C. M. (WI):– Test captain, *208, 238, 240*; 1 Test hundred, *225*; 23 d. in series, *188*; 5 c. in Test innings, *187*.

Ali Zia (UBL):– 2 hundreds in match (2), *136, 1096*.

Alikhan, R. I. (Sussex):– Career figures, *681*.

Alim-ud-Din (Pak.):– 2 Test hundreds, *219, 248*.

Allan, P. J. (Aust.):– 10 w. in innings, *154*.

Allcott, C. F. W. (NZ):– 190* for 8th wkt, *151*; Test p'ship record, *235*.

Allen, D. A. (Eng.):– 122 w. in Tests, *183*; Test p'ship records, *219*.

Allen, Sir G. O. (Eng.):– Test captain, *195, 208, 215*; Test cricket at 45, *193*; 1 Test hundred, *213*; 10 w. in innings, *154*; 10 w. or more in Test (1), *217*; Test p'ship record, *214*.

Alletson, E. B. (Notts.):– Fast scoring, *144*; 34 r. in over, *145*.

Alley, W. E. (Som.):– 3,019 r. in season, *138*.

Allom, M. J. C. (Eng.):– Test hat-trick, *185, 214*.

Allott, P. J. W. (Eng.):– Test p'ship record, *217*.

Altaf Shah (HBFC):– 355 for 5th wkt, *150*.

Amarnath, L. (Ind.):– Test captain, *229, 238, 247*; Hundred on Test début, *171, 172, 216*; 410 for 3rd wkt, *150*.

Amarnath, M. (Ind.):– 4,378 r. in Tests, *176*; 11 Test hundreds, *230, 239, 248, 250*; 2,234 r. in overseas season, *140*; 1,077 Test r. in year, *173*; Test p'ship records, *231, 240, 248, 250*.

Amarnath, S. (Ind.):– Hundred on Test début, *171, 243*; Test p'ship record, *243*.

Ambrose, C. E. L. (WI):– 123 for 9th wkt, *265*; 35 w. in WI domestic season, *1061*.

Ames, L. E. G. (Eng.):– 37,248 r., *141*; 2,434 r. in Tests, *174*; 1,000 r. (17), *139*; 3,058 r. in season, *139*; 102 hundreds, *137*; 8 Test hundreds, *196, 205, 209, 213*; 2 hundreds in match (3), *136*; 1,121 d., *165*; 100 d. in season (3), *164, 165*; 8 d. in Test, *187*; 2,482 r. and 104 d. in season, 1,919 r. and 122 d. in season, 1,795 r. and 128 d. in season, *163*; Test p'ship records, *206, 214*.

Amin Lakhani (Pak. Univs):– Double hat-trick, *157*.

Amir Elahi (Ind. and Pak.):– Test p'ship record, *249*.

Amiss, D. L. (Eng.):– 43,423 r., *141*; 7,040 r. in Sunday League, *793*; 3,612 r. in Tests, *174*; 1,379 Test r. in year, *173*; 1,000 r. (24), *139*; 102 hundreds, *137*; 11 Test hundreds, *209, 213, 216, 218*; 2 hundreds in match (2), *136*; 262* v West Indies, *170, 209*.

Anderson, J. H. (SA):– Test captain, *221*.

Anderson, R. W. (NZ):– Test p'ship record, *245*.

Andrew, K. V. (Eng.):– 7 d. in innings, *16[illegible]*.

Andrews, C. W. (Qld):– 335 for 7th wkt, *15[illegible]*.

Anil Dalpat (Pak.):– 10 d. in match, *164;* Test p'ship record, *246.*

Anwar Iqbal (H'bad):– Hit the ball twice, *153.*

Anwar Miandad (IDBP):– Hit the ball twice, *153.*

Appearances in Test cricket:– As captain, *127;* Most, *127*; Most consecutive, *193.*

Appleyard, R. (Eng.):– 200 w. in season, *158.*

Apte, M. L. (Ind.):– 1 Test hundred, *239.*

Archer, R. G. (Aust.):– 1 Test hundred, *225;* Test p'ship records, *226.*

Arkwright, H. A.:– 18 w. v Gentlemen of Kent, *156.*

Arif Butt (Pak.):– Test p'ship record, *246.*

Arif-ud-Din (UBL):– 10 d. in match, *164;* 7 d. in innings, *163.*

Armstrong, N. F. (Leics.):– 36 hundreds, *138.*

Armstrong, W. W. (Aust.):– Test captain, *195;* All-round, *162;* 2,863 r. in Tests, *175;* 2,172 r. v England, *203;* 45 hundreds, *138;* 6 Test hundreds, *198, 222;* Hundred and double-hundred, *135;* 303* v Somerset, *133;* Carrying bat in Test, *177;* 428 for 6th wkt, *150;* Test p'ship record, *223.*

Arnold, E. G. (Eng.):– All-round, *162;* Wkt with 1st ball on Test début, *184;* 393 for 5th wkt, *150.*

Arnold, G. G. (Eng.):– 115 w. in Tests, *183.*

Arnold, J. (Eng.):– 37 hundreds, *138.*

Arshad Ali (Sukkur):– Obstructing the field, *153.*

Arshad Pervez (HBL):– 35 hundreds, *138;* 426 for 2nd wkt, *149.*

Arun Lal (Ind.):– Test p'ship record, *250.*

Ashdown, W. H. (Kent):– Highest for Kent, *133;* 332 v Essex, *132;* 307* in day, *144;* 305* v Derbyshire, *133;* 39 hundreds, *138.*

Ashes, The:– *194-203;* History of, *84.*

Ashraf Ali (Pak.):– Test p'ship record, *252.*

Asif Iqbal (Pak.):– Test captain, *247;* 3,575 r. in Tests, *176;* 45 hundreds, *138;* 10 Test hundreds, *219, 232, 245, 248;* 350 for 4th wkt, *150;* 190 for 9th wkt, *151, 180, 219;* Test p'ship records, *219, 233, 242, 246.*

Asif Masood (Pak.):– Test p'ship record, *219.*

Aslam Ali (UBL):– 456 for 3rd wkt, *147, 150.*

Aslett, D. G. (Kent):– Hundred on début, *134.*

Astill, W. E. (Eng.):– All-round, *162, 163;* 2,431 w., *160;* 100 w. (9), *159.*

Athar Khan (Allied Bank):– Handled the ball, *152.*

Atherton, M. A. (CUCC & Lancs.):– Captain of Cambridge, *631.*

Athey, C. W. J. (Eng.):– Captain of Gloucestershire, *392;* 4 successive hundreds *136;* 1 Test hundred, *218.*

Atkins, P. D. (Surrey):– Hundred on début, *134, 264.*

Atkinson, D. St E. (WI):– Test hundred, *225;* All-round in Test, *186;* 347 for 7th wkt, *151, 226;* Test p'ship records, *226, 237.*

Atkinson, G. (Som.):– 1st wkt hundreds, *149.*

Attewell, W. (Eng.):– 1,950 w., *160;* 100 w. (10), *159.*

Australia:– Australia in Test cricket (*see p. 131*), B & H World Series Cup, *992-1002;* Bicentennial one-day international, *932;* Bicentennial Test, *930-2;* Definition of first-class matches, *1212;* Domestic season 1987-88, *1012-47;* Highest individual Test innings, *170;* Highest Test innings, *189;* Leading batsmen in Tests, *174-5;* Leading bowlers in Tests, *183;* Lowest Test innings, *191*; Most consecutive Test appearances, *193;* Most Test appearances, *127;* Most Test appearances as captain, *127;* Oldest Test player, *193;* Representative body, *1219;* Summary of Tests, *194;* Test cricketers (1877-1988), *97-105;* Youngest and oldest on Test début, *192.*

Australian Aboriginal Team:– In England, 1988, *798-800;* v MCC, *331.*

Ayling, J. R. (Hants):– Wkt with 1st ball in f-c cricket, *266.*

Azad, K. (Ind.):– Handled the ball, *152.*

Azhar Abbas (B'pur):– 10 d. in match, *164.*

Azharuddin, M. (Ind.):– 1,461 r. (avge 52.17) in Tests, *177;* 4 hundreds in succession, *136;* 6 Test hundreds, *172, 216, 248, 250;* Hundred on Test début, *172, 216;* 5 c. in innings, *266;* Test p'ship records, *217, 249, 250.*

Aziz Malik (Lahore Div.):– Hit the ball twice, *153.*

B

Bacchus, S. F. A. F. (WI):– 250 v India, *171, 238.*

Bacher, A. (SA):– Test captain, *221.*

Badcock, C. L. (Aust.):– 325 v Victoria, *132;* 1 Test hundred, *198.*

Badcock, F. T. (NZ):– Test p'ship record, *235.*

Baichan, L. (WI):– Hundred on Test début, *171, 241;* Hundred and double-hundred, *135*; 2 hundreds in match (2), *136.*

Baig, A. A. (Ind.):– Hundred on Test début, *171, 216;* Test p'ship record, *231.*

Bailey, T. E. (Eng.):– All-round, *162, 163, 186;* 28,641 r., *142;* 2,290 r. in Tests, *174;* 1,000 r. (17), *139;* 1 Test hundred, *213;* Slow batting in Test, *179;* 2,082 w., *160;* 132 w. in Tests, *182;* 100 w. (9), *159;* 10 w. in innings, *154;* 10 w. or more in Test (1), *211;* Test p'ship record, *219.*

Bainbridge, P. (Glos.):– 10,000 r., *267.*

Bain Clarkson Trophy, *837-8.*

Bairstow, D. L. (Eng.):– 1,063 d., *165;* 243 d. in Sunday League, *794;* 11 c. in match, *164;* 7 c. in innings, *163.*
Bakewell, A. H. (Eng.):– 1 Test hundred, *209;* 8 c. in match, *165.*
Balaskas, X. C. (SA):– 1 Test hundred, *235.*
Banerjee, S. N. (Ind.):– 249 for 10th wkt, *152.*
Banks, D. A. (Worcs.):– Hundred on début, *134.*
Bannerman, C. (Aust.):– Hundred on Test début, *171, 198.*
Bannister, J. D. (Warwicks.):– 10 w. in innings, *154.*
Baptiste, E. A. E. (WI):– 8 w. in innings, *288;* Test p'ship record, *211.*
Barber, R. W. (Eng.):– 1 Test hundred, *196;* Test p'ship record, *219.*
Bardsley, W. (Aust.):– Test captain, *196;* 2,469 r. in Tests, *175;* 53 hundreds, *138;* 6 Test hundreds, *198, 222;* 2 hundreds in same Test, *172, 198;* Carrying bat in Test, *177;* Test p'ship record, *223.*
Barker, G. (Essex):– 1,000 r. (15), *139;* Hundred on début, *134.*
Barlow, E. J. (SA):– 2,516 r. in Tests, *175;* 43 hundreds, *138;* 6 Test hundreds, *205, 222;* 341 for 3rd wkt, *150, 223.*
Barlow, R. G. (Eng.):– Hit the ball twice, *153;* 4 hat-tricks, *157.*
Barnes, S. F. (Eng.):– 189 w. in Tests, *182;* 106 w. v Australia, *203;* 104 w. in overseas season, *159;* 49 w. and 34 w. in series, *182, 208;* 17 w. in Test, *155, 181;* 14 w. in Test, *182;* 10 w. or more in Test (7), *201, 207;* 9 w. in Test innings, *180;* 8 w. in Test innings (2), *180, 181.*
Barnes, S. G. (Aust.):– 3 Test hundreds, *198, 230;* 405 for 5th wkt, *150, 180, 201;* Test p'ship records, *201, 230.*
Barnes, W. (Eng.):– 1 Test hundred, *196.*
Barnett, C. J. (Eng.):– 48 hundreds, *138;* 2 Test hundreds, *196;* 11 sixes in innings, *146.*
Barnett, K. J. (Eng.):– Captain of Derbyshire, *346;* 239* in 1988, *264;* Hundred before lunch, *264;* Cricketer of the Year, *52-3.*
Barratt, E. (Surrey):– 10 w. in innings, *153.*
Barrett, J. E. (Aust.):– Carrying bat in Test, *177.*
Barrington, K. F. (Eng.):– 31,714 r., *141;* 6,806 r. (avge 58.67) in Tests, *174, 177;* 2,111 r. v Australia, *203;* 1,039 Test r. in year, *173;* 1,000 r. (15), *139;* 76 hundreds, *137;* 20 Test hundreds, *177, 196, 205, 209, 213, 216, 218;* 256 v Australia, *171, 196;* 64 c. in season, *166;* Test p'ship records, *206, 214, 219.*
Barrow, I. (WI):– 1 Test hundred, *210.*
Bartlett, G. A. (NZ):– Test p'ship records, *235.*
Bartlett, R. J. (Som.):– Hundred on début, *134.*
Barton, P. T. (NZ):– 1 Test hundred, *235.*
Bates, W. (Eng.):– Test hat-trick, *185;* 14 w. in Test, *182, 201.*
Beck, J. E. F. (NZ):– Test p'ship record, *235.*
Bedfordshire, *802, 804-5.*
Bedi, B. S. (Ind.):– Test captain, *215, 229, 238, 242, 247;* 1,560 w., *160;* 266 w. in Tests, *184;* 10 w. or more in Test (1), *231;* Test p'ship records, *240, 244.*
Bedser, A. V. (Eng.):– 236 w. in Tests, *182;* 104 w. v Australia, *203;* 100 w. (11), *159;* 39 w. in series, *182;* 14 w. in Test, *182, 201;* 10 w. or more in Test (5), *201, 207, 217.*
Bell, A. J. (SA):– Test p'ship record, *207.*
Benaud, J. (Aust.):– 1 Test hundred, *232.*
Benaud, R. (Aust.):– Test captain, *195, 221, 224, 229, 231;* Fast scoring, *178;* 11 sixes in innings, *146;* 2,201 r. in Tests, *175;* 3 Test hundreds, *222, 225;* 248 w. in Tests, *183;* 106 w. in overseas season, *159;* 10 w. or more in Test (1), *231;* All-round in Tests, *185, 186;* Test p'ship records, *223, 226.*
Benefits in 1989, *800.*
Benjamin, S. (Rajasthan):– 7 d. in innings, *163.*
Benjamin, W. K. M. (WI):– Test p'ship record, *241.*
Benson and Hedges Cup:– *682-711;* Fixtures, 1989, *1255-8;* Rules, *1215-7.*
Benson and Hedges Trophy (SA), *1059-60.*
Benson and Hedges World Series Cup, *992-1002.*
Benson, M. R. (Eng.):– 10,000 r., *267.*
Bensted, E. C. (Qld):– 335 for 7th wkt, *151*
Berkshire, *658, 801, 803, 805-6.*
Berry, L. G. (Leics.):– 30,225 r., *141;* 1,000 r. (18), *139;* 45 hundreds, *138.*
Berry, R. (Eng.):– 10 w. in innings, *154.*
Bestwick, W. (Derbys.):– 10 w. in innings, *154.*
Betancourt, N. (WI):– Test captain, *208;* Oldest West Indian on début, *192.*
Bhandarkar, K. V. (M'tra):– 455 for 2nd wkt, *147, 149.*
Bhaskar Pillai, K. (Delhi):– 2 hundreds in match, *136, 1086.*
Bicknell, M. P. (Surrey):– 8 w. in innings, *265.*
Binks, J. G. (Eng.):– 1,071 d., *165;* 107 d. in season, *165;* 5 c. in Test innings, *188;* 41 consecutive Champ. appearances, *263.*
Binny, R. M. H. (Ind.):– 451 for 1st wkt, *14 148, 149;* Test p'ship record, *249.*
Bird, M. C. (Eng.):– 2 hundreds in match Eton, *333;* Test p'ship record, *206.*
Bisset, M. (SA):– Test captain, *204.*

Blackham, J. McC. (Aust.):– Test captain, *195-6;* Test p'ship record, *201.*
Blackie, D. D. (Aust.):– Test cricket at 46, *192;* Oldest Australian Test début, *192.*
Bland, C. H. G. (Sussex):– 10 w. in innings, *153.*
Bland, K. C. (SA):– 3 Test hundreds, *205, 222;* Test p'ship record, *235.*
Bligh, Hon. Ivo (Lord Darnley) (Eng.):– Test captain, *194;* The Ashes, *84.*
Blues:– Both universities, *336;* List of (1946-88), Cambridge, *645;* Oxford, *641.*
Blunt, R. C. (NZ):– 338* v Canterbury, *132, 144, 152;* 184 for 10th wkt, *152.*
Blythe, C. (Eng.):– 2,506 w., *160;* 215 w. in season, *158;* 100 w. (14), *159;* 100 w. in Tests, *183;* 17 w. in day, *156;* 17 w. in match, *155, 156;* 15 w. in Test, *181, 207;* 10 w. or more in Test (4), *201, 207;* 10 w. in innings, *154;* 8 w. in Test innings, *181.*
Board, J. H. (Eng.):– 1,207 d., *165.*
Bolus, J. B. (Eng.):– 39 hundreds, *138.*
Bonnor, G. J. (Aust.):– 1 Test hundred, *198.*
Boock, S. L. (NZ):– Test p'ship record, *228.*
Boon, D. C. (Aust.):– 6 Test hundreds, *198, 228, 230;* 2 hundreds in match, *136, 1039;* Carrying bat in Test, *178;* Test p'ship record, *230.*
Booth, A. (Lancs. II):– 253 v Lincolnshire, *261.*
Booth, B. C. (Aust.):– Test captain, *196;* 5 Test hundreds, *198, 221, 225.*
Booth, R. (Worcs.):– 1,126 d., *165;* 100 d. in season (2), *165.*
Borde, C. G. (Ind.):– Test captain, *229;* 3,061 r. in Tests, *176;* 1,604 r. in Indian season, *140;* 5 Test hundreds, *239, 243, 248.*
Border, A. R. (Aust.):– Test captain, *195, 224, 227, 229, 233;* 91 consecutive Tests, *193;* 18,810 r. (avge 54.20), *143;* 7,343 r. (avge 53.59) in Tests, *174, 177;* 4,316 r. in one-day ints, *256;* 2,392 r. v England, *203;* 1,099, 1,073 & 1,000 Test r. in year, *173;* 58 hundreds, *138;* 22 Test hundreds, *177, 198, 225, 228, 230, 232;* 4 hundreds in succession, *136;* 2 hundreds in same Test (2), *172;* 2 hundreds in match (2), *136, 172;* 104 c. in Tests, *189;* 65 c. in one-day ints, *258;* Test p'ship records, *228, 230, 233.*
Borland, A. F. (Natal):– 4 w. with consecutive balls, *156.*
Bosanquet, B. J. T. (Eng.):– All-round, *161;* 2 hundreds in match (2), *136;* 8 w. in Test innings, *181.*
Botham, I. T. (Eng.):– Test captain, *196, 208;* 65 consecutive Tests, *193;* 5,057 r. in Tests, *174;* 1,095 Test r. in year, *173;* 14 Test

Botham, I. T. (Eng.):– *contd* hundreds, *196, 213, 216, 218;* Fast scoring, *178, 179;* 32 r. and 30 r. in over, *145-6;* 80 sixes in season, *146;* 13 sixes in Sunday League innings, *793;* 12 sixes in innings, *145;* 1,000 w., *267;* 373 w. in Tests, *182;* 145 w. v Australia, *203;* 116 w. in one-day ints, *257;* 10 w. or more in Test (4), *201, 214, 217;* 8 w. in Test innings (2), *180-1;* 109 c. in Tests, *189;* All-round in Tests, *185, 186, 187;* All-round in one-day ints, *258;* Test p'ship record, *217*.

Bowden, M. P. (Eng.):– Test captain, *204*.

Bowes, W. E. (Eng.):– 1,639 w., *160;* 100 w. (9), *159*.

Bowler, P. D. (Leics. & Derbys.):– Hundred on début, *134;* Hundred on début for 2 counties, *264;* Carrying bat in 1988, *265*.

Bowley, E. H. (Eng.):– 28,378 r., *142;* 1,000 r. (15), *139;* 52 hundreds, *138;* 1 Test hundred, *213;* 490 for 1st wkt, *147, 148*.

Bowley, F. L. (Worcs.):– 38 hundreds, *138*.

Boyce, K. D. (WI):– 10 w. or more in Test (1), *211;* Best bowling in Sunday League, *794;* Test p'ship record, *240*.

Boycott, G. (Eng.):– Test captain, *212, 216;* 48,426 r. (avge 56.83), *141, 143;* 8,114 r. in Tests, *174;* 2,945 r. v Australia, *203;* 1,000 r. (26), *139-40;* 151 hundreds, *137;* 22 Test hundreds, *177, 196, 205, 209, 213, 216, 218;* 13 hundreds in season, *137;* 2 hundreds in match (3), *136;* Avge of 102.53 in English season, *140;* Carrying bat in Test, *178;* 1st wkt hundreds, *148-9;* Test p'ship record, *201*.

Boyd-Moss, R. J. (CUCC and Northants):– 2 hundreds in match (2), *136;* 3 hundreds v Oxford, *335*.

Bracewell, J. G. (NZ):– 1 Test hundred, *213;* 10 w. or more in Test, *229;* Test p'ship record, *214, 228*.

Bradley, W. M. (Eng.):– 3 hat-tricks, *157*.

Bradman, Sir D. G. (Aust.):– Test captain, *195, 229;* Fast scoring, *179;* 28,067 r. (avge 95.14), *142;* 6,996 r. (avge 99.94) in Tests, *174, 177;* 5,028 r. v England, *203;* 1,690 r. in Australian season, *140;* 1,025 Test r. in year, *173;* 1,000 r. (April 30-May 31), *145;* 1,000 r. (16), *139-40;* 974 r. in series, *173, 201;* 452* v Queensland, *132;* 369 v Tasmania, *132, 144;* 357 v Victoria, *132;* 340* v Victoria, *132;* 334 v England, *132, 133, 170, 198;* 309* in day, *144;* 304 v England, *133, 170, 198;* 300 r. in 213 min., *144;* 299* v South Africa, *170, 222;* 278 at Lord's, *260;* 270 and 254 v England, *170, 171, 198;* 117 hundreds, *137;* 29 Test hundreds, *177, 198, 222, 223, 230;* 13 hundreds in season, *137;* 6 hundreds in succession, *136;* 4 hundreds in succession, *136;* 2 hundreds in same Test, *172, 230;* 2 hundreds in match (4), *136;* Hundred and double-hundred, *136;* 10 successive fifties, *137;* Average of 115.66 in English season, *140;* 50 boundaries in innings, *147;* 30 r. in over, *146;* 451 for 2nd wkt, *147, 149, 180, 201;* 405 for 5th wkt, *150, 180, 201;* 346 for 6th wkt, *180, 201;* Test p'ship records, *201, 221, 230*.

Bradburn, W. P. (NZ):– Test p'ship record, *235*.

Bradley, W. M. (Eng.):– Wkt with 1st ball on Test début, *184*.

Brain, W. H. (Glos.):– w-k hat-trick, *157, 164*.

Bramall, Lord:– President of MCC, *328*.

Brassington, A. J. (Glos.):– Career figures, *681*.

Braund, L. C. (Eng.):– All-round, *162;* 3 Test hundreds, *196, 205;* 8 w. in Test innings, *181*.

Brayshaw, I. J. (W. Aust.):– 10 w. in innings *154*.

Brearley, J. M. (Eng.):– Test captain, *195 212, 215, 218;* 25,185 r., *142;* 312* v North Zone in day, *134, 144;* 45 hundreds, *138*.

Brearley, W. (Eng.):– 17 w. in match, *155;* 4 w. with consecutive balls, *156*.

Briasco, P. S. (C. Dist.):– 317 for 2nd wkt *149*.

Briers, N. E. (Leics.):– 10,000 r., *267*.

Briggs, J. (Eng.):– 1 Test hundred, *196;* Test hat-trick, *185;* 2,221 w., *160;* 118 w. in Tests, *183;* 100 w. (12), *159;* 15 w. in Test *181, 207;* 10 w. or more in Test (4), *20 207;* 10 w. in innings, *153;* 8 w. for 11 r. i Test innings, *180*.

Bright, R. J. (Aust.):– 10 w. or more in Tes (1), *233*.

Broad, B. C. (Eng.):– 6 Test hundreds, *19 213, 218*.

Brockwell, W. (Eng.):– 379 for 1st wkt, *14*

Bromfield, H. D. (SA):– Test p'ship recor *235*.

Bromley-Davenport, H. R. (Eng.):– Te p'ship record, *206*.

Brookes, D. (Eng.):– 30,874 r., *141;* 1,000 (17), *139;* 71 hundreds, *137*.

Brown, A. S. (Glos.):– 7 c. in innings, *16*

Brown, F. R. (Eng.):– Test captain, *195, 2 208, 212*.

Brown, G. (Eng.):– 37 hundreds, *138*.

Brown, J. (Scotland):– 7 d. in innings, *16*

Brown, J. T. (Eng.):– 1 Test hundred, *19* 311 v Sussex, *133;* 300 v Derbyshire, *13* 554 and 378 for 1st wkt, *147-8*.

Brown, K. R. (Middx):– 264 for 4th wkt, *2*

Brown, S. M. (Middx):– Obituary, *1155-* 1st wkt hundreds, *149*.

Brown, W. A. (Aust.):– Test captain, *227;* 13,838 r. (avge 51.44), *143;* 39 hundreds, *138;* 4 Test hundreds, *198, 222;* Carrying bat in Test, *177;* Test p'ship record, *223.*
Buckinghamshire, *662, 801, 803, 806.*
Burge, P. J. (Aust.):– Handled the ball, *152;* 2,290 r. in Tests, *175;* 38 hundreds, *138;* 4 Test hundreds, *198.*
Burgess, M. G. (NZ):– Test captain, *210, 227, 244;* 2,684 r. in Tests, *176;* 5 Test hundreds, *213, 237, 245;* Test p'ship records, *228, 243, 245.*
Burke, J. W. (Aust.):– 3 Test hundreds, *198, 222, 230;* Hundred on Test début, *171, 198;* Slow batting in Test, *179.*
Burke, S. F. (SA):– 10 w. or more in Test (1), *235.*
Burki, J. (Pak.):– Test captain, *218;* 3 Test hundreds, *219;* Test p'ship records, *219.*
Burns, W. B. (Worcs.):– 102* and hat-trick v Gloucestershire, *161;* 8 c. in match, *165;* 393 for 5th wkt, *150.*
Burton, G. (Eng.):– 10 w. in innings, *153.*
Butcher, B. F. (WI):– 3,104 r. in Tests, *176;* 7 Test hundreds, *210, 225, 238;* 335 for 5th wkt, *150.*
Butler, H. J. (Eng.):– 3 hat-tricks, *157.*
Butler, S. E. (OUCC):– All 10 Cambridge w., *153, 345;* 15 Cambridge w., *345.*
Butt, H. R. (Eng.):– 1,228 d., *165.*

C

Cairns, B. L. (NZ):– 130 w. in Tests, *184;* 10 w. or more in Test (1), *214;* Test p'ship record, *214.*
Callers-Pegasus Festival, *650.*
Calthorpe, Hon. F. S. G. (Eng.):– Test captain, *208.*
Camacho, G. S. (WI):– Slow scoring in Test, *179.*
Cambridge University 1988:– *631-640;* Blues, *645-8* (*Also see Oxford v Cambridge*).
Cambridgeshire, *666, 801, 802, 803, 804, 806-7;* v Cambridge Univ., *637.*
Cameron, F. J. (NZ):– Test p'ship record, *235.*
Cameron, H. B. (SA):– Test captain, *204;* Test p'ship record, *235.*
Canada:– Cricket in, *1102-3.*
Captains in Test cricket, *127* (*Also see individual series*).
Career records, *267;* of players not retained, *581.*
Carew, G. M. (WI):– 1 Test hundred, *210.*
Carew, M. C. (WI):– 1 Test hundred, *236;* Test p'ship record, *226.*
Carr, A. W. (Eng.):– Test captain, *195, 204;* 45 hundreds, *138.*
Carr, D. B. (Eng.):– Test captain, *215.*
Carrick, P. (Yorks.):– Captain of Yorkshire, *605.*
Carrying bat through innings:– in a Test match, *177-8;* in 1988, *265.*
Carson, W. N. (Auck.):– 445 for 3rd wkt, *150.*
Cartwright, T. W. (Eng.):– 1,536 w., *161;* 100 w. (8), *159.*
Catches in 1988, *266, 274.*
Catterall, R. H. (SA):– 3 Test hundreds, *205-6.*
Cave, H. B. (NZ):– Test captain, *236, 242, 244;* 239 for 9th wkt, *151.*
Central Lancashire League, 1988, *842-3.*
Chaman Lal (Mehandra College):– 502* v Government College, *261.*
Chandrasekhar, B. S. (Ind.):– 242 w. in Tests, *184;* 35 w. in series, *182;* 10 w. or more in Test (2), *231, 240;* 8 w. in Test innings, *181;* Test p'ship records, *217.*
Chapman, A. P. F. (Eng.):– Test captain, *195-6, 204, 208;* 1 Test hundred, *196;* Hundreds at Lord's, *335.*
Chapman, J. (Derbys.):– 283 for 9th wkt, *151.*
Chappell, G. S. (Aust.):– Test captain, *127, 195, 224, 227, 229, 231, 233;* 24,535 r. (avge 52.20), *143;* 7,110 r. (avge 53.86) in Tests, *174, 177;* 2,619 r. v England, *203;* 51 consecutive Tests, *193;* 74 hundreds, *137;* 24 Test hundreds, *177, 199, 225, 228, 230, 232;* 2 hundreds in same Test, *172, 225, 228;* 2 separate hundreds (4), *136;* Hundred and double-hundred, *135;* Hundred on Test début, *171, 198;* 122 c. in Tests, *189;* 14 c. in series, *189;* 7 c. in Test, *189;* Test p'ship records, *233.*
Chappell, I. M. (Aust.):– Test captain, *195-6, 224, 227, 231;* 5,345 r. in Tests, *174;* 2,138 r. v England, *203;* 71 consecutive Tests, *193;* 59 hundreds, *138;* 14 Test hundreds, *199, 225, 228, 230, 232;* 2 hundreds in same Test, *172, 228;* 2 hundreds in match (3), *136;* 105 c. in Tests, *189;* 6 c. in Test, *189;* Test p'ship records, *226, 228.*
Chapple, M. E. (NZ):– Test captain, *212;* Test p'ship record, *235.*
Chatfield, E. J. (NZ):– 136 w. in one-day ints, *257;* 115 w. in Tests, *184;* 10 w. or more in Test (1), *237.*
Chatterjee, P. (Bengal):– 10 w. in innings, *154.*
Chauhan, C. P. S. (Ind.):– 2,084 r. in Tests, *176;* 405 for 1st wkt, *148;* Test p'ship records, *217, 231, 240.*
Cheetham, J. E. (SA):– Test captain, *204, 221, 233;* Test p'ship records, *235.*
Cheshire, *659, 667-8, 801, 803-4, 807.*
Chidgey, G. J. (Free Foresters):– Hundred on début, *134.*

Chipperfield, A. G. (Aust.):– 1 Test hundred, *222;* Test p'ship record, *223.*

Christiani, R. J. (WI):– 1 Test hundred, *238.*

Christy, J. A. J. (SA):– 1 Test hundred, *235;* Test p'ship records, *235.*

Chubb, G. W. A. (SA):– Oldest South African Test début, *192.*

Clapp, R. J. (Som.):– Most w. in Sunday League season, *794.*

Clark, E. A. (Middx):– Hundred on début, *134.*

Clarke, S. T. (WI):– 8 w. in innings, *288;* 4 w. in 5 balls, *288;* Hat-trick, *288;* 3 hat-tricks, *157;* Test p'ship record, *241.*

Claughton, J. A. (OUCC):– Hundred on début, *134.*

Clay, J. C. (Eng.):– 17 w. in match, *155.*

Clinton, G. S. (Surrey):– 10,000 r., *267.*

Close, D. B. (Eng.):– Test captain, *208, 215, 218;* Test cricket at 45, *193;* Youngest England Test player, *192;* 34,994 r., *141;* 1,000 r. (20), *139;* 52 hundreds, *138;* 813 c., *166.*

Club Cricket Championship, *337, 652-3.*

Club Cricket Conference, *1220.*

Cockspur Cup, *337, 652-3.*

Coe, S. (Leics.):– Highest for Leicestershire, *134.*

Coen, S. K. (SA):– 305 for 2nd wkt, *149.*

Collinge, R. O. (NZ):– 116 w. in Tests, *184;* Test p'ship records, *180, 243, 245.*

Collins, A. E. J. (Clifton Coll.):– 628* v North Town, *261.*

Collins, G. C. (Kent):– 10 w. in innings, *154.*

Collins, H. L. (Aust.):– Test captain, *195, 221;* 4 Test hundreds, *199, 222;* Hundred on Test début, *171.*

Combined Services:– Address, *1220;* v Cambridge Univ., *640;* v NCA Young Cricketers, *337.*

Commaille, J. M. M. (SA):– 305 for 2nd wkt, *149.*

Compton, D. C. S. (Eng.):– Fast scoring, *144, 178;* 38,942 r. (avge 51.85), *141, 143;* 5,807 r. (avge 50.06) in Tests, *173, 177;* 3,816 r. in season, *138;* 1,159 Test r. in year, *173;* 1,000 r. (17), *139;* 753 r. in series, *207;* 123 hundreds, *137;* 18 hundreds in season, *137;* 17 Test hundreds, *196, 205, 209, 213, 218;* 4 successive hundreds, *136;* 2 hundreds in same Test, *172, 196;* 2 hundreds in match (3), *136;* 300 v NE Transvaal in 181 min., *133, 144;* 278 v Pakistan, *170, 218;* 273 r. in day v Pakistan, *179;* Avge of 90.85 in English season, *140;* 424* for 3rd wkt, *150;* Test p'ship records, *201, 206, 219.*

Coney, J. V. (NZ):– Test captain, *212, 227, 236, 244;* 2,668 r. in Tests, *176;* 3 Test hundreds, *213, 228, 245;* Test p'ship records, *214, 228, 237, 247.*

Congdon, B. E. (NZ):– Test captain, *212, 227, 236, 244;* 3,448 r. in Tests, *176;* 7 Test hundreds, *213, 228, 237;* Test p'ship records, *214, 229, 237, 243.*

Coningham, A. (Aust.):– Wkt with 1st ball on Test début, *184.*

Connolly, A. N. (Aust.):– 102 w. in Tests, *183.*

Consecutive Test appearances, *193.*

Constantine, Lord Learie (WI):– 107 and hat-trick, *161.*

Contractor, N. J. (Ind.):– Test captain, *215, 238, 247;* 1 Test hundred, *230;* 4 successive hundreds, *136;* 152 and 102* on début, *135.*

Cook, C. (Eng.):– 100 w. (9), *159.*

Cook, G. (Northants):– Captain o Northamptonshire, *490;* 203 in 1988, *264,* 90 c. in Sunday League, *795.*

Copson, W. H. (Derbys.):– 5 w. in 6 balls *157;* 4 w. with consecutive balls, *156;* 3 hat tricks, *157.*

Cornford, W. L., (Eng.):– 1,017 d., *165.*

Cornwall, *802, 803, 808.*

Corrall, P. (Leics.):– 10 d. in match, *164.*

Cosier, G. J. (Aust.):– 2 Test hundreds, *22 232;* Hundred on Test début, *171, 225;* Tes p'ship records, *231.*

Cosstick, S. (Vic.):– 6 w. for 1 r., *155.*

County caps in 1988, *538.*

County Championship:– *339-45;* Appea ances, *263;* Champion counties, *342* Constitution of, *263;* Fixtures, 1989, *125 60;* Match results 1864-1988, *343;* Ove rate and run-rate, *1106;* Positions 189 1988, *344-5.*

Cowdrey, C. S. (Eng.):– Test captain, *208* Captain of Kent, *426;* 10,000 r., *26* Discipline Committee hearing, *1222.*

Cowdrey, G. R. (Kent):– 222 for 7th wk *265.*

Cowdrey, M. C. (Eng.):– Test captain, *195- 204, 208, 215, 218;* 42,719 r., *141;* 7,624 r. Tests, *174;* 2,433 r. v Australia, *203;* 1,0 r. (27), *139-40;* 114 Tests, *127, 193;* 1 hundreds, *137;* 22 Test hundreds, *177, 19 7, 205, 209, 213, 216, 218;* 2 hundreds match (3), *136;* 307 v South Australia, *13* 120 c. in Tests, *189;* 6 c. in Test, *189;* 4 for 4th wkt v West Indies, *180, 211;* T p'ship records, *211, 214, 219.*

Cowie, J. (NZ):– 10 w. or more in Test (*214;* Test p'ship records, *214.*

Cowper, R. M. (Aust.):– 10,595 r. (av 53.78), *143;* 2,061 r. in Tests, *175;* 5 T hundreds, *199, 225, 230;* 307 v Engla *133, 170, 199;* Test p'ship record, *233.*

Cox, G. (Sussex):– 50 hundreds, *138.*

Cox, G. R. (Surrey):– 17 w. in match, *155* w. for 0 r., *155.*

Craig, I. D. (Aust.):– Test captain, *221;* Youngest Australian Test player, *192.*
Cranston, K. (Eng.):– Test captain, *208.*
Crapp, J. F. (Eng.):– 38 hundreds, *138.*
Crawford, W. P. A. (Aust.):– Test p'ship record, *230.*
Crawley, M. A. (OUCC):– Captain of Oxford, *621.*
Cricket associations and societies, *907-8.*
Cricket Council, *279.*
Cricketer Cup winners, *604.*
Cricketers of the Year, *70-5* (*See also* Births and Deaths of Cricketers).
Crisp, R. J. (SA):– 4 w. with consecutive balls (2), *156;* 3 hat-tricks, *157.*
Croft, C. E. H. (WI):– Slow scoring in Test, *179;* 125 w. in Tests, *183;* 8 w. in Test innings, *180;* Test p'ship records, *211, 226.*
Cromb, I. B. (NZ):– Test p'ship record, *235.*
Crowe, J. J. (NZ):– Test captain, *211, 226, 246;* 3 Test hundreds, *213, 237, 247;* Slow scoring in Test, *179;* Slow Test hundred, *179;* Test p'ship records, *237, 247.*
Crowe, M. D. (NZ):– 13,151 r. (avge 56.68), *143;* 2,774 r. in Tests, *176;* 1,676 r. in NZ season, *140;* 46 hundreds, *138;* 9 Test hundreds, *213, 228, 237;* Slow scoring in Test, *180;* Test p'ship records, *214, 228, 237.*
Cumberland, *667, 802, 803, 808-9.*
Cunis, R. S. (NZ):– Test p'ship records, *237, 245.*
Curran, K. M. (Glos.):– All-round in 1988, *266.*
Currie Cup (SA), *1048-9, 1051-4.*
Curtis, T. S. (Eng.):– 276 for 2nd wkt, *265.*

D

Dacre, C. C. (Auck.):– 2 hundreds in match (2), *136.*
Dalton, E. L. (SA):– 2 Test hundreds, *206;* Test p'ship record, *207.*
Daniel, W. W. (WI):– Best bowling in B & H Cup, *710.*
Darling, J. (Aust.):– Test captain, *195, 221;* 3 Test hundreds, *199.*
Dates of Formation of County Clubs, including Minor Counties, *262-3.*
Davidson, A. K. (Aust.):– 186 w. in Tests, *183;* 10 w. or more in Test (2), *227, 231;* All-round in Tests, *186;* Test p'ship record, *226.*
Davidson, G. (Derbys.):– Highest for Derbyshire, *134.*
Davies, D. E. (Glam.):– All-round, *162;* Highest for Glamorgan, *134;* 26,564 r., *142;* 1,000 r. (16), *139;* 139 and hat-trick v Leicestershire, *161;* 1st wkt hundreds, *149.*
Davies, T. (Glam.):– 6 d. in NWB Trophy innings, *680.*
Davis, C. A. (WI):– 4 Test hundreds, *210, 236, 238;* Test avge of 54.20, *177;* Test p'ship record, *237.*
Davis, I. C. (Aust.):– 1 Test hundred, *232;* Test p'ship record, *233.*
Davison, B. F. (Leics. and Tas.):– 27,453 r., *142;* 53 hundreds, *138.*
Dawkes, G. O. (Derbys.):– 1,043 d., *165;* w-k hat-trick, *157, 164.*
Dean, H. (Eng.):– 100 w. (8), *159;* 17 w. in match, *155.*
Deed, J. A. (Kent II):– 252 v Surrey II, *261.*
de Mel, A. L. F. (SL):– 59 w. in Tests, *184;* 59 w. in one-day ints, *257;* Test p'ship records, *250.*
Deloitte Ratings, *961.*
Dempster, C. S. (NZ):– 35 hundreds, *138;* 2 Test hundreds, *213;* Test p'ship record, *214.*
Denmark:– Cricket in, *1101;* in Canada, *1102.*
Denness, M. H. (Eng.):– Test captain, *195-6, 208, 212, 215, 218;* 25,886 r., *142;* 1,000 r. (15), *139;* 4 Test hundreds, *197, 213, 216;* Test p'ship record, *214.*
Dennett, G. E. (Glos.):– 2,147 w., *160;* 201 w. in season, *158;* 100 w. (12), *159;* 10 w. in innings, *154.*
Dennis, S. J. (Yorks.):– Career figures, *681.*
Denton, D. (Eng.):– 36,479 r., *141;* 1,000 r. (21), *139;* 69 hundreds, *137;* 1 Test hundred, *205;* 2 hundreds in match (3), *136.*
Depeiza, C. C. (WI):– 1 Test hundred, *225;* 347 for 7th wkt v Australia, *151, 226.*
Derbyshire:– *339, 346-60;* Championship positions, *344-5;* Highest score, *166;* Highest individual score, *134;* Lowest score, *167.*
Derbyshire II:– *820, 822-3.*
Desai, R. B. (Ind.):– Test p'ship records, *244, 249.*
Desai, S. (Karn.):– 451* for 1st wkt, *147, 148, 149.*
de Silva, D. S. (SL):– Test captain, *246;* Oldest Sri Lankan Test début, *192;* Test p'ship records, *250, 252.*
de Silva, E. A. R. (SL):– Test p'ship record, *250.*
de Silva, P. A. (SL):– 2 Test hundreds, *251;* Test p'ship records, *250, 252.*
Devon, *659-60, 802, 803, 809-10.*
Dexter, E. R. (Eng.):– Test captain, *195, 208, 212, 215, 218;* 4,502 r. in Tests, *174;* 1,038 Test r. in year, *173;* 51 hundreds, *138;* 8 Test hundreds, *197, 205, 209, 213, 216, 218;* Test p'ship records, *219.*

Dias, R. L. (SL):– 1,573 r. in one-day ints, *256;* 3 Test hundreds, *247, 250, 251;* Test p'ship records, *247, 250, 252.*
Dick, A. E. (NZ):– 23 d. in series, *188;* Test p'ship record, *235.*
Dilley, G. R. (Eng.):– 133 w. in Tests, *182.*
Dipper, A. E. (Glos.):– 1,000 r. (15), *139;* 53 hundreds, *138.*
Dodemaide, A. I. C. (Aust.):– Test p'ship record, *228.*
Doggart, G. H. G. (Eng.):– 215* on début, *134.*
D'Oliveira, B. L. (Eng.):– 2,484 r. in Tests, *174;* 43 hundreds, *138;* 5 Test hundreds, *197, 213, 216, 218.*
Dollery, H. E. (Eng.):– 1,000 r. (15), *139;* 50 hundreds, *138.*
Donnelly, M. P. (NZ):– 1 Test hundred, *213;* Hundreds at Lord's, *335.*
Dorreen, N. (Cant.):– 265 for 7th wkt, *151.*
Dorset, *801, 803, 804, 810.*
Doshi, D. R. (Ind.):– 114 w. in Tests, *184.*
Double, The, *162, 185-6, 266.*
Double-hundreds in 1988, *264.*
Douglas, J. (Middx):– 1st wkt hundreds, *149.*
Douglas, J. W. H. T. (Eng.):– Test captain, *195-6, 204;* All-round, *162;* 1 Test hundred, *205;* 3 hat-tricks, *157;* 1,893 w., *160;* Test p'ship record, *206.*
Dowling, G. T. (NZ):– Test captain, *212, 236, 242, 244;* 2,306 r. in Tests, *176;* 3 Test hundreds, *243;* Test p'ship records, *243.*
Downes, A. D. (Otago):– 4 w. with consecutive balls, *156.*
Downton, P. R. (Eng.):– 20 d. in series, *188.*
Drake, A. (Yorks.):– 10 w. in innings, *154;* 4 w. with consecutive balls, *156.*
Dredge, C. H. (Som.):– Career figures, *681.*
Ducat, A. (Eng.):– 52 hundreds, *138;* 306* v Oxford Univ., *133;* 50 boundaries in innings, *147.*
Duchess of Norfolk's XI:– v Sri Lankans, *317;* v West Indians, *286-7.*
Duckworth, G. (Eng.):– 1,095 d., *165;* 107 d. in season, *165.*
Duff, R. A. (Aust.):– 2 Test hundreds, *199;* Hundred on Test début, *171.*
Dujon, P. J. L. (WI):– 2,606 r. in Tests, *175;* 5 Test hundreds, *210, 225, 238, 241;* 174 d. in Tests, *188;* 150 d. in one-day ints, *257;* 20 d. in series (2), *188;* All-round in one-day ints, *258;* Test p'ship record, *241;* Cricketer of the Year, *53-5.*
Duleep Trophy (Ind.), *1076-8, 1086-7.*
Duleepsinhji, K. S. (Eng.):– Highest for Sussex, *134;* 50 hundreds, *138;* 4 successive hundreds, *137;* 3 Test hundreds, *197, 213;* 2 hundreds in match (3), *136;* Hundred and double-hundred, *135;* 333 v Northamptonshire, *132, 134.*
Dunell, O. R. (SA):– Test captain, *204.*
Durani, S. A. (Ind.):– 1 Test hundred, *239;* 10 w. or more in Test (1), *217.*
Durham, *660, 802, 803, 810-1.*
Dymock, G. (Aust.):– 10 w. or more in Test (1), *231.*
Dyson, A. H. (Glam.):– 305 consecutive Championship appearances, *263;* 1st wkt hundreds, *149.*
Dyson, J. (Aust.):– 2 Test hundreds, *199, 225.*

E

Eady, C. J. (Tas.):– 566 v Wellington, *261.*
East, D. E. (Essex):– 8 d. in innings, *163.*
East, R. J. (OFS):– 7 d. in innings, *163.*
Edgar, B. A. (NZ):– 3 Test hundreds, *228, 237, 245;* Slow scoring in Test, *179;* Tes p'ship record, *214, 228.*
Edmonds, P. H. (Eng.):– 125 w. in Tests, *183,* Test p'ship record, *217.*
Edrich, J. H. (Eng.):– Test captain, *196* 39,790 r., *141;* 5,138 r. in Tests, *174;* 2,64 r. v Australia, *203;* 1,000 r. (21), *139;* 10 hundreds, *137;* 12 Test hundreds, *197, 20 213, 216;* 2 hundreds in match (4), *136* 310* v New Zealand, *133, 170, 213;* 5 boundaries in innings, *147;* 1st wk hundreds, *148;* Test p'ship record, *214.*
Edrich, W. J. (Eng.):– 36,965 r., *141;* 3,539 (avge 80.43) in season, *138, 140;* 2,440 r. i Tests, *174;* 1,010 r. (April 30-May 31), *145* 1,000 r. (15), *139;* 86 hundreds, *137;* 6 Tes hundreds, *197, 205, 213;* 424* for 3rd wk *150;* Test p'ship records, *206.*
Edwards, R. (Aust.):– 2 Test hundreds, *19*
Elliott, G. (Vic.):– 9 w. for 2 r., *155.*
Elliott, H. (Eng.):– 1,206 d., *165;* 10 d. i match, *164.*
Ellison, R. M. (Eng.):– 10 w. or more in Te (1), *201.*
Emburey, J. E. (Eng.):– Test captain, *20* 1,000 w., *289;* 130 w. in Tests, *182;* A round in Tests, *186.*
Emmett, G. M. (Eng.):– 37 hundreds, *138;* hundreds in match (2), *136.*
Emmett, T. (Eng.):– 1,571 w., *160;* 16 w. day, *156.*
Endean, W. R. (SA):– Handled the ball, *15* 3 Test hundreds, *206, 222, 235;* Test p'sh records, *223, 235.*
Engineer, F. M. (Ind.):– 2,611 r. in Tes *176;* 2 Test hundreds, *216, 239;* Test p'sh records, *217, 244.*
England:– Definition of first-class match *555, 1212;* England in Test cricket (*see* *131*); England v Rest of the World, *22* Highest individual Test innings, *17* Highest Test innings, *189;* Hon. M members, *338;* Leading batsmen in Tes

England:– *contd*
174; Leading bowlers in Tests, *182*; Lowest Test innings, *191*; Most consecutive Test appearances, *191*; Most Test appearances, *127*; Most Test appearances as captain, *127*; Oldest Test player, *193*; Qualification and registration of players, *1213-4*; Representative body, *279*; Summary of Tests, *194*; Test cricketers (1877-1988), *85-97*; Youngest and oldest on Test début, *192*.
England Young Cricketers in Australia, *1007-11*.
English Schools Cricket Association:– Address, *1220*; 1988 season, *851-2, 854*.
Errata in *Wisden*, *1253*.
Essex:– *339, 361-76*; Championship positions, *344-5*; Highest score, *166*; Highest individual score, *134*; Lowest score, *167*; Ward Knockout Cup winners, *655-7*.
Essex II, *820, 822, 823-4*.
Esso/NAYC Under-19 County Festival, *849*.
Eton v Harrow, *332-3*.
Evans, T. G. (Eng.):– 2,439 r. in Tests, *174*; 2 Test hundreds, *209, 216*; Slow scoring in Test, *179*; 1,066 d., *165*; 219 d. in Tests, *188*; 75 d. v Australia, *203*; 20 d. in series, *188*.

F

'agg, A. E. (Eng.):– 27,291 r., *142*; 58 hundreds, *138*; 2 double-hundreds, *135*; 2 hundreds in match (2), *136*.
'airbairn, A. (Middx):– Hundred on début, *134*.
'alkner, N. J. (Surrey):– Hundred on début, *134*.
'amily connections, *254-5*.
ane, F. L. (Eng.):– Test captain, *196, 204*; 1 Test hundred, *205*.
arnes, K. (Eng.):– 10 w. or more in Test (1), *201*.
arrimond, W. (Eng.):– 7 d. in innings, *163*.
aulkner, G. A. (SA):– 4 Test hundreds, *206, 222*; All-round in Test, *185*.
avell, L. E. (Aust.):– 1 Test hundred, *230*; 2 hundreds in match (2), *136*.
azal Mahmood (Pak.):– Test captain, *231, 240, 247*; 139 w. in Tests, *184*; 10 w. or more in Test (3), *220, 233, 242*.
elton, N. A. (Som.):– Career figures, *681*.
ender, P. G. H. (Eng.):– All-round, *162*; Hundred in 35 minutes, *143*.
rguson, W. (WI):– 10 w. or more in Test (1), *211*.
rnandes, M. P. (WI):– Test captain, *208*.
rris, J. J. (Aust. and Eng.):– 10 w. or more in Test (1), *207*.
Fielder, A. (Eng.):– 10 w. in innings, *154*; 235 for 10th wkt, *152*.
Fielding statistics, 1988, *266, 274*.
Findlay, T. M. (WI):– Test p'ship record, *237*.
Fingleton, J. H. (Aust.):– 5 Test hundreds, *199, 222*; Test p'ship records, *201, 223*.
Finney, R. J. (Derbys):– Career figures, *681*.
First-class match defined, *555, 1211–2*.
First-wicket hundreds, *148-9*.
First-wicket partnerships, *148*.
Fisher, H. (Yorks.):– LBW hat-trick, *157*.
Fishlock, L. B. (Eng.):– 56 hundreds, *138*; 2 hundreds in match (4), *136*.
Flavell, J. A. (Eng.):– 1,529 w., *161*; 100 w. (8), *159*; 3 hat-tricks, *157*; LBW hat-trick, *157*.
Fleetwood-Smith, L. O'B. (Aust.):– 10 w. or more in Test (1), *202*.
Fletcher, K. W. R. (Eng.):– Test captain, *215, 220*; Captain of Essex, *361*; 37,665 r., *141*; 3,272 r. in Tests, *174*; 1,090 Test r. in year, *173*; 1,000 r. (20), *139*; 63 hundreds, *138*; 7 Test hundreds, *197, 209, 213, 216, 218*; Slow Test hundred, *180*; Test p'ship records, *214, 217*; Career figures, *681*.
Fletcher, S. D. (Yorks.):– 8 w. in innings, *265*.
Formation of counties, *262-3*.
Foster, F. R. (Eng.):– Highest for Warwickshire, *134*; 305* for Warwickshire, *133, 134*.
Foster, M. L. C. (WI):– 1 Test hundred, *225*; Test p'ship record, *226*.
Foster, N. A. (Eng.):– 10 w. or more in Test (1), *217*; 8 w. in Test innings, *181, 288*.
Foster, R. E. (Eng.):– Test captain, *203*; 2 hundreds in match (3), *136*; 287 v Australia on Test début, *133, 171, 172, 197*; Test p'ship record, *201*.
Foster, W. L. (Worcs.):– 2 hundreds in match, *136*.
Four w. with consecutive balls, *156*.
Fourth innings highest totals, *168*.
Fowler, G. (Eng.):– 3 Test hundreds, *209, 213, 216*; 251 for 4th wkt, *265*; Test p'ship records, *214, 217*.
Frank, C. N. (SA):– 1 Test hundred, *222*; Test p'ship record, *223*.
Fraser, A. R. C. (Middx):– Hat-trick in B & H Cup in 1988, *710*.
Fredericks, R. C. (WI):– 4,334 r. in Tests, *175*; 40 hundreds, *138*; 8 Test hundreds, *210, 225, 236, 238, 241*; 2 hundreds in match (3), *136*; Fast Test fifty, *178*; Fast Test hundred, *177*; Test p'ship records, *211, 237, 241*.
Free Foresters:– v Cambridge Univ., *640*; v Oxford Univ., *630*.
Freeman, A. P. (Eng.):– 3,776 w., *159*; 2,090 w. in eight seasons, *159*; 1,122 w. in four

Freeman, A. P. (Eng.):– *contd* seasons, *159;* 304 w. in season, *158;* 200 w. (8), *158;* 100 w. (17), *159;* 100 w. by June 13, *159;* 17 w. in match (2) *155;* 10 w. in innings (3), *154;* 10 w. or more in Test (3), *207, 211;* 3 hat-tricks, *157*.

Freeman, D. L. (NZ):– Youngest New Zealand Test player, *192*.

French, B. N. (Eng.):– 10 d. in match, *164*.

Fry, C. B. (Eng.):– Test captain, *195, 204;* 30,886 r. (avge 50.22), *141, 143;* Aggregate of 3,147 r., *139;* 94 hundreds, *137;* 13 hundreds in season, *139;* 6 & 4 successive hundreds, *136, 137;* 2 Test hundreds, *197, 205;* 2 hundreds in match (5), *135;* Hundred and double-hundred, *135;* Avge of 81.30 in English season, *140;* 1st wkt hundreds, *149*.

Funston, K. J. (SA):– Test p'ship record, *235*.

Future tours, *327*.

G

Gaekwad, A. D. (Ind.):– 2 Test hundreds, *239, 248;* Test p'ship record, *240*.

Gaekwad, D. K. (Ind.):– Test captain, *215*.

Ganteaume, A. G. (WI):– Hundred on Test début, *171, 210*.

Garner, J. (WI):– 259 w. in Tests, *183;* 146 w. in one-day ints, *257;* Test p'ship records, *226, 237, 241*.

Garnett, E. (Berks.):– 282 v Wiltshire, *261*.

Gartrell, R. B. (Tas.):– Handled the ball, *152*.

Gatting, M. W. (Eng.):– Test captain, *194, 208, 212, 215, 218;* Captain of Middlesex, *474*; 20,000 r., *267;* 3,848 r. in Tests, *174;* 50 hundreds, *138;* 9 Test hundreds, *197, 213, 216, 219*; 210 in 1988, *264;* 284 for 3rd wkt, *265;* 264 for 4th wkt, *265;* Test p'ship record, *217;* Discipline Committee hearing, *1222*.

Gavaskar, S. M. (Ind.):– "Sunil Gavaskar – The Little Master" by Tony Lewis, *76-81;* Test captain, *127, 215, 229, 238, 242, 247, 249;* 125 Tests, *127, 193;* 106 consecutive Tests, *193;* 25,834 r. (avge 51.46), *142, 143;* 10,122 r. (avge 51.12) in Tests, *176, 177;* 3,092 r. in one-day ints, *256;* 2,121 r. in overseas season, *140;* 1,555 & 1,310 Test r. in year, *173*; 774 r. in series, *173;* 81 hundreds, *137;* 34 Test hundreds, *177, 216, 230, 239, 243, 248, 250;* 2 hundreds in same Test (3), *136, 172, 239, 248;* Hundred and double-hundred, *135;* 236* v West Indies, *171, 239;* Slow scoring in Test, *179;* Carrying bat in Test, *178;* 340 v Bengal, *132;* 108 c. in Tests, *189;* 421 for 1st wkt, *148;* Test p'ship records, *217, 231, 240, 244, 248, 250*.

Geary, G. (Eng.):– 2,063 w., *160;* 100 w. (11), *159;* 10 w. in innings, *154;* 10 w. or more in Test (1), *207*.

Geddes Grant-Harrison Line Trophy (WI), *1061, 1066-7*.

Ghavri, K. D. (Ind.):– 109 w. in Tests, *184;* Test p'ship records, *231*.

Ghosh, A. (Bihar):– 10 d. in match, *164*.

Ghulam Ahmed (Ind.):– Test captain, *238, 242;* 10 w. or more in Test (1), *231;* Test p'ship record, *249*.

Gibb, P. A. (Eng.):– 2 Test hundreds, *205;* Hundred on Test début, *171;* Test p'ship record, *206*.

Gibb, P. J. M. (Tvl):– 342 for 4th wkt, *150*.

Gibbons, H. H. I. (Worcs.):– 44 hundreds, *138*.

Gibbs, G. L. R. (WI):– 390 for 1st wkt, *148, 149*.

Gibbs, L. R. (WI):– 309 w. in Tests, *183;* 10 w. or more in Test (2), *211-2;* 8 w. in Test innings, *181;* Hat-trick v Australia, *185*.

Giffen, G. (Aust.):– Test captain, *195;* All-round, *161, 162;* All-round in Tests, *186;* 1 Test hundred, *199;* 113 and hat-trick v Lancashire, *161;* 103 w. in Tests, *183, 203*, 17 w. in match, *155;* 10 w. in innings, *153*, 10 w. or more in Test (1), *202;* 3 hat-tricks *157*.

Gifford, N. (Eng.):– 2,068 w., *160;* 284 w. in Sunday League, *794;* Test p'ship records *214, 217;* Career figures, *681*.

Gilbert, D. R. (Aust.):– Test p'ship record *230*.

Gill, J. R. (Ireland):– Hundred on début, *134*

Gillette Cup winners, *680*.

Gilligan, A. E. R. (Eng.):– Test captain, *19*
204; 10 w. or more in Test (1), *207;* Tes p'ship record, *206*.

Gilligan, A. H. H. (Eng.):– Test captain, *21*

Gilmour, G. J. (Aust.):– 1 Test hundred, *22* Test p'ship records, *228*.

Gimblett, H. (Eng.):– 310 v Sussex, *133;* 5 hundreds, *138;* 2 hundreds in match (2 *136*.

Gladwin, C. (Eng.):– Obituary, *1161-2;* 1(w. (12), *159*.

Glamorgan:– *339, 377-91;* Championsh positions, *344-5;* Highest score, *16* Highest individual score, *134;* Lowe score, *167;* v Rest of the World XI, *65*

Glamorgan II, *820, 822, 824-5*.

Gloucestershire:– *339, 392-408;* Champio ship positions, *344-5;* Highest score, *16* Highest individual score, *133;* Lowe score, *167;* Tilcon Trophy, *649;* Wa Knockout Cup, *656*.

Gloucestershire II, *820, 822, 825-6*.

Goddard, J. D. C. (WI):– Test captain, *2(* *224, 236, 238;* 502* for 4th wkt, *146;* T p'ship record, *237*.

Goddard, T. L. (SA):– Test captain, *204, 221, 234;* 2,516 r. in Tests, *175;* 1 Test hundred, *206;* Carrying bat in Test, *178;* 123 w. in Tests, *183;* All-round in Tests, *186.*

Goddard, T. W. (Eng.):– 2,979 w., *159;* 200 w. (4), *158;* 100 w. (16), *159;* 17 w. in day, *156;* 17 w. in match, *155;* 10 w. in innings, *154;* 6 hat-tricks, *157;* Test hat-trick, *185.*

Goel, R. (Haryana):– 7 w. for 4 r., *155.*

Gomes, H. A. (WI):– 3,171 r. in Tests, *175;* 9 Test hundreds, *210, 225, 238;* Test p'ship records, *211, 226.*

Gomez, G. E. (WI):– Test captain, *208;* 1 Test hundred, *238;* 10 w. or more in Test (1), *227;* 434 for 3rd wkt, *150;* Test p'ship record, *240.*

Gooch, G. A. (Eng.):– Test captain, *208, 220;* Captain of Essex, *361;* 26,745 r, *142;* 4,541 r. in Tests, *174;* 66 hundreds, *137;* 8 Test hundreds, *197, 209, 213, 216;* 6 one-day int. hundreds, *256;* 275 in 1988, *264;* Hundred before lunch, *264;* 30 r. in over, *146;* Record score in B & H Cup, *710,* in Sunday League, *793;* 259 for 4th wkt, *265;* Test p'ship record, *220.*

Goonatillake, H. M. (SL):– Test p'ship record, *252.*

Gouldstone, M. R. (Northants):– Career figures, *681.*

Gover, A. R. (Eng.):– 200 w. (2), *158;* 100 w. (8), *159;* 4 w. with consecutive balls, *156.*

Gower, D. I. (Eng.):– Test captain, *195, 208, 215, 218, 220;* Captain of Leicestershire, *458;* 51 consecutive Tests, *193;* 7,000 r. in Tests, *174;* 2,479 r. v Australia, *203;* 1,061 and 1,059 Test r. in year, *173;* 2,905 r. in one-day ints, *256;* 40 hundreds, *138;* 14 Test hundreds, *197, 209, 213, 216, 219;* 7 one-day int. hundreds, *256;* Test p'ship record, *219.*

Grace, Dr E. M. (Eng.):– 192* and 10 w., *154, 161.*

Grace, Dr W. G. (Eng.):– Test captain, *195-6;* All-round, *162, 163;* Highest for Gloucestershire, *134;* Test cricket at 50, *193;* Throwing the cricket ball, *262;* 54,896 r., *141, 142, 163;* 2,739 r. in season, *139;* 1,000 r. (28), *139;* 1,000 r. in May, *145;* 126 hundreds, *137;* 2 Test hundreds, *197;* Hundred on Test début, *171;* 2 hundreds in match (3), *136;* 344 v Kent, *132;* 318* v Yorkshire, *132, 134;* 301 v Sussex, *133;* 130 and 102* at Canterbury, *135;* 123 and hat-trick v Kent, *161;* 104 and 10 w., *161;* 51 boundaries in innings, *147;* 2,876 w., *159, 161, 163;* 100 w. (10), *159;* 17 w. in match, *155;* 10 w. in innings, *153, 154;* 887 c., *166;* 1st wkt hundreds, *149.*

Graham, H. (Aust.):– 2 Test hundreds, *199;* Hundred on Test début, *171.*

Grant, G. C. (WI):– Test captain, *208, 224.*

Grant, R. S. (WI):– Test captain, *208.*

Graveney, D. A. (Glos.):– Captain of Gloucestershire, *392;* 14 w. in match, *265;* 8 w. in innings, *265.*

Graveney, J. K. (Glos.):– 10 w. in innings, *154.*

Graveney, T. W. (Eng.):– Test captain, *196;* 47,793 r., *141;* 4,882 r. in Tests, *174;* 1,000 r. (22), *139;* 122 hundreds, *137;* 11 Test hundreds, *197, 209, 216, 219;* 2 hundreds in match (3), *136;* 258 v West Indies, *171, 209;* Test p'ship records, *211, 219.*

Gray, E. J. (NZ):– 226 for 6th wkt, *151.*

Gray, J. R. (Hants):– 1st wkt hundreds, *149.*

Gray-Nicolls Trophy, 1988, *851.*

Greatbatch, M. J. (NZ):– 1 Test hundred, *213;* Hundred on Test début, *172, 936-7;* Test p'ship record, *214.*

Greenidge, C. G. (WI):– Test captain, *240;* Fast scoring, *179;* 34,440 r., *141;* 6,348 r. in Sunday League, *802;* 6,186 r. in Tests, *175;* 3,964 r. in one-day ints, *256;* 1,149 Test r. in year, *173;* 83 hundreds, *137;* 15 Test hundreds, *210, 225, 236, 237, 241;* 11 hundreds in Sunday League, *802;* 9 one-day int. hundreds, *256;* 4 successive hundreds, *137;* 2 hundreds in match (4), *136;* 2 hundreds in same Test, *172, 210;* Hundred on Test début, *171, 238;* 1,000 r. (16), *139;* Avge of 82.23 in English season, *140;* 13 sixes in innings (2), *146;* 311 for 3rd wkt, *288;* Test p'ship records, *211, 226, 237, 240, 241.*

Gregory, C. W. (Aust.):– 383 v Queensland, *132;* 318 r. in day, *144;* 55 boundaries in innings, *147.*

Gregory, D. W. (Aust.):– Test captain, *194.*

Gregory, J. M. (Aust.):– 2 Test hundreds, *199, 222;* Fastest Test hundred, *178;* All-round in Test, *185.*

Gregory, R. J. (Surrey):– 39 hundreds, *138.*

Gregory, S. E. (Aust.):– Test captain, *195, 221;* 2,282 r. in Tests, *175;* 2,193 r. v England, *203;* 4 Test hundreds, *199;* Test p'ship record, *201.*

Greig, A. W. (Eng.):– Test captain, *195, 208, 215;* 3,599 r. in Tests, *174;* 58 consecutive Tests, *193;* 8 Test hundreds, *197, 209, 213, 216;* 141 w. in Tests, *182;* 10 w. or more in Test (2), *211, 214;* 8 w. in Test innings, *181;* All-round in Tests, *185, 186;* 6 c. in Test, *189;* Test p'ship records, *211, 217.*

Greig, I. A. (Eng.):– Captain of Surrey, *539.*

Grieves, K. J. (Lancs.):– 63 c. in season, *166;* 8 c. in match, *165.*

Griffin, G. M. (SA):– Hat-trick v England, *185.*

Griffith, H. C. (WI):– 138 for 10th wkt, *152.*

Griffith, S. C. (Eng.):– Hundred on Test début, *171, 209*.
Grimmett, C. V. (Aust.):– 216 w. in Tests, *183;* 44 w. in series, *182;* 14 w. v South Africa, *182;* 10 w. in innings, *154;* 10 w. or more in Test (7), *202, 223, 227;* Test p'ship record, *223*.
Grounds, Test match, *252-3*.
Grout, A. T. W. (Aust.):– 187 d. in Tests, *188;* 76 d. v England, *203;* 23 d. in series, *188;* 8 d. in innings, *163;* 8 d. in Test, *187;* 6 d. in Test innings, *187*.
Guise, J. L. (Winchester):– 278 v Eton, *261*.
Gul Mahomed (Ind.):– 319 v Holkar, *132, 150;* 577 for 4th wkt, *147, 150*.
Gulfraz Khan (Pak. Rlwys):– 12 sixes in innings, *146;* 240 for 8th wkt, *151*.
Gunn, G. (Eng.):– Test cricket at 50, *193;* 35,208 r., *141;* 1,000 r. (20), *139;* 62 hundreds, *138;* 2 Test hundreds, *197;* 2 hundreds in match (3), *136;* Hundred on Test début, *171;* (and G. V. Gunn) Hundreds in same match, *136;* 1st wkt hundreds, *149*.
Gunn, J. (Eng.):– All-round, *162;* 40 hundreds, *138*.
Gunn, W. (Eng.):– 25,691 r., *142;* 48 hundreds, *138;* 1 Test hundred, *197*.
Gupte, M. S. (M'tra):– 405 for 1st wkt, *148*.
Gupte, S. P. (Ind.):– 149 w. in Tests, *184;* 10 w. in innings, *154;* 10 w. or more in Test (1), *240;* 9 w. in Test innings, *180, 240*.
Gurusinha, A. P. (SL):– 1 Test hundred, *251;* Test p'ship record, *252*.
Guy, J. W. (NZ):– 1 Test hundred, *243;* Test p'ship record, *243*.
Guystac Trophy (WI), *1066*.

H

Hadlee, D. R. (NZ):– Test p'ship records, *228, 245*.
Hadlee, R. J. (NZ):– All-round, *162;* All-round in Tests, *187;* All-round in one-day ints, *258;* 74 Tests, *127, 193;* 2,770 r. in Tests, *176;* 2 Test hundreds, *237, 247;* 373 w. in Tests, *184;* Most w. in Tests, *1087;* 143 w. in one-day ints, *257;* 15 w. in Test, *181, 229;* 10 w. or more in Test (8), *181, 214, 229, 237, 244;* 9 w. in Test innings, *180;* Hat-trick, *288;* Test p'ship records, *228, 245, 247*.
Hadlee, W. A. (NZ):– Test captain, *212, 227*.
Hafeez, A. (Ind. and Pak.), *see* Kardar, A. H.
Haig, N. E. (Eng.):– All-round, *162*.
Haigh, S. (Eng.):– 2,012 w., *160;* 100 w. (11), *159;* 5 hat-tricks, *157;* 4 w. with consecutive balls, *156*.
Hall, A. E. (SA):– 10 w. or more in Test (1), *207*.
Hall, W. W. (WI):– 192 w. in Tests, *183;* 10 w. or more in Test (1), *240;* Hat-trick v Pakistan, *185;* Test p'ship record, *240*.
Hallam, M. R. (Leics.):– 2 hundreds in match (3), *136;* Hundred and double-hundred (2), *135*.
Halliwell, E. A. (SA):– Test captain, *203, 220;* Test p'ship record, *222*.
Hallows, C. (Eng.):– 1,000 r. in May, *144;* 55 hundreds, *137;* 2 hundreds in match (2), *136;* 1st wkt hundreds, *148*.
Hamence, R. A. (Aust.):– 2 hundreds in match (2), *136*.
Hammond, W. R. (Eng.):– Test captain, *195, 204, 208, 212, 215;* 50,551 r. (avge 56.10), *141, 143;* 7,249 r. (avge 58.45) in Tests, *174, 177;* 3,323 r. in season, *138;* 2,852 r. v Australia, *203;* 1,042 r. in May, *145;* 1,000 r. (22), *139;* 905 r. in series, *173, 201;* 167 hundreds, *137;* 22 Test hundreds, *177, 197, 198, 205, 209, 213, 216;* 15 and 13 hundreds in season, *139;* 4 successive hundreds, *137;* 2 hundreds in match (7), *135;* 2 hundreds and 10 c. in match, *165;* 2 hundreds in same Test, *172, 197;* 336* v New Zealand, *132, 170, 213;* 317 v Nottinghamshire, *132;* 302* and 302 v Glamorgan, *133;* 295 r. in day in Test, *179;* 251 v Australia, *171;* Avge of 84.90 in English season, *140;* 819 c., *166;* 78 c. and 65 c. in season, *166;* 10 c. in match, *165;* Test p'ship records, *201, 206, 211, 214, 217*.
Hampshire:– *339, 409-25;* Benson & Hedges Cup winners, *709;* Championship positions, *344-5;* Highest score, *166;* Highest individual score, *134;* in Barbados, *1063;* in The Netherlands, *1102;* Lowest score, *167*.
Hampshire II:– *820, 822, 826-7*.
Hampshire, J. H. (Eng.):– 28,059 r., *142;* 1,000 r. (15), *139;* 43 hundreds, *138;* Hundred on Test début, *171, 209*.
Hanif Mohammad (Pak.):– Test captain, *218, 231, 244;* Test début at 17, *192;* Longest first-class innings, *132, 133;* 17,059 r. (avge 52.32), *143;* 3,915 r. in Tests, *176;* 55 hundreds, *138;* 12 Test hundreds, *219, 232, 241, 245, 248;* 2 hundreds in match (3), *136;* 2 hundreds in same Test, *172, 219,* 499 v Bahawalpur, *132;* 337 v West Indies, *132, 170, 241;* 64 boundaries in innings, *147;* Slow batting in Test, *179;* Test p'ship records, *219, 242, 246, 249*.
Hanumant Singh (Ind.):– Hundred on Test début, *171, 216;* Hundred and double-hundred, *135;* Test p'ship record, *244*.
Hardinge, H. T. W. (Eng.):– 33,519 r., *141;* 1,000 r. (18), *138;* 75 hundreds, *136;* 4 successive hundreds, *136;* 2 hundreds in

Hardinge, H. T. W. (Eng.):– *contd* match (4), *136;* Hundred and double-hundred, *135.*
Hardstaff, J. jun. (Eng.):– 31,847 r., *141;* 83 hundreds, *137;* 4 Test hundreds, *197, 213, 216;* Test p'ship records, *201, 214.*
Haroon Rashid (Pak.):– 3 Test hundreds, *219, 251;* Test p'ship records, *219, 252.*
Harper, R. A. (WI):– 217* in 1988, *264;* 227 for 6th wkt, *265;* 123 for 9th wkt, *265;* 12 sixes in innings, *146.*
Harris, 4th Lord (Eng.):– Test captain, *194.*
Harris, C. B. (Notts.):– 1st wkt hundreds, *149.*
Harris, M. J. (Middx and Notts.):– 41 hundreds, *138;* 2 hundreds in match (3), *136.*
Harris, P. G. Z. (NZ):– Test p'ship record, *235.*
Harrogate Festival, *649-50.*
Harrow v Eton, *332-3.*
Hart, R. T. (C. Dist.):– 317 for 2nd wkt, *149.*
Hartigan, R. J. (Aust.):– Hundred on Test début, *171, 199;* Test p'ship record, *201.*
Harvey, R. N. (Aust.):– Test captain, *196;* 21,699 r. (avge 50.93), *143;* 6,149 r. in Tests, *174;* 2,416 r. v England, *203;* 834 r. in series, *173;* 67 hundreds, *137;* 21 Test hundreds, *177, 199, 222, 225, 230;* 6 c. in Test, *189;* Test p'ship records, *223, 226.*
Harvey-Walker, A. J. (Derbys.):– Hundred on début, *133.*
Hassett, A. L. (Aust.):– Test captain, *195, 221, 224;* 16,890 r. (avge 58.24), *143;* 3,073 r. in Tests, *175;* 59 hundreds, *138;* 10 Test hundreds, *199, 222, 225, 230;* 2 hundreds in match (2), *136;* Test p'ship records, *201, 223.*
Hastings, B. F. (NZ):– 4 Test hundreds, *228, 237, 245;* Test p'ship records, *180, 228, 237, 245.*
Hathorn, C. M. H. (SA):– 1 Test hundred, *206.*
Hat-tricks:– *157;* Double, *157;* in one-day ints, *257;* in Test matches, *185;* All caught, *157;* All LBW, *157;* All stumped, *157;* Three and more, *157;* in 1988, *266.*
Havewalla, D. R. (BB and CI Rlwys):– 515 v St Xavier's, *261.*
Hawke, 7th Lord (Eng.):– Test captain, *204;* 292 for 8th wkt, *151.*
Hawke, N. J. N. (Aust.):– 10 w. or more in Tests (1), *227.*
Hawkesworth, W. (Otago):– 184 for 10th wkt, *152.*
Hayes, E. G. (Eng.):– 27,318 r., *142;* 1,000 r. (16), *139;* 48 hundreds, *138.*
Hayes, F. C. (Eng.):– Hundred on Test début, *171, 209;* 34 r. in over, *145.*
Hayes, J. A. (NZ):– Obstructing the field, *153.*
Hayhurst, A. N. (Lancs.):– 251 for 4th wkt, *265.*
Haynes, D. L. (WI):– 72 consecutive Tests, *193;* 10,000 r., *267;* 4,900 r. in one-day ints, *256;* 4,523 r. in Tests, *175;* 10 one-day int. hundreds, *256;* 9 Test hundreds, *210, 225, 236, 238;* Carrying bat in & batting through Test innings, *178;* Handled the ball, *152;* Test p'ship records, *226, 237, 240.*
Hayward, T. W. (Eng.):– 43,551 r., *141;* 3,518 r. in season, *138;* 1,000 r. (20), *139;* 1,000 r. (April 16-May 31), *145;* 104 hundreds, *137;* 13 hundreds in season, *137;* 4 successive hundreds, *136, 137;* 3 Test hundreds, *197, 205;* 2 hundreds in match (3), *136;* 315* v Lancashire, *133;* 1st wkt hundreds, *148-9.*
Hazare, V. S. (Ind.):– Test captain, *215, 238;* 18,621 r. (avge 58.19), *143;* 2,192 r. in Tests, *176;* 60 hundreds, *138;* 7 Test hundreds, *216, 230, 239, 248;* 2 hundreds in same Test, *172, 230;* 2 hundreds in match (3), *136;* 316* v Baroda, *132, 151;* 309 v Hindus, *133;* 577 for 4th wkt, *147, 150;* 245 for 9th wkt, *151;* Test p'ship records, *217, 231, 248.*
Headley, G. A. (WI):– Test captain, *208;* 2,190 r. (avge 60.83) in Tests, *175, 177;* 10 Test hundreds, *210, 225;* 2 hundreds in same Test, *172, 210;* 2 hundreds in match (2), *136;* 344* v Lord Tennyson's XI, *132, 150;* 270* v England, *170, 210;* Hundred on Test début, *171, 210;* 487* for 6th wkt, *147, 150.*
Headley, R. G. A. (WI):– 1st wkt hundreds, *148.*
Hearn, P. (Kent):– Hundred on début, *134.*
Hearne, J. T. (Eng.):– 3,061 w., *159;* 200 w. (3), *158;* 100 w. (15), *159;* 100 w. by June 12, *159;* 10 w. or more in Test (1), *201;* 4 hat-tricks, *157;* Hat-trick v Australia, *185;* Test p'ship record, *206.*
Hearne, J. W. (Eng.):– All-round, *162;* 37,252 r., *141;* 1,000 r. (19), *139;* 96 hundreds, *137;* 1 Test hundred, *197.*
Hemmings, E. E. (Eng.):– 10 w. in innings, *154.*
Henderson, M. (NZ):– Wkt with 1st ball on Test début, *184.*
Henderson, W. A. (NE Tvl):– 7 w. for 4 r., *155;* 5 w. in 6 balls, *157;* 4 w. with consecutive balls, *156.*
Hendren, E. H. (Eng.):– Test cricket at 46, *193;* 57,611 r. (avge 50.80), *141, 143;* 3,525 r. in Tests, *174;* 3,311 r. in season, *139;* 1,765 r. in West Indies, *140;* 1,000 r. (25), *139;* 170 hundreds, *137;* 13 hundreds in season, *137;* 7 Test hundreds, *197, 205,*

Hendren, E. H. (Eng.):– *contd* *209;* 2 hundreds in match (4), *136;* 301* v Worcestershire, *133;* 277* at Lord's, *260;* 754 c., *166;* Test p'ship record, *201.*

Hendriks, J. L. (WI):– Test p'ship record, *226.*

Hendry, H. L. (Aust.):– Obituary, *1162-3;* 1 Test hundred, *199;* 325* v New Zealanders, *132.*

Henry, O. (Boland):– 259 for 6th wkt, *151.*

Hertfordshire, *663, 802, 803, 811-2;* v Cambridge Univ., *640.*

Hick, G. A. (Zimb., Worcs. and N. Dist.):– "We Already Knew He Could Bat" by Peter Roebuck, *65-9;* 1,000 r. (April 17-May 29), *145, 264;* 410 r. in April, *264;* First to 2,000 r., *264;* Highest aggregate since 1969, *139;* Highest for Worcestershire, *134;* 405* v Somerset, *132, 264, 526;* 212 in 1988, *264;* Fastest hundred in 1988, *264;* 10 hundreds in 1988, *275;* 4 hundreds in NZ season, *1069;* 11 sixes in innings, *146, 264, 526;* 276 for 2nd wkt, *265;* 265 for 6th wkt, *265;* 205 for 7th wkt, *265;* 177* for 8th wkt, *265.*

Hickton, W. (Lancs.):– 10 w. in innings, *153.*

Hide, J. B. (Sussex):– 4 w. with consecutive balls, *156.*

Higgs, K. (Eng.):– 1,536 w., *160;* 3 hat-tricks, *157;* Test p'ship record, *211.*

Highest aggregates:– Individual, *138-9;* Team, *168, 191, 259.*

Highest individual scores:– *132-3, 260;* in Tests, *170-1;* in one-day ints, *256;* in 1988, *264.*

Highest innings totals:– in Tests, *189-90;* in one-day ints, *258;* in 1988, *267.*

Highest partnerships:– *147-52;* in one-day ints, *256*; in 1988, *265.*

Highest total for each county:– Individual, *134, 256;* Team, *166, 258.*

Hilditch, A. M. J. (Aust.):– 2 Test hundreds, *199, 225;* Handled the ball, *152.*

Hill, A. (Eng.):– 3 hat-tricks, *157.*

Hill, A. J. L. (Eng.):– 1 Test hundred, *205.*

Hill, C. (Aust.):– Test captain, *195, 221;* 3,412 r. in Tests, *174;* 2,660 r. v England, *203;* 1,061 Test r. in year, *173;* 45 hundreds, *138;* 7 Test hundreds, *199, 222;* 365* v NSW, *132, 151;* 232 for 9th wkt, *151;* Test p'ship records, *201.*

Hinds, F. (A. B. St Hill's XI):– 10 w. in innings, *154.*

Hinkly, E. (Kent):– 10 w. in innings, *153.*

Hirst, G. H. (Eng.):– All-round, *162, 163;* Highest for Yorkshire, *134;* 36,323 r., *141;* 1,000 r. (19), *139;* 60 hundreds, *138;* 341 v Leicestershire, *132, 134;* 2 hundreds and 5 w. twice v Somerset, *161;* 54 boundaries in innings, *147;* 2,739 w., *160;* 208 w. in season, *158;* 100 w. (15), *159.*

Hirwani, N. D. (Ind.):– 16 w. in Test, *181, 240, 957-8;* 8 w. in Test innings (2), *181.*

HMC Schools in 1988, *853-5.*

Hoad, E. L. G. (WI):– Test captain, *208;* 138 for 10th wkt, *152.*

Hobbs, Sir J. B. (Eng.):– Test cricket at 47, *193;* 61,237 r. (avge 50.65), *141, 143;* 5,410 r. (avge 56.94) in Tests, *174, 177;* 3,636 r. v Australia, *203;* 3,024 r. in season, *139;* 1,000 r. (26), *139;* 197 hundreds, *137;* 16 hundreds in season, *137;* 15 Test hundreds, *197, 205, 209;* 4 successive hundreds, *137;* 2 hundreds in match (6), *135;* 316* v Middlesex at Lord's, *132, 260;* Avge of 82 in English season, *140;* 428 for 1st wkt, *148;* 1st wkt hundreds, *148-9;* Test p'ship record, *201.*

Hobbs, R. N. S. (Eng.):– Hundred in 44 minutes, *144.*

Hogan, T. G. (Aust.):– Test p'ship record, *226.*

Hogg, R. M. (Aust.):– 123 w. in Tests, *183;* 41 w. in series, *182, 203;* 10 w. or more in Test (2), *202;* Test p'ship record, *226.*

Holder, V. A. (WI):– 109 w. in Tests, *183;* Test p'ship record, *241.*

Holding, M. A. (WI):– 249 w. in Tests, *183;* 142 w. in one-day ints, *257*; 14 w. in Test, *182, 212;* 11 w. in Test, *227;* 8 w. in Test innings, *181, 212;* Best bowling in NWB Trophy, *666, 679;* Test p'ship record, *211.*

Holford, D. A. J. (WI):– 1 Test hundred, *210;* Test p'ship records, *211, 226.*

Holland, R. G. (Aust.):– 10 w. or more in Test (2), *227, 229.*

Hollies, W. E. (Eng.):– 2,323 w., *160;* 100 w. (14), *159;* 10 w. in innings, *154.*

Holmes, G. C. (Glam.):– 2 hundreds in match, *264.*

Holmes, P. (Eng.):– Test cricket at 45, *193;* 30,573 r., *141;* 1,000 r. (15), *139;* 67 hundreds, *137;* 315* v Middlesex at Lord's, *133, 260;* 302* v Hampshire, *133;* 555 for 1st wkt, *147, 148, 149;* 1st wkt hundreds, *149.*

Holt, J. K. (WI):– 2 Test hundreds, *210, 238;* Test p'ship record, *211.*

Honours' List in 1988, *819.*

Hooker, J. E. H. (NSW):– 4 w. with consecutive balls, *156;* 307 for 10th wkt, *152.*

Hookes, D. W. (Aust.):– 1 Test hundred, *234;* 4 successive hundreds, *136, 137;* 2 hundreds in match (3), *136;* 306* v Tasmania, *133, 150;* Hundred in 43 minutes off 34 balls, *144;* 462* for 4th wkt *147, 150.*

Hooper, C. L. (WI):– 1 Test hundred, *238.*

Hopkins, J. A. (Glam.):– Career figures, *681*

Horan, T. (Aust.):– Test captain, *194;* 1 Test hundred, *199.*

Hornby, A. N. (Eng.):– Test captain, *194, 196.*
Hordern, H. V. (Aust.):– 10 w. or more in Test (2), *202.*
Horner, N. F. (Warwicks.):– 377* for 1st wkt, *148.*
Howard, N. D. (Eng.):– Test captain, *215.*
Howarth, G. P. (NZ):– Test captain, *212, 227, 236, 242, 244, 246;* 2,531 r. in Tests, *176;* 6 Test hundreds, *213, 237, 243, 245;* 2 hundreds in same Test, *172, 213;* Test p'ship records, *237, 245.*
Howarth, H. J. (NZ):– Test p'ship records, *228.*
Howell, H. (Eng.):– 10 w. in innings, *154.*
Howell, W. P. (Aust.):– 17 w. in match, *155;* 10 w. in innings, *153.*
Howorth, R. (Eng.):– All-round, *162;* 100 w. (9), *159;* Wkt with 1st ball on Test début, *184.*
Hubble, J. C. (Kent):– 10 d. in match, *164.*
Hughes, D. P. (Lancs.):– Captain of Lancashire, *442.*
Hughes, K. J. (Aust.):– Test captain, *195, 224, 229, 231;* 4,415 r. in Tests, *174;* 1,163 Test r. in year, *173;* 53 consecutive Tests, *193;* 9 Test hundreds, *199, 225, 230, 232;* Test p'ship records, *230, 233.*
Huish, F. H. (Kent):– 1,310 d., *165;* 100 d. in season (2), *165;* 10 d. in match, *164.*
Humpage, G. W. (Warwicks.):– 13 sixes in innings, *146;* 470 for 4th wkt, *147, 150.*
Hundreds:– In 1988, *275-8;* Before lunch in 1988, *264;* Fastest, *143;* Fastest in 1988, *264;* Fastest in Tests, *178;* Most individual (35 or more), *137-8;* Most in one-day ints, *256;* Most in season, *137;* Most in Tests, *177;* On début, *134-5, 172-3, 264;* Slowest in Tests, *179;* 4 or more in succession, *136-7;* 2 in match, *135-6, 264.*
Hundred and double-hundred in match, *136;* in a Test, *172.*
Hunte, C. C. (WI):– 3,245 r. in Tests, *175;* 8 Test hundreds, *210, 225, 238, 241;* Hundred on Test début, *171, 241;* 260 v Pakistan, *170, 241;* Carrying bat in Test, *178;* 446 for 2nd wkt, *149;* Test p'ship record, *241.*
Hunter, D. (Yorkshire):– 1,253 d., *165.*
Hussain, N. (Essex):– Hundred before lunch, *264.*
Hutchings, K. L. (Eng.):– 1 Test hundred, *197.*
Hutton, Sir Leonard (Eng.):– Test captain, *195, 208, 212, 215, 218;* 40,140 r. (avge 55.51), *141, 143;* 6,971 r. (avge 56.67) in Tests, *174, 177;* 3,429 r. in season, *138;* 2,428 r. v Australia, *203;* 1,294 r. and 1,050 r. in month, *145;* 1,000 r. (17), *139;* 129 hundreds, *137;* 19 Test hundreds, *197, 205, 209, 213, 216;* 2 hundreds in match (3), *136;* 364 v Australia, *132, 133, 170, 197;* Carrying bat in Test (2), *177-8;* Obstructing the field, *153;* 1st wkt hundreds, *148;* Test p'ship records, *201, 206, 211.*
Hydro Village Championship, *337-8, 653.*

I

Ibadulla, Khalid (Pak.):– Hundred on Test début, *171, 232;* Obstructing the field, *153;* 377* for 1st wkt, *148;* Test p'ship record, *233.*
Ibrahim, K. C. (Ind.):– 274 for 7th wkt, *151.*
Iddon, J. (Eng.):– 46 hundreds, *138.*
Ijaz Ahmed (Lahore Greens):– Obstructing the field, *153.*
Ijaz Ahmed (Pak.):– Test p'ship record, *219.*
Ijaz Butt (Pak.):– Slow batting in Test, *179.*
Ijaz Faqih (Pak.):– 1 Test hundred, *248;* 107 w. in Pakistan season, *159;* Test p'ship record, *249.*
Ikin, B. J. (Griq. West):– LBW hat-trick, *157.*
Illingworth, R. (Eng.):– Test captain, *195, 208, 212, 215, 218;* All-round, *162, 163;* All-round in Tests, *186;* 2 Test hundreds, *209, 216;* 2,072 w., *160;* 122 w. in Tests, *183;* 100 w. (10), *159;* Test p'ship record, *217.*
Illingworth, R. K. (Worcs.):– 117* for 8th wkt, *265;* 113 for 9th wkt, *265.*
Imran Khan (Pak.):– Test captain, *218, 231, 240, 247, 251;* 2,860 r. in Tests, *176;* 4 Test hundreds, *219, 241, 248;* 334 w. in Tests, *184;* 123 w. in one-day ints, *257;* 40 w. in series, *182;* 14 w. in Test, *182, 252;* 10 w. or more in Test (6), *220, 233, 242, 289, 252;* 8 w. in Test innings (2), *181, 249, 252;* All-round in one-day ints, *258;* All-round in Tests, *186, 187;* Test p'ship records, *233, 249, 252.*
Imtiaz Ahmed (Pak.):– Test captain, *218, 231;* 2,079 r. in Tests, *176;* 300* v Commonwealth XI, *133;* 3 Test hundreds, *241, 245, 248;* 308 for 7th wkt, *151, 246;* Test p'ship records, *246, 249.*
India:– Definition of first-class matches, *1212*; Domestic season 1987-88, *1076-87;* Highest individual Test innings, *171;* Highest Test innings, *189;* India in Test cricket (*see p. 131*); Leading batsmen in Tests, *176;* Leading bowlers in Tests, *184;* Lowest Test innings, *191;* Most consecutive Test appearances, *193;* Most Test appearances, *127;* Most Test appearances as captain, *127;* Representative body, *1219;* Sharjah Cup, *1003-6;* Summary of Tests, *194;* Test cricketers (1932-88), *118-22;* Youngest and oldest on Test début, *192.*
India v New Zealand, 1988-89, *1087.*

Indian Gymkhana Club:– v Sri Lankans, 316.

Individual hundreds (35 or more), 137-8.

Inman, C. C. (Leics.):– 50 in 8 min., 143; 32 r. in over, 145.

Insole, D. J. (Eng.):– 25,241 r., 142; 54 hundreds, 138; 1 Test hundred, 205.

International Cricket Conference:– Addresses of members, 1219-20; Constitution and Membership, 1210; Meetings, 48, 1221.

Intikhab Alam (Pak.):– Test captain, 218, 231, 240, 244; Test début at 17, 192; 1 Test hundred, 219; 1,571 w., 160; 125 w. in Tests, 184; 10 w. or more in Test (2), 246; Wkt with 1st ball on Test début, 184; All-round in Tests, 187; 190 for 9th wkt, 151, 180, 219; Test p'ship records, 219, 233, 246.

Iqbal Qasim (Pak.):– 159 w. in Tests, 184; 10 w. or more in Test (2), 233, 249; Test p'ship records, 233, 246, 249, 252.

Iqtidar Ali (Allied Bank):– Hit the ball twice, 153.

Irani Cup (Ind.), 1086.

Iredale, F. A. (Aust.):– 2 Test hundreds, 199.

Ireland:– v MCC, 650, 844; v Scotland, 652, 845; v Wales, 651, 845; v Worcestershire, 845; in NatWest Bank Trophy, 661-2; Representative body, 1220.

Irish Cricket in 1988, 844-6.

Ironmonger, H. (Aust.):– Oldest Australian Test player, 193; Test début at 46, 192; 10 w. or more in Test (2), 223, 227.

Irvine, B. L. (SA):– 1 Test hundred, 222.

Israr Ali (B'pur):– 6 w. for 1 r., 155.

I Zingari results, 1988, 850.

J

Jackman, R. D. (Eng.):– 234 w. in Sunday League, 794; 3 hat-tricks, 157.

Jackson, A. A. (Aust.):– Hundred v England on Test début, 171, 199.

Jackson, Hon. Sir F. S. (Eng.):– Test captain, 194; 5 Test hundreds, 197.

Jackson, H. L. (Eng.):– 1,733 w., 160; 100 w. (10), 159.

Jaisimha, M. L. (Ind.):– 2,056 r. in Tests, 176; 3 Test hundreds, 216, 230; Slow batting in Test, 179.

Jalal-ud-Din (Pak.):– Hat-trick in one-day int., 257; Handled the ball, 152.

Jameson, J. A. (Eng.):– 465* for 2nd wkt, 147, 149.

Jamshedji, R. J. D. (Ind.):– Oldest Indian Test début, 192.

Jardine, D. R. (Eng.):– Test captain, 195, 208, 212, 215; 35 hundreds, 138; 1 Test hundred, 209; Avge of 91.09 in English season, 140; Test p'ship record, 201.

Jarman, B. N. (Aust.):– Test captain, 196; 10 d. in match, 164; Test p'ship record, 230.

Jarvis, T. W. (NZ):– 1 Test hundred, 237; Slow batting in Test, 179; 387 for 1st wkt, 148, 149, 237; Test p'ship record, 237.

Javed Miandad (Pak.):– Test captain, 218, 231, 240, 244, 251; 92 Tests, 127, 193; 25,400 r. (avge 53.58), 142, 143; 6,621 r. (avge 53.82) in Tests, 176, 177; 4,482 r. in one-day ints, 256; 53 consecutive Tests, 193; 72 hundreds, 137; 17 Test hundreds, 219, 232, 241, 245, 248, 251; 6 hundreds in one-day ints, 256; 2 hundreds in match (4), 136; 2 hundreds in same Test, 172, 245; Hundred on Test début, 172, 245; 311 v National Bank, 133; 280* v India, 170, 248; 260 v England, 170, 219, 287; 211* v Sussex, 287; 8 c. in match, 165; 451 for 3rd wkt, 147; Test p'ship records, 219, 233, 245, 249, 252.

Javed Mohammad (Multan):– Hit the ball twice, 153.

Jefferies, S. T. (Hants and W. Prov.):– 10 w. in innings, 154; 8 w. in innings, 265; Best bowling in B & H Cup final, 709, 710; Man of the Match in B & H Cup final, 709.

Jenkins, R. O. (Eng.):– Double hat-trick, 157; 3 hat-tricks, 157.

Jennings, R. V. (Tvl):– 10 d. in match (3), 164.

Jessop, G. L. (Eng.):– All-round, 162; Fastest English Test hundred, 178, 197; Hundreds in 40 and 42 min., 143-4; 26,698 r., 142; 53 hundreds, 138; 2 hundreds in match (4), 136; 1 Test hundred, 178, 197; 200 r. in 120 min. and 130 min., 144.

Jesty, T. E. (Hants, Surrey and Lancs.):– 32 r. in over, 145; 248 w. in Sunday League, 248.

John Player League winners, 795.

Johnson, H. H. H. (WI):– 10 w. or more in Test (1), 212.

Johnson, I. W. (Aust.):– Test captain, 195, 224, 229, 231; 109 w. in Tests, 183; All-round in Tests, 186; Test p'ship records 226, 230.

Johnson, J. S. (Shropshire):– Hundred on début, 134.

Johnson, L. A. (Northants):– 10 d. in match (2), 164.

Johnson, T. F. (WI):– Wkt with 1st ball on Test début, 184.

Johnston, W. A. (Aust.):– Avge of 102 in English season, 140; 160 w. in Tests, 183

Jones, A. (Glam.):– 36,049 r., 141; 1,000 r (23), 139; 56 hundreds, 138; 2 hundreds in match (3), 136.

Jones, A. O. (Eng.):– Test captain, 195; 39 for 1st wkt, 148.

Jones, A. H. (NZ):– 1 Test hundred, 228 Test p'ship record, 228.

Jones, D. M. (Aust.):– 3 Test hundreds, *199, 230, 234;* Test p'ship record, *230.*
Jones, E. (Aust.):– 10 w. or more in Test (1), *202.*
Jones, E. W. (Glam.):– 223 d. in Sunday League, *794;* 7 d. in innings, *163.*
Jones, S. A. (Boland):– 259 for 6th wkt, *151.*
Jordon, R. C. (Vic):– 10 d. in match, *164.*
Joshi, P. G. (Ind.):– Test p'ship record, *249.*
Julien, B. D. (WI):– 2 Test hundreds, *210, 241;* Test p'ship records, *211, 241.*
Jupp, V. W. C. (Eng.):– All-round, *162;* 1,658 w., *160;* 102 and hat-trick, *161;* 100 w. (10), *159;* 5 hat-tricks, *157.*

K

Kallicharran, A. I. (WI):– Test captain, *224, 238;* 31,819 r., *141;* 4,399 r. in Tests, *175;* 85 hundreds, *137;* 12 Test hundreds, *210, 225, 236, 238, 241;* 2 hundreds in match (2), *136;* Hundred and double-hundred, *135;* Hundred on Test début, *171, 236;* Record score in NWB Trophy, *691;* 470 for 4th wkt, *147, 150;* Test p'ship records, *226, 237, 240.*
Kamal Najamuddin (Kar.):– 10 d. in match, *164;* 418 for 1st wkt, *148.*
Kambli, V. G. (Sharadashram Vidyamandir School):– 664* for 3rd wkt, *261, 1103.*
Kanhai, R. B. (WI):– Test captain, *208, 224;* 28,774 r., *142;* 6,227 r. in Tests, *175;* 61 consecutive Tests, *193;* 83 hundreds, *137;* 15 Test hundreds, *210, 225-6, 238-9, 241;* 256 v India, *171, 238;* 2 hundreds in same Test, *172, 225;* Avge of 82.53 in English season, *140;* 465* for 2nd wkt, *147, 149;* Test p'ship records, *226, 240, 241.*
Kapil Dev (Ind.):– Test captain, *215, 229, 238, 247, 249;* 3,889 r. in Tests, *176;* 66 consecutive Tests, *193;* 7 Test hundreds, *216, 230, 239, 250;* Fast Test fifty, *178;* 319 w. in Tests, *184;* 146 w. in one-day ints, *257;* 10 w. or more in Test (2), *240, 249;* 9 w. in Test innings, *180, 240;* 8 w. in Test innings (2), *181;* All-round in one-day ints, *258;* All-round in Tests, *187;* Test p'ship records, *217, 249, 250.*
Kardar, A. H. (Ind. and Pak.):– Test captain, *127, 218, 231, 240, 244, 247;* Test p'ship record, *242.*
Keeton, W. W. (Eng.):– Highest for Notts., *134;* 54 hundreds, *138;* 312* v Middlesex, *133, 134;* 1st wkt hundreds, *149.*
Kelleway, C. (Aust.):– 3 Test hundreds, *199, 222;* All-round in Test, *185;* Test p'ship records, *223.*
Kelly, J. J. (Aust.):– 8 d. in Test, *187.*
Kennedy, A. S. (Eng.):– All-round, *162;* 2,874 w., *159;* 205 w. in season, *158;* 100 w. (15), *159;* 10 w. in innings, *154;* 3 hat-tricks, *157.*
Kenny, R. B. (Ind.):– Test p'ship record, *231.*
Kent:– *339, 426-41;* Championship positions, *344-5;* Highest score, *166;* Highest individual score, *134;* Lowest score, *167.*
Kent II, *820, 822, 827-8;* Bain Clarkson Trophy finalists, *838.*
Kenyon, D. (Eng.):– 37,002 r., *141;* 1,000 r. (19), *139;* 74 hundreds, *137.*
Kerr, R. B. (Qld):– 388 for 1st wkt, *148.*
Khalid Alvi (Kar.):– 418 for 1st wkt, *148.*
Khalid Javed (Pak. Rlwys):– Obstructing the field, *153.*
Khalid Hassan (Pak.):– Test début at 16, *192.*
Khalid Irtiza (UBL):– 456 for 3rd wkt, *147, 150.*
Kilborn, M. J. (OUCC):– Captain of Oxford, *621.*
Killick, E. H. (Sussex):– 344 consecutive Championship appearances, *263.*
Kilner, R. (Eng.):– All-round, *162.*
King, C. L. (WI):– 1 Test hundred, *236.*
King, J. H. (Eng.):– Hit the ball twice, *153;* 25,121 r., *142;* 2 hundreds in match (2), *136.*
Kinneir, S. P. (Eng.):– Test début at 40, *192.*
Kippax, A. F. (Aust.):– 12,762 r. (avge 57.22), *143;* 43 hundreds, *138;* 2 Test hundreds, *199, 224;* 2 hundreds in match (2), *136;* 315* v Queensland, *133;* 307 for 10th wkt, *152.*
Kirmani, S. M. H. (Ind.):– 56 consecutive Tests, *193;* 2,759 r. in Tests, *176;* 2 Test hundreds, *215, 230;* 198 d. in Tests, *188;* 6 d. in Test innings, *187;* Test p'ship records, *217, 231, 240, 244, 249.*
Kirsten, N. (Border):– 7 d. in innings, *163.*
Kirsten, P. N. (Derbys. and W. Prov.):– 44 hundreds, *138;* 4 successive hundreds, *137;* 2 hundreds in match (3), *136.*
Kline, L. F. (Aust.):– Test hat-trick, *185.*
Knight, B. R. (Eng.):– All-round, *162;* 2 Test hundreds, *213, 216;* Test p'ship record, *214.*
Knott, A. P. E. (Eng.):– 4,389 r. in Tests, *174;* 65 consecutive Tests, *193;* 5 Test hundreds, *197, 209, 213, 219;* 1,344 d., *165;* 269 d. in Tests, *188;* 105 d. v Australia, *203;* 24 d. in series, *188;* 5 d. in Test innings, *187;* Test p'ship records, *201, 211, 214.*
Kripal Singh, A. G. (Ind.):– Hundred on Test début, *171, 243;* Test p'ship record, *244.*
Kunderan, B. K. (Ind.):– 2 Test hundreds, *216.*
Kuruppu, D. S. B. P. (SL):– Double-hundred on Test début, *172, 180, 247;* Slowest double-hundred, *180;* 201* v NZ, *171, 247.*

L

Lacey, Sir F. E. (Hants):– 323* v Norfolk, *261*.

Laird, B. M. (Aust.):– Test p'ship record, *228*.

Laker, J. C. (Eng.):– 1,944 w., *160;* 193 w. in Tests, *182;* 100 w. (11), *159;* 46 w. in series, *182, 202;* 19 w. in Test, *155, 181, 201;* 10 w. in innings (2), *154;* 10 w. in Test innings, *154, 180;* 10 w. or more in Test (3), *201, 207;* 9 w. in Test innings, *180;* 8 w. for 2 r., *155;* 4 hat-tricks, *157*.

Lamb, A. J. (Eng.):– Captain of Northamptonshire, *490;* 20,000 r., *267;* 2,969 r. in Tests, *174;* 55 hundreds, *138;* 8 Test hundreds, *209, 213, 216, 220;* 6 c. in Test, *189;* 30 r. in over, *146;* 355 for 5th wkt, *150, 1048;* 294 v Eastern Province, *1048*.

R. Lamba (Ind.):– 320 v West Zone, *132, 1077*.

Lambert, W. (Sussex):– 107 and 157 v Epsom (1817), *136*.

Lancashire:– *339, 442-57;* Championship positions, *344-5;* Highest score, *166;* Highest individual score, *133;* in Jamaica, *1063, 1066;* Lowest score, *167;* Refuge Assurance Cup winners, *797;* Ward Knockout Cup, *655-6*.

Lancashire II, *820, 822, 828;* Warwick Under-25 finalists, *839*.

Lancashire League, 1988, *842-3*.

Lance, H. R. (SA):– 174 for 10th wkt, *152;* Test p'ship record, *223*.

Langley, G. R. A. (Aust.):– 21 d. in series, *188;* 9 d. in Test, *187*.

Langridge, James (Eng.):– All-round, *162;* 31,716 r., *141;* 1,000 r. (20), *139;* 42 hundreds, *138;* 1,530 w., *161*.

Langridge, J. G. (Sussex):– 34,380 r., *141;* 1,000 r. (17), *139;* 76 hundreds, *137;* 4 successive hundreds, *137;* 2 hundreds in match (2), *136;* 784 c., *166;* 69 c. in season, *166;* 490 for 1st wkt, *147, 148*.

Langton, A. B. C. (SA):– Test p'ship record, *207*.

Larkins, W. (Eng.):– 42 hundreds, *138*.

Larsen, G. R. (Wgtn):– 341 for 5th wkt, *150, 1069*.

Larwood, H. (Eng.):– 100 w. (8), *159;* 10 w. or more in Test (1), *201;* Test p'ship record, *201*.

Laver, F. (Aust.):– 8 w. in Test innings, *180*.

Lawrence, G. B. (SA):– 8 w. in Test innings, *181*.

Lawrence Trophy, *264*.

Lawry, W. M. (Aust.):– Test captain, *195, 221, 224, 229;* 18,734 r. (avge 50.90), *143;* 5,234 r. in Tests, *174;* 2,233 r. v England, *203;* 1,056 Test r. in year, *173;* 50 hundreds, *138;* 13 Test hundreds, *199, 222, 225, 230;* Carrying bat in Test (2), *178;* 382 for 1st wkt, *148;* Test p'ship records, *201, 226*.

Lawson, G. F. (Aust.):– 145 w. in Tests, *183;* 10 w. or more in Test (2), *202, 227;* 8 w. in Test innings, *181;* Test p'ship record, *233*.

League Cricket Conference:– v Sri Lankans, *315-6*.

Le Couteur, P. R. (OUCC):– 160 and 11 w. v Cambridge, *336*.

Lee, F. S. (Som.):– 1st wkt hundreds, *149*.

Lee, H. W. (Eng.):– Test début at 40, *192;* 37 hundreds, *138;* 2 hundreds in match (2), *136*.

Lee, J. W. (Som.):– 1st wkt hundreds, *149*.

Lees, W. K. (NZ):– 1 Test hundred, *245;* 8 d. in Test, *187;* Test p'ship record, *245*.

Leggat, I. B. (NZ):– 239 for 9th wkt, *151*.

Legge, G. B. (Eng.):– 1 Test hundred, *213*.

Leicestershire:– *339, 458-73;* Championship positions, *344-5;* Highest score, *166;* Highest individual score, *134;* in The Netherlands, *1102;* Lowest score, *167*.

Leicestershire II, *821, 822, 828-9*.

Lester, E. (Yorks.):– 2 hundreds in match (2), *136*.

Lever, J. K. (Eng.):– 1,696 w., *160;* 365 w. in Sunday League, *794;* 10 w. or more in Test (1), *217*.

Lever, P. (Eng.):– Test p'ship records, *214, 217*.

Leveson Gower, Sir H. D. G. (Eng.):– Test captain, *204*.

Lewis, A. R. (Eng.):– Test captain, *215, 218;* 1 Test hundred, *216;* 1st wkt hundreds, *149*.

Leyland, M. (Eng.):– 33,660 r., *141;* 2,764 r. in Tests, *174;* 1,000 r. (17), *139;* 8 hundreds, *137;* 9 Test hundreds, *197, 205;* Test p'ship record, *201*.

Lillee, D. K. (Aust.):– 355 w. in Tests, *183;* 167 w. v England, *203;* 103 w. in one-day ints, *257;* 39 w. in series, *182;* 10 w. or more in Test (7), *202, 227, 229, 233;* Test p'ship record, *233*.

Lilley, A. A. (Eng.):– Hit the ball twice, *153;* 84 d. v Australia, *203*.

Lilley, A. W. (Essex):– Hundred on début, *134*.

Lillywhite, James jun. (Eng.):– Test captain, *194;* 10 w. in innings, *153*.

Lincolnshire, *802-3, 812*.

Lindsay, D. T. (SA):– 3 Test hundreds, *22* 30 r. in over, *146;* 24 d. in series, *188;* 8 d. in Test, *187;* 6 d. in Test innings, *18* All-round in Test, *186;* Test p'ship record, *223, 235*.

Lindsay, N. V. (SA):– 221 for 9th wkt, *15*

Lindwall, R. R. (Aust.):– Test captain, *229* Test hundreds, *199, 225;* 228 w. in Tes

Lindwall, R. R. (Aust.):– *contd* *183;* 114 w. v England, *203;* All-round in Tests, *186.*

Linton, G. N. (B'dos):– Handled the ball, *152.*

Llewellyn, C. B. (SA):– All-round, *162;* 10 w. or more in Test (1), *223;* 2 hundreds in match (2), *136;* Test p'ship record, *223.*

Lloyd, C. H. (WI):– Test captain, *127, 208, 224, 236, 238, 240;* 110 Tests, *127, 193;* 31,232 r., *141;* 7,515 r. in Tests, *175;* 79 hundreds, *137;* 19 Test hundreds, *210, 226, 239, 241;* Fast scoring, *144, 179;* 161 for 9th wkt, *151, 240;* 335 for 5th wkt, *150;* Test p'ship records, *240, 241.*

.loyd, D. (Eng.):– 38 hundreds, *138;* Double-hundred v India, *216.*

.loyd, T. A. (Eng.):– Captain of Warwickshire, *572.*

.oader, P. J. (Eng.):– Hat-trick v West Indies, *185.*

.ock, G. A. R. (Eng.):– 2,844 w., *160;* 200 w. in season (2), *158;* 174 w. in Tests, *182;* 100 w. (14), *159;* 10 w. in innings, *154;* 10 w. or more in Test (3), *211, 214;* 4 hat-tricks, *157;* 831 c., *166;* 64 c. in season, *166;* 8 c. in match, *165.*

ockwood, W. H. (Eng.):– 10 w. or more in Test (1), *201;* 3 hat-tricks, *157.*

ogie, A. L. (WI):– 2 Test hundreds, *239.*

ohmann, G. A. (Eng.):– Hat-trick v South Africa, *185;* 1,841 w., *160;* 200 w. (3), *158;* 112 w. in Tests, *183;* 100 w. (8), *159;* 35 w. in series, *182;* 15 w. in Test, *181;* 10 w. or more in Test (5), *201-2, 207;* 9 w. in Test innings, *180;* 8 w. in Test innings (3), *180-1.*

ong, A. (Surrey and Sussex):– 1,046 d., *165;* 11 d. in match, *164;* 7 d. in innings, *163.*

ords and Commons cricket, 1988, *1264.*

ord's Cricket Ground:– *260-1;* Matches in 1988, *329-38.*

oughborough Students:– v Cambridge Univ., *633.*

ve, J. D. (Yorks.):– 10,000 r., *267.*

west innings totals:– in Tests, *191;* in one-day ints, *259;* in 1988, *267.*

west match aggregates, *168, 192.*

wry, T. C. (NZ):– Test captain, *212.*

xton, S. J. E. (Aust.):– 1 Test hundred, *222.*

ckhurst, B. W. (Eng.):– 48 hundreds, *138;* 2 Test hundreds, *216, 219.*

mb, R. G. (Yorks.):– 1st wkt hundreds, *149.*

ons, J. J. (Aust.):– 1 Test hundred, *199.*

M

.cartney, C. G. (Aust.):– 2,131 r. in Tests, *'75;* 49 hundreds, *138;* 7 Test hundreds, *'99, 222;* 4 successive hundreds, *137;* 2 hundreds in match (2), *136;* 345 v Nottinghamshire, *132, 133, 144;* 300 r. in 205 min., *144;* 51 boundaries in innings, *147;* 10 w. or more in Test (1), *202.*

Macaulay, G. G. (Eng.):– 1,837 w., *160;* 211 w. in season, *158;* 100 w. (10), *159;* 4 hat-tricks, *157;* Wkt with 1st ball on Test début, *184.*

McCabe, S. J. (Aust.):– 2,748 r. in Tests, *175;* 6 Test hundreds, *199, 222.*

McCool, C. L. (Aust.):– 1 Test hundred, *199.*

McCosker, R. B. (Aust.):– 4 Test hundreds, *199, 225, 232;* 2 hundreds in match (3), *136.*

McCubbin, G. R. (Tvl):– 221 for 9th wkt, *151.*

McDermott, C. J. (Aust.):– 8 w. in Test innings, *181;* Test p'ship record, *228.*

McDonald, C. C. (Aust.):– 3,107 r. in Tests, *175;* 5 Test hundreds, *199, 222, 225;* Test p'ship records, *223, 226.*

McDonald, E. A. (Aust.):– 205 w. in season, *158;* 3 hat-tricks, *157.*

McDonald's Bicentennial Youth World Cup, *1007-11.*

McDonald's Cup (Aust.), *1046-7.*

McDonnell, P. S. (Aust.):– Test captain, *194;* 3 Test hundreds, *199.*

McEwan, K. S. (Essex and W. Prov.):– 69 hundreds, *137.*

McGibbon, A. R. (NZ):– Test p'ship record, *243.*

McGirr, H. M. (NZ):– Oldest New Zealand Test début, *192.*

McGlew, D. J. (SA):– Test captain, *204, 221, 234;* 2,440 r. in Tests, *175;* 7 Test hundreds, *206, 222, 235;* Slow Test hundred, *180;* 255* v New Zealand, *171, 235;* Carrying bat in Test, *178;* Test p'ship records, *223, 235.*

McGregor, S. N. (NZ):– 1 Test hundred, *245;* Test p'ship record, *235.*

Mackay, K. D. (Aust.):– Slow batting in Test, *179;* Test p'ship records, *223, 226.*

Mackay-Coghill, D. (Tvl):– 174 for 10th wkt, *152.*

McKenzie, G. D. (Aust.):– 246 w. in Tests, *183;* 10 w. or more in Tests (3), *227, 231;* 8 w. in Test innings, *181;* Test p'ship records, *223, 230.*

MacLaren, A. C. (Eng.):– Test captain, *195-6;* Highest for Lancashire, *134;* 47 hundreds, *138;* 5 Test hundreds, *197;* 424 v Somerset, *132, 134;* 65 boundaries in innings, *147.*

Maclean, J. A. (Aust.):– 7 d. in innings, *163.*

McLean, R. A. (SA):– 2,120 r. in Tests, *175;* 5 Test hundreds, *206, 235;* Test p'ship records, *235.*

McLeod, C. E. (Aust.):– 1 Test hundred, *199.*

McLeod, K. W. (Lancs.):– 5 w. for 8 r. v Leicestershire, *288*.
McMorris, E. D. A. (WI):– 1 Test hundred, *239;* Test p'ship record, *240*.
McSweeney, E. B. (Wgtn):– 341 for 5th wkt, *150, 1069*.
McWatt, C. A. (WI):– Test p'ship record, *211*.
Madan Lal (Ind.):– Test p'ship records, *217, 249, 250*.
Madugalle, R. S. (SL):– Test captain, *220, 233;* 1 Test hundred, *250;* Test p'ship records, *250, 252*.
Mahmood Rashid (UBL):– Obstructing the field, *153*.
Mailey, A. A. (Aust.):– 36 w. in series, *182, 202;* 10 w. in innings, *154;* 10 w. or more in Test (2), *202;* 9 w. in Test innings, *180;* Test p'ship record, *201*.
Majid Khan (Pak.):– Test captain, *218;* 27,444 r., *142;* 3,931 r. in Tests, *176;* 73 hundreds, *137;* 8 Test hundreds, *232, 241, 245;* Fast Test hundred, *178;* 30 r. in over, *146;* 13 sixes in innings, *146;* 389 for 1st wkt, *148;* Test p'ship records, *233, 242, 246, 252*.
Makepeace, H. (Eng.):– 25,799 r., *142;* 43 hundreds, *138;* 1 Test hundred, *197*.
Mallett, A. A. (Aust.):– 132 w. in Tests, *183;* 10 w. or more in Test (1), *231;* 8 w. in Test innings, *181*.
Maninder Singh (Ind.):– Test cricket at 17, *192;* 10 w. or more in Test (2), *249, 251*.
Manjrekar, V. L. (Ind.):– 3,208 r. in Tests, *176;* 38 hundreds, *138;* 7 Test hundreds, *216, 239, 243;* Test p'ship records, *217, 244*.
Mankad, A. V. (Ind.):– 12,980 r. (avge 50.90), *143*.
Mankad, V. (Ind.):– Test captain, *238, 247;* 2,109 r. in Tests, *176;* 5 Test hundreds, *216, 230, 243;* 162 w. in Tests, *184;* 10 w. or more in Test (2), *217, 249;* 8 w. in Test innings (2), *181, 217, 249;* All-round in Tests, *186, 187;* 413 for 1st wkt v New Zealand, *148, 180, 244*.
Mann, A. L. (Aust.):– 1 Test hundred, *230*.
Mann, F. G. (Eng.):– Test captain, *204, 212;* 1 Test hundred, *205*.
Mann, F. T. (Eng.):– Test captain, *204*.
Mansoor Akhtar (Pak.):– 1 Test hundred, *232;* 561 for 1st wkt, *147, 148, 149;* 389 for 1st wkt, *148;* Test p'ship record, *233*.
Maqsood Kundi (MCB):– 196* for 10th wkt, *152*.
Marks, V. J. (Eng.):– Captain of Somerset, *523;* 10,000 r., *289;* Test p'ship record, *219*.
Marriott, C. S. (Eng.):– 10 w. or more in Test (1), *211*.
Marsh, G. R. (Aust.):– 3 Test hundreds, *199, 228, 230;* 5 one-day int. hundreds, *256;* Test p'ship records, *228, 230*.
Marsh, S. A. (Kent):– 222 for 7th wkt, *265*.
Marsh, R. W. (Aust.):– 3,633 r. in Tests, *174;* 96 Tests, *127, 193;* 52 consecutive Tests, *193;* 3 Test hundreds, *199, 228, 232;* 355 d. in Tests, *188;* 148 d. v England, *203;* 1,220 r. and 123 d. in one-day ints, *258*; 28 d., 26 d., 23 d. and 21 d. in series, *188;* 11 d. and 10 d. in match, *164;* 9 d. and 8 d. (4) in Test, *187;* 6 d. in Test innings, *187*.
Marshall, M. D. (WI):– 290 w. in Tests, *183*, 115 w. in one-day ints, *257;* 10 w. or more in Test (3), *212, 227, 237;* 35 w. in series, *182;* Most w. since 1969, *159;* All-round in Tests, *186;* Test p'ship records, *237, 240*.
Marshall, R. E. (WI):– 35,725 r., *141;* 1,000 r (18), *139;* 68 hundreds, *137;* Fastes hundred in GC/NWB, *678;* 1st wk hundreds, *149*.
Martin, F. (Eng.):– 10 w. or more in Test (1), *202;* 4 w. with consecutive balls, *156*.
Martin, F. R. (WI):– 1 Test hundred, *226*.
Martin, J. W. (Aust.):– Test p'ship records, *226, 230*.
Martindale, E. A. (WI):– 255 for 8th wkt, *151*.
Marx, W. F. E. (Tvl):– 240 on début, *135*.
Marylebone Cricket Club, The:– *328-31*; England honorary members, *338;* v Ireland, *650, 844;* v Scotland, *331, 847*.
MCC Schools v National Association of Young Cricketers, *336*.
MCC Schools Festival, 1988, *852-5*.
Masood Anwar (R'pindi):– 8 c. in matc *165*.
Masood Iqbal (HBL):– 7 d. in innings, *16*
Massie, H. H. (Aust.):– Test captain, *196*.
Massie, R. A. L. (Aust.):– 16 w. in Test, *18* *202;* 10 w. or more in Test (1), *202;* 8 w. Test innings (2), *181, 202;* Test p'shi record, *233*.
Matthews, F. C. L. (Notts.):– 17 w. in matc *155*.
Matthews, G. R. J. (Aust.):– 3 Test hundrec *228, 230;* 10 w. or more in Test (1), *23* Test p'ship records, *228, 233*.
Matthews, T. J. (Aust.):– Double hat-trick Test, *157, 185;* 4 hat-tricks, *157*.
May, P. B. H. (Eng.):– Test captain, *127, 1* *204, 208, 212, 215;* 27,592 r. (avge 51.0 *142, 143;* 4,537 r. in Tests, *174;* consecutive Tests, *193;* 85 hundreds, *13* 13 Test hundreds, *197, 205, 210, 212, 216* successive hundreds, *137;* 2 hundreds match (3), *136;* Hundred on Test déb *171, 205;* 285* v West Indies, *170, 2* Test p'ship record, *180, 211*.
Maynard, M. P. (Eng.):– Hundred on déb *134;* Hundred before lunch, *264;* 50 in min., *143, 287;* 30 r. in over, *145;* You Cricketer of the Year, *425*.

Aayne, E. R. (Aust.):– 456 for 1st wkt, *147, 148, 149*.
Aead, C. P. (Eng.):– 55,061 r., *141;* 3,179 r. in season, *139;* 1,000 r. (27), *139;* 665 Championship appearances, *263;* 153 hundreds, *137;* 13 hundreds in season, *137;* 4 Test hundreds, *197, 205;* 2 hundreds in match (3), *136;* Hundred and double-hundred, *135*.
Aead, W. (Eng.):– 1,916 w., *160;* 100 w. (10), *159;* 17 w. in match, *155*.
Aeckiff, I. (Aust.):– Test p'ship record, *223*.
Aedlycott, K. T. (Surrey):– Hundred on début, *134;* 8 w. in innings, *265*.
Aeetings in 1988:– ICC, *1221;* MCC, *328-9;* TCCB, *1221, 1222;* TCCB Discipline Committee, *1222*.
Aehra, M. (Ind. Rlwys):– Obstructing the field, *153*.
Aehra, V. L. (Ind.):– Test cricket at 17, *192*.
Aelville, A. (SA):– Test captain, *204;* 4 Test hundreds, *206;* 2 hundreds in same Test, *172, 206;* 299 for 7th wkt, *151;* Test p'ship record, *206*.
Aendis, G. D. (Lancs.):– Carrying bat in 1988, *265*.
Aendis, L. R. D. (SL):– Test captain, *127, 220, 233, 246, 249, 251;* 24 Tests, *127, 193;* 4 Test hundreds, *220, 250;* 2 hundreds in same Test, *172, 250;* Test p'ship records, *220, 234, 250, 252*.
ercer, J. (Sussex, Glam. and Northants):– 1,591 w., *160;* 100 w. (9), *159;* 10 w. in innings, *154*.
erchant, U. M. (Bombay):– 360 for 5th wkt, *150*.
erchant, V. M. (Ind.):– 13,248 r. (avge 71.22), *142;* 4 successive hundreds, *137;* 44 hundreds, *138;* 3 Test hundreds, *216;* 359* v Maharashtra, *132, 151;* 142 and hat-trick, *161;* 371 for 6th wkt, *151*.
errick, T. A. (Warwicks.):– 6 w. in 10 balls, *265;* Hat-trick in 1988, *266*.
tcalfe, A. A. (Yorks.):– 216* in 1988, *264;* Hundred on début, *134*.
tson, C. P. (Glam.):– 6 d. in innings, *266*.
ddlesex:– *339, 474-89;* Championship positions, *344-5;* Highest score, *166;* Highest individual score, *134;* Lowest score, *167;* NatWest Bank Trophy winners, *677-8*.
ddlesex II, *821, 822, 829-30*.
burn, C. (Eng.):– 2 Test hundreds, *209, 219;* Test p'ship record, *211*.
ler, G. (Eng.):– Slow batting in Test, *179*.
ler, K. R. (Aust.):– 2,958 r. in Tests, *175;* 41 hundreds, *138;* 7 Test hundreds, *199, 225;* 170 w. in Tests, *183;* 10 w. or more in Test (1), *202;* All-round in Tests, *185, 186;* Test p'ship records, *223, 226*.
Mills, J. E. (NZ):– Hundred on Test début, *171, 213;* 190* for 8th wkt, *151;* Test p'ship record, *214*.
Mills, P. T. (Glos.):– 5 w. for 0 r., *155*.
Milton, C. A. (Eng.):– 32,150 r., *141;* 1,000 r. (16), *139;* 56 hundreds, *138;* 2 hundreds in match (2), *136;* Hundred on Test début, *171, 213;* 758 c., *166;* 63 c. in season, *166;* 8 c. in match, *165*.
Milton, W. H. (SA):– Test captain, *204*.
Minor Counties:– *801-19;* B & H Cup, *682, 688;* Championship winners, *803;* Fixtures, 1989, *1263-4;* Formation, *262-3;* Highest individual scores, *261;* NWB Trophy, *680;* Representative body, *1220;* Umpires, *311;* v Sri Lankans, *318-9;* v West Indians, *302-3*.
Miran Bux (Pak.):– Test début at 47, *192;* Oldest Pakistan Test player, *193*.
Mitchell, A. (Eng.):– 44 hundreds, *138;* 4 successive hundreds, *137*.
Mitchell, B. (SA):– 3,471 r. in Tests, *175;* 8 Test hundreds, *206, 235;* 2 hundreds in same Test, *172, 206;* 6 c. in Test, *189;* 299 for 7th wkt, *151;* Test p'ship records, *206-7, 235*.
Mitchell, F. (Eng. and SA):– Test captain, *204, 221*.
Mitchell, T. B. (Eng.):– 100 w. (10), *159;* 10 w. in innings, *154*.
Modi, R. S. (Ind.):– 1 Test hundred, *239;* 410 for 3rd wkt, *150;* 371 for 6th wkt, *151*.
Mohammad Farooq (Pak.):– Test p'ship record, *246*.
Mohammad Ilyas (Pak.):– 1 Test hundred, *245;* Test p'ship record, *246*.
Mohammad Iqbal (Muslim Model HS):– 475* v Islamia HS, *261*.
Mohapatra, S. (Orissa):– Hat-trick, *157, 1077*.
Mohol, S. N. (M'tra):– 4 w. with consecutive balls, *156*.
Mohsin Khan (Pak.):– 2,709 r. in Tests, *176;* 1,029 Test r. in year, *173;* 7 Test hundreds, *219, 232, 248, 251;* Handled the ball, *152;* 426 for 2nd wkt, *149;* Test p'ship records, *219, 233, 252*.
Mold, A. W. (Eng.):– 1,673 w., *160;* 200 w. (2), *158;* 100 w. (9), *159;* 4 w. with consecutive balls, *156*.
Moles, A. J. (Warwicks.):– Carrying bat in 1988, *265*.
Moloney, D. A. R. (NZ):– Test p'ship record, *214*.
Monkhouse, S. (Warwicks. and Glam.):– Career figures, *681*.
Mooney, F. L. H. (NZ):– Test p'ship record, *214*.
Moore, R. H. (Hants):– Highest for Hampshire, *134;* 316 v Warwickshire, *132, 134*.

More, K. S. (Ind.):– 5 st. in Test innings, *187, 958;* 6 st. in Test, *187, 958.*
Morgan, H. E. (Glam.):– 254 v Monmouthshire, *261.*
Morkel, D. P. B. (SA):– 222 for 8th wkt, *151.*
Moroney, J. R. (Aust.):– 2 hundreds in same Test, *172, 222.*
Morris, A. R. (Aust.):– Test captain, *196, 224;* 12,614 r. (avge 53.67), *143;* 3,533 r. in Tests, *174;* 2,080 r. v England, *203;* 46 hundreds, *138;* 12 Test hundreds, *199, 222, 225, 230;* 2 hundreds in same Test, *172, 199;* 2 hundreds in match (2), *136;* 148 and 111 on début, *135;* Test p'ship record, *230.*
Morris, H. (Glam.):– Captain of Glamorgan, *377.*
Morrison, J. F. M. (NZ):– 1 Test hundred, *228.*
Mortimore, J. B. (Eng.):– All-round, *162;* 1,807 w., *160.*
Moss, A. E. (Cant.):– 10 w. in innings on début, *153.*
Moss, J. K. (Aust.):– 390* for 3rd wkt, *150.*
Motz, R. C. (NZ):– 100 w. in Tests, *184.*
Moxon, M. D. (Yorks.):– Hundred on début, *134.*
Mudassar Nazar (Pak.):– 3,991 r. in Tests, *176;* 41 hundreds, *138;* 10 Test hundreds, *219, 245, 248;* Slowest Test hundred, *180;* 761 r. in series, *173;* Carrying bat in Test, *178;* 107 w. in one-day ints, *257;* All-round in one-day ints, *258;* Average of 82.50 in English season, *140;* 451 for 3rd wkt, *147;* 389 for 1st wkt, *148;* Test p'ship records, *219, 246, 249, 252.*
Murdoch, W. L. (Aust. and Eng.):– Test captain, *194-6;* 2 Test hundreds, *199;* 321 v Victoria, *132.*
Murray, A. R. A. (SA):– 1 Test hundred, *235;* Test p'ship record, *235.*
Murray, B. A. G. (NZ):– Test p'ship record, *243.*
Murray, D. A. (WI):– 10 d. in match, *164;* 9 d. in Test, *187.*
Murray, D. L. (WI):– Test captain, *223;* 189 d. in Tests, *188;* 24 d. in series, *188;* Test p'ship records, *226, 240, 241.*
Murray, J. T. (Eng.):– 1,025 r. and 104 d. in season, *163;* 1 Test hundred, *209;* Slow batting in Test, *179;* 1,527 d., *165;* 100 d. in season (2), *165;* 6 d. in Test innings, *187;* Test p'ship record, *211.*
Mushtaq Ali (Ind.):– 2 Test hundreds, *216, 239.*
Mushtaq Mohammad (Pak.):– Test captain, *231, 240, 241, 247;* Youngest Test player, *192;* 31,091 r., *141;* 3,643 r. in Tests, *176;* 1,000 r. (15), *139;* 72 hundreds, *137;* 10 Test hundreds, *219, 232, 241, 245, 248;* 303* v Karachi Univ., *133;* All-round in Tests, *186;* 350 for 4th wkt, *150;* Test p'ship records, *219, 242, 246.*
Mycroft, W. (Derbys.):– 17 w. in match, *155*

N

Nadeem Yousuf (MCB):– 196* for 10th wkt, *152.*
Nadkarni, R. G. (Ind.):– 1 Test hundred, *216;* 10 w. or more in Test (1), *231;* Test p'ship records, *217, 244.*
Nagarwalla, N. D. (M'tra):– 245 for 9th wkt, *151.*
Nanan, R. (WI):– Test p'ship record, *241;* 200 w. in WI domestic cricket, *1062.*
Nash, G. (Lancs.):– 4 w. with consecutive balls, *156.*
Nasim-ul-Ghani (Pak.):– Test début at 16, *192;* 1 Test hundred, *219;* Test p'ship record, *219.*
National Association of Young Cricketers:– v MCC Schools, *336.*
National Club Championship, *337, 653-4.*
National Cricket Association:– *279;* Address, *1220;* Young Cricketers v Combined Services, *337.*
National Village Championship, *337-8, 65*
NatWest Bank Trophy:– *658-81;* Fixtures 1989, *1257-60;* Rules, *1215-7.*
Nayudu, C. K. (Ind.):– Test captain, *215;* 1 sixes in innings, *146.*
Nazar Mohammad (Pak.):– 1 Test hundred, *248;* Carrying bat in Test, *178.*
Neale, P. A. (Worcs.):– Captain of Worcestershire, *588;* Cricketer of the Year, *55-7.*
Needham, A. (Surrey and Middx):– Career figures, *681.*
Netherlands, The, Cricket in, *1101-2.*
Netherlands XI:– v MCC, *331;* in New Zealand, *1101.*
Newell, M. (Notts.):– Carrying bat in 198 *265;* 345 for 4th wkt, *265.*
Newham, W. (Eng.):– 344 for 7th wkt, *15*
Newman, J. A. (Hants):– All-round, *16* 2,032 w., *160;* 100 w. (9), *159.*
Newman, P. G. (Derbys.):– 8 w. in innings, *265.*
Newport, P. J. (Eng.):– 205 for 7th wkt, *26* 8 w. in innings, *265.*
New South Wales:– in Zimbabwe, *1099-1*
New Zealand:– B & H World Series Cu *992-1002;* Definition of first-class match *1212;* Domestic season 1987-88, *1068-7* Highest individual Test innings, *17* Highest Test innings, *190;* Leading batsmen in Tests, *176;* Leading bowlers Tests, *184;* Lowest Test innings, *191;* M consecutive Test appearances, *193;* M Test appearances, *127;* Most Test appearances as captain, *127;* New Zealand in T cricket (*see p. 131*); Representative bo

New Zealand:– *contd*
1219; Sharjah Cup, *1003-6;* Summary of Tests, *194;* Test cricketers (1929-88), *114-8;* Youngest and Oldest on Test début, *192.*
Nicholas, M. C. J. (Hants):– Captain of Hampshire, *409;* 10,000 r., *267.*
Nicholls, R. B. (Glos.):– 1,000 r. (15), *139;* 395 for 1st wkt, *148.*
Nichols, M. S. (Eng.):– All-round, *162;* 1,833 w., *160;* 100 w. (11), *159.*
Nicolson, J. F. W. (Natal):– 424 for 1st wkt, *148, 149.*
Nimbalkar, B. B. (M'tra):– 443* v Western Indian States, *132, 149;* 50 boundaries in innings, *147;* 455 for 2nd wkt, *147, 149.*
Nissan Shield (SA), *1057-8.*
Noble, M. A. (Aust.):– Test captain, *194;* 37 hundreds, *138;* 1 Test hundred, *199;* 121 w. in Tests, *183;* 10 w. or more in Test (2), *202;* All-round in Tests, *186;* 428 for 6th wkt, *150.*
Noreiga, J. M. (WI):– 9 w. in Test innings, *180.*
Norfolk, *802, 803, 813;* v Cambridge Univ., *637.*
Northamptonshire:– *339, 490-506;* Championship positions, *344-5;* Highest score, *166;* Highest individual score, *134;* Lowest score, *167;* Tilcon Trophy, *649-50.*
Northamptonshire II, *821, 822, 830-1.*
Northumberland, *802, 803, 813-4.*
Nottinghamshire:– *339, 507-22;* Championship positions, *344-5;* Highest score, *166;* Highest individual score, *133;* Lowest score, *167.*
Nottinghamshire II, *821, 822, 831-2.*
Nourse, A. D. (SA):– Test captain, *204, 221;* 12,472 r. (avge 51.53), *143;* 2,960 r. (avge 53.81) in Tests, *175, 177;* 621 r. in series, *207;* 41 hundreds, *138;* 9 Test hundreds, *206, 222;* Test p'ship record, *206.*
Nourse, A. W. (SA):– Handled the ball, *152;* Oldest South African Test player, *193;* 2,234 r. in Tests, *175;* 38 hundreds, *138;* 1 Test hundred, *222;* 304* v Transvaal, *133;* 53 boundaries in innings, *147;* Test p'ship records, *223.*
Nunes, R. K. (WI):– Test captain, *208.*
Nupen, E. P. (SA):– Test captain, *204;* 10 w. or more in Test (1), *207;* Test p'ship record, *207.*
Nurse, S. M. (WI):– 2,523 r. in Tests, *175;* 6 Test hundreds, *210, 226, 236;* 258 v New Zealand, *171, 236;* Test p'ship record, *211.*

O

Oates, T. W. (Notts.):– 10 d. in match, *164.*
O'Brien, J. F. M. (Cheshire):– Hat-trick in NWB Trophy in 1988, *667, 679.*
O'Brien, Sir T. C. (Eng.):– Test captain, *204.*
Ochse, A. E. (SA):– Youngest South African Test player, *192.*
O'Connor, J. (Eng.):– 28,764 r., *142;* 1,000 r. (16), *139;* 72 hundreds, *137*
O'Keeffe, K. J. (Aust.):– Test p'ship records, *228, 233.*
Old, C. M. (Eng.):– Fast scoring, *143;* 143 w. in Tests, *182;* 4 w. in 5 balls v Pakistan, *220.*
Oldest players on Test début, *192.*
Oldest Test players, *193.*
Oldfield, N. (Eng.):– 38 hundreds, *138.*
Oldfield, W. A. (Aust.):– 130 d. in Tests, *188;* 90 d. v England, *203.*
Oldroyd, E. (Yorks.):– 36 hundreds, *138.*
O'Neill, N. C. (Aust.):– 13,859 r. (avge 50.95), *143;* 2,779 r. in Tests, *175;* 45 hundreds, *138*; 6 Test hundreds, *199, 225, 230, 232.*
O'Reilly, W. J. (Aust.):– 144 w. in Tests, *183;* 102 w. v England, *203;* 10 w. or more in Test (3), *202;* Test p'ship record, *223.*
Ormiston, R. W. (Wgtn):– 226 for 6th wkt, *151.*
O'Shaughnessy, S. J. (Lancs. and Worcs.):– Hundred in 35 minutes, *143-4.*
Over-rates in County Championship, *1106.*
Owen-Smith, H. G. (SA):– 1 Test hundred, *206;* Test p'ship record, *207.*
Oxford v Cambridge, *333-6.*
Oxford & Cambridge Universities:– v West Indians, *299-300;* in B & H Cup, *711.*
Oxford University 1988:– *621-30;* Blues, *641-4.*
Oxfordshire, *801, 803, 814.*

P

Page, M. L. (NZ):– Test captain, *212, 234;* 1 Test hundred, *213.*
Pairaudeau, B. H. (WI):– Hundred on Test début, *171, 239;* Test p'ship record, *240.*
Pakistan:– Definition of first-class matches, *1212;* Domestic season 1987-88, *1188-97;* Highest individual Test innings, *170;* Highest Test innings, *189;* Leading batsmen in Tests, *176;* Leading bowlers in Tests, *184;* Lowest Test innings, *191;* Most Test appearances, *127;* Most Test appearances as captain, *127;* Oldest Test player, *193;* Pakistan in Test cricket (*see p. 131*); Representative body, *1219;* Summary of Tests, *194;* Test cricketers (1952-88), *122-5;* Youngest and oldest on Test début, *192.*
Pakistan v Australia, 1988-89, *1097.*
Palmer, G. E. (Aust.):– 10 w. or more in Test (2), *202.*
Palmer, G. V. (Som.):– Career figures, *681.*
Pandya, A. (S'tra):– Handled the ball, *152.*

Parfitt, P. H. (Eng.):– 26,924 r., *142;* 1,000 r. (15), *139;* 58 hundreds, *138;* 7 Test hundreds, *205, 213, 216, 219;* 2 hundreds in match (2) *136;* Test p'ship records, *214, 219.*

Parkar, G. A. (Ind.):– 421 for 1st wkt, *148.*

Parkar, Z. (Bombay):– 10 d. in match, *164.*

Parker, C. W. L. (Glos.):– 3,278 w., *159;* 200 w. (5), *158;* 100 w. (16), *159;* 100 w. by June 12, *159;* 17 w. in match, *155;* 10 w. in innings, *154;* 6 hat-tricks, *157;* Double hat-trick, *157.*

Parker, J. M. (NZ):– Test captain, *244;* 3 Test hundreds, *213, 228, 243;* Test p'ship records, *228.*

Parker, P. W. G. (Eng.):– Captain of Sussex, *556;* 36 hundreds, *138;* 32 r. in over, *145.*

Parkhouse, W. G. A. (Eng.):– 1,000 r. (15), *139.*

Parkin, C. H. (Eng.):– 200 w. (2), *158.*

Parkinson's World XI, M.:– v MCC, *654-5;* v Yorkshire, *655.*

Parks, H. W. (Sussex):– 42 hundreds, *138.*

Parks, J. H. (Eng.):– All-round, *162;* 3,003 r. in season, *139*; 41 hundreds, *138.*

Parks, J. M. (Eng.):– 36,673 r., *141;* 1,000 r. (20), *139;* 51 hundreds, *138;* 2 Test hundreds, *205, 209;* 1,181 d., *165;* 114 d. in Tests, *188;* 8 d. in Test, *187;* Test p'ship records, *206, 211.*

Parks, R. J. (Hants):– 10 d. in match, *164.*

Parsons, Rev. J. H. (Warwicks.):– 38 hundreds, *138.*

Partnerships:– First-wicket, *148;* Highest, *147;* Highest for each country, *149-52;* Highest in one-day ints, *256;* Highest in Tests, *180* (*see individual series for records v countries*)*;* In 1988, *265.*

Passailaigue, C. C. (WI):– 487* for 6th wkt, *147, 150.*

Pataudi (sen.), Nawab of (Eng. and Ind.):– Test captain, *215;* 4 successive hundreds, *137;* Hundred on Test début, *171, 197.*

Pataudi (jun.), Nawab of (Ind.):– Test captain, *127, 215, 229, 238, 242;* 2,793 r. in Tests, *176;* 6 Test hundreds, *216, 230, 243;* 2 hundreds in match (2), *136;* Slow batting in Test, *179.*

Patel, B. P. (Ind.):– 37 hundreds, *138;* 1 Test hundred, *239;* Test p'ship records, *240, 244.*

Patel, J. M. (Ind.):– 14 w. in Test, *182, 231;* 9 w. in Test innings, *180, 231.*

Patil, S. M. (Ind.):– 4 Test hundreds, *216, 230, 248;* Test p'ship record, *249, 250.*

Patron's Trophy (Pak.), *1088, 1091-2.*

Patterson, B. M. W. (Scotland):– Hundred on début, *134, 264, 652, 847.*

Paynter, E. (Eng.):– 653 r. in series, *207;* 45 hundreds, *138;* 4 Test hundreds, *197, 205;* 2 hundreds in match (2), *136;* 2 hundreds ir same Test, *172, 205;* 322 v Sussex, *132* Test avge of 59.23, *177;* Test p'shi records, *201.*

Payton, W. R. D. (Notts.):– 39 hundreds *138.*

Peach, H. A. (Surrey):– Fast scoring, *144;* w. with consecutive balls, *156.*

Pearse, D. K. (Natal):– Handled the bal *152.*

Pearson, A. J. G. (CUCC and Som.):– 10 w in innings, *154.*

Peate, E. (Eng.):– 214 w. in season, *158;* 8 w for 5 r., *155.*

Peel, R. (Eng.):– 1,753 w., *160;* 102 w. i Tests, *183;* 100 w. (8), *159;* 10 w. or more i Test (2), *202;* 292 for 8th wkt, *151.*

Pegler, S. J. (SA):– Test p'ship record, *22*

Pellew, C. E. (Aust.):– 2 Test hundreds, *19*

Perks, R. T. D. (Worcs.):– 2,233 w., *160;* 10 w. (16), *159.*

Perrin, P. A. (Essex):– Highest for Esse *134;* 29,709 r., *142;* 1,000 r. (18), *139;* hundreds, *138;* 2 hundreds in match (4 *136;* 343* v Derbyshire, *132, 134;* 6 boundaries in innings, *147.*

Pervez Akhtar (Pak. Rlwys):– 337* v De Ismail Khan, *132.*

Petherick, P. J. (NZ):– Hat-trick v Pakista *185.*

Phadkar, D. G. (Ind.):– 2 Test hundreds, *21* *230.*

Philip, I. L. (Scotland):– Hundred on débu *134.*

Phillips, H. (Sussex):– 10 d. in match, *16*

Phillips, R. B. (Qld):– 7 d. in innings, *16*

Phillips, W. B. (Aust.):– Hundred on T début, *172, 232;* 2 Test hundreds, *225, 23* 462* for 4th wkt, *147, 150;* Test p'sh records, *228, 233.*

Pickett, H. (Essex):– 10 w. in innings, *15*

Pinch, C. (S. Aust.):– 2 hundreds in mat (2), *136.*

Pithey, A. J. (SA):– 1 Test hundred, *206;* T p'ship record, *207.*

Place, W. (Eng.):– 36 hundreds, *138;* 1 T hundred, *209.*

Playle, W. R. (NZ):– Slow Test batting, *1*

Pocock, P. I. (Eng.):– 1,607 w., *160;* 5 w. i balls, *157;* 4 w. with consecutive balls, *1* Test p'ship record, *211.*

Pollard, V. (NZ):– 2 Test hundreds, *2* Test p'ship records, *214, 237, 243.*

Pollock, P. M. (SA):– 116 w. in Tests, *183;* w. or more in Test (1), *207;* Test p's records, *223, 235.*

Pollock, R. G. (SA):– Handled the ball, *1* 20,940 r. (avge 54.67), *143;* 2,256 r. (a 60.97) in Tests, *175, 177;* 64 hundreds, *1* 7 Test hundreds, *206, 222;* 2 hundreds

Pollock, R. G. (SA):– *contd*
match (2), *136;* 274 v Australia, *170, 222;* 341 for 3rd wkt, *150;* Test p'ship records, *223.*
Ponsford, W. H. (Aust.):– 13,819 r. (avge 65.18), *142;* 2,122 r. in Tests, *175;* 47 hundreds, *138;* 7 Test hundreds, *199-200, 225;* Hundred on Test début, *171;* 437 v Queensland, *132;* 429 v Tasmania, *132;* 352 v New South Wales, *132;* 336 v South Australia, *132;* 334 r. in day, *144;* 281* at Lord's, *260;* 266 v England, *170, 199;* 456 for 1st wkt, *147, 148;* 375 for 1st wkt, *148;* 451 for 2nd wkt, *147, 149, 180, 201;* Test p'ship records, *180, 201.*
Pooley, E. (Surrey):– 12 d. and 10 d. in matches, *164.*
Poore, M. B. (NZ):– Test p'ship record, *235.*
Poore, R. M. (Hants):– 304 v Somerset, *133, 151;* Avge of 91.23 in English season, *140;* 411 for 6th wkt, *151.*
Popplewell, N. F. M. (Som.):– Hundred in 41 minutes, *143.*
Pougher, A. D. (Eng.):– 5 w. for 0 r., *155.*
Powell, J. L. (Cant.):– 265 for 7th wkt, *151.*
Prasanna, E. A. S. (Ind.):– 189 w. in Tests, *184;* 10 w. or more in Tests (2), *231, 244;* 8 w. in Test innings, *181, 244.*
Price, W. F. F. (Eng.):– 7 d. in innings, *163.*
Prideaux, R. M. (Eng.):– 25,136 r., *142;* 41 hundreds, *138;* 2 hundreds in match (2), *136;* 1st wkt hundreds, *149.*
ringle, D. R. (Eng.):– 259 for 4th wkt, *265.*
ritchard, T. L. (Warwicks.):– 3 hat-tricks, *157.*
rocter, M. J. (SA):– 48 hundreds, *138;* 6 successive hundreds, *136;* Hundred and hat-trick (2), *162;* 4 hat-tricks, *157;* LBW hat-trick (2), *157.*
rodger, J. M. (Kent):– 8 c. in match, *165.*
rout, J. A. (Wesley Coll.):– 459 v Geelong College, *261.*
ıblic Schools, highest score, *260.*
ıllar, G. (Eng.):– 41 hundreds, *138;* 4 Test hundreds, *205, 216, 219;* Test p'ship record, *219.*

Q

ısim Omar (Pak.):– 3 Test hundreds, *232, 248, 251;* 2 hundreds in match (2), *136;* Hundred and double-hundred, *135;* Test p'ship records, *233, 249, 252.*
ıaid-e-Azam Trophy (Pak.), *1088-9, 1092-7.*
ıaife, W. G. (Eng.):– 36,012 r., *141;* 1,000 r. (24), *139;* 72 hundreds, *137.*
alification of players for England, *1213, 1222.*
ıirk, T. (N. Tvl):– Obstructing the field, *153.*

R

Rabone, G. O. (NZ):– Test captain, *212, 234;* 1 Test hundred, *235;* Test p'ship record, *235.*
Rackemann, C. G. (Aust.):– 10 w. or more in Test (1), *233.*
Radford, N. V. (Eng.):– 113 for 9th wkt, *265.*
Radley, C. T. (Eng.):– 26,441 r., *142;* 6,650 r. in Sunday League, *793;* 1,000 r. (16), *139;* 46 hundreds, *138;* 2 Test hundreds, *213, 219;* Slow batting in Test, *179;* 500 c., *266;* 90 c. in Sunday League, *795.*
Rae, A. F. (WI):– 4 Test hundreds, *210, 239.*
Raiji, M. N. (Bombay):– 360 for 5th wkt, *150.*
Raja Sarfraz (R'pindi):– 240 for 8th wkt, *151.*
Ramadhin, S. (WI):– Most balls in single innings, *185;* Most balls in Test match, *185;* 188 w. in Tests, *183;* 10 w. or more in Test (1), *212;* Test p'ship record, *235.*
Ramaswami, C. (Ind.):– Test début at 40, *192.*
Ramchand, G. S. (Ind.):– Test captain, *229;* 2 Test hundreds, *230, 243;* Test p'ship record, *244.*
Ramiz Raja (Pak.):– 2 Test hundreds, *248, 251;* Slow scoring in Test, *179;* Test p'ship record, *252.*
Ramprakash, M. R. (Middx):– Man of the Match in NWB Trophy final, *677.*
Ranasinghe, A. N. (SL):– Test p'ship record, *250.*
Ranatunga, A. (SL):– 24 Tests, *127, 193;* 2 Test hundreds, *250, 251;* 1,354 r. in Tests, *176;* 739 r. in SL season, *140;* Test p'ship records, *234, 250, 252.*
Randall, D. W. (Eng.):– 2,470 r. in Tests, *174;* 41 hundreds, *138;* 7 Test hundreds, *197, 213, 216, 219;* Hundred and double-hundred, *135;* 237 in 1988, *264;* 345 for 4th wkt, *265;* Test p'ship record, *217.*
Rangnekar, K. M. (Ind.):– 274 for 7th wkt, *151.*
Ranji Trophy (Ind.), *1076-7, 1079-86.*
Ranjitsinhji, K. S. (HH the Jam Sahib of Nawanagar) (Eng.):– 24,692 r. (avge 56.37), *143;* 3,159 r. in season, *139;* 72 hundreds, *137;* 2 Test hundreds, *197;* Hundred on Test début, *171, 197;* Avge of 87.57 in English season, *140;* 344 for 7th wkt, *151.*
Ransford, V. S. (Aust.):– 1 Test hundred, *200;* Test p'ship records, *223.*
Rao, J. S. (Ind. Serv.):– Double hat-trick, *157;* 3 hat-tricks, *157.*
Rashid Israr (HBL):– 350 v National Bank, *132.*
Rashid Khan (Pak.):– Test p'ship records, *252.*
Ratnayake, R. J. (SL):– 9 w. in Test, *182;* Test p'ship records, *252.*

Ratnayeke, J. R. (SL):– 8 w. in Test innings, *181;* Test p'ship records, *250, 252.*

Read, W. W. (Eng.):– Test captain, *195, 204;* 338 v Oxford Univ., *132;* 38 hundreds, *138;* 1 Test hundred, *198;* Test p'ship record, *201.*

Record hit, *262.*

Red Stripe Cup (WI):– *1061-6.*

Redmond, R. E. (NZ):– Hundred on Test début, *171, 245;* Test p'ship record, *245.*

Redpath, I. R. (Aust.):– 4,737 r. in Tests, *174;* 8 Test hundreds, *200, 225, 228, 232;* Carrying bat in Test, *178;* 32 r. in over, *146.*

Refuge Assurance Cup:– *795-7;* 1989 Fixtures, *1260;* Rules, *1215-6, 1219.*

Refuge Assurance (Sunday) League:– *712-95;* 1989 Fixtures, *1261-2;* Rules, *1215-6, 1217-8.*

Registration of players, *1213-4.*

Reid, B. R. (Aust.):– Hat-trick in one-day int., *257.*

Reid, J. F. (NZ):– 6 Test hundreds, *228, 243, 245, 247;* Test p'ship records, *228, 245, 247.*

Reid, J. R. (NZ):– Test captain, *127, 212, 234, 236, 242, 244;* 3,428 r. in Tests, *176;* 2,188 r. in overseas season, *140;* 1,915 r. in South African season, *140;* 58 consecutive Tests, *193;* 39 hundreds, *138;* 6 Test hundreds, *213, 235, 243, 245;* 50 boundaries in innings, *147;* 15 sixes in innings, *146;* 324 for 4th wkt, *150;* Test p'ship records, *214, 235, 243, 245.*

Relations in Test cricket, *254-5.*

Relf, A. E. (Eng.):– All-round, *162;* 1,897 w., *160;* 100 w. (11), *159.*

Representative Bodies, Addresses, *1219-20.*

Rest of the World v England:– *221;* England players, *127.*

Rhodes, A. E. G. (Derbys.):– 5 hat-tricks, *157.*

Rhodes, S. J. (Worcs.):– 265 for 6th wkt, *265;* 6 d. in innings, *266;* 29 d. in Sunday League season, *794;* 4 st. in Sunday League innings, *795.*

Rhodes, W. (Eng.):– All-round, *162, 163;* All-round in Tests, *186;* Oldest Test player, *193;* 39,802 r., *141;* 2,325 r. in Tests, *174;* 1,000 r. (21), *139;* 763 Championship appearances, *263;* 58 hundreds, *138;* 2 hundreds in match (2), *136;* 2 Test hundreds, *198, 205;* 4,187 w., *159;* 200 w. (3), *158;* 127 w. in Tests, *182;* 109 w. v Australia, *203;* 100 w. (23), *159;* 15 Australian w. in match, *181, 201;* 10 w. or more in Test (1), *202;* 8 w. in Test innings, *181, 201;* 764 c., *166;* Test p'ship records, *201.*

Rice, C. E. B. (Notts. and Tvl):– 6,265 r. in Sunday League, *793;* 47 hundreds, *138;* Most r. in Sunday League season, *793;* Most w. in Sunday League season, *794.*

Rice, J. M. (Hants):– Record c. in Sunday League, *795.*

Richards, A. R. (SA):– Test captain, *204.*

Richards, B. A. (SA):– 28,358 r. (avge 54.74), *142, 143;* 1,000 r. (15), *139;* 80 hundreds, *137;* 2 Test hundreds, *222;* 2 hundreds in match (2), *136;* 356 v Western Australia, *132;* 325* in day, *144.*

Richards, C. J. (Eng.):– 1 Test hundred, *197;* 10 d. in match, *164;* 6 d. in innings, *266.*

Richards, I. V. A. (WI):– Test captain, *208* *224, 236, 238, 240;* 61 consecutive Tests, *193;* Highest for Somerset, *134;* 30,591 r., *141, 267;* 7,268 r. (avge 52.66) in Tests, *175* *177;* 5,869 r. in one-day ints, *256;* 1,71[illegible] Test r. in year, *173;* 1,000 r. (15), *139;* 829 r in series, *172;* 98 hundreds, *137;* 22 Tes[illegible] hundreds, *177, 210, 226, 236, 239, 241* 11 one-day int. hundreds, *256;* 322 [illegible] Warwickshire, *132, 134, 144;* 291 [illegible] England, *170, 210;* Fast scoring, *178, 179* Highest one-day int. score, *256;* 5[illegible] boundaries in innings, *147;* 26 sixes i[illegible] Sunday League season, *793;* 72 c. in one[illegible] day ints, *258;* 227 for 6th wkt, *265;* Te[illegible] p'ship records, *226, 237, 240.*

Richardson, A. J. (Aust.):– 280 v MCC, *133* 1 Test hundred, *200.*

Richardson, D. W. (Eng.):– 65 c. in seaso[illegible] *166.*

Richardson, P. E. (Eng.):– 26,055 r., *142* 2,061 r. in Tests, *173;* 44 hundreds, *138;* Test hundreds, *198, 205, 210, 213;* Slo[illegible] Test hundred, *180;* Test p'ship record, *21[illegible]*

Richardson, R. B. (WI):– 2,173 r. in Test *175;* 6 Test hundreds, *210, 226, 236;* Te[illegible] p'ship records, *226, 237.*

Richardson, T. (Eng.):– 2,104 w., *160;* 1,0[illegible] w. in four seasons, *159;* 200 w. (3), *158;* 1[illegible] w. (10), *159;* 10 w. or more in Test ([illegible] *201-2;* 10 w. in innings, *153;* 8 w. [illegible] Test innings, *181;* 4 hat-tricks, *157.*

Richardson, V. Y. (Aust.):– Test captai[illegible] *221;* 1 Test hundred, *200;* 6 c. in Test, *18[illegible]* 5 c. in Test innings, *188.*

Ridgway, F. (Eng.):– 4 w. with consecuti[illegible] balls, *156.*

Rigg, K. E. (Aust.):– 1 Test hundred, *22[illegible]*

Ripley, D. (Northants):– 6 d. in innings, *26[illegible]*

Ritchie, G. M. (Aust.):– 3 Test hundre[illegible] *200, 230, 232;* Slow Test batting, *179;* T[illegible] p'ship record, *228.*

Rixon, S. J. (Aust.):– 22 d. in series, *188;* 1[illegible] in match (2), *164.*

Rizwan-uz-Zaman (Pak.):– 2 hundreds [illegible] match (2), *136.*

Roach, C. A. (WI):– Obituary, *1174-5;* Test hundreds, *210.*

Roberts, A. M. E. (WI):– 202 w. in Tests, *183;* 10 w. or more in Test (2), *212, 240;* 161 for 9th wkt, *151, 240;* Test p'ship records, *226, 240.*
Roberts, A. W. (NZ):– Test p'ship record, *214.*
Robertson, J. D. (Eng.):– Highest for Middlesex, *134;* 31,914 r., *141;* 1,000 r. (15), *139;* 67 hundreds, *137;* 2 Test hundreds, *210, 213;* 331* v Worcestershire, *132, 134;* 331 r. in day, *144;* 1st wkt hundreds, *149.*
Robins, R. W. V. (Eng.):– Test captain, *212;* 1 Test hundred, *205.*
Robinson, R. T. (Eng.):– Captain of Nottinghamshire, *507;* 4 Test hundreds, *198, 216, 219;* Test p'ship record, *217.*
Roebuck, P. M. (Som.):– Captain of Somerset, *523.*
Roller, W. E. (Surrey):– 204 and hat-trick v Sussex, *161.*
Root, C. F. (Eng.):– 1,512 w., *161;* 219 w. in season, *158;* 100 w. (9), *159.*
owan, E. A. B. (SA):– 3 Test hundreds, *206, 222;* 306* v Natal, *133;* 342 for 4th wkt, *150;* Test p'ship record, *206.*
owe, L. G. (WI):– 2,047 r. in Tests, *175;* 7 Test hundreds, *210, 226, 236;* 4 successive hundreds, *137;* 2 hundreds on Test début, *135, 171-2, 236;* Hundred and double-hundred, *135, 136;* 302 v England, *133, 170, 210;* Test p'ship records, *211, 226, 237.*
oy, Pankaj (Ind.):– Test captain, *215;* 2,442 r. in Tests, *176;* 5 Test hundreds, *216, 239, 243;* 4 successive hundreds, *137;* 2 hundreds in match (2), *136;* 413 for 1st wkt v New Zealand, *148, 180, 244.*
in-rates in County Championship, *1106.*
ishby, T. (Surrey):– 10 w. in innings, *154.*
issell, A. C. (Eng.):– 27,358 r., *142;* 71 hundreds, *137;* 5 Test hundreds, *198, 205;* 2 hundreds in match (3), *136;* 2 hundreds in same Test, *172, 205;* Test p'ship record, *206.*
ssell, R. C. (Eng.):– w-k hat-trick, *164;* Test p'ship record, *220.*
ssell, W. E. (Eng.):– 25,525 r., *142;* 41 hundreds, *138.*
therford, K. R. (NZ):– 317 in day v D. B. Close's XI, *132, 144;* 53 boundaries in nnings, *147;* 1 Test hundred, *213;* Test 'ship records, *214, 228.*
all, R. J. (W. Prov.):– 10 d. in match, *164.*
der, J. (Aust.):– Test captain, *195;* 3 Test undreds, *200, 222;* Test avge of 51.62, *177.*

S

dat Ali (Income Tax):– Hundred and ouble-hundred, *135;* 1,649 r. in Pakistan ason, *140.*
SAB Bowl (SA), *1054-7.*
Sadiq Mohammad (Pak.):– 2,579 r. in Tests, *176;* 50 hundreds, *138;* 5 Test hundreds, *219, 232, 245;* 4 successive hundreds, *137;* 2 hundreds in match (3), *136;* Test p'ship record, *246.*
Saeed Ahmed (Pak.):– Test captain, *218;* 2,991 r. in Tests, *176;* 5 Test hundreds, *232, 241, 245, 248;* 4 successive hundreds, *137;* Test p'ship records, *242, 246.*
Saggers, R. A. (Aust.):– 21 d. in series, *188;* 10 d. in match, *164;* 7 d. in innings, *163.*
Salah-ud-Din (Pak.):– Hundred and double-hundred, *135;* 353 for 6th wkt, *151;* Test p'ship record, *246.*
Salim Malik (Pak.):– 2,140 r. in Tests, *176;* 6 Test hundreds, *219, 245, 248, 251;* Hundred on Test début, *172, 251;* Test p'ship records, *219, 233, 242, 248, 252.*
Salim Yousuf (Pak.):– Test p'ship records, *219, 242, 252.*
Sandham, A. (Eng.):– 41,284 r., *141;* 1,000 r. (20), *139;* 107 hundreds, *137;* 2 Test hundreds, *210;* 325 v West Indies, *132, 170, 210;* 219 v Australians, *133;* 428 for 1st wkt, *148;* 1st wkt hundreds, *148.*
Sandhu, B. S. (Ind.):– Test p'ship record, *240.*
Sardesai, D. N. (Ind.):– 2,001 r. in Tests, *176;* 5 Test hundreds, *239, 243;* Slow Test hundred, *179;* Test p'ship records, *240, 244.*
Sarfraz Nawaz (Pak.):– 177 w. in Tests, *184;* 10 w. or more in Test (1), *233;* 9 w. in Test innings, *180, 233;* All-round in Tests, *187;* Test p'ship records, *219, 242.*
Sarwate, C. T. (Ind.):– 236 for 8th wkt, *151;* 249 for 10th wkt, *152.*
Saxelby, K. (Notts.):– Career figures, *681.*
Scarborough Festival, *654-7;* Address of Secretary, *1220.*
Schofield, R. M. (C. Dist.):– 7 d. in innings, *163.*
Scotland:– v Ireland, *652, 847;* v MCC, *331, 847;* in B & H Cup, *682, 683, 846;* in NatWest Bank Trophy, *664, 846;* Representative body, *1220.*
Scott, C. W. (Notts.): 10 d. in match, *164, 266.*
Scott, H. J. H. (Aust.):– Test captain, *194;* 1 Test hundred, *200.*
Scottish Cricket in 1988, *846-8.*
Scotton, W. H. (Eng.):– Handled the ball, *152;* Test p'ship record, *201.*
Sealy, J. E. D. (WI):– Youngest West Indian Test player, *192.*
Second XI Championship:– *820-37;* Championship winners, *837.*
Serjeant, C. S. (Aust.):– 1 Test hundred, *225.*
Seymour, James (Kent):– 27,237 r., *142;* 1,000 r. (16), *139;* 53 hundreds, *138;* 2 hundreds in match (2), *136.*

Shackleton, D. (Eng.):– 2,857 w., *159;* 100 w. (20), *159;* 8 w. for 4 r., *155.*

Shacklock, F. J. (Notts.):– 4 w. with consecutive balls, *156.*

Shafiq Ahmed (Pak.):– 17,649 r. (avge 50.13), *143;* 49 hundreds, *138;* 2 hundreds in match (2), *136;* Hundred and double-hundred, *135;* 389 for 1st wkt, *148.*

Shahid Israr (Pak.):– 7 d. in innings, *163.*

Shahid Mahmood (Pak.):– 10 w. in innings, *154.*

Sharjah Cup, 1987-88, *1003-6.*

Sharma, Chetan (Ind.):– 10 w. or more in Test (1), *217;* Hat-trick in one-day int., *257;* Test p'ship records, *217, 250.*

Sharma, Gopal (Ind.):– Test p'ship record, *250.*

Sharma, R. (Derbys.):– 151 for 9th wkt, *288.*

Sharp, J. (Eng.):– 38 hundreds, *138;* 1 Test hundred, *198.*

Sharp, J. C. (Melb. GS):– 506* v Geelong College, *261.*

Sharpe, P. J. (Eng.):– 1 Test hundred, *213;* 71 c. in season, *166.*

Shastri, R. J. (Ind.):– Test captain, *238;* 2,568 r. in Tests, *176;* 7 Test hundreds, *216, 230, 239, 248;* 200 r. in 113 min., *144;* 36 r. in over, *145;* 13 sixes in innings, *146;* 127 w. in Tests, *184;* 101 w. in one-day ints, *257;* All-round in Tests, *187;* All-round in one-day ints, *258;* Test p'ship records, *217, 231, 240, 249.*

Shaw, A. (Eng.):– Test captain, *194;* 2,027 w., *160;* 201 w. in season, *158;* 100 w. (9), *159;* 10 w. in innings, *153;* Double hat-trick, *157;* 3 hat-tricks, *157.*

Sheahan, A. P. (Aust.):– 2 Test hundreds, *230, 232.*

Sheffield Shield (Aust.), *1012-46.*

Shell Cup (NZ), *1074-5.*

Shell Shield (WI):– Winners, *1066.*

Shell Trophy (NZ), *1068-9, 1071-4.*

Shepherd, D. J. (Glam.):– 2,218 w., *160;* 100 w. (12), *159.*

Shepherd, D. R. (Glos.):– Hundred on début, *134.*

Shepherd, J. N. (WI):– 267 w. in Sunday League, *794.*

Shepherd, T. F. (Surrey):– 42 hundreds, *138.*

Sheppard, Rt Rev. D. S. (Eng.):– Test captain, *218;* 45 hundreds, *138;* 3 Test hundreds, *198, 216.*

Sherwell, P. W. (SA):– Test captain, *204, 221;* 1 Test hundred, *206.*

Shillingford, G. C. (WI):– Test p'ship record, *237.*

Shillingford, I. T. (WI):– 1 Test hundred, *241.*

Shoaib Mohammad (Pak.):– 1 Test hundred, *248;* Test p'ship record, *219.*

Shodhan, D. H. (Ind.):– Hundred on Test début, *171, 248.*

Shrewsbury, A. (Eng.):– Test captain, *194-5;* 26,505 r., *142;* 59 hundreds, *138;* 3 Test hundreds, *198;* 6 c. in Test, *189;* 391 for 1st wkt, *148.*

Shropshire, *664-5, 801, 803, 815.*

Siedle, I. J. (SA):– 1 Test hundred, *206;* 424 for 1st wkt, *148, 149;* Test p'ship record, *206.*

Sikander Bakht (Pak.):– 10 w. or more in Test (1), *249;* 8 w. in Test innings, *181.*

Silva, S. A. R. (SL):– 2 Test hundreds, *220, 250;* 34 d. in Tests, *188;* 22 d. in series, *188,* 9 d. in Test (2), *187;* 6 d. in Test innings, *187;* All-round in Test, *186;* Test p'ship record, *250.*

Simmons, J. (Lancs.):– 1,000 w., *267;* 290 w in Sunday League, *794;* Most econ analysis in NWB Trophy, *679.*

Simpson, R. B. (Aust.):– Test captain, *19*… *221, 224, 229, 231;* 21,029 r. (avge 56.22), *143;* 4,869 r. in Tests, *174;* 2,063 r. i… overseas season, *140;* 1,381 Test r. in yea… *173;* 60 hundreds, *138;* 10 Test hundreds *200, 222, 225, 230, 232;* 2 hundreds in sam… Test, *172, 232;* 2 hundreds in match (2… *136;* 359 v Queensland, *132;* 311 … England, *133, 170, 200;* 110 c. in Test… *189;* 13 c. in series (2), *189;* 382 for 1st wk… *148, 226;* Test p'ship records, *201, 226.*

Simpson, R. T. (Eng.):– 30,546 r., *141;* … hundreds, *138;* 4 Test hundreds, *198, 20*… *213, 219;* Test p'ship records, *211, 214.*

Sims, Sir Arthur:– 433 for 8th wkt, *151.*

Sims, J. M. (Eng.):– 1,581 w., *160;* 100 w. (… *159;* 10 w. in innings, *154.*

Sinclair, B. W. (NZ):– Test captain, *212, 24*… 3 Test hundreds, *213, 235, 245;* Test p'sh… records, *235, 245.*

Sinclair, J. H. (SA):– 3 Test hundreds, *2*… *223;* All-round in Test, *185.*

Singh, R. P. (Holkar):– 236 for 8th wkt, *1*…

Sivaramakrishnan, L. (Ind.):– Young… Indian Test player, *192;* 10 w. or more… Test (1), *217;* Test p'ship record, *250.*

Slack, J. K. E. (CUCC):– Hundred on déb… *134.*

Slack, W. N. (Eng.):– 2 hundreds in mat… *264;* 284 for 3rd wkt, *265.*

Smailes, T. F. (Eng.):– 10 w. in innings, *1*…

Smales, K. (Notts.):– 10 w. in innings, *1*…

Small, G. C. (Eng.):– All-round, *266.*

Smart, C. C. (Glam.):– 32 r. in over, *14*…

Smith, A. C. (Eng.):– Test p'ship record, *2*…

Smith, C. Aubrey (Eng.):– Test captain, *2*…

Smith, C. L. (Eng.):– 35 hundreds, *138.*

Smith, D. M. (Eng.):– 10,000 r., *267.*

Smith, E. J. (Eng.):– 7 d. in innings, *16*…

Smith, H. D. (NZ):– Wkt with 1st ball … Test début, *184.*

Smith, I. D. S. (NZ):– 1 Test hundred, *214;* 120 d. in Tests, *188;* All-round in Test, *186;* Test p'ship record, *237.*
Smith, M. J. (Middx):– 40 hundreds, *138.*
Smith, M. J. K. (Eng.):– Test captain, *195, 204, 208, 212, 215;* 39,832 r., *141;* 3,245 r. in season, *139;* 2,278 r. in Tests, *174;* 1,000 r. (20), *139;* 69 hundreds, *137;* 3 Test hundreds, *205, 210, 216;* 3 hundreds v Cambridge, *335;* Test p'ship records, *211, 217.*
mith, M. S. (Natal):– 7 d. in innings, *163.*
mith, O. G. (WI):– 4 Test hundreds, *210, 226, 239;* Hundred on Test début, *171, 226;* All-round in Test, *186;* Test p'ship records, *237, 241.*
mith, R. (Essex):– All-round, *162.*
mith, S. G. (Northants):– All-round, *162;* 4 w. with consecutive balls, *156.*
mith, T. P. B. (Eng.):– 1,697 w., *160.*
mith, V. I. (SA):– 6 w. for 1 r., *155.*
mith, W. C. (Surrey):– 247 w. in season, *158.*
nooke, S. J. (SA):– Test captain, *204;* 1 Test hundred, *223;* 10 w. or more in Test (1), *207;* 8 w. in Test innings, *181.*
now, J. A. (Eng.):– 202 w. in Tests, *182;* 10 w. or more in Test (1), *211;* Test p'ship record, *211.*
bers, Sir G. S. (WI):– Test captain, *208, 224, 236, 238;* Test début at 17, *192;* 85 consecutive Tests, *193;* 28,315 r. (avge 54.87), *142, 143;* 8,032 r. (avge 57.78) in Tests, *175, 177;* 1,193 Test r. in year, *173;* 1,000 r. (15), *139-40;* 824 r. in series, *173;* 86 hundreds, *137;* 26 Test hundreds, *177, 210, 226, 236, 239, 241;* 2 hundreds in same Test, *172, 241;* 2 hundreds in match (2), *136;* 365* v Pakistan, *132, 149, 170, 241;* 36 r. in over, *145;* 235 w. in Tests, *183;* All-round in Tests, *186;* 109 c. in Tests, *189;* 6 c. in Test, *189;* 446 for 2nd wkt, *149;* Test p'ship records, *211, 237, 241.*
lkar, E. D. (Ind.):– 1 Test hundred, *239;* 5 c. in Test, *189;* Test p'ship record, *240.*
lomon, J. S. (WI):– 1 Test hundred, *239;* Hundreds in first three first-class innings, *135.*
merset:– *339, 523-38;* Championship positions, *344-5;* Highest score, *166;* Highest individual score, *134;* Lowest score, *167.*
merset II, *821, 822, 832-3.*
th Africa:– Domestic season 1987-88, *1048-60;* Highest individual Test innings, *170;* Highest Test innings, *190;* Leading batsmen in Tests, *175;* Leading bowlers in Tests, *183;* Lowest Test innings, *191;* Most Test appearances, *127;* Most Test appearances as captain, *127;* Oldest Test player, *193;* Representative bodies, *1219;* South Africa in Test cricket (*see p. 131*); Summary of Tests, *194;* Test cricketers (1888-1970), *105-9;* Youngest and oldest on Test début, *192.*
Southerton, J. (Eng.):– Oldest Test début, *192;* Test cricket at 49, *193;* 1,681 w., *160;* 210 w. in season, *159;* 100 w. (10), *159;* 16 w. in day, *156.*
Spofforth, F. R. (Aust.):– 207 w. in season, *158;* 14 England w. in match, *182, 202;* 10 w. or more in Test (4), *202;* 7 w. for 3 r., *155;* Test hat-trick, *185;* 4 hat-tricks, *157.*
Spooner, R. H. (Eng.):– 1 Test hundred, *205.*
Squires, H. S. (Surrey):– 37 hundreds, *138.*
Srikkanth, K. (Ind.):– 2 Test hundreds, *230, 248;* Test p'ship record, *248.*
Sri Lanka:– B & H World Series Cup, *992-1000;* Definition of first-class matches, *1212;* Domestic season 1987-88, *1198-9;* Highest individual Test innings, *171;* Highest Test innings, *190;* Leading batsmen in Tests, *176;* Leading bowlers in Tests, *184;* Lowest Test innings, *191;* Most Test appearances, *127;* Most Test appearances as captain, *127;* Representative body, *1219;* Sharjah Cup, *1003-5;* Sri Lanka in Test cricket (*see p. 131*); Summary of Tests, *194;* Test cricketers (1982-88), *126-7;* Oldest and youngest on Test début, *192.*
Sri Lanka B:– In Zimbabwe, *1099-100.*
Stackpole, K. R. (Aust.):– 2,807 r. in Tests, *175;* 7 Test hundreds, *200, 222, 225, 228, 230.*
Staffordshire, *665, 802, 803, 815-6.*
Standing, D. K. (Sussex):– Career figures, *681.*
Stanyforth, Lt-Col. R. T. (Eng.):– Test captain, *204.*
Statham, J. B. (Eng.):– 2,260 w., *160;* 252 w. in Tests, *182;* 100 w. (13), *159;* 10 w. or more in Test (1), *207;* 3 hat-tricks, *157.*
Status of matches in UK, *555.*
Steel, A. G. (Eng.):– Test captain, *194-6;* 2 Test hundreds, *198.*
Steele, D. S. (Eng.):– 1 Test hundred, *210.*
Steele, J. F. (Leics. and Glam.):– 101 c. in Sunday League, *795;* 390 for 1st wkt, *148.*
Stephenson, F. D. (Notts.):– Cricketer of the Year, *57-9;* All-round, *161, 162, 266;* 2 hundreds in match, *264;* 1st to 100 w. in 1988, *266.*
Stephenson, H. W. (Som.):– 1,082 d., *165.*
Stevens, G. T. S. (Eng.):– Test captain, *204;* 466* v Lambda, *261;* 10 w. or more in Test (1), *211.*
Stewart, A. J. (Surrey):– 6 d. in innings, *266.*
Stewart, M. J. (Eng.):– 26,492 r., *142;* 1,000 r. (15), *139;* 49 hundreds, *138;* 77 c. and 61 c. in season, *166;* 7 c. in innings, *165.*

Stewart, W. J. (Warwicks.):– 17 sixes in match, 146.
Steyn, S. S. L. (W. Prov.):– 222 for 8th wkt, 151.
Stimpson, P. J. (Worcs.):– 1st wkt hundreds, 148.
Stocks, F. W. (Notts.):– Hundred on début, 134.
Stoddart, A. E. (Eng.):– Test captain, 195-6; 2 Test hundreds, 198; 485 v Stoics, 261; 1st wkt hundreds, 149.
Stollmeyer, J. B. (WI):– Test captain, 208, 224, 238; 2,159 r. in Tests, 175; 4 Test hundreds, 226, 236, 239; 324 v British Guiana, 132, 150; 434 for 3rd wkt, 150.
Storie, A. C. (Northants and Warwicks.):– Hundred on début, 134; 5 c. in innings, 266; Career figures, 681.
Stricker, L. A. (SA):– Test p'ship record, 223.
Strudwick, H. (Eng.):– Test cricket at 46, 193; 1,497 d., 165; 21 d. in series, 188.
Strydom, J. J. (E. Prov.):– 355 for 5th wkt, 150, 1048.
Stumpings in 1988, 274.
Subba Row, R. (Eng.):– Chairman of Cricket Council and TCCB, 279; Highest for Northamptonshire, 134; 3 Test hundreds, 198, 210; 300 v Surrey, 133, 134; Test p'ship record, 217.
Suffolk, 663, 802, 803, 816.
Sunderam, P. (Rajasthan):– 10 w. in innings, 154.
Surrey:– 339, 539-55; Championship positions, 344-5; Highest score, 166; Highest individual score, 134; Lowest score, 167.
Surrey II, 821, 822, 833.
Sussex:– 339, 556-71; Championship positions, 344-5; Highest score, 166; Highest individual score, 134; Lowest score, 167.
Sussex II, 822, 833-4.
Sutcliffe, B. (NZ):– Test captain, 234, 236; 2,727 r. in Tests, 176; 44 hundreds, 138; 5 Test hundreds, 214, 243; 2 hundreds in match (4), 136; Hundred and double-hundred, 135; 385 v Canterbury, 132; 355 v Auckland, 132; 1st wkt hundreds, 148; Test p'ship records, 214, 235, 243.
Sutcliffe, H. (Eng.):– 50,138 r. (avge 51.95), 141, 143; 4,555 r. (avge 60.73) in Tests, 174, 177; 3,336 r. in season, 138; 2,741 r. v Australia, 203; 1,000 r. (24), 139; 149 hundreds, 137; 16 Test hundreds, 198, 205, 213; 13 and 14 hundreds in season, 137; 4 successive hundreds, 137; 2 hundreds in same Test (2), 172, 198, 205; 2 hundreds in match (4), 136; 313 v Essex, 133, 149; Avge of 96.96 in English season, 140; 1st wkt hundreds, 148-9; 555 for 1st wkt, 147, 148, 149.
Suttle, K. G. (Sussex):– 30,225 r., 142; 1,000 r. (17), 139; 49 hundreds, 138; 423 consecutive Championship appearances, 263.
Swansea Univ.:– UAU champions, 841.

T

Taber, H. B. (Aust.):– 20 d. in series, 188; 1[illegible] d. in match, 164; 8 d. in Test, 187; 7 d. i[illegible] innings, 163.
Taberer, H. M. (SA):– Test captain, 221.
Tahir Naqqash (Pak.):– Test p'ship record 252.
Talat Ali (Pak.):– Hundred and double hundred, 135.
Tallon, D. (Aust.):– 20 d. in series, 188; 12 d in match, 164; 7 d. in innings, 163.
Tancred, A. B. (SA):– Carrying bat in Tes[illegible] 177.
Tancred, L. J. (SA):– Test captain, 204, 221 Test p'ship record, 223.
Tarilton, P. H. (B'dos):– 304* v Trinida[illegible] 133.
Tariq Bashir (HBFC):– 355 for 5th wkt, 15[illegible]
Tarrant, F. A. (Vic. and Middx):– All-roun[illegible] 162; 100 w. (8), 159; 5 hat-tricks, 157; 4 w with consecutive balls, 156.
Taslim Arif (Pak.):– 1 Test hundred, 232; [illegible] d. in match, 164; 7 d. in innings, 163; Te[illegible] p'ship record, 233.
Tate, M. W. (Eng.):– All-round, 162, 16[illegible] All-round in Tests, 186; 1 Test hundre[illegible] 205; 2,784 w., 160; 200 w. (3), 158; 155 [illegible] in Tests, 182; 116 w. in overseas seaso[illegible] 159; 100 w. (14), 159; 38 w. in series, 20[illegible] 10 w. or more in Test (1), 202; 3 hat-trick[illegible] 157; Wkt with 1st ball on Test début, 18[illegible]
Tattersall, R. (Eng.):– 100 w. (8), 159; 10 [illegible] or more in Test (1), 207.
Tauseef Ahmed (Pak.):– Test p'ship reco[illegible] 252.
Tavaré, C. J. (Eng.):– 35 hundreds, 138[illegible] Test hundreds, 213, 216; Slow scoring Test, 179; 49 c. in season, 166; Test p's[illegible] record, 214.
Tayfield, H. J. (SA):– 170 w. in Tests, 183; [illegible] w. in series, 182, 208; 26 w. in series, 20[illegible] 13 w. in Test (2), 182, 207, 223; 9 w. in T[illegible] innings, 180; 8 w. in Test innings, 18[illegible] Test p'ship record, 235.
Taylor, B. (Essex):– 1,294 d., 165; 301 con[illegible] Championship appearances, 263.
Taylor, B. R. (NZ):– 2 Test hundreds, 2[illegible] 243; Hundred on Test début, 171, 243; [illegible] w. in Tests, 184; All-round in Test, 1[illegible] Test p'ship record, 243.
Taylor, D. D. (NZ):– 1st wkt hundreds, [illegible]
Taylor, H. W. (SA):– Test captain, 127, [illegible] 221; 2,936 r. in Tests, 175; 582 r. in se[illegible]

Taylor, H. W. (SA):– *contd*
207; 7 Test hundreds, *206;* Test p'ship record, *207.*

Taylor, J. M. (Aust.):– 1 Test hundred, *200;* Test p'ship record, *201.*

Taylor, N. R. (Kent):– Carrying bat in 1988, *265;* Hundred on début, *134.*

Taylor, R. W. (Eng.):– 1,649 d., *165;* 236 d. in Sunday League, *794;* 174 d. in Tests, *188;* 20 d. in series, *188;* 10 d. in Test, *187;* 10 d. in match (2), *164;* 7 d. in Test innings, *187;* 7 d. in innings (3), *163;* 7 d. in Sunday League innings, *795;* 6 d. in NWB Trophy innings, *680;* Test p'ship records, *217, 219.*

edstone, G. A. (Warwicks.):– Career figures, *681.*

endulkar, S. R. (Sharadashram Vidyamandir S.):– 664* for 3rd wkt, *261, 1103.*

ennyson, Hon. L. H. (Lord Tennyson) (Eng.):– Test captain, *195.*

est and County Cricket Board:– Meetings, *1221-2;* Officers, *279.*

est match grounds, *252-3.*

est matches, duration of and qualification for, *1210-1.*

exaco Trophy matches:– in 1988, *288-92, 326-7;* in 1989, *1256.*

homas, D. J. (Surrey and Glos.):– Career figures, *681.*

hompson, G. J. (Eng.):– 1,591 w., *160;* 100 w. (8), *159;* Hat-trick of c., *157.*

homson, J. R. (Aust.):– 200 w. in Tests, *183;* 100 w. v England, *203.*

omson, K. (NZ):– Test p'ship record, *243.*

omson, N. I. (Eng.):– 1,597 w., *160;* 100 w. (12), *159;* 10 w. in innings, *154.*

ousand runs in May, *145.*

rowing records, *262.*

ed matches, *169-70, 259.*

con Trophy:– *649-50;* Fixtures, 1989, *1257.*

mus, F. J. (Eng.):– All-round, *162, 163;* All-round in Tests, *186;* 2,830 w., *160;* 153 w. in Tests, *182;* 100 w. (16), *159.*

dd, L. J. (Kent):– 38 hundreds, *138.*

dd, P. A. (Notts. and Glam.):– Career igures, *681.*

chard, R. W. (Eng.):– 1,037 d., *165.*

ogood, G. J. (OUCC):– 149 and 10 w. v Cambridge, *336.*

hey, P. M. (Aust.):– 1 Test hundred, *225.*

hack, E. R. H. (Aust.):– 10 w. or more in est (1), *231.*

rs, Future, *327.*

vnsend, L. F. (Eng.):– All-round, *162.*

ns-Tasman Trophy, *227.*

e, G. E. (Aust.):– All-round, *162;* 100 w.), *159.*

up, G. B. (NZ):– 10 w. or more in Test (1), *37.*

t, A. E. (Aust. and Eng.):– All-round, *52;* Double hat-trick, *157;* Hit over Lord's Pavilion, *261;* 1,674 w., *160;* 200 w. (2), *158;* 10 w. in innings, *154;* 8 w. in Test innings, *181;* 4 w. with consecutive balls, *156.*

Trott, G. H. S. (Aust.):– Test captain, *195;* 1 Test hundred, *200.*

Trueman, F. S. (Eng.):– 2,304 w., *160;* 307 w. in Tests, *182;* 100 w. (12), *159;* 10 w. or more in Test (3), *202, 211;* 8 w. in Test innings, *180;* 4 hat-tricks, *157;* Test p'ship record, *219.*

Trumble, H. (Aust.):– Test captain, *196;* 141 w. in Tests, *183;* 10 w. or more in Test (3), *202;* 8 w. in Test innings, *181;* 2 Test hat-tricks, *185;* 3 hat-tricks, *157;* Test p'ship record, *201.*

Trumper, V. T. (Aust.):– 3,163 r. in Tests, *174;* 2,263 r. v England, *203;* 42 hundreds, *138;* 8 Test hundreds, *200, 222;* 300* v Sussex, *133;* 200 r. in 131 min., *144;* 433 for 8th wkt, *151;* Test p'ship record, *223.*

Tuckett, L. (SA):– Test p'ship record, *207.*

Tunnicliffe, J. (Yorks.):– 70 c., 66 c., 64 c. and 63 c. in season, *166;* 554 and 378 for 1st wkt, *147, 148.*

Turner, A. (Aust.):– 1 Test hundred, *225;* Test p'ship record, *233.*

Turner, C. T. B. (Aust.):– 283 w. in season, *158;* 106 w. in Australian season, *159;* 101 w. in Tests, *183, 203;* 17 w. in match, *155;* 10 w. or more in Test (2), *202.*

Turner, D. R. (Hants):– 6,429 r. in Sunday League, *793.*

Turner, G. M. (NZ):– Test captain, *227, 242, 244;* 34,346 r., *141;* 6,144 r. in Sunday League, *793;* 2,991 r. in Tests, *176;* 1,000 r. (18), *139;* 1,000 r. (April 24-May 31), *145;* 103 hundreds, *137;* 7 Test hundreds, *228, 237, 243, 245;* 2 hundreds in same Test, *172, 228;* 2 hundreds in match (6), *134;* 311* v Warwickshire in day, *133, 134, 144;* 259 v West Indies, *171, 237;* Avge of 90.07 in English season, *140;* Carrying bat in Test (2), *178;* 387 for 1st wkt, *148, 149, 237;* Test p'ship records, *228, 237, 245.*

Turner, J. B. (Minor Counties):– Hundred on début, *134.*

Turner, S. (Essex):– 303 w. in Sunday League, *794.*

Tyldesley, E. (Eng.):– 38,874 r., *141;* 3,024 r. in season, *139;* 1,000 r. (19), *139;* 102 hundreds, *137;* 3 Test hundreds, *205, 210;* 4 successive hundreds, *137;* 2 hundreds in match (2), *136;* 10 successive fifties, *137;* Test avge of 55.00, *177.*

Tyldesley, J. T. (Eng.):– 37,897 r., *141;* 3,041 r. in season, *139;* 1,000 r. (19), *139;* 86 hundreds, *137;* 4 Test hundreds, *198, 205;* 2 hundreds in match (3), *136.*

Tyldesley, R. K. (Eng.):– 1,509 w., *161;* 100 w. (10), *159;* 5 w. for 0 r., *155;* 4 w. with consecutive balls, *156.*
Tyler, E. J. (Som.):– 10 w. in innings, *153.*
Tyson, F. H. (Eng.):– 10 w. or more in Test (1), *202.*

U

UAU Championship, 1988, *840-1.*
Ulyett, G. (Eng.):– 1 Test hundred, *198;* 4 w. with consecutive balls, *156.*
Umpires for 1989, *311.*
Umpires, Association of Cricket, *1220.*
Umrigar, P. R. (Ind.):– Test captain, *229, 238, 242;* 16,154 r. (avge 52.28), *143;* 3,631 r. in Tests, *176;* 49 hundreds, *138;* 12 Test hundreds, *216-7, 239, 243, 248;* All-round in Test, *186;* Test p'ship records, *244, 248.*
Underwood, D. L. (Eng.):– 2,465 w., *160;* 346 w. in Sunday League, *794;* 297 w. in Tests, *182;* 105 w. v Australia, *203;* 100 w. (10), *159;* 10 w. or more in Test (6), *202, 214, 220;* 8 w. in Test innings, *181.*
Univ. of NSW:– v Cambridge Univ., *640.*

V

Valentine, A. L. (WI):– 139 w. in Tests, *183;* 10 w. or more in Test (2), *212;* 8 w. in Test innings, *181, 212.*
Valentine, B. H. (Eng.):– 35 hundreds, *138;* 2 Test hundreds, *205, 216;* Hundred on Test début, *171, 216.*
van der Bijl, P. G. V. (SA):– 1 Test hundred, *206.*
van der Merwe, P. L. (SA):– Test captain, *204, 221;* Test p'ship record, *223.*
Van Ryneveld, C. B. (SA):– Test captain, *204, 221;* Test p'ship record, *206.*
Veivers, T. R. (Aust.):– Test p'ship records, *230, 233.*
Vengsarkar, D. B. (Ind.):– Test captain, *238;* Avge of 101.66 in series, *944;* 14,270 r. (avge 51.89), *143;* 6,256 r. in Tests, *176;* 1,085 and 1,174 Test r. in year, *173;* 45 hundreds, *138;* 17 Test hundreds, *217, 230, 239, 248, 250;* Test p'ship records, *231, 240, 250.*
Venkataraghavan, S. (Ind.):– Test captain, *215, 238;* 156 w. in Tests, *184;* 10 w. or more in Test (1), *244;* 8 w. in Test innings, *181, 244.*
Verity, H. (Eng.):– 1,956 w., *160;* 200 w. (3), *158;* 144 w. in Tests, *182;* 100 w. (9), *159;* 17 w. in day, *156;* 17 w. in match, *155;* 15 Australian w. in match, *181, 202;* 10 w. in innings (2), *154;* 10 w. or more in Test (2), *181, 202, 217;* 8 w. in Test innings, *181, 202.*
Viljoen, K. G. (SA):– 2 Test hundreds, *206, 223.*
Village Championship, *337-8, 653.*
Vine, J. (Eng.):– 25,171 r., *142;* 399 consecutive Championship appearances, *263;* 1st wkt hundreds, *149;* Test p'ship record, *201.*
Virgin, R. T. (Som. and Northants):– 37 hundreds, *138;* 1st wkt hundreds, *149.*
Viswanath, G. R. (Ind.):– Test captain, *215, 247;* 87 consecutive Tests, *193;* 6,080 r. in Tests, *176;* 1,388 Test runs in year, *173;* 44 hundreds, *138;* 14 Test hundreds, *217, 230, 239, 243, 248;* Hundred on début, *135;* Hundred on Test début, *135, 171, 230;* 415 for 3rd wicket, *180, 217;* Test p'ship records, *217, 231, 240.*
Vivian, G. E. (NZ):– Test p'ship record, *243.*
Vivian, H. G. (NZ):– 1 Test hundred, *235,* Test p'ship record, *235.*
Vizianagram, Maharaj of (Ind.):– Tes captain, *215.*
Voce, W. (Eng.):– 1,558 w., *161;* 10 w. o more in Test (2), *202, 211.*
Vogler, A. E. E. (SA):– 36 w. in series, *182* 16 w. in day, *156;* 10 w. in innings, *154;* 1 w. or more in Test (1), *207;* 6 c. in Test, *189*

W

Wade, H. F. (SA):– Test captain, *204, 221*
Wade, W. W. (SA):– 1 Test hundred, *206.*
Wadekar, A. L. (Ind.):– Test captain, *21 238;* 2,113 r. in Tests, *176;* 36 hundred *138;* 1 Test hundred, *243;* 323 v Mysor *132;* Test p'ship record, *217.*
Wadsworth, K. J. (NZ):– Test p'ship recor *237.*
Waheed Mirza (Sind):– 324 v Quetta, *13 149;* 561 for 1st wkt, *147, 148, 149.*
Waite, J. H. B. (SA):– 2,405 r. in Tests, *17* 50 Tests, *127, 193;* 4 Test hundreds, *20 223, 235;* 141 d. in Tests, *188;* 26 d. series, *188;* Test p'ship records, *207, 22*
Walcott, C. L. (WI):– 11,820 r. (avge 56.5 *143;* 3,798 r. (avge 56.68) in Tests, *17 177;* 827 r. in series, *173;* 40 hundre *138;* 15 Test hundreds, *210, 226, 236, 2 241;* 2 hundreds in same Test, *172, 22* 2 hundreds in match (2), *136;* 314* Trinidad, *133, 150;* 574* for 4th wkt, *1 150;* Test p'ship records, *237, 240, 241.*
Wales:– in Minor Counties Championshi *802, 803, 816-7;* v Ireland, *651, 845;* MCC, *652.*
Walker, A. K. (Notts.):– 4 w. wi consecutive balls, *156.*
Walker, M. H. N. (Aust.):– 138 w. in Tes *183;* 8 w. in Test innings, *181;* Test p'sh record, *233.*

Walker, P. M. (Eng.):– 73 c., 69 c. and 65 c. in season, *166;* 8 c. in match, *165.*
Walker, V. E. (Middx):– 108 and 10 w., *161;* 10 w. in innings (2), *153.*
Walkley, E. (S. Aust.):– 232 for 9th wkt, *151.*
Wall, T. W. (Aust.):– 10 w. in innings, *154.*
Wallace, W. M. (NZ):– Test captain, *234;* 324 for 4th wkt, *150.*
Walters, C. F. (Eng.):– Test captain, *196;* 1 Test hundred, *216.*
Walters, K. D. (Aust.):– 5,357 r. in Tests, *174;* 45 hundreds, *138;* 15 Test hundreds, *200, 225, 228, 230, 232;* 2 hundreds in same Test, *172, 225;* Hundred and double-hundred, *135;* Hundred on Test début, *171, 200;* 250 v New Zealand, *171, 228;* Test p'ship records, *226, 228.*
Waqar Hassan (Pak.):– 1 Test hundred, *245;* 308 for 7th wkt v New Zealand, *151, 246.*
Ward, Alan (Eng.):– 4 w. in 4 balls in Sunday League, *794.*
Ward, Albert (Eng.):– 1 Test hundred, *198.*
Ward, J. T. (NZ):– Test p'ship record, *243.*
Ward Knockout Cup, *654-6.*
Ward, W. (MCC):– 278 at Lord's, *260.*
Wardle, J. H. (Eng.):– 1,846 w., *160;* 102 w. in Tests, *183;* 100 w. (10), *159;* 10 w. or more in Test (1), *207.*
Warnapura, B. (SL):– Test captain, *220, 249, 251.*
Warner, Sir Pelham F. (Eng.):– Test captain, *195, 204;* 29,028 r., *142;* 60 hundreds, *138;* Hundred on Test début, *171, 205;* Carrying bat in Test, *177.*
Warr, J. J. (Eng.):– President of MCC, *328.*
Warren, A. (Eng.):– 283 for 9th wkt, *151.*
Warwick Under-25 Competition:– *838-9.*
Warwickshire:– *339, 572-87;* Championship positions, *344-5;* Highest score, *166;* Highest individual score, *133;* Lowest score, *167;* Tilcon Trophy, *649-50.*
Warwickshire II, *822, 834-5;* Warwick Under-25 winners, *839.*
Washbrook, C. (Eng.):– 34,101 r., *141;* 2,569 r. in Tests, *174;* 1,000 r. (20), *139;* 76 hundreds, *137;* 6 Test hundreds, *198, 205, 210, 213;* 1st wkt hundreds, *148;* Test p'ship record, *206.*
Wasim Akram (Pak.):– Hat-trick in 1988, *266;* 10 w. or more in Test (1), *246;* Test p'ship record, *249.*
Wasim Bari (Pak.):– Test captain, *218;* 228 d. in Tests, *188;* 62 d. in one-day ints, *257;* 8 d. in Test, *187;* 7 d. in Test innings, *163, 187;* 7 d. in innings (2), *163;* Test p'ship records, *233, 242, 249.*
Wasim Raja (Pak.):– 2,821 r. in Tests, *176;* 4 Test hundreds, *219, 241, 248;* Test p'ship records, *242.*
Wass, T. G. (Notts.):– 1,666 w., *160;* 100 w. (10), *159;* 16 w. in day (2), *156.*
Wasu, H. (Vidarbha):– Obstructing the field, *153.*
Watkin, S. L. (Glam.):– 8 w. in innings, *265.*
Watkins, A. J. (Eng.):– 2 Test hundreds, *205, 216.*
Watkins, J. R. (Aust.):– Test p'ship record, *233.*
Watson, F. B. (Lancs.):– 50 hundreds, *138;* 300* v Surrey, *133;* 1st wkt hundreds, *149.*
Watson, W. (Eng.):– 25,670 r., *142;* 55 hundreds, *138;* 2 Test hundreds, *198, 210.*
Watson-Smith, R. (Border):– 183* and 125* in first two first-class innings, *135.*
Watts, E. A. (Surrey):– 10 w. in innings, *154.*
Waugh, S. R. (Aust.):– Cricketer of the Year, *59-60;* Test p'ship record, *228.*
Wazir Mohammad (Pak.):– Test p'ship records, *242.*
Weekes, E. D. (WI):– 12,010 r. (avge 55.34), *143;* 4,455 r. (avge 58.61) in Tests, *175, 177;* 779 r. in series, *173;* 36 hundreds, *138;* 15 Test hundreds, *210-1, 226, 236, 239, 241;* 5 successive hundreds, *136;* 2 hundreds in same Test, *172, 239;* 304* v Cambridge Univ., *133;* Avge of 79.65 in English season, *140;* Test p'ship records, *211, 237, 240, 241.*
Weekes, K. H. (WI):– 1 Test hundred, *210.*
Weerasinghe, C. D. U. S. (SL):– Youngest Sri Lankan Test player, *192.*
Wellard, A. W. (Eng.):– All-round, *162;* 1,614 w., *160;* 66 sixes in season, *146;* 30 r. and 31 r. in over, *146;* 100 w. (8), *159.*
Wellham, D. M. (Aust.):– Hundred on début, *135;* Hundred on Test début, *135, 172, 200.*
Wells, J. (Kent):– 4 w. with consecutive balls, *156.*
Wessels, K. C. (Aust.):– 15,827 r. (avge 50.08), *143;* 43 hundreds, *138;* 4 Test hundreds, *200, 225, 232, 234;* 2 hundreds in match (2), *136, 1051;* Hundred on Test début, *172, 200;* 388 for 1st wkt, *148;* Test p'ship record, *234.*
West Indies:– Definition of first-class matches, *1212;* Domestic season 1987-88, *1061-7;* Highest individual Test innings, *170;* Highest Test innings, *189;* Leading batsmen in Tests, *175;* Leading bowlers in Tests, *183;* Lowest Test innings, *191;* Most consecutive Test appearances, *193;* Most Test appearances, *127;* Most Test appearances as captain, *127;* Oldest Test player, *193;* Representative body, *1219;* Summary of Tests, *194;* Test cricketers (1928-88), *109-14;* West Indies in Test cricket (*see p. 131*); Youngest and oldest on Test début, *192.*
Wettimuny, S. (SL):– 2 Test hundreds, *220, 251;* 190 v England, *220, 260;* Carrying bat in Test, *178;* Longest innings in Lord's

Wettimuny, S. (SL):– *contd* Test, *260;* Test p'ship records, *220, 247, 250, 252.*

Whatmore, D. F. (Aust.):– 6 c. in Test, *189.*

White, C. de L. (Border):– Obituary, *1179;* Hat-trick of c., *157.*

White, G. C. (SA):– 2 Test hundreds, *206.*

White, J. C. (Eng.):– Test captain, *196, 204;* 2,356 w., *160;* 100 w. (14), *159;* 16 w. in day, *156;* 10 w. in innings, *154;* 10 w. or more in Test (1), *202;* 8 w. in Test innings, *181.*

Whitehead, H. (Leics.):– 380 for 1st wkt, *148.*

Whitehouse, J. (Warwicks.):– Hundred on début, *134.*

Whitelaw, P. E. (Auck.):– Obituary, *1179;* 445 for 3rd wkt, *150.*

Whittaker, G. J. (Surrey):– 253* v Gloucestershire II, *261.*

Whitty, W. J. (Aust.):– 37 w. in series, *182;* Test p'ship record, *223.*

Whysall, W. W. (Eng.):– 51 hundreds, *138;* 4 successive hundreds, *137;* 2 hundreds in match (2), *136;* 1st wkt hundreds, *149.*

Wicket-keeping records:– *163-5, 187-8, 257;* in 1988, *266, 274.*

Wicket records (1st to 10th), *149-52.*

Wiener, J. M. (Aust.):– 390* for 3rd wkt, *150.*

Wight, G. L. (British Guiana):– 390 for 1st wkt, *148, 149.*

Wijesuriya, R. G. C. E. (SL):– Test p'ship record, *252.*

Wiles, C. A. (WI):– Test début at 40, *192.*

Willey, P. (Eng.):– 5,975 r. in Sunday League, *793;* 42 hundreds, *138;* 2 Test hundreds, *210.*

William Younger Cup (National Club Championship), *337.*

Williams, A. B. (WI):– 2 Test hundreds, *226, 239;* Hundred on Test début, *172, 226.*

Williams, E. A. V. (WI):– 255 for 8th wkt, *151.*

Williams, R. G. (Northants):– 10,000 r., *267.*

Willis, R. G. D. (Eng.):– Test captain, *195, 212, 215, 218;* 325 w. in Tests, *182;* 128 w. v Australia, *203;* 8 w. in Test innings, *181;* Test p'ship records, *217, 219.*

Wills Cup (Pak.), *1088, 1097.*

Wilson, A. E. (Glos.):– 10 d. in match, *164.*

Wilson, D. (Eng.):– 30 r. in over, *146;* 3 hat-tricks, *157.*

Wilson, E. R. (Eng.):– Test début at 41, *192.*

Wilson, G. A. (Worcs.):– 3 hat-tricks, *157.*

Wilson, J. V. (Yorks.):– 61 c. in season, *166.*

Wiltshire, *660-1, 801, 803, 817-8;* v Cambridge Univ., *640.*

Winslow, P. L. (SA):– 1 Test hundred, *206;* 30 r. in over, *146;* Test p'ship record, *207.*

Wisden, J. (Sussex):– 10 w. in innings, *153.*

Wisden Trophy, *208.*

Women's Cricket Association, Address of Secretary, *1220.*

Wood, C. J. B. (Leics.):– 37 hundreds, *138;* 2 separate hundreds, *136;* 380 for 1st wkt, *148.*

Wood, G. M. (Aust.):– 3,109 r. in Tests, *175;* 8 Test hundreds, *200, 225, 228, 230, 232;* Test p'ship record, *228.*

Wood, H. (Eng.):– 1 Test hundred, *205;* Test p'ship record, *206.*

Woodfull, W. M. (Aust.):– Test captain, *195, 221, 224;* 13,388 r. (avge 64.99), *142;* 2,300 r. in Tests, *175;* 49 hundreds, *138;* 7 Test hundreds, *200, 222;* Carrying bat in Test (2), *177;* 375 for 1st wkt, *148.*

Woods, S. M. J. (Eng. and Aust.):– 10 w. in innings, *153.*

Woolley, C. N. (Northants):– 326 consecutive Championship appearances, *263.*

Woolley, F. E. (Eng.):– All-round, *162, 163;* Test cricket at 47, *193;* 58,969 r., *141;* 3,352 r. in season, *138;* 3,283 r. in Tests, *174;* 1,000 r. (28), *139;* 707 Championship appearances, *263;* 52 consecutive Test matches, *193;* 145 hundreds, *137;* 5 Test hundreds, *198, 205;* 4 successive hundreds, *137;* 305* v Tasmania, *133, 144;* 300 r. in 205 min., *144;* 2,068 w., *160;* 100 w. (8) *159;* 10 w. or more in Test (1), *202;* 1,018 c. *166;* 6 c. in Test, *187;* 235 for 10th wkt *152;* Test p'ship record, *201.*

Woolmer, R. A. (Eng.):– 3 Test hundreds *198.*

Wootton, G. (Notts.):– 10 w. in innings, *153*

Worcestershire:– *339, 588-604;* Championship positions, *344-5;* County champions *339;* Highest score, *166;* Highest individual score, *134;* Lowest score, *167* Refuge Assurance League winners, *712;* Ireland, *845.*

Worcestershire II, *822, 835-6.*

World Cup Finals, *259.*

World record partnership, *1102.*

Worrell, Sir F. M. M. (WI):– Test captain *208, 224, 238;* 15,025 r. (avge 54.24), *143* 3,860 r. in Tests, *175;* 39 hundreds, *138;* Test hundreds, *211, 226, 236, 239;* 308* Trinidad, *133;* 261 v England, *170, 21* Carrying bat in Test, *178;* 574* and 502 for 4th wkt, *147, 148, 150;* Test p'sh records, *211, 237, 240.*

Worrell, Frank, Trophy, *224.*

Worthington, T. S. (Eng.):– 1 Test hundre *216;* Test p'ship record, *217.*

Wright, C. W. (Eng.):– Test p'ship recor *206.*

Wright, D. V. P. (Eng.):– 2,056 w., *160;* 1 w. in Tests, *183;* 100 w. (10), *159;* 10 w. more in Test (1), *207;* 7 hat-tricks, *157*

Wright, J. G. (NZ):– Test captain, *21* 20,000 r., *267;* 3,343 r. in Tests, *176;* 2,9

Wright, J. G. (NZ):– *contd*
r. in one-day ints, *256*; 47 hundreds, *138*; 7 Test hundreds, *214, 228, 237, 243, 245*; Test p'ship records, *228, 237, 245*.
Wyatt, R. E. S. (Eng.):– Test captain, *195, 204, 208, 212*; 39,405 r., *141*; 1,000 r. (18), *139*; 85 hundreds, *137*; 2 Test hundreds, *205*; 124 and hat-trick v Ceylon, *161*.
Wynyard, E. G. (Eng.):– 411 for 6th wkt, *151*.

Y

Yadav, N. S. (Ind.):– 102 w. in Tests, *184*; Test p'ship record, *231, 244*.
Yajurvindra Singh (Ind.):– 7 c. in Test, *189*; 5 c. in Test innings, *188*.
Yallop, G. N. (Aust.):– Test captain, *195, 231*; 2,756 r. in Tests, *175*; 8 Test hundreds, *200, 230, 232*; 2 hundreds in match (2), *136*; 268 v Pakistan, *170, 232*; Test p'ship records, *233, 234*.
Yardley, B. (Aust.):– 126 w. in Tests, *183*; 10 w. or more in Test (1), *227*.
Yardley, N. W. D. (Eng.):– Test captain, *195-6, 204, 208*; Test p'ship record, *206*.
Yarnold, H. (Worcs.):– 110 d. in season, *164*; 7 d. in innings, *163*.
Yashpal Sharma (Ind.):– 2 Test hundreds, *217, 230*; Test p'ship records, *217, 240, 248*.
Yorkshire:– *339, 605-20*; Championship positions, *344-5*; Highest score, *166*; Highest individual score, *134*; Lowest score, *167*; v Michael Parkinson's World XI, *655*; v Yorkshire Exiles, *657*; Tilcon Trophy winners, *649-50*; Ward Knockout Cup, *656-7*.
Yorkshire II:– *822, 836-7*; Bain Clarkson Trophy winners, *838*.
Yorkshire Exiles:– v Yorkshire, *657*.
Young Cricketer of the Year, *425*.
Young, B. A. (N. Dist.):– 7 d. in innings, *163*.
Young, D. M. (Worcs. and Glos.):– 40 hundreds, *138*; 395 for 1st wkt, *148*.
Young, J. A. (Eng.):– 100 w. (8), *159*.
Youngest Test players, *192*.
Younis Ahmed (Pak.):– 26,063 r., *142*; 5,897 r. in Sunday League, *793*; 46 hundreds, *138*; Slow scoring in Test, *179*.
Youth World Cup, *1007-11*.
Yuile, B. W. (NZ):– Test p'ship record, *245*.

Z

Zaheer Abbas (Pak.):– Test captain, *218, 231, 244, 247*; 34,843 r. (avge 51.54), *141, 143*; 5,062 r. in Tests, *176*; 1,000 r. (17), *139*; 108 hundreds, *137*; 12 Test hundreds, *219, 232, 245, 248, 251*; 7 one-day int. hundreds, *256*; 4 successive hundreds, *137*; 2 hundreds in match (8), *135*; Hundred and double-hundred (4), *135, 136*; 274 v England, *170, 219*; Avge of 88.69 in English season, *140*; 30 r. in over, *146*; Fast scoring, *179*; Hit the ball twice, *153*; 353 for 6th wkt, *151*; Test p'ship records, *219, 233, 242, 249, 252*.
Zimbabwe:– 1987-88 season, *1099-1100*; Representative body, *1220*.
Zulch, J. W. (SA):– 2 Test hundreds, *223*; Carrying bat in Test, *177*.
Zulfiqar Ahmed (Pak.):– 10 w. or more in Test (1), *246*; Test p'ship record, *249*.

INDEX OF FILLERS

Addresses of Representative Bodies, *1219-20*.
Ashes, The, *84*.
A Suitable Case For Compo, *711*.
Career Figures of Players Retiring or Not Being Retained, *681*.
County Benefits Awarded in 1989, *800*.
County Caps Awarded in 1988, *538*.
Cricket Associations and Societies, *907-8*.
Cricketer Cup Winners, 1967-88, *604*.
Deloitte Ratings, *961*.
Errata in *Wisden*, *1253*.
Fielding in 1988, *274*.
First Real Tennis Court at Lord's, *489*.
Future Tours, *327*.
Honours' List, 1988, *819*.
India v New Zealand, 1988-89, *1087*.
I Zingari Results, 1988, *850*.
Lancashire Close Their Membership, *819*.
Lords and Commons Results, 1988, *1264*.
MCC England Honorary Cricket Members, *338*.
Overs Bowled and Runs Scored in the Britannic Assurance Championship, 1988, *1106*.
Pakistan v Australia, 1988-89, *1097*.
Status of Matches in UK, *555*.
Two Times Ten, *489*.
Umpires for 1989, *311*.
World Record Partnership, *1103*.
Young Cricketer of the Year, *425*.

NOTES BY THE EDITOR

Two years ago, when writing the Notes for the 1987 edition of *Wisden*, I took as a centrepiece the Palmer Report; the Report of the TCCB Enquiry into the Standards of Play of English Cricket in Test and First-class County Cricket. It would be appropriate to do so again, for the background to the enquiry remains as apt now as when it was first commissioned. It was the "widespread disappointment and genuine concern about the standards of play at Test and county level" following England's performances between 1982-83 and 1984. Given the wisdom contained in that report, there should be even greater concern that, in the two years following its publication, the problems and the causes which it highlights remain. Little has been done to solve the problems. In some instances, as with county pitches, there has been further deterioration rather than a serious attempt to bring about an improvement. But if it is any consolation, little of this is new. And because of that, it might be possible to look forward with a little optimism, if not necessarily with any great confidence.

A familiar story

Much was made of the fact that in 1988 England fielded as many as 2 players in the series against West Indies. For this, and for choosing fou captains for the five Tests, the England selectors were castigated. In 1966 when West Indies beat England by three Tests to one, and their victorie were as overwhelming as any achieved last year, England called on 2 players. (When John Price withdrew from the side for the final Test, whic England won, John Snow regained his place.) Moreover, of the three Englan captains that summer, M. J. K. Smith and Colin Cowdrey were replace following innings defeats inside the distance. Of England's captains la season, only John Emburey could be said to have lost the captaincy becaus of his form or because his side lost heavily.

"Before the summer ended, the selectors themselves came in for advers criticism", said Norman Preston in his Notes to the 1967 *Wisden*. But, h went on to say, "Examining the facts, one must remember that compare with other countries England have many more first-class players on the fring of Test standard, yet few who can be termed automatic choices". A simil view was expressed by Peter May, in an interview with the editor of t *Cricketer* magazine, following his retirement on November 25 after seve years as chairman of selectors. "We have more players of a certain standa than any other country", he said. "It's often easier to pick a team if you ha fewer players to choose from." What is of interest as much as the similarity views is that Mr May was also an England selector in 1966.

Critics of England's recent record, in which they went eighteen Tes without a win, might consider that from 1963 to 1966 England won only tw in eighteen home Tests against Australia, South Africa and West Indies. O of those victories was against West Indies at The Oval in 1966; the other, a against West Indies, was in 1963 at Edgbaston where Trueman had mat figures of twelve for 119, his best analysis in Test cricket. In that series, w 3-1 by West Indies, Trueman at the age of 32 took 34 wickets at 17.47 ea from 236.4 overs. This remained the record for an England-West Indies ser until last year, when Malcolm Marshall claimed 35 wickets at 12.65 fr

203.1 overs. By way of contrast, England's strike bowler, Graham Dilley, had fifteen wickets at 26.86 from 136.1 overs in his four Tests last year, although he did have fewer innings in which to bowl.

"The shortage of high-class batsmen and bowlers in English cricket could be a passing phase – or is it bound up with current conditions?" asked the editor of *Wisden* after the 1963 series. The old songs always were the best.

The consolation of history

It is because of what happened after 1966 that I ponder the possibility of looking ahead with some optimism. I am not necessarily forecasting success for England. There is no reason why, in a country where it is often impossible to have building work done or a motor car serviced properly, its sporting tradesmen should perform any better. But just as craftsmen can sometimes be found, so it is in sport. England, from defeat by West Indies in 1966, went on to win in the West Indies in 1967-68 and did not lose a series, home or away, until 1971, when India won at The Oval and brought to an end England's record run of 26 Test matches without defeat.

This summer brings an Ashes series and, against Australia, the chance for England to re-establish their credentials. For both countries it is an important series. But for England, at the end of it, there is the prospect of a tour of the West Indies, and this should not be ignored. I can see only too clearly a ituation in which England play well against Australia under Graham Gooch, nly to go to the Caribbean with a new captain.

he right captain for England

f anything constructive emerged from England's performances against West ndies, it was their attitude under Gooch's leadership at The Oval. There eemed to be a positiveness which, to me, had been absent in recent times. I an understand why the selectors wanted to retain him as captain, however isingenuous it was to expect the Indian government to accept him as a ouring captain. There is an authority about Gooch's batting which earns the espect of his colleagues and his opponents, and I think he has an ability to istance himself sufficiently from his team-mates to gain their respect also as leader. He will not need to be one of the lads. I do not share the concern at Gooch's batting will suffer from his being captain. Essex consider he is apable of doing the job, and they are a county who plan carefully and have a ommitment to success.

When, some twenty years ago, I first watched county cricket, what struck e was the discernible gap between the county game and a Test match. This ill sound as if I am stating the obvious. But it had not been obvious to me, om the game's literature or from the little international cricket I had seen, at first-class county cricketers did not play to their full potential day in, day t. I think I expected professional cricket to be like the professional theatre, which one could expect a first-class performance, even at a matinée. In ne I became accustomed to the inertia of county first-class cricket; the me, after all, has many charms. However, it has become more noticeable at players, when selected for England, are not bridging the gap. Their proach in Test match cricket seems little different from the way they play ich of their Championship cricket. It is imperative, therefore, that the captain and the cricket manager are men able to lift the players out of their usual mode and keep them playing to the peak of their ability over five days. Little I have seen convinces me that many players are capable of this transition on their own.

The county programme

Achieving this transition is not made easier in home Test matches by the county fixture list. The players have a day together before the Test match and are away to another county game soon after it finishes. The match becomes little more than an interim in what Peter Roebuck calls the "continuum" of county cricket. Given Test cricket's importance both to the financial welfare of the English game and to the morale of the country generally (remember 1981?), a Test match should be seen as more than just an occasion which brings in revenue. It should also be an occasion for pride; not for cynicism and despair.

There is a developing argument in favour of a sixteen-match, four-day County Championship. If the standard of English cricket is to be improved, it should be supported. Not all the county secretaries and treasurers will agree. If such a programme were implemented, it would mean eight fewer days of cricket per county. What will need to be resisted is any attempt to fill those eight days with more one-day cricket; indeed, cricket of any kind except net practice.

Men and women in other professional sports take time between fixtures to practise; the cricketers of other countries do not spend all their time playing and travelling. One would like to think that players could sort out their problems in the middle, but the modern game, in its various forms and with its pressures for success, does not allow this luxury. Consequently, English county cricket contains a good number of journeymen who make their way from one season to another contract by means of a satisfactory method rather than the techniques required for Test cricket. It is true that there are promising youngsters to encourage hope for the future. But other countries also have promising youngsters. As may be seen elsewhere in this Almanack, England, with a squad containing nine players with first class experience, finished fourth behind Australia, Pakistan and West Indies in the Youth World Cup in Australia last year.

If standards are to improve, so that English cricket is again an example to the world, it will require dedication and discipline. Players will need to work at their game with coaches who can pinpoint and correct the faults that creep in during the season. Matthew Maynard provides an example of this. When first saw him in 1986 he stood still at the crease, had time to move back or forward to play the ball, and he timed his strokes. He looked a potential Test cricketer. Last season, he was shuffling about at the crease as the bowler was delivering the ball. While some top-class batsmen do make an initial movement, few get away with fidgeting about like a tennis player receiving service.

County v country

It cannot be simply coincidence that a number of overseas players in county cricket have been critical of the commitment of their English colleagues. Career professionalism should be English cricket's strength, and yet it arguable that it is its weakness. In that it gives cricketers of other countries the opportunity to develop their skills, and do so in English conditions, it might be said to be a double weakness. Yet I would be reluctant to advocate a total restriction on overseas players. They remain an attraction, which was a reason for having them initially, and county cricket generally is richer for their presence. On the other hand, a limit of one overseas player per county does seem sensible. Unfortunately, while paying lip-service to a restriction, the chairmen and their committees put county before country as success is seen in a local rather than a national light.

It has been the same with pitches. When the ball behaves quite differently in a three-day game and a limited-overs game, yet at only a few strips' remove, something strange is happening. No-one, apart from batsmen perhaps, is looking for plumb pitches. But pitches which allow the ball to deviate laterally and bounce unevenly, as we have seen recently, serve only the ego and the averages of the bowlers. Certainly they do not help the selectors in their search for bowlers able to do something with the ball on a truer Test-match pitch.

For a batsman, it is important that he can trust the bounce, which means the pitch must be firm. I wonder if pitches are rolled sufficiently – and with a roller heavy enough to iron out the grasses which, we are told, produce erratic bounce. Most grounds I have seen in the last three years could afford also to get rid of some grass – not just from the pitch but from the outfield. The modern cricket ball, with its generous seam and longer-lasting shine, already favours the bowler whose ambition is to "hit the seam" and hope that the ball will deviate off the pitch. A less lush outfield would roughen the ball. Bowlers might then have to swing the ball, even the old ball, and in the absence of such artists there might be a place for the slow bowler. If wickets were hard, that slow bowler might also have to spin the ball and/or flight it. But all this has been said before. In the meantime, some action has been taken to penalise those counties whose pitches do not meet the TCCB's specifications. In the event of a pitch being found unsuitable, 25 points will be deducted from the home county's points in the Championship.

lot the happiest of years

hat decision was made at the Winter Meeting of the TCCB. Perhaps my ptimism is without foundation, but I felt after that meeting that the counties ere taking stock. After all, it had not been the happiest of years for the rofessional game.

In the train of England's tour of Pakistan late in 1987, England's presentative cricketers became the focus of media attention. This in itself ould have ensured exemplary behaviour. It did not. In Sydney, in ustralia's Bicentennial Test match, Chris Broad knocked down a stump ith his bat after being bowled and was fined; in New Zealand, Graham lley's language, when appeals for a catch were turned down, also resulted a fine. The trend was sufficiently disturbing for the TCCB to direct the ngland selectors to take into account a player's behaviour as well as his rm. "If you don't behave, you don't play" was the Board's message to the untry's cricketers.

None the less, when Broad was seen on television, expressing his obvious sappointment after his first-innings dismissal against West Indies at Lord's t summer, what happened? The England cricket manager, Micky Stewart, defended Broad on the grounds that he was "annoyed with himself", and Broad remained in the team for the Third Test, although he was subsequently omitted from the final eleven because of his poor form. The selectors are the appointees of the TCCB; indeed, Mr Stewart is an employee. The Board ought to ensure that its selectors are acting according to its instructions, not acting in isolation with no brief other than to select the best possible team. If that is the selectors' view, it is a blinkered one.

Gatting's term ends

Given the Board's strictures on behaviour, it was not surprising that Mike Gatting's position as captain of the England team became untenable when he was named in allegations of sexual impropriety by the *Sun* and *Today* newspapers. On June 8, the day after England had successfully fought to save the First Test, the *Sun* carried a story alleging a "sex orgy" involving two unnamed England players. The next morning, June 9, Gatting was named as one of the players, and that afternoon he was relieved of the captaincy. While he admitted inviting a young woman to his room on his birthday, June 6, Gatting denied that there had been any impropriety. The selectors, representing the Board, accepted Gatting's version of the events but, in the words of Mr May, felt that "Gatting had behaved irresponsibly during a Test match by inviting female company to his room for a drink in the late evening". Much wrath was directed at Mr May, the selectors and the TCCB.

I feel they had little option but to pursue the course they did if they were to expect certain standards from the England captain and his team. As it was to illustrate over the matter of English players working in South Africa, the TCCB has a responsibility wider than the playing of cricket. In this instance it had also to consider the game's sponsors, local as well as national, who are attracted to cricket because it has, or has had, an image with which they wish to be associated. What cricketers got up to in the past is irrelevant. There wa a time when the yellow press was prepared to wait until a celebrity ha written his or her memoirs before entering the bedroom. Today it makes the bed.

I suppose it is money that makes a newspaper prepared to destroy a man' name and his career. It cannot argue any public service in this case, becaus English cricket would have been better off without the revelations in the *Su* and *Today*. I suppose there is no connection between their proprietor bein an Australian, albeit a former Australian, and the fact that Australia, beate out of sight by M. W. Gatting's England team last time around, come [illegible] England this summer.

It was a journal from the same stable, the *Sunday Times*, which printed preview of Gatting's autobiography and landed him deeper in trouble wit the Test and County Cricket Board. The book, *Leading from the Fron* contained a chapter dealing with England's tour of Pakistan the previou winter; this had not been sanctioned by the Board as a player's tour contra excludes him from writing on recent tours. Gatting was asked to withdra the chapter, but this was not done. Instead it was rewritten, in the thir person, by Gatting's co-author, a subterfuge which did not pass muster wit the Board. Early in August it fined Gatting £5,000 for publishing the chapt without its consent. The sagas over the book and the barmaid ran more [illegible] less concurrently and placed a question mark over Gatting's suitability captain of the England team. Corollaries with other public figures will [illegible] resisted.

England's tour to India cancelled

Gatting did not play in the Second Test against West Indies, and after doing little in the Third, he asked the selectors not to consider him for the rest of the summer. He also withdrew from consideration for England's tour to India in the winter. Whether or not he would have been missed there became academic when the tour was cancelled on October 7. The Indian government would not grant visas to eight of the players whose names appeared on a list of sportsmen with links with South Africa, and the TCCB, holding to the International Cricket Conference's principle that no country should be allowed to influence the team selection of another, refused o replace those players. The team which England selected was as follows: G. A. Gooch (captain), J. E. Emburey (vice-captain), R. J. Bailey, K. J. Barnett, J. H. Childs, G. R. Dilley, N. A. Foster, D. I. Gower, E. E. Iemmings, A. J. Lamb, D. V. Lawrence, P. J. Newport, S. J. Rhodes, R. T. Robinson, R. C. Russell and R. A. Smith. The players about whom objections were raised were Gooch, Emburey, Bailey, Barnett, Dilley, Lamb, Newport and Robinson.

Even before the team was announced, on September 7, there had been peculation that the tour might be in jeopardy following the appointment the revious week of Gooch as captain. Gooch had captained the first of the rebel" tours to South Africa, for which he (and Emburey) had been banned rom Test cricket for three years. Both he and Emburey had been admitted nto India and Pakistan for the World Cup in 1987, an expediency which led accusations of hypocrisy. These did an injustice to the strength of feeling India against the apartheid policy of South Africa's elected government. Gooch and Emburey, with others, had gone virtually straight on to South Africa from a tour of India, which had been in doubt because the Indian overnment found unacceptable the inclusion of Geoffrey Boycott and Geoff ook, who had recently played in South Africa. Boycott moreover played part in setting up the team for South Africa, as well as being a member it. In the circumstances, it should not have been surprising when, on eptember 9, India's Foreign Ministry announced that no player "having or kely to have sporting contact with South Africa" would be granted a visa. Gooch, it was by now known, had intended spending the winter playing South Africa for Western Province, rather than touring India with ngland. When he was persuaded to tour as captain of England, he was leased from his South African contract. It was a situation made, if not signed, to aggravate the Indian government. In his interview with the *icketer*, Mr May was asked if he and his fellow selectors had considered political repercussions of appointing Gooch. His view was that the ectors' brief was to select the best possible team from the cricketing point view. "We don't pick teams for political reasons. In any case Graham ooch had been perfectly acceptable to India for the World Cup . . . ." ore apt, perhaps, to say that he had been an exception then rather than ceptable; and is it not naïve of the chairman and his selectors, at the end the 1980s, to think it unnecessary to look beyond the cricketing point of w? If the cricketing point of view were all that mattered, it would be ssible to ask why Gatting was stripped of the captaincy. Sad though it y be, cricket cannot operate as a business without an awareness of the ssy world beyond the boundary.

Pakistan refuse to play ball

When the tour of India was cancelled, the TCCB agreed to pay the players selected a substantial portion of their £12,000 tour fee. They also tried to arrange a replacement tour. With most countries already committed, this was not an easy task. Eventually, New Zealand arranged a seven-week tour in February and March incorporating two Test matches against England and a triangular limited-overs tournament involving Pakistan, their scheduled touring team. However, when Pakistan changed their mind and refused to play against England in New Zealand, this tour too had to be abandoned. New Zealand, whose finances had suffered the previous season, felt they could not afford to stage a secondary tour involving England which did not include the three-way one-day competition. Pakistan, like India, objected to the presence in the England team of players who had worked in South Africa; yet Pakistan's cricketers were playing at the time in Australia against at least one player, Terry Alderman, who had toured South Africa with "rebel" sides.

ICC decide on South African connections

India's decision to exclude "the England eight" left the TCCB in little doub that it would have to make concessions on the subject of links with Sout Africa if it was not to find itself isolated internationally. Certainly it was th opinion of the Board's executive that English cricket could not maintain it current financial health without a regular programme of Test matches a home and away. Some counties, no doubt, would have liked to call the bluf of those countries opposed to links with South Africa, but such thinking di not take into account the political opposition in the other ICC countries t apartheid. The reality of the situation demanded a solution. Only time wi tell if the solution agreed on will prevent further interference by government in the composition of touring teams.

At its meeting at Lord's on January 23 and 24, the ICC resolved that, a from April 1, 1989, any cricketer who visits South Africa as a player or coac or in an administrative capacity will automatically be suspended from Te cricket for the following terms according to the player's age: over sixteen an under nineteen, three years; nineteen and over, four years. In additio players participating in an organised tour will be suspended for five years. register of ineligible players will be kept by the ICC secretariat, and a secon or subsequent visit to South Africa could increase the suspension. Th resolution, which was proposed by West Indies and seconded by Sri Lank was unopposed and carried by 32 votes: two votes each by the seven fu members and one by each of the eighteen associate members. It was preced by much negotiating, and no doubt there were some on either side of t divide who saw it as a compromise. It is; and the test will come wh England tour West Indies this coming winter with players who worked South Africa before April 1. For the moment, England's cricketers can thankful that the resolution was not retrospective.

Nevertheless, an important principle has been conceded. If there remai any euphoria that international cricket has been saved – and with arguably, England's fully professional circuit with some four hundr employees – the citizens of the United Kingdom have had a freedom c tailed at the insistence of other countries. It can be argued that a freed which allows trade with an unjust society is not so valuable a freedom. None the less it is a freedom within British law. If it is expedient to accept restrictions on legal freedoms, how simple it will be to restrict freedom legally.

The future of cricket in South Africa

Freedom is a strange word to use in any context involving South Africa. Cricket, however, is not free of South Africa. There remains, as I write these Notes, the threat of legal action against the ICC and perhaps the TCCB, the cost of which will be borne by English cricket, not by those countries which instigated the ban on players who ply their trade in South Africa. There is also the possibility that South Africa will continue to attract cricketers from abroad. It would be ironic if this affected England less than other countries, whose seasons are the same as South Africa's. In a material age, money is a powerful persuader.

What the member countries of the ICC have not said in recent years is what they want of South Africa. Perhaps they hope that, as it is no longer on the agenda, the question of South Africa will cease to exist. I wonder if an opportunity has been lost by ignoring what is being done by the South African Cricket Union in taking cricket into the black townships. South Africa has to change if justice is to prevail and each child, regardless of colour, is to begin life equal with the next. That change can come through bloodshed or through the political will of the South African electorate. The second way will take time and education. I know nothing of the work of the South African Cricket Union except for what I have read. It may be propaganda. But if black South African children are being taught a game which brings them into regular contact with white South African children, might not the latter come to acknowledge the rights of the former and grow to vote out a government which maintains apartheid? Undue optimism? Probably, but I prefer subversion by the cricket bat to subversion by the Kalashnikov. If, however, the will of the voting class is not for change, no amount of cricket in the townships will destroy apartheid. And it is the ending of apartheid, not the number of black cricketers, which will influence world opinion.

Another problem to be solved

It is, of course, easier to ignore South Africa altogether, as the problem of short-pitched bowling has been ignored. At the moment it is primarily the West Indian fast bowlers who give cause for concern, but the day will come when some other country possesses similar firepower. Currently, countries try to counter the West Indians by preparing pitches unresponsive to fast bowling. This strikes as being just as contrary to the spirit of the game. Again, as in the past two editions, I advocate an independent panel of umpires for international cricket. Law 42.8 already empowers umpires to prevent such bowling, but as long as umpires are associated with the home authority, regardless of their neutrality they do not seem to find it easy to utilise these powers. Sadly it is no longer possible to expect all cricketers to respect the Laws or the spirit of the game. I am not suggesting that the game needs policemen; rather, men who understand cricket and cricketers; men who have played at least first-class cricket themselves.

A beautiful game

Cricket can still be a beautiful game. No-one at Lord's on the Saturday of the Second Test last year would surely deny that. As well as being a day of sunshine and marvellous batsmanship, it was the day when West Indies took from England the Test match and the series. It became obvious that, irrespective of England's successes in the Texaco Trophy one-day matches, West Indies were a better side. In the sometimes bitter analysis of England's defeats, this was often ignored. My personal memory of that match, though, was not West Indies' batting but David Gower's catch behind square leg to dismiss Ambrose in West Indies' first innings. There was a moment of suspension as he leapt up and twisted back that made the action graceful instead of hurried or snatched.

Two Tests later, at Headingley, Gower played in his 100th Test and reached 7,000 runs in Test cricket. Only two other Englishmen, Boycott and Cowdrey, have played in 100 Tests, and these two and Hammond are the only ones to have scored 7,000 runs. Gower reached his century of Tests in ten years, some three and a half years quicker than Cowdrey and seven years quicker than Boycott, who excused himself from the conflict for three years. In addition, Gower has played in 102 limited-overs internationals and, with 2,905 runs at an average of 31.92, is England's leading run-scorer. This is a remarkable achievement for someone who is said by his critics not to take the game seriously enough. It is also an indicator of the pressure he has lived with through his twenties, and perhaps it is worth asking if too much is expected of our truly gifted performers.

Worcestershire and Hick dominate the season

That Worcestershire were the team of the year is beyond dispute. They won the Britannic Assurance Championship, retained the Refuge Assurance League, and were runners-up in the finals of the NatWest Bank Trophy and Refuge Assurance Cup. In Graeme Hick, they had the cricketer of the year. His batting feats caught the imagination of the cricket world and led to calls for a reduction in the qualification period so that he could play for England. The TCCB Executive Committee proposed such a move, but it was rejected at the Board's Winter Meeting last December. The counties expressed their determination that, as far as possible, English county and Test cricket should be played by Englishmen; and presumably by the other nationalities of the United Kingdom.

The Oval is saved

Towards the end of last season, the Surrey members voted to allow their famous ground to be renamed the Foster's Oval as part of a sponsorship agreement with the brewers, Courage. For some time Surrey had been struggling to achieve the target of their "Save The Oval" appeal, and this sponsorship allowed them to commence work on their £5.8 million development planned for the ground. Without major renovations, it was said, The Oval's place as a Test match venue would be in jeopardy. Stands which were condemned by the fire authority are now being rebuilt, and the development plans include a cricket school and facilities which will benefit the local community. The ground will be known as the Foster's Oval for a period of fifteen years.

MCC honours Sir Donald Bradman

On the occasion of his 80th birthday, Sir Donald Bradman was invited by MCC to become an Honorary Life Vice-President of the Club "in recognition of his unique contribution to the game of cricket". J. G. W. Davies, the Club's President in 1985-86, was also elected an Honorary Life Vice-President last year, bringing to ten the number who have been accorded this honour. MCC's other Honorary Life Vice-Presidents have been Sir Pelham Warner (elected in 1961), R. H. Twining (1969), Captain The Lord Cornwallis (1971), Sir George Allen (1980), R. Aird (1982), F. R. Brown (1983), S. C. Griffith (1983) and C. G. A. Paris (1985).

Finally, these Notes should not end without a word of commendation for the work of Field-Marshal The Lord Bramall and the ICC secretariat at Lord's in helping to bring about a solution to the South African question. They have again shown that MCC, in its stewardship of the ICC, has a continuing and influential role in the affairs of world cricket. It is not a role the Club's members should discount lightly, although some might look upon it as an encumbrance. In international matters, MCC through the ICC is able to offer counsel which extends beyond parochial issues. Were it ever to content itself simply with its own affairs, MCC would be little more than a cricket club with a Long Room, a long tradition and a long waiting-list.

FIVE CRICKETERS OF THE YEAR

KIM BARNETT

Derbyshire took a considerable gamble in May 1983 when they appointed Kim Barnett as captain. Barnett was then 22 and still feeling his way as a player, but after a sequence of six different captains within the space of nine seasons, they were desperate for some kind of stability. Eddie Barlow had revived the county and Barry Wood had led them to victory in the 1981 NatWest Bank Trophy, their first success since the 1936 Championship. Wood became another to step down during a season, so Charles Elliott, then chairman of the cricket committee, and Philip Russell, the coach, persuaded others that Barnett offered the only hope of a long-term solution. It was a bold decision but, in 1988, Barnett was in his sixth season as captain, the longest Derbyshire reign since Donald Carr (1955 to 1962). Carr was also the last Derbyshire player to be picked for England as a batsman, on the 1951-52 tour of India, until Barnett's début against Sri Lanka last year.

There had, too, been talk of Barnett as a potential England captain; good progress for a man who describes himself as a glorified No. 7 and who joined Derbyshire as a leg-spinner. He has Derbyshire's admittedly modest batting records at his mercy. His 25 centuries for the county put him five behind Denis Smith's 30 and his 11,412 runs bring him within sight of Smith's 20,516, especially as he has established himself at around 1,500 runs a season.

KIM JOHN BARNETT, born in Stoke-on-Trent on July 17, 1960, grew up in Leek, a small Staffordshire town now on Derbyshire's extensive rota of Sunday venues. He was educated at Leek High School and, even before starting there, had played for Thomas Boltons' second team under the captaincy of his father, Derek. He graduated from the North Staffordshire League club to Leek, in the North Staffordshire and South Cheshire League, and came under the influence of the former England and Lancashire batsman, John Ikin, as he worked his way up the county representative teams. Ikin toughened his approach and Barnett continued to develop, first playing for England at Under-15 level as a leg-spinner. Counties began to pursue him. Barnett chose Derbyshire ahead of Northamptonshire and Warwickshire because he felt more at home there; and he could see more chance of winning a place. For a time he had worked for the National Westminster Bank, and two years after his début he would help Derbyshire win the trophy sponsored by his former employer.

Barlow had left Derbyshire before Barnett joined them in 1979, after heading the England Under-19 batting averages in Australia, but there was significant contact between them in 1982-83. It was the first of Barnett's three South African seasons for Boland, then led by Barlow. "I was impressed by Eddie's positive thinking about the game," Barnett says, "and he had a great effect on my career when I needed it. He taught me to channel my mental efforts and make the most of my strengths. He told me to make it clear to Derbyshire that I wanted the captaincy. I thought that was ridiculous, but it was due to Eddie that I was prepared when the opportunity came the following May."

Captaincy turned Barnett into an opening batsman because he felt, as leader of a largely inexperienced team, that he should go over the top first. He batted adventurously, chasing anything wide of the off stump with stroke which brought him many runs and, sometimes, accusations of rashness. Progress was recognised by selection as vice-captain of the 1985-86 England B tour of Zimbabwe, Bangladesh and Sri Lanka, but the fact that Barnett and others had played in South Africa turned it into a one-leg trip to Sri Lanka. The same problem cropped up when he was picked for last winter's tour of India, and Barnett was keener than most for the International Cricket Conference to produce a definitive ruling. He returned home early from Sri Lanka, a debilitating virus having caused alarming loss of weight, but he has maintained a high level of consistency for his county. When he missed a Championship match against Surrey at The Oval last June, it was his first absence for four years. It was ironic that a hand injury stopped him making his England début in the Fifth Test against West Indies, and a broken nose, suffered while fielding in a Sunday game at Old Trafford, caused further doubts before the Sri Lanka match.

The first England appearance was a logical result of increased maturity and a greater appetite for big scores. David Graveney described Barnett's 175 against Gloucestershire as one of the finest innings he had seen, and this was followed by 239 not out against Leicestershire. At this stage of the season, Barnett had evolved a technique of moving early, almost dancing at the crease. It looked odd but it obviously worked. He had often been vulnerable against medium-paced in-swing and felt that early movement pulled him nearer to the pitch of the ball. When he used this method for England, commentators came to the conclusion that he was primarily a front-foot player, but in fact he is stronger off the back foot. It is simply that he can adapt more easily and, with greater experience at international level, he may well fulfil the predictions made on his behalf. – Gerald Mortimer.

JEFFREY DUJON

As one who was to become an outstanding Test cricketer, Jeffrey Dujon began with two definite advantages. He was born and grew up in a cricketing environment, his interest and instinctive ball sense being nurtured at Jamaica's Test ground, Sabina Park, home of Kingston Cricket Club for which his father, Leroy, was an opening batsman good enough to gain selection to the island team. His education, sporting as well as academic, was received at a school with a long and celebrated cricket tradition, Wolmer's in Kingston. His advance from toddler at Sabina to Test player, from Wolmer's captain to the eighth old boy of the school to represent West Indies, was hardly unexpected by those who followed it. The only surprise was that the transition took as long as it did.

PETER JEFFREY LEROY DUJON, born in Kingston on May 28, 1956, was aged 25 before he was first chosen for West Indies on the 1981-82 tour of Australia. It had been a long wait. Jamaica captain in the annual West Indies youth championships and a member of the Young West Indies team to England in 1974 while still at Wolmer's, Dujon, not yet twenty, gathered Shell Shield hundreds in his first two first-class seasons in 1975 and 1976 against strong Barbados bowling. But this rapid progression was halted for the next five years by the well-meaning, yet misplaced, concern of the Jamaica selectors over how the young Dujon should develop. Although he was a wicket-keeper of unquestionable potential, it was felt by those who mattered that his batting was likely to deteriorate if he was saddled with any additional responsibility. It took Dujon many years to prove the theory a fallacy, and it probably cost him an earlier place in the West Indian team. "The West Indies middle-order batting was very strong at the time, and I realised my best way of breaking into a touring team was as a wicket-keeper who could bat", he says now. "I couldn't make it if I wasn't keeping."

It was not until 1981 that he was instated as Jamaica's wicket-keeper in the Shell Shield and he responded with his first century since 1976, an unbeaten 105 for a President's Young West Indies XI against the touring England team. This was followed a fortnight later by 135 not out (out of 263) for Jamaica against a Barbados attack headed by Malcolm Marshall (six for 75). His reward was an overdue place on the West Indians' tour to Australia as batsman and reserve wicket-keeper to David Murray. There, ability and luck combined to push him into the Test team. An unbeaten century against New South Wales and an injury to Gordon Greenidge brought him in as a specialist batsman for the First Test; an injury to Murray gave him his chance as wicket-keeper in the Third. Murray's decision to join the "rebel" tour of South Africa the following year meant that the position was his alone. Since then, he has become a permanent and essential fixture in the West Indies team, having missed only one Test – because of a fractured finger – in the 55 he had played to the end of the series in England in 1988.

Very few players in Test cricket's long history have managed to combine batting and keeping wicket as consistently and successfully as Dujon has. Statistics provide ample proof: 2,607 runs at an average of 38.91, five centuries, 174 catches and 5 stumpings by the end of the England series, in which his value was repeatedly emphasised. His four half-centuries in seven innings earned him an average of 50.83 and invariably steadied the innings; he held twenty catches and missed little.

Had the Jamaica selectors been guided by history, rather than hypothesis they would hardly have kept Dujon in the covers, rather than behind the stumps, for so long. Four previous West Indies wicket-keepers had been schooled at Wolmer's – Karl Nunes, the first Test captain in 1928, Ivan Barrow of the 1930s, and Gerry Alexander and Jackie Hendriks of more recent times. Dujon, in fact, took to keeping only in his later years at Wolmer's and was encouraged to do so, not by his famous predecessors but by his games master, Ron Jones, a Welshman, now a well-known sporting commentator on BBC radio. Even when he left school and turned out for Kingston in club cricket, Dujon found he had to forsake the gloves for a place in the outfield. The incumbent Jamaica wicket-keeper, Anthony Campbell, was in the Kingston team, and in any case the theory that he should specialise as a batsman had gained currency.

It was understandable, for he has always had the special touch which gav his batting the stamp of class. His build is slim and he lacks the sheer powe of those, such as Vivian Richards, Gordon Greenidge and Clive Lloyd, wh have come before him in the West Indies order. He was still at school whe his fellow Jamaican, Lawrence Rowe, was at his peak, and there is un mistakable evidence of Rowe's influence in his classically stylish play. He i beautifully balanced and co-ordinated and as adept against pace as agains spin. Two of his Test centuries have been gathered on the slow, turning pitc at Port-of-Spain's Queen's Park Oval, the second against Pakistan and Abd Qadir. Another was made on the contrasting fast and bouncy surface a Perth, during which he had to retire after a blow on the head from Terr

Alderman. That prompted him into the immediate, and continued, use of a helmet.

Behind the stumps, Dujon is nimble on his feet, acrobatic in his movements. The purists complain that he throws himself around, that he is too much of a showman. But much of his wicket-keeping has been practised standing back to the plethora of fast bowlers produced by West Indies, and his agility and reflexes have enabled him to snare some spectacular catches deflected off uncertain edges. He may be less certain standing up at the stumps, to spin, but he seldom gets the chance.

Dujon's all-round capacity – and his durability – have allowed West Indies to maintain their policy of including four fast bowlers in their eleven, an important element in their consistent success of the past dozen years. It is pertinent that, since Clive Lloyd succeeded Rohan Kanhai as captain in 1974, West Indies have required only three regular wicket-keepers – Deryck Murray until 1980, his unrelated namesake, David, between 1980 and 1982, and Dujon. It is a remarkable sequence.

Nor does it appear likely to end soon. Dujon's performance, with bat and gloves, has not diminished and, at 32, West Indies can anticipate several years service yet. Although he did spend a season with the Welsh club, Swansea, in 1975, Dujon has never had a professional contract in county or league cricket in England to make further demands on his stamina. For many years employed in the marketing department of the Shell Oil company in Kingston, he now resides in Barbados with his Barbadian wife and young son, playing cricket with the famous Pickwick club between tours and using squash to keep himself fit and fast on his feet. A prime mover behind the formation of the West Indies Players' Association, and its secretary, Dujon has taken on added responsibility in the past year. When his playing days are over, he is a likely candidate to move into administration. That, too, would be in the true tradition of Wolmer's, which has given the West Indies two Board presidents, Karl Nunes and Allan Rae, and two team managers and selectors, Gerry Alexander and Jackie Hendriks. – Tony Cozier.

PHIL NEALE

When Phil Neale was offered the captaincy of Worcestershire for the 1982 season, the county had reached a watershed. The time had arrived for the older guard, including former captains Glenn Turner and Norman Gifford, to fade into the background and for a younger generation to steer a new course. The choice of Neale was somewhat odd, for he was devoting half his year to professional soccer with Lincoln City. Six years later, when Worcestershire achieved the double of the County Championship and Sunday League titles, the decision to appoint a captain capable of handling a demanding schedule was to prove a wise one.

In 1988 Neale coped with calls on his time that would have floored a weaker or less organised man. In January he learnt that his son, Craig, then aged five, had contracted leukaemia and would require a protracted course of treatment. Around the same time he was laying the foundations for a benefit year that would involve attending more than 100 functions. When it became clear that Worcestershire could be challenging for all four major domestic honours, Neale had to live with the intense pressure of knowing that every decision he took as captain, every day of the week, would be crucial. He faltered just once, being admitted to hospital for viral tests only 72 hours before the NatWest Bank Trophy final early in September. Clearly still weak, he went to Lord's where, although losing the toss condemned Worcestershire to batting first on a damp wicket, he scored a patient 64 off 143 balls to prevent the match deteriorating into a one-sided contest.

PHILLIP ANTHONY NEALE was born in Scunthorpe, Lincolnshire, on June 5, 1954, and educated at Frederick Gough Grammar School and John Legott Sixth Form College. Much of his early cricket, however, was played in club rather than school surroundings. His father, Geoff, was an electrical engineer at the Appleby Frodingham Steelworks and Neale played for their junior sides from the age of thirteen. Although he pays tribute to schoolmaster Geoff Warburton, for early guidance, he claims never to have been coached formally.

He was, nevertheless, good enough to play for the Midlands ESCA Under-15 side, batting at No. 3, and he quickly progressed to the full English Schools and National Association of Young Cricketers sides. As a centre-forward, he represented Lincolnshire County Schools at soccer but, receiving no offers of a professional apprenticeship, he decided to make cricket a career and invest in education for his long-term future. With ten O and two A levels, he gained a place at Leeds University to read Russian Studies. "I thought of cricket as something to do, and a university education as something to go along with it", he says. "I chose Russian because, if at some stage I was to go into commerce, there could be huge opportunities if Russia ever opened up its massive markets to the West."

In three years at Leeds, Neale advanced his upright batting style, playing in the Bradford League for Pudsey St Lawrence and making the occasional appearance for Lincolnshire. Through the recommendation of a local reporter, Tommy Taylor, father of the Lincoln City manager, Graham, he also began his professional soccer career in 1974-75, switching from centre-forward to fullback. Neale is uncertain why he was particularly recommended to join Worcestershire, but he embarked on twin careers that were to leave him with no fitness problems for the next eleven years. He also had to forget thoughts of taking a holiday. Recalling the period from 1975, the year of his début for Worcestershire , to 1985, he says, "I did manage to plan one three-day break with my wife, Chris, to the Lake District, but I went down with food poisoning.

"At first I had an arrangement with Worcestershire and Lincoln City whereby I would join each team for the start of their respective seasons provided the one I was leaving early was not challenging for honours. In general terms it worked." Lincoln were twice promoted from the Fourth Division to the Third during a career in which Neale played over 350 games despite reported interest from Tottenham Hotspur, he remained a one-club man. When he quit soccer in 1985 he was the last of a breed to have played both sports at top level. "The seasons overlap so much now, and there is so much money involved in both sports, that I can't see anyone being able to hold down a first-team place in both soccer and cricket again", he says.

Neale's cricketing future was cemented with a maiden first-class century 143, against the West Indians in 1976. A month earlier he had appeared in the Benson and Hedges Cup final against Kent at Lord's. Perhaps the fact that he played two sports prevented him earning an England Test cap, but around the time he took over as captain at New Road Neale was in the selectors' minds. He was chosen for the England B side which faced Pakistan at Leicester in 1982, and after scoring 1,521 and 1,706 runs in successive summers he was shortlisted for an official England visit to Sharjah in the spring of 1985. Failing to make that trip, and with the knowledge that England's senior batsmen, who had just finished touring India, were unavailable, Neale recognised that his chances of a Test cap were gone.

"I think trends went against me. When I was a youngster, England were using experienced players. Later, as I got older, the selectors began to look at the generation behind me. But the next highest honour in the game must be leading your county. Winning the Sunday League twice and the County Championship has made that rewarding."

Last season, Worcestershire's batting was dominated by the brilliant scoring feats of Zimbabwe-born Graeme Hick. But following him in the order, Neale contributed significantly with 1,000 runs in a season for the eighth time and with four centuries, including a crucial one against Gloucestershire in the penultimate Championship match of the season.

Quiet but assertive as a captain on the field, Neale played an important role in the committee process which attracted such players as Neal Radford, Ian Botham and Graham Dilley to Worcestershire to blend with the youngsters and produce a winning side. "Some people were very wary of Botham", says Neale. "But we played against him at Weston-super-Mare as he was returning from his drugs ban. He scored a marvellous century in just over an hour, and apart from his being a great cricketer, I looked at Ian and thought that anyone who could walk from John O'Groats to Land's End for charity couldn't be all that bad." – Graham Otway.

FRANKLYN STEPHENSON

When Franklyn Stephenson cracked Neil Hartley past backward point for four on the last day of the 1988 season, it was the culmination of a remarkable achievement by Nottinghamshire's affable 29-year-old Barbadian. In completing the double, a feat performed just once before since the first-class programme was shortened twenty years ago, by Richard Hadlee in 1984, Stephenson also became only the third player ever to score two hundreds and take ten wickets in the same match. B. J. T. Bosanquet had been the first in 1905, George Hirst was the second a year later. A few hours before that final innings against Yorkshire at Trent Bridge, he had admitted that the double was unlikely; 99 runs to order was a demanding target, even for a middle-order batsman of Stephenson's disposition. In the event a punishing 117, including 92 in boundaries, followed a first innings of 111 and eleven wickets to secure a niche in history in his first full season of county cricket.

Surprisingly, those centuries were his first since his début for Barbados against Leeward Islands in Basseterre in March 1982. A night-watchman's innings of 165 against an attack spearheaded by Andy Roberts was described as one of the finest displays of clean hitting seen in the Shell Shield for many years. Last year he had hit seven fifties before his spectacular finale. Sometimes his concentration lapsed, and he became impatient batting at No. 7 when expecting a declaration. The Nottinghamshire captain, Tim Robinson, had refused to let him bat higher in the order.

"I've never respected bowlers", he says. "If I'm beaten, I try to smash the next ball out of the ground." As well as occasionally contributing to his downfall, this swashbuckling method caused him to miss two games after Gloucestershire's Kevin Curran broke his nose in May. Stephenson blamed himself. "It was a bad shot, not really a hook, more a reflex paddle." Physiotherapist Sheila Ball, surveying the damage, was told, "Fetch a plaster and my helmet".

His own bowling, however, wrought the most havoc, his 125 wickets being the most by a Nottinghamshire bowler since Bruce Dooland's 136 in 1957 The action determines stock in-movement, but swing and cut are not the prime elements; rather, it is bounce, from a height of 6ft 3½in, and pace which make him a true attacking bowler, astute at adapting to conditions and capable, also, of containment. Batsmen are forced to play regularly, and sometimes inadvisedly, when balls are delivered from wide of the crease and held up off the seam. Then, too, there is his regular employment of a slower ball which earned around a quarter of all his wickets, in addition to providing various comic cameos. "It's a versatile ball," he chuckles, "can bowl you overhead on the full [as happened to Derbyshire's Allan Warner] or under your nose, and is also good for sloggers – though it sometimes goes for six!"

Some critics attributed part of Stephenson's success to a wet summer and to bowlers' pitches generally. But while conceding that batting was at time unduly difficult he also gives credit to his opening foil, Kevin Cooper, the only other bowler to glean 100 wickets in 1988. Fast bowlers still hunt in pairs. Pointedly, given the recent reputation of Trent Bridge pitches, when Stephenson reached 100 wickets, exactly 50 had been captured away from Nottingham.

Ken Taylor, Nottinghamshire's manager, calls him a "thinking, intelligent cricketer, popular with players and supporters alike and a marvellous recruit". He dropped catches in the slips and sometimes bowled too short at the start, and his time-keeping was a constant source of irritation. However Stephenson's all-round success is best appreciated within its context; the balance of the county side had changed fundamentally, for Rice and Hadlee were seen as four players, the first four Championship games had been lost and inner conflict was rife. As Stephenson developed, so Nottinghamshire confidence grew.

Born on April 8, 1959, FRANKLYN DACOSTA STEPHENSON hails from Holders Hill, a cricket enclave on the west coast of Barbados, and as waiter he played initially for the Hotels team. Having toured England with the West Indies Young Cricketers in 1978, he joined a lineage of legends in the Central Lancashire League, superceding Joel Garner at Littleborough in 1979 before moving to Royton and representing Staffordshire in 198 Tasmania signed him for 1981-82 and a spectacular first-class début ensued six for 19 (ten for 46 in the match) against Victoria at the MCG. In 198 and 1983 he played for Gloucestershire in mid-week, fulfilling his league commitments at weekends, but he fell foul of a muddled arrangement exacerbated by Zaheer Abbas's involvement in a testimonial and the World Cup. Participation in the tours to South Africa by West Indian sides in 1982-83 and 1983-84 earned a life ban from West Indian cricket, although should be remembered that *vox populi* in Barbados favoured the tour.

Last season, in the shadow of Hadlee, was the ultimate test of his cricketing ability. He responded with 1,018 runs in addition to his 1 wickets, and he bowled more overs (819) than any bowler except the Somerset spinner, Vic Marks. In preparation for a repeat of the *annus mirabilis*, he spent last winter applying himself to playing more consiste innings, and swimming to eradicate the shoulder strain which occurred when he tried to york Gus Logie in the West Indians' tour match against Nottinghamshire. Stephenson follows the tradition of Trent Bridge's other Barbadian all-rounder, Sir Garfield Sobers, as a scratch golfer, and he is already laying the groundwork for an eventual alternative sporting career. *Aficionados* of true Caribbean style will hope it is delayed a little while yet. – Stephen Thorpe.

STEPHEN WAUGH

In the history of Somerset cricket, there has perhaps not been a more serious controversy than that which involved Viv Richards, Joel Garner and Ian Botham in the winter of 1986-87. Whatever the merits of their case, the feuding had to be stopped, the bad blood dissolved, and the West's worst dispute since the Monmouth rebellion laid to rest. In the summer of 1987 this was largely done when Martin Crowe batted as a highly impressive overseas player, and Somerset enjoyed a moderate yet substantial revival.

This progress continued until the morning of June 1, 1988. Crowe, after a long overnight drive from Old Trafford, where he had played another match-winning innings, woke up in Southampton to find that his back had given way. He had already hit two first-class centuries and Somerset's young, frail batting remained as dependent upon him as ever. This back trouble, involving stress fractures of the spine, ruled Crowe out for the rest of the season at almost exactly the time Botham was admitting to the same complaint. Somerset would have been in serious trouble if they had found themselves without a top overseas player; the whole controversy had, after all, turned upon Crowe and his future with the county. Most fortunately for them, Stephen Waugh came instantly to their rescue.

Summoned from Smethwick, where he was acting as a professional in the Birmingham and District League, the young Australian drove to Southampton and arrived just before lunch on the first morning. Soon he was going in, at No. 7, to confront a semi-crisis. He made a hundred against Hampshire, 115 not out, and in the dressing-room afterwards asked in his drily humorous manner: "Do you reckon I might get a game at Bath next week?" Waugh was almost as keen to play county cricket as Somerset were to have him.

After taking over from Crowe, and before his premature exit to prepare for Australia's tour of Pakistan, Waugh passed 1,000 runs in eleven completed innings and finished second in the national batting averages with six hundreds. In his three previous games for Somerset, in 1987, he had scored two centuries, which gave him eight in 30 first-class innings for the county. Not even Crowe, or Richards, had achieved such a level of consistency. What is more, Waugh had made only two other hundreds in first-class cricket to that point, for New South Wales in 1985-86.

STEPHEN RODGER WAUGH was born in Sydney on June 2, 1965, in the western suburbs. He and his twin brother, Mark, were soon involved not only in cricket but most sports, and Stephen was selected for Australia's youth football team. In batting ability there was little to choose between them: Mark was the more stylish, Steve the more quietly competitive, while a younger brother, Dean, watched admiringly and was not without talent of his own. It was Steve who won an Esso Scholarship to play for Essex Second XI in 1985, when he hit a century for Ilford against Chingford off 28 balls. On returning to Australia he found opportunities awaiting him, even though he was only twenty. Dennis Lillee, Rod Marsh and Greg Chappell had retired together; a "rebel" touring party of Australians had been signed up for South Africa. After just nine matches for New South Wales, Waugh was pitched into the Test team on the grounds of promise alone, making his début against India at Melbourne in December.

In such a deep end, only a man of great self-possession and talent could have avoided sinking. There was no luxury of apprenticeship. He had immediately to learn to bat in Test matches, one-day internationals and day/night internationals – and how to bowl his well-varied medium-pace. "I wouldn't have had it any other way", says Waugh. At times, however, he must privately have envied his twin – and Stan McCabe, to whom Steve is compared – for not having had to play over 50 internationals by the age of 22.

Far from being embarrassed, Waugh developed during this crash-course an extraordinary sang-froid. The last few overs of a one-day international are dreaded by most bowlers; they fear they will turn out to be the clown more often than the king. For this job, Waugh volunteered. In Australia's successful World Cup campaign, he bowled the final over against India and ensured that his country won their opening match by 1 run. When Australia reached the semi-final in Lahore, Waugh turned an overflowing crowd to the silence of stone by taking 18 runs off his side's last over and presenting Australia with a match-winning total. In the final, when England wanted 19 off two overs, two slower balls from Waugh, followed by his dismissal of Phillip DeFreitas, extinguished their challenge.

Nevertheless, Waugh by then had not got round to fulfilling his principal function of scoring Test match hundreds for Australia, which is why he accepted so keenly the chance offered by Somerset. He had to form the habit of century-making, and by batting at No. 4 – not No. 6 as he had for his country – he was able to do so. (Indeed, Somerset could not have given him greater scope as their batting was, without Crowe or him, beyond dispute the weakest in the Championship.) Waugh hit two centuries during the Bath Festival and never looked like doing otherwise. His 161 against Kent at Canterbury helped to give Somerset a startling innings victory over the Championship leaders. In general he found English pitches agreeably similar to those at the Sydney Cricket Ground; in fact, the "lower" the better, for the later he can play.

"Steve relishes responsibility in a way which an Englishman of his age wouldn't", said his new county captain, Vic Marks. "He plays his one-day innings so that he is in for the last five overs, and he expects to bowl 'at the death'." Somerset, unsurprisingly, are eager for Waugh's return in 1990. By then they are expecting him to have succeeded Allan Border as the foremost Australian batsman of his generation. – Scyld Berry.

THE PROBLEM OF PITCHES

By MIKE SELVEY

Shortly before the end of last year, there came forth from Lord's two decisions, independently made and announced yet inextricably linked, which together could have a profound effect on cricket in England, particularly at county level. Firstly, it was announced that the Test and County Cricket Board's Inspector of Pitches for the previous twelve years, Bernard Flack, would be retiring and would be replaced by The Oval's own dapper wizard of the wickets, Harry Brind, a younger and therefore more energetic man. Not long after, from the Board's winter meeting in early December, emanated the news that counties would run the risk of being docked 25 points if they contravened the Board's directive on "the preparation of pitches suitable for first-class cricket", and offered instead surfaces which – consciously or unconsciously, deliberately or otherwise – were plainly the opposite.

It was a move by the TCCB to recognise and do something about what has become a major, if sometimes over-emotive, issue in our domestic game; even in fact in the international game. For example, at Old Trafford last summer, the West Indian captain, Viv Richards, accused England of preparing a poor, turning pitch to suit themselves. There were denials, of course; and even if the accusation had been true, much good the policy did England. But, warned Richards, don't have a go at West Indies if Sabina Park is knee deep in grass. Similarly, countries touring India and Pakistan in recent years have been confronted with pitches taking turn very early in a Test match.

But in England it is the County Championship pitches which have given rise to the most adverse publicity. Largely because some groundsmen are more skilled than others, and not least because of the vagaries of the British weather, there has always been a difference in the qualities of surfaces provided. It has been regarded as an acceptable variable in the game; particularly so in the days of uncovered wickets. What is generally felt to be unacceptable now is the deliberate preparation – or under-preparation as it usually is – of surfaces specifically to ensure a result in county matches. It is not a new phenomenon. But in recent years, the practice appears to have become more prevalent.

What we need to understand initially is what is being done to pitches to make them so unacceptable, and also why counties have felt the need to take such measures. Conversely, we might ask what constitutes a good pitch in the first place. And from that arises the question of whether it is a bad thing anyway to provide pitches which, for all their faults, do at least produce some interesting cricket. Finally, if it is a bad thing, what can the counties, Harry Brind, and the TCCB Pitches Committee do about it?

On what constitutes a good pitch, the TCCB Pitches Committee is clear. Its 1983 report, soon to be revised, gives recommendations on the preparation of pitches suitable for first-class cricket. It opens with the following objective: "At the commencement of a match, the pitch should be completely dry, firm and true, providing pace and even bounce throughout the match." In an ideal world, therefore, given trouble-free weather, a pitch should be at its freshest at the start, encouraging the pace bowlers while being consistent enough not to discourage the batsmen. As the match progresses, natural wear and tear should allow the spinners to play an increasingly prominent part.

There should be an even but not excessive covering of grass, always bearing in mind that the true function of grass on cricket pitches is not to send seam bowlers into fits of ecstacy, but for the roots to bind the surface together. Preparation should begin ten days before the match, with careful watering and rolling by increasingly heavy rollers. The result – a "belter", ready for play, ideally, the day before the start.

Frequently, though, and increasingly it seems, these standards are not being met. The weather plays its part, of course. A groundsman rarely has the luxury of ten days of fine weather to control his preparation. As often as not, as soon as he has watered "copiously", as the directive suggests he should in a dry spell, the skies will open. But this, holes in the ozone layer and spacemen notwithstanding, has ever been so.

What is different, and consequently more insidious, is the frequency with which the standards are not met deliberately; and when not deliberate it is a sad reflection on the decline in some quarters to gang-mower, nine-to-five groundsmanship. Broadly speaking, a pitch can be affected deliberately in one of several ways. The most obvious of these is to raise the mower blades. This tactic, generally coinciding with the arrival of an overseas fast bowler, is so commonplace now that it seems almost churlish to single out any one county. But if Courtney Walsh can work the sort of miracle on my lawn that he managed, for example, at Cheltenham, I'd happily double his salary. An alternative to this is to remove any trace of grass whatsoever, even to the extent of scarifying the surface with the blades. Couple this with an absence of rolling – even a bit of discreet forking has not been unknown – and a pitch will turn from the off. At Calcutta in 1976-77, England were greeted with the disconcerting pre-match sight of groundstaff scrubbing the pitch with wire brushes! Just occasionally, the two techniques will be applied together – grass and rolling in the middle for the seamers, and the ends shaved.

Such pitches, however, are generally the product of skilled groundsmen. So too, can be those which are left discreetly damp, but more often they are a camouflage for incompetence. The damage such surfaces can do to the game as a spectacle has been seen in the major one-day finals, when the match is virtually decided in the first hour. Early starts, with the inherent problem of dew, play their part, but not to the extent that so many games should be won by the side batting second.

It is true that Lord's, by virtue of the amount of cricket played there particularly the number of show-piece games, has special problems. Th groundsman simply does not have the time to prepare pitches as well as h might. It is, in these circumstances, hard to get the watering right. Yet – an this is speaking from experience – in the latter part of the 1970s, both th county and one-day pitches there invariably began sodden, dried out durin play and then disintegrated. The top-dressing was wrong. Containing to little clay, it was incapable of holding the pitch together. This suite Middlesex, but essentially it was a disaster. The pitches for the one-day final began damp not because the watering had been timed badly, but to stop ther falling apart in front of a full house and television audience.

It is also true to say that at Lord's the authorities recognised that th pitches in general needed revamping, and MCC embarked on a programm of relaying, which appears now to be paying dividends. It is a course of actio which many other grounds will find necessary. Quite simply, throug constant use over the years and a gradual build-up of top-dressing from th original base, some pitches have become tired. An over-emphasis on ry grasses, which while strong-rooting tend, if not carefully managed, to grow in clumps, has not helped. They are a major cause of the variable pace in pitches and of the variable bounce which has resulted in the prevalence of hand injuries that plague the modern batsman.

If the poor quality of many pitches can be attributed to a combination of neglect and old age, and is thus beyond the control of administrators, might there perhaps be some justification for deliberately prepared "result" pitches? To put things in perspective, it might be worth quoting from the Editor's Notes in a previous *Wisden*. "It is a far smaller evil", Sydney Pardon wrote, "that the ball should jump up now and then, than that matches should be played under conditions that in fine weather give little hope of a definite result in three days. . . . No-one asks for a dangerous half-rolled wicket, but in three-day matches it is essential to have a pitch with a little life in it."

Considering this was penned in 1909, it shows a keen grasp of some of the problems facing the modern batsman in county cricket without, understandably, appreciating the overlying reason behind them. In the modern world, good cricket is insufficient on its own. The game survives on commercialism at all levels. To the counties, success on the field, which means winning, is paramount nowadays. Sponsors wish to be associated with a club not only for the prestige this brings but also because winning, however it might be achieved – and much success now can come from mediocrity – is often erroneously interpreted as excellence. Preparing pitches that aid this end is the easy option. Worcestershire now are a case in point. Few would argue that, at full strength, they are capable of winning any game they play. On good surfaces they would still be a decent bet for the Championship. Instead, just as Nottinghamshire have in recent years, they back their batsmen to give them enough runs, knowing that their bowlers can, by and large, outbowl the opposition on the pitches prepared.

One rationale given for four-day Championship cricket was that it would obviate the need for such practices, but in reality the four-day game will not change the attitude. If side A knows it can beat side B on a "result" pitch, it will continue to prepare the pitch accordingly, irrespective of the scheduled duration of the match. In fact, leading on from Sydney Pardon's theme, the possible alternative of flat, "nothing" wickets is equally if not more disheartening to players and spectators alike. Sporting pitches can provide magnificent entertainment, and if batsmen may disagree – occasionally they get things out of perspective, attributing their own incompetence to a supposedly poor surface – then they need also realise that they are employed in the entertainment business.

But the nub of the matter, away from commercialism and results, is whether the standard of the game is declining as a result of poor pitches. Already spinners are a protected species because of the preponderance of damp, green pitches which encourage seam bowling. Because pace and bounce are uneven, batting techniques have suffered. Quite simply, if cricketers are to perform their art to the full and, more importantly, learn with confidence, pitches have to be better than they are now, not only at first-class level but right through the system. You can see the problem, though. If we cannot get it right at Test level, what hope is there, say, at junior level?

The answer, in my view, has to be artificial surfaces, the technology of which is improving by the year. The vagaries of the pitch are one of the intrinsic charms of cricket, but players – batsmen and bowlers – should be allowed the chance to develop the skills needed to cope with this in some security. The day must surely come when, as a leader, one of our domestic competitions is played on artificial surfaces.

In the interim, the job of protecting our pitches rests with Harry Brind and the TCCB Pitches Committee. Brind's is a fair appointment; he is skilled, enthusiastic and knowledgeable. In the hope of raising both the quality of pitches and the standard of groundsmanship, his brief is to be educational – conducting seminars and counselling – as well as policing. But if the need arises, it is hoped that the justice of his committee will be swift. The job may not be easy, for the system is by no means without pitfalls. What, for example, if several pitches are reported on the same day? Then again, imagine a Nottinghamshire v Surrey cliffhanger, on a slightly flirty Trent Bridge pitch, with Surrey needing to haul back 25 points from Nottinghamshire to clinch the Championship title. Who polices the policeman? The answer, of course, is that Brind will make sure his own pitches at The Oval are above reproach and will expect the same of others. The 25-point penalty is designed to be a deterrent; but not to the extent that a regression to blandness becomes the order of the day. No-one will be thankful for that.

WEST INDIES RETAIN THE WISDEN TROPHY

[*Patrick Eagar*

rdon Greenidge, West Indies' acting-captain, receives the Wisden Trophy from Mr Fred Dinmore of Cornhill Insurance, sponsors of Test cricket in England.

THE ENGLAND TEAM FOR THE LORD'S TEST AGAINST WEST INDIES

[*Patrick Eagar*

The team which represented England at Lord's in the Second Test. Only two, Gooch and Pringle, were in the eleven for the final Test at The Oval. *Back row*: M. J. Stewart (*manager*), P. R. Downton, G. C. Small, B. C. Broad, D. R. Pringle, G. R. Dilley, M. D. Moxon, P. W. Jarvis, L. G. Brown [illegible]

THE 1988 WEST INDIAN TEAM IN ENGLAND

[*Patrick Eagar*

Back row: J. L. Hendriks (*manager*), D. Williams, K. L. T. Arthurton, C. L. Hooper, W. K. M. Benjamin, P. V. Simmons, I. R. Bishop, C. E. L. Ambrose, C. A. Walsh, R. A. Harper, B. P. Patterson, A. L. Logie, C. Wilkin (*assistant manager*). *Front row:* D. L. Haynes, M. D. Marshall, I. V. A. Richards (*captain*), C. G. Greenidge, P. J. L. Dujon, R. B. Richardson.

SERIES RECORDS FOR MARSHALL

[*Patrick Ea*

Malcolm Marshall, West Indies' strike bowler, captured 35 wickets against England in 198
record both for the series and for West Indies in all series.

TWO STALWARTS BOW OUT OF THE GAME

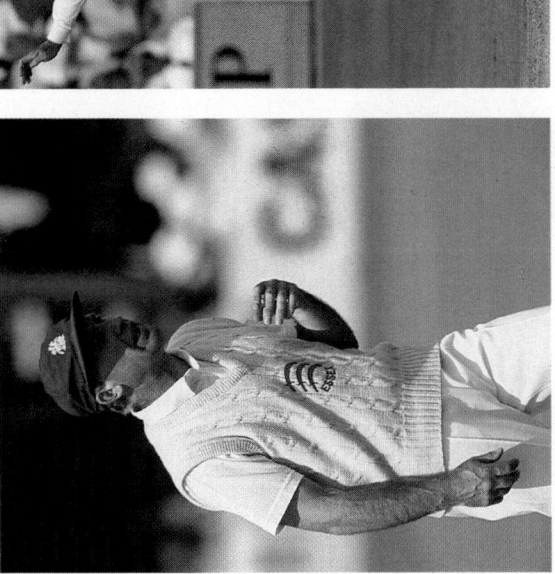

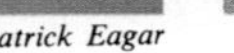

[*Patrick Eagar*

[*Patrick Eagar*

The 1988 season saw the retirement of two long-serving cricketers, Keith Fletcher (*left*) and Norman Gifford.

FOUR PLAYERS REHEARSE A DRAMA

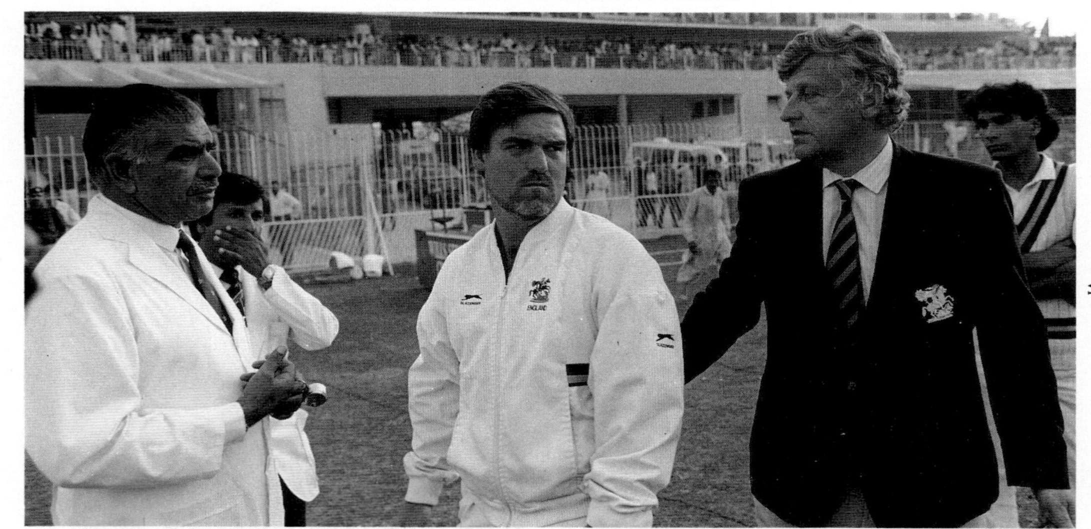

[*All-Sport/Adrian Murrell*

Team manager Peter Lush draws Mike Gatting, the England captain, away from a confrontation with umpires Shakoor Rana (*left*) and Shakeel Khan after the one-day international at Lahore in November 1987. They were soon to meet again. Shakeel Khan's umpiring in the First Test evoked criticism from [illegible] between Gatting and Shakoor Rana in the Second Test threatened the tour.

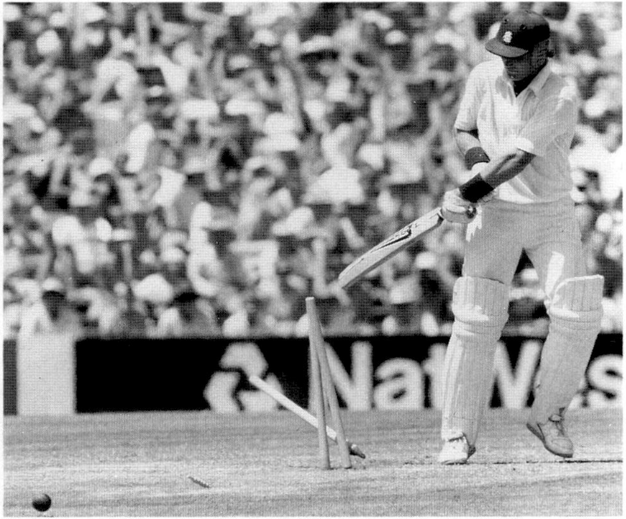

THE UNHAPPY ASPECT OF ENGLAND ABROAD

[*All-Sport/Adrian Murrell*

England's reputation was further sullied in 1987-88 by the behaviour of their opening batsman, Chris Broad. In the Lahore Test against Pakistan he refused to walk when given out by umpire Shakeel Khan and had to be persuaded to go by Graham Gooch. In the Bicentennial Test against Australia at Sydney, he showed his displeasure at being bowled (for 139) by flattening his leg stump.

FIVE CRICKETERS OF THE YEAR

[*David Mund*

K. J. Barnett (England and Derbyshire)

FIVE CRICKETERS OF THE YEAR

[*Patrick Eagar*

P. J. L. Dujon (West Indies)

FIVE CRICKETERS OF THE YEAR

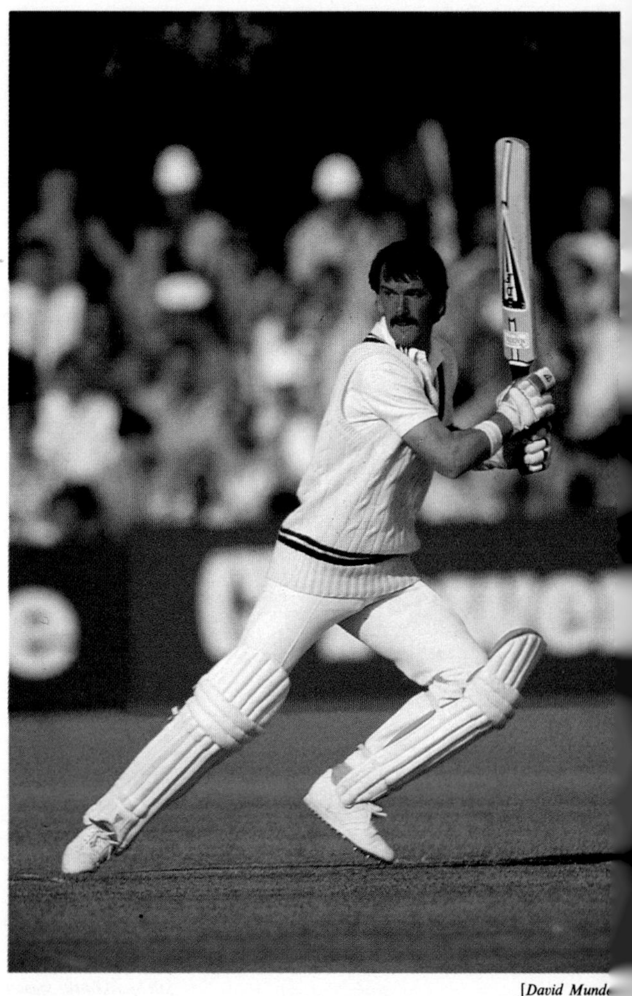

[*David Munde*

P. A. Neale (Worcestershire)

FIVE CRICKETERS OF THE YEAR

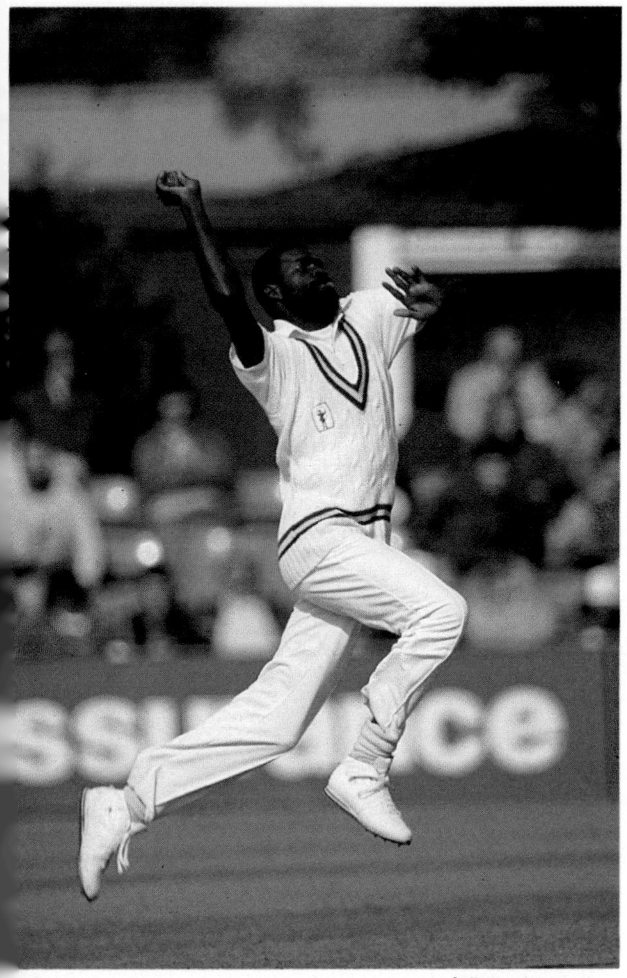

[*All-Sport/Adrian Murrell*

F. D. Stephenson (Nottinghamshire)

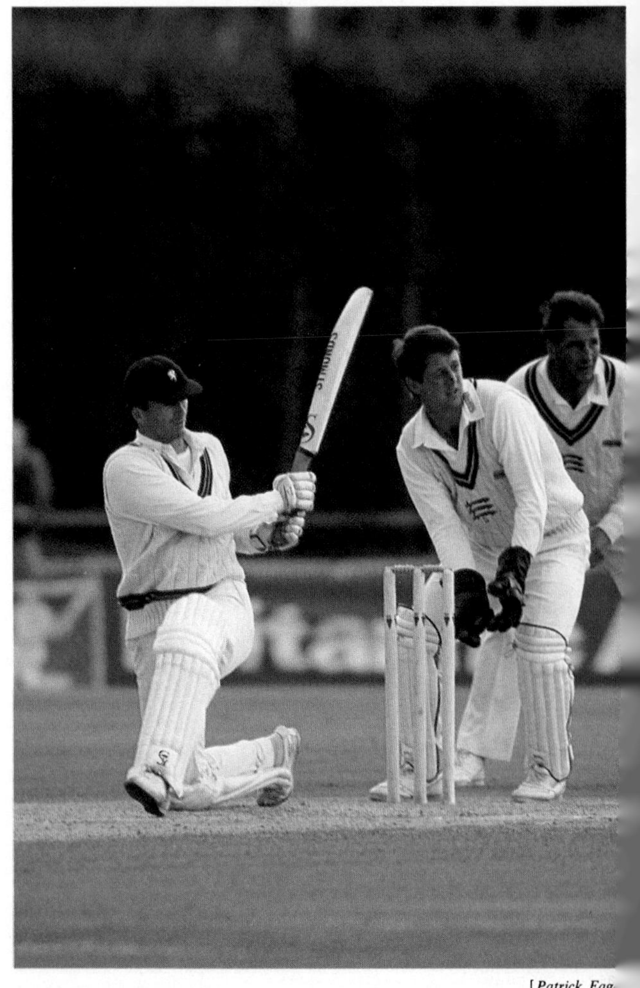

[*Patrick Eag*

S. R. Waugh (Somerset)

WE ALREADY KNEW HE COULD BAT

GRAEME HICK IN 1988

By PETER ROEBUCK

In 1895 one Archie MacLaren arrived in Taunton to meet a Somerset eleven led by Sammy Woods, a local legend. Archie hadn't faced any bowler over fourteen years of age for five weeks, but his dad was in the crowd so he wanted to do well. Only by a squeak did he survive his first ball. A day and a half later he lobbed a catch and walked off. He'd scored 424. Gamlin was the bowler, one of nine tried. Gamlin wasn't much of a cricketer. Sam told his chums at the Clarke's Tap that he was playing "on account of being good at rugby". Sam was that sort of bloke. Somerset was that sort of county. And he was very good – at rugby.

MacLaren's score sat in the record books, speaking of the time as might a snuff box in a museum. In a changed world it reminded us of a past of Free Foresters and Devon Dumplings. It could not be done again, could it? Golly, even Somerset rarely fielded total incompetents these days. Besides, the fielding had improved, the ball had shrunk (1927) and the stumps had grown (1931). Big scores were still possible. Gimblett had hit 310 in 1948 and Viv Richards 322 in 1985, but no-one had approached 400 in county cricket since the old Queen died.

Had Worcestershire not declared at tea (there were no tea intervals in Archie's day) on May 6, 1988, MacLaren's record would have been broken. It s not for this writer to decide if Somerset's tactics were quite as sound as hose of Mr Woods, but it can be taken that our selection was rather more onservative. Moreover our fielding was good and the bowling did not flag ntil the second afternoon when the captain, seeing that the horse had bolted nd emptied the yard besides, served up some atrocious swingers to which a iring and expansive batsman nearly fell. Nothing was given away easily. Yet Iick scored 405 not out.

One thing had changed in 1988. Four-day cricket was being tried. Batsmen ould bat for two days. Some were doing so. Already Gooch had plundered 75 off Kent; and that was just in the first innings. Hick was in form too, aking 212 off the Lancashire bowlers at Old Trafford. Around the counties, ricketers were staggered by the new scale of things. These scores were eyond contemplation. As it turned out, Hick was only warming up.

At Taunton, he was nearly out first ball, clipping a drive inches off the round in front of square leg. Our man was patrolling behind square. I'd onsidered moving him for Hick but had let it be for a minute, a fatal delay. nly by a narrow squeak did he avoid playing on a few minutes later. On 148 e was dropped in the gully where, ironically, he was to be caught twice in e return game a fortnight later. He never really gave Somerset a ghost of a ance until he'd passed 300. I never thought 300 could be written as if it ere a staging-post. It takes me a month to score 300 runs.

Once or twice his leg shots were lifted, but they were hit with a power that as efficient rather than savage and they thundered through or over the field. anding erect and immense yet never imperious, Hick boomed drives to id-off or through extra cover – "not a man move" shots – and he late-cut delicately. Throughout he ran fast between the wickets, throughout he used a bat so broad that bowlers felt as if they were trying to knock down a tank with a pea-shooter.

Yet there was never any sense of awesome personality in this awesome batting. Hick did not impose himself save as a batsman. From slip I saw a simple, straightforward fellow with a simple technique founded upon straight lines, power and fitness. Whenever possible he put his foot down the wicket and hit the ball hard. He was never as menacing as Viv Richards, whose saunter to the crease can have the effect upon a bowler that a bugle has upon a stag. Nor did Hick coil himself into an intensity of idea, execution and will as might Martin Crowe. No, he strode to the wicket as soon as Gordon Lord was out, took guard and began hitting the ball in order to score runs. He did not say much, and yet he was neither distant nor aloof. I never saw Walter Hammond bat, but I imagine he was something like this – authoritative, commanding, civil and durable.

At the crease Hick avoided flamboyance, eschewed the macho. Discipline was at the core of his game. If he was bowled a good ball he blocked it. Bad balls were hit. Unlike Richards or Botham he does not try to destroy a bowler's length. Unlike lesser batsmen he never gives his wicket away, whatever his score. Watching him, you cannot tell if he is on 10 or 210. He simply carries on. His game is as pure as a punched hole. It is this that frightens bowlers.

Most impressive of all, his 405 was a deeply unselfish innings. On a good pitch and in good weather his team had subsided to 132 for five. One mistake from Hick and they'd have been all out for a poor score. Yet after some hours of run-making Hick ran a fast 3 off the last ball of an over to give Newport an extra run and the strike. It was this sense of being in a team that caught our eye because it said so much about the man. We already knew he could bat.

Apart from its proportions, Hick's innings was not a masterpiece. He has acknowledged this. His hundred against a pounding West Indian attack on a dodgy Worcester wicket must have given him greater satisfaction, because there his technique, courage and temperament were stretched and did not break. And yet I wouldn't say this was his outstanding innings either however significant it was. Hick's most important innings of the season was his last one, at home against Glamorgan with Kent breathing down Worcestershire's neck and the Championship at stake.

To win the title Worcestershire had to score 300 runs in their 100 overs on an unreliable surface. Glamorgan had scored 244. Their bowlers were in top form. Upon Hick's innings hung the destiny of the Championship. Of course the game was closely followed around the counties. At Taunton, the lunch scores were read over the loudspeaker as we tucked into saddle of lamb in the dining-room. "Worcestershire 144 for three." A colleague had time to utter the word "Hick" before the announcer continued, "Graeme Hick 74 not out". A sigh went around the room, a reaction which spoke of the inevitability of things. It was as if we'd been told Liverpool had won the Football League. Whether joyful or sorry, no-one was surprised.

Hick scored 197 and Glamorgan were duly finished off next day. During the season Hick scored 3,684 runs in all cricket; 2,713 of them in all first-class matches, a record since fixtures were cut in 1969, and 2,443 in the Championship. His first-class total of 2,615 (average 79.24) for the county was only 39 runs short of Harold Gibbons's Worcestershire record of 2,65 (average 52.03) set in 1934. He equalled Glenn Turner's Worcestershire record by scoring ten hundreds, several of them on bad wickets, and his century against Glamorgan was the 34th first-class hundred of a young career. His strike-rate of innings per hundred is 5.29. Bradman's was 2.88, Ponsford and Woodfull's 5.00 and Vijay Merchant's 5.20; then comes Hick. Uniquely he holds four partnership records for Worcestershire – the second wicket with Curtis, sixth with Rhodes, seventh with Newport and the eighth with Illingworth. No other player holds more than three records for a county. Statistics trip off the page. And he's only 22. A retiring Somerset captain once said, "God help my successor". People bowling to Hick feel like that.

Hick suffered only two humps during the year. After his 405 not out, cameras followed him everywhere to record his reaching of 1,000 runs before the end of May. For a time he failed. Against Somerset at Worcester, he appeared agitated, rushing to the wicket, too aggressive. For once his batting was wild rather than measured. Accordingly he nearly didn't reach his target, and it was only his masterful innings against the West Indians that got him home. He needed 153 runs in that innings, an impossible target and yet, surviving one trenchant appeal, he reached it.

He failed in the NatWest Bank Trophy final. Fraser bowled fastish break-backs, searching for a crack between bat and pad and finding it with a scorcher. It was a good delivery. Fraser had denied Hick his drive, cramping him by banging the ball down the Lord's slope. So Hick did not mark a great occasion with a great innings. In fact, you'd hardly have known he was playing. Hick prefers it this way. Ego has no part in his cricket. He talks with his bat.

For Graeme Hick, though, it was a year of nearly undiluted success. He ould have done no more. Yet before he can be regarded as truly great he must take command at Test level. It will not be easy. Even at county level bowlers are probing for an Achilles' heel. Some captains think he occasionally lifts his head as he drives and set a man in gully accordingly. But this involves bowling to his strength, and is a risk economically and, to mid-ff, physically. Others try to contain him by angling the ball into his body, estricting his opportunities to hit on the rise, his particular joy. Hick pierces he off side as an arrow pierces a balloon, but his leg-side shots are a shade peculative. It is an area of hope, though the leg side is notoriously difficult to efend. Some consider Hick to be vulnerable to spin. One or two fast bowlers ancy rapping him on the gloves. To be frank it is all, like marriage, a iumph of hope over experience.

Test cricket awaits Hick. At Worcester Viv Richards saw a star on the rise. wonder what he thought. Imran Khan has said that Hick might not be so ffective at Test level because, like Zaheer Abbas, he is fundamentally a ont-foot player. Yet maybe Zaheer disappointed for other reasons as well. ick is a tough, strong character, a man with the courage to meet every allenge. He will, I believe, be a major force in Test cricket. After his nal innings of the 1988 season, one Glamorgan player said he was Unbelievable. I'd never seen anything like it. He played and missed only ree or four times. He didn't seem to get the balls others were getting."

I don't think he ever will.

G. A. HICK – FIRST-CLASS INNINGS IN 1988

Opponents	*Venue*	*Score*	*How out*	*Balls*	*Min.*	*Sixes*	*Fours*
Nottinghamshire (for MCC)	Lord's	61	ct	74	97	0	10
		37	ct	37	47	2	3
Lancashire	Manchester	212	b	312	345	4	25
Nottinghamshire	Worcester	86	ct	106	114	4	12
		14	ct	22	24	0	2
Somerset	Taunton	405*		469	553	11	35
Somerset	Worcester	8	ct	10	11	0	2
		11	ct	19	22	0	2
Leicestershire	Leicester	6	b	16	10	0	1
		7	b	10	16	0	1
West Indians	Worcester	172	ct	270	345	0	25
Lancashire	Worcester	0	ct	6	7	–	–
		8	ct	16	24	0	1
Middlesex	Lord's	78	b	92	120	0	12
Hampshire	Worcester	177	ct	223	265	2	19
Derbyshire	Derby	47	ct	58	62	0	8
		31	lbw	35	69	0	4
Gloucestershire	Worcester	20	b	37	58	0	3
Warwickshire	Birmingham	23	b	33	43	0	5
Nottinghamshire	Nottingham	8	lbw	22	34	0	1
		76	ct	111	146	1	8
Yorkshire	Worcester	198	ct	227	277	2	23
		17	b	26	25	0	3
Kent	Folkestone	21	ct	21	57	0	3
Northamptonshire	Worcester	132	ct	155	183	1	16
Sussex	Kidderminster	18	ct	43	69	0	3
		2*		3	5	–	–
Glamorgan	Abergavenny	46	b	76	92	0	6
		159	ct	186	222	5	15
Surrey	The Oval	41	ct	79	80	1	6
		127	ct	88	98	5	12
Essex	Worcester	34	ct	50	60	0	7
		20	ct	35	39	0	3
Warwickshire	Worcester	75	ct	141	175	0	12
Gloucestershire	Bristol	121	b	172	212	2	17
		18	lbw	26	36	0	3
Glamorgan	Worcester	197	ct	263	327	0	29
Matches 24, Not out 2,	Innings 37 Average 77.51	2,713		3,569	4,369	40	337

* *Signifies not out.*

NATWEST BANK TROPHY INNINGS

Opponents	*Venue*	*Score*	*How out*	*Balls*	*Min.*	*Sixes*	*Fou*
Cumberland	Worcester	138	b	143	170	4	13
Nottinghamshire	Nottingham	105	ct	110	134	2	7
Gloucestershire	Worcester	18	ct	52	54	0	[illegible]
Hampshire	Worcester	31	lbw	38	49	0	[illegible]
Middlesex	Lord's	4	b	26	38	–	1

BENSON AND HEDGES CUP INNINGS

Opponents	*Venue*	*Score*	*How out*	*Balls*	*Min.*	*Sixes*	*Fours*
Nottinghamshire	Worcester	20	ct	31	48	0	4
Northamptonshire	Northampton	47	ct	68	82	0	6
Yorkshire	Worcester	14	ct	18	27	0	2
Hampshire	Worcester	6	ct	26	35	0	0

REFUGE ASSURANCE CUP INNINGS

Middlesex	Worcester	74*	–	110	122	0	8
Lancashire	Birmingham	2	b	11	9	–	–

REFUGE ASSURANCE LEAGUE AGGREGATE

Matches 15,	Innings 14	512		519	614	9	38
Not out 2,	Average 42.66						

* *Signifies not out.*

Statistics compiled by Les Hatton.

WISDEN'S CRICKETERS OF THE YEAR

THE FIRST CENTURY

By ANTHONY BRADBURY

In his preface to the 1889 *Wisden*, the editor, Charles Pardon, wrote that to signalise the extraordinary success that bowlers had achieved in 1888, the Almanack was including six portraits specially taken by Messrs Hawkins of Brighton. Thus marked the start of the "Cricketers of the Year" feature in *Wisden*, which in 1989 now embarks on its second century. The articles have shown a consistency in two respects throughout the last hundred years. A player can be a Cricketer of the Year only once, and those selected are primarily chosen for their prowess during the English cricketing season. Success in other parts of the world may be only a marker for future consideration.

The Australians visited England in 1888. Their bowlers and some of their English counterparts had a remarkable season. Those whose medallion portraits enhanced the 1889 *Wisden* were, from Australia, J. J. Ferris, C. T. B. Turner and S. M. J. Woods, and from England, Lohmann, Briggs and Peel. Between them in eleven-a-side cricket in 1888 (not all first-class), they took 1,272 wickets at an average cost of 11.89. Turner alone had 314 victims.

For the 1890 *Wisden*, Charles Pardon recorded the decision of his proprietors to include portraits of Nine Great Professional Batsmen of the Year 1889. At that time the Almanack listed separately the averages of amateurs and professionals, and it may have been a brave move to show portraits of the professionals prior to any of the amateurs. The selected nine were W. Gunn, Shrewsbury and Barnes from Nottinghamshire, Albert Ward and Frank Sugg of Lancashire (two of the first Yorkshire exiles), Louis Hall from Yorkshire, and Abel, Maurice Read and Robert Henderson of Surrey. Henderson was a curious choice, for his highest score in 1889 had been 63 not out, but then five of the chosen nine had a season's average of less than 30.

Still ringing the changes, the 1891 *Wisden* included portraits of Five Great Wicket-keepers – Blackham from Australia, and Mordecai Sherwin, Gregor MacGregor, Harry Wood and Richard Pilling. The unfortunate Pilling had not played in 1890 and died of consumption before the 1891 season started.

The pattern of choosing five players each season was now established although it was to be some years before the nomenclature "Cricketers of the Year" was regularly used. In 1901 the title to the feature was "Mr R. E. Foster and Four Yorkshiremen" and in 1912 "Five Members of the MCC team in Australia".

On four occasions special portraits of one man have replaced the regular feature. In 1896 there was a single picture of W. G. Grace, following his triumphal progress through the 1895 season. The jubilee issue of the Almanack was in 1913, and for that year the editor, Sydney Pardon, chose a portrait of the founder, John Wisden. Pelham Warner was duly honoured in 1921 to mark his leadership of Middlesex to the County Championship in his last match in 1920. Finally, in 1926, to celebrate the achievement of Jack Hobbs in passing W. G. Grace's record number of centuries, a special photograph of "The Master" was printed.

Only world war has otherwise stopped the feature, proving wrong the forecast of Sydney Pardon in 1892 that there was no likelihood of the Almanack ever being published again without a portrait. In the slim volumes for 1916 and 1917 the dominant features were the lists of those who died in the Great War (the Roll of Honour) and there was no place for cricketing portraits. But for 1918 and 1919 Sydney Pardon decided that portraits of leading school players would lend attraction to otherwise gloomy volumes. Two of the ten chosen young men went on to play international cricket, A. P. F. Chapman and Greville Stevens. Seven of the others later played some first-class cricket, but the mists of time have closed on H. L. Calder of Cranleigh School. A generation later there were to be no Cricketers of the Year between 1940 and 1946, although there were photographic features of those who played in wartime teams.

Until 1920 the portraits were all produced by Hawkins & Compy from their small specialist premises in Brighton. The clarity of their early work shows their particular skill. Medallion portraits from other sources were used up to 1940, and in 1947 action photographs accompanied the descriptive material. In 1988 a new breakthrough occurred with colour photography in the Almanack. It is just a little sad that inset photographs also have had to be used to show the features of cricketers without their helmets.

In the first 100 years, nearly 450 men have been nominated a Cricketer of the Year. The majority have been Englishmen, but more than a hundred players from the combined strengths of Australia, South Africa and West Indies have also been chosen. It is surprising, in view of their current standing in world cricket, that New Zealand, India, Pakistan and Sri Lanka have less than 30 selections between them. That arithmetic is bound to change in the next century.

Inevitably, Test players dominate the list of Cricketers of the Year. However, not all distinguished Test players have been chosen. Sir George Allen is the only captain of an England team against Australia in the last century not to make the list. *Wisden* made up for this omission by including a special article upon the occasion of his knighthood. Philippe Edmonds is the only English Test player with more than 50 caps not to be chosen. Three distinguished county batsmen – Jack O'Connor of Essex (72 centuries), and Les Berry and Ken Suttle, who each scored more than 30,000 runs – were never chosen. Nor were those long-serving bowlers, R. T. D. Perks (Worcestershire) and E. G. Dennett (Gloucestershire), who took more than 4,000 wickets between them. From Australia no place was ever found for Doug Walters, who scored fifteen Test hundreds, four of them against but none of them in England. Nor for Jeff Thomson, whose partnership with Dennis Lillee was at its most prolific in Australia. Archie Jackson, Jack Fingleton and Ian Johnson were also never chosen.

Jack Cheetham, John Waite, Russell Endean, T. L. Goddard and Eddie Barlow are not on the South African list. From New Zealand no place was found for an outstanding leader, Geoff Howarth, and while Charlie Griffith was honoured for West Indies, his new-ball partner, Wes Hall, was not. V. S. Hazare, one-time captain of India, and surprisingly Viswanath, who played 91 times for his country, are not on the list, and Pakistan supporters will look in vain for Mohsin Khan, Sarfraz Nawaz and Intikhab Alam. Only one player, Sidath Wettimuny, has been chosen from Sri Lanka. Others must follow from that island.

In contrast are those players not of Test status who have been chosen over the last century, and who number in excess of 50. As they include Graeme Hick, Ken McEwan and Vintcent van der Bijl, one cannot say that they are not of Test class. Some well-known county captains have been chosen – Brian Sellers and Vic Wilson of Yorkshire, Stuart Surridge, Jack Bond, Ossie Wheatley and more recently David Hughes and Peter Roebuck. Then there are those who at times have been so close to the threshold of Test selection. Trevor Jesty is a notable recent example, as are Alan Jones and David Shepherd, both from Glamorgan. They were all unlucky not to play in official Tests. Other post-war stalwarts chosen from the county game have included John Langridge, Peter Sainsbury, Brian Taylor and Jack Simmons.

Pre-1939 seasons are reflected by some of the dashing amateurs who were outstanding on their day, and these include Hubert Ashton and Hugh Bartlett. Some players were selected on the strength of one outstanding performance; the Australians Bob Massie, with his sixteen Test wickets at Lord's in 1972, and Kim Hughes, who hit a wonderful hundred in the Centenary Test at Lord's in 1980, provide prime examples.

The editor's choice for each edition of *Wisden* must be subjective. Therein lies the fascination of the feature, for every cricketing enthusiast tries to read the editor's mind prior to each annual publication. Consider some of the decisions and choices made by different editors since 1945. The outstanding bowler of 1946 was a 43-year-old Yorkshireman, Arthur Booth, who had been for a generation in the shadow of Hedley Verity. That year he took 111 wickets at 11.61 apiece and headed the national bowling averages. However, he was not chosen as a Cricketer of the Year and his name no longer appears anywhere in the current *Wisden*.

In 1948 there was tremendous enthusiasm when Glamorgan won the County Championship for the first time. Yet not one of that splendid team ever became a Cricketer of the Year – not even Wilf Wooller or John Clay. Of course in 1948 the all-powerful Australians were in England, so no-one could complain at an editorial choice for the 1949 *Wisden* of Hassett, Lindwall, Johnston, Morris and Tallon. Even Keith Miller and Neil Harvey had to wait for another year. The 1951 *Wisden* recorded the first dominant year of West Indian cricket, and how fitting that to join Godfrey Evans should be the quartet of Weekes and Worrell, Ramadhin and Valentine. It was a shame in retrospect that no place could be found that year for Clyde Walcott, but his turn came subsequently.

Sometimes, rivals for places in the England team appear together as Cricketers of the Year. So it was that Johnny Wardle and Tony Lock appeared in the 1954 *Wisden*. Colin Bland of South Africa was a fielding star. Is he perhaps the only Cricketer of the Year chosen predominantly for that ability? Characteristically his photograph in 1966 shows him about to throw to a stump at lightning speed.

At times an editor has a chance to choose an international quintet of worldwide stature. In 1977 the selections were Mike Brearley, Vivian Richards, Gordon Greenidge, Michael Holding and Bob Taylor – every one of them a world leader in his branch of the game. Probably they narrowly shade the 1982 selection of Hadlee, Alderman, Miandad, Marsh and Border.

The permutations and the possibilities are endless. The decisions and choices remain difficult, but long may the Cricketers of the Year remain an essential feature of *Wisden Cricketers' Almanack*.

CRICKETERS OF THE YEAR, 1889-1988

In the list that follows, members of a touring team to England are denoted as such. Amateur cricketers prior to 1963 are indicated by the use of an asterisk, but not in the instance of members of a touring team.

889 *Six Great Bowlers of the Year:* J. Briggs, J. J. Ferris (Aust.), G. A. Lohmann, R. Peel, C. T. B. Turner (Aust.), S. M. J. Woods (Aust.).
890 *Nine Great Batsmen of the Year:* R. Abel, W. Barnes, W. Gunn, L. Hall, R. Henderson, J. M. Read, A. Shrewsbury, F. H. Sugg, A. Ward.
891 *Five Great Wicket-Keepers:* J. McC. Blackham (Aust.), *G. McGregor, R. Pilling, M. Sherwin, H. Wood.
892 *Five Great Bowlers:* W. Attewell, J. T. Hearne, F. Martin, A. W. Mold, J. W. Sharpe.
893 *Five Batsmen of the Year:* *H. T. Hewett, *L. C. H. Palairet, *W. W. Read, *S. W. Scott, *A. E. Stoddart.
894 *Five All-Round Cricketers:* G. Giffen (Aust.), A. Hearne, *F. S. Jackson, G. H. S. Trott (Aust.), E. Wainwright.
895 *Five Young Batsmen of the Season:* W. Brockwell, J. T. Brown, *C. B. Fry, T. W. Hayward, *A. C. MacLaren.
896 *W. G. Grace.
897 *Five Cricketers of the Season:* S. E. Gregory (Aust.), A. A. Lilley, *K. S. Ranjitsinhji, T. Richardson, H. Trumble (Aust.)
898 *Five Cricketers of the Year:* *F. G. Bull, W. R. Cuttell, *N. F. Druce, *G. L. Jessop, *J. R. Mason.
899 *Five Great Players of the Season:* W. H. Lockwood, W. Rhodes, W. Storer, *C. L. Townsend, A. E. Trott.
00 *Five Cricketers of the Season:* J. Darling (Aust.), C. Hill (Aust.), *A. O. Jones, M. A. Noble (Aust.), *Major R. M. Poore.
01 *Mr R. E. Foster and Four Yorkshiremen:* *R. E. Foster, S. Haigh, G. H. Hirst, *T. L. Taylor, J. Tunnicliffe.
02 L. C. Braund, *C. P. McGahey, *F. Mitchell, W. G. Quaife, J. T. Tyldesley.
03 W. W. Armstrong (Aust.), *C. J. Burnup, J. Iremonger, J. J. Kelly (Aust.), V. T. Trumper (Aust.).
04 C. Blythe, J. Gunn, A. E. Knight, W. Mead, *P. F. Warner.
05 *B. J. T. Bosanquet, E. A. Halliwell (SA), J. Hallows, *P. A. Perrin, *R. H. Spooner.
06 D. Denton, W. S. Lees, G. J. Thompson, J. Vine, *L. G. Wright.
07 *J. N. Crawford, A. Fielder, E. G. Hayes, *K. L. Hutchings, *N. A. Knox.
08 A. W. Hallam, R. O. Schwarz (SA), F. A. Tarrant, A. E. Vogler (SA), T. G. Wass.
09 *Lord Hawke and Four Cricketers of the Year:* *W. Brearley, *Lord Hawke, J. B. Hobbs, A. Marshal, J. T. Newstead.
10 W. Bardsley (Aust.), S. F. Barnes, *D. W. Carr, *A. P. Day, V. S. Ransford (Aust.).
11 *H. K. Foster, *A. Hartley, C. B. Llewellyn, W. C. Smith, F. E. Woolley.
12 *Five Members of the MCC's Team in Australia:* *F. R. Foster, J. W. Hearne, S. P. Kinneir, C. P. Mead, H. Strudwick.
13 John Wisden: Personal Recollections.
4 M. W. Booth, G. Gunn, J. W. Hitch, A. E. Relf, *Hon. L. H. Tennyson.
5 *J. W. H. T. Douglas, *P. G. H. Fender, H. T. W. Hardinge, *D. J. Knight, *S. G. Smith.
6-17 No portraits appeared.
8 *School Bowlers of the Year:* *P. H. Calder, *J. E. d'E. Firth, *C. H. Gibson, *G. A. Rotherham, *G. T. S. Stevens.
9 *Five Public School Cricketers of the Year:* *P. W. Adams, *A. P. F. Chapman, *A. C. Gore, *L. P. Hedges, *N. E. Partridge.
0 *Five Batsmen of the Year:* A. Ducat, E. H. Hendren, P. Holmes, H. Sutcliffe, E. Tyldesley.
1 *P. F. Warner.
2 *H. Ashton, *J. L. Bryan, J. M. Gregory (Aust.), C. G. Macartney (Aust.), E. A. McDonald (Aust.).
3 *A. W. Carr, A. P. Freeman, C. W. L. Parker, A. C. Russell, A. Sandham.

1924 *Five Bowlers of the Year:* *A. E. R. Gilligan, R. Kilner, G. G. Macaulay C. H. Parkin, M. W. Tate.

1925 R. H. Catterall (SA), *J. C. W. MacBryan, H. W. Taylor (SA), R. K. Tyldesley W. W. Whysall.

1926 J. B. Hobbs.

1927 G. Geary, H. Larwood, J. Mercer, W. A. Oldfield (Aust.) W. M. Woodfull (Aust.)

1928 R. C. Blunt (NZ), C. Hallows, W. R. Hammond, *D. R. Jardine, *V. W. C. Jupp

1929 L. E. G. Ames, G. Duckworth, M. Leyland, S. J. Staples, *J. C. White.

1930 E. H. Bowley, *K. S. Duleepsinhji, H. G. O. Owen-Smith (SA), *R. W. V. Robins *R. E. S. Wyatt.

1931 D. G. Bradman (Aust.), C. V. Grimmett (Aust.), *B. H. Lyon, *I. A. R. Peebles *M. J. Turnbull.

1932 W. E. Bowes, C. S. Dempster (NZ), James Langridge, *Nawab of Pataud H. Verity.

1933 W. E. Astill, *F. R. Brown, A. S. Kennedy, C. K. Nayudu (Ind.), W. Voce.

1934 A. H. Bakewell, G. A. Headley (WI), M. S. Nichols, L. F. Townsen *C. F. Walters.

1935 S. J. McCabe (Aust.), W. J. O'Reilly (Aust.), G. A. E. Paine, W. H. Ponsfo (Aust.), C. I. J. Smith.

1936 H. B. Cameron (SA), *E. R. T. Holmes, B. Mitchell (SA), D. Smith, A. W. Wellard

1937 C. J. Barnett, W. H. Copson, A. R. Gover, V. M. Merchant (Ind. T. S. Worthington.

1938 T. W. J. Goddard, J. Hardstaff jun., L. Hutton, J. H. Parks, E. Paynter.

1939 *H. T. Bartlett, W. H. Brown (Aust.), D. C. S. Compton, *K. Farnes, A. Woo

1940 L. N. Constantine (WI), W. J. Edrich, W. W. Keeton, *A. B. Seller D. V. P. Wright.

1941-46 No portraits appeared.

1947 A. V. Bedser, L. B. Fishlock, V. (M. H.) Mankad (Ind.), T. P. B. Smit C. Washbrook.

1948 *M. P. Donnelly, A. Melville (SA), A. D. Nourse (SA), J. D. Robertso *N. W. D. Yardley.

1949 A. L. Hassett, W. A. Johnston, R. R. Lindwall, A. R. Morris, D. Tallon (all Aust

1950 *T. E. Bailey, R. O. Jenkins, J. G. Langridge, *R. T. Simpson, B. Sutcliffe (NZ

1951 T. G. Evans, S. Ramadhin (WI), A. L. Valentine (WI), E. D. Weekes (W F. M. M. Worrell (WI).

1952 R. Appleyard, H. E. Dollery, J. C. Laker, *P. B. H. May, E. A. B. Rowan (SA

1953 H. Gimblett, T. W. Graveney, *D. S. Sheppard, *W. S. Surridge, F. S. Truema

1954 R. N. Harvey (Aust.), G. A. R. Lock, K. R. Miller (Aust.), J. H. Ward W. Watson.

1955 B. Dooland, Fazal Mahmood (Pak.), W. E. Hollies, J. B. Statham, G. E. Tribe

1956 *M. C. Cowdrey, *D. J. Insole, D. J. McGlew (SA), H. J. Tayfield (S F. H. Tyson.

1957 D. Brookes, J. W. Burke (Aust.), M. J. Hilton, G. R. A. Langley (Aus *P. E. Richardson.

1958 P. J. Loader, A. J. W. McIntyre, O. G. Smith (WI), M. J. Stewart, C. L. Walcott (W

1959 H. L. Jackson, R. E. Marshall, C. A. Milton, J. R. Reid (NZ), D. Shackleton.

1960 K. F. Barrington, *D. B. Carr, R. Illingworth, G. Pullar, *M. J. K. Smith.

1961 N. A. T. Adcock (SA), *E. R. Dexter, R. A. McLean (SA), *R. Subba R J. V. Wilson.

1962 W. E. Alley, R. Benaud (Aust.), A. K. Davidson (Aust.), W. M. Lawry (Aus N. C. O'Neill (Aust.).

1963 D. Kenyon, Mushtaq Mohammad (Pak.), P. H. Parfitt, P. J. Sharpe, F. J. Titm

1964 D. B. Close, C. C. Griffith (WI), C. C. Hunte (WI), R. B. Kanhai (W G. S. Sobers (WI).

1965 G. Boycott, P. J. Burge (Aust.), J. A. Flavell, G. D. McKenzie (Aus R. B. Simpson (Aust.).

1966 K. C. Bland (SA), J. H. Edrich, R. C. Motz (NZ), P. M. Pollock (SA), R. Pollock (SA).

1967 R. W. Barber, B. L. D'Oliveira, C. Milburn, J. T. Murray, S. M. Nurse (WI).

1968 Asif Iqbal (Pak.), Hanif Mohammad (Pak.), K. Higgs, J. M. Parks, Nawab Pataudi (Ind.).

1969 J. G. Binks, D. M. Green, B. A. Richards, D. L. Underwood, O. S. Wheatley

1970 B. F. Butcher (WI), A. P. E. Knott, Majid Khan, M. J. Procter, D. J. Shepherd.

1971 J. D. Bond, C. H. Lloyd, B. W. Luckhurst, G. M. Turner, R. T. Virgin.

1972 G. G. Arnold, B. S. Chandrasekhar (Ind.), L. R. Gibbs, B. Taylor, Zaheer Abbas (Pak.).

1973 G. S. Chappell (Aust.), D. K. Lillee (Aust.), R. A. L. Massie (Aust.), J. A. Snow, K. R. Stackpole (Aust.).

1974 K. D. Boyce (WI), B. E. Congdon (NZ), K. W. R. Fletcher, R. C. Fredericks (WI), P. J. Sainsbury.

1975 D. L. Amiss, M. H. Denness, N. Gifford, A. W. Greig, A. M. E. Roberts.

1976 I. M. Chappell (Aust.), P. G. Lee, R. B. McCosker (Aust.), D. S. Steele, R. A. Woolmer.

1977 J. M. Brearley, C. G. Greenidge (WI), M. A. Holding (WI), I. V. A. Richards (WI), R. W. Taylor.

1978 I. T. Botham, M. Hendrick, A. Jones, K. S. McEwan, R. G. D. Willis.

1979 D. I. Gower, J. K. Lever, C. M. Old, C. T. Radley, J. N. Shepherd.

1980 J. Garner, S. M. Gavaskar (Ind.), G. A. Gooch, D. W. Randall, B. C. Rose.

1981 K. J. Hughes (Aust.), R. D. Jackman, A. J. Lamb, C. E. B. Rice, V. A. P. van der Bijl.

1982 T. M. Alderman (Aust.), A. R. Border (Aust.), R. J. Hadlee, Javed Miandad, R. W. Marsh (Aust.).

1983 Imran Khan (Pak.), T. E. Jesty, A. I. Kallicharran, Kapil Dev (Ind.), M. D. Marshall.

1984 M. Amarnath (Ind.), J. V. Coney (NZ), J. E. Emburey, M. W. Gatting, C. L. Smith.

1985 M. D. Crowe, H. A. Gomes (WI), G. W. Humpage, J. Simmons, S. Wettimuny (SL).

1986 P. Bainbridge, R. M. Ellison, C. J. McDermott (Aust.), N. V. Radford, R. T. Robinson.

1987 J. H. Childs, G. A. Hick, D. B. Vengsarkar (Ind.), C. A. Walsh, J. J. Whitaker.

1988 J. P. Agnew, N. A. Foster, D. P. Hughes, P. M. Roebuck, Salim Malik (Pak.).

SUNIL GAVASKAR – THE LITTLE MASTER

By TONY LEWIS

It is tempting to write an appreciation of Sunil Gavaskar in extravagan language so that it matches the pinnacle to which he took his batsmanship. Reflect on the career of a man who played in more Test matches, scored more runs and hit more hundreds in Test cricket than any other and you think in heroic terms. Imagine his beginning in Bombay and the romance flows. It is 1951, he is two years old, up on the balcony of his parents' flat in the Chikalwadi district, defending a door with a toy bat as a tennis ball, gently propelled by Meena, his mother, bounces towards him. Link that to the fairy tale last appearance at Lord's, where he had never scored a century. In MCC's 200th-birthday match he constructed an innings of 188, all patienc and style, which demonstrated to many who had not seen him in his pom that here was art fined down, skills chiselled to something simple ye beautiful and lasting.

However, ornate language does not suit Sunil Gavaskar, even though Si Donald Bradman rightly described him as an ornament to cricket. Gavaska is a man who does not live in luxury though he could afford to. His middle class English accent is cultured and he is articulate, but he is frugal with hi words, often preferring silence. His eyes can twinkle and he has a relish c fun; he delivers the one-line joke like a knockout punch and is mischievous i mimicry. Yet Sunil Gavaskar's eyes can also turn to fire, his face burn wit anger, and deep in the small frame you can hear the fighting spirit of the o Marathas thunder.

It is impossible to think of Sunil without his wife, Marshniel, known to th cricket world and her friends as Pammi. Think of solid partnerships – Hutt and Washbrook, McGlew and Waite, Greenidge and Haynes, Mohsin ar Mudassar, Marsh and Boon, Contractor and Roy, and you would have to sa Gavaskar and Pammi. This is not because Sunil's opening partners ha changed so often, but because with Pammi, whom he married in 1974, l merges; he gossips and relaxes. Also he has someone to share his drive. On the objective was a massive collection of runs; now business ambition, whic has always floated just under the surface, gives them the purpose they ne in everyday life.

I first saw Sunil Gavaskar bat when I led MCC in India in 1972-73. V had been warned to expect something special by his incredible performanc in his first Test series in the West Indies in 1970-71. He scored 774 runs eight innings at an average of 154.80, including 124 and 220 in the Fifth Te at Port-of-Spain. He had not been as successful in England later in 1971 b now, about to play his first Test in India, he had the sub-continent longing greet a little master.

On the first day's cricket of that tour, against a President's XI, we bow to him until the final session, when he was run out for 86. The Fateh Maid in Hyderabad was hot and noisy and none too comfortable; the dragonfl buzzed low and we gulped down the salt drinks on the hour. The la crowd's roar never subsided but occasionally welled up to the accompanim of firecrackers. Gavaskar reminded me of Geoff Boycott – detached, insul totally within himself and not given to banter with players, umpires or ev his partners. He looked neat, 5ft $4\frac{3}{4}$in tall, and strong in the legs and forearr

His kit was clean, his appearance smart. Another Boycottism, I thought; preparation perfect for the pursuit of runs. And more Boycott in the sideways stance, the small first movement of the back foot, the sharp downward angling of the bat in the forward defensive stroke. He scored slowly, but t was important for him and for India that he took as much practice as possible against the English bowlers before the Test series began. His concentration was absolute.

Of course, Bombay already knew about Sunil Gavaskar's single-mindedness. His father, Manohar Gavaskar, had been a fine batsman and wicket-keeper in club cricket, and his maternal uncle, Madhav Mantri, had played four times for India. The former fired his enthusiasm, the second haped his thinking. By the age of twenty he had put away all childish strokeplay and made 327 for Bombay University in a trophy match. In our particular Test series runs eluded him, but that just meant that he had a more ealistic base from which to develop. Soon I was watching him from the ommentary boxes of the world and my pleasure in seeing him bat has not wavered over fifteen years.

Quite unforgettable was his 101 out of 246 against England at Old Trafford n 1974. Cold north-west winds drove in squalls, bringing only the seventh ay of rain in Manchester since mid-February. The pitch was firm and ouncy, Willis, Old and Hendrick were hostile, whacking in the short balls. Underwood and Greig were the slower bowlers and they gave nothing away. Gavaskar first demonstrated how brave he was. He kept his eye on the ball nd swayed either side of the high bounce, but when the ball was pitched up e was immediately forward to drive it straight. This is where Gavaskar was better player than Boycott overall. Boycott lost his strokes, or maybe rough parsimony he cut them out; Gavaskar reduced risk, too, but never st the spring off the back foot which sent him firmly into the drive.

Quite recently, in a BBC television interview, I asked him about that first ove back and across. He replied, "I just worked out the best method for my eight. If I had gone looking to play forward, I would have been hit on the ead all of the time. Playing back gave me options to sway, duck and drop e wrists or hook if I was in position to do so." That Saturday at Manchester certainly hooked many times – a shot he usually ignores – and with his other-in-law, Viswanath, he played handsome strokes with the debris of an nings around him.

Sunil Gavaskar has never been a dedicated net-player, and he never pears to thrive on too heavy a programme of cricket. It is interesting to te that he scored 39 per cent of his first-class runs in Test cricket, whereas ycott's percentage was 17. He has an independent mind and sees a much der world than cricket available to him. For example, when he joined merset in 1980 he was unhappy. At close of play the Somerset cricketers uld be off to the beer tent where they would chat about cricket. Sunil eferred to retreat from cricket to different conversations and take a quiet ss of wine with his dinner.

Gavaskar was India's Test captain 47 times. He won his first three series to 79-80 but later was accused of being too defensive. His final tally was nine ns, eight losses and 30 draws. Thoughtful and authoritative, he was easily best cricket brain in the Indian side for most of his career. Consequently was hard for him to accept the captaincy of the younger Kapil Dev, and the embarrassment of Indian players these two outstanding personalities shed. There have been many tales of their enmity, but I must write honestly that I have never witnessed it. If anything, the Kapil-Sunil impasse was fuelled as much by the media as by what went on behind dressing-room doors.

Indian cricket has now lost a great player. He became a better one-day cricketer as he came to enjoy the game more in his later days. He had proved everything and he delighted in leading India to victory in what was called the World Championship of Cricket in Australia in 1984-85. His perverse moments were now behind him: as when he walked off the field and took Chetan Chauhan with him as a demonstration against Australian umpiring; as when he called the Indian selectors "court jesters"; as when he refused ever to play again in Calcutta after he had delayed a declaration against David Gower's team and almost caused a riot.

Only the good thoughts will remain and they are precious. Sunil Gavaskar will be remembered for his rolling walk to the crease, his forearm padded against the fast bowlers. His deflections to fine leg will remain clearly etched, as will his firm pushes in a wide arc on the leg side, his drives, of course, and his lethal cut to square third man. But I will recall most the best player of spin bowling I have ever seen, always balanced, forever with time whether playing right out to the pitch of the ball or back to watch and wait. If he fell victim to Derek Underwood more often than he would have wished, it only praises Underwood's deception in the air which was often underrated.

As 1989 progresses, no doubt Sunil sits in his high-backed office chair in his beloved Bombay; around his neck will be hanging the locket on the gold chain given him by the religious man, Satya Sai Baba. I guess his patron and mentor, Virenchi Sagar of Nirlon, who gave the young Gavaskar security and a business future, will not be too far away. Sunil and I shared a car in Sharjah recently and he talked urgently about his ambitions in sports publishing video and television. He had that same resolute look in his eye; the second game has started. You would not wish to be Mr Gavaskar's opponent in any field.

S. M. GAVASKAR – FIRST-CLASS CAREER

	M	*I*	*NO*	*R*	*HI*	*100s*	*50s*	*Avge*
966-67	1	2	0	15	9	0	0	7.50
967-68	1	2	0	5	5	0	0	2.50
968-69	2	3	0	112	54	0	1	37.33
969-70	3	5	1	176	114	1	0	44.00
970-71	4	7	1	397	176	2	0	66.16
(Ceylon)	1	2	1	106	76*	0	1	106.00
(West Indies)	8	16	4	1,169	220	5	6	97.41
971 (England)	15	27	1	1,141	194	3	6	43.88
971-72	9	14	1	905	282	3	1	69.61
(Australia)	11	20	2	559	95	0	4	31.05
972-73	19	34	3	1,107	160	3	5	36.90
973-74	11	17	2	574	108	1	3	38.26
(Ceylon)	4	8	1	316	104	1	2	45.14
974 (England)	14	26	2	993	136	3	4	41.37
974-75	11	16	3	624	156*	1	3	48.00
975-76	8	11	1	948	203	4	1	94.80
(New Zealand)	6	11	1	313	116	1	1	31.30
(West Indies)	7	12	0	608	156	2	4	50.66
76-77	20	33	3	1,444	228	4	7	47.86
77-78	2	3	0	276	169	1	1	92.00
(Australia)	8	14	0	537	127	3	1	38.35
78-79	13	16	2	1,239	205	7	2	88.50
(Pakistan)	8	14	4	882	165*	3	4	88.20
79 (England)	13	20	1	1,062	221	3	5	55.89
79-80	20	32	2	1,518	166	4	7	50.36
30 (England)	15	23	3	686	155*	2	2	34.30
80-81	1	2	0	28	27	0	0	14.00
(Australia)	7	13	1	625	157	2	3	52.08
(New Zealand)	4	6	0	150	53	0	1	25.00
31-82	15	21	4	1,471	340	5	4	86.52
32 (England)	8	10	0	438	172	1	1	43.80
32-83	4	8	1	295	155	1	1	42.14
(Pakistan)	8	13	2	579	127*	1	5	52.63
(West Indies)	6	10	1	245	147*	1	0	27.22
33-84	15	24	5	1,310	236*	5	5	68.94
34-85	10	17	3	566	106	1	4	40.42
(Pakistan)	2	3	0	120	48	0	0	40.00
35-86	2	3	0	235	119	1	1	78.33
(Sri Lanka)	5	9	2	243	52	0	2	34.71
(Australia)	4	5	1	360	172	2	0	90.00
6 (England)	8	12	1	372	136*	1	1	33.81
6-87	14	17	0	897	176	2	6	52.76
7 (England)	1	2	0	188	188	1	0	94.00
	348	563	61	25,834	340	81	105	51.46

Signifies not out.

hest innings: 340, Bombay v Bengal at Bombay, 1981-82.

ling and Fielding: S. M. Gavaskar took 22 wickets during his career at a cost of 1,240 runs, verage 56.36. His best bowling figures were 3-43, President's XI v Ranji XI at Jamnagar, 972-73. He held 293 catches.

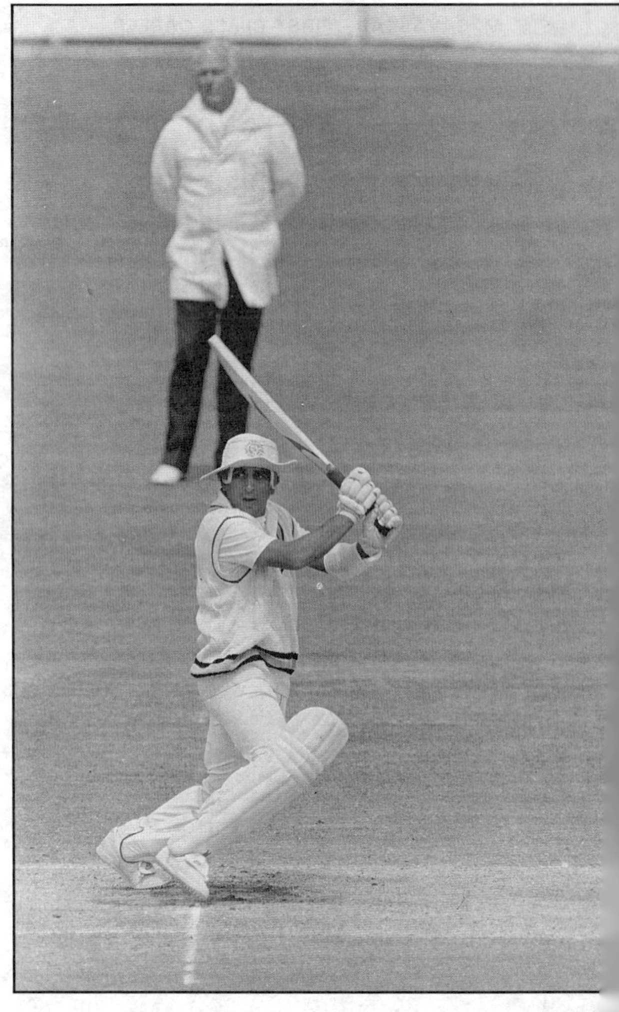

[*Patrick E*

Sunil Gavaskar's cut to square third man reveals the position, power and placement w
were the essence of his strokeplay.

S. M. GAVASKAR – TEST CAREER

	T	*I*	*NO*	*R*	*HI*	*100s*	*50s*	*Avge*
1970-71 v West Indies	4	8	3	774	220	4	3	154.80
1971 v England	3	6	0	144	57	0	2	24.00
1972-73 v †England	5	10	1	224	69	0	2	24.88
1974 v England	3	6	0	217	101	1	1	36.16
1974-75 v †West Indies	2	4	0	108	86	0	1	27.00
1975-76 v New Zealand	3	5	1	266	116	1	1	66.50
1975-76 v West Indies	4	7	0	390	156	2	1	55.71
1976-77 v †New Zealand	3	6	0	259	119	1	1	43.16
1976-77 v †England	5	10	0	394	108	1	2	39.40
1977-78 v Australia	5	9	0	450	127	3	0	50.00
1978-79 v Pakistan	3	6	1	447	137	2	2	89.40
1978-79 v †West Indies	6	9	1	732	205	4	1	91.50
1979 v England	4	7	0	542	221	1	4	77.42
1979-80 v †Australia	6	8	0	425	123	2	2	53.12
1979-80 v †Pakistan	6	11	1	529	166	1	2	52.90
1979-80 v †England	1	2	0	73	49	0	0	36.50
1980-81 v Australia	3	6	0	118	70	0	1	19.66
1980-81 v New Zealand	3	5	0	126	53	0	1	25.20
1981-82 v †England	6	9	1	500	172	1	3	62.50
1982 v England	3	3	0	74	48	0	0	24.66
1982-83 v †Sri Lanka	1	2	1	159	155	1	0	159.00
1982-83 v Pakistan	6	10	1	434	127*	1	3	48.22
1982-83 v West Indies	5	9	1	240	147*	1	0	30.00
1983-84 v †Pakistan	3	5	1	264	103*	1	2	66.00
1983-84 v †West Indies	6	11	1	505	236*	2	1	50.50
1984-85 v Pakistan	2	3	0	120	48	0	0	40.00
1984-85 v †England	5	8	0	140	65	0	1	17.50
1985-86 v Sri Lanka	3	6	1	186	52	0	2	37.20
1985-86 v Australia	3	4	1	352	172	2	0	117.33
1986 v England	3	6	0	175	54	0	1	29.16
1986-87 v †Australia	3	4	0	205	103	1	1	51.25
1986-87 v †Sri Lanka	3	3	0	255	176	1	1	85.00
1986-87 v †Pakistan	4	6	0	295	96	0	3	49.16
	125	214	16	10,122	236*	34	45	51.12

* *Signifies not out.* † *Signifies series played in India.*

Highest innings: 236* v West Indies at Madras, 1983-84.

Bowling and Fielding: S. M. Gavaskar took one wicket for 206 runs (380 balls). His only wicket was for 34 runs v Pakistan at Faisalabad, 1978-79. He held 108 catches.

S. M. GAVASKAR – LIMITED-OVERS CAREER

	M	*I*	*NO*	*R*	*HI*	*100s*	*50s*	*Avge*
One-day Internationals	107	102	14	3,092	103*	1	27	35.13

Highest innings: 103* v New Zealand at Nagpur, 1987-88. He held 22 catches.

	M	*I*	*NO*	*R*	*HI*	*100s*	*50s*	*Avge*
John Player League	11	11	1	262	57*	0	2	26.00
Benson and Hedges Cup	4	4	0	225	123	1	1	56.25
Gillette Cup	1	1	0	15	15	0	0	15.00

Statistics compiled by Philip Bailey.

ENGLAND v AUSTRALIA – THE BRAND LEADER?

By MATTHEW ENGEL

The first Australian team to visit England after the war was welcomed in the 1948 *Wisden* by the writer, Vivian Jenkins, who described the Test matches between the two nations as "an ever-recurring wonder that stirs the blood of each succeeding generation as they see it come to light anew". Jenkins's generation had just suffered a conflict infinitely more important than any game, and there was indeed a sense of wonder about the renewal of cricket. The Editor's Notes in that volume, referring to the 1947 season, were headed "A Wonderful Season" and the sub-headings included the phrases "Bowlers of Many Types", "Batsmen Excel", "Close Finishes" and "Great Crowds". Despite the present editor's best intentions, the 1989 edition is inevitably a little less upbeat.

This is, in part, the penalty for more than 40 years of peace. Sport has fallen into a routine. Every four years – immediately after leap year, the American presidential election and the quadrennial shellacking of English cricket by West Indies – the Australians arrive. Is that such a big deal any more?

Modern cricket, professional and problematical, cannot recapture the delight people felt in the late 1940s simply in being alive and, incidentally, involved in the game again. We have come to take the good things in life for granted. Players and journalists secretly rejoice when a tour is cancelled because it gives them a break from Test matches. Meanwhile, cricket has become a competing brand name in the leisure industry; it has to be sponsored, marketed and packaged for television.

England v Australia is a product. And if it remains the brand leader, it is hard to pretend that is anything to do with superior quality. It is highly improbable that the Test series this summer will be won by the world's best cricket team. If *Which?* magazine was conducting a survey, it would probably rate India against New Zealand a better buy. And yet. Ad-men understand better than anybody the importance of mystique, and in cricket we are absolute suckers for it. Somehow this spring is a little different from last spring, the one before and the one before that. The first grass cuttings smell just a mite sweeter; the tang of anticipation is that tiny bit keener. The Ashes are at stake. In spite of everything, England v Australia is an ever-recurring wonder, even in 1989.

But if it is to stay that way, we perhaps ought to understand the phenomenon a little better. It is probably 28 years since the two teams met as the best cricket teams on earth. Even so, there have been a stack of series and individual games since then that have stirred the blood in a way no other contest could have.

Part of this is because, somehow, England and Australia understand each other's cricket. Thinking about this, I wondered whether this might be something to do with the unfashionable concept of kith 'n' kin. But it is not. That rapport is never there with the New Zealanders. Lovely people, of course – but on a tour of New Zealand it soon becomes clear that everyone there would be far more interested if you were playing rugby or, worse, a best-of-50 one-day series. With England and Australia, there is a shared instinct For more than a century, cricket's founder-nations have managed to rub along together. The relationship has often been terse, even gruff, because both countries prefer it that way. But when problems have arisen – bodyline, the chuckers and drag artists of the fifties, even the Packer intervention – they have been settled in the end with a mutual regard and sympathy.

It happens that in the 1980s there has been a great deal of personal friendship between the dressing-rooms. This is partly a reaction to the sledging 1970s, and partly due to the personal qualities of the leading players of the era, Allan Border in particular. We have grown used to the sight of Australia's captain playing for Essex, though it would have been inconceivable for his predecessors. On the whole, I am inclined to think that it is a precedent which ought not be encouraged. This is nothing to do with the desperate theory that England's prospects of winning Test matches are being ruined by the small number of overseas players now allowed to appear in county cricket. It is everything to do with the freshness that Australians still bring to every fourth English summer.

Dean Jones, who was established as one of the world's leading players until he lost form in 1988, is still only a rumour to most English cricket-watchers. Ditto Bruce Reid. One feels that the appeal of the West Indians, for instance, would have been infinitely greater through the 1980s if the sight of Richards and Marshall had been rationed, instead of being on offer seven days a week, summer after summer, to those who bothered to turn up at Taunton and Southampton.

Australian touring teams really do arrive still, unlike Indians and West Indians who sort of coalesce over the course of a few days from exotic winter quarters in places like Oldham. Even with the Aussies, it is not quite the same as in the old days, when the liner would dock at Tilbury, and Woodfull or Bradman would stand on a windswept quayside in a full-length macintosh and make a brief but graceful speech (having had a month on board for preparation, with only formal dinners and deck quoits as distractions) about making friends, playing bright cricket and winning the series.

Nowadays, the players arrive at Heathrow, shortly after finishing their latest set of utterly forgettable one-day internationals against somebody or other. They will be driven to a hotel in central London and troop into a function room, probably with chandeliers. The team will be green-blazered, bleary-eyed, unshaven; if precedent is followed exactly, one or two may be suffering from very severe hangovers indeed. The captain will then make a brief but graceful speech about making friends, playing bright cricket and winning the series.

It is not necessary for anyone to believe this, even the captain. After all, in the past 25 years, Australia have won only one series in Britain – on the hastily arranged tour of 1975. However, he is probably being utterly insincere only if he says he intends to win all the county matches as well. The Australian tour, alone of them all, still retains a sense of occasion outside the Test matches; it remains an event when the team arrives in Northampton or Southampton. It would be an event in Hove or Canterbury, too, but this year Kent and Sussex are likely to get a fixture only by being knocked out of the NatWest Bank Trophy before the semi-finals, which is not something they are going to contrive on purpose. Among spectators, the enthusiasm remains; but it represents the triumph of hope and folk-memory over recent experience. The 1977, 1981 and 1985 Australians played 42 first-class matches between them outside the Tests and drew 31 of them. The last two visiting teams were unbeaten in first-class matches outside the Tests, just as the 1953 team was. It would be nice to see this as a tribute to their strength. Unfortunately, it has more to do with a truncated fixture list, appalling weather and pathetic attitudes on the part of both touring teams and counties.

I hereby propose a minor amendment to either the Laws of the Game or the tour conditions, to apply to (a) any touring captain who says he would have declared but thought that so-and-so needed the batting practice, and (b) any county captain who, on the first morning of the tourists' game, suddenly discovers that all his adult fast bowlers and front-line batsmen happen to have hay fever or groin strains; viz., that they should be taken at once to the traditional beneficiary's barbecue and served up roasted whole with the jacket potatoes.

However, these are the 1980s. If something is to be done, it will probably require a form of sponsorship. An attempt was made a decade ago, with an improbable £100,000 jackpot offered to the touring team if they won every county match. The 1980 West Indians actually got almost halfway – five wins out of eleven – towards scooping the pool before being confounded by that very wet summer. It seems to me that something similar may have to be devised again, this time with an equally juicy bone for the counties to gnaw.

Occasionally, a classic match still happens. For the opening game of first-class cricket on the 1985 tour, the Australians went to Taunton and there were 507 runs on the first day, a marvellous duel between Botham and the visiting attack, and then a burst of fast bowling from Jeff Thomson which implied that he and his team were ready to storm through the summer. It was an illusion, in various ways; but the tour as a whole was unforgettable none the less. One way or another, it always is. Pray heaven it always will be.

THE ASHES

"In affectionate remembrance of English cricket which died at The Oval, 29th August, 1882. Deeply lamented by a large circle of sorrowing friends and acquaintances, R.I.P. N.B. The body will be cremated and the Ashes taken to Australia."

Australia's first victory on English soil over the full strength of England, on August 29 1882, inspired a young London journalist, Reginald Shirley Brooks, to write this mock "obituary". It appeared in the *Sporting Times*.

Before England's defeat at The Oval, by 7 runs, arrangements had already been made fo the Hon. Ivo Bligh, afterwards Lord Darnley, to lead a team to Australia. Three weeks late they set out, now with the popular objective of recovering the Ashes. In the event, Australi won the first Test by nine wickets, but with England winning the next two it became generall accepted that they brought back the Ashes.

It was long accepted that the real Ashes – a small urn believed to contain the ashes of a ba used in the third match – were presented to Bligh by a group of Melbourne women. At th time of the 1982 centenary of The Oval Test match, however, evidence was produced whic suggested that these ashes were the remains of a ball and that they were given to the Englan captain by Sir William Clarke, the presentation taking place before the Test matches i Australia in 1883. The certain origin of the Ashes, therefore, is the subject of some dispute

After Lord Darnley's death in 1927, the urn was given to MCC by Lord Darnley Australian-born widow, Florence. It can be seen in the cricket museum at Lord's, togethe with a red and gold velvet bag, made specially for it, and the scorecard of the 1882 matcl

TEST CRICKETERS

FULL LIST FROM 1877 TO AUGUST 30, 1988

These lists have been compiled on a home and abroad basis, appearances abroad being printed in *italics*.

Abbreviations. E: England. A: Australia. SA: South Africa. WI: West Indies. NZ: New Zealand. In: India. P: Pakistan. SL: Sri Lanka.

All appearances are placed in this order of seniority. Hence, any England cricketer playing against Australia in England has that achievement recorded first and the remainder of his appearances at home (if any) set down before passing to matches abroad. Although the distinction between amateur and professional was abolished in 1963, initials of English professionals before that date are still given in brackets. The figures immediately following each name represent the total number of appearances in *all* Tests.

Where the season embraces two different years, the first year is given; i.e. 1876 indicates 1876-77.

When South Africa left the British Commonwealth in 1961 they ceased membership of the Imperial Cricket Conference, which in 1965 was renamed the International Cricket Conference. The rules of membership were changed then so that, although Pakistan have left the Commonwealth, they remain members of ICC.

ENGLAND

Number of Test cricketers: 536

Abel (R.) 13: v A 1888 (3) 1896 (3) 1902 (2); *v A 1891 (3); v SA 1888 (2)*

Absolom, C. A. 1: *v A 1878*

Agnew, J. P. 3: v A 1985 (1); v WI 1984 (1); v SL 1984 (1)

Allen (D. A.) 39: v A 1961 (4) 1964 (1); v SA 1960 (2); v WI 1963 (2) 1966 (1); v P 1962 (4); *v A 1962 (1) 1965 (4); v SA 1964 (4); v WI 1959 (5); v NZ 1965 (3); v In 1961 (5); v P 1961 (3)*

Allen, G. O. 25: v A 1930 (1) 1934 (2); v WI 1933 (1); v NZ 1931 (3); v In 1936 (3); *v A 1932 (5) 1936 (5); v WI 1947 (3); v NZ 1932 (2)*

Allom, M. J. C. 5: *v SA 1930 (1); v NZ 1929 (4)*

Allott, P. J. W. 13: v A 1981 (1) 1985 (4); v WI 1984 (3); v In 1982 (2); v SL 1984 (1); *v In 1981 (1); v SL 1981 (1)*

Ames (L. E. G.) 47: v A 1934 (5) 1938 (2); v SA 1929 (1) 1935 (4); v WI 1933 (3); v NZ 1931 (3) 1937 (3); v In 1932 (1); *v A 1932 (5) 1936 (5); v SA 1938 (5); v WI 1929 (4) 1934 (4); v NZ 1932 (2)*

Amiss, D. L. 50: v A 1968 (1) 1975 (2) 1977 (2); v WI 1966 (1) 1973 (3) 1976 (1); v NZ 1973 (3); v In 1967 (2) 1971 (1) 1974 (3); v P 1967 (1) 1971 (3) 1974 (3); *v A 1974 (5) 1976 (1); v WI 1973 (5) v NZ 1974 (2); v In 1972 (3) 1976 (5); v P 1972 (3)*

Andrew (K. V.) 2: v WI 1963 (1); *v A 1954 (1)*

Appleyard (R.) 9: v A 1956 (1); v SA 1955 (1); v P 1954 (1); *v A 1954 (4); v NZ 1954 (2)*

Archer, A. G. 1: *v SA 1898*

Armitage (T.) 2: *v A 1876 (2)*

Arnold (E. G.) 10: v A 1905 (4); v SA 1907 (2); *v A 1903 (4)*

Arnold, G. G. 34: v A 1972 (3) 1975 (1); v WI 1973 (3); v NZ 1969 (1) 1973 (3); v In 1974 (2); v P 1967 (2) 1974 (3); *v A 1974 (4); v WI 1973 (3); v NZ 1974 (2); v In 1972 (4); v P 1972 (3)*

rnold (J.) 1: v NZ 1931

still (W. E.) 9: *v SA 1927 (5); v WI 1929 (4)*

they, C. W. J. 23: v A 1980 (1); v WI 1988 (1); v NZ 1986 (3); v In 1986 (2); v P 1987 (4); *v A 1986 (5) 1987 (1); v WI 1980 (2); v NZ 1987 (1); v P 1987 (3)*

ttewell (W.) 10: v A 1890 (1); *v A 1884 (5) 1887 (1) 1891 (3)*

Bailey, R. J. 1: v WI 1988

Bailey, T. E. 61: v A 1953 (5) 1956 (4); v SA 1951 (2) 1955 (5); v WI 1950 (2) 1957 (4); v NZ 1949 (4) 1958 (4); v P 1954 (3); *v A 1950 (4) 1954 (5) 1958 (5); v SA 1956 (5); v WI 1953 (5); v NZ 1950 (2) 1954 (2)*

Bairstow, D. L. 4: v A 1980 (1); v WI 1980 (1); v In 1979 (1); *v WI 1980 (1)*

Bakewell (A. H.) 6: v SA 1935 (2); v WI 1933 (1); v NZ 1931 (2); *v In 1933 (1)*

Balderstone J. C. 2: v WI 1976 (2)

Barber, R. W. 28: v A 1964 (1) 1968 (1); v SA 1960 (1) 1965 (3); v WI 1966 (2); v NZ 1965 (3); *v A 1965 (5); v SA 1964 (4); v In 1961 (5); v P 1961 (3)*

Barber (W.) 2: v SA 1935 (2)

Barlow, G. D. 3: v A 1977 (1); *v In 1976 (2)*

Barlow (R. G.) 17: v A 1882 (1) 1884 (3) 1886 (3); *v A 1881 (4) 1882 (4) 1886 (2)*

Barnes (S. F.) 27: v A 1902 (1) 1909 (3) 1912 (3); v SA 1912 (3); *v A 1901 (3) 1907 (5) 1911 (5); v SA 1913 (4)*

Barnes (W.) 21: v A 1880 (1) 1882 (1) 1884 (2) 1886 (2) 1888 (3) 1890 (2); *v A 1882 (4) 1884 (5) 1886 (1)*

Barnett (C. J.) 20: v A 1938 (3) 1948 (1); v SA 1947 (3); v WI 1933 (1); v NZ 1937 (3); v In 1936 (1); *v A 1936 (5); v In 1933 (3)*

Barnett, K. J. 1: v SL 1988

Barratt (F.) 5: v SA 1929 (1); *v NZ 1929 (4)*

Barrington (K. F.) 82: v A 1961 (5) 1964 (5) 1968 (3); v SA 1955 (2) 1960 (4) 1965 (3); v WI 1963 (5) 1966 (2); v NZ 1965 (2); v In 1959 (5) 1967 (3); v P 1962 (4) 1967 (3); *v A 1962 (5) 1965 (5); v SA 1964 (5); v WI 1959 (5) 1967 (5); v NZ 1962 (3); v In 1961 (5) 1963 (1); v P 1961 (2)*

Barton (V. A.) 1: *v SA 1891*

Bates (W.) 15: *v A 1881 (4) 1882 (4) 1884 (5) 1886 (2)*

Bean (G.) 3: *v A 1891 (3)*

Bedser (A. V.) 51: v A 1948 (5) 1953 (5); v SA 1947 (2) 1951 (5) 1955 (1); v WI 1950 (3); v NZ 1949 (2); v In 1946 (3) 1952 (4); v P 1954 (2); *v A 1946 (5) 1950 (5) 1954 (1); v SA 1948 (5); v NZ 1946 (1) 1950 (2)*

Benson, M. R. 1: v In 1986

Berry (R.) 2: v WI 1950 (2)

Binks, J. G. 2: *v In 1963 (2)*

Bird M. C. 10: *v SA 1909 (5) 1913 (5)*

Birkenshaw J. 5: *v WI 1973 (2); v In 1972 (2); v P 1972 (1)*

Bligh, Hon. I. F. W. 4: *v A 1882 (4)*

Blythe (C.) 19: v A 1905 (1) 1909 (2); v SA 1907 (3); *v A 1901 (5) 1907 (1); v SA 1905 (5) 1909 (2)*

Board (J. H.) 6: *v SA 1898 (2) 1905 (4)*

Bolus, J. B. 7: v WI 1963 (2); *v In 1963 (5)*

Booth (M. W.) 2: *v SA 1913 (2)*

Bosanquet, B. J. T. 7: v A 1905 (3); *v A 1903 (4)*

Botham, I. T. 94: v A 1977 (2) 1980 (1) 1981 (6) 1985 (6); v WI 1980 (5) 1984 (5); v NZ 1978 (3) 1983 (4) 1986 (1); v In 1979 (4) 1982 (3); v P 1978 (3) 1982 (3) 1987 (5); v SL 1984 (1); *v A 1978 (6) 1979 (3) 1982 (5) 1986 (4); v WI 1980 (4) 1985 (5); v NZ 1977 (3) 1983 (3); v In 1979 (1) 198[illegible] (6); v P 1983 (1); v SL 1981 (1)*

Bowden, M. P. 2: *v SA 1888 (2)*

Bowes (W. E.) 15: v A 1934 (3) 1938 (2); v SA 1935 (4); v WI 1939 (2); v In 1932 (1) 1946 (1); *v A 1932 (1); v NZ 1932 (1)*

Bowley (E. H.) 5: v SA 1929 (2); *v NZ 1929 (3)*

Boycott, G. 108: v A 1964 (4) 1968 (3) 1972 (2) 1977 (3) 1980 (1) 1981 (6); v SA 1965 (2); v W 1966 (4) 1969 (3) 1973 (3) 1980 (5); v NZ 1965 (2) 1969 (3) 1973 (3) 1978 (2); v In 1967 (2) 197 (1) 1974 (1) 1979 (4); v P 1967 (1) 1971 (2); *v A 1965 (5) 1970 (5) 1978 (6) 1979 (3); v SA 196 (5); v WI 1967 (5) 1973 (5) 1980 (4); v NZ 1965 (2) 1977 (3); v In 1979 (1) 1981 (4); v P 1977 (3*

Bradley, W. M. 2: v A 1899 (2)

Braund (L. C.) 23: v A 1902 (5); v SA 1907 (3); *v A 1901 (5) 1903 (5) 1907 (5)*

Brearley, J. M. 39: v A 1977 (5) 1981 (4); v WI 1976 (2); v NZ 1978 (3); v In 1979 (4); v P 197 (3); *v A 1976 (1) 1978 (6) 1979 (3); v In 1976 (5) 1979 (1); v P 1977 (2)*

Brearley, W. 4: v A 1905 (2) 1909 (1); v SA 1912 (1)

Brennan, D. V. 2: v SA 1951 (2)

Briggs (John) 33: v A 1886 (3) 1888 (3) 1893 (2) 1896 (1) 1899 (1); *v A 1884 (5) 1886 (2) 1887 (1891 (3) 1894 (5) 1897 (5); v SA 1888 (2)*

Broad, B. C. 23: v WI 1984 (4) 1988 (2); v P 1987 (4); v SL 1984 (1); *v A 1986 (5) 1987 (1 v NZ 1987 (3); v P 1987 (3)*

Brockwell (W.) 7: v A 1893 (1) 1899 (1); *v A 1894 (5)*
Bromley-Davenport, H. R. 4: *v SA 1895 (3) 1898 (1)*
Brookes (D.) 1: *v WI 1947*
Brown (A.) 2: *v In 1961 (1); v P 1961 (1)*
Brown, D. J. 26: v A 1968 (4); v SA 1965 (2); v WI 1966 (1) 1969 (3); v NZ 1969 (1); v In 1967 (2): *v A 1965 (4); v WI 1967 (4); v NZ 1965 (2); v P 1968 (3)*
Brown, F. R. 22: v A 1953 (1); v SA 1951 (5); v WI 1950 (1); v NZ 1931 (2) 1937 (1) 1949 (2); v In 1932 (1); *v A 1950 (5); v NZ 1932 (2) 1950 (2)*
Brown (G.) 7: v A 1921 (3); *v SA 1922 (4)*
Brown (J. T.) 8: v A 1896 (2) 1899 (1); *v A 1894 (5)*
Buckenham (C. P.) 4: *v SA 1909 (4)*
Butcher, A. R. 1: v In 1979
Butcher, R. O. 3: *v WI 1980 (3)*
Butler (H. J.) 2: v SA 1947 (1); *v WI 1947 (1)*
Butt (H. R.) 3: *v SA 1895 (3)*

Calthorpe, Hon. F. S. G. 4: *v WI 1929 (4)*
Capel, D. J. 10: v WI 1988 (2); v P 1987 (1); *v A 1987 (1); v NZ 1987 (3); v P 1987 (3)*
Carr, A. W. 11: v A 1926 (4); v SA 1929 (2); *v SA 1922 (5)*
Carr, D. B. 2: *v In 1951 (2)*
Carr, D. W. 1: v A 1909
Cartwright, T. W. 5: v A 1964 (2); v SA 1965 (1); v NZ 1965 (1); *v SA 1964 (1)*
Chapman, A. P. F. 26: v A 1926 (4) 1930 (4); v SA 1924 (2); v WI 1928 (3); *v A 1924 (4) 1928 (4); v SA 1930 (5)*
Charlwood (H. R. J.) 2: *v A 1876 (2)*
Chatterton (W.) 1: *v SA 1891*
Childs, J. H. 2: v WI 1988 (2)
Christopherson, S. 1: v A 1884
Clark (E. W.) 8: v A 1934 (2); v SA 1929 (1); v WI 1933 (2); *v In 1933 (3)*
Clay, J. C. 1: v SA 1935
Close (D. B.) 22: v A 1961 (1); v SA 1955 (1); v WI 1957 (2) 1963 (5) 1966 (1) 1976 (3); v NZ 1949 (1); v In 1959 (1) 1967 (3); v P 1967 (3); *v A 1950 (1)*
Coldwell (L. J.) 7: v A 1964 (2); v P 1962 (2); *v A 1962 (2); v NZ 1962 (1)*
Compton (D. C. S.) 78: v A 1938 (4) 1948 (5) 1953 (5) 1956 (1); v SA 1947 (5) 1951 (4) 1955 (5); v WI 1939 (3) 1950 (1); v NZ 1937 (1) 1949 (4); v In 1946 (3) 1952 (2); v P 1954 (4); *v A 1946 (5) 1950 (4) 1954 (4); v SA 1948 (5) 1956 (5); v WI 1953 (5); v NZ 1946 (1) 1950 (2)*
Cook (C.) 1: v SA 1947
Cook, G. 7: v In 1982 (3); *v A 1982 (3); v SL 1981 (1)*
Cook, N. G. B. 12: v WI 1984 (3); v NZ 1983 (2); *v NZ 1983 (1); v P 1983 (3) 1987 (3)*
Cope, G. A. 3: *v P 1977 (3)*
Copson (W. H.) 3: v SA 1947 (1); v WI 1939 (2)
Cornford (W. L.) 4: *v NZ 1929 (4)*
Cottam, R. M. H. 4: *v In 1972 (2); v P 1968 (2)*
Coventry, Hon. C. J. 2: *v SA 1888 (2)*
Cowans, N. G. 19: v A 1985 (1); v WI 1984 (1); v NZ 1983 (4); *v A 1982 (4); v NZ 1983 (2); v In 1984 (5); v P 1983 (2)*
Cowdrey, C. S. 6: v WI 1988 (1); *v In 1984 (5)*
Cowdrey, M. C. 114: v A 1956 (5) 1961 (4) 1964 (3) 1968 (4); v SA 1955 (1) 1960 (5) 1965 (3); v WI 1957 (5) 1963 (2) 1966 (4); v NZ 1958 (4) 1965 (3); v In 1959 (5); v P 1962 (4) 1967 (2) 1971 (1); *v A 1954 (5) 1958 (5) 1962 (5) 1965 (4) 1970 (3) 1974 (5); v SA 1956 (5); v WI 1959 (5) 1967 (5); v NZ 1954 (2) 1958 (2) 1962 (3) 1965 (3) 1970 (1); v In 1963 (3); v P 1968 (3)*
Coxon (A.) 1: v A 1948
Cranston, J. 1: v A 1890
Cranston, K. 8: v A 1948 (1); v SA 1947 (3); *v WI 1947 (4)*
Crapp (J. F.) 7: v A 1948 (3); *v SA 1948 (4)*
Crawford, J. N. 12: v SA 1907 (2); *v A 1907 (5); v SA 1905 (5)*
Curtis, T. S. 2: v WI 1988 (2)
Cuttell (W. R.) 2: *v SA 1898 (2)*

Dawson, E. W. 5: *v SA 1927 (1); v NZ 1929 (4)*
Dean (H.) 3: v A 1912 (2); v SA 1912 (1)
DeFreitas, P. A. J. 12: v WI 1988 (3); v P 1987 (1); *v A 1986 (4); v NZ 1987 (2); v P 1987 (2)*

Denness, M. H. 28: v A 1975 (1); v NZ 1969 (1); v In 1974 (3); v P 1974 (3); *v A 1974 (5); v WI 1973 (5); v NZ 1974 (2); v In 1972 (5); v P 1972 (3)*

Denton (D.) 11: v A 1905 (1); *v SA 1905 (5) 1909 (5)*

Dewes, J. G. 5: v A 1948 (1); v WI 1950 (2); *v A 1950 (2)*

Dexter, E. R. 62: v A 1961 (5) 1964 (5) 1968 (2); v SA 1960 (5); v WI 1963 (5); v NZ 1958 (1) 1965 (2); v In 1959 (2); v P 1962 (5); *v A 1958 (2) 1962 (5); v SA 1964 (5); v WI 1959 (5); v NZ 1958 (2) 1962 (3); v In 1961 (5); v P 1961 (3)*

Dilley, G. R. 39: v A 1981 (3); v WI 1980 (3) 1988 (4); v NZ 1983 (1) 1986 (2); v In 1986 (2); v P 1987 (4); *v A 1979 (2) 1986 (4) 1987 (1); v WI 1980 (4); v NZ 1987 (3); v In 1981 (4); v P 1983 (1) 1987 (1)*

Dipper (A. E.) 1: v A 1921

Doggart, G. H. G. 2: v WI 1950 (2)

D'Oliveira, B. L. 44: v A 1968 (2) 1972 (5); v WI 1966 (4) 1969 (3); v NZ 1969 (3); v In 1967 (2) 1971 (3); v P 1967 (3) 1971 (3); *v A 1970 (6); v WI 1967 (5); v NZ 1970 (2); v P 1968 (3)*

Dollery (H. E.) 4: v A 1948 (2); v SA 1947 (1); v WI 1950 (1)

Dolphin (A.) 1: *v A 1920*

Douglas, J. W. H. T. 23: v A 1912 (1) 1921 (5); v SA 1924 (1); *v A 1911 (5) 1920 (5) 1924 (1); v SA 1913 (5)*

Downton, P. R. 30: v A 1981 (1) 1985 (6); v WI 1984 (5) 1988 (3); v In 1986 (1); v SL 1984 (1); *v WI 1980 (3) 1985 (5); v In 1984 (5)*

Druce, N. F. 5: *v A 1897 (5)*

Ducat (A.) 1: v A 1921

Duckworth (G.) 24: v A 1930 (5); v SA 1924 (1) 1929 (4) 1935 (1); v WI 1928 (1); v In 1936 (3); *v A 1928 (5); v SA 1930 (3); v NZ 1932 (1)*

Duleepsinhji, K. S. 12: v A 1930 (4); v SA 1929 (1); v NZ 1931 (3); *v NZ 1929 (4)*

Durston (F. J.) 1: v A 1921

Edmonds, P. H. 51: v A 1975 (2) 1985 (5); v NZ 1978 (3) 1983 (2) 1986 (3); v In 1979 (4) 1982 (3) 1986 (2); v P 1978 (3) 1987 (5); *v A 1978 (1) 1986 (5); v WI 1985 (3); v NZ 1977 (3); v In 1984 (5); v P 1977 (2)*

Edrich, J. H. 77: v A 1964 (3) 1968 (5) 1972 (5) 1975 (4); v SA 1965 (1); v WI 1963 (3) 1966 (1) 1969 (3) 1976 (2); v NZ 1965 (1) 1969 (3); v In 1967 (2) 1971 (3) 1974 (3); v P 1971 (3) 1974 (3); *v A 1965 (5) 1970 (6) 1974 (4); v WI 1967 (5); v NZ 1965 (3) 1970 (2) 1974 (2); v In 1963 (2); v P 1968 (3)*

Edrich, W. J. 39: v A 1938 (4) 1948 (5) 1953 (3); v SA 1947 (4); v WI 1950 (2); v NZ 1949 (4); v In 1946 (1); v P 1954 (1); *v A 1946 (5) 1954 (4); v SA 1938 (5); v NZ 1946 (1)*

Elliott (H.) 4: v WI 1928 (1); *v SA 1927 (1); v In 1933 (2)*

Ellison, R. M. 11: v A 1985 (2); v WI 1984 (1); v In 1986 (1); v SL 1984 (1); *v WI 1985 (3); v Ir 1984 (3)*

Emburey, J. E. 57: v A 1980 (1) 1981 (4) 1985 (6); v WI 1980 (3) 1988 (3); v NZ 1978 (1) 1986 (2) v In 1986 (3); v P 1987 (4); v SL 1988 (1); *v A 1978 (4) 1986 (5) 1987 (1) ; v WI 1980 (4) 1985 (4) v NZ 1987 (3); v In 1979 (1) 1981 (3); v P 1987 (3); v SL 1981 (1)*

Emmett (G. M.) 1: v A 1948

Emmett (T.) 7: *v A 1876 (2) 1878 (1) 1881 (4)*

Evans, A. J. 1: v A 1921

Evans (T. G.) 91: v A 1948 (5) 1953 (5) 1956 (5); v SA 1947 (5) 1951 (3) 1955 (3); v WI 1950 (3 1957 (5); v NZ 1949 (4) 1958 (5); v In 1946 (1) 1952 (4) 1959 (2); v P 1954 (4); *v A 1946 (4) 195 (5) 1954 (4) 1958 (3); v SA 1948 (3) 1956 (5); v WI 1947 (4) 1953 (4); v NZ 1946 (1) 1950 (1954 (2)*

Fagg (A. E.) 5: v WI 1939 (1); v In 1936 (2); *v A 1936 (2)*

Fairbrother, N. H. 4: v P 1987 (1); *v NZ 1987 (2); v P 1987 (1)*

Fane, F. L. 14: *v A 1907 (4); v SA 1905 (5) 1909 (5)*

Farnes, K. 15: v A 1934 (2) 1938 (4); *v A 1936 (2); v SA 1938 (5); v WI 1934 (2)*

Farrimond (W.) 4: v SA 1935 (1); *v SA 1930 (2); v WI 1934 (1)*

Fender, P. G. H. 13: v A 1921 (2); v SA 1924 (2) 1929 (1); *v A 1920 (3); v SA 1922 (5)*

Ferris, J. J. 1: *v SA 1891*

Fielder (A.) 6: *v A 1903 (2) 1907 (4)*

Fishlock (L. B.) 4: v In 1936 (2) 1946 (1); *v A 1946 (1)*

Flavell (J. A.) 4: v A 1961 (2) 1964 (2)

Fletcher, K. W. R. 59: v A 1968 (1) 1972 (1) 1975 (2); v WI 1973 (3); v NZ 1969 (2) 1973 (3); v 1971 (2) 1974 (3); v P 1974 (3); *v A 1970 (5) 1974 (5) 1976 (1); v WI 1973 (4); v NZ 1970 (1) 19 (2); v In 1972 (5) 1976 (3) 1981 (6); v P 1968 (3) 1972 (3); v SL 1981 (1)*

'lowers (W.) 8: v A 1893 (1); *v A 1884 (5) 1886 (2)*
'ord, F. G. J. 5: *v A 1894 (5)*
'oster, F. R. 11: v A 1912 (3); v SA 1912 (3); *v A 1911 (5)*
'oster, N. A. 25: v A 1985 (1); v WI 1984 (1) 1988 (2); v NZ 1983 (1) 1986 (1); v In 1986 (1); v P 1987 (5); v SL 1988 (1); *v A 1987 (1); v WI 1985 (3); v NZ 1983 (2); v In 1984 (2); v P 1983 (2) 1987 (2)*
'oster, R. E. 8: v SA 1907 (3); *v A 1903 (5)*
othergill (A. J.) 2: *v SA 1888 (2)*
owler, G. 21: v WI 1984 (5); v NZ 1983 (2); v P 1982 (1); v SL 1984 (1); *v A 1982 (3); v NZ 1983 (2); v In 1984 (5); v P 1983 (2)*
reeman (A. P.) 12: v SA 1929 (3); v WI 1928 (3); *v A 1924 (2); v SA 1927 (4)*
rench, B. N. 16: v NZ 1986 (3); v In 1986 (2); v P 1987 (4); *v A 1987 (1); v NZ 1987 (3); v P 1987 (3)*
'y, C. B. 26: v A 1899 (5) 1902 (3) 1905 (4) 1909 (3) 1912 (3); v SA 1907 (3) 1912 (3); *v SA 1895 (2)*

atting, M. W. 67: v A 1980 (1) 1981 (6) 1985 (6); v WI 1980 (4) 1984 (1) 1988 (2); v NZ 1983 (2) 1986 (3); v In 1986 (3); v P 1982 (3) 1987 (5); *v A 1986 (5) 1987 (1); v WI 1980 (1) 1985 (1); v NZ 1977 (1) 1983 (2) 1987 (3); v In 1981 (5) 1984 (5); v P 1977 (1) 1983 (3) 1987 (3)*
ay, L. H. 1: *v A 1894*
eary (G.) 14: v A 1926 (2) 1930 (1) 1934 (2); v SA 1924 (1) 1929 (2); *v A 1928 (4); v SA 1927 (2)*
ibb, P. A. 8: v In 1946 (2); *v A 1946 (1); v SA 1938 (5)*
fford, N. 15: v A 1964 (2) 1972 (3); v NZ 1973 (2); v In 1971 (2); v P 1971 (2); *v In 1972 (2); v P 1972 (2)*
lligan, A. E. R. 11: v SA 1924 (4); *v A 1924 (5); v SA 1922 (2)*
lligan, A. H. H. 4: *v NZ 1929 (4)*
mblett (H.) 3: v WI 1939 (1); v In 1936 (2)
adwin (C.) 8: v SA 1947 (2); v NZ 1949 (1); *v SA 1948 (5)*
ddard (T. W.) 8: v A 1930 (1); v WI 1939 (2); v NZ 1937 (2); *v SA 1938 (3)*
och, G. A. 68: v A 1975 (2) 1980 (1) 1981 (5) 1985 (6); v WI 1980 (5) 1988 (5); v NZ 1978 (3) 986 (3); v In 1979 (4) 1986 (3); v P 1978 (2); v SL 1988 (1); *v A 1978 (6) 1979 (2); v WI 1980 (4) 1985 (5); v In 1979 (1) 1981 (6); v P 1987 (3); v SL 1981 (1)*
ver (A. R.) 4: v NZ 1937 (2); v In 1936 (1) 1946 (1)
wer, D. I. 100: v A 1980 (1) 1981 (5) 1985 (6); v WI 1980 (1) 1984 (5) 1988 (4); v NZ 1978 (3) 983 (4) 1986 (3); v In 1979 (4) 1982 (3) 1986 (2); v P 1978 (3) 1982 (3) 1987 (5); v SL 1984 (1); *v 1 1978 (6) 1979 (3) 1982 (5) 1986 (5); v WI 1980 (4) 1985 (5); v NZ 1983 (3); v In 1979 (1) 1981 5) 1984 (5); v P 1983 (3); v SL 1981 (1)*
ace, E. M. 1: v A 1880
ace, G. F. 1: v A 1880
ace, W. G. 22: v A 1880 (1) 1882 (1) 1884 (3) 1886 (3) 1888 (3) 1890 (2) 1893 (2) 1896 (3) 1899 1); *v A 1891 (3)*
aveney (T. W.) 79: v A 1953 (5) 1956 (2) 1968 (5); v SA 1951 (1) 1955 (5); v WI 1957 (4) 1966 4) 1969 (1); v NZ 1958 (4); v In 1952 (4) 1967 (3); v P 1954 (3) 1962 (4) 1967 (3); *v A 1954 (2) 958 (5) 1962 (3); v WI 1953 (5) 1967 (5); v NZ 1954 (2) 1958 (2); v In 1951 (4); v P 1968 (3)*
enhough (T.) 4: v SA 1960 (1); v In 1959 (3)
enwood (A.) 2: *v A 1876 (2)*
ig, A. W. 58: v A 1972 (5) 1975 (4) 1977 (5); v WI 1973 (3) 1976 (5); v NZ 1973 (3); v In 1974); v P 1974 (3); *v A 1974 (6) 1976 (1); v WI 1973 (5); v NZ 1974 (2); v In 1972 (5) 1976 (5); v P 972 (3)*
ig, I. A. 2: v P 1982 (2)
eve, B. A. F. 2: *v SA 1888 (2)*
fith, S. C. 3: *v SA 1948 (2); v WI 1947 (1)*
n (G.) 15: v A 1909 (1); *v A 1907 (5) 1911 (5); v WI 1929 (4)*
n (J.) 6: v A 1905 (1); *v A 1901 (5)*
n (W.) 11: v A 1888 (2) 1890 (2) 1893 (3) 1896 (1) 1899 (1); *v A 1886 (2)*

, N. E. 5: v A 1921 (1); *v WI 1929 (4)*
h (S.) 11: v A 1905 (2) 1909 (1) 1912 (1); *v SA 1898 (2) 1905 (5)*
ws (C.) 2: v A 1921 (1); v WI 1928 (1)
mond, W. R. 85: v A 1930 (5) 1934 (5) 1938 (4); v SA 1929 (4) 1935 (5); v WI 1928 (3) 1933 1939 (3); v NZ 1931 (3) 1937 (3); v In 1932 (1) 1936 (2) 1946 (3); *v A 1928 (5) 1932 (5) 1936 1946 (4); v SA 1927 (5) 1930 (5) 1938 (5); v WI 1934 (4); v NZ 1932 (2) 1946 (1)*

Hampshire, J. H. 8: v A 1972 (1) 1975 (1); v WI 1969 (2); *v A 1970 (2); v NZ 1970 (2)*
Hardinge (H. T. W.) 1: v A 1921
Hardstaff (J.) 5: *v A 1907 (5)*
Hardstaff (J. jun.) 23: v A 1938 (2) 1948 (1); v SA 1935 (1); v WI 1939 (3); v NZ 1937 (3); v I 1936 (2) 1946 (2); *v A 1936 (5) 1946 (1); v WI 1947 (3)*
Harris, Lord 4: v A 1880 (1) 1884 (2); *v A 1878 (1)*
Hartley, J. C. 2: *v SA 1905 (2)*
Hawke, Lord 5: *v SA 1895 (3) 1898 (2)*
Hayes (E. G.) 5: v A 1909 (1); v SA 1912 (1); *v SA 1905 (3)*
Hayes, F. C. 9: v WI 1973 (3) 1976 (2); *v WI 1973 (4)*
Hayward (T. W.) 35: v A 1896 (2) 1899 (5) 1902 (1) 1905 (5) 1909 (1); v SA 1907 (3); *v A 1897 (. 1901 (5) 1903 (5); v SA 1895 (3)*
Hearne (A.) 1: *v SA 1891*
Hearne (F.) 2: *v SA 1888 (2)*
Hearne (G. G.) 1: *v SA 1891*
Hearne (J. T.) 12: v A 1896 (3) 1899 (3); *v A 1897 (5); v SA 1891 (1)*
Hearne (J. W.) 24: v A 1912 (3) 1921 (1) 1926 (1); v SA 1912 (2) 1924 (3); *v A 1911 (5) 1920 (1924 (4); v SA 1913 (3)*
Hemmings, E. E. 8: v P 1982 (2); *v A 1982 (3) 1987 (1); v NZ 1987 (1); v P 1987 (1)*
Hendren (E. H.) 51: v A 1921 (2) 1926 (5) 1930 (2) 1934 (4); v SA 1924 (5) 1929 (4); v WI 19 (1); *v A 1920 (5) 1924 (5) 1928 (5); v SA 1930 (5); v WI 1929 (4) 1934 (4)*
Hendrick, M. 30: v A 1977 (3) 1980 (1) 1981 (2); v WI 1976 (2) 1980 (2); v NZ 1978 (2); v In 19 (3) 1979 (4); v P 1974 (2); *v A 1974 (2) 1978 (5); v NZ 1974 (1) 1977 (1)*
Heseltine, C. 2: v SA 1895 (2)
Higgs, K. 15: v A 1968 (1); v WI 1966 (5); v SA 1965 (1); v In 1967 (1); v P 1967 (3); *v A 1965 (v NZ 1965 (3)*
Hill (A.) 2: *v A 1876 (2)*
Hill, A. J. L. 3: *v SA 1895 (3)*
Hilton (M. J.) 4: v SA 1951 (1); v WI 1950 (1); *v In 1951 (2)*
Hirst (G. H.) 24: v A 1899 (1) 1902 (4) 1905 (3) 1909 (4); v SA 1907 (3); *v A 1897 (4) 1903*
Hitch (J. W.) 7: v A 1912 (1) 1921 (1); v SA 1912 (1); *v A 1911 (3) 1920 (1)*
Hobbs (J. B.) 61: v A 1909 (3) 1912 (3) 1921 (1) 1926 (5) 1930 (5); v SA 1912 (3) 1924 (4) 1929 (v WI 1928 (2); *v A 1907 (4) 1911 (5) 1920 (5) 1924 (5) 1928 (5); v SA 1909 (5) 1913 (5*
Hobbs, R. N. S. 7: v In 1967 (3); v P 1967 (1) 1971 (1); *v WI 1967 (1); v P 1968 (1)*
Hollies (W. E.) 13: v A 1948 (1); v SA 1947 (3); v WI 1950 (2); v NZ 1949 (4); *v WI 1934*
Holmes, E. R. T. 5: v SA 1935 (1); *v WI 1934 (4)*
Holmes (P.) 7: v A 1921 (1); v In 1932 (1); *v SA 1927 (5)*
Hone, L. 1: *v A 1878*
Hopwood (J. L.) 2: v A 1934 (2)
Hornby, A. N. 3: v A 1882 (1) 1884 (1); *v A 1878 (1)*
Horton (M. J.) 2: v In 1959 (2)
Howard, N. D. 4: *v In 1951 (4)*
Howell (H.) 5: v A 1921 (1); v SA 1924 (1); *v A 1920 (3)*
Howorth (R.) 5: v SA 1947 (1); *v WI 1947 (4)*
Humphries (J.) 3: *v A 1907 (3)*
Hunter (J.) 5: *v A 1884 (5)*
Hutchings, K. L. 7: v A 1909 (2); *v A 1907 (5)*
Hutton (L.) 79: v A 1938 (3) 1948 (4) 1953 (5); v SA 1947 (5) 1951 (5); v WI 1939 (3) 1950 (3 NZ 1937 (3) 1949 (4); v In 1946 (3) 1952 (4); v P 1954 (2); *v A 1946 (5) 1950 (5) 1954 (5); v 1938 (4) 1948 (5); v WI 1947 (2) 1953 (5); v NZ 1950 (2) 1954 (2)*
Hutton, R. A. 5: v In 1971 (3); v P 1971 (2)

Iddon (J.) 5: v SA 1935 (1); *v WI 1934 (4)*
Ikin (J. T.) 18: v SA 1951 (3) 1955 (1); v In 1946 (2) 1952 (2); *v A 1946 (5); v NZ 1946 (1); v 1947 (4)*
Illingworth (R.) 61: v A 1961 (2) 1968 (3) 1972 (5); v SA 1960 (4); v WI 1966 (2) 1969 (3) 1973 v NZ 1958 (1) 1965 (1) 1969 (3) 1973 (3); v In 1959 (2) 1967 (3) 1971 (3); v P 1962 (1) 196 1971 (3); *v A 1962 (2) 1970 (6); v WI 1959 (5); v NZ 1962 (3) 1970 (2)*
Insole, D. J. 9: v A 1956 (1); v SA 1955 (1); v WI 1950 (1) 1957 (1); *v SA 1956 (5)*

Jackman, R. D. 4: v P 1982 (2); *v WI 1980 (2)*
Jackson, F. S. 20: v A 1893 (2) 1896 (3) 1899 (5) 1902 (5) 1905 (5)

'ackson (H. L.) 2: v A 1961 (1); v NZ 1949 (1)
'ameson, J. A. 4: v In 1971 (2); *v WI 1973 (2)*
'ardine, D. R. 22: v WI 1928 (2) 1933 (2); v NZ 1931 (3); v In 1932 (1); *v A 1928 (5) 1932 (5); v NZ 1932 (1); v In 1933 (3)*
'arvis, P. W. 4: v WI 1988 (2); *v NZ 1987 (2)*
'enkins (R. O.) 9: v WI 1950 (2); v In 1952 (2); *v SA 1948 (5)*
'essop, G. L. 18: v A 1899 (1) 1902 (4) 1905 (1) 1909 (2); v SA 1907 (3) 1912 (2); *v A 1901 (5)*
'ones, A. O. 12: v A 1899 (1) 1905 (2) 1909 (2); *v A 1901 (5) 1907 (2)*
'ones, I. J. 15: v WI 1966 (2); *v A 1965 (4); v WI 1967 (5); v NZ 1965 (3); v In 1963 (1)*
'upp (H.) 2: *v A 1876 (2)*
'upp, V. W. C. 8: v A 1921 (2); v WI 1928 (2); *v SA 1922 (4)*

eeton (W. W.) 2: v A 1934 (1); v WI 1939 (1)
ennedy (A. S.) 5: *v SA 1922 (5)*
enyon (D.) 8: v A 1953 (2); v SA 1955 (3); *v In 1951 (3)*
illick, E. T. 2: v SA 1929 (2)
ilner (R.) 9: v A 1926 (4); v SA 1924 (2); *v A 1924 (3)*
ing (J. H.) 1: v A 1909
inneir (S. P.) 1: *v A 1911*
night (A. E.) 3: *v A 1903 (3)*
night (B. R.) 29: v A 1968 (2); v WI 1966 (1) 1969 (3); v NZ 1969 (2); v P 1962 (2); *v A 1962 (1) 1965 (2); v NZ 1962 (3) 1965 (2); v In 1961 (4) 1963 (5); v P 1961 (2)*
night, D. J. 2: v A 1921 (2)
nott, A. P. E. 95: v A 1968 (5) 1972 (5) 1975 (4) 1977 (5) 1981 (2); v WI 1969 (3) 1973 (3) 1976 (5) 1980 (4); v NZ 1969 (3) 1973 (3); v In 1971 (3) 1974 (3); v P 1967 (2) 1971 (3) 1974 (3); *v A 1970 (6) 1974 (6) 1976 (1); v WI 1967 (2) 1973 (5); v NZ 1970 (1) 1974 (2); v In 1972 (5) 1976 (5); v P 1968 (3) 1972 (3)*
nox, N. A. 2: v SA 1907 (2)

ker (J. C.) 46: v A 1948 (3) 1953 (3) 1956 (5); v SA 1951 (2) 1955 (1); v WI 1950 (1) 1957 (4); v NZ 1949 (1) 1958 (4); v In 1952 (4); v P 1954 (1); *v A 1958 (4); v SA 1956 (5); v WI 1947 (4) 1953 (4)*
mb, A. J. 56: v A 1985 (6); v WI 1984 (5) 1988 (4); v NZ 1983 (4) 1986 (1); v In 1982 (3) 1986 (2); v P 1982 (3); v SL 1984 (1) 1988 (1); *v A 1982 (5) 1986 (5); v WI 1985 (5); v NZ 1983 (3); v In 1984 (5); v P 1983 (3)*
ngridge (James) 8: v SA 1935 (1); v WI 1933 (2); v In 1936 (1) 1946 (1); *v In 1933 (3)*
rkins, W. 6: v A 1981 (1); v WI 1980 (3); *v A 1979 (1); v In 1979 (1)*
rter (J. D. F.) 10: v SA 1965 (2); v NZ 1965 (1); v P 1962 (1); *v NZ 1962 (3); v In 1963 (3)*
rwood (H.) 21: v A 1926 (2) 1930 (3); v SA 1929 (3); v WI 1928 (2); v NZ 1931 (1); *v A 1928 (5) 1932 (5)*
wrence, D. V. 1: v SL 1988
dbeater (E.) 2: *v In 1951 (2)*
(H. W.) 1: *v SA 1930*
s (W. S.) 5: *v SA 1905 (5)*
ge G. B. 5: *v SA 1927 (1); v NZ 1929 (4)*
lie, C. F. H. 4: *v A 1882 (4)*
er, J. K. 21: v A 1977 (3); v WI 1980 (1); v In 1979 (1) 1986 (1); *v A 1976 (1) 1978 (1) 1979 (1); v NZ 1977 (1); v In 1976 (5) 1979 (1) 1981 (2); v P 1977 (3)*
er, P. 17: v A 1972 (1) 1975 (1); v In 1971 (1); v P 1971 (3); *v A 1970 (5) 1974 (2); v NZ 1970 (?) 1974 (2)*
eson Gower, H. D. G. 3: *v SA 1909 (3)*
ett, W. H. V. 1: *v In 1933*
is, A. R. 9: v NZ 1973 (1); *v In 1972 (5); v P 1972 (3)*
and (M.) 41: v A 1930 (3) 1934 (5) 1938 (1); v SA 1929 (5) 1935 (4); v WI 1928 (1) 1933 (1); v 1936 (2); *v A 1928 (1) 1932 (5) 1936 (5); v SA 1930 (5); v WI 1934 (3)*
y (A. A.) 35: v A 1896 (3) 1899 (4) 1902 (5) 1905 (5) 1909 (5); v SA 1907 (3); *v A 1901 (5) 03 (5)*
white (James jun.) 2: *v A 1876 (2)*
d, D. 9: v In 1974 (2); v P 1974 (3); *v A 1974 (4)*
d, T. A. 1: v WI 1984
der (P. J.) 13: v SA 1955 (1); v WI 1957 (2); v NZ 1958 (3); v P 1954 (1); *v A 1958 (2); v SA 56 (4)*

Lock (G. A. R.) 49: v A 1953 (2) 1956 (4) 1961 (3); v SA 1955 (3); v WI 1957 (3) 1963 (3); v NZ 1958 (5); v In 1952 (2); v P 1962 (3); *v A 1958 (4); v SA 1956 (1); v WI 1953 (5) 1967 (2); v NZ 1958 (2); v In 1961 (5); v P 1961 (2)*

Lockwood (W. H.) 12: v A 1893 (2) 1899 (1) 1902 (4); *v A 1894 (5)*

Lohmann (G. A.) 18: v A 1886 (3) 1888 (3) 1890 (2) 1896 (1); *v A 1886 (2) 1887 (1) 1891 (3); SA 1895 (3)*

Lowson (F. A.) 7: v SA 1951 (2) 1955 (1); *v In 1951 (4)*

Lucas, A. P. 5: v A 1880 (1) 1882 (1) 1884 (2); *v A 1878(1)*

Luckhurst, B. W. 21: v A 1972 (4); v WI 1973 (2); v In 1971 (3); v P 1971 (3); *v A 1970 (5); 197 (2); v NZ 1970 (2)*

Lyttelton, Hon. A. 4: v A 1880 (1) 1882 (1) 1884 (2)

Macaulay (G. G.) 8: v A 1926 (1); v SA 1924 (1); v WI 1933 (2); *v SA 1922 (4)*

MacBryan, J. C. W. 1: v SA 1924

McConnon (J. E.) 2: v P 1954 (2)

McGahey, C. P. 2: *v A 1901 (2)*

MacGregor, G. 8: v A 1890 (2) 1893 (3); *v A 1891 (3)*

McIntyre (A. J. W.) 3: v SA 1955 (1); v WI 1950 (1); *v A 1950 (10*

MacKinnon, F. A. 1: *v A 1878*

MacLaren, A. C. 35: v A 1896 (2) 1899 (4) 1902 (5) 1905 (4) 1909 (5); *v A 1894 (5) 1897 (1901 (5)*

McMaster, J. E. P. 1: *v SA 1888*

Makepeace (H.) 4: *v A 1920 (4)*

Mann, F. G. 7: v NZ 1949 (2); *v SA 1948 (5)*

Mann, F. T. 5: *v SA 1922 (5)*

Marks, V. J. 6: v NZ 1983 (1); v P 1982 (1); *v NZ 1983 (1); v P 1983 (3)*

Marriott, C. S. 1: v WI 1933

Martin (F.) 2: v A 1890 (1); *v SA 1891 (1)*

Martin, J. W. 1: v SA 1947

Mason, J. R. 5: *v A 1897 (5)*

Matthews (A. D. G.) 1: v NZ 1937

May, P. B. H. 66: v A 1953 (2) 1956 (5) 1961 (4); v SA 1951 (2) 1955 (5); v WI 1957 (5); v N 1958 (5); v In 1952 (4) 1959 (3); v P 1954 (4); *v A 1954 (5) 1958 (5); v SA 1956 (5); v WI 1953 1959 (3); v NZ 1954 (2) 1958 (2)*

Maynard, M. P. 1: v WI 1988

Mead (C. P.) 17: v A 1921 (2); *v A 1911 (4) 1928 (1); v SA 1913 (5) 1922 (5)*

Mead (W.) 1: v A 1899

Midwinter (W. E.) 4: *v A 1881 (4)*

Milburn, C. 9: v A 1968 (2); v WI 1966 (4); v In 1967 (1); v P 1967 (1); *v P 1968 (1)*

Miller, A. M. 1: *v SA 1895*

Miller, G. 34: v A 1977 (2); v WI 1976 (1) 1984 (2); v NZ 1978 (2); v In 1979 (3) 1982 (1); v 1978 (3) 1982 (1); *v A 1978 (6) 1979 (1) 1982 (5); v WI 1980 (1); v NZ 1977 (3); v P 1977*

Milligan, F. W. 2: *v SA 1898 (2)*

Millman (G.) 6: v P 1962 (2); *v In 1961 (2); v P 1961 (2)*

Milton (C. A.) 6: v NZ 1958 (2); v In 1959 (2); *v A 1958 (2)*

Mitchell (A.) 6: v SA 1935 (2); v In 1936 (1); *v In 1933 (3)*

Mitchell, F. 2: *v SA 1898 (2)*

Mitchell (T. B.) 5: v A 1934 (2); v SA 1935 (1); *v A 1932 (1); v NZ 1932 (1)*

Mitchell-Innes, N. S. 1: v SA 1935

Mold (A. W.) 3: v A 1893 (3)

Moon, L. J. 4: *v SA 1905 (4)*

Morley (F.) 4: v A 1880 (1); *v A 1882 (3)*

Mortimore (J. B.) 9: v A 1964 (1); v In 1959 (2); *v A 1958 (1); v NZ 1958 (2); v In 1963*

Moss (A. E.) 9: v A 1956 (1); v SA 1960 (2); v In 1959 (3); *v WI 1953 (1) 1959 (2)*

Moxon, M. D. 9: v WI 1988 (2); v NZ 1986 (2); v P 1987 (1); *v A 1987 (1); v NZ 1987*

Murdoch, W. L. 1: *v SA 1891*

Murray, J. T. 21: v A 1961 (5); v WI 1966 (1); v In 1967 (3); v P 1962 (3) 1967 (1); *v A 1962 (SA 1964 (1); v NZ 1962 (1) 1965 (1); v In 1961 (3); v P 1961 (1)*

Newham (W.) 1: *v A 1887*

Newport, P. J. 1: v SL 1988

Nichols (M. S.) 14: v A 1930 (1); v SA 1935 (4); v WI 1933 (1) 1939 (1); *v NZ 1929 (4); 1933 (3)*

ɔakman (A. S. M.) 2: v A 1956 (2)
)'Brien, T. C. 5: v A 1884 (1) 1888 (1); *v SA 1895 (3)*
)'Connor (J.) 4: v SA 1929 (1); *v WI 1929 (3)*
)ld, C. M. 46: v A 1975 (3) 1977 (2) 1980 (1) 1981 (2); v WI 1973 (1) 1976 (2) 1980 (1); v NZ 1973 (2) 1978 (1); v In 1974 (3); v P 1974 (3) 1978 (3); *v A 1974 (2) 1976 (1) 1978 (1); v WI 1973 (4) 1980 (1); v NZ 1974 (1) 1977 (2); v In 1972 (4) 1976 (4); v P 1972 (1) 1977 (1)*
)ldfield (N.) 1: v WI 1939

'adgett (D. E. V.) 2: v SA 1960 (2)
'aine (G. A. E.) 4: *v WI 1934 (4)*
'alairet, L. C. H. 2: v A 1902 (2)
'almer, C. H. 1: *v WI 1953*
almer, K. E. 1: *v SA 1964*
arfitt (P. H.) 37: v A 1964 (4) 1972 (3); v SA 1965 (2); v WI 1969 (1); v NZ 1965 (2); v P 1962 (5); *v A 1962 (2); v SA 1964 (5); v NZ 1962 (3) 1965 (3); v In 1961 (2) 1963 (3); v P 1961 (2)*
arker (C. W. L.) 1: v A 1921
ırker, P. W. G. 1: v A 1981
ırkhouse (W. G. A.) 7: v WI 1950 (2); v In 1959 (2); *v A 1950 (2); v NZ 1950 (1)*
ırkin (C. H.) 10: v A 1921 (4); v SA 1924 (1); *v A 1920 (5)*
ırks (J. H.) 1: v NZ 1937
ırks (J. M.) 46: v A 1964 (5); v SA 1960 (5) 1965 (3); v WI 1963 (4) 1966 (4); v NZ 1965 (3); v P 1954 (1); *v A 1965 (5); v SA 1964 (5); v WI 1959 (1) 1967 (3); v NZ 1965 (2); v In 1963 (5)*
ataudi, Nawab of, 3: v A 1934 (1); *v A 1932 (2)*
ıynter (E.) 20: v A 1938 (4); v WI 1939 (2); v NZ 1931 (1) 1937 (2); v In 1932 (1); *v A 1932 (3); v SA 1938 (5); v NZ 1932 (2)*
ːate (E.) 9: v A 1882 (1) 1884 (3) 1886 (1); *v A 1881 (4)*
ːebles, I. A. R. 13: v A 1930 (2); v NZ 1931 (3); *v SA 1927 (4) 1930 (4)*
ːel (R.) 20: v A 1888 (3) 1890 (1) 1893 (1) 1896 (1); *v A 1884 (5) 1887 (1) 1891 (3) 1894 (5)*
ːnn, F. 1: v A 1880
rks (R. T. D.) 2: v WI 1939 (1); *v SA 1938 (1)*
ıilipson, (H.) 5: *v A 1891 (1) 1894 (4)*
ɡott, A. C. S. 1: *v NZ 1983*
lling (R.) 8: v A 1884 (1) 1886 (1) 1888 (1); *v A 1881 (4) 1887 (1)*
ıce (W.) 3: *v WI 1947 (3)*
cock, P. I. 25: v A 1968 (1); v WI 1976 (2) 1984 (2); v SL 1984 (1); *v WI 1967 (2) 1973 (4); v In 1972 (4) 1984 (5); v P 1968 (1) 1972 (3)*
llard (R.) 4: v A 1948 (2); v In 1946 (1); *v NZ 1946 (1)*
ɔle (C. J.) 3: *v In 1951 (3)*
ɔe (G. H.) 1: v SA 1947
ıgher (A. D.) 1: *v SA 1891*
ce, J. S. E. 15: v A 1964 (2) 1972 (1); v In 1971 (3); v P 1971 (1); *v SA 1964 (4); v In 1963 (4)*
ːe (W. F. F.) 1: v A 1938
deaux, R. M. 3: v A 1968 (1); *v P 1968 (2)*
ıgle, D. R. 19: v WI 1984 (3) 1988 (4); v NZ 1986 (1); v In 1982 (3) 1986 (3); v P 1982 (1); v SL 988 (1); *v A 1982 (3)*
lar (G.) 28: v A 1961 (5); v SA 1960 (3); v In 1959 (3); v P 1962 (2); *v A 1962 (4); v WI 1959 5); v In 1961 (3); v P 1961 (3)*

ıife (W. G.) 7: v A 1899 (2); *v A 1901 (5)*

lford, N. V. 3: v NZ 1986 (1); v In 1986 (1); *v NZ 1987 (1)*
lley, C. T. 8: v NZ 1978 (3); v P 1978 (3); *v NZ 1977 (2)*
ıdall, D. W. 47: v A 1977 (5); v WI 1984 (1); v NZ 1983 (3); v In 1979 (3) 1982 (3); v P 1982); *v A 1976 (1) 1978 (6) 1979 (2) 1982 (4); v NZ 1977 (3) 1983 (3); v In 1976 (4); v P 1977 (3) 983 (3)*
jitsinhji, K. S. 15: v A 1896 (2) 1899 (5) 1902 (3); *v A 1897 (5)*
d, H. D. 1: v SA 1935
d (J. M.) 17: v A 1882 (1) 1890 (2) 1893 (1); *v A 1884 (5) 1886 (2) 1887 (1) 1891 (3); v SA 388 (2)*
d, W. W. 18: v A 1884 (2) 1886 (3) 1888 (3) 1890 (2) 1893 (2); *v A 1882 (4) 1887 (1); v SA 391 (1)*
(A. E.) 13: v A 1909 (1); *v A 1903 (2); v SA 1905 (5) 1913 (5)*

Rhodes (H. J.) 2: v In 1959 (2)
Rhodes (W.) 58: v A 1899 (3) 1902 (5) 1905 (4) 1909 (4) 1912 (3) 1921 (1) 1926 (1); v SA 1912 (3); *v A 1903 (5) 1907 (5) 1911 (5) 1920 (5); v SA 1909 (5) 1913 (5); v WI 1929 (4)*
Richards, C. J. 8: v WI 1988 (2); v P 1987 (1); *v A 1986 (5)*
Richardson (D. W.) 1: v WI 1957
Richardson (P. E.) 34: v A 1956 (5); v WI 1957 (5) 1963 (1); v NZ 1958 (4); *v A 1958 (4); v SA 1956 (5); v NZ 1958 (2); v In 1961 (5); v P 1961 (3)*
Richardson (T.) 14: v A 1893 (1) 1896 (3); *v A 1894 (5) 1897 (5)*
Richmond (T. L.) 1: v A 1921
Ridgway (F.) 5: *v In 1951 (5)*
Robertson (J. D.) 11: v SA 1947 (1); v NZ 1949 (1); *v WI 1947 (4); v In 1951 (5)*
Robins, R. W. V. 19: v A 1930 (2); v SA 1929 (1) 1935 (3); v WI 1933 (2); v NZ 1931 (1) 1937 (3); v In 1932 (1) 1936 (2); *v A 1936 (4)*
Robinson, R. T. 28: v A 1985 (6); v In 1986 (1); v P 1987 (5); v SL 1988 (1); *v A 1987 (1); v WI 1985 (4); v NZ 1987 (3); v In 1984 (5); v P 1987 (2)*
Roope, G. R. J. 21: v A 1975 (1) 1977 (2); v WI 1973 (1); v NZ 1973 (3) 1978 (1); v P 1978 (3); *v NZ 1977 (3); v In 1972 (2); v P 1972 (2) 1977 (3)*
Root (C. F.) 3: v A 1926 (3)
Rose, B. C. 9: v WI 1980 (3); *v WI 1980 (1); v NZ 1977 (2); v P 1977 (3)*
Royle, V. P. F. A. 1: *v A 1878*
Rumsey, F. E. 5: v A 1964 (1); v SA 1965 (1); v NZ 1965 (3)
Russell (A. C.) 10: v A 1921 (2); *v A 1920 (4); v SA 1922 (4)*
Russell, R. C. 1: v SL 1988
Russell, W. E. 10: v SA 1965 (1); v WI 1966 (2); v P 1967 (1); *v A 1965 (1); v NZ 1965 (3); v In 1961 (1); v P 1961 (1)*

Sandham (A.) 14: v A 1921 (1); v SA 1924 (2); *v A 1924 (2); v SA 1922 (5); v WI 1929 (4)*
Schultz, S. S. 1: *v A 1878*
Scotton (W. H.) 15: v A 1884 (1) 1886 (3); *v A 1881 (4) 1884 (5) 1886 (2)*
Selby (J.) 6: *v A 1876 (2) 1881 (4)*
Selvey, M. W. W. 3: v WI 1976 (2); *v In 1976 (1)*
Shackleton (D.) 7: v SA 1951 (1); v WI 1950 (1) 1963 (4); *v In 1951 (1)*
Sharp (J.) 3: v A 1909 (3)
Sharpe (J. W.) 3: v A 1890 (1); *v A 1891 (2)*
Sharpe, P. J. 12: v A 1964 (2); v WI 1963 (3) 1969 (3); v NZ 1969 (3); *v In 1963 (1)*
Shaw (A.) 7: v A 1880 (1); *v A 1876 (2) 1881 (4)*
Sheppard, Rev. D. S. 22: v A 1956 (2); v WI 1950 (1) 1957 (2); v In 1952 (2); v P 1954 (2) 19[illegible] (2); *v A 1950 (2) 1962 (5); v NZ 1950 (1) 1963 (3)*
Sherwin (M.) 3: v A 1888 (1); *v A 1886 (2)*
Shrewsbury (A.) 23: v A 1884 (2) 1886 (3) 1890 (2) 1893 (3); *v A 1881 (4) 1884 (5) 1886 (2) 1887 (*[illegible]
Shuter, J. 1: v A 1888
Shuttleworth, K. 5: v P 1971 (1); *v A 1970 (2); v NZ 1970 (2)*
Sidebottom, A. 1: v A 1985
Simpson, R. T. 27: v A 1953 (3); v SA 1951 (3); v WI 1950 (3); v NZ 1949 (2); v In 1952 (2); [illegible] 1954 (3); *v A 1950 (5) 1954 (1); v SA 1948 (1); v NZ 1950 (2) 1954 (2)*
Simpson-Hayward, G. H. 5: *v SA 1909 (5)*
Sims (J. M.) 4: v SA 1935 (1); v In 1936 (1); *v A 1936 (2)*
Sinfield (R. A.) 1: v A 1938
Slack, W. N. 3: v In 1986 (1); *v WI 1985 (2)*
Smailes (T. F.) 1: v In 1946
Small, G. C. 5: v WI 1988 (1); v NZ 1986 (2); *v A 1986 (2)*
Smith, A. C. 6: *v A 1962 (4); v NZ 1962 (2)*
Smith, C. A. 1: *v SA 1888*
Smith (C. I. J.) 5: v NZ 1937 (1); *v WI 1934 (4)*
Smith, C. L. 8: v NZ 1983 (2); v In 1986 (1); *v NZ 1983 (2); v P 1983 (3)*
Smith (D.) 2: v SA 1935 (2)
Smith D. M. 2: *v WI 1985 (2)*
Smith (D. R.) 5: *v In 1961 (5)*
Smith (D. V.) 3: v WI 1957 (3)
Smith (E. J.) 11: v A 1912 (3); v SA 1912 (3); *v A 1911 (4); v SA 1913 (1)*
Smith (H.) 1: v WI 1928

mith, M. J. K. 50: v A 1961 (1) 1972 (3); v SA 1960 (4) 1965 (3); v WI 1966 (1); v NZ 1958 (3) 1965 (3); v In 1959 (2); *v A 1965 (5); v SA 1964 (5); v WI 1959 (5); v NZ 1965 (3); v In 1961 (4) 1963 (5); v P 1961 (3)*
mith, R. A. 3: v WI 1988 (2); v SL 1988 (1)
mith (T. P. B.) 4: v In 1946 (1); *v A 1946 (2); v NZ 1946 (1)*
mithson (G. A.) 2: *v WI 1947 (2)*
now, J. A. 49: v A 1968 (5) 1972 (5) 1975 (4); v SA 1965 (1); v WI 1966 (3) 1969 (3) 1973 (1) 1976 (3); v NZ 1965 (1) 1969 (2) 1973 (3); v In 1967 (3) 1971 (2); v P 1967 (1); *v A 1970 (6); v WI 1967 (4); v P 1968 (2)*
outherton (J.) 2: *v A 1876 (2)*
pooner, R. H. 10: v A 1905 (2) 1909 (2) 1912 (3); v SA 1912 (3)
pooner (R. T.) 7: v SA 1955 (1); *v In 1951 (5); v WI 1953 (1)*
anyforth, R. T. 4: *v SA 1927 (4)*
aples (S. J.) 3: *v SA 1927 (3)*
atham (J. B.) 70: v A 1953 (1) 1956 (3) 1961 (4); v SA 1951 (2) 1955 (4) 1960 (5) 1965 (1); v WI 1957 (3) 1963 (2); v NZ 1958 (2); v In 1959 (3); v P 1954 (4) 1962 (3); *v A 1954 (5) 1958 (4) 1962 (5); v SA 1956 (4); v WI 1953 (4) 1959 (3); v NZ 1950 (1) 1954 (2); v In 1951 (5)*
eel, A. G. 13: v A 1880 (1) 1882 (1) 1884 (3) 1886 (3) 1888 (1); *v A 1882 (4)*
eele, D. S. 8: v A 1975 (3); v WI 1976 (5)
evens, G. T. S. 10: v A 1926 (2); *v SA 1922 (1) 1927 (5); v WI 1929 (2)*
evenson, G. B. 2: *v WI 1980 (1); v In 1979 (1)*
ewart (M. J.) 8: v WI 1963 (4); v P 1962 (2); *v In 1963 (2)*
oddart, A. E. 16: v A 1893 (3) 1896 (2); *v A 1887 (1) 1891 (3) 1894 (5) 1897 (2)*
orer (W.) 6: v A 1899 (1); *v A 1897 (5)*
eet (G. B.) 1: *v SA 1922*
udwick (H.) 28: v A 1921 (2) 1926 (5); v SA 1924 (1); *v A 1911 (1) 1920 (4) 1924 (5); v SA 1909 (5) 1913 (5)*
udd, C. T. 5: v A 1882 (1); *v A 1882 (4)*
udd, G. B. 4: *v A 1882 (4)*
bba Row, R. 13: v A 1961 (5); v SA 1960 (4); v NZ 1958 (1); v In 1959 (1); *v WI 1959 (2)*
gg (F. H.) 2: v A 1888 (2)
cliffe (H.) 54: v A 1926 (5) 1930 (4) 1934 (4); v SA 1924 (5) 1929 (5) 1935 (2); v WI 1928 (3) 933 (2); v NZ 1931 (2); v In 1932 (1); *v A 1924 (5) 1928 (4) 1932 (5); v SA 1927 (5); v NZ 932 (2)*
etman (R.) 11: v In 1959 (3); *v A 1958 (2); v WI 1959 (4); v NZ 1958 (2)*

e (F. W.) 1: v A 1902
e (M. W.) 39: v A 1926 (5) 1930 (5); v SA 1924 (5) 1929 (3) 1935 (1); v WI 1928 (3); v NZ 1931 1); *v A 1924 (5) 1928 (5); v SA 1930 (5); v NZ 1932 (1)*
tersall (R.) 16: v A 1953 (1); v SA 1951 (5); v P 1954 (1); *v A 1950 (2); v NZ 1950 (2); v In 951 (5)*
aré, C. J. 30: v A 1981 (2); v WI 1980 (2) 1984 (1); v NZ 1983 (4); v In 1982 (3); v P 1982 (3); SL 1984 (1); *v A 1982 (5); v NZ 1983 (2); v In 1981 (6); v SL 1981 (1)*
lor (K.) 3: v A 1964 (1); v In 1959 (2)
lor, L. B. 2: v A 1985 (2)
lor, R. W. 57: v A 1981 (3); v NZ 1978 (3) 1983 (4); v In 1979 (3) 1982 (3); v P 1978 (3) 1982); *v A 1978 (6) 1979 (3) 1982 (5); v NZ 1970 (1) 1977 (3) 1983 (3); v In 1979 (1) 1981 (6); v P 977 (3) 1983 (3); v SL 1981 (1)*
nyson, Hon. L. H. 9: v A 1921 (4); *v SA 1913 (5)*
ry, V. P. 2: v WI 1984 (2)
mas, J. G. 5: v NZ 1986 (1); *v WI 1985 (4)*
mpson (G. J.) 6: v A 1909 (1); *v SA 1909 (5)*
mson, N. I. 5: *v SA 1964 (5)*
nus (F. J.) 53: v A 1964 (5); v SA 1955 (2) 1965 (3); v WI 1963 (4) 1966 (3); v NZ 1965 (3); v P 62 (2) 1967 (2); *v A 1962 (5) 1965 (5) 1974 (4); v SA 1964 (5); v WI 1967 (2); v NZ 1962 (3); v 1963 (5)*
hard, R. W. 4: *v In 1976 (4)*
nsend, C. L. 2: v A 1899 (2)
nsend, D. C. H. 3: *v WI 1934 (3)*
nsend (L. F.) 4: *v WI 1929 (1); v In 1933 (3)*
nlett (M. F.) 3: *v WI 1947 (3)*
(A. E.) 2: *v SA 1898 (2)*

Trueman (F. S.) 67: v A 1953 (1) 1956 (2) 1961 (4) 1964 (4); v SA 1955 (1) 1960 (5); v WI 1957 (5 1963 (5); v NZ 1958 (5) 1965 (2); v In 1952 (4) 1959 (5); v P 1962 (4); *v A 1958 (3) 1962 (5); WI 1953 (3) 1959 (5); v NZ 1958 (2) 1962 (2)*

Tufnell, N. C. 1: *v SA 1909*

Turnbull, M. J. 9: v WI 1933 (2); v In 1936 (1); *v SA 1930 (5); v NZ 1929 (1)*

Tyldesley (E.) 14: v A 1921 (3) 1926 (1); v SA 1924 (1); v WI 1928 (3); *v A 1928 (1); v SA 1927 (5*

Tyldesley (J. T.) 31: v A 1899 (2) 1902 (5) 1905 (5) 1909 (4); v SA 1907 (3); *v A 1901 (5) 1903 (5); SA 1898 (2)*

Tyldesley (R. K.) 7: v A 1930 (2); v SA 1924 (4); *v A 1924 (1)*

Tylecote, E. F. S. 6: v A 1886 (2); *v A 1882 (4)*

Tyler (E. J.) 1: *v SA 1895*

Tyson (F. H.) 17: v A 1956 (1); v SA 1955 (2); v P 1954 (1); *v A 1954 (5) 1958 (2); v SA 1956 (2); NZ 1954 (2) 1958 (2)*

Ulyett (G.) 25: v A 1882 (1) 1884 (3) 1886 (3) 1888 (2) 1890 (1); *v A 1876 (2) 1878 (1) 1881 (4) 188 (5) 1887 (1); v SA 1888 (2)*

Underwood, D. L. 86: v A 1968 (4) 1972 (2) 1975 (4) 1977 (5); v WI 1966 (2) 1969 (2) 1973 (1976 (5) 1980 (1); v NZ 1969 (3) 1973 (1); v In 1971 (1) 1974 (3); v P 1967 (2) 1971 (1) 1974 (3 *v A 1970 (5) 1974 (5) 1976 (1) 1979 (3); v WI 1973 (4); v NZ 1970 (2) 1974 (2); v In 1972 (4) 19 (5) 1979 (1) 1981 (6); v P 1968 (3) 1972 (2); v SL 1981 (1)*

Valentine, B. H. 7: *v SA 1938 (5); v In 1933 (2)*

Verity (H.) 40: v A 1934 (5) 1938 (4); v SA 1935 (4); v WI 1933 (2) 1939 (1); v NZ 1931 (2) 19 (1); v In 1936 (3); *v A 1932 (4) 1936 (5); v SA 1938 (5); v NZ 1932 (1); v In 1933 (3)*

Vernon, G. F. 1: *v A 1882*

Vine (J.) 2: *v A 1911 (2)*

Voce (W.) 27: v NZ 1931 (1) 1937 (1); v In 1932 (1) 1936 (1) 1946 (1); *v A 1932 (4) 1936 (5) 19 (2); v SA 1930 (5); v WI 1929 (4); v NZ 1932 (2)*

Waddington (A.) 2: *v A 1920 (2)*

Wainwright (E.) 5: v A 1893 (1); *v A 1897 (4)*

Walker (P. M.) 3: v SA 1960 (3)

Walters, C. F. 11: v A 1934 (5); v WI 1933 (3); *v In 1933 (3)*

Ward, A. 5: v WI 1976 (1); v NZ 1969 (3); v P 1971 (1)

Ward (A.) 7: v A 1893 (2); *v A 1894 (5)*

Wardle (J. H.) 28: v A 1953 (3) 1956 (1); v SA 1951 (2) 1955 (3); v WI 1950 (1) 1957 (1); v P 19 (4); *v A 1954 (4); v SA 1956 (4); v WI 1947 (1) 1953 (2); v NZ 1954 (2)*

Warner, P. F. 15: v A 1909 (1) 1912 (1); v SA 1912 (1); *v A 1903 (5); v SA 1898 (2) 1905*

Warr, J. J. 2: *v A 1950 (2)*

Warren (A. R.) 1: v A 1905

Washbrook (C.) 37: v A 1948 (4) 1956 (3); v SA 1947 (5); v WI 1950 (2); v NZ 1937 (1) 1949 (v In 1946 (3); *v A 1946 (5) 1950 (5); v SA 1948 (5); v NZ 1946 (1) 1950 (1)*

Watkins (A. J.) 15: v A 1948 (1); v NZ 1949 (1); v In 1952 (3); *v SA 1948 (5); v In 1951*

Watson (W.) 23: v A 1953 (3) 1956 (2); v SA 1951 (5) 1955 (1); v NZ 1958 (2); v In 1952 (1); *1958 (2); v WI 1953 (5); v NZ 1958 (2)*

Webbe, A. J. 1: *v A 1878*

Wellard (A. W.) 2: v A 1938 (1); v NZ 1937 (1)

Wharton (A.) 1: v NZ 1949

Whitaker, J. J. 1: *v A 1986*

White (D. W.) 2: v *P 1961 (2)*

White, J. C. 15: v A 1921 (1) 1930 (1); v SA 1929 (3); v WI 1928 (1); *v A 1928 (5); v SA 1930*

Whysall (W. W.) 4: v A 1930 (1); *v A 1924 (3)*

Wilkinson (L. L.) 3: *v SA 1938 (3)*

Willey, P. 26: v A 1980 (1) 1981 (4) 1985 (1); v WI 1976 (2) 1980 (5); v NZ 1986 (1); v In 1979 *v A 1979 (3); v WI 1980 (4) 1985 (4)*

Willis, R. G. D. 90: v A 1977 (5) 1981 (6); v WI 1973 (1) 1976 (2) 1980 (4) 1984 (3); v NZ 1978 1983 (4); v In 1974 (1) 1979 (3) 1982 (3); v P 1974 (1) 1978 (3) 1982 (2); *v A 1970 (4) 197 1976 (1) 1978 (6) 1979 (3) 1982 (5); v WI 1973 (3); v NZ 1970 (1) 1977 (3) 1983 (3); v In 197 1981 (5); v P 1977 (3) 1983 (1); v SL 1981 (1)*

Wilson, C. E. M. 2: *v SA 1898 (2)*

Wilson, D. 6: *v NZ 1970 (1); v In 1963 (5)*

Wilson, E. R. 1: *v A 1920*

Vood (A.) 4: v A 1938 (1); v WI 1939 (3)
Vood, B. 12: v A 1972 (1) 1975 (3); v WI 1976 (1); v P 1978 (1); *v NZ 1974* (2); *v In 1972* (3); *v P 1972* (1)
Vood, G. E. C. 3: v SA 1924 (3)
Vood (H.) 4: v A 1888 (1); *v SA 1888* (2) *1891* (1)
Vood (R.) 1: *v A 1886*
Voods S. M. J. 3: *v SA 1895* (3)
Voolley (F. E.) 64: v A 1909 (1) 1912 (3) 1921 (5) 1926 (5) 1930 (2) 1934 (1); v SA 1912 (3) 1924 (5) 1929 (3); v NZ 1931 (1); v In 1932 (1); *v A 1911* (5) *1920* (5) *1924* (5); *v SA 1909* (5) *1913* (5) *1922* (5); *v NZ 1929* (4)
Voolmer, R. A. 19: v A 1975 (2) 1977 (5) 1981 (2); v WI 1976 (5) 1980 (2); *v A 1976* (1); *v In 1976* (2)
Vorthington (T. S.) 9: v In 1936 (2); *v A 1936* (3); *v NZ 1929* (4)
Vright, C. W. 3: *v SA 1895* (3)
Vright (D. V. P.) 34: v A 1938 (3) 1948 (1); v SA 1947 (4); v WI 1939 (3) 1950 (1); v NZ 1949 (1); v In 1946 (2); *v A 1946* (5) *1950* (5); *v SA 1938* (3) *1948* (3); *v NZ 1946* (1)
Vyatt, R. E. S. 40: v A 1930 (1) 1934 (4); v SA 1929 (2) 1935 (5); v WI 1933 (2); v In 1936 (1); *v A 1932* (5) *1936* (2); *v SA 1927* (5) *1930* (5); *v WI 1929* (2) *1934* (4); *v NZ 1932* (2)
Vynyard, E. G. 3: v A 1896 (1); *v SA 1905* (2)

ardley, N. W. D. 20: v A 1948 (5); v SA 1947 (5); v WI 1950 (3); *v A 1946* (5); *v SA 1938* (1); *v NZ 1946* (1)
oung (H. I.) 2: v A 1899 (2)
oung (J. A.) 8: v A 1948 (3); v SA 1947 (1); v NZ 1949 (2); *v SA 1948* (2)
oung, R. A. 2: *v A 1907* (2)

AUSTRALIA

Number of Test cricketers: 343

Beckett, E. L. 4: v E 1928 (2); v SA 1931 (1); *v E 1930* (1)
lderman, T. M. 22: v E 1982 (1); v WI 1981 (2) 1984 (3); v P 1981 (3); *v E 1981* (6); *v WI 1983* (3); *v NZ 1981* (3); *v P 1982* (1)
lexander, G. 2: v E 1884 (1); *v E 1880* (1)
lexander, H. H. 1: v E 1932
lan, F. E. 1: v E 1878
lan, P. J. 1: v E 1965
len, R. C. 1: v E 1886
ndrews, T. J. E. 16: v E 1924 (3); *v E 1921* (5) *1926* (5); *v SA 1921* (3)
cher, K. A. 5: v E 1950 (3); v WI 1951 (2)
cher, R. G. 19: v E 1954 (4); v SA 1952 (1); *v E 1953* (3) *1956* (5); *v WI 1954* (5); *v P 1956* (1)
mstrong, W. W. 50: v E 1901 (4) 1903 (3) 1907 (5) 1911 (5) 1920 (5); v SA 1910 (5); *v E 1902* (5) *1905* (5) *1909* (5) *1921* (5); *v SA 1902* (3)

dcock, C. L. 7: v E 1936 (3); *v E 1938* (4)
nnerman, A. C. 28: v E 1878 (1) 1881 (3) 1882 (4) 1884 (4) 1886 (1) 1887 (1) 1891 (3); *v E 1880* (1) *1882* (1) *1884* (3) *1888* (3) *1893* (3)
nnerman, C. 3: v E 1876 (2) 1878 (1)
dsley, W. 41: v E 1911 (4) 1920 (5) 1924 (3); v SA 1910 (5); *v E 1909* (5) *1912* (3) *1921* (5) *1926* (5); *v SA 1912* (3) *1921* (3)
nes, S. G. 13: v E 1946 (4); v In 1947 (3); *v E 1938* (1) *1948* (4); *v NZ 1945* (1)
nett, B. A. 4: *v E 1938* (4)
rett, J. E. 2: *v E 1890* (2)
rd, G. R. 3: *v P 1979* (3)
aud, J. 3: v P 1972 (2); *v WI 1972* (1)
aud, R. 63: v E 1954 (5) 1958 (5) 1962 (5); v SA 1952 (4) 1963 (4); v WI 1951 (1) 1960 (5); *v E 1953* (3) *1956* (5) *1961* (4); *v SA 1957* (5); *v WI 1954* (5); *v In 1956* (3) *1959* (5); *v P 1956* (1) *1959* (3)
nett, M. J. 3: v WI 1984 (2); *v E 1985* (1)

Blackham, J. McC. 35: v E 1876 (2) 1878 (1) 1881 (4) 1882 (4) 1884 (2) 1886 (1) 1887 (1) 1891 (3 1894 (1); *v E 1880 (1) 1882 (1) 1884 (3) 1886 (3) 1888 (3) 1890 (2) 1893 (3)*
Blackie, D. D. 3: v E 1928 (3)
Bonnor, G. J. 17: v E 1882 (4) 1884 (3); *v E 1880 (1) 1882 (1) 1884 (3) 1886 (2) 1888 (3)*
Boon, D. C. 28: v E 1986 (4) 1987 (1); v WI 1984 (3); v NZ 1985 (3) 1987 (3); v In 1985 (3) v SL 1987 (1); *v E 1985 (4); v NZ 1985 (3); v In 1986 (3)*
Booth, B. C. 29: v E 1962 (5) 1965 (3); v SA 1963 (4); v P 1964 (1); *v E 1961 (2) 1964 (5); v W 1964 (5); v In 1964 (3); v P 1964 (1)*
Border, A. R. 94: v E 1978 (3) 1979 (3) 1982 (5) 1986 (5) 1987 (1); v WI 1979 (3) 1981 (3) 1984 (5) v NZ 1980 (3) 1985 (3) 1987 (3); v In 1980 (3) 1985 (3); v P 1978 (2) 1981 (3) 1983 (5); v SL 198 (1); *v E 1980 (1) 1981 (6) 1985 (6); v WI 1983 (5); v NZ 1981 (3) 1985 (3); v In 1979 (6) 1986 (3) v P 1979 (3) 1982 (3); v SL 1982 (1)*
Boyle, H. F. 12: v E 1878 (1) 1881 (4) 1882 (1) 1884 (1); *v E 1880 (1) 1882 (1) 1884 (3)*
Bradman, D. G. 52: v E 1928 (4) 1932 (4) 1936 (5) 1946 (5); v SA 1931 (5); v WI 1930 (5); v I 1947 (5); *v E 1930 (5) 1934 (5) 1938 (4) 1948 (5)*
Bright, R. J. 25: v E 1979 (1); v WI 1979 (1); v NZ 1985 (1); v In 1985 (3); *v E 1977 (3) 1980 (1981 (5); v NZ 1985 (2); v In 1986 (3); v P 1979 (3) 1982 (2)*
Bromley, E. H. 2: v E 1932 (1); *v E 1934 (1)*
Brown, W. A. 22: v E 1936 (2); v In 1947 (3); *v E 1934 (5) 1938 (4) 1948 (2); v SA 1935 (5); v N 1945 (1)*
Bruce, W. 14: v E 1884 (2) 1891 (3) 1894 (4); *v E 1886 (2) 1893 (3)*
Burge, P. J. 42: v E 1954 (1) 1958 (1) 1962 (3) 1965 (4); v SA 1963 (5); v WI 1960 (2); *v E 1956 (1961 (5) 1964 (5); v SA 1957 (1); v WI 1954 (1); v In 1956 (3) 1959 (2) 1964 (3); v P 1959 (1964 (1)*
Burke, J. W. 24: v E 1950 (2) 1954 (2) 1958 (5); v WI 1951 (1); *v E 1956 (5); v SA 1957 (5); v 1956 (3); v P 1956 (1)*
Burn, K. E. 2: *v E 1890 (2)*
Burton, F. J. 2: v E 1886 (1) 1887 (1)

Callaway, S. T. 3: v E 1891 (2) 1894 (1)
Callen, I. W. 1: v In 1977
Carkeek, W. 6: *v E 1912 (3); v SA 1912 (3)*
Carlson, P. H. 2: v E 1978 (2)
Carter, H. 28: v E 1907 (5) 1911 (5) 1920 (2); v SA 1910 (5); *v E 1909 (5) 1921 (4); v SA 1921*
Chappell, G. S. 87: v E 1970 (5) 1974 (6) 1976 (1) 1979 (3) 1982 (5); v WI 1975 (6) 1979 (3) 19 (3); v NZ 1973 (3) 1980 (3); v In 1980 (3); v P 1972 (3) 1976 (3) 1981 (3) 1983 (5); *v E 1972 1975 (4) 1977 (5) 1980 (1); v WI 1972 (5); v NZ 1973 (3) 1976 (2) 1981 (3); v P 1979 (3); v 1982 (1)*
Chappell, I. M. 75: v E 1965 (2) 1970 (6) 1974 (6) 1979 (2); v WI 1968 (5) 1975 (6) 1979 (1); v N 1973 (3); v In 1967 (4); v P 1964 (1) 1972 (3); *v E 1968 (5) 1972 (5) 1975 (4); v SA 1966 (5) 19 (4); v WI 1972 (5); v NZ 1973 (3); v In 1969 (5)*
Chappell, T. M. 3: *v E 1981 (3)*
Charlton, P. C. 2: *v E 1890 (2)*
Chipperfield, A. G. 14: v E 1936 (3); *v E 1934 (5) 1938 (1); v SA 1935 (5)*
Clark, W. M. 10: v In 1977 (5); v P 1978 (1); *v WI 1977 (4)*
Colley, D. J. 3: *v E 1972 (3)*
Collins, H. L. 19: v E 1920 (5) 1924 (5); *v E 1921 (3) 1926 (3); v SA 1921 (3)*
Coningham, A. 1: v E 1894
Connolly, A. N. 29: v E 1965 (1) 1970 (1); v SA 1963 (3); v WI 1968 (5); v In 1967 (3); *v E 19 (5); v SA 1969 (4); v In 1964 (2); 1969 (5)*
Cooper, B. B. 1: v E 1876
Cooper, W. H. 2: v E 1881 (1) 1884 (1)
Corling, G. E. 5: *v E 1964 (5)*
Cosier, G. J. 18: v E 1976 (1) 1978 (2); v WI 1975 (3); v In 1977 (4); v P 1976 (3); *v WI 1977 v NZ 1976 (2)*
Cottam, W. J. 1: v E 1886
Cotter, A. 21: v E 1903 (2) 1907 (2) 1911 (4); v SA 1910 (5); *v E 1905 (3) 1909 (5)*
Coulthard, G. 1: v E 1881
Cowper, R. M. 27: v E 1965 (4); v In 1967 (4); v P 1964 (1); *v E 1964 (1) 1968 (4); v SA 1966 v WI 1964 (5); v In 1964 (2); v P 1964 (1)*
Craig, I. D. 11: v SA 1952 (1); *v E 1956 (2); v SA 1957 (5); v In 1956 (2); v P 1956 (1)*
Crawford, W. P. A. 4: *v E 1956 (1); v In 1956 (3)*

Darling, J. 34: v E 1894 (5) 1897 (5) 1901 (3); *v E 1896 (3) 1899 (5) 1902 (5) 1905 (5); v SA 1902 (3)*
Darling, L. S. 12: v E 1932 (2) 1936 (1); *v E 1934 (4): v SA 1935 (5)*
Darling, W. M. 14: v E 1978 (4); v In 1977 (1); v P 1978 (1); *v WI 1977 (3); v In 1979 (5)*
Davidson, A. K. 44: v E 1954 (3) 1958 (5) 1962 (5); v WI 1960 (4); *v E 1953 (5) 1956 (2) 1961 (5); v SA 1957 (5); v In 1956 (1) 1959 (5); v P 1956 (1) 1959 (3)*
Davis, I. C. 15: v E 1976 (1); v NZ 1973 (3); v P 1976 (3); *v E 1977 (3); v NZ 1973 (3) 1976 (2)*
Davis, S. P. 1: *v NZ 1985*
De Courcy, J. H. 3: *v E 1953 (3)*
Dell, A. R. 2: v E 1970 (1); v NZ 1973 (1)
Dodemaide, A. I. C. 3: v E 1987 (1); v NZ 1987 (1); v SL 1987 (1)
Donnan, H. 5: v E 1891 (2); *v E 1896 (3)*
Dooland, B. 3: v E 1946 (2); v In 1947 (1)
Duff, R. A. 22: v E 1901 (4) 1903 (5); *v E 1902 (5) 1905 (5); v SA 1902 (3)*
Duncan, J. R. F. 1: v E 1970
Dyer, G. C. 6: v E 1986 (1) 1987 (1); v NZ 1987 (3); v SL 1987 (1)
Dymock, G. 21: v E 1974 (1) 1978 (3) 1979 (3); v WI 1979 (2); v NZ 1973 (1); v P 1978 (1); *v NZ 1973 (2); v In 1979 (5); v P 1979 (3)*
Dyson, J. 30: v E 1982 (5); v WI 1981 (2) 1984 (3); v NZ 1980 (3); v In 1977 (3) 1980 (3); *v E 1981 (5); v NZ 1981 (3); v P 1982 (3)*

Eady, C. J. 2: v E 1901 (1); *v E 1896 (1)*
Eastwood, K. H. 1: v E 1970
Ebeling, H. I. 1: *v E 1934*
Edwards, J. D. 3: *v E 1888 (3)*
Edwards, R. 20: v E 1974 (5); v P 1972 (2); *v E 1972 (4) 1975 (4); v WI 1972 (5)*
Edwards, W. J. 3: v E 1974 (3)
Emery, S. H. 4: *v E 1912 (2); v SA 1912 (2)*
Evans, E. 6: v E 1881 (2) 1882 (1) 1884 (1); *v E 1886 (2)*

Fairfax, A. G. 10: v E 1928 (1); v WI 1930 (5); *v E 1930 (4)*
Favell, L. E. 19: v E 1954 (4) 1958 (2); v WI 1960 (4); *v WI 1954 (2); v In 1959 (4); v P 1959 (3)*
Ferris, J. J. 8: v E 1886 (2) 1887 (1); *v E 1888 (3) 1890 (2)*
Fingleton, J. H. 18: v E 1932 (3) 1936 (5); v SA 1931 (1); *v E 1938 (4); v SA 1935 (5)*
Fleetwood-Smith, L. O'B. 10: v E 1936 (3); *v E 1938 (4); v SA 1935 (3)*
Francis, B. C. 3: *v E 1972 (3)*
Freeman, E. W. 11: v WI 1968 (4); v In 1967 (2); *v E 1968 (2); v SA 1969 (2); v In 1969 (1)*
Freer, F. W. 1: v E 1946

Gannon, J. B. 3: v In 1977 (3)
Garrett, T. W. 19: v E 1876 (2) 1878 (1) 1881 (3) 1882 (3) 1884 (3) 1886 (2) 1887 (1); *v E 1882 (1) 1886 (3)*
Gaunt, R. A. 3: v SA 1963 (1); *v E 1961 (1); v SA 1957 (1)*
Gehrs, D. R. A. 6: v E 1903 (1); v SA 1910 (4); *v E 1905 (1)*
Giffen, G. 31: v E 1881 (3) 1882 (4) 1884 (3) 1891 (3) 1894 (5); *v E 1882 (1) 1884 (3) 1886 (3) 1893 (3) 1896 (3)*
Giffen, W. F. 3: v E 1886 (1) 1891 (2)
Gilbert, D. R. 9: v NZ 1985 (3); v In 1985 (2); *v E 1985 (1); v NZ 1985 (1); v In 1986 (2)*
Gilmour, G. J. 15: v E 1976 (1); v WI 1975 (5); v NZ 1973 (2); v P 1976 (3); *v E 1975 (1); v NZ 1973 (1) 1976 (2)*
Gleeson, J. W. 29: v E 1970 (5); v WI 1968 (5); v In 1967 (4); *v E 1968 (5) 1972 (3); v SA 1969 (4); v In 1969 (3)*
Graham, H. 6: v E 1894 (2); *v E 1893 (3) 1896 (1)*
Gregory, D. W. 3: v E 1876 (2) 1878 (1)
Gregory, E. J. 1: v E 1876
Gregory, J. M. 24: v E 1920 (5) 1924 (5) 1928 (1); *v E 1921 (5) 1926 (5); v SA 1921 (3)*
Gregory, R. G. 2: v E 1936 (2)
Gregory, S. E. 58: v E 1891 (1) 1894 (5) 1897 (5) 1901 (5) 1903 (4) 1907 (2) 1911 (1); *v E 1890 (2) 1893 (3) 1896 (3) 1899 (5) 1902 (5) 1905 (3) 1909 (5) 1912 (3); v SA 1902 (3) 1912 (3)*
Grimmett, C. V. 37: v E 1924 (1) 1928 (5) 1932 (3); v SA 1931 (5); v WI 1930 (5); *v E 1926 (3) 1930 (5) 1934 (5); v SA 1935 (5)*
Groube, T. U. 1: *v E 1880*

Grout, A. T. W. 51: v E 1958 (5) 1962 (2) 1965 (5); v SA 1963 (5); v WI 1960 (5); *v E 1961 (5) 1964 (5); v SA 1957 (5); v WI 1964 (5); v In 1959 (4) 1964 (1); v P 1959 (3) 1964 (1)*
Guest, C. E. J. 1: v E 1962

Hamence, R. A. 3: v E 1946 (1); v In 1947 (2)
Hammond, J. R. 5: *v WI 1972 (5)*
Harry, J. 1: v E 1894
Hartigan, R. J. 2: v E 1907 (2)
Hartkopf, A. E. V. 1: v E 1924
Harvey, M. R. 1: v E 1946
Harvey, R. N. 79: v E 1950 (5) 1954 (5) 1958 (5) 1962 (5); v SA 1952 (5); v WI 1951 (5) 1960 (4); v In 1947 (2); *v E 1948 (2) 1953 (5) 1956 (5) 1961 (5); v SA 1949 (5) 1957 (4); v WI 1954 (5); v In 1956 (3) 1959 (5); v P 1956 (1) 1959 (3)*
Hassett, A. L. 43: v E 1946 (5) 1950 (5); v SA 1952 (5); v WI 1951 (4); v In 1947 (4); *v E 1938 (4) 1948 (5) 1953 (5); v SA 1949 (5); v NZ 1945 (1)*
Hawke, N. J. N. 27: v E 1962 (1) 1965 (4); v SA 1963 (4); v In 1967 (1); v P 1964 (1); *v E 1964 (5) 1968 (2); v SA 1966 (2); v WI 1964 (5); v In 1964 (1); v P 1964 (1)*
Hazlitt, G. R. 9: v E 1907 (2) 1911 (1); *v E 1912 (3); v SA 1912 (3)*
Hendry, H. L. 11: v E 1924 (1) 1928 (4); *v E 1921 (4); v SA 1921 (2)*
Hibbert, P. A. 1: v In 1977
Higgs, J. D. 22: v E 1978 (5) 1979 (1); v WI 1979 (1); v NZ 1980 (3); v In 1980 (2); *v WI 1977 (4); v In 1979 (6)*
Hilditch, A. M. J. 18: v E 1978 (1); v WI 1984 (2); v NZ 1985 (1); v P 1978 (2); *v E 1985 (6); v In 1979 (6)*
Hill, C. 49: v E 1897 (5) 1901 (5) 1903 (5) 1907 (5) 1911 (5); v SA 1910 (5); *v E 1896 (3) 1899 (3) 1902 (5) 1905 (5); v SA 1902 (3)*
Hill, J. C. 3: *v E 1953 (2); v WI 1954 (1)*
Hoare, D. E. 1: v WI 1960
Hodges, J. H. 2: v E 1876 (2)
Hogan, T. G. 7: v P 1983 (1); *v WI 1983 (5); v SL 1982 (1)*
Hogg, R. M. 38: v E 1978 (6) 1982 (3); v WI 1979 (2) 1984 (4); v NZ 1980 (2); v In 1980 (2); v P 1978 (2) 1983 (4); *v E 1981 (2); v WI 1983 (4); v In 1979 (6); v SL 1982 (1)*
Hole, G. B. 18: v E 1950 (1) 1954 (3); v SA 1952 (4); v WI 1951 (5); *v E 1953 (5)*
Holland, R. G. 11: v WI 1984 (3); v NZ 1985 (3); v In 1985 (1); *v E 1985 (4)*
Hookes, D. W. 23: v E 1976 (1) 1982 (5); v WI 1979 (1); v NZ 1985 (2); v In 1985 (2); *v E 197. (5); v WI 1983 (5); v P 1979 (1); v SL 1982 (1)*
Hopkins, A. J. Y. 20: v E 1901 (2) 1903 (5); *v E 1902 (5) 1905 (3) 1909 (2); v SA 1902 (3)*
Horan, T. P. 15: v E 1876 (1) 1878 (1) 1881 (4) 1882 (4) 1884 (4); *v E 1882 (1)*
Hordern, H. V. 7: v E 1911 (5): v SA 1910 (2)
Hornibrook, P. M. 6: v E 1928 (1); *v E 1930 (5)*
Howell, W. P. 18: v E 1897 (3) 1901 (4) 1903 (3); *v E 1899 (5) 1902 (1); v SA 1902 (2)*
Hughes, K. J. 70: v E 1978 (6) 1979 (3) 1982 (5); v WI 1979 (3) 1981 (3) 1984 (4); v NZ 1980 (3); In 1977 (2) 1980 (3); v P 1978 (2) 1981 (3) 1983 (5); *v E 1977 (1) 1980 (1) 1981 (6); v WI 198 (5); v NZ 1981 (3); v In 1979 (6); v P 1979 (3) 1982 (3)*
Hughes, M. G. 7: v E 1986 (4); v NZ 1987 (1); v In 1985 (1); v SL 1987 (1)
Hunt, W. A. 1: v SA 1931
Hurst, A. G. 12: v E 1978 (6); v NZ 1973 (1); v In 1977 (1); v P 1978 (2); *v In 1979 (2)*
Hurwood, A. 2: v WI 1930 (2)

Inverarity, R. J. 6: v WI 1968 (1); *v E 1968 (2) 1972 (3)*
Iredale, F. A. 14: v E 1894 (5) 1897 (4); *v E 1896 (2) 1899 (3)*
Ironmonger, H. 14: v E 1928 (2) 1932 (4); v SA 1931 (4); v WI 1930 (4)
Iverson, J. B. 5: v E 1950 (5)

Jackson, A. 8: v E 1928 (2); v WI 1930 (4); *v E 1930 (2)*
Jarman, B. N. 19: v E 1962 (3); v WI 1968 (4); v In 1967 (4); v P 1964 (1); *v E 1968 (4); v In 19. (1); 1964 (2)*
Jarvis, A. H. 11: v E 1884 (3) 1894 (4); *v E 1886 (2) 1888 (2)*
Jenner, T. J. 9: v E 1970 (2) 1974 (2); v WI 1975 (1); *v WI 1972 (4)*
Jennings, C. B. 6: *v E 1912 (3); v SA 1912 (3)*
Johnson I. W. 45: v E 1946 (4) 1950 (5) 1954 (4); v SA 1952 (1); v WI 1951 (4); v In 1947 (4); *v 1948 (4) 1956 (5); v SA 1949 (5); v WI 1954 (5); v NZ 1945 (1); v In 1956 (2); v P 1956*
Johnson, L. J. 1: v In 1947

Johnston W. A. 40: v E 1950 (5) 1954 (4); v SA 1952 (5); v WI 1951 (5); v In 1947 (4); *v E 1948 (5) 1953 (3); v SA 1949 (5); v WI 1954 (4)*
Jones, D. M. 15: v E 1986 (5) 1987 (1); v NZ 1987 (3); v SL 1987 (1); *v WI 1983 (2); v In 1986 (3)*
Jones, E. 19: v E 1894 (1) 1897 (5) 1901 (2); *v E 1896 (3) 1899 (5) 1902 (2); v SA 1902 (1)*
Jones, S. P. 12: v E 1881 (2) 1884 (4) 1886 (1) 1887 (1); *v E 1882 (1) 1886 (3)*
Joslin, L. R. 1: v In 1967

Kelleway, C. 26: v E 1911 (4) 1920 (5) 1924 (5) 1928 (1); v SA 1910 (5); *v E 1912 (3); v SA 1912 (3)*
Kelly, J. J. 36: v E 1897 (5) 1901 (5) 1903 (5); *v E 1896 (3) 1899 (5) 1902 (5) 1905 (5); v SA 1902 (3)*
Kelly, T. J. D. 2: v E 1876 (1) 1878 (1)
Kendall, T. 2: v E 1876 (2)
Kent, M. F. 3: *v E 1981 (3)*
Kerr, R. B. 2: v NZ 1985 (2)
Kippax, A. F. 22: v E 1924 (1) 1928 (5) 1932 (1); v SA 1931 (4); v WI 1930 (5); *v E 1930 (5) 1934 (1)*
Kline L. F. 13: v E 1958 (2); v WI 1960 (2); *v SA 1957 (5); v In 1959 (3); v P 1959 (1)*

Laird, B. M. 21: v E 1979 (2); v WI 1979 (3) 1981 (3); v P 1981 (3); *v E 1980 (1); v NZ 1981 (3); v P 1979 (3) 1982 (3)*
Langley, G. R. A. 26: v E 1954 (2); v SA 1952 (5); v WI 1951 (5); *v E 1953 (4) 1956 (3); v WI 1954 (4); v In 1956 (2); v P 1956 (1)*
Laughlin, T. J. 3: v E 1978 (1); *v WI 1977 (2)*
Laver, F. 15: v E 1901 (1) 1903 (1); *v E 1899 (4) 1905 (5) 1909 (4)*
Lawry, W. M. 67: v E 1962 (5) 1965 (5) 1970 (5); v SA 1963 (5); v WI 1968 (5); v In 1967 (4); v P 1964 (1); *v E 1961 (5) 1964 (5) 1968 (4); v SA 1966 (5) 1969 (4); v WI 1964 (5); v In 1964 (3) 1969 (5); v P 1964 (1)*
Lawson, G. F. 37: v E 1982 (5) 1986 (1); v WI 1981 (1) 1984 (5); v NZ 1980 (1) 1985 (2); v P 1983 (5); *v E 1981 (3) 1985 (6); v WI 1983 (5); v P 1982 (3)*
Lee, P. K. 2: v E 1932 (1); v SA 1931 (1)
Lillee, D. K. 70: v E 1970 (2) 1974 (6) 1976 (1) 1979 (3) 1982 (1); v WI 1975 (5) 1979 (3) 1981 (3); v NZ 1980 (3); v In 1980 (3); v P 1972 (3) 1976 (3) 1981 (3) 1983 (5); *v E 1972 (5) 1975 (4) 1980 (1) 1981 (6); v WI 1972 (1); v NZ 1976 (2) 1981 (3); v P 1979 (3); v SL 1982 (1)*
Lindwall, R. R. 61: v E 1946 (4) 1950 (5) 1954 (4) 1958 (2); v SA 1952 (4); v WI 1951 (5); v In 1947 (5); *v E 1948 (5) 1953 (5) 1956 (4); v SA 1949 (4); v WI 1954 (5); v NZ 1945 (1); v In 1956 (3) 1959 (2); v P 1956 (1) 1959 (2)*
Love, H. S. B. 1: v E 1932
Loxton, S. J. E. 12: v E 1950 (3); v In 1947 (1); *v E 1948 (3); v SA 1949 (5)*
Lyons, J. J. 14: v E 1886 (1) 1891 (3) 1894 (3) 1897 (1); *v E 1888 (1) 1890 (2) 1893 (3)*

McAlister, P. A. 8: v E 1903 (2) 1907 (4); *v E 1909 (2)*
Macartney, C. G. 35: v E 1907 (5) 1911 (1) 1920 (2); v SA 1910 (4); *v E 1909 (5) 1912 (3) 1921 (5) 1926 (5); v SA 1912 (3) 1921 (2)*
McCabe, S. J. 39: v E 1932 (5) 1936 (5); v SA 1931 (5); v WI 1930 (5); *v E 1930 (5) 1934 (5) 1938 (4); v SA 1935 (5)*
McCool, C. L. 14: v E 1946 (5); v In 1947 (3); *v SA 1949 (5) v NZ 1945 (1)*
McCormick, E. L. 12: v E 1936 (4); *v E 1938 (3); v SA 1935 (5)*
McCosker, R. B. 25: v E 1974 (3) 1976 (1) 1979 (2); v WI 1975 (4) 1979 (1); v P 1976 (3); *v E 1975 (4) 1977 (5); v NZ 1976 (2)*
McDermott, C. J. 22: v E 1986 (1) 1987 (1); v WI 1984 (2); v NZ 1985 (2) 1987 (3); v In 1985 (2); v SL 1987 (1); *v E 1985 (6); v NZ 1985 (2); v In 1986 (2)*
McDonald, C. C. 47: v E 1954 (2) 1958 (5); v SA 1952 (5); v WI 1951 (1) 1960 (5); *v E 1956 (5) 1961 (3); v SA 1957 (5); v WI 1954 (5); v In 1956 (2) 1959 (5); v P 1956 (1) 1959 (3)*
McDonald, E. A. 11: v E 1920 (3); *v E 1921 (5); v SA 1921 (3)*
McDonnell, P. S. 19: v E 1881 (4) 1882 (3) 1884 (2) 1886 (2) 1887 (1); *v E 1880 (1) 1884 (3) 1888 (3)*
McIlwraith, J. 1: *v E 1886*
Mackay K. D. 37: v E 1958 (5) 1962 (3); v WI 1960 (5); *v E 1956 (3) 1961 (5); v SA 1957 (5); v In 1956 (3) 1959 (5); v P 1959 (3)*
McKenzie, G. D. 60: v E 1962 (5) 1965 (4) 1970 (3); v SA 1963 (5); v WI 1968 (5); v In 1967 (2); v P 1964 (1); *v E 1961 (3) 1964 (5) 1968 (5); v SA 1966 (5) 1969 (3); v WI 1964 (5); v In 1964 (3) 1969 (5); v P 1964 (1)*
McKibbin, T. R. 5: v E 1894 (1) 1897 (2); *v E 1896 (2)*

McLaren, J. W. 1: v E 1911
Maclean, J. A. 4: v E 1978 (4)
McLeod, C. E. 17: v E 1894 (1) 1897 (5) 1901 (2) 1903 (3); *v E 1899 (1) 1905 (5)*
McLeod, R. W. 6: v E 1891 (3); *v E 1893 (3)*
McShane, P. G. 3: v E 1884 (1) 1886 (1) 1887 (1)
Maddocks, L. V. 7: v E 1954 (3); *v E 1956 (2); v WI 1954 (1); v In 1956 (1)*
Maguire, J. N. 3: v P 1983 (1); *v WI 1983 (2)*
Mailey, A. A. 21: v E 1920 (5) 1924 (5); *v E 1921 (3) 1926 (5); v SA 1921 (3)*
Mallett, A. A. 38: v E 1970 (2) 1974 (5) 1979 (1); v WI 1968 (1) 1975 (6) 1979 (1); v NZ 1973 (3); v P 1972 (2); *v E 1968 (1) 1972 (2) 1975 (4) 1980 (1); v SA 1969 (1); v NZ 1973 (3); v In 1969 (5)*
Malone, M. F. 1: *v E 1977*
Mann, A. L. 4: v In 1977 (4)
Marr, A. P. 1: v E 1884
Marsh, G. R. 19: v E 1986 (5) 1987 (1); v NZ 1987 (3); v In 1985 (3); v SL 1987 (1); *v NZ 1985 (3); v In 1986 (3)*
Marsh, R. W. 96: v E 1970 (6) 1974 (6) 1976 (1) 1979 (3) 1982 (5); v WI 1975 (6) 1979 (3) 1981 (3); v NZ 1973 (3) 1980 (3); v In 1980 (3); v P 1972 (3) 1976 (3) 1981 (3) 1983 (5); *v E 1972 (5) 1975 (4) 1977 (5) 1980 (1) 1981 (6); v WI 1972 (5); v NZ 1973 (3) 1976 (2) 1981 (3); v P 1979 (3) 1982 (3)*
Martin, J. W. 8: v SA 1963 (1); v WI 1960 (3); *v SA 1966 (1); v In 1964 (2); v P 1964 (1)*
Massie, H. H. 9: v E 1881 (4) 1882 (3) 1884 (1); *v E 1882 (1)*
Massie, R. A. L. 6: v P 1972 (2); *v E 1972 (4)*
Matthews, C. D. 2: v E 1986 (2)
Matthews, G. R. J. 21: v E 1986 (4); v WI 1984 (1); v NZ 1985 (3); v In 1985 (3); v P 1983 (2); *v E 1985 (1); v WI 1983 (1); v NZ 1985 (3); v In 1986 (3)*
Matthews, T. J. 8: v E 1911 (2); *v E 1912 (3); v SA 1912 (3)*
May, T. B. A. 1: v NZ 1987
Mayne, E. R. 4: *v E 1912 (1); v SA 1912 (1) 1921 (2)*
Mayne, L. C. 6: *v SA 1969 (2); v WI 1964 (3); v In 1969 (1)*
Meckiff, I. 18: v E 1958 (4); v SA 1963 (1); v WI 1960 (2); *v SA 1957 (4); v In 1959 (5); v P 1959 (2)*
Meuleman, K. D. 1: *v NZ 1945*
Midwinter, W. E. 8: v E 1876 (2) 1882 (1) 1886 (2); *v E 1884 (3)*
Miller, K. R. 55: v E 1946 (5) 1950 (5) 1954 (4); v SA 1952 (4); v WI 1951 (5); v In 1947 (5); *v E 1948 (5) 1953 (5) 1956 (5); v SA 1949 (5); v WI 1954 (5); v NZ 1945 (1); v P 1956 (1)*
Minnett, R. B. 9: v E 1911 (5); *v E 1912 (1); v SA 1912 (3)*
Misson, F. M. 5: v WI 1960 (3); *v E 1961 (2)*
Moroney, J. R. 7: v E 1950 (1); v WI 1951 (1); *v SA 1949 (5)*
Morris, A. R. 46: v E 1946 (5) 1950 (5) 1954 (4); v SA 1952 (5); v WI 1951 (4); v In 1947 (4); *v E 1948 (5) 1953 (5); v SA 1949 (5); v WI 1954 (4)*
Morris, S. 1: v E 1884
Moses, H. 6: v E 1886 (2) 1887 (1) 1891 (2) 1894 (1)
Moss, J. K. 1: v P 1978
Moule, W. H. 1: *v E 1880*
Murdoch, W. L. 18: v E 1876 (1) 1878 (1) 1881 (4) 1882 (4) 1884 (1); *v E 1880 (1) 1882 (1) 1884 (3) 1890 (2)*
Musgrove, H. 1: v E 1884

Nagel, L. E. 1: v E 1932
Nash, L. J. 2: v E 1936 (1); v SA 1931 (1)
Nitschke, H. C. 2: v SA 1931 (2)
Noble, M. A. 42: v E 1897 (4) 1901 (5) 1903 (5) 1907 (5); *v E 1899 (5) 1902 (5) 1905 (5) 1909 (5); v SA 1902 (3)*
Noblet, G. 3: v SA 1952 (1); v WI 1951 (1); *v SA 1949 (1)*
Nothling, O. E. 1: v E 1928

O'Brien, L. P. J. 5: v E 1932 (2) 1936 (1); *v SA 1935 (2)*
O'Connor, J. D. A. 4: v E 1907 (3); *v E 1909 (1)*
O'Donnell, S. P. 6: v NZ 1985 (1); *v E 1985 (5)*
Ogilvie, A. D. 5: v In 1977 (3); *v WI 1977 (2)*
O'Keeffe, K. J. 24: v E 1970 (2) 1976 (1); v NZ 1973 (3); v P 1972 (2) 1976 (3); *v E 1977 (3); v WI 1972 (5); v NZ 1973 (3) 1976 (2)*

Oldfield, W. A. 54: v E 1920 (3) 1924 (5) 1928 (5) 1932 (4) 1936 (5); v SA 1931 (5); v WI 1930 (5); *v E 1921 (1) 1926 (5) 1930 (5) 1934 (5); v SA 1921 (1) 1935 (5)*

O'Neill, N. C. 42: v E 1958 (5) 1962 (5); v SA 1963 (4); v WI 1960 (5); *v E 1961 (5) 1964 (4); v WI 1964 (4); v In 1959 (5) 1964 (2); v P 1959 (3)*

O'Reilly, W. J. 27: v E 1932 (5) 1936 (5); v SA 1931 (2); *v E 1934 (5) 1938 (4); v SA 1935 (5); v NZ 1945 (1)*

Oxenham, R. K. 7: v E 1928 (3); v SA 1931 (1); v WI 1930 (3)

Palmer, G. E. 17: v E 1881 (4) 1882 (4) 1884 (2); *v E 1880 (1) 1884 (3) 1886 (3)*

Park, R. L. 1: v E 1920

Pascoe, L. S. 14: v E 1979 (2); v WI 1979 (1) 1981 (1); v NZ 1980 (3); v In 1980 (3); *v E 1977 (3) 1980 (1)*

Pellew, C. E. 10: v E 1920 (4); *v E 1921 (5); v SA 1921 (1)*

Phillips, W. B. 27: v WI 1984 (2); v NZ 1985 (3); v In 1985 (3); v P 1983 (5); *v E 1985 (6); v WI 1983 (5); v NZ 1985 (3)*

Philpott, P. I. 8: v E 1965 (3); *v WI 1964 (5)*

Ponsford, W. H. 29: v E 1924 (5) 1928 (2) 1932 (3); v SA 1931 (4); v WI 1930 (5); *v E 1926 (2) 1930 (4) 1934 (4)*

Pope, R. J. 1: v E 1884

Rackemann, C. G. 5: v E 1982 (1); v WI 1984 (1); v P 1983 (2); *v WI 1983 (1)*

Ransford, V. S. 20: v E 1907 (5) 1911 (5); v SA 1910 (5); *v E 1909 (5)*

Redpath, I. R. 66: v E 1965 (1) 1970 (6) 1974 (6); v SA 1963 (1); v WI 1968 (5) 1975 (6); v In 1967 (3); v P 1972 (3); *v E 1964 (5) 1968 (5); v SA 1966 (5) 1969 (4); v WI 1972 (5); v NZ 1973 (3); v In 1964 (2) 1969 (5); v P 1964 (1)*

Reedman, J. C. 1: v E 1894

Reid, B. A. 15: v E 1986 (5); v NZ 1987 (2); v In 1985 (3); *v NZ 1985 (3); v In 1986 (2)*

Renneberg, D. A. 8: v In 1967 (3); *v SA 1966 (5)*

Richardson, A. J. 9: v E 1924 (4); *v E 1926 (5)*

Richardson, V. Y. 19: v E 1924 (3) 1928 (2) 1932 (5); *v E 1930 (4); v SA 1935 (5)*

Rigg, K. E. 8: v E 1936 (3); v SA 1931 (4); v WI 1930 (1)

Ring, D. T. 13: v SA 1952 (5); v WI 1951 (5); v In 1947 (1); *v E 1948 (1) 1953 (1)*

Ritchie, G. M. 30: v E 1986 (4); v WI 1984 (1); v NZ 1985 (3); v In 1985 (2); *v E 1985 (6); v WI 1983 (5); v NZ 1985 (3); v In 1986 (3); v P 1982 (3)*

Rixon, S. J. 13: v WI 1984 (3); v In 1977 (5); *v WI 1977 (5)*

Robertson, W. R. 1: v E 1884

Robinson, R. D. 3: *v E 1977 (3)*

Robinson, R. H. 1: v E 1936

Rorke, G. F. 4: v E 1958 (2); *v In 1959 (2)*

Rutherford, J. W. 1: *v In 1956*

Ryder, J. 20: v E 1920 (5) 1924 (3) 1928 (5); *v E 1926 (4); v SA 1921 (3)*

Saggers, R. A. 6: *v E 1948 (1); v SA 1949 (5)*

Saunders, J. V. 14: v E 1901 (1) 1903 (2) 1907 (5); *v E 1902 (4); v SA 1902 (2)*

Scott, H. J. H. 8: v E 1884 (2); *v E 1884 (3) 1886 (3)*

Sellers, R. H. D. 1: *v In 1964*

Serjeant, C. S. 12: v In 1977 (4); *v E 1977 (3); v WI 1977 (5)*

Sheahan, A. P. 31: v E 1970 (2); v WI 1968 (5); v NZ 1973 (2); v In 1967 (4); v P 1972 (2); *v E 1968 (5) 1972 (2); v SA 1969 (4); v In 1969 (5)*

Shepherd, B. K. 9: v E 1962 (2); v SA 1963 (4); v P 1964 (1); *v WI 1964 (2)*

Sievers, M. W. 3: v E 1936 (3)

Simpson, R. B. 62: v E 1958 (1) 1962 (5) 1965 (3); v SA 1963 (5); v WI 1960 (5); v In 1967 (3) 1977 (5); v P 1964 (1); *v E 1961 (5) 1964 (5); v SA 1957 (5) 1966 (5); v WI 1964 (5) 1977 (5); v In 1964 (3); v P 1964 (1)*

Sincock, D. J. 3: v E 1965 (1); v P 1964 (1); *v WI 1964 (1)*

Slater, K. N. 1: v E 1958

Sleep, P. R. 11: v E 1986 (3) 1987 (1); v NZ 1987 (3); v P 1978 (1); *v In 1979 (2); v P 1982 (1)*

Slight, J. 1: *v E 1880*

Smith, D. B. M. 2: *v E 1912 (2)*

Smith, S. B. 3: *v WI 1983 (3)*

Spofforth, F. R. 18: v E 1876 (1) 1878 (1) 1881 (1) 1882 (4) 1884 (3) 1886 (1); *v E 1882 (1) 1884 (3) 1886 (3)*

Stackpole, K. R. 43: v E 1965 (2) 1970 (6); v WI 1968 (5); v NZ 1973 (3); v P 1972 (1); *v E 1972 (5); v SA 1966 (5) 1969 (4); v WI 1972 (4); v NZ 1973 (3); v In 1969 (5)*
Stevens, G. B. 4: *v In 1959 (2); v P 1959 (2)*

Taber, H. B. 16: v WI 1968 (1); *v E 1968 (1); v SA 1966 (5); 1969 (4); v In 1969 (5)*
Tallon, D. 21: v E 1946 (5) 1950 (5); v In 1947 (5); *v E 1948 (4) 1953 (1); v NZ 1945 (1)*
Taylor, J. M. 20: v E 1920 (5) 1924 (5); *v E 1921 (5) 1926 (3); v SA 1921 (2)*
Taylor, P. L. 3: v E 1986 (1) 1987 (1); v SL 1987 (1)
Thomas, G. 8: v E 1965 (3); *v WI 1964 (5)*
Thompson, N. 2: v E 1876 (2)
Thoms, G. R. 1: v WI 1951
Thomson, A. L. 4: v E 1970 (4)
Thomson, J. R. 51: v E 1974 (5) 1979 (1) 1982 (4); v WI 1975 (6) 1979 (1) 1981 (2); v In 1977 (5); v P 1972 (1) 1976 (1) 1981 (3); *v E 1975 (4) 1977 (5) 1985 (2); v WI 1977 (5); v NZ 1981 (3); v P 1982 (3)*
Thurlow, H. M. 1: v SA 1931
Toohey, P. M. 15: v E 1978 (5) 1979 (1); v WI 1979 (1); v In 1977 (5); *v WI 1977 (3)*
Toshack, E. R. H. 12: v E 1946 (5); v In 1947 (2); *v E 1948 (4); v NZ 1945 (1)*
Travers, J. P. F. 1: v E 1901
Tribe, G. E. 3: v E 1946 (3)
Trott, A. E. 3: v E 1894 (3)
Trott, G. H. S. 24: v E 1891 (3) 1894 (5) 1897 (5); *v E 1888 (3) 1890 (2) 1893 (3) 1896 (3)*
Trumble, H. 32: v E 1894 (1) 1897 (5) 1901 (5) 1903 (4); *v E 1890 (2) 1893 (3) 1896 (3) 1899 (5) 1902 (3); v SA 1902 (1)*
Trumble, J. W. 7: v E 1884 (4); *v E 1886 (3)*
Trumper, V. T. 48: v E 1901 (5) 1903 (5) 1907 (5) 1911 (5); v SA 1910 (5); *v E 1899 (5) 1902 (5) 1905 (5) 1909 (5); v SA 1902 (3)*
Turner, A. 14: v WI 1975 (6); v P 1976 (3); *v E 1975 (3); v NZ 1976 (2)*
Turner, C. T. B. 17: v E 1886 (2) 1887 (1) 1891 (3) 1894 (3); *v E 1888 (3) 1890 (2) 1893 (3)*

Veivers, T. R. 21: v E 1965 (4); v SA 1963 (3); v P 1964 (1); *v E 1964 (5); v SA 1966 (4); v In 196[illegible] (3); v P 1964 (1)*
Veletta, M. R. J. 5: v E 1987 (1); v NZ 1987 (3); v SL 1987 (1)

Waite, M. G. 2: *v E 1938 (2)*
Walker, M. H. N. 34: v E 1974 (6); 1976 (1); v WI 1975 (3); v NZ 1973 (1); v P 1972 (2) 1976 (2); *v E 1975 (4); 1977 (5); v WI 1972 (5); v NZ 1973 (3) 1976 (2)*
Wall, T. W. 18: v E 1928 (1) 1932 (4); v SA 1931 (3); v WI 1930 (1); *v E 1930 (5) 1934 (4)*
Walters, F. H. 1: v E 1884
Walters, K. D. 74: v E 1965 (5) 1970 (6) 1974 (6) 1976 (1); v WI 1968 (4); v NZ 1973 (3) 1980 (3); v In 1967 (2) 1980 (3); v P 1972 (1) 1976 (3); *v E 1968 (5) 1972 (4) 1975 (4) 1977 (5); v SA 196[illegible] (4); v WI 1972 (5); v NZ 1973 (3) 1976 (2); v In 1969 (5)*
Ward, F. A. 4: v E 1936 (3); *v E 1938 (1)*
Watkins, J. R. 1: v P 1972
Watson, G. D. 5: *v E 1972 (2); v SA 1966 (3)*
Watson, W. 4: v E 1954 (1); *v WI 1954 (3)*
Waugh, S. R. 18: v E 1986 (5) 1987 (1); v NZ 1987 (3); v In 1985 (2); v SL 1987 (1); *v NZ 19[illegible] (3); v In 1986 (3)*
Wellham, D. M. 6: v E 1986 (1); v WI 1981 (1); v P 1981 (2); *v E 1981 (1) 1985 (1)*
Wessels, K. C. 24: v E 1982 (4); v WI 1984 (5); v NZ 1985 (1); v P 1983 (5); *v E 1985 (6); v W[illegible] 1983 (2); v SL 1982 (1)*
Whatmore, D. F. 7: v P 1978 (2); *v In 1979 (5)*
Whitney, M. R. 3: v NZ 1987 (1); *v E 1981 (2)*
Whitty, W. J. 14: v E 1911 (2); v SA 1910 (5); *v E 1909 (1) 1912 (3); v SA 1912 (3)*
Wiener, J. M. 6: v E 1979 (2); v WI 1979 (2); *v P 1979 (2)*
Wilson, J. W. 1: *v In 1956*
Wood, G. M. 53: v E 1978 (6) 1982 (1); v WI 1981 (3) 1984 (5); v NZ 1980 (3); v In 1977 (1) 19[illegible] (3); v P 1978 (1) 1981 (3); *v E 1980 (1) 1981 (6) 1985 (5); v WI 1977 (5) 1983 (1); v NZ 1981 ([illegible] v In 1979 (2); v P 1982 (3); v SL 1982 (1)*
Woodcock, A. J. 1: v NZ 1973
Woodfull, W. M. 35: v E 1928 (5) 1932 (5); v SA 1931 (5); v WI 1930 (5); *v E 1926 (5) 1930 [illegible] 1934 (5)*

Woods, S. M. J. 3: *v E 1888 (3)*
Woolley, R. D. 2: *v WI 1983 (1); v SL 1982 (1)*
Worrall, J. 11: v E 1884 (1) 1887 (1) 1894 (1) 1897 (1); *v E 1888 (3) 1899 (4)*
Wright, K. J. 10: v E 1978 (2); v P 1978 (2); *v In 1979 (6)*

Yallop, G. N. 39: v E 1978 (6); v WI 1975 (3) 1984 (1); v In 1977 (1); v P 1978 (1) 1981 (1) 1983 (5); *v E 1980 (1) 1981 (6); v WI 1977 (4); v In 1979 (6); v P 1979 (3); v SL 1982 (1)*
Yardley, B. 33: v E 1978 (4) 1982 (5); v WI 1981 (3); v In 1977 (1) 1980 (2); v P 1978 (1) 1981 (3); *v WI 1977 (5); v NZ 1981 (3); v In 1979 (3); v P 1982 (2); v SL 1982 (1)*

Zoehrer, T. J. 10: v E 1986 (4); *v NZ 1985 (3); v In 1986 (3)*

SOUTH AFRICA

Number of Test cricketers: 235

Adcock, N. A. T. 26: v E 1956 (5); v A 1957 (5); v NZ 1953 (5) 1961 (2); *v E 1955 (4) 1960 (5)*
Anderson, J. H. 1: v A 1902
Ashley, W. H. 1: v E 1888

Bacher, A. 12: v A 1966 (5) 1969 (4); *v E 1965 (3)*
Balaskas, X. C. 9: v E 1930 (2) 1938 (1); v A 1935 (3); *v E 1935 (1); v NZ 1931 (2)*
Barlow, E. J. 30: v E 1964 (5); v A 1966 (5) 1969 (4); v NZ 1961 (5); *v E 1965 (3); v A 1963 (5); v NZ 1963 (3)*
Baumgartner, H. V. 1: v E 1913
Beaumont, R. 5: v E 1913 (2); *v E 1912 (1); v A 1912 (2)*
Begbie, D. W. 5: v E 1948 (3); v A 1949 (2)
Bell, A. J. 16: v E 1930 (3); *v E 1929 (3) 1935 (3); v A 1931 (5); v NZ 1931 (2)*
Bisset, M. 3: v E 1898 (2) 1909 (1)
Bissett, G. F. 4: v E 1927 (4)
Blanckenberg, J. M. 18: v E 1913 (5) 1922 (5); v A 1921 (3); *v E 1924 (5)*
Bland, K. C. 21: v E 1964 (5); v A 1966 (1); v NZ 1961 (5); *v E 1965 (3); v A 1963 (4); v NZ 1963 (3)*
Bock, E. G. 1: v A 1935
Bond, G. E. 1: v E 1938
Botten, J. T. 3: *v E 1965 (3)*
Brann, W. H. 3: v E 1922 (3)
Briscoe, A. W. 2: v E 1938 (1); v A 1935 (1)
Bromfield, H. D. 9: v E 1964 (3); v NZ 1961 (5); *v E 1965 (1)*
Brown, L. S. 2: *v A 1931 (1); v NZ 1931 (1)*
Burger, C. G. de V. 2: v A 1957 (2)
Burke, S. F. 2: v E 1964 (1); v NZ 1961 (1)
Buys, I. D. 1: v E 1922

Cameron, H. B. 26: v E 1927 (5) 1930 (5); *v E 1929 (4) 1935 (5); v A 1931 (5); v NZ 1931 (2)*
Campbell, T. 5: v E 1909 (4); *v E 1912 (1)*
Carlstein, P. R. 8: v A 1957 (1); *v E 1960 (5); v A 1963 (2)*
Carter, C. P. 10: v E 1913 (2); v A 1921 (3); *v E 1912 (2) 1924 (3)*
Catterall, R. H. 24: v E 1922 (5) 1927 (5) 1930 (4); *v E 1924 (5) 1929 (5)*
Chapman, H. W. 2: v E 1913 (1); v A 1921 (1)
Cheetham, J. E. 24: v E 1948 (1); v A 1949 (3); v NZ 1953 (5); *v E 1951 (5) 1955 (3); v A 1952 (5); v NZ 1952 (2)*
Chevalier, G. A. 1: v A 1969
Christy, J. A. J. 10: v E 1930 (1); *v E 1929 (2); v A 1931 (5); v NZ 1931 (2)*
Chubb, G. W. A. 5: *v E 1951 (5)*
Cochran, J. A. K. 1: v E 1930
Coen, S. K. 2: v E 1927 (2)
Commaille, J. M. M. 12: v E 1909 (5) 1927 (2); *v E 1924 (5)*
Conyngham, D. P. 1: v E 1922
Cook, F. J. 1: v E 1895
Cooper, A. H. C. 1: v E 1913

Cox, J. L. 3: v E 1913 (3)
Cripps, G. 1: v E 1891
Crisp, R. J. 9: v A 1935 (4); *v E 1935 (5)*
Curnow, S. H. 7: v E 1930 (3); *v A 1931 (4)*

Dalton, E. L. 15: v E 1930 (1) 1938 (4); v A 1935 (1); *v E 1929 (1) 1935 (4); v A 1931 (2); v NZ 1931 (2)*
Davies, E. Q. 5: v E 1938 (3); v A 1935 (2)
Dawson, O. C. 9: v E 1948 (4); *v E 1947 (5)*
Deane, H. G. 17: v E 1927 (5) 1930 (2); *v E 1924 (5) 1929 (5)*
Dixon, C. D. 1: v E 1913
Dower, R. R. 1: v E 1898
Draper, R. G. 2: v A 1949 (2)
Duckworth, C. A. R. 2: v E 1956 (2)
Dumbrill, R. 5: v A 1966 (2); *v E 1965 (3)*
Duminy, J. P. 3: v E 1927 (2); *v E 1929 (1)*
Dunell, O. R. 2: v E 1888 (2)
Du Preez, J. H. 2: v A 1966 (2)
Du Toit, J. F. 1: v E 1891
Dyer, D. V. 3: *v E 1947 (3)*

Elgie, M. K. 3: v NZ 1961 (3)
Endean, W. R. 28: v E 1956 (5); v A 1957 (5); v NZ 1953 (5); *v E 1951 (1) 1955 (5); v A 1952 (5); v NZ 1952 (2)*

Farrer, W. S. 6: v NZ 1961 (3); *v NZ 1963 (3)*
Faulkner, G. A. 25: v E 1905 (5) 1909 (5); *v E 1907 (3) 1912 (3) 1924 (1); v A 1910 (5) 1912 (3)*
Fellows-Smith, J. P. 4: *v E 1960 (4)*
Fichardt, C. G. 2: v E 1891 (1) 1895 (1)
Finlason, C. E. 1: v E 1888
Floquet, C. E. 1: v E 1909
Francis, H. H. 2: v E 1898 (2)
Francois, C. M. 5: v E 1922 (5)
Frank, C. N. 3: v A 1921 (3)
Frank, W. H. B. 1: v E 1895
Fuller, E. R. H. 7: v A 1957 (1); *v E 1955 (2); v A 1952 (2); v NZ 1952 (2)*
Fullerton, G. M. 7: v A 1949 (2); *v E 1947 (2) 1951 (3)*
Funston, K. J. 18: v E 1956 (3); v A 1957 (5); v NZ 1953 (3); *v A 1952 (5); v NZ 1952 (2)*

Gamsy, D. 2: v A 1969 (2)
Gleeson, R. A. 1: v E 1895
Glover, G. K. 1: v E 1895
Goddard, T. L. 41: v E 1956 (5) 1964 (5); v A 1957 (5) 1966 (5) 1969 (3); *v E 1955 (5) 1960 (5); v* *1963 (5); v NZ 1963 (3)*
Gordon, N. 5: v E 1938 (5)
Graham, R. 2: v E 1898 (2)
Grieveson, R. E. 2: v E 1938 (2)
Griffin, G. M. 2: *v E 1960 (2)*

Hall, A. E. 7: v E 1922 (4) 1927 (2) 1930 (1)
Hall, G. G. 1: v E 1964
Halliwell, E. A. 8: v E 1891 (1) 1895 (3) 1898 (1); v A 1902 (3)
Halse, C. G. 3: *v A 1963 (3)*
Hands, P. A. M. 7: v E 1913 (5); v A 1921 (1); *v E 1924 (1)*
Hands, R. H. M. 1: v E 1913
Hanley, M. A. 1: v E 1948
Harris, T. A. 3: v E 1948 (1); *v E 1947 (2)*
Hartigan, G. P. D. 5: v E 1913 (3); *v E 1912 (1); v A 1912 (1)*
Harvey, R. L. 2: v A 1935 (2)
Hathorn, C. M. H. 12: v E 1905 (5); v A 1902 (3); *v E 1907 (3); v A 1910 (1)*
Hearne, F. 4: v E 1891 (1) 1895 (3)
Hearne, G. A. L. 3: v E 1922 (2); *v E 1924 (1)*

Heine, P. S. 14: v E 1956 (5); v A 1957 (4); v NZ 1961 (1); *v E 1955 (4)*
Hime, C. F. W. 1: v E 1895
Hutchinson, P. 2: v E 1888 (2)

Ironside, D. E. J. 3: v NZ 1953 (3)
Irvine, B. L. 4: v A 1969 (4)

Johnson, C. L. 1: v E 1895

Keith, H. J. 8: v E 1956 (3); *v E 1955 (4); v A 1952 (1)*
Kempis, G. A. 1: v E 1888
Kotze, J. J. 3: v A 1902 (2); *v E 1907 (1)*
Kuys, F. 1: v E 1898

.ance, H. R. 13: v A 1966 (5) 1969 (3); v NZ 1961 (2); *v E 1965 (3)*
.angton, A. B. C. 15: v E 1938 (5); v A 1935 (5); *v E 1935 (5)*
.awrence, G. B. 5: v NZ 1961 (5)
.e Roux, F. le S. 1: v E 1913
.ewis, P. T. 1: v E 1913
.indsay, D. T. 19: v E 1964 (3); v A 1966 (5) 1969 (2); *v E 1965 (3); v A 1963 (3); v NZ 1963 (3)*
.indsay, J. D. 3: *v E 1947 (3)*
.indsay, N. V. 1: v A 1921
.ing, W. V. S. 6: v E 1922 (3); v A 1921 (3)
.lewellyn, C. B. 15: v E 1895 (1) 1898 (1); v A 1902 (3); *v E 1912 (3); v A 1910 (5) 1912 (2)*
.undie, E. B. 1: v E 1913

Iacaulay, M. J. 1: v E 1964
IcCarthy, C. N. 15: v E 1948 (5); v A 1949 (5); *v E 1951 (5)*
IcGlew, D. J. 34: v E 1956 (1); v A 1957 (5); v NZ 1953 (5) 1961 (5); *v E 1951 (2) 1955 (5) 1960 (5); v A 1952 (4); v NZ 1952 (2)*
IcKinnon, A. H. 8: v E 1964 (2); v A 1966 (2); v NZ 1961 (1); *v E 1960 (1) 1965 (2)*
IcLean, R. A. 40: v E 1956 (5) 1964 (2); v A 1957 (4); v NZ 1953 (4) 1961 (5); *v E 1951 (3) 1955 (5) 1960 (5); v A 1952 (5); v NZ 1952 (2)*
IcMillan, Q. 13: v E 1930 (5); *v E 1929 (2); v A 1931 (4); v NZ 1931 (2)*
Iann, N. B. F. 19: v E 1948 (5); v A 1949 (5); *v E 1947 (5) 1951 (4)*
Iansell, P. N. F. 13: *v E 1951 (2) 1955 (4); v A 1952 (5); v NZ 1952 (2)*
.arkham, L. A. 1: v E 1948
.arx, W. F. E. 3: v A 1921 (3)
Ieintjes, D. J. 2: v E 1922 (2)
.elle, M. G. 7: v A 1949 (2); *v E 1951 (1); v A 1952 (4)*
.elville, A. 11: v E 1938 (5) 1948 (1); *v E 1947 (5)*
.iddleton, J. 6: v E 1895 (2) 1898 (2); v A 1902 (2)
.ills, C. 1: v E 1891
.ilton, W. H. 3: v E 1888 (2) 1891 (1)
.itchell, B. 42: v E 1930 (5) 1938 (5) 1948 (5); v A 1935 (5); *v E 1929 (5) 1935 (5) 1947 (5); v A 1931 (5); v NZ 1931 (2)*
.itchell, F. 3: *v E 1912 (1); v A 1912 (2)*
.orkel, D. P. B. 16: v E 1927 (5); *v E 1929 (5); v A 1931 (5); v NZ 1931 (1)*
.urray, A. R. A. 10: v NZ 1953 (4); *v A 1952 (4); v NZ 1952 (2)*

.l, J. D. 6: v A 1949 (5) 1957 (1)
.wberry, C. 4: v E 1913 (4)
.wson, E. S. 3: v E 1930 (1) 1938 (2)
.cholson, F. 4: v A 1935 (4)
.colson, J. F. W. 3: v E 1927 (3)
.rton, N. O. 1: v E 1909
.urse, A. D. 34: v E 1938 (5) 1948 (5); v A 1935 (5) 1949 (5); *v E 1935 (4) 1947 (5) 1951 (5)*
.urse, A. W. 45: v E 1905 (5) 1909 (5) 1913 (5) 1922 (5); v A 1902 (3) 1921 (3); *v E 1907 (3) 1912 (3) 1924 (5); v A 1910 (5) 1912 (3)*
.pen, E. P. 17: v E 1922 (4) 1927 (5) 1930 (3); v A 1921 (2) 1935 (1); *v E 1924 (2)*

Ochse, A. E. 2: v E 1888 (2)
Ochse, A. L. 3: v E 1927 (1); *v E 1929 (2)*
O'Linn, S. 7: v NZ 1961 (2); *v E 1960 (5)*
Owen-Smith, H. G. 5: *v E 1929 (5)*

Palm, A. W. 1: v E 1927
Parker, G. M. 2: *v E 1924 (2)*
Parkin, D. C. 1: v E 1891
Partridge, J. T. 11: v E 1964 (3); *v A 1963 (5); v NZ 1963 (3)*
Pearse, O. C. 3: *v A 1910 (3)*
Pegler, S. J. 16: v E 1909 (1); *v E 1912 (3) 1924 (5); v A 1910 (4) 1912 (3)*
Pithey, A. J. 17: v E 1956 (3) 1964 (5); *v E 1960 (2); v A 1963 (4); v NZ 1963 (3)*
Pithey, D. B. 8: v A 1966 (2); *v A 1963 (3); v NZ 1963 (3)*
Plimsoll, J. B. 1: *v E 1947*
Pollock, P. M. 28: v E 1964 (5); v A 1966 (5) 1969 (4); v NZ 1961 (3); *v E 1965 (3); v A 1963 (5); v NZ 1963 (3)*
Pollock, R. G. 23: v E 1964 (5); v A 1966 (5) 1969 (4); *v E 1965 (3); v A 1963 (5); v NZ 1963 (1)*
Poore, R. M. 3: v E 1895 (3)
Pothecary, J. E. 3: *v E 1960 (3)*
Powell, A. W. 1: v E 1898
Prince, C. F. H. 1: v E 1898
Procter, M. J. 7: v A 1966 (3) 1969 (4)
Promnitz, H. L. E. 2: v E 1927 (2)

Quinn, N. A. 12: v E 1930 (1); *v E 1929 (4); v A 1931 (5); v NZ 1931 (2)*

Reid, N. 1: v A 1921
Richards, A. R. 1: v E 1895
Richards, B. A. 4: v A 1969 (4)
Richards, W. H. 1: v E 1888
Robertson, J. B. 3: v A 1935 (3)
Rose-Innes, A. 2: v E 1888 (2)
Routledge, T. W. 4: v E 1891 (1) 1895 (3)
Rowan, A. M. B. 15: v E 1948 (5); *v E 1947 (5) 1951 (5)*
Rowan, E. A. B. 26: v E 1938 (4) 1948 (4); v A 1935 (3); 1949 (5); *v E 1935 (5) 1951 (5)*
Rowe, G. A. 5: v E 1895 (2) 1898 (2); v A 1902 (1)

Samuelson, S. V. 1: v E 1909
Schwarz, R. O. 20: v E 1905 (5) 1909 (4); *v E 1907 (3) 1912 (1); v A 1910 (5) 1912 (2)*
Seccull, A. W. 1: v E 1895
Seymour, M. A. 7: v E 1964 (2); v A 1969 (1); *v A 1963 (4)*
Shalders, W. A. 12: v E 1898 (1) 1905 (5); v A 1902 (3); *v E 1907 (3)*
Shepstone, G. H. 2: v E 1895 (1) 1898 (1)
Sherwell, P. W. 13: v E 1905 (5); *v E 1907 (3); v A 1910 (5)*
Siedle, I. J. 18: v E 1927 (1) 1930 (5); v A 1935 (5); *v E 1929 (3) 1935 (4)*
Sinclair, J. H. 25: v E 1895 (3) 1898 (2) 1905 (5) 1909 (4); v A 1902 (3); *v E 1907 (3); v A 1910 (*
Smith, C. J. E. 3: v A 1902 (3)
Smith, F. W. 3: v E 1888 (2) 1895 (1)
Smith, V. I. 9: v A 1949 (3) 1957 (1); *v E 1947 (4) 1955 (1)*
Snooke, S. D. 1: *v E 1907*
Snooke, S. J. 26: v E 1905 (5) 1909 (5) 1922 (3); *v E 1907 (3) 1912 (3); v A 1910 (5) 1912 (*
Solomon, W. R. 1: v E 1898
Stewart, R. B. 1: v E 1888
Stricker, L. A. 13: v E 1909 (4); *v E 1912 (2); v A 1910 (5) 1912 (2)*
Susskind, M. J. 5: *v E 1924 (5)*

Taberer, H. M. 1: v A 1902
Tancred, A. B. 2: v E 1888 (2)
Tancred, L. J. 14: v E 1905 (5) 1913 (1); v A 1902 (3); *v E 1907 (1) 1912 (2); v A 1912 (*
Tancred, V. M. 1: v E 1898
Tapscott, G. L. 1: v E 1913
Tapscott, L. E. 2: v E 1922 (2)

Tayfield, H. J. 37: v E 1956 (5); v A 1949 (5) 1957 (5); v NZ 1953 (5); *v E 1955 (5) 1960 (5); v A 1952 (5); v NZ 1952 (2)*
Taylor, A. I. 1: v E 1956
Taylor, D. 2: v E 1913 (2)
Taylor, H. W. 42: v E 1913 (5) 1922 (5) 1927 (5) 1930 (4); v A 1921 (3); *v E 1912 (3) 1924 (5) 1929 (3); v A 1912 (3) 1931 (5); v NZ 1931 (1)*
Theunissen, N. H. G. de J. 1: v E 1888
Thornton, P. G. 1: v A 1902
Tomlinson, D. S. 1: *v E 1935*
Traicos, A. J. 3: v A 1969 (3)
Trimborn, P. H. J. 4: v A 1966 (3) 1969 (1)
Tuckett, L. 9: v E 1948 (4); *v E 1947 (5)*
Tuckett, L. R. 1: v E 1913
Twentyman-Jones, P. S. 1: v A 1902

van der Bijl, P. G. V. 5: v E 1938 (5)
Van der Merwe, E. A. 2: v A 1935 (1); *v E 1929 (1)*
Van der Merwe, P. L. 15: v E 1964 (2); v A 1966 (5); *v E 1965 (3); v A 1963 (3); v NZ 1963 (2)*
Van Ryneveld, C. B. 19: v E 1956 (5); v A 1957 (4); v NZ 1953 (5); *v E 1951 (5)*
Varnals, G. D. 3: v E 1964 (3)
Viljoen, K. G. 27: v E 1930 (3) 1938 (4) 1948 (2); v A 1935 (4); *v E 1935 (4) 1947 (5); v A 1931 (4); v NZ 1931 (1)*
'incent, C. L. 25: v E 1927 (5) 1930 (5); *v E 1929 (4) 1935 (4); v A 1931 (5); v NZ 1931 (2)*
'intcent, C. H. 3: v E 1888 (2) 1891 (1)
'ogler, A. E. E. 15: v E 1905 (5) 1909 (5); *v E 1907 (3); v A 1910 (2)*

Wade, H. F. 10: v A 1935 (5); *v E 1935 (5)*
Wade, W. W. 11: v E 1938 (3) 1948 (5); v A 1949 (3)
Waite, J. H. B. 50: v E 1956 (5); 1964 (2); v A 1957 (5); v NZ 1953 (5) 1961 (5); *v E 1951 (4) 1955 (5) 1960 (5); v A 1952 (5) 1963 (4); v NZ 1952 (2) 1963 (3)*
Walter, K. A. 2: v NZ 1961 (2)
Ward, T. A. 23: v E 1913 (5) 1922 (5); v A 1921 (3); *v E 1912 (2) 1924 (5); v A 1912 (3)*
'atkins, J. C. 15: v E 1956 (2); v A 1949 (3); v NZ 1953 (3); *v A 1952 (5); v NZ 1952 (2)*
'esley, C. 3: *v E 1960 (3)*
'estcott, R. J. 5: v A 1957 (2); v NZ 1953 (3)
'hite, G. C. 17: v E 1905 (5) 1909 (4); *v E 1907 (3) 1912 (2); v A 1912 (3)*
'illoughby, J. T. I. 2: v E 1895 (2)
'imble, C. S. 1: v E 1891
'inslow, P. L. 5: v A 1949 (2); *v E 1955 (3)*
'ynne, O. E. 6: v E 1948 (3); v A 1949 (3)

ulch, J. W. 16: v E 1909 (5) 1913 (3); v A 1921 (3); *v A 1910 (5)*

WEST INDIES

Number of Test cricketers: 193

hong, E. 6: v E 1929 (1) 1934 (2); *v E 1933 (3)*
exander, F. C. M. 25: v E 1959 (5); v P 1957 (5); *v E 1957 (2); v A 1960 (5); v In 1958 (5); v P 1958 (3)*
, Imtiaz 1: v In 1975
, Inshan 12: v E 1973 (2); v A 1972 (3); v In 1970 (1); v P 1976 (1); v NZ 1971 (3); *v E 1973 (1); v A 1975 (1)*
an, D. W. 5: v A 1964 (1); v In 1961 (2); *v E 1966 (2)*
nbrose, C. E. L. 8: v P 1987 (3); *v E 1988 (5)*
thurton, K. L. T. 1: *v E 1988*
garali, N. 2: *v E 1957 (2)*
kinson, D. St E. 22: v E 1953 (4); v A 1954 (4); v P 1957 (1); *v E 1957 (2); v A 1951 (2); v NZ 1951 (1) 1955 (4); v In 1948 (4)*

Atkinson, E. St E. 8: v P 1957 (3); *v In 1958 (3); v P 1958 (2)*
Austin, R. A. 2: v A 1977 (2)

Bacchus, S. F. A. F. 19: v A 1977 (2); *v E 1980 (5); v A 1981 (2); v In 1978 (6); v P 1980 (4)*
Baichan, L. 3: *v A 1975 (1); v P 1974 (2)*
Baptiste, E. A. E. 9: v A 1983 (3); *v E 1984 (5); v In 1983 (1)*
Barrow, I. 11: v E 1929 (1) 1934 (1); *v E 1933 (3) 1939 (1); v A 1930 (5)*
Barrett, A. G. 6: v E 1973 (2); v In 1970 (2); *v In 1974 (2)*
Bartlett, E. L. 5: *v E 1928 (1); v A 1930 (4)*
Benjamin, W. K. M. 7: v P 1987 (3); *v E 1988 (3); v In 1987 (1)*
Best, C. A. 3: v E 1985 (3)
Betancourt, N. 1: v E 1929
Binns, A. P. 5: v A 1954 (1); v In 1952 (1); *v NZ 1955 (3)*
Birkett, L. S. 4 *v A 1930 (4)*
Boyce, K. D. 21: v E 1973 (4); v A 1972 (4); v In 1970 (1); *v E 1973 (3); v A 1975 (4); v In 1974 (3); v P 1974 (2)*
Browne, C. R. 4: v E 1929 (2); *v E 1928 (2)*
Butcher, B. F. 44: v E 1959 (2) 1967 (5); v A 1964 (5); *v E 1963 (5) 1966 (5) 1969 (3); v A 1968 (5) v NZ 1968 (3); v In 1958 (5) 1966 (3); v P 1958 (3)*
Butler, L. 1: v A 1954
Butts, C. G. 7: v NZ 1984 (1); *v NZ 1986 (1); v In 1987 (3); v P 1986 (2)*
Bynoe, M. R. 4: *v In 1966 (3); v P 1958 (1)*

Camacho, G. S. 11: v E 1967 (5); v In 1970 (2); *v E 1969 (2); v A 1968 (2)*
Cameron, F. J. 5: *v In 1948 (5)*
Cameron, J. H. 2: *v E 1939 (2)*
Carew, G. M. 4: v E 1934 (1) 1947 (2); *v In 1948 (1)*
Carew, M. C. 19: v E 1967 (1); v NZ 1971 (3); v In 1970 (3); *v E 1963 (2) 1966 (1) 1969 (1); v 1968 (5); v NZ 1968 (3)*
Challenor, G. 3: *v E 1928 (3)*
Chang, H. S. 1: *v In 1978*
Christiani, C. M. 4: v E 1934 (4)
Christiani, R. J. 22: v E 1947 (4) 1953 (1); v In 1952 (2); *v E 1950 (4); v A 1951 (5); v NZ 1951 (1) v In 1948 (5)*
Clarke, C. B. 3: *v E 1939 (3)*
Clarke, S. T. 11: v A 1977 (1); *v A 1981 (1); v In 1978 (5); v P 1980 (4)*
Constantine, L. N. 18: v E 1929 (3) 1934 (3); *v E 1928 (3) 1933 (1) 1939 (3); v A 1930 (5)*
Croft, C. E. H. 27: v E 1980 (4); v A 1977 (2); v P 1976 (5); *v E 1980 (3); v A 1979 (3) 1981 (3); NZ 1979 (3); v P 1980 (4)*

Da Costa, O. C. 5: v E 1929 (1) 1934 (1); *v E 1933 (3)*
Daniel, W. W. 10: v A 1983 (2); v In 1975 (1); *v E 1976 (4) v In 1983 (3)*
Davis, B. A. 4: v A 1964 (4)
Davis, C. A. 15: v A 1972 (2); v NZ 1971 (5); v In 1970 (4); *v E 1969 (3); v A 1968 (1)*
Davis, W. W. 15: v A 1983 (1); v NZ 1984 (2); v In 1982 (1); *v E 1984 (1); v In 1983 (6) 1987 (*
De Caires, F. I. 3: v E 1929 (3)
Depeiza, C. C. 5: v A 1954 (3); *v NZ 1955 (2)*
Dewdney, T. 9: v A 1954 (2); v P 1957 (3); *v E 1957 (1); v NZ 1955 (3)*
Dowe, U. G. 4: v A 1972 (1); v NZ 1971 (1); v In 1970 (2)
Dujon, P. J. L. 55: v E 1985 (4); v A 1983 (5); v NZ 1984 (4); v In 1982 (5); v P 1987 (3); *v E 19 (5) 1988 (5); v A 1981 (3) 1984 (5); v NZ 1986 (3); v In 1983 (6) 1987 (4); v P 1986 (3)*

Edwards, R. M. 5: *v A 1968 (2); v NZ 1968 (3)*

Ferguson, W. 8: v E 1947 (4) 1953 (1); *v In 1948 (3)*
Fernandes, M. P. 2: v E 1929 (1); *v E 1928 (1)*
Findlay, T. M. 10: v A 1972 (1); v NZ 1971 (5); v In 1970 (2); *v E 1969 (2)*
Foster, M. L. C. 14: v E 1973 (1); v A 1972 (4) 1977 (1); v NZ 1971 (3); v In 1970 (2); v P 19 (1); *v E 1969 (1) 1973 (1)*
Francis, G. N. 10: v E 1929 (1); *v E 1928 (3) 1933 (1); v A 1930 (5)*
Frederick, M. C. 1: v E 1953

Fredericks, R. C. 59: v E 1973 (5); v A 1972 (5); v NZ 1971 (5); v In 1970 (4) 1975 (4); v P 1976 (5); *v E 1969 (3) 1973 (3) 1976 (5); v A 1968 (4) 1975 (6); v NZ 1968 (3); v In 1974 (5); v P 1974 (2)*
Fuller, R. L. 1: v E 1934
Furlonge, H. A. 3: v A 1954 (1); *v NZ 1955 (2)*

Ganteaume, A. G. 1: v E 1947
Garner, J. 58: v E 1980 (4) 1985 (5); v A 1977 (2) 1983 (5); v NZ 1984 (4); v In 1982 (4); v P 1976 (5); *v E 1980 (5) 1984 (5); v A 1979 (3) 1981 (3) 1984 (5); v NZ 1979 (3) 1986 (2); v P 1980 (3)*
Gaskin, B. B. M. 2: v E 1947 (2)
Gibbs, G. L. R. 1: v A 1954
Gibbs, L. R. 79: v E 1967 (5) 1973 (5); v A 1964 (5) 1972 (5); v NZ 1971 (2); v In 1961 (5) 1970 (1); v P 1957 (4); *v E 1963 (5) 1966 (5) 1969 (3) 1973 (3); v A 1960 (3) 1968 (5) 1975 (6); v NZ 1968 (3); v In 1958 (1) 1966 (3) 1974 (5); v P 1958 (3) 1974 (2)*
Gilchrist, R. 13: v P 1957 (5); *v E 1957 (4); v In 1958 (4)*
Gladstone, G. 1: v E 1929
Goddard, J. D. C. 27: v E 1947 (4); *v E 1950 (4) 1957 (5); v A 1951 (4); v NZ 1951 (2) 1955 (3); v In 1948 (5)*
Gomes, H. A. 60: v E 1980 (4) 1985 (5); v A 1977 (3) 1983 (2); v NZ 1984 (4); v In 1982 (5); *v E 1976 (2) 1984 (5); v A 1981 (3) 1984 (5); v NZ 1986 (3); v In 1978 (6) 1983 (6); v P 1980 (4) 1986 (3)*
Gomez, G. E. 29: v E 1947 (4) 1953 (4); v In 1952 (4); *v E 1939 (2) 1950 (4); v A 1951 (5); v NZ 1951 (1); v In 1948 (5)*
Grant, G. C. 12: v E 1934 (4); *v E 1933 (3); v A 1930 (5)*
Grant, R. S. 7: v E 1934 (4); *v E 1939 (3)*
Gray, A. H. 5: *v NZ 1986 (2); v P 1986 (3)*
Greenidge, A. E. 6: v A 1977 (2); *v In 1978 (4)*
Greenidge, C. G. 87: v E 1980 (4) 1985 (5); v A 1977 (2) 1983 (5); v NZ 1984 (4); v In 1982 (5); v P 1976 (5) 1987 (3); *v E 1976 (5) 1980 (5) 1984 (5) 1988 (4); v A 1975 (2) 1979 (3) 1981 (2) 1984 (5); v NZ 1979 (3) 1986 (3); v In 1974 (5) 1983 (6) 1987 (3); v P 1986 (3)*
Greenidge, G. A. 5: v A 1972 (3); v NZ 1971 (2)
Grell, M. G. 1: v E 1929
Griffith, C. C. 28: v E 1959 (1) 1967 (4); v A 1964 (5); *v E 1963 (5) 1966 (5); v A 1968 (3); v NZ 1968 (2); v In 1966 (3)*
Griffith, H. C. 13: v E 1929 (3); *v E 1928 (3) 1933 (2); v A 1930 (5)*
Guillen, S. C. 5: *v A 1951 (3); v NZ 1951 (2)*

Hall, W. W. 48: v E 1959 (5) 1967 (4); v A 1964 (5); v In 1961 (5); *v E 1963 (5) 1966 (5); v A 1960 (5) 1968 (2); v NZ 1968 (1); v In 1958 (5) 1966 (3); v P 1958 (3)*
Harper, R. A. 23: v E 1985 (2); v A 1983 (4); v NZ 1984 (1); *v E 1984 (5) 1988 (3); v A 1984 (2); v In 1983 (2) 1987 (1); v P 1986 (3)*
Haynes, D. L. 76: v E 1980 (4) 1985 (5); v A 1977 (2) 1983 (5); v NZ 1984 (4); v In 1982 (5); v P 1987 (3); *v E 1980 (5) 1984 (5) 1988 (4); v A 1979 (3) 1981 (3) 1984 (5); v NZ 1979 (3) 1986 (3); v In 1983 (6) 1987 (4); v P 1980 (4) 1986 (3)*
Headley, G. A. 22: v E 1929 (4) 1934 (4) 1947 (1) 1953 (1); *v E 1933 (3) 1939 (3); v A 1930 (5); v In 1948 (1)*
Headley, R. G. A. 2: *v E 1973 (2)*
Hendriks, J. L. 20: v A 1964 (4); v In 1961 (1); *v E 1966 (3) 1969 (1); v A 1968 (5); v NZ 1968 (3); v In 1966 (3)*
Hoad, E. L. G. 4: v E 1929 (1); *v E 1928 (1) 1933 (2)*
Holder, V. A. 40: v E 1973 (1); v A 1972 (3) 1977 (3); v NZ 1971 (4); v In 1970 (3) 1975 (1); v P 1976 (1); *v E 1969 (3) 1973 (2) 1976 (4); v A 1975 (3); v In 1974 (4) 1978 (6); v P 1974 (2)*
Holding, M. A. 60: v E 1980 (4) 1985 (4); v A 1983 (3); v NZ 1984 (3); v In 1975 (4) 1982 (5); *v E 1976 (4) 1980 (5) 1984 (4); v A 1975 (5) 1979 (3) 1981 (3) 1984 (3); v NZ 1979 (3) 1986 (1); v In 1983 (6)*
Holford, D. A. J. 24: v E 1967 (4); v NZ 1971 (5); v In 1970 (1) 1975 (2); v P 1976 (1); *v E 1966 (5); v A 1968 (2); v NZ 1968 (3); v In 1966 (1)*
Holt, J. K. 17: v E 1953 (5); v A 1954 (5); *v In 1958 (5); v P 1958 (2)*
Hooper, C. L. 11: v P 1987 (3); *v E 1988 (5); v In 1987 (3)*
Howard, A. B. 1: v NZ 1971
Hunte, C. C. 44: v E 1959 (5); v A 1964 (5); v In 1961 (5); v P 1957 (5); *v E 1963 (5) 1966 (5); v A 1960 (5); v In 1958 (5) 1966 (3); v P 1958 (1)*

Hunte, E. A. C. 3: v E 1929 (3)
Hylton, L. G. 6: v E 1934 (4); *v E 1939 (2)*

Johnson, H. H. H. 3: v E 1947 (1); *v E 1950 (2)*
Johnson, T. F. 1: *v E 1939*
Jones, C. M. 4: v E 1929 (1) 1934 (3)
Jones, P. E. 9: v E 1947 (1); *v E 1950 (2); v A 1951 (1); v In 1948 (5)*
Julien, B. D. 24: v E 1973 (5); v In 1975 (4); v P 1976 (1); *v E 1973 (3) 1976 (2); v A 1975 (3); v In 1974 (4); v P 1974 (2)*
Jumadeen, R. R. 12: v A 1972 (1) 1977 (2); v NZ 1971 (1); v In 1975 (4); v P 1976 (1); *v E 1976 (1); v In 1978 (2)*

Kallicharran, A. I. 66: v E 1973 (5); v A 1972 (5) 1977 (5); v NZ 1971 (2); v In 1975 (4); v P 1976 (5); *v E 1973 (3) 1976 (3) 1980 (5); v A 1975 (6) 1979 (3); v NZ 1979 (3); v In 1974 (5) 1978 (6); v P 1974 (2) 1980 (4)*
Kanhai, R. B. 79: v E 1959 (5) 1967 (5) 1973 (5); v A 1964 (5) 1972 (5); v In 1961 (5) 1970 (5); v P 1957 (5); *v E 1957 (5) 1963 (5) 1966 (5) 1973 (3); v A 1960 (5) 1968 (5); v In 1958 (5) 1966 (3); v P 1958 (3)*
Kentish, E. S. M. 2: v E 1947 (1) 1953 (1)
King, C. L. 9: v P 1976 (1); *v E 1976 (3) 1980 (1); v A 1979 (1); v NZ 1979 (3)*
King, F. M. 14: v E 1953 (3); v A 1954 (4); v In 1952 (5); *v NZ 1955 (2)*
King, L. A. 2: v E 1967 (1); v In 1961 (1)

Lashley, P. D. 4: *v E 1966 (2); v A 1960 (2)*
Legall, R. 4: v In 1952 (4)
Lewis, D. M. 3: v In 1970 (3)
Lloyd, C. H. 110: v E 1967 (5) 1973 (5) 1980 (4); v A 1972 (3) 1977 (2) 1983 (4); v NZ 1971 (2); v In 1970 (5) 1975 (4) 1982 (5); v P 1976 (5); *v E 1969 (3) 1973 (3) 1976 (5) 1980 (4) 1984 (5); v A 1968 (4) 1975 (6) 1979 (2) 1981 (3) 1984 (5); v NZ 1968 (3) 1979 (3); v In 1966 (3) 1974 (5) 1983 (6); v P 1974 (2) 1980 (4)*
Logie, A. L. 28: v A 1983 (1); v NZ 1984 (4); v In 1982 (5); v P 1987 (3); *v E 1988 (5); v NZ 1986 (3); v In 1983 (3) 1987 (4)*

McMorris, E. D. A. 13: v E 1959 (4); v In 1961 (4); v P 1957 (1); *v E 1963 (2) 1966 (2)*
McWatt, C. A. 6: v E 1953 (5); v A 1954 (1)
Madray, I. S. 2: v P 1957 (2)
Marshall, M. D. 58: v E 1980 (1) 1985 (5); v A 1983 (4); v NZ 1984 (4); v In 1982 (5); v P 1987 (2); *v E 1980 (4) 1984 (4) 1988 (5); v A 1984 (5); v NZ 1986 (3); v In 1978 (3) 1983 (6); v P 1980 (4) 1986 (3)*
Marshall, N. E. 1: v A 1954
Marshall, R. E. 4: *v A 1951 (2); v NZ 1951 (2)*
Martin, F. R. 9: v E 1929 (1); *v E 1928 (3); v A 1930 (5)*
Martindale, E. A. 10: v E 1934 (4); *v E 1933 (3) 1939 (3)*
Mattis, E. H. 4: v E 1980 (4)
Mendonca, I. L. 2: v In 1961 (2)
Merry, C. A. 2: *v E 1933 (2)*
Miller, R. 1: v In 1952
Moodie, G. H. 1: v E 1934
Murray, D. A. 19: v E 1980 (4); v A 1977 (3); *v A 1981 (2); v In 1978 (6); v P 1980 (4)*
Murray, D. L. 62: v E 1967 (5) 1973 (5); v A 1972 (4) 1977 (2); v In 1975 (4); v P 1976 (5); *v E 1963 (5) 1973 (3) 1976 (5) 1980 (5); v A 1975 (6) 1979 (3); v NZ 1979 (3); v In 1974 (5); v P 1974 (2)*

Nanan, R. 1: *v P 1980*
Neblett, J. M. 1: v E 1934
Noreiga, J. M. 4: v In 1970 (4)
Nunes, R. K. 4: v E 1929 (1); *v E 1928 (3)*
Nurse, S. M. 29: v E 1959 (1) 1967 (5); v A 1964 (4); v In 1961 (1); *v E 1966 (5); v A 1960 (3) 196[illegible] (5); v NZ 1968 (3); v In 1966 (2)*

Padmore, A. L. 2: v In 1975 (1); *v E 1976 (1)*
Pairaudeau, B. H. 13: v E 1953 (2); v In 1952 (5): *v E 1957 (2); v NZ 1955 (4)*

Parry, D. R. 12: v A 1977 (5); *v NZ 1979 (1); v In 1978 (6)*
Passailaigue, C. C. 1: v E 1929
Patterson, B. P. 13: v E 1985 (5); v P 1987 (1); *v E 1988 (2); v In 1987 (4); v P 1986 (1)*
Payne, T. R. O. 1: v E 1985
Phillip, N. 9: v A 1977 (3); *v In 1978 (6)*
Pierre, L. R. 1: v E 1947

Rae, A. F. 15: v In 1952 (2); *v E 1950 (4); v A 1951 (3); v NZ 1951 (1); v In 1948 (5)*
Ramadhin, S. 43: v E 1953 (5) 1959 (4); v A 1954 (4); v In 1952 (4); *v E 1950 (4) 1957 (5); v A 1951 (5) 1960 (2); v NZ 1951 (2) 1955 (4); v In 1958 (2); v P 1958 (2)*
Richards, I. V. A. 99: v E 1980 (4) 1985 (5); v A 1977 (2) 1983 (5); v NZ 1984 (4); v In 1975 (4) 1982 (5); v P 1976 (5) 1987 (2); *v E 1976 (4) 1980 (5) 1984 (5) 1988 (5); v A 1975 (6) 1979 (3) 1981 (3) 1984 (5); v NZ 1986 (3); v In 1974 (5) 1983 (6) 1987 (4); v P 1974 (2) 1980 (4) 1986 (3)*
Richardson, R. B. 36: v E 1985 (5); v A 1983 (5); v NZ 1984 (4); v P 1987 (3); *v E 1988 (3); v A 1984 (5); v NZ 1986 (3); v In 1983 (1) 1987 (4); v P 1986 (3)*
Rickards, K. R. 2: v E 1947 (1); *v A 1951 (1)*
Roach, C. A. 16: v E 1929 (4) 1934 (1); *v E 1928 (3) 1933 (3); v A 1930 (5)*
Roberts, A. M. E. 47: v E 1973 (1) 1980 (3); v A 1977 (2); v In 1975 (2) 1982 (5); v P 1976 (5); *v E 1976 (5) 1980 (3); v A 1975 (5) 1979 (3) 1981 (2); v NZ 1979 (2); v In 1974 (5) 1983 (2); v P 1974 (2)*
Roberts, A. T. 1: *v NZ 1955*
Rodriguez, W. V. 5: v E 1967 (1); v A 1964 (1); v In 1961 (2); *v E 1963 (1)*
Rowe, L. G. 30: v E 1973 (5); v A 1972 (3); v NZ 1971 (4); v In 1975 (4); *v E 1976 (2); v A 1975 (6) 1979 (3); v NZ 1979 (3)*

t Hill, E. L. 2: v E 1929 (2)
t Hill, W. H. 3: v E 1929 (1); *v E 1928 (2)*
carlett, R. O. 3: v E 1959 (3)
cott, A. P. H. 1: v In 1952
cott, O. C. 8: v E 1929 (1); *v E 1928 (2); v A 1930 (5)*
ealey, B. J. 1: *v E 1933*
ealy, J. E. D. 11: v E 1929 (2) 1934 (4); *v E 1939 (3); v A 1930 (2)*
hepherd, J. N. 5: v In 1970 (2); *v E 1969 (3)*
hillingford, G. C. 7: v NZ 1971 (2); v In 1970 (3); *v E 1969 (2)*
hillingford, I. T. 4: v A 1977 (1); v P 1976 (3)
hivnarine, S. 8: v A 1977 (3); *v In 1978 (5)*
mmons, P. V. 2: v P 1987 (1); *v In 1987 (1)*
ngh, C. K. 2: v E 1959 (2)
mall, J. A. 3: v E 1929 (1); *v E 1928 (2)*
mall, M. A. 2: v A 1983 (1); *v E 1984 (1)*
nith, C. W. 5: v In 1961 (1); *v A 1960 (4)*
nith, O. G. 26: v A 1954 (4); v P 1957 (5); *v E 1957 (5); v NZ 1955 (4); v In 1958 (5); v P 1958 (3)*
bers, G. S. 93: v E 1953 (1) 1959 (5) 1967 (5) 1973 (4); v A 1954 (4) 1964 (5); v NZ 1971 (5); v In 1961 (5); 1970 (5); v P 1957 (5); *v E 1957 (5) 1963 (5) 1966 (5) 1969 (3) 1973 (3); v A 1960 (5) 1968 (5); v NZ 1955 (4) 1968 (3); v In 1958 (5) 1966 (3); v P 1958 (3)*
lomon, J. S. 27: v E 1959 (2); v A 1964 (4); v In 1961 (4); *v E 1963 (5); v A 1960 (5); v In 1958 (4); v P 1958 (3)*
ayers, S. C. 4: v In 1961 (4)
ollmeyer, J. B. 32: v E 1947 (2) 1953 (5); v A 1954 (2); v In 1952 (5); *v E 1939 (3) 1950 (4); v A 1951 (5); v NZ 1951 (2); v In 1948 (4)*
ollmeyer, V. H. 1: *v E 1939*

ylor, J. 3: v P 1957 (1); *v In 1958 (1); v P 1958 (1)*
im, J. 4: v E 1947 (1); *v A 1951 (1); v In 1948 (2)*

lentine, A. L. 36: v E 1953 (3); v A 1954 (3); v In 1952 (5) 1961 (2); v P 1957 (1); *v E 1950 (4) 1957 (2); v A 1951 (5) 1960 (5); v NZ 1951 (2) 1955 (4)*
lentine, V. A. 2: *v E 1933 (2)*

lcott, C. L. 44: v E 1947 (4) 1953 (5) 1959 (2); v A 1954 (5); v In 1952 (5); v P 1957 (4); *v E 1950 (4) 1957 (5); v A 1951 (3); v NZ 1951 (2); v In 1948 (5)*
lcott, L. A. 1: v E 1929

Walsh, C. A. 25: v E 1985 (1); v NZ 1984 (1); v P 1987 (3); *v E 1988 (5); v A 1984 (5); v NZ 1986 (3); v In 1987 (4); v P 1986 (3)*
Watson, C. 7: v E 1959 (5); v In 1961 (1); *v A 1960 (1)*
Weekes, E. D. 48: v E 1947 (4) 1953 (4); v A 1954 (5) v In 1952 (5); v P 1957 (5); *v E 1950 (4) 1957 (5); v A 1951 (5); v NZ 1951 (2) 1955 (4); v In 1948 (5)*
Weekes, K. H. 2: *v E 1939 (2)*
White, W. A. 2: v A 1964 (2)
Wight, C. V. 2: v E 1929 (1); *v E 1928 (1)*
Wight, G. L. 1: v In 1952
Wiles, C. A. 1: *v E 1933*
Willett, E. T. 5: v A 1972 (3); *v In 1974 (2)*
Williams, A. B. 7: v A 1977 (3); *v In 1978 (4)*
Williams, E. A. V. 4: v E 1947 (3); *v E 1939 (1)*
Wishart, K. L. 1: v E 1934
Worrell, F. M. M. 51: v E 1947 (3) 1953 (4) 1959 (4); v A 1954 (4); v In 1952 (5) 1961 (5); *v E 1950 (4) 1957 (5) 1963 (5); v A 1951 (5) 1960 (5); v NZ 1951 (2)*

NEW ZEALAND

Number of Test cricketers: 166

Alabaster, J. C. 21: v E 1962 (2); v WI 1955 (1); v In 1967 (4); *v E 1958 (2); v SA 1961 (5); v WI 1971 (2); v In 1955 (4); v P 1955 (1)*
Allcott, C. F. W. 6: v E 1929 (2); v SA 1931 (1); *v E 1931 (3)*
Anderson, R. W. 9: v E 1977 (3); *v E 1978 (3); v P 1976 (3)*
Anderson, W. M. 1: v A 1945
Andrews, B. 2: *v A 1973 (2)*

Badcock, F. T. 7: v E 1929 (3) 1932 (2); v SA 1931 (2)
Barber, R. T. 1: v WI 1955
Bartlett, G. A. 10: v E 1965 (2); v In 1967 (2); v P 1964 (1); *v SA 1961 (5)*
Barton, P. T. 7: v E 1962 (3); *v SA 1961 (4)*
Beard, D. D. 4: v WI 1951 (2) 1955 (2)
Beck, J. E. F. 8: v WI 1955 (4); *v SA 1953 (4)*
Bell, W. 2: *v SA 1953 (2)*
Bilby, G. P. 2: v E 1965 (2)
Blain, T. E. 1: *v E 1986*
Blair, R. W. 19: v E 1954 (1) 1958 (2) 1962 (2); v SA 1952 (2) 1963 (3); v WI 1955 (2) *v E 1958 (3) v SA 1953 (4)*
Blunt, R. C. 9: v E 1929 (4); v SA 1931 (2); *v E 1931 (3)*
Bolton, B. A. 2: v E 1958 (2)
Boock, S. L. 29: v E 1977 (3) 1983 (2) 1987 (1); v WI 1979 (3) 1986 (2); v P 1978 (3) 1984 (2); *v 1978 (3); v A 1985 (1); v WI 1984 (3); v P 1984 (3); v SL 1983 (3)*
Bracewell, B. P. 6: v P 1978 (1) 1984 (1); *v E 1978 (3); v A 1980 (1)*
Bracewell, J. G. 30: v E 1987 (3); v A 1985 (2); v WI 1986 (3); v In 1980 (1); *v E 1983 (4) 1986 (3 v A 1980 (3) 1985 (2) 1987 (3); v WI 1984 (1); v P 1984 (2); v SL 1983 (2) 1986 (1)*
Bradburn, W. P. 2: v SA 1963 (2)
Brown, V. R. 2: *v A 1985 (2)*
Burgess, M. G. 50: v E 1970 (1) 1977 (3); v A 1973 (1) 1976 (2); v WI 1968 (2); v In 1967 (4) 19 (3); v P 1972 (3) 1978 (3); *v E 1969 (2) 1973 (3) 1978 (3); v A 1980 (3); v WI 1971 (5); v In 19 (3) 1976 (3); v P 1969 (3) 1976 (3)*
Burke, C. 1: v A 1945
Burtt, T. B. 10: v E 1946 (1) 1950 (2); v SA 1952 (1); v WI 1951 (2); *v E 1949 (4)*
Butterfield, L. A. 1: v A 1945

Cairns, B. L. 43: v E 1974 (1) 1977 (1) 1983 (3); v A 1976 (1) 1981 (3); v WI 1979 (3); v In 1975 1980 (3); v P 1978 (3) 1984 (3); v SL 1982 (2); *v E 1978 (2) 1983 (4); v A 1973 (1) 1980 (3) 19 (1); v WI 1984 (2); v In 1976 (2); v P 1976 (2); v SL 1983 (2)*
Cameron, F. J. 19: v E 1962 (3); v SA 1963 (3); v P 1964 (3); *v E 1965 (2); v SA 1961 (5); v In 19 (1); v P 1964 (2)*

Cave, H. B. 19: v E 1954 (2); v WI 1955 (3); *v E 1949 (4) 1958 (2); v In 1955 (5); v P 1955 (3)*
Chapple, M. E. 14: v E 1954 (1) 1965 (1); v SA 1952 (1) 1963 (3); v WI 1955 (1); *v SA 1953 (5) 1961 (2)*
Chatfield, E. J. 38: v E 1974 (1) 1977 (1) 1983 (3) 1987 (3); v A 1976 (2) 1981 (1) 1985 (3); v WI 1986 (3); v P 1984 (3); v SL 1982 (2); *v E 1983 (3) 1986 (1); v A 1985 (2) 1987 (2); v WI 1984 (4); v P 1984 (1); v SL 1983 (2) 1986 (1)*
Cleverley, D. C. 2: v SA 1931 (1); v A 1945 (1)
Collinge, R. O. 35: v E 1970 (2) 1974 (2) 1977 (3); v A 1973 (3); v In 1967 (2) 1975 (3); v P 1964 (3) 1972 (2); *v E 1965 (3) 1969 (1) 1973 (3) 1978 (1); v In 1964 (2) 1976 (1); v P 1964 (2) 1976 (2)*
Colquhoun, I. A. 2: v E 1954 (2)
Coney, J. V. 52: v E 1983 (3); v A 1973 (2) 1981 (3) 1985 (3); v WI 1979 (3) 1986 (3); v In 1980 (3); v P 1978 (3) 1984 (3); v SL 1982 (2); *v E 1983 (4) 1986 (3); v A 1973 (2) 1980 (2) 1985 (3); v WI 1984 (4); v P 1984 (3); v SL 1983 (3)*
Congdon, B. E. 61: v E 1965 (3) 1970 (2) 1974 (2) 1977 (3); v A 1973 (3) 1976 (2); v WI 1968 (3); v In 1967 (4) 1975 (3); v P 1964 (3) 1972 (3); *v E 1965 (3) 1969 (3) 1973 (3) 1978 (3); v A 1973 (3); v WI 1971 (5); v In 1964 (3) 1969 (3); v P 1964 (1) 1969 (3)*
Cowie, J. 9: v E 1946 (1); v A 1945 (1); *v E 1937 (3) 1949 (4)*
Cresswell G. F. 3: v E 1950 (2); *v E 1949 (1)*
Cromb, I. B. 5: v SA 1931 (2); *v E 1931 (3)*
Crowe, J. J. 35: v E 1983 (3) 1987 (2); v WI 1986 (3); v P 1984 (3); v SL 1982 (2); *v E 1983 (2) 1986 (3); v A 1985 (3) 1987 (3); v WI 1984 (4); v P 1984 (3); v SL 1983 (3) 1986 (1)*
Crowe, M. D. 42: v E 1983 (3) 1987 (3); v A 1981 (3) 1985 (3); v WI 1986 (3); v P 1984 (3); *v E 1983 (4) 1986 (3); v A 1985 (3) 1987 (3); v WI 1984 (4); v P 1984 (3); v SL 1983 (3) 1986 (1)*
Cunis, R. S. 20: v E 1965 (3) 1970 (2); v SA 1963 (1); v WI 1968 (3); *v E 1969 (1); v WI 1971 (5); v In 1969 (3); v P 1969 (2)*

D'Arcy, J. W. 5: *v E 1958 (5)*
Dempster, C. S. 10: v E 1929 (4) 1932 (2); v SA 1931 (2); *v E 1931 (2)*
Dempster, E. W. 5: v SA 1952 (1); *v SA 1953 (4)*
Dick, A. E. 17: v E 1962 (3); v SA 1963 (2); v P 1964 (2); *v E 1965 (2); v SA 1961 (5); v P 1964 (3)*
Dickinson, G. R. 3: v E 1929 (2); v SA 1931 (1)
Donnelly, M. P. 7: *v E 1937 (3) 1949 (4)*
Dowling, G. T. 39: v E 1962 (3) 1970 (2); v In 1967 (4); v SA 1963 (1); v WI 1968 (3); v P 1964 (2); *v E 1965 (3) 1969 (3); v SA 1961 (4); v WI 1971 (2); v In 1964 (4) 1969 (3); v P 1964 (2) 1969 (3)*
Dunning, J. A. 4: v E 1932 (1); *v E 1937 (3)*

dgar, B. A. 39: v E 1983 (3); v A 1981 (3) 1985 (3); v WI 1979 (3); v In 1980 (3); v P 1978 (3); v SL 1982 (2); *v E 1978 (3) 1983 (4) 1986 (3); v A 1980 (3) 1985 (3); v P 1984 (3)*
dwards, G. N. 8: v E 1977 (1); v A 1976 (2); v In 1980 (3); *v E 1978 (2)*
mery, R. W. G. 2: v WI 1951 (2)

isher, F. E. 1: v SA 1952
oley, H. 1: v E 1929
ranklin, T. J. 5: v E 1987 (3); v A 1985 (1); *v E 1983 (1)*
reeman, D. L. 2: v E 1932 (2)

allichan, N. 1: *v E 1937*
edye, S. G. 4: v SA 1963 (3); v P 1964 (1)
illespie, S. R. 1: v A 1985
ray, E. J. 9: *v E 1983 (2) 1986 (3); v A 1987 (1); v P 1984 (2); v SL 1986 (1)*
reatbatch, M. J. 2: v E 1987 (2)
uillen, S. C. 3: v WI 1955 (3)
uy, J. W. 12: v E 1958 (2); v WI 1955 (2); *v SA 1961 (2); v In 1955 (5); v P 1955 (1)*

adlee, D. R. 26: v E 1974 (2) 1977 (1); v A 1973 (3) 1976 (1); v In 1975 (3); v P 1972 (2); *v E 1969 (2) 1973 (3); v A 1973 (3); v In 1969 (3); v P 1969 (3)*
adlee, R. J. 74: v E 1977 (3) 1983 (3) 1987 (1); v A 1973 (2) 1976 (2) 1981 (3) 1985 (3); v WI 1979 (3) 1986 (3); v In 1975 (2) 1980 (3); v P 1972 (1) 1978 (3) 1984 (3); v SL 1982 (2); *v E 1973 (1) 1978 (3) 1983 (4) 1986 (3); v A 1973 (3) 1980 (3) 1985 (3) 1987 (3); v WI 1984 (4); v In 1976 (3); v P 1976 (3); v SL 1983 (3) 1986 (1)*
adlee, W. A. 11: v E 1946 (1) 1950 (2); v A 1945 (1); *v E 1937 (3) 1949 (4)*

Harford, N. S. 8: *v E 1958 (4); v In 1955 (2); v P 1955 (2)*
Harford, R. I. 3: v In 1967 (3)
Harris, P. G. Z. 9: v P 1964 (1); *v SA 1961 (5); v In 1955 (1); v P 1955 (2)*
Harris, R. M. 2: v E 1958 (2)
Hastings, B. F. 31: v E 1974 (2); v A 1973 (3); v WI 1968 (3); v In 1975 (1); v P 1972 (3); *v E 1969 (3) 1973 (3); v A 1973 (3); v WI 1971 (5); v In 1969 (2); v P 1969 (3)*
Hayes, J. A. 15: v E 1950 (2) 1954 (1); v WI 1951 (2); *v E 1958 (4); v In 1955 (5); v P 1955 (1)*
Henderson, M. 1: v E 1929
Horne, P. A. 3: v WI 1986 (1); *v A 1987 (1); v SL 1986 (1)*
Hough, K. W. 2: v E 1958 (2)
Howarth, G. P. 47: v E 1974 (2) 1977 (3) 1983 (3); v A 1976 (2) 1981 (3); v WI 1979 (3); v In 1980 (3); v P 1978 (3) 1984 (3); v SL 1982 (2); *v E 1978 (3) 1983 (4); v A 1980 (2); v WI 1984 (4); v In 1976 (2); v P 1976 (2); v SL 1983 (3)*
Howarth, H. J. 30: v E 1970 (2) 1974 (2); v A 1973 (3) 1976 (2); v In 1975 (2); v P 1972 (3); *v E 1969 (3) 1973 (2); v WI 1971 (5); v In 1969 (3); v P 1969 (3)*

James, K. C. 11: v E 1929 (4) 1932 (2); v SA 1931 (2); *v E 1931 (3)*
Jarvis, T. W. 13: v E 1965 (1); v P 1972 (3); *v WI 1971 (4); v In 1964 (2); v P 1964 (3)*
Jones, A. H. 5: v E 1987 (1); *v A 1987 (3); v SL 1986 (1)*

Kerr, J. L. 7: v E 1932 (2); v SA 1931 (1); *v E 1931 (2) 1937 (2)*

Lees, W. K. 21: v E 1977 (2); v A 1976 (1); v WI 1979 (3); v P 1978 (3); v SL 1982 (2); *v E 1983 (2); v A 1980 (2); v In 1976 (3); v P 1976 (3)*
Leggat, I. B. 1: *v SA 1953*
Leggat, J. G. 9: v E 1954 (1); v SA 1952 (1); v WI 1951 (1) 1955 (1); *v In 1955 (3); v P 1955 (2)*
Lissette, A. F. 2: v WI 1955 (2)
Lowry, T. C. 7: v E 1929 (4); *v E 1931 (3)*

MacGibbon, A. R. 26: v E 1950 (2) 1954 (2); v SA 1952 (1); v WI 1955 (3); *v E 1958 (5); v SA 1953 (5); v In 1955 (5); v P 1955 (3)*
McEwan, P. E. 4: v WI 1979 (1); *v A 1980 (2); v P 1984 (1)*
McGirr, H. M. 2: v E 1929 (2)
McGregor, S. N. 25: v E 1954 (2) 1958 (2); v SA 1963 (3); v WI 1955 (4); v P 1964 (2); *v SA 1961 (5); v In 1955 (4); v P 1955 (3)*
McLeod E. G. 1: v E 1929
McMahon T. G. 5: v WI 1955 (1); *v In 1955 (3); v P 1955 (1)*
McRae, D. A. N. 1: v A 1945
Matheson, A. M. 2: v E 1929 (1); *v E 1931 (1)*
Meale, T. 2: *v E 1958 (2)*
Merritt, W. E. 6: v E 1929 (4); *v E 1931 (2)*
Meuli, E. M. 1: v SA 1952
Milburn, B. D. 3: v WI 1968 (3)
Miller, L. S. M. 13: v SA 1952 (2); v WI 1955 (3); *v E 1958 (4); v SA 1953 (4)*
Mills, J. E. 7: v E 1929 (3) 1932 (1); *v E 1931 (3)*
Moir, A. M. 17: v E 1950 (2) 1954 (2) 1958 (2); v SA 1952 (1); v WI 1951 (2) 1955 (1); *v E 195[illegible] (2); v In 1955 (2); v P 1955 (3)*
Moloney D. A. R. 3: *v E 1937 (3)*
Mooney, F. L. H. 14: v E 1950 (2); v SA 1952 (2); v WI 1951 (2); *v E 1949 (3); v SA 1953 (5*
Morgan, R. W. 20: v E 1965 (2) 1970 (2); v WI 1968 (1); v P 1964 (2); *v E 1965 (3); v WI 1971 (3) v In 1964 (4); v P 1964 (3)*
Morrison, B. D. 1: v E 1962
Morrison, D. K. 6: v E 1987 (3); *v A 1987 (3)*
Morrison, J. F. M. 17: v E 1974 (2); v A 1973 (3) 1981 (3); v In 1975 (3); *v A 1973 (3); v In 19[illegible] (1); v P 1976 (2)*
Motz, R. C. 32: v E 1962 (2) 1965 (3); v SA 1963 (2); v WI 1968 (3): v In 1967 (4); v P 1964 (3 *v E 1965 (3) 1969 (3); v SA 1961 (5); v In 1964 (3); v P 1964 (1)*
Murray, B. A. G. 13: v E 1970 (1); v In 1967 (4); *v E 1969 (2); v In 1969 (3); v P 1969 (3*

Newman J. 3: v E 1932 (2); v SA 1931 (1)

O'Sullivan, D. R. 11: v In 1975 (1); v P 1972 (1); *v A 1973 (3); v In 1976 (3); v P 1976 (*
Overton, G. W. F. 3: *v SA 1953 (3)*

Page, M. L. 14: v E 1929 (4) 1932 (2); v SA 1931 (2); *v E 1931 (3) 1937 (3)*
Parker, J. M. 36: v E 1974 (2) 1977 (3); v A 1973 (3) 1976 (2); v WI 1979 (3); v In 1975 (3); v P 1972 (1) 1978 (2); *v E 1973 (3) 1978 (2); v A 1973 (3) 1980 (3); v In 1976 (3); v P 1976 (3)*
Parker, N. M. 3: *v In 1976 (2); v P 1976 (1)*
Patel, D. N. 6: v WI 1986 (3); *v A 1987 (3)*
Petherick, P. J. 6: v A 1976 (1); *v In 1976 (3); v P 1976 (2)*
Petrie, E. C. 14: v E 1958 (2) 1965 (3); *v E 1958 (5); v In 1955 (2); v P 1955 (2)*
Playle, W. R. 8: v E 1962 (3); *v E 1958 (5)*
Pollard, V. 32: v E 1965 (3) 1970 (1); v WI 1968 (3); v In 1967 (4); v P 1972 (1); *v E 1965 (3) 1969 (3) 1973 (3); v In 1964 (4) 1969 (1); v P 1964 (3) 1969 (3)*
Poore, M. B. 14: v E 1954 (1); v SA 1952 (1); *v SA 1953 (5); v In 1955 (4); v P 1955 (3)*
Puna, N. 3: v E 1965 (3)

Rabone, G. O. 12: v E 1954 (2); v SA 1952 (1); v WI 1951 (2); *v E 1949 (4); v SA 1953 (3)*
Redmond, R. E. 1: v P 1972
Reid, J. F. 19: v A 1985 (3); v In 1980 (3); v P 1978 (1) 1984 (3); *v A 1985 (3); v P 1984 (3); v SL 1983 (3)*
Reid, J. R. 58: v E 1950 (2) 1954 (2) 1958 (2) 1962 (3); v SA 1952 (2) 1963 (3); v WI 1951 (2) 1955 (4); v P 1964 (3); *v E 1949 (2) 1958 (5) 1965 (3); v SA 1953 (5) 1961 (5); v In 1955 (5) 1964 (4); v P 1955 (3) 1964 (3)*
Roberts, A. D. G. 7: v In 1975 (2); *v In 1976 (3); v P 1976 (2)*
Roberts, A. W. 5: v E 1929 (1); v SA 1931 (2); *v E 1937 (2)*
Robertson, G. K. 1: v A 1985
Rowe, C. G. 1: v A 1945
Rutherford, K. R. 14: v E 1987 (2); v A 1985 (3); v WI 1986 (2); *v E 1986 (1); v A 1987 (1); v WI 1984 (4); v SL 1986 (1)*

Scott, R. H. 1: v E 1946
Scott, V. J. 10: v E 1946 (1) 1950 (2); v A 1945 (1); v WI 1951 (2); *v E 1949 (4)*
Shrimpton, M. J. F. 10: v E 1962 (2) 1965 (3) 1970 (2); v SA 1963 (1); *v A 1973 (2)*
Sinclair, B. W. 21: v E 1962 (3) 1965 (3); v SA 1963 (3); v In 1967 (2); v P 1964 (2); *v E 1965 (3); v In 1964 (2); v P 1964 (3)*
inclair, I. M. 2: v WI 1955 (2)
mith, F. B. 4: v E 1946 (1); v WI 1951 (1); *v E 1949 (2)*
mith, H. D. 1: v E 1932
mith, I. D. S. 43: v E 1983 (3) 1987 (3); v A 1981 (3) 1985 (3); v WI 1986 (3); v In 1980 (3); v P 1984 (3); *v E 1983 (2) 1986 (2); v A 1980 (1) 1985 (3) 1987 (3); v WI 1984 (4); v P 1984 (3); v SL 1983 (3) 1986 (1)*
nedden, C. A. 1: v E 1946
nedden, M. C. 16: v E 1983 (1) 1987 (2); v A 1981 (3); v WI 1986 (1); v In 1980 (3); v SL 1982 (2); *v E 1983 (1); v A 1985 (1) 1987 (1); v SL 1986 (1)*
parling, J. T. 11: v E 1958 (2) 1962 (1); v SA 1963 (2); *v E 1958 (3); v SA 1961 (3)*
tirling, D. A. 6: *v E 1986 (2); v WI 1984 (1); v P 1984 (3)*
utcliffe, B. 42: v E 1946 (1) 1950 (2) 1954 (2) 1958 (2); v SA 1952 (2); v WI 1951 (2) 1955 (2); *v E 1949 (4) 1958 (4) 1965 (1); v SA 1953 (5); v In 1955 (5) 1964 (4); v P 1955 (3) 1964 (3)*

aylor, B. R. 30: v E 1965 (1); v WI 1968 (3); v In 1967 (3); v P 1972 (3); *v E 1965 (2) 1969 (2) 1973 (3); v WI 1971 (4); v In 1964 (3) 1969 (2); v P 1964 (3) 1969 (1)*
aylor, D. D. 3: v E 1946 (1); v WI 1955 (2)
homson, K. 2: v In 1967 (2)
indill, E. W. T. 5: v E 1946 (1); v A 1945 (1); *v E 1937 (3)*
roup, G. B. 15: v A 1981 (2) 1985 (2); v WI 1979 (3); v In 1980 (2); v P 1978 (2); *v A 1980 (2); v WI 1984 (1); v In 1976 (1)*
ruscott, P. B. 1: v P 1964
urner, G. M. 41: v E 1970 (2) 1974 (2); v A 1973 (3) 1976 (2); v WI 1968 (3); v In 1975 (3); v P 1972 (3); v SL 1982 (2); *v E 1969 (2) 1973 (3); v A 1973 (2); v WI 1971 (5); v In 1969 (3) 1976 (3); v P 1969 (1) 1976 (2)*

ance, R. H. 1: v E 1987
vian, G. E. 5: *v WI 1971 (4); v In 1964 (1)*
vian, H. G. 7: v E 1932 (1); v SA 1931 (1); *v E 1931 (2) 1937 (3)*

Wadsworth, K. J. 33: v E 1970 (2) 1974 (2); v A 1973 (3); v In 1975 (3); v P 1972 (3); *v E 1969 (3) 1973 (3); v A 1973 (3); v WI 1971 (5); v In 1969 (3); v P 1969 (3)*
Wallace, W. M. 13: v E 1946 (1) 1950 (2); v A 1945 (1); v SA 1952 (2); *v E 1937 (3) 1949 (4)*
Ward, J. T. 8: v SA 1963 (1); v In 1967 (1); v P 1964 (1); *v E 1965 (1); v In 1964 (4)*
Watson, W. 2: *v E 1986 (2)*
Watt, L. 1: v E 1954
Webb, M. G. 3: v E 1970 (1); v A 1973 (1); *v WI 1971 (1)*
Webb, P. N. 2: v WI 1979 (2)
Weir, G. L. 11: v E 1929 (3) 1932 (2); v SA 1931 (2); *v E 1931 (3) 1937 (1)*
Whitelaw, P. E. 2: v E 1932 (2)
Wright, J. G. 58: v E 1977 (3) 1983 (3) 1987 (3); v A 1981 (3) 1985 (2); v WI 1979 (3) 1986 (3); v In 1980 (3); v P 1978 (3) 1984 (3); v SL 1982 (2); *v E 1978 (2) 1983 (3) 1986 (3); v A 1980 (3) 1985 (3) 1987 (3); v WI 1984 (4); v P 1984 (3); v SL 1983 (3)*

Yuile, B. W. 17: v E 1962 (2); v WI 1968 (3); v In 1967 (1); v P 1964 (3); *v E 1965 (1); v In 1964 (3) 1969 (1); v P 1964 (1) 1969 (2)*

INDIA

Number of Test cricketers: 182

Abid Ali, S. 29: v E 1972 (4); v A 1969 (1); v WI 1974 (2); v NZ 1969 (3); *v E 1971 (3) 1974 (3); v A 1967 (4); v WI 1970 (5); v NZ 1967 (4)*
Adhikari, H. R. 21: v E 1951 (3); v A 1956 (2); v WI 1948 (5) 1958 (1); v P 1952 (2); *v E 1952 (3); v A 1947 (5)*
Amarnath, L. 24: v E 1933 (3) 1951 (3); v WI 1948 (5); v P 1952 (5); *v E 1946 (3); v A 1947 (5)*
Amarnath, M. 69: v E 1976 (2) 1984 (5); v A 1969 (1) 1979 (1) 1986 (3); v WI 1978 (2) 1983 (3) 1987 (3); v NZ 1976 (3); v P 1983 (2) 1986 (5); v SL 1986 (2); *v E 1979 (2) 1986 (2); v A 1977 (5) 1985 (3); v WI 1975 (4) 1982 (5); v NZ 1975 (3); v P 1978 (3) 1982 (6) 1984 (2); v SL 1985 (2)*
Amarnath, S. 10: v E 1976 (2): *v WI 1975 (2); v NZ 1975 (3); v P 1978 (3)*
Amar Singh 7: v E 1933 (3); *v E 1932 (1) 1936 (3)*
Amir Elahi 1: *v A 1947*
Apte, A. L. 1: *v E 1959*
Apte, M. L. 7: v P 1952 (2); *v WI 1952 (5)*
Arshad Ayub 4: v WI (4)
Arun, B. 2: v SL 1986 (2)
Arun Lal 9: v WI 1987 (4); v P 1986 (1); v SL 1982 (1); *v P 1982 (3)*
Azad, K. 7: v E 1981 (3); v WI 1983 (2); v P 1983 (1); *v NZ 1980 (1)*
Azharuddin, M. 24: v E 1984 (3); v A 1986 (3); v WI 1987 (3); v P 1986 (5); v SL 1986 (1); *v E 1986 (3); v A 1985 (3); v SL 1985 (3)*

Baig, A. A. 10: v A 1959 (3); v WI 1966 (2); v P 1960 (3); *v E 1959 (2)*
Banerjee, S. A. 1: v WI 1948
Banerjee, S. N. 1: v WI 1948
Baqa Jilani, M. 1: *v E 1936*
Bedi, B. S. 67: v E 1972 (5) 1976 (5); v A 1969 (5); v WI 1966 (2) 1974 (4) 1978 (3); v NZ 1969 (3) 1976 (3); *v E 1967 (3) 1971 (3) 1974 (3) 1979 (3); v A 1967 (2) 1977 (5); v WI 1970 (5) 1975 (4); v NZ 1967 (4) 1975 (2); v P 1978 (3)*
Bhandari, P. 3: v A 1956 (1); v NZ 1955 (1); *v P 1954 (1)*
Bhat, A. R. 2: v WI 1983 (1); v P 1983 (1)
Binny, R. M. H. 27: v E 1979 (1); v WI 1983 (6); v P 1979 (6) 1983 (2) 1986 (3); *v E 1986 (3); v A 1980 (1) 1985 (2); v NZ 1980 (1); v P 1984 (1); v SL 1985 (1)*
Borde, C. G. 55: v E 1961 (5) 1963 (5); v A 1959 (5) 1964 (3) 1969 (1); v WI 1958 (4) 1966 (3); v NZ 1964 (4); v P 1960 (5); *v E 1959 (4) 1967 (3); v A 1967 (4); v WI 1961 (5); v NZ 1967 (4)*

Chandrasekhar, B. S. 58: v E 1963 (4) 1972 (5) 1976 (5); v A 1964 (2); v WI 1966 (3) 1974 (4) 19[illegible] (4); v NZ 1964 (2) 1976 (3); *v E 1967 (3) 1971 (3) 1974 (2) 1979 (1); v A 1967 (2) 1977 (5); v W[illegible] 1975 (4); v NZ 1975 (3); v P 1978 (3)*
Chauhan, C. P. S. 40: v E 1972 (2); v A 1969 (1) 1979 (6); v WI 1978 (6); v NZ 1969 (2); v P 19[illegible] (6); *v E 1979 (4); v A 1977 (4) 1980 (3); v NZ 1980 (3); v P 1978 (3)*

Chowdhury, N. R. 2: v E 1951 (1); v WI 1948 (1)
Colah, S. H. M. 2: v E 1933 (1); *v E 1932 (1)*
Contractor, N. J. 31: v E 1961 (5); v A 1956 (1) 1959 (5); v WI 1958 (5); v NZ 1955 (4); v P 1960 (5); *v E 1959 (4); v WI 1961 (2)*

Dani, H. T. 1: v P 1952
Desai, R. B. 28: v E 1961 (4) 1963 (2); v A 1959 (3); v WI 1958 (1); v NZ 1964 (3); v P 1960 (5); *v E 1959 (5); v A 1967 (1); v WI 1961 (3); v NZ 1967 (1)*
Dilawar Hussain 3: v E 1933 (2); *v E 1936 (1)*
Divecha, R. V. 5: v E 1951 (2); v P 1952 (1); *v E 1952 (2)*
Doshi, D. R. 33: v E 1979 (1) 1981 (6); v A 1979 (6); v P 1979 (6) 1983 (1); v SL 1982 (1); *v E 1982 (3); v A 1980 (3); v NZ 1980 (2); v P 1982 (4)*
Durani, S. A. 29: v E 1961 (5) 1963 (5) 1972 (3); v A 1959 (1) 1964 (3); v WI 1966 (1); v NZ 1964 (3); *v WI 1961 (5) 1970 (3)*

Engineer, F. M. 46: v E 1961 (4) 1972 (5); v A 1969 (5); v WI 1966 (1) 1974 (5); v NZ 1964 (4) 1969 (2); *v E 1967 (3) 1971 (3) 1974 (3); v A 1967 (4); v WI 1961 (3); v NZ 1967 (4)*

Gadkari, C. V. 6: *v WI 1952 (3); v P 1954 (3)*
Gaekwad, A. D. 40: v E 1976 (4) 1984 (3); v WI 1974 (3) 1978 (5) 1983 (6); v NZ 1976 (3); v P 1983 (3); *v E 1979 (2); v A 1977 (1); v WI 1975 (3) 1982 (5); v P 1984 (2)*
Gaekwad, D. K. 11: v WI 1958 (1); v P 1952 (2) 1960 (1); *v E 1952 (1) 1959 (4); v WI 1952 (2)*
Gaekwad, H. G. 1: v P 1952
Gandotra, A. 2: v A 1969 (1); v NZ 1969 (1)
Gavaskar, S. M. 125: v E 1972 (5) 1976 (5) 1979 (1) 1981 (6) 1984 (5); v A 1979 (6) 1986 (3); v WI 1974 (2) 1978 (6) 1983 (6); v NZ 1976 (3); v P 1979 (6) 1983 (3) 1986 (4); v SL 1982 (1) 1986 (3); *v E 1971 (3) 1974 (3) 1979 (4) 1982 (3) 1986 (3); v A 1977 (5) 1980 (3) 1985 (3); v WI 1970 (4) 1975 (4) 1982 (5); v NZ 1975 (3) 1980 (3); v P 1978 (3) 1982 (6) 1984 (2); v SL 1985 (3)*
Ghavri, K. D. 39: v E 1976 (3) 1979 (1); v A 1979 (6); v WI 1974 (3) 1978 (6); v NZ 1976 (2); v P 1979 (6); *v E 1979 (4); v A 1977 (3) 1980 (3); v NZ 1980 (1); v P 1978 (1)*
Ghorpade, J. M. 8: v A 1956 (1); v WI 1958 (1); v NZ 1955 (1); *v E 1959 (3); v WI 1952 (2)*
Ghulam Ahmed 22: v E 1951 (2); v A 1956 (2); v WI 1948 (3) 1958 (2); v NZ 1955 (1); v P 1952 (4); *v E 1952 (4); v P 1954 (4)*
Gopalan, M. J. 1: v E 1933
Gopinath, C. D. 8: v E 1951 (3); v A 1959 (1); v P 1952 (1); *v E 1952 (1); v P 1954 (2)*
Guard, G. M. 2: v A 1959 (1); v WI 1958 (1)
Guha, S. 4: v A 1969 (3); *v E 1967 (1)*
Gul Mahomed 8: v P 1952 (2); *v E 1946 (1); v A 1947 (5)*
Gupte, B. P. 3: v E 1963 (1); v NZ 1964 (1); v P 1960 (1)
Gupte, S. P. 36: v E 1951 (1) 1961 (2); v A 1956 (3); v WI 1958 (5); v NZ 1955 (5); v P 1952 (2) 1960 (3); *v E 1959 (5); v WI 1952 (5); v P 1954 (5)*

Hafeez, A. 3: *v E 1946 (3)*
Hanumant Singh 14: v E 1963 (2); v A 1964 (3); v WI 1966 (2); v NZ 1964 (4) 1969 (1); *v E 1967 (2)*
Hardikar, M. S. 2: v WI 1958 (2)
Hazare, V. S. 30: v E 1951 (5); v WI 1948 (5); v P 1952 (3); *v E 1946 (3) 1952 (4); v A 1947 (5); v WI 1952 (5)*
Hindlekar, D. D. 4: *v E 1936 (1) 1946 (3)*
Hirwani, N. D. 1: v WI 1987

Ibrahim, K. C. 4: v WI 1948 (4)
Indrajitsinhji, K. S. 4: v A 1964 (3); v NZ 1969 (1)
Irani, J. K. 2: *v A 1947 (2)*

Jahangir Khan, M. 4: *v E 1932 (1) 1936 (3)*
Jai, L. P. 1: v E 1933
Jaisimha, M. L. 39: v E 1961 (5) 1963 (5); v A 1959 (1) 1964 (3); v WI 1966 (2); v NZ 1964 (4) 1969 (1); v P 1960 (4); *v E 1959 (1); v A 1967 (2); v WI 1961 (4) 1970 (3); v NZ 1967 (4)*
Jamshedji, R. J. 1: v E 1933
Jayantilal, K. 1: *v WI 1970*

Joshi, P. G. 12: v E 1951 (2); v A 1959 (1); v WI 1958 (1); v P 1952 (1) 1960 (1); *v E 1959 (3); v WI 1952 (3)*

Kanitkar, H. S. 2: v WI 1974 (2)
Kapil Dev 92: v E 1979 (1) 1981 (6) 1984 (4); v A 1979 (6) 1986 (3); v WI 1978 (6) 1983 (6) 198 (4); v P 1979 (6) 1983 (3) 1986 (5); v SL 1982 (1) 1986 (3); *v E 1979 (4) 1982 (3) 1986 (3); v A 1980 (3) 1985 (3); v WI 1982 (5); v NZ 1980 (3); v P 1978 (3) 1982 (6) 1984 (2); v SL 1985 (3)*
Kardar, A. H. (*see* Hafeez)
Kenny, R. B. 5: v A 1959 (4); v WI 1958 (1)
Kirmani, S. M. H. 88: v E 1976 (5) 1979 (1) 1981 (6) 1984 (5); v A 1979 (6); v WI 1978 (6) 198 (6); v NZ 1976 (3); v P 1979 (6) 1983 (3); v SL 1982 (1); *v E 1982 (3); v A 1977 (5) 1980 (3) 198 (3); v WI 1975 (4) 1982 (5); v NZ 1975 (3) 1980 (3); v P 1978 (3) 1982 (6) 1984 (2)*
Kischenchand, G. 5: v P 1952 (1); *v A 1947 (4)*
Kripal Singh, A. G. 14: v E 1961 (3) 1963 (2); v A 1956 (2) 1964 (1); v WI 1958 (1); v NZ 195 (4); *v E 1959 (1)*
Krishnamurthy, P. 5: *v WI 1970 (5)*
Kulkarni, R. R. 3: v A 1986 (1); v P 1986 (2)
Kulkarni, U. N. 4: *v A 1967 (3); v NZ 1967 (1)*
Kumar, V. V. 2: v E 1961 (1); v P 1960 (1)
Kunderan, B. K. 18: v E 1961 (1) 1963 (5); v A 1959 (3); v WI 1966 (2); v NZ 1964 (1); v P 196 (2); *v E 1967 (2); v WI 1961 (2)*

Lall Singh 1: *v E 1932*
Lamba, R. 4: v WI 1987 (1); v SL 1986 (3)

Madan Lal 39: v E 1976 (2) 1981 (6); v WI 1974 (2) 1983 (3); v NZ 1976 (1); v P 1983 (3); v S 1982 (1); *v E 1974 (2) 1982 (3) 1986 (1); v A 1977 (2); v WI 1975 (4) 1982 (2); v NZ 1975 (3); v 1982 (3) 1984 (1)*
Maka, E. S. 2: v P 1952 (1); *v WI 1952 (1)*
Malhotra, A. 7: v E 1981 (2) 1984 (1); v WI 1983 (3); *v E 1982 (1)*
Maninder Singh 31: v A 1986 (3); v WI 1983 (4) 1987 (3); v P 1986 (4); v SL 1986 (3); *v E 19 (3); v WI 1982 (3); v P 1982 (5) 1984 (1); v SL 1985 (2)*
Manjrekar, S. V. 1: v WI 1987
Manjrekar, V. L. 55: v E 1951 (2) 1961 (5) 1963 (4); v A 1956 (3) 1964 (3); v WI 1958 (4); v N 1955 (5) 1964 (1); v P 1952 (3) 1960 (5); *v E 1952 (4) 1959 (2); v WI 1952 (4) 1961 (5); v 1954 (5)*
Mankad, A. V. 22: v E 1976 (1); v A 1969 (5); v WI 1974 (1); v NZ 1969 (2) 1976 (3); *v E 1971 1974 (1); v A 1977 (3); v WI 1970 (3)*
Mankad, V. 44: v E 1951 (5); v A 1956 (3); v WI 1948 (5) 1958 (2); v NZ 1955 (4); v P 1952 (4) *E 1946 (3) 1952 (3); v A 1947 (5); v WI 1952 (5); v P 1954 (5)*
Mansur Ali Khan (*see* Pataudi)
Mantri, M. K. 4: v E 1951 (1); *v E 1952 (2); v P 1954 (1)*
Meherhomji, K. R. 1: *v E 1936*
Mehra, V. L. 8: v E 1961 (1) 1963 (2); v NZ 1955 (2); *v WI 1961 (3)*
Merchant, V. M. 10: v E 1933 (3) 1951 (1); *v E 1936 (3) 1946 (3)*
Milkha Singh, A. G. 4: v E 1961 (1); v A 1959 (1); v P 1960 (2)
Modi, R. S. 10: v E 1951 (1); v WI 1948 (5); v P 1952 (1); *v E 1946 (3)*
More, K. S. 17: v A 1986 (2); v WI 1987 (4); v P 1986 (5); v SL 1986 (3); *v E 1986 (3)*
Muddiah, V. M. 2: v A 1959 (1); v P 1960 (1)
Mushtaq Ali, S. 11: v E 1933 (2) 1951 (1); v WI 1948 (3); *v E 1936 (3) 1946 (2)*

Nadkarni, R. G. 41: v E 1961 (1) 1963 (5); v A 1959 (5) 1964 (3); v WI 1958 (1) 1966 (1); v 1955 (1) 1964 (4); v P 1960 (4); *v E 1959 (4); v A 1967 (3); v WI 1961 (5); v NZ 1967*
Naik, S. S. 3: v WI 1974 (2); *v E 1974 (1)*
Naoomal Jeoomal 3: v E 1933 (2); *v E 1932 (1)*
Narasimha Rao, M. V. 4: v A 1979 (2); v WI 1978 (2)
Navle, J. G. 2: v E 1933 (1); *v E 1932 (1)*
Nayak, S. V. 2: *v E 1982 (2)*
Nayudu, C. K. 7: v E 1933 (3); *v E 1932 (1) 1936 (3)*
Nayudu, C. S. 11: v E 1933 (2) 1951 (1); *v E 1936 (2) 1946 (2); v A 1947 (4)*
Nazir Ali, S. 2: v E 1933 (1); *v E 1932 (1)*
Nissar, Mahomed 6: v E 1933 (2); *v E 1932 (1) 1936 (3)*
Nyalchand, S. 1: v P 1952

Pai, A. M. 1: v NZ 1969
Palia, P. E. 2: *v E 1932 (1) 1936 (1)*
Pandit, C. S. 3: v A 1986 (2); *v E 1986 (1)*
Parkar, G. A. 1: *v E 1982*
Parkar, R. D. 2: v E 1972 (2)
Parsana, D. D. 2: v WI 1978 (2)
Patankar, C. T. 1: v NZ 1955
Pataudi sen., Nawab of, 3: *v E 1946 (3)*
Pataudi jun., Nawab of (now Mansur Ali Khan) 46: v E 1961 (3) 1963 (5) 1972 (3); v A 1964 (3) 1969 (5); v WI 1966 (3) 1974 (4); v NZ 1964 (4) 1969 (3); *v E 1967 (3); v A 1967 (3); v WI 1961 (3); v NZ 1967 (4)*
Patel, B. P. 21: v E 1976 (5); v WI 1974 (3); v NZ 1976 (3); *v E 1974 (2); v A 1977 (2); v WI 1975 (3); v NZ 1975 (3)*
Patel, J. M. 7: v A 1956 (2) 1959 (3); v NZ 1955 (1); *v P 1954 (1)*
Patiala, Yuvraj of, 1: v E 1933
Patil, S. M. 29: v E 1979 (1) 1981 (4) 1984 (2); v WI 1983 (2); v P 1979 (2) 1983 (3); v SL 1982 (1); *v E 1982 (2); v A 1980 (3); v NZ 1980 (3); v P 1982 (4) 1984 (2)*
Patil, S. R. 1: v NZ 1955
Phadkar, D. G. 31: v E 1951 (4); v A 1956 (1); v WI 1948 (4) 1958 (1); v NZ 1955 (4); v P 1952 (2); *v E 1952 (4); v A 1947 (4); v WI 1952 (4); v P 1954 (3)*
Prabhakar, M. 2: v E 1984 (2)
Prasanna, E. A. S. 49: v E 1961 (1) 1972 (3) 1976 (4); v A 1969 (5); v WI 1966 (1) 1974 (5); v NZ 1969 (3); *v E 1967 (3) 1974 (2); v A 1967 (4) 1977 (4); v WI 1961 (1) 1970 (3) 1975 (1); v NZ 1967 (4) 1975 (3); v P 1978 (2)*
Punjabi, P. H. 5: *v P 1954 (5)*

Rai Singh, K. 1: *v A 1947*
Rajinder Pal 1: v E 1963
Rajindernath, V. 1: v P 1952
Rajput, L. S. 2: *v SL 1985 (2)*
Raman, W. V. 1: v WI 1987
Ramaswami, C. 2: *v E 1936 (2)*
Ramchand, G. S. 33: v A 1956 (3) 1959 (5); v WI 1958 (3); v NZ 1955 (5); v P 1952 (3); *v E 1952 (4); v WI 1952 (5); v P 1954 (5)*
Ramji, L. 1: v E 1933
Rangachary, C. R. 4: v WI 1948 (2); *v A 1947 (2)*
Rangnekar, K. M. 3: *v A 1947 (3)*
Ranjane, V. B. 7: v E 1961 (3) 1963 (1); v A 1964 (1); v WI 1958 (1); *v WI 1961 (1)*
Reddy, B. 4: *v E 1979 (4)*
Rege, M. R. 1: v WI 1948
Roy, A. 4: v A 1969 (2); v NZ 1969 (2)
Roy, Pankaj 43: v E 1951 (5); v A 1956 (3) 1959 (5); v WI 1958 (5); v NZ 1955 (3); v P 1952 (3) 1960 (1); *v E 1952 (4) 1959 (5); v WI 1952 (4); v P 1954 (5)*
Roy, Pranab 2: v E 1981 (2)

Sandhu, B. S. 8: v WI 1983 (1); *v WI 1982 (4); v P 1982 (3)*
Sardesai, D. N. 30: v E 1961 (1) 1963 (5) 1972 (1); v A 1964 (3) 1969 (1); v WI 1966 (2); v NZ 1964 (3); *v E 1967 (1) 1971 (3); v A 1967 (2); v WI 1961 (3) 1970 (5)*
Sarwate, C. T. 9: v E 1951 (1); v WI 1948 (2); *v E 1946 (1); v A 1947 (5)*
Saxena, R. C. 1: *v E 1967*
Sekar, T. A. P. 2: *v P 1982 (2)*
Sen, P. 14: v E 1951 (2); v WI 1948 (5); v P 1952 (2); *v E 1952 (2); v A 1947 (3)*
Sengupta, A. K. 1: v WI 1958
Sharma, Ajay 1: v WI 1987
Sharma, Chetan 19: v E 1984 (3); v A 1986 (2); v WI 1987 (3); v SL 1986 (2); *v E 1986 (2); v A 1985 (2); v P 1984 (2); v SL 1985 (3)*
Sharma, Gopal 4: v E 1984 (1); v P 1986 (2); *v SL 1985 (1)*
Sharma, P. 5: v E 1976 (2); v WI 1974 (2); *v WI 1975 (1)*
Shastri, R. J. 58: v E 1981 (6) 1984 (5); v A 1986 (3); v WI 1983 (6) 1987 (4); v P 1983 (2) 1986 (5); v SL 1986 (3); *v E 1982 (3) 1986 (3); v A 1985 (3); v WI 1982 (5); v NZ 1980 (3); v P 1982 (2) 1984 (2); v SL 1985 (3)*
Shinde, S. G. 7: v E 1951 (3); v WI 1948 (1); *v E 1946 (1) 1952 (2)*

Shodhan, R. H. 3: v P 1952 (1); *v WI 1952 (2)*
Shukla, R. C. 1: v SL 1982
Sidhu, N. S. 2: v WI 1983 (2)
Sivaramakrishnan, L. 9: v E 1984 (5); *v A 1985 (2); v WI 1982 (1); v SL 1985 (1)*
Sohoni, S. W. 4: v E 1951 (1); *v E 1946 (2); v A 1947 (1)*
Solkar, E. D. 27: v E 1972 (5) 1976 (1); v A 1969 (4); v WI 1974 (4); v NZ 1969 (1); *v E 1971 (3) 1974 (3); v WI 1970 (5) 1975 (1)*
Sood, M. M. 1: v A 1959
Srikkanth, K. 32: v E 1981 (4) 1984 (2); v A 1986 (3); v WI 1987 (4); v P 1986 (5); v SL 1986 (3); *v E 1986 (3); v A 1985 (3); v P 1982 (2); v SL 1985 (3)*
Srinivasan, T. E. 1: *v NZ 1980*
Subramanya, V. 9: v WI 1966 (2); v NZ 1964 (1); *v E 1967 (2); v A 1967 (2); v NZ 1967 (2)*
Sunderram, G. 2: v NZ 1955 (2)
Surendranath, R. 11: v A 1959 (2); v WI 1958 (2); v P 1960 (2); *v E 1959 (5)*
Surti, R. F. 26: v E 1963 (1); v A 1964 (2) 1969 (1); v WI 1966 (2); v NZ 1964 (1) 1969 (2); v P 1960 (2); *v E 1967 (2); v A 1967 (4); v WI 1961 (5); v NZ 1967 (4)*
Swamy, V. N. 1: v NZ 1955

Tamhane, N. S. 21: v A 1956 (3) 1959 (1); v WI 1958 (4); v NZ 1955 (4); v P 1960 (2); *v E 1959 (2); v P 1954 (5)*
Tarapore, K. K. 1: v WI 1948

Umrigar, P. R. 59: v E 1951 (5) 1961 (4); v A 1956 (3) 1959 (3); v WI 1948 (1) 1958 (5); v NZ 1955 (5); v P 1952 (5) 1960 (5); *v E 1952 (4) 1959 (4); v WI 1952 (5) 1961 (5); v P 1954 (5*

Vengsarkar, D. B. 98: v E 1976 (1) 1979 (1) 1981 (6) 1984 (5); v A 1979 (6) 1986 (2); v WI 1978 (6 1983 (5) 1987 (3); v P 1979 (5) 1983 (1) 1986 (5); v SL 1982 (1) 1986 (3); *v E 1979 (4) 1982 (3 1986 (3); v A 1977 (5) 1980 (3) 1985 (3); v WI 1975 (2) 1982 (5); v NZ 1975 (3) 1980 (3); v P 197 (3) 1982 (6) 1984 (2); v SL 1985 (3)*
Venkataraghavan, S. 57: v E 1972 (2) 1976 (1); v A 1969 (5) 1979 (3); v WI 1966 (2) 1974 (2) 197 (6); v NZ 1964 (4) 1969 (2) 1976 (3); v P 1983 (2); *v E 1967 (1) 1971 (3) 1974 (2) 1979 (4); v 1977 (1); v WI 1970 (5) 1975 (3) 1982 (5); v NZ 1975 (1)*
Viswanath, G. R. 91: v E 1972 (5) 1976 (5) 1979 (1) 1981 (6); v A 1969 (4) 1979 (6); v WI 1974 (1978 (6); v NZ 1976 (3); v SL 1982 (1); v P 1979 (6); *v E 1971 (3) 1974 (3) 1979 (4) 1982 (3); v 1977 (5) 1980 (3); v WI 1970 (3) 1975 (4); v NZ 1975 (3) 1980 (3); v P 1978 (3) 1982 (6*
Viswanath, S. 3: *v SL 1985 (3)*
Vizianagram, Maharaj Sir Vijaya 3: *v E 1936 (3)*

Wadekar, A. L. 37: v E 1972 (5); v A 1969 (5); v WI 1966 (2); v NZ 1969 (3); *v E 1967 (3) 1971 (1974 (3); v A 1967 (4); v WI 1970 (5); v NZ 1967 (4)*
Wazir Ali, S. 7: v E 1933 (3); *v E 1932 (1) 1936 (3)*

Yadav, N. S. 35: v E 1979 (1) 1981 (1) 1984 (4); v A 1979 (5) 1986 (3); v WI 1983 (3); v P 1979 (1986 (4); v SL 1986 (2); *v A 1980 (2) 1985 (3); v NZ 1980 (1); v P 1984 (1)*
Yajurvindra Singh 4: v E 1976 (2); v A 1979 (1); *v E 1979 (1)*
Yashpal Sharma 37: v E 1979 (1) 1981 (2); v A 1979 (6); v WI 1983 (1); v P 1979 (6) 1983 (v SL 1982 (1); *v E 1979 (3) 1982 (3); v A 1980 (3); v WI 1982 (5); v NZ 1980 (1); v P 1982*
Yograj Singh 1: *v NZ 1980*

Note: Hafeez, on going later to Oxford University, took his correct name, Kardar.

PAKISTAN

Number of Test cricketers: 108

Aamer Malik 3: v E 1987 (2); *v WI 1987 (1)*
Abdul Kadir 4: v A 1964 (1); *v A 1964 (1); v NZ 1964 (2)*
Abdul Qadir 54: v E 1977 (3) 1983 (3) 1987 (3); v A 1982 (3); v WI 1980 (2) 1986 (3); v NZ 1 (3); v In 1982 (5) 1984 (1); v SL 1985 (3); *v E 1982 (3) 1987 (4); v A 1983 (5); v WI 1987 v NZ 1984 (2); v In 1979 (3) 1986 (3); v SL 1985 (2)*

ˋfaq Hussain 2: v E 1961 (1); *v A 1964 (1)*
ˋftab Baloch 2: v WI 1974 (1); v NZ 1969 (1)
ˋftab Gul 6: v E 1968 (2); v NZ 1969 (1); *v E 1971 (3)*
ˋgha Saadat Ali 1: v NZ 1955
ˋgha Zahid 1: v WI 1974
ˋlim-ud-Din 25: v E 1961 (2); v A 1956 (1) 1959 (1); v WI 1958 (1); v NZ 1955 (3); v In 1954 (5); *v E 1954 (3) 1962 (3); v WI 1957 (5); v In 1960 (1)*
mir Elahi 5: *v In 1952 (5)*
nil Dalpat 9: v E 1983 (3); v NZ 1984 (3); *v NZ 1984 (3)*
nwar Hussain 4: *v In 1952 (4)*
nwar Khan 1: *v NZ 1978*
rif Butt 3: *v A 1964 (1); v NZ 1964 (2)*
shraf Ali 8: v E 1987 (3); v In 1984 (2); v SL 1981 (2) 1985 (1)
sif Iqbal 58: v E 1968 (3) 1972 (3); v A 1964 (1); v WI 1974 (2); v NZ 1964 (3) 1969 (3) 1976 (3); v In 1978 (3); *v E 1967 (3) 1971 (3) 1974 (3); v A 1964 (1) 1972 (3) 1976 (3) 1978 (2); v WI 1976 (5); v NZ 1964 (3) 1972 (3) 1978 (2); v In 1979 (6)*
sif Masood 16: v E 1968 (2) 1972 (1); v WI 1974 (2); v NZ 1969 (1); *v E 1971 (3) 1974 (3); v A 1972 (3) 1976 (1)*
sif Mujtaba 3: v E 1987 (1); v WI 1986 (2)
zeem Hafeez 18: v E 1983 (2); v NZ 1984 (3); v In 1984 (2); *v A 1983 (5); v NZ 1984 (3); v In 1983 (3)*
zhar Khan 1: v A 1979
zmat Rana 1: v A 1979

rki, J. 25: v E 1961 (3); v A 1964 (1); v NZ 1964 (3) 1969 (1); *v E 1962 (5) 1967 (3); v A 1964 (1); v NZ 1964 (3); v In 1960 (5)*

Souza, A. 6: v E 1961 (2); v WI 1958 (1); *v E 1962 (3)*

tesham-ud-Din 5: v A 1979 (1); *v E 1982 (1); v In 1979 (3)*

rooq Hamid 1: *v A 1964*
rrukh Zaman 1: v NZ 1976
zal Mahmood 34: v E 1961 (1); v A 1956 (1) 1959 (2); v WI 1958 (3); v NZ 1955 (2); v In 1954 4); *v E 1954 (4) 1962 (2); v WI 1957 (5); v In 1952 (5) 1960 (5)*

azali, M. E. Z. 2: *v E 1954 (2)*
ulam Abbas 1: *v E 1967*
l Mahomed 1: v A 1956

nif Mohammad 55: v E 1961 (3) 1968 (3); v A 1956 (1) 1959 (3) 1964 (1); v WI 1958 (1); v NZ 955 (3) 1964 (3) 1969 (1); v In 1954 (5); *v E 1954 (4) 1962 (5) 1967 (3); v A 1964 (1); v WI 1957 5); v NZ 1964 (3); v In 1952 (5) 1960 (5)*
oon Rashid 23: v E 1977 (3); v A 1979 (2) 1982 (3); v In 1982 (1); v SL 1981 (2); *v E 1978 (3) 982 (1); v A 1976 (1) 1978 (1); v WI 1976 (5); v NZ 1978 (1)*
eeb Ahsan 12: v E 1961 (2); v A 1959 (1); v WI 1958 (1); *v WI 1957 (3); v In 1960 (5)*

dulla, K. 4: v A 1964 (1); *v E 1967 (2); v NZ 1964 (1)*
Ahmed 10: v E 1987 (3); *v E 1987 (4); v WI 1987 (2); v In 1986 (1)*
Butt 8: v A 1959 (2); v WI 1958 (3); *v E 1962 (3)*
Faqih 5: v WI 1980 (1); *v A 1981 (1); v WI 1987 (2); v In 1986 (1)*
an Khan 73: v A 1979 (2) 1982 (3); v WI 1980 (4) 1986 (3); v NZ 1976 (3); v In 1978 (3) 1982); v SL 1981 (1) 1985 (3); *v E 1971 (1) 1974 (3) 1982 (3) 1987 (5); v A 1976 (3) 1978 (2) 1981 (3) 83 (2); v WI 1976 (5) 1987 (3); v NZ 1978 (2); v In 1979 (5) 1986 (5); v SL 1985 (3)*
az Ahmed 41: v E 1961 (3); v A 1956 (1) 1959 (3); v WI 1958 (3); v NZ 1955 (3); v In 1954); *v E 1954 (4) 1962 (4); v WI 1957 (5); v In 1952 (5) 1960 (5)*
thab Alam 47: v E 1961 (2) 1968 (3) 1972 (3); v A 1959 (1) 1964 (1); v WI 1974 (2); v NZ 64 (3) 1969 (3) 1976 (3); *v E 1962 (3) 1967 (3) 1971 (3) 1974 (3); v A 1964 (1) 1972 (3); v WI 76 (1); v NZ 1964 (3) 1972 (3); v In 1960 (3)*
l Qasim 47: v E 1977 (3) 1987 (3); v A 1979 (3) 1982 (2); v WI 1980 (4); v NZ 1984 (3); v In 78 (3) 1982 (2); v SL 1981 (3); *v E 1978 (3); v A 1976 (3) 1981 (2); v WI 1976 (2); v NZ 1984 ; v In 1979 (6) 1983 (1) 1986 (3)*
Ali 4: v A 1959 (2); *v In 1952 (2)*

Jalal-ud-Din 6: v A 1982 (1); v In 1982 (2) 1984 (2); v SL 1985 (1)
Javed Akhtar 1: *v E 1962*
Javed Miandad 92: v E 1977 (3) 1987 (3); v A 1979 (3) 1982 (3); v WI 1980 (4) 1986 (3); v NZ 1976 (3) 1984 (3); v In 1978 (3) 1982 (6) 1984 (2); v SL 1981 (3) 1985 (3); *v E 1978 (3) 1982 (3) 1987 (5); v A 1976 (3) 1978 (2) 1981 (3) 1983 (5); v WI 1976 (1) 1987 (3); v NZ 1978 (3) 1984 (3); v In 1979 (6) 1983 (3) 1986 (4); v SL 1985 (3)*

Kardar, A. H. 23: v A 1956 (1); v NZ 1955 (3); v In 1954 (5); *v E 1954 (4); v WI 1957 (5); v In 1952 (5)*
Khalid Hassan 1: *v E 1954*
Khalid Wazir 2: *v E 1954 (2)*
Khan Mohammad 13: v A 1956 (1); v NZ 1955 (3); v In 1954 (4); *v E 1954 (2); v WI 1957 (2); v In 1952 (1)*

Liaqat Ali 5: v E 1977 (2); v WI 1974 (1); *v E 1978 (2)*

Mahmood Hussain 27: v E 1961 (1); v WI 1958 (3); v NZ 1955 (1); v In 1954 (5); *v E 1954 (2) 1962 (3); v WI 1957 (3); v In 1952 (4) 1960 (5)*
Majid Khan 63: v E 1968 (3) 1972 (3); v A 1964 (1) 1979 (3); v WI 1974 (2) 1980 (4); v NZ 1964 (3) 1976 (3); v In 1978 (3) 1982 (1); v SL 1981 (1); *v E 1967 (3) 1971 (2) 1974 (3) 1982 (1); v A 1972 (3) 1976 (3) 1978 (2) 1981 (3); v WI 1976 (5); v NZ 1972 (3) 1978 (2); v In 1979 (6)*
Mansoor Akhtar 18: v A 1982 (3); v WI 1980 (2); v In 1982 (3); v SL 1981 (1); *v E 1982 (3) 1987 (5); v A 1981 (1)*
Manzoor Elahi 4: v NZ 1984 (1); v In 1984 (1); *v In 1986 (2)*
Maqsood Ahmed 16: v NZ 1955 (2); v In 1954 (5); *v E 1954 (4); v In 1952 (5)*
Mathias, Wallis 21: v E 1961 (1); v A 1956 (1) 1959 (2); v WI 1958 (3); v NZ 1955 (1); *v E 1962 (3); v WI 1957 (5); v In 1960 (5)*
Miran Bux 2: v In 1954 (2)
Mohammad Aslam 1: *v E 1954*
Mohammad Farooq 7: v NZ 1964 (3); *v E 1962 (2); v In 1960 (2)*
Mohammad Ilyas 10: v E 1968 (2); v NZ 1964 (3); *v E 1967 (1); v A 1964 (1); v NZ 1964 (3)*
Mohammad Munaf 4: v E 1961 (2); v A 1959 (2)
Mohammad Nazir 14: v E 1972 (1); v WI 1980 (4); v NZ 1969 (3); *v A 1983 (3); v In 1983 (3)*
Mohsin Kamal 7: v E 1983 (1); v SL 1985 (1); *v E 1987 (4); v SL 1985 (1)*
Mohsin Khan 48: v E 1977 (1) 1983 (3); v A 1982 (3); v WI 1986 (3); v NZ 1984 (2); v In 1982 (6) 1984 (2); v SL 1981 (2) 1985 (2); *v E 1978 (3) 1982 (3); v A 1978 (1) 1981 (2) 1983 (5); v NZ 1978 (1) 1984 (3); v In 1983 (3); v SL 1985 (3)*
Mudassar Nazar 71: v E 1977 (3) 1983 (1) 1987 (3); v A 1979 (3) 1982 (3); v WI 1986 (2); v NZ 1984 (3); v In 1978 (2) 1982 (6) 1984 (2); v SL 1981 (1) 1985 (3) ; *v E 1978 (3) 1982 (3) 1987 (5); v A 1976 (1) 1978 (1) 1981 (3) 1983 (5); v WI 1987 (3); v NZ 1978 (1) 1984 (3); v In 1979 (5) 1983 (3); v SL 1985 (3)*
Mufasir-ul-Haq 1: *v NZ 1964*
Munir Malik 3: v A 1959 (1); *v E 1962 (2)*
Mushtaq Mohammad 57: v E 1961 (3) 1968 (3) 1972 (3); v WI 1958 (1) 1974 (2); v NZ 1969 (2) 1976 (3); v In 1978 (3); *v E 1962 (5) 1967 (3) 1971 (3) 1974 (3); v A 1972 (3) 1976 (3) 1978 (2); v WI 1976 (5); v NZ 1972 (2) 1978 (3); v In 1960 (5)*

Nasim-ul-Ghani 29: v E 1961 (2); v A 1959 (2) 1964 (1); v WI 1958 (3); *v E 1962 (5) 1967 (2); v A 1964 (1) 1972 (1); v WI 1957 (5); v NZ 1964 (3); v In 1960 (4)*
Naushad Ali 6: v NZ 1964 (3); *v NZ 1964 (3)*
Nazar Mohammad 5: *v In 1952 (5)*
Nazir Junior (*see* Mohammad Nazir)
Niaz Ahmed 2: v E 1968 (1); *v E 1967 (1)*

Pervez Sajjad 19: v E 1968 (1) 1972 (2); v A 1964 (1); v NZ 1964 (3) 1969 (3); *v E 1971 (3); v NZ 1964 (3) 1972 (3)*

Qasim Omar 26: v E 1983 (3); v WI 1986 (3); v NZ 1984 (3); v In 1984 (2); v SL 1985 (3); *v A 1983 (5); v NZ 1984 (3); v In 1983 (1); v SL 1985 (3)*

Ramiz Raja 22: v E 1983 (2) 1987 (3); v WI 1986 (3); v SL 1985 (1); *v E 1987 (2); v WI 1987 (3); v In 1986 (5); v SL 1985 (3)*

Rashid Khan 4: v SL 1981 (2); *v A 1983 (1); v NZ 1984 (1)*
Rehman, S. F. 1: *v WI 1957*
Rizwan-uz-Zaman 9: v WI 1986 (1); v SL 1981 (2); *v A 1981 (1); v In 1986 (5)*

adiq Mohammad 41: v E 1972 (3) 1977 (2); v WI 1974 (1) 1980 (3); v NZ 1969 (3) 1976 (3); v In 1978 (1); *v E 1971 (3) 1974 (3) 1978 (3); v A 1972 (3) 1976 (2); v WI 1976 (5); v NZ 1972 (3); v In 1979 (3)*
aeed Ahmed 41: v E 1961 (3) 1968 (3); v A 1959 (3) 1964 (1); v WI 1958 (3); v NZ 1964 (3); *v E 1962 (5) 1967 (3) 1971 (1); v A 1964 (1) 1972 (2); v WI 1957 (5); v NZ 1964 (3); v In 1960 (5)*
alah-ud-Din 5: v E 1968 (1); v NZ 1964 (3) 1969 (1)
aleem Jaffer 5: v E 1987 (1); v WI 1986 (1); *v WI 1987 (1); v In 1986 (2)*
alim Altaf 21: v E 1972 (3); v NZ 1969 (2); v In 1978 (1); *v E 1967 (2) 1971 (2); v A 1972 (3) 1976 (2); v WI 1976 (3); v NZ 1972 (3)*
alim Malik 47: v E 1983 (3) 1987 (3); v WI 1986 (1); v NZ 1984 (3); v In 1982 (6) 1984 (2); v SL 1981 (2) 1985 (3); *v E 1987 (5); v A 1983 (3); v WI 1987 (3); v NZ 1984 (3); v In 1983 (2) 1986 (5); v SL 1985 (3)*
alim Yousuf 19: v WI 1986 (3); v SL 1981 (1) 1985 (2); *v E 1987 (5); v WI 1987 (3); v In 1986 (5)*
arfraz Nawaz 55: v E 1968 (1) 1972 (2) 1977 (2) 1983 (3); v A 1979 (3); v WI 1974 (2) 1980 (2); v NZ 1976 (3); v In 1978 (3) 1982 (6); *v E 1974 (3) 1978 (2) 1982 (1); v A 1972 (2) 1976 (2) 1978 (2) 1981 (3) 1983 (3); v WI 1976 (4); v NZ 1972 (3) 1978 (3)*
afiq Ahmad 6: v E 1977 (3); v WI 1980 (2); *v E 1974 (1)*
afqat Rana 5: v E 1968 (2); v A 1964 (1); v NZ 1969 (2)
ahid Israr 1: v NZ 1976
ahid Mahmood 1: *v E 1962*
arpe, D. 3: v A 1959 (3)
oaib Mohammad 17: v E 1983 (1) 1987 (1) ; v NZ 1984 (1); v SL 1985 (1); *v E 1987 (4); v WI 1987 (3); v NZ 1984 (1); v In 1983 (2) 1986 (3)*
uja-ud-Din 19: v E 1961 (2); v A 1959 (3); v WI 1958 (3); v NZ 1955 (3); v In 1954 (5); *v E 1954 (3)*
kander Bakht 26: v E 1977 (2); v WI 1980 (1); v NZ 1976 (1); v In 1978 (2) 1982 (1); *v E 1978 (3) 1982 (2); v A 1978 (2) 1981 (3); v WI 1976 (1); v NZ 1978 (3); v In 1979 (5)*

hir Naqqash 15: v A 1982 (3); v In 1982 (2); v SL 1981 (3); *v E 1982 (2); v A 1983 (1); v NZ 1984 (1); v In 1983 (3)*
at Ali 10: v E 1972 (3); *v E 1978 (2); v A 1972 (1); v NZ 1972 (1) 1978 (3)*
slim Arif 6: v A 1979 (3); v WI 1980 (2); *v In 1979 (1)*
useef Ahmed 24: v E 1983 (2) 1987 (2); v A 1979 (3); v WI 1986 (3); v NZ 1984 (1); v In 1984 1); v SL 1981 (3) 1985 (1); *v E 1987 (2); v In 1986 (4); v SL 1985 (2)*

qar Hassan 21: v A 1956 (1) 1959 (1); v WI 1958 (1); v NZ 1955 (3); v In 1954 (5); *v E 1954 4); v WI 1957 (1); v In 1952 (5)*
sim Akram 25: v E 1987 (2); v WI 1986 (2); v SL 1985 (3); *v E 1987 (5); v WI 1987 (3); v NZ 984 (2); v In 1986 (5); v SL 1985 (3)*
sim Bari 81: v E 1968 (3) 1972 (3) 1977 (3); v A 1982 (3); v WI 1974 (2) 1980 (2); v NZ 1969 3) 1976 (2); v In 1978 (3) 1982 (6); *v E 1967 (3) 1971 (3) 1974 (3) 1978 (3) 1982 (3); v A 1972 (3) 976 (3) 1978 (2) 1981 (3) 1983 (5); v WI 1976 (5); v NZ 1972 (3) 1978 (3); v In 1979 (6); 1983 3)*
sim Raja 57: v E 1972 (1) 1977 (3) 1983 (3); v A 1979 (3); v WI 1974 (2) 1980 (4); v NZ 1976) 1984 (1); v In 1982 (1) 1984 (1); v SL 1981 (3); *v E 1974 (2) 1978 (3) 1982 (1); v A 1978 (1) 981 (3) 1983 (2); v WI 1976 (5); v NZ 1972 (3) 1978 (3) 1984 (2); v In 1979 (6) 1983 (3)*
zir Mohammad 20: v A 1956 (1) 1959 (1); v WI 1958 (3); v NZ 1955 (2); v In 1954 (5); *v E 954 (2); v WI 1957 (5); v In 1952 (1)*

nis Ahmed 4: v NZ 1969 (2); *v In 1986 (2)*

eer Abbas 78: v E 1972 (2) 1983 (3); v A 1979 (2) 1982 (3); v WI 1974 (2) 1980 (3); v NZ 1969) 1976 (3) 1984 (3); v In 1978 (3) 1982 (6) 1984 (2); v SL 1981 (1) 1985 (2); *v E 1971 (3) 1974 (3) 982 (3); v A 1972 (3) 1976 (3) 1978 (2) 1981 (2) 1983 (5); v WI 1976 (3); v NZ 1972 (3) 1978 (2) 984 (2); v In 1979 (5) 1983 (3)*
r Khan 1: *v SL 1985*
qar Ahmed 9: v A 1956 (1); v NZ 1955 (3); *v E 1954 (2); v In 1952 (3)*
arnain 3: *v SL 1985 (3)*

SRI LANKA

Number of Test cricketers: 42

Ahangama, F. S. 3: v In 1985 (3)
Amalean, K. N. 2: v P 1985 (1); *v A 1987 (1)*
Amerasinghe, A. M. J. G. 2: v NZ 1983 (2)
Anurasiri, S. D. 4: v NZ 1986 (1); v P 1985 (2); *v In 1986 (1)*
de Alwis, R. G. 11: v A 1982 (1); v NZ 1983 (3); v P 1985 (2); *v A 1987 (1); v NZ 1982 (1); v I 1986 (3)*
de Mel, A. L. F. 17: v E 1981 (1); v A 1982 (1); v In 1985 (3); v P 1985 (3); *v E 1984 (1); v In 198 (1) 1986 (1); v P 1981 (3) 1985 (3)*
de Silva, D. S. 12: v E 1981 (1); v A 1982 (1); v NZ 1983 (3); *v E 1984 (1); v NZ 1982 (2); v I 1982 (1); v P 1981 (3)*
de Silva, E. A. R. 5: v In 1985 (1); v P 1985 (1); *v In 1986 (3)*
de Silva, G. R. A. 4: v E 1981 (1); *v In 1982 (1); v P 1981 (2)*
de Silva, P. A. 15: v In 1985 (3); v P 1985 (3); *v E 1984 (1) 1988 (1); v A 1987 (1); v In 1986 (3 v P 1985 (3)*
Dias, R. L. 20: v E 1981 (1); v A 1982 (1); v NZ 1983 (2) 1986 (1); v In 1985 (3); v P 1985 (1); *v 1984 (1); v In 1982 (1) 1986 (3); v P 1981 (3) 1985 (3)*

Fernando, E. R. N. S. 5: v A 1982 (1); v NZ 1983 (2); *v NZ 1982 (2)*

Goonatillake, H. M. 5: v E 1981 (1); *v In 1982 (1); v P 1981 (3)*
Gunasekera, Y. 2: *v NZ 1982 (2)*
Guneratne, R. P. W. 1: v A 1982
Gurusinha, A. P. 7: v NZ 1986 (1); v P 1985 (2); *v In 1986 (3); v P 1985 (1)*

Jayasekera, R. S. A. 1: *v P 1981*
Jeganathan, S. 2: *v NZ 1982 (2)*
John, V. B. 6: v NZ 1983 (3); *v E 1984 (1); v NZ 1982 (2)*
Jurangpathy, B. R. 2: v In 1985 (1); *v In 1986 (1)*

Kaluperuma, L. W. 2: v E 1981 (1); *v P 1981 (1)*
Kaluperuma, S. M. S. 4: v NZ 1983 (3); *v A 1987 (1)*
Kuruppu, D. S. B. P. 3: v NZ 1986 (1); *v E 1988 (1); v A 1987 (1)*
Kuruppuarachchi, A. K. 2: v NZ 1986 (1); v P 1985 (1)

Labrooy, G. F. 3: *v E 1988 (1); v A 1987 (1); v In 1986 (1)*

Madugalle, R. S. 21: v E 1981 (1); v A 1982 (1); v NZ 1983 (3) 1986 (1); v In 1985 (3); *v E 1984 1988 (1); v A 1987 (1); v NZ 1982 (2); v In 1982 (1); v P 1981 (3) 1985 (3)*
Madurasinghe, A. W. R. 1: *v E 1988*
Mahanama, R. S. 4: v NZ 1986 (1); v P 1985 (2); *v A 1987 (1)*
Mendis, L. R. D. 24: v E 1981 (1); v A 1982 (1); v NZ 1983 (3) 1986 (1); v In 1985 (3); v P 1 (3); *v E 1984 (1) 1988 (1); v In 1982 (1) 1986 (3); v P 1981 (3) 1985 (3)*

Ramanayake, C. P. H. 2: *v E 1988 (1); v A 1987 (1)*
Ranasinghe, A. N. 2: *v In 1982 (1); v P 1981 (1)*
Ranatunga, A. 24: v E 1981 (1); v A 1982 (1); v NZ 1983 (3) 1986 (1); v In 1985 (3); v P 1985 *v E 1984 (1) 1988 (1); v A 1987 (1); v In 1982 (1) 1986 (3); v P 1981 (2) 1985 (3)*
Ratnayake, R. J. 14: v A 1982 (1); v NZ 1983 (1) 1986 (1); v In 1985 (3); v P 1985 (1); *v NZ (2); v In 1986 (2); v P 1985 (3)*
Ratnayeke, J. R. 20: v NZ 1983 (2) 1986 (1); v P 1985 (3); *v E 1984 (1) 1988 (1); v A 1987 v NZ 1982 (2); v In 1982 (1) 1986 (3); v P 1981 (2) 1985 (3)*

Samarasekera, M. A. R. 1: *v E 1988*
Silva, S. A. R. 9: v In 1985 (3); v P 1985 (1); *v E 1984 (1) 1988 (1); v NZ 1982 (1); v P 1985*

Warnapura, B. 4: v E 1981 (1); *v In 1982 (1); v P 1981 (2)*
Warnaweera, K. P. J. 1: v P 1985

Weerasinghe, C. D. U. S. 1: v In 1985
Wettimuny, M. D. 2: *v NZ 1982 (2)*
Wettimuny, S. 23: v E 1981 (1); v A 1982 (1); v NZ 1983 (3); v In 1985 (3); v P 1985 (3); *v E 1984 (1); v NZ 1982 (2); v In 1986 (3); v P 1981 (3) 1985 (3)*
Wijesuriya, R. G. C. E. 4: *v P 1981 (1) 1985 (3)*

TWO COUNTRIES

Twelve cricketers have appeared for two countries in Test matches, namely:

Amir Elahi, *India and Pakistan.*
J. J. Ferris, *Australia and England.*
S. C. Guillen, *West Indies and NZ.*
Gul Mahomed, *India and Pakistan.*
F. Hearne, *England and South Africa.*
A. H. Kardar, *India and Pakistan.*
W. E. Midwinter, *England and Australia.*
F. Mitchell, *England and South Africa.*
W. L. Murdoch, *Australia and England.*
Nawab of Pataudi, sen., *England and India.*
A. E. Trott, *Australia and England.*
S. M. J. Woods, *Australia and England.*

MOST TEST APPEARANCES FOR EACH COUNTRY

England: M. C. Cowdrey 114.
Australia: R. W. Marsh 96.
outh Africa: J. H. B. Waite 50.
West Indies: C. H. Lloyd 110.
New Zealand: R. J. Hadlee 74.
India: S. M. Gavaskar 125.
Pakistan: Javed Miandad 92.
Sri Lanka: L. R. D. Mendis and A. Ranatunga 24.

MOST TEST APPEARANCES AS CAPTAIN FOR EACH COUNTRY

ngland: P. B. H. May 41.
ustralia: G. S. Chappell 48.
outh Africa: H. W. Taylor 18.
'est Indies: C. H. Lloyd 74.
New Zealand: J. R. Reid 34.
India: S. M. Gavaskar 47.
Pakistan: Imran Khan 33.
Sri Lanka: L. R. D. Mendis 19.

ENGLAND v REST OF THE WORLD

he following were awarded England caps for playing against the Rest of the World in England 1970, although the five matches played are now generally considered not to have rated as full sts: D. L. Amiss (1), G. Boycott (2), D. J. Brown (2), M. C. Cowdrey (4), M. H. Denness (1), L. D'Oliveira (4), J. H. Edrich (2), K. W. R. Fletcher (4), A. W. Greig (3), R. Illingworth (5), Jones (1), A. P. E. Knott (5), P. Lever (1), B. W. Luckhurst (5), C. M. Old (2), P. J. Sharpe (1), Shuttleworth (1), J. A. Snow (5), D. L. Underwood (3), A. Ward (1), D. Wilson (2).

CRICKET RECORDS

Amended by BILL FRINDALL to end of the 1988 season in England

Unless stated to be of a minor character, all records apply only to first-class cricket including some performances in the distant past which have always been recognised as of exceptional merit.

* Denotes not out or an unbroken partnership.

(A), (SA), (WI), (NZ), (I), (P) or (SL) indicates either the nationality of the player, or the country in which the record was made.

FIRST-CLASS RECORDS

BATTING RECORDS

Highest Individual Scores 132
Highest Scores in England and Australia 133
Highest for Each First-class County 134
Hundred on Début in British Isles 134
Two Double-Hundreds in a Match 135
Hundred and Double-Hundred in a Match 135
Two Separate Hundreds in a Match 135
Four Hundreds or More in Succession 136
Most Hundreds in a Season 137
Most Hundreds in a Career 13
3,000 Runs in a Season 13
1,000 Runs in a Season Most Times 139
Highest Aggregates Outside England 14
Highest Averages in an English Season 14
25,000 Runs in a Career 14
Career Average over 50 14
Fast Scoring 14
300 Runs in One Day 14
1,000 Runs in May 14
1,000 Runs in Two Separate Months 14
Most Runs Scored off One Over 14
Most Sixes in an Innings 14
Most Sixes in a Season 14
Most Boundaries in an Innings 14
Highest Partnerships 14
Partnerships for First Wicket 14
First-Wicket Hundreds in Both Innings 14
Partnership Records for All Countries 14
Out Handled the Ball 15
Out Obstructing the Field 15
Out Hit the Ball Twice 1

BOWLING RECORDS

Ten Wickets in One Innings 1
Outstanding Analyses 1
Most Wickets in a Match 1
Sixteen or More Wickets in a Day 1
Four Wickets with Consecutive Balls . . . . .
Hat-tricks . . . . .
200 Wickets in a Season . . . . .
100 Wickets in a Season Most Times . . . . .
100 Wickets in a Season Outside England . . . . .
1,500 Wickets in a Career . . . . .

ALL-ROUND RECORDS

Iundred and Ten Wickets in One Innings ... 161
wo Hundred Runs and Sixteen Wickets ... 161
Iundred in Each Innings and Five Wickets Twice ... 161
Iundred in Each Innings and Ten Wickets ... 161
Iundred and Hat-trick ... 161
eason Doubles ... 162
),000 Runs and 2,000 Wickets in a Career ... 163

WICKET-KEEPING RECORDS

Iost Dismissals in an Innings ... 163
icket-keepers' Hat-tricks ... 164
ost Dismissals in a Match ... 164
ost Dismissals in a Season ... 164
ost Dismissals in a Career ... 165

FIELDING RECORDS

ost Catches in an Innings ... 165
ost Catches in a Match ... 165
ost Catches in a Season ... 166
ost Catches in a Career ... 166

TEAM RECORDS

ghest Totals ... 166
ghest for Each First-class County ... 166
west Totals ... 167
west for Each First-class County ... 167
ghest Match Aggregates ... 168
west Match Aggregate ... 168
ghest Fourth Innings Totals ... 168
gest Victories ... 168
d Matches ... 169
tches Begun and Finished on First Day ... 170

TEST MATCH RECORDS

BATTING RECORDS

hest Individual Test Innings ... 170
dred on Test Début ... 171
Runs in First Test ... 172
Separate Hundreds in a Test ... 172
dred and Double-Hundred in Same Test ... 172
t Runs in a Series ... 173
) Test Runs in a Calendar Year ... 173
t Runs in a Career ... 174
est Averages ... 177
t Hundreds ... 177
ying Bat Through Test Innings ... 177

Fastest Fifties 17
Fastest Hundreds 17
Fastest Double-Hundreds 17
Fastest Triple-Hundreds 17
Most Runs in a Day by a Batsman 17
Slowest Individual Batting 17
Slowest Hundreds 18
Highest Wicket Partnerships 18

BOWLING RECORDS

Most Wickets in an Innings, in a Match and in a Series 18
Most Wickets in a Career 18
Wicket with First Ball in Test Cricket 18
Hat-tricks 18
Most Balls Bowled in a Test 18

ALL-ROUND RECORDS

100 Runs and Five Wickets in an Innings 1
100 Runs and Five Dismissals in an Innings 1
100 Runs and Ten Wickets in a Test 1
1,000 Runs and 100 Wickets in a Career 1
1,000 Runs, 100 Wickets and 100 Catches 1

WICKET-KEEPING RECORDS

Most Dismissals in an Innings, in a Match, in a Series and in a Career ....

FIELDING RECORDS

Most Catches in an Innings, in a Match, in a Series and in a Career ....

TEAM RECORDS

Highest Innings Totals ....
Highest Fourth Innings Totals ....
Most Runs in a Day (Both Sides and One Side) ....
Most Wickets in One Day ....
Highest Match Aggregates ....
Lowest Innings Totals ....
Fewest Runs in a Full Day's Play ....
Lowest Match Aggregates ....
Youngest Test Players ....
Oldest Players on Test Début ....
Oldest Test Players ....
Most Test Match Appearances ....
Most Consecutive Test Appearances ....

TEST SERIES

ummary of All Test Matches 194
ngland v Australia 194
ngland v South Africa 204
ngland v West Indies 208
ngland v New Zealand 212
ngland v India 215
ngland v Pakistan 218
ngland v Sri Lanka 220
ngland v Rest of the World 221
ustralia v South Africa 221
ustralia v West Indies 224
ustralia v New Zealand 227
ustralia v India 229
ustralia v Pakistan 231
ustralia v Sri Lanka 233
outh Africa v New Zealand 234
est Indies v New Zealand 236
est Indies v India 238
est Indies v Pakistan 240
ew Zealand v India 242
ew Zealand v Pakistan 244
ew Zealand v Sri Lanka 246
dia v Pakistan 247
dia v Sri Lanka 249
kistan v Sri Lanka 251
st Match Grounds 252
milies in Test Cricket 254

LIMITED-OVERS INTERNATIONAL RECORDS

00 or More Runs 256
ghest Individual Score for Each Country 256
ve or More Hundreds 256
ghest Partnership for Each Wicket 256
) or More Wickets 257
st Bowling for Each Country 257
t-tricks 257
cket-keeping and Fielding Records 257
-round 258
ghest Innings Totals 258
ghest Totals Batting Second 259
ghest Match Aggregates 259
west Innings Totals 259
gest Victories 259
d Match 259
rld Cup Finals 259

MISCELLANEOUS

ge Attendances 260
d's Cricket Ground 260
hest Scores in Minor Counties and Other Matches 261
hest Partnership in Minor Cricket 261
ord Hit 262
owing the Cricket Ball 262
mation Dates of County and Minor County Clubs 262
stitution of County Championship 263
t County Championship Appearances 263
t Consecutive County Championship Appearances 263

FIRST-CLASS RECORDS

BATTING RECORDS

HIGHEST INDIVIDUAL SCORES

499	Hanif Mohammad	Karachi v Bahawalpur at Karachi	1958-5
452*	D. G. Bradman	NSW v Queensland at Sydney	1929-3
443*	B. B. Nimbalkar	Maharashtra v Kathiawar at Poona	1948-4
437	W. H. Ponsford	Victoria v Queensland at Melbourne	1927-2
429	W. H. Ponsford	Victoria v Tasmania at Melbourne	1922-2
428	Aftab Baloch	Sind v Baluchistan at Karachi	1973-7
424	A. C. MacLaren	Lancashire v Somerset at Taunton	189
405*	G. A. Hick	Worcestershire v Somerset at Taunton	198
385	B. Sutcliffe	Otago v Canterbury at Christchurch	1952-
383	C. W. Gregory	NSW v Queensland at Brisbane	1906-0
369	D. G. Bradman	South Australia v Tasmania at Adelaide	1935-3
365*	C. Hill	South Australia v NSW at Adelaide	1900-0
365*	G. S. Sobers	West Indies v Pakistan at Kingston	1957-
364	L. Hutton	England v Australia at The Oval	19
359*	V. M. Merchant	Bombay v Maharashtra at Bombay	1943-
359	R. B. Simpson	NSW v Queensland at Brisbane	1963-
357*	R. Abel	Surrey v Somerset at The Oval	18
357	D. G. Bradman	South Australia v Victoria at Melbourne	1935-
356	B. A. Richards	South Australia v W. Australia at Perth	1970-
355	B. Sutcliffe	Otago v Auckland at Dunedin	1949-
352	W. H. Ponsford	Victoria v NSW at Melbourne	1926-
350	Rashid Israr	Habib Bank v National Bank at Lahore	1976-
345	C. G. Macartney	Australians v Nottinghamshire at Nottingham	19
344*	G. A. Headley	Jamaica v Lord Tennyson's XI at Kingston	1931-
344	W. G. Grace	MCC v Kent at Canterbury	18
343*	P. A. Perrin	Essex v Derbyshire at Chesterfield	19
341	G. H. Hirst	Yorkshire v Leicestershire at Leicester	19
340*	D. G. Bradman	NSW v Victoria at Sydney	1928-
340	S. M. Gavaskar	Bombay v Bengal at Bombay	1981
338*	R. C. Blunt	Otago v Canterbury at Christchurch	1931-
338	W. W. Read	Surrey v Oxford University at The Oval	18
337*	Pervez Akhtar	Railways v Dera Ismail Khan at Lahore	1964
337†	Hanif Mohammad	Pakistan v West Indies at Bridgetown	1957
336*	W. R. Hammond	England v New Zealand at Auckland	1932
336	W. H. Ponsford	Victoria v South Australia at Melbourne	1927
334	D. G. Bradman	Australia v England at Leeds	19
333	K. S. Duleepsinhji	Sussex v Northamptonshire at Hove	19
332	W. H. Ashdown	Kent v Essex at Brentwood	19
331*	J. D. Robertson	Middlesex v Worcestershire at Worcester	19
325*	H. L. Hendry	Victoria v New Zealanders at Melbourne	1925
325	A. Sandham	England v West Indies at Kingston	1929
325	C. L. Badcock	South Australia v Victoria at Adelaide	1935
324	J. B. Stollmeyer	Trinidad v British Guiana at Port-of-Spain	1946
324	Waheed Mirza	Karachi Whites v Quetta at Karachi	1976
323	A. L. Wadekar	Bombay v Mysore at Bombay	1966
322	E. Paynter	Lancashire v Sussex at Hove	1
322	I. V. A. Richards	Somerset v Warwickshire at Taunton	1
321	W. L. Murdoch	NSW v Victoria at Sydney	188
320	R. Lamba	North Zone v West Zone at Bhilai	198
319	Gul Mahomed	Baroda v Holkar at Baroda	194
318*	W. G. Grace	Gloucestershire v Yorkshire at Cheltenham	1
317	W. R. Hammond	Gloucestershire v Nottinghamshire at Gloucester	1
317	K. R. Rutherford	New Zealanders v D. B. Close's XI at Scarborough	1
316*	J. B. Hobbs	Surrey v Middlesex at Lord's	1
316*	V. S. Hazare	Maharashtra v Baroda at Poona	193
316	R. H. Moore	Hampshire v Warwickshire at Bournemouth	1

315*	T. W. Hayward	Surrey v Lancashire at The Oval	1898
315*	P. Holmes	Yorkshire v Middlesex at Lord's	1925
315*	A. F. Kippax	NSW v Queensland at Sydney	1927-28
14*	C. L. Walcott	Barbados v Trinidad at Port-of-Spain	1945-46
13	H. Sutcliffe	Yorkshire v Essex at Leyton	1932
12*	W. W. Keeton	Nottinghamshire v Middlesex at The Oval‡	1939
12*	J. M. Brearley	MCC Under 25 v North Zone at Peshawar	1966-67
11*	G. M. Turner	Worcestershire v Warwickshire at Worcester	1982
11	J. T. Brown	Yorkshire v Sussex at Sheffield	1897
11	R. B. Simpson	Australia v England at Manchester	1964
11	Javed Miandad	Karachi Whites v National Bank at Karachi	1974-75
10*	J. H. Edrich	England v New Zealand at Leeds	1965
10	H. Gimblett	Somerset v Sussex at Eastbourne	1948
09	V. S. Hazare	The Rest v Hindus at Bombay	1943-44
08*	F. M. M. Worrell	Barbados v Trinidad at Bridgetown	1943-44
07	M. C. Cowdrey	MCC v South Australia at Adelaide	1962-63
07	R. M. Cowper	Australia v England at Melbourne	1965-66
06*	A. Ducat	Surrey v Oxford University at The Oval	1919
06*	E. A. B. Rowan	Transvaal v Natal at Johannesburg	1939-40
06*	D. W. Hookes	South Australia v Tasmania at Adelaide	1986-87
05*	F. E. Woolley	MCC v Tasmania at Hobart	1911-12
05*	F. R. Foster	Warwickshire v Worcestershire at Dudley	1914
05*	W. H. Ashdown	Kent v Derbyshire at Dover	1935
04*	A. W. Nourse	Natal v Transvaal at Johannesburg	1919-20
04*	P. H. Tarilton	Barbados v Trinidad at Bridgetown	1919-20
04*	E. D. Weekes	West Indians v Cambridge University at Cambridge	1950
4	R. M. Poore	Hampshire v Somerset at Taunton	1899
4	D. G. Bradman	Australia v England at Leeds	1934
3*	W. W. Armstrong	Australians v Somerset at Bath	1905
3*	Mushtaq Mohammad	Karachi Blues v Karachi University at Karachi	1967-68
3*	Abdul Azeem	Hyderabad v Tamil Nadu at Hyderabad	1986-87
2*	P. Holmes	Yorkshire v Hampshire at Portsmouth	1920
2*	W. R. Hammond	Gloucestershire v Glamorgan at Bristol	1934
2	W. R. Hammond	Gloucestershire v Glamorgan at Newport	1939
2	L. G. Rowe	West Indies v England at Bridgetown	1973-74
1*	E. H. Hendren	Middlesex v Worcestershire at Dudley	1933
1	W. G. Grace	Gloucestershire v Sussex at Bristol	1896
0*	V. T. Trumper	Australians v Sussex at Hove	1899
0*	F. B. Watson	Lancashire v Surrey at Manchester	1928
0*	Imtiaz Ahmed	PM's XI v Commonwealth XI at Bombay	1950-51
0	J. T. Brown	Yorkshire v Derbyshire at Chesterfield	1898
0	D. C. S. Compton	MCC v N. E. Transvaal at Benoni	1948-49
0	R. Subba Row	Northamptonshire v Surrey at The Oval	1958

† Hanif Mohammad batted for 16 hours 10 minutes – the longest innings in first-class cricket.
‡ Played at The Oval because Lord's was required for Eton v Harrow.

HIGHEST FOR TEAMS

English Teams in Australia

	M. C. Cowdrey	MCC v South Australia at Adelaide	1962-63
	R. E. Foster	England v Australia at Sydney	1903-04

inst Australians in England

	L. Hutton	England v Australia at The Oval	1938
	A. Sandham	Surrey at The Oval (record for any county)	1934

Australian Teams in England

	C. G. Macartney	v Nottinghamshire at Nottingham	1921
	D. G. Bradman	Australia v England at Leeds	1930

inst English Teams in Australia

	R. M. Cowper	Australia v England at Melbourne	1965-66
	A. J. Richardson	South Australia v MCC at Adelaide	1922-23

For Each First-Class County

Derbyshire	274	G. Davidson v Lancashire at Manchester	1896
Essex	343*	P. A. Perrin v Derbyshire at Chesterfield	1904
Glamorgan	287*	D. E. Davies v Gloucestershire at Newport	1939
Gloucestershire	318*	W. G. Grace v Yorkshire at Cheltenham	1876
Hampshire	316	R. H. Moore v Warwickshire at Bournemouth	1937
Kent	332	W. H. Ashdown v Essex at Brentwood	1934
Lancashire	424	A. C. MacLaren v Somerset at Taunton	1895
Leicestershire	252*	S. Coe v Northamptonshire at Leicester	1914
Middlesex	331*	J. D. Robertson v Worcestershire at Worcester	1949
Northamptonshire	300	R. Subba Row v Surrey at The Oval	1958
Nottinghamshire	312*	W. W. Keeton v Middlesex at The Oval†	1939
Somerset	322	I. V. A. Richards v Warwickshire at Taunton	1985
Surrey	357*	R. Abel v Somerset at The Oval	1899
Sussex	333	K. S. Duleepsinhji v Northamptonshire at Hove	1930
Warwickshire	305*	F. R. Foster v Worcestershire at Dudley	1914
Worcestershire	405*	G. A. Hick v Somerset at Taunton	1988
Yorkshire	341	G. H. Hirst v Leicestershire at Leicester	190

† *Played at The Oval because Lord's was required for Eton v Harrow.*

HUNDRED ON DEBUT IN BRITISH ISLES

(The following list does not include instances of players who have previously appeared in firs class cricket outside the British Isles or who performed the feat before 1946. Particulars of th latter are in *Wisdens* prior to 1984.)

114	F. W. Stocks	Nottinghamshire v Kent at Nottingham	194
108	A. Fairbairn	Middlesex v Somerset at Taunton	†‡194
124	P. Hearn	Kent v Warwickshire at Gillingham	194
215*	G. H. G. Doggart	Cambridge University v Lancashire at Cambridge	194
106	J. R. Gill	Ireland v MCC at Dublin	194
107*	G. Barker	Essex v Canadians at Clacton	†195
135	J. K. E. Slack	Cambridge University v Middlesex at Cambridge	195
100*	E. A. Clark	Middlesex v Cambridge University at Cambridge	195
113	G. J. Chidgey	Free Foresters v Cambridge U. at Cambridge	196
108	D. R. Shepherd	Gloucestershire v Oxford University at Oxford	196
110*	A. J. Harvey-Walker	Derbyshire v Oxford University at Burton upon Trent	†197
173	J. Whitehouse	Warwickshire v Oxford University at Oxford	197
106	J. B. Turner	Minor Counties v Pakistanis at Jesmond	197
112	J. A. Claughton	Oxford University v Gloucestershire at Oxford	†19
100*	A. W. Lilley	Essex v Nottinghamshire at Nottingham	19
146*	J. S. Johnson	Minor Counties v Indians at Wellington	19
110	N. R. Taylor	Kent v Sri Lankans at Canterbury	19
146*	D. G. Aslett	Kent v Hampshire at Bournemouth	19
116	M. D. Moxon	Yorkshire v Essex at Leeds	†19
100	D. A. Banks	Worcestershire v Oxford University at Oxford	19
122	A. A. Metcalfe	Yorkshire v Nottinghamshire at Bradford	19
117*	K. T. Medlycott	Surrey v Cambridge University at Banstead	§19
101*	N. J. Falkner		
106	A. C. Storie	Northamptonshire v Hampshire at Northampton	†19
102	M. P. Maynard	Glamorgan v Yorkshire at Swansea	19
117*	R. J. Bartlett	Somerset v Oxford University at Oxford	19
100*	P. D. Bowler	Leicestershire v Hampshire at Leicester	19
145	I. L. Philip	Scotland v Ireland at Glasgow	19
114*	P. D. Atkins	Surrey v Cambridge University at The Oval	19
100	B. M. W. Patterson	Scotland v Ireland at Dumfries	19

† *In his second innings.*

‡ *A. Fairbairn (Middlesex) in 1947 scored hundreds in the second innings of his first two matc in first-class cricket: 108 as above, 110* Middlesex v Nottinghamshire at Nottingham.*

§ *The only instance in England of two players performing the feat in the same match.*

Notes: A number of players abroad have also made a hundred on a first appearance.

The highest innings on début was hit by W. F. E. Marx when he made 240 for Transvaal against Griqualand West at Johannesburg in 1920-21.

There are three instances of a cricketer making two separate hundreds on début: A. R. Morris, New South Wales, 148 and 111 against Queensland in 1940-41, N. J. Contractor, Gujarat, 152 and 102* against Baroda in 1952-53, and Aamer Malik, Lahore "A", 132* and 110* against Railways in 1979-80.

J. S. Solomon, British Guiana, scored a hundred in each of his first three innings in first-class cricket: 114* v Jamaica; 108 v Barbados in 1956-57; 121 v Pakistanis in 1957-58.

R. Watson-Smith, Border, scored 310 runs before he was dismissed in first-class cricket, including not-out centuries in his first two innings: 183* v Orange Free State and 125* v Griqualand West in 1969-70.

G. R. Viswanath and D. M. Wellham alone have scored a hundred on both their début in first-class cricket and in Test cricket. Viswanath scored 230 for Mysore v Andhra in 1967-68 and 137 for India v Australia in 1969-70. Wellham scored 100 for New South Wales v Victoria in 1980-81 and 103 for Australia v England in 1981.

TWO DOUBLE-HUNDREDS IN A MATCH

. E. Fagg	244	202*	Kent v Essex at Colchester	1938

HUNDRED AND DOUBLE-HUNDRED IN A MATCH

. B. Fry	125	229	Sussex v Surrey at Hove	1900
/. W. Armstrong	157*	245	Victoria v South Australia at Melbourne	1920-21
. T. W. Hardinge	207	102*	Kent v Surrey at Blackheath	1921
. P. Mead	113	224	Hampshire v Sussex at Horsham	1921
. S. Duleepsinhji	115	246	Sussex v Kent at Hastings	1929
. G. Bradman	124	225	Woodfull's XI v Ryder's XI at Sydney	1929-30
. Sutcliffe	243	100*	New Zealanders v Essex at Southend	1949
. R. Hallam	210*	157	Leicestershire v Glamorgan at Leicester	1959
. R. Hallam	203*	143*	Leicestershire v Sussex at Worthing	1961
anumant Singh	109	213*	Rajasthan v Bombay at Bombay	1966-67
alah-ud-Din	256	102*	Karachi v East Pakistan at Karachi	1968-69
. D. Walters	242	103	Australia v West Indies at Sydney	1968-69
M. Gavaskar	124	220	India v West Indies at Port-of-Spain	1970-71
G. Rowe	214	100*	West Indies v New Zealand at Kingston	1971-72
. S. Chappell	247*	133	Australia v New Zealand at Wellington	1973-74
Baichan	216*	102	Berbice v Demerara at Georgetown	1973-74
heer Abbas	216*	156*	Gloucestershire v Surrey at The Oval	1976
heer Abbas	230*	104*	Gloucestershire v Kent at Canterbury	1976
heer Abbas	205*	108*	Gloucestershire v Sussex at Cheltenham	1977
adat Ali	141	222	Income Tax v Multan at Multan	1977-78
lat Ali	214*	104	PIA v Punjab at Lahore	1978-79
afiq Ahmed	129	217*	National Bank v MCB at Karachi	1978-79
W. Randall	209	146	Nottinghamshire v Middlesex at Nottingham	1979
heer Abbas	215*	150*	Gloucestershire v Somerset at Bath	1981
sim Omar	210*	110	MCB v Lahore at Lahore	1982-83
I. Kallicharran	200*	117*	Warwickshire v Northamptonshire at Birmingham	1984

TWO SEPARATE HUNDREDS IN A MATCH

Eight times: Zaheer Abbas.
Seven times: W. R. Hammond.
Six times: J. B. Hobbs, G. M. Turner.
Five times: C. B. Fry.

Four times: D. G. Bradman, G. S. Chappell, J. H. Edrich, L. B. Fishlock, T. W. Graveney, C. G. Greenidge, H. T. W. Hardinge, E. H. Hendren, Javed Miandad, G. L. Jessop, P. A. Perrin, B. Sutcliffe, H. Sutcliffe.

Three times: L. E. G. Ames, G. Boycott, I. M. Chappell, D. C. S. Compton, M. C. Cowdrey, D. Denton, K. S. Duleepsinhji, R. E. Foster, R. C. Fredericks, S. M. Gavaskar, W. G. Grace, G. Gunn, M. R. Hallam, Hanif Mohammad, M. J. Harris, T. W. Hayward, V. S. Hazare, D. W. Hookes, L. Hutton, A. Jones, P. N. Kirsten, R. B. McCosker, P. B. H. May, C. P. Mead, A. C. Russell, Sadiq Mohammad, J. T. Tyldesley.

Twice: Agha Zahid, Ali Zia, D. L. Amiss, L. Baichan, A. R. Border, B. J. T. Bosanquet, R. J. Boyd-Moss, C. C. Dacre, G. M. Emmett, A. E. Fagg, L. E. Favell, H. Gimblett, C. Hallows, R. A. Hamence, A. L. Hassett, G. A. Headley, A. I. Kallicharran, J. H. King, A. F. Kippax, J. G. Langridge, H. W. Lee, E. Lester, C. B. Llewellyn, C. G. Macartney, C. A. Milton, A. R. Morris, P. H. Parfitt, Nawab of Pataudi jun., E. Paynter, C. Pinch, R. G. Pollock, R. M. Prideaux, Qasim Omar, W. Rhodes, B. A. Richards, Rizwan-uz-Zaman, Pankaj Roy, James Seymour, Shafiq Ahmed, R. B. Simpson, G. S. Sobers, E. Tyldesley, C. L. Walcott, K. C. Wessels, W. W. Whysall, G. N. Yallop.

Notes: W. Lambert scored 107 and 157 for Sussex v Epsom at Lord's in 1817 and it was not until W. G. Grace made 130 and 102* for South of the Thames v North of the Thames at Canterbury in 1868 that the feat was repeated.

T. W. Hayward (Surrey) set up a unique record in 1906 when in one week – six days – he hit four successive hundreds, 144 and 100 v Nottinghamshire at Nottingham and 143 and 125 v Leicestershire at Leicester.

D. W. Hookes (South Australia) scored four successive hundreds in eleven days at Adelaide in 1976-77: 185 and 105 v Queensland (tied match) and 135 and 156 v New South Wales.

L. G. Rowe is alone in scoring hundreds in each innings on his first appearance in Test cricket: 214 and 100* for West Indies v New Zealand at Kingston in 1971-72.

Zaheer Abbas (Gloucestershire) set a unique record in 1976 by twice scoring a double hundred and a hundred in the same match without being dismissed: 216* and 156* v Surrey at The Oval and 230* and 104* v Kent at Canterbury. In 1977 he achieved this feat for a third time, scoring 205* and 108* v Sussex at Cheltenham, and in 1981 for a fourth time, scoring 215* and 150* v Somerset at Bath.

M. R. Hallam (Leicestershire), opening the batting each time, achieved the following trebles: 210* and 157 v Glamorgan at Leicester, 1959; 203* and 143* v Sussex at Worthing, 1961; 107* and 149* v Worcestershire at Leicester, 1965. In the last two matches he was on the field the whole time.

C. J. B. Wood, 107* and 117* for Leicestershire against Yorkshire at Bradford, 1911, is alone in carrying his bat and scoring hundreds in each innings.

W. L. Foster, 140 and 172*, and R. E. Foster, 134 and 101*, for Worcestershire v Hampshire at Worcester in July 1899, were the first brothers each to score two separate hundreds in the same first-class match.

The brothers I. M. Chappell, 145 and 121, and G. S. Chappell, 247* and 133, for Australia v New Zealand at Wellington in 1973-74, became the first players on the same side each to score a hundred in each innings of a Test match.

G. Gunn, 183, and G. V. Gunn, 100*, for Nottinghamshire v Warwickshire at Birmingham in 1931, provide the only instance of father and son each hitting a century in the same innings of a first-class match.

Most recent instances

In 1987-88

K. Bhaskar Pillai	129	103*	North Zone v East Zone at Jodhpur.
K. C. Wessels	101	130	Eastern Province v OFS at Bloemfontein.
D. C. Boon	108	143	Tasmania v Queensland at Launceston.
Ali Zia	112	103	United Bank v Railways at Lahore.

In 1988: See Features of 1988.

FOUR HUNDREDS OR MORE IN SUCCESSION

Six in succession: C. B. Fry 1901; D. G. Bradman 1938-39; M. J. Procter 1970-71.

Five in succession: E. D. Weekes 1955-56.

Four in succession: C. W. J. Athey 1987; M. Azharuddin 1984-85; A. R. Border 1985; D. G. Bradman 1931-32, 1948-49; D. C. S. Compton 1946-47; N. J. Contractor 1957-58; K.

Duleepsinhji 1931; C. B. Fry 1911; C. G. Greenidge 1986; W. R. Hammond 1936-37, 1945-46; H. T. W. Hardinge 1913; T. W. Hayward 1906; J. B. Hobbs 1920, 1925; D. W. Hookes 1976-77; P. N. Kirsten 1976-77; J. G. Langridge 1949; C. G. Macartney 1921; K. S. McEwan 1977; P. B. H. May 1956-57; V. M. Merchant 1941-42; A. Mitchell 1933; Nawab of Pataudi sen. 1931; L. G. Rowe 1971-72; Pankaj Roy 1962-63; Sadiq Mohammad 1976; Saeed Ahmed 1961-62; H. Sutcliffe 1931, 1939; E. Tyldesley 1926; W. W. Whysall 1930; F. E. Woolley 1929; Zaheer Abbas 1970-71, 1982-83.

Note: The most fifties in consecutive innings is ten – by E. Tyldesley in 1926 and by D. G. Bradman in the 1947-48 and 1948 seasons.

MOST HUNDREDS IN A SEASON

Eighteen: D. C. S. Compton in 1947. These included six hundreds against the South Africans n which matches his average was 84.78. His aggregate for the season was 3,816, also a record.

Sixteen: J. B. Hobbs in 1925, when aged 42, played 16 three-figure innings in first-class natches. It was during this season that he exceeded the number of hundreds obtained in first-lass cricket by W. G. Grace.

Fifteen: W. R. Hammond in 1938.

Fourteen: H. Sutcliffe in 1932.

Thirteen: G. Boycott in 1971, D. G. Bradman in 1938, C. B. Fry in 1901, W. R. Hammond in 933 and 1937, T. W. Hayward in 1906, E. H. Hendren in 1923, 1927 and 1928, C. P. Mead in 928, and H. Sutcliffe in 1928 and 1931.

MOST HUNDREDS IN A CAREER

(35 or More)

	Hundreds		100th		Hundreds		100th
	Total	*Abroad*	*100*		*Total*	*Abroad*	*100*
B. Hobbs	197	22	1923	D. G. Bradman	117	41†	1947-48
H. Hendren	170	19	1928-29	Zaheer Abbas	108	70†	1982-83
. R. Hammond	167	33	1935	M. C. Cowdrey	107	27	1973
P. Mead	153	8	1927	A. Sandham	107	20	1935
Boycott	151	27	1977	T. W. Hayward	104	4	1913
Sutcliffe	149	14	1932	J. H. Edrich	103	13	1977
E. Woolley	145	10	1929	G. M. Turner	103	85†	1982
Hutton	129	24	1951	L. E. G. Ames	102	13	1950
. G. Grace	126	1	1895	D. L. Amiss	102	15	1986
C. S. Compton	123	31	1952	E. Tyldesley	102	8	1934
W. Graveney	122	31	1964				

† "Abroad" for D. G. Bradman is outside Australia; for Zaheer Abbas, outside Pakistan; for M. Turner, outside New Zealand.

E. H. Hendren and D. G. Bradman scored their 100th hundreds in Australia, Zaheer Abbas scored in Pakistan. Zaheer Abbas and G. Boycott did so in Test matches.

V. A. Richards	98	M. Leyland	80	J. O'Connor	72
W. Hearne	96	B. A. Richards	80	W. G. Quaife	72
B. Fry	94	C. H. Lloyd	79	K. S. Ranjitsinhji	72
J. Edrich	86	K. F. Barrington	76	D. Brookes	71
S. Sobers	86	J. G. Langridge	76	A. C. Russell	71
T. Tyldesley	86	C. Washbrook	76	D. Denton	69
I. Kallicharran	85	H. T. W. Hardinge	75	K. S. McEwan	69
B. H. May	85	R. Abel	74	M. J. K. Smith	69
E. S. Wyatt	85	G. S. Chappell	74	R. E. Marshall	68
G. Greenidge	83	D. Kenyon	74	R. N. Harvey	67
Hardstaff, jun.	83	Majid Khan	73	P. Holmes	67
B. Kanhai	83	Javed Miandad	72	J. D. Robertson	67
M. Gavaskar	81	Mushtaq Mohammad	72	G. A. Gooch	66

P. A. Perrin 66
R. G. Pollock 64
R. T. Simpson 64
K. W. R. Fletcher 63
G. Gunn 62
V. S. Hazare 60
G. H. Hirst 60
R. B. Simpson 60
P. F. Warner 60
I. M. Chappell 59
A. L. Hassett 59
A. Shrewsbury 59
A. R. Border 58
A. E. Fagg 58
P. H. Parfitt 58
W. Rhodes 58
L. B. Fishlock 56
A. Jones 56
C. A. Milton 56
C. Hallows 55
Hanif Mohammad 55
A. J. Lamb 55
W. Watson 55
D. J. Insole 54
W. W. Keeton 54
W. Bardsley 53
B. F. Davison 53
A. E. Dipper 53
G. L. Jessop 53
James Seymour 53
E. H. Bowley 52
D. B. Close 52
A. Ducat 52
E. R. Dexter 51
J. M. Parks 51
W. W. Whysall 51
G. Cox jun. 50
H. E. Dollery 50
K. S. Duleepsinhji 50
M. W. Gatting 50
H. Gimblett 50
W. M. Lawry 50
Sadiq Mohammad 50
F. B. Watson 50
C. G. Macartney 49
Shafiq Ahmed 49
M. J. Stewart 49
K. G. Suttle 49
P. M. Umrigar 49
W. M. Woodfull 49

C. J. Barnett 48
W. Gunn 48
E. G. Hayes 48
B. W. Luckhurst 48
M. J. Procter 48
A. C. MacLaren 47
W. H. Ponsford 47
C. E. B. Rice 47
J. G. Wright 47
M. D. Crowe 46
J. Iddon 46
A. R. Morris 46
C. T. Radley 46
Younis Ahmed 46
W. W. Armstrong 45
Asif Iqbal 45
L. G. Berry 45
J. M. Brearley 45
A. W. Carr 45
C. Hill 45
N. C. O'Neill 45
E. Paynter 45
Rev. D. S. Sheppard 45
K. D. Walters 45
D. B. Vengsarkar 45
H. H. I. Gibbons 44
P. N. Kirsten 44
V. M. Merchant 44
A. Mitchell 44
P. E. Richardson 44
B. Sutcliffe 44
G. R. Viswanath 44
E. J. Barlow 43
B. L. D'Oliveira 43
J. H. Hampshire 43
A. F. Kippax 43
H. Makepeace 43
K. C. Wessels 43
James Langridge 42
W. Larkins 42
H. W. Parks 42
T. F. Shepherd 42
V. T. Trumper 42
P. Willey 42
M. J. Harris 41
K. R. Miller 41
Mudassar Nazar 41
A. D. Nourse 41
J. H. Parks 41

R. M. Prideaux 41
G. Pullar 41
D. W. Randall 41
W. E. Russell 41
R. C. Fredericks 40
D. I. Gower 40
J. Gunn 40
M. J. Smith 4
C. L. Walcott 4
D. M. Young 4
W. H. Ashdown 3
J. B. Bolus 3
W. A. Brown 3
R. J. Gregory 3
W. R. D. Payton 3
J. R. Reid 3
F. M. M. Worrell 3
F. L. Bowley 3
P. J. Burge 3
J. F. Crapp 3
D. Lloyd 3
V. L. Manjrekar ....
A. W. Nourse ....
N. Oldfield ....
Rev. J. H. Parsons ....
W. W. Read ....
J. Sharp ....
L. J. Todd ....
J. Arnold ....
G. Brown ....
G. M. Emmett ....
H. W. Lee ....
M. A. Noble ....
B. P. Patel ....
H. S. Squires ....
R. T. Virgin ....
C. J. B. Wood ....
N. F. Armstrong ....
E. Oldroyd ....
P. W. G. Parker ....
W. Place ....
A. L. Wadekar ....
E. D. Weekes ....
Arshad Pervez ....
C. S. Dempster ....
D. R. Jardine ....
C. L. Smith ....
C. J. Tavaré ....
B. H. Valentine ....

3,000 RUNS IN A SEASON

	Season	*I*	*NO*	*R*	*HI*	*100s*	*A*
D. C. S. Compton	1947	50	8	3,816	246	18	90
W. J. Edrich	1947	52	8	3,539	267*	12	80
T. W. Hayward	1906	61	8	3,518	219	13	66
L. Hutton	1949	56	6	3,429	269*	12	68
F. E. Woolley	1928	59	4	3,352	198	12	60
H. Sutcliffe	1932	52	7	3,336	313	14	74
W. R. Hammond	1933	54	5	3,323	264	13	67

	Season	*I*	*NO*	*R*	*HI*	*100s*	*Avge*
E. H. Hendren	1928	54	7	3,311	209*	13	70.44
R. Abel	1901	68	8	3,309	247	7	55.15
W. R. Hammond	1937	55	5	3,252	217	13	65.04
M. J. K. Smith	1959	67	11	3,245	200*	8	57.94
E. H. Hendren	1933	65	9	3,186	301*	11	56.89
C. P. Mead	1921	52	6	3,179	280*	10	69.10
T. W. Hayward	1904	63	5	3,170	203	11	54.65
K. S. Ranjitsinhji	1899	58	8	3,159	197	8	63.18
C. B. Fry	1901	43	3	3,147	244	13	78.67
K. S. Ranjitsinhji	1900	40	5	3,065	275	11	87.57
L. E. G. Ames	1933	57	5	3,058	295	9	58.80
J. T. Tyldesley	1901	60	5	3,041	221	9	55.29
C. P. Mead	1928	50	10	3,027	180	13	75.67
J. B. Hobbs	1925	48	5	3,024	266*	16	70.32
E. Tyldesley	1928	48	10	3,024	242	10	79.57
W. E. Alley	1961	64	11	3,019	221*	11	56.96
W. R. Hammond	1938	42	2	3,011	271	15	75.27
E. H. Hendren	1923	51	12	3,010	200*	13	77.17
H. Sutcliffe	1931	42	11	3,006	230	13	96.96
J. H. Parks	1937	63	4	3,003	168	11	50.89
H. Sutcliffe	1928	44	5	3,002	228	13	76.97

Notes: W. G. Grace scored 2,739 runs in 1871 – the first batsman to reach 2,000 runs in a season. He made ten hundreds and twice exceeded 200, with an average of 78.25 in all first-class matches. At the time, the over consisted of four balls.

The highest aggregate in a season since the reduction of County Championship matches in 1969 is 2,713 by G. A. Hick (37 innings) in 1988.

1,000 RUNS IN A SEASON MOST TIMES

(Includes Overseas Tours and Seasons)

28 times: W. G. Grace 2,000 (6); F. E. Woolley 3,000 (1), 2,000 (12).
27 times: M. C. Cowdrey 2,000 (2); C. P. Mead 3,000 (2), 2,000 (9).
26 times: G. Boycott 2,000 (3); J. B. Hobbs 3,000 (1), 2,000 (16).
25 times: E. H. Hendren 3,000 (3), 2,000 (12).
24 times: D. L. Amiss 2,000 (3); W. G. Quaife 2,000 (1); H. Sutcliffe 3,000 (3), 2,000 (12).
23 times: A. Jones.
22 times: T. W. Graveney 2,000 (7); W. R. Hammond 3,000 (3), 2,000 (9).
21 times: D. Denton 2,000 (5); J. H. Edrich 2,000 (6); W. Rhodes 2,000 (2).
20 times: D. B. Close; K. W. R. Fletcher; G. Gunn; T. W. Hayward 3,000 (2), 2,000 (8); James Langridge 2,000 (1); J. M. Parks 2,000 (3); A. Sandham 2,000 (8); M. J. K. Smith 3,000 (1), 2,000 (5); C. Washbrook 2,000 (2).
19 times: J. W. Hearne 2,000 (4); G. H. Hirst 2,000 (3); D. Kenyon 2,000 (7); E. Tyldesley 3,000 (1), 2,000 (5); J. T. Tyldesley 3,000 (1), 2,000 (4).
18 times: L. G. Berry 2,000 (1); H. T. W. Hardinge 2,000 (5); R. E. Marshall 2,000 (6); P. A. Perrin; G. M. Turner 2,000 (3); R. E. S. Wyatt 2,000 (5).
17 times: L. E. G. Ames 3,000 (1), 2,000 (5); T. E. Bailey 2,000 (1); D. Brookes 2,000 (6); D. C. S. Compton 3,000 (1), 2,000 (5); L. Hutton 3,000 (1), 2,000 (8); J. G. Langridge 2,000 (11); M. Leyland 2,000 (3); K. G. Suttle 2,000 (1), Zaheer Abbas 2,000 (2).
16 times: D. G. Bradman 2,000 (4); D. E. Davies 2,000 (1); C. G. Greenidge 2,000 (1); E. G. Hayes 2,000 (2); C. A. Milton 2,000 (1); J. O'Connor 2,000 (4); C. T. Radley; James Seymour 2,000 (1).
15 times: G. Barker; K. F. Barrington 2,000 (3); E. H. Bowley 2,000 (4); M. H. Denness; A. E. Cooper 2,000 (5); H. E. Dollery 2,000 (2); W. J. Edrich 3,000 (1), 2,000 (8); J. H. Hampshire; P. Holmes 2,000 (7); Mushtaq Mohammad; R. B. Nicholls 2,000 (1); P. H. Parfitt 2,000 (3); W. G. A. Parkhouse 2,000 (1); B. A. Richards 2,000 (1); I. V. A. Richards 2,000 (1); J. D. Robertson 2,000 (9); G. S. Sobers; M. J. Stewart 2,000 (1).

Notes: F. E. Woolley reached 1,000 runs in 28 consecutive seasons (1907-1938). C. P. Mead did so 27 seasons in succession (1906-1936).

Outside England, 1,000 runs in a season has been reached most times by D. G. Bradman (in 12 seasons in Australia).

Three batsmen have scored 1,000 runs in a season in each of four different countries: G. S. Sobers in West Indies, England, India and Australia; M. C. Cowdrey and G. Boycott in England, South Africa, West Indies and Australia.

HIGHEST AGGREGATES OUTSIDE ENGLAND

	Season	I	NO	R	HI	100s	Avge
In Australia							
D. G. Bradman	1928-29	24	6	1,690	340*	7	93.88
In South Africa							
J. R. Reid	1961-62	30	2	1,915	203	7	68.39
In West Indies							
E. H. Hendren	1929-30	18	5	1,765	254*	6	135.76
In New Zealand							
M. D. Crowe	1986-87	21	3	1,676	175*	8	93.11
In India							
C. G. Borde	1964-65	28	3	1,604	168	6	64.1
In Pakistan							
Saadat Ali	1983-84	27	1	1,649	208	4	63.4
In Sri Lanka							
A. Ranatunga	1985-86	16	2	739	135*	3	52.7

Note: In more than one country, the following aggregates of over 2,000 runs have bee recorded.

	Season	I	NO	R	HI	100s	Avge
M. Amarnath (P/I/WI)	1982-83	34	6	2,234	207	9	79.7
J. R. Reid (SA/A/NZ).	1961-62	40	2	2,188	203	7	57.5
S. M. Gavaskar (I/P) .	1978-79	30	6	2,121	205	10	88.3
R. B. Simpson (I/P/A/WI)	1964-65	34	4	2,063	201	8	68.7

HIGHEST AVERAGES IN AN ENGLISH SEASON

(Qualification: 12 innings)

	Season	I	NO	R	HI	100s	Avg
D. G. Bradman	1938	26	5	2,429	278	13	115.
G. Boycott	1979	20	5	1,538	175*	6	102.
W. A. Johnston	1953	17	16	102	28*	0	102.
G. Boycott	1971	30	5	2,503	233	13	100.
D. G. Bradman	1930	36	6	2,960	334	10	98.
H. Sutcliffe	1931	42	11	3,006	230	13	96.
R. M. Poore	1899	21	4	1,551	304	7	91.
D. R. Jardine	1927	14	3	1,002	147	5	91.
D. C. S. Compton	1947	50	8	3,816	246	18	90.
G. M. Turner	1982	16	3	1,171	311*	5	90.
D. G. Bradman	1948	31	4	2,428	187	11	89.
Zaheer Abbas	1981	36	10	2,306	215*	10	88.
K. S. Ranjitsinhji	1900	40	5	3,065	275	11	87.
D. R. Jardine	1928	17	4	1,133	193	3	87.
W. R. Hammond	1946	26	5	1,783	214	7	84.
D. G. Bradman	1934	27	3	2,020	304	7	84.
R. B. Kanhai	1975	22	9	1,073	178*	3	82.
Mudassar Nazar	1982	16	6	825	211*	4	82
C. G. Greenidge	1984	16	3	1,069	223	4	82
J. B. Hobbs	1928	38	7	2,542	200*	12	82
C. B. Fry	1903	40	7	2,683	234	9	81
W. J. Edrich	1947	52	8	3,539	267*	12	80

25,000 RUNS IN A CAREER

Dates in italics denote the first half of an overseas season; i.e. *1945* denotes the 1945-46 season.

	Career	*R*	*I*	*NO*	*HI*	*100s*	*Avge*
J. B. Hobbs	1905-34	61,237	1,315	106	316*	197	50.65
F. E. Woolley	1906-38	58,969	1,532	85	305*	145	40.75
E. H. Hendren	1907-38	57,611	1,300	166	301*	170	50.80
C. P. Mead	1905-36	55,061	1,340	185	280*	153	47.67
†W. G. Grace	1865-1908	54,896	1,493	105	344	126	39.55
W. R. Hammond	1920-51	50,551	1,005	104	336*	167	56.10
H. Sutcliffe	1919-45	50,138	1,088	123	313	149	51.95
G. Boycott	1962-86	48,426	1,014	162	261*	151	56.83
T. W. Graveney	1948-*71*	47,793	1,223	159	258	122	44.91
T. W. Hayward	1893-1914	43,551	1,138	96	315*	104	41.79
D. L. Amiss	1960-87	43,423	1,139	126	262*	102	42.86
M. C. Cowdrey	1950-76	42,719	1,130	134	307	107	42.89
A. Sandham	1911-*37*	41,284	1,000	79	325	107	44.82
L. Hutton	1934-60	40,140	814	91	364	129	55.51
M. J. K. Smith	1951-75	39,832	1,091	139	204	69	41.84
W. Rhodes	1898-1930	39,802	1,528	237	267*	58	30.83
. H. Edrich	1956-78	39,790	979	104	310*	103	45.47
. E. S. Wyatt	1923-57	39,405	1,141	157	232	85	40.04
. C. S. Compton	1936-64	38,942	839	88	300	123	51.85
. Tyldesley	1909-36	38,874	961	106	256*	102	45.46
T. Tyldesley	1895-1923	37,897	994	62	295*	86	40.66
. W. R. Fletcher	1962-88	37,665	1,167	170	228*	63	37.77
W. Hearne	1909-36	37,252	1,025	116	285*	96	40.98
E. G. Ames	1926-51	37,248	951	95	295	102	43.51
. Kenyon	1946-67	37,002	1,159	59	259	74	33.63
. J. Edrich	1934-58	36,965	964	92	267*	86	42.39
M. Parks	1949-76	36,673	1,227	172	205*	51	34.76
Denton	1894-1920	36,479	1,163	70	221	69	33.37
. H. Hirst	1891-1929	36,323	1,215	151	341	60	34.13
Jones	1957-83	36,049	1,168	72	204*	56	32.89
. G. Quaife	1894-1928	36,012	1,203	185	255*	72	35.37
E. Marshall	*1945*-72	35,725	1,053	59	228*	68	35.94
Gunn	1902-32	35,208	1,061	82	220	62	35.96
B. Close	1949-86	34,994	1,225	173	198	52	33.26
heer Abbas	*1965-86*	34,843	768	92	274	108	51.54
G. Greenidge	1970-88	34,440	817	69	273*	83	46.04
G. Langridge	1928-55	34,380	984	66	250*	76	37.45
M. Turner	*1964-82*	34,346	792	101	311*	103	49.70
Washbrook	1933-64	34,101	906	107	251*	76	42.67
Leyland	1920-48	33,660	932	101	263	80	40.50
T. W. Hardinge	1902-33	33,519	1,021	103	263*	75	36.51
Abel	1881-1904	33,124	1,007	73	357*	74	35.46
A. Milton	1948-74	32,150	1,078	125	170	56	33.73
D. Robertson	1937-59	31,914	897	46	331*	67	37.50
Hardstaff, jun.	1930-55	31,847	812	94	266	83	44.35
I. Kallicharran	*1966*-88	31,819	798	83	243*	85	44.50
nes Langridge	1924-53	31,716	1,058	157	167	42	35.20
F. Barrington	1953-68	31,714	831	136	256	76	45.63
H. Lloyd	*1963*-86	31,232	730	96	242*	79	49.26
shtaq Mohammad	*1956*-85	31,091	843	104	303*	72	42.07
B. Fry	1892-*1921*	30,886	658	43	258*	94	50.22
Brookes	1934-59	30,874	925	70	257	71	36.10
V. A. Richards	*1971*-88	30,591	656	43	322	98	49.90
Holmes	1913-35	30,573	810	84	315*	67	42.11
T. Simpson	*1944*-63	30,546	852	55	259	64	38.32
G. Berry	1924-51	30,225	1,056	57	232	45	30.25

	Career	*R*	*I*	*NO*	*HI*	*100s*	*Avge*
K. G. Suttle	1949-71	30,225	1,064	92	204*	49	31.09
P. A. Perrin	1896-1928	29,709	918	91	343*	66	35.92
P. F. Warner	1894-1929	29,028	875	75	244	60	36.28
R. B. Kanhai	*1954-81*	28,774	669	82	256	83	49.01
J. O'Connor	1921-39	28,764	903	79	248	72	34.90
T. E. Bailey	1945-67	28,641	1,072	215	205	28	33.42
E. H. Bowley	1912-34	28,378	859	47	283	52	34.94
B. A. Richards	*1964-82*	28,358	576	58	356	80	54.74
G. S. Sobers	*1952*-74	28,315	609	93	365*	86	54.87
A. E. Dipper	1908-32	28,075	865	69	252*	53	35.27
D. G. Bradman	*1927-48*	28,067	338	43	452*	117	95.14
J. H. Hampshire	1961-84	28,059	924	112	183*	43	34.55
P. B. H. May	1948-63	27,592	618	77	285*	85	51.00
B. F. Davison	*1967-87*	27,453	766	79	189	53	39.96
Majid Khan	*1961-84*	27,444	700	62	241	73	43.01
A. C. Russell	1908-30	27,358	717	59	273	71	41.57
E. G. Hayes	1896-1926	27,318	896	48	276	48	32.2
A. E. Fagg	1932-57	27,291	803	46	269*	58	36.0
James Seymour	1900-26	27,237	911	62	218*	53	32.0
P. H. Parfitt	1956-*73*	26,924	845	104	200*	58	36.3
G. A. Gooch	1973-88	26,745	660	52	275	66	43.9
G. L. Jessop	1894-1914	26,698	855	37	286	53	32.6
D. E. Davies	1924-54	26,564	1,032	80	287*	32	27.9
A. Shrewsbury	1875-1902	26,505	813	90	267	59	36.6
M. J. Stewart	1954-72	26,492	898	93	227*	49	32.9
C. T. Radley	1964-87	26,441	880	134	200	46	35.4
Younis Ahmed	*1961-86*	26,063	762	118	221*	46	40.4
P. E. Richardson	1949-65	26,055	794	41	185	44	34.6
M. H. Denness	1959-80	25,886	838	65	195	33	33.4
S. M. Gavaskar	*1966*-87	25,834	563	61	340	81	51.4
H. Makepeace	1906-30	25,799	778	66	203	43	36.2
W. Gunn	1880-1904	25,691	850	72	273	48	33.0
W. Watson	1939-64	25,670	753	109	257	55	39.
G. Brown	1908-33	25,649	1,012	52	232*	37	26.7
G. M. Emmett	1936-59	25,602	865	50	188	37	31.
J. B. Bolus	1956-75	25,598	833	81	202*	39	34.
W. E. Russell	1956-72	25,525	796	64	193	41	34.
Javed Miandad	*1973-87*	25,400	562	88	311	72	53.
C. J. Barnett	1927-*53*	25,389	821	45	259	48	32.
L. B. Fishlock	1931-52	25,376	699	54	253	56	39.
D. J. Insole	1947-63	25,241	743	72	219*	54	37.
J. M. Brearley	1961-83	25,185	768	102	312*	45	37.
J. Vine	1896-1922	25,171	920	79	202	34	29.
R. M. Prideaux	1958-*74*	25,136	808	75	202*	41	34.
J. H. King	1895-1926	25,122	988	69	227*	34	27.

† *Some statisticians have removed from W. G. Grace's record a number of matches which th consider not to have been first-class. The above figures are those which became universally accep upon appearance in W. G. Grace's obituary in the* Wisden *of 1916. Some works of reference give career record as being 54,211–1,478–104–344–124–39.45. These figures also appeared in the 19 edition of* Wisden.

CAREER AVERAGE OVER 50

(Qualification: 10,000 runs)

Avge		*Career*	*I*	*NO*	*R*	*HI*	*10*
95.14	D. G. Bradman	*1927-48*	338	43	28,067	452*	1
71.22	V. M. Merchant	*1929-51*	229	43	13,248	359*	
65.18	W. H. Ponsford	*1920-34*	235	23	13,819	437	
64.99	W. M. Woodfull	*1921-34*	245	39	13,388	284	

Avge		*Career*	*I*	*NO*	*R*	*HI*	*100s*
58.24	A. L. Hassett	*1932-53*	322	32	16,890	232	59
58.19	V. S. Hazare	*1934-66*	365	45	18,621	316*	60
57.22	A. F. Kippax	*1918-35*	256	33	12,762	315*	43
56.83	G. Boycott	1962-86	1,014	162	48,426	261*	151
56.68	M. D. Crowe	*1979*-88	274	42	13,151	242*	46
56.55	C. L. Walcott	*1941-63*	238	29	11,820	314*	40
56.37	K. S. Ranjitsinhji	1893-1920	500	62	24,692	285*	72
56.22	R. B. Simpson	*1952-77*	436	62	21,029	359	60
56.10	W. R. Hammond	1920-51	1,005	104	50,551	336*	167
55.51	L. Hutton	1934-60	814	91	40,140	364	129
55.34	E. D. Weekes	*1944*-64	241	24	12,010	304*	36
54.87	G. S. Sobers	*1952*-74	609	93	28,315	365*	86
54.74	B. A. Richards	*1964-82*	576	58	28,358	356	80
54.67	R. G. Pollock	*1960-86*	437	54	20,940	274	64
4.24	F. M. M. Worrell	*1941*-64	326	49	15,025	308*	39
4.20	A. R. Border	*1976*-88	409	62	18,810	205	58
3.78	R. M. Cowper	*1959-69*	228	31	10,595	307	26
3.67	A. R. Morris	*1940-63*	250	15	12,614	290	46
3.58	Javed Miandad	*1973-87*	562	88	25,400	311	72
2.32	Hanif Mohammad	*1951-75*	371	45	17,059	499	55
2.27	P. R. Umrigar	*1944-67*	350	41	16,154	252*	49
2.20	G. S. Chappell	*1966-83*	542	72	24,535	247*	74
1.95	H. Sutcliffe	1919-45	1,088	123	50,138	313	149
.89	D. B. Vengsarkar	*1975-87*	317	42	14,270	210	45
.85	D. C. S. Compton	1936-64	839	88	38,942	300	123
.54	Zaheer Abbas	*1965-86*	768	92	34,843	274	108
.53	A. D. Nourse	*1931-52*	269	27	12,472	260*	41
.46	S. M. Gavaskar	*1966*-87	563	61	25,834	340	81
.44	W. A. Brown	*1932-49*	284	15	13,838	265*	39
.00	P. B. H. May	1948-63	618	77	27,592	285*	85
).95	N. C. O'Neill	*1955-67*	306	34	13,859	284	45
.93	R. N. Harvey	*1946-62*	461	35	21,699	231*	67
.90	W. M. Lawry	*1955-71*	417	49	18,734	266	50
.90	A. V. Mankad	*1963-82*	326	71	12,980	265	31
.80	E. H. Hendren	1907-38	1,300	166	57,611	301*	170
.65	J. B. Hobbs	1905-34	1,315	106	61,237	316*	197
.22	C. B. Fry	1892-*1921*	658	43	30,886	258*	94
.13	Shafiq Ahmed	*1967-87*	400	48	17,649	217*	49
.08	K. C. Wessels	*1973-87*	343	27	15,827	254	43

FAST FIFTIES

inutes

† C. C. Inman (57) Leicestershire v Nottinghamshire at Nottingham . . . 1965
C. I. J. Smith (66) Middlesex v Gloucestershire at Bristol 1938
S. J. Pegler (50) South Africans v Tasmania at Launceston 1910-11
F. T. Mann (53) Middlesex v Nottinghamshire at Lord's 1921
H. B. Cameron (56) Transvaal v Orange Free State at Johannesburg . . . 1934-35
C. I. J. Smith (52) Middlesex v Kent at Maidstone 1935
M. P. Maynard (61*) Glamorgan v Yorkshire at Cardiff 1987

† *Full tosses were bowled to expedite a declaration.*

FASTEST HUNDREDS

nutes

P. G. H. Fender (113*) Surrey v Northamptonshire at Northampton . . 1920
S. J. O'Shaughnessy (105) Lancashire v Leicestershire at Manchester 1983
C. M. Old (107) Yorkshire v Warwickshire at Birmingham 1977
G. L. Jessop (101) Gloucestershire v Yorkshire at Harrogate 1897
N. F. M. Popplewell (143) Somerset v Gloucestershire at Bath 1983

Minutes			
42	G. L. Jessop (191)	Gentlemen of South v Players of South at Hastings	1907
43	A. H. Hornby (106)	Lancashire v Somerset at Manchester	1905
43	D. W. Hookes (107)	South Australia v Victoria at Adelaide	1982-83
44	R. N. S. Hobbs (100)	Essex v Australians at Chelmsford	1975

Notes: The fastest recorded hundred in terms of balls received was scored off 34 balls by D. W. Hookes (above).

Research of the scorebook has shown that P. G. H. Fender scored his hundred from between 40 and 46 balls. He contributed 113 to an unfinished sixth-wicket partnership of 171 in 42 minutes with H. A. Peach.

S. J. O'Shaughnessy scored his hundred on the final afternoon of the season and against a succession of long-hops and full-tosses offered by occasional bowlers to expedite a declaration.

E. B. Alletson (Nottinghamshire) scored 189 out of 227 runs in 90 minutes against Sussex at Hove in 1911. It has been estimated that his last 139 runs took 37 minutes.

FASTEST DOUBLE-HUNDREDS

Minutes			
113	R. J. Shastri (200*)	Bombay v Baroda at Bombay	1984-8
120	G. L. Jessop (286)	Gloucestershire v Sussex at Hove	190
120	C. H. Lloyd (201*)	West Indians v Glamorgan at Swansea	197
130	G. L. Jessop (234)	Gloucestershire v Somerset at Bristol	190
131	V. T. Trumper (293)	Australians v Canterbury at Christchurch	1913-1

FASTEST TRIPLE-HUNDREDS

Minutes			
181	D. C. S. Compton (300)	MCC v N. E. Transvaal at Benoni	1948-4
205	F. E. Woolley (305*)	MCC v Tasmania at Hobart	1911-1
205	C. G. Macartney (345)	Australians v Nottinghamshire at Nottingham	192
213	D. G. Bradman (369)	South Australia v Tasmania at Adelaide	1935-3

300 RUNS IN ONE DAY

345	C. G. Macartney	Australians v Nottinghamshire at Nottingham	19
334	W. H. Ponsford	Victoria v New South Wales at Melbourne	1926-
333	K. S. Duleepsinhji	Sussex v Northamptonshire at Hove	19
331*	J. D. Robertson	Middlesex v Worcestershire at Worcester	19
325*	B. A. Richards	S. Australia v W. Australia at Perth	1970-
322†	E. Paynter	Lancashire v Sussex at Hove	19
322	I. V. A. Richards	Somerset v Warwickshire at Taunton	19
318	C. W. Gregory	New South Wales v Queensland at Brisbane	1906-
317	K. R. Rutherford	New Zealanders v D. B. Close's XI at Scarborough	19
316†	R. H. Moore	Hampshire v Warwickshire at Bournemouth	19
315*	R. C. Blunt	Otago v Canterbury at Christchurch	1931-
312*	J. M. Brearley	MCC Under 25 v North Zone at Peshawar	1966-
311*	G. M. Turner	Worcestershire v Warwickshire at Worcester	19
309*	D. G. Bradman	Australia v England at Leeds	1
307*	W. H. Ashdown	Kent v Essex at Brentwood	1
306*	A. Ducat	Surrey v Oxford University at The Oval	1
305*	F. R. Foster	Warwickshire v Worcestershire at Dudley	1

† *E. Paynter's 322 and R. H. Moore's 316 were scored on the same day: July 28, 1937.*

1,000 RUNS IN MAY

	Runs	Avge
W. G. Grace, May 9 to May 30, 1895 (22 days):		
13, 103, 18, 25, 288, 52, 257, 73*, 18, 169	1,016	112.88
Grace was within two months of completing his 47th year.		
W. R. Hammond, May 7 to May 31, 1927 (25 days):		
27, 135, 108, 128, 17, 11, 99, 187, 4, 30, 83, 7, 192, 14	1,042	74.42
Hammond scored his 1,000th run on May 28, thus equalling Grace's record of 22 days.		
C. Hallows, May 5 to May 31, 1928 (27 days):		
100, 101, 51*, 123, 101*, 22, 74, 104, 58, 34*, 232	1,000	125.00

1,000 RUNS IN APRIL AND MAY

T. W. Hayward, April 16 to May 31, 1900:		
120*, 55, 108, 131*, 55, 193, 120, 5, 6, 3, 40, 146, 92	1,074	97.63
D. G. Bradman, April 30 to May 31, 1930:		
236, 185*, 78, 9, 48*, 66, 4, 44, 252*, 32, 47*	1,001	143.00
On April 30 Bradman scored 75 not out.		
D. G. Bradman, April 30 to May 31, 1938:		
258, 58, 137, 278, 2, 143, 145*, 5, 30*	1,056	150.85
Bradman scored 258 on April 30, and his 1,000th run on May 27.		
W. J. Edrich, April 30 to May 31, 1938:		
104, 37, 115, 63, 20*, 182, 71, 31, 53*, 45, 15, 245, 0, 9, 20*	1,010	84.16
Edrich scored 21 not out on April 30. All his runs were scored at Lord's.		
G. M. Turner, April 24 to May 31, 1973:		
41, 151*, 143, 85, 7, 8, 17*, 81, 13, 53, 44, 153*, 3, 2, 66*, 30, 10*, 111	1,018	78.30
G. A. Hick, April 17 to May 29, 1988:		
61, 37, 212, 86, 14, 405*, 8, 11, 6, 7, 172	1,019	101.90
Hick scored a record 410 runs in April, and his 1,000th run on May 28.		

1,000 RUNS IN TWO SEPARATE MONTHS

Only four batsmen, C. B. Fry, K. S. Ranjitsinhji, H. Sutcliffe and L. Hutton, have scored over 1,000 runs in each of two months in the same season. L. Hutton, by scoring 1,294 in June 1949, made more runs in a single month than anyone else. He also made 1,050 in August 1949.

MOST RUNS SCORED OFF ONE OVER

(All instances refer to six-ball overs)

6	G. S. Sobers	off M. A. Nash, Nottinghamshire v Glamorgan at Swansea (six 6s)	1968
6	R. J. Shastri	off Tilak Raj, Bombay v Baroda at Bombay (six 6s)	1984-85
4	E. B. Alletson	off E. H. Killick, Nottinghamshire v Sussex at Hove (46604446; including two no-balls)	1911
4	F. C. Hayes	off M. A. Nash, Lancashire v Glamorgan at Swansea (646666)	1977
2	I. T. Botham	off I. R. Snook, England XI v Central Districts at Palmerston North (466466)	1983-84
2	C. C. Inman	off N. W. Hill, Leicestershire v Nottinghamshire at Nottingham (466664; full tosses were provided for him to hit)	1965
2	T. E. Jesty	off R. J. Boyd-Moss, Hampshire v Northamptonshire at Southampton (666662)	1984
2	P. W. G. Parker	off A. I. Kallicharran, Sussex v Warwickshire at Birmingham (466664)	1982

32	I. R. Redpath	off N. Rosendorff, Australians v Orange Free State at Bloemfontein (666644)	1969-70
32	C. C. Smart	off G. Hill, Glamorgan v Hampshire at Cardiff (664664)	1935
31	M. H. Bowditch (1) and M. J. Procter (30)	off A. A. Mallett, Western Province v Australians at Cape Town (Procter hit five 6s)	1969-70
31	A. W. Wellard	off F. E. Woolley, Somerset v Kent at Wells (666661)	1938
30	I. T. Botham	off P. A. Smith, Somerset v Warwickshire at Taunton (4466460 including one no-ball)	1982
30	D. G. Bradman	off A. P. Freeman, Australians v England XI at Folkestone (466464)	1934
30	H. B. Cameron	off H. Verity, South Africans v Yorkshire at Sheffield (444666)	1935
30	G. A. Gooch	off S. R. Gorman, Essex v Cambridge U. at Cambridge (662664)	1985
30	A. J. Lamb	off A. I. Kallicharran, Northamptonshire v Warwickshire at Birmingham (644664)	1982
30	D. T. Lindsay	off W. T. Greensmith, South African Fezela XI v Essex at Chelmsford (066666 to win the match)	1961
30	Majid Khan	off R. C. Davis, Pakistanis v Glamorgan at Swansea (606666)	1967
30	M. P. Maynard	off K. Sharp, Glamorgan v Yorkshire at Cardiff (464466)	1987
30	A. W. Wellard	off T. R. Armstrong, Somerset v Derbyshire at Wells (066666)	1936
30	D. Wilson	off R. N. S. Hobbs, Yorkshire v MCC at Scarborough (466266)	1966
30	P. L. Winslow	off J. T. Ikin, South Africans v Lancashire at Manchester (446646)	1955
30	Zaheer Abbas	off D. Breakwell, Gloucestershire v Somerset at Taunton (466626)	1979

Note: The greatest number of runs scored off an eight-ball over is 34 (40446664) by R. M. Edwards off M. C. Carew, Governor-General's XI v West Indians at Auckland, 1968-69.

MOST SIXES IN AN INNINGS

15	J. R. Reid (296)	Wellington v N. Districts at Wellington	1962-63
13	Majid Khan (147*)	Pakistanis v Glamorgan at Swansea	1967
13	C. G. Greenidge (273*)	D. H. Robins' XI v Pakistanis at Eastbourne	1974
13	C. G. Greenidge (259)	Hampshire v Sussex at Southampton	1975
13	G. W. Humpage (254)	Warwickshire v Lancashire at Southport	1982
13	R. J. Shastri (200*)	Bombay v Baroda at Bombay	1984-85
12	Gulfraz Khan (207)	Railways v Universities at Lahore	1976-77
12	I. T. Botham (138*)	Somerset v Warwickshire at Birmingham	198
12	R. A. Harper (234)	Northamptonshire v Gloucestershire at Northampton	198
11	C. K. Nayudu (153)	Hindus v MCC at Bombay	1926-2
11	C. J. Barnett (194)	Gloucestershire v Somerset at Bath	193
11	R. Benaud (135)	Australians v T. N. Pearce's XI at Scarborough	195
11	G. A. Hick (405*)	Worcestershire v Somerset at Taunton	198

Note: W. J. Stewart (Warwickshire) hit seventeen sixes in the match v Lancashire, a Blackpool, 1959; ten in his first innings of 155 and seven in his second innings of 125.

MOST SIXES IN A SEASON

80	I. T. Botham	1985	66	A. W. Wellard	19

Note: A. W. Wellard hit 50 or more sixes in a season four times. His number of sixes in 19 has in the past been given as 72, but recent research has caused this to be adjusted.

MOST BOUNDARIES IN AN INNINGS

68	P. A. Perrin (343*)	Essex v Derbyshire at Chesterfield	1904
65	A. C. MacLaren (424)	Lancashire v Somerset at Taunton	1895
64	Hanif Mohammad (499)	Karachi v Bahawalpur at Karachi	1958-59
57	J. H. Edrich (310*)	England v New Zealand at Leeds	1965
55	C. W. Gregory (383)	NSW v Queensland at Brisbane	1906-07
54	G. H. Hirst (341)	Yorkshire v Leicestershire at Leicester	1905
53	A. W. Nourse (304*)	Natal v Transvaal at Johannesburg	1919-20
53	K. R. Rutherford (317)	New Zealanders v D. B. Close's XI at Scarborough.	1986
51	C. G. Macartney (345)	Australians v Nottinghamshire at Nottingham	1921
50	D. G. Bradman (369)	South Australia v Tasmania at Adelaide	1935-36
50	A. Ducat (306*)	Surrey v Oxford University at The Oval	1919
50	B. B. Nimbalkar (443*)	Maharashtra v Kathiawar at Poona	1948-49
50	J. R. Reid (296)	Wellington v N. Districts at Wellington	1962-63
50	I. V. A. Richards (322)	Somerset v Warwickshire at Taunton	1985

Note: Boundaries include sixes.

HIGHEST PARTNERSHIPS

577 V. S. Hazare (288) and Gul Mahomed (319), fourth wicket, Baroda v Holkar at Baroda ... 1946-47

574* F. M. M. Worrell (255*) and C. L. Walcott (314*), fourth wicket, Barbados v Trinidad at Port-of-Spain ... 1945-46

561 Waheed Mirza (324) and Mansoor Akhtar (224*), first wicket, Karachi Whites v Quetta at Karachi ... 1976-77

555 P. Holmes (224*) and H. Sutcliffe (313), first wicket, Yorkshire v Essex at Leyton ... 1932

554 J. T. Brown (300) and J. Tunnicliffe (243), first wicket, Yorkshire v Derbyshire at Chesterfield ... 1898

502* F. M. M. Worrell (308*) and J. D. C. Goddard (218*), fourth wicket, Barbados v Trinidad at Bridgetown ... 1943-44

490 E. H. Bowley (283) and J. G. Langridge (195), first wicket, Sussex v Middlesex at Hove ... 1933

487* G. A. Headley (344*) and C. C. Passailaigue (261*), sixth wicket, Jamaica v Lord Tennyson's XI at Kingston ... 1931-32

470 A. I. Kallicharran (230*) and G. W. Humpage (254), fourth wicket, Warwickshire v Lancashire at Southport ... 1982

465* J. A. Jameson (240*) and R. B. Kanhai (213*), second wicket, Warwickshire v Gloucestershire at Birmingham ... 1974

462* D. W. Hookes (306*) and W. B. Phillips (213*), fourth wicket, South Australia v Tasmania at Adelaide ... 1986-87

456 W. H. Ponsford (248) and E. R. Mayne (209), first wicket, Victoria v Queensland at Melbourne ... 1923-24

456 Khalid Irtiza (290) and Aslam Ali (236), third wicket, United Bank v Multan at Karachi ... 1975-76

455 K. V. Bhandarkar (205) and B. B. Nimbalkar (443*), second wicket, Maharashtra v Kathiawar at Poona ... 1948-49

451 D. G. Bradman (244) and W. H. Ponsford (266), second wicket, Australia v England, Fifth Test, at The Oval ... 1934

451* S. Desai (218*) and R. M. H. Binny (211*), first wicket, Karnataka v Kerala at Chikmagalur ... 1977-78

451 Mudassar Nazar (231) and Javed Miandad (280*), third wicket, Pakistan v India, Fourth Test, at Hyderabad ... 1982-83

PARTNERSHIPS FOR FIRST WICKET

561	Waheed Mirza and Mansoor Akhtar, Karachi Whites v Quetta at Karachi	1976-77
555	P. Holmes and H. Sutcliffe, Yorkshire v Essex at Leyton	1932
554	J. T. Brown and J. Tunnicliffe, Yorkshire v Derbyshire at Chesterfield	1898
490	E. H. Bowley and J. G. Langridge, Sussex v Middlesex at Hove	1933
456	E. R. Mayne and W. H. Ponsford, Victoria v Queensland at Melbourne	1923-24
451*	S. Desai and R. M. H. Binny, Karnataka v Kerala at Chikmagalur	1977-78
428	J. B Hobbs and A. Sandham, Surrey v Oxford University at The Oval	1926
424	J. F. W. Nicholson and I. J. Siedle, Natal v Orange Free State at Bloemfontein	1926-27
421	S. M. Gavaskar and G. A. Parkar, Bombay v Bengal at Bombay	1981-82
418	Kamal Najamuddin and Khalid Alvi, Karachi v Railways at Karachi	1980-81
413	V. Mankad and Pankaj Roy, India v New Zealand at Madras (world Test record)	1955-56
405	C. P. S. Chauhan and M. S. Gupte, Maharashtra v Vidarbha at Poona	1972-73
395	D. M. Young and R. B. Nicholls, Gloucestershire v Oxford University at Oxford	1962
391	A. O. Jones and A. Shrewsbury, Nottinghamshire v Gloucestershire at Bristol	1899
390	G. L. Wight and G. L. R. Gibbs, B. Guiana v Barbados at Georgetown	1951-52
390	B. Dudleston and J. F. Steele, Leicestershire v Derbyshire at Leicester	1979
389	Majid Khan and Shafiq Ahmed, Punjab A v Sind A at Karachi	1974-75
389	Mudassar Nazar and Mansoor Akhtar, United Bank v Rawalpindi at Lahore	1981-82
388	K. C. Wessels and R. B. Kerr, Queensland v Victoria at St Kilda, Melbourne	1982-83
387	G. M. Turner and T. W. Jarvis, New Zealand v West Indies at Georgetown	1971-72
382	R. B. Simpson and W. M. Lawry, Australia v West Indies at Bridgetown	1964-65
380	H. Whitehead and C. J. B. Wood, Leicestershire v Worcestershire at Worcester	1906
379	R. Abel and W. Brockwell, Surrey v Hampshire at The Oval	1897
378	J. T. Brown and J. Tunnicliffe, Yorkshire v Sussex at Sheffield	1897
377*	N. F. Horner and Khalid Ibadulla, Warwickshire v Surrey at The Oval	1960
375	W. H. Ponsford and W. M. Woodfull, Victoria v New South Wales at Melbourne	1926-27

FIRST-WICKET HUNDREDS IN BOTH INNINGS

B. Sutcliffe and D. D. Taylor, for Auckland v Canterbury in 1948-49, scored for the first wicke[t] 220 in the first innings and 286 in the second innings. This is the only instance of two double century opening stands in the same match.

T. W. Hayward and J. B. Hobbs in 1907 accomplished a performance without parallel b[y] scoring over 100 together for Surrey's first wicket four times in one week: 106 and 125 [v] Cambridge University at The Oval, and 147 and 105 v Middlesex at Lord's.

L. Hutton and C. Washbrook, in three consecutive Test match innings which they opene[d] together for England v Australia in 1946-47, made 138 in the second innings at Melbourne, an[d] 137 and 100 at Adelaide. They also opened with 168 and 129 at Leeds in 1948.

J. B. Hobbs and H. Sutcliffe, in three consecutive Test match innings which they opene[d] together for England v Australia in 1924-25, made 157 and 110 at Sydney and 283 at Melbourn[e]. On 26 occasions – 15 times in Test matches – Hobbs and Sutcliffe took part in a three-figu[re] first-wicket partnership. Seven of these stands exceeded 200.

G. Boycott and J. H. Edrich, in three consecutive Test match innings which they opene[d] together for England v Australia in 1970-71, made 161* in the second innings at Melbourne, an[d] 107 and 103 at Adelaide.

In 1971 R. G. A. Headley and P. J. Stimpson of Worcestershire shared in first-wick[et] hundred partnerships on each of the first four occasions they opened the innings together: 1[?] and 147 v Northamptonshire at Worcester, 102 and 128* v Warwickshire at Birmingham[.]

J. B. Hobbs during his career, which extended from 1905 to 1934, helped to make 100 or mo[re] for the first wicket in first-class cricket 166 times – 15 of them in 1926, when in consecuti[ve] innings he helped to make 428, 182, 106 and 123 before a wicket fell. As many as 117 of the 1[66] stands were made for Surrey. In all first-class matches Hobbs and A. Sandham shared 66 fir[st-]wicket partnerships of 100 or more runs.

P. Holmes and H. Sutcliffe made 100 or more runs for the first wicket of Yorkshire on 69 occasions; J. B. Hobbs and A. Sandham for Surrey on 63 occasions; W. W. Keeton and C. B. Harris of Nottinghamshire on 46; T. W. Hayward and J. B. Hobbs of Surrey on 40; G. Gunn and W. W. Whysall of Nottinghamshire on 40; J. D. Robertson and S. M. Brown of Middlesex on 34; C. B. Fry and J. Vine of Sussex on 33; R. E. Marshall and J. R. Gray of Hampshire on 33; D. E. Davies and A. H. Dyson of Glamorgan on 32; and G. Boycott and R. G. Lumb of Yorkshire on 27.

J. Douglas and A. E. Stoddart in 1896 scored over 150 runs for the Middlesex first wicket three times within a fortnight. In 1901, J. Iremonger and A. O. Jones obtained over 100 for the Nottinghamshire first wicket four times within eight days, scoring 134 and 144* v Surrey at The Oval, 238 v Essex at Leyton, and 119 v Derbyshire at Welbeck.

J. W. Lee and F. S. Lee, brothers, for Somerset in 1934, scored over 100 runs thrice in succession in the County Championship.

W. G. Grace and A. E. Stoddart, in three consecutive innings against the Australians in 1893, made over 100 runs for each opening partnership.

C. Hallows and F. B. Watson, in consecutive innings for Lancashire in 1928, opened with 200, 202, 107, 118; reached three figures twelve times, 200 four times.

H. Sutcliffe, in the period 1919-1939 inclusive, shared in 145 first-wicket partnerships of 100 runs or more.

There were four first-wicket hundred partnerships in the match between Somerset and Cambridge University at Taunton in 1960. G. Atkinson and R. T. Virgin scored 172 and 112 for Somerset and R. M. Prideaux and A. R. Lewis 198 and 137 for Cambridge University.

PARTNERSHIP RECORDS FOR ALL COUNTRIES

Best First-Wicket Stands

Pakistan	561	Waheed Mirza (324) and Mansoor Akhtar (224*), Karachi Whites v Quetta at Karachi	1976-77
English	555	P. Holmes (224*) and H. Sutcliffe (313), Yorkshire v Essex at Leyton	1932
Australian	456	W. H. Ponsford (248) and E. R. Mayne (209), Victoria v Queensland at Melbourne	1923-24
Indian	451*	S. Desai (218*) and R. M. H. Binny (211*), Karnataka v Kerala at Chikmagalur	1977-78
South African	424	J. F. W. Nicolson (252*) and I. J. Siedle (174), Natal v Orange Free State at Bloemfontein	1926-27
West Indian	390	G. L. Wight (262*) and G. L. R. Gibbs (216), British Guiana v Barbados at Georgetown	1951-52
New Zealand	387	G. M. Turner (259) and T. W. Jarvis (182), New Zealand v West Indies at Georgetown	1971-72

Best Second-Wicket Stands

English	465*	J. A. Jameson (240*) and R. B. Kanhai (213*), Warwickshire v Gloucestershire at Birmingham	1974
Indian	455	K. V. Bhandarkar (205) and B. B. Nimbalkar (443*), Maharashtra v Kathiawar at Poona	1948-49
Australian	451	W. H. Ponsford (266) and D. G. Bradman (244), Australia v England at The Oval	1934
West Indian	446	C. C. Hunte (260) and G. S. Sobers (365*), West Indies v Pakistan at Kingston	1957-58
Pakistan	426	Arshad Pervez (220) and Mohsin Khan (220), Habib Bank v Income Tax Dept at Lahore	1977-78
New Zealand	317	R. T. Hart (167*) and P. S. Briasco (157), Central Districts v Canterbury at New Plymouth	1983-84
South African	305	S. K. Coen (165) and J. M. M Commaille (186), Orange Free State v Natal at Bloemfontein	1926-27

Best Third-Wicket Stands

Pakistan	456	Khalid Irtiza (290) and Aslam Ali (236), United Bank v Multan at Karachi	1975-76
New Zealand	445	P. E. Whitelaw (195) and W. N. Carson (290), Auckland v Otago at Dunedin (in 268 minutes)	1936-37
West Indian	434	J. B. Stollmeyer (324) and G. E. Gomez (190), Trinidad v British Guiana at Port-of-Spain	1946-47
English	424*	W. J. Edrich (168*) and D. C. S. Compton (252*), Middlesex v Somerset at Lord's	1948
Indian	410	L. Amarnath (262) and R. S. Modi (156), India in England v The Rest at Calcutta	1946-47
Australian	390*	J. M. Wiener (221*) and J. K. Moss (200*), Victoria v Western Australia at St Kilda, Melbourne	1981-82
South African	341	E. J. Barlow (201) and R. G. Pollock (175), South Africa v Australia at Adelaide	1963-64

Best Fourth-Wicket Stands

Indian	577	V. S. Hazare (288) and Gul Mahomed (319), Baroda v Holkar at Baroda	1946-47
West Indian	574*	C. L. Walcott (314*) and F. M. M. Worrell (255*), Barbados v Trinidad at Port-of-Spain	1945-4
English	470	A. I. Kallicharran (230*) and G. W. Humpage (254), Warwickshire v Lancashire at Southport	198
Australian	462*	D. W. Hookes (306*) and W. B. Phillips (213*), South Australia v Tasmania at Adelaide	1986-87
Pakistan	350	Mushtaq Mohammad (201) and Asif Iqbal (175), Pakistan v New Zealand at Dunedin	1972-7
South African	342	E. A. B. Rowan (196) and P. J. M. Gibb (203), Transvaal v N. E. Transvaal at Johannesburg	1952-5
New Zealand	324	J. R. Reid (188*) and W. M. Wallace (197), New Zealanders v Cambridge University at Cambridge	194

Best Fifth-Wicket Stands

Australian	405	S. G. Barnes (234) and D. G. Bradman (234), Australia v England at Sydney	1946-4
English	393	E. G. Arnold (200*) and W. B. Burns (196), Worcestershire v Warwickshire at Birmingham	190
Indian	360	U. M. Merchant (217) and M. N. Raiji (170), Bombay v Hyderabad at Bombay	1947-4
Pakistan	355	Altaf Shah (276) and Tariq Bashir (196), House Building Finance Corporation v Multan at Multan	1976-7
South African	355	A. J. Lamb (294) and J. J. Strydom (107), OFS v Eastern Province at Bloemfontein	1987-8
New Zealand	341	G. R. Larsen (161) and E. B. McSweeney (205*), Wellington v Central Districts at Levin	1987-
West Indian	335	B. F. Butcher (151) and C. H. Lloyd (201*), West Indians v Glamorgan at Swansea	19

Best Sixth-Wicket Stands

West Indian	487*	G. A. Headley (344*) and C. C. Passailaigue (261*), Jamaica v Lord Tennyson's XI at Kingston	1931-
Australian	428	M. A. Noble (284) and W. W. Armstrong (172*), Australians v Sussex at Hove	19

English	411	R. M. Poore (304) and E. G. Wynyard (225), Hampshire v Somerset at Taunton	1899
Indian	371	V. M. Merchant (359*) and R. S. Modi (168), Bombay v Maharashtra at Bombay	1943-44
Pakistan	353	Salah-ud-Din (256) and Zaheer Abbas (197), Karachi v East Pakistan at Karachi	1968-69
South African	259	S. A. Jones (209*) and O. Henry (125), Boland v Border at East London	1987-88
New Zealand	226	E. J. Gray (126) and R. W. Ormiston (93), Wellington v Central Districts at Wellington	1981-82

Best Seventh-Wicket Stands

West Indian	347	D. St E. Atkinson (219) and C. C. Depeiza (122), West Indies v Australia at Bridgetown	1954-55
English	344	K. S. Ranjitsinhji (230) and W. Newham (153), Sussex v Essex at Leyton	1902
Australian	335	C. W. Andrews (253) and E. C. Bensted (155), Queensland v New South Wales at Sydney	1934-35
Pakistan	308	Waqar Hassan (189) and Imtiaz Ahmed (209), Pakistan v New Zealand at Lahore	1955-56
South African	299	B. Mitchell (159) and A. Melville (153), Transvaal v Griqualand West at Kimberley	1946-47
ndian	274	K. C. Ibrahim (250) and K. M. Rangnekar (138), Bijapur XI v Bengal XI at Bombay	1942-43
New Zealand	265	J. L. Powell (164) and N. Dorreen (105*), Canterbury v Otago at Christchurch	1929-30

Best Eighth-Wicket Stands

ustralian	433	A. Sims (184*) and V. T. Trumper (293), An Australian XI v Canterbury at Christchurch	1913-14
nglish	292	R. Peel (210*) and Lord Hawke (166), Yorkshire v Warwickshire at Birmingham	1896
Vest Indian	255	E. A. V. Williams (131*) and E. A. Martindale (134), Barbados v Trinidad at Bridgetown	1935-36
akistan	240	Gulfraz Khan (207) and Raja Sarfraz (102), Railways v Universities at Lahore	1976-77
dian	236	C. T. Sarwate (235) and R. P. Singh (88), Holkar v Delhi and District at Delhi	1949-50
outh African	222	D. P. B. Morkel (114) and S. S. L. Steyn (261*), Western Province v Border at Cape Town	1929-30
ew Zealand	190*	J. E. Mills (104*) and C. F. W. Allcott (102*), New Zealanders v Civil Service at Chiswick	1927

est Ninth-Wicket Stands

nglish	283	J. Chapman (165) and A. Warren (123), Derbyshire v Warwickshire at Blackwell	1910
dian	245	V. S. Hazare (316*) and N. D. Nagarwalla (98), Maharashtra v Baroda at Poona	1939-40
ew Zealand	239	H. B. Cave (118) and I. B. Leggat (142*), Central Districts v Otago at Dunedin	1952-53
stralian	232	C. Hill (365*) and E. Walkley (53), South Australia v New South Wales at Adelaide	1900-01
uth African	221	N. V. Lindsay (160*) and G. R. McCubbin (97), Transvaal v Rhodesia at Bulawayo	1922-23
kistan	190	Asif Iqbal (146) and Intikhab Alam (51), Pakistan v England at The Oval	1967
est Indian	161	C. H. Lloyd (161*) and A. M. E. Roberts (68), West Indies v India at Calcutta	1983-84

Best Tenth-Wicket Stands

Australian	307	A. F. Kippax (260*), and J. E. H. Hooker (62), New South Wales v Victoria at Melbourne	1928-29
Indian	249	C. T. Sarwate (124*) and S. N. Banerjee (121), Indians v Surrey at The Oval	1946
English	235	F. E. Woolley (185) and A. Fielder (112*), Kent v Worcestershire at Stourbridge	1909
Pakistan	196*	Nadim Yousuf (202*) and Maqsood Kundi (109*) Muslim Commercial Bank v National Bank at Lahore	1981-82
New Zealand	184	R. C. Blunt (338*) and W. Hawkesworth (21), Otago v Canterbury at Christchurch	1931-32
South African	174	H. R. Lance (168) and D. Mackay-Coghill (57*), Transvaal v Natal at Johannesburg	1965-66
West Indian	138	E. L. G. Hoad (149*) and H. C. Griffith (84), West Indians v Sussex at Hove	1933

Note: All the English record wicket partnerships were made in the County Championship.

OUT HANDLED THE BALL

J. Grundy	MCC v Kent at Lord's	1857
G. Bennett	Kent v Sussex at Hove	1872
W. H. Scotton	Smokers v Non-Smokers at East Melbourne	1886-87
C. W. Wright	Nottinghamshire v Gloucestershire at Bristol	1893
E. Jones	South Australia v Victoria at Melbourne	1894-95
A. W. Nourse	South Africans v Sussex at Hove	1907
E. T. Benson	MCC v Auckland at Auckland	1929-30
A. W. Gilbertson	Otago v Auckland at Auckland	1952-53
W. R. Endean	South Africa v England at Cape Town	1956-57
P. J. Burge	Queensland v New South Wales at Sydney	1958-59
Dildar Awan	Services v Lahore at Lahore	1959-60
Mahmood-ul-Hasan	Karachi University v Railways-Quetta at Karachi	1960-61
Ali Raza	Karachi Greens v Hyderabad at Karachi	1961-6
Mohammad Yusuf	Rawalpindi v Peshawar at Peshawar	1962-6
A. Rees	Glamorgan v Middlesex at Lord's	196
Pervez Akhtar	Multan v Karachi Greens at Sahiwal	1971-7
Javed Mirza	Railways v Punjab at Lahore	1972-7
R. G. Pollock	Eastern Province v Western Province at Cape Town	1973-7
C. I. Dey	Northern Transvaal v Orange Free State at Bloemfontein	1973-7
Nasir Valika	Karachi Whites v National Bank at Karachi	1974-7
Haji Yousuf	National Bank v Railways at Lahore	1974-7
Masood-ul-Hasan	PIA v National Bank B at Lyallpur	1975-7
D. K. Pearse	Natal v Western Province at Cape Town	1978-7
A. M. J. Hilditch	Australia v Pakistan at Perth	1978-7
Musleh-ud-Din	Railways v Lahore at Lahore	1979-8
Jalal-ud-Din	IDBP v Habib Bank at Bahawalpur	1981-8
Mohsin Khan	Pakistan v Australia at Karachi	1982-8
D. L. Haynes	West Indies v India at Bombay	1983-
K. Azad	Delhi v Punjab at Amritsar	1983-8
Athar A. Khan	Allied Bank v HBFC at Sialkot	1983-
A. Pandya	Saurashtra v Baroda at Baroda	1984-
G. N. Linton	Barbados v Windward Islands at Bridgetown	1985-
R. B. Gartrell	Tasmania v Victoria at Melbourne	1986-

OUT OBSTRUCTING THE FIELD

C. A. Absolom	Cambridge University v Surrey at The Oval	18
T. Straw	Worcestershire v Warwickshire at Worcester	18
T. Straw	Worcestershire v Warwickshire at Birmingham	19
J. P. Whiteside	Leicestershire v Lancashire at Leicester	19

L. Hutton	England v South Africa at The Oval	1951
J. A. Hayes	Canterbury v Central Districts at Christchurch	1954-55
D. D. Deshpande	Madhya Pradesh v Uttar Pradesh at Benares	1956-57
M. Mehra	Railways v Delhi at Delhi	1959-60
K. Ibadulla	Warwickshire v Hampshire at Coventry	1963
Qaiser Khan	Dera Ismail Khan v Railways at Lahore	1964-65
Ijaz Ahmed	Lahore Greens v Lahore Blues at Lahore	1973-74
Qasim Feroze	Bahawalpur v Universities at Lahore	1974-75
T. Quirk	Northern Transvaal v Border at East London	1978-79
Mahmood Rashid	United Bank v Muslim Commercial Bank at Bahawalpur	1981-82
Arshad Ali	Sukkur v Quetta at Quetta	1983-84
H. Wasu	Vidarbha v Rajasthan at Akola	1984-85
Khalid Javed	Railways v Lahore at Lahore	1985-86

OUT HIT THE BALL TWICE

H. E. Bull	MCC v Oxford University at Lord's	1864
H. R. J. Charlwood	Sussex v Surrey at Hove	1872
R. G. Barlow	North v South at Lord's	1878
P. S. Wimble	Transvaal v Griqualand West at Kimberley	1892-93
G. B. Nicholls	Somerset v Gloucestershire at Bristol	1896
A. A. Lilley	Warwickshire v Yorkshire at Birmingham	1897
. H. King	Leicestershire v Surrey at The Oval	1906
A. P. Binns	Jamaica v British Guiana at Georgetown	1956-57
. Bavanna	Andhra v Mysore at Guntur	1963-64
aheer Abbas	PIA A v Karachi Blues at Karachi	1969-70
nwar Miandad	IDBP v United Bank at Lahore	1979-80
nwar Iqbal	Hyderabad v Sukkur at Hyderabad	1983-84
qtidar Ali	Allied Bank v Muslim Commercial Bank at Lahore	1983-84
ziz Malik	Lahore Division v Faisalabad at Sialkot	1984-85
aved Mohammad	Multan v Karachi Whites at Sahiwal	1986-87

BOWLING RECORDS

TEN WICKETS IN ONE INNINGS

	O	*M*	*R*		
Hinkly (Kent)				v England at Lord's	1848
. Wisden (North)				v South at Lord's	1850
E. Walker (England)	43	17	74	v Surrey at The Oval	1859
E. Walker (Middlesex)	44.2	5	104	v Lancashire at Manchester	1865
Wootton (All England)	31.3	9	54	v Yorkshire at Sheffield	1865
. Hickton (Lancashire)	36.2	19	46	v Hampshire at Manchester	1870
E. Butler (Oxford)	24.1	11	38	v Cambridge at Lord's	1871
mes Lillywhite (South)	60.2	22	129	v North at Canterbury	1872
Shaw (MCC)	36.2	8	73	v North at Lord's	1874
Barratt (Players)	29	11	43	v Australians at The Oval	1878
Giffen (Australian XI)	26	10	66	v The Rest at Sydney	1883-84
G. Grace (MCC)	36.2	17	49	v Oxford University at Oxford	1886
Burton (Middlesex)	52.3	25	59	v Surrey at The Oval	1888
. E. Moss (Canterbury)	21.3	10	28	v Wellington at Christchurch	1889-90
M. J. Woods (Cambridge U.)	31	6	69	v Thornton's XI at Cambridge	1890
Richardson (Surrey)	15.3	3	45	v Essex at The Oval	1894
Pickett (Essex)	27	11	32	v Leicestershire at Leyton	1895
J. Tyler (Somerset)	34.3	15	49	v Surrey at Taunton	1895
P. Howell (Australians)	23.2	14	28	v Surrey at The Oval	1899
H. G. Bland (Sussex)	25.2	10	48	v Kent at Tonbridge	1899
Briggs (Lancashire)	28.5	7	55	v Worcestershire at Manchester	1900
E. Trott (Middlesex)	14.2	5	42	v Somerset at Taunton	1900
Hinds (A. B. St Hill's XI)	19.1	6	36	v Trinidad at Port-of-Spain	1900-01

	O	M	R		
A. Fielder (Players)	24.5	1	90	v Gentlemen at Lord's	1906
E. G. Dennett (Gloucestershire)	19.4	7	40	v Essex at Bristol	1906
A. E. E. Vogler (E. Province)	12	2	26	v Griqualand West at Johannesburg	1906-07
C. Blythe (Kent)	16	7	30	v Northamptonshire at Northampton	1907
A. Drake (Yorkshire)	8.5	0	35	v Somerset at Weston-super-Mare	1914
W. Bestwick (Derbyshire)	19	2	40	v Glamorgan at Cardiff	1921
A. A. Mailey (Australians)	28.4	5	66	v Gloucestershire at Cheltenham	1921
C. W. L. Parker (Glos.)	40.3	13	79	v Somerset at Bristol	1921
T. Rushby (Surrey)	17.5	4	43	v Somerset at Taunton	1921
J. C. White (Somerset)	42.2	11	76	v Worcestershire at Worcester	1921
G. C. Collins (Kent)	19.3	4	65	v Nottinghamshire at Dover	192
H. Howell (Warwickshire)	25.1	5	51	v Yorkshire at Birmingham	192
A. S. Kennedy (Players)	22.4	10	37	v Gentlemen at The Oval	192
G. O. Allen (Middlesex)	25.3	10	40	v Lancashire at Lord's	192
A. P. Freeman (Kent)	42	9	131	v Lancashire at Maidstone	192
G. Geary (Leicestershire)	16.2	8	18	v Glamorgan at Pontypridd	192
C. V. Grimmett (Australians)	22.3	8	37	v Yorkshire at Sheffield	193
A. P. Freeman (Kent)	30.4	8	53	v Essex at Southend	193
H. Verity (Yorkshire)	18.4	6	36	v Warwickshire at Leeds	193
A. P. Freeman (Kent)	36.1	9	79	v Lancashire at Manchester	193
V. W. C. Jupp (Northants)	39	6	127	v Kent at Tunbridge Wells	193
H. Verity (Yorkshire)	19.4	16	10	v Nottinghamshire at Leeds	193
T. W. Wall (South Australia)	12.4	2	36	v New South Wales at Sydney	1932-3
T. B. Mitchell (Derbyshire)	19.1	4	64	v Leicestershire at Leicester	193
J. Mercer (Glamorgan)	26	10	51	v Worcestershire at Worcester	193
T. W. Goddard (Glos.)	28.4	4	113	v Worcestershire at Cheltenham	193
T. F. Smailes (Yorkshire)	17.1	5	47	v Derbyshire at Sheffield	193
E. A. Watts (Surrey)	24.1	8	67	v Warwickshire at Birmingham	193
*W. E. Hollies (Warwickshire)	20.4	4	49	v Nottinghamshire at Birmingham	194
J. M. Sims (East)	18.4	2	90	v West at Kingston	194
T. E. Bailey (Essex)	39.4	9	90	v Lancashire at Clacton	194
J. K. Graveney (Glos.)	18.4	2	66	v Derbyshire at Chesterfield	194
R. Berry (Lancashire)	36.2	9	102	v Worcestershire at Blackpool	19
S. P. Gupte (President's XI)	24.2	7	78	v Combined XI at Bombay	1954-
J. C. Laker (Surrey)	46	18	88	v Australians at The Oval	19
J. C. Laker (England)	51.2	23	53	v Australia at Manchester	19
G. A. R. Lock (Surrey)	29.1	18	54	v Kent at Blackheath	19
K. Smales (Nottinghamshire)	41.3	20	66	v Gloucestershire at Stroud	19
P. Chatterjee (Bengal)	19	11	20	v Assam at Jorhat	1956-
J. D. Bannister (Warwickshire)	23.3	11	41	v Comb. Services at Birmingham	19
A. J. G. Pearson (Cambridge University)	30.3	8	78	v Leicestershire at Loughborough	19
N. I. Thomson (Sussex)	34.2	19	49	v Warwickshire at Worthing	19
P. J. Allan (Queensland)	15.6	3	61	v Victoria at Melbourne	1965-
I. J. Brayshaw (W. Australia)	17.6	4	44	v Victoria at Perth	1967-
Shahid Mahmood (Karachi Whites)	25	5	58	v Khairpur at Karachi	1969-
E. E. Hemmings (International XI)	49.3	14	175	v West Indies XI at Kingston	1982-
P. Sunderam (Rajasthan)	22	5	78	v Vidarbha at Jodhpur	1985-
S. T. Jefferies (W. Province)	22.5	7	59	v Orange Free State at Cape Town	1987-

* *J. Wisden and W. E. Hollies achieved the feat without the direct assistance of a fielder. Wisden's were all bowled; Hollies bowled seven and had three leg-before-wicket.*

† *On debut in first-class cricket.*

Note: The following instances were achieved in 12-a-side matches:

E. M. Grace (MCC)	32.2	7	69	v Gents of Kent at Canterbury	1
W. G. Grace (MCC)	46.1	15	92	v Kent at Canterbury	1

OUTSTANDING ANALYSES

	O	*M*	*R*	*W*		
H. Verity (Yorkshire)	19.4	16	10	10	v Nottinghamshire at Leeds	1932
G. Elliott (Victoria)	19	17	2	9	v Tasmania at Launceston	1857-58
Ahad Khan (Railways)	6.3	4	7	9	v Dera Ismail Khan at Lahore	1964-65
. C. Laker (England)	14	12	2	8	v The Rest at Bradford	1950
D. Shackleton (Hampshire)	11.1	7	4	8	v Somerset at Weston-super-Mare	1955
E. Peate (Yorkshire)	16	11	5	8	v Surrey at Holbeck	1883
. R. Spofforth (Australians)	8.3	6	3	7	v England XI at Birmingham	1884
W. A. Henderson (N.E. Transvaal)	9.3	7	4	7	v Orange Free State at Bloemfontein	1937-38
Rajinder Goel (Haryana)	7	4	4	7	v Jammu and Kashmir at Chandigarh	1977-78
. I. Smith (South Africans)	4.5	3	1	6	v Derbyshire at Derby	1947
. Cosstick (Victoria)	21.1	20	1	6	v Tasmania at Melbourne	1868-69
srar Ali (Bahawalpur)	11	10	1	6	v Dacca U. at Bahawalpur	1957-58
. D. Pougher (MCC)	3	3	0	5	v Australians at Lord's	1896
. R. Cox (Sussex)	6	6	0	5	v Somerset at Weston-super-Mare	1921
. K. Tyldesley (Lancashire)	5	5	0	5	v Leicestershire at Manchester	1924
. T. Mills (Gloucestershire)	6.4	6	0	5	v Somerset at Bristol	1928

MOST WICKETS IN A MATCH

-90	J. C. Laker	England v Australia at Manchester	1956
-48	C. Blythe	Kent v Northamptonshire at Northampton	1907
-50	C. T. B. Turner	Australians v England XI at Hastings	1888
-54	W. P. Howell	Australians v Western Province at Cape Town	1902-03
-56	C. W. L. Parker	Gloucestershire v Essex at Gloucester	1925
-67	A. P. Freeman	Kent v Sussex at Hove	1922
-89	W. G. Grace	Gloucestershire v Nottinghamshire at Cheltenham	1877
-89	F. C. L. Matthews	Nottinghamshire v Northants at Nottingham	1923
91	H. Dean	Lancashire v Yorkshire at Liverpool	1913
-91	H. Verity	Yorkshire v Essex at Leyton	1933
92	A. P. Freeman	Kent v Warwickshire at Folkestone	1932
103	W. Mycroft	Derbyshire v Hampshire at Southampton	1876
106	G. R. Cox	Sussex v Warwickshire at Horsham	1926
106	T. W. Goddard	Gloucestershire v Kent at Bristol	1939
119	W. Mead	Essex v Hampshire at Southampton	1895
137	W. Brearley	Lancashire v Somerset at Manchester	1905
159	S. F. Barnes	England v South Africa at Johannesburg	1913-14
201	G. Giffen	South Australia v Victoria at Adelaide	1885-86
212	J. C. Clay	Glamorgan v Worcestershire at Swansea	1937

es: H. A. Arkwright took eighteen wickets for 96 runs in a 12-a-side match for Gentlemen of
C v Gentlemen of Kent at Canterbury in 1861.

V. Mead took seventeen wickets for 205 runs for Essex v Australians at Leyton in 1893, the
r before Essex were raised to first-class status.

. P. Fenner took seventeen wickets for Cambridge Town Club v University of Cambridge at
nbridge in 1844.

SIXTEEN OR MORE WICKETS IN A DAY

17-48	C. Blythe	Kent v Northamptonshire at Northampton	1907
17-91	H. Verity	Yorkshire v Essex at Leyton	1933
17-106	T. W. Goddard	Gloucestershire v Kent at Bristol	1939
16-38	T. Emmett	Yorkshire v Cambridgeshire at Hunslet	1869
16-52	J. Southerton	South v North at Lord's	1875
16-69	T. G. Wass	Nottinghamshire v Lancashire at Liverpool	1906
16-38	A. E. E. Vogler	E. Province v Griqualand West at Johannesburg	1906-07
16-103	T. G. Wass	Nottinghamshire v Essex at Nottingham	1908
16-83	J. C. White	Somerset v Worcestershire at Bath	1919

FOUR WICKETS WITH CONSECUTIVE BALLS

J. Wells	Kent v Sussex at Brighton	1862
G. Ulyett	Lord Harris's XI v New South Wales at Sydney	1878-79
G. Nash	Lancashire v Somerset at Manchester	1882
J. B. Hide	Sussex v MCC and Ground at Lord's	1890
F. J. Shacklock	Nottinghamshire v Somerset at Nottingham	1893
A. D. Downes	Otago v Auckland at Dunedin	1893-94
F. Martin	MCC and Ground v Derbyshire at Lord's	1895
A. W. Mold	Lancashire v Nottinghamshire at Nottingham	1895
W. Brearley†	Lancashire v Somerset at Manchester	1905
S. Haigh	MCC v Army XI at Pretoria	1905-06
A. E. Trott‡	Middlesex v Somerset at Lord's	1907
F. A. Tarrant	Middlesex v Gloucestershire at Bristol	1907
A. Drake	Yorkshire v Derbyshire at Chesterfield	191
S. G. Smith	Northamptonshire v Warwickshire at Birmingham	191
H. A. Peach	Surrey v Sussex at The Oval	192
A. F. Borland	Natal v Griqualand West at Kimberley	1926-2
J. E. H. Hooker†	New South Wales v Victoria at Sydney	1928-2
R. K. Tyldesley†	Lancashire v Derbyshire at Derby	192
R. J. Crisp	Western Province v Griqualand West at Johannesburg	1931-3
R. J. Crisp	Western Province v Natal at Durban	1933-3
A. R. Gover	Surrey v Worcestershire at Worcester	193
W. H. Copson	Derbyshire v Warwickshire at Derby	193
W. A. Henderson	N.E. Transvaal v Orange Free State at Bloemfontein	1937-3
F. Ridgway	Kent v Derbyshire at Folkestone	195
A. K. Walker§	Nottinghamshire v Leicestershire at Leicester	195
S. N. Mohol	Board of Control President's XI v Minister for Small Savings' XI at Poona	1965-6
P. I. Pocock	Surrey v Sussex at Eastbourne	197

† *Not all in the same innings.*

‡ *Trott achieved another hat-trick in the same innings of this, his benefit match.*

§ *Walker dismissed Firth with the last ball of the first innings and Lester, Tompkin and Smiths with the first three balls of the second innings, a feat without parallel.*

Notes: In their match with England at The Oval in 1863, Surrey lost four wickets in the course a four-ball over from G. Bennett.

Sussex lost five wickets in the course of the final (six-ball) over of their match with Surrey Eastbourne in 1972. P. I. Pocock, who had taken three wickets in his previous over, captur four more, taking in all seven wickets with eleven balls, a feat unique in first-class matches. (T eighth wicket fell to a run-out.)

HAT-TRICKS

Double Hat-Trick

Besides Trott's performance, which is given in the preceding section, the following instances are recorded of players having performed the hat-trick twice in the same match, Rao doing so in the same innings.

A. Shaw	Nottinghamshire v Gloucestershire at Nottingham	1884
T. J. Matthews	Australia v South Africa at Manchester	1912
C. W. L. Parker	Gloucestershire v Middlesex at Bristol	1924
R. O. Jenkins	Worcestershire v Surrey at Worcester	1949
J. S. Rao	Services v Northern Punjab at Amritsar	1963-64
Amin Lakhani	Combined XI v Indians at Multan	1978-79

Five Wickets with Six Consecutive Balls

W. H. Copson	Derbyshire v Warwickshire at Derby	1937
W. A. Henderson	NE Transvaal v Orange Free State at Bloemfontein	1937-38
P. I. Pocock	Surrey v Sussex at Eastbourne	1972

Most Hat-Tricks

Seven times: D. V. P. Wright.
Six times: T. W. Goddard, C. W. L. Parker.
Five times: S. Haigh, V. W. C. Jupp, A. E. G. Rhodes, F. A. Tarrant.
Four times: R. G. Barlow, J. T. Hearne, J. C. Laker, G. A. R. Lock, G. G. Macaulay, T. J. Matthews, M. J. Procter, T. Richardson, F. R. Spofforth, F. S. Trueman.
Three times: W. M. Bradley, H. J. Butler, S. T. Clarke, W. H. Copson, R. J. Crisp, J. W. H. T. Douglas, J. A. Flavell, A. P. Freeman, G. Giffen, K. Higgs, A. Hill, W. A. Humphries, R. D. Jackman, R. O. Jenkins, A. S. Kennedy, W. H. Lockwood, E. A. McDonald, T. L. Pritchard, J. S. Rao, A. Shaw, J. B. Statham, M. W. Tate, H. Trumble, D. Wilson, G. A. Wilson.

Unusual Hat-Tricks

All "Stumped":	by W. H. Brain off C. L. Townsend, Gloucestershire v Somerset at Cheltenham	1893
All "Caught":	by G. J. Thompson off S. G. Smith, Northamptonshire v Warwickshire at Birmingham	1914
	by Cyril White off R. Beesly, Border v Griqualand West at Queenstown	1946-47
	by G. O. Dawkes (wicket-keeper) off H. L. Jackson, Derbyshire v Worcestershire at Kidderminster	1958
All "LBW":	H. Fisher, Yorkshire v Somerset at Sheffield	1932
	J. A. Flavell, Worcestershire v Lancashire at Manchester	1963
	M. J. Procter, Gloucestershire v Essex at Westcliff	1972
	B. J. Ikin, Griqualand West v OFS at Kimberley	1973-74
	M. J. Procter, Gloucestershire v Yorkshire at Cheltenham	1979
	Aamer Wasim, Zone C v Lahore at Lahore	1985-86

Most recent instances

1987-88

Mohapatra — Orissa v Tripura at Cuttack.

1988: See Features of 1988.

200 WICKETS IN A SEASON

	Season	*O*	*M*	*R*	*W*	*Avge*
A. P. Freeman	1928	1,976.1	423	5,489	304	18.05
A. P. Freeman	1933	2,039	651	4,549	298	15.26
T. Richardson	1895‡	1,690.1	463	4,170	290	14.37
C. T. B. Turner**	1888†	2,427.2	1,127	3,307	283	11.68
A. P. Freeman	1931	1,618	360	4,307	276	15.60
A. P. Freeman	1930	1,914.3	472	4,632	275	16.84
T. Richardson	1897‡	1,603.4	495	3,945	273	14.45
A. P. Freeman	1929	1,670.5	381	4,879	267	18.27
W. Rhodes	1900	1,553	455	3,606	261	13.81
J. T. Hearne	1896	2,003.1	818	3,670	257	14.28
A. P. Freeman	1932	1,565.5	404	4,149	253	16.39
W. Rhodes	1901	1,565	505	3,797	251	15.12
T. W. Goddard	1937	1,478.1	359	4,158	248	16.76
W. C. Smith	1910	1,423.3	420	3,225	247	13.05
T. Richardson	1896‡	1,656.2	526	4,015	246	16.32
A. E. Trott	1899‡	1,772.4	587	4,086	239	17.09
T. W. Goddard	1947	1,451.2	344	4,119	238	17.30
M. W. Tate	1925	1,694.3	472	3,415	228	14.97
J. T. Hearne	1898‡	1,802.2	781	3,120	222	14.05
C. W. L. Parker	1925	1,512.3	478	3,311	222	14.91
G. A. Lohmann	1890‡	1,759.1	737	2,998	220	13.62
M. W. Tate	1923	1,608.5	331	3,061	219	13.97
C. F. Root	1925	1,493.2	416	3,770	219	17.21
C. W. L. Parker	1931	1,320.4	386	3,125	219	14.2
H. Verity	1936	1,289.3	463	2,847	216	13.1
G. A. R. Lock	1955	1,408.4	497	3,109	216	14.3
C. Blythe	1909	1,273.5	343	3,128	215	14.5
E. Peate	1882†	1,853.1	868	2,466	214	11.5
A. W. Mold	1895‡	1,629	598	3,400	213	15.9
W. Rhodes	1902	1,306.3	405	2,801	213	13.1
C. W. L. Parker	1926	1,739.5	556	3,920	213	18.4
J. T. Hearne	1893‡	1,741.4	667	3,492	212	16.4
A. P. Freeman	1935	1,503.2	320	4,562	212	21.5
G. A. R. Lock	1957	1,194.1	449	2,550	212	12.0
A. E. Trott	1900	1,547.1	363	4,923	211	23.3
G. G. Macaulay	1925	1,338.2	307	3,268	211	15.4
H. Verity	1935	1,279.2	453	3,032	211	14.3
J. Southerton	1870†	1,876.5	709	3,074	210	14.6
G. A. Lohmann	1888†	1,649.1	783	2,280	209	10.9
C. H. Parkin	1923	1,356.2	356	3,543	209	16.9
G. H. Hirst	1906	1,306.1	271	3,434	208	16.5
F. R. Spofforth	1884†	1,577	653	2,654	207	12.8
A. W. Mold	1894‡	1,288.3	456	2,548	207	12.3
C. W. L. Parker	1922	1,294.5	445	2,712	206	13.
A. S. Kennedy	1922	1,346.4	366	3,444	205	16.8
M. W. Tate	1924	1,469.5	465	2,818	205	13.
E. A. McDonald	1925	1,249.4	282	3,828	205	18.
A. P. Freeman	1934	1,744.4	440	4,753	205	23.
C. W. L. Parker	1924	1,303.5	411	2,913	204	14.
G. A. Lohmann	1889‡	1,614.1	646	2,714	202	13.
H. Verity	1937	1,386.2	487	3,168	202	15.
A. Shaw	1878†	2,630	1,586	2,201	201	10.
E. G. Dennett	1907	1,216.2	305	3,227	201	16.
A. R. Gover	1937	1,219.4	191	3,816	201	18.
C. H. Parkin	1924	1,162.5	357	2,735	200	13.
T. W. Goddard	1935	1,553	384	4,073	200	20.
A. R. Gover	1936	1,159.2	185	3,547	200	17.
T. W. Goddard	1939§	819	139	2,973	200	14
R. Appleyard	1951	1,313.2	391	2,829	200	14.

† *Indicates 4-ball overs;* ‡ *5-ball overs. All others were 6-ball overs except* § *8-ball overs.*
** *Exclusive of matches not reckoned as first-class.*

Notes: In four consecutive seasons (1928-31), A. P. Freeman took 1,122 wickets, and in eight consecutive seasons (1928-35), 2,090 wickets. In each of these eight seasons he took over 200 wickets.

T. Richardson took 1,005 wickets in four consecutive seasons (1894-97).

In 1896, J. T. Hearne took his 100th wicket as early as June 12. In 1931, C. W. L. Parker did the same and A. P. Freeman obtained his 100th wicket a day later.

The most wickets in a season since the reduction of Championship matches in 1969 is 134 by M. D. Marshall (822 overs) in 1982.

100 WICKETS IN A SEASON MOST TIMES

(Includes Overseas Tours and Seasons)

23 times: W. Rhodes 200 wkts (3).

20 times: D. Shackleton (In successive seasons – 1949 to 1968 inclusive).

17 times: A. P. Freeman 300 wkts (1), 200 wkts (7).

16 times: T. W. Goddard 200 wkts (4), C. W. L. Parker 200 wkts (5), R. T. D. Perks, '. J. Titmus.

15 times: J. T. Hearne 200 wkts (3), G. H. Hirst 200 wkts (1), A. S. Kennedy 200 wkts (1).

14 times: C. Blythe 200 wkts (1), W. E. Hollies, G. A. R. Lock 200 wkts (2), M. W. Tate 200 vkts (3), J. C White.

13 times: J. B. Statham.

12 times: J. Briggs, E. G. Dennett 200 wkts (1), C. Gladwin, D. J. Shepherd, N. I. Thomson, '. S. Trueman.

11 times: A. V. Bedser, G. Geary, S. Haigh, J. C. Laker, M. S. Nichols, A. E. Relf.

10 times: W. Attewell, W. G. Grace, R. Illingworth, H. L. Jackson, V. W. C. Jupp, G. G. facaulay 200 wkts (1), W. Mead, T. B. Mitchell, T. Richardson 200 wkts (3), J. Southerton 200 'kts (1), R. K. Tyldesley, D. L. Underwood, J. H. Wardle, T. G. Wass, D. V. P. Wright.

9 times: W. E. Astill, T. E. Bailey, W. E. Bowes, C. Cook, R. Howorth, J. Mercer, A. W. Mold 00 wkts (2), J. Newman, C. F. Root 200 wkts (1), A. Shaw 200 wkts (1), H. Verity 200 wkts (3).

8 times: T. W. Cartwright, H. Dean, J. A. Flavell, A. R. Gover 200 wkts (2), H. Larwood, . A. Lohmann 200 wkts (3), R. Peel, J. M. Sims, F. A. Tarrant, R. Tattersall, G. J. Thompson, . E. Tribe, A. W. Wellard, F. E. Woolley, J. A. Young.

100 WICKETS IN A SEASON OUTSIDE ENGLAND

V		Season	Country	R	Avge
'6	M. W. Tate	1926-27	India/Ceylon	1,599	13.78
7	Ijaz Faqih	1985-86	Pakistan	1,719	16.06
6	C. T. B. Turner ...	1887-88	Australia	1,441	13.59
6	R. Benaud	1957-58	South Africa	2,056	19.39
4	S. F. Barnes	1913-14	South Africa	1,117	10.74
3	Abdul Qadir	1982-83	Pakistan	2,367	22.98

1,500 WICKETS IN A CAREER

ates in italics denote the first half of an overseas season; i.e. *1970* denotes the 1970-71 season.

	Career	W	R	Avge
. Rhodes	1898-1930	4,187	69,993	16.71
P. Freeman	1914-36	3,776	69,577	18.42
W. L. Parker	1903-35	3,278	63,817	19.46
T. Hearne	1888-1923	3,061	54,352	17.75
W. Goddard	1922-52	2,979	59,116	19.84
'. G. Grace	1865-1908	2,876	51,545	17.92
S. Kennedy	1907-36	2,874	61,034	21.23
Shackleton	1948-69	2,857	53,303	18.65

	Career	*W*	*R*	*Avge*
G. A. R. Lock	1946-*70*	2,844	54,709	19.23
F. J. Titmus	1949-82	2,830	63,313	22.37
M. W. Tate	1912-37	2,784	50,571	18.16
G. H. Hirst	1891-1929	2,739	51,282	18.72
C. Blythe	1899-1914	2,506	42,136	16.81
D. L. Underwood	1963-87	2,465	49,993	20.28
W. E. Astill	1906-39	2,431	57,783	23.76
J. C. White	1909-37	2,356	43,759	18.57
W. E. Hollies	1932-57	2,323	48,656	20.94
F. S. Trueman	1949-69	2,304	42,154	18.29
J. B. Statham	1950-68	2,260	36,995	16.36
R. T. D. Perks	1930-55	2,233	53,770	24.07
J. Briggs	1879-1900	2,221	35,430	15.95
D. J. Shepherd	1950-72	2,218	47,302	21.32
E. G. Dennett	1903-26	2,147	42,571	19.82
T. Richardson	1892-1905	2,104	38,794	18.43
T. E. Bailey	1945-67	2,082	48,170	23.1
R. Illingworth	1951-83	2,072	42,023	20.28
N. Gifford	1960-88	2,068	48,731	23.56
F. E. Woolley	1906-38	2,068	41,066	19.85
G. Geary	1912-38	2,063	41,339	20.0
D. V. P. Wright	1932-57	2,056	49,307	23.98
J. Newman	1906-30	2,032	51,111	25.1
‡A. Shaw	1864-97	2,027	24,579	12.1
S. Haigh	1895-1913	2,012	32,091	15.9
H. Verity	1930-39	1,956	29,146	14.9
W. Attewell	1881-1900	1,950	29,896	15.3
J. C. Laker	1946-*64*	1,944	35,791	18.4
A. V. Bedser	1939-60	1,924	39,279	20.4
W. Mead	1892-1913	1,916	36,388	18.9
A. E. Relf	1900-21	1,897	39,724	20.9
P. G. H. Fender	1910-36	1,894	47,458	25.0
J. W. H. T. Douglas	1901-30	1,893	44,159	23.3
J. H. Wardle	1946-*67*	1,846	35,027	18.9
G. R. Cox	1895-1928	1,843	42,136	22.8
G. A. Lohmann	1884-*97*	1,841	25,295	13.7
J. W. Hearne	1909-36	1,839	44,926	24.4
G. G. Macaulay	1920-35	1,837	32,440	17.6
M. S. Nichols	1924-39	1,833	39,666	21.6
J. B. Mortimore	1950-75	1,807	41,904	23.1
C. Cook	1946-64	1,782	36,578	20.
R. Peel	1882-99	1,753	28,442	16.
H. L. Jackson	1947-63	1,733	30,101	17.
T. P. B. Smith	1929-52	1,697	45,059	26.
J. K. Lever	1967-88	1,696	41,016	24.
J. Southerton	1854-79	1,681	24,290	14.
A. E. Trott	*1892*-1911	1,674	35,317	21.
A. W. Mold	1889-1901	1,673	26,010	15.
T. G. Wass	1896-1920	1,666	34,092	20.
V. W. C. Jupp	1909-38	1,658	38,166	23.
C. Gladwin	1939-58	1,653	30,265	18.
W. E. Bowes	1928-47	1,639	27,470	16.
A. W. Wellard	1927-50	1,614	39,302	24.
P. I. Pocock	1964-86	1,607	42,648	26.
N. I. Thomson	1952-72	1,597	32,867	20.
J. Mercer	1919-47	1,591	37,210	23.
G. J. Thompson	1897-1922	1,591	30,058	18.
J. M. Sims	1929-53	1,581	39,401	24.
T. Emmett	1866-88	1,571	21,314	13.
Intikhab Alam	*1957*-82	1,571	43,474	27
B. S. Bedi	*1961-80*	1,560	33,843	21.

	Career	*W*	*R*	*Avge*
W. Voce	1927-52	1,558	35,961	23.08
A. R. Gover	1928-48	1,555	36,753	23.63
T. W. Cartwright	1952-77	1,536	29,357	19.11
K. Higgs	1958-86	1,536	36,267	23.61
James Langridge	1924-53	1,530	34,524	22.56
J. A. Flavell	1949-67	1,529	32,847	21.48
C. F. Root	1910-33	1,512	31,933	21.11
R. K. Tyldesley	1919-35	1,509	25,980	17.21

† *Some statisticians have removed from W. G. Grace's record a number of matches which they consider not to have been first-class. The above figures are those which became universally accepted upon appearance in W. G. Grace's obituary in the* Wisden *of 1916. Some works of reference gave his career record as being 2,809–50,999–18.15 (these figures also appeared in the 1981 edition of* Wisden), *and subsequently it has been amended to 2,808–50,982–18.15.*

‡ *The figures for A. Shaw exclude one wicket for which no analysis is available.*

ALL-ROUND RECORDS

HUNDRED AND TEN WICKETS IN ONE INNINGS

/. E. Walker, England v Surrey at The Oval; 20*, 108, ten for 74, and four for 17. 1859

V. G. Grace, MCC v Oxford University at Oxford; 104, two for 60, and ten for 49. 1886

lote: E. M. Grace, for MCC v Gentlemen of Kent in a 12-a-side match at Canterbury in 1862, cored 192* and took five for 77 and ten for 69.

TWO HUNDRED RUNS AND SIXTEEN WICKETS

. Giffen, South Australia v Victoria at Adelaide; 271, nine for 96, and seven for 70. 1891-92

HUNDRED IN EACH INNINGS AND FIVE WICKETS TWICE

. H. Hirst, Yorkshire v Somerset at Bath; 111, 117*, six for 70, and five for 45. 1906

HUNDRED IN EACH INNINGS AND TEN WICKETS

J. T. Bosanquet, Middlesex v Sussex at Lord's; 103, 100*, three for 75, and eight for 53 1905

D. Stephenson, Nottinghamshire v Yorkshire at Nottingham; 111, 117, four for 105, and seven for 117 1988

HUNDRED AND HAT-TRICK

Giffen, Australians v Lancashire at Manchester; 13, 113, and six for 55 including hat-trick 1884

E. Roller, Surrey v Sussex at The Oval; 204, four for 28 including hat-trick, and two for 16. (Unique instance of 200 and hat-trick.) 1885

B. Burns, Worcestershire v Gloucestershire at Worcester; 102*, three for 56, ncluding hat-trick, and two for 21 1913

W. C. Jupp, Sussex v Essex at Colchester; 102, six for 61, including hat-trick, and ix for 78 1921

E. S. Wyatt, MCC v Ceylon at Colombo; 124 and five for 39 including hat-trick. 1926-27

N. Constantine, West Indians v Northamptonshire at Northampton; seven for 45, ncluding hat-trick, 107 (five 6s), and six for 67 1928

E. Davies, Glamorgan v Leicestershire at Leicester; 139, four for 27, and three for 1 including hat-trick 1937

M. Merchant, Dr C. R. Pereira's XI v Sir Homi Mehta's XI at Bombay; 1, 142, hree for 31 including hat-trick, and no wicket for 17 1946-47

M. J. Procter, Gloucestershire v Essex at Westcliff-on-Sea; 51, 102, three for 43, and five for 30 including hat-trick (all lbw) 1972

M. J. Procter, Gloucestershire v Leicestershire at Bristol; 122, no wkt for 32, and seven for 26 including hat-trick 1979

Note: W. G. Grace, for MCC v Kent in a 12-a-side match at Canterbury in 1874, scored 123 and took five for 82 and six for 47 including a hat-trick.

SEASON DOUBLES

2,000 RUNS AND 200 WICKETS

1906 G. H. Hirst 2,385 runs and 208 wickets

3,000 RUNS AND 100 WICKETS

1937 J. H. Parks 3,003 runs and 101 wickets

2,000 RUNS AND 100 WICKETS

	Season	*R*	*W*		*Season*	*R*	*W*
W. G. Grace	1873	2,139	106	F. E. Woolley	1914	2,272	12
W. G. Grace	1876	2,622	129	J. W. Hearne	1920	2,148	14
C. L. Townsend ...	1899	2,440	101	V. W. C. Jupp	1921	2,169	12
G. L. Jessop	1900	2,210	104	F. E. Woolley	1921	2,101	16
G. H. Hirst	1904	2,501	132	F. E. Woolley	1922	2,022	16
G. H. Hirst	1905	2,266	110	F. E. Woolley	1923	2,091	10
W. Rhodes	1909	2,094	141	L. F. Townsend ...	1933	2,268	10
W. Rhodes	1911	2,261	117	D. E. Davies	1937	2,012	10
F. A. Tarrant	1911	2,030	111	James Langridge ..	1937	2,082	10
J. W. Hearne	1913	2,036	124	T. E Bailey	1959	2,011	10
J. W. Hearne	1914	2,116	123				

1,000 RUNS AND 200 WICKETS

	Season	*R*	*W*		*Season*	*R*	*W*
A. E. Trott	1899	1,175	239	M. W. Tate	1923	1,168	2[illegible]
A. E. Trott	1900	1,337	211	M. W. Tate	1924	1,419	2[illegible]
A. S. Kennedy	1922	1,129	205	M. W. Tate	1925	1,290	2[illegible]

1,000 RUNS AND 100 WICKETS

Sixteen times: W. Rhodes.

Fourteen times: G. H. Hirst.

Ten times: V. W. C. Jupp.

Nine times: W. E. Astill.

Eight times: T. E. Bailey, W. G. Grace, M. S. Nichols, A. E. Relf, F. A. Tarra M. W. Tate†, F. J. Titmus, F. E. Woolley.

Seven times: G. E. Tribe.

Six times: P. G. H. Fender, R. Illingworth, James Langridge.

Five times: J. W. H. T. Douglas, J. W. Hearne, A. S. Kennedy, J. Newman.

Four times: E. G. Arnold, J. Gunn, R. Kilner, B. R. Knight.

Three times: W. W. Armstrong (Australians), L. C. Braund, G. Giffen (Australians), N. Haig, R. Howorth, C. B. Llewellyn, J. B. Mortimore, Ray Smith, S. G. Smith, L. Townsend, A. W. Wellard.

† *M. W. Tate also scored 1,193 runs and took 116 wickets for MCC in first-class matches on 1926-27 MCC tour of India and Ceylon.*

Note: R. J. Hadlee (1984) and F. D. Stephenson (1988) are the only players to perform the f since the reduction of County Championship matches. A complete list of those performing feat before then will be found on p. 202 of the 1982 *Wisden.*

WICKET-KEEPERS' DOUBLE

	Season	*R*	*D*
L. E. G. Ames	1928	1,919	122
L. E. G. Ames	1929	1,795	128
L. E. G. Ames	1932	2,482	104
J. T. Murray	1957	1,025	104

20,000 RUNS AND 2,000 WICKETS IN A CAREER

	Career	*R*	*Avge*	*W*	*Avge*	*'Doubles'*
W. E. Astill	1906-39	22,731	22.55	2,431	23.76	9
T. E. Bailey	1945-67	28,642	33.42	2,082	23.13	8
W. G. Grace	1865-1908	54,896	39.55	2,876	17.92	8
G. H. Hirst	1891-1929	36,323	34.13	2,739	18.72	14
R. Illingworth	1951-83	24,134	28.06	2,072	20.28	6
W. Rhodes	1898-1930	39,802	30.83	4,187	16.71	16
M. W. Tate	1912-37	21,717	25.01	2,784	18.16	8
F. J. Titmus	1949-82	21,588	23.11	2,830	22.37	8
F. E. Woolley	1906-38	58,969	40.75	2,068	19.85	8

WICKET-KEEPING RECORDS

MOST DISMISSALS IN AN INNINGS

(all ct)	A. T. W. Grout	Queensland v Western Australia at Brisbane	1959-60
(all ct)	D. E. East	Essex v Somerset at Taunton	†1985
(4ct, 3st)	E. J. Smith	Warwickshire v Derbyshire at Birmingham	1926
(6ct, 1st)	W. Farrimond	Lancashire v Kent at Manchester	1930
(all ct)	W. F. F. Price	Middlesex v Yorkshire at Lord's	1937
(3ct, 4st)	D. Tallon	Queensland v Victoria at Brisbane	1938-39
(all ct)	R. A. Saggers	New South Wales v Combined XI at Brisbane	1940-41
(1ct, 6st)	H. Yarnold	Worcestershire v Scotland at Dundee	1951
(4ct, 3st)	J. Brown	Scotland v Ireland at Dublin	1957
(6ct, 1st)	N. Kirsten	Border v Rhodesia at East London	1959-60
(all ct)	M. S. Smith	Natal v Border at East London	1959-60
(all ct)	K. V. Andrew	Northamptonshire v Lancashire at Manchester	1962
(all ct)	A. Long	Surrey v Sussex at Hove	1964
(all ct)	R. M. Schofield	Central Districts v Wellington at Wellington	1964-65
(all ct)	R. W. Taylor	Derbyshire v Glamorgan at Derby	1966
(6ct, 1st)	H. B. Taber	New South Wales v South Australia at Adelaide	1968-69
(6ct, 1st)	E. W. Jones	Glamorgan v Cambridge University at Cambridge	1970
(6ct, 1st)	S. Benjamin	Central Zone v North Zone at Bombay	1973-74
(all ct)	R. W. Taylor	Derbyshire v Yorkshire at Chesterfield	1975
(6ct, 1st)	Shahid Israr	Karachi Whites v Quetta at Karachi	1976-77
(4ct, 3st)	Wasim Bari	PIA v Sind at Lahore	1977-78
(all ct)	J. A. Maclean	Queensland v Victoria at Melbourne	1977-78
(5ct, 2st)	Taslim Arif	National Bank v Punjab at Lahore	1978-79
(all ct)	Wasim Bari	Pakistan v New Zealand at Auckland	1978-79
(all ct)	R. W. Taylor	England v India at Bombay	1979-80
(all ct)	D. L. Bairstow	Yorkshire v Derbyshire at Scarborough	1982
(6ct, 1st)	R. B. Phillips	Queensland v New Zealanders at Bundaberg	1982-83
(3ct, 4st)	Masood Iqbal	Habib Bank v Lahore at Lahore	1982-83
(3ct, 4st)	Arif-ud-Din	United Bank v PACO at Sahiwal	1983-84
(6ct, 1st)	R. J. East	OFS v Western Province B at Cape Town	1984-85
(all ct)	B. A. Young	Northern Districts v Canterbury at Christchurch	1986-87

† *The first eight wickets to fall.*

WICKET-KEEPERS' HAT-TRICKS

W. H. Brain, Gloucestershire v Somerset at Cheltenham, 1893 – three stumpings off successive balls from C. L. Townsend.
G. O. Dawkes, Derbyshire v Worcestershire at Kidderminster, 1958 – three catches off successive balls from H. L. Jackson.
R. C. Russell, Gloucestershire v Surrey at The Oval, 1986 – three catches off successive balls from C. A. Walsh and D. V. Lawrence (2).

MOST DISMISSALS IN A MATCH

12 (8ct, 4st)	E. Pooley	Surrey v Sussex at The Oval	1868
12 (9ct, 3st)	D. Tallon	Queensland v New South Wales at Sydney	1938-39
12 (9ct, 3st)	H. B. Taber	New South Wales v South Australia at Adelaide	1968-69
11 (all ct)	A. Long	Surrey v Sussex at Hove	1964
11 (all ct)	R. W. Marsh	Western Australia v Victoria at Perth	1975-76
11 (all ct)	D. L. Bairstow	Yorkshire v Derbyshire at Scarborough	1982
10 (5ct, 5st)	H. Phillips	Sussex v Surrey at The Oval	1872
10 (2ct, 8st)	E. Pooley	Surrey v Kent at The Oval	1878
10 (9ct, 1st)	T. W. Oates	Nottinghamshire v Middlesex at Nottingham	1906
10 (1ct, 9st)	F. H. Huish	Kent v Surrey at The Oval	1911
10 (9ct, 1st)	J. C. Hubble	Kent v Gloucestershire at Cheltenham	1923
10 (8ct, 2st)	H. Elliott	Derbyshire v Lancashire at Manchester	1935
10 (7ct, 3st)	P. Corrall	Leicestershire v Sussex at Hove	1936
10 (9ct, 1st)	R. A. Saggers	New South Wales v Combined XI at Brisbane	1940-41
10 (all ct)	A. E. Wilson	Gloucestershire v Hampshire at Portsmouth	1953
10 (7ct, 3st)	B. N. Jarman	South Australia v New South Wales at Adelaide	1961-62
10 (all ct)	L. A. Johnson	Northamptonshire v Sussex at Worthing	1963
10 (all ct)	R. W. Taylor	Derbyshire v Hampshire at Chesterfield	1963
10 (8ct, 2st)	L. A. Johnson	Northamptonshire v Warwickshire at Birmingham	1965
10 (9ct, 1st)	R. C. Jordon	Victoria v South Australia at Melbourne	1970-71
10 (all ct)	R. W. Marsh†	Western Australia v South Australia at Perth	1976-77
10 (6ct, 4st)	Taslim Arif	National Bank v Punjab at Lahore	1978-79
10 (9ct, 1st)	Arif-ud-Din	United Bank v Karachi B at Karachi	1978-79
10 (all ct)	R. W. Taylor	England v India at Bombay	1979-8
10 (all ct)	R. J. Parks	Hampshire v Derbyshire at Portsmouth	198
10 (9ct, 1st)	A. Ghosh	Bihar v Assam at Bhagalpur	1981-8
10 (8ct, 2st)	Z. Parkar	Bombay v Maharashtra at Bombay	1981-8
10 (all ct)	R. V. Jennings	Transvaal v Arosa Sri Lankans at Johannesburg	1982-8
10 (9ct, 1st)	Kamal Najamuddin	Karachi v Lahore at Multan	1982-8
10 (all ct)	D. A. Murray	West Indies XI v South Africa at Port Elizabeth	1983-8
10 (7ct, 3st)	Azhar Abbas	Bahawalpur v Lahore City Greens at Bahawalpur	1983-8
10 (7ct, 3st)	B. N. French	Nottinghamshire v Oxford University at Oxford	198
10 (8ct, 2st)	R. J. Ryall	Western Province v Transvaal at Cape Town	1984-8
10 (all ct)	S. J. Rixon	Australian XI v South Africa at Johannesburg	1985-8
10 (8ct, 2st)	Anil Dalpat	Karachi v United Bank at Lahore	1985-8
10 (all ct)	R. V. Jennings	Transvaal v Northern Transvaal at Verwoerdburg	1986-8
10 (all ct)	S. J. Rixon	Australian XI v South Africa at Johannesburg	1986-8
10 (all ct)	R. V. Jennings	Transvaal v Orange Free State at Johannesburg	1986-8
10 (9ct, 1st)	C. J. Richards	Surrey v Sussex at Guildford	198
10 (all ct)	C. W. Scott	Nottinghamshire v Derbyshire at Derby	198

† *Marsh also scored a hundred (104), a unique "double".*

MOST DISMISSALS IN A SEASON

128 (79ct, 49st)	L. E. G. Ames	Kent	19
122 (70ct, 52st)	L. E. G. Ames	Kent	19
110 (63ct, 47st)	H. Yarnold	Worcestershire	19

107 (77ct, 30st)	G. Duckworth	Lancashire	1928
107 (96ct, 11st)	J. G. Binks	Yorkshire	1960
104 (40ct, 64st)	L. E. G. Ames	Kent	1932
104 (82ct, 22st)	J. T. Murray	Middlesex	1957
102 (69ct, 33st)	F. H. Huish	Kent	1913
102 (95ct, 7st)	J. T. Murray	Middlesex	1960
101 (62ct, 39st)	F. H. Huish	Kent	1911
101 (85ct, 16st)	R. Booth	Worcestershire	1960
100 (91ct, 9st)	R. Booth	Worcestershire	1964

MOST DISMISSALS IN A CAREER

Dates in italics denote the first half of an overseas season; i.e. *1914* denotes the 1914-15 season.

	Career	*M*	*Ct*	*St*	*Total*
R. W. Taylor	1960-88	639	1,473	176	1,649
J. T. Murray	1952-75	635	1,270	257	1,527
H. Strudwick	1902-27	675	1,242	255	1,497
A. P. E. Knott	1964-85	511	1,211	133	1,344
F. H. Huish	1895-1914	497	933	377	1,310
B. Taylor	1949-73	572	1,083	211	1,294
D. Hunter	1889-1909	548	906	347	1,253
H. R. Butt	1890-1912	550	953	275	1,228
J. H. Board	1891-*1914*	525	852	355	1,207
H. Elliott	1920-47	532	904	302	1,206
J. M. Parks	1949-76	739	1,088	93	1,181
R. Booth	1951-70	468	948	178	1,126
L. E. G. Ames	1926-51	593	703	418	1,121
G. Duckworth	1923-47	504	753	342	1,095
H. W. Stephenson	1948-64	462	748	334	1,082
J. G. Binks	1955-75	502	895	176	1,071
T. G. Evans	1939-69	465	816	250	1,066
D. L. Bairstow	1970-88	442	926	137	1,063
A. Long	1960-80	452	922	124	1,046
G. O. Dawkes	1937-61	482	895	148	1,043
R. W. Tolchard	1965-83	483	912	125	1,037
W. L. Cornford	1921-47	496	675	342	1,017

FIELDING RECORDS

(Excluding wicket-keepers)

Most Catches in an Innings

7	M. J. Stewart	Surrey v Northamptonshire at Northampton	1957
7	A. S. Brown	Gloucestershire v Nottinghamshire at Nottingham	1966

Most Catches in a Match

10	W. R. Hammond	Gloucestershire v Surrey at Cheltenham	†1928
8	W. B. Burns	Worcestershire v Yorkshire at Bradford	1907
8	A. H. Bakewell	Northamptonshire v Essex at Leyton	1928
	W. R. Hammond	Gloucestershire v Worcestershire at Cheltenham	1932
	K. J. Grieves	Lancashire v Sussex at Manchester	1951
	C. A. Milton	Gloucestershire v Sussex at Hove	1952
	G. A. R. Lock	Surrey v Warwickshire at The Oval	1957
	J. M. Prodger	Kent v Gloucestershire at Cheltenham	1961
	P. M. Walker	Glamorgan v Derbyshire at Swansea	1970
	Javed Miandad	Habib Bank v Universities at Lahore	1977-78
	Masood Anwar	Rawalpindi v Lahore Division at Rawalpindi	1983-84

† *Hammond also scored a hundred in each innings.*

Most Catches in a Season

78	W. R. Hammond	1928
77	M. J. Stewart	1957
73	P. M. Walker	1961
71	P. J. Sharpe	1962
70	J. Tunnicliffe	1901
69	J. G. Langridge	1955
69	P. M. Walker	1960
66	J. Tunnicliffe	1895
65	W. R. Hammond	1925
65	P. M. Walker	1959
65	D. W. Richardson	1961
64	K. F. Barrington	1957
64	G. A. R. Lock	1957
63	J. Tunnicliffe	1896
63	J. Tunnicliffe	1904
63	K. J. Grieves	1950
63	C. A. Milton	1956
61	J. V. Wilson	1955
61	M. J. Stewart	1958

Note: The most catches by a fielder since the reduction of County Championship matches in 1969 is 49 by C. J. Tavaré in 1979.

Most Catches in a Career

Dates in italics denote the first half of an overseas season; i.e. *1970* denotes the 1970-71 season.

1,018	F. E. Woolley (1906-38)
887	W. G. Grace (1865-1908)
831	G. A. R. Lock (1946-*70*)
819	W. R. Hammond (1920-51)
813	D. B. Close (1949-86)
784	J. G. Langridge (1928-55)
764	W. Rhodes (1898-1930)
758	C. A. Milton (1948-74)
754	E. H. Hendren (1907-38)

TEAM RECORDS

HIGHEST TOTALS

1,107	Victoria v New South Wales at Melbourne	1926-27
1,059	Victoria v Tasmania at Melbourne	1922-23
951-7 dec.	Sind v Baluchistan at Karachi	1973-74
918	New South Wales v South Australia at Sydney	1900-01
912-8 dec.	Holkar v Mysore at Indore	1945-46
910-6 dec.	Railways v Dera Ismail Khan at Lahore	1964-65
903-7 dec.	England v Australia at The Oval	1938
887	Yorkshire v Warwickshire at Birmingham	1896
849	England v West Indies at Kingston	1929-30
843	Australians v Oxford and Cambridge Universities Past and Present at Portsmouth	1893

Note: North Zone totalled 868 v West Zone at Bhilai in 1987-88. However, this included 68 penalty points for West Zone's failure to meet (by 17 overs) the statutory over-rate.

HIGHEST FOR EACH FIRST-CLASS COUNTY

Derbyshire	645	v Hampshire at Derby	1898
Essex	692	v Somerset at Taunton	189
Glamorgan	587-8	v Derbyshire at Cardiff	195
Gloucestershire	653-6	v Glamorgan at Bristol	192
Hampshire	672-7	v Somerset at Taunton	189
Kent	803-4	v Essex at Brentwood	193
Lancashire	801	v Somerset at Taunton	189
Leicestershire	701-4	v Worcestershire at Worcester	190
Middlesex	642-3	v Hampshire at Southampton	192
Northamptonshire	557-6	v Sussex at Hove	191
Nottinghamshire	739-7	v Leicestershire at Nottingham	190
Somerset	675-9	v Hampshire at Bath	192
Surrey	811	v Somerset at The Oval	189
Sussex	705-8	v Surrey at Hastings	190
Warwickshire	657-6	v Hampshire at Birmingham	189
Worcestershire	633	v Warwickshire at Worcester	190
Yorkshire	887	v Warwickshire at Birmingham	189

LOWEST TOTALS

12	Oxford University v MCC and Ground at Oxford	†1877
12	Northamptonshire v Gloucestershire at Gloucester	1907
13	Auckland v Canterbury at Auckland	1877-78
13	Nottinghamshire v Yorkshire at Nottingham	1901
14	Surrey v Essex at Chelmsford	1983
15	MCC v Surrey at Lord's	1839
15	Victoria v MCC at Melbourne	†1903-04
15	Northamptonshire v Yorkshire at Northampton	†1908
15	Hampshire v Warwickshire at Birmingham (Following on, Hampshire scored 521 and won by 155 runs.)	1922
16	MCC and Ground v Surrey at Lord's	1872
16	Derbyshire v Nottinghamshire at Nottingham	1879
16	Surrey v Nottinghamshire at The Oval	1880
16	Warwickshire v Kent at Tonbridge	1913
16	Trinidad v Barbados at Bridgetown	1942-43
16	Border v Natal at East London (first innings)	1959-60
17	Gentlemen of Kent v Gentlemen of England at Lord's	1850
17	Gloucestershire v Australians at Cheltenham	1896
18	The Bs v England at Lord's	1831
18	Kent v Sussex at Gravesend	†1867
18	Tasmania v Victoria at Melbourne	1868-69
18	Australians v MCC and Ground at Lord's	†1896
18	Border v Natal at East London (second innings)	1959-60
19	Sussex v Surrey at Godalming	1830
19	Sussex v Nottinghamshire at Hove	†1873
19	MCC and Ground v Australians at Lord's	1878
19	Wellington v Nelson at Nelson	1885-86

† *Signifies that one man was absent.*

ote: At Lord's in 1810, The Bs, with one man absent, were dismissed by England for 6.

LOWEST TOTAL IN A MATCH

4	(16 and 18) Border v Natal at East London	1959-60
2	(27 and 15) Northamptonshire v Yorkshire at Northampton	1908

ote: Northamptonshire batted one man short in each innings.

LOWEST FOR EACH FIRST-CLASS COUNTY

erbyshire	16	v Nottinghamshire at Nottingham	1879
ssex	30	v Yorkshire at Leyton	1901
lamorgan	22	v Lancashire at Liverpool	1924
loucestershire	17	v Australians at Cheltenham	1896
ampshire	15	v Warwickshire at Birmingham	1922
ent	18	v Sussex at Gravesend	1867
ncashire	25	v Derbyshire at Manchester	1871
icestershire	25	v Kent at Leicester	1912
ddlesex	20	v MCC at Lord's	1864
rthamptonshire	12	v Gloucestershire at Gloucester	1907
ttinghamshire	13	v Yorkshire at Nottingham	1901
merset	25	v Gloucestershire at Bristol	1947
rrey	14	v Essex at Chelmsford	1983
ssex	19	v Nottinghamshire at Hove	1873
arwickshire	16	v Kent at Tonbridge	1913
orcestershire	24	v Yorkshire at Huddersfield	1903
rkshire	23	v Hampshire at Middlesbrough	1965

HIGHEST MATCH AGGREGATES

2,376 for 38 wickets	Maharashtra v Bombay at Poona	1948-49
2,078 for 40 wickets	Bombay v Holkar at Bombay	1944-45
1,981 for 35 wickets	England v South Africa at Durban	1938-39
1,929 for 39 wickets	New South Wales v South Australia at Sydney	1925-26
1,911 for 34 wickets	New South Wales v Victoria at Sydney	1908-09
1,905 for 40 wickets	Otago v Wellington at Dunedin	1923-24

In England

1,723 for 31 wickets	England v Australia at Leeds	1948
1,601 for 29 wickets	England v Australia at Lord's	1930
1,570 for 29 wickets	Essex v Kent at Chelmsford	1988
1,507 for 28 wickets	England v West Indies at The Oval	1976
1,502 for 28 wickets	MCC v New Zealanders at Lord's	1927
1,499 for 31 wickets	T. N. Pearce's XI v Australians at Scarborough	1961
1,496 for 24 wickets	England v Australia at Nottingham	1938
1,494 for 37 wickets	England v Australia at The Oval	1934

LOWEST MATCH AGGREGATE

105 for 31 wickets	MCC v Australians at Lord's	1878

Note: The lowest aggregate since 1900 is 158 for 22 wickets, Surrey v Worcestershire at Th Oval, 1954.

HIGHEST FOURTH INNINGS TOTALS

(Unless otherwise stated, the side making the runs won the match.)

654-5 England v South Africa at Durban ... 1938-3
(After being set 696 to win. The match was left drawn on the tenth day.)

604 Maharashtra v Bombay at Poona ... 1948-4
(After being set 959 to win.)

576-8 Trinidad v Barbados at Port-of-Spain ... 1945-4
(After being set 672 to win. Match drawn on fifth day.)

572 New South Wales v South Australia at Sydney ... 1907-0
(After being set 593 to win.)

529-9 Combined XI v South Africans at Perth ... 1963-6
(After being set 579 to win. Match drawn on fourth day.)

518 Victoria v Queensland at Brisbane ... 1926-2
(After being set 753 to win.)

507-7 Cambridge University v MCC and Ground at Lord's ... 189

502-6 Middlesex v Nottinghamshire at Nottingham ... 192
(Game won by an unfinished stand of 271; a county record.)

502-8 Players v Gentlemen at Lord's ... 190

500-7 South African Universities v Western Province at Stellenbosch ... 1978-

LARGEST VICTORIES

Largest Innings Victories

Inns and 851 runs:	Railways (910-6 dec.) v Dera Ismail Khan (Lahore)	1964-
Inns and 666 runs:	Victoria (1,059) v Tasmania (Melbourne)	1922-
Inns and 656 runs:	Victoria (1,107) v New South Wales (Melbourne)	1926-
Inns and 605 runs:	New South Wales (918) v South Australia (Sydney)	1900-
Inns and 579 runs:	England (903-7 dec.) v Australia (The Oval)	19
Inns and 575 runs:	Sind (951-7 dec.) v Baluchistan (Karachi)	1973-
Inns and 527 runs:	New South Wales (713) v South Australia (Adelaide)	1908-
Inns and 517 runs:	Australians (675) v Nottinghamshire (Nottingham)	19

Largest Victories by Runs Margin

685 runs: New South Wales (235 and 761-8 dec.) v Queensland (Sydney) ... 1929-30
675 runs: England (521 and 342-8 dec.) v Australia (Brisbane) ... 1928-29
638 runs: New South Wales (304 and 770) v South Australia (Adelaide) ... 1920-21
625 runs: Sargodha (376 and 416) v Lahore Municipal Corporation (Faisalabad) 1978-79
609 runs: Muslim Commercial Bank (575 and 282-0 dec.) v WAPDA (Lahore). 1977-78
571 runs: Victoria (304 and 649) v South Australia (Adelaide) ... 1926-27
562 runs: Australia (701 and 327) v England (The Oval) ... 1934

Victory Without Losing a Wicket

Lancashire (166-0 dec. and 66-0) beat Leicestershire by ten wickets (Manchester) 1956
Karachi A (277-0 dec.) beat Sind A by an innings and 77 runs (Karachi) ... 1957-58
Railways (236-0 dec. and 16-0) beat Jammu and Kashmir by ten wickets (Srinagar) 1960-61
Karnataka (451-0 dec.) beat Kerala by an innings and 186 runs (Chikmagalur) . 1977-78

TIED MATCHES IN FIRST-CLASS CRICKET

There have been 35 tied matches since the First World War.

Somerset v Sussex at Taunton ... 1919
(The last Sussex batsman not allowed to bat under Law 45 [subsequently Law 17 and now Law 31])
Orange Free State v Eastern Province at Bloemfontein ... 1925-26
(Eastern Province had two wickets to fall.)
Essex v Somerset at Chelmsford ... 1926
(Although Essex had one man to go in, MCC ruled that the game should rank as a tie. The ninth wicket fell half a minute before time.)
Gloucestershire v Australians at Bristol ... 1930
Victoria v MCC at Melbourne ... 1932-33
(Victoria's third wicket fell to the last ball of the match when one run was needed to win.)
Worcestershire v Somerset at Kidderminster ... 1939
Southern Punjab v Baroda at Patiala ... 1945-46
Essex v Northamptonshire at Ilford ... 1947
Hampshire v Lancashire at Bournemouth ... 1947
D. G. Bradman's XI v A. L. Hassett's XI at Melbourne ... 1948-49
Hampshire v Kent at Southampton ... 1950
Sussex v Warwickshire at Hove ... 1952
Essex v Lancashire at Brentwood ... 1952
Northamptonshire v Middlesex at Peterborough ... 1953
Yorkshire v Leicestershire at Huddersfield ... 1954
Sussex v Hampshire at Eastbourne ... 1955
Victoria v New South Wales at Melbourne ... 1956-57
T. N. Pearce's XI v New Zealanders at Scarborough ... 1958
Essex v Gloucestershire at Leyton ... 1959
Australia v West Indies (First Test) at Brisbane ... 1960-61
Bahawalpur v Lahore B at Bahawalpur ... 1961-62
Hampshire v Middlesex at Portsmouth ... 1967
England XI v England Under-25 XI at Scarborough ... 1968
Yorkshire v Middlesex at Bradford ... 1973
Sussex v Essex at Hove ... 1974
South Australia v Queensland at Adelaide ... 1976-77
Central Districts v England XI at New Plymouth ... 1977-78
Victoria v New Zealanders at Melbourne ... 1982-83
Muslim Commercial Bank v Railways at Sialkot ... 1983-84
Sussex v Kent at Hastings ... 1984
Northamptonshire v Kent at Northampton ... 1984
Eastern Province B v Boland at Albany SC, Port Elizabeth ... 1985-86
Natal B v Eastern Province B at Pietermaritzburg ... 1985-86
India v Australia (First Test) at Madras ... 1986-87
Gloucestershire v Derbyshire at Bristol ... 1987

Note: Since 1948 a tie has been recognised only when the scores are level with all the wickets down in the fourth innings. This ruling applies to all grades of cricket, and in the case of a one-day match to the second innings, provided that the match has not been brought to a further conclusion.

MATCHES BEGUN AND FINISHED ON FIRST DAY

Since 1900. A fuller list may be found in the Wisden of 1981 and preceding editions.

Yorkshire v Worcestershire at Bradford, May 7	1900
MCC and Ground v London County at Lord's, May 20	1903
Transvaal v Orange Free State at Johannesburg, December 30	1906
Middlesex v Gentlemen of Philadelphia at Lord's, July 20	1908
Gloucestershire v Middlesex at Bristol, August 26	1909
Eastern Province v Orange Free State at Port Elizabeth, December 26	1912
Kent v Sussex at Tonbridge, June 21	1919
Lancashire v Somerset at Manchester, May 21	1925
Madras v Mysore at Madras, November 4	1934
Ireland v New Zealanders at Dublin, September 11	1937
Derbyshire v Somerset at Chesterfield, June 11	1947
Lancashire v Sussex at Manchester, July 12	1950
Surrey v Warwickshire at The Oval, May 16	1953
Somerset v Lancashire at Bath, June 6 (H. T. F. Buse's benefit)	1953
Kent v Worcestershire at Tunbridge Wells, June 15	1960

TEST MATCH RECORDS

BATTING RECORDS

HIGHEST INDIVIDUAL INNINGS

365*	G. S. Sobers, West Indies v Pakistan at Kingston	1957-58
364	L. Hutton, England v Australia at The Oval	1938
337	Hanif Mohammad, Pakistan v West Indies at Bridgetown	1957-58
336*	W. R. Hammond, England v New Zealand at Auckland	1932-33
334	D. G. Bradman, Australia v England at Leeds	193
325	A. Sandham, England v West Indies at Kingston	1929-30
311	R. B. Simpson, Australia v England at Manchester	1964
310*	J. H. Edrich, England v New Zealand at Leeds	196
307	R. M. Cowper, Australia v England at Melbourne	1965-66
304	D. G. Bradman, Australia v England at Leeds	193
302	L. G. Rowe, West Indies v England at Bridgetown	1973-7
299*	D. G. Bradman, Australia v South Africa at Adelaide	1931-3
291	I. V. A. Richards, West Indies v England at The Oval	197
287	R. E. Foster, England v Australia at Sydney	1903-0
285*	P. B. H. May, England v West Indies at Birmingham	195
280*	Javed Miandad, Pakistan v India at Hyderabad	1982-8
278	D. C. S. Compton, England v Pakistan at Nottingham	195
274	R. G. Pollock, South Africa v Australia at Durban	1969-7
274	Zaheer Abbas, Pakistan v England at Birmingham	197
270*	G. A. Headley, West Indies v England at Kingston	1934-3
270	D. G. Bradman, Australia v England at Melbourne	1936-3
268	G. N. Yallop, Australia v Pakistan at Melbourne	1983-8
266	W. H. Ponsford, Australia v England at The Oval	193
262*	D. L. Amiss, England v West Indies at Kingston	1973-7
261	F. M. M. Worrell, West Indies v England at Nottingham	19
260	C. C. Hunte, West Indies v Pakistan at Kingston	1957-5
260	Javed Miandad, Pakistan v England at The Oval	19

259	G. M. Turner, New Zealand v West Indies at Georgetown	1971-72
258	T. W. Graveney, England v West Indies at Nottingham	1957
258	S. M. Nurse, West Indies v New Zealand at Christchurch	1968-69
256	R. B. Kanhai, West Indies v India at Calcutta	1958-59
256	K. F. Barrington, England v Australia at Manchester	1964
255*	D. J. McGlew, South Africa v New Zealand at Wellington	1952-53
254	D. G. Bradman, Australia v England at Lord's	1930
251	W. R. Hammond, England v Australia at Sydney	1928-29
250	K. D. Walters, Australia v New Zealand at Christchurch	1976-77
250	S. F. A. F. Bacchus, West Indies v India at Kanpur	1978-79

The highest individual innings for other countries are:

236*	S. M. Gavaskar, India v West Indies at Madras	1983-84
201*	D. S. B. P. Kuruppu, Sri Lanka v New Zealand at Colombo (CCC)	1986-87

HUNDRED ON TEST DEBUT

C. Bannerman (165*)	Australia v England at Melbourne	1876-77
W. G. Grace (152)	England v Australia at The Oval	1880
H. Graham (107)	Australia v England at Lord's	1893
K. S. Ranjitsinhji (154*)	England v Australia at Manchester	1896
P. F. Warner (132*)	England v South Africa at Johannesburg	1898-99
R. A. Duff (104)	Australia v England at Melbourne	1901-02
R. E. Foster (287)	England v Australia at Sydney	1903-04
G. Gunn (119)	England v Australia at Sydney	1907-08
R. J. Hartigan (116)	Australia v England at Adelaide	1907-08
H. L. Collins (104)	Australia v England at Sydney	1920-21
W. H. Ponsford (110)	Australia v England at Sydney	1924-25
A. A. Jackson (164)	Australia v England at Adelaide	1928-29
G. A. Headley (176)	West Indies v England at Bridgetown	1929-30
J. E. Mills (117)	New Zealand v England at Wellington	1929-30
Nawab of Pataudi (102)	England v Australia at Sydney	1932-33
B. H. Valentine (136)	England v India at Bombay	1933-34
L. Amarnath (118)	India v England at Bombay	1933-34
P. A. Gibb (106)	England v South Africa at Johannesburg	1938-39
S. C. Griffith (140)	England v West Indies at Port-of-Spain	1947-48
A. G. Ganteaume (112)	West Indies v England at Port-of-Spain	1947-48
J. W. Burke (101*)	Australia v England at Adelaide	1950-51
P. B. H. May (138)	England v South Africa at Leeds	1951
R. H. Shodhan (110)	India v Pakistan at Calcutta	1952-53
B. H. Pairaudeau (115)	West Indies v India at Port-of-Spain	1952-53
O. G. Smith (104)	West Indies v Australia at Kingston	1954-55
A. G. Kripal Singh (100*)	India v New Zealand at Hyderabad	1955-56
C. C. Hunte (142)	West Indies v Pakistan at Bridgetown	1957-58
C. A. Milton (104*)	England v New Zealand at Leeds	1958
A. A. Baig (112)	India v England at Manchester	1959
Hanumant Singh (105)	India v England at Delhi	1963-64
Khalid Ibadulla (166)	Pakistan v Australia at Karachi	1964-65
. R. Taylor (105)	New Zealand v India at Calcutta	1964-65
. D. Walters (155)	Australia v England at Brisbane	1965-66
. H. Hampshire (107)	England v West Indies at Lord's	1969
G. R. Viswanath (137)	India v Australia at Kanpur	1969-70
G. S. Chappell (108)	Australia v England at Perth	1970-71
. G. Rowe (214, 100*)	West Indies v New Zealand at Kingston	1971-72
. I. Kallicharran (100*)	West Indies v New Zealand at Georgetown	1971-72
. E. Redmond (107)	New Zealand v Pakistan at Auckland	1972-73
. C. Hayes (106*)	England v West Indies at The Oval	1973
. G. Greenidge (107)	West Indies v India at Bangalore	1974-75
Baichan (105*)	West Indies v Pakistan at Lahore	1974-75
. J. Cosier (109)	Australia v West Indies at Melbourne	1975-76

S. Amarnath (124)	India v New Zealand at Auckland	1975-76
Javed Miandad (163)	Pakistan v New Zealand at Lahore	1976-77
†A. B. Williams (100)	West Indies v Australia at Georgetown	1977-78
†D. M. Wellham (103)	Australia v England at The Oval	1981
†Salim Malik (100*)	Pakistan v Sri Lanka at Karachi	1981-82
K. C. Wessels (162)	Australia v England at Brisbane	1982-83
W. B. Phillips (159)	Australia v Pakistan at Perth	1983-84
§M. Azharuddin (110)	India v England at Calcutta	1984-85
D. S. B. P. Kuruppu (201*)	Sri Lanka v New Zealand at Colombo (CCC)	1986-87
†M. J. Greatbatch (107*)	New Zealand v England at Auckland	1987-88

† *In his second innings of the match.*

‡ *L. G. Rowe is the only batsman to score a hundred in each innings on début.*

§ *M. Azharuddin is the only batsman to score hundreds in each of his first three Tests.*

L. Amarnath and S. Amarnath provide the only instance of a father and son scoring a hundre on début.

300 RUNS IN FIRST TEST

314	L. G. Rowe (214, 100*)	West Indies v New Zealand at Kingston	1971-7
306	R. E. Foster (287, 19)	England v Australia at Sydney	1903-0

TWO SEPARATE HUNDREDS IN A TEST

Three times: S. M. Gavaskar v West Indies (1970-71), v Pakistan (1978-79), v West Indie (1978-79).

Twice in one series: C. L. Walcott v Australia (1954-55).

Twice: H. Sutcliffe v Australia (1924-25), v South Africa (1929); G. A. Headley v Englan (1929-30 and 1939); G. S. Chappell v New Zealand (1973-74), v West Indies (1975-76); ‡A. Border v Pakistan (1979-80), v New Zealand (1985-86).

Once: W. Bardsley v England (1909); A. C. Russell v South Africa (1922-23); W. Hammond v Australia (1928-29); E. Paynter v South Africa (1938-39); D. C. S. Compton Australia (1946-47); A. R. Morris v England (1946-47); A. Melville v England (1947); Mitchell v England (1947); D. G. Bradman v India (1947-48); V. S. Hazare v Australia (194 48); E. D. Weekes v India (1948-49); J. Moroney v South Africa (1949-50); G. S. Sobers Pakistan (1957-58); R. B. Kanhai v Australia (1960-61); Hanif Mohammad v England (196 62); R. B. Simpson v Pakistan (1964-65); K. D. Walters v West Indies (1968-69); †L. G. Rowe New Zealand (1971-72); I. M. Chappell v New Zealand (1973-74); G. M. Turner v Austral (1973-74); C. G. Greenidge v England (1976); G. P. Howarth v England (1977-78); L. R. Mendis v India (1982-83); Javed Miandad v New Zealand (1984-85).

† *L. G. Rowe's two hundreds were on his Test début.*

‡ *A. R. Border scored 150* and 153 against Pakistan to become the first batsman to score 150 each innings of a Test match.*

HUNDRED AND DOUBLE-HUNDRED IN SAME TEST

K. D. Walters (Australia)	242 and 103 v West Indies at Sydney	1968-
S. M. Gavaskar (India)	124 and 220 v West Indies at Port-of-Spain	1970-
†L. G. Rowe (West Indies)	214 and 100* v New Zealand at Kingston	1971-
G. S. Chappell (Australia)	247* and 133 v New Zealand at Wellington	1973-

† *On Test début.*

MOST RUNS IN A SERIES

	T	*I*	*NO*	*R*	*HI*	*100s*	*Avge*		
D. G. Bradman . . .	5	7	0	974	334	4	139.14	A v E	1930
W. R. Hammond .	5	9	1	905	251	4	113.12	E v A	1928-29
R. N. Harvey	5	9	0	834	205	4	92.66	A v SA	1952-53
I. V. A. Richards .	4	7	0	829	291	3	118.42	WI v E	1976
C. L. Walcott	5	10	0	827	155	5	82.70	WI v A	1954-55
G. S. Sobers	5	8	2	824	365*	3	137.33	WI v P	1957-58
D. G. Bradman . . .	5	9	0	810	270	3	90.00	A v E	1936-37
D. G. Bradman . . .	5	5	1	806	299*	4	201.50	A v SA	1931-32
E. D. Weekes	5	7	0	779	194	4	111.28	WI v I	1948-49
†S. M. Gavaskar . .	4	8	3	774	220	4	154.80	I v WI	1970-71
Mudassar Nazar . .	6	8	2	761	231	4	126.83	P v I	1982-83
D. G. Bradman . . .	5	8	0	758	304	2	94.75	A v E	1934
D. C. S. Compton	5	8	0	753	208	4	94.12	E v SA	1947

† *Gavaskar's aggregate was achieved in his first Test series.*

1,000 TEST RUNS IN A CALENDAR YEAR

	T	*I*	*NO*	*R*	*HI*	*100s*	*Avge*	*Year*
V. A. Richards (*West Indies*) .	11	19	0	1,710	291	7	90.00	1976
. M. Gavaskar (*India*)	18	27	1	1,555	221	5	59.80	1979
. R. Viswanath (*India*)	17	26	3	1,388	179	5	60.34	1979
. B. Simpson (*Australia*)	14	26	3	1,381	311	3	60.04	1964
. L. Amiss (*England*)	13	22	2	1,379	262*	5	68.95	1974
M. Gavaskar (*India*)	18	32	4	1,310	236*	5	46.78	1983
. S. Sobers (*West Indies*)	7	12	3	1,193	365*	5	132.55	1958
. B. Vengsarkar (*India*)	18	27	4	1,174	146*	5	51.04	1979
. J. Hughes (*Australia*)	15	28	4	1,163	130*	2	48.45	1979
. C. S. Compton (*England*) . . .	9	15	1	1,159	208	6	82.78	1947
G. Greenidge (*West Indies*) .	14	22	4	1,149	223	4	63.83	1984
R. Border (*Australia*)	11	20	3	1,099	196	4	64.64	1985
T. Botham (*England*)	14	22	0	1,095	208	3	49.77	1982
. W. R. Fletcher (*England*) . . .	13	22	4	1,090	178	2	60.55	1973
B. Vengsarkar (*India*)	11	16	4	1,085	166	5	90.41	1987
. Amarnath (*India*)	14	24	1	1,077	120	4	46.82	1983
R. Border (*Australia*)	14	27	3	1,073	162	3	44.70	1979
Hill (*Australia*)	12	21	2	1,061	142	2	55.78	1902
I. Gower (*England*)	14	25	2	1,061	114	1	46.13	1982
I. Gower (*England*)	14	25	1	1,059	136	2	44.12	1986
M. Lawry (*Australia*)	14	27	2	1,056	157	2	42.24	1964
M. Gavaskar (*India*)	9	15	2	1,044	205	4	80.30	1978
F. Barrington (*England*)	12	22	2	1,039	132*	3	51.95	1963
R. Dexter (*England*)	11	15	1	1,038	205	2	74.14	1962
F. Barrington (*England*)	10	17	4	1,032	172	4	79.38	1961
ohsin Khan (*Pakistan*)	10	17	3	1,029	200	4	73.50	1982
G. Bradman (*Australia*)	8	13	4	1,025	201	5	113.88	1948
M. Gavaskar (*India*)	11	20	1	1,024	156	4	53.89	1976
R. Border (*Australia*)	11	19	3	1,000	140	5	62.50	1986

e: The earliest date for completing 1,000 runs is May 3 by M. Amarnath in 1983.

MOST RUNS IN A CAREER

(Qualification: 2,000 runs)

ENGLAND

	T	*I*	*NO*	*R*	*HI*	*100s*	*Avge*
G. Boycott	108	193	23	8,114	246*	22	47.72
M. C. Cowdrey	114	188	15	7,624	182	22	44.06
W. R. Hammond	85	140	16	7,249	336*	22	58.45
D. I. Gower	100	172	13	7,000	215	14	44.02
L. Hutton	79	138	15	6,971	364	19	56.67
K. F. Barrington	82	131	15	6,806	256	20	58.67
D. C. S. Compton	78	131	15	5,807	278	17	50.06
J. B. Hobbs	61	102	7	5,410	211	15	56.94
J. H. Edrich	77	127	9	5,138	310*	12	43.54
I. T. Botham	94	150	5	5,057	208	14	34.87
T. W. Graveney	79	123	13	4,882	258	11	44.38
H. Sutcliffe	54	84	9	4,555	194	16	60.73
G. A. Gooch	68	123	4	4,541	196	8	38.15
P. B. H. May	66	106	9	4,537	285*	13	46.77
E. R. Dexter	62	102	8	4,502	205	9	47.89
A. P. E. Knott	95	149	15	4,389	135	5	32.75
M. W. Gatting	67	115	14	3,848	207	9	38.09
D. L. Amiss	50	88	10	3,612	262*	11	46.3
A. W. Greig	58	93	4	3,599	148	8	40.4
E. H. Hendren	51	83	9	3,525	205*	7	47.6
F. E. Woolley	64	98	7	3,283	154	5	36.0
K. W. R. Fletcher	59	96	14	3,272	216	7	39.9
A. J. Lamb	56	98	9	2,969	137*	8	33.3
M. Leyland	41	65	5	2,764	187	9	46.0
C. Washbrook	37	66	6	2,569	195	6	42.8
B. L. D'Oliveira	44	70	8	2,484	158	5	40.0
D. W. Randall	47	79	5	2,470	174	7	33.3
W. J. Edrich	39	63	2	2,440	219	6	40.0
T. G. Evans	91	133	14	2,439	104	2	20.4
L. E. G. Ames	47	72	12	2,434	149	8	40.5
W. Rhodes	58	98	21	2,325	179	2	30.1
T. E. Bailey	61	91	14	2,290	134*	1	29.7
M. J. K. Smith	50	78	6	2,278	121	3	31.6
P. E. Richardson	34	56	1	2,061	126	5	37.4

AUSTRALIA

	T	*I*	*NO*	*R*	*HI*	*100s*	*Avg*
A. R. Border	94	164	27	7,343	205	22	53.
G. S. Chappell	87	151	19	7,110	247*	24	53.
D. G. Bradman	52	80	10	6,996	334	29	99.
R. N. Harvey	79	137	10	6,149	205	21	48.
K. D. Walters	74	125	14	5,357	250	15	48.
I. M. Chappell	75	136	10	5,345	196	14	42.
W. M. Lawry	67	123	12	5,234	210	13	47.
R. B. Simpson	62	111	7	4,869	311	10	46.
I. R. Redpath	66	120	11	4,737	171	8	43.
K. J. Hughes	70	124	6	4,415	213	9	37.
R. W. Marsh	96	150	13	3,633	132	3	26.
A. R. Morris	46	79	3	3,533	206	12	46.
C. Hill	49	89	2	3,412	191	7	39.
V. T. Trumper	48	89	8	3,163	214*	8	39

	T	*I*	*NO*	*R*	*HI*	*100s*	*Avge*
G. M. Wood	53	101	5	3,109	172	8	32.38
C. C. McDonald	47	83	4	3,107	170	5	39.32
A. L. Hassett	43	69	3	3,073	198*	10	46.56
K. R. Miller	55	87	7	2,958	147	7	36.97
W. W. Armstrong	50	84	10	2,863	159*	6	38.68
K. R. Stackpole	43	80	5	2,807	207	7	37.42
N. C. O'Neill	42	69	8	2,779	181	6	45.55
G. N. Yallop	39	70	3	2,756	268	8	41.13
S. J. McCabe	39	62	5	2,748	232	6	48.21
W. Bardsley	41	66	5	2,469	193*	6	40.47
W. M. Woodfull	35	54	4	2,300	161	7	46.00
P. J. Burge	42	68	8	2,290	181	4	38.16
S. E. Gregory	58	100	7	2,282	201	4	24.53
R. Benaud	63	97	7	2,201	122	3	24.45
C. G. Macartney	35	55	4	2,131	170	7	41.78
W. H. Ponsford	29	48	4	2,122	266	7	48.22
R. M. Cowper	27	46	2	2,061	307	5	46.84

SOUTH AFRICA

	T	*I*	*NO*	*R*	*HI*	*100s*	*Avge*
. Mitchell	42	80	9	3,471	189*	8	48.88
. D. Nourse	34	62	7	2,960	231	9	53.81
. W. Taylor	42	76	4	2,936	176	7	40.77
. J. Barlow	30	57	2	2,516	201	6	45.74
. L. Goddard	41	78	5	2,516	112	1	34.46
. J. McGlew	34	64	6	2,440	255*	7	42.06
H. B. Waite	50	86	7	2,405	134	4	30.44
. G. Pollock	23	41	4	2,256	274	7	60.97
. W. Nourse	45	83	8	2,234	111	1	29.78
. A. McLean	40	73	3	2,120	142	5	30.28

WEST INDIES

	T	*I*	*NO*	*R*	*HI*	*100s*	*Avge*
. S. Sobers	93	160	21	8,032	365*	26	57.78
H. Lloyd	110	175	14	7,515	242*	19	46.67
V. A. Richards	99	147	9	7,268	291	22	52.66
B. Kanhai	79	137	6	6,227	256	15	47.53
G. Greenidge	87	146	14	6,186	223	15	46.86
L. Haynes	76	129	15	4,523	184	9	39.67
D. Weekes	48	81	5	4,455	207	15	58.61
I. Kallicharran	66	109	10	4,399	187	12	44.43
C. Fredericks	59	109	7	4,334	169	8	42.49
M. M. Worrell	51	87	9	3,860	261	9	49.48
L. Walcott	44	74	7	3,798	220	15	56.68
C. Hunte	44	78	6	3,245	260	8	45.06
A. Gomes	60	91	11	3,171	143	9	39.63
F. Butcher	44	78	6	3,104	209*	7	43.11
J. L. Dujon	55	76	9	2,607	139	5	38.91
M. Nurse	29	54	1	2,523	258	6	47.60
A. Headley	22	40	4	2,190	270*	10	60.83
B. Richardson	36	59	6	2,173	185	6	41.00
B. Stollmeyer	32	56	5	2,159	160	4	42.33
G. Rowe	30	49	2	2,047	302	7	43.55

NEW ZEALAND

	T	*I*	*NO*	*R*	*HI*	*100s*	*Avge*
B. E. Congdon	61	114	7	3,448	176	7	32.22
J. R. Reid	58	108	5	3,428	142	6	33.28
J. G. Wright	58	103	4	3,343	141	7	33.76
G. M. Turner	41	73	6	2,991	259	7	44.64
M. D. Crowe	42	70	6	2,774	188	9	43.34
R. J. Hadlee	74	118	17	2,770	151*	2	27.42
B. Sutcliffe	42	76	8	2,727	230*	5	40.10
M. G. Burgess	50	92	6	2,684	119*	5	31.20
J. V. Coney	52	85	14	2,668	174*	3	37.57
G. P. Howarth	47	83	5	2,531	147	6	32.44
G. T. Dowling	39	77	3	2,306	239	3	31.16

INDIA

	T	*I*	*NO*	*R*	*HI*	*100s*	*Avge*
S. M. Gavaskar	125	214	16	10,122	236*	34	51.12
D. B. Vengsarkar	98	158	22	6,256	166	17	46.00
G. R. Viswanath	91	155	10	6,080	222	14	41.93
M. Amarnath	69	113	10	4,378	138	11	42.50
Kapil Dev	92	133	12	3,889	163	6	32.14
P. R. Umrigar	59	94	8	3,631	223	12	42.2
V. L. Manjrekar	55	92	10	3,208	189*	7	39.1
C. G. Borde	55	97	11	3,061	177*	5	35.5
Nawab of Pataudi jun.	46	83	3	2,793	203*	6	34.9
S. M. H. Kirmani	88	124	22	2,759	102	2	27.04
F. M. Engineer	46	87	3	2,611	121	2	31.08
R. J. Shastri	58	86	12	2,568	142	7	34.7
Pankaj Roy	43	79	4	2,442	173	5	32.5
V. S. Hazare	30	52	6	2,192	164*	7	47.6
A. L. Wadekar	37	71	3	2,113	143	1	31.0
V. Mankad	44	72	5	2,109	231	5	31.4
C. P. S. Chauhan	40	68	2	2,084	97	0	31.5
M. L. Jaisimha	39	71	4	2,056	129	3	30.6
D. N. Sardesai	30	55	4	2,001	212	5	39.2

PAKISTAN

	T	*I*	*NO*	*R*	*HI*	*100s*	*Avg*
Javed Miandad	92	141	18	6,621	280*	17	53.8
Zaheer Abbas	78	124	11	5,062	274	12	44.7
Mudassar Nazar	71	109	8	3,991	231	10	39.
Majid Khan	63	106	5	3,931	167	8	38.
Hanif Mohammad ...	55	97	8	3,915	337	12	43.
Mushtaq Mohammad .	57	100	7	3,643	201	10	39.
Asif Iqbal	58	99	7	3,575	175	11	38.
Saeed Ahmed	41	78	4	2,991	172	5	40.
Imran Khan	73	106	18	2,860	135*	4	32.
Wasim Raja	57	92	14	2,821	125	4	36.
Mohsin Khan	48	79	6	2,709	200	7	37.
Sadiq Mohammad	41	74	2	2,579	166	5	35.
Salim Malik	47	65	11	2,140	119*	6	39.
Imtiaz Ahmed	41	72	1	2,079	209	3	29.

SRI LANKA: The highest aggregate is 1,537, average 37.48, by A. Ranatunga in 24 Test

HIGHEST AVERAGES

(Qualification: 20 innings)

Avge		*T*	*I*	*NO*	*R*	*HI*	*100s*
99.94	D. G. Bradman (*A*)	52	80	10	6,996	334	29
60.97	R. G. Pollock (*SA*)........	23	41	4	2,256	274	7
60.83	G. A. Headley (*WI*)........	22	40	4	2,190	270*	10
60.73	H. Sutcliffe (*E*)...........	54	84	9	4,555	194	16
59.23	E. Paynter (*E*)	20	31	5	1,540	243	4
58.67	K. F. Barrington (*E*)	82	131	15	6,806	256	20
58.61	E. D. Weekes (*WI*)	48	81	5	4,455	207	15
58.45	W. R. Hammond (*E*)	85	140	16	7,249	336*	22
57.78	G. S. Sobers (*WI*)	93	160	21	8,032	365*	26
56.94	J. B. Hobbs (*E*)	61	102	7	5,410	211	15
56.68	C. L. Walcott (*WI*)	44	74	7	3,798	220	15
56.67	L. Hutton (*E*)	79	138	15	6,971	364	19
55.00	E. Tyldesley (*E*)	14	20	2	990	122	3
54.20	C. A. Davis (*WI*)	15	29	5	1,301	183	4
53.86	G. S. Chappell (*A*)	87	151	19	7,110	247*	24
53.82	Javed Miandad (*P*)	92	141	18	6,621	280*	17
3.81	A. D. Nourse (*SA*)	34	62	7	2,960	231	9
3.59	A. R. Border (*A*)	94	164	27	7,343	205	22
2.66	I. V. A. Richards (*WI*)	99	147	9	7,268	291	22
1.62	J. Ryder (*A*)	20	32	5	1,394	201*	3
1.12	S. M. Gavaskar (*I*)	125	214	16	10,122	236*	34
0.06	D. C. S. Compton (*E*)	78	131	15	5,807	278	17

MOST HUNDREDS

otal		*E*	*A*	*SA*	*WI*	*NZ*	*I*	*P*	*SL*
34	S. M. Gavaskar (*India*)	4	8	—	13	2	—	5	2
29	D. G. Bradman (*Australia*)	19	—	4	2	—	4	—	—
26	G. S. Sobers (*West Indies*)	10	4	—	—	1	8	3	—
24	G. S. Chappell (*Australia*)...........	9	—	—	5	3	1	6	0
22	W. R. Hammond (*England*)	—	9	6	1	4	2	—	—
22	M. C. Cowdrey (*England*)	—	5	3	6	2	3	3	—
22	G. Boycott (*England*)	—	7	1	5	2	4	3	—
22	A. R. Border (*Australia*)	7	—	—	2	4	4	5	0
22	I. V. A. Richards (*West Indies*)	8	4	—	—	1	7	2	—
21	R. N. Harvey (*Australia*)............	6	—	8	3	—	4	0	—
20	K. F. Barrington (*England*)..........	—	5	2	3	3	3	4	—

CARRYING BAT THROUGH TEST INNINGS

(Figures in brackets show side's total)

B. Tancred	26*	(47)	South Africa v England at Cape Town ..	1888-89
E. Barrett	67*	(176)	Australia v England at Lord's	1890
Abel	132*	(307)	England v Australia at Sydney	1891-92
F. Warner	132*	(237)	England v South Africa at Johannesburg .	1898-99
W. Armstrong ..	159*	(309)	Australia v South Africa at Johannesburg	1902-03
W. Zulch	43*	(103)	South Africa v England at Cape Town ..	1909-10
Bardsley	193*	(383)	Australia v England at Lord's	1926
M. Woodfull ...	30*	(66)‡	Australia v England at Brisbane	1928-29
M. Woodfull ...	73*	(193)†	Australia v England at Adelaide	1932-33
A. Brown	206*	(422)	Australia v England at Lord's	1938
Hutton	202*	(344)	England v West Indies at The Oval	1950

L. Hutton	156* (272)	England v Australia at Adelaide	1950-51
Nazar Mohammad	124* (331)	Pakistan v India at Lucknow	1952-53
F. M. M. Worrell	191* (372)	West Indies v England at Nottingham	1957
T. L. Goddard	56* (99)	South Africa v Australia at Cape Town	1957-58
D. J. McGlew	127* (292)	South Africa v New Zealand at Durban	1961-62
C. C. Hunte	60* (131)	West Indies v Australia at Port-of-Spain	1964-65
G. M. Turner	43* (131)	New Zealand v England at Lord's	1969
W. M. Lawry	49* (107)	Australia v India at Delhi	1969-70
W. M. Lawry	60* (116)†	Australia v England at Sydney	1970-71
G. M. Turner	223* (386)	New Zealand v West Indies at Kingston	1971-72
I. R. Redpath	159* (346)	Australia v New Zealand at Auckland	1973-74
G. Boycott	99* (215)	England v Australia at Perth	1979-80
S. M. Gavaskar	127* (286)	India v Pakistan at Faisalabad	1982-83
Mudassar Nazar	152* (323)	Pakistan v India at Lahore	1982-83
S. Wettimuny	63* (144)	Sri Lanka v New Zealand at Christchurch	1982-83
D. C. Boon	58* (103)	Australia v New Zealand at Auckland	1985-86
D. L. Haynes	88* (211)	West Indies v Pakistan at Karachi	1986-87

† *One man absent.* ‡ *Two men absent.*

Notes: G. M. Turner (223*) holds the record for the highest score by a player carrying his bat through a Test innings. He is also the youngest player to do so, being 22 years 63 days old when he first achieved the feat (1969).

Nazar Mohammad and Mudassar Nazar provide the only instance of a father and son carrying their bat through a Test innings.

D. L. Haynes (55 and 105) opened the batting and was last man out in each innings for West Indies v New Zealand at Dunedin, 1979-80.

FASTEST FIFTIES

Minutes			
28	J. T. Brown	England v Australia at Melbourne	1894-95
29	S. A. Durani	India v England at Kanpur	1963-64
30	E. A. V. Williams	West Indies v England at Bridgetown	1947-48
30	B. R. Taylor	New Zealand v West Indies at Auckland	1968-69
33	C. A. Roach	West Indies v England at The Oval	1933
34	C. R. R. Browne	West Indies v England at Georgetown	1929-30

The fastest fifties in terms of balls received (where recorded) are:

Balls			
32	I. T. Botham	England v New Zealand at The Oval	198
33	R. C. Fredericks	West Indies v Australia at Perth	1975-7
33	Kapil Dev	India v England at Manchester	198
33	I. V. A. Richards	West Indies v England at St John's	1985-8

FASTEST HUNDREDS

Minutes			
70	J. M. Gregory	Australia v South Africa at Johannesburg	1921-2
75	G. L. Jessop	England v Australia at The Oval	190
78	R. Benaud	Australia v West Indies at Kingston	1954-5
80	J. H. Sinclair	South Africa v Australia at Cape Town	1902-0
81	I. V. A. Richards	West Indies v England at St John's	1985-8
86	B. R. Taylor	New Zealand v West Indies at Auckland	1968-6

The fastest hundreds in terms of balls received (where recorded) are:

Balls			
56	I. V. A. Richards	West Indies v England at St John's	1985-
67	J. M. Gregory	Australia v South Africa at Johannesburg	1921-
71	R. C. Fredericks	West Indies v Australia at Perth	1975-
76	G. L. Jessop	England v Australia at The Oval	19
77	Majid Khan	Pakistan v New Zealand at Karachi	1976-

FASTEST DOUBLE-HUNDREDS

Minutes			
214	D. G. Bradman	Australia v England at Leeds	1930
223	S. J. McCabe	Australia v England at Nottingham	1938
226	V. T. Trumper	Australia v South Africa at Adelaide	1910-11
234	D. G. Bradman	Australia v England at Lord's	1930
240	W. R. Hammond	England v New Zealand at Auckland	1932-33
241	S. E. Gregory	Australia v England at Sydney	1894-95
245	D. C. S. Compton	England v Pakistan at Nottingham	1954

The fastest double-hundreds in terms of balls received (where recorded) are:

Balls			
219	I. T. Botham	England v India at The Oval	1982
233	C. G. Greenidge	West Indies v England at Lord's	1984
240	C. H. Lloyd	West Indies v India at Bombay	1974-75
241	Zaheer Abbas	Pakistan v India at Lahore	1982-83
242	D. G. Bradman	Australia v England at The Oval	1934
242	I. V. A. Richards	West Indies v Australia at Melbourne	1984-85

FASTEST TRIPLE-HUNDREDS

Minutes			
288	W. R. Hammond	England v New Zealand at Auckland	1932-33
336	D. G. Bradman	Australia v England at Leeds	1930

MOST RUNS IN A DAY BY A BATSMAN

09	D. G. Bradman	Australia v England at Leeds	1930
95	W. R. Hammond	England v New Zealand at Auckland	1932-33
73	D. C. S. Compton	England v Pakistan at Nottingham	1954
71	D. G. Bradman	Australia v England at Leeds	1934

SLOWEST INDIVIDUAL BATTING

* in 80 minutes	C. E. H. Croft, West Indies v Australia at Brisbane	1979-80
* in 100 minutes	J. T. Murray, England v Australia at Sydney	1962-63
in 102 minutes	Nawab of Pataudi jun, India v England at Bombay	1972-73
in 123 minutes	G. Miller, England v Australia at Melbourne	1978-79
in 125 minutes	T. W. Jarvis, New Zealand v India at Madras	1964-65
* in 133 minutes	T. G. Evans, England v Australia at Adelaide	1946-47
in 188 minutes	G. M. Ritchie, Australia v New Zealand at Sydney	1985-86
in 194 minutes	W. R. Playle, New Zealand v England at Leeds	1958
in 217 minutes	M. D. Crowe, New Zealand v Sri Lanka at Colombo (SSC)	1983-84
* in 250 minutes	J. W. Burke, Australia v England at Brisbane	1958-59
in 264 minutes	K. D. Mackay, Australia v England at Lord's	1956
* in 271 minutes	Younis Ahmed, Pakistan v India at Ahmedabad	1986-87
in 332 minutes	C. J. Tavaré, England v India at Madras	1981-82
in 336 minutes	B. A. Edgar, New Zealand v Australia at Wellington	1981-82
in 346 minutes	G. S. Camacho, West Indies v England at Bridgetown	1967-68
in 367 minutes	Ijaz Butt, Pakistan v Australia at Karachi	1959-60
in 390 minutes	D. N. Sardesai, India v West Indies at Bridgetown	1961-62
in 408 minutes	Ramiz Raja, Pakistan v West Indies at Karachi	1986-87
in 458 minutes	T. E. Bailey, England v Australia at Brisbane	1958-59
in 505 minutes	M. L. Jaisimha, India v Pakistan at Kanpur	1960-61
5 in 575 minutes	D. J. McGlew, South Africa v Australia at Durban	1957-58
4 in 591 minutes	Mudassar Nazar, Pakistan v England at Lahore	1977-78
)* in 609 minutes	J. J. Crowe, New Zealand v Sri Lanka, Colombo (CCC)	1986-87
3 in 648 minutes	C. T. Radley, England v New Zealand at Auckland	1977-78
2 in 708 minutes	S. M. Gavaskar, India v England at Bangalore	1981-82
7 in 970 minutes	Hanif Mohammad, Pakistan v West Indies at Bridgetown	1957-58

SLOWEST HUNDREDS

557 minutes	Mudassar Nazar, Pakistan v England at Lahore	1977-78
545 minutes	D. J. McGlew, South Africa v Australia at Durban	1957-58
515 minutes	J. J. Crowe, New Zealand v Sri Lanka, Colombo (CCC)	1986-87
488 minutes	P. E. Richardson, England v South Africa at Johannesburg	1956-57

Notes: The slowest hundred for any Test in England is 458 minutes (329 balls) by K. W. R. Fletcher, England v Pakistan, The Oval, 1974.

The slowest double-hundred in a Test was scored in 776 minutes (517 balls) by D. S. B. P. Kuruppu for Sri Lanka v New Zealand at Colombo (CCC), 1986-87, on his début. It is also the slowest-ever first-class double-hundred.

HIGHEST WICKET PARTNERSHIPS

413 for 1st	V. Mankad (231) and Pankaj Roy (173) for India v New Zealand at Madras	1955-56
451 for 2nd	W. H. Ponsford (266) and D. G. Bradman (244) for Australia v England at The Oval	1934
451 for 3rd	Mudassar Nazar (231) and Javed Miandad (280*) for Pakistan v India at Hyderabad	1982-83
411 for 4th	P. B. H. May (285*) and M. C. Cowdrey (154) for England v West Indies at Birmingham	1957
405 for 5th	S. G. Barnes (234) and D. G. Bradman (234) for Australia v England at Sydney	1946-47
346 for 6th	J. H. W. Fingleton (136) and D. G. Bradman (270) for Australia v England at Melbourne	1936-37
347 for 7th	D. St E. Atkinson (219) and C. C. Depeiza (122) for West Indies v Australia at Bridgetown	1954-55
246 for 8th	L. E. G. Ames (137) and G. O. Allen (122) for England v New Zealand at Lord's	1931
190 for 9th	Asif Iqbal (146) and Intikhab Alam (51) for Pakistan v England at The Oval	1967
151 for 10th	B. F. Hastings (110) and R. O. Collinge (68*) for New Zealand v Pakistan at Auckland	1972-73

BOWLING RECORDS

MOST WICKETS IN AN INNINGS

10-53	J. C. Laker	England v Australia at Manchester	195
9-28	G. A. Lohmann	England v South Africa at Johannesburg	1895-9
9-37	J. C. Laker	England v Australia at Manchester	195
9-52	R. J. Hadlee	New Zealand v Australia at Brisbane	1985-8
9-56	Abdul Qadir	Pakistan v England at Lahore	1987-8
9-69	J. M. Patel	India v Australia at Kanpur	1959-6
9-83	Kapil Dev	India v West Indies at Ahmedabad	1983-8
9-86	Sarfraz Nawaz	Pakistan v Australia at Melbourne	1978-7
9-95	J. M. Noreiga	West Indies v India at Port-of-Spain	1970-7
9-102	S. P. Gupte	India v West Indies at Kanpur	1958-5
9-103	S. F. Barnes	England v South Africa at Johannesburg	1913-1
9-113	H. J. Tayfield	South Africa v England at Johannesburg	1956-5
9-121	A. A. Mailey	Australia v England at Melbourne	1920-2
8-7	G. A. Lohmann	England v South Africa at Port Elizabeth	1895-9
8-11	J. Briggs	England v South Africa at Cape Town	1888-8
8-29	S. F. Barnes	England v South Africa at The Oval	19
8-29	C. E. H. Croft	West Indies v Pakistan at Port-of-Spain	1976-
8-31	F. Laver	Australia v England at Manchester	19
8-31	F. S. Trueman	England v India at Manchester	19
8-34	I. T. Botham	England v Pakistan at Lord's	19
8-35	G. A. Lohmann	England v Australia at Sydney	1886-

8-38	L. R. Gibbs	West Indies v India at Bridgetown	1961-62
8-43†	A. E. Trott	Australia v England at Adelaide	1894-95
8-43	H. Verity	England v Australia at Lord's	1934
8-43	R. G. D. Willis	England v Australia at Leeds	1981
8-51	D. L. Underwood	England v Pakistan at Lord's	1974
8-52	V. Mankad	India v Pakistan at Delhi	1952-53
8-53	G. B. Lawrence	South Africa v New Zealand at Johannesburg	1961-62
8-53†	R. A. L. Massie	Australia v England at Lord's	1972
8-55	V. Mankad	India v England at Madras	1951-52
8-56	S. F. Barnes	England v South Africa at Johannesburg	1913-14
8-58	G. A. Lohmann	England v Australia at Sydney	1891-92
8-58	Imran Khan	Pakistan v Sri Lanka at Lahore	1981-82
8-59	C. Blythe	England v South Africa at Leeds	1907
8-59	A. A. Mallett	Australia v Pakistan at Adelaide	1972-73
8-60	Imran Khan	Pakistan v India at Karachi	1982-83
8-61†	N. D. Hirwani	India v West Indies at Madras	1987-88
8-65	H. Trumble	Australia v England at The Oval	1902
8-68	W. Rhodes	England v Australia at Melbourne	1903-04
8-69	H. J. Tayfield	South Africa v England at Durban	1956-57
8-69	Sikander Bakht	Pakistan v India at Delhi	1979-80
8-70	S. J. Snooke	South Africa v England at Johannesburg	1905-06
-71	G. D. McKenzie	Australia v West Indies at Melbourne	1968-69
-72	S. Venkataraghavan	India v New Zealand at Delhi	1964-65
-75†	N. D. Hirwani	India v West Indies at Madras	7-88
-76	E. A. S. Prasanna	India v New Zealand at Auckland	1975-76
-79	B. S. Chandrasekhar	India v England at Delhi	1972-73
-81	L. C. Braund	England v Australia at Melbourne	1903-04
-83	J. R. Ratnayeke	Sri Lanka v Pakistan at Sialkot	1985-86
-84†	R. A. L. Massie	Australia v England at Lord's	1972
-85	Kapil Dev	India v Pakistan at Lahore	1982-83
-86	A. W. Greig	England v West Indies at Port-of-Spain	1973-74
-92	M. A. Holding	West Indies v England at The Oval	1976
-94	T. Richardson	England v Australia at Sydney	1897-98
-103	I. T. Botham	England v West Indies at Lord's	1984
-104†	A. L. Valentine	West Indies v England at Manchester	1950
-106	Kapil Dev	India v Australia at Adelaide	1985-86
-107	B. J. T. Bosanquet	England v Australia at Nottingham	1905
-107	N. A. Foster	England v Pakistan at Leeds	1987
-112	G. F. Lawson	Australia v West Indies at Adelaide	1984-85
-126	J. C. White	England v Australia at Adelaide	1928-29
-141	C. J. McDermott	Australia v England at Manchester	1985
-143	M. H. N. Walker	Australia v England at Melbourne	1974-75

† *On Test début.*

MOST WICKETS IN A MATCH

-90	J. C. Laker	England v Australia at Manchester	1956
-159	S. F. Barnes	England v South Africa at Johannesburg	1913-14
-136†	N. D. Hirwani	India v West Indies at Madras	1987-88
-137†	R. A. L. Massie	Australia v England at Lord's	1972
-28	J. Briggs	England v South Africa at Cape Town	1888-89
-45	G. A. Lohmann	England v South Africa at Port Elizabeth	1895-96
99	C. Blythe	England v South Africa at Leeds	1907
104	H. Verity	England v Australia at Lord's	1934
123	R. J. Hadlee	New Zealand v Australia at Brisbane	1985-86
124	W. Rhodes	England v Australia at Melbourne	1903-04

14-90	F. R. Spofforth	Australia v England at The Oval	1882
14-99	A. V. Bedser	England v Australia at Nottingham	1953
14-102	W. Bates	England v Australia at Melbourne	1882-83
14-116	Imran Khan	Pakistan v Sri Lanka at Lahore	1981-82
14-124	J. M. Patel	India v Australia at Kanpur	1959-60
14-144	S. F. Barnes	England v South Africa at Durban	1913-14
14-149	M. A. Holding	West Indies v England at The Oval	1976
14-199	C. V. Grimmett	Australia v South Africa at Adelaide	1931-32

† *On Test début.*

Notes: The best for South Africa is 13-165 by H. J. Tayfield against Australia at Melbourne, 1952-53.

The best for Sri Lanka is 9-125 by R. J. Ratnayake against India at Colombo (PSO), 1985-86.

MOST WICKETS IN A SERIES

	T	*R*	*W*	*Avge*		
S. F. Barnes	4	536	49	10.93	England v South Africa	1913-14
J. C. Laker	5	442	46	9.60	England v Australia	1956
C. V. Grimmett	5	642	44	14.59	Australia v South Africa	1935-36
T. M. Alderman	6	893	42	21.26	Australia v England	1981
R. M. Hogg	6	527	41	12.85	Australia v England	1978-79
Imran Khan	6	558	40	13.95	Pakistan v India	1982-83
A. V. Bedser	5	682	39	17.48	England v Australia	1953
D. K. Lillee	6	870	39	22.30	Australia v England	1981
M. W. Tate	5	881	38	23.18	England v Australia	1924-25
W. J. Whitty	5	632	37	17.08	Australia v South Africa	1910-1
H. J. Tayfield	5	636	37	17.18	South Africa v England	1956-57
A. E. E. Vogler	5	783	36	21.75	South Africa v England	1909-1
A. A. Mailey	5	946	36	26.27	Australia v England	1920-2
G. A. Lohmann	3	203	35	5.80	England v South Africa	1895-9
B. S. Chandrasekhar	5	662	35	18.91	India v England	1972-7
M. D. Marshall	5	443	35	12.65	West Indies v England	198

MOST WICKETS IN A CAREER

(Qualification: 100 wickets)

ENGLAND

	T	*Balls*	*R*	*W*	*Avge*	*5 W/i*	*10 W/m*
I. T. Botham	94	20,801	10,392	373	27.86	27	4
R. G. D. Willis	90	17,357	8,190	325	25.20	16	—
F. S. Trueman	67	15,178	6,625	307	21.57	17	3
D. L. Underwood	86	21,862	7,674	297	25.83	17	6
J. B. Statham	70	16,056	6,261	252	24.84	9	1
A. V. Bedser	51	15,918	5,876	236	24.89	15	5
J. A. Snow	49	12,021	5,387	202	26.66	8	1
J. C. Laker	46	12,027	4,101	193	21.24	9	3
S. F. Barnes	27	7,873	3,106	189	16.43	24	7
G. A. R. Lock	49	13,147	4,451	174	25.58	9	3
M. W. Tate	39	12,523	4,055	155	26.16	7	1
F. J. Titmus	53	15,118	4,931	153	32.22	7	—
H. Verity	40	11,173	3,510	144	24.37	5	2
C. M. Old	46	8,858	4,020	143	28.11	4	—
A. W. Greig	58	9,802	4,541	141	32.20	6	2
G. R. Dilley	39	7,682	3,789	133	28.48	6	—
T. E. Bailey	61	9,712	3,856	132	29.21	5	1
J. E. Emburey	57	13,315	4,763	130	36.63	6	—
W. Rhodes	58	8,231	3,425	127	26.96	6	1

	T	*Balls*	*R*	*W*	*Avge*	*5 W/i*	*10 W/m*
P. H. Edmonds	51	12,028	4,273	125	34.18	2	—
D. A. Allen	39	11,297	3,779	122	30.97	4	—
R. Illingworth	61	11,934	3,807	122	31.20	3	—
. Briggs	33	5,332	2,094	118	17.74	9	4
G. G. Arnold	34	7,650	3,254	115	28.29	6	—
G. A. Lohmann	18	3,821	1,205	112	10.75	9	5
D. V. P. Wright	34	8,135	4,224	108	39.11	6	1
R. Peel	20	5,216	1,715	102	16.81	6	2
. H. Wardle	28	6,597	2,080	102	20.39	5	1
C. Blythe	19	4,546	1,863	100	18.63	9	4

AUSTRALIA

	T	*Balls*	*R*	*W*	*Avge*	*5 W/i*	*10 W/m*
. K. Lillee	70	18,467	8,493	355	23.92	23	7
. Benaud	63	19,108	6,704	248	27.03	16	1
. D. McKenzie	60	17,681	7,328	246	29.78	16	3
. R. Lindwall	61	13,650	5,251	228	23.03	12	—
. V. Grimmett	37	14,513	5,231	216	24.21	21	7
R. Thomson	51	10,535	5,601	200	28.00	8	—
. K. Davidson	44	11,587	3,819	186	20.53	14	2
. R. Miller	55	10,461	3,906	170	22.97	7	1
. A. Johnston	40	11,048	3,826	160	23.91	7	—
. F. Lawson	37	8,705	4,420	145	30.48	10	2
. J. O'Reilly	27	10,024	3,254	144	22.59	11	3
Trumble	32	8,099	3,072	141	21.78	9	3
. H. N. Walker	34	10,094	3,792	138	27.47	6	—
A. Mallett	38	9,990	3,940	132	29.84	6	1
Yardley	33	8,909	3,986	126	31.63	6	1
M. Hogg	38	7,633	3,503	123	28.47	6	2
. A. Noble	42	7,159	3,025	121	25.00	9	2
W. Johnson	45	8,780	3,182	109	29.19	3	—
Giffen	31	6,391	2,791	103	27.09	7	1
N. Connolly	29	7,818	2,981	102	29.22	4	—
T. B. Turner	17	5,179	1,670	101	16.53	11	2

SOUTH AFRICA

	T	*Balls*	*R*	*W*	*Avge*	*5 W/i*	*10 W/m*
J. Tayfield	37	13,568	4,405	170	25.91	14	2
L. Goddard	41	11,736	3,226	123	26.22	5	—
M. Pollock	28	6,522	2,806	116	24.18	9	1
A. T. Adcock	26	6,391	2,195	104	21.10	5	—

WEST INDIES

	T	*Balls*	*R*	*W*	*Avge*	*5 W/i*	*10 W/m*
R. Gibbs	79	27,115	8,989	309	29.09	18	2
D. Marshall	58	13,047	5,921	290	20.41	18	3
Garner	58	13,169	5,433	259	20.97	7	—
A. Holding	60	12,680	5,898	249	23.68	13	2
S. Sobers	93	21,599	7,999	235	34.03	6	—
M. E. Roberts	47	11,136	5,174	202	25.61	11	2
W. Hall	48	10,421	5,066	192	26.38	9	1
Ramadhin	43	13,939	4,579	158	28.98	10	1
L. Valentine	36	12,953	4,215	139	30.32	8	2
E. H. Croft	27	6,165	2,913	125	23.30	3	—
A. Holder	40	9,095	3,627	109	33.27	3	—

NEW ZEALAND

	T	*Balls*	*R*	*W*	*Avge*	*5 W/i*	*10 W/m*
R. J. Hadlee	74	19,135	8,379	373	22.46	32	8
B. L. Cairns	43	10,628	4,280	130	32.92	6	1
R. O. Collinge	35	7,689	3,392	116	29.24	3	—
E. J. Chatfield	38	9,016	3,457	115	30.06	3	1
B. R. Taylor	30	6,334	2,953	111	26.60	4	—
R. C. Motz	32	7,034	3,148	100	31.48	5	—

INDIA

	T	*Balls*	*R*	*W*	*Avge*	*5 W/i*	*10 W/r*
Kapil Dev	92	19,225	9,454	319	29.63	19	2
B. S. Bedi	67	21,364	7,637	266	28.71	14	1
B. S. Chandrasekhar ..	58	15,963	7,199	242	29.74	16	2
E. A. S. Prasanna	49	14,353	5,742	189	30.38	10	2
V. Mankad	44	14,686	5,236	162	32.32	8	2
S. Venkataraghavan ..	57	14,877	5,634	156	36.11	3	1
S. P. Gupte	36	11,284	4,403	149	29.55	12	1
R. J. Shastri	58	13,051	4,911	127	38.66	2	—
D. R. Doshi	33	9,322	3,502	114	30.71	6	—
K. D. Ghavri	39	7,042	3,656	109	33.54	4	—
N. S. Yadav	35	8,349	3,580	102	35.09	3	—

PAKISTAN

	T	*Balls*	*R*	*W*	*Avge*	*5 W/i*	*10 W/*
Imran Khan	73	17,137	7,319	334	21.91	23	6
Abdul Qadir	54	14,425	6,483	205	31.62	14	5
Sarfraz Nawaz	55	13,927	5,798	177	32.75	4	1
Iqbal Qasim	47	12,396	4,629	159	29.11	7	2
Fazal Mahmood	34	9,834	3,434	139	24.70	13	4
Intikhab Alam	47	10,474	4,494	125	35.95	5	2

SRI LANKA: The highest aggregate is 59 wickets, average 36.94, by A. L. F. de Mel in 17 Te

WICKET WITH FIRST BALL IN TEST CRICKET

	Batsman dismissed			
A. Coningham	A. C. MacLaren	A v E	Melbourne	1894
W. M. Bradley	F. Laver	E v A	Manchester	1
E. G. Arnold	V. T. Trumper	E v A	Sydney	190
G. G. Macaulay	G. A. L. Hearne	E v SA	Cape Town	192
M. W. Tate	M. J. Susskind	E v SA	Birmingham	1
M. Henderson	E. W. Dawson	NZ v E	Christchurch	192
H. D. Smith	E. Paynter	NZ v E	Christchurch	193
T. F. Johnson	W. W. Keeton	WI v E	The Oval	
R. Howorth	D. V. Dyer	E v SA	The Oval	
Intikhab Alam	C. C. McDonald	P v A	Karachi	195

HAT-TRICKS

. R. Spofforth	Australia v England at Melbourne	1878-79
V. Bates	England v Australia at Melbourne	1882-83
. Briggs	England v Australia at Sydney	1891-92
. A. Lohmann	England v South Africa at Port Elizabeth	1895-96
. T. Hearne	England v Australia at Leeds	1899
I. Trumble	Australia v England at Melbourne	1901-02
I. Trumble	Australia v England at Melbourne	1903-04
. J. Matthews† / . J. Matthews	Australia v South Africa at Manchester	1912
I. J. C. Allom‡	England v New Zealand at Christchurch	1929-30
. W. Goddard	England v South Africa at Johannesburg	1938-39
. J. Loader	England v West Indies at Leeds	1957
. F. Kline	Australia v South Africa at Cape Town	1957-58
V. W. Hall	West Indies v Pakistan at Lahore	1958-59
. M. Griffin	South Africa v England at Lord's	1960
. R. Gibbs	West Indies v Australia at Adelaide	1960-61
. J. Petherick‡	New Zealand v Pakistan at Lahore	1976-77

† *T. J. Matthews did the hat-trick in each innings of the same match.*
‡ *On Test début.*

MOST BALLS BOWLED IN A TEST

Ramadhin (West Indies) sent down 774 balls in 129 overs against England at Birmingham, 57. It was the most delivered by any bowler in a Test, beating H. Verity's 766 for England ainst South Africa at Durban, 1938-39. In this match Ramadhin also bowled the most balls 88) in any single first-class innings, including Tests.

It should be noted that six balls were bowled to the over in the Australia v England Test series 1928-29 and 1932-33, when the eight-ball over was otherwise in force in Australia.

ALL-ROUND RECORDS

100 RUNS AND FIVE WICKETS IN AN INNINGS

gland					
W. Greig	148	6-164	v West Indies	Bridgetown	1973-74
T. Botham	103	5-73	v New Zealand	Christchurch	1977-78
T. Botham	108	8-34	v Pakistan	Lord's	1978
T. Botham	114	6-58 / 7-48	v India	Bombay	1979-80
T. Botham	149*	6-95	v Australia	Leeds	1981
T. Botham	138	5-59	v New Zealand	Wellington	1983-84
stralia					
Kelleway	114	5-33	v South Africa	Manchester	1912
M. Gregory	100	7-69	v England	Melbourne	1920-21
R. Miller	109	6-107	v West Indies	Kingston	1954-55
Benaud	100	5-84	v South Africa	Johannesburg	1957-58
th Africa					
I. Sinclair	106	6-26	v England	Cape Town	1898-99
A. Faulkner	123	5-120	v England	Johannesburg	1909-10

West Indies					
D. St E. Atkinson	219	5-56	v Australia	Bridgetown	1954-5
O. G. Smith	100	5-90	v India	Delhi	1958-5
G. S. Sobers	104	5-63	v India	Kingston	1961-6
G. S. Sobers	174	5-41	v England	Leeds	196
New Zealand					
B. R. Taylor†	105	5-86	v India	Calcutta	1964-6
India					
V. Mankad	184	5-196	v England	Lord's	195
P. R. Umrigar	172*	5-107	v West Indies	Port-of-Spain	1961-6
Pakistan					
Mushtaq Mohammad	201	5-49	v New Zealand	Dunedin	1972-7
Mushtaq Mohammad	121	5-28	v West Indies	Port-of-Spain	1976-7
Imran Khan	117	6-98 } 5-82 }	v India	Faisalabad	1982-8

† *On début.*

100 RUNS AND FIVE DISMISSALS IN AN INNINGS

D. T. Lindsay	182	6ct	SA v A	Johannesburg	1966-6
I. D. S. Smith	113*	4ct, 1st	NZ v E	Auckland	1983-8
S. A. R. Silva	111	5ct	SL v I	Colombo (PSO)	1985-8

100 RUNS AND TEN WICKETS IN A TEST

A. K. Davidson	44 80	5-135 } 6-87 }	A v WI	Brisbane	1960-
I. T. Botham	114	6-58 } 7-48 }	E v I	Bombay	1979-
Imran Khan	117	6-98 } 5-82 }	P v I	Faisalabad	1982-

1,000 RUNS AND 100 WICKETS IN A CAREER

	Tests	*Runs*	*Wkts*	*Tests for Double*
England				
T. E. Bailey	61	2,290	132	47
I. T. Botham	94	5,057	373	21
J. E. Emburey	57	1,409	130	46
A. W. Greig	58	3,599	141	37
R. Illingworth	61	1,836	122	47
W. Rhodes	58	2,325	127	44
M. W. Tate	39	1,198	155	33
F. J. Titmus	53	1,449	153	40
Australia				
R. Benaud	63	2,201	248	32
A. K. Davidson	44	1,328	186	34
G. Giffen	31	1,238	103	30
I. W. Johnson	45	1,000	109	45
R. R. Lindwall	61	1,502	228	38
K. R. Miller	55	2,958	170	33
M. A. Noble	42	1,997	121	27
South Africa				
T. L. Goddard	41	2,516	123	36
West Indies				
M. D. Marshall	58	1,278	290	49
G. S. Sobers	93	8,032	235	48

	Tests	Runs	Wkts	Tests for Double
ew Zealand				
. J. Hadlee	74	2,770	373	28
dia				
apil Dev	92	3,889	319	25
Mankad	44	2,109	162	23
. J. Shastri	58	2,568	127	44
akistan				
nran Khan	73	2,860	334	30
tikhab Alam	47	1,493	125	41
rfraz Nawaz	55	1,045	177	55

1,000 RUNS, 100 WICKETS AND 100 CATCHES

	Tests	Runs	Wkts	Ct
I. T. Botham	94	5,057	373	109
G. S. Sobers	93	8,032	235	109

WICKET-KEEPING RECORDS

ost Dismissals in an Innings

all ct)	Wasim Bari	Pakistan v New Zealand at Auckland	1978-79
all ct)	R. W. Taylor	England v India at Bombay	1979-80
all ct)	A. T. W. Grout	Australia v South Africa at Johannesburg	1957-58
5ct, 1st)	S. M. H. Kirmani	India v New Zealand at Christchurch	1975-76
ll ct)	D. T. Lindsay	South Africa v Australia at Johannesburg	1966-67
ll ct)	R. W. Marsh	Australia v England at Brisbane	1982-83
ll ct)	J. T. Murray	England v India at Lord's	1967
ll ct)	S. A. R. Silva	Sri Lanka v India at Colombo (SSC)	1985-86

'e: The most stumpings in an innings is 5 by K. S. More for India v West Indies at Madras 1987-88.

ost Dismissals in One Test

all ct)	R. W. Taylor	England v India at Bombay	1979-80
8ct, 1st)	G. R. A. Langley	Australia v England at Lord's	1956
all ct)	R. W. Marsh	Australia v England at Brisbane	1982-83
ll ct)	D. A. Murray	West Indies v Australia at Melbourne	1981-82
all ct)	S. A. R. Silva	Sri Lanka v India at Colombo (SSC)	1985-86
8ct, 1st)	S. A. R. Silva	Sri Lanka v India at Colombo (PSO)	1985-86
5ct, 2st)	L. E. G. Ames	England v West Indies at The Oval	1933
5ct, 2st)	A. T. W. Grout	Australia v Pakistan at Lahore	1959-60
all ct)	A. T. W. Grout	Australia v England at Lord's	1961
all ct)	J. J. Kelly	Australia v England at Sydney	1901-02
ll ct)	G. R. A. Langley	Australia v West Indies at Kingston	1954-55
ll ct)	W. K. Lees	New Zealand v Sri Lanka at Wellington	1982-83
ll ct)	D. T. Lindsay	South Africa v Australia at Johannesburg	1966-67
ll ct)	R. W. Marsh	Australia v West Indies at Melbourne	1975-76
ll ct)	R. W. Marsh	Australia v New Zealand at Christchurch	1976-77
'ct, 1st)	R. W. Marsh	Australia v India at Sydney	1980-81
ll ct)	R. W. Marsh	Australia v England at Adelaide	1982-83
ll ct)	J. M. Parks	England v New Zealand at Christchurch	1965-66
'ct, 1st)	H. B. Taber	Australia v South Africa at Johannesburg	1966-67
ll ct)	Wasim Bari	Pakistan v England at Leeds	1971

s: S. A. R. Silva made 18 dismissals in two successive Tests.
e most stumpings in a match is 6 by K. S. More for India v West Indies at Madras in -88.

Most Dismissals in a Series

(*Played in 5 Tests unless otherwise stated*)

28 (all ct)	R. W. Marsh	Australia v England	1982-8
26 (all ct)	R. W. Marsh	Australia v West Indies (6 Tests)	1975-7
26 (23ct, 3st)	J. H. B. Waite	South Africa v New Zealand	1961-6
24 (21ct, 3st)	A. P. E. Knott	England v Australia (6 Tests)	1970-7
24 (all ct)	D. T. Lindsay	South Africa v Australia	1966-6
24 (22ct, 2st)	D. L. Murray	West Indies v England	196
23 (22ct, 1st)	F. C. M. Alexander.	West Indies v England	1959-6
23 (21ct, 2st)	A. E. Dick	New Zealand v South Africa	1961-6
23 (20ct, 3st)	A. T. W. Grout ...	Australia v West Indies	1960-6
23 (22ct, 1st)	A. P. E. Knott	England v Australia (6 Tests)	1974-7
23 (21ct, 2st)	R. W. Marsh	Australia v England	197
23 (all ct)	R. W. Marsh	Australia v England (6 Tests)	198
23 (16ct, 7st)	J. H. B. Waite	South Africa v New Zealand	1953-5
22 (all ct)	S. J. Rixon	Australia v India	1977-7
22 (21ct, 1st)	S. A. R. Silva	Sri Lanka v India (3 Tests)	1985-8
21 (20ct, 1st)	A. T. W. Grout ...	Australia v England	19
21 (16ct, 5st)	G. R. A. Langley ..	Australia v West Indies	1951-
21 (all ct)	R. W. Marsh	Australia v Pakistan	1983-8
21 (13ct, 8st)	R. A. Saggers	Australia v South Africa	1949-
21 (15ct, 6st)	H. Strudwick	England v South Africa	1913-
20 (19ct, 1st)	P. R. Downton	England v Australia (6 Tests)	19
20 (19ct, 1st)	P. J. L. Dujon	West Indies v Australia	1983-
20 (all ct)	P. J. L. Dujon	West Indies v England	19
20 (18ct, 2st)	T. G. Evans	England v South Africa	1956-
20 (17ct, 3st)	A. T. W. Grout ...	Australia v England	1958-
20 (16ct, 4st)	G. R. A. Langley ..	Australia v West Indies (4 Tests)	1954-
20 (19ct, 1st)	H. B. Taber	Australia v South Africa	1966-
20 (16ct, 4st)	D. Tallon	Australia v England	1946-
20 (18ct, 2st)	R. W. Taylor	England v Australia (6 Tests)	1978-

Most Dismissals in a Career

	T	*Ct*	*St*	*To*
R. W. Marsh (Australia)	96	343	12	35
A. P. E. Knott (England)	95	250	19	26
Wasim Bari (Pakistan)	81	201	27	22
T. G. Evans (England)	91	173	46	21
S. M. H. Kirmani (India)	88	160	38	19
D. L. Murray (West Indies)	62	181	8	18
A. T. W. Grout (Australia)	51	163	24	1
P. J. L. Dujon (West Indies)	55	174	5	1
R. W. Taylor (England)	57	167	7	1
J. H. B. Waite (South Africa)	50	124	17	1
W. A. Oldfield (Australia)	54	78	52	1
I. D. S. Smith (New Zealand)	43	120	7	1
J. M. Parks (England)	46	103	11	1

Notes: The records for P. J. L. Dujon and J. M. Parks each include two catches taken w
not keeping wicket in two and three Tests respectively.

S. A. R. Silva (33 ct, 1 st) has made most dismissals for Sri Lanka.

FIELDING RECORDS

(Excluding wicket-keepers)

Most Catches in an Innings

5	V. Y. Richardson	Australia v South Africa at Durban	193
5	Yajurvindra Singh	India v England at Bangalore	197

Most Catches in One Test

G. S. Chappell	Australia v England at Perth	1974-75
Yajurvindra Singh	India v England at Bangalore	1976-77
A. Shrewsbury	England v Australia at Sydney	1887-88
A. E. E. Vogler	South Africa v England at Durban	1909-10
F. E. Woolley	England v Australia at Sydney	1911-12
J. M. Gregory	Australia v England at Sydney	1920-21
B. Mitchell	South Africa v Australia at Melbourne	1931-32
V. Y. Richardson	Australia v South Africa at Durban	1935-36
R. N. Harvey	Australia v England at Sydney	1962-63
M. C. Cowdrey	England v West Indies at Lord's	1963
E. D. Solkar	India v West Indies at Port-of-Spain	1970-71
G. S. Sobers	West Indies v England at Lord's	1973
I. M. Chappell	Australia v New Zealand at Adelaide	1973-74
A. W. Greig	England v Pakistan at Leeds	1974
D. F. Whatmore	Australia v India at Kanpur	1979-80
A. J. Lamb	England v New Zealand at Lord's	1983

Most Catches in a Series

J. M. Gregory	Australia v England	1920-21
G. S. Chappell	Australia v England (6 Tests)	1974-75
R. B. Simpson	Australia v South Africa	1957-58
R. B. Simpson	Australia v West Indies	1960-61

Most Catches in a Career

G. S. Chappell (Australia)	122 in 87 matches
M. C. Cowdrey (England)	120 in 114 matches
R. B. Simpson (Australia)	110 in 62 matches
W. R. Hammond (England)	110 in 85 matches
G. S. Sobers (West Indies)	109 in 93 matches
I. T. Botham (England)	109 in 94 matches
S. M. Gavaskar (India)	108 in 125 matches
I. M. Chappell (Australia)	105 in 75 matches
A. R. Border (Australia)	102 in 94 matches

TEAM RECORDS

HIGHEST INNINGS TOTALS

-7 dec.	England v Australia at The Oval	1938
	England v West Indies at Kingston	1929-30
-3 dec.	West Indies v Pakistan at Kingston	1957-58
-8 dec.	Australia v West Indies at Kingston	1954-55
-6 dec.	Australia v England at Lord's	1930
	Pakistan v England at The Oval	1987
	Australia v England at The Oval	1934
	Australia v England at The Oval	1930
-8 dec.	West Indies v England at The Oval	1976
-8 dec.	West Indies v England at Port-of-Spain	1953-54
-7	India v Sri Lanka at Kanpur	1986-87
-6	Pakistan v India at Faisalabad	1984-85
	Australia v India at Adelaide	1947-48
	Australia v West Indies at Bridgetown	1954-55
-8 dec.	Australia v England at Sydney	1946-47
-8 dec.	England v Australia at Nottingham	1938
8 dec.	Pakistan v West Indies at Bridgetown	1957-58
8 dec.	Australia v England at Manchester	1964
5	England v South Africa at Durban	1938-39
7 dec.	England v India at Madras	1984-85
8 dec.	West Indies v England at Lord's	1973
	Pakistan v India at Faisalabad	1982-83
6 dec.	Australia v West Indies at Bridgetown	1964-65

The highest innings for the countries not mentioned on previous page are:

622-9 dec. South Africa v Australia at Durban ... 1969-7
553-7 dec. New Zealand v Australia at Brisbane ... 1985-8
491-7 dec. Sri Lanka v England at Lord's ... 198

HIGHEST FOURTH INNINGS TOTALS

To win

406-4 India v West Indies at Port-of-Spain ... 1975-7
404-3 Australia v England at Leeds ... 19
362-7 Australia v West Indies at Georgetown ... 1977-7
348-5 West Indies v New Zealand at Auckland ... 1968-6
344-1 West Indies v England at Lord's ... 19

To tie

347 India v Australia at Madras ... 1986-8

To draw

654-5 England (needing 696 to win) v South Africa at Durban ... 1938-
429-8 India (needing 438 to win) v England at The Oval ... 19
423-7 South Africa (needing 451 to win) v England at The Oval ... 19
408-5 West Indies (needing 836 to win) v England at Kingston ... 1929-

To lose

445 India (lost by 47 runs) v Australia at Adelaide ... 1977-
440 New Zealand (lost by 38 runs) v England at Nottingham ... 19
417 England (lost by 45 runs) v Australia at Melbourne ... 1976-
411 England (lost by 193 runs) v Australia at Sydney ... 1924-

MOST RUNS IN A DAY (BOTH SIDES)

588 England (398-6), India (190-0) at Manchester (2nd day) ... 1
522 England (503-2), South Africa (19-0) at Lord's (2nd day) ... 1
508 England (221-2), South Africa (287-6) at The Oval (3rd day) ... 1

MOST RUNS IN A DAY (ONE SIDE)

503 England (503-2) v South Africa at Lord's (2nd day) ... 1
494 Australia (494-6) v South Africa at Sydney (1st day) ... 191
475 Australia (475-2) v England at The Oval (1st day) ...
471 England (471-8) v India at The Oval (1st day) ...
458 Australia (458-3) v England at Leeds (1st day) ...
455 Australia (455-1) v England at Leeds (2nd day) ...

MOST WICKETS IN ONE DAY

27 England (18-3 to 53 out and 62) v Australia (60) at Lord's (2nd day) ...
25 Australia (112 and 48-5) v England (61) at Melbourne (1st day) ... 190

HIGHEST MATCH AGGREGATES

uns	*Wkts*			*Days played*
,981	35	South Africa v England at Durban	1938-39	10†
,815	34	West Indies v England at Kingston	1929-30	9‡
,764	39	Australia v West Indies at Adelaide	1968-69	5
,753	40	Australia v England at Adelaide	1920-21	6
,723	31	England v Australia at Leeds	1948	5
,661	36	West Indies v Australia at Bridgetown	1954-55	6

† *No play on one day.* ‡ *No play on two days.*

LOWEST INNINGS TOTALS

	New Zealand v England at Auckland	1954-55
	South Africa v England at Port Elizabeth	1895-96
	South Africa v England at Birmingham	1924
	South Africa v England at Cape Town	1898-99
	Australia v England at Birmingham	1902
	South Africa v Australia at Melbourne	1931-32
	Australia v England at Sydney	1887-88
	New Zealand v Australia at Wellington	1945-46
†	India v England at Lord's	1974
	South Africa v England at Cape Town	1888-89
	Australia v England at The Oval	1896
	England v Australia at Sydney	1886-87
	South Africa v Australia at Melbourne	1931-32
	South Africa v England at Cape Town	1888-89
	New Zealand v England at Lord's	1958

The lowest innings for the countries not mentioned above are:

West Indies v Pakistan at Faisalabad	1986-87
Pakistan v Australia at Perth	1981-82
Sri Lanka v New Zealand at Wellington	1982-83

† *Batted one man short.*

FEWEST RUNS IN A FULL DAY'S PLAY

At Karachi, October 11, 1956. Australia 80 all out; Pakistan 15 for two (first day, 5½ hours).

At Karachi, December 8, 1959. Pakistan 0 for no wicket to 104 for five v Australia (fourth day, 5½ hours).

At Brisbane, December 9, 1958. England 92 for two to 198 all out v Australia (fourth day, 5 hours). *England were dismissed five minutes before the close of play, leaving no time for Australia to start their second innings.*

At Karachi, October 15, 1956. Australia 138 for six to 187 all out; Pakistan 63 for one (fourth day, 5½ hours).

At Madras, October 19, 1956. India 117 for five v Australia (first day, 5½ hours).

At Colombo (SSC), March 21, 1984. New Zealand 6 for no wicket to 123 for four (fifth day, 5 hours, 47 minutes).

England

At Lord's, August 26, 1978. England 175 for two to 289 all out; New Zealand 37 for seven (third day, 6 hours).

At Leeds, July 10, 1971. Pakistan 208 for four to 350 all out; England 17 for one (third day, 6 hours).

LOWEST MATCH AGGREGATES

(For a completed match)

Runs	*Wkts*			*Days playea*
234	29	Australia v South Africa at Melbourne	1931-32	3†
291	40	England v Australia at Lord's	1888	2
295	28	New Zealand v Australia at Wellington	1945-46	2
309	29	West Indies v England at Bridgetown	1934-35	3
323	30	England v Australia at Manchester	1888	2

† *No play on one day.*

YOUNGEST TEST PLAYERS

Years	*Days*			
15	124	Mushtaq Mohammad . . .	Pakistan v West Indies at Lahore . . .	1958-5
16	191	Aftab Baloch	Pakistan v New Zealand at Dacca . .	1969-7
16	248	Nasim-ul-Ghani	Pakistan v West Indies at Bridgetown	1957-5
16	352	Khalid Hassan	Pakistan v England at Nottingham . .	19
17	118	L. Sivaramakrishnan . . .	India v West Indies at St John's	1982-8
17	122	J. E. D. Sealy	West Indies v England at Bridgetown	1929-3
17	189	C. D. U. S. Weerasinghe	Sri Lanka v India at Colombo (PSO)	1985-8
17	193	Maninder Singh	India v Pakistan at Karachi	1982-
17	239	I. D. Craig	Australia v South Africa at Melbourne	1952-
17	245	G. S. Sobers	West Indies v England at Kingston . .	1953-
17	265	V. L. Mehra	India v New Zealand at Bombay . . .	1955-
17	300	Hanif Mohammad	Pakistan v India at Delhi	1952-
17	341	Intikhab Alam	Pakistan v Australia at Karachi	1959-

Note: The youngest Test players for countries not mentioned above are: England – D. Close, 18 years 149 days, v New Zealand at Manchester, 1949; New Zealand – D. L. Freema 18 years 197 days, v England at Christchurch, 1932-33; South Africa – A. E. Ochse, 19 yea 1 day, v England at Port Elizabeth, 1888-89.

OLDEST PLAYERS ON TEST DEBUT

Years	*Days*			
49	119	J. Southerton	England v Australia at Melbourne . . .	1876
47	284	Miran Bux	Pakistan v India at Lahore	1954
46	253	D. D. Blackie	Australia v England at Sydney	1928
46	237	H. Ironmonger	Australia v England at Brisbane	1928
42	242	N. Betancourt	West Indies v England at Port-of-Spain	1929
41	337	E. R. Wilson	England v Australia at Sydney	1920
41	27	R. J. D. Jamshedji	India v England at Bombay	1933
40	345	C. A. Wiles	West Indies v England at Manchester	1
40	216	S. P. Kinneir	England v Australia at Sydney	1911
40	110	H. W. Lee	England v South Africa at Johannesburg	1930
40	56	G. W. A. Chubb	South Africa v England at Nottingham.	1
40	37	C. Ramaswami	India v England at Manchester	1

Note: The oldest Test player on début for New Zealand was H. M. McGirr, 38 years 101 d v England at Auckland, 1929-30; for Sri Lanka, D. S. de Silva, 39 years 251 days, v Englan Colombo (PSO), 1981-82.

OLDEST TEST PLAYERS

(Age on final day of their last Test match)

Years	*Days*			
52	165	W. Rhodes	England v West Indies at Kingston	1929-30
50	327	H. Ironmonger	Australia v England at Sydney	1932-33
50	320	W. G. Grace	England v Australia at Nottingham	1899
50	303	G. Gunn	England v West Indies at Kingston	1929-30
49	139	J. Southerton	England v Australia at Melbourne	1876-77
47	302	Miran Bux	Pakistan v India at Peshawar	1954-55
47	249	J. B. Hobbs	England v Australia at The Oval	1930
47	87	F. E. Woolley	England v Australia at The Oval	1934
46	309	D. D. Blackie	Australia v England at Adelaide	1928-29
46	206	A. W. Nourse	South Africa v England at The Oval	1924
46	202	H. Strudwick	England v Australia at The Oval	1926
46	41	E. H. Hendren	England v West Indies at Kingston	1934-35
45	245	G. O. Allen	England v West Indies at Kingston	1947-48
45	215	P. Holmes	England v India at Lord's	1932
45	140	D. B. Close	England v West Indies at Manchester	1976

MOST TEST MATCH APPEARANCES

For	*Total*		*E*	*A*	*SA*	*WI*	*NZ*	*I*	*P*	*SL*
ngland	114	M. C. Cowdrey	—	43	14	21	18	8	10	—
ustralia	96	R. W. Marsh	42	—	—	17	14	3	20	—
outh Africa	50	J. H. B. Waite	21	14	—	—	15	—	—	—
'est Indies	110	C. H. Lloyd	34	29	—	—	8	28	11	—
ew Zealand	74	R. J. Hadlee	18	22	—	10	—	8	10	6
dia	125	S. M. Gavaskar	38	20	—	27	9	—	24	7
akistan	92	Javed Miandad	17	19	—	11	12	24	—	9
i Lanka	24	L. R. D. Mendis	3	1	—	—	4	7	9	—
	24	A. Ranatunga	3	2	—	—	4	7	8	—

MOST CONSECUTIVE TEST APPEARANCES

6	S. M. Gavaskar (*India*)	Bombay 1974-75 to Madras 1986-87
1	A. R. Border (*Australia*)	Melbourne 1978-79 to Perth 1987-88
7	G. R. Viswanath (*India*)	Georgetown 1970-71 to Karachi 1982-83
5	G. S. Sobers (*West Indies*)	Port-of-Spain 1954-55 to Port-of-Spain 1971-72
2	D. L. Haynes (*West Indies*)	Brisbane 1979-80 to Lord's 1988
1	I. M. Chappell (*Australia*)	Adelaide 1965-66 to Melbourne 1975-76
5	Kapil Dev (*India*)	Faisalabad 1978-79 to Delhi 1984-85
5	I. T. Botham (*England*)	Wellington 1977-78 to Karachi 1983-84
5	A. P. E. Knott (*England*)	Auckland 1970-71 to The Oval 1977
1	R. B. Kanhai (*West Indies*)	Birmingham 1957 to Sydney 1968-69
1	I. V. A. Richards (*West Indies*)	Nottingham 1980 to Madras 1987-88
3†	A. W. Greig (*England*)	Manchester 1972 to The Oval 1977
3†	J. R. Reid (*New Zealand*)	Manchester 1949 to Leeds 1965
[illegible]	S. M. H. Kirmani (*India*)	Madras 1979-80 to Kanpur 1984-85
[illegible]	K. J. Hughes (*Australia*)	Brisbane 1978-79 to Sydney 1982-83
[illegible]	Javed Miandad (*Pakistan*)	Lahore 1977-78 to Sydney 1983-84
[illegible]	R. W. Marsh (*Australia*)	Brisbane 1970-71 to The Oval 1977
[illegible]	P. B. H. May (*England*)	The Oval 1953 to Leeds 1959
[illegible]	F. E. Woolley (*England*)	The Oval 1909 to The Oval 1926
	G. S. Chappell (*Australia*)	Perth 1970-71 to The Oval 1977
	D. I. Gower (*England*)	Bombay 1981-82 to Lord's 1986

Indicates complete Test career.

SUMMARY OF ALL TEST MATCHES

To end of 1988 season in England

		Tests	Won by								Tied	Drawn
			E	*A*	*SA*	*WI*	*NZ*	*I*	*P*	*SL*		
England	v Australia	263	88	97	–	–	–	–	–	–	–	78
	v South Africa	102	46	–	18	–	–	–	–	–	–	38
	v West Indies	95	21	–	–	39	–	–	–	–	–	35
	v New Zealand	66	30	–	–	–	4	–	–	–	–	32
	v India	75	30	–	–	–	–	11	–	–	–	34
	v Pakistan	47	13	–	–	–	–	–	5	–	–	29
	v Sri Lanka	3	2	–	–	–	–	–	–	0	–	1
Australia	v South Africa	53	–	29	11	–	–	–	–	–	–	13
	v West Indies	62	–	27	–	19	–	–	–	–	1	15
	v New Zealand	24	–	10	–	–	5	–	–	–	–	9
	v India	45	–	20	–	–	–	8	–	–	1	16
	v Pakistan	28	–	11	–	–	–	–	8	–	–	9
	v Sri Lanka	2	–	2	–	–	–	–	–	0	–	0
South Africa	v New Zealand	17	–	–	9	–	2	–	–	–	–	6
West Indies	v New Zealand	24	–	–	–	8	4	–	–	–	–	12
	v India	58	–	–	–	23	–	6	–	–	–	29
	v Pakistan	25	–	–	–	9	–	–	6	–	–	10
New Zealand	v India	25	–	–	–	–	4	10	–	–	–	11
	v Pakistan	27	–	–	–	–	3	–	10	–	–	14
	v Sri Lanka	6	–	–	–	–	4	–	–	0	–	2
India	v Pakistan	40	–	–	–	–	–	4	7	–	–	29
	v Sri Lanka	7	–	–	–	–	–	2	–	1	–	4
Pakistan	v Sri Lanka	9	–	–	–	–	–	–	5	1	–	3
		1,103	230	196	38	98	26	41	41	2	2	429

	Tests	*Won*	*Lost*	*Drawn*	*Tied*	*Toss Won*
England	651	230	174	247	–	323
Australia	477	196	139	140	2	240
South Africa	172	38	77	57	–	80
West Indies	264	98	64	101	1	141
New Zealand	189	26	77	86	–	93
India	250	41	85	123	1	123
Pakistan	176	41	41	94	–	90
Sri Lanka	27	2	15	10	–	13

ENGLAND v AUSTRALIA

	Captains					
Season	*England*	*Australia*	*T*	*E*	*A*	*D*
1876-77	James Lillywhite	D. W. Gregory	2	1	1	0
1878-79	Lord Harris	D. W. Gregory	1	0	1	0
1880	Lord Harris	W. L. Murdoch	1	1	0	0
1881-82	A. Shaw	W. L. Murdoch	4	0	2	2
1882	A. N. Hornby	W. L. Murdoch	1	0	1	0

THE ASHES

	Captains						
Season	*England*	*Australia*	*T*	*E*	*A*	*D*	*Held*
1882-83	Hon. Ivo Bligh	W. L. Murdoch	4*	2	2	0	E
1884	Lord Harris[1]	W. L. Murdoch	3	1	0	2	E
1884-85	A. Shrewsbury	T. Horan[2]	5	3	2	0	E
1886	A. G. Steel	H. J. H. Scott	3	3	0	0	E

Season	*England*	*Australia*	*T*	*E*	*A*	*D*	*Held by*
	Captains						
1886-87	A. Shrewsbury	P. S. McDonnell	2	2	0	0	E
1887-88	W. W. Read	P. S. McDonnell	1	1	0	0	E
1888	W. G. Grace[3]	P. S. McDonnell	3	2	1	0	E
890†	W. G. Grace	W. L. Murdoch	2	2	0	0	E
891-92	W. G. Grace	J. McC. Blackham	3	1	2	0	A
893	W. G. Grace[4]	J. McC. Blackham	3	1	0	2	E
894-95	A. E. Stoddart	G. Giffen[5]	5	3	2	0	E
896	W. G. Grace	G. H. S. Trott	3	2	1	0	E
897-98	A. E. Stoddart[6]	G. H. S. Trott	5	1	4	0	A
899	A. C. MacLaren[7]	J. Darling	5	0	1	4	A
901-02	A. C. MacLaren	J. Darling[8]	5	1	4	0	A
902	A. C. MacLaren	J. Darling	5	1	2	2	A
903-04	P. F. Warner	M. A. Noble	5	3	2	0	E
905	Hon. F. S. Jackson	J. Darling	5	2	0	3	E
907-08	A. O. Jones[9]	M. A. Noble	5	1	4	0	A
909	A. C. MacLaren	M. A. Noble	5	1	2	2	A
911-12	J. W. H. T. Douglas	C. Hill	5	4	1	0	E
912	C. B. Fry	S. E. Gregory	3	1	0	2	E
920-21	J. W. H. T. Douglas	W. W. Armstrong	5	0	5	0	A
921	Hon. L. H. Tennyson[10]	W. W. Armstrong	5	0	3	2	A
924-25	A. E. R. Gilligan	H. L. Collins	5	1	4	0	A
926	A. W. Carr[11]	H. L. Collins[12]	5	1	0	4	E
928-29	A. P. F. Chapman[13]	J. Ryder	5	4	1	0	E
30	A. P. F. Chapman[14]	W. M. Woodfull	5	1	2	2	A
32-33	D. R. Jardine	W. M. Woodfull	5	4	1	0	E
34	R. E. S. Wyatt[15]	W. M. Woodfull	5	1	2	2	A
36-37	G. O. Allen	D. G. Bradman	5	2	3	0	A
38†	W. R. Hammond	D. G. Bradman	4	1	1	2	A
46-47	W. R. Hammond[16]	D. G. Bradman	5	0	3	2	A
48	N. W. D. Yardley	D. G. Bradman	5	0	4	1	A
50-51	F. R. Brown	A. L. Hassett	5	1	4	0	A
53	L. Hutton	A. L. Hassett	5	1	0	4	E
54-55	L. Hutton	I. W. Johnson[17]	5	3	1	1	E
56	P. B. H. May	I. W. Johnson	5	2	1	2	E
58-59	P. B. H. May	R. Benaud	5	0	4	1	A
61	P. B. H. May[18]	R. Benaud[19]	5	1	2	2	A
62-63	E. R. Dexter	R. Benaud	5	1	1	3	A
64	E. R. Dexter	R. B. Simpson	5	0	1	4	A
65-66	M. J. K. Smith	R. B. Simpson[20]	5	1	1	3	A
68	M. C. Cowdrey[21]	W. M. Lawry[22]	5	1	1	3	A
70-71†	R. Illingworth	W. M. Lawry[23]	6	2	0	4	E
72	R. Illingworth	I. M. Chappell	5	2	2	1	E
74-75	M. H. Denness[24]	I. M. Chappell	6	1	4	1	A
75	A. W. Greig[25]	I. M. Chappell	4	0	1	3	A
76-77‡	A. W. Greig	G. S. Chappell	1	0	1	0	—
7	J. M. Brearley	G. S. Chappell	5	3	0	2	E
8-79	J. M. Brearley	G. N. Yallop	6	5	1	0	E
9-80‡	J. M. Brearley	G. S. Chappell	3	0	3	0	—
0‡	I. T. Botham	G. S. Chappell	1	0	0	1	—
1	J. M. Brearley[26]	K. J. Hughes	6	3	1	2	E
2-83	R. G. D. Willis	G. S. Chappell	5	1	2	2	A
5	D. I. Gower	A. R. Border	6	3	1	2	E
6-87	M. W. Gatting	A. R. Border	5	2	1	2	E
7-88‡	M. W. Gatting	A. R. Border	1	0	0	1	—
	In Australia		140	51	67	22	
	In England		123	37	30	56	
	Totals		263	88	97	78	

* *The Ashes were awarded in 1882-83 after a series of three matches which England won 2-1. A fourth unofficial match was played, each innings being played on a different pitch, and this was won by Australia.*

† *The matches at Manchester in 1890 and 1938 and at Melbourne (Third Test) in 1970-71 were abandoned without a ball being bowled and are excluded.*

‡ *The Ashes were not at stake in these series.*

Notes: The following deputised for the official touring captain or were appointed by the home authority for only a minor proportion of the series:

[1]A. N. Hornby (First). [2]W. L. Murdoch (First), H. H. Massie (Third), J. McC. Blackham (Fourth). [3]A. G. Steel (First). [4]A. E. Stoddart (First). [5]J. McC. Blackham (First). [6]A. C. MacLaren (First, Second and Fifth). [7]W. G. Grace (First). [8]H. Trumble (Fourth and Fifth). [9]F. L. Fane (First, Second and Third). [10]J. W. H. T. Douglas (First and Second). [11]A. P. F. Chapman (Fifth). [12]W. Bardsley (Third and Fourth). [13]J. C. White (Fifth). [14]R. E. S. Wya (Fifth). [15]C. F. Walters (First). [16]N. W. D. Yardley (Fifth). [17]A. R. Morris (Second). [18]M. C. Cowdrey (First and Second). [19]R. N. Harvey (Second). [20]B. C. Booth (First and Third). [21]T. W. Graveney (Fourth). [22]B. N. Jarman (Fourth). [23]I. M. Chappell (Seventh). [24]J. H. Edric (Fourth). [25]M. H. Denness (First). [26]I. T. Botham (First and Second).

HIGHEST INNINGS TOTALS

For England in England: 903-7 dec. at The Oval	193
in Australia: 636 at Sydney	1928-2
For Australia in England: 729-6 dec. at Lord's	193
in Australia: 659-8 dec. at Sydney	1946-4

LOWEST INNINGS TOTALS

For England in England: 52 at The Oval	194
in Australia: 45 at Sydney	1886-8
For Australia in England: 36 at Birmingham	190
in Australia: 42 at Sydney	1887-8

INDIVIDUAL HUNDREDS

For England (187)

132*‡	R. Abel, Sydney	1891-92
120	L. E. G. Ames, Lord's	1934
185	R. W. Barber, Sydney	1965-66
134	W. Barnes, Adelaide	1884-85
129	C. J. Barnett, Adelaide	1936-37
126	C. J. Barnett, Nottingham	1938
132*	K. F. Barrington, Adelaide	1962-63
101	K. F. Barrington, Sydney	1962-63
256	K. F. Barrington, Manchester	1964
102	K. F. Barrington, Adelaide	1965-66
115	K. F. Barrington, Melbourne	1965-66
119*	I. T. Botham, Melbourne	1979-80
149*	I. T. Botham, Leeds	1981
118	I. T. Botham, Manchester	1981
138	I. T. Botham, Brisbane	1986-87
113	G. Boycott, The Oval	1964
142*	G. Boycott, Sydney	1970-71
119*	G. Boycott, Adelaide	1970-71
107	G. Boycott, Nottingham	1977
191	G. Boycott, Leeds	19
128*	G. Boycott, Lord's	19
137	G. Boycott, The Oval	19
103*	L. C. Braund, Adelaide	1901
102	L. C. Braund, Sydney	1903
121	J. Briggs, Melbourne	1884
162	B. C. Broad, Perth	1986
116	B. C. Broad, Adelaide	1986
112	B. C. Broad, Melbourne	1986
139	B. C. Broad, Sydney	1987
140	J. T. Brown, Melbourne	1894
121	A. P. F. Chapman, Lord's	19
102†	D. C. S. Compton, Nottingham	1
147 103*	D. C. S. Compton, Adelaide	1946
184	D. C. S. Compton, Nottingham	1
145*	D. C. S. Compton, Manchester	1
102	M. C. Cowdrey, Melbourne	1954

100* M. C. Cowdrey, Sydney ... 1958-59
113 M. C. Cowdrey, Melbourne ... 1962-63
104 M. C. Cowdrey, Melbourne ... 1965-66
04 M. C. Cowdrey, Birmingham ... 1968
88 M. H. Denness, Melbourne 1974-75
80 E. R. Dexter, Birmingham . 1961
174 E. R. Dexter, Manchester . 1964
58 B. L. D'Oliveira, The Oval . 1968
17 B. L. D'Oliveira, Melbourne ... 1970-71
73† K. S. Duleepsinhji, Lord's . 1930
20† J. H. Edrich, Lord's ... 1964
09 J. H. Edrich, Melbourne .. 1965-66
03 J. H. Edrich, Sydney ... 1965-66
64 J. H. Edrich, The Oval ... 1968
15* J. H. Edrich, Perth ... 1970-71
30 J. H. Edrich, Adelaide ... 1970-71
75 J. H. Edrich, Lord's ... 1975
19 W. J. Edrich, Sydney ... 1946-47
11 W. J. Edrich, Leeds ... 1948
46 K. W. R. Fletcher, Melbourne ... 1974-75
87† R. E. Foster, Sydney ... 1903-04
44 C. B. Fry, The Oval ... 1905
60 M. W. Gatting, Manchester 1985
00* M. W. Gatting, Birmingham 1985
00 M. W. Gatting, Adelaide .. 1986-87
6 G. A. Gooch, The Oval ... 1985
2 D. I. Gower, Perth ... 1978-79
4 D. I. Gower, Adelaide ... 1982-83
6 D. I. Gower, Nottingham . 1985
5 D. I. Gower, Birmingham . 1985
7 D. I. Gower, The Oval ... 1985
6 D. I. Gower, Perth ... 1986-87
2† W. G. Grace, The Oval ... 1880
0 W. G. Grace, The Oval ... 1886
1 T. W. Graveney, Sydney .. 1954-55
0 A. W. Greig, Brisbane ... 1974-75
9† G. Gunn, Sydney ... 1907-08
2* G. Gunn, Sydney ... 1907-08
2* W. Gunn, Manchester ... 1893
W. R. Hammond, Sydney . 1928-29
W. R. Hammond, Melbourne ... 1928-29
* } W. R. Hammond, Adelaide 1928-29
W. R. Hammond, Leeds .. 1930
W. R. Hammond, Sydney . 1932-33
W. R. Hammond, Sydney . 1932-33
* W. R. Hammond, Sydney . 1936-37
W. R. Hammond, Lord's .. 1938
* J. Hardstaff jun., The Oval 1938
T. W. Hayward, Manchester ... 1899
T. W. Hayward, The Oval . 1899
J. W. Hearne, Melbourne . 1911-12
* E. H. Hendren, Lord's ... 1926
E. H. Hendren, Brisbane .. 1928-29
E. H. Hendren, Manchester 1934

126* J. B. Hobbs, Melbourne ... 1911-12
187 J. B. Hobbs, Adelaide ... 1911-12
178 J. B. Hobbs, Melbourne ... 1911-12
107 J. B. Hobbs, Lord's ... 1912
122 J. B. Hobbs, Melbourne ... 1920-21
123 J. B. Hobbs, Adelaide ... 1920-21
115 J. B. Hobbs, Sydney ... 1924-25
154 J. B. Hobbs, Melbourne ... 1924-25
119 J. B. Hobbs, Adelaide ... 1924-25
119 J. B. Hobbs, Lord's ... 1926
100 J. B. Hobbs, The Oval ... 1926
142 J. B. Hobbs, Melbourne ... 1928-29
126 K. L. Hutchings, Melbourne ... 1907-08
100† L. Hutton, Nottingham ... 1938
364 L. Hutton, The Oval ... 1938
122* L. Hutton, Sydney ... 1946-47
156*‡ L. Hutton, Adelaide ... 1950-51
145 L. Hutton, Lord's ... 1953
103 Hon. F. S. Jackson, The Oval ... 1893
118 Hon. F. S. Jackson, The Oval ... 1899
128 Hon. F. S. Jackson, Manchester ... 1902
144* Hon. F. S. Jackson, Leeds . 1905
113 Hon. F. S. Jackson, Manchester ... 1905
104 G. L. Jessop, The Oval ... 1902
106* A. P. E. Knott, Adelaide .. 1974-75
135 A. P. E. Knott, Nottingham 1977
137† M. Leyland, Melbourne ... 1928-29
109 M. Leyland, Lord's ... 1934
153 M. Leyland, Manchester .. 1934
110 M. Leyland, The Oval ... 1934
126 M. Leyland, Brisbane ... 1936-37
111* M. Leyland, Melbourne ... 1936-37
187 M. Leyland, The Oval ... 1938
131 B. W. Luckhurst, Perth ... 1970-71
109 B. W. Luckhurst, Melbourne ... 1970-71
120 A. C. MacLaren, Melbourne ... 1894-95
109 A. C. MacLaren, Sydney .. 1897-98
124 A. C. MacLaren, Adelaide ... 1897-98
116 A. C. MacLaren, Sydney .. 1901-02
140 A. C. MacLaren, Nottingham ... 1905
117 H. Makepeace, Melbourne . 1920-21
104 P. B. H. May, Sydney ... 1954-55
101 P. B. H. May, Leeds ... 1956
113 P. B. H. May, Melbourne . 1958-59
182* C. P. Mead, The Oval ... 1921
102† Nawab of Pataudi, Sydney . 1932-33
216* E. Paynter, Nottingham ... 1938
174† D. W. Randall, Melbourne 1976-77
150 D. W. Randall, Sydney ... 1978-79
115 D. W. Randall, Perth ... 1982-83
154*† K. S. Ranjitsinhji, Manchester ... 1896
175 K. S. Ranjitsinhji, Sydney . 1897-98

117	W. W. Read, The Oval	1884
179	W. Rhodes, Melbourne	1911-12
133	C. J. Richards, Perth	1986-87
104	P. E. Richardson, Manchester	1956
175†	R. T. Robinson, Leeds	1985
148	R. T. Robinson, Birmingham	1985
135*	A. C. Russell, Adelaide	1920-21
101	A. C. Russell, Manchester	1921
102*	A. C. Russell, The Oval	1921
105	J. Sharp, The Oval	1909
113	Rev. D. S. Sheppard, Manchester	1956
113	Rev. D. S. Sheppard, Melbourne	1962-63
105*	A. Shrewsbury, Melbourne	1884-85
164	A. Shrewsbury, Lord's	1886
106	A. Shrewsbury, Lord's	1893
156*	R. T. Simpson, Melbourne	1950-51
135*	A. G. Steel, Sydney	1882-83
148	A. G. Steel, Lord's	1884
134	A. E. Stoddart, Adelaide	1891-92
173	A. E. Stoddart, Melbourne	1894-95
112†	R. Subba Row, Birmingham	1961
137	R. Subba Row, The Oval	1961
115†	H. Sutcliffe, Sydney	1924-25
176 / 127	H. Sutcliffe, Melbourne	1924-25
143	H. Sutcliffe, Melbourne	1924-25
161	H. Sutcliffe, The Oval	1926
135	H. Sutcliffe, Melbourne	1928-29
161	H. Sutcliffe, The Oval	1930
194	H. Sutcliffe, Sydney	1932-33
138	J. T. Tyldesley, Birmingham	1902
100	J. T. Tyldesley, Leeds	1905
112*	J. T. Tyldesley, The Oval	1905
149	G. Ulyett, Melbourne	1881-82
117	A. Ward, Sydney	1894-95
112	C. Washbrook, Melbourne	1946-47
143	C. Washbrook, Leeds	1948
109†	W. Watson, Lord's	195
133*	F. E. Woolley, Sydney	1911-1
123	F. E. Woolley, Sydney	1924-2
149	R. A. Woolmer, The Oval	197
120	R. A. Woolmer, Lord's	197
137	R. A. Woolmer, Manchester	197

† *Signifies hundred on first appearance in England–Australia Tests.*
‡ *Carried his bat.*

Note: In consecutive innings in 1928-29, W. R. Hammond scored 251 at Sydney, 200 and 32 a Melbourne, and 119* and 177 at Adelaide.

For Australia (204)

133*	W. W. Armstrong, Melbourne	1907-08
158	W. W. Armstrong, Sydney	1920-21
121	W. W. Armstrong, Adelaide	1920-21
123*	W. W. Armstrong, Melbourne	1920-21
118	C. L. Badcock, Melbourne	1936-37
165*†	C. Bannerman, Melbourne	1876-77
136 / 130	W. Bardsley, The Oval	1909
193*‡	W. Bardsley, Lord's	1926
234	S. G. Barnes, Sydney	1946-47
141	S. G. Barnes, Lord's	1948
128	G. J. Bonnor, Sydney	1884-85
103	D. C. Boon, Adelaide	1986-87
184*	D. C. Boon, Sydney	1987-88
112	B. C. Booth, Brisbane	1962-63
103	B. C. Booth, Melbourne	1962-63
115	A. R. Border, Perth	1979-80
123*	A. R. Border, Manchester	1981
106*	A. R. Border, The Oval	1981
196	A. R. Border, Lord's	1985
146*	A. R. Border, Manchester	1985
125	A. R. Border, Perth	1986-87
100*	A. R. Border, Adelaide	1986-87
112	D. G. Bradman, Melbourne	1928-29
123	D. G. Bradman, Melbourne	1928-29
131	D. G. Bradman, Nottingham	193
254	D. G. Bradman, Lord's	193
334	D. G. Bradman, Leeds	193
232	D. G. Bradman, The Oval	193
103*	D. G. Bradman, Melbourne	1932-3
304	D. G. Bradman, Leeds	193
244	D. G. Bradman, The Oval	193
270	D. G. Bradman, Melbourne	1936-
212	D. G. Bradman, Adelaide	1936-
169	D. G. Bradman, Melbourne	1936-
144*	D. G. Bradman, Nottingham	19
102*	D. G. Bradman, Lord's	19
103	D. G. Bradman, Leeds	19
187	D. G. Bradman, Brisbane	1946-
234	D. G. Bradman, Sydney	1946-
138	D. G. Bradman, Nottingham	19
173*	D. G. Bradman, Leeds	19
105	W. A. Brown, Lord's	19
133	W. A. Brown, Nottingham	19
206*‡	W. A. Brown, Lord's	19
181	P. J. Burge, The Oval	19
103	P. J. Burge, Sydney	1962
160	P. J. Burge, Leeds	19
120	P. J. Burge, Melbourne	1965-

101*†	J. W. Burke, Adelaide	1950-51
108†	G. S. Chappell, Perth	1970-71
131	G. S. Chappell, Lord's	1972
113	G. S. Chappell, The Oval	1972
144	G. S. Chappell, Sydney	1974-75
102	G. S. Chappell, Melbourne	1974-75
112	G. S. Chappell, Manchester	1977
114	G. S. Chappell, Melbourne	1979-80
117	G. S. Chappell, Perth	1982-83
115	G. S. Chappell, Adelaide	1982-83
111	I. M. Chappell, Melbourne	1970-71
104	I. M. Chappell, Adelaide	1970-71
118	I. M. Chappell, The Oval	1972
192	I. M. Chappell, The Oval	1975
104†	H. L. Collins, Sydney	1920-21
162	H. L. Collins, Adelaide	1920-21
114	H. L. Collins, Sydney	1924-25
307	R. M. Cowper, Melbourne	1965-66
101	J. Darling, Sydney	1897-98
178	J. Darling, Adelaide	1897-98
160	J. Darling, Sydney	1897-98
104†	R. A. Duff, Melbourne	1901-02
46	R. A. Duff, The Oval	1905
02	J. Dyson, Leeds	1981
170*	R. Edwards, Nottingham	1972
15	R. Edwards, Perth	1974-75
00	J. H. Fingleton, Brisbane	1936-37
36	J. H. Fingleton, Melbourne	1936-37
61	G. Giffen, Sydney	1894-95
07†	H. Graham, Lord's	1893
05	H. Graham, Sydney	1894-95
00	J. M. Gregory, Melbourne	1920-21
01	S. E. Gregory, Sydney	1894-95
03	S. E. Gregory, Lord's	1896
17	S. E. Gregory, The Oval	1899
12	S. E. Gregory, Adelaide	1903-04
16†	R. J. Hartigan, Adelaide	1907-08
12†	R. N. Harvey, Leeds	1948
22	R. N. Harvey, Manchester	1953
52	R. N. Harvey, Brisbane	1954-55
57	R. N. Harvey, Melbourne	1958-59
14	R. N. Harvey, Birmingham	1961
54	R. N. Harvey, Adelaide	1962-63
28	A. L. Hassett, Brisbane	1946-47
37	A. L. Hassett, Nottingham	1948
5	A. L. Hassett, Nottingham	1953
04	A. L. Hassett, Lord's	1953
12	H. L. Hendry, Sydney	1928-29
19	A. M. J. Hilditch, Leeds	1985
38	C. Hill, Melbourne	1897-98
5	C. Hill, Lord's	1899
9	C. Hill, Sheffield	1902
0	C. Hill, Adelaide	1907-08
4	T. P. Horan, Melbourne	1881-82
9	K. J. Hughes, Brisbane	1978-79
7	K. J. Hughes, Lord's	1980
137	K. J. Hughes, Sydney	1982-83
140	F. A. Iredale, Adelaide	1894-95
108	F. A. Iredale, Manchester	1896
164†	A. A. Jackson, Adelaide	1928-29
184*	D. M. Jones, Sydney	1986-87
147	C. Kelleway, Adelaide	1920-21
100	A. F. Kippax, Melbourne	1928-29
130	W. M. Lawry, Lord's	1961
102	W. M. Lawry, Manchester	1961
106	W. M. Lawry, Manchester	1964
166	W. M. Lawry, Brisbane	1965-66
119	W. M. Lawry, Adelaide	1965-66
108	W. M. Lawry, Melbourne	1965-66
135	W. M. Lawry, The Oval	1968
100	R. R. Lindwall, Melbourne	1946-47
134	J. J. Lyons, Sydney	1891-92
170	C. G. Macartney, Sydney	1920-21
115	C. G. Macartney, Leeds	1921
133*	C. G. Macartney, Lord's	1926
151	C. G. Macartney, Leeds	1926
109	C. G. Macartney, Manchester	1926
187*	S. J. McCabe, Sydney	1932-33
137	S. J. McCabe, Manchester	1934
112	S. J. McCabe, Melbourne	1936-37
232	S. J. McCabe, Nottingham	1938
104*	C. L. McCool, Melbourne	1946-47
127	R. B. McCosker, The Oval	1975
107	R. B. McCosker, Nottingham	1977
170	C. C. McDonald, Adelaide	1958-59
133	C. C. McDonald, Melbourne	1958-59
147	P. S. McDonnell, Sydney	1881-82
103	P. S. McDonnell, The Oval	1884
124	P. S. McDonnell, Adelaide	1884-85
112	C. E. McLeod, Melbourne	1897-98
110†	G. R. Marsh, Brisbane	1986-87
110*	R. W. Marsh, Melbourne	1976-77
141*	K. R. Miller, Adelaide	1946-47
145*	K. R. Miller, Sydney	1950-51
109	K. R. Miller, Lord's	1953
155	A. R. Morris, Melbourne	1946-47
122 / 124*	A. R. Morris, Adelaide	1946-47
105	A. R. Morris, Lord's	1948
182	A. R. Morris, Leeds	1948
196	A. R. Morris, The Oval	1948
206	A. R. Morris, Adelaide	1950-51
153	A. R. Morris, Brisbane	1954-55
153*	W. L. Murdoch, The Oval	1880
211	W. L. Murdoch, The Oval	1884
133	M. A. Noble, Sydney	1903-04
117	N. C. O'Neill, The Oval	1961
100	N. C. O'Neill, Adelaide	1962-63
116	C. E. Pellew, Melbourne	1920-21
104	C. E. Pellew, Adelaide	1920-21
110†	W. H. Ponsford, Sydney	1924-25

128	W. H. Ponsford, Melbourne	1924-25
110	W. H. Ponsford, The Oval	1930
181	W. H. Ponsford, Leeds	1934
266	W. H. Ponsford, The Oval	1934
143*	V. S. Ransford, Lord's	1909
171	I. R. Redpath, Perth	1970-71
105	I. R. Redpath, Sydney	1974-75
100	A. J. Richardson, Leeds	1926
138	V. Y. Richardson, Melbourne	1924-25
146	G. M. Ritchie, Nottingham	1985
201*	J. Ryder, Adelaide	1924-25
112	J. Ryder, Melbourne	1928-29
102	H. J. H. Scott, The Oval	1884
311	R. B. Simpson, Manchester	1964
225	R. B. Simpson, Adelaide	1965-66
207	K. R. Stackpole, Brisbane	1970-71
136	K. R. Stackpole, Adelaide	1970-71
114	K. R. Stackpole, Nottingham	1972
108	J. M. Taylor, Sydney	1924-25
143	G. H. S. Trott, Lord's	1896
135*	V. T. Trumper, Lord's	1899
104	V. T. Trumper, Manchester	1902
185*	V. T. Trumper, Sydney	1903-04
113	V. T. Trumper, Adelaide	1903-04
166	V. T. Trumper, Sydney	1907-08
113	V. T. Trumper, Sydney	1911-12
155†	K. D. Walters, Brisbane	1965-66
115	K. D. Walters, Melbourne	1965-66
112	K. D. Walters, Brisbane	1970-71
103	K. D. Walters, Perth	1974-75
103†	D. M. Wellham, The Oval	1981
162†	K. C. Wessels, Brisbane	1982-83
100	G. M. Wood, Melbourne	1978-79
112	G. M. Wood, Lord's	1980
172	G. M. Wood, Nottingham	1985
141	W. M. Woodfull, Leeds	1926
117	W. M. Woodfull, Manchester	1926
111	W. M. Woodfull, Sydney	1928-29
107	W. M. Woodfull, Melbourne	1928-29
102	W. M. Woodfull, Melbourne	1928-29
155	W. M. Woodfull, Lord's	1930
102†	G. N. Yallop, Brisbane	1978-79
121	G. N. Yallop, Sydney	1978-79
114	G. N. Yallop, Manchester	1981

† *Signifies hundred on first appearance in England–Australia Tests.*

‡ *Carried his bat.*

Notes: D. G. Bradman's scores in 1930 were 8 and 131 at Nottingham, 254 and 1 at Lord's, 334 at Leeds, 14 at Manchester, and 232 at The Oval.

D. G. Bradman scored a hundred in eight successive Tests against England in which he batted – three in 1936-37, three in 1938 and two in 1946-47. He was injured and unable to bat at The Oval in 1938.

W. H. Ponsford and K. D. Walters each hit hundreds in their first two Tests.

C. Bannerman and H. Graham each scored their maiden hundred in first-class cricket in their first Test.

No right-handed batsman has obtained two hundreds for Australia in a Test match against England, and no left-handed batsman for England against Australia.

H. Sutcliffe, in his first two games for England, scored 59 and 115 at Sydney and 176 and 127 at Melbourne in 1924-25. In the latter match, which lasted into the seventh day, he was on the field throughout except for 86 minutes, namely 27 hours and 52 minutes.

C. Hill made 98 and 97 at Adelaide in 1901-02, and F. E. Woolley 95 and 93 at Lord's in 1921.

H. Sutcliffe in 1924-25, C. G. Macartney in 1926 and A. R. Morris in 1946-47 made three hundreds in consecutive innings.

J. B. Hobbs and H. Sutcliffe shared eleven first-wicket three-figure partnerships.

L. Hutton and C. Washbrook twice made three-figure stands in each innings, at Adelaide in 1946-47 and at Leeds in 1948.

H. Sutcliffe, during his highest score of 194, v Australia in 1932-33, took part in three stands each exceeding 100, viz. 112 with R. E. S. Wyatt for the first wicket, 188 with W. R. Hammond for the second wicket, and 123 with the Nawab of Pataudi for the third wicket. In 1903-04 R. E. Foster, in his historic innings of 287, added 192 for the fifth wicket with L. C. Braund, 115 for the ninth with A. E. Relf, and 130 for the tenth with W. Rhodes.

When L. Hutton scored 364 at The Oval in 1938 he added 382 for the second wicket with M. Leyland, 135 for the third wicket with W. R. Hammond and 215 for the sixth wicket with J. Hardstaff jun.

D. C. S. Compton and A. R. Morris at Adelaide in 1946-47 provide the only instance of a player on each side hitting two separate hundreds in a Test match.

G. S. and I. M. Chappell at The Oval in 1972 provide the first instance in Test matches of brothers each scoring hundreds in the same innings.

RECORD PARTNERSHIPS FOR EACH WICKET

For England

323 for 1st	J. B. Hobbs and W. Rhodes at Melbourne	1911-12
382 for 2nd†	L. Hutton and M. Leyland at The Oval	1938
262 for 3rd	W. R. Hammond and D. R. Jardine at Adelaide	1928-29
222 for 4th	W. R. Hammond and E. Paynter at Lord's	1938
206 for 5th	E. Paynter and D. C. S. Compton at Nottingham	1938
215 for 6th	L. Hutton and J. Hardstaff jun. at The Oval	1938
	G. Boycott and A. P. E. Knott at Nottingham	1977
143 for 7th	F. E. Woolley and J. Vine at Sydney	1911-12
124 for 8th	E. H. Hendren and H. Larwood at Brisbane	1928-29
151 for 9th	W. H. Scotton and W. W. Read at The Oval	1884
130 for 10th†	R. E. Foster and W. Rhodes at Sydney	1903-04

For Australia

244 for 1st	R. B. Simpson and W. M. Lawry at Adelaide	1965-66
451 for 2nd†	W. H. Ponsford and D. G. Bradman at The Oval	1934
276 for 3rd	D. G. Bradman and A. L. Hassett at Brisbane	1946-47
388 for 4th†	W. H. Ponsford and D. G. Bradman at Leeds	1934
405 for 5th†‡	S. G. Barnes and D. G. Bradman at Sydney	1946-47
346 for 6th†	J. H. Fingleton and D. G. Bradman at Melbourne	1936-37
65 for 7th	C. Hill and H. Trumble at Melbourne	1897-98
243 for 8th†	R. J. Hartigan and C. Hill at Adelaide	1907-08
54 for 9th†	S. E. Gregory and J. McC. Blackham at Sydney	1894-95
27 for 10th†	J. M. Taylor and A. A. Mailey at Sydney	1924-25

† *Denotes record partnership against all countries.*
‡ *Record fifth-wicket partnership in first-class cricket.*

MOST RUNS IN A SERIES

ngland in England	732 (average 81.33)	D. I. Gower	1985
ngland in Australia	905 (average 113.12)	W. R. Hammond	1928-29
ustralia in England	974 (average 139.14)	D. G. Bradman	1930
ustralia in Australia	810 (average 90.00)	D. G. Bradman	1936-37

TEN WICKETS OR MORE IN A MATCH

For England (37)

-163 (6-42, 7-121)	S. F. Barnes, Melbourne	1901-02
-102 (7-28, 7-74)	W. Bates, Melbourne	1882-83
-105 (5-46, 5-59)	A. V. Bedser, Melbourne	1950-51
-99 (7-55, 7-44)	A. V. Bedser, Nottingham	1953
-102 (6-44, 5-58)	C. Blythe, Birmingham	1909
-176 (6-78, 5-98)	I. T. Botham, Perth	1979-80
-253 (6-125, 4-128)	I. T. Botham, The Oval	1981
-74 (5-29, 6-45)	J. Briggs, Lord's	1886
-136 (6-49, 6-87)	J. Briggs, Adelaide	1891-92
-148 (5-34, 5-114)	J. Briggs, The Oval	1893
104 (6-77, 4-27)†	R. M. Ellison, Birmingham	1985
179 (5-102, 5-77)†	K. Farnes, Nottingham	1934
60 (6-41, 4-19)	J. T. Hearne, The Oval	1896
113 (5-58, 6-55)	J. C. Laker, Leeds	1956
90 (9-37, 10-53)	J. C. Laker, Manchester	1956
124 (5-96, 5-28)	H. Larwood, Sydney	1932-33
76 (6-48, 5-28)	W. H. Lockwood, Manchester	1902
104 (7-36, 5-68)	G. A. Lohmann, The Oval	1886
87 (8-35, 2-52)	G. A. Lohmann, Sydney	1886-87

10-142 (8-58, 2-84) G. A. Lohmann, Sydney 1891-92
12-102 (6-50, 6-52)† F. Martin, The Oval 1890
10-58 (5-18, 5-40) R. Peel, Sydney 1887-88
11-68 (7-31, 4-37) R. Peel, Manchester 1888
15-124 (7-56, 8-68) W. Rhodes, Melbourne 1903-04
10-156 (5-49, 5-107)† T. Richardson, Manchester 1893
11-173 (6-39, 5-134) T. Richardson, Lord's 1896
13-244 (7-168, 6-76) T. Richardson, Manchester 1896
10-204 (8-94, 2-110) T. Richardson, Sydney 1897-98
11-228 (6-130, 5-98)† M. W. Tate, Sydney 1924-25
11-88 (5-58, 6-30) F. S. Trueman, Leeds 1961
10-130 (4-45, 6-85) F. H. Tyson, Sydney 1954-55
10-82 (4-37, 6-45) D. L. Underwood, Leeds 1972
11-215 (7-113, 4-102) D. L. Underwood, Adelaide 1974-75
15-104 (7-61, 8-43) H. Verity, Lord's 1934
10-57 (6-41, 4-16) W. Voce, Brisbane 1936-37
13-256 (5-130, 8-126) J. C. White, Adelaide 1928-29
10-49 (5-29, 5-20) F. E. Woolley, The Oval 1912

For Australia (35)

10-239 (4-129, 6-110) L. O'B. Fleetwood-Smith, Adelaide 1936-37
10-160 (4-88, 6-72) G. Giffen, Sydney 1891-92
11-82 (5-45, 6-37)† C. V. Grimmett, Sydney 1924-25
10-201 (5-107, 5-94) C. V. Grimmett, Nottingham 1930
10-122 (5-65, 5-57) R. M. Hogg, Perth 1978-79
10-66 (5-30, 5-36) R. M. Hogg, Melbourne 1978-79
12-175 (5-85, 7-90)† H. V. Hordern, Sydney 1911-1
10-161 (5-95, 5-66) H. V. Hordern, Sydney 1911-1
10-164 (7-88, 3-76) E. Jones, Lord's 189
11-134 (6-47, 5-87) G. F. Lawson, Brisbane 1982-8
10-181 (5-58, 5-123) D. K. Lillee, The Oval 197
11-165 (6-26, 5-139) D. K. Lillee, Melbourne 1976-7
11-138 (6-60, 5-78) D. K. Lillee, Melbourne 1979-80
11-159 (7-89, 4-70) D. K. Lillee, The Oval 198
11-85 (7-58, 4-27) C. G. Macartney, Leeds 190
10-302 (5-160, 5-142) A. A. Mailey, Adelaide 1920-2
13-236 (4-115, 9-121) A. A. Mailey, Melbourne 1920-2
16-137 (8-84, 8-53)† R. A. L. Massie, Lord's 197
10-152 (5-72, 5-80) K. R. Miller, Lord's 195
13-77 (7-17, 6-60) M. A. Noble, Melbourne 1901-0
11-103 (5-51, 6-52) M. A. Noble, Sheffield 190
10-129 (5-63, 5-66) W. J. O'Reilly, Melbourne 1932-3
11-129 (4-75, 7-54) W. J. O'Reilly, Nottingham 193
10-122 (5-66, 5-56) W. J. O'Reilly, Leeds 193
11-165 (7-68, 4-97) G. E. Palmer, Sydney 1881-8
10-126 (7-65, 3-61) G. E. Palmer, Melbourne 1882-8
13-110 (6-48, 7-62) F. R. Spofforth, Melbourne 1878-7
14-90 (7-46, 7-44) F. R. Spofforth, The Oval 188
11-117 (4-73, 7-44) F. R. Spofforth, Sydney 1882-8
10-144 (4-54, 6-90) F. R. Spofforth, Sydney 1884-8
12-89 (6-59, 6-30) H. Trumble, The Oval 189
10-128 (4-75, 6-53) H. Trumble, Manchester 190
12-173 (8-65, 4-108) H. Trumble, The Oval 190
12-87 (5-44, 7-43) C. T. B. Turner, Sydney 1887-
10-63 (5-27, 5-36) C. T. B. Turner, Lord's 18

† *Signifies ten wickets or more on first appearance in England–Australia Tests.*

Note: J. Briggs, J. C. Laker, T. Richardson in 1896, R. M. Hogg, A. A. Mailey, H. Trumble a C. T. B. Turner took ten wickets or more in successive Tests. J. Briggs was omitted, howev from the England team for the first Test match in 1893.

MOST WICKETS IN A SERIES

England in England	46 (average 9.60)	J. C. Laker	1956
England in Australia	38 (average 23.18)	M. W. Tate	1924-25
Australia in England	42 (average 21.26)	T. M. Alderman (6 Tests)	1981
Australia in Australia	41 (average 12.85)	R. M. Hogg (6 Tests)	1978-79

WICKET-KEEPING – MOST DISMISSALS

	M	*Ct*	*St*	*Total*
†R. W. Marsh (Australia)	42	141	7	148
A. P. E. Knott (England)	34	97	8	105
†W. A. Oldfield (Australia)	38	59	31	90
A. A. Lilley (England)	32	65	19	84
A. T. W. Grout (Australia)	22	69	7	76
T. G. Evans (England)	31	63	12	75

† *The number of catches by R. W. Marsh (141) and stumpings by W. A. Oldfield (31) are respective records in England–Australia Tests.*

SCORERS OF OVER 2,000 RUNS

	T	*I*	*NO*	*R*	*HI*	*Avge*
D. G. Bradman	37	63	7	5,028	334	89.78
J. B. Hobbs	41	71	4	3,636	187	54.26
G. Boycott	38	71	9	2,945	191	47.50
W. R. Hammond	31	58	3	2,852	251	51.85
H. Sutcliffe	27	46	5	2,741	194	66.85
C. Hill	41	76	1	2,660	188	35.46
J. H. Edrich	32	57	3	2,644	175	48.96
G. S. Chappell	35	65	8	2,619	144	45.94
D. I. Gower	31	56	3	2,479	215	46.77
M. C. Cowdrey	43	75	4	2,433	113	34.26
L. Hutton	27	49	6	2,428	364	56.46
R. N. Harvey	37	68	5	2,416	167	38.34
A. R. Border	30	57	14	2,392	196	55.62
V. T. Trumper	40	74	5	2,263	185*	32.79
W. M. Lawry	29	51	5	2,233	166	48.54
. E. Gregory	52	92	7	2,193	201	25.80
V. W. Armstrong	42	71	9	2,172	158	35.03
. M. Chappell	30	56	4	2,138	192	41.11
K. F. Barrington	23	39	6	2,111	256	63.96
A. R. Morris	24	43	2	2,080	206	50.73

BOWLERS WITH 100 WICKETS

	T	*Balls*	*R*	*W*	*5 W/i*	*Avge*
D. K. Lillee	29	8,516	3,507	167	11	21.00
T. Botham	33	7,999	3,852	145	9	26.56
H. Trumble	31	7,895	2,945	141	9	20.88
. G. D. Willis	35	7,294	3,346	128	7	26.14
M. A. Noble	39	6,845	2,860	115	9	24.86
. R. Lindwall	29	6,728	2,559	114	6	22.44
W. Rhodes	41	5,791	2,616	109	6	24.00
. F. Barnes	20	5,749	2,288	106	12	21.58
. V. Grimmett	22	9,224	3,439	106	11	32.44
. L. Underwood	29	8,000	2,770	105	4	26.38
. V. Bedser	21	7,065	2,859	104	7	27.49
. Giffen	31	6,325	2,791	103	7	27.09
. J. O'Reilly	19	7,864	2,587	102	8	25.36
. Peel	20	5,216	1,715	102	6	16.81
T. B. Turner	17	5,195	1,670	101	11	16.53
R. Thomson	21	4,951	2,418	100	5	24.18

ENGLAND v SOUTH AFRICA

Season	England (Captains)	South Africa (Captains)	T	E	SA	D
1888-89	C. A. Smith[1]	O. R. Dunell[2]	2	2	0	0
1891-92	W. W. Read	W. H. Milton	1	1	0	0
1895-96	Lord Hawke[3]	E. A. Halliwell[4]	3	3	0	0
1898-99	Lord Hawke	M. Bisset	2	2	0	0
1905-06	P. F. Warner	P. W. Sherwell	5	1	4	0
1907	R. E. Foster	P. W. Sherwell	3	1	0	2
1909-10	H. D. G. Leveson Gower[5]	S. J. Snooke	5	2	3	0
1912	C. B. Fry	F. Mitchell[6]	3	3	0	0
1913-14	J. W. H. T. Douglas	H. W. Taylor	5	4	0	1
1922-23	F. T. Mann	H. W. Taylor	5	2	1	2
1924	A. E. R. Gilligan[7]	H. W. Taylor	5	3	0	2
1927-28	R. T. Stanyforth[8]	H. G. Deane	5	2	2	1
1929	J. C. White[9]	H. G. Deane	5	2	0	3
1930-31	A. P. F. Chapman	H. G. Deane[10]	5	0	1	4
1935	R. E. S. Wyatt	H. F. Wade	5	0	1	4
1938-39	W. R. Hammond	A. Melville	5	1	0	4
1947	N. W. D. Yardley	A. Melville	5	3	0	2
1948-49	F. G. Mann	A. D. Nourse	5	2	0	3
1951	F. R. Brown	A. D. Nourse	5	3	1	1
1955	P. B. H. May	J. E. Cheetham[11]	5	3	2	0
1956-57	P. B. H. May	C. B. van Ryneveld[12]	5	2	2	1
1960	M. C. Cowdrey	D. J. McGlew	5	3	0	2
1964-65	M. J. K. Smith	T. L. Goddard	5	1	0	4
1965	M. J. K. Smith	P. L. van der Merwe	3	0	1	2
	In South Africa		58	25	13	20
	In England		44	21	5	18
	Totals		102	46	18	38

Notes: The following deputised for the official touring captain or were appointed by the hom authority for only a minor proportion of the series:

[1]M. P. Bowden (Second). [2]W. H. Milton (Second). [3]Sir T. C. O'Brien (First). [4]A. R. Richard (Third). [5]F. L. Fane (Fourth and Fifth). [6]L. J. Tancred (Second and Third). [7]J. W. H. T Douglas (Fourth). [8]G. T. S. Stevens (Fifth). [9]A. W. Carr (Fourth and Fifth). [10]E. P. Nupe (First), H. B. Cameron (Fourth and Fifth). [11]D. J. McGlew (Third and Fourth). [12]D. J McGlew (Second).

HIGHEST INNINGS TOTALS

For England in England: 554-8 dec. at Lord's 194
in South Africa: 654-5 at Durban 1938-3
For South Africa in England: 538 at Leeds 195
in South Africa: 530 at Durban 1938-3

LOWEST INNINGS TOTALS

For England in England: 76 at Leeds 190
in South Africa: 92 at Cape Town 1898-9
For South Africa in England: 30 at Birmingham 192
in South Africa: 30 at Port Elizabeth 1895-9

INDIVIDUAL HUNDREDS

For England (87)

120	R. Abel, Cape Town	1888-89
148*	L. E. G. Ames, The Oval	1935
115	L. E. G. Ames, Cape Town	1938-39
148*	K. F. Barrington, Durban	1964-65
121	K. F. Barrington, Johannesburg	1964-65
117	G. Boycott, Port Elizabeth	1964-65
104†	L. C. Braund, Lord's	1907
208	D. C. S. Compton, Lord's	1947
163†	D. C. S. Compton, Nottingham	1947
115	D. C. S. Compton, Manchester	1947
113	D. C. S. Compton, The Oval	1947
114	D. C. S. Compton, Johannesburg	1948-49
12	D. C. S. Compton, Nottingham	1951
58	D. C. S. Compton, Manchester	1955
01	M. C. Cowdrey, Cape Town	1956-57
55	M. C. Cowdrey, The Oval	1960
05	M. C. Cowdrey, Nottingham	1965
04	D. Denton, Johannesburg	1909-10
72	E. R. Dexter, Johannesburg	1964-65
19†	J. W. H. T. Douglas, Durban	1913-14
19	W. J. Edrich, Durban	1938-39
91	W. J. Edrich, Manchester	1947
89	W. J. Edrich, Lord's	1947
43	F. L. Fane, Johannesburg	1905-06
29	C. B. Fry, The Oval	1907
06†	P. A. Gibb, Johannesburg	1938-39
20	P. A. Gibb, Durban	1938-39
38*	W. R. Hammond, Birmingham	1929
01*	W. R. Hammond, The Oval	1929
36*	W. R. Hammond, Durban	1930-31
31	W. R. Hammond, Cape Town	1938-39
20	W. R. Hammond, Durban	1938-39
40	W. R. Hammond, Durban	1938-39
22	T. W. Hayward, Johannesburg	1895-96
32	E. H. Hendren, Leeds	1924
2	E. H. Hendren, The Oval	1924
4	A. J. L. Hill, Cape Town	1895-96
7	J. B. Hobbs, Cape Town	1909-10
1	J. B. Hobbs, Lord's	1924
0	L. Hutton, Leeds	1947
8	L. Hutton, Johannesburg	1948-49
3	L. Hutton, Johannesburg	1948-49
100	L. Hutton, Leeds	1951
110*	D. J. Insole, Durban	1956-57
102	M. Leyland, Lord's	1929
161	M. Leyland, The Oval	1935
136*	F. G. Mann, Port Elizabeth	1948-49
138†	P. B. H. May, Leeds	1951
112	P. B. H. May, Lord's	1955
117	P. B. H. May, Manchester	1955
102	C. P. Mead, Johannesburg	1913-14
117	C. P. Mead, Port Elizabeth	1913-14
181	C. P. Mead, Durban	1922-23
122*	P. H. Parfitt, Johannesburg	1964-65
108*	J. M. Parks, Durban	1964-65
117† } 100 }	E. Paynter, Johannesburg	1938-39
243	E. Paynter, Durban	1938-39
175	G. Pullar, The Oval	1960
152	W. Rhodes, Johannesburg	1913-14
117†	P. E. Richardson, Johannesburg	1956-57
108	R. W. V. Robins, Manchester	1935
140 } 111 }	A. C. Russell, Durban	1922-23
137	R. T. Simpson, Nottingham	1951
121	M. J. K. Smith, Cape Town	1964-65
119†	R. H. Spooner, Lord's	1912
122	H. Sutcliffe, Lord's	1924
102	H. Sutcliffe, Johannesburg	1927-28
114	H. Sutcliffe, Birmingham	1929
100	H. Sutcliffe, Lord's	1929
104 } 109* }	H. Sutcliffe, The Oval	1929
100*	M. W. Tate, Lord's	1929
122†	E. Tyldesley, Johannesburg	1927-28
100	E. Tyldesley, Durban	1927-28
112	J. T. Tyldesley, Cape Town	1898-99
112	B. H. Valentine, Cape Town	1938-39
132*†‡	P. F. Warner, Johannesburg	1898-99
195	C. Washbrook, Johannesburg	1948-49
111	A. J. Watkins, Johannesburg	1948-49
134*	H. Wood, Cape Town	1891-92
115*	F. E. Woolley, Johannesburg	1922-23
134*	F. E. Woolley, Lord's	1924
154	F. E. Woolley, Manchester	1929
113	R. E. S. Wyatt, Manchester	1929
149	R. E. S. Wyatt, Nottingham	1935

For South Africa (58)

8	E. J. Barlow, Cape Town	1964-65
4*	K. C. Bland, Johannesburg	1964-65
127	K. C. Bland, The Oval	1965
120	R. H. Catterall, Birmingham	1924

120	R. H. Catterall, Lord's	1924
119	R. H. Catterall, Durban	1927-28
117	E. L. Dalton, The Oval	1935
102	E. L. Dalton, Johannesburg	1938-39
116*	W. R. Endean, Leeds	1955
123	G. A. Faulkner, Johannesburg	1909-10
112	T. L. Goddard, Johannesburg	1964-65
102	C. M. H. Hathorn, Johannesburg	1905-06
104*	D. J. McGlew, Manchester	1955
133	D. J. McGlew, Leeds	1955
142	R. A. McLean, Lord's	1955
100	R. A. McLean, Durban	1956-57
109	R. A. McLean, Manchester	1960
103	A. Melville, Durban	1938-39
189 104*	A. Melville, Nottingham	1947
117	A. Melville, Lord's	1947
123	B. Mitchell, Cape Town	1930-31
164*	B. Mitchell, Lord's	1935
128	B. Mitchell, The Oval	1935
109	B. Mitchell, Durban	1938-39
120 189*	B. Mitchell, The Oval	1947
120	B. Mitchell, Cape Town	1948-49
120	A. D. Nourse, Cape Town	1938-39
103	A. D. Nourse, Durban	1938-39
149	A. D. Nourse, Nottingham	1947
115	A. D. Nourse, Manchester	1947
129*	A. D. Nourse, Johannesburg	1948-49
112	A. D. Nourse, Cape Town	1948-49
208	A. D. Nourse, Nottingham	1951
129	H. G. Owen-Smith, Leeds	1929
154	A. J. Pithey, Cape Town	1964-65
137	R. G. Pollock, Port Elizabeth	1964-65
125	R. G. Pollock, Nottingham	1965
156*	E. A. B. Rowan, Johannesburg	1948-49
236	E. A. B. Rowan, Leeds	1951
115	P. W. Sherwell, Lord's	1907
141	I. J. Siedle, Cape Town	1930-31
106	J. H. Sinclair, Cape Town	1898-99
109	H. W. Taylor, Durban	1913-14
176	H. W. Taylor, Johannesburg	1922-23
101	H. W. Taylor, Johannesburg	1922-23
102	H. W. Taylor, Durban	1922-23
101	H. W. Taylor, Johannesburg	1927-28
121	H. W. Taylor, The Oval	1929
117	H. W. Taylor, Cape Town	1930-31
125	P. G. V. van der Bijl, Durban	1938-39
124	K. G. Viljoen, Manchester	1935
125	W. W. Wade, Port Elizabeth	1948-49
113	J. H. B. Waite, Manchester	1955
147	G. C. White, Johannesburg	1905-06
118	G. C. White, Durban	1909-10
108	P. L. Winslow, Manchester	195

† *Signifies hundred on first appearance in England–South Africa Tests.*
‡ *P. F. Warner carried his bat through the second innings.*

Notes: The highest score by a South African batsman on début is 93* by A. W. Nourse a Johannesburg in 1905-06.

P. N. F. Mansell made 90 at Leeds in 1951, the best on début in England.

A. Melville's four hundreds were made in successive Test innings.

H. Wood scored the only hundred of his career in a Test match.

RECORD PARTNERSHIP FOR EACH WICKET

For England

359 for 1st†	L. Hutton and C. Washbrook at Johannesburg	1948-4
280 for 2nd	P. A. Gibb and W. J. Edrich at Durban	1938-3
370 for 3rd†	W. J. Edrich and D. C. S. Compton at Lord's	194
197 for 4th	W. R. Hammond and L. E. G. Ames at Cape Town	1938-3
237 for 5th	D. C. S. Compton and N. W. D. Yardley at Nottingham	194
206* for 6th	K. F. Barrington and J. M. Parks at Durban	1964-6
115 for 7th	M. C. Bird and J. W. H. T. Douglas at Durban	1913-1
154 for 8th	C. W. Wright and H. R. Bromley-Davenport at Johannesburg	1895-9
71 for 9th	H. Wood and J. T. Hearne at Cape Town	1891-9
92 for 10th	A. C. Russell and A. E. R. Gilligan at Durban	1922-2

For South Africa

260 for 1st†	I. J. Siedle and B. Mitchell at Cape Town	1930-3
198 for 2nd†	E. A. B. Rowan and C. B. van Ryneveld at Leeds	195
319 for 3rd	A. Melville and A. D. Nourse at Nottingham	194

214 for 4th†	H. W. Taylor and H. G. Deane at The Oval	1929
157 for 5th†	A. J. Pithey and J. H. B. Waite at Johannesburg	1964-65
171 for 6th	J. H. B. Waite and P. L. Winslow at Manchester	1955
123 for 7th	H. G. Deane and E. P. Nupen at Durban	1927-28
109* for 8th	B. Mitchell and L. Tuckett at The Oval	1947
137 for 9th†	E. L. Dalton and A. B. C. Langton at The Oval	1935
103 for 10th†	H. G. Owen-Smith and A. J. Bell at Leeds	1929

† *Denotes record partnership against all countries.*

MOST RUNS IN A SERIES

England in England	753 (average 94.12)	D. C. S. Compton	1947
England in South Africa	653 (average 81.62)	E. Paynter	1938-39
South Africa in England	621 (average 69.00)	A. D. Nourse	1947
South Africa in South Africa	582 (average 64.66)	H. W. Taylor	1922-23

TEN WICKETS OR MORE IN A MATCH

For England (23)

1-110 (5-25, 6-85)†	S. F. Barnes, Lord's	1912
0-115 (6-52, 4-63)	S. F. Barnes, Leeds	1912
3-57 (5-28, 8-29)	S. F. Barnes, The Oval	1912
0-105 (5-57, 5-48)	S. F. Barnes, Durban	1913-14
7-159 (8-56, 9-103)	S. F. Barnes, Johannesburg	1913-14
4-144 (7-56, 7-88)	S. F. Barnes, Durban	1913-14
2-112 (7-58, 5-54)	A. V. Bedser, Manchester	1951
1-118 (6-68, 5-50)	C. Blythe, Cape Town	1905-06
5-99 (8-59, 7-40)	C. Blythe, Leeds	1907
0-104 (7-46, 3-58)	C. Blythe, Cape Town	1909-10
5-28 (7-17, 8-11)	J. Briggs, Cape Town	1888-89
3-91 (6-54, 7-37)†	J. J. Ferris, Cape Town	1891-92
0-207 (7-115, 3-92)	A. P. Freeman, Leeds	1929
2-171 (7-71, 5-100)	A. P. Freeman, Manchester	1929
2-130 (7-70, 5-60)	G. Geary, Johannesburg	1927-28
1-90 (6-7, 5-83)	A. E. R. Gilligan, Birmingham	1924
0-119 (4-64, 6-55)	J. C. Laker, The Oval	1951
5-45 (7-38, 8-7)†	G. A. Lohmann, Port Elizabeth	1895-96
2-71 (9-28, 3-43)	G. A. Lohmann, Johannesburg	1895-96
1-97 (6-63, 5-34)	J. B. Statham, Lord's	1960
2-101 (7-52, 5-49)	R. Tattersall, Lord's	1951
2-89 (5-53, 7-36)	J. H. Wardle, Cape Town	1956-57
0-175 (5-95, 5-80)	D. V. P. Wright, Lord's	1947

For South Africa (6)

-112 (4-49, 7-63)†	A. E. Hall, Cape Town	1922-23
-150 (5-63, 6-87)	E. P. Nupen, Johannesburg	1930-31
-87 (5-53, 5-34)	P. M. Pollock, Nottingham	1965
-127 (4-57, 8-70)	S. J. Snooke, Johannesburg	1905-06
-192 (4-79, 9-113)	H. J. Tayfield, Johannesburg	1956-57
-181 (5-87, 7-94)	A. E. E. Vogler, Johannesburg	1909-10

† *Signifies ten wickets or more on first appearance in England–South Africa Tests.*

ote: S. F. Barnes took ten wickets or more in his first five Tests v South Africa and in six of his ven Tests v South Africa. A. P. Freeman and G. A. Lohmann took ten wickets or more in ccessive matches.

MOST WICKETS IN A SERIES

England in England	34 (average 8.29)	S. F. Barnes	1912
England in South Africa	49 (average 10.93)	S. F. Barnes	1913-14
South Africa in England	26 (average 21.84)	H. J. Tayfield	1955
South Africa in England	26 (average 22.57)	N. A. T. Adcock ..	1960
South Africa in South Africa .	37 (average 17.18)	H. J. Tayfield	1956-57

ENGLAND v WEST INDIES

	Captains					
Season	*England*	*West Indies*	*T*	*E*	*WI*	*D*
1928	A. P. F. Chapman	R. K. Nunes	3	3	0	0
1929-30	Hon. F. S. G. Calthorpe	E. L. G. Hoad[1]	4	1	1	2
1933	D. R. Jardine[2]	G. C. Grant	3	2	0	1
1934-35	R. E. S. Wyatt	G. C. Grant	4	1	2	1
1939	W. R. Hammond	R. S. Grant	3	1	0	2
1947-48	G. O. Allen[3]	J. D. C. Goddard[4]	4	0	2	2
1950	N. W. D. Yardley[5]	J. D. C. Goddard	4	1	3	0
1953-54	L. Hutton	J. B. Stollmeyer	5	2	2	1
1957	P. B. H. May	J. D. C. Goddard	5	3	0	2
1959-60	P. B. H. May[6]	F. C. M. Alexander	5	1	0	4

THE WISDEN TROPHY

	Captains						
Season	*England*	*West Indies*	*T*	*E*	*WI*	*D*	*Held b*
1963	E. R. Dexter	F. M. M. Worrell	5	1	3	1	WI
1966	M. C. Cowdrey[7]	G. S. Sobers	5	1	3	1	WI
1967-68	M. C. Cowdrey	G. S. Sobers	5	1	0	4	E
1969	R. Illingworth	G. S. Sobers	3	2	0	1	E
1973	R. Illingworth	R. B. Kanhai	3	0	2	1	WI
1973-74	M. H. Denness	R. B. Kanhai	5	1	1	3	WI
1976	A. W. Greig	C. H. Lloyd	5	0	3	2	WI
1980	I. T. Botham	C. H. Lloyd[8]	5	0	1	4	WI
1980-81†	I. T. Botham	C. H. Lloyd	4	0	2	2	WI
1984	D. I. Gower	C. H. Lloyd	5	0	5	0	WI
1985-86	D. I. Gower	I. V. A. Richards	5	0	5	0	WI
1988	J. E. Emburey[9]	I. V. A. Richards	5	0	4	1	WI
	In England		54	14	24	16	
	In West Indies		41	7	15	19	
	Totals		95	21	39	35	

† *The Test match at Georgetown, scheduled as the second of the series, was cancelled owing political pressure.*

Notes: The following deputised for the official touring captain or were appointed by the hor authority for only a minor proportion of the series:

[1]N. Betancourt (Second), M. P. Fernandes (Third), R. K. Nunes (Fourth). [2]R. E. S. Wy (Third). [3]K. Cranston (First). [4]G. A. Headley (First), G. E. Gomez (Second). [5]F. R. Brov (Fourth). [6]M. C. Cowdrey (Fourth and Fifth). [7]M. J. K. Smith (First), D. B. Close (Fift [8]I. V. A. Richards (Fifth). [9]M. W. Gatting (First), C. S. Cowdrey (Fourth), G. A. Goo (Fifth).

HIGHEST INNINGS TOTALS

For England	in England: 619-6 dec. at Nottingham	1957
	in West Indies: 849 at Kingston	1929-30
For West Indies	in England: 687-8 dec. at The Oval	1976
	in West Indies: 681-8 dec. at Port-of-Spain	1953-54

LOWEST INNINGS TOTALS

For England	in England: 71 at Manchester	1976
	in West Indies: 103 at Kingston	1934-35
For West Indies	in England: 86 at The Oval	1957
	in West Indies: 102 at Bridgetown	1934-35

INDIVIDUAL HUNDREDS

For England (83)

105	L. E. G. Ames, Port-of-Spain	1929-30
49	L. E. G. Ames, Kingston	1929-30
26	L. E. G. Ames, Kingston	1934-35
74	D. L. Amiss, Port-of-Spain	1973-74
62*	D. L. Amiss, Kingston	1973-74
18	D. L. Amiss, Georgetown	1973-74
03	D. L. Amiss, The Oval	1976
07†	A. H. Bakewell, The Oval	1933
28†	K. F. Barrington, Bridgetown	1959-60
21	K. F. Barrington, Port-of-Spain	1959-60
43	K. F. Barrington, Port-of-Spain	1967-68
16	G. Boycott, Georgetown	1967-68
28	G. Boycott, Manchester	1969
06	G. Boycott, Lord's	1969
12	G. Boycott, Port-of-Spain	1973-74
4*	G. Boycott, St John's	1980-81
0†	D. C. S. Compton, Lord's	1939
3	D. C. S. Compton, Port-of-Spain	1953-54
4†	M. C. Cowdrey, Birmingham	1957
2	M. C. Cowdrey, Lord's	1957
4	M. C. Cowdrey, Kingston	1959-60
9	M. C. Cowdrey, Port-of-Spain	1959-60
1	M. C. Cowdrey, Kingston	1967-68
8	M. C. Cowdrey, Port-of-Spain	1967-68
6*†	E. R. Dexter, Bridgetown	1959-60
0	E. R. Dexter, Georgetown	1959-60
6	J. H. Edrich, Bridgetown	1967-68
4	T. G. Evans, Manchester	1950
9*	K. W. R. Fletcher, Bridgetown	1973-74
[illegible]	G. Fowler, Lord's	1984
[illegible]	G. A. Gooch, Lord's	1980
[illegible]	G. A. Gooch, Bridgetown	1980-81
153	G. A. Gooch, Kingston	1980-81
146	G. A. Gooch, Nottingham	1988
154*	D. I. Gower, Kingston	1980-81
258	T. W. Graveney, Nottingham	1957
164	T. W. Graveney, The Oval	1957
109	T. W. Graveney, Nottingham	1966
165	T. W. Graveney, The Oval	1966
118	T. W. Graveney, Port-of-Spain	1967-68
148	A. W. Greig, Bridgetown	1973-74
121	A. W. Greig, Georgetown	1973-74
116	A. W. Greig, Leeds	1976
140†	S. C. Griffith, Port-of-Spain	1947-48
138	W. R. Hammond, The Oval	1939
107†	J. H. Hampshire, Lord's	1969
106*†	F. C. Hayes, The Oval	1973
205*	E. H. Hendren, Port-of-Spain	1929-30
123	E. H. Hendren, Georgetown	1929-30
159	J. B. Hobbs, The Oval	1928
196†	L. Hutton, Lord's	1939
165*	L. Hutton, The Oval	1939
202*‡	L. Hutton, The Oval	1950
169	L. Hutton, Georgetown	1953-54
205	L. Hutton, Kingston	1953-54
113	R. Illingworth, Lord's	1969
127	D. R. Jardine, Manchester	1933
116	A. P. E. Knott, Leeds	1976
110	A. J. Lamb, Lord's	1984
100	A. J. Lamb, Leeds	1984
100*	A. J. Lamb, Manchester	1984
113	A. J. Lamb, Lord's	1988
135	P. B. H. May, Port-of-Spain	1953-54
285*	P. B. H. May, Birmingham	1957
104	P. B. H. May, Nottingham	1957
126*	C. Milburn, Lord's	1966
112†	J. T. Murray, The Oval	1966
101*†	J. M. Parks, Port-of-Spain	1959-60
107	W. Place, Kingston	1947-48

126 P. E. Richardson, Nottingham ... 1957
107 P. E. Richardson, The Oval 1957
133 J. D. Robertson, Port-of-Spain ... 1947-48
152† A. Sandham, Bridgetown .. 1929-30
325 A. Sandham, Kingston 1929-30
108 M. J. K. Smith, Port-of-Spain ... 1959-60
106† D. S. Steele, Nottingham .. 1976
100† R. Subba Row, Georgetown ... 1959-60
122† E. Tyldesley, Lord's 1928
114† C. Washbrook, Lord's 1950
102 C. Washbrook, Nottingham ... 1950
116† W. Watson, Kingston 1953-54
100* P. Willey, The Oval 1980
102* P. Willey, St John's 1980-81

For West Indies (92)

105 I. Barrow, Manchester 1933
133 B. F. Butcher, Lord's 1963
209* B. F. Butcher, Nottingham 1966
107 G. M. Carew, Port-of-Spain 1947-48
103 C. A. Davis, Lord's 1969
101 P. J. Dujon, Manchester .. 1984
150 R. C. Fredericks, Birmingham ... 1973
138 R. C. Fredericks, Lord's ... 1976
109 R. C. Fredericks, Leeds ... 1976
112† A. G. Ganteaume, Port-of-Spain ... 1947-48
143 H. A. Gomes, Birmingham 1984
104* H. A. Gomes, Leeds 1984
134 } 101 } C. G. Greenidge, Manchester ... 1976
115 C. G. Greenidge, Leeds ... 1976
214* C. G. Greenidge, Lord's ... 1984
223 C. G. Greenidge, Manchester ... 1984
103 C. G. Greenidge, Lord's ... 1988
184 D. L. Haynes, Lord's 1980
125 D. L. Haynes, The Oval ... 1984
131 D. L. Haynes, St John's ... 1985-86
176† G. A. Headley, Bridgetown 1929-30
114 } 112 } G. A. Headley, Georgetown 1929-30
223 G. A. Headley, Kingston .. 1929-30
169* G. A. Headley, Manchester 1933
270* G. A. Headley, Kingston .. 1934-35
106 } 107 } G. A. Headley, Lord's 1939
105* D. A. J. Holford, Lord's ... 1966
166 J. K. Holt, Bridgetown 1953-54
182 C. C. Hunte, Manchester .. 1963
108* C. C. Hunte, The Oval 1963
135 C. C. Hunte, Manchester .. 1966
121 B. D. Julien, Lord's 1973
158 A. I. Kallicharran, Port-of-Spain ... 1973-74
119 A. I. Kallicharran, Bridgetown ... 1973-74
110 R. B. Kanhai, Port-of-Spain 1959-60
104 R. B. Kanhai, The Oval 1966
153 R. B. Kanhai, Port-of-Spain 1967-68
150 R. B. Kanhai, Georgetown 1967-68
157 R. B. Kanhai, Lord's 1973
118† C. H. Lloyd, Port-of-Spain . 1967-68
113* C. H. Lloyd, Bridgetown .. 1967-68
132 C. H. Lloyd, The Oval 1973
101 C. H. Lloyd, Manchester .. 1980
100 C. H. Lloyd, Bridgetown .. 1980-81
137 S. M. Nurse, Leeds 1966
136 S. M. Nurse, Port-of-Spain 1967-68
106 A. F. Rae, Lord's 1950
109 A. F. Rae, The Oval 1950
232† I. V. A. Richards, Nottingham ... 1976
135 I. V. A. Richards, Manchester ... 1976
291 I. V. A. Richards, The Oval ... 1976
145 I. V. A. Richards, Lord's .. 198
182* I. V. A. Richards, Bridgetown ... 1980-81
114 I. V. A. Richards, St John's 1980-81
117 I. V. A. Richards, Birmingham ... 198
110* I. V. A. Richards, St John's 1985-8
102 R. B. Richardson, Port-of-Spain ... 1985-8
160 R. B. Richardson, Bridgetown ... 1985-8
122 C. A. Roach, Bridgetown .. 1929-3
209 C. A. Roach, Georgetown . 1929-3
120 L. G. Rowe, Kingston 1973-7
302 L. G. Rowe, Bridgetown .. 1973-7
123 L. G. Rowe, Port-of-Spain . 1973-7
161† O. G. Smith, Birmingham . 195
168 O. G. Smith, Nottingham . 195
226 G. S. Sobers, Bridgetown .. 1959-6
147 G. S. Sobers, Kingston 1959-6
145 G. S. Sobers, Georgetown . 1959-6
102 G. S. Sobers, Leeds 196
161 G. S. Sobers, Manchester .. 196
163* G. S. Sobers, Lord's 196
174 G. S. Sobers, Leeds 196
113* G. S. Sobers, Kingston 1967-6
152 G. S. Sobers, Georgetown . 1967-6
150* G. S. Sobers, Lord's 19
168* C. L. Walcott, Lord's 19
220 C. L. Walcott, Bridgetown . 1953-
124 C. L. Walcott, Port-of-Spain ... 1953-
116 C. L. Walcott, Kingston ... 1953-
141 E. D. Weekes, Kingston ... 1947-
129 E. D. Weekes, Nottingham 19
206 E. D. Weekes, Port-of-Spain ... 1953-
137 K. H. Weekes, The Oval .. 19

131* F. M. M. Worrell, Georgetown ... 1947-48
261 F. M. M. Worrell, Nottingham ... 1950
138 F. M. M. Worrell, The Oval ... 1950
167 F. M. M. Worrell, Port-of-Spain ... 1953-54
191*‡ F. M. M. Worrell, Nottingham ... 1957
197* F. M. M. Worrell, Bridgetown ... 1959-60

† Signifies hundred on first appearance in England–West Indies Tests. S. C. Griffith provides the nly instance for England of a player hitting his maiden century in first-class cricket in his first Test.
‡ Carried his bat.

RECORD PARTNERSHIPS FOR EACH WICKET

For England

12 for 1st	C. Washbrook and R. T. Simpson at Nottingham	1950
66 for 2nd	P. E. Richardson and T. W. Graveney at Nottingham	1957
64 for 3rd	L. Hutton and W. R. Hammond at The Oval	1939
11 for 4th†	P. B. H. May and M. C. Cowdrey at Birmingham	1957
30* for 5th	C. Milburn and T. W. Graveney at Lord's	1966
63 for 6th	A. W. Greig and A. P. E. Knott at Bridgetown	1973-74
97 for 7th†	M. J. K. Smith and J. M. Parks at Port-of-Spain	1959-60
17 for 8th	T. W. Graveney and J. T. Murray at The Oval	1966
09 for 9th	G. A. R. Lock and P. I. Pocock at Georgetown	1967-68
28 for 10th	K. Higgs and J. A. Snow at The Oval	1966

For West Indies

6 for 1st	R. C. Fredericks and L. G. Rowe at Kingston	1973-74
7* for 2nd	C. G. Greenidge and H. A. Gomes at Lord's	1984
8 for 3rd†	E. D. Weekes and F. M. M. Worrell at Port-of-Spain	1953-54
9 for 4th†	G. S. Sobers and F. M. M. Worrell at Bridgetown	1959-60
5 for 5th†	S. M. Nurse and G. S. Sobers at Leeds	1966
4* for 6th†	G. S. Sobers and D. A. J. Holford at Lord's	1966
5* for 7th‡	G. S. Sobers and B. D. Julien at Lord's	1973
for 8th	C. A. McWatt and J. K. Holt at Georgetown	1953-54
0 for 9th	E. A. E. Baptiste and M. A. Holding at Birmingham	1984
* for 10th	M. A. Holding and C. E. H. Croft at St John's	1980-81

† Denotes record partnership against all countries.
‡ 231 runs were added for this wicket in two separate partnerships: G. S. Sobers retired ill and was laced by K. D. Boyce when 155 had been added.

TEN WICKETS OR MORE IN A MATCH

For England (10)

98 (7-44, 4-54)	T. E. Bailey, Lord's	1957
93 (5-54, 5-39)	A. P. Freeman, Manchester	1928
156 (8-86, 5-70)	A. W. Greig, Port-of-Spain	1973-74
48 (5-28, 6-20)	G. A. R. Lock, The Oval	1957
96 (5-37, 6-59)†	C. S. Marriott, The Oval	1933
142 (4-82, 6-60)	J. A. Snow, Georgetown	1967-68
195 (5-105, 5-90)†	G. T. S. Stevens, Bridgetown	1929-30
152 (6-100, 5-52)	F. S. Trueman, Lord's	1963
19 (5-75, 7-44)	F. S. Trueman, Birmingham	1963
49 (4-79, 7-70)	W. Voce, Port-of-Spain	1929-30

For West Indies (11)

47 (5-70, 6-77)†	K. D. Boyce, The Oval	1973
29 (5-137, 6-92)	W. Ferguson, Port-of-Spain	1947-48
57 (5-59, 6-98)†	L. R. Gibbs, Manchester	1963

10-106 (5-37, 5-69)	L. R. Gibbs, Manchester	1966
14-149 (8-92, 6-57)	M. A. Holding, The Oval	1976
10-96 (5-41, 5-55)†	H. H. H. Johnson, Kingston	1947-48
10-92 (6-32, 4-60)	M. D. Marshall, Lord's	1988
11-152 (5-66, 6-86)	S. Ramadhin, Lord's	1950
10-123 (5-60, 5-63)	A. M. E. Roberts, Lord's	1976
11-204 (8-104, 3-100)†	A. L. Valentine, Manchester	1950
10-160 (4-121, 6-39)	A. L. Valentine, The Oval	1950

† *Signifies ten wickets or more on first appearance in England–West Indies Tests.*

Note: F. S. Trueman took ten wickets or more in successive matches.

ENGLAND v NEW ZEALAND

Captains

Season	*England*	*New Zealand*	*T*	*E*	*NZ*	*D*
1929-30	A. H. H. Gilligan	T. C. Lowry	4	1	0	
1931	D. R. Jardine	T. C. Lowry	3	1	0	
1932-33	D. R. Jardine[1]	M. L. Page	2	0	0	
1937	R. W. V. Robins	M. L. Page	3	1	0	
1946-47	W. R. Hammond	W. A. Hadlee	1	0	0	
1949	F. G. Mann[2]	W. A. Hadlee	4	0	0	
1950-51	F. R. Brown	W. A. Hadlee	2	1	0	
1954-55	L. Hutton	G. O. Rabone	2	2	0	
1958	P. B. H. May	J. R. Reid	5	4	0	
1958-59	P. B. H. May	J. R. Reid	2	1	0	
1962-63	E. R. Dexter	J. R. Reid	3	3	0	
1965	M. J. K. Smith	J. R. Reid	3	3	0	
1965-66	M. J. K. Smith	B. W. Sinclair[3]	3	0	0	
1969	R. Illingworth	G. T. Dowling	3	2	0	
1970-71	R. Illingworth	G. T. Dowling	2	1	0	
1973	R. Illingworth	B. E. Congdon	3	2	0	
1974-75	M. H. Denness	B. E. Congdon	2	1	0	
1977-78	G. Boycott	M. G. Burgess	3	1	1	
1978	J. M. Brearley	M. G. Burgess	3	3	0	
1983	R. G. D. Willis	G. P. Howarth	4	3	1	
1983-84	R. G. D. Willis	G. P. Howarth	3	0	1	
1986	M. W. Gatting	J. V. Coney	3	0	1	
1987-88	M. W. Gatting	J. J. Crowe[4]	3	0	0	
	In New Zealand		32	11	2	
	In England		34	19	2	
	Totals		66	30	4	

Notes: The following deputised for the official touring captain or were appointed by the ho authority for only a minor proportion of the series:

[1]R. E. S. Wyatt (Second). [2]F. R. Brown (Third and Fourth). [3]M. E. Chapple (First). [4]J. Wright (Third).

HIGHEST INNINGS TOTALS

For England in England: 546-4 dec. at Leeds		19
	in New Zealand: 593-6 dec. at Auckland	1974-
For New Zealand in England: 551-9 dec. at Lord's		19
	in New Zealand: 537 at Wellington	1983-

LOWEST INNINGS TOTALS

For England in England: 187 at Manchester		19
	in New Zealand: 64 at Wellington	1977
For New Zealand in England: 47 at Lord's		19
	in New Zealand: 26 at Auckland	1954

INDIVIDUAL HUNDREDS

For England (69)

122†	G. O. Allen, Lord's	1931
137†	L. E. G. Ames, Lord's	1931
103	L. E. G. Ames, Christchurch	1932-33
138*†	D. L. Amiss, Nottingham	1973
64*	D. L. Amiss, Christchurch	1974-75
34*	T. E. Bailey, Christchurch	1950-51
26†	K. F. Barrington, Auckland	1962-63
63	K. F. Barrington, Leeds	1965
37	K. F. Barrington, Birmingham	1965
03	I. T. Botham, Christchurch	1977-78
03	I. T. Botham, Nottingham	1983
38	I. T. Botham, Wellington	1983-84
09	E. H. Bowley, Auckland	1929-30
15	G. Boycott, Leeds	1973
31	G. Boycott, Nottingham	1978
14†	B. C. Broad, Christchurch	1987-88
14	D. C. S. Compton, Leeds	1949
16	D. C. S. Compton, Lord's	1949
28*	M. C. Cowdrey, Wellington	1962-63
9	M. C. Cowdrey, Lord's	1965
81	M. H. Denness, Auckland	1974-75
41	E. R. Dexter, Christchurch	1958-59
0	B. L. D'Oliveira, Christchurch	1970-71
7	K. S. Duleepsinhji, Auckland	1929-30
9	K. S. Duleepsinhji, The Oval	1931
0*†	J. H. Edrich, Leeds	1965
5	J. H. Edrich, Lord's	1969
5	J. H. Edrich, Nottingham	1969
0	W. J. Edrich, The Oval	1949
8	K. W. R. Fletcher, Lord's	1973
6	K. W. R. Fletcher, Auckland	1974-75
5†	G. Fowler, The Oval	1983
	M. W. Gatting, The Oval	1986
183	G. A. Gooch, Lord's	1986
111†	D. I. Gower, The Oval	1978
112*	D. I. Gower, Leeds	1983
108	D. I. Gower, Lord's	1983
131	D. I. Gower, The Oval	1986
139†	A. W. Greig, Nottingham	1973
100*	W. R. Hammond, The Oval	1931
227	W. R. Hammond, Christchurch	1932-33
336*	W. R. Hammond, Auckland	1932-33
140	W. R. Hammond, Lord's	1937
114†	J. Hardstaff jun., Lord's	1937
103	J. Hardstaff jun., The Oval	1937
100	L. Hutton, Manchester	1937
101	L. Hutton, Leeds	1949
206	L. Hutton, The Oval	1949
125†	B. R. Knight, Auckland	1962-63
101	A. P. E. Knott, Auckland	1970-71
102*†	A. J. Lamb, The Oval	1983
137*	A. J. Lamb, Nottingham	1983
196	G. B. Legge, Auckland	1929-30
113*	P. B. H. May, Leeds	1958
101	P. B. H. May, Manchester	1958
124*	P. B. H. May, Auckland	1958-59
104*†	C. A. Milton, Leeds	1958
131*†	P. H. Parfitt, Auckland	1962-63
158	C. T. Radley, Auckland	1977-78
164	D. W. Randall, Wellington	1983-84
104	D. W. Randall, Auckland	1983-84
100†	P. E. Richardson, Birmingham	1958
121†	J. D. Robertson, Lord's	1949
111	P. J. Sharpe, Nottingham	1969
103†	R. T. Simpson, Manchester	1949
117†	H. Sutcliffe, The Oval	1931
109*	H. Sutcliffe, Manchester	1931
109†	C. J. Tavaré, The Oval	1983
103*	C. Washbrook, Leeds	1949

For New Zealand (33)

	J. G. Bracewell, Nottingham	1986
	M. G. Burgess, Auckland	1970-71
	M. G. Burgess, Lord's	1973
*	J. V. Coney, Wellington	1983-84
	B. E. Congdon, Christchurch	1965-66
	B. E. Congdon, Nottingham	1973
	B. E. Congdon, Lord's	1973
	J. J. Crowe, Auckland	1983-84
	M. D. Crowe, Wellington	1983-84
	M. D. Crowe, Lord's	1986
	M. D. Crowe, Wellington	1987-88
	C. S. Dempster, Wellington	1929-30
	C. S. Dempster, Lord's	1931
	M. P. Donnelly, Lord's	1949
107*†	M. J. Greatbatch, Auckland	1987-88
116	W. A. Hadlee, Christchurch	1946-47
122 102	G. P. Howarth, Auckland	1977-78
123	G. P. Howarth, Lord's	1978
117†	J. E. Mills, Wellington	1929-30
104	M. L. Page, Lord's	1931
121	J. M. Parker, Auckland	1974-75
116	V. Pollard, Nottingham	1973
105*	V. Pollard, Lord's	1973
100	J. R. Reid, Christchurch	1962-63
107*	K. R. Rutherford, Wellington	1987-88
114	B. W. Sinclair, Auckland	1965-66

113* I. D. S. Smith, Auckland .. 1983-84
101 B. Sutcliffe, Manchester ... 1949
116 B. Sutcliffe, Christchurch .. 1950-51
130 J. G. Wright, Auckland ... 1983-84
119 J. G. Wright, The Oval ... 1986
103 J. G. Wright, Auckland ... 1987-88

† *Signifies hundred on first appearance in England–New Zealand Tests.*

RECORD PARTNERSHIPS FOR EACH WICKET

For England

223 for 1st G. Fowler and C. J. Tavaré at The Oval 198
369 for 2nd J. H. Edrich and K. F. Barrington at Leeds 196
245 for 3rd W. R. Hammond and J. Hardstaff jun. at Lord's 193
266 for 4th M. H. Denness and K. W. R. Fletcher at Auckland 1974-7
242 for 5th W. R. Hammond and L. E. G. Ames at Christchurch 1932-3
240 for 6th† P. H. Parfitt and B. R. Knight at Auckland 1962-6
149 for 7th A. P. E. Knott and P. Lever at Auckland 1970-7
246 for 8th† L. E. G. Ames and G. O. Allen at Lord's 193
163* for 9th† M. C. Cowdrey and A. C. Smith at Wellington 1962-6
59 for 10th A. P. E. Knott and N. Gifford at Nottingham 197

For New Zealand

276 for 1st C. S. Dempster and J. E. Mills at Wellington 1929-3
131 for 2nd B. Sutcliffe and J. R. Reid at Christchurch 1950-5
210 for 3rd B. A. Edgar and M. D. Crowe at Lord's 198
155 for 4th M. D. Crowe and M. J. Greatbatch at Wellington 1987-8
177 for 5th B. E. Congdon and V. Pollard at Nottingham 197
134 for 6th K. R. Rutherford and J. G. Bracewell at Wellington 1987-8
104 for 7th B. Sutcliffe and V. Pollard at Birmingham 196
104 for 8th A. W. Roberts and D. A. R. Moloney at Lord's 193
118 for 9th† J. V. Coney and B. L. Cairns at Wellington 1983-8
57 for 10th F. L. H. Mooney and J. Cowie at Leeds 194

† *Denotes record partnership against all countries.*

TEN WICKETS OR MORE IN A MATCH

For England (7)

11-140 (6-101, 5-39) I. T. Botham, Lord's 19
10-149 (5-98, 5-51) A. W. Greig, Auckland 1974-
11-65 (4-14, 7-51) G. A. R. Lock, Leeds 19
11-84 (5-31, 6-53) G. A. R. Lock, Christchurch 1958-
11-70 (4-38, 7-32)† D. L. Underwood, Lord's 19
12-101 (6-41, 6-60) D. L. Underwood, The Oval 19
12-97 (6-12, 6-85) D. L. Underwood, Christchurch 1970-

For New Zealand (4)

10-144 (7-74, 3-70) B. L. Cairns, Leeds 19
10-140 (4-73, 6-67) J. Cowie, Manchester 19
10-100 (4-74, 6-26) R. J. Hadlee, Wellington 1977-
10-140 (6-80, 4-60) R. J. Hadlee, Nottingham 19

† *Signifies ten wickets or more on first appearance in England–New Zealand Tests.*

Note: D. L. Underwood took twelve wickets in successive matches against New Zealand 1969 and 1970-71.

HAT-TRICK AND FOUR WICKETS IN FIVE BALLS

M. J. C. Allom, in his first Test match, v New Zealand at Christchurch in 1929-30, dismis C. S. Dempster, T. C. Lowry, K. C. James, and F. T. Badcock to take four wickets in balls (w-www).

ENGLAND v INDIA

	Captains					
Season	*England*	*India*	*T*	*E*	*I*	*D*
1932	D. R. Jardine	C. K. Nayudu	1	1	0	0
1933-34	D. R. Jardine	C. K. Nayudu	3	2	0	1
1936	G. O. Allen	Maharaj of Vizianagram	3	2	0	1
1946	W. R. Hammond	Nawab of Pataudi sen.	3	1	0	2
1951-52	N. D. Howard[1]	V. S. Hazare	5	1	1	3
1952	L. Hutton	V. S. Hazare	4	3	0	1
1959	P. B. H. May[2]	D. K. Gaekwad[3]	5	5	0	0
961-62	E. R. Dexter	N. J. Contractor	5	0	2	3
963-64	M. J. K. Smith	Nawab of Pataudi jun.	5	0	0	5
967	D. B. Close	Nawab of Pataudi jun.	3	3	0	0
971	R. Illingworth	A. L. Wadekar	3	0	1	2
972-73	A. R. Lewis	A. L. Wadekar	5	1	2	2
974	M. H. Denness	A. L. Wadekar	3	3	0	0
976-77	A. W. Greig	B. S. Bedi	5	3	1	1
979	J. M. Brearley	S. Venkataraghavan	4	1	0	3
979-80	J. M. Brearley	G. R. Viswanath	1	1	0	0
981-82	K. W. R. Fletcher	S. M. Gavaskar	6	0	1	5
982	R. G. D. Willis	S. M. Gavaskar	3	1	0	2
984-85	D. I. Gower	S. M. Gavaskar	5	2	1	2
986	M. W. Gatting[4]	Kapil Dev	3	0	2	1
	In England		35	20	3	12
	In India		40	10	8	22
	Totals		75	30	11	34

otes: The 1932 Indian touring team was captained by the Maharaj of Porbandar but he did not ay in the Test match.

The following deputised for the official touring captain or were appointed by the home thority for only a minor proportion of the series:

[1]D. B. Carr (Fifth). [2]M. C. Cowdrey (Fourth and Fifth). [3]Pankaj Roy (Second). [4]D. I. Gower irst).

HIGHEST INNINGS TOTALS

r England in England: 633-5 dec. at Birmingham 1979
in India: 652-7 dec. at Madras 1984-85

r India in England: 510 at Leeds 1967
in India: 553-8 dec. at Kanpur 1984-85

LOWEST INNINGS TOTALS

England in England: 101 at The Oval 1971
in India: 102 at Bombay 1981-82

India in England: 42 at Lord's 1974
in India: 83 at Madras 1976-77

INDIVIDUAL HUNDREDS

For England (61)

188	D. L. Amiss, Lord's	1974
179	D. L. Amiss, Delhi	1976-77
151*	K. F. Barrington, Bombay	1961-62
172	K. F. Barrington, Kanpur	1961-62
113*	K. F. Barrington, Delhi	1961-62
137	I. T. Botham, Leeds	1979
114	I. T. Botham, Bombay	1979-80
142	I. T. Botham, Kanpur	1981-82
128	I. T. Botham, Manchester	1982
208	I. T. Botham, The Oval	1982
246*†	G. Boycott, Leeds	1967
155	G. Boycott, Birmingham	1979
125	G. Boycott, The Oval	1979
105	G. Boycott, Delhi	1981-82
160	M. C. Cowdrey, Leeds	1959
107	M. C. Cowdrey, Calcutta	1963-64
151	M. C. Cowdrey, Delhi	1963-64
118	M. H. Denness, Lord's	1974
100	M. H. Denness, Birmingham	1974
126*	E. R. Dexter, Kanpur	1961-62
109†	B. L. D'Oliveira, Leeds	1967
100*	J. H. Edrich, Manchester	1974
104	T. G. Evans, Lord's	1952
113	K. W. R. Fletcher, Bombay	1972-73
123*	K. W. R. Fletcher, Manchester	1974
201	G. Fowler, Madras	1984-85
136	M. W. Gatting, Bombay	1984-85
207	M. W. Gatting, Madras	1984-85
183*	M. W. Gatting, Birmingham	1986
129	G. A. Gooch, Madras	1981-82
114	G. A. Gooch, Lord's	1986
200*†	D. I. Gower, Birmingham	1979
175†	T. W. Graveney, Bombay	1951-52
151	T. W. Graveney, Lord's	1967
148	A. W. Greig, Bombay	1972-73
106	A. W. Greig, Lord's	1974
103	A. W. Greig, Calcutta	1976-77
167	W. R. Hammond, Manchester	1936
217	W. R. Hammond, The Oval	1936
205*	J. Hardstaff jun., Lord's	1946
150	L. Hutton, Lord's	195
104	L. Hutton, Manchester	195
107	R. Illingworth, Manchester	197
127	B. R. Knight, Kanpur	1963-6
107	A. J. Lamb, The Oval	198
125	A. R. Lewis, Kanpur	1972-7
214*	D. Lloyd, Birmingham	197
101	B. W. Luckhurst, Manchester	197
106	P. B. H. May, Nottingham	195
121	P. H. Parfitt, Kanpur	1963-6
131	G. Pullar, Manchester	195
119	G. Pullar, Kanpur	1961-6
126	D. W. Randall, Lord's	198
160	R. T. Robinson, Delhi	1984-8
119	D. S. Sheppard, The Oval	195
100†	M. J. K. Smith, Manchester	195
149	C. J. Tavaré, Delhi	1981-8
136†	B. H. Valentine, Bombay	1933-3
102	C. F. Walters, Madras	1933-3
137*†	A. J. Watkins, Delhi	1951-5
128	T. S. Worthington, The Oval	19

For India (50)

118†	L. Amarnath, Bombay	1933-34
110†	M. Azharuddin, Calcutta	1984-85
105	M. Azharuddin, Madras	1984-85
122	M. Azharuddin, Kanpur	1984-85
112†	A. A. Baig, Manchester	1959
121	F. M. Engineer, Bombay	1972-73
101	S. M. Gavaskar, Manchester	1974
108	S. M. Gavaskar, Bombay	1976-77
221	S. M. Gavaskar, The Oval	1979
172	S. M. Gavaskar, Bangalore	1981-82
105†	Hanumant Singh, Delhi	1963-64
164*	V. S. Hazare, Delhi	1951-52
155	V. S. Hazare, Bombay	1951-52
127	M. L. Jaisimha, Delhi	1961-62
129	M. L. Jaisimha, Calcutta	1963-64
116	Kapil Dev, Kanpur	1981-82
102	S. M. H. Kirmani, Bombay	1984-85
192	B. K. Kunderan, Madras	1963-64
100	B. K. Kunderan, Delhi	1963-64
133	V. L. Manjrekar, Leeds	1952
189*	V. L. Manjrekar, Delhi	1961-62
108	V. L. Manjrekar, Madras	1963-
184	V. Mankad, Lord's	19
114	V. M. Merchant, Manchester	19
128	V. M. Merchant, The Oval	19
154	V. M. Merchant, Delhi	1951-
112	Mushtaq Ali, Manchester	19
122*	R. G. Nadkarni, Kanpur	1963-
103	Nawab of Pataudi jun., Madras	1961-
203*	Nawab of Pataudi jun., Delhi	1963
148	Nawab of Pataudi jun., Leeds	19
129*	S. M. Patil, Manchester	19
115	D. G. Phadkar, Calcutta	1951-
140	Pankaj Roy, Bombay	1951
111	Pankaj Roy, Madras	1951
142	R. J. Shastri, Bombay	1984
111	R. J. Shastri, Calcutta	1984
130*	P. R. Umrigar, Madras	1951
118	P. R. Umrigar, Manchester	1

47*	P. R. Umrigar, Kanpur	1961-62	113	G. R. Viswanath, Bombay	1972-73
03	D. B. Vengsarkar, Lord's	1979	113	G. R. Viswanath, Lord's	1979
57	D. B. Vengsarkar, Lord's	1982	107	G. R. Viswanath, Delhi	1981-82
37	D. B. Vengsarkar, Kanpur	1984-85	222	G. R. Viswanath, Madras	1981-82
26*	D. B. Vengsarkar, Lord's	1986	140	Yashpal Sharma, Madras	1981-82
02*	D. B. Vengsarkar, Leeds	1986			

† *Signifies hundred on first appearance in England–India Tests.*

ote: M. Azharuddin scored hundreds in each of his first three Tests.

RECORD PARTNERSHIPS FOR EACH WICKET

For England

8 for 1st	G. Fowler and R. T. Robinson at Madras	1984-85
1 for 2nd	G. Fowler and M. W. Gatting at Madras	1984-85
9 for 3rd	R. Subba Row and M. J. K. Smith at The Oval	1959
6 for 4th	W. R. Hammond and T. S. Worthington at The Oval	1936
4 for 5th†	K. W. R. Fletcher and A. W. Greig at Bombay	1972-73
1 for 6th	I. T. Botham and R. W. Taylor at Bombay	1979-80
5 for 7th	D. W. Randall and P. H. Edmonds at Lord's	1982
8 for 8th	R. Illingworth and P. Lever at Manchester	1971
for 9th	K. W. R. Fletcher and N. Gifford at Madras	1972-73
for 10th	P. J. W. Allott and R. G. D. Willis at Lord's	1982

For India

3 for 1st	S. M. Gavaskar and C. P. S. Chauhan at The Oval	1979
2 for 2nd	F. M. Engineer and A. L. Wadekar at Bombay	1972-73
5 for 3rd†‡	G. R. Viswanath and Yashpal Sharma at Madras	1981-82
2 for 4th†	V. S. Hazare and V. L. Manjrekar at Leeds	1952
4 for 5th†	M. Azharuddin and R. J. Shastri at Calcutta	1984-85
) for 6th	S. M. H. Kirmani and Kapil Dev at The Oval	1982
5 for 7th†	R. J. Shastri and S. M. H. Kirmani at Bombay	1984-85
for 8th	R. J. Shastri and S. M. H. Kirmani at Delhi	1981-82
for 9th	R. J. Shastri and Madan Lal at Delhi	1981-82
for 10th	R. G. Nadkarni and B. S. Chandrasekhar at Calcutta	1963-64
	S. M. H. Kirmani and C. Sharma at Madras	1984-85

Denotes record partnership against all countries.

415 runs were added between the fall of the 2nd and 3rd wickets: D. B. Vengsarkar retired hurt n he and Viswanath had added 99 runs.

TEN WICKETS OR MORE IN A MATCH

For England (7)

8 (5-35, 5-43)†	G. O. Allen, Lord's	1936
45 (7-49, 4-96)†	A. V. Bedser, Lord's	1946
3 (4-41, 7-52)	A. V. Bedser, Manchester	1946
06 (6-58, 7-48)	I. T. Botham, Bombay	1979-80
63 (6-104, 5-59)†	N. A. Foster, Madras	1984-85
0 (7-46, 3-24)†	J. K. Lever, Delhi	1976-77
53 (7-49, 4-104)	H. Verity, Madras	1933-34

For India (4)

77 (6-105, 4-72)	S. A. Durani, Madras	1961-62
08 (8-55, 4-53)	V. Mankad, Madras	1951-52
88 (4-130, 6-58)	Chetan Sharma, Birmingham	1986
31 (6-64, 6-117)†	L. Sivaramakrishnan, Bombay	1984-85

Signifies ten wickets or more on first appearance in England–India Tests.

: A. V. Bedser took eleven wickets in a match in the first two Tests of his career.

ENGLAND v PAKISTAN

Captains

Season	*England*	*Pakistan*	*T*	*E*	*P*	*D*
1954	L. Hutton[1]	A. H. Kardar	4	1	1	
1961-62	E. R. Dexter	Imtiaz Ahmed	3	1	0	
1962	E. R. Dexter[2]	Javed Burki	5	4	0	
1967	D. B. Close	Hanif Mohammad	3	2	0	
1968-69	M. C. Cowdrey	Saeed Ahmed	3	0	0	
1971	R. Illingworth	Intikhab Alam	3	1	0	
1972-73	A. R. Lewis	Majid Khan	3	0	0	
1974	M. H. Denness	Intikhab Alam	3	0	0	
1977-78	J. M. Brearley[3]	Wasim Bari	3	0	0	
1978	J. M. Brearley	Wasim Bari	3	2	0	
1982	R. G. D. Willis[4]	Imran Khan	3	2	1	
1983-84	R. G. D. Willis[5]	Zaheer Abbas	3	0	1	
1987	M. W. Gatting	Imran Khan	5	0	1	
1987-88	M. W. Gatting	Javed Miandad	3	0	1	
	In England		29	12	3	1
	In Pakistan		18	1	2	1
	Totals		47	13	5	2

Notes: The following deputised for the official touring captain or were appointed by the hom authority for only a minor proportion of the series:

[1]D. S. Sheppard (Second and Third). [2]M. C. Cowdrey (Third). [3]G. Boycott (Thir [4]D. I. Gower (Second). [5]D. I. Gower (Second and Third).

HIGHEST INNINGS TOTALS

For England in England: 558-6 dec. at Nottingham 19
in Pakistan: 546-8 dec. at Faisalabad 1983-

For Pakistan in England: 708 at The Oval 19
in Pakistan: 569-9 dec. at Hyderabad 1972-

LOWEST INNINGS TOTALS

For England in England: 130 at The Oval 19
in Pakistan: 130 at Lahore 1987-

For Pakistan in England: 87 at Lord's 19
in Pakistan: 191 at Faisalabad 1987

INDIVIDUAL HUNDREDS

For England (41)

112 D. L. Amiss, Lahore 1972-73
158 D. L. Amiss, Hyderabad .. 1972-73
183 D. L. Amiss, The Oval 1974
123 C. W. J. Athey, Lord's 1987
139† K. F. Barrington, Lahore .. 1961-62
148 K. F. Barrington, Lord's .. 1967
109* K. F. Barrington, Nottingham 1967
142 K. F. Barrington, The Oval 1967
100† I. T. Botham, Birmingham . 1978
108 I. T. Botham, Lord's 1978
121* G. Boycott, Lord's 1971
112 G. Boycott, Leeds 1971
100* G. Boycott, Hyderabad 1977
116 B. C. Broad, Faisalabad ... 1987
278 D. C. S. Compton, Nottingham 1
159† M. C. Cowdrey, Birmingham 1
182 M. C. Cowdrey, The Oval . 1
100 M. C. Cowdrey, Lahore ... 1968
205 E. R. Dexter, Karachi 196
172 E. R. Dexter, The Oval ... 1
114* B. L. D'Oliveira, Dacca ... 196
122 K. W. R. Fletcher, The Oval ....

124	M. W. Gatting, Birmingham	1987
50*	M. W. Gatting, The Oval	1987
52	D. I. Gower, Faisalabad	1983-84
73*	D. I. Gower, Lahore	1983-84
53	T. W. Graveney, Lord's	1962
14	T. W. Graveney, Nottingham	1962
05	T. W. Graveney, Karachi	1968-69
16	A. P. E. Knott, Birmingham	1971
08*†	B. W. Luckhurst, Birmingham	1971
139	C. Milburn, Karachi	1968-69
111	P. H. Parfitt, Karachi	1961-62
101*	P. H. Parfitt, Birmingham	1962
119	P. H. Parfitt, Leeds	1962
101*	P. H. Parfitt, Nottingham	1962
165	G. Pullar, Dacca	1961-62
106†	C. T. Radley, Birmingham	1978
105	D. W. Randall, Birmingham	1982
166†	R. T. Robinson, Manchester	1987
101	R. T. Simpson, Nottingham	1954

For Pakistan (30)

09	Alim-ud-Din, Karachi	1961-62
46	Asif Iqbal, The Oval	1967
04*	Asif Iqbal, Birmingham	1971
02	Asif Iqbal, Lahore	1972-73
11 / 04	Hanif Mohammad, Dacca	1961-62
87*	Hanif Mohammad, Lord's	1967
22†	Haroon Rashid, Lahore	1977-78
08	Haroon Rashid, Hyderabad	1977-78
18	Imran Khan, The Oval	1987
38	Intikhab Alam, Hyderabad	1972-73
38†	Javed Burki, Lahore	1961-62
40	Javed Burki, Dacca	1961-62
01	Javed Burki, Lord's	1962
60	Javed Miandad, The Oval	1987
0	Mohsin Khan, Lord's	1982
4	Mohsin Khan, Lahore	1983-84
114†	Mudassar Nazar, Lahore	1977-78
124	Mudassar Nazar, Birmingham	1987
120	Mudassar Nazar, Lahore	1987-88
100*	Mushtaq Mohammad, Nottingham	1962
100	Mushtaq Mohammad, Birmingham	1971
157	Mushtaq Mohammad, Hyderabad	1972-73
101	Nasim-ul-Ghani, Lord's	1962
119	Sadiq Mohammad, Lahore	1972-73
116	Salim Malik, Faisalabad	1983-84
102	Salim Malik, The Oval	1987
112	Wasim Raja, Faisalabad	1983-84
274†	Zaheer Abbas, Birmingham	1971
240	Zaheer Abbas, The Oval	1974

† *Signifies hundred on first appearance in England–Pakistan Tests.*

ote: Three batsmen – Majid Khan, Mushtaq Mohammad and D. L. Amiss – were dismissed r 99 at Karachi, 1972-73: the only instance in Test matches.

RECORD PARTNERSHIPS FOR EACH WICKET

For England

8 for 1st	G. Pullar and R. W. Barber at Dacca	1961-62
8 for 2nd	M. C. Cowdrey and E. R. Dexter at The Oval	1962
for 3rd	K. F. Barrington and T. W. Graveney at Lord's	1967
3 for 4th	E. R. Dexter and P. H. Parfitt at Karachi	1961-62
2 for 5th	D. C. S. Compton and T. E. Bailey at Nottingham	1954
3* for 6th	P. H. Parfitt and D. A. Allen at Birmingham	1962
7 for 7th	D. I. Gower and V. J. Marks at Faisalabad	1983-84
for 8th	P. H. Parfitt and D. A. Allen at Leeds	1962
for 9th	T. W. Graveney and F. S. Trueman at Lord's	1962
for 10th	R. W. Taylor and R. G. D. Willis at Birmingham	1982

For Pakistan

for 1st	Mohsin Khan and Shoaib Mohammad at Lahore	1983-84
for 2nd†	Zaheer Abbas and Mushtaq Mohammad at Birmingham	1971
for 3rd	Mudassar Nazar and Haroon Rashid at Lahore	1977-78
for 4th	Javed Miandad and Salim Malik at The Oval	1987
for 5th	Javed Burki and Nasim-ul-Ghani at Lord's	1962
for 6th	Mushtaq Mohammad and Intikhab Alam at Hyderabad	1972-73
for 7th	Ijaz Ahmed and Salim Yousuf at The Oval	1987
for 8th†	Hanif Mohammad and Asif Iqbal at Lord's	1967
for 9th†	Asif Iqbal and Intikhab Alam at The Oval	1967
for 10th	Sarfraz Nawaz and Asif Masood at Leeds	1974

Denotes record partnership against all countries.

TEN WICKETS OR MORE IN A MATCH

For England (2)

11-83 (6-65, 5-18)†	N. G. B. Cook, Karachi	1983-84
13-71 (5-20, 8-51)	D. L. Underwood, Lord's	1974

For Pakistan (5)

10-194 (5-84, 5-110)	Abdul Qadir, Lahore	1983-84
13-101 (9-56, 4-45)	Abdul Qadir, Lahore	1987-88
10-186 (5-88, 5-98)	Abdul Qadir, Karachi	1987-88
12-99 (6-53, 6-46)	Fazal Mahmood, The Oval	1954
10-77 (3-37, 7-40)	Imran Khan, Leeds	1987

† *Signifies ten wickets or more on first appearance in England–Pakistan Tests.*

FOUR WICKETS IN FIVE BALLS

C. M. Old, v Pakistan at Birmingham in 1978, dismissed Wasim Raja, Wasim Bari, Iqbal Qasim and Sikander Bakht to take four wickets in five balls (ww-ww).

ENGLAND v SRI LANKA

	Captains				
Season	*England*	*Sri Lanka*	*T*	*E*	*SL*
1981-82	K. W. R. Fletcher	B. Warnapura	1	1	0
1984	D. I. Gower	L. R. D. Mendis	1	0	0
1988	G. A. Gooch	R. S. Madugalle	1	1	0
	In England		2	1	0
	In Sri Lanka		1	1	0
	Totals		3	2	0

Highest innings total for England: 429 at Lord's ... 198
for Sri Lanka: 491-7 dec. at Lord's ... 198

Lowest innings total for England: 223 at Colombo (PSO) ... 1981-
for Sri Lanka: 175 at Colombo (PSO) ... 1981-

INDIVIDUAL HUNDREDS

For England (1)

107† A. J. Lamb, Lord's ... 1984

For Sri Lanka (3)

111 L. R. D. Mendis, Lord's ... 19
102*† S. A. R. Silva, Lord's ... 19
190 S. Wettimuny, Lord's ... 19

† *Signifies hundred on first appearance in England–Sri Lanka Tests.*

Best bowling in an innings for England: 6-33 by J. E. Emburey at Colombo (PSO) 1981
for Sri Lanka: 4-70 by A. L. F. de Mel at Colombo (PSO) 1981

Best wicket partnership for England: 131 for 2nd by G. A. Gooch and R. C. Russell at Lord's ... 1
for Sri Lanka: 150 for 5th‡ by S. Wettimuny and L. R. D. Mendis at Lord's ... 1

‡ *Denotes record partnership against all countries.*

ENGLAND v REST OF THE WORLD

In 1970, owing to the cancellation of the South African tour to England, a series of matches was arranged, with the trappings of a full Test series, between England and the Rest of the World. It was played for the Guinness Trophy.

The following players represented the Rest of the World: E. J. Barlow (5), F. M. Engineer (2), L. R. Gibbs (4), Intikhab Alam (5), R. B. Kanhai (5), C. H. Lloyd (5), G. D. McKenzie (3), D. L. Murray (3), Mushtaq Mohammad (2), P. M. Pollock (1), R. G. Pollock (5), M. J. Procter (5), B. A. Richards (5), G. S. Sobers (5).

A list of players who appeared for England in these matches may be found on page 127.

AUSTRALIA v SOUTH AFRICA

	Captains					
Season	*Australia*	*South Africa*	*T*	*A*	*SA*	*D*
1902-03*S*	J. Darling	H. M. Taberer[1]	3	2	0	1
1910-11*A*	C. Hill	P. W. Sherwell	5	4	1	0
1912*E*	S. E. Gregory	F. Mitchell[2]	3	2	0	1
1921-22*S*	H. L. Collins	H. W. Taylor	3	1	0	2
1931-32*A*	W. M. Woodfull	H. B. Cameron	5	5	0	0
1935-36*S*	V. Y. Richardson	H. F. Wade	5	4	0	1
1949-50*S*	A. L. Hassett	A. D. Nourse	5	4	0	1
1952-53*A*	A. L. Hassett	J. E. Cheetham	5	2	2	1
1957-58*S*	I. D. Craig	C. B. van Ryneveld[3]	5	3	0	2
1963-64*A*	R. B. Simpson[4]	T. L. Goddard	5	1	1	3
1966-67*S*	R. B. Simpson	P. L. van der Merwe	5	1	3	1
1969-70*S*	W. M. Lawry	A. Bacher	4	0	4	0
	In South Africa		30	15	7	8
	In Australia		20	12	4	4
	In England		3	2	0	1
	Totals		53	29	11	13

S Played in South Africa. A Played in Australia. E Played in England.

Notes: The following deputised for the official touring captain or were appointed by the home authority for only a minor proportion of the series:

[1]J. H. Anderson (Second), E. A. Halliwell (Third). [2]L. J. Tancred (Third). [3]D. J. McGlew (First). [4]R. Benaud (First).

HIGHEST INNINGS TOTALS

For Australia in Australia:	578 at Melbourne	1910-11
in South Africa:	549-7 dec. at Port Elizabeth	1949-50
For South Africa in Australia:	595 at Adelaide	1963-64
in South Africa:	622-9 dec. at Durban	1969-70

LOWEST INNINGS TOTALS

For Australia in Australia:	153 at Melbourne	1931-32
in South Africa:	75 at Durban	1949-50
For South Africa in Australia:	36† at Melbourne	1931-32
in South Africa:	85 at Johannesburg	1902-03

† Scored 45 in the second innings giving the smallest aggregate of 81 (12 extras) in Test cricket.

INDIVIDUAL HUNDREDS

For Australia (55)

159*‡	W. W. Armstrong, Johannesburg	1902-03
132	W. W. Armstrong, Melbourne	1910-11
132†	W. Bardsley, Sydney	1910-11
121	W. Bardsley, Manchester	1912
164	W. Bardsley, Lord's	1912
122	R. Benaud, Johannesburg	1957-58
100	R. Benaud, Johannesburg	1957-58
169†	B. C. Booth, Brisbane	1963-64
102*	B. C. Booth, Sydney	1963-64
226†	D. G. Bradman, Brisbane	1931-32
112	D. G. Bradman, Sydney	1931-32
167	D. G. Bradman, Melbourne	1931-32
299*	D. G. Bradman, Adelaide	1931-32
121	W. A. Brown, Cape Town	1935-36
189	J. W. Burke, Cape Town	1957-58
109†	A. G. Chipperfield, Durban	1935-36
203	H. L. Collins, Johannesburg	1921-22
112	J. H. Fingleton, Cape Town	1935-36
108	J. H. Fingleton, Johannesburg	1935-36
118	J. H. Fingleton, Durban	1935-36
119	J. M. Gregory, Johannesburg	1921-22
178	R. N. Harvey, Cape Town	1949-50
151*	R. N. Harvey, Durban	1949-50
116	R. N. Harvey, Port Elizabeth	1949-50
100	R. N. Harvey, Johannesburg	1949-50
109	R. N. Harvey, Brisbane	1952-53
190	R. N. Harvey, Sydney	1952-53
116	R. N. Harvey, Adelaide	1952-53
205	R. N. Harvey, Melbourne	1952-5
112†	A. L. Hassett, Johannesburg	1949-5
167	A. L. Hassett, Port Elizabeth	1949-5
163	A. L. Hassett, Adelaide	1952-5
142†	C. Hill, Johannesburg	1902-0
191	C. Hill, Sydney	1910-1
100	C. Hill, Melbourne	1910-1
114	C. Kelleway, Manchester	191
102	C. Kelleway, Lord's	191
157	W. M. Lawry, Melbourne	1963-6
101†	S. J. E. Loxton, Johannesburg	1949-5
137	C. G. Macartney, Sydney	1910-1
116	C. G. Macartney, Durban	1921-2
149	S. J. McCabe, Durban	1935-3
189*	S. J. McCabe, Johannesburg	1935-3
154	C. C. McDonald, Adelaide	1952-5
118 / 101*	J. Moroney, Johannesburg	1949-5
111	A. R. Morris, Johannesburg	1949-
157	A. R. Morris, Port Elizabeth	1949-
127†	K. E. Rigg, Sydney	1931-
142	J. Ryder, Cape Town	1921-
153	R. B. Simpson, Cape Town	1966-
134	K. R. Stackpole, Cape Town	1966-
159	V. T. Trumper, Melbourne	1910-
214*	V. T. Trumper, Adelaide	1910-
161	W. M. Woodfull, Melbourne	1931-

For South Africa (36)

114†	E. J. Barlow, Brisbane	1963-64
109	E. J. Barlow, Melbourne	1963-64
201	E. J. Barlow, Adelaide	1963-64
127	E. J. Barlow, Cape Town	1969-70
110	E. J. Barlow, Johannesburg	1969-70
126	K. C. Bland, Sydney	1963-64
162*	W. R. Endean, Melbourne	1952-53
204	G. A. Faulkner, Melbourne	1910-11
115	G. A. Faulkner, Adelaide	1910-11
122*	G. A. Faulkner, Manchester	1912
152	C. N. Frank, Johannesburg	1921-22
102	B. L. Irvine, Port Elizabeth	1969-70
182	D. T. Lindsay, Johannesburg	1966-67
137	D. T. Lindsay, Durban	1966-67
131	D. T. Lindsay, Johannesburg	1966-67
108	D. J. McGlew, Johannesburg	1957
105	D. J. McGlew, Durban	1957
231	A. D. Nourse, Johannesburg	1935
114	A. D. Nourse, Cape Town	1949
111	A. W. Nourse, Johannesburg	1921
122	R. G. Pollock, Sydney	1963
175	R. G. Pollock, Adelaide	1963
209	R. G. Pollock, Cape Town	1966
105	R. G. Pollock, Port Elizabeth	1966
274	R. G. Pollock, Durban	1969
140	B. A. Richards, Durban	1969
126	B. A. Richards, Port Elizabeth	1969
143	E. A. B. Rowan, Durban	1949

101	J. H. Sinclair, Johannesburg	1902-03
104	J. H. Sinclair, Cape Town	1902-03
103	S. J. Snooke, Adelaide	1910-11
11	K. G. Viljoen, Melbourne	1931-32
115	J. H. B. Waite, Johannesburg	1957-58
134	J. H. B. Waite, Durban	1957-58
105	J. W. Zulch, Adelaide	1910-11
150	J. W. Zulch, Sydney	1910-11

† *Signifies hundred on first appearance in Australia–South Africa Tests.*
‡ *Carried his bat.*

RECORD PARTNERSHIPS FOR EACH WICKET

For Australia

33 for 1st	J. H. Fingleton and W. A. Brown at Cape Town	1935-36
75 for 2nd	C. C. McDonald and A. L. Hassett at Adelaide	1952-53
42 for 3rd	C. Kelleway and W. Bardsley at Lord's	1912
68 for 4th	R. N. Harvey and K. R. Miller at Sydney	1952-53
43 for 5th	W. W. Armstrong and V. T. Trumper at Melbourne	1910-11
07 for 6th	C. Kelleway and V. S. Ransford at Melbourne	1910-11
60 for 7th	R. Benaud and G. D. McKenzie at Sydney	1963-64
3 for 8th	A. G. Chipperfield and C. V. Grimmett at Durban	1935-36
3 for 9th	D. G. Bradman and W. J. O'Reilly at Adelaide	1931-32
	K. D. Mackay and I. Meckiff at Johannesburg	1957-58
2 for 10th	V. S. Ransford and W. J. Whitty at Melbourne	1910-11

For South Africa

76 for 1st	D. J. McGlew and T. L. Goddard at Johannesburg	1957-58
73 for 2nd	L. J. Tancred and C. B. Llewellyn at Johannesburg	1902-03
1 for 3rd†	E. J. Barlow and R. G. Pollock at Adelaide	1963-64
6 for 4th	C. N. Frank and A. W. Nourse at Johannesburg	1921-22
9 for 5th	J. H. B. Waite and W. R. Endean at Johannesburg	1957-58
0 for 6th†	R. G. Pollock and H. R. Lance at Durban	1969-70
1 for 7th	D. T. Lindsay and P. L. van der Merwe at Johannesburg	1966-67
4 for 8th†	A. W. Nourse and E. A. Halliwell at Johannesburg	1902-03
for 9th	R. G. Pollock and P. M. Pollock at Cape Town	1966-67
for 10th	L. A. Stricker and S. J. Pegler at Adelaide	1910-11

† *Denotes record partnership against all countries.*

TEN WICKETS OR MORE IN A MATCH

For Australia (5)

199 (7-116, 7-83)	C. V. Grimmett, Adelaide	1931-32
88 (5-32, 5-56)	C. V. Grimmett, Cape Town	1935-36
110 (3-70, 7-40)	C. V. Grimmett, Johannesburg	1935-36
173 (7-100, 6-73)	C. V. Grimmett, Durban	1935-36
24 (5-6, 6-18)	H. Ironmonger, Melbourne	1931-32

For South Africa (2)

16 (5-43, 5-73)	C. B. Llewellyn, Johannesburg	1902-03
65 (6-84, 7-81)	H. J. Tayfield, Melbourne	1952-53

e: C. V. Grimmett took ten wickets or more in three consecutive matches in 1935-36.

AUSTRALIA v WEST INDIES

	Captains						
Season	*Australia*	*West Indies*	*T*	*A*	*WI*	*T*	*D*
1930-31*A*	W. M. Woodfull	G. C. Grant	5	4	1	0	0
1951-52*A*	A. L. Hassett[1]	J. D. C. Goddard[2]	5	4	1	0	0
1954-55*W*	I. W. Johnson	D. S. Atkinson[3]	5	3	0	0	2
1960-61*A*	R. Benaud	F. M. M. Worrell	5	2	1	1	1

THE FRANK WORRELL TROPHY

	Captains							
Season	*Australia*	*West Indies*	*T*	*A*	*WI*	*T*	*D*	*Held b*
1964-65*W*	R. B. Simpson	G. S. Sobers	5	1	2	0	2	WI
1968-69*A*	W. M. Lawry	G. S. Sobers	5	3	1	0	1	A
1972-73*W*	I. M. Chappell	R. B. Kanhai	5	2	0	0	3	A
1975-76*A*	G. S. Chappell	C. H. Lloyd	6	5	1	0	0	A
1977-78*W*	R. B. Simpson	A. I. Kallicharran[4]	5	1	3	0	1	WI
1979-80*A*	G. S. Chappell	C. H. Lloyd[5]	3	0	2	0	1	WI
1981-82*A*	G. S. Chappell	C. H. Lloyd	3	1	1	0	1	WI
1983-84*W*	K. J. Hughes	C. H. Lloyd[6]	5	0	3	0	2	WI
1984-85*A*	A. R. Border[7]	C. H. Lloyd	5	1	3	0	1	WI
	In Australia		37	20	11	1	5	
	In West Indies		25	7	8	0	10	
	Totals		62	27	19	1	15	

A Played in Australia. W Played in West Indies.

Notes: The following deputised for the official touring captain or were appointed by the ho authority for only a minor proportion of the series:

[1]A. R. Morris (Third). [2]J. B. Stollmeyer (Fifth). [3]J. B. Stollmeyer (Second and Third). [4]C. Lloyd (First and Second). [5]D. L. Murray (First). [6]I. V. A. Richards (Second). [7]K. J. Hugh (First and Second).

HIGHEST INNINGS TOTALS

For Australia in Australia: 619 at Sydney 1968
in West Indies: 758-8 dec. at Kingston 1954
For West Indies in Australia: 616 at Adelaide 1968
in West Indies: 573 at Bridgetown 1964

LOWEST INNINGS TOTALS

For Australia in Australia: 76 at Perth 1984
in West Indies: 90 at Port-of-Spain 1977
For West Indies in Australia: 78 at Sydney 1951
in West Indies: 109 at Georgetown 1972

INDIVIDUAL HUNDREDS

For Australia (64)

28	R. G. Archer, Kingston	1954-55
21	R. Benaud, Kingston	1954-55
17	B. C. Booth, Port-of-Spain	1964-65
26	A. R. Border, Adelaide	1981-82
00*	A. R. Border, Port-of-Spain	1983-84
23	D. G. Bradman, Brisbane	1930-31
52	D. G. Bradman, Melbourne	1930-31
06	G. S. Chappell, Bridgetown	1972-73
23 09*	‡G. S. Chappell, Brisbane	1975-76
32*	G. S. Chappell, Sydney	1975-76
24	G. S. Chappell, Brisbane	1979-80
7†	I. M. Chappell, Brisbane	1968-69
5	I. M. Chappell, Melbourne	1968-69
6*	I. M. Chappell, Bridgetown	1972-73
9	I. M. Chappell, Georgetown	1972-73
6	I. M. Chappell, Perth	1975-76
9†	G. J. Cosier, Melbourne	1975-76
3	R. M. Cowper, Port-of-Spain	1964-65
2	R. M. Cowper, Bridgetown	1964-65
7*†	J. Dyson, Sydney	1981-82
3	R. N. Harvey, Kingston	1954-55
3	R. N. Harvey, Port-of-Spain	1954-55
4	R. N. Harvey, Kingston	1954-55
2	A. L. Hassett, Sydney	1951-52
2	A. L. Hassett, Melbourne	1951-52
3†	A. M. J. Hilditch, Melbourne	1984-85
0*†	K. J. Hughes, Brisbane	1979-80
*	K. J. Hughes, Melbourne	1981-82
5†	A. F. Kippax, Adelaide	1930-31
)	W. M. Lawry, Bridgetown	1964-65
5	W. M. Lawry, Brisbane	1968-69
	W. M. Lawry, Melbourne	1968-69
	W. M. Lawry, Sydney	1968-69
118	R. R. Lindwall, Bridgetown	1954-55
109*	R. B. McCosker, Melbourne	1975-76
110	C. C. McDonald, Port-of-Spain	1954-55
127	C. C. McDonald, Kingston	1954-55
129	K. R. Miller, Sydney	1951-52
147	K. R. Miller, Kingston	1954-55
137	K. R. Miller, Bridgetown	1954-55
109	K. R. Miller, Kingston	1954-55
111	A. R. Morris, Port-of-Spain	1954-55
181†	N. C. O'Neill, Brisbane	1960-61
120	W. B. Phillips, Bridgetown	1983-84
183	W. H. Ponsford, Sydney	1930-31
109	W. H. Ponsford, Brisbane	1930-31
132	I. R. Redpath, Sydney	1968-69
102	I. R. Redpath, Melbourne	1975-76
103	I. R. Redpath, Adelaide	1975-76
101	I. R. Redpath, Melbourne	1975-76
124	C. S. Serjeant, Georgetown	1977-78
201	R. B. Simpson, Bridgetown	1964-65
142	K. R. Stackpole, Kingston	1972-73
122	P. M. Toohey, Kingston	1977-78
136	A. Turner, Adelaide	1975-76
118	K. D. Walters, Sydney	1968-69
110	K. D. Walters, Adelaide	1968-69
242 103	K. D. Walters, Sydney	1968-69
102*	K. D. Walters, Bridgetown	1972-73
112	K. D. Walters, Port-of-Spain	1972-73
173	K. C. Wessels, Sydney	1984-85
126	G. M. Wood, Georgetown	1977-78

G. S. Chappell is the only player to score hundreds in both innings of his first Test as captain.

For West Indies (63)

	F. C. M. Alexander, Sydney	1960-61
	D. St E. Atkinson, Bridgetown	1954-55
	B. F. Butcher, Port-of-Spain	1964-65
	B. F. Butcher, Sydney	1968-69
	B. F. Butcher, Adelaide	1968-69
	C. C. Depeiza, Bridgetown	1954-55
	P. J. L. Dujon, Port-of-Spain	1983-84
	P. J. L. Dujon, Perth	1984-85
	M. L. C. Foster, Kingston	1972-73
	R. C. Fredericks, Perth	1975-76
	H. A. Gomes, Georgetown	1977-78
	H. A. Gomes, Kingston	1977-78
	H. A. Gomes, Sydney	1981-82
	H. A. Gomes, Adelaide	1981-82
	H. A. Gomes, Perth	1984-85
	H. A. Gomes, Adelaide	1984-85
120*	C. G. Greenidge, Georgetown	1983-84
127	C. G. Greenidge, Kingston	1983-84
103*	D. L. Haynes, Georgetown	1983-84
145	D. L. Haynes, Bridgetown	1983-84
102*	G. A. Headley, Brisbane	1930-31
105	G. A. Headley, Sydney	1930-31
110	C. C. Hunte, Melbourne	1960-61
101	A. I. Kallicharran, Brisbane	1975-76
127	A. I. Kallicharran, Port-of-Spain	1977-78
126	A. I. Kallicharran, Kingston	1977-78
106	A. I. Kallicharran, Adelaide	1979-80
117 115	R. B. Kanhai, Adelaide	1960-61

129	R. B. Kanhai, Bridgetown	1964-65
121	R. B. Kanhai, Port-of-Spain	1964-65
105	R. B. Kanhai, Bridgetown	1972-73
129†	C. H. Lloyd, Brisbane	1968-69
178	C. H. Lloyd, Georgetown	1972-73
149	C. H. Lloyd, Perth	1975-76
102	C. H. Lloyd, Melbourne	1975-76
121	C. H. Lloyd, Adelaide	1979-80
114	C. H. Lloyd, Brisbane	1984-85
123*	F. R. Martin, Sydney	1930-31
201	S. M. Nurse, Bridgetown	1964-65
137	S. M. Nurse, Sydney	1968-69
101	I. V. A. Richards, Adelaide	1975-76
140	I. V. A. Richards, Brisbane	1979-80
178	I. V. A. Richards, St John's	1983-84
208	I. V. A. Richards, Melbourne	1984-85
131*	R. B. Richardson, Bridgetown	1983-84
154	R. B. Richardson, St John's	1983-8
138	R. B. Richardson, Brisbane.	1984-8
107	L. G. Rowe, Brisbane	1975-7
104†	O. G. Smith, Kingston	1954-5
132	G. S. Sobers, Brisbane	1960-6
168	G. S. Sobers, Sydney	1960-6
110	G. S. Sobers, Adelaide	1968-6
113	G. S. Sobers, Sydney	1968-6
104	J. B. Stollmeyer, Sydney	1951-5
108	C. L. Walcott, Kingston	1954-5
126 / 110	C. L. Walcott, Port-of-Spain	1954-5
155 / 110	C. L. Walcott, Kingston	1954-5
139	E. D. Weekes, Port-of-Spain	1954-5
100†	A. B. Williams, Georgetown	1977-7
108	F. M. M. Worrell, Melbourne	1951-5

† *Signifies hundred on first appearance in Australia–West Indies Tests.*

Note: F. C. M. Alexander and C. C. Depeiza scored the only hundreds of their careers in Test match.

RECORD PARTNERSHIPS FOR EACH WICKET

For Australia

382 for 1st†	W. M. Lawry and R. B. Simpson at Bridgetown	1964-
298 for 2nd	W. M. Lawry and I. M. Chappell at Melbourne	1968-
295 for 3rd†	C. C. McDonald and R. N. Harvey at Kingston	1954-
336 for 4th	W. M. Lawry and K. D. Walters at Sydney	1968-
220 for 5th	K. R. Miller and R. G. Archer at Kingston	1954-
206 for 6th	K. R. Miller and R. G. Archer at Bridgetown	1954-
134 for 7th	A. K. Davidson and R. Benaud at Brisbane	1960-
137 for 8th	R. Benaud and I. W. Johnson at Kingston	1954-
97 for 9th	K. D. Mackay and J. W. Martin at Melbourne	1960-
97 for 10th	T. G. Hogan and R. M. Hogg at Georgetown	1983-

For West Indies

250* for 1st	C. G. Greenidge and D. L. Haynes at Georgetown	1983
165 for 2nd	M. C. Carew and R. B. Kanhai at Brisbane	1968
308 for 3rd	R. B. Richardson and I. V. A. Richards at St John's	1983
198 for 4th	L. G. Rowe and A. I. Kallicharran at Brisbane	1975
210 for 5th	R. B. Kanhai and M. L. C. Foster at Kingston	1972
165 for 6th	R. B. Kanhai and D. L. Murray at Bridgetown	1972
347 for 7th†‡	D. St E. Atkinson and C. C. Depeiza at Bridgetown	1954
82 for 8th	H. A. Gomes and A. M. E. Roberts at Adelaide	1981
122 for 9th	D. A. J. Holford and J. L. Hendriks at Adelaide	1968
56 for 10th	J. Garner and C. E. H. Croft at Brisbane	1979

† *Denotes record partnership against all countries.*
‡ *Record seventh-wicket partnership in first-class cricket.*

TEN WICKETS OR MORE IN A MATCH

For Australia (9)

11-222 (5-135, 6-87)†	A. K. Davidson, Brisbane	1960-61
11-183 (7-87, 4-96)†	C. V. Grimmett, Adelaide	1930-31
10-115 (6-72, 4-43)	N. J. N. Hawke, Georgetown	1964-65
10-144 (6-54, 4-90)	R. G. Holland, Sydney	1984-85
11-79 (7-23, 4-56)	H. Ironmonger, Melbourne	1930-31
11-181 (8-112, 3-69)	G. F. Lawson, Adelaide	1984-85
10-127 (7-83, 3-44)	D. K. Lillee, Melbourne	1981-82
10-159 (8-71, 2-88)	G. D. McKenzie, Melbourne	1968-69
10-185 (3-87, 7-98)	B. Yardley, Sydney	1981-82

For West Indies (3)

0-113 (7-55, 3-58)	G. E. Gomez, Sydney	1951-52
1-107 (5-45, 6-62)	M. A. Holding, Melbourne	1981-82
0-107 (5-69, 5-38)	M. D. Marshall, Adelaide	1984-85

† *Signifies ten wickets or more on first appearance in Australia–West Indies Tests.*

AUSTRALIA v NEW ZEALAND

	Captains					
eason	*Australia*	*New Zealand*	*T*	*A*	*NZ*	*D*
945-46*N*	W. A. Brown	W. A. Hadlee	1	1	0	0
973-74*A*	I. M. Chappell	B. E. Congdon	3	2	0	1
973-74*N*	I. M. Chappell	B. E. Congdon	3	1	1	1
976-77*N*	G. S. Chappell	G. M. Turner	2	1	0	1
980-81*A*	G. S. Chappell	G. P. Howarth[1]	3	2	0	1
981-82*N*	G. S. Chappell	G. P. Howarth	3	1	1	1

TRANS-TASMAN TROPHY

	Captains						
ason	*Australia*	*New Zealand*	*T*	*A*	*NZ*	*D*	*Held by*
85-86*A*	A. R. Border	J. V. Coney	3	1	2	0	NZ
85-86*N*	A. R. Border	J. V. Coney	3	0	1	2	NZ
87-88*A*	A. R. Border	J. J. Crowe	3	1	0	2	A
	In Australia		12	6	2	4	
	In New Zealand		12	4	3	5	
	Totals		24	10	5	9	

Played in Australia. N Played in New Zealand.

te: The following deputised for the official touring captain: [1]M. G. Burgess (Second).

HIGHEST INNINGS TOTALS

r Australia in Australia: 496 in Adelaide 1987-88
in New Zealand: 552 at Christchurch 1976-77

r New Zealand in Australia: 553-7 dec. at Brisbane 1985-86
in New Zealand: 484 at Wellington 1973-74

LOWEST INNINGS TOTALS

r Australia in Australia: 162 at Sydney 1973-74
in New Zealand: 103 at Auckland 1985-86

New Zealand in Australia: 121 at Perth 1980-81
in New Zealand: 42 at Wellington 1945-46

INDIVIDUAL HUNDREDS

For Australia (22)

143	D. C. Boon, Brisbane	1987-88
152*	A. R. Border, Brisbane	1985-86
140, 114*	A. R. Border, Christchurch	1985-86
205	A. R. Border, Adelaide	1987-88
247*, 133	G. S. Chappell, Wellington	1973-74
176	G. S. Chappell, Christchurch	1981-82
145, 121	I. M. Chappell, Wellington	1973-74
101	G. J. Gilmour, Christchurch	1976-77
118	G. R. Marsh, Auckland	1985-86
132	R. W. Marsh, Adelaide	1973-74
115†	G. R. J. Matthews, Brisbane	1985-86
130	G. R. J. Matthews, Wellington	1985-86
159*‡	I. R. Redpath, Auckland	1973-74
122†	K. R. Stackpole, Melbourne	1973-74
104*	K. D. Walters, Auckland	1973-74
250	K. D. Walters, Christchurch	1976-7
107	K. D. Walters, Melbourne	1980-81
111†	G. M. Wood, Brisbane	1980-81
100	G. M. Wood, Auckland	1981-8

For New Zealand (15)

101*	J. V. Coney, Wellington	1985-86
132	B. E. Congdon, Wellington	1973-74
107*	B. E. Congdon, Christchurch	1976-77
188	M. D. Crowe, Brisbane	1985-86
137	M. D. Crowe, Christchurch	1985-86
137	M. D. Crowe, Adelaide	1987-88
161	B. A. Edgar, Auckland	1981-82
101	B. F. Hastings, Wellington	1973-7
150	A. H. Jones, Adelaide	1987-8
117	J. F. M. Morrison, Sydney	1973-7
108	J. M. Parker, Sydney	1973-7
108†	J. F. Reid, Brisbane	1985-8
101, 110*	G. M. Turner, Christchurch	1973-7
141	J. G. Wright, Christchurch	1981-8

† *Signifies hundred on first appearance in Australia–New Zealand Tests.*
‡ *Carried his bat.*

Notes: G. S. and I. M. Chappell at Wellington in 1973-74 provide the only instance in Te matches of brothers both scoring a hundred in each innings and in the same Test.

G. S. Chappell's match aggregate of 380 (247* and 133) for Australia at Wellington in 1973-7 is the record in Test matches.

RECORD PARTNERSHIPS FOR EACH WICKET

For Australia

106 for 1st	B. M. Laird and G. M. Wood at Auckland	1981-8
168 for 2nd	G. R. Marsh and W. B. Phillips at Auckland	1985-8
264 for 3rd	I. M. Chappell and G. S. Chappell at Wellington	1973-
116 for 4th	A. R. Border and S. R. Waugh at Adelaide	1987-8
213 for 5th	G. M. Ritchie and G. R. J. Matthews at Wellington	1985-8
197 for 6th	A. R. Border and G. R. J. Matthews at Brisbane	1985-8
217 for 7th†	K. D. Walters and G. J. Gilmour at Christchurch	1976-
93 for 8th	G. J. Gilmour and K. J. O'Keeffe at Auckland	1976-
61 for 9th	A. I. C. Dodemaide and C. J. McDermott at Adelaide	1987-
60 for 10th	K. D. Walters and J. D. Higgs at Melbourne	1980-

For New Zealand

107 for 1st	G. M. Turner and J. M. Parker at Auckland	1973-
128 for 2nd	J. G. Wright and A. H. Jones at Adelaide	1987-
224 for 3rd	J. F. Reid and M. D. Crowe at Brisbane	1985-
229 for 4th†	B. E. Congdon and B. F. Hastings at Wellington	1973-
88 for 5th	J. V. Coney and M. G. Burgess at Perth	1980
109 for 6th	K. R. Rutherford and J. V. Coney at Wellington	1985
132* for 7th	J. V. Coney and R. J. Hadlee at Wellington	1985
53 for 8th	B. A. Edgar and R. J. Hadlee at Brisbane	1980
73 for 9th	H. J. Howarth and D. R. Hadlee at Christchurch	1976
124 for 10th	J. G. Bracewell and S. L. Boock at Sydney	1985

† *Denotes record partnership against all countries.*

TEN WICKETS OR MORE IN A MATCH

For Australia (2)

10-174 (6-106, 4-68)	R. G. Holland, Sydney	1985-86
11-123 (5-51, 6-72)	D. K. Lillee, Auckland	1976-77

For New Zealand (4)

10-106 (4-74, 6-32)	J. G. Bracewell, Auckland	1985-86
15-123 (9-52, 6-71)	R. J. Hadlee, Brisbane	1985-86
11-155 (5-65, 6-90)	R. J. Hadlee, Perth	1985-86
10-176 (5-109, 5-67)	R. J. Hadlee, Melbourne	1987-88

AUSTRALIA v INDIA

Captains

eason	*Australia*	*India*	*T*	*A*	*I*	*T*	*D*
947-48*A*	D. G. Bradman	L. Amarnath	5	4	0	0	1
956-57*I*	I. W. Johnson[1]	P. R. Umrigar	3	2	0	0	1
959-60*I*	R. Benaud	G. S. Ramchand	5	2	1	0	2
964-65*I*	R. B. Simpson	Nawab of Pataudi jun.	3	1	1	0	1
967-68*A*	R. B. Simpson[2]	Nawab of Pataudi jun.[3]	4	4	0	0	0
969-70*I*	W. M. Lawry	Nawab of Pataudi jun.	5	3	1	0	1
977-78*A*	R. B. Simpson	B. S. Bedi	5	3	2	0	0
979-80*I*	K. J. Hughes	S. M. Gavaskar	6	0	2	0	4
980-81*A*	G. S. Chappell	S. M. Gavaskar	3	1	1	0	1
985-86*A*	A. R. Border	Kapil Dev	3	0	0	0	3
986-87*I*	A. R. Border	Kapil Dev	3	0	0	1	2
	In Australia		20	12	3	0	5
	In India		25	8	5	1	11
	Totals		45	20	8	1	16

Played in Australia. I Played in India.

otes: The following deputised for the official touring captain or were appointed by the home thority for only a minor proportion of the series:

[1]R. R. Lindwall (Second). [2]W. M. Lawry (Third and Fourth). [3]C. G. Borde (First).

HIGHEST INNINGS TOTALS

r Australia in Australia: 674 at Adelaide	1947-48
in India: 574-7 dec. at Madras	1986-87
r India in Australia: 600-4 dec. at Sydney	1985-86
in India: 517-5 dec. at Bombay	1986-87

LOWEST INNINGS TOTALS

r Australia in Australia: 83 at Melbourne	1980-81
in India: 105 at Kanpur	1959-60
r India in Australia: 58 at Brisbane	1947-48
in India: 135 at Delhi	1959-60

INDIVIDUAL HUNDREDS

For Australia (45)

112	S. G. Barnes, Adelaide	1947-48
123†	D. C. Boon, Adelaide	1985-86
131	D. C. Boon, Sydney	1985-86
122	D. C. Boon, Madras	1986-87
162†	A. R. Border, Madras	1979-80
124	A. R. Border, Melbourne	1980-81
163	A. R. Border, Melbourne	1985-86
106	A. R. Border, Madras	1986-87
185†	D. G. Bradman, Brisbane	1947-48
132 127*	D. G. Bradman, Melbourne	1947-48
201	D. G. Bradman, Adelaide	1947-48
161	J. W. Burke, Bombay	1956-57
204†	G. S. Chappell, Sydney	1980-81
151	I. M. Chappell, Melbourne	1967-68
138	I. M. Chappell, Delhi	1969-70
108	R. M. Cowper, Adelaide	1967-68
165	R. M. Cowper, Sydney	1967-68
101	L. E. Favell, Madras	1959-60
153	R. N. Harvey, Melbourne	1947-48
140	R. N. Harvey, Bombay	1956-57
114	R. N. Harvey, Delhi	1959-60
102	R. N. Harvey, Bombay	1959-60
198*	A. L. Hassett, Adelaide	1947-48
100	K. J. Hughes, Madras	1979-80
213	K. J. Hughes, Adelaide	1980-81
210†	D. M. Jones, Madras	1986-87
100	W. M. Lawry, Melbourne	1967-68
105	A. L. Mann, Perth	1977-78
101	G. R. Marsh, Bombay	1986-87
100*	G. R. J. Matthews, Melbourne	1985-86
100*	A. R. Morris, Melbourne	1947-48
163	N. C. O'Neill, Bombay	1959-60
113	N. C. O'Neill, Calcutta	1959-60
128†	G. M. Ritchie, Adelaide	1985-86
114	A. P. Sheahan, Kanpur	1969-70
103	R. B. Simpson, Adelaide	1967-68
109	R. B. Simpson, Melbourne	1967-68
176	R. B. Simpson, Perth	1977-78
100	R. B. Simpson, Adelaide	1977-78
103†	K. R. Stackpole, Bombay	1969-70
102	K. D. Walters, Madras	1969-70
125	G. M. Wood, Adelaide	1980-81
121†	G. N. Yallop, Adelaide	1977-78
167	G. N. Yallop, Calcutta	1979-80

For India (31)

100	M. Amarnath, Perth	1977-78
138	M. Amarnath, Sydney	1985-86
108	N. J. Contractor, Bombay	1959-60
113†	S. M. Gavaskar, Brisbane	1977-78
127	S. M. Gavaskar, Perth	1977-78
118	S. M. Gavaskar, Melbourne	1977-78
115	S. M. Gavaskar, Delhi	1979-80
123	S. M. Gavaskar, Bombay	1979-80
166*	S. M. Gavaskar, Adelaide	1985-86
172	S. M. Gavaskar, Sydney	1985-86
103	S. M. Gavaskar, Bombay	1986-87
116 145	V. S. Hazare, Adelaide	1947-48
101	M. L. Jaisimha, Brisbane	1967-68
119	Kapil Dev, Madras	1986-87
101*	S. M. H. Kirmani, Bombay	1979-80
116	V. Mankad, Melbourne	1947-48
111	V. Mankad, Melbourne	1947-48
128*†	Nawab of Pataudi, Madras	1964-6
174	S. M. Patil, Adelaide	1980-8
123	D. G. Phadkar, Adelaide	1947-48
109	G. S. Ramchand, Bombay	1956-5
121*	R. J. Shastri, Bombay	1986-8
116	K. Srikkanth, Sydney	1985-8
112	D. B. Vengsarkar, Bangalore	1979-8
164*	D. B. Vengsarkar, Bombay	1986-8
137†	G. R. Viswanath, Kanpur	1969-7
161*	G. R. Viswanath, Bangalore	1979-8
131	G. R. Viswanath, Delhi	1979-8
114	G. R. Viswanath, Melbourne	1980-8
100*	Yashpal Sharma, Delhi	1979-8

† *Signifies hundred on first appearance in Australia–India Tests.*

RECORD PARTNERSHIPS FOR EACH WICKET

For Australia

217 for 1st	D. C. Boon and G. R. Marsh at Sydney	1985-8
236 for 2nd	S. G. Barnes and D. G. Bradman at Adelaide	1947-4
222 for 3rd	A. R. Border and K. J. Hughes at Madras	1979-
178 for 4th	D. M. Jones and A. R. Border at Madras	1986-
223* for 5th	A. R. Morris and D. G. Bradman at Melbourne	1947-
151 for 6th	T. R. Veivers and B. N. Jarman at Bombay	1964-
64 for 7th	T. R. Veivers and J. W. Martin at Madras	1964-
73 for 8th	T. R. Veivers and G. D. McKenzie at Madras	1964-
87 for 9th	I. W. Johnson and W. P. A. Crawford at Madras	1956-
77 for 10th	A. R. Border and D. R. Gilbert at Melbourne	1985-

For India

192 for 1st	S. M. Gavaskar and C. P. S. Chauhan at Bombay	1979-80
224 for 2nd	S. M. Gavaskar and M. Amarnath at Sydney	1985-86
159 for 3rd	S. M. Gavaskar and G. R. Viswanath at Delhi	1979-80
159 for 4th	D. B. Vengsarkar and G. R. Viswanath at Bangalore	1979-80
109 for 5th	A. A. Baig and R. B. Kenny at Bombay	1959-60
298* for 6th†	D. B. Vengsarkar and R. J. Shastri at Bombay	1986-87
132 for 7th	V. S. Hazare and H. R. Adhikari at Adelaide	1947-48
127 for 8th	S. M. H. Kirmani and K. D. Ghavri at Bombay	1979-80
57 for 9th	S. M. H. Kirmani and K. D. Ghavri at Sydney	1980-81
94 for 10th	S. M. Gavaskar and N. S. Yadav at Adelaide	1985-86

† *Denotes record partnership against all countries.*

TEN WICKETS OR MORE IN A MATCH

For Australia (8)

1-105 (6-52, 5-53)	R. Benaud, Calcutta	1956-57
2-124 (5-31, 7-93)	A. K. Davidson, Kanpur	1959-60
2-166 (5-99, 7-67)	G. Dymock, Kanpur	1979-80
0-91 (6-58, 4-33)†	G. D. McKenzie, Madras	1964-65
0-151 (7-66, 3-85)	G. D. McKenzie, Melbourne	1967-68
0-144 (5-91, 5-53)	A. A. Mallett, Madras	1969-70
0-249 (5-103, 5-146)	G. R. J. Matthews, Madras	1986-87
1-31 (5-2, 6-29)†	E. R. H. Toshack, Brisbane	1947-48

For India (6)

0-194 (5-89, 5-105)	B. S. Bedi, Perth	1977-78
2-104 (6-52, 6-52)	B. S. Chandrasekhar, Melbourne	1977-78
0-130 (7-49, 3-81)	Ghulam Ahmed, Calcutta	1956-57
1-122 (5-31, 6-91)	R. G. Nadkarni, Madras	1964-65
4-124 (9-69, 5-55)	J. M. Patel, Kanpur	1959-60
0-174 (4-100, 6-74)	E. A. S. Prasanna, Madras	1969-70

† *Signifies ten wickets or more on first appearance in Australia–India Tests.*

AUSTRALIA v PAKISTAN

ason	*Captains* *Australia*	*Pakistan*	*T*	*A*	*P*	*D*
56-57 *P*	I. W. Johnson	A. H. Kardar	1	0	1	0
59-60 *P*	R. Benaud	Fazal Mahmood[1]	3	2	0	1
64-65 *P*	R. B. Simpson	Hanif Mohammad	1	0	0	1
64-65 *A*	R. B. Simpson	Hanif Mohammad	1	0	0	1
72-73 *A*	I. M. Chappell	Intikhab Alam	3	3	0	0
76-77 *A*	G. S. Chappell	Mushtaq Mohammad	3	1	1	1
78-79 *A*	G. N. Yallop[2]	Mushtaq Mohammad	2	1	1	0
79-80 *P*	G. S. Chappell	Javed Miandad	3	0	1	2
81-82 *A*	G. S. Chappell	Javed Miandad	3	2	1	0
82-83 *P*	K. J. Hughes	Imran Khan	3	0	3	0
83-84 *A*	K. J. Hughes	Imran Khan[3]	5	2	0	3
	In Pakistan		11	2	5	4
	In Australia		17	9	3	5
	Totals		28	11	8	9

Played in Australia. P Played in Pakistan.

tes: The following deputised for the official touring captain or were appointed by the home hority for only a minor proportion of the series:

Imtiaz Ahmed (Second). [2]K. J. Hughes (Second). [3]Zaheer Abbas (First, Second and Third).

HIGHEST INNINGS TOTALS

For Australia in Australia: 585 at Adelaide 1972-73
in Pakistan: 617 at Faisalabad 1979-80
For Pakistan in Australia: 624 at Adelaide 1983-84
in Pakistan: 501-6 dec. at Faisalabad 1982-83

LOWEST INNINGS TOTALS

For Australia in Australia: 125 at Melbourne 1981-82
in Pakistan: 80 at Karachi 1956-57
For Pakistan in Australia: 62 at Perth 1981-82
in Pakistan: 134 at Dacca 1959-60

INDIVIDUAL HUNDREDS

For Australia (32)

142	J. Benaud, Melbourne	1972-73
105†	A. R. Border, Melbourne	1978-79
150* 153	A. R. Border, Lahore	1979-80
118	A. R. Border, Brisbane	1983-84
117*	A. R. Border, Adelaide	1983-84
116*	G. S. Chappell, Melbourne	1972-73
121	G. S. Chappell, Melbourne	1976-77
235	G. S. Chappell, Faisalabad	1979-80
201	G. S. Chappell, Brisbane	1981-82
150*	G. S. Chappell, Brisbane	1983-84
182	G. S. Chappell, Sydney	1983-84
196	I. M. Chappell, Adelaide	1972-73
168	G. J. Cosier, Melbourne	1976-77
105†	I. C. Davis, Adelaide	1976-77
106	K. J. Hughes, Perth	1981-82
106	K. J. Hughes, Adelaide	1983-84
105	R. B. McCosker, Melbourne	1976-7
118†	R. W. Marsh, Adelaide	1972-7
134	N. C. O'Neill, Lahore	1959-6
159†	W. B. Phillips, Perth	1983-8
135	I. R. Redpath, Melbourne	1972-7
106*	G. M. Ritchie, Faisalabad	1982-8
127	A. P. Sheahan, Melbourne	1972-7
153† 115	R. B. Simpson, Karachi	1964-6
107	K. D. Walters, Adelaide	1976-7
179	K. C. Wessels, Adelaide	1983-8
100	G. M. Wood, Melbourne	1981-8
172	G. N. Yallop, Faisalabad	1979-8
141	G. N. Yallop, Perth	1983-8
268	G. N. Yallop, Melbourne	1983-8

For Pakistan (25)

152*	Asif Iqbal, Adelaide	1976-77
120	Asif Iqbal, Sydney	1976-77
134*	Asif Iqbal, Perth	1978-79
101*	Hanif Mohammad, Karachi	1959-60
104	Hanif Mohammad, Melbourne	1964-65
129*	Javed Miandad, Perth	1978-79
106*	Javed Miandad, Faisalabad	1979-80
138	Javed Miandad, Lahore	1982-83
131	Javed Miandad, Adelaide	1983-84
166†	Khalid Ibadulla, Karachi	1964-65
158	Majid Khan, Melbourne	1972-73
108	Majid Khan, Melbourne	1978-79
110*	Majid Khan, Lahore	1979-80
111	Mansoor Akhtar, Faisalabad	1982-83
135	Mohsin Khan, Lahore	1982-
149	Mohsin Khan, Adelaide	1983-
152	Mohsin Khan, Melbourne	1983-
121	Mushtaq Mohammad, Sydney	1972
113	Qasim Omar, Adelaide	1983-
137	Sadiq Mohammad, Melbourne	1972
105	Sadiq Mohammad, Melbourne	1976
166	Saeed Ahmed, Lahore	1959
210*	Taslim Arif, Faisalabad	1979
101	Zaheer Abbas, Adelaide	1976
126	Zaheer Abbas, Faisalabad	1982

† *Signifies hundred on first appearance in Australia–Pakistan Tests.*

RECORD PARTNERSHIPS FOR EACH WICKET

For Australia

134 for 1st	I. C. Davis and A. Turner at Melbourne	1976-77
259 for 2nd	W. B. Phillips and G. N. Yallop at Perth	1983-84
203 for 3rd	G. N. Yallop and K. J. Hughes at Melbourne	1983-84
217 for 4th	G. S. Chappell and G. N. Yallop at Faisalabad	1979-80
171 for 5th	G. S. Chappell and G. J. Cosier at Melbourne	1976-77
	A. R. Border and G. S. Chappell at Brisbane	1983-84
139 for 6th	R. M. Cowper and T. R. Veivers at Melbourne	1964-65
185 for 7th	G. N. Yallop and G. R. J. Matthews at Melbourne	1983-84
117 for 8th	G. J. Cosier and K. J. O'Keeffe at Melbourne	1976-77
83 for 9th	J. R. Watkins and R. A. L. Massie at Sydney	1972-73
52 for 10th	D. K. Lillee and M. H. N. Walker at Sydney	1976-77
	G. F. Lawson and T. M. Alderman at Lahore	1982-83

For Pakistan

49 for 1st†	Khalid Ibadulla and Abdul Kadir at Karachi	1964-65
33 for 2nd	Mohsin Khan and Qasim Omar at Adelaide	1983-84
23* for 3rd	Taslim Arif and Javed Miandad at Faisalabad	1979-80
55 for 4th	Mansoor Akhtar and Zaheer Abbas at Faisalabad	1982-83
86 for 5th	Javed Miandad and Salim Malik at Adelaide	1983-84
15 for 6th	Asif Iqbal and Javed Miandad at Sydney	1976-77
04 for 7th	Intikhab Alam and Wasim Bari at Adelaide	1972-73
11 for 8th	Majid Khan and Imran Khan at Lahore	1979-80
6 for 9th	Intikhab Alam and Afaq Hussain at Melbourne	1964-65
7 for 10th	Asif Iqbal and Iqbal Qasim at Adelaide	1976-77

† *Denotes record partnership against all countries.*

TEN WICKETS OR MORE IN A MATCH

For Australia (2)

-111 (7-87, 3-24)†	R. J. Bright, Karachi	1979-80
-135 (6-82, 4-53)	D. K. Lillee, Melbourne	1976-77
-118 (5-32, 6-86)†	C. G. Rackemann, Perth	1983-84

For Pakistan (5)

-218 (4-76, 7-142)	Abdul Qadir, Faisalabad	1982-83
-114 (6-34, 7-80)†	Fazal Mahmood, Karachi	1956-57
-165 (6-102, 6-63)	Imran Khan, Sydney	1976-77
-118 (4-69, 7-49)	Iqbal Qasim, Karachi	1979-80
-125 (2-39, 9-86)	Sarfraz Nawaz, Melbourne	1978-79

† *Signifies ten wickets or more on first appearance in Australia–Pakistan Tests.*

AUSTRALIA v SRI LANKA

	Captains					
ason	*Australia*	*Sri Lanka*	*T*	*A*	*SL*	*D*
82-83*SL*	G. S. Chappell	L. R. D. Mendis	1	1	0	0
87-88*A*	A. R. Border	R. S. Madugalle	1	1	0	0
	Totals		2	2	0	0

Played in Australia. SL Played in Sri Lanka.

INDIVIDUAL HUNDREDS

For Australia (3)

143*†	D. W. Hookes, Kandy ...	1982-83	
102†	D. M. Jones, Perth	1987-88	
141†	K. C. Wessels, Kandy ...	1982-83	

† *Signifies hundred on first appearance in Australia–Sri Lanka Tests.*

Highest score for Sri Lanka: 96 by S. Wettimuny at Kandy, 1982-83

Best bowling in an innings for Australia: 5-66 by T. G. Hogan at Kandy 1982-83
for Sri Lanka: 4-97 by K. N. Amalean at Perth 1987-88

Best wicket partnership for Australia: 170 for the 2nd by K. C. Wessels and G. N. Yallop at Kandy 1982-83
for Sri Lanka: 96 for the 5th by L. R. D. Mendis and A. Ranatunga at Kandy 1982-83

Highest innings total for Australia: 514-4 dec. at Kandy 1982-83
for Sri Lanka: 271 at Kandy 1982-83

SOUTH AFRICA v NEW ZEALAND

Captains

Season	*South Africa*	*New Zealand*	*T*	*SA*	*NZ*
1931-32*N*	H. B. Cameron	M. L. Page	2	2	0
1952-53*N*	J. E. Cheetham	W. M. Wallace	2	1	0
1953-54*S*	J. E. Cheetham	G. O. Rabone[1]	5	4	0
1961-62*S*	D. J. McGlew	J. R. Reid	5	2	2
1963-64*N*	T. L. Goddard	J. R. Reid	3	0	0
	In New Zealand		7	3	0
	In South Africa		10	6	2
	Totals		17	9	2

N Played in New Zealand. S Played in South Africa.

Note: The following deputised for the official touring captain:
[1]B. Sutcliffe (Fourth and Fifth).

HIGHEST INNINGS TOTALS

For South Africa in South Africa: 464 at Johannesburg 1961-
in New Zealand: 524-8 at Wellington 1952-

For New Zealand in South Africa: 505 at Cape Town 1953-
in New Zealand: 364 at Wellington 1931-

LOWEST INNINGS TOTALS

For South Africa in South Africa: 148 at Johannesburg 1953-
in New Zealand: 223 at Dunedin 1963-

For New Zealand in South Africa: 79 at Johannesburg 1953-
in New Zealand: 138 at Dunedin 1963-

INDIVIDUAL HUNDREDS

For South Africa (11)

22* X. C. Balaskas, Wellington ... 1931-32
03† J. A. J. Christy, Christchurch ... 1931-32
16 W. R. Endean, Auckland ... 1952-53
55*† D. J. McGlew, Wellington ... 1952-53
27*‡ D. J. McGlew, Durban ... 1961-62
20 D. J. McGlew, Johannesburg ... 1961-62
101 R. A. McLean, Durban ... 1953-54
113 R. A. McLean, Cape Town ... 1961-62
113† B. Mitchell, Christchurch ... 1931-32
109† A. R. A. Murray, Wellington ... 1952-53
101 J. H. B. Waite, Johannesburg ... 1961-62

For New Zealand (7)

09 P. T. Barton, Port Elizabeth ... 1961-62
01 P. G. Z. Harris, Cape Town ... 1961-62
07 G. O. Rabone, Durban ... 1953-54
135 J. R. Reid, Cape Town ... 1953-54
142 J. R. Reid, Johannesburg ... 1961-62
138 B. W. Sinclair, Auckland ... 1963-64
100† H. G. Vivian, Wellington ... 1931-32

† *Signifies hundred on first appearance in South Africa–New Zealand Tests.*
‡ *Carried his bat.*

RECORD PARTNERSHIPS FOR EACH WICKET

For South Africa

6 for 1st	J. A. J. Christy and B. Mitchell at Christchurch	1931-32
for 2nd	J. A. J. Christy and H. B. Cameron at Wellington	1931-32
2 for 3rd	D. J. McGlew and R. A. McLean at Johannesburg	1961-62
5 for 4th	K. J. Funston and R. A. McLean at Durban	1953-54
0 for 5th	W. R. Endean and J. E. Cheetham at Auckland	1952-53
for 6th	K. C. Bland and D. T. Lindsay at Auckland	1963-64
6 for 7th†	D. J. McGlew and A. R. A. Murray at Wellington	1952-53
for 8th	J. E. Cheetham and H. J. Tayfield at Cape Town	1953-54
for 9th	P. M. Pollock and N. A. T. Adcock at Port Elizabeth	1961-62
for 10th	D. J. McGlew and H. D. Bromfield at Port Elizabeth	1961-62

For New Zealand

6 for 1st	G. O. Rabone and M. E. Chapple at Cape Town	1953-54
for 2nd	W. P. Bradburn and B. W. Sinclair at Dunedin	1963-64
for 3rd	M. B. Poore and B. Sutcliffe at Cape Town	1953-54
for 4th	B. W. Sinclair and S. N. McGregor at Auckland	1963-64
4 for 5th	J. R. Reid and J. E. F. Beck at Cape Town	1953-54
for 6th	H. G. Vivian and F. T. Badcock at Wellington	1931-32
for 7th	J. R. Reid and G. A. Bartlett at Johannesburg	1961-62
for 8th	P. G. Z. Harris and G. A. Bartlett at Durban	1961-62
for 9th	C. F. W. Allcott and I. B. Cromb at Wellington	1931-32
* for 10th	A. E. Dick and F. J. Cameron at Cape Town	1961-62

† *Denotes record partnership against all countries.*

TEN WICKETS OR MORE IN A MATCH

For South Africa (1)

196 (6-128, 5-68)† S. F. Burke, Cape Town ... 1961-62

Signifies ten wickets or more on first appearance in South Africa–New Zealand Tests.

e: The best match figures by a New Zealand bowler are 8-180 (4-61, 4-119), J. C. Alabaster Cape Town, 1961-62.

WEST INDIES v NEW ZEALAND

Captains

Season	*West Indies*	*New Zealand*	*T*	*WI*	*NZ*	*D*
1951-52*N*	J. D. C. Goddard	B. Sutcliffe	2	1	0	1
1955-56*N*	D. St E. Atkinson	J. R. Reid[1]	4	3	1	0
1968-69*N*	G. S. Sobers	G. T. Dowling	3	1	1	1
1971-72*W*	G. S. Sobers	G. T. Dowling[2]	5	0	0	5
1979-80*N*	C. H. Lloyd	G. P. Howarth	3	0	1	2
1984-85*W*	I. V. A. Richards	G. P. Howarth	4	2	0	2
1986-87*N*	I. V. A. Richards	J. V. Coney	3	1	1	1
	In New Zealand		15	6	4	
	In West Indies		9	2	0	[illegible]
	Totals		24	8	4	1[illegible]

N Played in New Zealand. W Played in West Indies.

Notes: The following deputised for the official touring captain or were appointed by the hom authority for only a minor proportion of the series:
[1]H. B. Cave (First). [2]B. E. Congdon (Third, Fourth and Fifth).

HIGHEST INNINGS TOTALS

For West Indies in West Indies: 564-8 at Bridgetown 1971-7
in New Zealand: 546-6 dec. at Auckland 1951-5

For New Zealand in West Indies: 543-3 dec. at Georgetown 1971-7
in New Zealand: 460 at Christchurch 1979-8

LOWEST INNINGS TOTALS

For West Indies in West Indies: 133 at Bridgetown 1971-7
in New Zealand: 77 at Auckland 1955-5

For New Zealand in West Indies: 94 at Bridgetown 1984-8
in New Zealand: 74 at Dunedin 1955-5

INDIVIDUAL HUNDREDS

By West Indies (25)

109† M. C. Carew, Auckland ... 1968-69
183 C. A. Davis, Bridgetown .. 1971-72
163 R. C. Fredericks, Kingston 1971-72
100 C. G. Greenidge, Port-of-Spain 1984-85
213 C. G. Greenidge, Auckland 1986-87
105† D. L. Haynes, Dunedin ... 1979-80
122 D. L. Haynes, Christchurch 1979-80
121 D. L. Haynes, Wellington . 1986-87
100*† A. I. Kallicharran, Georgetown 1971-72
101 A. I. Kallicharran, Port-of-Spain 1971-72
100* C. L. King, Christchurch .. 1979-80
168† S. M. Nurse, Auckland ... 1968-69
258 S. M. Nurse, Christchurch . 1968
105 I. V. A. Richards, Bridgetown 1984
185 R. B. Richardson, Georgetown 1984
214† }
100* } L. G. Rowe, Kingston 1971
100 L. G. Rowe, Christchurch . 1979
142 G. S. Sobers, Bridgetown .. 1971
152 J. B. Stollmeyer, Auckland . 1951
115 C. L. Walcott, Auckland .. 1951
123 E. D. Weekes, Dunedin ... 1955
103 E. D. Weekes, Christchurch 1955
156 E. D. Weekes, Wellington . 1955
100 F. M. M. Worrell, Auckland 1951

By New Zealand (17)

01	M. G. Burgess, Kingston	1971-72	117*	B. F. Hastings, Christchurch	1968-69
66*	B. E. Congdon, Port-of-Spain	1971-72	105	B. F. Hastings, Bridgetown	1971-72
26	B. E. Congdon, Bridgetown	1971-72	147	G. P. Howarth, Christchurch	1979-80
12	J. J. Crowe, Kingston	1984-85	182	T. W. Jarvis, Georgetown	1971-72
88	M. D. Crowe, Georgetown	1984-85	124†	B. R. Taylor, Auckland	1968-69
19	M. D. Crowe, Wellington	1986-87	223*‡	G. M. Turner, Kingston	1971-72
04	M. D. Crowe, Auckland	1986-87	259	G. M. Turner, Georgetown	1971-72
27	B. A. Edgar, Auckland	1979-80	138	J. G. Wright, Wellington	1986-87
03	R. J. Hadlee, Christchurch	1979-80			

† *Signifies hundred on first appearance in West Indies–New Zealand Tests.*
‡ *Carried his bat.*

otes: E. D. Weekes in 1955-56 made three hundreds in consecutive innings.
L. G. Rowe and A. I. Kallicharran each scored hundreds in their first two innings in Test icket, Rowe being the only batsman to do so in his first match.

RECORD PARTNERSHIPS FOR EACH WICKET

For West Indies

5 for 1st	C. G. Greenidge and D. L. Haynes at Christchurch	1979-80
9 for 2nd	R. C. Fredericks and L. G. Rowe at Kingston	1971-72
5 for 3rd	C. G. Greenidge and R. B. Richardson at Port-of-Spain	1984-85
2 for 4th	E. D. Weekes and O. G. Smith at Dunedin	1955-56
	C. G. Greenidge and A. I. Kallicharran at Christchurch	1979-80
9 for 5th	F. M. M. Worrell and C. L. Walcott at Auckland	1951-52
4 for 6th	C. A. Davis and G. S. Sobers at Bridgetown	1971-72
3 for 7th	D. St E. Atkinson and J. D. C. Goddard at Christchurch	1955-56
for 8th	I. V. A. Richards and M. D. Marshall at Bridgetown	1984-85
for 9th	M. D. Marshall and J. Garner at Bridgetown	1984-85
for 10th	T. M. Findlay and G. C. Shillingford at Bridgetown	1971-72

For New Zealand

7 for 1st†	G. M. Turner and T. W. Jarvis at Georgetown	1971-72
0 for 2nd†	G. P. Howarth and J. J. Crowe at Kingston	1984-85
1 for 3rd†	J. G. Wright and M. D. Crowe at Wellington	1986-87
5 for 4th	B. E. Congdon and B. F. Hastings at Bridgetown	1971-72
2 for 5th	M. D. Crowe and J. V. Coney at Georgetown	1984-85
0 for 6th	G. M. Turner and K. J. Wadsworth at Kingston	1971-72
3 for 7th	M. D. Crowe and I. D. S. Smith at Georgetown	1984-85
for 8th†	B. E. Congdon and R. S. Cunis at Port-of-Spain	1971-72
for 9th	V. Pollard and R. S. Cunis at Auckland	1968-69
for 10th	B. E. Congdon and J. C. Alabaster at Port-of-Spain	1971-72

Denotes record partnership against all countries.

TEN WICKETS OR MORE IN A MATCH

For West Indies (1)

20 (4-40, 7-80)	M. D. Marshall, Bridgetown	1984-85

For New Zealand (3)

24 (4-51, 6-73)†	E. J. Chatfield, Port-of-Spain	1984-85
02 (5-34, 6-68)†	R. J. Hadlee, Dunedin	1979-80
66 (4-71, 6-95)	G. B. Troup, Auckland	1979-80

Signifies ten wickets or more on first appearance in West Indies–New Zealand Tests.

WEST INDIES v INDIA

	Captains					
Season	*West Indies*	*India*	*T*	*WI*	*I*	*D*
1948-49*I*	J. D. C. Goddard	L. Amarnath	5	1	0	4
1952-53*W*	J. B. Stollmeyer	V. S. Hazare	5	1	0	4
1958-59*I*	F. C. M. Alexander	Ghulam Ahmed[1]	5	3	0	2
1961-62*W*	F. M. M. Worrell	N. J. Contractor[2]	5	5	0	0
1966-67*I*	G. S. Sobers	Nawab of Pataudi jun.	3	2	0	[illegible]
1970-71*W*	G. S. Sobers	A. L. Wadekar	5	0	1	4
1974-75*I*	C. H. Lloyd	Nawab of Pataudi jun.[3]	5	3	2	0
1975-76*W*	C. H. Lloyd	B. S. Bedi	4	2	1	[illegible]
1978-79*I*	A. I. Kallicharran	S. M. Gavaskar	6	0	1	[illegible]
1982-83*W*	C. H. Lloyd	Kapil Dev	5	2	0	[illegible]
1983-84*I*	C. H. Lloyd	Kapil Dev	6	3	0	[illegible]
1987-88*I*	I. V. A. Richards	D. B. Vengsarkar[4]	4	1	1	[illegible]
	In India		34	13	4	1[illegible]
	In West Indies		24	10	2	1[illegible]
	Totals		58	23	6	2[illegible]

I Played in India. W Played in West Indies.

Notes: The following deputised for the official touring captain or were appointed by the hom authority for only a minor proportion of the series:

[1]P. R. Umrigar (First), V. Mankad (Fourth), H. R. Adhikari (Fifth). [2]Nawab of Pataudi jur (Third, Fourth and Fifth). [3]S. Venkataraghavan (Second). [4]R. J. Shastri (Fourth).

HIGHEST INNINGS TOTALS

For West Indies in West Indies: 631-8 dec. at Kingston 1961-6
in India: 644-8 dec. at Delhi 1958-5

For India in West Indies: 469-7 at Port-of-Spain 1982-8
in India: 644-7 dec. at Kanpur 1978-7

LOWEST INNINGS TOTALS

For West Indies in West Indies: 214 at Port-of-Spain 1970-7
in India: 127 at Delhi 1987-8

For India in West Indies: 97† at Kingston 1975-
in India: 75 at Delhi 1987-

† *Five men absent hurt.*

INDIVIDUAL HUNDREDS

For West Indies (71)

250	S. F. A. F. Bacchus, Kanpur	1978-79
103	B. F. Butcher, Calcutta	1958-59
142	B. F. Butcher, Madras	1958-59
107†	R. J. Christiani, Delhi	1948-49
125*	C. A. Davis, Georgetown	1970-71
105	C. A. Davis, Port-of-Spain	1970-71
110	P. J. L. Dujon, St John's	1982-83
100	R. C. Fredericks, Calcutta	1974-75
104	R. C. Fredericks, Bombay	1974-75
123	H. A. Gomes, Port-of-Spain	1982-83
101†	G. E. Gomez, Delhi	1948-49
107†	C. G. Greenidge, Bangalore	1974-75
154*	C. G. Greenidge, St John's	1982
194	C. G. Greenidge, Kanpur	1983
141	C. G. Greenidge, Calcutta	1987
136	D. L. Haynes, St John's	1982
123	J. K. Holt, Delhi	1958
100*	C. L. Hooper, Calcutta	1987
101	C. C. Hunte, Bombay	1966
124†	A. I. Kallicharran, Bangalore	1974
103*	A. I. Kallicharran, Port-of-Spain	1975
187	A. I. Kallicharran, Bombay	1978
256	R. B. Kanhai, Calcutta	1958

138	R. B. Kanhai, Kingston	1961-62
139	R. B. Kanhai, Port-of-Spain	1961-62
158*	R. B. Kanhai, Kingston	1970-71
163	C. H. Lloyd, Bangalore	1974-75
242*	C. H. Lloyd, Bombay	1974-75
102	C. H. Lloyd, Bridgetown	1975-76
143	C. H. Lloyd, Port-of-Spain	1982-83
106	C. H. Lloyd, St John's	1982-83
103	C. H. Lloyd, Delhi	1983-84
161*	C. H. Lloyd, Calcutta	1983-84
130	A. L. Logie, Bridgetown	1982-83
101	A. L. Logie, Calcutta	1987-88
125†	E. D. A. McMorris, Kingston	1961-62
15†	B. H. Pairaudeau, Port-of-Spain	1952-53
04	A. F. Rae, Bombay	1948-49
09	A. F. Rae, Madras	1948-49
92*	I. V. A. Richards, Delhi	1974-75
42	I. V. A. Richards, Bridgetown	1975-76
30	I. V. A. Richards, Port-of-Spain	1975-76
77	I. V. A. Richards, Port-of-Spain	1975-76
09	I. V. A. Richards, Georgetown	1982-83
20	I. V. A. Richards, Bombay	1983-84
09*	I. V. A. Richards, Delhi	1987-88
100	O. G. Smith, Delhi	1958-59
142*†	G. S. Sobers, Bombay	1958-59
198	G. S. Sobers, Kanpur	1958-59
106*	G. S. Sobers, Calcutta	1958-59
153	G. S. Sobers, Kingston	1961-62
104	G. S. Sobers, Kingston	1961-62
108*	G. S. Sobers, Georgetown	1970-71
178*	G. S. Sobers, Bridgetown	1970-71
132	G. S. Sobers, Port-of-Spain	1970-71
100*	J. S. Solomon, Delhi	1958-59
160	J. B. Stollmeyer, Madras	1948-49
104*	J. B. Stollmeyer, Port-of-Spain	1952-53
152†	C. L. Walcott, Delhi	1948-49
108	C. L. Walcott, Calcutta	1948-49
125	C. L. Walcott, Georgetown	1952-53
118	C. L. Walcott, Kingston	1952-53
128†	E. D. Weekes, Delhi	1948-49
194	E. D. Weekes, Bombay	1948-49
162 101	E. D. Weekes, Calcutta	1948-49
207	E. D. Weekes, Port-of-Spain	1952-53
161	E. D. Weekes, Port-of-Spain	1952-53
109	E. D. Weekes, Kingston	1952-53
111	A. B. Williams, Calcutta	1978-79
237	F. M. M. Worrell, Kingston	1952-53

For India (52)

14*†	H. R. Adhikari, Delhi	1948-49
01*	M. Amarnath, Kanpur	1978-79
17	M. Amarnath, Port-of-Spain	1982-83
16	M. Amarnath, St John's	1982-83
63*	M. L. Apte, Port-of-Spain	1952-53
09	C. G. Borde, Delhi	1958-59
21	C. G. Borde, Bombay	1966-67
25	C. G. Borde, Madras	1966-67
04	S. A. Durani, Port-of-Spain	1961-62
09	F. M. Engineer, Madras	1966-67
02	A. D. Gaekwad, Kanpur	1978-79
6	S. M. Gavaskar, Georgetown	1970-71
7*	S. M. Gavaskar, Bridgetown	1970-71
4 0	S. M. Gavaskar, Port-of-Spain	1970-71
6	S. M. Gavaskar, Port-of-Spain	1975-76
2	S. M. Gavaskar, Port-of-Spain	1975-76
5	S. M. Gavaskar, Bombay	1978-79
7 2*	S. M. Gavaskar, Calcutta	1978-79
0	S. M. Gavaskar, Delhi	1978-79
7*	S. M. Gavaskar, Georgetown	1982-83
1	S. M. Gavaskar, Delhi	1983-84
5*	S. M. Gavaskar, Madras	1983-84
4*	V. S. Hazare, Bombay	1948-49
122	V. S. Hazare, Bombay	1948-49
126*	Kapil Dev, Delhi	1978-79
100*	Kapil Dev, Port-of-Spain	1982-83
109	Kapil Dev, Madras	1987-88
118	V. L. Manjrekar, Kingston	1952-53
112	R. S. Modi, Bombay	1948-49
106†	Mushtaq Ali, Calcutta	1948-49
115*	B. P. Patel, Port-of-Spain	1975-76
150	P. Roy, Kingston	1952-53
212	D. N. Sardesai, Kingston	1970-71
112	D. N. Sardesai, Port-of-Spain	1970-71
150	D. N. Sardesai, Bridgetown	1970-71
102	R. J. Shastri, St John's	1982-83
102	E. D. Solkar, Bombay	1974-75
130	P. R. Umrigar, Port-of-Spain	1952-53
117	P. R. Umrigar, Kingston	1952-53
172*	P. R. Umrigar, Port-of-Spain	1961-62
157*	D. B. Vengsarkar, Calcutta	1978-79
109	D. B. Vengsarkar, Delhi	1978-79
159	D. B. Vengsarkar, Delhi	1983-84
100	D. B. Vengsarkar, Bombay	1983-84
102	D. B. Vengsarkar, Delhi	1987-88
102*	D. B. Vengsarkar, Calcutta	1987-88
139	G. R. Viswanath, Calcutta	1974-75
112	G. R. Viswanath, Port-of-Spain	1975-76
124	G. R. Viswanath, Madras	1978-79
179	G. R. Viswanath, Kanpur	1978-79

† *Signifies hundred on first appearance in West Indies–India Tests.*

RECORD PARTNERSHIPS FOR EACH WICKET

For West Indies

296 for 1st†	C. G. Greenidge and D. L. Haynes at St John's	1982-83
255 for 2nd	E. D. A. McMorris and R. B. Kanhai at Kingston	1961-62
220 for 3rd	I. V. A. Richards and A. I. Kallicharran at Bridgetown	1975-76
267 for 4th	C. L. Walcott and G. E. Gomez at Delhi	1948-49
219 for 5th	E. D. Weekes and B. H. Pairaudeau at Port-of-Spain	1952-53
250 for 6th	C. H. Lloyd and D. L. Murray at Bombay	1974-75
130 for 7th	C. G. Greenidge and M. D. Marshall at Kanpur	1983-84
124 for 8th†	I. V. A. Richards and K. D. Boyce at Delhi	1974-75
161 for 9th†	C. H. Lloyd and A. M. E. Roberts at Calcutta	1983-84
98* for 10th†	F. M. M. Worrell and W. W. Hall at Port-of-Spain	1961-62

For India

153 for 1st	S. M. Gavaskar and C. P. S. Chauhan at Bombay	1978-79
344* for 2nd†	S. M. Gavaskar and D. B. Vengsarkar at Calcutta	1978-79
159 for 3rd	M. Amarnath and G. R. Viswanath at Port-of-Spain	1975-76
172 for 4th	G. R. Viswanath and A. D. Gaekwad at Kanpur	1978-79
204 for 5th	S. M. Gavaskar and B. P. Patel at Port-of-Spain	1975-76
170 for 6th	S. M. Gavaskar and R. J. Shastri at Madras	1983-84
186 for 7th	D. N. Sardesai and E. D. Solkar at Bridgetown	1970-71
107 for 8th	Yashpal Sharma and B. S. Sandhu at Kingston	1982-83
143* for 9th	S. M. Gavaskar and S. M. H. Kirmani at Madras	1983-84
62 for 10th	D. N. Sardesai and B. S. Bedi at Bridgetown	1970-71

† *Denotes record partnership against all countries.*

TEN WICKETS OR MORE IN A MATCH

For West Indies (2)

11-126 (6-50, 5-76)	W. W. Hall, Kanpur	1958-59
12-121 (7-64, 5-57)	A. M. E. Roberts, Madras	1974-75

For India (4)

11-235 (7-157, 4-78)†	B. S. Chandrasekhar, Bombay	1966-67
10-223 (9-102, 1-121)	S. P. Gupte, Kanpur	1958-59
16-136 (8-61, 8-75)†	N. D. Hirwani, Madras	1987-88
10-135 (1-52, 9-83)	Kapil Dev, Ahmedabad	1983-8

† *Signifies ten wickets or more on first appearance in West Indies–India Tests.*

WEST INDIES v PAKISTAN

Captains

Season	*West Indies*	*Pakistan*	*T*	*WI*	*P*
1957-58*W*	F. C. M. Alexander	A. H. Kardar	5	3	1
1958-59*P*	F. C. M. Alexander	Fazal Mahmood	3	1	2
1974-75*P*	C. H. Lloyd	Intikhab Alam	2	0	0
1976-77*W*	C. H. Lloyd	Mushtaq Mohammad	5	2	1
1980-81*P*	C. H. Lloyd	Javed Miandad	4	1	0
1986-87*P*	I. V. A. Richards	Imran Khan	3	1	1
1987-88*W*	I. V. A. Richards[1]	Imran Khan	3	1	1
	In West Indies		13	6	3
	In Pakistan		12	3	3
	Totals		25	9	6

P Played in Pakistan. W Played in West Indies.

Note: The following was appointed by the home authority for only a minor proportion of t series:

[1]C. G. Greenidge (First).

HIGHEST INNINGS TOTALS

For West Indies in West Indies: 790-3 dec. at Kingston 1957-58
in Pakistan: 493 at Karachi 1974-75

For Pakistan in West Indies: 657-8 dec. at Bridgetown 1957-58
in Pakistan: 406-8 dec. at Karachi 1974-75

LOWEST INNINGS TOTALS

For West Indies in West Indies: 154 at Port-of-Spain 1976-77
in Pakistan: 53 at Faisalabad 1986-87

For Pakistan in West Indies: 106 at Bridgetown 1957-58
in Pakistan: 77 at Lahore 1986-87

INDIVIDUAL HUNDREDS

For West Indies (19)

105*†	L. Baichan, Lahore	1974-75
06*	P. J. L. Dujon, Port-of-Spain	1987-88
20	R. C. Fredericks, Port-of-Spain	1976-77
00	C. G. Greenidge, Kingston	1976-77
42†	C. C. Hunte, Bridgetown	1957-58
60	C. C. Hunte, Kingston	1957-58
14	C. C. Hunte, Georgetown	1957-58
01	B. D. Julien, Karachi	1974-75
15	A. I. Kallicharran, Karachi	1974-75
17	R. B. Kanhai, Lahore	1958-59
157	C. H. Lloyd, Bridgetown	1976-77
120*	I. V. A. Richards, Multan	1980-81
123	I. V. A. Richards, Port-of-Spain	1987-88
120	I. T. Shillingford, Georgetown	1976-77
365*	G. S. Sobers, Kingston	1957-58
125 } 109* }	G. S. Sobers, Georgetown	1957-58
145	C. L. Walcott, Georgetown	1957-58
197†	E. D. Weekes, Bridgetown	1957-58

Pakistan (16)

35	Asif Iqbal, Kingston	1976-77
37†	Hanif Mohammad, Bridgetown	1957-58
03	Hanif Mohammad, Karachi	1958-59
22	Imtiaz Ahmed, Kingston	1957-58
23	Imran Khan, Lahore	1980-81
4	Javed Miandad, Georgetown	1987-88
2	Javed Miandad, Port-of-Spain	1987-88
0	Majid Khan, Karachi	1974-75
7	Majid Khan, Georgetown	1976-77
123	Mushtaq Mohammad, Lahore	1974-75
121	Mushtaq Mohammad, Port-of-Spain	1976-77
150	Saeed Ahmed, Georgetown	1957-58
107*	Wasim Raja, Karachi	1974-75
117*	Wasim Raja, Bridgetown	1976-77
106	Wazir Mohammad, Kingston	1957-58
189	Wazir Mohammad, Port-of-Spain	1957-58

† *Signifies hundred on first appearance in West Indies–Pakistan Tests.*

RECORD PARTNERSHIPS FOR EACH WICKET

For West Indies

2 for 1st	R. C. Fredericks and C. G. Greenidge at Kingston	1976-77
5 for 2nd†	C. C. Hunte and G. S. Sobers at Kingston	1957-58
2 for 3rd	R. B. Kanhai and G. S. Sobers at Lahore	1958-59
8* for 4th	G. S. Sobers and C. L. Walcott at Kingston	1957-58
5 for 5th	E. D. Weekes and O. G. Smith at Bridgetown	1957-58
1 for 6th	C. H. Lloyd and D. L. Murray at Bridgetown	1976-77
for 7th	C. H. Lloyd and J. Garner at Bridgetown	1976-77
for 8th	B. D. Julien and V. A. Holder at Karachi	1974-75
* for 9th	P. J. L. Dujon and W. K. M. Benjamin at Bridgetown	1987-88
for 10th	R. Nanan and S. T. Clarke at Faisalabad	1980-81

For Pakistan

159 for 1st‡	Majid Khan and Zaheer Abbas at Georgetown	1976-77
178 for 2nd	Hanif Mohammad and Saeed Ahmed at Karachi	1958-59
169 for 3rd	Saeed Ahmed and Wazir Mohammad at Port-of-Spain	1957-58
154 for 4th	Wazir Mohammad and Hanif Mohammad at Port-of-Spain	1957-58
87 for 5th	Mushtaq Mohammad and Asif Iqbal at Kingston	1976-77
166 for 6th	Wazir Mohammad and A. H. Kardar at Kingston	1957-58
128 for 7th	Wasim Raja and Wasim Bari at Karachi	1974-75
94 for 8th	Salim Malik and Salim Yousuf at Port-of-Spain	1987-88
73 for 9th	Wasim Raja and Sarfraz Nawaz at Bridgetown	1976-77
133 for 10th†	Wasim Raja and Wasim Bari at Bridgetown	1976-77

† *Denotes record partnership against all countries.*

‡ *219 runs were added for this wicket in two separate partnerships: Sadiq Mohammad retired hurt and was replaced by Zaheer Abbas when 60 had been added. The highest partnership by two opening batsmen is 152 by Hanif Mohammad and Imtiaz Ahmed at Bridgetown, 1957-58.*

TEN WICKETS OR MORE IN A MATCH

For Pakistan (2)

12-100 (6-34, 6-66)	Fazal Mahmood, Dacca	1958-59
11-121 (7-80, 4-41)	Imran Khan, Georgetown	1987-88

Note: The best match figures by a West Indian bowler are 9-95 (8-29, 1-66) by C. E. H. Croft a Port-of-Spain, 1976-77.

NEW ZEALAND v INDIA

Captains

Season	*New Zealand*	*India*	*T*	*NZ*	*I*	*L*
1955-56*I*	H. B. Cave	P. R. Umrigar[1]	5	0	2	
1964-65*I*	J. R. Reid	Nawab of Pataudi jun.	4	0	1	
1967-68*N*	G. T. Dowling[2]	Nawab of Pataudi jun.	4	1	3	
1969-70*I*	G. T. Dowling	Nawab of Pataudi jun.	3	1	1	
1975-76*N*	G. M. Turner	B. S. Bedi[3]	3	1	1	
1976-77*I*	G. M. Turner	B. S. Bedi	3	0	2	
1980-81*N*	G. P. Howarth	S. M. Gavaskar	3	1	0	
	In India		15	1	6	
	In New Zealand		10	3	4	
	Totals		25	4	10	1

I Played in India. N Played in New Zealand.

Notes: The following deputised for the official touring captain or were appointed by the hon authority for a minor proportion of the series:

[1]Ghulam Ahmed (First). [2]B. W. Sinclair (First). [3]S. M. Gavaskar (First).

HIGHEST INNINGS TOTALS

For New Zealand in New Zealand: 502 at Christchurch	1967-
in India: 462-9 dec. at Calcutta	1964-
450-2 dec. at Delhi	1955-
For India in New Zealand: 414 at Auckland	1975-
in India: 537-3 dec. at Madras	1955-

LOWEST INNINGS TOTALS

For New Zealand in New Zealand: 100 at Wellington 1980-81
in India: 127 at Bombay 1969-70

For India in New Zealand: 81 at Wellington 1975-76
in India: 88 at Bombay 1964-65

INDIVIDUAL HUNDREDS

For New Zealand (16)

120	G. T. Dowling, Bombay	1964-65
143	G. T. Dowling, Dunedin	1967-68
239	G. T. Dowling, Christchurch	1967-68
102†	J. W. Guy, Hyderabad	1955-56
137*	G. P. Howarth, Wellington	1980-81
104	J. M. Parker, Bombay	1976-77
123*	J. F. Reid, Christchurch	1980-81
119*	J. R. Reid, Delhi	1955-56
120	J. R. Reid, Calcutta	1955-56
137*†	B. Sutcliffe, Hyderabad	1955-56
230*	B. Sutcliffe, Delhi	1955-56
151*	B. Sutcliffe, Calcutta	1964-65
105†	B. R. Taylor, Calcutta	1964-65
117	G. M. Turner, Christchurch	1975-76
113	G. M. Turner, Kanpur	1976-77
110	J. G. Wright, Auckland	1980-81

For India (20)

124†	S. Amarnath, Auckland	1975-76
109	C. G. Borde, Bombay	1964-65
116†	S. M. Gavaskar, Auckland	1975-76
119	S. M. Gavaskar, Bombay	1976-77
100*†	A. G. Kripal Singh, Hyderabad	1955-56
118†	V. L. Manjrekar, Hyderabad	1955-56
77	V. L. Manjrekar, Delhi	1955-56
02*	V. L. Manjrekar, Madras	1964-65
23	V. Mankad, Bombay	1955-56
31	V. Mankad, Madras	1955-56
153	Nawab of Pataudi jun., Calcutta	1964-65
113	Nawab of Pataudi jun., Delhi	1964-65
106*	G. S. Ramchand, Calcutta	1955-56
100	Pankaj Roy, Calcutta	1955-56
173	Pankaj Roy, Madras	1955-56
200*	D. N. Sardesai, Bombay	1964-65
106	D. N. Sardesai, Delhi	1964-65
223†	P. R. Umrigar, Hyderabad	1955-56
103*	G. R. Viswanath, Kanpur	1976-77
143	A. L. Wadekar, Wellington	1967-68

† *Signifies hundred on first appearance in New Zealand–India Tests. B. R. Taylor provides the nly instance for New Zealand of a player scoring his maiden hundred in first-class cricket in his first est.*

RECORD PARTNERSHIPS FOR EACH WICKET

For New Zealand

26 for 1st	B. A. G. Murray and G. T. Dowling at Christchurch	1967-68
55 for 2nd	G. T. Dowling and B. E. Congdon at Dunedin	1967-68
22* for 3rd	B. Sutcliffe and J. R. Reid at Delhi	1955-56
3 for 4th	G. T. Dowling and M. G. Burgess at Christchurch	1967-68
9 for 5th	G. T. Dowling and K. Thomson at Christchurch	1967-68
for 6th	J. W. Guy and A. R. MacGibbon at Hyderabad	1955-56
3 for 7th	B. Sutcliffe and B. R. Taylor at Calcutta	1964-65
for 8th	V. Pollard and G. E. Vivian at Calcutta	1964-65
for 9th	M. G. Burgess and J. C. Alabaster at Dunedin	1967-68
for 10th	J. T. Ward and R. O. Collinge at Madras	1964-65

For India

413 for 1st†	V. Mankad and Pankaj Roy at Madras	1955-56
204 for 2nd	S. M. Gavaskar and S. Amarnath at Auckland	1975-76
238 for 3rd	P. R. Umrigar and V. L. Manjrekar at Hyderabad	1955-56
171 for 4th	P. R. Umrigar and A. G. Kripal Singh at Hyderabad	1955-56
127 for 5th	V. L. Manjrekar and G. S. Ramchand at Delhi	1955-56
193* for 6th	D. N. Sardesai and Hanumant Singh at Bombay	1964-65
116 for 7th	B. P. Patel and S. M. H. Kirmani at Wellington	1975-76
143 for 8th†	R. G. Nadkarni and F. M. Engineer at Madras	1964-65
105 for 9th	S. M. H. Kirmani and B. S. Bedi at Bombay	1976-77
	S. M. H. Kirmani and N. S. Yadav at Auckland	1980-81
57 for 10th	R. B. Desai and B. S. Bedi at Dunedin	1967-68

† *Denotes record partnership against all countries.*

TEN WICKETS OR MORE IN A MATCH

For New Zealand (1)

11-58 (4-35, 7-23)	R. J. Hadlee, Wellington	1975-76

For India (2)

11-140 (3-64, 8-76)	E. A. S. Prasanna, Auckland	1975-76
12-152 (8-72, 4-80)	S. Venkataraghavan, Delhi	1964-65

NEW ZEALAND v PAKISTAN

	Captains					
Season	*New Zealand*	*Pakistan*	*T*	*NZ*	*P*	*D*
1955-56*P*	H. B. Cave	A. H. Kardar	3	0	2	1
1964-65*N*	J. R. Reid	Hanif Mohammad	3	0	0	3
1964-65*P*	J. R. Reid	Hanif Mohammad	3	0	2	1
1969-70*P*	G. T. Dowling	Intikhab Alam	3	1	0	2
1972-73*N*	B. E. Congdon	Intikhab Alam	3	0	1	2
1976-77*P*	G. M. Turner[1]	Mushtaq Mohammad	3	0	2	1
1978-79*N*	M. G. Burgess	Mushtaq Mohammad	3	0	1	2
1984-85*P*	J. V. Coney	Zaheer Abbas	3	0	2	1
1984-85*N*	G. P. Howarth	Javed Miandad	3	2	0	1
	In Pakistan		15	1	8	6
	In New Zealand		12	2	2	8
	Totals		27	3	10	14

N Played in New Zealand. P Played in Pakistan.

Note: The following deputised for the official touring captain:
[1]J. M. Parker (Third).

HIGHEST INNINGS TOTALS

For New Zealand in New Zealand 492 at Wellington	1984-8
in Pakistan: 482-6 dec. at Lahore	1964-6
For Pakistan in New Zealand: 507-6 dec. at Dunedin	1972-7
in Pakistan: 565-9 dec. at Karachi	1976-7
561 at Lahore	1955-5

LOWEST INNINGS TOTALS

For New Zealand in New Zealand: 156 at Dunedin	1972-7
in Pakistan: 70 at Dacca	1955-5
For Pakistan in New Zealand: 169 at Auckland	1984-8
in Pakistan: 114 at Lahore	1969-7

INDIVIDUAL HUNDREDS

For New Zealand (16)

119* M. G. Burgess, Dacca 1969-70
111 M. G. Burgess, Lahore 1976-77
111* J. V. Coney, Dunedin 1984-85
129† B. A. Edgar, Christchurch . 1978-79
110 B. F. Hastings, Auckland .. 1972-73
114 G. P. Howarth, Napier ... 1978-79
152 W. K. Lees, Karachi 1976-77
111 S. N. McGregor, Lahore .. 1955-56
107† R. E. Redmond, Auckland . 1972-73
106 J. F. Reid, Hyderabad 1984-85
148 J. F. Reid, Wellington 1984-85
158* J. F. Reid, Auckland 1984-85
128 J. R. Reid, Karachi 1964-65
130 B. W. Sinclair, Lahore 1964-65
110† G. M. Turner, Dacca 1969-70
107 J. G. Wright, Karachi 1984-85

For Pakistan (26)

175 Asif Iqbal, Dunedin 1972-73
166 Asif Iqbal, Lahore 1976-77
104 Asif Iqbal, Napier 1978-79
103 Hanif Mohammad, Dacca . 1955-56
100* Hanif Mohammad, Christchurch 1964-65
203* Hanif Mohammad, Lahore 1964-65
209 Imtiaz Ahmed, Lahore 1955-56
63† Javed Miandad, Lahore ... 1976-77
206 Javed Miandad, Karachi .. 1976-77
60* Javed Miandad, Christchurch 1978-79
04 } Javed Miandad, Hyderabad 1984-85
03* }
10 Majid Khan, Auckland ... 1972-73
12 Majid Khan, Karachi 1976-77
19* Majid Khan, Napier 1978-79
126 Mohammad Ilyas, Karachi 1964-65
106 Mudassar Nazar, Hyderabad 1984-85
201 Mushtaq Mohammad, Dunedin 1972-73
101 Mushtaq Mohammad, Hyderabad 1976-77
107 Mushtaq Mohammad, Karachi 6-77
166 Sadiq Mohammad, Wellington 1972-73
103* Sadiq Mohammad, Hyderabad 1976-77
172 Saeed Ahmed, Karachi 1964-65
119* Salim Malik, Karachi 1984-85
189 Waqar Hassan, Lahore 1955-56
135 Zaheer Abbas, Auckland .. 1978-79

† *Signifies hundred on first appearance in New Zealand–Pakistan Tests.*

ote: Mushtaq and Sadiq Mohammad, at Hyderabad in 1976-77, provide the fourth instance in est matches, after the Chappells (thrice), of brothers each scoring hundreds in the same nnings.

RECORD PARTNERSHIPS FOR EACH WICKET

For New Zealand

9 for 1st	R. E. Redmond and G. M. Turner at Auckland	1972-73
5 for 2nd	J. G. Wright and G. P. Howarth at Napier	1978-79
8 for 3rd	B. W. Sinclair and J. R. Reid at Lahore	1964-65
8 for 4th	B. F. Hastings and M. G. Burgess at Wellington	1972-73
3 for 5th†	M. G. Burgess and R. W. Anderson at Lahore	1976-77
5 for 6th	J. F. Reid and R. J. Hadlee at Wellington	1984-85
6 for 7th†	W. K. Lees and R. J. Hadlee at Karachi	1976-77
0 for 8th	B. W. Yuile and D. R. Hadlee at Karachi	1969-70
for 9th	M. G. Burgess and R. S. Cunis at Dacca	1969-70
1 for 10th†	B. F. Hastings and R. O. Collinge at Auckland	1972-73

For Pakistan

147 for 1st‡	Sadiq Mohammad and Majid Khan at Karachi	1976-77
114 for 2nd	Mohammad Ilyas and Saeed Ahmed at Rawalpindi	1964-65
212 for 3rd	Mudassar Nazar and Javed Miandad at Hyderabad	1984-85
350 for 4th†	Mushtaq Mohammad and Asif Iqbal at Dunedin	1972-73
281 for 5th†	Javed Miandad and Asif Iqbal at Lahore	1976-77
217 for 6th†	Hanif Mohammad and Majid Khan at Lahore	1964-65
308 for 7th†	Waqar Hassan and Imtiaz Ahmed at Lahore	1955-56
89 for 8th	Anil Dalpat and Iqbal Qasim at Karachi	1984-85
52 for 9th	Intikhab Alam and Arif Butt at Auckland	1964-65
65 for 10th	Salah-ud-Din and Mohammad Farooq at Rawalpindi	1964-65

† *Denotes record partnership against all countries.*

‡ *In the preceding Test of this series, at Hyderabad, 164 runs were added for this wicket by Sadiq Mohammad, Majid Khan and Zaheer Abbas. Sadiq Mohammad retired hurt after 136 had been scored.*

TEN WICKETS OR MORE IN A MATCH

For Pakistan (4)

10-182 (5-91, 5-91)	Intikhab Alam, Dacca	1969-70
11-130 (7-52, 4-78)	Intikhab Alam, Dunedin	1972-73
10-128 (5-56, 5-72)	Wasim Akram, Dunedin	1984-85
11-79 (5-37, 6-42)†	Zulfiqar Ahmed, Karachi	1955-56

† *Signifies ten wickets or more on first appearance in New Zealand–Pakistan Tests.*

Note: The best match figures by a New Zealand bowler are 9-70 (4-36, 5-34), F. J. Cameron a[t] Auckland, 1964-65.

NEW ZEALAND v SRI LANKA

	Captains					
Season	*New Zealand*	*Sri Lanka*	*T*	*NZ*	*SL*	*L*
1982-83*N*	G. P. Howarth	D. S. de Silva	2	2	0	
1983-84*S*	G. P. Howarth	L. R. D. Mendis	3	2	0	
1986-87*S*†	J. J. Crowe	L. R. D. Mendis	1	0	0	
	In New Zealand		2	2	0	
	In Sri Lanka		4	2	0	
	Totals		6	4	0	

N Played in New Zealand. S Played in Sri Lanka.

† *The Second and Third Tests were cancelled owing to civil disturbances.*

HIGHEST INNINGS TOTALS

For New Zealand in New Zealand: 344 at Christchurch 1982-8
in Sri Lanka: 459 at Colombo (CCC) 1983-8

For Sri Lanka in New Zealand: 240 at Wellington 1982-8
in Sri Lanka: 397-9 dec. at Colombo (CCC) 1986-8

LOWEST INNINGS TOTALS

For New Zealand in New Zealand: 201 at Wellington 1982-
in Sri Lanka: 198 at Colombo (SSC) 1983-

For Sri Lanka in New Zealand: 93 at Wellington 1982-
in Sri Lanka: 97 at Kandy 1983-

INDIVIDUAL HUNDREDS

For New Zealand (3)

20* J. J. Crowe, Colombo (CCC) 1986-87
51* R. J. Hadlee, Colombo (CCC) 1986-87
80 J. F. Reid, Colombo (CCC) 1983-84

For Sri Lanka (2)

108† R. L. Dias, Colombo (SSC) 1983-84
201*† D. S. B. P. Kuruppu, Colombo (CCC) 1986-87

† *Signifies hundred on first appearance in New Zealand–Sri Lanka Tests.*

est wicket partnership for New Zealand: 246* for the 6th† by J. J. Crowe and R. J. Hadlee at Colombo (CCC) 1986-87
for Sri Lanka: ‡159* for the 3rd by S. Wettimuny and R. L. Dias at Colombo (SSC) 1983-84

† *Denotes record partnership against all countries.*

‡ *163 runs were added for this wicket in two separate partnerships: S. Wettimuny retired hurt and as replaced by L. R. D. Mendis when 159 had been added.*

TEN WICKETS OR MORE IN A MATCH

For New Zealand (1)

-102 (5-73, 5-29) R. J. Hadlee, Colombo (CCC) 1983-84

Note: The best match figures by a Sri Lankan bowler are 8-159 (5-86, 3-73), V. B. John at andy, 1983-84.

INDIA v PAKISTAN

	Captains					
ason	*India*	*Pakistan*	*T*	*I*	*P*	*D*
52-53*I*	L. Amarnath	A. H. Kardar	5	2	1	2
54-55*P*	V. Mankad	A. H. Kardar	5	0	0	5
60-61*I*	N. J. Contractor	Fazal Mahmood	5	0	0	5
78-79*P*	B. S. Bedi	Mushtaq Mohammad	3	0	2	1
79-80*I*	S. M. Gavaskar[1]	Asif Iqbal	6	2	0	4
82-83*P*	S. M. Gavaskar	Imran Khan	6	0	3	3
33-84*I*	Kapil Dev	Zaheer Abbas	3	0	0	3
34-85*P*	S. M. Gavaskar	Zaheer Abbas	2	0	0	2
36-87*I*	Kapil Dev	Imran Khan	5	0	1	4
	In India		24	4	2	18
	In Pakistan		16	0	5	11
	Totals		40	4	7	29

layed in India. P Played in Pakistan.

te: The following was appointed by the home authority for only a minor proportion of the es:
G. R. Viswanath (Sixth).

HIGHEST INNINGS TOTALS

India in India: 539-9 dec. at Madras 1960-61
in Pakistan: 500 at Faisalabad 1984-85

Pakistan in India: 487-9 dec. at Madras 1986-87
in Pakistan: 674-6 at Faisalabad 1984-85

LOWEST INNINGS TOTALS

For India in India: 106 at Lucknow 1952-53
in Pakistan: 145 at Karachi 1954-55
For Pakistan in India: 116 at Bangalore 1986-87
in Pakistan: 158 at Dacca 1954-55

INDIVIDUAL HUNDREDS

For India (28)

109*	M. Amarnath, Lahore	1982-83
120	M. Amarnath, Lahore	1982-83
103*	M. Amarnath, Karachi	1982-83
101*	M. Amarnath, Lahore	1984-85
141	M. Azharuddin, Calcutta ..	1986-87
110	M. Azharuddin, Jaipur	1986-87
177*	C. G. Borde, Madras	1960-61
201	A. D. Gaekwad, Jullundur .	1983-84
111 137	S. M. Gavaskar, Karachi ..	1978-79
166	S. M. Gavaskar, Madras ..	1979-80
127*‡	S. M. Gavaskar, Faisalabad	1982-83
103*	S. M. Gavaskar, Bangalore	1983-84
146*	V. S. Hazare, Bombay	1952-53
127	S. M. Patil, Faisalabad	1984-85
128	R. J. Shastri, Karachi	1982-8
139	R. J. Shastri, Faisalabad ..	1984-8
125	R. J. Shastri, Jaipur	1986-8
110†	R. H. Shodhan, Calcutta ..	1952-5
123	K. Srikkanth, Madras	1986-8
102	P. R. Umrigar, Bombay ...	1952-5
108	P. R. Umrigar, Peshawar ..	1954-5
115	P. R. Umrigar, Kanpur ...	1960-6
117	P. R. Umrigar, Madras ...	1960-6
112	P. R. Umrigar, Delhi	1960-6
146*	D. B. Vengsarkar, Delhi ..	1979-8
109	D. B. Vengsarkar, Ahmedabad	1986-8
145†	G. R. Viswanath, Faisalabad	1978-7

For Pakistan (35)

103*	Alim-ud-Din, Karachi	1954-55
104†	Asif Iqbal, Faisalabad	1978-79
142	Hanif Mohammad, Bahawalpur	1954-55
160	Hanif Mohammad, Bombay	1960-61
105†	Ijaz Faqih, Ahmedabad ...	1986-87
135	Imtiaz Ahmed, Madras ...	1960-61
117	Imran Khan, Faisalabad ..	1982-83
135*	Imran Khan, Madras	1986-87
154*†	Javed Miandad, Faisalabad	1978-79
100	Javed Miandad, Karachi ..	1978-79
126	Javed Miandad, Faisalabad	1982-83
280*	Javed Miandad, Hyderabad	1982-83
101*†	Mohsin Khan, Lahore	1982-83
126	Mudassar Nazar, Bangalore	1979-80
119	Mudassar Nazar, Karachi .	1982-83
231	Mudassar Nazar, Hyderabad	1982-83
152*†	Mudassar Nazar, Lahore ..	1982-8
152	Mudassar Nazar, Karachi .	1982-8
199	Mudassar Nazar, Faisalabad	1984-
101	Mushtaq Mohammad, Delhi	1960-
124*‡	Nazar Mohammad, Lucknow	1952-
210	Qasim Omar, Faisalabad ..	1984-
114	Ramiz Raja, Jaipur	1986-
121†	Saeed Ahmed, Bombay ...	1960-
103	Saeed Ahmed, Madras	1960-
107	Salim Malik, Faisalabad ..	1982-
102*	Salim Malik, Faisalabad ..	1984-
101	Shoaib Mohammad, Madras	1986-
125	Wasim Raja, Jullundur	1983-
176†	Zaheer Abbas, Faisalabad .	1978-
235*	Zaheer Abbas, Lahore	1978-
215	Zaheer Abbas, Lahore	1982
186	Zaheer Abbas, Karachi ...	1982-
168	Zaheer Abbas, Faisalabad .	1982
168*	Zaheer Abbas, Lahore	1984

† *Signifies hundred on first appearance in India–Pakistan Tests.*
‡ *Carried his bat.*

RECORD PARTNERSHIPS FOR EACH WICKET

For India

200 for 1st	S. M. Gavaskar and K. Srikkanth at Madras	1986
125 for 2nd	S. M. Gavaskar and M. Amarnath at Hyderabad	1982
190 for 3rd	M. Amarnath and Yashpal Sharma at Lahore	1982
183 for 4th	V. S. Hazare and P. R. Umrigar at Bombay	1952

200 for 5th	S. M. Patil and R. J. Shastri at Faisalabad	1984-85
143 for 6th	M. Azharuddin and Kapil Dev at Calcutta	1986-87
155 for 7th	R. M. H. Binny and Madan Lal at Bangalore	1983-84
122 for 8th	S. M. H. Kirmani and Madan Lal at Faisalabad	1982-83
149 for 9th†	P. G. Joshi and R. B. Desai at Bombay	1960-61
109 for 10th†	H. R. Adhikari and Ghulam Ahmed at Delhi	1952-53

For Pakistan

162 for 1st	Hanif Mohammad and Imtiaz Ahmed at Madras	1960-61
250 for 2nd	Mudassar Nazar and Qasim Omar at Faisalabad	1984-85
451 for 3rd†	Mudassar Nazar and Javed Miandad at Hyderabad	1982-83
287 for 4th	Javed Miandad and Zaheer Abbas at Faisalabad	1982-83
213 for 5th	Zaheer Abbas and Mudassar Nazar at Karachi	1982-83
207 for 6th	Salim Malik and Imran Khan at Faisalabad	1982-83
54 for 7th	Imran Khan and Ijaz Faqih at Ahmedabad	1986-87
12 for 8th	Imran Khan and Wasim Akram at Madras	1986-87
0 for 9th	Wasim Bari and Iqbal Qasim at Bangalore	1979-80
04 for 10th	Zulfiqar Ahmed and Amir Elahi at Madras	1952-53

† *Denotes record partnership against all countries.*

TEN WICKETS OR MORE IN A MATCH

For India (3)

1-146 (4-90, 7-56)	Kapil Dev, Madras	1979-80
0-126 (7-27, 3-99)	Maninder Singh, Bangalore	1986-87
3-131 (8-52, 5-79)†	V. Mankad, Delhi	1952-53

For Pakistan (5)

2-94 (5-52, 7-42)	Fazal Mahmood, Lucknow	1952-53
1-79 (3-19, 8-60)	Imran Khan, Karachi	1982-83
1-180 (6-98, 5-82)	Imran Khan, Faisalabad	1982-83
0-175 (4-135, 6-40)	Iqbal Qasim, Bombay	1979-80
1-190 (8-69, 3-121)	Sikander Bakht, Delhi	1979-80

† *Signifies ten wickets or more on first appearance in India–Pakistan Tests.*

INDIA v SRI LANKA

	Captains					
ason	*India*	*Sri Lanka*	*T*	*I*	*SL*	*D*
82-83*I*	S. M. Gavaskar	B. Warnapura	1	0	0	1
85-86*S*	Kapil Dev	L. R. D. Mendis	3	0	1	2
86-87*I*	Kapil Dev	L. R. D. Mendis	3	2	0	1
	In India		4	2	0	2
	In Sri Lanka		3	0	1	2
	Totals		7	2	1	4

'layed in India. S Played in Sri Lanka.

HIGHEST INNINGS TOTALS

r India in India: 676-7 at Kanpur 1986-87
in Sri Lanka: 325-5 dec. at Kandy 1985-86

: Sri Lanka in India: 420 at Kanpur 1986-87
in Sri Lanka: 385 at Colombo (PSO) 1985-86

LOWEST INNINGS TOTALS

For India in India: 400 at Cuttack 1986-87
in Sri Lanka: 198 at Colombo (PSO) 1985-86
For Sri Lanka in India: 141 at Nagpur 1986-87
in Sri Lanka: 198 at Kandy 1985-86

INDIVIDUAL HUNDREDS

For India (9)

116*	M. Amarnath, Kandy	1985-86	163	Kapil Dev, Kanpur	1986-8
131	M. Amarnath, Nagpur	1986-87	114*†	S. M. Patil, Madras	1982-8
199	M. Azharuddin, Kanpur	1986-87	153	D. B. Vengsarkar, Nagpur	1986-8
155†	S. M. Gavaskar, Madras	1982-83	166	D. B. Vengsarkar, Cuttack	1986-8
176	S. M. Gavaskar, Kanpur	1986-87			

For Sri Lanka (7)

106	R. L. Dias, Kandy	1985-86	124	L. R. D. Mendis, Kandy	1985-8
103	R. S. Madugalle, Colombo (SSC)	1985-86	111	A. Ranatunga, Colombo (SSC)	1985-8
105, 105	†L. R. D. Mendis, Madras	1982-83	111	S. A. R. Silva, Colombo (PSO)	1985-8

† *Signifies hundred on first appearance in India–Sri Lanka Tests.*

RECORD PARTNERSHIPS FOR EACH WICKET

For India

156 for 1st	S. M. Gavaskar and Arun Lal at Madras	1982-8
173 for 2nd	S. M. Gavaskar and D. B. Vengsarkar at Madras	1982-8
173 for 3rd	M. Amarnath and D. B. Vengsarkar at Nagpur	1986-8
163 for 4th	S. M. Gavaskar and M. Azharuddin at Kanpur	1986-
78 for 5th	M. Amarnath and M. Azharuddin at Kandy	1985-
272 for 6th	M. Azharuddin and Kapil Dev at Kanpur	1986-
78* for 7th	S. M. Patil and Madan Lal at Madras	1982-
70 for 8th	Kapil Dev and L. Sivaramakrishnan at Colombo (PSO)	1985-
16 for 9th	S. M. Gavaskar and Gopal Sharma at Colombo (SSC)	1985-
29 for 10th	Kapil Dev and Chetan Sharma at Colombo (PSO)	1985-

For Sri Lanka

159 for 1st†	S. Wettimuny and J. R. Ratnayeke at Kanpur	1986-
95 for 2nd	S. A. R. Silva and R. S. Madugalle at Colombo (PSO)	1985-
153 for 3rd	R. L. Dias and L. R. D. Mendis at Madras	1982
216 for 4th	R. L. Dias and L. R. D. Mendis at Kandy	1985
144 for 5th	R. S. Madugalle and A. Ranatunga at Colombo (SSC)	1985
89 for 6th	L. R. D. Mendis and A. N. Ranasinghe at Madras	1982
77 for 7th†	R. S. Madugalle and D. S. de Silva at Madras	1982
40* for 8th	P. A. de Silva and A. L. F. de Mel at Kandy	1985
42 for 9th	J. R. Ratnayeke and A. L. F. de Mel at Madras	1982
44 for 10th	R. J. Ratnayake and E. A. R. de Silva at Nagpur	1986

† *Denotes record partnership against all countries.*

TEN WICKETS OR MORE IN A MATCH

For India (1)

0-107 (3-56, 7-51) Maninder Singh, Nagpur 1986-87

ote: The best match figures by a Sri Lankan bowler are 9-125 (4-76, 5-49) by R. J. Ratnayake gainst India at Colombo (PSO), 1985-86.

PAKISTAN v SRI LANKA

	Captains					
eason	*Pakistan*	*Sri Lanka*	*T*	*P*	*SL*	*D*
981-82*P*	Javed Miandad	B. Warnapura[1]	3	2	0	1
85-86*P*	Javed Miandad	L. R. D. Mendis	3	2	0	1
985-86*S*	Imran Khan	L. R. D. Mendis	3	1	1	1
	In Pakistan		6	4	0	2
	In Sri Lanka		3	1	1	1
	Totals		9	5	1	3

Played in Pakistan. S Played in Sri Lanka.

ote: [1]L. R. D. Mendis captained in the Second Test.

HIGHEST INNINGS TOTALS

r Pakistan in Pakistan: 555-3 at Faisalabad 1985-86
in Sri Lanka: 318 at Colombo (PSO) 1985-86

r Sri Lanka in Pakistan: 479 at Faisalabad 1985-86
in Sri Lanka: 323-3 at Colombo (PSO) 1985-86

LOWEST INNINGS TOTALS

r Pakistan in Pakistan: 259 at Sialkot 1985-86
in Sri Lanka: 132 at Colombo (CCC) 1985-86

Sri Lanka in Pakistan: 149 at Karachi 1981-82
in Sri Lanka: 101 at Kandy 1985-86

INDIVIDUAL HUNDREDS

For Pakistan (7)

†	Haroon Rashid, Karachi .	1981-82
*	Javed Miandad, Faisalabad	1985-86
	Mohsin Khan, Lahore ...	1981-82
†	Qasim Omar, Faisalabad .	1985-86
122	Ramiz Raja, Colombo (PSO)	1985-86
100*†	Salim Malik, Karachi	1981-82
134†	Zaheer Abbas, Lahore ...	1981-82

For Sri Lanka (6)

·	P. A. de Silva, Faisalabad	1985-86
	P. A. de Silva, Karachi ..	1985-86
	R. L. Dias, Lahore	1981-82
*	A. P. Gurusinha, Colombo (PSO)	1985-86
135*	A. Ranatunga, Colombo (PSO)	1985-86
157	S. Wettimuny, Faisalabad	1981-82

Signifies hundred on first appearance in Pakistan–Sri Lanka Tests.

RECORD PARTNERSHIPS FOR EACH WICKET

For Pakistan

98* for 1st	Mudassar Nazar and Mohsin Khan at Karachi	1985-8
151 for 2nd	Mohsin Khan and Majid Khan at Lahore	1981-8
397 for 3rd	Qasim Omar and Javed Miandad at Faisalabad	1985-8
162 for 4th	Salim Malik and Javed Miandad at Karachi	1981-8
102 for 5th	Mudassar Nazar and Salim Malik at Kandy	1985-8
100 for 6th	Zaheer Abbas and Imran Khan at Lahore	1981-8
104 for 7th	Haroon Rashid and Tahir Naqqash at Karachi	1981-8
29 for 8th	Ashraf Ali and Iqbal Qasim at Faisalabad	1981-8
	Salim Yousuf and Abdul Qadir at Sialkot	1985-8
	Salim Yousuf and Abdul Qadir at Karachi	1985-8
127 for 9th	Haroon Rashid and Rashid Khan at Karachi	1981-8
48 for 10th	Rashid Khan and Tauseef Ahmed at Faisalabad	1981-8

For Sri Lanka

77 for 1st	S. Wettimuny and H. M. Goonatillake at Faisalabad	1981-8
217 for 2nd†	S. Wettimuny and R. L. Dias at Faisalabad	1981-8
85 for 3rd	S. Wettimuny and R. L. Dias at Faisalabad	1985-8
240* for 4th†	A. P. Gurusinha and A. Ranatunga at Colombo (PSO)	1985-8
58 for 5th	R. L. Dias and L. R. D. Mendis at Lahore	1981-8
121 for 6th	A. Ranatunga and P. A. de Silva at Faisalabad	1985-8
66 for 7th	P. A. de Silva and J. R. Ratnayeke at Faisalabad	1985-8
61 for 8th†	R. S. Madugalle and D. S. de Silva at Faisalabad	1981-8
52 for 9th†	P. A. de Silva and R. J. Ratnayake at Faisalabad	1985-8
36 for 10th	R. J. Ratnayake and R. G. C. E. Wijesuriya at Faisalabad	1985-

† *Denotes record partnership against all countries.*

TEN WICKETS OR MORE IN A MATCH

For Pakistan (1)

14-116 (8-58, 6-58)	Imran Khan, Lahore	1981-

Note: The best match figures by a Sri Lankan bowler are 9-162 (4-103, 5-59), D. S. de Silva Faisalabad, 1981-82.

TEST MATCH GROUNDS

In Chronological Sequence

City and Ground	*Date of First Test*	*Match*
1. Melbourne, Melbourne Cricket Ground	March 15, 1877	Australia v England
2. London, Kennington Oval	September 6, 1880	England v Australia
3. Sydney, Sydney Cricket Ground (No. 1)	February 17, 1882	Australia v England
4. Manchester, Old Trafford	July 11, 1884	England v Australia
This match was due to have started on July 10, but rain prevented any play.		
5. London, Lord's	July 21, 1884	England v Australia
6. Adelaide, Adelaide Oval	December 12, 1884	Australia v England
7. Port Elizabeth, St George's Park	March 12, 1889	South Africa v Englan
8. Cape Town, Newlands	March 25, 1889	South Africa v Engla
9. Johannesburg, Old Wanderers*	March 2, 1896	South Africa v Engla
10. Nottingham, Trent Bridge	June 1, 1899	England v Australia

	City and Ground	*Date of First Test*	*Match*
.1.	Leeds, Headingley	June 29, 1899	England v Australia
2.	Birmingham, Edgbaston	May 29, 1902	England v Australia
3.	Sheffield, Bramall Lane*	July 3, 1902	England v Australia
4.	Durban, Lord's*	January 21, 1910	South Africa v England
5.	Durban, Kingsmead	January 18, 1923	South Africa v England
6.	Brisbane, Exhibition Ground*	November 30, 1928	Australia v England
7.	Christchurch, Lancaster Park	January 10, 1930	New Zealand v England
8.	Bridgetown, Kensington Oval	January 11, 1930	West Indies v England
9.	Wellington, Basin Reserve	January 24, 1930	New Zealand v England
0.	Port-of-Spain, Queen's Park Oval	February 1, 1930	West Indies v England
1.	Auckland, Eden Park	February 17, 1930	New Zealand v England

This match was due to have started on February 14, but rain prevented any play on the first two ays. February 16 was a Sunday.

2.	Georgetown, Bourda	February 21, 1930	West Indies v England
3.	Kingston, Sabina Park	April 3, 1930	West Indies v England
4.	Brisbane, Woolloongabba	November 27, 1931	Australia v South Africa
5.	Bombay, Gymkhana Ground*	December 15, 1933	India v England
6.	Calcutta, Eden Gardens	January 5, 1934	India v England
7.	Madras, Chepauk (Chidambaram Stadium)	February 10, 1934	India v England
8.	Delhi, Feroz Shah Kotla	November 10, 1948	India v West Indies
9.	Bombay, Brabourne Stadium*	December 9, 1948	India v West Indies
.	Johannesburg, Ellis Park*	December 27, 1948	South Africa v England
.	Kanpur, Green Park (Modi Stadium)	January 12, 1952	India v England
.	Lucknow, University Ground*	October 25, 1952	India v Pakistan
.	Dacca, Dacca Stadium*	January 1, 1955	Pakistan v India
.	Bahawalpur, Dring Stadium	January 15, 1955	Pakistan v India
.	Lahore, Lawrence Gardens (Bagh-i-Jinnah)*	January 29, 1955	Pakistan v India
.	Peshawar, Peshawar Club Ground	February 13, 1955	Pakistan v India
.	Karachi, National Stadium	February 26, 1955	Pakistan v India
.	Dunedin, Carisbrook	March 11, 1955	New Zealand v England
.	Hyderabad, Fateh Maidan (Lal Bahadur Stadium)	November 19, 1955	India v New Zealand
.	Madras, Corporation Stadium*	January 6, 1956	India v New Zealand
.	Johannesburg, New Wanderers	December 24, 1956	South Africa v England
	Lahore, Gaddafi Stadium	November 21, 1959	Pakistan v Australia
	Rawalpindi, Rawalpindi Club Ground	March 27, 1965	Pakistan v New Zealand
.	Nagpur, Vidarbha Cricket Association Ground	October 3, 1969	India v New Zealand
	Perth, Western Australian Cricket Association Ground	December 11, 1970	Australia v England
	Hyderabad, Niaz Stadium	March 16, 1973	Pakistan v England
	Bangalore, Karnataka State Cricket Association Ground	November 22, 1974	India v West Indies
	Bombay, Wankhede Stadium	January 23, 1975	India v West Indies
	Faisalabad, Iqbal Park	October 16, 1978	Pakistan v India
	Napier, McLean Park	February 16, 1979	New Zealand v Pakistan
	Multan, Ibn-e-Qasim Bagh Stadium	December 30, 1980	Pakistan v West Indies
	St John's (Antigua), Recreation Ground	March 27, 1981	West Indies v England
	Colombo, P. Saravanamuttu Oval	February 17, 1982	Sri Lanka v England
	Kandy, Asgiriya Stadium	April 22, 1983	Sri Lanka v Australia
	Jullundur, Burlton Park	September 24, 1983	India v Pakistan
	Ahmedabad, Gujarat Stadium	November 12, 1983	India v West Indies
	Colombo, Singhalese Sports Club Ground	March 16, 1984	Sri Lanka v New Zealand
	Colombo, Colombo Cricket Club Ground	March 24, 1984	Sri Lanka v New Zealand
	Sialkot, Jinnah Park	October 27, 1985	Pakistan v Sri Lanka
	Cuttack, Barabati Stadium	January 4, 1987	India v Sri Lanka
	Jaipur, Sawai Mansingh Stadium	February 21, 1987	India v Pakistan

Denotes no longer used for Test matches. In some instances the ground is no longer in existence.

FAMILIES IN TEST CRICKET

FATHERS AND SONS

England
M. C. Cowdrey (114 Tests, 1954-55–1974-75) and C. S. Cowdrey (6 Tests, 1984-85–1988).
J. Hardstaff (5 Tests, 1907-08) and J. Hardstaff jun. (23 Tests, 1935–1948).
L. Hutton (79 Tests, 1937–1954-55) and R. A. Hutton (5 Tests, 1971).
F. T. Mann (5 Tests, 1922-23) and F. G. Mann (7 Tests, 1948-49–1949).
J. H. Parks (1 Test, 1937) and J. M. Parks (46 Tests, 1954–1967-68).
F. W. Tate (1 Test, 1902) and M. W. Tate (39 Tests, 1924–1935).
C. L. Townsend (2 Tests, 1899) and D. C. H. Townsend (3 Tests, 1934-35).

Australia
E. J. Gregory (1 Test, 1876-77) and S. E. Gregory (58 Tests, 1890–1912).

South Africa
F. Hearne (4 Tests, 1891-92–1895-96) and G. A. L. Hearne (3 Tests, 1922-23–1924).
F. Hearne also played 2 Tests for England in 1888-89.
J. D. Lindsay (3 Tests, 1947) and D. T. Lindsay (19 Tests, 1963-64–1969-70).
A. W. Nourse (45 Tests, 1902-03–1924) and A. D. Nourse (34 Tests, 1935–1951).
L. R. Tuckett (1 Test, 1913-14) and L. Tuckett (9 Tests, 1947–1948-49).

West Indies
G. A. Headley (22 Tests, 1929-30–1953-54) and R. G. A. Headley (2 Tests, 1973).
O. C. Scott (8 Tests, 1928–1930-31) and A. P. H. Scott (1 Test, 1952-53).

New Zealand
W. M. Anderson (1 Test, 1945-46) and R. W. Anderson (9 Tests, 1976-77–1978).
W. A. Hadlee (11 Tests, 1937–1950-51) and D. R. Hadlee (26 Tests, 1969–1977-78); R. Hadlee (74 Tests, 1972-73–1987-88).
H. G. Vivian (7 Tests, 1931–1937) and G. E. Vivian (5 Tests, 1964-65–1971-72).

India
L. Amarnath (24 Tests, 1933-34–1952-53) and M. Amarnath (69 Tests, 1969-70–1987-8 S. Amarnath (10 Tests, 1975-76–1978-79).
D. K. Gaekwad (11 Tests, 1952–1960-61) and A. D. Gaekwad (40 Tests, 1974-75–1984-8
Nawab of Pataudi (Iftikhar Ali Khan) (3 Tests, 1946) and Nawab of Pataudi (Mansur Khan) (46 Tests, 1961-62–1974-75).
Nawab of Pataudi sen. also played 3 Tests for England, 1932-33–1934.
V. Mankad (44 Tests, 1946–1958-59) and A. V. Mankad (22 Tests, 1969-70–1977-78).
Pankaj Roy (43 Tests, 1951-52–1960-61) and Pranab Roy (2 Tests, 1981-82).

India and Pakistan
M. Jahangir Khan (4 Tests, 1932–1936) and Majid Khan (63 Tests, 1964-65–1982-83).
S. Wazir Ali (7 Tests, 1932–1936) and Khalid Wazir (2 Tests, 1954).

Pakistan
Hanif Mohammad (55 Tests, 1954–1969-70) and Shoaib Mohammad (17 Tests, 1983- 1987-88).
Nazar Mohammad (5 Tests, 1952-53) and Mudassar Nazar (71 Tests, 1976- 1987-88).

GRANDFATHERS AND GRANDSONS

Australia
V. Y. Richardson (19 Tests, 1924-25–1935-36) and G. S. Chappell (87 Tests, 1970-71–1983- I. M. Chappell (75 Tests, 1964-65–1979-80); T. M. Chappell (3 Tests, 1981).

GREAT-GRANDFATHER AND GREAT-GRANDSON

Australia

W. H. Cooper (2 Tests, 1881-82 and 1884-85) and A. P. Sheahan (31 Tests, 1967-68–1973-74).

BROTHERS IN SAME TEST TEAM

England

E. M., G. F. and W. G. Grace: 1 Test, 1880.
C. T. and G. B. Studd: 4 Tests, 1882-83.
A. and G. G. Hearne: 1 Test, 1891-92.
F. Hearne, their brother, played in this match for South Africa.
D. W. and P. E. Richardson: 1 Test, 1957.

Australia

E. J. and D. W. Gregory: 1 Test, 1876-77.
C. and A. C. Bannerman: 1 Test, 1878-79.
G. and W. F. Giffen: 2 Tests, 1891-92.
G. H. S. and A. E. Trott: 3 Tests, 1894-95.
I. M. and G. S. Chappell: 43 Tests, 1970-71–1979-80.

South Africa

S. J. and S. D. Snooke: 1 Test, 1907.
D. and H. W. Taylor: 2 Tests, 1913-14.
R. H. M. and P. A. M. Hands: 1 Test, 1913-14.
E. A. B. and A. M. B. Rowan: 9 Tests, 1948-49–1951.
P. M. and R. G. Pollock: 23 Tests, 1963-64–1969-70.
A. J. and D. B. Pithey: 5 Tests, 1963-64.

West Indies

G. C. and R. S. Grant: 4 Tests, 1934-35.
J. B. and V. H. Stollmeyer: 1 Test, 1939.
D. St E. and E. St E. Atkinson: 1 Test, 1957-58.

New Zealand

J. J. and M. D. Crowe: 33 Tests, 1983–1987-88.
D. R. and R. J. Hadlee: 10 Tests, 1973–1977-78.
H. J. and G. P. Howarth: 4 Tests, 1974-75–1976-77.
J. M. and N. M. Parker: 3 Tests, 1976-77.
B. P. and J. G. Bracewell: 1 Test, 1980-81.

India

S. Wazir Ali and S. Nazir Ali: 2 Tests, 1932–1933-34.
L. Ramji and Amar Singh: 1 Test, 1933-34.
C. K. and C. S. Nayudu: 4 Tests, 1933-34–1936.
A. G. Kripal Singh and A. G. Milkha Singh: 1 Test, 1961-62.
S. and M. Amarnath: 8 Tests, 1975-76–1978-79.

Pakistan

Wazir and Hanif Mohammad: 18 Tests, 1952-53–1959-60.
Wazir and Mushtaq Mohammad: 1 Test, 1958-59.
Hanif and Mushtaq Mohammad: 19 Tests, 1960-61–1969-70.
Hanif, Mushtaq and Sadiq Mohammad: 1 Test, 1969-70.
Mushtaq and Sadiq Mohammad: 26 Tests, 1969-70–1978–79.
Wasim and Ramiz Raja: 2 Tests, 1983-84.

Sri Lanka

M. D. and S. Wettimuny: 2 Tests, 1982-83.

LIMITED-OVERS INTERNATIONAL RECORDS

Note: Limited-overs international matches do not have first-class status.

3,000 OR MORE RUNS

	M	*I*	*NO*	*R*	*HI*	*100s*	*Avge*
I. V. A. Richards (*West Indies*)	149	135	21	5,869	189*	11	51.48
D. L. Haynes (*West Indies*)	139	138	17	4,900	148	10	40.4
Javed Miandad (*Pakistan*)	131	126	29	4,482	119*	6	46.2
A. R. Border (*Australia*)	170	160	22	4,316	127*	3	31.2
C. G. Greenidge (*West Indies*)	97	96	9	3,964	133*	9	45.5
S. M. Gavaskar (*India*)	107	102	14	3,092	103*	1	35.1
Leading run-scorers for other countries							
J. G. Wright (*New Zealand*)	110	109	1	2,926	101	1	27.0
D. I. Gower (*England*)	102	99	8	2,905	158	7	31.9
R. L. Dias (*Sri Lanka*)	57	54	5	1,573	121	2	32.1

HIGHEST INDIVIDUAL SCORE FOR EACH COUNTRY

189*	I. V. A. Richards	**West Indies** v England at Manchester	198
175*	Kapil Dev	**India** v Zimbabwe at Tunbridge Wells	198
171*	G. M. Turner	**New Zealand** v East Africa at Birmingham	197
158	D. I. Gower	**England** v New Zealand at Brisbane	1982-8
138*	G. S. Chappell	**Australia** v New Zealand at Sydney	1980-8
123	Zaheer Abbas	**Pakistan** v Sri Lanka at Lahore	1981-8
121	R. L. Dias	**Sri Lanka** v India at Bangalore	1982-8

FIVE OR MORE HUNDREDS

Total		*E*	*A*	*WI*	*NZ*	*I*	*P*	*SL*	*Other*
11	I. V. A. Richards (*West Indies*)	3	3	–	1	3	0	1	0
10	D. L. Haynes (*West Indies*)	0	6	–	2	0	1	1	0
9	C. G. Greenidge (*West Indies*)	0	1	–	3	2	1	1	1
7	D. I. Gower (*England*)	–	2	0	3	0	1	1	0
7	Zaheer Abbas (*Pakistan*)	0	2	0	1	3	–	1	0
6	G. A. Gooch (*England*)	–	3	1	0	1	1	0	0
6	Javed Miandad (*Pakistan*)	1	0	1	0	3	–	1	0
5	G. R. Marsh (*Australia*)	0	–	0	2	3	0	0	0

HIGHEST PARTNERSHIP FOR EACH WICKET

212 for 1st	G. R. Marsh (104) and D. C. Boon (111), Australia v India at Jaipur	1986
221 for 2nd	C. G. Greenidge (115) and I. V. A. Richards (149), West Indies v India at Jamshedpur	1983
224* for 3rd	D. M. Jones (99*) and A. R. Border (118*), Australia v Sri Lanka at Adelaide	1984
173 for 4th	D. M. Jones (121) and S. R. Waugh (82), Australia v Pakistan at Perth	1986
152 for 5th	I. V. A. Richards (98) and C. H. Lloyd (89*), West Indies v Sri Lanka at Brisbane	1984

44 for 6th	Imran Khan (102*) and Shahid Mahboob (77), Pakistan v Sri Lanka at Leeds	1983
15 for 7th	P. J. L. Dujon (57*) and M. D. Marshall (66), West Indies v Pakistan at Gujranwala	1986-87
17 for 8th	D. L. Houghton (141) and I. P. Butchart (54), Zimbabwe v New Zealand at Hyderabad (Pakistan)	1987-88
26* for 9th	Kapil Dev (175*) and S. M. H. Kirmani (24*), India v Zimbabwe at Tunbridge Wells	1983
)6* for 10th	I. V. A. Richards (189*) and M. A. Holding (12*), West Indies v England at Manchester	1984

100 OR MORE WICKETS

	M	*Balls*	*R*	*W*	*BB*	*4W/i*	*Avge*
Garner (*West Indies*)	98	5,330	2,752	146	5-31	5	18.84
apil Dev (*India*)	123	6,315	3,948	146	5-43	2	27.04
J. Hadlee (*New Zealand*)	107	5,717	3,130	143	5-25	5	21.88
. A. Holding (*West Indies*)	102	5,473	3,034	142	5-26	6	21.36
J. Chatfield (*New Zealand*)	108	5,759	3,420	136	5-34	3	25.14
ıran Khan (*Pakistan*)	106	4,430	2,788	123	6-14	4	22.66
T. Botham (*England*)	95	5,076	3,398	116	4-56	1	29.29
D. Marshall (*West Indies*)	90	4,787	2,654	115	4-23	3	23.07
ıdassar Nazar (*Pakistan*)	112	4,453	3,147	107	5-28	2	29.41
K. Lillee (*Australia*)	63	3,593	2,145	103	5-34	6	20.82
J. Shastri (*India*)	101	4,796	3,283	101	4-38	2	32.50
ading bowler for Sri Lanka							
L. F. de Mel	56	2,681	2,201	59	5-32	2	37.30

BEST BOWLING FOR EACH COUNTRY

1	W. W. Davis	**West Indies** v Australia at Leeds	1983
4	G. J. Gilmour	**Australia** v England at Leeds	1975
4	Imran Khan	**Pakistan** v India at Sharjah	1984-85
0	V. J. Marks	**England** v New Zealand at Wellington	1983-84
3	R. O. Collinge	**New Zealand** v India at Christchurch	1975-76
6	U. S. H. Karnain	**Sri Lanka** v New Zealand at Moratuwa	1983-84
3	Kapil Dev	**India** v Australia at Nottingham	1983

HAT-TRICKS

ıl-ud-Din	Pakistan v Australia at Hyderabad	1982-83
A. Reid	Australia v New Zealand at Sydney	1985-86
ıtan Sharma	India v New Zealand at Nagpur	1987-88

MOST DISMISSALS IN A MATCH

ll ct)	R. W. Marsh	Australia v England at Leeds	1981
ll ct)	R. G. de Alwis	Sri Lanka v Australia at Colombo (PSO)	1982-83
ıl ct)	S. M. H. Kirmani	India v Zimbabwe at Leicester	1983
ct, 2 st)	S. Viswanath	India v England at Sydney	1984-85
ct, 2 st)	K. S. More	India v New Zealand at Sharjah	1987-88

50 OR MORE DISMISSALS

	M	*Ct*	*St*	*Total*
L. Dujon (*West Indies*)	120	135	15	150
V. Marsh (*Australia*)	91	119	4	123
ım Bari (*Pakistan*)	51	52	10	62

MOST CATCHES IN A MATCH

(Excluding wicket-keepers)

4	Salim Malik	Pakistan v New Zealand at Sialkot	1984-8
4	S. M. Gavaskar	India v Pakistan at Sharjah	1984-8

Note: While fielding as substitute, J. G. Bracewell held 4 catches for New Zealand v Austral at Adelaide, 1980-81.

50 OR MORE CATCHES

	M	*Ct*		*M*	*Ct*
I. V. A. Richards (*West Indies*)	149	72	A. R. Border (*Australia*)	170	65

ALL-ROUND

1,000 Runs and 100 Wickets

	M	*R*	*W*
I. T. Botham (*England*)	95	1,693	116
R. J. Hadlee (*New Zealand*)	107	1,601	143
Imran Khan (*Pakistan*)	106	1,898	123
Kapil Dev (*India*)	123	2,615	146
Mudassar Nazar (*Pakistan*)	112	2,438	107
R. J. Shastri (*India*).............	101	2,067	101

1,000 Runs and 100 Dismissals

	M	*R*	*D*
P. J. L. Dujon (*West Indies*)	120	1,303	150
R. W. Marsh (*Australia*)	91	1,220	123

HIGHEST INNINGS TOTALS

360-4	(50 overs)	**West Indies** v Sri Lanka at Karachi	1987
338-5	(60 overs)	**Pakistan** v Sri Lanka at Swansea	1
334-4	(60 overs)	**England** v India at Lord's	1
333-8	(45 overs)	West Indies v India at Jamshedpur	1983
333-9	(60 overs)	England v Sri Lanka at Taunton	1
330-6	(60 overs)	Pakistan v Sri Lanka at Nottingham	1
328-5	(60 overs)	**Australia** v Sri Lanka at The Oval	1
323-2	(50 overs)	Australia v Sri Lanka at Adelaide	1984
322-6	(60 overs)	England v New Zealand at The Oval	1
320-8	(55 overs)	England v Australia at Birmingham	1
320-9	(60 overs)	Australia v India at Nottingham	1
315-4	(47 overs)	West Indies v Pakistan at Port-of-Spain	198
313-9	(50 overs)	West Indies v Australia at St John's	197
309-6	(50 overs)	West Indies v Sri Lanka at Perth	198
309-5	(60 overs)	**New Zealand** v East Africa at Birmingham	1
304-5	(50 overs)	New Zealand v Sri Lanka at Auckland	198
302-8	(50 overs)	Australia v New Zealand at Melbourne	198

Note: The highest score by **India** is 299-4 (40 overs) v Sri Lanka at Bombay, 1986-87, anc highest by **Sri Lanka** is 289-7 (40 overs) v India at Bombay, 1986-87.

HIGHEST TOTALS BATTING SECOND

Winning

297-6 (48.5 overs) New Zealand v England at Adelaide 1982-83

Losing

289-7 (40 overs) Sri Lanka v India at Bombay 1986-87
288-9 (60 overs) Sri Lanka v Pakistan at Swansea 1983

HIGHEST MATCH AGGREGATES

26-14 (120 overs) Pakistan v Sri Lanka at Swansea 1983
19-19 (118 overs) England v Sri Lanka at Taunton 1983
04-9 (120 overs) Australia v Sri Lanka at The Oval 1975

LOWEST INNINGS TOTALS

5 (40.3 overs) Canada v England at Manchester 1979
5 (28.3 overs) **Sri Lanka** v West Indies at Sharjah 1986-87
3 (25.5 overs) **India** v Australia at Sydney 1980-81
4 (35.5 overs) **New Zealand** v Pakistan at Sharjah 1985-86
) (25.2 overs) **Australia** v England at Birmingham 1977
) (26.3 overs) Australia v New Zealand at Adelaide 1985-86
4 (29 overs) New Zealand v Australia at Wellington 1981-82
8 (24.1 overs) India v Sri Lanka at Kanpur 1986-87
) (34.2 overs) India v Pakistan at Sialkot 1978-79
5 (47 overs) **Pakistan** v England at Manchester 1978
5 (37.2 overs) Sri Lanka v West Indies at Manchester 1975
7 (32.5 overs) Pakistan v India at Sharjah 1984-85
(35.5 overs) Sri Lanka v Australia at Adelaide 1984-85
(35.4 overs) Australia v West Indies at Perth 1986-87
(36.2 overs) **England** v Australia at Leeds 1975
(31.7 overs) England v Australia at Melbourne 1978-79
(52.3 overs) East Africa v England at Birmingham 1975
(41 overs) Sri Lanka v India at Sharjah 1983-84

ote: This section does not take into account those matches in which the number of overs was duced.

The lowest innings total by **West Indies** is 111 (41.4 overs) v Pakistan at Melbourne, 1983-84.

LARGEST VICTORIES

runs Australia (323-2 in 50 overs) v Sri Lanka (91 in 35.5 overs) at Adelaide 1984-85
runs New Zealand (276-7 in 50 overs) v Australia (70 in 26.3 overs) at Adelaide 1985-86
runs England (334-4 in 60 overs) v India (132-3 in 60 overs) at Lord's 1975

ten wickets: There have been seven instances of victory by ten wickets.

TIED MATCH

st Indies 222-5 (50 overs), Australia 222-9 (50 overs) at Melbourne 1983-84

WORLD CUP FINALS

5 (60 overs) West Indies (291-8) beat Australia (274) by 17 runs at Lord's.
) (60 overs) West Indies (286-9) beat England (194) by 92 runs at Lord's.
(60 overs) India (183) beat West Indies (140) by 43 runs at Lord's.
7 (50 overs) Australia (253-5) beat England (246-8) by 7 runs at Calcutta.

MISCELLANEOUS

LARGE ATTENDANCES

Test Series

943,000	Australia v England (5 Tests)	1936-37
In England		
549,650	England v Australia (5 Tests)	1953

Test Match

†350,534	Australia v England, Melbourne (Third Test)	1936-37
325,000+	India v England, Calcutta (Second Test)	1972-73
In England		
158,000+	England v Australia, Leeds (Fourth Test)	1948
137,915	England v Australia, Lord's (Second Test)	195

Test Match Day

90,800	Australia v West Indies, Melbourne (Fifth Test, 2nd day)	1960-6

Other First-Class Matches in England

80,000+	Surrey v Yorkshire, The Oval (3 days)	190
78,792	Yorkshire v Lancashire, Leeds (3 days)	190
76,617	Lancashire v Yorkshire, Manchester (3 days)	192

One-day International

86,133‡	Australia v West Indies, Melbourne	1983-8

† *Although no official figures are available, the attendance at the Fourth Test between India ar England at Calcutta, 1981-82, was thought to have exceeded this figure.*

‡ *It is estimated that a crowd of more than 90,000 attended the one-day international betwe India and Pakistan at Calcutta, 1986-87. However, this figure has not been confirmed.*

LORD'S CRICKET GROUND

Lord's and the MCC were founded in 1787. The Club has enjoyed an uninterrupted career sin that date, but there have been three grounds known as Lord's. The first (1787-1810) was situa where Dorset Square now is; the second (1809-13), at North Bank, had to be abandoned ow to the cutting of the Regent's Canal; and the third, opened in 1814, is the present one at St Joh Wood. It was not until 1866 that the freehold of Lord's was secured by the MCC. The pres pavilion was erected in 1890 at a cost of £21,000.

HIGHEST INDIVIDUAL SCORES MADE AT LORD'S

316*	J. B. Hobbs	Surrey v Middlesex	19
315*	P. Holmes	Yorkshire v Middlesex	19
281*	W. H. Ponsford	Australians v MCC	19
278	W. Ward	MCC v Norfolk (with E. H. Budd, T. Vigne and F. Ladbroke)	18
278	D. G. Bradman	Australians v MCC	1
277*	E. H. Hendren	Middlesex v Kent	1

Note: The longest innings in a Test match at Lord's was played by S. Wettimuny (642 minu 190 runs) for Sri Lanka v England, 1984.

HIGHEST TOTALS OBTAINED AT LORD'S

First-Class Matches

729-6	Australia v England	1930
665	West Indians v Middlesex	1939
652-8	West Indies v England	1973
629	England v India	1974
612-8	Middlesex v Nottinghamshire	1921
610-5	Australians v Gentlemen	1948
609-8	Cambridge University v MCC and Ground	1913
608-7	Middlesex v Hampshire	1919
607	MCC and Ground v Cambridge University	1902

Minor Match

735-9	MCC and Ground v Wiltshire	1888

BIGGEST HIT AT LORD'S

The only known instance of a batsman hitting a ball over the present pavilion at Lord's occurred when A. E. Trott, appearing for MCC against Australians on July 31, August 1, 2, 1899, drove M. A. Noble so far and high that the ball struck a chimney pot and fell behind the building.

HIGHEST SCORE IN A MINOR COUNTY MATCH

23*	F. E. Lacey	Hampshire v Norfolk at Southampton	1887

HIGHEST SCORE IN MINOR COUNTIES CHAMPIONSHIP

32	E. Garnett	Berkshire v Wiltshire at Reading	1908
54	H. E. Morgan	Glamorgan v Monmouthshire at Cardiff	1901
53*	G. J. Whittaker	Surrey II v Gloucestershire II at The Oval	1950
53	A. Booth	Lancashire II v Lincolnshire at Grimsby	1950
52	J. A. Deed	Kent II v Surrey II at The Oval (on début)	1924

HIGHEST SCORE FOR ENGLISH PUBLIC SCHOOL

78	J. L. Guise	Winchester v Eton at Eton	1921

HIGHEST SCORES IN OTHER MATCHES

28*	A. E. J. Collins, Clark's House v North Town at Clifton College. (A Junior House match. His innings of 6 hours 50 minutes was spread over four afternoons.)	1899
6	C. J. Eady, Break-o'-Day v Wellington at Hobart	1901-02
5	D. R. Havewalla, B.B. and C.I. Rly v St Xavier's at Bombay	1933-34
6*	J. C. Sharp, Melbourne GS v Geelong College at Melbourne	1914-15
2*	Chaman Lal, Mehandra Coll., Patiala v Government Coll., Rupar at Patiala	1956-57
5	A. E. Stoddart, Hampstead v Stoics at Hampstead	1886
5*	Mohammad Iqbal, Muslim Model HS v Islamia HS, Sialkot at Lahore	1958-59
5*	G. T. S. Stevens, Beta v Lambda (University College School House match) at Neasden	1919
9	J. A. Prout, Wesley College v Geelong College at Geelong	1908-09

HIGHEST PARTNERSHIP IN MINOR CRICKET

* for 3rd	V. G. Kambli and S. R. Tendulkar, Sharadashram Vidyamandir School v St Xavier's High School at Bombay	1987-88

RECORD HIT

The Rev. W. Fellows, while at practice on the Christ Church ground at Oxford in 1856, drove a ball bowled by Charles Rogers 175 yards from hit to pitch.

THROWING THE CRICKET BALL

140 yards 2 feet, Robert Percival, on the Durham Sands, Co. Durham Racecourse c1882
140 yards 9 inches, Ross Mackenzie, at Toronto 1872

Notes: W. F. Forbes, on March 16, 1876, threw 132 yards at the Eton College sports. He was then eighteen years of age.

Onochie Onuorah, on June 5, 1987, threw a $4\frac{3}{4}$oz ball 100 yards 1 foot $8\frac{1}{2}$ inches (91.94 metres) at The Abbey School, Westgate, sports. He was then thirteen years of age.

William Yardley, while a boy at Rugby, threw 100 yards with his right hand and 78 yards with his left .

Charles Arnold, of Cambridge, once threw 112 yards with the wind and 108 against.

W. H. Game, at The Oval in 1875, threw the ball 111 yards and then back the same distance. W. G. Grace threw 109 yards one way and back 105, and George Millyard 108 with the wind and 103 against. At The Oval in 1868, W. G. Grace made three successive throws of 116, 11[illegible] and 118 yards, and then threw back over 100 yards. D. G. Foster (Warwickshire) threw 13[illegible] yards, and in 1930 he made a Danish record with 120.1 metres – about 130 yards.

DATES OF FORMATION OF COUNTY CLUBS NOW FIRST-CLASS

County	First known county organisation	Present Club Original date	Present Club Reorganisation, if substantial
Derbyshire	November 4, 1870	November 4, 1870	—
Essex	By May, 1790	January 14, 1876	—
Glamorgan	1863	July 6, 1888	—
Gloucestershire	November 3, 1863	1871	—
Hampshire	April 3, 1849	August 12, 1863	July, 1879
Kent	August 6, 1842	March 1, 1859	December 6, 1870
Lancashire	January 12, 1864	January 12, 1864	—
Leicestershire	By August, 1820	March 25, 1879	—
Middlesex	December 15, 1863	February 2, 1864	—
Northamptonshire	1820	1820	July 31, 1878
Nottinghamshire	March/April, 1841	March/April, 1841	December 11, 1866
Somerset	October 15, 1864	August 18, 1875	—
Surrey	August 22, 1845	August 22, 1845	—
Sussex	June 16, 1836	March 1, 1839	August, 1857
Warwickshire	May, 1826	1882	—
Worcestershire	1844	March 5, 1865	—
Yorkshire	March 7, 1861	January 8, 1863	December 10, 1891

DATES OF FORMATION OF CLUBS IN THE CURRENT MINOR COUNTIES CHAMPIONSHIP

County	First known county organisation	Present Club
Bedfordshire	May, 1847	November 3, 1899
Berkshire	By May, 1841	March 17, 1895
Buckinghamshire	November, 1864	January 15, 1891
Cambridgeshire	March 13, 1844	June 6, 1891
Cheshire	1819	September 29, 1908

County	*First known county organisation*	*Present Club*
Cornwall	1813	November 12, 1894
Cumberland	January 2, 1884	April 10, 1948
Devon	1824	November 26, 1899
Dorset	1862 *or* 1871	February 5, 1896
Durham	January 24, 1874	May 10, 1882
Hertfordshire	1838	March 8, 1876
Lincolnshire	1853	September 28, 1906
Norfolk	January 11, 1827	October 14, 1876
Northumberland	1834	December, 1895
Oxfordshire	1787	December 14, 1921
Shropshire	1819 or 1829	June 28, 1956
Staffordshire	November 24, 1871	November 24, 1871
Suffolk	July 27, 1864	August, 1932
Wiltshire	February 24, 1881	January, 1893

CONSTITUTION OF COUNTY CHAMPIONSHIP

here are references in the sporting press to a champion county as early as 1825, but the list is ot continuous and in some years only two counties contested the title. The earliest reference in ıy cricket publication is from 1864, and at this time there were eight leading counties who have ɔme to be regarded as first-class from that date – Cambridgeshire, Hampshire, Kent, liddlesex, Nottinghamshire, Surrey, Sussex and Yorkshire. The newly formed Lancashire club ɛgan playing inter-county matches in 1865, Gloucestershire in 1870 and Derbyshire in 1871, ıd they are therefore regarded as first-class from these respective dates. Cambridgeshire ropped out after 1871, Hampshire, who had not played inter-county matches in certain ıasons, after 1885, and Derbyshire after 1887. Somerset, who had played matches against the rst-class counties since 1879, were regarded as first-class from 1882 to 1885, and were admitted ırmally to the Championship in 1891. In 1894, Derbyshire, Essex, Leicestershire and /arwickshire were granted first-class status, but did not compete in the Championship until 395 when Hampshire returned. Worcestershire, Northamptonshire and Glamorgan were lmitted to the Championship in 1899, 1905 and 1921 respectively and are regarded as first-ıss from these dates. An invitation in 1921 to Buckinghamshire to enter the Championship ıs declined, owing to the lack of necessary playing facilities, and an application by Devon in 48 was unsuccessful.

MOST COUNTY CHAMPIONSHIP APPEARANCES

763	W. Rhodes	Yorkshire	1898-1930
707	F. E. Woolley	Kent	1906-38
665	C. P. Mead	Hampshire	1906-36

OST CONSECUTIVE COUNTY CHAMPIONSHIP APPEARANCES

423	K. G. Suttle	Sussex	1954-69
412	J. G. Binks	Yorkshire	1955-69
399	J. Vine	Sussex	1899-1914
344	E. H. Killick	Sussex	1898-1912
326	C. N. Woolley	Northamptonshire	1913-31
305	A. H. Dyson	Glamorgan	1930-47
301	B. Taylor	Essex	1961-72

tes: J. Vine made 417 consecutive appearances for Sussex in all first-class matches between y 1900 and September 1914.

G. Binks did not miss a Championship match for Yorkshire between making his début in ıe 1955 and retiring at the end of the 1969 season.

FEATURES OF 1988

Double-Hundreds

K. J. Barnett	239*	Derbyshire v Leicestershire at Leicester.
G. Cook	203	Northamptonshire v Yorkshire at Scarborough.
M. W. Gatting	210	Middlesex v Nottinghamshire at Lord's.
G. A. Gooch	275	Essex v Kent at Chelmsford.
R. A. Harper	217*	West Indians v Sussex at Hove.
G. A. Hick (2)	212	Worcestershire v Lancashire at Manchester.
	405*	Worcestershire v Somerset at Taunton.
A. A. Metcalfe	216*	Yorkshire v Middlesex at Leeds.
D. W. Randall	237	Nottinghamshire v Derbyshire at Nottingham.

Hundred in Each Innings of a Match

G. C. Holmes	100*	107	Glamorgan v Somerset at Taunton.
W. N. Slack	163*	105*	Middlesex v Glamorgan at Lord's.
F. D. Stephenson ...	111	117	Nottinghamshire v Yorkshire at Nottingham.

Fastest Hundred

(*For the Walter Lawrence Trophy*)

G. A. Hick .... 79 balls Worcestershire v Surrey at The Oval.
In 91 minutes and including four sixes and nine fours.

Hundred Before Lunch

K. J. Barnett	Derbyshire v Gloucestershire at Derby (1st day).
G. A. Gooch	Essex v Surrey at Chelmsford (1st day).
N. Hussain	Essex v Leicestershire at Chelmsford (2nd day).
M. P. Maynard	Glamorgan v Worcestershire at Abergavenny (3rd day).

Eleven Sixes in an Innings

G. A. Hick .... Worcestershire v Somerset at Taunton.

Hundred on First-Class Début

P. D. Atkins	114*	Surrey v Cambridge University at The Oval.
B. M. W. Patterson .	100	Scotland v Ireland at Dumfries.

P. D. Bowler scored 155* on début for Derbyshire (v Cambridge University at Cambridg Having scored 100* for Leicestershire on his first-class début, v Hampshire in 1986, became the first to score hundreds on début for two counties.

First to 1,000 Runs

G. A. Hick (Worcestershire) on May 28.

Hick became the eighth batsman to score 1,000 runs before June and set a record aggreg for the month of April with 410 runs, average 82.00.

First to 2,000 Runs

G. A. Hick (Worcestershire) on August 16.

Carrying Bat Through Completed Innings

P. D. Bowler	159* (340)	Derbyshire v Essex at Chesterfield.
G. D. Mendis	65* (163)	Lancashire v Glamorgan at Swansea.
A. J. Moles	67* (107†)	Warwickshire v Kent at Birmingham.
M. Newell	10* (44†)	Nottinghamshire v Warwickshire at Birmingham.
N. R. Taylor	67* (121)	Kent v Leicestershire at Leicester.

† *One or more batsmen absent. Innings totals shown in brackets.*

Notable Partnerships

Second Wicket

276 T. S. Curtis/G. A. Hick, Worcestershire v Hampshire at Worcester.

Third Wicket

284 W. N. Slack/M. W. Gatting, Middlesex v Glamorgan at Lord's.

Fourth Wicket

345 M. Newell/D. W. Randall, Nottinghamshire v Derbyshire at Nottingham.
264 M. W. Gatting/K. R. Brown, Middlesex v Nottinghamshire at Lord's.
259 G. A. Gooch/D. R. Pringle, Essex v Kent at Chelmsford.
251 G. Fowler/A. N. Hayhurst, Lancashire v Derbyshire at Derby.

Sixth Wicket

265† G. A. Hick/S. J. Rhodes, Worcestershire v Somerset at Taunton.
227 I. V. A. Richards/R. A. Harper, West Indians v Sussex at Hove.

Seventh Wicket

222 G. R. Cowdrey/S. A. Marsh, Kent v Essex at Chelmsford.
205† G. A. Hick/P. J. Newport, Worcestershire v Yorkshire at Worcester.

Eighth Wicket

177*† G. A. Hick/R. K. Illingworth, Worcestershire v Somerset at Taunton.

Ninth Wicket

123 R. A. Harper/C. E. L. Ambrose, West Indians v Sussex at Hove.
113 R. K. Illingworth/N. V. Radford, Worcestershire v Nottinghamshire at Nottingham.

* *Unbroken partnership.* † *County record.*

Fourteen Wickets in a Match

D. A. Graveney .... 14-165 Gloucestershire v Worcestershire at Bristol.

Eight Wickets in an Innings

T. M. Alderman	8-59	Gloucestershire v Somerset at Taunton.
M. P. Bicknell	9-45	Surrey v Cambridge University at The Oval.
S. D. Fletcher	8-58	Yorkshire v Essex at Sheffield.
D. A. Graveney	8-127	Gloucestershire v Worcestershire at Bristol.
S. T. Jefferies	8-97	Hampshire v Gloucestershire at Gloucester.
K. T. Medlycott	8-52	Surrey v Sussex at Hove.
P. G. Newman	8-29	Derbyshire v Yorkshire at Leeds.
P. J. Newport	8-52	Worcestershire v Middlesex at Lord's.
S. L. Watkin	8-59	Glamorgan v Warwickshire at Birmingham.

Six Wickets in Ten Balls

T. A. Merrick ...... Warwickshire v Derbyshire at Derby.

Hat-Tricks

T. A. Merrick .... Warwickshire v Derbyshire at Derby.
Wasim Akram ..... Lancashire v Surrey at Southport.

Wicket with First Ball in First-Class Cricket

J. R. Ayling .... Hampshire v Oxford University at Oxford.

First to 100 Wickets

F. D. Stephenson (Nottinghamshire) on August 22.

The Season's Double

F. D. Stephenson (Nottinghamshire) 1,018 runs and 125 wickets.

1,000 Runs and 50 Wickets

K. M. Curran (Gloucestershire) 1,005 runs and 65 wickets.

Match Double (100 runs and 10 wickets)

G. C. Small	31, 69; 6-79, 6-42	Warwickshire v Glamorgan at Birmingham.
F. D. Stephenson	111,117; 4-105, 7-117	Nottinghamshire v Yorkshire at Nottingham.

Ten Wicket-Keeping Dismissals in a Match

C. W. Scott (10 ct) .... Nottinghamshire v Derbyshire at Derby.

Six Wicket-Keeping Dismissals in an Innings

C. P. Metson (6 ct) .... Glamorgan v Leicestershire at Neath.
S. J. Rhodes (6 ct) .... Worcestershire v Sussex at Kidderminster.
C. J. Richards (6 ct) .... Surrey v Warwickshire at The Oval.
D. Ripley (6 ct) .... Northamptonshire v Sussex at Northampton.
A. J. Stewart (6 ct)......... Surrey v Lancashire at Southport.

Stumped by a Substitute

C. L. Hooper (West Indians) by W. Noon (Northamptonshire) at Northampton.

Five Catches in the Field in an Innings

A. C. Storie .... Warwickshire v Leicestershire at Birmingham.

Highest Innings Totals

628-7 dec. . . . Worcestershire v Somerset at Taunton.
616 . . . . Essex v Kent at Chelmsford.
614 . . . . Nottinghamshire v Derbyshire at Nottingham.
561-9 dec. . . . West Indians v Sussex at Hove.
553 . . . . Surrey v Sussex at Hove.
543-8 dec. . . . Glamorgan v Somerset at Cardiff.
539-3 dec. . . . Kent v Oxford University at Oxford.
505-5 dec. . . . Middlesex v Nottinghamshire at Lord's.

Lowest Innings Totals

44† . . . . Nottinghamshire v Warwickshire at Birmingham.
47 . . . . Glamorgan v Lancashire at Swansea.
65 . . . . Nottinghamshire v Kent at Dartford.
68 . . . . Oxford University v Leicestershire at Oxford.
71 . . . . Sussex v Kent at Hastings.
74 . . . . Warwickshire v Surrey at The Oval.

† *One man absent.*

Highest Match Aggregate

1,570 (29 wickets) . . . Essex v Kent at Chelmsford.

The record aggregate for a County Championship match.

Four Hundreds in an Innings

Kent (539-3 dec.) v Oxford University at Oxford.
S. G. Hinks 138, R. F. Pienaar 127, C. J. Tavaré 138*, C. S. Cowdrey 124*.

In the second innings, S. A. Marsh (100*) scored Kent's fifth hundred of the match.

Victory after Following On

Northamptonshire (170 & 363) v Warwickshire (415 & 112) at Northampton.

Career Aggregate Milestones†

[illegible],000 runs . . . . I. V. A. Richards.
[illegible],000 runs . . . . M. W. Gatting, A. J. Lamb, J. G. Wright.
[illegible],000 runs . . . . P. Bainbridge, M. R. Benson, N. E. Briers, G. C. Clinton, C. S. Cowdrey, D. L. Haynes, J. D. Love, M. C. J. Nicholas, D. M. Smith, R. G. Williams.
[illegible]000 wickets . . . . . . I. T. Botham, J. Simmons.

† *Achieved since September 1987.*

FIRST-CLASS AVERAGES, 1988

BATTING

(Qualification: 8 innings, average 10.00)

** Signifies not out. † Denotes a left-handed batsman.*

	M	*I*	*NO*	*R*	*HI*	*100s*	*50s*	*Avge*
G. A. Hick (*Worcs.*)	24	37	2	2,713	405*	10	5	77.51
S. R. Waugh (*Somerset*)	15	24	6	1,314	161	6	4	73.00
C. W. J. Athey (*Glos.*)	13	22	6	1,064	168*	2	6	66.50
G. A. Gooch (*Essex*)	21	37	1	2,324	275	6	15	64.55
M. D. Crowe (*Somerset*)	5	9	1	487	136*	2	2	60.87
†A. R. Border (*Essex*)	20	32	8	1,393	169*	6	4	58.04
K. J. Barnett (*Derbys.*)	19	30	2	1,623	239*	5	8	57.96
A. J. Lamb (*Northants*)	16	27	5	1,163	155	5	5	52.86
M. A. Atherton (*CUCC & Lancs.*)	16	27	4	1,121	152*	4	3	48.73
N. Hussain (*Essex*)	9	13	3	486	165*	1	2	48.60
†D. M. Smith (*Surrey*)	11	18	5	630	157*	2	1	48.46
M. W. Gatting (*Middx*)	20	33	2	1,469	210	3	9	47.38
M. R. Ramprakash (*Middx*)	9	13	4	421	68*	0	3	46.77
P. D. Bowler (*Derbys.*)	24	42	5	1,725	159*	4	9	46.62
D. L. Haynes (*WI & World XI*)	15	25	4	964	158	1	7	45.90
†W. N. Slack (*Middx*)	19	32	5	1,228	163*	3	6	45.48
†G. S. Clinton (*Surrey*)	18	29	5	1,054	158	4	4	43.91
R. C. Ontong (*Glam.*)	17	25	8	734	120*	1	4	43.17
†J. G. Wright (*Derbys.*)	11	20	1	815	154*	1	5	42.89
C. J. Tavaré (*Kent*)	22	36	2	1,430	138*	4	5	42.05
C. J. Richards (*Surrey*)	20	25	4	874	102*	1	6	41.61
M. D. Moxon (*Yorks.*)	21	39	3	1,485	191	3	8	41.25
M. P. Maynard (*Glam.*)	23	42	6	1,485	126	3	11	41.25
R. A. Smith (*Hants*)	21	42	8	1,356	141*	4	4	39.88
M. A. Lynch (*Surrey*)	21	29	4	996	103*	2	4	39.84
P. A. Neale (*Worcs.*)	21	31	5	1,036	167	4	2	39.84
T. S. Curtis (*Worcs.*)	22	38	4	1,337	131	2	7	39.32
D. W. Randall (*Notts.*)	21	37	4	1,286	237	2	9	38.96
P. W. G. Parker (*Sussex*)	21	40	5	1,359	124	5	5	38.82
P. J. Prichard (*Essex*)	24	39	8	1,202	97	0	9	38.77
†D. I. Gower (*Leics.*)	22	38	4	1,317	172	2	5	38.7
R. T. Robinson (*Notts.*)	21	35	4	1,194	134*	4	4	38.5
Asif Din (*Warwicks.*)	23	41	4	1,425	158*	2	8	38.5
A. A. Metcalfe (*Yorks.*)	22	40	5	1,320	216*	2	8	37.7
J. E. Morris (*Derbys.*)	23	37	5	1,204	175	2	6	37.6
K. M. Curran (*Glos.*)	19	34	7	1,005	142	2	4	37.2
R. F. Pienaar (*Kent*)	21	35	2	1,228	144	3	7	37.2
R. J. Bailey (*Northants*)	24	42	2	1,448	127*	3	8	36.2
†T. A. Lloyd (*Warwicks*)	24	43	3	1,448	160*	4	3	36.2
P. Bainbridge (*Glos.*)	23	38	1	1,334	169	4	6	36.0
J. J. Whitaker (*Leics.*)	23	39	5	1,223	145	3	5	35.9
C. L. Smith (*Hants*)	22	43	3	1,436	124*	3	8	35.9
G. D. Mendis (*Lancs.*)	24	42	4	1,364	151	2	8	35.8
P. D. Atkins (*Surrey*)	6	11	1	357	114*	1	1	35.7
G. C. Holmes (*Glam.*)	20	32	4	999	117	4	4	35.6
P. Johnson (*Notts.*)	24	42	3	1,389	140	3	7	35.6
†D. R. Turner (*Hants*)	22	40	6	1,204	150*	2	6	35.4
J. D. Carr (*Middx*)	24	43	6	1,297	144	2	7	35.6
A. W. Stovold (*Glos.*)	21	39	2	1,296	136	2	6	35.
A. P. Wells (*Sussex*)	23	42	5	1,286	120	1	9	34.
A. J. Stewart (*Surrey*)	22	32	3	1,006	133	2	6	34.

	M	*I*	*NO*	*R*	*HI*	*100s*	*50s*	*Avge*
N. E. Briers (*Leics.*)	24	41	2	1,335	125*	2	9	34.23
M. R. Benson (*Kent*)	21	37	1	1,227	110	2	8	34.08
R. J. Shastri (*Glam.*)	12	19	2	575	157	1	2	33.82
†A. R. Butcher (*Glam.*)	23	40	2	1,282	166	1	9	33.73
R. G. Williams (*Northants*)	20	34	9	842	119	1	4	33.68
D. J. Capel (*Northants*)	21	36	5	1,040	92	0	7	33.54
A. J. Moles (*Warwicks.*)	18	31	2	968	115	1	5	33.37
P. J. Hartley (*Yorks.*)	13	17	6	364	127*	1	0	33.09
†S. T. Jefferies (*Hants*)	14	19	5	462	60	0	2	33.00
L. Potter (*Leics.*)	23	34	7	885	107	1	5	32.77
A. Needham (*Middx*)	8	12	3	293	66*	0	2	32.55
†I. J. Gould (*Sussex*)	19	31	4	875	82*	0	6	32.40
P. R. Downton (*Middx*)	18	24	5	614	120	1	2	32.31
P. E. Robinson (*Yorks.*)	24	40	3	1,173	129*	1	8	31.70
D. M. Ward (*Surrey*)	25	36	6	942	126	1	8	31.40
†R. C. Russell (*Glos.*)	24	36	8	870	94	0	6	31.07
†Wasim Akram (*Lancs.*)	10	18	2	496	116*	1	3	31.00
A. J. Wright (*Glos.*)	24	42	1	1,268	137	2	5	30.92
I. D. Austin (*Lancs.*)	6	9	2	216	64	0	2	30.85
†N. H. Fairbrother (*Lancs.*)	23	41	4	1,134	111	2	6	30.64
†G. Fowler (*Lancs.*)	21	38	1	1,134	172	2	5	30.64
R. O. Butcher (*Middx*)	19	29	3	796	134	1	4	30.61
S. C. Goldsmith (*Derbys.*)	24	39	4	1,071	89	0	7	30.60
P. Carrick (*Yorks.*)	23	34	7	815	81	0	2	30.18
P. A. Cottey (*Glam.*)	13	23	3	603	92	0	5	30.15
†A. I. Kallicharran (*Warwicks.*)	9	15	1	418	117*	1	2	29.85
M. C. J. Nicholas (*Hants*)	25	47	3	1,301	132*	2	5	29.56
V. P. Terry (*Hants*)	23	43	3	1,182	190	3	5	29.55
B. J. M. Maher (*Derbys.*)	24	39	6	974	121*	1	5	29.51
R. J. Harden (*Somerset*)	6	11	1	295	78	0	3	29.50
†S. G. Hinks (*Kent*)	16	27	1	764	138	1	3	29.38
G. Cook (*Northants*)	18	30	1	850	203	2	3	29.31
J. P. Stephenson (*Essex*)	18	31	4	791	99	0	6	29.29
J. E. Emburey (*Middx*)	20	27	4	673	102	1	4	29.26
F. D. Stephenson (*Notts.*)	22	35	0	1,018	117	2	7	29.08
C. S. Cowdrey (*Kent*)	21	36	7	843	124*	2	2	29.06
J. D. Love (*Yorks.*)	18	28	2	751	93*	0	6	28.88
T. E. Jesty (*Lancs.*)	15	27	3	693	73	0	3	28.87
†N. A. Felton (*Somerset*)	14	27	2	720	127	1	4	28.80
R. Sharma (*Derbys.*)	10	14	3	315	80	0	1	28.63
G. R. Cowdrey (*Kent*)	20	33	4	830	145	1	4	28.62
P. M. Roebuck (*Somerset*)	12	19	3	454	112*	1	1	28.37
K. R. Brown (*Middx*)	21	34	5	822	131*	2	2	28.34
D. A. Hagan (*OUCC*)	7	13	2	306	59	0	1	27.81
G. J. Lord (*Worcs.*)	20	33	2	862	101	1	4	27.80
H. Morris (*Glam.*)	19	33	3	832	87	0	6	27.73
A. Fordham (*Northants*)	16	29	6	637	125*	1	3	27.69
K. W. R. Fletcher (*Essex*)	12	14	3	303	58	0	2	27.54
A. Sidebottom (*Yorks.*)	18	24	5	517	55	0	2	27.21
N. R. Taylor (*Kent*)	21	37	3	925	114	2	4	27.20
M. J. Weston (*Worcs.*)	18	24	5	514	95*	0	3	27.05
M. J. Kilborn (*OUCC*)	7	13	0	351	78	0	2	27.00
A. W. Lilley (*Essex*)	21	33	3	803	80*	0	5	26.76
P. Pollard (*Notts.*)	9	17	1	428	142	1	1	26.75
P. W. Romaines (*Glos.*)	21	39	3	955	101*	1	6	26.52
N. A. Stanley (*Northants*)	8	12	2	263	66	0	3	26.30
P. J. Newport (*Worcs.*)	22	25	8	447	77*	0	1	26.29
B. Roberts (*Derbys.*)	24	39	4	919	71	0	7	26.25
W. Larkins (*Northants*)	23	41	2	1,024	134	2	4	26.25
N. D. Burns (*Somerset*)	23	34	7	708	133*	1	2	26.22
S. J. Rhodes (*Worcs.*)	23	33	10	597	108	1	1	25.95

	M	*I*	*NO*	*R*	*HI*	*100s*	*50s*	*Avge*
†J. J. E. Hardy (*Somerset*)	22	39	3	927	97	0	6	25.75
A. C. S. Pigott (*Sussex*)	20	34	8	668	56	0	3	25.69
†B. C. Broad (*Notts.*)	20	34	0	872	73	0	5	25.64
R. J. Bartlett (*Somerset*)	19	31	3	707	102*	1	3	25.25
G. C. Small (*Warwicks.*)	20	29	7	554	70	0	3	25.18
P. Willey (*Northants*)	24	40	1	978	130	2	3	25.07
†R. J. Scott (*Hants*)	9	16	1	374	107*	1	2	24.93
I. L. Pont (*Essex*)	8	8	2	149	68	0	1	24.83
V. J. Marks (*Somerset*)	23	31	2	719	68	0	3	24.79
†D. Byas (*Yorks.*)	14	25	1	592	112	1	4	24.66
S. A. Marsh (*Kent*)	23	35	6	713	120	2	1	24.58
C. M. Wells (*Sussex*)	24	41	4	908	109*	1	4	24.54
J. G. Thomas (*Glam.*)	16	26	5	515	110	2	0	24.52
J. R. Ayling (*Hants*)	19	33	4	711	88*	0	4	24.51
N. J. Lenham (*Sussex*)	18	32	2	733	74	0	3	24.43
D. A. Banks (*Warwicks.*)	7	9	1	195	61	0	1	24.37
J. F. Sykes (*Middx*)	9	13	1	292	88	0	2	24.33
J. A. Hopkins (*Glam.*)	13	23	1	534	87	0	4	24.27
R. A. Cobb (*Leics.*)	11	20	2	432	65	0	2	24.00
D. E. East (*Essex*)	20	30	2	669	134	1	2	23.89
A. M. Green (*Sussex*)	16	29	2	639	68	0	4	23.66
D. A. Thorne (*Warwicks.*)	15	25	1	566	76	0	4	23.58
P. A. Smith (*Warwicks.*)	16	27	4	542	84*	0	3	23.56
A. N. Hayhurst (*Lancs.*)	14	23	2	492	107	1	2	23.42
S. A. Almaer (*OUCC*)	6	11	0	256	67	0	1	23.27
J. G. Wyatt (*Somerset*)	15	26	1	578	69	0	3	23.12
K. T. Medlycott (*Surrey*)	23	29	5	554	77*	0	4	23.08
T. J. Boon (*Leics.*)	15	23	1	505	131	1	2	22.95
†C. Penn (*Kent*)	20	31	12	436	40	0	0	22.94
M. A. Feltham (*Surrey*)	22	25	9	367	74	0	1	22.93
R. I. Alikhan (*Sussex*)	10	19	0	429	98	0	3	22.57
†K. Sharp (*Yorks.*)	12	19	0	428	128	1	1	22.52
R. K. Illingworth (*Worcs.*)	23	22	4	404	60	0	2	22.44
R. J. Blakey (*Yorks.*)	16	24	4	446	85*	0	2	22.30
N. V. Radford (*Worcs.*)	18	15	6	200	65	0	1	22.22
N. J. Pringle (*Somerset*)	8	15	4	244	54	0	1	22.18
G. Miller (*Essex*)	19	21	4	377	77	0	1	22.17
B. R. Hardie (*Essex*)	13	20	3	377	58	0	2	22.17
J. D. Birch (*Notts.*)	24	39	4	776	114*	1	2	22.17
M. Newell (*Notts.*)	20	37	3	740	105	1	2	21.76
C. K. Bullen (*Surrey*)	12	14	2	261	59*	0	2	21.7
M. R. Gouldstone (*Northants*)	7	12	1	239	71	0	2	21.7
M. Watkinson (*Lancs.*)	24	39	4	759	85*	0	6	21.6
D. A. Reeve (*Warwicks.*)	16	23	3	431	103	1	0	21.5
P. A. J. DeFreitas (*Leics.*)	17	25	1	517	113	1	3	21.5
M. A. Roseberry (*Middx*)	14	21	3	386	67	0	1	21.4
J. C. M. Atkinson (*CUCC*)	7	12	0	257	73	0	1	21.4
P. Whitticase (*Leics.*)	23	32	10	469	71	0	2	21.3
†A. Walker (*Northants*)	18	20	10	213	40*	0	0	21.3
T. R. Ward (*Kent*)	10	17	0	362	72	0	3	21.2
C. C. Lewis (*Leics.*)	16	23	4	400	40	0	0	21.0
D. L. Bairstow (*Yorks.*)	14	23	3	416	94*	0	2	20.8
I. G. Swallow (*Yorks.*)	11	19	2	352	48*	0	0	20.7
N. F. Williams (*Middx*)	8	11	2	186	63*	0	1	20.6
†J. W. Lloyds (*Glos.*)	16	24	3	433	102*	1	1	20.6
S. J. W. Andrew (*Hants*)	11	9	7	41	12*	0	0	20.5
W. W. Davis (*Northants*)	15	18	3	306	43	0	0	20.4
K. P. Evans (*Notts.*)	15	24	4	406	54	0	1	20.3
G. D. Rose (*Somerset*)	20	25	6	385	69*	0	1	20.2
J. Simmons (*Lancs.*)	21	27	9	362	57*	0	1	20.1
D. J. R. Martindale (*Notts.*)	9	14	1	261	52*	0	1	20.0

	M	I	NO	R	HI	100s	50s	Avge
S. P. Hughes (*Middx*)	18	21	5	321	53	0	1	20.06
M. P. Speight (*Sussex*)	7	13	0	258	58	0	2	19.84
I. A. Greig (*Surrey*)	23	28	1	529	67	0	1	19.59
†G. J. Parsons (*Warwicks.*)	10	13	4	174	52	0	1	19.33
D. R. Pringle (*Essex*)	19	27	0	516	128	1	3	19.11
D. J. Bicknell (*Surrey*)	11	19	1	343	62	0	2	19.05
G. A. Tedstone (*Warwicks.*)	4	8	0	151	50	0	1	18.87
M. W. Pooley (*Glos.*)	8	13	5	149	38	0	0	18.62
G. D. Reynolds (*OUCC*)	6	9	1	147	69	0	1	18.37
D. A. Leatherdale (*Worcs.*)	10	15	1	255	34*	0	0	18.21
P. Moores (*Sussex*)	14	24	2	395	97*	0	1	17.95
D. P. Hughes (*Lancs.*)	22	34	4	522	62	0	3	17.40
A. P. Igglesden (*Kent*)	7	8	2	103	41	0	0	17.16
I. Folley (*Lancs.*)	19	20	14	102	30	0	0	17.00
A. C. Storie (*Warwicks.*)	9	17	2	255	68	0	1	17.00
C. W. Scott (*Notts.*)	19	27	6	356	63*	0	1	16.95
T. J. G. O'Gorman (*Derbys.*)	5	9	0	152	78	0	1	16.88
D. Ripley (*Northants*)	25	33	6	451	49	0	0	16.70
P. J. Bakker (*Hants*)	10	11	8	50	16	0	0	16.66
N. J. Falkner (*Sussex*)	7	14	0	232	55	0	1	16.57
G. W. Humpage (*Warwicks.*)	17	26	1	411	80	0	3	16.44
†R. M. Ellison (*Kent*)	20	27	6	345	50*	0	1	16.42
E. E. Hemmings (*Notts.*)	17	25	10	245	31*	0	0	16.33
†D. J. Wild (*Northants*)	18	27	1	423	75	0	2	16.26
W. K. Hegg (*Lancs.*)	24	34	5	467	76	0	1	16.10
†K. D. James (*Hants*)	12	22	2	320	77	0	1	16.00
R. Bate (*CUCC*)	7	12	2	160	45	0	0	16.00
†P. A. Booth (*Yorks.*)	5	8	2	96	33*	0	0	16.00
C. P. Metson (*Glam.*)	23	30	8	351	48	0	0	15.95
A. E. Warner (*Derbys.*)	19	25	6	300	45	0	0	15.78
S. T. Clarke (*Surrey*)	12	10	1	141	28	0	0	15.66
R. J. Parks (*Hants*)	23	35	8	420	38*	0	0	15.55
D. A. Graveney (*Glos.*)	23	24	9	231	47	0	0	15.40
S. D. Weale (*OUCC*)	6	9	0	136	40	0	0	15.11
M. W. Alleyne (*Glos.*)	14	21	1	300	56	0	1	15.00
T. D. Topley (*Essex*)	16	22	6	235	56*	0	1	14.68
D. J. Foster (*Somerset*)	13	14	9	72	20	0	0	14.40
P. G. Newman (*Derbys.*)	16	19	6	187	39	0	0	14.38
S. D. Heath (*CUCC*)	5	8	1	100	33*	0	0	14.28
T. A. Merrick (*Warwicks.*)	16	21	3	256	34	0	0	14.22
A. R. Clarke (*Sussex*)	21	32	8	337	68	0	1	14.04
T. M. Tremlett (*Hants*)	7	10	2	111	38	0	0	13.87
B. N. French (*Notts.*)	7	11	1	135	28	0	0	13.50
D. K. Lillee (*Northants*)	8	11	2	120	22	0	0	13.33
D. B. D'Oliveira (*Worcs.*)	8	11	1	132	37	0	0	13.20
C. Shaw (*Yorks.*)	21	25	12	170	31	0	0	13.07
S. J. Noyes (*CUCC*)	8	14	1	170	38	0	0	13.07
M. A. Holding (*Derbys.*)	11	12	2	129	30*	0	0	12.90
J. P. Agnew (*Leics.*)	24	29	8	271	38	0	0	12.90
P. J. W. Allott (*Lancs.*)	19	28	4	308	31*	0	0	12.83
R. J. Maru (*Hants*)	23	29	5	302	74	0	1	12.58
A. R. C. Fraser (*Middx*)	23	28	10	223	41	0	0	12.38
T. M. Alderman (*Glos.*)	20	22	11	135	43*	0	0	12.27
N. A. Mallender (*Somerset*)	17	20	7	158	44	0	0	12.15
N. H. Peters (*Surrey*)	12	15	8	85	25*	0	0	12.14
R. J. Turner (*CUCC*)	8	14	1	155	27	0	0	11.92
G. J. F. Ferris (*Leics.*)	18	20	8	139	36*	0	0	11.58
O. H. Mortensen (*Derbys.*)	12	12	8	46	15	0	0	11.50
M. D. Harman (*Kent*)	12	13	6	80	17*	0	0	11.42
G. A. Pointer (*CUCC*)	7	12	2	114	18*	0	0	11.40
A. R. K. Pierson (*Warwicks.*)	9	12	7	57	18*	0	0	11.40

	M	*I*	*NO*	*R*	*HI*	*100s*	*50s*	*Avge*
†G. R. Dilley (*Worcs.*)	13	15	2	147	36	0	0	11.30
†K. E. Cooper (*Notts.*)	24	34	9	282	39	0	0	11.28
L. B. Taylor (*Leics.*)	17	16	6	111	60	0	1	11.10
J. M. Tremellen (*CUCC*)	7	12	0	131	33	0	0	10.91
A. A. Donald (*Warwicks.*)	7	10	3	74	29	0	0	10.57
†J. H. Childs (*Essex*)	20	19	12	73	25*	0	0	10.42
J. Derrick (*Glam.*)	21	28	6	229	50*	0	1	10.40
N. A. Foster (*Essex*)	16	21	4	171	34	0	0	10.05
†A. N. Jones (*Somerset*)	20	21	8	130	38	0	0	10.00

BOWLING

(Qualification: 10 wickets in 10 innings)

† *Denotes a left-arm bowler.*

	O	*M*	*R*	*W*	*BB*	*5 W/i*	*Avge*
O. H. Mortensen (*Derbys.*)	233.3	73	464	34	6-35	4	13.64
S. T. Clarke (*Surrey*)	396.4	108	913	63	6-52	4	14.49
N. F. Williams (*Middx*)	178.3	33	511	30	6-42	2	17.03
P. W. Jarvis (*Yorks.*)	233.2	52	651	37	6-40	2	17.59
N. G. Cowans (*Middx*)	491.5	123	1,290	71	6-49	3	18.16
F. D. Stephenson (*Notts.*)	819.1	196	2,289	125	7-56	10	18.31
G. J. Parsons (*Warwicks.*)	228	69	553	29	7-16	1	19.06
A. R. C. Fraser (*Middx*)	697.1	195	1,550	80	6-68	6	19.37
P. J. Newport (*Worcs.*)	600.3	129	1,844	93	8-52	7	19.82
G. C. Small (*Warwicks.*)	628.1	170	1,605	80	7-15	8	20.06
A. A. Donald (*Warwicks.*)	180.4	40	534	26	5-57	1	20.53
P. J. W. Allott (*Lancs.*)	590.2	162	1,378	67	6-59	5	20.56
A. Sidebottom (*Yorks.*)	513.2	135	1,303	63	7-89	3	20.68
N. A. Mallender (*Somerset*)	433.1	111	1,037	50	5-12	1	20.74
K. M. Curran (*Glos.*)	414.2	86	1,385	65	7-54	4	21.30
†Wasim Akram (*Lancs.*)	291.4	76	666	31	7-53	2	21.48
K. E. Cooper (*Notts.*)	816	220	2,179	101	5-41	5	21.57
A. P. Igglesden (*Kent*)	234.3	46	805	37	6-34	3	21.75
†K. D. James (*Hants*)	298.5	73	763	35	5-25	2	21.80
†R. K. Illingworth (*Worcs.*)	597.4	189	1,274	58	5-46	4	21.96
W. W. Davis (*Northants*)	538.2	91	1,614	73	7-52	7	22.10
T. A. Merrick (*Warwicks.*)	475.3	105	1,437	65	6-29	5	22.10
S. D. Fletcher (*Yorks.*)	412	66	1,308	59	8-58	2	22.16
G. J. F. Ferris (*Leics.*)	452.1	82	1,380	62	5-47	2	22.25
P. J. Bakker (*Hants*)	293.4	86	670	30	5-54	1	22.33
G. R. Dilley (*Worcs.*)	387.1	70	1,098	49	5-46	4	22.40
T. A. Munton (*Warwicks.*)	425.1	126	1,047	46	6-21	2	22.76
N. A. Foster (*Essex*)	598.3	122	1,822	80	6-53	5	22.77
T. M. Alderman (*Glos.*)	601	135	1,711	75	8-59	3	22.81
M. A. Robinson (*Northants*)	402.4	85	1,055	46	4-19	0	22.93
T. M. Tremlett (*Hants*)	125.3	35	326	14	4-19	0	23.28
I. A. Greig (*Surrey*)	402.3	83	1,143	49	6-34	2	23.3[illegible]
J. R. Ayling (*Hants*)	432.1	97	1,098	47	4-57	0	23.36
P. A. Smith (*Warwicks.*)	164.3	20	540	23	3-7	0	23.4[illegible]
M. D. Harman (*Kent*)	266.4	86	593	25	5-55	2	23.7[illegible]
R. M. Ellison (*Kent*)	603.4	171	1,697	71	7-75	3	23.9[illegible]
†N. G. B. Cook (*Northants*)	768.2	264	1,635	68	6-56	2	24.0[illegible]
†K. T. Medlycott (*Surrey*)	593.1	159	1,660	69	8-52	6	24.0[illegible]
P. A. J. DeFreitas (*Leics.*)	557.3	127	1,555	64	5-38	5	24.2[illegible]
C. Penn (*Kent*)	646.1	144	1,989	81	7-70	6	24.5[illegible]
J. Simmons (*Lancs.*)	629	159	1,548	63	5-53	2	24.5[illegible]

	O	*M*	*R*	*W*	*BB*	*5 W/i*	*Avge*
S. J. W. Andrew (*Hants*)	268.5	68	765	31	5-36	1	24.67
N. V. Radford (*Worcs.*)	570.5	101	1,770	71	7-73	3	24.92
J. P. Agnew (*Leics.*)	783.5	166	2,367	93	7-61	8	25.45
†J. H. Childs (*Essex*)	654.5	208	1,582	62	6-92	4	25.51
†D. A. Graveney (*Glos.*)	612.2	179	1,353	53	8-127	2	25.52
A. Walker (*Northants*)	465.5	98	1,380	54	5-64	1	25.55
T. D. Topley (*Essex*)	538.3	87	1,663	65	7-75	4	25.58
·J. K. Lever (*Essex*)	422.4	90	1,120	43	4-61	0	26.04
A. E. Warner (*Derbys.*)	445	104	1,151	44	4-22	0	26.15
D. R. Pringle (*Essex*)	515.2	111	1,492	57	6-39	4	26.17
J. E. Emburey (*Middx*)	671.5	215	1,543	58	6-24	2	26.60
M. J. Weston (*Worcs.*)	124	31	320	12	4-24	0	26.66
G. D. Rose (*Somerset*)	504.5	116	1,526	57	6-47	1	26.77
P. G. Newman (*Derbys.*)	339.5	81	950	35	8-29	1	27.14
C. A. Connor (*Hants*)	495.3	92	1,497	55	5-70	1	27.21
D. V. Lawrence (*Glos.*)	647.2	103	2,296	84	7-47	4	27.33
L. B. Taylor (*Leics.*)	324.3	70	967	35	6-49	1	27.62
N. H. Peters (*Surrey*)	278.2	50	954	34	6-31	1	28.05
A. C. S. Pigott (*Sussex*)	627	108	2,078	74	6-100	2	28.08
C. K. Bullen (*Surrey*)	107.1	25	316	11	4-56	0	28.72
C. C. Lewis (*Leics.*)	391.4	83	1,210	42	6-22	2	28.80
H. R. J. Trump (*Somerset*)	270	74	696	24	4-17	0	29.00
M. W. Cleal (*Somerset*)	168	25	582	20	4-41	0	29.10
V. J. Marks (*Somerset*)	862.5	222	2,214	76	7-118	5	29.13
C. S. Cowdrey (*Kent*)	391.2	96	1,141	39	5-46	1	29.25
M. W. Pooley (*Glos.*)	128.4	30	384	13	4-80	0	29.53
K. J. Barnett (*Derbys.*)	161.1	37	414	14	3-63	0	29.57
R. G. Williams (*Northants*)	331	72	980	33	5-86	1	29.69
. Folley (*Lancs.*)	614.3	168	1,701	57	6-20	2	29.84
D. E. Malcolm (*Derbys.*)	488.1	93	1,676	56	6-68	2	29.92
M. A. Feltham (*Surrey*)	584.1	135	1,679	56	5-45	2	29.98
A. N. Jones (*Somerset*)	512	86	1,658	55	7-30	1	30.14
G. Miller (*Essex*)	434.1	106	1,177	39	5-76	1	30.17
M. P. Bicknell (*Surrey*)	516.2	136	1,511	50	9-45	1	30.22
G. A. Hick (*Worcs.*)	204	43	642	21	4-114	0	30.57
. L. Watkin (*Glam.*)	527.3	129	1,423	46	8-59	2	30.93
. Carrick (*Yorks.*)	593	179	1,551	50	5-46	2	31.02
. E. Hemmings (*Notts.*)	508.5	139	1,312	42	4-50	0	31.23
D. A. Reeve (*Warwicks.*)	292	71	750	24	4-50	0	31.25
. J. Wild (*Northants*)	187.5	37	563	18	4-18	0	31.27
N. Gifford (*Warwicks.*)	425.1	121	976	31	3-66	0	31.48
. P. Pridgeon (*Worcs.*)	266.3	58	662	21	3-68	0	31.52
G. Thomas (*Glam.*)	422.2	62	1,531	48	6-68	2	31.89
Derrick (*Glam.*)	540.1	138	1,511	47	6-54	1	32.14
. A. Bunting (*Sussex*)	400	69	1,320	41	5-44	3	32.19
. F. Pienaar (*Kent*)	404.2	99	1,162	36	5-27	1	32.27
. N. Hayhurst (*Lancs.*)	181.3	41	553	17	4-45	0	32.52
Shaw (*Yorks.*)	507.5	110	1,522	46	4-17	0	33.08
L. Pont (*Essex*)	220	30	795	24	5-103	1	33.12
. M. Babington (*Sussex*)	554.5	112	1,628	49	4-66	0	33.22
R. Barwick (*Glam.*)	408.5	112	1,064	32	5-37	1	33.25
J. Base (*Derbys.*)	195	20	735	22	4-74	0	33.40
M. Such (*Leics.*)	123.5	22	340	10	4-81	0	34.00
M. Wells (*Sussex*)	534.4	119	1,469	43	4-43	0	34.16
Watkinson (*Lancs.*)	647.3	153	1,779	52	6-43	2	34.21
A. Holding (*Derbys.*)	279.1	49	827	24	4-74	0	34.45
C. W. Fenton (*CUCC*)	271.4	65	726	21	4-64	0	34.57
J. Capel (*Northants*)	436.1	76	1,451	41	4-40	0	35.39
J. Shastri (*Glam.*)	304.2	91	709	20	7-49	1	35.45
T. Jefferies (*Hants*)	355.1	53	1,216	34	8-97	2	35.76
J. Maru (*Hants*)	701	201	1,792	50	5-69	1	35.84

	O	*M*	*R*	*W*	*BB*	*5 W/i*	*Avge*
P. J. Hartley (*Yorks.*)	307.3	32	1,219	34	5-85	1	35.85
D. J. Millns (*Notts.*)	179	22	683	19	3-37	0	35.94
D. K. Lillee (*Northants*)	245	45	778	21	6-68	1	37.04
†R. P. Davis (*Kent*)	563	177	1,409	38	5-132	1	37.07
D. J. Foster (*Somerset*)	299.3	46	1,044	28	4-46	0	37.28
A. R. Clarke (*Sussex*)	618	157	1,650	44	5-60	2	37.50
K. P. Evans (*Notts.*)	258.5	49	829	22	3-22	0	37.68
G. A. Gooch (*Essex*)	152	39	401	10	2-29	0	40.1
G. C. Holmes (*Glam.*)	121.2	15	445	11	5-38	1	40.4
P. Willey (*Northants*)	341	106	803	19	4-153	0	42.2
†P. C. R. Tufnell (*Middx*)	433.2	120	1,058	25	4-88	0	42.3
R. C. Ontong (*Glam.*)	395.1	94	1,128	26	4-38	0	43.3
S. P. Hughes (*Middx*)	441.3	84	1,258	27	4-39	0	46.5
M. R. Sygrove (*OUCC*)	215.4	34	848	18	3-91	0	47.1
K. Saxelby (*Notts.*)	245.2	42	837	17	3-21	0	49.2
J. W. Lloyds (*Glos.*)	239.3	42	757	13	2-22	0	58.2
P. Bainbridge (*Glos.*)	324	62	1,054	17	5-33	1	62.0
J. N. Perry (*CUCC*)	211	44	643	10	3-72	0	64.3
M. A. Atherton (*CUCC & Lancs.*)	269.1	42	807	11	3-32	0	73.3

The following bowlers took ten wickets but bowled in fewer than ten innings:

	O	*M*	*R*	*W*	*BB*	*5 W/i*	*Avge*
Imran Khan (*Sussex*)	122.3	27	310	13	5-50	1	23.8
I. D. Austin (*Lancs.*)	137.1	43	367	15	5-79	1	24.4
C. L. Cairns (*Notts.*)	109	16	384	15	4-70	0	25.6
H. L. Alleyne (*Kent*)	94.3	17	322	12	5-54	1	26.8
N. G. Cowley (*Hants*)	157.1	47	337	11	3-39	0	30.6
M. Frost (*Surrey*)	99.5	23	326	10	4-56	0	32.6
†P. A. Booth (*Yorks.*)	135.4	35	361	11	5-98	1	32.8
F. A. Griffith (*Derbys.*)	99.3	20	347	10	4-47	0	34.7
†A. M. G. Scott (*CUCC*)	120	26	385	11	4-66	0	35.0
A. M. Green (*Sussex*)	151.5	40	392	10	6-82	1	39.2

FIELDING IN 1988

(Qualification: 20 dismissals)

87 D. Ripley (80 ct, 7 st)
78 S. J. Rhodes (70 ct, 8 st)
73 R. J. Parks (63 ct, 10 st)
73 P. Whitticase (69 ct, 4 st)
69 R. C. Russell (57 ct, 12 st)
66 D. E. East (60 ct, 6 st)
65 C. J. Richards (64 ct, 1 st)
61 B. J. M. Maher (60 ct, 1 st)
61 S. A. Marsh (56 ct, 5 st)
60 W. K. Hegg (52 ct, 8 st)
60 C. P. Metson (52 ct, 8 st)
59 N. D. Burns (57 ct, 2 st)
57 G. W. Humpage (56 ct, 1 st)
51 C. W. Scott (49 ct, 2 st)
45 P. R. Downton (40 ct, 5 st)
39 D. L. Bairstow (38 ct, 1 st)
33 C. S. Cowdrey
33 I. J. Gould
33 P. Moores (30 ct, 3 st)
33 V. P. Terry
32 K. R. Brown
31 R. J. Maru
29 C. J. Tavaré
28 R. J. Blakey (26 ct, 2 st)
28 G. A. Gooch
28 G. A. Hick
28 M. Newell
27 A. R. Border
27 K. T. Medlycott
25 D. P. Hughes
25 A. J. Stewart
24 J. E. Emburey
23 R. J. Bailey
23 J. J. E. Hardy
23 W. Larkins
23 M. D. Moxon
22 R. A. Harper
22 M. P. Maynard
22 G. Miller
21 J. D. Carr
21 T. S. Curtis
21 P. E. Robinson
21 D. M. Ward
20 J. W. Lloyds
20 S. R. Waugh

INDIVIDUAL SCORES OF 100 AND OVER

There were 235 three-figure innings in first-class cricket in 1988, nine fewer than in 1987. The following list includes 186 hit in the County Championship, and 35 in other first-class games, but not the nine hit by the West Indian touring team, nor the five hit by the Sri Lankan touring team, which can be found in their respective sections.

* *Signifies not out.*

G. A. Hick (10)
405* Worcs. v Somerset, Taunton
212 Worcs. v Lancs., Manchester
98 Worcs. v Yorks., Worcester
97 Worcs. v Glam., Worcester
77 Worcs. v Hants, Worcester
72 Worcs. v West Indians, Worcester
59 Worcs. v Glam., Abergavenny
32 Worcs. v Northants, Worcester
27 Worcs. v Surrey, The Oval
21 Worcs. v Glos., Bristol

R. Border (6)
69* Essex v Derbys., Chesterfield
68 Essex v Kent, Canterbury
61 Essex v Sussex, Ilford
30* Essex v Notts., Colchester
12 Essex v Warwicks., Birmingham
10* Essex v Northants, Northampton

A. Gooch (6)
75 Essex v Kent, Chelmsford
46 England v West Indies, Nottingham
9 Essex v Surrey, Chelmsford
3 Essex v Surrey, The Oval
3 Essex v Sussex, Ilford
8 Essex v Northants, Chelmsford

R. Waugh (6)
1 Somerset v Kent, Canterbury
7 Somerset v Sussex, Bath
5* Somerset v Hants, Southampton
2* Somerset v Middx, Uxbridge
3* Somerset v Warwicks., Bath
1* Somerset v Glam., Taunton

J. Barnett (5)
9* Derbys. v Leics., Leicester
5 Derbys. v Glos., Derby
7 Derbys. v Lancs., Derby
Derbys. v Cambridge U., Cambridge
Derbys. v Yorks., Chesterfield

J. Lamb (5)
Northants v Essex, Chelmsford
Northants v Glos., Bristol
England v West Indies, Lord's
* Northants v Glam., Wellingborough School
* Northants v Oxford U., Oxford

P. W. G. Parker (5)
124 Sussex v Kent, Maidstone
117 Sussex v Kent, Hastings
104* Sussex v Hants, Eastbourne
101* Sussex v Somerset, Hove
101* Sussex v Somerset, Bath

M. A. Atherton (4)
152* Lancs. v Sussex, Hove
151* Cambridge U. v Middx, Cambridge
115* Lancs. v Derbys., Manchester
100* Cambridge U. v Surrey, Cambridge

P. Bainbridge (4)
169 Glos. v Yorks., Cheltenham
124 Glos. v Worcs., Bristol
119 Glos. v Oxford U., Oxford
119 Glos. v Warwicks., Cheltenham

P. D. Bowler (4)
159* Derbys. v Essex, Chesterfield
158 Derbys. v Surrey, The Oval
155* Derbys. v Cambridge U., Cambridge
134 Derbys. v Lancs., Derby

G. S. Clinton (4)
158 Surrey v Sussex, Hove
102 Surrey v Glos., Cheltenham
101 Surrey v Yorks., Harrogate
100 Surrey v Middx, Lord's

G. C. Holmes (4)
117 Glam. v Glos., Bristol
108 Glam. v Somerset, Cardiff
100* } Glam. v Somerset, Taunton
107 }

T. A. Lloyd (4)
160* Warwicks. v Hants, Birmingham
151 Warwicks. v Somerset, Bath
121 Warwicks. v Northants, Birmingham
101 Warwicks. v Middx, Uxbridge

P. A. Neale (4)
167 Worcs. v Sussex, Kidderminster
125 Worcs. v Derbys., Derby
108* Worcs. v Kent, Folkestone
102* Worcs. v Glos., Bristol

R. T. Robinson (4)
134* Notts. v Essex, Colchester
129 Notts. v MCC, Lord's
115 Notts. v Lancs., Nottingham
107* Notts. v Worcs., Nottingham

R. A. Smith (4)
141* Hants v Glos., Gloucester
119 Hants v Sussex, Southampton
118 Hants v Oxford U., Oxford
104* Hants v Sri Lankans, Southampton

C. J. Tavaré (4)
138* Kent v Oxford U., Oxford
129* Kent v Glam., Cardiff
119 Kent v Derbys., Chesterfield
103 Kent v Warwicks., Birmingham

R. J. Bailey (3)
127* Northants v Sussex, Northampton
110 Northants v Derbys., Northampton
101 Northants v Oxford U., Oxford

M. W. Gatting (3)
210 Middx v Notts., Lord's
180 Middx v Glam., Lord's
104 Middx v Hants, Basingstoke

P. Johnson (3)
140 Notts. v Hants, Southampton
124 Notts. v Yorks., Sheffield
104 Notts. v Oxford U., Oxford

M. P. Maynard (3)
126 Glam. v Glos., Bristol
122 Glam. v Somerset, Cardiff
108* Glam. v Worcs., Abergavenny

M. D. Moxon (3)
191 Yorks. v Northants, Scarborough
132 Yorks. v Sri Lankans, Leeds
106 Yorks. v Worcs., Worcester

R. F. Pienaar (3)
144 Kent v Yorks., Canterbury
128 Kent v Leics., Canterbury
127 Kent v Oxford U., Oxford

W. N. Slack (3)
163* } Middx v Glam., Lord's
105* }
144 Middx v Yorks., Lord's

C. L. Smith (3)
124* Hants v Lancs., Liverpool
117 Hants v Notts., Southampton
103* Hants v Essex, Portsmouth

V. P. Terry (3)
190 Hants v Sri Lankans, Southampton
126* Hants v Surrey, Guildford
106 Hants v Somerset, Southampton

J. J. Whitaker (3)
145 Leics. v Derbys., Derby
126 Leics. v Glam., Neath
100* Leics. v Worcs., Leicester

Asif Din (2)
158* Warwicks. v Cambridge U., Cambridge
131 Warwicks. v Northants, Northampton

C. W. J. Athey (2)
168* Glos. v Northants, Bristol
123 Glos. v Glam., Bristol

M. R. Benson (2)
110 Kent v Essex, Chelmsford
110 Kent v Middx, Tunbridge Wells

N. E. Briers (2)
125* Leics. v Derbys., Leicester
119 Leics. v Essex, Leicester

K. R. Brown (2)
131* Middx v Notts., Lord's
107* Middx v Sri Lankans, Lord's

J. D. Carr (2)
144 Middx v Leics., Leicester
106 Middx v Notts., Lord's

G. Cook (2)
203 Northants v Yorks., Scarborough
124* Northants v Middx, Luton

C. S. Cowdrey (2)
124* Kent v Oxford U., Oxford
108 Kent v Derbys., Chesterfield

M. D. Crowe (2)
136* Somerset v Lancs., Manchester
132 Somerset v Worcs., Worcester

K. M. Curran (2)
142 Glos. v Middx, Lord's
101 Glos. v Surrey, Cheltenham

T. S. Curtis (2)
131 Worcs. v Hants, Worcester
108 Worcs. v Middx, Lord's

N. H. Fairbrother (2)
111 Lancs. v Essex, Southend
101 Lancs. v Notts., Nottingham

G. Fowler (2)
172 Lancs. v Derbys., Derby
104 Lancs. v Essex, Southend

D. I. Gower (2)
172 Leics. v Essex, Chelmsford
146 Leics. v Notts., Leicester

W. Larkins (2)
134 Northants v Glos., Bristol
112* Northants v Kent, Northampton

. A. Lynch (2)
103* Surrey v Cambridge U., Cambridge
03 Surrey v Lancs., The Oval

. A. Marsh (2)
20 Kent v Essex, Chelmsford
00* Kent v Oxford U., Oxford

. D. Mendis (2)
51 Lancs. v Glos., Manchester
39 Lancs. v Oxford U., Oxford

. A. Metcalfe (2)
16* Yorks. v Middx, Leeds
15 Yorks. v Derbys., Chesterfield

E. Morris (2)
75 Derbys. v Glam., Swansea
06 Derbys. v Notts., Nottingham

. C. J. Nicholas (2)
32* Hants v Glam., Bournemouth
02* Hants v Essex, Portsmouth

D. W. Randall (2)
237 Notts. v Derbys., Nottingham
134 Notts. v Leics., Worksop

D. M. Smith (2)
157* Surrey v Hants, Guildford
131 Surrey v Sussex, The Oval

F. D. Stephenson (2)
111 } Notts. v Yorks., Nottingham
117 }

A. J. Stewart (2)
133 Surrey v Essex, The Oval
119 Surrey v Sussex, Hove

A. W. Stovold (2)
136 Glos. v Sussex, Bristol
133 Glos. v Somerset, Taunton

N. R. Taylor (2)
114 Kent v Surrey, Guildford
112* Kent v Glam., Cardiff

J. G. Thomas (2)
110 Glam. v Warwicks., Birmingham
100* Glam. v Worcs., Abergavenny

D. R. Turner (2)
150* Hants v Middx, Basingstoke
100* Hants v Somerset, Southampton

P. Willey (2)
130 Leics. v Sussex, Leicester
104 Leics. v Yorks., Leeds

A. J. Wright (2)
137 Glos. v Sri Lankans, Bristol
136 Glos. v Derbys., Derby

The following each played one three-figure innings:

D. Atkins, 114*, Surrey v Cambridge U., The Oval.

J. Bartlett, 102*, Somerset v Kent, Canterbury; J. D. Birch, 114*, Notts. v Oxford U., Oxford; T. J. Boon, 131, Leics. v Kent, Leicester; N. D. Burns, 133*, Somerset v Sussex, Hove; A. R. Butcher, 166, Glam. v Cambridge U., Cambridge; R. O. Butcher, 134, Middx v Sussex, Hove; D. Byas, 112, Yorks. v Glos., Cheltenham.

R. Cowdrey, 145, Kent v Essex, Chelmsford.

A. J. DeFreitas, 113, Leics. v Notts., Worksop; P. R. Downton, 120, Middx v Lancs., Manchester.

E. East, 134, Essex v Glos., Ilford; J. E. Emburey, 102, Middx v Warwicks., Uxbridge.

A. Felton, 127, Somerset v Glos., Taunton; A. Fordham, 125*, Northants v Surrey, The Oval.

J. Hartley, 127*, Yorks. v Lancs., Manchester; A. N. Hayhurst, 107, Lancs. v Derbys., Derby; S. G. Hinks, 138, Kent v Oxford U., Oxford; N. Hussain, 165*, Essex v Leics., Chelmsford.

I. Kallicharran, 117*, Warwicks. v Cambridge U., Cambridge.

W. Lloyds, 102*, Glos. v Oxford U., Oxford; G. J. Lord, 101, Worcs. v Glos., Bristol.

J. M. Maher, 121*, Derbys. v Leics., Derby; A. J. Moles, 115, Warwicks. v Lancs., Nuneaton.

M. Newell, 105, Notts. v Derbys., Nottingham.
R. C. Ontong, 120*, Glam. v Kent, Cardiff.
B. M. W. Patterson, 100, Scotland v Ireland, Dumfries; P. Pollard, 142, Notts. v Kent, Dartford; L. Potter, 107, Leics. v Derbys., Derby; D. R. Pringle, 128, Essex v Kent, Chelmsford.
D. A. Reeve, 103, Warwicks. v Northants, Northampton; S. J. Rhodes, 108, Worcs. v Derbys., Derby; C. J. Richards, 102*, Surrey v Sussex, The Oval; P. E. Robinson, 129*, Yorks. v Notts., Sheffield; P. M. Roebuck, 112*, Somerset v Glam., Taunton; P. W. Romaines, 101*, Glos. v Lancs., Manchester.
R. J. Scott, 107*, Hants v Sri Lankans, Southampton; K. Sharp, 128, Yorks. v Sri Lankans, Leeds; R. J. Shastri, 157, Glam. v Somerset, Cardiff.
G. P. Thorpe, 100*, Surrey v Cambridge U., The Oval.
D. M. Ward, 126, Surrey v Glam., Swansea; Wasim Akram, 116*, Lancs. v Somerset, Manchester; A. P. Wells, 120, Sussex v Warwicks., Hove; C. M. Wells, 109*, Sussex v Surrey, The Oval; R. G. Williams, 119, Northants v Essex, Northampton; J. G. Wright, 154*, Derbys. v Warwicks., Derby.

TEN WICKETS IN A MATCH

There were 35 instances of bowlers taking ten or more wickets in a match in first-class cricket in 1988, fifteen more than in 1987. The list includes 33 in the County Championship, one in another first-class match and one by the West Indian touring team.

K. M. Curran (3)
12-162 Glos. v Derbys., Derby
11-109 Glos. v Leics., Gloucester
10-82 Glos. v Hants, Southampton

K. T. Medlycott (3)
12-105 Surrey v Sussex, Hove
10-88 Surrey v Somerset, Weston-super-Mare
10-192 Surrey v Kent, Guildford

F. D. Stephenson (3)
12-103 Notts. v Derbys., Derby
11-222 Notts. v Yorks., Nottingham
10-95 Notts. v Northants, Nottingham

S. T. Clarke (2)
11-107 Surrey v Glos., Cheltenham
10-89 Surrey v Lancs., The Oval

W. W. Davis (2)
10-136 Northants v Sussex, Northampton
10-185 Northants v Warwicks., Northampton

N. A. Foster (2)
10-86 Essex v Yorks., Sheffield
10-128 Essex v Worcs., Worcester

A. R. C. Fraser (2)
11-102 Middx v Hants, Basingstoke
10-117 Middx v Notts., Lord's

R. K. Illingworth (2)
10-132 Worcs. v Glos., Bristol
10-153 Worcs. v Lancs., Manchester

G. C. Small (2)
12-121 Warwicks. v Glam., Birmingham
10-84 Warwicks. v Yorks., Birmingham

The following each took ten wickets in a match on one occasion:

J. P. Agnew, 11-122, Leics. v Northants, Leicester.
J. H. Childs, 11-180, Essex v Leics., Chelmsford; N. G. Cowans, 10-97, Middx v Warwicks., Uxbridge.
D. A. Graveney, 14-165, Glos. v Worcs., Bristol.
A. P. Igglesden, 10-91, Kent v Hants, Bournemouth.
P. W. Jarvis, 10-115, Yorks. v Kent, Canterbury.
C. C. Lewis, 10-70, Leics. v Oxford U., Oxford.
V. J. Marks, 10-116, Somerset v Notts., Taunton; M. D. Marshall, 10-92, West Indies v England, Lord's; T. A. Merrick, 10-69, Warwicks. v Hants, Birmingham.
P. J. Newport, 10-109, Worcs. v Somerset, Taunton.
N. H. Peters, 10-67, Surrey v Warwicks., The Oval.
R. J. Shastri, 11-90, Glam. v Lancs., Swansea.
T. D. Topley, 12-179, Essex v Derbys., Chesterfield.

THE CRICKET COUNCIL

he Cricket Council, which was set up in 1968 and reconstituted in 1974 and 1983, acts s the governing body for cricket in the British Isles. It comprises the following, the officers sted being those for 1987-88.

'hairman: R. Subba Row.
'ice-Chairman: J. D. Robson.
Representatives of the Test and County Cricket Board: R. Subba Row, C. R. M. Atkinson, D. J. Insole, F. G. Mann, D. N. Perry, H. J. Pocock, A. D. Steven, F. M. Turner.
Representatives of the National Cricket Association: J. D. Robson, F. R. Brown, F. H. Elliott, E. K. Ingman, J. G. Overy.
Representatives of the Marylebone Cricket Club: Field-Marshal The Lord Bramall, G. H. G. Doggart, N. E. J. Pocock.
Representative (non-voting) of the Minor Counties Cricket Association: G. L. B. August.
Representative (non-voting) of the Irish Cricket Union: D. Scott.
Representative (non-voting) of the Scottish Cricket Union: R. W. Barclay.

cretary: A. C. Smith.

THE TEST AND COUNTY CRICKET BOARD

e TCCB was set up in 1968 to be responsible for Test matches, official tours, and first-class d minor county competitions. It is composed of representatives of the seventeen first-ss counties; Marylebone Cricket Club; Minor Counties Cricket Association; Oxford iversity Cricket Club, Cambridge University Cricket Club, the Irish Cricket Union and Scottish Cricket Union.

fficers 1987-88

airman: R. Subba Row.

irmen of Committees: R. Subba Row (Executive); D. B. Carr (County Pitches); O. S. Vheatley (Cricket), D. J. Insole (Overseas Tours); P. R. Bromage (Discipline); A. D. teven (Finance); C. R. M. Atkinson (PR and Marketing); D. R. W. Silk (Registration); '. B. H. May (Selection); A. C. Smith (Umpires); M. D. Vockins (Under-25 and Second XI 'ompetitions).

ef Executive: A. C. Smith. *Cricket Secretary:* T. M. Lamb. *Assistant Secretary Administration):* B. Langley. *Accountant:* C. A. Barker. *Marketing Manager:* K. Deshayes. *ngland Tour Manager:* P. M. Lush. *England Team Manager:* M. J. Stewart.

THE NATIONAL CRICKET ASSOCIATION

h the setting up of the Cricket Council in 1968 it was necessary to form a separate nisation to represent the interests of all cricket below the first-class game, and it is the ional Cricket Association that carries out this function. It comprises representatives from ounty cricket associations and seventeen national cricketing organisations.

'icers 1987-88

ident: F. R. Brown.
rman: J. D. Robson.
Chairman: F. H. Elliott.
Chief Executive: K. V. Andrew.
General Secretary: B. J. Aspital.
Hon. Treasurer: D. W. Carter.

THE WEST INDIANS IN ENGLAND, 1988

The morale and reputation of English cricket has seldom been as severel bruised as it was during the 1988 Cornhill Insurance Test series against Wes Indies. Another resounding loss, with four consecutive and heavy defea after a drawn First Test, was not unusual – the margins in the previous serie between the countries, in 1984 and 1985-86, had been complete; 5-0 to We Indies each time. England even had the satisfaction, brief and illusory thoug it might have been, of winning all three one-day internationals for the Texac Trophy. The euphoria ended there and the season was quickly transforme into a sequence of traumatic events, on and off the field.

It began with the dismissal after the First Test of Mike Gatting, th captain since 1986, on the evidence of obscene allegations in the tabloid pre of his nocturnal relationship with a young barmaid during the match. Th affair, filled with sordid controversy, shook the foundations of Englis cricket, undermined the confidence of the team, and opened the selecto under the continued chairmanship of Peter May, to harsh and widespre criticism. It was certainly not the only reason for yet another humiliati demise, for West Indies again proved powerful and confident opponents. Y England's problems multiplied rapidly after it; under Vivian Richard increasingly assured captaincy, and with Malcolm Marshall's irresistible fa swing bowling, the West Indians took fullest advantage.

England's selectors did not seem to know where to turn, either for a n captain or for a settled team. Their confusion was evident even in t dismissal of Gatting. While accepting his assertion that nothing impro had taken place with the young woman, they removed him all the same "improper behaviour". After that, they appointed John Emburey for t Second and Third Tests, even though Emburey's place in the team w increasingly tenuous. When they decided that Emburey was not their m they chose Christopher Cowdrey on the basis of his influence in Ke current success in the County Championship. Cowdrey, son of a gr batsman and former England captain, as well as May's godson, came w well-founded doubts over his ability as a player of Test quality. It v generally taken almost as a blessing in disguise when, after England had heavily under him at Headingley, he injured his foot in a county match was ruled out of the final Test at The Oval. With most of their m candidates exhausted, the selectors made Graham Gooch their fourth capt of the summer. Gooch, a cricketer of vast experience, had relinquished captaincy of Essex at the end of the previous season in order to concent on his batting.

England did somewhat better under him but lost nevertheless, by e wickets. He confirmed that he remained one of the finest batsmen in game and was the only Englishman to play in all five Tests, although A Lamb, along with him the only century-maker, and Graham Dilley, leading wicket-taker, were prevented from doing so only by injury. E David Gower was dropped after reaching the rare landmark of 7,000 run his 100th Test, at Headingley. In all, 23 players were chosen for the five T which was a manifesto for failure, especially against opponents quic spot and exploit the slightest weakness. At the end, England were wit either an obvious captain or a single player who had established hi during the series.

The West Indians arrived in May after seven months of demanding cricket during which they struggled to come to terms with the retirements of three of their most influential players, the fast bowlers, Joel Garner and Michael Holding, and the left-handed batsman, Larry Gomes. They had been eliminated from the World Cup in India and Pakistan before the semi-finals, shared the subsequent Test series in India when beaten in the final Test, and salvaged a draw against Pakistan in an exciting home series by winning the Third Test by two wickets. Several players were still unknown quantities, and Richards was yet to assert himself as captain, even three years after succeeding Clive Lloyd. Defeat in all three one-day internationals, when the unreliability of their batting on damp, green pitches was exposed, England's determined fight to save the First Test, and the loss of five wickets before lunch on the first day of the Second Test provided a stern examination of the West Indians' character. As England faltered and Richards's stature as a mature leader grew, they showed they were made of stern stuff.

Marshall, already justifiably numbered among the great fast bowlers, was again the dominant individual, his 35 wickets at 12.65 each creating an overall record for the series. Speed and hostility had been his stock-in-trade in 1984 and 1985-86, when he had a total of 51 wickets and physically damaged several batsmen. Now he revealed a new side to his bowling, moving the ball – late, appreciably and both ways – to suit pitches left slow and holding by a wet summer. He hardly resorted to a bouncer for he had no need to. A rib injury reduced him to thirteen overs in England's second innings of the First Test, probably costing West Indies victory as well as prompting his change of style.

Marshall had long stood tall in international company, but of those who came in support, only Courtney Walsh could be counted as an established Test bowler. It did not take long for Curtly Ambrose, a tall Antiguan who shot to prominence only a few months earlier in the West Indies season, to demonstrate that he was a ready-made replacement for Garner. The height of his delivery, the bounce he could generate, and his direct method made him a constant menace and earned him 22 wickets. Walsh, Winston Benjamin and Patrick Patterson, all with English county experience, were capable back-ups, yet the most exciting prospect was not required in the Tests. Like Ambrose, Ian Bishop, aged twenty, was on his first tour. He possessed all the attributes for bowling fast – size, strength, stamina, speed and a model action. Counties were queuing to offer him contracts long before the tour was over. Derbyshire eventually secured his signature as Northamptonshire had earlier gained Ambrose.

Yet again, West Indies' emphasis was on fast bowling, almost to the complete exclusion of spin. As it was, the only specialist spinner, Roger Harper, fell into such a muddle over his action that he had to seek remedial attention at the MCC Indoor School and was ineffective for much of the tour. In the interim, he compensated with improved batting to the extent that he headed the tour averages and played two important innings in the Tests. Additionally, he claimed five wickets in the final Test, a measure of his determination to overcome a problem and of his cricketing intelligence.

The West Indian batting was unpredictable, with the middle order lacking its old reliability. Gordon Greenidge's masterful century at Lord's was the only three-figure Test innings. Both Richards and Desmond Haynes went through a series in England without a century for the first time, Richie Richardson's technique made him vulnerable to the moving ball, and it often required the last half of the order to repair early damage. Gus Logie, Jeffrey Dujon, Harper, Marshall and even Ambrose featured in such revivals.

Logie's unrestrained response to even the deepest crisis was typically West Indian, but he now added the consistency that he had lacked at the highest level. Dujon, elegant in his strokeplay, level-headed in his approach, was a joy to watch in whatever he did, whether as batsman or wicket-keeper. His century partnerships with Logie in each innings at Lord's were critical to the balance of the match, arguably of the series even.

Carl Hooper, 21, and the left-handed Keith Arthurton, 23, were two young batsmen on their first tours of England. The latter was included as the seventeenth player at the request of the selectors to gain experience. Hooper's potential, already revealed against India and Pakistan, was evident in his high-class 84 in the First Test, but injuries to Greenidge, Haynes and Richardson, following that to Philip Simmons earlier, elevated him to the unaccustomed No. 3 position for the last three Tests, in which his form declined markedly. The injuries also opened the way for Arthurton to make his Test début at Headingley. The success of bringing him on the tour was reflected in two outstanding, unbeaten innings of 101 and 78 in the final match against Essex. Arthurton's fielding in the covers was in keeping with the high standards long since set by West Indies and maintained by thi team, in which Harper, in any position, and Logie, under the bat at short leg were exceptional.

The third batsman new to England, the third opener, Simmons, had hi tour cut short by a blow on the head during his only first-class innings against Gloucestershire at Bristol. Hit by a ball from the fast bowler Lawrence, while batting in poor light on a lively pitch and without a helmet Simmons developed a blood clot on the brain, and only a quick operation a the nearby Frenchay Hospital, one of Britain's finest neurosurgical units saved his life.

As in 1984, the former Test wicket-keeper, Jackie Hendriks, was a capabl and popular manager, assisted by a fellow-member of the selection pane Calvin Wilkin of the Leeward Islands. Happily, there was little of th criticism of the over-rate and short-pitched bowling which was directed at th 1984 team, simply because there was very little of the latter and the forme was covered by the Playing Conditions which set 90 overs as the minimum t be bowled in a day. With rain and bad light constantly intervening, and th option to extend play by an hour often being utilised, it rarely ended on tim It was not unusual for play to continue until after seven o'clock; once carried on to 7.40 p.m.

The days when counties regarded matches against the touring team as highlight of the season – and counties such as Surrey and Yorkshire wou present as much of a challenge as England – have long gone. Now there w little point to them. The West Indians used them principally for practice, th counties viewed them as an unwanted intrusion into a crowded programm when key players should be rested. Kent, leading the Championship at th time, were without seven of their regular first-team players in a match th duly lost by an innings in two days. Never pressed in any county match, th West Indians would have won many more if that had been their object. spite of this, however, and of England's depressing plight, the tour prov highly profitable, with Lord's recording takings of over £1 million, the fi time for a Test in England. Corporate sponsorship provided much of t revenue but led to complaints in the media that the genuine lover of the game was being turned away by increased entrance fees. Certainly, the formerly high level of attendance by the West Indian immigrant population was noticeably diminished. – Tony Cozier.

WEST INDIAN TOUR RESULTS

est matches – Played 5: Won 4, Drawn 1.
irst-class matches – Played 16: Won 6, Drawn 10.
Vins – England (4), Kent, Somerset.
raws – England, Essex, Glamorgan, Gloucestershire, Lancashire, Leicestershire, Northamptonshire, Nottinghamshire, Sussex, Worcestershire.
ne-day internationals – Played 3: Lost 3.
ther non first-class matches – Played 4: Won 3, Drawn 1. *Wins* – Hampshire, Lavinia, Duchess of Norfolk's XI, Oxford and Cambridge Universities. *Draw* – Minor Counties.

TEST MATCH AVERAGES

ENGLAND – BATTING

	T	*I*	*NO*	*R*	*HI*	*100s*	*Avge*
A. Gooch	5	10	0	459	146	1	45.90
J. Lamb	4	8	2	254	113	1	42.33
I. Gower	4	8	1	211	88*	0	30.14
A. Smith	2	4	0	106	57	0	26.50
R. Downton	3	5	1	84	27	0	21.00
W. Jarvis	2	3	1	42	29*	0	21.00
C. Broad	2	4	0	71	54	0	17.75
S. Curtis	2	4	0	69	30	0	17.25
A. Foster	2	4	1	49	34	0	16.33
D. Moxon	2	4	0	55	26	0	13.75
R. Dilley	4	7	1	58	28	0	9.66
W. Gatting	2	4	0	38	29	0	9.50
E. Emburey	3	5	0	46	30	0	9.20
R. Pringle	4	7	0	52	39	0	7.42
J. Capel	2	4	0	29	16	0	7.25
A. J. DeFreitas	3	5	0	36	18	0	7.20
J. Richards	2	4	0	13	8	0	3.25
H. Childs	2	4	4	2	2*	0	0.00

Played in one Test: C. W. J. Athey 16, 11; R. J. Bailey 43, 3; C. S. Cowdrey 0, 5; M. P. Maynard 3, 10; G. C. Small 5*, 7.

Signifies not out.

BOWLING

	O	*M*	*R*	*W*	*BB*	*Avge*
R. Dilley	136.1	26	403	15	5-55	26.86
A. Foster	73.2	12	250	9	5-64	27.77
R. Pringle	119	33	326	11	5-95	29.63
C. Small	37.5	6	140	4	4-64	35.00
V. Jarvis	57.1	6	217	6	4-107	36.16

Also bowled: D. J. Capel 22–2–79–1; J. H. Childs 86–29–183–3; C. S. Cowdrey 0–21–0; P. A. J. DeFreitas 92–16–253–3; J. E. Emburey 62–14–228–3.

WEST INDIES – BATTING

	T	*I*	*NO*	*R*	*HI*	*100s*	*Avge*
A. L. Logie	5	7	2	364	95*	0	72.8
P. J. L. Dujon	5	7	1	305	67	0	50.8
R. A. Harper	3	3	0	147	74	0	49.0
C. G. Greenidge	4	6	0	282	103	1	47.0
D. L. Haynes	4	7	2	235	77*	0	47.0
I. V. A. Richards ...	5	6	0	223	80	0	37.1
M. D. Marshall	5	6	1	135	72	0	27.0
C. L. Hooper	5	7	0	166	84	0	23.7
C. E. L. Ambrose ...	5	6	2	75	43	0	18.7
R. B. Richardson ...	3	4	0	71	26	0	17.7
C. A. Walsh	5	5	3	26	9*	0	13.0
W. K. M. Benjamin .	3	2	0	9	9	0	4.5
B. P. Patterson	2	2	0	2	2	0	1.0

Played in one Test: K. L. T. Arthurton 27.

* *Signifies not out.*

BOWLING

	O	*M*	*R*	*W*	*BB*	*Avg*
W. K. M. Benjamin ...	67	17	151	12	4-52	12.
R. A. Harper	29	11	63	5	3-50	12.
M. D. Marshall	203.1	49	443	35	7-22	12.
C. E. L. Ambrose	203.1	56	445	22	4-53	20.
C. A. Walsh	157.2	40	412	12	4-46	34.
B. P. Patterson	74.5	13	270	4	2-100	67.

Also bowled: C. L. Hooper 24–3–57–0; I. V. A. Richards 10–1–28–0.

WEST INDIAN AVERAGES – FIRST-CLASS MATCHES

BATTING

	M	*I*	*NO*	*R*	*HI*	*100s*	*Av*
R. A. Harper	12	13	5	622	217*	1	77.
C. G. Greenidge	11	16	1	762	111	3	50
P. J. L. Dujon	12	16	4	601	141	1	50
K. L. T. Arthurton ...	10	13	3	499	121	2	49
D. L. Haynes	14	23	4	903	158	1	47
A. L. Logie	13	18	4	586	95*	0	41
I. V. A. Richards	13	16	1	624	128	1	41
C. L. Hooper	14	20	1	625	87	0	32
M. D. Marshall	9	10	1	289	76	0	32
C. E. L. Ambrose	13	15	3	278	59	0	23
D. Williams	8	10	1	182	51	0	20
R. B. Richardson	10	14	0	279	82	0	19
W. K. M. Benjamin ..	10	10	4	102	21*	0	17
I. R. Bishop	8	6	2	56	23	0	14
B. P. Patterson	9	7	2	60	23*	0	12
C. A. Walsh	9	7	3	31	9*	0	7

Played in one match: P. V. Simmons 53*.

* *Signifies not out.*

BOWLING

	O	*M*	*R*	*W*	*BB*	*5W/i*	*Avge*
M. D. Marshall	245.4	56	553	42	7-22	3	13.16
W. K. M. Benjamin ...	183.1	43	467	33	4-20	0	14.15
. R. Bishop	142	30	406	21	6-39	2	19.33
:. E. L. Ambrose	329.1	86	733	35	4-27	0	20.94
R. A. Harper	227.3	70	521	21	4-10	0	24.80
3. P. Patterson	196	33	632	25	5-39	1	25.28
:. L. Hooper	106.1	16	303	9	3-61	0	33.66
:. A. Walsh	232.2	55	622	18	5-49	1	34.55

Also bowled: K. L. T. Arthurton 27.1–8–80–3; I. V. A. Richards 45.4–10–122–3; R. B. :ichardson 4–0–22–0.

FIELDING

1 – P. J. L. Dujon (31 ct); 22 – R. A. Harper; 12 – D. Williams (11 ct, 1 st); 10 – substitutes; – C. L. Hooper, A. L. Logie, I. V. A. Richards, R. B. Richardson; 8 – K. L. T. Arthurton; – W. K. M. Benjamin, C. G. Greenidge, D. L. Haynes; 3 – M. D. Marshall; 1 – C. E. L. ,mbrose, I. R. Bishop, B. P. Patterson.

HUNDREDS FOR WEST INDIANS

he following twelve three-figure innings were played for the West Indians, nine in first-class ·atches and three in non first-class matches.

. G. Greenidge (4)
111 v Essex, Chelmsford
103 v England, Lord's (Second Test)
·103 v Hants, Southampton
101 v Notts., Nottingham

. L. T. Arthurton (2)
121 v Northants, Northampton
101* v Essex, Chelmsford

J. L. Dujon (1)
141 v Glam., Swansea

R. A. Harper (1)
217* v Sussex, Hove

D. L. Haynes (1)
158 v Sussex, Hove

C. L. Hooper (1)
†140* v Minor Counties, Trowbridge

A. L. Logie (1)
†100 v Minor Counties, Trowbridge

I. V. A. Richards (1)
128 v Sussex, Hove

* *Signifies not out.* † *Not first-class.*

Note: Those matches which follow which were not first-class are signified by the use of :agger.

SUSSEX v WEST INDIANS

Hove, May 7, 9, 10. Drawn. Toss: Sussex. The West Indians, having bowled out Sussex .hin 50 minutes on the final morning, eschewed enforcing the follow-on in favour of batting ,ctice. Bishop in particular, lively and hostile down the slope, had shown the touring team be capable of forcing victory. Instead, Haynes and Richardson put on 197 for the second ·ket, with Haynes staying for just over three and threequarter hours. He had already batted most of the first morning, when the young Sussex seam bowlers reduced their visitors to for five at lunch. But by then Richards had already hit Clarke for two sixes, one breaking ·indow in the south stand, and after lunch he hit two more plus fifteen fours as he and :rper were adding 227 for the sixth wicket. Harper's hundred came from 197 balls –

Richards's, his 98th, had taken 128 – and in all he batted for 396 minutes, hitting 25 fours in his double-century. He and Ambrose hit 123 for the ninth wicket as 167 runs came from the second morning's play. In the afternoon, Parker batted stylishly and with some authority, hitting thirteen fours in a stay of two and a half hours.

Close of play: First day, West Indians 394-7 (R. A. Harper 133*, D. Williams 18*); Second day, Sussex 211-6 (I. J. Gould 8*, M. W. Pringle 8*).

West Indians

C. G. Greenidge c Gould b Bunting	15	– b Pringle	2
D. L. Haynes c Gould b Babington	36	– c Clarke b Alikhan	158
R. B. Richardson c Parker b Bunting	20	– c Babington b Clarke	82
C. L. Hooper c Parker b Bunting	7	– c Parker b A. P. Wells	34
A. L. Logie lbw b Clarke	3	– not out	10
*I. V. A. Richards c A. P. Wells b Pringle	128		
R. A. Harper not out	217		
W. K. M. Benjamin c Clarke b C. M. Wells	10	– (7) not out	
†D. Williams c Gould b Bunting	28	– (6) lbw b Alikhan	
C. E. L. Ambrose c Gould b Bunting	59		
I. R. Bishop not out	9		
B 9, l-b 4, w 7, n-b 9	29	B 1, l-b 6, n-b 6	1
1/22 2/54 3/75 4/80 5/94 6/321 7/349 8/411 9/534 (9 wkts dec.)	561	1/13 2/210 3/281 4/285 5/300 (5 wkts dec.)	30

Bowling: *First Innings*—Bunting 35–3–161–5; Pringle 23–2–98–1; Babington 30–3–91–1; Clarke 30–3–118–1; C. M. Wells 22–5–57–1; Lenham 6–1–23–0. *Second Innings*—Bunting 14–0–71–0; Pringle 10–2–37–1; Babington 10–1–41–0; C. M. Wells 7–2–13–0; Clarke 11–1–51–1; Lenham 3–0–18–0; A. P. Wells 9–1–43–1; Alikhan 7–0–19–2; Green 3–1–5–0.

Sussex

R. I. Alikhan c Richardson b Bishop	29
A. M. Green c Richards b Bishop	32
*P. W. G. Parker c Haynes b Hooper	89
A. P. Wells b Benjamin	17
C. M. Wells c Williams b Benjamin	1
N. J. Lenham c Benjamin b Ambrose	12
†I. J. Gould c Williams b Hooper	33
M. W. Pringle b Bishop	14
A. R. Clarke c Logie b Bishop	
R. A. Bunting not out	
A. M. Babington c Bishop b Hooper	
B 5, l-b 5, w 4, n-b 4	
1/57 2/79 3/145 4/147 5/195 6/195 7/239 8/245 9/245	2

Bowling: Ambrose 14–4–42–1; Benjamin 15–4–38–2; Harper 10–3–24–0; Bishop 14–1–55–4; Richards 8–1–22–0; Hooper 16.5–2–61–3.

Umpires: B. J. Meyer and N. T. Plews.

†LAVINIA, DUCHESS OF NORFOLK'S XI v WEST INDIANS

At Arundel, May 8. West Indians won by 66 runs. Toss: West Indians.

West Indians

D. L. Haynes c Lenham b Pocock	50
P. V. Simmons lbw b Rice	0
C. L. Hooper c Lenham b Babington	52
A. L. Logie run out	53
K. L. T. Arthurton not out	35
*I. V. A. Richards c Rice b Babington	
B 2, l-b 2	
1/0 2/87 3/119 4/181 5/201 (5 wkts, 40 overs)	

M. D. Marshall, †D. Williams, C. A. Walsh, I. R. Bishop and C. E. L. Ambrose did not bat.

Bowling: Imran 5–3–2–0; Rice 8–1–34–1; Turner 4–0–23–0; Pocock 7–0–47–1; Underwood 8–1–49–0; Babington 8–1–42–2.

Lavinia, Duchess of Norfolk's XI

P. W. G. Parker b Hooper	39
N. J. Lenham b Ambrose	4
D. L. Amiss b Marshall	5
C. T. Radley lbw b Marshall	1
C. E. B. Rice b Marshall	0
*Imran Khan not out	56
†I. J. Gould not out	20
B 2, l-b 5, w 1, n-b 2	10
1/11 2/25 3/27 4/27 5/77 (5 wkts, 40 overs)	135

S. Turner, D. L. Underwood, P. I. Pocock and A. M. Babington did not bat.

Bowling: Ambrose 7–0–17–1; Bishop 8–0–32–0; Walsh 5–0–9–0; Marshall 6–2–7–3; Hooper 8–2–19–1; Richards 4–0–17–0; Haynes 1–0–16–0; Arthurton 1–0–11–0.

Umpires: C. Cook and J. G. Langridge.

†HAMPSHIRE v WEST INDIANS

At Southampton, May 12. West Indians won by 93 runs. Toss: Hampshire. Greenidge hit ·ight sixes as he scored his century before lunch.

West Indians

:. G. Greenidge c R. A. Smith b Cowley	103
'. V. Simmons c James b Cowley	55
R. B. Richardson c Parks b Connor	8
:. L. Hooper c R. A. Smith b Connor	56
I. V. A. Richards c James b Jefferies	13
A. L. Logie not out	21
R. A. Harper not out	6
L-b 10, w 7	17
1/116 2/157 3/183 4/227 5/253 (5 wkts, 50 overs)	279

D. Williams, M. D. Marshall, C. A. Walsh and B. P. Patterson did not bat.

Bowling: Jefferies 10–0–44–1; Connor 10–2–67–2; James 10–1–51–0; Andrew 10–0–46–0; :owley 10–0–61–2.

Hampshire

. J. Scott c Harper b Walsh	12
'. L. Smith lbw b Walsh	18
. A. Smith run out	37
'. R. Turner c and b Walsh	47
M. C. J. Nicholas c Richards b Simmons	9
. D. James c Richardson b Hooper	16
†R. J. Parks not out	13
S. T. Jefferies not out	10
L-b 4, w 9, n-b 11	24
1/41 2/48 3/115 4/139 5/146 6/164 (6 wkts, 50 overs)	186

. G. Cowley, C. A. Connor and S. J. W. Andrew did not bat.

Bowling: Marshall 8–0–20–0; Patterson 8–0–30–0; Harper 10–0–41–0; Walsh 9–1–30–3; mmons 8–0–32–1; Richards 4–0–20–0; Hooper 3–1–9–1.

Umpires: H. D. Bird and J. Birkenshaw.

SOMERSET v WEST INDIANS

: Taunton, May 14, 15. West Indians won by ten wickets. Toss: Somerset. On a pitch mpathetic to seam bowling, the additional pace and hostility of the West Indians dominated e match. Marks's lively 42 from 65 balls, partly against the spinners, saved Somerset from innings defeat, but even so the West Indians won easily just before the end of the second y. Wyatt, with a gritty if fortunate 55-ball 42, took Somerset to 64 for one on the first day, : then Ambrose and Benjamin tore the innings apart. Half-centuries from Haynes, Hooper d Harper gave the West Indians their security, although determined seam bowling, led by eal, an eighteen-year-old making his first-class début, always kept them in check.

Close of play: First day, West Indians 168-5 (C. L. Hooper 50*, M. D. Marshall 9*).

Somerset

J. G. Wyatt c Dujon b Benjamin	42	– c Arthurton b Walsh	4
N. A. Felton c Greenidge b Ambrose	10	– c Harper b Ambrose	4
J. J. E. Hardy c Harper b Ambrose	17	– c Haynes b Ambrose	8
M. D. Crowe c Harper b Ambrose	2	– c Dujon b Marshall	12
S. R. Waugh lbw b Benjamin	1	– c Arthurton b Benjamin	27
*V. J. Marks c and b Benjamin	4	– b Hooper	42
†N. D. Burns c Harper b Ambrose	0	– c Dujon b Benjamin	0
G. D. Rose c Benjamin b Marshall	12	– run out	14
M. W. Cleal c Dujon b Benjamin	6	– c Harper b Hooper	19
C. H. Dredge c Richardson b Marshall	4	– run out	5
D. J. Foster not out	6	– not out	2
L-b 1, n-b 8	9	B 1, l-b 5, n-b 3	9
1/46 2/64 3/74 4/75 5/77 6/77 7/83 8/102 9/102	113	1/9 2/13 3/17 4/59 5/59 6/59 7/92 8/125 9/142	146

Bowling: *First Innings*—Marshall 8.4–3–23–2; Walsh 8–0–28–0; Ambrose 13–3–27–4; Benjamin 13–5–34–4. *Second Innings*—Marshall 13–0–31–1; Walsh 10–4–21–1; Ambrose 8–1–26–2; Benjamin 4–0–11–2; Harper 14–5–26–0; Hooper 7.2–1–25–2.

West Indians

*C. G. Greenidge lbw b Foster	22	– not out	4
D. L. Haynes c Cleal b Rose	50	– not out	8
R. B. Richardson c Burns b Cleal	26		
C. L. Hooper c Waugh b Rose	54		
K. L. T. Arthurton c Burns b Foster	1		
†P. J. L. Dujon c Felton b Cleal	5		
M. D. Marshall b Foster	9		
R. A. Harper not out	53		
W. K. M. Benjamin b Rose	8		
C. E. L. Ambrose b Cleal	12		
C. A. Walsh c Rose b Cleal	4		
L-b 5, n-b 2	7		
1/33 2/74 3/131 4/149 5/157 6/168 7/184 8/219 9/243	251	(no wkt)	1

Bowling: *First Innings*—Rose 21–4–71–3; Foster 17–2–77–3; Cleal 15–3–41–4; Dredg 15–5–44–0; Marks 6–2–13–0. *Second Innings*—Wyatt 1–0–4–0; Felton 0.5–0–8–0.

Umpires: D. J. Constant and D. R. Shepherd.

†ENGLAND v WEST INDIES

First Texaco Trophy Match

At Birmingham, May 19. England won by six wickets. Toss: England. A professional displa brought England their seventh victory in their last eight limited-overs games against We Indies. In contrast, the West Indians lacked the necessary discipline. Put in, on a mornin that began cloudy but brightened later, they made a flying start. When Simmons was caugh it was still only the sixth over and 34 runs were on the board. Small, in the eleventh over, h first, bowled Greenidge with one that nipped back, and in his second over Richards w brilliantly caught by Emburey off a full-blooded square slash. In the intermediate ove Richards had struck Dilley (6–0–41–1) for three fours. When Pringle dismissed Richardson the fourteenth over, Logie and Hooper set about saving the innings. But the wicket was slo and with Small and Pringle moving the ball about, their stand of 97 took 29 overs. Each fac 96 deliveries for his 51. When England batted, Walsh and Ambrose bowled erratically and came from the first ten overs. Greenidge at slip took a fine catch, low to his left, to remo

Broad in the sixteenth over, but Gatting, after a hesitant start, played excellently. Gooch (93 balls) was caught at second slip in the 30th over, and after an unhappy début for Lynch, the captain (125 balls, seven fours) and Pringle saw England home without further alarm. Pringle, a much criticised inclusion, justified the selectors' decision with his steady bowling and untroubled batting.

Man of the Match: G. C. Small. *Attendance:* 17,450; *receipts* £198,650.

West Indies

C. G. Greenidge b Small	18	C. E. L. Ambrose b Emburey	1
P. V. Simmons c Lamb b Dilley	22	C. A. Walsh not out	2
R. B. Richardson lbw b Pringle	11		
*I. V. A. Richards c Emburey b Small	13	L-b 2, w 3, n-b 6	11
A. L. Logie c Downton b Small	51		—
C. L. Hooper c Emburey b Small	51	1/34 (2) 2/50 (1) (55 overs)	217
P. J. L. Dujon run out	27	3/66 (4) 4/72 (3) 5/169 (6)	
R. A. Harper b Emburey	4	6/180 (5) 7/195 (8) 8/209 (9)	
M. D. Marshall c Lamb b DeFreitas	6	9/212 (10) 10/217 (7)	

Bowling: DeFreitas 11–2–45–1; Dilley 11–0–64–1; Small 11–0–31–4; Pringle 11–5–26–1; Emburey 11–1–49–2.

England

G. A. Gooch c Harper b Ambrose	43	D. R. Pringle not out	23
B. C. Broad c Greenidge b Marshall	35	B 2, l-b 10, w 7, n-b 6	25
*M. W. Gatting not out	82		—
M. A. Lynch run out	0	1/70 (2) 2/119 (1) (4 wkts, 53 overs)	219
A. J. Lamb b Hooper	11	3/121 (4) 4/153 (5)	

†P. R. Downton, J. E. Emburey, P. A. J. DeFreitas, G. C. Small and G. R. Dilley did not bat.

Bowling: Ambrose 11–1–39–1; Walsh 11–1–50–0; Richards 7–1–29–0; Marshall 11–1–32–1; Harper 7–0–33–0; Hooper 6–0–24–1.

Umpires: J. Birkenshaw and B. J. Meyer.

†ENGLAND v WEST INDIES

Second Texaco Trophy Match

At Leeds, May 21. England won by 47 runs to win the Texaco Trophy and also their first one-day series against West Indies in England. Toss: West Indies. A pitch providing uneven bounce and, in generally sunny conditions, encouraging movement was not ideal for a limited-overs match. Against tighter fast bowling than at Edgbaston, England's batsmen found runs hard to come by, although Gooch (95 balls) played with sure judgement. When Richards unaccountably gave Simmons and himself seventeen overs, Pringle (55 balls) and Downton (47 balls) took advantage of the respite, adding 66 in thirteen overs. Having Gooch caught at sheepish gully with the first ball after lunch had given Simmons, at a whippy medium pace, figures of 4–2–3–2; but it made no sense for Marshall and Ambrose to have six overs unbowled at the end. Bishop, taking two for 9 in his last five overs, impressed. Less impressive was an over-rate of more than four minutes. England's opening attack was fast and hostile, and in support Small and Pringle exploited the conditions with accurate bowling. Richards looked as if he was intent on a match-winning innings until Gatting, recalling Edgbaston, brought back Dilley in the hope of tempting him. Richards hit the first three balls for four, then was dropped by Broad at mid-off. Several overs later, his concentration broken, he dragged a ball from Small on to his stumps. When Logie was caught at mid-wicket in the next over from a ball that "stopped", West Indies were 67 for five in the nineteenth. After 30 overs they were 105 for eight, but Ambrose and Walsh stayed for fourteen overs to prolong the match. When Greenidge moved from 11 to 15, he became the fifth batsman to score 4,000 runs in one-day internationals.

Man of the Match: D. R. Pringle. *Attendance:* 17,000; *receipts* £185,000.

England

G. A. Gooch c Greenidge b Simmons . 32
B. C. Broad c Dujon b Ambrose 13
*M. W. Gatting c Richards b Marshall. 18
M. A. Lynch lbw b Marshall 2
A. J. Lamb c Dujon b Simmons 2
D. R. Pringle c Dujon b Walsh 39
†P. R. Downton c Dujon b Bishop 30
J. E. Emburey c Ambrose b Bishop ... 8
P. A. J. DeFreitas not out 15
G. C. Small not out 7
B 3, l-b 1, w 3, n-b 13 20

1/29 (2) 2/64 (3) 3/72 (4) 4/80 (5) 5/83 (1) 6/149 (6) 7/154 (7) 8/169 (8) (8 wkts, 55 overs) 186

G. R. Dilley did not bat.

Bowling: Walsh 11–0–39–1; Ambrose 7–2–19–1; Marshall 9–1–29–2; Bishop 11–1–32–2; Simmons 9–2–30–2; Richards 8–0–33–0.

West Indies

C. G. Greenidge c Downton b Small .. 21
P. V. Simmons b DeFreitas 1
R. B. Richardson c Downton b Dilley . 1
*I. V. A. Richards b Small 31
A. L. Logie c Lynch b Dilley 8
C. L. Hooper lbw b Pringle 12
†P. J. L. Dujon b Pringle 12
M. D. Marshall c Downton b Gooch .. 1
C. E. L. Ambrose c Downton b Pringle 23
C. A. Walsh b Emburey 18
I. R. Bishop not out 2
L-b 3, w 3, n-b 3 9

1/2 (2) 2/11 (3) 3/38 (1) 4/67 (4) 5/67 (5) 6/83 (7) 7/84 (8) 8/104 (6) 9/132 (9) 10/139 (10) (46.3 overs) 139

Bowling: Dilley 11–0–45–2; DeFreitas 9–2–29–1; Small 9–2–11–2; Pringle 11–0–30–3; Gooch 3–0–12–1; Emburey 3.3–0–9–1.

Umpires: D. J. Constant and D. R. Shepherd.

†ENGLAND v WEST INDIES

Third Texaco Trophy Match

At Lord's, May 23, 24. England won by seven wickets. Toss: England. West Indies finished day of stoppages for rain and bad light 125 for six after 50 overs, Dujon 15 and Marshall being not out. Next morning, however, these two attacked the bowling with such panache tha England were set a target which the conditions made sufficiently challenging. Small, s accurate throughout the series, was hit for 17 in one over. The pressure on the West India batsmen was reflected by their three self-inflicted run-outs. DeFreitas had an especially fir match: his first five overs were maidens, he took a low catch on the square-leg boundary t dismiss Greenidge (94 balls), and he ran out Hooper from long-leg. England could afford n to take risks and batted sensibly against a much improved attack, spearheaded by Marsha Only when victory was in sight did Gatting (58 balls) and Lamb step up the tempo. Walsh first six overs cost only 1 run and his final figures were the most economical in a one-da international between Test-match countries. But the West Indians were profligate with wid and no-balls, bowling 21 in all and twice seeing Gooch "dismissed" by a no-ball.

Man of the Match: P. A. J. DeFreitas. *Attendance:* 20,680; *receipts* £354,546.

Men of the Series: England – M. W. Gatting; West Indies – M. D. Marshall.

West Indies

C. G. Greenidge c DeFreitas b Emburey 39
D. L. Haynes run out 10
R. B. Richardson c Downton b Pringle. 13
*I. V. A. Richards c Emburey b DeFreitas . 9
A. L. Logie run out 0
C. L. Hooper run out 12
†P. J. L. Dujon not out 30
M. D. Marshall b Emburey ....
B 2, l-b 10, w 12 ....

1/40 (2) 2/75 (1) 3/79 (3) 4/79 (5) 5/95 (4) 6/111 (6) 7/178 (8) (7 wkts, 55 overs)

W. K. M. Benjamin, C. A. Walsh and I. R. Bishop did not bat.

TEXACO TROPHY
TEXACO

Bowling: DeFreitas 11–5–20–1; Radford 11–2–29–0; Small 10–1–34–0; Pringle 11–4–27–1; Emburey 10–1–53–2; Gooch 2–1–3–0.

England

G. A. Gooch st Dujon b Hooper 28
B. C. Broad b Bishop 34
*M. W. Gatting not out 40
M. A. Lynch b Bishop 6
A. J. Lamb not out 30
B 6, l-b 17, w 5, n-b 14 42

1/71 (1) 2/108 (2) (3 wkts, 50 overs) 180
3/124 (4)

D. R. Pringle, †P. R. Downton, J. E. Emburey, P. A. J. DeFreitas, G. C. Small and N. V. Radford did not bat.

Bowling: Marshall 9–2–21–0; Walsh 11–5–11–0; Bishop 11–1–33–2; Benjamin 9–0–38–0; Hooper 10–0–54–1.

Umpires: H. D. Bird and N. T. Plews.

GLOUCESTERSHIRE v WEST INDIANS

At Bristol, May 25, 26, 27. Drawn. Toss: West Indians. A serious accident to Simmons, whic could have had fatal consequences, cast a shadow over this match. He was batting without helmet in poor light on the second day when he lost sight of a short ball from Lawrence an was struck on the head. The seriousness of his condition was quickly recognised and he wa rushed to Frenchay Hospital, where he was operated on immediately to relieve pressu caused by a blood clot on the brain. The operation was successful, but it was decided tha Simmons should take no further part in the tour. Although only 23 overs had been possible c the opening day, the helpful bowling conditions made a result seem a possibility. Glouceste shire's Barbadian, Greene, made good use of them, and then Patterson, bowling at great pac to an array of close fieldsmen, caused havoc when the home side batted. Only Wright courageous 49 and a large ration of extras enabled Gloucestershire to make some semblance a reply. Richards, however, settled for batting practice on the final day, and he contributed dismissive 63 from 68 balls, hitting ten fours and a six.

Close of play: First day, West Indians 90-2 (P. V. Simmons 41*, A. L. Logie 20*); Secor day, Gloucestershire 140.

West Indians

D. L. Haynes c Russell b Greene .... 19 – lbw b Lawrence ....
P. V. Simmons retired hurt .... 53 – absent injured
R. B. Richardson b Greene .... 2 – (2) c Wright b Lawrence ......
A. L. Logie b Greene .... 38 – (3) c Greene b Thomas ....
K. L. T. Arthurton c Russell b Greene ..... 10 – (4) b Thomas ....
*I. V. A. Richards b Lawrence .... 10 – (5) c Alleyne b Lawrence ......
M. D. Marshall st Russell b Lloyds .... 46 – (6) b Greene ....
†D. Williams lbw b Greene .... 20 – (7) st Russell b Lloyds ....
C. E. L. Ambrose c Romaines b Thomas ...... 25 – (8) c Russell b Lloyds ....
I. R. Bishop c Bainbridge b Thomas .... 7 – (9) not out ....
B. P. Patterson not out .... 5 – (10) c Bainbridge b Graveney ..
L-b 4, w 1, n-b 17 .... 22 B 4, l-b 5, n-b 10 ....

1/32 2/37 3/127 4/145 5/145 257 1/33 2/46 3/58 4/72 5/149 2
6/173 7/224 8/245 9/257 6/161 7/197 8/216 9/233

Bowling: *First Innings*—Lawrence 18–0–87–1; Greene 22–8–53–5; Thomas 14–3–46–2; Bainbridge 14–1–61–0; Lloyds 2–1–6–1. *Second Innings*—Lawrence 13–0–61–3; Greene 12–5–37–1; Thomas 10–0–57–2; Bainbridge 13–1–47–0; Lloyds 9–1–22–2; Graveney 2.3–2–0–1.

Gloucestershire

A. J. Wright c sub b Marshall . . . . 49 – not out 50
I. P. Butcher c sub b Patterson . . . . 0 – run out 4
P. W. Romaines c Marshall b Patterson . . . . 2 – not out 31
P. Bainbridge c Richards b Patterson 2
J. W. Lloyds c Williams b Patterson 0
†R. C. Russell c Marshall b Patterson 19
M. W. Alleyne run out 8
D. J. Thomas b Marshall 10
V. S. Greene c Logie b Marshall 0
*D. A. Graveney not out 4
D. V. Lawrence b Marshall 4
B 8, l-b 10, n-b 24 . . . . 42 L-b 1, n-b 12 13

1/13 2/15 3/27 4/31 5/70 140 1/14 (1 wkt) 98
6/93 7/119 8/119 9/136

Bowling: *First Innings*—Patterson 8–0–39–5; Ambrose 6–0–18–0; Bishop 6–0–25–0; Richards 7–2–24–0; Marshall 4.5–1–14–4; Arthurton 3–1–2–0. *Second Innings*—Patterson 5–0–20–0; Ambrose 5–0–20–0; Bishop 5–1–23–0; Richardson 4–0–22–0; Marshall 3–0–5–0; Richards 2–0–7–0.

Umpires: A. A. Jones and M. J. Kitchen.

WORCESTERSHIRE v WEST INDIANS

At Worcester, May 28, 29, 30. Drawn. Toss: West Indians. After four successive failures, Hick arrived at the wicket in the second over, needing 153 runs in the match to become the second batsman since the war to score 1,000 runs before the end of May. At the end of the first day he was still there, unbeaten on 172 after an unbroken second-wicket stand of 284 with the acting-captain, Curtis. Hick completed the first century of the summer against the tourists from 194 deliveries in 267 minutes. News that he was on course for 1,000 runs swelled the crowd to more than 3,000 by 5.30 p.m. when in the 83rd over he cut Ambrose for his 22nd boundary to reach 153. Among the crowd were his parents, who had arrived from Zimbabwe that day. Only W. G. Grace and D. G. Bradman attained the milestone in fewer than Hick's seven innings, in which he received 1,345 deliveries and hit 118 fours and 21 sixes. Only Bradman was younger than Hick, who was just five days into his 23rd year. Rain interrupted the second day's play after 65 minutes, and when the match resumed at half past two on the third day, only Haynes, Richards and Logie obtained the batting practice the West Indians were looking for before the First Test.

Close of play: First day, Worcestershire 284-1 (T. S. Curtis 78*, G. A. Hick 172*); Second day, Worcestershire 321-3 dec.

Worcestershire

T. S. Curtis b Patterson 82
J. Lord b Ambrose 0
G. A. Hick c Dujon b Patterson 172
P. Vorster not out 16
S. J. O'Shaughnessy not out 9
B 1, l-b 13, w 2, n-b 26 42

1/0 2/284 3/293 (3 wkts dec.) 321

J. Weston, †S. J. Rhodes, P. J. Newport, R. K. Illingworth, S. M. McEwan and R. M. Ellcock did not bat.

Bowling: Patterson 19.1–6–59–2; Ambrose 19–4–59–1; Walsh 22–4–78–0; Bishop -2–32–0; Hooper 14–1–46–0; Richards 9–1–33–0.

West Indians

C. G. Greenidge c Hick b Newport	2	†P. J. L. Dujon not out	4
D. L. Haynes lbw b Illingworth	71		
R. B. Richardson c Rhodes b Ellcock	5	N-b 2	2
*I. V. A. Richards b Ellcock	50		—
C. L. Hooper c Weston b Illingworth	7	1/4 2/9 3/99	(5 wkts) 170
A. L. Logie not out	29	4/114 5/155	

C. A. Walsh, B. P. Patterson, I. R. Bishop and C. E. L. Ambrose did not bat.

Bowling: Newport 9–1–40–1; Ellcock 13–2–51–2; McEwan 7–0–21–0; Illingworth 19–5–45–2; Weston 4–0–4–0; O'Shaughnessy 2–0–9–0.

Umpires: D. O. Oslear and K. E. Palmer.

ENGLAND v WEST INDIES

First Cornhill Test

At Nottingham, June 2, 3, 4, 6, 7. Drawn. Toss: England. Helped by a combination of bad light and rain – which accounted for more than a day's play – an anaesthetised pitch, and some excellent batting by Gooch, in both innings, and Gower, in the second, England ended their losing sequence of ten Tests against West Indies. But with Marshall exposing worrying frailties in England's batsmen, and Richards quickly re-establishing his dominance over their bowlers, it was an uneasy feeling of equality.

Both sides approached the match tentatively. England were desperate to throw off their inferiority complex at the start of a new series; West Indies had been unusually erratic in the first weeks of the tour, and Marshall, on whom so much rested, had not fully recovered from a side strain suffered in the recent series against Pakistan. Apart from Gower and Jarvis, who replaced Lynch and Small, England fielded the side which won the first two one-day internationals. Hemmings and Thomas were omitted from the squad selected. West Indies adopted their trusted formula, choosing four fast bowlers with Hooper as the emergency spinner.

Gatting's decision to bat first seemed completely justified when Gooch and Broad put on 125 for the first wicket, allowing England a glimpse of unexpected security on a pitch which apart from some variable bounce, gave little help to the faster bowlers nor much to the strokemaker. England's openers adapted accordingly, working hard for every run, while the West Indians were so put out by the behaviour of the pitch that they resorted to Hooper's off spin well before lunch. When Gooch reached 29, he became the sixteenth England batsman to score 4,000 Test runs. Otherwise, the morning passed with a comforting lack of incident fo the disappointingly small crowd.

That changed quickly in mid-afternoon when Marshall, slowing his pace, gained jus reward for a classic spell of medium-fast swing bowling. In seven overs, he took four for 1 and picked up a warning for running on the pitch. Gooch was the first to go, dragging a intended off-drive on to his stumps after a stay of 175 minutes which featured eight fours Gatting soon followed, his weakness against the in-swinger ruthlessly exploited as he gave simple catch to short leg, and in the last over before tea, Broad played on after 241 minutes c dogged concentration. Lamb was lbw to a wicked in-swinger two balls later. When Gowe gave Ambrose his first wicket of the series, England's top five batsmen, with 300 cap between them, had gone in the space of 61 runs. Pringle and Downton steadied the innings fc the day, but it took Ambrose and Marshall just thirteen overs to take the remaining fiv wickets for 25 runs the following morning.

Despite the collapse, England would still have been moderately pleased with their total on pitch of increasingly uncertain bounce and movement, which the early West Indian batsme found equally difficult to master. Greenidge was dropped at slip by Emburey off Jarvis befo edging the same bowler to Downton five balls later, and Emburey quickly had Richardsc caught at forward short leg. But an innings of calculated savagery by Richards change the balance of the match and laid the foundation for a large West Indies total, built ov three days between frequent interruptions for rain. Richards announced himself with fo fours on the second evening; his real assault came on Saturday when he singled o Emburey for particular punishment, hitting one huge six over long on. Hooper, using h feet beautifully against Emburey, joined in the attack, and in 30 overs on Saturday West Indies made 138 for the loss of Haynes and Richards. Poor Emburey, having taken a wicket in his first over, conceded 62 runs off his first seven overs.

Hooper, classically, Marshall, gleefully – with three sixes of Emburey – and Ambrose, inelegantly, made sure that the captain's initiative was capitalised on as England plugged away with a lack of imagination and enthusiasm that at times bordered on the careless. Pringle and Jarvis kept their rhythm admirably, but on Monday it seemed from fairly early on that England had settled for a draw. Given their fragility in the first innings, this seemed a perilous course. However, it was aided by Richards, who delayed his declaration until after tea, leaving England with a day plus 31 overs to survive. They lost Broad before the close, but Gooch's solidity was reassuring and he batted 6 hours 50 minutes, facing 303 balls and hitting fifteen fours. Gatting stayed with him for more than two hours, and then Gower joined him in a three-hour partnership of 161 for the third wicket. Marshall left the field with a recurrence of his side injury early in the afternoon, and long before the end Richards had accepted the draw. Although avoiding defeat, England had now gone a record fourteen Tests without a win since beating Australia at Melbourne in December 1986. Their previous sequence of thirteen had run from January 1984 to December 1984. – Andrew Longmore.

Man of the Match: M. D. Marshall. *Attendance:* 24,608; *receipts* £285,005.

Close of play: First day, England 220-5 (D. R. Pringle 39*, P. R. Downton 9*); Second day, West Indies 126-2 (D. L. Haynes 53*, I. V. A. Richards 22*); Third day, West Indies 264-4 (C. L. Hooper 47*, A. L. Logie 18*); Fourth day, England 67-1 (G. A. Gooch 38*, M. W. Gatting 8*).

England

G. A. Gooch b Marshall	73	– c Dujon b Patterson	146
B. C. Broad b Marshall	54	– c Dujon b Ambrose	16
*M. W. Gatting c Logie b Marshall	5	– b Marshall	29
D. I. Gower c Dujon b Ambrose	18	– not out	88
A. J. Lamb lbw b Marshall	0	– not out	6
D. R. Pringle b Marshall	39		
†P. R. Downton not out	16		
J. E. Emburey c Dujon b Marshall	0		
P. A. J. DeFreitas b Ambrose	3		
P. W. Jarvis b Ambrose	6		
G. R. Dilley b Ambrose	2		
L-b 13, w 5, n-b 11	29	L-b 10, n-b 6	16
1/125 (1) 2/141 (3) 3/161 (2) 4/161 (5) 5/186 (4) 6/223 (6) 7/223 (8) 8/235 (9) 9/243 (10) 10/245 (11)	245	1/39 (2) 2/116 (3) 3/277 (1)	(3 wkts) 301

Bowling: *First Innings*—Marshall 30–4–69–6; Patterson 16–2–49–0; Ambrose 6–10–53–4; Walsh 20–4–39–0; Hooper 8–1–20–0; Richards 1–0–2–0. *Second Innings*—Marshall 13–4–23–1; Patterson 24–6–69–1; Ambrose 23–4–56–1; Walsh 25–5–84–0; Richards –1–26–0; Hooper 14–1–33–0.

West Indies

C. G. Greenidge c Downton b Jarvis	25
D. L. Haynes c Downton b Jarvis	60
R. B. Richardson c Gatting b Emburey	17
I. V. A. Richards c Gooch b DeFreitas	80
C. L. Hooper c Downton b DeFreitas	84
A. L. Logie c Gooch b Pringle	20
†P. J. L. Dujon c and b Dilley	16
M. D. Marshall b Emburey	72
C. E. L. Ambrose run out	43
C. A. Walsh not out	3
B 6, l-b 8, n-b 14	28
1/54 (1) 2/84 (3) 3/159 (2) 4/231 (4) 5/271 (6) 6/309 (7) 7/334 (5) 8/425 (8) 9/448 (9)	(9 wkts dec.) 448

B. P. Patterson did not bat.

Bowling: Dilley 34–5–101–1; DeFreitas 27–5–93–2; Jarvis 18.1–1–63–2; Pringle –11–82–1; Emburey 16–4–95–2.

Umpires: H. D. Bird and J. Birkenshaw.

LANCASHIRE v WEST INDIANS

At Manchester, June 8, 9, 10. Drawn. Toss: Lancashire. In a gloomy, almost totally meaningless match severely curtailed by rain, the West Indians batted for the first two days and Lancashire for the third. After sharing in an opening partnership of 133 with Greenidge, Haynes went on to get within 7 runs of his second century of the summer. He played attractively, but it was Arthurton, who had scored only 15 runs in three previous innings, who took the eye with his attractive strokeplay.

Close of play: First day, West Indians 172-3 (D. L. Haynes 77*, K. L. T. Arthurton 2*); Second day, West Indians 287-5 (P. J. L. Dujon 35*, R. A. Harper 0*).

West Indians

*C. G. Greenidge c Murphy b Watkinson . 67
D. L. Haynes c Hayhurst b Folley 93
R. B. Richardson run out 16
A. L. Logie lbw b Matthews 0
K. L. T. Arthurton c Abrahams b Matthews . 60
P. J. L. Dujon not out 35
R. A. Harper not out 0
B 5, l-b 5, w 2, n-b 4 16

1/133 2/159 3/160 4/221 5/283 (5 wkts dec.) 287

†D. Williams, W. K. M. Benjamin, I. R. Bishop and B. P. Patterson did not bat.

Bowling: Matthews 17.2–2–48–2; Murphy 24–5–58–0; Watkinson 19–2–68–1; Folley 27–10–60–1; Fitton 16–3–43–0.

Lancashire

G. D. Mendis c Harper b Bishop 59
A. N. Hayhurst b Benjamin 7
J. Abrahams c Harper b Patterson 9
T. E. Jesty c Arthurton b Harper 43
*N. H. Fairbrother not out 44
M. Watkinson c Harper b Bishop 4
†W. K. Hegg c Greenidge b Arthurton . 19
J. D. Fitton not out 11
L-b 16, w 5, n-b 21 42

1/29 2/52 3/148 4/148 5/166 6/207 (6 wkts) 238

C. D. Matthews, I. Folley and A. J. Murphy did not bat.

Bowling: Patterson 12–2–34–1; Benjamin 15–2–39–1; Harper 29–10–57–1; Bishop 14–1–61–2; Arthurton 10–3–31–1.

Umpires: K. E. Palmer and D. S. Thompsett.

NORTHAMPTONSHIRE v WEST INDIANS

At Northampton, June 11, 12, 13. Drawn. Toss: Northamptonshire. The West Indian decision to bat through the last day, although understandable in view of the forthcoming Te match, ensured a meaningless day's play in terms of a contest. Arthurton took advantage c the perfect weather and a depleted county attack to score his first hundred of the tour, hittin three sixes and sixteen fours in 239 minutes at the crease. Hooper joined him in a stand of 1C before being stumped by Noon, Northamptonshire's seventeen-year-old reserve wicke keeper, who, contrary to the Playing Conditions for First-class Matches, took over whe Ripley left the field with a damaged thumb. On the first day, Haynes held the innings togeth with a solid 72, Richards played some extravagant strokes in his 39 off 54 balls, and Harp added 81 with Williams in 26 overs of bright and purposeful batting. Northamptonshire soc ran into trouble against Walsh, who previously had taken only one first-class wicket on t tour. They recovered through Stanley, who batted for three and a half hours after a shaky sta and was well supported by Cook. Hoffman, the former Warwickshire pace bowler, batted ar bowled usefully on his first-class début for Northamptonshire.

Close of play: First day, Northamptonshire 40-2 (R. J. Bailey 12*, A. J. Lamb 4*); Secor day, West Indians 49-2 (C. L. Hooper 20*, A. L. Logie 5*).

West Indians

D. L. Haynes b Cook	72	– c Lamb b Cook	22
R. B. Richardson b Cook	42	– lbw b Capel	0
C. L. Hooper c Ripley b Hoffman	0	– st sub b Bailey	74
A. L. Logie lbw b Robinson	23	– lbw b Capel	10
K. L. T. Arthurton run out	3	– b Larkins	121
*I. V. A. Richards b Capel	39	– c and b Bailey	6
R. A. Harper c Ripley b Wild	44	– b Cook	5
†D. Williams c Ripley b Wild	44	– c and b Hoffman	51
C. E. L. Ambrose run out	1	– not out	14
W. K. M. Benjamin not out	1	– not out	21
C. A. Walsh b Cook	1		
B 4, l-b 10, w 1, n-b 3	18	B 6, l-b 13, n-b 2	21
1/76 2/83 3/115 4/130 5/189 6/203 7/284 8/286 9/287	288	1/2 2/44 3/63 4/167 5/175 6/214 7/305 8/309	(8 wkts dec.) 345

Bowling: *First Innings*—Capel 12–2–51–1; Robinson 17–3–52–1; Cook 29.2–7–66–3; Hoffman 13–3–43–1; Wild 18–2–62–2. *Second Innings*—Capel 15–2–35–2; Robinson 10–3–15–0; Hoffman 19–3–54–1; Cook 25–6–90–2; Bailey 17–2–77–2; Wild 5–2–15–0; Larkins 10–3–21–1; Lamb 4–0–19–0.

Northamptonshire

A. Fordham c Richards b Walsh	10
*W. Larkins lbw b Walsh	7
R. J. Bailey lbw b Benjamin	45
A. J. Lamb c Hooper b Walsh	6
D. J. Capel c Harper b Walsh	2
D. J. Wild b Benjamin	15
N. A. Stanley st Williams b Hooper	55
†D. Ripley c Williams b Walsh	8
N. G. B. Cook c Harper b Hooper	24
D. S. Hoffman not out	20
M. A. Robinson lbw b Benjamin	5
B 6, l-b 17, w 4, n-b 8	35
1/16 2/23 3/52 4/60 5/91 6/112 7/135 8/202 9/223	232

Bowling: Walsh 22–3–49–5; Benjamin 19.2–4–44–3; Ambrose 14–6–23–0; Harper 25–7–58–0; Hooper 12–4–35–2.

Umpires: B. Dudleston and A. G. T. Whitehead.

ENGLAND v WEST INDIES

Second Cornhill Test

At Lord's, June 16, 17, 18, 20, 21. West Indies won by 134 runs. Toss: West Indies. Dilley, with six boundaries in his 28, and Jarvis added 53 for England's last wicket to keep the game going until just after lunch on the fifth day. Later, the England manager, M. J. Stewart, found some solace in England's last-day batting, suggesting that on a good pitch, and with the sun shining, West Indies' bowlers had not looked unbeatable. This was self-deluding. Once Lamb had reached his first Test hundred since 1984, the West Indians did little more than stroll through the closing stages.

Throughout the match, batting was easier while the sun shone. When it went behind the clouds, the ball swung and seamed, tipping the balance firmly in the bowlers' favour. When it did shine for any length of time, as on the Saturday, West Indies had the good fortune to be batting; and it was on the Saturday, in their second innings, that their resplendent batting took the match beyond England's reach. Greenidge was the linchpin, adding 83 with Richardson and 83 with Richards. The off-driven four off Small with which he reached his fifteenth Test hundred was imperious. It was his fourteenth boundary, and he batted in all for four hours, facing 192 balls; when 49, he became the fifth West Indian to score 6,000 runs in Tests. Richards's 81-ball 72 contained an early six off Emburey and twelve fours – four of them struck successively off Small to pass 50. Finally, Logie and Dujon batted stylishly for their second century partnership of the match. Their 130 together on the opening day had rescued West Indies from a position at lunch of 66 for five.

It was the start England needed after the troubled events that followed Trent Bridge. Gatting, the victim of unsavoury allegations in the press, had been replaced as captain by Emburey and as a batsman by Moxon. Small came in for DeFreitas, but on the third afternoon he limped off the field and virtually out of the series with a recurrence of the thigh strain that had prevented him from playing at Nottingham. West Indies were unchanged, and when Richards won the toss, he chose, after a long deliberation, to bat on a pitch well shorn of grass. The sun was shining then; when Haynes was caught by Moxon, throwing himself forward at short leg, the cloud covered it. Dilley was swinging the ball away on a remorseless line and also obtaining lift. His next three wickets came from catches behind the bat, and at lunch, having bowled throughout the morning, he had figures of 13–4–35–4. He would have taken five had Pringle at first slip caught Logie when he was 10.

This was a decisive miss, for Logie took the attack excitingly to the bowlers, reaching his half-century with his twelfth four. Dujon's fifty was more classically compiled. On the point of tea, Emburey squeezed the ball between his defensive bat and pad, and soon afterwards clung to Logie's square slash at point. Gower rose gracefully and twisted back behind square leg to catch Ambrose, but Walsh and Patterson held on for twenty minutes and saw the score past 200. England had only 6.5 overs of batting before bad light stopped play with thirteen overs remaining, and in that time they lost Broad, beaten by Marshall's pace and a low bounce. He left looking unhappy, and his expression of disappointment, caught by the television camera, was to cost him his Test place.

The second day, again overcast, belonged to Marshall, who finished with six for 32, the best return by a West Indian at Lord's. He was fast, varied his line and pace, moved the ball late, and was often unplayable as he took five of England's last seven wickets. Gower batted in the Logie mode either side of lunch and the stoppage that preceded it, overtook Gooch, who was 100 minutes in the 30s, and ultimately perished when an attempted pull from outside off stump became a lob towards square leg. For England, it was the beginning of the end. Bad light interrupted West Indies' second innings three times before the close, but next day, Saturday, they set out a feast of batting delights. Any joy England had on Monday morning at taking their last five wickets in eleven overs was tempered by the knowledge that, 441 runs behind, they had to bat for 172 overs to save the match. Dujon reached his second fifty, but the collapse that followed his dismissal left Logie 5 runs short of a well-merited century, having faced 124 balls, hit twelve boundaries, and provided great entertainment.

But for Lamb, on his 34th birthday, and the hour lost to bad light and drizzle, the match would have been over that day – a long, slow one, with West Indies' over-rate averaging 11.21 and play continuing until 7.40 p.m. Lamb's innings was a testimony to his character and technique. His first 39 runs came somewhat adventurously from 39 balls, but with confidence he settled into the form which had been eluding him at Test level. Moxon stayed with him for almost two hours, Downton for an hour and a quarter, and Emburey in 32 balls found the boundary six times before a full toss hit first his thumb and then his stumps. Lamb, 99 overnight, needed 25 minutes (23 balls) next morning to reach 100, and when Hooper brought his innings to a close with a thrilling pick-up and throw on the run, he had batted for 338 minutes, faced 213 balls, and hit fifteen fours. Marshall, who had begun England's decline finished with ten wickets for the third time in a Test.

For the first time in England, the match receipts exceeded £1 million, being £1,031,262.50 from an attendance of 77,923. – G.W.

Man of the Match: A. L. Logie.

Close of play: First day, England 20-1 (G. A. Gooch 17*, M. D. Moxon 3*); Second day West Indies 16-0 (C. G. Greenidge 12*, D. L. Haynes 4*); Third day, West Indies 354- (A. L. Logie 69*, P. J. L. Dujon 45*); Fourth day, England 214-7 (A. J. Lamb 99* G. C. Small 0*).

West Indies

C. G. Greenidge c Downton b Dilley	22	– c Emburey b Dilley	10
D. L. Haynes c Moxon b Dilley	12	– c Downton b Dilley	
R. B. Richardson c Emburey b Dilley	5	– lbw b Pringle	2
*I. V. A. Richards c Downton b Dilley	6	– b Pringle	7
C. L. Hooper c Downton b Small	3	– c Downton b Jarvis	1
A. L. Logie c Emburey b Small	81	– not out	9
†P. J. L. Dujon b Emburey	53	– b Jarvis	5
M. D. Marshall c Gooch b Dilley	11	– b Jarvis	
C. E. L. Ambrose c Gower b Small	0	– b Dilley	
C. A. Walsh not out	9	– b Dilley	
B. P. Patterson b Small	0	– c Downton b Jarvis	
L-b 6, n-b 1	7	L-b 19, w 1, n-b 5	2
1/21 (2) 2/40 (1) 3/47 (3) 4/50 (5) 5/54 (4) 6/184 (7) 7/199 (6) 8/199 (8) 9/199 (9) 10/209 (11)	209	1/32 (2) 2/115 (3) 3/198 (1) 4/226 (4) 5/240 (5) 6/371 (7) 7/379 (8) 8/380 (9) 9/384 (10) 10/397 (11)	39

Bowling: *First Innings*—Dilley 23–6–55–5; Jarvis 13–2–47–0; Small 18.5–5–64–4; Pringle 7–3–20–0; Emburey 6–2–17–1. *Second Innings*—Dilley 27–6–73–4; Small 19–1–76–0; Jarvis 26–3–107–4; Emburey 15–1–62–0; Pringle 21–4–60–2.

England

G. A. Gooch b Marshall	44	– lbw b Marshall	16
B. C. Broad lbw b Marshall	0	– c Dujon b Marshall	1
M. D. Moxon c Richards b Ambrose	26	– run out	14
D. I. Gower c sub (K. L. T. Arthurton) b Walsh	46	– c Richardson b Patterson	1
A. J. Lamb lbw b Marshall	10	– run out	113
D. R. Pringle c Dujon b Walsh	1	– lbw b Walsh	0
†P. R. Downton lbw b Marshall	11	– lbw b Marshall	27
*J. E. Emburey b Patterson	7	– b Ambrose	30
G. C. Small not out	5	– c Richards b Marshall	7
P. W. Jarvis c Haynes b Marshall	7	– not out	29
G. R. Dilley b Marshall	0	– c Richardson b Patterson	28
L-b 6, n-b 2	8	B 5, l-b 20, w 2, n-b 14	41
1/13 (2) 2/58 (3) 3/112 (4) 4/129 (1) 5/134 (6) 6/140 (5) 7/153 (8) 8/157 (7) 9/165 (10) 10/165 (11)	165	1/27 (1) 2/29 (2) 3/31 (4) 4/104 (3) 5/105 (6) 6/161 (7) 7/212 (8) 8/232 (9) 9/254 (5) 10/307 (11)	307

Bowling: *First Innings*—Marshall 18–5–32–6; Patterson 13–3–52–1; Ambrose 12–1–39–1; Walsh 16–6–36–2. *Second Innings*—Marshall 25–5–60–4; Patterson 21.5–2–100–2; Walsh 20–1–75–1; Ambrose 20–4–47–1.

Umpires: K. E. Palmer and D. R. Shepherd.

†OXFORD & CAMBRIDGE UNIVERSITIES v WEST INDIANS

At Cambridge, June 23, 24. West Indians won by an innings and 172 runs. Toss: West Indians. The West Indian fast bowlers needed just five hours to win this two-day fixture against a Universities side which found that first-class experience against the counties counted for little when the opposition meant business. Only Atherton looked to have the class and technique to make his mark. On the first day the tourists batted freely and attractively until the declaration left the Universities with 55 minutes' batting. Logie struck thirteen fours in his 57 from 42 deliveries.

Close of play: First day, Oxford & Cambridge Universities 14-4 (D. A. Hagan 6*, R. J. Turner 0*).

West Indians

C. G. Greenidge b Sygrove	5	I. R. Bishop not out	39
R. B. Richardson c Turner b Fenton	12	B. P. Patterson lbw b Perry	12
C. L. Hooper c Atkinson b Perry	51		
A. L. Logie c Turner b Perry	57	L-b 2, w 2	4
K. L. T. Arthurton c Hagan b Atherton	70		
R. A. Harper c Atkinson b Perry	15	1/15 2/17 3/100	(9 wkts dec.) 355
D. Williams c Atherton b Sygrove	84	4/142 5/181 6/244	
W. K. M. Benjamin c Fenton b Atherton	6	7/251 8/323 9/355	

C. A. Walsh did not bat.

Bowling: Fenton 20–4–61–1; Sygrove 25–5–95–2; Perry 18.3–0–82–4; Weale 11–3–53–0; Atherton 18–4–62–2.

Oxford & Cambridge Universities

Batsman	1st inns	2nd inns	
P. A. C. Bail b Patterson	0	lbw b Benjamin	15
M. A. Crawley c Hooper b Benjamin	1	c Benjamin b Patterson	1
*M. A. Atherton c Williams b Patterson	1	c Williams b Benjamin	45
M. J. Kilborn b Harper	6	c Logie b Benjamin	4
D. A. Hagan c Hooper b Bishop	6	c Richardson b Benjamin	5
†R. J. Turner c Williams b Benjamin	0	(7) c Arthurton b Bishop	4
J. C. M. Atkinson c Patterson b Bishop	5	(6) c Benjamin b Bishop	38
S. D. Weale b Benjamin	4	c Patterson b Hooper	8
J. N. Perry not out	14	c Hooper b Bishop	0
M. R. Sygrove c Williams b Bishop	0	c Walsh b Hooper	5
N. C. W. Fenton b Bishop	1	not out	2
		B 16, l-b 2	18
1/0 2/2 3/2 4/8 5/14 6/14 7/22 8/26 9/30	38	1/6 2/50 3/54 4/70 5/101 6/121 7/129 8/129 9/138	145

Bowling: *First Innings*—Patterson 4–3–2–2; Benjamin 10–5–23–3; Bishop 8.5–5–12–4; Harper 2–1–1–1. *Second Innings*—Walsh 7–2–17–0; Patterson 7–1–21–1; Harper 17–3–59–0; Hooper 3.3–1–3–2; Benjamin 10–3–18–4; Bishop 4–2–9–3.

Umpires: R. Julian and K. Taylor.

KENT v WEST INDIANS

At Canterbury, June 25, 26. West Indians won by an innings and 43 runs. Toss: Kent. Put in to bat, the touring team began uncertainly against a Kent side short of seven first-team players being rested because of injury. Hooper, batting for 190 minutes and hitting a six and fourteen fours, held the innings together before Harper and the lower-order batsmen scored enterprisingly. On the second day, Sunday, the below-strength county side was shot out twice. The fast bowlers did the early damage and Harper's off-spin completed the rout of the first innings. Pienaar resisted for 34 overs in the second innings, but Bishop, with formidable pace, and Harper brought more discomfort to Kent. The county's only consolation was a bold half-century by Kelleher, who hit four sixes and five fours in reaching 50 off 42 balls.

Close of play: First day, West Indians 275.

West Indians

D. L. Haynes b Alleyne	10
R. B. Richardson c Farbrace b Kelleher	5
C. L. Hooper c Farbrace b G. R. Cowdrey	87
K. L. T. Arthurton c Sabine b Davis	22
*I. V. A. Richards c Wells b Pienaar	7
P. J. L. Dujon c Harman b Wells	10
R. A. Harper not out	56
†D. Williams b Kelleher	1[illegible]
C. E. L. Ambrose c Harman b Davis	1[illegible]
W. K. M. Benjamin b Alleyne	1[illegible]
I. R. Bishop run out	2[illegible]
L-b 6, w 1, n-b 1	[illegible]
1/10 2/20 3/82 4/105 5/140 6/146 7/168 8/199 9/232	27[illegible]

Bowling: Alleyne 20–4–62–2; Kelleher 22–5–41–2; Sabine 10–4–29–0; Pienaar 14–2–51–1 Davis 9.4–3–20–2; Cowdrey 5–1–14–1; Wells 14–4–51–1; Harman 1–0–1–0.

Kent

Batsman	1st inns	2nd inns	
R. F. Pienaar c Arthurton b Ambrose	0	c Richardson b Bishop	3[illegible]
T. R. Ward c Dujon b Ambrose	8	c Arthurton b Ambrose	[illegible]
*S. G. Hinks c Harper b Benjamin	1	c Hooper b Bishop	1
G. R. Cowdrey b Harper	9	b Bishop	[illegible]
V. J. Wells c Harper b Benjamin	0	c Harper b Bishop	
D. J. Sabine c Williams b Benjamin	7	c Arthurton b Bishop	
†P. Farbrace c Richardson b Bishop	6	c Dujon b Bishop	
D. J. M. Kelleher c Richardson b Harper	13	c Ambrose b Harper	5[illegible]
M. D. Harman b Harper	7	c Williams b Harper	
R. P. Davis not out	10	not out	
H. L. Alleyne b Harper	2	c sub b Harper	
B 11, l-b 7	18	B 4, l-b 6, n-b 1	1[illegible]
1/0 2/9 3/9 4/9 5/21 6/31 7/35 8/54 9/71	81	1/12 2/34 3/64 4/73 5/75 6/85 7/86 8/115 9/144	1[illegible]

Bowling: *First Innings*—Ambrose 8–3–6–2; Benjamin 7–2–23–3; Bishop 11–3–24–1; Harper 10.5–7–10–4. *Second Innings*—Ambrose 7–3–11–1; Benjamin 8–4–14–0; Harper 20.5–6–51–3; Bishop 15–3–39–6; Hooper 2–1–1–0; Arthurton 2–0–25–0.

Umpires: J. H. Hampshire and K. J. Lyons.

ENGLAND v WEST INDIES

Third Cornhill Test

At Manchester, June 30, July 1, 2, 4, 5. West Indies won by an innings and 156 runs. Toss: England. With England unable to cope for any length of time with the West Indian fast bowlers, and in particular with Marshall, a Test match which had been scheduled for a minimum of 455 overs ended after 243.1 had been bowled. The game lasted until the fifth day only because of constant interruptions for bad light and rain. In terms of the fifteen-overs-per-hour equation of the Playing Conditions for the series, the match theoretically finished shortly before tea on the third day.

England made four changes. Broad was dropped, ostensibly for his consistent failure to make runs in home Tests, but there was always a suspicion that he was being disciplined for the incident at Lord's when he was spotted by a television camera mouthing his disappointment at an lbw decision. Moxon was promoted to open, Gatting came back into the side, all-rounder Capel replaced Pringle, and DeFreitas returned in the absence through injury of Jarvis and Small. When Cook, the Northamptonshire slow left-armer, failed a fitness test, Childs, a slow left-arm spinner with Essex, became at 36 years and 320 days England's oldest débutant for more than 40 years. A hamstring injury ended Haynes's run of 72 consecutive Tests for West Indies, who included a spinner, Harper, for the first time in the series and brought in Benjamin for Patterson.

Under overcast skies, England on the opening morning slumped to 55 for four by lunch and thereafter were always staring at a defeat. Marshall, although rumoured to be carrying a rib injury, lanced his way through Moxon's defences and, recalling memories of Lord's in 1984, trapped Gatting leg-before without the batsman offering a shot. Gower edged Walsh into the safe hands of Harper at slip, and when Gooch edged Benjamin to the wicket-keeper, West Indies were firmly in command. Lamb and Downton provided brief resistance as the afternoon saw a series of stoppages for rain, but England's innings of 135 lasted only 60.2 overs. Walsh, who at the start of the summer was struggling to hold his place, was the pick of the bowlers with four for 46.

Emburey, who had claimed the wicket of stand-in opener Richardson on several occasions, took the new ball. And in the three overs before the close of play, England missed two catches that might just have made the West Indians struggle. Instead, for the next two and a half days, as the rain continued to sweep in from the west, England were kept in the field while their opponents cruised to a first-innings lead with only three wickets down and then stamped their complete authority on the match. Although the pitch provided some movement off the seam and the bounce was erratic, England's pace attack lacked the skill and extra yard of pace to take advantage. Childs accounted for Hooper with his fourteenth ball in international cricket, and for a time managed to subdue Richards, but his control and steadiness were inadequate compensation for the lack of penetration that was England's main weakness. The West Indian innings owed much to a partnership of 94 for the sixth wicket between Harper and Dujon. The former had shown excellent form in recent games, while Dujon was merely confirming a return to form after two lean years.

No play was possible before lunch on the fourth day, and with the forecasts predicting little improvement in the weather, Richards was faced with a dilemma over the timing of his declaration. Eventually, when play was due to resume at 4.15 p.m. after a second stoppage, he decided that a lead of 249 would be sufficient for his fast bowlers in the possible 136 overs that remained. Although his decision could not be regarded as erring towards caution, the events that followed showed that he could have let West Indies' innings follow its natural course.

By the close of play, England were 60 for three, with Marshall accounting for Gooch and Gatting and Benjamin having Moxon caught at slip. One refreshing factor of the day's play had been the sight of the umpires carrying out inspections wearing their white coats. They were able to signal to the dressing-rooms when conditions were fit for play to restart, instead of following the time-honoured, and time-wasting, tradition of walking back to the pavilion to inform the teams of their intentions.

On the final morning, England's only chance of survival lay with the weather, but Manchester dawned bright and steamy. In a shade over an hour, England lost their last seven wickets while only 33 runs were added – and then it rained. Marshall, maintaining a strike-rate of a wicket every 26 balls in the series, was the chief destroyer, sending back five Englishmen to finish with a career-best seven for 22, while Lamb and Emburey fell to the fast-improving Ambrose. The 6ft 7in, 24-year-old Leeward Islander, although unknown to most English followers, was not without local knowledge, having taken more than 100 wickets the previous year in the Central Lancashire League. He kept the ball well up to the bat and relied on pace and movement. The same could be said of Marshall. England could not blame this defeat on the hostility of fast short-pitched bowling. Their undoing was the intelligent use of the conditions by a far superior force. – Graham Otway.

Man of the Match: M. D. Marshall. *Attendance:* 45,854; *receipts* £414,474.

Close of play: First day, West Indies 4-0 (C. G. Greenidge 4*, R. B. Richardson 0*); Second day, West Indies 242-5 (P. J. L. Dujon 35*, R. A. Harper 23*); Third day, West Indies 357-6 (R. A. Harper 61*, M. D. Marshall 37*); Fourth day, England 60-3 (D. I. Gower 24*, A. J. Lamb 6*).

England

G. A. Gooch c Dujon b Benjamin	27	– lbw b Marshall	1
M. D. Moxon b Marshall	0	– c Richards b Benjamin	15
M. W. Gatting lbw b Marshall	0	– c Richardson b Marshall	4
D. I. Gower c Harper b Walsh	9	– c Richardson b Marshall	34
A. J. Lamb c Greenidge b Ambrose	33	– c Logie b Ambrose	9
D. J. Capel b Benjamin	1	– c sub (K. L. T. Arthurton) b Marshall	0
†P. R. Downton c Greenidge b Walsh	24	– c Harper b Marshall	6
*J. E. Emburey c Dujon b Walsh	1	– c Logie b Ambrose	8
P. A. J. DeFreitas c Greenidge b Ambrose	15	– c Harper b Marshall	0
G. R. Dilley c Harper b Walsh	14	– b Marshall	4
J. H. Childs not out	2	– not out	0
L-b 4, n-b 5	9	B 1, l-b 10, n-b 1	12
1/12 (2) 2/14 (3) 3/33 (4) 4/55 (1) 5/61 (6) 6/94 (5) 7/98 (8) 8/113 (7) 9/123 (9) 10/135 (10)	135	1/6 (1) 2/22 (3) 3/36 (2) 4/73 (4) 5/73 (6) 6/73 (5) 7/87 (7) 8/87 (9) 9/93 (8) 10/93 (10)	93

Bowling: *First Innings*—Marshall 12–5–19–2; Ambrose 17–5–35–2; Walsh 18.2–4–46–4; Benjamin 13–4–31–2. *Second Innings*—Marshall 15.4–5–22–7; Ambrose 16–4–36–2; Walsh 4–1–10–0; Benjamin 4–1–6–1; Harper 2–1–4–0; Hooper 1–0–4–0.

West Indies

C. G. Greenidge lbw b DeFreitas	45
R. B. Richardson b Dilley	23
C. L. Hooper lbw b Childs	15
*I. V. A. Richards b Capel	47
A. L. Logie lbw b Dilley	39
†P. J. L. Dujon c Capel b Dilley	67
R. A. Harper b Dilley	74
M. D. Marshall not out	43
C. E. L. Ambrose not out	7
L-b 21, n-b 3	24
1/35 (2) 2/77 (3) 3/101 (1) 4/175 (4) 5/187 (5) 6/281 (6) 7/373 (7) (7 wkts dec.)	384

W. K. M. Benjamin and C. A. Walsh did not bat.

Bowling: Dilley 28.1–4–99–4; Emburey 25–7–54–0; DeFreitas 35–5–81–1; Capel 12–2–38–1; Childs 40–12–91–1.

Umpires: D. J. Constant and N. T. Plews.

†MINOR COUNTIES v WEST INDIANS

At Trowbridge, July 9, 10. Drawn. Toss: West Indians. Rain prevented any play on the second day, when the match was called off soon after lunch. Logie took the spectators' mind off the dull weather on the first day, racing to his half-century in 42 minutes and to his hundred in 89 off 96 balls with fifteen fours. Richards hit four sixes in 21 balls, and a the time Hooper (three sixes, fifteen fours) held the innings together. The Minor Counties bowlers had done well to restrict the West Indians to 79 for two from 42 overs before lunch, with Turner, the former Essex player, conceding only 16 runs from his first thirteen overs. They were made to pay for their temerity in the afternoon.

West Indians

D. L. Haynes c Olley b Evans 33
W. K. M. Benjamin run out 11
C. L. Hooper not out 140
A. L. Logie b Turner 100
K. L. T. Arthurton c Greensword b Turner . 7
*I. V. A. Richards c Merry b Evans . . . 34
R. A. Harper not out 14
B 2, l-b 7, n-b 10 19

1/13 2/73 3/242 4/263 5/313 (5 wkts dec.) 358

C. E. L. Ambrose, I. R. Bishop, †D. Williams and B. P. Patterson did not bat.

Bowling: Turner 20–3–41–2; Merry 13–2–34–0; Burrow 7–2–16–0; Greensword 12–0–37–0; Evans 19–1–87–2; O'Brien 18–1–117–0; Plumb 3–0–17–0.

Minor Counties

C. J. Stockdale not out 5
*S. G. Plumb c Williams b Benjamin . . 0
N. A. Folland not out 12
L-b 1 1

1/2 (1 wkt) 18

P. R. Oliver, S. Greensword, S. Burrow, †M. W. C. Olley, S. Turner, R. A. Evans, W. G. Merry and J. F. M. O'Brien did not bat.

Bowling: Patterson 3–1–4–0; Benjamin 3–1–13–1.

Umpires: D. J. Halfyard and R. C. Tolchard.

GLAMORGAN v WEST INDIANS

At Swansea, July 13, 14, 15. Drawn. Toss: West Indians. With the first day lost following heavy rain, there was keen disappointment among Welsh cricket supporters. Next day, however, they were treated to a splendidly controlled innings from Dujon, in the unaccustomed role of opening batsman, some big hitting by Hooper, and a brisk assault by Richards, whose five fours in his 23 not out included four in one over off Thomas. Hooper despatched North, the left-arm slow bowler, for two sixes in an over. When asked how far he would like mid-off pushed back, North crisply requested, "Ilfracombe!" Dujon, who also pulled the spinner for six, struck 22 fours in his 141 in four and threequarter hours. On a bland pitch, Barwick bowled with control and movement in the morning, conceding just 5 runs off his first eleven overs. Hopkins was the only batsman to come to terms with the tourists' fast bowlers and made his highest score of the season, 87, in a little short of five hours, hitting fifteen fours and facing 191 deliveries. He was twice struck on the helmet with considerable impact, but it was a badly bruised finger that kept him off the field after Morris declared the Glamorgan innings closed 122 runs behind.

Close of play: First day, No play; Second day, Glamorgan 43-0 (A. R. Butcher 12*, A. Hopkins 22*).

West Indians

D. L. Haynes c Morris b Ontong . . . . 14 – not out 28
†P. J. L. Dujon c Butcher b Ontong . . . . .141 – c Derrick b Thomas 16
C. L. Hooper st Metson b Derrick . . . . 49 – not out 18
K. L. T. Arthurton not out 45
*I. V. A. Richards not out 23
B 10, l-b 12, w 3, n-b 5 . . . . 30 L-b 1, n-b 4 5

1/57 2/160 3/265 (3 wkts dec.) 302 1/23 (1 wkt) 67

D. Williams, R. A. Harper, I. R. Bishop, M. D. Marshall, B. P. Patterson and C. A. Walsh did not bat.

Bowling: *First Innings*—Thomas 14–2–52–0; Barwick 20–9–37–0; Derrick 18–5–49–1; Ontong 19–6–50–2; North 16–3–74–0; Butcher 2–0–18–0. *Second Innings*—Thomas 8–0–35–1; Barwick 5–1–13–0; North 6–4–14–0; Derrick 4–2–4–0.

Glamorgan

A. R. Butcher c Hooper b Patterson . . . 18
J. A. Hopkins c Arthurton b Harper . . . 87
*H. Morris c Williams b Bishop 12
M. P. Maynard c Harper b Bishop 12
G. C. Holmes not out 8
R. C. Ontong c Arthurton b Harper . . . 0
J. G. Thomas not out 0
B 20, l-b 8, w 5, n-b 10 43

1/65 2/116 3/153 4/179 5/179 (5 wkts dec.) 180

P. D. North, †C. P. Metson, J. Derrick and S. R. Barwick did not bat.

Bowling: Patterson 19–6–35–1; Bishop 20–6–56–2; Harper 8–2–12–2; Marshall 6–3–15–0; Walsh 13–4–34–0.

Umpires: J. C. Balderstone and P. B. Wight.

LEICESTERSHIRE v WEST INDIANS

At Leicester, July 16, 17, 18. Drawn. Toss: Leicestershire. The West Indians, as expected, dominated this match from the outset. Rain curtailed the first day's play soon after Richards, to the disappointment of the crowd, was bowled without scoring by DeFreitas, but his side went on to score 370 in an effortless way. Dujon hit six fours in reaching his half-century from 86 balls, and Greenidge, who had been ill the previous day, resumed to finish with two sixes and seven fours as the last three wickets added 126. Thereafter, the story was a familiar one as English batsmen collapsed before the West Indian fast bowlers. While the tourists had batted, the pitch seemed the most benign Grace Road had offered all season. When it was Leicestershire's turn, it transformed into one offering pace, movement and bounce, such was the gulf between the two attacks. There was, however, a twist to the tale, and it was provided by Potter, who played two of his strangest yet perhaps most heroic innings. Coming in at No. 5 he twice remained undefeated, batting in all for 275 minutes. Almost single-handedly he had saved his side from defeat when, with twenty overs remaining, Richards decided not to pursue victory.

Close of play: First day, West Indians 150-4 (C. L. Hooper 54*, P. J. L. Dujon 20*); Second day, Leicestershire 33-4 (L. Potter 6*, C. C. Lewis 2*).

West Indians

C. G. Greenidge c Taylor b Potter 75
D. L. Haynes b Agnew 16
C. L. Hooper c Whitticase b DeFreitas . 62
A. L. Logie b Lewis 18
K. L. T. Arthurton c Whitticase b Taylor 3
*I. V. A. Richards b DeFreitas 0
†P. J. L. Dujon c Willey b Taylor 51
R. A. Harper c Whitticase b Potter . . . 47
C. E. L. Ambrose c sub b Willey 1
W. K. M. Benjamin c and b Agnew . . . 1
B. P. Patterson not out 2
L-b 16, w 2, n-b 20 3

1/30 2/81 3/87 4/90 5/169 6/210 7/244 8/271 9/309 37

C. G. Greenidge, when 16, retired ill at 49 and resumed at 244.

Bowling: DeFreitas 23–3–81–2; Agnew 29–3–114–2; Lewis 17–6–38–1; Taylor 22–4–69–2 Willey 8–2–28–1; Potter 5.3–1–24–2.

Leicestershire

Batsman	First innings		Second innings	
T. J. Boon c Dujon b Patterson	2	–	c Hooper b Benjamin	1
*N. E. Briers c Dujon b Patterson	4	–	c Harper b Richards	20
P. Willey lbw b Ambrose	3	–	c Dujon b Patterson	21
J. J. Whitaker c Patterson b Ambrose	8	–	b Patterson	2
L. Potter not out	16	–	not out	19
C. C. Lewis c Haynes b Benjamin	27	–	c Harper b Patterson	0
P. A. J. DeFreitas lbw b Patterson	1	–	c Benjamin b Harper	22
†P. Whitticase c Richards b Patterson	2	–	not out	14
J. P. Agnew c Richards b Benjamin	8			
P. M. Such b Benjamin	2			
L. B. Taylor c Richards b Benjamin	0			
B 4, l-b 2, n-b 11	17		N-b 4	4
1/2 2/5 3/9 4/24 5/67 6/68 7/72 8/88 9/90	90		1/2 2/39 3/45 4/48 5/48 6/71	(6 wkts) 103

Bowling: *First Innings*—Patterson 16–1–44–4; Ambrose 10–2–19–2; Benjamin 15–1–20–4; Harper 2–1–1–0. *Second Innings*—Ambrose 12–3–19–0; Benjamin 10–3–24–1; Patterson 10–1–29–3; Richards 5–2–7–1; Harper 13–6–23–1; Hooper 2–1–1–0.

Umpires: J. H. Harris and B. Hassan.

ENGLAND v WEST INDIES

Fourth Cornhill Test

At Leeds, July 21, 22, 23, 25, 26. West Indies won by ten wickets. Toss: West Indies. Victory gave the West Indians the series 3-0, the fourth time in a row they had either won or regained the Wisden Trophy at Headingley. Yet just before tea on the Monday, England had visions of their first home victory over West Indies for nineteen years; the tourists' first-innings lead had been wiped out, with Curtis the only casualty, and Gooch was threatening the half-century mark. But it was an apparition, just like Macbeth's dagger, provoked by a guilty conscience for the performance to come. When England went to grab their chance, it evaporated as quickly as it had appeared; maybe it never really existed. Less than two hours later, England's last nine wickets had departed for 58 runs, making the West Indians' win a formality.

England came to Headingley with four survivors from the original Old Trafford thirteen – Gooch, Gower, Lamb and Dilley. Athey, Richards and Pringle were recalled, Foster was fit at last, and Curtis and Robin Smith were given their first taste of Test cricket. Cowdrey had already been appointed England's third captain of the series. The selectors had met several times after the heavy Manchester defeat to discuss the captaincy; twice they had delayed their decision. In the end, Emburey was not reappointed and Cowdrey, who had taken Kent to the top of the Championship table, was given the job for the two remaining West Indies Tests. "We believe Cowdrey's style of leadership is what is now required", claimed England's chairman of selectors, P. B. H. May, who was also Cowdrey's godfather. But England's captaincy shuffle was too much for the gateman at Headingley. He did not recognise the new skipper and refused him entry to the car park on Wednesday.

Cowdrey's five previous Tests, on Gower's tour of India in 1984-85, had brought him 96 runs and four wickets. Colin and Chris Cowdrey became the second father-son combination to lead England, after F. T. and F. G. Mann. Ironically, the last time England had used three captains in a series, against West Indies in 1966, Cowdrey senior took over from

M. J. K. Smith before being replaced by D. B. Close. News of Cowdrey's appointment came four hours after Gatting had notified the selectors of his indefinite withdrawal from Test cricket. Gatting, who the day before had been referred to the full disciplinary committee of the TCCB over publication of his autobiography, *Leading From the Front*, insisted that he was not in the right frame of mind to play in a Test match against West Indies.

The touring team had more traditional worries, with Greenidge and Richardson, their openers in the Third Test, both ruled out because of injury. But Haynes was fit again and Dujon was promoted to join him, with Arthurton making his Test début. England, as expected, made Childs twelfth man. The first day was dominated not by West Indies' bowlers, or even the notorious Headingley pitch, but by the Headingley drains. Play, having started 50 minutes late, was halted after two overs, this time for two hours, when the bowler's run-up at the Rugby Club End was found to be flooded. Umpire Bird had always had a keen eye for dangerous elements above, but this attack from below caught him unawares. The drains had been blocked before the Test to try to retain moisture in the square. But the Yorkshire club insisted that all drains were functioning properly by the start of the match and put the cause of the trouble on the volume of overnight rain.

West Indies had won the toss, and their reluctance to ignore this inconvenience and get at England's new batting line-up was curious, especially when the home side were later reduced to 80 for four. Marshall gave Gooch no chance, while Benjamin ended Curtis's dogged 94 minute stay and spoilt Gower's 100th Test match. But the arrival of Robin Smith to join Lamb brightened England's day. By Friday morning, West Indies were showing signs of apprehension for the first time in the series; even Marshall was reduced to using the weapon of more mortal fast bowlers when frustrated – the short-pitched delivery. Tragically for England, though, Lamb tore the calf muscle in his right leg, the mood and moment were lost, and they were back on the defensive. Lamb limped off just before noon with England 183 for four; 47 minutes and 58 balls later, they had been dismissed for 201, the last wicket pair, Foster and Dilley, having added 16 of those last 18 runs. England's new captain lasted twelve balls and neither he, Richards nor Pringle, now batting at No. 9 after going in at No. 6 in the first two Tests, looked like delaying the West Indian bowlers for long.

West Indies' batsmen had a tough time, though, and finished the day at 156 for five, Haynes having taken 40 overs for his 54. Foster made a good return to claim the wickets of Hooper and Richards, the latter brilliantly caught by Curtis, diving to intercept a certai boundary at square leg. By Saturday night, West Indies had reached 238 for eight after rai had restricted play to 23.4 overs. Pringle was the only participant to make much of the thir day, taking all three wickets for 20 in six overs, but England's three missed slip chances we to prove especially expensive and frustrating. Yorkshire had hoped for better weathe Headingley loses its automatic right to a Test match in 1990. Gate receipts and attendanc were down, its pitch – and now its drains – had gained something of a dubious reputation ov the years, and, once again, the West Indian players were the subject of racial abuse from t Yorkshire crowd. Richards, not for the first time, was the target in an incident described b Mr Hendriks, the team's manager, as "unfortunate and most distasteful".

West Indies were all out for 275 at midday on Monday, their total boosted by a stubbo knock of two and threequarter hours from Harper. Pringle finished with his best Te figures, five for 95, and if England had let the tourists off by dropping catches, they we back in the game after making up the deficit with one wicket down. But then Gooch chas a wide delivery from Walsh, Gower added only the 2 runs he needed for his 7,000 in Te before flicking Marshall down the leg side to Dujon, and Walsh produced a beauty to dism Athey; 80 for one had become 85 for four and England were finished. Only a heroic kno from Lamb, batting at No. 8, took the match into the last day. Richards, Cowdrey a Pringle all failed again; their six innings produced only 18 runs. Dujon and Haynes had trouble scoring the 65 runs needed for victory and the match was over inside eight overs Tuesday morning. England's humiliation was complete. Had it not been for the rain a drain, this Test match would not have lasted beyond tea on Saturday. – David Norrie.

Man of the Match: C. E. L. Ambrose. *Attendance:* 44,350; *receipts* £400,014.

Close of play: First day, England 137-4 (A. J. Lamb 45*, R. A. Smith 23*); Second d West Indies 156-5 (K. L. T. Arthurton 1*, R. A. Harper 0*); Third day, West Indies 23 (R. A. Harper 31*, W. K. M. Benjamin 7*); Fourth day, West Indies 27-0 (D. L. Hay 10*, P. J. L. Dujon 17*).

England

G. A. Gooch c Dujon b Marshall	9	– c Hooper b Walsh	50
T. S. Curtis lbw b Benjamin	12	– b Ambrose	12
C. W. J. Athey lbw b Ambrose	16	– c Dujon b Walsh	11
D. I. Gower c Dujon b Benjamin	13	– c Dujon b Marshall	2
A. J. Lamb retired hurt	64	– (8) c Dujon b Ambrose	19
R. A. Smith c Dujon b Ambrose	38	– (5) lbw b Marshall	11
C. S. Cowdrey lbw b Marshall	0	– (6) b Walsh	5
C. J. Richards b Ambrose	2	– (7) b Ambrose	8
D. R. Pringle c Dujon b Marshall	0	– b Benjamin	3
N. A. Foster not out	8	– c Hooper b Benjamin	0
G. R. Dilley c Hooper b Ambrose	8	– not out	2
B 1, l-b 18, w 6, n-b 6	31	B 3, l-b 8, n-b 4	15
/14 (1) 2/43 (2) 3/58 (4) 4/80 (3) /183 (6) 6/183 (7) 7/185 (9) /185 (8) 9/201 (11)	201	1/56 (2) 2/80 (1) 3/85 (4) 4/85 (3)5/105 (5) 6/105 (6) 7/127 (7) 8/132 (9) 9/132 (10) 10/138 (8)	138

Bowling: *First Innings*—Marshall 23–8–55–3; Ambrose 25.1–8–58–4; Benjamin 9–2–27–2; Walsh 12–4–42–0. *Second Innings*—Marshall 17–4–47–2; Ambrose 19.5–4–40–3; Walsh)–9–38–3; Benjamin 5–4–2–2.

West Indies

. L. Haynes lbw b Pringle	54	– not out	25
P. J. L. Dujon c Smith b Dilley	13	– not out	40
. L. Hooper lbw b Foster	19		
. V. A. Richards c Curtis b Foster	18		
. L. Logie c Foster b Pringle	44		
. L. T. Arthurton c Richards b Pringle	27		
. A. Harper c Gower b Foster	56		
. D. Marshall c Gooch b Pringle	3		
E. L. Ambrose lbw b Pringle	8		
. K. M. Benjamin run out	9		
A. Walsh not out	9		
L-b 15	15	L-b 2	2
15 (2) 2/61 (3) 3/97 (4) 4/137 (1) 156 (5) 6/194 (6) 7/210 (8) 222 (9) 9/245 (10) 10/275 (7)	275		(no wkt) 67

Bowling: *First Innings*—Dilley 20–5–59–1; Foster 32.2–6–98–3; Pringle 27–7–95–5; wdrey 2–0–8–0. *Second Innings*—Dilley 4–0–16–0; Foster 7–1–36–0; Cowdrey 3.3–0–13–0.

Umpires: H. D. Bird and D. R. Shepherd.

NOTTINGHAMSHIRE v WEST INDIANS

Nottingham, July 27, 28, 29. Drawn. Toss: West Indians. Callaghan, a South African from tern Province, marked his English first-class début by taking a wicket with his first very. Greenidge played a patient innings of 316 minutes for his century, but Richards ted the bowling with disdain, hitting twelve fours in his 75. In between showers on the nd day, Nottinghamshire lost five wickets, but Stephenson and Scott formed a productive nership of 93 on the third. The former batted for 176 minutes for his 56, the latter four utes longer for his unbeaten 63. Cooper played sensibly to ensure that the follow-on was ided. When the West Indians batted again for two overs, Scott made his bowling début. *lose of play:* First day, West Indians 321-7 (R. A. Harper 20*, W. K. M. Benjamin 7*); ond day, Nottinghamshire 91-5 (J. D. Birch 14*, F. D. Stephenson 0*).

West Indians

C. G. Greenidge b Cooper 101
P. J. L. Dujon b Cairns .... 18 – (1) not out 16
C. L. Hooper c Scott b Cairns 3
K. L. T. Arthurton b Callaghan 24
*I. V. A. Richards c Scott b Stephenson 75
A. L. Logie c Johnson b Millns 53
R. A. Harper lbw b Millns 28
†D. Williams lbw b Stephenson .... 2 – (2) not out 1
W. K. M. Benjamin not out 17
I. R. Bishop lbw b Cairns 6
B. P. Patterson b Cairns 16
L-b 10, w 2, n-b 7 19

1/42 2/56 3/108 4/223 5/265 6/303 7/305 8/330 9/341 — 362 — (no wkt) 17

Bowling: *First Innings*—Millns 29–7–102–2; Stephenson 18–3–49–2; Cairns 24–5–82–4; Cooper 19–3–60–1; Callaghan 17–1–59–1. *Second Innings*—Birch 1–0–7–0; Scott 1–0–10–0.

Nottinghamshire

M. Newell c Williams b Patterson 0
*R. T. Robinson c Williams b Patterson 6
P. Johnson c Dujon b Benjamin 3
D. J. R. Martindale b Harper 32
D. J. Callaghan c Benjamin b Harper .. 29
J. D. Birch b Patterson 23
F. D. Stephenson c and b Harper 56
†C. W. Scott not out 63
C. L. Cairns run out ....
K. E. Cooper b Richards 1
D. J. Millns b Richards ....
B 5, l-b 3, n-b 5 ....

1/0 2/11 3/11 4/66 5/82 6/102 7/195 8/201 9/239 — 24

Bowling: Patterson 15–3–45–3; Benjamin 17–1–69–1; Harper 39–11–87–3; Bisho 12–7–11–0; Arthurton 10–3–21–0; Hooper 5–2–5–0; Richards 4.4–3–1–2.

Umpires: M. J. Kitchen and R. Palmer.

ESSEX v WEST INDIANS

At Chelmsford, July 30, 31, August 1. Drawn. Toss: West Indians. The tourists were subject to slow handclapping by the crowd after delaying their declaration, which left Essex with th impossible task of trying to score 409 for victory in 100 minutes plus twenty overs. In th event, Gooch used the time to record his second half-century of the game. Both West Indi innings were dominated by Greenidge and Arthurton. Greenidge followed up his 81 (one s twelve fours) with 111 made from 176 balls, four of which he hit for six, while Arthurt emerged from the match unbeaten with scores of 101 and 78. Bishop bowled with mu hostility during Essex's first innings, claiming four of his wickets in a 30-ball sp which cost just 7 runs.

Close of play: First day, Essex 8-1 (G. A. Gooch 0*, T. D. Topley 0*); Second day, W Indians 70-0 (C. G. Greenidge 35*, D. L. Haynes 32*).

West Indians

*C. G. Greenidge c Miller b Topley .... 81 – st East b Gooch 1
D. L. Haynes c East b Pont .... 14 – c East b Pringle ....
C. L. Hooper c and b Pont .... 34 – c Childs b Miller ....
A. L. Logie c Border b Childs 13
K. L. T. Arthurton not out ....101 – (4) not out ....
R. A. Harper b Pringle .... 6 – (5) not out ....
M. D. Marshall st East b Miller 76
†D. Williams lbw b Pont 1
C. E. L. Ambrose run out 31
I. R. Bishop b Topley 0
B. P. Patterson lbw b Topley 0
B 4, l-b 3, w 3, n-b 11 .... 21 L-b 5, n-b 2 ....

1/24 2/97 3/139 4/171 5/189 6/299 7/300 8/358 9/378 — 378 — 1/83 2/145 3/225 (3 wkts dec.)

Bowling: *First Innings*—Pont 17–3–78–3; Topley 24.3–3–91–3; Pringle 19–2–64–1; Gooch 9–1–35–0; Childs 14–3–46–1; Miller 16–5–57–1. *Second Innings*—Pont 7–0–38–0; Topley 14–3–52–0; Childs 17–3–53–0; Border 8–1–39–0; Pringle 7–2–24–1; Miller 10–0–45–1; Gooch 8–1–24–1.

Essex

*G. A. Gooch c Hooper b Harper	56	– not out	67
†D. E. East b Bishop	5	– b Bishop	16
T. D. Topley c Logie b Patterson	2	– (5) b Arthurton	0
A. W. Lilley c sub b Bishop	68		
A. R. Border c Williams b Bishop	32	– (7) not out	0
P. J. Prichard not out	52	– b Arthurton	2
N. Hussain c sub b Bishop	0	– (3) lbw b Hooper	17
D. R. Pringle c Williams b Bishop	1	– (4) c sub b Hooper	3
J. Miller c Hooper b Patterson	16		
L. Pont c sub b Harper	5		
L-b 2, w 1, n-b 10	13	B 1, l-b 1, n-b 6	8
/8 2/29 3/114 4/173 5/182 /192 7/194 8/244 9/250 (9 wkts dec.)	250	1/51 2/91 3/111 4/111 5/113 (5 wkts)	113

H. Childs did not bat.

Bowling: *First Innings*—Bishop 22–5–49–5; Patterson 11–1–33–2; Ambrose 10–' '8–0; Harper 17.5–0–68–2; Hooper 15–0–58–0; Marshall 7–0–22–0. *Second Innings*—Bishop 9–1–31–1; Patterson 6–0–24–0; Harper 9–1–41–0; Hooper 8–1–14–2; Arthurton 2.1–1–1–2.

Umpires: B. Leadbeater and R. A. White.

ENGLAND v WEST INDIES

Fifth Cornhill Test

t The Oval, August 4, 5, 6, 8. West Indies won by eight wickets. Toss: England. As Logie on-ove DeFreitas for the winning boundary nineteen minutes after tea on the fourth day, the g of St George fluttered at half-mast on the pavilion roof, a sad symbol of England's failure compete on the same plane as a formidable team re-emerging as the world's best. It was ngland's eighteenth successive Test without a victory. Nevertheless, Gooch, captaining ngland for the first time, could derive comfort from his own staunch batting and from ngland's commitment until lunch on the third day, when it was conceivable that they could ve forced a winning position. From there, however, West Indies stepped firmly on the ottle and were uncatchable.

The days leading up to the match were a test of fortitude for the beleaguered England ectors. They had chosen a side containing two uncapped players in Barnett and Maynard, hough the latter was intended as cover for Lamb, who was still struggling for fitness after injury at Headingley. Athey and Gower were omitted; Small and Capel were recalled. t no sooner had the team been announced than Dilley withdrew with a stress problem in right knee. His place was taken by DeFreitas, who had recently been the subject of ciplinary measures by his county. Next Cowdrey, the captain, and Barnett withdrew, fering respectively from a foot and a hand injury. Finally, on the eve of the match, Lamb nitted defeat after a perfunctory fitness test. Bailey, the tall Northamptonshire batsman, s drafted in to make his Test début alongside Maynard. Gooch was named as the fourth gland captain of the series in his 67th Test; only four men had played more matches before ding England for the first time. West Indies had Greenidge available again and Arthurton od down. England left out Small.

Gooch, winning the toss, decided to bat first on a pitch containing bounce and reasonable e. It did not, initially, disclose the movement it was to provide for the quicker bowlers. in the eighth over, Gooch received an unplayable ball from Ambrose and immediately inexperienced middle order was exposed. Maynard apart, they acquitted themselves mmendably without threatening to usurp the authority of the West Indian bowlers. tis, having taken half an hour to get off the mark, delved into his reservoir of concentration to remain for two and a half hours and Bailey used his height to minimise the short ball. Their stand of 65 did much to dampen West Indies' firepower. Smith announced himself with a pull off Benjamin which almost carried for six, then settled down to bat fo almost three and a half hours. But a rash stroke from Maynard broke the heart of the resistance and England ended the first day 203 for nine, dejected and vulnerable.

Next morning, Foster lifted their morale with a spectacular piece of fast bowling whic removed West Indies' first five batsmen. On the hottest day of the series, he went to work from the Vauxhall End and the ultimate result was a small but significant first-innings lead o 22, England's first over West Indies in thirteen matches. As at Lord's, England met determined response from Logie and Dujon, who added 69 in 93 minutes, a stand elegantl stage-managed by Dujon. When Pringle had him lbw, shuffling across the crease, the nex four wickets subsided for 28.

As their openers put on 50, England had cause to hope that an overdue victory in a summe of disillusion was within their compass. Alas, they lost Curtis, Bailey and Smith inside ha an hour, Smith being lbw without offering a stroke. When Marshall dismissed Curtis, h increased to 35 his wickets for the series, surpassing the 34 of F. S. Trueman in 1963, th previous best in an England–West Indies rubber. It was also the premier achievement by West Indian in any series, confirming Marshall's status as the world's leading strike bowler

Gooch held centre stage on the Saturday, allying grim determination to his solid techniqu without ever finding his best touch or timing. Having entered the arena at five o'clock o Friday afternoon, he left it some 24 hours later, having batted through the innings and sper seven hours eight minutes over his 84. It was the longest he had batted without making hundred; with the ball moving about disconcertingly, it was also an immense feat c concentration. Only Foster, as night-watchman, supported him with any vigour, striking fearless 34 in 106 minutes (80 balls).

When Gooch led England out on Saturday evening with a disappointing lead of 224 defend, it was amid an atmosphere of inevitability. Within seven balls, he was back in th pavilion, having badly dislocated the third finger of his left hand in attempting to catc Haynes at first slip, ironically from a no-ball by DeFreitas. He took no further part ar Pringle, in his eighteenth Test, took over. He was to discover the difficulty of setting a fie for Greenidge at his attacking best. The West Indian vice-captain moved quickly ar ruthlessly to his fifty before the close, to all intents and purposes closing the door on Englan West Indies resumed on Monday needing another 154 with all their wickets in hand, althou Richards was in hospital and could not have batted. Greenidge fell first ball after lunc but by then Haynes was firmly entrenched and their twelfth century opening partnersh had smoothed the path to victory in the only Test of the series not interrupted by t weather. – David Field.

Man of the Match: P. J. L. Dujon. *Attendance:* 53,057; *receipts* £652,413.

Men of the Series: England – G. A. Gooch; West Indies – M. D. Marshall.

Close of play: First day, England 203-9 (N. A. Foster 5*, J. H. Childs 0*); Second da England 64-3 (G. A. Gooch 38*, N. A. Foster 1*); Third day, West Indies 71-0 (C. Greenidge 53*, D. L. Haynes 15*).

England

*G. A. Gooch c Logie b Ambrose . . . . 9 – c Greenidge b Ambrose . . . . . .
T. S. Curtis c Dujon b Benjamin . . . . 30 – lbw b Marshall . . . .
R. J. Bailey c Dujon b Ambrose . . . . 43 – b Benjamin . . . .
R. A. Smith c Harper b Marshall . . . . 57 – lbw b Benjamin . . . .
M. P. Maynard c Dujon b Ambrose . . . . 3 – (6) c and b Benjamin . . . .
D. J. Capel c Marshall b Harper . . . . 16 – (7) lbw b Walsh . . . .
†C. J. Richards c Logie b Harper . . . . 0 – (8) c Dujon b Walsh . . . .
D. R. Pringle c Dujon b Marshall . . . . 1 – (9) b Harper . . . .
P. A. J. DeFreitas c Haynes b Harper . . . . 18 – (10) c Haynes b Harper . . . .
N. A. Foster c sub (K. L. T. Arthurton)
b Marshall . 7 – (5) c Logie b Benjamin . . . .
J. H. Childs not out . . . . 0 – not out . . . .
L-b 6, n-b 15 . . . . 21 B 3, l-b 15, n-b 15 . . . . . .

1/12 (1) 2/77 (2) 3/116 (3) 4/121 (5) 5/160 (6) 6/160 (7) 7/165 (8) 8/196 (9) 9/198 (4) 10/205 (10) — 205

1/50 (2) 2/55 (3) 3/55 (4) 4/108 (5) 5/125 (6) 6/139 (7) 7/157 (8) 8/175 (9) 9/177 (10) 10/202 (1)

Bowling: *First Innings*—Marshall 24.3–3–64–3; Ambrose 20–6–31–3; Walsh 10–1–21–0; Benjamin 14–2–33–1; Harper 21–7–50–3; Hooper 1–1–0–0. *Second Innings*—Marshall 25–6–52–1; Ambrose 24.1–10–50–1; Benjamin 22–4–52–4; Walsh 12–5–21–2; Harper 5–3–9–2.

West Indies

	First innings		Second innings	
. G. Greenidge c DeFreitas b Foster	10	– c Richards b Childs	77
. L. Haynes c Richards b Foster	2	– not out	77
. L. Hooper c Gooch b Foster	11	– b Foster	23
I. V. A. Richards c Curtis b Foster	0		
. L. Logie c Gooch b Foster	47	– (4) not out	38
P. J. L. Dujon lbw b Pringle	64		
. A. Harper run out	17		
1. D. Marshall c and b Childs	0		
. E. L. Ambrose not out	17		
V. K. M. Benjamin b Pringle	0		
. A. Walsh c DeFreitas b Pringle	5		
L-b 7, w 1, n-b 2	10	B 2, l-b 3, n-b 6	11
9 (2) 2/16 (1) 3/16 (4) 4/57 (3) 126 (5) 6/155 (6) 7/156 (8) 167 (7) 9/168 (10) 10/183 (11)	183	1/131 (1) 2/162 (3)	(2 wkts) 226

Bowling: *First Innings*—Foster 16–2–64–5; DeFreitas 13–4–33–0; Pringle 17–4–45–3 apel -0–21–0; Childs 6–1–13–1. *Second Innings*—Foster 18–3–52–1; DeFreitas 17–2–46–0, ilds)–16–79–1; Pringle 13–4–24–0; Capel 3–0–20–0.

Umpires: H. D. Bird and K. E. Palmer.

UMPIRES FOR 1989

TEST MATCH UMPIRES

J. Constant, who stood in 36 Test matches from 1971 to 1988, was omitted from the Test atch panel for the 1989 series between England and Australia. His place on the seven-man nel is taken by the former England, Yorkshire and Derbyshire batsman, J. H. Hampshire, o has been on the first-class list since 1985, while B. J. Meyer returns after a year's absence place of J. Birkenshaw. The panel is: H. D. Bird, J. H. Hampshire, J. W. Holder, B. J. eyer, K. E. Palmer, N. T. Plews and D. R. Shepherd.

FIRST-CLASS UMPIRES

J. Eele, B. Hassan and D. S. Thompsett have been promoted from the Reserve list to join list of first-class umpires for 1989. The number on the list was increased by two to help ilitate the decision of the TCCB to have a first-class umpire standing in Second Eleven ampionship matches, and a vacancy occurred when J. Birkenshaw took up a position with nerset. The full list is: J. C. Balderstone, H. D. Bird, J. D. Bond, D. J. Constant, Dudleston, P. J. Eele, D. G. L. Evans, J. H. Hampshire, J. H. Harris, B. Hassan, V. Holder, A. A. Jones, R. Julian, M. J. Kitchen, B. Leadbeater, K. J. Lyons, B. J. Meyer, O. Oslear, K. E. Palmer, R. Palmer, N. T. Plews, D. R. Shepherd, D. S. Thompsett, A. White, A. G. T. Whitehead and P. B. Wight. *Reserves:* M. J. Harris, V. A. Holder, J. Rhodes and K. Taylor.

MINOR COUNTIES UMPIRES

Adams, N. P. Atkins, R. Bell, K. Bray, C. J. Chapman, D. J. Dennis, D. Fawkner-Corbett, H. Gillingham, D. J. Halfyard, D. B. Harrison, B. Knight, T. Lynan, G. I. McLean, G. A. Morley, D. Norton, M. K. Reed, K. S. Shenton, C. Smith, C. T. Spencer, A. Stickley, A. R. Tayler, R. C. Tolchard, R. Walker, T. V. Wilkins, R. T. Wilson and G. Wilson. *Reserves:* P. Brown, K. Coburn, R. K. Curtis, R. M. Davison, R. F. Elliott, . Foulkes, P. Gray, D. H. Halewood, M. A. Johnson, R. Pattinson, C. T. Puckett, . Stevens, J. Stobart, J. D. Thornton and B. H. Willey.

THE SRI LANKANS IN ENGLAND, 1988

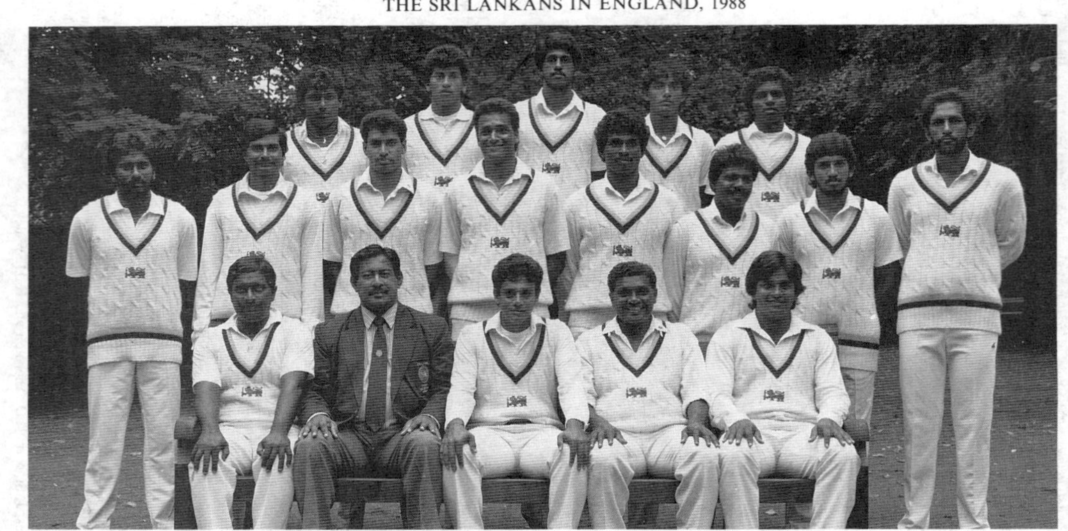

[*Bill Smith*

Back row: P. A. de Silva, R. S. Mahanama, A. W. R. Madurasinghe, H. P. Tillekeratne, S. D. Anurasiri. *Middle row:* F. S. Ahangama, D. S. B. P. Kuruppu, [illegible] M. A. R. Samarasekera, C. P. H. Ramanayake, S. A. R. Silva, B. E. A. Rajadurai, J. R. Ratnayeke. *Front row:* L. R. D. Mendis,

THE SRI LANKANS IN ENGLAND, 1988

Sri Lanka arrived in England for their third visit of the 1980s, and their econd as a Test-match country, almost unnoticed owing to the attention eing given to the England-West Indies series and England's attendant roblems. They began their fourteen-match tour with a leisurely fixture gainst the League Cricket Conference at Oxton on the Wirral and ended it vith a one-day international at The Oval on the Sunday after the NatWest Bank Trophy final. The tour ran concurrently with the Sri Lankan Schooloys Under-17 tour of England and Wales.

At all times the Sri Lankans played with great enthusiasm. However, they vere often troubled by injuries and illness, and the poor summer did not help hem either come to terms with English conditions or gain the match practice hey needed so badly. Sri Lanka's cricket in recent years had been severely estricted by the island's political disturbances, which prevented them from ntertaining other countries. Of the nine first-class matches, all were drawn ave the Cornhill Test match, which England won by seven wickets. The Sri ankans were in a strong position against Yorkshire, but rain on the last day revented any play until the afternoon, when Blakey thwarted them with his ighest score of the season so far.

The touring party of sixteen players was captained by Ranjan Madugalle, ith Arjuna Ranatunga as his vice-captain. Duleep Mendis, who captained e 1984 side, was back again, but there was no place for his vice-captain en, Roy Dias. One of his country's most experienced players, Dias had led e Sri Lankan B team with much success in Zimbabwe earlier in the year. here was even speculation that he might have captained this team to ngland; instead, he spent the summer coaching in Holland.

Eight of the party had no previous experience of first-class cricket in ngland, although four of them had played Test cricket: the seam bowlers, liya Ahangama, Champaka Ramanayake and Graeme Labrooy, plus oshan Mahanama, an opening batsman of exciting promise. Athula marasekera, a tall all-rounder, and Hashan Tillekeratne, a left-handed iddle-order batsman who at 21 was the youngest of the tourists, had played one-day internationals and, like the off-spinner, Ranjith Madurasinghe, d been with the B team in Zimbabwe. Brian Rajadurai, a leg-spinner, was e other newcomer.

It became apparent as the tour progressed that their strength was their tting. Those with memories of 1984, when Sri Lanka put on 491 for seven ainst England after being asked to bat first, hoped that the tourists would ain produce an exhibition of their true cricketing ability, despite their ent disadvantages. Logic prevailed over romance; again put in at Lord's, y were unable to do themselves justice in conditions that were ideal for ing bowling. But in their second innings, 235 runs behind and facing an ings defeat, they did show their ability to fight back and to score runs ertainingly, making England bat again and taking the match into the al day.

f the Sri Lankan batsmen proved they could hold their heads high at this el, the bowling was less convincing. Predominantly seam, it lacked pace l penetration, although Labrooy seemed to improve with every outing and duced some inspired spells against the counties. Ahangama, of rather gentle pace, was nevertheless difficult to get away and bowled a good line anc length whenever given the opportunity. Ravi Ratnayeke, who had been sucl a power in the past, proved to be more of a hard-hitting batsman. Yet giver the opportunity to play regularly at international level, Sri Lanka might wel establish an attack to match the calibre of their batting.

The team was managed by Mr Abu Fuard, with Mr Ranjit Fernando, wh had played for Sri Lanka in the first World Cup, as cricket manage Throughout the tour, the considerable knowledge and experience of Mendi was always evident, and it is to be hoped that he will continue to assist in th development of the younger players. – William Powell.

SRI LANKAN TOUR RESULTS

Test match – Played 1: Lost 1.
First-class matches – Played 9: Lost 1, Drawn 8.
Loss – England.
Draws – Derbyshire, Gloucestershire, Hampshire, Middlesex, Nottinghamshire, Surre Warwickshire, Yorkshire.
One-day international – Played 1: Lost 1.
Other non first-class matches – Played 4: Won 1, Drawn 3. *Win* – Indian Gymkhana Club *Draws* – Lavinia, Duchess of Norfolk's XI, League Cricket Conference, Minor Counties.

SRI LANKAN AVERAGES – FIRST-CLASS MATCHES

BATTING

	M	*I*	*NO*	*R*	*HI*	*100s*	*Av*
J. R. Ratnayeke	8	10	5	311	60*	0	62.
P. A. de Silva	6	9	3	333	117*	1	55.
D. S. B. P. Kuruppu	6	10	1	438	158	1	48.
R. S. Madugalle	8	11	2	403	97	0	44.
L. R. D. Mendis	9	12	2	362	124	1	36.
A. Ranatunga	8	9	1	271	84	0	33.
M. A. R. Samarasekera	9	15	2	401	104	1	30.
R. S. Mahanama	5	8	2	179	46*	0	29.
S. A. R. Silva	8	14	1	338	112	1	26
G. F. Labrooy	7	4	1	73	42	0	24
H. P. Tillekeratne	5	6	1	121	50*	0	24
A. W. R. Madurasinghe	6	7	2	75	30	0	15

Played in five matches: F. S. Ahangama 0*, 3*. Played in four matches: C. P. Ramanayake 18, 0, 2. Played in three matches: S. D. Anurasiri 4*. Played in two match B. E. A. Rajadurai did not bat.

* *Signifies not out.*

BOWLING

	O	*M*	*R*	*W*	*BB*	*5W/i*	*A*
F. S. Ahangama	99.2	22	321	12	4-51	0	2(
G. F. Labrooy	203.5	30	665	20	6-61	1	3:
M. A. R. Samarasekera	127.4	14	406	10	3-31	0	4(
C. P. H. Ramanayake	87.2	11	315	7	2-36	0	4:
J. R. Ratnayeke	231.5	36	687	15	3-47	0	4:
A. W. R. Madurasinghe	144.4	35	376	6	3-50	0	6:

Also bowled: S. D. Anurasiri 62–16–175–2; P. A. de Silva 14–5–42–1; B. E. A. Rajad 20–3–65–1; A. Ranatunga 50.4–11–153–2; H. P. Tillekeratne 9–1–35–1.

FIELDING

5 – S. A. R. Silva (15 ct); 5 – M. A. R. Samarasekera; 4 – R. S. Madugalle, H. P. ʼillekeratne; 3 – P. A. de Silva, A. Ranatunga; 2 – D. S. B. P. Kuruppu (1 ct, 1 st); G. F. ‚abrooy, A. W. R. Madurasinghe, L. R. D. Mendis; 1 – F. S. Ahangama, S. D. Anurasiri, ‘. S. Mahanama, J. R. Ratnayeke.

HUNDREDS FOR SRI LANKANS

he following five three-figure innings were played for the Sri Lankans in first-class matches.

. A. de Silva (1)
117* v Warwicks., Birmingham

. S. B. P. Kuruppu (1)
158 v Notts., Nottingham

. R. D. Mendis (1)
124 v Surrey, The Oval

M. A. R. Samarasekera (1)
104 v Surrey, The Oval

S. A. R. Silva (1)
112 v Yorks., Leeds

* *Signifies not out.*

Note: Those matches which follow which were not first-class are signified by the use of dagger.

†LEAGUE CRICKET CONFERENCE v SRI LANKANS

Oxton CC, Birkenhead, July 20, 21. Drawn. Toss: Sri Lankans. The possibility of an eresting finish was spoilt when rain fell before the Sri Lankans could begin their attempt to re 130 in 65 minutes. Play had not started until 2.30 p.m., when the League Cricket nference put on 120 in 115 minutes following the touring team's declaration at their ernight score. On the opening day, they had not batted with such freedom, especially iinst the leg-spinner, Rajadurai. The tempo quickened when the Sri Lankan batsmen and sun came out after an early tea was taken. A six off Hall took Samarasekera to 50 from 69 lls, and in addition he hit eleven fours in his 74 from 130 balls.

'lose of play: First day, Sri Lankans 138-3 (P. A. de Silva 37*, A. Ranatunga 0*).

ague Cricket Conference

Foster b Rajadurai	28	– c Silva b Ahangama	11
R. J. Veletta lbw b Ranatunga	29	– c Rajadurai b Madurasinghe	22
Ingham c Ranatunga b Rajadurai	4	– (4) not out	34
ɜordon c Tillekeratne b Rajadurai	27	– (3) c Silva b Rajadurai	43
Smith c Tillekeratne b Samarasekera	1		
Walker c Mahanama b Ranatunga	0	– not out	1
Cottee b Ahangama	16		
\. Moseley lbw b Ratnayeke	24		
Macauley not out	2		
). Matthews not out	6	– (5) c Ahangama b Madurasinghe	4
B 5, l-b 3, n-b 2	10	L-b 3, n-b 2	5
2/60 3/74 4/75 5/78 7 7/119 8/141	(8 wkts dec.) 147	1/17 2/56 3/95 4/103	(4 wkts dec.) 120

Iall did not bat.

ɔwling: *First Innings*—Ratnayeke 13–3–32–1; Ahangama 13–4–37–1; Rajadurai –43–3; Samarasekera 11–5–16–1; Ranatunga 5–1–11–2; Madurasinghe 1–1–0–0. *Second ıgs*—Ratnayeke 7–1–29–0; Ahangama 9–2–29–1; Madurasinghe 10–2–37–2; Rajadurai -22–1.

Sri Lankans

R. S. Mahanama lbw b Moseley 0
†S. A. R. Silva c Hall b Cottee 24
M. A. R. Samarasekera c Veletta b Hall 74
P. A. de Silva not out 37
*A. Ranatunga not out 0
L-b 3 3

1/4 2/85 3/119 (3 wkts dec.) 138

J. R. Ratnayeke, F. S. Ahangama, L. R. D. Mendis, H. P. Tillekeratne, B. E. A. Rajadura and A. W. R. Madurasinghe did not bat.

Bowling: Moseley 11–1–35–1; Matthews 9–4–23–0; Cottee 14–2–37–1; Hall 16–5–40–1.

Umpires: M. J. Leddy and F. Maddison.

†At Osterley, July 27. Sri Lankans won by nine wickets. Indian Gymkhana Club 88 (44. overs) (G. F. Labrooy three for 7); Sri Lankans 89 for one (26 overs) (R. S. Mahanama 3 not out).

WARWICKSHIRE v SRI LANKANS

At Birmingham, July 23, 25, 26. Drawn. Toss: Sri Lankans. Eleven hours were lost to rain in match of which the highlight was an attractive unbeaten 117 from de Silva. He hit three six and 21 fours off 149 deliveries, although the disappointing modern trend of resting key playe for games against touring teams meant that the Sri Lankans faced a reserve attack. Silva, wi whom de Silva added 137 for the third wicket, batted just over three hours for his 62.

Close of play: First day, No play; Second day, Sri Lankans 13-1 (S. A. R. Silva 1 M. A. R. Samarasekera 5*).

Warwickshire

†G. W. Humpage c Samarasekera b Labrooy . 14
A. C. Storie c Samarasekera b Ratnayeke 22
Asif Din c Silva b Ramanayake 59
D. A. Banks b Labrooy 61
D. A. Thorne c Labrooy b Ramanayake 5
S. D. Myles lbw b Labrooy 21
N. M. K. Smith b Rajadurai 3
*T. A. Lloyd not out ....
G. J. Parsons not out ....
B 6, l-b 14, n-b 7 ....

1/23 2/82 3/134 4/146 5/209 6/212 7/212 (7 wkts dec.)

A. A. Donald and J. E. Benjamin did not bat.

Bowling: Ratnayeke 14–4–26–1; Labrooy 13–4–45–3; Samarasekera 9–0–32 Ramanayake 13–2–36–2; Rajadurai 11–1–28–1; Ranatunga 4–0–25–0.

Sri Lankans

R. S. Mahanama run out 6
†S. A. R. Silva run out 62
M. A. R. Samarasekera c Banks b Parsons . 21
P. A. de Silva not out 117
*R. S. Madugalle not out ....
L-b 3, n-b 5 ....

1/6 2/44 3/181 (3 wkts)

A. Ranatunga, L. R. D. Mendis, J. R. Ratnayeke, G. F. Labrooy, C. P. H. Ramanayake B. E. A. Rajadurai did not bat.

Bowling: Donald 13–4–27–0; Benjamin 17–6–53–0; Parsons 9–1–24–1; Myles 12–2–3 Smith 5–2–20–0; Asif Din 10–1–61–0; Banks 1–1–0–0; Storie 1–1–0–0.

Umpires: M. J. Harris and J. W. Holder.

†LAVINIA, DUCHESS OF NORFOLK'S XI v SRI LANKANS

At Arundel, July 29. Drawn. Toss: Sri Lankans. Rain again beset the touring team's programme, a downpour at tea ending any prospect of further play. Earlier, Parker had needed just 69 balls for his half-century, which included three sixes and two fours, while Clinton batted for three and a half hours, hitting eight fours and a six.

Lavinia, Duchess of Norfolk's XI

G. S. Clinton c Rajadurai b Samarasekera . 107
. F. Sykes st Kuruppu b Rajadurai . . . 41
. W. G. Parker b Ramanayake 50
A. J. Stewart not out 4
L-b 3, n-b 9 12

1/96 2/199 3/214 (3 wkts dec.) 214

R. D. V. Knight, I. A. Greig, J. R. T. Barclay, †R. J. Parks, A. R. Clarke, S. P. Hughes and M. P. Bicknell did not bat.

Bowling: Labrooy 8–0–25–0; Ramanayake 12–0–52–1; Rajadurai 16–3–58–1; Samarasekera 9.2–2–29–1; Anurasiri 10–1–47–0.

Sri Lankans

. S. Mahanama not out 12
D. S. B. P. Kuruppu not out 9
L-b 2 2

(no wkt) 23

. A. R. Samarasekera, P. A. de Silva, *R. S. Madugalle, A. Ranatunga, L. R. D. Mendis, C. P. H. Ramanayake, B. E. A. Rajadurai, S. D. Anurasiri and G. F. Labrooy did not bat.

Bowling: Bicknell 6–3–15–0; Hughes 5–2–6–0.

Umpires: J. G. Langridge and D. O. Oslear.

MIDDLESEX v SRI LANKANS

t Lord's, July 30, August 1, 2. Drawn. Toss: Middlesex. Samarasekera showed the way as Sri nka's medium-pace bowlers asserted themselves against the Middlesex top-order batsmen. kes, assisted first by Emburey and then by Fraser, effected the recovery. Sri Lanka's hero is the elegant Ranatunga, whose 84, with a six and nine fours, recalled his identical score in e Lord's Test four years earlier. On a mundane third day, Brown likewise revived memories a previous deed when he matched his century against the 1985 Australians. The target of 5 in a minimum of 43 overs – although Middlesex would have bowled more – was not alistic against a team unaccustomed to pacing a run-chase. In any case, losing three cheap ckets persuaded the Sri Lankans to take the safe way home.

Close of play: First day, Sri Lankans 3-0 (R. S. Mahanama 1*, S. A. R. Silva 2*); Second y, Middlesex 19-0 (J. D. Carr 10*, K. R. Brown 6*).

iddlesex

R. Brown c Silva b Samarasekera . . . . 17 – (2) not out 107
D. Carr c Silva b Samarasekera . . . . 21 – (1) b Samarasekera 39
R. Ramprakash c Mahanama b Samarasekera 0 – lbw b Ratnayeke 20
O. Butcher c Ranatunga b Ramanayake . . . . 41 – not out 10
A. Roseberry c Silva b Ratnayeke 11
R. Downton b Ramanayake 24
E. Emburey c Ranatunga b Madurasinghe . . 43
. Sykes c Madugalle b Ratnayeke 88
P. Hughes lbw b Madurasinghe 8
R. C. Fraser c Mendis b Ratnayeke 41
C. R. Tufnell not out 1
L-b 12, w 1, n-b 16 . . . . 29 L-b 2, n-b 7 9

) 2/40 3/47 4/64 5/113 324 1/110 2/166 (2 wkts dec.) 185
26 7/204 8/224 9/315

Bowling: *First Innings*—Ratnayeke 24.5–6–77–3; Ramanayake 23–3–81–2; Samarasekera 21–2–77–3; Ranatunga 2–1–5–0; Anurasiri 13–0–53–0; Madurasinghe 9–1–19–2. *Second Innings*—Ratnayeke 19–0–66–1; Ramanayake 5–0–36–0; Anurasiri 10–4–17–0; Samarasekera 9–0–29–1; Ranatunga 8–2–12–0; Madurasinghe 4–0–23–0.

Sri Lankans

R. S. Mahanama c Emburey b Tufnell . . . . 40 – c Brown b Emburey 18
†S. A. R. Silva c Downton b Emburey . . . . 42 – c Brown b Emburey 13
M. A. R. Samarasekera lbw b Emburey . . . . 17 – c Emburey b Tufnell 1
P. A. de Silva c Ramprakash b Tufnell . . . . 5 – not out 2
*R. S. Madugalle c Brown b Tufnell 3
A. Ranatunga lbw b Fraser 84
L. R. D. Mendis c Butcher b Fraser . . . . 10 – (5) not out 1
J. R. Ratnayeke c Tufnell b Fraser 2
C. P. H. Ramanayake c Butcher b Hughes 18
A. W. R. Madurasinghe b Emburey 30
S. D. Anurasiri not out 4
B 2, l-b 2, n-b 6 10   B 2, l-b 2 . . . .

1/77 2/104 3/107 4/111 5/123   265   1/23 2/40 3/44   (3 wkts) 8
6/146 7/152 8/192 9/261

Bowling: *First Innings*—Fraser 23–5–66–3; Hughes 19–5–61–1; Emburey 33.4–19–50–; Carr 6–3–13–0; Tufnell 28–7–71–3. *Second Innings*—Hughes 6–3–7–0; Carr 5–3–6–; Emburey 13–5–26–2; Tufnell 14–5–37–1; Ramprakash 1–1–0–0.

Umpires: J. H. Hampshire and A. A. Jones.

†MINOR COUNTIES v SRI LANKANS

At Sleaford, August 4, 5. Drawn. Toss: Sri Lankans. Silva set the tone for a match containi much entertaining batting, hitting fourteen fours in his 76 from 163 balls. He had some luc being dropped twice at third slip. Plumb hit 59 from 60 balls in the Minor Counties reply, a when he declared first thing next morning, Silva (104 balls) hit his second fifty as he a Mahanama (150 balls) put on 108 in 110 minutes. After lunch Samarasekera struck a six a six fours as he raced to 38 from 23 balls with the declaration in the offing. Minor Count were set to score 281 in 115 minutes plus twenty overs, and while Plumb was hitting 108 fr 112 balls (one six, fifteen fours) they always had a chance. Ramanayake's return at the start the last twenty overs, when 135 were still needed, proved crucial, for he removed Fell and th Plumb in the fourth and eighth of them. Garnham kept going, but there were no easy runs Ramanayake and Anurasiri conceded just 27 from the last nine overs.

Close of play: First day, Minor Counties 184-5 (M. A. Garnham 0*).

Sri Lankans

R. S. Mahanama c Plumb b Hale . . . . 13 – lbw b Evans . . . .
†S. A. R. Silva st Garnham b Evans . . . . 76 – lbw b Evans . . . .
D. S. B. P. Kuruppu b Hale . . . . 52 – (6) not out . . . .
L. R. D. Mendis not out . . . . 44 – (5) not out . . . .
*A. Ranatunga c Henderson b Evans 3
H. P. Tillekeratne not out . . . . 8 – (3) lbw b Evans . . . .
M. A. R. Samarasekera (did not bat) . . . . – (4) st Garnham b Blank . . . . . .
B 8, l-b 8, w 1, n-b 11 28   L-b 3, w 5, n-b 7 . . . . . .

1/29 2/133 3/175 4/191   (4 wkts dec.) 224   1/108 2/167 3/223   (4 wkts dec.)
4/223

H. C. P. Ramanayake, F. S. Ahangama, B. E. A. Rajadurai and S. D. Anurasiri did not b

Bowling: *First Innings*—Hale 15–1–71–2; Blank 19–6–44–0; Evans 18–2–45–2; Tho 5–2–18–0; O'Brien 9–3–30–0. *Second Innings*—Hale 6–0–33–0; Blank 12–1–65–1; Ev 24–5–66–3; O'Brien 18–2–73–0.

Minor Counties

. J. Stockdale c Mendis b Ahangama	29 – c Silva b Ramanayake	2
S. G. Plumb c Silva b Samarasekera	59 – c Tillekeratne b Ramanayake	108
N. A. Folland lbw b Anurasiri	25 – lbw b Ahangama	1
. P. Henderson lbw b Tillekeratne	31 – c Samarasekera b Anurasiri	39
. A. Fell c Rajadurai b Anurasiri	29 – lbw b Ramanayake	25
M. A. Garnham not out	0 – not out	37
. R. Thomas (did not bat)	– b Ramanayake	1
. C. Blank (did not bat)	– run out	4
. A. Hale (did not bat)	– not out	6
B 1, l-b 2, w 1, n-b 7	11 L-b 10, n-b 1	11
44 2/118 3/118 4/169 5/184 (5 wkts dec.)	184 1/18 2/23 3/124 4/175 5/204 6/209 7/223 (7 wkts)	234

. A. Evans and J. F. M. O'Brien did not bat.

Bowling: *First Innings*—Ramanayake 5–0–26–0; Ahangama 11–1–37–1; Rajadurai -0–21–0; Anurasiri 10–0–47–2; Samarasekera 9–2–26–1; Ranatunga 4–1–11–0; illekeratne 1–0–13–1. *Second Innings*—Ramanayake 19–4–80–4; Ahangama 10–1–47–1; nurasiri 12–1–59–1; Samarasekera 5–0–38–0.

Umpires: C. Smith and R. T. Wilson.

NOTTINGHAMSHIRE v SRI LANKANS

Nottingham, August 6, 7, 8. Drawn. Toss: Nottinghamshire. Fielding a weak side, the unty put the touring team in to bat and spent most of the day in the field. Kuruppu's innings 158 in 315 minutes, with 28 fours, formed the backbone of his team's total; Madugalle hit elve fours in his 72. Nottinghamshire lost Pollard in the fifteen overs faced on the first ening. Sunday, the second day, was very hot and the tempo of the batting was tedious as oad tried to recapture his form and Newell spent 151 minutes over 25. Millns caught the ary Sri Lankans unawares before the close, but instead of leading to a possible run-chase, last day amounted to little more than batting practice. Newell picked up two wickets with leg-breaks and Broad bowled both right- and left-arm. Indeed, the cricket became less ious as the day wore on. When the Sri Lankans eventually declared, Pollard and Newell put 101 for the first wicket in two hours.

Close of play: First day, Nottinghamshire 41-1 (B. C. Broad 12*, M. Newell 7*); Second y, Sri Lankans 54-4 (R. S. Madugalle 5*, H. P. Tillekeratne 5*).

i Lankans

S. B. P. Kuruppu c Scott b Birch	158 – b Millns	4
A. R. Silva c K. P. Evans b Cairns	3 – c Scott b Millns	1
A. R. Samarasekera lbw b Cairns	0 – c sub b Millns	28
R. D. Mendis c Scott b Millns	24 – run out	1
S. Madugalle c Scott b K. P. Evans	72 – c Scott b Newell	77
P. Tillekeratne c Scott b Cairns	5 – run out	32
. Ratnayeke not out	17 – c Scott b Newell	35
S. Mahanama b Newell	8 – not out	37
W. R. Madurasinghe (did not bat)	– not out	8
B 2, l-b 9, n-b 9	20 L-b 5, w 4, n-b 12	21
2/12 3/45 4/210 5/222 4 7/307 (7 wkts dec.)	307 1/8 2/25 3/30 4/40 5/110 6/197 7/200 (7 wkts dec.)	244

F. Labrooy and F. S. Ahangama did not bat.

owling: *First Innings*—Millns 15–0–95–1; Cairns 19–2–70–3; Saxelby 4.2–2–8–0; K. P. ns 22–8–66–1; Birch 17.4–6–44–1; Newell 2.4–0–13–1. *Second Innings*—Cairns –53–0; Millns 14–2–45–3; Birch 9–4–25–0; K. P. Evans 8–2–20–0; Newell 11–2–38–2; . Evans 5–1–23–0; Broad 4–0–30–0; Pollard 1.5–0–5–0.

Nottinghamshire

B. C. Broad c Tillekeratne b Madurasinghe 73
P. Pollard c Tillekeratne b Labrooy .... 16 – (1) not out 62
M. Newell c Madugalle b Ahangama .... 25 – (2) not out 3
D. J. R. Martindale lbw b Madurasinghe 23
*J. D. Birch c and b Madurasinghe 20
R. J. Evans not out 50
K. P. Evans not out 18
L-b 6, w 2, n-b 17 .... 25 B 1, l-b 2, n-b 5 ....

1/26 2/107 3/152 4/157 5/202 (5 wkts dec.) 250 (no wkt) 10

†C. W. Scott, C. L. Cairns, K. Saxelby and D. J. Millns did not bat.

Bowling: *First Innings*—Ratnayeke 17–4–53–0; Labrooy 20–2–57–1; Madurasingh 29.2–14–50–3; Ahangama 17–5–41–1; Samarasekera 12–1–36–0; Tillekeratne 2–0–7–(*Second Innings*—Ratnayeke 7–1–16–0; Labrooy 9–0–38–0; Ahangama 6–2–19–(Madurasinghe 6–1–20–0; Samarasekera 1–0–5–0.

Umpires: B. Dudleston and A. G. T. Whitehead.

YORKSHIRE v SRI LANKANS

At Leeds, August 10, 11, 12. Drawn. Toss: Yorkshire. A massive partnership between Moxc and Sharp, who added 237 for the second wicket from 56 overs, punished some modera bowling by the Sri Lankans, who also conceded runs by setting attacking field-placings th were not justified. Moxon batted for three hours, hitting a six and sixteen fours in 197 ball while Sharp received 208 balls and hit sixteen fours. The Sri Lankan batsmen also enjoyed t ideal conditions provided by the old Headingley Test strip, which had not been used for t England-West Indies Test match because of large cracks. Silva made a stylish 112 from 2 deliveries with fourteen boundaries. However, the game took an unexpected turn wh Yorkshire began their second innings that evening. Labrooy had three for 10 in 22 balls at o stage as the county slumped to 41 for six. Heavy rain prevented further play until t afternoon on the last day, but the tourists might still have won had they not dropped Blak from a relatively straightforward chance to short leg when he was 36. He made the most this escape to add 56 from eighteen overs with Booth and reach an unbeaten 85, his best sc of the season to date. The Sri Lankans had nineteen overs in which to score 163, but the ra returned to deny them even a tilt.

Close of play: First day, Yorkshire 297-5 (R. J. Blakey 5*, C. S. Pickles 3*); Second da Yorkshire 41-6 (R. J. Blakey 16*, P. Carrick 0*).

Yorkshire

M. D. Moxon lbw b Ahangama ....132 – b Labrooy ....
D. Byas c Silva b Ratnayeke .... 4 – b Ratnayeke ....
K. Sharp b Ahangama ....128 – c Madugalle b Labrooy ....
P. E. Robinson c Silva b Ahangama .... 0 – b Labrooy ....
N. G. Nicholson c Silva b Ahangama .... 15 – lbw b Ahangama ....
†R. J. Blakey not out .... 5 – not out ....
C. S. Pickles not out .... 3 – lbw b Labrooy ....
*P. Carrick (did not bat) .... – c Tillekeratne b Ratnayeke .....
P. A. Booth (did not bat) .... – b Ratnayeke ....
S. J. Dennis (did not bat) .... – lbw b Labrooy ....
P. N. Anderson (did not bat) .... – b Labrooy ....
B 1, l-b 5, n-b 4 .... 10 B 2, l-b 8, w 3, n-b 7 ....

1/11 2/248 3/250 4/287 5/292 (5 wkts dec.) 297 1/3 2/15 3/16 4/18 5/38
6/41 7/78 8/134 9/152

Bowling: *First Innings*—Ratnayeke 16–1–61–1; Labrooy 13–0–71–0; Ahang 16.1–2–51–4; Samarasekera 5–1–21–0; Ranatunga 4–0–12–0; Madurasinghe 26–6–6 Tillekeratne 2–0–14–0. *Second Innings*—Ratnayeke 21–5–47–3; Labrooy 16.5–1–6 Ahangama 11–4–23–1; Madurasinghe 2–0–11–0.

Sri Lankans

). S. B. P. Kuruppu c Anderson b Booth ..... 19 – c Blakey b Dennis 0
'S. A. R. Silva c Byas b Carrick ....112 – not out 3
I. A. R. Samarasekera c Byas b Dennis ...... 40 – not out 4
\. Ranatunga c Pickles b Booth 27
'R. S. Madugalle b Anderson 48
.. R. D. Mendis not out..................... 20
B 9, l-b 9, n-b 3 21

/47 2/128 3/192 4/229 5/287 (5 wkts dec.) 287 1/0 (1 wkt) 7

I. P. Tillekeratne, J. R. Ratnayeke, A. W. R. Madurasinghe, F. S. Ahangama and G. F. Labrooy did not bat.

Bowling: *First Innings*—Dennis 16–5–44–1; Anderson 17.3–4–47–1; Booth 26–8–80–2; ickles 15–5–53–0; Carrick 17–3–45–1. *Second Innings*—Dennis 2–1–2–1; Pickles 1.2–0–5–0.

Umpires: D. O. Oslear and N. T. Plews.

SURREY v SRI LANKANS

t The Oval, August 13, 14, 15. Drawn. Toss: Surrey. Although the Sri Lankans settled for itting practice, rather than set Surrey a target on the last afternoon, the match did provide e county with an opportunity to give their young players experience. Frost, making his cond first-class appearance, began with the early wicket of Kuruppu, but Samarasekera iickly settled and, being fierce on any delivery pitched up, raced to his hundred from 124 ills. His 104 contained two sixes and fourteen fours. Labrooy took three for 1 in twelve liveries with the new ball to give the Sri Lankans the initiative at the end of the first day, t spirited lower-order batting swelled Surrey's score from 94 for seven to a first-innings lead 23. On a pitch still showing a hint of green, the limitations of the Sri Lankan attack were posed by Medlycott, Bullen and Martin Bicknell. On the final day, Kuruppu and Mendis th atoned for their first-day failures, with Mendis's punishing 124 off 114 balls including ır sixes and fourteen fours.

Close of play: First day, Surrey 49-4 (G. E. Brown 9*, Zahid Sadiq 2*); Second day, Sri nkans 43-0 (D. S. B. P. Kuruppu 21*, S. A. R. Silva 17*).

i Lankans

S. B. P. Kuruppu c Stewart b Frost .... 5 – b Medlycott 87
A. R. Silva lbw b M. P. Bicknell .... 3 – c Stewart b M. P. Bicknell 24
A. R. Samarasekera c Bullen b Feltham ....104 – c Feltham b M. P. Bicknell 1
Ranatunga c Medlycott b M. P. Bicknell ... 9 – retired hurt 0
. S. Madugalle c Brown b Feltham .... 44 – c Stewart b Frost 22
R. D. Mendis lbw b Frost .... 0 – b Bullen 124
P. Tillekeratne run out .... 22 – b Medlycott 7
R. Ratnayeke b Bullen .... 5 – not out 15
W. R. Madurasinghe b Feltham .... 3 – not out 1
F. Labrooy b M. P. Bicknell 18
S. Ahangama not out 0
B 4, l-b 2 .... 6 B 4, l-b 10, w 3, n-b 2 ... 19

2/10 3/36 4/152 5/155 219 1/54 2/62 3/106 (6 wkts dec.) 300
33 7/192 8/197 9/219 4/205 5/235 6/298

owling: *First Innings*—Frost 10–2–28–2; M. P. Bicknell 22–4–66–3; Feltham 22.3–6–52–3; inson 3–0–16–0; Bullen 13–5–14–1; Medlycott 6–0–37–0. *Second Innings*—Frost 5–78–1; M. P. Bicknell 26–9–78–2; Feltham 17–4–40–0; Medlycott 13–3–67–2; Robinson -22–0; Bullen 5–5–0–1; Stewart 1–1–0–0; D. J. Bicknell 1–0–1–0; Ward 1–1–0–0.

Surrey

D. J. Bicknell c Madugalle b Labrooy . 5
J. D. Robinson c Silva b Labrooy 18
*A. J. Stewart c Silva b Labrooy 1
D. M. Ward c Silva b Ahangama 10
†G. E. Brown c Ahangama b Labrooy . 10
Zahid Sadiq b Ahangama 16
K. T. Medlycott c Madurasinghe b Ratnayeke . 51
M. A. Feltham c Labrooy b Samarasekera . 15
C. K. Bullen not out 59
M. P. Bicknell c Silva b Samarasekera . 33
M. Frost c Tillekeratne b Samarasekera . 7
B 1, l-b 8, w 2, n-b 6 17

1/21 2/27 3/28 4/44 5/51 6/75 7/94 8/154 9/208 242

Bowling: Ratnayeke 20–2–59–1; Labrooy 29–6–86–4; Ahangama 13–3–36–2; Samarasekera 15.4–4–31–3; Madurasinghe 13–5–21–0.

Umpires: D. J. Constant and K. Taylor.

GLOUCESTERSHIRE v SRI LANKANS

At Bristol, August 17, 18, 19. Drawn. Toss: Sri Lankans. Gloucestershire, without five firs[t] team regulars, gave a first-class début to Ball, an eighteen-year-old off-spin bowler, an[d] Ibadulla had his first match of the season. Ball took a wicket in his fifth over, and whe[n] Pooley struck twice, ending a lively effort by Samarasekera, the Sri Lankans faced th[e] prospect of being bowled out cheaply. However, Mendis began a recovery which wa[s] completed by Tillekeratne and Ratnayeke with an unbroken partnership of 109. Wright an[d] Romaines feasted on some friendly bowling until rain washed out the second day's play aft[er] lunch, and on the third day Wright went on to 137, with seventeen fours, having batted f[or] four and a quarter hours. Gloucestershire's declaration allowed de Silva and Mahanama tim[e] for batting practice, and while Alleyne kept wicket Russell patrolled the boundaries un[til] given the chance to bowl an over of leg-spin.

Close of play: First day, Gloucestershire 48-1 (A. J. Wright 35*, P. W. Romaines 8*); Second day, Gloucestershire 147-1 (A. J. Wright 98*, P. W. Romaines 40*).

Sri Lankans

R. S. Mahanama b Greene . . . . 12 – not out 4
†D. S. B. P. Kuruppu b Ball 39
M. A. R. Samarasekera c Russell b Pooley 53
P. A. de Silva c Russell b Pooley . . . . 13 – (2) not out . . . .
*A. Ranatunga run out 4
L. R. D. Mendis lbw b Greene 39
H. P. Tillekeratne not out 50
J. R. Ratnayeke not out 60
L-b 10, w 1, n-b 4 . . . . 15 L-b 1 . . . .

1/30 2/102 3/127 4/128 5/132 6/176 (6 wkts dec.) 285 (no wkt) 1

C. P. H. Ramanayake, B. E. A. Rajadurai and S. D. Anurasiri did not bat.

Bowling: *First Innings*—Greene 12–2–29–2; Jarvis 15–2–48–0; Pooley 18–5–52–2; Alley[ne] 7–2–21–0; Ball 29–5–88–1; Graveney 19–5–37–0. *Second Innings*—Greene 5–1–12–0; Jar[vis] 5–2–7–0; Pooley 5–0–18–0; Ibadulla 8–0–49–0; Graveney 4–0–13–0; Russell 1–0–12–0.

Gloucestershire

A. J. Wright b Ramanayake 137
I. P. Butcher lbw b Ratnayeke 0
P. W. Romaines c Anurasiri b Ratnayeke 62
M. W. Alleyne not out 32
K. B. K. Ibadulla not out . . . .
L-b 6, n-b 7 . . . .

1/3 2/184 3/230 (3 wkts dec.)

†R. C. Russell, M. W. Pooley, V. S. Greene, *D. A. Graveney, M. C. J. Ball and K. B. Jarvis did not bat.

Bowling: Ratnayeke 23–5–59–2; Ramanayake 19–3–76–1; Rajadurai 9–2–37–0; Anurasiri 12–3–38–0; Ranatunga 6–1–30–0.

Umpires: M. J. Harris and P. B. Wight.

HAMPSHIRE v SRI LANKANS

At Southampton, August 20, 21, 22. Drawn. Toss: Hampshire. Terry and Smith took advantage of a good batting wicket, putting on 225 for the third wicket against an attack which lacked both pace and penetration. Terry batted 354 minutes for his career-best 190, an innings which included 21 fours and took him past 1,000 runs for the season. The touring team were sent reeling on the second morning, losing four wickets in the first half-hour as James evoked memories of his six for 22 against the Australians in 1985. Madugalle rescued his side, hitting a six and eleven fours before narrowly missing his hundred. Scott drove and pulled his way to a maiden first-class century, and Hampshire's declaration set the Sri Lankans a target of 274 from a minimum of 47 overs. Instead, they settled for batting practice. Silva took 82 minutes over his 19, but Samarasekera provided some late entertainment by hitting four sixes off Maru.

Close of play: First day, Sri Lankans 13-0 (R. S. Mahanama 6*, S. A. R. Silva 3*); Second day, Hampshire 36-0 (R. J. Scott 27*, T. C. Middleton 9*).

Hampshire

V. P. Terry lbw b Ahangama	190		
T. C. Middleton lbw b Labrooy	5	– lbw b Ahangama	23
M. C. J. Nicholas c Silva b Ratnayeke	57		
R. A. Smith not out	104	– not out	23
R. J. Scott (did not bat)		– (1) not out	107
K. D. James (did not bat)		– (3) c Ratnayeke b Madurasinghe	25
L-b 6, w 1, n-b 5	12	L-b 4, n-b 3	7
1/8 2/143 3/368 (3 wkts dec.)	368	1/78 2/136 (2 wkts dec.)	185

N. G. Cowley, †A. N. Aymes, T. M. Tremlett, R. J. Maru and C. A. Connor did not bat.

Bowling: *First Innings*—Ratnayeke 19–2–66–1; Labrooy 18–4–68–1; Samarasekera 15–0–53–0; Ahangama 11.1–2–55–1; Madurasinghe 21–1–75–0; de Silva 1–0–10–0; Ranatunga 9–0–35–0. *Second Innings*—Ratnayeke 12–2–34–0; Labrooy 17–1–52–0; Madurasinghe 18.2–3–55–1; Ahangama 6–1–26–1; Ranatunga 3–0–14–0.

Sri Lankans

R. S. Mahanama b Connor	12		
S. A. R. Silva c Aymes b James	3	– (1) c Smith b Maru	19
M. A. R. Samarasekera c Terry b James	0	– not out	40
P. A. de Silva c Terry b James	14		
R. S. Madugalle c Terry b Maru	97		
A. Ranatunga c Aymes b James	39		
L. R. D. Mendis lbw b James	0		
J. R. Ratnayeke c Aymes b Tremlett	41	– (2) not out	45
A. W. R. Madurasinghe c Smith b Connor	27		
G. F. Labrooy b Maru	4		
C. P. S. Ahangama not out	3		
B 12, l-b 14, w 1, n-b 13	40	L-b 1, n-b 1	2
1/13 2/13 3/33 4/33 5/139 6/139 7/222 8/252 9/264	280	1/45 (1 wkt)	106

Bowling: *First Innings*—Connor 18.4–3–42–2; James 21–3–80–5; Maru 22–8–46–2; Tremlett 17–4–43–1; Cowley 12–4–29–0; Scott 6–1–14–0. *Second Innings*—Connor 6–3–4–0; James 4–2–14–0; Cowley 16–7–23–0; Maru 12–1–52–1; Tremlett 3–2–2–0; Smith 1–0–1–0; Middleton 1–0–9–0.

Umpires: J. C. Balderstone and M. J. Kitchen.

ENGLAND v SRI LANKA

Cornhill Test Match

At Lord's, August 25, 26, 27, 29, 30. England won by seven wickets. Toss: England. England's dismal run of eighteen Test matches without a win had to end sooner or later, and when Sri Lanka, put in, were 63 for six nine minutes before lunch, there was much talk of the match being over no later than Saturday, with the England players returning to their counties for the next round of four-day Championship matches due to start the following Tuesday. In the end, Sri Lanka kept them at the ground until after lunch on the final day.

It was certainly an undistinguished morning for the Sri Lankans. Silva, dropped at the wicket off Lawrence in the sixth over, was less fortunate in the seventh when he gave Russell, one of four new players in the England team, a more straightforward chance. Lawrence, who bowled with speed and hostility, Newport and Barnett were the other newcomers. Sri Lanka had two new caps in Samarasekera and Madurasinghe, and it was the former who was next to go, having spent more than half an hour at the crease without scoring. Meanwhile Kuruppu had been looking anything but the compiler of the slowest-ever double-hundred. He had scored 46 of the first 49 runs off the bat when he gave Gooch an easy chance at second slip and Newport his first Test wicket. The same combination disposed of de Silva, and two leg before decisions accelerated the Sri Lankan decline.

The first hour of the afternoon went better for Sri Lanka until Mendis, playing with increasing flamboyance, was caught in a well-baited trap at deep third man. It was an injudicious shot, and was made to appear more so as his team slipped to 130 for nine. Unexpectedly, when Labrooy joined Ratnayeke, England met the first show of genuine defiance. In 86 minutes they added 64 for the last wicket, a record for Sri Lanka against a countries, with Labrooy surprising perhaps even himself with the quality of his strokeplay. H straight-drove Lawrence for one of his six boundaries and the partnership caused Gooch t make five bowling changes in 21 overs before Pringle eventually took the wicket.

If the Sri Lankan batting had been disappointing in the morning, their bowling was eve more modest. The England openers appeared to have the opportunity to score at will, and so i was a surprise when Robinson, changing his mind halfway through the stroke, chippe Ratnayeke to mid-wicket. With only sixteen deliveries remaining in the day, Russell appeare as night-watchman. On Friday, he outscored Gooch 35-30 during the first session, albe having much more of the strike, and it did not come as a surprise when Gooch was the first t go, having batted for four hours nineteen minutes and faced 194 balls for his 75.

This heralded the arrival of Barnett, who was soon into his attractive stride as well a nursing Russell through hitherto uncharted territory – the 80s and 90s. Impatience was th downfall of Russell. When only 6 runs short of what would have been his maiden first-cla century, he chased a wide ball from Labrooy and was caught at cover. He had faced 202 ba in 277 minutes at the crease and his 94 included eleven boundaries. Barnett and Lamb (balls) were both out when a century seemed there for the taking, and Smith must have bee disappointed when he deflected a very wide ball on to his stumps. Even more disappointe was Emburey, who came into the match with a Championship hundred behind him but hol out at cover.

It was a tribute to the perseverance of the Sri Lankan attack that England were bowled o and a tribute to their determination and technique that they batted so much better in t second innings. At the press conference held at the start of the tour, both the captain a manager had said that Sri Lankan cricket had regressed during the past four years becau of their having played so few Test matches. Their ghastly experience of the first day w obviously put to good use on the third and fourth days. At times, the England capta appeared concerned as to where the next wicket was coming from. Samarasekera (110 ba one six, seven fours) and Ranatunga particularly batted very well, and Ranatunga could f hard done by as three straight drives, two off the front foot and one off the back, struck stumps at the far end, almost certainly depriving him of a dozen runs. As it was, there we ten fours in his 78 from 181 balls, and Mendis struck eight fours in his 98-ball half-centu

Sri Lanka restored their pride and won many friends with their second-innings displ They certainly frustrated England by taking the match into the fifth day. The end was without its bizarre note as the players went to lunch with England just 1 run short of vict when most people on the ground thought that the clock had not quite reached one o'clo Gooch had been an hour and a half over his 36 while Robinson was still there on 34, havi batted for two hours twelve minutes and received 109 balls. When play resumed, only four deliveries were required before Smith struck the winning boundary and England won a Test match at Lord's for the first time in five years. – Norman de Mesquita.

Men of the Match: England – P. J. Newport; Sri Lanka – J. R. Ratnayeke.

Attendance: 31,855; *receipts* £250,418.

Close of play: First day, England 47-1 (G. A. Gooch 24*, R. C. Russell 2*); Second day, England 278-3 (K. J. Barnett 55*, A. J. Lamb 20*); Third day, Sri Lanka 92-2 (M. A. R. Samarasekera 30*, P. A. de Silva 15*); Fourth day, England 8-0 (G. A. Gooch 1*, R. T. Robinson 4*).

Sri Lanka

D. S. B. P. Kuruppu c Gooch b Newport	46	– c Barnett b Foster	25
†S. A. R. Silva c Russell b Foster	1	– c Russell b Newport	16
M. A. R. Samarasekera c Russell b Foster	0	– lbw b Emburey	57
P. A. de Silva c Gooch b Newport	3	– lbw b Lawrence	18
*R. S. Madugalle lbw b Foster	3	– b Foster	20
A. Ranatunga lbw b Newport	5	– b Newport	78
L. R. D. Mendis c Smith b Lawrence	21	– lbw b Pringle	56
J. R. Ratnayeke not out	59	– c Lamb b Lawrence	32
A. W. R. Madurasinghe run out	4	– b Newport	2
C. P. H. Ramanayake lbw b Pringle	0	– (11) c Gooch b Newport	2
G. F. Labrooy lbw b Pringle	42	– (10) not out	9
B 1, l-b 7, n-b 2	10	L-b 8, n-b 8	16
1/7 (2) 2/44 (3) 3/52 (1) 4/53 (4) 5/61 (5) 6/63 (6) 7/122 (7) 8/127 (9) 9/130 (10) 10/194 (11)	194	1/43 (1) 2/51 (2) 3/96 (4) 4/145 (5) 5/147 (3) 6/251 (7) 7/309 (6) 8/311 (9) 9/323 (8) 10/331 (11)	331

Bowling: *First Innings*—Foster 21–5–51–3; Lawrence 15–4–37–1; Newport 21–4–77–3; Pringle 6.5–1–17–2; Emburey 2–1–4–0. *Second Innings*—Foster 33–10–98–2; Lawrence 21–5–74–2; Newport 26.3–7–87–4; Pringle 11–2–30–1; Emburey 18–9–34–1.

England

*G. A. Gooch lbw b Ratnayeke	75	– c Silva b Samarasekera	36
R. T. Robinson c Samarasekera b Ratnayeke	19	– not out	34
†R. C. Russell c Samarasekera b Labrooy	94		
K. J. Barnett c Ranatunga b Labrooy	66	– (3) c Silva b Samarasekera	0
A. J. Lamb b Labrooy	63	– (4) c de Silva b Ranatunga	8
R. A. Smith b Ranatunga	31	– (5) not out	8
D. R. Pringle c Silva b Labrooy	14		
J. E. Emburey c de Silva b Samarasekera	0		
P. J. Newport c de Silva b Ramanayake	26		
N. A. Foster not out	14		
D. V. Lawrence c Mendis b Ramanayake	4		
B 1, l-b 3, w 2, n-b 17	23	L-b 8, w 2, n-b 4	14
1/40 (2) 2/171 (1) 3/233 (3) 4/320 (4) 5/358 (5) 6/373 (6) 7/378 (8) 8/383 (7) 9/420 (9) 10/429 (11)	429	1/73 (1) 2/73 (3) 3/82 (4)	(3 wkts) 100

Bowling: *First Innings*—Ratnayeke 32–3–107–2; Labrooy 40–7–119–4; Ramanayake 7.2–3–86–2; Madurasinghe 16–4–41–0; Samarasekera 22–5–66–1; Ranatunga 6–3–6–1. *Second Innings*—Ratnayeke 7–1–16–0; Labrooy 9–0–24–0; Samarasekera 10–0–38–2; Ranatunga 8.4–4–14–1.

Umpires: D. J. Constant and J. W. Holder.

DERBYSHIRE v SRI LANKANS

At Derby, August 31, September 1, 2. Drawn. Toss: Derbyshire. Maher led Derbyshire for the first time. The highlight of the first day was a stylish innings by de Silva, who faced only balls and hit 58 of his 76 runs in boundaries, a six and thirteen fours. Rain washed out the second day and, with the Texaco one-day international pending, both teams were prepared to play a limited-overs game. The TCCB refused permission, although when Derbyshire's game against the Australians in 1985 was similarly spoiled, an overs game was played on the fourth day. While the decision condemned spectators to some meaningless cricket, it did allow Goldsmith to complete 1,000 runs in his début season for the county, emulating Bowler.

Close of play: First day, Derbyshire 15-1 (P. D. Bowler 7*, B. J. M. Maher 5*); Second day, No play.

Sri Lankans

D. S. B. P. Kuruppu not out 55
S. A. R. Silva lbw b Newman 36
M. A. R. Samarasekera c Base b Griffith 25
P. A. de Silva c Jean-Jacques b Base . . 76
H. P. Tillekeratne b Jean-Jacques 5
A. Ranatunga c Maher b Base 25
L. R. D. Mendis c Morris b Roberts . . 55
*†R. S. Madugalle not out 6
L-b 3, w 1, n-b 10 14

1/74 2/125 3/162 4/183 5/206 6/282 (6 wkts dec.) 297

S. D. Anurasiri, G. F. Labrooy and F. S. Ahangama did not bat.

D. S. B. P. Kuruppu, when 21, retired hurt at 37 and resumed at 183.

Bowling: Newman 15–5–48–1; Base 20–4–60–2; Griffith 19–3–79–1; Jean-Jacques 17–2–66–1; Sharma 10–2–34–0; Roberts 4–1–7–1.

Derbyshire

P. D. Bowler lbw b Ahangama 7
T. J. G. O'Gorman hit wkt b Labrooy . 0
*†B. J. M. Maher b Tillekeratne 54
J. E. Morris c Kuruppu b Anurasiri . . . 25
S. C. Goldsmith b Ahangama 60
B. Roberts c Samarasekera b Anurasiri . 16
F. A. Griffith st Kuruppu b de Silva . . . 18
R. Sharma not out 40
P. G. Newman not out 13
L-b 2, w 1, n-b 11 14

1/1 2/16 3/51 4/152 5/152 6/187 7/187 (7 wkts dec.) 247

S. J. Base and M. Jean-Jacques did not bat.

Bowling: Labrooy 19–5–44–1; Ahangama 19–3–70–2; Anurasiri 27–9–67–2; de Silva 13–5–32–1; Samarasekera 8–1–18–0; Tillekeratne 5–1–14–1.

Umpires: B. Dudleston and D. O. Oslear.

†ENGLAND v SRI LANKA

Texaco Trophy Match

At The Oval, September 4. England won by five wickets. Toss: England. Put in on an ide[illegible] batting wicket, in bright sunshine, Sri Lanka made a promising start. Kuruppu hit a fine [illegible] from 66 balls and then Ranatunga (62 balls) and Mendis added 69 in less than an hou[illegible] Mendis hit six fours and a mighty six while scoring 60 from 65 balls. If 242 seemed a usef[illegible] score, at one stage it had looked as if England would have to chase 270 or more. Small was th[illegible] pick of the England bowlers, Gooch was economical, but Marks on his return to the Englan[illegible] team proved expensive. England lost Gooch in the second over and Robinson in the eleventh[illegible] but Barnett (146 balls) and Lamb set about the bowling with ease. In a stand of 118 in [illegible] minutes, Lamb had made 66 from 70 balls, including an effortless straight-driven six into th[illegible] Pavilion, when he was smartly caught at square leg by the substitute, Rajadurai, who fielde[illegible] for Mendis throughout the innings. Bailey again gave evidence of his potential with [illegible] unbeaten 43 from 34 balls and Pringle hit 19 off eleven balls to hasten the win. Sri Lanka use[illegible] seven bowlers, and the inclusion of Madurasinghe, whose three overs cost 24, ahead [illegible] Ahangama, who had been difficult to score off on the tour, seemed a puzzling selection.

Men of the Match: England – K. J. Barnett; Sri Lanka – L. R. D. Mendis.

Attendance: 9,066; *receipts* £106,170.

Sri Lanka

†D. S. B. P. Kuruppu lbw b Gooch . . . 38
M. A. R. Samarasekera b Small 10
P. A. de Silva b Gooch 16
A. Ranatunga run out 37
L. R. D. Mendis b Small 60
*R. S. Madugalle c Foster b Pringle . . . 17
J. R. Ratnayeke c Pringle b Small 19
H. P. Tillekeratne not out 15
G. F. Labrooy not out 10
B 1, l-b 10, w 8, n-b 1 20

1/21 (2) 2/54 (3) 3/75 (1) 4/144 (4) 5/190 (6) 6/193 (5) 7/224 (7) (7 wkts, 55 overs) 242

A. W. R. Madurasinghe and S. D. Anurasiri did not bat.

Bowling: Foster 11–0–47–0; Small 11–1–44–3; Gooch 11–1–35–2; Pringle 11–0–46–1; Marks 11–0–59–0.

England

*G. A. Gooch c de Silva b Labrooy . . . 7
R. T. Robinson lbw b Ratnayeke 13
K. J. Barnett run out 84
A. J. Lamb c sub (B. E. A. Rajadurai) b Labrooy . 66
R. A. Smith c Kuruppu b Labrooy 9
R. J. Bailey not out 43
D. R. Pringle not out 19
W 3, l-b 1 4

1/9 (1) 2/22 (2) 3/140 (4) 4/154 (5) 5/213 (3) (5 wkts, 52.4 overs) 245

†R. C. Russell, V. J. Marks, N. A. Foster and G. C. Small did not bat.

Bowling: Ratnayeke 9.4–3–37–1; Labrooy 10–0–40–3; Samarasekera 11–0–52–0; Ranatunga 11–0–42–0; Anurasiri 6–0–31–0; de Silva 2–0–19–0; Madurasinghe 3–0–24–0.

Umpires: J. W. Holder and K. E. Palmer.

FUTURE TOURS

989	Australians to England
989-90	Sri Lankans and Pakistanis to Australia Indians to Pakistan England to West Indies Indians to New Zealand and Sri Lanka Australians to New Zealand
990	New Zealanders and Indians to England
990-91	New Zealanders to Pakistan England to Australia West Indians to Sri Lanka* and India Sri Lankans to Pakistan New Zealanders to Australia* Pakistanis to India* Sri Lankans to New Zealand* Australians to West Indies
91	West Indians to England
1991-92	New Zealanders to Australia* Indians to Australia* West Indians to Australia England to Pakistan and New Zealand* Sri Lankans to India
1992	Sri Lankans and Pakistanis to England*
1992-93	West Indians to Australia England to India* Indians to West Indies
1993	Australians to England*
1993-94	Indians to Pakistan* Indians to Sri Lanka
1994	Indians to England*
1994-95	England to Australia

* *Signifies unconfirmed.*

THE MARYLEBONE CRICKET CLUB, 1988

Patron – HER MAJESTY THE QUEEN

President – J. J. WARR

President Designate – FIELD-MARSHAL THE LORD BRAMALL

Treasurer – G. H. G. DOGGART

Chairman of Finance – SIR ANTHONY TUKE

*Trustees – D. J. INSOLE, F. G. MANN, SIR OLIVER POPPLEWELL

Life Vice-Presidents – SIR GEORGE ALLEN, F. R. BROWN, S. C. GRIFFITH, C. G. A. PARIS

Secretary – LT-COL. J. R. STEPHENSON
(Lord's Cricket Ground, St John's Wood, NW8 8QN)

ASSISTANT SECRETARIES – LT-COL. L. G. JAMES (Administration), M. R. BLOW (Finance), WG-CDR V. J. W. M. LAWRENCE (Marketing & Personnel)

Curator – S. E. A. GREEN

Ground Administrator – A. W. P. FLEMING

MCC Committee for 1987-88: J. J. Warr (President), Field-Marshal The Lor Bramall, M. C. Cowdrey, G. H. G. Doggart, C. A. Fry, D. L. Hud A. C. D. Ingleby-Mackenzie, D. J. Insole, I. C. MacLaurin, D. R. Mal P. B. H. May, M. E. L. Melluish, M. M. Morton, N. E. J. Pococ D. R. W. Silk, Sir Anthony Tuke, J. A. F. Vallance.

* *Trustees retire annually in rotation but are eligible for re-election. In the capacity as Trustees they are entitled to attend MCC Committee meetings but a ineligible to vote.*

Although their posts do not involve membership of the MCC Committe the following were chairmen of current MCC Standing Sub-Committee A. J. B. Mason (Tennis & Squash), M. E. L. Melluish (Indoor Schoo T. M. B. Sissons (Arts & Library).

At the 201st Annual General Meeting of MCC, held at Lord's on May 1988, at which the President took the chair, D. J. Insole was appointed Trustee for a further three years and Sir Anthony Tuke was appoint Chairman of Finance for a further five years. Under the Rules of the Cl each had to retire on September 30, 1988, and each had expressed h willingness to stand for re-election.

In his statement to members, the President said that much thought and work had been expended on improving the facilities at Lord's, both for members and the general public. This was reflected in the accounts, which recorded a deficit of £28,000 even though income had again increased. Maintenance of buildings was a major item of expenditure. Refurbishments of the Pavilion had continued and the exterior had been redecorated; individual bucket seats had been installed in the Warner, Tavern and Grand Stand balconies; a permanent stand had been built in front of the Tavern; and the previously mentioned three stands had been rewired to comply with the Safety of Sports Grounds Act. There had also been improvements to the drainage of the ground and new covers had been purchased to replace the existing covers, all of which had been destroyed during the storm of October 16, 1987.

A management consultant from McKinsey was examining the way the club was organised and managed, and he would make recommendations for improvements. In addition, a working party was undertaking a major revision of the Rules of the Club. It was hoped to present the amended rules to the Annual Meeting in 1989.

The President, J. J. Warr, named Field-Marshal The Lord Bramall to succeed him on October 1, 1988. Lord Bramall, Lord Lieutenant of Greater London, was Chief of the Defence Staff from 1982 to 1985. Captain of Eton in 1942 and vice-captain that year of the Public Schools XI at Lord's, he had maintained his interest in the game through a long association with Services cricket and latterly as an MCC committee member.

Because there were more nominations than vacancies for the committee, a postal ballot was held among members, as a result of which M. J. K. Smith, D. G. Trelford, J. C. Woodcock and H. M. Wyndham were elected to join the committee from October 1, 1988. Those due for rotational retirement on September 30, 1988 were A. C. D. Ingleby-Mackenzie, D. J. Insole, P. B. H. May and M. M. Morton.

At Special General Meetings which followed the Annual Meeting, members approved the refurbishment of Q Stand and its use by Middlesex CCC for their home matches, and also approved increases in the annual subscription for full, out-match and associate members from January 1, 1989. Earlier, approval had been given to the introduction of a registration fee of half the annual subscription for all existing and future candidates for membership. The waiting list stood at 13,452 and was increasing by approximately 1,500 a year. In a normal year, places came available for some 150 candidates, with the balance made up by the election of qualified probationary cricket candidates. In 1987, 410 vacancies occurred, owing to 204 deaths, 102 resignations and 104 lapsed memberships.

The membership of the club on December 31, 1987 was 19,794, made up of 17,829 full members and 1,965 associate members. These comprised the following: 10,739 full and 1,519 associate town members, 2,280 full and 251 associate country members, 3,383 at the over-65 rate, 165 full and 156 associate members at the under-25 rate, 276 full and 21 associate at the special schoolmasters' rate, 685 full and 18 associate members on the abroad list, 59 life members, 19 60-year life members, 38 honorary cricket members and 185 honorary life members.

MCC v NOTTINGHAMSHIRE

At Lord's, April 16, 17, 18. Drawn. Toss: Nottinghamshire. The season began as it meant to continue, with the opening day affected by rain and bad light. Robinson was dropped twice during the play that was possible, but on the second day, with the sun on his back, he moved smoothly to the first century of the season. In a stay of four and a half hours he hit two sixes and eleven fours. Nottinghamshire declared midway through the afternoon, whereupon Hick gave the Sunday crowd good value for their free admission by hitting 61 off 74 balls. Williams apart, however, the other MCC batsmen failed to do justice to a good batting pitch. Agnew extracted life and lift from it on the final morning to remove both Nottinghamshire openers, but for the second time Johnson was untroubled in reaching 50. The third declaration of the match set MCC 279 to win in 215 minutes. The loss of Fowler and Hick effectively ended their chance of victory, while Nottinghamshire spoilt their own prospects by dropping five catches.

Close of play: First day, Nottinghamshire 125-1 (R. T. Robinson 62*, M. Newell 5*); Second day, MCC 159-7 (R. G. Williams 35*, G. C. Small 21*).

Nottinghamshire

B. C. Broad b Williams	49	– c Russell b Agnew	32
*R. T. Robinson c Russell b Agnew	129	– c Maynard b Agnew	18
M. Newell run out	23	– not out	26
P. Johnson not out	61	– not out	59
J. D. Birch not out	23		
B 2, l-b 9, w 1, n-b 1	13	L-b 2, w 2	4
1/110 2/170 3/233 (3 wkts dec.)	298	1/46 2/53 (2 wkts dec.)	139

F. D. Stephenson, †B. N. French, E. E. Hemmings, R. A. Pick, K. E. Cooper and K. Saxelby did not bat.

Bowling: *First Innings*—Agnew 25–5–71–1; Small 20–9–48–0; Cook 20–2–62–0; Wells 10–3–40–0; Williams 17–4–45–1; Maynard 9–2–21–0. *Second Innings*—Agnew 11–2–43–2; Small 6–3–16–0; Maynard 4–0–21–0; Cook 11–4–23–0; Williams 10–2–34–0.

MCC

T. S. Curtis b Stephenson	13	– b Stephenson	18
G. Fowler lbw b Pick	0	– b Hemmings	73
G. A. Hick c Birch b Pick	61	– c and b Pick	37
*M. C. J. Nicholas lbw b Pick	12	– c Johnson b Cooper	27
M. P. Maynard c Stephenson b Saxelby	1	– run out	32
R. G. Williams not out	35	– not out	[illegible]
†R. C. Russell c Hemmings b Saxelby	7	– not out	1[illegible]
C. M. Wells c French b Saxelby	1		
G. C. Small not out	21		
L-b 3, n-b 5	8	B 1, l-b 7, n-b 6	1[illegible]
1/2 2/49 3/85 4/92 5/92 6/100 7/116 (7 wkts dec.)	159	1/66 2/121 3/142 4/192 5/201 (5 wkts)	22[illegible]

N. G. B. Cook and J. P. Agnew did not bat.

Bowling: *First Innings*—Stephenson 15–1–58–1; Pick 11–5–37–3; Cooper 10–3–40–[illegible] Saxelby 7–2–21–3. *Second Innings*—Stephenson 10–1–21–1; Pick 12–2–61–1; Coop[illegible] 11–1–44–1; Saxelby 6–0–41–0; Hemmings 13–2–47–1.

Umpires: B. Dudleston and J. H. Harris.

†At Lord's, May 11. MCC Young Cricketers won by three wickets. Toss: MCC. MCC 192 f[illegible] six dec. (J. R. T. Barclay 58, R. P. Hodson 30 not out); MCC Young Cricketers 194 f[illegible] seven (R. G. Twose 54, J. R. Wood 37, C. H. H. Pegg 36, A. D. Towse 44).

†At Cambridge, May 17. MCC drew with Cambridge University (See Cambridge Univers[illegible] section).

†At Oxford, June 8, 9, 10. MCC lost to Oxford University by 153 runs (See Oxford University section).

†At Downpatrick, June 11, 12, 13. MCC drew with Ireland (See Other Matches, 1988).

†At Lord's, June 24. Netherlands XI won by nine wickets. Toss: MCC. MCC 238 for four dec. (P. W. Romaines 105, J. W. van Alkemade 72; H. Visee three for 56); Netherlands XI 239 for one (C. Ruskamp 117 not out, R. Lifmann 69, C. M. Kuggeleijn 35 not out).

†MCC v ABORIGINAL CRICKET ASSOCIATION

At Lord's, June 28. Drawn. Toss: MCC. The match, the final fixture of the Australian Aboriginals' tour of the United Kingdom, was abandoned at 3.30 p.m. after rain had earlier interrupted play.

MCC

. D. David b Mainhardt	6
B. Knowles not out	41
D. M. Jones lbw b Mainhardt	3
. J. F. Hutchinson not out	13
B 1, l-b 3, w 5	9
/21 2/41	(2 wkts) 72

N. D. Maxwell, R. J. Doughty, †P. A. Nixon, D. R. Gilbert, A. W. Lyon, T. M. Lamb and D. Wilson did not bat.

Bowling: Mainhardt 9–1–35–2; Thompson 5–0–27–0; Bagshaw 3–0–6–0.

Aboriginal Cricket Association

J. P. McGuire, D. E. Breckenridge, J. A. Marsh, S. C. Appoo, E. V. Graham-Vanderbyl, P. D. Bagshaw, N. J. Bulger, †M. R. Williams, M. S. Mainhardt, D. M. Thompson and B. F. Pearce.

Umpires: R. E. A. Frost and D. W. G. Lloyd.

At Lord's, July 14, 15. Drawn. Toss: MCC. MCC 219 (Sadiq Mohammad 42, R. J. Lanchbury 42, S. C. Wundke 51; O. Henry six for 54) and 161 for two dec. (W. A. Donald 30, Sadiq Mohammad 45, R. J. Lanchbury 51 not out); Scotland 147 for five dec. (B. M. W. Patterson 36 not out, O. Henry 69).

At Lord's, July 20. MCC won by 23 runs. Toss: MCC. MCC 137 (Sadiq Mohammad 37; M. C. J. Ball five for 42); MCC Schools 114 (D. Wilson six for 22).

At Swansea, August 22, 23, 24. MCC drew with Wales (See Other Matches, 1988).

At Scarborough, August 31, September 1, 2. MCC lost to Michael Parkinson's World XI by 32 runs (See Other Matches, 1988).

OTHER MATCHES AT LORD'S, 1988

May 23. Third Texaco Trophy match. ENGLAND beat WEST INDIES by seven wickets (See West Indian tour section).

June 16, 17, 18, 20, 21. Second Cornhill Test. ENGLAND lost to WEST INDIES by 134 runs (See West Indian tour section).

ETON v HARROW

June 25. Drawn. Toss: Eton. Eton, left with 48 overs in which to score 216, were 19 runs shor at the end of a thrilling chase. They had lost their openers either side of tea, but as St Georg and Carr were adding 123 by means of ringing shots and adventurous running, Harrow's dela in declaring became more understandable. Carr's dismissal was the break the Harrow me needed. The Eton momentum was lost and 51 from the last four overs proved too great a task Harrow's innings was a solid affair, with Boralessa taking more than three hours over hi 42. Keey and Bourne batted attractively, and in retrospect Harrow were thankful for Raper' dashing 24 at the end.

Harrow

*C. Keey lbw b Johnson 37
H. Boralessa c Martin b Fleming 42
M. B. T. de Souza-Girao c Martin b Fleming . 8
J. K. Bourne c Petre b Fleming 67
†C. A. Abraham c Trusted b Erith 10
C. Raper not out 24
R. D. Nelson b Erith 0
J. T. G. Allen b Erith ....
G. R. C. Bucknall not out ....
B 4, l-b 8, w 4, n-b 6 2

1/69 2/80 3/142 4/183 5/183 6/195 7/195 (7 wkts dec.) 21

J. A. R. Hill and J. E. Oppenheimer did not bat.

Bowling: Erith 19–8–34–3; Sullivan 16–4–50–0; Johnson 15–2–55–1; Fleming 30–10–64–

Eton

A. G. Bignell c Abraham b Hill 12
S. R. B. Martin run out 14
C. H. G. St George not out 84
J. E. Carr run out 51
T. M. Fleming b Bucknall 1
H. R. E. Petre c Keey b Bucknall 7
J. C. Prichard run out ....
†J. T. Trusted not out ....
B 6, l-b 8, n-b 1 ....

1/25 2/32 3/155 4/157 5/167 6/188 (6 wkts) 1

E. B. J. Johnson, *J. K. Erith and J. P. Sullivan did not bat.

Bowling: Oppenheimer 3–1–8–0; Raper 16–3–45–0; Hill 18–1–84–1; Boralessa 4–0–16– Bucknall 7–0–30–2.

Umpires: P. Adams and D. J. Dennis.

ETON v HARROW, RESULTS AND HUNDREDS

Of the 153 matches played Eton have won 50, Harrow 44 and 59 have been drawn. This is generally published record, but Harrow men object strongly to the first game in 1805 be treated as a regular contest between the two schools, contending that it is no more correct count that one than the fixture of 1857 which has been rejected.

The matches played during the war years 1915-18 and 1940-45 are not reckoned belonging to the regular series.

Results since 1950:

1950	Drawn
1951	Drawn
1952	Harrow won by seven wickets
1953	Eton won by ten wickets
1954	Harrow won by nine wickets
1955	Eton won by 38 runs
1956	Drawn
1957	Drawn
1958	Drawn
1959	Drawn
1960	Harrow won by 124 runs
1961	Harrow won by an innings and 12 runs
1962	Drawn
1963	Drawn
1964	Eton won by eight wickets
1965	Harrow won by 48 runs
1966	Drawn
1967	Drawn
1968	Harrow won by seven wickets
1969	Drawn
1970	Eton won by 97 runs
1971	Drawn
1972	Drawn
1973	Drawn
1974	Harrow won by eight wickets
1975	Harrow won by an innings and 151 runs
1976	Drawn
1977	Eton won by six wickets
1978	Drawn
1979	Drawn
1980	Drawn
1981	Drawn
1982	Drawn
1983	Drawn
1984	Drawn
1985	Eton won by 3 runs
1986	Drawn
1987	Drawn
1988	Drawn

Forty-five three-figure innings have been played in matches between these two schools. Those since 1918:

61*	M. K. Fosh	1975 Harrow
59	E. W. Dawson	1923 Eton
58	I. S. Akers-Douglas	1928 Eton
53	N. S. Hotchkin	1931 Eton
51	R. M. Tindall	1976 Harrow
35	J. C. Atkinson-Clark	1930 Eton
15	E. Crutchley	1939 Harrow
12	A. W. Allen	1931 Eton
12*	T. M. H. James	1978 Harrow
11	R. A. A. Holt	1937 Harrow
09	K. F. H. Hale	1929 Eton
09	N. S. Hotchkin	1932 Eton
07	W. N. Coles	1946 Eton
106	D. M. Smith	1966 Eton
104	R. Pulbrook	1932 Harrow
103	L. G. Crawley	1921 Harrow
103	T. Hare	1947 Eton
102*	P. H. Stewart-Brown	1923 Harrow
102	R. V. C. Robins	1953 Eton
100	R. H. Cobbold	1923 Eton
100*	P. V. F. Cazalet	1926 Eton
100	A. N. A. Boyd	1934 Eton
100*	P. M. Studd	1935 Harrow
100	S. D. D. Sainsbury	1947 Eton
100	M. J. J. Faber	1968 Eton

* *Signifies not out.*

In 1904, D. C. Boles of Eton, making 183, set a record for the match, beating the 152 otained for Eton in 1841 by Emilius Bayley, afterwards the Rev. Sir John Robert Laurie milius Bayley Laurie. M. C. Bird, Harrow, in 1907, scored 100 not out and 131, the only atsman who has made two 100s in the match. N. S. Hotchkin, Eton, played the following nings: 1931, 153; 1932, 109 and 96; 1933, 88 and 12.

OXFORD UNIVERSITY v CAMBRIDGE UNIVERSITY

Lord's, July 2, 3, 4. Abandoned. For the first time, Sunday play had been scheduled in the niversity Match, but heavy rain in London made any prospect of play impossible on all ree days. The umpires made their decision to abandon what would have been the 144th niversity Match early on the third morning, so creating another piece of history. It was the st time the match, the oldest fixture on the first-class calendar, had been called off without a ll bowled. Blues were awarded as follows:

Oxford University

S. A. Almaer (*Ilford County HS and St Catherine's*), M. A. Crawley (*Manchester GS and Oriel*), *M. J. Kilborn (*Farrer Agric. HS, Univ. of NSW and St John's*), D. A. Hagan (*Trinity, Leamington Spa and St Edmund Hall*), T. B. Jack (*Aquinas Coll., Univ of WA and Keble*), M. E. O. Brown (*Diocesan Coll., Univ. of Cape Town and Worcester*), S. D. Weale (*Westminster City and Keble*), †G. D. Reynolds (*Wellington Coll. and University*), J. D. Nuttall (*Pocklington and St Peter's*), P. G. Edwards (*Canford and Christ Church*), M. R. Sygrove (*Lutterworth GS and St John's*).

Cambridge University

P. A. C. Bail (*Millfield and Downing*), †R. J. Turner (*Millfield and Magdalene*), *M. A. Atherton (*Manchester GS and Downing*), S. J. Noyes (*RGS High Wycombe and Homerton*), J. C. M. Atkinson (*Millfield and Downing*), J. M. Tremellen (*Bradfield and St Catharine's*), S. D. Heath (*King Edward's, Birmingham and Trinity*), R. Bate (*Haberdashers' Aske's and Pembroke*), J. N. Perry (*Ampleforth and Trinity*), G. A. Pointer (*St Dunstan's and St John's*), N. C. W. Fenton (*Rugby and Magdalene*).

OXFORD v CAMBRIDGE, RESULTS AND HUNDREDS

The University match dates back to 1827. Altogether there have been 143 official matches, Cambridge winning 54 and Oxford 46, with 43 drawn. The 1988 match was abandoned without a ball bowled. Results since 1950:

1950	Drawn
1951	Oxford won by 21 runs
1952	Drawn
1953	Cambridge won by two wickets
1954	Drawn
1955	Drawn
1956	Drawn
1957	Cambridge won by an innings and 186 runs
1958	Cambridge won by 99 runs
1959	Oxford won by 85 runs
1960	Drawn
1961	Drawn
1962	Drawn
1963	Drawn
1964	Drawn
1965	Drawn
1966	Oxford won by an innings and 9 runs
1967	Drawn
1968	Drawn
1969	Drawn
1970	Drawn
1971	Drawn
1972	Cambridge won by an innings and 25 runs
1973	Drawn
1974	Drawn
1975	Drawn
1976	Oxford won by ten wickets
1977	Drawn
1978	Drawn
1979	Cambridge won by an innings and 52 runs
1980	Drawn
1981	Drawn
1982	Cambridge won by seven wickets
1983	Drawn
1984	Oxford won by five wickets
1985	Drawn
1986	Cambridge won by five wickets
1987	Drawn
1988	Abandoned

Ninety-three three-figure innings have been played in the University matches. For those scored before 1919 see 1940 *Wisden*. Those subsequent to 1919 include the seven highest:

238*	Nawab of Pataudi, sen.	1931	Oxford
211	G. Goonesena	1957	Cam.
201*	M. J. K. Smith	1954	Oxford
201	A. Ratcliffe	1931	Cam.
200	Majid Khan	1970	Cam.
193	D. C. H. Townsend	1934	Oxford
174	P. A. C. Bail	1986	Cam.
170	M. Howell	1919	Oxford
167	B. W. Hone	1932	Oxford
158	P. M. Roebuck	1975	Cam.
157	D. R. Wilcox	1932	Cam.
155	F. S. Goldstein	1968	Oxford
149	J. T. Morgan	1929	Cam.
149	G. J. Toogood	1985	Oxford
146	R. O'Brien	1956	Cam.
146	D. R. Owen-Thomas	1971	Cam.
145*	H. E. Webb	1948	Oxford
145	D. P. Toft	1967	Oxford

142	M. P. Donnelly	1946 Oxford
140	M. A. Crawley	1987 Oxford
139	R. J. Boyd-Moss	1983 Cam.
136	E. T. Killick	1930 Cam.
135	H. A. Pawson	1947 Oxford
131	Nawab of Pataudi, jun.	1960 Oxford
129	H. J. Enthoven	1925 Cam.
128*	A. J. T. Miller	1984 Oxford
127	D. S. Sheppard	1952 Cam.
124	A. K. Judd	1927 Cam.
124	A. Ratcliffe	1932 Cam.
124	R. J. Boyd-Moss	1983 Cam.
122	P. A. Gibb	1938 Cam.
121	J. N. Grover	1937 Oxford
119	J. M. Brearley	1964 Cam.
118	H. Ashton	1921 Cam.
118	D. R. W. Silk	1954 Cam.
117	M. J. K. Smith	1956 Oxford
116*	D. R. W. Silk	1953 Cam.
116	M. C. Cowdrey	1953 Oxford
115	A. W. Allen	1934 Cam.
114*	D. R. Owen-Thomas	1972 Cam.
114	J. F. Pretlove	1955 Cam.
113*	J. M. Brearley	1962 Cam.
113	E. R. T. Holmes	1927 Oxford
112*	E. D. Fursdon	1975 Oxford
111*	G. W. Cook	1957 Cam.
109	C. H. Taylor	1923 Oxford
109	G. J. Toogood	1984 Oxford
108	F. G. H. Chalk	1934 Oxford
106	Nawab of Pataudi, sen.	1929 Oxford
105	E. J. Craig	1961 Cam.
104*	D. A. Thorne	1986 Oxford
104	H. J. Enthoven	1924 Cam.
104	M. J. K. Smith	1955 Oxford
103*	A. R. Lewis	1962 Cam.
103*	D. R. Pringle	1979 Cam.
102*	A. P. F. Chapman	1922 Cam.
101*	R. W. V. Robins	1928 Cam.
101	N. W. D. Yardley	1937 Cam.
100*	M. Manasseh	1964 Oxford
100	P. J. Dickinson	1939 Cam.
100	N. J. Cosh	1967 Cam.
100	R. J. Boyd-Moss	1982 Cam.

* *Signifies not out.*

Highest Totals

503	Oxford	1900
457	Oxford	1947
453-8	Oxford	1931
432-9	Cambridge	1936
431	Cambridge	1932
425	Cambridge	1938

Lowest Totals

2	Oxford	1878
9	Cambridge	1858
42	Oxford	1890
47	Cambridge	1838

otes: A. P. F. Chapman and M. P. Donnelly enjoy the following distinction: Chapman cored a century at Lord's in the University match (102*, 1922); for Gentlemen v Players (160, 922), (108, 1926); and for England v Australia (121, 1930). M. P. Donnelly scored a century Lord's in the University match (142, 1946); for Gentlemen v Players (162*, 1947); and for ew Zealand v England (206, 1949).

A. Ratcliffe's 201 for Cambridge in 1931 remained a record for the match for only one day, eing beaten by the Nawab of Pataudi's 238* for Oxford next day.

M. J. K. Smith (Oxford) and R. J. Boyd-Moss (Cambridge) are the only players who have ored three hundreds. Smith scored 201* in 1954, 104 in 1955, and 117 in 1956; Boyd-Moss ored 100 in 1982 and 139 and 124 in 1983. His aggregate of 489 surpassed Smith's previous cord of 477.

The following players have scored two hundreds: W. Yardley (Cambridge) 100 in 1870 and 0 in 1872; H. J. Enthoven (Cambridge) 104 in 1924 and 129 in 1925; Nawab of Pataudi xford) 106 in 1929 and 238* in 1931; A. Ratcliffe (Cambridge) 201 in 1931 and 124 1932; D. R. W. Silk (Cambridge) 116* in 1953 and 118 in 1954; J. M. Brearley (Camidge) 113* in 1962 and 119 in 1964; D. R. Owen-Thomas (Cambridge) 146 in 1971 and 4* in 1972; G. J. Toogood (Oxford) 109 in 1984 and 149 in 1985.

F. C. Cobden, in the Oxford v Cambridge match in 1870, performed the hat-trick by taking e last three wickets and won an extraordinary game for Cambridge by 2 runs. The feat is thout parallel in first-class cricket. Other hat-tricks, all for Cambridge, have been credited A. G. Steel (1879), P. H. Morton (1880), J. F. Ireland (1911), and R. G. H. Lowe (1926).

S. E. Butler, in the 1871 match, took all the wickets in the Cambridge first innings. The feat unique in University matches. He bowled 24.1 overs. In the follow-on he took five wickets 57, giving him match figures of fifteen for 95 runs.

The best all-round performances in the history of the match have come from P. R. Le Couteur, who scored 160 and took eleven Cambridge wickets for 66 runs in 1910, and G. J. Toogood, who in 1985 scored 149 and took ten Cambridge wickets for 93.

D. W. Jarrett (Oxford 1975, Cambridge 1976), S. M. Wookey (Cambridge 1975-76, Oxford 1978) and G. Pathmanathan (Oxford 1975-78, Cambridge 1983) are alone in gaining cricket Blues for both Universities.

July 9. Benson and Hedges Cup final. HAMPSHIRE beat DERBYSHIRE by seven wickets (See Benson and Hedges Cup section).

July 20. MCC beat MCC Schools by 23 runs (See MCC section).

MCC SCHOOLS v NATIONAL ASSOCIATION OF YOUNG CRICKETERS

July 21. MCC Schools won by six wickets. Toss: National Association of Young Cricketers. The Schools matches at Lord's followed the format introduced for the MCC Bicentenary, when two one-day matches were scheduled in place of the two-day match against NAYC. For this, the second of their two matches, MCC Schools brought in Derbyshire in place of I. J. Houseman (Harrogate GS), who had played against MCC the previous day. Ilott, bowling quickish left-arm, and Shahid, a leg-spinner, both with Essex, provided a contrasting check on the NAYC innings. They took seven of the eight wickets which fell before the declaration. MCC Schools began steadily with a half-century opening partnership from Knight and Lewis, and when Habib was bowled after a promising 60, just 6 runs were needed from the last three overs. A feature of both MCC Schools matches was the impeccable wicket-keeping of Kellaway.

National Association of Young Cricketers

P. Simmonite (*Lancashire*) c Ellison b Ilott . 18
P. Lunn (*Oxfordshire*) c and b Shahid . . 29
M. Bailey (*Staffordshire*) b Ball 34
A. Smith (*Surrey*) b Shahid 7
I. G. Steer (*Warwickshire*) c Ellison b Shahid . 17
P. J. Rendall (*Somerset*) c Kellaway b Ilott . 21
J. Meadows (*Gloucestershire*) c Knight b Shahid . 6
M. Saxelby (*Nottinghamshire*) b Ilott . . . 20
*†G. R. Sanders (*Nottinghamshire*) not out . 17
D. W. Headley (*Worcestershire*) not out . 1
L-b 10, w 2 1

1/31 2/89 3/95 4/106 5/119 6/131 7/163 8/178 (8 wkts dec.) 19

C. Cowell (*Surrey*) did not bat.

Bowling: Derbyshire 3–1–20–0; Ilott 22–3–72–3; Ellison 8–3–16–0; Ball 9–3–22–1; Shahi 21–11–51–4.

MCC Schools

J. J. Lewis (*King Edward VI, Chelmsford*) lbw b Lunn . 27
*N. V. Knight (*Felsted*) b Smith 26
D. A. Graham (*Chipping Campden*) c Bailey b Rendall . 35
A. Habib (*Taunton*) b Headley 60
N. J. Gregory (*Ipswich*) not out 1
N. Shahid (*Ipswich*) not out . . . .
B 2, l-b 19, n-b 7 . . . .

1/57 2/81 3/131 4/186 (4 wkts) 19

B. C. A. Ellison (*Rugby*), †M. J. Kellaway (*Eastleigh C of E*), M. C. J. Ball (*Bath C of E* N. A. Derbyshire (*Ampleforth*) and M. C. Ilott (*Francis Combe*) did not bat.

Bowling: Saxelby 9.3–0–32–0; Headley 9–0–35–1; Lunn 8–3–17–1; Cowell 5–2–25–0; Smi 13–2–40–1; Rendall 5–0–22–1.

Umpires: D. B. Harman and B. Wilson.

The National Cricket Association selected the following to play for NCA Young Cricketers against Combined Services: *N. V. Knight (*Essex*), J. J. Lewis (*Essex*), P. Simmonite (*Lancashire*), D. A. Graham (*Gloucestershire*), A. Habib (*Somerset*), N. Shahid (*Essex*), G. R. Sanders (*Nottinghamshire*), M. C. J. Ball (*Gloucestershire*), M. Saxelby (*Nottinghamshire*), I. J. Houseman (*Yorkshire*) and M. C. Ilott (*Essex*).

July 22. Drawn. Toss: NCA Young Cricketers. Combined Services 228 for five dec. (J. N. Doherty 50, J. P. Barrett 73, M. V. Fleming 51); NCA Young Cricketers 113 for four (P. Simmonite 62 not out).

WOLVERHAMPTON v ENFIELD

Cockspur Cup Final

August 19. Abandoned. Toss: Wolverhampton. Enfield 104 for two (30 overs) (M. Morgan 51 not out, A. J. Moulding 32 not out). The match was replayed at Birmingham on August 24 (See Other Matches, 1988).

NATIONAL CLUB CHAMPIONSHIP WINNERS 1969-88

1969 HAMPSTEAD beat Pocklington Pixies by 14 runs.
1970 CHELTENHAM beat Stockport by three wickets.
1971 BLACKHEATH beat Ealing by eight wickets.
1972 SCARBOROUGH beat Brentham by six wickets.
1973 WOLVERHAMPTON beat The Mote by five wickets.
1974 SUNBURY beat Tunbridge Wells by seven wickets.
1975 YORK beat Blackpool by six wickets.
1976 SCARBOROUGH beat Dulwich by five wickets.
1977 SOUTHGATE beat Bowdon by six wickets.
1978 CHELTENHAM beat Bishop's Stortford by 15 runs.
1979 SCARBOROUGH beat Reading by two wickets.
1980 MOSELEY beat Gosport Borough by nine wickets.
1981 SCARBOROUGH beat Blackheath by 57 runs.
1982 SCARBOROUGH beat Finchley by 4 runs.
1983 SHREWSBURY beat Hastings and St Leonards Priory by 2 runs.
1984 OLD HILL beat Bishop's Stortford by five wickets.
1985 OLD HILL beat Reading by nine wickets.
1986 STOURBRIDGE beat Weston-super-Mare by four wickets.
1987 OLD HILL beat Teddington by five wickets.
1988 ENFIELD beat Wolverhampton by nine wickets.

From 1969 to 1975, the Championship was contested for the D. H. Robins Trophy, from 1976 to 1982 for the John Haig Trophy, from 1983 to 1986 for the William Younger Cup, and since 1987 for the Cockspur Cup.

GOATACRE v HIMLEY

Hydro Village Championship Final

August 20. Abandoned. Himley 207 for six (40 overs) (S. A. Walker 44, J. E. Hughes 35); Goatacre 0 for no wkt. The match was replayed at Beckenham on August 21 (See Other Matches, 1988).

VILLAGE CHAMPIONSHIP WINNERS 1972-88

1972 TROON (Cornwall) beat Astwood Bank (Worcestershire) by seven wickets.
1973 TROON (Cornwall) beat Gowerton (Glamorgan) by 12 runs.
1974 BOMARSUND (Northumberland) beat Collingham (Nottinghamshire) by three wickets.
(Played at Edgbaston after being rained off at Lord's).
1975 GOWERTON (Glamorgan) beat Isleham (Cambridgeshire) by six wickets.
1976 TROON (Cornwall) beat Sessay (Yorkshire) by 18 runs.
1977 COOKLEY (Worcestershire) beat Lindal Moor (Cumbria) by 28 runs.
1978 LINTON PARK (Kent) beat Toft (Cheshire) by four wickets.
1979 EAST BIERLEY (Yorkshire) beat Ynysygerwn (Glamorgan) by 92 runs.
1980 MARCHWIEL (Clwyd) beat Longparish (Hampshire) by 79 runs.
1981 ST FAGANS (Glamorgan) beat Broad Oak (Yorkshire) by 22 runs.
1982 ST FAGANS (Glamorgan) beat Collingham (Nottinghamshire) by six wickets.
1983 QUARNDON (Derbyshire) beat Troon (Cornwall) by eight wickets.
1984 MARCHWIEL (Clwyd) beat Hursley Park (Hampshire) by 8 runs.
1985 FREUCHIE (Fife) beat Rowledge (Surrey) by virtue of fewer wickets lost with the scores level.
1986 FORGE VALLEY (Yorkshire) beat Ynysygerwn (Glamorgan) by 5 runs.
1987 LONGPARISH (Hampshire) beat Treeton Welfare (Yorkshire) by 76 runs.
1988 GOATACRE (Wiltshire) beat Himley (West Midlands) by four wickets.

From 1972 to 1977, the Village Championship was sponsored by John Haig Ltd, in 1978 by The Cricketer, *from 1979 to 1984 by Samuel Whitbread and Co. Ltd, and since 1986 by Hydro Fertilizers. There was no sponsor in 1985.*

August 25, 26, 27, 29, 30. Cornhill Test. ENGLAND beat SRI LANKA by seven wickets (See Sri Lankan tour section).

September 3. NatWest Bank Trophy final. MIDDLESEX beat WORCESTERSHIRE by three wickets (See NatWest Bank Trophy section).

MCC ENGLAND HONORARY CRICKET MEMBERS

C. J. Barnett
H. Larwood
L. E. G. Ames, CBE
Sir Leonard Hutton
D. C. S. Compton, CBE
D. V. P. Wright
T. G. Evans, CBE
C. Washbrook
A. V. Bedser, CBE
P. B. H. May, CBE
W. Watson
P. E. Richardson
T. E. Bailey
M. J. K. Smith, OBE
J. Hardstaff
J. B. Statham, CBE
F. S. Trueman
T. W. Graveney, OBE
G. A. R. Lock
C. Milburn
D. A. Allen
R. W. Barber
E. R. Dexter
P. H. Parfitt
F. H. Tyson
M. C. Cowdrey, CBE
J. T. Murray, MBE
J. M. Parks
D. B. Close, CBE
B. L. D'Oliveira, OBE
R. Illingworth, CBE
G. Pullar
F. J. Titmus, MBE
D. J. Brown
M. H. Denness
J. M. Brearley, OBE
R. W. Taylor, MBE
R. G. D. Willis, MBE
J. H. Edrich, MBE
A. P. E. Knott
C. M. Old
J. A. Snow

BRITANNIC ASSURANCE COUNTY CHAMPIONSHIP, 1988

The new-format County Championship came to an exciting climax, with three counties seeking maximum points from their last game in their bid to win the title: Worcestershire (266 points) to maintain their one-point lead at the top of the table if Kent also took 24 points; Kent (265 points) to take advantage should Worcestershire fail; Essex (261 points) to snatch the title should the front-runners falter. In the event, both Worcestershire and Kent finished the season in the manner of champions, winning by an innings with a day to spare and a full complement of points. Not even a puerile attempt to sabotage the pitch at Worcester could halt Worcestershire's defeat of bottom-placed Glamorgan, while Kent finally came to terms with the four-day game to defeat fourth-placed Surrey. Essex remained in third place and Nottinghamshire, the defending champions, finished fifth to claim a share of the prizemoney.

For the first time, some Championship matches were played over four days, and this had a significant bearing on the outcome. Each county played sixteen three-day matches – against the other sixteen counties – and six four-day matches, making a Championship programme of 22 fixtures. In most cases, three four-day games were played at the start and three at the end of the season, but Glamorgan, Hampshire, Surrey, Sussex and Yorkshire each played four at the end. This proved to be to Surrey's liking, helping them jump from tenth in mid-August to fourth, a repeat of their 1987 placing. Three of their seven wins came in four-day games, although ironically not one of these matches went into the fourth day.

Continued over

BRITANNIC ASSURANCE CHAMPIONSHIP

					Bonus points		
Win = 16 points	*Played*	*Won*	*Lost*	*Drawn*	*Batting*	*Bowling*	*Points*
1 – Worcestershire (9)	22	10	3	9	55	75	290
2 – Kent (14)	22	10	5	7	57	72	289
3 – Essex (12)	22	9	5	8	61	69	282
4 – Surrey (4)	22	7	5	10	57	72	241
5 – Nottinghamshire (1)	22	8	8	6	34	71	229
6 – Warwickshire (15)	22	6	8	8	48	74	218
7 – Middlesex (16)	22	7	3	12	49	54	215
8 – Leicestershire (3)	22	6	3	13	56	63	215
9 – Lancashire (2)	22	6	7	9	41	67	212
10 – Gloucestershire (10)	21	6	7	8	52	59	207
11 – Somerset (11)	22	5	6	11	48	65	201
12 – Northamptonshire (7)	22	5	7	10	48	71	199
13 – Yorkshire (8)	22	4	6	12	48	65	177
14 – Derbyshire (6)	22	4	3	15	53	54	171
15 – Hampshire (5)	22	4	6	12	33	69	166
16 – Sussex (17)	22	3	11	8	37	65	150
17 – Glamorgan (13)	21	1	8	12	42	53	111

1987 positions are shown in brackets.
The total for Nottinghamshire includes 12 points for a win in a one-innings match, and those for Essex, Lancashire and Somerset include 8 points for levelling the scores in a drawn match.

The following match was abandoned and is not included in the above table: May 28, 30, 31 – Glamorgan v Gloucestershire at Swansea.

Worcestershire, with their batting centred on the immense talent of Hick, were formidable in the four-day game, winning five of their six matches. Kent's bustling, aggressive approach, built on teamwork rather than individual talents, was better suited to the three-day game. Seven of their nine wins in three-day fixtures came when chasing a target, but they could win only one four-day game, their last. In the four-day matches, Worcestershire gained 85 per cent of the maximum points available, Kent only 34 per cent; yet in the three-day games, Kent gained 62 per cent to Worcestershire's 43 per cent. Third-placed Essex, with 59 per cent in the four-day games (three wins) and 51 per cent in the three-day games (six wins), were the county least affected by the new format. Nottinghamshire won seven three-day games – only Kent won more – but just one four-day match.

At the end of the first three rounds of four-day matches, Worcestershire headed the table with 69 points from Middlesex, Leicestershire and Essex. Kent were fifteenth with just 13 points, but they won their next six games to lead the table in mid-June. Apart from four days in August, they remained there until the penultimate round. Middlesex replaced Worcestershire at the top from mid-May until early June but fell to tenth before three wins in August lifted them back to fifth. In the end, they had to settle for seventh. Warwickshire were fourth in August, but three defeats in four games saw them slip out of the reckoning for the prizemoney. Lancashire, the previous season's runners-up, were fifteenth at the end of May, hinted at a challenge when moving into fourth at the beginning of August, but failed to sustain it and finished ninth.

The preparation of pitches to favour counties' bowling strengths continued to attract concern and criticism. Worcestershire's pitches were among those mentioned, but this should not detract from their achievement throughout the season. They were always one of the top three in the table, and such consistency over five months made them worthy champions.

REGULATIONS FOR BRITANNIC ASSURANCE CHAMPIONSHIP

(As applied in 1988)

1. Prizemoney

First (Worcestershire)	£35,00
Second (Kent)	£17,50
Third (Essex)	£10,00
Fourth (Surrey)	£5,00
Fifth (Nottinghamshire)	£2,50
Winner of each match	£21
Championship Player of the Year (F. D. Stephenson)	£50
County of the Month	£75
Player of the Month	£25

2. Scoring of Points

(*a*) For a win, sixteen points, plus any points scored in the first innings.

(*b*) In a tie, each side to score eight points, plus any points scored in the first innings.

(*c*) If the scores are equal in a drawn match, the side batting in the fourth innings to sco eight points, plus any points scored in the first innings.

(*d*) **First Innings Points** (awarded only for performances **in the first 100 overs** of each fir innings and retained whatever the result of the match).

(i) A maximum of four batting points to be available as under:
150 to 199 runs – 1 point; 200 to 249 runs – 2 points; 250 to 299 runs – 3 points; 300 runs or over – 4 points.

(ii) A maximum of four bowling points to be taken as under:
3 to 4 wickets taken – 1 point; 5 to 6 wickets taken – 2 points; 7 to 8 wickets taken – 3 points; 9 to 10 wickets taken – 4 points.

(*e*) If play starts when fewer than eight hours' playing time remains and a one innings match is played, no first innings points shall be scored. The side winning on the one innings to score twelve points.

(*f*) The side which has the highest aggregate of points gained at the end of the season shall be the Champion County. Should any sides in the Championship table be equal on points the side with most wins will have priority.

3. Hours of Play

1st, 2nd [3rd] days . . . 11.00 a.m. to 6.30 p.m. or after 110 overs, whichever is the later. (For Sunday play, the home county may decide to play from 12 noon to 7.30 p.m.)

Final day . . . . 11.00 a.m. to 6.00 p.m. or after 102 overs, whichever is the later.

(*a*) If play is suspended (including any interval between innings) the minimum number of overs to be bowled in a day to be reduced by one over for each 3½ minutes or part thereof of such suspension or suspensions in aggregate.

(*b*) If at 5.00 p.m. on the final day, nineteen overs or fewer remain to be bowled, the umpires shall indicate that play shall continue until a minimum of a further twenty overs has been bowled, or until 6.00 p.m., whichever is the later. Play may cease on the final day at any time between 5.30 p.m. and 6.00 p.m. by mutual agreement of the captains. Should an innings end between 4.50 p.m. and 5.00 p.m., the time at the end of the ten-minute interval shall replace 5.00 p.m.

(*c*) The captains may agree or, in the event of disagreement, the umpires may decide to play 30 minutes (or minimum ten overs) extra time at the end of the first and/or second day's play (and/or the third day of four) if, in their opinion, it would bring about a definite result on that day. In the event of the possibility of a finish disappearing before the full period has expired, the whole period must be played out. Any time so claimed does not affect the timing for cessation of play on the final day.

(*d*) If an innings ends during the course of an over, that part shall count as a full over so far as the minimum number of overs per day is concerned.

(*e*) If play is suspended for the day in the middle of an over, that over must be completed next day in addition to the minimum overs required that day.

Intervals

Lunch: 1.15 p.m. to 1.55 p.m. (1st, 2nd [3rd] days), 2.15 p.m. to 2.55 p.m. on Sundays when play commences at 12 noon
1.00 p.m. to 1.40 p.m. (final day)

Tea: 4.10 p.m. to 4.30 p.m. (1st, 2nd [3rd] days), 5.10 p.m. to 5.30 p.m. on Sundays when play commences at 12 noon, or when 40 overs remain to be bowled, whichever is the later.
3.40 p.m. to 4.00 p.m. (final day), or when 40 overs remain to be bowled, whichever is the later.

4. Substitutes

A substitute shall be allowed as of right in the event of a cricketer currently playing in a Championship match being required to join the England team for a Test match (or one-day international). Such substitutes may be permitted to bat or bowl in that match, subject to the approval of the TCCB. The player who is substituted may not take further part in the match, even though he might not be required by England. If batting at the time, the player substituted shall be retired "not out" and his substitute may be permitted to bat subject to the approval of the TCCB.

The opposing captain shall have no right of objection to any player acting as substitute in the field, nor as to where he shall field. However, no substitute may act as wicket-keeper.

No substitute may take the field until the player for whom he is to substitute has been absent from the field for five consecutive complete overs.

5. New ball

The captain of the fielding side shall have the choice of taking the new ball after 100 overs have been bowled with the old one.

6. Covering of Pitches and Bowler's Run-up

The whole pitch shall be covered:

(*a*) The night before a match and, if necessary, until the first ball is bowled.

(*b*) On each night of a match and, if necessary, throughout Sunday. In the event of play being suspended because of bad light or rain, during the hours of play.

The bowler's run-up shall be covered to a distance of at least ten yards, with a width of four yards.

7. Declarations

Law 14 will apply, but, in addition, a captain may also forfeit his first innings, subject to the provisions set out in Law 14.2. If, owing to weather conditions, the match has not started when fewer than eight hours of playing time remain, the first innings of each side shall automatically be forfeited and a one-innings match played.

CHAMPION COUNTY SINCE 1864

Note: The earliest county champions were decided usually by the fewest matches lost, but in 1888 an unofficial points system was introduced. In 1890, the Championship was constituted officially. From 1977 to 1983 it was sponsored by Schweppes, and since 1984 by Britannic Assurance.

1864	Surrey
1865	Nottinghamshire
1866	Middlesex
1867	Yorkshire
1868	Nottinghamshire
1869	Nottinghamshire Yorkshire
1870	Yorkshire
1871	Nottinghamshire
1872	Nottinghamshire
1873	Gloucestershire Nottinghamshire
1874	Gloucestershire
1875	Nottinghamshire
1876	Gloucestershire
1877	Gloucestershire
1878	Undecided
1879	Nottinghamshire Lancashire
1880	Nottinghamshire
1881	Lancashire
1882	Nottinghamshire Lancashire
1883	Nottinghamshire
1884	Nottinghamshire
1885	Nottinghamshire
1886	Nottinghamshire
1887	Surrey
1888	Surrey
1889	Surrey Lancashire Nottinghamshire
1890	Surrey
1891	Surrey
1892	Surrey
1893	Yorkshire
1894	Surrey
1895	Surrey
1896	Yorkshire
1897	Lancashire
1898	Yorkshire
1899	Surrey
1900	Yorkshire
1901	Yorkshire
1902	Yorkshire
1903	Middlesex
1904	Lancashire
1905	Yorkshire
1906	Kent
1907	Nottinghamshire
1908	Yorkshire
1909	Kent
1910	Kent
1911	Warwickshire
1912	Yorkshire
1913	Kent
1914	Surrey
1919	Yorkshire
1920	Middlesex
1921	Middlesex
1922	Yorkshire
1923	Yorkshire
1924	Yorkshire
1925	Yorkshire
1926	Lancashire
1927	Lancashire
1928	Lancashire
1929	Nottinghamshire
1930	Lancashire
1931	Yorkshire
1932	Yorkshire
1933	Yorkshire
1934	Lancashire
1935	Yorkshire
1936	Derbyshire
1937	Yorkshire
1938	Yorkshire
1939	Yorkshire
1946	Yorkshire
1947	Middlesex
1948	Glamorgan
1949	Middlesex Yorkshire
1950	Lancashire Surrey
1951	Warwickshire
1952	Surrey
1953	Surrey
1954	Surrey
1955	Surrey
1956	Surrey
1957	Surrey
1958	Surrey
1959	Yorkshire
1960	Yorkshire
1961	Hampshire
1962	Yorkshire
1963	Yorkshire
1964	Worcestershire
1965	Worcestershire
1966	Yorkshire
1967	Yorkshire
1968	Yorkshire
1969	Glamorgan
1970	Kent
1971	Surrey
1972	Warwickshire
1973	Hampshire
1974	Worcestershire
1975	Leicestershire
1976	Middlesex
1977	Middlesex Kent
1978	Kent
1979	Essex
1980	Middlesex
1981	Nottinghamshire
1982	Middlesex
1983	Essex
1984	Essex
1985	Middlesex
1986	Essex
1987	Nottinghamshire
1988	Worcestershire

Notes: The title has been won outright as follows: Yorkshire 31 times, Surrey 18, Nottinghamshire 14, Middlesex 9, Lancashire 8, Kent 6, Essex 4, Worcestershire 4, Gloucestershire 3, Warwickshire 3, Glamorgan 2, Hampshire 2, Derbyshire 1, Leicestershire 1.

Eight times the title has been shared as follows: Nottinghamshire 5, Lancashire 4, Middlesex 2, Surrey 2, Yorkshire 2, Gloucestershire 1, Kent 1.

The earliest date the Championship has been won in any season since it was expanded in 1895 was August 12, 1910, by Kent.

BRITANNIC ASSURANCE CHAMPIONSHIP STATISTICS FOR 1988

	For			*Against*		
County	*Runs*	*Wickets*	*Avge*	*Runs*	*Wickets*	*Avge*
Derbyshire	9,748	308	31.64	8,490	256	33.16
Essex	9,324	278	33.53	9,143	333	27.45
Glamorgan	8,417	295	28.53	9,046	256	35.33
Gloucestershire	9,067	311	29.15	9,175	318	28.85
Hampshire	8,957	332	26.97	8,597	294	29.24
Kent	9,208	324	28.41	9,591	344	27.88
Lancashire	8,622	334	25.81	8,747	318	27.50
Leicestershire	8,464	299	28.30	8,347	304	27.45
Middlesex	8,829	275	32.10	8,072	297	27.17
Northamptonshire	8,611	320	26.90	9,220	337	27.35
Nottinghamshire	8,618	362	23.80	8,542	333	25.65
Somerset	8,462	291	29.07	9,682	327	29.60
Surrey	7,853	266	29.52	8,321	313	26.58
Sussex	9,013	355	25.38	9,343	296	31.56
Warwickshire	8,389	342	24.52	8,596	333	25.81
Worcestershire	9,014	269	33.50	8,347	325	25.68
Yorkshire	9,100	313	29.07	8,437	290	29.09
	149,696	5,274	28.38	149,696	5,274	28.38

COUNTY CHAMPIONSHIP – MATCH RESULTS, 1864-1988

County	*Years of Play*	*Played*	*Won*	*Lost*	*Tied*	*Drawn*
erbyshire	1871-87; 1895-1988	2,068	505	756	1	806
ssex	1895-1988	2,031	564	592	5	870
lamorgan	1921-1988	1,565	338	542	0	685
loucestershire	1870-1988	2,306	684	849	2	771
ampshire	1864-85; 1895-1988	2,140	558	740	4	838
ent	1864-1988	2,428	889	737	4	798
ancashire	1865-1988	2,506	937	509	3	1,057
eicestershire	1895-1988	1,998	431	746	1	820
iddlesex	1864-1988	2,208	823	567	5	813
orthamptonshire	1905-1988	1,765	418	626	3	718
ottinghamshire	1864-1988	2,337	713	610	0	1,014
merset	1882-85; 1891-1988	2,038	478	841	3	716
rrey	1864-1988	2,585	1,034	564	4	983
ssex	1864-1988	2,477	695	857	5	920
arwickshire	1895-1988	2,012	523	592	1	896
orcestershire	1899-1988	1,953	474	699	1	779
rkshire	1864-1988	2,606	1,186	423	2	995
mbridgeshire	1864-69; 1871	19	8	8	0	3
		18,521	11,258	11,258	22	7,241

tes: Matches abandoned without a ball bowled are wholly excluded.

Counties participated in the years shown, except that there were no matches in the years 5-18 and 1940-45; Hampshire did not play inter-county matches in 1868-69, 1871-74 and 9; Worcestershire did not take part in the Championship in 1919.

COUNTY CHAMPIONSHIP – FINAL POSITIONS, 1890-1988

	Derbyshire	Essex	Glamorgan	Gloucestershire	Hampshire	Kent	Lancashire	Leicestershire	Middlesex	Northamptonshire	Nottinghamshire	Somerset	Surrey	Sussex	Warwickshire	Worcestershire	Yorkshire
1890	—	—	—	6	—	3	2	—	7	—	5	—	1	8	—	—	3
1891	—	—	—	9	—	5	2	—	3	—	4	5	1	7	—	—	8
1892	—	—	—	7	—	7	4	—	5	—	2	3	1	9	—	—	6
1893	—	—	—	9	—	4	2	—	3	—	6	8	5	7	—	—	1
1894	—	—	—	9	—	4	4	—	3	—	7	6	1	8	—	—	2
1895	5	9	—	4	10	14	2	12	6	—	12	8	1	11	6	—	3
1896	7	5	—	10	8	9	2	13	3	—	6	11	4	14	12	—	1
1897	14	3	—	5	9	12	1	13	8	—	10	11	2	6	7	—	4
1898	9	5	—	3	12	7	6	13	2	—	8	13	4	9	9	—	1
1899	15	6	—	9	10	8	4	13	2	—	10	13	1	5	7	12	3
1900	13	10	—	7	15	3	2	14	7	—	5	11	7	3	6	12	1
1901	15	10	—	14	7	7	3	12	2	—	9	12	6	4	5	11	1
1902	10	13	—	14	15	7	5	11	12	—	3	7	4	2	6	9	1
1903	12	8	—	13	14	8	4	14	1	—	5	10	11	2	7	6	3
1904	10	14	—	9	15	3	1	7	4	—	5	12	11	6	7	13	2
1905	14	12	—	8	16	6	2	5	11	13	10	15	4	3	7	8	1
1906	16	7	—	9	8	1	4	15	11	11	5	11	3	10	6	14	2
1907	16	7	—	10	12	8	6	11	5	15	1	14	4	13	9	2	2
1908	14	11	—	10	9	2	7	13	4	15	8	16	3	5	12	6	1
1909	15	14	—	16	8	1	2	13	6	7	10	11	5	4	12	8	3
1910	15	11	—	12	6	1	4	10	3	9	5	16	2	7	14	13	8
1911	14	6	—	12	11	2	4	15	3	10	8	16	5	13	1	9	7
1912	12	15	—	11	6	3	4	13	5	2	8	14	7	10	9	16	1
1913	13	15	—	9	10	1	8	14	6	4	5	16	3	7	11	12	2
1914	12	8	—	16	5	3	11	13	2	9	10	15	1	6	7	14	4
1919	9	14	—	8	7	2	5	9	13	12	3	5	4	11	15	—	1
1920	16	9	—	8	11	5	2	13	1	14	7	10	3	6	12	15	4
1921	12	15	17	7	6	4	5	11	1	13	8	10	2	9	16	14	3
1922	11	8	16	13	6	4	5	14	7	15	2	10	3	9	12	17	1
1923	10	13	16	11	7	5	3	14	8	17	2	9	4	6	12	15	1
1924	17	15	13	6	12	5	4	11	2	16	6	8	3	10	9	14	1
1925	14	7	17	10	9	5	3	12	6	11	4	15	2	13	8	16	1
1926	11	9	8	15	7	3	1	13	6	16	4	14	5	10	12	17	[illegible]
1927	5	8	15	12	13	4	1	7	9	16	2	14	6	10	11	17	[illegible]
1928	10	16	15	5	12	2	1	9	8	13	3	14	6	7	11	17	4
1929	7	12	17	4	11	8	2	9	6	13	1	15	10	4	14	16	[illegible]
1930	9	6	11	2	13	5	1	12	16	17	4	13	8	7	15	10	
1931	7	10	15	2	12	3	6	16	11	17	5	13	8	4	9	14	
1932	10	14	15	13	8	3	6	12	10	16	4	7	5	2	9	17	
1933	6	4	16	10	14	3	5	17	12	13	8	11	9	2	7	15	
1934	3	8	13	7	14	5	1	12	10	17	9	15	11	2	4	16	
1935	2	9	13	15	16	10	4	6	3	17	5	14	11	7	8	12	
1936	1	9	16	4	10	8	11	15	2	17	5	7	6	14	13	12	
1937	3	6	7	4	14	12	9	16	2	17	10	13	8	5	11	15	
1938	5	6	16	10	14	9	4	15	2	17	12	7	3	8	13	11	
1939	9	4	13	3	15	5	6	17	2	16	12	14	8	10	11	7	
1946	15	8	6	5	10	6	3	11	2	16	13	4	11	17	14	8	
1947	5	11	9	2	16	4	3	14	1	17	11	11	6	9	15	7	
1948	6	13	1	8	9	15	5	11	3	17	14	12	2	16	7	10	
1949	15	9	8	7	16	13	11	17	1	6	11	9	5	13	4	3	

	Derbyshire	Essex	Glamorgan	Gloucestershire	Hampshire	Kent	Lancashire	Leicestershire	Middlesex	Northamptonshire	Nottinghamshire	Somerset	Surrey	Sussex	Warwickshire	Worcestershire	Yorkshire
1950	5	17	11	7	12	9	1	16	14	10	15	7	1	13	4	6	3
1951	11	8	5	12	9	16	3	15	7	13	17	14	6	10	1	4	2
1952	4	10	7	9	12	15	3	6	5	8	16	17	1	13	10	14	2
1953	6	12	10	6	14	16	3	3	5	11	8	17	1	2	9	15	12
1954	3	15	4	13	14	11	10	16	7	7	5	17	1	9	6	11	2
1955	8	14	16	12	3	13	9	6	5	7	11	17	1	4	9	15	2
1956	12	11	13	3	6	16	2	17	5	4	8	15	1	9	14	9	7
1957	4	5	9	12	13	14	6	17	7	2	15	8	1	9	11	16	3
958	5	6	15	14	2	8	7	12	10	4	17	3	1	13	16	9	11
959	7	9	6	2	8	13	5	16	10	11	17	12	3	15	4	14	1
960	5	6	11	8	12	10	2	17	3	9	16	14	7	4	15	13	1
961	7	6	14	5	1	11	13	9	3	16	17	10	15	8	12	4	2
962	7	9	14	4	10	11	16	17	13	8	15	6	5	12	3	2	1
963	17	12	2	8	10	13	15	16	6	7	9	3	11	4	4	14	1
964	12	10	11	17	12	7	14	16	6	3	15	8	4	9	2	1	5
965	9	15	3	10	12	5	13	14	6	2	17	7	8	16	11	1	4
966	9	16	14	15	11	4	12	8	12	5	17	3	7	10	6	2	1
967	6	15	14	17	12	2	11	2	7	9	15	8	4	13	10	5	1
968	8	14	3	16	5	2	6	9	10	13	4	12	15	17	11	7	1
969	16	6	1	2	5	10	15	14	11	9	8	17	3	7	4	12	13
970	7	12	2	17	10	1	3	15	16	14	11	13	5	9	7	6	4
971	17	10	16	8	9	4	3	5	6	14	12	7	1	11	2	15	13
972	17	5	13	3	9	2	15	6	8	4	14	11	12	16	1	7	10
973	16	8	11	5	1	4	12	9	13	3	17	10	2	15	7	6	14
974	17	12	16	14	2	10	8	4	6	3	15	5	7	13	9	1	11
975	15	7	9	16	3	5	4	1	11	8	13	12	6	17	14	10	2
976	15	6	17	3	12	14	16	4	1	2	13	7	9	10	5	11	8
977	7	6	14	3	11	1	16	5	1	9	17	4	14	8	10	13	12
978	14	2	13	10	8	1	12	6	3	17	7	5	16	9	11	15	4
979	16	1	17	10	12	5	13	6	14	11	9	8	3	4	15	2	7
980	9	8	13	7	17	16	15	10	1	12	3	5	2	4	14	11	6
81	12	5	14	13	7	9	16	8	4	15	1	3	6	2	17	11	10
82	11	7	16	15	3	13	12	2	1	9	4	6	5	8	17	14	10
83	9	1	15	12	3	7	12	4	2	6	14	10	8	11	5	16	17
84	12	1	13	17	15	5	16	4	3	11	2	7	8	6	9	10	14
85	13	4	12	3	2	9	14	16	1	10	8	17	6	7	15	5	11
86	11	1	17	2	6	8	15	7	12	9	4	16	3	14	12	5	10
87	6	12	13	10	5	14	2	3	16	7	1	11	4	17	15	9	8
88	14	3	17	10	15	2	9	8	7	12	5	11	4	16	6	1	13

te: From 1969 onwards, positions have been given in accordance with the Championship gulations which state that "Should *any* sides in the table be equal on points the side with ost wins will have priority".

DERBYSHIRE

President: The Duke of Devonshire
Chairman: C. N. Middleton
Chairman, Cricket Committee: G. L. Willatt
Secretary: I. Edwards
County Ground, Nottingham Road, Derby DE2 6DA (Telephone: 0332-383211)
Captain: K. J. Barnett
Coach: P. E. Russell

Derbyshire's best days came early in the season, culminating in thei Benson and Hedges Cup semi-final victory over Glamorgan at Swansea It proved to be their peak although, until then, they had played som excellent cricket in three competitions. Derbyshire flopped in the Benso and Hedges final at Lord's and the acknowledged importance of the tos could not disguise that. The quarter-final of the NatWest Bank Trophy in which they again lost to Hampshire, was their last glimpse of success and from that point there was an increasing sense that they were drifting Their overall performance in the Refuge Assurance League was poo and they slipped in the Britannic Assurance Championship, from sixt in 1987 to an undistinguished fourteenth. Derbyshire found it hard t dismiss opponents twice and, although they lost only three games, a tota of fifteen draws was the highest in the Championship. Pitches at Derb and Chesterfield tended to be too bland, lacking the essential balanc between bat and ball. Coupled with moderate bowling, this produce some dull cricket in home games.

Michael Holding was a giant in the knockout games and established world record for limited-overs cricket when he took eight for 21 in th NatWest Trophy elimination of Sussex at Hove. It was a marvellou piece of bowling and his contributions with bat as well as ball were vit to success in the Benson and Hedges Cup. But he had a thin time in th Championship. Although Paul Newman began with a match-winnir eight for 29 against Yorkshire and Allan Warner provided reliab support, the only consistently effective bowler was Ole Mortensen. H 34 wickets cost 13.64 each, and his command of length and dire tion echoed the highest traditions of Derbyshire seam bowling. Unfo tunately, a series of injuries limited him to twelve Championsh matches. On occasions, Devon Malcolm was startlingly fast; at othe his tendency to pitch consistently short led to severe punishment a there seemed to be no middle ground.

Kim Barnett led the team with his usual verve and optimism. H batting matured significantly and his ability to play longer innin suggested an increased appetite for runs. His 175 against Gloucestershi was a remarkable display of complete domination, and his unbeaten 2 against Leicestershire was the third-highest score in Derbyshire's histo The batting was strengthened by two newcomers, Peter Bowler and Ste Goldsmith. Bowler immediately settled with a century on his déb against Cambridge University, completing a unique double as he h scored 100 not out on his first appearance for Leicestershire in 19

Before he joined Derbyshire, Bowler had played in only ten first-class natches; in 1988 he scored four hundreds in a total of 1,725 first-class runs and provided much-needed stability in a potentially volatile batting order. In the process, he eclipsed the previous best total in a début season for Derbyshire, 1,510 by Chris Wilkins in 1970. Goldsmith had played wice for Kent in the Championship before being released and, in contrast to Bowler's patient accumulation, attacked vigorously, if not always with total discretion. Goldsmith can play thrilling strokes and it was a notable feat to score 1,071 runs in his first season.

Unfortunately for Derbyshire, cracks appeared elsewhere. John Morris had a respectable season but, it was felt in Derbyshire, one of nder-achievement. He has the talent, range of strokes and strength to be major force in the English game. Bruce Roberts declined sharply after ollowing an excellent season in 1987 with a good winter for Transvaal. He began to score runs with any degree of consistency only after ropping down the order. That move meant a promotion for Bernie Maher, who also maintained his wicket-keeping standards and has ecome a very useful county cricketer. Tim O'Gorman, who was tudying law at Durham University, showed promise, and Chris Adams, ne only Derbyshire-born player retained on the staff for 1989, made an ncouraging début. Opportunities were limited for Rajeshwar Sharma, Frank Griffith showed all-round promise late in the season, but Martin ean-Jacques has not developed as quickly as Derbyshire had hoped.

Derbyshire made a third signing during the winter and, as a result, ound themselves appearing before the TCCB discipline committee. hey engaged seam bowler Simon Base from Glamorgan and were fined 2,000 for making an illegal approach, a penalty which may be regarded the future as cricket's first transfer fee. In addition, Base was ispended until July 1, and only in the closing weeks of the season did he egin to show why Derbyshire were so keen to have him.

At the end of 1988, John Wright and Roger Finney retired from ounty cricket. Wright, one of the finest batsmen in Derbyshire's history, ined the county in 1977 and was seen at his best in partnership with the outh African, Peter Kirsten. After the arrival of Holding and the troduction of a limitation on the number of overseas players, Wright as seen less often, but at Weston-super-Mare he had the satisfaction of ading Derbyshire to one of their four Championship victories. Finney as one of the young players who helped Barnett to re-establish the team d developed into a valued all-rounder. In 1987, he lost his ability to owl a sharp left-arm in-swing and became a spinner. Last season, his w style also deserted him and he decided to leave the game. For 1989, erbyshire have engaged the promising West Indian fast bowler, Ian shop, fighting off competition from several other counties. One of the tractions for Bishop was the prospect of learning from Holding, and erbyshire will be hoping that one of the greatest of all West Indian fast wlers has another good season left. Hoping, too, that their pitches can ow more legitimate life. – Gerald Mortimer.

DERBYSHIRE 1988

[*Bill Smith*

Back row: F. A. Griffith, K. M. Krikken, T. J. G. O'Gorman, D. E. Malcolm, S. J. Base, P. D. Bowler, M. Wakefield, C. J. Adams. *Middle row:* S. W. Tacey (*scorer*), M. Jean-Jacques, R. Sharma, A. E. Warner, B. J. M. Maher, M. Beardshall, S. C. Goldsmith, I. Edwards (*secretary*), J. D. Brown (*youth coaching organiser*). *Front row:* B. Roberts, P. G. Newman, J. E. Morris, A. Hill (*assistant coach*), K. J. Barnett (*captain*), P. E. Russell (*coach*), R. J. Finney,

DERBYSHIRE RESULTS

All first-class matches – Played 24: Won 5, Lost 3, Drawn 16.

County Championship matches – Played 22: Won 4, Lost 3, Drawn 15.

Bonus points – Batting 53, Bowling 54.

Competition placings – Britannic Assurance County Championship, 14th; NatWest Bank Trophy, q-f; Benson and Hedges Cup, finalists; Refuge Assurance League, 12th equal.

BRITANNIC ASSURANCE CHAMPIONSHIP AVERAGES

BATTING

	Birthplace	*M*	*I*	*NO*	*R*	*HI*	*Avge*
‡K. J. Barnett	*Stoke-on-Trent*	17	27	2	1,406	239*	56.24
‡R. J. Finney	*Darley Dale*	3	5	2	142	52*	47.33
P. D. Bowler	*Plymouth*	22	40	4	1,563	159*	43.41
‡J. G. Wright	*Darfield, NZ*	11	20	1	815	154*	42.89
‡J. E. Morris	*Crewe*	21	35	5	1,163	175	38.76
S. C. Goldsmith	*Ashford, Kent*	22	37	4	956	89	28.96
‡B. J. M. Maher	*Hillingdon*	22	38	6	920	121*	28.75
‡B. Roberts	*Lusaka, N. Rhodesia*	22	37	4	903	71	27.36
R. Sharma	*Nairobi, Kenya*	9	13	2	275	80	25.00
T. J. G. O'Gorman	*Woking*	4	8	0	152	78	19.00
F. A. Griffith	*Whipps Cross, London*	4	6	1	87	37	17.40
‡A. E. Warner	*Birmingham*	18	25	6	300	45	15.78
‡P. G. Newman	*Leicester*	14	18	5	174	39	13.38
‡M. A. Holding	*Kingston, Jamaica*	11	12	2	129	30*	12.90
‡O. H. Mortensen	*Vejle, Denmark*	12	12	8	46	15	11.50
S. J. Base	*Maidstone*	7	9	3	51	15	8.50
D. E. Malcolm	*Kingston, Jamaica*	19	21	5	119	22	7.43
M. Jean-Jacques	*Soufrière, Dominica*	3	4	0	5	5	1.25

Also batted: C. J. Adams (*Whitwell*) (1 match) 21.

* *Signifies not out.* ‡ *Denotes county cap.* § *Not qualified for England.*

he following played a total of eleven three-figure innings for Derbyshire in County hampionship matches – K. J. Barnett 4, P. D. Bowler 3, J. E. Morris 2, B. J. M. Maher 1, G. Wright 1.

BOWLING

	O	*M*	*R*	*W*	*BB*	*5W/i*	*Avge*
H. Mortensen	233.3	73	464	34	6-35	4	13.64
G. Newman	306.5	70	877	32	8-29	1	27.40
E. Warner	416	92	1,091	37	4-36	0	29.48
J. Barnett	158.1	35	411	13	3-63	0	31.61
E. Malcolm	468	85	1,642	50	6-68	2	32.84
A. Holding	279.1	49	827	24	4-74	0	34.45
J. Base	165	12	654	17	4-74	0	38.47

Also bowled: P. D. Bowler 169.5–28–577–7; R. J. Finney 45–8–131–0; S. C. Goldsmith -8–125–0; F. A. Griffith 80.3–17–268–9; M. Jean-Jacques 84.1–14–262–8; J. E. Morris -0–19–0; B. Roberts 99–21–300–8; R. Sharma 208.2–47–559–7.

cket-keeper: B. J. M. Maher 51 ct, 1 st.

ading Fielder: S. C. Goldsmith 16.

At Cambridge, April 16, 17, 18. DERBYSHIRE beat CAMBRIDGE UNIVERSITY by ar innings and 214 runs.

DERBYSHIRE v LEICESTERSHIRE

At Derby, April 21, 22, 23, 25. Drawn. Derbyshire 4 pts, Leicestershire 7 pts. Toss: Leicester shire. Impressive bowling by Agnew, Taylor and, particularly, Lewis soon had Derbyshire i trouble, but they were rescued by Maher's fine century. He reached 100 in 255 minutes from 222 balls with eleven fours as Derbyshire's last four wickets added 231. Derbyshire did nc bowl well as bitter cold gripped the match. Potter and Whitaker shared a fifth-wicke partnership of 199 and both scored centuries, Potter's first for Leicestershire coming in 23 minutes from 219 balls with a six and thirteen fours. In all, Whitaker batted for 312 minutes faced 303 balls and hit nineteen fours. Leicestershire having established a lead of 158, Derby shire could not think in terms of a declaration until they had ensured their own safety. Afte an opening partnership of 121 between Wright and Bowler, a draw became increasingly likely especially as Agnew did not bowl on the last day because of a shoulder injury.

Close of play: First day, Derbyshire 289-9 (B. J. M. Maher 101*, D. E. Malcolm 7*); Secon day, Leicestershire 231-4 (J. J. Whitaker 52*, L. Potter 3*); Third day, Derbyshire 66-0 (P. D Bowler 24*, J. G. Wright 42*).

Derbyshire

P. D. Bowler c Whitticase b Lewis	30	– b DeFreitas	4
J. G. Wright c Whitticase b Agnew	6	– b Willey	8
B. Roberts c Willey b Taylor	0	– c Potter b Taylor	4
J. E. Morris c and b Taylor	4	– st Whitticase b Willey	
*K. J. Barnett c Whitticase b Lewis	38	– c Gower b Willey	2
S. C. Goldsmith c Whitticase b Lewis	0	– c Lewis b DeFreitas	4
†B. J. M. Maher not out	121	– lbw b Lewis	1
R. J. Finney c Whitticase b Willey	33	– not out	5
A. E. Warner b Lewis	39	– c and b DeFreitas	
P. G. Newman lbw b Agnew	26	– not out	
D. E. Malcolm b Lewis	22		
L-b 4, w 1	5	L-b 7, w 2	
1/19 2/28 3/40 4/58 5/58 6/93 7/152 8/215 9/272	324	1/121 2/133 3/143 4/189 5/193 6/257 7/266 8/279	(8 wkts dec.) 3

Bonus points – Derbyshire 3, Leicestershire 3 (Score at 100 overs: 255-8).

Bowling: *First Innings*—Agnew 27–9–57–2; DeFreitas 30–7–94–0; Taylor 20–4–78–2; Lev 26.5–5–73–5; Willey 15–8–11–1; Potter 1–0–7–0. *Second Innings*—DeFreitas 39–14–93- Agnew 6–3–8–0; Lewis 30–7–109–1; Willey 43–17–62–3; Taylor 17–5–43–1; Potter 5–2–9-

Leicestershire

T. J. Boon c Goldsmith b Warner	31
N. E. Briers lbw b Bowler	90
P. Willey c Maher b Newman	34
*D. I. Gower run out	14
J. J. Whitaker b Warner	145
L. Potter c Barnett b Newman	107
P. A. J. DeFreitas c Maher b Newman	17
C. C. Lewis run out	1
†P. Whitticase not out	
J. P. Agnew not out	
L-b 8, n-b 6	
1/63 2/108 3/127 4/219 5/418 6/446 7/450 8/452	(8 wkts dec.) 4

L. B. Taylor did not bat.

Bonus points – Leicestershire 4, Derbyshire 1 (Score at 100 overs: 311-4).

Bowling: Newman 33–7–105–3; Malcolm 21–1–103–0; Finney 42–8–117–0; War 38–11–95–2; Bowler 22–3–54–1.

Umpires: H. D. Bird and J. H. Hampshire.

At Leeds, April 28, 29, 30. DERBYSHIRE beat YORKSHIRE by five wickets.

DERBYSHIRE v ESSEX

At Chesterfield, May 5, 6, 7, 9. Drawn. Derbyshire 3 pts, Essex 8 pts. Toss: Derbyshire. A fine match of fluctuating fortunes contained three outstanding performances and reached a thrilling climax which illustrated many virtues of the four-day game on a good pitch. Derbyshire made a good start with an opening partnership of 101; that they failed to take advantage of it was largely because of Topley's excellent bowling, seven for 75 being the best performance of his career. Border showed exactly the right approach with a masterly unbeaten 169, his highest for the county, although he finished with a runner after a blow from Malcolm. He batted for 409 minutes, faced 364 balls and hit a six and 24 fours. Essex were 156 ahead, but Bowler carried his bat for 159 (422 minutes, 344 balls, thirteen fours), negotiated Topley, who took his match figures to twelve for 179, and enabled Derbyshire to leave a target of 185 in what became 60 overs. Gooch soon became Essex's only hope, and when he was out they were obliged to hold on, with Topley and Pont surviving the last four overs.

Close of play: First day, Derbyshire 188-6 (S. C. Goldsmith 21*, D. E. Malcolm 0*); Second day, Essex 314-4 (A. R. Border 141*, J. P. Stephenson 66*); Third day, Derbyshire 261-6 (P. D. Bowler 120*, D. E. Malcolm 1*).

Derbyshire

'K. J. Barnett b Topley	52	– c East b Topley	23
'. D. Bowler b Topley	42	– not out	159
. Roberts lbw b Topley	31	– c Stephenson b Topley	14
. E. Morris c Border b Gooch	22	– c East b Gooch	18
. C. Goldsmith c and b Topley	22	– (7) c Fletcher b Pont	52
B. J. M. Maher c Topley b Gooch	4	– (5) lbw b Topley	13
I. Jean-Jacques c East b Pont	5	– (11) c East b Lever	0
). E. Malcolm c East b Topley	12	– c East b Topley	7
1. A. Holding c Prichard b Topley	3	– (10) b Lever	12
'. G. Newman c Gooch b Topley	5	– (9) c Fletcher b Lever	18
. E. Warner not out	9	– (6) c Gooch b Topley	3
B 2, l-b 4, n-b 5	11	B 1, l-b 10, n-b 10	21
/101 2/108 3/141 4/156 5/166 '/188 7/194 8/203 9/204	218	1/29 2/61 3/118 4/159 5/171 6/260 7/275 8/312 9/340	340

Bonus points – Derbyshire 2, Essex 4.

Bowling: *First Innings*—Lever 27–11–45–0; Pont 14–2–60–1; Topley 26.3–6–75–7; Gooch -2–29–2; Border 2–0–3–0. *Second Innings*—Lever 33.3–2–103–3; Topley 45–11–104–5; ooch 14–5–29–1; Pont 27–0–93–1.

ssex

. A. Gooch c Barnett b Malcolm	85	– lbw b Holding	56
R. Hardie c Newman b Holding	1	– c Roberts b Newman	5
J. Prichard c Malcolm b Newman	2	– lbw b Warner	11
R. Border not out	169	– (5) lbw b Malcolm	0
W. Lilley c Roberts b Malcolm	1	– (6) c Maher b Malcolm	8
P. Stephenson c Maher b Holding	74	– (4) run out	11
. W. R. Fletcher c Maher b Holding	0	– c Jean-Jacques b Warner	3
). E. East c Maher b Holding	0	– c Bowler b Warner	1
L. Pont b Jean-Jacques	6	– (11) not out	0
D. Topley b Jean-Jacques	5	– (9) not out	5
K. Lever c Barnett b Jean-Jacques	4	– (10) b Malcolm	0
B 1, l-b 10, w 8, n-b 8	27	L-b 10, n-b 1	11
' 2/12 3/145 4/151 5/329 29 7/332 8/360 9/370	374	1/12 2/37 3/55 4/55 5/70 6/82 7/86 8/107 9/108	(9 wkts) 111

Bonus points – Essex 4, Derbyshire 1 (Score at 100 overs: 326-4).

Bowling: *First Innings*—Holding 24–1–74–4; Newman 28–10–59–1; Malcolm 22–5–63–2; Jean-Jacques 19.4–5–49–3; Warner 19–2–67–0; Bowler 6–0–38–0; Roberts 5–1–13–0. *Second Innings*—Holding 14–4–28–1; Newman 11–2–21–1; Malcolm 18–5–33–3; Warner 16–5–19–3; Jean-Jacques 1–1–0–0.

Umpires: J. C. Balderstone and A. G. T. Whitehead.

At Swansea, May 21, 23, 24. DERBYSHIRE drew with GLAMORGAN.

DERBYSHIRE v NOTTINGHAMSHIRE

At Derby, May 28, 30, 31. Drawn. Derbyshire 4 pts, Nottinghamshire 5 pts. Toss: Nottinghamshire. There was movement for the seam bowlers and Stephenson made excellent use of it. Derbyshire did not have enough batsmen to emulate Bowler's application. Scott took five catches in the first innings and went on to equal the Nottinghamshire record of ten dismissals in a match, previously shared by T. W. Oates (1906) and B. N. French (1984). When Nottinghamshire replied, Mortensen, in his first Championship game of the season, also exploited the conditions to take five for 24 and limit their lead to 41 after six wickets fell for the addition of 48 runs. Bowler, continuing an excellent start for his new county, produced the only substantial innings when Derbyshire batted again, and they were just 118 ahead when rain ended the match after eighteen overs on the third day. Stephenson followed his best bowling for Nottinghamshire with another six wickets and match figures of twelve for 103, one of them coming when Warner was bowled, ducking under a slower ball.

Close of play: First day, Nottinghamshire 124-4 (D. W. Randall 19*, J. D. Birch 23*); Second day, Derbyshire 122-3 (P. D. Bowler 61*, S. C. Goldsmith 19*).

Derbyshire

	First innings		Second innings	
*K. J. Barnett c Scott b Stephenson	2	–	c Scott b Saxelby	19
P. D. Bowler c Scott b Stephenson	50	–	c Scott b Stephenson	84
B. Roberts c Scott b Stephenson	0	–	c Scott b Stephenson	19
J. E. Morris b Saxelby	24	–	c Scott b Stephenson	[illegible]
S. C. Goldsmith lbw b Birch	3	–	c Scott b Stephenson	2[illegible]
†B. J. M. Maher c Scott b Cooper	13	–	lbw b Stephenson	[illegible]
A. E. Warner c Scott b Cooper	16	–	b Stephenson	[illegible]
P. G. Newman lbw b Stephenson	0	–	not out	[illegible]
M. A. Holding lbw b Stephenson	18	–	not out	[illegible]
D. E. Malcolm c Saxelby b Stephenson	5			
O. H. Mortensen not out	0			
B 4, l-b 8	12		B 2, l-b 1, n-b 1	[illegible]
1/4 2/4 3/56 4/61 5/96 6/108 7/109 8/117 9/132	143		1/34 2/60 3/62 4/138 5/156 6/156 7/159 (7 wkts)	15[illegible]

Bonus points – Nottinghamshire 4.

Bowling: *First Innings*—Stephenson 21.2–9–44–6; Cooper 19–5–54–2; Saxelby 8–1–16–[illegible] Birch 7–2–15–1; Hemmings 3–1–2–0. *Second Innings*—Stephenson 22.3–5–59–6; Coop[illegible] 13–5–19–0; Saxelby 22–4–71–1; Hemmings 2–0–7–0.

Nottinghamshire

B. C. Broad c Maher b Holding	41
P. Pollard lbw b Holding	0
*R. T. Robinson b Mortensen	25
P. Johnson c Maher b Mortensen	3
D. W. Randall c Mortensen b Malcolm	24
J. D. Birch c Maher b Malcolm	31
F. D. Stephenson c Maher b Malcolm	0
†C. W. Scott not out	16
E. E. Hemmings lbw b Mortensen	[illegible]
K. E. Cooper c and b Mortensen	[illegible]
K. Saxelby b Mortensen	[illegible]
L-b 8, w 7, n-b 2	[illegible]
1/9 2/60 3/72 4/85 5/136 6/136 7/139 8/158 9/182	[illegible]

Bonus points – Nottinghamshire 1, Derbyshire 4.

Bowling: Holding 21–6–49–2; Malcolm 20–6–54–3; Newman 10–1–32–0; Mortensen 16.2–7–24–5; Warner 7–2–17–0.

Umpires: D. J. Constant and D. G. L. Evans.

At Horsham, June 4, 6, 7. DERBYSHIRE beat SUSSEX by one wicket.

DERBYSHIRE v GLOUCESTERSHIRE

At Derby, June 11, 13, 14. Gloucestershire won by four wickets. Gloucestershire 24 pts, Derbyshire 6 pts. Toss: Derbyshire. Barnett played magnificently to score a century before lunch, for the second time in his career, having sixteen minutes to spare. He went on to a career-highest 175 in 237 minutes, from 200 balls with 28 fours. It was a brilliant display but, Roberts apart, the other Derbyshire batsmen made little of Curran's controlled swing as he took six wickets for the first time. After a professional display by Wright, who hit eleven fours in a century scored from 236 balls, Graveney declared 21 behind. Curran improved his best return for match figures of twelve for 162 and his bowling was decisive against brittle batting. Gloucestershire had 78 overs in which to score 204, and although they were in difficulty at 123 for six, Curran and Russell batted soundly to steer them to maximum points.

Close of play: First day, Gloucestershire 43-0 (A. W. Stovold 24*, A. J. Wright 17*); Second day, Derbyshire 128-3 (J. E. Morris 24*, S. C. Goldsmith 43*).

Derbyshire

First innings		Second innings	
*K. J. Barnett c Wright b Lawrence	175	– c Curran b Alderman	5
P. D. Bowler lbw b Alderman	0	– lbw b Alderman	23
B. Roberts c and b Alderman	69	– c Athey b Alderman	24
J. E. Morris c Lloyds b Curran	3	– c and b Curran	28
S. C. Goldsmith c Russell b Lawrence	5	– c Bainbridge b Curran	63
†B. J. M. Maher c Athey b Curran	3	– c Athey b Curran	0
R. Sharma b Curran	3	– b Lawrence	10
A. E. Warner c and b Curran	22	– lbw b Curran	5
M. A. Holding c Lloyds b Curran	16	– c Alderman b Curran	9
D. E. Malcolm b Curran	17	– b Curran	1
D. H. Mortensen not out	1	– not out	0
B 1, l-b 2, w 5, n-b 7	15	B 4, l-b 2, w 1, n-b 7	14
/18 2/203 3/250 4/258 5/259 /262 7/286 8/292 9/326	329	1/5 2/58 3/63 4/132 5/132 6/154 7/165 8/178 9/182	182

Bonus points – Derbyshire 4, Gloucestershire 4.

Bowling: *First Innings*—Lawrence 18–2–80–2; Alderman 19–2–81–2; Curran 26.1–3–103–6; ainbridge 12–3–37–0; Graveney 7–3–25–0. *Second Innings*—Lawrence 16–4–38–1; Alderman 3–2–45–3; Curran 14.3–2–59–6; Graveney 11–2–23–0; Lloyds 2–0–11–0.

iloucestershire

First innings		Second innings	
. W. Stovold b Holding	37	– b Malcolm	1
. J. Wright c Morris b Bowler	136	– c Holding b Malcolm	13
. W. Romaines c Maher b Roberts	27	– c Sharma b Mortensen	30
. W. J. Athey c Maher b Malcolm	18	– b Warner	47
. Bainbridge lbw b Barnett	75	– c Holding b Mortensen	12
. M. Curran not out	8	– (7) not out	40
W. Lloyds not out	0	– (6) c Holding b Sharma	12
R. C. Russell (did not bat)		– not out	36
B 1, l-b 3, n-b 3	7	L-b 9, w 1, n-b 3	13
77 2/123 3/168 4/281 5/303	(5 wkts dec.) 308	1/2 2/31 3/79 4/100 5/121 6/123	(6 wkts) 204

D. A. Graveney, T. M. Alderman and D. V. Lawrence did not bat.

Bonus points – Gloucestershire 4, Derbyshire 2.

Bowling: *First Innings*—Holding 22–3–55–1; Malcolm 15–2–53–1; Mortensen 6–1–11–0; Sharma 19–9–54–0; Warner 15–2–47–0; Roberts 10–1–45–1; Bowler 6–0–24–1; Barnett 4–0–15–1. *Second Innings*—Holding 16–3–56–0; Malcolm 11–4–27–2; Mortensen 13–3–36–2; Warner 12–0–46–1; Sharma 10–2–18–1; Barnett 4–1–12–0.

Umpires: J. Birkenshaw and N. T. Plews.

DERBYSHIRE v WORCESTERSHIRE

At Derby, June 18, 20, 21. Drawn. Derbyshire 6 pts, Worcestershire 7 pts. Toss: Worcestershire. Mortensen having collapsed with a damaged calf muscle at the end of his third over, Derbyshire's attack was stretched as Neale and Rhodes added 206 for the sixth wicket. Neale, who scored his first century of the season, was out in the 121st over of the day after hitting a six and thirteen fours from 288 balls in 301 minutes. And when Worcestershire batted into the second day, Rhodes completed his maiden century in 154 minutes from 192 balls with a six and seven fours. Maher's unbeaten 76 helped Derbyshire to maximum batting points after avoiding the follow-on had presented problems, and some undemanding bowling enabled Worcestershire to set a target of 246 in what could have been 59 overs, even after a brief interruption for rain. Derbyshire, requiring 75 an hour on a turning pitch, did not come close to the required rate.

Close of play: First day, Worcestershire 332-6 (S. J. Rhodes 97*); Second day, Derbyshire 322-9 (B. J. M. Maher 76*, O. H. Mortensen 1*).

Worcestershire

T. S. Curtis c Sharma b Mortensen . . . . 0 – b Bowler 76
G. J. Lord c Maher b Newman . . . . 28 – c Goldsmith b Bowler 53
G. A. Hick c Goldsmith b Roberts . . . . 47 – lbw b Sharma 31
D. B. D'Oliveira c Goldsmith b Roberts . . . . . . 0 – not out 20
*P. A. Neale lbw b Newman . . . . .125 – not out 8
M. J. Weston c Maher b Newman 20
†S. J. Rhodes c Wright b Jean-Jacques 108
P. J. Newport c Bowler b Newman 8
R. K. Illingworth lbw b Jean-Jacques 0
N. V. Radford not out 9
S. M. McEwan c Roberts b Jean-Jacques 6
B 1, l-b 13, w 2 . . . . 16 B 2, l-b 9, n-b 1 12

1/1 2/61 3/61 4/86 5/126 367 1/128 2/154 3/176 (3 wkts dec.) 200
6/332 7/352 8/352 9/352

Bonus points – Worcestershire 3, Derbyshire 2 (Score at 100 overs: 252-5).

Bowling: *First Innings*—Newman 36–12–108–4; Mortensen 3–2–1–1; Jean-Jacque[illegible] 34.3–4–106–3; Roberts 24–3–68–2; Goldsmith 19–6–27–0; Sharma 19–7–43–0. *Secon[illegible] Innings*—Newman 5.2–1–22–0; Jean-Jacques 5–0–11–0; Goldsmith 6–1–28–0; Sharm[illegible] 17–1–65–1; Bowler 17–0–63–2.

Derbyshire

P. D. Bowler c Rhodes b Newport . . . . 5 – c Radford b Illingworth . . . . 1[illegible]
J. G. Wright c Radford b McEwan . . . . 12 – c Rhodes b Illingworth . . . . 3[illegible]
B. Roberts c and b Illingworth . . . . 65 – c Curtis b Hick . . . . [illegible]
J. E. Morris c Hick b Illingworth . . . . 46 – not out . . . . 3[illegible]
S. C. Goldsmith b Radford . . . . 30 – st Rhodes b Illingworth . . . . 1[illegible]
†B. J. M. Maher not out . . . . 76 – not out . . . . [illegible]
*K. J. Barnett c Rhodes b Illingworth 22
R. Sharma c Hick b McEwan 12
P. G. Newman b Hick 39
M. Jean-Jacques lbw b Hick 0
O. H. Mortensen not out 1
B 4, l-b 5, n-b 5 . . . . 14 B 4, l-b 4 . . . . [illegible]

1/5 2/32 3/113 4/148 5/166 (9 wkts dec.) 322 1/58 2/59 3/62 4/93 (4 wkts) 11[illegible]
6/194 7/221 8/297 9/297

Bonus points – Derbyshire 4, Worcestershire 4.

Bowling: *First Innings*—Radford 17–1–50–1; Newport 17–4–66–1; McEwan 13–0–61–2; Illingworth 41–10–108–3; Hick 10–2–28–2. *Second Innings*—Radford 9–0–27–0; Newport 5–1–13–0; Illingworth 20–11–27–3; Hick 14–3–33–1; Curtis 2–0–7–0.

Umpires: R. Julian and B. J. Meyer.

At The Oval, June 25, 27, 28. DERBYSHIRE drew with SURREY.

DERBYSHIRE v MIDDLESEX

At Derby, July 2, 4, 5. Drawn. Derbyshire 4 pts. Toss: Derbyshire. Rain took a firm grip of the game. Middlesex reached 92 for three by lunch on the first day but did not resume until the third morning, when Mortensen hustled them out by taking five for 16 in eleven overs. Although Derbyshire forfeited their first innings, further rain ruined any hopes of a positive finish.

Close of play: First day, Middlesex 92-3 (A. Needham 41*, K. R. Brown 7*); Second day, No play.

Middlesex

W. N. Slack run out	4		
J. D. Carr c Bowler b Mortensen	12	(1) not out	23
A. Needham not out	66	(2) not out	17
*R. O. Butcher c Maher b Roberts	17		
†K. R. Brown c Maher b Mortensen	12		
I. J. F. Hutchinson lbw b Mortensen	3		
M. A. Roseberry lbw b Mortensen	5		
J. F. Sykes c Maher b Newman	2		
S. P. Hughes lbw b Mortensen	1		
A. R. C. Fraser lbw b Mortensen	0		
N. G. Cowans b Newman	0		
B 1, l-b 9, w 6	16		
1/21 2/23 3/76 4/105 5/109 6/117 7/124 8/129 9/133	138	(no wkt)	40

Bonus points – Derbyshire 4.

Bowling: *First Innings*—Holding 2–0–4–0; Malcolm 11–6–10–0; Mortensen 21–8–35–6; Newman 19.1–3–53–2; Warner 5–0–14–0; Roberts 3–0–12–1. *Second Innings*—Barnett 3–1–16–0; Bowler 5–0–24–0.

Derbyshire

Derbyshire forfeited their first innings.

K. J. Barnett, P. D. Bowler, B. Roberts, J. E. Morris, S. C. Goldsmith, †B. J. M. Maher, P. G. Newman, A. E. Warner, M. A. Holding, O. H. Mortensen and D. E. Malcolm.

Umpires: J. W. Holder and K. J. Lyons.

At Southend, July 13, 14, 15. DERBYSHIRE lost to ESSEX by nine wickets.

DERBYSHIRE v NORTHAMPTONSHIRE

At Derby, July 16, 17, 18. Derbyshire won by 144 runs. Derbyshire 20 pts, Northamptonshire pts. Toss: Northamptonshire. Rain interfered with play on the first two days, costing a total of seven hours and 40 minutes. Derbyshire, recovering from the early loss of two wickets, were still batting on the third morning when Barnett declared. Northamptonshire forfeited their first innings and Derbyshire their second, leaving the former to score 309 in a minimum 90 overs. However, improved weather meant that the pitch, affected by the water which ran under the covers on Saturday night and Sunday morning, was drying when Northamptonshire began their innings. Such conditions suited Mortensen, and he made excellent use of them as the visitors lost their first five wickets before lunch. He claimed five wickets for the third time in eight innings and Derbyshire won with 90 minutes to spare.

Close of play: First day, Derbyshire 146-3 (P. D. Bowler 44*, K. J. Barnett 10*); Second day, Derbyshire 283-5 (B. J. M. Maher 33*, S. C. Goldsmith 17*).

Derbyshire

P. D. Bowler lbw b Walker 61
J. G. Wright lbw b Capel 5
B. Roberts c Ripley b Davis 0
J. E. Morris b N. G. B. Cook 79
*K. J. Barnett b Wild 73
†B. J. M. Maher lbw b N. G. B. Cook . 48
S. C. Goldsmith not out 25
B 3, l-b 9, w 2, n-b 3 17

1/6 2/7 3/129 4/196 5/239 6/308 (6 wkts dec.) 308

A. E. Warner, P. G. Newman, O. H. Mortensen and S. J. Base did not bat.

Bonus points – Derbyshire 4, Northamptonshire 2 (Score at 100 overs: 303-5).

Bowling: Davis 25–4–71–1; Capel 16–2–48–1; N. G. B. Cook 23.3–10–39–2; Walker 21–3–70–1; Wild 11–0–47–1; Williams 5–0–21–0.

Derbyshire forfeited their second innings.

Northamptonshire

Northamptonshire forfeited their first innings.

*G. Cook c Roberts b Newman 0
W. Larkins c Maher b Mortensen 22
R. J. Bailey c Maher b Mortensen 5
A. J. Lamb c Warner b Mortensen 10
D. J. Capel lbw b Mortensen 47
R. G. Williams lbw b Base 0
D. J. Wild c Barnett b Mortensen 25
†D. Ripley b Newman 22
N. G. B. Cook b Newman .... [illegible]
W. W. Davis c Mortensen b Base 17
A. Walker not out 6
L-b 3, n-b 6 9

1/6 2/25 3/36 4/39 5/41 6/99 7/129 8/130 9/149 16[illegible]

Bowling: Newman 20.1–7–57–3; Mortensen 18–8–28–5; Base 14–1–46–2; Warne[r] 12–2–30–0.

Umpires: J. D. Bond and R. Julian.

At Leicester, July 20, 21, 22. DERBYSHIRE drew with LEICESTERSHIRE.

At Portsmouth, July 23, 25, 26. DERBYSHIRE drew with HAMPSHIRE.

DERBYSHIRE v WARWICKSHIRE

At Derby, July 30, August 1, 2. Drawn. Derbyshire 5 pts, Warwickshire 7 pts. Toss: Warwic[k]shire. When rain interrupted play on the first day, Derbyshire were 161 for four. Three and [a] half overs after the resumption, they were all out for 166 and Merrick had taken six wickets [in] ten balls without a run being scored off him. Only P. I. Pocock, six wickets in nine balls f[or] Surrey against Sussex at Eastbourne in 1972, on his way to seven in eleven, could claim a mo[re] potent spell. Merrick performed the hat-trick, dismissing Goldsmith, Barnett and Newma[n] with the third, fourth and fifth balls of his twelfth over. Mortensen was out to the first ball [of] Merrick's next over and Base survived three balls before he and Malcolm were bowle[d]. Malcolm, who took four wickets in seven balls, helped to limit Warwickshire's lead to 119. [A] Sunday injury put Barnett out of the game, and delayed his Test début, but Wright, who h[ad] retired hurt on the second day after Merrick had hit him on the right knee, saw Derbyshire [to] safety with his 27th and last century for the county. Wright reached 100 from 188 balls in 2[illegible] minutes with a six and thirteen fours.

Close of play: First day, Warwickshire 30-0 (T. A. Lloyd 19*, A. J. Moles 9*); Second da[y], Derbyshire 99-3 (J. E. Morris 3*, B. Roberts 6*).

Derbyshire

	First innings		Second innings	
P. D. Bowler lbw b Small		3	b Gifford	33
J. G. Wright b Gifford		48	not out	154
†B. J. M. Maher b Small		39	b Merrick	18
J. E. Morris not out		54	(5) c Merrick b Gifford	31
B. Roberts c Asif Din b Gifford		9	(6) b Munton	60
S. C. Goldsmith lbw b Merrick		0	(7) c Asif Din b Gifford	84
*K. J. Barnett c Humpage b Merrick		0		
P. G. Newman lbw b Merrick		0	(4) b Merrick	0
O. H. Mortensen c Moles b Merrick		0	(8) lbw b Reeve	15
S. J. Base b Merrick		0	(9) not out	11
D. E. Malcolm b Merrick		0		
L-b 10, n-b 3		13	B 4, l-b 8, w 6, n-b 4	22
1/9 2/84 3/111 4/161 5/162 6/162 7/162 8/166 9/166		166	1/74 2/75 3/78 4/171 5/193 6/378 7/412 (7 wkts dec.)	428

Bonus points – Derbyshire 1, Warwickshire 4.

In the second innings J. G. Wright, when 24, retired hurt at 38 and resumed at 171.

Bowling: *First Innings*—Small 19–5–42–2; Merrick 13–6–29–6; Munton 9–3–21–0; Gifford 19–4–52–2; Reeve 5–1–12–0. *Second Innings*—Merrick 30–6–96–2; Small 20–5–56–0; Reeve 15–6–29–1; Munton 14–5–36–1; Gifford 50–15–125–3; Lloyd 4–0–29–0; Asif Din 10–0–35–0; Humpage 3–0–10–0.

Warwickshire

*T. A. Lloyd b Malcolm	27
A. J. Moles not out	50
Asif Din b Newman	52
D. A. Banks c Maher b Mortensen	41
D. A. Thorne lbw b Malcolm	35
†G. W. Humpage c and b Base	52
D. A. Reeve lbw b Malcolm	17
G. C. Small c Maher b Malcolm	0
T. A. Merrick b Malcolm	0
T. A. Munton b Malcolm	0
N. Gifford b Newman	0
L-b 4, w 3, n-b 4	11
1/52 2/122 3/171 4/234 5/242 6/282 7/282 8/284 9/284	285

Bonus points – Warwickshire 3, Derbyshire 4.

A. J. Moles, when 26, retired hurt at 64 and resumed at 242.

Bowling: Base 21–4–79–1; Malcolm 18–4–68–6; Mortensen 19–0–60–1; Newman 13.2–2–41–2; Bowler 4–0–27–0; Roberts 1–0–6–0.

Umpires: K. J. Lyons and P. B. Wight.

At Weston-super-Mare, August 6, 8, 9. DERBYSHIRE beat SOMERSET by 183 runs.

DERBYSHIRE v KENT

t Chesterfield, August 13, 15, 16. Drawn. Derbyshire 6 pts, Kent 8 pts. Toss: Kent. Chris owdrey, forced to miss the Fifth Test because of injury, returned for Kent, as did Igglesden, ho had been out since April with knee trouble. Derbyshire's batting was uneven, although a tand of 83 between Roberts and Sharma steered them to a respectable total. On the second ay, Kent flayed the bowling. Malcolm, consistently pitching short, was treated savagely. avaré completed 1,000 runs after reaching his century, with seventeen fours, from 115 balls nd Cowdrey's century was scored at a run a ball, his second 50 coming from 28. By batting ıt the 100 overs to establish a lead of 204, Kent limited the options on the final day, specially on such a placid batting surface. Bowler and O'Gorman began with a partnership of 68, Derbyshire's best for any wicket against Kent, and with Goldsmith making his highest ore, against his former county, the game was saved comfortably.

Close of play: First day, Derbyshire 262; Second day, Derbyshire 35-0 (P. D. Bowler 24*, J. G. O'Gorman 10*).

Derbyshire

Batsman	First innings		Second innings	
P. D. Bowler	c Marsh b Penn	53	c Benson b Pienaar	84
T. J. G. O'Gorman	c Hinks b Ellison	27	c Hinks b Pienaar	78
†B. J. M. Maher	lbw b Igglesden	22	c Tavaré b Igglesden	13
J. E. Morris	c Penn b Pienaar	1	c Marsh b Pienaar	0
S. C. Goldsmith	c Davis b Penn	33	c Ellison b Taylor	89
B. Roberts	lbw b Igglesden	58	run out	15
R. Sharma	c Marsh b Ellison	43	not out	16
A. E. Warner	lbw b Igglesden	0	not out	4
*M. A. Holding	c Marsh b Penn	7		
O. H. Mortensen	not out	3		
D. E. Malcolm	c Hinks b Penn	6		
	L-b 4, w 3, n-b 2	9	L-b 7, w 1, n-b 10	18
1/48 2/87 3/88 4/125 5/148 6/231 7/231 8/247 9/255		262	1/168 2/175 3/175 4/213 5/267 6/313 (6 wkts dec.)	317

Bonus points – Derbyshire 3, Kent 4.

Bowling: *First Innings*—Igglesden 21–4–47–3; Penn 24.4–12–43–4; Ellison 18–4–89–2; Pienaar 19–3–57–1; Davis 3–0–8–0; Cowdrey 5–1–14–0. *Second Innings*—Igglesden 20–3–85–1; Penn 14–1–56–0; Davis 20–8–51–0; Cowdrey 6–2–19–0; Ellison 13–3–53–0; Pienaar 18–7–40–3; Taylor 6–3–6–1.

Kent

M. R. Benson	c Holding b Warner	30
N. R. Taylor	c Sharma b Mortensen	5
R. F. Pienaar	c Maher b Warner	52
C. J. Tavaré	c Bowler b Mortensen	119
S. G. Hinks	c Mortensen b Bowler	35
*C. S. Cowdrey	c Bowler b Roberts	108
†S. A. Marsh	c Maher b Holding	39
R. M. Ellison	run out	18
C. Penn	not out	22
A. P. Igglesden	not out	22
	L-b 11, n-b 5	16
1/14 2/81 3/91 4/216 5/288 6/382 7/415 8/421	(8 wkts dec.)	466

R. P. Davis did not bat.

Bonus points – Kent 4, Derbyshire 3.

Bowling: Holding 19–0–77–1; Mortensen 18–3–42–2; Malcolm 17–3–131–0; Warner 21–0–92–2; Bowler 16–6–57–1; Roberts 9–0–56–1.

Umpires: J. C. Balderstone and D. R. Shepherd.

DERBYSHIRE v YORKSHIRE

At Chesterfield, August 17, 18, 19. Drawn. Derbyshire 4 pts, Yorkshire 5 pts. Toss: Derby shire. Metcalfe held together Yorkshire's first innings and reached 100 from 155 balls in 20 minutes with seventeen fours. It was his first century of the season and helped him into a goo spell. In reply, Barnett reached 50 from only 39 balls, but his dismissal was the only incident c note on the second day, when rain restricted play to twenty minutes. The third morning wa also lost, but after two declarations Derbyshire were set 244 to win in what two furthe interruptions turned into 50 overs. While Barnett was in, Derbyshire were likely winners. H hit a six and ten fours in his century, reached in 130 minutes from 124 balls. When he wa bowled by Fletcher, however, Derbyshire had nobody who could dominate in similar fashio and finished 28 runs short.

Close of play: First day, Derbyshire 71-2 (K. J. Barnett 57*, B. J. M. Maher 7*); Secon day, Derbyshire 83-3 (B. J. M. Maher 10*, J. E. Morris 0*).

Yorkshire

M. D. Moxon b Malcolm	0		
A. A. Metcalfe c O'Gorman b Warner	115	– (1) not out	9
D. Byas lbw b Malcolm	17	– (2) not out	16
P. E. Robinson c Maher b Warner	10		
K. Sharp b Base	1		
†R. J. Blakey c Maher b Base	38		
*P. Carrick c Goldsmith b Malcolm	10		
A. Sidebottom not out	51		
S. J. Dennis c Barnett b Malcolm	0		
C. Shaw c Roberts b Holding	24		
S. D. Fletcher b Warner	8		
B 4, l-b 4, w 1, n-b 18	27		
1/9 2/55 3/92 4/94 5/179 6/216 7/216 8/216 9/254	301	(no wkt dec.)	25

Bonus points – Yorkshire 4, Derbyshire 4.

Bowling: *First Innings*—Holding 23–5–81–1; Malcolm 23–5–78–4; Base 23–0–86–2; Warner 18.2–6–48–3. *Second Innings*—Barnett 2–0–10–0; Bowler 1.5–0–15–0.

Derbyshire

*K. J. Barnett c Blakey b Sidebottom	64	– b Fletcher	109
P. D. Bowler c Sharp b Dennis	3	– b Dennis	26
T. J. G. O'Gorman c Blakey b Shaw	4	– b Sidebottom	16
†B. J. M. Maher not out	10		
J. E. Morris not out	0	– (4) c Robinson b Fletcher	7
S. C. Goldsmith (did not bat)		– (5) c Carrick b Sidebottom	17
B. Roberts (did not bat)		– (6) not out	17
M. A. Holding (did not bat)		– (7) c Sharp b Sidebottom	9
A. E. Warner (did not bat)		– (8) not out	1
N-b 2	2	L-b 7, n-b 7	14
1/21 2/50 3/82	(3 wkts dec.) 83	1/82 2/155 3/165 4/173 5/198 6/214	(6 wkts) 216

S. J. Base and D. E. Malcolm did not bat.

Bonus point – Yorkshire 1.

Bowling: *First Innings*—Dennis 11–1–27–1; Fletcher 3–0–29–0; Shaw 6–1–18–1; Carrick 2–0–2–0; Sidebottom 2.2–0–7–1. *Second Innings*—Sidebottom 13.5–3–54–3; Dennis 16–1–61–1; Shaw 6–0–35–0; Fletcher 7–2–15–2; Carrick 6–0–44–0.

Umpires: J. H. Hampshire and D. R. Shepherd.

At Manchester, August 20, 22, 23. DERBYSHIRE drew with LANCASHIRE.

At Northampton, August 25, 26, 27, 29. DERBYSHIRE drew with NORTHAMPTONSHIRE.

At Derby, August 31, September 1, 2. DERBYSHIRE drew with SRI LANKANS (See Sri Lankan tour section).

At Nottingham, September 9, 10, 11, 12. DERBYSHIRE lost to NOTTINGHAMSHIRE by an innings and 41 runs.

DERBYSHIRE v LANCASHIRE

At Derby, September 14, 15, 16, 17. Drawn. Derbyshire 5 pts, Lancashire 5 pts. Toss: Lancashire. On a green pitch which never gave the promised help to bowlers, the first innings followed similar courses. Barnett, dropped twice, batted with power for his fifth century of the season, reaching 100 from 165 balls in 161 minutes with thirteen fours. Maher helped him to add 173, but Derbyshire did not make the most of their good start. Nor did Lancashire build on Fowler's 172, which took him past 1,000 runs. Fowler hit fifteen fours in reaching his century from 200 balls and he shared a fourth-wicket partnership of 251 with Hayhurst, whose maiden century came from 276 balls with eleven fours. Lancashire's last six wickets added only 51 runs, giving Base reward for a good spell, whereupon Bowler raised the fourth century of the game and his fourth of the season in 302 minutes with twelve fours. Lancashire were set 300 to win in what became 76 overs, but when they fell out of contention Derbyshire could not part Watkinson and Hegg, who stayed together for 23 overs.

Close of play: First day, Derbyshire 311-4 (B. J. M. Maher 88*, B. Roberts 17*); Second day, Lancashire 264-3 (G. Fowler 139*, A. N. Hayhurst 80*); Third day, Derbyshire 165-3 (P. D. Bowler 69*, S. J. Base 0*).

Derbyshire

*K. J. Barnett c Lloyd b Folley	157	– c Fowler b Folley	55
P. D. Bowler c Atherton b Hayhurst	23	– st Hegg b Atherton	134
†B. J. M. Maher c Hegg b Watkinson	92	– b Austin	24
T. J. G. O'Gorman c Fowler b Folley	8	– lbw b Folley	2
S. C. Goldsmith c Fowler b Folley	5	– (6) b Austin	11
B. Roberts lbw b Hayhurst	27	– (7) not out	18
R. Sharma b Murphy	17		
F. A. Griffith b Watkinson	1		
M. A. Holding not out	30		
S. J. Base lbw b Murphy	0	– (5) b Watkinson	10
D. E. Malcolm b Murphy	0	– (8) not out	18
B 1, l-b 6, n-b 6	13	B 8, l-b 9, n-b 5	22
1/69 2/242 3/260 4/272 5/325 6/325 7/326 8/369 9/369	373	1/110 2/153 3/164 4/197 5/209 6/271 (6 wkts dec.)	294

Bonus points – Derbyshire 4, Lancashire 1 (Score at 100 overs: 307-4).

Bowling: *First Innings*—Murphy 19.1–3–70–3; Watkinson 28–6–70–2; Hayhurst 19–4–56–2; Austin 20–7–41–0; Folley 31–9–103–3; Atherton 11–4–26–0. *Second Innings*—Watkinson 14–4–36–1; Murphy 9–2–41–0; Hayhurst 3–2–2–0; Folley 37–10–91–2; Atherton 14–5–51–1; Austin 30–12–56–2.

Lancashire

G. D. Mendis b Malcolm	6	– c and b Barnett	60
G. Fowler c Bowler b Malcolm	172	– c Maher b Holding	19
M. A. Atherton c Maher b Griffith	17	– lbw b Base	7
*N. H. Fairbrother b Griffith	0	– c O'Gorman b Base	0
A. N. Hayhurst c Roberts b Holding	107	– lbw b Barnett	47
G. D. Lloyd c and b Base	22	– b Sharma	0
M. Watkinson lbw b Base	6	– not out	27
I. D. Austin lbw b Base	0	– c Sharma b Barnett	0
†W. K. Hegg lbw b Base	2	– not out	22
I. Folley not out	1		
A. J. Murphy c O'Gorman b Holding	3		
B 5, l-b 7, n-b 20	32	B 7, n-b 6	13
1/15 2/66 3/66 4/317 5/336 6/352 7/352 8/355 9/363	368	1/30 2/48 3/48 4/144 5/145 6/147 7/147 (7 wkts)	195

Bonus points – Lancashire 4, Derbyshire 1 (Score at 100 overs: 300-3).

Bowling: *First Innings*—Holding 25.1–3–48–2; Malcolm 21–2–69–2; Base 19–0–74–4; Griffith 16–2–53–2; Roberts 6–1–19–0; Sharma 30–7–66–0; Barnett 13–3–27–0. *Second Innings*—Holding 14–4–39–1; Base 11–0–50–2; Malcolm 2–1–4–0; Barnett 28–10–63–3; Sharma 21–10–32–1.

Umpires: A. A. Jones and B. J. Meyer.

ESSEX

President: T. N. Pearce
Chairman: D. J. Insole
Chairman, Cricket Committee: G. J. Saville
Secretary/General Manager: P. J. Edwards
County Ground, New Writtle Street,
Chelmsford CM2 0PG
(Telephone: 0245-354533)
Captain: 1988 – K. W. R. Fletcher
1989 – G. A. Gooch

That Essex did not emerge with at least one trophy in 1988 would have been interpreted as failure in some quarters. Certainly, their inability to beat Hampshire in the semi-final of the Benson and Hedges Cup, followed by the second-round defeat by Surrey in the NatWest Bank Trophy, both at Chelmsford, brought acute disappointment. And there was little satisfaction in a mid-table position in the Refuge Assurance League. There was, however, much comfort to be gained from Essex's third place behind Worcestershire and Kent, both of whom they beat, in he Britannic Assurance Championship.

A knee injury had ruled out Neil Foster for the first six weeks of the season; and when the strike bowler was fit enough to return, he soon found himself in the England dressing-room alongside his county colleagues, Graham Gooch, Derek Pringle and John Childs. This meant Essex had to call on a number of relatively young, inexperienced players to remain in the Championship race – at a time when Brian Hardie was out with a broken arm, having been struck by Surrey's Clarke in the NatWest tie. That they succeeded in keeping their title hopes alive until the final match of the season says much for their efforts.

The summer resulted in another bountiful harvest for Gooch. Ironically, having given up the Essex captaincy at the end of 1987 ecause he felt it affected his batting, he discovered in 1988 that he could shoulder such responsibility and still make runs. Gooch, because of Keith Fletcher's decision to leave himself out for half the season, plus the ailure of others to live up to expectations at Test level, found himself aptaining both club and country. His figures show he did not find a burden. He scored 2,324 first-class runs at an average of nearly 5, starting with a career-best 275 in the opening match against Kent and ending with 108, his sixth century, in the final game against Northamptonshire. In between, he reached his 1,000 runs in just ten nnings, one fewer than Worcestershire's Hick needed to achieve the feat efore the end of May. Gooch also hit fifteen half-centuries, and in only ve out of 21 matches did he fail to reach 50 in an innings.

Allan Border, who returned to Australia in late August to prepare for eir tour to Pakistan, also scored six centuries, and it was refreshing to e Paul Prichard achieve 1,000 runs in the Championship after missing ost of 1987 with a bad hand injury. Yet Prichard remained something an enigma; talented but not doing himself justice. He failed to register hundred, and while four of his nine half-centuries were not out, on a number of other occasions he was dismissed in the 30s and 40s. That is something he must overcome if he is to progress to a greater stage. The more experienced Alan Lilley was another batsman who often failed to translate encouraging starts into substantial innings.

Of the younger players, John Stephenson and Nasser Hussain went some way to confirming that the county's future is in safe hands. Hardie's prolonged absence gave Stephenson an extended run as opener, and in compiling nearly 800 first-class runs he had three unbeaten scores of 78 or more, in addition to missing his maiden century by just 1 run in the penultimate round of the Championship. Twenty-year-old Hussain, on vacation from Durham University, was thrust into the middle order as Fletcher stepped aside, and he rewarded his captain's confidence with a Championship average of 58.62. The elegance with which he scored his maiden first-class hundred, 165 not out against Leicestershire, suggested many more to follow in the years ahead.

Foster, although not fully fit, performed admirably for both Essex and England. He would surely have collected 100 wickets for the second time in three seasons but for his unavailability in the opening weeks. With John Lever nearing the end of a distinguished career, it was generally left to Pringle or Don Topley to share the new ball with Foster. Topley, with his unquenchable enthusiasm, took 102 wickets in all matches and was awarded his county cap. Pringle was a formidable bowler when the conditions suited him, but he continued to disappoint with the bat, only three times reaching 50 after beginning the season with a personal-best 128 against Kent. Childs, the left-arm spinner, again proved a match winner when he discovered a pitch to his liking, and at the age of 3[illegible] found himself elevated to Test status. Geoff Miller, after an indifferent season, accepted a new contract and was awarded his county cap. He and Childs will again comprise the spin department without a challenger in sight.

David East performed competently behind the stumps, in addition to proving a more than useful lower-order batsman. Mark Waugh, twin of the Australian and Somerset player, Stephen, and Essex's overseas replacement for Border, did not disappoint when called in for the last few games. He launched his county career with a century on his début in the Sunday League against Nottinghamshire at Colchester – and averaged 44.50 in his three Championship games.

In November, an era in Essex cricket passed with Fletcher's retirement from the first-class game – though not from the club's activities. In 27 seasons, he scored 29,434 runs for the county, with an average of 36.88 and 45 hundreds. Under his captaincy, Essex became one of the leading sides of modern times, winning both the County Championship and Sunday League three times and the knockout trophies once each. Now he looks on from the wings as Gooch again steps into the limelight. – Nigel Fuller.

ESSEX 1988

[*Bill Smith*

Back row: P. J. Prichard, G. Miller, A. W. Lilley, J. P. Stephenson, I. L. Pont, J. H. Childs, T. D. Topley, N. A. Foster. *Front row:* A. R. Border, B. R. Hardie, J. K. Lever, K. W. R. Fletcher (*captain*), G. A. Gooch, D. R. Pringle, D. E. East. *Inset:* M. E. Waugh.

ESSEX RESULTS

All first-class matches – Played 24: Won 10, Lost 5, Drawn 9.

County Championship matches – Played 22: Won 9, Lost 5, Drawn 8.

Bonus points – Batting 61, Bowling 69.

Competition placings – Britannic Assurance County Championship, 3rd; NatWest Bank Trophy, 2nd round; Benson and Hedges Cup, s-f; Refuge Assurance League, 10th equal.

BRITANNIC ASSURANCE CHAMPIONSHIP AVERAGES

BATTING

	Birthplace	*M*	*I*	*NO*	*R*	*HI*	*Avge*
‡G. A. Gooch	*Leytonstone*	14	23	0	1,631	275	70.91
§‡A. R. Border	*Sydney, Australia*	19	30	7	1,361	169*	59.17
N. Hussain	*Madras, India*	8	11	3	469	165*	58.62
§M. E. Waugh	*Sydney, Australia*	3	4	0	178	86	44.50
‡P. J. Prichard	*Billericay*	22	36	7	1,051	80	36.24
‡K. W. R. Fletcher	*Worcester*	12	14	3	303	58	27.54
J. P. Stephenson	*Stebbing*	17	29	3	707	99	27.19
‡D. R. Pringle	*Nairobi, Kenya*	13	17	0	446	128	26.2
‡A. W. Lilley	*Ilford*	19	30	2	730	80*	26.0
‡D. E. East	*Clapton*	18	26	2	580	134	24.1
‡B. R. Hardie	*Stenhousemuir*	12	19	3	353	58	22.0
‡G. Miller	*Chesterfield*	17	19	4	329	77	21.9
I. L. Pont	*Brentwood*	6	6	2	76	29	19.0
‡T. D. Topley	*Canterbury*	15	20	6	233	56*	16.6
‡J. H. Childs	*Plymouth*	16	15	8	71	25*	10.1
‡N. A. Foster	*Colchester*	13	16	2	108	22	7.7
A. D. Brown	*Clacton on Sea*	4	5	3	13	6*	6.5
‡J. K. Lever	*Stepney*	13	13	1	53	20	4.4

Also batted: M. C. Ilott (*Watford*) (1 match) 6.

* *Signifies not out.* ‡ *Denotes county cap.* § *Not qualified for England.*

The following played a total of fourteen three-figure innings for Essex in Count Championship matches – A. R. Border 6, G. A. Gooch 5, D. E. East 1, N. Hussain D. R. Pringle 1.

BOWLING

	O	*M*	*R*	*W*	*BB*	*5W/i*	*Avg*
N. A. Foster	471.1	95	1,423	66	6-53	4	21.
T. D. Topley	500	81	1,520	62	7-75	4	24.
D. R. Pringle	352.3	71	1,031	41	6-39	3	25.
J. H. Childs	505.2	160	1,239	49	6-92	3	25.
J. K. Lever	422.4	90	1,120	43	4-61	0	26.
G. Miller	376.1	95	1,025	35	5-76	1	29.
I. L. Pont	158	16	591	16	5-103	1	36.

Also bowled: G. A. Gooch 135–37–342–9; J. P. Stephenson 59.2–12–187–4; A. R. Bord 28–8–74–1; A. W. Lilley 11–0–119–0; P. J. Prichard 1–0–7–0; N. Hussain 9–0–47– M. C. Ilott 15–1–48–0; M. E. Waugh 12–0–75–0.

Wicket-keepers: D. E. East 53 ct, 4 st; A. D. Brown 9 ct, 2 st.

Leading Fielders: A. R. Border 26, G. A. Gooch 19, G. Miller 18, A. W. Lilley 16.

ESSEX v KENT

At Chelmsford, April 21, 22, 23, 25. Essex won by eight wickets. Essex 21 pts, Kent 4 pts. Toss: Kent. This game produced a record number of runs for a County Championship match, 1,570, before Essex emerged victors with 22 balls to spare. Their target had been 169 in 25 overs. Benson and Taylor shared in a double-century stand to lay the foundation for Kent's total, to which Gooch responded with a career-best 275 that included four sixes among his 31 boundaries. He batted for 466 minutes and faced 399 deliveries. Pringle, with whom he shared a stand of 259 for the fourth wicket, also posted a career-best score, with the aid of nineteen fours, while Fletcher became the highest run-maker for Essex, overtaking the 29,172 runs scored by P. A. Perrin. Kent looked in danger of an innings defeat when they lost their captain at 122, but Graham Cowdrey and Marsh both hit maiden first-class hundreds to set up an exciting finish.

Close of play: First day, Kent 303-4 (C. S. Cowdrey 36*, G. R. Cowdrey 1*); Second day, Essex 279-3 (G. A. Gooch 126*, D. R. Pringle 88*); Third day, Kent 76-4 (R. P. Davis 0*, C. S. Cowdrey 24*).

Kent

First innings		Second innings	
M. R. Benson c East b Topley	110	– c Gooch b Topley	13
N. R. Taylor b Topley	94	– c Miller b Childs	24
S. G. Hinks c Prichard b Gooch	35	– st East b Miller	10
C. J. Tavaré c East b Topley	13	– c East b Childs	0
*C. S. Cowdrey c Border b Pringle	48	– (6) c Gooch b Childs	54
G. R. Cowdrey c Gooch b Lever	35	– (7) b Topley	145
†S. A. Marsh lbw b Lever	7	– (8) c Border b Lever	120
C. Penn not out	25	– (9) c Prichard b Topley	1
R. P. Davis not out	10	– (5) c Border b Childs	1
A. P. Igglesden (did not bat)		– c Fletcher b Childs	3
H. L. Alleyne (did not bat)		– not out	0
B 2, l-b 15, w 1, n-b 5	23	B 3, l-b 10	13
1/208 2/209 3/254 4/295 5/327 6/352 7/363 (7 wkts dec.)	400	1/27 2/49 3/49 4/49 5/89 6/122 7/344 8/357 9/372	384

Bonus points – Kent 3, Essex 1 (Score at 100 overs: 259-3).

Bowling: *First Innings*—Lever 33–11–62–2; Topley 39–6–124–3; Pringle 37–7–77–1; Gooch 9–3–19–1; Childs 24–6–65–0; Miller 7–1–30–0; Border 3–1–6–0. *Second Innings*—Lever 19–4–85–1; Topley 21.2–5–57–3; Childs 45–16–113–5; Miller 28–6–95–1; Border 4–0–21–0.

Essex

First innings		Second innings	
G. A. Gooch b Davis	275	– lbw b Davis	73
B. R. Hardie c C. S. Cowdrey b Penn	20	– c Taylor b C. S. Cowdrey	22
P. J. Prichard c Benson b Penn	0	– (4) not out	15
A. R. Border c Marsh b C. S. Cowdrey	31	– (3) not out	55
D. R. Pringle c Marsh b Alleyne	128		
K. W. R. Fletcher c sub b Davis	58		
G. Miller b Davis	16		
D. E. East c Tavaré b Davis	29		
T. D. Topley c Marsh b Penn	1		
J. K. Lever not out	13		
J. H. Childs b Davis	7		
B 6, l-b 24, w 1, n-b 7	38	B 1, l-b 4	5
1/33 2/33 3/126 4/385 5/539 6/543 7/591 8/594 9/606	616	1/53 2/150 (2 wkts)	170

Bonus points – Essex 4, Kent 1 (Score at 100 overs: 361-3).

Bowling: *First Innings*—Igglesden 13–2–57–0; Alleyne 20–2–80–1; Penn 41–7–160–3; C. S. Cowdrey 31–3–93–1; Davis 39.5–8–132–5; G. R. Cowdrey 17–1–64–0. *Second Innings*—C. S. Cowdrey 7–0–59–1; Alleyne 6–0–40–0; Davis 4.2–0–34–1; G. R. Cowdrey 4–0–32–0.

Umpires: R. Julian and K. J. Lyons.

At Lord's, April 28, 29, 30, May 2. ESSEX lost to MIDDLESEX by 176 runs.

At Chesterfield, May 5, 6, 7, 9. ESSEX drew with DERBYSHIRE.

At Cambridge, May 18, 19, 20. ESSEX beat CAMBRIDGE UNIVERSITY by 135 runs.

At Birmingham, May 21, 23, 24. ESSEX lost to WARWICKSHIRE by five wickets.

ESSEX v SURREY

At Chelmsford, May 28, 30, 31. Essex won by 195 runs. Essex 20 pts, Surrey 4 pts. Toss: Essex. Left with a minimum of 90 overs in which to score 326 for victory, Surrey were easily brushed aside as Pringle returned his best figures of the season to date on a pitch which helped the seam bowlers – although not to the degree the visitors' batting indicated. Two declarations on the final morning set up a definite result after rain washed out the second day's play. The first had been dominated by Gooch, who reached a century before lunch and went on to make 139 from 184 balls in 195 minutes, hitting nineteen fours and a six.

Close of play: First day, Surrey 22-0 (G. S. Clinton 12*, D. M. Smith 10*); Second day, No play.

Essex

	First innings		Second innings	
G. A. Gooch b Feltham	139			
B. R. Hardie c Richards b Clarke	36			
P. J. Prichard b Medlycott	0			
A. R. Border c Lynch b Medlycott	4			
D. R. Pringle c Clarke b Medlycott	7			
*K. W. R. Fletcher c Lynch b Feltham	9			
G. Miller not out	39			
†D. E. East lbw b Greig	21			
I. L. Pont c Medlycott b Greig	0	–	(1) not out	25
T. D. Topley c and b Mays	17	–	(2) not out	15
J. H. Childs c Mays b Feltham	13			
B 6, l-b 9, w 1, n-b 1	17		L-b 3, n-b 2	5
1/138 2/139 3/155 4/177 5/209 6/210 7/240 8/240 9/264	302		(no wkt dec.)	45

Bonus points – Essex 4, Surrey 4 (Score at 100 overs: 300-9).

Bowling: *First Innings*—Clarke 19–4–46–1; Greig 10–1–33–2; Feltham 17.2–3–56–3 Medlycott 44–11–116–3; Mays 11–1–36–1. *Second Innings*—Stewart 4.1–0–16–0; Richard 4–1–26–0.

Surrey

	First innings		Second innings	
G. S. Clinton not out	12	–	b Miller	1
D. M. Smith not out	10	–	c East b Pringle	3
A. J. Stewart (did not bat)		–	c East b Pringle	
M. A. Lynch (did not bat)		–	b Pringle	2
D. M. Ward (did not bat)		–	b Pringle	
†C. J. Richards (did not bat)		–	b Miller	
*I. A. Greig (did not bat)		–	c Prichard b Miller	1
K. T. Medlycott (did not bat)		–	c and b Topley	
M. A. Feltham (did not bat)		–	lbw b Pringle	2
C. S. Mays (did not bat)		–	not out	1
S. T. Clarke (did not bat)		–	c Gooch b Pringle	
			L-b 2, n-b 6	
(no wkt dec.)	22		1/42 2/42 3/46 4/48 5/69 6/71 7/93 8/94 9/130	13

Bowling: *First Innings*—Pont 4–2–2–0; Pringle 2–1–4–0; Childs 4–1–6–0; Miller 3–1–10–0. *Second Innings*—Pont 6–0–15–0; Topley 8–0–27–1; Miller 23–8–47–3; Pringle 16–4–39–6.

Umpires: J. W. Holder and B. Leadbeater.

ESSEX v SUSSEX

At Ilford, June 11, 13, 14. Essex won by an innings and 173 runs. Essex 24 pts, Sussex 3 pts. Toss: Sussex. Essex coasted to their third Championship victory of the summer, winning before lunch on the final day with Foster, in his first Championship match after his winter knee operation, completing a five-wicket haul. On the opening day Miller exploited a dampish pitch for his best figures of the season, and then Gooch emphasised his good form with a century which, containing sixteen fours, signalled his 1,000 runs for the season. He had taken only ten innings, one fewer than Hick of Worcestershire, who had achieved the feat on May 28. An enterprising Prichard provided good support for the second wicket, paving the way for Border to underline his class with 161 from 220 deliveries. He struck twenty boundaries in egistering his first hundred on Essex soil. When umpire Bird was forced to retire on the econd day because of illness, he was replaced initially by G. Clark, a member of the Association of Cricket Umpires, and the Sussex coach, J. A. Jameson, who had previously been on the first-class umpires' list.

Close of play: First day, Essex 197-1 (G. A. Gooch 113*, P. J. Prichard 69*); Second day, Sussex 77-5 (Imran Khan 16*, A. R. Clarke 3*).

Sussex

R. I. Alikhan c East b Foster	11	– b Foster	18
A. M. Green c Fletcher b Miller	23	– c Gooch b Foster	23
*P. W. G. Parker c Hardie b Miller	28	– c East b Pringle	1
A. P. Wells c Miller b Childs	4	– b Topley	9
C. M. Wells b Miller	27	– c Miller b Foster	0
Imran Khan c Prichard b Miller	11	– c Topley b Foster	16
N. J. Lenham c Prichard b Miller	9	– (8) st East b Miller	27
I. J. Gould c Pringle b Childs	13	– (9) b Miller	26
A. C. S. Pigott run out	24	– (10) c Hardie b Foster	3
J. S. Kimber not out	0	– (11) not out	0
A. R. Clarke c Border b Childs	0	– (7) c East b Pringle	3
B 4, l-b 1	5	B 1, l-b 7	8
1/18 2/62 3/67 4/67 5/94 6/117 7/118 8/154 9/155	155	1/32 2/37 3/55 4/57 5/63 6/77 7/77 8/117 9/134	134

Bonus points – Sussex 1, Essex 4.

Bowling: *First Innings*—Foster 8–3–12–1; Pringle 6–1–16–0; Childs 23.1–9–46–3; Miller 2–4–76–5. *Second Innings*—Foster 23–5–61–5; Pringle 18–7–41–2; Childs 4–3–4–0; Topley 0–9–1; Miller 6.2–2–11–2.

Essex

A. Gooch c and b Green	113
D. E. East c Alikhan b C. M. Wells	13
J. Prichard lbw b Imran	80
R. Border run out	161
R. Hardie c Green b Clarke	17
R. Pringle b Clarke	1
Miller b Imran	17
N. A. Foster lbw b Imran	0
T. D. Topley not out	56
L-b 4	4
1/38 2/198 3/208 4/266 5/280 6/319 7/321 8/462	(8 wkts dec.) 462

K. W. R. Fletcher and J. H. Childs did not bat.

Bonus points – Essex 4, Sussex 2 (Score at 100 overs: 301-5).

Bowling: Imran 29–4–92–3; Pigott 10–1–53–0; C. M. Wells 20–3–49–1; Clarke 5–14–115–2; Green 24–1–90–1; Kimber 12–1–59–0.

Umpires: J. C. Balderstone and H. D. Bird
(subsequently G. Clark, J. A. Jameson and D. O. Oslear).

ESSEX v GLOUCESTERSHIRE

At Ilford, June 15, 16, 17. Gloucestershire won by eight wickets. Gloucestershire 24 pts, Essex 4 pts. Toss: Gloucestershire. Essex, depleted by Test calls and injuries, were easily beaten, providing Border with an unhappy first match as captain. Only Lilley and Topley, who shared an eighth-wicket stand of 105, offered any resistance to Alderman in the first innings. When Essex followed on, it needed an exhilarating century from East to save them from an innings defeat after Lawrence had made a breakthrough with four wickets in nine balls. His career-best 134 came from just 113 balls and contained five sixes and nineteen fours. Batting first on a slow pitch, Gloucestershire had assembled a formidable total consistently with Athey and Russell providing the backbone.

Close of play: First day, Gloucestershire 361-8 (R. C. Russell 64*, D. V. Lawrence 2*); Second day, Essex 41-1 (B. R. Hardie 24*, P. J. Prichard 2*).

Gloucestershire

First innings		Second innings	
A. W. Stovold b Lever	15	c Foster b Miller	28
A. J. Wright c Miller b Topley	42	c East b Childs	19
P. W. Romaines c Stephenson b Foster	3	not out	12
C. W. J. Athey c Foster b Miller	76	not out	9
P. Bainbridge c Lever b Foster	37		
K. M. Curran c East b Foster	21		
J. W. Lloyds c Prichard b Topley	32		
†R. C. Russell c Lilley b Miller	64		
*D. A. Graveney b Lever	47		
D. V. Lawrence c Border b Miller	10		
T. M. Alderman not out	1		
B 4, l-b 12, w 4, n-b 2	22	L-b 1	1
1/18 2/21 3/74 4/152 5/183 6/206 7/243 8/359 9/361	370	1/32 2/50 (2 wkts)	69

Bonus points – Gloucestershire 4, Essex 3 (Score at 100 overs: 336-7).

Bowling: *First Innings*—Lever 23–5–84–2; Foster 26–4–99–3; Topley 19–2–59–2; Child 18–6–54–0; Miller 24.1–7–44–3; Stephenson 3–0–14–0. *Second Innings*—Foster 6–1–9–0 Lever 2–0–12–0; Childs 8–1–24–1; Miller 4.3–0–23–1.

Essex

First innings		Second innings	
B. R. Hardie c Stovold b Alderman	16	c Lloyds b Lawrence	36
J. P. Stephenson c Athey b Alderman	1	lbw b Alderman	1
P. J. Prichard c Curran b Alderman	6	c Alderman b Lawrence	
*A. R. Border lbw b Alderman	14	c Alderman b Lawrence	
A. W. Lilley not out	80	c Russell b Lawrence	
G. Miller c Athey b Lawrence	6	c Bainbridge b Alderman	2
N. A. Foster c Stovold b Curran	3	(8) c Stovold b Lawrence	1
†D. E. East c Lawrence b Curran	0	(7) c Romaines b Lawrence	13
T. D. Topley c Stovold b Curran	44	c Russell b Lawrence	2
J. K. Lever c Russell b Alderman	0	b Alderman	
J. H. Childs lbw b Alderman	0	not out	
L-b 11, n-b 7	18	L-b 3, n-b 4	
1/18 2/24 3/40 4/51 5/74 6/83 7/83 8/188 9/188	188	1/31 2/54 3/54 4/54 5/57 6/104 7/138 8/211 9/212	24

Bonus points – Essex 1, Gloucestershire 4.

Bowling: *First Innings*—Lawrence 19–6–58–1; Alderman 19–6–41–6; Curran 16–4–28– Lloyds 10–0–43–0; Graveney 4–0–7–0. *Second Innings*—Alderman 20–2–84–3; Lawren 17.5–4–85–7; Curran 10–0–68–0; Bainbridge 2–0–9–0.

Umpires: J. C. Balderstone and K. J. Lyons.

At Sheffield, June 18, 20. ESSEX beat YORKSHIRE by nine wickets.

ESSEX v MIDDLESEX

At Chelmsford, June 25, 27, 28. Drawn. Essex 7 pts, Middlesex 5 pts. Toss: Middlesex. Rain washed out all but 23 overs of the final day's play after Essex had gained a slender first-innings lead of 37 on the second. Hardie, with his first Championship half-century of the summer, and Miller batted with great resolution; the most enterprising innings came from Lilley, whose 61 included ten boundaries. Fraser and Emburey bowled with commendable accuracy on a slowish pitch, as had Foster and Childs when Middlesex were made to graft for runs on the opening day. Only Gatting and Williams batted with any real fluency, the former reaching his fifty off 77 balls.

Close of play: First day, Essex 27-0 (G. A. Gooch 14*, B. R. Hardie 12*); Second day, Essex 296.

Middlesex

W. N. Slack b Foster	23	– c Brown b Lever	13
J. D. Carr c Pringle b Foster	29	– c Gooch b Foster	14
*M. W. Gatting c Border b Foster	67		
R. O. Butcher c Border b Foster	6	– retired hurt	23
K. R. Brown lbw b Pringle	12	– (3) b Lever	9
†P. R. Downton b Childs	27	– (5) not out	7
J. E. Emburey c Hardie b Lever	7	– (6) not out	0
N. F. Williams not out	63		
A. R. C. Fraser c Hardie b Childs	17		
P. C. R. Tufnell c Hardie b Childs	1		
N. G. Cowans b Childs	4		
B 1, l-b 1, n-b 1	3		
1/43 2/61 3/67 4/99 5/144 6/164 7/184 8/225 9/239	259	1/18 2/28 3/43	(3 wkts) 66

Bonus points – Middlesex 3, Essex 4.

In the second innings R. O. Butcher retired hurt at 64.

Bowling: *First Innings*—Lever 18–3–64–1; Foster 22–5–64–4; Childs 21.1–7–52–4; Pringle 20–4–49–1; Gooch 5–1–19–0; Miller 2–0–9–0. *Second Innings*—Foster 12–2–36–1; Lever 8–1–23–2; Pringle 3.1–0–7–0.

Essex

*G. A. Gooch c Brown b Tufnell	29
B. R. Hardie c and b Emburey	58
A. R. Border c Butcher b Emburey	20
A. W. Lilley c Emburey b Cowans	61
D. R. Pringle c Carr b Emburey	0
G. Miller lbw b Fraser	47
N. A. Foster c Emburey b Fraser	22
P. J. Prichard c Downton b Fraser	34
J. K. Lever c Emburey b Fraser	0
†A. D. Brown not out	6
J. H. Childs c Downton b Fraser	0
B 1, l-b 16, n-b 2	19
1/60 2/92 3/159 4/159 5/197 6/221 7/263 8/263 9/296	296

Bonus points – Essex 3, Middlesex 2 (Score at 100 overs: 254-6).

Bowling: Fraser 28–7–59–5; Cowans 15–4–43–1; Williams 1–0–4–0; Emburey 47–16–86–3; Tufnell 27–7–87–1.

Umpires: B. J. Meyer and N. T. Plews.

At Canterbury, June 29, 30, July 1. ESSEX drew with KENT.

At Taunton, July 2, 4, 5. ESSEX drew with SOMERSET.

ESSEX v DERBYSHIRE

At Southend, July 13, 14, 15. Essex won by nine wickets. Essex 22 pts, Derbyshire 5 pts. Toss: Derbyshire. An unbroken partnership of 135 between Stephenson and Prichard carried Essex to victory after Derbyshire had lost their last seven wickets cheaply on the final day to leave the home side with 73 overs to score 173. Wright, with a dozen boundaries, batted attractively for Derbyshire on the opening day, as did Morris (one six, eight fours) and Barnett (201 balls, fifteen fours). The Derbyshire captain failed by 1 run to join the ranks of those who have scored hundreds against all the other competing first-class counties. He was undone by the hostility of Foster, who claimed nine wickets in the match. A robust 53 from Gooch in 64 balls and a stylish, unbeaten 85 in 150 balls from Border enabled Essex to record maximum batting points by the 80th over.

Close of play: First day, Derbyshire 332-8 (A. E. Warner 9*, S. J. Base 2*); Second day, Derbyshire 55-3 (P. G. Newman 0*, S. J. Base 2*).

Derbyshire

P. D. Bowler lbw b Gooch	11	– c East b Lever	1
J. G. Wright c Lilley b Gooch	82	– c East b Miller	34
B. Roberts c Gooch b Foster	6	– lbw b Foster	17
J. E. Morris c Miller b Childs	56	– (6) lbw b Lever	36
*K. J. Barnett c East b Foster	99	– (7) c Border b Foster	10
†B. J. M. Maher c Miller b Foster	2	– (8) c Border b Foster	0
S. C. Goldsmith c East b Lever	47	– (9) c Foster b Childs	15
P. G. Newman c Lilley b Foster	6	– (4) b Childs	8
A. E. Warner c Childs b Foster	11	– (10) c and b Lever	6
S. J. Base not out	4	– (5) b Childs	7
D. E. Malcolm c Border b Foster	0	– not out	0
B 2, l-b 9, w 1	12	B 1, l-b 1	2
1/22 2/37 3/120 4/181 5/204 6/310 7/314 8/329 9/334	336	1/12 2/49 3/53 4/66 5/73 6/96 7/96 8/129 9/131	136

Bonus points – Derbyshire 3, Essex 2 (Score at 100 overs: 278-5).

Bowling: *First Innings*—Foster 29–7–96–6; Lever 22–4–72–1; Gooch 14–5–33–2; Miller 22–8–46–0; Childs 28–7–64–1; Stephenson 3–0–14–0. *Second Innings*—Lever 7.4–1–18–3; Foster 22–4–47–3; Childs 21–7–62–3; Miller 5–2–7–1.

Essex

*G. A. Gooch lbw b Warner	53	– lbw b Warner	17
J. P. Stephenson b Newman	16	– not out	78
P. J. Prichard c Bowler b Warner	28	– not out	65
A. R. Border not out	85		
A. W. Lilley b Newman	37		
N. Hussain run out	47		
G. Miller not out	9		
L-b 5, w 2, n-b 18	25	L-b 10, n-b 5	15
1/44 2/92 3/125 4/202 5/283	(5 wkts dec.) 300	1/40	(1 wkt) 175

†D. E. East, N. A. Foster, J. H. Childs and J. K. Lever did not bat.

Bonus points – Essex 4, Derbyshire 2.

Bowling: *First Innings*—Newman 16–2–41–2; Malcolm 14–1–58–0; Base 18–1–99–0; Warner 12–2–30–2; Bowler 13–2–49–0; Barnett 6.5–0–18–0. *Second Innings*—Malcolm 9–1–44–0; Newman 6–1–18–0; Warner 11–7–19–1; Bowler 15–2–47–0; Base 9–1–28–0; Barnett 2.3–0–9–0.

Umpires: D. J. Constant and K. E. Palmer.

ESSEX v LANCASHIRE

At Southend, July 16, 18, 19. Lancashire won by four wickets. Lancashire 20 pts, Essex 7 pts. Toss: Essex. Lancashire reached their target of 289 from 82 overs with five balls to spare, having recovered from losing their first three wickets in eight balls with the scoreboard showing 32 runs. Fairbrother, whose 111 spanned 190 balls and included thirteen fours and a six, led the recovery in a stand of 144 in 42 overs with Watkinson, whose 70 featured nine fours and a six. Following Watkinson's departure, Hughes provided Fairbrother with more valuable support. Twenty-year-old Hussain, playing his second Championship match of the season, was one of four to record half-centuries in the Essex first innings; Stephenson held his side together in the second as Allott reaped the major rewards while quick runs were sought. Fowler, ninth out, and Jesty batted with resolution in Lancashire's first innings.

Close of play: First day, Essex 346-7 (N. Hussain 80*, D. E. East 0*); Second day, Essex 74-1 (J. P. Stephenson 28*, P. J. Prichard 44*).

Essex

*G. A. Gooch b Simmons	96	– lbw b Allott	2
J. P. Stephenson b Simmons	55	– not out	84
P. J. Prichard c Fowler b Hayhurst	4	– lbw b Allott	44
A. R. Border run out	0	– c Hegg b Simmons	10
A. W. Lilley lbw b Simmons	16	– st Hegg b Simmons	2
N. Hussain not out	80	– c and b Allott	14
G. Miller b Folley	77	– (9) b Allott	1
N. A. Foster c Hegg b Simmons	11	– c Hegg b Simmons	3
†D. E. East not out	0	– (7) b Allott	0
D. R. Pringle (did not bat)		– b Allott	7
L-b 5, n-b 2	7	L-b 2	2
1/104 2/123 3/123 4/160 5/182 6/331 7/344 (7 wkts dec.)	346	1/2 2/74 3/113 4/115 5/150 6/150 7/153 8/159 9/169 (9 wkts dec.)	169

J. H. Childs did not bat.

Bonus points – Essex 3, Lancashire 2 (Score at 100 overs: 273-5).

Bowling: *First Innings*—Allott 16–2–46–0; Watkinson 20–7–55–0; Folley 25–5–96–1; Hayhurst 16–4–61–1; Simmons 34–7–83–4. *Second Innings*—Allott 20–4–59–6; Watkinson 6–1–28–0; Folley 5–1–11–0; Simmons 16–2–69–3.

Lancashire

G. D. Mendis c Lilley b Foster	0	– (2) run out	13
G. Fowler c Stephenson b Foster	104	– (1) c Border b Miller	17
T. E. Jesty c and b Childs	73	– b Childs	0
N. H. Fairbrother c East b Foster	23	– c Stephenson b Childs	111
M. Watkinson b Childs	1	– b Childs	70
*D. P. Hughes b Childs	0	– c Border b Pringle	45
A. N. Hayhurst c Lilley b Miller	1	– not out	14
†W. K. Hegg c Hussain b Miller	4		
P. J. W. Allott lbw b Miller	4	– (8) not out	8
Simmons c Miller b Childs	3		
Folley not out	0		
L-b 12, w 1, n-b 1	14	L-b 11	11
/0 2/119 3/160 4/171 5/171 /174 7/198 8/206 9/227	227	1/32 2/32 3/32 4/176 5/261 6/281 (6 wkts)	289

Bonus points – Lancashire 2, Essex 4.

Bowling: *First Innings*—Foster 19–3–47–3; Pringle 11–2–48–0; Gooch 8–3–15–0; Childs 29.4–8–63–4; Miller 20–5–42–3. *Second Innings*—Foster 12–1–54–0; Childs 28.1–8–79–3; Pringle 10–0–38–1; Miller 23–3–91–1; Border 8–3–16–0.

Umpires: D. J. Constant and K. E. Palmer.

At Portsmouth, July 20, 21, 22. ESSEX drew with HAMPSHIRE.

At Leicester, July 23, 25, 26. ESSEX drew with LEICESTERSHIRE.

At Chelmsford, July 30, 31, August 1. ESSEX drew with WEST INDIANS (See West Indian tour section).

At Northampton, August 3, 4, 5. ESSEX beat NORTHAMPTONSHIRE by four wickets.

ESSEX v NOTTINGHAMSHIRE

At Colchester, August 13, 15, 16. Nottinghamshire won by two wickets. Nottinghamshire 24 pts, Essex 6 pts. Toss: Essex. In a thrilling finish, Robinson hit Foster for 2 runs off each of the last two deliveries to secure victory and complete a fine recovery after his side had lost four early wickets. The Nottinghamshire captain, who included eighteen boundaries in his unbeaten 217-ball stay, shared a century stand with Birch, whose 75 contained thirteen fours. Border, with his sixth century of the summer, held the Essex first innings together, finally adding 49 with Childs for the last wicket, while Gooch batted attractively in the second. Robinson had earlier shown his class in Nottinghamshire's first innings, when Randall's 76 not out came from 129 deliveries. Pringle captured three of his six wickets in his first four overs as Nottinghamshire set off to meet a target of 274 in 69 overs, but Robinson was to have the final word.

Close of play: First day, Essex 347-9 (A. R. Border 130*, J. H. Childs 25*); Second day, Essex 68-1 (G. A. Gooch 54*, A. W. Lilley 7*).

Essex

*G. A. Gooch lbw b Cooper	36	– c Cooper b Evans	90
J. P. Stephenson b Cooper	3	– c Scott b Cooper	0
A. W. Lilley b Hemmings	29	– c Broad b Hemmings	42
A. R. Border not out	130	– c Stephenson b Evans	11
P. J. Prichard c Evans b Hemmings	32	– not out	33
D. R. Pringle c Broad b Evans	12	– c Scott b Stephenson	31
G. Miller c Randall b Cooper	10		
N. A. Foster c Scott b Cooper	0	– not out	5
†D. E. East b Stephenson	43	– (7) c Martindale b Hemmings	2
T. D. Topley lbw b Stephenson	0		
J. H. Childs not out	25		
B 2, l-b 10, w 5, n-b 10	27	B 6, l-b 4, n-b 2	12
1/35 2/63 3/105 4/168 5/207 6/230 7/230 8/292 9/298 (9 wkts dec.)	347	1/16 2/132 3/152 4/152 5/204 6/207 (6 wkts dec.)	226

Bonus points – Essex 4, Nottinghamshire 4 (Score at 100 overs: 307-9).

Bowling: *First Innings*—Stephenson 30–7–74–2; Cooper 30–5–114–4; Evans 15–1–31–1; Hemmings 35–7–116–2. *Second Innings*—Stephenson 9–0–43–1; Cooper 14–3–54–1; Hemmings 22–2–88–2; Evans 8–1–31–2.

Nottinghamshire

	First innings		Second innings	
B. C. Broad c Prichard b Childs	33	– c Gooch b Pringle	2
*R. T. Robinson c Foster b Miller	63	– not out	134
P. Johnson c Miller b Foster	23	– lbw b Pringle	5
D. J. R. Martindale c Foster b Miller	18	– c Miller b Pringle	10
D. W. Randall not out	76	– lbw b Foster	1
J. D. Birch b Pringle	9	– c East b Pringle	75
F. D. Stephenson c Border b Foster	35	– c East b Pringle	18
K. P. Evans not out	31	– lbw b Foster	3
E. E. Hemmings (did not bat)		– b Pringle	13
†C. W. Scott (did not bat)		– not out	1
L-b 6, n-b 6	12	B 3, l-b 6, n-b 3	12
1/64 2/105 3/142 4/158 5/179 6/248 (6 wkts dec.)	300	1/3 2/15 3/37 4/39 5/164 6/215 7/245 8/266 (8 wkts)	274

K. E. Cooper did not bat.

Bonus points – Nottinghamshire 4, Essex 2.

Bowling: *First Innings*—Foster 24–4–78–2; Pringle 15–3–40–1; Childs 18.2–2–61–1; Miller 21–2–74–2; Topley 11–1–41–0. *Second Innings*—Foster 20–2–88–2; Pringle 19–1–82–6; Miller 15–2–59–0; Childs 14–2–36–0; Border 1–1–0–0.

Umpires: B. Dudleston and J. H. Harris.

ESSEX v GLAMORGAN

At Colchester, August 17, 18, 19. Drawn. Essex 14 pts, Glamorgan 5 pts. Toss: Glamorgan. The match ended in confusion when Pringle was run out attempting the winning run from the final delivery. With the injured Miller absent from the ground, and therefore unable to bat if required, Glamorgan argued that they should be awarded an additional eight points for a tied match. The umpires, however, deemed the result was a draw, and an adjudication from the TCCB upheld their decision. Pringle, with his second six-wicket haul in successive days, made the Welsh county struggle in their first innings, but Butcher and Ontong provided substance in the second. Gooch, following his half-century in Essex's first innings, again batted with great authority as his side chased a target of 273 in two hours plus twenty overs. Pringle's late heroics saw him gather 54 from 56 balls, but the loss of eight overs through rain immediately after tea had been detrimental to Essex's chances.

Close of play: First day, Essex 96-1 (G. A. Gooch 61*, A. W. Lilley 25*); Second day, Glamorgan 154-4 (G. C. Holmes 0*, R. C. Ontong 0*).

Glamorgan

	First innings	Second innings	
A. R. Butcher c Border b Pringle	17	– run out	66
P. A. Cottey c Lilley b Foster	1	– c East b Childs	47
*H. Morris lbw b Topley	22	– c East b Gooch	31
M. P. Maynard c East b Pringle	26	– st East b Childs	0
G. C. Holmes c Border b Pringle	36	– c Pringle b Childs	8
R. C. Ontong c Lilley b Childs	34	– not out	83
I. G. Thomas b Pringle	9	– c East b Border	19
†C. P. Metson b Childs	3	– c Stephenson b Topley	7
J. Derrick c Stephenson b Pringle	15	– not out	16
P. D. North not out	15		
S. L. Watkin c Border b Pringle	0		
B 2, l-b 5, n-b 7	14	B 5, l-b 5, n-b 4	14
1/8 2/45 3/47 4/80 5/143 6/155 7/157 8/162 9/192	192	1/79 2/154 3/154 4/154 5/172 6/218 7/253 (7 wkts dec.)	291

Bonus points – Glamorgan 1, Essex 4.

Bowling: *First Innings*—Foster 20–5–52–1; Pringle 21.4–7–51–6; Topley 14–1–48–1; Gooch 12–7–17–0; Childs 9–5–17–2. *Second Innings*—Foster 16–4–56–0; Pringle 16–6–30–0; Topley 18–2–63–1; Childs 40–17–91–3; Gooch 8–2–21–1; Border 5–0–20–1.

Essex

First innings		Second innings	
*G. A. Gooch b Watkin	65	b Ontong	72
J. P. Stephenson c Thomas b Watkin	4	c Morris b Ontong	31
A. W. Lilley c Metson b Watkin	41	(4) b Holmes	45
A. R. Border c Maynard b Thomas	1	(3) c Metson b Watkin	23
P. J. Prichard c Cottey b Ontong	43	(6) b Holmes	13
D. R. Pringle lbw b Watkin	3	(5) run out	54
N. A. Foster c Metson b North	3	(8) st Metson b Holmes	5
†D. E. East not out	39	(7) c Butcher b Holmes	5
T. D. Topley c Holmes b North	2	c Maynard b Holmes	1
J. H. Childs c Maynard b North	0	not out	4
G. Miller absent injured			
B 1, l-b 3, w 1, n-b 5	10	B 6, l-b 11, n-b 2	19
1/24 2/100 3/101 4/149 5/157 6/165 7/182 8/209 9/211	211	1/82 2/115 3/147 4/205 5/225 6/237 7/248 8/260 9/272	(9 wkts) 272

Bonus points – Essex 2, Glamorgan 4.

Bowling: *First Innings*—Thomas 14–2–61–1; Watkin 23–5–56–4; Derrick 8–1–29–0; Ontong 18–5–37–1; North 10.5–3–24–3. *Second Innings*—Thomas 7–0–48–0; Watkin 12–0–55–1; North 4–0–20–0; Ontong 13–0–71–2; Derrick 4–0–23–0; Holmes 7–0–38–5.

Umpires: B. Dudleston and J. H. Harris.

At Worcester, August 20, 22, 23. ESSEX beat WORCESTERSHIRE by 77 runs.

At The Oval, August 30, 31, September 1, 2. ESSEX drew with SURREY.

ESSEX v LEICESTERSHIRE

At Chelmsford, September 9, 10, 11. Essex won by an innings and 83 runs with a day to spare. Essex 24 pts, Leicestershire 5 pts. Toss: Essex. After Stephenson missed his maiden centur by 1 run, Hussain gathered his with a delightful innings, full of punishing strokes. On th second day, he scored a hundred before lunch, and in all he hit 21 fours and a six from 21 balls. Waugh, on his home Championship début, Prichard and East all scored freely. Gower' response was to record his best in the Championship, a magnificent innings full of exquisi timing which brought him 22 fours and a six during a stay of 254 minutes and 240 deliveries Despite his immense contribution, however, Leicestershire were forced to follow on 32 behind and were once again undone by Childs, who found enough turn and bounce to finis the match with eleven wickets. The highlight of Leicestershire's second innings was a spirite maiden half-century by Taylor, whose 60 came from 42 balls in less than half an hour an contained six sixes and five fours.

Close of play: First day, Essex 362-6 (N. Hussain 35*, G. Miller 0*); Second da Leicestershire 218-4 (D. I. Gower 143*, P. N. Hepworth 9*).

Essex

*G. A. Gooch b Ferris	23	†D. E. East c Gower b Taylor	66
J. P. Stephenson c Briers b Willey	99	N. A. Foster not out	6
A. W. Lilley lbw b Willey	21		
M. E. Waugh c Briers b Willey	86	B 2, l-b 9, w 2, n-b 25	38
P. J. Prichard b Willey	59		
N. Hussain not out	165	1/45 2/117 3/199 (8 wkts dec.)	592
D. R. Pringle run out	12	4/282 5/335 6/358	
G. Miller b Lewis	17	7/422 8/571	

J. H. Childs did not bat.

Bonus points – Essex 4, Leicestershire 2 (Score at 100 overs: 353-5).

Bowling: Ferris 29–2–117–1; Agnew 31–2–122–0; Taylor 19–2–80–1; Lewis 22–4–109–1; Willey 43–6–153–4.

Leicestershire

*D. I. Gower lbw b Childs	172	– c East b Foster	37
N. E. Briers c East b Foster	6	– c Miller b Childs	25
P. Willey run out	11	– b Childs	13
J. J. Whitaker c Miller b Childs	30	– c Prichard b Foster	1
T. J. Boon c Hussain b Childs	11	– not out	63
P. N. Hepworth c Lilley b Childs	9	– lbw b Foster	4
C. C. Lewis c Prichard b Miller	5	– c Foster b Childs	0
†P. Whitticase b Foster	10	– c Stephenson b Childs	9
J. P. Agnew c Waugh b Childs	2	– c Prichard b Pringle	4
G. J. F. Ferris b Foster	0	– st East b Childs	25
L. B. Taylor not out	0	– c Hussain b Childs	60
B 1, l-b 10, w 1	12		
1/14 2/77 3/120 4/163 5/238 6/249 7/263 8/268 9/268	268	1/62 2/62 3/72 4/81 5/90 6/91 7/117 8/122 9/169	241

Bonus points – Leicestershire 3, Essex 4.

Bowling: *First Innings*—Foster 18–4–73–3; Pringle 7–0–41–0; Childs 39.2–11–88–5; Miller 29–10–48–1; Gooch 3–1–7–0. *Second Innings*—Foster 14–3–64–3; Pringle 13–2–54–1; Miller 5–0–31–0; Childs 23.3–4–92–6.

Umpires: D. J. Constant and M. J. Kitchen.

ESSEX v NORTHAMPTONSHIRE

At Chelmsford, September 14, 15, 16, 17. Essex won by six wickets. Essex 21 pts, Northamptonshire 7 pts. Toss: Northamptonshire. Given a target of 272 in 61 overs, Essex won with an over to spare to finish third in the Championship table behind Worcestershire and Kent, these two having won their final matches the previous day. Gooch twice pulled Nick Cook for six and struck nine other boundaries as he hit his sixth century of the summer from 118 balls. Prichard ensured victory by completing his fifty in less than an hour. Lamb dominated Northamptonshire's first innings, collecting twenty fours and two sixes in just over four hours, and Fordham and Williams batted attractively in the second. Nick Cook, the left-arm spinner, returned his best figures for Northamptonshire as Essex made steady progress in their first innings, his six for 56 being achieved while he nursed a broken right thumb, suffered in the previous match against Yorkshire.

Close of play: First day, Northamptonshire 301-6 (D. J. Wild 40*, D. Ripley 0*); Second day, Essex 199-5 (N. Hussain 2*, D. R. Pringle 0*); Third day, Northamptonshire 200-6 (R. G. Williams 45*, D. Ripley 4*).

Northamptonshire

First Innings		Second Innings	
*G. Cook b Foster	3	b Childs	6
A. Fordham c East b Stephenson	34	c East b Foster	70
R. J. Bailey c East b Childs	15	c Pringle b Childs	39
A. J. Lamb b Childs	155	c Gooch b Childs	16
D. J. Capel lbw b Foster	10	lbw b Childs	0
R. G. Williams b Childs	28	not out	63
D. J. Wild c Gooch b Pringle	46	c Lilley b Foster	13
†D. Ripley c East b Foster	9	c Waugh b Pringle	11
D. K. Lillee c Gooch b Pringle	2	c Miller b Foster	13
M. A. Robinson not out	19	not out	2
N. G. B. Cook b Foster	3		
L-b 8, n-b 8	16	B 2, l-b 6, n-b 2	10
1/6 2/37 3/69 4/113 5/200 6/295 7/310 8/312 9/326	340	1/19 2/90 3/115 4/115 5/166 6/190 7/213 8/240 (8 wkts dec.)	243

Bonus points – Northamptonshire 4, Essex 2 (Score at 100 overs: 306-6).

Bowling: *First Innings*—Foster 33.4–4–106–4; Pringle 22–3–69–2; Childs 31–14–55–3; Gooch 5–1–18–0; Stephenson 7–0–27–1; Miller 16–1–57–0. *Second Innings*—Foster 21–2–68–3; Pringle 12–2–30–1; Childs 33–11–87–4; Miller 10–2–33–0; Gooch 6–0–17–0.

Essex

First Innings		Second Innings	
*G. A. Gooch c Ripley b Lillee	35	b N. G. B. Cook	108
J. P. Stephenson c Robinson b N. G. B. Cook	38	lbw b Lillee	1
A. W. Lilley lbw b Lillee	48	c Wild b N. G. B. Cook	43
M. E. Waugh b N. G. B. Cook	35	c Ripley b N. G. B. Cook	28
P. J. Prichard b Lillee	27	not out	55
N. Hussain b Williams	52	not out	17
D. R. Pringle st Ripley b N. G. B. Cook	12		
G. Miller c Bailey b N. G. B. Cook	10		
†D. E. East c Williams b N. G. B. Cook	24		
N. A. Foster c Fordham b N. G. B. Cook	2		
J. H. Childs not out	3		
B 8, l-b 14, n-b 4	26	B 10, l-b 13	23
1/55 2/89 3/131 4/193 5/198 6/257 7/277 8/285 9/289	312	1/5 2/134 3/180 4/227 (4 wkts)	275

Bonus points – Essex 3, Northamptonshire 3 (Score at 100 overs: 287-8).

Bowling: *First Innings*—Lillee 27–3–101–3; Robinson 16–3–48–0; N. G. B. Cook 42.2–18–56–6; Capel 5–1–29–0; Williams 19–5–56–1. *Second Innings*—Lillee 9–2–28–1 Robinson 5–1–14–0; N. G. B. Cook 25–2–100–3; Williams 15–1–74–0; Bailey 6–0–36–0.

Umpires: D. G. L. Evans and R. Palmer.

GLAMORGAN

Patron: HRH The Prince of Wales
President: His Honour Rowe Harding
Chairman: A. R. Lewis
Chairman, Cricket Committee: A. R. Lewis
Chief Executive: P. G. Carling
Secretary: A. P. Dilloway
Sophia Gardens, Cardiff CF1 9XR
(Telephone: 0222-343478)
Captain: H. Morris
Senior Coach: A. Jones

ottom of the Britannic Assurance Championship table in their entenary season was a bitter disappointment for Glamorgan. "We have good batting side on paper, but unfortunately we did not produce the oods", summed up Hugh Morris, the captain. "We should have scored a ot more runs and it was frustrating when we failed to capitalise on some xcellent starts. None of our bowlers took 50 wickets, and so we must ccept that it was a season when we did not do ourselves justice. Iowever, we made some significant strides in limited-overs matches. We nished fifth in the Refuge Assurance League, which is our highest osition. We reached the semi-finals of the Benson and Hedges Cup for e first time, and we went to the quarter-finals of the NatWest Bank rophy. Having achieved that, I think there are some very bright spots n the horizon."

Matthew Maynard was the season's brightest spot. He finished top of e Glamorgan first-class averages for the second consecutive season, nd in 120 innings in just over three years he has scored 30 half-centuries r his county and eight centuries. He made his Test début against West dies at The Oval, and while some critics suggested he had been thrown too soon, others considered he should have been in the England side om the one-day internationals as the most exciting attacking young tsman in the country.

His moment of greatest grief, however, came with a bizarre dismissal the Benson and Hedges semi-final, which Derbyshire won by 14 runs Swansea. As he twisted to play a delivery from Holding, his shoulder ocked his helmet off and it fell on to his wicket. "I had not been earing my chin-strap and nobody let me forget it for weeks", he called. "This got to me eventually and I lost my confidence."

For the first time, Glamorgan spent a week of preparation in the nshine of southern Spain. The benefit of this quickly materialised. In e first home Championship fixture, Glamorgan scored 543 for eight, e record score at Sophia Gardens and the seventh highest in the unty's history. Alas, the high promise could not be maintained. Morris, ving started off well, went through a bad spell and had no sooner covered form than a torn knee cartilage put him out. In August, dney Ontong and Steve Barwick were involved in a car crash while velling from Colchester to Wellingborough, and both missed the last e Championship games. With Ravi Shastri also on the injury list, amorgan played Leicestershire at Neath without their four leading wlers.

Although Shastri's bowling faded to a surprising degree, his clea hitting was always refreshing, and he finished well ahead of his rivals a the top of the Refuge Assurance League six-hit table. Geoff Holmes, wh missed two matches because of injury, failed by 1 run to complete 1,00 in first-class matches. A notable achievement was his century in eac innings at Taunton. Alan Butcher was the only batsman, other tha Maynard, to reach 1,000 runs, with nine half-centuries and 166 agains Cambridge University at Fenner's. His experience was invaluabl especially after John Hopkins, his opening partner, had lost his place an announced that he would retire at the end of the season. Hopkins serve the county with outstanding dedication since his début in 1970 and hi 230 at Worcester in 1977 is the highest post-war innings for the count Always a popular figure, Hopkins, scorer of 13,610 first-class runs an eighteen centuries for Glamorgan, announced his retirement on the da that Gregory Thomas scored his maiden century.

Anthony Cottey proved a valuable performer with his efficient strok play and outstanding fielding while given his longest run in the fir team. Glamorgan also were delighted with the reliable contribution John Derrick as a medium-pacer and awarded him his county cap. H batting fell away, but he took 45 Championship wickets at 31.51 ru each and his four for 36 brought a Sunday victory over Yorkshire to kee Glamorgan in the race for a top position. Colin Metson, despite son patchy days, displayed alertness and enthusiasm in claiming dismissals behind the stumps. He shows great promise, but nee consistency.

The bowling left a great deal to be desired. However, Steve Watkin, tall 23 year old, made the most of his opportunities and finished top the averages with 46 first-class wickets at just under 31 runs eac Accuracy of line and length brought its reward and he took eight for in Warwickshire's first innings at Edgbaston. Thomas declined to rene his contract for 1989 after his plea to be released before the 1988 seas had been rejected by one vote. His 48 wickets cost almost 32 runs eac but he hit two centuries late in the season to leave a lasting memo Corrie van Zyl returned to South Africa when he was dropped from first-team squad, Steve Bastien took five for 90 against Leicestershire Neath on his début, but Barwick was dogged by injuries. The spinn had few pickings. Generally, pitches at Cardiff and Swansea were sl and of low bounce.

Tony Lewis took over as the club's centenary-year chairman, and advice of other former players, Don Shepherd and Peter Walker, w sought while sharpening up coaching and development. Late in season, an administrative reshaping resulted in Philip Carling, secretary, becoming chief executive, with Tony Dilloway the n secretary and Mike Fatkin appointed assistant-secretary. – John Bill

[*Bill Smith*

Back row: G. N. Lewis (*scorer*), G. C. Holmes, J. Derrick, S. L. Watkin, R. J. Shastri, J. G. Thomas, M. P. Maynard, C. P. Metson. *Front row:* S. R. Barwick, J. A. Hopkins, H. Morris (*captain*), A. R. Butcher, R. C. Ontong.

GLAMORGAN RESULTS

All first-class matches – Played 23: Won 1, Lost 8, Drawn 14. Abandoned 1.

County Championship matches – Played 21: Won 1, Lost 8, Drawn 12. Abandoned 1.

Bonus points – Batting 42, Bowling 53.

Competition placings – Britannic Assurance County Championship, 17th; NatWest Bank Trophy, q-f; Benson and Hedges Cup, s-f; Refuge Assurance League, 5th equal.

BRITANNIC ASSURANCE CHAMPIONSHIP AVERAGES

BATTING

	Birthplace	*M*	*I*	*NO*	*R*	*HI*	*Avge*
‡M. P. Maynard	*Oldham*	19	35	6	1,361	126	46.9
‡R. C. Ontong	*Johannesburg, SA*	16	24	8	734	120*	45.8
§‡R. J. Shastri	*Bombay, India*	12	19	2	575	157	33.8
‡G. C. Holmes	*Newcastle-upon-Tyne*	18	30	3	912	117	33.7
‡A. R. Butcher	*Croydon*	21	38	2	1,098	93	30.5
‡H. Morris	*Cardiff*	18	32	3	820	87	28.2
P. D. North	*Newport*	5	7	3	107	41*	26.7
P. A. Cottey	*Swansea*	12	21	3	443	73	24.6
‡J. G. Thomas	*Trebanos*	15	25	4	515	110	24.5
‡J. A. Hopkins	*Maesteg*	11	20	1	368	71	19.3
‡C. P. Metson	*Goffs Oak*	21	29	7	347	48	15.7
P. G. P. Roebuck	*Bath*	2	4	0	60	46	15.0
S. Bastien	*Stepney, London*	4	6	2	57	36*	14.2
M. J. Cann	*Cardiff*	6	7	0	78	28	11.1
‡J. Derrick	*Cwmaman*	19	26	5	212	50*	10.0
S. L. Watkin	*Maesteg*	15	19	7	115	23	9.5
‡S. R. Barwick	*Neath*	12	7	2	40	30	8.0
§C. J. P. G. van Zyl	*Bloemfontein, SA*	3	5	1	30	11	7.5

Also batted: S. Monkhouse (*Bury*) (2 matches) 0*.

* *Signifies not out.* ‡ *Denotes county cap.* § *Not qualified for England.*

The following played a total of eleven three-figure innings for Glamorgan in Coun Championship matches – G. C. Holmes 4, M. P. Maynard 3, J. G. Thomas 2, R. C. Ontong R. J. Shastri 1.

BOWLING

	O	*M*	*R*	*W*	*BB*	*5W/i*	*Av*
S. L. Watkin	505.3	125	1,347	44	8-59	2	30.
J. G. Thomas	400.2	60	1,444	47	6-68	2	30.
J. Derrick	504.1	123	1,418	45	6-54	1	31.
S. R. Barwick	383.5	102	1.014	32	5-37	1	31.
R. J. Shastri	304.2	91	709	20	7-49	1	35.
G. C. Holmes	116.2	12	440	11	5-38	1	40.
R. C. Ontong	376.1	88	1,078	24	4-38	0	44

Also bowled: S. Bastien 119.1–35–289–8; A. R. Butcher 47–8–172–5; M. J. Ca 14–2–63–4; J. A. Hopkins 5–1–46–0; M. P. Maynard 5–2–13–0; S. Monkhouse 44–8–118 H. Morris 4.3–0–58–0; P. D. North 64.5–12–195–5; C. J. P. G. van Zyl 99.1–27–291–2.

Wicket-keeper: C. P. Metson 51 ct, 6 st.

Leading Fielder: M. P. Maynard 21.

At Bristol, April 21, 22, 23, 25. GLAMORGAN lost to GLOUCESTERSHIRE by six wickets.

GLAMORGAN v SOMERSET

At Cardiff, April 28, 29, 30, May 2. Drawn. Glamorgan 8 pts, Somerset 4 pts. Toss: Somerset. Glamorgan's 543 for eight, after they had been asked to bat on a low, slow pitch, was the highest total at Sophia Gardens, surpassing Northamptonshire's 529 for eight declared in 1983. Curiously, it came about because of bad light. Glamorgan, resuming on the second day in the late afternoon, were overtaken by gathering darkness as the cloud ceiling dropped dramatically. Had they declared, Somerset unhesitatingly would have appealed against the light, so Morris kept his batsmen out in the gloom while the runs accumulated. Maynard's 122 in 187 minutes, with one six and seventeen fours, was his second century in successive matches; Shastri's 157 in five hours (nineteen fours) was his highest Championship innings; and Holmes also repeated his century of the previous match at Bristol, making 108 in 207 minutes (ten fours). Not since E. Davies, W. G. A. Parkhouse and A. J. Watkins at Trent Bridge in 1949 had three Glamorgan batsmen hit hundreds in one innings, while Glamorgan's total was their seventh highest and their biggest score for 37 years. When Somerset did bat, they were forced to follow on on the fourth day, but with the rain still interrupting, play was severely restricted.

Close of play: First day, Glamorgan 400-4 (R. J. Shastri 138*, G. C. Holmes 31*); Second day, Glamorgan 543-8 (C. P. Metson 31*, S. L. Watkin 7*); Third day, Somerset 243-8 (N. A. Mallender 20*, A. N. Jones 0*).

Glamorgan

.. R. Butcher c Burns b Waugh	48	†C. P. Metson not out	31
. A. Hopkins c Mallender b Waugh	42	S. L. Watkin not out	7
H. Morris c and b Mallender	6		
. P. Maynard c and b Rose	122	L-b 3, n-b 12	15
. J. Shastri b Roebuck	157		
. C. Holmes b Foster	108	1/91 2/96 3/113 (8 wkts dec.)	543
.. C. Ontong c Burns b Rose	5	4/329 5/460 6/473	
G. Thomas b Rose	2	7/475 8/527	

R. Barwick did not bat.

Bonus points – Glamorgan 4, Somerset 1 (Score at 100 overs: 356-4).

Bowling: Mallender 24–7–79–1; Jones 22–2–65–0; Rose 24–2–96–3; Foster 17–1–84–1; Marks 33–7–107–0; Waugh 11–1–33–2; Harden 14–1–50–0; Roebuck 11–0–26–1.

Somerset

A. Felton b Thomas	8 – not out	64
. M. Roebuck c Metson b Barwick	40 – not out	24
J. E. Hardy b Thomas	0	
R. Waugh c Metson b Ontong	53	
J. Harden b Barwick	0	
J. Marks b Butcher	8	
. D. Burns lbw b Butcher	66	
D. Rose c Metson b Barwick	27	
A. Mallender not out	29	
N. Jones c Metson b Thomas	6	
J. Foster b Thomas	9	
B 6, l-b 4, n-b 11	21	B 4, l-b 4, n-b 4 12
28 2/32 3/76 4/82 5/98 .44 7/220 8/236 9/251	267	(no wkt) 100

Bonus points – Somerset 3, Glamorgan 4.

Bowling: *First Innings*—Thomas 24.2–6–74–4; Watkin 19–4–59–0; Barwick 26–6–74–3; Holmes 3–0–9–0; Butcher 10–1–28–2; Ontong 9–4–8–1; Maynard 2–0–5–0. *Second Innings*—Thomas 4–0–14–0; Barwick 5–2–11–0; Butcher 2–0–6–0; Shastri 6–2–14–0; Watkin 7–3–8–0; Ontong 9–3–12–0; Holmes 5–1–19–0; Maynard 3–2–8–0.

Umpires: A. A. Jones and M. J. Kitchen.

At Cambridge, May 5, 6, 7. GLAMORGAN drew with CAMBRIDGE UNIVERSITY.

At Bournemouth, May 18, 19, 20. GLAMORGAN drew with HAMPSHIRE.

GLAMORGAN v DERBYSHIRE

At Swansea, May 21, 23, 24. Drawn. Glamorgan 2 pts, Derbyshire 4 pts. Toss: Derbyshire Rain prevented play after lunch on the second and third days. Derbyshire batted on until jus before lunch on the second, accumulating their highest score against the Welsh county an allowing Morris to take his score to 175 (two sixes, twenty fours) in just under six and a ha hours. On the opening day, he and Wright added a punishing 192 for the third wicket on placid pitch after Thomas in his fourth over had dismissed Bowler and Roberts. Thoma developed a strain in his side and could not bowl after lunch on the first day, and Glamorga were further handicapped when Shastri retired, feeling unwell. When Glamorgan battec Cottey reached his highest Championship score with an unbeaten 49 before rain ended pla on the last morning.

Close of play: First day, Derbyshire 356-6 (J. E. Morris 159*, R. J. Finney 31*); Second da Glamorgan 2-0 (J. A. Hopkins 1*, P. A. Cottey 1*).

Derbyshire

P. D. Bowler c Morris b Thomas 10	P. G. Newman c Butcher b Barwick . . 2
J. G. Wright c Metson b Derrick 79	A. E. Warner not out 2
B. Roberts b Thomas 0	D. E. Malcolm b Derrick 1
J. E. Morris c Hopkins b Barwick 175	
*K. J. Barnett c Morris b Derrick 0	B 12, l-b 13, w 6, n-b 9 . . . . . .
S. C. Goldsmith run out 25	
†B. J. M. Maher lbw b Barwick 14	1/14 2/14 3/206 4/206 5/261 4
R. J. Finney c Hopkins b Barwick 45	6/296 7/382 8/389 9/428

Bonus points – Derbyshire 4, Glamorgan 2 (Score at 100 overs: 327-6).

Bowling: Thomas 7–2–16–2; Barwick 41–12–130–4; Derrick 38.2–7–116–3; Onto 20–7–71–0; Butcher 9–2–27–0; Shastri 9–2–41–0; Holmes 9–1–27–0.

Glamorgan

J. A. Hopkins not out 30
P. A. Cottey not out 49
B 4, l-b 1, w 1, n-b 4 10

(no wkt) 89

A. R. Butcher, *H. Morris, R. J. Shastri, G. C. Holmes, R. C. Ontong, J. Derrick, J. Thomas, †C. P. Metson and S. R. Barwick did not bat.

Bowling: Malcolm 11–3–23–0; Newman 9–1–22–0; Warner 8–3–9–0; Roberts 7–2–16– Finney 3–0–14–0.

Umpires: M. J. Kitchen and P. B. Wight.

GLAMORGAN v GLOUCESTERSHIRE

\t Swansea, May 28, 30, 31. Abandoned.

GLAMORGAN v KENT

\t Cardiff, June 4, 6, 7. Kent won by four wickets. Kent 21 pts, Glamorgan 1 pt. Toss: ;lamorgan. Glamorgan received permission from the TCCB to use a shaved pitch to see if onditions would encourage spin bowling. Both captains agreed to the experiment, but it esulted only in a pitch of low bounce and slow turn which so restricted strokeplay that ;lamorgan raised just one batting point. There were three unbeaten centuries and three eclarations, with Kent set a target of 270 in what turned out to be 66 overs. They lost their rst three wickets cheaply and their interest had to be rekindled by spinners feeding runs enerously. Tavaré guided them to victory with fourteen balls to spare, his unbeaten 129 in ıst over three hours containing one six and fifteen fours. The other unbeaten century-makers ere Ontong in the home side's first innings with 120 (five sixes, seven fours) off 220 balls in 31 minutes, and Taylor in the Kent first innings. His 112 included ten fours and took a little ver four hours before they declared 117 runs behind.

Close of play: First day, Glamorgan 274-7 (R. C. Ontong 76*, J. Derrick 5*); Second day, lamorgan 16-1 (A. R. Butcher 2*, C. P. Metson 8*).

;lamorgan

R. Butcher c Harman b G. R. Cowdrey	52	– c Taylor b Pienaar	8
A. Hopkins c Davis b C. S. Cowdrey	61	– c Taylor b Ellison	5
I. Morris b C. S. Cowdrey	0	– (4) c Tavaré b Harman	38
. P. Maynard b Pienaar	1	– (5) c and b Davis	5
J. Shastri st Marsh b Davis	20	– (6) c G. R. Cowdrey b Harman	5
. C. Holmes b Harman	34	– (7) c C. S. Cowdrey b Davis	10
C. Ontong not out	120	– (8) not out	12
G. Thomas c Marsh b Davis	14	– (9) not out	10
Derrick not out	50		
:. P. Metson (did not bat)		– (3) b Davis	48
B 11, l-b 5, n-b 1	17	B 3, l-b 2, w 3, n-b 3	11
38 2/97 3/104 4/139 5/162 194 7/253 (7 wkts dec.)	369	1/8 2/34 3/96 4/110 5/116 6/121 7/136 (7 wkts dec.)	152

R. Barwick did not bat.

Bonus points – Glamorgan 1, Kent 2 (Score at 100 overs: 197-6)

Bowling: *First Innings*—Ellison 27–9–69–0; Pienaar 20–3–53–1; Davis 36–11–94–2; C. S. wdrey 24–6–66–2; Harman 20–5–51–1; G. R. Cowdrey 15–8–20–1. *Second Innings*—Ellison -1–53–1; Pienaar 10–3–19–1; Davis 13–5–32–3; C. S. Cowdrey 6–1–19–0; Harman -24–2.

ent

R. Benson b Shastri	54	– run out	5
R. Taylor not out	112	– c Shastri b Barwick	6
G. Hinks lbw b Shastri	72	– c Maynard b Thomas	17
J. Tavaré (did not bat)		– not out	129
F. Pienaar (did not bat)		– c Holmes b Shastri	34
. S. Cowdrey (did not bat)		– lbw b Thomas	49
R. Cowdrey (did not bat)		– b Barwick	6
A. Marsh (did not bat)		– not out	19
B 4, l-b 6, n-b 4	14	L-b 6	6
3 2/252 (2 wkts dec.)	252	1/7 2/11 3/29 4/114 5/224 6/239 (6 wkts)	271

M. Ellison, M. D. Harman and R. P. Davis did not bat.

Bonus points – Kent 3.

Bowling: *First Innings*—Thomas 13–1–37–0; Barwick 15–5–31–0; Ontong 20–1–80–0; Shastri 23.4–2–59–2; Derrick 4–2–10–0; Butcher 7–2–25–0. *Second Innings*—Thomas 14–2–43–2; Barwick 10–0–43–2; Shastri 21.4–6–89–1; Ontong 14–0–65–0; Butcher 4–0–25–0

Umpires: J. D. Bond and D. J. Constant.

At Nottingham, June 11, 13, 14. GLAMORGAN lost to NOTTINGHAMSHIRE by 14 runs.

At Leicester, June 15, 16, 17. GLAMORGAN drew with LEICESTERSHIRE.

GLAMORGAN v LANCASHIRE

At Swansea, June 25, 27, 28. Lancashire won by 72 runs. Lancashire 21 pts, Glamorgan 5 pts. Toss: Lancashire. Batting last was always going to be an ordeal on a pitch designed to rende maximum assistance to the spinners, and Glamorgan, requiring 120 to win, failed dismally o the final day. The previous day, Shastri had found bounce as well as turn and was virtual unplayable in Lancashire's second innings, which was dominated by Mendis's magnifice defiance. He carried his bat for 65, faced 283 balls, and stayed for four and a quarter hour He should have been run out for 31; indeed was so far down the pitch that he made no effo to get back – until Maynard's return was too high for the wicket-keeper to gather cleanly Shastri's best figures for the county, seven for 49, gave him a match analysis of eleven for 9 But the final day belonged to Simmons and Folley. Simmons, who had taken his 1,000 wicket in first-class cricket when he bowled Derrick in the first innings, finished with four f 9 as all Glamorgan's batsmen were dismissed while 23 runs were added to the openin partnership of 24. Folley's share, six for 20, included four of the top five batsmen. The innin lasted fewer than 90 minutes, and the Welsh county's total was their lowest since Ke dismissed them for 46 at Cardiff in 1979.

Close of play: First day, Glamorgan 127-5 (R. J. Shastri 8*); Second day, Lancashire 16

Lancashire

G. D. Mendis c Maynard b Watkin	13	– (2) not out
G. Fowler c Metson b Thomas	13	– (1) c Butcher b Shastri
T. E. Jesty c Maynard b Shastri	37	– c Butcher b Shastri
N. H. Fairbrother c Morris b Watkin	8	– c Metson b Ontong
M. Watkinson c Metson b Shastri	9	– c Maynard b Ontong
*D. P. Hughes b Ontong	7	– c Maynard b Shastri
Wasim Akram b Ontong	10	– lbw b Ontong
†W. K. Hegg lbw b Shastri	6	– c Maynard b Shastri
P. J. W. Allott b Thomas	25	– c Metson b Shastri
J. Simmons c Metson b Shastri	14	– lbw b Shastri
I. Folley not out	4	– c Thomas b Shastri
L-b 6, n-b 3	9	B 5, l-b 12, n-b 2
1/21 2/29 3/52 4/74 5/93 6/99 7/109 8/113 9/145	155	1/45 2/61 3/76 4/82 5/105 6/110 7/117 8/145 9/157 1

Bonus points – Lancashire 1, Glamorgan 4.

Bowling: *First Innings*—Thomas 11–3–41–2; Watkin 8–1–16–2; Shastri 21.1–7–41 Ontong 18–5–51–2. *Second Innings*—Thomas 2–0–7–0; Shastri 45.1–22–49–7; Wat 4–0–8–0; Ontong 40–11–82–3.

Duncan Fearnley
Eye to Perfection
Duncan Fearnley Cricket Sales Ltd.
Perfection in Cricket Equipment
SANSOME PLACE WORCESTER
Telephone: STD 0905 612981 Telex: 946240

Glamorgan

A. R. Butcher c Hegg b Simmons	36 – c Fowler b Folley	16
J. A. Hopkins c Hughes b Allott	8 – b Simmons	7
*H. Morris c Fowler b Allott	7 – (4) c Fairbrother b Folley	1
M. P. Maynard b Simmons	40 – (3) c Hegg b Folley	10
G. C. Holmes lbw b Folley	18 – c Fowler b Folley	1
R. J. Shastri b Simmons	41 – b Simmons	0
R. C. Ontong b Wasim	3 – c Fairbrother b Simmons	3
J. G. Thomas c Fairbrother b Simmons	14 – c Hegg b Folley	0
J. Derrick b Simmons	0 – c Wasim b Folley	0
†C. P. Metson lbw b Folley	2 – not out	4
S. L. Watkin not out	0 – c Fairbrother b Simmons	0
B 8, l-b 21, n-b 1	30 B 4, l-b 1	5
1/15 2/29 3/96 4/103 5/127 6/136 7/196 8/196 9/199	199 1/24 2/24 3/34 4/35 5/36 6/38 7/39 8/39 9/39	47

Bonus points – Glamorgan 1, Lancashire 4.

Bowling: *First Innings*—Wasim 21–10–31–1; Allott 9–2–18–2; Simmons 31.1–14–53–5; Folley 30–10–68–2. *Second Innings*—Wasim 3–1–5–0; Allott 3–0–8–0; Folley 9–4–20–6; Simmons 8.5–4–9–4.

Umpires: J. Birkenshaw and J. H. Harris.

At Taunton, June 29, 30, July 1. GLAMORGAN drew with SOMERSET.

At Swansea, July 13, 14, 15. GLAMORGAN drew with WEST INDIANS (See West Indian tour section).

At Lord's, July 16, 18, 19. GLAMORGAN drew with MIDDLESEX.

GLAMORGAN v WARWICKSHIRE

At Cardiff, July 20, 21, 22. Drawn. Glamorgan 5 pts, Warwickshire 7 pts. Toss: Warwickshire. Holmes and Shastri pulled the Glamorgan innings together with an aggressive century stand after the home side had been asked to bat, and Asif Din performed a similar service for Warwickshire with vigorous strokeplay. Watkin, deputising for the injured Thomas, returned career-best figures. Rain interrupted play and returned on the final day to spoil what promised to be an exciting finish. With Lloyd feeding runs for the Glamorgan declaration, Butcher, with clean hitting, struck two sixes and eleven fours in his 93 off 101 deliveries and Morris weighed in with a half-century, hoisting the first of a succession of lost balls into the river-bank shrubbery. Maynard was responsible for most of those that followed as he hastened to an unbeaten 72 in 50 minutes off 55 deliveries. He hit four sixes and eight fours. Warwickshire, set to score 270 in three hours, were interested, but the rain came yet again.

Close of play: First day, Warwickshire 50-1 (A. J. Moles 20*, Asif Din 6*); Second day, Warwickshire 255-8 dec.

Glamorgan

A. R. Butcher lbw b Reeve	47	– c Asif Din b Lloyd 93
J. A. Hopkins c Thorne b Donald	0	– b Donald 5
*H. Morris c Humpage b Donald	21	– c Reeve b Lloyd 51
M. P. Maynard c Donald b Reeve	0	– not out 72
R. J. Shastri c and b Reeve	52	– b Pierson 15
G. C. Holmes lbw b Small	79	
R. C. Ontong lbw b Donald	6	– (6) not out 23
J. Derrick b Small	7	
†C. P. Metson c Donald b Pierson	20	
S. L. Watkin b Small	1	
S. Monkhouse not out	0	
L-b 2, w 1, n-b 10	13	B 8, l-b 5, w 3, n-b 3 19
1/5 2/70 3/71 4/78 5/179 6/200 7/223 8/234 9/240	246	1/24 2/165 3/177 4/222 (4 wkts dec.) 278

Bonus points – Glamorgan 2, Warwickshire 4.

Bowling: *First Innings*—Small 16–4–53–3; Donald 17–4–44–3; Munton 16–5–56–0; Reeve 19–4–51–3; Pierson 13.4–3–36–1; Asif Din 3–1–4–0. *Second Innings*—Donald 8–1–26–1; Small 4–1–5–0; Munton 7–0–30–0; Pierson 21–3–86–1; Lloyd 15–1–107–2; Thorne 3–0–11–0.

Warwickshire

*T. A. Lloyd c Metson b Watkin	17	– (2) not out 13
A. J. Moles c Morris b Watkin	33	– (1) c Metson b Watkin 15
Asif Din lbw b Derrick	65	– not out 1
D. A. Banks c Metson b Monkhouse	19	
D. A. Thorne b Watkin	20	
†G. W. Humpage c Ontong b Watkin	19	
D. A. Reeve b Derrick	26	
G. C. Small st Metson b Derrick	29	
A. A. Donald not out	1	
A. R. K. Pierson not out	2	
B 3, l-b 11, n-b 10	24	L-b 2, n-b 1 3
1/32 2/82 3/145 4/157 5/192 6/192 7/244 8/251	(8 wkts dec.) 255	1/31 (1 wkt) 32

T. A. Munton did not bat.

Bonus points – Warwickshire 3, Glamorgan 3.

Bowling: *First Innings*—Watkin 31–11–66–4; Monkhouse 24–4–72–1; Shastri 9–5–15–0; Derrick 22–3–52–3; Holmes 4–2–14–0; Ontong 7–1–22–0. *Second Innings*—Watki 4.3–0–15–1; Monkhouse 4–0–15–0.

Umpires: A. A. Jones and M. J. Kitchen.

GLAMORGAN v YORKSHIRE

At Cardiff, July 23, 25, 26. Drawn. Glamorgan 2 pts, Yorkshire 2 pts. Toss: Glamorgan. Aft Saturday's play had been washed out, Yorkshire, put in, decided to bat throughout the secor day, and not even Glamorgan's use of their friendly bowlers could encourage a declaration. was a frustrating exercise on an equally frustrating pitch where bounce was minimal and ofte marginal. For a long period, Yorkshire failed to maintain a scoring-rate of 2 runs per ove The final day was a particularly dismal one for Butcher, who faced five balls in the fir innings and just two in the second, being dismissed twice in the space of 45 minutes, lbw eac time to a shooter. Maynard struck nine fours in his unbeaten 60 after rain had wrecked t original target of 303 runs from a minimum of 90 overs. As a match, it did not do much f cricket.

Close of play: First day, No play; Second day, Yorkshire 322-9 (P. J. Hartley 30*, C. Sha 26*).

Yorkshire

M. D. Moxon b Watkin	0	P. J. Hartley not out	30
A. A. Metcalfe c Derrick b Watkin	2	S. D. Fletcher c Morris b Butcher	13
K. Sharp b Derrick	24	C. Shaw not out	26
J. D. Love b Monkhouse	52	B 1, l-b 9, w 2, n-b 10	22
P. E. Robinson lbw b Watkin	63		——
I. G. Swallow c Ontong b Derrick	43	1/0 2/21 3/33 (9 wkts dec.)	322
†D. L. Bairstow c Shastri b Cann	33	4/126 5/170 6/235	
*P. Carrick b Cann	14	7/237 8/250 9/263	

Bonus points – Yorkshire 2, Glamorgan 2 (Score at 100 overs: 207-5).

Bowling: Watkin 31–12–47–3; Monkhouse 16–4–31–1; Derrick 34–8–90–2; Ontong 18–7–32–0; Shastri 17–5–37–0; Cann 6–0–43–2; Butcher 4–0–32–1.

Yorkshire forfeited their second innings.

Glamorgan

A. R. Butcher lbw b Love	4	– lbw b Hartley 0
P. A. Cottey not out	5	– c Bairstow b Shaw 45
*H. Morris not out	7	– c Swallow b Shaw 44
M. P. Maynard (did not bat)		– not out 60
R. J. Shastri (did not bat)		– c Fletcher b Carrick 8
R. C. Ontong (did not bat)		– not out 4
B 4	4	B 8, l-b 8, n-b 2 18
	——	——
1/4 (1 wkt dec.)	20	1/0 2/95 3/100 4/124 (4 wkts) 179

M. J. Cann, J. Derrick, S. Monkhouse, †C. P. Metson and S. L. Watkin did not bat.

Bowling: *First Innings*—Love 2.3–0–11–1; Metcalfe 2–0–5–0. *Second Innings*—Hartley 10–0–27–1; Fletcher 14–2–37–0; Shaw 14–4–18–2; Carrick 19–9–27–1; Swallow 13–3–54–0.

Umpires: R. Julian and B. J. Meyer.

At Eastbourne, July 30, August 1, 2. GLAMORGAN drew with SUSSEX.

At Swansea, August 3. GLAMORGAN lost to WORLD INVITATION XI by 47 runs (See Other Matches, 1988).

GLAMORGAN v SURREY

At Swansea, August 6, 8, 9. Drawn. Glamorgan 5 pts, Surrey 6 pts. Toss: Surrey. Ward's 126 off 300 deliveries, with eighteen fours, marked a rare day of searing sunshine when there was never a great deal of urgency on a slow pitch. On the second day, the home side made a confident start with their first century opening partnership of the summer in the Championship, Butcher and Cottey selecting their shots shrewdly, and Morris shored up his team's innings after three wickets fell for the addition of 11 runs. On the last day, Barwick took four wickets for 4 runs in twenty balls, and with six wickets down for 99 Surrey, only 134 ahead, looked to Greig to stabilise events. He did so steadfastly, assembling 45 runs in 81 minutes and dashing Welsh hopes of their first Championship victory. Butcher was prepared to make an assault on the target of 207 from what would have been 31 overs, but when three wickets went down for 36, Glamorgan decided that further risks were unjustified.

Close of play: First day, Surrey 293-8 (C. K. Bullen 24*, N. H. Peters 0*); Second day, Glamorgan 249-9 (J. Derrick 13*).

Surrey

First innings		Second innings	
D. J. Bicknell c Morris b Barwick	8	c Derrick b Barwick	21
P. D. Atkins c Butcher b Shastri	28	c Shastri b Ontong	41
†A. J. Stewart lbw b Shastri	1	(8) c Holmes b Ontong	18
M. A. Lynch c Derrick b Ontong	22	(9) not out	24
D. M. Ward st Metson b Shastri	126	(3) c Metson b Barwick	0
*I. A. Greig c Shastri b Ontong	25	c Cann b Barwick	45
K. T. Medlycott c Derrick b Watkin	43	(5) c Shastri b Barwick	4
M. A. Feltham c Metson b Watkin	0	(7) c Holmes b Ontong	0
C. K. Bullen c Metson b Barwick	24	(4) lbw b Barwick	3
N. H. Peters not out	3	c Cann b Ontong	0
J. Boiling b Barwick	1	not out	8
L-b 8, w 4, n-b 4	16	B 4, l-b 3	7
1/11 2/25 3/54 4/77 5/130 6/222 7/222 8/288 9/293	297	1/50 2/52 3/56 4/60 5/99 6/99 7/138 8/142 9/142	(9 wkts dec.) 171

Bonus points – Surrey 2, Glamorgan 2 (Score at 100 overs: 222-5).

Bowling: *First Innings*—Watkin 26–9–69–2; Barwick 22.5–9–44–3; Shastri 40–11–80–3; Ontong 24–8–53–2; Derrick 11–1–43–0. *Second Innings*—Watkin 15–0–49–0; Barwick 17–3–37–5; Shastri 26.4–12–40–0; Ontong 15–4–38–4.

Glamorgan

First innings		Second innings	
A. R. Butcher c Bicknell b Medlycott	54	not out	65
P. A. Cottey b Feltham	50	lbw b Feltham	2
*H. Morris c Greig b Feltham	51	(5) not out	19
G. C. Holmes c and b Feltham	1	(3) c Stewart b Peters	2
R. J. Shastri lbw b Greig	27	(4) run out	7
R. C. Ontong lbw b Medlycott	16		
M. J. Cann c Feltham b Medlycott	0		
†C. P. Metson b Medlycott	23		
J. Derrick not out	19		
S. L. Watkin lbw b Greig	1		
S. R. Barwick st Stewart b Medlycott	7		
B 4, n-b 9	13	W 1, n-b 2	3
1/109 2/117 3/120 4/164 5/199 6/205 7/224 8/246 9/249	262	1/14 2/29 3/36	(3 wkts) 98

Bonus points – Glamorgan 3, Surrey 4.

Bowling: *First Innings*—Feltham 24–6–58–3; Peters 5–1–9–0; Medlycott 40.5–8–122–5; Greig 15–3–36–2; Boiling 7–1–19–0; Bullen 4–1–14–0. *Second Innings*—Feltham 5–0–27–1; Peters 2–0–18–1; Medlycott 7–1–25–0; Boiling 8–2–21–0; Bullen 2–0–3–0; Greig 2–1–4–0.

Umpires: B. J. Meyer and D. O. Oslear.

GLAMORGAN v WORCESTERSHIRE

At Abergavenny, August 13, 15, 16. Worcestershire won by five wickets. Worcestershi 22 pts, Glamorgan 5 pts. Toss: Worcestershire. Victory with four balls to spare enabl Worcestershire to overtake Kent and become the new Championship leaders. On a sma ground and an easy-paced pitch – and in hot sunshine on the last two days – a third-day ru chase was inevitable from the moment Neale won the toss and asked the home side to ba Morris entered into the spirit of the match and declared his second innings at lunch, by whi time Maynard had completed his century, made during the morning session in 84 minu (103 balls) with three sixes and nine fours. He became the first Glamorgan batsman to pa 1,000 first-class runs during the season. In the home side's first innings, Thomas had scor his maiden century (two sixes, nine fours) in just over four hours to rescue Glamorgan af the first six wickets had fallen for 92. As anticipated by a large and appreciative crowd, final afternoon provided another memorable Hick innings. In less than three and a half hours, he struck five sixes and fifteen fours (three balls were lost beyond the trees and his hitting ensured that the graceful hang-gliders kept a respectful distance), and during the course of his assault he became the first to pass 2,000 first-class runs for the season. When he left, caught alongside the sightscreen for 159 from 186 balls, only 28 runs were needed. Curtis, with his well-constructed 86, and Neale, with nine fours in 51 from 55 balls, also helped shape a notable victory. Indeed, Worcestershire, chasing 341 at just under 5 runs an over, paced their performance superbly.

Close of play: First day, Glamorgan 192-7 (J. G. Thomas 59*, C. P. Metson 5*); Second day, Glamorgan 22-0 (A. R. Butcher 10*, P. A. Cottey 12*).

Glamorgan

A. R. Butcher lbw b Ellcock	15	– c Newport b O'Shaughnessy	41
P. A. Cottey c Hick b Newport	8	– lbw b Curtis	59
*H. Morris b Newport	24	– b Weston	3
M. P. Maynard b Newport	10	– not out	108
R. J. Shastri c Hick b Pridgeon	14		
G. C. Holmes c Rhodes b Pridgeon	1	– (5) not out	17
R. C. Ontong b Illingworth	43		
J. G. Thomas not out	100		
†C. P. Metson b Ellcock	43		
S. L. Watkin c Neale b Illingworth	23		
S. R. Barwick not out	0		
L-b 10, w 1, n-b 6	17	B 4, l-b 2, w 3, n-b 5	14
1/12 2/38 3/61 4/72 5/77 6/92 7/169 8/235 9/290 (9 wkts dec.)	298	1/63 2/66 3/165 (3 wkts dec.)	242

Bonus points – Glamorgan 3, Worcestershire 4 (Score at 100 overs: 295-9).

Bowling: *First Innings*—Newport 31.4–4–108–3; Ellcock 19–3–75–2; Pridgeon 24–6–48–2; Illingworth 17–7–31–2; Weston 4–1–6–0; O'Shaughnessy 6–1–20–0. *Second Innings*—Newport 3–0–9–0; Ellcock 3–0–13–0; Weston 9–0–51–1; O'Shaughnessy 9–1–35–1; Hick 4–0–13–0; Neale 14–1–62–0; Curtis 10.2–0–53–1.

Worcestershire

T. S. Curtis c and b Barwick	24	– c sub b Holmes	86
G. J. Lord c Maynard b Ontong	56	– c Butcher b Thomas	2
G. A. Hick b Holmes	46	– c Ontong b Watkin	159
S. J. O'Shaughnessy c Holmes b Ontong	0	– b Holmes	0
*P. A. Neale not out	46	– b Watkin	51
M. J. Weston b Thomas	1	– not out	28
†S. J. Rhodes not out	19	– not out	1
B 1, l-b 1, n-b 6	8	L-b 13, w 2, n-b 2	17
1/82 2/82 3/82 4/170 5/171 (5 wkts dec.)	200	1/4 2/196 3/196 4/313 5/324 (5 wkts)	344

P. J. Newport, R. K. Illingworth, R. M. Ellcock and A. P. Pridgeon did not bat.

Bonus points – Worcestershire 2, Glamorgan 2.

Bowling: *First Innings*—Thomas 11–0–62–1; Watkin 15–6–28–0; Barwick 12–4–22–1; Ontong 19–3–69–2; Holmes 5–0–17–1. *Second Innings*—Thomas 13–1–69–1; Watkin 18–2–90–2; Barwick 14–1–61–0; Ontong 12–0–43–0; Holmes 14.2–1–68–2.

Umpires: D. G. L. Evans and A. G. T. Whitehead.

At Colchester, August 17, 18, 19. GLAMORGAN drew with ESSEX.

At Wellingborough School, August 20, 22, 23. GLAMORGAN lost to NORTHAMPTONSHIRE by seven wickets.

GLAMORGAN v LEICESTERSHIRE

At Neath, August 25, 26, 27, 29. Drawn. Glamorgan 1 pt, Leicestershire 3 pts. Toss: Leicestershire. Less than an hour's play was possible on the second day and none at all on the last two days. Whitaker effected Leicestershire's recovery on the opening day with a chanceless 126, hitting two sixes and sixteen fours in a little more than four hours. Potter helped him in a stand worth 164, a Leicestershire record for the fifth wicket against the Welsh county. Bastien, a 25-year-old seam bowler from Stepney Green in London, marked his first-class début by taking five wickets, and there were six catches by Metson behind the stumps. Glamorgan were without their four leading bowlers, seamers Thomas and Barwick and spinners Ontong and Shastri. Barwick and Ontong had been injured in a car accident while travelling to the previous match at Wellingborough.

Close of play: First day, Leicestershire 301-6 (J. P. Agnew 14*, P. Whitticase 2*); Second day, Glamorgan 11-2 (H. Morris 1*, M. P. Maynard 1*); Third day, No play.

Leicestershire

T. J. Boon c Metson b Watkin	9
N. E. Briers hit wkt b Derrick	6
P. Willey c Metson b Bastien	28
*D. I. Gower c Metson b North	39
J. J. Whitaker c Butcher b Bastien	126
L. Potter c Metson b Watkin	66
J. P. Agnew c Metson b Bastien	21
†P. Whitticase c Maynard b Watkin	6
L. B. Taylor c Metson b Bastien	0
G. J. F. Ferris c Cottey b Bastien	2
P. M. Such not out	0
B 1, l-b 4, w 1, n-b 5	11
1/10 2/36 3/48 4/112 5/276 6/294 7/312 8/312 9/314	314

Bonus points – Leicestershire 3, Glamorgan 1 (Score at 100 overs: 268-4).

Bowling: Watkin 37–10–86–3; Bastien 28.1–4–90–5; Derrick 23–9–47–1; Holmes 12–1–42–0; North 17–4–35–1; Butcher 4–0–9–0.

Glamorgan

A. R. Butcher lbw b Ferris	1
P. A. Cottey lbw b Ferris	8
*H. Morris not out	1
M. P. Maynard not out	1
1/9 2/10	(2 wkts) 11

G. C. Holmes, M. J. Cann, S. Bastien, J. Derrick, †C. P. Metson, P. D. North and S. L. Watkin did not bat.

Bowling: Ferris 3–1–9–2; Agnew 2–1–2–0.

Umpires: H. D. Bird and D. R. Shepherd.

At Birmingham, August 30, 31, September 1, 2. GLAMORGAN beat WARWICKSHIRE by 4 runs.

GLAMORGAN v HAMPSHIRE

At Cardiff, September 9, 10, 11, 12. Hampshire won by two wickets. Hampshire 19 pts, Glamorgan 7 pts. Toss: Hampshire. Twice Glamorgan's middle order collapsed and Hampshire, 133 runs behind on first innings, winched their way back into the game to gain a notable victory. On an easy-paced pitch, Butcher and Cottey launched the home side with their most impressive start of the summer; but after Maynard's half-century, five wickets tumbled while 1 run was added. Although Hampshire failed against Thomas's pace, their hopes were raised by Glamorgan's persistence in surrendering the initiative. Butcher and Maynard again made attractive runs, but the last five second-innings wickets contributed only 46 runs in a disastrous 45 minutes. And when Hampshire batted again, with more than a day to score 368, Glamorgan missed seven chances in the field. Terry and Robin Smith, who struck ten fours in his 65, shaped the victory, and then Ayling, Hampshire's 6ft 4in seam bowler, compounded the home team's distress by defying them for two and threequarter hours, facing 168 deliveries for an unbeaten half-century. Defeat doomed Glamorgan to finish at the bottom of the table.

Close of play: First day, Hampshire 10-1 (V. P. Terry 10*, R. J. Maru 0*); Second day, Glamorgan 187-4 (M. P. Maynard 71*, C. P. Metson 2*); Third day, Hampshire 267-5 (D. R. Turner 17*, J. R. Ayling 4*).

Glamorgan

*A. R. Butcher c Turner b Maru	74	– b James	56
P. A. Cottey run out	73	– c Maru b Bakker	8
P. G. P. Roebuck c Terry b Connor	0	– b Connor	46
M. P. Maynard lbw b James	50	– lbw b Connor	71
G. C. Holmes c Parks b James	6	– c Parks b Bakker	0
J. Derrick lbw b Maru	0	– (7) lbw b Connor	1
J. G. Thomas c C. L. Smith b Maru	0	– (8) c Nicholas b Maru	26
†C. P. Metson not out	21	– (6) c Maru b Bakker	2
P. D. North lbw b James	0	– b Connor	4
S. L. Watkin c R. A. Smith b Connor	8	– not out	11
S. Bastien b Connor	0	– b Maru	4
B 12, l-b 12, n-b 3	27	L-b 1, n-b 4	5
1/147 2/150 3/180 4/223 5/224 6/224 7/224 8/224 9/259	259	1/22 2/107 3/153 4/164 5/188 6/188 7/194 8/208 9/226	234

Bonus points – Glamorgan 3, Hampshire 3 (Score at 100 overs: 250-8).

Bowling: *First Innings*—Connor 18–4–56–3; Bakker 17–5–27–0; Ayling 17–6–32–0; James 23–5–54–3; Maru 29–9–66–3. *Second Innings*—Connor 23–7–61–4; Bakker 20–8–41–3; Ayling 7–2–25–0; James 15–3–58–1; Maru 15.3–4–48–2.

Hampshire

V. P. Terry c North b Thomas	21	– c Metson b North	66
C. L. Smith c Metson b Watkin	0	– lbw b Watkin	34
R. J. Maru c Metson b Thomas	3	– (9) c Maynard b Thomas	28
*M. C. J. Nicholas c Metson b Bastien	21	– (3) b Derrick	47
R. A. Smith lbw b Thomas	0	– (4) lbw b Derrick	65
D. R. Turner not out	40	– (5) lbw b Derrick	24
K. D. James lbw b Thomas	0	– (6) lbw b Thomas	1
J. R. Ayling c Thomas b Watkin	17	– (7) not out	54
†R. J. Parks b Watkin	0	– (8) b Watkin	12
C. A. Connor b Derrick	1	– not out	5
P. J. Bakker lbw b Derrick	7		
B 1, l-b 5, n-b 10	16	L-b 19, w 4, n-b 11	34
1/2 2/17 3/50 4/50 5/50 6/51 7/87 8/87 9/108	126	1/85 2/139 3/206 4/258 5/259 6/290 7/309 8/365	(8 wkts) 370

Bonus points – Glamorgan 4.

Bowling: *First Innings*—Thomas 20–3–67–4; Watkin 15–5–28–3; Bastien 10–3–19–1; Derrick 8.1–3–6–2. *Second Innings*—Thomas 28–6–69–2; Watkin 35–11–87–2; Derrick 36.4–8–96–3; Bastien 27–11–67–0; North 12–2–32–1.

Umpires: R. Julian and R. A. White.

At Worcester, September 14, 15, 16. GLAMORGAN lost to WORCESTERSHIRE by an innings and 76 runs.

GLOUCESTERSHIRE

Patron: HRH The Princess of Wales
President: R. J. Bereley
Chairman: D. N. Perry
Chairman, Cricket Committee: D. A. Allen
Secretary: P. G. M. August
Phoenix County Ground, Nevil Road, Bristol BS7 9EJ (Telephone: 0272-245216)
Captain: 1988 – D. A. Graveney
1989 – C. W. J. Athey
Senior Coach: J. N. Shepherd
Youth Coach: G. G. Wiltshire

Near the end of a somewhat disappointing yet far from disastrous season, Gloucestershire shot themselves in the foot when the cricket committee, under the chairmanship of David Allen, voted 4-1 to dismiss David Graveney as captain and replace him with Bill Athey. Unfortunately, the decision was made public as Graveney was engaged in taking fourteen wickets against Worcestershire in a Championship match at Bristol. The timing of the announcement and the insensitive way it was handled upset not only Graveney, one of the most popular cricketers in the county game, but also the players and many members. It caused at least one potential sponsor to break off negotiations.

Don Perry, the club chairman, did his best to defuse a difficult situation by announcing that the cricket committee had, in fact, no power to dismiss the captain but could only forward a recommendation to the management committee, which was in turn answerable to the annual meeting. He apologised to Graveney for the "distress and embarrassment" caused to someone who had given the club such "magnificent service". With some members calling for the cricket committee's resignation, Graveney, offered first a one-year and then a two-year contract, decided to give himself a few months before deciding about his future. He was at pains to stress that he still had the best interests of the club at heart.

Advocates of change pointed out that the side had again failed to win a major trophy and that a new captain might get more out of the players. Graveney had been captain for eight years; a long time given the stresses imposed by the modern game. He had often felt obliged to play when not fully fit and had suffered a frustrating series of near misses in the pursuit of honours.

The latest of these came in the Refuge Assurance League, in which Gloucestershire finished second to Worcestershire. This was the county's highest placing since the Sunday competition began. The policy of playing a different side on Sundays – Alderman and Lawrence were always rested, with Jarvis and Greene taking over and Thomas, when fit, also playing – proved a success.

In the Britannic Assurance Championship, the record also showed improvement, if only a marginal one. There were six wins out of 21 games played, compared with five wins and a tie from 24 games in 1987 although the final position of tenth was unchanged. Gloucestershire did not live up to the expectations raised in June when good, positive cricket brought successive away wins over Derbyshire and Essex. Instead, they slowly slipped from third during a run of twelve games without a win.

Jeremy Lloyds's loss of form, which cost him his place, upset the balance of the side, and Kassim Ibadulla, who might have been a useful stand-in, was out of action for a time with a broken thumb. But that said, it was not easy to pinpoint the reason for such a decline. Terry Alderman, still a top-quality performer in English conditions, proved a more than satisfactory replacement for Courtney Walsh, missing only one Championship game and finishing with 75 wickets. David Lawrence had his best season, gaining in accuracy and variety without sacrificing hostility, constantly encouraging his colleagues even when the tide was running against them. Kevin Curran, unable to bowl for two seasons because of fitness problems, came back so strongly that he was the county's leading bowler in the first-class averages, in addition to being econd to Athey in the batting.

Athey was having a successful summer until he had his knuckles roken by Clarke of Surrey at Cheltenham at the beginning of August. He was one of five batsmen who passed 1,000 runs. Andy Stovold njoyed a new lease of life, Phil Bainbridge showed a marked improvement, and Tony Wright played some solid innings as foil to the lashing Stovold. Paul Romaines, with no young batsman emerging to hallenge him for his place, maintained his average, but Mark Alleyne ailed to live up to the high hopes held for him. He became something of bits and pieces player with his best efforts reserved for Sundays. Flaws n his batting technique condemned him to a series of low scores in Championship cricket. Later in the season, Malcolm Pooley, a YTS rainee and Young England all-rounder, was often preferred. His seam owling commanded respect and he sold his wicket dearly. Of the new ecruits, Ian Butcher made scant use of limited opportunities and David Thomas was forced into retirement by a back injury.

Gloucestershire's ambitions in the Benson and Hedges Cup ended omewhat unexpectedly. With qualification from their group seemingly ssured, they were dismissed cheaply on a poor pitch at Swansea and assed over on scoring-rate. They ran Worcestershire close in the third ound of the NatWest Bank Trophy and might have won had Graveney een able to call on another spin bowler. Although the weather was often oor, Gloucestershire's home games were blessed with the best of the ummer, and the Cheltenham Festival coincided with the nearest thing a heatwave 1988 produced. It is doubtful if there was a better pitch in ngland last season than that at the College Ground for the match with orkshire.

The selection of Jack Russell and Lawrence for the Test match gainst Sri Lanka made them the first Gloucestershire-born players to ay for England while on the county staff since 1966, when David llen played one match against West Indies. Both did well enough to be lected for the subsequently cancelled tour of India. Earlier in the ason, Graveney had been asked about his availability to play against est Indies, but he had doubted whether he was fit enough for five-day icket. – Geoffrey Wheeler.

GLOUCESTERSHIRE 1988

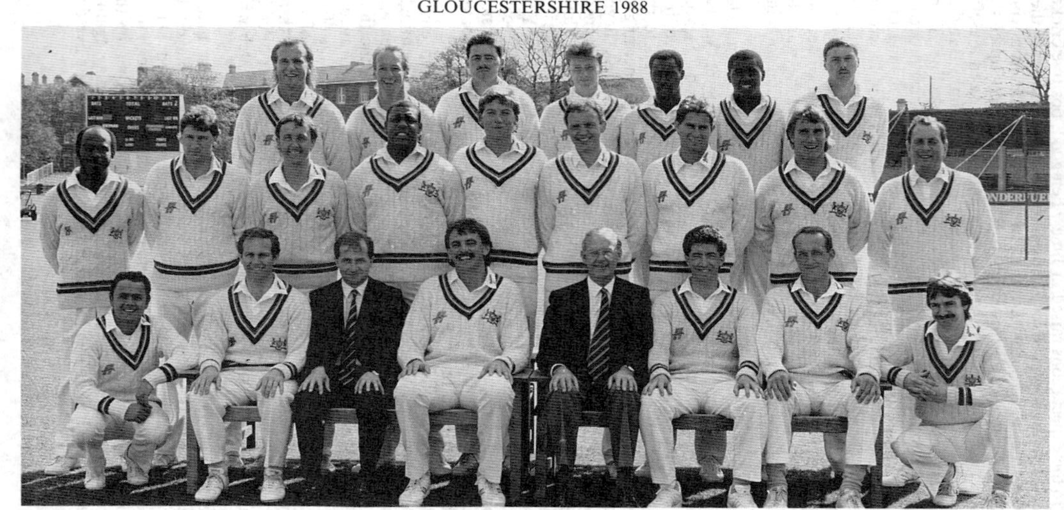

[*Bill Smith*

Back row: I. P. Butcher, J. W. Lloyds, A. J. Wright, M. W. Pooley, V. S. Greene, M. W. Alleyne, P. W. Romaines. *Middle row:* J. N. Shepherd (*senior coach*), D. J. Thomas, A. J. Brassington, D. V. Lawrence, D. J. Chubbs, K. B. S. Jarvis, T. M. Alderman, K. M. Curran, G. G. Wiltshire (*youth* [illegible] K. B. K. Ibadulla, A. W. Stovold, P. G. M. August (*secretary*), D. A. Graveney (*captain*), D. N. Perry (*chairman*), P. Bainbridge,

GLOUCESTERSHIRE RESULTS

All first-class matches – Played 24: Won 6, Lost 7, Drawn 11. Abandoned 1.

County Championship matches – Played 21: Won 6, Lost 7, Drawn 8. Abandoned 1.

Bonus points – Batting 52, Bowling 59.

Competition placings – Britannic Assurance County Championship, 10th; NatWest Bank Trophy, q-f; Benson and Hedges Cup, 3rd in Group D; Refuge Assurance League, 2nd; Refuge Assurance Cup, s-f.

BRITANNIC ASSURANCE CHAMPIONSHIP AVERAGES

BATTING

	Birthplace	*M*	*I*	*NO*	*R*	*HI*	*Avge*
‡C. W. J. Athey	*Middlesbrough*	12	20	6	1,037	168*	74.07
§‡K. M. Curran	*Rusape, S. Rhodesia*	19	34	7	1,005	142	37.22
‡A. W. Stovold	*Bristol*	21	39	2	1,296	136	35.02
‡P. Bainbridge	*Stoke-on-Trent*	21	36	1	1,213	169	34.65
K. B. K. Ibadulla	*Birmingham*	3	6	2	122	77	30.50
‡R. C. Russell	*Stroud*	19	30	6	658	72	27.41
‡A. J. Wright	*Stevenage*	21	38	0	1,023	136	26.92
‡P. W. Romaines	*Bishop Auckland*	18	34	2	859	101*	26.84
M. W. Pooley	*Truro*	6	12	4	146	38	18.25
‡J. W. Lloyds	*Penang, Malaya*	14	22	2	331	68	16.55
‡D. A. Graveney	*Bristol*	20	23	8	227	47	15.13
M. W. Alleyne	*Tottenham, London*	11	18	0	224	56	12.44
§T. M. Alderman	*Perth, Australia*	20	22	11	135	43*	12.27
‡D. V. Lawrence	*Gloucester*	20	24	3	217	29	10.33

Also batted: (1 match each): M. C. J. Ball (*Bristol*) 2; ‡A. J. Brassington (*Bagnall, Staffs.*) ; I. P. Butcher (*Farnborough, Kent*) 11, 8; §V. S. Greene (*Christ Church, Barbados*) 2; K. B. S. arvis (*Dartford*) 1*; D. J. Thomas (*Solihull*) 7, 3.

** Signifies not out.   ‡ Denotes county cap.   § Not qualified for England.*

he following played a total of eleven three-figure innings for Gloucestershire in County hampionship matches – P. Bainbridge 3, C. W. J. Athey 2, K. M. Curran 2, A. W. Stovold P. W. Romaines 1, A. J. Wright 1.

BOWLING

	O	*M*	*R*	*W*	*BB*	*5W/i*	*Avge*
. M. Curran	414.2	86	1,385	65	7-54	4	21.30
M. Alderman	601	135	1,711	75	8-59	3	22.81
. A. Graveney	561.5	163	1,268	49	8-127	2	25.87
. V. Lawrence	580.2	94	2,037	77	7-47	4	26.45
. W. Pooley	104.4	25	311	11	4-80	0	28.27
Bainbridge	284.4	58	913	12	3-85	0	76.08

Also bowled: M. W. Alleyne 61–11–206–6; C. W. J. Athey 5–0–20–0; M. C. J. Ball 3–2–1; V. S. Greene 18–3–49–0; K. B. K. Ibadulla 26.2–6–94–3; K. B. S. Jarvis -1–104–1; J. W. Lloyds 214.3–37–696–9; P. W. Romaines 0.1–0–6–0; D. J. Thomas 4–5–66–3.

icket-keepers: R. C. Russell 46 ct, 9 st; M. W. Alleyne 4 ct, 1 st; A. J. Brassington 1 ct, 1 st.

ading Fielders: J. W. Lloyds 20, C. W. J. Athey 18, K. M. Curran 15.

GLOUCESTERSHIRE v GLAMORGAN

At Bristol, April 21, 22, 23, 25. Gloucestershire won by six wickets. Gloucestershire 21 pts, Glamorgan 5 pts. Toss: Gloucestershire. Three declarations produced a fourth-day situation which left Gloucestershire to score 328 at just over 4 runs an over, a target comfortably achieved with seventeen balls to spare. Batsmen thrived on a mild pitch, particularly Maynard for Glamorgan and Athey for Gloucestershire. Maynard hit the first Championship hundred of the season after Alderman had caused early problems. Full of dashing strokes, his 126 included a six and eighteen fours; Holmes's century was more sedately made. Athey, who had finished 1987 with a hundred against the same opponents, controlled Gloucestershire's first innings and then the later stages of their run-chase after Wright and Alleyne, each missed early on, had added 120 for the second wicket.

Close of play: First day, Glamorgan 330-6 (G. C. Holmes 104*, J. G. Thomas 17*); Second day, Gloucestershire 265-6 (J. W. Lloyds 19*, R. C. Russell 0*); Third day, Glamorgan 217-5 (G. C. Holmes 12*, J. Derrick 0*).

Glamorgan

A. R. Butcher c Russell b Alderman .... 16 – lbw b Alderman 4
J. A. Hopkins c Wright b Alderman .... 1 – st Russell b Alleyne 27
*H. Morris c Wright b Lawrence .... 26 – b Alleyne 84
M. P. Maynard c and b Graveney ....126 – lbw b Alleyne 68
G. C. Holmes b Alderman ....117 – c Lloyds b Curran 36
R. C. Ontong c Russell b Lloyds .... 11 – b Alleyne 9
J. Derrick lbw b Alleyne .... 12 – run out ....
J. G. Thomas c Athey b Alderman .... 31 – not out 3
C. J. P. G. van Zyl b Lawrence .... 5 – c Russell b Lawrence ....
†C. P. Metson not out .... 5 – not out ....
B 1, l-b 7, n-b 14 22   B 5, l-b 9, w 1, n-b 9 2

1/3 2/28 3/115 4/243 5/283 6/304 7/354 8/361 9/372 (9 wkts dec.) 372   1/5 2/83 3/192 4/195 5/217 6/241 7/270 8/283 (8 wkts dec.) 29

S. R. Barwick did not bat.

Bonus points – Glamorgan 3, Gloucestershire 2 (Score at 100 overs: 290-5).

Bowling: *First Innings*—Lawrence 31–4–94–2; Alderman 31–9–70–4; Bainbridge 16–3–59–0; Curran 12–2–49–0; Graveney 23–10–44–1; Alleyne 8–1–28–1; Lloyds 7–1–20– *Second Innings*—Lawrence 27–6–76–1; Alderman 23–7–56–1; Curran 14–1–45–1; Graveney 7–2–16–0; Alleyne 18–7–48–4; Lloyds 14–3–41–0.

Gloucestershire

A. W. Stovold c Morris b Derrick .... 52 – c Metson b Thomas ....
A. J. Wright c Morris b Thomas .... 0 – run out ....
M. W. Alleyne lbw b Thomas .... 0 – b Butcher ....
C. W. J. Athey c Morris b Derrick ....123 – not out ....
P. Bainbridge b van Zyl 52
K. M. Curran c Hopkins b Holmes .... 1 – not out ....
J. W. Lloyds c Metson b Derrick .... 68 – (5) lbw b Holmes ....
†R. C. Russell not out 23
B 1, l-b 6, n-b 15 22   L-b 4, n-b 10 ....

1/1 2/4 3/163 4/206 5/214 6/264 7/341 (7 wkts dec.) 341   1/14 2/134 3/169 4/263 (4 wkts) 3

*D. A. Graveney, D. V. Lawrence and T. M. Alderman did not bat.

Bonus points – Gloucestershire 3, Glamorgan 2 (Score at 100 overs: 292-6).

Bowling: *First Innings*—Thomas 22–5–78–2; van Zyl 26–10–72–1; Barwick 24–7–73– Derrick 24.1–5–65–3; Ontong 11–4–35–0; Holmes 6–2–11–1. *Second Innings*—Thomas 13–0–72–1; van Zyl 16.1–2–63–0; Barwick 12–1–48–0; Derrick 11–1–51–0; Holmes 17–0–73–1; Ontong 4–0–14–0; Butcher 2–0–4–1.

Umpires: D. G. L. Evans and D. S. Thompsett.

GLOUCESTERSHIRE v SUSSEX

At Bristol, April 28, 29, 30, May 2. Drawn. Gloucestershire 5 pts, Sussex 7 pts. Toss: Gloucestershire. Rain prevented any play on the final day, by which time Sussex had worked themselves into a useful position, being 188 runs ahead with six second-innings wickets in hand. They had batted consistently, if rather slowly, in their first innings until Alderman, the pick of the Gloucestershire bowlers, made short work of the tail. Bunting, making his début, and Pringle combined to reduce Gloucestershire to 19 for three before Stovold, who played with confidence from the start, and Bainbridge added 138 in a sprightly fourth-wicket partnership. However, the later batsmen surrendered tamely.

Close of play: First day, Sussex 284-7 (M. W. Pringle 23*, A. R. Clarke 0*); Second day, Gloucestershire 76-3 (A. W. Stovold 50*, P. Bainbridge 18*); Third day, Sussex 116-4 (P. W. G. Parker 55*, N. J. Lenham 8*).

Sussex

R. I. Alikhan lbw b Alderman	46	– lbw b Alderman	7
A. M. Green lbw b Curran	18	– lbw b Lawrence	9
*P. W. G. Parker c Wright b Curran	18	– not out	55
A. P. Wells c Stovold b Graveney	69	– st Brassington b Graveney	24
C. M. Wells c Alleyne b Graveney	33	– c Brassington b Graveney	0
N. J. Lenham c Lloyds b Graveney	32	– not out	8
†I. J. Gould c Athey b Alderman	20		
M. W. Pringle c Lloyds b Alderman	35		
A. R. Clarke b Alderman	9		
R. A. Bunting not out	11		
A. M. Babington c Athey b Alderman	1		
B 4, l-b 10, n-b 18	32	L-b 3, n-b 10	13
/45 2/81 3/134 4/186 5/224 /254 7/278 8/304 9/318	324	1/14 2/31 3/99 4/103	(4 wkts) 116

Bonus points – Sussex 3, Gloucestershire 2 (Score at 100 overs: 259-6).

Bowling: *First Innings*—Lawrence 20–5–55–0; Alderman 31–9–75–5; Curran 17–2–50–2; Bainbridge 14–3–49–0; Graveney 26–7–50–3; Alleyne 2–0–9–0; Lloyds 12–4–22–0. *Second Innings*—Lawrence 8–2–29–1; Alderman 10–1–23–1; Curran 7–2–19–0; Bainbridge 6–0–16–0; Alleyne 6–2–17–0; Graveney 8–5–6–2; Lloyds 4–3–3–0.

Gloucestershire

A. W. Stovold c Alikhan b Bunting	136
A. J. Wright lbw b Bunting	1
M. W. Alleyne c Gould b Bunting	2
. W. J. Athey b Pringle	0
Bainbridge c and b Clarke	49
. M. Curran c Lenham b Clarke	20
W. Lloyds c A. P. Wells b Pringle	8
D. A. Graveney c Gould b Bunting	9
D. V. Lawrence c Clarke b Bunting	9
T. M. Alderman not out	2
†A. J. Brassington lbw b Clarke	1
B 2, l-b 7, n-b 6	15
1/5 2/18 3/19 4/157 5/189 6/212 7/228 8/238 9/251	252

Bonus points – Gloucestershire 3, Sussex 4.

Bowling: Bunting 25–4–86–5; Pringle 17–4–51–2; Clarke 22.2–3–47–3; Babington –2–59–0.

Umpires: B. Dudleston and R. Palmer.

Northampton, May 5, 6, 7, 9. GLOUCESTERSHIRE lost to NORTHAMPTONSHIRE by 49 runs.

At Nottingham, May 18, 19, 20. GLOUCESTERSHIRE beat NOTTINGHAMSHIRE by six wickets.

At Bristol, May 25, 26, 27. GLOUCESTERSHIRE drew with WEST INDIANS (See West Indian tour section).

At Swansea, May 28, 30, 31. GLAMORGAN v GLOUCESTERSHIRE. Abandoned.

At Oxford, June 1, 2, 3. GLOUCESTERSHIRE drew with OXFORD UNIVERSITY.

At Derby, June 11, 13, 14. GLOUCESTERSHIRE beat DERBYSHIRE by four wickets.

At Ilford, June 15, 16, 17. GLOUCESTERSHIRE beat ESSEX by eight wickets.

At Manchester, June 18, 20, 21. GLOUCESTERSHIRE drew with LANCASHIRE.

GLOUCESTERSHIRE v LEICESTERSHIRE

At Gloucester, June 25, 27, 28. Leicestershire won by 80 runs. Leicestershire 21 pts Gloucestershire 4 pts. Toss: Gloucestershire. Not one over of spin was called for in a match played on a well-grassed pitch. A crucial factor in Leicestershire's victory was the plucky batting of Briers, who passed 50 in each innings. No other batsman scored one half-century and only Athey, who twice played soundly for Gloucestershire, reached 40. Sixteen wickets fell on the first day and when, on the second, Briers and Cobb added 80 to a first-innings lead of 47, it seemed certain that Gloucestershire's final target [225 in 93 overs] would be too stiff So it proved, although as Wright and Athey added 69 there was just a flicker of hope. It wa snuffed out by DeFreitas, who took nine wickets in the match for Leicestershire.

Close of play: First day, Gloucestershire 92-6 (J. W. Lloyds 5*, K. M. Curran 1*); Secon day, Leicestershire 162-7 (C. C. Lewis 2*, P. Whitticase 3*).

Leicestershire

R. A. Cobb run out	7	– lbw b Curran	3
N. E. Briers c Lloyds b Curran	53	– b Curran	5
P. Willey c Athey b Lawrence	12	– c Stovold b Curran	2
*D. I. Gower c Russell b Curran	10	– lbw b Curran	
J. J. Whitaker lbw b Curran	0	– c Lloyds b Lawrence	
L. Potter lbw b Lawrence	35	– c Stovold b Curran	
P. A. J. DeFreitas b Curran	7	– c Stovold b Alderman	2
C. C. Lewis c Russell b Lawrence	12	– c Russell b Lawrence	
†P. Whitticase run out	10	– c Russell b Curran	1
J. P. Agnew lbw b Alderman	11	– not out	
G. J. F. Ferris not out	8	– lbw b Curran	
L-b 11, w 7, n-b 6	24	B 1, l-b 7, n-b 7	1
1/16 2/37 3/48 4/56 5/119 6/137 7/150 8/155 9/166	189	1/80 2/101 3/124 4/125 5/125 6/144 7/155 8/169 9/175	17

Bonus points – Leicestershire 1, Gloucestershire 4.

Bowling: *First Innings*—Lawrence 24–4–67–3; Alderman 17.2–6–35–1; Curran 25–8–55– Bainbridge 10–3–21–0. *Second Innings*—Lawrence 14–3–34–2; Alderman 15–3–40–1; Curra 17.2–4–54–7; Bainbridge 20–8–41–0.

Gloucestershire

A. W. Stovold b Ferris	23	– c Willey b Agnew	6
A. J. Wright lbw b Ferris	5	– lbw b DeFreitas	34
P. W. Romaines b Ferris	10	– b Agnew	6
C. W. J. Athey c Cobb b DeFreitas	35	– c Whitticase b DeFreitas	41
P. Bainbridge b Lewis	5	– c Whitticase b DeFreitas	30
†R. C. Russell c Whitaker b DeFreitas	1	– (8) c Potter b Agnew	4
. W. Lloyds c Whitticase b DeFreitas	6	– c Gower b Agnew	9
K. M. Curran c Briers b Lewis	29	– (6) c Cobb b DeFreitas	0
*D. A. Graveney c Whitticase b DeFreitas	8	– c Whitticase b Agnew	7
D. V. Lawrence c Cobb b DeFreitas	8	– c Lewis b Agnew	0
T. M. Alderman not out	2	– not out	0
B 1, l-b 3, w 1, n-b 5	10	B 4, l-b 2, n-b 1	7
/24 2/37 3/44 4/79 5/80 /91 7/106 8/127 9/135	142	1/9 2/19 3/88 4/95 5/95 6/114 7/120 8/140 9/144	144

Bonus points – Leicestershire 4.

Bowling: *First Innings*—Ferris 9–0–36–3; Agnew 9–3–15–0; DeFreitas 14.3–5–41–5; Lewis 4–3–46–2. *Second Innings*—DeFreitas 20–2–63–4; Agnew 20.2–6–39–6; Ferris 4–0–13–0; ewis 8–1–23–0.

Umpires: B. Dudleston and D. R. Shepherd.

GLOUCESTERSHIRE v HAMPSHIRE

t Gloucester, June 29, 30, July 1. Drawn. Gloucestershire 5 pts, Hampshire 8 pts. Toss: ampshire. This game was played on a pitch far more favourable to batsmen, although loucestershire twice had to be rescued by Russell, who hit twelve boundaries in a career-best 2 and followed it with 69. Robin Smith's commanding 141 not out (seventeen fours) saw ampshire achieve their first full hand of batting points for the season. Maru, one of the two ght-watchmen, enjoyed a career-best 74 in a fourth-wicket partnership of 153 in 39 overs, nd then Turner joined Smith in another century partnership. When Gloucestershire batted gain, the spotlight fell on another of Hampshire's South Africans, Jefferies, who was on urse to take ten wickets in an innings for the second time in six months as he claimed their st eight wickets. Fortunately for Gloucestershire he tired, and Alderman stayed with ussell for two hours so that Hampshire were left with only 49 overs in which to score 241. hris Smith, hitting fourteen fours, looked to be leading Hampshire to victory until he fell to awrence, whose late, accurate spell did much to ensure that they finished 15 runs short.

Close of play: First day, Hampshire 15-2 (R. J. Maru 1*, C. A. Connor 0*); Second day, loucestershire 105-4 (C. W. J. Athey 17*, K. M. Curran 16*).

loucestershire

W. Stovold b Andrew	25	– c Parks b Jefferies	37
J. Wright c Parks b Jefferies	13	– c Maru b Jefferies	16
W. Romaines c Parks b Connor	0	– c Turner b Jefferies	4
W. J. Athey c R. A. Smith b Ayling	23	– c Terry b Jefferies	22
. Bainbridge c Parks b Ayling	43	– b Jefferies	8
M. Curran b Ayling	48	– c Terry b Jefferies	16
W. Lloyds c Parks b Andrew	30	– lbw b Jefferies	10
. C. Russell c Maru b Ayling	72	– c Parks b Connor	69
V. Lawrence st Parks b Maru	24	– c and b Jefferies	13
M. Alderman not out	1	– c Nicholas b Connor	33
B. S. Jarvis (did not bat)		– not out	1
B 6, l-b 11, w 2, n-b 9	28	L-b 7, w 1, n-b 11	19
6 2/31 3/56 4/111 5/113 78 7/219 8/299 9/307	(9 wkts dec.) 307	1/55 2/62 3/65 4/73 5/112 6/113 7/138 8/165 9/241	248

Bonus points – Gloucestershire 4, Hampshire 4.

Bowling: *First Innings*—Andrew 14–5–50–2; Connor 19–4–76–1; Jefferies 20–2–76–1; Ayling 23–5–57–4; Maru 12.4–2–31–1. *Second Innings*—Andrew 4–2–25–0; Connor 9.3–1–26–2; Jefferies 28–3–97–8; Maru 31–9–76–0; Ayling 12–4–17–0.

Hampshire

V. P. Terry c Athey b Lawrence	4	– lbw b Alderman	10
C. L. Smith b Lawrence	9	– c Russell b Lawrence	94
R. J. Maru c Athey b Lloyds	74	– (8) not out	3
C. A. Connor lbw b Lawrence	8		
R. A. Smith not out	141	– (4) lbw b Curran	2
D. R. Turner not out	64	– (5) c Romaines b Jarvis	40
*M. C. J. Nicholas (did not bat)		– (3) b Curran	19
S. T. Jefferies (did not bat)		– (6) not out	29
J. R. Ayling (did not bat)		– (7) b Lawrence	8
B 1, l-b 10, n-b 4	15	B 6, l-b 9, n-b 6	21
1/10 2/15 3/25 4/178 (4 wkts dec.)	315	1/26 2/75 3/81 4/173 5/185 6/215 (6 wkts)	226

†R. J. Parks and S. J. W. Andrew did not bat.

Bonus points – Hampshire 4, Gloucestershire 1.

Bowling: *First Innings*—Lawrence 9–2–45–3; Alderman 12–4–34–0; Jarvis 18–1–72–0; Curran 8–3–26–0; Lloyds 30–5–91–1; Bainbridge 10–2–21–0; Athey 3–0–15–0. *Secon[d] Innings*—Lawrence 14.4–1–47–2; Alderman 8–2–18–1; Lloyds 10–0–58–0; Curran 11–2–50–2; Jarvis 4–0–32–1; Bainbridge 1–0–6–0.

Umpires: B. Dudleston and D. R. Shepherd.

At Worcester, July 2, 4, 5. GLOUCESTERSHIRE drew with WORCESTERSHIRE.

GLOUCESTERSHIRE v NORTHAMPTONSHIRE

At Bristol, July 13, 14, 15. Northamptonshire won by 1 run. Northamptonshire 20 p[ts], Gloucestershire 2 pts. Toss: Gloucestershire. Three splendid centuries, two forfeitures, an[d] pulsating finish made up for the loss of the first day. Geoff Cook and Larkins found no per[il] in the pitch as they produced their first century opening of the season, with Larkins very mu[ch] the dominant partner. He needed only 164 balls for his 134, hitting a six and 24 fours, yet w[as] subsequently upstaged by Lamb, who raced to his hundred from just 86 deliveries, hitti[ng] twenty boundaries along the way. Gloucestershire, chasing 350 in 98 overs, were wrong-foo[ted] by Davis before Athey, missed at slip when 38, developed their challenge in partnerships w[ith] Romaines and Bainbridge. Even though Davis, who bowled demandingly throughout, a[nd] Nick Cook combined to swing the game back in Northamptonshire's favour, he kept [the] momentum going. The last over arrived with 15 needed and the last pair together. Athey to[ok] 12 from Cook's first three balls; the fifth went to Walker, whose accurate throw from lo[ng]-off narrowly beat Alderman's attempt to complete a second run to tie the scores. At[hey] remained unbeaten with 168, having batted for almost five and threequarter hours, faced deliveries and hit three sixes and seventeen fours.

Close of play: First day, No play; Second day, Northamptonshire 347-5 (D. J. Capel 2[…], D. J. Wild 2*).

Northamptonshire

*G. Cook lbw b Curran 32
W. Larkins c Lloyds b Curran 134
R. J. Bailey c Russell b Alderman 21
A. J. Lamb st Russell b Graveney 117
D. J. Capel not out 28
R. G. Williams b Graveney 0
D. J. Wild not out 2
B 1, l-b 5, w 1, n-b 8 15

1/106 2/150 3/255 4/337 5/337 (5 wkts dec.) 349

†D. Ripley, N. G. B. Cook, W. W. Davis and A. Walker did not bat.

Bonus points – Northamptonshire 4, Gloucestershire 2.

Bowling: Lawrence 12–2–76–0; Alderman 16–2–68–1; Curran 23–3–80–2; Bainbridge 15–2–79–0; Graveney 16–6–38–2; Athey 1–0–2–0.

Northamptonshire forfeited their second innings.

Gloucestershire

Gloucestershire forfeited their first innings.

A. W. Stovold c Lamb b Davis 0
A. J. Wright c Ripley b Davis 7
P. W. Romaines c Ripley b Davis 55
C. W. J. Athey not out 168
P. Bainbridge b N. G. B. Cook 55
K. M. Curran b Davis 1
J. W. Lloyds c Bailey b Davis 0
†R. C. Russell st Ripley b N. G. B. Cook 4
*D. A. Graveney b Davis 17
D. V. Lawrence b N. G. B. Cook 6
T. M. Alderman run out 5
B 4, l-b 14, w 1, n-b 11 30

1/8 2/19 3/114 4/214 5/233 6/233 7/241 8/297 9/326 348

Bowling: Davis 27–3–92–6; Capel 20–3–62–0; Wild 12–3–44–0; N. G. B. Cook 31.5–10–103–3; Walker 7–1–29–0.

Umpires: M. J. Kitchen and B. Leadbeater.

GLOUCESTERSHIRE v SOMERSET

At Bristol, July 16, 18, 19. Somerset won by eight wickets. Somerset 21 pts, Gloucestershire 5 pts. Toss: Gloucestershire. Despite the loss of nearly all of the first day, an unreliable pitch allowed time to be made up and Somerset won with ease. Gloucestershire's first innings of 168 represented a notable recovery from 22 for four, Athey and Curran staging the only partnership of substance, and Somerset found batting hazardous against Gloucestershire's quick bowlers. They gained a valuable lead of 27 as Jones hit hard and cleanly for 38, his best score. Gloucestershire's second-innings collapse began when Athey played on to Marks, who obtained considerable turn, but there were some poor strokes played as the last seven wickets tumbled for 43 runs. With Hardy chancing his arm successfully, Somerset made light of scoring 93 to win.

Close of play: First day, Gloucestershire 10-2 (P. W. Romaines 7*); Second day, Somerset 166-8 (N. J. Pringle 42*, A. N. Jones 19*).

Gloucestershire

Batsman	First innings		Second innings	
A. W. Stovold c Bartlett b Mallender	3	– c Burns b Rose	29
A. J. Wright b Mallender	0	– c Hardy b Jones	0
P. W. Romaines c Burns b Jones	7	– b Rose	19
C. W. J. Athey lbw b Jones	56	– b Marks	18
P. Bainbridge b Mallender	4	– c Hardy b Rose	13
K. M. Curran c Waugh b Rose	39	– c Hardy b Marks	11
M. W. Alleyne c Burns b Rose	4	– c Hardy b Marks	6
†R. C. Russell c Hardy b Foster	8	– c Burns b Marks	9
*D. A. Graveney lbw b Mallender	22	– lbw b Mallender	4
D. V. Lawrence b Jones	11	– not out	2
T. M. Alderman not out	1	– b Mallender	0
L-b 7, n-b 6	13	L-b 5, n-b 3	8
1/3 2/10 3/12 4/22 5/91 6/98 7/114 8/148 9/162	168	1/1 2/42 3/72 4/76 5/93 6/101 7/103 8/117 9/119	119

Bonus points – Gloucestershire 1, Somerset 4.

Bowling: *First Innings*—Jones 11.3–4–47–3; Mallender 16–0–47–4; Marks 2–0–11–0; Rose 8–0–20–2; Foster 12–2–36–1. *Second Innings*—Jones 6–1–26–1; Mallender 9.3–2–20–2; Rose 12–2–31–3; Marks 10–3–25–4; Foster 2–0–12–0.

Somerset

J. J. E. Hardy c Russell b Alderman	6	– not out	52
*P. M. Roebuck c Russell b Alderman	22	– c Alderman b Curran	26
N. J. Pringle c Curran b Lawrence	42	– st Russell b Graveney	0
S. R. Waugh c Russell b Alderman	33	– not out	1
R. J. Bartlett c Lawrence b Bainbridge	6		
†N. D. Burns lbw b Alderman	5		
V. J. Marks b Curran	21		
G. D. Rose lbw b Curran	0		
N. A. Mallender c Russell b Curran	0		
A. N. Jones c Russell b Lawrence	38		
D. J. Foster not out	9		
B 1, l-b 7, n-b 5	13	B 4, l-b 2, n-b 8	14
1/25 2/34 3/84 4/96 5/103 6/133 7/135 8/135 9/185	195	1/89 2/90	(2 wkts) 93

Bonus points – Somerset 1, Gloucestershire 4.

Bowling: *First Innings*—Lawrence 11.1–3–30–2; Alderman 23–4–75–4; Curran 17–2–64–3; Bainbridge 11–3–16–1; Graveney 6–4–2–0. *Second Innings*—Lawrence 6–1–38–0; Alderman 9–1–19–0; Graveney 7–2–18–1; Curran 3.1–1–12–1.

Umpires: M. J. Kitchen and B. Leadbeater.

At Hove, July 20, 21, 22. GLOUCESTERSHIRE drew with SUSSEX.

GLOUCESTERSHIRE v SURREY

At Cheltenham, July 30, August 1, 2. Surrey won by 21 runs. Surrey 24 pts, Gloucestershire 5 pts. Toss: Gloucestershire. A heroic stand by Curran and Alderman came close to producing an astonishing victory for Gloucestershire who, set 265, looked well beaten at 132 for eight with Athey unable to bat. The last-wicket pair added 111, and Surrey had the boundary fully manned to prevent Curran from running away with the game. Finally, the tireless Clarke claimed his wicket soon after Curran had completed a memorable century which included fifteen fours. Clarke, with a match return of eleven for 107 – plus two warnings for persistent short-pitched bowling – and Clinton were the key performers for Surrey. The opening batsman's century on the first day was a courageous effort, for he was handicapped by a leg strain as he soldiered on for nearly six hours, and Gloucestershire had good reason to regret missing him twice. Clarke, gaining tremendous lift from the very fast pitch, broke two knuckles in Athey's right hand in Gloucestershire's first innings, but Athey had to go in again briefly to help Alderman save the follow-on. Lawrence, working up a great pace, produced a career-best seven for 47 to rout Surrey in their second innings, and then Stovold and Wright kept Clarke at bay while adding 74. The subsequent collapse, however, left Curran and Alderman with just too much to do.

Close of play: First day, Gloucestershire 12-3 (C. W. J. Athey 1*, D. A. Graveney 1*); Second day, Gloucestershire 55-0 (A. W. Stovold 30*, A. J. Wright 24*).

Surrey

First innings		Second innings	
G. S. Clinton c Stovold b Lawrence	102	(8) not out	18
P. D. Atkins c Stovold b Alderman	17	(1) c Russell b Lawrence	0
A. J. Stewart c Alleyne b Lawrence	21	c Curran b Lawrence	0
M. A. Lynch c Wright b Curran	45	c Curran b Alderman	0
D. M. Ward c Russell b Curran	43	c Wright b Lawrence	4
†C. J. Richards c Russell b Alderman	43	b Lawrence	18
*I. A. Greig c Athey b Alderman	0	c Stovold b Alderman	35
K. T. Medlycott c Wright b Alderman	1	(2) c Russell b Curran	17
N. H. Peters c Russell b Curran	8	b Lawrence	0
S. T. Clarke b Curran	16	c Alleyne b Lawrence	11
M. P. Bicknell not out	8	c and b Lawrence	5
L-b 7, n-b 1	8	L-b 2, w 1, n-b 4	7
1/32 2/55 3/116 4/249 5/264 6/265 7/267 8/280 9/300	312	1/0 2/1 3/4 4/17 5/41 6/46 7/94 8/96 9/108	115

Bonus points – Surrey 4, Gloucestershire 4.

In the first innings D. M. Ward, when 31, retired hurt at 166 and resumed at 249.

Bowling: *First Innings*—Lawrence 21–3–85–2; Alderman 20–1–81–4; Bainbridge 14–2–40–0; Curran 23.2–6–62–4; Graveney 12–1–37–0. *Second Innings*—Lawrence 14.5–0–47–7; Alderman 8–1–42–2; Curran 6–1–24–1.

Gloucestershire

First innings		Second innings	
A. W. Stovold c Stewart b Bicknell	5	c Stewart b Clarke	46
A. J. Wright c Richards b Clarke	1	c Ward b Clarke	27
P. Bainbridge c Medlycott b Bicknell	3	(4) c sub b Clarke	0
C. W. J. Athey not out	25	absent injured	
*D. A. Graveney c Clarke b Bicknell	13	(8) c Richards b Clarke	5
P. W. Romaines c Ward b Clarke	33	(3) c Peters b Clarke	2
K. M. Curran c Ward b Clarke	52	(5) c sub b Clarke	101
M. W. Alleyne b Peters	10	(6) c Richards b Peters	8
†R. C. Russell c Richards b Clarke	4	(7) c Clarke b Peters	5
D. V. Lawrence c Bicknell b Clarke	4	(9) c Stewart b Peters	0
T. M. Alderman not out	1	(10) not out	43
B 6, l-b 5, n-b 1	12	L-b 3, w 1, n-b 2	6
1/5 2/9 3/9 4/37 5/141 6/144 7/151 8/155 9/162 (9 wkts dec.)	163	1/74 2/75 3/75 4/82 5/103 6/109 7/125 8/132 9/243	243

Bonus points – Gloucestershire 1, Surrey 4.

In the first innings C. W. J. Athey, when 25, retired hurt at 62 and resumed at 162.

Bowling: *First Innings*—Clarke 21.1–5–44–5; Bicknell 14–4–49–3; Peters 13–3–44–1; Greig 5–1–13–0; Medlycott 1–0–2–0. *Second Innings*—Clarke 32.1–14–63–6; Bicknell 20–2–68–0; Peters 20–1–96–3; Greig 6–2–13–0.

Umpires: D. J. Constant and B. J. Meyer.

GLOUCESTERSHIRE v WARWICKSHIRE

At Cheltenham, August 3, 4, 5. Drawn. Gloucestershire 7 pts, Warwickshire 6 pts. Toss: Warwickshire. Gloucestershire were well placed to record their first win since mid-June when Warwickshire, set 284 to win in 61 overs, subsided to 101 for six, having also lost Banks with a broken thumb. However, the home county were baulked by a brave partnership between Smith, later found to have batted with a broken finger, and Parsons. Smith remained until the last ball of the penultimate over, and Merrick played out the last six balls. Despite these injuries – in addition, Stovold retired after being hit on the helmet by a bouncer – the pitch was not as lively as against Surrey. Stovold launched the Gloucestershire first innings in dashing style, and then Bainbridge and Romaines flourished in a partnership of 160. Romaines fell for 99 for the second Cheltenham Festival in succession, the ball spinning back from a defensive stroke to hit his stumps. Asif Din was in fluent form for Warwickshire, hitting sixteen fours in a rapid 84, while Bainbridge and Romaines again led the way in Gloucestershire's second innings.

Close of play: First day, Gloucestershire 325-5 (P. Bainbridge 109*, M. W. Pooley 10*); Second day, Gloucestershire 55-1 (P. W. Romaines 24*, P. Bainbridge 15*).

Gloucestershire

First innings		Second innings	
A. W. Stovold c Thorne b Reeve	52	– retired hurt	16
A. J. Wright c Munton b Reeve	9	– c Humpage b Parsons	0
P. W. Romaines b Reeve	99	– lbw b Parsons	50
P. Bainbridge c Humpage b Munton	119	– c Reeve b Parsons	70
M. W. Alleyne c Reeve b Parsons	15	– (6) c Humpage b Reeve	21
K. M. Curran c Humpage b Reeve	5	– (5) c Lloyd b Smith	2
M. W. Pooley c Humpage b Parsons	11	– not out	25
D. V. Lawrence c Smith b Munton	10	– (9) c Merrick b Asif Din	0
†R. C. Russell not out	4	– (8) c Thorne b Asif Din	41
*D. A. Graveney (did not bat)		– not out	3
B 4, l-b 22, w 2, n-b 4	32	L-b 4, n-b 2	6
1/48 2/69 3/229 4/256 5/279 6/340 7/342 8/356 (8 wkts dec.)	356	1/16 2/118 3/121 4/152 5/167 6/225 7/226 (7 wkts dec.)	234

T. M. Alderman did not bat.

Bonus points – Gloucestershire 4, Warwickshire 2 (Score at 100 overs: 305-5).

Bowling: *First Innings*—Merrick 20–3–89–0; Parsons 31–9–67–2; Reeve 33–9–71–4; Munton 25–5–66–2; Smith 5–0–25–0; Asif Din 4–1–12–0. *Second Innings*—Merrick 8–3–34–0; Parsons 15–3–47–3; Asif Din 10–2–48–2; Munton 6–1–49–0; Smith 7–2–20–1; Reeve 6–2–18–1; Lloyd 1–0–14–0.

Warwickshire

First innings		Second innings	
A. J. Moles c Russell b Alderman	41	– (2) c Alderman b Curran	1
*T. A. Lloyd c Graveney b Lawrence	10	– (1) c Alleyne b Lawrence	0
Asif Din c Russell b Curran	84	– c Wright b Lawrence	26
D. A. Banks c Bainbridge b Curran	1	– retired hurt	24
D. A. Thorne st Russell b Graveney	74	– c Alleyne b Pooley	14
†G. W. Humpage b Alderman	0	– c sub b Graveney	11
D. A. Reeve lbw b Alderman	11	– c Alleyne b Lawrence	14
P. A. Smith not out	50	– c Pooley b Lawrence	32
G. J. Parsons not out	23	– c Russell b Alderman	52
T. A. Merrick (did not bat)		– not out	6
T. A. Munton (did not bat)		– not out	0
B 4, l-b 2, n-b 7	13	B 4, l-b 4, n-b 3	11
1/29 2/142 3/142 4/146 5/147 6/169 7/257 (7 wkts dec.)	307	1/0 2/16 3/42 4/76 5/86 6/101 7/171 8/187 (8 wkts)	191

Bonus points – Warwickshire 4, Gloucestershire 3.

Bowling: *First Innings*—Lawrence 14–1–56–1; Alderman 18–2–62–3; Curran 20–5–82–2 Graveney 17.3–5–50–1; Bainbridge 4–0–29–0; Pooley 7–1–22–0. *Second Innings*—Lawrenc 21–3–71–4; Curran 10–1–47–1; Pooley 6–1–9–1; Alderman 7.5–2–20–1; Graveney 16–6–36–1

Umpires: D. J. Constant and B. J. Meyer.

GLOUCESTERSHIRE v YORKSHIRE

At Cheltenham, August 6, 8, 9. Drawn. Gloucestershire 5 pts, Yorkshire 8 pts. Toss: Gloucestershire. Graveney's gamble in putting Yorkshire in on an excellent batting pitch came badly unstuck, as did Carrick's decision to impose the follow-on. Although Alderman bowled a fine spell to leave Yorkshire 103 for four at lunch on the first day, Byas, with a maiden century, took the sting out of the bowling in assured style, and the lower-order batsmen took their cue with some vigorous hitting. How Gloucestershire allowed themselves to be bowled out for 214 on the hottest of days, despite some demanding bowling by Sidebottom, was a mystery in view of their second-innings display. Bainbridge, whose 169 (26 fours) was his highest first-class score, and Curran (eighteen fours) did much as they liked in a third-wicket partnership of 218, scoring 154 together on the final morning. Graveney's declaration, which asked 252 in 160 minutes, was a tempting one in such fast-scoring conditions, but with their early batsmen again upset by Alderman, and with Love nursing a knee injury, Yorkshire seemed to have little interest in the chase.

Close of play: First day, Gloucestershire 21-0 (A. J. Wright 13*, P. W. Romaines 6*); Second day, Gloucestershire 148-2 (P. Bainbridge 73*, K. M. Curran 32*).

Yorkshire

M. D. Moxon lbw b Alderman	31	– lbw b Alderman	21
A. A. Metcalfe lbw b Pooley	15	– c Russell b Alderman	33
D. Byas st Russell b Bainbridge	112	– run out	9
J. D. Love c Russell b Alderman	2		
P. E. Robinson c Curran b Alderman	5	– (4) c Curran b Alderman	6
†R. J. Blakey c Russell b Lawrence	40	– (5) not out	13
*P. Carrick c Wright b Pooley	81	– (6) not out	17
A. Sidebottom not out	37		
P. J. Hartley st Russell b Graveney	20		
C. Shaw not out	3		
B 8, l-b 11, w 1, n-b 1	21	B 1, l-b 2, n-b 2	5
1/38 2/85 3/97 4/103 5/183 6/270 7/320 8/360 (8 wkts dec.)	367	1/49 2/64 3/67 4/73 (4 wkts)	104

S. D. Fletcher did not bat.

Bonus points – Yorkshire 4, Gloucestershire 3 (Score at 100 overs: 364-8).

Bowling: *First Innings*—Lawrence 13–3–43–1; Curran 7–0–50–0; Pooley 19–7–56–2; Alderman 19–5–52–3; Bainbridge 13–2–58–1; Graveney 24.4–6–71–1; Alleyne 5–0–18–0. *Second Innings*—Lawrence 6–0–17–0; Alderman 12–3–37–3; Pooley 9–1–26–0; Curran 6–2–10–0; Graveney 6–2–11–0.

Gloucestershire

A. J. Wright c Moxon b Sidebottom	33	– b Hartley	34
P. W. Romaines c Robinson b Sidebottom	35	– c Blakey b Sidebottom	4
P. Bainbridge b Sidebottom	1	– c Blakey b Hartley	169
K. M. Curran b Hartley	10	– run out	98
M. W. Alleyne c Blakey b Shaw	19	– c Blakey b Carrick	30
M. W. Pooley c Blakey b Carrick	10	– (7) not out	25
A. W. Stovold c Hartley b Sidebottom	49	– (8) not out	30
†R. C. Russell c Love b Sidebottom	29	– (6) c Moxon b Carrick	1
*D. A. Graveney not out	7		
D. V. Lawrence b Hartley	4		
T. M. Alderman c Sidebottom b Hartley	0		
L-b 8, w 1, n-b 8	17	B 2, l-b 7, w 1, n-b 3	13
1/67 2/69 3/91 4/91 5/108 6/134 7/181 8/205 9/214	214	1/6 2/84 3/302 4/319 5/320 6/349 (6 wkts dec.)	404

Bonus points – Gloucestershire 2, Yorkshire 4.

Bowling: *First Innings*—Hartley 17–1–66–3; Fletcher 13–3–48–0; Carrick 14–7–21–1; Sidebottom 17–4–34–5; Shaw 15–5–37–1. *Second Innings*—Hartley 23–1–105–2; Sidebottom 14–5–30–1; Shaw 20–2–87–0; Carrick 32–7–106–2; Fletcher 6–0–30–0; Byas 3–0–25–0; Robinson 1.2–0–12–0.

Umpires: R. Julian and P. B. Wight.

At Lord's, August 13, 15, 16. GLOUCESTERSHIRE lost to MIDDLESEX by nine wickets.

At Bristol, August 17, 18, 19. GLOUCESTERSHIRE drew with SRI LANKANS (See Sri Lankan tour section).

GLOUCESTERSHIRE v KENT

At Bristol, August 20, 22, 23. Drawn. Gloucestershire 5 pts, Kent 7 pts. Toss: Kent. Despite the weather being against them – three hours were lost on the first day and the third day was also shortened by rain and bad light – Kent went close to achieving the win that would have consolidated their position as Championship leaders. Their four batting points were gained comfortably, and then, although Chris Cowdrey was hit for 38 in three overs by Bainbridge and Romaines, five Gloucestershire wickets were captured for 140. However, Ibadulla and Russell held on for 37 overs, adding 112, and Graveney was able to declare. The loss of 22 overs early on the third day made Kent's dash for runs more hectic than anticipated, but they came quickly enough for Gloucestershire to be given a target of 227 from 45 overs. Ellison reduced them to 43 for four, Romaines and Russell had to be tempted out of a defensive frame of mind by the occasional bowlers, and when Ellison and Harman came back to regain control, Graveney and Pooley had to defend grimly. With four overs remaining, Igglesden was summoned, but the umpires ruled that the light was too poor for a fast bowler to be used and the players trooped off.

Close of play: First day, Kent 202-3 (R. F. Pienaar 39*, C. S. Cowdrey 8*); Second day, Gloucestershire 259-7 dec.

Kent

M. R. Benson b Pooley	70	– b Pooley	58
N. R. Taylor c Alderman b Lawrence	41	– c Russell b Pooley	8
R. F. Pienaar c Curran b Graveney	51	– c Alderman b Bainbridge	14
C. J. Tavaré c Curran b Graveney	35	– c Russell b Bainbridge	13
*C. S. Cowdrey retired ill	8	– lbw b Pooley	2
G. R. Cowdrey b Pooley	50	– lbw b Bainbridge	17
S. G. Hinks not out	26	– b Pooley	44
†S. A. Marsh not out	5	– not out	25
L-b 7, w 1, n-b 7	15	B 2, n-b 1	3
1/116 2/117 3/184 4/242 5/296 (5 wkts dec.)	301	1/21 2/54 3/77 4/80 5/99 6/113 7/184 (7 wkts dec.)	184

R. M. Ellison, M. D. Harman and A. P. Igglesden did not bat.

Bonus points – Kent 4, Gloucestershire 2.

Bowling: *First Innings*—Lawrence 13–2–54–1; Alderman 23–6–72–0; Graveney 26.1–8–65–2; Curran 10–3–19–0; Pooley 18–2–54–2; Ibadulla 8–3–30–0. *Second Innings*—Lawrence 4–1–7–0; Curran 3–1–10–0; Pooley 15.4–2–80–4; Bainbridge 15–1–85–3.

Gloucestershire

	First Innings		Second Innings	
A. W. Stovold b Igglesden	14	–	c Tavaré b Ellison	12
A. J. Wright b Igglesden	22	–	c Tavaré b Ellison	5
P. W. Romaines c Ellison b Pienaar	42	–	b Ellison	61
P. Bainbridge c Marsh b Harman	55	–	c G. R. Cowdrey b Harman	8
K. M. Curran c Igglesden b Harman	0	–	b Ellison	4
†R. C. Russell not out	34	–	c C. S. Cowdrey b Harman	34
K. B. K. Ibadulla c C. S. Cowdrey b G. R. Cowdrey	77	–	c C. S. Cowdrey b Ellison	14
M. W. Pooley c Marsh b Harman	3	–	(9) not out	15
*D. A. Graveney (did not bat)		–	(8) not out	2
B 3, l-b 4, n-b 5	12		B 3, l-b 2, w 1	6
1/26 2/61 3/140 4/140 5/140 6/252 7/259 (7 wkts dec.)	259		1/16 2/19 3/28 4/43 5/128 6/144 7/144 (7 wkts)	161

D. V. Lawrence and T. M. Alderman did not bat.

Bonus points – Gloucestershire 3, Kent 3.

Bowling: *First Innings*—Igglesden 14–2–54–2; Ellison 19–5–66–0; Pienaar 17–5–41–1; C. S. Cowdrey 3–0–38–0; Harman 20–7–48–3; G. R. Cowdrey 2–0–5–1. *Second Innings*—Igglesden 4–0–15–0; Ellison 16–5–46–5; Harman 14–7–31–2; Pienaar 2–1–1–0; Benson 3–0–35–0; Hinks 2–0–28–0.

Umpires: J. H. Hampshire and J. H. Harris.

At Southampton, August 30, 31, September 1, 2. GLOUCESTERSHIRE beat HAMPSHIRE by five wickets.

GLOUCESTERSHIRE v WORCESTERSHIRE

At Bristol, September 9, 10, 11, 12. Worcestershire won by 114 runs. Worcestershire 23 pts, Gloucestershire 6 pts. Toss: Worcestershire. Worcestershire took up the running in the race for the County Championship, winning a match which contained four centuries and was notable for the slow bowlers taking 32 of the 40 wickets. Graveney claimed the honours in this latter department with the best figures of his seventeen-year career, only to learn afterwards that the county had decided to replace him as captain. On the first day, he had prevented Worcestershire from taking maximum batting points after a chanceless century by Hick, his ninth of the season. Yet in spite of Hick's 121 (two sixes, seventeen fours) Worcestershire from 217 for six needed Neale and the tailenders to extend the innings beyond 400 – runs which were to prove crucial. For Gloucestershire, Bainbridge (twelve fours) batted splendidly for three and threequarter hours, but with Illingworth taking Graveney's lead, the last pair were together when the follow-on was saved. Lord's century, his first for Worcestershire, ensured that Gloucestershire's target would be a formidable one; he batted for more than five hours against demanding spin bowling before he was last out. On the final day Curran hit some powerful blows and, following a break for rain, Russell and Lawrence frolicked for half an hour. Worcestershire, however, always had the match well in hand.

Close of play: First day, Worcestershire 344-8 (P. A. Neale 73*, G. R. Dilley 11*); Second day, Worcestershire 4-0 (T. S. Curtis 4*, G. J. Lord 0*); Third day, Gloucestershire 78-3 (K. M. Curran 11*, T. M. Alderman 0*).

Worcestershire

First innings		Second innings	
T. S. Curtis lbw b Alderman	2	not out	13
G. J. Lord c Alderman b Graveney	41	c Curran b Graveney	101
G. A. Hick b Graveney	121	lbw b Lawrence	18
D. A. Leatherdale c Russell b Graveney	25	c Russell b Lawrence	8
*P. A. Neale not out	102	c Russell b Graveney	4
M. J. Weston c Lloyds b Graveney	0	b Lloyds	12
†S. J. Rhodes st Russell b Graveney	1	c Lloyds b Graveney	24
R. K. Illingworth c Alderman b Graveney	38	c Lloyds b Graveney	8
N. V. Radford lbw b Graveney	15	b Lloyds	1
G. R. Dilley c Curran b Lloyds	36	c and b Graveney	3
A. P. Pridgeon c Lloyds b Graveney	1	c Russell b Graveney	1
B 3, l-b 14, n-b 5	22	L-b 1, w 3, n-b 2	6
1/3 2/115 3/163 4/209 5/213 6/217 7/283 8/315 9/400	404	1/53 2/65 3/80 4/108 5/163 6/185 7/186 8/190 9/196	199

Bonus points – Worcestershire 3, Gloucestershire 3 (Score at 100 overs: 283-7).

In the second innings T. S. Curtis, when 13, retired hurt at 21 and resumed at 196.

Bowling: *First Innings*—Lawrence 22–2–75–0; Alderman 23–5–66–1; Pooley 5–1–16–0; Graveney 57.3–14–127–8; Lloyds 25–5–89–1; Bainbridge 9–4–14–0. *Second Innings*—Lawrence 12–2–45–2; Alderman 11–1–31–0; Lloyds 32–5–84–2; Graveney 30.2–11–38–6.

Gloucestershire

First innings		Second innings	
A. W. Stovold b Dilley	4	c Weston b Pridgeon	0
A. J. Wright lbw b Pridgeon	39	c Rhodes b Hick	39
P. W. Romaines b Dilley	0	c Radford b Hick	20
P. Bainbridge c Hick b Illingworth	124	(6) b Illingworth	27
K. M. Curran c Curtis b Illingworth	8	(4) c Rhodes b Illingworth	57
J. W. Lloyds st Rhodes b Illingworth	47	(7) lbw b Hick	1
M. W. Pooley c Hick b Illingworth	1	(8) c Radford b Hick	0
†R. C. Russell c Rhodes b Illingworth	1	(9) c sub b Illingworth	41
D. V. Lawrence b Hick	6	(10) c Lord b Illingworth	29
T. M. Alderman lbw b Radford	7	(5) c Weston b Illingworth	0
*D. A. Graveney not out	2	not out	4
B 1, l-b 9, n-b 13	23	B 3, l-b 2, n-b 4	9
1/8 2/12 3/95 4/116 5/214 6/237 7/246 8/247 9/253	262	1/2 2/62 3/71 4/88 5/143 6/146 7/152 8/152 9/213	227

Bonus points – Gloucestershire 3, Worcestershire 4.

Bowling: *First Innings*—Dilley 11–2–43–2; Radford 9.1–0–37–1; Illingworth 31–12–69–5; Pridgeon 16–6–39–1; Hick 20–3–54–1; Weston 2–0–7–0; Leatherdale 1–0–3–0. *Second Innings*—Radford 10–4–20–0; Pridgeon 9–1–25–1; Illingworth 35.1–13–63–5; Hick 32–9–114–4.

Umpires: J. W. Holder and A. A. Jones.

At Taunton, September 14, 15, 16, 17. GLOUCESTERSHIRE beat SOMERSET by four wickets.

HAMPSHIRE

President: C. G. A. Paris
Chairman: D. Rich
Chairman, Cricket Committee: C. J. Knott
Chief Executive: A. F. Baker
Northlands Road, Southampton SO9 2TY
(Telephone: 0703-333788)
Captain: M. C. J. Nicholas
Coach: P. J. Sainsbury

n Hampshire, 1988 will be remembered as the year when they at last rid hemselves of the tag of being the only county not to have appeared in a ord's final. Moreover, it was the year in which they won their first nockout trophy, for on their first visit to Lord's they beat Derbyshire andsomely by seven wickets to lift the Benson and Hedges Cup. Their outh African opening bowler, Steve Jefferies, had set up the victory ith a return of five for 13, the best figures in a Lord's final. A month ter, Hampshire could have made it two finals in the same season but ent down by 29 runs in the NatWest Bank Trophy semi-finals to orcestershire, the county they had beaten in the quarter-finals of the enson and Hedges Cup.

However, Hampshire's successful season in the two knockout competitions contrasted strongly with their performances in the Britannic ssurance Championship and the Refuge Assurance League. In the hampionship, they rarely played to their full potential and, with just ur wins, finished fifteenth, a drop of ten places and their lowest placing nce 1984 when, as last season, they were without Gordon Greenidge d Malcolm Marshall. Yet even without their two West Indians, ampshire had hoped to do better in the Sunday League. Instead, after ree of the first four games were lost, their challenge never got off the ound. A late run, which saw them win their last four games, lifted them ninth.

Hampshire's Championship campaign also started disappointingly th defeat by Surrey at Southampton inside two of the scheduled four ys. They came back well to beat Kent at Canterbury with a day to are, but it was mid-July before their next win in a contrived finish ainst Surrey at Guildford. They ended the season by beating amorgan and Sussex, the counties below them in the table.

For the first time in some years, Hampshire's vaunted batting line-up led to prosper. They secured fewer batting bonus points than any other unty and went without one in eight of their 22 games. Whereas six tsmen averaged over 40 in the Championship in 1987, only Nigel wley (four games) did so in 1988. Paul Terry's Championship form s in marked contrast to his superb batting in the Benson and Hedges p, in which he won three Gold Awards. Before his unbeaten 126 at ildford, he had scored just 358 runs in 21 Championship innings at an rage of 17.90, and it was not until he reached 187 in his career-best against the Sri Lankans, in late August, that he completed his 1,000 t-class runs.

Chris Smith was his usual reliable self, scoring three hundreds an eight fifties in 1,436 runs, although there was a period in August when h managed just 13 runs from six consecutive Championship innings. Th veteran left-hander, David Turner, achieved 1,000 runs for the nint time, while Mark Nicholas, the captain, and Robin Smith also reache four figures. Although capped by England, Robin Smith again failed t capitalise on his apparent ability, passing 50 only four times in 3 Championship innings.

Richard Scott, a young left-hander, made an inauspicious start to hi Championship career with three successive ducks, all at Portsmouth. Bu a maiden first-class hundred against the touring Sri Lankans and tw Championship half-centuries marked him as a good prospect for th future. It was largely due to the need to bring on young players lik Scott that Hampshire decided not to offer a new contract to Gordo Greenidge, still one of the world's great batsmen.

Allied to the inconsistency of the batting was an attack which ofte lacked penetration, particularly on home pitches. It was not helped b injuries to Jefferies, Tim Tremlett and Stephen Andrew, or the loss o form of the slow left-armer, Rajesh Maru. Jefferies, a well-built left-ar swing bowler, signed on a two-year contract as cover for Marsha enjoyed a purple patch in mid-summer, anticipating his match-winnir spell at Lord's with eight for 97 in Gloucestershire's second innings a Gloucester; but he missed the last six Championship games. He was t leading wicket-taker, with 40, in the one-day competitions.

Cardigan Connor, who was awarded his county cap early in t season, had a much improved year with 55 first-class wickets, and Pau Jan Bakker, the Dutchman, coming into the side in July, proved he cou be a competent seam bowler in the first-class game. But the big success the season was 21-year-old, Hampshire-born Jon Ayling, who was giv his chance early on because of Tremlett's injury and responded with a outstanding début season. Helped by four half-centuries, one a matc winning effort at Cardiff, he scored 711 first-class runs and took wickets at 23.36 apiece. Blessed with a superb temperament, he show himself to be a fine striker of the ball, hitting three sixes and four fou in making 44 off 59 balls to help Hampshire beat Sussex in the fir Championship match.

Cowley's role was limited mostly to the one-day games, in which tightly controlled off-breaks conceded an average of 3.54 runs per ov in 207 overs and captured eighteen wickets. His economy in the Bens and Hedges Cup, 2.15 runs per over in the seven matches, was qu remarkable. – Victor Isaacs.

[*Patrick Eagar*

Back row: R. J. Maru, C. A. Connor, R. A. Smith, J. R. Ayling, S. J. W. Andrew, S. T. Jefferies, K. D. James, R. J. Parks. *Front row:* C. L. Smith, D. R. Turner, M. C. J. Nicholas (*captain*), V. P. Terry, N. G. Cowley.

HAMPSHIRE RESULTS

All first-class matches – Played 24: Won 4, Lost 6, Drawn 14.

County Championship matches – Played 22: Won 4, Lost 6, Drawn 12.

Bonus points – Batting 33, Bowling 69.

Competition placings – Britannic Assurance County Championship, 15th; NatWest Bank Trophy, s-f; Benson and Hedges Cup, winners; Refuge Assurance League, 9th.

BRITANNIC ASSURANCE CHAMPIONSHIP AVERAGES

BATTING

	Birthplace	*M*	*I*	*NO*	*R*	*HI*	*Avg*
‡N. G. Cowley	*Shaftesbury*	4	5	2	139	55	46.3
‡C. L. Smith	*Durban, SA*	22	43	3	1,436	124*	35.9
‡D. R. Turner	*Chippenham*	21	38	5	1,121	150*	33.9
§S. T. Jefferies	*Cape Town, SA*	14	19	5	462	60	33.0
‡R. A. Smith	*Durban, SA*	16	32	4	912	141*	32.5
‡M. C. J. Nicholas	*London*	22	42	3	1,146	132*	29.3
‡V. P. Terry	*Osnabruck, WG*	22	42	3	992	126*	25.4
J. R. Ayling	*Portsmouth*	18	31	4	667	88*	24.7
S. J. W. Andrew	*London*	10	9	7	41	12*	20.5
R. J. Scott	*Bournemouth*	7	13	0	255	58	19.6
§P. J. Bakker	*Vlaardingen, Netherlands*	10	11	8	50	16	16.6
‡R. J. Parks	*Cuckfield*	22	33	8	392	38*	15.6
K. D. James	*Lambeth, London*	10	19	2	238	77	14.0
‡T. M. Tremlett	*Wellington, Somerset*	6	10	2	111	38	13.8
‡R. J. Maru	*Nairobi, Kenya*	21	28	5	302	74	13.1
‡C. A. Connor	*The Valley, Anguilla*	17	22	4	135	24	7.

* *Signifies not out.* ‡ *Denotes county cap.* § *Not qualified for England.*

The following played a total of eleven three-figure innings for Hampshire in Cour Championship matches – C. L. Smith 3, M. C. J. Nicholas 2, R. A. Smith 2, V. P. Terry D. R. Turner 2.

BOWLING

	O	*M*	*R*	*W*	*BB*	*5W/i*	*Av*
T. M. Tremlett	105.3	29	281	13	4-19	0	21.
P. J. Bakker	293.4	86	670	30	5-54	1	22.
J. R. Ayling	409.1	84	1,065	45	4-57	0	23.
K. D. James	250.5	56	639	26	5-25	1	24
S. J. W. Andrew	233.3	60	681	26	4-52	0	26
C. A. Connor	470.5	86	1,451	53	5-70	1	27
S. T. Jefferies	355.1	53	1,216	34	8-97	2	35
R. J. Maru	622	171	1,618	45	5-69	1	35

Also bowled: N. G. Cowley 96.1–22–246–8; M. C. J. Nicholas 33–3–114–1; R. J. S 13.3–2–52–0; C. L. Smith 49–1–171–5; R. A. Smith 5.1–1–34–0; D. R. Turner 0.2–0–8–0

Wicket-keeper: R. J. Parks 59 ct, 10 st.

Leading Fielders: R. J. Maru 30, V. P. Terry 30, M. C. J. Nicholas 18.

HAMPSHIRE v SURREY

At Southampton, April 21, 22. Surrey won by nine wickets with two days to spare. Surrey 22 pts, Hampshire 4 pts. Toss: Hampshire. Poor batting by Hampshire on a pitch offering some help to the seam bowlers resulted in a comfortable victory for Surrey, who claimed the extra half-hour to complete their task at the end of the second day. Jefferies, making his début for the home county, soon impressed with his left-arm fast bowling, but it was Connor, beating the bat regularly, who posed the bigger threat. Surrey, in some trouble at 120 for five, recovered well thanks mainly to Richards. Clarke and Peters, another newcomer, were too much for the Hampshire batsmen, who were soon being asked to bat again. They were saved from an innings defeat only by an eighth-wicket stand of 92 between Jefferies and Tremlett. Greig, the Surrey captain, returned his best figures for the county as he kept Hampshire under pressure in their second innings.

Close of play: First day, Hampshire 44-3 (R. A. Smith 9*, R. J. Maru 4*).

Surrey

	First innings		Second innings	
G. S. Clinton c C. L. Smith b Jefferies	11	– run out	3
D. M. Smith c Parks b Connor	4	– not out	32
A. J. Stewart c Maru b Tremlett	14	– not out	6
M. A. Lynch c Tremlett b Connor	39		
D. M. Ward c Maru b Tremlett	6		
C. J. Richards c Terry b Connor	61		
I. A. Greig lbw b James	34		
K. T. Medlycott lbw b Connor	37		
M. A. Feltham c Parks b Jefferies	15		
N. H. Peters c Maru b Jefferies	0		
S. T. Clarke not out	14		
B 1, l-b 8, n-b 2	11	L-b 6	6
1/8 2/26 3/30 4/39 5/120 6/161 7/201 8/231 9/231	246	1/29	(1 wkt) 47

Bonus points – Surrey 2, Hampshire 4.

Bowling: *First Innings*—Jefferies 21.1–6–64–3; Connor 27–7–71–4; Tremlett 13–2–41–2; James 16–4–35–1; Maru 13–4–26–0. *Second Innings*—Jefferies 3–0–23–0; Connor 3–0–14–0; R. A. Smith 0.1–0–4–0.

Hampshire

	First innings		Second innings	
V. P. Terry c Ward b Clarke	4	– c Richards b Clarke	49
C. L. Smith c Stewart b Peters	3	– lbw b Greig	9
M. C. J. Nicholas c Lynch b Clarke	18	– lbw b Greig	0
R. A. Smith c Clinton b Peters	21	– b Greig	8
R. J. Maru c Medlycott b Peters	4	– (10) c Stewart b Greig	9
I. R. Turner c Clinton b Peters	7	– (5) c Richards b Feltham	1
K. D. James c Stewart b Clarke	0	– (6) b Greig	2
R. J. Parks not out	12	– (7) c Ward b Clarke	14
S. T. Jefferies c Lynch b Feltham	8	– (8) lbw b Greig	60
T. M. Tremlett lbw b Feltham	3	– (9) c Richards b Peters	38
C. A. Connor c Richards b Feltham	0	– not out	0
L-b 4, w 3, n-b 4	11	L-b 1, w 1, n-b 6	8
1/7 2/12 3/38 4/58 5/65 6/68 7/68 8/87 9/91	91	1/12 2/12 3/25 4/28 5/43 6/77 7/96 8/188 9/192	198

Bonus points – Surrey 4.

Bowling: *First Innings*—Clarke 18–8–27–3; Peters 16–3–47–4; Greig 4–1–7–0; Feltham 4–0–6–3. *Second Innings*—Clarke 18–8–36–2; Peters 11–2–45–1; Feltham 21–8–60–1; Greig 23–4–56–6.

Umpires: B. Hassan and P. B. Wight.

At Canterbury, April 28, 29, 30. HAMPSHIRE beat KENT by seven wickets.

At Oxford, May 5, 6, 7. HAMPSHIRE drew with OXFORD UNIVERSITY.

At Southampton, May 12. HAMPSHIRE lost to WEST INDIANS by 93 runs (See Wes Indian tour section).

HAMPSHIRE v GLAMORGAN

At Bournemouth, May 18, 19, 20. Drawn. Hampshire 6 pts, Glamorgan 7 pts. Toss Hampshire. On a slow, rain-affected pitch, both sides struggled for runs against some tigh seam and spin bowling. And with much time lost to rain and bad light, a draw looked the mos likely result until the initiative of the captains provided an entertaining last afternoon. Aide by some friendly bowling which produced 100 runs in eight overs, Hampshire were ab to set Glamorgan a target of 201 in two hours, or a minimum of 39 overs. Maru an the Championship débutant, Ayling, quickened Hampshire's hopes of a win, but the lat Glamorgan batsmen held on bravely for a draw after Parks had made three stumpings in th space of eight deliveries.

Close of play: First day, Glamorgan 4-1 (A. R. Butcher 3*, C. P. Metson 0*); Second da Hampshire 10-1 (C. L. Smith 2*).

Hampshire

V. P. Terry c Metson b Thomas . . . . 13 – c van Zyl b Thomas . . . .
C. L. Smith c Metson b van Zyl . . . . 0 – c Butcher b Derrick 2
*M. C. J. Nicholas b Derrick . . . . 45 – not out 1
R. A. Smith c Metson b Barwick . . . . 20 – not out . . . .
D. R. Turner c Hopkins b Ontong 38
J. R. Ayling run out 0
†R. J. Parks c Metson b Thomas 2
S. T. Jefferies c Derrick b Ontong 39
R. J. Maru b Ontong 37
C. A. Connor b Ontong 0
S. J. W. Andrew not out 4
B 2, l-b 15, n-b 2 . . . . 19 B 1, n-b 2 . . . .

1/5 2/27 3/63 4/125 5/125 6/133 7/139 8/198 9/198 — 217 1/10 2/64 (2 wkts dec.) 2

Bonus points – Hampshire 2, Glamorgan 4.

Bowling: *First Innings*—Thomas 20–2–70–2; van Zyl 13–5–20–1; Derrick 16–10–23- Barwick 16–3–40–1; Ontong 20.2–7–47–4. *Second Innings*—Thomas 9–1–29–1; van 15–4–36–0; Derrick 14–5–35–1; Barwick 11–5–24–0; Ontong 11–1–30–0; Butcher 2–2–0 Hopkins 5–1–46–0; Morris 4.3–0–58–0.

Glamorgan

A. R. Butcher c Maru b Connor	34	– c Terry b Connor	19
J. A. Hopkins c Parks b Jefferies	1	– lbw b Ayling	47
†C. P. Metson lbw b Ayling	32	– (10) not out	2
*H. Morris c Terry b Ayling	39	– (3) c Jefferies b Maru	37
M. P. Maynard c Nicholas b Andrew	39	– (4) c Turner b Ayling	23
G. C. Holmes c Terry b Connor	12	– (5) c Parks b Maru	7
R. C. Ontong not out	60	– (6) st Parks b Maru	9
J. G. Thomas b Connor	2	– (7) st Parks b Ayling	19
J. Derrick c Terry b Ayling	4	– st Parks b Maru	0
C. J. P. G. van Zyl b Andrew	11	– (8) not out	7
S. R. Barwick b Jefferies	30		
B 5, l-b 2, n-b 5	12	L-b 4, n-b 3	7
1/2 2/66 3/72 4/145 5/166 6/166 7/169 8/178 9/206	276	1/44 2/99 3/133 4/133 5/141 6/168 7/172 8/172	(8 wkts) 177

Bonus points – Glamorgan 3, Hampshire 4.

Bowling: *First Innings*—Connor 32–9–67–3; Jefferies 14.2–3–59–2; Andrew 17–3–58–2; Ayling 20–6–38–3; Maru 14–3–47–0. *Second Innings*—Jefferies 4–0–22–0; Connor 9.5–1–36–1; Maru 15–5–70–4; Ayling 9–1–45–3.

Umpires: J. H. Harris and R. Palmer.

At Middlesbrough, May 28, 30, 31. HAMPSHIRE drew with YORKSHIRE.

HAMPSHIRE v SOMERSET

At Southampton, June 1, 2, 3. Drawn. Hampshire 4 pts, Somerset 6 pts. Toss: Somerset. When Crowe declared himself unfit an hour before the start, Somerset called up Waugh, their other overseas player, from Smethwick. By the time he reached the County Ground at Southampton, his side were in some trouble at 64 for four, but his arrival at the crease marked a revival. Not out 94 by the close, next day he moved on to his first Championship hundred of the season; his unbeaten 115 included a six and nine fours. When Hampshire batted, Jones caused havoc with a spell of seven for 18 in twelve overs. Only Nicholas and Jefferies resisted to any effect, and despite the sterling efforts of Connor and Andrew, Hampshire failed by 3 runs to avoid the follow-on. However, with the wicket and the weather both easing, batting proved less of a problem second time around. Terry (sixteen fours) and Chris Smith opened with a century stand, and Turner reached his century with a four off the last ball of the match.

Close of play: First day, Somerset 262-8 (S. R. Waugh 94*, A. N. Jones 0*); Second day, Hampshire 23-0 (V. P. Terry 10*, C. L. Smith 12*).

Somerset

N. A. Felton c Ayling b Connor	18	G. D. Rose lbw b Jefferies	13
J. G. Wyatt c and b Andrew	20	A. N. Jones c Terry b Connor	3
J. E. Hardy c Terry b Connor	0	D. J. Foster c R. A. Smith b Ayling	20
R. J. Bartlett st Parks b Ayling	19		
N. D. Burns c Parks b Connor	47	B 4, l-b 9, w 2, n-b 5	20
V. J. Marks b Jefferies	20		
S. R. Waugh not out	115	1/36 2/38 3/60 4/64 5/106 6/157 7/220 8/253 9/278	308
R. W. Cleal c sub b Ayling	13		

Bonus points – Somerset 2, Hampshire 3 (Score at 100 overs: 248-7).

Bowling: Jefferies 33–8–93–2; Andrew 18–5–44–1; Connor 34–3–89–4; Ayling 24–8–46–3; Maru 11–1–23–0.

Hampshire

V. P. Terry c Waugh b Jones	5	– c Jones b Rose	106
C. L. Smith c Hardy b Jones	11	– c Burns b Marks	47
*M. C. J. Nicholas b Jones	47	– b Marks	(
R. A. Smith c Waugh b Jones	7	– c Felton b Marks	1:
D. R. Turner c Waugh b Jones	0	– not out	10(
J. R. Ayling c Hardy b Jones	0	– not out	6
†R. J. Parks c Bartlett b Jones	0		
S. T. Jefferies c Burns b Rose	39		
R. J. Maru c Burns b Foster	13		
C. A. Connor not out	22		
S. J. W. Andrew c Wyatt b Rose	6		
L-b 5, w 1	6	B 1, l-b 2, n-b 1	
1/6 2/17 3/31 4/31 5/35 6/35 7/91 8/108 9/138	156	1/124 2/128 3/148 4/192	(4 wkts) 33

Bonus points – Hampshire 1, Somerset 4.

Bowling: *First Innings*—Jones 18–9–30–7; Foster 16–2–41–1; Rose 16.3–5–53–2; Cle 9–3–27–0. *Second Innings*—Rose 15–3–44–1; Cleal 13–2–59–0; Foster 15–3–40–0; Mar 46–11–111–3; Jones 13–2–42–0; Bartlett 7–0–37–0.

Umpires: J. C. Balderstone and R. Palmer.

At Liverpool, June 4, 6, 7. HAMPSHIRE lost to LANCASHIRE by four wickets.

At Worcester, June 11, 13, 14. HAMPSHIRE lost to WORCESTERSHIRE by ten wicke

HAMPSHIRE v MIDDLESEX

At Basingstoke, June 15, 16, 17. Drawn. Hampshire 4 pts, Middlesex 4 pts. Toss: Hampshi Choosing to bat first on a wicket that offered help to the seam bowlers throughout the f day, Hampshire struggled. Cowans, having dismissed Terry with the first ball of the mat took three wickets for 0 in eight balls just when it looked as if Nicholas and Robin Sm might overcome the conditions, and the tall Middlesex seamer, Fraser, maintained pressure with straight, demanding bowling. However, Hampshire fought back well to ta seven Middlesex wickets before the close of an enthralling day. Turner emulated his fea the previous home match by scoring 0 – one of four to fall first ball on the opening day – in the second innings hitting an unbeaten century. He was one of the few Hampshire batsm to master Fraser – who followed his five wickets of the first innings with six in the secon and his 150, including twenty fours, enabled Hampshire to make a challenging declarati Middlesex needed 300 in a minimum of 71 overs but, to the disappointment of the larger t usual crowd, Gatting seemed to settle for batting practice. His own century, an attractive c featured eighteen fours.

Close of play: First day, Middlesex 121-7 (S. P. Hughes 21*, A. R. C. Fraser 7*); Sec day, Hampshire 226-7 (D. R. Turner 93*, R. J. Maru 10*).

Hampshire

V. P. Terry c Olley b Cowans	0 – lbw b Fraser	6
C. L. Smith c Carr b Fraser	8 – c Carr b Tufnell	19
*M. C. J. Nicholas lbw b Cowans	39 – c Olley b Tufnell	48
R. A. Smith c Carr b Fraser	33 – b Cowans	18
D. R. Turner b Cowans	0 – not out	150
J. R. Ayling c Butcher b Cowans	0 – (8) c Brown b Fraser	12
K. D. James b Fraser	15 – (6) lbw b Fraser	0
†R. J. Parks c and b Hughes	7 – (7) c Carr b Fraser	0
R. J. Maru c Olley b Fraser	0 – lbw b Fraser	27
C. A. Connor c Gatting b Fraser	5 – c Olley b Fraser	1
S. J. W. Andrew not out	12 – not out	4
B 4, l-b 6, n-b 7	17 B 5, l-b 16, n-b 6	27
1/0 2/28 3/69 4/69 5/71 6/110 7/115 8/115 9/119	136 1/17 2/34 3/56 4/173 5/182 6/184 7/203 8/271 9/273	(9 wkts dec.) 312

Bonus points – Middlesex 4.

Bowling: *First Innings*—Cowans 14–6–33–4; Hughes 18–2–54–1; Fraser 21.4–5–34–5; Tufnell 4–1–5–0. *Second Innings*—Cowans 11–0–26–1; Fraser 32–9–68–6; Hughes '8.2–5–63–0; Tufnell 39–10–96–2; Gatting 8–1–21–0; Sykes 4–0–17–0.

Middlesex

W. N. Slack c Nicholas b Connor	19 – c Terry b Maru	42
. D. Carr c Parks b Andrew	8 – c Parks b Connor	6
M. W. Gatting c Maru b Ayling	18 – st Parks b Maru	104
R. O. Butcher lbw b Connor	24 – (5) not out	17
K. R. Brown c Parks b Andrew	10 – (6) not out	2
M. W. C. Olley b Ayling	4	
. F. Sykes lbw b Ayling	0 – (4) c Parks b Andrew	6
. P. Hughes run out	34	
A. R. C. Fraser c R. A. Smith b Connor	16	
N. G. Cowans not out	0	
. C. R. Tufnell c Parks b Connor	2	
L-b 4, n-b 10	14 L-b 2, w 1, n-b 6	9
'20 2/36 3/67 4/78 5/86 '86 7/96 8/147 9/147	149 1/10 2/92 3/111 4/181	(4 wkts) 186

Bonus points – Hampshire 4.

Bowling: *First Innings*—Andrew 18–10–24–2; Connor 21.5–5–61–4; Ayling 12–1–39–3; Maru 4–1–5–0; James 4–0–14–0; C. L. Smith 1–0–2–0. *Second Innings*—Andrew 15–6–25–1; Connor 14–4–36–1; Maru 21–8–57–2; Ayling 7–1–22–0; James 6–1–21–0; C. L. Smith -0–9–0; R. A. Smith 1–0–14–0.

Umpires: J. H. Hampshire and R. A. White.

HAMPSHIRE v NOTTINGHAMSHIRE

: Southampton, June 18, 20, 21. Drawn. Hampshire 7 pts, Nottinghamshire 3 pts. Toss: ottinghamshire. The bowling of Connor, who took five wickets on a good pitch, and the bsequent batting of Chris Smith (one six, fourteen fours), the in-form Turner and Cowley w Hampshire hold a considerable advantage by the end of the second day. However, an :ractive 140 from Johnson (sixteen fours) and a painstaking 80 by Newell, who batted for 5 urs 22 minutes, saved Nottinghamshire by ensuring that Hampshire were not left an easy get. Certainly, the task of scoring 168 in twenty overs proved too much for them and five :kets were lost before the match finished.

Close of play: First day, Hampshire 112-2 (C. L. Smith 69*, R. A. Smith 7*); Second day, ttinghamshire 70-2 (M. Newell 12*, P. Johnson 8*).

Nottinghamshire

P. Pollard c Parks b Andrew	8	– b Maru 34
M. Newell c Terry b Connor	24	– c Parks b Connor 80
P. Johnson c Maru b Ayling	49	– (4) c C. L. Smith b Maru 140
F. D. Stephenson c Nicholas b Connor	10	– (5) c C. L. Smith b Maru 0
D. W. Randall c Parks b Andrew	6	– (6) lbw b Andrew 26
*J. D. Birch b Connor	36	– (7) lbw b Ayling 8
K. P. Evans c Maru b Andrew	6	– (9) c Terry b Cowley 34
†C. W. Scott b Connor	5	– (3) c Parks b Maru 0
E. E. Hemmings c Cowley b Connor	13	– (8) b Andrew 5
K. E. Cooper lbw b Cowley	21	– c Maru b Ayling 0
D. J. Millns not out	7	– not out 5
L-b 7, w 1, n-b 4	12	B 4, l-b 13, n-b 10 27
1/10 2/68 3/86 4/101 5/111 6/125 7/147 8/167 9/172	197	1/59 2/59 3/270 4/270 5/287 6/299 7/308 8/319 9/324 359

Bonus points – Nottinghamshire 1, Hampshire 4.

Bowling: *First Innings*—Andrew 18–2–54–3; Connor 22–5–70–5; Ayling 19–5–39–1; Mar 12–3–27–0; Cowley 1.1–1–0–1. *Second Innings*—Andrew 20–3–53–2; Connor 17–4–48–1 Ayling 16–5–24–2; Maru 43–10–132–4; Cowley 27.1–7–67–1; C. L. Smith 3–0–16–0; Nichola 1–0–2–0.

Hampshire

V. P. Terry c Newell b Hemmings	23	– (5) not out
C. L. Smith c Newell b Hemmings	117	– c Evans b Cooper 1
*M. C. J. Nicholas lbw b Hemmings	2	– (4) c Randall b Cooper
R. A. Smith c Newell b Stephenson	20	– (1) c Scott b Stephenson
D. R. Turner lbw b Stephenson	75	– (3) b Stephenson
J. R. Ayling lbw b Cooper	12	– c Newell b Hemmings
†R. J. Parks c Stephenson b Cooper	24	– not out
N. G. Cowley b Evans	55	
R. J. Maru c Scott b Millns	5	
C. A. Connor b Hemmings	18	
S. J. W. Andrew not out	8	
B 6, l-b 15, w 4, n-b 5	30	B 3, l-b 1
1/64 2/73 3/134 4/219 5/248 6/290 7/304 8/329 9/375	389	1/8 2/18 3/35 4/37 5/45 (5 wkts) 4

Bonus points – Hampshire 3, Nottinghamshire 2 (Score at 100 overs: 262-5).

Bowling: *First Innings*—Stephenson 29–5–91–2; Cooper 29–10–67–2; Millns 17–5–53- Hemmings 37–10–96–4; Evans 13.3–1–61–1. *Second Innings*—Stephenson 7–4–25–2; Coop 6–3–15–2; Hemmings 5–4–1–1.

Umpires: J. H. Hampshire and R. A. White.

At Gloucester, June 29, 30, July 1. HAMPSHIRE drew with GLOUCESTERSHIRE.

At Guildford, July 13, 14, 15. HAMPSHIRE beat SURREY by eight wickets.

At Birmingham, July 16, 18, 19. HAMPSHIRE lost to WARWICKSHIRE by an innings a 21 runs.

HAMPSHIRE v ESSEX

\t Portsmouth, July 20, 21, 22. Drawn. Hampshire 5 pts, Essex 6 pts. Toss: Essex. Iampshire, having been put in, were made to struggle for runs on a green pitch by Lever and 'opley, who were unplayable at times. Nicholas held the Hampshire innings together with a rave 66 in a stay of two and threequarter hours. Essex also found runs hard to get, but Border showed his class with a half-century before the second afternoon was lost to the eather. Fletcher, too, coped well with the conditions. With so much time already lost, and he start delayed on the third day, the captains negotiated in the hope of achieving a result. cott was the unlucky Hampshire batsman, bagging a pair on his Championship début before ne declaration bowlers were introduced. Smith and Nicholas both enjoyed hundreds, their nbeaten 210 for the second wicket including 178 in 45 minutes. Essex's target was 213 in 44 vers. Jefferies caused an initial setback, but Stephenson and Lilley (54 balls) added 84 in venty overs before the weather stopped the chase with an hour remaining.

Close of play: First day, Essex 118-5 (A. R. Border 43*, K. W. R. Fletcher 1*); Second day, ssex 203-7 (K. W. R. Fletcher 45*).

Iampshire

J. Scott c East b Lever	0	– c East b Lever	0
. L. Smith lbw b Lever	27	– not out	103
M. C. J. Nicholas c East b Lever	66	– not out	102
P. Terry lbw b Topley	6		
. R. Turner c Prichard b Topley	6		
R. J. Parks c Lilley b Lever	18		
M. Tremlett c Lilley b Miller	28		
T. Jefferies c East b Topley	6		
J. Maru lbw b Topley	5		
A. Connor b Stephenson	24		
J. Bakker not out	0		
B 4, l-b 5, w 1, n-b 5	15	B 5, l-b 1, n-b 3	9
) 2/67 3/87 4/102 5/120 135 7/143 8/158 9/201	201	1/4 (1 wkt dec.)	214

Bonus points – Hampshire 2, Essex 4.

Bowling: *First Innings*—Lever 24–4–61–4; Topley 28–2–88–4; Pont 10–4–26–0; Stephenson !–3–10–1; Miller 3–0–7–1. *Second Innings*—Lever 8–3–14–1; Topley 7–1–16–0; Stephenson)–5–0; Lilley 11–0–119–0; Hussain 9–0–47–0; Prichard 1–0–7–0.

ssex

J. Prichard c Maru b Bakker	5	– (3) hit wkt b Bakker	0
P. Stephenson c Terry b Bakker	4	– (1) not out	34
W. Lilley c Scott b Connor	35	– (5) not out	53
R. Border b Bakker	55	– c Nicholas b Jefferies	9
Hussain c Parks b Bakker	19		
D. Topley c Terry b Bakker	3		
. W. R. Fletcher not out	45		
Miller c Maru b Tremlett	19		
. E. East (did not bat)		– (2) b Jefferies	10
B 8, l-b 8, n-b 2	18	L-b 10, w 1	11
2/15 3/66 4/103 5/115 38 7/203 (7 wkts dec.)	203	1/11 2/20 3/33 (3 wkts)	117

. Pont and J. K. Lever did not bat.

Bonus points – Essex 2, Hampshire 3.

owling: *First Innings*—Jefferies 24.4–4–59–0; Bakker 20–5–54–5; Connor 7.2–1–20–1; mlett 12.3–3–44–1; Maru 11–7–5–0; Scott 3–1–5–0. *Second Innings*—Jefferies 10–3–37–2; ker 13–1–42–1; Maru 4–1–11–0; Tremlett 6–1–17–0.

Umpires: J. Birkenshaw and J. D. Bond.

HAMPSHIRE v DERBYSHIRE

At Portsmouth, July 23, 25, 26. Drawn. Hampshire 3 pts, Derbyshire 3 pts. Toss: Derbyshir After rain had prevented a start until three o'clock on the second day, both sides made ever effort to achieve a result. Scott fell for his third successive nought but Smith and Turner eac hit half-centuries, Ayling went for quick runs, and Hampshire were able to declare o attaining a third bonus point. The original plan was that Derbyshire would forfeit their firs innings; instead, with Barnett not trusting the pitch, they batted for seventeen overs befo declaring and, after Hampshire had forfeited their second innings, had a target of 207 in minimum of 52 overs. Maher, who hit two sixes and seven fours in his 62, kept Derbyshire the hunt until he was sixth out, one of three stumpings by Parks off Maru, whose control ar turn on a helpful pitch persuaded Barnett to play out the last two overs rather than try f the runs.

Close of play: First day, No play; Second day, Hampshire 141-4 (D. R. Turner 50*, J. Ayling 5*).

Hampshire

R. J. Scott lbw b Malcolm 0
C. L. Smith lbw b Mortensen 53
*M. C. J. Nicholas b Malcolm 4
V. P. Terry c Goldsmith b Warner 20
D. R. Turner b Newman 62
J. R. Ayling c Mortensen b Barnett ... 48
†R. J. Parks c Maher b Newman 0
S. T. Jefferies not out ....
T. M. Tremlett not out ....
B 2, l-b 3, w 2, n-b 6 ....

1/0 2/10 3/42 4/132 5/157 6/157 7/226 (7 wkts dec.) 2

R. J. Maru and P. J. Bakker did not bat.

Bonus points – Hampshire 3, Derbyshire 3.

Bowling: Malcolm 19–3–64–2; Mortensen 12–5–15–1; Warner 15–4–35–1; Barn 29.2–8–74–1; Newman 14–3–37–2; Bowler 7–1–21–0.

Hampshire forfeited their second innings.

Derbyshire

P. D. Bowler not out .... 19 – c Terry b Maru ....
J. G. Wright lbw b Ayling .... 23 – c Smith b Bakker ....
†B. J. M. Maher not out .... 1 – st Parks b Maru ....
J. E. Morris (did not bat) .... – b Bakker ....
B. Roberts (did not bat) .... – b Maru ....
S. C. Goldsmith (did not bat) .... – st Parks b Maru ....
*K. J. Barnett (did not bat) .... – not out ....
A. E. Warner (did not bat) .... – st Parks b Maru ....
P. G. Newman (did not bat) .... – not out ....
W 1, n-b 1 .... 2 L-b 13, n-b 1 ....

1/44 (1 wkt dec.) 45 1/27 2/50 3/90 4/113 5/137 6/170 7/178 (7 wkts)

D. E. Malcolm and O. H. Mortensen did not bat.

Bowling: *First Innings*—Jefferies 3–0–12–0; Bakker 5–2–7–0; Tremlett 6–4–13–0; Ay 3.3–1–13–1. *Second Innings*—Jefferies 5.4–0–26–0; Bakker 14–6–21–2; Maru 20–2–69 Tremlett 4–0–15–0; Ayling 8–0–38–0.

Umpires: J. Birkenshaw and J. D. Bond.

At Eastbourne, August 3, 4, 5. HAMPSHIRE drew with SUSSEX.

At Leicester, August 6, 8, 9. HAMPSHIRE drew with LEICESTERSHIRE.

HAMPSHIRE v NORTHAMPTONSHIRE

At Bournemouth, August 13, 15, 16. Drawn. Hampshire 6 pts, Northamptonshire 6 pts. Toss: Hampshire. Terry and Chris Smith, with their second century opening stand of the season, provided the backbone of Hampshire's first innings on a seamers' pitch. Hampshire's makeshift opening attack of Bakker and James, back after injuries, supported by Tremlett, who was returning after a three-month absence, restricted the visitors to 205. Geoff Cook battled for almost three hours, Gouldstone for two and a half, and Nick Cook and Walker took twenty overs to add 46 for the eighth wicket. Robinson's seam bowling again impressed as Hampshire struggled under cloud cover in the second innings, but a fighting half-century from Turner and a late flurry from Parks enabled them to set a target of 199 from a minimum of 46 overs. Once Tremlett had unhinged the top half of Northamptonshire's batting with a spell of four for 9 in 3.4 overs, this was never a likely proposition. Maru took seven catches in the match to equal the county's record for a fielder.

Close of play: First day, Northamptonshire 27-0 (G. Cook 12*, W. Larkins 13*); Second day, Hampshire 61-3 (R. A. Smith 14*, R. J. Maru 1*).

Hampshire

First innings		Second innings	
'. P. Terry b Capel	82	c Larkins b Lillee	24
'. L. Smith b Robinson	59	c Ripley b N. G. B. Cook	6
M. C. J. Nicholas c Fordham b Robinson	5	c Larkins b Robinson	15
'. A. Smith c Walker b Robinson	12	c Ripley b Robinson	16
. R. Turner c Larkins b Bailey	27	(6) c Larkins b Bailey	51
. R. Ayling lbw b Lillee	5	(7) b N. G. B. Cook	10
.. D. James c Ripley b Lillee	13	(8) c N. G. B. Cook b Lillee	1
R. J. Parks c Larkins b N. G. B. Cook	4	(9) not out	31
. M. Tremlett c and b N. G. B. Cook	6	(10) c Ripley b Robinson	2
. J. Maru not out	11	(5) c Fordham b Robinson	1
J. Bakker c and b N. G. B. Cook	1	not out	0
B 1, l-b 5, w 2, n-b 6	14	L-b 4, n-b 3	7
118 2/128 3/150 4/177 5/195 201 7/218 8/220 9/238	239	1/30 2/30 3/60 4/62 5/68 6/88 7/103 8/139 9/154	(9 wkts dec.) 164

Bonus points – Hampshire 2, Northamptonshire 4.

Bowling: *First Innings*—Lillee 22–1–75–2; Walker 15–3–42–0; Robinson 16–4–33–3; Capel 5–3–27–1; N. G. B. Cook 26–11–45–3; Bailey 2.1–0–11–1. *Second Innings*—Lillee '–5–43–2; Walker 7–0–34–0; N. G. B. Cook 31–17–33–2; Robinson 18–4–38–4; Bailey 0–12–1.

Northamptonshire

First innings		Second innings	
;. Cook c Maru b Ayling	50	c Ayling b Tremlett	14
. Larkins b Tremlett	17	c Turner b Tremlett	25
J. Bailey c Parks b Bakker	6	c Maru b Tremlett	4
Fordham c Maru b James	2	not out	19
. R. Gouldstone c Maru b Tremlett	36	c Ayling b Tremlett	0
. Ripley c Nicholas b Bakker	12	c Maru b Ayling	31
J. Capel c Tremlett b Bakker	23	c Nicholas b Ayling	0
G. B. Cook c Parks b Ayling	23	c Maru b Ayling	6
Walker c Ayling b Maru	20	not out	3
K. Lillee c and b Maru	0		
A. Robinson not out	0		
B 8, l-b 4, n-b 4	16	B 5, l-b 1	6
0 2/59 3/62 4/98 5/117 47 7/159 8/205 9/205	205	1/29 2/43 3/46 4/46 5/90 6/90 7/100	(7 wkts) 108

Bonus points – Northamptonshire 2, Hampshire 4.

Bowling: *First Innings*—Bakker 27–7–50–3; James 19–3–46–1; Maru 22–8–38–2; Ayling 16.2–5–35–2; Tremlett 15–5–24–2. *Second Innings*—Bakker 10–6–18–0; James 3–1–7–0; Maru 20.4–9–35–0; Tremlett 7–2–19–4; R. A. Smith 3–1–7–0; Ayling 5–2–12–3; C. L. Smith 3–1–4–0.

Umpires: H. D. Bird and M. J. Kitchen.

HAMPSHIRE v KENT

At Bournemouth, August 17, 18, 19. Kent won by 91 runs. Kent 22 pts, Hampshire 4 pts. Toss: Kent. Kent did well to score 240 on a pitch which helped the seam bowlers throughout. Wicket-keeper Marsh showed his batting skills by making the only half-century of the match and Pienaar passed 1,000 runs for the season while making an attractive 47. Ayling was the pick of the Hampshire bowlers and Tremlett showed his customary economy. Hampshire in reply struggled against the Kent seam attack, notably Igglesden, who marked his return from injury by taking five for 40, his best figures to date. Robin Smith batted two hours for his 34. Even the loss of five hours to rain on the second day was not to deny Kent. When they batted again, a belligerent fourth-wicket stand of 72 between Tavaré and Chris Cowdrey allowed a lunchtime declaration which left Hampshire a target of 242. Igglesden, well supported by Ellison, destroyed their batting for a second time to finish with match figures of ten for 91 and put Kent back at the top of the Championship table. Only Cowley, making a rare first-class appearance, offered any real resistance.

Close of play: First day, Hampshire 45-4 (R. A. Smith 2*, D. R. Turner 1*); Second day, Kent 9-0 (M. R. Benson 9*, N. R. Taylor 0*).

Kent

M. R. Benson c Nicholas b Tremlett	19	– c Maru b Tremlett	3
N. R. Taylor c R. A. Smith b Cowley	29	– b Tremlett	1
R. F. Pienaar c R. A. Smith b Cowley	47	– c R. A. Smith b Ayling	
C. J. Tavaré c Parks b Ayling	29	– c Tremlett b Bakker	4
*C. S. Cowdrey b Bakker	3	– not out	3
G. R. Cowdrey b Maru	11	– not out	
†S. A. Marsh c Terry b Ayling	50		
R. M. Ellison c Terry b Tremlett	20		
C. Penn c Parks b Ayling	10		
A. P. Igglesden c Bakker b Ayling	13		
M. D. Harman not out	4		
L-b 5	5	L-b 5	
1/29 2/86 3/101 4/108 5/143 6/143 7/180 8/208 9/231	240	1/49 2/58 3/64 4/136 (4 wkts dec.)	14

Bonus points – Kent 2, Hampshire 4.

Bowling: *First Innings*—Bakker 19–7–40–1; Tremlett 17–8–32–2; Ayling 21.3–2–62–; Maru 20–4–57–1; Cowley 21–6–44–2. *Second Innings*—Bakker 10.5–0–64–1; Tremle 11–2–32–2; Ayling 8–1–30–1; Maru 2–0–9–0.

Hampshire

V. P. Terry c Marsh b Penn	20	– (6) lbw b Ellison	
C. L. Smith c Marsh b Igglesden	5	– b Igglesden	
*M. C. J. Nicholas c Harman b Penn	13	– (1) c Marsh b Ellison	
R. J. Maru lbw b Igglesden	0	– (10) b Igglesden	
R. A. Smith c and b Harman	34	– (3) c Marsh b Igglesden	
D. R. Turner c C. S. Cowdrey b Ellison	2	– (4) c Penn b Ellison	
J. R. Ayling c Marsh b Igglesden	23	– (5) b Ellison	
†R. J. Parks c Marsh b Igglesden	9	– (7) c C. S. Cowdrey b Igglesden	
N. G. Cowley c Taylor b Ellison	21	– (8) not out	
T. M. Tremlett b Igglesden	2	– (9) c Marsh b C. S. Cowdrey	
P. J. Bakker not out	0	– c G. R. Cowdrey b Igglesden	
L-b 4, w 1, n-b 5	10	B 9, l-b 3, n-b 4	
1/21 2/41 3/41 4/41 5/51 6/93 7/110 8/133 9/137	139	1/1 2/17 3/44 4/54 5/58 6/71 7/75 8/111 9/120	1

Bonus points – Kent 4.

Bowling: *First Innings*—Penn 14–2–40–2; Igglesden 20–7–40–5; Ellison 14.3–5–32–2; Pienaar 7–4–14–0; Harman 4–1–9–1. *Second Innings*—Igglesden 13.2–2–51–5; Penn 8–2–27–0; Ellison 9–0–29–4; Harman 6–2–9–0; C. S. Cowdrey 7–0–22–1.

Umpires: H. D. Bird and M. J. Kitchen.

At Southampton, August 20, 21, 22. HAMPSHIRE drew with SRI LANKANS (See Sri Lankan tour section).

At Taunton, August 25, 26, 27, 29. HAMPSHIRE drew with SOMERSET.

HAMPSHIRE v GLOUCESTERSHIRE

At Southampton, August 30, 31, September 1, 2. Gloucestershire won by five wickets. Gloucestershire 20 pts, Hampshire 4 pts. Toss: Hampshire. Only bad weather prevented Hampshire from losing inside two days, as was the case in the opening four-day game on the same ground in April. Smith's battling 46 in the second innings provided the only resistance to Curran, who bowled well on a helpful pitch for match figures of ten for 82. James returned Championship-best figures of five for 25 in Gloucestershire's first innings to restrict their lead to 25, and when they began their second innings, needing 126 for victory, Bakker provided an early scare by taking two quick wickets. However, Curran sealed a fine all-round performance by hitting an unbeaten 28 to see Gloucestershire home before tea.

Close of play: First day, Gloucestershire 134-8 (M. W. Pooley 7*, M. C. J. Ball 0*); Second day, Hampshire 113-6 (R. J. Maru 2*, J. R. Ayling 1*); Third day, No play.

Hampshire

. P. Terry c Alleyne b Curran	18	– lbw b Curran	14
. L. Smith lbw b Curran	0	– c Alderman b Ball	46
M. C. J. Nicholas lbw b Curran	10	– c Romaines b Curran	0
. R. Turner b Pooley	1	– c Curran b Pooley	17
R. J. Scott c Pooley b Bainbridge	28	– c Alleyne b Bainbridge	13
. D. James lbw b Bainbridge	11	– c Pooley b Curran	13
. R. Ayling st Alleyne b Graveney	6	– (8) b Alderman	21
R. J. Parks b Graveney	12	– (9) c Alleyne b Curran	0
. J. Maru lbw b Curran	6	– (7) c Alleyne b Curran	2
. A. Connor c Wright b Graveney	7	– lbw b Curran	0
. J. Bakker not out	0	– not out	13
B 5, l-b 5, w 2, n-b 2	14	L-b 1, n-b 10	11
4 2/29 3/34 4/38 5/57 70 7/95 8/101 9/113	113	1/32 2/32 3/55 4/89 5/110 6/112 7/114 8/116 9/116	150

Bonus points – Gloucestershire 4.

Bowling: *First Innings*—Alderman 12–3–27–0; Curran 17–8–24–4; Pooley 8–4–10–1; ainbridge 9–2–20–2; Graveney 9.1–1–22–3. *Second Innings*—Alderman 16.1–2–38–1; Curran –5–58–6; Pooley 11–5–26–1; Bainbridge 10–5–10–1; Graveney 10–4–15–0; Ball 5–3–2–1.

Gloucestershire

A. W. Stovold c Parks b Connor	21	– c Parks b Bakker	18
A. J. Wright b Connor	19	– c Parks b Bakker	0
P. W. Romaines b Connor	7	– c Scott b Ayling	33
P. Bainbridge c Parks b James	47	– c Maru b Bakker	19
K. M. Curran b James	19	– not out	28
K. B. K. Ibadulla c Parks b James	0	– (7) not out	10
†M. W. Alleyne lbw b Ayling	0		
M. W. Pooley not out	9	– (6) b Connor	8
*D. A. Graveney c Scott b James	3		
M. C. J. Ball c Parks b Connor	2		
T. M. Alderman b James	0		
L-b 1, n-b 10	11	L-b 8, w 2, n-b 2	12
1/31 2/43 3/56 4/105 5/114 6/119 7/123 8/133 9/137	138	1/12 2/19 3/74 4/93 5/113	(5 wkts) 128

Bonus points – Hampshire 4.

Bowling: *First Innings*—Bakker 14–5–37–0; Connor 13–1–43–4; Ayling 9–1–22–1; Maru 5–1–10–0; James 12–3–25–5. *Second Innings*—Connor 9.4–0–40–1; Bakker 11–5–15–3; Ayling 11–0–35–1; James 8–1–24–0; Maru 5–0–6–0.

Umpires: A. G. T. Whitehead and P. B. Wight.

At Cardiff, September 9, 10, 11, 12. HAMPSHIRE beat GLAMORGAN by two wickets.

HAMPSHIRE v SUSSEX

At Southampton, September 14, 15, 16, 17. Hampshire won by four wickets. Hampshire 22 pts, Sussex 5 pts. Toss: Sussex. Electing to bat first, Sussex struggled early on, especially against Bakker, and owed much to the return to form of Colin Wells. A remarkable feature of the match was the success enjoyed by two occasional off-spinners, Green and Chris Smith. Both took advantage of the rough at one end caused by James's following through on the wicket in Sussex's first innings, and they each returned career-best figures. After Smith, who had not captured a wicket all season, had taken five in Sussex's second innings, Hampshire were left to make 297 with almost a day and a half remaining. They looked in some danger of being defeated at 71 for three, but Robin Smith and Scott took them to within 82 runs of victory with a fourth-wicket stand of 144. Combining caution with aggression, Smith scored his 119 off 222 balls and hit seventeen fours. Ayling's 44, made off 59 balls, included three sixes and four fours and saw Hampshire almost home.

Close of play: First day, Hampshire 0-0 (V. P. Terry 0*, C. L. Smith 0*); Second day, Sussex 23-1 (M. P. Speight 13*, P. W. G. Parker 0*); Third day, Hampshire 165-3 (R. A. Smith 85*, R. J. Scott 30*).

Sussex

M. P. Speight c C. L. Smith b Bakker	16	– (2) c and b C. L. Smith	5
A. M. Green c C. L. Smith b James	9	– (4) b C. L. Smith	
*P. W. G. Parker c Scott b Bakker	1	– b James	2
A. P. Wells lbw b James	40	– (5) b C. L. Smith	1
I. J. Gould c Parks b James	44	– (6) c Parks b Ayling	5
C. M. Wells c sub b James	92	– (7) run out	3
A. C. S. Pigott c R. A. Smith b Maru	24	– (8) c James b C. L. Smith	1
†P. Moores c Parks b Ayling	2	– (1) b Maru	
A. R. Clarke c Terry b Maru	12	– not out	2
R. A. Bunting not out	17	– c and b C. L. Smith	
A. M. Babington c Connor b Maru	12	– run out	
B 3, l-b 5, n-b 1	9	B 3, l-b 5	
1/23 2/25 3/31 4/103 5/141 6/204 7/211 8/242 9/254	278	1/19 2/60 3/81 4/102 5/121 6/180 7/212 8/214 9/225	24

Bonus points – Sussex 3, Hampshire 4 (Score at 100 overs: 260-9).

Bowling: *First Innings*—Connor 16–2–48–0; Bakker 16.2–4–29–2; James 25–4–70–4; Maru 25.3–8–49–3; Ayling 16.4–3–48–1; Scott 4–0–26–0. *Second Innings*—Connor 13–0–48–0; Maru 24–7–67–1; James 11–1–36–1; C. L. Smith 19–0–69–5; Ayling 5–0–12–1.

Hampshire

V. P. Terry b Green	25	– b Pigott	11
C. L. Smith st Moores b Green	59	– c Pigott b Green	1
*M. C. J. Nicholas c Moores b Green	31	– c Gould b Green	30
R. A. Smith lbw b Clarke	41	– b Babington	119
R. J. Scott b Clarke	7	– c Gould b Clarke	56
J. R. Ayling c Gould b Green	9	– c Speight b Babington	44
K. D. James b Pigott	14	– not out	22
†R. J. Parks not out	22	– not out	5
R. J. Maru c Pigott b Green	0		
C. A. Connor c C. M. Wells b Green	1		
P. J. Bakker absent injured			
B 6, l-b 4, n-b 3	13	B 5, l-b 5	10
1/48 2/122 3/131 4/164 5/181 6/193 7/213 8/216 9/222	222	1/12 2/12 3/71 4/215 5/243 6/292	(6 wkts) 298

Bonus points – Hampshire 2, Sussex 2 (Score at 100 overs: 207-6).

Bowling: *First Innings*—Pigott 17–4–47–1; Babington 11–0–17–0; Green 45.5–16–82–6; Clarke 22–10–32–2; C. M. Wells 6–0–14–0; Bunting 6–0–20–0. *Second Innings*—Pigott 21–2–67–1; Babington 19.2–3–51–2; Green 32–10–104–2; Clarke 19–9–46–1; Gould 5–0–20–0.

Umpires: R. Julian and K. J. Lyons.

YOUNG CRICKETER OF THE YEAR

(*Elected by the Cricket Writers Club*)

1950	R. Tattersall	1970	C. M. Old
1951	P. B. H. May	1971	J. Whitehouse
1952	F. S. Trueman	1972	D. R. Owen-Thomas
1953	M. C. Cowdrey	1973	M. Hendrick
1954	P. J. Loader	1974	P. H. Edmonds
1955	K. F. Barrington	1975	A. Kennedy
1956	B. Taylor	1976	G. Miller
1957	M. J. Stewart	1977	I. T. Botham
1958	A. C. D. Ingleby-Mackenzie	1978	D. I. Gower
1959	G. Pullar	1979	P. W. G. Parker
1960	D. A. Allen	1980	G. R. Dilley
1961	P. H. Parfitt	1981	M. W. Gatting
1962	P. J. Sharpe	1982	N. G. Cowans
1963	G. Boycott	1983	N. A. Foster
1964	J. M. Brearley	1984	R. J. Bailey
1965	A. P. E. Knott	1985	D. V. Lawrence
1966	D. L. Underwood	1986	A. A. Metcalfe
1967	A. W. Greig	1986	J. J. Whitaker
1968	R. M. H. Cottam	1987	R. J. Blakey
1969	A. Ward	1988	M. P. Maynard

An additional award, in memory of Norman Preston, Editor of *Wisden* from 1952 to 1980, was made to C. W. J. Athey in 1980.

KENT

Patron: HRH The Duke of Kent
President: H. J. Pocock
Chairman: P. H. Edgley
Chairman, Cricket Committee:
A. J. P. Woodhouse
Secretary: D. B. Dalby
St Lawrence Ground, Old Dover Road,
Canterbury CT1 3NZ
(Telephone: 0227-456886)
Captain: C. S. Cowdrey
Director of Coaching: J. C. T. Page
Cricket Administrator: B. W. Luckhurst

For Kent, it had all the trappings of a Championship-winning season – almost bottom of the table after three successive defeats; a team meeting at which there was plenty of straight talking. Such facets had been present in 1970, albeit at the halfway stage of the summer, and the title was won. In 1988 it was lost, by the agonising margin of one point, after the field had been led since the middle of June. Disappointment? Of course. But there was pride, too, at finishing second and confounding the critics who had written off the side early in the season.

Certainly there was excuse enough for doing so. The first three Britannic Assurance Championship matches, all four-day affairs, had been lost, two of them in three days. Injuries abounded. Alan Igglesden, the home-bred pace-bowling hope, sustained a serious knee injury in the opening game. During the third match, the West Indian fast bowler, Hartley Alleyne, in his first season with the county, sustained a heel injury; he never played another Championship match. In the first five games the side did not finish with eleven fit men.

On the last evening of the third Championship match at Leicester, the county's new cricket chairman, Jim Woodhouse, presided at a team meeting at which the poor start was analysed and resolutions were made. Fielding was high on the agenda, for whatever limitations any side might have in batting or bowling, fielding was something it could work on. Kent certainly did. They quickly became recognised as one of the finest fielding sides in the country. They held important catches consistently, often spectacularly. Another important decision was to obtain cricket guidance for the first team. Colin Page and Alan Ealham were not able to be with them enough to fill this role, and so the former Australian Test batsman, John Inverarity, was appointed cricket adviser. That paid off handsomely as the players' confidence was boosted and maintained.

The excitement mounted from late May, when at Canterbury Kent squeezed home with a three-wicket win over Yorkshire and began a winning sequence of six Championship matches in succession, the best since 1920. The last of these was at Edgbaston, where in the Warwickshire first innings Kent gained only three bonus bowling points instead of four because they could take only eight wickets. Warwickshire had two batsmen injured. It was a point that rankled all season, but the authorities were insistent that the rule stated that the fourth bonus point was awarded only when a side took the ninth wicket.

Seven wins out of eleven was the first-half achievement, but unfortunately this could not be sustained in the second half of the campaign. Somerset inflicted an innings defeat in the first game of Canterbury Week, which attracted some marvellous attendances, and a month later Kent were beaten by Sussex at Maidstone. The Somerset defeat produced only one bonus point, and if anybody wanted to pinpoint when the title was lost, that game could well have been the moment.

Whereas no-one really expected Kent to go anywhere near the title, so the formation of the side proved surprising too. Injuries saw to that. Chris Penn emerged as the county's leading strike bowler, sharing the new ball, gaining confidence from doing so, and being rewarded with his best-ever return of 80 Championship wickets. Roy Pienaar, the South African batsman signed in an emergency the previous summer because he also bowled medium-fast, batted superbly and took wickets at important stages of matches. His fine season compensated for some of the other batting disappointments. The left-handed Simon Hinks lost his place midway through the season, giving Trevor Ward the chance to show his promise, but Hinks had returned to the side and to form by the end of the summer. Graham Cowdrey began with a maiden century in the first match of the season but then endured a frustrating run before enjoying a more productive and consistent period. His bowling was shown to greater advantage in limited-overs cricket than in the Championship.

Chris Cowdrey, for whom the season's achievements were a great joy as captain, had his problems with the bat. But his bowling played an important part in the successes during the first half of the season. In the second half of the summer, or to be more precise, the second part of that, the bowling honours fell to Igglesden. He returned to take 37 wickets in six matches, leaving himself and all Kent wondering what might have been achieved had he been fit all summer. Fortunately for the county, Richard Ellison returned after missing the 1987 season to take a best-ever 71 first-class wickets, a tremendous performance. The left-arm spin of Richard Davis and the off-spin of Mark Harman proved useful, while Steven Marsh kept wicket consistently and also began the season with his maiden hundred.

The batting was led, appropriately in his benefit year, by Chris Tavaré. Starting slowly, he scored four centuries, was twice dismissed in the 90s, and played with assurance and confidence. Mark Benson followed Tavaré and Pienaar past 1,000 runs, and Neil Taylor might have done so but for injury causing him to miss the last two matches. The season was dominated by the Championship success, because in the one-day competitions Kent were disappointing. They failed to qualify for the Benson and Hedges quarter-finals, were beaten by Middlesex in the quarter-finals of the NatWest Bank Trophy, and were never really in the hunt for the Refuge Assurance League. Yet the confidence derived from the summer's Championship performance will surely stand the side in good stead in 1989. – Dudley Moore.

KENT 1988

[*Bill Smith*

Back row: J. I. Longley, R. F. Pienaar, T. R. Ward, V. J. Wells, D. J. Sabine. *Middle row:* J. Foley (*scorer*), A. G. E. Ealham (*coach*), G. R. Cowdrey, R. P. Davis, A. P. Igglesden, D. J. M. Kelleher, P. Farbrace, M. D. Harman, G. Popplewell (*physiotherapist*), J. C. T. Page (*director of coaching*), C. Lewis (*scorer*). *Front row:* S. A. Marsh, M. R. Benson, N. R. Taylor, C. J. Tavaré, C. S. Cowdrey (*captain*), R. M. Ellison, S. G. Hinks, H. L. Alleyne, C. Penn.

KENT RESULTS

All first-class matches – Played 24: Won 10, Lost 6, Drawn 8.

County Championship matches – Played 22: Won 10, Lost 5, Drawn 7.

Bonus points – Batting 57, Bowling 72.

Competition placings – Britannic Assurance County Championship, 2nd; NatWest Bank Trophy, q-f; Benson and Hedges Cup, 3rd in Group C; Refuge Assurance League, 7th.

BRITANNIC ASSURANCE CHAMPIONSHIP AVERAGES

BATTING

	Birthplace	*M*	*I*	*NO*	*R*	*HI*	*Avge*
‡C. J. Tavaré	*Orpington*	21	35	1	1,292	129*	38.00
§‡R. F. Pienaar	*Johannesburg, SA*	19	32	2	1,070	144	35.66
‡M. R. Benson	*Shoreham*	21	37	1	1,227	110	34.08
‡G. R. Cowdrey	*Farnborough, Kent*	18	29	4	790	145	31.60
‡N. R. Taylor	*Orpington*	20	36	2	915	114	26.91
‡S. G. Hinks	*Northfleet*	14	24	1	611	92	26.56
‡C. S. Cowdrey	*Farnborough, Kent*	19	33	6	714	108	26.44
T. R. Ward	*Farningham*	9	15	0	345	72	23.00
‡C. Penn	*Dover*	19	30	12	407	40	22.61
D. J. M. Kelleher	*Southwark, London*	4	5	1	86	43*	21.50
‡S. A. Marsh	*Westminster, London*	22	34	5	613	120	21.13
A. P. Igglesden	*Farnborough, Kent*	7	8	2	103	41	17.16
‡R. M. Ellison	*Ashford, Kent*	19	27	6	345	50*	16.42
M. D. Harman	*Aylesbury, Bucks*	10	11	6	71	17*	14.20
R. P. Davis	*Margate*	17	19	6	103	23	7.92
§H. L. Alleyne	*Bridgetown, Barbados*	3	5	1	16	9	4.00

* *Signifies not out.* ‡ *Denotes county cap.* § *Not qualified for England.*

The following played a total of twelve three-figure innings for Kent in County Championship matches – C. J. Tavaré 3, M. R. Benson 2, R. F. Pienaar 2, N. R. Taylor 2, C. S. Cowdrey 1, G. R. Cowdrey 1, S. A. Marsh 1.

BOWLING

	O	*M*	*R*	*W*	*BB*	*5W/i*	*Avge*
A. P. Igglesden	234.3	46	805	37	6-34	3	21.75
R. M. Ellison	571.4	156	1,652	69	7-75	3	23.94
C. Penn	629.1	142	1,918	80	7-70	6	23.97
H. L. Alleyne	74.3	13	260	10	5-54	1	26.00
M. D. Harman	238.4	76	537	20	5-68	1	26.85
C. S. Cowdrey	384.5	96	1,114	39	5-46	1	28.56
R. F. Pienaar	368.2	90	1,055	32	5-27	1	32.96
R. P. Davis	529.2	163	1,333	34	5-132	1	39.20

Also bowled: M. R. Benson 3.3–0–39–0; G. R. Cowdrey 88.4–17–351–5; S. G. Hinks 2–0–28–0; D. J. M. Kelleher 72–18–188–7; N. R. Taylor 8–4–7–1; T. R. Ward 4–1–4–0.

Wicket-keeper: S. A. Marsh 51 ct, 5 st.

Leading Fielders: C. S. Cowdrey 31, C. J. Tavaré 29, N. R. Taylor 15.

At Chelmsford, April 21, 22, 23, 25. KENT lost to ESSEX by eight wickets.

KENT v HAMPSHIRE

At Canterbury, April 28, 29, 30. Hampshire won by seven wickets. Hampshire 21 pts, Kent 6 pts. Toss: Kent. Having elected to bat, Kent never really settled against the pace of Jefferies and Andrew. Chris Cowdrey hit six fours in his 53-minute 48 and Kelleher batted for 160 minutes as the last three wickets added 84. When Hampshire batted, Kelleher was forced out of the attack after six overs with a hamstring injury sustained while fielding, but a career-best bowling performance by Cowdrey, after Alleyne had done the early damage, enabled Kent to take a 60-run lead. Hampshire hit back before the close, however, and the rout of Kent was completed on the third morning when Parks claimed his 500th first-class dismissal. A second-wicket stand of 129 off 48 overs between Chris Smith and Nicholas set up an easy Hampshire victory with well over a day to spare. Nicholas hit eleven fours in his 139-minute innings while Smith hit seven fours in a stay of 167 minutes.

Close of play: First day, Hampshire 41-1 (C. L. Smith 20*, M. C. J. Nicholas 18*); Second day, Kent 61-7 (R. P. Davis 5*, M. D. Harman 4*).

Kent

M. R. Benson c Parks b Jefferies	8	– c Jefferies b Andrew	18
N. R. Taylor c Maru b Andrew	27	– b Connor	0
S. G. Hinks c Parks b Jefferies	34	– c Terry b Connor	7
G. R. Cowdrey c Parks b Andrew	0	– c Parks b Andrew	10
T. R. Ward run out	11	– c Terry b Connor	2
*C. S. Cowdrey b Jefferies	48	– c Parks b James	12
†S. A. Marsh c Terry b Andrew	9	– (8) lbw b Andrew	0
D. J. M. Kelleher not out	43	– (11) c Parks b James	0
M. D. Harman c Parks b Andrew	12	– not out	17
R. P. Davis c Parks b James	16	– (7) c Terry b James	23
H. L. Alleyne lbw b Jefferies	9	– (10) lbw b James	0
L-b 3, n-b 10	13	B 2, l-b 1, w 1, n-b 6	10
1/14 2/56 3/56 4/86 5/119 6/144 7/146 8/186 9/213	230	1/6 2/24 3/28 4/37 5/52 6/56 7/56 8/99 9/99	99

Bonus points – Kent 2, Hampshire 4.

Bowling: *First Innings*—Jefferies 20.5–1–80–4; Connor 14–3–46–0; Andrew 19–6–52–4; James 17–6–31–1; Maru 13–7–17–0; Nicholas 2–1–1–0. *Second Innings*—Jefferies 13–4–29–0; Connor 18–8–23–3; Andrew 10–3–21–3; James 11.5–2–22–4; Maru 4–3–1–0.

Hampshire

V. P. Terry lbw b Alleyne	1	– lbw b Alleyne	2
C. L. Smith c Harman b Alleyne	30	– run out	62
*M. C. J. Nicholas c Ward b Alleyne	18	– st Marsh b Harman	74
R. A. Smith c Benson b C. S. Cowdrey	23	– not out	9
D. R. Turner lbw b C. S. Cowdrey	31	– not out	6
K. D. James lbw b C. S. Cowdrey	26		
†R. J. Parks c and b Davis	33		
S. T. Jefferies b C. S. Cowdrey	4		
R. J. Maru run out	0		
C. A. Connor c sub b C. S. Cowdrey	0		
S. J. W. Andrew not out	0		
B 2, l-b 1, w 1	4	L-b 5, w 1, n-b 1	7
1/1 2/41 3/62 4/81 5/119 6/160 7/166 8/170 9/170	170	1/12 2/141 3/149	(3 wkts) 160

Bonus points – Hampshire 1, Kent 4.

Bowling: *First Innings*—Kelleher 6–3–7–0; Alleyne 20–6–58–3; Davis 11–5–22–1; C. S. Cowdrey 24.2–10–46–5; Harman 8–3–7–0; G. R. Cowdrey 10–1–27–0. *Second Innings*—C. S. Cowdrey 13–2–27–0; Alleyne 10–0–28–1; Davis 21–7–40–0; Harman 12–3–35–1; G. R. Cowdrey 4–1–21–0; Benson 0.3–0–4–0.

Umpires: D. J. Constant and D. O. Oslear.

At Leicester, May 5, 6, 7. KENT lost to LEICESTERSHIRE by an innings and 47 runs.

At Oxford, May 18, 19, 20. KENT drew with OXFORD UNIVERSITY.

KENT v YORKSHIRE

At Canterbury, May 21, 23, 24. Kent won by three wickets. Kent 22 pts, Yorkshire 3 pts. Toss: Yorkshire. Yorkshire failed to turn to advantage a sound and productive start. Metcalfe and Swallow, promoted to No. 3 from No. 9, laid a good foundation with a second-wicket stand of 83 in 34 overs, but a mid-innings collapse saw four wickets crash for 9 runs in six overs as the swing and seam bowlers gained the upper hand. A superb century by Pienaar, who hit a six and thirteen fours in a stay of almost five and threequarter hours, helped Kent take an important 30-run lead, and when Yorkshire batted again, they failed badly against Penn's career-best performance and Ellison. Sidebottom, the night-watchman, did best for Yorkshire; Robinson had a nightmare match, run out in the first innings without facing and dismissed first ball in the second. Needing 104 for victory, Kent were made to struggle by Jarvis, whose sustained fast bowling brought him six of the seven wickets and a match return of ten for 115.

Close of play: First day, Kent 18-1 (R. F. Pienaar 3*, R. P. Davis 0*); Second day, Yorkshire 11-1 (M. D. Moxon 8*, A. Sidebottom 2*).

Yorkshire

M. D. Moxon c Cowdrey b Pienaar	26	– lbw b Ellison	15
A. A. Metcalfe lbw b Ellison	67	– c Tavaré b Penn	0
I. G. Swallow c Tavaré b Harman	46	– (4) lbw b Ellison	0
K. Sharp c Hinks b Davis	57	– (5) c Tavaré b Davis	14
J. D. Love c sub b Harman	6	– (6) b Ellison	19
P. E. Robinson run out	0	– (7) lbw b Penn	0
†D. L. Bairstow b Davis	1	– (8) lbw b Penn	0
*P. Carrick c Marsh b Penn	3	– (9) lbw b Penn	26
A. Sidebottom b Ellison	16	– (3) b Penn	41
P. W. Jarvis c Harman b Penn	13	– lbw b Penn	0
C. Shaw not out	3	– not out	8
B 1, l-b 3, w 2	6	L-b 8, n-b 2	10
1/45 2/128 3/174 4/192 5/192 6/197 7/201 8/215 9/240	244	1/7 2/45 3/45 4/71 5/77 6/77 7/77 8/109 9/109	133

Bonus points – Yorkshire 2, Kent 3 (Score at 100 overs: 231-8).

Bowling: *First Innings*—Ellison 24–9–55–2; Penn 20–7–55–2; Cowdrey 14–5–30–0; Pienaar 10–2–40–1; Harman 19–6–37–2; Davis 16–3–23–2. *Second Innings*—Penn 24–6–66–6; Ellison 18.4–3–41–3; Harman 4–2–7–0; Davis 9–4–11–1.

Kent

N. R. Taylor c Bairstow b Sidebottom	13	– c Bairstow b Jarvis	18
R. F. Pienaar b Jarvis	144	– c Metcalfe b Jarvis	0
R. P. Davis c Bairstow b Jarvis	2		
S. G. Hinks c Robinson b Shaw	66	– (3) c Carrick b Sidebottom	34
C. J. Tavaré c Robinson b Shaw	18	– (4) b Jarvis	21
*C. S. Cowdrey c Moxon b Jarvis	1	– (5) lbw b Jarvis	2
†S. A. Marsh c Swallow b Shaw	13	– (6) c Metcalfe b Jarvis	4
R. M. Ellison not out	4	– (7) b Jarvis	11
C. Penn c Bairstow b Shaw	0	– not out	0
M. D. Harman c Bairstow b Jarvis	1		
M. R. Benson (did not bat)		– (8) not out	5
B 4, l-b 6, n-b 2	12	B 4, l-b 5	9
1/18 2/21 3/169 4/249 5/256 6/261 7/273 8/273 9/274 (9 wkts dec.)	274	1/5 2/54 3/62 4/65 5/81 6/88 7/103 (7 wkts)	104

Bonus points – Kent 3, Yorkshire 1 (Score at 100 overs: 256-4).

Bowling: *First Innings*—Jarvis 25.2–3–75–4; Sidebottom 19–7–38–1; Shaw 21–6–56–4; Moxon 4–2–7–0; Carrick 24–7–56–0; Swallow 13–4–32–0. *Second Innings*—Jarvis 16.3–7–40–6; Sidebottom 13–8–21–1; Shaw 7–1–34–0.

Umpires: J. C. Balderstone and J. H. Harris.

KENT v NOTTINGHAMSHIRE

At Dartford, June 1, 2, 3. Kent won by two wickets. Kent 23 pts, Nottinghamshire 3 pts. Toss: Nottinghamshire. The swing and seam bowling of Ellison, Penn and Cowdrey, complemented by the left-arm spin of Davis, was too much for Nottinghamshire. They lost their last six wickets for 11 runs in fourteen overs with only Robinson, their captain, providing any resistance. Kent started badly, but Benson reached his half-century out of 69 from 72 balls, and then Tavaré and Pienaar added 79 off 32 overs. On the second morning Marsh, Ellison and Penn all batted enterprisingly. Robinson and Pollard gave Nottinghamshire a good start with 122 off 51 overs, and on the third day Pollard (eleven fours) extended his innings to 471 minutes, having recorded his maiden century. Ellison took four wickets for 9 runs in 5.2 overs to finish the innings and return career-best figures. Kent, needing 111 in 24 overs, collapsed against the pace of Cooper and Saxelby, but Cowdrey steered them to victory with one ball to spare, scoring 10 off four balls in the final over.

Close of play: First day, Kent 175-6 (R. F. Pienaar 53*, S. A. Marsh 5*); Second day, Nottinghamshire 154-2 (P. Pollard 69*, P. Johnson 3*).

Nottinghamshire

*R. T. Robinson c Marsh b Cowdrey	31	– c Taylor b Harman	56
P. Pollard c Cowdrey b Ellison	2	– c Tavaré b Ellison	142
D. W. Randall c Harman b Penn	7	– (5) lbw b Ellison	44
P. Johnson c and b Penn	0	– c Hinks b Davis	30
D. J. R. Martindale c Cowdrey b Davis	6	– (3) b Ellison	15
J. D. Birch lbw b Cowdrey	5	– c Marsh b Ellison	0
†C. W. Scott c Ellison b Davis	1	– (8) lbw b Ellison	21
C. L. Cairns not out	7	– (7) b Davis	15
K. E. Cooper c Hinks b Davis	3	– not out	5
K. Saxelby b Davis	0	– lbw b Ellison	1
J. A. Afford lbw b Penn	0	– c Benson b Ellison	0
L-b 3	3	B 16, l-b 8, n-b 4	28
1/17 2/24 3/28 4/40 5/54 6/57 7/57 8/60 9/60	65	1/122 2/149 3/190 4/276 5/276 6/313 7/348 8/349 9/355	357

Bonus points – Kent 4.

Bowling: *First Innings*—Ellison 13–5–17–1; Penn 10–4–23–3; Davis 14–8–12–4; Cowdrey 7–3–9–2; Harman 1–0–1–0. *Second Innings*—Penn 9–1–41–0; Ellison 40.2–14–75–7; Davis 56–23–106–2; Cowdrey 12–6–15–0; Harman 29–6–72–1; Pienaar 7–0–24–0.

Kent

M. R. Benson c Martindale b Afford	52 – c Pollard b Cooper	16
N. R. Taylor lbw b Cooper	2 – b Saxelby	5
S. G. Hinks c Pollard b Cairns	7 – c Scott b Cooper	8
C. J. Tavaré b Birch	42 – b Cooper	4
R. F. Pienaar c Scott b Cairns	53 – lbw b Cooper	14
*C. S. Cowdrey c Robinson b Cairns	0 – not out	35
R. P. Davis lbw b Cairns	0	
†S. A. Marsh c Cooper b Birch	49 – (7) b Cooper	14
R. M. Ellison not out	50 – (8) c Johnson b Saxelby	3
C. Penn lbw b Cooper	40 – not out	0
M. D. Harman (did not bat)	– (9) b Saxelby	6
B 5, l-b 9, n-b 3	17 L-b 5, n-b 1	6
1/20 2/31 3/73 4/152 5/161 6/161 7/175 8/253 9/312	(9 wkts dec.) 312 1/22 2/24 3/29 4/44 5/51 6/83 7/90 8/99	(8 wkts) 111

Bonus points – Kent 3, Nottinghamshire 3 (Score at 100 overs: 263-8).

Bowling: *First Innings*—Cooper 30–10–51–2; Cairns 19–3–70–4; Afford 25–6–73–1; Saxelby 20–1–52–0; Birch 17–2–52–2. *Second Innings*—Saxelby 12–1–45–3; Cooper 11.5–0–61–5.

Umpires: R. Julian and A. G. T. Whitehead.

\t Cardiff, June 4, 6, 7. KENT beat GLAMORGAN by four wickets.

KENT v MIDDLESEX

\t Tunbridge Wells, June 11, 13, 14. Kent won by six wickets. Kent 20 pts, Middlesex 4 pts. 'oss: Kent. Pace and seam were so on top on the first day that Middlesex were batting again efore the close. Put in, they had lost half their first-innings batting for 56 in nineteen overs. Kent fared even worse, with half the side out for 42 in twelve overs, but their lower-order atsmen took them to a lead of 18 runs. Gatting, with ten fours in his 94-minute half-century, nd Downton, who batted for three hours and hit eleven fours, ensured that Middlesex could ave Kent some kind of target. Pienaar, taking three for 24 in fourteen overs of medium pace, nished with his best figures for Kent. An opening stand of 98 off 44 overs was the solid start ent needed. Benson reached his century in 284 minutes, having hit twelve fours, and ienaar, who passed 50 in 115 minutes with seven fours, saw Kent to a fine victory.

Close of play: First day, Middlesex 16-0 (W. N. Slack 14*, J. D. Carr 2*); Second day, Kent 5-0 (M. R. Benson 25*, N. R. Taylor 20*).

ʼiddlesex

. N. Slack c C. S. Cowdrey b Ellison	0 – lbw b Ellison	28
D. Carr lbw b Penn	0 – c Benson b Ellison	6
1. W. Gatting c G. R. Cowdrey b Penn	20 – c Benson b C. S. Cowdrey	76
O. Butcher c Tavaré b Ellison	9 – c G. R. Cowdrey b Ellison	7
R. Brown c Marsh b C. S. Cowdrey	25 – c Hinks b Pienaar	13
. R. Downton lbw b C. S. Cowdrey	6 – c Ellison b Pienaar	74
E. Emburey c Marsh b Penn	4 – c Marsh b Pienaar	39
F. Williams c Hinks b C. S. Cowdrey	0 – lbw b C. S. Cowdrey	9
R. C. Fraser not out	8 – not out	7
G. Cowans b Penn	0 – c Marsh b Pienaar	0
C. R. Tufnell b C. S. Cowdrey	9 – c Tavaré b Pienaar	6
L-b 4, w 3, n-b 4	11 L-b 3, w 1, n-b 3	7
2/4 3/29 4/31 5/56 1 7/71 8/77 9/77	92 1/23 2/57 3/72 4/115 5/165 6/239 7/252 8/262 9/262	272

Bonus points – Kent 4.

Bowling: *First Innings*—Ellison 8–1–15–2; Penn 13–3–36–4; C. S. Cowdrey 11.2–5–16–4; Pienaar 6–1–21–0. *Second Innings*—Ellison 23–4–89–3; Penn 21–6–61–0; C. S. Cowdrey 22–6–59–2; Pienaar 16.1–7–27–5; Davis 14–5–33–0.

Kent

M. R. Benson c Downton b Cowans . . . . 10 – c Slack b Cowans 110
N. R. Taylor c Emburey b Williams . . . . 0 – c Downton b Cowans 52
S. G. Hinks lbw b Cowans . . . . 4 – c Carr b Cowans 4
C. J. Tavaré c Slack b Williams . . . . 2 – b Emburey 15
R. F. Pienaar lbw b Fraser . . . . 16 – not out 58
*C. S. Cowdrey c Emburey b Fraser . . . . 16 – not out 7
G. R. Cowdrey c Brown b Fraser 4
†S. A. Marsh c Downton b Fraser 23
R. M. Ellison c Carr b Emburey 17
C. Penn not out 15
R. P. Davis run out 0
L-b 3 . . . . 3 L-b 6, n-b 3 9

1/10 2/14 3/14 4/20 5/42 6/50 7/55 8/82 9/104 — 110
1/98 2/104 3/133 4/210 — (4 wkts) 255

Bonus points – Middlesex 4.

Bowling: *First Innings*—Cowans 10–3–29–2; Williams 10–3–32–2; Fraser 11–3–30–4; Emburey 6–0–16–1. *Second Innings*—Cowans 21–6–48–3; Williams 9–2–23–0; Emburey 37–15–70–1; Tufnell 18–4–53–0; Fraser 14–4–54–0; Carr 0.1–0–1–0.

Umpires: A. A. Jones and B. J. Meyer.

KENT v LANCASHIRE

At Tunbridge Wells, June 15, 16, 17. Kent won by five wickets. Kent 23 pts, Lancashire 5 pts. Toss: Kent. A spell of three for 29 in 28 balls by Chris Cowdrey arrested Lancashire' reasonable start, and when Jesty was out, having hit ten fours in his 71-minute 47, Ken gained control. Pienaar's damaging second spell brought him four wickets for 36 in eigh overs. Allott's two for 3 in twelve balls on the second morning surprised Kent, but Tavaré resolution provided them with the springboard to take a vital first-innings lead of 5 Lancashire lost five wickets in clearing the arrears, but their lower order stretched Kent' winning target to 151. Although Wasim Akram was unable to bowl because of a thro infection, Kent were faltering at 114 for five before the Cowdrey brothers made sure of the fifth consecutive Championship victory.

Close of play: First day, Kent 120-3 (C. J. Tavaré 12*, R. P. Davis 1*); Second day Lancashire 90-5 (T. E. Jesty 29*, Wasim Akram 11*).

Lancashire

G. D. Mendis b C. S. Cowdrey . . . . 38 – c C. S. Cowdrey b Pienaar . . . . . [illegible]
G. Fowler c Tavaré b C. S. Cowdrey . . . . 10 – c C. S. Cowdrey b Penn . . . .
T. E. Jesty c Pienaar b Davis . . . . 47 – c Marsh b Penn . . . . [illegible]
N. H. Fairbrother c Taylor b C. S. Cowdrey . . . 4 – c Marsh b C. S. Cowdrey . . . . . . [illegible]
M. Watkinson c Hinks b Penn . . . . 18 – c Tavaré b Penn . . . .
*D. P. Hughes c Tavaré b Pienaar . . . . 17 – c Davis b C. S. Cowdrey . . . . . .
Wasim Akram c Marsh b Pienaar . . . . 16 – c Taylor b Penn . . . . [illegible]
†W. K. Hegg c Marsh b C. S. Cowdrey . . . . 25 – c Hinks b Pienaar . . . . [illegible]
P. J. W. Allott c Taylor b Pienaar . . . . 11 – c Hinks b Pienaar . . . . [illegible]
J. Simmons lbw b Pienaar . . . . 10 – not out . . . . [illegible]
I. Folley not out . . . . 0 – lbw b Penn . . . .
L-b 2, n-b 1 . . . . 3 L-b 6, w 1, n-b 1 . . . .

1/36 2/67 3/84 4/120 5/120 6/152 7/153 8/175 9/197 — 199
1/25 2/25 3/34 4/46 5/51 6/91 7/125 8/126 9/179 — [illegible]

Bonus points – Lancashire 1, Kent 4.

Bowling: *First Innings*—Penn 21–6–68–1; Pienaar 21–6–77–4; C. S. Cowdrey 11.1–2–36–4;)avis 4–1–16–1. *Second Innings*—Penn 22.5–7–60–5; Pienaar 26–7–96–3; C. S. Cowdrey 3–1–41–2.

Kent

1. R. Benson b Watkinson	48	– c Hughes b Allott	38
'. R. Taylor c Hegg b Allott	25	– c Hegg b Watkinson	17
G. Hinks lbw b Allott	16	– c and b Watkinson	24
. J. Tavaré b Wasim	63	– c Hughes b Watkinson	4
. F. Pienaar c Fowler b Simmons	19	– lbw b Allott	21
. P. Davis c Hegg b Allott	4		
'. R. Cowdrey c Hughes b Allott	6	– (6) not out	20
C. S. Cowdrey c Watkinson b Allott	37	– (7) not out	18
S. A. Marsh c Hegg b Allott	5		
. Penn lbw b Watkinson	8		
'. D. Harman not out	0		
L-b 13, w 2, n-b 6	21	L-b 8, n-b 4	12
36 2/89 3/116 4/134 5/144 195 7/211 8/237 9/246	252	1/57 2/76 3/86 4/93 5/114	(5 wkts) 154

Bonus points – Kent 3, Lancashire 4.

the first innings M. R. Benson, when 36, retired hurt at 61 and resumed at 195.

Bowling: *First Innings*—Wasim 27–9–44–1; Allott 36.3–9–86–6; Watkinson 27–6–76–2; nmons 8–2–33–1. *Second Innings*—Allott 23–8–56–2; Watkinson 20.3–3–69–3; Folley 0–21–0.

Umpires: A. A. Jones and B. J. Meyer.

Birmingham, June 18, 20. KENT beat WARWICKSHIRE by an innings and 46 runs.

Canterbury, June 25, 26. KENT lost to WEST INDIANS by an innings and 43 runs (See Vest Indian tour section).

KENT v ESSEX

Canterbury, June 29, 30, July 1. Drawn. Kent 4 pts, Essex 7 pts. Toss: Essex. After Essex made a poor start, the rescue operation was launched by Border, who batted superbly on a ‹et seemingly assisting the seam bowlers. He batted for 371 minutes, hitting 27 fours, and cher helped hir. in a stand of 134 from 48 overs. Essex became the first side to score 300 in an innings at Canterbury in 1988, and Kent began as if they would follow suit. Ward e an impressive 70 out of an opening stand of 109 in 106 minutes before becoming the of Pringle's three wickets in nine deliveries. Kent promised to recover, but the off-spin of er produced three wickets in eight balls as they lost four batsmen for 3 runs in seven overs. prevented any play before tea on the final day, spoiling what could have been an esting finish.

ose of play: First day, Essex 330; Second day, Kent 221-9 (C. S. Cowdrey 34*, R. P. ıs 1*).

Essex

J. P. Stephenson c Davis b Ellison . . . . 0 – (2) c Marsh b Davis 43
B. R. Hardie lbw b Penn . . . . 4 – (1) not out 35
P. J. Prichard b Davis 45
A. R. Border c C. S. Cowdrey b Davis 168
A. W. Lilley run out 10
D. R. Pringle c C. S. Cowdrey b Ellison 13
*K. W. R. Fletcher c Marsh b Pienaar 36
G. Miller b Pienaar 16
N. A. Foster c Ward b Davis 21
†A. D. Brown not out . . . . 2 – (3) not out . . . .
J. K. Lever c Tavaré b Pienaar 1
B 1, l-b 7, w 1, n-b 5 . . . . 14 L-b 4 . . . .

1/5 2/5 3/81 4/92 5/117 330 1/82 (1 wkt dec.) 8
6/251 7/305 8/307 9/328

Bonus points – Essex 3, Kent 2 (Score at 100 overs: 273-6).

Bowling: *First Innings*—Penn 27–9–69–1; Ellison 21–6–47–2; C. S. Cowdrey 16–6–45–
Pienaar 23.3–5–86–3; Davis 17–4–55–3; G. R. Cowdrey 5–1–20–0. *Second Innings*—G. R.
Cowdrey 5–0–31–0; Pienaar 7–2–23–0; Davis 10–4–19–1; Ward 4–1–4–0; Taylor 2–1–1–0.

Kent

N. R. Taylor c Miller b Foster 77
T. R. Ward lbw b Pringle 70
S. G. Hinks c Miller b Pringle 0
C. J. Tavaré c Brown b Pringle 0
R. F. Pienaar lbw b Miller 20
G. R. Cowdrey st Brown b Miller 13
*C. S. Cowdrey not out 43
†S. A. Marsh st Brown b Miller 0
R. M. Ellison b Miller . . . .
C. Penn b Lever . . . .
R. P. Davis b Foster . . . .
B 1, l-b 4 . . . .

1/109 2/109 3/109 4/152 5/176 2
6/206 7/208 8/208 9/209

Bonus points – Kent 2, Essex 4.

Bowling: Lever 16–3–38–1; Foster 24.2–8–51–2; Pringle 15–4–42–3; Miller 39–12–95–4

Umpires: J. H. Hampshire and K. J. Lyons.

At Hastings, July 2, 4, 5. KENT beat SUSSEX by four wickets.

At Guildford, July 16, 18, 19. KENT drew with SURREY.

At Northampton, July 20, 21, 22. KENT beat NORTHAMPTONSHIRE by one wicke

KENT v WORCESTERSHIRE

At Folkestone, July 23, 25, 26. Drawn. Kent 5 pts, Worcestershire 6 pts. Toss: K Worcestershire, put in on a pitch which looked to be helping the seam bowlers, lost half t batting for 62 runs in the first twenty overs to Penn and Ellison. Neale received useful sup from Newport in a stand of 33 off ten overs, and Illingworth was settling in when rain cam limit the day's play to 41.4 overs. On the second morning Neale and Illingworth made t stand worth 87 off 28 overs, and Neale went on to complete his century in 220 minutes balls) with fifteen fours. Kent began soundly before rain again ended play early. On final day they collapsed badly, but there was no time for Worcestershire to conjure a re

Close of play: First day, Worcestershire 132-7 (P. A. Neale 38*, R. K. Illingworth 1 Second day, Kent 41-0 (M. R. Benson 22*, N. R. Taylor 17*).

Worcestershire

P. Bent c Benson b Penn	5	– b Ellison	2
G. J. Lord c Penn b Ellison	0	– c Taylor b Ellison	13
G. A. Hick c Taylor b Ellison	21		
D. A. Leatherdale c Marsh b Ellison	22	– not out	34
*P. A. Neale not out	108		
M. J. Weston c Tavaré b Ellison	0		
†S. J. Rhodes lbw b Penn	7	– (3) not out	31
P. J. Newport c Ward b Pienaar	16		
R. K. Illingworth c Marsh b Ellison	34		
N. V. Radford c Tavaré b Penn	6		
A. P. Pridgeon c Tavaré b Ellison	4		
L-b 11, w 2, n-b 2	15	L-b 1	1
1/6 2/23 3/39 4/60 5/62 6/71 7/104 8/191 9/217	238	1/15 2/16	(2 wkts dec.) 81

Bonus points – Worcestershire 2, Kent 4.

Bowling: *First Innings*—Penn 25–5–74–3; Ellison 29.2–6–99–6; Kelleher 3–0–6–0; Pienaar -4–16–1; Davis 14–3–32–0. *Second Innings*—Penn 5–1–9–0; Ellison 4–2–13–2; Davis 4–5–29–0; Pienaar 5–0–6–0; Kelleher 6–0–18–0; Cowdrey 2–0–5–0.

Kent

M. R. Benson c Hick b Radford	28	C. Penn c Rhodes b Newport	16
S. R. Taylor c Hick b Radford	40	D. J. M. Kelleher c Illingworth b Newport	6
T. R. Ward lbw b Radford	1	R. P. Davis not out	5
C. J. Tavaré c Hick b Illingworth	14	L-b 5, w 1, n-b 1	7
R. F. Pienaar c Rhodes b Newport	6		
G. R. Cowdrey c Weston b Illingworth	7		
S. A. Marsh c Rhodes b Newport	8	1/64 2/68 3/79 4/91 5/92 6/108 7/108 8/140 9/140	152
R. M. Ellison c Newport b Illingworth	14		

Bonus points – Kent 1, Worcestershire 4.

Bowling: Radford 20–4–40–3; Newport 23.3–7–50–4; Pridgeon 17–6–32–0; Illingworth -6–25–3.

Umpires: R. Palmer and R. A. White.

KENT v SOMERSET

Canterbury, July 30, August 1, 2. Somerset won by an innings and 146 runs. Somerset pts, Kent 1 pts. Toss: Somerset. One of the finest innings played on the St Lawrence ground during the season came from the Australian, Waugh, who figured in a tremendous fourth-wicket stand of 205 in 47 overs with Bartlett. Earlier, Roebuck and Pringle had needed overs to add 97, but Waugh quickly reached 52 out of 81 off just 73 balls. He finally batted 198 minutes, hitting 23 fours in his 161 off 172 balls. On the second day Bartlett completed maiden Championship hundred off 204 balls in 231 minutes with ten fours. Kent responded disastrously. They lost half their side for 48 runs in thirteen overs, undone by the pace of Jones and Mallender, and the off-spin of Trump rounded off their innings as he enjoyed a spell of three for 1 in nine balls. Following on, Kent fared just as badly, with the first five failing to make an impression. Graham Cowdrey went on to a battling half-century on the final morning, but it was only a matter of time before Kent suffered their first defeat in five Championship games. Their captain, Chris Cowdrey, went in at No. 11 because of a blow on the foot from the bowling of Jones in the first innings, and he subsequently withdrew from the England team for the Oval Test.

Close of play: First day, Somerset 385-4 (R. J. Bartlett 71*, N. D. Burns 10*); Second day, Kent 109-5 (G. R. Cowdrey 20*, S. A. Marsh 12*).

Somerset

J. J. E. Hardy lbw b Penn	14	†N. D. Burns not out	4
*P. M. Roebuck b Penn	68	B 3, l-b 4, n-b 1	8
N. J. Pringle lbw b C. S. Cowdrey	54		—
S. R. Waugh b Pienaar	161	1/26 2/123 3/162 (4 wkts dec.)	45
R. J. Bartlett not out	102	4/367	

V. J. Marks, G. D. Rose, N. A. Mallender, A. N. Jones and H. R. J. Trump did not bat.

Bonus points – Somerset 3, Kent 1 (Score at 100 overs: 295-3).

Bowling: Penn 30–3–107–2; Ellison 8–3–14–0; Davis 38–7–114–0; C. S. Cowdre 29–11–81–1; Pienaar 18–1–75–1; G. R. Cowdrey 10–1–54–0.

Kent

M. R. Benson b Mallender	6	– c Burns b Mallender	1
N. R. Taylor lbw b Mallender	3	– lbw b Jones	1
T. R. Ward b Jones	17	– lbw b Mallender	
C. J. Tavaré c Waugh b Trump	33	– b Mallender	2
R. F. Pienaar c Waugh b Jones	6	– b Trump	1
*C. S. Cowdrey b Jones	8	– (11) b Mallender	
G. R. Cowdrey c Trump b Marks	12	– (6) not out	6
†S. A. Marsh c Pringle b Trump	0	– (7) lbw b Jones	1
R. M. Ellison c Pringle b Trump	0	– (8) b Marks	1
C. Penn c Burns b Trump	18	– (9) b Marks	1
R. P. Davis not out	17	– (10) b Mallender	
L-b 1	1	B 5, l-b 2, w 1, n-b 5	1
	—		—
1/7 2/16 3/26 4/32 5/48 6/84 7/86 8/86 9/86	121	1/22 2/34 3/37 4/50 5/91 6/119 7/152 8/180 9/181	18

Bonus points – Somerset 4.

Bowling: *First Innings*—Jones 9–3–33–3; Mallender 7–1–19–2; Rose 7–2–14–0; Ma 13–3–37–1; Trump 7.5–1–17–4. *Second Innings*—Jones 15–4–33–2; Mallender 17.4–12–12– Marks 29–8–68–2; Rose 3–1–7–0; Trump 21–4–53–1; Pringle 2–0–5–0.

Umpires: J. Birkenshaw and R. Julian.

KENT v LEICESTERSHIRE

At Canterbury, August 3, 4, 5. Drawn. Kent 8 pts, Leicestershire 5 pts. Toss: Kent. A century by the South African all-rounder, Pienaar, held the Kent innings together, and received good support from Tavaré and Graham Cowdrey. Kent achieved their four bat points on the first day, and had Leicestershire in early trouble on the second. Gower, howe played superbly, scoring two-thirds of his runs in boundaries, and as Kent tried to dismiss Leicestershire tail quickly, their former batsman, Potter, held them up for two and a hours. On the final day Kent set Leicestershire 221 to win in a minimum of 58 overs, an one stage Gower and Whitaker, adding 84 off seventeen overs, looked to be putting then course. In the event, the off-spin of Harman, who returned Championship-best figures, sw the game Kent's way and Leicestershire had to hold on to save it.

Close of play: First day, Kent 318-8 (S. A. Marsh 25*, M. D. Harman 2*); Second Leicestershire 247.

Kent

First innings		Second innings	
M. R. Benson c Gower b Ferris	44	– c Whitticase b Ferris	15
N. R. Taylor lbw b Agnew	13	– c Briers b Willey	22
R. F. Pienaar st Whitticase b Willey	128	– st Whitticase b Such	23
*C. J. Tavaré b Agnew	36	– c Briers b Such	17
T. R. Ward b Agnew	0	– c Potter b Ferris	12
G. R. Cowdrey b Taylor	32	– not out	35
†S. A. Marsh not out	30		
R. M. Ellison lbw b Agnew	19	– (7) c Whitticase b Ferris	1
C. Penn lbw b Agnew	1	– (8) not out	7
M. D. Harman c Gower b Agnew	4		
R. P. Davis lbw b Agnew	0		
B 2, l-b 10, n-b 8	20	B 3, l-b 3, n-b 2	8
/31 2/102 3/206 4/206 5/262 /272 7/299 8/301 9/327	327	1/23 2/58 3/76 4/86 5/108 6/116 (6 wkts dec.)	140

Bonus points – Kent 4, Leicestershire 3 (Score at 100 overs: 303-8).

Bowling: *First Innings*—Ferris 21–4–77–1; Agnew 28.4–8–61–7; Such 17–4–47–0; Taylor 9–6–53–1; Willey 25–7–61–1; Potter 5–0–16–0. *Second Innings*—Agnew 17–3–55–0; Ferris 3–3–42–3; Such 7–1–25–2; Willey 4–0–12–1.

.eicestershire

First innings		Second innings	
. J. Boon lbw b Penn	0	– c Ward b Harman	33
. E. Briers c Taylor b Penn	17	– b Harman	20
. Willey run out	39	– b Davis	16
D. I. Gower c Marsh b Harman	90	– st Marsh b Harman	43
J. Whitaker st Marsh b Harman	36	– c and b Davis	48
. Potter not out	30	– c Cowdrey b Harman	14
P. Whitticase b Penn	19	– (8) not out	11
P. Agnew b Penn	0	– (7) b Harman	3
. B. Taylor lbw b Penn	0		
. J. F. Ferris lbw b Ellison	3	– (9) not out	4
M. Such lbw b Ellison	0		
B 4, l-b 7, w 1, n-b 1	13	B 3, l-b 7, w 1	11
0 2/25 3/88 4/172 5/193 228 7/228 8/228 9/247	247	1/54 2/65 3/73 4/157 5/183 6/185 7/193 (7 wkts)	203

Bonus points – Leicestershire 2, Kent 4.

Bowling: *First Innings*—Penn 23–7–68–5; Ellison 17.4–4–47–2; Harman 22–9–36–2; enaar 13–2–32–0; Davis 24–8–53–0. *Second Innings*—Penn 6–2–10–0; Ellison 2–0–14–0; avis 28–6–101–2; Harman 24.4–5–68–5.

Umpires: J. Birkenshaw and R. Julian.

Chesterfield, August 13, 15, 16. KENT drew with DERBYSHIRE.

Bournemouth, August 17, 18, 19. KENT beat HAMPSHIRE by 91 runs.

Bristol, August 20, 22, 23. KENT drew with GLOUCESTERSHIRE.

KENT v SUSSEX

At Maidstone, August 25, 26, 27, 29. Sussex won by 63 runs. Sussex 21 pts, Kent 6 pts. Toss: Kent. Put in to bat, Sussex managed only 114 runs for the loss of five wickets in 50 overs, with the Kent pace bowlers very much on top. Pigott hit an unbeaten 47 to extend the Sussex first innings, but by the close Kent had made a steady start. However, the eventual lead of 49 was disappointing, especially when Sussex batted much better second time around. Lenham and Parker put on 168 in 49 overs, and Parker, batting for 202 minutes and hitting eighteen fours hit his best score of the summer. Kent collapsed on the third evening, losing four wickets for 17 runs before they were rescued by Tavaré and Graham Cowdrey, who on the final day took their stand to 96. Tavaré, batting for 255 minutes and hitting thirteen fours, held the Ken innings together, but he could not prevent the Sussex seam attack bowling their side to thei third victory of the season.

Close of play: First day, Kent 87-1 (M. R. Benson 23*, R. F. Pienaar 47*); Second day Sussex 160-1 (N. J. Lenham 66*, P. W. G. Parker 77*); Third day, Kent 76-4 (C. J. Tavar 28*, G. R. Cowdrey 36*).

Sussex

N. J. Lenham c Marsh b C. S. Cowdrey . . . . . . 28 – c Tavaré b Penn 7
A. M. Green c C. S. Cowdrey b Igglesden . . . . . 9 – c C. S. Cowdrey b Pienaar . . . . .
*P. W. G. Parker c C. S. Cowdrey b Igglesden . 0 – b Penn .12
A. P. Wells c C. S. Cowdrey b Pienaar . . . . 39 – c C. S. Cowdrey b Pienaar 3
I. J. Gould c Tavaré b Pienaar . . . . 23 – c Penn b Igglesden 5
C. M. Wells lbw b Ellison . . . . 13 – c sub b Igglesden 2
A. C. S. Pigott not out . . . . 47 – c G. R. Cowdrey b Penn 2
†P. Moores c Marsh b Penn . . . . 8 – c C. S. Cowdrey b Penn . . . .
A. R. Clarke c Pienaar b Igglesden . . . . 4 – c Tavaré b Igglesden . . . .
R. A. Bunting c Marsh b Igglesden . . . . 0 – b Igglesden . . . .
A. M. Babington c C. S. Cowdrey b Penn . . . . . 0 – not out . . . .
B 1, l-b 2, w 4, n-b 6 . . . . 13 B 1, l-b 10, w 1, n-b 4 . . .

1/23 2/24 3/66 4/108 5/114 6/137 7/164 8/169 9/169 — 184
1/36 2/204 3/233 4/274 5/317 6/324 7/346 8/347 9/350 — 3

Bonus points – Sussex 1, Kent 4.

Bowling: *First Innings*—Igglesden 19–5–53–4; Penn 20.5–1–53–2; Ellison 16–5–34–1; C. Cowdrey 10–1–28–1; Harman 1–1–0–0; Pienaar 10–4–13–2. *Second Innings*—Pe 31–10–100–4; Igglesden 30.2–4–105–4; Ellison 8–0–28–0; Pienaar 25–8–45–2; C. S. Cowd 10–2–30–0; Harman 15–5–40–0.

Kent

M. R. Benson c Gould b Pigott . . . . 30 – c Moores b Pigott . . . .
N. R. Taylor c Moores b Pigott . . . . 10 – lbw b Babington . . . .
R. F. Pienaar c Moores b Babington . . . . 72 – c Moores b Pigott . . . .
C. J. Tavaré c Moores b Pigott . . . . 47 – b Bunting . . . .
*C. S. Cowdrey lbw b Babington . . . . 10 – c Green b Babington . . . .
G. R. Cowdrey lbw b C. M. Wells . . . . 0 – b Babington . . . .
†S. A. Marsh lbw b Babington . . . . 0 – lbw b Bunting . . . .
R. M. Ellison c Moores b C. M. Wells . . . . 32 – (11) not out . . . .
C. Penn b C. M. Wells . . . . 16 – (8) c Babington b Pigott . . . .
M. D. Harman not out . . . . 1 – (9) c Moores b C. M. Wells . . . .
A. P. Igglesden b C. M. Wells . . . . 1 – (10) c Green b Pigott . . . .
L-b 10, w 4 . . . . 14 L-b 6, w 3, n-b 4 . . . .

1/21 2/96 3/140 4/162 5/163 6/164 7/190 8/226 9/231 — 233
1/0 2/2 3/12 4/17 5/113 6/193 7/202 8/240 9/242

Bonus points – Kent 2, Sussex 4.

Bowling: *First Innings*—Pigott 24–3–77–3; Bunting 20–7–40–0; C. M. Wells 19.1–5–43–4; Babington 25–6–63–3. *Second Innings*—Pigott 29.4–5–86–4; Babington 27–8–58–3; C. M. Wells 25–7–55–1; Bunting 14–4–39–2; Clarke 3–2–3–0.

Umpires: D. G. L. Evans and N. T. Plews.

At Lord's, September 9, 10, 11, 12. KENT drew with MIDDLESEX.

KENT v SURREY

At Canterbury, September 14, 15, 16. Kent won by an innings and 66 runs. Kent 24 pts, Surrey 4 pts. Toss: Kent. A third-wicket partnership of 104 off 29 overs between Hinks and Tavaré set Kent on course for maximum batting points and the innings was given a final fillip by a last-wicket stand of 82 in sixteen overs between Ellison and Igglesden. Igglesden followed his career-best score with a career-best bowling return as Surrey collapsed from 100 for two to 109, taking six for 4 in 23 balls. Greig retired hurt after being hit in the face by a ball from Penn, and his injury prevented him from batting when Surrey followed on. They again started reasonably, but on the third morning Penn brought about another slump with a spell of three for 4 in sixteen balls. Kent returned briefly to the top of the Championship table before the news came in that Worcestershire had beaten Glamorgan, also with a day to spare.

Close of play: First day, Kent 307-9 (R. M. Ellison 23*, A. P. Igglesden 12*); Second day, Surrey 79-2 (G. S. Clinton 42*, M. A. Lynch 17*).

Kent

M. R. Benson lbw b Frost 7	†S. A. Marsh b Feltham 0
S. G. Hinks c and b Frost 92	C. Penn c Richards b Feltham 19
T. R. Ward b M. P. Bicknell 8	R. M. Ellison not out 38
C. J. Tavaré c Richards b M. P. Bicknell 60	A. P. Igglesden b Feltham 41
R. F. Pienaar c Richards b M. P. Bicknell . 25	B 8, l-b 6, w 1, n-b 6 21
*C. S. Cowdrey lbw b Feltham 9	1/25 2/59 3/163 4/191 5/202 354
G. R. Cowdrey c Lynch b Feltham 34	6/216 7/216 8/269 9/272

Bonus points – Kent 4, Surrey 4.

Bowling: Frost 17–3–64–2; M. P. Bicknell 37–12–111–3; Feltham 34.2–3–124–5; Greig –0–23–0; Medlycott 6–1–18–0.

Surrey

D. J. Bicknell b Igglesden	37	– c C. S. Cowdrey b Penn 5
G. S. Clinton c Ward b C. S. Cowdrey	31	– c Benson b Igglesden 43
. J. Stewart b Ellison	11	– b C. S. Cowdrey 13
M. A. Lynch run out	8	– c Pienaar b Penn 36
. M. Ward b Igglesden	4	– b Penn 7
C. J. Richards c Marsh b Igglesden	2	– not out 35
. A. Greig retired hurt	1	– absent injured
. T. Medlycott b Igglesden	0	– (7) c C. S. Cowdrey b Penn 5
. A. Feltham lbw b Igglesden	0	– (8) c Marsh b Igglesden 15
. P. Bicknell not out	0	– (9) b Ellison 3
. Frost lbw b Igglesden	0	– (10) c G. R. Cowdrey b Ellison . 4
B 2, n-b 13	15	L-b 2, w 1, n-b 10 13
70 2/86 3/100 4/100 5/105	109	1/15 2/56 3/90 4/108 5/119 179
108 7/109 8/109 9/109		6/133 7/164 8/167 9/179

Bonus points – Kent 4.

Bowling: *First Innings*—Penn 12–3–37–0; Igglesden 11–3–34–6; Ellison 8–4–16–1; C. S. wdrey 6–0–20–1. *Second Innings*—Penn 15–2–44–4; Igglesden 13–2–61–2; Ellison .1–2–39–2; C. S. Cowdrey 10–1–28–1; Pienaar 2–0–5–0.

Umpires: M. J. Kitchen and P. B. Wight.

LANCASHIRE

Patron: HM The Queen
President: C. Washbrook
Chairman: R. Bennett
Secretary: C. D. Hassell
County Cricket Ground, Old Trafford,
Manchester M16 0PX
(Telephone: 061-848 7021)
Captain: D. P. Hughes
Coach: J. A. Ormrod

Lancashire's decision in the closing weeks of the season to reappoint David Hughes as captain for a third term in 1989 was a reflection of the continuing progress the county had made after the revival of 1987. Slipping from second to ninth in the Britannic Assurance Championship might not seem much like progress, but the encouraging aspect of Lancashire's play throughout the summer was the continuing good spirit, dedication and determination to succeed. The atmosphere around Old Trafford was again clear and positive. There was a good feel to the place, and once again Lancashire kept interest in the season alive right through to the final match.

This time their strong suit was the 40-over Sunday game, the competition in which they excelled in its opening years as the John Player League. They finished third in the Refuge Assurance League their highest position since 1971 and one which qualified them for the new Refuge Assurance Cup. In this, they beat Gloucestershire and, in the final at Edgbaston, Worcestershire. Sunday cricket proved to be full of adventure and high drama, with six of their victories coming in the last three balls. For all this, though, the spectators did not gather in anything like the numbers that saw Lancashire march through the opposition in the first years of 40-over cricket.

Unfortunately, Lancashire could not extend their Sunday success t the longer limited-overs games. They failed to get past the second roun of the NatWest Bank Trophy for the fifth time in seven years and wer out of the Benson and Hedges Cup at the qualifying stage for the fourt successive season since winning it in 1984.

Lancashire's magnificent performance of finishing runners-up t Nottinghamshire in the Championship of 1987 after eleven years in th bottom six probably worked against them in 1988. Too much seemed t be expected of them. I for one was just happy that they did not slide bac into the basement, and although they finished ninth and did not win match at Old Trafford, they kept alive their hopes of a top place unt three matches from the end. Their run-in for the Championship in 198 saw them win the last six matches; in 1988 they won only one of the la nine. They were unlucky to lose Wasim Akram through injury for the la seven weeks of the season, and once he had gone they won just o Championship match, against Sussex at Hove.

Wasim in fact, in his first season of county cricket, played in on ten of the 22 Championship matches. He was late arriving, owing Pakistan's Test series against West Indies, and was troubled by inju which resulted in a minor groin operation towards the end of the summer. In those few matches, however, he showed his capabilities with 31 wickets at 21.48 runs each, and 496 runs (31.00). He scored a century in his second game for the club, and in an outstanding individual performance, against Surrey at Southport, he scored 58 and 98 and took eight wickets in the match, including Lancashire's first hat-trick since Jack Simmons's in 1977.

Four bowlers, Allott, Simmons, Folley and Watkinson, took more than 50 wickets and four batsmen, Mendis, Fairbrother, Fowler and Atherton – whose summer was again shared between Cambridge University and Lancashire – topped 1,000 runs. Graeme Fowler, whose 1,800 runs were second in total only to Hick's in English first-class cricket in 1987, nearly did not make it to four figures in 1988. He had had a poor year, relieved only by three good scores in four innings in the middle of the season, when he went into the last three games with a total of 810 runs. He then scored a fine, fighting 97 against Surrey at The Oval and, having saved his best innings of the summer for the end, a magnificent 172 against Derbyshire at Derby.

Another player who fell away in 1988 was Ian Folley, the left-arm spinner. He exceeded 50 wickets again, yet had a poor, dispiriting year as he lost so much of the control and confidence of 1987. Gehan Mendis was the third player behind Hick and Gooch to reach 1,000 runs but in the end would have been disappointed at not getting 1,500, and Neil Fairbrother, who finished with a pair against Derbyshire in his first Championship match as captain, had his worst season since establishing himself in the team. Andy Hayhurst continued his gradual progress, and his maiden century in the final match might persuade Lancashire to try him at No. 3 at the start of the summer until Michael Atherton has finished his studies at Cambridge.

Paul Allott was again the outstanding bowler, willing and economical, and Simmons, at 47, earned himself a further one-year contract with yet another season of highly skilled off-spin bowling, becoming the thirteenth Lancashire bowler to take 1,000 wickets. Mike Watkinson had an outstanding all-round season with 759 first-class runs to go with his 52 wickets, although too much was probably expected of him batting at No. 5. Hughes again found runs hard to come by, and by the end of the season he had slipped to No. 8 in the order. But his captaincy was again forceful and positive and played the most significant part in an interesting, successful season. His fielding was outstanding and belied his 41 years.

Lancashire released only one player, David Makinson, who has been troubled with a back injury, and towards the end of the season they beat several other counties in signing Phillip DeFreitas from Leicestershire. He is the first ready-made English Test cricketer Lancashire have obtained, and with Wasim Akram and Patrick Patterson also available, they have high hopes for the 1989 season. – Brian Bearshaw.

LANCASHIRE 1988

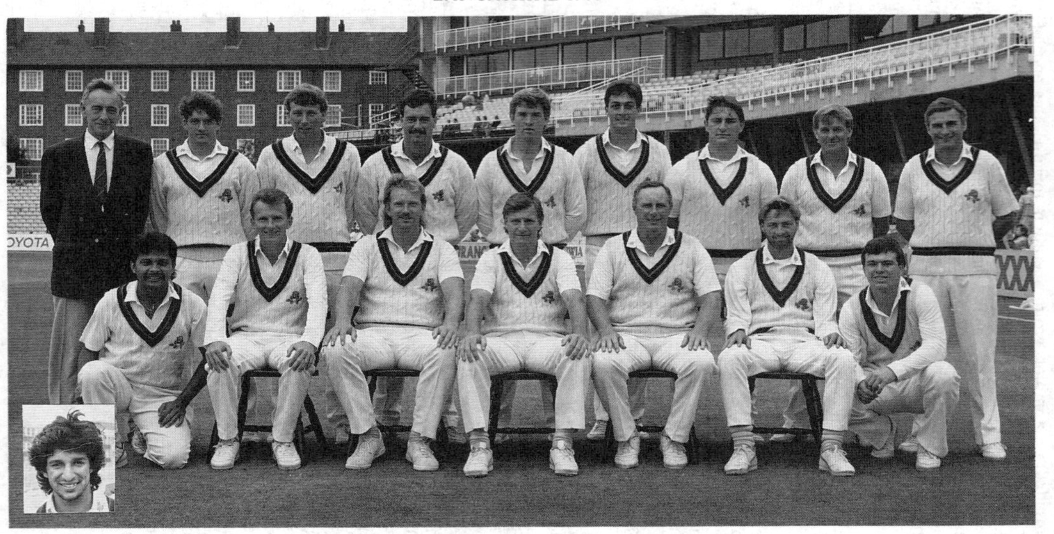

[*Bill Smith*

Back row: W. Davies (*scorer*), I. Folley, M. A. Atherton, A. J. Murphy, A. N. Hayhurst, M. Watkinson, I. D. Austin, T. E. Jesty, J. A. Ormrod
[illegible] G. D. Mendis, N. H. Fairbrother, P. J. W. Allott, D. P. Hughes (*captain*), J. Simmons, G. Fowler, W. K. Hegg. *Inset:* Wasim Akram.

LANCASHIRE RESULTS

All first-class matches – Played 24: Won 6, Lost 7, Drawn 11.

County Championship matches – Played 22: Won 6, Lost 7, Drawn 9.

Bonus points – Batting 41, Bowling 67.

Competition placings – Britannic Assurance County Championship, 9th; NatWest Bank Trophy, 2nd round; Benson and Hedges Cup, 4th in Group A; Refuge Assurance League, 3rd; Refuge Assurance Cup, winners.

BRITANNIC ASSURANCE CHAMPIONSHIP AVERAGES

BATTING

	Birthplace	*M*	*I*	*NO*	*R*	*HI*	*Avge*
M. A. Atherton	*Manchester*	8	14	2	456	152*	38.00
‡G. D. Mendis	*Colombo, Ceylon*	22	40	4	1,166	151	32.38
§Wasim Akram	*Lahore, Pakistan*	10	18	2	496	116*	31.00
I. D. Austin	*Haslingden*	6	9	2	216	64	30.85
‡G. Fowler	*Accrington*	20	36	1	1,061	172	30.31
‡N. H. Fairbrother	*Warrington*	22	40	3	1,090	111	29.45
T. E. Jesty	*Gosport*	13	25	3	587	73	26.68
A. N. Hayhurst	*Manchester*	12	21	2	477	107	25.10
‡M. Watkinson	*Westhoughton*	22	37	4	725	85*	21.96
‡J. Simmons	*Clayton-le-Moors*	20	26	9	335	57*	19.70
‡D. P. Hughes	*Newton-le-Willows*	21	33	3	465	62	15.50
W. K. Hegg	*Whitefield*	22	32	5	406	76	15.03
‡I. Folley	*Burnley*	17	19	13	90	30	15.00
‡P. J. W. Allott	*Altrincham*	19	28	4	308	31*	12.83

Also batted: ‡J. Abrahams (*Cape Town, SA*) (1 match) 9, 1; J. D. Fitton (*Littleborough*) (1 match) 36; §C. D. Matthews (*Cunderdin, Australia*) (2 matches) 7, 0, 31; G. D. Lloyd (*Accrington*) (1 match) 22, 0; A. J. Murphy (*Manchester*) (2 matches) 0, 0, 3; N. J. Speak (*Manchester*) (1 match) 35, 10.

* *Signifies not out.* ‡ *Denotes county cap.* § *Not qualified for England.*

The following played a total of nine three-figure innings for Lancashire in County Championship matches – M. A. Atherton 2, N. H. Fairbrother 2, G. Fowler 2, A. N. Hayhurst 1, G. D. Mendis 1, Wasim Akram 1.

BOWLING

	O	*M*	*R*	*W*	*BB*	*5W/i*	*Avge*
P. J. W. Allott	590.2	162	1,378	67	6-59	5	20.56
Wasim Akram	291.4	76	666	31	7-53	2	21.48
J. Simmons	585	150	1,457	60	5-53	2	24.28
I. D. Austin	137.1	43	367	15	5-79	1	24.46
I. Folley	547.3	142	1,564	52	6-20	2	30.07
M. Watkinson	600.3	149	1,632	50	6-43	2	32.64
A. N. Hayhurst	159.3	31	518	15	4-45	0	34.53

Also bowled: M. A. Atherton 89.5–23–242–4; N. H. Fairbrother 10.1–0–59–0; J. D. Fitton 42–13–77–7; T. E. Jesty 25–10–56–0; C. D. Matthews 60–16–177–5; G. D. Mendis 8–0–35–0; A. J. Murphy 47.1–7–184–3.

Wicket-keeper: W. K. Hegg 50 ct, 8 st.

Leading Fielders: D. P. Hughes 25, G. Fowler 19.

LANCASHIRE v WORCESTERSHIRE

At Manchester, April 21, 22, 23, 25. Worcestershire won by ten wickets. Worcestershire 23 pts, Lancashire 1 pt. Toss: Worcestershire. After losing by 117 runs on a spinners' wicket in 1987, Worcestershire gained revenge on a pitch taking spin on the first morning in the opening four-day Championship match at Old Trafford. Hick looked in a class apart from any other batsman in the match and his innings was the dominating, deciding feature. He faced 312 balls, batted 345 minutes, and hit 25 fours and four sixes. Neale provided the main support for 264 minutes in a partnership of 202. Dilley started Lancashire's first-innings decline; Illingworth completed it and, with five wickets in each innings, recorded his first ten-wicket match return in the Championship. Lancashire provided sterner resistance in the second innings, and a last-wicket stand between Simmons and Folley put on 89 to deny Worcestershire an innings victory. This was their first Championship win at Old Trafford for twenty years.

Close of play: First day, Worcestershire 142-3 (G. A. Hick 48*, P. A. Neale 0*); Second day, Lancashire 11-2 (W. K. Hegg 4*, T. E. Jesty 2*); Third day, Lancashire 161-4 (M. Watkinson 9*, D. P. Hughes 0*).

Worcestershire

T. S. Curtis b Folley	49	– not out	11
G. J. Lord b Simmons	30		
G. A. Hick b Simmons	212		
D. B. D'Oliveira c Mendis b Matthews	11		
*P. A. Neale c Hegg b Folley	40		
†S. J. Rhodes c Hughes b Simmons	28	– (2) not out	10
I. T. Botham c Hughes b Folley	3		
P. J. Newport not out	13		
L-b 21, w 1, n-b 1	23	L-b 8	8
1/70 2/94 3/138 4/340 5/368 6/375 7/409 (7 wkts dec.)	409	(no wkt)	29

R. K. Illingworth, N. V. Radford and G. R. Dilley did not bat.

Bonus points – Worcestershire 3, Lancashire 1 (Score at 100 overs: 261-3).

Bowling: *First Innings*—Matthews 24–7–78–1; Allott 26–10–44–0; Watkinson 13–4–37–0; Folley 38–8–116–3; Simmons 43–9–113–3. *Second Innings*—Jesty 9–4–11–0; Folley 8.3–5–10–0.

Lancashire

G. D. Mendis c Radford b Dilley	3	– c Rhodes b Illingworth	19
G. Fowler c Hick b Dilley	0	– c sub b Illingworth	50
†W. K. Hegg c Rhodes b Dilley	8	– (7) c Curtis b Illingworth	0
T. E. Jesty c Rhodes b Illingworth	13	– (3) c Radford b Hick	12
N. H. Fairbrother b Illingworth	10	– (4) lbw b Illingworth	56
M. Watkinson st Rhodes b Illingworth	6	– (5) c Curtis b Hick	68
*D. P. Hughes c Hick b Radford	3	– (6) c Curtis b Illingworth	20
P. J. W. Allott c Rhodes b Hick	7	– b Hick	1
J. Simmons b Illingworth	32	– not out	57
C. D. Matthews c Curtis b Illingworth	7	– c Dilley b Hick	0
I. Folley not out	0	– b Dilley	30
B 4, l-b 4, n-b 4	12	B 6, l-b 4, w 3, n-b 10	23
1/3 2/5 3/19 4/40 5/41 6/48 7/52 8/83 9/100	101	1/40 2/53 3/128 4/161 5/242 6/244 7/244 8/247 9/247	336

Bonus points – Worcestershire 4.

Bowling: *First Innings*—Dilley 9–2–14–3; Radford 10–2–25–1; Illingworth 22.4–4–46–5 Hick 6–2–8–1. *Second Innings*—Dilley 11.5–1–31–1; Radford 8–2–12–0; Illingworth 59–14–107–5; Hick 44–10–138–4; Newport 6–0–38–0.

Umpires: J. W. Holder and D. O. Oslear.

LANCASHIRE v WARWICKSHIRE

At Manchester, April 28, 29, 30, May 2. Drawn. Lancashire 6 pts, Warwickshire 5 pts. Toss: Warwickshire. A game of fluctuating fortunes ended with Lancashire in the stronger position, needing 153 more for victory with nine wickets standing, when rain ended play. Smith led Warwickshire's first-innings recovery from 14 for five after thirteen overs, and with Small and Merrick tearing through the Lancashire batting later in the day, the first day surprisingly belonged to Warwickshire. But Lancashire's last three wickets, inspired by Hegg, put on 135 and Warwickshire themselves needed some strong lower-order batting, notably from Small, to set Lancashire a target of 236 in at least 91 overs. Three stoppages for rain on the final day meant that only 43.4 overs were bowled.

Close of play: First day, Lancashire 85-7 (W. K. Hegg 12*, J. Simmons 0*); Second day, Warwickshire 153-4 (T. A. Lloyd 61*, P. A. Smith 19*); Third day, Warwickshire 291-8 (G. C. Small 69*, A. R. K. Pierson 3*).

Warwickshire

*T. A. Lloyd b Matthews	0	– c Fowler b Allott	64
A. J. Moles c Simmons b Allott	0	– c Folley b Allott	22
Asif Din c Hegg b Matthews	4	– run out	3
A. I. Kallicharran lbw b Allott	1	– b Simmons	36
†G. W. Humpage c Fowler b Matthews	4	– lbw b Allott	1
P. A. Smith c Hughes b Allott	68	– c Mendis b Simmons	22
D. A. Reeve c Hughes b Watkinson	11	– lbw b Allott	36
G. C. Small b Matthews	14	– st Hegg b Folley	70
T. A. Merrick c Fowler b Folley	23	– c Watkinson b Folley	19
A. R. K. Pierson not out	13	– lbw b Allott	8
N. Gifford b Simmons	12	– not out	0
L-b 3, n-b 2	5	B 9, l-b 5, w 1, n-b 1	16
/0 2/4 3/6 4/6 5/14 6/38 /89 8/117 9/131	155	1/42 2/60 3/104 4/107 5/159 6/161 7/236 8/287 9/297	297

Bonus points – Warwickshire 1, Lancashire 4.

Bowling: *First Innings*—Matthews 15–3–47–4; Allott 18–6–33–3; Watkinson 18–6–37–1; esty 3–0–16–0; Folley 10–2–19–1; Simmons 3.5–3–0–1. *Second Innings*—Matthews 1–6–52–0; Allott 32.5–7–65–5; Watkinson 23–4–48–0; Folley 26–11–57–2; Simmons 4–18–61–2.

ancashire

G. D. Mendis c Pierson b Small	10	– not out	41
G. Fowler c Humpage b Merrick	6	– lbw b Gifford	23
. E. Jesty b Small	2	– not out	17
N. H. Fairbrother c Humpage b Merrick	0		
M. Watkinson b Small	19		
D. P. Hughes lbw b Small	13		
W. K. Hegg b Merrick	76		
. J. W. Allott c Asif Din b Merrick	15		
Simmons b Small	20		
. D. Matthews b Merrick	31		
Folley not out	3		
B 4, l-b 8, w 4, n-b 6	22	L-b 1, w 1	2
12 2/15 3/16 4/20 5/55 58 7/82 8/127 9/211	217	1/46	(1 wkt) 83

Bonus points – Lancashire 2, Warwickshire 4.

Bowling: *First Innings*—Small 25–4–60–5; Merrick 22.5–4–67–5; Smith 6–0–21–0; Reeve 2–11–0; Gifford 22–10–24–0; Asif Din 3–1–22–0. *Second Innings*—Small 9–3–15–0; errick 8–1–11–0; Reeve 6–0–17–0; Pierson 10.4–4–19–0; Gifford 10–3–20–1.

Umpires: H. D. Bird and N. T. Plews.

At Nottingham, May 5, 6, 7, 9. LANCASHIRE beat NOTTINGHAMSHIRE by 51 runs.

At Oxford, May 21, 23, 24. LANCASHIRE drew with OXFORD UNIVERSITY.

LANCASHIRE v SOMERSET

At Manchester, May 28, 30, 31. Somerset won by two wickets. Somerset 22 pts, Lancashire 5 pts. Toss: Lancashire. A maiden first-class century from Wasim Akram, the Pakistan fast bowler, in only his second first-class match for Lancashire, enabled his county's last five wickets to put on 202 runs. Crowe dominated the second day, hitting twenty fours and a six and scoring his unbeaten 136 from 217 balls. Lancashire, without Fowler who had slipped on the stairs in the pavilion and hurt his back on Saturday, batted badly on the final day and Somerset were left with a comfortable 55-over target of 202 for victory. However, it needed another fine innings from Crowe, with support from Marks, to lift them from 46 for four, and the final over arrived with Somerset needing 4 runs and Lancashire two wickets. Wasim started with two bouncers, the second of which was hit to the boundary by Rose to secure an exciting victory.

Close of play: First day, Lancashire 329-9 (Wasim Akram 116*, I. Folley 4*); Second day, Lancashire 25-2 (G. D. Mendis 7*, N. H. Fairbrother 9*).

Lancashire

G. D. Mendis c Bartlett b Foster	36	– c Burns b Foster	28
G. Fowler c Burns b Rose	8	– absent injured	
T. E. Jesty b Marks	15	– (2) c and b Rose	5
N. H. Fairbrother c Wyatt b Marks	0	– b Cleal	36
M. Watkinson c Marks b Cleal	52	– b Cleal	3
*D. P. Hughes b Marks	42	– c Wyatt b Foster	4
Wasim Akram not out	116	– st Burns b Marks	13
†W. K. Hegg b Marks	10	– not out	30
J. Simmons c sub b Marks	23	– (10) b Rose	0
P. J. W. Allott run out	18	– (9) c Burns b Rose	13
I. Folley not out	4	– (3) b Rose	0
L-b 2, w 1, n-b 2	5	B 4, l-b 3, w 2, n-b 4	13
1/17 2/41 3/41 4/83 5/127 6/214 7/226 8/276 9/306	(9 wkts dec.) 329	1/7 2/7 3/74 4/80 5/80 6/88 7/116 8/145 9/145	145

Bonus points – Lancashire 3, Somerset 3 (Score at 100 overs: 293-8).

Bowling: *First Innings*—Mallender 4–2–2–0; Foster 25–3–96–1; Rose 17.2–0–75–1; Clea 22–4–63–1; Marks 40.4–11–91–5; Bartlett 1–1–0–0. *Second Innings*—Rose 13.2–2–39–4; Foste 19–4–58–2; Cleal 9–2–27–2; Marks 7–3–14–1.

Somerset

J. G. Wyatt c Hughes b Simmons	47	– (2) c Hegg b Allott	
N. A. Felton c Allott b Wasim	0	– (1) lbw b Allott	1
J. J. E. Hardy b Wasim	30	– c Jesty b Simmons	1
M. D. Crowe not out	136	– b Simmons	8
R. J. Bartlett c Watkinson b Simmons	31	– c Hegg b Wasim	
*V. J. Marks c Allott b Watkinson	8	– run out	3
†N. D. Burns not out	16	– c Hughes b Simmons	
M. W. Cleal (did not bat)		– c Fairbrother b Simmons	
N. A. Mallender (did not bat)		– not out	
G. D. Rose (did not bat)		– not out	
L-b 1, n-b 4	5	L-b 7	
1/1 2/42 3/114 4/210 5/221	(5 wkts dec.) 273	1/10 2/25 3/34 4/46 5/128 6/159 7/179 8/189	(8 wkts) 2

D. J. Foster did not bat.

Bonus points – Somerset 3, Lancashire 2.

Bowling: *First Innings*—Wasim 15–5–27–2; Allott 16–6–47–0; Watkinson 25–3–66–1; Simmons 30–4–94–2; Folley 5–0–38–0. *Second Innings*—Wasim 22.2–7–66–1; Allott 12–0–39–2; Simmons 13–0–58–4; Watkinson 7–0–32–0.

Umpires: B. Dudleston and J. H. Hampshire.

At Worcester, June 1, 2, 3. LANCASHIRE drew with WORCESTERSHIRE.

LANCASHIRE v HAMPSHIRE

At Liverpool, June 4, 6, 7. Lancashire won by four wickets. Lancashire 21 pts, Hampshire 4 pts. Toss: Hampshire. In a game of three declarations, Lancashire achieved their second Championship win of the season with fourteen balls to spare after being set to score 256 in 57 overs. Hampshire, 216 for five after 100 overs, laboured through their first innings with Terry batting for 72 overs and Ayling missing his first century by 12 runs in his third Championship match. After Hampshire had batted on for nine overs on the second morning, Lancashire declared 69 behind and helped organise the run-chase with friendly bowling from Mendis and Fairbrother. However, nothing should detract from the quality of Chris Smith's century after Hampshire had been 10 for three on the second evening. Lancashire's first six batsmen all reached double figures but the main contributors to the victory were Jesty and Watkinson, both of whom benefited from dropped catches.

Close of play: First day, Hampshire 285-6 (J. R. Ayling 68*, S. T. Jefferies 26*); Second day, Hampshire 10-3 (C. L. Smith 0*, R. A. Smith 0*).

Hampshire

First innings		Second innings	
V. P. Terry c Mendis b Hayhurst	74	lbw b Allott	0
C. L. Smith c Hughes b Simmons	24	not out	124
*M. C. J. Nicholas st Hegg b Simmons	31	b Folley	10
R. A. Smith run out	29	(5) lbw b Simmons	18
D. R. Turner b Watkinson	11	(6) b Folley	13
J. R. Ayling not out	88		
†R. J. Parks lbw b Folley	11		
S. T. Jefferies not out	39	(7) not out	19
R. J. Maru (did not bat)		(4) lbw b Folley	0
B 2, l-b 11	13	L-b 1, w 1	2
1/36 2/114 3/163 4/167 5/198 6/237 (6 wkts dec.)	320	1/0 2/10 3/10 4/63 5/102 (5 wkts dec.)	186

C. A. Connor and S. J. W. Andrew did not bat.

Bonus points – Hampshire 2, Lancashire 2 (Score at 100 overs: 216-5).

Bowling: *First Innings*—Wasim 18–5–41–0; Allott 21–8–31–0; Watkinson 13–4–32–1; Simmons 25–4–82–2; Folley 39–7–103–1; Hayhurst 8–1–18–1. *Second Innings*—Allott -4–12–1; Watkinson 8–5–7–0; Folley 23–8–56–3; Simmons 9–5–11–1; Wasim 4–0–16–0; Mendis 8–0–35–0; Fairbrother 7.3–0–48–0.

Lancashire

First innings		Second innings	
G. D. Mendis c Parks b Andrew	22	c Parks b Connor	17
A. N. Hayhurst c Ayling b Maru	80	b Maru	33
N. H. Fairbrother c Terry b Maru	69	(4) c Connor b Jefferies	13
T. E. Jesty c R. A. Smith b Jefferies	8	(3) lbw b Maru	60
M. Watkinson b Connor	6	not out	73
†W. K. Hegg not out	1		
Wasim Akram not out	46	b Connor	7
D. P. Hughes (did not bat)		(6) c Terry b Maru	17
P. J. W. Allott (did not bat)		(8) not out	31
B 2, l-b 7, w 2, n-b 8	19	B 1, l-b 2, w 1, n-b 4	8
1/28 2/139 3/155 4/203 5/203 (5 wkts dec.)	251	1/33 2/86 3/106 4/126 5/169 6/209 (6 wkts)	259

Folley and J. Simmons did not bat.

Bonus points – Lancashire 3, Hampshire 2.

Bowling: *First Innings*—Andrew 14–1–52–1; Connor 11–1–49–1; Jefferies 19–6–34–1; Maru 34.1–13–79–2; C. L. Smith 1–0–1–0; Ayling 8–2–27–0. *Second Innings*—Andrew 4–1–16–0; Connor 11.4–0–60–2; Maru 21–3–106–3; Jefferies 11–0–54–1; C. L. Smith 7–0–20–0.

Umpires: J. H. Harris and K. E. Palmer.

At Manchester, June 8, 9, 10. LANCASHIRE drew with WEST INDIANS (See West Indian tour section).

At Tunbridge Wells, June 15, 16, 17. LANCASHIRE lost to KENT by five wickets.

LANCASHIRE v GLOUCESTERSHIRE

At Manchester, June 18, 20, 21. Drawn. Lancashire 4 pts, Gloucestershire 5 pts. Toss: Lancashire. Gloucestershire's last pair held out for twenty balls to earn a draw after a bold attempt to score 331 off 67 overs had been sustained until the fall of the ninth wicket. Mendis had dominated the opening day for five and a half hours, and Romaines batted for three and a half hours on the second, both of them registering their first Championship centuries of the summer. After Gloucestershire had declared 73 behind, Lawrence bowled with fire to force Mendis to retire and take five of Lancashire's second-innings wickets. Both teams had weakened attacks, which meant that Gloucestershire's target was stiffer than might have been expected. Consistent batting kept them on course, but superb bowling by Simmons and the running out of Bainbridge caused Gloucestershire to falter and settle for a draw.

Close of play: First day, Gloucestershire 19-0 (A. W. Stovold 11*, A. J. Wright 8*); Second day, Lancashire 134-3 (N. H. Fairbrother 53*, D. P. Hughes 21*).

Lancashire

G. D. Mendis c Romaines b Alleyne	151	– not out	26
G. Fowler c Athey b Bainbridge	17	– b Lawrence	23
N. J. Speak c Wright b Lloyds	35	– lbw b Lawrence	10
N. H. Fairbrother b Lawrence	54	– c Athey b Lawrence	54
M. Watkinson lbw b Lawrence	0	– c Lloyds b Lawrence	0
*D. P. Hughes c Alleyne b Graveney	22	– c and b Graveney	55
A. N. Hayhurst not out	21	– b Lawrence	5
I. D. Austin not out	9	– st Russell b Lloyds	43
†W. K. Hegg (did not bat)		– not out	27
B 4, l-b 10, w 1, n-b 5	20	B 2, l-b 4, n-b 8	14
1/64 2/148 3/236 4/236 5/294 6/302 (6 wkts dec.)	329	1/51 2/71 3/72 4/144 5/155 6/216 7/224 (7 wkts dec.)	257

J. Simmons and I. Folley did not bat.

Bonus points – Lancashire 4, Gloucestershire 2 (Score at 100 overs: 307-6).

In the second innings G. D. Mendis, when 19, retired hurt at 46 and resumed at 224.

Bowling: *First Innings*—Lawrence 16–5–50–2; Greene 18–3–49–0; Bainbridge 13–2–49–1; Alleyne 13–0–44–1; Lloyds 19–4–66–1; Graveney 26–4–57–1. *Second Innings*—Lawrence 20–4–54–5; Bainbridge 20–4–59–0; Alleyne 5–0–30–0; Lloyds 13–0–48–1; Graveney 18–5–51–1; Athey 1–0–3–0; Romaines 0.1–0–6–0.

Gloucestershire

A. W. Stovold c Hughes b Watkinson	32	– c Speak b Simmons	72
A. J. Wright lbw b Austin	36	– c Hegg b Watkinson	14
P. W. Romaines not out	101	– st Hegg b Folley	46
C. W. J. Athey not out	72	– c Speak b Simmons	58
J. W. Lloyds (did not bat)		– b Simmons	12
P. Bainbridge (did not bat)		– run out	48
M. W. Alleyne (did not bat)		– st Hegg b Simmons	21
†R. C. Russell (did not bat)		– not out	13
V. S. Greene (did not bat)		– b Simmons	2
*D. A. Graveney (did not bat)		– c Watkinson b Folley	0
D. V. Lawrence (did not bat)		– not out	1
B 11, l-b 3, w 1	15	L-b 9	9
1/55 2/99 (2 wkts dec.)	256	1/33 2/128 3/140 4/156 5/243 6/277 7/282 8/285 9/294 (9 wkts)	296

Bonus points – Gloucestershire 3.

Bowling: *First Innings*—Watkinson 16–4–65–1; Hayhurst 14–1–53–0; Austin 12.2–2–45–1; Folley 23–5–44–0; Simmons 14–3–35–0. *Second Innings*—Watkinson 8–1–29–1; Hayhurst 4–0–26–0; Austin 6–2–23–0; Simmons 26–5–81–5; Folley 23–0–128–2.

Umpires: J. C. Balderstone and D. G. L. Evans (3rd day, B. Leadbeater).

At Swansea, June 25, 27, 28. LANCASHIRE beat GLAMORGAN by 72 runs.

At Nuneaton, June 29, 30, July 1. LANCASHIRE beat WARWICKSHIRE by six wickets.

At Northampton, July 2, 4, 5. LANCASHIRE drew with NORTHAMPTONSHIRE.

LANCASHIRE v LEICESTERSHIRE

At Manchester, July 13, 14, 15. Drawn. Lancashire 5 pts, Leicestershire 4 pts. Toss: Lancashire. Another exciting finish saw Lancashire again come within one wicket of winning, Such keeping out the last two balls after Leicestershire had been set to score 251 in 68 overs. Watkinson led a late assault on the bowling as Lancashire scored 144 in the final session of the opening day, and Gower, whose 96 featured thirteen fours, batted delightfully on the second day, when rain restricted play to 56 overs. Mendis became the third player in the country after Hick and Gooch to reach 1,000 runs for the season as Lancashire built on their lead of 131 before declaring. Leicestershire had lost only two wickets by tea but then collapsed against the spin bowling of Folley, who took four wickets in twelve balls, and Simmons. Whitticase led the fight for a draw with 27 runs in 27 overs.

Close of play: First day, Lancashire 304-8 (M. Watkinson 85*, J. Simmons 27*); Second day, Leicestershire 173-6 (P. A. J. DeFreitas 10*, P. Whitticase 4*).

Lancashire

G. D. Mendis c Whitticase b DeFreitas	25	– c sub b Potter	51
G. Fowler b Ferris	75	– c Whitaker b Such	15
T. E. Jesty c Gower b Such	14	– not out	44
N. H. Fairbrother c Whitaker b Such	43	– not out	3
M. Watkinson not out	85		
*D. P. Hughes b Such	9		
A. N. Hayhurst c Whitaker b Willey	4		
†W. K. Hegg c Cobb b Such	0		
P. J. W. Allott c Potter b Willey	6		
J. Simmons not out	27		
B 5, l-b 4, n-b 7	16	B 5, l-b 1	6
1/47 2/83 3/157 4/175 5/206 6/223 7/223 8/250 (8 wkts dec.)	304	1/28 2/105 (2 wkts dec.)	119

I. Folley did not bat.

Bonus points – Lancashire 3, Leicestershire 3 (Score at 100 overs: 254-8).

Bowling: *First Innings*—Ferris 17–3–52–1; Agnew 15–2–53–0; DeFreitas 22–6–67–1; Willey 24–9–42–2; Such 29–4–81–4. *Second Innings*—Ferris 3–2–2–0; Agnew 3–1–5–0; Willey 14–5–26–0; Such 20–0–66–1; Potter 6–2–14–1.

Leicestershire

R. A. Cobb c Hegg b Allott	2	– (7) b Allott	5
N. E. Briers c Hughes b Watkinson	2	– c Allott b Folley	37
P. Willey c Watkinson b Simmons	40	– c Hughes b Simmons	6
*D. I. Gower c Watkinson b Folley	96	– c Fairbrother b Folley	23
J. J. Whitaker c and b Simmons	1	– st Hegg b Folley	0
L. Potter b Folley	4	– (1) c Jesty b Simmons	29
P. A. J. DeFreitas not out	10	– (6) c Hegg b Folley	0
†P. Whitticase not out	4	– lbw b Simmons	27
J. P. Agnew (did not bat)		– lbw b Simmons	2
G. J. F. Ferris (did not bat)		– not out	0
P. M. Such (did not bat)		– not out	0
B 7, l-b 3, n-b 4	14	B 3, l-b 1	4
1/6 2/8 3/114 4/124 5/155 6/160 (6 wkts dec.)	173	1/45 2/55 3/95 4/97 5/97 6/98 7/105 8/124 9/133 (9 wkts)	133

Bonus points – Leicestershire 1, Lancashire 2.

Bowling: *First Innings*—Allott 12–3–32–1; Watkinson 12–3–40–1; Simmons 22–5–66–2; Folley 10–4–25–2. *Second Innings*—Allott 10–4–35–1; Watkinson 3–0–11–0; Simmons 28–12–42–4; Folley 27–11–41–4.

Umpires: J. Birkenshaw and J. H. Hampshire.

At Southend, July 16, 18, 19. LANCASHIRE beat ESSEX by four wickets.

LANCASHIRE v SURREY

At Southport, July 20, 21, 22. Drawn. Lancashire 12 pts, Surrey 7 pts. Toss: Lancashire. An eventful opening day was the prelude to yet another game of high excitement. Atkins deputising for Smith who was injured, narrowly failed to score a century in his firs Championship appearance, having already marked his first-class début with a hundred. A second-wicket partnership of 152 with Stewart was followed by the fall of eight wickets for 6 runs, five of them to Wasim Akram, who with the wickets of Greig, Medlycott and Felthan took the first hat-trick by a Lancashire player for eleven years. Wasim followed this feat b steering Lancashire clear of the follow-on on the second day and conducting the challenge that almost brought victory on the third. Lancashire, set to score 272 in 70 overs, looked to have lost hope until Wasim went in at 129 for five and with four sixes and nine fours led the onslaught which left him on strike with 1 run needed and three balls remaining. His attempt for the boundary that would have given him the season's fastest century in 78 balls produced a boundary-edge catch, and Simmons was unable to hit the last two balls from Greig, both of which were down the leg side. Lancashire did, however, have the consolation of gaining eight points as the batting side in the fourth innings with the scores equal.

Close of play: First day, Lancashire 8-0 (G. D. Mendis 5*, G. Fowler 3*); Second day, Surrey 51-2 (A. J. Stewart 18*, M. A. Lynch 7*).

Surrey

G. S. Clinton b Simmons	15	– c Folley b Wasim	12
P. D. Atkins lbw b Watkinson	99	– c Fowler b Wasim	9
†A. J. Stewart c Folley b Watkinson	73	– run out	45
M. A. Lynch lbw b Wasim	19	– c Hughes b Allott	29
D. M. Ward not out	23	– c Hegg b Watkinson	6
*I. A. Greig lbw b Wasim	0	– c Watkinson b Allott	23
K. T. Medlycott b Wasim	0	– c Fairbrother b Wasim	24
M. A. Feltham b Wasim	0	– not out	0
C. K. Bullen lbw b Watkinson	4		
N. H. Peters run out	6		
M. P. Bicknell b Wasim	1		
B 1, l-b 10, n-b 2	13	B 2, l-b 4, w 1, n-b 3	10
1/34 2/186 3/213 4/221 5/222 6/222 7/222 8/227 9/251	253	1/17 2/38 3/88 4/109 5/109 6/156 7/158 (7 wkts dec.)	158

Bonus points – Surrey 3, Lancashire 4 (Score at 100 overs: 251-9).

Bowling: *First Innings*—Wasim 27.2–6–58–5; Allott 15–4–33–0; Simmons 16–3–45–1; Watkinson 25–8–54–3; Folley 16–5–44–0; Jesty 3–1–8–0. *Second Innings*—Wasim 13–0–58–3; Allott 22.4–8–52–2; Watkinson 10–1–42–1.

Lancashire

G. D. Mendis lbw b Bicknell	9	– lbw b Bicknell	22
G. Fowler c Stewart b Greig	19	– c Stewart b Greig	12
T. E. Jesty c Stewart b Peters	1	– b Bicknell	4
N. H. Fairbrother b Peters	0	– b Peters	64
M. Watkinson c Stewart b Bicknell	19	– lbw b Bicknell	28
*D. P. Hughes lbw b Greig	0	– c Greig b Peters	12
Wasim Akram c Stewart b Bicknell	58	– c Ward b Greig	98
P. J. W. Allott b Greig	11	– run out	17
†W. K. Hegg c Stewart b Greig	8	– (10) run out	0
J. Simmons c Stewart b Feltham	2	– (9) not out	6
I. Folley not out	4		
L-b 5, n-b 4	9	L-b 8	8
1/24 2/28 3/28 4/51 5/51 6/59 7/72 8/102 9/122	140	1/33 2/39 3/47 4/85 5/129 6/204 7/261 8/271 9/271 (9 wkts)	271

Bonus points – Surrey 4.

Bowling: *First Innings*—Bicknell 20.1–7–35–3; Peters 20–7–35–2; Greig 21–10–26–4; Feltham 8–1–39–1. *Second Innings*—Peters 21–6–70–2; Bicknell 16–2–36–3; Greig 19–4–89–2; Feltham 13–2–64–0; Medlycott 1–0–4–0.

Umpires: J. H. Hampshire and D. O. Oslear.

At Leeds, July 30, August 1. LANCASHIRE lost to YORKSHIRE by ten wickets.

LANCASHIRE v MIDDLESEX

At Manchester, August 6, 8, 9. Middlesex won by ten wickets. Middlesex 22 pts, Lancashire 6 pts. Toss: Lancashire. Consistent batting, followed by good bowling from Folley, who reduced Middlesex to 60 for four on a wicket taking spin, put Lancashire in apparent control early on the second day. Yet Middlesex fought back so spiritedly that victory was almost theirs by the end of the day after the extra half-hour had been claimed. Downton, the night-watchman, hit his first century of the season in an innings which lasted almost four and a half hours before he was last out, having shared in partnerships of 81, 72 and 63 with Butcher, Brown and Cowans as Folley lost his rhythm and Simmons tired. Emburey took four wickets and Cowans three before the close of a triumphant day for Middlesex, who secured their first victory in twelve matches the following morning when Cowans took the remaining two wickets.

Close of play: First day, Middlesex 48-3 (P. R. Downton 1*); Second day, Lancashire 98-8 (W. K. Hegg 12*, J. Simmons 1*).

Lancashire

G. D. Mendis b Tufnell	30	– c Downton b Cowans	9
G. Fowler c Downton b Fraser	12	– c Needham b Cowans	2
M. A. Atherton b Emburey	42	– lbw b Fraser	4
N. H. Fairbrother c Downton b Emburey	19	– st Downton b Emburey	15
M. Watkinson b Tufnell	50	– lbw b Cowans	34
*D. P. Hughes c Needham b Tufnell	0	– c Tufnell b Emburey	2
A. N. Hayhurst b Emburey	37	– c Gatting b Emburey	0
†W. K. Hegg c Gatting b Fraser	21	– b Cowans	41
P. J. W. Allott c Needham b Fraser	5	– c Needham b Emburey	14
J. Simmons b Fraser	0	– b Cowans	11
I. Folley not out	3	– not out	3
B 10, l-b 3, n-b 3	16	B 4, l-b 3	7
1/36 2/55 3/89 4/135 5/152 6/167 7/208 8/222 9/222	235	1/10 2/11 3/23 4/41 5/47 6/65 7/67 8/84 9/133	142

Bonus points – Lancashire 2, Middlesex 3 (Score at 100 overs: 220-7).

Bowling: *First Innings*—Fraser 15–4–37–4; Cowans 4–1–16–0; Emburey 41.1–17–70–3; Tufnell 38–13–84–3; Needham 9–4–15–0. *Second Innings*—Fraser 13–1–48–1; Cowans 14.1–2–48–5; Emburey 19–10–26–4; Tufnell 6–2–13–0.

Middlesex

W. N. Slack b Allott	12	– not out	37
J. D. Carr b Folley	19	– not out	35
A. Needham b Folley	15		
†P. R. Downton c Mendis b Allott	120		
*M. W. Gatting c Allott b Folley	8		
R. O. Butcher c Hegg b Watkinson	49		
K. R. Brown c Mendis b Atherton	38		
J. E. Emburey c Watkinson b Simmons	0		
A. R. C. Fraser c Hughes b Atherton	2		
P. C. R. Tufnell c Watkinson b Atherton	2		
N. G. Cowans not out	27		
B 5, l-b 6, n-b 2	13	N-b 1	1
1/23 2/43 3/48 4/60 5/141 6/213 7/215 8/232 9/242	305	(no wkt)	73

Bonus points – Middlesex 3, Lancashire 4 (Score at 100 overs: 293-9).

Bowling: *First Innings*—Allott 16.2–1–43–2; Watkinson 13–4–31–1; Simmons 37–6–120–1; Folley 20–3–68–3; Atherton 17–5–32–3. *Second Innings*—Allott 3–1–5–0; Watkinson 3–0–8–0; Atherton 10–2–36–0; Simmons 10–4–24–0.

Umpires: B. Leadbeater and D. R. Shepherd.

At Hove, August 13, 15, 16. LANCASHIRE beat SUSSEX by eight wickets.

LANCASHIRE v NOTTINGHAMSHIRE

At Lytham, August 17, 18, 19. Nottinghamshire won by 151 runs. Nottinghamshire 19 pts, Lancashire 4 pts. Toss: Nottinghamshire. A deluge that washed out play on the second day led to a double forfeiture of innings on the third, which gave Lancashire a victory target of 273 in 84 overs. Stephenson, exploiting the difficult wicket, made the target academic by removing the first five batsmen to take his haul for the season to 99 and leave Lancashire 55 for five. Cooper took four of the last five wickets to put Nottinghamshire in joint fifth place in the Championship with Lancashire. Nottinghamshire had done well to reach 272 on the opening day, helped mainly by an eighth-wicket partnership of 73 between Scott and Evans and several dropped catches by Lancashire.

Close of play: First day, Nottinghamshire 272; Second day, No play.

Nottinghamshire

B. C. Broad c Allott b Austin	17	†C. W. Scott lbw b Simmons	40
*R. T. Robinson c and b Allott	19	E. E. Hemmings c Hegg b Allott	9
P. Johnson c Fowler b Simmons	38	K. E. Cooper not out	13
D. J. R. Martindale c Allott b Austin	2		
D. W. Randall c Allott b Folley	28	L-b 6	6
J. D. Birch c Hughes b Watkinson	48		—
F. D. Stephenson c Hegg b Folley	17	1/29 2/49 3/51 4/79 5/134	272
K. P. Evans c Hegg b Allott	35	6/170 7/170 8/243 9/251	

Bonus points – Nottinghamshire 3, Lancashire 4 (Score at 100 overs: 264-9).

Bowling: Allott 27.5–7–62–3; Watkinson 18–3–53–1; Austin 15–5–42–2; Simmons 24–4–56–2; Folley 17–3–53–2.

Nottinghamshire forfeited their second innings.

Lancashire

Lancashire forfeited their first innings.

G. D. Mendis c Johnson b Stephenson	3	P. J. W. Allott b Cooper	3
G. Fowler c Scott b Stephenson	17	J. Simmons c Birch b Cooper	5
M. A. Atherton c Evans b Stephenson	0	I. Folley not out	1
N. H. Fairbrother c Evans b Cooper	31		
M. Watkinson c Johnson b Stephenson	4	L-b 6, n-b 7	13
*D. P. Hughes c Scott b Stephenson	3		—
I. D. Austin c Martindale b Hemmings	39	1/8 2/8 3/42 4/49 5/55	121
†W. K. Hegg c Scott b Cooper	2	6/107 7/111 8/111 9/119	

Bowling: Stephenson 17–8–25–5; Cooper 19–4–42–4; Hemmings 13–7–31–1; Evans 7–2–17–0.

Umpires: J. Birkenshaw and J. W. Holder.

LANCASHIRE v DERBYSHIRE

At Manchester, August 20, 22, 23. Drawn. Lancashire 2 pts, Derbyshire 5 pts. Toss: Lancashire. No play was possible on Saturday, although the teams did manage to take the field before the rain drove them off. After Barnett broke his nose during the Refuge Assurance League match on the Sunday, Lancashire agreed to his being replaced by Griffith for the remaining two days of the Championship match. They paid for their generosity. Griffith, twenty years old and making his Championship début, took four wickets in the space of four overs on a pitch of easy pace and on which Wright and Bowler replied with an opening stand of 127. Derbyshire declared 40 behind on the final morning, whereupon Atherton and

Fairbrother, assisted in the later stages by some helpful bowling, shared in an unbroken stand of 124 to leave Derbyshire with 64 overs in which to score 261 to win. An opening spell of five for 22 from Watkinson had Derbyshire reeling at 43 for six, but an unselfish, grafting innings of 201 minutes by Morris enabled them to hang on for a draw.

Close of play: First day, No play; Second day, Derbyshire 157-3 (P. D. Bowler 51*, S. C. Goldsmith 4*).

Lancashire

G. D. Mendis b Warner	14		
G. Fowler c Roberts b Base	38	– (1) c Griffith b Bowler	40
M. A. Atherton c Maher b Warner	5	– (2) not out	115
N. H. Fairbrother c Warner b Base	15	– (3) not out	50
M. Watkinson b Griffith	8		
I. D. Austin lbw b Sharma	64		
*D. P. Hughes b Griffith	2		
†W. K. Hegg lbw b Griffith	7		
P. J. W. Allott c Roberts b Griffith	0		
J. Simmons lbw b Malcolm	5		
I. Folley not out	17		
B 1, l-b 4, w 3, n-b 14	22	B 2, l-b 2, w 2, n-b 9	15
1/50 2/58 3/79 4/83 5/97 6/102 7/114 8/114 9/141	197	1/96 (1 wkt dec.)	220

Bonus points – Lancashire 1, Derbyshire 4.

Bowling: *First Innings*—Malcolm 20–4–62–1; Warner 23–5–40–2; Base 13–2–43–2; Griffith 9–1–47–4; Sharma 0.1–0–0–1. *Second Innings*—Malcolm 3–0–17–0; Warner 4–0–20–0; Base 4–0–26–0; Griffith 5–0–24–0; Sharma 10–2–30–0; Bowler 8–1–56–1; Morris 5.1–0–19–0; Goldsmith 5–1–24–0.

Derbyshire

P. D. Bowler not out	51	– c Fairbrother b Watkinson	1
*J. G. Wright c Atherton b Folley	82	– c Fowler b Watkinson	10
A. E. Warner b Simmons	17	– (8) c and b Simmons	20
D. E. Malcolm b Simmons	0		
S. C. Goldsmith not out	4	– b Simmons	4
†B. J. M. Maher (did not bat)		– (3) c Hughes b Watkinson	0
J. E. Morris (did not bat)		– (4) not out	86
B. Roberts (did not bat)		– (6) c Hegg b Watkinson	1
R. Sharma (did not bat)		– (7) c Allott b Watkinson	0
F. A. Griffith (did not bat)		– (9) c Folley b Watkinson	15
S. J. Base (did not bat)		– (10) not out	0
N-b 3	3	N-b 5	5
1/127 2/149 3/149 (3 wkts dec.)	157	1/1 2/1 3/20 4/40 5/43 6/43 7/99 8/133 (8 wkts)	142

Bonus points – Derbyshire 1, Lancashire 1.

Bowling: *First Innings*—Allott 7–0–24–0; Watkinson 12–2–50–0; Austin 4–1–21–0; Simmons 10–1–35–2; Folley 8–0–27–1. *Second Innings*—Allott 7–2–19–0; Watkinson 17–6–50–6; Simmons 21–7–39–2; Folley 9–4–17–0; Atherton 9.5–4–17–0.

Umpires: B. J. Meyer and A. G. T. Whitehead.

At The Oval, August 25, 26, 27. LANCASHIRE lost to SURREY by an innings and 1 run.

LANCASHIRE v YORKSHIRE

At Manchester, August 30, 31, September 1, 2. Drawn. Lancashire 6 pts, Yorkshire 6 pts. Toss: Yorkshire. Play started at 10.30 a.m. each day to accommodate television schedules. It was believed to be the earliest start ever for a Championship match, but that was no excuse for Yorkshire's dismal start in which they lost six wickets, four of them to Allott, for 37 runs. A maiden century from Hartley, who batted 248 minutes and hit eleven fours and a six, plus staunch support from Fletcher, who shared in a last-wicket stand of 91, enabled Yorkshire to reach 224. Fifteen wickets fell to spinners on the second day, which ended with Yorkshire precariously placed, 125 ahead with seven wickets down. Five of them had fallen to the off-spinner, Fitton, who was standing in for the injured Simmons and playing in his second Championship match. Only 85 minutes' play was possible on the third day, and the prospect of an interesting finish was washed out, along with the fourth day, by rain.

Close of play: First day, Lancashire 38-2 (I. Folley 0*, M. A. Atherton 0*); Second day, Yorkshire 119-7 (P. J. Hartley 35*, P. A. Booth 1*); Third day, Yorkshire 171-8 (P. A. Booth 33*, C. Shaw 16*).

Yorkshire

	First innings		Second innings	
M. D. Moxon b Allott	2	–	c Fowler b Fitton	24
A. A. Metcalfe c Hughes b Watkinson	11	–	c and b Folley	18
D. Byas lbw b Allott	0	–	b Fitton	3
P. E. Robinson c Mendis b Allott	9	–	c Hegg b Fitton	4
J. D. Love b Allott	8	–	c Mendis b Fitton	31
†R. J. Blakey c Hughes b Watkinson	3	–	lbw b Fitton	0
*P. Carrick c Atherton b Allott	36	–	c Hughes b Folley	0
P. J. Hartley not out	127	–	b Fitton	38
P. A. Booth lbw b Folley	4	–	not out	33
C. Shaw b Folley	2	–	not out	16
S. D. Fletcher c Fowler b Fitton	17			
L-b 4, n-b 1	5		L-b 4	4
1/6 2/6 3/20 4/22 5/29 6/37 7/100 8/113 9/133	224		1/34 2/43 3/52 4/55 5/55 6/56 7/118 8/135 (8 wkts)	171

Bonus points – Yorkshire 2, Lancashire 4.

Bowling: *First Innings*—Allott 29–8–70–5; Watkinson 20–6–60–2; Folley 19–6–52–2; Hayhurst 2–1–2–0; Fitton 11–4–18–1; Atherton 5–0–18–0. *Second Innings*—Allott 8–3–13–0; Watkinson 3–2–1–0; Folley 20–6–58–2; Fitton 31–9–59–6; Atherton 17–2–36–0.

Lancashire

G. D. Mendis c Moxon b Carrick	16
G. Fowler b Booth	16
I. Folley c Love b Carrick	10
M. A. Atherton c Blakey b Carrick	34
N. H. Fairbrother c Hartley b Carrick	21
A. N. Hayhurst c Robinson b Booth	57
M. Watkinson c Hartley b Booth	0
*D. P. Hughes lbw b Booth	0
†W. K. Hegg c Moxon b Carrick	8
J. D. Fitton c Moxon b Booth	36
P. J. W. Allott not out	6
B 2, l-b 7, w 1, n-b 4	14
1/32 2/37 3/66 4/96 5/111 6/120 7/126 8/143 9/199	218

Bonus points – Lancashire 2, Yorkshire 4.

Bowling: Hartley 2–0–15–0; Fletcher 5–1–14–0; Shaw 7–1–20–0; Carrick 42–17–62–5; Booth 37.4–9–98–5.

Umpires: R. Julian and M. J. Kitchen.

At Derby, September 14, 15, 16, 17. LANCASHIRE drew with DERBYSHIRE.

LEICESTERSHIRE

Chairman: C. H. Palmer
Chairman, Cricket Committee: J. J. Palmer
Chief Executive: F. M. Turner
County Cricket Ground, Grace Road,
Leicester LE2 8AD
(Telephone: 0533-831880/832128)
Captain: D. I. Gower
Coach: K. Higgs

Leicestershire's season provided an excellent example of how deceptive appearances can be in the modern county game. Their squad possessed a seam-bowling attack which was one of the strongest in the country, even allowing for the absence of the fastest bowler, Winston Benjamin, with the West Indian touring side. Their batting line-up looked similarly impressive, with players of contrasting talents suited to all the permutations that competitive cricket requires. Moreover, having finished third in the Britannic Assurance Championship and reached the semi-finals of the NatWest Bank Trophy in 1987, the players had become attuned to the pressures of challenge. On paper, the 1988 season suggested salutations, success and silverware.

After Leicestershire's first two home matches, against Northamptonshire and Kent, the form book seemed to be right. Both games, four-day fixtures, were won convincingly with a day and a half to spare. So impressive was the nature of those victories that it was difficult not to believe that here were the champions-elect, playing to the full extent of their considerable potential. However, Leicestershire, like their neighbours Nottinghamshire in recent seasons, were often equipped with pitches favourable to their attack. And while no concrete complaints were lodged by visiting teams, it was not unusual for a Grace Road track to resemble in some way the verdant outfield. As it is often pointed out such things are the same for both sides; and in their third successive Championship match at Grace Road, Leicestershire were beaten by eight wickets by Middlesex.

There followed some indifferent performances, and as May became June, Leicestershire slipped from third to tenth and the prospect of a fruitless season began to take shape. Consecutive victories over Sussex a home and Gloucestershire away arrested the slide and lifted them back t third place in the table, yet the impression remained that in a run-chas Leicestershire were not going to shape up. This happened on thre occasions and left the county needing good results in their last three four day matches. Instead, the first two were ruined by the weather, Esse beat them at Chelmsford, and eighth was the final placing.

The gloomy finale was lightened somewhat by the glorious batting c David Gower, who had resumed the captaincy following the resignatio of Peter Willey in the winter. As he had the previous season, Gowe saved his best until the last. His innings of 172 at Chelmsford, followin a courageous 146 against Nottinghamshire, took him past 1,000 runs i the Championship and to the top of the Leicestershire averages. In bot matches he opened the innings and, without any diminution of his innate flair, he batted with a resolve that had not always been apparent from the boundary.

Willey, for the first time since joining Leicestershire in 1984, failed to reach four figures and will be hoping to make amends in 1989. Nigel Briers, who led the side well in Gower's absence, compiled his highest aggregate in eighteen years with the county, as did Laurie Potter batting usually at No. 6. But James Whitaker, although scoring his 1,000 runs and hitting three centuries, failed to build on a promising start. None the less, if the batting largely left something to be desired, it is ironic, given the county's bowling strength, that only three counties gained more batting bonus points, whereas only four counties gained fewer bowling points.

What the attack lacked was balance, as is reflected in the fact that the seamers accounted for 267 of the 299 Championship wickets taken by the bowlers. Moreover, the 32 that fell to the spinners cost almost 43 runs each. Once again Jon Agnew, with 93 first-class wickets, was the pick of the attack; and again it remained a mystery that he was ignored by the national selectors. He played in every Championship match and only Stephenson, Cooper and Marks bowled more overs. His club was no doubt grateful for his constant availability, and Agnew is of a suitably philosophical disposition not to let the selectors' oversight affect his dedication. Behind the stumps, Phil Whitticase, with 69 catches and four stumpings, recorded the highest number of dismissals by a Leicestershire wicket-keeper for 21 years.

If the county's performance in the Championship was disappointing, their displays in the limited-overs competitions were lamentable. They finished next to last in the Refuge Assurance League, they failed to qualify for the knockout stages of the Benson and Hedges Cup for the third year running since winning the final, and in the NatWest Trophy they were eliminated by Gloucestershire in the second round. As these competitions provide a considerable source of revenue, and so are vital to any sort of financial stability, much improvement is needed in this area.

To that end, the departure of Phillip DeFreitas may seem a bitter blow. For the second year he was dropped from the first team for lack of effort, and it was no surprise when he asked to leave. He subsequently joined Lancashire after being released with one year of his contract still to run. To replace him, the county re-signed Gordon Parsons from Warwickshire. While he is not in the DeFreitas class as an all-round performer, his presence may instil a more harmonious feeling in the dressing-room.

Otherwise, the make-up of the side should remain similar. No doubt the expectations that rest on the playing staff's shoulders will likewise remain. It is to be hoped that the positive prognostications that come from the side's strength on paper will this time manifest themselves on the field into something tangible. – James Hunt.

LEICESTERSHIRE 1988

[*Bill Smith*

Back row: M. Bailey, M. I. Gidley, W. G. Lovell, L. Tennant, R. A. Cobb, P. Whitticase. *Middle row:* C. Mortimer (*physiotherapist*), G. R. Blackburn (*scorer*), T. J. Boon, P. M. Such, L. Potter, G. J. F. Ferris, C. C. Lewis, R. Edmunds, J. D. R. Benson, P. N. Hepworth, K. Higgs (*coach*). Front row: P. A. J. DeFreitas, J. J. Whitaker, N. E. Briers, C. H. Palmer (*president*), D. I. Gower (*captain*), F. M. Turner (*chief executive*),

LEICESTERSHIRE RESULTS

All first-class matches – Played 24: Won 7, Lost 3, Drawn 14.

County Championship matches – Played 22: Won 6, Lost 3, Drawn 13.

Bonus points – Batting 56, Bowling 63.

Competition placings – Britannic Assurance County Championship, 8th; NatWest Bank Trophy, 2nd round; Benson and Hedges Cup, 3rd in Group A; Refuge Assurance League, 14th equal.

BRITANNIC ASSURANCE CHAMPIONSHIP AVERAGES

BATTING

	Birthplace	*M*	*I*	*NO*	*R*	*HI*	*Avge*
‡D. I. Gower	*Tunbridge Wells*	17	29	3	1,080	172	41.53
‡J. J. Whitaker	*Skipton*	21	36	5	1,160	145	37.41
‡N. E. Briers	*Leicester*	22	38	2	1,231	125*	34.19
‡L. Potter	*Bexleyheath*	21	31	4	796	107	29.48
‡P. A. J. DeFreitas	*Scotts Head, Dominica*	12	17	1	458	113	28.62
‡P. Willey	*Sedgefield*	22	37	1	946	130	26.27
‡T. J. Boon	*Doncaster*	13	20	1	459	131	24.15
‡R. A. Cobb	*Leicester*	11	20	2	432	65	24.00
P. M. Hepworth	*Ackworth*	4	6	0	132	51	22.00
‡P. Whitticase	*Solihull*	21	30	9	453	71	21.57
C. C. Lewis	*Georgetown, Guyana*	14	20	3	337	40	19.82
‡J. P. Agnew	*Macclesfield*	22	28	8	263	38	13.15
‡L. B. Taylor	*Earl Shilton*	15	15	6	111	60	12.33
‡G. J. F. Ferris	*Urlings Village, Antigua*	18	20	8	139	36*	11.58
P. M. Such	*Helensburgh*	6	5	2	7	6	2.33

Also batted: (1 match each): L. Tennant (*Walsall*) 3, 0*; J. D. R. Benson (*Dublin, Ireland*) . M. A. Garnham (*Johannesburg, SA*) did not bat.

* *Signifies not out.* ‡ *Denotes county cap.* § *Not qualified for England.*

he following played a total of twelve three-figure innings for Leicestershire in County hampionship matches – J. J. Whitaker 3, N. E. Briers 2, D. I. Gower 2, P. Willey 2, T. J. ɔon 1, P. A. J. DeFreitas 1, L. Potter 1.

BOWLING

	O	*M*	*R*	*W*	*BB*	*5W/i*	*Avge*
A. J. DeFreitas	412.3	91	1,188	54	5-38	5	22.00
. J. F. Ferris	452.1	82	1,380	62	5-47	2	22.25
P. Agnew	718.5	156	2,139	88	7-61	8	24.30
B. Taylor	283.3	58	850	31	6-49	1	27.41
C. Lewis	342.2	68	1,102	31	5-73	1	35.54
Willey	333	104	775	18	4-153	0	43.05

Also bowled: L. Potter 93.1–25–269–6; P. M. Such 115–20–331–8; L. Tennant 7–2–19–1.

icket-keepers: P. Whitticase 60 ct, 4 st; M. A. Garnham 2 ct.

ading Fielders: N. E. Briers 14, D. I. Gower 14.

At Oxford, April 16, 18, 19. LEICESTERSHIRE beat OXFORD UNIVERSITY by an innings and 153 runs.

At Derby, April 21, 22, 23, 25. LEICESTERSHIRE drew with DERBYSHIRE.

LEICESTERSHIRE v NORTHAMPTONSHIRE

At Leicester, April 28, 29, 30. Leicestershire won by an innings and 51 runs. Leicestershire 23 pts, Northamptonshire 4 pts. Toss: Leicestershire. With conducive conditions for their seam attack and a favourable toss, Leicestershire dominated play from the start and completed their innings victory with five sessions of play remaining. The reason for such an emphatic win on a slow, green and awkward pitch was plain to see as Northamptonshire's top-order batsmen, with at times unnecessarily extravagant strokeplay, perished against bowlers keeping the ball up. Agnew, carrying on from the previous season, finished off the visitors' first innings with a spell of five for 10 in 33 balls and completed the match with career-best figures of eleven for 122. He shared the second-innings wickets with DeFreitas, who also enjoyed himself with the bat, hitting a breezy 66 which built on solid half-centuries from Briers and Willey as Leicestershire amassed a winning 327.

Close of play: First day, Leicestershire 70-1 (N. E. Briers 27*, P. Willey 7*); Second day, Northamptonshire 17-1 (W. Larkins 9*, R. J. Bailey 1*).

Northamptonshire

*G. Cook c Whitticase b DeFreitas	8	– c Whitticase b DeFreitas	7
W. Larkins c Whitticase b Lewis	32	– c Gower b DeFreitas	9
R. J. Bailey c Gower b Lewis	27	– c Lewis b Agnew	1
A. J. Lamb b Agnew	54	– b Agnew	47
R. G. Williams c Whitticase b Agnew	6	– lbw b DeFreitas	9
N. A. Stanley lbw b Lewis	22	– c Whitticase b DeFreitas	4
†D. Ripley lbw b Agnew	1	– lbw b Agnew	0
N. G. B. Cook c Gower b Agnew	0	– c Whitticase b Agnew	10
W. W. Davis not out	14	– b Agnew	4
S. J. Brown c Whitticase b Agnew	0	– c Whitticase b DeFreitas	5
M. A. Robinson lbw b Agnew	1	– not out	0
L-b 9, w 2	11	L-b 4	4
1/8 2/66 3/95 4/110 5/158 6/160 7/160 8/163 9/168	176	1/8 2/17 3/17 4/36 5/54 6/59 7/79 8/83 9/94	10

Bonus points – Northamptonshire 1, Leicestershire 4.

Bowling: *First Innings*—DeFreitas 12–3–22–1; Agnew 20.3–3–66–6; Lewis 22–5–75–3; Taylor 3–1–4–0. *Second Innings*—DeFreitas 16–5–40–5; Agnew 15.1–2–56–5.

Leicestershire

T. J. Boon c and b Davis	22
N. E. Briers c Bailey b Robinson	63
P. Willey c G. Cook b Davis	56
*D. I. Gower c N. G. B. Cook b Brown	7
L. Potter c Ripley b Davis	2
J. D. R. Benson c G. Cook b Davis	3
P. A. J. DeFreitas c Stanley b Robinson	66
C. C. Lewis c Bailey b N. G. B. Cook	8
†P. Whitticase not out	1
J. P. Agnew c Williams b Brown	3
L. B. Taylor c Brown b N. G. B. Cook	
L-b 14, n-b 27	4
1/48 2/124 3/139 4/149 5/158 6/202 7/247 8/271 9/312	32

Bonus points – Leicestershire 3, Northamptonshire 3 (Score at 100 overs: 286-8).

Bowling: Davis 36–5–115–4; Brown 33–5–107–2; Robinson 27–5–82–2; N. G. B. Cook 16.2–9–9–2.

Umpires: J. Birkenshaw and B. J. Meyer.

LEICESTERSHIRE v KENT

At Leicester, May 5, 6, 7. Leicestershire won by an innings and 47 runs. Leicestershire 23 pts, Kent 3 pts. Toss: Leicestershire. There was a feeling of *déjà vu* about Leicestershire's second four-day Championship match at Grace Road, with the visiting side being beaten by an innings with a day to spare. As in the previous match, it was meticulous seam bowling which laid the foundations; Kent were put in and bowled out for 121 in 2 hours 40 minutes. Again Agnew proved the merit of bowling to a full length, taking six wickets after coming on as second change. Apart from Taylor, who carried his bat for the second time in his career, the Kent batsmen revealed an inability to deal with movement off the seam and at one stage they were 39 for five. In contrast, a dogged 131 in five and a half hours by Boon, whose first hundred for two years contained thirteen fours, provided an ideal platform for Leicestershire. When Kent batted a second time, DeFreitas and Agnew again picked up the lion's share of the wickets.

Close of play: First day, Leicestershire 12-0 (T. J. Boon 1*, N. E. Briers 10*); Second day, Kent 17-3 (R. P. Davis 6*).

Kent

M. R. Benson b Ferris	5	– c Willey b Ferris	1
N. R. Taylor not out	67	– c Potter b Agnew	2
S. G. Hinks b Ferris	1	– lbw b Agnew	5
C. J. Tavaré c Potter b Lewis	4	– (5) c Lewis b DeFreitas	13
*C. S. Cowdrey c Gower b Lewis	0	– (6) c Whitticase b Agnew	16
G. R. Cowdrey lbw b Agnew	0	– absent injured	
†S. A. Marsh c Whitaker b Agnew	15	– lbw b DeFreitas	26
R. M. Ellison c Boon b Agnew	6	– c Potter b DeFreitas	27
C. Penn c and b Agnew	2	– not out	19
R. P. Davis lbw b Agnew	2	– (4) c Boon b DeFreitas	10
H. L. Alleyne b Agnew	7	– (10) b Lewis	0
B 1, l-b 1, w 6, n-b 4	12	L-b 3, w 1, n-b 5	9
1/14 2/23 3/38 4/38 5/39 6/82 7/96 8/103 9/111	121	1/2 2/10 3/17 4/29 5/47 6/65 7/85 8/118 9/128	128

Bonus points – Leicestershire 4.

Bowling: *First Innings*—DeFreitas 8–2–14–0; Ferris 10–1–31–2; Lewis 10–2–37–2; Agnew 3.2–1–37–6. *Second Innings*—Ferris 5–1–4–1; Agnew 18–4–45–3; DeFreitas 18–4–52–4; Lewis 4.2–0–24–1.

Leicestershire

T. J. Boon c Davis b Alleyne	131
N. E. Briers c Marsh b Alleyne	21
P. Willey lbw b Alleyne	4
D. I. Gower c Marsh b Ellison	1
J. J. Whitaker lbw b C. S. Cowdrey	7
L. Potter lbw b Ellison	9
P. A. J. DeFreitas c C. S. Cowdrey b Alleyne	60
C. C. Lewis lbw b Ellison	40
†P. Whitticase c Marsh b Ellison	6
J. P. Agnew c Marsh b Alleyne	2
G. J. F. Ferris not out	0
L-b 7, w 4, n-b 4	15
1/29 2/41 3/42 4/51 5/96 6/192 7/265 8/292 9/296	296

Bonus points – Leicestershire 3, Kent 3 (Score at 100 overs: 292-7).

Bowling: Alleyne 18.3–5–54–5; Ellison 24–7–90–4; C. S. Cowdrey 23–7–56–1; Penn –7–66–0; Davis 14–4–23–0.

Umpires: J. W. Holder and D. S. Thompsett.

LEICESTERSHIRE v MIDDLESEX

At Leicester, May 18, 19, 20. Middlesex won by eight wickets. Middlesex 24 pts, Leicestershire 4 pts. Toss: Middlesex. On an easy-paced wicket which had odd moments of disconcerting bounce, Leicestershire were undone by the very formula which had served them so well in their first two home matches. Losing the toss did not help their cause, but neither did their batsmen, only four of whom managed double figures in the first innings as the Middlesex seamers bowled consistently and aggressively straight. Leicestershire lost their last six wickets for just 10 runs in five overs, and their feeble showing was put into perspective by Carr. His century came off 114 balls and included fourteen fours and 6 runs courtesy of an overthrow. Middlesex's total was a commendable effort against Leicestershire's strong bowling attack, especially as they were without three players on England duty and Slack, who had fainted at the wicket and been rushed to hospital for tests. Leicestershire also lost a player when Whitticase, their wicket-keeper, was struck in the face by a rising delivery from Lewis, who took over the gloves himself after a sojourn by Whitaker. Batting again, Leicestershire looked as if they might be beaten inside two days, but Gower, with a flourishing 74, arrested the slide. He could not, however, prevent defeat.

Close of play: First day, Middlesex 212-1 (J. D. Carr 136*, S. P. Hughes 0*); Second day, Leicestershire 201-4 (J. J. Whitaker 45*, L. Potter 18*).

Leicestershire

R. A. Cobb c Brown b Cowans	31	– c Olley b Williams	14
N. E. Briers b Williams	20	– b Williams	35
*D. I. Gower b Williams	6	– c Olley b Williams	74
P. Willey b Cowans	27	– c Carr b Cowans	0
J. J. Whitaker b Fraser	13	– b Hughes	55
L. Potter c Carr b Williams	2	– not out	39
C. C. Lewis c Olley b Williams	1	– b Williams	5
†P. Whitticase lbw b Fraser	0	– absent injured	
J. P. Agnew not out	3	– (8) b Hughes	1
G. J. F. Ferris c Olley b Fraser	0	– (9) b Cowans	12
L. B. Taylor c Brown b Williams	4	– (10) c Brown b Cowans	8
B 1, n-b 6	7	B 1, l-b 10, n-b 11	22
1/38 2/46 3/83 4/89 5/104 6/105 7/106 8/108 9/109	114	1/51 2/68 3/76 4/157 5/218 6/223 7/227 8/245 9/265	265

Bonus points – Middlesex 4.

Bowling: *First Innings*—Cowans 16–6–22–2; Williams 13.5–2–46–5; Fraser 12–2–16–3 Hughes 10–3–28–0; Sykes 1–0–1–0. *Second Innings*—Cowans 21.3–2–75–3; Hughes 18–4–51–2; Fraser 26–10–55–0; Williams 20–5–60–4; Sykes 1–0–13–0.

Middlesex

W. N. Slack retired ill	4		
J. D. Carr c Willey b Ferris	144	– (1) not out	3[illegible]
K. R. Brown lbw b Agnew	58	– b Taylor	[illegible]
S. P. Hughes b Agnew	19		
*R. O. Butcher b Lewis	5		
M. A. Roseberry lbw b Agnew	24	– (4) not out	[illegible]
J. F. Sykes c Lewis b Taylor	1	– (2) c Willey b Ferris	[illegible]
N. F. Williams lbw b Agnew	1		
A. R. C. Fraser b Agnew	2		
†M. W. C. Olley b Agnew	16		
N. G. Cowans not out	17		
B 8, l-b 8, n-b 22	38	B 1, l-b 1, n-b 3	[illegible]
1/212 2/233 3/245 4/281 5/288 6/292 7/293 8/298 9/329	329	1/16 2/17	(2 wkts) 5[illegible]

Bonus points – Middlesex 4, Leicestershire 4.

In the first innings W. N. Slack retired ill at 12.

Bowling: *First Innings*—Ferris 23–3–90–1; Agnew 24–6–67–6; Lewis 17–1–72–1; Taylor 18–3–58–1; Willey 10–1–26–0. *Second Innings*—Ferris 7–0–22–1; Agnew 2–0–2–0; Taylor 6.3–1–20–1; Potter 2–0–6–0.

Umpires: A. A. Jones and R. A. White.

LEICESTERSHIRE v WORCESTERSHIRE

At Leicester, May 21, 23, 24. Drawn. Leicestershire 5 pts, Worcestershire 5 pts. Toss: Leicestershire. Solid innings from Neale and Curtis thwarted the Leicestershire seam bowlers, who bowled too short a length on a green pitch offering movement. Gower's response, in an effort to contrive a victory, was to declare while still in arrears, and in coming to this decision he was helped by two factors. The first was some spirited batting by Whitaker, who reached his second century of the season in 159 minutes, having hit ten fours; the second was Hick's ineligibility to bat for at least five overs because he had been off the field with a thigh injury. The portents for Leicestershire were encouraging when Worcestershire were 32 for four at the end of the second day. But Curtis, this time with Illingworth, again batted with fortitude and common sense. When Leicestershire were eventually asked to score 234 runs after tea, the tables were almost embarrassingly turned.

Close of play: First day, Worcestershire 286-7 (P. J. Newport 2*, R. K. Illingworth 6*); Second day, Worcestershire 32-4 (T. S. Curtis 7*, R. K. Illingworth 3*).

Worcestershire

	First innings		Second innings	
T. S. Curtis lbw b Taylor	57	– c Gower b Potter	78
G. J. Lord c Potter b Ferris	43	– c Garnham b Agnew	1
G. A. Hick b Ferris	6	– (7) b Lewis	7
S. J. O'Shaughnessy c Potter b Taylor	5	– (3) b Agnew	5
*P. A. Neale c Briers b Taylor	72	– (4) c Willey b Ferris	2
D. A. Leatherdale c Garnham b Willey	27	– (5) b Potter	11
†S. J. Rhodes b Lewis	20	– (8) not out	31
P. J. Newport c Briers b Ferris	6	– (9) not out	6
R. K. Illingworth c Briers b Ferris	6	– (6) lbw b Lewis	60
R. M. Ellcock b Ferris	0		
A. P. Pridgeon not out	1		
B 5, l-b 13, w 8, n-b 22	48	B 2, l-b 14, n-b 5	21
1/103 2/116 3/129 4/141 5/192 6/269 7/279 8/286 9/286	291	1/4 2/10 3/14 4/29 5/126 6/142 7/210	(7 wkts dec.) 222

Bonus points – Worcestershire 3, Leicestershire 2 (Score at 100 overs: 259-5).

Bowling: *First Innings*—Ferris 21.2–6–47–5; Agnew 30–10–73–0; Lewis 23–3–65–1; Taylor 23–6–53–3; Willey 15–5–35–1. *Second Innings*—Ferris 18–4–36–1; Agnew 21–5–36–2; Potter 16–3–32–2; Willey 13–4–25–0; Lewis 23–3–60–2; Taylor 5–1–17–0.

Leicestershire

	First innings		Second innings	
R. A. Cobb c Pridgeon b O'Shaughnessy	22	– (7) not out	6
N. E. Briers lbw b Newport	23	– (2) c Illingworth b Pridgeon	8
*D. I. Gower c O'Shaughnessy b Newport	46	– b Illingworth	12
P. Willey c Curtis b O'Shaughnessy	23	– (5) c O'Shaughnessy b Newport	14
J. J. Whitaker not out	100	– (4) b Newport	24
L. Potter c Rhodes b Ellcock	15	– (1) run out	6
C. C. Lewis not out	35	– (6) not out	29
B 4, l-b 7, n-b 5	16		
1/50 2/101 3/103 4/164 5/223	(5 wkts dec.) 280	1/12 2/15 3/46 4/54 5/71	(5 wkts) 99

†M. A. Garnham, J. P. Agnew, G. J. F. Ferris and L. B. Taylor did not bat.

Bonus points – Leicestershire 3, Worcestershire 2.

Bowling: *First Innings*—Ellcock 17–2–72–1; Pridgeon 23–6–60–0; Newport 15–4–49–2; O'Shaughnessy 12–1–55–2; Illingworth 12–1–33–0. *Second Innings*—Pridgeon 7–0–19–1; Ellcock 6–1–19–0; Newport 10–2–39–2; Illingworth 9–3–22–1.

Umpires: A. A. Jones and R. A. White.

At Northampton, May 28, 30, 31. LEICESTERSHIRE drew with NORTHAMPTONSHIRE.

At The Oval, June 11, 13, 14. LEICESTERSHIRE drew with SURREY.

LEICESTERSHIRE v GLAMORGAN

At Leicester, June 15, 16, 17. Drawn. Leicestershire 8 pts, Glamorgan 5 pts. Toss: Glamorgan. With the pitch less responsive than expected on the first day, Leicestershire managed maximum batting points. Potter, Whitaker and Willey, who hit eight fours in a 54-ball innings of 42, made the most of the Glamorgan bowling. Such were the vagaries of the weather, though, that on the second day conditions worsened, with the result that the Leicestershire seam bowlers found considerable help in the pitch. At 66 for four, Glamorgan looked to be in some difficulty, but Hopkins, batting bravely despite suffering several blows to the body, occupied the crease for four and a half hours. Leicestershire's lead was kept to 67, and an indifferent second innings, during which Derrick took a career-best six for 54, left them a minimum of 44 overs in which to bowl Glamorgan out a second time. The visitors, perhaps not surprisingly, showed little interest in a target of 232.

Close of play: First day, Glamorgan 12-1 (J. A. Hopkins 4*, C. P. Metson 0*); Second day, Leicestershire 14-0 (R. A. Cobb 2*, N. E. Briers 12*).

Leicestershire

R. A. Cobb c Hopkins b Thomas	15	– c Maynard b Thomas	8
*N. E. Briers c Cottey b Thomas	7	– c Maynard b Barwick	59
P. Willey c Maynard b Barwick	42	– c Maynard b Barwick	0
J. J. Whitaker b Derrick	68	– c Butcher b Derrick	43
L. Potter c and b Ontong	96	– c Butcher b Barwick	23
P. N. Hepworth b Ontong	32	– (8) b Derrick	1
C. C. Lewis not out	26	– (6) b Derrick	9
J. P. Agnew st Metson b Ontong	5	– (7) c Thomas b Derrick	12
†P. Whitticase not out	10	– c and b Derrick	0
G. J. F. Ferris (did not bat)		– b Derrick	5
L. B. Taylor (did not bat)		– not out	0
B 4, l-b 6, w 1, n-b 1	12	L-b 2, w 1, n-b 1	4
1/13 2/40 3/88 4/166 5/251 6/276 7/290 (7 wkts dec.)	313	1/22 2/23 3/99 4/137 5/146 6/146 7/147 8/147 9/153	164

Bonus points – Leicestershire 4, Glamorgan 3.

Bowling: *First Innings*—Thomas 19–3–73–2; van Zyl 18–4–67–0; Barwick 24–8–58–1 Derrick 20–6–57–1; Ontong 17–4–41–3; Butcher 1–0–7–0. *Second Innings*—Thomas 10–4–26–1; van Zyl 11–2–33–0; Barwick 22–5–49–3; Derrick 18.3–6–54–6.

Glamorgan

	First innings		Second innings	
A. R. Butcher lbw b Agnew	6	–	not out	23
J. A. Hopkins c Whitaker b Ferris	71	–	b Ferris	7
†C. P. Metson b Agnew	27			
*H. Morris c Cobb b Lewis	1	–	(3) c Whitticase b Lewis	15
M. P. Maynard c Whitticase b Lewis	6	–	(4) not out	13
P. A. Cottey c Whitticase b Lewis	18			
R. C. Ontong not out	66			
J. G. Thomas b Ferris	24			
J. Derrick b Agnew	0			
C. J. P. G. van Zyl b Ferris	5			
S. R. Barwick c Whitticase b Ferris	0			
B 1, l-b 8, w 3, n-b 10	22		B 4, l-b 3, w 3, n-b 3	13
1/11 2/59 3/60 4/66 5/118 6/180 7/235 8/236 9/246	246		1/11 2/46 (2 wkts)	71

Bonus points – Glamorgan 2, Leicestershire 4.

Bowling: *First Innings*—Ferris 26.4–9–51–4; Agnew 36–8–94–3; Lewis 23–7–55–3; Taylor 9–2–31–0; Willey 1–0–6–0. *Second Innings*—Ferris 9–0–23–1; Agnew 9–4–16–0; Lewis 5.1–1–22–1; Taylor 2–1–3–0.

Umpires: J. D. Bond and D. O. Oslear.

LEICESTERSHIRE v SUSSEX

At Leicester, June 18, 20, 21. Leicestershire won by eight wickets. Leicestershire 23 pts, Sussex 4 pts. Toss: Leicestershire. In accordance with a familiar pattern established at Grace Road on Leicestershire's winning the toss, Sussex were asked to bat on a greenish strip and were soon dismissed for 159. DeFreitas took the bowling honours with five for 38, but his figures disguised a rather sulky performance. Both Ferris and Agnew exploited the conditions much better without the all-rounder's good fortune. After a shaky start, Leicestershire's victory bid was stepped up a pace or two by Willey and the 21-year-old Hepworth, who was making his second appearance. Together they added 148 for the fifth wicket, with Willey scoring a splendid 130, his century coming up in 259 minutes as he hit Kimber successively for three of his fourteen fours. This was only his second score above 50 for the season, and it was completed after having a tooth damaged from a blow to the vizor by a bouncer from Imran Khan. Alan Wells, Green and Lenham were not so fortunate, all having to retire after being struck by the Leicestershire pacemen. This resulted in Sussex's second innings petering out at 210, which left Leicestershire with the simple task of scoring 61.

Close of play: First day, Leicestershire 102-4 (P. Willey 52*, P. N. Hepworth 31*); Second day, Sussex 101-3 (C. M. Wells 38*, N. J. Lenham 25*).

Sussex

	First innings		Second innings	
R. I. Alikhan b Agnew	9	–	c Whitticase b Ferris	0
A. M. Green c Lewis b Agnew	9	–	retired hurt	18
*P. W. G. Parker b Ferris	4	–	lbw b Agnew	3
A. P. Wells not out	8	–	absent injured	
Imran Khan c Whitticase b Agnew	55	–	(4) c Whitticase b Agnew	0
C. M. Wells b DeFreitas	4	–	(5) c Whitticase b Agnew	41
N. J. Lenham hit wkt b DeFreitas	6	–	(6) retired hurt	36
†P. Moores lbw b DeFreitas	2	–	(7) b Lewis	15
A. C. S. Pigott b Ferris	11	–	(8) c Cobb b Agnew	56
S. J. S. Kimber c Whitaker b DeFreitas	8	–	(9) run out	1
A. R. Clarke b DeFreitas	14	–	(10) not out	14
B 4, l-b 10, n-b 15	29		L-b 8, n-b 18	26
1/17 2/26 3/29 4/73 5/85 6/94 7/122 8/144 9/144	159		1/15 2/25 3/25 4/106 5/162 6/170 7/210	210

Bonus points – Sussex 1, Leicestershire 4.

In the first innings A. P. Wells, when 8, retired hurt at 55 and resumed at 144-9.
In the second innings A. M. Green retired hurt at 29 and N. J. Lenham at 125.

Bowling: *First Innings*—Ferris 14–2–41–2; Agnew 15–3–50–3; DeFreitas 13.3–1–38–5; Lewis 12–7–16–0. *Second Innings*—Ferris 18–2–65–1; Agnew 19.1–3–70–4; DeFreitas 15–2–38–0; Lewis 11–5–20–1; Potter 13–8–9–0.

Leicestershire

R. A. Cobb lbw b Imran	1	– not out	22
*N. E. Briers c Parker b Pigott	12	– c Parker b Imran	12
P. Willey c Kimber b C. M. Wells	130	– c Parker b Kimber	6
J. J. Whitaker b Pigott	0	– not out	17
L. Potter lbw b Pigott	1		
P. N. Hepworth lbw b C. M. Wells	51		
P. A. J. DeFreitas b Clarke	34		
C. C. Lewis c Moores b Pigott	23		
†P. Whitticase not out	21		
J. P. Agnew c Alikhan b Pigott	22		
G. J. F. Ferris b Pigott	3		
B 2, l-b 3, w 1, n-b 5	11	B 4	4
1/4 2/22 3/22 4/27 5/175 6/233 7/239 8/265 9/305	309	1/17 2/28	(2 wkts) 61

Bonus points – Leicestershire 3, Sussex 3 (Score at 100 overs: 259-7).

Bowling: *First Innings*—Imran 26–10–45–1; Pigott 35.4–5–100–6; C. M. Wells 24–7–66–2; Kimber 14–3–63–0; Clarke 14–5–30–1. *Second Innings*—Imran 7–2–7–1; Kimber 9–4–17–1; C. M. Wells 5–2–15–0; Clarke 3–1–11–0; Alikhan 0.3–0–7–0.

Umpires: J. D. Bond and D. O. Oslear.

At Gloucester, June 25, 27, 28. LEICESTERSHIRE beat GLOUCESTERSHIRE by 80 runs.

At Leeds, July 2, 4, 5. LEICESTERSHIRE lost to YORKSHIRE by four wickets.

At Manchester, July 13, 14, 15. LEICESTERSHIRE drew with LANCASHIRE.

At Leicester, July 16, 17, 18. LEICESTERSHIRE drew with WEST INDIANS (See West Indian tour section).

LEICESTERSHIRE v DERBYSHIRE

At Leicester, July 20, 21, 22. Drawn. Leicestershire 4 pts, Derbyshire 5 pts. Toss: Leicestershire. The Derbyshire captain, Barnett, who in some quarters was looked upon as the man to ease the England side's batting problems, provided valuable support for his cause with a peerless, unbeaten innings of 239. At the same time he passed 1,000 runs for the season, surpassed his personal best of 175, set the previous month, and became the third-highest-scoring Derbyshire batsman. He hit a six and nineteen fours on his way to the double-century, which was reached in 379 minutes. For Leicestershire, there was a solid century from the acting-captain, Briers, his first of the season, which came in 231 minutes and included twelve fours and a six. He declared at the overnight score, no doubt after consultation with Barnett as the follow-on was still enforceable, and in turn Derbyshire left the home side to chase 301 in a minimum of 64 overs. On a pitch which had already produced 808 runs, this seemed a safe target, yet it nearly brought victory for Derbyshire before Potter and Agnew steered Leicestershire to safety in the gloom.

Close of play: First day, Derbyshire 348-4 (K. J. Barnett 200*, B. J. M. Maher 10*); Second day, Leicestershire 254-3 (N. E. Briers 125*, P. Willey 13*).

Derbyshire

*K. J. Barnett not out	239	– c Cobb b Lewis	16
P. D. Bowler c Whitticase b Ferris	20	– lbw b Agnew	5
B. Roberts c Whitticase b Ferris	33	– c and b Lewis	16
J. E. Morris c Cobb b Willey	18	– c Briers b Potter	42
S. C. Goldsmith c Whitticase b Potter	45	– not out	40
†B. J. M. Maher c Willey b Agnew	14	– lbw b Potter	5
P. G. Newman c Lewis b Agnew	0	– not out	0
A. E. Warner not out	28		
L-b 9, w 3, n-b 20	32	L-b 1	1
1/90 2/217 3/249 4/326 5/360 6/366 (6 wkts dec.)	429	1/17 2/31 3/39 4/105 5/123 (5 wkts dec.)	125

M. A. Holding, D. E. Malcolm and O. H. Mortensen did not bat.

Bonus points – Derbyshire 4, Leicestershire 1 (Score at 100 overs: 326-3).

Bowling: *First Innings*—Agnew 31–8–122–2; Ferris 17–2–66–2; DeFreitas 22–5–81–0; Lewis 9–0–34–0; Willey 35–11–75–1; Potter 21–5–42–1. *Second Innings*—Agnew 12–2–36–1; Ferris 3–2–3–0; Lewis 16–4–43–2; Potter 7.1–2–42–2.

Leicestershire

R. A. Cobb b Holding	19	– run out	11
*N. E. Briers not out	125	– b Barnett	60
T. J. Boon c and b Barnett	70	– c Maher b Holding	5
J. J. Whitaker lbw b Barnett	12	– (5) c sub b Newman	22
P. Willey not out	13	– (4) c Warner b Newman	7
L. Potter (did not bat)		– not out	41
C. C. Lewis (did not bat)		– c Goldsmith b Barnett	0
†P. Whitticase (did not bat)		– lbw b Holding	16
P. A. J. DeFreitas (did not bat)		– c Goldsmith b Holding	6
J. P. Agnew (did not bat)		– not out	0
B 4, l-b 3, w 1, n-b 7	15	B 3, l-b 6, n-b 6	15
1/27 2/176 3/221 (3 wkts dec.)	254	1/39 2/46 3/58 4/112 5/120 6/133 7/169 8/180 (8 wkts)	183

G. J. F. Ferris did not bat.

Bonus points – Leicestershire 3, Derbyshire 1.

Bowling: *First Innings*—Holding 10–2–35–1; Mortensen 15–3–33–0; Malcolm 11–1–60–0; Warner 8–2–24–0; Newman 8–2–23–0; Bowler 16–4–33–0; Barnett 19–5–39–2. *Second Innings*—Holding 13–4–33–3; Malcolm 8–0–28–0; Mortensen 8–3–6–0; Newman 13–0–71–2; Warner 5–0–17–0; Barnett 11–4–15–2; Bowler 6–4–4–0.

Umpires: J. H. Harris and B. Hassan.

LEICESTERSHIRE v ESSEX

At Leicester, July 23, 25, 26. Drawn. Leicestershire 5 pts, Essex 6 pts. Toss: Essex. More trouble behind the scenes at Grace Road resulted in DeFreitas being dropped for this match. Briers, the acting-captain, felt that the England all-rounder had failed to give 100 per cent in the previous match against Derbyshire and should, therefore, be disciplined. It was the second time in his brief career that such action had been taken, and it was to prove decisive for both club and player. Briers's hard line transferred itself on to the pitch as he batted for 238 minutes for his second century in successive matches, hitting just seven boundaries. Torrential overnight rain had caused the loss of 30 overs on the opening day, and the match was dogged by bad weather throughout. Essex declared in arrears on the second day in the hope of being set a target, only for further rain to negate any prospect of play after lunch on the last day. Briers, unbeaten on 63, was showing the potential to become the first Leicestershire player since 1965 to score a hundred in each innings.

Close of play: First day, Leicestershire 226-6 (N. E. Briers 118*, P. Whitticase 17*); Second day, Leicestershire 42-1 (N. E. Briers 18*, P. Whitticase 0*).

Leicestershire

	First innings		Second innings	
R. A. Cobb c East b Pont	29	– c Miller b Pont	20
*N. E. Briers c and b Topley	119	– not out	63
T. J. Boon lbw b Lever	2		
P. Willey run out	6		
J. J. Whitaker lbw b Lever	12		
L. Potter c Miller b Topley	10		
C. C. Lewis c Lilley b Pont	18		
†P. Whitticase not out	50	– (3) not out	40
J. P. Agnew b Topley	18		
G. J. F. Ferris c Border b Lever	18		
L. B. Taylor not out	0		
L-b 5, w 4, n-b 9	18	L-b 6	6
1/57 2/62 3/78 4/109 5/140 6/177 7/237 8/259 9/293	(9 wkts dec.) 300	1/42	(1 wkt) 129

Bonus points – Leicestershire 4, Essex 4.

Bowling: *First Innings*—Lever 26.2–4–75–3; Topley 29–5–100–3; Stephenson 11–3–26–0; Pont 20–1–86–2; Miller 2–1–8–0. *Second Innings*—Lever 11–0–32–0; Topley 17–3–54–0; Pont 11–1–37–1; Miller 1–1–0–0.

Essex

†D. E. East c Whitticase b Agnew	41
G. Miller c Whitticase b Agnew	1
A. W. Lilley c Cobb b Ferris	9
A. R. Border not out	65
P. J. Prichard not out	71
L-b 2, w 3, n-b 8	13
1/2 2/14 3/89	(3 wkts dec.) 200

J. P. Stephenson, N. Hussain, *K. W. R. Fletcher, T. D. Topley, I. L. Pont and J. K. Lever did not bat.

Bonus points – Essex 2, Leicestershire 1.

Bowling: Ferris 8–0–51–1; Agnew 15.2–3–43–2; Lewis 4–1–14–0; Taylor 12–2–42–0; Willey 16–4–44–0; Potter 1–0–4–0.

Umpires: K. J. Lyons and P. B. Wight.

At Worksop, July 30, August 1, 2. LEICESTERSHIRE drew with NOTTINGHAMSHIRE.

At Canterbury, August 3, 4, 5. LEICESTERSHIRE drew with KENT.

LEICESTERSHIRE v HAMPSHIRE

At Leicester, August 6, 8, 9. Drawn. Leicestershire 6 pts, Hampshire 7 pts. Toss: Leicestershire. Taylor, with a season's-best six for 49, almost brought about an improbable victory for Leicestershire after Hampshire had been set to score 251 in 50 overs. The visitors seemed well in control as the final hour approached, needing a further 113 runs with nine wickets in hand, but Taylor changed all that, at one point taking three wickets in nine balls. Although Scott got the innings going again, in the end Hampshire were grateful that Maru and Bakker survived the last nine balls to achieve the draw. After Leicestershire had elected to bat first on the flattest Grace Road pitch of the season, Willey with 98 prevented the innings from falling apart. Ferris hit a career-best 36 not out as he and Such added 43 in 44 balls for the last wicket. Hampshire owed much to their night-watchman, James, who batted for four hours and the lower order, while Leicestershire needed the stimulus of Whitaker's unbeaten 87 to return the compliment of Nicholas's declaration.

Close of play: First day, Hampshire 10-1 (C. L. Smith 3*, K. D. James 0*); Second day, Leicestershire 32-1 (N. E. Briers 15*, P. Willey 8*).

Leicestershire

First innings		Second innings	
T. J. Boon c Parks b Bakker	2	– lbw b Bakker	2
N. E. Briers c Smith b Jefferies	28	– c Maru b Bakker	23
P. Willey c Nicholas b Maru	98	– c Jefferies b Nicholas	56
*D. I. Gower c Parks b Jefferies	10	– c Turner b Ayling	13
J. J. Whitaker b Maru	28	– not out	87
L. Potter lbw b Jefferies	26	– not out	23
†P. Whitticase c Parks b Jefferies	34		
J. P. Agnew c Nicholas b Jefferies	14		
L. B. Taylor st Parks b Maru	6		
G. J. F. Ferris not out	36		
P. M. Such run out	1		
B 4, l-b 5, n-b 6	15	L-b 8	8
1/6 2/50 3/74 4/120 5/191 6/217 7/247 8/248 9/255	298	1/2 2/40 3/59 4/128 (4 wkts dec.)	212

Bonus points – Leicestershire 3, Hampshire 4 (Score at 100 overs: 293-9).

Bowling: *First Innings*—Jefferies 30.3–3–126–5; Bakker 13–5–35–1; Maru 31–7–69–3; Ayling 14–4–34–0; James 12–4–25–0. *Second Innings*—Bakker 12–3–21–2; Maru 23–5–49–0; Smith 13–0–50–0; Ayling 8–1–26–1; Nicholas 18–1–58–1.

Hampshire

First innings		Second innings	
R. J. Scott b Ferris	2	– (5) c Whitaker b Agnew	41
C. L. Smith b Taylor	28	– (2) b Taylor	68
K. D. James b Agnew	77	– (8) c Boon b Agnew	10
*M. C. J. Nicholas lbw b Ferris	3	– c Potter b Taylor	6
V. P. Terry lbw b Ferris	0	– (1) b Agnew	39
D. R. Turner c Whitticase b Agnew	30	– (3) b Taylor	32
J. R. Ayling run out	5	– (6) c Briers b Taylor	9
S. T. Jefferies c and b Taylor	15	– (7) b Taylor	8
†R. J. Parks not out	38	– b Taylor	4
R. J. Maru not out	34	– not out	1
P. J. Bakker (did not bat)		– not out	5
B 2, l-b 9, w 3, n-b 14	28	L-b 5, n-b 5	10
1/7 2/67 3/94 4/94 5/150 6/163 7/163 8/199 (8 wkts dec.)	260	1/86 2/145 3/151 4/152 5/202 6/204 7/219 8/223 9/228 (9 wkts)	233

Bonus points – Hampshire 3, Leicestershire 3.

Bowling: *First Innings*—Ferris 24–5–58–3; Agnew 25.3–3–63–2; Willey 26–11–51–0; Taylor 15–3–48–2; Such 7–2–29–0. *Second Innings*—Agnew 16–1–79–3; Ferris 13–3–52–0; Willey 3–0–24–0; Such 7–1–24–0; Taylor 11–0–49–6.

Umpires: J. H. Harris and N. T. Plews.

At Birmingham, August 13, 15, 16. LEICESTERSHIRE beat WARWICKSHIRE by one wicket.

LEICESTERSHIRE v SOMERSET

At Hinckley, August 20, 22, 23. Leicestershire won by seven wickets. Leicestershire 22 pts, Somerset 5 pts. Toss: Somerset. Although only 51.2 overs were possible on the first day because of the indifferent weather, it was time enough for the Leicestershire seamers to enhance their reputations. Ferris dismissed Hardy first ball, but Agnew and DeFreitas did most of the damage as Somerset were reduced to 158 for nine. DeFreitas was also attracting attention off the field with the news that Leicestershire had agreed to release him after two unhappy years. Potter and Whitticase, however, put these matters behind them as they established a winning position. Potter reached his half-century from 107 balls, while Whitticase's 71 was a personal best. Somerset fared little better second time around against Ferris, Agnew and DeFreitas, and Leicestershire, needing only 102, accomplished their victory with 31 overs to spare.

Close of play: First day, Somerset 158-9 (M. W. Cleal 6*, A. N. Jones 4*); Second day, Somerset 62-3 (P. M. Roebuck 10*, M. W. Cleal 3*).

Somerset

First innings		Second innings	
J. J. E. Hardy c Whitticase b Ferris	0	– c Whitticase b Ferris	2
N. A. Felton c Whitaker b DeFreitas	11	– c Boon b Willey	24
J. G. Wyatt c Willey b Agnew	57	– b DeFreitas	14
*P. M. Roebuck c Whitticase b DeFreitas	5	– c Boon b Ferris	10
R. J. Bartlett c Willey b Agnew	38	– (6) c Whitaker b Ferris	0
†N. D. Burns c Potter b Agnew	11	– (7) b DeFreitas	17
V. J. Marks lbw b Agnew	0	– (8) b Agnew	50
G. D. Rose c Whitticase b Ferris	0	– (9) c Whitticase b Ferris	6
M. W. Cleal not out	8	– (5) c Whitticase b Taylor	13
N. A. Mallender c Potter b Agnew	3	– c Whitticase b Agnew	9
A. N. Jones b DeFreitas	7	– not out	1
L-b 12, w 1, n-b 11	24	L-b 9, w 3, n-b 12	24
1/0 2/36 3/72 4/93 5/138 6/138 7/141 8/142 9/148	164	1/3 2/43 3/59 4/64 5/64 6/86 7/106 8/158 9/160	170

Bonus points – Somerset 1, Leicestershire 4.

Bowling: *First Innings*—Ferris 11–2–19–2; Agnew 19–7–51–5; DeFreitas 17–4–57–3; Taylor 8–0–25–0. *Second Innings*—Ferris 16–2–36–4; Agnew 12.5–2–34–2; DeFreitas 14–1–51–2; Taylor 17–4–30–1; Willey 6–3–10–1.

Leicestershire

First innings		Second innings	
T. J. Boon lbw b Jones	13	– b Jones	19
N. E. Briers b Mallender	22	– run out	19
P. Willey c Mallender b Rose	10	– c Wyatt b Rose	22
*D. I. Gower lbw b Cleal	10	– not out	28
J. J. Whitaker c Rose b Jones	22	– not out	10
L. Potter c Roebuck b Marks	52		
P. A. J. DeFreitas c Rose b Cleal	13		
†P. Whitticase c Felton b Rose	71		
J. P. Agnew c Bartlett b Marks	0		
G. J. F. Ferris c Felton b Marks	8		
L. B. Taylor not out	0		
B 4, l-b 2, n-b 6	12	L-b 2, n-b 2	4
1/23 2/44 3/55 4/62 5/96 6/119 7/205 8/205 9/233	233	1/38 2/49 3/77	(3 wkts) 10

Bonus points – Leicestershire 2, Somerset 4.

Bowling: *First Innings*—Mallender 17–3–49–1; Jones 15–1–55–2; Cleal 11–2–43–2; Ros 17–6–40–2; Marks 13.4–3–34–3; Wyatt 1–0–6–0. *Second Innings*—Mallender 7–0–20–0; Jone 9–2–40–1; Rose 10–2–40–1; Marks 2–2–0–0.

Umpires: B. Leadbeater and P. B. Wight.

At Neath, August 25, 26, 27, 29. LEICESTERSHIRE drew with GLAMORGAN.

LEICESTERSHIRE v NOTTINGHAMSHIRE

At Leicester, August 30, 31, September 1, 2. Drawn. Leicestershire 8 pts, Nottinghamshire 3 pts. Toss: Nottinghamshire. Gower, in a mood of fierce determination, rescued a disappointing season with an innings of incomparable majesty and style against the country's eading fast bowlers. Having lost the toss and been put in in conditions highly favourable to he seamers, the Leicestershire captain decided to open the innings himself. His colleagues struggled against the seaming ball early on, but Gower, with effortless drives and powerful cuts, advanced to the 39th hundred of his career, hitting Stephenson for a six and then a four. He faced 219 balls for his 146 and hit 21 fours as well as that six. Nottinghamshire lacked anyone of Gower's class and the Leicestershire seam attack once more made the most of the onditions, dismissing the visitors for 133 and giving Gower the satisfaction of enforcing the ollow-on. Although rain had robbed Leicestershire of half the second day's play and all of the hird, victory was in sight until Randall, with a defiant, unbeaten 90, convinced Gower that he match had been saved.

Close of play: First day, Leicestershire 314-7 (P. Whitticase 8*, J. P. Agnew 4*); Second ay, Nottinghamshire 118-8 (B. N. French 16*, E. E. Hemmings 13*); Third day, No play.

.eicestershire

D. I. Gower c Pollard b Stephenson	146	J. P. Agnew not out	15
I. E. Briers c Evans b Cooper	4	G. J. F. Ferris b Stephenson	0
'. Willey c Evans b Cooper	1		
. J. Whitaker c Pollard b Evans	5	L-b 6, n-b 1	7
. J. Boon b Stephenson	15		
. Potter c French b Hemmings	85	1/38 2/53 3/71 4/112 (9 wkts dec.)	332
. C. Lewis c French b Hemmings	39	5/217 6/293 7/310	
P. Whitticase b Stephenson	15	8/332 9/332	

. B. Taylor did not bat.

Bonus points – Leicestershire 4, Nottinghamshire 3 (Score at 100 overs: 310-7).

Bowling: Stephenson 30.4–7–107–4; Cooper 28–8–80–2; Evans 24–4–73–1; Hemmings 3–8–66–2.

Nottinghamshire

. C. Broad lbw b Agnew	20	– c Whitticase b Agnew 52
Pollard lbw b Ferris	0	– c Whitticase b Ferris 0
Johnson lbw b Agnew	7	– lbw b Taylor 74
. Newell b Taylor	12	– c Boon b Ferris 6
. W. Randall b Ferris	3	– not out 90
. D. Birch b Agnew	11	– b Lewis 16
D. Stephenson b Taylor	6	– c Boon b Lewis 7
P. Evans c Whitticase b Ferris	24	– c Whitticase b Lewis 0
3. N. French b Ferris	23	– not out 0
E. Hemmings not out	18	
E. Cooper c Briers b Ferris	2	
N-b 7	7	B 3, l-b 6, n-b 4 13
' 2/28 3/29 4/34 5/45	133	1/1 2/128 3/134 4/157 (7 wkts) 258
37 7/79 8/89 9/126		5/206 6/220 7/225

Bonus points – Leicestershire 4.

Bowling: *First Innings*—Ferris 15.4–4–49–5; Agnew 19–4–59–3; Taylor 8–3–16–2; Lewis 4–9–0. *Second Innings*—Ferris 15–1–60–2; Agnew 19–7–64–1; Taylor 21–2–57–1; Lewis -2–67–3; Willey 2–1–1–0.

Umpires: K. J. Lyons and R. Palmer.

Chelmsford, September 9, 10, 11. LEICESTERSHIRE lost to ESSEX by an innings and 3 runs.

MIDDLESEX

Patron: HRH The Duke of Edinburgh
President: F. G. Mann
Chairman: M. P. Murray
Chairman, Cricket Committee: M. O. C. Sturt
Secretary: Lt-Col. P. F. Packham
Lord's Cricket Ground, St John's Wood,
London NW8 8QN (Telephone: 01-289 1300)
Captain: M. W. Gatting
Coach: D. Bennett

Middlesex returned to the winner's enclosure, after a rare year on th outside, when they beat Worcestershire in the NatWest Bank Troph final. It was the fifth time in his six years as captain that Mike Gattin had accepted a prize and it provided a gratifying end to an encouragin season. Middlesex were seventh in the Britannic Assurance Champion ship, quarter-finalists in the Benson and Hedges Cup, and fourth in th Refuge Assurance League. They led the Sunday table throughout mid summer, but four "no results" asked too much of them at the end. victory from just one of the "no results" would have seen them finis runners-up. Nevertheless, they did qualify for the new Refuge Assuranc Cup, only to be eliminated by Worcestershire several days after th NatWest final.

The position in the Championship reflected a considerable improv ment from sixteenth in 1987, and there were hints that Middlesex migh challenge for the title sooner than was expected during two previou mediocre seasons. They led the table by mid-May, having won their fir four matches, three of them by huge margins in four-day fixtures. But th next win did not come until early August. Two more wins were banke that month to ensure a final place in the top half of the table. Th June/July slump, which brought a tumble to twelfth, could be attribute to the weather and England calls. Gatting, Paul Downton and Joh Emburey were often absent, although having begun the West Indi series with three Middlesex players, England ended it with none. Oth factors were unreliable batting and a scarcity of wickets from spin un Emburey abruptly rediscovered the edges of opponents' bats after losi the England leadership.

In the NatWest final, two of the young players responsible for t renewed optimism, Mark Ramprakash and Angus Fraser, demonstrat their talents to a wide audience. In 1987 most areas of the team had giv cause for concern; last season, Fraser and Ramprakash helped ea anxieties about the pace bowling and the batting.

In April, Middlesex had almost an abundance of quick bowlers. B Neil Williams's back problems returned after he had bowled marv lously in the early wins, Wayne Daniel failed to complete the only t matches for which he could be selected, and Simon Hughes w depressingly ineffective. Daniel's failure to regain fitness meant downbeat end to his dozen years at Lord's; and it also meant th Middlesex's efforts were achieved without an overseas player. Giv these circumstances, it was not only welcome but also necessary th

-raser should develop into a high-class opening bowler. He hit the pitch ıard, moved the ball about, and was naggingly accurate. He resembled hose big, strong fast-medium bowlers of the 1950s and 1960s; he eminded Gatting most of Vintcent van der Bijl, the South African who owled Middlesex to the 1980 Championship. Fraser's advance showed n his Championship figures: 77 wickets at 19.27, compared with 44 at 2.27. His new-ball partner, Norman Cowans, relished full fitness. A ouch slower than earlier in his career, he was none the less dangerous on oth hard and spongy pitches.

Ramprakash's increased value was, like Fraser's, obvious from his Championship record: 401 runs at 57.28 against 321 at 29.18. A-level tudies restricted him to eight matches in each of his first two seasons, ut he now turns his attention fully to cricket. Ramprakash's strokeplay nd temperament earned him a considered tribute from Gatting after is innings in the NatWest final: "He plays as well as any seasoned rofessional. He is better than I was at eighteen."

As usual, Middlesex's season centred on Gatting. For some years he as returned to Middlesex between Tests to thrash a century. Last year as different. Losing the Test captaincy after a newspaper-inflamed :andal, and his conflict with the TCCB over his autobiography, ıfluenced him to stand down twice from the England side and he played ı only two Tests. He described his summer as one of anguish and ırment, but he had the perfect balm for external troubles by playing for county enjoying varied success. He repeatedly expressed his gratitude ır the good wishes received from colleagues, the committee and ıpporters.

In his unusual season, Gatting batted in a normal, even traditional, ay for Middlesex. Off county attacks he hammered 1,431 runs at 53, ıd his overall Championship average in the 1980s is a remarkable '.33. A weakness was an increasing involvement in run-outs, two of hich jeopardised the NatWest semi-final and final victories. Gatting as not necessarily at fault, but as the captain and senior batsman he ust organise the right man to duplicate the essential noisy authority of ırlow or Radley which made Middlesex supreme as runners.

Wilf Slack had an excellent season, overcoming a mysterious affliction ıich caused him to faint three times on the field. But the other main tsmen will not be content with their outputs. Though John Carr's iving can be the highlight of the Middlesex innings, and he did pass)00 runs, his form was patchy. His urgent approach often betrayed m. He experimented with medium-pace bowling, his off-spin having serted him, and his new style was usefully employed in limited-overs ıtches. Another important change bowler was Andy Needham, whose ıef interlude with Middlesex ended with a satisfying return of -3–84–3 in the final three rounds of the NatWest Trophy.

Roland Butcher had a typical year, which unhappily is not praise. There re far too few first-class runs for one of his gifts, although he did play the innings in the quarter- and semi-finals of the NatWest. Keith Brown 1 Mike Roseberry gave no firm hints that they will secure long-term ces. So Middlesex were again grateful for the ability of Emburey and wnton to pull the innings out of trouble; Downton with calm, orthodox okeplay and Emburey with his unique jabbing, clubbing, powerful ıts. As in 1987, both averaged over 35. – Terry Cooper.

MIDDLESEX 1988

[*Bill Smith*

Back row: A. A. Barnett, M. R. Ramprakash, A. Needham, I. J. F. Hutchinson, P. N. Weekes, T. A. Radford, M. W. C. Olley, J. Davis (*physiotherapist*), A. Jones (*scorer*). *Middle row:* H. Sharp (*scorer*), D. Bennett (*coach*), K. R. Brown, A. G. J. Fraser, M. A. Roseberry, A. R. C. Fraser, J. F. Sykes, P. C. R. Tufnell, N. R. MacLaurin, C. T. Radley (*assistant coach*). *Front row:* J. D. Carr, N. F. Williams, P. R. Downton, W. W. Daniel, M. W. Gatting

MIDDLESEX RESULTS

All first-class matches – Played 24: Won 7, Lost 3, Drawn 14.

County Championship matches – Played 22: Won 7, Lost 3, Drawn 12.

Bonus points – Batting 49, Bowling 54.

Competition placings – Britannic Assurance County Championship, 7th; NatWest Bank Trophy, winners; Benson and Hedges Cup, q-f; Refuge Assurance League, 4th; Refuge Assurance Cup, s-f.

BRITANNIC ASSURANCE CHAMPIONSHIP AVERAGES

BATTING

	Birthplace	*M*	*I*	*NO*	*R*	*HI*	*Avge*
M. R. Ramprakash ..	*Bushey*	8	11	4	401	68*	57.28
M. W. Gatting	*Kingsbury*	18	29	2	1,431	210	53.00
W. N. Slack	*Troumaca, St Vincent*	19	32	5	1,228	163*	45.48
̣. E. Emburey	*Peckham*	15	20	4	584	102	36.50
. D. Carr	*St John's Wood*	22	39	6	1,194	144	36.18
P. R. Downton	*Farnborough, Kent*	14	18	4	506	120	36.14
A. Needham	*Calow*	7	10	3	231	66*	33.00
R. O. Butcher	*East Point, Barbados*	17	25	2	673	134	29.26
K. R. Brown	*Edmonton*	19	30	4	668	131*	25.69
M. A. Roseberry	*Houghton-le-Spring*	12	18	3	357	67	23.80
N. F. Williams	*Hope Well, St Vincent*	8	11	2	186	63*	20.66
S. P. Hughes	*Kingston-upon-Thames*	16	18	5	248	34	19.07
. F. Sykes	*Shoreditch*	7	10	1	164	86	18.22
. J. F. Hutchinson ..	*Welshpool*	3	4	0	48	25	12.00
A. R. C. Fraser	*Billinge*	22	27	10	182	17	10.70
N. G. Cowans	*Enfield St Mary, Jamaica*	20	21	7	119	27*	8.50
. C. R. Tufnell	*Barnet*	9	10	2	41	20	5.12

Also batted: A. A. Barnett (*Malaga, Spain*) (1 match) 10; §‡W. W. Daniel (*St Philip, rbados*) (2 matches) 0, 0; M. W. C. Olley (*Romford*) (3 matches) 16, 16, 4.

* *Signifies not out.* ‡ *Denotes county cap.* § *Not qualified for England.*

e following played a total of twelve three-figure innings for Middlesex in County ampionship matches – M. W. Gatting 3, W. N. Slack 3, J. D. Carr 2, K. R. Brown 1, O. Butcher 1, P. R. Downton 1, J. E. Emburey 1.

BOWLING

	O	*M*	*R*	*W*	*BB*	*5W/i*	*Avge*
F. Williams	178.3	33	511	30	6-42	2	17.03
G. Cowans	491.5	123	1,290	71	6-49	3	18.16
R. C. Fraser	674.1	190	1,484	77	6-68	6	19.27
E. Emburey	543.1	167	1,201	49	6-24	2	24.51
C. R. Tufnell	349.2	90	876	19	4-88	0	46.10
P. Hughes	385.3	70	1,136	22	3-45	0	51.63

Also bowled: A. A. Barnett 27–9–65–0; K. R. Brown 1–1–0–0; J. D. Carr 65.1–15–154–5; W. Daniel 16–2–37–2; M. W. Gatting 96–21–287–4; A. Needham 113.4–19–399–8; M. R. mprakash 8–0–53–0; M. A. Roseberry 11.4–1–61–2; W. N. Slack 2–1–14–0; J. F. Sykes 0–142–0.

cket-keepers: P. R. Downton 30 ct, 5 st; K. R. Brown 13 ct; M. W. C. Olley 8 ct.

ding Fielders: J. D. Carr 20, J. E. Emburey 19, K. R. Brown 15.

MIDDLESEX v NOTTINGHAMSHIRE

At Lord's, April 21, 22, 23, 25. Middlesex won by 241 runs. Middlesex 19 pts, Nottingham shire 7 pts. Toss: Middlesex. Middlesex provided a perfect illustration of how, in a four-da match, a bad start can be transformed into an overwhelming victory. The previous summer' status of the two counties appeared to be confirmed as Nottinghamshire controlled th opening two innings. Each of their pace quartet had a hand in Middlesex's early slide befor Butcher and Emburey added 121 in two hours. Emburey expended minimum effort as h included eleven fours in his 61. Fraser picked up two wickets on the first evening, and he an Newell fought each other to a standstill on the second. Newell batted for more than six hou and Fraser's lengthy toils brought him career-best figures. Stephenson's flamboyant inning gave Nottinghamshire a substantial advantage. Gatting was in early on the third day and soo treated an undemanding attack with disdain, hitting the ball all around Lord's as he collecte 35 fours in his 285-ball double-century. He and Carr added 161 in 31 overs, with Carr hittin fourteen fours in his century; with Brown, who hit his first Championship hundred and h highest score, Gatting added 264 in 63 overs. Set 397, Nottinghamshire did not hint at challenge. Robinson was injured in the opening overs, Johnson's defiance was isolated, an Middlesex's three quick bowlers easily compensated for Daniel's absence with an injure back. Another Middlesex casualty was Butcher, who was struck in the face by a cut fro Stephenson and required stitches.

Close of play: First day, Nottinghamshire 102-3 (M. Newell 23*, P. Johnson 1*); Secon day, Middlesex 50-1 (J. D. Carr 18*, A. R. C. Fraser 4*); Third day, Nottinghamshire 10 (B. C. Broad 8*, R. T. Robinson 1*).

Middlesex

J. D. Carr c Broad b Pick	16	– c Stephenson b Saxelby	10
†P. R. Downton c Newell b Stephenson	0	– lbw b Pick	2
*M. W. Gatting b Saxelby	7	– (4) c Robinson b Stephenson	21
K. R. Brown c Johnson b Cooper	14	– (5) not out	13
R. O. Butcher c Stephenson b Cooper	73	– (6) lbw b Stephenson	
M. A. Roseberry c Broad b Cooper	0		
J. E. Emburey c French b Cooper	61	– not out	
A. R. C. Fraser c Robinson b Stephenson	7	– (3) c Johnson b Pick	
S. P. Hughes not out	4		
N. G. Cowans b Stephenson	6		
W. W. Daniel lbw b Cooper	0		
B 4, l-b 7	11	L-b 11, n-b 3	
1/21 2/21 3/46 4/46 5/46 6/167 7/182 8/188 9/198	199	1/41 2/51 3/212 4/476 5/482 (5 wkts dec.)	5

Bonus points – Middlesex 1, Nottinghamshire 4.

Bowling: *First Innings*—Stephenson 19–3–52–3; Pick 13–2–46–1; Cooper 20.5–6–52- Saxelby 11–2–31–1; Hemmings 4–1–7–0. *Second Innings*—Stephenson 34–4–121–2; P 23–2–128–2; Cooper 22–3–96–0; Saxelby 22–4–81–1; Hemmings 8–1–40–0; Birch 8–2–28-

Nottinghamshire

B. C. Broad c Downton b Fraser	68	– lbw b Cowans	
*R. T. Robinson lbw b Cowans	1	– lbw b Fraser	
M. Newell c Butcher b Cowans	80	– c Emburey b Fraser	
R. A. Pick c Downton b Fraser	0	– (9) b Hughes	
P. Johnson c Brown b Fraser	13	– (4) b Fraser	
J. D. Birch c Carr b Fraser	10	– (5) b Cowans	
F. D. Stephenson lbw b Gatting	63	– (6) c Downton b Cowans	
†B. N. French c Downton b Fraser	21	– (7) c Downton b Fraser	
E. E. Hemmings not out	28	– (8) run out	
K. Saxelby c Brown b Hughes	8	– c Brown b Hughes	
K. E. Cooper b Fraser	0	– not out	
B 4, l-b 4, n-b 8	16	L-b 5, w 2, n-b 1	
1/12 2/97 3/97 4/117 5/127 6/240 7/258 8/291 9/307	308	1/16 2/27 3/32 4/106 5/106 6/110 7/114 8/154 9/154	

Bonus points – Nottinghamshire 3, Middlesex 2 (Score at 100 overs: 250-6).

Bowling: *First Innings*—Cowans 27–9–52–2; Daniel 3–0–18–0; Hughes 33–10–81–1; Emburey 21–6–51–0; Fraser 37.2–13–75–6; Gatting 8–1–23–1. *Second Innings*—Cowans 16–4–38–3; Fraser 18–5–42–4; Hughes 10.1–3–25–2; Emburey 7–0–40–0; Gatting 1–0–5–0.

Umpires: D. J. Constant and A. A. Jones.

MIDDLESEX v ESSEX

At Lord's, April 28, 29, 30, May 2. Middlesex won by 176 runs. Middlesex 23 pts, Essex 5 pts. Toss: Essex. Lever gave two glimpses of his masterly control in taking the important wickets of Slack and, first ball, Gatting. Carr sustained the innings, his 66 containing the high proportion of twelve boundaries, and the middle order held off the seam bowlers to see the total to espectability. Williams's three wickets were the highlights of a second day restricted to 35 overs. His line and movement put a stranglehold on the batsmen, and three more wickets on the hird day gave him his best figures for Middlesex. His previous best, five for 15, had also been gainst Essex. Despite again dismissing Gatting cheaply, Essex slipped further out of con- ention as Slack, Downton and Emburey built up the lead. And set 352 in a day, they failed to nake half that. Prichard and East showed that survival was possible, but run-scoring was eyond everybody on a pitch offering bounce and lateral movement.

Close of play: First day, Essex 62-1 (G. A. Gooch 34*, P. J. Prichard 16*); Second day, Essex 127-5 (A. W. Lilley 7*, K. W. R. Fletcher 8*); Third day, Middlesex 275-8 (J. E. Emburey 76*, A. R. C. Fraser 7*).

Middlesex

W. N. Slack lbw b Lever	5	–	lbw b Lever	65
D. Carr c East b Gooch	66	–	c Gooch b Pringle	5
*M. W. Gatting b Lever	0	–	lbw b Pringle	16
.. R. Brown c Gooch b Pringle	13	–	lbw b Topley	20
.. O. Butcher lbw b Gooch	22	–	c East b Topley	19
†P. R. Downton c Pringle b Topley	39	–	c Border b Topley	35
E. Emburey c Gooch b Pringle	18	–	not out	76
. F. Williams c Border b Lever	44	–	lbw b Topley	2
P. Hughes c Border b Pringle	19	–	b Topley	16
.. R. C. Fraser not out	14	–	not out	7
. G. Cowans lbw b Pringle	1			
B 4, l-b 6, w 1, n-b 11	22		L-b 4, w 1, n-b 9	14
18 2/22 3/46 4/117 5/126 172 7/189 8/245 9/253	263		1/6 2/32 3/89 4/132 5/132 6/211 7/213 8/251 (8 wkts dec.)	275

Bonus points – Middlesex 3, Essex 4.

Bowling: *First Innings*—Lever 23–8–47–3; Topley 17–2–74–1; Pringle 22.4–3–90–4; Gooch –4–38–2; Childs 4–2–4–0. *Second Innings*—Lever 19–3–47–1; Pringle 20–2–67–2; Topley –1–94–5; Gooch 20–1–63–0.

ssex

A. Gooch b Williams	43	–	c Downton b Williams	12
R. Hardie lbw b Cowans	6	–	c sub b Cowans	5
J. Prichard c Emburey b Fraser	16	–	b Cowans	25
R. Border lbw b Williams	30	–	c sub b Hughes	19
W. Lilley b Williams	52	–	(6) c Downton b Cowans	18
R. Pringle c Cowans b Williams	6	–	(5) c Cowans b Hughes	20
.. W. R. Fletcher c Downton b Hughes	14	–	c Downton b Hughes	9
). E. East c Downton b Williams	1	–	b Williams	20
D. Topley c Brown b Hughes	1	–	lbw b Fraser	7
K. Lever c Emburey b Williams	0	–	b Cowans	20
H. Childs not out	0	–	not out	1
L-b 13, n-b 5	18		B 2, l-b 11, n-b 6	19
7 2/62 3/92 4/105 5/113 46 7/155 8/168 9/178	187		1/21 2/29 3/70 4/80 5/101 6/113 7/128 8/148 9/169	175

Bonus points – Essex 1, Middlesex 4.

Bowling: *First Innings*—Cowans 21–7–54–1; Fraser 13–7–14–1; Hughes 25–6–63–2; Williams 22.2–5–42–6; Gatting 1–0–1–0. *Second Innings*—Cowans 19.4–5–45–4; Fraser 24–6–44–1; Williams 16–3–28–2; Hughes 17–4–45–3.

Umpires: D. G. L. Evans and J. H. Hampshire.

At The Oval, May 5, 6, 7. MIDDLESEX beat SURREY by 148 runs.

At Leicester, May 18, 19, 20. MIDDLESEX beat LEICESTERSHIRE by eight wickets.

At Cambridge, May 21, 22, 23. MIDDLESEX drew with CAMBRIDGE UNIVERSITY.

MIDDLESEX v SUSSEX

At Lord's, May 28, 30, 31. Drawn. Middlesex 3 pts, Sussex 4 pts. Toss: Middlesex. Imra Khan returned to Championship duty with an excellent analysis that included the wicket c Gatting, the Middlesex captain again revealing his weakness at defending a ball moving int his stumps. Carr, hitting twelve fours in his 76, played the leading role in his stand of 104 wi Gatting. Middlesex struck quickly on Saturday evening, but rain did not permit any play afte the weekend.

Middlesex

K. R. Brown c Gould b Imran 14
J. D. Carr b Pigott 76
*M. W. Gatting b Imran 31
R. O. Butcher c Gould b Bunting 30
†P. R. Downton c Gould b C. M. Wells 19
M. A. Roseberry lbw b C. M. Wells . . . 11
J. E. Emburey lbw b Babington 1
N. F. Williams not out 34
S. P. Hughes c Gould b Imran . . . .
A. R. C. Fraser b Imran . . . .
N. G. Cowans b Imran . . . .
B 6, l-b 7, w 1, n-b 8 . . . .

1/24 2/128 3/128 4/174 5/188 2
6/193 7/199 8/221 9/251

Bonus points – Middlesex 3, Sussex 4.

Bowling: Imran 22.3–7–50–5; Pigott 19–3–66–1; C. M. Wells 14–4–39–2; Babingt 16–3–62–1; Bunting 9–1–27–1; Heseltine 1–0–4–0.

Sussex

D. K. Standing lbw b Williams 4
A. M. Green not out 28
N. J. Lenham lbw b Cowans 0
A. P. Wells not out 17

1/7 2/8 (2 wkts) 49

*C. M. Wells, Imran Khan, †I. J. Gould, A. C. S. Pigott, P. A. W. Heseltine, R. A. Bunt and A. M. Babington did not bat.

Bowling: Cowans 6–2–8–1; Williams 8–4–25–1; Fraser 6–3–7–0; Hughes 3–0–5 Emburey 2–1–4–0.

Umpires: J. C. Balderstone and R. Julian.

MIDDLESEX v WORCESTERSHIRE

At Lord's, June 4, 6, 7. Worcestershire won by 209 runs. Worcestershire 19 pts, Middlesex 3 pts. Toss: Worcestershire. The contest between the Championship leaders became a voluntary one-innings match when the first day was washed out. Hick continued his May form with glorious batting which, producing twelve fours, emphasised the problems of his colleagues. Curtis toiled for over six hours and Lord, his opening partner, had needed 80 minutes to make 17. Two forfeitures gave Middlesex a day in which to make 334, but Newport, extracting everything from a pitch which gave little to the other pace bowlers, had his team on top of the table by mid-afternoon. The course of the innings was determined in his first two overs when he had Carr and Roseberry caught at slip and Butcher caught behind, hooking first ball. The fifth-wicket stand between Brown and Sykes provided token resistance before Newport worked his way through the innings to record career-best figures.

Close of play: First day, No play; Second day, Worcestershire 333-8 (S. J. Rhodes 22*, N. V. Radford 7*).

Worcestershire

T. S. Curtis run out 108
G. J. Lord b Fraser 17
G. A. Hick b Hughes 78
D. B. D'Oliveira b Cowans 37
*P. A. Neale c Brown b Fraser 12
M. J. Weston b Fraser 1
†S. J. Rhodes not out 22
P. J. Newport c Sykes b Hughes 1
R. K. Illingworth c and b Williams ... 12
N. V. Radford not out 7
B 5, l-b 23, n-b 10 38

1/46 2/156 3/235 4/260 5/262 6/287 7/299 8/318 (8 wkts dec.) 333

S. M. McEwan did not bat.

Bonus points – Worcestershire 3, Middlesex 3 (Score at 100 overs: 299-7).

Bowling: Cowans 21–3–66–1; Williams 24–3–65–1; Fraser 31–11–56–3; Hughes 29–5–92–2; Sykes 5–0–26–0.

Worcestershire forfeited their second innings.

Middlesex

Middlesex forfeited their first innings.

D. Carr c Hick b Newport 0
R. Brown c Rhodes b Illingworth .. 31
A. Roseberry c D'Oliveira b Newport 1
R. O. Butcher c Rhodes b Newport .. 0
Needham c Rhodes b Newport 6
F. Sykes c Rhodes b Newport 32
F. Williams b Newport 5
P. Hughes c Weston b Newport 20
†M. W. C. Olley b Radford 16
A. R. C. Fraser b Newport 0
N. G. Cowans not out 2
B 2, l-b 7, w 1, n-b 1 11

1/2 2/4 3/4 4/15 5/65 6/74 7/85 8/112 9/112 124

Bowling: Radford 19–5–37–1; Newport 22–6–52–8; McEwan 5–1–13–0; Weston 3–1–4–0; Illingworth 6–2–9–1.

Umpires: B. Leadbeater and N. T. Plews.

At Tunbridge Wells, June 11, 13, 14. MIDDLESEX lost to KENT by six wickets.

At Basingstoke, June 15, 16, 17. MIDDLESEX drew with HAMPSHIRE.

At Luton, June 18, 20, 21. MIDDLESEX drew with NORTHAMPTONSHIRE.

At Chelmsford, June 25, 27, 28. MIDDLESEX drew with ESSEX.

MIDDLESEX v YORKSHIRE

At Lord's, June 29, 30, July 1. Drawn. Middlesex 8 pts, Yorkshire 3 pts. Toss: Middlesex. Daniel marked his return after two months' absence through injury with two early wickets, but Yorkshire's middle and lower order fought back effectively. Middlesex took advantage of Carr's bright start and were closing fast on Yorkshire's total on the first evening. Slack batted well on a second day reduced by 43 overs. His leg-side play and straightish driving were powerful and productive; he hit nineteen fours and received 251 balls. Joining him for the sixth wicket, Sykes achieved his Championship-best score. Butcher, leading Middlesex, decided to amass a large lead and go for an innings win, but he may have regretted this tactic when the weather took 53 overs from the final day. The top Yorkshire batsmen, though still struggling against the pace bowlers, survived longer second time round. Bairstow, who had injured a finger keeping wicket (Robinson deputised and took three catches), was not allowed to bat until the fall of the fifth wicket in accordance with the TCCB's new playing conditions.

Close of play: First day, Middlesex 171-3 (W. N. Slack 65*, K. R. Brown 38*); Second day, Yorkshire 5-0 (I. G. Swallow 5*, D. Byas 0*).

Yorkshire

I. G. Swallow b Daniel	5	– lbw b Cowans	12
D. Byas c Brown b Cowans	4	– lbw b Fraser	14
A. A. Metcalfe lbw b Daniel	0	– b Hughes	12
P. E. Robinson c Carr b Hughes	8	– not out	19
S. N. Hartley c Butcher b Hughes	22	– c Brown b Fraser	12
†D. L. Bairstow c Brown b Fraser	41		
*P. Carrick c Roseberry b Cowans	24	– (6) not out	4
A. Sidebottom c Carr b Hughes	28		
P. J. Hartley not out	16		
C. Shaw c Brown b Fraser	0		
S. D. Fletcher c Butcher b Cowans	18		
L-b 8, n-b 13	21	B 4, l-b 1, w 1, n-b 1	7
1/7 2/9 3/9 4/35 5/53 6/84 7/150 8/154 9/154	187	1/18 2/40 3/51 4/75 (4 wkts)	80

Bonus points – Yorkshire 1, Middlesex 4.

Bowling: *First Innings*—Cowans 15.1–3–39–3; Daniel 12–2–16–2; Fraser 18–2–56–2 Hughes 16–2–68–3. *Second Innings*—Cowans 8–3–21–1; Fraser 17–6–32–2; Daniel 1–0–3–0 Hughes 11–4–19–1.

Middlesex

W. N. Slack c Robinson b P. J. Hartley	144
J. D. Carr c Bairstow b Fletcher	30
M. A. Roseberry lbw b Fletcher	0
*R. O. Butcher lbw b Shaw	22
†K. R. Brown c Robinson b Fletcher	39
I. J. F. Hutchinson c Robinson b Sidebottom	7
J. F. Sykes b Shaw	86
S. P. Hughes not out	1
A. R. C. Fraser c Byas b Shaw	
N. G. Cowans b Fletcher	
W. W. Daniel b Shaw	
B 9, l-b 10, w 1, n-b 13	3
1/44 2/44 3/91 4/176 5/190 6/334 7/367 8/379 9/387	38

Bonus points – Middlesex 4, Yorkshire 2 (Score at 100 overs: 341-6).

Bowling: Sidebottom 18–6–51–1; Fletcher 22–0–108–4; P. J. Hartley 19–2–75–1; Sha 22.3–3–54–4; Carrick 20–4–55–0; Swallow 8–1–26–0.

Umpires: R. A. White and P. B. Wight.

At Derby, July 2, 4, 5. MIDDLESEX drew with DERBYSHIRE.

At Nottingham, July 13, 14, 15. MIDDLESEX lost to NOTTINGHAMSHIRE by 40 runs.

MIDDLESEX v GLAMORGAN

At Lord's, July 16, 18, 19. Drawn. Middlesex 5 pts, Glamorgan 4 pts. Toss: Middlesex. As they did the previous season, Middlesex compiled a huge Saturday score against Glamorgan. Gatting had made himself unavailable for the Test team for the second time in the summer, saying he was not in "the right frame of mind", but he certainly relished playing for his county. With Thomas unfit and Barwick injured during the day, batting seemed a simple task on a good pitch. Gatting, who came to the crease after a marvellous piece of wicket-keeping by Metson, reached the 50th century of his career before Slack, who had begun two hours earlier, passed 100. He hit 23 fours and faced 199 balls for his 180, whereas Slack found the boundary thirteen times from his 307 balls. The second day contained 125 overs as the spinners worked unsuccessfully against some quality batting from Butcher, Morris and Maynard. The first two made their highest Championship scores of the season to date and shared in a stand of 162 in 66 overs. On the third day Slack made his second unbeaten century of the match as a prelude to Glamorgan's being set a target of 314 in two sessions. Two quick wickets by Cowans put them out of contention, although Maynard and Shastri played sparkling innings as they tried to repair the damage. Middlesex narrowly failed largely because Emburey was not as dangerous as Needham, who, having his first bowl of the season, delivered 28 consecutive overs.

Close of play: First day, Glamorgan 17-1 (A. R. Butcher 7*, H. Morris 6*); Second day, Middlesex 58-0 (J. D. Carr 32*, W. N. Slack 24*).

Middlesex

W. N. Slack not out ....163 – (2) not out 105
J. D. Carr b Barwick .... 13 – (1) st Metson b Derrick 53
A. Needham st Metson b Derrick 35
*M. W. Gatting c Watkin b Holmes..........180
K. R. Brown not out 11
M. R. Ramprakash (did not bat) .... – (3) not out 24
B 2, l-b 14, n-b 2 .... 18 B 3, l-b 5, n-b 1 9

1/23 2/96 3/380 (3 wkts dec.) 420 1/98 (1 wkt dec.) 191

†P. R. Downton, J. E. Emburey, S. P. Hughes, A. R. C. Fraser and N. G. Cowans did not bat.

Bonus points – Middlesex 4, Glamorgan 1 (Score at 100 overs: 401-3).

Bowling: *First Innings*—Barwick 16–6–34–1; Watkin 17–4–54–0; Derrick 23–1–98–1; Ontong 21–1–91–0; Shastri 11–0–66–0; Holmes 15–2–61–1. *Second Innings*—Watkin 14–2–53–0; Derrick 17–3–45–1; Holmes 11–0–46–0; Ontong 11.3–5–28–0; Shastri 4–1–11–0.

Glamorgan

A. R. Butcher b Fraser .... 83 – c Carr b Cowans 9
. A. Hopkins c Downton b Fraser .... 2 – b Cowans 7
H. Morris c Gatting b Emburey .... 87 – c Slack b Needham 15
M. P. Maynard b Needham .... 71 – b Needham 64
R. J. Shastri not out .... 35 – c Emburey b Needham 34
G. C. Holmes not out .... 5 – c Fraser b Needham 50
R. C. Ontong (did not bat).................. – c Slack b Needham 37
. Derrick (did not bat) .... – c and b Emburey 13
C. P. Metson (did not bat) .... – not out 19
. L. Watkin (did not bat) .... – not out 0
B 4, l-b 6, w 1, n-b 4 .... 15 L-b 15, n-b 2 17

/3 2/165 3/211 4/284 (4 wkts dec.) 298 1/20 2/23 3/59 4/138 (8 wkts) 265
5/145 6/213 7/237 8/265

R. Barwick did not bat.

Bonus points – Glamorgan 3, Middlesex 1 (Score at 100 overs: 254-3).

Bowling: *First Innings*—Fraser 20–5–42–2; Cowans 14–1–36–0; Emburey 36–8–91–1; Gatting 13–2–41–0; Hughes 11–4–27–0; Needham 20–3–51–1; Brown 1–1–0–0. *Second Innings*—Cowans 7–3–11–2; Fraser 13–2–32–0; Emburey 29–8–78–1; Hughes 2–0–4–0; Needham 28–1–125–5.

Umpires: J. W. Holder and R. Palmer.

MIDDLESEX v SURREY

At Lord's, July 23, 25, 26. Drawn. Middlesex 2 pts, Surrey 3 pts. Toss: Middlesex. Rain at either end of the game prevented the possibility of a result. Only four overs were bowled on the first day, and with 23 having been lost on the second, Surrey batted into Tuesday. Clinton shared in a series of useful stands, but his second fifty was twice as long as the first and he faced 217 balls in all for his century. Middlesex made a few runs towards their eventual target before their declaration and Surrey's forfeiture left them to score 307 in 60 overs. Despite a short delay in starting their attempt, they were progressing promisingly, with Carr outscoring Gatting in an aggressive partnership. After tea, however, there were only four overs. Carr, who had hit sixteen fours, could manage only three singles from the three balls he received in the final spell of play and so narrowly missed his hundred.

Close of play: First day, Surrey 19-0 (G. S. Clinton 14*, P. D. Atkins 5*); Second day, Surrey 232-4 (D. M. Ward 18*, Zahid Sadiq 13*).

Surrey

G. S. Clinton c Carr b Emburey	100	N. H. Peters not out	24
P. D. Atkins c Downton b Cowans	25	S. T. Clarke c Slack b Needham	5
†A. J. Stewart b Emburey	44	M. P. Bicknell not out	3
M. A. Lynch c Downton b Emburey	24	B 4, l-b 12, w 1	17
D. M. Ward st Downton b Emburey	57		
Zahid Sadiq c Needham b Emburey	13	1/67 2/145 3/198 (9 wkts dec.)	334
*I. A. Greig b Emburey	20	4/201 5/239 6/271	
C. K. Bullen run out	2	7/274 8/319 9/324	

Bonus points – Surrey 3, Middlesex 2 (Score at 100 overs: 274-6).

Bowling: Cowans 12–4–43–1; Fraser 13–2–29–0; Hughes 9–0–33–0; Emburey 43–12–94–6; Gatting 9–2–26–0; Needham 29.4–8–93–1.

Surrey forfeited their second innings.

Middlesex

J. D. Carr not out	22	– not out	97
W. N. Slack retired ill	0		
A. Needham not out	5	– (2) c Stewart b Bicknell	0
*M. W. Gatting (did not bat)		– (3) c Lynch b Bullen	55
R. O. Butcher (did not bat)		– (4) b Clarke	8
M. R. Ramprakash (did not bat)		– (5) not out	15
L-b 1	1	B 5, l-b 3, w 1, n-b 1	10
(no wkt dec.)	28	1/0 2/148 3/163 (3 wkts)	185

†P. R. Downton, J. E. Emburey, S. P. Hughes, A. R. C. Fraser and N. G. Cowans did not bat.

Bowling: *First Innings*—Bicknell 4–1–8–0; Peters 3–0–14–0; Bullen 1–0–5–0. *Second Innings*—Clarke 11.3–2–45–1; Bicknell 11–2–49–1; Peters 6–0–29–0; Greig 2–0–18–0; Bullen 8–1–36–1.

Umpires: J. C. Balderstone and D. O. Oslear.

At Lord's, July 30, August 1, 2. MIDDLESEX drew with SRI LANKANS (See Sri Lankan tour section).

At Manchester, August 6, 8, 9. MIDDLESEX beat LANCASHIRE by ten wickets.

MIDDLESEX v GLOUCESTERSHIRE

At Lord's, August 13, 15, 16. Middlesex won by nine wickets. Middlesex 22 pts, Gloucestershire 6 pts. Toss: Gloucestershire. The effect of Cowans's hostile overture was cancelled out by Curran's aggression, which brought him more than half of Gloucestershire's runs. His 142, a career best, came off 271 balls and included nineteen fours. On the second morning, Slack and Gatting countered high-class pace bowling with determined strokeplay, but Middlesex were in some difficulty when Butcher, against predictions, limped in. He saw Emburey thrash a typical reviving innings which featured thirteen fierce fours and a square-cut six off Lawrence. Gatting declared in arrears, hoping no doubt to be set a target, but his bowlers pre-empted the need for any deal by striking crucially to tilt the match before the close. Next morning Gloucestershire's innings was rounded up with great efficiency by Emburey (four for 5 in seven overs) and Tufnell. Gatting and Carr joined forces soon after noon and by three o'clock had knocked off the runs in 32.3 overs of magnificent shots. Gatting hit twelve fours and one six and scored 87 of the last 113 runs.

Close of play: First day, Middlesex 11-1 (W. N. Slack 9*; S. P. Hughes 1*); Second day, Gloucestershire 142-5 (M. W. Alleyne 9*, M. W. Pooley 0*).

Gloucestershire

A. W. Stovold c Downton b Cowans	1	– c Downton b Fraser	33
A. J. Wright lbw b Carr	40	– c Downton b Tufnell	43
P. W. Romaines c Carr b Cowans	1	– c Slack b Emburey	17
P. Bainbridge c Brown b Cowans	2	– b Emburey	3
K. M. Curran st Downton b Tufnell	142	– (6) run out	33
M. W. Alleyne c Gatting b Emburey	0	– (5) c Gatting b Emburey	14
†R. C. Russell c Emburey b Hughes	13	– (8) st Downton b Emburey	13
M. W. Pooley b Emburey	38	– (7) b Emburey	1
*D. A. Graveney c Hughes b Tufnell	16	– c Gatting b Tufnell	0
D. V. Lawrence not out	1	– c Gatting b Emburey	0
T. M. Alderman lbw b Emburey	2	– not out	0
L-b 6, n-b 6	12	B 1, l-b 1, n-b 2	4
1/1 2/20 3/22 4/103 5/104 6/122 7/228 8/259 9/265	268	1/69 2/94 3/99 4/100 5/142 6/147 7/156 8/161 9/161	161

Bonus points – Gloucestershire 3, Middlesex 3 (Score at 100 overs: 252-7).

Bowling: *First Innings*—Fraser 23–7–51–0; Cowans 13–3–50–3; Hughes 18–2–46–1; Carr 7–2–20–1; Emburey 21–7–46–3; Tufnell 24–4–49–2. *Second Innings*—Cowans 5–0–19–0; Hughes 6–0–45–0; Fraser 7–2–13–1; Tufnell 26.3–9–58–2; Emburey 21–9–24–6.

Middlesex

W. N. Slack c Russell b Curran	56	– lbw b Alderman	0
J. D. Carr c Romaines b Lawrence	0	– not out	58
S. P. Hughes c Romaines b Lawrence	3		
*M. W. Gatting st Russell b Graveney	51	– (3) not out	93
K. R. Brown lbw b Curran	3		
†P. R. Downton b Curran	6		
J. E. Emburey lbw b Alderman	82		
R. O. Butcher c Pooley b Graveney	24		
A. R. C. Fraser not out	8		
N. G. Cowans not out	15		
L-b 8, n-b 5	13	B 4, l-b 11, n-b 3	18
1/1 2/26 3/82 4/90 5/127 6/127 7/200 8/242	(8 wkts dec.) 261	1/5	(1 wkt) 169

P. C. R. Tufnell did not bat.

Bonus points – Middlesex 3, Gloucestershire 3.

Bowling: *First Innings*—Lawrence 14–0–72–2; Alderman 16–3–46–1; Curran 16–2–65–3; Pooley 3–0–4–0; Bainbridge 1–0–3–0; Graveney 14–2–63–2. *Second Innings*—Lawrence 8–2–30–0; Alderman 7–2–18–1; Graveney 11.3–0–65–0; Curran 8–2–33–0; Pooley 3–1–8–0.

Umpires: J. D. Bond and K. E. Palmer.

MIDDLESEX v SOMERSET

At Uxbridge, August 17, 18, 19. Drawn. Middlesex 6 pts, Somerset 6 pts. Toss: Somerset. Emburey entered the attack after only nine overs and took two wickets in his fifth. Waugh and Felton denied the spin bowlers in a skilful stand of 160 in 50 overs, only for Tufnell and Emburey to regain control after their dismissal. Brown, Roseberry and Ramprakash all played solidly, but Middlesex were disrupted by Downton's hamstring injury and Gatting's bruised hand, which forced him to bat down the order. On the third day Waugh signed off his summer with Somerset with a century, although the last 77 runs came off "declaration" bowling. Rain for 80 minutes, just as Somerset were about to declare, complicated the captains' equation, and more rain made Middlesex's target 253 in 35 overs. Two wickets in the first three overs made a difficult job impossible, but Somerset had a glimpse of victory before Gatting and Ramprakash saved the match after coming together with 75 minutes left.

Close of play: First day, Middlesex 26-2 (K. R. Brown 13*, A. R. C. Fraser 10*); Second day, Somerset 13-1 (J. J. E. Hardy 2*, J. G. Wyatt 3*).

Somerset

J. J. E. Hardy c Brown b Emburey	26	– c Emburey b Carr	28
N. A. Felton c Slack b Emburey	88	– b Cowans	7
J. G. Wyatt b Emburey	0	– c Slack b Emburey	19
S. R. Waugh b Tufnell	83	– not out	112
R. J. Bartlett c Carr b Tufnell	9	– c Cowans b Roseberry	35
†N. D. Burns st Downton b Tufnell	7	– not out	13
*V. J. Marks b Cowans	34		
G. D. Rose retired hurt	6		
H. R. J. Trump c and b Tufnell	2		
N. A. Mallender not out	11		
A. N. Jones c Emburey b Fraser	3		
L-b 2, n-b 4	6	B 4, l-b 11, w 1, n-b 2	18
1/38 2/38 3/198 4/208 5/215 6/216 7/238 8/268 9/275	275	1/7 2/51 3/73 4/168 (4 wkts dec.)	232

Bonus points – Somerset 3, Middlesex 3 (Score at 100 overs: 270-8).

Bowling: *First Innings*—Fraser 20.2–7–52–1; Cowans 16–5–36–1; Emburey 34–6–97–3; Tufnell 34–6–88–4. *Second Innings*—Cowans 9–3–20–1; Fraser 13–1–37–0; Tufnell 8–2–17–0; Emburey 14–4–30–1; Carr 2–0–4–1; Roseberry 7.1–1–41–1; Ramprakash 5–0–46–0; Gatting 1–0–8–0; Slack 1–0–14–0.

Middlesex

J. D. Carr run out	0	– run out	20
W. N. Slack lbw b Mallender	1	– c and b Jones	0
K. R. Brown c Waugh b Jones	73	– c Burns b Mallender	1
A. R. C. Fraser b Mallender	12	– (8) not out	0
M. A. Roseberry lbw b Jones	48	– (4) c Burns b Mallender	21
M. R. Ramprakash c Rose b Marks	45	– (5) not out	43
†P. R. Downton retired hurt	7		
*M. W. Gatting b Trump	27	– (7) c Burns b Trump	51
J. E. Emburey c Wyatt b Marks	13	– (6) b Mallender	0
N. G. Cowans not out	15		
P. C. R. Tufnell not out	0		
B 7, l-b 4, w 1, n-b 2	14	B 1, l-b 6, n-b 6	13
1/2 2/5 3/36 4/134 5/145 6/199 7/231 8/235 (8 wkts dec.)	255	1/0 2/1 3/37 4/45 5/45 6/145 (6 wkts)	149

Bonus points – Middlesex 3, Somerset 3.

Bowling: *First Innings*—Mallender 14–0–52–2; Jones 17–3–55–2; Marks 13–3–52–2; Rose 11–2–44–0; Trump 22–7–41–1. *Second Innings*—Mallender 8–2–43–3; Jones 7–0–30–1; Marks 12.4–4–41–0; Rose 2–1–4–0; Trump 5–1–24–1.

Umpires: K. J. Lyons and R. Palmer.

MIDDLESEX v WARWICKSHIRE

At Uxbridge, August 20, 22, 23. Middlesex won by seven wickets. Middlesex 23 pts, Warwickshire 6 pts. Toss: Warwickshire. Lloyd, whose 101 came out of 156 with nineteen fours, stood virtually alone as Cowans exploited a pitch that encouraged his style. Middlesex's faltering start contained one of Gatting's late-summer run-outs, and for the second consecutive Monday Emburey shifted the balance of a match that was sliding away from them. He had to adapt his unique batting method to Gifford's pitching the ball in the rough outside the leg stump, with the result that the third century of his career was slower than might have been expected. He hit thirteen fours from his 193 balls. Before the close, Cowans increased Middlesex's grip with two lbws, and Emburey completed a successful day with the wickets of Lloyd and Pierson. Warwickshire began the final day 1 run ahead and were only 27 in front when their seventh wicket went soon after noon. Reeve, helped by Munton, ensured that the match was prolonged into the second session, and then Small and Munton shook Middlesex with early wickets. At 14 for three, and with Small almost unplayable, Middlesex needed the hard work of Gatting and Roseberry, who saw them home without further anxiety.

Close of play: First day, Middlesex 66-2 (W. N. Slack 39*, M. A. Roseberry 4*); Second day, Warwickshire 63-4 (D. A. Thorne 10*, D. A. Reeve 3*).

Warwickshire

J. D. Ratcliffe lbw b Cowans	5	– lbw b Cowans	4
*T. A. Lloyd c Gatting b Emburey	101	– c Gatting b Emburey	41
Asif Din c Brown b Cowans	18	– lbw b Cowans	4
D. A. Thorne c Brown b Fraser	6	– lbw b Cowans	26
D. A. Reeve c Sykes b Cowans	14	– (6) b Emburey	41
S. D. Myles c Brown b Cowans	0	– (7) b Fraser	3
†G. A. Tedstone c Brown b Cowans	34	– (8) b Fraser	0
G. C. Small lbw b Emburey	4	– (9) lbw b Fraser	5
A. R. K. Pierson c Brown b Fraser	1	– (5) lbw b Emburey	0
T. A. Munton not out	9	– not out	24
N. Gifford c Sykes b Cowans	7	– c Emburey b Cowans	0
B 2, l-b 5, n-b 6	13	L-b 6, w 1, n-b 3	10
1/21 2/57 3/78 4/148 5/148 6/156 7/160 8/172 9/199	212	1/11 2/25 3/57 4/59 5/84 6/88 7/89 8/106 9/152	158

Bonus points – Warwickshire 2, Middlesex 4.

Bowling: *First Innings*—Cowans 17.2–2–49–6; Fraser 26–11–61–2; Emburey 25–9–54–2; Carr 7–1–25–0; Tufnell 3–1–16–0. *Second Innings*—Fraser 19–7–25–3; Cowans 22.1–6–48–4; Emburey 17–6–35–3; Tufnell 25–8–44–0.

Middlesex

J. D. Carr c and b Small	4	– lbw b Small	0
W. N. Slack b Reeve	44	– b Munton	4
†K. R. Brown b Gifford	16	– c Tedstone b Small	2
M. A. Roseberry c Tedstone b Small	12	– (5) not out	41
*M. W. Gatting run out	4	– (4) not out	45
M. R. Ramprakash c Thorne b Gifford	33		
J. E. Emburey c and b Small	102		
J. F. Sykes b Gifford	25		
A. R. C. Fraser lbw b Small	14		
N. G. Cowans b Small	0		
P. C. R. Tufnell not out	0		
B 9, l-b 7, w 1, n-b 3	20	B 1, l-b 2, w 2	5
1/18 2/50 3/77 4/84 5/85 6/150 7/220 8/265 9/265	274	1/0 2/6 3/14	(3 wkts) 97

Bonus points – Middlesex 3, Warwickshire 4.

Bowling: *First Innings*—Small 27.2–5–74–5; Munton 11–4–40–0; Gifford 34–10–68–3; Pierson 11–2–38–0; Reeve 15–2–38–1. *Second Innings*—Small 12–5–16–2; Munton 8–2–14–1; Gifford 8–2–24–0; Pierson 3–0–24–0; Asif Din 2–0–16–0.

Umpires: D. G. L. Evans and R. Palmer.

At Leeds, August 25, 26, 27, 29. MIDDLESEX drew with YORKSHIRE.

At Hove, August 30, 31, September 1, 2. MIDDLESEX drew with SUSSEX.

MIDDLESEX v KENT

At Lord's, September 9, 10, 11, 12. Drawn. Middlesex 5 pts, Kent 7 pts. Toss: Middlesex. Kent arrived at Lord's looking for the win that would take them to the verge of the Championship. But missing a fourth batting point was an ominous prelude to drawing the game – a result which was crucial in Kent's failure to take the title. Carr, reprieved at the Pavilion steps when the umpires decided that Slack rather than he had been run out, repaired Middlesex's early problems in an attractive stand of 136 with Butcher. Kent, nevertheless, gathered full bowling points, and Benson and Tavaré guaranteed them a good lead. Their run-rate, however, left the Cowdrey brothers too much to do. Benson spent four hours over his 81 and Tavaré was nearly two hours moving from his half-century to 78. Carr and Slack comfortably erased the deficit, but Penn ended the third day with a burst of four for 15 in 38 balls; when Gatting went first ball next morning, Kent looked likely winners. Rain, however, extracted twenty overs, and the later batsmen endured endlessly with Tufnell's career-best 20 in a last-wicket stand of 46 bringing Kent's frustration to a peak. Requiring 230 from 29 overs, Kent attacked with a complete disregard for wickets, the outcome being that Middlesex came closer to winning. The eighth wicket fell with eleven overs left, the ninth with six, but Igglesden and Harman proved equal to the occasion.

Close of play: First day, Kent 26-0 (M. R. Benson 20*, S. G. Hinks 5*); Second day, Kent 367-6 (G. R. Cowdrey 80*, C. Penn 30*); Third day, Middlesex 230-5 (M. W. Gatting 35* A. R. C. Fraser 9*).

Middlesex

W. N. Slack run out	5	– c Marsh b Penn	8
J. D. Carr c G. R. Cowdrey b Ellison	92	– c Ellison b Penn	6
*M. W. Gatting c Marsh b Ellison	26	– lbw b Igglesden	3
M. A. Roseberry lbw b Ellison	0	– (6) c Penn b C. S. Cowdrey	1
R. O. Butcher b C. S. Cowdrey	59	– lbw b Penn	1
M. R. Ramprakash lbw b Igglesden	54	– (4) c Tavaré b Penn	
J. E. Emburey c C. S. Cowdrey b Ellison	6	– (9) lbw b Penn	2
†P. R. Downton not out	22	– not out	5
A. R. C. Fraser c Benson b Igglesden	7	– (7) b Penn	1
N. G. Cowans b Igglesden	6	– c Tavaré b Penn	
P. C. R. Tufnell lbw b Penn	1	– b Igglesden	2
B 4, l-b 1, w 2, n-b 5	12	B 8, l-b 6, w 1, n-b 11	2
1/7 2/54 3/54 4/190 5/192 6/207 7/267 8/281 9/287	290	1/151 2/158 3/165 4/185 5/219 6/230 7/249 8/301 9/305	35

Bonus points – Middlesex 3, Kent 4.

Bowling: *First Innings*—Igglesden 22–3–86–3; Penn 15.3–2–52–1; Pienaar 17–2–56– Ellison 17–5–49–4; Harman 14–6–27–0; C. S. Cowdrey 6–2–15–1. *Second Innings*—Igglesde 33.5–9–117–2; Penn 30–5–70–7; Ellison 27–7–80–0; Pienaar 5–1–16–0; Harman 19–7–35– C. S. Cowdrey 11–5–19–1.

Kent

M. R. Benson b Cowans	81	– c Butcher b Fraser	25
S. G. Hinks c Butcher b Fraser	20	– b Fraser	23
R. F. Pienaar lbw b Cowans	4	– b Cowans	2
C. J. Tavaré run out	78	– c Tufnell b Emburey	11
*C. S. Cowdrey c Roseberry b Tufnell	37	– c Butcher b Fraser	5
G. R. Cowdrey c Butcher b Cowans	86	– lbw b Fraser	10
†S. A. Marsh c Gatting b Carr	21	– c Ramprakash b Fraser	1
C. Penn c Downton b Fraser	30	– b Emburey	30
R. M. Ellison c Downton b Cowans	6	– c Roseberry b Emburey	3
A. P. Igglesden b Cowans	17	– not out	1
M. D. Harman not out	14	– not out	0
L-b 17, n-b 1	18	B 7, l-b 11	18
1/44 2/51 3/168 4/214 5/241 6/276 7/368 8/378 9/381	412	1/39 2/52 3/68 4/73 5/76 6/92 7/93 8/128 9/128	(9 wkts) 129

Bonus points – Kent 3, Middlesex 2 (Score at 100 overs: 260-5).

Bowling: *First Innings*—Fraser 38–10–89–2; Cowans 35.5–9–105–5; Emburey 31–5–80–0; Carr 10–2–25–1; Tufnell 24–3–86–1; Gatting 5–1–10–0. *Second Innings*—Fraser 9–2–27–5; Cowans 4–0–30–1; Emburey 10–5–42–3; Tufnell 6–4–12–0.

Umpires: J. C. Balderstone and B. Leadbeater.

FIRST REAL TENNIS COURT AT LORD'S

In June 1989 occurs the 150th anniversary of the opening of the first real tennis court at Lord's. The foundation of the court was laid in the area of the Mound Stand in October 1838 and the building was completed and opened in June 1839.

TWO TIMES TEN

Andy Langston, an opening bowler for the Alexandra Park club in North London, performed a remarkable double feat inside one week in June 1988. On June 18, playing for Buckingham Palace, his former employer, he took all ten wickets for 59 in 20.3 overs against the Royal Household at Windsor Great Park. Five days later, on June 23, playing for Alexandra Park in a match celebrating their centenary, he took all ten wickets for 77 in 25.1 overs against a Club Cricket Conference President's XI.

NORTHAMPTONSHIRE

Patron: The Earl of Dalkeith
President: D. C. Lucas
Chairman: W. R. F. Chamberlain
Chairman, Cricket Committee: A. P. Arnold
Secretary/Manager: S. P. Coverdale
County Ground, Wantage Road,
Northampton NN1 4TJ
(Telephone: 0604-32917)
Captain: 1988 – G. Cook
1989 – A. J. Lamb
Coach: R. M. Carter
Cricket Development Officer: B. L. Reynolds

After the near misses of the previous year, Northamptonshire's failure to challenge for any of the major trophies in 1988 was especially disappointing. Nothing better served to illustrate the unfulfilled hopes of the season than the striking contrast between the high-profile arrival in May of Dennis Lillee, thrusting the club into the national spotlight, and the small, low-key press conference to witness Geoff Cook's resignation as captain in September.

The decision of Cook, a leader respected throughout the county game, to stand down after eight years in charge was hardly a surprise following a season in which little had gone right for him, or his team. Twelfth in the Britannic Assurance Championship, a drop of five places from 1987, was Northamptonshire's lowest placing since 1981 – the year Cook took over from Jim Watts – and recent one-day successes became distant memories as the side failed to qualify for the knockout stages of the Benson and Hedges Cup, lost in the first round of the NatWest Bank Trophy to a minor county, Cheshire, and managed only four wins in the Refuge Assurance League.

Injuries and Test calls contributed to the club's difficulties. Cook himself (broken jaw), Lillee (damaged ankle) and Richard Williams (knee ligament trouble) were all sidelined for significant periods, and Allan Lamb made only nine Championship appearances around international duties and a month away with a pulled calf muscle. Yet these factors can only partially explain why Northamptonshire suffered so many reverses in 1988. Cook readily admitted that the side had been found wanting in commitment and application, hence his desire for someone with "fresh ideas and fresh motivation" to replace him. Certainly, the fighting qualities which enabled Northamptonshire to beat Warwickshire after following on four weeks into the season were displayed all too rarely thereafter.

When available, Lamb, who averaged 59.85 in all first-class games for the county, was easily the most consistent performer in a batting line-up which produced a frustrating mixture of meritorious and unconvincing efforts. Both David Capel and Williams shone on occasions, but Duncan Wild had a harrowing season. Robert Bailey alone topped 1,000 Championship runs, and he earned his Test début against West Indies. His fight to overcome a bad patch in mid-season was not helped by a quirk of the fixture list which allowed Northamptonshire's batsmen only a possible six first-class innings in four weeks. Too often, though, Bailey found himself facing a newer ball and fresher bowlers than he would have liked, after the almost inevitable fall of an early wicket. In the Championship, Northamptonshire's opening stands averaged only 22.

Wayne Larkins was seldom able to combine his ability with the concentration necessary to build a long innings. Apart from two typically dazzling centuries against Gloucestershire and Kent, his form slipped to such a degree that Cook, in a controversial move which added greatly to the captain's personal burden, dropped his long-time opening partner for the last two matches. Ironically, when Cook was out of action for five weeks early in the season, Larkins had led the side and proved a capable leader, popular with his fellow players. Alan Fordham took the opportunities offered to him as a result of Cook's injury, Larkins's demotion, and the premature retirement of Robin Boyd-Moss to play several responsible and valuable innings.

The emergence of Fordham and the Hull-born seamer, Mark Robinson, gave most cause for satisfaction. Having served a two-year apprenticeship in the Second XI, Robinson was eager for success and finished with 42 wickets from thirteen Championship games, looking the most dangerous member of the pace attack from the beginning of August onwards. Inevitably, the 21 year old benefited from the presence of Lillee, who earned much admiration for his determination to fight back from an injury which threatened to end his career within three weeks of his taking six for 68 in the second innings of his Championship début against Gloucestershire. He was an admirable ambassador for the club, liberal with his advice to colleagues and opponents alike.

Lillee's lengthy absence meant a heavier work-load for Winston Davis than had been envisaged. The West Indian responded splendidly with 73 wickets, three more than in 1987. He bowled more overs than anyone else except the left-arm spinner, Nick Cook, whose tally of 66 wickets for Northamptonshire was, in turn, second only to Davis's. Northamptonshire owed much to these two contrasting bowlers, for Capel, troubled by injury at either end of the season, and Walker marked time. Williams's off-spin could have been decisive on more than one occasion during his spell out of the side, and even when he was fit his bowling opportunities were unduly limited.

The attack could not complain at the quality of support given from behind the stumps by David Ripley. The young Yorkshireman's 81 dismissals have only once been exceeded for Northamptonshire – by K. V. Andrew in 1962 – and, following the departure of Stuart Waterton at the end of the previous season, Ripley appeared more relaxed with very few "off days".

Northamptonshire's new captain in 1989 will face the testing task of getting the best out of a talented group of players which includes several strong personalities. He will, however, have at his disposal not only the experience of Geoff Cook, who accepted a new two-year playing contract, but also the choice of two outstanding overseas fast bowlers in Davis and Curtly Ambrose. Looking further ahead, though, some of the shortcomings of 1988 require urgent attention. Additional spin bowling and experienced batting cover would balance the squad, and fostering a stronger sense of pride in performance must be high on any list of priorities. – Andrew Radd.

NORTHAMPTONSHIRE 1988

[*Bill Smith*

Back row: A. Roberts, W. Noon, M. R. Baker, A. Penberthy, D. S. Hoffman, M. A. Robinson, N. A. Stanley, G. Smith. *Middle row:* R. Norman (*physiotherapist*), A. Fordham, M. R. Gouldstone, S. J. Brown, D. Ripley, W. W. Davis, D. J. Wild, A. Walker, R. M. Carter (*coach*). *Front row:* [illegible] W. Larkins, R. G. Williams, N. G. B. Cook. *Inset:* D. K. Lillee.

NORTHAMPTONSHIRE RESULTS

All first-class matches – Played 24: Won 6, Lost 7, Drawn 11.

County Championship matches – Played 22: Won 5, Lost 7, Drawn 10.

Bonus points – Batting 48, Bowling 71.

Competition placings – Britannic Assurance County Championship, 12th; NatWest Bank Trophy, 1st round; Benson and Hedges Cup, 3rd in Group B; Refuge Assurance League, 14th equal.

BRITANNIC ASSURANCE CHAMPIONSHIP AVERAGES

BATTING

	Birthplace	*M*	*I*	*NO*	*R*	*HI*	*Avge*
‡A. J. Lamb	*Langebaanweg, SA*	9	15	2	731	155	56.23
‡D. J. Capel	*Northampton*	17	29	4	981	92	39.24
‡R. J. Bailey	*Biddulph*	20	36	1	1,203	127*	34.37
‡R. G. Williams	*Bangor*	18	31	7	770	119	32.08
‡G. Cook	*Middlesbrough*	17	29	1	836	203	29.85
A. Fordham	*Bedford*	15	28	6	627	125*	28.50
‡W. Larkins	*Roxton*	20	37	2	905	134	25.85
‡A. Walker	*Emley*	16	19	10	208	40*	23.11
M. R. Gouldstone	*Bishop's Stortford*	7	12	1	239	71	21.72
§‡W. W. Davis	*Sion Hill, St Vincent*	15	18	3	306	43	20.40
N. A. Stanley	*Bedford*	6	10	2	142	62	17.75
‡D. J. Wild	*Northampton*	17	26	1	408	75	16.32
‡D. Ripley	*Leeds*	22	30	5	390	49	15.60
§D. K. Lillee	*Perth, Australia*	7	10	2	98	22	12.25
S. J. Brown	*Cleadon*	3	6	1	34	25*	6.80
‡N. G. B. Cook	*Leicester*	20	24	1	133	24	5.78
M. A. Robinson	*Hull*	13	16	7	32	19*	3.55

* *Signifies not out.* ‡ *Denotes county cap.* § *Not qualified for England.*

The following played a total of eleven three-figure innings for Northamptonshire in County Championship matches – A. J. Lamb 3, R. J. Bailey 2, G. Cook 2, W. Larkins 2, A. Fordham 1, R. G. Williams 1.

BOWLING

	O	*M*	*R*	*W*	*BB*	*5W/i*	*Avge*
W. W. Davis	538.2	91	1,614	73	7-52	7	22.10
M. A. Robinson	347.4	72	932	42	4-19	0	22.19
N. G. B. Cook	632.2	228	1,285	56	6-56	2	22.94
A. Walker	406.1	81	1,240	46	5-64	1	26.95
R. G. Williams	295	61	888	31	5-86	1	28.64
D. J. Wild	164.5	33	486	16	4-18	0	30.37
D. J. Capel	371.4	68	1,235	34	4-40	0	36.32
D. K. Lillee	232	42	731	20	6-68	1	36.55

Also bowled: R. J. Bailey 59.1–8–201–5; S. J. Brown 65–13–176–4; G. Cook 5–1–7–0; W. Larkins 5–1–8–0.

Wicket-keeper: D. Ripley 66 ct, 6 st.

Leading Fielders: W. Larkins 23, R. J. Bailey 19.

At Oxford, April 20, 21, 22. NORTHAMPTONSHIRE beat OXFORD UNIVERSITY by an innings and 157 runs.

At Leicester, April 28, 29, 30. NORTHAMPTONSHIRE lost to LEICESTERSHIRE by an innings and 51 runs.

NORTHAMPTONSHIRE v GLOUCESTERSHIRE

At Northampton, May 5, 6, 7, 9. Northamptonshire won by 49 runs. Northamptonshire 22 pts, Gloucestershire 5 pts. Toss: Gloucestershire. Lillee marked his first Championship appearance by bowling Northamptonshire to victory with a masterly display on the fourth afternoon. Maintaining an impeccable line and exploiting the helpful conditions, he wrapped up Gloucestershire's second innings by taking four for 16 in a seven-over spell after lunch to finish with six wickets, all captured without assistance from the field. On the second day, he had bowled Stovold with his eighth ball in county cricket. The fast bowlers dominated throughout, although in the opening stages Bailey played positively for two and a half hours, and Wright battled through 42 overs for his 36. Northamptonshire's first-innings advantage was pressed home first by Williams and Ripley, in a stand of 82, and then by Lillee and Brown, who added 40 for the ninth wicket in an hour. Chasing 251 to win in four complete sessions, Gloucestershire looked on course at 118 for two with Wright again batting steadily. But Walker claimed three of their next four wickets in the space of six overs and set the scene for Lillee to apply the *coup de grâce* with a skill undiminished by the passing years.

Close of play: First day, Northamptonshire 164-6 (D. Ripley 15*, N. G. B. Cook 5*); Second day, Northamptonshire 54-2 (R. J. Bailey 21*, A. J. Lamb 18*); Third day, Gloucestershire 103-2 (A. J. Wright 40*, T. M. Alderman 8*).

Northamptonshire

First innings		Second innings	
*G. Cook lbw b Alderman	3	– c Russell b Thomas	12
W. Larkins c Bainbridge b Lawrence	9	– b Alderman	0
R. J. Bailey c Russell b Bainbridge	66	– c Romaines b Lawrence	21
A. J. Lamb b Thomas	11	– c Bainbridge b Alderman	30
D. J. Capel c Athey b Alderman	40	– c Lloyds b Alderman	3
R. G. Williams c Lloyds b Graveney	5	– c Lloyds b Graveney	51
†D. Ripley c Graveney b Alderman	15	– lbw b Alderman	35
N. G. B. Cook c Russell b Lawrence	5	– c Russell b Graveney	3
S. J. Brown c Wright b Alderman	4	– not out	25
D. K. Lillee b Lawrence	22	– c Athey b Graveney	22
A. Walker not out	11	– c Athey b Thomas	3
L-b 5, w 1, n-b 9	15	L-b 7, n-b 4	11
1/11 2/19 3/57 4/123 5/136 6/147 7/164 8/168 9/183	206	1/2 2/21 3/59 4/70 5/79 6/161 7/161 8/165 9/205	216

Bonus points – Northamptonshire 2, Gloucestershire 4.

Bowling: *First Innings*—Lawrence 16–3–54–3; Alderman 24–7–52–4; Thomas 11–3–27–1; Bainbridge 15–1–40–1; Graveney 15–6–22–1; Lloyds 2–1–6–0. *Second Innings*—Lawrence 18–2–59–1; Alderman 22–6–52–4; Thomas 13.4–2–39–2; Bainbridge 10–3–27–0; Graveney 22–11–32–3.

Gloucestershire

	First innings		Second innings	
A. W. Stovold b Lillee	4	– c N. G. B. Cook b Capel	40
A. J. Wright b Walker	36	– c Larkins b Walker	48
P. W. Romaines c Ripley b Brown	6	– lbw b Lillee	7
C. W. J. Athey c Williams b Capel	27	– (5) b Lillee	40
P. Bainbridge c Bailey b Walker	9	– (6) b Walker	2
J. W. Lloyds c Brown b Capel	2	– (7) c Ripley b Walker	0
†R. C. Russell c Capel b N. G. B. Cook	29	– (8) lbw b Lillee	10
D. J. Thomas b Brown	7	– (9) b Lillee	3
*D. A. Graveney c Ripley b Walker	20	– (10) not out	1
D. V. Lawrence b Walker	10	– (11) b Lillee	23
T. M. Alderman not out	3	– (4) b Lillee	14
B 4, l-b 12, n-b 3	19	B 7, l-b 6	13
1/8 2/28 3/82 4/96 5/101 6/110 7/124 8/152 9/161	172	1/64 2/86 3/118 4/120 5/127 6/127 7/160 8/176 9/177	201

Bonus points – Gloucestershire 1, Northamptonshire 4.

Bowling: *First Innings*—Lillee 16–4–39–1; Capel 16–6–35–2; Brown 15–3–27–2; Walker 17.2–5–50–4; Larkins 2–1–1–0; N. G. B. Cook 5–3–4–1. *Second Innings*—Lillee 29–8–68–6; Capel 14–3–32–1; N. G. B. Cook 7–3–12–0; Walker 20–3–68–3; Brown 3–0–8–0.

Umpires: D. J. Constant and R. A. White.

NORTHAMPTONSHIRE v WARWICKSHIRE

At Northampton, May 17, 18, 19, 20. Northamptonshire won by 6 runs. Northamptonshire 19 pts, Warwickshire 7 pts. Toss: Warwickshire. Four days of absorbing cricket ended dramatically at 3.45 on the last afternoon when Larkins caught Gifford at slip to give Northamptonshire their first victory after following on since winning at Worcester in 1906. Warwickshire required only 119 to win, but lost four wickets for 38 in threequarters of an hour before lunch, and when Smith departed soon afterwards, half the side was out for 51. Asif Din and Reeve, the first-innings century-makers, tilted the balance back in Warwickshire's favour, but Davis and Williams broke through for the second and decisive time. This was all in stark contrast to the first two days. First Asif Din (232 minutes, seventeen fours) and Reeve (331 minutes, nine fours) steered Warwickshire to their highest total at Northampton; and then Merrick and Smith made inroads into the home side's batting, the latter claiming his three wickets in six balls. Northamptonshire followed on 245 behind with two days remaining, but a greatly improved performance, featuring an 89-run partnership for the ninth wicket between Ripley and Davis, gave the bowlers an outside chance. As Warwickshire's confidence ebbed away, they eagerly grasped it.

Close of play: First day, Warwickshire 320-7 (D. A. Reeve 75*, T. A. Merrick 6*); Second day, Northamptonshire 14-0 (A. Fordham 6*, W. Larkins 3*); Third day, Northamptonshire 331-8 (D. Ripley 29*, W. W. Davis 36*).

Warwickshire

	First innings		Second innings	
*T. A. Lloyd b Davis	10	– c Bailey b Walker	2
A. J. Moles b Davis	7	– lbw b Davis	9
Asif Din c Ripley b Walker	131	– c Walker b Williams	48
A. I. Kallicharran lbw b Davis	0	– lbw b Walker	0
†G. W. Humpage lbw b Walker	3	– c and b Davis	3
P. A. Smith lbw b Davis	47	– c Williams b Walker	5
D. A. Reeve b Williams	103	– c Fordham b Davis	12
G. J. Parsons c Ripley b Davis	18	– not out	8
T. A. Merrick b Davis	34	– b Williams	1
A. R. K. Pierson not out	18	– b Davis	1
N. Gifford b Williams	12	– c Larkins b Williams	3
B 1, l-b 8, w 9, n-b 14	32	B 8, l-b 2, n-b 10	20
1/12 2/41 3/41 4/58 5/147 6/254 7/289 8/366 9/399	415	1/3 2/22 3/24 4/38 5/51 6/98 7/103 8/104 9/105	112

Bonus points – Warwickshire 3, Northamptonshire 2 (Score at 100 overs: 269-6).

Bowling: *First Innings*—Davis 36–5–141–6; Capel 22–5–75–0; Walker 25–9–67–2; Cook 34–11–57–0; Brown 14–5–34–0; Wild 9–0–22–0; Williams 3.2–0–10–2. *Second Innings*—Davis 19–3–44–4; Walker 14–1–40–3; Cook 1–0–3–0; Capel 1–0–6–0; Williams 6.4–3–9–3.

Northamptonshire

A. Fordham lbw b Merrick	6	– lbw b Parsons	26
*W. Larkins c Humpage b Parsons	19	– c Humpage b Reeve	33
R. J. Bailey lbw b Smith	76	– c Lloyd b Gifford	60
D. J. Capel c Reeve b Gifford	9	– c Moles b Smith	37
R. G. Williams c Humpage b Pierson	8	– c Humpage b Merrick	13
D. J. Wild b Merrick	17	– c and b Smith	58
†D. Ripley not out	14	– c Lloyd b Reeve	47
N. G. B. Cook lbw b Smith	0	– lbw b Merrick	1
S. J. Brown b Smith	0	– c Humpage b Merrick	0
W. W. Davis c Asif Din b Gifford	6	– c Gifford b Smith	43
A. Walker c Moles b Merrick	0	– not out	3
B 2, l-b 5, n-b 8	15	B 5, l-b 10, w 5, n-b 22	42
1/11 2/49 3/78 4/105 5/132 6/149 7/149 8/151 9/163	170	1/58 2/92 3/170 4/184 5/242 6/264 7/268 8/268 9/357	363

Bonus points – Northamptonshire 1, Warwickshire 4.

Bowling: *First Innings*—Merrick 19.5–3–48–3; Parsons 9–2–26–1; Gifford 18–7–38–2; Reeve 6–1–16–0; Pierson 12–3–27–1; Smith 6–0–8–3. *Second Innings*—Merrick 39–7–115–3; Parsons 17–5–36–1; Reeve 18.3–6–30–2; Smith 18–1–49–3; Gifford 28–11–68–1; Pierson 19–8–39–0; Asif Din 8–3–11–0.

Umpires: D. G. L. Evans and J. W. Holder.

At The Oval, May 21, 23, 24. NORTHAMPTONSHIRE drew with SURREY.

NORTHAMPTONSHIRE v LEICESTERSHIRE

At Northampton, May 28, 30, 31. Drawn. Northamptonshire 8 pts, Leicestershire 2 pts. Toss: Leicestershire. Rain docked 90 minutes from the final day's play and, in all probability, cost Northamptonshire their first Championship victory over Leicestershire for twelve years. Put in on a green-looking pitch which did not produce the expected degree of movement for the seam bowlers, Northamptonshire moved comfortably to maximum batting points thanks to Bailey, Lamb and, most impressively, Capel (thirteen fours). Larkins declared before the start on the second day and then saw his seamers work steadily through a Leicestershire side lacking the necessary application. Capel sent back Whitaker, Potter and Willey in successive overs, but in the follow-on Cobb defended sensibly for four hours. The visitors' cause was helped not only by the weather, which brought about four stoppages on the third day, but also by an ankle injury to Lillee, who stumbled in the field and suffered a hairline fracture and ligament damage. Late resistance from Agnew, absent in the first innings with flu, left Northamptonshire to chase 81 in eight overs, a target which proved beyond them although they made a spirited attempt.

Close of play: First day, Northamptonshire 327-8 (R. G. Williams 33*, D. K. Lillee 4*) Second day, Leicestershire 117-2 (R. A. Cobb 38*, P. Willey 23*).

Northamptonshire

A. Fordham c Whitticase b Lewis	25	– (7) not out	0
*W. Larkins lbw b DeFreitas	42	– c Whitticase b Ferris	0
R. J. Bailey c DeFreitas b Ferris	55	– (1) run out	18
A. J. Lamb lbw b Ferris	70	– (3) c and b DeFreitas	14
D. J. Capel c Gower b Willey	75	– (4) b Ferris	8
R. G. Williams not out	33	– (5) b DeFreitas	12
D. J. Wild b Willey	0	– (6) c DeFreitas b Ferris	4
†D. Ripley c Whitaker b Willey	4	– not out	1
N. G. B. Cook b Lewis	2		
D. K. Lillee not out	4		
L-b 11, w 1, n-b 5	17	L-b 3, w 1, n-b 1	5
1/67 2/102 3/165 4/210 5/306 6/306 7/314 8/319	(8 wkts dec.) 327	1/1 2/33 3/42 4/45 5/57 6/61	(6 wkts) 62

A. Walker did not bat.

Bonus points – Northamptonshire 4, Leicestershire 2 (Score at 100 overs: 306-6).

Bowling: *First Innings*—Ferris 18–7–25–2; Agnew 24–5–86–0; DeFreitas 26–6–65–1; Lewis 27–4–86–2; Potter 1–0–1–0; Willey 14–4–53–3. *Second Innings*—Ferris 4–0–32–3; DeFreitas 4–0–27–2.

Leicestershire

R. A. Cobb lbw b Wild	20	– b Walker	64
N. E. Briers c Cook b Capel	23	– run out	10
*D. I. Gower b Wild	20	– c Williams b Walker	38
P. Willey c Ripley b Capel	21	– c Bailey b Capel	27
J. J. Whitaker c sub b Capel	4	– c Ripley b Cook	25
L. Potter c Ripley b Capel	5	– b Cook	27
P. A. J. DeFreitas c Wild b Walker	14	– lbw b Capel	2
C. C. Lewis c Williams b Walker	20	– c Ripley b Walker	29
†P. Whitticase b Walker	2	– c Fordham b Capel	0
G. J. F. Ferris not out	5	– (11) not out	2
J. P. Agnew absent ill		– (10) b Walker	23
L-b 6, n-b 3	9	B 4, l-b 5, w 2, n-b 6	17
1/40 2/67 3/76 4/91 5/99 6/100 7/122 8/128 9/143	143	1/18 2/72 3/125 4/169 5/184 6/190 7/218 8/219 9/251	264

Bonus points – Northamptonshire 4.

Bowling: *First Innings*—Lillee 12–1–39–0; Walker 15–5–40–3; Capel 14–3–40–4; Wild 1–3–18–2. *Second Innings*—Lillee 2–1–9–0; Walker 26.1–5–59–4; Capel 31–9–72–3; Wild :1–3–61–0; Larkins 3–0–17–0; Williams 6–3–4–0; Cook 31–18–33–2.

Umpires: J. H. Harris and K. J. Lyons.

NORTHAMPTONSHIRE v YORKSHIRE

t Northampton, June 1, 2, 3. Drawn. Northamptonshire 4 pts, Yorkshire 5 pts. Toss: 'orkshire. The condition of the pitch overshadowed everything else after Larkins and the ijured Geoff Cook had chosen to play on the same one used in the match against Leicester- iire on the preceding days. Their decision attracted much criticism. Carrick reported it as ınfit" after fifteen wickets fell on the first day, and the TCCB's Inspector of Pitches was ılled in the following afternoon. Ironically, batting became easier as the match progressed. .itially no-one had succeeded in mastering the variable bounce and prodigious movement off e seam as Davis and Capel for Northamptonshire and Shaw, Sidebottom and Fletcher for

Yorkshire took full advantage. Beginning their second innings 25 runs ahead, Yorkshire were put in a strong position by an opening stand of 62 between Moxon and Blakey, and a shrewd blend of attack and defence by Carrick enabled him to set Northamptonshire to score 254 in a minimum of 72 overs, the highest total of the match. While Bailey and Capel were adding 115 in 40 overs, this looked possible, but the odd delivery still misbehaved and it was Yorkshire who were closer to victory when two heavy showers in the last hour washed out thirteen overs.

Close of play: First day, Northamptonshire 96-5 (D. J. Wild 21*, M. R. Gouldstone 4*); Second day, Yorkshire 119-4 (K. Sharp 10*).

Yorkshire

First innings		Second innings	
M. D. Moxon b Capel	1	c Larkins b Williams	44
†R. J. Blakey c Ripley b Wild	24	b Cook	27
I. G. Swallow c Ripley b Davis	6	b Capel	27
K. Sharp b Davis	8	c Fordham b Williams	48
J. D. Love c Gouldstone b Davis	8	b Capel	0
P. E. Robinson run out	18	c Bailey b Davis	3
D. L. Bairstow not out	15	(9) not out	4
*P. Carrick b Capel	29	(7) c Bailey b Robinson	47
A. Sidebottom b Davis	36	(8) run out	4
C. Shaw b Capel	0	c and b Williams	0
S. D. Fletcher lbw b Davis	0	not out	5
B 1, l-b 5, n-b 4	10	B 2, l-b 4, w 1, n-b 12	19
1/1 2/20 3/44 4/46 5/67 6/82 7/150 8/150 9/152	155	1/62 2/103 3/111 4/119 5/125 6/204 7/217 8/220 9/220 (9 wkts dec.)	228

Bonus points – Yorkshire 1, Northamptonshire 4.

Bowling: *First Innings*—Davis 20.4–6–54–5; Capel 11–5–12–3; Wild 15–4–45–1; Cook 6–3–10–0; Robinson 8–1–28–0. *Second Innings*—Davis 21–6–49–1; Capel 21–2–65–2; Robinson 15–2–53–1; Cook 14–7–25–1; Williams 13–3–30–3.

Northamptonshire

First innings		Second innings	
A. Fordham c Blakey b Fletcher	23	lbw b Sidebottom	6
*W. Larkins c Moxon b Shaw	14	c Swallow b Sidebottom	12
R. J. Bailey c Sidebottom b Shaw	19	c Blakey b Sidebottom	72
D. J. Capel lbw b Sidebottom	6	lbw b Fletcher	46
R. G. Williams b Sidebottom	1	c Sharp b Swallow	25
D. J. Wild c Fletcher b Sidebottom	32	b Fletcher	0
M. R. Gouldstone b Shaw	5	c Blakey b Carrick	2
†D. Ripley hit wkt b Fletcher	6	(9) not out	0
N. G. B. Cook c Blakey b Fletcher	2		
W. W. Davis not out	12	(8) not out	16
M. A. Robinson lbw b Shaw	0		
B 2, l-b 3, n-b 5	10	B 3, l-b 4, n-b 6	13
1/26 2/63 3/63 4/65 5/86 6/105 7/111 8/118 9/129	130	1/19 2/26 3/141 4/155 5/155 6/170 7/178 (7 wkts)	192

Bonus points – Yorkshire 4.

Bowling: *First Innings*—Sidebottom 19–4–48–3; Shaw 23.5–8–50–4; Carrick 3–1–3–0 Fletcher 16–5–24–3. *Second Innings*—Sidebottom 16–1–51–3; Shaw 13–1–53–0; Fletcher 15–3–45–2; Carrick 14–7–34–1; Swallow 1–0–2–1.

Umpires: J. H. Harris and K. J. Lyons.

At Taunton, June 4, 6, 7. NORTHAMPTONSHIRE beat SOMERSET by seven wickets.

At Northampton, June 11, 12, 13. NORTHAMPTONSHIRE drew with WEST INDIANS (See West Indian tour section).

NORTHAMPTONSHIRE v MIDDLESEX

At Luton, June 18, 20, 21. Drawn. Northamptonshire 8 pts, Middlesex 6 pts. Toss: Northamptonshire. Once again, Wardown Park provided an excellent pitch for Luton's annual Championship game – true in bounce with help for the spin bowlers later on – and both sides played some attractive cricket. Capel, hitting twelve boundaries in his 92 from 127 balls, dominated Northamptonshire's first innings with a flawless display, and Stanley, Ripley and Davis pressed on to secure the fourth batting point. Half-centuries from Gatting and Butcher kept Middlesex's arrears to 61, while Hutchinson, a 23 year old making his first-class début, underlined his potential with a polished 25. However, the best batting of the match came from Geoff Cook, who celebrated his return after five weeks' absence through a broken jaw by hitting his highest Championship score for two years. Made in just under four hours, his unbeaten 124 included fifteen fours. His declaration at lunch on the third day offered Middlesex 297 to win, and much depended on Gatting. He took up the challenge with 34 off 37 balls, but when he and Slack both fell to Walker, the remaining batsmen were left with too much to do.

Close of play: First day, Middlesex 38-0 (W. N. Slack 23*, J. D. Carr 15*); Second day, Northamptonshire 122-1 (G. Cook 54*, R. J. Bailey 40*).

Northamptonshire

*G. Cook c Gatting b Williams	3	– not out	124
W. Larkins c Roseberry b Gatting	38	– c Brown b Williams	25
R. J. Bailey lbw b Fraser	19	– c Carr b Williams	48
D. J. Capel c Brown b Hughes	92	– c Roseberry b Tufnell	21
R. G. Williams c Brown b Williams	14	– c Gatting b Tufnell	1
D. J. Wild c Gatting b Fraser	1	– c Brown b Carr	7
N. A. Stanley c Tufnell b Fraser	62	– not out	5
†D. Ripley c Slack b Tufnell	49		
N. G. B. Cook c Butcher b Fraser	6		
W. W. Davis c Carr b Tufnell	40		
A. Walker not out	1		
B 6, w 1, n-b 6	13	L-b 2, n-b 2	4
1/4 2/41 3/111 4/160 5/161 6/189 7/263 8/274 9/336	338	1/50 2/145 3/191 4/199 5/228 (5 wkts dec.)	235

Bonus points – Northamptonshire 4, Middlesex 3 (Score at 100 overs: 323-8).

Bowling: *First Innings*—Williams 20–3–77–2; Fraser 24–6–58–4; Hughes 18–1–79–1; Gatting 10–2–42–1; Tufnell 32.5–10–76–2. *Second Innings*—Williams 15–2–43–2; Fraser 5–1–18–0; Tufnell 34–6–92–2; Hughes 17–1–67–0; Carr 4–0–13–1.

Middlesex

W. N. Slack b Davis	44	– c Ripley b Walker	54
J. D. Carr c and b Davis	21	– c Larkins b Capel	15
M. W. Gatting c Davis b N. G. B. Cook	54	– c Larkins b Walker	34
R. O. Butcher st Ripley b N. G. B. Cook	61	– c Larkins b Williams	17
K. R. Brown c Stanley b N. G. B. Cook	0	– (6) run out	33
M. A. Roseberry c Larkins b Davis	9	– (7) not out	42
J. F. Hutchinson c Walker b Williams	25	– (5) c Bailey b Williams	13
S. P. Hughes c Walker b N. G. B. Cook	28	– not out	22
N. F. Williams c Ripley b Davis	19		
A. R. C. Fraser not out	4		
P. C. R. Tufnell c Wild b Davis	0		
L-b 6, w 1, n-b 5	12	B 1, l-b 2, w 1	4
1/50 2/82 3/142 4/142 5/156 6/223 7/227 8/270 9/275	277	1/60 2/95 3/108 4/122 5/155 6/191 (6 wkts)	234

Bonus points – Middlesex 3, Northamptonshire 4.

Bowling: *First Innings*—Davis 22.1–2–54–5; Capel 12–2–52–0; Wild 6–0–28–0; N. G. B. Cook 29–4–61–4; Walker 5–0–12–0; Williams 18–4–64–1. *Second Innings*—Davis 11–4–22–0; Capel 12–2–40–1; N. G. B. Cook 29–4–73–0; Walker 4–1–20–2; Williams 19–3–76–2.

Umpires: D. J. Constant and D. S. Thompsett.

At Nottingham, June 25, 27, 28. NORTHAMPTONSHIRE lost to NOTTINGHAMSHIRE by 191 runs.

NORTHAMPTONSHIRE v LANCASHIRE

At Northampton, July 2, 4, 5. Drawn. Northamptonshire 3 pts, Lancashire 7 pts. Toss: Northamptonshire. The loss of all but 25 minutes' play on the second day denied Lancashire the opportunity to press home their advantage, earned by Wasim Akram's lively pace and skilfully controlled movement. In one of the quickest spells seen at Northampton during the season, the Pakistani claimed five for 36 in his opening fourteen overs and returned after lunch to dismiss Williams, who together with Ripley offered the only real resistance, and Davis. Apart from Mendis's retirement with a jarred hand, the visitors made relatively untroubled progress in reply, Fowler batting fluently for three hours. However, the intervention of the weather left Hughes with little alternative but to pursue batting points and trust to another Northamptonshire collapse. This did not materialise and the match ended quietly with Fordham completing a well-organised half-century.

Close of play: First day, Lancashire 107-0 (G. Fowler 48*, T. E. Jesty 23*); Second day, Lancashire 128-0 (G. Fowler 53*, T. E. Jesty 37*).

Northamptonshire

*G. Cook c Hegg b Wasim	10		
W. Larkins c Watkinson b Wasim	17	– c Hegg b Watkinson	36
R. J. Bailey c Hegg b Wasim	8	– st Hegg b Folley	10
A. Fordham lbw b Wasim	0	– (1) not out	50
R. G. Williams b Wasim	39	– (4) not out	33
N. A. Stanley c Allott b Watkinson	4		
D. J. Wild lbw b Wasim	1		
†D. Ripley not out	43		
W. W. Davis lbw b Wasim	0		
A. Walker c Hegg b Allott	9		
M. A. Robinson b Allott	0		
B 5, l-b 10, w 1	16	L-b 2, n-b 3	5
1/17 2/31 3/35 4/50 5/59 6/68 7/111 8/111 9/147	147	1/41 2/55 (2 wkts)	134

Bonus points – Lancashire 4.

Bowling: *First Innings*—Wasim 25–6–53–7; Allott 10.4–1–22–2; Watkinson 13–3–36–1; Folley 3–1–8–0; Simmons 11–5–13–0. *Second Innings*—Wasim 12–3–24–0; Allott 5–1–18–0; Watkinson 8–1–30–1; Folley 11–3–22–1; Simmons 9–1–25–0; Jesty 6–4–13–0.

Lancashire

G. Fowler run out	78
G. D. Mendis c Cook b Robinson	34
T. E. Jesty c Ripley b Robinson	39
N. H. Fairbrother b Robinson	1
M. Watkinson c Ripley b Walker	12
*D. P. Hughes not out	45
Wasim Akram b Williams	5
†W. K. Hegg lbw b Williams	3
P. J. W. Allott not out	5
B 8, l-b 6, w 1, n-b 13	28
1/132 2/165 3/173 4/174 5/195 6/210 7/234 (7 wkts dec.)	250

J. Simmons and I. Folley did not bat.

Bonus points – Lancashire 3, Northamptonshire 3.

G. D. Mendis, when 24, retired hurt at 63 and resumed at 132.

Bowling: Davis 21–0–66–0; Walker 18–3–63–1; Robinson 22–6–63–3; Williams 19.2–5–28–2; Wild 4–0–16–0.

Umpires: M. J. Kitchen and D. R. Shepherd.

At Bristol, July 13, 14, 15. NORTHAMPTONSHIRE beat GLOUCESTERSHIRE by 1 run.

At Derby, July 16, 17, 18. NORTHAMPTONSHIRE lost to DERBYSHIRE by 144 runs.

NORTHAMPTONSHIRE v KENT

At Northampton, July 20, 21, 22. Kent won by one wicket. Kent 22 pts, Northamptonshire 7 pts. Toss: Northamptonshire. In a splendid finish, with both sides pressing for victory right to the end, Marsh pushed Williams for the winning single off the fourth ball of the last over after Kent had been set 288 in 63 overs. The two Northamptonshire spinners, Williams and Nick Cook, operated for most of the innings and the advantage switched back and forth during an intriguing last afternoon. Ultimately, Kent could thank Ward, with 59 off 72 balls, Graham Cowdrey, who opened his account with two sixes, and Marsh for seeing the chase to its successful conclusion and maintaining their push for Championship honours. On an easy-paced pitch, batsmen on both sides prospered in the early stages. Bailey, Williams and Wild all played with authority for the home side, and Pienaar timed the ball sweetly for the visitors. The outstanding batting, though, came from Larkins on the third morning; he struck a six and sixteen fours in the course of his 40th century for the county. With fine support from Fordham and Capel, Larkins enabled Northamptonshire to add 172 in two hours before lunch to precipitate Geoff Cook's well-balanced declaration.

Close of play: First day, Northamptonshire 289-6 (R. G. Williams 46*, D. Ripley 0*); Second day, Northamptonshire 18-2 (W. Larkins 8*, A. Fordham 0*).

Northamptonshire

*G. Cook c Kelleher b Penn	17	– c Ward b Penn	6
W. Larkins b Penn	2	– not out	112
R. J. Bailey c Marsh b Ellison	63	– lbw b Kelleher	4
A. Fordham c and b Kelleher	30	– lbw b Cowdrey	52
D. J. Capel lbw b Ellison	44	– not out	39
R. G. Williams not out	71		
D. J. Wild c Davis b Penn	75		
†D. Ripley run out	0		
N. G. B. Cook b Davis	13		
D. K. Lillee c Pienaar b Penn	0		
M. A. Robinson lbw b Penn	0		
L-b 9, n-b 5	14	B 2, l-b 6, w 1, n-b 4	13
1/6 2/66 3/94 4/162 5/163 6/286 7/293 8/327 9/329	329	1/8 2/15 3/165 (3 wkts dec.)	226

Bonus points – Northamptonshire 4, Kent 3 (Score at 100 overs: 302-7).

Bowling: *First Innings*—Ellison 19–5–59–2; Penn 30.5–7–82–5; Kelleher 21–4–58–1; Davis 27–7–73–1; Pienaar 13–3–48–0. *Second Innings*—Penn 10–2–38–1; Kelleher 12–1–57–1; Ellison 9–4–23–0; Davis 12–2–47–0; Cowdrey 7.4–0–53–1.

Kent

M. R. Benson c G. Cook b Williams . . . . 65 – c Lillee b Williams 30
N. R. Taylor b Capel . . . . 0 – b N. G. B. Cook 17
T. R. Ward lbw b Lillee . . . . 23 – lbw b Williams 59
*C. J. Tavaré b Williams . . . . 40 – b N. G. B. Cook 37
R. F. Pienaar not out . . . . 74 – c Fordham b N. G. B. Cook . . . 5
G. R. Cowdrey b Williams . . . . 35 – c and b N. G. B. Cook 49
†S. A. Marsh c Lillee b Williams . . . . 5 – not out 38
R. M. Ellison c Bailey b Williams . . . . 2 – b N. G. B. Cook 13
C. Penn not out . . . . 9 – lbw b Williams 10
D. J. M. Kelleher (did not bat) . . . . – c Capel b Williams 17
R. P. Davis (did not bat) . . . . – not out 0
B 5, l-b 6, n-b 4 . . . . 15 L-b 13 13

1/2 2/38 3/128 4/141 5/209 (7 wkts dec.) 268 1/36 2/71 3/129 (9 wkts) 288
6/239 7/252 4/138 5/187 6/212
7/240 8/257 9/287

Bonus points – Kent 3, Northamptonshire 3.

Bowling: *First Innings*—Lillee 11–2–43–1; Capel 13–2–52–1; Robinson 3–0–10–0; N. G. B. Cook 32–12–63–0; Williams 24–3–86–5; Bailey 2–0–3–0. *Second Innings*—Lillee 9–3–26–0; Capel 7–1–31–0; N. G. B. Cook 26–4–105–5; Williams 20.4–0–113–4.

Umpires: B. Dudleston and K. E. Palmer.

NORTHAMPTONSHIRE v SUSSEX

At Northampton, July 23, 25, 26. Drawn. Northamptonshire 6 pts, Sussex 4 pts. Toss: Northamptonshire. Rain docked the equivalent of a full day's play from a match dominated by the pace bowling of Davis and Capel on the first day, and an outstanding hundred from Bailey on the second. Sussex always looked likely to struggle after being inserted on a green pitch under heavy skies, and in between six interruptions Northamptonshire's new-ball pair, bowling unchanged, worked their way through the visitors' batting. Davis returned career-best figures and Ripley held six catches behind the stumps. Larkins departed before the close, bringing in Bailey, who survived two early chances off Imran and proceeded to bat on Monday with skill, application and scant support. He drove strongly off the front and back foot for fifteen fours in four and a half hours. For Sussex, Bunting had the satisfaction of a wicket in his first over at Northampton since leaving the county staff four years earlier. Beginning their second innings 115 runs adrift, Sussex edged towards safety thanks to sensible batting from Lenham and the Wells brothers. Davis and Robinson triggered a collapse to 207 for seven on the last afternoon, but Gould and Imran, aided by another stoppage for rain thwarted Northamptonshire.

Close of play: First day, Northamptonshire 26-1 (G. Cook 7*, R. J. Bailey 14*); Second day Sussex 68-1 (N. J. Lenham 36*, A. R. Clarke 0*).

Sussex

N. J. Falkner c Ripley b Capel . . . . 8 – (2) c Bailey b N. G. B. Cook . . . 2
N. J. Lenham c Ripley b Davis . . . . 15 – (1) run out 5
C. M. Wells lbw b Davis . . . . 3 – (4) lbw b Davis 6
A. P. Wells c Ripley b Davis . . . . 6 – (5) lbw b Davis 3
*P. W. G. Parker c Larkins b Davis . . . . 13 – (6) lbw b Robinson 4
Imran Khan c Ripley b Capel . . . . 4 – (7) not out 3
M. P. Speight c Robinson b Davis . . . . 10 – (8) b Robinson 4
†I. J. Gould b Davis . . . . 8 – (9) c Ripley b Capel 3
A. C. S. Pigott c Ripley b Capel . . . . 0 – (10) not out 1
A. R. Clarke not out . . . . 24 – (3) b Davis . . . .
R. A. Bunting c Ripley b Davis 3
B 1, l-b 6, w 9, n-b 8 . . . . 24 L-b 11, n-b 14 2

1/16 2/33 3/34 4/45 5/53 118 1/68 2/79 3/103 (8 wkts dec.) 28
6/62 7/83 8/88 9/88 4/175 5/201 6/201
7/207 8/269

Bonus points – Northamptonshire 4.

Bowling: *First Innings*—Davis 16.5–0–52–7; Capel 16–2–59–3. *Second Innings*—Davis 24–5–84–3; Capel 15–2–67–1; Williams 21–8–43–0; N. G. B. Cook 8–4–13–1; Robinson 17–1–64–2; Bailey 5–2–5–0.

Northamptonshire

*G. Cook b C. M. Wells 10
W. Larkins c Speight b Imran 0
R. J. Bailey not out 127
A. Fordham c A. P. Wells b Imran ... 0
D. J. Capel lbw b C. M. Wells 7
R. G. Williams c Clarke b Bunting 28
D. J. Wild lbw b Pigott 10
†D. Ripley b Imran 5
N. G. B. Cook run out 1
W. W. Davis c Speight b Pigott 26
M. A. Robinson lbw b Clarke 0
B 5, l-b 11, w 2, n-b 1 19

1/9 2/57 3/58 4/79 5/127 6/160 7/173 8/180 9/223 — 233

Bonus points – Northamptonshire 2, Sussex 4.

Bowling: Imran 25–3–61–3; Pigott 21–2–79–2; C. M. Wells 14–1–45–2; Bunting 8–2–24–1; Clarke 4.5–0–8–1.

Umpires: B. Dudleston and K. E. Palmer.

At Worcester, July 30, August 1, 2. NORTHAMPTONSHIRE drew with WORCESTERSHIRE.

NORTHAMPTONSHIRE v ESSEX

At Northampton, August 3, 4, 5. Essex won by four wickets. Essex 22 pts, Northamptonshire 7 pts. Toss: Northamptonshire. The home county took the early honours, only for irresolute batting on a deteriorating pitch to offer Essex a chance of victory. Not without a few alarms, they grasped it. Fourteen wickets fell on the first day, but Williams (212 minutes, 21 fours) gave a fine exhibition of strokeplay, although forced to employ a runner for the last 21 runs because of a wrenched knee – an injury which, significantly in the event, prevented him from bowling. He added 110 with late replacement Gouldstone, recalled that morning from a Second XI match in Harrow to cover for Test calls and illness. Williams's effort was matched by Border, who was at his most skilful and combative in a five-hour stay. He hit fifteen boundaries and rescued Essex from a perilous position at the close of the first day. Good support from Hussain ensured a deficit of only 45, and then Northamptonshire fell apart against Miller and Topley, several of their batsmen being undone by treacherous low bounce. Essex needed 135, but Northamptonshire badly needed spin support for Nick Cook to maintain the pressure. In the absence of Williams, a solid innings from Prichard proved decisive.

Close of play: First day, Essex 48-4 (A. R. Border 12*, P. J. Prichard 0*); Second day, Northamptonshire 60-5 (A. Fordham 27*, N. G. B. Cook 0*).

Northamptonshire

G. Cook c East b Topley	16 – c East b Lever	0
. Larkins lbw b Lever	10 – c East b Topley	2
. Fordham c Fletcher b Topley	1 – lbw b Topley	31
. G. Williams c Lilley b Miller	119 – (8) lbw b Topley	0
. J. Wild b Lever	14 – (4) c Hussain b Miller	20
. R. Gouldstone b Miller	71 – (5) c Hussain b Miller	10
D. Ripley b Miller	8 – (6) c East b Miller	0
. G. B. Cook lbw b Topley	0 – (7) lbw b Topley	5
. W. Davis c East b Lever	18 – lbw b Topley	18
Walker b Miller	8 – not out	2
. A. Robinson not out	0 – run out	0
B 2, l-b 12, n-b 4	18 B 1	1
15 2/22 3/37 4/117 5/227 256 7/257 8/261 9/283	283 1/0 2/6 3/38 4/58 5/58 6/66 7/66 8/85 9/88	89

Bonus points – Northamptonshire 3, Essex 4.

Bowling: *First Innings*—Lever 21.4–3–60–3; Topley 32–6–100–3; Ilott 15–1–48–0; Miller 19–7–36–4; Stephenson 7–1–25–0. *Second Innings*—Lever 11–2–14–1; Topley 21–8–37–5; Miller 19.1–9–37–3.

Essex

†D. E. East c Fordham b Walker	17	– c Larkins b N. G. B. Cook	34
J. P. Stephenson lbw b Davis	5	– c G. Cook b N. G. B. Cook	14
A. W. Lilley lbw b Walker	4	– b N. G. B. Cook	0
A. R. Border not out	110	– c Ripley b Davis	0
T. D. Topley lbw b Walker	2		
P. J. Prichard c Ripley b Davis	21	– (5) not out	44
N. Hussain c Fordham b Davis	45	– (6) b Walker	1
*K. W. R. Fletcher c Larkins b Robinson	1	– (7) c Fordham b Davis	20
G. Miller lbw b Robinson	0	– (8) not out	4
J. K. Lever run out	3		
M. C. Ilott b Robinson	6		
L-b 5, w 1, n-b 18	24	B 1, l-b 13, n-b 4	18
1/16 2/22 3/37 4/48 5/94 6/164 7/167 8/171 9/192	238	1/42 2/42 3/50 4/64 5/73 6/111	(6 wkts) 13

Bonus points – Essex 2, Northamptonshire 4.

Bowling: *First Innings*—Davis 28–6–102–3; Walker 24–6–68–3; N. G. B. Cook 17–6–29–0 Robinson 18.3–3–34–3. *Second Innings*—Davis 23–6–41–2; Walker 13–1–32–1; Robinso 7.1–1–18–0; N. G. B. Cook 21–9–30–3.

Umpires: B. Leadbeater and A. G. T. Whitehead.

At Birmingham, August 6, 8, 9. NORTHAMPTONSHIRE lost to WARWICKSHIRE b six wickets.

At Bournemouth, August 13, 15, 16. NORTHAMPTONSHIRE drew with HAMPSHIRI

NORTHAMPTONSHIRE v GLAMORGAN

At Wellingborough School, August 20, 22, 23. Northamptonshire won by seven wicke Northamptonshire 22 pts, Glamorgan 3 pts. Toss: Glamorgan. Glamorgan, handicapped the absence of Ontong and Barwick, who were both badly shaken in a road accident ne Colchester the evening before the match, were rarely in contention after running into ea trouble against effective seam bowling from Walker and Robinson. Holmes battled gamely more than four hours, and either side of a 37-over stoppage for rain on Saturday he added for the ninth wicket with North to carry the innings into the second day. Northamptonsh wasted no time obtaining two batting points, Larkins leading the way with 67 off 86 balls, a they snatched the initiative before the close when Bailey's occasional off-spin accounted Butcher, Cottey and Morris in quick succession and Robinson held an outstanding ret catch to dismiss Holmes. The rest of the batting disintegrated on the last morning as Robins improved his career-best figures for the third time in as many weeks. Only a 41-run flour from North and Watkin gave Glamorgan's attack anything to bowl at. In fact, 177 in complete sessions proved a straightforward task with Lamb (138 minutes, one six, fift fours) in dominant form, although Thomas generated impressive pace on a slow pitch and not concede defeat without a fight.

Close of play: First day, Glamorgan 168-8 (G. C. Holmes 64*, P. D. North 15*); Sec day, Glamorgan 87-4 (M. P. Maynard 7*, C. P. Metson 1*).

Glamorgan

A. R. Butcher c Larkins b Walker	7	– c Lamb b Bailey	40
P. A. Cottey lbw b Walker	2	– c Gouldstone b Bailey	30
*H. Morris c Bailey b Walker	8	– lbw b Bailey	2
M. P. Maynard c Ripley b Robinson	22	– c Ripley b Robinson	8
G. C. Holmes c N. G. B. Cook b Walker	83	– c and b Robinson	4
M. J. Cann b N. G. B. Cook	7	– (7) c Larkins b Davis	6
J. G. Thomas c Ripley b Robinson	10	– (8) c G. Cook b Robinson	7
†C. P. Metson c Ripley b Robinson	3	– (6) lbw b Robinson	1
J. Derrick c Ripley b Walker	13	– c Ripley b N. G. B. Cook	5
P. D. North not out	41	– not out	19
S. L. Watkin lbw b N. G. B. Cook	1	– c and b N. G. B. Cook	20
B 4, l-b 8, n-b 11	23	L-b 9, n-b 6	15
1/8 2/12 3/32 4/61 5/82 6/106 7/115 8/140 9/211	220	1/71 2/73 3/82 4/86 5/89 6/90 7/104 8/110 9/116	157

Bonus points – Glamorgan 2, Northamptonshire 4.

Bowling: *First Innings*—Davis 28–7–66–0; Walker 21–4–64–5; Robinson 27–10–48–3; N. G. B. Cook 12.4–6–30–2. *Second Innings*—Davis 14–2–42–1; Walker 7–0–26–0; Bailey 9–0–27–3; Robinson 12–2–19–4; N. G. B. Cook 23–12–34–2.

Northamptonshire

*G. Cook c Butcher b Watkin	75	– b Thomas	32
W. Larkins b Derrick	67	– lbw b Thomas	7
R. J. Bailey c Morris b Butcher	31	– c Cann b Derrick	17
A. J. Lamb not out	20	– not out	104
A. Fordham not out	0	– not out	13
L-b 3, w 1, n-b 4	8	B 1, l-b 4	5
1/101 2/180 3/183 (3 wkts dec.)	201	1/13 2/46 3/84 (3 wkts)	178

M. R. Gouldstone, †D. Ripley, N. G. B. Cook, W. W. Davis, A. Walker and M. A. Robinson did not bat.

Bonus points – Northamptonshire 2, Glamorgan 1.

Bowling: *First Innings*—Thomas 10–0–39–0; Watkin 14–4–33–1; Derrick 16.5–3–57–1; North 9–0–46–0; Holmes 6–1–14–0; Butcher 2–1–9–1. *Second Innings*—Thomas 14–2–44–2; Watkin 15–4–36–0; Derrick 16.4–4–55–1; North 10–1–38–0.

Umpires: B. Dudleston and R. Julian.

NORTHAMPTONSHIRE v DERBYSHIRE

At Northampton, August 25, 26, 27, 29. Drawn. Northamptonshire 5 pts, Derbyshire 7 pts. Toss: Derbyshire. The visitors threatened only briefly to approach their target of 296 in 71 overs, and it was left to Griffith and Mortensen to play out the final 13.4 overs for the draw. Derbyshire's seamers found a well-grassed pitch to their liking early on, and Northamptonshire were indebted to Bailey, just released from the England team at Lord's, and Wild for a useful-looking total in such favourable bowling conditions. Their efforts were put into perspective as Derbyshire lost half their wickets for 101 before the close, only for Morris, Griffith and Roberts to stage an even more effective recovery than Northamptonshire's and secure a lead of 67. Bad light and rain interrupted the home side's second innings, but with Mortensen in the pavilion with a back injury, Geoff Cook and Bailey (280 minutes, thirteen fours) wiped off the arrears in a second-wicket stand of 133. Valuable runs from Gouldstone and the tail, clearly indicating the extent to which the pitch had eased, paved the way for Cook's comparatively cautious declaration, although his caution appeared justified as Wright and Bowler collected runs briskly. The complexion of the game was transformed, however, by Bowler's dismissal, and with the middle order crumbling in a welter of injudicious strokes, the ninth-wicket pair had to negotiate a testing 50 minutes.

Close of play: First day, Derbyshire 102-5 (J. E. Morris 28*, F. A. Griffith 0*); Second day, Northamptonshire 111-1 (G. Cook 45*, R. J. Bailey 47*); Third day, Northamptonshire 93-7 (M. R. Gouldstone 24*, A. Walker 16*).

Northamptonshire

First innings		Second innings	
*G. Cook c Maher b Mortensen	20	– lbw b Griffith	69
W. Larkins lbw b Malcolm	5	– c Maher b Warner	8
D. J. Capel lbw b Mortensen	18	– (4) lbw b Malcolm	26
M. R. Gouldstone b Warner	0	– (5) not out	47
D. J. Wild b Mortensen	41	– (6) c Morris b Roberts	4
†D. Ripley c Maher b Griffith	14	– (7) run out	1
R. J. Bailey c Maher b Mortensen	51	– (3) c Griffith b Roberts	110
N. G. B. Cook c Maher b Mortensen	4	– c O'Gorman b Malcolm	10
A. Walker b Warner	21	– c O'Gorman b Malcolm	33
D. K. Lillee b Mortensen	12	– c Morris b Griffith	22
M. A. Robinson not out	0		
L-b 5, w 1, n-b 1	7	B 6, l-b 14, w 6, n-b 6	32
1/7 2/44 3/45 4/51 5/87 6/132 7/150 8/173 9/193	193	1/11 2/144 3/222 4/241 5/249 6/251 7/277 8/318 9/362 (9 wkts dec.)	362

Bonus points – Northamptonshire 1, Derbyshire 4.

Bowling: *First Innings*—Mortensen 26.1–13–40–6; Malcolm 20–1–83–1; Warner 11–0–42–2; Griffith 5–0–23–1. *Second Innings*—Warner 36–6–91–1; Malcolm 37–6–109–3; Griffith 33.3–12–67–2; Roberts 11–4–17–2; Goldsmith 13–0–46–0; Bowler 9–1–12–0.

Derbyshire

First innings		Second innings	
P. D. Bowler lbw b Walker	10	– b Walker	42
*J. G. Wright c Ripley b Robinson	28	– c Bailey b N. G. B. Cook	28
†B. J. M. Maher lbw b Lillee	24	– c Lillee b N. G. B. Cook	[illegible]
J. E. Morris c Larkins b Lillee	45	– c Larkins b Walker	[illegible]
S. C. Goldsmith c Bailey b Lillee	0	– lbw b Robinson	[illegible]
T. J. G. O'Gorman b Robinson	5	– (7) lbw b Robinson	[illegible]
F. A. Griffith c Ripley b Walker	37	– (8) not out	[illegible]
B. Roberts c Ripley b N. G. B. Cook	71	– (6) st Ripley b N. G. B. Cook	[illegible]
A. E. Warner b Walker	6	– c Walker b Robinson	[illegible]
O. H. Mortensen not out	13	– not out	
D. E. Malcolm b N. G. B. Cook	0		
B 2, l-b 8, n-b 11	21	L-b 5, w 4, n-b 4	[illegible]
1/39 2/47 3/87 4/87 5/101 6/135 7/187 8/193 9/260	260	1/50 2/100 3/100 4/100 5/110 6/153 7/157 8/159 (8 wkts)	17[illegible]

Bonus points – Derbyshire 3, Northamptonshire 4.

Bowling: *First Innings*—Lillee 28–1–96–3; Walker 26–6–68–3; Robinson 23–4–61–[illegible] N. G. B. Cook 15.3–8–25–2. *Second Innings*—Lillee 20–5–58–0; Walker 10.5–1–43–[illegible] N. G. B. Cook 21–9–40–3; Robinson 16–4–24–3; G. Cook 3–1–2–0.

Umpires: B. Leadbeater and D. O. Oslear.

At Scarborough, September 9, 10, 11, 12. NORTHAMPTONSHIRE drew wi[illegible] YORKSHIRE.

At Chelmsford, September 14, 15, 16, 17. NORTHAMPTONSHIRE lost to ESSEX by [illegible] wickets.

NOTTINGHAMSHIRE

President: J. W. Baddiley
Chairman: C. W. Gillott
Chairman, Cricket Committee: R. T. Simpson
Secretary: B. Robson
County Cricket Ground, Trent Bridge,
Nottingham NG2 6AG
(Telephone: 0602-821525)
Cricket Manager: K. A. Taylor
Captain: R. T. Robinson

Few supporters of Nottinghamshire imagined that, in the season mmediately following the departure of their two inspirational overseas cricketers, Richard Hadlee and Clive Rice, the county would have an easy time in 1988. Yet by the end of a summer which was not without its raumas, Nottinghamshire had achieved levels of success that even the nost optimistic Trent Bridge regular would have doubted at the outset. n finishing fifth in the Britannic Assurance Championship, and so laiming a share of the prizemoney, they won only one game fewer than hey did in winning the title twelve months earlier. And in the West ndian all-rounder, Franklyn Stephenson, they had the Championship Player of the Year.

The season was barely weeks old when some alarming collapses gave ise to the possibility of a dramatic return to the days when avoiding lefeat was regarded as a moral victory. They lost their first four Championship games, and when in mid-June they beat Glamorgan by 42 runs, their Championship record read nine matches played, two von and six lost. Certainly, life did not always run smoothly for im Robinson, the man charged with the responsibility of keeping Nottinghamshire to the forefront of English cricket. His problems ame to a head amid rumblings that he was not getting the support e requested – and needed – from some of his colleagues. But, as ottinghamshire have always done under the astute management of Ken aylor, the problems were aired fairly and honestly in public. Chris road, seen as a chief agitator, manfully accepted his contribution to the nhappy affair and the dust settled without further recriminations.

Out of that mid-season turbulence, Nottinghamshire's health blos-omed, thanks largely to the marvellous bowling of the new-ball pair, ephenson and Kevin Cooper. Both topped 100 wickets, and not since e days before the Championship programme was reduced in 1969 has y county boasted such an achievement. For Stephenson, heading the t of first-class wicket-takers in the country with 125 was just part of remarkable performance in his first season on the staff. He had been gned as a replacement for Hadlee, indeed had been recommended by adlee himself, but no-one expected him to emulate his predecessor's eat successes. How wrong everyone was. Stephenson, as self-motivated Hadlee, proved his all-round ability by repeating the New Zealander's eviously unique double of 1984 and so became the second player to ore 1,000 runs and take 100 wickets in a season since 1969. Moreover, ephenson completed the feat in two fewer games, and he did so in style, taking two hundreds off Yorkshire in the last game of the season. Onl once before had he reached three figures.

Stephenson gained maximum support from Cooper, who, relishing th chance to use the new ball regularly, emerged from the shadows to clain 101 first-class wickets and prove that he had developed into one of th game's most respected swing and seam bowlers. Without such a sterlin contribution from these two, though, Nottinghamshire would have bee in difficulty, for their back-up bowlers were all too often ruled ou because of injury. Andy Pick had an operation on his hand and made bu a few appearances, Kevin Saxelby struggled throughout to regain fitness and when Eddie Hemmings joined Andy Afford, who had back trouble on the injury list, Nottinghamshire did not have a spin bowler Hemmings, at 39, captured 41 wickets in the Championship, but apar from Stephenson, Cooper and Chris Cairns, the fast-bowling son of th former New Zealand Test player, no bowler averaged under 30 in th Championship.

Sadly, Nottinghamshire's batting line-up, regarded as their stronge suit in any pre-season analysis, did not match the accomplishments of th strike bowlers. They plummeted disastrously to be dismissed for 65 b Kent and 44 by Warwickshire in successive matches at the beginnin of June, and only occasionally did they bat as a cohesive unit. Y there were some individual performances to enjoy, particularly Dere Randall's career-best 237 against Derbyshire at Trent Bridge. It was a innings of such quality that one was left wondering why he was not st an England cricketer. In addition to Stephenson, he, Paul Johnson ar Robinson all passed 1,000 runs for Nottinghamshire.

Randall was one of the few players to avoid injury during the course the season. At one time, the county was without five or six regulars. addition to the bowlers who were unavailable, Bruce French had decid that the time had come for surgery on a two-year-old injury to a finge Nottinghamshire were fortunate in having a ready understudy behir the stumps in Chris Scott, who equalled the county record by taking t catches against Derbyshire at Derby.

The return from the limited-overs competitions left much to desired. Runners-up in the Refuge Assurance League in 1987, Nottin hamshire finished bottom in 1988 with only three wins. They we beaten in the quarter-finals of the Benson and Hedges Cup Glamorgan, and their defence of the NatWest Bank Trophy came to acrimonious end when the umpires' decision to abandon play on t third day handed Worcestershire their second-round tie on scoring-ra Even when they were in winning positions they invariably specialised self-destruction, and in 1989 they will want to put last season's one-d experiences as far behind them as possible. – John Lawson.

NOTTINGHAMSHIRE 1988

[*Bill Smith*

Back row: P. Pollard, R. J. Evans, C. D. Fraser-Darling, K. P. Evans, J. A. Afford, G. W. Mike. *Middle row:* D. J. R. Martindale, C. W. Scott, R. A. Pick, K. Saxelby, F. D. Stephenson, D. J. Millns, M. Newell. *Front row:* B. N. French, M. K. Bore, E. E. Hemmings, D. W. Randall, R. T. Robinson (*captain*), K. A. Taylor (*manager*), B. C. Broad, J. D. Birch, K. E. Cooper, P. Johnson. *Inset:* C. L. Cairns.

NOTTINGHAMSHIRE RESULTS

All first-class matches – Played 26: Won 8, Lost 8, Drawn 10.

County Championship matches – Played 22: Won 8, Lost 8, Drawn 6.

Bonus points – Batting 34, Bowling 71.

Competition placings – Britannic Assurance County Championship, 5th; NatWest Bank Trophy, 2nd round; Benson and Hedges Cup, q-f; Refuge Assurance League, 17th.

BRITANNIC ASSURANCE CHAMPIONSHIP AVERAGES

BATTING

	Birthplace	*M*	*I*	*NO*	*R*	*HI*	*Avge*
‡D. W. Randall	*Retford*	21	37	4	1,286	237	38.9
‡R. T. Robinson	*Sutton-in-Ashfield*	18	30	3	988	134*	36.5
‡P. Johnson	*Newark*	21	37	0	1,104	140	29.8
§‡F. D. Stephenson	*St James, Barbados*	20	34	0	962	117	28.2
P. Pollard	*Nottingham*	7	13	0	323	142	24.8
‡B. C. Broad	*Bristol*	16	27	0	647	68	23.9
‡M. Newell	*Blackburn*	16	30	1	619	105	21.3
K. P. Evans	*Calverton*	13	22	3	359	54	18.8
‡J. D. Birch	*Nottingham*	20	35	2	596	75	18.0
‡E. E. Hemmings	*Leamington Spa*	16	25	10	245	31*	16.3
‡B. N. French	*Warsop*	6	11	1	135	28	13.5
‡C. W. Scott	*Thorpe-on-the-Hill*	16	25	4	273	47*	13.0
D. J. R. Martindale	*Harrogate*	6	10	0	125	46	12.5
‡K. E. Cooper	*Hucknall*	22	33	9	263	39	10.9
‡R. A. Pick	*Nottingham*	2	4	1	31	19	10.3
§C. L. Cairns	*Picton, NZ*	2	4	1	29	15	9.6
‡K. Saxelby	*Worksop*	7	12	1	41	17	3.7
D. J. Millns	*Mansfield*	8	11	5	19	7*	3.
J. A. Afford	*Crowland*	4	8	3	4	3	0.8

Also batted: ‡M. K. Bore (*Hull*) (1 match) 5, 0.

* *Signifies not out.* ‡ *Denotes county cap.* § *Not qualified for England.*

The following played a total of eleven three-figure innings for Nottinghamshire in Coun Championship matches – R. T. Robinson 3, P. Johnson 2, D. W. Randall 2, F. D. Stephens 2, M. Newell 1, P. Pollard 1.

BOWLING

	O	*M*	*R*	*W*	*BB*	*5W/i*	*Avge*
F. D. Stephenson	776.1	191	2,161	121	7-56	10	17.
K. E. Cooper	776	213	2,035	99	5-41	5	20.
E. E. Hemmings	495.5	137	1,265	41	4-50	0	30.
D. J. Millns	101	13	374	12	3-37	0	31.
K. P. Evans	201.5	34	665	18	3-22	0	36.
K. Saxelby	193	29	690	12	3-30	0	57.

Also bowled: J. A. Afford 83–19–270–9; J. D. Birch 68.4–16–226–5; M. K. Bore 9–2–41– C. L. Cairns 49–6–179–8; M. Newell 1–0–11–0; R. A. Pick 51–7–236–5; R. T. Robins 4–0–38–0.

Wicket-keepers: C. W. Scott 39 ct, 2 st; B. N. French 12 ct.

Leading Fielders: M. Newell 28, K. P. Evans 18, R. T. Robinson 17.

At Lord's, April 16, 17, 18. NOTTINGHAMSHIRE drew with MCC.

At Lord's, April 21, 22, 23, 25. NOTTINGHAMSHIRE lost to MIDDLESEX by 241 runs.

At Worcester, April 28, 29, 30. NOTTINGHAMSHIRE lost to WORCESTERSHIRE by six wickets.

NOTTINGHAMSHIRE v LANCASHIRE

At Nottingham, May 5, 6, 7, 9. Lancashire won by 51 runs. Lancashire 22 pts, Nottinghamshire 6 pts. Toss: Lancashire. Rain delayed the start until 1.25 p.m., but thereafter wickets fell quickly once Cooper had made the initial breakthrough. However, Fairbrother defied the bowlers and the damp pitch. Undefeated at the close with 91, he went on to a well-deserved hundred next morning. Nottinghamshire also began badly and were not helped by Robinson having to retire early with a foreign body in his eye. When he returned, he assisted Stephenson in a useful stand and a first-innings lead of 2 was achieved. With Mendis and Hughes making fifties, the home side required 288 from a minimum of 97 overs. No-one, however, could stay with the captain, and when he was last out Nottinghamshire were still more than 50 runs in arrears.

Close of play: First day, Lancashire 190-8 (N. H. Fairbrother 91*, J. Simmons 7*); Second day, Lancashire 3-0 (G. D. Mendis 1*, G. Fowler 1*); Third day, Lancashire 289-7 (T. E. Jesty 26*, D. P. Hughes 62*).

Lancashire

G. D. Mendis c Scott b Stephenson	33	– b Afford	87
G. Fowler lbw b Cooper	2	– c Robinson b Cooper	6
T. E. Jesty b Cooper	4	– retired ill	26
N. H. Fairbrother c Newell b Cooper	101	– c Scott b Hemmings	49
M. Watkinson c Newell b Hemmings	22	– c Stephenson b Hemmings	6
D. P. Hughes b Cooper	2	– c Robinson b Stephenson	62
W. K. Hegg c Robinson b Afford	11	– st Scott b Afford	8
Wasim Akram lbw b Cooper	7	– c Birch b Afford	0
J. W. Allott c and b Hemmings	4	– lbw b Cooper	25
Simmons c Afford b Hemmings	21	– not out	0
Folley not out	5	– b Stephenson	0
B 4, l-b 2, w 2, n-b 1	9	B 7, l-b 11, n-b 2	20
4 2/19 3/48 4/87 5/90 139 7/164 8/169 9/207	221	1/19 2/144 3/164 4/187 5/211 6/223 7/263 8/289 9/289	289

Bonus points – Lancashire 2, Nottinghamshire 4.

the second innings T. E. Jesty, when 18, retired ill at 52 and resumed at 263.

Bowling: *First Innings*—Stephenson 24–7–47–1; Cooper 32–11–60–5; Birch 7–2–18–0; emmings 27.3–7–62–3; Afford 6–0–28–1. *Second Innings*—Stephenson 27.2–5–73–2; Cooper –6–47–2; Hemmings 44–16–71–2; Afford 28–7–80–3.

Nottinghamshire

B. C. Broad b Allott	4	– c Hughes b Folley	32
*R. T. Robinson b Folley	44	– c Fowler b Simmons	115
M. Newell b Wasim	0	– c Hegg b Folley	0
P. Johnson hit wkt b Folley	17	– hit wkt b Simmons	4
D. W. Randall c and b Folley	9	– b Folley	10
J. D. Birch b Simmons	36	– c Wasim b Folley	19
F. D. Stephenson c and b Simmons	79	– lbw b Simmons	15
†C. W. Scott b Folley	0	– b Wasim	11
E. E. Hemmings not out	11	– lbw b Wasim	1
K. E. Cooper b Wasim	2	– b Folley	13
J. A. Afford b Wasim	3	– not out	0
B 7, l-b 9, n-b 2	18	B 3, l-b 8, w 1, n-b 4	16
1/11 2/16 3/54 4/61 5/124 6/171 7/171 8/215 9/218	223	1/66 2/66 3/73 4/96 5/128 6/155 7/184 8/188 9/228	236

Bonus points – Nottinghamshire 2, Lancashire 4.

In the first innings R. T. Robinson, when 19, retired hurt at 38 and resumed at 124.

Bowling: *First Innings*—Wasim 17–4–34–3; Allott 12–5–21–1; Folley 24–5–79–4; Simmons 22–7–53–2; Watkinson 12–4–20–0. *Second Innings*—Wasim 16–5–50–2; Allott 8–3–10–0; Watkinson 6–2–10–0; Simmons 30.4–6–66–3; Folley 24–6–89–5.

Umpires: M. J. Kitchen and B. Leadbeater.

NOTTINGHAMSHIRE v GLOUCESTERSHIRE

At Nottingham, May 18, 19, 20. Gloucestershire won by six wickets. Gloucestershire 23 pts, Nottinghamshire 4 pts. Toss: Gloucestershire. Twenty wickets fell on the opening day Curran and Stovold were the only senior batsmen to master Nottinghamshire's all-seam attack, but Gloucestershire's tail was most effective in pushing the total past the third bonus point. When Nottinghamshire lost both openers cheaply, then saw Johnson and Randall foolishly run out, they were 22 for four. Stephenson, who suffered a broken nose when struck attempting to hook Curran, and Scott prevented a total rout. The follow-on was enforced, and on the second day Nottinghamshire began in a more determined manner. Robinson batted 9 minutes for his 45. The lower order, however, was brushed aside by Lawrence, and when ba light ended play early, Gloucestershire were on the brink of victory. Good bowling by Stephenson on Friday morning meant that Nottinghamshire made their opponents work har for victory, but Gloucestershire had won by lunch.

Close of play: First day, Nottinghamshire 97; Second day, Gloucestershire 31-1 (A. W Stovold 27*, I. P. Butcher 1*).

Gloucestershire

A. W. Stovold c Newell b Stephenson	84	– c Newell b Cooper	2
A. J. Wright b Stephenson	5	– c Newell b Stephenson	
I. P. Butcher c Scott b Cooper	11	– c Newell b Stephenson	
P. Bainbridge b Pick	4	– (5) not out	1
K. M. Curran c Cooper b Pick	41	– (4) c and b Stephenson	1
J. W. Lloyds c Scott b Stephenson	0	– not out	1
M. W. Alleyne lbw b Cooper	12		
†R. C. Russell lbw b Evans	29		
*D. A. Graveney not out	20		
D. V. Lawrence b Stephenson	27		
T. M. Alderman c Robinson b Cooper	11		
L-b 8, w 1, n-b 1	10	L-b 2, n-b 1	
1/21 2/38 3/53 4/145 5/145 6/151 7/195 8/195 9/241	254	1/27 2/42 3/42 4/60	(4 wkts) 8

Bonus points – Gloucestershire 3, Nottinghamshire 4.

Bowling: *First Innings*—Stephenson 25–6–80–4; Pick 15–3–62–2; Cooper 20.2–5–56–3; Evans 11–0–48–1. *Second Innings*—Stephenson 13.1–4–36–3; Cooper 13–5–42–1.

Nottinghamshire

First innings		Second innings	
*R. T. Robinson lbw b Lawrence	0	lbw b Curran	45
M. Newell lbw b Alderman	2	lbw b Graveney	25
D. W. Randall run out	2	c Russell b Lawrence	58
P. Johnson run out	14	lbw b Curran	24
J. D. Birch b Lawrence	6	c Butcher b Alderman	41
F. D. Stephenson lbw b Curran	35	b Lawrence	13
K. P. Evans lbw b Alderman	4	lbw b Alderman	3
†C. W. Scott lbw b Curran	20	b Lawrence	3
K. E. Cooper c Russell b Lawrence	5	b Lawrence	0
R. A. Pick not out	1	c Butcher b Lawrence	11
J. A. Afford b Lawrence	0	not out	0
L-b 5, w 2, n-b 1	8	L-b 5, w 2, n-b 4	11
1/0 2/2 3/10 4/22 5/45 6/50 7/84 8/88 9/89	97	1/67 2/85 3/132 4/163 5/193 6/199 7/213 8/213 9/225	234

Bonus points – Gloucestershire 4.

In the first innings F. D. Stephenson, when 30, retired hurt at 71 and resumed at 89.

Bowling: *First Innings*—Lawrence 14–2–36–4; Alderman 10–4–26–2; Bainbridge 2–0–13–0; Curran 5.1–1–17–2. *Second Innings*—Lawrence 17.5–1–73–5; Alderman 22–6–48–2; Bainbridge 9–2–23–0; Curran 19–6–36–2; Graveney 17–5–37–1; Alleyne 4–1–12–0.

Umpires: J. D. Bond and P. B. Wight.

NOTTINGHAMSHIRE v SUSSEX

At Nottingham, May 21, 23, 24. Nottinghamshire won by 67 runs. Nottinghamshire 23 pts, Sussex 5 pts. Toss: Nottinghamshire. The reigning county champions gained their first win of 1988 in their fifth match, having lost the previous four. With Broad playing for England, Pollard opened and made a good impression. Stephenson and Randall later combined to produce the only hundred partnership of the match. Cooper soon reduced Sussex to 19 for four by the close, but an innings of three hours by Alan Wells kept the visitors in the game. Nottinghamshire gave a poor display in their second innings, and Sussex had virtually all the last day in which to make 239. They reached 52 for the loss of Standing, but with the pitch helping the bowlers, the middle order went cheaply. There was a brief flourish from the tailenders, notably Clarke, before Nottinghamshire won with some ease.

Close of play: First day, Sussex 19-4 (A. M. Green 14*); Second day, Nottinghamshire 148-9 (K. E. Cooper 10*, J. A. Afford 1*).

Nottinghamshire

First innings		Second innings	
P. Pollard b Bunting	44	c Pigott b C. M. Wells	19
M. Newell b C. M. Wells	14	b Babington	26
*R. T. Robinson b C. M. Wells	46	lbw b C. M. Wells	8
P. Johnson c Gould b Pigott	20	c Parker b Bunting	24
D. W. Randall b Pigott	64	c Gould b Bunting	15
J. D. Birch b Pigott	1	lbw b Pigott	24
F. D. Stephenson b Pigott	63	b Pigott	1
†C. W. Scott lbw b C. M. Wells	5	c A. P. Wells b Bunting	7
K. Saxelby c A. P. Wells b Pigott	0	c C. M. Wells b Pigott	0
K. E. Cooper not out	0	c Lenham b Pigott	12
J. A. Afford lbw b C. M. Wells	0	not out	1
L-b 9, w 3, n-b 1	13	B 4, l-b 4, w 5	13
1/39 2/104 3/115 4/145 5/147 6/257 7/266 8/270 9/270	270	1/37 2/53 3/73 4/97 5/101 6/104 7/123 8/124 9/139	150

Bonus points – Nottinghamshire 3, Sussex 4.

Bowling: *First Innings*—Pigott 24–12–46–5; Bunting 14–2–50–1; Babington 20–3–73–0; Clarke 14–3–33–0; C. M. Wells 24.5–5–59–4. *Second Innings*—Pigott 18.1–3–40–4; Bunting 12–3–39–3; C. M. Wells 12–5–23–2; Babington 6–0–40–1.

Sussex

N. J. Lenham lbw b Stephenson	1	– (6) c and b Stephenson	33
A. M. Green c Stephenson b Afford	54	– b Saxelby	28
*P. W. G. Parker b Cooper	0	– c Robinson b Saxelby	22
A. R. Clarke c Robinson b Cooper	0	– (9) c Newell b Stephenson	26
R. A. Bunting lbw b Cooper	0	– (10) c Scott b Cooper	3
D. K. Standing c Newell b Stephenson	0	– (1) b Stephenson	9
A. P. Wells c Saxelby b Stephenson	74	– (4) c Cooper b Afford	0
C. M. Wells c Birch b Saxelby	21	– (5) c Scott b Saxelby	0
†I. J. Gould c Robinson b Cooper	6	– (7) c Birch b Afford	20
A. C. S. Pigott c Afford b Cooper	0	– (8) b Afford	23
A. M. Babington not out	6	– not out	0
L-b 10, w 4, n-b 6	20	B 1, l-b 5, n-b 1	7
1/8 2/11 3/19 4/19 5/19 6/87 7/136 8/145 9/151	182	1/24 2/52 3/65 4/65 5/65 6/92 7/134 8/142 9/171	171

Bonus points – Sussex 1, Nottinghamshire 4.

Bowling: *First Innings*—Stephenson 19.1–8–45–3; Cooper 23–7–41–5; Birch 1–1–0–0; Saxelby 13–2–57–1; Afford 10–3–29–1. *Second Innings*—Stephenson 18.3–7–56–3; Cooper 14–7–19–1; Saxelby 10–2–30–3; Afford 14–3–60–3.

Umpires: J. D. Bond and K. E. Palmer.

At Derby, May 28, 30, 31. NOTTINGHAMSHIRE drew with DERBYSHIRE.

At Dartford, June 1, 2, 3. NOTTINGHAMSHIRE lost to KENT by two wickets.

At Birmingham, June 4, 6, 7. NOTTINGHAMSHIRE lost to WARWICKSHIRE by 161 runs.

NOTTINGHAMSHIRE v GLAMORGAN

At Nottingham, June 11, 13, 14. Nottinghamshire won by 142 runs. Nottinghamshire 21 pts, Glamorgan 4 pts. Toss: Glamorgan. Put in to bat, Nottinghamshire lost Broad second ball. Pollard and Newell raised the score to 70, but the home side owed almost everything to Randall as Thomas returned career-best figures. On the second morning, eight Glamorgan wickets fell in quick succession – the last five for 7 runs – to the bowling of Cooper, Stephenson and Millns, a 23-year-old seam bowler from Clipstone, making his début. The Nottinghamshire batsmen fared little better in their second innings, five wickets falling for 77. However, Stephenson and the lower order almost trebled the total. Glamorgan began the last day needing 309 with eight wickets in hand, but within an hour they were 38 for five and it looked as if the players would be going home for lunch. A sound innings by Butcher delayed the finish until mid-afternoon.

Close of play: First day, Glamorgan 44-2 (H. Morris 2*); Second day, Glamorgan 9-2 (C. P. Metson 0*, H. Morris 1*).

Nottinghamshire

B. C. Broad b Thomas	2	– b Barwick	15
P. Pollard c Ontong b Thomas	39	– c Metson b Thomas	1
M. Newell c Cottey b Derrick	26	– lbw b Derrick	0
*J. D. Birch c Metson b Thomas	7	– (5) c Maynard b Barwick	0
D. W. Randall b Thomas	67	– (4) run out	30
F. D. Stephenson b Derrick	6	– c Hopkins b Barwick	65
K. P. Evans c Metson b Barwick	1	– c and b Barwick	29
†C. W. Scott c Metson b Thomas	2	– c Ontong b Derrick	34
E. E. Hemmings not out	15	– c Butcher b Derrick	12
K. E. Cooper c Ontong b Barwick	0	– not out	23
D. J. Millns b Thomas	0	– c Hopkins b Derrick	7
B 4, l-b 4, w 2, n-b 3	13	L-b 9, w 3, n-b 2	14
1/2 2/70 3/79 4/94 5/115 6/122 7/130 8/175 9/178	178	1/20 2/20 3/27 4/36 5/77 6/145 7/150 8/169 9/214	230

Bonus points – Nottinghamshire 1, Glamorgan 4.

Bowling: *First Innings*—Thomas 22.2–6–68–6; Barwick 26–11–31–2; Ontong 7–2–17–0; Shastri 15–6–30–0; Derrick 14–5–24–2. *Second Innings*—Thomas 15–1–57–1; Barwick 30–7–93–4; Derrick 27.5–8–67–4; Shastri 2–1–4–0.

Glamorgan

A. R. Butcher c Newell b Cooper	27	– (5) c Evans b Millns	65
J. A. Hopkins c Randall b Hemmings	10	– (1) c Scott b Cooper	1
*H. Morris c Scott b Cooper	25	– (4) c Broad b Stephenson	1
M. P. Maynard b Stephenson	0	– (6) lbw b Millns	10
R. J. Shastri b Millns	1	– (7) c Millns b Hemmings	36
P. A. Cottey not out	12	– (2) b Stephenson	4
R. C. Ontong c Randall b Cooper	5	– (8) b Hemmings	25
J. G. Thomas c Pollard b Stephenson	0	– (9) run out	14
J. Derrick b Stephenson	0	– (10) not out	4
†C. P. Metson c Scott b Stephenson	1	– (3) c Evans b Cooper	3
S. R. Barwick c Hemmings b Stephenson	0	– b Millns	1
L-b 9, n-b 1	10	B 1, l-b 5, w 1, n-b 4	11
1/24 2/44 3/46 4/47 5/72 6/84 7/88 8/88 9/91	91	1/7 2/7 3/12 4/16 5/38 6/92 7/123 8/162 9/171	175

Bonus points – Nottinghamshire 4.

Bowling: *First Innings*—Stephenson 22–7–42–5; Cooper 17–10–15–3; Hemmings 5–2–10–1; Millns 3–1–15–1. *Second Innings*—Stephenson 13–5–26–2; Cooper 18–3–60–2; Millns 10–1–37–3; Evans 6–2–12–0; Hemmings 15–6–34–2.

Umpires: B. Leadbeater and P. B. Wight.

At Oxford, June 15, 16, 17. NOTTINGHAMSHIRE drew with OXFORD UNIVERSITY.

At Southampton, June 18, 20, 21. NOTTINGHAMSHIRE drew with HAMPSHIRE.

NOTTINGHAMSHIRE v NORTHAMPTONSHIRE

At Nottingham, June 25, 27, 28. Nottinghamshire won by 191 runs. Nottinghamshire 20 pts, Northamptonshire 4 pts. Toss: Northamptonshire. Nottinghamshire's third successive home victory led to some complaints about the pitch from Cook, the Northamptonshire captain. On the first day, when the atmosphere was conducive to swing, nineteen wickets fell to the seam bowlers with only 228 runs coming from the bat. Newell alone showed the necessary application and concentration and, having opened the innings, he was last man out. Runs came more freely on a cold Monday. Birch, still deputising for Robinson, batted in his best vein, adding 132 with Stephenson, whose defensive innings lasted 160 minutes. Birch himself batted for 140 minutes and hit a six and eight fours. Northamptonshire had 95 overs in which to score the 314 runs needed for victory. But Stephenson, who with Cooper bowled unchanged, returned career-best figures and the match was Nottinghamshire's before tea.

Close of play: First day, Nottinghamshire 0-0 (B.C. Broad 0*, M. Newell 0*); Second day, Nottinghamshire 265-9 (K. P. Evans 3*, D. J. Millns 0*).

Nottinghamshire

B. C. Broad lbw b Capel	3	– lbw b Wild	47
M. Newell b Wild	44	– b Walker	21
P. Johnson b Wild	31	– c Bailey b Capel	32
F. D. Stephenson c Ripley b Wild	0	– (5) run out	47
D. W. Randall b Walker	10	– (4) c Ripley b Wild	0
*J. D. Birch lbw b Walker	0	– lbw b Capel	75
E. E. Hemmings b Wild	6	– c Ripley b Capel	10
K. P. Evans c Ripley b Davis	4	– not out	13
†C. W. Scott c Ripley b Davis	0	– c Cook b Davis	3
K. E. Cooper run out	30	– b Davis	0
D. J. Millns not out	0	– b Davis	0
B 2, l-b 10, w 2, n-b 1	15	B 1, l-b 19, w 2, n-b 5	27
1/4 2/45 3/45 4/63 5/63 6/76 7/94 8/94 9/142	143	1/55 2/106 3/110 4/114 5/246 6/250 7/259 8/265 9/265	275

Bonus points – Northamptonshire 4.

Bowling: *First Innings*—Capel 13–3–35–1; Davis 15–3–42–2; Walker 13–4–36–2; Wild 10.1–5–18–4. *Second Innings*—Davis 20–5–43–3; Capel 23–2–68–3; Wild 28–5–77–2; Walker 15–4–50–1; Williams 7–2–17–0.

Northamptonshire

*G. Cook b Cooper	18	– c Hemmings b Stephenson	23
W. Larkins c Evans b Stephenson	4	– b Stephenson	15
R. J. Bailey c Randall b Millns	14	– c Birch b Cooper	4
A. J. Lamb b Millns	0	– lbw b Stephenson	7
D. J. Capel c Broad b Evans	9	– c Newell b Stephenson	6
R. G. Williams b Stephenson	28	– c Scott b Stephenson	2
N. A. Stanley lbw b Stephenson	3	– lbw b Cooper	5
D. J. Wild c Birch b Cooper	9	– b Stephenson	1
†D. Ripley not out	8	– c Millns b Stephenson	16
W. W. Davis b Cooper	7	– c Scott b Cooper	34
A. Walker lbw b Cooper	0	– not out	4
L-b 5	5	B 2, l-b 2, n-b 1	5
1/17 2/31 3/36 4/43 5/62 6/75 7/88 8/95 9/105	105	1/23 2/41 3/48 4/55 5/59 6/64 7/68 8/68 9/117	122

Bonus points – Nottinghamshire 4.

Bowling: *First Innings*—Stephenson 16–5–39–3; Cooper 15–5–25–4; Millns 6–1–21–2; Evans 6–3–8–1; Hemmings 5–2–7–0. *Second Innings*—Stephenson 18–4–56–7; Coope 17–6–62–3.

Umpires: J. C. Balderstone and J. W. Holder.

NOTTINGHAMSHIRE v MIDDLESEX

At Nottingham, July 13, 14, 15. Nottinghamshire won by 40 runs. Nottinghamshire 12 pts. Toss: Middlesex. No play was possible on the first day, and it was not until 4.33 p.m. on the second that the ground had recovered sufficiently from the rain for a single-innings match to start. After 75 minutes, however, the rain returned to prevent further play that day. Randall completed 50 off 89 balls on the third morning, but with the remaining batsmen failing to make much impression, Middlesex seemed to have an easy task – 174 off 61 overs. Stephenson and Cooper, using the seam, had other ideas, and though Slack held out for 178 minutes, being seventh out at 118, all the visiting batsmen succumbed to the two pace bowlers. Nottinghamshire won with ten overs in hand.

Close of play: First day, No play; Second day, Nottinghamshire 60-3 (P. Johnson 12*, D. W. Randall 4*).

Nottinghamshire

B. C. Broad c Downton b Fraser	24	†C. W. Scott c Slack b Fraser	5
M. Newell c Emburey b Fraser	2	K. E. Cooper c Emburey b Fraser	0
*R. T. Robinson lbw b Cowans	11	D. J. Millns not out	0
P. Johnson lbw b Cowans	32		
D. W. Randall b Hughes	50	L-b 8, n-b 8	16
J. D. Birch c Emburey b Cowans	0		
F. D. Stephenson c Emburey b Hughes	1	1/3 2/40 3/51 4/96 5/96	173
K. P. Evans lbw b Fraser	32	6/99 7/143 8/168 9/170	

Bowling: Fraser 21.1–4–43–5; Cowans 21–5–60–3; Emburey 5–0–13–0; Hughes 11–0–49–2.

Middlesex

J. D. Carr b Stephenson	4	S. P. Hughes b Stephenson	3
W. N. Slack c Scott b Stephenson	46	A. R. C. Fraser not out	0
A. Needham lbw b Stephenson	5	N. G. Cowans b Stephenson	4
*M. W. Gatting c Evans b Cooper	7		
K. R. Brown lbw b Cooper	21	L-b 15, n-b 16	31
M. R. Ramprakash c Evans b Cooper	0		
†P. R. Downton c Birch b Cooper	0	1/4 2/16 3/35 4/88 5/92	133
J. E. Emburey b Stephenson	12	6/92 7/118 8/119 9/129	

Bowling: Stephenson 18–2–45–6; Cooper 14–2–34–4; Evans 15–4–24–0; Millns 4–0–15–0.

Umpires: N. T. Plews and R. A. White.

NOTTINGHAMSHIRE v WORCESTERSHIRE

At Nottingham, July 16, 18, 19. Nottinghamshire won by six wickets. Nottinghamshire 20 pts, Worcestershire 5 pts. Toss: Worcestershire. Continuing where they left off the previous afternoon, Stephenson and Cooper quickly made Neale regret his decision to bat on a morning when the atmosphere made the ball swing. By lunch the visitors were 50 for eight. Directly after the interval, Robinson missed a difficult chance off Radford and the ninth-wicket pair went on to add 113 in 105 minutes. When rain ended play at 4.03 p.m., Nottinghamshire were 3 without loss. The home side's first innings followed the pattern set by Worcestershire, with Cooper and Scott adding 76 for the ninth wicket after Dilley and Radford had swept aside the early batting. Hick batted in commanding fashion on the second afternoon, hitting eight fours in his 76, but Nottinghamshire had the whole of the last day in which to score 224. Recalling the earlier batting, the pundits forecast a Worcestershire win; Robinson, however, made a chanceless, unbeaten 107, including fourteen fours, and victory for the home side came at 4.40 p.m.

Close of play: First day, Nottinghamshire 3-0 (B. C. Broad 1*, M. Newell 2*); Second day, Worcestershire 199.

Worcestershire

T. S. Curtis c Birch b Stephenson	2	c Newell b Stephenson	19
S. J. O'Shaughnessy c Broad b Cooper	0	b Stephenson	12
G. A. Hick lbw b Cooper	8	c Scott b Evans	76
*P. A. Neale c Broad b Stephenson	0	c Newell b Millns	2
M. J. Weston b Cooper	6	c Randall b Millns	8
D. A. Leatherdale c Newell b Cooper	0	c Millns b Evans	28
†S. J. Rhodes lbw b Millns	5	b Stephenson	0
P. J. Newport c Broad b Stephenson	1	c Johnson b Millns	28
R. K. Illingworth c Evans b Stephenson	58	lbw b Cooper	10
N. V. Radford lbw b Stephenson	65	not out	0
G. R. Dilley not out	4	lbw b Cooper	0
B 1, l-b 3, w 1, n-b 5	10	B 2, l-b 7, n-b 7	16
1/2 2/6 3/11 4/16 5/19 6/20 7/23 8/39 9/152	159	1/22 2/59 3/68 4/81 5/155 6/156 7/160 8/199 9/199	199

Bonus points – Worcestershire 1, Nottinghamshire 4.

Bowling: *First Innings*—Stephenson 21–6–52–5; Cooper 20–5–40–4; Millns 9–3–26–1; Evans 11–1–37–0. *Second Innings*—Stephenson 20–6–42–3; Cooper 19.5–2–71–2; Millns 13–0–40–3; Evans 10–4–37–2.

Nottinghamshire

B. C. Broad c Rhodes b Dilley	7	c Illingworth b Radford	4
M. Newell c Rhodes b Radford	8	(3) c Weston b Illingworth	24
*R. T. Robinson c Radford b Dilley	5	(2) not out	107
P. Johnson c Hick b Dilley	10	lbw b Dilley	3
D. W. Randall c Illingworth b Radford	0	c Hick b Radford	33
J. D. Birch c Illingworth b Radford	0	not out	34
F. D. Stephenson b Dilley	1		
K. P. Evans b Radford	11		
†C. W. Scott not out	47		
K. E. Cooper c Leatherdale b Dilley	39		
D. J. Millns lbw b Radford	0		
L-b 3, n-b 4	7	B 3, l-b 12, n-b 6	21
1/10 2/20 3/26 4/32 5/32 6/33 7/33 8/47 9/123	135	1/13 2/78 3/83 4/140	(4 wkts) 226

Bonus points – Worcestershire 4.

Bowling: *First Innings*—Dilley 17–2–46–5; Radford 21.3–0–67–5; Newport 5–0–19–0. *Second Innings*—Dilley 15–7–25–1; Radford 15–5–46–2; Newport 13–2–37–0; Weston 8–1–33–0; Illingworth 21–9–41–1; Hick 6–0–18–0; O'Shaughnessy 1–0–7–0; Curtis 0.3–0–4–0.

Umpires: N. T. Plews and R. A. White.

At Taunton, July 23, 25, 26. NOTTINGHAMSHIRE drew with SOMERSET.

At Nottingham, July 27, 28, 29. NOTTINGHAMSHIRE drew with WEST INDIANS (See West Indian tour section).

NOTTINGHAMSHIRE v LEICESTERSHIRE

At Worksop, July 30, August 1, 2. Drawn. Nottinghamshire 8 pts, Leicestershire 6 pts. Toss: Leicestershire. Stephenson soon had the visitors in disarray, but between three breaks for rain, DeFreitas followed the example of Whitaker. The England all-rounder's hundred came in 95 minutes off 82 balls, and when he was out shortly before the close, he had hit fourteen fours and six sixes. Monday belonged to Randall. The former Test cricketer recorded his first hundred at Worksop and was at the crease for 208 minutes. Nineteen fours and two sixes illuminated his innings, and with Birch and Stephenson also hitting out brightly, the Nottinghamshire scoring-rate was more than 4 runs per over. Although play began on time on the third day, rain arrived at lunch, and when the cricketers were able to resume, there was little point to the proceedings. A dog interrupted play for several minutes.

Close of play: First day, Leicestershire 257-9 (P. M. Such 6*, L. B. Taylor 6*); Second day, Leicestershire 50-1 (N. E. Briers 21*, P. Whitticase 2*).

Leicestershire

T. J. Boon b Stephenson	8	– b Cooper	21
N. E. Briers c Robinson b Cooper	24	– c Scott b Cooper	34
P. Willey c Broad b Stephenson	0	– (4) lbw b Cooper	1
*D. I. Gower b Stephenson	4	– (5) not out	72
J. J. Whitaker b Stephenson	61	– (6) c Robinson b Hemmings	36
L. Potter c Robinson b Hemmings	9	– (7) c and b Hemmings	9
P. A. J. DeFreitas c Randall b Cooper	113	– (8) c Johnson b Hemmings	1
†P. Whitticase b Stephenson	0	– (3) lbw b Stephenson	5
J. P. Agnew c Scott b Stephenson	10	– not out	9
P. M. Such run out	6		
L. B. Taylor not out	6		
L-b 11, n-b 5	16	B 1, l-b 10, n-b 1	12
1/16 2/16 3/20 4/80 5/98 6/139 7/144 8/178 9/249	257	1/48 2/59 3/60 4/81 5/146 6/156 7/164	(7 wkts) 200

Bonus points – Leicestershire 3, Nottinghamshire 4.

Bowling: *First Innings*—Stephenson 24.1–4–66–6; Cooper 18–5–55–2; Hemmings 25–6–101–1; Millns 5–0–24–0. *Second Innings*—Millns 4–0–16–0; Cooper 23–9–59–3; Hemmings 21–7–47–3; Stephenson 20–1–67–1.

Nottinghamshire

B. C. Broad lbw b Agnew	17
*R. T. Robinson lbw b Agnew	35
P. Johnson lbw b Agnew	25
D. J. R. Martindale c Whitticase b Agnew	12
D. W. Randall c Potter b Agnew	134
J. D. Birch b DeFreitas	44
F. D. Stephenson c Whitticase b Agnew	57
†C. W. Scott not out	18
K. E. Cooper b DeFreitas	5
E. E. Hemmings not out	13
L-b 1, n-b 6	7
1/42 2/67 3/93 4/96 5/162 6/281 7/343 8/352	(8 wkts dec.) 367

D. J. Millns did not bat.

Bonus points – Nottinghamshire 4, Leicestershire 3.

Bowling: DeFreitas 19–3–62–2; Agnew 28–2–117–6; Taylor 6–1–30–0; Such 12–4–34–0; Potter 11–1–74–0; Willey 10–1–49–0.

Umpires: D. R. Shepherd and A. G. T. Whitehead.

At Sheffield, August 3, 4, 5. NOTTINGHAMSHIRE drew with YORKSHIRE.

At Nottingham, August 6, 7, 8. NOTTINGHAMSHIRE drew with SRI LANKANS (See Sri Lankan tour section).

At Colchester, August 13, 15, 16. NOTTINGHAMSHIRE beat ESSEX by two wickets.

At Lytham, August 17, 18, 19. NOTTINGHAMSHIRE beat LANCASHIRE by 151 runs.

NOTTINGHAMSHIRE v SURREY

At Nottingham, August 20, 22, 23. Surrey won by nine wickets. Surrey 23 pts, Nottinghamshire 4 pts. Toss: Surrey. In between showers and handicapped by poor light, Nottinghamshire made little progress against Clarke, Feltham and Bicknell, though the tenth wicket added a valuable 31 runs. In easier conditions on Monday, Stewart batted 184 minutes for 76, while Richards hit gaily for his 80 in 66 minutes, Evans being the main sufferer. Stephenson became the first bowler to reach 100 wickets in 1988 when he had Medlycott leg before – one of the few moments of cheer for the home crowd. Nottinghamshire could not improve on their first innings when they batted a second time, but a curiosity was that their tenth wicket again raised the best partnership. It ended when a ball from Clarke struck Cooper on the helmet, forcing him to retire hurt and allowing Surrey to win the match before lunch. French returned to the Nottinghamshire side after an absence of nearly three months as the result of a damaged hand.

Close of play: First day, Nottinghamshire 122-9 (K. P. Evans 23*, K. E. Cooper 5*); Second day, Nottinghamshire 67-3 (M. Newell 13*, B. N. French 0*).

Nottinghamshire

Batsman	1st	2nd innings	2nd
B. C. Broad c Lynch b Clarke	19	– c Richards b Bicknell	11
*R. T. Robinson b Feltham	13	– b Clarke	2
P. Johnson c Robinson b Bicknell	23	– c Lynch b Clarke	30
M. Newell c Richards b Bicknell	11	– c Richards b Bicknell	18
D. W. Randall c Richards b Bicknell	0	– (6) c Richards b Clarke	2
J. D. Birch c Medlycott b Clarke	0	– (7) c Richards b Clarke	10
F. D. Stephenson c Richards b Bicknell	6	– (8) c Clarke b Bicknell	1
K. P. Evans not out	33	– (9) c Ward b Clarke	4
†B. N. French c Clarke b Feltham	11	– (5) b Clarke	0
E. E. Hemmings c Greig b Feltham	2	– not out	31
K. E. Cooper c Bullen b Feltham	14	– retired hurt	7
B 6, l-b 4, w 2	12	B 2, l-b 10, w 2, n-b 1	15
1/24 2/42 3/58 4/62 5/63 6/75 7/90 8/107 9/113	144	1/11 2/33 3/67 4/67 5/69 6/83 7/87 8/88 9/91	131

Bonus points – Surrey 4.

Bowling: *First Innings*—Clarke 23–5–47–2; Feltham 17.1–6–43–4; Bicknell 24–9–34–4; Greig 5–1–10–0. *Second Innings*—Clarke 21–5–52–6; Bicknell 18–4–67–3; Medlycott 2–2–0–0.

Surrey

Batsman	1st	2nd innings	2nd
C. K. Bullen lbw b Cooper	2	– c French b Evans	3
J. D. Robinson b Evans	20	– not out	4
A. J. Stewart c Evans b Cooper	76	– not out	2
M. A. Lynch c Robinson b Hemmings	11		
D. M. Ward c Newell b Hemmings	10		
†C. J. Richards c Broad b Hemmings	80		
*I. A. Greig c French b Cooper	10		
K. T. Medlycott lbw b Stephenson	0		
S. T. Clarke b Stephenson	2		
M. P. Bicknell c Cooper b Evans	25		
M. A. Feltham not out	24		
B 1, l-b 4, n-b 4	9	L-b 1	1
1/5 2/43 3/71 4/91 5/202 6/204 7/207 8/213 9/217	269	1/3	(1 wkt) 10

Bonus points – Surrey 3, Nottinghamshire 4.

Bowling: *First Innings*—Stephenson 22–5–66–2; Cooper 22–5–90–3; Evans 10.5–0–59–2; Hemmings 16–3–49–3. *Second Innings*—Birch 2–0–5–0; Evans 1.3–1–4–1.

Umpires: H. D. Bird and J. Birkenshaw.

At Leicester, August 30, 31, September 1, 2. NOTTINGHAMSHIRE drew with LEICESTERSHIRE.

NOTTINGHAMSHIRE v DERBYSHIRE

At Nottingham, September 9, 10, 11, 12. Nottinghamshire won by an innings and 41 runs. Nottinghamshire 22 pts, Derbyshire 4 pts. Toss: Derbyshire. The contrasting styles of Bowler and Morris were features of the first day. The former spent 175 minutes over 50, whereas Morris was in twelve minutes longer for 106 (eighteen fours). Saturday saw Randall at his best. With Newell holding one end, the Retford batsman scored all round the wicket, doing as he pleased, and when the partnership ended on the third day, it was worth 345. Newell had batted 373 minutes for 105. Randall was out four minutes later after 297 minutes and 36 fours, having passed by 28 his previous highest score. Stephenson and Evans continued Derbyshire's agony with 117 for the seventh wicket, both recording their highest innings for the county, and Nottinghamshire went on to their highest total for 40 years. By the close on Sunday, Cooper had reached his 100th wicket for the season when he dismissed Barnett. In contrast to the first three days, Monday was cold with a bitter wind, and it was a relief to the players when the game ended early in the afternoon.

Close of play: First day, Derbyshire 327-7 (B. Roberts 54*, M. A. Holding 5*); Second day, Nottinghamshire 387-3 (M. Newell 95*, D. W. Randall 202*); Third day, Derbyshire 116-5 (B. J. M. Maher 26*, S. J. Base 0*).

Derbyshire

*K. J. Barnett c Hemmings b Cooper	19	– lbw b Cooper	45
P. D. Bowler c Evans b Stephenson	50	– c Birch b Cooper	11
†B. J. M. Maher c Newell b Stephenson	33	– c Evans b Hemmings	37
J. E. Morris c and b Hemmings	106	– c French b Stephenson	16
S. C. Goldsmith b Hemmings	30	– b Stephenson	6
B. Roberts c Newell b Stephenson	62	– b Evans	3
R. Sharma c and b Hemmings	3	– (8) c Robinson b Evans	41
F. A. Griffith c Evans b Cooper	10	– (9) c French b Stephenson	19
M. A. Holding b Stephenson	12	– (10) lbw b Evans	4
S. J. Base c Evans b Stephenson	4	– (7) b Stephenson	15
D. E. Malcolm not out	1	– not out	6
B 2, l-b 8, n-b 7	17	B 5, l-b 9, w 4, n-b 5	23
1/29 2/107 3/132 4/185 5/294 6/299 7/316 8/338 9/346	347	1/50 2/62 3/98 4/106 5/116 6/141 7/151 8/194 9/219	226

Bonus points – Derbyshire 3, Nottinghamshire 2 (Score at 100 overs: 299-6).

Bowling: *First Innings*—Stephenson 33–11–91–5; Cooper 37–6–88–2; Evans 17–2–64–0; Hemmings 33–7–87–3; Birch 2–0–7–0. *Second Innings*—Stephenson 30–11–76–4; Cooper 15–2–49–2; Hemmings 39–15–65–1; Evans 10.5–4–22–3.

Nottinghamshire

B. C. Broad b Base	48
*R. T. Robinson lbw b Holding	11
M. Newell c Goldsmith b Sharma	105
P. Johnson b Base	11
D. W. Randall b Malcolm	237
J. D. Birch c Barnett b Malcolm	11
F. D. Stephenson b Barnett	83
K. P. Evans lbw b Base	54
†B. N. French c Maher b Base	11
E. E. Hemmings not out	7
K. E. Cooper c and b Barnett	1
B 10, l-b 13, n-b 12	35
1/41 2/75 3/90 4/435 5/439 6/476 7/593 8/595 9/607	614

Bonus points – Nottinghamshire 4, Derbyshire 1 (Score at 100 overs: 388-3).

Bowling: Holding 27–3–95–1; Malcolm 31–2–146–2; Base 33–3–123–4; Sharma 44–3–129–1; Griffith 12–2–54–0; Barnett 15.3–1–44–2.

Umpires: J. Birkenshaw and R. Palmer.

NOTTINGHAMSHIRE v YORKSHIRE

At Nottingham, September 14, 15, 16, 17. Yorkshire won by 127 runs. Yorkshire 24 pts, Nottinghamshire 5 pts. Toss: Yorkshire. The game will go down in history as "Stephenson's Match". It was perhaps appropriate that in the year celebrating the 150th anniversary of Trent Bridge, the final match of the season should produce a feat never before seen on the ground. Only twice before in first-class cricket had a player scored, as Stephenson did against

Yorkshire, two hundreds and taken ten wickets in a match: B. J. T. Bosanquet, Middlesex v Surrey at Lord's in 1905, and G. H. Hirst, Yorkshire v Somerset at Bath in 1906. At the start of the match, Stephenson required 210 runs to complete the "double" for the season. Bearing in mind that he had never scored a hundred for Nottinghamshire, the feat appeared beyond him. In the first innings, however, when only Johnson among his colleagues mastered the bowling, he hit 111 in 157 minutes, including a six and eighteen fours. In the second innings, his 117 came in 137 minutes with twenty fours and two sixes, and while he chanced his arm, he gave no actual chances. Nine minutes after he was lbw to the persevering Fletcher, the match was over. Stephenson's all-round brilliance swamped the rest of the match details, but Bairstow, returning to the Yorkshire side after six matches, reached 1,000 dismissals for his county when he caught Johnson in the first innings. He then came close to celebrating his achievement with a century, hitting fifteen fours and a six as he raced to 94 from 99 balls before the close. Instead, Carrick declared at the overnight score to leave his bowlers all day to dismiss Nottinghamshire.

Close of play: First day, Yorkshire 260-4 (P. E. Robinson 59*, D. L. Bairstow 19*); Second day, Nottinghamshire 256-5 (F. D. Stephenson 96*, K. P. Evans 30*); Third day, Yorkshire 340-7 (D. L. Bairstow 94*, P. J. Hartley 3*).

Yorkshire

M. D. Moxon c Broad b Cooper	68	– c Newell b Stephenson	40
A. A. Metcalfe c Johnson b Evans	74	– b Stephenson	18
D. Byas c French b Saxelby	26	– b Stephenson	12
P. E. Robinson c Robinson b Evans	98	– c French b Stephenson	80
J. D. Love lbw b Stephenson	6	– b Stephenson	38
†D. L. Bairstow run out	26	– not out	94
*P. Carrick b Stephenson	0	– b Stephenson	37
A. Sidebottom c Saxelby b Stephenson	41	– c Evans b Stephenson	5
P. J. Hartley c Newell b Stephenson	7	– not out	3
P. A. Booth not out	15		
S. D. Fletcher c French b Evans	1		
L-b 14, n-b 4	18	B 4, l-b 7, n-b 2	13
1/123 2/165 3/178 4/193 5/282 6/282 7/341 8/359 9/363	380	1/29 2/54 3/93 4/193 5/198 6/284 7/318 (7 wkts dec.)	340

Bonus points – Yorkshire 4, Nottinghamshire 2 (Score at 100 overs: 305-6).

Bowling: *First Innings*—Stephenson 37–7–105–4; Cooper 22–5–70–1; Saxelby 15–1–69–1 Evans 18.1–2–62–3; Hemmings 29–8–60–0. *Second Innings*—Stephenson 34–2–117–7; Coope[illegible] 13–5–37–0; Evans 17–2–75–0; Hemmings 10–2–35–0; Saxelby 14–2–65–0.

Nottinghamshire

B. C. Broad lbw b Sidebottom	35	– c Bairstow b Sidebottom	1[illegible]
*R. T. Robinson c Moxon b Sidebottom	10	– c Love b Hartley	1[illegible]
M. Newell b Sidebottom	11	– c Bairstow b Hartley	2[illegible]
P. Johnson c Bairstow b Sidebottom	59	– c Sidebottom b Fletcher	2[illegible]
D. W. Randall c and b Carrick	7	– c Bairstow b Fletcher	5[illegible]
F. D. Stephenson c Carrick b Sidebottom	111	– lbw b Fletcher	11[illegible]
K. P. Evans b Sidebottom	30	– c Bairstow b Fletcher	[illegible]
†B. N. French lbw b Sidebottom	11	– c Booth b Hartley	2[illegible]
E. E. Hemmings lbw b Hartley	6	– not out	[illegible]
K. E. Cooper b Hartley	1	– b Fletcher	[illegible]
K. Saxelby not out	5	– c Sidebottom b Fletcher	[illegible]
L-b 2, w 2, n-b 6	10	L-b 10, n-b 7	1[illegible]
1/39 2/59 3/81 4/106 5/166 6/264 7/273 8/285 9/286	296	1/25 2/29 3/79 4/83 5/188 6/206 7/280 8/293 9/293	29[illegible]

Bonus points – Nottinghamshire 3, Yorkshire 4.

Bowling: *First Innings*—Hartley 14.4–3–51–2; Fletcher 18–3–59–0; Sidebottom 26–4–89–[illegible] Carrick 14–3–53–1; Booth 13–3–42–0. *Second Innings*—Sidebottom 12–2–43–1; Hartle[illegible] 16–0–85–3; Fletcher 18.5–3–74–6; Booth 4–2–9–0; Carrick 15–2–76–0.

Umpires: J. C. Balderstone and K. E. Palmer (2nd, 3rd and 4th days, B. Hassan).

SOMERSET

President: C. R. M. Atkinson
Chairman: J. Gardner
Chairman, Cricket Committee: R. E. Marshall
Secretary: 1988 – A. S. Brown
Chief Executive: 1989 – P. W. Anderson
The County Ground, St James's Street,
Taunton TA1 1JT
(Telephone: 0823-272946/253666)
Captain: 1988 – P. M. Roebuck
1989 – V. J. Marks
Coach: P. J. Robinson

Although never in contention for titles, Somerset, often fielding young and inexperienced sides, recovered from a depressing start to retain eleventh position in the Britannic Assurance Championship; moreover, with three more victories than in 1987. They achieved little in the limited-overs competitions, but if results were unexciting, the spirit of the side maintained an encouragingly high level. However bad the situation, Somerset kept going with great determination.

Peter Roebuck, in his third year as captain, can take the credit for much of the rebuilding success since 1986. He said at the start of last season that he intended to stretch the team; to make maximum demands on their fitness and prowess, as he always has on himself. He wanted to win more games, and in acknowledging that this could mean losing more he was right. Unhappily, in a season bedevilled by early illness, a broken wrist and, at the start of August, a nagging finger injury, his own form was not consistent. When the finger injury prompted him to vacate the captaincy for the last few matches, his vice-captain and most reliable player, Victor Marks, took over.

The first eleven matches, of all sorts, brought nine defeats, several of them heavy, and a solitary victory over Combined Universities in the Benson and Hedges Cup. Here was a severe test of character, for their luck, be it toss, weather or decisions, seemed regularly to be out. Then, following a nasty dose of flu, Martin Crowe returned with some superb batting, the young bowlers responded, and, despite losing the toss at Worcester and Old Trafford, so conceding two excellent starts, Somerset produced two prized wins. It says much for the fighting quality of the side that their five Championship victories owed virtually nothing to declarations. Three of the final top four teams were beaten fair and square, and Somerset went close to victory against Warwickshire (twice), Sussex and Nottinghamshire.

Several times, injuries seriously complicated matters. Richard Harden was out for a long time, and Crowe's back trouble reached crisis point in late May with him being advised to have four months' rest. When he left, the Australian, Stephen Waugh, stepped in to provide some magnificent batting. He took over the run-scoring at Bath, as Crowe had in 1984 and 1987, he made 1,000 runs in all cricket in June, and he was prominent as Somerset won five Sunday victories in seven starts in mid-season. By early August, they had climbed to fourth in the Championship. The committee's wisdom in re-signing Waugh was generally overlooked, and with Crowe's future at Taunton in doubt, there are hopes that Waugh will return in 1990. As cover for 1989, meanwhile, the Transvaal opening batsman, Jimmy Cook, was given a one-year contract on the assumption that neither Crowe nor Waugh would be available.

Although all the batsmen had days of achievement, only Waugh reached 1,000 first-class runs, and only Crowe and Waugh averaged more than 30. But perhaps this was a reflection on the quality of the pitches, for the bowlers generally had useful figures. After a poor start, Neil Mallender came back marvellously to end with 50 first-class wickets at 20.74 each. As usual, Marks led the bowlers with 76 wickets at 29.13, while Graham Rose had 57 at 26.77 and Adrian Jones, sometimes outstanding, 55 at 30.14. Darren Foster's 28 wickets again offered promise for the future. Neil Burns, playing in every match for the second season in succession – his first full seasons in the game – kept up a high standard of wicket-keeping, batting and enthusiasm throughout.

Three young men made distinctive marks for the future. Ricky Bartlett, given an extended trial, overcame the trauma of an early "king pair" to score 707 first-class runs, including a maiden Championship century, and 410 runs in the one-day matches. Matthew Cleal, a nineteen-year-old medium-pace bowler, showed considerable ability and application, and Harvey Trump, whose off-spinning compared well with that of Marks when they played together, displayed a warming amount of cricketing virtue.

There was one irony when the "non-retained" list arrived. Nigel Felton, who was on it, completed his eighth and one of his best centuries the day it was published. Colin Dredge, a faithful seamer all through the great years since 1976, left after a good benefit and several years in the shadow of injury. The Cambridge University batsman, Paul Bail, and the left-arm spinners, Robert Woolston and Tim Scriven, also left the staff.

In the final few weeks some people, including a number still disgruntled by the affairs of 1986, contrived to find sinister significance in an unusual three-pronged coincidence. The secretary, Tony Brown, transferred to a post at Lord's; the cricket manager, Brian Rose, having considered moving out of cricket for several years, found a job in industry; and Roebuck resigned the captaincy, to be replaced by Marks. The club, however, was not disintegrating. The excellent weather and cricket at Bath and Weston-super-Mare largely atoned for the early heavy defeats, the later awful weather, and some absurd arranging of fixtures at Taunton by the TCCB. Considering all things, membership and sponsorship held up pretty well. – Eric Hill.

SOMERSET 1988

[*Bill Smith*

Back row: M. Douglas, D. J. Foster, R. J. Harden, N. J. Pringle, R. J. Bartlett. *Middle row:* P. J. Robinson (*coach*), G. D. Rose, G. Townsend, M. W. Cleal, A. R. Phillips, G. V. Palmer, J. G. Wyatt, R. G. Woolston, J. J. E. Hardy, A. N. Jones. *Front row:* N. D. Burns, N. A. Felton, M. D. Crowe, V. J. Marks, P. M. Roebuck (*captain*), B. C. Rose, C. H. Dredge, N. A. Mallender, T. Gard. *Insets:* S. R. Waugh, H. R. J. Trump.

SOMERSET RESULTS

All first-class matches – Played 23: Won 5, Lost 7, Drawn 11.

County Championship matches – Played 22: Won 5, Lost 6, Drawn 11.

Bonus points – Batting 48, Bowling 65.

Competition placings – Britannic Assurance County Championship, 11th; NatWest Bank Trophy, 2nd round; Benson and Hedges Cup, 4th in Group D; Refuge Assurance League, 12th equal.

BRITANNIC ASSURANCE CHAMPIONSHIP AVERAGES

BATTING

	Birthplace	*M*	*I*	*NO*	*R*	*HI*	*Avge*
§‡S. R. Waugh	*Sydney, Australia*	14	22	6	1,286	161	80.37
§‡M. D. Crowe	*Auckland, NZ*	4	7	1	473	136*	78.83
‡N. A. Felton	*Guildford*	13	25	2	706	127	30.69
R. J. Harden	*Bridgwater*	6	11	1	295	78	29.50
‡P. M. Roebuck	*Oxford*	12	19	3	454	112*	28.37
‡N. D. Burns	*Chelmsford*	22	32	7	708	133*	28.32
‡J. J. E. Hardy	*Nakaru, Kenya*	21	37	3	902	97	26.52
‡V. J. Marks	*Middle Chinnock*	22	29	2	673	68	24.92
R. J. Bartlett	*Ash Priors*	18	29	3	648	102*	24.92
J. G. Wyatt	*Paulton*	14	24	1	532	69	23.13
N. J. Pringle	*Weymouth*	8	15	4	244	54	22.18
‡G. D. Rose	*Tottenham, London*	19	23	6	359	69*	21.11
‡C. H. Dredge	*Frome*	2	4	0	73	37	18.25
D. J. Foster	*Tottenham, London*	12	12	7	64	20	12.80
‡N. A. Mallender	*Kirk Sandall*	16	19	6	157	44	12.07
‡A. N. Jones	*Woking*	20	21	8	130	38	10.00
M. W. Cleal	*Yeovil*	8	10	1	72	13	8.00
H. R. J. Trump	*Taunton*	8	10	1	62	48	6.88

Also batted: G. V. Palmer (*Taunton*) (1 match) 0, 23; T. J. A. Scriven (*High Wycombe*) (2 matches) 7, 4.

* *Signifies not out.* ‡ *Denotes county cap.* § *Not qualified for England.*

The following played a total of twelve three-figure innings for Somerset in County Championship matches – S. R. Waugh 6, M. D. Crowe 2, R. J. Bartlett 1, N. D. Burns 1, N. A. Felton 1, P. M. Roebuck 1.

BOWLING

	O	*M*	*R*	*W*	*BB*	*5W/i*	*Avge*
N. A. Mallender	411.1	108	969	47	5-12	1	20.61
G. D. Rose	483.5	112	1,455	54	6-47	1	26.94
H. R. J. Trump	258	70	653	23	4-17	0	28.39
V. J. Marks	856.5	220	2,201	76	7-118	5	28.96
A. N. Jones	512	86	1,658	55	7-30	1	30.14
M. W. Cleal	153	22	541	16	3-16	0	33.81
D. J. Foster	282.3	44	967	25	4-46	0	38.68

Also bowled: R. J. Bartlett 30–4–145–4; C. H. Dredge 53.5–15–181–3; R. J. Harden 16–1–61–0; J. J. E. Hardy 0.3–0–12–0; G. V. Palmer 18.2–2–54–1; N. J. Pringle 13–1–40–1; P. M. Roebuck 28.4–2–106–1; T. J. A. Scriven 96–25–237–3; S. R. Waugh 23–5–60–3; J. G. Wyatt 9–4–30–1.

Wicket-keeper: N. D. Burns 55 ct, 2 st.

Leading Fielders: J. J. E. Hardy 23, S. R. Waugh 19.

At Hove, April 21, 22, 23, 25. SOMERSET lost to SUSSEX by seven wickets.

At Cardiff, April 28, 29, 30, May 2. SOMERSET drew with GLAMORGAN.

SOMERSET v WORCESTERSHIRE

At Taunton, May 5, 6, 7, 9. Worcestershire won by an innings and 214 runs. Worcestershire 23 pts, Somerset 4 pts. Toss: Worcestershire. All else in the match was overshadowed by the immense achievement of the Worcestershire batsman, Hick, who seventeen days before his 22nd birthday became one of only seven batsmen to score 400 in an innings. W. H. Ponsford performed the feat twice. Hick went in at 78 for one, and having steered his side from the dangers of 132 for five – Rose had taken three for 9 in 27 balls – he dominated play until tea on the second day. Worcestershire then declared, with Hick 19 runs short of A. C. MacLaren's highest score in England, made in 1895, also against Somerset at Taunton. The highest score in England this century, and a record for Worcestershire, his unbeaten 405 came from 469 balls and in 555 minutes; he hit 35 fours and eleven sixes. The first hundred came from 126 balls (153 minutes), the second from 151 balls (189 minutes), the third from 134 balls (142 minutes) and the fourth from 58 balls (71 minutes, eight sixes, six fours). The weather was fine when he batted and, on a pitch encouraging movement off the seam, he survived very sharp chances when 67, 101 and 141. Yet there were only two other scores over 50 in the match. The first, by Rhodes, occupied 274 balls as a new Worcestershire record was set for the sixth wicket (265); the county's eighth-wicket record was also broken as Hick and Illingworth added 177 before the declaration. Radford and Hick made inroads in the Somerset reply. Then, on the third and fourth days, under heavy cloud, Newport and Radford steadily overcame considerable defiance by the Somerset batsmen in adverse conditions. The match finished 90 minutes into the final day.

Close of play: First day, Worcestershire 312-5 (G. A. Hick 179*, S. J. Rhodes 40*); Second day, Somerset 103-4 (M. D. Crowe 11*, V. J. Marks 20*); Third day, Somerset 143-6 (M. D. Crowe 47*, G. D. Rose 13*).

Worcestershire

T. S. Curtis b Rose	27
G. J. Lord c Mallender b Dredge	49
G. A. Hick not out	405
D. B. D'Oliveira c Roebuck b Rose	0
*P. A. Neale c Marks b Mallender	0
. T. Botham b Rose	7
†S. J. Rhodes c Felton b Dredge	56
P. J. Newport b Marks	27
R. K. Illingworth not out	31
B 6, l-b 16, n-b 4	26
1/78 2/112 3/112 4/119 5/132 6/397 7/451 (7 wkts dec.)	628

N. V. Radford and G. R. Dilley did not bat.

Bonus points – Worcestershire 3, Somerset 2 (Score at 100 overs: 287-5).

Bowling: Jones 32–4–97–0; Mallender 32–9–86–1; Marks 50–6–141–1; Rose 31–8–101–3; Dredge 34.5–8–133–2; Roebuck 10–0–48–0.

Somerset

	First innings		Second innings	
N. A. Felton c Radford b Hick	24	c Rhodes b Newport	36
P. M. Roebuck lbw b Radford	0	lbw b Radford	17
J. E. Hardy c Rhodes b Radford	39	b Newport	0
M. D. Crowe c Rhodes b Newport	28	c Lord b Radford	53
. J. Harden lbw b Hick	2	lbw b Newport	3
. J. Marks c Botham b Newport	42	c Hick b Newport	7
N. D. Burns c Botham b Radford	32	c Illingworth b Hick	11
G. D. Rose c Curtis b Newport	12	c Rhodes b Newport	30
N. A. Mallender c Rhodes b Newport	3	lbw b Radford	1
. H. Dredge b Radford	16	c Curtis b Newport	17
. N. Jones not out	8	not out	3
L-b 6, n-b 10	16	B 2, l-b 1, n-b 11	14
1 2/70 3/70 4/75 5/147 152 7/166 8/173 9/203	222	1/49 2/59 3/62 4/74 5/90 6/111 7/154 8/167 9/185	192

Bonus points – Somerset 2, Worcestershire 4.

Bowling: *First Innings*—Dilley 12–0–40–0; Radford 23.5–1–77–4; Newport 17–4–59–4; Hick 8–3–18–2; Illingworth 1–0–4–0; Botham 9–3–18–0. *Second Innings*—Dilley 14–2–40–0; Botham 6–2–25–0; Radford 17–6–39–3; Newport 15.3–3–50–6; Illingworth 11–4–20–0; Hick 11–4–15–1.

Umpires: R. Julian and R. Palmer.

At Taunton, May 14, 15. SOMERSET lost to WEST INDIANS by ten wickets (See West Indian tour section).

At Worcester, May 18, 19, 20. SOMERSET beat WORCESTERSHIRE by nine wickets.

At Manchester, May 28, 30, 31. SOMERSET beat LANCASHIRE by two wickets.

At Southampton, June 1, 2, 3. SOMERSET drew with HAMPSHIRE.

SOMERSET v NORTHAMPTONSHIRE

At Taunton, June 4, 6, 7. Northamptonshire won by seven wickets. Northamptonshire 23 pts, Somerset 6 pts. Toss: Northamptonshire. A green pitch heavily favoured seam bowling, especially under the thick cloud that prevailed for most of Somerset's two innings. Twenty wickets fell on the second day and the match finished within the first hour of the third. Davis and his supporters dominated both Somerset innings, although there was spirited resistance from Wyatt, who batted throughout the second innings, Waugh, Marks and Dredge. After Somerset had been put in and bowled out on the opening day, Bailey and Capel laid sound foundations for Northamptonshire in bright evening conditions. Next day, however, Jones began a collapse to 160 for seven, but Williams hit a dashing 55 from 68 balls, and Cook and Walker, the latter in spite of muscle trouble which stopped him bowling, added a valuable 48 for the last wicket. Northamptonshire began their second innings needing 134 to win, but Jones, with three wickets in one over, and many other close calls, gave Somerset hope. In the end, Larkins (87 balls, thirteen fours) and Williams survived the murky Monday evening and smoothly won the match on a fine Tuesday with the highest partnership of it.

Close of play: First day, Northamptonshire 129-3 (R. J. Bailey 58*, D. J. Capel 29*); Second day, Northamptonshire 59-3 (W. Larkins 41*, R. G. Williams 11*).

Somerset

N. A. Felton c Bailey b Davis . . . . 5 – c Ripley b Davis 2
J. G. Wyatt c Bailey b Wild . . . . 30 – b Capel 69
J. J. E. Hardy c Ripley b Davis . . . . 12 – c Ripley b Davis . . . . [illegible]
S. R. Waugh c Larkins b Davis . . . . 37 – c Ripley b Davis 40
R. J. Bartlett lbw b Wild . . . . 0 – lbw b Wild . . . . [illegible]
†N. D. Burns lbw b Capel . . . . 8 – hit wkt b Davis . . . . [illegible]
*V. J. Marks c Fordham b Davis . . . . 43 – c Ripley b Wild . . . . 1[illegible]
G. D. Rose c Ripley b Capel . . . . 5 – lbw b Wild . . . . 1[illegible]
C. H. Dredge b Davis . . . . 37 – c Cook b Capel . . . . [illegible]
A. N. Jones c Larkins b Wild . . . . 10 – c Bailey b Capel . . . . [illegible]
D. J. Foster not out . . . . 8 – not out . . . . [illegible]
B 4, l-b 14, w 1, n-b 1 . . . . 20 L-b 11, w 11 . . . . 2[illegible]

1/7 2/37 3/95 4/95 5/95 215 1/10 2/10 3/84 4/85 5/103 17[illegible]
6/121 7/143 8/177 9/201 6/132 7/166 8/173 9/175

Bonus points – Somerset 2, Northamptonshire 4.

Bowling: *First Innings*—Davis 24–5–92–5; Capel 17–3–52–2; Wild 14.4–3–38–3; Walke[illegible] 2–1–5–0; Cook 4–1–7–0; Williams 2–0–3–0. *Second Innings*—Davis 15–0–54–4; Cap[illegible] 10.5–0–63–3; Wild 17–6–50–3.

Northamptonshire

A. Fordham c Waugh b Rose	4	– lbw b Jones	3
*W. Larkins c Hardy b Rose	7	– not out	81
R. J. Bailey c Bartlett b Jones	59	– b Jones	0
M. R. Gouldstone c Burns b Waugh	16	– c Hardy b Jones	0
D. J. Capel c Burns b Rose	33		
R. G. Williams c Felton b Foster	55	– (5) not out	38
D. J. Wild c Rose b Jones	7		
†D. Ripley c Burns b Jones	0		
N. G. B. Cook run out	24		
W. W. Davis c Felton b Dredge	5		
A. Walker not out	21		
B 2, l-b 6, w 1, n-b 20	29	B 3, l-b 3, n-b 6	12
1/5 2/16 3/53 4/135 5/135 6/156 7/160 8/206 9/212	260	1/15 2/15 3/15	(3 wkts) 134

Bonus points – Northamptonshire 3, Somerset 4.

Bowling: *First Innings*—Jones 20–1–81–3; Foster 13–5–25–1; Rose 28–8–81–3; Dredge 15–7–34–1; Waugh 9–3–17–1; Marks 8–5–14–0. *Second Innings*—Jones 9–1–49–3; Foster 10–0–41–0; Rose 4–0–18–0; Dredge 4–0–14–0; Marks 1–0–6–0.

Umpires: B. J. Meyer and P. B. Wight.

SOMERSET v WARWICKSHIRE

At Bath, June 11, 13, 14. Drawn. Somerset 4 pts, Warwickshire 4 pts. Toss: Warwickshire. In cool, cloudy weather Lloyd, with one six and thirteen fours in his 151 from 311 balls, dominated the first day. But the innings fell away as Rose returned remarkable figures on a slow pitch. Waugh, in warm conditions, responded next day, hitting twelve fours in his hundred from 154 balls. Hardy (196 balls) provided excellent support and Somerset declared 31 behind. Attack proved costly for Warwickshire against Marks and Cleal, and Somerset were left wanting 241 from a minimum of 45 overs. Hardy and Wyatt provided the right start with 51 in twelve overs, and while Waugh and Wyatt were adding 89 in sixteen, victory looked possible. However, with Gifford and Small bowling well, Warwickshire could themselves glimpse victory when Waugh (86 balls) was seventh out. Cleal, Jones and Foster blocked out the final 28 deliveries of an enthralling day's play to save the game for Somerset.

Close of play: First day, Warwickshire 315-9 (A. R. K. Pierson 1*, N. Gifford 1*); Second day, Warwickshire 36-1 (T. A. Lloyd 23*, Asif Din 2*).

Warwickshire

*T. A. Lloyd c and b Marks	151	– (2) c Waugh b Marks	30
A. J. Moles lbw b Rose	27	– (1) lbw b Jones	11
Asif Din c Bartlett b Marks	45	– c Burns b Foster	44
A. C. Storie c Burns b Rose	32	– lbw b Foster	22
†G. W. Humpage b Marks	9	– c Jones b Cleal	23
P. A. Smith c Jones b Rose	17	– c Bartlett b Marks	31
D. A. Reeve lbw b Rose	1	– not out	26
G. C. Small c Wyatt b Rose	6	– c Cleal b Marks	14
A. A. Donald b Rose	0	– c Waugh b Marks	0
A. R. K. Pierson not out	1	– c Pringle b Cleal	0
N. Gifford not out	1	– c Burns b Cleal	1
B 7, l-b 10, w 1, n-b 7	25	L-b 6, n-b 1	7
1/62 2/168 3/273 4/285 5/289 6/304 7/309 8/309 9/314	(9 wkts dec.) 315	1/32 2/57 3/103 4/136 5/136 6/176 7/196 8/198 9/203	209

Bonus points – Warwickshire 3, Somerset 1 (Score at 100 overs: 285-4).

Bowling: *First Innings*—Jones 11–0–53–0; Foster 17–5–43–0; Marks 46–13–108–3; Rose 22–6–47–6; Cleal 15–3–47–0. *Second Innings*—Jones 12–2–35–1; Foster 12–0–40–2; Marks 28–8–75–4; Rose 12–4–29–0; Cleal 6.3–1–24–3.

Somerset

J. J. E. Hardy b Pierson	81 – lbw b Small	29
J. G. Wyatt lbw b Small	7 – run out	59
R. J. Bartlett lbw b Pierson	28 – lbw b Small	0
S. R. Waugh not out	103 – b Gifford	79
N. J. Pringle not out	41 – st Humpage b Gifford	2
†N. D. Burns (did not bat)	– c Humpage b Donald	9
*V. J. Marks (did not bat)	– b Small	7
G. D. Rose (did not bat)	– b Gifford	2
M. W. Cleal (did not bat)	– lbw b Small	5
A. N. Jones (did not bat)	– not out	8
D. J. Foster (did not bat)	– not out	0
B 7, l-b 12, w 1, n-b 4	24 B 3, l-b 9, w 1, n-b 2	15
1/26 2/91 3/179 (3 wkts dec.)	284 1/51 2/55 3/144 4/157 5/180 6/200 7/202 8/203 9/211 (9 wkts)	215

Bonus points – Somerset 3, Warwickshire 1 (Score at 100 overs: 276-3).

Bowling: *First Innings*—Small 14–4–31–1; Donald 11–4–34–0; Gifford 26–4–54–0; Reeve 14–5–23–0; Pierson 28–4–84–2; Asif Din 3–0–20–0; Smith 8–1–19–0. *Second Innings*—Donald 11–0–66–1; Small 13–4–32–4; Pierson 6–0–23–0; Gifford 16–1–67–3; Reeve 2–0–15–0.

Umpires: D. G. L. Evans and R. Julian.

SOMERSET v SUSSEX

At Bath, June 15, 16, 17. Drawn. Somerset 13 pts, Sussex 4 pts. Toss: Sussex. The first three innings on a slow pitch were largely dominated by three batsmen: Alikhan, whose 98 (293 balls, fifteen fours) was his highest score, Waugh (258 balls), and Parker, whose smooth unbeaten century from 159 balls set up the declaration that left Somerset to score 251 in 172 minutes. When the first 22 overs produced only 65 runs, for two wickets, a draw seemed inevitable. But Bartlett accelerated and Waugh took charge. Two sixes and six fours decorated the Australian's 91-ball 85, and when he was caught on the boundary, 19 were needed off the last eleven balls. Pringle and Mallender kept going, but the latter, needing 3 from the last ball, could manage only 2 to level the scores and so win Somerset the extra eight points. Another compelling last session was made possible in no small part by Parker's policy of bowling the leg-spinner, Clarke, throughout the final hour.

Close of play: First day, Sussex 286-6 (I. J. Gould 47*, S. J. S. Kimber 21*); Second day, Sussex 12-1 (R. I. Alikhan 2*).

Sussex

R. I. Alikhan lbw b Marks	98 – b Mallender	20
A. M. Green lbw b Jones	7 – lbw b Marks	10
*P. W. G. Parker c Pringle b Rose	1 – not out	101
A. P. Wells lbw b Marks	64 – lbw b Scriven	38
C. M. Wells lbw b Mallender	0 – not out	30
N. J. Lenham run out	31	
†I. J. Gould not out	69	
S. J. S. Kimber not out	32	
L-b 4, n-b 14	18 L-b 3, n-b 4	7
1/17 2/26 3/125 4/134 5/204 6/242 (6 wkts dec.)	320 1/12 2/56 3/139 (3 wkts dec.)	206

A. R. Clarke, R. A. Bunting and P. W. Threlfall did not bat.

Bonus points – Sussex 2, Somerset 2 (Score at 100 overs: 230-5).

Bowling: *First Innings*—Jones 13–3–36–1; Mallender 24–6–75–1; Rose 19–6–63–1; Waugh 3–1–10–0; Scriven 32–6–71–0; Marks 34–11–61–2. *Second Innings*—Jones 8–0–29–0; Marks 23–4–81–1; Mallender 7–1–21–1; Rose 6–0–30–0; Scriven 16–4–42–1.

Somerset

First innings		Second innings	
J. J. E. Hardy c Green b Bunting	1	b Clarke	40
J. G. Wyatt c A. P. Wells b C. M. Wells	16	b Bunting	4
R. J. Bartlett c A. P. Wells b C. M. Wells	38	b Kimber	35
S. R. Waugh b Clarke	137	c Kimber b C. M. Wells	85
N. J. Pringle b Green	40	(8) not out	20
†N. D. Burns b Clarke	13	(7) c Parker b C. M. Wells	2
G. D. Rose not out	10	(6) b Clarke	0
*V. J. Marks not out	15	(5) c Green b Clarke	40
N. A. Mallender (did not bat)		not out	8
B 1, l-b 5	6	B 10, l-b 6	16
1/1 2/43 3/62 4/184 5/205 6/258 (6 wkts dec.)	276	1/16 2/65 3/114 4/200 5/200 6/203 7/232 (7 wkts)	250

A. N. Jones and T. J. A. Scriven did not bat.

Bonus points – Somerset 3, Sussex 2 (Score at 100 overs: 251-5).

Bowling: *First Innings*—Threlfall 8–2–13–0; Bunting 16–6–48–1; C. M. Wells 18–4–50–2; Kimber 13–4–28–0; Clarke 35.5–6–90–2; Green 15–2–41–1. *Second Innings*—Threlfall 4–1–18–0; Bunting 5–1–14–1; C. M. Wells 17–2–69–2; Clarke 21–1–98–3; Kimber 7–0–35–1.

Umpires: D. G. L. Evans and R. Julian.

SOMERSET v GLAMORGAN

At Taunton, June 29, 30, July 1. Drawn. Somerset 5 pts, Glamorgan 3 pts. Toss: Glamorgan. Before a thunderstorm flooded the ground and reduced the first day's play to 68 overs, Glamorgan had struggled on a lively, greenish pitch. Hopkins fought well to prop up the early innings, and Holmes carried his fine performance over into the second day. He had just reached his half-century when Metson was out, but with Watkin helping him add 67 he moved on to his hundred, scored from 207 balls. After some early difficulties, Roebuck (100 in 182 balls) and Waugh (133 balls) gave Somerset a chance to force a win with a stand of 179 in 43 overs. Glamorgan collapsed before the close. Next day, however, Morris and Maynard, despite being hit by lifting balls, increased their partnership to a vital 80 from 22 overs before Maynard retired with a hand injury. Glamorgan were only 93 runs ahead with 285 minutes remaining, but Holmes again came to their rescue, boldly reaching his second century of the match in 133 balls (fifteen fours). With Shastri he added 99 in 27 overs, and Somerset were further frustrated by the showers which reduced the day's play by 22 overs.

Close of play: First day, Glamorgan 162-7 (G. C. Holmes 45*, C. P. Metson 3*); Second day, Glamorgan 36-3 (H. Morris 5*, M. P. Maynard 26*).

Glamorgan

First innings		Second innings	
A. R. Butcher c Marks b Rose	4	run out	2
. A. Hopkins b Foster	36	b Foster	0
H. Morris c Burns b Marks	11	lbw b Rose	24
M. P. Maynard b Foster	0	(5) retired hurt	53
R. J. Shastri run out	20	(6) c Waugh b Wyatt	30
G. C. Holmes not out	100	(7) b Bartlett	107
R. C. Ontong c Burns b Foster	17	(8) not out	12
. Derrick c Bartlett b Marks	0	(9) run out	0
C. P. Metson c Burns b Foster	17	(4) c Hardy b Mallender	1
. L. Watkin not out	15	not out	3
B 1, l-b 14, w 1, n-b 16	32	L-b 7, w 3, n-b 5	15
/19 2/56 3/56 4/66 5/112 /138 7/141 8/185 (8 wkts dec.)	252	1/2 2/2 3/3 4/84 5/183 6/242 7/244 (7 wkts dec.)	247

R. Barwick did not bat.

Bonus points – Glamorgan 3, Somerset 3.

Bowling: *First Innings*—Jones 14.2–1–48–0; Mallender 21–8–33–0; Rose 19–7–40–1; Foster 23–5–72–4; Marks 20–5–43–2; Roebuck 2–1–1–0. *Second Innings*—Mallender 15–3–53–1; Foster 12–1–52–1; Marks 17–7–37–0; Rose 10–3–16–1; Jones 10–2–49–0; Roebuck 1–1–0–0; Wyatt 8–4–24–1; Bartlett 5–3–9–1.

Somerset

J. J. E. Hardy c Morris b Barwick 12
*P. M. Roebuck not out 112
J. G. Wyatt c Hopkins b Derrick 6
S. R. Waugh not out 101
B 5, l-b 3, n-b 4 12

1/38 2/64 (2 wkts dec.) 243

R. J. Bartlett, V. J. Marks, †N. D. Burns, G. D. Rose, N. A. Mallender, A. N. Jones and D. J. Foster did not bat.

Bonus points – Somerset 2.

Bowling: Barwick 17–2–51–1; Watkin 20–3–57–0; Derrick 14–2–58–1; Shastri 15–0–49–0; Ontong 3.2–0–20–0.

Umpires: J. D. Bond and A. G. T. Whitehead.

SOMERSET v ESSEX

At Taunton, July 2, 4, 5. Drawn. Somerset 3 pts, Essex 3 pts. Toss: Essex. Despite the best efforts of all concerned, the rain which limited play to 51 overs on the first two days had the final word. Hardie (108 balls) and Pringle (101 balls) underpinned the Essex innings before the occasional bowlers came on to set up a declaration. Somerset's target was 259 in 79 overs, but storms gradually altered the situation and a final grand downpour ended matters at 3.50 p.m.

Close of play: First day, Essex 43-1 (B. R. Hardie 13*, P. J. Prichard 11*); Second day, Essex 170-5 (D. R. Pringle 42*, A. D. Brown 0*).

Essex

B. R. Hardie b Rose 50
J. P. Stephenson c Hardy b Mallender . 9
P. J. Prichard lbw b Rose 23
A. R. Border b Foster 1
A. W. Lilley b Marks 25
D. R. Pringle c Roebuck b Bartlett 75
†A. D. Brown b Marks 3
*K. W. R. Fletcher not out 35
G. Miller not out 15
B 1, l-b 11, n-b 10 22

1/15 2/73 3/78 4/109 5/157 6/199 7/215 (7 wkts dec.) 258

N. A. Foster and J. K. Lever did not bat.

Bonus points – Essex 3, Somerset 3.

Bowling: Jones 11.4–2–33–0; Mallender 8–3–13–1; Marks 17–2–49–2; Rose 11.2–1–41–2; Foster 14–0–62–1; Bartlett 5–0–20–1; Roebuck 3–0–16–0; Hardy 0.3–0–12–0.

Essex forfeited their second innings.

Somerset

Somerset forfeited their first innings.

J. J. E. Hardy c Brown b Lever 6
*P. M. Roebuck run out 24
J. G. Wyatt retired hurt 2
S. R. Waugh not out 33
R. J. Bartlett not out 1
L-b 5 ....

1/15 2/43 (2 wkts) 8

V. J. Marks, †N. D. Burns, G. D. Rose, N. A. Mallender, A. N. Jones and D. J. Foster di not bat.

Bowling: Foster 18–3–48–0; Lever 6–2–13–1; Pringle 4–1–10–0; Miller 7–1–9–0.

Umpires: J. D. Bond and A. G. T. Whitehead.

At Bristol, July 16, 18, 19. SOMERSET beat GLOUCESTERSHIRE by eight wickets.

SOMERSET v NOTTINGHAMSHIRE

At Taunton, July 23, 25, 26. Drawn. Somerset 5 pts, Nottinghamshire 6 pts. Toss: Nottinghamshire. Only 67 overs were possible on the Saturday, when after a promising opening the visitors slipped to 107 for four. Johnson and Stephenson revived the innings with 79 in 24 overs, but after the latter's dismissal came the first of the match's remarkable collapses. On a day when twenty wickets fell, Somerset's reply was undermined by Stephenson, who promptly took three wickets for 5 runs in eighteen balls. Sturdy batting from Hardy and Bartlett steadied the innings, but Hemmings reduced it to 84 for seven before the nineteen-year-old Trump confirmed the excellent impression already created on his début by his bowling and fielding. With Rose, he added 66 in 23 overs. On Tuesday morning, in the easiest batting conditions of the match, Nottinghamshire's last five wickets fell for 1 run in thirteen balls as Marks took four wickets with his last seven balls. Somerset had 82 overs in which to score 148, but they had barely started when the first of two heavy storms reached the ground. The umpires waited until 4.55 p.m. before abandoning the match.

Close of play: First day, Nottinghamshire 173-4 (P. Johnson 45*, F. D. Stephenson 30*); Second day, Nottinghamshire 51-4 (D. J. R. Martindale 22*, F. D. Stephenson 2*).

Nottinghamshire

First innings		Second innings	
M. Newell c Burns b Marks	21	c Burns b Jones	2
*R. T. Robinson c Trump b Mallender	50	c Rose b Marks	13
P. Johnson b Trump	73	c Burns b Jones	0
D. J. R. Martindale c Burns b Mallender	10	lbw b Marks	46
D. W. Randall c Waugh b Marks	0	lbw b Mallender	4
F. D. Stephenson lbw b Marks	31	b Jones	19
K. P. Evans c Burns b Marks	3	c Pringle b Mallender	5
†C. W. Scott run out	0	c Waugh b Marks	1
E. E. Hemmings c Waugh b Marks	1	not out	0
K. E. Cooper not out	0	c Bartlett b Marks	0
D. J. Millns c Hardy b Trump	0	c Mallender b Marks	0
B 8, l-b 3, w 1, n-b 10	22	L-b 6, n-b 7	13
1/76 2/86 3/106 4/107 5/186 6/196 7/208 8/211 9/211	211	1/10 2/10 3/37 4/42 5/85 6/102 7/102 8/103 9/103	103

Bonus points – Nottinghamshire 2, Somerset 4.

Bowling: *First Innings*—Jones 7–0–28–0; Mallender 21–6–49–2; Rose 10–1–31–0; Marks 32–10–73–5; Trump 14–8–17–2; Bartlett 1–0–2–0. *Second Innings*—Jones 14–3–42–3; Mallender 8–3–8–2; Marks 12–1–43–5; Rose 3–1–4–0; Trump 1–1–0–0.

Somerset

First innings		Second innings	
J. J. E. Hardy c Johnson b Hemmings	25	not out	15
*P. M. Roebuck b Stephenson	0	c Scott b Cooper	5
N. J. Pringle c Scott b Stephenson	3	not out	6
S. R. Waugh lbw b Stephenson	0		
R. J. Bartlett c Newell b Hemmings	39		
†N. D. Burns b Hemmings	0		
V. J. Marks lbw b Hemmings	9		
G. D. Rose c Newell b Stephenson	22		
H. R. J. Trump lbw b Cooper	48		
N. A. Mallender b Cooper	1		
A. N. Jones not out	2		
B 2, l-b 8, n-b 8	18	L-b 1	1
1/0 2/11 3/11 4/43 5/47 6/65 7/84 8/150 9/160	167	1/6	(1 wkt) 27

Bonus points – Somerset 1, Nottinghamshire 4.

Bowling: *First Innings*—Cooper 18.1–7–40–2; Stephenson 18–3–41–4; Hemmings 23–7–50–4; Millns 5–0–26–0. *Second Innings*—Stephenson 4.3–1–20–0; Cooper 2–0–3–1; Hemmings 2–0–3–0.

Umpires: D. J. Constant and J. H. Harris.

At Canterbury, July 30, August 1, 2. SOMERSET beat KENT by an innings and 146 runs.

SOMERSET v SURREY

At Weston-super-Mare, August 3, 4, 5. Somerset won by five wickets. Somerset 21 pts, Surrey 4 pts. Toss: Surrey. On a slow pitch, offering increasing turn and bounce, the bowlers remained on top until the last session. Seventeen wickets fell on each of the first two days. Waugh and Bartlett, in Somerset's first innings, put together the highest stand of the match when they added 55 in fourteen overs. Somerset, with a day and 65 minutes in which to score 109 for victory, began their second innings at a racing pace, but after ten overs had brought 46 runs Medlycott took four wickets in three overs. Next morning he caught and bowled Bartlett to increase his match return to ten wickets, but a splendidly controlled 47 in 133 balls from Roebuck, and a thoughtfully attacking 25 from 34 balls by Burns brought victory before lunch.

Close of play: First day, Somerset 119-7 (N. D. Burns 8*); Second day, Somerset 55-4 (P. M. Roebuck 21*, R. J. Bartlett 0*).

Surrey

G. S. Clinton c and b Trump	16	– not out	10
P. D. Atkins lbw b Mallender	10	– c Waugh b Jones	6
†A. J. Stewart c Burns b Mallender	0	– lbw b Marks	13
D. M. Ward c and b Trump	17	– b Marks	28
Zahid Sadiq c Hardy b Jones	37	– c Hardy b Marks	0
*I. A. Greig b Marks	20	– c Pringle b Marks	22
K. T. Medlycott lbw b Jones	0	– c Waugh b Trump	21
M. A. Feltham lbw b Mallender	18	– lbw b Marks	2
C. K. Bullen lbw b Mallender	10	– lbw b Mallender	7
N. H. Peters not out	8	– c Pringle b Mallender	0
M. P. Bicknell b Trump	5	– c Hardy b Mallender	2
L-b 2, n-b 5	7	L-b 4, n-b 4	8
1/20 2/20 3/40 4/53 5/98 6/98 7/112 8/126 9/135	148	1/15 2/55 3/55 4/64 5/99 6/104 7/116 8/116 9/117	119

Bonus points – Somerset 4.

In the second innings G. S. Clinton, when 9, retired hurt at 15 and resumed at 116-7.

Bowling: *First Innings*—Jones 11–2–36–2; Mallender 19–6–22–4; Marks 16–4–32–1; Trump 19.1–7–32–3; Foster 5–0–24–0. *Second Innings*—Jones 13–3–29–1; Mallender 16–5–18–3; Foster 4–0–18–0; Marks 20–7–41–5; Trump 7–3–9–1.

Somerset

J. J. E. Hardy b Greig	23	– b Medlycott	26
*P. M. Roebuck lbw b Greig	10	– not out	47
N. J. Pringle lbw b Greig	9	– c Bullen b Medlycott	0
S. R. Waugh b Feltham	31	– c Stewart b Medlycott	4
R. J. Bartlett c Bullen b Medlycott	25	– (6) c and b Medlycott	3
†N. D. Burns lbw b Greig	35	– (7) not out	25
V. J. Marks c Feltham b Medlycott	0		
H. R. J. Trump c Ward b Medlycott	4		
N. A. Mallender c Ward b Medlycott	5	– (5) c Stewart b Medlycott	0
A. N. Jones c and b Medlycott	4		
D. J. Foster not out	4		
B 3, l-b 6	9	L-b 5	5
1/32 2/45 3/52 4/107 5/107 6/111 7/119 8/129 9/141	159	1/46 2/46 3/50 4/54 5/60	(5 wkts) 11

Bonus points – Somerset 1, Surrey 4.

Bowling: *First Innings*—Bicknell 7–2–20–0; Peters 4–0–16–0; Greig 20.1–4–40–4; Medlycott 24–10–55–5; Feltham 6–1–19–1. *Second Innings*—Bicknell 2–0–10–0; Peters 2–0–16–0; Feltham 3–0–11–0; Greig 12–2–21–0; Medlycott 15–5–33–5; Bullen 6–1–14–0.

Umpires: J. C. Balderstone and R. A. White.

SOMERSET v DERBYSHIRE

At Weston-super-Mare, August 6, 8, 9. Derbyshire won by 183 runs. Derbyshire 22 pts, Somerset 5 pts. Toss: Derbyshire. The pitch, although looking the same as that used in the previous match, played quite differently and the bat dominated until Somerset's final demise against the pace of Warner and Malcolm. On the opening day, Sharma (162 balls) and Roberts (112 balls) enabled Derbyshire to recover from 124 for five. Somerset, with Hardy and Bartlett especially in the vanguard, replied soundly before declaring 43 runs behind. Roebuck, who had sustained a hand injury in the Sunday match, could not bat. Encouraged by Somerset's occasional bowlers, Derbyshire were able to set a target of 266 in 230 minutes, but after Hardy and Pringle had added 35 in eight overs, Somerset collapsed completely and unaccountably. They lost their last seven wickets inside an hour, leaving Derbyshire the winners with two hours to spare.

Close of play: First day, Derbyshire 324-8 (A. E. Warner 45*, O. H. Mortensen 6*); Second day, Derbyshire 58-0 (P. D. Bowler 29*, J. G. Wright 27*).

Derbyshire

P. D. Bowler b Marks	27	– b Trump	34
*J. G. Wright run out	31	– c Marks b Scriven	59
†B. J. M. Maher c Hardy b Trump	0	– lbw b Bartlett	30
J. E. Morris c Waugh b Mallender	24	– not out	59
S. C. Goldsmith c Burns b Marks	37	– b Pringle	22
B. Roberts c Mallender b Trump	62	– not out	16
R. Sharma c Roebuck b Scriven	80		
P. G. Newman c Pringle b Trump	5		
A. E. Warner c Waugh b Mallender	45		
O. H. Mortensen not out	6		
D. E. Malcolm c Waugh b Mallender	0		
B 3, l-b 4	7	L-b 1, n-b 1	2
1/58 2/58 3/62 4/122 5/124 6/256 7/269 8/277 9/324	324	1/93 2/99 3/156 4/183 (4 wkts dec.)	222

Bonus points – Derbyshire 3, Somerset 2 (Score at 100 overs: 262-6).

Bowling: *First Innings*—Jones 14–4–58–0; Mallender 20.5–7–29–3; Marks 28–5–61–2; Trump 31–9–81–3; Scriven 25–6–84–1; Pringle 1–0–4–0. *Second Innings*—Jones 3–1–14–0; Mallender 5–2–7–0; Marks 5–0–18–0; Scriven 23–9–40–1; Trump 17–2–58–1; Pringle 9–1–25–1; Bartlett 7–0–48–1; Roebuck 1–0–11–0.

Somerset

J. J. E. Hardy b Sharma	60	– c Maher b Malcolm	25
†N. D. Burns c Maher b Newman	33	– c Mortensen b Warner	2
N. J. Pringle retired hurt	4	– c Maher b Malcolm	9
S. R. Waugh c Maher b Warner	44	– lbw b Warner	1
R. J. Bartlett c Bowler b Malcolm	66	– lbw b Malcolm	8
V. J. Marks run out	46	– c Bowler b Malcolm	11
H. R. J. Trump b Malcolm	8	– (8) c Goldsmith b Warner	0
T. J. A. Scriven b Bowler	7	– (9) lbw b Sharma	4
N. A. Mallender not out	2	– (7) b Warner	4
A. N. Jones c Goldsmith b Malcolm	0	– not out	9
P. M. Roebuck (did not bat)		– absent injured	
L-b 10, n-b 1	11	L-b 2, w 2, n-b 5	9
1/64 2/142 3/157 4/220 5/234 6/271 7/281 8/281 (8 wkts dec.)	281	1/5 2/40 3/41 4/43 5/59 6/66 7/66 8/67 9/82	82

Bonus points – Somerset 3, Derbyshire 3.

Bowling: *First Innings*—Malcolm 17.3–4–63–3; Newman 12–3–46–1; Mortensen 16–5–44–0; Warner 13–4–42–1; Sharma 15–2–63–1; Bowler 5–1–13–1. *Second Innings*—Warner 13–2–37–4; Malcolm 12–1–43–4; Sharma 0.2–0–0–1.

Umpires: J. C. Balderstone and R. A. White.

At Scarborough, August 13, 15, 16. SOMERSET drew with YORKSHIRE.

At Uxbridge, August 17, 18, 19. SOMERSET drew with MIDDLESEX.

At Hinckley, August 20, 22, 23. SOMERSET lost to LEICESTERSHIRE by seven wickets.

SOMERSET v HAMPSHIRE

At Taunton, August 25, 26, 27, 29. Drawn. Somerset 5 pts, Hampshire 7 pts. Toss: Hampshire. After early difficulties on a variable pitch, Turner (144 balls, fourteen fours) and Nicholas launched a determined recovery. On the second day, Somerset faltered against the swinging ball as James took three for 4 in 23 deliveries. Marks, Bartlett and finally Rose made sure that the follow-on was avoided, and when Hampshire batted again, Rose and Jones struck. From 80 for eight, they were rescued by Maru who, dropped when 4, added a vital 44 in nine overs with Connor. Somerset were set 255 in 62 overs, which was soon reduced to 60 overs by the rain which had seriously interrupted all four days. Hardy and Felton put on 108 in 36 overs in poor light, and Bartlett, declining an offer to go off, kept going until the final downpour.

Close of play: First day, Hampshire 303-7 (R. J. Parks 38*, R. J. Maru 9*); Second day, Somerset 191-9 (G. D. Rose 34*, A. N. Jones 7*); Third day, Hampshire 42-5 (K. D. James 0*, J. R. Ayling 0*).

Hampshire

V. P. Terry c Burns b Cleal	17	– c Hardy b Rose	7
C. L. Smith b Rose	2	– b Rose	0
K. D. James c Burns b Jones	2	– (6) c Burns b Jones	2
D. R. Turner c Burns b Rose	93	– lbw b Jones	13
*M. C. J. Nicholas lbw b Marks	35	– (3) b Rose	10
R. J. Scott lbw b Trump	40	– (5) c Harden b Cleal	5
J. R. Ayling run out	49	– c Rose b Jones	24
†R. J. Parks c Bartlett b Jones	38	– c Burns b Jones	11
R. J. Maru c Burns b Rose	13	– not out	19
C. A. Connor c Rose b Jones	9	– c Burns b Rose	21
P. J. Bakker not out	0	– not out	8
B 1, l-b 11, n-b 11	23	B 5, l-b 6, w 1, n-b 3	15
1/6 2/27 3/33 4/108 5/192 6/212 7/284 8/303 9/321	321	1/6 2/9 3/28 (9 wkts dec.) 4/41 5/42 6/51 7/75 8/80 9/124	13

Bonus points – Hampshire 3, Somerset 3 (Score at 100 overs: 294-7).

Bowling: *First Innings*—Jones 21.3–3–66–3; Rose 23–9–56–3; Cleal 16–2–63–1; Marl 26–5–61–1; Trump 24–4–63–1. *Second Innings*—Jones 23–5–77–4; Rose 23.2–6–47–4; Cle 1–1–0–1.

Somerset

J. J. E. Hardy lbw b Bakker	19	– c Terry b Ayling	50
N. A. Felton c Parks b James	36	– run out	57
J. G. Wyatt b James	8	– c Maru b Connor	5
R. J. Bartlett c Maru b Connor	23	– not out	17
R. J. Harden c Parks b James	0	– not out	4
†N. D. Burns lbw b Ayling	9		
*V. J. Marks c Terry b Ayling	42		
G. D. Rose c Smith b Bakker	34		
M. W. Cleal c Parks b Maru	1		
H. R. J. Trump c Scott b Maru	0		
A. N. Jones not out	17		
L-b 11, n-b 2	13	B 4, l-b 9, n-b 3	16
/38 2/59 3/72 4/72 5/83 /128 7/165 8/178 9/178	202	1/108 2/127 3/127 (3 wkts)	149

Bonus points – Somerset 2, Hampshire 4.

Bowling: *First Innings*—Bakker 21.3–4–37–2; Connor 15–4–52–1; James 24–7–46–3; Ayling 6–4–32–2; Scott 4–1–8–0; Maru 10–3–16–2. *Second Innings*—Bakker 8–2–19–0; Connor –2–33–1; James 11–3–22–0; Maru 10.5–0–42–0; Ayling 7–0–20–1.

Umpires: J. D. Bond and J. H. Hampshire.

At Birmingham, September 9, 10, 11, 12. SOMERSET drew with WARWICKSHIRE.

SOMERSET v GLOUCESTERSHIRE

At Taunton, September 14, 15, 16, 17. Gloucestershire won by four wickets. Gloucestershire pts, Somerset 6 pts. Toss: Somerset. Despite three batting collapses, a first-morning injury to artlett, and the absence through injury of two main bowlers, Somerset remained in contention ntil the fourth day. Defiant batting by Harden and Burns, who added 128 in the first innings, a vely 50 from Marks, and a partnership of 161 in the second by Felton and Harden held up loucestershire after early breakthroughs. Stovold (231 balls) and Wright gave the visitors superb start with 180 in 60 overs, but the persistence of Marks and Trump kept the first nings in check. Only Bainbridge prospered thereafter as the lead was held to 58. Felton, the ay after being told that he was not being re-engaged, made a brilliant 127 from 187 balls after escape at 30, but Alderman's spell of six for 9 in 47 deliveries proved the decisive factor. kept Gloucestershire's target to 157, none too easy on an awkward, turning pitch. Rose d the spinners removed six batsmen for 113, but Curran, with a patient 51 from 141 balls, sed his side to victory. His final strokes took him to 1,000 runs for the season.

Close of play: First day, Gloucestershire 44-0 (A. W. Stovold 30*, A. J. Wright 13*); Second ay, Somerset 31-1 (N. A. Felton 20*, M. W. Cleal 1*); Third day, Gloucestershire 99-4 . M. Curran 20*, J. W. Lloyds 10*).

omerset

J. E. Hardy c Russell b Lawrence	5	– b Lloyds	10
A. Felton b Lawrence	21	– b Graveney	127
G. Wyatt b Lawrence	23	– (4) lbw b Alderman	0
J. Bartlett c and b Ibadulla	3	– (10) c Bainbridge b Alderman	0
J. Harden b Ibadulla	78	– c Romaines b Alderman	52
. D. Burns c Stovold b Lloyds	56	– c Lloyds b Alderman	2
. J. Marks c Romaines b Ibadulla	50	– c Lloyds b Alderman	3
D. Rose c Romaines b Graveney	14	– lbw b Alderman	8
W. Cleal c Stovold b Graveney	9	– (3) c Russell b Alderman	3
R. J. Trump c Stovold b Graveney	0	– (9) not out	0
J. Foster not out	0	– c Lloyds b Alderman	2
B 5, l-b 5, n-b 8	18	L-b 3, n-b 4	7
4 2/34 3/55 4/183 5/235 56 7/268 8/276 9/276	277	1/25 2/35 3/35 4/196 5/197 6/201 7/208 8/211 9/211	214

Bonus points – Somerset 3, Gloucestershire 2 (Score at 100 overs: 262-6).

the first innings R. J. Bartlett, when 2, retired hurt at 37 and resumed at 276-9.

Bowling: *First Innings*—Lawrence 20–4–75–3; Alderman 12–4–44–0; Graveney 46–16–66–3; Lloyds 12–4–30–1; Bainbridge 4–0–9–0; Ibadulla 12.2–2–43–3. *Second Innings*—Lawrence 11–0–37–0; Alderman 27.2–7–59–8; Lloyds 9–2–28–1; Graveney 29–6–66–1 Ibadulla 6–1–21–0.

Gloucestershire

A. W. Stovold c Hardy b Marks	133	– lbw b Rose	18
A. J. Wright lbw b Marks	52	– c Trump b Marks	26
P. W. Romaines c Hardy b Marks	7	– b Marks	18
P. Bainbridge c Burns b Trump	57	– c and b Trump	1
K. M. Curran c Hardy b Marks	1	– not out	5
J. W. Lloyds c Rose b Marks	22	– c Hardy b Rose	1
K. B. K. Ibadulla c Burns b Trump	9	– (8) not out	1
†R. C. Russell c sub b Marks	1	– (7) c Burns b Rose	
D. V. Lawrence run out	16		
*D. A. Graveney not out	14		
T. M. Alderman c Burns b Marks	5		
B 5, l-b 9, n-b 4	18	B 2, l-b 8	1
1/180 2/200 3/211 4/217 5/285 6/289 7/292 8/311 9/328	335	1/28 2/57 3/60 4/72 5/107 6/113	(6 wkts) 15

Bonus points – Gloucestershire 3, Somerset 3 (Score at 100 overs: 292-7).

Bowling: *First Innings*—Rose 15–3–43–0; Foster 6–1–34–0; Marks 50.2–14–118–7; Trum 39–10–96–2; Cleal 7–0–30–0. *Second Innings*—Rose 19–5–50–3; Foster 3–2–10–0; Mar 30–10–62–2; Trump 14–4–25–1.

Umpires: J. W. Holder and R. A. White.

COUNTY CAPS AWARDED IN 1988

Essex	G. Miller, T. D. Topley.
Glamorgan	J. Derrick, R. J. Shastri.
Hampshire	C. A. Connor.
Kent	G. R. Cowdrey, R. F. Pienaar.
Leicestershire	G. J. F. Ferris, L. Potter.
Middlesex	A. R. C. Fraser.
Nottinghamshire	C. W. Scott, F. D. Stephenson.
Somerset	G. D. Rose, S. R. Waugh.
Surrey	K. T. Medlycott.
Warwickshire	T. A. Merrick.
Yorkshire	S. D. Fletcher, P. E. Robinson.

No caps were awarded by Derbyshire, Gloucestershire, Lancashire, Northamptonshire, Susse Worcestershire.

SURREY

Patron: HM The Queen
President: 1988 – Sir Michael Sandberg
1989 – C. G. Howard
Chairman: D. H. Newton
Chairman, Cricket Committee: J. A. Fulford
Secretary: D. G. Seward
Kennington Oval, London SE11 5SS
(Telephone: 01-582 6660)
Captain: I. A. Greig
Coaches: G. G. Arnold and C. E. Waller

A theme of ancient and modern threads itself indelibly through Surrey's ummer. While the decaying Oval's status as England's oldest Test match enue was secured by an emotive appeal to cricket lovers and opulently ustained by sponsorship from a leading brewery, the exuberance of outh served Surrey admirably to maintain a satisfying status quo for Ian ireig's enthusiastic side. But for a frozen performance against Midlesex in their NatWest Bank Trophy semi-final, in which the shortfall n experience was strikingly evident, Surrey's fledglings would have inished the season with a feeling of greater stature.

Fourth place in the Britannic Assurance Championship equalled urrey's 1987 performance, albeit leaving members with a familiar eeling of unfulfilled promise. There had, however, been a wider vailability of seasoned performers in the previous season, whereas on ccasions last season Greig took the field with only four capped players. s the Surrey coach, Geoff Arnold, said when summing up the season, It was another example of getting to the last hurdle and not clearing it. ut to keep the same position in the Championship and reach a seminal, as we also did in 1987, with so many youngsters made it a satisfying eason on which the club can build." Surrey's problem was that they left eir run too late. They were twelfth in mid-August before winning three ut of four Championship matches by huge margins. When title conenders Kent demolished them by an innings in two and a half days at anterbury in the last match of the campaign, there were enough points reserve to claim a share of the prizemoney.

The portents for the season looked ominous when only one win came a strong Benson and Hedges Cup group in May. Their lack of bowling ariety, among other reasons, left them without a chance in the 55-over mpetition. But a consistent challenge was mounted in the Refuge ssurance League. Despite losing two of their last three matches, they tained fifth place, an improvement of two and a considerable nprovement on four seasons earlier when they languished in bottom sition. Arnold, his number two, Chris Waller, and Greig, all once with ssex, have clearly instilled into Surrey the one-day traditions of their rmer county.

With Sylvester Clarke restricted to twelve Championship matches by jury and a club suspension for failing to report for the match at ansea, and Tony Gray not bowling a single over in the Championship, was left to Martin Bicknell, Nick Peters, Mark Feltham, Mark Frost,

Keith Medlycott and Chris Bullen, all uncapped, to sustain the attack. Clarke and Gray, the West Indian overseas players, had successfully operated in rotation in the previous three seasons. Clarke, on his day, remained the country's most feared quick bowler and captured 63 wickets, but Gray was seemingly unable to regain his form of recent years. He had suffered a broken arm in net practice during the previous autumn's World Cup, but after struggling for a time in the West Indies Red Stripe tournament he had played in the one-day series against Pakistan. However, he was passed over for the tour of England in favour of his fellow Trinidadian, Ian Bishop. Surrey, hardly surprisingly, did not offer him a new contract; nor the left-handed batsman, David Smith, who when told the news gave vent to his feelings by thrashing an unbeaten 157 against Hampshire at Guildford.

Less expected was the announcement in November that the wicket-keeper, Jack Richards, was being released on the recommendation of the cricket sub-committee with a year of his contract still to run. His batting had been a bonus early in the season, when Surrey were often pinned below the halfway mark in the Championship; he had been effective in the Sunday League opening the innings; and he topped their Championship averages with 861 runs at 50.64. The England selectors had recalle him for the last two Test matches against the West Indians.

Bicknell served another rewarding term of apprenticeship, and hi nine for 45 against Cambridge University in mid-June remained th country's best bowling of the season. Medlycott's left-arm spin, blossoming batting and outstanding close-catching, after Monte Lynch's hand had been badly bruised and Alec Stewart had broken a thumb, took hir close to England recognition. His self-belief and eagerness to spin th ball earned him 69 wickets, the second-highest slow-bowling retur behind Marks of Somerset, but at a lower cost.

Only Grahame Clinton and Stewart reached 1,000 runs, a routin achievement not secured until September 16. But the bonus poin showed that the load was spread evenly. Surrey collected 57 for battin as many as Kent and two more than the champions, Worcestershir Lynch just failed to record four figures, having started the summer a a member of England's Texaco Trophy squad and ending it limpin towards a knee operation.

A "Save The Oval" appeal brought in essential finance for the urge development and general maintenance of the ground. But mar members were startled by a proposed sponsorship from Courage L which involved renaming the ground "The Foster's Oval". The cas input was believed to be around £2 million; progress held sway ov tradition and agreement was carried by 1,738 votes to 322 at a Speci General Meeting. The club were thus able to commence their £5 million West Side building programme, and the smiles were spread wi among Surrey officials when the bulldozers rumbled in halfway throug September. – David Field.

SURREY 1988

[*Bill Smith*

Back row: N. M. Kendrick, A. D. Brown, J. D. Robinson, J. Boiling, M. Frost, N. H. Peters, G. P. Thorpe. *Middle row:* G. G. Arnold (*coach*), G. E. Brown, K. T. Medlycott, D. J. Bicknell, M. P. Bicknell, M. A. Feltham, D. M. Ward, P. D. Atkins, Zahid Sadiq, C. E. Waller (*coach*). *Front row:* C. K. Bullen, D. M. Smith, S. T. Clarke, C. J. Richards, I. A. Greig (*captain*), G. S. Clinton, M. A. Lynch, A. J. Stewart. *Insets:* A. H. Gray, C. S. Mays.

SURREY RESULTS

All first-class matches – Played 25: Won 9, Lost 5, Drawn 11.

County Championship matches – Played 22: Won 7, Lost 5, Drawn 10.

Bonus points – Batting 57, Bowling 72.

Competition placings – Britannic Assurance County Championship, 4th; NatWest Bank Trophy, s-f; Benson and Hedges Cup, 5th in Group C; Refuge Assurance League, 5th equal.

BRITANNIC ASSURANCE CHAMPIONSHIP AVERAGES

BATTING

	Birthplace	*M*	*I*	*NO*	*R*	*HI*	*Avge*
‡C. J. Richards	*Penzance*	17	21	4	861	102*	50.64
‡D. M. Smith	*Balham*	10	17	5	585	157*	48.7
‡G. S. Clinton	*Sidcup*	17	28	5	980	158	42.6
‡A. J. Stewart	*Merton*	20	30	3	992	133	36.7
‡M. A. Lynch	*Georgetown, BG*	20	28	3	893	103	35.7
D. M. Ward	*Croydon*	22	31	5	835	126	32.1
P. D. Atkins	*Aylesbury*	5	9	0	235	99	26.1
M. A. Feltham	*St John's Wood*	20	24	9	352	74	23.4
‡K. T. Medlycott	*Whitechapel*	21	27	4	483	77*	21.0
J. D. Robinson	*Epsom*	2	4	2	37	20	18.5
‡I. A. Greig	*Queenstown, SA*	22	27	1	462	47	17.7
G. P. Thorpe	*Farnham*	2	4	1	50	19	16.6
D. J. Bicknell	*Guildford*	9	16	1	247	50	16.4
§‡S. T. Clarke	*Christ Church, Barbados*	12	10	1	141	28	15.6
N. H. Peters	*Guildford*	11	14	7	83	25*	11.8
C. K. Bullen	*Clapham*	9	11	1	101	24	10.1
M. P. Bicknell	*Guildford*	15	12	3	60	25	6.6

Also batted: J. Boiling (*New Delhi, India*) (1 match) 1, 8*; G. E. Brown (*Balham*) (1 match 0; M. Frost (*Barking*) (2 matches) 0, 0, 4; C. S. Mays (*Brighton*) (2 matches) 13*; Zahid Sadi (*Nairobi, Kenya*) (2 matches) 13, 37, 0.

* *Signifies not out.* ‡ *Denotes county cap.* § *Not qualified for England.*

The following played a total of eleven three-figure innings for Surrey in Count Championship matches – G. S. Clinton 4, D. M. Smith 2, A. J. Stewart 2, M. A. Lynch C. J. Richards 1, D. M. Ward 1.

BOWLING

	O	*M*	*R*	*W*	*BB*	*5W/i*	*Avg*
S. T. Clarke	396.4	108	913	63	6-52	4	14.4
K. T. Medlycott	522.1	143	1,445	62	8-52	6	23.
I. A. Greig	371.3	74	1,082	41	6-56	1	26.
N. H. Peters	263.2	48	907	34	6-31	1	26.
M. A. Feltham	521.4	116	1,536	51	5-45	2	30.
M. P. Bicknell	439.2	115	1,280	36	4-34	0	35.

Also bowled: D. J. Bicknell 1–0–18–0; J. Boiling 15–3–40–0; C. K. Bullen 60.1–7–209– G. S. Clinton 0.4–0–16–0; M. Frost 28–4–115–2; M. A. Lynch 29.2–8–88–4; C. S. Ma 25–2–102–1; C. J. Richards 4–1–26–0; J. D. Robinson 13–1–67–3; A. J. Stewart 13.1–2–45– G. P. Thorpe 24–2–60–3; D. M. Ward 5–0–31–0.

Wicket-keepers: C. J. Richards 59 ct, 1 st; A. J. Stewart 11 ct, 1 st; G. E. Brown 1 ct 1

Leading Fielders: K. T. Medlycott 25, M. A. Lynch 16, I. A. Greig 16, D. M. Ward 16.

At Southampton, April 21, 22. SURREY beat HAMPSHIRE by nine wickets.

At Cambridge, April 28, 29, 30. SURREY beat CAMBRIDGE UNIVERSITY by 97 runs.

SURREY v MIDDLESEX

At The Oval, May 5, 6, 7. Middlesex won by 148 runs. Middlesex 22 pts, Surrey 4 pts. Toss: Aiddlesex. Middlesex managed only 207 on a pitch of variable bounce, and when Surrey ollowed their example by struggling to 43 for three by the end of the first day, bad weather lone looked like extending the match to its scheduled conclusion. Neither side seemed to ppreciate it was engaged in one of the experimental four-day fixtures, and the impression vas confirmed when Surrey declined to 97 early on the second day. Gatting, with a grafting, wo-phased 52, held the Middlesex first innings together after being dropped at slip, by Greig ff Clarke, first ball. His luck held again in the second innings, when he was dropped twice uring his 79 on a day when fifteen wickets fell. To win, Surrey required 327 on a pitch rovoking suspicion; only an explosive innings from Lynch promised that they would even pproach it. Cowans smoothed Middlesex's path to victory with four of the first five wickets nd the match was over by tea on the third day.

Close of play: First day, Surrey 43-3 (D. M. Smith 20*, D. M. Ward 2*); Second day, Iiddlesex 196-8 (J. E. Emburey 33*).

Aiddlesex

. D. Carr b Clarke	0	c Lynch b Peters	7
V. N. Slack c Richards b Feltham	21	b Peters	11
M. W. Gatting c Richards b Peters	52	c Richards b Clarke	79
. R. Brown lbw b Greig	6	c Richards b Medlycott	41
. O. Butcher lbw b Peters	29	lbw b Medlycott	3
P. R. Downton c Stewart b Feltham	32	c and b Medlycott	12
E. Emburey c Richards b Greig	9	c Ward b Medlycott	41
. F. Williams c Lynch b Feltham	8	lbw b Clarke	1
P. Hughes not out	25	c Peters b Medlycott	2
. R. C. Fraser c Medlycott b Clarke	5	not out	6
. G. Cowans hit wkt b Clarke	6	b Clarke	5
B 4, l-b 4, w 4, n-b 2	14	L-b 8	8
0 2/36 3/58 4/106 5/126 155 7/164 8/165 9/196	207	1/16 2/21 3/89 4/103 5/143 6/161 7/171 8/196 9/211	216

Bonus points – Middlesex 2, Surrey 4.

Bowling: *First Innings*—Clarke 22.2–5–69–3; Peters 18–1–63–2; Feltham 22–7–32–3; Greig -6–35–2. *Second Innings*—Clarke 28.1–7–60–3; Peters 14–4–28–2; Greig 2–0–16–0; edlycott 34–10–82–5; Feltham 10–2–22–0.

urrey

S. Clinton c Brown b Williams	2	lbw b Cowans	3
M. Smith c Carr b Emburey	28	c Downton b Emburey	8
J. Stewart b Williams	3	lbw b Cowans	6
A. Lynch b Emburey	15	b Williams	73
M. Ward b Emburey	14	c Carr b Cowans	10
. J. Richards not out	13	lbw b Cowans	6
A. Greig lbw b Cowans	2	b Fraser	30
T. Medlycott c Butcher b Cowans	0	b Emburey	5
A. Feltham c Brown b Cowans	0	c Downton b Williams	1
T. Clarke c Cowans b Williams	15	(11) b Fraser	22
H. Peters run out	2	(10) not out	5
L-b 2, n-b 1	3	B 3, l-b 3, n-b 3	9
2/14 3/41 4/61 5/70 3 7/75 8/75 9/95	97	1/4 2/14 3/22 4/95 5/109 6/120 7/125 8/128 9/156	178

Bonus points – Middlesex 4.

Bowling: *First Innings*—Williams 8.2–1–28–3; Cowans 15–5–22–3; Hughes 3–0–7–0; Emburey 21–8–31–3; Fraser 9–5–7–0. *Second Innings*—Cowans 14–5–20–4; Fraser 13.4–2–36–2; Emburey 30–6–78–2; Williams 11–0–38–2.

Umpires: J. H. Harris and P. B. Wight.

SURREY v NORTHAMPTONSHIRE

At The Oval, May 21, 23, 24. Drawn. Surrey 4 pts, Northamptonshire 5 pts. Toss: Surrey Fordham's six-hour maiden hundred, which included only seven boundaries, and the first o two innings of 80 by Capel gave Northamptonshire the initiative after Greig had put them in But rain after just four balls on the second morning prevented their capitalising on Saturday' sound basis; Larkins was obliged to declare if he wanted the match to take a positive course Clinton made 50 out of 71, and then Richards, deputising at No. 3 because of a hand injury t Stewart, drove powerfully until a tired stroke saw him fall 15 runs short of his century Following Surrey's declaration at their overnight score, Clarke claimed three early wicket before Capel and Williams pulled the innings round with an unbroken stand of 144. Surrey' target was 258 in 54 overs, and fierce hitting by Greig and Ward gave them an outside chance In the end, however, Cook's tight left-arm spin kept them some way short of the target.

Close of play: First day, Northamptonshire 298-5 (A. Fordham 125*, N. A. Stanley 18*) Second day, Surrey 215-6 (D. M. Ward 51*, M. A. Feltham 4*).

Northamptonshire

A. Fordham not out	125	– (2) c Greig b Clarke	
*W. Larkins c Greig b Clarke	2	– (1) c Richards b Clarke	2
R. J. Bailey lbw b Feltham	48	– c D. J. Bicknell b Clarke	
D. J. Capel b Clarke	81	– not out	8
R. G. Williams b Clarke	0	– not out	4
D. J. Wild b Feltham	7		
N. A. Stanley not out	18		
B 5, l-b 11, n-b 1	17	B 8, l-b 7, n-b 4	
1/3 2/91 3/210 4/212 5/229 (5 wkts dec.)	298	1/10 2/10 3/30 (3 wkts dec.)	17

†D. Ripley, N. G. B. Cook, W. W. Davis and A. Walker did not bat.

Bonus points – Northamptonshire 3, Surrey 2 (Score at 100 overs: 260-5).

Bowling: *First Innings*—Clarke 24–5–48–3; M. P. Bicknell 23.4–10–44–0; Greig 20–3–48– Feltham 30–9–90–2; Medlycott 13–3–52–0. *Second Innings*—Clarke 8–4–11–3; M. P. Bickn 14–2–60–0; Feltham 9–4–33–0; Greig 7–0–36–0; Medlycott 9.3–4–19–0.

Surrey

G. S. Clinton c Walker b Davis	50	– c Stanley b Davis
D. J. Bicknell lbw b Capel	2	– b Davis
†C. J. Richards b Cook	85	– c Ripley b Cook
D. M. Smith lbw b Walker	0	– st Ripley b Cook
D. M. Ward not out	51	– b Cook
*I. A. Greig b Cook	9	– c Walker b Cook
K. T. Medlycott c and b Cook	12	– (8) not out
M. A. Feltham not out	4	– (9) not out
A. J. Stewart (did not bat)		– (7) c Ripley b Williams
L-b 1, n-b 1	2	B 1, l-b 7
1/5 2/71 3/72 4/165 5/181 6/205 (6 wkts dec.)	215	1/27 2/40 3/59 4/74 5/140 6/156 7/162 (7 wkts)

S. T. Clarke and M. P. Bicknell did not bat.

Bonus points – Surrey 2, Northamptonshire 2.

Bowling: *First Innings*—Davis 14–2–51–1; Capel 16–3–43–1; Walker 14–2–51–1; Wild 3–0–12–0; Cook 18–5–48–3; Williams 5–1–9–0. *Second Innings*—Davis 12.4–3–31–2; Capel 5–1–13–0; Walker 7–2–19–0; Cook 19–4–68–4; Williams 10–1–49–1.

Umpires: J. H. Hampshire and R. Julian.

At Chelmsford, May 28, 30, 31. SURREY lost to ESSEX by 195 runs.

SURREY v SUSSEX

At The Oval, June 1, 2, 3. Surrey won by an innings and 11 runs. Surrey 24 pts, Sussex 2 pts. Toss: Surrey. The Sussex bowling, worn down by Smith's punishing hundred – Surrey's first of the season in the Championship – was brought to the point of submission by Richards's glorious 102 not out from 98 balls. At the time the season's fastest hundred, it included a six and fifteen fours. Greig declared first thing on the second day, and when Sussex lost half their batting for 49, the prospect of an innings defeat became a distinct possibility. A typically defiant 82 not out from Gould cut Surrey's lead to 279 before the follow-on was enforced, and in the second innings Colin Wells, refusing to capitulate, hit a brave, four-hour hundred. Unfortunately, with Sussex only 11 runs short of making Surrey bat again, he was struck on the wrist by a brutal ball from Clarke and, unable to grip his bat, was forced to retire. Feltham quickly bowled his ninth-wicket partner, Heseltine, to complete Surrey's victory.

Close of play: First day, Surrey 467-5 (C. J. Richards 102*); Second day; Sussex 94-3 (N. J. Lenham 34*, C. M. Wells 22*).

Surrey

G. S. Clinton c Pigott b Babington	10	†C. J. Richards not out	102
D. M. Smith c Lenham b Heseltine	131	L-b 15, n-b 11	26
A. J. Stewart lbw b Babington	39		
M. A. Lynch c Alikhan b Pringle	93	1/52 2/133 3/278 (5 wkts dec.)	467
D. M. Ward c C. M. Wells b Pigott	66	4/405 5/467	

*I. A. Greig, K. T. Medlycott, M. A. Feltham, S. T. Clarke and M. P. Bicknell did not bat.

Bonus points – Surrey 4, Sussex 1 (Score at 100 overs: 387-3).

Bowling: Pigott 20–2–107–1; Pringle 19–0–82–1; Babington 25–2–84–2; C. M. Wells 9–5–77–0; Heseltine 27–5–102–1.

Sussex

. I. Alikhan b Greig	9 – lbw b Feltham	8
. M. Green c Richards b Clarke	5 – c Greig b Bicknell	9
. J. Lenham c Smith b Clarke	2 – c Richards b Feltham	40
. P. Wells c Richards b Clarke	34 – c Richards b Greig	11
C. M. Wells c Greig b Bicknell	2 – retired hurt	109
. Moores c Clinton b Bicknell	0 – lbw b Greig	35
I. J. Gould not out	82 – b Medlycott	11
. C. S. Pigott lbw b Greig	20 – b Greig	1
. W. Pringle c Richards b Greig	0 – c Stewart b Medlycott	19
. A. W. Heseltine b Greig	6 – b Feltham	8
. M. Babington c Richards b Bicknell	9 – not out	0
B 5, l-b 1, w 4, n-b 9	19 B 1, l-b 7, w 3, n-b 6	17
20 2/22 3/24 4/44 5/49	188 1/16 2/27 3/45 4/107 5/175	268
103 7/149 8/149 9/171	6/205 7/206 8/229 9/268	

Bonus points – Sussex 1, Surrey 4.

Bowling: *First Innings*—Clarke 13–5–36–3; Bicknell 20.5–1–66–3; Greig 17–4–44–4; eltham 8–0–36–0. *Second Innings*—Clarke 17–6–31–0; Feltham 26.4–8–70–3; Bicknell –5–47–1; Greig 21–2–74–3; Medlycott 20–7–36–2; Stewart 2–1–2–0.

Umpires: J. W. Holder and N. T. Plews.

At Harrogate, June 4, 6, 7. SURREY drew with YORKSHIRE.

SURREY v LEICESTERSHIRE

At The Oval, June 11, 13, 14. Drawn. Surrey 4 pts, Leicestershire 7 pts. Toss: Leicestershire. DeFreitas, sharp and incisive, claimed five wickets to support Gower's decision to give his seam bowlers first use of a helpful pitch. Clinton fought hard to hold Surrey's innings together, but the inadequacy of their 179 was emphasised as Briers and Cobb fashioned an opening stand of 96. Cobb, without a first-class hundred in a career dating from 1980, was to bat for four and a quarter hours. Surrey's eighteen-year-old all-rounder, Thorpe, celebrated his first-class début with the wickets of Willey and Gower. Medlycott and Smith sustained Surrey's middle order after Leicestershire's declaration, but at 227 for eight – a lead of 151 – their position was vulnerable. Peters and Feltham removed the danger, adding a vital 64, and when Greig declared, setting a target of 216 in 29 overs, Peters quickly struck twice, leaving Leicestershire to settle for the draw.

Close of play: First day, Leicestershire 23-0 (R. A. Cobb 8*, N. E. Briers 12*); Second day, Surrey 60-2 (K. T. Medlycott 8*, M. A. Lynch 26*).

Surrey

D. J. Bicknell b Ferris	0	– b Ferris	7
G. S. Clinton c Willey b Ferris	59	– c Whitticase b DeFreitas	13
D. M. Smith c Ferris b DeFreitas	15	– (5) c Whitticase b DeFreitas	59
M. A. Lynch b Agnew	5	– lbw b DeFreitas	34
D. M. Ward st Whitticase b Such	27	– (6) c Whitticase b Agnew	1
*I. A. Greig lbw b Ferris	2	– (7) b DeFreitas	2
K. T. Medlycott b DeFreitas	24	– (3) c Briers b Agnew	71
G. P. Thorpe c Whitticase b DeFreitas	15	– c Whitticase b Agnew	16
M. A. Feltham lbw b DeFreitas	17	– not out	34
N. H. Peters not out	2	– not out	25
†G. E. Brown c Willey b DeFreitas	0		
B 4, l-b 6, n-b 3	13	B 4, l-b 11, w 1, n-b 13	29
1/0 2/42 3/65 4/95 5/97 6/136 7/144 8/166 9/179	179	1/18 2/26 3/102 4/170 5/174 6/185 7/227 8/227 (8 wkts dec.)	29

Bonus points – Surrey 1, Leicestershire 4.

Bowling: *First Innings*—Ferris 16–3–43–3; Agnew 27–8–63–1; DeFreitas 21.3–7–43–5; Suc 10–2–20–1. *Second Innings*—Ferris 21–4–54–1; DeFreitas 30–3–114–4; Such 6–2–5–0; Agne 20–3–88–3; Willey 5–1–6–0; Potter 3–2–9–0.

Leicestershire

R. A. Cobb c Feltham b Greig	65		
N. E. Briers lbw b Greig	49	– c Medlycott b Peters	
*D. I. Gower lbw b Thorpe	3	– (1) not out	1
P. Willey c Lynch b Thorpe	10	– (3) b Peters	
J. J. Whitaker c Feltham b Medlycott	40	– (4) not out	1
L. Potter c Brown b Feltham	13		
P. A. J. DeFreitas st Brown b Medlycott	30		
J. P. Agnew not out	18		
†P. Whitticase not out	9		
B 1, l-b 10, w 4, n-b 3	18		
1/96 2/99 3/117 4/182 5/184 6/226 7/226 (7 wkts dec.)	255	1/3 2/11 (2 wkts)	

G. J. F. Ferris and P. M. Such did not bat.

Bonus points – Leicestershire 3, Surrey 3.

Bowling: *First Innings*—Peters 19–4–59–0; Feltham 26–9–57–1; Greig 21–3–50–2; Thorpe 14–2–33–2; Medlycott 17.4–9–45–2. *Second Innings*—Peters 5–1–18–2; Feltham 5–1–17–0; Medlycott 1–0–3–0.

Umpires: K. J. Lyons and R. Palmer.

SURREY v CAMBRIDGE UNIVERSITY

At The Oval, June 15, 16, 17. Surrey won by 149 runs. Toss: Surrey. Surrey paraded the products of their youth policy and had good reason for satisfaction. Two maiden hundreds provided the interest on the opening day, and on the third nineteen-year-old Martin Bicknell took nine wickets as Cambridge were swept aside for 86. Atkins became the seventh Surrey player to score a hundred on début, and there was a stylish performance from Thorpe who, driving delightfully, moved from 50 to his first hundred in just 31 balls. The University were sustained by the considerable talent of Atherton and by Atkinson in their first innings, but they had nothing to offer against Bicknell's pace when Bullen's second declaration of the match asked them to score 236 in approximately 45 overs.

Close of play: First day, Cambridge University 8-0 (R. J. Turner 1*, S. J. Noyes 2*); Second day, Surrey 10-0 (D. J. Bicknell 5*, C. K. Bullen 5*).

Surrey

D. J. Bicknell c Tremellen b Perry	62	– c Atherton b Pointer	29
P. D. Atkins not out	114	– (5) c Atherton b Fenton	8
D. M. Ward b Perry	12	– c Turner b Perry	1
Zahid Sadiq c Turner b Perry	5	– c Atherton b Fenton	64
G. P. Thorpe not out	100	– (6) run out	8
*C. K. Bullen (did not bat)		– (2) c Atherton b Tremellen	56
N. M. Kendrick (did not bat)		– not out	8
N. H. Peters (did not bat)		– not out	2
B 6, l-b 8, n-b 2	16	L-b 15, w 1	16
/124 2/166 3/172 (3 wkts dec.)	309	1/49 2/63 3/117 4/166 5/178 6/184 (6 wkts dec.)	192

A. H. Gray, M. P. Bicknell and †G. E. Brown did not bat.

Bowling: *First Innings*—Fenton 22–8–45–0; Pointer 17–1–70–0; Perry 25–4–72–3; Hart 2–1–71–0; Atherton 11–0–37–0. *Second Innings*—Fenton 18–4–49–2; Perry 11–3–47–1; Pointer 9–1–39–1; Tremellen 5–0–13–1; Atherton 8–1–29–0.

Cambridge University

R. J. Turner c Brown b Thorpe	9	– (7) c Brown b M. P. Bicknell	6
. J. Noyes b Gray	38	– c Thorpe b M. P. Bicknell	2
M. A. Atherton c Peters b Bullen	86	– c Brown b M. P. Bicknell	5
M. Tremellen c and b Bullen	15	– (1) c Brown b Gray	2
. C. M. Atkinson b Bullen	73	– (4) c Zahid b M. P. Bicknell	22
D. Heath c Thorpe b Bullen	13	– (5) c Zahid b M. P. Bicknell	11
. Bate c Bullen b Kendrick	2	– (6) b M. P. Bicknell	0
. A. Pointer not out	12	– c Kendrick b M. P. Bicknell	11
N. Perry (did not bat)		– b M. P. Bicknell	26
. J. Hart (did not bat)		– not out	0
. C. W. Fenton (did not bat)		– b M. P. Bicknell	0
B 1, l-b 9, w 1, n-b 7	18	N-b 1	1
30 2/94 3/146 4/189 5/247 252 7/266 (7 wkts dec.)	266	1/4 2/9 3/10 4/27 5/27 6/49 7/50 8/81 9/86	86

Bowling: *First Innings*—Gray 17–10–17–1; M. P. Bicknell 16–5–42–0; Peters 13–2–32–0; horpe 6–1–17–1; Kendrick 26.5–6–92–1; Bullen 18–4–56–4. *Second Innings*—Gray 3–21–1; M. P. Bicknell 13–3–45–9; Peters 2–0–15–0; Kendrick 2–1–5–0.

Umpires: R. Palmer and H. J. Rhodes.

SURREY v DERBYSHIRE

At The Oval, June 25, 27, 28. Drawn. Surrey 5 pts, Derbyshire 6 pts. Toss: Derbyshire. The match, although condemned by the weather to end in a draw, was a personal triumph for Bowler. The Derbyshire opening batsman handsomely sustained them throughout the first day, his unbeaten 143 being almost half their score. Bowler had gone to his hundred with a six off Medlycott, and on the second morning he proceeded to his third score of 150 since joining his new county. Derbyshire's bowlers, however, could not match that kind of consistency, and bristling efforts by Richards and Lynch enabled Greig to close his first innings challengingly 79 runs in arrears. Bad light and rain on the third day sent the match meandering towards a stalemate, even though Derbyshire, batting mostly in gloom, endeavoured to set Surrey a realistic target. Bowler hit another half-century in an opening stand of 122 with Maher, and 251 in 50 overs appeared a reasonable objective until the weather gave Surrey no chance to pursue it.

Close of play: First day, Derbyshire 289-6 (P. D. Bowler 143*, P. G. Newman 8*); Second day, Surrey 250-8 dec.

Derbyshire

P. D. Bowler c Greig b Clarke	158	– not out	57
†B. J. M. Maher b Clarke	1	– b Lynch	75
B. Roberts c Richards b Greig	39	– not out	30
J. E. Morris c Medlycott b Greig	18		
S. C. Goldsmith b Thorpe	4		
R. Sharma c and b Medlycott	34		
C. J. Adams c Thorpe b Bullen	21		
P. G. Newman not out	23		
A. E. Warner c Greig b Clarke	8		
M. Jean-Jacques b Feltham	0		
B 3, l-b 10, w 2, n-b 8	23	L-b 8, n-b 1	9
1/5 2/65 3/104 4/111 5/192 6/266 7/316 8/326 9/329 (9 wkts dec.)	329	1/122 (1 wkt dec.)	171

*M. A. Holding did not bat.

Bonus points – Derbyshire 3, Surrey 2 (Score at 100 overs: 279-6).

Bowling: *First Innings*—Clarke 32–6–92–3; Feltham 22.3–4–66–1; Greig 19–5–52–2 Thorpe 7–0–21–1; Medlycott 25–9–51–1; Bullen 13–2–34–1. *Second Innings*—Felthar 8–1–19–0; Greig 7–2–21–0; Medlycott 8–0–34–0; Thorpe 3–0–6–0; Bullen 5–0–18–0; Clark 1–0–10–0; Ward 4–0–28–0; Lynch 2–0–9–1; Bicknell 1–0–18–0.

Surrey

D. J. Bicknell c Adams b Newman	16	– b Jean-Jacques	2
G. S. Clinton c Maher b Warner	31	– not out	1
G. P. Thorpe c Morris b Warner	19	– not out	
M. A. Lynch lbw b Holding	56		
D. M. Ward c Sharma b Warner	0		
†C. J. Richards c Goldsmith b Jean-Jacques	77		
K. T. Medlycott c Holding b Warner	0		
*I. A. Greig c Bowler b Holding	12		
C. K. Bullen not out	18		
M. A. Feltham not out	7		
B 1, l-b 10, w 2, n-b 1	14	L-b 1	
1/46 2/62 3/91 4/91 5/145 6/146 7/168 8/235 (8 wkts dec.)	250	1/47 (1 wkt)	4

S. T. Clarke did not bat.

Bonus points – Surrey 3, Derbyshire 3.

Bowling: *First Innings*—Holding 18–2–63–2; Newman 19–5–51–1; Warner 16–6–36–4; Jean-Jacques 16–2–77–1; Sharma 3.5–0–12–0. *Second Innings*—Newman 2–0–7–0; Jean-Jacques 8–2–19–1; Bowler 7–3–20–0.

Umpires: H. D. Bird and D. O. Oslear.

SURREY v WARWICKSHIRE

At The Oval, July 2, 4, 5. Surrey won by an innings and 43 runs. Surrey 22 pts, Warwickshire 2 pts. Toss: Warwickshire. A ten-wicket return by Peters, in only his fourth Championship match, played a major part in Warwickshire's third innings defeat in succession at The Oval. Supported by Clarke's hostility, the twenty-year-old fast bowler exploited the moisture in the pitch to capture six for 31 as the visitors' batting crumpled in their first innings. By the close Surrey had moved comfortably ahead, prompted by a vibrant 63 from Lynch, but with all of Monday's play lost to the weather, quick runs were essential on the final day. Ward and Richards provided them, whereupon Peters and Clarke, each with another four wickets, sealed meek Warwickshire's fate.

Close of play: First day, Surrey 146-4 (D. M. Ward 28*, C. J. Richards 3*); Second day, No play.

Warwickshire

A. J. Moles c and b Clarke	25	– c Richards b Peters	2
*T. A. Lloyd c Richards b Peters	11	– (4) b Clarke	18
Asif Din c Richards b Clarke	2	– (5) b Clarke	8
A. C. Storie c Clarke b Peters	0	– (2) c Greig b Peters	4
†G. W. Humpage c Richards b Peters	1	– (6) c Richards b Clarke	3
P. A. Smith c Medlycott b Clarke	0	– (7) c Medlycott b Peters	0
D. A. Thorne c Richards b Peters	10	– (3) c Feltham b Clarke	7
G. C. Small c Clarke b Peters	5	– c Clinton b Greig	32
T. A. Merrick c Richards b Clarke	8	– lbw b Peters	1
T. A. Munton c Richards b Peters	0	– c Peters b Greig	16
A. R. K. Pierson not out	0	– not out	8
L-b 3, w 6, n-b 3	12	B 2, l-b 7, w 3, n-b 5	17
1/25 2/34 3/46 4/50 5/50 6/51 7/58 8/74 9/74	74	1/11 2/15 3/36 4/48 5/54 6/55 7/57 8/60 9/102	116

Bonus points – Surrey 4.

Bowling: *First Innings*—Clarke 16–2–40–4; Peters 15.2–5–31–6. *Second Innings*—Clarke 9–5–40–4; Peters 16–4–36–4; Greig 4.5–1–15–2; Feltham 2–0–16–0.

Surrey

G. S. Clinton c Lloyd b Munton	23
D. M. Smith c Moles b Munton	19
J. Stewart c Humpage b Munton	0
M. A. Lynch b Munton	63
D. M. Ward not out	62
C. J. Richards b Munton	49
*I. A. Greig c Merrick b Pierson	7
B 4, l-b 5, n-b 1	10
1/36 2/36 3/58 4/137 5/220 6/233 (6 wkts dec.)	233

K. T. Medlycott, M. A. Feltham, S. T. Clarke and N. H. Peters did not bat.

Bonus points – Surrey 2, Warwickshire 2.

Bowling: Merrick 14–2–61–0; Small 19–4–76–0; Munton 17–4–50–5; Smith 2–0–18–0; Pierson 3.3–0–19–1.

Umpires: J. H. Hampshire and K. E. Palmer.

SURREY v HAMPSHIRE

At Guildford, July 13, 14, 15. Hampshire won by eight wickets. Hampshire 16 pts, Surrey 5 pts. Toss: Hampshire. The match did not start until two o'clock because of muddy patches on the square, but Smith's hundred from 125 balls made up for the time lost. Surrey's strongly built left-hander struck thirteen boundaries as he raced to 82, and then his tempo changed as he went to 100 in singles before a storm brought an early close. Next morning Stewart, who had shown such good form the previous day, was undone by Maru's bounce, but Smith took his score to 157 (217 balls, 21 fours). Hampshire struggled initially. However, Nicholas staged a recovery and then opened up the game by forsaking bonus points in the hope of a challenging target. Greig's response was 299 in a minimum of 69 overs, which proved none too difficult a task on a traditionally fast-scoring ground that was celebrating 50 years of county cricket. Some poor bowling gave Terry the latitude to make an attractive, finely paced hundred, and Nicholas hit seventeen fours as they put on 160 for the second wicket. The win was Hampshire's first at Guildford in fourteen attempts.

Close of play: First day, Surrey 181-1 (D. M. Smith 101*, A. J. Stewart 63*); Second day, Hampshire 125-4 (M. C. J. Nicholas 57*, J. R. Ayling 7*).

Surrey

D. J. Bicknell c Terry b Connor .... 6 – c Terry b Jefferies 15
D. M. Smith not out .... 157 – b Jefferies 23
A. J. Stewart c Nicholas b Maru .... 72 – c Parks b Ayling 27
M. A. Lynch not out .... 48 – not out 44
D. M. Ward (did not bat) .... – not out 6
L-b 10, n-b 8 .... 18 L-b 2, n-b 5 7

1/22 2/190 (2 wkts dec.) 301 1/38 2/46 3/98 (3 wkts dec.) 122

†C. J. Richards, *I. A. Greig, K. T. Medlycott, M. A. Feltham, M. P. Bicknell and N. H. Peters did not bat.

Bonus points – Surrey 4.

Bowling: *First Innings*—Jefferies 5–0–38–0; Connor 19–2–57–1; Andrew 15–0–77–0; Maru 24–3–85–1; Ayling 14–3–34–0. *Second Innings*—Jefferies 8–0–37–2; Connor 6–0–20–0 Andrew 2–0–6–0; Maru 8.4–1–33–0; Ayling 8–2–24–1.

Hampshire

V. P. Terry c Ward b Peters .... 4 – not out 126
C. L. Smith c Richards b Peters .... 16 – c and b Medlycott 44
*M. C. J. Nicholas not out .... 57 – c and b Medlycott 97
R. A. Smith c Feltham b M. P. Bicknell .... 3 – not out 17
D. R. Turner b Feltham 30
J. R. Ayling not out 7
L-b 2, n-b 6 .... 8 L-b 5, n-b 10 15

1/10 2/34 3/40 4/115 (4 wkts dec.) 125 1/98 2/258 (2 wkts) 299

S. T. Jefferies, †R. J. Parks, R. J. Maru, C. A. Connor and S. J. W. Andrew did not bat.

Bonus point – Surrey 1.

Bowling: *First Innings*—Peters 11–1–33–2; M. P. Bicknell 16–7–34–1; Feltham 16–3–36–1 Greig 3–0–20–0. *Second Innings*—M. P. Bicknell 13–1–68–0; Peters 9–0–53–0; Greig 7–0–37–0; Feltham 13–2–43–0; Medlycott 20–2–78–2; Lynch 1.5–0–15–0.

Umpires: A. A. Jones and A. G. T. Whitehead.

SURREY v KENT

At Guildford, July 16, 18, 19. Drawn. Surrey 8 pts, Kent 7 pts. Toss: Kent. Smith, who wa forced to retire in Surrey's first innings, heroically blunted Kent's attempt to win their eight Championship match out of nine, a run which had taken them to the top of the tabl Cowdrey, who two days earlier had been named captain of England, elected to bat first an

Ward, a young prospect, unveiled a wide range of off-side strokes in his 72. It was an outstanding slip catch by Medlycott that robbed him of the chance of a maiden hundred. Cowdrey declared before the start on Monday, and Smith began with three powerfully hit boundaries before aggravating a back injury. However, half-centuries from Stewart and Surrey's Ward ensured that full batting points were obtained by the time Greig declared, 21 behind. As Kent worked towards a declaration, Taylor, who hit seventeen fours, reached his second Championship century of the summer and Medlycott, nagging away skilfully, took his match return to ten for 192. Surrey's target was 310 from 53 overs, and Feltham, promoted to open, gave them a flying start before Penn began to profit from the increasingly low bounce. Clinton resisted throughout, and finally Smith, in obvious pain, came in at No. 9 to see Surrey through the final seventeen overs.

Close of play: First day, Kent 324-9 (C. Penn 31*, R. P. Davis 5*); Second day, Kent 63-0 (M. R. Benson 34*, N. R. Taylor 17*).

Kent

First innings		Second innings	
M. R. Benson c Medlycott b Feltham	24	– c Richards b Peters	66
N. R. Taylor c Richards b Bicknell	7	– c Lynch b Medlycott	114
T. R. Ward c Medlycott b Bicknell	72	– c sub b Medlycott	32
C. J. Tavaré lbw b Medlycott	34	– c Medlycott b Peters	0
R. F. Pienaar lbw b Medlycott	88	– c Greig b Medlycott	5
*C. S. Cowdrey run out	4	– c Richards b Medlycott	0
G. R. Cowdrey lbw b Feltham	28	– c and b Medlycott	26
†S. A. Marsh lbw b Medlycott	1	– c Peters b Medlycott	11
R. M. Ellison c Greig b Medlycott	12	– not out	2
C. Penn not out	31	– not out	2
R. P. Davis not out	5		
B 1, l-b 11, n-b 6	18	B 16, l-b 3, w 1, n-b 10	30
1/14 2/82 3/141 4/163 5/167 6/215 7/232 8/282 9/301 (9 wkts dec.)	324	1/133 2/191 3/191 4/206 5/206 6/259 7/276 8/280 (8 wkts dec.)	288

Bonus points – Kent 4, Surrey 4.

Bowling: *First Innings*—Bicknell 24–3–84–2; Peters 14–2–51–0; Greig 16–6–45–0; Feltham 13–1–52–2; Medlycott 28–8–80–4. *Second Innings*—Bicknell 14–5–44–0; Peters 19–3–96–2; Greig 3–1–8–0; Medlycott 27–2–112–6; Stewart 3–0–9–0.

Surrey

First innings		Second innings	
G. S. Clinton lbw b Ellison	43	– (2) not out	71
D. M. Smith retired hurt	15	– (9) not out	10
A. J. Stewart c Benson b Ellison	56	– c and b Davis	17
M. A. Lynch c Benson b Ellison	10	– run out	3
D. M. Ward not out	70	– b Penn	0
·C. J. Richards c Taylor b C. S. Cowdrey	30	– c Marsh b Penn	2
K. T. Medlycott c Taylor b G. R. Cowdrey	10	– (8) b Penn	0
*I. A. Greig c Davis b Pienaar	19	– (7) c Ward b Davis	6
M. A. Feltham lbw b Davis	31	– (1) c Marsh b Penn	48
N. H. Peters not out	0		
L-b 9, w 1, n-b 9	19	L-b 4, w 3, n-b 4	11
/117 2/128 3/131 4/185 5/210 /241 7/298 (7 wkts dec.)	303	1/78 2/110 3/114 4/117 5/119 6/133 7/139 (7 wkts)	168

ɅI. P. Bicknell did not bat.

Bonus points – Surrey 4, Kent 3.

Bowling: *First Innings*—Ellison 20–5–47–3; Penn 5–0–40–0; C. S. Cowdrey 12–1–66–1;)avis 26.3–7–96–1; Pienaar 10–2–31–1; G. R. Cowdrey 4–2–14–1. *Second Innings*—Pienaar 0.4–2–41–0; Ellison 10–3–37–0; C. S. Cowdrey 2–0–9–0; Davis 19–8–36–2; Penn 11–0–41–4.

Umpires: A. A. Jones and A. G. T. Whitehead.

At Southport, July 20, 21, 22. SURREY drew with LANCASHIRE.

At Lord's, July 23, 25, 26. SURREY drew with MIDDLESEX.

At Cheltenham, July 30, August 1, 2. SURREY beat GLOUCESTERSHIRE by 21 runs.

At Weston-super-Mare, August 3, 4, 5. SURREY lost to SOMERSET by five wickets.

At Swansea, August 6, 8, 9. SURREY drew with GLAMORGAN.

At The Oval, August 13, 14, 15. SURREY drew with SRI LANKANS (See Sri Lankan tour section).

SURREY v WORCESTERSHIRE

At The Oval, August 17, 18, 19. Drawn. Surrey 6 pts, Worcestershire 6 pts. Toss: Worcestershire. There was an air of inevitability about Hick making his mark on the match, Worcestershire's first as Championship leaders for two months. He served his county's strategy brilliantly, hitting the fastest hundred of the season in just 79 balls (91 minutes) and going on to 127 from 88 balls, his 98-minute innings including five sixes and twelve fours. When 47, he completed 3,000 runs in all competitions for the season. Expecting the pitch to take spin, Worcestershire chipped out a solid first-innings total, although missing a fourth batting point. Curtis was 4 hours 21 minutes over his 86 before being bowled by Robinson in his first over of Championship cricket. Surrey, at one time 51 for four, declared just 1 run behind thanks to Stewart, an aggressively determined Richards and Medlycott. Lord and Neale played willing supporting roles in Hick's command performance, but rain washed out any chance of Surrey making a response to a target of 253 in 51 overs.

Close of play: First day, Worcestershire 289-8 (P. J. Newport 33*, R. M. Ellcock 0*); Second day, Surrey 302-7 dec.

Worcestershire

T. S. Curtis b Robinson	86	– c Greig b Feltham	17
G. J. Lord c Richards b Feltham	13	– c M. P. Bicknell b Feltham	43
G. A. Hick c Richards b Medlycott	41	– c Ward b Robinson	127
S. J. O'Shaughnessy c Feltham b Robinson	30	– run out	2
*P. A. Neale b Feltham	36	– b Bullen	35
M. J. Weston b Medlycott	14	– not out	14
†S. J. Rhodes run out	15	– not out	2
P. J. Newport c Stewart b M. P. Bicknell	33		
R. K. Illingworth b Bullen	3		
R. M. Ellcock c Medlycott b Feltham	9		
A. P. Pridgeon not out	4		
L-b 5, n-b 14	19	L-b 8, n-b 3	1[illegible]
1/47 2/109 3/178 4/199 5/234 6/238 7/280 8/288 9/291	303	1/50 2/65 3/71 4/198 5/238 (5 wkts dec.)	25[illegible]

Bonus points – Worcestershire 3, Surrey 2 (Score at 100 overs: 269-6).

Bowling: *First Innings*—M. P. Bicknell 23–9–53–1; Feltham 24–5–59–3; Greig 6–0–27–0; Bullen 11–2–31–1; Medlycott 41–10–87–2; Robinson 9–1–41–2. *Second Innings*—M. P. Bicknell 7–0–40–0; Feltham 11–4–28–2; Medlycott 15–1–91–0; Greig 3–0–14–0; Bullen 8–0–44–1; Robinson 4–0–26–1.

Surrey

D. J. Bicknell c and b Newport	11 – not out	5
J. D. Robinson c Rhodes b Illingworth	13 – not out	0
A. J. Stewart c Neale b Newport	77	
M. A. Lynch c Ellcock b Newport	4	
D. M. Ward c Rhodes b Pridgeon	1	
†C. J. Richards c Rhodes b Hick	87	
K. T. Medlycott not out	77	
*I. A. Greig c Weston b Hick	26	
M. A. Feltham not out	1	
L-b 2, n-b 3	5	
1/24 2/40 3/49 4/51 5/149 6/245 7/285	(7 wkts dec.) 302	(no wkt) 5

C. K. Bullen and M. P. Bicknell did not bat.

Bonus points – Surrey 4, Worcestershire 3.

Bowling: *First Innings*—Ellcock 10–0–45–0; Newport 17.5–3–70–3; Illingworth 28–5–70–1; Pridgeon 12–1–44–1; Hick 11–0–71–2. *Second Innings*—Newport 1–0–5–0.

Umpires: J. D. Bond and D. G. L. Evans.

At Nottingham, August 20, 22, 23. SURREY beat NOTTINGHAMSHIRE by nine wickets.

SURREY v LANCASHIRE

At The Oval, August 25, 26, 27. Surrey won by an innings and 1 run with more than a day to spare. Surrey 24 pts, Lancashire 4 pts. Toss: Lancashire. Stirring fast bowling by Clarke helped Surrey to their second successive Championship victory. His second ten-wicket return of the summer took his haul to eighteen wickets in the nine days after being fined a week's wages for failing to arrive at Swansea for the match against Glamorgan. Lancashire made a sound enough start but lost their last nine wickets for 44 runs and were all out by lunch on the first day. In contrast was the stand of 164 between Stewart and Lynch in the afternoon. Lynch's 103 contained a six and eighteen fours, and Lancashire did themselves no favours by dropping him in the slips when he was 25 and 60. However, they atoned for their earlier shortcomings by reaching 150 for two at the end of the second day, with Fowler underpinning the fightback. Unfortunately, the Bank Holiday Saturday found their resistance wanting. Needing 97 to make Surrey bat again, they could manage only 96 as the last eight wickets fell.

Close of play: First day, Surrey 231-4 (D. M. Ward 7*, C. J. Richards 14*); Second day, Lancashire 150-2 (G. Fowler 92*, N. H. Fairbrother 4*).

Lancashire

G. D. Mendis c Greig b Clarke	29	– c Bullen b Clarke	0
G. Fowler c Richards b Clarke	20	– c Stewart b Clarke	97
M. A. Atherton c Clarke b Feltham	3	– c Richards b Clarke	49
N. H. Fairbrother c Richards b Feltham	0	– c Richards b Bicknell	44
M. Watkinson c Richards b Feltham	1	– c Ward b Clarke	0
A. N. Hayhurst c Medlycott b Bicknell	9	– c Stewart b Bicknell	17
I. D. Austin c Bicknell b Feltham	0	– c Greig b Medlycott	4
*D. P. Hughes b Clarke	9	– not out	6
†W. K. Hegg c Clinton b Feltham	6	– c Richards b Medlycott	0
J. Simmons not out	2	– hit wkt b Clarke	13
A. J. Murphy b Clarke	0	– b Clarke	0
B 2, w 1, n-b 2	5	B 7, l-b 8, n-b 1	16
1/27 2/40 3/40 4/56 5/56 6/66 7/66 8/76 9/84	84	1/0 2/136 3/163 4/175 5/209 6/218 7/222 8/223 9/246	246

Bonus points – Surrey 4.

Bowling: *First Innings*—Clarke 13.4–3–29–4; Bicknell 5–2–8–1; Feltham 14–3–45–5. *Second Innings*—Clarke 28.4–9–60–6; Feltham 23–5–72–0; Bicknell 16–7–37–2; Greig 8–1–31–0; Medlycott 11–3–31–2.

Surrey

C. K. Bullen c Hegg b Watkinson 20
G. S. Clinton c Hegg b Austin 7
A. J. Stewart c Hegg b Watkinson 70
M. A. Lynch c Hegg b Watkinson 103
D. M. Ward c Watkinson b Austin 32
†C. J. Richards c Fairbrother b Austin . 38
*I. A. Greig lbw b Austin 2
K. T. Medlycott c Murphy b Simmons . 1
M. A. Feltham not out 15
S. T. Clarke b Austin 28
M. P. Bicknell b Simmons 2
B 5, l-b 7, n-b 1 13

1/20 2/38 3/202 4/211 5/274 6/283 7/284 8/284 9/316 — 331

Bonus points – Surrey 4, Lancashire 4 (Score at 100 overs: 319-9).

Bowling: Murphy 19–2–73–0; Watkinson 25–7–57–3; Austin 23–4–79–5; Hayhurst 14–3–52–0; Simmons 19–7–40–2; Atherton 3–1–18–0.

Umpires: A. A. Jones and R. A. White.

SURREY v ESSEX

At The Oval, August 30, 31, September 1, 2. Drawn. Surrey 6 pts, Essex 6 pts. Toss: Essex. Gooch's somewhat bizarre entry overshadowed Stewart's first century of the summer for Surrey. History of a kind was made on the first day, when Gooch appeared on two scorecards on the same day. He captained England to their first win in nineteen attempts in the Test match against Sri Lanka, six miles away at Lord's, and then dashed across the river to take up the place left for him by Essex in the knowledge that the Test was due to finish early that day. Although not unlawful, the practice was seen as questionable in some quarters and was to be considered later by the TCCB. Essex fielded with ten men until Gooch took the field some 45 minutes after lunch, Greig quite rightly not permitting the use of a substitute. Foster and Pringle, also involved at Lord's, remained absentees, which gave Surrey the latitude to gain maximum batting points and build a challenging score. Stewart's 133 lasted 268 minutes and included 21 fours. Gooch masterminded the Essex reply with an unbeaten 78 in the 36 overs of batting that the weather allowed Essex on the second day. But their title ambitions received a setback when further rain washed out the third day and permitted only 36 overs on the fourth.

Close of play: First day, Surrey 360-9 (M. A. Feltham 16*, M. P. Bicknell 5*); Second day, Essex 118-2 (G. A. Gooch 78*, M. E. Waugh 24*); Third day, No play.

Surrey

D. J. Bicknell c East b Pont 50
C. K. Bullen c Fletcher b Topley 8
A. J. Stewart c Topley b Pont 133
M. A. Lynch c and b Pont 14
D. M. Ward lbw b Topley 50
†C. J. Richards c Gooch b Pont 31
*I. A. Greig c and b Stephenson 7
K. T. Medlycott c Gooch b Stephenson 6
M. A. Feltham not out 18
S. T. Clarke c Fletcher b Pont 28
M. P. Bicknell b Topley 5
L-b 7, w 2, n-b 3 12

1/18 2/123 3/143 4/249 5/277 6/304 7/304 8/311 9/350 — 362

Bonus points – Surrey 4, Essex 3 (Score at 100 overs: 329-8).

Bowling: Pont 29–4–103–5; Topley 26.5–5–70–3; Waugh 12–0–75–0; Childs 19–6–41–0; Stephenson 22–5–66–2; Gooch 1–1–0–0.

Essex

G. A. Gooch b M. P. Bicknell	123	*K. W. R. Fletcher not out	9
J. P. Stephenson c Bullen b Clarke	2	B. R. Hardie not out	0
A. W. Lilley b M. P. Bicknell	4	B 1, l-b 8, w 1, n-b 7	17
M. E. Waugh c Clarke b M. P. Bicknell	29		
P. J. Prichard b Medlycott	33	1/41 2/61 3/133 (6 wkts dec.)	257
†D. E. East c Clarke b Bullen	40	4/201 5/207 6/257	

T. D. Topley, I. L. Pont and J. H. Childs did not bat.

Bonus points – Essex 3, Surrey 2.

Bowling: Clarke 10–0–27–1; M. P. Bicknell 21–4–80–3; Feltham 16–3–58–0; Medlycott 14–2–62–1; Greig 4–0–11–0; Bullen 2.1–0–10–1.

Umpires: H. D. Bird and A. A. Jones.

At Hove, September 9, 10, 11. SURREY beat SUSSEX by an innings and 119 runs.

At Canterbury, September 14, 15, 16. SURREY lost to KENT by an innings and 66 runs.

STATUS OF MATCHES IN THE UK

(*a*) **Automatic First-Class Matches**

The following matches of three or more days' duration should automatically be considered first-class:

(i) County Championship matches.
(ii) Official representative tourist matches from Full Member Countries, unless specifically excluded.
(iii) MCC v any First-Class County.
(iv) Oxford v Cambridge and either University against First-Class Counties.
(v) Scotland v Ireland.

(*b*) **Excluded from First-Class Status**

The following matches of three or more days' duration should not normally be accorded first-class status:

(i) County "friendly" matches.
(ii) Matches played by Scotland or Ireland, other than their annual match against each other.
(iii) Unofficial tourist matches, unless circumstances are exceptional.
(iv) MCC v Oxford/Cambridge.
(v) Matches involving privately raised teams, unless included officially in a touring team's itinerary.

(*c*) **Consideration of Doubtful Status**

Matches played by unofficial touring teams of exceptional ability can be considered in advance and decisions taken accordingly.

Certain other matches comprising 22 recognised first-class cricketers might also be considered in advance.

SUSSEX

President: The Marquess of Abergavenny
Chairman: R. M. Leadley
Secretary: N. Bett
County Ground, Eaton Road,
Hove BN3 3AN
(Telephone: 0273-732161)
Captain: P. W. G. Parker
Coach: 1988 – J. A. Jameson

Although Sussex managed only three wins in the Britannic Assurance Championship, and infrequent limited-overs successes, there was considerable encouragement for the new administration and management team at Hove. The convincing defeat in August of the then Championship leaders, Kent, was a great boost to an inexperienced side. And it showed that, despite their final position of sixteenth, they were capable of entertaining and effective cricket. By the end of the 1988 season, there was a genuine belief that Sussex were on the way up.

Much of the credit for this must go to the new captain, Paul Parker. Passed over when John Barclay resigned in 1986, Parker proved to be an enthusiastic and caring leader while retaining all his brilliance in the field. In addition, he was the mainstay of a generally weak batting line-up, hitting five hundreds in the Championship and averaging 37.35. However, only one of those hundreds, against Somerset in April, came in the first innings. Parker handled his inexperienced bowling attack successfully enough for Sussex to obtain 65 bowling bonus points, and the leg-spinner, Andy Clarke, in his first season, could not have wished for a more supportive captain.

Parker's task in leading a side in which uncapped players were always in the majority – no caps were awarded in 1988 – could have been eased by a significant contribution from Imran Khan. In the event, Imran appeared in only four Championship matches, although making a useful enough contribution to the one-day effort. A contract which bound him to one-day games but to only a handful of Championship matches of his own choosing was clearly inadequate and became something of an embarrassment to the club. Matters came to a head during Eastbourne Week when Imran arrived late for the Refuge Assurance League match against Glamorgan. While his apology was accepted, the next day it was announced that he would not play again until the last match of the season – and he missed that through injury. It was a sad end to Imran's Sussex career, during which he scored 7,216 first-class runs and took 407 wickets.

Of Sussex's three other capped batsmen, Alan Wells was a consistent and attractive middle-order player. But it was a disappointing year for his brother, Colin, and the opening batsman, Allan Green. Colin Wells, who in 1987 scored more than 1,400 Championship runs, finished 92 runs short of his 1,000 runs from all first-class matches last season, though he continued to bowl his seamers with great accuracy and was particularly useful in the Sunday League. Green, of whom so much was expected a few years ago, missed seven weeks in mid-season after being struck on the hand in the match against Leicestershire. Against Derbyshire at Horsham, he had the unusual distinction of being out first ball in both innings without recording a "king pair"; he was run out in the second innings, going for a second run.

In contrast, Tony Pigott, who to add to his past injury problems was diagnosed as a diabetic before the start of the season, had a marvellous summer, scoring 668 runs and taking 74 wickets in the Championship. He bowled at least 100 overs more than any other Sussex seam bowler, undertaking a greater work-load than might have been expected of him at a stronger county.

With Green either out of action or struggling to recapture his form, Parker was forced to experiment with his opening batsmen. Neil Lenham, despite finger and shoulder injuries, played some attractive innings, but has still to live up to his promise, while inconsistent form and a back injury restricted Nick Falkner, recruited from Surrey, to seven matches. Down the order, Ian Gould also had injury worries and towards the end of the season did not keep wicket. As ever, he was an exciting batsman to watch. His replacement as wicket-keeper was Peter Moores, who did all that was expected of him and scored a battling 97 not out against Lancashire. If it seemed something of a luxury for Sussex to include both Gould and Moores, the side contained three wicket-keepers when the Durham University 'keeper, Martin Speight, was drafted in as a batsman. He batted brightly, hitting two first-class fifties, but he lacked the discipline required of an opening batsman when tried there towards the end of the season.

Before the season started, it looked as if Sussex, without Garth le Roux and with Imran an infrequent starter, would struggle to bowl sides out. While this was sometimes the case, on the whole they were served admirably by their inexperienced bowlers. Andy Babington took 48 Championship wickets with his fast-medium away-swing, and if Rodney Bunting, in his first year of first-class cricket, was less accurate, he still produced three five-wicket returns. The first was on his début, the second against the West Indians. Tall and with a high action, on occasions he looked a very good prospect.

Most interest, however, centred on Clarke, the 26-year-old leg-spinner, who joined the staff in 1988 after several successful seasons in the local leagues. He took 42 Championship wickets, with a best of five for 60 against Hampshire. Relying more on accuracy than spin, he was particularly effective in limited-overs cricket and ended the season third in the Sunday League averages with seventeen wickets at 15.70. Philip Threlfall, given a two-year contract midway through the season, showed the potential to bowl fast in the Second XI but played just once, without success, for the first team. Simon Kimber fought his way into the side halfway through the season but with seven wickets in four Championship matches failed to keep his place. He appeared regularly in the one-day fixtures. Four players were not re-engaged: Rehan Alikhan, Meyrick Pringle, Peter Heseltine and David Standing. – Jack Arlidge.

SUSSEX 1988

[*Bill Smith*

Back row: M. P. Speight, P. A. W. Heseltine, K. Greenfield, N. J. Lenham, R. I. Alikhan, N. J. Falkner, A. R. Clarke. *Middle row:* L. V. Chandler (*scorer*), C. P. Cale (*assistant coach*), A. M. Babington, P. V. Boarer, M. W. Pringle, R. A. Bunting, S. J. S. Kimber, J. W. Hall, P. Moores, I. C. Waring (*assistant coach*), J. A. Jameson (*coach*). *Front row:* D. K. Standing, A. M. Green, C. M. Wells, P. W. G. Parker (*captain*), A. C. S. Pigott, A. P. Wells, I. J. Gould. *Inset:* Imran Khan.

SUSSEX RESULTS

All first-class matches – Played 23: Won 3, Lost 11, Drawn 9.

County Championship matches – Played 22: Won 3, Lost 11, Drawn 8.

Bonus points – Batting 37, Bowling 65.

Competition placings – Britannic Assurance County Championship, 16th; NatWest Bank Trophy, 1st round; Benson and Hedges Cup, 4th in Group C; Refuge Assurance League, 14th equal.

BRITANNIC ASSURANCE CHAMPIONSHIP AVERAGES

BATTING

	Birthplace	*M*	*I*	*NO*	*R*	*HI*	*Avge*
‡P. W. G. Parker	*Bulawayo, S. Rhodesia*	20	39	5	1,270	124	37.35
‡A. P. Wells	*Newhaven*	22	41	5	1,269	120	35.25
‡I. J. Gould	*Slough*	18	30	4	842	82*	32.38
‡C. M. Wells	*Newhaven*	22	39	4	906	109*	25.88
‡A. C. S. Pigott	*London*	20	34	8	668	56	25.69
N. J. Lenham	*Worthing*	17	31	2	721	74	24.86
‡A. M. Green	*Pulborough*	15	28	2	607	68	23.34
§‡Imran Khan	*Lahore, Pakistan*	4	6	1	116	55	23.20
R. I. Alikhan	*London*	9	18	0	400	98	22.22
M. P. Speight	*Walsall*	7	13	0	258	58	19.84
P. Moores	*Macclesfield*	14	24	2	395	97*	17.95
N. J. Falkner	*Redhill*	7	14	0	232	55	16.57
§M. W. Pringle	*Adelaide, SA*	4	6	0	90	35	15.00
A. R. Clarke	*Patcham*	20	31	8	336	68	14.60
S. J. S. Kimber	*Ormskirk*	4	7	3	54	32*	13.50
R. A. Bunting	*East Winch*	16	20	4	92	17*	5.75
A. M. Babington	*London*	18	25	8	85	12	5.00

Also batted: P. A. W. Heseltine (*Barnsley*) (2 matches) 6, 8; D. K. Standing (*Brighton*) (2 matches) 0, 9, 4. P. W. Threlfall (*Barrow-in-Furness*) (1 match) did not bat.

* *Signifies not out.* ‡ *Denotes county cap.* § *Not qualified for England.*

The following played a total of seven three-figure innings for Sussex in County Championship matches – P. W. G. Parker 5, A. P. Wells 1, C. M. Wells 1.

BOWLING

	O	*M*	*R*	*W*	*BB*	*5W/i*	*Avge*
Imran Khan	109.3	26	255	13	5-50	1	19.61
A. C. S. Pigott	627	108	2,078	74	6-100	2	28.08
R. A. Bunting	351	66	1,088	36	5-44	2	30.22
A. M. Babington	514.5	108	1,496	48	4-66	0	31.16
C. M. Wells	495.4	109	1,359	42	4-43	0	32.35
A. R. Clarke	577	153	1,481	42	5-60	2	35.26
A. M. Green	148.5	39	387	10	6-82	1	38.70

Also bowled: R. I. Alikhan 0.3–0–7–0; I. J. Gould 21–2–84–2; P. A. W. Heseltine 28–5–106–1; S. J. S. Kimber 83–19–272–7; N. J. Lenham 19.5–2–60–3; P. Moores 1–0–6–0; P. W. G. Parker 1–0–1–1; M. W. Pringle 98–19–323–6; M. P. Speight 0.3–0–2–1; P. W. Threlfall 12–3–31–0; A. P. Wells 5–1–11–0.

Wicket-keepers: P. Moores 30 ct, 3 st; I. J. Gould 18 ct.

Leading Fielders: A. P. Wells 17, A. C. S. Pigott 16.

SUSSEX v SOMERSET

At Hove, April 21, 22, 23, 25. Sussex won by seven wickets. Sussex 23 pts, Somerset 4 pts. Toss: Sussex. Sussex began their Championship programme in fine style, with Parker, the season's beneficiary, in splendid form, scoring 101 not out in the first innings and 71 not out in the second. This was his first match as the club's captain and Sussex's first Championship victory at their county ground since 1986. On the debit side, Pigott was carried off with a hamstring injury after pulling up sharply in his run-up while bowling the thirteenth over of the third day. Burns's 133 not out in Somerset's second innings, his highest score to date, saved the visitors from a heavier defeat after Babington had upset their middle order with four wickets for 6 runs in 32 balls.

Close of play: First day, Sussex 139-5 (P. W. G. Parker 44*, I. J. Gould 3*); Second day, Somerset 183-6 (N. D. Burns 54*, G. V. Palmer 13*); Third day, Sussex 68-1 (A. M. Green 43*, P. W. G. Parker 13*).

Somerset

Batsman	First innings		Second innings	
N. A. Felton	c Green b Babington	39	lbw b Pigott	0
*P. M. Roebuck	c Gould b Babington	12	b Babington	19
N. J. Pringle	lbw b Pigott	4	lbw b Babington	10
M. D. Crowe	c Gould b Babington	19	lbw b Babington	25
R. J. Harden	b Pringle	5	run out	45
V. J. Marks	c Parker b Pigott	23	lbw b Babington	0
†N. D. Burns	not out	16	not out	133
G. V. Palmer	b Pigott	0	c Parker b Pigott	23
N. A. Mallender	b Clarke	2	lbw b Lenham	44
A. N. Jones	c Pringle b Clarke	0	b Lenham	6
D. J. Foster	c A. P. Wells b Pigott	9	c Gould b Lenham	1
	L-b 3, n-b 10	13	B 8, l-b 10, w 3, n-b 6	27
	1/54 2/57 3/68 4/87 5/89 6/119 7/119 8/126 9/126	142	1/0 2/34 3/45 4/66 5/66 6/167 7/197 8/316 9/327	333

Bonus points – Sussex 4.

Bowling: *First Innings*—Pigott 20.3–5–55–4; Pringle 14–2–35–1; Clarke 20–6–34–2; Babington 13–7–15–3. *Second Innings*—Pigott 18.1–7–42–2; Pringle 21–6–58–0; Lenham 17.5–2–57–3; Babington 33.5–9–66–4; Clarke 42–13–74–0; Green 8–5–7–0; A. P. Wells 5–1–11–0.

Sussex

Batsman	First innings		Second innings	
R. I. Alikhan	b Foster	18	lbw b Marks	6
A. M. Green	c Crowe b Foster	29	b Marks	44
*P. W. G. Parker	not out	101	not out	71
A. P. Wells	c Crowe b Foster	4	lbw b Mallender	25
C. M. Wells	c Burns b Mallender	24	not out	49
N. J. Lenham	lbw b Mallender	6		
†I. J. Gould	c Mallender b Marks	13		
A. C. S. Pigott	c Burns b Jones	28		
M. W. Pringle	b Foster	4		
A. R. Clarke	c Marks b Jones	19		
A. M. Babington	lbw b Palmer	0		
	B 6, l-b 4, w 2, n-b 8	20	B 3, l-b 7, n-b 8	18
	1/44 2/64 3/68 4/115 5/127 6/155 7/200 8/206 9/266	266	1/40 2/74 3/122 (3 wkts)	213

Bonus points – Sussex 3, Somerset 4.

Bowling: *First Innings*—Jones 12–2–49–2; Mallender 27–7–59–2; Foster 16–1–67–4; Marks 18–4–55–1; Palmer 8.2–0–26–1. *Second Innings*—Mallender 17–3–46–1; Jones 15–2–35–0; Palmer 10–2–28–0; Foster 8–1–35–0; Marks 17–6–49–2; Pringle 1–0–6–0; Roebuck 0.4–0–4–0.

Umpires: J. H. Harris and A. G. T. Whitehead.

At Bristol, April 28, 29, 30, May 2. SUSSEX drew with GLOUCESTERSHIRE.

At Hove, May 7, 9, 10. SUSSEX drew with WEST INDIANS (See West Indian tour section).

At Nottingham, May 21, 23, 24. SUSSEX lost to NOTTINGHAMSHIRE by 67 runs.

At Lord's, May 28, 30, 31. SUSSEX drew with MIDDLESEX.

At The Oval, June 1, 2, 3. SUSSEX lost to SURREY by an innings and 11 runs.

SUSSEX v DERBYSHIRE

At Horsham, June 4, 6, 7. Derbyshire won by one wicket. Derbyshire 22 pts, Sussex 7 pts. Toss: Sussex. In a thrilling finish, Derbyshire won off the last ball. Chasing a target of 178 in a minimum of 50 overs, they still needed 8 runs when the last man, Malcolm, joined Sharma in he penultimate over. He immediately hit Clarke for four, but Pigott allowed only two singles from five balls. Sharma swung at the final delivery, got an edge that just evaded Green at second slip, and the batsmen scrambled 2 runs to provide a final thrill to an entertaining game. Morris, with the highest score of the match, 71 including eight fours, had put Derbyshire in a good position before Pigott, with three wickets, gave Sussex their chance. A pitch with more than a hint of green had encouraged the seam bowlers throughout, and the wicket-keepers, Maher and Gould, reaped a rich harvest, effecting seven dismissals each.

Close of play: First day, Sussex 247-6 (I. J. Gould 21*, S. J. S. Kimber 8*); Second day, Sussex 33-2 (P. W. G. Parker 26*, A. P. Wells 2*).

Sussex

R. I. Alikhan lbw b Warner	56	– b Malcolm	1
A. M. Green c Barnett b Malcolm	0	– run out	1
P. W. G. Parker c Barnett b Malcolm	25	– c Roberts b Mortensen	48
A. P. Wells lbw b Barnett	36	– c Roberts b Mortensen	2
C. M. Wells st Maher b Barnett	16	– c Goldsmith b Warner	7
N. J. Lenham c Maher b Mortensen	62	– c Maher b Malcolm	21
I. J. Gould b Malcolm	32	– c Maher b Mortensen	10
S. J. S. Kimber c Maher b Malcolm	8	– c Maher b Mortensen	5
A. C. S. Pigott c Goldsmith b Malcolm	12	– not out	45
A. R. Clarke not out	0	– c Maher b Warner	3
A. M. Babington c Goldsmith b Warner	0	– b Warner	1
B 1, l-b 10, w 2, n-b 12	25	B 1, l-b 5, w 3, n-b 2	11
1/4 2/30 3/84 4/112 5/197 6/229 7/255 8/271 9/272	272	1/1 2/11 3/35 4/61 5/77 6/89 7/95 8/126 9/147	155

Bonus points – Sussex 3, Derbyshire 3 (Score at 100 overs: 259-7).

Bowling: *First Innings*—Mortensen 22–8–32–1; Malcolm 19–5–52–5; Warner 20.2–6–42–2; Roberts 5–2–14–0; Barnett 17–2–69–2; Sharma 14–3–32–0; Bowler 6–0–20–0. *Second Innings*—Malcolm 14–6–19–2; Warner 19.2–4–52–3; Mortensen 20–4–57–4; Sharma ·1–15–0; Roberts 9–6–6–0.

Derbyshire

First innings		Second innings	
P. D. Bowler c Gould b Pigott	62	– c Green b C. M. Wells	29
J. G. Wright run out	9	– c Parker b C. M. Wells	0
B. Roberts c Gould b Kimber	28	– c Pigott b Kimber	1
J. E. Morris c Gould b Kimber	0	– c Pigott b Kimber	71
S. C. Goldsmith c Pigott b Kimber	0	– c Gould b Babington	9
†B. J. M. Maher c Gould b Babington	38	– lbw b Pigott	28
R. Sharma lbw b Pigott	0	– (8) not out	16
*K. J. Barnett c A. P. Wells b Pigott	67	– (7) c Gould b Pigott	12
A. E. Warner not out	26	– c Gould b Pigott	0
D. E. Malcolm lbw b Pigott	0	– (11) not out	5
O. H. Mortensen b C. M. Wells	2	– (10) b Clarke	2
B 4, l-b 8, w 2, n-b 4	18	L-b 2, n-b 3	5
1/28 2/70 3/74 4/80 5/132 6/132 7/204 8/247 9/247	250	1/1 2/12 3/75 4/92 5/142 6/146 7/162 8/162 9/170	(9 wkts) 178

Bonus points – Derbyshire 3, Sussex 4.

Bowling: *First Innings*—Pigott 16–3–60–4; Babington 12–1–55–1; C. M. Wells 20–9–46–1; Kimber 20–7–44–3; Clarke 10–3–30–0; Lenham 2–0–3–0. *Second Innings*—C. M. Wells 14–3–47–2; Pigott 14–3–54–3; Kimber 8–0–26–2; Clarke 8.3–2–22–1; Babington 8.3–1–27–1.

Umpires: A. A. Jones and D. R. Shepherd.

At Ilford, June 11, 13, 14. SUSSEX lost to ESSEX by an innings and 173 runs.

At Bath, June 15, 16, 17. SUSSEX drew with SOMERSET.

At Leicester, June 18, 20, 21. SUSSEX lost to LEICESTERSHIRE by eight wickets.

SUSSEX v YORKSHIRE

At Hove, June 25, 27, 28. Yorkshire won by three wickets. Yorkshire 22 pts, Sussex 7 pts. Toss: Sussex. Yorkshire, after losing half their wickets for 72, reached a target of 186 wit thirteen balls to spare to secure their first Championship win of the season. Moxon put the on course with a responsible innings of 61 in 160 minutes, adding 70 for the sixth wicket wi Carrick. Sidebottom, who hit the winning run in the gloom, had earlier in the day joined wi Fletcher in bowling out Sussex after rain, which held up play for more than an hour, ha freshened the pitch. Sussex lost six wickets in 10.1 overs, and 105 was their lowest total of th season thus far. They had scored 299 in their first innings, with the opening pair, Falkner ar Alikhan, putting on 91. Falkner marked his first-class début for Sussex with a half-centur and Alikhan went on to what proved to be the highest innings of the match.

Close of play: First day, Yorkshire 10-0 (M. D. Moxon 8*, I. G. Swallow 2*); Second da Sussex 26-2 (N. J. Falkner 14*, A. P. Wells 5*).

Sussex

R. I. Alikhan b Carrick	71	– lbw b Jarvis	1
N. J. Falkner c Bairstow b Jarvis	55	– lbw b Jarvis	14
*P. W. G. Parker c Robinson b Jarvis	29	– b Jarvis	2
A. P. Wells c Bairstow b Fletcher	20	– lbw b Sidebottom	37
C. M. Wells c Bairstow b Fletcher	9	– c Byas b Jarvis	10
M. P. Speight c Bairstow b Carrick	8	– b Sidebottom	3
†P. Moores b Carrick	22	– c Bairstow b Sidebottom	2
A. C. S. Pigott c Swallow b Shaw	35	– c Byas b Fletcher	5
M. W. Pringle b Carrick	17	– b Fletcher	15
A. R. Clarke not out	7	– not out	6
A. M. Babington c Moxon b Shaw	10	– c Shaw b Sidebottom	1
B 4, l-b 5, n-b 7	16	L-b 2, n-b 7	9
/91 2/161 3/167 4/189 5/196 /205 7/256 8/274 9/286	299	1/8 2/21 3/26 4/44 5/55 6/58 7/64 8/96 9/98	105

Bonus points – Sussex 3, Yorkshire 4 (Score at 100 overs: 293-9).

Bowling: *First Innings*—Jarvis 15–2–52–2; Sidebottom 18–4–62–0; Fletcher 20–4–50–2; haw 18–4–55–2; Carrick 30–10–71–4. *Second Innings*—Jarvis 11–5–21–4; Sidebottom 6.1–2–47–4; Fletcher 6–0–35–2.

orkshire

. D. Moxon b Babington	13	– c Pigott b Clarke	61
G. Swallow b C. M. Wells	30	– c Moores b Pigott	21
. Byas lbw b Pringle	16	– c Alikhan b Pigott	0
. A. Metcalfe b Clarke	9	– c A. P. Wells b Pringle	22
. E. Robinson c sub b C. M. Wells	49	– c Pigott b C. M. Wells	0
D. L. Bairstow c Moores b C. M. Wells	5	– b C. M. Wells	0
P. Carrick c Alikhan b Clarke	38	– b Babington	43
. Sidebottom not out	37	– not out	27
. W. Jarvis b Babington	0	– not out	6
. Shaw c and b Babington	4		
D. Fletcher lbw b Babington	1		
L-b 5, n-b 12	17	L-b 4, n-b 2	6
24 2/64 3/64 4/122 5/127 144 7/185 8/196 9/203	219	1/23 2/28 3/71 4/72 5/72 6/142 7/170	(7 wkts) 186

Bonus points – Yorkshire 2, Sussex 4.

Bowling: *First Innings*—Pigott 9–2–14–0; C. M. Wells 19–2–40–3; Babington 20–1–66–4; ringle 17–4–62–1; Clarke 18–6–32–2. *Second Innings*—Pigott 17–1–67–2; Babington .5–1–45–1; C. M. Wells 12–4–23–2; Pringle 10–3–35–1; Clarke 5–0–12–1.

Umpires: R. Palmer and A. G. T. Whitehead.

SUSSEX v KENT

Hastings, July 2, 4, 5. Kent won by four wickets. Kent 23 pts, Sussex 4 pts. Toss: Sussex. ent made hard work of reaching a modest target of 106 from 35 overs; it was the final over en Penn pulled a delivery from Colin Wells to the fine-leg boundary for the winning runs. e victory, Kent's seventh Championship win in eight games, owed much to their opener, nson, who compiled a solid 54 before being sixth out at 102. Sussex were dismissed for a mal 71 on the first day. Penn claimed the first five wickets for only 16 runs in 8.1 overs, and lleher saw to the tailenders to finish with four for 24. Tavaré, batting for 251 minutes and ting six fours, narrowly missed out on a painstaking century as Kent built up a lead of 217. wever, Sussex fought back gamely and went into the last day needing 95 to avoid an ings defeat with seven wickets in hand. Parker's aggressive 117 included sixteen firmly ck boundaries, and he put on 59 for the sixth wicket with Speight, whose 50 was a eer best.

lose of play: First day, Kent 219-6 (C. J. Tavaré 87*, R. M. Ellison 8*); Second day, ssex 122-3 (P. W. G. Parker 31*, A. R. Clarke 2*).

Sussex

R. I. Alikhan b Penn	0	– (2) c Tavaré b Kelleher	21
N. J. Falkner lbw b Penn	5	– (1) c Pienaar b Penn	45
*P. W. G. Parker c Benson b Penn	10	– c Tavaré b Cowdrey	117
A. P. Wells c Tavaré b Penn	10	– c Benson b Pienaar	11
C. M. Wells c Marsh b Penn	0	– (6) c Taylor b Pienaar	15
M. P. Speight c Tavaré b Ellison	14	– (7) st Marsh b Davis	50
A. C. S. Pigott c Marsh b Kelleher	2	– (8) c Ward b Cowdrey	8
†P. Moores c Marsh b Kelleher	1	– (9) c Cowdrey b Davis	28
A. R. Clarke not out	12	– (5) c Cowdrey b Ellison	4
R. A. Bunting c Taylor b Kelleher	5	– c Ward b Ellison	1
A. M. Babington c Cowdrey b Kelleher	4	– not out	0
L-b 3, n-b 5	8	L-b 12, n-b 10	22
1/1 2/10 3/28 4/28 5/30 6/38 7/49 8/56 9/67	71	1/61 2/81 3/118 4/148 5/191 6/250 7/258 8/315 9/322	322

Bonus points – Kent 4.

Bowling: *First Innings*—Penn 12–3–29–5; Ellison 9–5–15–1; Kelleher 13–6–24–4. *Second Innings*—Ellison 31–10–78–2; Penn 24–2–106–1; Davis 24.4–10–41–2; Kelleher 11–4–18–1; Pienaar 17–4–38–2; Cowdrey 13–4–29–2.

Kent

M. R. Benson c A. P. Wells b Pigott	0	– c Babington b Clarke	54
N. R. Taylor lbw b Babington	21	– c Moores b Babington	5
T. R. Ward c Alikhan b Pigott	27	– c Falkner b Bunting	10
C. J. Tavaré run out	95		
R. F. Pienaar lbw b C. M. Wells	37	– (4) lbw b Babington	9
*C. S. Cowdrey c Moores b C. M. Wells	8	– (5) c Moores b C. M. Wells	9
†S. A. Marsh lbw b Babington	21	– (6) st Moores b Clarke	5
R. M. Ellison b Pigott	20	– (7) not out	8
C. Penn not out	24	– (8) not out	4
D. J. M. Kelleher b C. M. Wells	20		
R. P. Davis c Alikhan b C. M. Wells	4		
B 1, l-b 6, w 3, n-b 1	11	L-b 2	2
1/0 2/48 3/52 4/132 5/148 6/193 7/237 8/246 9/280	288	1/14 2/29 3/43 4/72 5/87 6/102	(6 wkts) 10

Bonus points – Kent 3, Sussex 4.

Bowling: *First Innings*—Pigott 29–5–78–3; C. M. Wells 33.3–7–94–4; Babingto 15–3–47–2; Bunting 13–1–39–0; Clarke 7–0–23–0. *Second Innings*—Pigott 4–0–8–0; Babingto 12–3–23–2; Bunting 4–1–18–1; C. M. Wells 9.1–0–37–1; Clarke 5–0–18–2.

Umpires: A. A. Jones and B. Leadbeater.

SUSSEX v GLOUCESTERSHIRE

At Hove, July 20, 21, 22. Drawn. Sussex 5 pts, Gloucestershire 5 pts. Toss: Sussex. Glouceste shire set Sussex 257 to win in a minimum of 59 overs and the home side were struggling at 1 for seven when, following two earlier interruptions for rain, bad light ended play with 8 overs remaining. Sussex had lost half their wickets for 93 after Lenham and Falkner ga them a useful start with 43, but Alan Wells, top scorer in the first innings, played responsib again for 100 minutes, his 54 including a six and five fours. He was one of three victims for t lively Lawrence, who took four for 38 in the first innings, when he was warned twice f running on the wicket. After Gloucestershire had been put in, and again when they we batting to set a target, Stovold led the way. His 77 off 74 balls in the second innings contain thirteen fours.

Close of play: First day, Sussex 20-0 (N. J. Falkner 11*, N. J. Lenham 7*); Second da Sussex 161-6 (A. P. Wells 69*, A. C. S. Pigott 0*).

Gloucestershire

A. W. Stovold c Pigott b Bunting	63 – c Moores b C. M. Wells	77
A. J. Wright b Pigott	50	
P. W. Romaines c Lenham b Pigott	36 – c Parker b Pigott	2
P. Bainbridge c Lenham b Bunting	11 – c Moores b Pigott	2
K. M. Curran c Speight b Clarke	27 – not out	42
M. W. Alleyne lbw b Clarke	6 – c Moores b C. M. Wells	0
J. W. Lloyds c A. P. Wells b Babington	0 – (2) c Parker b Pigott	0
†R. C. Russell b Bunting	50 – (7) not out	11
*D. A. Graveney c Moores b Bunting	3	
D. V. Lawrence run out	3	
T. M. Alderman not out	4	
L-b 15, w 8	23	B 3, l-b 4 — 7
1/112 2/134 3/146 4/166 5/169 6/197 7/259 8/267 9/269	276	1/15 2/23 3/33 4/114 5/116 (5 wkts dec.) 141

Bonus points – Gloucestershire 3, Sussex 4.

In the first innings A. J. Wright, when 11, retired hurt at 30 and resumed at 197.

Bowling: *First Innings*—Pigott 21–2–74–2; Babington 21–2–44–1; Bunting 19.1–2–59–4; C. M. Wells 15–3–48–0; Clarke 20–11–36–2. *Second Innings*—Pigott 11–1–40–3; Babington 5–1–26–0; Bunting 4–0–33–0; Clarke 6–0–17–0; C. M. Wells 5–2–18–2.

Sussex

N. J. Falkner c Alderman b Lawrence	20 – (2) lbw b Lawrence	18
N. J. Lenham c Russell b Lawrence	8 – (1) c Russell b Curran	38
*P. W. G. Parker b Lawrence	12 – lbw b Lawrence	6
A. P. Wells not out	69 – c Wright b Lawrence	54
C. M. Wells c Romaines b Lawrence	2 – b Graveney	13
M. P. Speight lbw b Graveney	35 – c Romaines b Bainbridge	0
†P. Moores lbw b Graveney	4 – c and b Bainbridge	22
A. C. S. Pigott not out	0 – not out	8
A. R. Clarke (did not bat)	– not out	6
B 4, l-b 5, w 1, n-b 1	11	L-b 6, n-b 3 — 9
1/22 2/42 3/47 4/61 5/151 6/161 (6 wkts dec.)	161	1/43 2/57 3/65 4/88 5/93 6/145 7/166 (7 wkts) 174

R. A. Bunting and A. M. Babington did not bat.

Bonus points – Sussex 1, Gloucestershire 2.

Bowling: *First Innings*—Lawrence 13–2–38–4; Alderman 13.2–3–36–0; Curran 7–0–32–0; Bainbridge 8.4–2–31–0; Graveney 8–4–15–2. *Second Innings*—Lawrence 11–1–48–3; Curran .4–1–48–1; Graveney 11–3–23–1; Bainbridge 11–1–49–2.

Umpires: R. Palmer and P. B. Wight.

At Northampton, July 23, 25, 26. SUSSEX drew with NORTHAMPTONSHIRE.

SUSSEX v GLAMORGAN

Eastbourne, July 30, August 1, 2. Drawn. Sussex 7 pts, Glamorgan 7 pts. Toss: Glamorgan. e first match of the Eastbourne Festival petered out after Sussex had been set 246 to win in ninimum of 39 overs. Despite generally fine weather and a fast outfield, neither side had hieved a run-rate above 3 an over in the first innings, which made Glamorgan's declaration, cing Sussex to score at 6 an over, hardly a generous one. Nevertheless, the match did duce some good cricket. In Glamorgan's first innings, Maynard hit nine fours in his 68 m 78 balls, and Ontong batted stoutly for three hours nineteen minutes before being last out for 89. Watkin returned career-best figures when Sussex batted, and it needed Pigott's 52, containing seven fours, to prevent Glamorgan from gaining a decisive advantage. Glamorgan, needing to push the score along, found the going slow. Morris faced 133 balls for his 63, and by the time he declared, midway through the afternoon, the match was condemned to a draw.

Close of play: First day, Sussex 11-2 (N. J. Lenham 2*, R. A. Bunting 2*); Second day, Glamorgan 75-3 (H. Morris 25*, C. P. Metson 0*).

Glamorgan

A. R. Butcher c Moores b Pigott . . . . 0 – c Falkner b C. M. Wells 0
*H. Morris c A. P. Wells b Clarke . . . . 56 – b C. M. Wells 63
M. P. Maynard c A. P. Wells b Bunting . . . . . . 68 – b Pigott 27
G. C. Holmes c Moores b Bunting . . . . 8 – c Bunting b Pigott 19
R. J. Shastri b Pigott . . . . 19 – (6) not out 54
R. C. Ontong b Pigott . . . . 89 – (7) c C. M. Wells b Clarke 42
J. G. Thomas c Pigott b Bunting . . . . 21 – (8) not out 8
J. Derrick run out 1
†C. P. Metson lbw b Pigott . . . . 3 – (5) c Moores b Bunting 7
S. L. Watkin lbw b Clarke 6
S. R. Barwick not out 2
L-b 3, w 3, n-b 4 . . . . 10 L-b 3, w 1, n-b 3 7

1/4 2/96 3/107 4/146 5/175 6/225 7/232 8/243 9/275 283 1/1 2/48 3/73 4/86 5/135 6/192 (6 wkts dec.) 22

Bonus points – Glamorgan 3, Sussex 4 (Score at 100 overs: 275-9).

Bowling: *First Innings*—Pigott 25.1–5–82–4; Babington 13–3–37–0; Clarke 24–6–58–2; C. M. Wells 22–5–54–0; Bunting 20–4–49–3. *Second Innings*—Pigott 18–6–56–2; C. M. Wells 14–2–36–2; Babington 16–5–56–0; Bunting 10–2–30–1; Clarke 15–1–46–1.

Sussex

N. J. Falkner c Derrick b Watkin . . . . 6 – (2) c Maynard b Shastri . . . .
N. J. Lenham c Metson b Thomas . . . . 40 – (1) c Metson b Watkin 2
A. R. Clarke c Derrick b Watkin 0
R. A. Bunting lbw b Barwick 11
*P. W. G. Parker c Morris b Shastri . . . . 46 – (3) lbw b Watkin . . . .
A. P. Wells c Metson b Shastri . . . . 50 – (4) not out 4
C. M. Wells c Metson b Watkin 7
I. J. Gould c Maynard b Watkin . . . . 1 – (5) not out 3
A. C. S. Pigott c Metson b Watkin 52
†P. Moores not out 38
A. M. Babington run out 2
L-b 7, w 1, n-b 4 . . . . 12 L-b 9 . . . .

1/9 2/9 3/30 4/64 5/138 6/153 7/159 8/174 9/250 265 1/26 2/27 3/40 (3 wkts) 1

Bonus points – Sussex 3, Glamorgan 4.

Bowling: *First Innings*—Thomas 10–2–26–1; Watkin 28–5–89–5; Barwick 20–4–57–; Shastri 24–7–58–2; Derrick 8–3–19–0; Ontong 6–2–9–0. *Second Innings*—Watkin 15–4–53–; Barwick 3–1–3–0; Shastri 14–2–26–1; Ontong 8–3–12–0; Derrick 1–0–12–0.

Umpires: D. G. L. Evans and D. O. Oslear.

SUSSEX v HAMPSHIRE

At Eastbourne, August 3, 4, 5. Drawn. Sussex 5 pts, Hampshire 7 pts. Toss: Sussex. Parker Hampshire to score 252 at just over 5 runs an over, and after an opening stand of 75 betwe Scott, who hit a maiden first-class fifty, and Smith, Terry with his second half-century of match took them to within 45 runs of the target. The match produced an outstand performance from Clarke, the Sussex leg-spinner. Coming to the crease when Sussex in th first innings were 188 for seven, he exceeded by 42 his previous highest score, hitting ten fo in his 68. And as Hampshire chased their target, he delighted the loyal Eastbourne crowd, already enjoying three days of unremitting sunshine, with his flighted leg-spin. Clarke claimed the first five wickets, effectively stifled Hampshire's bid for victory, and finished with career-best figures of five for 60. In Hampshire's first innings, Ayling hit seventeen fours in his 86 (120 balls) to consolidate the good work of Terry and Turner and allow Nicholas to make a challenging declaration. Parker then hit an elegant hundred – his fourth of the season – off 223 balls before setting up the interesting finish.

Close of play: First day, Hampshire 8-0 (R. J. Scott 3*, C. L. Smith 5*); Second day, Sussex 65-1 (N. J. Lenham 38*, P. W. G. Parker 12*).

Sussex

N. J. Lenham c Scott b Jefferies	24	– c Smith b Bakker	47
N. J. Falkner b Bakker	10	– c Scott b Bakker	4
*P. W. G. Parker c Scott b Ayling	45	– not out	104
A. P. Wells c Terry b Ayling	56	– c Scott b James	7
. J. Gould c Parks b Jefferies	5	– b James	4
C. M. Wells lbw b Jefferies	11	– c Smith b Maru	11
A. C. S. Pigott c Parks b Ayling	16	– not out	35
†P. Moores c Parks b Bakker	15		
A. R. Clarke c James b Ayling	68		
R. A. Bunting c and b Maru	5		
A. M. Babington not out	0		
B 5, l-b 10, w 1, n-b 8	24	L-b 4, w 1, n-b 8	13
/28 2/80 3/97 4/113 5/129 /179 7/188 8/229 9/266	279	1/18 2/85 3/113 4/131 5/154 (5 wkts dec.)	225

Bonus points – Sussex 3, Hampshire 4 (Score at 100 overs: 267-9).

Bowling: *First Innings*—Jefferies 30–4–79–3; Bakker 26–8–70–2; James 11–4–36–0; Ayling 2.3–4–57–4; Maru 14–8–22–1. *Second Innings*—Jefferies 6–0–22–0; Bakker 16–3–43–2; ames 22–4–67–2; Ayling 9–2–25–0; Maru 16–2–46–1; Nicholas 1–0–5–0; Scott 2.3–0–13–0.

Hampshire

. J. Scott lbw b Babington	5	– b Clarke	58
. L. Smith c Moores b Babington	5	– c Babington b Clarke	27
M. C. J. Nicholas c Moores b Bunting	20	– st Moores b Clarke	17
. P. Terry c Moores b Babington	53	– not out	50
. R. Turner c Pigott b Babington	45	– b Clarke	0
R. Ayling c Pigott b Bunting	86	– c C. M. Wells b Clarke	2
. D. James not out	17	– (8) c Falkner b Gould	12
T. Jefferies not out	11	– (7) c C. M. Wells b Gould	22
R. J. Parks (did not bat)		– not out	11
B 1, l-b 6, w 2, n-b 2	11	L-b 6, n-b 2	8
10 2/11 3/66 4/108 5/197 236 (6 wkts dec.)	253	1/75 2/98 3/109 4/109 5/129 6/168 7/191 (7 wkts)	207

J. Maru and P. J. Bakker did not bat.

Bonus points – Hampshire 3, Sussex 2.

Bowling: *First Innings*—Pigott 13–2–37–0; Clarke 15–8–27–0; Babington 23.5–8–70–4; nting 21–5–65–2; C. M. Wells 13–1–47–0. *Second Innings*—Pigott 4–1–25–0; Babington 2–23–0; C. M. Wells 13–2–33–0; Clarke 20.4–6–60–5; Bunting 4–1–12–0; Gould 9–1–48–2.

Umpires: D. G. L. Evans and D. O. Oslear.

Kidderminster, August 6, 8, 9. SUSSEX lost to WORCESTERSHIRE by nine wickets.

SUSSEX v LANCASHIRE

At Hove, August 13, 15, 16. Lancashire won by eight wickets. Lancashire 24 pts, Sussex 3 pts. Toss: Sussex. Only a career-best 97 not out by the Sussex wicket-keeper, Moores, who dominated a last-wicket stand of 70 with Babington, ensured that the match went into the final session. Moores hit thirteen fours in his innings of 166 balls, while Babington faced 55 balls with his runs coming from his sole scoring stroke. Generally, however, the honours went to Lancashire, who had lost their previous two games by ten wickets, and in particular to Atherton. The Cambridge University captain batted five and a half hours for his chanceless, career-best 152 not out (274 balls, one six, seventeen fours), stepping up the tempo at the end as he went from 100 to 152 in 37 deliveries. He and Austin, whose unbeaten 57 came off 85 balls with a six and six fours, put on 132 in 26 overs before the declaration. Lancashire's 337 in 100 overs represented a fine recovery from 137 for five. Sussex, Colin Wells apart, crumbled in the face of consistent seam bowling after Watkinson had taken three wickets in five balls. At the close of the second day, Sussex, following on, were still 17 behind with only four wickets in hand. Next day they lost Colin Wells early on, but the late-order batting fough hard to set Lancashire something of a target – 111 in 55 overs. Mendis made light of it, hitting nine fours in his 53, and Lancashire romped to their sixth win of the season.

Close of play: First day, Sussex 4-1 (N. J. Lenham 0*, A. R. Clarke 0*); Second day, Susse 148-6 (C. M. Wells 24*, P. Moores 5*).

Lancashire

G. D. Mendis run out .... 14 – c A. P. Wells b Babington 5
G. Fowler b Pigott .... 26 – not out 3
M. A. Atherton not out ....152 – c Clarke b Parker 1
N. H. Fairbrother b Bunting .... 18 – not out .... (
M. Watkinson c Parker b Pigott 18
*D. P. Hughes lbw b Bunting 0
A. N. Hayhurst c Green b C. M. Wells 30
I. D. Austin not out 57
L-b 16, w 4, n-b 2 .... 22 B 1, l-b 2, w 2, n-b 3 ....

1/33 2/62 3/93 4/130 (6 wkts dec.) 337 1/74 2/109 (2 wkts) 11
5/137 6/205

†W. K. Hegg, P. J. W. Allott and J. Simmons did not bat.

Bonus points – Lancashire 4, Sussex 2.

Bowling: *First Innings*—Pigott 23–3–102–2; Bunting 21–3–58–2; Babington 18–9–45–(C. M. Wells 15–3–35–1; Clarke 23–4–81–0. *Second Innings*—Pigott 7–0–32–0; Buntir 6–1–20–0; C. M. Wells 4–0–21–0; Babington 5–0–31–1; Clarke 2–1–3–0; Parker 1–0–1–1.

Sussex

N. J. Lenham c Atherton b Watkinson .... 8 – lbw b Watkinson ....
A. M. Green b Allott .... 3 – lbw b Allott 2
A. R. Clarke lbw b Watkinson .... 22 – (9) c Hayhurst b Allott ....
*P. W. G. Parker b Austin .... 6 – (3) c Hegg b Hayhurst ....
A. P. Wells lbw b Watkinson .... 0 – (4) lbw b Hayhurst ....
I. J. Gould b Austin .... 22 – (5) c Hegg b Hayhurst ....
C. M. Wells b Austin .... 68 – (6) c Hegg b Watkinson ....
A. C. S. Pigott run out .... 18 – (7) c Simmons b Hayhurst .....
†P. Moores c Hegg b Allott .... 5 – (8) not out ....
R. A. Bunting c and b Allott .... 5 – c Fowler b Austin ....
A. M. Babington not out .... 7 – c Simmons b Austin ....
L-b 3, n-b 5 .... 8 L-b 5, n-b 3 ....

1/3 2/35 3/36 4/36 5/48 172 1/9 2/52 3/84 4/92 5/103 2
6/92 7/129 8/137 9/151 6/137 7/175 8/184 9/205

Bonus points – Sussex 1, Lancashire 4.

Bowling: *First Innings*—Allott 23–9–61–3; Watkinson 23–6–60–3; Austin 11–5–20 Hayhurst 8–3–22–0; Simmons 2–1–6–0. *Second Innings*—Allott 23–7–58–2; Watkins 21–4–69–2; Hayhurst 20–2–78–4; Austin 15.5–5–40–2; Atherton 3–0–8–0; Simmo 8–1–17–0.

Umpires: B. Leadbeater and B. J. Meyer.

SUSSEX v WARWICKSHIRE

At Hove, August 17, 18, 19. Sussex won by 160 runs. Sussex 22 pts, Warwickshire 7 pts. Toss: Sussex. Inspired seam bowling by Bunting, ably supported by Pigott, took Sussex to their first Championship win of the season since the opening match. Set 257 to win in 47 overs, Warwickshire had collapsed to 63 for seven by the start of the last twenty overs and were all out for 96. The result was all the more surprising in that, until the final afternoon, runs had come easily for the batsmen. Sussex, having won the toss, batted well to reach 224 for two, only to lose their way. Alan Wells, with eight fifties already during the season, finally reached a century; his 120 came from 222 balls and included two sixes and twelve fours. With Parker, who was hampered by a leg injury, he added 175 in 50 overs. In reply, Warwickshire achieved maximum batting points before declaring. Asif Din retired ill with heatstroke, but after his return he added 74 with Tedstone and dominated a stand of 55 in eight overs with Small. Rain prevented Sussex from batting again until the third day, when Parker hit a brilliant 61 and Alan Wells and Gould put on 146 in 39 overs before the declaration.

Close of play: First day, Warwickshire 11-0 (A. C. Storie 4*, J. D. Ratcliffe 6*); Second day, Warwickshire 303-8 dec.

Sussex

N. J. Lenham c Ratcliffe b Small	0	– c Asif Din b Small	4
A. M. Green b Gifford	22	– run out	38
*P. W. G. Parker b Gifford	79	– c Ratcliffe b Gifford	61
A. P. Wells c Gifford b Munton	120	– not out	74
I. J. Gould c Thorne b Gifford	9	– not out	69
C. M. Wells c Tedstone b Munton	1		
A. C. S. Pigott not out	23		
†P. Moores c Thorne b Asif Din	8		
A. R. Clarke st Tedstone b Asif Din	4		
R. A. Bunting c Thorne b Asif Din	6		
B 8, l-b 19, n-b 1	28	B 2, l-b 9, w 2	13
1/10 2/49 3/224 4/236 5/255 6/261 7/270 8/280 9/300	(9 wkts dec.) 300	1/6 2/106 3/113	(3 wkts dec.) 259

A. M. Babington did not bat.

Bonus points – Sussex 3, Warwickshire 3 (Score at 100 overs: 287-8).

Bowling: *First Innings*—Small 21–6–67–1; Merrick 9.2–1–30–0; Munton 23.4–2–53–2; Gifford 34–10–66–3; Asif Din 15–2–57–3. *Second Innings*—Small 6–0–31–1; Munton 7–1–22–0; Gifford 11–1–46–1; Asif Din 17–5–43–0; Lloyd 11–0–58–0; Storie 6–2–20–0; Myles 6–0–28–0.

Warwickshire

A. C. Storie c Gould b Pigott	7	– (2) c Gould b Bunting	15
. D. Ratcliffe c Moores b Pigott	16	– (1) c Green b Pigott	6
Asif Din c Babington b Clarke	84	– c Babington b Bunting	8
T. A. Lloyd c Gould b Babington	19	– c and b Bunting	1
D. A. Thorne c Moores b Bunting	50	– c Parker b Bunting	5
. D. Myles lbw b Pigott	16	– c Moores b Pigott	13
G. A. Tedstone run out	50	– lbw b Babington	17
G. C. Small b Pigott	29	– lbw b Babington	0
. A. Merrick not out	3	– c Pigott b Bunting	16
. A. Munton not out	15	– c Gould b Pigott	4
N. Gifford (did not bat)		– not out	0
B 1, l-b 9, w 2, n-b 2	14	B 6, l-b 3, w 1, n-b 1	11
1/18 2/35 3/73 4/118 5/144 6/218 7/273 8/288	(8 wkts dec.) 303	1/17 2/25 3/27 4/34 5/41 6/62 7/62 8/86 9/92	96

Bonus points – Warwickshire 4, Sussex 3.

In the first innings Asif Din, when 22, retired ill at 50 and resumed at 144.

Bowling: *First Innings*—Pigott 23–2–96–4; Bunting 17–2–47–1; Clarke 29–9–85–1; Babington 16–3–29–1; C. M. Wells 7–0–21–0; Green 7–1–15–0. *Second Innings*—Pigott 11.4–1–27–3; Bunting 14–4–44–5; Clarke 5–1–9–0; Green 4–3–1–0; Babington 4–3–6–2.

Umpires: B. Leadbeater and B. J. Meyer.

At Maidstone, August 25, 26, 27, 29. SUSSEX beat KENT by 63 runs.

SUSSEX v MIDDLESEX

At Hove, August 30, 31, September 1, 2. Drawn. Sussex 3 pts, Middlesex 5 pts. Toss: Middlesex. A strange and disappointing match was ruined as a spectacle, and indeed as a contest, by the loss of all the third day to rain and the unwillingness of both captains to risk defeat in the pursuit of victory. Middlesex's 471 for nine, in 160 overs, owed much to Butcher's 134 from 196 balls (three sixes, fifteen fours), a promising 66 from Ramprakash – with whom Butcher added 155 in 38 overs – and an entertaining 73 from 78 balls by Emburey. The England off-spinner, who had arrived from the Lord's Test match at tea on the first afternoon, hit four sixes, two of them over extra cover, and four fours. The Sussex reply took until 5.10 p.m. on the fourth day. Green, facing 147 balls for his 52, made a welcome return to form, and Colin Wells's unbeaten 86 included two sixes and eight fours. Middlesex's seventeen-year-old left-arm spinner, Barnett, conceded just 65 runs from 27 overs in an impressive début. There was just time at the end for Speight, one of three wicket-keepers in the Sussex side, to take his first wicket in first-class cricket.

Close of play: First day, Middlesex 280-4 (R. O. Butcher 92*, M. R. Ramprakash 35*); Second day, Sussex 97-1 (A. M. Green 49*, P. W. G. Parker 6*); Third day, No play.

Middlesex

	First innings		Second innings	
W. N. Slack c Gould b Bunting	40			
J. D. Carr lbw b C. M. Wells	31			
*M. W. Gatting c Speight b Bunting	39			
M. A. Roseberry c Parker b Pigott	36			
R. O. Butcher c Moores b Pigott	134			
M. R. Ramprakash run out	66			
†P. R. Downton b Babington	17			
J. E. Emburey not out	73			
S. P. Hughes b Pigott	7		(1) not out	6
A. A. Barnett b Pigott	10			
A. R. C. Fraser not out	4		(2) c Gould b Speight	2
B 1, l-b 7, w 3, n-b 3	14			
1/50 2/106 3/111 4/186 5/341 6/369 7/385 8/415 9/443	(9 wkts dec.) 471	1/8		(1 wkt dec.) 8

Bonus points – Middlesex 3, Sussex 1 (Score at 100 overs: 266-4).

Bowling: *First Innings*—Pigott 40–9–139–4; Babington 37–9–88–1; Bunting 24–3–100–2; C. M. Wells 32–12–60–1; Clarke 27–8–76–0. *Second Innings*—Moores 1–0–6–0; Speigh 0.3–0–2–1.

Sussex

M. P. Speight c Slack b Emburey	27
A. M. Green c Downton b Fraser	52
*P. W. G. Parker b Gatting	32
A. P. Wells c Hughes b Emburey	16
I. J. Gould lbw b Emburey	30
C. M. Wells not out	86
A. C. S. Pigott run out	16
†P. Moores c Butcher b Fraser	12
A. R. Clarke b Hughes	[illegible]
R. A. Bunting c Butcher b Fraser	[illegible]
A. M. Babington b Roseberry	[illegible]
B 13, l-b 9, w 2, n-b 11	3
1/71 2/123 3/136 4/186 5/189 6/211 7/253 8/271 9/290	32

Bonus points – Sussex 2, Middlesex 2 (Score at 100 overs: 237-6).

Bowling: Fraser 25–6–65–3; Hughes 27–4–79–1; Gatting 11–3–23–1; Emburey 26–9–45–3 Barnett 27–9–65–0; Carr 8–2–14–0; Ramprakash 2–0–6–0; Roseberry 0.3–0–1–1.

Umpires: J. C. Balderstone and J. H. Hampshire.

SUSSEX v SURREY

At Hove, September 9, 10, 11. Surrey won by an innings and 119 runs. Surrey 24 pts, Sussex 3 pts. Toss: Surrey. With a day to spare, Surrey completed their second innings victory over Sussex in 1988. The match was a personal triumph for their left-arm spinner, Medlycott, whose second-innings and match figures were career-best returns. Surrey were always in a formidable position after scoring 553 in 170 overs. Centuries from Stewart (one six, nineteen fours) and Clinton (267 minutes, thirteen fours) dwarfed other useful contributions from Ward, Feltham, Greig and Medlycott. Clarke's five wickets were just reward for his persistance. Despite Green's 68, his highest first-class score of the summer, and a useful 47 from Gould, Sussex could not avoid the follow-on. Medlycott exploited the wearing pitch well, while Lynch, an occasional off-spinner, surprised everyone with three for 10. The Sussex second innings began in bizarre fashion. On account of the gloomy light, Stewart opened the bowling and with his first ball dismissed Speight, hit wicket – his first first-class wicket. More sound batting from Green and Gould was all Sussex could offer as Medlycott, who bowled all but seven of the overs bowled from the sea end on the third day, worked his way through the innings.

Close of play: First day, Surrey 364-4 (G. S. Clinton 137*, M. A. Feltham 10*); Second day, Sussex 144-4 (I. J. Gould 16*, A. R. Clarke 0*).

Surrey

D. J. Bicknell lbw b Babington	19
G. S. Clinton b Babington	158
A. J. Stewart c C. M. Wells b Clarke	119
M. A. Lynch c A. P. Wells b C. M. Wells	13
D. M. Ward c Parker b Babington	56
M. A. Feltham c Gould b Clarke	74
†C. J. Richards c A. P. Wells b Pigott	11
*I. A. Greig c Babington b Clarke	42
K. T. Medlycott not out	45
M. P. Bicknell b Clarke	1
M. Frost c and b Clarke	0
L-b 12, n-b 3	15
1/36 2/223 3/246 4/341 5/417 6/459 7/463 8/532 9/545	553

Bonus points – Surrey 4, Sussex 1 (Score at 100 overs: 303-3).

Bowling: Pigott 42–5–137–1; Babington 30–5–100–3; Bunting 29–5–73–0; C. M. Wells 18–2–51–1; Clarke 38–5–133–5; Green 13–1–47–0.

Sussex

M. P. Speight lbw b Greig	33	– hit wkt b Stewart	0
A. M. Green c Lynch b Medlycott	68	– c Greig b Medlycott	53
*P. W. G. Parker c Richards b Medlycott	1	– c Ward b Medlycott	24
A. P. Wells b Lynch	21	– lbw b Medlycott	9
I. J. Gould c D. J. Bicknell b Medlycott	47	– c Lynch b Medlycott	40
A. R. Clarke lbw b Medlycott	11	– (9) c Clinton b Medlycott	7
C. M. Wells c Richards b Feltham	9	– (6) c Lynch b Medlycott	13
A. C. S. Pigott c Richards b Feltham	0	– (7) not out	22
†P. Moores b Lynch	22	– (8) c Richards b Medlycott	19
R. A. Bunting not out	3	– c Lynch b Medlycott	0
A. M. Babington b Lynch	0	– c Richards b M. P. Bicknell	4
B 6, l-b 4, w 1, n-b 3	14	L-b 8, n-b 6	14
1/102 2/103 3/112 4/142 5/162 6/197 7/197 8/198 9/229	229	1/0 2/76 3/89 4/98 5/136 6/155 7/179 8/191 9/200	205

Bonus points – Sussex 2, Surrey 4.

Bowling: *First Innings*—Frost 5–1–23–0; M. P. Bicknell 22–4–65–0; Greig 12–2–34–1; Medlycott 31–16–53–4; Feltham 16–3–34–2; Lynch 5.3–1–10–3. *Second Innings*—Stewart 4–1–18–1; Medlycott 27–7–52–8; M. P. Bicknell 7.4–1–23–1; Frost 6–0–28–0; Lynch 14–5–40–0; Feltham 8–0–36–0.

Umpires: J. H. Harris and K. J. Lyons.

At Southampton, September 14, 15, 16, 17. SUSSEX lost to HAMPSHIRE by four wickets.

WARWICKSHIRE

President: The Earl of Aylesford
Chairman: R. J. Evans
Chairman, Cricket Committee: M. J. K. Smith
Secretary: D. M. W. Heath
County Ground, Edgbaston,
Birmingham B5 7QU
(Telephone: 021-440 4292)
Cricket Manager/Coach: R. M. H. Cottam
Captain: T. A. Lloyd

Their committee having narrowly survived a vote of no confidence at a Special General Meeting the previous November, Warwickshire began the 1988 season with a new club chairman, captain and coach. These were sweeping changes, but if results are anything to go by, they were effective ones. A much improved performance on the field saw Warwickshire advance from fifteenth in 1987 to a creditable sixth in the Britannic Assurance Championship and from seventeenth to tenth in the Refuge Assurance League. Perhaps the best indicator of the new attitude at Edgbaston was their record in the major county competitions: fifteen wins from 43 games in 1988 compared with eight from 43 games the previous year.

The encouraging resurgence in the playing fortunes, brought about by the enthusiastic approach of the new captain, Andy Lloyd, came frustratingly close to tangible success in the Championship. In addition to their six wins, five close finishes all went against Warwickshire. The biggest disappointment, early in the season, was losing to Northamptonshire by 6 runs after enforcing the follow-on and needing only 119 to win. Subsequent failures to capture the last wicket in the fixtures against Somerset and Leicestershire, a 4-run defeat by Glamorgan, and an 11-run shortfall against Somerset in their last match of the season combined to keep Warwickshire out of the prizemoney by just twelve points. They were fourth in the table at the beginning of September, but their nearest rivals, Surrey and Nottinghamshire, both had a game in hand.

Warwickshire's welcome success was built around the penetrative new-ball attack of Gladstone Small and Tony Merrick on the most helpful pitches seen at Edgbaston since the war. Only the champions, Worcestershire, finished with more bowling bonus points. Small lost fitness and form after the Lord's Test against West Indies in mid-June but rallied magnificently to complete his best season with ball and bat. His 80 first-class wickets at 20.06 apiece took him past 500 in his career, and the three half-centuries he scored in his 554 runs, at an average per innings of 25.18, emphasised how close he was to becoming a genuine all-rounder. Merrick finished with 64 wickets from fifteen Championship matches, but his occasional waywardness – he conceded 3.02 runs per over in the Championship compared with Small's 2.5 – lent weight to the view that the other overseas fast bowler, Allan Donald, might have played more than six games.

Of the supporting seam bowlers, Tim Munton's 46 wickets underlined his steady progress, but the new signing, Dermot Reeve, had a moderate first season. Troubled by a shoulder injury, he bowled only 292 overs in sixteen Championship games for his 24 wickets at 31.25 each.

The poorly prepared pitches around the country, with Edgbaston sadly not exempt from criticism, meant a light work-load for the spinners, Norman Gifford and Adrian Pierson, who bowled only 571 Championship overs between them for 40 wickets. Gifford's long career came to a close in the last home match of the season against Somerset, with his 2,068th and final wicket being that of another England slow bowler, Vic Marks. In a career spanning 29 years and 710 first-class matches, he is one of only ten bowlers to take more than 2,000 wickets since 1945, with the final one putting him level with F. E. Woolley in 27th position in the all-time list of wicket-takers.

Much was expected of Alvin Kallicharran after he had been forced to miss the whole of 1987. But a poor start to the summer, followed by a finger injury, resulted in such a disappointing season for the former West Indian batsman, now England-qualified, that he passed 50 only twice in fourteen Championship innings which yielded 301 runs. With Geoff Humpage losing form so badly that he could manage only 397 runs from 25 Championship innings, the Warwickshire batting, therefore, depended heavily on Lloyd, who responded well with four hundreds in his 1,439 runs. Asif Din was the only other batsman to reach 1,000 runs, however, and so it was not surprising that Warwickshire suffered from a crucial shortage of runs. Nor could this be explained away solely by the poor pitches.

Andy Moles, after a prolific winter for Griqualand West in South Africa, fell away, while the potential of Paul Smith and David Thorne remained unfulfilled. Other than Asif Din and Lloyd, only Moles averaged more than 30, and the time is rapidly approaching when either the younger players must shoulder greater responsibility or make way for other batsmen. Hand injuries to Kallicharran, Moles and Reeve disrupted the side, but was it really essential for Warwickshire to select as many as 22 players in the Championship campaign? Among these were the former Worcestershire batsman, David Banks, a new signing, and the Taunton School wicket-keeper, Piran Holloway.

The batting weaknesses were exposed in the Refuge Assurance League, in which Warwickshire scored an aggregate of 2,360 runs in their fourteen completed matches. They could exceed 200 only four times, although scores of 133 for four and 110 for three against Essex and Leicestershire respectively were winning totals. Having qualified for the quarter-finals of the Benson and Hedges Cup, the side was no match for Essex at Chelmsford, and another hot-bed of one-day cricket, Canterbury, brought about their second-round exit from the NatWest Bank Trophy after they had scored 144 on a tricky but far from difficult pitch.

On balance, 1988 was a successful season. But the departure of Gifford, the loss of form by Humpage, and the brittle middle-order batting does threaten major problems in the near future. If last season is anything to go by, there is much too much reliance on the new-ball bowling. – Jack Bannister.

WARWICKSHIRE 1988

[*Bill Smith*

Back row: G. A. Tedstone, G. D. Hodgson, R. S. Weir, G. P. Williamson, N. M. K. Smith, J. E. Benjamin, S. J. Green, A. J. Moles, O. Chagar. *Middle row:* Asif Din, D. A. Reeve, G. J. Parsons, A. R. K. Pierson, T. A. Munton, J. D. Ratcliffe, R. D. O. Earl, D. A. Thorne, E. T. Milburn, A. C. Storie. *Front row:* R. N. Abberley (*youth coach*), G. C. Small, G. W. Humpage, T. A. Lloyd (*captain*), R. M. H. Cottam (*cricket manager/coach*), N. Gifford, A. I. Kallicharran, P. A. Smith.

WARWICKSHIRE RESULTS

All first-class matches – Played 24: Won 6, Lost 8, Drawn 10.
County Championship matches – Played 22: Won 6, Lost 8, Drawn 8.
Bonus points – Batting 48, Bowling 74.
Competition placings – Britannic Assurance County Championship, 6th; NatWest Bank Trophy, 2nd round; Benson and Hedges Cup, q-f; Refuge Assurance League, 10th equal.

BRITANNIC ASSURANCE CHAMPIONSHIP AVERAGES

BATTING

	Birthplace	*M*	*I*	*NO*	*R*	*HI*	*Avge*
‡T. A. Lloyd	*Oswestry*	22	41	2	1,439	160*	36.89
‡Asif Din	*Kampala, Uganda*	21	39	3	1,208	131	33.55
‡A. J. Moles	*Solihull*	17	30	2	873	115	31.17
‡G. C. Small	*St George, Barbados*	17	26	5	521	70	24.80
D. A. Thorne	*Coventry*	14	24	1	561	76	24.39
‡P. A. Smith	*Jesmond*	15	27	4	542	84*	23.56
D. A. Reeve	*Kowloon, Hong Kong*	16	23	3	431	103	21.55
‡A. I. Kallicharran	*Paidama, BG*	8	14	0	301	63	21.50
‡G. J. Parsons	*Slough*	8	12	3	174	52	19.33
D. A. Banks	*Pensnett*	6	8	1	134	47	19.14
G. A. Tedstone	*Southport*	4	8	0	151	50	18.87
A. C. Storie	*Bishopbriggs, Glasgow*	8	16	2	233	68	16.64
‡G. W. Humpage	*Birmingham*	15	25	1	397	80	16.54
S. D. Myles	*Mansfield*	3	6	0	90	39	15.00
§‡T. A. Merrick	*St John's, Antigua*	15	21	3	256	34	14.22
A. R. K. Pierson	*Enfield*	8	12	7	57	18*	11.40
§A. A. Donald	*Bloemfontein, SA*	6	10	3	74	29	10.57
T. A. Munton	*Melton Mowbray*	16	22	7	131	24*	8.73
P. C. L. Holloway	*Helston*	3	5	0	40	16	8.00
J. D. Ratcliffe	*Solihull*	2	4	0	31	16	7.75
‡N. Gifford	*Ulverston*	17	25	11	104	23*	7.42

Also batted: S. J. Green (*Bloxwich*) (1 match) 0, 28.

* *Signifies not out.* ‡ *Denotes county cap.* § *Not qualified for England.*

The following played a total of seven three-figure innings for Warwickshire in County Championship matches – T. A. Lloyd 4, Asif Din 1, A. J. Moles 1, D. A. Reeve 1.

BOWLING

	O	*M*	*R*	*W*	*BB*	*5W/i*	*Avge*
G. C. Small	550.2	146	1,380	75	7-15	8	18.40
A. A. Donald	167.4	36	507	26	5-57	1	19.50
T. A. Merrick	468	104	1,416	64	6-29	5	22.12
T. A. Munton	425.1	126	1,047	46	6-21	2	22.76
P. A. Smith	157.3	20	525	22	3-7	0	23.86
G. J. Parsons	203	61	513	21	3-17	0	24.42
D. A. Reeve	292	71	750	24	4-50	0	31.25
N. Gifford	422.1	120	971	31	3-66	0	31.32

Also bowled: Asif Din 91–16–326–6; G. W. Humpage 3–0–10–0; T. A. Lloyd 31–1–208–2; . D. Myles 6–0–28–0; A. R. K. Pierson 148.5–35–431–9; A. C. Storie 6–2–20–0; D. A. Thorne 3–0–11–0.

Wicket-keepers: G. W. Humpage 52 ct, 1 st; P. C. L. Holloway 8 ct, 1 st; G. A. Tedstone ct, 1 st.

Leading Fielders: Asif Din 18, D. A. Thorne 17.

At Cambridge, April 20, 21, 22. WARWICKSHIRE drew with CAMBRIDGE UNIVERSITY.

At Manchester, April 28, 29, 30, May 2. WARWICKSHIRE drew with LANCASHIRE.

WARWICKSHIRE v YORKSHIRE

At Birmingham, May 5, 6, 7. Warwickshire won by seven wickets. Warwickshire 22 pts, Yorkshire 5 pts. Toss: Warwickshire. The home county outplayed Yorkshire on a slow seamer's pitch to win with more than a day to spare. With Small and Warwickshire's new signing, Reeve, reducing the visitors to 50 for five, Lloyd's decision to field first was soon justified. Bairstow and Carrick gave the Yorkshire total a degree of respectability by putting on 106 for the sixth wicket with some attacking batting. Yorkshire struck back before the close, but next day Humpage anchored the Warwickshire reply with a splendid 80 (one six, thirteen fours) from 155 deliveries. When Yorkshire batted again, Small achieved his first ten-wicket match return, and then Asif Din's unbeaten 62 ensured that Warwickshire were not troubled in completing their first Championship victory of the season.

Close of play: First day, Warwickshire 50-4 (A. I. Kallicharran 2*, G. W. Humpage 0*); Second day, Yorkshire 122-6 (P. E. Robinson 36*, P. Carrick 6*).

Yorkshire

M. D. Moxon c Humpage b Reeve	21	– c Asif Din b Small	16
A. A. Metcalfe c Humpage b Small	3	– c Humpage b Merrick	29
R. J. Blakey c Humpage b Small	14	– c Reeve b Merrick	5
J. D. Love lbw b Parsons	0	– lbw b Small	21
P. E. Robinson lbw b Reeve	2	– c Humpage b Small	36
†D. L. Bairstow c Humpage b Small	68	– c Moles b Small	1
*P. Carrick c Humpage b Reeve	64	– (8) not out	28
A. Sidebottom c Asif Din b Small	0	– (9) b Merrick	1
P. J. Hartley b Reeve	4	– (10) b Merrick	11
P. W. Jarvis lbw b Small	1	– (11) c Kallicharran b Parsons	13
C. Shaw not out	2	– (7) c Kallicharran b Small	0
B 1, l-b 8, n-b 6	15	L-b 11, n-b 3	14
1/10 2/33 3/36 4/46 5/50 6/156 7/156 8/171 9/182	194	1/16 2/53 3/56 4/105 5/111 6/111 7/126 8/131 9/156	175

Bonus points – Yorkshire 1, Warwickshire 4.

Bowling: *First Innings*—Small 23–10–29–5; Merrick 15–2–40–0; Parsons 22–8–52–1; Reeve 16.5–5–50–4; Smith 3–0–13–0; Gifford 2–1–1–0. *Second Innings*—Small 22–7–55–5; Merrick 23–5–77–4; Reeve 10–5–9–0; Parsons 12.3–4–23–1.

Warwickshire

*T. A. Lloyd c Moxon b Hartley	22	– c Moxon b Hartley	39
A. J. Moles lbw b Sidebottom	5	– lbw b Jarvis	11
Asif Din lbw b Hartley	4	– not out	62
A. I. Kallicharran lbw b Sidebottom	37	– lbw b Hartley	0
G. J. Parsons b Shaw	10		
†G. W. Humpage b Jarvis	80	– (5) not out	22
P. A. Smith c Hartley b Jarvis	31		
D. A. Reeve lbw b Jarvis	0		
G. C. Small c Love b Hartley	22		
T. A. Merrick b Sidebottom	8		
N. Gifford not out	0		
B 9, l-b 3, n-b 4	16	L-b 1	1
1/23 2/30 3/37 4/50 5/133 6/179 7/181 8/204 9/235	235	1/39 2/62 3/64	(3 wkts) 135

Bonus points – Warwickshire 2, Yorkshire 4.

Bowling: *First Innings*—Jarvis 20–8–38–3; Sidebottom 27–11–56–3; Hartley 23–7–69–3; Shaw 16–6–45–1; Carrick 2–0–15–0. *Second Innings*—Jarvis 13–3–40–1; Sidebottom 3–1–13–0; Hartley 10–1–40–2; Shaw 9–2–31–0; Moxon 2–0–8–0; Metcalfe 0.5–0–2–0.

Umpires: K. J. Lyons and D. R. Shepherd.

At Northampton, May 17, 18, 19, 20. WARWICKSHIRE lost to NORTHAMPTONSHIRE by 6 runs.

WARWICKSHIRE v ESSEX

At Birmingham, May 21, 23, 24. Warwickshire won by five wickets. Warwickshire 21 pts, Essex 5 pts. Toss: Warwickshire. Another green pitch allowed the seam bowlers to dominate throughout the match. Sixteen wickets fell on the opening day, when Border was unable to continue and needed stitches after being struck on the left side of the head by Merrick. Warwickshire's first innings lasted 38 deliveries fewer than Essex's, and when Essex were only 83 runs ahead with five wickets down, it did not look as if the match would enter the third day. However, Border, batting bravely, added 140 in 148 minutes with Fletcher to tilt the balance in Essex's favour; his 112 in 225 minutes came from 193 balls and included ten fours. Warwickshire were left requiring the highest score of the match, 254, on the final day. Lloyd (134 balls) and Moles gave them confidence with a century opening stand, Asif Din batted attractively while adding 70 with his captain, and Warwickshire emerged victors shortly after tea.

Close of play: First day, Warwickshire 118-7 (D. A. Reeve 19*, T. A. Merrick 8*); Second day, Essex 247.

Essex

B. R. Hardie c Humpage b Parsons	2	– (5) c Humpage b Munton	4
J. P. Stephenson lbw b Munton	32	– (1) lbw b Merrick	3
P. J. Prichard c Humpage b Merrick	29	– c Kallicharran b Parsons	0
A. R. Border retired hurt	4	– c Reeve b Merrick	112
A. W. Lilley b Merrick	0	– (6) lbw b Parsons	22
*K. W. R. Fletcher c Humpage b Merrick	7	– (7) c Humpage b Munton	57
†D. E. East c and b Merrick	15	– (2) c Asif Din b Merrick	9
I. L. Pont c Moles b Smith	29	– run out	16
T. D. Topley c Humpage b Smith	16	– c Moles b Munton	1
J. K. Lever c Humpage b Smith	6	– b Smith	5
J. H. Childs not out	2	– not out	0
B 1, l-b 12, n-b 11	24	L-b 12, w 1, n-b 5	18
1/7 2/46 3/76 4/84 5/94 6/110 7/145 8/158 9/166	166	1/11 2/12 3/12 4/42 5/77 6/217 7/227 8/228 9/247	247

Bonus points – Essex 1, Warwickshire 4.

Bowling: *First Innings*—Merrick 20–6–39–4; Parsons 12–3–48–1; Munton 16–2–47–1; Reeve 4–2–12–0; Smith 5.3–1–7–3. *Second Innings*—Merrick 26–7–72–3; Parsons 11–4–25–2; Munton 19–3–62–3; Smith 7.1–0–45–1; Reeve 12–2–31–0.

Warwickshire

A. J. Moles c East b Lever	30	– c Hardie b Lever	41
*T. A. Lloyd c sub b Topley	18	– c East b Pont	86
Asif Din c East b Lever	2	– c East b Pont	33
A. I. Kallicharran b Lever	6	– lbw b Topley	24
†G. W. Humpage c Hardie b Topley	22	– c East b Pont	14
P. A. Smith c East b Pont	0	– not out	32
D. A. Reeve b Topley	36	– not out	2
G. J. Parsons lbw b Topley	4		
T. A. Merrick c Fletcher b Pont	24		
T. A. Munton c Fletcher b Pont	0		
N. Gifford not out	6		
L-b 6, w 1, n-b 5	12	B 1, l-b 9, w 4, n-b 8	22
1/46 2/54 3/57 4/70 5/71 6/92 7/110 8/147 9/147	160	1/106 2/176 3/178 4/204 5/232	(5 wkts) 254

Bonus points – Warwickshire 1, Essex 4.

Bowling: *First Innings*—Lever 16–5–32–3; Pont 17–1–65–3; Topley 18.1–1–57–4. *Second Innings*—Lever 15–4–48–1; Topley 22.1–4–71–1; Pont 20–1–104–3; Childs 10–3–21–0.

Umpires: J. Birkenshaw and B. Dudleston.

WARWICKSHIRE v NOTTINGHAMSHIRE

At Birmingham, June 4, 6, 7. Warwickshire won by 161 runs. Warwickshire 22 pts, Nottinghamshire 5 pts. Toss: Nottinghamshire. Three declarations left Nottinghamshire to score 206 in a minimum of 49 overs, but on a pitch where the bounce was uncertain, and without Robinson, they were no match for Small. As the England seam bowler returned career-best figures of seven for 15, Nottinghamshire plunged to the lowest score of the season in 87 minutes, losing their last seven wickets for 12 runs. Only Newell survived; his 10 not out was the sixth-lowest score by a player carrying his bat. Half-centuries from Storie and Humpage, plus valuable contributions from Smith, Reeve and Small, had helped the home side establish a good position after rain had robbed the first day of almost three hours' play. Robinson suffered a broken finger from a ball from Smith and, Randall apart, the Nottinghamshire batsmen did not find the going easy. Nevertheless, nothing that had gone before gave any indication of the dramatic collapse that brought Warwickshire their third successive home win.

Close of play: First day, Warwickshire 185-4 (A. C. Storie 56*, P. A. Smith 35*); Second day, Nottinghamshire 146-5 (D. W. Randall 34*, C. W. Scott 0*).

Warwickshire

A. J. Moles c Scott b Cooper	5	– c Pollard b Cooper	27
*T. A. Lloyd c Newell b Cairns	11	– c Hemmings b Cooper	29
Asif Din b Cairns	6	– c Birch b Cooper	14
A. C. Storie c Newell b Cooper	68	– not out	9
†G. W. Humpage c Saxelby b Cairns	58	– st Scott b Hemmings	22
P. A. Smith lbw b Cairns	38	– not out	0
D. A. Reeve lbw b Cooper	24		
G. C. Small not out	45		
T. A. Merrick lbw b Hemmings	19		
T. A. Munton not out	4		
B 3, l-b 11, w 3, n-b 5	22	B 5, l-b 5	10
1/17 2/25 3/38 4/124 5/190 6/228 7/229 8/288	(8 wkts dec.) 300	1/58 2/63 3/77 4/106	(4 wkts dec.) 111

N. Gifford did not bat.

Bonus points – Warwickshire 4, Nottinghamshire 3.

Nottinghamshire

P. Pollard lbw b Reeve	28	– lbw b Small 6
M. Newell c Smith b Small	18	– not out 10
*R. T. Robinson retired hurt	23	– absent injured
P. Johnson c Humpage b Small	18	– hit wkt b Merrick 19
D. W. Randall not out	69	– b Small 1
J. D. Birch c Humpage b Munton	3	– b Small 1
C. L. Cairns c Asif Din b Merrick	7	– b Smith 0
†C. W. Scott c Reeve b Gifford	22	– (3) b Small 0
E. E. Hemmings not out	1	– (8) lbw b Small 1
K. E. Cooper (did not bat)		– (9) c Humpage b Small 3
K. Saxelby (did not bat)		– (10) c Asif Din b Small 0
B 1, l-b 9, w 3, n-b 4	17	L-b 1, n-b 2 3
1/54 2/69 3/95 4/110 5/127 6/203 (6 wkts dec.)	206	1/7 2/7 3/32 4/33 5/38 6/39 7/40 8/44 9/44 44

Bonus points – Nottinghamshire 2, Warwickshire 2.

Bowling: *First Innings*—Merrick 23–8–55–1; Small 21–7–33–2; Munton 13–5–29–1; Reeve 23–8–52–1; Smith 6–2–11–0; Gifford 4–0–16–1. *Second Innings*—Small 11.2–5–15–7; Merrick 5–0–23–1; Reeve 3–0–3–0; Smith 3–1–2–1.

Umpires: M. J. Kitchen and A. G. T. Whitehead.

At Bath, June 11, 13, 14. WARWICKSHIRE drew with SOMERSET.

At Leeds, June 15, 16, 17. WARWICKSHIRE beat YORKSHIRE by seven wickets.

WARWICKSHIRE v KENT

At Birmingham, June 18, 20. Kent won by an innings and 46 runs. Kent 23 pts, Warwickshire 2 pts. Toss: Warwickshire. Little went right for Warwickshire from the time Lloyd won the toss and put Kent in. Missing the usual new-ball pairing of Merrick and Small, their attack failed to exploit another helpful pitch; catches were dropped, with Tavaré benefiting when still in single figures and twice after he had passed 50; and in both innings they had only nine batsmen. This last factor was to have a bearing on the outcome of the County Championship for it meant that Kent, although dismissing Warwickshire, qualified for only three bonus points, having taken only eight wickets. Kallicharran broke a finger while fielding on Saturday and Reeve broke a thumb during practice before the Sunday League game. Tavaré's 103 (271 minutes, eight fours) and his partnership of 169 for the sixth wicket with his captain, Cowdrey, provided the substance of the Kent innings. Kent's medium-pace attack made much more effective use of the pitch on the second day, when they twice bowled out Warwickshire. Moles batted throughout the first innings, hitting eleven fours in an unbeaten 67, as Warwickshire succumbed in a little under two and a half hours.

Close of play: First day, Kent 327.

Kent

M. R. Benson b Smith	37
N. R. Taylor lbw b Donald	6
. G. Hinks b Smith	27
C. J. Tavaré c Humpage b Parsons	103
R. F. Pienaar c Humpage b Donald	19
G. R. Cowdrey c Donald b Smith	4
C. S. Cowdrey b Gifford	78
S. A. Marsh c Humpage b Parsons	4
R. M. Ellison c Reeve b Parsons	5
C. Penn c Donald b Gifford	2
R. P. Davis not out	2
B 6, l-b 16, w 9, n-b 9	40
1/9 2/83 3/88 4/121 5/136 6/305 7/309 8/323 9/323	327

Bonus points – Kent 4, Warwickshire 2 (Score at 100 overs: 305-5).

Bowling: Donald 20–3–45–2; Munton 18–6–33–0; Reeve 19–4–90–0; Smith 22–2–58–3; Parsons 25–8–71–3; Gifford 5.5–3–8–2.

Warwickshire

*T. A. Lloyd c C. S. Cowdrey b Penn	10	– (2) c Tavaré b C. S. Cowdrey	40
A. J. Moles not out	67	– (1) c Davis b Ellison	21
Asif Din b C. S. Cowdrey	10	– b Penn	52
P. A. Smith c Tavaré b C. S. Cowdrey	1	– c and b Ellison	8
†G. W. Humpage b Ellison	0	– c Penn b Ellison	1
G. J. Parsons c and b G. R. Cowdrey	12	– lbw b C. S. Cowdrey	17
A. A. Donald c Marsh b Penn	0	– (8) not out	18
T. A. Munton c C. S. Cowdrey b Ellison	1	– (7) b C. S. Cowdrey	1
N. Gifford c Ellison b Penn	1	– b Penn	8
A. I. Kallicharran absent injured		– absent injured	
D. A. Reeve absent injured		– absent injured	
L-b 1, w 1, n-b 3	5	L-b 1, w 7	8
1/14 2/40 3/45 4/58 5/100 6/101 7/104 8/107	107	1/34 2/84 3/98 4/104 5/141 6/142 7/157 8/174	174

Bonus points – Kent 3.

Bowling: *First Innings*—Ellison 12–2–38–2; Penn 12.5–4–32–3; C. S. Cowdrey 10–1–31–2; G. R. Cowdrey 3–2–5–1. *Second Innings*—Ellison 14–3–56–3; Penn 17.4–3–55–2; Pienaar 5–1–14–0; C. S. Cowdrey 10–2–48–3.

Umpires: J. W. Holder and N. T. Plews.

WARWICKSHIRE v LANCASHIRE

At Nuneaton, June 29, 30. July 1. Lancashire won by six wickets. Lancashire 22 pts, Warwickshire 6 pts. Toss: Lancashire. Moles hit his first hundred of the season to frustrate Lancashire, who had put Warwickshire in on a slow, seaming pitch. The opener's 115 came off 218 deliveries in a stay of 277 minutes and he hit sixteen fours; but a remarkable collapse in which five wickets fell at 222 saw the benefits of his innings eroded. Although good bowling by Small and Munton earned Warwickshire a narrow lead, Wasim Akram and Watkinson broke through before the close, and Watkinson's sustained spell of medium-pace bowling on the final day ensured that Lancashire required only 151 with 62 overs in which to score the runs. With Mendis hitting nine fours in his unbeaten 56, and attacking innings coming from Jesty and Fairbrother, Lancashire raced to victory in half the time.

Close of play: First day, Lancashire 51-1 (G. Fowler 21*, W. K. Hegg 0*); Second day, Warwickshire 64-4 (A. C. Storie 30*, T. A. Munton 0*).

Warwickshire

A. J. Moles c Hegg b Hayhurst	115	– (2) c Mendis b Watkinson	17
*T. A. Lloyd lbw b Simmons	39	– (7) b Watkinson	3
A. C. Storie c Hughes b Allott	6	– (1) c Hegg b Watkinson	35
†G. W. Humpage c Hegg b Wasim	21	– b Wasim	8
P. A. Smith lbw b Wasim	0	– c Fowler b Watkinson	3
D. A. Thorne c Hegg b Allott	21	– (3) c Hegg b Wasim	3
S. J. Green lbw b Hayhurst	0	– (8) lbw b Allott	28
G. C. Small c Allott b Hayhurst	0	– (9) c Mendis b Watkinson	6
T. A. Merrick c Jesty b Allott	0	– (10) c Simmons b Allott	11
T. A. Munton not out	9	– (6) c Hegg b Watkinson	3
N. Gifford c Watkinson b Hayhurst	3	– not out	4
B 2, l-b 13, w 3, n-b 2	20	L-b 3, w 2, n-b 3	8
1/96 2/123 3/160 4/160 5/222 6/222 7/222 8/222 9/222	234	1/29 2/32 3/44 4/55 5/70 6/76 7/77 8/95 9/117	129

Bonus points – Warwickshire 2, Lancashire 4.

Bowling: *First Innings*—Wasim 19–4–48–2; Allott 24–6–59–3; Watkinson 18–2–52–0; Hayhurst 17.3–2–45–4; Simmons 3–0–7–1; Jesty 4–1–8–0. *Second Innings*—Wasim 21–5–43–2; Allott 12.3–1–40–2; Watkinson 25–8–43–6.

Lancashire

	First innings		Second innings	
G. D. Mendis c Humpage b Merrick	27	– not out		56
G. Fowler c Thorne b Munton	31	– run out		5
†W. K. Hegg b Small	13			
T. E. Jesty c Gifford b Munton	12	– (3) b Munton		38
N. H. Fairbrother c Thorne b Merrick	46	– (4) c Thorne b Munton		30
A. N. Hayhurst b Munton	1	– (5) lbw b Merrick		1
M. Watkinson c Humpage b Munton	11	– (6) not out		4
*D. P. Hughes not out	23			
Wasim Akram b Small	22			
P. J. W. Allott lbw b Small	2			
J. Simmons lbw b Smith	2			
L-b 12, w 4, n-b 7	23	B 5, l-b 6, w 4, n-b 3		18
1/51 2/69 3/85 4/97 5/112 6/156 7/158 8/186 9/192	213	1/21 2/90 3/141 4/147	(4 wkts)	152

Bonus points – Lancashire 2, Warwickshire 4.

Bowling: *First Innings*—Small 26–7–59–3; Merrick 29–7–86–2; Munton 25–5–55–4; Smith 1–0–1–1. *Second Innings*—Small 8–0–32–0; Merrick 11.4–2–56–1; Smith 4–0–32–0; Munton 8–2–21–2.

Umpires: J. Birkenshaw and D. O. Oslear.

At The Oval, July 2, 4, 5. WARWICKSHIRE lost to SURREY by an innings and 43 runs.

WARWICKSHIRE v WORCESTERSHIRE

At Birmingham, July 13, 14, 15. Drawn. Warwickshire 7 pts, Worcestershire 4 pts. Toss: Worcestershire. With no play at all on the second day, and 530 minutes in all lost to the weather, both sides settled for bonus points. In this contest, Warwickshire had the better of the argument. On a pitch which offered assistance to spin and seam, albeit at a slow pace, Munton combined hostility and accuracy to return career-best figures, having begun with three for 1 from his first twelve overs. Pierson, with his off-spin, lent good support. The Warwickshire innings was a dogged effort by batsmen desperately trying to recover form, and a good crowd had a frustrating day.

Close of play: First day, Warwickshire 16-0 (T. A. Lloyd 13*, A. J. Moles 1*); Second day, No play.

Worcestershire

	First innings		Second innings	
T. S. Curtis b Pierson	26	– not out		5
S. J. O'Shaughnessy c Thorne b Smith	4			
G. A. Hick b Pierson	23			
*P. A. Neale b Pierson	1			
M. J. Weston c Holloway b Munton	1			
D. A. Leatherdale b Munton	12			
†S. J. Rhodes c Asif Din b Munton	1			
P. J. Newport b Munton	1			
R. K. Illingworth c Holloway b Munton	13	– (2) not out		8
N. V. Radford not out	13			
G. R. Dilley c Moles b Munton	17			
L-b 14, w 4	18	N-b 1		1
1/39 2/68 3/69 4/70 5/70 6/79 7/81 8/95 9/108	130		(no wkt)	14

Bonus points – Warwickshire 4.

Bowling: *First Innings*—Small 11–3–32–0; Merrick 8–3–12–0; Pierson 20–8–33–3; Smith 4–0–18–1; Munton 19–12–21–6. *Second Innings*—Small 4–1–11–0; Merrick 4–2–3–0.

Warwickshire

*T. A. Lloyd lbw b Newport	46
A. J. Moles c Rhodes b Illingworth	42
Asif Din lbw b Illingworth	14
D. A. Banks c and b Hick	47
D. A. Thorne c and b Weston	36
P. A. Smith c and b Weston	20
†P. C. L. Holloway c O'Shaughnessy b Hick	2
G. C. Small lbw b Weston	1
T. A. Merrick not out	23
T. A. Munton b Weston	0
A. R. K. Pierson not out	5
B 1, l-b 7, n-b 6	14
1/65 2/86 3/126 4/179 5/206 6/217 7/219 8/220 9/221	(9 wkts dec.) 250

Bonus points – Warwickshire 3, Worcestershire 4.

Bowling: Dilley 8–1–25–0; Radford 18–2–55–0; Newport 9–3–24–1; Illingworth 30.2–7–58–2; Hick 20–4–56–2; Weston 10–0–24–4.

Umpires: H. D. Bird and B. Dudleston.

WARWICKSHIRE v HAMPSHIRE

At Birmingham, July 16, 18, 19. Warwickshire won by an innings and 21 runs. Warwickshire 24 pts, Hampshire 1 pt. Toss: Warwickshire. Only seventeen overs were possible on the first day, but Warwickshire had sufficient time to achieve their fifth Championship victory of the season. The West Indian fast bowler, Merrick, a fearsome prospect on another untrustworthy Edgbaston pitch, was their matchwinner with ten wickets for 69 from 35.1 overs. Only the Smith brothers played him with any confidence. On Monday, Lloyd and Moles enforced the advantage with an opening partnership of 203. Lloyd's unbeaten 160, his best of the summer, came from 228 deliveries in a stay of 266 minutes, during which he hit seventeen fours. By the close Merrick had decided Hampshire's fate.

Close of play: First day, Hampshire 63-4 (R. A. Smith 6*, J. R. Ayling 0*); Second day, Hampshire 9-3 (C. L. Smith 2*, R. A. Smith 0*).

Hampshire

V. P. Terry b Small	26	– lbw b Merrick	5
C. L. Smith lbw b Merrick	21	– c Munton b Reeve	46
*M. C. J. Nicholas c Humpage b Merrick	3	– (4) b Merrick	0
R. A. Smith lbw b Small	14	– (5) b Small	32
D. R. Turner c Banks b Merrick	1	– (6) c Humpage b Merrick	22
J. R. Ayling b Merrick	7	– (7) c Humpage b Munton	26
S. T. Jefferies c Humpage b Munton	13	– (8) c Lloyd b Munton	14
†R. J. Parks lbw b Merrick	3	– (9) lbw b Munton	2
T. M. Tremlett c Banks b Merrick	15	– (10) not out	4
R. J. Maru lbw b Munton	2	– (3) c Banks b Merrick	0
C. A. Connor not out	7	– c Merrick b Small	0
L-b 3, w 2, n-b 5	10	L-b 2, w 1, n-b 3	6
1/35 2/52 3/56 4/62 5/77 6/79 7/87 8/100 9/108	122	1/9 2/9 3/9 4/75 5/111 6/111 7/133 8/145 9/156	157

Bonus points – Warwickshire 4.

Bowling: *First Innings*—Small 14–3–57–2; Merrick 19.1–7–40–6; Munton 6–0–22–2. *Second Innings*—Small 22.2–6–55–2; Merrick 16–6–29–4; Munton 19–10–34–3; Reeve 11–2–34–1; Pierson 1–0–3–0.

Warwickshire

A. J. Moles c Nicholas b Ayling 60	D. A. Thorne not out 32
*T. A. Lloyd not out 160	B 5, l-b 23, n-b 6 34
Asif Din c Nicholas b Maru 13	——
D. A. Banks c C. L. Smith b Maru 1	1/203 2/233 3/237 (3 wkts dec.) 300

†G. W. Humpage, D. A. Reeve, G. C. Small, T. A. Merrick, T. A. Munton and A. R. K. Pierson did not bat.

Bonus points – Warwickshire 4, Hampshire 1.

Bowling: Jefferies 17–1–60–0; Connor 18–1–72–0; Tremlett 14–2–44–0; Maru 12–3–44–2; Nicholas 5–0–25–0; Ayling 7–2–27–1.

Umpires: B. Dudleston and B. J. Meyer.

At Cardiff, July 20, 21, 22. WARWICKSHIRE drew with GLAMORGAN.

At Birmingham, July 23, 25, 26. WARWICKSHIRE drew with SRI LANKANS (See Sri Lankan tour section).

At Derby, July 30, August 1, 2. WARWICKSHIRE drew with DERBYSHIRE.

At Cheltenham, August 3, 4, 5. WARWICKSHIRE drew with GLOUCESTERSHIRE.

WARWICKSHIRE v NORTHAMPTONSHIRE

At Birmingham, August 6, 8, 9. Warwickshire won by six wickets. Warwickshire 23 pts, Northamptonshire 7 pts. Toss: Warwickshire. Nine wickets from Merrick spearheaded Warwickshire's second successive home win to maintain their Championship challenge. Batting was never easy on an uncertain pitch. Moles suffered a broken thumb on the first evening, and Warwickshire needed another inspiring hundred from Lloyd to hold their first innings together in the face of some hostile fast bowling from Davis on the second day. The captain's 121 included seventeen fours off 213 deliveries faced, and subsequent events proved its worth. Seventeen wickets fell after lunch as first Warwickshire were bowled out and then Merrick and Parsons routed the visitors between tea and the close.

Close of play: First day, Warwickshire 73-0 (T. A. Lloyd 44*, A. J. Moles 26*); Second day, Northamptonshire 86-9 (A. Walker 4*, M. A. Robinson 0*).

Northamptonshire

*G. Cook b Merrick	37	– c Asif Din b Merrick	6
W. Larkins c Lloyd b Merrick	49	– (7) b Merrick	2
A. Fordham lbw b Reeve	10	– (2) c Humpage b Parsons	20
D. J. Wild lbw b Reeve	0	– (3) c Humpage b Merrick	14
M. R. Gouldstone b Gifford	50	– (4) lbw b Reeve	2
N. A. Stanley c Asif Din b Reeve	14	– (5) c and b Small	5
†D. Ripley c Thorne b Small	11	– (6) b Parsons	15
N. G. B. Cook c Humpage b Merrick	9	– lbw b Merrick	0
W. W. Davis c Humpage b Merrick	9	– c Small b Parsons	8
A. Walker not out	40	– not out	10
M. A. Robinson c Humpage b Parsons	4	– b Merrick	2
B 4, l-b 12, n-b 12	28	B 4, l-b 10	14
	——		——
1/79 2/96 3/96 4/123 5/149 6/179 7/199 8/209 9/217	261	1/7 2/27 3/37 4/42 5/57 6/74 7/74 8/76 9/82	98

Bonus points – Northamptonshire 3, Warwickshire 4.

Bowling: *First Innings*—Small 19–4–51–1; Merrick 26–7–85–4; Reeve 18–2–55–3; Parsons 12.3–5–22–1; Gifford 14–6–32–1. *Second Innings*—Small 14–5–27–1; Merrick 14.2–2–26–5; Reeve 7–1–14–1; Parsons 8–3–17–3.

Warwickshire

First innings		Second innings	
A. J. Moles lbw b Walker	35		
*T. A. Lloyd c Fordham b Davis	121	(1) b Walker	11
A. C. Storie lbw b Davis	2	(2) c Ripley b Davis	7
Asif Din lbw b Robinson	26	(3) not out	31
D. A. Thorne c Ripley b Davis	8	(4) c Ripley b Davis	8
†G. W. Humpage c Ripley b Walker	2	(5) c Ripley b Walker	8
D. A. Reeve c N. G. B. Cook b Davis	1	(6) not out	15
G. J. Parsons c and b Davis	0		
G. C. Small c Gouldstone b Robinson	11		
T. A. Merrick c Gouldstone b N. G. B. Cook	34		
N. Gifford not out	1		
B 7, l-b 15, w 2, n-b 13	37	L-b 2	2
1/80 2/153 3/177 4/184 5/189 6/211 7/213 8/246 9/274	278	1/17 2/21 3/33 4/50	(4 wkts) 82

Bonus points – Warwickshire 3, Northamptonshire 4.

In the first innings A. J. Moles, when 26, retired hurt at 73 and resumed at 246; D. A. Thorne, when 7, retired hurt at 174 and resumed at 211.

Bowling: *First Innings*—Davis 27–4–76–5; Walker 23–2–86–2; Robinson 23–4–68–2; N. G. B. Cook 15.1–2–26–1. *Second Innings*—Davis 11–1–32–2; Walker 14.3–6–28–2; Robinson 6–1–13–0; N. G. B. Cook 2–1–7–0.

Umpires: J. W. Holder and A. A. Jones.

WARWICKSHIRE v LEICESTERSHIRE

At Birmingham, August 13, 15, 16. Leicestershire won by one wicket. Leicestershire 22 pts, Warwickshire 5 pts. Toss: Warwickshire. A low-scoring match produced a thrilling climax, with Leicestershire winning off the last ball with their last pair at the wicket. Afternoon rain restricted the first day to 53 overs, in which time it was evident that another Edgbaston pitch was offering over-generous help to the faster bowlers. Only Asif Din, Thorne and Myles, in his first Championship match for Warwickshire, looked like coming to terms with the demands of the conditions. The match turned on the sixth-wicket stand of 59 between the steadfast Whitaker and DeFreitas, whose 55 off 71 balls included a six and ten fours. When the home side were bowled out for 173, Leicestershire were left with 41 overs in which to score 149. Merrick made an immediate breakthrough, Briers, Gower and Whitaker provided the substance of the innings, and when Taylor was run out going for the winning run, Agnew was left with three balls from which to win the match. Off Gifford's final delivery he scampered a run to mid-wicket to do so.

Close of play: First day, Warwickshire 117-6 (S. D. Myles 15*, G. J. Parsons 6*); Second day, Warwickshire 22-0 (T. A. Lloyd 18*, A. C. Storie 3*).

Warwickshire

First innings		Second innings	
*T. A. Lloyd c Briers b DeFreitas	1	c Whitticase b DeFreitas	34
A. C. Storie lbw b DeFreitas	7	c Briers b DeFreitas	11
Asif Din c and b DeFreitas	40	run out	30
D. A. Thorne b DeFreitas	31	b Taylor	15
D. A. Reeve b Taylor	3	lbw b Taylor	0
S. D. Myles c Gower b Taylor	39	b Taylor	19
†G. A. Tedstone b Taylor	4	c Gower b Agnew	32
G. J. Parsons c Whitticase b DeFreitas	11	(9) lbw b Agnew	5
G. C. Small not out	29	(10) not out	0
T. A. Merrick lbw b Taylor	0	(8) lbw b Tennant	22
N. Gifford c Whitticase b Agnew	1	b Agnew	0
L-b 7, w 2, n-b 6	15	L-b 1, n-b 4	5
1/1 2/46 3/61 4/75 5/102 6/109 7/134 8/174 9/174	181	1/41 2/61 3/90 4/90 5/95 6/143 7/153 8/173 9/173	173

Bonus points – Warwickshire 1, Leicestershire 4.

Bowling: *First Innings*—Agnew 29.2–7–62–1; DeFreitas 32–5–74–5; Tennant 6–1–19–0; Taylor 14–5–19–4. *Second Innings*—DeFreitas 19–6–52–2; Agnew 18.4–3–65–3; Taylor 18–6–48–3; Willey 9–6–3–0; Potter 1–0–4–0; Tennant 1–1–0–1.

Leicestershire

T. J. Boon c Storie b Merrick	2	– c Reeve b Merrick	0
N. E. Briers c Storie b Merrick	0	– c Storie b Gifford	54
P. Willey c Tedstone b Reeve	37	– lbw b Merrick	3
*D. I. Gower c Storie b Small	20	– c Thorne b Reeve	20
J. J. Whitaker lbw b Merrick	27	– (7) c Thorne b Asif Din	36
L. Potter c Asif Din b Gifford	6	– (5) c Reeve b Gifford	2
P. A. J. DeFreitas c Storie b Merrick	55	– (6) c Parsons b Small	9
†P. Whitticase b Gifford	35	– run out	8
J. P. Agnew c Tedstone b Merrick	0	– not out	5
L. Tennant c Storie b Merrick	3	– (11) not out	0
L. B. Taylor not out	14	– (10) run out	2
B 2, l-b 5	7	B 4, l-b 4, w 1, n-b 1	10
1/3 2/4 3/49 4/68 5/77 6/136 7/167 8/167 9/179	206	1/0 2/13 3/69 4/74 5/84 6/106 7/129 8/143 9/148	(9 wkts) 149

Bonus points – Leicestershire 2, Warwickshire 4.

Bowling: *First Innings*—Merrick 19–4–64–6; Small 14–4–38–1; Gifford 15.1–7–32–2; Reeve 15–2–47–1; Parsons 5–0–18–0. *Second Innings*—Merrick 6–0–34–2; Small 10.2–2–30–1; Gifford 15–4–42–2; Reeve 3.4–0–8–1; Asif Din 6–0–27–1.

Umpires: R. Julian and R. Palmer.

At Hove, August 17, 18, 19. WARWICKSHIRE lost to SUSSEX by 160 runs.

At Uxbridge, August 20, 22, 23. WARWICKSHIRE lost to MIDDLESEX by seven wickets.

At Worcester, August 25, 26, 27, 29. WARWICKSHIRE drew with WORCESTERSHIRE.

WARWICKSHIRE v GLAMORGAN

At Birmingham, August 30, 31, September 1, 2. Glamorgan won by 4 runs. Glamorgan 23 pts, Warwickshire 6 pts. Toss: Glamorgan. With Thomas having a splendid all-round match, and Watkin returning career-best figures in Warwickshire's first innings, Glamorgan secured their first Championship win of the season. On the first day, Thomas hit his second first-class hundred in a fortnight to rescue his side after Donald had taken four wickets for 10 runs in seven overs; on the last, when Warwickshire needed 194 for victory, he took six wickets. For Glamorgan, having had Warwickshire 107 for nine, winning was a close-run thing, however. Small, the innings' top-scorer, and Gifford added 82 before Thomas made the final breakthrough; had they not been parted, it would have been the highest tenth-wicket stand in first-class cricket to win a match. Small, in addition to his 100 runs in the match, celebrated his return to top form with figures of twelve for 121, and Kallicharran's 63 was his Championship best in an injury-marred comeback to county cricket.

Close of play: First day, Glamorgan 268-9 (J. G. Thomas 108*, S. Bastien 35*); Second day, Glamorgan 3-0 (A. R. Butcher 1*, P. A. Cottey 1*); Third day, Glamorgan 127-8 (J. Derrick 17*, S. L. Watkin 2*).

Glamorgan

*A. R. Butcher c Holloway b Donald	11 – c Holloway b Small	11
P. A. Cottey c Small b Donald	1 – b Donald	3
M. J. Cann c Holloway b Donald	6 – c Holloway b Small	22
M. P. Maynard lbw b Small	63 – c Thorne b Small	36
G. C. Holmes lbw b Donald	0 – lbw b Small	4
J. Derrick lbw b Small	4 – b Donald	21
J. G. Thomas c and b Small	110 – b Munton	0
†C. P. Metson b Small	19 – c Asif Din b Small	1
P. D. North c Holloway b Small	7 – c Banks b Donald	21
S. L. Watkin b Small	0 – c Holloway b Small	5
S. Bastien not out	36 – not out	2
L-b 11, n-b 4	15 B 2, l-b 1, w 3, n-b 4	10
1/9 2/24 3/27 4/27 5/41 6/114 7/173 8/189 9/189	272 1/18 2/18 3/67 4/81 5/82 6/85 7/86 8/123 9/134	136

Bonus points – Glamorgan 3, Warwickshire 4.

Bowling: *First Innings*—Donald 21–4–59–4; Small 26.5–4–79–6; Munton 28–12–68–0; Smith 7–1–51–0; Gifford 1–0–4–0. *Second Innings*—Donald 15–5–51–3; Small 23.4–9–42–6; Smith 3–0–17–0; Munton 10–3–23–1; Gifford 2–2–0–0.

Warwickshire

*T. A. Lloyd c Maynard b Watkin	45 – b Thomas	10
P. A. Smith lbw b Watkin	5 – c Holmes b Thomas	1
Asif Din c North b Watkin	21 – b Derrick	33
D. A. Thorne c Maynard b Watkin	1 – lbw b Thomas	0
A. I. Kallicharran c Metson b Watkin	63 – c Metson b Derrick	18
D. A. Banks c Cann b Watkin	0 – c Cann b Derrick	1
†P. C. L. Holloway lbw b Derrick	16 – c Metson b Thomas	14
G. C. Small lbw b Watkin	31 – lbw b Thomas	69
A. A. Donald b Bastien	9 – b Derrick	7
T. A. Munton c Metson b Watkin	3 – c Metson b Thomas	6
N. Gifford not out	0 – not out	23
B 8, l-b 8, w 3, n-b 2	21 B 4, l-b 2, n-b 1	7
1/16 2/70 3/76 4/77 5/77 6/118 7/192 8/201 9/215	215 1/11 2/16 3/16 4/45 5/55 6/77 7/83 8/100 9/107	189

Bonus points – Warwickshire 2, Glamorgan 4.

Bowling: *First Innings*—Thomas 15–4–54–0; Watkin 31–10–59–8; Bastien 23–11–37–1; Derrick 20–6–48–1; North 2–2–0–0; Holmes 2–1–1–0. *Second Innings*—Watkin 17–2–55–0; Thomas 16.4–0–70–6; Bastien 6–1–11–0; Derrick 21–6–47–4.

Umpires: J. D. Bond and R. A. White.

WARWICKSHIRE v SOMERSET

At Birmingham, September 9, 10, 11, 12. Drawn. Warwickshire 4 pts, Somerset 6 pts. Toss Somerset. Half-centuries from Thorne and the admirable Small, after Lloyd and Moles had begun with 132, took Warwickshire close to their seventh win of the season. Their target, se after rain had prevented any play on the last morning, was 301 from 68 overs, and from the last ten overs 89 were needed. In the end they finished 11 runs short with Gifford, in his 710th first-class appearance, marking his retirement by playing out the last three balls from Mark to deny Somerset victory. On an easy-paced pitch, the bowlers had to work harder for thei wickets than in some earlier games at Edgbaston. Some batsmen, too, found the goin difficult, and at times the crowd had good reason for their impatience at the slow scoring

Hardy was 33 overs in scoring 23 in Somerset's second innings, when Warwickshire were handicapped by injuries which prevented Merrick and Smith from bowling. The latter had broken his index finger for the second time in five weeks while compiling his highest Championship score of the season.

Close of play: First day, Somerset 321-8 (G. D. Rose 0*); Second day, Warwickshire 184-5 (P. A. Smith 65*, P. C. L. Holloway 0*); Third day, Somerset 174-5 (N. D. Burns 46*, V. J. Marks 11*).

Somerset

First innings		Second innings	
J. J. E. Hardy b Gifford	40	st Holloway b Gifford	23
N. A. Felton b Small	17	b Small	0
J. G. Wyatt b Small	29	b Munton	26
R. J. Bartlett hit wkt b Merrick	67	b Munton	4
R. J. Harden b Smith	63	lbw b Munton	43
†N. D. Burns c Thorne b Merrick	1	not out	48
*V. J. Marks c Asif Din b Small	68	c Thorne b Gifford	11
G. D. Rose not out	37	not out	6
M. W. Cleal lbw b Smith	0		
N. A. Mallender b Munton	6		
A. N. Jones b Munton	5		
B 4, l-b 18, w 2, n-b 15	39	B 7, l-b 13, n-b 4	24
1/50 2/78 3/121 4/178 5/189 6/321 7/321 8/321 9/344	372	1/6 2/53 3/63 4/63 5/159 6/174 (6 wkts dec.)	185

Bonus points – Somerset 3, Warwickshire 2 (Score at 100 overs: 270-5).

Bowling: *First Innings*—Small 29–10–56–3; Merrick 18.5–0–95–2; Munton 21.3–7–38–2; Gifford 34–8–68–1; Smith 27–7–68–2; Asif Din 8–0–25–0. *Second Innings*—Small 18–4–26–1; Munton 29–7–50–3; Gifford 34.1–4–83–2; Asif Din 2–1–6–0.

Warwickshire

First innings		Second innings	
*T. A. Lloyd lbw b Jones	7	(2) c Burns b Marks	69
A. J. Moles c Burns b Jones	20	(1) c Burns b Jones	64
Asif Din c Burns b Cleal	23	lbw b Jones	14
D. A. Thorne c Burns b Cleal	11	c Burns b Rose	54
A. I. Kallicharran c Harden b Marks	47	lbw b Jones	8
P. A. Smith not out	84	(8) c Jones b Rose	1
†P. C. L. Holloway c Bartlett b Jones	3	(9) c Bartlett b Marks	5
G. C. Small c Harden b Mallender	22	(6) not out	56
T. A. Merrick b Marks	4	(7) lbw b Rose	0
T. A. Munton st Burns b Marks	10	b Marks	2
N. Gifford b Mallender	6	not out	0
B 12, l-b 2, w 1, n-b 5	20	L-b 12, w 1, n-b 4	17
1/8 2/37 3/58 4/66 5/181 6/198 7/207 8/223 9/231	257	1/132 2/148 3/168 4/184 5/234 6/234 7/255 8/272 9/289 (9 wkts)	290

Bonus points – Warwickshire 2, Somerset 3 (Score at 100 overs: 230-8).

In the first innings P. A. Smith, when 65, retired hurt at 184 and resumed at 231.

Bowling: *First Innings*—Mallender 18–3–42–2; Jones 21–5–45–3; Rose 13–4–28–0; Cleal 14–0–51–2; Marks 39.3–17–66–3; Harden 2–0–11–0. *Second Innings*—Jones 13–0–45–3; Rose 13–1–56–3; Marks 30–4–115–3; Cleal 9–0–42–0; Bartlett 3–0–20–0.

Umpires: J. H. Hampshire and N. T. Plews.

WORCESTERSHIRE

Patron: The Duke of Westminster
President: D. Kenyon
Chairman: C. D. Fearnley
Chairman, Cricket Committee: M. G. Jones
Secretary: M. D. Vockins
County Ground, New Road, Worcester WR2 4QQ (Telephone: 0905-422694)
Captain: P. A. Neale
Coach: B. L. D'Oliveira

It was the season Worcestershire had planned for. And but for the toss of a coin, it might have been possible to argue that, in 1988, theirs was the most successful side of modern times. Instead, exposed to batting first on an autumnal morning at Lord's, they lost the NatWest Bank Trophy final to Middlesex by three wickets, and with it the chance of an unprecedented treble. The previous Sunday, they had retained their Refuge Assurance League title, having claimed 38 of the possible 40 points from their last ten games; a fortnight later, despite an attempt to sabotage the pitch at New Road, they were the Britannic Assurance county champions. A compensatory third trophy awaited them in the new Refuge Assurance Cup, but as at Lord's they failed to overcome the early dismissal of Graeme Hick and lost to Lancashire by 52 runs. Their official winnings for the year, however, had been boosted to a record £80,000 from the five county competitions. In the Benson and Hedges Cup, they had been knocked out in the quarter-finals by Hampshire, the eventual winners.

Few counties have been as indebted to one player over the course of a season as Worcestershire were to Hick. In their final Championship match, against Glamorgan, they required 24 points to be certain of pipping Kent. It was Hick's 197 on the second day that secured maximum batting points and left the bowlers with almost two days in which to win the match. Yet Worcestershire were by no means a one-man team. Far from it.

Neal Radford and Graham Dilley started the year as England tourists; Tim Curtis and Phil Newport graduated to the Test team during the season; and Steven Rhodes's contribution was recognised with selection for the ill-fated winter tour of India. Radford's 71 wickets increased his tally in the Championship to 356 in 81 matches since his "free transfer" from Lancashire, while Dilley, although restricted by injuries and England calls to just nine Championship appearances, weighed in with 34 wickets. Newport, meanwhile, went from strength to strength. His 85 Championship wickets included five or more in an innings seven times, with a career-best eight for 52 in the win over Middlesex. Curtis passed 1,000 runs for the fifth successive season, and succeeded in occupying the crease for as long as most in the final two Tests against West Indies. His non-selection for India was viewed at New Road as yet another of the anomalies of a muddled selection process. Rhodes was second in the national wicket-keeping list with 78 first-class dismissals, including a county record-equalling nine catches against Sussex at Kidderminster. In the Sunday League, he broke J. T. Murray's thirteen-year record with 29 dismissals.

Phil Neale's contribution, in his benefit season, was a significant one, both as a respected captain and with the bat. His 1,036 first-class runs contained four hundreds, including a career-highest 167 against Sussex. Richard Illingworth, the left-arm spinner, enjoyed his best season to date, twice taking ten wickets in a match, and the long-serving Paul Pridgeon, although unable to command a regular place in the Championship side, topped the Sunday League averages with 26 wickets at just 12.58 each. Also in the Sunday competition, both Hick and Curtis scored more than 500 runs. David Leatherdale, as he showed in the NatWest final, has both the ability and temperament to strengthen the middle-order batting; only 21, he was voted the club's uncapped player of the year. Martin Weston, meanwhile, proved an adequate replacement for Ian Botham in the all-rounder's role, particularly in the limited-overs matches.

Botham appeared in just four Championship, four Refuge Assurance and three Benson and Hedges matches before announcing on May 20 that, because of a back condition, he required an operation to fuse two vertebrae. And yet, such was the depth of talent assembled at New Road, he was probably missed more by England than by Worcestershire. Nevertheless, his unavailability, combined with Damian D'Oliveira's unexpected loss of form, left a void of experienced batting in the middle order. D'Oliveira had a top score of 37 in eight Championship matches before being omitted for the rest of the season. Worcestershire also had a problem at the top of the order, where neither Gordon Lord nor Steve O'Shaughnessy could make the other opener's position his own. They generally shared the role as Curtis's partner, with Lord being preferred mostly in the Championship and O'Shaughnessy taking over in the one-day games. Lord, however, did prove his value with a crucial century on a difficult wicket in the penultimate Championship match at Bristol.

And so to Hick, whose season is chronicled in more detail earlier in this edition. Suffice it, here, to record that he scored 3,586 runs for the county in all cricket; that his first-class aggregate of 2,713 runs beat G. A. Gooch's previous record of 2,559, the highest aggregate since the Championship was reduced in 1969; and that his ten hundreds equalled G. M. Turner's record for Worcestershire in 1970. He also hit a maiden hundred in the Refuge Assurance League and two successive hundreds in the NatWest Bank Trophy. His monumental 405 not out at Taunton was the second-highest innings in the history of the County Championship and erased from the record books Turner's 311 not out against Warwickshire in 1982, the previous highest score by a Worcestershire batsman.

When the West Indians took the field at Worcester on May 28, Hick needed a further 153 runs to become the first player since Turner in 1973 to reach 1,000 runs by the end of May. He got them, from 253 balls, and went on to make 172. One man might not make a team, but no-one at New Road was prepared to suggest what Worcestershire would have achieved in 1988 without Graeme Hick. – Chris Moore.

WORCESTERSHIRE 1988

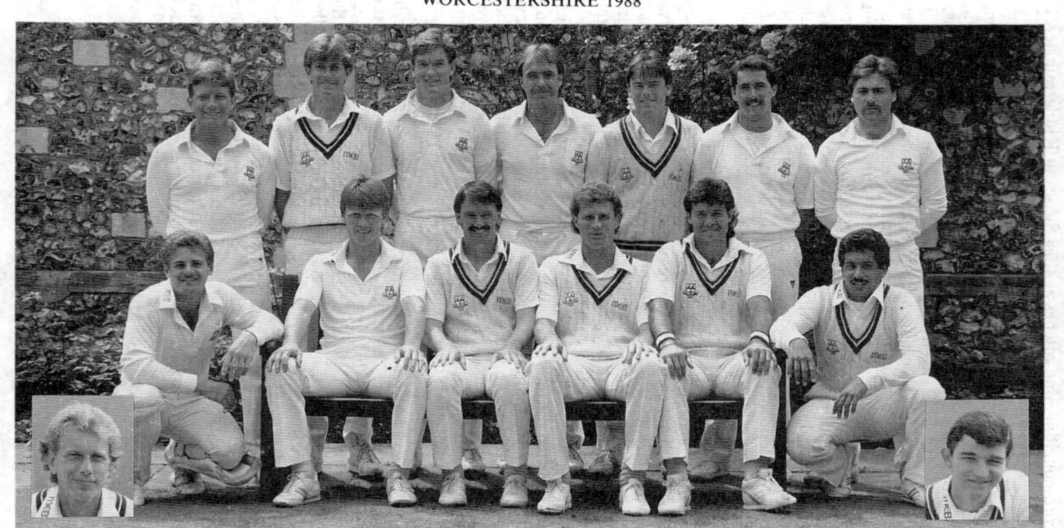

[*Bill Smith*

Back row: G. J. Lord, P. J. Newport, G. A. Hick, M. J. Weston, S. M. McEwan, R. K. Illingworth, S. J. O'Shaughnessy. *Front row:* S. J. Rhodes, T. S. Curtis, P. A. Neale (*captain*), A. P. Pridgeon, N. V. Radford, D. B. D'Oliveira. *Insets:* G. R. Dilley, D. A. Leatherdale.

WORCESTERSHIRE RESULTS

All first-class matches – Played 23: Won 10, Lost 3, Drawn 10.
County Championship matches – Played 22: Won 10, Lost 3, Drawn 9.
Bonus points – Batting 55, Bowling 75.
Competition placings – Britannic Assurance County Championship, winners; NatWest Bank Trophy, finalists; Benson and Hedges Cup, q-f; Refuge Assurance League, winners; Refuge Assurance Cup, finalists.

BRITANNIC ASSURANCE CHAMPIONSHIP AVERAGES

BATTING

	Birthplace	*M*	*I*	*NO*	*R*	*HI*	*Avge*
§‡G. A. Hick	*Salisbury, Rhodesia*	22	34	2	2,443	405*	76.34
‡T. S. Curtis	*Chislehurst*	18	31	4	1,155	131	42.77
‡P. A. Neale	*Scunthorpe*	21	31	5	1,036	167	39.84
G. J. Lord	*Birmingham*	19	32	2	862	101	28.73
‡M. J. Weston	*Worcester*	17	24	5	514	95*	27.05
‡P. J. Newport	*High Wycombe*	20	24	8	421	77*	26.31
‡S. J. Rhodes	*Bradford*	22	33	10	597	108	25.95
‡R. K. Illingworth	*Bradford*	22	22	4	404	60	22.44
‡N. V. Radford	*Luanshya, N. Rhodesia*	18	15	6	200	65	22.22
P. Bent	*Worcester*	3	6	1	111	50	22.20
D. A. Leatherdale	*Bradford*	10	15	1	255	34*	18.21
‡D. B. D'Oliveira	*Cape Town, SA*	8	11	1	132	37	13.20
‡G. R. Dilley	*Dartford*	9	8	1	89	36	12.71
R. M. Ellcock	*Bridgetown, Barbados*	4	4	1	27	13	9.00
S. J. O'Shaughnessy	*Bury*	10	17	0	133	44	7.82
‡I. T. Botham	*Heswall*	4	4	0	18	7	4.50
‡A. P. Pridgeon	*Wall Heath*	10	11	3	31	11	3.87

Also batted: S. M. McEwan (*Worcester*) (5 matches) 0*, 6.

* *Signifies not out.* ‡ *Denotes county cap.* § *Not qualified for England.*

The following played a total of seventeen three-figure innings for Worcestershire in County Championship matches – G. A. Hick 9, P. A. Neale 4, T. S. Curtis 2, G. J. Lord 1, S. J. Rhodes 1.

BOWLING

	O	*M*	*R*	*W*	*BB*	*5W/i*	*Avge*
P. J. Newport	544	117	1,640	85	8-52	7	19.29
G. R. Dilley	251	44	695	34	5-46	3	20.44
R. K. Illingworth	578.4	184	1,229	56	5-46	4	21.94
N. V. Radford	570.5	101	1,770	71	7-73	3	24.92
M. J. Weston	120	31	316	12	4-24	0	26.33
G. A. Hick	204	43	642	21	4-114	0	30.57
A. P. Pridgeon	266.3	58	662	21	3-68	0	31.52

Also bowled: I. T. Botham 43–11–125–1; T. S. Curtis 14.5–1–74–1; R. M. Ellcock 1.1–8–328–7; D. A. Leatherdale 7–3–20–1; S. M. McEwan 79–7–289–8; P. A. Neale 4–1–62–0; S. J. O'Shaughnessy 34–3–152–4.

Wicket-keeper: S. J. Rhodes 69 ct, 8 st.

Leading Fielders: G. A. Hick 27, T. S. Curtis 19, R. K. Illingworth 18.

At Manchester, April 21, 22, 23, 25. WORCESTERSHIRE beat LANCASHIRE by ten wickets.

WORCESTERSHIRE v NOTTINGHAMSHIRE

At Worcester, April 28, 29, 30. Worcestershire won by six wickets. Worcestershire 23 pts, Nottinghamshire 4 pts. Toss: Nottinghamshire. There was a certain irony in Nottinghamshire's demise on the second day when Dilley and Radford bowled them out twice on a green, untrustworthy pitch. Dilley, with a burst of four for 9 in 23 balls, precipitated the initial collapse, and then Radford weighed in with five for 29 in his second spell as Nottinghamshire were dismissed for 132 before lunch. Following on 158 in arrears, they were again given the benefit of a half-century opening stand by Broad and Robinson. But after both fell to Radford in successive overs, Dilley, generating excessive lift and movement, took four for 23 in 26 deliveries. The visitors were 155 for seven at tea, and a win inside two of the scheduled four days was on the cards until Randall, 69 off 73 balls, and Cooper helped the last three wickets produce 94 runs. Hick, with four sixes and twelve fours, had dominated the first morning's play, scoring 86 of the lunch total of 120 for one. But needing 14 runs to become the first Worcestershire batsman to hit a century in five successive Championship matches, he departed to Cooper's fourth ball of the afternoon.

Close of play: First day, Nottinghamshire 13-0 (B. C. Broad 9*, R. T. Robinson 3*); Second day, Nottinghamshire 248.

Worcestershire

T. S. Curtis c Robinson b Stephenson	34	– c Birch b Cooper	20
G. J. Lord c Newell b Cooper	1	– not out	41
G. A. Hick c Broad b Cooper	86	– c French b Stephenson	14
D. B. D'Oliveira c Birch b Cooper	4	– c Stephenson b Birch	6
S. J. O'Shaughnessy b Stephenson	44	– lbw b Cooper	1
*I. T. Botham c and b Cooper	4		
†S. J. Rhodes lbw b Cooper	17	– (6) not out	6
P. J. Newport c French b Birch	33		
R. K. Illingworth b Stephenson	9		
G. R. Dilley lbw b Stephenson	21		
N. V. Radford not out	28		
L-b 8, n-b 1	9	L-b 3, n-b 1	4
1/8 2/120 3/126 4/130 5/138 6/162 7/223 8/238 9/241	290	1/36 2/59 3/71 4/82	(4 wkts) 92

Bonus points – Worcestershire 3, Nottinghamshire 4.

Bowling: *First Innings*—Stephenson 29–7–99–4; Cooper 29–10–75–5; Saxelby 18–3–58–0; Bore 9–2–41–0; Birch 4–1–9–1. *Second Innings*—Stephenson 15–8–29–1; Saxelby 6–1–23–0; Cooper 12–4–25–2; Birch 3.1–2–12–1.

Nottinghamshire

B. C. Broad c Rhodes b Dilley	53	– c Hick b Radford	27
*R. T. Robinson b Dilley	8	– lbw b Radford	22
M. Newell c Rhodes b Dilley	1	– c Rhodes b Newport	2
P. Johnson c Newport b Dilley	7	– c Botham b Dilley	38
D. W. Randall c D'Oliveira b Radford	10	– c Hick b Dilley	69
J. D. Birch lbw b Radford	0	– b Dilley	13
F. D. Stephenson c Rhodes b Radford	8	– lbw b Dilley	0
†B. N. French c Hick b Radford	17	– c Botham b Dilley	13
K. Saxelby c Illingworth b Newport	4	– lbw b Radford	17
K. E. Cooper not out	3	– not out	33
M. K. Bore c Newport b Radford	5	– c Curtis b Newport	0
B 2, l-b 8, w 1, n-b 5	16	L-b 9, w 1, n-b 4	14
1/53 2/58 3/66 4/77 5/80 6/90 7/113 8/124 9/124	132	1/55 2/56 3/79 4/106 5/126 6/126 7/154 8/207 9/233	248

Bonus points – Worcestershire 4.

Bowling: *First Innings*—Dilley 11–0–37–4; Radford 13.2–2–55–5; Botham 4–1–14–0; Newport 7–1–16–1. *Second Innings*—Dilley 21–1–80–5; Radford 20–2–95–3; Newport 8.4–0–36–2; Botham 6–0–28–0.

Umpires: D. R. Shepherd and D. S. Thompsett.

At Taunton, May 5, 6, 7, 9. WORCESTERSHIRE beat SOMERSET by an innings and 214 runs.

WORCESTERSHIRE v SOMERSET

At Worcester, May 18, 19, 20. Somerset won by nine wickets. Somerset 24 pts, Worcestershire 6 pts. Toss: Worcestershire. Worcestershire's first defeat of the season, which cost them their place at the top of the Championship table, paled into insignificance against the announcement later that Botham required immediate surgery on his back and was likely to miss the remainder of the season. On the second day, he had just taken his first Championship wicket of the summer when he fell awkwardly, diving to stop a ball in the slips. He left the field and thereafter took no further part. Already without Dilley and Radford, who were on England duty, Worcestershire slumped to 119 all out on the final morning, leaving Somerset to score 33 runs for a victory which provided full revenge for their crushing defeat at Taunton two weeks earlier. Crowe's chanceless century in 225 minutes (thirteen fours) on a deteriorating wicket had turned the match in Somerset's favour.

Close of play: First day, Somerset 35-1 (P. M. Roebuck 7*, J. J. E. Hardy 11*); Second day, Worcestershire 52-3 (S. J. O'Shaughnessy 16*, P. A. Neale 8*).

Worcestershire

T. S. Curtis c Roebuck b Rose	70	– lbw b Foster	1
G. J. Lord c Crowe b Marks	64	– lbw b Foster	4
G. A. Hick c Hardy b Jones	8	– c Hardy b Jones	11
S. J. O'Shaughnessy c Roebuck b Foster	1	– lbw b Jones	17
*P. A. Neale b Rose	8	– c Crowe b Jones	10
I. T. Botham c Wyatt b Foster	4	– absent injured	
†S. J. Rhodes b Rose	35	– (6) b Cleal	11
P. J. Newport c Burns b Cleal	11	– (7) c Burns b Cleal	16
R. K. Illingworth c Wyatt b Foster	8	– (8) not out	12
R. M. Ellcock not out	5	– (9) c Marks b Rose	13
A. P. Pridgeon b Foster	2	– (10) c Marks b Cleal	2
L-b 11, w 2, n-b 11	24	L-b 7, w 8, n-b 7	22
1/131 2/140 3/155 4/167 5/174 6/174 7/193 8/220 9/236	240	1/7 2/15 3/21 4/56 5/66 6/83 7/90 8/117 9/119	119

Bonus points – Worcestershire 2, Somerset 4.

Bowling: *First Innings*—Jones 19–1–43–1; Foster 18.3–2–46–4; Cleal 13–2–49–1; Rose 19–5–51–3; Marks 22–6–40–1. *Second Innings*—Jones 14–3–28–3; Foster 15–6–31–2; Rose 7–1–37–1; Cleal 7.3–0–16–3.

Somerset

N. A. Felton c Illingworth b Ellcock	16	– not out	13
*P. M. Roebuck c Curtis b Botham	8	– c Rhodes b Ellcock	5
J. J. E. Hardy lbw b Newport	70	– not out	8
M. D. Crowe c Curtis b Pridgeon	132		
J. G. Wyatt c Curtis b Newport	45		
V. J. Marks c Illingworth b Newport	6		
†N. D. Burns c Rhodes b Newport	3		
G. D. Rose c and b Pridgeon	20		
M. W. Cleal c Rhodes b Ellcock	8		
A. N. Jones c Curtis b Ellcock	0		
D. J. Foster not out	0		
L-b 3, w 1, n-b 15	19	L-b 5, w 1, n-b 1	7
1/20 2/50 3/125 4/227 5/262 6/283 7/312 8/325 9/325	327	1/11	(1 wkt) 33

Bonus points – Somerset 4, Worcestershire 4.

Bowling: *First Innings*—Ellcock 21–2–86–3; Botham 18–5–40–1; Newport 24–3–97–4; Pridgeon 18.3–2–68–2; Illingworth 6–1–33–0. *Second Innings*—Ellcock 5.1–0–18–1; Pridgeon 5–1–10–0.

Umpires: B. Leadbeater and K. J. Lyons.

At Leicester, May 21, 23, 24. WORCESTERSHIRE drew with LEICESTERSHIRE.

At Worcester, May 28, 29, 30. WORCESTERSHIRE drew with WEST INDIANS (See West Indian tour section).

WORCESTERSHIRE v LANCASHIRE

At Worcester, June 1, 2, 3. Drawn. Worcestershire 4 pts, Lancashire 5 pts. Toss: Worcestershire. The TCCB's Inspector of Pitches was directed to New Road after nineteen wickets fell on the second day on a pitch which had been used for the previous week's Benson and Hedges Cup quarter-final. Worcestershire lost their last seven first-innings wickets for 50 runs in two hours and then bowled out Lancashire in their second innings for 147. As the pitch turned spiteful with its variations in bounce, batting became little more than a lottery, and a target of 218 always looked beyond Worcestershire's reach, especially once they lost Hick early on. When the rain ceased on the third day, they resumed at 47 for two with only 25 overs remaining, and a match-saving stand of 62 between Leatherdale and Weston provided the final frustration for the visitors. Newport was heading for career-best figures in Lancashire's first innings after taking four wickets in nineteen balls without conceding a run, but Wasim Akram rescued them, hitting three sixes and six fours in a half-century off only 33 balls. Allott, in turn, had a spell of four for 11 in 10.3 overs as Worcestershire were hustled out 70 runs behind.

Close of play: First day, Worcestershire 69-3 (P. A. Neale 2*, D. A. Leatherdale 1*); Second day, Worcestershire 36-2 (T. S. Curtis 16*, P. A. Neale 10*).

Lancashire

G. D. Mendis c Rhodes b Radford	17	– lbw b Radford	15
A. N. Hayhurst c Rhodes b Newport	8	– b Radford	1
T. E. Jesty b Newport	48	– c Radford b Newport	32
N. H. Fairbrother b Weston	2	– c Rhodes b McEwan	24
J. Abrahams c Rhodes b Newport	9	– b McEwan	1
M. Watkinson lbw b Newport	4	– c Rhodes b McEwan	21
*D. P. Hughes c Rhodes b Newport	1	– lbw b Radford	18
Wasim Akram c Radford b Newport	55	– b McEwan	4
†W. K. Hegg c Weston b McEwan	5	– c Lord b Newport	6
P. J. W. Allott lbw b Radford	14	– c Hick b Newport	19
J. Simmons not out	1	– not out	1
B 4, l-b 8, w 4, n-b 9	25	L-b 4, n-b 1	5
1/22 2/60 3/65 4/92 5/97 6/99 7/102 8/116 9/187	189	1/17 2/18 3/73 4/75 5/75 6/105 7/118 8/123 9/146	147

Bonus points – Lancashire 1, Worcestershire 4.

Bowling: *First Innings*—Radford 14–1–52–2; Newport 21–8–51–6; McEwan 14–2–61–1; Weston 6–2–13–1. *Second Innings*—Radford 12–1–39–3; Newport 15.5–1–61–3; McEwan 11–0–43–4.

Worcestershire

T. S. Curtis b Hayhurst	43	– b Allott	20
G. J. Lord lbw b Watkinson	21	– c Hughes b Allott	1
G. A. Hick c Abrahams b Hayhurst	0	– c Hegg b Allott	8
*P. A. Neale lbw b Watkinson	6	– lbw b Watkinson	17
D. A. Leatherdale c Simmons b Watkinson	3	– lbw b Allott	20
M. J. Weston c Hegg b Allott	18	– b Watkinson	45
†S. J. Rhodes c Hegg b Allott	13	– not out	0
P. J. Newport c Hegg b Watkinson	0	– not out	5
R. K. Illingworth c Simmons b Allott	10		
N. V. Radford lbw b Allott	1		
S. M. McEwan not out	0		
B 1, l-b 2, w 1	4	L-b 2	2
1/66 2/66 3/66 4/71 5/76 6/106 7/107 8/111 9/118	119	1/2 2/12 3/47 4/51 5/113 6/113	(6 wkts) 118

Bonus points – Lancashire 4.

Bowling: *First Innings*—Wasim 9–2–25–0; Allott 20.3–10–29–4; Watkinson 20–6–37–4; Hayhurst 14–4–25–2. *Second Innings*—Wasim 7–2–11–0; Allott 20.3–5–43–4; Watkinson 20–8–31–2; Hayhurst 3–0–22–0; Simmons 1–0–9–0.

Umpires: D. O. Oslear and K. E. Palmer.

At Lord's, June 4, 6, 7. WORCESTERSHIRE beat MIDDLESEX by 209 runs.

WORCESTERSHIRE v HAMPSHIRE

At Worcester, June 11, 13, 14. Worcestershire won by ten wickets. Worcestershire 24 pts, Hampshire 3 pts. Toss: Worcestershire. A record second-wicket stand for Worcestershire against Hampshire of 276 in 77 overs provided the platform for the comprehensive victory which consolidated Worcestershire's position at the top of the table and also provided some consolation for their defeat by Hampshire in the quarter-finals of the Benson and Hedges

Cup. Hick reached his fourth century of the season off 153 balls and his 177 (223 balls) contained two sixes and nineteen fours. Curtis, again a model of patience and composure, registered his second successive Championship hundred, off 277 deliveries with twelve boundaries, and remained unbeaten at the close. Newport's fourth five-wicket return of the summer enabled Neale to enforce the follow-on, and in spite of Chris Smith's valiant 87 (fifteen fours), Worcestershire needed only 17 runs for victory. Cowley was unable to bat in Hampshire's second innings because of a wrist injury.

Close of play: First day, Worcestershire 354-3 (T. S. Curtis 127*, P. A. Neale 13*); Second day, Hampshire 66-1 (C. L. Smith 39*, C. A. Connor 0*).

Worcestershire

T. S. Curtis b Connor	131	– not out	13
G. J. Lord lbw b Andrew	20	– not out	4
G. A. Hick c Parks b Cowley	177		
D. B. D'Oliveira c R. A. Smith b Ayling	0		
*P. A. Neale lbw b Andrew	38		
M. J. Weston b Connor	5		
†S. J. Rhodes lbw b Connor	0		
P. J. Newport not out	6		
B 4, l-b 13, w 2, n-b 1	20		
1/36 2/312 3/314 4/361 5/385 6/385 7/397 (7 wkts dec.)	397	(no wkt)	17

R. K. Illingworth, N. V. Radford and G. R. Dilley did not bat.

Bonus points – Worcestershire 4, Hampshire 1 (Score at 100 overs: 325-3).

Bowling: *First Innings*—Connor 19–5–66–3; Andrew 26.3–8–78–2; Jefferies 15–0–59–0; Ayling 25–1–68–1; Cowley 30–5–86–1; Nicholas 6–1–23–0. *Second Innings*—R. A. Smith 1–0–9–0; Turner 0.2–0–8–0.

Hampshire

V. P. Terry b Newport	14	– lbw b Weston	24
C. L. Smith b Radford	4	– lbw b Radford	87
*M. C. J. Nicholas c D'Oliveira b Newport	23	– (4) c Rhodes b Dilley	13
R. A. Smith c Rhodes b Weston	45	– (5) b Radford	4
D. R. Turner c Hick b Dilley	3	– (6) lbw b Dilley	15
J. R. Ayling lbw b Radford	13	– (7) lbw b Radford	1
S. T. Jefferies c Rhodes b Newport	53	– (8) b Dilley	24
†R. J. Parks c Neale b Weston	22	– (9) c Rhodes b Dilley	13
C. A. Connor b Newport	1	– (3) b Dilley	0
S. J. W. Andrew c D'Oliveira b Newport	2	– not out	4
N. G. Cowley not out	10	– absent injured	
L-b 10, n-b 3	13	B 6, l-b 7, w 6, n-b 6	25
1/8 2/34 3/81 4/90 5/111 6/112 7/153 8/176 9/192	203	1/66 2/72 3/116 4/135 5/139 6/142 7/186 8/187 9/210	210

Bonus points – Hampshire 2, Worcestershire 4.

Bowling: *First Innings*—Dilley 17–4–37–1; Radford 16–3–62–2; Newport 20–3–61–5; Weston 12–4–26–2; Illingworth 2–0–7–0. *Second Innings*—Radford 28–3–82–3; Newport 14–3–45–0; Dilley 23.1–5–65–5; Illingworth 5–4–1–0; Weston 6–4–4–1.

Umpires: D. J. Constant and J. W. Holder.

At Derby, June 18, 20, 21. WORCESTERSHIRE drew with DERBYSHIRE.

WORCESTERSHIRE v GLOUCESTERSHIRE

At Worcester, July 2, 4, 5. Drawn. Worcestershire 1 pt, Gloucestershire 4 pts. Toss: Gloucestershire. With no play possible on the second day because of rain, both sides forfeited an innings after Gloucestershire had batted on after lunch on the final afternoon. Worcestershire's target was an imposing 333 in a minimum of 60 overs. But just as Hick and Curtis were rising to the challenge on the easiest New Road pitch of the season, they lost three wickets with the score at 70. Curran struck twice with successive deliveries in his first over, effectively ending the game as a contest. Weston's first Championship half-century of the summer, off 64 balls, arrested the slide, and Newport and Rhodes played out the final seventeen overs. It was Worcestershire's least productive game of the Championship campaign to date. Athey was the mainstay of the Gloucestershire innings, his unbeaten 91 coming off 167 balls and containing ten fours.

Close of play: First day, Gloucestershire 188-2 (P. W. Romaines 33*, C. W. J. Athey 22*); Second day, No play.

Gloucestershire

A. W. Stovold c O'Shaughnessy b Radford . 42
A. J. Wright c Illingworth b Newport . 69
P. W. Romaines b O'Shaughnessy 59
C. W. J. Athey not out 91
P. Bainbridge b McEwan 38
K. M. Curran not out 5
L-b 18, n-b 10 28

1/66 2/141 3/234 4/294 (4 wkts dec.) 332

J. W. Lloyds, †R. C. Russell, *D. A. Graveney, D. V. Lawrence and T. M. Alderman did not bat.

Bonus points – Gloucestershire 4, Worcestershire 1 (Score at 100 overs: 321-4).

Bowling: Radford 23–5–85–1; Newport 24–5–59–1; McEwan 15–1–49–1; Illingworth 23–5–55–0; Weston 7–2–16–0; O'Shaughnessy 6–0–35–1; Leatherdale 2–0–5–0; Curtis 2–1–10–0.

Gloucestershire forfeited their second innings.

Worcestershire

Worcestershire forfeited their first innings.

T. S. Curtis c Graveney b Curran 41
S. J. O'Shaughnessy lbw b Alderman . . 6
G. A. Hick b Alderman 20
*P. A. Neale lbw b Curran 0
M. J. Weston c Curran b Graveney . . . 65
D. A. Leatherdale c Athey b Graveney . 26
†S. J. Rhodes not out 26
P. J. Newport not out 40
B 3, l-b 1, n-b 5 9

1/31 2/70 3/70 4/70 5/136 6/167 (6 wkts) 233

R. K. Illingworth, N. V. Radford and S. M. McEwan did not bat.

Bowling: Lawrence 13–2–59–0; Alderman 11–2–38–2; Curran 5–3–6–2; Graveney 20–2–70–2; Lloyds 13.3–0–56–0.

Umpires: J. C. Balderstone and J. Birkenshaw.

At Birmingham, July 13, 14, 15. WORCESTERSHIRE drew with WARWICKSHIRE.

At Nottingham, July 16, 18, 19. WORCESTERSHIRE lost to NOTTINGHAMSHIRE by six wickets.

WORCESTERSHIRE v YORKSHIRE

At Worcester, July 20, 21, 22. Worcestershire won by 21 runs. Worcestershire 22 pts, Yorkshire 7 pts. Toss: Worcestershire. Yorkshire, needing 57 runs from the last ten overs, were within sight of their first win at New Road for 21 years, but they lost their last five wickets for 28 runs and Worcestershire scraped home with thirteen balls to spare. Worcestershire owed much to another towering innings from Hick. His 198 on the first day, with two sixes and 23 fours, came off 226 balls and transformed Worcestershire's innings after they had slipped to 114 for five. His stand of 205 off 54 overs for the seventh wicket with Newport was a Worcestershire record, giving Hick a share in four of the county's first eight partnership records. His century, in his 71st Championship appearance, also left him only three short of a full set of hundreds against the counties, Derbyshire, Leicestershire and Kent being the remaining trio. Yorkshire declared 54 runs in arrears, having achieved maximum batting points for the first time in 1988, and following an opening stand of 107 between Lord, with his highest score for Worcestershire, and Bent, who marked his Championship début with a maiden half-century, they were set a victory target of 270 in a minimum of 63 overs. Moxon hit eleven boundaries in compiling the first Championship hundred of the summer by a Yorkshire batsman, only to see the innings fold after he was caught at long-off off Illingworth.

Close of play: First day, Yorkshire 21-0 (M. D. Moxon 11*, A. A. Metcalfe 8*); Second day, Worcestershire 48-0 (P. Bent 27*, G. J. Lord 21*).

Worcestershire

P. Bent c Bairstow b Hartley ... 31 – c Robinson b Carrick ... 50
G. J. Lord c Love b Shaw ... 11 – c Robinson b Carrick ... 85
S. J. O'Shaughnessy lbw b Hartley ... 2 – lbw b Shaw ... 4
G. A. Hick c Robinson b Shaw ... 198 – c Carrick ... 17
*P. A. Neale c Love b Shaw ... 0 – not out ... 19
M. J. Weston b Sidebottom ... 10 – not out ... 24
†S. J. Rhodes c Bairstow b Carrick ... 5
P. J. Newport not out ... 77
B 5, l-b 6, w 2, n-b 9 ... 22 B 9, l-b 5, n-b 2 ... 16

1/32 2/55 3/56 4/74 5/114 6/151 7/356 (7 wkts dec.) 356 1/107 2/131 3/166 4/167 (4 wkts dec.) 215

R. K. Illingworth, N. V. Radford and S. M. McEwan did not bat.

Bonus points – Worcestershire 4, Yorkshire 3.

Bowling: *First Innings*—Hartley 18–1–92–2; Sidebottom 19–2–62–1; Shaw 25.2–3–93–3 Carrick 28–11–67–1; Swallow 8–0–31–0. *Second Innings*—Sidebottom 5–1–15–0; Shaw 17–3–52–1; Hartley 6–0–33–0; Swallow 8–0–38–0; Carrick 14–1–52–3; Sharp 1–0–11–0.

Yorkshire

M. D. Moxon b Radford ... 39 – c McEwan b Illingworth ... 106
A. A. Metcalfe c Neale b Newport ... 28 – c Rhodes b Radford ... [illegible]
K. Sharp c Illingworth b Newport ... 12 – b Illingworth ... 1[illegible]
J. D. Love lbw b Illingworth ... 36 – b Illingworth ... 1[illegible]
P. E. Robinson c Radford b Illingworth ... 51 – b Newport ... 3[illegible]
I. G. Swallow not out ... 48 – (10) run out ...
†D. L. Bairstow st Rhodes b Hick ... 9 – (6) lbw b Radford ... 2[illegible]
*P. Carrick not out ... 46 – (7) c Illingworth b Radford ... 2[illegible]
A. Sidebottom (did not bat) ... – (8) b Radford ...
P. J. Hartley (did not bat) ... – (9) c and b Illingworth ...
C. Shaw (did not bat) ... – not out ...
L-b 13, w 3, n-b 17 ... 33 B 1, l-b 9, w 1, n-b 10 ... 2[illegible]

1/69 2/85 3/109 4/172 5/222 6/239 (6 wkts dec.) 302 1/3 2/42 3/81 4/152 5/208 6/220 7/238 8/239 9/239 24[illegible]

Bonus points – Yorkshire 4, Worcestershire 2.

Bowling: *First Innings*—Radford 16–3–50–1; Newport 24.2–9–53–2; Illingworth 28–11–67–2; McEwan 15–2–51–0; Weston 5–0–14–0; Hick 10–0–54–1. *Second Innings*—Radford 13.5–3–60–4; Newport 14–3–54–1; McEwan 6–1–11–0; Illingworth 24–2–82–4; Weston 7–0–31–0.

Umpires: N. T. Plews and A. G. T. Whitehead.

At Folkestone, July 23, 25, 26. WORCESTERSHIRE drew with KENT.

WORCESTERSHIRE v NORTHAMPTONSHIRE

At Worcester, July 30, August 1, 2. Drawn. Worcestershire 8 pts, Northamptonshire 3 pts. Toss: Northamptonshire. A dispute between the captains, Neale and Cook, over whether or not Northamptonshire had been asked to follow on late on the second day, had to be settled by a TCCB ruling, which found in Worcestershire's favour. With a first-innings lead of 171, Neale insisted he had signalled to the Northamptonshire dressing-room that they should bat again. Cook was equally adamant he had not been notified, either officially or unofficially, and after taking his team into the middle, to be joined by the Worcestershire eleven, he refused to accept that his side should bat again. Umpires Bond and Harris eventually led the players off with the matter being referred to Lord's. Play for the day was finally called off at 7.25 p.m., with the official ruling that the four overs still due to be bowled should be added on to the final day. Having lost the argument, Northamptonshire succeeded in staving off defeat, Cook batting 158 minutes for a defiant 32. Hick, with the 30th first-class century of his career, and Radford, with a season's-best seven for 73, including a spell of six for 10 in 40 balls, had taken the honours on the first two days.

Close of play: First day, Worcestershire 321-5 (M. J. Weston 12*, S. J. Rhodes 14*); Second day, Northamptonshire 191.

Worcestershire

T. S. Curtis c Larkins b Lillee	45	†S. J. Rhodes b Capel	23
G. J. Lord c Larkins b Robinson	47	P. J. Newport not out	6
G. A. Hick c Ripley b Robinson	132	L-b 8, w 2, n-b 7	17
D. A. Leatherdale lbw b Robinson	11		—
*P. A. Neale lbw b Robinson	44	1/96 2/96 3/135 (6 wkts dec.)	362
M. J. Weston not out	37	4/274 5/301 6/340	

R. K. Illingworth, N. V. Radford and A. P. Pridgeon did not bat.

Bonus points – Worcestershire 4, Northamptonshire 2.

Bowling: Lillee 30–6–106–1; Capel 20–3–92–1; Robinson 29–7–102–4; N. G. B. Cook 15–5–38–0; Williams 3–0–6–0; Wild 3–1–10–0.

Northamptonshire

*G. Cook b Radford	0	– lbw b Radford	32
W. Larkins c Hick b Pridgeon	21	– c Rhodes b Newport	5
R. J. Bailey lbw b Pridgeon	20	– c Curtis b Pridgeon	48
A. Fordham c Weston b Illingworth	44	– lbw b Leatherdale	29
D. J. Capel lbw b Radford	70	– not out	51
R. G. Williams lbw b Radford	10	– not out	15
D. J. Wild c Weston b Radford	0		
†D. Ripley c Curtis b Radford	0		
N. G. B. Cook c Hick b Radford	3		
D. K. Lillee not out	1		
M. A. Robinson b Radford	4		
B 1, l-b 11, n-b 6	18	B 1, l-b 17, n-b 7	25
	—		—
1/0 2/36 3/58 4/147 5/162 6/162 7/162 8/184 9/185	191	1/12 2/85 3/111 4/155 (4 wkts)	205

Bonus points – Northamptonshire 1, Worcestershire 4.

Bowling: *First Innings*—Radford 24.4–7–73–7; Newport 17–1–63–0; Pridgeon 14–8–20–2; Weston 3–1–8–0; Illingworth 7–4–15–1. *Second Innings*—Radford 29.2–7–73–1; Newport 19.4–9–26–1; Pridgeon 20–6–29–1; Weston 4–2–8–0; Illingworth 16–5–39–0; Leatherdale 4–3–12–1.

Umpires: J. D. Bond and J. H. Harris.

WORCESTERSHIRE v SUSSEX

At Kidderminster, August 6, 8, 9. Worcestershire won by nine wickets. Worcestershire 24 pts, Sussex 2 pts. Toss: Sussex. Even without Dilley, who was refused permission to play by the England selectors, having the week before pulled out of the final Test against West Indies because of a knee injury, Worcestershire required only 75 minutes of the last day to complete a comprehensive victory. Fittingly, it was virtually secured by Rhodes, equalling the club record of nine dismissals in a match; the same catch gave Newport a match analysis of nine for 128. Worcestershire's first-innings lead of 224 followed a stand of 181 in 54 overs between Weston (fifteen fours) and Neale, whose 167 beat his previous career-best score of 163 not out against Nottinghamshire in 1979. He claimed 102 of his runs in boundaries with 24 fours and one six. Defiant half-centuries from Alan Wells and Pigott enabled Sussex to avert an innings defeat, but it took Worcestershire only 23 balls to score the 14 runs needed for victory.

Close of play: First day, Worcestershire 179-4 (P. A. Neale 66*, M. J. Weston 42*); Second day, Sussex 221-8 (A. R. Clarke 8*).

Sussex

N. J. Lenham b Newport	36	– (2) c Rhodes b Newport	7
N. J. Falkner c Rhodes b Radford	1	– (1) c Rhodes b Pridgeon	12
*P. W. G. Parker lbw b Radford	4	– c Pridgeon b Newport	12
A. P. Wells c Radford b Newport	1	– c Rhodes b Newport	65
I. J. Gould b Illingworth	60	– c Rhodes b Pridgeon	6
C. M. Wells c Hick b Pridgeon	2	– run out	26
A. C. S. Pigott c Rhodes b Newport	12	– lbw b Radford	55
†P. Moores c Rhodes b Newport	3	– c Rhodes b Radford	24
A. R. Clarke c Neale b Newport	4	– c Lord b Radford	10
R. A. Bunting not out	1	– c Rhodes b Newport	4
A. M. Babington c Leatherdale b Illingworth	10	– not out	6
B 4, l-b 4, n-b 4	12	B 1, l-b 6, w 2, n-b 1	10
1/2 2/20 3/27 4/68 5/75 6/110 7/128 8/134 9/136	146	1/15 2/25 3/31 4/40 5/121 6/133 7/205 8/221 9/227	237

Bonus points – Worcestershire 4.

Bowling: *First Innings*—Radford 10–1–29–2; Newport 21–4–62–5; Pridgeon 8–1–19–1 Illingworth 8.3–2–28–2. *Second Innings*—Newport 24.1–6–66–4; Pridgeon 17–3–48–2 Illingworth 16–3–36–0; Radford 23–7–66–3; Hick 3–0–14–0.

Worcestershire

P. Bent c C. M. Wells b Pigott	16	– not out	
G. J. Lord lbw b Babington	10	– c Moores b Babington	
G. A. Hick c Lenham b Babington	18	– not out	
D. A. Leatherdale c A. P. Wells b Clarke	24		
*P. A. Neale c Pigott b Babington	167		
M. J. Weston c Moores b Clarke	94		
†S. J. Rhodes c Lenham b Clarke	6		
P. J. Newport b Pigott	18		
R. K. Illingworth not out	2		
N. V. Radford c and b Pigott	1		
A. P. Pridgeon c Falkner b Babington	11		
L-b 3	3		
1/28 2/28 3/62 4/82 5/263 6/303 7/350 8/358 9/359	370	1/7	(1 wkt) 1

Bonus points – Worcestershire 4, Sussex 2 (Score at 100 overs: 306-6).

Bowling: *First Innings*—Pigott 21–3–85–3; Babington 26.3–5–83–4; Clarke 34–9–92–3; Bunting 14–1–47–0; C. M. Wells 12–2–44–0; Gould 7–1–16–0. *Second Innings*—Babington 2–0–7–1; Bunting 1.5–1–7–0.

Umpires: D. J. Constant and J. H. Hampshire.

At Abergavenny, August 13, 15, 16. WORCESTERSHIRE beat GLAMORGAN by five wickets.

At The Oval, August 17, 18, 19. WORCESTERSHIRE drew with SURREY.

WORCESTERSHIRE v ESSEX

At Worcester, August 20, 22, 23. Essex won by 77 runs. Essex 23 pts, Worcestershire 4 pts. Toss: Essex. Worcestershire, having been set a target of 295 in 80 overs on a deteriorating pitch, finally succumbed with 22 balls remaining. Victory took Essex to within five points of the home county as they began the run-in for the Championship. Newport underlined the all-round qualities that earned him his first England call-up during the game, following a match return of nine for 126 by resisting for the final two hours in making an unbeaten 34. Foster took the last two wickets in three balls to finish with an even better ten for 128. Rain had caused the loss of 22 overs on the opening day, when Gooch occupied the crease for 3 hours 27 minutes until he was brilliantly stumped by Rhodes, standing up to Pridgeon, for 72.

Close of play: First day, Essex 230-6 (D. R. Pringle 43*, D. E. East 15*); Second day, Essex 100-6 (P. J. Prichard 43*, N. A. Foster 1*).

Essex

*G. A. Gooch st Rhodes b Pridgeon	72	– c Neale b Radford	14
J. P. Stephenson b Radford	20	– lbw b Newport	10
A. W. Lilley c Curtis b Newport	9	– lbw b Radford	2
A. R. Border lbw b Newport	34	– lbw b Newport	1
P. J. Prichard c Rhodes b Newport	13	– c Rhodes b Pridgeon	80
N. Hussain c Newport b Pridgeon	4	– c D'Oliveira b Weston	25
D. R. Pringle b Radford	63	– c Rhodes b Pridgeon	2
†D. E. East c Radford b Newport	16	– (9) c Hick b Pridgeon	0
N. A. Foster c Rhodes b Newport	0	– (8) c Hick b Newport	16
T. D. Topley not out	5	– not out	15
. H. Childs (did not bat)		– c Rhodes b Newport	11
B 1, l-b 21, n-b 4	26	L-b 3, w 1, n-b 2	6
1/29 2/59 3/139 4/165 5/165 6/185 7/232 8/232 9/262	(9 wkts dec.) 262	1/12 2/21 3/26 4/30 5/72 6/77 7/130 8/132 9/163	182

Bonus points – Essex 3, Worcestershire 3 (Score at 100 overs: 261-8).

Bowling: *First Innings*—Radford 30.1–8–80–2; Newport 31–9–70–5; Pridgeon 26–7–61–2; Illingworth 14–5–29–0. *Second Innings*—Radford 14–3–39–2; Newport 21.5–3–56–4; Pridgeon 19–2–68–3; Weston 7–3–16–1.

Worcestershire

T. S. Curtis lbw b Foster	10	– c Stephenson b Topley	33
G. J. Lord c East b Pringle	15	– c Border b Foster	1
G. A. Hick c Foster b Topley	34	– c Lilley b Pringle	20
D. B. D'Oliveira c Topley b Foster	8	– c sub b Foster	29
*P. A. Neale b Foster	0	– c Border b Childs	31
M. J. Weston b Topley	4	– c Border b Topley	10
†S. J. Rhodes b Foster	17	– c Lilley b Pringle	11
P. J. Newport b Topley	5	– not out	34
R. K. Illingworth c Gooch b Foster	31	– lbw b Pringle	20
N. V. Radford c Stephenson b Foster	18	– lbw b Foster	11
A. P. Pridgeon not out	0	– b Foster	0
B 1, l-b 5, n-b 2	8	L-b 17	17
1/27 2/27 3/59 4/59 5/73 6/73 7/85 8/118 9/149	150	1/5 2/48 3/88 4/94 5/112 6/123 7/163 8/190 9/211	217

Bonus points – Worcestershire 1, Essex 4.

Bowling: *First Innings*—Foster 22.4–5–67–6; Pringle 17–5–32–1; Topley 12–2–44–3; Childs 1–0–1–0. *Second Innings*—Foster 22.2–3–61–4; Pringle 25–6–74–3; Topley 14–4–31–2; Gooch 3–1–17–0; Childs 7–3–9–1; Border 5–3–8–0.

Umpires: J. D. Bond and D. R. Shepherd.

WORCESTERSHIRE v WARWICKSHIRE

At Worcester, August 25, 26, 27, 29. Drawn. Worcestershire 7 pts, Warwickshire 5 pts. Toss: Warwickshire. On the last day, Warwickshire made Worcestershire pay a price for the resounding ten-wicket victory of the previous afternoon, with which they retained the Refuge Assurance League title, keeping them in the field until Lloyd declared 75 minutes before the close with a lead of 235. The return of the rain, which had caused the loss of the last 21 overs on the second afternoon and all of the third day, meant that Worcestershire did not have to bat again. Weston's unbeaten 95 on the second day, including 72 of the last 80 runs scored off the bat, had taken Worcestershire to a first-innings lead of 83. Warwickshire had wiped out the deficit before the rain, and on the Monday Thorne, with his best score for Warwickshire, and Kallicharran steered Warwickshire to a position of safety.

Close of play: First day, Worcestershire 40-3 (G. A. Hick 14*, R. K. Illingworth 0*); Second day, Warwickshire 83-2 (Asif Din 20*, D. A. Thorne 22*); Third day, No play.

Warwickshire

D. A. Reeve lbw b Dilley	3	– (7) b Radford	
*T. A. Lloyd c Rhodes b Dilley	45	– (1) st Rhodes b Illingworth	
Asif Din c Rhodes b Weston	26	– c Rhodes b Dilley	
D. A. Thorne b Dilley	18	– c Weston b Illingworth	
A. I. Kallicharran c Rhodes b Dilley	1	– b Radford	
†G. A. Tedstone lbw b Radford	10	– (2) c Weston b Radford	
P. A. Smith lbw b Illingworth	26	– (6) c O'Shaughnessy b Illingworth	
G. C. Small c Weston b Pridgeon	0	– not out	
A. A. Donald c Neale b Pridgeon	29	– not out	
T. A. Munton c D'Oliveira b Illingworth	11		
N. Gifford not out	15		
L-b 5, w 1, n-b 8	14	B 11, l-b 14, w 4, n-b 5	
1/20 2/64 3/88 4/98 5/99 6/113 7/114 8/160 9/175	198	1/22 2/42 3/147 4/191 5/237 6/279 7/302	(7 wkts dec.) 3

Bonus points – Warwickshire 1, Worcestershire 4.

Bowling: *First Innings*—Dilley 24–7–53–4; Radford 18–4–72–1; Weston 15–7–25–1; Pridgeon 16–1–39–2; Illingworth 13.4–10–4–2. *Second Innings*—Dilley 28–3–75–1; Radford 32–3–126–3; Illingworth 28–9–51–3; Pridgeon 15–1–33–0; Hick 5–3–8–0.

Worcestershire

S. J. O'Shaughnessy lbw b Small 0
G. J. Lord lbw b Donald 0
G. A. Hick c Small b Gifford 75
D. B. D'Oliveira b Munton 17
R. K. Illingworth c Tedstone b Donald . 15
*P. A. Neale b Small 23
M. J. Weston not out 95
†S. J. Rhodes c Tedstone b Small 0
N. V. Radford lbw b Small 15
G. R. Dilley c Lloyd b Donald 3
A. P. Pridgeon b Small 5
B 3, l-b 15, w 5, n-b 10 33

1/1 2/14 3/40 4/75 5/151 6/157 7/159 8/179 9/196 — 281

Bonus points – Worcestershire 3, Warwickshire 4.

Bowling: Small 27.3–5–95–5; Donald 23–4–89–3; Munton 12–3–46–1; Gifford 19–7–33–1.

Umpires: J. H. Harris and M. J. Kitchen.

At Bristol, September 9, 10, 11, 12. WORCESTERSHIRE beat GLOUCESTERSHIRE by 114 runs.

WORCESTERSHIRE v GLAMORGAN

At Worcester, September 14, 15, 16. Worcestershire won by an innings and 76 runs. Worcestershire 24 pts, Glamorgan 4 pts. Toss: Glamorgan. Not even a vandal's attempt at sabotage could prevent Worcestershire from taking the maximum points needed to clinch their first Championship title for fourteen years. Play on the third day was delayed for an hour while a mixture of petroleum jelly and engine oil, spread over the pitch during the night, was cleared with the help of industrial heaters. Then, after Worcestershire had extended their lead to 179, Glamorgan were promptly dismissed for 103 in 36 overs, leaving Worcestershire victors with more than a day to spare. Newport's five wickets came in a spell of 26 balls in which he conceded just 2 runs, and took his tally for the season to 93. But once again it was Hick, with a majestic 197, containing 29 fours, who made it all possible. His fourteenth first-class hundred of the year equalled G. M. Turner's record of ten in a season for Worcestershire, set in 1970. And in guiding Worcestershire to their essential fourth batting point with only seventeen balls to spare, he also went past G. A. Gooch's 1984 aggregate of 2,559 runs, the previous highest since the Championship was reduced in 1969.

Close of play: First day, Worcestershire 19-0 (T. S. Curtis 2*, G. J. Lord 10*); Second day, Worcestershire 380-6 (S. J. Rhodes 45*, P. J. Newport 25*).

Glamorgan

A. R. Butcher b Newport . . . . 35 – c Illingworth b Dilley 9
. A. Cottey c Illingworth b Weston . . . . 13 – lbw b Radford 5
. G. P. Roebuck c Rhodes b Newport . . . . 13 – c Illingworth b Dilley 1
M. P. Maynard c Newport b Illingworth . . . . . . 69 – (7) st Rhodes b Illingworth 19
G. C. Holmes b Radford . . . . 6 – (4) c Hick b Newport 33
M. J. Cann st Rhodes b Illingworth . . . . 28 – (5) c Rhodes b Newport 9
. G. Thomas b Radford . . . . 40 – (6) c Neale b Newport 0
Derrick not out . . . . 21 – c Curtis b Newport 0
C. P. Metson b Radford . . . . 1 – c and b Newport 0
L. Watkin c Illingworth b Radford . . . . 1 – not out 13
Bastien c Curtis b Illingworth . . . . 5 – c Leatherdale b Illingworth 10
B 2, l-b 4, n-b 6 . . . . 12 B 1, l-b 1, w 2 4

32 2/62 3/63 4/77 5/153 178 7/225 8/227 9/231 — 244
1/14 2/14 3/24 4/58 5/58 6/72 7/72 8/80 9/80 — 103

Bonus points – Glamorgan 2, Worcestershire 4.

Bowling: *First Innings*—Dilley 21–4–54–0; Radford 28–5–84–4; Newport 15–2–53–2; Weston 7–2–16–1; Illingworth 25–14–31–3. *Second Innings*—Dilley 8–3–30–2; Radford 8–2–16–1; Newport 10–2–23–5; Weston 5–1–14–0; Illingworth 4.2–1–18–2.

Worcestershire

T. S. Curtis b Thomas	8
G. J. Lord b Derrick	42
G. A. Hick c sub b Thomas	197
D. A. Leatherdale c Metson b Bastien	4
*P. A. Neale c Roebuck b Cann	29
M. J. Weston c Bastien b Cann	2
†S. J. Rhodes c Thomas b Watkin	46
P. J. Newport c Metson b Thomas	30
R. K. Illingworth c sub b Derrick	16
N. V. Radford not out	10
G. R. Dilley b Derrick	5
B 5, l-b 21, w 2, n-b 6	34
1/28 2/101 3/110 4/253 5/263 6/342 7/382 8/386 9/417	423

Bonus points – Worcestershire 4, Glamorgan 2 (Score at 100 overs: 314-5).

Bowling: Thomas 36–4–130–3; Watkin 34–8–91–1; Derrick 32–7–91–3; Bastien 25–5–65–1; Cann 8–2–20–2.

Umpires: B. Dudleston and B. Leadbeater.

THE CRICKETER CUP WINNERS, 1967-1988

Sponsored by The Cricketer

1967	REPTON PILGRIMS	beat Radley Rangers by 96 runs.

Final Sponsored by Champagne Mercier

1968	OLD MALVERNIANS	beat Harrow Wanderers by five wickets.
1969	OLD BRIGHTONIANS	beat Stowe Templars by 156 runs.
1970	OLD WYKEHAMISTS	beat Old Tonbridgians by 94 runs.

Final Sponsored by Moët & Chandon

1971	OLD TONBRIDGIANS	beat Charterhouse Friars on faster scoring-rate
1972	OLD TONBRIDGIANS	beat Old Malvernians by 114 runs.
1973	RUGBY METEORS	beat Old Tonbridgians by five wickets.
1974	OLD WYKEHAMISTS	beat Old Alleynians on faster scoring-rate.
1975	OLD MALVERNIANS	beat Harrow Wanderers by 97 runs.
1976	OLD TONBRIDGIANS	beat Old Blundellians by 170 runs.
1977	SHREWSBURY SARACENS	beat Oundle Rovers by nine wickets.
1978	CHARTERHOUSE FRIARS	beat Oundle Rovers by nine wickets.
1979	OLD TONBRIDGIANS	beat Uppingham Rovers by 5 runs.
1980	MARLBOROUGH BLUES	beat Old Wellingtonians by 31 runs.
1981	CHARTERHOUSE FRIARS	beat Old Wykehamists by nine wickets.
1982	OLD WYKEHAMISTS	beat Old Malvernians on faster scoring-rate.
1983	REPTON PILGRIMS	beat Haileybury Hermits by seven wickets.
1984	OLD TONBRIDGIANS	beat Old Malvernians by seven wickets.
1985	OUNDLE ROVERS	beat Repton Pilgrims by three wickets.
1986	OLD MALVERNIANS	beat Downside Wanderers by six wickets.
1987	SHREWSBURY SARACENS	beat Old Cliftonians by 58 runs.
1988	OUNDLE ROVERS	beat Shrewsbury Saracens by 19 runs.

From 1967 to 1983 the final was played at Burton Court, Chelsea. Since then, it has been played a Vincent Square, Westminster.

YORKSHIRE

Patron: HRH The Duchess of Kent
President: The Viscount Mountgarret
Chairman: B. Walsh
Chairman, Cricket Committee: D. B. Close
Secretary: J. Lister
Headingley Cricket Ground, Leeds LS6 3BU
(Telephone: 0532-787394)
Captain: P. Carrick

Yorkshire endured one of the worst seasons in their history, with all the high hopes encouraged by their success in the 1987 Benson and Hedges Cup dashed. They disappeared from that competition in the qualifying stages, slumped from eighth to thirteenth in the Britannic Assurance Championship, were comprehensively beaten in the second round of the NatWest Bank Trophy, and could do no better than eighth in the Refuge Assurance League.

Before the end of May they were under considerable pressure, for, in addition to surrendering the Benson and Hedges Cup, they lost their first three Championship games, reaching 200 only once in six innings. It was a sorry start from which they never fully recovered, although the second half of the programme brought about some improvement. Having lost five of the first eleven games, and winning two, they picked up in July, August and September to the extent of losing only once more while gaining another two victories.

Unfortunately, Phil Carrick did not have a good season as captain. He batted extremely well in testing circumstances when the top half of the order was struggling, but he failed to give the team the necessary sense of direction and erred on the cautious side when faced with a challenge. His relaxed style of leadership, which allows for a good deal of free expression, worked well when Yorkshire were reasonably successful, but it did not match up to requirements when things were going badly. There is little doubt that collectively the players failed to do themselves justice.

The initial difficulties concerned an acute shortage of runs, and Yorkshire had claimed a mere eleven batting points at the halfway stage of the Championship. Only Martyn Moxon looked capable of coping with some unsatisfactory pitches, and the lack of overall consistency was reflected in the fact that Yorkshire used seven different combinations to cover the first three places in the order in eleven fixtures. Richard Blakey was the principal victim of the chopping and changing and was unable to find the form that made him the leading personality the previous year. He soon found himself with the Colts and, although having a spell as replacement for David Bairstow behind the stumps, was dropped five times in all.

The county had to wait until mid-July before Moxon registered their first century, but his breakthrough inspired others. His first-wicket partner, Ashley Metcalfe, emerged from the shadows to play some sparkling innings, and also revealed unexpected patience in compiling a career-best unbeaten 216 against Middlesex at Headingley.

Moxon and Metcalfe comfortably topped the 1,000-run mark, as did Phil Robinson in his first full season. Robinson also had to battle his way through a barren spell, with twenty Championship innings yielding 346 runs for an average of 18.21, but he established himself and duly earned his cap. The two senior members of the middle order, Jim Love and Kevin Sharp, again failed to make the expected contributions, the latter losing his place to David Byas, another left-hander, who showed power and promise. Byas had difficulty in settling in at the wicket and failed to reach double figures in ten out of 22 innings, but he appeared to learn from his mistakes, applied himself thoughtfully, and should benefit from the experience of an extended run at first-class level.

The attack was clearly weakened by the absence of Paul Jarvis, who dropped out with a serious back strain at the end of June and did not play again. Earlier he had bowled with genuine hostility, achieving an impressive strike-rate of a wicket every 34.09 balls. Arnie Sidebottom, in his benefit year, responded to the extra demands put on him with an admirable all-round effort. He often found himself having to organise late resistance with the bat and rarely failed to put a sting in the Yorkshire tail; with the ball he caused even the leading batsmen some anxious moments.

The support came largely from Stuart Fletcher and Chris Shaw. Fletcher, who was capped in late September, could not force his way into the team early on, but he had the satisfaction of recording career-best figures of eight for 58 against Essex at Sheffield and also was Yorkshire's leading wicket-taker in the Sunday League with 25 at 20.04 each. Realistically, though, Yorkshire leant heavily on Jarvis and Sidebottom to provide the essential cutting edge. Peter Hartley met with mixed fortunes, proving expensive with the ball but compiling his maiden first-class hundred in the shadow of a Roses crisis at Old Trafford.

Yorkshire continued with the policy of relying largely on medium-pace, with Carrick supplying the spin. In late August, however, a turning pitch at Old Trafford brought the slow left-arm of Paul Booth back into the picture. He had appeared in only one Championship game in three years, but promptly took five wickets and subsequently, in less accommodating circumstances, continued to impress with his willingness to give the ball some air in an attempt to force errors from the opposing batsmen.

Another casualty in Yorkshire's decline was Bairstow, the unchallenged wicket-keeper for eighteen years, who reluctantly resumed the captaincy on a temporary basis when Carrick pulled a rib muscle at the start of the campaign. That decision underlined his position as senior professional, but on August 13 he was dropped for the first time since his junior days. He had struggled all summer with the bat and then he badly strained his back at Sheffield during the Nottinghamshire match. He was, however, recalled for the final fixture, at Trent Bridge, and duly claimed his 1,000th first-class victim for the county – only the third man to achieve this feat. He also hit a spectacular unbeaten 94 to remind everyone of his explosive talent in this area. – John Callaghan.

YORKSHIRE 1988

[*Bill Smith*

Back row: I. G. Swallow, P. J. Berry, P. A. Booth, C. S. Pickles, C. Shaw, S. D. Fletcher, P. E. Robinson. *Middle row*: W. Morton (*physiotherapist*), S. N. Hartley, M. D. Moxon, P. J. Hartley, D. Byas, S. J. Dennis, P. W. Jarvis, N. G. Nicholson, S. Oldham, D. E. V. Padgett (*coach*). *Front row*: A. A. Metcalfe, J. D. Love, D. L. Bairstow, P. Carrick (*captain*), A. Sidebottom, K. Sharp, R. J. Blakey.

YORKSHIRE RESULTS

All first-class matches – Played 24: Won 5, Lost 6, Drawn 13.

County Championship matches – Played 22: Won 4, Lost 6, Drawn 12.

Bonus points – Batting 48, Bowling 65.

Competition placings – Britannic Assurance County Championship, 13th; NatWest Bank Trophy, 2nd round; Benson and Hedges Cup, 4th in Group B; Refuge Assurance League, 8th.

BRITANNIC ASSURANCE CHAMPIONSHIP AVERAGES

BATTING

	Birthplace	*M*	*I*	*NO*	*R*	*HI*	*Avge*
‡M. D. Moxon	*Barnsley*	18	33	3	1,297	191	43.23
‡A. A. Metcalfe	*Horsforth*	21	39	5	1,268	216*	37.29
‡P. E. Robinson	*Keighley*	22	37	3	1,132	129*	33.29
‡P. J. Hartley	*Keighley*	13	17	6	364	127*	33.09
‡P. Carrick	*Armley*	21	32	7	795	81	31.80
‡J. D. Love	*Leeds*	17	27	2	744	93*	29.76
‡A. Sidebottom	*Barnsley*	18	24	5	517	55	27.2
D. Byas	*Kilham*	12	22	1	515	112	24.52
‡D. L. Bairstow	*Bradford*	14	23	3	416	94*	20.80
I. G. Swallow	*Barnsley*	11	19	2	352	48*	20.70
‡R. J. Blakey	*Huddersfield*	14	21	2	347	51	18.26
‡K. Sharp	*Leeds*	11	17	0	297	57	17.4
P. A. Booth	*Huddersfield*	4	7	2	82	33*	16.4
C. Shaw	*Hemsworth*	21	25	12	170	31	13.0
‡S. D. Fletcher	*Keighley*	16	14	3	79	18	7.1
‡P. W. Jarvis	*Redcar*	5	9	1	55	13	6.8

Also batted: (2 matches each): ‡S. J. Dennis (*Scarborough*) 0, 14*, 0; ‡S. N. Hartle (*Shipley*) 22, 12, 26*.

* *Signifies not out.* ‡ *Denotes county cap.*

The following played a total of seven three-figure innings for Yorkshire in Count Championship matches – A. A. Metcalfe 2, M. D. Moxon 2, D. Byas 1, P. J. Hartley P. E. Robinson 1.

BOWLING

	O	*M*	*R*	*W*	*BB*	*5W/i*	*Avg*
P. W. Jarvis	176.1	46	434	31	6-40	2	14.0
A. Sidebottom	513.2	135	1,303	63	7-89	3	20.
S. D. Fletcher	384.4	59	1,252	53	8-58	2	23.
C. Shaw	507.5	110	1,522	46	4-17	0	33.
P. Carrick	546	163	1,447	42	5-46	2	34.
P. J. Hartley	307.3	32	1,219	34	5-85	1	35.

Also bowled: P. A. Booth 109.4–27–281–9; D. Byas 9.2–0–49–0; S. J. Dennis 63–9–196– S. N. Hartley 5–1–25–0; J. D. Love 2.3–0–11–1; A. A. Metcalfe 2.5–0–7–0; M. D. Mox 6–2–15–0; P. E. Robinson 1.2–0–12–0; K. Sharp 1–0–11–0; I. G. Swallow 88–15–311–2.

Wicket-keepers: D. L. Bairstow 38 ct, 1 st; R. J. Blakey 19 ct, 2 st.

Leading Fielders: M. D. Moxon 22, P. E. Robinson 19.

YORKSHIRE v DERBYSHIRE

At Leeds, April 28, 29, 30. Derbyshire won by five wickets. Derbyshire 21 pts, Yorkshire 5 pts. Toss: Yorkshire. Yorkshire's batsmen never mastered the problems of an easy-paced pitch which provided movement off the seam. Moxon resisted for 252 minutes (219 balls) while making 79, but no-one else suggested permanence. Derbyshire were in trouble, too, until Goldsmith held the innings together at a crucial time, his unbeaten 51 coming from 87 balls. Newman then took three wickets for 2 runs in twelve balls at the start of Yorkshire's second innings and went on to achieve career-best figures. Sidebottom, however, showed what could be achieved by a well-organised batsman. He hit seven boundaries in his 91-ball innings and added 68 in twenty overs with Hartley for the eighth wicket. Derbyshire, with plenty of time in which to get the 184 needed for victory, were never under pressure and, despite rain, completed the job with a day to spare.

Close of play: First day, Derbyshire 80-3 (P. D. Bowler 27*, P. G. Newman 7*); Second day, Derbyshire 20-0 (K. J. Barnett 15*, P. D. Bowler 3*).

Yorkshire

First innings		Second innings	
M. D. Moxon c Barnett b Warner	79	– lbw b Newman	0
A. A. Metcalfe c Morris b Holding	11	– c Maher b Newman	8
R. J. Blakey b Malcolm	4	– c Bowler b Newman	0
J. D. Love c Holding b Malcolm	9	– lbw b Warner	46
P. E. Robinson c Roberts b Holding	18	– c Holding b Newman	24
*†D. L. Bairstow c Goldsmith b Holding	14	– c Maher b Newman	5
A. Sidebottom c Maher b Roberts	2	– c Barnett b Newman	48
P. W. Jarvis lbw b Warner	11	– c Bowler b Newman	0
P. J. Hartley c Maher b Malcolm	2	– c Barnett b Holding	37
P. A. Booth c Roberts b Malcolm	0	– c Roberts b Newman	2
C. Shaw not out	0	– not out	6
B 3, l-b 2, w 2, n-b 4	11	L-b 9, w 4, n-b 3	16
1/18 2/30 3/44 4/99 5/121 6/126 7/158 8/161 9/161	161	1/1 2/5 3/8 4/84 5/84 6/92 7/92 8/160 9/185	192

Bonus points – Yorkshire 1, Derbyshire 4.

Bowling: *First Innings*—Holding 15–6–23–3; Newman 15–3–34–0; Malcolm 12.3–3–36–4; Warner 19–6–35–2; Roberts 9–1–28–1. *Second Innings*—Holding 16–3–67–1; Newman 16.5–5–29–8; Warner 19–5–45–1; Malcolm 11–0–42–0.

Derbyshire

First innings		Second innings	
*K. J. Barnett lbw b Jarvis	14	– lbw b Jarvis	52
P. D. Bowler lbw b Sidebottom	37	– lbw b Shaw	28
B. Roberts b Shaw	11	– c Bairstow b Jarvis	23
T. E. Morris c Hartley b Jarvis	19	– b Hartley	6
P. G. Newman lbw b Sidebottom	8		
S. C. Goldsmith not out	51	– (5) c Moxon b Shaw	42
†B. J. M. Maher lbw b Sidebottom	0	– (6) not out	13
R. J. Finney b Jarvis	10	– (7) not out	2
A. E. Warner c Moxon b Hartley	0		
M. A. Holding c Love b Jarvis	9		
D. E. Malcolm lbw b Jarvis	0		
B 4, l-b 3, n-b 4	11	B 3, l-b 15	18
1/18 2/37 3/72 4/90 5/103 6/103 7/145 8/152 9/169	170	1/62 2/97 3/106 4/122 5/173	(5 wkts) 184

Bonus points – Derbyshire 1, Yorkshire 4.

Bowling: *First Innings*—Jarvis 23–6–49–5; Sidebottom 19–5–28–3; Shaw 16–4–32–1; Hartley 16–0–54–1; Booth 1–1–0–0. *Second Innings*—Jarvis 17–1–38–2; Shaw 18.5–3–65–2; Sidebottom 15–7–18–0; Hartley 16–6–45–1.

Umpires: J. D. Bond and B. Leadbeater.

At Birmingham, May 5, 6, 7. YORKSHIRE lost to WARWICKSHIRE by seven wickets.

At Canterbury, May 21, 23, 24. YORKSHIRE lost to KENT by three wickets.

YORKSHIRE v HAMPSHIRE

At Middlesbrough, May 28, 30, 31. Drawn. Yorkshire 6 pts, Hampshire 4 pts. Toss: Hampshire. Hampshire gained no advantage from having first use of a pitch which gave help to the spinners in the later stages. They batted badly, losing wickets to some wild strokes against no more than steady seam bowling. Metcalfe thrashed 28 in 23 balls when Yorkshire replied, but with Moxon and Swallow surrendering the initiative, the innings became bogged down. Parks claimed his 500th first-class dismissal for Hampshire when he caught Love, and players on each side suffered from injury. Metcalfe, although wearing a helmet with a visor, took the full force of a firm stroke in the face when fielding at short leg to Chris Smith, and Cowley cracked a bone in his thumb as he attempted to hold a fierce return chance from Jarvis. Hampshire were soon in difficulty when they batted a second time, 109 in arrears, but Chris Smith, missed by Robinson at slip when 36 off Jarvis, batted outstandingly. He showed both judgement and courage as he took some knocks in batting for 212 minutes (186 balls) to score an unbeaten 88, which included twelve boundaries. The weather also frustrated Yorkshire, with only fourteen overs possible between the showers on the last day.

Close of play: First day, Yorkshire 89-2 (M. D. Moxon 37*, K. Sharp 10*); Second day, Hampshire 129-4 (C. L. Smith 72*, R. J. Parks 15*).

Hampshire

First innings		Second innings	
V. P. Terry c Robinson b Sidebottom	2	– c Sharp b Jarvis	8
C. L. Smith c Bairstow b Jarvis	5	– not out	88
*M. C. J. Nicholas c Moxon b Shaw	8	– c Robinson b Shaw	7
R. A. Smith c Bairstow b Jarvis	36	– st Bairstow b Carrick	1
D. R. Turner lbw b Carrick	30	– c Bairstow b Jarvis	20
†R. J. Parks lbw b Sidebottom	13	– not out	18
S. T. Jefferies c Bairstow b Sidebottom	14		
N. G. Cowley b Sidebottom	10		
R. J. Maru lbw b Sidebottom	0		
C. A. Connor c Shaw b Carrick	5		
S. J. W. Andrew not out	1		
L-b 2, n-b 4	6	B 1, l-b 2, n-b 4	7
1/8 2/11 3/34 4/85 5/85 6/112 7/115 8/119 9/124	130	1/12 2/25 3/31 4/84 (4 wkts)	149

Bonus points – Yorkshire 4.

Bowling: *First Innings*—Jarvis 16–5–36–2; Sidebottom 18.2–6–30–5; Shaw 10–3–27–1 Carrick 18–4–35–2. *Second Innings*—Jarvis 19.2–6–45–2; Sidebottom 14–2–32–0; Shaw 6–1–17–1; Carrick 21–9–33–1; Swallow 4–0–19–0.

Yorkshire

M. D. Moxon c Connor b Cowley	40
A. A. Metcalfe c Nicholas b Andrew	28
I. G. Swallow c Nicholas b Maru	7
K. Sharp c Nicholas b Connor	36
J. D. Love c Parks b Connor	6
P. E. Robinson lbw b Andrew	38
†D. L. Bairstow c Nicholas b Cowley	0
*P. Carrick not out	46
A. Sidebottom c Parks b Cowley	[illegible]
P. W. Jarvis c Maru b Andrew	1[illegible]
C. Shaw c and b Maru	[illegible]
L-b 6, n-b 12	1[illegible]
1/33 2/65 3/113 4/126 5/132 6/135 7/194 8/203 9/232	23[illegible]

Bonus points – Yorkshire 2, Hampshire 4.

Bowling: Andrew 19–5–46–3; Jefferies 13–5–30–0; Connor 21–2–63–2; Maru 20–7–45–2 Cowley 16.5–3–49–3.

Umpires: B. J. Meyer and R. A. White.

At Northampton, June 1, 2, 3. YORKSHIRE drew with NORTHAMPTONSHIRE.

YORKSHIRE v SURREY

At Harrogate, June 4, 6, 7. Drawn. Yorkshire 1 pt, Surrey 8 pts. Toss: Yorkshire. Another careless batting performance left Yorkshire in a hopeless position after only eighteen overs, at which point they were 18 for five. Greig, the Surrey captain, had taken three wickets in nine balls. Robinson resisted stoutly, well supported by Sidebottom, but a total of 142 represented a feeble effort on a good batting pitch. Surrey made the most of the situation, with Clinton batting for five hours (250 balls, eleven fours) to provide a solid foundation. Yorkshire were handicapped when Sidebottom limped off with a groin strain after bowling only 6.3 overs, but his absence hardly excused a dreadful performance in the field. Five straightforward catches were put down, three of them by Moxon. Stewart had to retire with a broken thumb, but the runs flowed, particularly at the expense of the spinners, Carrick and Swallow, who were cut time and again. Yorkshire were left to save the game on the last day, which they did comfortably enough. The most important stand involved Metcalfe and Love, who put on 105 in 37 overs. The latter had an unusual escape on 22 when a delivery from Feltham clipped the off stump quite hard without dislodging a bail, and he went on to end a lean spell with his 200-minute 93 not out.

Close of play: First day, Yorkshire 103-7 (P. E. Robinson 41*, A. Sidebottom 22*); Second day, Surrey 342-4 (C. J. Richards 60*, K. T. Medlycott 54*).

Yorkshire

M. D. Moxon c Smith b Bicknell	5	– lbw b Greig	44
A. A. Metcalfe c Richards b Feltham	3	– st Richards b Greig	87
†R. J. Blakey c Medlycott b Greig	4	– c Richards b Feltham	27
K. Sharp lbw b Greig	2	– c Clinton b Feltham	5
J. D. Love c Ward b Greig	0	– not out	93
P. E. Robinson c Ward b Medlycott	58	– run out	10
I. G. Swallow c and b Medlycott	17	– c and b Medlycott	2
*P. Carrick c Feltham b Medlycott	3	– not out	6
A. Sidebottom c sub b Medlycott	36		
C. Shaw c Medlycott b Feltham	2		
S. D. Fletcher not out	0		
B 4, l-b 4, n-b 4	12	B 15, l-b 5, w 2, n-b 14	36
1/6 2/11 3/15 4/15 5/18 6/49 7/56 8/139 9/142	142	1/57 2/131 3/143 4/248 5/276 6/281 (6 wkts dec.)	310

Bonus points – Surrey 4.

Bowling: *First Innings*—Bicknell 16–8–28–1; Feltham 21–5–52–2; Greig 9–1–28–3; Medlycott 10.1–4–19–4; Mays 2–0–7–0. *Second Innings*—Bicknell 6–1–12–0; Feltham 26–7–56–2; Medlycott 29–8–83–1; Greig 16–3–47–2; Mays 12–1–59–0; Lynch 6–2–14–0; Ward 1–0–3–0; Clinton 0.4–0–16–0.

Surrey

G. S. Clinton b Swallow	101
D. M. Smith c Sharp b Fletcher	34
A. J. Stewart retired hurt	31
M. A. Lynch lbw b Fletcher	36
D. M. Ward c Blakey b Shaw	17
†C. J. Richards not out	60
K. T. Medlycott not out	54
B 2, l-b 5, n-b 2	9
1/59 2/169 3/195 4/263 (4 wkts dec.)	342

*I. A. Greig, M. A. Feltham, C. S. Mays and M. P. Bicknell did not bat.

Bonus points – Surrey 4, Yorkshire 1 (Score at 100 overs: 335-4).

Bowling: Sidebottom 6.3–2–19–0; Shaw 21–2–84–1; Swallow 25–6–91–1; Fletcher 24.3–5–52–2; Carrick 24–6–89–0.

Umpires: K. J. Lyons and D. O. Oslear.

At Cambridge, June 11, 12, 13. YORKSHIRE beat CAMBRIDGE UNIVERSITY by ten wickets.

YORKSHIRE v WARWICKSHIRE

At Leeds, June 15, 16, 17. Warwickshire won by seven wickets. Warwickshire 20 pts, Yorkshire 5 pts. Toss: Warwickshire. Donald, bowling with great pace and hostility, cut through the Yorkshire innings on a pitch offering some encouragement. Only the inexperienced Byas, who batted for 150 minutes (117 balls, eight fours), offered much resistance after his second-wicket stand with Sharp, worth 84 in 24 overs, had been broken. Warwickshire fell into even greater confusion as their batsmen played a series of careless strokes, and Yorkshire's second innings followed the same sorry pattern. Metcalfe, the one batsman to apply himself, was on 21 for 50 minutes, but his caution went unrewarded. Munton, who removed him, bowled a marathon spell of 24 overs broken only by lunch. Finally, Warwickshire put the conditions into perspective. An opening stand of 93 in 29 overs set them on the right path, and Asif Din played extremely well in making the top score of a low-key game. Punishing every bowling error, he hit thirteen fours in his 77 from 141 balls. Munton, the night-watchman, remained unbeaten, facing 90 deliveries in all as Warwickshire moved smoothly to victory.

Close of play: First day, Yorkshire 9-0 (A. A. Metcalfe 9*, D. Byas 0*); Second day, Warwickshire 112-2 (Asif Din 12*, T. A. Munton 0*).

Yorkshire

A. A. Metcalfe b Donald	4	– lbw b Munton	25
D. Byas c Moles b Munton	57	– c Humpage b Donald	6
K. Sharp c Humpage b Smith	33	– b Donald	0
J. D. Love lbw b Parsons	1	– c Moles b Parsons	0
P. E. Robinson b Smith	9	– lbw b Munton	13
†D. L. Bairstow c Humpage b Donald	27	– (7) b Donald	10
*P. Carrick lbw b Munton	2	– (8) b Munton	19
I. G. Swallow not out	7	– (6) b Munton	8
A. Sidebottom c Humpage b Donald	5	– b Donald	15
S. J. Dennis b Donald	0	– not out	14
C. Shaw c Asif Din b Donald	4	– c Humpage b Smith	2
B 2, l-b 4, n-b 8	14	L-b 9, w 1, n-b 1	11
1/5 2/89 3/96 4/109 5/123 6/143 7/145 8/152 9/152	163	1/28 2/30 3/30 4/43 5/56 6/61 7/85 8/89 9/108	123

Bonus points – Yorkshire 1, Warwickshire 4.

Bowling: *First Innings*—Donald 19.4–2–57–5; Munton 13–5–26–2; Reeve 3–0–14–0; Parsons 12–5–26–1; Smith 9–1–34–2. *Second Innings*—Donald 22–9–36–4; Munton 25–12–35–4; Parsons 11–2–35–1; Smith 3.5–1–8–1.

Warwickshire

*T. A. Lloyd lbw b Dennis	2	– (2) b Shaw	49
A. J. Moles lbw b Shaw	27	– (1) lbw b Sidebottom	43
Asif Din c Bairstow b Sidebottom	5	– c Swallow b Shaw	77
A. C. Storie c Bairstow b Dennis	4	– (5) not out	4
†G. W. Humpage lbw b Shaw	10		
P. A. Smith c Robinson b Shaw	0		
D. A. Reeve c Sharp b Shaw	13		
G. J. Parsons not out	14		
A. A. Donald c Bairstow b Dennis	1		
T. A. Munton c Sharp b Sidebottom	0	– (4) not out	13
N. Gifford lbw b Sidebottom	0		
L-b 4, n-b 1	5	B 10, l-b 8, n-b 2	20
1/3 2/9 3/14 4/37 5/37 6/60 7/63 8/78 9/79	81	1/93 2/112 3/201	(3 wkts) 206

Bonus points – Yorkshire 4.

Bowling: *First Innings*—Sidebottom 15.2–7–25–3; Dennis 17–3–35–3; Shaw 12–5–17–4. *Second Innings*—Sidebottom 18–7–43–1; Dennis 19–4–73–0; Shaw 23.4–10–46–2; Carrick 8–5–10–0; Byas 4–0–16–0.

Umpires: J. Birkenshaw and B. Hassan.

YORKSHIRE v ESSEX

At Sheffield, June 18, 20. Essex won by nine wickets. Essex 21 pts, Yorkshire 4 pts. Toss: Yorkshire. Poor batting characterised the game on a pitch which Border, captaining Essex, described as the best he had seen in the season. Foster's opening spell of 12–5–19–3 broke the back of Yorkshire's resistance, although Swallow prevented a complete collapse. Essex appeared to be heading for a big lead until Fletcher produced a spell of four wickets for 2 runs on his way to a career-best return. He became the first Yorkshire bowler for eight years to take eight wickets in an innings. Sadly his batsmen wasted the opportunity afforded them by this splendid effort. Lever and Foster soon reduced Yorkshire to 11 for four, and every delivery which bounced a little or moved off the seam seemed to bring a wicket. Robinson and Swallow briefly promised a recovery by adding 54 in 25 overs, but Essex were left with an easy target to win inside two days.

Close of play: First day, Essex 135-7 (J. K. Lever 1*, T. D. Topley 2*).

Yorkshire

A. A. Metcalfe c Hardie b Foster	6	– c Border b Lever	5
D. Byas c Brown b Lever	4	– lbw b Lever	0
R. J. Blakey c Hardie b Foster	4	– c Border b Foster	1
K. Sharp b Topley	22	– c Miller b Foster	5
P. E. Robinson c Miller b Foster	8	– (6) b Topley	33
†D. L. Bairstow c Brown b Lever	7	– (7) c Childs b Foster	14
*P. Carrick c Brown b Lever	1	– (8) c Brown b Lever	11
I. G. Swallow c Brown b Foster	37	– (5) c Lilley b Topley	27
A. Sidebottom lbw b Foster	24	– c Topley b Foster	2
C. Shaw not out	6	– c Brown b Topley	0
S. D. Fletcher c Childs b Foster	0	– not out	8
B 2, l-b 5, n-b 7	14	L-b 1, n-b 6	7
1/12 2/12 3/27 4/39 5/54 6/54 7/67 8/108 9/129	133	1/5 2/6 3/8 4/11 5/65 6/89 7/96 8/98 9/99	113

Bonus points – Essex 4.

Bowling: *First Innings*—Foster 22.1–7–53–6; Lever 17–4–30–3; Topley 13–1–39–1; Childs 2–1–4–0. *Second Innings*—Foster 16–6–33–4; Lever 15.3–3–41–3; Topley 15–2–38–3.

Essex

B. R. Hardie c Bairstow b Fletcher	3	– (2) not out	33
J. P. Stephenson b Fletcher	12	– (1) lbw b Sidebottom	9
P. J. Prichard c Metcalfe b Fletcher	54	– not out	39
*A. R. Border lbw b Shaw	39		
A. W. Lilley c Bairstow b Fletcher	13		
G. Miller lbw b Fletcher	1		
J. K. Lever b Fletcher	1		
N. A. Foster c Bairstow b Fletcher	1		
T. D. Topley not out	17		
†A. D. Brown c Bairstow b Fletcher	2		
J. H. Childs c Byas b Sidebottom	4		
B 5, l-b 3, w 1, n-b 2	11	L-b 4, n-b 4	8
1/7 2/26 3/100 4/125 5/130 6/131 7/133 8/136 9/140	158	1/25	(1 wkt) 89

Bonus points – Essex 1, Yorkshire 4.

Bowling: *First Innings*—Fletcher 24–6–58–8; Sidebottom 15.5–3–35–1; Shaw 12–1–33–1; Swallow 8–1–18–0; Carrick 4–2–6–0. *Second Innings*—Fletcher 6–0–35–0; Sidebottom 8–0–29–1; Shaw 5–0–13–0; Byas 2.2–0–8–0.

Umpires: J. Birkenshaw and B. Hassan.

At Hove, June 25, 27, 28. YORKSHIRE beat SUSSEX by three wickets.

At Lord's, June 29, 30, July 1. YORKSHIRE drew with MIDDLESEX.

YORKSHIRE v LEICESTERSHIRE

At Leeds, July 2, 4, 5. Yorkshire won by four wickets. Yorkshire 19 pts, Leicestershire 2 pts. Toss: Yorkshire. Leicestershire made steady progress after being put in on an easy-paced pitch, although bad light and rain cut 36 overs from the first day. Rain washed out the second day, and on the third Willey went on to complete his first century at Headingley in his 23rd season of county cricket. He made his 104 from 213 balls in 235 minutes, hitting twelve boundaries. Carrick also enjoyed a surprising personal achievement in taking five wickets for the first time at Headingley, having been playing for Yorkshire since 1970. Both sides forfeited an innings to leave Yorkshire with 68 overs in which to score 254. Leicestershire set the pattern for a poor day in the field when Metcalfe was missed behind the wicket off Ferris in the first over. Love escaped a sharp chance to Willey in the gully off Lewis when 15 and also chopped Agnew firmly on to his stumps without dislodging a bail as he played the match-winning innings – 68 from 81 deliveries with two sixes and six fours. Leicestershire appeared to have gained the advantage when the fifth Yorkshire wicket fell at 143, but Agnew was wayward in terms of length and line, and Hartley played well as the home side won with nine balls to spare.

Close of play: First day, Leicestershire 155-4 (P. Willey 91*, P. N. Hepworth 1*); Second day, No play.

Leicestershire

*N. E. Briers c Byas b Fletcher	5
R. A. Cobb c Love b Sidebottom	38
P. Willey c Robinson b Shaw	104
J. J. Whitaker c Robinson b Carrick	0
L. Potter c Byas b Sidebottom	10
P. N. Hepworth c Blakey b Sidebottom	35
C. C. Lewis st Blakey b Carrick	35
J. P. Agnew b Carrick	0
†P. Whitticase b Carrick	0
G. J. F. Ferris not out	8
L. B. Taylor st Blakey b Carrick	4
L-b 5, w 1, n-b 8	14
1/7 2/120 3/121 4/151 5/175 6/235 7/236 8/236 9/243	253

Bonus points – Leicestershire 2, Yorkshire 3 (Score at 100 overs: 236-7).

Bowling: Sidebottom 33–12–60–3; Fletcher 22–3–78–1; Hartley 5–1–25–0; Shaw 14–3–39–1; Carrick 33.5–13–46–5.

Leicestershire forfeited their second innings.

Yorkshire

Yorkshire forfeited their first innings.

A. A. Metcalfe c Whitaker b Taylor	21
D. Byas c Whitticase b Ferris	28
†R. J. Blakey c and b Taylor	51
K. Sharp c Lewis b Ferris	10
P. E. Robinson c Whitaker b Ferris	0
J. D. Love c Cobb b Ferris	68
S. N. Hartley not out	26
*P. Carrick not out	22
L-b 15, w 3, n-b 12	30
1/38 2/83 3/105 4/105 5/143 6/224	(6 wkts) 256

A. Sidebottom, S. D. Fletcher and C. Shaw did not bat.

Bowling: Ferris 19.3–4–74–4; Agnew 20–4–78–0; Lewis 15–2–43–0; Taylor 12–0–46–2.

Umpires: H. D. Bird and P. J. Eele.

At Worcester, July 20, 21, 22. YORKSHIRE lost to WORCESTERSHIRE by 21 runs.

At Cardiff, July 23, 25, 26. YORKSHIRE drew with GLAMORGAN.

YORKSHIRE v LANCASHIRE

At Leeds, July 30, August 1. Yorkshire won by ten wickets. Yorkshire 23 pts, Lancashire 5 pts. Toss: Lancashire. Lancashire appeared to be building a useful score on an easy-paced pitch when they reached 114 with only three wickets down. At that point, however, Watkinson was lbw to Sidebottom and his dismissal started a major collapse. Sidebottom took four for 4 in 21 balls as Lancashire lost six wickets for 12 runs in nine overs of irresponsible batting. Mendis, the only batsman to achieve any degree of permanence, battled for three hours before being eighth out. Lancashire were handicapped by the absence of Wasim Akram with a groin strain on the second day, but Allott bravely overcame the pain from a damaged foot to lead their attack with great spirit. Yorkshire did not, in fact, take full advantage of a favourable situation and were still 2 runs behind when their sixth wicket fell, despite a sound contribution from Love, who had fourteen fours in his 116-ball 77. Sidebottom and Carrick, however, added 78 in 24 overs and ensured a good lead. Lancashire failed to do themselves justice for a second time, Sidebottom taking two wickets in his second over to undermine their resolve. Fairbrother attempted to stop the rot with a determined innings which included seven boundaries and occupied a little over two hours, but once again wild strokeplay gave away wickets. By claiming the extra half-hour, Yorkshire were able to win in two days, thus ending a sequence of twelve draws between the counties.

Close of play: First day, Yorkshire 90-3 (J. D. Love 45*, P. E. Robinson 17*).

Lancashire

G. D. Mendis c Bairstow b Sidebottom	58	– c Bairstow b Sidebottom	0
G. Fowler b Hartley	0	– c Blakey b Shaw	24
M. A. Atherton c Love b Shaw	13	– c Bairstow b Sidebottom	0
N. H. Fairbrother c Moxon b Fletcher	15	– c Bairstow b Hartley	43
M. Watkinson lbw b Sidebottom	20	– lbw b Fletcher	11
*D. P. Hughes c Moxon b Sidebottom	3	– c Robinson b Hartley	5
Wasim Akram lbw b Sidebottom	0	– b Hartley	6
A. N. Hayhurst c Sidebottom b Shaw	1	– b Fletcher	3
†W. K. Hegg not out	13	– b Fletcher	31
P. J. W. Allott c Moxon b Shaw	1	– c Hartley b Fletcher	0
J. Simmons c Love b Hartley	18	– not out	7
L-b 10, w 1, n-b 1	12	B 6, l-b 13, w 1, n-b 6	26
1/4 2/37 3/55 4/114 5/120 6/120 7/121 8/125 9/126	154	1/3 2/3 3/48 4/69 5/82 6/92 7/115 8/117 9/140	156

Bonus points – Lancashire 1, Yorkshire 4.

Bowling: *First Innings*—Sidebottom 14–2–32–4; Hartley 8.5–1–29–2; Fletcher 10–2–36–1; Shaw 18–7–47–3. *Second Innings*—Sidebottom 8–4–17–2; Hartley 15–1–65–3; Fletcher 13–3–36–4; Shaw 5–1–19–1.

Yorkshire

M. D. Moxon c Hegg b Wasim	2	– not out	9
A. A. Metcalfe c Atherton b Allott	13	– not out	9
R. J. Blakey lbw b Wasim	12		
J. D. Love c Hegg b Allott	77		
P. E. Robinson lbw b Allott	27		
†D. L. Bairstow b Hayhurst	15		
*P. Carrick lbw b Allott	37		
A. Sidebottom lbw b Allott	55		
P. J. Hartley c Hughes b Simmons	27		
S. D. Fletcher run out	7		
C. Shaw not out	6		
L-b 15	15		
1/12 2/18 3/34 4/115 5/148 6/152 7/230 8/249 9/282	293		(no wkt) 18

Bonus points – Yorkshire 3, Lancashire 4.

Bowling: *First Innings*—Wasim 15–2–32–2; Allott 32–7–85–5; Watkinson 27–5–100–0; Hayhurst 14–3–49–1; Simmons 5.3–0–12–1. *Second Innings*—Hayhurst 3–1–7–0; Fairbrother 2.4–0–11–0.

Umpires: J. W. Holder and R. Palmer.

YORKSHIRE v NOTTINGHAMSHIRE

At Sheffield, August 3, 4, 5. Drawn. Yorkshire 8 pts, Nottinghamshire 5 pts. Toss: Yorkshire. The game was dogged by rain, which badly affected the first two days and made it almost impossible to bring about a positive finish. Robinson, compiling his career-best score, dominated the Yorkshire innings, batting for almost five hours, receiving 276 balls and hitting eleven fours. He and Love added 79 in 24 overs at an important stage, and later, with Shaw, he made sure of a fourth batting point in a last-wicket stand of 78 in twenty overs. Nottinghamshire collapsed in good batting conditions and at 142 for eight were in danger of being asked to follow on. Johnson, who was badly missed at slip by Carrick off Shaw when 34, batted defiantly, the nature of his innings being reflected in the fact that his 124 came from 129 balls and included a six and ten fours. Yorkshire were given runs in order to set up a fourth-innings chase on the last afternoon, and Nottinghamshire's target became 262 in 53 overs. When Broad and Robinson used 34 of them while putting on 119 for the first wicket, their colleagues were left with too much to do, particularly as Yorkshire adopted defensive measures in the field.

Close of play: First day, Yorkshire 182-5 (P. E. Robinson 53*, P. Carrick 8*); Second day, Nottinghamshire 110-6 (P. Johnson 69*, C. W. Scott 11*).

Yorkshire

M. D. Moxon c Randall b Cooper	12	– not out	64
A. A. Metcalfe b Hemmings	27	– not out	51
R. J. Blakey c Johnson b Cooper	5		
J. D. Love c Randall b Millns	69		
P. E. Robinson not out	129		
†D. L. Bairstow c Cooper b Hemmings	4		
*P. Carrick b Stephenson	26		
I. G. Swallow c Millns b Stephenson	2		
P. J. Hartley lbw b Hemmings	23		
S. D. Fletcher c Scott b Hemmings	1		
C. Shaw b Stephenson	31		
B 1, l-b 6, n-b 1	8	B 1, l-b 3	4
1/21 2/37 3/64 4/143 5/163 6/203 7/207 8/257 9/259	337		(no wkt dec.) 119

Bonus points – Yorkshire 4, Nottinghamshire 4 (Score at 100 overs: 302-9).

Bowling: *First Innings*—Stephenson 31.5–7–91–3; Cooper 33–7–83–2; Millns 19–1–83–1; Hemmings 25–4–73–4. *Second Innings*—Stephenson 3–0–13–0; Millns 6–1–18–0; Birch 7.3–1–46–0; Robinson 4–0–38–0.

Nottinghamshire

	First innings		Second innings	
B. C. Broad lbw b Fletcher	1	–	b Fletcher	45
*R. T. Robinson lbw b Hartley	6	–	b Fletcher	67
P. Johnson c Blakey b Shaw	124	–	lbw b Fletcher	2
D. J. R. Martindale lbw b Hartley	0	–	c Blakey b Fletcher	6
D. W. Randall c Blakey b Shaw	12	–	not out	29
J. D. Birch c Bairstow b Hartley	0	–	(7) not out	18
F. D. Stephenson c Bairstow b Shaw	10	–	(6) run out	13
†C. W. Scott c Bairstow b Fletcher	11			
E. E. Hemmings c Blakey b Hartley	3			
K. E. Cooper b Hartley	16			
D. J. Millns not out	0			
L-b 7, w 1, n-b 4	12		B 6, l-b 12	18
1/3 2/15 3/23 4/45 5/50 6/84 7/129 8/142 9/191	195		1/119 2/121 3/136 4/137 5/165	(5 wkts) 198

Bonus points – Nottinghamshire 1, Yorkshire 4.

Bowling: *First Innings*—Hartley 21–3–85–5; Fletcher 18–2–59–2; Shaw 15.4–1–44–3. *Second Innings*—Hartley 8–0–40–0; Fletcher 12–0–48–4; Shaw 12–1–41–0; Carrick 17–1–51–0.

Umpires: A. A. Jones and D. R. Shepherd.

At Cheltenham, August 6, 8, 9. YORKSHIRE drew with GLOUCESTERSHIRE.

At Leeds, August 10, 11, 12. YORKSHIRE drew with SRI LANKANS (See Sri Lankan tour section).

YORKSHIRE v SOMERSET

At Scarborough, August 13, 15, 16. Drawn. Yorkshire 7 pts, Somerset 3 pts. Toss: Yorkshire. Yorkshire scored steadily throughout the first day on a pitch which gave the bowlers no assistance, yet only just managed the fourth batting point in the 100th over. Somerset, after a good start, surprisingly lost their way as Carrick chipped away in a marathon spell. Hardy, who became the third batsman to get out in the 90s, made his 97 from 206 balls, hitting twelve fours, and Rose contributed important runs as the follow-on was avoided. Yorkshire, given a lead of 99, sacrificed wickets in return for quick runs, although at 104 for five they were in some danger of being bowled out too cheaply. However, Blakey and Carrick added 50 in eight overs and Somerset were finally set a reasonable target of 282 in what became 65 overs. They scored much too slowly in the early stages, managing only 3 an over in the first half of their innings, in addition to which Yorkshire were negative in their field-placings. The match was drifting quietly towards a draw when Fletcher took two wickets with the first two balls of the final over to reduce Somerset to 241 for nine, but Jones survived the remaining four deliveries.

Close of play: First day, Yorkshire 369-3 (P. E. Robinson 81*); Second day, Yorkshire 33-0 (M. D. Moxon 10*, A. A. Metcalfe 22*).

Yorkshire

M. D. Moxon c Jones b Trump	81	– b Mallender	10
A. A. Metcalfe c Burns b Rose	98	– c Mallender b Trump	31
D. Byas c Jones b Mallender	98	– lbw b Mallender	0
P. E. Robinson not out	81	– c Wyatt b Marks	53
K. Sharp (did not bat)		– run out	5
†R. J. Blakey (did not bat)		– c Trump b Marks	30
*P. Carrick (did not bat)		– c Jones b Bartlett	43
A. Sidebottom (did not bat)		– not out	0
P. J. Hartley (did not bat)		– not out	5
L-b 2, w 1, n-b 8	11	L-b 1, n-b 4	5
1/162 2/195 3/369	(3 wkts dec.) 369	1/43 2/44 3/44 4/104 5/104 6/154 7/177	(7 wkts dec.) 182

C. Shaw and S. D. Fletcher did not bat.

Bonus points – Yorkshire 4 (Score at 100 overs: 300-2).

Bowling: *First Innings*—Jones 20–5–71–0; Mallender 17.1–3–46–1; Rose 16–3–71–1; Marks 31–6–98–0; Trump 26–6–81–1. *Second Innings*—Mallender 11–4–19–2; Jones 8–0–26–0; Trump 10–3–56–1; Marks 14–2–63–2; Rose 4–2–8–0; Bartlett 1–0–9–1.

Somerset

J. J. E. Hardy c Sharp b Carrick	97	– c and b Fletcher	10
N. A. Felton b Sidebottom	21	– b Carrick	61
†N. D. Burns c Blakey b Carrick	15	– (6) c Moxon b Carrick	3
S. R. Waugh lbw b Sidebottom	2	– b Fletcher	31
R. J. Bartlett c Blakey b Carrick	0	– b Carrick	33
G. D. Rose not out	69	– (8) c Sharp b Carrick	8
*V. J. Marks lbw b Fletcher	25	– not out	33
J. G. Wyatt c Moxon b Carrick	1	– (3) c Byas b Sidebottom	44
H. R. J. Trump lbw b Sidebottom	0	– (10) lbw b Fletcher	0
N. A. Mallender not out	23	– (9) b Fletcher	3
A. N. Jones (did not bat)		– not out	0
L-b 9, n-b 8	17	L-b 5, n-b 10	15
1/86 2/117 3/128 4/135 5/149 6/196 7/203 8/214	(8 wkts dec.) 270	1/24 2/124 3/134 4/190 5/194 6/218 7/231 8/241 9/241	(9 wkts) 241

Bonus points – Somerset 3, Yorkshire 3 (Score at 100 overs: 260-8).

Bowling: *First Innings*—Sidebottom 24–6–50–3; Hartley 8–1–34–0; Shaw 17–4–60–0; Fletcher 15–2–40–1; Carrick 38–13–77–4. *Second Innings*—Sidebottom 19–2–63–1; Fletcher 15–1–40–4; Hartley 5–0–24–0; Shaw 5–1–14–0; Carrick 21–2–95–4.

Umpires: J. H. Hampshire and N. T. Plews.

At Chesterfield, August 17, 18, 19. YORKSHIRE drew with DERBYSHIRE.

YORKSHIRE v MIDDLESEX

At Leeds, August 25, 26, 27, 29. Drawn. Yorkshire 4 pts, Middlesex 4 pts. Toss: Yorkshire. Yorkshire occupied the crease for more than nine hours in their first innings. The pitch was very slow and Metcalfe batted with tremendous concentration, receiving 508 balls and hitting one six and twenty fours in his career-best, unbeaten 216. Yorkshire managed just two batting points, although Love brought about some acceleration with 70 from 86 deliveries to dominate a stand of 125 in 25 overs. Steady bowling by Carrick caused a minor collapse in the Middlesex reply as three wickets fell for 5 runs in six overs to raise the prospect of the follow-on; but Roseberry and Ramprakash responded with a stand worth 110 in 30 overs. They played with style and flair, and Gatting was able to declare 148 behind. Yorkshire were then given cheap runs to set up a declaration which demanded 334 in 81 overs. Slack gave the run-chase a positive start, his 83 coming from 129 balls, and Middlesex sacrificed wickets in a determined bid for victory. They required 114 from the last twenty overs and 40 from the final five. An exciting finish reached its climax when Cowans, the last man, survived after deflecting the ball on to his stumps without dislodging a bail.

Close of play: First day, Yorkshire 215-2 (A. A. Metcalfe 109*, P. E. Robinson 30*); Second day, Middlesex 164-2 (A. Needham 23*, M. A. Roseberry 6*); Third day, Yorkshire 92-0 (M. D. Moxon 33*, A. A. Metcalfe 44*).

Yorkshire

M. D. Moxon b Gatting	57	– not out	89
A. A. Metcalfe not out	216	– not out	78
D. Byas lbw b Carr	0		
P. E. Robinson b Needham	88		
J. D. Love not out	70		
B 4, l-b 20, w 1, n-b 7	32	L-b 9, w 5, n-b 4	18
1/134 2/135 3/338 (3 wkts dec.)	463	(no wkt dec.)	185

†R. J. Blakey, *P. Carrick, A. Sidebottom, P. J. Hartley, C. Shaw and S. D. Fletcher did not bat.

Bonus points – Yorkshire 2 (Score at 100 overs: 215-2).

Bowling: *First Innings*—Cowans 20–5–52–0; Fraser 30–11–50–0; Hughes 31–5–86–0; Slack 1–1–0–0; Carr 27–8–52–1; Gatting 20–7–36–1; Needham 20–3–78–1; Sykes 19–0–85–0. *Second Innings*—Fraser 7–1–22–0; Cowans 6–1–26–0; Hughes 14–5–20–0; Gatting 9–2–51–0; Needham 7–0–37–0; Roseberry 4–0–19–0; Ramprakash 1–0–1–0.

Middlesex

W. N. Slack c Metcalfe b Carrick	75	– c Blakey b Fletcher	83
J. D. Carr c Carrick b Sidebottom	48	– c Blakey b Fletcher	18
A. Needham c Fletcher b Carrick	29	– b Fletcher	53
M. A. Roseberry c Robinson b Fletcher	67	– (5) c Love b Hartley	27
*M. W. Gatting b Carrick	1	– (4) c Moxon b Shaw	41
†K. R. Brown c Hartley b Carrick	2	– (7) not out	18
M. R. Ramprakash not out	68	– (6) c Moxon b Hartley	49
J. F. Sykes not out	3	– b Carrick	1
S. P. Hughes (did not bat)		– run out	13
A. R. C. Fraser (did not bat)		– run out	2
N. G. Cowans (did not bat)		– not out	3
B 2, l-b 6, w 5, n-b 9	22	L-b 8, w 1, n-b 5	14
1/122 2/145 3/179 4/180 5/184 6/294 (6 wkts dec.)	315	1/45 2/159 3/168 4/209 5/285 6/285 7/286 8/311 9/313 (9 wkts)	322

Bonus points – Middlesex 4, Yorkshire 2.

Bowling: *First Innings*—Sidebottom 22–5–74–1; Hartley 17–2–61–0; Carrick 28–9–67–4; Fletcher 17.2–5–56–1; Shaw 15–6–49–0. *Second Innings*—Hartley 18–1–66–2; Fletcher 19–1–55–3; Carrick 21–2–89–1; Shaw 18–2–77–1; Sidebottom 5–0–27–0.

Umpires: J. Birkenshaw and K. J. Lyons.

At Manchester, August 30, 31, September 1, 2. YORKSHIRE drew with LANCASHIRE.

†At Scarborough, September 7. YORKSHIRE lost to YORKSHIRE EXILES by eight wickets (See Other Matches, 1988).

YORKSHIRE v NORTHAMPTONSHIRE

At Scarborough, September 9, 10, 11, 12. Drawn. Yorkshire 5 pts, Northamptonshire 7 pts. Toss: Yorkshire. On a pitch offering the bowlers not the slightest hint of assistance, Yorkshire batted carelessly. Robinson, claiming three for 17 in a spell of 46 deliveries, brought about a minor collapse and the last seven wickets went down for 80 runs in 30 overs. Geoff Cook, missed at slip off Booth when 24, went on to a career-best 203 from 404 balls, hitting one six and 25 other boundaries. He and Capel put on 170 in 49 overs as Northamptonshire gained a lead of 144. Left-arm spinner Booth, in one of his rare appearances, was particularly impressive for Yorkshire as he flighted the ball intelligently. Yorkshire were left with nothing but the draw to play for and Moxon held their rearguard action together with his highest score. The opener resisted for more than six and a half hours, facing 393 balls and hitting 27 fours. By mid-afternoon Northamptonshire, who were handicapped by the absence of Nick Cook, who broke his thumb while batting, had accepted the inevitability of a draw – the twelfth in succession in Championship matches at Scarborough.

Close of play: First day, Northamptonshire 1-0 (G. Cook 0*, A. Fordham 0*); Second day, Northamptonshire 218-3 (G. Cook 97*, D. J. Capel 12*); Third day, Yorkshire 136-1 (M. D. Moxon 72*, D. Byas 25*).

Yorkshire

M. D. Moxon c Ripley b Williams	86	– c Lamb b Williams	191
A. A. Metcalfe c and b Williams	56	– lbw b Robinson	26
D. Byas c Ripley b Williams	21	– c Lamb b Williams	72
P. E. Robinson c Capel b N. G. B. Cook	32	– b Robinson	17
J. D. Love c G. Cook b Robinson	45	– lbw b Robinson	14
†R. J. Blakey c Ripley b Robinson	0	– not out	45
*P. Carrick c Ripley b Robinson	12		
P. J. Hartley st Ripley b Williams	1	– not out	12
P. A. Booth c Capel b Davis	28	– (7) c Fordham b Williams	0
C. Shaw not out	19		
S. D. Fletcher c G. Cook b Walker	0		
L-b 5, n-b 15	20	B 3, l-b 3, n-b 14	20
1/102 2/158 3/174 4/240 5/241 6/258 7/267 8/276 9/312	320	1/79 2/245 3/281 4/311 5/356 6/356	(6 wkts) 397

Bonus points – Yorkshire 4, Northamptonshire 3 (Score at 100 overs: 301-8).

Bowling: *First Innings*—Davis 18–2–67–1; Walker 10–1–43–1; Robinson 19–3–53–3; N. G. B. Cook 22–7–46–1; Williams 30–7–80–4; Capel 5–0–26–0. *Second Innings*—Davis 9–2–31–0; Capel 6–0–39–0; Williams 48–12–110–3; Robinson 20–6–59–3; N. G. B. Cook 9–3–13–0; Bailey 33–6–107–0; Walker 11.2–2–27–0; G. Cook 2–0–5–0.

Northamptonshire

*G. Cook b Fletcher	203
A. Fordham c Moxon b Hartley	3
R. J. Bailey c Fletcher b Booth	17
A. J. Lamb c Byas b Booth	76
D. J. Capel c Carrick b Shaw	69
R. G. Williams c Fletcher b Booth	14
†D. Ripley c Blakey b Carrick	12
N. G. B. Cook retired hurt	2
W. W. Davis c Fletcher b Carrick	29
A. Walker b Booth	13
M. A. Robinson not out	0
B 4, l-b 14, w 1, n-b 7	26
1/19 2/55 3/180 4/350 5/387 6/417 7/421 8/458 9/464	464

Bonus points – Northamptonshire 4, Yorkshire 1 (Score at 100 overs: 306-3).

Bowling: Hartley 16–1–58–1; Fletcher 25–3–91–1; Shaw 23–5–60–1; Booth 54–12–132–4; Carrick 33.1–11–105–2.

Umpires: D. O. Oslear and P. B. Wight.

At Nottingham, September 14, 15, 16, 17. YORKSHIRE beat NOTTINGHAMSHIRE by 127 runs.

THE UNIVERSITIES IN 1988

OXFORD

President: M. J. K. Smith (St Edmund Hall)
Hon. Treasurer: Dr S. R. Porter (Nuffield College)

Captain: M. J. Kilborn (Farrer Agric. HS, University of New South Wales and St John's)
Secretary: S. D. Weale (Westminster City and Keble)

Captain for 1989: M. A. Crawley (Manchester GS and Oriel)
Secretary: P. G. Edwards (Canford and Christ Church)

Oxford University lost only two of their first-class matches in another depressingly wet season at The Parks, but the record conceals weaknesses which have persisted over the last five years. On account of an unbending admissions policy, Oxford cannot compete with other universities, notably Durham, for the promising, up-and-coming cricketer who is pursuing a university education. Until it is relaxed, they will continue to be the poor relations amongst the universities.

After being beaten comprehensively in their first two matches, Oxford drew their remaining five first-class matches through a combination of improved batting in the second innings, rain, and the counties' preference for batting practice in the second innings rather than enforcing the follow-on. The Dark Blues are most vulnerable in the early part of the season, and the defeats by an innings and more than 150 runs by Leicestershire and Northamptonshire underlined the weakness, which was increased by an injury to all-rounder Mark Crawley. He missed the first half of the season with a dislocated collarbone, the result of a cycling mishap, and his absence considerably weakened the batting.

Nevertheless, what strength Oxford possessed was in the batting. Twice, against Hampshire and Lancashire, they had to bat throughout the last day, and they did so well that the counties conceded draws before the end of the match. They were well served by their openers, Simon Almaer and David Hagan, and Mike Kilborn, the captain, provided the backbone of the innings. Almaer and Hagan were most consistent, regularly giving the innings a start of 50 or more, and the 102 against Lancashire in the second innings was Oxford's first century opening partnership for two years.

Almaer, a Freshman, batted for two and a half hours for 4 runs on his début against Northamptonshire, and throughout the season he revealed great concentration and endurance. Kilborn batted with the same freedom as in the previous year but suffered the same affliction of getting out when looking set for a big score. Crawley's 98 against Nottinghamshire in the last match was the Dark Blues' highest individual score, and the 120 he put on with Kilborn in the same match was the best partnership.

The opening bowling was the main weakness. Iain Henderson was woefully inaccurate and he again failed to overcome the problem of overstepping. Malcolm Sygrove and John Nuttall bore the brunt of the opening bowling, and although both were rewarded on occasions, the county batsmen accumulated thirteen centuries between them. The two slow left-arm

OXFORD UNIVERSITY 1988

[Bill Smith

Back row: R. G. M. Carter (*coach*), G. D. Reynolds, M. E. O. Brown, J. D. Nuttall, M. R. Sygrove, T. B. Jack, S. A. Almaer, D. A. Polkinghorne.
Front row: M. A. Crawley, S. D. Weale, M. J. Kilborn (*captain*), D. A. Hagan, P. G. Edwards.

bowlers, Patrick Edwards and Simon Weale, toiled tirelessly, but both suffered from too many dropped catches. Overall the fielding again did not measure up to the standard set by their opponents.

The future of Oxford cricket cannot be viewed with any great optimism. It is so different from the fortunes of the Boat Club and Rugby Club, who can compete and hold their own at the highest level. Perhaps the cricket hierarchy have something to learn from the other clubs. – Paton Fenton.

OXFORD UNIVERSITY RESULTS

First-class matches – Played 7: Lost 2, Drawn 5. Abandoned 1.

FIRST-CLASS AVERAGES

BATTING AND FIELDING

	Birthplace	*M*	*I*	*NO*	*R*	*HI*	*Avge*	*Ct/St*
M. A. Crawley	*Newton-le-Willows*	4	7	2	177	98	35.40	2
D. A. Hagan	*Wide Open*	7	13	2	306	59	27.81	3
M. J. Kilborn	*Gunnedah, Australia*	7	13	0	351	78	27.00	5
D. A. Polkinghorne ...	*Durban, SA*	3	4	1	72	45*	24.00	2
M. E. O. Brown	*Durban, SA*	3	5	2	71	47	23.66	0
S. A. Almaer	*Wanstead*	6	11	0	256	67	23.27	2
G. D. Reynolds	*Wegburg, WG*	6	9	1	147	69	18.37	6
S. D. Weale	*Knightsbridge*	6	9	0	136	40	15.11	3
J. D. Nuttall	*Fulford*	5	6	2	52	35	13.00	2
I. M. Henderson	*Glapthorn*	5	7	1	55	21*	9.16	1
P. G. Edwards	*Bradford-on-Avon*	5	7	3	32	9	8.00	2
M. R. Sygrove	*Lutterworth*	7	8	3	29	8*	5.80	0
R. E. Morris	*St Asaph*	4	8	0	39	21	4.87	1
A. N. S. Hampton	*Burton upon Trent*	3	6	0	22	12	3.66	0

Also batted: N. H. Green (*South Norwood*) (1 match) 9 (1 ct); N. Heppel (*Hampton Court*) (1 match) 14*; T. B. Jack (*Perth, Australia*) (2 matches) 29, 5, 23 (1 ct); A. M. Searle (*Stamford*) (1 match) 2; J. E. B. Cope (*Leigh-on-Sea*) (1 match) (1 ct) did not bat.

* *Signifies not out.*

BOWLING

	O	*M*	*R*	*W*	*BB*	*Avge*
M. J. Kilborn	41.5	8	185	5	3-37	37.00
M. R. Sygrove	215.4	34	848	18	3-91	47.11
J. D. Nuttall	116	20	410	7	2-64	58.57
P. G. Edwards	171.3	43	560	9	3-88	62.22
I. M. Henderson ...	71	10	316	5	3-104	63.20
S. D. Weale	200	41	681	8	3-130	85.12

Also bowled: D. A. Hagan 3–0–21–0; M. A. Crawley 38–7–136–0; A. M. Searle 17–2–76–0; N. Heppel 14–0–74–0.

OXFORD UNIVERSITY v LEICESTERSHIRE

At Oxford, April 16, 18, 19. Leicestershire won by an innings and 153 runs. Toss: Leicestershire. Only Kilborn reached double figures when the University were put in and dismissed for 98. Beginning the second day at 66 for three, they lost their remaining wickets for 32 runs in 22.2 overs. Leicestershire, passing Oxford's score for the loss of one wicket, declared with a lead of 221. Briers and Boon gave the innings a sound start with 83 and later Whitaker and Potter hit half-centuries. Oxford fared even worse in their second innings and were shot out for 68, with Lewis taking five wickets in an innings and ten in a match for the first time. Green had suffered a broken finger and did not bat again.

Close of play: First day, Oxford University 66-3 (M. J. Kilborn 40*, N. H. Green 4*); Second day, Leicestershire 177-3 (N. E. Briers 67*, J. J. Whitaker 19*).

Oxford University

D. A. Hagan c Whitticase b DeFreitas	9	– lbw b DeFreitas	18
R. E. Morris c Whitaker b Taylor	1	– (7) c Whitaker b Such	1
*M. J. Kilborn b DeFreitas	48	– c Whitticase b Lewis	8
†G. D. Reynolds c Whitticase b Taylor	7	– (2) c Whitticase b Lewis	13
N. H. Green c Whitaker b Lewis	9	– absent injured	
A. N. S. Hampton c Whitticase b DeFreitas	0	– (5) c DeFreitas b Lewis	7
S. D. Weale c Whitaker b DeFreitas	8	– (6) c and b Lewis	12
I. M. Henderson c Whitticase b Lewis	1	– (4) c sub b Lewis	0
P. G. Edwards not out	5	– (8) c Boon b Lewis	1
M. R. Sygrove c Potter b Lewis	4	– b Such	1
J. D. Nuttall b Lewis	1	– (9) not out	2
L-b 3, n-b 2	5	B 1, l-b 2, n-b 2	5
1/2 2/20 3/43 4/79 5/79 6/81 7/88 8/88 9/92	98	1/24 2/33 3/33 4/47 5/50 6/62 7/64 8/67 9/68	68

Bowling: *First Innings*—DeFreitas 22–13–15–4; Taylor 10–3–32–2; Lewis 19.2–4–48–4. *Second Innings*—DeFreitas 8–4–18–1; Taylor 9–5–16–0; Lewis 13–5–22–6; Such 8.5–2–9–2.

Leicestershire

T. J. Boon c Green b Sygrove	43
N. E. Briers c Reynolds b Sygrove	80
*D. I. Gower b Sygrove	26
P. Willey c Kilborn b Edwards	8
J. J. Whitaker c Nuttall b Edwards	53
L. Potter not out	54
P. A. J. DeFreitas c Kilborn b Weale	0
C. C. Lewis not out	36
B 3, l-b 6, n-b 10	19
1/83 2/126 3/139 4/206 5/244 6/244 (6 wkts dec.)	319

†P. Whitticase, P. M. Such and L. B. Taylor did not bat.

Bowling: Henderson 7–0–35–0; Nuttall 13–1–70–0; Sygrove 23–4–91–3; Edwards 31–7–74–2; Weale 15–5–40–1.

Umpires: J. D. Bond and N. T. Plews.

OXFORD UNIVERSITY v NORTHAMPTONSHIRE

At Oxford, April 20, 21, 22. Northamptonshire won by an innings and 157 runs. Toss: Northamptonshire. Oxford failed to benefit from an opening partnership of 53 by Almaer and Hagan. It took Almaer, who was making his first-class début, two and a half hours to score 4, but his determination failed to inspire the remaining batsmen and the innings closed at 137. Henderson dismissed Cook and Larkins, the county openers, for 45, but Bailey and Lamb put Northamptonshire in a commanding position with a stand that was worth 180 when Lamb retired hurt. Bailey's 101 contained three sixes and eleven fours, while Lamb hit a six and fourteen fours before falling heavily and injuring a shoulder. Northamptonshire declared on the third morning, 252 ahead with five hours remaining, and Almaer and Hagan gave Oxford hope of holding out for a draw by staying for an hour. After lunch, however, Cook and Brown captured seven wickets and Walker polished off the innings with a spell of three for 8.

Close of play: First day, Northamptonshire 5-0 (G. Cook 2*, W. Larkins 2*); Second day, Northamptonshire 336-4 (N. A. Stanley 51*, D. Ripley 21*).

Oxford University

D. A. Hagan c Bailey b Larkins	43	– c Ripley b Brown	36
S. A. Almaer c Bailey b Robinson	4	– b N. G. B. Cook	9
*M. J. Kilborn c Ripley b Robinson	7	– c Lamb b Brown	6
†G. D. Reynolds lbw b Brown	1	– (6) c Stanley b N. G. B. Cook	1
R. E. Morris c G. Cook b Williams	21	– (4) lbw b N. G. B. Cook	5
A. N. S. Hampton c Ripley b Robinson	12	– (5) lbw b N. G. B. Cook	2
S. D. Weale c G. Cook b N. G. B. Cook	14	– c N. G. B. Cook b Brown	10
I. M. Henderson c Ripley b Brown	9	– c Bailey b Walker	6
P. G. Edwards c Ripley b Walker	9	– not out	8
J. D. Nuttall b Walker	0	– b Walker	0
M. R. Sygrove not out	0	– c Ripley b Walker	8
B 3, l-b 2, w 1, n-b 11	17	L-b 3, n-b 1	4
1/53 2/61 3/66 4/67 5/96 6/113 7/119 8/135 9/137	137	1/34 2/50 3/57 4/61 5/63 6/64 7/74 8/83 9/83	95

Bowling: *First Innings*—Walker 22–9–40–2; Brown 21–13–25–2; Robinson 21–5–43–3; N. G. B. Cook 15–8–18–1; Larkins 9–9–0–1; Williams 4–3–6–1. *Second Innings*—Walker 12.4–5–20–3; Brown 16–8–20–3; N. G. B. Cook 24–7–32–4; Williams 5–2–7–0; Robinson 7–2–13–0.

Northamptonshire

*G. Cook c Hagan b Henderson	14
W. Larkins c Reynolds b Henderson	9
R. J. Bailey lbw b Henderson	101
A. J. Lamb retired hurt	101
R. G. Williams c Almaer b Weale	28
N. A. Stanley c Reynolds b Nuttall	66
†D. Ripley not out	41
N. G. B. Cook not out	14
B 2, l-b 5, w 1, n-b 7	15
1/15 2/45 3/236 4/306 5/360	(5 wkts dec.) 389

S. J. Brown, M. A. Robinson and A. Walker did not bat.

A. J. Lamb retired hurt at 225.

Bowling: Sygrove 16–3–57–0; Henderson 34–8–104–3; Edwards 23–3–85–0; Nuttall 23–5–59–1; Weale 35–13–66–1; Hagan 1–0–4–0; Kilborn 1–0–7–0.

Umpires: J. D. Bond and N. T. Plews.

OXFORD UNIVERSITY v HAMPSHIRE

At Oxford, May 5, 6, 7. Drawn. Toss: Hampshire. Oxford paid heavily for a dropped catch. Smith was put down when 10 off Henderson, who had dismissed Scott in the second over, and he went on to score 118, which included eighteen fours. Smith added 107 with Nicholas for the second wicket and 87 for the third with Turner, who went on to score 76. When Oxford batted, Hagan was struck on the elbow by Andrew's first ball of the innings and had to retire. Kilborn joined Almaer in a partnership of 50, but three wickets fell in four balls. Later, Ayling took a wicket with his first ball in first-class cricket when he dismissed another making his début, Polkinghorne. Although Hampshire led by 252, Nicholas did not enforce the follow-on, and the county's second declaration left Oxford with 380 minutes' batting. After losing Morris for 1, Almaer and Kilborn added 63, followed by 59 for the third wicket by Almaer and Hagan. The Dark Blues lost three quick wickets to the spinners, but Polkinghorne and Reynolds defied Hampshire with an unbroken partnership of 69.

Close of play: First day, Oxford University 38-0 (S. A. Almaer 12*, M. J. Kilborn 23*); second day, Oxford University 4-1 (S. A. Almaer 0*, M. J. Kilborn 3*).

Hampshire

First innings		Second innings	
R. J. Scott b Henderson	1	c Morris b Weale	11
*M. C. J. Nicholas c Weale b Edwards	40	c Henderson b Sygrove	19
R. A. Smith c Hagan b Edwards	118	(8) not out	54
D. R. Turner c Kilborn b Edwards	76	(9) not out	7
K. D. James c Reynolds b Sygrove	42	(4) c Polkinghorne b Kilborn	15
†R. J. Parks c Kilborn b Sygrove	23	(5) c Kilborn b Edwards	5
J. R. Ayling c Edwards b Sygrove	41	c Almaer b Kilborn	3
N. G. Cowley not out	16	(3) lbw b Sygrove	13
R. J. Maru (did not bat)		(6) lbw b Kilborn	0
L-b 3, n-b 10	13	L-b 1, n-b 2	3
1/5 2/112 3/199 4/260 5/306 6/313 7/370 (7 wkts dec.)	370	1/31 2/33 3/52 4/61 5/61 6/69 7/87 (7 wkts dec.)	130

S. J. W. Andrew and A. D. Mullally did not bat.

Bowling: *First Innings*—Sygrove 23.4–3–95–3; Henderson 13–2–66–1; Weale 31–4–101–0; Edwards 25–4–88–3; Hagan 2–0–17–0. *Second Innings*—Sygrove 11–1–35–2; Weale 6–0–24–1; Edwards 15–4–33–1; Kilborn 11–5–37–3.

Oxford University

First innings		Second innings	
D. A. Hagan b Andrew	0	(4) lbw b Cowley	42
S. A. Almaer c Maru b Andrew	16	lbw b Cowley	36
*M. J. Kilborn c Scott b James	30	c Mullally b Cowley	40
A. N. S. Hampton lbw b Andrew	0	(5) c Parks b Maru	1
R. E. Morris lbw b James	8	(1) c Smith b James	1
D. A. Polkinghorne c Parks b Ayling	12	not out	45
S. D. Weale c Parks b James	0	c James b Maru	7
†G. D. Reynolds b Ayling	14	not out	29
I. M. Henderson c Parks b Andrew	18		
P. G. Edwards not out	8		
M. R. Sygrove b Andrew	0		
B 1, l-b 4, n-b 7	12	L-b 4, w 1	5
1/50 2/50 3/50 4/52 5/62 6/66 7/83 8/99 9/118	118	1/1 2/64 3/123 4/124 5/124 6/137 (6 wkts)	206

In the first innings D. A. Hagan, when 0, retired hurt at 0 and resumed at 50-2.

Bowling: *First Innings*—Andrew 16.2–4–36–5; Mullally 12–1–44–0; Maru 8–6–4–0; James 10–6–15–3; Ayling 13–8–14–2; Cowley 2–2–0–0. *Second Innings*—Andrew 19–4–48–0; James 13–6–15–1; Mullally 8–4–8–0; Maru 37–15–72–2; Ayling 10–5–19–0; Cowley 31–12–39–3; Nicholas 1–0–1–0.

Umpires: B. Dudleston and P. J. Eele.

OXFORD UNIVERSITY v KENT

At Oxford, May 18, 19, 20. Drawn. Toss: Oxford University. Kent's batsmen took a fearfu toll of Oxford University's bowlers after they were put in. Pienaar, a South African, anc Hinks scored centuries in an opening partnership of 226, and Tavaré and Chris Cowdrey completed unbeaten centuries during a fourth-wicket stand of 248 before Cowdrey declared a a massive 539 for three. Almaer and Hagan made a positive reply with 64, Kilborn hit 51, an there was unexpected resistance from the tail on the last day. Reynolds, with a career-best 69 and Nuttall added 77 for the ninth wicket, the Dark Blues' best partnership, and Sygrov helped Nuttall put on 30 for the last wicket. Kent, 262 ahead, batted again and declare immediately Marsh completed a century. This, however, left Oxford with only 90 minutes batting.

Close of play: First day, Kent 322-3 (C. J. Tavaré 35*, C. S. Cowdrey 14*); Second day Oxford University 160-6 (M. J. Kilborn 51*).

Kent

S. G. Hinks c Weale b Nuttall	138		
R. F. Pienaar c Crawley b Nuttall	127		
C. J. Tavaré not out	138		
G. R. Cowdrey b Edwards	4	(1) b Sygrove	18
*C. S. Cowdrey not out	124		
†S. A. Marsh (did not bat)	–	(2) not out	100
C. Penn (did not bat)	–	(3) c Weale b Edwards	29
N. R. Taylor (did not bat)	–	(4) not out	10
B 3, l-b 5	8	B 6, l-b 3, w 1, n-b 1	11
1/226 2/270 3/291 (3 wkts dec.)	539	1/60 2/136 (2 wkts dec.)	168

R. M. Ellison, R. P. Davis and M. D. Harman did not bat.

Bowling: *First Innings*—Sygrove 21–4–76–0; Nuttall 24–2–105–2; Edwards 30–9–129–1; Kilborn 7–1–33–0; Weale 34–3–188–0. *Second Innings*—Sygrove 12–3–39–1; Weale 6–1–21–0; Crawley 11–1–41–0; Edwards 11.3–2–35–1; Nuttall 6–1–23–0.

Oxford University

D. A. Hagan c Marsh b Harman	33	(5) not out	6
S. A. Almaer c Marsh b Davis	24	c Marsh b Ellison	3
*M. J. Kilborn c C. S. Cowdrey b Harman	51	c Marsh b Pienaar	3
M. A. Crawley b Harman	0	not out	10
R. E. Morris b Harman	0	(1) c Taylor b Pienaar	2
D. A. Polkinghorne c Penn b Davis	9		
S. D. Weale c Marsh b Penn	21		
†G. D. Reynolds c Taylor b Pienaar	69		
P. G. Edwards c C. S. Cowdrey b Harman	0		
J. D. Nuttall c Hinks b Ellison	35		
M. R. Sygrove not out	8		
B 5, l-b 9, w 1, n-b 12	27	L-b 2, w 2	4
1/64 2/95 3/96 4/96 5/121 6/160 7/160 8/170 9/247	277	1/5 2/5 3/10 (3 wkts)	28

Bowling: *First Innings*—Ellison 24–12–36–1; Penn 17–2–71–1; Pienaar 14–3–39–1; Harman 27–10–55–5; Davis 24–11–56–2; C. S. Cowdrey 1–0–6–0. *Second Innings*—Ellison 8–3–9–1; Pienaar 8–4–17–2.

Umpires: R. C. Tolchard and A. G. T. Whitehead.

OXFORD UNIVERSITY v LANCASHIRE

At Oxford, May 21, 23, 24. Drawn. Toss: Oxford University. Oxford University produced their most consistent batting and earned a comfortable draw. They were given a sound start by Almaer and Hagan, and with Kilborn, Brown, Jack and Weale making useful contributions, the innings closed at 230. Lancashire passed the score for the loss of Abrahams, who put on 97 with Mendis. Mendis, who was dropped when 14, went on to hit 139, including sixteen fours, adding 141 in a second-wicket stand with Jesty. Hughes and Watkinson later plundered the tiring attack, which conceded 134 runs off 34 overs before Lancashire declared with a lead of 199. On the last day Almaer and Hagan began with 102 – Oxford's first century opening partnership for two years. Almaer hit a career-best 67, Hagan, dropped when 1, scored 59, and when Kilborn weighed in with 45, Oxford were safe. Hughes brought his players off with eleven overs left.

Close of play: First day, Lancashire 19-0 (G. D. Mendis 10*, J. Abrahams 8*); Second day, Lancashire 429-7 (D. P. Hughes 57*, I. Folley 12*).

Oxford University

D. A. Hagan b Hayhurst	30 – c Mendis b Simmons	59
S. A. Almaer lbw b Watkinson	16 – c Simmons b Folley	67
*M. J. Kilborn c and b Makinson	32 – c Watkinson b Folley	45
M. A. Crawley b Murphy	6 – not out	14
T. B. Jack b Folley	29 – b Hayhurst	5
M. E. O. Brown c Watkinson b Folley	47 – not out	6
†G. D. Reynolds c Hegg b Simmons	3	
S. D. Weale c Hegg b Murphy	40	
I. M. Henderson lbw b Simmons	0	
P. G. Edwards c Simmons b Murphy	1	
M. R. Sygrove not out	6	
B 1, l-b 12, w 1, n-b 6	20 L-b 13, n-b 4	17
1/46 2/69 3/88 4/99 5/166 6/174 7/182 8/189 9/215	230 1/102 2/179 3/187 4/198	(4 wkts) 213

Bowling: *First Innings*—Murphy 17.4–5–45–3; Watkinson 15–1–47–1; Makinson 15–9–28–1; Folley 20–7–43–2; Hayhurst 12–5–21–1; Simmons 16–3–33–2. *Second Innings*—Murphy 12–1–31–0; Makinson 12–5–22–0; Watkinson 13–1–32–0; Simmons 28–6–58–1; Hayhurst 10–5–14–1; Folley 20–9–34–2; Mendis 4–1–9–0.

Lancashire

G. D. Mendis c Crawley b Weale	139
J. Abrahams c Reynolds b Edwards	39
T. E. Jesty c Hagan b Sygrove	63
†W. K. Hegg c Edwards b Weale	42
J. Simmons b Weale	27
*D. P. Hughes not out	57
M. Watkinson b Sygrove	30
A. N. Hayhurst lbw b Sygrove	8
I. Folley not out	12
B 1, l-b 4, w 2, n-b 5	12
1/97 2/238 3/272 4/299 5/333 6/390 7/404	(7 wkts dec.) 429

D. J. Makinson and A. J. Murphy did not bat.

Bowling: Sygrove 33–7–113–3; Weale 35–6–130–3; Edwards 36–14–116–1; Henderson 3–0–19–0; Crawley 8–3–19–0; Kilborn 4–0–27–0.

Umpires: R. C. Tolchard and A. G. T. Whitehead.

OXFORD UNIVERSITY v GLOUCESTERSHIRE

At Oxford, June 1, 2, 3. Drawn. Toss: Oxford University. Gloucestershire lost Romaines at 19, but on an easy wicket the Oxford bowling was put in perspective by Butcher and Bainbridge, who added 171 for the second wicket. There were seventeen fours in Bainbridge's first century of the season, and later Lloyds and Alleyne plundered 123 for the fourth wicket. Immediately Lloyds (fifteen fours) completed his century, Gloucestershire declared. Apart from Almaer and Jack, the Dark Blues disappointed. Jack's dismissal signalled an alarming collapse and Oxford were all out for 117. Bainbridge and Graveney did the damage. Although Gloucestershire led by 243, they batted again and had scored 141 for three by lunch on the third day when heavy rain prevented any further play.

Close of play: First day, Oxford University 5-0 (T. B. Jack 5*, S. A. Almaer 0*); Second day, Gloucestershire 20-1 (A. J. Wright 8*, R. C. Russell 12*).

Gloucestershire

	First innings		Second innings	
I. P. Butcher c Jack b Nuttall	75			
P. W. Romaines lbw b Sygrove	1	– lbw b Kilborn	0
P. Bainbridge b Nuttall	119			
J. W. Lloyds not out	102			
M. W. Alleyne b Sygrove	36			
†R. C. Russell not out	11	– (3) b Kilborn	69
A. J. Wright (did not bat)		– (1) c Reynolds b Sygrove	9
D. J. Thomas (did not bat)		– (4) not out	57
M. W. Pooley (did not bat)		– (5) not out	3
B 4, l-b 8, n-b 4	16	L-b 1, w 1, n-b 1	3
1/19 2/190 3/205 4/328	(4 wkts dec.) 360	1/3 2/22 3/133	(3 wkts dec.) 141

*D. A. Graveney and K. B. S. Jarvis did not bat.

Bowling: *First Innings*—Sygrove 19–4–91–2; Nuttall 20–5–64–2; Heppel 14–0–74–0; Searle 17–2–76–0; Crawley 6–0–25–0; Kilborn 4.5–0–18–0. *Second Innings*—Sygrove 13–2–79–1; Kilborn 12–2–59–2; Crawley 1–0–2–0.

Oxford University

T. B. Jack b Graveney	23
S. A. Almaer c Alleyne b Bainbridge	35
*M. J. Kilborn c Russell b Graveney	1
M. A. Crawley b Lloyds	8
D. A. Hagan c Alleyne b Bainbridge	10
M. E. O. Brown c Alleyne b Bainbridge	2
†G. D. Reynolds lbw b Bainbridge	10
A. M. Searle c Thomas b Graveney	2
N. Heppel not out	14
M. R. Sygrove st Russell b Bainbridge	2
J. D. Nuttall absent ill	
L-b 2, n-b 8	10
1/40 2/46 3/63 4/84 5/86 6/89 7/97 8/101 9/117	117

Bowling: Bainbridge 12.2–2–33–5; Pooley 1–0–3–0; Jarvis 5–2–6–0; Thomas 5–1–5–0; Lloyds 14–3–33–1; Graveney 25–9–35–3.

Umpires: P. J. Eele and D. G. L. Evans.

†At Oxford, June 8, 9, 10. Oxford University won by 153 runs, their first victory of the season. Oxford University 226 for seven dec. (M. J. Kilborn 101) and 77 for four dec.; MCC 0 for no wkt dec. and 150 (M. J. Kilborn five for 28).

OXFORD UNIVERSITY v NOTTINGHAMSHIRE

At Oxford, June 15, 16, 17. Drawn. Toss: Oxford University. After Nottinghamshire lost Newell and Pollard for 64 on a perfect batting pitch, Johnson and Martindale responded with 100 for the third wicket. Johnson needed just 109 balls for his 104, which contained seventeen fours. Birch reached his hundred on the second day, and after his declaration Oxford made a good reply in their last first-class match at The Parks. An opening partnership of 70 by Almaer and Crawley was followed by 120 from Kilborn and Crawley, who fell when 2 runs short of a century. The Dark Blues declared at their overnight score and again quickly accounted for the county openers, only for Johnson and Martindale to raise their second century partnership of the match. Nottinghamshire's declaration set Oxford to score 301 in a little over four hours, but they faced defeat when half the side was out for 75. A stubborn eighth-wicket stand by Henderson and Nuttall, who negotiated ten overs, earned them a draw.

Close of play: First day, Nottinghamshire 350-7 (J. D. Birch 85*, C. W. Scott 3*); Second day, Oxford University 228-3 (D. A. Hagan 16*, M. E. O. Brown 0*).

Nottinghamshire

P. Pollard lbw b Nuttall	16	– lbw b Nuttall	11
M. Newell lbw b Henderson	16	– lbw b Sygrove	0
P. Johnson c Nuttall b Weale	104	– (4) not out	58
D. J. R. Martindale c Polkinghorne b Weale	29	– (3) not out	52
*J. D. Birch not out	114		
R. J. Evans lbw b Sygrove	21		
C. D. Fraser-Darling c Cope b Sygrove	18		
K. P. Evans run out	29		
†C. W. Scott retired hurt	20		
K. Saxelby not out	6		
B 3, l-b 6, w 11, n-b 12	32	L-b 2	2
1/40 2/64 3/164 4/193 5/261 6/293 7/336	(7 wkts dec.) 405	1/9 2/15	(2 wkts dec.) 123

D. J. Millns did not bat.

Bowling: *First Innings*—Sygrove 32–2–112–2; Henderson 14–0–92–1; Nuttall 25–5–77–1; Crawley 10–3–37–0; Weale 30–9–74–2; Kilborn 2–0–4–0. *Second Innings*—Sygrove 12–1–60–1; Nuttall 5–1–12–1; Weale 8–0–37–0; Crawley 2–0–12–0.

Oxford University

S. A. Almaer lbw b K. P. Evans	21	– (7) lbw b Birch	25
M. A. Crawley lbw b K. P. Evans	98	– c Fraser-Darling b R. J. Evans	41
*M. J. Kilborn b Millns	78	– c Scott b Saxelby	2
D. A. Hagan not out	16	– (1) c R. J. Evans b Saxelby	4
M. E. O. Brown not out	0	– (4) c R. J. Evans b K. P. Evans	16
D. A. Polkinghorne (did not bat)		– (5) c Birch b R. J. Evans	6
S. D. Weale (did not bat)		– (6) c Fraser-Darling b R. J. Evans	24
I. M. Henderson (did not bat)		– not out	21
J. D. Nuttall (did not bat)		– not out	14
B 6, l-b 5, w 4	15	B 4, l-b 4, n-b 1	9
1/70 2/190 3/221	(3 wkts dec.) 228	1/26 2/30 3/54 4/66 5/75 6/96 7/142	(7 wkts) 162

†J. E. B. Cope and M. R. Sygrove did not bat.

Bowling: *First Innings*—Saxelby 18–5–42–0; Millns 15–0–52–1; K. P. Evans 17–4–52–2; Fraser-Darling 2–0–8–0; Birch 19–4–63–0. *Second Innings*—Saxelby 17–4–35–2; Millns 5–0–15–0; K. P. Evans 10–1–26–1; Fraser-Darling 10–4–22–0; R. J. Evans 20–8–40–3; Newell 3–2–1–0; Birch 8–5–14–1; Johnson 2–1–1–0.

Umpires: P. J. Eele and P. B. Wight.

†At Oxford, June 18, 20, 21. Drawn. Oxford University just managed to hold out for a draw after being set to score 225 in 135 minutes. Free Foresters 320 for nine dec. (C. J. C. Rowe 103, G. D. Reynolds 60) and 222 for nine dec.; Oxford University 318 (S. A. Almaer 99, D. A. Hagan 55) and 209 for nine (D. A. Hagan 50).

†At Oxford, June 22. Aboriginal Cricket Association won by 40 runs. Aboriginal Cricket Association 195 for seven (50 overs) (G. James 51, P. Bagshaw 56); Oxford University 15 (47 overs) (M. J. Kilborn 58).

At Lord's, July 2, 3, 4. OXFORD UNIVERSITY v CAMBRIDGE UNIVERSITY. Abandoned.

CAMBRIDGE

President: Lord Butterfield (Downing)

Captain: M. A. Atherton (Manchester GS and Downing)
Secretary: G. A. Pointer (St Dunstan's and St John's)

Captain for 1989: M. A. Atherton
Secretary: R. J. Turner (Millfield and Magdalene)

Michael Atherton's 665 first-class runs, which included two hundreds, did much to brighten another disappointing Cambridge season. The biggest disappointment, however, came at Lord's when the 144th University Match was abandoned without a ball being bowled – the first time in the 161-year history of the fixture that this had happened. It denied several players probably their only chance to play in a first-class match at cricket's most famous ground.

Although the weather did not have an undue influence on the relatively short Fenner's season, it did present problems for the groundsman in his preparation. The pitches, although providing a little more bounce than in recent seasons, generally helped the bowlers. Perhaps because of this, Nigel Fenton, despite an ungainly action, emerged as one of the most effective new-ball bowlers at Cambridge since the departure of Derek Pringle. But such was the shortage of good seam bowling that when injuries and examinations took their toll, Alastair Scott, who had graduated the previous year, was called back from his desk in the City to play in three first-class games. His eleven wickets, taking his University career total to 72, made him the second-highest wicket-taker of the term after Fenton. Jon Perry took ten and Graham Pointer, the secretary, only seven. The slow bowling was mainly in the hands of Atherton, who earned seven wickets with his leg-spin.

But the captain's outstanding contribution was his batting. With an unbeaten 151 against Middlesex and 100 not out against Surrey, he stood out from his team-mates for the quality of his technique and his mature approach when all around him was crumbling. Jonathon Atkinson, a Freshman with some previous first-class experience with Somerset, was the only other batsman to make a first-class fifty, scoring 73 against Surrey at The Oval in the last first-class match before Lord's. The rest of the batting was less convincing. Paul Bail, who preferred to play for Somerset Second XI for a short time after examinations, was again unable to produce the form that in his first season had marked him as such an exciting young batsman. As did the others, he scored runs freely in the non first-class games but struggled against the county attacks.

University cricket in 1988 was played against the continuing threat of the loss of first-class status. This prospect has prompted Cambridge to look seriously at an admissions policy which does not assist young sportsmen to gain places. Although such matters are strictly outside the control of the Cricket Club, Atherton has made it a priority, following his re-election as captain, to seek a way of opening more academic doors for promising young cricketers. Certainly, it is only a more enlightened admissions policy which will enable the standard of cricket played at Fenner's to improve. – David Hallett.

CAMBRIDGE UNIVERSITY 1988

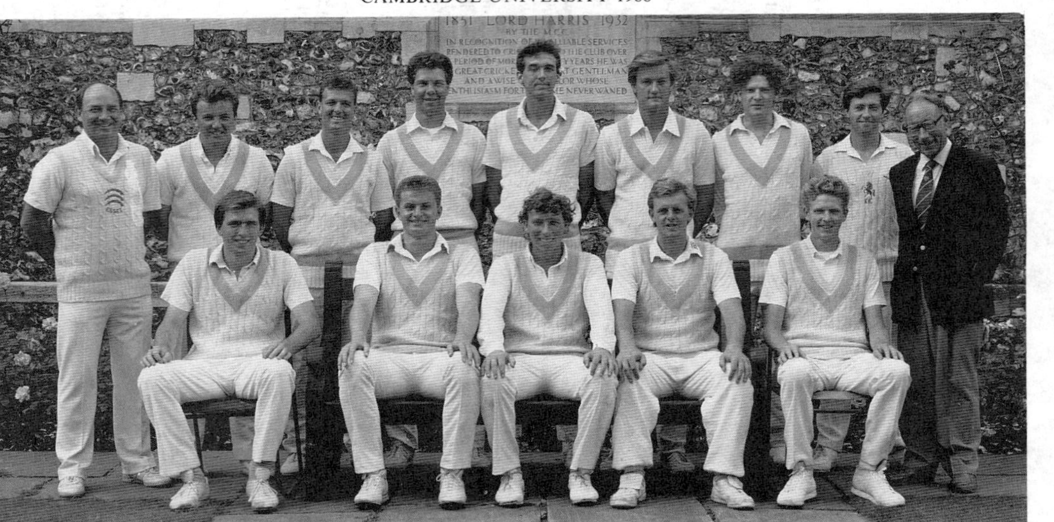

[*Bill Smith*

Back row: G. J. Saville (*coach*), R. Bate, S. J. Noyes, R. J. Turner, N. C. W. Fenton, J. C. M. Atkinson, S. D. Heath, R. J. Hart, A. R. May (*scorer*). *Front* [illegible] M. A. Atherton (*captain*), P. A. C. Bail, J. N. Perry.

CAMBRIDGE UNIVERSITY RESULTS

First-class matches – Played 8: Lost 5, Drawn 3. Abandoned 1.

FIRST-CLASS AVERAGES

BATTING AND FIELDING

	Birthplace	*M*	*I*	*NO*	*R*	*HI*	*Avge*	*Ct/St*
M. A. Atherton	*Manchester*	8	13	2	665	151*	60.45	10
J. C. M. Atkinson ...	*Butleigh*	7	12	0	257	73	21.41	4
P. A. C. Bail	*Burnham-on-Sea*	4	6	0	102	44	17.00	1
R. Bate	*Finchley*	7	12	2	160	45	16.00	1
S. D. Heath	*Bristol*	5	8	1	100	33*	14.28	2
S. J. Noyes	*High Wycombe*	8	14	1	170	38	13.07	0
R. J. Turner	*Malvern*	8	14	1	155	27	11.92	9/2
G. A. Pointer	*Lewisham*	7	12	2	114	18*	11.40	0
J. M. Tremellen	*Pendine*	7	12	0	131	33	10.91	3
J. N. Perry	*Frimley*	7	9	1	73	26	9.12	3
A. M. G. Scott	*Guildford*	3	5	1	9	8	2.25	0
R. J. Hart	*Beckenham*	3	5	1	7	6	1.75	0
N. C. W. Fenton	*Bradford*	7	9	3	4	2	0.66	1

Also batted: A. K. Golding (*Colchester*) (1 match) 18* (2 ct); R. Heap (*Leeds*) (1 match) 0, 15 (2 ct); A. M. Hooper (*Perivale*) (2 matches) 3, 2, 0; R. A. Pyman (*Changi, Singapore*) (2 matches) 3, 0, 4 (2 ct); J. M. C. Stenner (*RAF Newton*) (1 match) 10, 13.

* *Signifies not out.*

M. A. Atherton played the two three-figure innings for Cambridge University.

BOWLING

	O	*M*	*R*	*W*	*BB*	*Avge*
N. C. W. Fenton ..	271.4	65	726	21	4-64	34.57
A. M. G. Scott	120	26	385	11	4-66	35.00
J. N. Perry	211	44	643	10	3-72	64.30
M. A. Atherton ...	179.2	19	565	7	2-38	80.71
G. A. Pointer	184.5	24	663	7	3-31	94.71

Also bowled: J. C. M. Atkinson 17–1–86–1; P. A. C. Bail 14–1–71–1; A. K. Golding 23–11–43–0; R. J. Hart 67–11–231–4; J. M. Tremellen 5–0–13–1.

†At Cambridge, April 14. Middlesex won by 72 runs. Middlesex 178 for seven (50 overs) (K. R. Brown 65 not out); Cambridge University 106 for eight (50 overs) (P. C. R. Tufnell four for 12).

†At Cambridge, April 15. Loughborough Students won by five wickets. Cambridge University 193 for five (50 overs) (P. A. C. Bail 64); Loughborough Students 194 for five (G. D. Hodgson 51).

CAMBRIDGE UNIVERSITY v DERBYSHIRE

At Cambridge, April 16, 17, 18. Derbyshire won by an innings and 214 runs. Toss: Derbyshire. The start of the first-class season was delayed by rain until after tea on the first day, and within an hour on the second morning Cambridge had been dismissed for 86. There followed an opening partnership of 238 between Barnett, the county captain, and Bowler, his new recruit, who achieved a unique double. Having hit a century on his début for Leicestershire in 1986, he now scored one on his first appearance for Derbyshire. Barnett faced 166 balls and hit twelve fours in his century, while altogether he faced 240 deliveries in compiling his highest score, hitting sixteen fours and one six. Bowler faced 310 balls for his century, hitting only five boundaries, and in all he batted for more than a day's play for his career-best score. The pace of Malcolm was a factor in Cambridge's second-innings failure, with only Bail, batting at No. 7, making any progress.

Close of play: First day, Cambridge University 73-4 (M. A. Atherton 43*, S. J. Noyes 6*); Second day, Derbyshire 275-3 (P. D. Bowler 92*, S. J. Base 5*).

Cambridge University

P. A. C. Bail lbw b Malcolm	7	– (7) c Roberts b Malcolm	44
A. M. Hooper c Maher b Newman	3	– (1) c Maher b Malcolm	2
*M. A. Atherton c Maher b Warner	44	– c Maher b Malcolm	3
J. M. Tremellen lbw b Base	1	– c Maher b Base	8
J. C. M. Atkinson c Roberts b Base	0	– c and b Warner	25
S. J. Noyes c Maher b Warner	6	– c Bowler b Finney	2
†R. J. Turner not out	2	– (2) c Maher b Newman	3
R. J. Hart c Barnett b Warner	0	– c Barnett b Warner	1
J. N. Perry b Warner	6	– c Maher b Warner	4
G. A. Pointer lbw b Malcolm	0	– b Barnett	5
N. C. W. Fenton b Malcolm	1	– not out	0
B 2, l-b 6, w 2, n-b 6	16	B 2, l-b 2, w 1, n-b 4	9
1/10 2/18 3/31 4/31 5/73 6/74 7/74 8/80 9/81	86	1/3 2/9 3/9 4/30 5/45 6/52 7/53 8/70 9/94	106

Bowling: *First Innings*—Newman 11–5–12–1; Malcolm 14–6–21–3; Base 8–3–20–2; Warne 18–11–22–4; Finney 7–5–3–0. *Second Innings*—Newman 7–1–13–1; Malcolm 6.1–2–13–3 Base 2–1–1–1; Warner 11–1–38–3; Finney 7–2–34–1; Barnett 3–2–3–1.

Derbyshire

*K. J. Barnett lbw b Fenton	151	S. C. Goldsmith lbw b Fenton	5
P. D. Bowler not out	155	B 4, l-b 8, w 5, n-b 4	2
B. Roberts c and b Fenton	0		
J. E. Morris c Turner b Perry	16	1/238 2/244 3/265	(5 wkts dec.) 40
S. J. Base c Tremellen b Atherton	8	4/282 5/406	

†B. J. M. Maher, R. J. Finney, P. G. Newman, A. E. Warner and D. E. Malcolm did not bat

Bowling: Fenton 35.4–4–102–3; Pointer 19–3–55–0; Perry 22–4–84–1; Hart 25–1–94–0 Atherton 26–5–59–1.

Umpires: J. C. Balderstone and B. J. Meyer.

CAMBRIDGE UNIVERSITY v WARWICKSHIRE

At Cambridge, April 20, 21, 22. Drawn. Toss: Warwickshire. Kallicharran marked his retur to county cricket, following his qualification as English, with a hundred made from 18 deliveries and containing a six and ten fours. He shared an unbroken partnership of 216 fo the third wicket with Asif Din, who reached his century in 201 deliveries, having hit eleve fours. The University had mustered only 78 in their first innings, totally unable to cope wi the movement obtained in helpful conditions by Parsons, who in one eighteen-ball spell too five wickets without conceding a run. They were saved from further humiliation by the rai which prevented any play on the third day.

Close of play: First day, Warwickshire 174-1 (A. J. Moles 83*, Asif Din 73*); Second da Warwickshire 405-2 (Asif Din 158*, A. I. Kallicharran 117*).

Cambridge University

P. A. C. Bail lbw b Small	4	J. N. Perry not out	14
†R. J. Turner c Humpage b Parsons	27	G. A. Pointer c Kallicharran b Parsons	0
*M. A. Atherton c Humpage b Smith	11	N. C. W. Fenton b Merrick	1
J. M. Tremellen c Humpage b Parsons	18		
J. C. M. Atkinson c Moles b Parsons	0	N-b 3	3
S. J. Noyes c Moles b Parsons	0		
A. M. Hooper c Humpage b Parsons	0	1/6 2/35 3/58 4/58 5/58	78
R. Bate b Parsons	0	6/58 7/58 8/69 9/77	

Bowling: Small 14–6–21–1; Merrick 7.3–1–21–1; Smith 7–0–15–1; Parsons 16–7–16–7; Gifford 3–1–5–0.

Warwickshire

*T. A. Lloyd c Atherton b Fenton	9
A. J. Moles c Atherton b Fenton	95
Asif Din not out	158
A. I. Kallicharran not out	117
B 5, l-b 12, w 4, n-b 5	26
1/26 2/189 (2 wkts)	405

†G. W. Humpage, P. A. Smith, G. J. Parsons, T. A. Merrick, G. C. Small, A. R. K. Pierson and N. Gifford did not bat.

Bowling: Fenton 39–7–118–2; Pointer 28–2–91–0; Perry 30–8–84–0; Atherton 9–1–54–0; Bail 2–0–15–0; Atkinson 5–0–26–0.

Umpires: J. C. Balderstone and B. J. Meyer.

CAMBRIDGE UNIVERSITY v SURREY

At Cambridge, April 28, 29, 30. Surrey won by 97 runs. Toss: Surrey. Lynch scored a hard-hitting century, containing a six and fourteen fours, from 122 balls. He batted with ease against a Cambridge attack that included Scott who, although having graduated, returned to help his university in an injury crisis. Fenton had been included in the eleven when the captains tossed, but when he was injured during fielding practice, Greig gave permission for Scott to come in as his replacement. Greig, a former Cambridge captain, found movement off the pitch to take six for 34, and only Atherton made any significant impression as his side was dismissed for 176. By the end of the day, the Surrey captain had added a half-century to his six wickets. Atherton's second-innings hundred, made from 229 balls with ten fours and a six, was not enough to stave off defeat as Frost, on his first-class début, and Medlycott each took four wickets for the county.

Close of play: First day, Surrey 310-3 (M. A. Lynch 103*, D. M. Ward 53*); Second day, Surrey 85-0 (C. K. Bullen 30*, I. A. Greig 54*).

Surrey

. S. Clinton c Atherton b Scott	74		
. M. Smith c Turner b Scott	45		
. J. Stewart c Perry b Atherton	13		
. A. Lynch not out	103		
. M. Ward not out	53	– (3) st Turner b Atherton	31
. K. Bullen (did not bat)		– (1) lbw b Atkinson	45
. A. Greig (did not bat)		– (2) lbw b Scott	67
. T. Medlycott (did not bat)		– (4) not out	20
B 8, l-b 10, w 1, n-b 3	22	L-b 3	3
104 2/145 3/157 (3 wkts dec.)	310	1/99 2/127 3/166 (3 wkts dec.)	166

. J. Richards, M. A. Feltham and M. Frost did not bat.

Bowling: *First Innings*—Pointer 25–4–89–0; Perry 20–3–62–0; Atkinson 3–1–8–0; Atherton 19–1–56–1; Scott 20–5–77–2. *Second Innings*—Pointer 7–1–33–0; Scott 12–2–46–1; Perry 8–4–21–0; Atherton 5.3–0–20–1; Atkinson 7–0–43–1.

Cambridge University

P. A. C. Bail lbw b Greig	27	– c Lynch b Frost	13
†R. J. Turner c Ward b Greig	23	– c Greig b Frost	7
*M. A. Atherton c Ward b Greig	46	– not out	100
J. M. Tremellen lbw b Greig	0	– c Smith b Medlycott	7
J. C. M. Atkinson c Ward b Frost	11	– lbw b Frost	35
S. J. Noyes lbw b Medlycott	10	– lbw b Medlycott	17
R. Bate c Medlycott b Feltham	28	– c Ward b Medlycott	0
S. D. Heath c Richards b Feltham	12	– lbw b Greig	1
J. N. Perry c Clinton b Greig	2	– lbw b Greig	0
G. A. Pointer lbw b Greig	0	– c Ward b Medlycott	7
A. M. G. Scott not out	1	– c Richards b Frost	0
B 4, l-b 3, w 4, n-b 5	16	B 2, l-b 5, n-b 9	16
1/40 2/70 3/70 4/89 5/116 6/138 7/169 8/172 9/172	176	1/17 2/35 3/50 4/126 5/168 6/170 7/177 8/177 9/202	203

Bowling: *First Innings*—Frost 17–7–49–1; Feltham 23–9–51–2; Greig 19–8–34–6; Medlycott 16–4–35–1. *Second Innings*—Frost 23.5–5–56–4; Greig 12–1–27–2; Medlycott 36–9–76–4 Bullen 11–4–37–0.

Umpires: B. Hassan and R. Julian.

CAMBRIDGE UNIVERSITY v GLAMORGAN

At Cambridge, May 5, 6, 7. Drawn. Toss: Cambridge University. Butcher, captaining th county, batted throughout the first day, finishing with his highest score for Glamorgan. H reached his century in 230 balls, having hit thirteen fours. When he did not appear on th second morning, the umpires declared him "retired out". Cambridge replied with great spiri batting right down the order. They easily avoided the follow-on and then extended thei innings well into the third day. The county, having failed in the gamble to bowl out th University twice, were left to bat out the match in unsatisfactory fashion.

Close of play: First day, Glamorgan 331-3 (A. R. Butcher 166*, G. C. Holmes 53*); Secon day, Cambridge University 195-5 (S. J. Noyes 26*, R. Bate 32*).

Glamorgan

*A. R. Butcher retired, out	166		
J. A. Hopkins b Perry	11	– c Bail b Pointer	6
P. A. Cottey c Atkinson b Bail	68	– (1) c Heath b Atherton	9
M. P. Maynard b Fenton	19	– (3) b Perry	4
G. C. Holmes run out	79		
J. Derrick not out	10	– (4) b Perry	
†C. P. Metson (did not bat)		– (5) not out	
B 3, l-b 4, w 6, n-b 2	15	B 5, l-b 6, w 3	
1/20 2/160 3/197 4/331 5/368	(5 wkts dec.) 368	1/114 2/194 3/222 4/232	(4 wkts dec.) 23

C. J. P. G. van Zyl, P. D. North, S. L. Watkin and S. Monkhouse did not bat.

Bowling: *First Innings*—Fenton 34–12–66–1; Pointer 18.1–4–58–0; Perry 27–4–100– Atherton 30–4–97–0; Atkinson 1–0–4–0; Bail 7–1–36–1. *Second Innings*—Fenton 7–2–14– Pointer 21–3–73–1; Atherton 21.3–0–66–1; Perry 16–2–43–2; Atkinson 1–0–5–0; Ba 5–0–20–0.

Cambridge University

P. A. C. Bail lbw b Monkhouse	7
†R. J. Turner c Hopkins b Watkin	17
*M. A. Atherton lbw b North	16
J. M. Tremellen c Derrick b van Zyl	33
J. C. M. Atkinson lbw b Monkhouse	42
S. J. Noyes b Monkhouse	33
R. Bate run out	45
S. D. Heath not out	33
J. N. Perry c Metson b Watkin	7
G. A. Pointer st Metson b North	17
N. C. W. Fenton b Derrick	0
B 6, l-b 12, w 1, n-b 9	28
1/9 2/31 3/64 4/94 5/125 6/214 7/221 8/229 9/260	278

Bowling: van Zyl 15–3–48–1; Monkhouse 23–9–37–3; North 26–13–46–2; Derrick 14–8–40–1; Watkin 22–4–76–2; Butcher 5–2–8–0; Holmes 5–3–5–0.

Umpires: J. H. Hampshire and H. J. Rhodes.

†At Cambridge, May 9. Cambridge University won by 110 runs. Cambridge University 277 for seven (50 overs) (P. A. C. Bail 74, M. A. Atherton 68, J. C. M. Atkinson 53); Norfolk 167 for six (50 overs) (D. R. Thomas 56 not out).

†At Cambridge, May 10. Cambridge University won by 2 runs. Cambridge University 189 (P. A. C. Bail 68; R. Haywood four for 42); Cambridgeshire 187 for nine (55 overs) (N. T. Gadsby 94).

†At Cambridge, May 17. Drawn. MCC 228 for three dec. (P. W. G. Parker 108 not out); Cambridge University 220 for eight (P. A. C. Bail 72, S. J. Noyes 52).

CAMBRIDGE UNIVERSITY v ESSEX

At Cambridge, May 18, 19, 20. Essex won by 135 runs. Toss: Essex. Fenton was the pick of the Cambridge bowlers, troubling all the batsmen to earn his best figures. Prichard delighted the Essex followers with his strokeplay, hitting thirteen fours in his innings of 97 from 168 balls. Once again Atherton was the main runmaker for Cambridge, facing 139 balls for his half-century and batting in all for four hours, while Noyes was five minutes short of three hours over his 33. Childs took five wickets in his last 42 deliveries after an hour-long stoppage because of rain. Stephenson and East hit ten fours apiece to set up Essex's second declaration, and Cambridge were soon in trouble against the seam bowling of Pont and Ilott and the left-arm spin of Childs, who finished with match figures of nine for 61.

Close of play: First day, Cambridge University 3-1 (S. J. Noyes 2*, A. M. G. Scott 0*); second day, Cambridge University 188.

Essex

B. R. Hardie c Pyman b Fenton	24		
P. Stephenson lbw b Scott	5	(1) not out	79
J. Prichard c Heap b Fenton	97		
W. Lilley b Fenton	0	(3) not out	5
Miller c Tremellen b Pointer	32		
D. E. East lbw b Fenton	13	(2) c Heap b Pointer	55
L. Pont st Turner b Atherton	68		
N. Pook b Scott	6		
C. Seymour not out	33		
B 2, l-b 9, w 10	21	L-b 4, w 2	6
1/12 2/84 3/86 4/152 5/175 6/182 7/215 8/299 (8 wkts dec.)	299	1/115 (1 wkt dec.)	145

H. Childs and M. C. Ilott did not bat.

Bowling: *First Innings*—Fenton 29–5–78–4; Scott 31–8–80–2; Pointer 19–1–87–1; Atherton 12.5–2–43–1. *Second Innings*—Fenton 8–0–41–0; Scott 8–1–41–0; Atherton 14–3–39–0; Pointer 7–2–20–1.

Cambridge University

†R. J. Turner lbw b Pont . . . . 0 – c Miller b Ilott 6
S. J. Noyes lbw b Stephenson . . . . 33 – c Miller b Pont 3
A. M. G. Scott c East b Ilott . . . . 0 – (10) c East b Childs 0
*M. A. Atherton c East b Childs . . . . 84 – b Pont 9
J. M. Tremellen c Pook b Miller . . . . 21 – c East b Pont 22
R. Bate c Stephenson b Childs . . . . 6 – c Pook b Childs 9
S. D. Heath c East b Childs . . . . 8 – c Stephenson b Childs 16
R. Heap c Pook b Miller . . . . 0 – (3) lbw b Ilott 15
R. A. Pyman c Miller b Childs . . . . 3 – (8) b Pont 0
G. A. Pointer c Stephenson b Childs . . . . 16 – (9) not out 18
N. C. W. Fenton not out . . . . 0 – b Childs 2
B 6, l-b 8, w 3 . . . . 17 B 3, l-b 5, w 2, n-b 11 . . . 21

1/0 2/6 3/83 4/141 5/156 6/161 7/169 8/169 9/188 — 188
1/12 2/12 3/36 4/48 5/62 6/85 7/88 8/102 9/113 — 121

Bowling: *First Innings*—Pont 18–8–30–1; Ilott 22–11–40–1; Childs 18.2–7–36–5; Miller 25–5–43–2; Stephenson 12–4–25–1. *Second Innings*—Pont 20–3–58–4; Ilott 12–3–23–2; Miller 7–1–7–0; Childs 14.1–6–25–4.

Umpires: V. A. Holder and D. O. Oslear.

CAMBRIDGE UNIVERSITY v MIDDLESEX

At Cambridge, May 21, 22, 23. Drawn. Toss: Cambridge University. Put in, Middlesex needed some sound and sensible batting from Butcher and Needham to retrieve the good position established by the openers before Scott took his four wickets. Hughes punished a tiring attack either side of tea. Atherton was outstanding in his side's reply, dominating a third-wicket stand of 92 with Turner and one of 83 with Golding for the eighth wicket before declaring. He reached his second hundred of the season from 255 balls and then moved on to a career-best 151 not out, batting in all for five hours four minutes, facing 321 balls, and hitting a six and seventeen fours. Middlesex's declaration left the University to score 221 in an hour plus twenty overs and they batted out comfortably for the draw.

Close of play: First day, Cambridge University 7-1 (R. J. Turner 4*, A. M. G. Scott 0*) Second day, Middlesex 31-2 (K. R. Brown 18*, M. A. Roseberry 3*).

Middlesex

J. F. Sykes c Atherton b Scott . . . . 37 – c Atkinson b Fenton . . . . [illegible]
J. D. Carr lbw b Scott . . . . 38 – c Atherton b Scott . . . . [illegible]
K. R. Brown c Heath b Scott . . . . 0 – lbw b Perry . . . . 3[illegible]
*R. O. Butcher c Perry b Scott . . . . 52 – (6) b Perry . . . . 2[illegible]
M. A. Roseberry run out . . . . 2 – (4) c Atkinson b Fenton . . . . 1[illegible]
N. R. C. MacLaurin c Golding b Fenton . . . . 2 – (5) lbw b Fenton . . . . 3[illegible]
A. Needham c Turner b Fenton . . . . 44 – c Pyman b Fenton . . . . 1[illegible]
S. P. Hughes run out . . . . 53 – c Turner b Scott . . . . 1[illegible]
†M. W. C. Olley c Atkinson b Atherton . . . . 6 – not out . . . . 2[illegible]
A. G. J. Fraser c Golding b Atherton . . . . 14 – not out . . . . [illegible]
P. C. R. Tufnell not out 2
B 2, l-b 5, w 1, n-b 4 . . . . 12 B 17, l-b 3, w 4 . . . . 2[illegible]

1/72 2/75 3/84 4/96 5/107 6/172 7/189 8/205 9/238 — 262
1/4 2/12 3/59 4/78 5/117 6/121 7/151 8/162 — (8 wkts dec.) 19[illegible]

Bowling: *First Innings*—Fenton 28–10–72–2; Scott 27–7–66–4; Perry 14–2–42–0; Golding 16–7–37–0; Atherton 10–0–38–2. *Second Innings*—Fenton 22–5–64–4; Scott 22–3–75–2; Perry 12–2–25–2; Golding 7–4–6–0; Atherton 4–2–5–0.

Cambridge University

First Innings		Second Innings	
†R. J. Turner lbw b Sykes	24	– lbw b Tufnell	16
S. J. Noyes lbw b Hughes	1	– (3) not out	24
A. M. G. Scott c Brown b Fraser	8		
*M. A. Atherton not out	151		
J. C. M. Atkinson lbw b Hughes	5	– (2) run out	26
R. Bate c Olley b Hughes	1	– (4) not out	12
S. D. Heath c Carr b Hughes	6		
R. A. Pyman b Tufnell	4		
A. K. Golding not out	18		
B 10, l-b 5, w 2, n-b 2	19	B 8, l-b 4	12
1/1 2/17 3/109 4/116 5/122 6/133 7/154 (7 wkts dec.)	237	1/45 2/60 (2 wkts)	90

J. N. Perry and N. C. W. Fenton did not bat.

Bowling: *First Innings*—Hughes 24–6–39–4; Fraser 22–5–57–1; Tufnell 35–17–52–1; Carr 8–1–23–0; Sykes 23–8–51–1; Brown 1–1–0–0. *Second Innings*—Hughes 7–0–15–0; Fraser 6–1–25–0; Sykes 7–1–12–0; Tufnell 7–1–22–1; MacLaurin 1–0–4–0.

Umpires: V. A. Holder and D. O. Oslear.

CAMBRIDGE UNIVERSITY v YORKSHIRE

At Cambridge, June 11, 12, 13. Yorkshire won by ten wickets. Toss: Yorkshire. Atherton again dominated Cambridge's batting, and once he departed the tail had little to offer against Carrick's spin. Yorkshire lost early wickets to Fenton, but Metcalfe, Robinson and Byas gave the innings its impetus before Pointer and Hart curtailed it. Cambridge made little headway in their second innings, although Atherton resisted for almost two hours. Yorkshire claimed the extra half-hour in an attempt to win in two days, only to be held up by the tail. They had to return for 26 minutes on the third day to complete their ten-wicket win.

Close of play: First day, Yorkshire 121-4 (D. Byas 1*); Second day, Yorkshire 9-0 (P. J. Berry 7*, N. G. Nicholson 1*).

Cambridge University

First Innings		Second Innings	
†R. J. Turner c Nicholson b Dennis	0	– c Carrick b Fletcher	15
S. J. Noyes b Fletcher	0	– b Towse	1
*M. A. Atherton c Byas b Berry	75	– c Robinson b Carrick	35
M. Tremellen lbw b Fletcher	2	– lbw b Fletcher	2
J. C. M. Atkinson b Towse	15	– b Fletcher	3
M. C. Stenner c Berry b Carrick	10	– c Blakey b Towse	13
R. Bate not out	28	– c Love b Berry	29
R. J. Hart c Nicholson b Carrick	0	– c Nicholson b Carrick	6
G. A. Pointer c Towse b Carrick	15	– c Metcalfe b Carrick	13
J. N. Perry c Dennis b Carrick	7	– c Byas b Fletcher	7
N. C. W. Fenton c Robinson b Berry	0	– not out	0
L-b 4	4	B 3, l-b 8	11
1/0 2/0 3/2 4/35 5/59 6/120 7/120 8/142 9/152	156	1/2 2/24 3/30 4/36 5/56 6/82 7/110 8/110 9/135	135

Bowling: *First Innings*—Dennis 9–4–20–1; Fletcher 15–5–31–2; Towse 9–2–24–1; Carrick 18–7–42–4; Berry 15.2–5–35–2. *Second Innings*—Fletcher 12.2–2–25–4; Towse 11–5–26–2; Berry 23–8–56–1; Carrick 12–6–17–3.

Yorkshire

†R. J. Blakey c Turner b Fenton	9		
A. A. Metcalfe c Turner b Fenton	52		
J. D. Love lbw b Fenton	7		
P. E. Robinson c Perry b Hart	40		
D. Byas b Pointer	69		
N. G. Nicholson c Bate b Hart	16	– (2) not out	12
*P. Carrick b Hart	0		
P. J. Berry c Turner b Pointer	4	– (1) not out	23
S. J. Dennis not out	36		
S. D. Fletcher c Atherton b Hart	2		
A. D. Towse b Pointer	1		
B 3, l-b 7, w 1, n-b 4	15	B 4, l-b 2	6
1/16 2/40 3/115 4/121 5/178 6/178 7/199 8/217 9/240	251		(no wkt) 41

Bowling: *First Innings*—Fenton 25–8–65–3; Perry 25–8–61–0; Pointer 10.4–2–31–3; Hart 30–9–66–4; Atherton 8–0–18–0. *Second Innings*—Pointer 4–0–17–0; Perry 1–0–2–0; Fenton 4–0–12–0; Atherton 0.3–0–4–0.

Umpires: B. Hassan and R. A. White.

At The Oval, June 15, 16, 17. CAMBRIDGE UNIVERSITY lost to SURREY by 149 runs.

†At Cambridge, June 18, 19, 20. Drawn. Cambridge University 360 for five dec. (J. C. M. Atkinson 112, S. J. Noyes 101, R. J. Turner 52) and 182 for seven dec. (J. C. M. Atkinson 53; M. V. Fleming four for 40); Combined Services 212 (J. P. Barrett 82; J. N. Perry four for 57) and 312 for nine (E. C. Gordon-Lennox 122 not out; M. A. Atherton four for 135).

†At Cambridge, June 21. University of New South Wales won by 6 runs. University of New South Wales 180 for eight (50 overs) (A. Shaw 66); Cambridge University 174 (M. A. Atherton 74).

†At Cambridge, June 22. Cambridge University won by 10 runs. Cambridge University 234 for four (50 overs) (S. J. Noyes 102 not out, S. D. Heath 60); University of New South Wales 224 for eight (50 overs) (P. L. Solari 94, A. Pratt 58).

†At Cambridge, June 25. Drawn. Cambridge University 174 (M. A. Atherton 57; A. R. Wingfield Digby five for 60); Free Foresters 145 for nine (G. A. Pointer four for 35).

†At Cambridge, June 26. Cambridge University won by six wickets. Quidnuncs 244 for five dec. (J. P. C. Mills 97 not out, D. C. Holliday 60); Cambridge University 245 for four (J. M. Tremellen 80 not out, S. J. Noyes 62 not out, R. J. Turner 59).

†At Devizes, June 27, 28. Drawn. Cambridge University 247 for eight dec. (M. A. Atherton 112, S. D. Heath 62) and 138 for three; Wiltshire 137 (M. A. Watts 57; N. C. W. Fenton four for 13) and 138 for four (R. Greatorix 66).

†At Bishop's Stortford, June 29. Hertfordshire Under-25 won by 38 runs. Hertfordshire Under-25 91 (M. A. Atherton five for 28); Cambridge University 53 (P. O'Reilly five for 15).

†At Bishop's Stortford, June 30. Drawn. Cambridge University 159 for six v Hertfordshire Under-25.

At Lord's, July 2, 3, 4. OXFORD UNIVERSITY v CAMBRIDGE UNIVERSITY. Abandoned.

OXFORD AND CAMBRIDGE BLUES

From 1946 to 1988, and some others

A full list of Blues from 1837 may be found in all *Wisdens* published between 1923 and 1939. Between 1948 and 1972 the list was confined to all those who had won Blues after 1880, plus some of "special interest for personal or family reasons". Between 1972 and 1982 the list was restricted to those who had won Blues since 1919. Such adjustments have been necessary owing to the exigencies of space.

OXFORD

Aamer Hameed (Central Model HS and Punjab U.) 1979
Abell, G. E. B. (Marlborough) 1924, 1926-27
Allan, J. M. (Edinburgh Academy) 1953-56
Allerton, J. W. O. (Stowe) 1969
Allison, D. F. (Greenmore Coll.) 1970
Almaer, S. A. (Ilford County HS) 1988
Altham, H. S. (Repton) 1911-12
Arenhold, J. A. (Diocesan Coll., SA) 1954

Baig, A. A. (Aliya and Osmania U., India) 1959-62
Baig, M. A. (Osmania U., India) 1962-64
Bailey, J. A. (Christ's Hospital) (Capt. in 1958) 1956-58
Barber, A. T. (Shrewsbury) (Capt. in 1929) 1927-29
Barker, A. H. (Charterhouse) 1964-65, 1967
Bartlett, J. H. (Chichester) 1946, 1951
Beech, A. R. (John XXIII Coll., Perth and Univ. of Western Australia) 1987
Bettington, R. H. B. (The King's School, Parramatta) (Capt. in 1923) 1920-23
Bird, W. S. (Malvern) (Capt. in 1906) 1904-06
Birrell, H. B. (St Andrews, SA) 1953-54
Blake, P. D. S. (Eton) (Capt. in 1952) 1950-52
Bloy, N. C. F. (Dover) 1946-47
Boobbyer, B. (Uppingham) 1949-52
Bosanquet, B. J. T. (Eton) 1898-1900
Botton, N. D. (King Edward's, Bath) 1974
Bowman, R. C. (Fettes) 1957
Brettell, D. N. (Cheltenham) 1977
Bristowe, W. R. (Charterhouse) 1984-85
Brooks, R. A. (Quintin and Bristol U.) 1967
Brown, M. E. O. (Diocesan Coll. and Univ. of Cape Town) 1988
Burchnall, R. L. (Winchester) 1970-71
Burki, J. (St Mary's, Rawalpindi and Punjab U.) 1958-60
Burton, M. St J. W. (Umtali HS, Rhodesia and Rhodes U.) (Capt. in 1970) 1969-71
Bury, T. E. O. (Charterhouse) 1980
Bush, J. E. (Magdalen Coll. Sch.) 1952

Campbell, A. N. (Berkhamsted) 1970
Campbell, I. P. (Canford) 1949-50
Campbell, I. P. F. (Repton) (Capt. in 1913) 1911-13
Cantlay, C. P. T. (Radley) 1975
Carr, D. B. (Repton) (Capt. in 1950) 1949-51
Carr, J. D. (Repton) 1983-85
Carroll, P. R. (Newington Coll. and Sydney U.) 1971
Chalk, F. G. H. (Uppingham) (Capt. in 1934) 1931-34
Chesterton, G. H. (Malvern) 1949
Claughton, J. A. (King Edward's, Birmingham) (Capt. in 1978) 1976-79
Clements, S. M. (Ipswich) (Capt. in 1979) 1976, 1979
Clube, S. V. M. (St John's, Leatherhead) 1956
Cope, J. E. B. (St John's, Leatherhead) 1986-87
Corlett, S. C. (Worksop) 1971-72
Corran, A. J. (Gresham's) 1958-60
Coutts, I. D. F. (Dulwich) 1952
Cowan, R. S. (Lewes Priory CS) 1980-82
Cowdrey, M. C. (Tonbridge) (Capt. in 1954) 1952-54
Coxon, A. J. (Harrow CS) 1952
Crawley, A. M. (Harrow) 1927-30
Crawley, M. A. (Manchester GS) 1987-88
Crutchley, G. E. V. (Harrow) 1912
Cullinan, M. R. (Hilton Coll., SA) 1983-84
Curtis, I. J. (Whitgift) 1980, 1982
Cushing, V. G. B. (KCS Wimbledon) 1973
Cuthbertson, J. L. (Rugby) 1962-63

Davidson, W. W. (Brighton) 1947-48
Davis, F. J. (Blundell's) 1963
Dawson, T. A. J. (Mill Hill) 1986
Delisle, G. P. S. (Stonyhurst) 1955-56
de Saram, F. C. (Royal Coll., Colombo) 1934-35
Divecha, R. V. (Podar HS and Bombay U.) 1950-51
Dixon, E. J. H. (St Edward's, Oxford) (Capt. in 1939) 1937-39
Donnelly, M. P. (New Plymouth BHS and Canterbury U., NZ) (Capt. in 1947) 1946-47
Dowding, A. L. (St Peter's, Adelaide) (Capt. in 1953) 1952-53

Drybrough, C. D. (Highgate) (Capt. in 1961-62) 1960-62
Duff, A. R. (Radley) 1960-61
Dyer, A. W. (Mill Hill) 1965-66
Dyson, E. M. (QEGS, Wakefield) 1958

Eagar, M. A. (Rugby) 1956-59
Easter, J. N. C. (St Edward's, Oxford) 1967-68
Edbrooke, R. M. (Queen Elizabeth's Hospital) 1984
Edwards, P. G. (Canford) 1987-88
Ellis, R. G. P. (Haileybury) (Capt. in 1982) 1981-83
Elviss, R. W. (Leeds GS) 1966-67
Ezekowitz, R. A. B. (Westville BHS, Durban and Cape Town U., SA) 1980-81

Faber, M. J. J. (Eton) 1972
Fane, F. L. (Charterhouse) 1897-98
Fasken, D. K. (Wellington) 1953-55
Fellows-Smith, J. P. (Durban HS, SA) 1953-55
Fillary, E. W. J. (St Lawrence) 1963-65
Findlay, W. (Eton) (Capt. in 1903) 1901-03
Firth, T. (Stockport GS) 1987
Fisher, P. B. (St Ignatius, Enfield) 1975-78
Foster, G. N. (Malvern) 1905-08
Foster, H. K. (Malvern) 1894-96
Foster, R. E. (Malvern) (Capt. in 1900) 1897-1900
Franks, J. G. (Stamford) 1984-85
Fry, C. A. (Repton) 1959-61
Fry, C. B. (Repton) (Capt. in 1894) 1892-95
Fursdon, E. D. (Sherborne) 1974-75

Gamble, N. W. (Stockport GS) 1967
Garofall, A. R. (Latymer Upper) 1967-68
Gibbs, P. J. K. (Hanley GS) 1964-66
Gibson, I. (Manchester GS) 1955-58
Gilliat, R. M. C. (Charterhouse) (Capt. in 1966) 1964-67
Gilligan, F. W. (Dulwich) (Capt. in 1920) 1919-20
Glover, T. R. (Lancaster RGS) (Capt. in 1975) 1973-75
Goldstein, F. S. (Falcon Coll., Bulawayo) (Capt. in 1968-69) 1966-69
Green, D. M. (Manchester GS) 1959-61
Grover, J. N. (Winchester) (Capt. in 1938) 1936-38
Groves, M. G. M. (Diocesan Coll., SA) 1964-66
Guest, M. R. J. (Rugby) 1964-66
Guise, J. L. (Winchester) (Capt. in 1925) 1924-25
Gurr, D. R. (Aylesbury GS) 1976-77

Hagan, D. A. (Trinity, Leamington Spa) 1986, 1988
Halliday, S. J. (Downside) 1980
Hamblin, C. B. (King's, Canterbury) 1971-73
Hamilton, A. C. (Charterhouse) 1975
Harris, C. R. (Buckingham RLS) 1964
Harris, Hon. G. R. C. (Lord Harris) (Eton) 1871-72, 1874
Hayes, K. A. (QEGS, Blackburn) (Capt. in 1984) 1981-84
Heal, M. G. (St Brendan's, Bristol) 1970, 1972
Heard, H. (QE Hosp. Sch.) 1969-70
Henderson, D. (St Edward's, Oxford) 1950
Henderson, I. M. (Laxton) 1987
Henley, D. F. (Harrow) 1947
Heseltine, P. J. (Holgate GS) 1983
Hiller, R. B. (Bec) 1966
Hobbs, J. A. D. (Liverpool Coll.) 1957
Hofmeyr, M. B. (Pretoria, SA) (Capt. in 1951) 1949-51
Holmes, E. R. T. (Malvern) (Capt. in 1927) 1925-27
Hone, B. W. (Adelaide U.) (Capt. in 1933) 1931-33
Howell, M. (Repton) (Capt. in 1919) 1914, 1919
Huxford, P. N. (Richard Hale) 1981

Imran Khan (Aitchison Coll., Lahore and Worcester RGS) (Capt. in 1974) 1973-75

Jack, T. B. (Aquinas Coll. and Univ. of WA) 1988
Jakobson, T. R. (Charterhouse) 1961
Jardine, D. R. (Winchester) 1920-21, 1923
Jardine, M. R. (Fettes) (Capt. in 1891) 1889-92
Jarrett, D. W. (Wellington) 1975
Johns, R. L. (St Albans and Keele U.) 1970
Jones, A. K. C. (Solihull) (Capt. in 1973) 1971-73
Jones, P. C. H. (Milton HS, Rhodesia and Rhodes U.) (Capt. in 1972) 1971-72
Jose, A. D. (Adelaide U.) 1950-51
Jowett, D. C. P. R. (Sherborne) 1952-55
Jowett, R. L. (Bradford GS) 1957-59

Kamm, A. (Charterhouse) 1954
Kardar, A. H. (Islamia Coll. and Punjab U.) 1947-49
Kayum, D. A. (Selhurst GS and Chatham House GS) 1977-78
Keighley, W. G. (Eton) 1947-48
Kentish, E. S. M. (Cornwall Coll., Jamaica) 1956
Khan, A. J. (Aitchison Coll., Lahore and Punjab U.) 1968-69
Kilborn, M. J. (Farrer Agric. HS and Univ. of NSW) (Capt. in 1988) 1986-88
Kingsley, P. G. T. (Winchester) (Capt. in 1930) 1928-30

Kinkead-Weekes, R. C. (Eton) 1972
Knight, D. J. (Malvern) 1914, 1919
Knight, J. M. (Oundle) 1979
Knott, C. H. (Tonbridge) (Capt. in 1924) 1922-24
Knott, F. H. (Tonbridge) (Capt. in 1914) 1912-14
Knox, F. P. (Dulwich) (Capt. in 1901) 1899-1901

Lamb, Hon. T. M. (Shrewsbury) 1973-74
Lawrence, M. P. (Manchester GS) 1984-86
Lee, R. J. (Church of England GS and Sydney U.) 1972-74
Legge, G. B. (Malvern) (Capt. in 1926) 1925-26
L'Estrange, M. G. (St Aloysius Coll. and Sydney U.) 1977, 1979
Leveson Gower, H. D. G. (Winchester) (Capt. in 1896) 1893-96
Lewis, D. J. (Cape Town U.) 1951
Lloyd, M. F. D. (Magdalen Coll. Sch.) 1974
Luddington, R. S. (KCS, Wimbledon) 1982

McCanlis, M. A. (Cranleigh) (Capt. in 1928) 1926-28
Macindoe, D. H. (Eton) (Capt. in 1946) 1937-39, 1946
McKinna, G. H. (Manchester GS) 1953
MacLarnon, P. C. (Loughborough GS) 1985
Majendie, N. L. (Winchester) 1962-63
Mallett, A. W. H. (Dulwich) 1947-48
Mallett, N. V. H. (St Andrew's Coll. and Cape Town U.) 1981
Manasseh, M. (Epsom) 1964
Marie, G. V. (Western Australia U. and Reading U.) (Capt. in 1979, but injury prevented him playing v Cambridge) 1978
Marks, V. J. (Blundell's) (Capt. in 1976-77) 1975-78
Marsden, R. (Merchant Taylors', Northwood) 1982
Marshall, J. C. (Rugby) 1953
Marsham, C. D. B. (Private) (Capt. in 1857-58) 1854-58
Marsham, C. H. B. (Eton) (Capt. in 1902) 1900-02
Marsham, C. J. B. (Private) 1851
Marsham, R. H. B. (Private) 1856
Marsland, G. P. (Rossall) 1954
Martin, J. D. (Magdalen Coll. Sch.) (Capt. in 1965) 1962-63, 1965
Maudsley, R. H. (Malvern) 1946-47
May, B. (Prince Edward's, Salisbury and Cape Town U.) (Capt. in 1971) 1970-72
Mee, A. A. G. (Merchant Taylors', Northwood) 1986
Melville, A. (Michaelhouse, SA) (Capt. in 1931-32) 1930-33
Melville, C. D. M. (Michaelhouse, SA) 1957
Metcalfe, S. G. (Leeds GS) 1956
Millener, D. J. (Auckland GS and Auckland U.) 1969-70
Miller, A. J. T. (Haileybury) (Capt. in 1985) 1983-85
Minns, R. E. F. (King's, Canterbury) 1962-63
Mitchell, W. M. (Dulwich) 1951-52
Mitchell-Innes, N. S. (Sedbergh) (Capt. in 1936) 1934-37
Moore, D. N. (Shrewsbury) (Capt. in 1931, when he did not play v Cambridge owing to illness) 1930
Morgan, A. H. (Hastings GS) 1969
Morrill, N. D. (Sandown GS and Millfield) 1979
Morris, R. E. (Dyffryn Conwy, Llanrwst) 1987
Moulding, R. P. (Haberdashers' Aske's) (Capt. in 1981) 1978-83
Mountford, P. N. G. (Bromsgrove) 1963

Neate, F. W. (St Paul's) 1961-62
Newton-Thompson, J. O. (Diocesan Coll., SA) 1946
Niven, R. A. (Berkhamsted) 1968-69, 1973
Nuttall, J. D. (Pocklington) 1988

O'Brien, T. C. (St Charles' College, Notting-Hill) 1884-85
Orders, J. O. D. (Winchester) 1978-81
Owen-Smith, H. G. (Diocesan College, SA) 1931-33

Palairet, L. C. H. (Repton) (Capt. in 1892-93) 1890-93
Pataudi, Nawab of (Chief's College, Lahore) 1929-31
Pataudi, Nawab of (Winchester) (Capt. in 1961, when he did not play v Cambridge owing to a car accident and 1963) 1960, 1963
Pathmanathan, G. (Royal Coll., Colombo and Sri Lanka U.) 1975-78
Paver, R. G. L. (Fort Victoria HS and Rhodes U.) 1973-74
Pawson, A. C. (Winchester) 1903
Pawson, A. G. (Winchester) (Capt. in 1910) 1908-11
Pawson, H. A. (Winchester) (Capt. in 1948) 1947-48
Pearce, J. P. (Ampleforth) 1979
Peebles, I. A. R. (Glasgow Academy) 1930
Petchey, M. D. (Latymer Upper) 1983
Phillips, J. B. M. (King's, Canterbury) 1955
Piachaud, J. D. (St Thomas's, Colombo) 1958-61
Pithey, D. B. (Plumtree HS and Cape Town U.) 1961-62
Porter, S. R. (Peers School) 1973
Potter, I. C. (King's, Canterbury) 1961-62
Potts, H. J. (Stand GS) 1950

Price, V. R. (Bishop's Stortford) (Capt. in 1921) 1919-22
Pycroft, J. (Bath) 1836

Quinlan, J. D. (Sherborne) 1985

Rawlinson, H. T. (Eton) 1983-84
Raybould, J. G. (Leeds GS) 1959
Reynolds, G. D. (Wellington Coll.) 1988
Ridge, S. P. (Dr Challenor's GS) 1982
Ridley, G. N. S. (Milton HS, Rhodesia) (Capt. in 1967) 1965-68
Ridley, R. M. (Clifton) 1968-70
Robertson-Glasgow, R. C. (Charterhouse) 1920-23
Robinson, G. A. (Preston Cath. Coll.) 1971
Robinson, H. B. O. (North Shore Coll., Vancouver) 1947-48
Rogers, J. J. (Sedbergh) 1979-81
Ross, C. J. (Wanganui CS and Wellington U., NZ) (Capt. in 1980) 1978-80
Rudd, C. R. D. (Eton) 1949
Rumbold, J. S. (St Andrew's Coll., NZ) 1946
Rutnagur, R. S. (Westminster) 1985-86
Rydon, R. A. (Sherborne) 1986

Sabine, P. N. B. (Marlborough) 1963
Sale, R. (Repton) 1910
Sale, R. (Repton) 1939, 1946
Salvi, N. V. (Rossall) 1986
Sanderson, J. F. W. (Westminster) 1980
Sardesai, R. D. (St Xavier's Coll., Bombay and Univ. of Bombay) 1987
Saunders, C. J. (Lancing) 1964
Savage, R. Le Q. (Marlborough) 1976-78
Sayer, D. M. (Maidstone GS) 1958-60
Scott, M. D. (Winchester) 1957
Singleton, A. P. (Shrewsbury) (Capt. in 1937) 1934-37
Siviter, K. (Liverpool) 1976
Smith, A. C. (King Edward's, Birmingham) (Capt. in 1959-60) 1958-60
Smith, G. O. (Charterhouse) 1895-96
Smith, M. J. K. (Stamford) (Capt. in 1956) 1954-56
Stallibrass, M. J. D. (Lancing) 1974
Stevens, G. T. S. (UCS) (Capt. in 1922) 1920-23
Sutcliffe, S. P. (King George V GS, Southport) 1980-81
Sutton, M. A. (Ampleforth) 1946
Sygrove, M. R. (Lutterworth GS) 1988

Tavaré, C. J. (Sevenoaks) 1975-77
Taylor, C. H. (Westminster) 1923-26
Taylor, T. J. (Stockport GS) 1981-82
Thackeray, P. R. (St Edward's, Oxford and Exeter U.) 1974
Thomas, R. J. A. (Radley) 1965
Thorne, D. A. (Bablake) (Capt. in 1986) 1984-86
Toft, D. P. (Tonbridge) 1966-67
Toogood, G. J. (N. Bromsgrove HS) (Capt. in 1983) 1982-85
Tooley, C. D. M. (St Dunstan's) (Capt. in 1987) 1985-87
Topham, R. D. N. (Shrewsbury and Australian National U., Canberra) 1976
Travers, B. H. (Sydney U.) 1946, 1948
Twining, R. H. (Eton) (Capt. in 1912) 1910-13

van der Bijl, P. G. (Diocesan Coll., SA) 1932
Van Ryneveld, C. B. (Diocesan Coll., SA) (Capt. in 1949) 1948-50
Varey, J. G. (Birkenhead) 1982-83

Wagstaffe, M. C. (Rossall and Exeter U.) 1972
Walford, M. M. (Rugby) 1936, 1938
Walker, D. F. (Uppingham) (Capt. in 1935) 1933-35
Waller, G. de W. (Hurstpierpoint) 1974
Walsh, D. R. (Marlborough) 1967-69
Walshe, A. P. (Milton HS, Rhodesia) 1953, 1955-56
Walton, A. C. (Radley) (Capt. in 1957) 1955-57
Ward, J. M. (Newcastle-under-Lyme HS) 1971-73
Warner, P. F. (Rugby) 1895-96
Watson, A. G. M. (St Lawrence) 1965-66, 1968
Weale, S. D. (Westminster City) 1987-88
Webb, H. E. (Winchester) 1948
Webbe, A. J. (Harrow) (Capt. in 1877-78) 1875-78
Wellings, E. M. (Cheltenham) 1929, 1931
Westley, S. A. (Lancaster RGS) 1968-69
Wheatley, G. A. (Uppingham) 1946
Whitcombe, P. A. (Winchester) 1947-49
Whitcombe, P. J. (Worcester RGS) 1951-52
Wiley, W. G. A. (Diocesan Coll., SA) 1952
Williams, C. C. P. (Westminster) (Capt. in 1955) 1953-55
Wilson, P. R. B. (Milton HS, Rhodesia and Cape Town U.) 1968, 1970
Wilson, R. W. (Warwick) 1957
Wingfield Digby, A. R. (Sherborne) 1971, 1975-77
Winn, C. E. (KCS, Wimbledon) 1948-51
Woodcock, R. G. (Worcester RGS) 1957-58
Wookey, S. M. (Malvern and Cambridge U.) 1978
Wordsworth, Chas. (Harrow) (Capt. both years, first Oxford Capt.) 1827, 1829
Worsley, D. R. (Bolton) (Capt. in 1964) 1961-64
Wrigley, M. H. (Harrow) 1949

CAMBRIDGE

Acfield, D. L. (Brentwood) 1967-68
Aers, D. R. (Tonbridge) 1967
Ahluwalia, M. S. (Latymer Upper) 1986
Aird, R. (Eton) 1923
Alexander, F. C. M. (Wolmer's Coll., Jamaica) 1952-53
Allbrook, M. E. (Tonbridge) 1975-78
Allen, G. O. (Eton) 1922-23
Allom, M. J. C. (Wellington) 1927-28
Andrew, C. R. (Barnard Castle) (Capt. in 1985) 1984-85
Ashton, C. T. (Winchester) (Capt. in 1923) 1921-23
Ashton, G. (Winchester) (Capt. in 1921) 1919-21
Ashton, H. (Winchester) (Capt. in 1922) 1920-22
Atherton, M. A. (Capt. in 1988) (Manchester GS) 1987-88
Atkins, G. (Dr Challenor's GS) 1960
Atkinson, J. C. M. (Millfield) 1988
Aworth, C. J. (Tiffin) (Capt. in 1975) 1973-75

Bail, P. A. C. (Millfield) 1986-88
Bailey, T. E. (Dulwich) 1947-48
Baker, R. K. (Brentwood) 1973-74
Bannister, C. S. (Caterham) 1976
Barber, R. W. (Ruthin) 1956-57
Barford, M. T. (Eastbourne) 1970-71
Barrington, W. E. J. (Lancing) 1982
Bartlett, H. T. (Dulwich) (Capt. in 1936) 1934-36
Bate, R. (Haberdashers' Aske's) 1988
Beaumont, D. J. (West Bridgford GS and Bramshill Coll.) 1978
Benke, A. F. (Cheltenham) 1962
Bennett, B. W. P. (Welbeck and RMA Sandhurst) 1979
Bennett, C. T. (Harrow) (Capt. in 1925) 1923, 1925
Bernard, J. R. (Clifton) 1958-60
Bhatia, A. N. (Doon School, India) 1969
Bligh, Hon. Ivo F. W. (Lord Darnley) (Eton) (Capt. in 1881) 1878-81
Blofeld, H. C. (Eton) 1959
Bodkin, P. E. (Bradfield) (Capt. in 1946) 1946
Boyd-Moss, R. J. (Bedford) 1980-83
Brearley, J. M. (City of London) (Capt. in 1963-64) 1961-64
Breddy, M. N. (Cheltenham GS) 1984
Brodie, J. B. (Union HS, SA) 1960
Brodrick, P. D. (Royal GS, Newcastle) 1961
Bromley, R. C. (Christ's Coll. and Canterbury U., NZ) 1970
Brooker, M. E. W. (Lancaster RGS and Burnley GS) 1976
Brown, A. D. (Clacton HS) 1986
Brown, F. R. (The Leys) 1930-31
Browne, D. W. (Stamford) 1986
Burnett, A. C. (Lancing) 1949
Burnley, I. D. (Queen Elizabeth, Darlington) 1984
Bushby, M. H. (Dulwich) (Capt. in 1954) 1952-54

Calthorpe, Hon. F. S. G. (Repton) 1912-14, 1919
Cameron, J. H. (Taunton) 1935-37
Cangley, B. G. M. (Felsted) 1947
Carling, P. G. (Kingston GS) 1968, 1970
Chambers, R. E. J. (Forest) 1966
Chapman, A. P. F. (Oakham and Uppingham) 1920-22
Close, P. A. (Haileybury) 1965
Cobden, F. C. (Harrow) 1870-72
Cockett, J. A. (Aldenham) 1951
Coghlan, T. B. L. (Rugby) 1960
Conradi, E. R. (Oundle) 1946
Cook, G. W. (Dulwich) 1957-58
Cooper, N. H. C. (St Brendan's, Bristol and East Anglia U.) 1979
Cosh, N. J. (Dulwich) 1966-68
Cotterell, T. A. (Downside) 1983-85
Cottrell, G. A. (Kingston GS) (Capt. in 1968) 1966-68
Cottrell, P. R. (Chislehurst and Sidcup GS) 1979
Coverdale, S. P. (St Peter's, York) 1974-77
Craig, E. J. (Charterhouse) 1961-63
Crawford, N. C. (Shrewsbury) 1979-80
Crawley, E. (Harrow) 1887-89
Crawley, L. G. (Harrow) 1923-25
Croft, P. D. (Gresham's) 1955
Crookes, D. V. (Michaelhouse, SA) 1953
Curtis, T. S. (Worcester RGS) 1983

Daniell, J. (Clifton) 1899-1901
Daniels, D. M. (Rutlish) 1964-65
Datta, P. B. (Asutosh Coll., Calcutta) 1947
Davies, A. G. (Birkenhead) 1984-85
Davies, J. G. W. (Tonbridge) 1933-34
Davidson, J. E. (Penglais) 1985-86
Dawson, E. W. (Eton) (Capt. in 1927) 1924-27
Day, S. H. (Malvern) (Capt. in 1901) 1899-1902
Dewes, A. R. (Dulwich) 1978
Dewes, J. G. (Aldenham) 1948-50
Dexter, E. R. (Radley) (Capt. in 1958) 1956-58
Dickinson, D. C. (Clifton) 1953
Doggart, A. G. (Bishop's Stortford) 1921-22
Doggart, G. H. G. (Winchester) (Capt. in 1950) 1948-50
Doggart, S. J. G. (Winchester) 1980-83
Douglas-Pennant, S. (Eton) 1959

Duleepsinhji, K. S. (Cheltenham) 1925-26, 1928

Edmonds, P. H. (Gilbert Rennie HS, Lusaka, Skinner's and Cranbrook) (Capt. in 1973) 1971-73
Edwards, T. D. W. (Sherborne) 1981
Elgood, B. C. (Bradfield) 1948
Ellison, C. C. (Tonbridge) 1982-83, 1985-86
Enthoven, H. J. (Harrow) (Capt. in 1926) 1923-26
Estcourt, N. S. D. (Plumtree, Southern Rhodesia) 1954

Falcon, M. (Harrow) (Capt. in 1910) 1908-11
Farnes, K. (Royal Liberty School, Romford) 1931-33
Fell, D. J. (John Lyon) 1985-87
Fenton, N. C. W. (Rugby) 1988
Field, M. N. (Bablake) 1974
Fitzgerald, J. F. (St Brendan's, Bristol) 1968
Ford, A. F. J. (Repton) 1878-81
Ford, F. G. J. (Repton) (Capt. in 1889) 1887-90
Ford, W. J. (Repton) 1873
Fosh, M. K. (Harrow) 1977-78

Gardiner, S. J. (St Andrew's, Bloemfontein) 1978
Garlick, P. L. (Sherborne) 1984
Gibb, P. A. (St Edward's, Oxford) 1935-38
Gibson, C. H. (Eton) 1920-21
Gilligan, A. E. R. (Dulwich) 1919-20
Goldie, C. F. E. (St Paul's) 1981-82
Golding, A. K. (Colchester GS) 1986
Goodfellow, A. (Marlborough) 1961-62
Goonesena, G. (Royal Coll., Colombo) (Capt. in 1957) 1954-57
Gorman, S. R. (St Peter's, York) 1985, 1987
Grace, W. G., jun. (Clifton) 1895-96
Grant, G. C. (Trinidad) 1929-30
Grant, R. S. (Trinidad) 1933
Green, D. J. (Burton GS) (Capt. in 1959) 1957-59
Greig, I. A. (Queen's Coll., SA) (Capt. in 1979) 1977-79
Grierson, H. (Bedford GS) 1911
Grimes, A. D. H. (Tonbridge) 1984
Griffith, M. G. (Marlborough) 1963-65
Griffith, S. C. (Dulwich) 1935
Griffiths, W. H. (Charterhouse) 1946-48

Hadley, R. J. (Sanfields CS) 1971-73
Hall, J. E. (Ardingly) 1969
Hall, P. J. (Geelong) 1949
Harvey, J. R. W. (Marlborough) 1965
Hawke, Hon. M. B. (Eton) (Capt. in 1885) 1882-83, 1885
Hayes, P. J. (Brighton) 1974-75, 1977
Hays, D. L. (Highgate) 1966, 1968
Hayward, W. I. D. (St Peter's Coll., Adelaide) 1950-51, 1953
Haywood, D. C. (Nottingham HS) 1968
Hazelrigg, A. G. (Eton) (Capt. in 1932) 1930-32
Heath, S. D. (King Edward's, Birmingham) 1988
Henderson, S. P. (Downside and Durham U.) (Capt. in 1983) 1982-83
Hewitt, S. G. P. (Bradford GS) 1983
Hignell, A. J. (Denstone) (Capt. in 1977-78) 1975-78
Hobson, B. S. (Taunton) 1946
Hodgson, K. I. (Oundle) 1981-83
Hodson, R. P. (QEGS, Wakefield) 1972-73
Holliday, D. C. (Oundle) 1979-81
Hooper, A. M. (Latymer Upper) 1987
Howat, M. G. (Abingdon) 1977, 1980
Howland, C. B. (Dulwich) (Capt. in 1960) 1958-60
Hughes, G. (Cardiff HS) 1965
Human, J. H. (Repton) (Capt. in 1934) 1932-34
Hurd, A. (Chigwell) 1958-60
Hutton, R. A. (Repton) 1962-64
Huxter, R. J. A. (Magdalen Coll. Sch.) 1981

Insole, D. J. (Monoux, Walthamstow) (Capt. in 1949) 1947-49

Jackson, E. J. W. (Winchester) 1974-76
Jackson, F. S. (Harrow) (Capt. in 1892-93) 1890-93
Jahangir Khan (Lahore), 1933-36
James, R. M. (St John's, Leatherhead) 1956-58
Jameson, T. E. N. (Taunton and Durham U.) 1970
Jarrett, D. W. (Wellington and Oxford U.) 1976
Jefferson, R. I. (Winchester) 1961
Jenner, Herbert (Eton) (Capt. in 1827, First Cambridge Capt.) 1827
Jessop, G. L. (Cheltenham GS) (Capt. in 1899) 1896-99
Johnson, P. D. (Nottingham HS) 1970-72
Jones, A. O. (Bedford Modern) 1893
Jorden, A. M. (Monmouth) (Capt. in 1969-70) 1968-70

Kelland, P. A. (Repton) 1950
Kemp-Welch, G. D. (Charterhouse) (Capt. in 1931) 1929-31
Kendall, M. P. (Gillingham GS) 1972
Kenny, C. J. M. (Ampleforth) 1952
Kerslake, R. C. (Kingswood) 1963-64
Killick, E. T. (St Paul's) 1928-30
Kirby, D. (St Peter's, York) (Capt. in 1961) 1959-61
Kirkman, M. C. (Dulwich) 1963
Knight, R. D. V. (Dulwich) 1967-70
Knightley-Smith, W. (Highgate) 1953

Lacey, F. E. (Sherborne) 1882
Lacy-Scott, D. G. (Marlborough) 1946
Lea, A. E. (High Arcal GS) 1984-86
Lewis, A. R. (Neath GS) (Capt. in 1962) 1960-62
Lewis, L. K. (Taunton) 1953
Littlewood, D. J. (Enfield GS) 1978
Lowry, T. C. (Christ's College, NZ) (Capt. in 1924) 1923-24
Lumsden, V. R. (Munro College, Jamaica) 1953-55
Lyttelton, 4th Lord (Eton) 1838
Lyttelton, Hon. Alfred (Eton) (Capt. in 1879) 1876-79
Lyttelton, Hon. C. F. (Eton) 1908-09
Lyttelton, Hon. C. G. (Lord Cobham) (Eton) 1861-64
Lyttelton, Hon. Edward (Eton) (Capt. in 1878) 1875-78
Lyttelton, Hon. G. W. S. (Eton) 1866-67

McAdam, K. P. W. J. (Prince of Wales, Nairobi and Millfield) 1965-66
MacBryan, J. C. W. (Exeter) 1920
McCarthy, C. N. (Maritzburg Coll., SA) 1952
McDowall, J. I. (Rugby) 1969
MacGregor, G. (Uppingham) (Capt. in 1891) 1888-91
McLachlan, A. A. (St Peter's, Adelaide) 1964-65
McLachlan, I. M. (St Peter's, Adelaide) 1957-58
Majid Khan (Aitchison Coll., Lahore and Punjab U.) (Capt. in 1971-72) 1970-72
Malalasekera, V. P. (Royal Coll., Colombo) 1966-67
Mann, E. W. (Harrow) (Capt. in 1905) 1903-05
Mann, F. G. (Eton) 1938-39
Mann, F. T. (Malvern) 1909-11
Marlar, R. G. (Harrow) (Capt. in 1953) 1951-53
Marriott, C. S. (St Columba's) 1920-21
Mathews, K. P. A. (Felsted) 1951
May, P. B. H. (Charterhouse) 1950-52
Melluish, M. E. L. (Rossall) (Capt. in 1956) 1954-56
Meyer, R. J. O. (Haileybury) 1924-26
Middleton, M. R. (Harrow) 1987
Miller, M. E. (Prince Henry GS, Hohne, WG) 1963
Mills, J. M. (Oundle) (Capt. in 1948) 1946-48
Mills, J. P. C. (Oundle) (Capt. in 1982) 1979-82
Mischler, N. M. (St Paul's) 1946-47
Mitchell, F. (St Peter's, York) (Capt. in 1896) 1894-97
Morgan, J. T. (Charterhouse) (Capt. in 1930) 1928-30
Morgan, M. N. (Marlborough) 1954
Morris, R. J. (Blundell's) 1949
Morrison, J. S. F. (Charterhouse) (Capt. in 1919) 1912, 1914, 1919
Moses, G. H. (Ystalyfera GS) 1974
Moylan, A. C. D. (Clifton) 1977
Mubarak, A. M. (Royal Coll., Colombo and Sri Lanka U.) 1978-80
Murray, D. L. (Queen's RC, Trinidad) (Capt. in 1966) 1965-66
Murrills, T. J. (The Leys) (Capt. in 1976) 1973-74, 1976

Nevin, M. R. S. (Winchester) 1969
Norris, D. W. W. (Harrow) 1967-68
Noyes, S. J. (Royal GS, High Wycombe) 1988

O'Brien, R. P. (Wellington) 1955-56
Odendaal, A. (Queen's Coll. and Stellenbosch U., SA) 1980
Owen-Thomas, D. R. (KCS, Wimbledon) 1969-72

Palfreman, A. B. (Nottingham HS) 1966
Palmer, R. W. M. (Bedford) 1982
Parker, G. W. (Crypt, Gloucester) (Capt. in 1935) 1934-35
Parker, P. W. G. (Collyer's GS) 1976-78
Parsons, A. B. D. (Brighton) 1954-55
Pathmanathan, G. (Royal Coll., Colombo, Sri Lanka U. and Oxford U.) 1983
Paull, R. K. (Millfield) 1967
Payne, M. W. (Wellington) (Capt. in 1907) 1904-07
Pearman, H. (King Alfred's and St Andrew's U.) 1969
Pearson, A. J. G. (Downside) 1961-63
Peck, I. G. (Bedford) (Capt. in 1980-81) 1980-81
Pepper, J. (The Leys) 1946-48
Perry, J. N. (Ampleforth) 1987-88
Pieris, P. I. (St Thomas's, Colombo) 1957-58
Pointer, G. A. (St Dunstan's) 1987-88
Pollock, A. J. (Shrewsbury) (Capt. in 1984) 1982-84
Ponniah, C. E. M. (St Thomas's, Colombo) 1967-69
Ponsonby, Hon. F. G. B. (Lord Bessborough) (Harrow) 1836
Popplewell, N. F. M. (Radley) 1977-79
Popplewell, O. B. (Charterhouse) 1949-51
Pretlove, J. F. (Alleyn's) 1954-56
Price, D. G. (Haberdashers' Aske's) (Capt. in 1986-87) 1984-87
Prideaux, R. M. (Tonbridge) 1958-60
Pringle, D. R. (Felsted) (Capt. in 1982, when he did not play v Oxford owing to Test selection) 1979-81
Pritchard, G. C. (King's, Canterbury) 1964
Pryer, B. J. K. (City of London) 1948
Pyemont, C. P. (Marlborough) 1967

Ranjitsinhji, K. S. (Rajkumar Coll., India) 1893
Ratcliffe, A. (Rydal) 1930-32
Reddy, N. S. K. (Doon School, India) 1959-61
Rimell, A. G. J. (Charterhouse) 1949-50
Robins, R. W. V. (Highgate) 1926-28
Roebuck, P. G. P. (Millfield) 1984-85
Roebuck, P. M. (Millfield) 1975-77
Roopnaraine, R. (Queen's RC, BG) 1965-66
Rose, M. H. (Pocklington) 1963-64
Ross, N. P. G. (Marlborough) 1969
Roundell, J. (Winchester) 1973
Russell, D. P. (West Park GS, St Helens) 1974-75
Russell, S. G. (Tiffin) (Capt. in 1967) 1965-67
Russom, N. (Huish's GS) 1980-81

Scott, A. M. G. (Seaford Head) 1985-87
Seabrook, F. J. (Haileybury) (Capt. in 1928) 1926-28
Seager, C. P. (Peterhouse, Rhodesia) 1971
Selvey, M. W. W. (Battersea GS and Manchester U.) 1971
Sheppard, D. S. (Sherborne) (Capt. in 1952) 1950-52
Short, R. L. (Denstone) 1969
Shuttleworth, G. M. (Blackburn GS) 1946-48
Silk, D. R. W. (Christ's Hospital) (Capt. in 1955) 1953-55
Singh, S. (Khalsa Coll. and Punjab U.) 1955-56
Sinker, N. D. (Winchester) 1966
Slack, J. K. E. (UCS) 1954
Smith, C. S. (William Hulme's GS) 1954-57
Smith, D. J. (Stockport GS) 1955-56
Smyth, R. I. (Sedbergh) 1973-75
Snowden, W. (Merchant Taylors', Crosby) (Capt. in 1974) 1972-75
Spencer, J. (Brighton and Hove GS) 1970-72
Steele, H. K. (King's Coll., NZ) 1971-72
Stevenson, M. H. (Rydal) 1949-52
Studd, C. T. (Eton) (Capt. in 1883) 1880-83
Studd, G. B. (Eton) (Capt. in 1882) 1879-82
Studd, J. E. K. (Eton) (Capt. in 1884) 1881-84
Studd, P. M. (Harrow) (Capt. in 1939) 1937-39
Studd, R. A. (Eton) 1895
Subba Row, R. (Whitgift) 1951-53
Surridge, D. (Richard Hale and Southampton U.) 1979
Swift, B. T. (St Peter's, Adelaide) 1957

Taylor, C. R. V. (Birkenhead) 1971-73
Thomson, R. H. (Bexhill) 1961-62
Thwaites, I. G. (Eastbourne) 1964
Tindall, M. (Harrow) (Capt. in 1937) 1935-37
Tordoff, G. G. (Normanton GS) 1952
Trapnell, B. M. W. (UCS) 1946
Tremellen, J. M. (Bradfield) 1987-88
Turnbull, M. J. (Downside) (Capt. in 1929) 1926, 1928-29
Turner, R. J. (Millfield) 1988

Urquhart, J. R. (King Edward VI School, Chelmsford) 1948

Valentine, B. H. (Repton) 1929
Varey, D. W. (Birkenhead) 1982-83

Wait, O. J. (Dulwich) 1949, 1951
Warr, J. J. (Ealing County GS) (Capt. in 1951) 1949-52
Watts, H. E. (Downside) 1947
Webster, W. H. (Highgate) 1932
Weedon, M. J. H. (Harrow) 1962
Wells, T. U. (King's Coll., NZ) 1950
Wheatley, O. S. (King Edward's, Birmingham) 1957-58
Wheelhouse, A. (Nottingham HS) 1959
White, R. C. (Hilton Coll., SA) (Capt. in 1965) 1962-65
Wilcox, D. R. (Dulwich) (Capt. in 1933) 1931-33
Wilenkin, B. C. G. (Harrow) 1956
Wilkin, C. L. A. (St Kitts GS) 1970
Willard, M. J. L. (Judd) 1959-61
Willatt, G. L. (Repton) (Capt. in 1947) 1946-47
Windows, A. R. (Clifton) 1962-64
Wood, G. E. C. (Cheltenham) (Capt. in 1920) 1914, 1919-20
Wookey, S. M. (Malvern) 1975-76
Wooller, W. (Rydal) 1935-36
Wright, S. (Mill Hill) 1973

Yardley, N. W. D. (St Peter's, York) (Capt. in 1938) 1935-38
Young, R. A. (Repton) (Capt. in 1908) 1905-08

OTHER MATCHES, 1988

THE TILCON TROPHY

†GLOUCESTERSHIRE v WARWICKSHIRE

At Harrogate, June 8. Warwickshire won by 2 runs. Toss: Gloucestershire. Rain and high winds delayed the start of the match, which was reduced to twenty overs a side.

Man of the Match: D. A. Reeve.

Warwickshire

*T. A. Lloyd c Athey b Jarvis	28	J. E. Benjamin run out	1
A. C. Storie c Russell b Lawrence	2	A. A. Donald b Bainbridge	0
Asif Din c Wright b Jarvis	31	L-b 4, w 5	9
P. A. Smith c Stovold b Curran	18		—
†G. W. Humpage b Greene	19	1/4 2/60 3/68 (8 wkts, 20 overs)	152
D. A. Reeve not out	35	4/100 5/105 6/128	
G. J. Parsons c Greene b Curran	9	7/144 8/152	

T. A. Munton and N. Gifford did not bat.

Bowling: Alderman 4–0–31–0; Lawrence 4–0–26–1; Jarvis 2–0–13–2; Greene 4–0–27–1; Curran 4–0–28–2; Bainbridge 2–0–23–1.

Gloucestershire

A. W. Stovold run out	49	V. S. Greene run out	0
C. W. J. Athey c Storie b Benjamin	4		
K. M. Curran c Parsons b Benjamin	11	B 1, l-b 10, w 4, n-b 4	19
D. V. Lawrence c Humpage b Parsons	6		—
*P. Bainbridge c Benjamin b Parsons	36	1/12 2/33 3/39 (6 wkts, 20 overs)	150
J. W. Lloyds not out	25	4/103 5/149 6/150	

A. J. Wright, †R. C. Russell, T. M. Alderman and K. B. S. Jarvis did not bat.

Bowling: Donald 4–0–10–0; Benjamin 4–0–18–2; Parsons 4–0–39–2; Smith 2–0–23–0; Gifford 4–0–33–0; Reeve 2–0–16–0.

Umpires: K. J. Lyons and D. O. Oslear.

†YORKSHIRE v NORTHAMPTONSHIRE

At Harrogate, June 9. Yorkshire won by 128 runs. Toss: Northamptonshire.

Man of the Match: A. A. Metcalfe.

Yorkshire

M. D. Moxon c Bailey b Cook	33	P. W. Jarvis c Ripley b Wild	0
A. A. Metcalfe c Capel b Cook	81	S. J. Dennis c Ripley b Hoffman	22
†R. J. Blakey c Ripley b Hoffman	0	C. Shaw not out	2
K. Sharp b Wild	25	L-b 10, w 1	11
P. E. Robinson st Ripley b Bailey	32		—
S. N. Hartley c Bailey b Cook	20	1/107 2/116 3/121 (9 wkts, 55 overs)	283
I. G. Swallow c Gouldstone b Cook	13	4/171 5/183 6/211	
*P. Carrick not out	44	7/218 8/228 9/271	

Bowling: Davis 8–1–18–0; Robinson 11–3–46–0; Wild 9–0–51–2; Hoffman 11–0–71–2; Cook 9–0–52–4; Bailey 7–0–35–1.

Northamptonshire

A. Fordham lbw b Dennis 30
M. R. Gouldstone c Hartley b Jarvis . . 1
R. J. Bailey c Sharp b Hartley 50
D. J. Capel c Swallow b Moxon 16
D. J. Wild b Dennis 1
*W. Larkins c Robinson b Moxon 24
†D. Ripley c Blakey b Swallow 0
W. W. Davis c Blakey b Shaw 11
N. G. B. Cook not out 11
D. S. Hoffman c sub b Shaw 2
M. A. Robinson c Robinson b Shaw . . . 3
B 2, l-b 2, w 2 6

1/1 2/79 3/84 (40.3 overs) 155
4/86 5/114 6/125
7/127 8/139 9/151

Bowling: Jarvis 6–2–13–1; Shaw 7.3–2–21–3; Hartley 6–0–25–1; Dennis 6–1–32–2; Swallow 10–0–42–1; Moxon 5–0–18–2.

Umpires: K. J. Lyons and D. O. Oslear.

FINAL

†YORKSHIRE v WARWICKSHIRE

At Harrogate, June 10. Yorkshire won by two wickets. Toss: Yorkshire.
Man of the Match: A. A. Metcalfe.

Warwickshire

A. C. Storie c Carrick b Dennis 59
*T. A. Lloyd c Moxon b Shaw 18
Asif Din b Fletcher 1
P. A. Smith c Moxon b Fletcher 19
†G. W. Humpage b Swallow 13
D. A. Reeve c Blakey b Fletcher 17
G. J. Parsons c Blakey b Shaw 8
A. A. Donald c Metcalfe b Shaw 12
J. E. Benjamin b Fletcher 1
T. A. Munton not out 3
N. Gifford not out 1
B 1, w 4, n-b 2 7

1/18 2/33 3/56 (9 wkts, 55 overs) 159
4/82 5/125 6/136
7/145 8/151 9/155

Bowling: Dennis 11–4–38–1; Shaw 10–5–25–3; Fletcher 10–0–38–4; Swallow 11–1–30–1; Hartley 3–0–13–0; Carrick 10–4–14–0.

Yorkshire

M. D. Moxon c Humpage b Munton . . 17
A. A. Metcalfe lbw b Reeve 89
†R. J. Blakey c Humpage b Reeve 7
K. Sharp c Humpage b Donald 3
P. E. Robinson c Reeve b Asif Din . . . 20
S. N. Hartley b Donald 5
I. G. Swallow c Humpage b Smith 1
*P. Carrick st Humpage b Asif Din . . . 0
S. J. Dennis not out 0
C. Shaw not out 4
B 1, l-b 8, w 3, n-b 2 14

1/105 2/117 3/124 (8 wkts, 40.1 overs) 160
4/129 5/145 6/155
7/155 8/155

S. D. Fletcher did not bat.

Bowling: Donald 11–3–23–2; Benjamin 5–0–27–0; Gifford 3–0–14–0; Munton 6–0–35–1; Reeve 5–0–21–2; Parsons 7–0–25–0; Asif Din 2–1–1–2; Smith 1.1–0–5–1.

Umpires: K. J. Lyons and D. O. Oslear.

†At Downpatrick, June 11, 12, 13. Drawn. Ireland 138 (M. F. Cohen 51, G. D. Harrison 32; W. A. Donald three for 30, N. D. Maxwell four for 15) and 345 for nine dec. (S. J. S. Warke 64, M. F. Cohen 55, M. A. Masood 57, P. B. Jackson 43, G. D. Harrison 42, Extras 33; J. Simmons four for 77); MCC 217 (S. Ducat 53, N. D. Maxwell 30; D. A. Lewis three for 44) and 206 for seven (G. D. Mendis 36, A. J. T. Miller 94; G. D. Harrison three for 22).

†At Dublin, July 17, 18, 19. Drawn. Ireland 307 for six dec. (S. J. S. Warke 83, M. F. Cohen 75, D. A. Lewis 53 not out) and 233 for seven dec. (D. A. Lewis 54, D. A. Vincent 52 not out); Wales 259 (D. A. Francis 85, A. C. Puddle 59; A. N. Nelson four for 68, H. Milling four for 71) and 233 for nine (D. A. Francis 69, C. M. Elward 67; G. D. Harrison four for 72).

CALLERS-PEGASUS FESTIVAL

†At Jesmond, July 28. England XI v Rest of the World XI. Abandoned.

†ENGLAND XI v REST OF THE WORLD XI

At Jesmond, July 29. England XI won by 2 runs. Toss: Rest of the World XI.
Man of the Match: N. H. Fairbrother.

England XI

*G. A. Gooch c Border b Lillee	2
M. D. Moxon c Corby b Imran	15
N. H. Fairbrother c Salim b Miandad	81
P. Willey b Maninder	26
R. A. Smith b Lawson	47
D. J. Capel c Jones b Miandad	9
†D. L. Bairstow not out	29
P. A. J. DeFreitas c Jones b Miandad	6
N. A. Foster c Jones b Miandad	0
G. C. Small not out	0
B 1, l-b 10, w 5, n-b 2	18
1/2 2/35 3/83 4/162 5/195 6/196 7/214 8/216 (8 wkts, 45 overs)	233

D. L. Underwood did not bat.

Bowling: Lillee 6–0–17–1; Imran 7–3–14–1; Maninder 8–0–62–1; Lawson 9–3–32–1; Mudassar 9–0–54–0; Miandad 3–0–10–4; Salim 3–0–33–0.

Rest of the World XI

*Imran Khan b Foster	3
Salim Malik b Underwood	67
D. M. Jones c DeFreitas b Capel	37
A. R. Border c Willey b Underwood	22
Javed Miandad c Bairstow b Capel	18
S. R. Waugh b Foster	43
Mudassar Nazar c sub b Small	20
G. F. Lawson c Bairstow b Foster	8
†K. C. Corby not out	1
Maninder Singh not out	0
B 3, l-b 6, w 1, n-b 2	12
1/7 2/115 3/117 4/154 5/156 6/198 7/220 8/229 (8 wkts, 45 overs)	231

D. K. Lillee did not bat.

Bowling: DeFreitas 9–0–46–0; Foster 8–2–30–3; Small 9–0–52–1; Underwood 9–0–49–2; Capel 7–2–23–2; Willey 3–0–22–0.

Umpires: S. Levison and G. McLean.

†At Swansea, August 3 (day/night). Rest of the World XI won by 47 runs. Rest of the World XI 255 for nine (40 overs) (D. M. Jones 89, M. J. Greatbatch 94); Glamorgan 208 (38.4 overs) (H. Morris 36; P. L. Taylor three for 36, Maninder Singh four for 52).

One of the events held to mark Glamorgan's centenary season, this match was played in the centre of the rugby ground at St Helen's. Nineteen sixes spiced the occasion, with one of them, by Javed Miandad off R. C. Ontong, going out of the ground.

SCOTLAND v IRELAND

At Dumfries, August 20, 21, 22. Scotland won by an innings and 43 runs. Toss: Ireland. Scotland's winning margin in this, the centenary of the first match between Scotland and Ireland, was the biggest since 1926. On a ground new to first-class cricket, Nunholm, the visitors struggled from the time Jackson invited Scotland to bat first on a wicket which played well throughout the match. Scotland quickly made up for the loss of the first morning to rain, and two subsequent stoppages, with Swan and Patterson adding 95 in 84 minutes for the third wicket. Swan's 77 off 113 balls included a six and ten fours, and when he was out Patterson went on to reach a hundred on his first-class début from exactly 200 balls. Ireland lost two wickets in the first three overs and in two and a quarter hours struggled to 75 for eight before Thompson, Halliday and Nelson added 93. Following on, they had to bat for most of the third day if they were to save the match. They began encouragingly, and Rea resisted for almost three hours. But the Scottish spinners, Govan and Morton, always had time on their side and completed their task with an hour and a quarter to spare.

Close of play: First day, Scotland 241-4 (B. M. W. Patterson 48*, M. J. Smith 18*); Second day, Ireland 143-9 (M. Halliday 22*, A. N. Nelson 5*).

Scotland

I. L. Philip c Nelson b Thompson	27
G. B. J. McGurk lbw b Halliday	63
*R. G. Swan b Nelson	77
B. M. W. Patterson c Cohen b Nelson	100
D. L. Snodgrass c Jackson b Wallace	2
M. J. Smith lbw b Nelson	40
W. Morton b Nelson	7
J. W. Govan st Jackson b Halliday	4
†D. J. Haggo st Jackson b Halliday	45
J. E. Ker b Wallace	5
A. Bee not out	11
B 1, l-b 7, w 4, n-b 3	15
1/72 2/112 3/207 4/210 5/286 6/310 7/319 8/337 9/360	396

Bowling: Nelson 32–8–100–4; Wallace 25–5–91–2; Halliday 30–1–97–3; Thompson 17–2–59–1; Harrison 12–0–41–0.

Ireland

S. J. S. Warke c McGurk b Ker	4	– c Patterson b Smith	42
M. F. Cohen b Ker	5	– c McGurk b Smith	7
D. A. Vincent c Morton b Bee	8	– c Haggo b Govan	16
G. D. Harrison c Haggo b Govan	25	– c Swan b Govan	0
D. A. Lewis st Haggo b Govan	17	– c Patterson b Govan	0
M. P. Rea run out	0	– c Smith b Morton	53
N. E. Thompson c Bee b Morton	38	– c Morton b Govan	14
P. Wallace b Govan	0	– (11) lbw b Govan	0
*†P. B. Jackson c Patterson b Govan	0	– (10) not out	2
M. Halliday not out	29	– (8) b Morton	26
A. N. Nelson b Bee	22	– (9) c McGurk b Morton	4
B 4, l-b 5, w 5, n-b 6	20	B 7, l-b 5, w 4, n-b 5	21
1/4 2/11 3/23 4/50 5/50 6/75 7/75 8/75 9/136	168	1/43 2/69 3/69 4/71 5/71 6/109 7/170 8/181 9/184	185

Bowling: *First Innings*—Ker 13–2–36–2; Bee 8.1–0–20–2; Smith 10–2–21–0; Govan 27–11–38–4; Morton 18–6–44–1. *Second Innings*—Ker 5–1–12–0; Bee 9–2–35–0; Govan 29.5–14–54–5; Smith 13–1–30–2; Morton 22–9–35–3; Snodgrass 4–2–7–0.

Umpires: J. Breslin and D. Walker.

†At Swansea, August 22, 23, 24. Drawn. MCC 338 for eight dec. (C. J. C. Rowe 57, A. T. van Lint 53, S. C. Wundke 101, C. F. E. Goldie 61; B. J. Lloyd four for 90); Wales 187 (M. Tremellen 75; R. M. O. Cooke three for 56, C. J. C. Rowe four for 45) and 88 for three (M. A. R. Jones 32).

†GOATACRE v HIMLEY

Hydro Village Championship

At Beckenham, August 21. Goatacre won by four wickets. Toss: Goatacre. The match, a replay of the final which had been abandoned the previous day at Lord's because of storms, was a personal triumph for Kevin Iles, the Goatacre captain and a grandson of the club's founder. His four wickets and a run-out prevented Himley from building on a platform of 150 for three, and after Goatacre had been held to 36 by tight bowling, he came to the crease in the eighteenth over and was soon striking the ball to all parts of the ground, raising his half-century off 43 balls. Goatacre needed 8 runs to win off the last over, and when Butler scored boundaries from the first two balls, Iles remained unbeaten with 91, the highest individual score in a village final. It included six sixes and three fours. (See also Other Matches at Lord's, 1988.)

Himley

†S. A. Walker b K. M. Iles 75
*A. Shorter c Dolman b Rose 16
D. J. Shorter c Wilkins b Turner 24
J. E. Hughes c G. R. Iles b Turner 30
J. K. Day lbw b K. M. Iles 9
D. Meageen run out 4
J. A. Crawford c G. R. Iles b K. M. Iles 3
M. J. Soley run out 6
C. H. Norris b K. M. Iles 2
K. R. Gerrish not out 2
R. Robinson c Angell b Rose 4
B 4, l-b 5, w 7, n-b 1 17

1/25 2/69 3/150 4/157 5/168 6/173 7/177 8/186 9/187 (39.4 overs) 192

Bowling: Rose 8.4–1–38–2; Angell 6–0–36–0; Turner 9–1–32–2; K. M. Iles 9–0–46–4; Dolman 7–0–31–0.

Goatacre

J. B. Turner c D. J. Shorter b Robinson 0
A. S. Walters c Meageen b Norris 9
M. Hunt c D. J. Shorter b Meageen ... 28
*K. M. Iles not out 91
P. D. Rose run out 19
J. I. N. Angell st Walker b Gerrish ... 18
†J. Wilkins b Gerrish 2
K. J. Butler not out 9
L-b 10, w 7 17

1/0 2/36 3/57 4/117 5/172 6/178 (6 wkts, 39.2 overs) 193

G. R. Iles, J. C. Haines and P. Dolman did not bat.

Bowling: Robinson 9–2–16–1; Norris 9–1–27–1; Meageen 4–0–24–1; Day 9–0–58–0; D. J. Shorter 6.2–1–46–0; Gerrish 2–0–12–2.

Umpires: R. A. J. Lovegrove and M. K. Reed.

†ENFIELD v WOLVERHAMPTON

Cockspur Cup Final

At Birmingham, August 24. Enfield won by nine wickets. Toss: Wolverhampton. The Edgbaston groundstaff made light of the occasional squalls of rain and, after the scheduled final at Lord's had been abandoned the previous Friday, the National Club Championship was decided in this replay. Allen, Enfield's most prolific scorer in 1988, took full advantage of the "life" he was given by the London weather. Out lbw to Williams for 1 at Lord's, he now hit an unbeaten 119, playing the dominant role in an opening partnership of 141 before Sandrock was bowled in the 33rd over. Wolverhampton had begun well after electing to bat, only to be tied down by the off-spin of Morgan, the Enfield captain, and Keable. When the Midlanders needed to accelerate, they found the seam attack of Roach and Higgs too accurate. (See also Other Matches at Lord's, 1988.)

Wolverhampton

R. Griffin c Brown b Roach	48	C. Horton b Roach	4
D. Lampitt b Morgan	30	J. Turner not out	0
†D. Manning b Keable	15	D. Barnes not out	1
G. Williams b Higgs	14	B 2, l-b 4, w 2, n-b 1	9
J. Hughes b Higgs	1		
R. Wood run out	23	1/54 2/85 3/113 (9 wkts, 45 overs)	164
T. Heap lbw b Higgs	4	4/115 5/117 6/131	
*P. Jones lbw b Roach	15	7/154 8/159 9/163	

Bowling: Carter 5–2–20–0; Lester 5–0–22–0; Morgan 9–3–17–1; Keable 9–2–24–1; Roach 9–0–35–3; Higgs 8–1–40–3.

Enfield

J. A. Allen not out	119
G. W. Sandrock b Jones	30
*M. Morgan not out	2
B 3, l-b 7, w 2, n-b 2	14
1/141 (1 wkt, 34.5 overs)	165

A. J. Moulding, P. D. Keable, A. S. E. Roach, A. K. Higgs, M. H. Walton, †G. Brown, R. M. Carter and M. R. Lester did not bat.

Bowling: Turner 7.5–2–37–0; Williams 7–0–38–0; Barnes 5–0–22–0; Jones 9–0–33–1; Horton 6–0–25–0.

Umpires: N. P. Grainger and P. Stevens.

MICHAEL PARKINSON'S WORLD XI v MCC

At Scarborough, August 31, September 1, 2. Michael Parkinson's World XI won by 32 runs. Toss: World XI. A festival spirit of goodwill made up for the loss of the second day to rain. Knight, the MCC captain, declared at Wednesday night's score and later gave his spinners a generous spell. Hookey, a 21-year-old left-hander from New South Wales and currently playing in the Northern League, kept the fielders' and spectators' hands warm on a blustery day with his highest first-class score. His 90 included a six and twelve fours. Imran's declaration invited MCC to score 205 in 75 minutes and twenty overs, which looked feasible while Larkins and Bartlett were going well. When Lawson dismissed Larkins and Bailey in quick succession, the match soon swung the way of the World XI. It was not a result that had looked likely on the first day, when the World XI, electing to bat, had been bowled out cheaply on a pitch which looked better than their batting suggested.

Close of play: First day, MCC 137-2 (R. J. Bailey 48*, D. J. Capel 28*); Second day, No play.

Michael Parkinson's World XI

Mudassar Nazar run out	20	– c Ripley b Mallender	4
S. G. Hookey c Ripley b Walker	28	– (3) lbw b Cook	90
D. L. Haynes c Bartlett b Capel	15	– (2) c Cook b Trump	46
M. J. Greatbatch b Larkins	6	– not out	26
*Imran Khan lbw b Mallender	13		
B. L. Cairns c Ripley b Capel	3	– (5) st Ripley b Cook	19
Chetan Sharma lbw b Mallender	27		
G. F. Lawson b Walker	2		
D. K. Lillee c Ripley b Walker	22		
†R. W. Taylor c Ripley b Capel	4		
Maninder Singh not out	2		
L-b 1	1	B 4, l-b 9	13
1/44 2/63 3/70 4/74 5/83 6/108 7/115 8/117 9/139	143	1/4 2/92 3/178 4/198 (4 wkts dec.)	198

Bowling: *First Innings*—Mallender 15–3–40–2; Walker 20–3–57–3; Capel 12.3–2–33–3; Larkins 8–5–7–1; Cook 1–0–5–0. *Second Innings*—Mallender 7–0–28–1; Walker 5–0–23–0; Larkins 3–0–19–0; Capel 3–0–18–0; Trump 12–4–43–1; Cook 10.4–2–54–2.

MCC

W. Larkins c Greatbatch b Maninder	51	– c sub b Lawson	52
R. J. Bartlett lbw b Lillee	3	– st Taylor b Maninder	56
R. J. Bailey not out	48	– c and b Lawson	5
D. J. Capel not out	28	– b Maninder	0
M. J. Robinson (did not bat)		– lbw b Cairns	19
*R. D. V. Knight (did not bat)		– lbw b Lawson	1
†D. Ripley (did not bat)		– c Maninder b Cairns	12
N. G. B. Cook (did not bat)		– b Cairns	10
A. Walker (did not bat)		– c Mudassar b Maninder	5
H. R. J. Trump (did not bat)		– c Lawson b Cairns	0
N. A. Mallender (did not bat)		– not out	1
L-b 1, n-b 6	7	B 1, l-b 8, w 1, n-b 1	11
1/6 2/82 (2 wkts dec.)	137	1/95 2/118 3/119 4/126 5/133 6/151 7/160 8/169 9/171	172

Bowling: *First Innings*—Imran 6–0–21–0; Lillee 6–2–15–1; Maninder 8–2–24–1; Lawson 8–3–16–0; C. Sharma 8–1–27–0; Mudassar 8–3–33–0. *Second Innings*—Lillee 7–1–32–0; Imran 7–1–34–0; Maninder 12–0–52–3; Lawson 9–1–34–3; Cairns 3–0–11–4.

Umpires: J. Birkenshaw and B. Leadbeater.

†At Scarborough, September 3. Yorkshire won by 7 runs. Toss: Michael Parkinson's World XI. Yorkshire 265 for four (50 overs) (M. D. Moxon 63, D. Byas 111, P. E. Robinson 60); Michael Parkinson's World XI 258 for nine (50 overs) (A. J. Lamb 36, Imran Khan 40, D. K. Lillee 51 not out, N. G. B. Cook 30; S. D. Fletcher three for 26).

WARD KNOCKOUT CUP

†ESSEX v LANCASHIRE

At Scarborough, September 4. Essex won by 27 runs. Toss: Essex. Lilley hit four sixes and ten fours in his 111 from 109 deliveries.

Man of the Match: A. W. Lilley.

Essex

*B. R. Hardie b Folley	42
J. P. Stephenson c Hegg b Makinson	26
A. W. Lilley b Matthews	111
M. E. Waugh c and b Folley	2
P. J. Prichard c and b Watkinson	45
†D. E. East b Murphy	5
I. L. Pont not out	3
T. D. Topley b Matthews	0
L-b 13, w 3	16
1/51 2/96 3/102 4/206 5/228 6/250 7/250 (7 wkts, 50 overs)	250

N. Hussain, G. Miller and J. K. Lever did not bat.

Bowling: Murphy 8–1–34–1; Watkinson 10–1–45–1; Makinson 10–1–38–1; Folley 10–1–27–2; Abrahams 4–0–31–0; Matthews 8–0–62–2.

Lancashire

G. D. Mendis b Topley	46
A. N. Hayhurst b Topley	32
J. Abrahams c Pont b Miller	33
T. E. Jesty c Prichard b Topley	36
*N. H. Fairbrother c and b Miller	2
M. Watkinson b Waugh	9
†W. K. Hegg c Stephenson b Pont	33
C. D. Matthews c Hardie b Pont	1
D. J. Makinson b Lever	9
I. Folley not out	2
A. J. Murphy b Lever	1
B 3, l-b 10, w 6	19
1/76 2/107 3/161 4/165 5/165 6/176 7/195 8/219 9/220 (48 overs)	223

Bowling: Pont 9–0–58–2; Lever 9–1–35–2; Miller 10–1–30–2; Topley 10–1–39–3; Waugh 7–1–38–1; Stephenson 3–0–10–0.

Umpires: J. Birkenshaw and B. Leadbeater.

†YORKSHIRE v GLOUCESTERSHIRE

At Scarborough, September 5. Yorkshire won by 73 runs. Toss: Gloucestershire.
Man of the Match: P. Carrick.

Yorkshire

M. D. Moxon c Graveney b Greene . . . 15
A. A. Metcalfe c Greene b Curran 47
K. Sharp b Curran 17
P. E. Robinson b Curran 9
J. D. Love c Alleyne b Pooley 1
†D. L. Bairstow b Jarvis 16
*P. Carrick c Wright b Graveney 35
P. J. Hartley b Jarvis 16
C. S. Pickles c Wright b Graveney 8
S. J. Dennis not out 6
P. J. Berry b Greene 0
B 2, l-b 12, w 1 15

1/39 2/79 3/88 4/93 5/97 6/134 7/152 8/175 9/181 (47.4 overs) 185

Bowling: Jarvis 10–0–66–2; Greene 8.4–1–24–2; Pooley 9–1–24–1; Curran 10–4–20–3; Graveney 10–1–37–2.

Gloucestershire

A. W. Stovold c Bairstow b Hartley . . . 4
A. J. Wright c Dennis b Carrick 28
P. W. Romaines c Bairstow b Dennis . . 2
C. W. J. Athey c Metcalfe b Pickles . . . 6
K. M. Curran b Pickles 6
D. J. Thomas c Dennis b Berry 4
†M. W. Alleyne b Carrick 9
M. W. Pooley not out 23
V. S. Greene run out 13
*D. A. Graveney b Carrick 1
K. B. S. Jarvis b Dennis 4
B 5, l-b 4, w 2, n-b 1 12

1/5 2/8 3/21 4/39 5/44 6/59 7/73 8/103 9/105 (44.2 overs) 112

Bowling: Dennis 7.2–1–9–2; Hartley 5–1–5–1; Pickles 10–3–22–2; Berry 10–1–30–1; Carrick 10–2–30–3; Love 2–0–7–0.

Umpires: J. Birkenshaw and B. Leadbeater.

FINAL

†YORKSHIRE v ESSEX

At Scarborough, September 6. Essex won by 94 runs. Toss: Yorkshire.
Man of the Match: J. P. Stephenson.

Essex

N. Hussain lbw b Dennis 0
J. P. Stephenson c Berry b Carrick 50
M. E. Waugh c Metcalfe b Carrick 36
A. W. Lilley c Hartley b Berry 4
P. J. Prichard c Berry b Pickles 41
†D. E. East c Robinson b Pickles 10
*B. R. Hardie b Hartley 9
I. L. Pont c Bairstow b Hartley 13
G. Miller not out 14
T. D. Topley not out 6
B 2, l-b 13, w 8 23

1/0 2/81 3/93 4/107 5/151 6/163 7/183 8/188 (8 wkts, 50 overs) 206

J. K. Lever did not bat.

Bowling: Dennis 10–1–41–1; Hartley 10–1–43–2; Pickles 10–1–37–2; Berry 10–1–37–1; Carrick 10–2–33–2.

Yorkshire

M. D. Moxon c Lever b Miller 31
A. A. Metcalfe c Prichard b Topley . . . 15
K. Sharp c Waugh b Topley 6
P. E. Robinson c and b Topley 7
J. D. Love run out 16
†D. L. Bairstow lbw b Stephenson 0
*P. Carrick st East b Miller 9
P. J. Hartley c Prichard b Miller 8
C. S. Pickles st East b Miller 11
S. J. Dennis b Stephenson 2
P. J. Berry not out 0
L-b 6, w 1 7

1/27 2/39 3/59 4/69 5/71 6/84 7/91 8/104 9/108 (39.5 overs) 112

Bowling: Pont 6–1–14–0; Lever 6–2–12–0; Topley 7–1–18–3; Waugh 5–0–20–0; Stephenson 7–1–14–2; Miller 8.5–0–28–4.

Umpires: J. Birkenshaw and B. Leadbeater.

†YORKSHIRE v YORKSHIRE EXILES

At Scarborough, September 8. Yorkshire Exiles won by eight wickets. Toss: Yorkshire. *Man of the Match:* G. Cook.

Yorkshire

M. D. Moxon c Rhodes b Oldham 30
A. A. Metcalfe c Rhodes b Walker 17
D. Byas c Walker b Beardshall 17
P. E. Robinson b Oldham 2
J. D. Love b Beardshall 23
†R. J. Blakey b Walker 29
*P. Carrick not out 24
P. J. Hartley c Ripley b Mallender 1
A. Sidebottom not out 7
L-b 5, w 2, n-b 1 8

1/22 2/53 3/62 4/75 5/120 6/130 7/133 (7 wkts, 50 overs) 158

C. Shaw and S. D. Fletcher did not bat.

Bowling: Mallender 10–2–28–1; Walker 10–1–34–2; Beardshall 10–0–34–2; Oldham 10–2–30–2; Illingworth 10–1–27–0.

Yorkshire Exiles

*G. Cook not out 56
T. J. Boon c Metcalfe b Shaw 15
D. J. R. Martindale b Carrick 7
J. J. Whitaker not out 58
B 4, l-b 9, w 8, n-b 5 26

1/43 2/70 (2 wkts, 46.1 overs) 162

D. Ripley, †S. J. Rhodes, R. K. Illingworth, A. Walker, M. Beardshall, N. A. Mallender and S. Oldham did not bat.

Bowling: Hartley 8–1–35–0; Sidebottom 10–1–28–0; Fletcher 8–2–32–0; Shaw 10–2–21–1; Carrick 10–2–29–1; Metcalfe 0.1–0–4–0.

Umpires: J. Birkenshaw and B. Leadbeater.

Devon

K. G. Rice c Scott b Hemmings 28
R. P. Twose b Stephenson 1
N. R. Gaywood c Newell b Cooper . . . 9
G. Wallen c Scott b Evans 27
*J. H. Edwards c Evans b Stephenson . 4
R. G. Twose c Scott b Evans 56
P. A. Brown not out 67
†R. C. Turpin not out 29
L-b 14, w 2, n-b 1 17

1/5 2/24 3/56 4/76 5/114 6/161 (6 wkts, 60 overs) 238

A. W. Allin, M. A. Cottam and M. C. Woodman did not bat.

Bowling: Stephenson 10–5–24–2; Cooper 12–3–25–1; Saxelby 12–0–48–0; Hemmings 12–3–38–1; Evans 11–1–48–2; Randall 1–0–20–0; Johnson 1–0–11–0; Newell 1–0–10–0.

Umpires: D. J. Halfyard and R. Palmer.

DURHAM v SOMERSET

At Darlington, June 22. Somerset won by 34 runs. Toss: Durham.
Man of the Match: J. J. E. Hardy.

Somerset

*P. M. Roebuck b Greensword 47
J. J. E. Hardy run out 100
J. G. Wyatt run out 8
S. R. Waugh st Fothergill b Conn 21
G. V. Palmer b Conn 17
V. J. Marks b Cairns 21
G. D. Rose st Fothergill b Conn 8
R. J. Bartlett not out 6
†N. D. Burns not out 1
B 2, l-b 1, w 4, n-b 4 11

1/96 2/105 3/166 4/200 5/214 6/227 7/233 (7 wkts, 60 overs) 240

N. A. Mallender and A. N. Jones did not bat.

Bowling: Johnston 12–1–28–0; Tindale 5–1–17–0; Cairns 12–0–60–1; Greensword 12–2–44–1; Conn 12–2–34–3; Patel 7–1–54–0.

Durham

J. W. Lister c Rose b Waugh 46
W. Johnson c Burns b Palmer 16
P. Burn lbw b Palmer 0
*N. A. Riddell c Waugh b Palmer 0
A. S. Patel run out 14
S. Greensword lbw b Mallender 19
B. L. Cairns c Wyatt b Mallender 54
J. Tindale st Burns b Waugh 30
I. E. Conn not out 4
†A. R. Fothergill not out 3
B 1, l-b 9, w 9, n-b 1 20

1/55 2/59 3/64 4/72 5/102 6/113 7/196 8/200 (8 wkts, 60 overs) 206

J. Johnston did not bat.

Bowling: Jones 5–0–41–0; Mallender 11–1–35–2; Rose 9–3–27–0; Palmer 12–3–24–3 Marks 12–3–24–0; Waugh 11–3–45–2.

Umpires: D. B. Harrison and D. O. Oslear.

ESSEX v WILTSHIRE

At Chelmsford, June 22. Essex won by 291 runs. Toss: Wiltshire. Essex's total was a county record for the 60-overs competition and the third-highest overall, while their margin of victory was the second-greatest in the competition.
Man of the Match: D. R. Pringle.

Essex

*G. A. Gooch c and b Simpkins 70
B. R. Hardie c and b Simpkins 77
P. J. Prichard c Dixon b Cooper 77
A. R. Border c Savage b Meehan 35
D. R. Pringle not out 80
A. W. Lilley c Cullip b Dixon 7
J. P. Stephenson not out 31
B 1, l-b 5, w 3 9

1/112 2/162 3/234 4/300 5/309 (5 wkts, 60 overs) 386

G. Miller, †A. D. Brown, J. K. Lever and T. D. Topley did not bat.

Bowling: Dixon 12–0–59–1; Watts 12–0–97–0; Simpkins 12–2–33–2; Meehan 12–0–97–1; Cooper 12–0–94–1.

Wiltshire

B. H. White c Border b Lever 1
†J. J. Cullip lbw b Topley 3
K. H. Foyle run out 6
D. J. M. Mercer run out 13
R. R. Savage c and b Miller 32
J. J. Newman c Gooch b Pringle 2
*R. C. Cooper c Pringle b Gooch 6
J. H. Dixon c Stephenson b Miller 12
D. P. Simpkins not out 4
M. A. Watts lbw b Gooch 3
P. Meehan c Brown b Miller 1
L-b 10, w 1, n-b 1 12

1/4 2/6 3/25 4/26 5/40 6/71 7/81 8/83 9/86 (41.3 overs) 95

Bowling: Lever 8–2–17–1; Topley 9–1–17–1; Pringle 7–2–9–1; Gooch 9–3–19–2; Miller 8.3–2–23–3.

Umpires: J. D. Bond and B. Dudleston.

GLOUCESTERSHIRE v IRELAND

At Bristol, June 22. Gloucestershire won by nine wickets. Toss: Ireland.
Man of the Match: A. W. Stovold.

reland

. J. S. Warke lbw b Alderman 2
/I. F. Cohen lbw b Lawrence 66
/I. A. Masood c Alleyne b Alderman . . 35
. D. Harrison c Athey b Alderman . . 0
. A. Lewis b Bainbridge 28
. A. McCollum b Bainbridge 13
. D. Garth run out 8
†P. B. Jackson not out 6
M. Halliday c Athey b Alderman 3
A. N. Nelson run out 0
H. Milling c Russell b Alderman 0
B 4, l-b 13, w 5, n-b 3 25

1/8 2/62 3/62 4/142 5/153 6/175 7/178 8/184 9/185 (59.5 overs) 186

Bowling: Lawrence 12–2–25–1; Alderman 11.5–0–34–5; Curran 12–1–35–0; Bainbridge 2–2–42–2; Graveney 12–1–33–0.

loucestershire

. W. Stovold not out 104
. J. Wright c Halliday b Harrison 55
. W. Romaines not out 18
L-b 6, w 7 13

/116 (1 wkt, 39.4 overs) 190

. W. J. Athey, P. Bainbridge, K. M. Curran, M. W. Alleyne, †R. C. Russell, *D. A. Graveney, D. V. Lawrence and T. M. Alderman did not bat.

Bowling: Milling 7–1–32–0; Nelson 5–1–19–0; Garth 9.4–0–45–0; Halliday 7–0–32–0; arrison 5–0–21–1; Lewis 6–0–35–0.

Umpires: D. J. Dennis and A. G. T. Whitehead.

KENT v BUCKINGHAMSHIRE

At Canterbury, June 22. Kent won by eight wickets. Toss: Kent.
Man of the Match: R. F. Pienaar.

Buckinghamshire

A. R. Harwood c Marsh b Pienaar 17
M. J. Roberts run out 2
T. Butler c Marsh b C. S. Cowdrey 44
S. Burrow c Tavaré b G. R. Cowdrey .. 1
*N. G. Hames c Marsh b Pienaar 8
T. J. A. Scriven c Marsh b Pienaar 2
K. I. Hodgson c Davis b G. R. Cowdrey 5
G. R. Black b Davis 14
†D. J. Goldsmith c Marsh b Davis 1
A. W. Lyon c Pienaar b Davis 2
C. D. Booden not out 0
L-b 2, w 13, n-b 2 17

1/11 2/43 3/44 4/63 5/65 6/70 7/110 8/110 9/112 (56 overs) 113

Bowling: Penn 10–1–22–0; Ellison 7–1–15–0; C. S. Cowdrey 8–0–16–1; Pienaar 12–2–19–3; G. R. Cowdrey 12–7–20–2; Davis 7–2–19–3.

Kent

M. R. Benson c Booden b Burrow 38
N. R. Taylor lbw b Black 5
S. G. Hinks not out 64
C. J. Tavaré not out 6
W 2 2

1/26 2/84 (2 wkts, 40.2 overs) 115

R. F. Pienaar, *C. S. Cowdrey, G. R. Cowdrey, †S. A. Marsh, R. M. Ellison, C. Penn and R. P. Davis did not bat.

Bowling: Booden 5–2–13–0; Black 7–0–23–1; Lyon 9–0–27–0; Scriven 12–0–27–0; Burrow 6.2–0–16–1; Hodgson 1–0–9–0.

Umpires: C. T. Spencer and P. B. Wight.

LANCASHIRE v LINCOLNSHIRE

At Manchester, June 22. Lancashire won by 158 runs. Toss: Lincolnshire.
Man of the Match: N. H. Fairbrother.

Lancashire

G. D. Mendis c and b French 64
G. Fowler run out 38
T. E. Jesty c Fell b Kelk 37
N. H. Fairbrother not out 80
M. Watkinson run out 2
*D. P. Hughes b Fell 23
Wasim Akram b Fell 14
A. N. Hayhurst c Kelk b Fell 35
†W. K. Hegg b Butler 6
P. J. W. Allott c Fell b Butler 0
J. Simmons b Butler 0
L-b 4, w 2 6

1/60 2/131 3/145 4/159 5/214 6/239 7/287 8/304 9/305 (59.5 overs) 30[illegible]

Bowling: Kelk 9–1–54–1; French 12–0–56–1; Marshall 12–1–67–0; Burton 12–1–54–0 Fell 12–0–50–3; Butler 2.5–0–20–3.

Lincolnshire

J. G. Franks c Fairbrother b Simmons . 42
G. J. Carsberg c Jesty b Wasim 1
C. Wicks c Hughes b Allott 12
M. A. Fell c Simmons b Hayhurst 27
P. R. Butler lbw b Simmons 33
N. French b Wasim 1
*H. Pougher lbw b Wasim 0
D. Marshall c Hegg b Watkinson 4
†N. P. Dobbs b Wasim .... [illegible]
R. L. Burton b Hayhurst .... [illegible]
S. D. Kelk not out .... [illegible]
L-b 8, w 10, n-b 1 .... 1[illegible]

1/5 2/47 3/77 4/90 5/109 6/109 7/119 8/130 9/139 (53 overs) 14[illegible]

Bowling: Wasim 12–2–27–4; Allott 9–2–24–1; Watkinson 12–2–37–1; Hayhurst 11–2–24–2; Simmons 9–1–27–2.

Umpires: J. C. Balderstone and B. J. Meyer.

LEICESTERSHIRE v SUFFOLK

At Leicester, June 22. Leicestershire won by 87 runs. Toss: Suffolk.
Man of the Match: D. I. Gower.

Leicestershire

N. E. Briers st Halliday b Gladwin	42	J. P. Agnew c Wright b Bailey	1
R. A. Cobb b Green	14	†P. Whitticase not out	5
P. Willey c Gladwin b Bailey	15		
*D. I. Gower b Bailey	99	B 2, l-b 15, w 8, n-b 1	26
J. J. Whitaker c Hayes b Gladwin	14		
L. Potter c Caley b Gladwin	22	1/42 2/70 3/119 (9 wkts, 60 overs)	255
P. A. J. DeFreitas b Green	7	4/161 5/199 6/208	
C. C. Lewis b Green	10	7/249 8/250 9/255	

G. J. F. Ferris did not bat.

Bowling: Green 12–0–44–3; Wright 6–1–26–0; Bailey 12–3–42–3; Hayes 10–2–22–0; Caley –0–40–0; Gladwin 12–0–64–3.

Suffolk

C. Gladwin c Whitticase b DeFreitas	14	P. J. Hayes not out	26
. W. Edrich c Whitticase b Ferris	22	P. J. Caley not out	4
M. S. A. McEvoy b Potter	35	B 1, l-b 5, w 5, n-b 3	14
. D. Barker c Gower b Lewis	0		
G. Morgan b Lewis	40	1/16 2/76 3/77 (6 wkts, 60 overs)	168
S. J. Halliday run out	13	4/83 5/106 6/158	

M. J. W. Wright, *M. D. Bailey and R. C. Green did not bat.

Bowling: DeFreitas 8–1–14–1; Agnew 7–1–25–0; Ferris 6–0–28–1; Lewis 12–1–32–2; Potter 2–4–31–1; Willey 12–1–24–0; Whitaker 2–0–4–0; Gower 1–0–4–0.

Umpires: R. H. Duckett and M. J. Kitchen.

MIDDLESEX v HERTFORDSHIRE

t Lord's, June 22. Middlesex won by eight wickets. Toss: Hertfordshire.
Man of the Match: P. C. R. Tufnell.

ertfordshire

. J. T. Miller c and b Tufnell	44	T. S. Smith not out	4
. P. G. Wright c Emburey b Tufnell	8	W. G. Merry not out	4
P. Henderson lbw b Tufnell	17	B 2, l-b 19, w 5, n-b 2	28
. Gilbert c Emburey b Fraser	4		
E. P. Neal b Williams	0	1/50 2/75 3/92 (7 wkts, 60 overs)	142
. C. G. Wright lbw b Emburey	19	4/92 5/93	
M. W. C. Olley c Downton b Williams	14	6/121 7/134	

Surridge and R. J. Hailey did not bat.

Bowling: Williams 11–3–22–2; Fraser 12–3–25–1; Gatting 5–2–14–0; Hughes 8–2–16–0; ıfnell 12–4–29–3; Emburey 12–6–15–1.

Middlesex

J. D. Carr c Olley b Merry 42
W. N. Slack c Olley b Merry 0
*M. W. Gatting not out 80
R. O. Butcher not out 13
L-b 4, w 4 8

1/8 2/115 (2 wkts, 24.5 overs) 143

K. R. Brown, †P. R. Downton, J. E. Emburey, S. P. Hughes, N. F. Williams, A. R. C. Fraser and P. C. R. Tufnell did not bat.

Bowling: Surridge 6.5–0–35–0; Merry 9–0–33–2; Hailey 3–0–22–0; Smith 3–0–21–0; Neal 3–0–28–0.

Umpires: J. H. Harris and D. S. Thompsett.

SCOTLAND v GLAMORGAN

At Edinburgh, June 22. Glamorgan won by 85 runs. Toss: Scotland. Shastri's analysis of fiv for 13 was the best by a Glamorgan bowler in the 60-overs competition. Morris held fou catches in the field to equal the record for the competition.

Man of the Match: R. J. Shastri.

Glamorgan

A. R. Butcher c Swan b Govan 47
J. A. Hopkins c Fleming b Rice 12
*H. Morris c Rice b Govan 17
M. P. Maynard b Rice 35
G. C. Holmes c Fleming b Ker 15
R. J. Shastri c Rice b Ker 11
R. C. Ontong c Philip b Parfitt 8
J. G. Thomas c and b Rice 0
J. Derrick c Swan b Rice ....
†C. P. Metson b Parfitt ....
S. R. Barwick not out ....
B 15, l-b 9, w 6 3

1/28 2/89 3/104 4/143 5/149 6/174 7/174 8/174 9/179 (59.2 overs) 17

Bowling: Rice 12–2–29–4; Ker 12–3–36–2; Parfitt 11.2–5–11–2; Govan 12–3–29–2 McIntyre 12–1–50–0.

Scotland

I. L. Philip c Morris b Thomas 0
G. B. J. McGurk lbw b Shastri 36
R. G. Swan c Metson b Ontong 9
*C. E. B. Rice c and b Derrick 6
M. J. Smith c Metson b Shastri 17
B. M. W. Patterson c Morris b Shastri . 5
J. W. Govan c Morris b Shastri 0
†D. Fleming c Morris b Shastri 0
J. E. Ker c Metson b Barwick ....
E. J. McIntyre c Holmes b Barwick ...
C. L. Parfitt not out ....
L-b 5 ....

1/0 2/23 3/34 4/69 5/72 6/72 7/74 8/79 9/79 (45.2 overs) 9

Bowling: Thomas 6–0–14–1; Barwick 10.2–3–23–2; Ontong 12–0–27–1; Derrick 6–2–12– Shastri 11–2–13–5.

Umpires: B. Leadbeater and J. van Geloven.

SHROPSHIRE v HAMPSHIRE

At Telford, June 22. Hampshire won by 86 runs. Toss: Shropshire.

Man of the Match: C. L. Smith.

Hampshire

V. P. Terry c Johnson b Edmunds 83
C. L. Smith c Johnson b Wormald 117
D. R. Turner lbw b Barnard 0
R. A. Smith c Ashley b Maninder 40
S. T. Jefferies c Roberts b Wormald ... 39
N. G. Cowley not out 1
J. R. Ayling not out 1
B 1, l-b 5, w 7 13

1/163 2/163 3/225 4/291 5/292 (5 wkts, 60 overs) 294

*M. C. J. Nicholas, †R. J. Parks, S. J. W. Andrew and C. A. Connor did not bat.

Bowling: Wormald 12–1–85–2; Roberts 12–2–28–0; Maninder 12–2–59–1; Edmunds 12–0–67–1; Barnard 12–0–49–1.

Shropshire

*J. Foster b Jefferies 21
J. B. R. Jones run out 83
J. S. Johnson b Jefferies 0
T. Parton run out 33
M. R. Davies run out 16
P. B. Wormald c R. A. Smith b C. L. Smith . 14
Maninder Singh not out 3
†D. J. Ashley st Parks b C. L. Smith .. 8
B 2, l-b 22, w 3, n-b 3 30

1/51 2/51 3/165 4/165 5/187 6/197 7/208 (7 wkts, 60 overs) 208

G. Edmunds, A. S. Barnard and J. S. Roberts did not bat.

Bowling: Andrew 12–1–32–0; Connor 10–3–20–0; Jefferies 12–1–40–2; Ayling 11–5–26–0; Cowley 12–0–39–0; C. L. Smith 2–0–24–2; Nicholas 1–0–3–0.

Umpires: A. A. Jones and K. J. Lyons.

STAFFORDSHIRE v SURREY

At Burton upon Trent, June 22. Surrey won by 55 runs. Toss: Staffordshire.
Man of the Match: D. A. Banks.

Surrey

G. S. Clinton c Banks b Perryman 30
D. M. Smith c Griffiths b Blank 44
A. J. Stewart c Griffiths b Banks 54
M. A. Lynch c Waterhouse b Banks ... 48
D. M. Ward b Dutton 2
†C. J. Richards b Blank 50
*I. A. Greig c Waterhouse b Webster .. 22
S. T. Clarke b Blank 1
C. K. Bullen run out 0
M. A. Feltham not out 16
M. P. Bicknell not out 1
B 1, l-b 9, w 5, n-b 2 17

1/59 2/91 3/174 4/187 5/189 6/226 7/228 8/229 9/284 (9 wkts, 60 overs) 285

Bowling: Webster 12–1–54–1; Perryman 12–2–34–1; Dutton 12–1–31–1; Blank 12–1–75–3; Flower 4–0–32–0; Banks 8–0–49–2.

Staffordshire

S. J. Dean c Richards b Feltham 17
*N. J. Archer c Bicknell b Bullen 45
J. A. Waterhouse c Richards b Clarke . 52
D. A. Banks not out 62
P. R. Oliver c Ward b Greig 5
A. Dutton b Clarke 20
†A. Griffiths lbw b Clarke 0
D. C. Blank run out 1
A. J. Webster c Bullen b Clarke 4
S. P. Perryman not out 1
B 4, l-b 12, w 5, n-b 2 23

1/48 2/98 3/153 4/170 5/207 6/207 7/208 8/225 (8 wkts, 60 overs) 230

R. W. Flower did not bat.

Bowling: Clarke 12–0–27–4; Bicknell 8–2–36–0; Greig 10–4–28–1; Feltham 12–1–59–1; Bullen 12–2–39–1; Lynch 6–0–25–0.

Umpires: H. D. Bird and B. Hassan.

SUSSEX v DERBYSHIRE

At Hove, June 22. Derbyshire won by six wickets. Toss: Sussex. Holding's return of eight for 21 was the best in any limited-overs competition. His figures include nine no-balls debited against him.

Man of the Match: M. A. Holding.

Sussex

R. I. Alikhan c Sharma b Holding 9
D. K. Standing c Roberts b Holding ... 4
*P. W. G. Parker c Maher b Holding .. 0
Imran Khan c Barnett b Holding 0
C. M. Wells c Maher b Holding 0
A. P. Wells c Roberts b Holding 0
†P. Moores c Holding b Newman 20
A. C. S. Pigott c Roberts b Holding ... 53
S. J. S. Kimber c Maher b Newman ... 0
A. R. Clarke c Maher b Holding 24
A. M. Babington not out 0
L-b 4, w 7, n-b 13 24

1/7 2/9 3/10 4/22 5/27 6/27 7/95 8/95 9/129 (46.1 overs) 134

Bowling: Holding 10.1–2–21–8; Newman 9–4–15–2; Warner 8–2–27–0; Jean-Jacques 10–0–46–0; Sharma 6–1–16–0; Roberts 3–0–5–0.

Derbyshire

*K. J. Barnett lbw b Babington 49
P. D. Bowler c Moores b Pigott 6
B. Roberts c Alikhan b Imran 9
J. E. Morris not out 43
S. C. Goldsmith c Moores b C. M. Wells 3
†B. J. M. Maher not out 21
L-b 1, w 2, n-b 1 4

1/35 2/60 3/74 4/79 (4 wkts, 29.1 overs) 135

R. Sharma, M. Jean-Jacques, A. E. Warner, P. G. Newman and M. A. Holding did not bat.

Bowling: Imran 10.1–1–49–1; Pigott 7–1–34–1; Babington 6–0–32–1; C. M. Wells 6–0–19–1.

Umpires: P. J. Eele and R. A. White.

WARWICKSHIRE v CAMBRIDGESHIRE

At Birmingham, June 22. Warwickshire won by 67 runs. Toss: Warwickshire.

Man of the Match: M. A. Garnham.

Warwickshire

*T. A. Lloyd run out 121
A. J. Moles c Wykes b Stephenson 25
Asif Din c Stephenson b Wykes 25
†G. W. Humpage c Gadsby b Wykes .. 2
P. A. Smith b Wykes 6
A. C. Storie b Turner 1
S. J. Green b Collard 1
G. J. Parsons not out 15
T. A. Merrick run out 13
N. Gifford not out 3
B 11, l-b 10, w 6, n-b 1 28

1/115 2/168 3/189 4/200 5/201 6/203 7/204 8/224 (8 wkts, 60 overs) 240

T. A. Munton did not bat.

Bowling: Turner 12–1–23–1; Rice 12–1–46–0; Wykes 12–0–36–3; Stephenson 12–0–59–1; Collard 12–0–55–1.

Cambridgeshire

I. S. Lawrence c Humpage b Merrick .. 0
*N. T. Gadsby lbw b Smith 18
†M. A. Garnham c and b Asif Din 110
P. A. Redfarn c Humpage b Smith 6
P. J. Dicks st Humpage b Gifford 13
S. Turner run out 3
C. W. A. Thornely not out .... 1[illegible]
G. S. Rice not out .... [illegible]
B 2, l-b 7, w 1, n-b 2 .... 1[illegible]

1/0 2/51 3/71 4/102 5/105 6/166 (6 wkts, 60 overs) 17[illegible]

M. G. Stephenson, D. C. Collard and A. P. A. Wykes did not bat.

Bowling: Merrick 9–6–3–1; Munton 12–1–42–0; Parsons 12–0–35–0; Smith 12–0–54–2; Gifford 12–0–27–1; Asif Din 3–1–3–1.

Umpires: J. W. Holder and N. T. Plews.

WORCESTERSHIRE v CUMBERLAND

At Worcester, June 22. Worcestershire won by 108 runs. Toss: Worcestershire.
Man of the Match: G. A. Hick.

Worcestershire

T. S. Curtis b Reidy	40	†S. J. Rhodes not out	2
G. J. Lord c Dutton b Halliwell	0		
G. A. Hick b Halliwell	138	B 1, l-b 8, w 4	13
D. B. D'Oliveira lbw b Reidy	0		
*P. A. Neale c Dutton b Halliwell	98	1/1 2/85 3/95 (5 wkts, 60 overs)	336
M. J. Weston not out	45	4/247 5/326	

P. J. Newport, N. V. Radford, G. R. Dilley and A. P. Pridgeon did not bat.

Bowling: Halliwell 12–1–58–3; Scothern 12–0–93–0; Wall 12–3–68–0; Reidy 12–1–54–2; Woods 12–0–54–0.

Cumberland

C. J. Stockdale c Rhodes b Weston	51	S. Wall c Hick b Curtis	11
S. Sharp b Radford	16	M. G. Scothern not out	2
K. A. Hayes b Weston	29		
B. W. Reidy c Rhodes b Hick	2	B 8, l-b 2, w 7, n-b 1	18
G. J. Clarke c Lord b Pridgeon	36		
*J. R. Moyes lbw b Hick	2	1/21 2/93 3/96 (8 wkts, 60 overs)	228
†S. M. Dutton c Neale b Newport	40	4/102 5/115 6/189	
M. D. Woods not out	21	7/191 8/207	

D. Halliwell did not bat.

Bowling: Dilley 6–1–15–0; Radford 6–0–25–1; Pridgeon 10–1–35–1; Newport 10–0–35–1; Weston 12–1–53–2; Hick 12–1–37–2; Curtis 2–1–6–1; D'Oliveira 2–0–12–0.

Umpires: C. Cook and J. H. Hampshire.

SECOND ROUND

CHESHIRE v DERBYSHIRE

At Chester, July 6, 7, 8. Derbyshire won by 87 runs. Toss: Cheshire. A hat-trick by John O'Brien, Cheshire's left-arm spinner, initiated a collapse in which Derbyshire's last seven wickets fell for 19 runs. His first hat-trick, and the first by a minor county player in the competition, comprised the dismissal of Morris to the last ball of one over and of Goldsmith and Malcolm (caught at long-off) at the start of his next. Fox completed Derbyshire's demise with a spell of four for 5 in fifteen balls. Cheshire were 78 for three (Mudassar Nazar 26*, N. T. O'Brien 19*) when poor light stopped play after 34.5 overs of their reply, but their hopes of reaching the quarter-finals were dashed by Mortensen, who took four for 0 in sixteen balls as Derbyshire won inside an hour on Friday. There was no play on the second day.
Man of the Match: O. H. Mortensen.

Derbyshire

*K. J. Barnett b Mudassar 1
P. D. Bowler c Smith b J. F. M. O'Brien 46
B. Roberts c J. F. M. O'Brien b Blackburn . 57
J. E. Morris c and b J. F. M. O'Brien . 41
S. C. Goldsmith c Smith b J. F. M. O'Brien . 8
M. A. Holding c Blackburn b Fox 1
D. E. Malcolm c Cockbain b J. F. M. O'Brien . 0
†B. J. M. Maher lbw b Fox 4
P. G. Newman b Fox 3
R. Sharma c Cockbain b Fox 4
O. H. Mortensen not out 0
B 8, l-b 8, w 8, n-b 1 25

1/1 2/110 3/136 4/171 5/174 6/174 7/178 8/186 9/187 (58.4 overs) 190

Bowling: Fox 10.4–1–24–4; Mudassar 7–3–9–1; N. T. O'Brien 12–2–28–0; Wood 12–2–38–0; Blackburn 7–0–35–1; J. F. M. O'Brien 10–1–40–4.

Cheshire

B. Wood lbw b Holding 6
D. W. Varey c and b Mortensen 17
I. Cockbain c Maher b Newman 1
Mudassar Nazar c Holding b Mortensen 32
*N. T. O'Brien b Sharma 21
J. J. Hitchmough b Mortensen 12
S. T. Crawley c Maher b Mortensen . . . 1
G. J. Blackburn c Mortensen b Newman 1
†N. Smith b Mortensen 0
A. Fox run out 0
J. F. M. O'Brien not out 1
B 1, l-b 5, w 4, n-b 1 11

1/15 2/25 3/39 4/85 5/93 6/99 7/100 8/100 9/101 (48.5 overs) 103

Bowling: Holding 8–4–8–1; Malcolm 10–2–24–0; Newman 8.5–2–19–2; Mortensen 12–4–15–5; Bowler 3–0–14–0; Sharma 7–1–17–1.

Umpires: M. J. Kitchen and D. R. Shepherd.

ESSEX v SURREY

At Chelmsford, July 6, 7. Surrey won by three wickets. Toss: Essex. When play got under way after tea, Essex put on 30 before Clarke, in his fourth over, forced Hardie's retirement with a fractured left arm and, two balls later, bowled Prichard. Thereafter, only Gooch showed any measure of command on a pitch which looked better than the scores indicate. Surrey, 24 for one overnight after nine overs (D. M. Smith 2*, C. K. Bullen 4*), struggled in turn but always had overs and wickets in hand.

Man of the Match: G. A. Gooch.

Essex

G. A. Gooch c Greig b Bullen 71
B. R. Hardie retired hurt 11
P. J. Prichard b Clarke 0
A. R. Border c Lynch b Peters 1
D. R. Pringle c Richards b Peters 6
A. W. Lilley lbw b Greig 1
*K. W. R. Fletcher lbw b Feltham 0
G. Miller c Richards b Greig 9
N. A. Foster c Richards b Clarke 12
†D. E. East c and b Clarke 20
J. K. Lever not out 1
L-b 1, w 6, n-b 2 9

1/30 2/36 3/42 4/49 5/63 6/77 7/105 8/130 9/141 (45 overs) 141

Bowling: Clarke 9–1–29–3; Peters 9–2–28–2; Greig 7–2–19–2; Feltham 12–1–43–1; Bullen 8–1–21–1.

Surrey

G. S. Clinton c East b Lever 17
D. M. Smith c Prichard b Miller 5
C. K. Bullen lbw b Foster 22
A. J. Stewart lbw b Lever 31
M. A. Lynch c Miller b Foster 17
D. M. Ward b Foster 0
†C. J. Richards not out 30
*I. A. Greig c East b Gooch 1
M. A. Feltham not out 7
B 4, l-b 4, w 4 12

1/19 2/28 3/64 4/92 5/92 6/107 7/114 (7 wkts, 48.5 overs) 142

S. T. Clarke and N. H. Peters did not bat.

Bowling: Foster 12–0–51–3; Lever 9–4–15–2; Miller 12–2–21–1; Pringle 7.5–0–26–0; Gooch 8–0–21–1.

Umpires: K. E. Palmer and P. B. Wight.

GLAMORGAN v LANCASHIRE

At Cardiff, July 6, 7. Glamorgan won by 31 runs. Toss: Lancashire. A slow outfield and a pitch of uncertain bounce made this a difficult match for batsmen. Glamorgan owed much to partnerships of 108 in 35 overs between the left-handers, Butcher (131 balls) and Morris, and of 55 in nine overs – the product of some good running – from Holmes and Shastri. On the second day, it was the tight control of the Glamorgan bowlers that frustrated Lancashire, who overnight had been 8 for one after six overs (G. Fowler 2*, W. K. Hegg 0*). Hegg took 27 overs over his 20, and only when Hayhurst and Allott were adding 47 in five overs did Glamorgan's hold on the match look uncertain.

Man of the Match: A. R. Butcher.

Glamorgan

A. R. Butcher run out	80	J. G. Thomas not out	10
J. A. Hopkins lbw b Allott	0		
*H. Morris c and b Simmons	39	L-b 14, w 9, n-b 1	24
M. P. Maynard c Simmons b Watkinson	22		—
G. C. Holmes run out	38	1/1 2/109 3/141 (5 wkts, 60 overs)	246
R. J. Shastri not out	33	4/174 5/229	

R. C. Ontong, J. Derrick, †C. P. Metson and S. R. Barwick did not bat.

Bowling: Allott 9–1–21–1; Wasim 8–0–38–0; Hayhurst 8–1–29–0; Simmons 12–2–35–1; Jesty 11–1–48–0; Watkinson 12–0–61–1.

Lancashire

G. D. Mendis lbw b Barwick	4	A. N. Hayhurst not out	38
G. Fowler b Derrick	35	P. J. W. Allott b Shastri	14
†W. K. Hegg b Shastri	20	J. Simmons c and b Thomas	6
T. E. Jesty b Ontong	0	B 11, l-b 3, w 10, n-b 3	27
N. H. Fairbrother c Shastri b Derrick	35		—
M. Watkinson b Shastri	9	1/7 2/57 3/58 (57.5 overs)	215
*D. P. Hughes b Derrick	18	4/76 5/103 6/135	
Wasim Akram b Derrick	9	7/144 8/159 9/206	

Bowling: Barwick 11–5–22–1; Thomas 10.5–1–39–1; Derrick 12–1–57–4; Ontong 12–0–31–1; Shastri 12–0–52–3.

Umpires: J. H. Harris and R. A. White.

HAMPSHIRE v SOMERSET

At Southampton, July 6, 7. Hampshire won by five wickets. Toss: Hampshire. Morning rain delayed the start until after two o'clock on both days. Bartlett, dropped when 15 and 30, hit two sixes and five fours in his 85 from 131 balls and Marks prompted the total to 227. At the close, Hampshire were 42 for one after nineteen overs (C. L. Smith 18*, M. C. J. Nicholas [illegible]4*). With twenty overs remaining, they required 117 with eight wickets in hand, and when [illegible]8 were needed from the last seven overs, Jefferies eased the pressure with 31 from 23 balls. Chris Smith, who when 26 had slipped, suffered a groin strain and been forced to bat with a runner (Terry), missed out on a well-deserved century when Waugh's last delivery went for [illegible] byes to give Hampshire victory.

Man of the Match: C. L. Smith.

Somerset

J. J. E. Hardy c Parks b Jefferies	12	G. D. Rose c Parks b Jefferies	3
*P. M. Roebuck c Connor b Andrew	22	G. V. Palmer not out	10
R. J. Bartlett c Connor b Ayling	85	L-b 10, w 2, n-b 3	15
S. R. Waugh c Parks b Andrew	0		—
N. J. Pringle c Parks b Connor	17	1/26 2/68 3/68 (7 wkts, 60 overs)	227
†N. D. Burns b Ayling	18	4/110 5/152	
V. J. Marks not out	45	6/183 7/201	

N. A. Mallender and A. N. Jones did not bat.

Bowling: Connor 12–1–42–1; Jefferies 12–0–65–2; Andrew 12–2–37–2; Ayling 12–2–35–2; Cowley 12–3–38–0.

Hampshire

V. P. Terry c Pringle b Marks	9	N. G. Cowley not out	1
C. L. Smith not out	99		
*M. C. J. Nicholas c Hardy b Waugh	32	B 4, l-b 11, w 5, n-b 1	21
R. A. Smith c Bartlett b Rose	36		—
D. R. Turner lbw b Rose	0	1/15 2/80 3/180 (5 wkts, 59 overs)	229
S. T. Jefferies b Waugh	31	4/180 5/224	

J. R. Ayling, †R. J. Parks, C. A. Connor and S. J. W. Andrew did not bat.

Bowling: Jones 11–4–37–0; Mallender 12–0–41–0; Marks 12–3–31–1; Rose 12–0–46–2; Waugh 11–0–51–2; Palmer 1–0–8–0.

Umpires: J. D. Bond and R. Julian.

KENT v WARWICKSHIRE

At Canterbury, July 6. Kent won by seven wickets. Toss: Kent. A confident all-round display took Kent through to the quarter-finals. Warwickshire's chances fell away in the seven overs after lunch, when they lost three wickets for 18 runs, undoing the good repair work of Lloyd and Asif Din in adding 58 for the third wicket. Kent also began badly, with Merrick's first ball bowling Benson, but Taylor held the innings together while first Ward and then Pienaar batted fluently.

Man of the Match: R. F. Pienaar.

Warwickshire

A. J. Moles lbw b Penn	0	G. C. Small b Davis	12
*T. A. Lloyd c Marsh b G. R. Cowdrey	38	T. A. Merrick run out	2
A. C. Storie lbw b Ellison	3	T. A. Munton not out	0
Asif Din c Marsh b Penn	28	B 2, l-b 8, w 2	12
†G. W. Humpage run out	11		—
D. A. Thorne st Marsh b G. R. Cowdrey	20	1/0 2/11 3/69 (55.3 overs)	144
P. A. Smith lbw b Penn	5	4/86 5/87 6/92	
D. A. Reeve b Pienaar	13	7/121 8/141 9/143	

Bowling: Penn 12–3–30–3; Ellison 10–2–18–1; C. S. Cowdrey 10–1–31–0; Pienaar 12–3–25–1; G. R. Cowdrey 7–0–19–2; Davis 4.3–1–11–1.

Kent

M. R. Benson b Merrick	1	S. G. Hinks not out	8
N. R. Taylor c Thorne b Merrick	41	L-b 2, w 1, n-b 3	6
T. R. Ward b Smith	34		—
R. F. Pienaar not out	58	1/1 2/53 3/118 (3 wkts, 48.4 overs)	148

*C. S. Cowdrey, †S. A. Marsh, R. M. Ellison, C. Penn, G. R. Cowdrey and R. P. Davis did not bat.

Bowling: Small 10–1–32–0; Merrick 12–1–36–2; Munton 9.4–2–41–0; Reeve 3–2–2–0; Smith 9–3–19–1; Asif Din 5–0–16–0.

Umpires: A. A. Jones and B. Leadbeater.

LEICESTERSHIRE v GLOUCESTERSHIRE

At Leicester, July 6, 7. Gloucestershire won by 73 runs. Toss: Leicestershire. Resuming on the second day at 46 for one from twenty overs (N. E. Briers 12*, P. Willey 1*), Leicestershire lost both overnight batsmen in the first six overs and Whitaker first ball. Lewis hit his first fifty for the county from 32 balls (two sixes, four fours) and added 56 in seven overs with Whitticase to show what might have been achieved. Four stoppages on the first day failed to disturb Gloucestershire's batsmen. Athey and Bainbridge (103 balls) put on 112 in 25 overs, and with Curran in sparkling form, 97 runs came from the last eleven overs.

Man of the Match: K. M. Curran.

Gloucestershire

A. W. Stovold run out 11	M. W. Alleyne not out 2
A. J. Wright b Agnew 9	
P. W. Romaines c Whitticase b Lewis . 20	L-b 15, w 5, n-b 2 22
C. W. J. Athey b Ferris 62	—
P. Bainbridge b Lewis 89	1/18 2/41 3/64 (5 wkts, 60 overs) 273
K. M. Curran not out 58	4/176 5/257

†R. C. Russell, *D. A. Graveney, D. V. Lawrence and T. M. Alderman did not bat.

Bowling: Agnew 12–2–37–1; Ferris 12–2–62–1; DeFreitas 12–0–37–0; Lewis 12–1–54–2; Willey 12–0–68–0.

Leicestershire

N. E. Briers c Graveney b Bainbridge . 16	†P. Whitticase c Graveney b Alderman 23
R. A. Cobb run out 28	G. J. F. Ferris not out 1
P. Willey c and b Lawrence 7	J. P. Agnew absent injured
*D. I. Gower c Athey b Graveney 28	L-b 6, w 4, n-b 1 11
J. J. Whitaker c Alderman b Curran . . 0	—
L. Potter c Romaines b Alderman 22	1/44 2/50 3/66 (47.2 overs) 200
P. A. J. DeFreitas c Russell b Curran . 11	4/72 5/92 6/108
C. C. Lewis c Russell b Curran 53	7/137 8/193 9/200

Bowling: Alderman 10.2–2–47–2; Lawrence 7–0–24–1; Bainbridge 12–3–19–1; Alleyne 6–1–37–0; Curran 7–1–31–3; Graveney 5–0–36–1.

Umpires: D. O. Oslear and R. Palmer.

NOTTINGHAMSHIRE v WORCESTERSHIRE

At Nottingham, July 6, 7, 8. Worcestershire won on faster scoring-rate. Toss: Nottinghamshire. The holders, Nottinghamshire, were eliminated when the umpires, considering an area some 60 yards from the pitch to be unfit for play, abandoned the match at 4.30 p.m. on Friday. There had been no play at all during the day, but Nottinghamshire felt that the conditions were adequate for a resumption and registered a complaint to the TCCB. On the first day, only 18.4 overs were bowled before rain stopped play (Worcestershire 51-1; T. S. Curtis 31*, G. A. Hick 1*); on the second, which began at 12.55 p.m., heavy rain just before six o'clock interrupted Nottinghamshire's reply, but not before Worcestershire had bowled the important twenty overs, latterly in poor light. Hick's 105, from 110 balls, contained two sixes and six fours, and there were seven fours in Curtis's 120 from 182 balls. Their partnership of 186 was a record for Worcestershire's second wicket in the competition.

Man of the Match: T. S. Curtis.

Worcestershire

T. S. Curtis c Randall b Saxelby 120
S. J. O'Shaughnessy lbw b Hemmings . . 17
G. A. Hick c Broad b Cooper 105
*P. A. Neale c Cooper b Saxelby 12
M. J. Weston b Stephenson 12
D. A. Leatherdale not out 6
†S. J. Rhodes not out 2
B 2, l-b 6, w 3 11

1/45 2/231 3/253 4/276 5/282 (5 wkts, 60 overs) 285

P. J. Newport, N. V. Radford, G. R. Dilley and A. P. Pridgeon did not bat.

Bowling: Stephenson 12–2–50–1; Cooper 12–0–50–1; Saxelby 12–0–68–2; Hemmings 12–0–67–1; Evans 12–2–42–0.

Nottinghamshire

B. C. Broad c Rhodes b Dilley 2
*R. T. Robinson c Radford b Newport . 30
P. Johnson run out 29
D. W. Randall not out 4
J. D. Birch not out 1
L-b 3, w 3, n-b 2 8

1/2 2/51 3/72 (3 wkts, 20.3 overs) 74

F. D. Stephenson, K. P. Evans, †C. W. Scott, E. E. Hemmings, K. E. Cooper and K. Saxelby did not bat.

Bowling: Dilley 5–2–16–1; Radford 5–0–20–0; Weston 5.3–2–14–0; Newport 4–0–20–1; Hick 1–0–1–0.

Umpires: J. C. Balderstone and B. Dudleston.

YORKSHIRE v MIDDLESEX

At Leeds, July 6, 7, 8. Middlesex won by 37 runs. Toss: Yorkshire. A stand of 119 in 31 overs between Gatting and Downton helped Middlesex build a good total for the conditions on a day twice interrupted by rain. Gatting was twenty overs scoring 22 but later was the driving force. On the second day, Yorkshire were struggling at 59 for four (J. D. Love 14*, D. L. Bairstow 2*) when bad light, followed by rain, stopped play after 25 overs. Taking their partnership to 94 from 27 overs, the overnight pair left Yorkshire to score 76 from ten overs, but after Love's dismissal the next five wickets managed only 38 in eight overs.

Man of the Match: M. W. Gatting.

Middlesex

W. N. Slack c Metcalfe b P. J. Hartley. 5
J. D. Carr b Sidebottom 7
A. Needham c Bairstow b Shaw 30
*M. W. Gatting b P. J. Hartley 74
†P. R. Downton c S. N. Hartley b Shaw 43
J. E. Emburey c Moxon b Shaw 16
K. R. Brown c Bairstow b Shaw 11
N. F. Williams not out 8
S. P. Hughes not out 3
B 4, l-b 17, w 3, n-b 4 28

1/13 2/37 3/53 4/172 5/182 6/208 7/210 (7 wkts, 60 overs) 225

A. R. C. Fraser and N. G. Cowans did not bat.

Bowling: Fletcher 12–0–51–0; Sidebottom 12–1–29–1; P. J. Hartley 12–0–37–2; Shaw 12–4–29–4; Carrick 10–1–46–0; S. N. Hartley 2–0–12–0.

Yorkshire

M. D. Moxon lbw b Fraser 9
A. A. Metcalfe c Needham b Cowans . 0
K. Sharp b Hughes 21
J. D. Love c sub b Fraser 67
S. N. Hartley c Needham b Carr 4
†D. L. Bairstow c and b Emburey 36
*P. Carrick c Needham b Cowans 14
A. Sidebottom c Brown b Hughes 10
P. J. Hartley not out 5
S. D. Fletcher c Downton b Fraser 2
C. Shaw c Downton b Fraser 1
L-b 4, w 10, n-b 5 19

1/1 2/26 3/48 4/55 5/150 6/159 7/177 8/182 9/186 (58 overs) 188

Bowling: Cowans 11–1–29–2; Williams 1.1–1–2–0; Gatting 5.5–0–17–0; Emburey 12–0–49–1; Fraser 12–2–34–4; Hughes 10–0–33–2; Carr 6–0–20–1.

Umpires: P. J. Eele and B. J. Meyer.

QUARTER-FINALS

DERBYSHIRE v HAMPSHIRE

At Derby, July 27. Hampshire won by four wickets. Toss: Hampshire. Hampshire completed a hat-trick of one-day victories over Derbyshire in the three competitions in 1988 and only a late thrust by Mortensen, who took three wickets in ten balls, caused a falter. Hampshire's bowling on a soft pitch was accurate rather than penetrative, but they worked their way through Derbyshire's batting. Cowley was particularly economical. Derbyshire lacked a major contribution from any of their leading batsmen and their total seemed even less adequate when Terry set off in style. He hit nine fours, only one short of Derbyshire's total, and put Hampshire firmly in control. Mortensen refused to concede the match, but there were sixteen balls to spare when James edged him for the winning boundary.

Man of the Match: V. P. Terry.

Derbyshire

*K. J. Barnett c R. A. Smith b Jefferies 32
P. D. Bowler c Parks b James 13
†B. J. M. Maher run out 44
J. E. Morris b Cowley 16
B. Roberts c C. L. Smith b James 21
S. C. Goldsmith run out 10
M. A. Holding c Cowley b Ayling 0
P. G. Newman run out 15
A. E. Warner c R. A. Smith b Bakker . 9
D. E. Malcolm b Bakker 0
O. H. Mortensen not out 0
L-b 23, w 7, n-b 1 31

1/25 2/74 3/107 4/146 5/152 6/152 7/173 8/190 9/191 (59.5 overs) 191

Bowling: Jefferies 12–1–32–1; Bakker 11.5–1–36–2; James 12–2–37–2; Ayling 12–2–42–1; Cowley 12–2–21–1.

Hampshire

V. P. Terry lbw b Holding 67
C. L. Smith lbw b Malcolm 23
D. R. Turner c Mortensen b Warner . . 7
R. A. Smith c Maher b Mortensen 38
*M. C. J. Nicholas c Maher b Mortensen 31
S. T. Jefferies c Maher b Mortensen . . . 5
J. R. Ayling not out 7
K. D. James not out 4
L-b 7, w 4 11

1/67 2/91 3/107 4/168 5/171 6/180 (6 wkts, 57.2 overs) 193

†R. J. Parks, N. G. Cowley and P. J. Bakker did not bat.

Bowling: Holding 12–2–31–1; Mortensen 10.2–5–35–3; Warner 12–3–38–1; Newman 12–2–34–0; Malcolm 11–1–48–1.

Umpires: K. J. Lyons and N. T. Plews.

MIDDLESEX v KENT

At Lord's, July 27. Middlesex won by five wickets. Toss: Middlesex. Put in on a pitch containing enough moisture to encourage the Middlesex seam bowlers, Kent struggled to make progress against an attack in which Fraser set a high standard of accuracy. Taylor was nineteen overs over his 7 runs, and Kent were looking to Tavaré and Pienaar, who had added 5 in twelve overs, when the South African essayed a reverse sweep against Emburey and was bowled. The Middlesex early batting also foundered against the seaming ball, but Butcher provided the platform that was needed. Recalled to the side after a spell out because of poor form, he flourished against the change bowlers, hitting his 64 from 73 balls. Brown and Downton, left with overs in hand, had no need to take risks as they picked off the 41 runs required for victory.

Man of the Match: R. O. Butcher.

Kent

M. R. Benson c Gatting b Fraser 7
N. R. Taylor c Downton b Gatting 7
T. R. Ward c Downton b Cowans 1
C. J. Tavaré c Downton b Fraser 49
R. F. Pienaar b Emburey 34
*C. S. Cowdrey c Downton b Needham 10
G. R. Cowdrey lbw b Cowans 25
R. M. Ellison run out 21
†S. A. Marsh not out 24
C. Penn b Hughes 0
R. P. Davis run out 0
L-b 7, w 9, n-b 1 17

1/7 2/8 3/38 4/93 5/115 6/122 7/165 8/185 9/190 (59.3 overs) 195

Bowling: Cowans 10–2–32–2; Fraser 12–3–20–2; Hughes 9–0–39–1; Gatting 5–0–17–1; Needham 12–1–36–1; Emburey 11.3–1–44–1.

Middlesex

W. N. Slack c Marsh b Ellison 1
J. D. Carr b Penn 16
A. Needham c Benson b Pienaar 27
*M. W. Gatting c Marsh b Pienaar . . . 24
R. O. Butcher c Davis b Penn 64
K. R. Brown not out 37
†P. R. Downton not out 18
L-b 5, w 7 12

1/9 2/25 3/66 4/79 5/155 (5 wkts, 50.5 overs) 199

J. E. Emburey, S. P. Hughes, A. R. C. Fraser and N. G. Cowans did not bat.

Bowling: Ellison 11.5–1–53–1; Penn 10–2–25–2; Pienaar 11–0–46–2; C. S. Cowdrey 8–0–27–0; G. R. Cowdrey 3–0–10–0; Davis 7–0–33–0.

Umpires: K. E. Palmer and A. G. T. Whitehead.

SURREY v GLAMORGAN

At The Oval, July 27. Surrey won by four wickets. Toss: Surrey. Surrey were guided into the semi-finals by the methodical talent of Atkins, making his limited-overs début, and the hard hitting of Lynch. Glamorgan, with only one victory in limited-overs matches at The Oval in 25 years, failed to score sufficient runs for the conditions. Maynard, true to his free-scoring reputation, bustled to 64 in 88 deliveries before an impetuous stroke sent the ball into long-on's hands. Ontong, after a lethargic start, hit 40 from 46 balls and Shastri fashioned an unbeaten 59 in 77 deliveries as the last ten overs produced 83 runs. Yet Glamorgan might just have been able to defend their total had Lynch not been dropped twice and Atkins once, this a sharp chance to Maynard at second slip before he had scored. The 22-year-old newcomer stayed almost to the end for his 82 from 149 balls, while Lynch, despite being troubled by cramp in his right thigh, scored his 61 at a run a ball as they added 102 in twenty overs.

Man of the Match: P. D. Atkins.

Glamorgan

*A. R. Butcher c Atkins b Greig 26
J. A. Hopkins c Richards b Bicknell . . . 3
P. A. Todd b Peters 2
M. P. Maynard c Bicknell b Bullen 64
G. C. Holmes c Bullen b Greig 13
R. J. Shastri not out 59
R. C. Ontong c Bullen b Clarke 4
J. G. Thomas not out 1
B 1, l-b 8, w 7 1

1/14 2/24 3/55 4/87 5/134 6/218 (6 wkts, 60 overs) 23

J. Derrick, †C. P. Metson and S. R. Barwick did not bat.

Bowling: Clarke 12–0–36–1; Bicknell 11–0–50–1; Peters 12–1–50–1; Greig 12–0–48–2 Bullen 12–0–29–1; Lynch 1–0–13–0.

Surrey

G. S. Clinton lbw b Barwick	3	*I. A. Greig not out	13
P. D. Atkins c Shastri b Holmes	82	C. K. Bullen not out	3
A. J. Stewart b Derrick	22	L-b 8, w 10, n-b 3	21
M. A. Lynch c Derrick b Ontong	61		
D. M. Ward run out	27	1/11 2/45 3/147 (6 wkts, 57 overs)	236
†C. J. Richards lbw b Thomas	4	4/197 5/210 6/229	

N. H. Peters, S. T. Clarke and M. P. Bicknell did not bat.

Bowling: Thomas 12–1–44–1; Barwick 12–1–40–1; Derrick 12–1–47–1; Shastri 8–0–38–0; Ontong 8–0–42–1; Holmes 5–0–17–1.

Umpires: J. H. Hampshire and J. W. Holder.

WORCESTERSHIRE v GLOUCESTERSHIRE

At Worcester, July 27. Worcestershire won by four wickets. Toss: Worcestershire. The loss of five wickets for 29 runs in thirteen overs either side of lunch left Gloucestershire perilously placed at 113 for seven and virtually decided a low-key quarter-final played before a capacity, all-ticket crowd. Illingworth and Hick did the initial damage, finishing their 24 overs with combined figures of four for 50. Graveney and Curran, with a stand of 52 off twelve overs, ensured there would be a total to defend, and Graveney followed up with three wickets, including that of Hick, who batted almost an hour for his 18. Worcestershire, 87 for four at tea, were steadied by a match-winning stand of 74 between Neale and Weston and won with thirteen balls to spare.

Man of the Match: P. A. Neale.

Gloucestershire

A. W. Stovold c Rhodes b Illingworth	48	*D. A. Graveney c Neale b Radford	22
A. J. Wright lbw b Dilley	2	D. V. Lawrence not out	2
P. W. Romaines st Rhodes b Illingworth	18	T. M. Alderman b Radford	0
C. W. J. Athey lbw b Hick	11	B 5, l-b 5, w 3	13
P. Bainbridge b Hick	12		
K. M. Curran run out	53	1/7 2/54 3/84 (60 overs)	185
M. W. Alleyne lbw b Dilley	0	4/90 5/104 6/105	
†R. C. Russell c Rhodes b Dilley	4	7/113 8/165 9/185	

Bowling: Dilley 12–1–30–3; Radford 12–0–55–2; Newport 10–2–34–0; Illingworth 12–0–28–2; Hick 12–2–22–2; Weston 2–1–6–0.

Worcestershire

T. S. Curtis b Alderman	11	†S. J. Rhodes b Alderman	6
S. J. O'Shaughnessy c Athey b Graveney	42	P. J. Newport not out	10
G. A. Hick c Alderman b Graveney	18	B 6, l-b 9, w 2, n-b 1	18
D. A. Leatherdale c Athey b Graveney	0		
*P. A. Neale c Alderman b Curran	45	1/19 2/67 3/67 (6 wkts, 57.5 overs)	189
M. J. Weston not out	39	4/86 5/160 6/168	

R. K. Illingworth, N. V. Radford and G. R. Dilley did not bat.

Bowling: Alderman 12–4–46–2; Lawrence 12–2–33–0; Graveney 12–5–23–3; Curran 10.5–0–48–1; Bainbridge 11–2–24–0.

Umpires: D. J. Constant and R. Julian.

SEMI-FINALS

SURREY v MIDDLESEX

At The Oval, August 10. Middlesex won by 70 runs. Toss: Middlesex. Middlesex, losers in five previous 60-overs encounters at The Oval, enjoyed a comfortable passage to their fifth September final. The only challenge to their authority was mounted by Stewart, who hit an impeccable unbeaten hundred. His colleagues seemed to forget the basic one-day tactic of picking up singles and turning ones into twos when the bowling is uncompromising; it was soon clear that Middlesex's 258 was beyond Surrey. That score was based on a solid half-century from Slack, a dashing 65 in 80 balls by Butcher, and a stand of 49 in seven overs as Downton and Brown provided the necessary late impetus. However, Slack was fortunate to survive a run-out involving Gatting. A misunderstanding left both batsmen running to the same end, and Gatting was ahead when Bullen's throw hit the stumps. Slack started to depart, but the Surrey players insisted that Gatting was the one to go. Umpire Meyer agreed.

Man of the Match: R. O. Butcher.

Middlesex

J. D. Carr c Richards b Clarke	8	J. E. Emburey not out	10
W. N. Slack lbw b Bullen	56	S. P. Hughes not out	4
A. Needham c Stewart b Bullen	24	B 1, l-b 5, w 7	13
*M. W. Gatting run out	18		—
R. O. Butcher c Ward b Bicknell	65	1/17 2/63 3/99 (7 wkts, 60 overs)	258
†P. R. Downton c Richards b Clarke	40	4/154 5/189	
K. R. Brown b Clarke	20	6/238 7/243	

A. R. C. Fraser and N. G. Cowans did not bat.

Bowling: Clarke 12–1–49–3; Bicknell 12–0–38–1; Feltham 12–3–58–0; Greig 12–0–52–0; Bullen 12–0–55–2.

Surrey

G. S. Clinton st Downton b Needham	17	C. K. Bullen lbw b Cowans	7
P. D. Atkins c Downton b Cowans	0	S. T. Clarke b Cowans	3
A. J. Stewart not out	107	M. P. Bicknell b Fraser	1
M. A. Lynch b Carr	15	L-b 6, w 8, n-b 1	15
D. M. Ward b Carr	4		—
†C. J. Richards b Cowans	10	1/2 2/51 3/104 (56.4 overs)	188
*I. A. Greig run out	9	4/112 5/129 6/148	
M. A. Feltham c Gatting b Fraser	0	7/149 8/175 9/185	

Bowling: Fraser 10.4–3–29–2; Cowans 12–0–45–4; Hughes 6–0–26–0; Needham 12–1–23–1; Emburey 11–2–40–0; Carr 5–0–19–2.

Umpires: J. Birkenshaw and B. J. Meyer.

WORCESTERSHIRE v HAMPSHIRE

At Worcester, August 10. Worcestershire won by 29 runs. Toss: Hampshire. After three successive semi-final defeats in recent years, Worcestershire reached their first Lord's final for twelve years, winning a marathon tie which ended in virtual darkness at 8.25 p.m. Hampshire spurned three offers to go off for bad light as they fought to keep alive their chance of becoming the first county to win both Lord's finals in the same season. Worcestershire, however, always held the upper hand, particularly after Newport had accounted for Terry (141 balls) and Turner, who had put on 98 for the second wicket. This left Hampshire needing to score at more than 8 an over for fourteen overs, which was too demanding in the conditions. Earlier, Curtis (159 balls) and O'Shaughnessy (107 balls) had aroused thoughts of a total exceeding 300. Their stand of 148 off 40 overs was the highest for Worcestershire's first wicket against first-class opponents in the 60-overs competition. But after Hick and Leatherdale had added 49 in seven overs, Worcestershire lost their last seven wickets for 24 runs in 25 deliveries.

Man of the Match: T. S. Curtis.

Worcestershire

T. S. Curtis c Nicholas b James 74	P. J. Newport c Parks b Jefferies 1
S. J. O'Shaughnessy c R. A. Smith b Cowley . 62	R. K. Illingworth not out 2
G. A. Hick lbw b Ayling 31	G. R. Dilley b Bakker 1
D. A. Leatherdale b Jefferies 43	B 1, l-b 20, w 5, n-b 5 31
*P. A. Neale c R. A. Smith b Ayling .. 9	
M. J. Weston c and b Jefferies 2	1/148 2/169 3/218 (59.5 overs) 268
†S. J. Rhodes c Ayling b Bakker 9	4/244 5/251 6/254
N. V. Radford c R. A. Smith b Bakker. 3	7/257 8/259 9/266

Bowling: Jefferies 12–0–67–3; Bakker 11.5–2–34–3; James 11–1–45–1; Ayling 12–0–51–2; Cowley 12–0–47–1; C. L. Smith 1–0–3–0.

Hampshire

V. P. Terry c Rhodes b Newport 80	N. G. Cowley lbw b Hick 1
C. L. Smith c Illingworth b Hick 29	†R. J. Parks not out 18
D. R. Turner b Newport 35	P. J. Bakker c and b Hick 2
R. A. Smith c Rhodes b Weston 1	L-b 2, w 6 8
*M. C. J. Nicholas c Curtis b Hick ... 20	
S. T. Jefferies c Hick b Weston 8	1/49 2/147 3/148 (58.3 overs) 239
J. R. Ayling c Neale b Dilley 25	4/153 5/164 6/196
K. D. James b Dilley 12	7/206 8/210 9/236

Bowling: Dilley 11–2–50–2; Radford 7–0–24–0; Newport 12–1–37–2; Illingworth 12–2–44–0; Hick 11.3–0–54–4; Weston 5–0–28–2.

Umpires: J. H. Hampshire and A. G. T. Whitehead.

FINAL

MIDDLESEX v WORCESTERSHIRE

At Lord's, September 3. Middlesex won by three wickets. Toss: Middlesex. Winning the toss gave Middlesex a decisive advantage on a pitch containing sufficient moisture to help the seam bowlers throughout the day. Atrocious weather in the days preceding the final had not helped the groundsman in his preparations, although the match itself was played in fine weather. If indication were needed that this would not be an easy pitch for batsmen, 42 balls passed without a run before Hick, who replaced Curtis in the second over, broke the deadlock with a handsome cover drive. It was to be his only scoring stroke; in the twelfth over Fraser brought the ball back between his pad and bat. When Gatting changed his bowlers, Fraser's figures were 7–5–9–2, Cowans's 9–6–9–1. Leatherdale, with good footwork against the spinners and some neat strokes, helped Neale rebuild the innings until he was bowled in the 40th over, just two overs away from lunch. They had added 62, and in the afternoon Neale and Weston put on 66. The Worcestershire captain, who earlier in the week had been in hospital recovering from a stomach infection, remained until the 57th over, when he became Hughes's second wicket in his spell of four for 7 in thirteen balls. Neale hit five fours in his 64 from 143 balls.

By bowling their overs quickly, Middlesex had ensured they would not have to bat in near-darkness. And when Dilley, bowling with pace and hostile accuracy, dismissed Carr, Needham and Slack in his first spell (8–3–14–3), Middlesex must have been relieved they had adopted such a policy. Furthermore, Gatting had also gone, run out without facing a ball. O'Shaughnessy, seeing that Gatting was more interested in Slack's safety than his own, threw down the striker's wicket from some distance behind the bowler's stumps. When Butcher ran himself out, Middlesex were 64 for five in the 29th over. However, Ramprakash, two days away from his nineteenth birthday, took them to within 3 runs of victory, batting throughout in his cap with confidence, style and a rare charm. Emburey stayed with him till the 53rd over, by which time Ramprakash had reached 50 from 118 balls. His 56, from 123 balls, contained four fours – one superbly struck on the up off the back foot – and, for the non-partisan, was adequate compensation for the disappointment of Hick's failure.

Man of the Match: M. R. Ramprakash.

Attendance: 19,014 (excluding members); *receipts* £353,017.

Worcestershire

T. S. Curtis b Fraser	4	R. K. Illingworth not out	6
S. J. O'Shaughnessy c Downton b Cowans	1	G. R. Dilley not out	2
G. A. Hick b Fraser	4	L-b 7, w 1, n-b 2	10
D. A. Leatherdale b Needham	29		
*P. A. Neale b Hughes	64	1/5 (1) 2/9 (2) (9 wkts, 60 overs)	161
M. J. Weston c Downton b Fraser	31	3/9 (3) 4/71 (4)	
†S. J. Rhodes c Emburey b Hughes	1	5/137 (6) 6/140 (7)	
P. J. Newport b Hughes	4	7/145 (5) 8/148 (8)	
N. V. Radford b Hughes	5	9/153 (9)	

Bowling: Cowans 12–6–23–1; Fraser 12–5–36–3; Carr 4–1–9–0; Hughes 8–0–30–4; Needham 12–1–25–1; Emburey 12–3–31–0.

Middlesex

W. N. Slack b Dilley	14	S. P. Hughes not out	0
J. D. Carr c Rhodes b Dilley	1		
A. Needham b Dilley	6	B 4, l-b 5, w 7, n-b 2	18
*M. W. Gatting run out	0		
R. O. Butcher run out	24	1/3 (2) 2/21 (3) (7 wkts, 55.3 overs)	162
M. R. Ramprakash c Radford b Dilley	56	3/21 (4) 4/25 (1)	
J. E. Emburey b Dilley	35	5/64 (5) 6/149 (7)	
†P. R. Downton not out	8	7/159 (6)	

A. R. C. Fraser and N. G. Cowans did not bat.

Bowling: Dilley 12–3–29–5; Radford 11.3–3–37–0; Illingworth 12–4–24–0; Newport 10–1–20–0; Weston 2–0–9–0; Hick 5–0–19–0; O'Shaughnessy 3–0–15–0.

Umpires: H. D. Bird and D. R. Shepherd.

NATWEST BANK TROPHY RECORDS

(Including Gillette Cup, 1963-80)

Batting

Highest individual scores: 206, A. I. Kallicharran, Warwickshire v Oxfordshire, Birmingham, 1984; 177, C. G. Greenidge, Hampshire v Glamorgan, Southampton, 1975; 172 not out, G. A. Hick, Worcestershire v Devon, Worcester, 1987; 165 not out, V. P. Terry, Hampshire v Berkshire, Southampton, 1985; 158, G. D. Barlow, Middlesex v Lancashire, Lord's, 1984; 158, Zaheer Abbas, Gloucestershire v Leicestershire, Leicester, 1983; 156, D. I. Gower, Leicestershire v Derbyshire, Leicester, 1984; 155, J. J. Whitaker, Leicestershire v Wiltshire, Swindon, 1984; 154, P. Willey, Leicestershire v Hampshire, Leicester, 1987; 153, A. Hill, Derbyshire v Cornwall, Derby, 1986. (93 hundreds were scored in the Gillette Cup; 69 hundreds have been scored in the NatWest Bank Trophy.)

Fastest hundred: R. E. Marshall in 77 minutes, Hampshire v Bedfordshire at Goldington, 1968.

Highest innings totals (off 60 overs): 404 for three, Worcestershire v Devon, Worcester, 1987; 392 for five, Warwickshire v Oxfordshire, Birmingham, 1984; 386 for five, Essex v Wiltshire, Chelmsford, 1988; 371 for four, Hampshire v Glamorgan, Southampton, 1975; 365 for three, Derbyshire v Cornwall, Derby, 1986; 354 for seven, Leicestershire v Wiltshire, Swindon, 1984; 349 for six, Lancashire v Gloucestershire, Bristol, 1984; 341 for six, Leicestershire v Hampshire, Leicester, 1987; 339 for four, Hampshire v Berkshire, Southampton, 1985; 336 for five, Worcestershire v Cumberland, Worcester, 1988; 330 for four, Somerset v Glamorgan, Cardiff, 1978; 329 for five, Warwickshire v Buckinghamshire, Birmingham, 1987; 327 for seven, Gloucestershire v Berkshire, Reading, 1966; 327 for six, Essex v Scotland, Chelmsford, 1984; 326 for six, Leicestershire v Worcestershire, Leicester, 1979; 326 for nine, Hampshire v Leicestershire, Leicester, 1987; 321 for four, Hampshire v Bedfordshire, Goldington, 1968. *In the final:* 317 for four, Yorkshire v Surrey, 1965.

Highest innings total by a minor county: 256 off 58 overs, Oxfordshire v Warwickshire, Birmingham, 1983.

Highest innings by a side batting first and losing: 302 for five (60 overs), Leicestershire v Gloucestershire, Leicester, 1983. *In the final:* 242 for eight (60 overs), Lancashire v Sussex, 1986.

Highest totals by a side batting second: 326 for nine (60 overs), Hampshire v Leicestershire, Leicester, 1987; 306 for six (59.3 overs), Gloucestershire v Leicestershire, Leicester, 1983; 298 (59 overs), Lancashire v Worcestershire, Manchester, 1985; 297 for four (57.1 overs), Somerset v Warwickshire, Taunton, 1978; 296 for four (58 overs), Kent v Surrey, Canterbury, 1985; 290 for seven (59.3 overs), Yorkshire v Worcestershire, Leeds, 1982; 287 for six (59 overs), Warwickshire v Glamorgan, Birmingham, 1976; 287 (60 overs), Essex v Somerset, Taunton, 1978; 282 for nine (60 overs), Leicestershire v Gloucestershire, Leicester, 1975. *In the final:* 279 for five (60 overs), Nottinghamshire v Essex, 1985.

Highest total by a side batting second and winning: 306 for six (59.3 overs), Gloucestershire v Leicestershire, Leicester, 1983. *In the final:* 243 for three (58.2 overs), Sussex v Lancashire, 1986.

Highest total by a side batting second and losing: 326 for nine (60 overs), Hampshire v Leicestershire, Leicester, 1987.

Lowest innings in the final at Lord's: 118 (60 overs), Lancashire v Kent, 1974.

Lowest completed innings totals: 39 (26.4 overs), Ireland v Sussex, Hove, 1985; 41 (20 overs), Cambridgeshire v Buckinghamshire, Cambridge, 1972; 41 (19.4 overs), Middlesex v Essex, Westcliff, 1972; 41 (36.1 overs), Shropshire v Essex, Wellington, 1974.

Lowest total by a side batting first and winning: 98 (56.2 overs), Worcestershire v Durham, Chester-le-Street, 1968.

Shortest innings: 10.1 overs (60 for one), Worcestershire v Lancashire, Worcester, 1963.

Matches re-arranged on a reduced number of overs are excluded from the above.

Record partnerships for each wicket

227 for 1st	R. E. Marshall and B. L. Reed, Hampshire v Bedfordshire at Goldington	1968
286 for 2nd	I. S. Anderson and A. Hill, Derbyshire v Cornwall at Derby	1986
209 for 3rd	P. Willey and D. I. Gower, Leicestershire v Ireland at Leicester	1986
234* for 4th	D. Lloyd and C. H. Lloyd, Lancashire v Gloucestershire at Manchester	1978
166 for 5th	M. A. Lynch and G. R. J. Roope, Surrey v Durham at The Oval	1982
105 for 6th	G. S. Sobers and R. A. White, Nottinghamshire v Worcestershire at Worcester	1974
160* for 7th	C. J. Richards and I. R. Payne, Surrey v Lincolnshire at Sleaford	1983
71* for 8th	R. C. Ontong and T. Davies, Glamorgan v Staffordshire at Stone	1986
87 for 9th	M. A. Nash and A. E. Cordle, Glamorgan v Lincolnshire at Swansea	1974
81 for 10th	S. Turner and R. E. East, Essex v Yorkshire at Leeds	1982

Bowling

Hat-tricks (7): J. D. F. Larter, Northamptonshire v Sussex, Northampton, 1963; D. A. D. Sydenham, Surrey v Cheshire, Hoylake, 1964; R. N. S. Hobbs, Essex v Middlesex, Lord's, 1968; N. M. McVicker, Warwickshire v Lincolnshire, Birmingham, 1971; G. S. le Roux, Sussex v Ireland, Hove, 1985; M. Jean-Jacques, Derbyshire v Nottinghamshire, Derby, 1987; J. F. M. O'Brien, Cheshire v Derbyshire, Chester, 1988.

Four wickets in five balls: D. A. D. Sydenham, Surrey v Cheshire, Hoylake, 1964.

Best bowling: eight for 21, M. A. Holding, Derbyshire v Sussex, Hove, 1988; eight for 31, D. L. Underwood, Kent v Scotland, Edinburgh, 1987; seven for 15, A. L. Dixon, Kent v Surrey, The Oval, 1967; seven for 30, P. J. Sainsbury, Hampshire v Norfolk, Southampton, 1965; seven for 32, S. P. Davis, Durham v Lancashire, Chester-le-Street, 1983; seven for 33, R. D. Jackman, Surrey v Yorkshire, Harrogate, 1970; seven for 37, N. A. Mallender, Northamptonshire v Worcestershire, Northampton, 1984.

Most economical analysis: 12–9–3–1, J. Simmons, Lancashire v Suffolk, Bury St Edmunds, 1985.

Wicket-keeping and Fielding

Most dismissals in an innings: 6 (5 ct, 1 st), R. W. Taylor, Derbyshire v Essex, Derby, 1981; 6 (4 ct, 2 st), T. Davies, Glamorgan v Staffordshire, Stone, 1986.

Most catches by a fielder: (4) A. S. Brown, Gloucestershire v Middlesex, Bristol, 1963; G. Cook, Northamptonshire v Glamorgan, Northampton, 1972; C. G. Greenidge, Hampshire v Cheshire, Southampton, 1981; D. C. Jackson, Durham v Northamptonshire, Darlington, 1984; T. S. Smith, Hertfordshire v Somerset, St Albans, 1984; H. Morris, Glamorgan v Scotland, Edinburgh, 1988.

Results

Largest victories in runs: Worcestershire by 299 runs v Devon, Worcester, 1987; Essex by 291 runs v Wiltshire, Chelmsford, 1988; Sussex by 244 runs v Ireland, Hove, 1985; Warwickshire by 227 runs v Oxfordshire, Birmingham, 1984; Essex by 226 runs v Oxfordshire, Chelmsford, 1985; Leicestershire by 214 runs v Staffordshire, Longton, 1975; Hampshire by 209 runs v Dorset, Southampton, 1987; Derbyshire by 204 runs v Cornwall, Derby, 1986; Warwickshire by 201 runs v Buckinghamshire, Birmingham, 1987; Sussex by 200 runs v Durham, Hove, 1964. *In the final:* 175 runs, Yorkshire v Surrey, Lord's, 1965.

Victories by ten wickets (7): Northamptonshire v Leicestershire, Leicester, 1964; Warwickshire v Cambridgeshire, Birmingham, 1965; Sussex v Derbyshire, Hove, 1968; Hampshire v Nottinghamshire, Southampton, 1977; Middlesex v Worcestershire, Worcester, 1980; Yorkshire v Cheshire, Birkenhead, 1985; Yorkshire v Berkshire, Finchampstead, 1988.

Earliest finishes: both at 2.20 p.m. Worcestershire beat Lancashire by nine wickets at Worcester, 1963; Essex beat Middlesex by eight wickets at Westcliff, 1972.

Scores level: Nottinghamshire 215, Somerset 215 for nine at Taunton, 1964; Surrey 196, Sussex 196 for eight at The Oval, 1970; Somerset 287 for six, Essex 287 at Taunton, 1978; Surrey 195 for seven, Essex 195 at Chelmsford, 1980; Essex 149, Derbyshire 149 for eight at Derby, 1981; Northamptonshire 235 for nine, Derbyshire 235 for six in the final at Lord's, 1981; Middlesex 222 for nine, Somerset 222 for eight at Lord's, 1983; Hampshire 224 for eight, Essex 224 for seven at Southampton, 1985. Under the rules the side which lost fewer wickets won.

Wins by a minor county over a first-class county (7): Durham v Yorkshire (by five wickets), Harrogate, 1973; Lincolnshire v Glamorgan (by six wickets), Swansea, 1974; Hertfordshire v Essex (by 33 runs), 2nd round, Hitchin, 1976; Shropshire v Yorkshire (by 37 runs), Telford, 1984; Durham v Derbyshire (by seven wickets), Derby, 1985; Buckinghamshire v Somerset (by 7 runs), High Wycombe, 1987; Cheshire v Northamptonshire (by one wicket), Chester, 1988.

WINNERS

Gillette Cup

1963 SUSSEX beat Worcestershire by 14 runs.
1964 SUSSEX beat Warwickshire by eight wickets.
1965 YORKSHIRE beat Surrey by 175 runs.
1966 WARWICKSHIRE beat Worcestershire by five wickets.
1967 KENT beat Somerset by 32 runs.
1968 WARWICKSHIRE beat Sussex by four wickets.
1969 YORKSHIRE beat Derbyshire by 69 runs.
1970 LANCASHIRE beat Sussex by six wickets.
1971 LANCASHIRE beat Kent by 24 runs.
1972 LANCASHIRE beat Warwickshire by four wickets.
1973 GLOUCESTERSHIRE beat Sussex by 40 runs.
1974 KENT beat Lancashire by four wickets.
1975 LANCASHIRE beat Middlesex by seven wickets.
1976 NORTHAMPTONSHIRE beat Lancashire by four wickets.
1977 MIDDLESEX beat Glamorgan by five wickets.
1978 SUSSEX beat Somerset by five wickets.
1979 SOMERSET beat Northamptonshire by 45 runs.
1980 MIDDLESEX beat Surrey by seven wickets.

NatWest Bank Trophy

1981 DERBYSHIRE beat Northamptonshire by losing fewer wickets with the scores level.
1982 SURREY beat Warwickshire by nine wickets.
1983 SOMERSET beat Kent by 24 runs.
1984 MIDDLESEX beat Kent by four wickets.
1985 ESSEX beat Nottinghamshire by 1 run.
1986 SUSSEX beat Lancashire by seven wickets.
1987 NOTTINGHAMSHIRE beat Northamptonshire by three wickets.
1988 MIDDLESEX beat Worcestershire by three wickets.

CAREER FIGURES OF PLAYERS RETIRING OR NOT RETAINED

BATTING

	M	*I*	*NO*	*R*	*HI*	*100s*	*Avge*	*1,000r/ season*
R. I. Alikhan	69	103	8	2,350	98	0	24.73	0
A. J. Brassington	128	156	46	882	35	0	8.01	0
S. J. Dennis	72	71	27	456	53*	0	10.36	0
C. H. Dredge	194	224	68	2,182	56*	0	13.98	0
N. A. Felton	108	180	7	4,987	173*	8	28.82	2
R. J. Finney	114	168	29	2,856	82	0	20.54	0
K. W. R. Fletcher	730	1,167	170	37,665	228*	63	37.77	20
N. Gifford	710	805	264	7,047	89	0	13.02	0
M. R. Gouldstone	8	13	1	274	71	0	22.83	0
J. A. Hopkins ...	305	535	32	13,742	230	18	27.32	7
S. Monkhouse ...	11	12	5	30	15	0	4.28	0
A. Needham	109	156	23	3,077	138	4	23.13	1
G. V. Palmer	54	70	11	903	78	0	15.30	0
K. Saxelby	121	120	36	989	59*	0	11.77	0
D. K. Standing ..	43	70	10	1,130	65	0	18.83	0
A. C. Storie	45	75	12	1,350	106	1	21.42	0
G. A. Tedstone ..	32	45	7	641	67*	0	16.86	0
D. J. Thomas ...	150	193	41	3,044	119	2	20.02	0
P. A. Todd	171	302	16	7,663	178	9	26.79	3

* *Signifies not out.*

BOWLING AND FIELDING

	R	*W*	*BB*	*Avge*	*5W/i*	*10W/m*	*Ct/St*
R. I. Alikhan	124	3	2-19	41.33	0	0	34
A. J. Brassington	—	—	—	—	—	—	216/49
S. J. Dennis	6,061	194	5-35	31.24	5	0	20
C. H. Dredge	13,338	443	6-37	30.10	12	0	85
N. A. Felton	15	0	—	—	—	-	46
R. J. Finney	6,297	202	7-54	31.17	8	0	28
K. W. R. Fletcher	2,296	51	5-41	45.01	1	0	644
N. Gifford	48,731	2,068	8-28	23.56	93	14	319
M. R. Gouldstone	—	—	—	—	—	—	4
J. A. Hopkins ...	148	0	—	—	—	—	213/1
S. Monkhouse ...	576	18	3-37	32.00	0	0	2
A. Needham	5,373	124	6-30	43.33	6	0	50
G. V. Palmer	4,107	92	5-38	44.64	1	0	30
K. Saxelby	8,628	275	6-49	31.37	6	1	24
D. K. Standing ..	725	6	2-28	120.83	0	0	17
A. C. Storie	71	0	—	—	—	—	29
G. A. Tedstone ..	—	—	—	—	—	—	49/10
D. J. Thomas ...	11,415	336	6-36	33.97	7	1	50
P. A. Todd	7	0	—	—	—	—	119

Note: N. Gifford, four times, was the only bowler from this list to take 100 wickets in a season.

BENSON AND HEDGES CUP, 1988

Hampshire, who had been the only first-class county not to appear in a Lord's final, won the Benson and Hedges Cup with considerable ease, having taken six Derbyshire wickets before lunch. Derbyshire's total of 117 was the lowest in either of the two major finals at Lord's.

In becoming the eleventh county to win the trophy, Hampshire also won £21,000 in prizemoney, while Derbyshire received £10,500 as runners-up. Essex and Glamorgan, the losing semi-finalists, each received £5,000, and the losing quarter-finalists, Middlesex, Nottinghamshire, Warwickshire and Worcestershire, received £2,500 each. In addition, the winners of the group matches received £725.

Steve Jefferies's return of five for 13 from his ten overs, the best figures in a Benson and Hedges Cup final, made C. H. Lloyd's task of nominating the Gold Award winner at Lord's a simple one. Jefferies received £550, while the Gold Award winners in the semi-finals received £275 each, in the quarter-finals £200 each, and in the group matches £125 each.

Total prizemoney for the competition was £87,400, an increase of £2,500 over the previous year. Benson and Hedges increased their total sponsorship to the TCCB for 1988 to £456,425.

FINAL GROUP TABLE

	Played	*Won*	*Lost*	*No Result*	*Pts*	*Run-rate*
Group A						
DERBYSHIRE	4	3	0	1	7	64.89
WARWICKSHIRE	4	2	1	1	5	75.15
Leicestershire	4	2	1	1	5	60.10
Lancashire	4	1	3	0	2	68.25
Scotland	4	0	3	1	1	50.10
Group B						
WORCESTERSHIRE	4	2	1	1	5	68.78
NOTTINGHAMSHIRE	4	2	1	1	5	65.36
Northamptonshire	4	2	1	1	5	56.46
Yorkshire	4	1	1	2	4	59.19
Minor Counties	4	0	3	1	1	50.20
Group C						
ESSEX	4	3	1	0	6	72.15
MIDDLESEX	4	3	1	0	6	70.01
Kent	4	2	2	0	4	73.53
Sussex	4	1	3	0	2	60.90
Surrey	4	1	3	0	2	58.89
Group D						
GLAMORGAN	4	3	1	0	6	63.36
HAMPSHIRE	4	3	1	0	6	62.61
Gloucestershire	4	3	1	0	6	60.94
Somerset	4	1	3	0	2	67.47
Combined Universities	4	0	4	0	0	48.63

The two top teams in each group qualified for the quarter-finals.

Where two or more teams finished with the same number of points, the position in the group was based on faster run-rate.

GROUP A

LEICESTERSHIRE v LANCASHIRE

At Leicester, April 26, 27. Leicestershire won by 46 runs. Toss: Lancashire. Close of play: Lancashire 46-6 (19 overs) (T. E. Jesty 25*, W. K. Hegg 3*).
Gold Award: T. E. Jesty.

Leicestershire

N. E. Briers c Hegg b Allott 1
T. J. Boon b Allott 53
P. Willey c Watkinson b Jesty 59
*D. I. Gower c Simmons b Watkinson . 14
L. Potter c Hegg b Jesty 19
J. D. R. Benson not out 37
P. A. J. DeFreitas c Mendis b Jesty . . . 1
C. C. Lewis c Hegg b Jesty 2
†P. Whitticase c Hegg b Jesty 4
J. P. Agnew not out 5
B 2, l-b 6, w 9, n-b 1 18

1/8 2/128 3/131 4/152 5/172 6/174 7/182 8/190 (8 wkts, 55 overs) 213

L. B. Taylor did not bat.

Bowling: Matthews 5–0–17–0; Allott 11–4–19–2; Watkinson 10–0–48–1; Hayhurst 8–1–27–0; Simmons 10–0–55–0; Jesty 11–0–39–5.

Lancashire

G. Fowler c Lewis b DeFreitas 0
G. D. Mendis b DeFreitas 1
*D. P. Hughes b Lewis 12
N. H. Fairbrother c Whitticase b DeFreitas . 0
T. E. Jesty b DeFreitas 57
M. Watkinson lbw b Lewis 0
A. N. Hayhurst lbw b Taylor 3
†W. K. Hegg lbw b Willey 11
P. J. W. Allott c Taylor b Lewis 6
J. Simmons not out 31
C. D. Matthews c Benson b Willey 43
W 3 3

1/1 2/2 3/5 4/30 5/30 6/33 7/71 8/78 9/98 (41.5 overs) 167

Bowling: DeFreitas 9–0–27–4; Agnew 9–1–42–0; Lewis 9–0–41–3; Taylor 5–0–23–1; Willey 9.5–1–34–2.

Umpires: D. O. Oslear and R. A. White.

SCOTLAND v DERBYSHIRE

At Glasgow, April 26. Derbyshire won by seven wickets. Toss: Derbyshire.
Gold Award: K. J. Barnett.

Scotland

I. L. Philip c Morris b Holding 3
K. Scott c Morris b Mortensen 0
R. G. Swan b Newman 13
*C. E. B. Rice c Maher b Newman . . . 32
D. B. Pauline c Maher b Holding 42
†M. J. Smith b Warner 20
J. W. Govan c and b Holding 12
P. G. Duthie not out 5
D. Fleming b Warner 4
E. J. McIntyre run out 6
L-b 8, w 2, n-b 1 11

1/5 2/5 3/44 4/58 5/100 6/128 7/132 8/137 9/148 (9 wkts, 55 overs) 148

C. L. Parfitt did not bat.

Bowling: Holding 11–2–22–3; Mortensen 11–2–31–1; Newman 11–2–21–2; Warner 11–1–37–2; Bowler 11–3–29–0.

Derbyshire

*K. J. Barnett c Govan b McIntyre	66	S. C. Goldsmith not out	27
P. D. Bowler c Rice b Parfitt	19	B 3, l-b 6, w 1, n-b 1	11
B. Roberts c Swan b Parfitt	7		—
J. E. Morris not out	19	1/71 2/90 3/104 (3 wkts, 45 overs)	149

†B. J. M. Maher, R. J. Finney, P. G. Newman, A. E. Warner, M. A. Holding and O. H. Mortensen did not bat.

Bowling: Rice 9–1–31–0; Duthie 7–1–28–0; Govan 7–1–31–0; Parfitt 11–3–27–2; McIntyre 11–3–23–1.

Umpires: J. D. Bond and B. Leadbeater.

DERBYSHIRE v WARWICKSHIRE

At Derby, May 3, 4. No result. Toss: Derbyshire. There was no play on the second day.

Warwickshire

*T. A. Lloyd c Maher b Mortensen	36	D. A. Reeve not out	9
A. J. Moles c Maher b Finney	34		
Asif Din not out	67	L-b 16, w 9, n-b 4	29
A. I. Kallicharran c Holding b Bowler	2		—
†G. W. Humpage c Goldsmith b Warner	13	1/66 2/92 3/98 (5 wkts, 55 overs)	233
P. A. Smith c Barnett b Holding	43	4/121 5/201	

G. J. Parsons, G. C. Small, T. A. Merrick and N. Gifford did not bat.

Bowling: Holding 11–1–59–1; Mortensen 11–0–39–1; Warner 11–2–48–1; Newman 11–0–33–0; Bowler 10–0–33–1; Finney 1–0–5–1.

Derbyshire

*K. J. Barnett, P. D. Bowler, B. Roberts, J. E. Morris, S. C. Goldsmith, †B. J. M. Maher, R. J. Finney, P. G. Newman, A. E. Warner, M. A. Holding and O. H. Mortensen.

Umpires: J. W. Holder and R. A. White.

SCOTLAND v LEICESTERSHIRE

At Glasgow, May 3, 4. No result.

LANCASHIRE v DERBYSHIRE

At Liverpool, May 10. Derbyshire won by five wickets. Toss: Lancashire.
Gold Award: K. J. Barnett.

Lancashire

G. D. Mendis lbw b Warner	55	I. D. Austin c Morris b Holding	9
G. Fowler c Maher b Warner	50	P. J. W. Allott not out	0
J. Abrahams run out	7	L-b 14, w 10	24
M. Watkinson not out	70		—
Wasim Akram c Maher b Malcolm	23	1/106 2/117 3/122 (7 wkts, 55 overs)	257
*D. P. Hughes run out	7	4/162 5/181	
A. N. Hayhurst c Morris b Warner	12	6/231 7/252	

J. Simmons and †W. K. Hegg did not bat.

Bowling: Holding 11–1–49–1; Malcolm 11–1–40–1; Mortensen 11–0–50–0; Newman 11–0–52–0; Warner 11–0–52–3.

Derbyshire

*K. J. Barnett c Wasim b Simmons ... 85	M. A. Holding not out 35
P. D. Bowler b Allott 64	
B. Roberts c Hegg b Allott 0	B 1, l-b 6, w 6 13
J. E. Morris not out 48	—
S. C. Goldsmith lbw b Simmons 12	1/140 2/140 3/167 (5 wkts, 53.4 overs) 258
†B. J. M. Maher b Austin 1	4/196 5/197

D. E. Malcolm, P. G. Newman, A. E. Warner and O. H. Mortensen did not bat.

Bowling: Allott 10–1–42–2; Wasim 10.4–0–45–0; Hayhurst 7–0–33–0; Simmons 11–2–41–2; Watkinson 6–0–45–0; Austin 9–0–45–1.

Umpires: H. D. Bird and J. H. Hampshire.

WARWICKSHIRE v SCOTLAND

At Birmingham, May 10. Warwickshire won by 123 runs. Toss: Warwickshire. Warwickshire's total was their highest in the competition.

Gold Award: A. I. Kallicharran.

Warwickshire

*T. A. Lloyd c Rice b McIntyre 93	D. A. Reeve not out 1
A. J. Moles lbw b Rice 6	B 1, l-b 6, w 4 11
Asif Din c Scott b Duthie 107	—
A. I. Kallicharran not out 90	1/17 2/155 3/302 (4 wkts, 55 overs) 308
P. A. Smith c McGurk b Rice 0	4/302

†G. A. Tedstone, G. C. Small, G. J. Parsons, T. A. Merrick and N. Gifford did not bat.

Bowling: Rice 11–3–58–2; Duthie 11–1–75–1; Pauline 11–0–50–0; Parfitt 11–0–54–0; McIntyre 11–0–64–1.

Scotland

I. L. Philip b Gifford 51	G. B. J. McGurk not out 2
K. Scott c Small b Gifford 30	
R. G. Swan run out 1	L-b 13, w 1, n-b 5 19
*C. E. B. Rice b Moles 56	—
D. B. Pauline b Gifford 7	1/85 2/92 3/97 (5 wkts, 55 overs) 185
M. J. Smith not out 19	4/138 5/172

†D. Fleming, E. J. McIntyre, C. L. Parfitt and P. G. Duthie did not bat.

Bowling: Small 6–0–15–0; Merrick 8–1–17–0; Parsons 7–0–28–0; Reeve 6–1–17–0; Smith 10–0–45–0; Gifford 11–5–23–3; Asif Din 5–0–16–0; Moles 2–0–11–1.

Umpires: K. J. Lyons and D. R. Shepherd.

LANCASHIRE v SCOTLAND

At Manchester, May 12, 13. Lancashire won by 154 runs. Toss: Lancashire. Lancashire's total was their highest in the competition. Fairbrother's unbeaten 116, which came off 82 balls and contained four sixes and six fours, was his third hundred in four consecutive innings in eight days. Close of play: Scotland 57-1 (28 overs) (K. Scott 28*, R. G. Swan 7*).

Gold Award: N. H. Fairbrother.

Lancashire

G. D. Mendis run out 61
G. Fowler c and b McIntyre 66
N. H. Fairbrother not out 116
M. Watkinson c McIntyre b Ker 18
Wasim Akram b Ker 8
*D. P. Hughes b Rice 19
P. J. W. Allott not out 14
B 6, l-b 5, n-b 4 15

1/122 2/152 3/195 4/231 5/282 (5 wkts, 55 overs) 317

A. N. Hayhurst, I. D. Austin, J. Simmons and †W. K. Hegg did not bat.

Bowling: Rice 11–0–59–1; Duthie 11–0–96–0; Ker 11–1–77–2; Parfitt 11–1–30–0; McIntyre 11–0–44–1.

Scotland

I. L. Philip c Mendis b Austin 20
K. Scott c and b Allott 34
R. G. Swan not out 60
G. B. J. McGurk b Hayhurst 33
M. J. Smith not out 4
B 1, l-b 2, w 9 12

1/38 2/76 3/158 (3 wkts, 55 overs) 163

*C. E. B. Rice, E. J. McIntyre, †D. Fleming, P. G. Duthie, C. L. Parfitt and J. E. Ker did not bat.

Bowling: Wasim 9–0–27–0; Allott 9–5–15–1; Austin 10–3–17–1; Watkinson 11–1–38–0; Hayhurst 7–1–29–1; Simmons 7–2–26–0; Hughes 2–0–8–0.

Umpires: R. Julian and K. J. Lyons.

LEICESTERSHIRE v WARWICKSHIRE

At Leicester, May 12. Leicestershire won by 9 runs. Toss: Warwickshire.
Gold Award: G. J. F. Ferris.

Leicestershire

T. J. Boon c Humpage b Reeve 37
N. E. Briers c Humpage b Merrick 44
*D. I. Gower c Moles b Parsons 53
P. Willey c Humpage b Merrick 2
J. J. Whitaker c Humpage b Munton .. 16
L. Potter c Humpage b Parsons 10
P. A. J. DeFreitas c Parsons b Merrick. 4
C. C. Lewis not out 13
†P. Whitticase b Merrick 2
J. P. Agnew run out 3
G. J. F. Ferris not out 1
B 1, l-b 7, w 1, n-b 2 11

1/68 2/114 3/117 4/146 5/165 6/174 7/178 8/183 9/188 (9 wkts, 55 overs) 196

Bowling: Small 11–3–38–0; Merrick 11–3–24–4; Munton 11–0–42–1; Parsons 11–1–39–2; Reeve 11–0–45–1.

Warwickshire

*T. A. Lloyd b Ferris 1
A. J. Moles lbw b DeFreitas 33
Asif Din c Potter b Ferris 40
A. I. Kallicharran c Whitticase b DeFreitas . 79
†G. W. Humpage c Briers b Willey ... 11
P. A. Smith lbw b Lewis 0
D. A. Reeve lbw b Agnew 1
G. J. Parsons b Ferris 3
G. C. Small c Willey b Ferris 1
T. A. Merrick b Ferris 8
T. A. Munton not out 3
L-b 3, w 4 7

1/9 2/56 3/128 4/151 5/159 6/171 7/173 8/174 9/178 (54 overs) 187

Bowling: Ferris 11–2–28–5; Agnew 11–1–49–1; Lewis 11–1–39–1; DeFreitas 10–1–27–2; Willey 11–1–41–1.

Umpires: J. D. Bond and R. Palmer.

DERBYSHIRE v LEICESTERSHIRE

At Derby, May 14. Derbyshire won by six wickets. Toss: Derbyshire.
Gold Award: K. J. Barnett.

Leicestershire

T. J. Boon retired hurt	6	P. A. J. DeFreitas c Goldsmith b Holding	57
N. E. Briers b Holding	5	C. C. Lewis not out	8
*D. I. Gower c Goldsmith b Warner	15	L-b 6, w 4, n-b 4	14
P. Willey b Bowler	37		
J. J. Whitaker c Maher b Newman	7	1/14 2/56 3/76 (5 wkts, 55 overs)	186
L. Potter not out	37	4/76 5/169	

†P. Whitticase, J. P. Agnew and G. J. F. Ferris did not bat.

Bowling: Holding 11–1–34–2; Malcolm 9–0–32–0; Newman 11–1–33–1; Warner 8–1–33–1; Bowler 11–2–30–1; Finney 5–0–18–0.

Derbyshire

*K. J. Barnett b Willey	71	M. A. Holding not out	17
P. D. Bowler c and b DeFreitas	55	L-b 4, w 1, n-b 4	9
B. Roberts not out	29		
J. E. Morris run out	9	1/114 2/146 (4 wkts, 54.4 overs)	190
S. C. Goldsmith b Ferris	0	3/160 4/161	

†B. J. M. Maher, R. J. Finney, A. E. Warner, P. G. Newman and D. E. Malcolm did not bat.

Bowling: Ferris 10–1–42–1; Agnew 5–0–22–0; Lewis 8–1–29–0; DeFreitas 9.4–0–39–1; Willey 11–0–26–1; Potter 11–1–28–0.

Umpires: J. H. Hampshire and A. A. Jones.

WARWICKSHIRE v LANCASHIRE

At Birmingham, May 14. Warwickshire won by 89 runs. Toss: Lancashire.
Gold Award: A. R. K. Pierson.

Warwickshire

*T. A. Lloyd c Austin b Simmons	31	T. A. Merrick b Allott	6
A. J. Moles c Fowler b Allott	68	A. R. K. Pierson not out	3
Asif Din c Hegg b Hayhurst	27	N. Gifford b Wasim	0
A. I. Kallicharran run out	45	L-b 9, w 9	18
†G. W. Humpage c Fowler b Allott	14		
P. A. Smith run out	17	1/75 2/121 3/150 (55 overs)	249
D. A. Reeve b Wasim	18	4/173 5/198 6/232	
G. C. Small lbw b Wasim	2	7/234 8/241 9/249	

Bowling: Wasim 11–1–37–3; Allott 11–0–57–3; Austin 9–0–50–0; Simmons 11–0–50–1; Watkinson 11–1–35–0; Hayhurst 2–0–11–1.

Lancashire

G. Fowler lbw b Reeve	10	I. D. Austin b Gifford	20
G. D. Mendis b Pierson	39	P. J. W. Allott b Gifford	0
A. N. Hayhurst run out	0	J. Simmons not out	8
N. H. Fairbrother c Merrick b Pierson	27	L-b 1, w 14	15
M. Watkinson lbw b Pierson	14		
*D. P. Hughes b Gifford	15	1/54 2/55 3/66 (47.5 overs)	160
Wasim Akram run out	11	4/96 5/100 6/122	
†W. K. Hegg b Merrick	1	7/126 8/134 9/134	

Bowling: Small 9–0–26–0; Merrick 8–1–27–1; Pierson 11–1–34–3; Reeve 9–1–36–1; Gifford 10.5–0–36–3.

Umpires: J. C. Balderstone and D. O. Oslear.

GROUP B

NOTTINGHAMSHIRE v MINOR COUNTIES

At Nottingham, April 26. Nottinghamshire won by eight wickets. Toss: Minor Counties. *Gold Award:* K. Saxelby.

Minor Counties

D. W. Varey c Newell b Saxelby	5
C. J. Stockdale c French b Stephenson	9
R. D. V. Knight lbw b Pick	18
S. P. Henderson b Saxelby	6
*S. G. Plumb c French b Saxelby	21
G. R. J. Roope c Robinson b Saxelby	18
†M. A. Garnham c French b Stephenson	0
S. Turner c French b Saxelby	2
S. Greensword c Saxelby b Stephenson	21
A. J. Webster b Stephenson	12
S. J. Edwards not out	2
L-b 12, w 6, n-b 1	19
1/13 2/24 3/43 4/51 5/89 6/90 7/92 8/92 9/130 (54.2 overs)	133

Bowling: Stephenson 10.2–2–14–4; Pick 11–2–41–1; Cooper 11–4–28–0; Saxelby 11–4–21–5; Hemmings 11–2–17–0.

Nottinghamshire

B. C. Broad b Knight	52
*R. T. Robinson c Roope b Plumb	24
M. Newell not out	31
P. Johnson not out	22
B 1, l-b 3, w 1, n-b 3	8
1/62 2/98 (2 wkts, 31 overs)	137

D. W. Randall, F. D. Stephenson, †B. N. French, E. E. Hemmings, R. A. Pick, K. Saxelby and K. E. Cooper did not bat.

Bowling: Webster 5–0–19–0; Turner 6–0–21–0; Edwards 4–1–23–0; Plumb 9–0–34–1; Knight 7–0–36–1.

Umpires: H. D. Bird and B. J. Meyer.

YORKSHIRE v NORTHAMPTONSHIRE

At Leeds, April 26, 27. No result. Toss: Northamptonshire. Close of play: Yorkshire 116-0 (27 overs) (M. D. Moxon 57*, A. A. Metcalfe 53*).

Yorkshire

M. D. Moxon not out	82
A. A. Metcalfe c Ripley b Walker	70
J. D. Love not out	4
L-b 5, w 5, n-b 7	17
1/166 (1 wkt, 37.2 overs)	173

R. J. Blakey, P. E. Robinson, *†D. L. Bairstow, A. Sidebottom, P. J. Hartley, P. W. Jarvis, C. Shaw and S. D. Fletcher did not bat.

Bowling: Davis 8–1–37–0; Brown 7–0–33–0; Williams 2–0–7–0; N. G. B. Cook 7–0–31–0; Larkins 7–0–31–0; Walker 6.2–0–29–1.

Northamptonshire

*G. Cook, W. Larkins, R. J. Bailey, A. J. Lamb, R. G. Williams, N. A. Stanley, †D. Ripley, N. G. B. Cook, S. J. Brown, W. W. Davis and A. Walker.

Umpires: J. C. Balderstone and J. W. Holder.

MINOR COUNTIES v WORCESTERSHIRE

At Old Hill CC, May 3, 4. No result.

NOTTINGHAMSHIRE v YORKSHIRE

At Nottingham, May 3, 4. No result. Toss: Nottinghamshire. There was no play on the second day.

Yorkshire

M. D. Moxon not out 3
A. A. Metcalfe not out 5

(no wkt, 3 overs) 8

R. J. Blakey, J. D. Love, P. E. Robinson, *†D. L. Bairstow, A. Sidebottom, P. J. Hartley, P. W. Jarvis, S. D. Fletcher and C. Shaw did not bat.

Bowling: Stephenson 2–1–2–0; Pick 1–0–6–0.

Nottinghamshire

*R. T. Robinson, B. C. Broad, D. W. Randall, J. D. Birch, P. Johnson, F. D. Stephenson, †B. N. French, E. E. Hemmings, R. A. Pick, K. E. Cooper and K. P. Evans.

Umpires: R. Julian and D. O. Oslear.

MINOR COUNTIES v NORTHAMPTONSHIRE

At Darlington, May 10. Northamptonshire won by 44 runs. Toss: Northamptonshire.
Gold Award: R. A. Evans.

Northamptonshire

*G. Cook run out 18
W. Larkins c Roope b Burrow 70
R. J. Bailey b Webster 57
A. J. Lamb run out 19
D. J. Capel b Webster 7
R. G. Williams not out 10
N. A. Stanley st Garnham b Plumb . . . 5
†D. Ripley not out 4
B 1, l-b 6, w 5 12

1/54 2/136 3/167 4/176 5/187 6/197 (6 wkts, 55 overs) 202

N. G. B. Cook, D. K. Lillee and A. Walker did not bat.

Bowling: Webster 11–1–43–2; Busby 7–1–19–0; Evans 11–5–21–0; Greensword 7–0–26–0; Plumb 10–1–43–1; Burrow 9–0–43–1.

Minor Counties

. J. Stockdale b Walker 25
S. G. Plumb lbw b N. G. B. Cook . . . 16
. P. Addison c Ripley b Walker 2
. R. Oliver c Walker b Williams 31
G. R. J. Roope c G. Cook b Williams . 1
M. A. Garnham c Capel b Williams . . 11
. Greensword lbw b Lillee 20
. Burrow c Lillee b Stanley 20
A. J. Webster c Lamb b N. G. B. Cook 4
R. A. Evans not out 3
R. N. Busby st Ripley b Lamb 9
B 1, l-b 9, w 4, n-b 2 16

1/46 2/46 3/50 4/72 5/86 6/104 7/137 8/140 9/144 (55 overs) 158

Bowling: Lillee 9–2–23–1; Capel 11–2–35–0; Walker 8–2–21–2; N. G. B. Cook 11–4–21–2; Williams 11–1–27–3; Bailey 3–0–7–0; Stanley 1–0–3–1; Lamb 1–0–11–1.

Umpires: J. D. Bond and B. Leadbeater.

WORCESTERSHIRE v NOTTINGHAMSHIRE

At Worcester, May 10, 11. Nottinghamshire won by one wicket. Toss: Nottinghamshire. Close of play: Nottinghamshire 124-3 (36.4 overs) (D. W. Randall 58*, J. D. Birch 14*).

Gold Award: D. W. Randall.

Worcestershire

T. S. Curtis b Stephenson 0
G. J. Lord c Johnson b Evans 15
G. A. Hick c Scott b Cooper 20
*P. A. Neale c Johnson b Evans 8
D. B. D'Oliveira c Robinson b Pick ... 35
I. T. Botham c Cooper b Evans 4
†S. J. Rhodes b Hemmings 21
P. J. Newport run out 6
N. V. Radford not out 37
G. R. Dilley c Evans b Cooper 16
A. P. Pridgeon not out 5
B 3, l-b 9, w 9, n-b 10 31

1/0 2/33 3/47 4/56 5/73 6/104 7/123 8/144 9/186 (9 wkts, 55 overs) 198

Bowling: Stephenson 11–3–31–1; Pick 11–1–48–1; Cooper 11–0–55–2; Evans 11–1–36–3; Hemmings 11–2–16–1.

Nottinghamshire

B. C. Broad lbw b Radford 27
*R. T. Robinson c Rhodes b Dilley ... 2
D. W. Randall c Rhodes b Newport ... 69
P. Johnson c Neale b Radford 9
J. D. Birch run out 15
F. D. Stephenson run out 2
K. P. Evans c Rhodes b Pridgeon 18
†C. W. Scott lbw b Botham 5
E. E. Hemmings not out 21
K. E. Cooper b Botham 9
R. A. Pick not out 1
L-b 5, w 6, n-b 13 24

1/9 2/83 3/93 4/138 5/143 6/149 7/167 8/169 9/197 (9 wkts, 55 overs) 202

Bowling: Dilley 11–0–40–1; Radford 11–1–45–2; Pridgeon 11–1–35–1; Newport 11–1–29–1; Botham 11–1–48–2.

Umpires: D. O. Oslear and A. G. T. Whitehead.

NORTHAMPTONSHIRE v WORCESTERSHIRE

At Northampton, May 12. Worcestershire won by 125 runs. Toss: Northamptonshire.

Gold Award: G. A. Hick.

Worcestershire

T. S. Curtis b N. G. B. Cook 52
G. J. Lord lbw b Capel 2
G. A. Hick c Capel b Wild 47
D. B. D'Oliveira c Capel b Lillee 34
*P. A. Neale c Ripley b Capel 7
I. T. Botham c Capel b Lillee 43
†S. J. Rhodes b Walker 10
P. J. Newport c G. Cook b Lillee 9
N. V. Radford not out .... [illegible]
R. K. Illingworth not out .... [illegible]
B 7, l-b 18, w 12, n-b 2 ...... 3[illegible]

1/10 2/122 3/134 4/147 5/217 6/225 7/241 8/243 (8 wkts, 55 overs) 25[illegible]

G. R. Dilley did not bat.

Bowling: Lillee 11–0–61–3; Capel 10–0–39–2; Walker 11–0–59–1; Williams 7–1–21–0 Wild 8–0–34–1; N. G. B. Cook 8–2–17–1.

Northamptonshire

*G. Cook retired hurt 0
W. Larkins lbw b Radford 0
R. J. Bailey lbw b Radford 22
A. J. Lamb lbw b Radford 6
D. J. Capel lbw b Radford 25
R. G. Williams b Botham 9
D. J. Wild b Newport 0
†D. Ripley b Dilley 30
N. G. B. Cook run out 8
D. K. Lillee b Dilley 7
A. Walker not out 0
B 1, l-b 9, w 6, n-b 8 24

1/5 2/21 3/38 4/55 5/57 6/97 7/121 8/128 9/131 (40.3 overs) 131

Bowling: Dilley 8.3–2–32–2; Radford 11–1–25–4; Newport 6–1–18–1; Botham 6–1–11–1; Illingworth 6–0–27–0; Hick 3–0–8–0.

Umpires: A. A. Jones and P. B. Wight.

YORKSHIRE v MINOR COUNTIES

At Leeds, May 12. Yorkshire won by six wickets. Toss: Yorkshire.
Gold Award: M. D. Moxon.

Minor Counties

C. J. Stockdale c Blakey b Shaw 21
*S. G. Plumb hit wkt b Jarvis 1
R. D. V. Knight c Bairstow b Shaw . . . 38
P. R. Oliver c Bairstow b Hartley 48
G. R. J. Roope lbw b Moxon 39
S. Burrow c Robinson b Hartley 28
†M. A. Garnham not out 13
S. Greensword not out 2
B 6, l-b 5, w 2, n-b 3 16

1/3 2/41 3/108 4/121 5/183 6/201 (6 wkts, 55 overs) 206

A. J. Webster, R. N. Busby and R. A. Evans did not bat.

Bowling: Jarvis 10–1–43–1; Sidebottom 11–1–23–0; Shaw 11–3–30–2; Hartley 11–1–55–2; Carrick 11–0–38–0; Moxon 1–0–6–1.

Yorkshire

M. D. Moxon c and b Evans 83
A. A. Metcalfe lbw b Knight 21
R. J. Blakey st Garnham b Greensword 9
J. D. Love not out 45
P. E. Robinson lbw b Busby 34
†D. L. Bairstow not out 8
B 5, l-b 2, n-b 1 8

1/73 2/109 3/123 4/200 (4 wkts, 52 overs) 208

*P. Carrick, A. Sidebottom, P. J. Hartley, P. W. Jarvis and C. Shaw did not bat.

Bowling: Webster 11–0–42–0; Busby 8–1–43–1; Knight 10–1–38–1; Greensword 11–3–28–1; Evans 11–0–44–1; Plumb 1–0–6–0.

Umpires: D. O. Oslear and N. T. Plews.

NORTHAMPTONSHIRE v NOTTINGHAMSHIRE

At Northampton, May 14. Northamptonshire won by 12 runs. Toss: Nottinghamshire.
Gold Award: D. J. Wild.

Northamptonshire

R. J. Bailey c and b Evans 89
*W. Larkins c Stephenson b Cooper . . . 5
A. J. Lamb lbw b Cooper 8
D. J. Capel run out 23
R. G. Williams b Saxelby 75
D. J. Wild c Evans b Hemmings 1
M. A. Stanley b Stephenson 8
W. W. Davis run out 8
†D. Ripley not out 4
N. G. B. Cook not out 1
B 2, w 1, n-b 1 4

1/16 2/26 3/75 4/190 5/195 6/212 7/220 8/223 (8 wkts, 55 overs) 226

A. Walker did not bat.

Bowling: Stephenson 11–0–39–1; Cooper 11–2–36–2; Saxelby 11–1–58–1; Evans 11–1–45–1; Hemmings 11–1–46–1.

Nottinghamshire

B. C. Broad b Capel 22
*R. T. Robinson b Wild 47
D. W. Randall lbw b Capel 5
P. Johnson c and b Wild 30
J. D. Birch c Walker b Wild 14
F. D. Stephenson c Stanley b Wild 9
K. P. Evans not out 31
†C. W. Scott b Davis 18
E. E. Hemmings c Capel b Davis 5
K. E. Cooper b Walker 4
K. Saxelby lbw b Walker 1
B 4, l-b 17, w 4, n-b 3 28

1/56 2/62 3/114 4/119 5/142 6/145 7/190 8/206 9/212 (55 overs) 214

Bowling: Davis 11–0–40–2; Capel 9–0–33–2; Walker 11–2–34–2; Cook 11–0–34–0; Williams 5–0–20–0; Wild 8–0–32–4.

Umpires: D. G. L. Evans and J. W. Holder.

WORCESTERSHIRE v YORKSHIRE

At Worcester, May 14. Worcestershire won by 55 runs. Toss: Yorkshire. The partnership of 121 between Neale and Rhodes was a record for the sixth wicket in the Benson and Hedges Cup. Neale took 28 off one over from Hartley, in which he hit two sixes and four fours before being caught off the seventh delivery. An earlier delivery had been a no-ball.

Gold Award: P. A. Neale.

Worcestershire

T. S. Curtis c Bairstow b Fletcher 5
S. J. O'Shaughnessy c Bairstow b Fletcher . 8
G. A. Hick c Robinson b Hartley 14
D. B. D'Oliveira lbw b Moxon 28
*P. A. Neale c Sharp b Hartley 91
I. T. Botham c Hartley b Fletcher 7
†S. J. Rhodes not out 43
P. J. Newport not out 11
B 2, l-b 9, w 6, n-b 3 20

1/16 2/18 3/41 4/76 5/90 6/211 (6 wkts, 55 overs) 227

N. V. Radford, G. R. Dilley and A. P. Pridgeon did not bat.

Bowling: Sidebottom 11–4–32–0; Shaw 11–3–30–0; Fletcher 11–1–55–3; Hartley 11–2–72–2; Carrick 2–0–10–0; Moxon 9–1–17–1.

Yorkshire

M. D. Moxon lbw b Botham 7
A. A. Metcalfe lbw b Radford 8
K. Sharp c Radford b Newport 75
J. D. Love c Neale b Pridgeon 17
P. E. Robinson c Rhodes b Dilley 6
†D. L. Bairstow b Botham 13
*P. Carrick b Botham 15
P. J. Hartley c Curtis b Botham 12
A. Sidebottom run out 2
C. Shaw not out 4
S. D. Fletcher c Rhodes b Botham 1
L-b 6, w 6 12

1/12 2/24 3/71 4/116 5/123 6/149 7/154 8/167 9/167 (52 overs) 172

Bowling: Dilley 9–3–10–1; Radford 10–1–39–1; Newport 11–1–42–1; Botham 11–2–41–5; Pridgeon 11–1–34–1.

Umpires: J. D. Bond and B. Dudleston.

GROUP C

ESSEX v SURREY

At Chelmsford, April 26. Essex won by eight wickets. Toss: Surrey.
Gold Award: T. D. Topley.

Surrey

G. S. Clinton c East b Topley 10
D. M. Smith st East b Miller 29
A. J. Stewart c Miller b Pringle 21
M. A. Lynch c Pringle b Topley 23
D. M. Ward c East b Gooch 2
†C. J. Richards c Topley b Lever 19
*I. A. Greig c Miller b Topley 8
C. K. Bullen c East b Lever 21
M. A. Feltham c Topley b Lever 1
S. T. Clarke c Border b Topley 4
N. H. Peters not out 1
L-b 4 4

1/29 2/61 3/61 4/65 5/95 6/105 7/120 8/129 9/135 (52.1 overs) 143

Bowling: Lever 9.1–1–22–3; Topley 11–2–22–4; Miller 11–2–29–1; Pringle 11–1–29–1; Gooch 10–2–37–1.

Essex

G. A. Gooch b Clarke 43
B. R. Hardie c Bullen b Peters 0
P. J. Prichard not out 68
A. R. Border not out 19
B 4, l-b 5, w 5 14

1/4 2/101 (2 wkts, 39.5 overs) 144

*K. W. R. Fletcher, A. W. Lilley, D. R. Pringle, G. Miller, †D. E. East, J. K. Lever and T. D. Topley did not bat.

Bowling: Clarke 10–1–23–1; Peters 8–1–24–1; Feltham 8–1–22–0; Greig 6–1–33–0; Bullen 7.5–1–33–0.

Umpires: K. J. Lyons and R. Julian.

SUSSEX v KENT

At Hove, April 26. Kent won by seven wickets. Toss: Sussex.
Gold Award: S. G. Hinks.

Sussex

A. M. Green c Marsh b Kelleher 24
N. J. Lenham c Marsh b Alleyne 8
*P. W. G. Parker b C. S. Cowdrey 10
A. P. Wells st Marsh b Davis 53
C. M. Wells b Davis 1
†I. J. Gould c Hinks b C. S. Cowdrey 19
S. J. S. Kimber c C. S. Cowdrey b G. R. Cowdrey 9
D. K. Standing not out 42
M. W. Pringle not out 19
L-b 12, w 3, n-b 7 22

1/23 2/37 3/51 4/61 5/96 6/113 7/154 (7 wkts, 55 overs) 207

R. A. Bunting and A. M. Babington did not bat.

Bowling: Ellison 11–3–30–0; Alleyne 9–0–43–1; C. S. Cowdrey 10–1–40–2; Kelleher 11–2–43–1; Davis 10–1–33–2; G. R. Cowdrey 4–2–6–1.

Kent

M. R. Benson c Gould b Pringle 14
N. R. Taylor lbw b Kimber 31
S. G. Hinks not out 78
C. J. Tavaré b Bunting 31
*C. S. Cowdrey not out 40
B 2, l-b 5, w 1, n-b 6 14

1/24 2/70 3/119 (3 wkts, 49.2 overs) 208

G. R. Cowdrey, †S. A. Marsh, R. M. Ellison, D. J. M. Kelleher, R. P. Davis and H. L. Alleyne did not bat.

Bowling: Pringle 9–2–33–1; Bunting 11–0–36–1; Standing 4–1–17–0; Babington 11–0–43–0; Kimber 11–1–42–1; Lenham 2–0–18–0; A. P. Wells 1–0–9–0; Parker 0.2–0–3–0.

Umpires: J. H. Harris and A. G. T. Whitehead.

MIDDLESEX v SUSSEX

At Lord's, May 3, 4. Middlesex won by five wickets. Toss: Middlesex. Fraser became the tenth bowler in the competition, and the second for Middlesex, to take a hat-trick when he dismissed Kimber, Imran Khan and Bunting. Close of play: Middlesex 62-1 (22 overs) (J. D. Carr 34*, A. R. C. Fraser 1*).

Gold Award: M. W. Gatting.

Sussex

A. M. Green c Downton b Cowans . . . 7
N. J. Lenham b Hughes 55
*P. W. G. Parker c Downton b Williams 3
Imran Khan b Fraser 71
†I. J. Gould b Williams 1
C. M. Wells run out 8
A. P. Wells c Cowans b Emburey 8
S. J. S. Kimber c Williams b Fraser . . . 15
D. K. Standing not out 0
R. A. Bunting b Fraser 0
L-b 7, w 6, n-b 1 14

1/19 2/30 3/117 4/122 5/138 6/155 7/182 8/182 9/182 (9 wkts, 55 overs) 182

A. M. Babington did not bat.

Bowling: Cowans 11–3–28–1; Williams 11–2–21–2; Hughes 11–2–29–1; Fraser 11–3–39–3; Emburey 11–0–58–1.

Middlesex

W. N. Slack b Bunting 16
J. D. Carr b Lenham 62
A. R. C. Fraser c Gould b Bunting 13
*M. W. Gatting not out 56
K. R. Brown c Bunting b Kimber 7
R. O. Butcher c Gould b Babington . . . 5
†P. R. Downton not out 2
W 16, n-b 6 22

1/55 2/91 3/149 4/164 5/175 (5 wkts, 47.5 overs) 183

J. E. Emburey, N. F. Williams, S. P. Hughes and N. G. Cowans did not bat.

Bowling: Imran 11–1–26–0; Bunting 11–0–52–2; Babington 11–0–48–1; Kimber 10–2–34–1; Lenham 4–0–17–1; A. P. Wells 0.5–0–6–0.

Umpires: D. J. Constant and J. H. Hampshire.

SURREY v KENT

At The Oval, May 3, 4. Surrey won by nine wickets. Toss: Surrey. Clinton's score was the highest by a Surrey batsman, while Taylor's was the highest against Surrey in the competition. Close of play: Surrey 182-1 (45 overs) (G. S. Clinton 94*, A. J. Stewart 22*).

Gold Award: N. R. Taylor.

Kent

M. R. Benson lbw b Greig 6
N. R. Taylor c Clarke b Peters 137
S. G. Hinks c Lynch b Greig 4
C. J. Tavaré c Smith b Feltham 26
*C. S. Cowdrey c Clarke b Feltham . . . 4
G. R. Cowdrey c Ward b Clarke 11
†S. A. Marsh lbw b Greig 17
R. M. Ellison c Richards b Clarke 17
C. Penn not out . . . . [illegible]
R. P. Davis not out . . . . [illegible]
L-b 13, w 5 . . . . [illegible]

1/31 2/37 3/150 4/182 5/196 6/207 7/238 8/242 (8 wkts, 55 overs) [illegible]

H. L. Alleyne did not bat.

Bowling: Clarke 11–3–32–2; Peters 11–0–44–1; Greig 11–2–24–3; Feltham 11–1–42–[illegible] Bullen 5–0–48–0; Lynch 6–0–42–0.

Surrey

G. S. Clinton not out 121
D. M. Smith b Ellison 55
A. J. Stewart not out 57
L-b 8, w 8 16

1/136 (1 wkt, 53.1 overs) 249

M. A. Lynch, D. M. Ward, †C. J. Richards, *I. A. Greig, C. K. Bullen, M. A. Feltham, S. T. Clarke and N. H. Peters did not bat.

Bowling: Alleyne 10–2–39–0; Ellison 10–1–44–1; Penn 10–0–46–0; C. S. Cowdrey 11–2–38–0; Davis 10.1–0–63–0; G. R. Cowdrey 2–0–11–0.

Umpires: D. G. L. Evans and R. Palmer.

KENT v ESSEX

At Canterbury, May 10, 11. Kent won by six wickets. Toss: Kent. The stand of 180 between Benson and Taylor was a record for the first wicket for Kent in the competition. Close of play: Kent 6-0 (2.4 overs) (M. R. Benson 3*, N. R. Taylor 2*).
Gold Award: M. R. Benson.

:ssex

ɜ. A. Gooch not out 120
. R. Hardie c Marsh b Cowdrey 51
. R. Border c and b Ellison 12
. J. Prichard c Marsh b Penn 8
). R. Pringle c Marsh b Penn 5
K. W. R. Fletcher b Cowdrey 38
. W. Lilley lbw b Alleyne 7
†D. E. East c Cowdrey b Ellison 12
G. Miller not out 0
B 1, l-b 13, w 10, n-b 5 29

1/122 2/142 3/157 (7 wkts, 55 overs) 282
4/172 5/231
6/247 7/268

. D. Topley and J. K. Lever did not bat.

Bowling: Ellison 11–0–58–2; Alleyne 11–0–62–1; Cowdrey 11–0–50–2; Penn 11–1–40–2; Vells 3–0–18–0; Davis 8–1–40–0.

ent

. R. Benson run out 113
. R. Taylor c Border b Topley 87
G. Hinks b Topley 2
. J. Tavaré c East b Gooch 16
C. S. Cowdrey not out 21
R. M. Ellison not out 22
L-b 15, w 7 22

1/180 2/186 3/224 (4 wkts, 54.1 overs) 283
4/253

. J. Wells, †S. A. Marsh, C. Penn, R. P. Davis and H. L. Alleyne did not bat.

Bowling: Lever 10.1–3–36–0; Pringle 11–1–46–0; Topley 11–0–41–2; Gooch 11–0–59–1; :iller 4–0–38–0; Border 7–0–48–0.

Umpires: M. J. Kitchen and R. A. White.

SURREY v MIDDLESEX

. The Oval, May 10. Middlesex won by 1 run. Toss: Surrey.
Gold Award: M. A. Lynch.

Middlesex

J. D. Carr lbw b Clarke 0
W. N. Slack b Peters 8
*M. W. Gatting c Clinton b Bullen 72
R. O. Butcher b Bullen 49
†P. R. Downton lbw b Clarke 28
J. E. Emburey c Clarke b Feltham 9
K. R. Brown not out 32
N. F. Williams b Greig 3
S. P. Hughes run out 1
A. R. C. Fraser run out 0
N. G. Cowans not out 1
B 2, l-b 11, w 8 21

1/0 2/21 3/112 4/171 5/172 6/186 7/217 8/218 9/221 (9 wkts, 55 overs) 224

Bowling: Clarke 11–1–38–2; Peters 11–2–33–1; Greig 11–3–31–1; Feltham 11–0–54–1; Bullen 11–0–55–2.

Surrey

G. S. Clinton c and b Hughes 8
D. M. Smith run out 85
A. J. Stewart c Carr b Williams 49
M. A. Lynch not out 63
*I. A. Greig lbw b Fraser 0
D. M. Ward b Hughes 3
†C. J. Richards not out ....
B 4, l-b 6, w 1, n-b 3 1

1/37 2/121 3/194 4/200 5/218 (5 wkts, 55 overs) 22

C. K. Bullen, M. A. Feltham, S. T. Clarke and N. H. Peters did not bat.

Bowling: Williams 11–1–42–1; Cowans 11–1–30–0; Hughes 11–1–55–2; Emburey 11–2–29–0; Fraser 11–1–57–1.

Umpires: J. H. Harris and P. B. Wight.

ESSEX v SUSSEX

At Chelmsford, May 12. Essex won by two wickets. Toss: Essex.
Gold Award: D. R. Pringle.

Sussex

N. J. Falkner c Pringle b Miller 15
A. M. Green c Hardie b Pringle 53
*P. W. G. Parker run out 64
A. P. Wells c Hardie b Pringle 38
C. M. Wells c East b Topley 10
†I. J. Gould b Lever 14
Imran Khan not out ....
N. J. Lenham not out ....
L-b 11, w 8 ....

1/37 2/94 3/161 4/184 5/213 6/216 (6 wkts, 55 overs) 2

S. J. S. Kimber, D. K. Standing and A. M. Babington did not bat.

Bowling: Lever 11–2–45–1; Pringle 11–1–43–2; Topley 11–0–50–1; Gooch 11–1–33–; Miller 11–1–35–1.

Essex

G. A. Gooch b Kimber 20
B. R. Hardie b Kimber 51
P. J. Prichard lbw b Babington 0
A. R. Border b Kimber 29
D. R. Pringle c Falkner b C. M. Wells . 51
*K. W. R. Fletcher b Imran 6
A. W. Lilley c Gould b C. M. Wells ... 28
†D. E. East c Kimber b Standing 5
G. Miller not out ....
T. D. Topley not out ....
L-b 15, w 4, n-b 2 ....

1/49 2/58 3/107 4/122 5/137 6/201 7/206 8/210 (8 wkts, 54.5 overs) 2

J. K. Lever did not bat.

Bowling: Imran 11–1–43–1; Kimber 11–1–36–3; C. M. Wells 11–0–51–2; Babingt 9–0–35–1; Standing 9.5–0–27–1; Lenham 3–0–11–0.

Umpires: J. C. Balderstone and B. J. Meyer.

KENT v MIDDLESEX

At Canterbury, May 12. Middlesex won by six wickets, becoming the first county to qualify for the quarter-finals. Toss: Middlesex.
Gold Award: J. E. Emburey.

Kent

M. R. Benson b Hughes	61
N. R. Taylor c Brown b Emburey	38
S. G. Hinks lbw b Cowans	28
C. J. Tavaré b Emburey	15
*C. S. Cowdrey c Downton b Cowans	6
R. M. Ellison c Downton b Emburey	10
V. J. Wells not out	15
†S. A. Marsh b Emburey	3
C. Penn b Fraser	3
H. L. Alleyne not out	8
L-b 16, w 2, n-b 1	19
1/94 2/136 3/143 4/159 5/164 6/183 7/191 8/197 (8 wkts, 55 overs)	206

R. P. Davis did not bat.

Bowling: Cowans 11–0–21–2; Williams 11–0–45–0; Hughes 11–2–49–1; Fraser 11–3–33–1; Emburey 11–1–42–4.

Middlesex

W. N. Slack c Marsh b Penn	47
J. D. Carr run out	35
*M. W. Gatting b Ellison	68
R. O. Butcher c Taylor b Cowdrey	36
†P. R. Downton not out	6
J. E. Emburey not out	2
B 2, l-b 4, w 4, n-b 3	13
1/54 2/116 3/183 4/205 (4 wkts, 44.3 overs)	207

K. R. Brown, N. F. Williams, S. P. Hughes, A. R. C. Fraser and N. G. Cowans did not bat.

Bowling: Ellison 9.3–0–39–1; Alleyne 6–0–40–0; Cowdrey 9–0–38–1; Davis 11–0–43–0; Penn 5–0–26–1; Wells 4–1–15–0.

Umpires: M. J. Kitchen and R. A. White.

MIDDLESEX v ESSEX

At Lord's, May 14. Essex won by five wickets. Toss: Essex.
Gold Award: A. R. Border.

Middlesex

W. N. Slack c East b Topley	23
J. D. Carr b Topley	29
*M. W. Gatting lbw b Gooch	38
R. O. Butcher c Pringle b Gooch	75
†P. R. Downton lbw b Lever	6
K. R. Brown lbw b Pringle	2
J. E. Emburey c Lilley b Topley	17
N. F. Williams c Lever b Pringle	3
S. P. Hughes c East b Gooch	0
A. R. C. Fraser not out	13
N. G. Cowans not out	4
B 3, l-b 15, w 6, n-b 2	26
1/49 2/65 3/139 4/169 5/174 6/208 7/208 8/208 9/230 (9 wkts, 55 overs)	236

Bowling: Lever 11–1–25–1; Pont 7–0–44–0; Pringle 11–2–30–2; Topley 11–0–53–3; Gooch 11–2–44–3; Border 4–0–22–0.

Essex

G. A. Gooch b Hughes	57
B. R. Hardie c Brown b Emburey	36
P. J. Prichard run out	7
A. R. Border not out	75
D. R. Pringle c Emburey b Hughes	40
K. W. R. Fletcher b Hughes	4
A. W. Lilley not out	4
L-b 6, w 7, n-b 1	14
1/87 2/99 3/106 4/211 5/215 (5 wkts, 53.5 overs)	237

D. E. East, I. L. Pont, T. D. Topley and J. K. Lever did not bat.

Bowling: Williams 11–0–57–0; Cowans 10.5–0–44–0; Fraser 11–1–54–0; Emburey 10–0–37–1; Hughes 11–0–39–3.

Umpires: R. Palmer and P. B. Wight.

SUSSEX v SURREY

At Hove, May 14. Sussex won by 42 runs. Toss: Sussex. Although Essex's victory over Middlesex was to decide the group's other qualifier for the quarter-finals, Surrey began their innings knowing that victory in 22 overs would put them second on run-rate if Essex lost at Lord's. In the attempt, they were bowled out in 21.4 overs, the shortest completed innings in the history of the competition. Sussex were also involved in the previous shortest innings – 22.2 overs by Minor Counties (108) at Slough in 1981.

Gold Award: I. J. Gould.

Sussex

N. J. Lenham c Richards b Feltham . . . 22
A. M. Green b Feltham 29
*P. W. G. Parker lbw b Feltham 0
A. P. Wells lbw b Bicknell 26
C. M. Wells c Richards b Bicknell 26
Imran Khan c Smith b Greig 30
†I. J. Gould b Clarke 37
A. C. S. Pigott run out 1
S. J. S. Kimber not out 2
D. K. Standing st Richards b Greig . . . 1
A. M. Babington not out 4
L-b 11, w 7, n-b 2 20

1/54 2/54 3/59 4/115 5/117 6/180 7/184 8/189 9/190 — (9 wkts, 55 overs) 198

Bowling: Clarke 11–1–27–1; Bicknell 11–1–46–2; Greig 11–1–33–2; Feltham 11–0–35–3; Bullen 11–0–46–0.

Surrey

G. S. Clinton lbw b C. M. Wells 14
D. M. Smith c Pigott b Imran 18
A. J. Stewart b Babington 23
M. A. Lynch c Standing b Babington . . 46
D. M. Ward b Babington 7
†C. J. Richards b Babington 3
*I. A. Greig c Green b Standing 0
S. T. Clarke c Babington b Standing . . 32
C. K. Bullen not out 4
M. A. Feltham lbw b Imran 2
M. P. Bicknell b Imran 0
B 2, l-b 4, w 1 7

1/31 2/33 3/87 4/109 5/111 6/112 7/143 8/149 9/156 — (21.4 overs) 156

Bowling: Imran 5.4–0–43–3; Pigott 1–0–14–0; C. M. Wells 5–0–35–1; Babington 6–0–29–4; Standing 4–0–29–2.

Umpires: J. Birkenshaw and M. J. Kitchen.

GROUP D

The Combined Universities' squad of thirteen named for the competition was: M. A Atherton (Cambridge) (*captain*), J. C. M. Atkinson (Cambridge), P. A. C. Bail (Cambridge), T. M. Barry (Loughborough), J. Boiling (Durham), N. C. W. Fenton (Cambridge), G. D Harding (Durham), M. P. Hickson (Loughborough), N. Hussain (Durham), M. J. Kilborr (Oxford), T. J. G. O'Gorman (Durham), M. A. Smith (Exeter) and M. P. Speight (Durham)

GLOUCESTERSHIRE v COMBINED UNIVERSITIES

At Bristol, April 26, 27. Gloucestershire won by 60 runs. Toss: Gloucestershire. Close of play Combined Universities 139-7 (41 overs) (M. P. Speight 46*, M. A. Smith 0*).

Gold Award: C. W. J. Athey.

Gloucestershire

A. W. Stovold c Hussain b Boiling 42
A. J. Wright c Atkinson b Barry 11
M. W. Alleyne b Fenton 9
C. W. J. Athey c Hussain b Barry 82
J. W. Lloyds c Bail b Harding 20
K. M. Curran c Atherton b Boiling ... 1
P. Bainbridge c Boiling b Barry 47
D. J. Thomas not out 12
*D. A. Graveney not out 2
L-b 8, w 8 16

1/43 2/55 3/83 4/120 5/135 6/220 7/232 (7 wkts, 55 overs) 242

†A. J. Brassington and T. M. Alderman did not bat.

Bowling: Fenton 11–0–31–1; Smith 11–2–45–0; Barry 10–0–52–3; Harding 11–0–54–1; Boiling 11–0–44–2; Atherton 1–0–8–0.

Combined Universities

P. A. C. Bail lbw b Alderman 0
T. J. G. O'Gorman lbw b Alderman ... 14
*M. A. Atherton lbw b Curran 0
N. Hussain c Athey b Bainbridge 44
J. C. M. Atkinson run out 24
†M. P. Speight b Alleyne 83
T. M. Barry c Alderman b Alleyne 6
G. D. Harding b Alleyne 0
M. A. Smith c Lloyds b Alleyne 0
J. Boiling c Brassington b Alleyne 3
N. C. W. Fenton not out 0
L-b 4, w 2, n-b 2 8

1/0 2/8 3/18 4/69 5/93 6/115 7/126 8/139 9/167 (51.1 overs) 182

Bowling: Alderman 7–2–14–2; Curran 6–0–24–1; Bainbridge 10–1–34–1; Thomas 8–0–45–0; Graveney 11–2–34–0; Alleyne 9.1–2–27–5.

Umpires: D. G. L. Evans and D. S. Thompsett.

SOMERSET v HAMPSHIRE

At Taunton, April 26. Hampshire won by five wickets. Toss: Somerset.
Gold Award: S. T. Jefferies.

Somerset

N. A. Felton b Jefferies 50
P. M. Roebuck c Parks b Jefferies ... 42
J. J. E. Hardy c R. A. Smith b Jefferies 8
. R. Waugh b Andrew 7
. J. Harden b Andrew 7
. J. Marks lbw b Connor 9
N. D. Burns c Parks b James 5
G. D. Rose not out 22
G. V. Palmer c Cowley b James 14
N. A. Mallender not out 16
L-b 9, w 7, n-b 1 17

1/91 2/105 3/108 4/118 5/128 6/138 7/141 8/158 (8 wkts, 55 overs) 197

A. N. Jones did not bat.

Bowling: Jefferies 11–0–44–3; Connor 11–3–32–1; James 11–1–37–2; Andrew 11–1–47–2; Cowley 11–4–28–0.

Hampshire

. P. Terry c Burns b Rose 47
. L. Smith c Roebuck b Mallender ... 13
M. C. J. Nicholas lbw b Palmer 72
. A. Smith c Marks b Jones 8
. R. Turner run out 3
. D. James not out 21
†R. J. Parks not out 23
L-b 10, w 3, n-b 1 14

1/22 2/107 3/138 4/144 5/155 (5 wkts, 53.5 overs) 201

T. Jefferies, N. G. Cowley, S. J. W. Andrew and C. A. Connor did not bat.

Bowling: Jones 10–0–33–1; Mallender 10–3–20–1; Rose 11–1–47–1; Waugh 7–0–35–0; Marks 10.5–1–42–0; Palmer 5–0–14–1.

Umpires: D. J. Constant and B. Hassan.

COMBINED UNIVERSITIES v SOMERSET

At Oxford, May 3, 4. Somerset won by 70 runs in a match reduced by poor weather to 41 overs a side. Toss: Combined Universities. There was no play on the first day.
Gold Award: S. R. Waugh.

Somerset

N. A. Felton c Speight b Hickson 9
*P. M. Roebuck c Atherton b Fenton . . 4
J. J. E. Hardy run out 34
S. R. Waugh c Boiling b Barry 79
R. J. Harden c Smith b Boiling 13
V. J. Marks c Speight b Smith 15
G. D. Rose c Atherton b Smith 6
G. V. Palmer not out 5
†N. D. Burns b Smith 2
N. A. Mallender b Smith 0
A. N. Jones not out 1
B 1, l-b 2, w 7, n-b 4 14

1/11 2/19 3/92 (9 wkts, 41 overs) 182
4/115 5/145 6/169
7/173 8/179 9/179

Bowling: Fenton 9–1–26–1; Hickson 8–1–27–1; Boiling 8–0–27–1; Barry 8–0–50–1; Smith 8–0–49–4.

Combined Universities

P. A. C. Bail c Burns b Jones 1
T. J. G. O'Gorman c Roebuck b Waugh 39
*M. A. Atherton c Roebuck b Waugh . 29
N. Hussain c Burns b Jones 4
J. C. M. Atkinson run out 5
†M. P. Speight c Mallender b Palmer . . 17
T. M. Barry c Hardy b Jones 6
M. P. Hickson lbw b Jones 4
M. A. Smith b Palmer 1
J. Boiling not out 2
N. C. W. Fenton b Mallender 0
L-b 3, w 1 4

1/1 2/63 3/74 (38.3 overs) 112
4/79 5/93 6/99
7/108 8/108 9/111

Bowling: Mallender 6.3–0–17–1; Jones 9–1–19–4; Marks 5–0–19–0; Rose 8–0–29–0; Waugh 5–1–16–2; Palmer 5–2–9–2.

Umpires: D. R. Shepherd and D. S. Thompsett.

HAMPSHIRE v GLAMORGAN

At Southampton, May 3. Hampshire won by ten wickets. Toss: Hampshire.
Gold Award: V. P. Terry.

Glamorgan

*A. R. Butcher b Jefferies 14
J. A. Hopkins c Jefferies b James 8
R. C. Ontong c R. A. Smith b Andrew . 0
M. P. Maynard c Connor b Andrew . . . 4
R. J. Shastri c Terry b James 55
G. C. Holmes c C. L. Smith b Connor . 18
P. A. Cottey c C. L. Smith b Jefferies . 15
J. G. Thomas c Terry b James 14
†C. P. Metson b Connor 1
S. L. Watkin not out . . . .
S. R. Barwick not out . . . .
B 1, l-b 4, w 2, n-b 4 1

1/21 2/24 3/24 (9 wkts, 55 overs) 15
4/38 5/70 6/104
7/135 8/139 9/153

Bowling: Connor 11–2–28–2; Jefferies 11–0–36–2; Andrew 11–0–26–2; James 11–2–31–3 Cowley 11–3–31–0.

Hampshire

V. P. Terry not out 80
C. L. Smith not out 70
L-b 5, n-b 3 8

(no wkt, 47 overs) 158

R. A. Smith, D. R. Turner, *M. C. J. Nicholas, K. D. James, †R. J. Parks, S. T. Jefferies N. G. Cowley, S. J. W. Andrew and C. A. Connor did not bat.

Bowling: Thomas 9–1–25–0; Barwick 10–1–18–0; Watkin 3–0–25–0; Butcher 7–2–19–0; Shastri 8–0–29–0; Ontong 5–0–20–0; Holmes 3–0–11–0; Maynard 2–0–6–0.

Umpires: B. Dudleston and M. J. Kitchen.

HAMPSHIRE v GLOUCESTERSHIRE

At Southampton, May 10. Gloucestershire won by six wickets. Toss: Gloucestershire.
Gold Award: P. Bainbridge.

Hampshire

R. J. Scott b Graveney 41
C. L. Smith c Curran b Bainbridge 18
D. R. Turner b Graveney 29
R. A. Smith b Graveney 2
*M. C. J. Nicholas c Stovold b Alderman 48
K. D. James c Lloyds b Curran 25
S. T. Jefferies c Athey b Lawrence 1
†R. J. Parks b Lawrence 9
N. G. Cowley b Alderman 7
C. A. Connor not out 5
S. J. W. Andrew not out 4
L-b 12, w 2, n-b 2 16

1/43 2/74 3/84 4/114 5/172 6/177 7/178 8/191 9/197 (9 wkts, 55 overs) 205

Bowling: Lawrence 11–1–36–2; Alderman 11–2–38–2; Curran 11–2–34–1; Bainbridge 6–1–27–1; Alleyne 7–0–23–0; Graveney 9–0–35–3.

Gloucestershire

A. W. Stovold b Connor 13
A. J. Wright c Parks b Jefferies 1
P. Bainbridge c C. L. Smith b Connor . 96
C. W. J. Athey run out 37
K. M. Curran not out 32
J. W. Lloyds not out 7
L-b 14, w 5, n-b 2 21

1/18 2/20 3/125 4/197 (4 wkts, 53.5 overs) 207

M. W. Alleyne, †R. C. Russell, *D. A. Graveney, D. V. Lawrence and T. M. Alderman did not bat.

Bowling: Jefferies 11–0–55–1; Connor 10.5–1–38–2; James 10–1–41–0; Andrew 11–0–46–0; Cowley 11–3–13–0.

Umpires: J. Birkenshaw and A. A. Jones.

SOMERSET v GLAMORGAN

At Taunton, May 10. Glamorgan won by six wickets. Toss: Somerset.
Gold Award: M. P. Maynard.

Somerset

G. Wyatt c Metson b Derrick 44
N. A. Felton b Derrick 13
J. E. Hardy b Thomas 60
R. Waugh not out 75
J. Harden b Thomas 30
B 1, l-b 4, w 1 6

1/51 2/66 3/158 4/228 (4 wkts, 55 overs) 228

V. J. Marks, †N. D. Burns, G. D. Rose, G. V. Palmer, N. A. Mallender and A. N. Jones did not bat.

Bowling: Thomas 11–1–40–2; Barwick 11–2–57–0; Derrick 11–1–27–2; Ontong 11–1–47–0; Shastri 11–0–52–0.

Glamorgan

A. R. Butcher c Waugh b Marks 57
J. A. Hopkins b Rose 22
*H. Morris c Mallender b Rose 5
M. P. Maynard c Felton b Rose 71
R. J. Shastri not out 39
G. C. Holmes not out 19
L-b 13, w 1, n-b 2 16

1/48 2/56 3/162 4/175 (4 wkts, 53.2 overs) 229

R. C. Ontong, J. Derrick, J. G. Thomas, †C. P. Metson and S. R. Barwick did not bat.

Bowling: Mallender 11–2–28–0; Jones 8–0–55–0; Rose 11–2–32–3; Palmer 10.2–0–50–0; Marks 11–1–39–1; Waugh 2–0–12–0.

Umpires: R. Julian and R. Palmer.

GLAMORGAN v COMBINED UNIVERSITIES

At Cardiff, May 12. Glamorgan won by 84 runs. Toss: Combined Universities. Maynard, who reached his hundred off 75 balls, equalled H. Morris's record for a Glamorgan batsman in the Benson and Hedges Cup, and Glamorgan's total was their highest in the competition.

Gold Award: M. P. Maynard.

Glamorgan

A. R. Butcher c Hussain b Fenton 12
J. A. Hopkins run out 50
*H. Morris run out 15
M. P. Maynard b Fenton 115
R. J. Shastri c Speight b Fenton 0
G. C. Holmes not out 59
R. C. Ontong b Smith 19
J. G. Thomas not out 16
B 2, l-b 7, w 6, n-b 1 16

1/23 2/44 3/152 4/186 5/219 6/260 (6 wkts, 55 overs) 302

J. Derrick, †C. P. Metson and S. R. Barwick did not bat.

Bowling: Fenton 11–0–44–3; Hickson 11–0–64–0; Boiling 11–2–51–0; Atkinson 7–0–46–0 Smith 10–0–59–1; Kilborn 5–0–29–0.

Combined Universities

*M. A. Atherton c Metson b Derrick . . 17
T. J. G. O'Gorman b Derrick 43
M. J. Kilborn b Derrick 10
N. Hussain not out 76
P. A. C. Bail lbw b Derrick 13
J. C. M. Atkinson c Ontong b Shastri . 6
†M. P. Speight c Maynard b Holmes . . 8
M. P. Hickson c Shastri b Ontong 10
M. A. Smith lbw b Morris . . . .
J. Boiling not out . . . .
B 4, l-b 12, w 5, n-b 2 2

1/38 2/81 3/82 4/120 5/129 6/153 7/176 8/196 (8 wkts, 55 overs) 21

N. C. W. Fenton did not bat.

Bowling: Thomas 5–1–6–0; Barwick 6–2–21–0; Ontong 11–2–43–1; Derrick 11–3–53–4 Shastri 11–2–24–1; Holmes 9–1–41–1; Morris 2–0–14–1.

Umpires: B. Dudleston and D. G. L. Evans.

GLOUCESTERSHIRE v SOMERSET

At Bristol, May 12. Gloucestershire won by six wickets. Toss: Gloucestershire.

Gold Award: A. W. Stovold.

Somerset

J. G. Wyatt b Curran 55
N. A. Felton b Bainbridge 10
J. J. E. Hardy not out 70
M. D. Crowe b Alleyne 24
R. J. Harden c Lawrence b Graveney .. 19
*V. J. Marks b Alderman 16
G. D. Rose c Russell b Curran 18
G. V. Palmer not out 1
B 1, l-b 10, w 3 14

1/49 2/75 3/118 (6 wkts, 55 overs) 227
4/148 5/173 6/218

†N. D. Burns, D. J. Foster and N. A. Mallender did not bat.

Bowling: Lawrence 4–0–24–0; Alderman 11–1–57–1; Curran 11–2–42–2; Bainbridge 11–3–29–1; Alleyne 10–0–35–1; Graveney 8–1–29–1.

Gloucestershire

A. W. Stovold run out 78
A. J. Wright c Crowe b Foster 66
P. Bainbridge c Wyatt b Rose 6
C. W. J. Athey not out 27
K. M. Curran c Burns b Mallender 30
J. W. Lloyds not out 8
L-b 3, w 3, n-b 7 13

1/137 2/151 3/166 (4 wkts, 48.4 overs) 228
4/220

†R. C. Russell, M. W. Alleyne, *D. A. Graveney, D. V. Lawrence and T. M. Alderman did not bat.

Bowling: Mallender 9.4–0–36–1; Foster 11–0–57–1; Rose 11–0–50–1; Palmer 8–1–40–0; Marks 9–0–42–0.

Umpires: D. J. Constant and A. G. T. Whitehead.

COMBINED UNIVERSITIES v HAMPSHIRE

At Cambridge, May 14. Hampshire won by seven wickets. Toss: Combined Universities. *Gold Award:* V. P. Terry.

Combined Universities

T. J. G. O'Gorman c Parks b Andrew . 12
*M. A. Atherton b Cowley 38
M. J. Kilborn c Nicholas b Jefferies ... 14
N. Hussain run out 2
P. A. C. Bail lbw b Connor 18
†M. P. Speight c Parks b Andrew 20
T. M. Barry c Parks b Andrew 8
G. D. Harding c Parks b Jefferies 3
J. Boiling not out 2
M. A. Smith run out 1
N. C. W. Fenton not out 1
L-b 8, w 2, n-b 1 11

1/25 2/66 3/69 (9 wkts, 55 overs) 130
4/75 5/105 6/106
7/125 8/125 9/129

Bowling: Jefferies 11–2–28–2; Connor 11–4–16–1; James 11–1–35–0; Andrew 11–4–20–3; Cowley 11–2–23–1.

Hampshire

R. A. Smith c Atherton b Fenton 8
V. P. Terry not out 68
D. R. Turner c and b Boiling 14
*M. C. J. Nicholas c and b Boiling 18
C. L. Smith not out 14
L-b 7, w 2 9

1/25 2/51 3/91 (3 wkts, 29.1 overs) 131

K. D. James, †R. J. Parks, S. T. Jefferies, N. G. Cowley, C. A. Connor and S. J. W. Andrew did not bat.

Bowling: Fenton 9–2–21–1; Smith 7–1–36–0; Boiling 9.1–0–48–2; Harding 4–0–19–0.

Umpires: B. Leadbeater and N. T. Plews.

GLAMORGAN v GLOUCESTERSHIRE

At Swansea, May 14. Glamorgan won by five wickets. Toss: Glamorgan.
Gold Award: R. C. Ontong.

Gloucestershire

A. W. Stovold b Thomas	0
A. J. Wright c Ontong b Barwick	9
P. Bainbridge b Barwick	11
C. W. J. Athey c Barwick b Ontong	31
K. M. Curran b Derrick	0
J. W. Lloyds run out	1
M. W. Alleyne b Derrick	2
†R. C. Russell b Shastri	11
D. V. Lawrence c Cottey b Ontong	6
*D. A. Graveney not out	5
T. M. Alderman b Thomas	8
B 4, l-b 9, w 3, n-b 1	17
1/0 2/14 3/27 4/32 5/35 6/48 7/73 8/82 9/84 (50.4 overs)	101

Bowling: Thomas 8.4–4–22–2; Barwick 11–4–10–2; Derrick 11–6–12–2; Holmes 5–0–16–0; Shastri 9–2–17–1; Ontong 6–2–11–2.

Glamorgan

A. R. Butcher c Russell b Lawrence	0
P. A. Cottey c Lloyds b Alderman	14
*H. Morris c Athey b Alderman	11
M. P. Maynard c Russell b Curran	15
R. J. Shastri c Athey b Curran	7
G. C. Holmes not out	29
R. C. Ontong not out	24
B 1, w 2, n-b 3	6
1/0 2/26 3/27 4/47 5/52 (5 wkts, 45.3 overs)	106

J. Derrick, J. G. Thomas, †C. P. Metson and S. R. Barwick did not bat.

Bowling: Lawrence 11–5–15–1; Alderman 11–2–24–2; Curran 11–2–27–2; Bainbridge 8–0–23–0; Graveney 2.3–1–7–0; Alleyne 2–1–9–0.

Umpires: J. H. Harris and K. J. Lyons.

QUARTER-FINALS

DERBYSHIRE v MIDDLESEX

At Derby, May 25, 26. Derbyshire won by nine wickets. Toss: Derbyshire. Derbyshire took an early grip on the game when Holding dismissed Carr, Gatting (already dropped at square leg) and Butcher in his first three overs. Middlesex never recovered fully, although Brown, Emburey and Sykes suggested they might pin the innings together. Malcolm's second spell (3–0–10–4) finished Middlesex and the only threat to Derbyshire came from the weather. The third interruption left them 33 without loss after eight overs (K. J. Barnett 22*, P. D. Bowler 10*) and they could not resume until 5.30 p.m. on the second day. Barnett saw them through with his fourth consecutive score of 50 or more in the competition.
Gold Award: D. E. Malcolm.

Middlesex

J. D. Carr lbw b Holding	0
K. R. Brown c Sharma b Bowler	32
*M. W. Gatting lbw b Holding	5
R. O. Butcher c Goldsmith b Holding	0
†P. R. Downton lbw b Malcolm	9
J. E. Emburey b Newman	18
J. F. Sykes b Malcolm	24
N. F. Williams c Bowler b Malcolm	12
S. P. Hughes c Bowler b Malcolm	2
A. R. C. Fraser not out	1
N. G. Cowans b Malcolm	0
L-b 2, w 5	7
1/0 2/8 3/8 4/40 5/50 6/77 7/102 8/106 9/109 (46 overs)	110

Bowling: Holding 9–3–13–3; Newman 9–2–13–1; Malcolm 9–0–27–5; Warner 8–1–25–0 Bowler 6–2–18–1; Roberts 5–1–12–0.

Derbyshire

*K. J. Barnett not out 69
P. D. Bowler lbw b Fraser 26
B. Roberts not out 4
B 2, l-b 9, n-b 1 12

1/93 (1 wkt, 30.3 overs) 111

J. E. Morris, S. C. Goldsmith, †B. J. M. Maher, A. E. Warner, P. G. Newman, M. A. Holding, R. Sharma and D. E. Malcolm did not bat.

Bowling: Williams 4–0–21–0; Cowans 4–1–12–0; Emburey 3–0–14–0; Fraser 10–2–27–1; Hughes 4–0–16–0; Gatting 4.3–1–10–0; Brown 1–1–0–0.

Umpires: J. Birkenshaw and K. E. Palmer.

ESSEX v WARWICKSHIRE

At Chelmsford, May 25. Essex won by nine wickets. Toss: Warwickshire. With Small unable to play because of a thigh strain and Reeve having injured his shoulder while batting, Warwickshire lacked the resources to apply the brake to Gooch and Hardie as they put on 157 for the first wicket in 35 overs. Gooch went on to his second unbeaten Benson and Hedges Cup century of the season, hitting fourteen fours in all and receiving 167 deliveries. His Gold Award was his fourteenth, three more than any other player had received. Earlier, Warwickshire had always struggled to make progress against a tight attack, with Lloyd needing almost 54 overs for his 87.

Gold Award: G. A. Gooch.

Warwickshire

*T. A. Lloyd c Miller b Pringle 87
A. J. Moles c and b Lever 7
Asif Din c Gooch b Foster 5
A. I. Kallicharran c Foster b Pringle .. 42
†G. W. Humpage c Border b Pringle .. 14
P. A. Smith c Pringle b Gooch 16
D. A. Reeve not out 20
T. A. Merrick run out 0
A. R. K. Pierson not out 4
L-b 15, w 7, n-b 2 24

1/18 2/36 3/104 4/131 5/175 6/203 7/203 (7 wkts, 55 overs) 219

T. A. Munton and N. Gifford did not bat.

Bowling: Lever 11–1–58–1; Foster 11–2–38–1; Gooch 11–2–30–1; Pringle 11–0–56–3; Miller 11–3–22–0.

Essex

G. A. Gooch not out 117
B. R. Hardie c Humpage b Asif Din .. 53
P. J. Prichard not out 30
B 2, l-b 10, w 5, n-b 6 23

1/157 (1 wkt, 47.2 overs) 223

A. R. Border, D. R. Pringle, *K. W. R. Fletcher, A. W. Lilley, G. Miller, †D. E. East, N. A. Foster and J. K. Lever did not bat.

Bowling: Merrick 11–2–27–0; Munton 11–0–37–0; Smith 5.2–0–38–0; Gifford 7–1–33–0; Pierson 5–0–30–0; Moles 4–0–20–0; Asif Din 4–0–26–1.

Umpires: J. H. Hampshire and N. T. Plews.

GLAMORGAN v NOTTINGHAMSHIRE

At Cardiff, May 25, 26. Glamorgan won by six wickets. Toss: Nottinghamshire. Maynard, who had fractured the tip of the index finger on his left hand the previous week at Bournemouth while trying to take a catch in the outfield, played against medical advice and hit a match-winning 108 off 111 deliveries (one six, seven fours). With Hopkins, who was the sheet-anchor in the partnership, he added 187 in 35 overs after Glamorgan had lost two wickets in the first ten overs. In contrast to Glamorgan's start, Robinson and Broad had launched Nottinghamshire's innings with 108 at almost 4 runs an over once play began at 1.30 p.m. on the second scheduled day. But when caution took over against accurate bowling and top-class fielding, the innings lost its momentum. It was the first time Glamorgan had qualified for the semi-finals in the seventeen years of the competition.

Gold Award: M. P. Maynard.

Nottinghamshire

*R. T. Robinson c Metson b Thomas	60
B. C. Broad c Morris b Shastri	45
D. W. Randall run out	23
P. Johnson c Holmes b Barwick	37
J. D. Birch lbw b Derrick	4
F. D. Stephenson b Derrick	10
K. P. Evans c Derrick b Thomas	11
E. E. Hemmings run out	0
†C. W. Scott not out	5
K. E. Cooper not out	2
B 4, l-b 12, w 6, n-b 1	23
1/108 2/126 3/152 4/171 5/191 6/199 7/204 8/211 (8 wkts, 55 overs)	220

K. Saxelby did not bat.

Bowling: Thomas 11–1–34–2; Barwick 11–1–46–1; Derrick 11–0–39–2; Ontong 11–1–34–0; Shastri 11–0–51–1.

Glamorgan

A. R. Butcher b Cooper	1
J. A. Hopkins c Cooper b Birch	81
*H. Morris lbw b Cooper	9
M. P. Maynard c Hemmings b Evans	108
R. J. Shastri not out	0
G. C. Holmes not out	2
B 2, l-b 12, w 6	20
1/13 2/32 3/219 4/219 (4 wkts, 49.2 overs)	221

R. C. Ontong, J. G. Thomas, J. Derrick, †C. P. Metson and S. R. Barwick did not bat.

Bowling: Stephenson 9–0–27–0; Cooper 9–2–20–2; Saxelby 9–0–46–0; Hemmings 11–0–51–0; Evans 9.2–0–55–1; Birch 2–1–8–1.

Umpires: D. R. Shepherd and P. B. Wight.

WORCESTERSHIRE v HAMPSHIRE

At Worcester, May 25, 26, 27. Hampshire won by three wickets. Toss: Hampshire. An unbeaten 87 from Robin Smith, which he described as "the most satisfying innings of my life", steered Hampshire home against the odds on a devilish wicket. After rain had prevented a start until 4.50 p.m. on the second afternoon, Weston and Rhodes rescued Worcestershire from 67 for five with a stand of 69. Worcestershire were 111 for five overnight after 42 overs (M. J. Weston 34*, S. J. Rhodes 7*). Hampshire, in turn, slumped to 84 for six as the pitch provided extravagant assistance to Radford, Dilley and Newport. But when the score was 114, Smith, who was using his feet effectively to smother the vagaries of the bounce, was joined by Cowley for a match-winning stand of 56.

Gold Award: R. A. Smith.

Worcestershire

T. S. Curtis b Connor	3	N. V. Radford not out	9
G. J. Lord b Jefferies	6	G. R. Dilley b Connor	9
G. A. Hick c Jefferies b Ayling	6	A. P. Pridgeon c Parks b Jefferies	1
*P. A. Neale lbw b Andrew	26	B 1, l-b 9, w 13, n-b 4	27
S. J. O'Shaughnessy c Parks b Andrew	12		
M. J. Weston run out	50	1/12 2/14 3/29 (54.2 overs)	169
†S. J. Rhodes lbw b Jefferies	16	4/65 5/67 6/136	
P. J. Newport c and b Jefferies	4	7/145 8/147 9/168	

Bowling: Jefferies 10.2–0–34–4; Connor 11–1–33–2; Andrew 11–0–33–2; Ayling 11–3–36–1; Cowley 11–1–23–0.

Hampshire

V. P. Terry lbw b Radford	5	S. T. Jefferies c Hick b Radford	7
C. L. Smith c Hick b Newport	10	N. G. Cowley not out	18
*M. C. J. Nicholas b Radford	5	B 4, l-b 8, w 12, n-b 1	25
R. A. Smith not out	87		
D. R. Turner c Rhodes b Dilley	11	1/5 2/20 3/38 (7 wkts, 53.1 overs)	170
J. R. Ayling c Weston b Dilley	1	4/75 5/83	
†R. J. Parks c Hick b Weston	1	6/84 7/114	

C. A. Connor and S. J. W. Andrew did not bat.

Bowling: Dilley 11–1–36–2; Radford 11–3–29–3; Newport 11–0–40–1; Pridgeon 11–4–22–0; Weston 8.1–0–27–1; O'Shaughnessy 1–0–4–0.

Umpires: H. D. Bird and B. Leadbeater.

SEMI-FINALS

ESSEX v HAMPSHIRE

At Chelmsford, June 8, 9. Hampshire won by seven wickets. Toss: Hampshire. Terry, with his first century in the competition, was the guiding light as Hampshire reached a one-day final at Lord's for the first time. He scored 109 from 174 balls, hitting nine fours, and his side were just 7 runs short of victory when Pringle dismissed him. The Essex batsmen had never been able to break free against an accurate attack supported by fine work in the field. Terry and Chris Smith responded with an opening stand of 118 in 33 overs before rain ended the day's play with Hampshire 192 for one from 46 overs (V. P. Terry 88*, D. R. Turner 28*). Six hours were then lost on the second day before Hampshire could pop the champagne corks in celebration.

Gold Award: V. P. Terry.

Essex

G. A. Gooch b Ayling	41	A. W. Lilley b Connor	29
B. R. Hardie lbw b Cowley	40	N. A. Foster not out	9
P. J. Prichard c Jefferies b Cowley	14	B 1, l-b 12, w 7, n-b 3	23
A. R. Border b Connor	38		
D. R. Pringle b Jefferies	4	1/88 2/92 3/125 (6 wkts, 55 overs)	238
*K. W. R. Fletcher not out	40	4/137 5/169 6/228	

†D. E. East, T. D. Topley and J. K. Lever did not bat.

Bowling: Connor 11–1–41–2; Andrew 11–2–48–0; Jefferies 11–0–63–1; Ayling 11–2–42–1; Cowley 11–0–31–2.

Hampshire

V. P. Terry lbw b Pringle 109	*M. C. J. Nicholas not out 1
C. L. Smith c East b Gooch 56	L-b 15, w 6, n-b 1 22
D. R. Turner c East b Foster 31	—
R. A. Smith not out 20	1/118 2/197 3/232 (3 wkts, 53.4 overs) 239

J. R. Ayling, †R. J. Parks, S. T. Jefferies, N. G. Cowley, C. A. Connor and S. J. W. Andrew did not bat.

Bowling: Foster 11–4–30–1; Lever 10–1–36–0; Topley 11–0–56–0; Gooch 11–0–46–1; Pringle 10.4–0–56–1.

Umpires: B. Dudleston and A. G. T. Whitehead.

GLAMORGAN v DERBYSHIRE

At Swansea, June 8, 9, 10. Derbyshire won by 14 runs. Toss: Glamorgan. An absorbing match took three days to complete because, after rain had delayed the start and bad light had prevented a completion on Wednesday, the second day was lost entirely. On Friday, play could not begin until three o'clock, when in bright sunshine Glamorgan resumed at 130 for five (R. C. Ontong 14*, G. C. Holmes 5*). They were to find the task of scoring at just over 7 runs an over for twelve overs beyond them, Holding finishing off their challenge by taking three wickets for 8 runs in eight deliveries. The bizarre dismissal of Maynard on the first day had dashed the home side's hopes. Butcher, with some lovely shots, and Hopkins had set Glamorgan off to a brisk start with 58 in eighteen overs, and Maynard had struck four boundaries in his 22 when, as he played a ball from Holding, his helmet fell on to his stumps. Ontong bowled his off-breaks particularly accurately after Derbyshire had been asked to bat on a slow, turning pitch. There was a splendid innings by Barnett until he was run out by Thomas's throw from long leg, and Roberts contributed a valuable 44, but in the end Derbyshire were most indebted to Holding, who finished with his best figures in the competition.

Gold Award: M. A. Holding.

Derbyshire

*K. J. Barnett run out 43	P. G. Newman not out 15
P. D. Bowler st Metson b Derrick 23	D. E. Malcolm not out 0
B. Roberts c Metson b Derrick 44	
J. E. Morris b Derrick 19	B 1, l-b 4, w 13, n-b 1 19
S. C. Goldsmith c Shastri b Barwick . . 25	—
†B. J. M. Maher b Barwick 1	1/50 2/88 3/131 (8 wkts, 55 overs) 217
M. A. Holding c Hopkins b Thomas . . 15	4/140 5/143 6/174
A. E. Warner c Morris b Barwick 13	7/197 8/200

O. H. Mortensen did not bat.

Bowling: Thomas 11–0–54–1; Barwick 11–3–45–3; Ontong 11–1–19–0; Derrick 11–0–52–3; Shastri 11–2–42–0.

Glamorgan

A. R. Butcher lbw b Mortensen 31	J. Derrick b Holding 4
J. A. Hopkins b Bowler 18	†C. P. Metson c Bowler b Holding 9
M. P. Maynard hit wkt b Holding 22	S. R. Barwick not out 0
*H. Morris c Maher b Holding 3	L-b 16, w 11, n-b 1 28
R. J. Shastri c Holding b Malcolm 16	—
R. C. Ontong c Roberts b Warner 26	1/58 2/70 3/83 (54.2 overs) 203
G. C. Holmes c Goldsmith b Newman . 28	4/98 5/116 6/167
J. G. Thomas c Goldsmith b Holding . . 18	7/173 8/187 9/203

Bowling: Holding 10.2–1–31–5; Malcolm 11–1–25–1; Newman 8–0–36–1; Mortensen 11–0–28–1; Bowler 3–0–15–1; Warner 11–1–52–1.

Umpires: B. Leadbeater and B. J. Meyer.

FINAL

DERBYSHIRE v HAMPSHIRE

At Lord's, July 9. Hampshire won by seven wickets. A spell of four wickets for 1 run in eight balls by Jefferies, helped by some inept batting against the in-swinging ball, decided the match in the first hour. And when Maher, pulling across the line, and Holding, driving the ball straight to Turner in front of the Pavilion, got themselves out, Derbyshire went to lunch at 80 for six. Much depended on Morris, who had been dropped first ball by Chris Smith at slip, a low, hard chance to his left which would have given Jefferies a hat-trick. The South African, bowling left arm over the wicket, had bowled Barnett, driving, off his pads with the last ball of the sixth over and had Bowler caught off bat and pad with the first ball of the eighth over. Nicholas had just positioned himself at forward short leg, and he took a second catch there when Roberts propped forward later in the same over. Winning the toss was proving to be a distinct advantage to Hampshire, but it was Jefferies's ability to swing the ball, as much as the morning conditions, which was the decisive factor. Morris (79 balls) played well until, having seen Derbyshire to 100, he needlessly sought a second run and was beaten by Cowley's throw from long leg. Jefferies came back to take his fifth wicket and so return the best figures in a Benson and Hedges Cup final; he conceded only 9 runs off the bat, and one of those was from the missed hat-trick catch. Connor, having begun his eighth over with three wides, brought the innings to a close with successive deliveries.

Derbyshire's bowlers, with nothing to defend, had to attack. Barnett set four slips and a gully for Holding and Malcolm, but Chris Smith (51 balls) and Nicholas (88 balls) could afford to be patient. There was a delightful innings, full of powerful strokes, from Robin Smith (27 balls, seven fours), and a magnificent tumbling catch to dismiss him by Goldsmith, who sprinted 40 to 50 yards from long leg to hold a top-edged hook. Light rain at 4.50 p.m. threatened to hold up Hampshire, but ten minutes later, with the scores level, umpire Constant no-balled Warner. Hampshire, previously the only county never to have played in a Lord's final, had won there at their first attempt.

Gold Award: S. T. Jefferies.

Attendance: 18,476 (excluding members); *receipts* £338,989.

Derbyshire

*K. J. Barnett b Jefferies	13
P. D. Bowler c Nicholas b Jefferies	4
B. Roberts c Nicholas b Jefferies	0
J. E. Morris run out	42
S. C. Goldsmith lbw b Jefferies	0
†B. J. M. Maher b Ayling	8
M. A. Holding c Turner b Cowley	7
P. G. Newman b Connor	10
A. E. Warner b Jefferies	4
O. H. Mortensen not out	0
D. E. Malcolm b Connor	0
L-b 14, w 12, n-b 3	29
1/27 (1) 2/28 (2) 3/29 (3) 4/32 (5) 5/71 (6) 6/80 (7) 7/101 (4) 8/114 (9) 9/117 (8) 10/117 (11) (46.3 overs)	117

Bowling: Connor 7.3–1–27–2; Jefferies 10–3–13–5; Andrew 9–0–25–0; Ayling 9–2–21–1; Cowley 11–2–17–1.

Hampshire

V. P. Terry c Roberts b Malcolm	2
C. L. Smith c Maher b Mortensen	20
*M. C. J. Nicholas not out	35
R. A. Smith c Goldsmith b Warner	38
D. R. Turner not out	7
L-b 8, w 3, n-b 5	16
1/10 (1) 2/44 (2) 3/90 (4) (3 wkts, 31.5 overs)	118

J. R. Ayling, S. T. Jefferies, †R. J. Parks, N. G. Cowley, C. A. Connor and S. J. W. Andrew did not bat.

Bowling: Holding 11–2–36–0; Malcolm 7–2–25–1; Newman 3–1–11–0; Mortensen 5–1–19–1; Warner 5.5–0–19–1.

Umpires: D. J. Constant and N. T. Plews.

BENSON AND HEDGES CUP RECORDS

Highest individual scores: 198 not out, G. A. Gooch, Essex v Sussex, Hove, 1982; 173 not out, C. G. Greenidge, Hampshire v Minor Counties (South), Amersham, 1973; 158 not out, B. F. Davison, Leicestershire v Warwickshire, Coventry, 1972; 155 not out, M. D. Crowe, Somerset v Hampshire, Southampton, 1987; 154 not out, M. J. Procter, Gloucestershire v Somerset, Taunton, 1972. (158 hundreds have been scored in the competition.)

Highest totals in 55 overs: 350 for three, Essex v Oxford & Cambridge Univs, Chelmsford, 1979; 333 for four, Essex v Oxford & Cambridge Univs, Chelmsford, 1985; 327 for four, Leicestershire v Warwickshire, Coventry, 1972; 327 for two, Essex v Sussex, Hove, 1982; 321 for one, Hampshire v Minor Counties (South), Amersham, 1973. *In the final:* 290 for six, Essex v Surrey, 1979.

Highest total by a side batting second and winning: 291 for five (53.5 overs), Warwickshire v Lancashire, Manchester, 1981. *In the final:* 244 for six (55 overs), Yorkshire v Northamptonshire, 1987.

Highest total by a side batting second and losing: 300 (55 overs), Northamptonshire v Derbyshire, Derby, 1987. *In the final:* 255 (51.4 overs), Surrey v Essex, 1979.

Highest match aggregate: 601 for thirteen wickets, Somerset (307-6) v Gloucestershire (294-7), Taunton, 1982.

Lowest totals: 56 in 26.2 overs, Leicestershire v Minor Counties, Wellington, 1982; 59 in 34 overs, Oxford & Cambridge Univs v Glamorgan, Cambridge, 1983; 60 in 26 overs, Sussex v Middlesex, Hove, 1978; 62 in 26.5 overs, Gloucestershire v Hampshire, Bristol, 1975. *In the final:* 117 in 46.3 overs, Derbyshire v Hampshire, 1988.

Shortest completed innings: 21.4 overs (156), Surrey v Sussex, Hove, 1988.

Record partnership for each wicket

241 for 1st	S. M. Gavaskar and B. C. Rose, Somerset v Kent at Canterbury ...	1980
285* for 2nd	C. G. Greenidge and D. R. Turner, Hampshire v Minor Counties (South) at Amersham ...	1973
269* for 3rd	P. M. Roebuck and M. D. Crowe, Somerset v Hampshire at Southampton ...	1987
184* for 4th	D. Lloyd and B. W. Reidy, Lancashire v Derby at Chesterfield ...	1980
160 for 5th	A. J. Lamb and D. J. Capel, Northamptonshire v Leicestershire at Northampton ...	1986
121 for 6th	P. A. Neale and S. J. Rhodes, Worcestershire v Yorkshire at Worcester	1988
149* for 7th	J. D. Love and C. M. Old, Yorkshire v Scotland at Bradford ...	1981
109 for 8th	R. E. East and N. Smith, Essex v Northamptonshire at Chelmsford.	1977
83 for 9th	P. G. Newman and M. A. Holding, Derbyshire v Nottinghamshire at Nottingham ...	1985
80* for 10th	D. L. Bairstow and M. Johnson, Yorkshire v Derbyshire at Derby ..	1981

Best bowling: Seven for 12, W. W. Daniel, Middlesex v Minor Counties (East), Ipswich, 1978; seven for 22, J. R. Thomson, Middlesex v Hampshire, Lord's, 1981; seven for 32, R. G. D. Willis, Warwickshire v Yorkshire, Birmingham, 1981. *In the final:* Five for 13, S. T. Jefferies, Hampshire v Derbyshire, 1988.

Hat-tricks (10): G. D. McKenzie, Leicestershire v Worcestershire, Worcester, 1972; K. Higgs, Leicestershire v Surrey in the final, Lord's, 1974; A. A. Jones, Middlesex v Essex, Lord's, 1977; M. J. Procter, Gloucestershire v Hampshire, Southampton, 1977; W. Larkins, Northamptonshire v Oxford & Cambridge Univs, Northampton, 1980; E. A. Moseley, Glamorgan v Kent, Cardiff, 1981; G. C. Small, Warwickshire v Leicestershire, Leicester, 1984; N. A. Mallender, Somerset v Combined Univs, Taunton, 1987; W. K. M. Benjamin, Leicestershire v Nottinghamshire, Leicester, 1987; A. R. C. Fraser, Middlesex v Sussex, Lord's, 1988.

WINNERS 1972-88

1972 LEICESTERSHIRE beat Yorkshire by five wickets.
1973 KENT beat Worcestershire by 39 runs.
1974 SURREY beat Leicestershire by 27 runs.
1975 LEICESTERSHIRE beat Middlesex by five wickets.
1976 KENT beat Worcestershire by 43 runs.
1977 GLOUCESTERSHIRE beat Kent by 64 runs.
1978 KENT beat Derbyshire by six wickets.
1979 ESSEX beat Surrey by 35 runs.
1980 NORTHAMPTONSHIRE beat Essex by 6 runs.
1981 SOMERSET beat Surrey by seven wickets.
1982 SOMERSET beat Nottinghamshire by nine wickets.
1983 MIDDLESEX beat Essex by 4 runs.
1984 LANCASHIRE beat Warwickshire by six wickets.
1985 LEICESTERSHIRE beat Essex by five wickets.
1986 MIDDLESEX beat Kent by 2 runs.
1987 YORKSHIRE beat Northamptonshire, having taken more wickets with the scores tied.
1988 HAMPSHIRE beat Derbyshire by seven wickets.

WINS BY OXFORD AND CAMBRIDGE UNIVERSITIES

1973 OXFORD beat Northamptonshire at Northampton by two wickets.
1975 OXFORD & CAMBRIDGE beat Worcestershire at Cambridge by 66 runs.
1975 OXFORD & CAMBRIDGE beat Northamptonshire at Oxford by three wickets.
1976 OXFORD & CAMBRIDGE beat Yorkshire at Barnsley by seven wickets.
1984 OXFORD & CAMBRIDGE beat Gloucestershire at Bristol by 27 runs.

WINS BY MINOR COUNTIES AND SCOTLAND

1980 MINOR COUNTIES beat Gloucestershire at Chippenham by 3 runs.
1981 MINOR COUNTIES beat Hampshire at Southampton by 3 runs.
1982 MINOR COUNTIES beat Leicestershire at Wellington by 131 runs.
1986 SCOTLAND beat Lancashire at Perth by 3 runs.
1987 MINOR COUNTIES beat Glamorgan at Oxford (Christ Church) by seven wickets.

A SUITABLE CASE FOR COMPO

Five consecutive run-outs off the last five balls of the final over turned round the fortunes of Hatfield Town and Barnly Dun in their Doncaster and District Premier Division match on May 21, 1988. With seven balls remaining, Hatfield Town were 160 for four in reply to Barnly Dun's 166 for nine off 44 overs. Seven balls later they were all out for 164, leaving Barnly Dun the winners by 2 runs.

REFUGE ASSURANCE LEAGUE, 1988

Worcestershire retained the Refuge Assurance League title, having been unbeaten in their last ten games and taken 38 points from a possible 40. They went into their final match with Lancashire and Middlesex two points behind them, but it was their closest rivals, not they, who faltered. Worcestershire beat Warwickshire convincingly by ten wickets; Lancashire and Middlesex both lost, allowing Gloucestershire, who won at Chelmsford, to leapfrog over them from fourth place to second. All three had 44 points, but Middlesex had won one game less than the other two and Gloucestershire had won one away game more than Lancashire.

The introduction of a new competition, the Refuge Assurance Cup, to be contested by the first four counties in the League, gave an added dimension to the Sunday competition. It also meant an earlier start and finish to the League programme to accommodate the Cup semi-finals and final.

Worcestershire, in contrast to their start in the County Championship, began their defence of the Sunday League with defeats by Lancashire and Nottinghamshire. After that, however, they lost only to Middlesex, at Lord's on June 5. That win put unbeaten Middlesex on top of the table ahead of Lancashire and the previous leaders, Surrey, and they stayed there for eleven weeks until Worcestershire displaced them on August 21 after the penultimate round of matches. Middlesex could look back on four games lost to the weather which cost them a possible eight points.

Continued over

REFUGE ASSURANCE LEAGUE

		P	*W*	*L*	*T*	*NR*	*Pts*	*Sixes*	*4W*	*Away Wins*
1	Worcestershire (1)	15	12	3	0	1	50	27	6	6
2	Gloucestershire (3)	14	10	4	0	2	44	31	2	4
3	Lancashire (9)	15	10	4	0	2	44	25	2	3
4	Middlesex (10)	15	9	3	0	4	44	24	1	3
5	Surrey (7)	15	8	5	1	2	38	28	3	4
	Glamorgan (14)	15	8	5	1	2	38	30	2	4
7	Kent (6)	14	7	6	0	3	34	27	3	3
8	Yorkshire (12)	15	7	7	0	2	32	29	5	3
9	Hampshire (7)	15	7	8	0	1	30	11	3	3
10	Essex (14)	15	6	8	1	1	28	24	3	2
	Warwickshire (17)	14	6	8	0	2	28	14	3	2
12	Somerset (4)	15	6	9	0	1	26	23	1	3
	Derbyshire (5)	16	5	8	1	2	26	30	1	3
14	Northamptonshire (10)	14	4	9	0	3	22	23	0	2
	Sussex (14)	15	4	9	2	1	22	15	1	1
	Leicestershire (12)	14	4	9	0	3	22	13	3	1
17	Nottinghamshire (2)	14	3	11	0	2	16	13	1	1

1987 positions in brackets.

When two or more counties finish with an equal number of points for any of the first four places, the positions are decided by the most wins or, if still equal, the most away wins.

No play was possible in the following eleven matches: May 8 – Leicestershire v Kent. May 29 – Gloucestershire v Warwickshire. July 3 – Kent v Nottinghamshire, Northamptonshire v Lancashire, Somerset v Essex, Surrey v Warwickshire, Sussex v Hampshire, Worcestershire v Gloucestershire. July 10 – Northamptonshire v Yorkshire, Nottinghamshire v Leicestershire. July 17 – Middlesex v Glamorgan.

Lancashire, like Middlesex, took 28 points from their first nine games, but two consecutive defeats kept them out of the top four from July 17 to August 7. Gloucestershire, third in 1987, improved one place to maintain their marked improvement in the 40-overs game. The strength of their batting was such that their captain, Graveney, went to the crease only twice. Essex, Surrey, Kent and Yorkshire all featured at some stage of the season, only to fall from contention before the competition reached the final rounds.

Worcestershire's success reflected the team's strength in all departments. Hick top-scored for them with 512 runs (average 42.67) and Curtis was not far behind with 504 (average 45.82). Pridgeon, who played in fewer than half of their Championship matches, bowled impressively in the Refuge Assurance League, taking 26 wickets at 12.58 apiece, while Rhodes, with 26 catches and 3 stumpings, broke the record for dismissals in a season, 28, set by J. T. Murray of Middlesex in 1975. In addition, D'Oliveira's 31-ball 50 against Nottinghamshire earned him the BBC award for the fastest televised half-century.

Turner, of Hampshire, was the season's leading batsman; his 573 runs put him third in the Sunday League's career list with 6,429. Against Kent, he became the first left-hander to pass 6,000 runs and Hampshire became the first county to total 50,000 runs in the League. Greig, Surrey's captain, was the season's leading bowler with 28 wickets. Stephen and Mark Waugh, from New South Wales, became the first brothers to register hundreds in the League. Mark, playing for Essex, became the first player to hit a Sunday League hundred on début, 103 against Nottinghamshire, and Stephen's 109 not out for Somerset against Northamptonshire was the 300th century in the Sunday competition. Zaheer Abbas, of Gloucestershire, scored the 100th in 1976 and V. P. Terry, of Hampshire, the 200th in 1983. Another Australian, Matthews of Lancashire, took a wicket with his first ball in the League, dismissing Curtis of Worcestershire to emulate a feat previously achieved only by C. J. Armishaw and E. J. Barlow, both of Derbyshire. The Yorkshire wicket-keeper, Bairstow, overtook R. W. Taylor's 236 dismissals when he caught the Hampshire captain, Nicholas, at Middlesbrough.

DISTRIBUTION OF PRIZEMONEY

The total prizemoney was £77,450.

£21,000 and Refuge Assurance Trophy: WORCESTERSHIRE.
£10,500 to runners-up: GLOUCESTERSHIRE.
£4,750 for third place: LANCASHIRE.
£2,750 for fourth place: MIDDLESEX.
£275 each match to the winners – shared if tied or no result.

Batting award: £400 to R. J. Shastri (Glamorgan) who hit fourteen sixes in the season.

Other leading six-hitters:

9 – R. O. Butcher (Middlesex), S. C. Goldsmith (Derbyshire), G. A. Hick (Worcestershire).
8 – M. W. Alleyne (Gloucestershire).
7 – W. Larkins (Northamptonshire), A. A. Metcalfe (Yorkshire), D. A. Reeve (Warwickshire), P. W. Romaines (Gloucestershire), A. J. Stewart (Surrey), D. J. Wild (Northamptonshire).
6 – D. Byas (Yorkshire), N. H. Fairbrother (Lancashire), M. A. Holding (Derbyshire), A. W. Lilley (Essex), M. A. Lynch (Surrey), D. W. Randall (Nottinghamshire), N. R. Taylor (Kent), S. R. Waugh (Somerset).

5 – P. Bainbridge (Gloucestershire), P. Carrick (Yorkshire), C. S. Cowdrey (Kent), G. R. Cowdrey (Kent), D. E. East (Essex), R. M. Ellison (Kent), A. N. Hayhurst (Lancashire), P. A. Neale (Worcestershire), C. J. Richards (Surrey), M. Watkinson (Lancashire), A. J. Wright (Gloucestershire).

A total of 387 sixes was hit in the League in 1988.

Fastest televised fifty: £250 to D. B. D'Oliveira (Worcestershire) – 31 balls v Nottinghamshire at Worcester on May 1.

Bowling award: £400 to S. D. Fletcher (Yorkshire) who took four wickets or more in an innings three times.

P. J. Bakker (Hampshire), A. P. Pridgeon (Worcestershire), D. A. Reeve (Warwickshire) and T. D. Topley (Essex) each took four wickets or more in an innings twice.

S. J. W. Andrew (Hampshire), P. Carrick (Yorkshire), A. R. Clarke (Sussex), S. T. Clarke (Surrey), C. S. Cowdrey (Kent), K. M. Curran (Gloucestershire), P. A. J. DeFreitas (Leicestershire), J. Derrick (Glamorgan), G. J. F. Ferris (Leicestershire), N. A. Foster (Essex), A. H. Gray (Surrey), V. S. Greene (Gloucestershire), I. A. Greig (Surrey), P. J. Hartley (Yorkshire), A. N. Hayhurst (Lancashire), G. A. Hick (Worcestershire), M. A. Holding (Derbyshire), C. C. Lewis (Leicestershire), S. M. McEwan (Worcestershire), N. A. Mallender (Somerset), C. Penn (Kent), R. F. Pienaar (Kent), N. V. Radford (Worcestershire), G. C. Small (Warwickshire), F. D. Stephenson (Nottinghamshire), J. G. Thomas (Glamorgan), M. Watkinson (Lancashire), M. J. Weston (Worcestershire) and N. F. Williams (Middlesex) each took four wickets or more in an innings once.

DERBYSHIRE

DERBYSHIRE v LEICESTERSHIRE

At Derby, April 24. Derbyshire won by nine wickets. Toss: Derbyshire.

Leicestershire

L. Potter c Maher b Newman	2
N. E. Briers st Maher b Bowler	42
*D. I. Gower c Maher b Mortensen	5
J. J. Whitaker b Warner	4
P. Willey c Barnett b Bowler	27
T. J. Boon c Maher b Mortensen	22
P. A. J. DeFreitas c Roberts b Holding	37
C. C. Lewis not out	14
†P. Whitticase b Warner	1
J. P. Agnew run out	3
L. B. Taylor b Warner	1
L-b 7, w 3	10
1/6 2/13 3/29 4/81 5/91 6/146 7/148 8/153 9/156 (37.3 overs)	168

Bowling: Newman 8–1–23–1; Mortensen 8–0–34–2; Finney 4–0–16–0; Warner 5.3–0–21–3; Holding 7–0–38–1; Bowler 5–0–29–2.

Derbyshire

*K. J. Barnett not out	77
P. D. Bowler b Taylor	32
B. Roberts not out	47
B 2, l-b 7, w 4, n-b 2	15
1/53 (1 wkt, 39.3 overs)	171

J. E. Morris, †B. J. M. Maher, S. C. Goldsmith, P. G. Newman, A. E. Warner, M. A. Holding, O. H. Mortensen and R. J. Finney did not bat.

Bowling: Agnew 8–0–26–0; DeFreitas 7.3–1–22–0; Lewis 8–0–39–0; Willey 8–0–29–0; Taylor 8–0–46–1.

Umpires: H. D. Bird and J. H. Hampshire.

At Leeds, May 1. YORKSHIRE v DERBYSHIRE. No result.

DERBYSHIRE v ESSEX

At Derby, May 8. Essex won by 59 runs. Toss: Derbyshire.

Essex

G. A. Gooch b Holding	54	J. P. Stephenson not out	8
B. R. Hardie run out	64		
P. J. Prichard c Maher b Newman	18	B 4, l-b 8, w 3, n-b 2	17
D. R. Pringle lbw b Newman	0		
*K. W. R. Fletcher b Newman	11	1/87 2/129 3/129 (5 wkts, 40 overs)	201
A. W. Lilley not out	29	4/147 5/178	

G. Miller, †D. E. East, T. D. Topley and J. K. Lever did not bat.

Bowling: Mortensen 8–0–35–0; Jean-Jacques 6–0–35–0; Newman 8–1–30–3; Warner 8–0–38–0; Holding 8–1–43–1; Bowler 2–0–8–0.

Derbyshire

*K. J. Barnett c East b Pringle	1	P. G. Newman b Pringle	8
P. D. Bowler c Lever b Topley	7	M. Jean-Jacques b Topley	7
B. Roberts b Topley	8	O. H. Mortensen lbw b Topley	2
M. A. Holding c Stephenson b Miller	14		
J. E. Morris run out	39	L-b 3, w 8	11
S. C. Goldsmith c Pringle b Topley	7		
A. E. Warner lbw b Miller	11	1/1 2/17 3/18 4/38 5/54 (34.4 overs)	142
†B. J. M. Maher not out	27	6/84 7/100 8/121 9/138	

Bowling: Lever 6–0–15–0; Pringle 6–0–19–2; Miller 8–0–44–2; Topley 7.4–0–25–5; Gooch 7–0–36–0.

Umpires: J. C. Balderstone and A. G. T. Whitehead.

At Newport, May 22. DERBYSHIRE lost to GLAMORGAN by 25 runs.

DERBYSHIRE v NOTTINGHAMSHIRE

At Derby, May 29. Derbyshire won by nine wickets after being set a revised target of 93 from twenty overs, rain during Nottinghamshire's innings having earlier caused the match to be reduced to 34 overs a side. Toss: Derbyshire.

Nottinghamshire

B. C. Broad c Roberts b Mortensen	20	K. P. Evans not out	1
*R. T. Robinson lbw b Warner	25	†C. W. Scott not out	1
D. W. Randall b Holding	59	L-b 9, w 3	12
J. D. Birch lbw b Holding	4		
P. Pollard run out	25	1/43 2/63 3/70 (7 wkts, 34 overs)	158
F. D. Stephenson c and b Holding	7	4/141 5/152	
E. E. Hemmings b Holding	4	6/154 7/157	

K. E. Cooper and K. Saxelby did not bat.

Bowling: Newman 7–0–38–0; Mortensen 8–0–29–1; Bowler 4–0–18–0; Warner 8–0–42–1; Holding 7–0–22–4.

Derbyshire

*K. J. Barnett c Birch b Stephenson	38
J. E. Morris not out	50
B. Roberts not out	0
B 4, l-b 1	5
1/86 (1 wkt, 16 overs)	93

P. D. Bowler, S. C. Goldsmith, †B. J. M. Maher, M. A. Holding, A. E. Warner, P. G. Newman, R. Sharma and O. H. Mortensen did not bat.

Bowling: Stephenson 5–1–20–1; Cooper 4–0–22–0; Saxelby 3–0–20–0; Evans 2–0–15–0; Hemmings 2–0–11–0.

Umpires: D. J. Constant and D. G. L. Evans.

At Horsham, June 5. DERBYSHIRE beat SUSSEX by 5 runs.

DERBYSHIRE v GLOUCESTERSHIRE

At Heanor, June 12. Gloucestershire won by 42 runs. Toss: Gloucestershire.

Gloucestershire

A. W. Stovold c Maher b Sharma	7	†R. C. Russell c sub b Warner	20
C. W. J. Athey lbw b Roberts	55	V. S. Greene not out	2
*P. Bainbridge c Goldsmith b Roberts	63		
K. M. Curran run out	20	L-b 9, w 10	19
J. W. Lloyds c Barnett b Newman	8		—
P. W. Romaines c Barnett b Roberts	1	1/17 2/137 3/142 (8 wkts, 40 overs)	258
A. J. Wright lbw b Holding	14	4/158 5/161 6/183	
M. W. Alleyne not out	49	7/187 8/243	

K. B. S. Jarvis did not bat.

Bowling: Sharma 4–0–19–1; Mortensen 6–0–24–0; Newman 8–0–29–1; Warner 8–0–82–1; Holding 8–0–40–1; Roberts 6–1–55–3.

Derbyshire

*K. J. Barnett b Alleyne	33	P. G. Newman b Curran	7
P. D. Bowler c and b Alleyne	28	†B. J. M. Maher c Russell b Curran	0
B. Roberts run out	53	O. H. Mortensen not out	1
J. E. Morris run out	0	L-b 10, w 5	15
S. C. Goldsmith b Alleyne	14		—
M. A. Holding c Russell b Bainbridge	21	1/59 2/73 3/73 (36.5 overs)	216
A. E. Warner c Jarvis b Bainbridge	14	4/129 5/157 6/162	
R. Sharma b Curran	30	7/192 8/214 9/215	

Bowling: Jarvis 8–0–47–0; Curran 6.5–0–54–3; Greene 6–0–27–0; Bainbridge 8–0–42–2; Alleyne 8–1–36–3.

Umpires: J. Birkenshaw and N. T. Plews.

DERBYSHIRE v WORCESTERSHIRE

At Knypersley, June 19. Worcestershire won by 69 runs. Toss: Derbyshire. The fifth-wicket stand of 123 between Neale and Weston was a record for Worcestershire in the Sunday League, while the partnership of 40 between Maher and Jean-Jacques was a record for Derbyshire's tenth wicket in all one-day cricket.

Worcestershire

T. S. Curtis b Jean-Jacques	2	N. V. Radford not out	21
†S. J. Rhodes b Warner	36	S. M. McEwan c Sharma b Roberts	0
G. A. Hick c Roberts b Warner	18	A. P. Pridgeon not out	2
D. B. D'Oliveira c and b Warner	0	L-b 7, w 5, n-b 4	16
*P. A. Neale c Goldsmith b Holding	91		—
M. J. Weston c Warner b Newman	72	1/3 2/38 3/39 (9 wkts, 40 overs)	280
S. J. O'Shaughnessy c Warner b Roberts	21	4/76 5/199 6/240	
P. J. Newport c and b Roberts	1	7/249 8/268 9/269	

Bowling: Newman 8–0–63–1; Jean-Jacques 8–0–52–1; Warner 8–1–34–3; Holding 8–0–46–1; Sharma 2–0–20–0; Roberts 4–0–35–3; Goldsmith 2–0–23–0.

Derbyshire

*K. J. Barnett run out 30
P. D. Bowler lbw b Weston 4
B. Roberts c Rhodes b Radford 32
J. E. Morris c Curtis b Pridgeon 47
S. C. Goldsmith c Weston b McEwan . 19
M. A. Holding b McEwan 3
A. E. Warner lbw b McEwan 16
†B. J. M. Maher not out 36
R. Sharma c Rhodes b McEwan 0
P. G. Newman b Pridgeon 1
M. Jean-Jacques c Rhodes b Newport . 13
L-b 6, w 4 10

1/5 2/65 3/77 (36.4 overs) 211
4/105 5/111 6/135
7/165 8/166 9/171

Bowling: Weston 5–0–36–1; Newport 4.4–0–21–1; Pridgeon 8–0–43–2; Radford 6–0–28–1; McEwan 8–0–37–4; O'Shaughnessy 5–0–40–0.

Umpires: R. Julian and B. J. Meyer.

At The Oval, June 26. DERBYSHIRE tied with SURREY.

DERBYSHIRE v MIDDLESEX

At Repton School, July 3. No result. Toss: Middlesex.

Derbyshire

*K. J. Barnett b Cowans 6
P. D. Bowler b Fraser 0
B. Roberts b Fraser 14
J. E. Morris b Cowans 0
S. C. Goldsmith b Hughes 61
M. A. Holding c Sykes b Hughes 1
A. E. Warner c Brown b Fraser 5
†B. J. M. Maher c Butcher b Sykes ... 9
P. G. Newman b Sykes 15
S. J. Base c Hughes b Needham 0
O. H. Mortensen not out 0
B 2, l-b 6, w 11 19

1/0 2/9 3/10 (37.1 overs) 130
4/95 5/95 6/97
7/102 8/124 9/126

Bowling: Cowans 7–1–12–2; Fraser 8–2–8–3; Hughes 8–0–29–2; Slack 3–0–25–0; Sykes 6.1–0–26–2; Carr 1–0–13–0; Needham 4–0–9–1.

Middlesex

W. N. Slack not out 13
J. D. Carr not out 15
L-b 2, w 2 4

(no wkt, 10.2 overs) 32

†K. R. Brown, *R. O. Butcher, M. A. Roseberry, J. F. Sykes, A. Needham, S. P. Hughes, A. R. C. Fraser, I. J. F. Hutchinson and N. G. Cowans did not bat.

Bowling: Newman 2–0–11–0; Mortensen 5–1–10–0; Warner 3.2–0–9–0.

Umpires: J. W. Holder and K. J. Lyons.

At Portsmouth, July 24. DERBYSHIRE lost to HAMPSHIRE by four wickets.

DERBYSHIRE v WARWICKSHIRE

At Derby, July 31. Warwickshire won by 8 runs. Toss: Derbyshire.

Warwickshire

*T. A. Lloyd b Base	29	D. A. Thorne not out	59
†G. W. Humpage c Maher b Base	25	B 1, l-b 5, n-b 2	8
Asif Din c Mortensen b Roberts	38		
D. A. Banks not out	51	1/42 2/84 3/115 (3 wkts, 40 overs)	210

P. A. Smith, D. A. Reeve, G. C. Small, T. A. Munton, A. A. Donald and A. R. K. Pierson did not bat.

Bowling: Newman 8–0–65–0; Mortensen 5–0–19–0; Base 8–1–20–2; Griffith 8–0–37–0; Roberts 4–0–15–1; Bowler 7–0–48–0.

Derbyshire

J. G. Wright c Donald b Smith	15	F. A. Griffith not out	4
*K. J. Barnett c Humpage b Small	74		
†B. J. M. Maher b Small	27	B 1, l-b 7, w 9, n-b 2	19
J. E. Morris run out	37		
B. Roberts c Smith b Small	4	1/42 2/130 3/137 (5 wkts, 40 overs)	202
S. C. Goldsmith not out	22	4/155 5/184	

P. D. Bowler, P. G. Newman, S. J. Base and O. H. Mortensen did not bat.

Bowling: Munton 7–0–36–0; Donald 8–0–51–0; Smith 5–0–17–1; Pierson 4–0–16–0; Reeve 8–0–48–0; Small 8–0–26–3.

Umpires: K. J. Lyons and P. B. Wight.

At Weston-super-Mare, August 7. DERBYSHIRE beat SOMERSET by 2 runs.

DERBYSHIRE v KENT

At Chesterfield, August 14. Kent won by six wickets. Toss: Kent.

Derbyshire

P. D. Bowler lbw b G. R. Cowdrey	42	A. E. Warner b Alleyne	0
J. E. Morris b Davis	20	F. A. Griffith b Alleyne	9
†B. J. M. Maher b Davis	6	S. J. Base not out	1
S. C. Goldsmith c G. R. Cowdrey b Ellison	23	L-b 8, w 3	11
*M. A. Holding c Marsh b G. R. Cowdrey	2	1/55 2/68 3/76 (8 wkts, 40 overs)	184
B. Roberts not out	40	4/80 5/104 6/163	
R. Sharma c Marsh b Alleyne	30	7/163 8/175	

O. H. Mortensen did not bat.

Bowling: Alleyne 8–0–34–3; Penn 4–0–20–0; G. R. Cowdrey 8–0–20–2; Davis 8–0–22–2; Ellison 5–0–40–1; C. S. Cowdrey 7–0–40–0.

Kent

M. R. Benson c Roberts b Griffith	8	G. R. Cowdrey not out	50
†S. A. Marsh c Maher b Mortensen	6	L-b 8, w 6, n-b 2	16
C. J. Tavaré not out	82		
*C. S. Cowdrey c Sharma b Base	20	1/18 2/18 3/52 (4 wkts, 37.3 overs)	186
S. G. Hinks c Holding b Base	4	4/67	

N. R. Taylor, H. L. Alleyne, C. Penn, R. M. Ellison and R. P. Davis did not bat.

Bowling: Mortensen 8–2–15–1; Holding 6.3–0–45–0; Griffith 8–0–50–1; Base 8–0–30–2; Warner 7–0–38–0.

Umpires: J. C. Balderstone and D. R. Shepherd.

At Manchester, August 21. DERBYSHIRE lost to LANCASHIRE by 2 runs.

At Northampton, August 28. DERBYSHIRE beat NORTHAMPTONSHIRE by 5 runs.

ESSEX

ESSEX v KENT

At Chelmsford, April 24. Essex won by nine wickets. Toss: Kent.

Kent

M. R. Benson c East b Topley	9
R. F. Pienaar c East b Lever	6
C. J. Tavaré b Miller	23
*C. S. Cowdrey c Lever b Miller	11
S. G. Hinks c Border b Topley	55
G. R. Cowdrey b Gooch	45
N. R. Taylor c Border b Topley	7
†S. A. Marsh c Fletcher b Pont	9
R. M. Ellison not out	14
D. J. M. Kelleher not out	7
B 1, l-b 7, w 7	15
1/9 2/29 3/50 4/74 5/151 6/166 7/169 8/185 (8 wkts, 40 overs)	201

R. P. Davis did not bat.

Bowling: Lever 8–0–43–1; Pont 8–0–41–1; Topley 8–0–46–3; Miller 8–2–29–2; Gooch 8–1–34–1.

Essex

G. A. Gooch b Davis	90
B. R. Hardie not out	78
A. R. Border not out	26
L-b 7, n-b 1	8
1/145 (1 wkt, 36.3 overs)	202

P. J. Prichard, *K. W. R. Fletcher, I. L. Pont, G. Miller, †D. E. East, T. D. Topley, J. K. Lever and A. W. Lilley did not bat.

Bowling: Kelleher 6–0–31–0; Ellison 8–0–40–0; Pienaar 4–0–23–0; Davis 7.3–1–41–1; C. S. Cowdrey 6–0–42–0; G. R. Cowdrey 5–0–18–0.

Umpires: R. Julian and K. J. Lyons.

At Lord's, May 1. ESSEX lost to MIDDLESEX by 26 runs.

At Derby, May 8. ESSEX beat DERBYSHIRE by 59 runs.

ESSEX v NORTHAMPTONSHIRE

At Chelmsford, May 15. Essex won by 24 runs. Toss: Northamptonshire. Larkins hit his 100th six in the Sunday League, the fifth to do so after I. V. A. Richards, C. G. Greenidge, C. H. Lloyd and I. T. Botham.

Essex

G. A. Gooch b Wild	50	†D. E. East not out	10
B. R. Hardie c Wild b Williams	87	G. Miller not out	7
A. R. Border st Ripley b Cook	5	B 1, l-b 12, w 2, n-b 1	16
D. R. Pringle c and b Wild	7		
P. J. Prichard c Stanley b Williams	15	1/113 2/128 3/143 (7 wkts, 40 overs)	214
A. W. Lilley run out	8	4/172 5/180	
*K. W. R. Fletcher c Bailey b Walker	9	6/194 7/197	

J. K. Lever and T. D. Topley did not bat.

Bowling: Davis 8–0–37–0; Capel 8–0–36–0; Wild 8–0–39–2; Walker 4–0–29–1; Cook 8–0–29–1; Williams 4–0–31–2.

Northamptonshire

*W. Larkins c Fletcher b Pringle	37	D. J. Wild not out	6
R. J. Bailey c East b Pringle	20		
A. J. Lamb b Gooch	16	L-b 10, w 1, n-b 1	12
D. J. Capel c Border b Pringle	38		
R. G. Williams b Lever	55	1/54 2/71 3/86 (5 wkts, 40 overs)	190
W. W. Davis not out	6	4/178 5/178	

N. A. Stanley, †D. Ripley, N. G. B. Cook and A. Walker did not bat.

Bowling: Lever 8–0–43–1; Topley 8–1–41–0; Gooch 8–0–43–1; Pringle 8–0–31–3; Miller 8–1–22–0.

Umpires: B. Leadbeater and N. T. Plews.

At Birmingham, May 22. ESSEX lost to WARWICKSHIRE by six wickets.

ESSEX v SURREY

At Chelmsford, May 29. Surrey won by eight wickets in a match reduced by rain to 32 overs a side. Toss: Surrey. Richards hit two sixes and nine fours, reaching his century off 94 balls.

Essex

G. A. Gooch c Richards b Greig	1	†D. E. East c Zahid b Gray	14
B. R. Hardie c Bullen b Greig	5	G. Miller not out	16
A. R. Border c Bullen b Gray	30		
D. R. Pringle b Bicknell	6	B 1, l-b 4, w 1	6
P. J. Prichard b Bicknell	0		
*K. W. R. Fletcher b Gray	21	1/1 2/12 3/23 (8 wkts, 32 overs)	138
A. W. Lilley not out	38	4/25 5/57 6/71	
N. A. Foster c Zahid b Gray	1	7/73 8/101	

J. K. Lever did not bat.

Bowling: Bicknell 8–1–14–2; Greig 8–0–43–2; Feltham 8–0–20–0; Gray 8–0–56–4.

Surrey

†C. J. Richards not out	105
D. M. Smith lbw b Lever	7
A. J. Stewart lbw b Pringle	7
M. A. Lynch not out	8
L-b 11, w 1	12
1/25 2/57 (2 wkts, 26.3 overs)	139

D. M. Ward, *I. A. Greig, Zahid Sadiq, C. K. Bullen, M. A. Feltham, A. H. Gray and M. P. Bicknell did not bat.

Bowling: Lever 6.3–0–18–1; Foster 8–0–26–0; Gooch 4–0–31–0; Miller 3–0–25–0; Pringle 5–0–28–1.

Umpires: J. W. Holder and B. Leadbeater.

ESSEX v SUSSEX

At Ilford, June 12. Tied. Toss: Essex.

Sussex

A. M. Green b Gooch . . . 57
A. P. Wells c East b Childs . . . 27
†I. J. Gould b Pringle . . . 27
*P. W. G. Parker c Pringle b Lever . . . 10
C. M. Wells not out . . . 36
Imran Khan c Gooch b Pringle . . . 19
A. C. S. Pigott b Lever . . . 4
P. Moores not out . . . 4
B 1, l-b 17, w 2 . . . 20

1/53 2/108 3/121 4/143 5/189 6/193 (6 wkts, 40 overs) 204

N. J. Lenham, S. J. S. Kimber and A. R. Clarke did not bat.

Bowling: Lever 8–1–34–2; Topley 8–0–35–0; Childs 8–0–44–1; Gooch 8–0–35–1; Pringle 8–0–38–2.

Essex

G. A. Gooch c Pigott b Kimber . . . 4
B. R. Hardie c Parker b Clarke . . . 39
A. R. Border c Gould b Pigott . . . 77
D. R. Pringle b Clarke . . . 0
P. J. Prichard st Gould b Clarke . . . 3
*K. W. R. Fletcher c Clarke b Pigott . . . 14
A. W. Lilley c Lenham b Imran . . . 23
†D. E. East c Parker b Pigott . . . 24
T. D. Topley run out . . . 1
J. K. Lever not out . . . 3
J. H. Childs not out . . . 1
B 7, l-b 5, w 3 . . . 15

1/10 2/85 3/85 4/97 5/127 6/168 7/190 8/198 9/202 (9 wkts, 40 overs) 204

Bowling: Imran 8–0–50–1; Kimber 8–0–41–1; C. M. Wells 8–0–35–0; Clarke 8–0–32–3; Pigott 8–0–34–3.

Umpires: J. C. Balderstone and H. D. Bird.

At Sheffield, June 19. ESSEX lost to YORKSHIRE by four wickets.

At Bournemouth, June 26. ESSEX beat HAMPSHIRE by eight wickets.

At Taunton, July 3. SOMERSET v ESSEX. No result.

ESSEX v GLAMORGAN

At Chelmsford, July 10. Glamorgan won by six wickets. Toss: Glamorgan.

Essex

G. A. Gooch c Metson b Thomas . . . 12
P. J. Prichard c Metson b Barwick . . . 10
A. R. Border run out . . . 73
A. W. Lilley c Butcher b Ontong . . . 5
*K. W. R. Fletcher c and b Shastri . . . 2
N. Hussain run out . . . 38
N. A. Foster run out . . . 1
J. P. Stephenson c Derrick b Barwick . . . 8
†D. E. East not out . . . 23
T. D. Topley c Holmes b Barwick . . . 0
J. K. Lever run out . . . 1
B 3, l-b 18, w 8, n-b 2 . . . 31

1/21 2/39 3/53 4/78 5/166 6/167 7/169 8/201 9/202 (40 overs) 204

Bowling: Thomas 8–0–40–1; Barwick 8–0–38–3; Derrick 8–0–27–0; Ontong 8–1–39–1; Shastri 8–1–39–1.

Glamorgan

J. A. Hopkins b Gooch	50	A. R. Butcher not out	5
*H. Morris c Gooch b Topley	22	B 2, l-b 6, w 5	13
M. P. Maynard c Border b Gooch	9		—
G. C. Holmes c Lever b Foster	47	1/55 2/87 3/98 (4 wkts, 39.2 overs)	206
R. J. Shastri not out	60	4/190	

R. C. Ontong, J. G. Thomas, J. Derrick, †C. P. Metson and S. R. Barwick did not bat.

Bowling: Foster 8–0–18–1; Lever 8–0–41–0; Stephenson 8–0–42–0; Gooch 8–0–55–2; Topley 7.2–0–42–1.

Umpires: A. A. Jones and R. Palmer.

ESSEX v LANCASHIRE

At Southend, July 17. Essex won by six wickets. Toss: Essex.

Lancashire

G. D. Mendis c Border b Foster	16	P. J. W. Allott c Border b Foster	3
G. Fowler b Miller	14	†W. K. Hegg not out	9
T. E. Jesty c Border b Foster	0	J. Simmons not out	1
N. H. Fairbrother c East b Miller	7	L-b 14, w 1, n-b 2	17
A. N. Hayhurst c Miller b Lever	20		—
M. Watkinson c Pringle b Foster	49	1/26 2/26 3/43 (9 wkts, 40 overs)	170
*D. P. Hughes b Pringle	27	4/50 5/76 6/142	
Wasim Akram c Border b Pringle	7	7/149 8/154 9/161	

Bowling: Foster 8–1–25–4; Lever 8–0–54–1; Miller 8–1–18–2; Gooch 8–1–32–0; Pringle 8–1–27–2.

Essex

G. A. Gooch c Hegg b Watkinson	7	*K. W. R. Fletcher not out	10
P. J. Prichard b Simmons	22	L-b 5, w 1, n-b 1	7
A. R. Border not out	72		—
A. W. Lilley c Watkinson b Simmons	31	1/17 2/48 3/100 (4 wkts, 38.1 overs)	171
N. Hussain c Hegg b Watkinson	22	4/151	

D. R. Pringle, G. Miller, †D. E. East, N. A. Foster and J. K. Lever did not bat.

Bowling: Allott 8–2–26–0; Watkinson 7.1–1–41–2; Simmons 8–0–43–2; Wasim 8–0–22–0; Hayhurst 7–1–34–0.

Umpires: D. J. Constant and K. E. Palmer.

At Leicester, July 24. ESSEX lost to LEICESTERSHIRE by eight wickets.

ESSEX v NOTTINGHAMSHIRE

At Colchester, August 14. Essex won by 77 runs. Toss: Nottinghamshire.

Essex

G. A. Gooch c Newell b Cooper 2
P. J. Prichard c Newell b Mike 36
M. E. Waugh c Fraser-Darling b K. P. Evans . 103
D. R. Pringle c Newell b K. P. Evans . 8
A. W. Lilley c Newell b K. P. Evans . . 11
N. Hussain b Stephenson 30
†D. E. East not out 29
N. A. Foster not out 0
B 1, l-b 11, w 4, n-b 1 17

1/5 2/47 3/57 4/89 5/199 6/225 (6 wkts, 40 overs) 236

*K. W. R. Fletcher, G. Miller and T. D. Topley did not bat.

Bowling: Cooper 8–0–39–1; Fraser-Darling 8–0–48–0; Mike 8–1–57–1; K. P. Evans 8–1–26–3; Stephenson 8–0–54–1.

Nottinghamshire

B. C. Broad c East b Topley 11
*R. T. Robinson c Hussain b Waugh . . 49
†M. Newell run out 9
D. W. Randall c East b Waugh 0
J. D. Birch c Gooch b Topley 21
R. J. Evans c Gooch b Topley 7
F. D. Stephenson not out 41
C. D. Fraser-Darling c Fletcher b Topley 10
K. P. Evans lbw b Topley 2
G. W. Mike lbw b Topley 0
K. E. Cooper not out 3
L-b 5, w 1 6

1/24 2/52 3/52 4/73 5/101 6/101 7/138 8/148 9/148 (9 wkts, 40 overs) 159

Bowling: Topley 8–0–33–6; Foster 7–1–15–0; Pringle 7–0–18–0; Miller 8–1–36–0; Waugh 4–0–16–2; Gooch 5–0–33–0; Lilley 1–0–3–0.

Umpires: B. Dudleston and J. H. Harris.

At Worcester, August 21. ESSEX lost to WORCESTERSHIRE by 18 runs.

ESSEX v GLOUCESTERSHIRE

At Chelmsford, August 28. Gloucestershire won by five wickets in a match reduced by rain to 27 overs a side. Toss: Gloucestershire.

Essex

B. R. Hardie c Alleyne b Jarvis 7
J. P. Stephenson c Alleyne b Jarvis 4
M. E. Waugh b Pooley 5
P. J. Prichard b Bainbridge 8
A. W. Lilley c Greene b Bainbridge . . . 26
*K. W. R. Fletcher b Bainbridge 12
†D. E. East b Greene 5
I. L. Pont run out 15
T. D. Topley b Greene 6
J. K. Lever b Greene 0
J. H. Childs not out 2
B 3, l-b 7, w 2 12

1/13 2/20 3/24 4/38 5/62 6/63 7/79 8/95 9/95 (27 overs) 102

Bowling: Jarvis 5–0–14–2; Greene 6–0–13–3; Pooley 5–0–19–1; Bainbridge 5–0–21–3; Curran 6–0–25–0.

Gloucestershire

A. W. Stovold b Topley 12
A. J. Wright b Lever 4
P. Bainbridge c Waugh b Childs 3
K. M. Curran not out 30
). J. Thomas b Childs 4
P. W. Romaines b Pont 32
†M. W. Alleyne not out 9
B 2, l-b 7, w 2 11

1/15 2/20 3/22 4/28 5/84 (5 wkts, 25.3 overs) 105

V. S. Greene, *D. A. Graveney, M. W. Pooley and K. B. S. Jarvis did not bat.

Bowling: Lever 6–0–22–1; Childs 6–1–14–2; Pont 4.3–0–19–1; Topley 5–0–17–1; Waugh –0–24–0.

Umpires: R. Julian and A. G. T. Whitehead.

GLAMORGAN

At Bristol, April 24. GLAMORGAN lost to GLOUCESTERSHIRE by five wickets.

GLAMORGAN v SOMERSET

At Cardiff, May 1. Glamorgan won by eight wickets in a match reduced by rain to sixteen overs a side. Toss: Glamorgan.

Somerset

N. A. Felton b Holmes 8
*P. M. Roebuck run out 31
S. R. Waugh b Shastri 29
R. J. Harden c Morris b Thomas 15
J. J. E. Hardy st Metson b Shastri 0
G. D. Rose not out 38
G. V. Palmer not out 1
B 1, l-b 8, w 3 12

1/34 2/74 3/77 4/77 5/131 (5 wkts, 16 overs) 134

†N. D. Burns, V. J. Marks, A. N. Jones and N. A. Mallender did not bat.

Bowling: Thomas 4–0–25–1; Watkin 2–0–16–0; Barwick 3–0–27–0; Holmes 3–0–25–1; Shastri 3–0–19–2; Derrick 1–0–13–0.

Glamorgan

M. P. Maynard c Roebuck b Palmer .. 27
G. C. Holmes b Mallender 43
R. J. Shastri not out 53
J. G. Thomas not out 9
B 1, w 5 6

1/55 2/108 (2 wkts, 16 overs) 138

S. L. Watkin, *H. Morris, A. R. Butcher, R. C. Ontong, J. Derrick, †C. P. Metson and S. R. Barwick did not bat.

Bowling: Rose 3–0–23–0; Mallender 4–0–41–1; Palmer 3–0–26–1; Jones 3–0–27–0; Waugh 3–0–20–0.

Umpires: A. A. Jones and M. J. Kitchen.

At Southampton, May 8. GLAMORGAN lost to HAMPSHIRE by 60 runs.

At Birmingham, May 15. GLAMORGAN beat WARWICKSHIRE by ten wickets.

GLAMORGAN v DERBYSHIRE

At Newport, May 22. Glamorgan won by 25 runs. Toss: Derbyshire. Barnett became the third player to carry his bat through a completed innings with ten wickets down, the others being D. H. K. Smith, 36 not out in a total of 109 for Derbyshire v Kent at Chesterfield in 1969, and J. H. Hampshire, 77 not out in a total of 142 for Yorkshire v Essex at Leyton in 1976.

Glamorgan

J. A. Hopkins lbw b Newman 60
*H. Morris run out 10
P. A. Todd c Roberts b Bowler 9
R. J. Shastri c Barnett b Roberts 26
G. C. Holmes c Warner b Newman . . . 15
J. G. Thomas b Warner 5
A. R. Butcher not out 34
R. C. Ontong c Maher b Holding 0
J. Derrick b Holding 10
†C. P. Metson not out 9
L-b 16, w 4, n-b 1 21

1/33 2/48 3/103 4/134 5/136 6/156 7/168 8/188 (8 wkts, 40 overs) 199

S. R. Barwick did not bat.

Bowling: Newman 8–0–31–2; Mortensen 8–0–38–0; Warner 7–0–40–1; Bowler 4–1–16–1; Holding 8–1–30–2; Roberts 5–0–28–1.

Derbyshire

*K. J. Barnett not out 90
P. D. Bowler lbw b Thomas 5
B. Roberts c Metson b Thomas 0
J. E. Morris c Ontong b Barwick 5
S. C. Goldsmith c Hopkins b Derrick . . 1
M. A. Holding c Todd b Ontong 19
†B. J. M. Maher c Todd b Shastri 4
R. J. Finney b Shastri 15
P. G. Newman c Derrick b Holmes . . . 6
A. E. Warner c Todd b Holmes 11
O. H. Mortensen run out 5
B 1, l-b 5, w 7 13

1/16 2/16 3/29 4/30 5/65 6/81 7/117 8/140 9/159 (39.2 overs) 174

Bowling: Thomas 7–1–27–2; Barwick 6–0–19–1; Derrick 8–1–41–1; Ontong 8–2–29–1; Shastri 8–0–34–2; Holmes 2.2–0–18–2.

Umpires: M. J. Kitchen and P. B. Wight.

GLAMORGAN v KENT

At Merthyr Tydfil, June 5. Kent won by five wickets. Toss: Glamorgan. This was the first county match at this venue.

Glamorgan

J. A. Hopkins c Taylor b Wells 8
*H. Morris lbw b C. S. Cowdrey 23
M. P. Maynard c C. S. Cowdrey b Ellison 1
R. J. Shastri c Marsh b Davis 2
G. C. Holmes c Wells b C. S. Cowdrey 17
A. R. Butcher c G. R. Cowdrey b C. S. Cowdrey . 34
R. C. Ontong c Ellison b Pienaar 7
J. G. Thomas b Pienaar 2
J. Derrick b C. S. Cowdrey 15
†C. P. Metson c Hinks b Ellison 2
S. R. Barwick not out 4
B 2, l-b 6, w 10, n-b 1 19

1/27 2/27 3/36 4/61 5/61 6/80 7/97 8/114 9/122 (39.4 overs) 134

Bowling: Ellison 8–1–37–2; Wells 6–0–15–1; Davis 8–0–21–1; Pienaar 8–1–20–2; C. S. Cowdrey 6.4–1–20–4; G. R. Cowdrey 3–0–13–0.

Kent

M. R. Benson b Barwick 4
N. R. Taylor st Metson b Shastri 62
C. J. Tavaré b Holmes 25
S. G. Hinks c Morris b Derrick 1
*C. S. Cowdrey c Hopkins b Derrick . . 14
R. F. Pienaar not out 11
G. R. Cowdrey not out 14
L-b 3, w 1 4

1/6 2/57 3/58 4/86 5/116 (5 wkts, 38 overs) 135

R. M. Ellison, †S. A. Marsh, V. J. Wells and R. P. Davis did not bat.

Bowling: Thomas 7–2–17–0; Barwick 8–2–10–1; Ontong 2–0–18–0; Shastri 7–0–42–1; Holmes 6–0–24–1; Derrick 8–1–21–2.

Umpires: J. D. Bond and D. J. Constant.

At Nottingham, June 12. GLAMORGAN beat NOTTINGHAMSHIRE by 5 runs.

GLAMORGAN v LANCASHIRE

At Pontypridd, June 26. No result. Toss: Lancashire.

Glamorgan

J. A. Hopkins c Jesty b Watkinson	26
*H. Morris c Hegg b Watkinson	22
M. P. Maynard lbw b Watkinson	3
G. C. Holmes b Hayhurst	15
R. J. Shastri c Hughes b Simmons	19
R. C. Ontong c Simmons b Hayhurst	29
J. G. Thomas c Hughes b Hayhurst	25
J. Derrick b Hayhurst	3
†C. P. Metson c Hegg b Wasim	5
S. L. Watkin not out	1
S. R. Barwick not out	3
L-b 11, w 1	12
1/48 2/54 3/57 4/90 5/97 6/145 7/153 8/155 9/159 (9 wkts, 38 overs)	163

Bowling: Allott 8–0–28–0; Wasim 8–0–32–1; Watkinson 8–1–22–3; Simmons 7–0–28–1; Hayhurst 6–0–37–4; Jesty 1–0–5–0.

Lancashire

G. D. Mendis c Metson b Barwick	1
G. Fowler c Metson b Barwick	6
T. E. Jesty not out	14
N. H. Fairbrother c Metson b Barwick	0
M. Watkinson not out	0
L-b 5, n-b 2	7
1/1 2/28 3/28 (3 wkts, 8 overs)	28

*D. P. Hughes, A. N. Hayhurst, P. J. W. Allott, J. Simmons, Wasim Akram and †W. K. Hegg did not bat.

Bowling: Thomas 4–0–15–0; Barwick 4–0–8–3.

Umpires: J. Birkenshaw and J. H. Harris.

At Chelmsford, July 10. GLAMORGAN beat ESSEX by six wickets.

At Lord's, July 17. MIDDLESEX v GLAMORGAN. No result.

GLAMORGAN v YORKSHIRE

At Cardiff, July 24. Glamorgan won by 15 runs. Toss: Yorkshire. Two interruptions by rain during Glamorgan's innings caused the match to be reduced to 28 overs a side.

Glamorgan

J. A. Hopkins c Bairstow b Shaw	21
*H. Morris lbw b Sidebottom	2
M. P. Maynard c Hartley b Carrick	63
P. A. Todd lbw b Shaw	0
R. J. Shastri not out	50
A. R. Butcher not out	11
L-b 11, w 2	13
1/8 2/42 3/42 4/130 (4 wkts, 28 overs)	160

R. C. Ontong, S. L. Watkin, J. Derrick, †C. P. Metson and S. R. Barwick did not bat.

Bowling: Fletcher 8–0–48–0; Sidebottom 6–2–26–1; Shaw 6–0–36–2; Carrick 8–1–39–1.

Yorkshire

K. Sharp c Todd b Derrick 30
A. A. Metcalfe c Metson b Barwick ... 0
P. E. Robinson b Derrick 49
D. Byas b Derrick 22
J. D. Love c Maynard b Derrick 3
†D. L. Bairstow b Watkin 6
S. N. Hartley b Watkin 2
*P. Carrick not out 4
A. Sidebottom not out 6
B 7, l-b 15, w 1 23

1/2 2/58 3/119 4/126 5/126 6/134 7/135 (7 wkts, 28 overs) 145

C. Shaw and S. D. Fletcher did not bat.

Bowling: Watkin 7–1–19–2; Barwick 8–0–34–1; Derrick 8–1–36–4; Ontong 5–0–34–0.

Umpires: R. Julian and B. J. Meyer.

At Eastbourne, July 31. GLAMORGAN tied with SUSSEX.

GLAMORGAN v SURREY

At Ebbw Vale, August 7. Glamorgan won by 8 runs. Toss: Glamorgan.

Glamorgan

J. A. Hopkins c Ward b Bullen 12
*H. Morris c Bullen b Medlycott 51
A. R. Butcher c Ward b Bullen 27
G. C. Holmes c Bicknell b Feltham ... 33
R. J. Shastri b Greig 18
R. C. Ontong c Zahid b Feltham 35
J. G. Thomas c Ward b Greig 2
†C. P. Metson not out 10
J. Derrick not out 0
L-b 3, w 6 9

1/41 2/91 3/99 4/146 5/148 6/158 7/196 (7 wkts, 40 overs) 197

S. L. Watkin and S. R. Barwick did not bat.

Bowling: Peters 5–0–20–0; Greig 8–0–44–2; Thorpe 4–1–25–0; Bullen 8–0–26–2; Medlycott 8–0–43–1; Feltham 7–0–36–2.

Surrey

†A. J. Stewart b Ontong 34
P. D. Atkins lbw b Barwick 2
D. M. Ward c Metson b Thomas 1
Zahid Sadiq lbw b Watkin 20
D. J. Bicknell b Holmes 31
*I. A. Greig c Barwick b Watkin 9
G. P. Thorpe st Metson b Derrick 15
K. T. Medlycott c Shastri b Thomas ... 34
M. A. Feltham b Thomas 19
C. K. Bullen b Thomas 1
N. H. Peters not out 4
B 5, l-b 9, w 5 19

1/11 2/12 3/55 4/69 5/100 6/116 7/151 8/184 9/184 (39.2 overs) 189

Bowling: Barwick 7–2–18–1; Thomas 6.2–1–31–4; Shastri 2–0–14–0; Watkin 8–0–28–2; Ontong 8–1–29–1; Holmes 5–0–30–1; Derrick 3–0–25–1.

Umpires: B. J. Meyer and D. O. Oslear.

GLAMORGAN v WORCESTERSHIRE

At Swansea, August 14. Worcestershire won by seven wickets. Toss: Worcestershire. After rain had delayed the start by two hours, a match of 22 overs a side was started, in which Glamorgan, put in, had reached 73 for one when another heavy shower interrupted the tenth over. This match was then abandoned and another of eleven overs a side was started when the weather cleared.

Glamorgan

J. A. Hopkins c D'Oliveira b Pridgeon . 9
M. P. Maynard c Curtis b Pridgeon . . . 11
R. J. Shastri c and b O'Shaughnessy . . . 18
G. C. Holmes not out 28
R. C. Ontong c Rhodes b Hick 1
J. G. Thomas c Pridgeon b O'Shaughnessy . 7
*H. Morris not out 4
L-b 1, w 2 3

1/13 2/25 3/61 4/63 5/72 (5 wkts, 11 overs) 81

S. L. Watkin, J. Derrick, †C. P. Metson and S. R. Barwick did not bat.

Bowling: Newport 1–0–10–0; Pridgeon 2–0–11–2; Illingworth 3–0–22–0; McEwan 1–0–14–0; O'Shaughnessy 2–0–12–2; Hick 2–0–11–1.

Worcestershire

G. A. Hick not out 42
S. J. O'Shaughnessy c Shastri b Derrick 25
D. B. D'Oliveira c Maynard b Ontong . 1
*P. A. Neale c Metson b Thomas 8
M. J. Weston not out 3
L-b 2, w 4 6

1/43 2/45 3/76 (3 wkts, 10.1 overs) 85

T. S. Curtis, †S. J. Rhodes, P. J. Newport, R. K. Illingworth, S. M. McEwan and A. P. Pridgeon did not bat.

Bowling: Thomas 2–0–13–1; Barwick 2–0–13–0; Ontong 3–0–17–1; Watkin 1–0–13–0; Derrick 2–0–23–1; Holmes 0.1–0–4–0.

Umpires: D. G. L. Evans and A. G. T. Whitehead.

At Wellingborough School, August 21. GLAMORGAN beat NORTHAMPTONSHIRE by six wickets.

GLAMORGAN v LEICESTERSHIRE

At Llanelli, August 28. Leicestershire won by eight wickets in a match reduced by rain to thirteen overs a side. Toss: Leicestershire.

Glamorgan

J. A. Hopkins b Agnew 28
M. P. Maynard c Boon b Ferris 4
G. C. Holmes c Whitaker b Tennant . . 3
R. J. Shastri c Gower b Agnew 12
A. R. Butcher lbw b Taylor 2
J. G. Thomas b Ferris 13
*H. Morris b Ferris 7
†C. P. Metson not out 3
L-b 3, w 2 5

1/9 2/15 3/51 4/51 5/59 6/72 7/77 (7 wkts, 13 overs) 7

J. Derrick, S. L. Watkin and S. R. Barwick did not bat.

Bowling: Ferris 3–0–9–3; Tennant 2–0–14–1; Willey 2–0–18–0; Agnew 3–0–13–2; Taylo 3–0–20–1.

Leicestershire

L. Potter run out 4
N. E. Briers not out 37
*D. I. Gower c Metson b Watkin 2
J. J. Whitaker not out 30
L-b 3, w 2 5

1/9 2/23 (2 wkts, 12.1 overs) 78

P. Willey, T. J. Boon, G. J. F. Ferris, †P. Whitticase, J. P. Agnew, L. Tennant and L. B. Taylor did not bat.

Bowling: Thomas 2.1–0–10–0; Barwick 3–0–21–0; Watkin 3–0–17–1; Holmes 1–0–8–0; Derrick 1–0–5–0; Shastri 2–0–14–0.

Umpires: H. D. Bird and D. R. Shepherd.

GLOUCESTERSHIRE

GLOUCESTERSHIRE v GLAMORGAN

At Bristol, April 24. Gloucestershire won by five wickets. Toss: Gloucestershire.

Glamorgan

J. A. Hopkins b Jarvis	8	R. C. Ontong c Russell b Greene	7
*H. Morris c Stovold b Alleyne	37	J. G. Thomas not out	0
M. P. Maynard c and b Greene	1	B 4, l-b 9, w 4, n-b 2	19
A. R. Butcher b Curran	2		
R. J. Shastri not out	84	1/16 2/21 3/28 (6 wkts, 40 overs)	176
G. C. Holmes b Jarvis	18	4/86 5/119 6/164	

†C. P. Metson, S. R. Barwick and J. Derrick did not bat.

Bowling: Jarvis 8–0–18–2; Greene 8–2–42–2; Curran 8–1–32–1; Thomas 8–0–33–0; Alleyne 8–0–38–1.

Gloucestershire

A. W. Stovold b Holmes	41	D. J. Thomas not out	1
C. W. J. Athey b Derrick	67		
K. M. Curran not out	34	L-b 9, w 4	13
J. W. Lloyds c and b Barwick	13		
P. W. Romaines b Thomas	8	1/109 2/119 3/147 (5 wkts, 39 overs)	177
M. W. Alleyne c Metson b Holmes	0	4/165 5/171	

V. S. Greene, †R. C. Russell, *D. A. Graveney and K. B. S. Jarvis did not bat.

Bowling: Thomas 8–2–23–1; Barwick 6–0–32–1; Ontong 7–0–31–0; Derrick 8–0–39–1; Shastri 4–0–23–0; Holmes 6–1–20–2.

Umpires: D. G. L. Evans and D. S. Thompsett.

GLOUCESTERSHIRE v SUSSEX

At Bristol, May 1. Gloucestershire won by seven wickets in a match reduced by rain to ten overs a side. Toss: Gloucestershire.

Sussex

Imran Khan b Bainbridge	6	S. J. S. Kimber not out	1
†I. J. Gould c Romaines b Alleyne	6		
P. W. G. Parker run out	12	L-b 6	6
C. M. Wells c Romaines b Curran	12		
A. P. Wells run out	25	1/8 2/19 3/36 (5 wkts, 10 overs)	69
A. M. Green not out	1	4/46 5/67	

N. J. Lenham, D. K. Standing, A. M. Babington and R. A. Bunting did not bat.

Bowling: Jarvis 2–0–11–0; Alleyne 2–0–12–1; Bainbridge 2–0–9–1; Green 2–0–14–0; Curran 2–0–17–1.

Gloucestershire

C. W. J. Athey not out 32
K. M. Curran c Gould b Bunting 2
J. W. Lloyds lbw b Bunting 2
P. W. Romaines b Babington 27
*P. Bainbridge not out 4
B 2, n-b 1 4
1/9 2/16 3/63 (3 wkts, 9.1 overs) 71

M. W. Alleyne, †R. C. Russell, D. J. Thomas, V. S. Greene, M. W. Pooley and K. B. S. Jarvis did not bat.

Bowling: Imran 2–0–9–0; Bunting 2–0–8–2; Babington 2–0–14–1; Standing 2–0–21–0; Kimber 1.1–0–17–0.

Umpires: B. Dudleston and R. Palmer.

At Northampton, May 8. GLOUCESTERSHIRE lost to NORTHAMPTONSHIRE by one wicket.

At Nottingham, May 15. GLOUCESTERSHIRE beat NOTTINGHAMSHIRE by two wickets.

GLOUCESTERSHIRE v WARWICKSHIRE

At Bristol, May 29. No result.

At Heanor, June 12. GLOUCESTERSHIRE beat DERBYSHIRE by 42 runs.

At Manchester, June 19. GLOUCESTERSHIRE lost to LANCASHIRE by one wicket.

GLOUCESTERSHIRE v LEICESTERSHIRE

At Gloucester, June 26. Gloucestershire won by 63 runs. Toss: Leicestershire.

Gloucestershire

A. W. Stovold c Whitticase b Agnew . . 23
C. W. J. Athey b Agnew 12
*P. Bainbridge b Lewis 37
K. M. Curran c Willey b Lewis 8
P. W. Romaines c Whitticase b DeFreitas . 67
M. W. Alleyne c DeFreitas b Ferris . . . 13
A. J. Wright lbw b DeFreitas 12
J. W. Lloyds c Willey b DeFreitas 4
†R. C. Russell c Gower b DeFreitas . . . 0
V. S. Greene not out 6
K. B. S. Jarvis not out 1
L-b 14, w 2, n-b 3 19
1/37 2/40 3/62 (9 wkts, 40 overs) 202
4/139 5/164 6/178
7/194 8/194 9/198

Bowling: Ferris 8–0–45–1; Agnew 8–0–24–2; DeFreitas 8–0–33–4; Lewis 8–0–46–2; Willey 8–0–40–0.

Leicestershire

L. Potter run out 1
N. E. Briers c and b Alleyne 54
*D. I. Gower lbw b Jarvis 0
J. J. Whitaker b Curran 11
P. Willey c Bainbridge b Alleyne 21
P. N. Hepworth b Bainbridge 16
P. A. J. DeFreitas c Athey b Curran . . 1
C. C. Lewis lbw b Curran 1
†P. Whitticase c Stovold b Curran . . . .
J. P. Agnew b Curran . . . .
G. J. F. Ferris not out . . . .
L-b 10, w 6 . . . . 1[illegible]
1/9 2/11 3/37 (36.1 overs) 13[illegible]
4/82 5/118 6/118
7/120 8/121 9/133

Bowling: Jarvis 8–1–16–1; Greene 6–1–19–0; Curran 6.1–1–15–5; Alleyne 8–0–37–2; Bainbridge 8–0–42–1.

Umpires: B. Dudleston and D. R. Shepherd.

At Hereford, July 3. WORCESTERSHIRE v GLOUCESTERSHIRE. No result.

At Southampton, July 10. GLOUCESTERSHIRE beat HAMPSHIRE on faster scoring-rate.

GLOUCESTERSHIRE v SOMERSET

At Bristol, July 17. Gloucestershire won by seven wickets. Toss: Gloucestershire.

Somerset

G. D. Rose c Graveney b Jarvis 15
*P. M. Roebuck c Russell b Greene . . . 14
S. R. Waugh b Bainbridge 30
R. J. Bartlett c Greene b Alleyne 28
J. J. E. Hardy c and b Jarvis 10
N. J. Pringle c Russell b Alleyne 15
V. J. Marks lbw b Jarvis 2
†N. D. Burns run out 34
G. V. Palmer b Greene 3
N. A. Mallender not out 10
B 1, l-b 18, w 4 23

1/34 2/34 3/81 4/101 5/113 6/123 7/138 8/164 9/184 (9 wkts, 40 overs) 184

A. N. Jones did not bat.

Bowling: Jarvis 8–1–28–3; Greene 8–0–38–2; Bainbridge 8–0–27–1; Curran 8–0–39–0; Alleyne 8–0–33–2.

Gloucestershire

A. W. Stovold b Jones 10
C. W. J. Athey c Burns b Mallender . . 39
P. Bainbridge not out 73
K. M. Curran c Waugh b Jones 41
P. W. Romaines not out 14
L-b 5, w 3 8

1/23 2/65 3/156 (3 wkts, 37.5 overs) 185

A. J. Wright, M. W. Alleyne, †R. C. Russell, V. S. Greene, *D. A. Graveney and K. B. S. Jarvis did not bat.

Bowling: Jones 8–0–43–2; Rose 8–0–30–0; Marks 8–0–42–0; Mallender 7–0–32–1; Palmer 4.5–0–23–0; Pringle 2–0–10–0.

Umpires: M. J. Kitchen and B. Leadbeater.

GLOUCESTERSHIRE v SURREY

At Cheltenham, July 31. Surrey won by eight wickets. Toss: Surrey. Surrey were set a revised target of 163 off 25 overs after rain interrupted their innings when they were 62 for two off twelve overs.

Gloucestershire

A. W. Stovold c Richards b Bicknell . . 28
C. W. J. Athey b Feltham 50
P. Bainbridge c Stewart b Peters 38
K. M. Curran b Greig 13
P. W. Romaines c Richards b Peters . . 21
A. J. Wright not out 49
M. W. Alleyne not out 21
L-b 4, w 4 8

1/50 2/111 3/120 4/149 5/155 (5 wkts, 35 overs) 228

†R. C. Russell, V. S. Greene, *D. A. Graveney and K. B. S. Jarvis did not bat.

Bowling: Bicknell 7–0–31–1; Greig 7–0–38–1; Peters 5–0–38–2; Feltham 7–0–46–1; Clarke 7–0–51–0; Bullen 2–0–20–0.

Surrey

M. A. Feltham c Bainbridge b Jarvis .. 1
†C. J. Richards not out 72
A. J. Stewart c Russell b Greene 0
M. A. Lynch not out 85
L-b 3, w 2, n-b 1 6

1/3 2/6 (2 wkts, 21.2 overs) 164

D. M. Ward, Zahid Sadiq, *I. A. Greig, C. K. Bullen, M. P. Bicknell, S. T. Clarke and N. H. Peters did not bat.

Bowling: Greene 6–0–28–1; Jarvis 7–1–58–1; Bainbridge 3–0–33–0; Curran 5.2–0–42–0.

Umpires: D. J. Constant and B. J. Meyer.

GLOUCESTERSHIRE v YORKSHIRE

At Cheltenham, August 7. Gloucestershire won by three wickets. Toss: Gloucestershire.

Yorkshire

A. A. Metcalfe run out 33
D. Byas c Russell b Jarvis 13
P. E. Robinson c Russell b Jarvis 4
J. D. Love lbw b Jarvis 3
S. N. Hartley c and b Graveney 28
*P. Carrick c and b Greene 41
A. Sidebottom lbw b Bainbridge 3
†R. J. Blakey not out 40
P. J. Hartley run out .... [illegible]
C. Shaw not out .... [illegible]
L-b 11, w 2, n-b 4 .... 1[illegible]

1/25 2/33 3/45 4/69 5/110 6/115 7/168 8/173 (8 wkts, 40 overs) 19[illegible]

S. D. Fletcher did not bat.

Bowling: Jarvis 8–2–27–3; Greene 7–0–35–1; Curran 8–1–43–0; Bainbridge 8–1–28–1 Thomas 4–0–23–0; Graveney 5–0–24–1.

Gloucestershire

A. J. Wright b P. J. Hartley 36
P. W. Romaines c Metcalfe b P. J. Hartley . 15
P. Bainbridge c Blakey b P. J. Hartley . 7
K. M. Curran c Blakey b P. J. Hartley . 7
D. J. Thomas run out 29
J. W. Lloyds c S. N. Hartley b Shaw .. 18
†R. C. Russell b Fletcher 28
M. W. Alleyne not out .... 2[illegible]
V. S. Greene not out .... 1[illegible]
B 4, l-b 13 .... 1[illegible]

1/44 2/60 3/69 4/82 5/113 6/125 7/172 (7 wkts, 39 overs) 19[illegible]

*D. A. Graveney and K. B. S. Jarvis did not bat.

Bowling: Sidebottom 8–0–41–0; Shaw 8–0–21–1; Fletcher 7–0–41–1; P. J. Hartle[illegible] 8–1–27–4; Carrick 8–0–46–0.

Umpires: R. Julian and P. B. Wight.

At Lord's, August 14. GLOUCESTERSHIRE lost to MIDDLESEX on scoring-rate.

GLOUCESTERSHIRE v KENT

At Moreton-in-Marsh, August 21. Gloucestershire won by 80 runs. Toss: Kent.

Gloucestershire

A. W. Stovold c Marsh b Alleyne 4
A. J. Wright c Ellison b Harman 81
P. Bainbridge c Davis b G. R. Cowdrey 81
K. M. Curran c Tavaré b Davis 12
P. W. Romaines c Alleyne
b C. S. Cowdrey . 42
M. W. Alleyne b Alleyne 1
†R. C. Russell run out 21
V. S. Greene c Davis b Harman 11
*D. A. Graveney not out 1
M. W. Pooley not out 1
L-b 3, w 8, n-b 3 14

1/10 2/176 3/181 (8 wkts, 40 overs) 269
4/225 5/228 6/234
7/255 8/267

K. B. S. Jarvis did not bat.

Bowling: Ellison 6–1–22–0; Alleyne 8–0–42–2; Harman 6–0–58–2; G. R. Cowdrey 5–0–39–1; Davis 8–0–50–1; C. S. Cowdrey 7–0–55–1.

Kent

M. R. Benson b Jarvis 3
†S. A. Marsh c Russell b Greene 9
C. J. Tavaré b Bainbridge 6
*C. S. Cowdrey b Curran 30
S. G. Hinks b Bainbridge 25
G. R. Cowdrey b Graveney 22
R. M. Ellison c and b Graveney 18
H. L. Alleyne c Wright b Curran 25
N. R. Taylor c Wright b Greene 22
M. D. Harman not out 8
R. P. Davis lbw b Curran 0
L-b 15, w 6 21

1/16 2/16 3/45 (36.1 overs) 189
4/88 5/92 6/124
7/135 8/174 9/182

Bowling: Jarvis 5–0–22–1; Greene 7–0–16–2; Bainbridge 8–0–47–2; Curran 6.1–0–24–3; Graveney 7–0–45–2; Pooley 3–0–20–0.

Umpires: J. H. Hampshire and J. H. Harris.

At Chelmsford, August 28. GLOUCESTERSHIRE beat ESSEX by five wickets.

HAMPSHIRE

HAMPSHIRE v SURREY

At Southampton, April 24. Surrey won by 22 runs. Toss: Hampshire.

Surrey

†C. J. Richards c R. A. Smith b Connor 30
D. M. Smith lbw b Tremlett 75
A. J. Stewart c R. A. Smith b James .. 53
M. A. Lynch run out 25
D. M. Ward c R. A. Smith b Nicholas 8
Zahid Sadiq c Terry b Tremlett 0
I. A. Greig c James b Jefferies 5
C. K. Bullen c Nicholas b Tremlett ... 11
M. A. Feltham b Connor 18
S. T. Clarke not out 2
N. H. Peters not out 1
L-b 7, w 1 8

1/53 2/149 3/185 (9 wkts, 39 overs) 236
4/193 5/194 6/202
7/205 8/232 9/234

Bowling: Jefferies 8–2–26–1; Tremlett 7–0–48–3; Connor 7–0–40–2; James 8–0–46–1; Cowley 3–0–23–0; Nicholas 6–0–46–1.

Hampshire

R. A. Smith c Bullen b Peters 6
V. P. Terry c Clarke b Feltham 43
*M. C. J. Nicholas b Greig 2
D. R. Turner not out 103
C. L. Smith c Ward b Bullen 10
S. T. Jefferies c Peters b Greig 39
N. G. Cowley not out 1
L-b 10 10

1/12 2/25 3/84 (5 wkts, 39 overs) 214
4/113 5/208

†R. J. Parks, T. M. Tremlett, C. A. Connor and K. D. James did not bat.

Bowling: Peters 8–1–22–1; Greig 8–0–27–2; Feltham 8–0–57–1; Bullen 8–0–51–1; Clarke 7–0–47–0.

Umpires: B. Hassan and P. B. Wight.

At Canterbury, May 1. HAMPSHIRE lost to KENT by two wickets.

HAMPSHIRE v GLAMORGAN

At Southampton, May 8. Hampshire won by 60 runs. Toss: Glamorgan.

Hampshire

R. A. Smith b Shastri 28
†R. J. Parks c Metson b Barwick 3
D. R. Turner c Cottey b Shastri 43
*M. C. J. Nicholas not out 63
C. L. Smith b Barwick 44
K. D. James hit wkt b Thomas 3
S. T. Jefferies not out 12
B 1, l-b 9, w 4, n-b 2 16

1/9 2/57 3/94 4/188 5/191 (5 wkts, 40 overs) 212

J. R. Ayling, N. G. Cowley, S. J. W. Andrew and C. A. Connor did not bat.

Bowling: Barwick 8–1–29–2; Butcher 5–0–25–0; Shastri 8–0–33–2; Thomas 8–0–48–1; Ontong 8–0–43–0; Holmes 3–0–24–0.

Glamorgan

*A. R. Butcher c Parks b Jefferies 0
P. A. Cottey run out 4
M. P. Maynard c Andrew b Cowley ... 24
R. J. Shastri c R. A. Smith b Cowley .. 31
G. C. Holmes c Nicholas b Ayling 17
J. A. Hopkins not out 40
R. C. Ontong c James b Ayling 13
J. G. Thomas c R. A. Smith b Ayling . 3
J. Derrick c Parks b Connor 6
†C. P. Metson not out 0
L-b 8, w 5, n-b 1 14

1/0 2/15 3/46 4/76 5/90 6/118 7/129 8/144 (8 wkts, 40 overs) 152

S. R. Barwick did not bat.

Bowling: Jefferies 4–0–8–1; Connor 6–2–11–1; James 8–0–41–0; Andrew 6–0–22–0; Cowley 8–0–31–2; Ayling 8–0–31–3.

Umpires: B. J. Meyer and N. T. Plews.

HAMPSHIRE v MIDDLESEX

At Southampton, May 15. Middlesex won by 29 runs. Toss: Middlesex.

Middlesex

J. D. Carr c C. L. Smith b Andrew ... 30
W. N. Slack c Parks b Connor 12
†P. R. Downton c Parks b James 7
R. O. Butcher c C. L. Smith b Andrew. 7
*J. E. Emburey c Parks b Jefferies 12
K. R. Brown c Terry b Cowley 14
J. F. Sykes c Parks b Andrew 57
N. F. Williams not out 28
N. G. Cowans b Andrew .... [illegible]
S. P. Hughes not out .... [illegible]
B 1, l-b 6, w 8, n-b 1 .... 1[illegible]

1/15 2/40 3/60 4/64 5/85 6/108 7/173 8/179 (8 wkts, 40 overs) 18[illegible]

A. R. C. Fraser did not bat.

Bowling: Jefferies 8–0–48–1; Connor 8–1–29–1; James 8–0–28–1; Andrew 8–0–50–4; Cowley 8–0–27–1.

Hampshire

R. A. Smith c Downton b Fraser 12
V. P. Terry b Cowans 0
D. R. Turner c Cowans b Hughes 61
*M. C. J. Nicholas lbw b Hughes 11
C. L. Smith c Butcher b Sykes 13
K. D. James c Downton b Fraser 0
†R. J. Parks not out 35
S. T. Jefferies c Brown b Emburey 4
N. G. Cowley c and b Fraser 11
C. A. Connor not out 4
B 4, l-b 3, w 1, n-b 1 9

1/1 2/17 3/63 4/89 5/90 6/102 7/110 8/145 (8 wkts, 40 overs) 160

S. J. W. Andrew did not bat.

Bowling: Cowans 8–0–33–1; Fraser 8–1–19–3; Emburey 8–1–22–1; Williams 2–0–18–0; Sykes 6–0–29–1; Hughes 8–0–32–2.

Umpires: D. G. L. Evans and J. W. Holder.

At Middlesbrough, May 29. HAMPSHIRE beat YORKSHIRE by seven wickets.

At Manchester, June 5. HAMPSHIRE lost to LANCASHIRE by six wickets.

At Worcester, June 12. HAMPSHIRE lost to WORCESTERSHIRE by 151 runs.

HAMPSHIRE v NOTTINGHAMSHIRE

At Basingstoke, June 19. Hampshire won by 5 runs. Toss: Nottinghamshire.

Hampshire

V. P. Terry c Birch b Cooper 2
C. L. Smith c Scott b Saxelby 0
R. A. Smith b Evans 46
D. R. Turner b Stephenson 79
*M. C. J. Nicholas c Scott b Cooper .. 14
T. R. Ayling c Johnson b Saxelby 10
K. D. James c Scott b Saxelby 8
N. G. Cowley not out 19
†R. J. Parks not out 10
B 1, l-b 9, w 7, n-b 1 18

1/0 2/6 3/110 4/141 5/158 6/174 7/175 (7 wkts, 40 overs) 206

C. A. Connor and S. J. W. Andrew did not bat.

Bowling: Cooper 8–1–35–2; Saxelby 8–0–38–3; Hemmings 8–0–40–0; Evans 8–0–37–1; Stephenson 8–1–46–1.

Nottinghamshire

P. Pollard c Ayling b James 18
M. Newell lbw b Connor 3
P. Johnson b Cowley 82
J. D. Birch b Ayling 54
D. W. Randall not out 19
F. D. Stephenson c Terry b Connor ... 1
E. E. Hemmings not out 2
B 1, l-b 9, w 7, n-b 5 22

1/6 2/56 3/159 4/184 5/193 (5 wkts, 40 overs) 201

K. Saxelby, K. P. Evans, †C. W. Scott and K. E. Cooper did not bat.

Bowling: Connor 8–2–33–2; Andrew 8–0–44–0; James 8–1–33–1; Ayling 8–0–32–1; Cowley –0–49–1.

Umpires: J. H. Hampshire and R. A. White.

HAMPSHIRE v ESSEX

At Bournemouth, June 26. Essex won by eight wickets. Toss: Essex. Rain in the 26th over, when Hampshire were 113 for two, caused their innings to be reduced to 34 overs. Following further rain between innings, Essex were set a revised target of 102 off twenty overs.

Hampshire

V. P. Terry c Hussain b Gooch 40
*M. C. J. Nicholas c Hardie b Topley . 31
R. A. Smith b Pringle 41
D. R. Turner c Miller b Pringle 13
S. T. Jefferies b Lever 14
C. L. Smith not out 19
J. R. Ayling lbw b Pringle 0
N. G. Cowley run out 3
L-b 10, w 1 11

1/60 2/91 3/121 4/144 5/150 6/150 7/172 (7 wkts, 34 overs) 172

†R. J. Parks, C. A. Connor and S. J. W. Andrew did not bat.

Bowling: Lever 8–0–36–1; Pringle 8–0–40–3; Miller 8–1–36–0; Topley 4–0–21–1; Gooch 6–0–29–1.

Essex

*G. A. Gooch c Parks b Connor 16
B. R. Hardie c R. A. Smith b Jefferies . 32
A. R. Border not out 44
D. R. Pringle not out 8
L-b 1, w 1 2

1/27 2/87 (2 wkts, 17.5 overs) 102

J. P. Stephenson, A. W. Lilley, N. Hussain, G. Miller, †A. D. Brown, T. D. Topley and J. K. Lever did not bat.

Bowling: Connor 6–0–42–1; Andrew 2–0–12–0; Jefferies 6.5–0–22–1; Ayling 2–0–16–0; Cowley 1–0–9–0.

Umpires: M. J. Kitchen and D. S. Thompsett.

At Hastings, July 3. SUSSEX v HAMPSHIRE. No result.

HAMPSHIRE v GLOUCESTERSHIRE

At Southampton, July 10. Gloucestershire won on faster scoring-rate when rain ended play. Toss: Gloucestershire.

Hampshire

V. P. Terry c Jarvis b Alleyne 31
*M. C. J. Nicholas retired hurt 0
R. A. Smith c Athey b Jarvis 57
D. R. Turner run out 5
J. R. Ayling c Stovold b Curran 24
K. D. James c Russell b Alleyne 0
S. T. Jefferies not out 15
N. G. Cowley not out 16
L-b 5, w 3, n-b 1 9

1/87 2/94 3/111 4/112 5/131 (5 wkts, 40 overs) 157

†R. J. Parks, T. M. Tremlett and C. A. Connor did not bat.

Bowling: Jarvis 8–0–27–1; Greene 8–0–46–0; Curran 8–0–33–1; Bainbridge 8–2–14–0 Alleyne 8–0–32–2.

Gloucestershire

A. W. Stovold not out	43
C. W. J. Athey st Parks b Cowley	31
P. Bainbridge c James b Cowley	0
K. M. Curran not out	13
B 4, l-b 12, w 1, n-b 2	19
1/79 2/85 (2 wkts, 26 overs)	106

P. W. Romaines, A. J. Wright, M. W. Alleyne, †R. C. Russell, V. S. Greene, *D. A. Graveney and K. B. S. Jarvis did not bat.

Bowling: Jefferies 3–0–13–0; Connor 4–0–6–0; Ayling 6–1–16–0; Tremlett 2–0–8–0; Cowley 7–1–32–2; James 4–0–15–0.

Umpires: J. H. Harris and D. O. Oslear.

At Birmingham, July 17. HAMPSHIRE lost to WARWICKSHIRE by 111 runs.

HAMPSHIRE v DERBYSHIRE

At Portsmouth, July 24. Hampshire won by four wickets. Toss: Hampshire.

Derbyshire

*K. J. Barnett c Parks b Jefferies	1
P. D. Bowler lbw b Ayling	33
B. Roberts c Parks b Bakker	1
J. E. Morris c Terry b Tremlett	32
S. C. Goldsmith lbw b Bakker	26
M. A. Holding c Terry b Ayling	14
A. E. Warner run out	1
†B. J. M. Maher c Ayling b Bakker	13
P. G. Newman not out	0
S. J. Base b Bakker	3
O. H. Mortensen lbw b Bakker	0
L-b 5, w 2, n-b 2	9
1/1 2/2 3/60 4/83 5/103 6/105 7/128 8/128 9/133 (38.5 overs)	133

Bowling: Bakker 7.5–1–26–5; Jefferies 7–2–11–1; Ayling 8–0–36–2; James 8–0–20–0; Tremlett 8–0–35–1.

Hampshire

V. P. Terry c Maher b Holding	23
R. J. Scott run out	6
D. R. Turner b Mortensen	0
*M. C. J. Nicholas c Holding b Base	9
C. L. Smith c Maher b Holding	0
S. T. Jefferies c Mortensen b Newman	30
J. R. Ayling not out	41
K. D. James not out	15
B 2, l-b 3, w 4, n-b 1	10
1/26 2/30 3/30 4/30 5/54 6/92 (6 wkts, 35.5 overs)	134

†R. J. Parks, T. M. Tremlett and P. J. Bakker did not bat.

Bowling: Newman 7–0–26–1; Mortensen 8–2–19–1; Holding 8–1–25–2; Warner 3.5–0–13–0; Base 7–1–30–1; Bowler 2–0–16–0.

Umpires: J. Birkenshaw and J. D. Bond.

At Leicester, August 7. HAMPSHIRE beat LEICESTERSHIRE by 63 runs.

HAMPSHIRE v NORTHAMPTONSHIRE

At Bournemouth, August 14. Hampshire won by eight wickets in a match reduced by rain to twenty overs a side. Toss: Hampshire.

Northamptonshire

R. J. Bailey c C. L. Smith b James 12
W. Larkins b Bakker 3
A. Fordham run out 23
D. J. Wild lbw b James 0
*G. Cook c R. A. Smith b Ayling 37
M. R. Gouldstone c R. A. Smith b Bakker . 11
†D. Ripley not out 2
L-b 5, w 1 6

1/10 2/16 3/18 4/67 5/91 6/94 (6 wkts, 20 overs) 94

S. J. Brown, D. K. Lillee, N. G. B. Cook and A. Walker did not bat.

Bowling: James 5–0–10–2; Bakker 8–0–44–2; Tremlett 2–0–6–0; Ayling 5–0–29–1.

Hampshire

V. P. Terry c Lillee b Brown 20
D. R. Turner not out 47
R. A. Smith c Larkins b N. G. B. Cook 21
C. L. Smith not out 4
L-b 4, w 1 5

1/48 2/93 (2 wkts, 18.4 overs) 97

*M. C. J. Nicholas, J. R. Ayling, K. D. James, †A. N. Aymes, T. M. Tremlett, N. G. Cowley and P. J. Bakker did not bat.

Bowling: Lillee 6–0–31–0; Walker 4–0–17–0; Brown 5–0–26–1; N. G. B. Cook 3.4–0–19–1.

Umpires: H. D. Bird and M. J. Kitchen.

At Taunton, August 28. HAMPSHIRE beat SOMERSET by 62 runs.

KENT

At Chelmsford, April 24. KENT lost to ESSEX by nine wickets.

KENT v HAMPSHIRE

At Canterbury, May 1. Kent won by two wickets. D. R. Turner became the sixth player to pass 6,000 runs in the Sunday League. Toss: Kent.

Hampshire

R. A. Smith c Marsh b C. S. Cowdrey . 18
V. P. Terry c Marsh b Ellison 15
D. R. Turner b Pienaar 54
*M. C. J. Nicholas b C. S. Cowdrey ... 9
C. L. Smith st Marsh b Davis 70
K. D. James c Pienaar b Davis 14
S. T. Jefferies run out 5
N. G. Cowley b Davis 0
†R. J. Parks not out 4
C. A. Connor c Hinks b Penn 2
S. J. W. Andrew not out 1
L-b 14, w 3, n-b 6 23

1/30 2/42 3/68 4/162 5/192 6/203 7/207 8/208 9/211 (9 wkts, 40 overs) 215

Bowling: Ellison 8–2–29–1; Penn 8–0–39–1; C. S. Cowdrey 8–0–39–2; Pienaar 7–0–49–1; Davis 8–2–36–3; G. R. Cowdrey 1–0–9–0.

Kent

M. R. Benson c R. A. Smith b Cowley	44	R. M. Ellison not out	34
R. F. Pienaar c Parks b Jefferies	2	C. Penn not out	3
C. J. Tavaré b Connor	3		
S. G. Hinks b Cowley	8	B 4, l-b 12, w 11, n-b 4	31
*C. S. Cowdrey c Parks b Andrew	12		—
G. R. Cowdrey c Cowley b James	9	1/5 2/14 3/30 (8 wkts, 39.5 overs)	218
N. R. Taylor b Jefferies	68	4/51 5/80 6/94	
†S. A. Marsh run out	4	7/116 8/209	

R. P. Davis did not bat.

Bowling: Jefferies 8–1–31–2; Connor 7.5–0–48–1; James 8–1–23–1; Andrew 8–0–31–1; Cowley 7–0–53–2; Nicholas 1–0–16–0.

Umpires: D. J. Constant and D. O. Oslear.

At Leicester, May 8. LEICESTERSHIRE v KENT. No result.

KENT v LANCASHIRE

At Canterbury, May 15. Kent won by seven wickets. Toss: Kent.

Lancashire

G. D. Mendis b C. S. Cowdrey	19	P. J. W. Allott c Hinks b Ellison	30
G. Fowler c Tavaré b Penn	0	J. Simmons not out	2
A. N. Hayhurst lbw b Ellison	4	†W. K. Hegg c G. R. Cowdrey b Penn	1
N. H. Fairbrother c Marsh b Penn	6	B 1, l-b 4, w 5	10
M. Watkinson c and b G. R. Cowdrey	48		—
*D. P. Hughes c Taylor b C. S. Cowdrey	5	1/2 2/9 3/17 (39.1 overs)	169
Wasim Akram c Davis b G. R. Cowdrey	24	4/46 5/72 6/110	
I. D. Austin c Benson b Penn	20	7/113 8/165 9/167	

Bowling: Ellison 8–0–27–2; Penn 7.1–0–22–4; Davis 2–0–12–0; C. S. Cowdrey 8–0–34–2; Pienaar 8–0–48–0; G. R. Cowdrey 6–0–21–2.

Kent

M. R. Benson b Austin	11	*C. S. Cowdrey not out	10
N. R. Taylor lbw b Wasim	85	L-b 10, w 2, n-b 1	13
C. J. Tavaré c Wasim b Austin	17		—
S. G. Hinks not out	36	1/29 2/71 3/152 (3 wkts, 35 overs)	172

G. R. Cowdrey, R. F. Pienaar, †S. A. Marsh, R. M. Ellison, C. Penn and R. P. Davis did not bat.

Bowling: Allott 6–0–11–0; Wasim 6–0–31–1; Austin 8–0–28–2; Watkinson 8–0–36–0; Simmons 3–0–20–0; Hayhurst 4–0–36–0.

Umpires: R. Palmer and P. B. Wight.

KENT v YORKSHIRE

At Canterbury, May 22. Yorkshire won by 43 runs. Toss: Kent.

Yorkshire

M. D. Moxon b Ellison	0	*P. Carrick not out	38
A. A. Metcalfe c Marsh b Penn	8	A. Sidebottom not out	6
K. Sharp c G. R. Cowdrey b Wells	44	L-b 16, w 8	24
P. E. Robinson c Marsh b Pienaar	2		—
†D. L. Bairstow b Pienaar	7	1/0 2/23 3/33 (6 wkts, 40 overs)	159
S. N. Hartley b Penn	30	4/58 5/89 6/141	

S. D. Fletcher, P. W. Jarvis and C. Shaw did not bat.

Bowling: Ellison 8–2–34–1; Penn 8–0–39–2; Pienaar 8–0–22–2; C. S. Cowdrey 8–2–16–0; Wells 4–0–14–1; G. R. Cowdrey 4–0–18–0.

Kent

R. F. Pienaar c Bairstow b Moxon	13	C. Penn b Fletcher	8
N. R. Taylor c Carrick b Shaw	12	V. J. Wells not out	10
C. J. Tavaré b Fletcher	3	R. P. Davis lbw b Fletcher	0
S. G. Hinks b Sidebottom	32	L-b 13, w 6, n-b 1	20
*C. S. Cowdrey c Bairstow b Fletcher	9		—
G. R. Cowdrey lbw b Shaw	1	1/28 2/32 3/48 (36.4 overs)	116
R. M. Ellison c Sharp b Shaw	3	4/62 5/65 6/77	
†S. A. Marsh run out	5	7/98 8/98 9/116	

Bowling: Jarvis 8–2–27–0; Sidebottom 6–1–14–1; Fletcher 6.4–0–11–4; Shaw 8–0–24–3; Moxon 3–0–9–1; Carrick 5–0–18–0.

Umpires: J. C. Balderstone and J. H. Harris.

At Northampton, May 29. NORTHAMPTONSHIRE v KENT. No result.

At Merthyr Tydfil, June 5. KENT beat GLAMORGAN by five wickets.

At Birmingham, June 19. KENT beat WARWICKSHIRE by four wickets.

KENT v NOTTINGHAMSHIRE

At Canterbury, July 3. No result.

KENT v MIDDLESEX

At Canterbury, July 10. Middlesex won by two wickets. Toss: Middlesex.

Kent

T. R. Ward c Emburey b Sykes	25	G. R. Cowdrey not out	22
N. R. Taylor b Needham	22		
C. J. Tavaré c Emburey b Needham	8	L-b 7, w 1, n-b 1	9
*C. S. Cowdrey not out	61		—
R. F. Pienaar b Hughes	34	1/37 2/55 3/66 (5 wkts, 40 overs)	187
S. G. Hinks b Emburey	6	4/114 5/125	

†S. A. Marsh, C. Penn, R. M. Ellison and R. P. Davis did not bat.

Bowling: Fraser 7–2–34–0; Cowans 5–1–11–0; Sykes 7–1–32–1; Needham 6–1–24–2; Emburey 8–1–36–1; Hughes 7–0–43–1.

Middlesex

W. N. Slack run out 12
A. Needham c Davis b Pienaar 36
*M. W. Gatting c Marsh b Pienaar . . . 18
†P. R. Downton c and b Pienaar 7
K. R. Brown b G. R. Cowdrey 14
R. O. Butcher c G. R. Cowdrey b Pienaar . 11
J. E. Emburey c Hinks b Ellison 15
J. F. Sykes run out 9
S. P. Hughes not out 18
A. R. C. Fraser not out 30
L-b 12, w 8, n-b 1 21

1/52 2/67 3/77 4/86 5/111 6/115 7/132 8/141 (8 wkts, 39.3 overs) 191

N. G. Cowans did not bat.

Bowling: Penn 7–0–46–0; Ellison 7.3–0–33–1; C. S. Cowdrey 8–0–25–0; Davis 4–0–19–0; Pienaar 8–0–34–4; G. R. Cowdrey 5–0–22–1.

Umpires: M. J. Kitchen and A. G. T. Whitehead.

At The Oval, July 17. KENT lost to SURREY by five wickets.

KENT v WORCESTERSHIRE

At Folkestone, July 24. Worcestershire won by seven wickets. Toss: Worcestershire.

Kent

M. R. Benson c Bent b Pridgeon 66
N. R. Taylor run out 20
T. R. Ward c Radford b Pridgeon 5
R. F. Pienaar c Rhodes b Pridgeon 9
G. R. Cowdrey c Pridgeon b O'Shaughnessy . 6
*C. J. Tavaré not out 34
R. M. Ellison not out 37
L-b 11, w 3 14

1/57 2/74 3/100 4/110 5/114 (5 wkts, 40 overs) 191

†S. A. Marsh, C. Penn, D. J. M. Kelleher and R. P. Davis did not bat.

Bowling: Newport 6–0–20–0; Weston 8–0–30–0; Radford 8–0–44–0; Illingworth 8–0–34–0; Pridgeon 8–0–39–3; O'Shaughnessy 2–0–13–1.

Worcestershire

P. Bent c Pienaar b Ellison 13
S. J. O'Shaughnessy c Cowdrey b Kelleher . 41
G. A. Hick c Penn b Kelleher 22
D. A. Leatherdale not out 62
*P. A. Neale not out 41
B 1, l-b 9, w 2, n-b 1 13

1/24 2/80 3/82 (3 wkts, 38 overs) 192

M. J. Weston, †S. J. Rhodes, P. J. Newport, R. K. Illingworth, N. V. Radford and A. P. Pridgeon did not bat.

Bowling: Penn 8–0–41–0; Ellison 7–0–45–1; Davis 8–2–16–0; Pienaar 5–0–30–0; Kelleher 7–1–27–2; Cowdrey 3–0–23–0.

Umpires: R. Palmer and R. A. White.

KENT v SOMERSET

At Canterbury, July 31. Kent won by seven wickets. Toss: Kent.

Somerset

G. D. Rose c Alleyne b C. S. Cowdrey . 38
*P. M. Roebuck b Alleyne 1
S. R. Waugh b C. S. Cowdrey 39
R. J. Bartlett st Marsh b Davis 2
J. C. M. Atkinson c Taylor b G. R. Cowdrey . 2
V. J. Marks b Wells 2
†N. D. Burns c C. S. Cowdrey b Wells . 9
H. R. J. Trump c and b G. R. Cowdrey 4
N. A. Mallender c C. S. Cowdrey b Wells 5
C. H. Dredge b Alleyne 13
D. J. Foster not out 2
L-b 8 8

1/8 2/73 3/88 (39.2 overs) 125
4/88 5/92 6/95
7/100 8/110 9/111

Bowling: Kelleher 5–1–18–0; Alleyne 6.2–0–19–2; Davis 8–1–23–1; C. S. Cowdrey 5–0–27–2; G. R. Cowdrey 8–1–13–2; Wells 7–1–17–3.

Kent

N. R. Taylor lbw b Mallender 21
T. R. Ward c Bartlett b Rose 20
C. J. Tavaré not out 30
*C. S. Cowdrey c Bartlett b Dredge . . . 46
S. G. Hinks not out 0
L-b 4, w 2, n-b 3 9

1/48 2/48 3/120 (3 wkts, 29.4 overs) 126

H. L. Alleyne, G. R. Cowdrey, †S. A. Marsh, V. J. Wells, D. J. M. Kelleher and R. P. Davis did not bat.

Bowling: Foster 7–1–32–0; Dredge 6.4–0–38–1; Marks 6–1–29–0; Mallender 5–0–10–1; Rose 5–0–13–1.

Umpires: J. Birkenshaw and R. Julian.

At Chesterfield, August 14. KENT beat DERBYSHIRE by six wickets.

At Moreton-in-Marsh, August 21. KENT lost to GLOUCESTERSHIRE by 80 runs.

KENT v SUSSEX

At Maidstone, August 28. Kent won by four wickets in a match reduced by rain to 23 overs a side. Toss: Kent.

Sussex

A. P. Wells st Marsh b G. R. Cowdrey. 40
*P. W. G. Parker lbw b Wells 6
C. M. Wells c Marsh b Wells 8
M. P. Speight c Davis b Fleming 31
I. J. Gould b Davis 6
A. M. Green st Marsh b C. S. Cowdrey 8
†P. Moores c and b Davis 4
A. R. Clarke st Marsh b Davis 7
S. J. S. Kimber not out 2
R. A. Bunting not out 5
B 1, l-b 7 8

1/23 2/35 3/86 (8 wkts, 23 overs) 125
4/94 5/100 6/110
7/118 8/118

A. M. Babington did not bat.

Bowling: Wells 5–0–22–2; Sabine 5–0–19–0; G. R. Cowdrey 4–1–16–1; Fleming 5–0–34–1; Davis 3–0–19–3; C. S. Cowdrey 1–0–7–1.

Kent

N. R. Taylor b Clarke 10
T. R. Ward c Green b Babington 6
R. F. Pienaar c and b Green 44
G. R. Cowdrey b Clarke 7
S. G. Hinks not out 33
*C. S. Cowdrey st Moores b Green 9
†S. A. Marsh st Moores b Green 0
M. V. Fleming not out 3
L-b 4, w 9, n-b 1 14

1/14 2/51 3/70 (6 wkts, 22.4 overs) 126
4/107 5/117 6/117

V. J. Wells, D. J. Sabine and R. P. Davis did not bat.

Bowling: Bunting 4–0–23–0; Babington 5–0–19–1; Clarke 5–1–16–2; Kimber 3–0–28–0; C. M. Wells 3–0–20–0; Green 2.4–1–16–3.

Umpires: D. G. L. Evans and N. T. Plews.

LANCASHIRE

LANCASHIRE v WORCESTERSHIRE

At Manchester, April 24. Lancashire won by seven wickets. Toss: Lancashire. Matthews, having Curtis caught behind, became the third bowler to take a wicket with his first ball in the Sunday League.

Worcestershire

T. S. Curtis c Hegg b Matthews 1
I. T. Botham b Watkinson 39
G. A. Hick run out 9
D. B. D'Oliveira c Hegg b Watkinson . 7
*P. A. Neale run out 31
S. J. O'Shaughnessy c Simmons b Matthews . 50
†S. J. Rhodes lbw b Allott 16
P. J. Newport run out 5
N. V. Radford not out 3
R. K. Illingworth not out 0
B 1, l-b 10 11

1/5 2/21 3/46 4/75 5/100 6/150 7/167 8/169 (8 wkts, 40 overs) 172

G. R. Dilley did not bat.

Bowling: Allott 8–1–24–1; Matthews 8–0–44–2; Watkinson 8–0–33–2; Hayhurst 8–0–30–0; Simmons 8–1–30–0.

Lancashire

G. D. Mendis lbw b Botham 42
G. Fowler c Rhodes b Botham 43
T. E. Jesty b Illingworth 33
N. H. Fairbrother not out 40
M. Watkinson not out 4
L-b 4, w 8, n-b 2 14

1/92 2/95 3/172 (3 wkts, 36.2 overs) 176

*D. P. Hughes, A. N. Hayhurst, C. D. Matthews, †W. K. Hegg, P. J. W. Allott and J. Simmons did not bat.

Bowling: Dilley 8–0–30–0; Newport 8–0–33–0; Illingworth 6.2–0–37–1; Radford 4–0–22–0; Botham 8–0–36–2; O'Shaughnessy 2–0–14–0.

Umpires: J. W. Holder and D. O. Oslear.

LANCASHIRE v WARWICKSHIRE

At Manchester, May 1. Lancashire won by one wicket, having been set a revised target of 143 off 25 overs after rain interrupted play. Toss: Lancashire.

Warwickshire

*T. A. Lloyd c Hegg b Matthews 11
†G. W. Humpage b Hayhurst 46
A. I. Kallicharran c Watkinson b Simmons . 63
A. J. Moles run out 7
P. A. Smith b Watkinson 48
Asif Din not out 17
D. A. Reeve not out 6
L-b 12, w 2 14

1/35 2/80 3/98 4/165 5/200 (5 wkts, 37.1 overs) 212

G. C. Small, T. A. Merrick, N. Gifford and A. R. K. Pierson did not bat.

Bowling: Allott 7–0–21–0; Matthews 6.1–0–27–1; Watkinson 8–0–46–1; Hayhurst 8–0–59–1; Simmons 8–0–47–1.

Lancashire

G. D. Mendis c Humpage b Merrick	1	P. J. W. Allott c Smith b Small	43
G. Fowler run out	14	J. Simmons not out	20
T. E. Jesty b Small	9	C. D. Matthews not out	1
N. H. Fairbrother c Merrick b Small	5	L-b 8, w 3, n-b 1	12
M. Watkinson b Gifford	6		
*D. P. Hughes run out	2	1/1 2/14 3/22 (9 wkts, 24.3 overs)	144
A. N. Hayhurst b Small	24	4/39 5/44 6/57	
†W. K. Hegg b Gifford	7	7/75 8/110 9/127	

Bowling: Small 8–0–44–4; Merrick 7.3–0–41–1; Gifford 5–0–22–2; Reeve 4–0–29–0.

Umpires: H. D. Bird and N. T. Plews.

At Nottingham, May 8. LANCASHIRE beat NOTTINGHAMSHIRE by two wickets.

At Canterbury, May 15. LANCASHIRE lost to KENT by seven wickets.

LANCASHIRE v LEICESTERSHIRE

At Manchester, May 29. Lancashire won on faster scoring-rate after rain ended play. Toss: Leicestershire.

Lancashire

G. D. Mendis b Ferris	0	P. J. W. Allott c Whitticase b Ferris	3
A. N. Hayhurst c Taylor b Ferris	84	I. D. Austin not out	1
T. E. Jesty c Whitticase b Ferris	10	L-b 6, w 8, n-b 2	16
N. H. Fairbrother c Whitticase b Taylor	43		
M. Watkinson c Willey b Potter	30	1/0 2/30 3/108 (7 wkts, 40 overs)	214
*D. P. Hughes run out	6	4/178 5/184	
Wasim Akram not out	21	6/196 7/202	

J. Simmons and †W. K. Hegg did not bat.

Bowling: Ferris 7–1–24–4; DeFreitas 8–0–41–0; Lewis 8–0–40–0; Willey 8–0–33–0; Taylor 7–0–53–1; Potter 2–0–17–1.

Leicestershire

N. E. Briers not out	36
L. Potter c Hegg b Wasim	51
*D. I. Gower not out	1
L-b 4, w 7	11
1/94 (1 wkt, 22.3 overs)	99

J. J. Whitaker, P. Willey, P. A. J. DeFreitas, †P. Whitticase, C. C. Lewis, J. D. R. Benson, L. B. Taylor and G. J. F. Ferris did not bat.

Bowling: Wasim 4.3–0–16–1; Allott 8–1–26–0; Austin 4–1–13–0; Watkinson 3–0–19–0; Simmons 3–0–21–0.

Umpires: B. Dudleston and J. H. Hampshire.

LANCASHIRE v HAMPSHIRE

At Manchester, June 5. Lancashire won by six wickets. Toss: Lancashire.

Hampshire

C. L. Smith c Hughes b Watkinson	20	K. D. James not out	24
V. P. Terry lbw b Wasim	3	S. T. Jefferies not out	21
R. A. Smith b Austin	51	L-b 8, w 2	10
D. R. Turner b Watkinson	34		—
*M. C. J. Nicholas b Austin	3	1/6 2/51 3/100 (6 wkts, 40 overs)	196
J. R. Ayling b Wasim	30	4/106 5/125 6/163	

†R. J. Parks, S. J. W. Andrew and C. A. Connor did not bat.

Bowling: Allott 8–0–43–0; Wasim 8–0–33–2; Watkinson 8–0–36–2; Austin 8–1–34–2; Simmons 8–0–42–0.

Lancashire

G. D. Mendis lbw b Ayling	48	*D. P. Hughes not out	7
A. N. Hayhurst run out	34	L-b 6, w 2, n-b 1	9
T. E. Jesty b Jefferies	2		—
N. H. Fairbrother not out	57	1/78 2/81 3/103 (4 wkts, 39.4 overs)	197
M. Watkinson c Nicholas b Jefferies	40	4/186	

I. D. Austin, Wasim Akram, P. J. W. Allott, †W. K. Hegg and J. Simmons did not bat.

Bowling: Connor 8–2–32–0; James 7.4–0–51–0; Andrew 8–0–43–0; Ayling 8–0–28–1; Jefferies 8–1–37–2.

Umpires: J. H. Harris and K. E. Palmer.

LANCASHIRE v GLOUCESTERSHIRE

At Manchester, June 19. Lancashire won by one wicket. Toss: Gloucestershire.

Gloucestershire

A. W. Stovold lbw b Allott	9	M. W. Alleyne not out	37
C. W. J. Athey run out	26	L-b 14, n-b 1	15
P. Bainbridge b Austin	21		—
A. J. Wright c Hughes b Simmons	20	1/22 2/55 3/67 (4 wkts, 40 overs)	206
P. W. Romaines not out	78	4/107	

J. W. Lloyds, *D. A. Graveney, †R. C. Russell, V. S. Greene and K. B. S. Jarvis did not bat.

Bowling: Watkinson 8–0–38–0; Allott 8–0–38–1; Austin 8–0–37–1; Simmons 8–0–29–1; Hayhurst 8–0–50–0.

Lancashire

G. D. Mendis lbw b Jarvis	50	J. Simmons lbw b Greene	0
G. Fowler c Alleyne b Jarvis	14	I. D. Austin not out	19
T. E. Jesty run out	39	†W. K. Hegg not out	3
N. H. Fairbrother c and b Jarvis	15	L-b 8, w 2	10
M. Watkinson c Wright b Greene	24		—
*D. P. Hughes c Wright b Greene	6	1/17 2/81 3/110 (9 wkts, 39.4 overs)	209
A. N. Hayhurst c Greene b Alleyne	27	4/137 5/147 6/174	
P. J. W. Allott b Greene	2	7/177 8/177 9/196	

Bowling: Jarvis 8–0–36–3; Greene 8–0–25–4; Alleyne 8–1–47–1; Bainbridge 7.4–0–56–0; Graveney 8–1–37–0.

Umpires: J. C. Balderstone and D. G. L. Evans.

At Pontypridd, June 26. GLAMORGAN v LANCASHIRE. No result.

At Tring, July 3. NORTHAMPTONSHIRE v LANCASHIRE. No result.

LANCASHIRE v SOMERSET

At Manchester, July 10. Somerset won by 6 runs in a match reduced to 34 overs a side. Toss: Lancashire.

Somerset

*P. M. Roebuck lbw b Allott	13
J. J. E. Hardy b Wasim	25
S. R. Waugh st Hegg b Simmons	37
R. J. Bartlett c Wasim b Watkinson	55
N. J. Pringle c Hegg b Hayhurst	10
V. J. Marks b Wasim	20
G. D. Rose b Wasim	2
G. V. Palmer not out	4
†N. D. Burns not out	1
B 5, l-b 16, w 2	23
1/32 2/82 3/92 4/119 5/163 6/171 7/185 (7 wkts, 34 overs)	190

N. A. Mallender and A. N. Jones did not bat.

Bowling: Watkinson 7–0–36–1; Allott 7–0–28–1; Wasim 7–1–24–3; Simmons 7–0–42–1; Hayhurst 6–0–39–1.

Lancashire

G. D. Mendis c Burns b Jones	4
G. Fowler c Burns b Rose	5
T. E. Jesty lbw b Waugh	41
A. N. Hayhurst b Marks	37
N. H. Fairbrother not out	51
M. Watkinson c Rose b Marks	2
*D. P. Hughes c Hardy b Palmer	3
Wasim Akram c Roebuck b Mallender	12
P. J. W. Allott run out	15
†W. K. Hegg not out	0
B 5, l-b 3, w 6	14
1/11 2/17 3/94 4/94 5/99 6/110 7/141 8/184 (8 wkts, 34 overs)	184

J. Simmons did not bat.

Bowling: Jones 5–0–21–1; Rose 4–0–17–1; Mallender 7–0–35–1; Marks 7–0–26–2; Waugh 7–0–47–1; Palmer 4–0–30–1.

Umpires: R. Julian and R. A. White.

At Southend, July 17. LANCASHIRE lost to ESSEX by six wickets.

At Scarborough, July 31. LANCASHIRE beat YORKSHIRE by two wickets.

LANCASHIRE v MIDDLESEX

At Blackpool, August 7. Lancashire won by 52 runs. Toss: Middlesex.

Lancashire

G. D. Mendis c and b Carr	86
G. Fowler b Fraser	16
T. E. Jesty c Fraser b Needham	28
N. H. Fairbrother c Carr b Needham	6
M. Watkinson c Needham b Hughes	41
*D. P. Hughes b Emburey	0
A. N. Hayhurst c Gatting b Hughes	11
I. D. Austin b Hughes	1
P. J. W. Allott run out	0
J. Simmons not out	9
†W. K. Hegg b Fraser	0
L-b 4, w 3, n-b 2	9
1/22 2/100 3/114 4/179 5/180 6/186 7/198 8/198 9/204 (40 overs)	207

Bowling: Fraser 8–1–27–2; Cowans 6–0–24–0; Hughes 8–0–43–3; Emburey 8–0–41–1; Carr 5–0–30–1; Needham 5–0–38–2.

Middlesex

W. N. Slack b Watkinson 11
J. D. Carr c Hughes b Watkinson 2
A. Needham c Fairbrother b Watkinson 3
*M. W. Gatting lbw b Allott 3
R. O. Butcher c Austin b Simmons 21
K. R. Brown c Hegg b Austin 0
J. E. Emburey c Simmons b Allott 50
†P. R. Downton run out 32
S. P. Hughes not out 16
A. R. C. Fraser c and b Simmons 0
N. G. Cowans c Fairbrother b Watkinson 10
B 1, l-b 5, w 1 7

1/4 2/8 3/15 4/25 5/26 6/53 7/121 8/130 9/131 (37.4 overs) 155

Bowling: Allott 7–0–19–2; Watkinson 7.4–2–17–4; Austin 8–0–27–1; Simmons 8–1–36–2; Hayhurst 7–0–50–0.

Umpires: B. Leadbeater and D. R. Shepherd.

At Hove, August 14. LANCASHIRE beat SUSSEX by five wickets.

LANCASHIRE v DERBYSHIRE

At Manchester, August 21. Lancashire won by 2 runs. Toss: Derbyshire.

Lancashire

G. D. Mendis run out 9
G. Fowler b Sharma 13
A. N. Hayhurst c Base b Warner 77
N. H. Fairbrother c Maher b Base 5
T. E. Jesty c Base b Bowler 31
M. Watkinson b Base 1
I. D. Austin run out 41
*D. P. Hughes not out 1
P. J. W. Allott not out 11
L-b 5, w 4, n-b 2 11

1/20 2/33 3/43 4/102 5/106 6/185 7/187 (7 wkts, 40 overs) 200

†W. K. Hegg and J. Simmons did not bat.

Bowling: Holding 8–1–35–0; Warner 8–0–68–1; Sharma 8–2–22–1; Base 8–0–21–2; Barnett 4–0–22–0; Griffith 1–0–8–0; Bowler 3–0–19–1.

Derbyshire

P. D. Bowler b Austin 44
J. E. Morris b Allott 2
†B. J. M. Maher c Hegg b Austin 20
S. C. Goldsmith b Austin 5
M. A. Holding c Fowler b Simmons 53
B. Roberts st Hegg b Simmons 37
R. Sharma c Watkinson b Hayhurst 0
A. E. Warner not out 16
F. A. Griffith run out 8
*K. J. Barnett run out 3
S. J. Base run out 0
B 2, l-b 8 10

1/4 2/52 3/64 4/88 5/155 6/156 7/167 8/186 9/197 (39.5 overs) 198

Bowling: Watkinson 8–1–33–0; Allott 7.5–1–21–1; Simmons 8–0–45–2; Austin 8–1–34–3; Hayhurst 8–0–55–1.

Umpires: B. J. Meyer and A. G. T. Whitehead.

At The Oval, August 28. LANCASHIRE lost to SURREY by six wickets.

LEICESTERSHIRE

At Derby, April 24. LEICESTERSHIRE lost to DERBYSHIRE by nine wickets.

LEICESTERSHIRE v NORTHAMPTONSHIRE

At Leicester, May 1. Leicestershire won on scoring-rate when Northamptonshire failed by 49 runs to achieve a revised target of 161 off 37 overs. Toss: Northamptonshire.

Leicestershire

N. E. Briers c Ripley b Davis 7
L. Potter run out 49
*D. I. Gower c Walker b Robinson . . . 14
J. J. Whitaker c G. Cook b N. G. B. Cook . 13
P. Willey c and b N. G. B. Cook 2
P. A. J. DeFreitas b Walker 1
C. C. Lewis lbw b Walker 40
J. P. Agnew c Stanley b Williams 16
†P. Whitticase not out 19
L. B. Taylor not out 5
L-b 3, w 3, n-b 1 7

1/17 2/36 3/79 4/83 5/87 6/91 7/131 8/150 (8 wkts, 40 overs) 173

G. J. F. Ferris did not bat.

Bowling: Davis 8–0–47–1; Robinson 8–0–35–1; N. G. B. Cook 8–1–19–2; Walker 8–0–41–2; Williams 8–0–28–1.

Northamptonshire

*G. Cook lbw b Ferris 8
W. Larkins b Ferris 0
A. J. Lamb c Willey b Agnew 26
R. J. Bailey lbw b Agnew 17
R. G. Williams c Whitticase b Agnew . 9
N. A. Stanley run out 12
†D. Ripley c Whitticase b Taylor 12
N. G. B. Cook not out 13
W. W. Davis run out 0
A. Walker c Whitticase b Taylor 4
M. A. Robinson lbw b Taylor 0
L-b 3, w 5, n-b 3 11

1/10 2/11 3/50 4/65 5/66 6/94 7/95 8/98 9/112 (32.5 overs) 112

Bowling: Ferris 7–0–30–2; DeFreitas 5–1–11–0; Lewis 6–0–16–0; Agnew 8–0–32–3; Taylor 6.5–0–20–3.

Umpires: J. Birkenshaw and B. J. Meyer.

LEICESTERSHIRE v KENT

At Leicester, May 8. No result.

LEICESTERSHIRE v WORCESTERSHIRE

At Leicester, May 22. Worcestershire won by four wickets. Toss: Worcestershire.

Leicestershire

L. Potter c Rhodes b Pridgeon 5
N. E. Briers c Rhodes b Weston 2
*D. I. Gower c Leatherdale b McEwan. 50
J. J. Whitaker c O'Shaughnessy b McEwan . 31
P. Willey c Weston b Newport 43
C. C. Lewis c Rhodes b Illingworth . . . 5
J. D. R. Benson c and b Pridgeon 19
†M. A. Garnham b Pridgeon 0
J. P. Agnew not out 8
L. B. Taylor b Pridgeon 1
G. J. F. Ferris not out 13
L-b 9, w 9, n-b 2 20

1/4 2/40 3/79 4/112 5/131 6/171 7/173 8/174 9/178 (9 wkts, 40 overs) 197

Bowling: Newport 8–0–49–1; Weston 8–0–28–1; Pridgeon 8–1–36–4; Illingworth 8–0–43–1; McEwan 8–0–32–2.

Worcestershire

T. S. Curtis lbw b Willey 50
†S. J. Rhodes b Willey 25
G. A. Hick b Ferris 66
S. J. O'Shaughnessy lbw b Willey 0
*P. A. Neale b Agnew 9
D. A. Leatherdale b Ferris 13
M. J. Weston not out 14
P. J. Newport not out 0
L-b 15, w 7, n-b 2 24

1/83 2/103 3/103 4/129 5/178 6/185 (6 wkts, 39.4 overs) 201

S. M. McEwan, R. K. Illingworth and A. P. Pridgeon did not bat.

Bowling: Ferris 8–0–36–2; Agnew 8–1–37–1; Taylor 8–0–42–0; Lewis 7.4–0–40–0; Willey 6–2–20–3; Potter 2–0–11–0.

Umpires: A. A. Jones and R. A. White.

At Manchester, May 29. LEICESTERSHIRE lost to LANCASHIRE on scoring-rate.

At The Oval, June 12. LEICESTERSHIRE lost to SURREY by four wickets.

LEICESTERSHIRE v SUSSEX

At Leicester, June 19. Sussex won by 3 runs. Toss: Sussex.

Sussex

A. M. Green c Lewis b Taylor 24
*P. W. G. Parker b Lewis 78
Imran Khan c Whitticase b Lewis 15
C. M. Wells not out 22
A. C. S. Pigott c Lewis b Ferris 22
†P. Moores not out 1
L-b 7, w 4, n-b 9 20

1/71 2/129 3/140 4/175 (4 wkts, 40 overs) 182

R. I. Alikhan, N. J. Lenham, R. A. Bunting, S. J. S. Kimber and A. R. Clarke did not bat.

Bowling: Ferris 8–0–30–1; Agnew 8–0–38–0; DeFreitas 8–0–43–0; Lewis 8–1–26–2; Taylor 8–0–38–1.

Leicestershire

*N. E. Briers lbw b Clarke 48
L. Potter lbw b C. M. Wells 10
J. J. Whitaker lbw b Kimber 13
C. C. Lewis c Pigott b Kimber 4
P. A. J. DeFreitas c Moores b Kimber . 3
J. D. R. Benson b Pigott 35
P. N. Hepworth run out 38
J. P. Agnew not out 0
G. J. F. Ferris not out 0
L-b 24, w 3, n-b 1 28

1/42 2/89 3/89 4/95 5/96 6/179 7/179 (7 wkts, 40 overs) 179

†P. Whitticase and L. B. Taylor did not bat.

Bowling: Imran 7–0–38–0; Kimber 7–0–35–3; C. M. Wells 8–3–11–1; Pigott 8–1–27–1; Bunting 2–0–18–0; Clarke 8–1–26–1.

Umpires: J. D. Bond and D. O. Oslear.

At Gloucester, June 26. LEICESTERSHIRE lost to GLOUCESTERSHIRE by 63 runs.

At Hull, July 3. LEICESTERSHIRE lost to YORKSHIRE by six wickets.

At Nottingham, July 10. NOTTINGHAMSHIRE v LEICESTERSHIRE. No result.

LEICESTERSHIRE v ESSEX

At Leicester, July 24. Leicestershire won by eight wickets. Toss: Leicestershire.

Essex

J. P. Stephenson c Whitticase b Lewis . 0
P. J. Prichard lbw b Agnew 10
A. R. Border c Whitticase b Lewis 3
A. W. Lilley b Taylor 22
N. Hussain c Briers b Taylor 14
*K. W. R. Fletcher run out 24
G. Miller c Briers b Taylor 31
†D. E. East c and b Tennant 2
I. L. Pont c Whitticase b Lewis 6
T. D. Topley c Agnew b Lewis 3
J. K. Lever not out 2
L-b 14, w 1, n-b 1 16

1/1 2/6 3/28 4/55 5/72 6/103 7/105 8/120 9/128 (40 overs) 133

Bowling: Lewis 8–0–13–4; Tennant 8–0–36–1; Agnew 8–2–15–1; Willey 8–1–24–0; Taylor 8–0–31–3.

Leicestershire

*N. E. Briers c and b Miller 26
L. Potter not out 66
P. Willey c Hussain b Topley 5
J. J. Whitaker not out 25
B 1, l-b 8, w 3, n-b 3 15

1/74 2/84 (2 wkts, 37 overs) 137

T. J. Boon, P. N. Hepworth, C. C. Lewis, †P. Whitticase, J. P. Agnew, L. Tennant and L. B. Taylor did not bat.

Bowling: Topley 7–0–23–1; Lever 6–1–23–0; Miller 8–1–23–1; Pont 8–0–32–0; Stephenson 0.2–0–4–0; Border 7.4–1–23–0.

Umpires: K. J. Lyons and P. B. Wight.

LEICESTERSHIRE v MIDDLESEX

At Leicester, July 31. No result. Toss: Middlesex. The match had been reduced to 27 overs per side because of rain.

Leicestershire

L. Potter run out 19
N. E. Briers run out 0
*D. I. Gower c Butcher b Cowans 15
J. J. Whitaker c Carr b Emburey 51
P. Willey c Downton b Fraser 4
T. J. Boon run out 11
P. A. J. DeFreitas b Hughes 8
†P. Whitticase c Butcher b Emburey . . 1
J. P. Agnew b Emburey 10
L. B. Taylor run out 1
L. Tennant not out 1
B 1, l-b 5, w 3 9

1/0 2/22 3/70 4/78 5/104 6/108 7/118 8/128 9/128 (27 overs) 130

Bowling: Cowans 5–0–22–1; Hughes 3–0–19–1; Gatting 4–0–26–0; Needham 6–0–25–0; Fraser 6–0–17–1; Emburey 3–0–15–3.

Middlesex

W. N. Slack, J. D. Carr, A. Needham, *M. W. Gatting, R. O. Butcher, K. R. Brown, J. E. Emburey, †P. R. Downton, S. P. Hughes, A. R. C. Fraser and N. G. Cowans.

Umpires: D. R. Shepherd and A. G. T. Whitehead.

LEICESTERSHIRE v HAMPSHIRE

At Leicester, August 7. Hampshire won by 63 runs. Toss: Hampshire.

Hampshire

V. P. Terry c Ferris b Such 40
*M. C. J. Nicholas c Such b Willey ... 18
D. R. Turner c Taylor b Such 51
J. R. Ayling b Ferris 34
C. L. Smith c Benson b Taylor 47
S. T. Jefferies not out 18
B 11, l-b 10, w 8, n-b 3 32

1/56 2/116 3/156 4/206 5/240 (5 wkts, 40 overs) 240

N. G. Cowley, †R. J. Parks, P. J. Bakker, R. J. Maru and K. D. James did not bat.

Bowling: Ferris 8–0–34–1; Tennant 8–0–46–0; Willey 8–0–27–1; Taylor 8–0–55–1; Such 7–0–53–2; Potter 1–0–4–0.

Leicestershire

N. E. Briers b Ayling 32
L. Potter c Nicholas b Cowley 52
*D. I. Gower c Terry b Ayling 4
J. J. Whitaker run out 0
P. Willey st Parks b Maru 16
†J. D. R. Benson not out 42
T. J. Boon c and b Maru 11
G. J. F. Ferris b Maru 2
L. Tennant not out 5
L-b 8, w 4, n-b 1 13

1/85 2/91 3/91 4/104 5/113 6/136 7/148 (7 wkts, 40 overs) 177

P. M. Such and L. B. Taylor did not bat.

Bowling: Jefferies 4–0–15–0; Bakker 6–0–20–0; James 6–0–31–0; Ayling 7–0–38–2; Cowley 8–0–31–1; Maru 8–0–30–3; Nicholas 1–0–4–0.

Umpires: J. H. Harris and N. T. Plews.

At Birmingham, August 14. LEICESTERSHIRE lost to WARWICKSHIRE by seven wickets.

LEICESTERSHIRE v SOMERSET

At Leicester, August 21. Leicestershire won by two wickets, having been set a revised target of 142 runs off 30 overs. Toss: Leicestershire.

Somerset

G. D. Rose b Tennant 11
J. J. E. Hardy c Whitticase b Agnew .. 40
J. G. Wyatt c Whitticase b Tennant ... 3
R. J. Bartlett c Tennant b Agnew 50
R. J. Harden c DeFreitas b Taylor 32
V. J. Marks not out 14
†N. D. Burns not out 16
L-b 5, w 2, n-b 2 9

1/21 2/36 3/65 4/140 5/147 (5 wkts, 37 overs) 175

*P. M. Roebuck, N. A. Mallender, A. N. Jones and C. H. Dredge did not bat.

Bowling: DeFreitas 7–0–37–0; Tennant 8–0–29–2; Willey 8–0–46–0; Agnew 8–0–34–2; Taylor 6–0–24–1.

Leicestershire

L. Potter c Burns b Dredge 0
N. E. Briers c Marks b Rose 30
*D. I. Gower b Dredge 1
J. J. Whitaker lbw b Rose 11
P. Willey c Rose b Marks 18
J. D. R. Benson b Marks 10
P. A. J. DeFreitas c Jones b Marks ... 4
†P. Whitticase c Wyatt b Mallender ... 21
J. P. Agnew not out 19
L. Tennant not out 17
B 1, l-b 10, w 1 12

1/0 2/5 3/41 4/66 5/76 6/85 7/90 8/115 (8 wkts, 29.5 overs) 143

L. B. Taylor did not bat.

Bowling: Dredge 6–0–17–2; Mallender 5.5–0–35–1; Marks 6–0–19–3; Jones 4–0–28–0; Rose 8–0–33–2.

Umpires: J. D. Bond and B. Leadbeater.

At Llanelli, August 28. LEICESTERSHIRE beat GLAMORGAN by eight wickets.

MIDDLESEX

MIDDLESEX v NOTTINGHAMSHIRE

At Lord's, April 24. Middlesex won by four wickets. Toss: Middlesex.

Nottinghamshire

B. C. Broad c Gatting b Williams 18
*R. T. Robinson run out 40
P. Johnson c Brown b Williams 2
D. W. Randall c Downton b Williams . 12
J. D. Birch not out 35
F. D. Stephenson c Emburey b Sykes .. 12
†B. N. French b Fraser 23
K. P. Evans b Fraser 6
R. A. Pick not out 1
B 2, l-b 10, w 4 16

1/40 2/46 3/74 4/82 5/106 6/149 7/164 (7 wkts, 40 overs) 165

K. E. Cooper and K. Saxelby did not bat.

Bowling: Cowans 4–0–21–0; Fraser 8–0–23–2; Williams 8–0–28–3; Emburey 7–0–25–0; Sykes 6–1–22–1; Hughes 7–0–34–0.

Middlesex

J. D. Carr lbw b Stephenson 8
*M. W. Gatting b Cooper 0
†P. R. Downton run out 49
R. O. Butcher b Evans 0
J. E. Emburey b Evans 47
K. R. Brown c French b Cooper 10
J. F. Sykes not out 33
N. F. Williams not out 11
L-b 6, w 1, n-b 1 8

1/1 2/33 3/34 4/86 5/103 6/133 (6 wkts, 38.1 overs) 166

S. P. Hughes, A. R. C. Fraser and N. G. Cowans did not bat.

Bowling: Pick 8–0–46–0; Cooper 8–1–22–2; Stephenson 7.1–1–23–1; Evans 8–0–32–2; Saxelby 7–0–37–0.

Umpires: D. J. Constant and A. A. Jones.

MIDDLESEX v ESSEX

At Lord's, May 1. Middlesex won by 26 runs, in a match reduced by rain to 34 overs a side. Toss: Essex.

Middlesex

W. N. Slack c Hardie b Miller 41	N. G. Cowans c Prichard b Pont 0
*M. W. Gatting c East b Miller 28	A. R. C. Fraser not out 0
†P. R. Downton c Fletcher b Miller . . . 14	
R. O. Butcher c Lever b Gooch 30	B 5, l-b 10, w 10, n-b 3 28
J. E. Emburey c and b Gooch 16	—
K. R. Brown c Lever b Pont 27	1/59 2/87 3/97 (8 wkts, 34 overs) 198
J. F. Sykes run out 0	4/143 5/149 6/154
N. F. Williams not out 14	7/195 8/195

S. P. Hughes did not bat.

Bowling: Lever 7–0–29–0; Pont 7–0–42–2; Gooch 7–0–49–2; Miller 7–0–34–3; Topley 6–0–29–0.

Essex

G. A. Gooch b Hughes 33	I. L. Pont not out 29
B. R. Hardie c Butcher b Cowans 5	T. D. Topley c Sykes b Williams 23
A. R. Border c Downton b Cowans . . . 5	J. K. Lever b Hughes 0
D. R. Pringle c Gatting b Cowans 40	L-b 6, w 7, n-b 2 15
P. J. Prichard c Slack b Emburey 10	—
*K. W. R. Fletcher run out 0	1/10 2/17 3/83 (33.3 overs) 172
†D. E. East c Slack b Williams 9	4/103 5/103 6/103
G. Miller c Downton b Williams 3	7/115 8/115 9/172

Bowling: Fraser 7–0–24–0; Cowans 7–0–29–3; Hughes 6.3–0–38–2; Williams 6–0–30–3; Emburey 7–0–45–1.

Umpires: D. G. L. Evans and J. H. Hampshire.

At The Oval, May 8. SURREY v MIDDLESEX. No result.

At Southampton, May 15. MIDDLESEX beat HAMPSHIRE by 29 runs.

MIDDLESEX v SUSSEX

At Lord's, May 29. Middlesex won by 53 runs. Toss: Sussex.

Middlesex

J. D. Carr b Babington 21	J. F. Sykes not out 2
*M. W. Gatting c Pigott b Babington . . 51	
†P. R. Downton c Pigott b C. M. Wells 27	L-b 4, w 1, n-b 1 6
R. O. Butcher b Pigott 77	—
J. E. Emburey c Gould b Imran 18	1/41 2/96 3/111 (5 wkts, 38 overs) 213
K. R. Brown not out 11	4/175 5/211

N. F. Williams, S. P. Hughes, A. R. C. Fraser and N. G. Cowans did not bat.

Bowling: Imran 8–1–37–1; Pigott 8–0–36–1; Babington 8–0–47–2; C. M. Wells 6–0–52–1; Kimber 8–0–37–0.

Sussex

A. M. Green b Fraser 13	S. J. S. Kimber not out 14
A. P. Wells c Brown b Williams 6	N. J. Lenham not out 12
*C. M. Wells lbw b Emburey 25	B 3, l-b 12, w 5, n-b 1 21
Imran Khan run out 30	—
†I. J. Gould c Cowans b Williams 26	1/14 2/40 3/49 (7 wkts, 38 overs) 160
P. Moores c Downton b Hughes 8	4/105 5/115
A. C. S. Pigott st Downton b Emburey . 5	6/130 7/134

D. K. Standing and A. M. Babington did not bat.

Bowling: Williams 8–0–33–2; Cowans 6–0–23–0; Fraser 7–0–18–1; Emburey 8–1–30–2; Hughes 7–0–33–1; Sykes 2–0–8–0.

Umpires: J. C. Balderstone and R. Julian.

MIDDLESEX v WORCESTERSHIRE

At Lord's, June 5. Middlesex won by 45 runs. Toss: Worcestershire.

Middlesex

J. D. Carr b O'Shaughnessy	69	J. F. Sykes not out	4
A. Needham c Radford b Newport	39		
M. A. Roseberry c Rhodes b Newport	13	B 1, l-b 11, w 15, n-b 2	29
*R. O. Butcher b Radford	47		—
†K. R. Brown lbw b Radford	21	1/78 2/97 3/157 (5 wkts, 40 overs)	237
N. R. C. MacLaurin not out	15	4/203 5/217	

N. F. Williams, S. P. Hughes, A. R. C. Fraser and N. G. Cowans did not bat.

Bowling: Weston 8–0–25–0; Radford 8–0–58–2; Pridgeon 6–0–19–0; McEwan 4–0–33–0; Newport 8–0–46–2; Hick 3–0–26–0; O'Shaughnessy 3–0–18–1.

Worcestershire

T. S. Curtis c Brown b Hughes	41	N. V. Radford b Cowans	3
†S. J. Rhodes c Fraser b Cowans	10	S. M. McEwan not out	0
G. A. Hick c and b Sykes	22		
D. B. D'Oliveira b Hughes	12	B 2, l-b 8, w 7, n-b 1	18
*P. A. Neale run out	8		—
M. J. Weston b Hughes	42	1/17 2/51 3/86 (8 wkts, 40 overs)	192
S. J. O'Shaughnessy run out	26	4/100 5/107 6/163	
P. J. Newport not out	10	7/184 8/192	

A. P. Pridgeon did not bat.

Bowling: Cowans 8–1–28–2; Williams 8–0–37–0; Fraser 8–0–50–0; Sykes 8–0–41–1; Hughes 8–0–26–3.

Umpires: B. Leadbeater and N. T. Plews.

At Luton, June 19. MIDDLESEX beat NORTHAMPTONSHIRE by eight wickets.

MIDDLESEX v SOMERSET

At Lord's, June 26. Somerset won by 27 runs. Toss: Somerset. The stand of 132 between Brown and Williams was a record for the seventh wicket in the Sunday League.

Somerset

*P. M. Roebuck b Fraser	31	V. J. Marks not out	8
J. J. E. Hardy b Williams	1		
J. G. Wyatt c Downton b Williams	1	L-b 4, w 3, n-b 3	10
S. R. Waugh not out	140		—
R. J. Bartlett c Butcher b Williams	50	1/14 2/20 3/62 (5 wkts, 40 overs)	247
G. D. Rose b Fraser	6	4/203 5/210	

†N. D. Burns, G. V. Palmer, N. A. Mallender and A. N. Jones did not bat.

Bowling: Cowans 8–0–42–0; Williams 8–1–38–3; Fraser 8–0–48–2; Hughes 8–0–72–0; Emburey 8–0–43–0.

Middlesex

W. N. Slack lbw b Mallender	12	S. P. Hughes not out	3
J. D. Carr c Wyatt b Jones	1	N. G. Cowans c Bartlett b Rose	0
*M. W. Gatting c and b Rose	33	A. R. C. Fraser not out	0
R. O. Butcher c Burns b Mallender	2	L-b 12, w 4, n-b 1	17
J. E. Emburey c Burns b Mallender	2		
†P. R. Downton run out	5	1/11 2/37 3/39 (9 wkts, 40 overs)	220
K. R. Brown c Hardy b Rose	102	4/43 5/50 6/74	
N. F. Williams b Mallender	43	7/206 8/218 9/219	

Bowling: Mallender 8–1–31–4; Jones 7–0–56–1; Marks 8–1–26–0; Rose 7–0–34–3; Palmer 8–0–41–0; Waugh 2–0–20–0.

Umpires: B. J. Meyer and N. T. Plews.

At Repton School, July 3. DERBYSHIRE v MIDDLESEX. No result.

At Canterbury, July 10. MIDDLESEX beat KENT by two wickets.

MIDDLESEX v GLAMORGAN

At Lord's, July 17. No result.

MIDDLESEX v WARWICKSHIRE

At Lord's, July 24. Middlesex won by six wickets. Toss: Middlesex.

Warwickshire

*T. A. Lloyd b Emburey	34	A. A. Donald not out	18
†G. W. Humpage b Hughes	36	A. R. K. Pierson not out	5
Asif Din c Butcher b Emburey	5		
D. A. Banks b Fraser	15	B 2, l-b 13, w 4	19
D. A. Thorne c Brown b Fraser	29		
D. A. Reeve b Fraser	10	1/68 2/84 3/86 (8 wkts, 40 overs)	184
S. J. Green b Tufnell	0	4/121 5/141 6/142	
G. C. Small b Emburey	13	7/145 8/166	

T. A. Munton did not bat.

Bowling: Fraser 8–0–30–3; Cowans 4–0–22–0; Hughes 6–0–32–1; Emburey 8–0–31–3; Tufnell 6–0–32–1; Needham 8–0–22–0.

Middlesex

W. N. Slack not out	77	J. E. Emburey not out	4
*M. W. Gatting b Reeve	37	L-b 16, w 1	17
A. Needham run out	15		
R. O. Butcher b Donald	30	1/77 2/106 3/164 (4 wkts, 38.2 overs)	187
K. R. Brown run out	7	4/175	

†P. R. Downton, S. P. Hughes, A. R. C. Fraser, P. C. R. Tufnell and N. G. Cowans did not bat.

Bowling: Donald 8–0–31–1; Munton 8–1–29–0; Small 8–0–46–0; Reeve 7.2–1–16–1; Pierson 7–0–49–0.

Umpires: J. C. Balderstone and D. O. Oslear.

At Leicester, July 31. LEICESTERSHIRE v MIDDLESEX. No result.

At Blackpool, August 7. MIDDLESEX lost to LANCASHIRE by 52 runs.

MIDDLESEX v GLOUCESTERSHIRE

At Lord's, August 14. Middlesex won on scoring-rate when Gloucestershire failed by 5 runs to achieve their revised target of 173 off 34 overs. Rain had interrupted their innings after fourteen overs. Toss: Gloucestershire.

Middlesex

W. N. Slack b Pooley	53	S. P. Hughes run out	13
J. D. Carr c Curran b Bainbridge	37	A. R. C. Fraser not out	9
*M. W. Gatting b Bainbridge	10		
R. O. Butcher c Romaines b Pooley	14	L-b 16, w 2	18
J. E. Emburey run out	6		
†P. R. Downton not out	36	1/75 2/89 3/110 (8 wkts, 40 overs)	203
K. R. Brown c Russell b Curran	2	4/124 5/137 6/149	
J. F. Sykes lbw b Curran	5	7/157 8/187	

N. G. Cowans did not bat.

Bowling: Greene 8–0–48–0; Jarvis 8–1–38–0; Curran 8–0–31–2; Bainbridge 8–0–30–2; Pooley 8–0–40–2.

Gloucestershire

A. W. Stovold b Cowans	24	M. W. Alleyne not out	24
†R. C. Russell run out	2	V. S. Greene not out	5
P. Bainbridge c and b Emburey	17	L-b 7, w 5	12
K. M. Curran c Sykes b Emburey	32		
P. W. Romaines b Hughes	6	1/8 2/38 3/64 (6 wkts, 34 overs)	168
A. J. Wright c Brown b Fraser	46	4/86 5/106 6/161	

M. W. Pooley, *D. A. Graveney and K. B. S. Jarvis did not bat.

Bowling: Fraser 6–0–24–1; Cowans 8–0–27–1; Emburey 8–0–31–2; Hughes 8–0–51–1; Sykes 4–0–28–0.

Umpires: J. D. Bond and K. E. Palmer.

At Leeds, August 28. MIDDLESEX lost to YORKSHIRE by four wickets.

NORTHAMPTONSHIRE

At Leicester, May 1. NORTHAMPTONSHIRE lost to LEICESTERSHIRE on scoring-rate.

NORTHAMPTONSHIRE v GLOUCESTERSHIRE

At Northampton, May 8. Northamptonshire won by one wicket. Toss: Northamptonshire.

Gloucestershire

A. W. Stovold b Walker	27	V. S. Greene not out	7
C. W. J. Athey b N. G. B. Cook	51	†R. C. Russell not out	0
K. M. Curran c Bailey b Williams	16	L-b 11, w 1, n-b 1	13
J. W. Lloyds c G. Cook b Williams	1		—
P. W. Romaines run out	5	1/10 2/86 3/102 (7 wkts, 40 overs)	169
P. Bainbridge c Lamb b Walker	17	4/110 5/115	
M. W. Alleyne c Ripley b Davis	32	6/138 7/168	

*D. A. Graveney and K. B. S. Jarvis did not bat.

Bowling: Davis 8–0–41–1; Capel 4–0–16–0; Walker 8–0–32–2; N. G. B. Cook 8–1–28–1; Larkins 8–0–31–0; Williams 4–0–10–2.

Northamptonshire

R. J. Bailey b Greene	9	†D. Ripley run out	1
W. Larkins c Russell b Greene	37	N. G. B. Cook c Greene b Jarvis	2
A. J. Lamb st Russell b Graveney	59	A. Walker not out	4
D. J. Capel c Russell b Curran	8	B 2, l-b 15, w 13, n-b 1	31
R. G. Williams lbw b Curran	0		—
*G. Cook c Russell b Jarvis	5	1/19 2/126 3/141 (9 wkts, 40 overs)	172
N. A. Stanley not out	14	4/141 5/141 6/158	
W. W. Davis run out	2	7/164 8/166 9/168	

Bowling: Jarvis 8–1–30–2; Greene 8–1–22–2; Curran 8–0–27–2; Bainbridge 6–1–37–0; Alleyne 4–0–19–0; Graveney 6–1–20–1.

Umpires: D. J. Constant and R. A. White.

At Chelmsford, May 15. NORTHAMPTONSHIRE lost to ESSEX by 24 runs.

At The Oval, May 22. NORTHAMPTONSHIRE lost to SURREY by seven wickets.

NORTHAMPTONSHIRE v KENT

At Northampton, May 29. No result. Rain interrupted a match of twenty overs a side, and when the weather cleared it was later than the time permitted to begin a match of ten overs a side. Toss: Northamptonshire.

Kent

N. R. Taylor c Wild b Cook	29	*C. S. Cowdrey not out	14
R. F. Pienaar b Cook	38	L-b 4, w 7	11
C. J. Tavaré not out	40		—
S. G. Hinks b Davis	11	1/67 2/77 3/111 (3 wkts, 16 overs)	143

G. R. Cowdrey, R. M. Ellison, †S. A. Marsh, C. Penn, V. J. Wells and R. P. Davis did not bat.

Bowling: Capel 4–0–27–0; Wild 4–0–38–0; Cook 4–0–34–2; Walker 2–0–22–0; Davis 2–0–18–1.

Northamptonshire

*W. Larkins, R. J. Bailey, A. J. Lamb, D. J. Capel, R. G. Williams, D. J. Wild, A. Fordham, †D. Ripley, N. G. B. Cook, W. W. Davis and A. Walker.

Umpires: J. H. Harris and K. J. Lyons.

At Taunton, June 5. NORTHAMPTONSHIRE lost to SOMERSET by two wickets.

NORTHAMPTONSHIRE v MIDDLESEX

At Luton, June 19. Middlesex won by eight wickets. Toss: Middlesex. The second-wicket stand of 154 between Slack and Gatting was a record for Middlesex in the Sunday League. Larkins became the first Northamptonshire player to score 5,000 runs in the Sunday League.

Northamptonshire

R. J. Bailey c Brown b Gatting	24
W. Larkins c MacLaurin b Hughes	65
D. J. Capel c Brown b Fraser	22
R. G. Williams c Brown b Hughes	0
*G. Cook c Butcher b Williams	26
D. J. Wild b Fraser	3
N. A. Stanley st Brown b Sykes	4
†D. Ripley not out	11
W. W. Davis c Butcher b Sykes	34
N. G. B. Cook not out	0
L-b 5, w 6	11
1/52 2/107 3/110 4/131 5/145 6/150 7/155 8/194 (8 wkts, 40 overs)	200

A. Walker did not bat.

Bowling: Fraser 8–1–21–2; Williams 7–1–19–1; Gatting 4–0–29–1; Tufnell 8–1–30–0; Hughes 8–1–58–2; Sykes 5–0–38–2.

Middlesex

W. N. Slack c Bailey b Wild	65
J. D. Carr c Ripley b Davis	9
*M. W. Gatting not out	105
R. O. Butcher not out	17
L-b 3, w 2	5
1/16 2/170 (2 wkts, 36.5 overs)	201

†K. R. Brown, N. R. C. MacLaurin, J. F. Sykes, N. F. Williams, S. P. Hughes, A. R. C. Fraser and P. C. R. Tufnell did not bat.

Bowling: Davis 8–1–29–1; Capel 6–1–26–0; Wild 8–1–45–1; Walker 5–0–32–0; N. G. B. Cook 7.5–0–51–0; Williams 2–0–15–0.

Umpires: D. J. Constant and D. S. Thompsett.

At Nottingham, June 26. NORTHAMPTONSHIRE beat NOTTINGHAMSHIRE by seven wickets.

NORTHAMPTONSHIRE v LANCASHIRE

At Tring, July 3. No result.

NORTHAMPTONSHIRE v YORKSHIRE

At Northampton, July 10. No result.

NORTHAMPTONSHIRE v SUSSEX

At Northampton, July 24. Northamptonshire won by five wickets. Toss: Northamptonshire. The match was moved from Finedon to the County Ground because the pitch at Finedon was waterlogged.

Sussex

*P. W. G. Parker run out	10	M. P. Speight lbw b Lillee	12
A. P. Wells run out	32	A. C. S. Pigott not out	3
C. M. Wells b Wild	27	L-b 9, w 2, n-b 1	12
Imran Khan not out	45		
N. J. Falkner b Williams	2	1/32 2/59 3/91 (6 wkts, 40 overs)	152
†I. J. Gould b Walker	9	4/101 5/125 6/145	

S. J. S. Kimber, A. R. Clarke and A. M. Babington did not bat.

Bowling: Lillee 7–0–18–1; Walker 8–0–33–1; N. G. B. Cook 8–1–21–0; Capel 8–0–31–0; Wild 3–0–18–1; Williams 6–0–22–1.

Northamptonshire

R. J. Bailey lbw b C. M. Wells	3	N. A. Stanley not out	1
W. Larkins c Parker b Babington	1		
D. J. Capel c Parker b Imran	83	L-b 11, w 6	17
R. G. Williams c Gould b Pigott	22		
*G. Cook lbw b Clarke	8	1/6 2/10 3/89 (5 wkts, 39.3 overs)	153
D. J. Wild not out	18	4/120 5/145	

†D. Ripley, D. K. Lillee, A. Walker and N. G. B. Cook did not bat.

Bowling: Imran 7.3–0–24–1; C. M. Wells 8–3–25–1; Babington 6–0–15–1; Clarke 6–0–27–1; Kimber 4–0–12–0; Pigott 8–0–39–1.

Umpires: B. Dudleston and K. E. Palmer.

At Worcester, July 31. NORTHAMPTONSHIRE lost to WORCESTERSHIRE by six wickets.

At Birmingham, August 7. NORTHAMPTONSHIRE beat WARWICKSHIRE by five wickets.

At Bournemouth, August 14. NORTHAMPTONSHIRE lost to HAMPSHIRE by eight wickets.

NORTHAMPTONSHIRE v GLAMORGAN

At Wellingborough School, August 21. Glamorgan won by six wickets. Toss: Glamorgan.

Northamptonshire

R. J. Bailey c Metson b Derrick	19	S. J. Brown b Watkin	1
W. Larkins c Butcher b Thomas	3	D. K. Lillee not out	6
A. J. Lamb b North	35		
D. J. Wild c Shastri b Thomas	54	B 3, l-b 12, w 6	21
*G. Cook st Metson b North	7		
M. R. Gouldstone c Metson b North	0	1/15 2/40 3/77 (8 wkts, 40 overs)	171
†D. Ripley b Watkin	20	4/96 5/96 6/155	
N. G. B. Cook not out	5	7/161 8/165	

M. A. Robinson did not bat.

Bowling: Thomas 7–1–30–2; Watkin 8–1–28–2; Holmes 6–0–24–0; Derrick 5–0–23–1; Shastri 7–0–31–0; North 7–2–20–3.

Glamorgan

J. A. Hopkins b Lillee	10	A. R. Butcher not out	7
*H. Morris c Bailey b Robinson	32	L-b 5, w 8	13
M. P. Maynard st Ripley b Wild	44		—
G. C. Holmes b Brown	9	1/17 2/82 3/95 (4 wkts, 37.3 overs)	172
R. J. Shastri not out	57	4/117	

P. D. North, J. G. Thomas, J. Derrick, †C. P. Metson and S. L. Watkin did not bat.

Bowling: Lillee 8–2–21–1; Robinson 8–0–41–1; N. G. B. Cook 8–1–24–0; Brown 7.3–0–36–1; Wild 6–0–45–1.

Umpires: B. Dudleston and R. Julian.

NORTHAMPTONSHIRE v DERBYSHIRE

At Northampton, August 28. Derbyshire won by 5 runs. Toss: Northamptonshire.

Derbyshire

J. E. Morris c Larkins b N. G. B. Cook	65	F. A. Griffith b Walker	0
P. D. Bowler run out	38	†B. J. M. Maher not out	1
T. J. G. O'Gorman b N. G. B. Cook	14		
S. C. Goldsmith lbw b Davis	43	B 5, l-b 10, w 10, n-b 1	26
*M. A. Holding c Capel b Walker	10		—
B. Roberts b Brown	3	1/108 2/125 3/133 (8 wkts, 40 overs)	227
R. Sharma not out	23	4/159 5/171 6/208	
A. E. Warner c Walker b Davis	4	7/219 8/225	

S. J. Base did not bat.

Bowling: Davis 8–0–43–2; Walker 8–0–33–2; Brown 8–0–44–1; N. G. B. Cook 8–0–40–2; Wild 7–0–48–0; G. Cook 1–0–4–0.

Northamptonshire

R. J. Bailey b Warner	24	†W. Noon lbw b Holding	6
W. Larkins c Goldsmith b Griffith	9	A. Walker lbw b Holding	1
D. J. Capel c Base b Griffith	10	L-b 7, w 3, n-b 2	12
D. J. Wild c Base b Holding	91		—
*G. Cook b Base	43	1/21 2/45 3/48 (8 wkts, 40 overs)	222
M. R. Gouldstone run out	10	4/154 5/199 6/199	
W. W. Davis not out	16	7/220 8/222	

N. G. B. Cook and S. J. Brown did not bat.

Bowling: Base 8–1–32–1; Griffith 8–2–27–2; Warner 8–0–60–1; Bowler 5–0–31–0; Holding 8–0–35–3; Roberts 3–0–30–0.

Umpires: B. Leadbeater and D. O. Oslear.

NOTTINGHAMSHIRE

At Lord's, April 24. NOTTINGHAMSHIRE lost to MIDDLESEX by four wickets.

At Worcester, May 1. NOTTINGHAMSHIRE beat WORCESTERSHIRE by five wickets.

NOTTINGHAMSHIRE v LANCASHIRE

At Nottingham, May 8. Lancashire won by two wickets. Toss: Lancashire.

Nottinghamshire

*R. T. Robinson lbw b Hayhurst 23
B. C. Broad c Hegg b Wasim 1
D. W. Randall c Allott b Austin 54
P. Johnson c Mendis b Hayhurst 21
J. D. Birch b Simmons 14
F. D. Stephenson b Allott 43
†B. N. French c Hegg b Wasim 18
K. P. Evans not out 8
E. E. Hemmings not out 12
L-b 8 8

1/3 2/67 3/93 4/114 5/122 6/175 7/181 (7 wkts, 40 overs) 202

R. A. Pick and K. E. Cooper did not bat.

Bowling: Wasim 8–1–37–2; Allott 8–0–32–1; Watkinson 4–0–33–0; Hayhurst 6–0–28–2; Austin 8–0–34–1; Simmons 6–1–30–1.

Lancashire

G. D. Mendis c French b Cooper 4
G. Fowler c Johnson b Hemmings 26
A. N. Hayhurst lbw b Cooper 2
N. H. Fairbrother not out 116
M. Watkinson c French b Pick 16
*D. P. Hughes c French b Evans 4
. D. Austin run out 4
Wasim Akram c Johnson b Stephenson 13
P. J. W. Allott b Stephenson 11
J. Simmons not out 1
B 2, l-b 8, n-b 1 11

1/4 2/14 3/59 4/98 5/120 6/136 7/172 8/201 (8 wkts, 40 overs) 208

†W. K. Hegg did not bat.

Bowling: Cooper 8–0–39–2; Pick 8–0–30–1; Stephenson 8–0–50–2; Hemmings 8–0–26–1; Evans 8–0–53–1.

Umpires: M. J. Kitchen and B. Leadbeater.

NOTTINGHAMSHIRE v GLOUCESTERSHIRE

At Nottingham, May 15. Gloucestershire won by two wickets. Toss: Gloucestershire.

Nottinghamshire

*R. T. Robinson c Russell b Curran 50
. C. Broad c and b Alleyne 43
D. W. Randall b Bainbridge 27
. Johnson b Greene 33
. D. Birch c Curran b Bainbridge 19
. D. Stephenson lbw b Bainbridge 0
. P. Evans c Curran b Greene 11
E. E. Hemmings not out 2
L-b 8, w 14, n-b 1 23

1/99 2/107 3/167 4/171 5/171 6/199 7/208 (7 wkts, 40 overs) 208

C. W. Scott, K. E. Cooper and K. Saxelby did not bat.

Bowling: Jarvis 8–0–48–0; Greene 8–0–42–2; Curran 8–0–23–1; Bainbridge 8–0–43–3; Alleyne 8–0–44–1.

Gloucestershire

. W. Stovold c Scott b Cooper 2
. W. J. Athey c Robinson b Evans 48
. J. Wright c Johnson b Cooper 11
. M. Curran b Stephenson 2
Bainbridge c Scott b Evans 17
W. Romaines c and b Saxelby 25
M. W. Alleyne c Johnson b Stephenson 45
R. C. Russell c Evans b Stephenson 17
V. S. Greene not out 21
*D. A. Graveney not out 4
L-b 9, w 6, n-b 2 17

1/3 2/20 3/31 4/58 5/116 6/120 7/182 8/184 (8 wkts, 39.5 overs) 209

. B. S. Jarvis did not bat.

Bowling: Cooper 8–2–27–2; Saxelby 8–0–60–1; Stephenson 7.5–0–37–3; Evans 8–0–30–2; Hemmings 8–0–46–0.

Umpires: J. H. Hampshire and A. A. Jones.

NOTTINGHAMSHIRE v SUSSEX

At Nottingham, May 22. Nottinghamshire won by six wickets. Toss: Nottinghamshire.

Sussex

A. P. Wells c Robinson b Fraser-Darling 19
†I. J. Gould c Johnson b Stephenson .. 12
*P. W. G. Parker c Johnson b Cooper . 1
Imran Khan c Scott b Saxelby 10
C. M. Wells lbw b Birch 47
P. Moores b Stephenson 33
A. M. Green b Stephenson 9
N. J. Lenham not out 4
S. J. S. Kimber c Randall b Saxelby ... 3
D. K. Standing not out ....
B 1, l-b 4, w 4, n-b 1 1
1/30 2/33 3/33 (8 wkts, 40 overs) 15
4/60 5/119 6/135
7/142 8/146

A. M. Babington did not bat.

Bowling: Cooper 8–0–19–1; Stephenson 8–1–33–3; Fraser-Darling 7–0–40–1; Saxelby 8–1–18–2; Evans 6–0–20–0; Birch 3–0–17–1.

Nottinghamshire

*R. T. Robinson c Parker b Babington . 18
D. W. Randall c Gould b Imran 18
P. Johnson b Lenham 15
J. D. Birch not out 65
P. Pollard lbw b Standing 25
F. D. Stephenson not out ....
B 2, l-b 4, w 1 ....
1/25 2/42 3/64 (4 wkts, 38.1 overs) 15
4/144

†C. W. Scott, K. P. Evans, K. E. Cooper, C. D. Fraser-Darling and K. Saxelby did not bat

Bowling: C. M. Wells 6–0–26–0; Imran 8–2–22–1; Kimber 6–0–28–0; Babington 6–0–18–1; Lenham 4–0–16–1; Standing 8–0–36–1; Parker 0.1–0–4–0.

Umpires: J. D. Bond and K. E. Palmer.

At Derby, May 29. NOTTINGHAMSHIRE lost to DERBYSHIRE by nine wickets.

At Birmingham, June 5. NOTTINGHAMSHIRE lost to WARWICKSHIRE by 29 runs.

NOTTINGHAMSHIRE v GLAMORGAN

At Nottingham, June 12. Glamorgan won by 5 runs. Toss: Nottinghamshire.

Glamorgan

J. A. Hopkins b Stephenson 2
*H. Morris c Scott b Evans 16
M. P. Maynard c and b Birch 75
P. A. Todd b Stephenson 38
R. J. Shastri not out 52
J. G. Thomas not out ....
L-b 9, w 4 ....
1/5 2/66 3/139 (4 wkts, 40 overs) 19
4/166

P. A. Cottey, R. C. Ontong, J. Derrick, †C. P. Metson and S. R. Barwick did not bat.

Bowling: Cooper 8–0–36–0; Stephenson 8–2–17–2; Fraser-Darling 5–0–46–0; Evans 8–1–23–1; Hemmings 8–1–33–0; Birch 3–0–34–1.

Nottinghamshire

B. C. Broad c Cottey b Thomas 61
M. Newell st Metson b Derrick 44
D. W. Randall c Metson b Shastri 12
P. Johnson lbw b Shastri 14
*J. D. Birch run out 30
F. D. Stephenson b Barwick 0
C. D. Fraser-Darling not out 10
E. E. Hemmings b Barwick 3
K. P. Evans not out 0
L-b 15, w 3, n-b 1 19

1/90 2/107 3/127 4/171 5/176 6/180 7/186 (7 wkts, 40 overs) 193

†C. W. Scott and K. E. Cooper did not bat.

Bowling: Thomas 8–0–40–1; Barwick 8–0–46–2; Shastri 8–0–33–2; Ontong 8–1–18–0; Derrick 8–0–41–1.

Umpires: B. Leadbeater and P. B. Wight.

At Basingstoke, June 19. NOTTINGHAMSHIRE lost to HAMPSHIRE by 5 runs.

NOTTINGHAMSHIRE v NORTHAMPTONSHIRE

At Nottingham, June 26. Northamptonshire won by seven wickets. Toss: Northamptonshire.

Nottinghamshire

. C. Broad not out 96
M. Newell c Ripley b Walker 58
. Johnson b Walker 17
. W. Randall c N. G. B. Cook b Walker 32
*J. D. Birch not out 1
B 5, l-b 4, w 7 16

1/129 2/167 3/210 (3 wkts, 40 overs) 220

. D. Stephenson, K. P. Evans, †C. W. Scott, E. E. Hemmings, D. J. Millns and K. Saxelby did not bat.

Bowling: Capel 8–0–22–0; Davis 8–2–40–0; Larkins 2–0–11–0; Wild 6–0–31–0; Walker -0–60–3; N. G. B. Cook 8–0–47–0.

Northamptonshire

. J. Bailey c Scott b Millns 75
. Larkins c Hemmings b Evans 32
. J. Lamb c Randall b Stephenson . . . 79
. J. Capel not out 2
R. G. Williams not out 12
L-b 12, w 11 23

1/55 2/203 3/210 (3 wkts, 38.4 overs) 223

G. Cook, D. J. Wild, †D. Ripley, W. W. Davis, N. G. B. Cook and A. Walker did not bat.

Bowling: Saxelby 7.4–0–48–0; Millns 7–0–55–1; Stephenson 8–0–36–1; Evans 8–0–33–1; Hemmings 8–0–39–0.

Umpires: J. C. Balderstone and J. W. Holder.

At Canterbury, July 3. KENT v NOTTINGHAMSHIRE. No result.

NOTTINGHAMSHIRE v LEICESTERSHIRE

At Nottingham, July 10. No result.

NOTTINGHAMSHIRE v YORKSHIRE

At Nottingham, July 17. Yorkshire won by seven wickets. Toss: Yorkshire.

Nottinghamshire

B. C. Broad c Robinson b Fletcher 19
*R. T. Robinson st Bairstow b Carrick . 15
P. Johnson b Carrick 5
D. W. Randall c Love b Fletcher 44
J. D. Birch c Love b Shaw 3
F. D. Stephenson c Sharp b Carrick ... 1
K. P. Evans run out 11
†C. W. Scott not out 13
K. E. Cooper b Fletcher ....
K. Saxelby not out ....
L-b 8, w 3, n-b 1 1

1/39 2/39 3/50 4/59 5/60 6/96 7/119 8/119 (8 wkts, 28 overs) 12

D. J. Millns did not bat.

Bowling: Hartley 6–0–22–0; Sidebottom 5–0–22–0; Fletcher 6–0–27–3; Shaw 5–0–30–1 Carrick 6–0–16–3.

Yorkshire

K. Sharp b Stephenson 41
A. A. Metcalfe lbw b Cooper 5
P. E. Robinson c Cooper b Millns 41
D. Byas not out 9
J. D. Love not out 1
L-b 9, w 2 1

1/8 2/94 3/95 (3 wkts, 25.1 overs) 12

†D. L. Bairstow, *P. Carrick, A. Sidebottom, P. J. Hartley, C. Shaw and S. D. Fletch did not bat.

Bowling: Stephenson 6–1–13–1; Cooper 6–0–17–1; Millns 6–0–31–1; Saxelby 4–0–28–(Evans 3.1–0–28–0.

Umpires: N. T. Plews and R. A. White.

At Taunton, July 24. NOTTINGHAMSHIRE lost to SOMERSET by nine wickets.

At Colchester, August 14. NOTTINGHAMSHIRE lost to ESSEX by 77 runs.

NOTTINGHAMSHIRE v SURREY

At Nottingham, August 21. Nottinghamshire won on scoring-rate when Surrey failed 4 runs to achieve their revised target of 164 off 28 overs. Toss: Surrey.

Nottinghamshire

M. Newell b Bullen 30
*R. T. Robinson c Bicknell b Greig ...100
D. W. Randall b Greig 60
P. Johnson run out 19
F. D. Stephenson not out 12
J. D. Birch not out ....
L-b 6, w 4 ....

1/89 2/169 3/213 4/226 (4 wkts, 40 overs) 2

†B. N. French, K. P. Evans, G. W. Mike, C. D. Fraser-Darling and D. J. Millns did not ba

Bowling: Bicknell 8–0–36–0; Greig 8–0–48–2; Robinson 7.2–1–47–0; Feltham 1.4–0–7– Clarke 8–0–50–0; Bullen 7–0–39–1.

Surrey

C. J. Richards c Stephenson b Fraser-Darling . 41
. D. Robinson c Johnson b Stephenson 14
. J. Stewart b Stephenson 25
M. A. Lynch c Stephenson b Evans ... 9
. M. Ward c Johnson b Evans 2
I. A. Greig c Mike b Fraser-Darling .. 21
. T. Medlycott c Stephenson b Fraser-Darling . 2
C. K. Bullen b Stephenson 23
S. T. Clarke not out 12
M. P. Bicknell b Stephenson 1
M. A. Feltham not out 4
L-b 5, w 1 6

1/20 2/80 3/83 4/92 5/95 6/108 7/122 8/154 9/156 (9 wkts, 28 overs) 160

Bowling: Millns 4–0–22–0; Stephenson 8–3–23–4; Mike 4–0–24–0; Evans 8–0–63–2; raser-Darling 4–0–23–3.

Umpires: H. D. Bird and J. Birkenshaw.

SOMERSET

t Hove, April 24. SOMERSET lost to SUSSEX by five wickets.

t Cardiff, May 1. SOMERSET lost to GLAMORGAN by eight wickets.

SOMERSET v WORCESTERSHIRE

t Taunton, May 8. Worcestershire won by seven wickets. Toss: Somerset.

omerset

G. Wyatt c D'Oliveira b Radford ... 2
. M. Roebuck c and b Botham 18
. D. Crowe c Rhodes b Pridgeon 2
. J. Harden b Pridgeon 4
J. E. Hardy lbw b Illingworth 21
. J. Marks b Newport 25
. D. Rose c Curtis b Newport 10
. V. Palmer not out 25
†N. D. Burns lbw b Botham 6
N. A. Mallender not out 23
B 1, l-b 5, w 3 9

1/8 2/15 3/25 4/29 5/74 6/76 7/92 8/114 (8 wkts, 40 overs) 145

N. Jones did not bat.

Bowling: Radford 8–0–31–1; Pridgeon 8–1–12–2; Botham 8–2–32–2; Newport 8–0–35–2; ingworth 8–0–29–1.

Vorcestershire

S. Curtis b Mallender 63
T. Botham c Palmer b Marks 10
. A. Hick c Rose b Palmer 29
B. D'Oliveira not out 24
*P. A. Neale not out 10
L-b 9, w 3 12

1/34 2/87 3/133 (3 wkts, 35.3 overs) 148

J. O'Shaughnessy, †S. J. Rhodes, P. J. Newport, R. K. Illingworth, N. V. Radford and A. P. Pridgeon did not bat.

Bowling: Jones 6–0–34–0; Mallender 7–3–11–1; Rose 8–0–26–0; Marks 8–2–23–1; Palme 6.3–0–45–1.

Umpires: R. Julian and R. Palmer.

SOMERSET v NORTHAMPTONSHIRE

At Taunton, June 5. Somerset won by two wickets. Toss: Somerset.

Northamptonshire

R. J. Bailey b Palmer 78
*W. Larkins c Jones b Marks 42
D. J. Capel st Burns b Marks 18
R. G. Williams c Waugh b Rose 7
D. J. Wild c Dredge b Palmer 11
M. R. Gouldstone run out 7
W. W. Davis b Jones 12
A. Fordham lbw b Jones 0
†D. Ripley not out . . . .
N. G. B. Cook c Bartlett b Palmer . . . .
M. A. Robinson run out . . . .
B 2, l-b 14, w 3, n-b 4 2

1/60 2/127 3/140 4/170 5/171 6/188 7/195 8/196 9/210 (39.4 overs) 21

Bowling: Jones 6–0–53–2; Foster 3–0–14–0; Dredge 8–1–18–0; Marks 8–1–36–2; Ros 8–0–37–1; Palmer 6.4–0–37–3.

Somerset

J. G. Wyatt c Cook b Davis 11
J. J. E. Hardy run out 1
R. J. Bartlett run out 25
S. R. Waugh not out 109
G. D. Rose b Wild 19
*V. J. Marks b Wild 16
G. V. Palmer b Wild 0
†N. D. Burns c Ripley b Williams 2
C. H. Dredge b Williams . . . .
A. N. Jones not out 1
L-b 7, w 3, n-b 1 1

1/6 2/28 3/72 4/98 5/138 6/139 7/142 8/146 (8 wkts, 39.4 overs) 21

D. J. Foster did not bat.

Bowling: Davis 8–1–28–1; Capel 6–0–29–0; Robinson 5.4–0–37–0; Cook 4–0–18–0; Wil 8–0–28–3; Williams 8–0–65–2.

Umpires: B. J. Meyer and P. B. Wight.

SOMERSET v WARWICKSHIRE

At Bath, June 12. Warwickshire won by 32 runs. Toss: Warwickshire.

Warwickshire

*T. A. Lloyd st Burns b Marks 40
P. A. Smith c Hardy b Foster 29
Asif Din lbw b Rose 36
†G. W. Humpage b Rose 16
A. J. Moles c Rose b Palmer 13
D. A. Reeve c Bartlett b Palmer 31
N. M. K. Smith c Palmer b Jones 2
G. C. Small c Burns b Palmer 8
A. A. Donald not out . . . .
N. Gifford not out . . . .
B 1, l-b 21, w 4, n-b 1 2

1/50 2/95 3/118 4/145 5/165 6/179 7/202 8/202 (8 wkts, 40 overs) 2(

T. A. Munton did not bat.

Bowling: Jones 7–0–41–1; Foster 6–0–18–1; Dredge 5–0–18–0; Marks 8–0–35–1; Ro 8–0–41–2; Palmer 6–1–27–3.

Somerset

J. G. Wyatt c Humpage b Munton 4
J. J. E. Hardy run out 14
R. J. Bartlett b Gifford 26
S. R. Waugh c Lloyd b Small 68
G. D. Rose c Moles b Small 14
*V. J. Marks c and b P. A. Smith 7
G. V. Palmer c P. A. Smith b Donald . 4
†N. D. Burns c Lloyd b Reeve 17
C. H. Dredge b Reeve 5
A. N. Jones run out 2
D. J. Foster not out 0
L-b 4, w 4, n-b 1 9

1/9 2/27 3/61 4/96 5/114 6/144 7/148 8/162 9/170 (38.2 overs) 170

Bowling: Donald 7–2–30–1; Munton 8–2–17–1; Reeve 7.2–1–26–2; Gifford 5–0–28–1; Small 8–0–40–2; P. A. Smith 3–0–25–1.

Umpires: D. G. L. Evans and R. Julian.

SOMERSET v SURREY

At Bath, June 19. Somerset won by 17 runs. Toss: Surrey.

Somerset

. J. E. Hardy c Greig b Bicknell 15
*P. M. Roebuck c Richards b Clarke .. 64
. G. Wyatt b Greig 77
. R. Waugh b Bullen 11
. J. Bartlett lbw b Feltham 10
N. D. Burns b Clarke 30
. J. Marks not out 12
. D. Rose c and b Greig 2
G. V. Palmer b Clarke 1
N. A. Mallender b Clarke 0
L-b 9, w 2 11

1/54 2/114 3/143 4/183 5/201 6/227 7/230 8/231 9/233 (9 wkts, 40 overs) 233

. N. Jones did not bat.

Bowling: Bicknell 8–0–32–1; Greig 8–0–47–2; Feltham 8–0–53–1; Bullen 8–0–54–1; Clarke –2–38–4.

Surrey

C. J. Richards c Waugh b Marks 29
. M. Smith run out 17
ahid Sadiq lbw b Waugh 7
. A. Lynch b Marks 28
. M. Ward c and b Rose 34
. A. Greig c Waugh b Palmer 29
. T. Medlycott c Burns b Jones 17
. K. Bullen c Burns b Palmer 1
S. T. Clarke c Bartlett b Mallender 8
M. P. Bicknell not out 9
M. A. Feltham not out 20
B 1, l-b 7, w 7, n-b 2 17

1/49 2/53 3/78 4/94 5/150 6/158 7/162 8/185 9/188 (9 wkts, 40 overs) 216

Bowling: Jones 7–0–40–1; Mallender 8–0–38–1; Rose 7–0–55–1; Waugh 8–0–27–1; Marks –1–31–2; Palmer 2–0–17–2.

Umpires: B. Dudleston and A. A. Jones.

t Lord's, June 26. SOMERSET beat MIDDLESEX by 27 runs.

SOMERSET v ESSEX

t Taunton, July 3. No result.

t Manchester, July 10. SOMERSET beat LANCASHIRE by 6 runs.

At Bristol, July 17. SOMERSET lost to GLOUCESTERSHIRE by seven wickets.

SOMERSET v NOTTINGHAMSHIRE

At Taunton, July 24. Somerset won by nine wickets. Toss: Somerset.

Nottinghamshire

M. Newell c Burns b Foster 8
*R. T. Robinson c Burns b Foster 4
P. Johnson c Dredge b Foster 3
D. W. Randall c Burns b Mallender ... 68
D. J. R. Martindale lbw b Marks 39
F. D. Stephenson c Bartlett b Rose 14
K. P. Evans lbw b Rose 0
†C. W. Scott c Marks b Mallender 9
K. E. Cooper run out 1
K. Saxelby not out 2
D. J. Millns not out 0
L-b 10, n-b 4 14

1/8 2/13 3/20 (9 wkts, 40 overs) 162
4/119 5/145 6/146
7/147 8/148 9/158

Bowling: Foster 8–0–28–3; Dredge 8–1–14–0; Rose 8–1–21–2; Mallender 8–0–41–2; Marks 6–0–29–1; Palmer 2–0–19–0.

Somerset

G. D. Rose not out 93
*P. M. Roebuck b Millns 35
R. J. Bartlett not out 27
L-b 7, w 1 8

1/109 (1 wkt, 30.3 overs) 163

S. R. Waugh, J. C. M. Atkinson, V. J. Marks, G. V. Palmer, †N. D. Burns, N. A. Mallender C. H. Dredge and D. J. Foster did not bat.

Bowling: Stephenson 6–1–31–0; Cooper 6–0–19–0; Saxelby 7–0–39–0; Millns 6–0–37–1 Evans 5.3–0–30–0.

Umpires: D. J. Constant and J. H. Harris.

At Canterbury, July 31. SOMERSET lost to KENT by seven wickets.

SOMERSET v DERBYSHIRE

At Weston-super-Mare, August 7. Derbyshire won by 2 runs. Toss: Somerset.

Derbyshire

*J. G. Wright lbw b Mallender 4
P. D. Bowler run out 21
J. E. Morris lbw b Marks 34
†B. J. M. Maher c Bartlett b Jones 6
S. C. Goldsmith b Marks 6
B. Roberts b Jones 25
R. Sharma c Burns b Jones 33
P. G. Newman not out ....
A. E. Warner c Wyatt b Mallender 1
L-b 15, w 2, n-b 1 1

1/8 2/61 3/68 (8 wkts, 40 overs) 17
4/78 5/78 6/134
7/147 8/174

S. J. Base and O. H. Mortensen did not bat.

Bowling: Mallender 8–0–43–2; Dredge 8–1–28–0; Cleal 8–0–49–0; Marks 8–2–8–2; Jone 8–0–31–3.

Somerset

V. J. Marks c Base b Sharma	80	M. W. Cleal run out	1
*P. M. Roebuck lbw b Warner	28	A. N. Jones not out	2
J. G. Wyatt c Wright b Sharma	2		
S. R. Waugh c Sharma b Warner	33	B 1, l-b 9, w 4	14
R. J. Bartlett c Bowler b Newman	0		
N. J. Pringle st Maher b Sharma	9	1/65 2/71 3/134 (9 wkts, 40 overs)	172
†N. D. Burns c Wright b Roberts	0	4/140 5/163 6/163	
N. A. Mallender c Goldsmith b Roberts	3	7/167 8/167 9/172	

C. H. Dredge did not bat.

Bowling: Mortensen 8–3–22–0; Newman 8–0–27–1; Base 8–0–33–0; Warner 8–0–35–2; Sharma 6–1–35–3; Roberts 2–0–10–2.

Umpires: J. C. Balderstone and R. A. White.

At Scarborough, August 14. SOMERSET beat YORKSHIRE by 2 runs.

At Leicester, August 21. SOMERSET lost to LEICESTERSHIRE by two wickets.

SOMERSET v HAMPSHIRE

At Taunton, August 28. Hampshire won by 62 runs. Toss: Somerset.

Hampshire

V. P. Terry b Dredge	77	K. D. James not out	2
*M. C. J. Nicholas b Mallender	36		
D. R. Turner c Burns b Rose	37	B 4, l-b 4, w 4	12
C. L. Smith not out	28		
R. J. Scott lbw b Jones	4	1/96 2/148 3/164 (5 wkts, 40 overs)	207
J. R. Ayling c Roebuck b Jones	11	4/169 5/193	

N. G. Cowley, †R. J. Parks, C. A. Connor and P. J. Bakker did not bat.

Bowling: Mallender 8–0–34–1; Dredge 8–0–37–1; Jones 8–1–47–2; Marks 8–0–39–0; Rose 8–0–42–1.

Somerset

G. D. Rose c Connor b James	17	N. A. Mallender lbw b Bakker	0
P. M. Roebuck c Parks b Bakker	3	A. N. Jones not out	7
J. J. E. Hardy c Parks b Bakker	0	C. H. Dredge b Bakker	0
J. G. Wyatt st Parks b Ayling	72	B 1, l-b 5, w 2	8
R. J. Bartlett run out	23		
R. J. Harden lbw b Cowley	6	1/16 2/16 3/26 (35.4 overs)	145
*V. J. Marks b Ayling	4	4/83 5/107 6/120	
†N. D. Burns c Bakker b James	5	7/134 8/134 9/142	

Bowling: Connor 6–1–15–0; Bakker 5.4–1–15–4; James 8–1–24–2; Ayling 8–0–31–2; Cowley 8–0–54–1.

Umpires: J. D. Bond and J. H. Hampshire.

SURREY

At Southampton, April 24. SURREY beat HAMPSHIRE by 22 runs.

SURREY v MIDDLESEX

At The Oval, May 8. No result, a thunderstorm having ended play. Toss: Middlesex.

Surrey

†C. J. Richards c Downton b Cowans	0	M. A. Feltham b Emburey	2
D. M. Smith c Slack b Hughes	54	M. P. Bicknell c and b Fraser	2
A. J. Stewart c Brown b Williams	33	N. H. Peters run out	0
M. A. Lynch c Carr b Williams	48	B 1, l-b 15, w 4, n-b 5	25
D. M. Ward lbw b Hughes	1		
Zahid Sadiq lbw b Williams	18	1/10 2/50 3/142 (40 overs)	200
*I. A. Greig not out	17	4/146 5/175 6/181	
C. K. Bullen c Downton b Williams	0	7/181 8/195 9/198	

Bowling: Cowans 6–1–24–1; Fraser 8–2–21–1; Emburey 8–0–35–1; Williams 8–0–39–4; Hughes 8–0–43–2; Gatting 2–0–22–0.

Middlesex

J. D. Carr c Richards b Peters	0	R. O. Butcher not out	13
W. N. Slack not out	9	L-b 1, w 1	2
*M. W. Gatting c Zahid b Peters	6		
†P. R. Downton lbw b Greig	1	1/1 2/14 3/15 (3 wkts, 8.5 overs)	31

J. E. Emburey, K. R. Brown, A. R. C. Fraser, N. F. Williams, S. P. Hughes and N. G. Cowans did not bat.

Bowling: Peters 4.5–0–16–2; Greig 4–0–14–1.

Umpires: J. H. Harris and P. B. Wight.

At Hove, May 15. SURREY beat SUSSEX by seven wickets.

SURREY v NORTHAMPTONSHIRE

At The Oval, May 22. Surrey won by seven wickets. Toss: Surrey.

Northamptonshire

R. J. Bailey c Clarke b Bicknell	5	N. G. B. Cook b Clarke	11
*W. Larkins b Bullen	40	W. W. Davis run out	9
D. J. Wild lbw b Greig	2	A. Walker not out	1
D. J. Capel c Greig b Bicknell	12	L-b 3, w 4	7
R. G. Williams c Richards b Clarke	18		
A. Fordham c Bicknell b Greig	14	1/10 2/14 3/36 (39.4 overs)	133
N. A. Stanley c Richards b Greig	2	4/82 5/82 6/87	
†D. Ripley c Bullen b Feltham	12	7/107 8/132 9/132	

Bowling: Bicknell 8–0–24–2; Greig 8–1–20–3; Feltham 8–0–38–1; Bullen 8–1–23–1; Clarke 7.4–0–25–2.

Surrey

†C. J. Richards lbw b Capel	1	*I. A. Greig not out	56
D. M. Smith c Ripley b Capel	15	L-b 9, w 3	12
A. J. Stewart c Fordham b Walker	15		
D. M. Ward not out	38	1/3 2/32 3/32 (3 wkts, 38 overs)	137

Zahid Sadiq, K. T. Medlycott, C. K. Bullen, M. A. Feltham, S. T. Clarke and M. P. Bicknell did not bat.

Bowling: Davis 8–1–22–0; Capel 8–0–16–2; Walker 7–2–28–1; Wild 7–2–12–0; Cook 3–0–20–0; Larkins 2–0–9–0; Williams 3–0–21–0.

Umpires: J. H. Hampshire and R. Julian.

At Chelmsford, May 29. SURREY beat ESSEX by eight wickets.

At Leeds, June 5. SURREY lost to YORKSHIRE by four wickets.

SURREY v LEICESTERSHIRE

At The Oval, June 12. Surrey won by four wickets. Toss: Surrey.

Leicestershire

N. E. Briers b Clarke	29	J. P. Agnew not out	18
L. Potter c and b Bullen	41	G. J. F. Ferris not out	1
*D. I. Gower b Bullen	2		
J. J. Whitaker c Smith b Greig	24	L-b 6, w 2, n-b 1	9
P. Willey c and b Bullen	2		
J. D. R. Benson b Feltham	13	1/66 2/75 3/80 (8 wkts, 40 overs)	158
P. A. J. DeFreitas b Clarke	19	4/84 5/114 6/124	
†P. Whitticase run out	0	7/128 8/155	

L. Tennant did not bat.

Bowling: Bicknell 8–0–27–0; Greig 8–1–38–1; Feltham 8–0–37–1; Bullen 8–1–27–3; Clarke 8–0–23–2.

Surrey

†C. J. Richards b Ferris	4	K. T. Medlycott not out	29
D. M. Smith c Whitticase b Agnew	16	C. K. Bullen not out	7
Zahid Sadiq c Whitticase b Willey	53	B 1, l-b 8, w 2, n-b 2	13
M. A. Lynch c Whitticase b Willey	12		
D. M. Ward b DeFreitas	23	1/9 2/25 3/58 (6 wkts, 39.2 overs)	159
*I. A. Greig c and b Willey	2	4/111 5/115 6/121	

M. A. Feltham, S. T. Clarke and M. P. Bicknell did not bat.

Bowling: Ferris 8–2–30–1; DeFreitas 7.2–1–24–1; Agnew 8–1–34–1; Tennant 8–1–27–0; Willey 8–0–35–3.

Umpires: K. J. Lyons and R. Palmer.

At Bath, June 19. SURREY lost to SOMERSET by 17 runs.

SURREY v DERBYSHIRE

At The Oval, June 26. Tied. Toss: Derbyshire.

Surrey

†C. J. Richards run out	24	*I. A. Greig not out	35
G. S. Clinton c Jean-Jacques b Roberts	47	B 1, l-b 5, w 5	11
Zahid Sadiq c and b Warner	10		
M. A. Lynch run out	50	1/51 2/69 3/118 (4 wkts, 40 overs)	225
D. M. Ward not out	48	4/155	

K. T. Medlycott, C. K. Bullen, M. A. Feltham, S. T. Clarke and M. P. Bicknell did not bat.

Bowling: Newman 8–1–35–0; Roberts 4–0–25–1; Jean-Jacques 8–0–42–0; Holding 8–1–30–0; Warner 8–0–61–1; Sharma 4–0–26–0.

Derbyshire

*K. J. Barnett c Clinton b Bullen	72	R. Sharma run out	0
P. D. Bowler c Bullen b Bicknell	25	P. G. Newman not out	0
B. Roberts c Zahid b Bullen	26		
J. E. Morris c Lynch b Feltham	1	B 3, l-b 5, w 2	10
S. C. Goldsmith b Clarke	21		
M. A. Holding c Zahid b Greig	40	1/39 2/126 3/128 (8 wkts, 40 overs)	225
A. E. Warner b Greig	7	4/128 5/192 6/194	
†B. J. M. Maher not out	23	7/216 8/217	

M. Jean-Jacques did not bat.

Bowling: Bicknell 8–0–32–1; Greig 8–0–46–2; Feltham 8–0–45–1; Bullen 8–0–48–2; Clarke 8–0–46–1.

Umpires: H. D. Bird and D. O. Oslear.

SURREY v WARWICKSHIRE

At The Oval, July 3. No result.

SURREY v WORCESTERSHIRE

At The Oval, July 10. Worcestershire won by 39 runs. Toss: Surrey.

Worcestershire

T. S. Curtis c Zahid b Greig	97	N. V. Radford not out	4
S. J. O'Shaughnessy c Stewart b Peters	25	R. K. Illingworth run out	0
G. A. Hick c Smith b Bullen	29		
*P. A. Neale c Richards b Greig	19	B 1, l-b 6, w 2, n-b 1	10
M. J. Weston run out	1		
D. A. Leatherdale c Richards b Clarke	2	1/55 2/111 3/142 (9 wkts, 40 overs)	205
†S. J. Rhodes c and b Clarke	8	4/147 5/150 6/188	
P. J. Newport c Bullen b Greig	10	7/195 8/204 9/205	

G. R. Dilley did not bat.

Bowling: Peters 8–0–34–1; Greig 8–0–51–3; Bicknell 8–0–47–0; Clarke 8–0–28–2; Bullen 8–0–38–1.

Surrey

†C. J. Richards c Curtis b Weston	17	M. P. Bicknell c O'Shaughnessy b Dilley	1
D. M. Smith b Illingworth	32	S. T. Clarke not out	2
A. J. Stewart run out	33	N. H. Peters b Newport	0
M. A. Lynch c Rhodes b O'Shaughnessy	17	L-b 14, w 2, n-b 3	19
D. M. Ward b Radford	0		
Zahid Sadiq c O'Shaughnessy b Radford	10	1/37 2/70 3/103 (39.2 overs)	166
*I. A. Greig c Newport b O'Shaughnessy	16	4/104 5/120 6/126	
C. K. Bullen run out	19	7/162 8/163 9/165	

Bowling: Weston 8–1–28–1; Dilley 7–0–36–1; Newport 5.2–0–17–1; Illingworth 3–0–19–1; Radford 8–0–26–2; O'Shaughnessy 8–0–26–2.

Umpires: J. C. Balderstone and B. Dudleston.

SURREY v KENT

At The Oval, July 17. Surrey won by five wickets. Toss: Surrey.

Kent

N. R. Taylor lbw b Greig 1
T. R. Ward c Feltham b Greig 0
C. J. Tavaré b Bicknell 9
R. F. Pienaar run out 84
*C. S. Cowdrey c Feltham b Bullen ... 6
G. R. Cowdrey lbw b Bullen 3
S. G. Hinks b Greig 16
R. M. Ellison c Lynch b Greig 44
†S. A. Marsh not out 7
C. Penn c Bullen b Greig 2
B 1, l-b 6, w 4 11

1/0 2/1 3/21 4/38 5/55 6/95 7/162 8/180 9/183 (9 wkts, 40 overs) 183

R. P. Davis did not bat.

Bowling: Bicknell 8–3–11–1; Greig 8–1–30–5; Clarke 8–0–43–0; Feltham 8–0–33–0; Bullen 8–0–59–2.

Surrey

†C. J. Richards c Marsh b Penn 6
G. S. Clinton c G. R. Cowdrey b Penn. 16
A. J. Stewart c Tavaré b G. R. Cowdrey 26
M. A. Lynch not out 67
D. M. Ward b Pienaar 6
Zahid Sadiq c Ward b Pienaar 13
*I. A. Greig not out 30
L-b 13, w 9, n-b 1 23

1/22 2/29 3/85 4/109 5/127 (5 wkts, 38.5 overs) 187

C. K. Bullen, M. A. Feltham, S. T. Clarke and M. P. Bicknell did not bat.

Bowling: Penn 8–0–20–2; Ellison 8–0–36–0; Pienaar 8–0–38–2; C. S. Cowdrey 7–0–34–0; G. R. Cowdrey 5–0–37–1; Davis 2.5–0–9–0.

Umpires: A. A. Jones and A. G. T. Whitehead.

At Cheltenham, July 31. SURREY beat GLOUCESTERSHIRE by eight wickets.

At Ebbw Vale, August 7. SURREY lost to GLAMORGAN by 8 runs.

At Nottingham, August 21. SURREY lost to NOTTINGHAMSHIRE on scoring-rate.

SURREY v LANCASHIRE

At The Oval, August 28. Surrey won by six wickets in a match reduced by rain to 31 overs a side. Toss: Surrey.

Lancashire

G. D. Mendis c Bullen b Greig 5
G. Fowler c Ward b Feltham 70
A. N. Hayhurst st Richards b Medlycott 44
N. H. Fairbrother c Clinton b Medlycott 22
M. Watkinson st Richards b Feltham .. 9
T. E. Jesty not out 18
I. D. Austin not out 6
L-b 4, w 3 7

1/15 2/100 3/146 4/147 5/156 (5 wkts, 31 overs) 181

*D. P. Hughes, P. J. W. Allott, J. Simmons and †W. K. Hegg did not bat.

Bowling: Bicknell 5–0–15–0; Greig 4–0–15–1; Robinson 2–0–23–0; Feltham 6–0–52–2; Bullen 7–0–31–0; Medlycott 6–0–29–2; Lynch 1–0–12–0.

Surrey

†C. J. Richards c and b Simmons	71	*I. A. Greig not out	29
G. S. Clinton run out	17	L-b 7, n-b 2	9
A. J. Stewart lbw b Simmons	7		—
M. A. Lynch not out	43	1/63 2/90 3/107 (4 wkts, 30.2 overs)	182
D. M. Ward run out	6	4/131	

J. D. Robinson, C. K. Bullen, M. A. Feltham, K. T. Medlycott and M. P. Bicknell did not bat.

Bowling: Allott 5.2–0–31–0; Watkinson 6–0–49–0; Austin 6–0–42–0; Simmons 7–0–29–2; Hayhurst 6–0–24–0.

Umpires: A. A. Jones and R. A. White.

SUSSEX

SUSSEX v SOMERSET

At Hove, April 24. Sussex won by five wickets. Toss: Somerset.

Somerset

N. A. Felton b Pringle	0	G. D. Rose not out	29
*P. M. Roebuck b Pringle	10	G. V. Palmer not out	14
J. J. E. Hardy c C. M. Wells b Standing	45	B 5, w 2, n-b 1	8
R. J. Harden b Lenham	52		—
†N. D. Burns c and b Standing	6	1/3 2/20 3/102 (6 wkts, 40 overs)	191
V. J. Marks b Pringle	27	4/110 5/133 6/154	

N. A. Mallender, A. N. Jones and D. J. Foster did not bat.

Bowling: Babington 8–2–31–0; Pringle 8–0–37–3; Kimber 7–1–32–0; Clarke 4–1–18–0; Lenham 8–0–31–1; Standing 5–0–37–2.

Sussex

†I. J. Gould c Burns b Jones	0	S. J. S. Kimber not out	15
N. J. Lenham b Foster	33		
*P. W. G. Parker c Rose b Jones	90	B 2, l-b 10, w 5, n-b 2	19
C. M. Wells lbw b Rose	1		—
A. P. Wells c Palmer b Marks	15	1/10 2/77 3/86 (5 wkts, 39 overs)	195
A. M. Green not out	22	4/131 5/169	

A. R. Clarke, M. W. Pringle, D. K. Standing and A. M. Babington did not bat.

Bowling: Jones 8–0–41–2; Mallender 7–0–29–0; Palmer 3–0–15–0; Marks 8–0–27–1; Foster 5–0–31–1; Rose 8–0–40–1.

Umpires: J. H. Harris and A. G. T. Whitehead.

At Bristol, May 1. SUSSEX lost to GLOUCESTERSHIRE by seven wickets.

SUSSEX v SURREY

At Hove, May 15. Surrey won by seven wickets. Toss: Surrey.

Sussex

†I. J. Gould c Clarke b Bicknell	5	A. M. Green run out	19
N. J. Lenham c Lynch b Bullen	39	A. C. S. Pigott not out	20
*P. W. G. Parker c Stewart b Bullen	13	L-b 3, w 1, n-b 1	5
Imran Khan c and b Bicknell	0		
C. M. Wells c Bullen b Clarke	47	1/9 2/42 3/42 4/74 (7 wkts, 40 overs)	154
A. P. Wells c Lynch b Greig	6	5/93 6/123 7/154	

D. K. Standing, S. J. S. Kimber and A. M. Babington did not bat.

Bowling: Bicknell 8–0–28–2; Greig 8–0–35–1; Bullen 8–0–30–2; Feltham 8–1–24–0; Clarke 8–0–34–1.

Surrey

†C. J. Richards c A. P. Wells b Imran	5	D. M. Ward not out	27
D. M. Smith b Pigott	33	L-b 5, w 7, n-b 1	13
A. J. Stewart lbw b Pigott	46		
M. A. Lynch not out	31	1/7 2/88 3/89 (3 wkts, 36 overs)	155

Zahid Sadiq, *I. A. Greig, C. K. Bullen, M. A. Feltham, S. T. Clarke and M. P. Bicknell did not bat.

Bowling: Imran 8–2–27–1; C. M. Wells 8–0–31–0; Pigott 7–0–38–2; Kimber 8–0–31–0; Babington 3–0–10–0; Standing 2–0–13–0.

Umpires: J. Birkenshaw and M. J. Kitchen.

At Nottingham, May 22. SUSSEX lost to NOTTINGHAMSHIRE by six wickets.

At Lord's, May 29. SUSSEX lost to MIDDLESEX by 53 runs.

SUSSEX v DERBYSHIRE

At Horsham, June 5. Derbyshire won by 5 runs. Toss: Sussex.

Derbyshire

*K. J. Barnett c Imran b Pigott	50	R. Sharma run out	5
P. D. Bowler c Gould b Babington	9	P. G. Newman not out	1
B. Roberts c Parker b Kimber	59		
J. E. Morris b Pigott	43	L-b 8, w 4, n-b 1	13
S. C. Goldsmith c Moores b Imran	11		
M. A. Holding b Pigott	6	1/40 2/88 3/158 (8 wkts, 40 overs)	213
A. E. Warner c Moores b Imran	0	4/170 5/180 6/181	
†B. J. M. Maher not out	16	7/205 8/210	

O. H. Mortensen did not bat.

Bowling: Imran 8–0–33–2; Kimber 8–0–49–1; Alikhan 8–0–42–0; Babington 8–1–33–1; Pigott 8–0–48–3.

Sussex

A. M. Green c Sharma b Mortensen	2	N. J. Lenham not out	18
A. P. Wells c Roberts b Newman	2	R. I. Alikhan not out	0
*P. W. G. Parker c Goldsmith b Roberts	80		
Imran Khan c Maher b Mortensen	0	L-b 10, w 4, n-b 1	15
P. Moores c Warner b Roberts	34		
†I. J. Gould c and b Newman	2	1/6 2/6 3/8 (8 wkts, 40 overs)	208
S. J. S. Kimber b Holding	15	4/69 5/76 6/129	
A. C. S. Pigott c Newman b Warner	40	7/149 8/206	

A. M. Babington did not bat.

Bowling: Mortensen 8–1–18–2; Newman 8–1–34–2; Warner 8–1–37–1; Sharma 3–0–13–0; Holding 8–0–43–1; Roberts 5–0–53–2.

Umpires: A. A. Jones and D. R. Shepherd.

At Ilford, June 12. SUSSEX tied with ESSEX.

At Leicester, June 19. SUSSEX beat LEICESTERSHIRE by 3 runs.

SUSSEX v YORKSHIRE

At Hove, June 26. Sussex won by seven wickets. Toss: Sussex.

Yorkshire

M. D. Moxon b Clarke	30
A. A. Metcalfe c Parker b C. M. Wells	4
K. Sharp b C. M. Wells	10
D. Byas b Kimber	46
P. E. Robinson c Parker b Pigott	1
S. N. Hartley not out	43
†D. L. Bairstow c Moores b Pigott	1
*P. Carrick c Kimber b Clarke	15
A. Sidebottom c C. M. Wells b Pigott	6
C. Shaw not out	8
L-b 8, w 3, n-b 1	12
1/6 2/38 3/82 4/89 5/101 6/104 7/137 8/152 (8 wkts, 40 overs)	176

S. D. Fletcher did not bat.

Bowling: Imran 8–0–24–0; C. M. Wells 8–0–25–2; Babington 6–0–19–0; Clarke 6–0–34–2; Pigott 8–0–42–3; Kimber 4–0–24–1.

Sussex

A. P. Wells c Robinson b Hartley	22
*P. W. G. Parker b Carrick	54
C. M. Wells not out	57
Imran Khan c Sharp b Sidebottom	15
A. C. S. Pigott not out	15
L-b 11, w 2, n-b 1	14
1/63 2/117 3/161 (3 wkts, 39.2 overs)	177

R. I. Alikhan, †P. Moores, M. P. Speight, S. J. S. Kimber, A. R. Clarke and A. M. Babington did not bat.

Bowling: Fletcher 8–0–34–0; Sidebottom 7.2–0–22–1; Moxon 5–0–22–0; Shaw 8–2–46–0; Hartley 4–0–10–1; Carrick 7–0–32–1.

Umpires: R. Palmer and A. G. T. Whitehead.

SUSSEX v HAMPSHIRE

At Hastings, July 3. No result.

SUSSEX v WARWICKSHIRE

At Hove, July 10. Sussex won by 8 runs. Toss: Warwickshire.

Sussex

*P. W. G. Parker c N. M. K. Smith b Merrick	52	A. C. S. Pigott not out	16
A. P. Wells c N. M. K. Smith b Munton	4	†P. Moores not out	3
C. M. Wells c Holloway b Reeve	0	L-b 14, w 3, n-b 5	22
Imran Khan c Reeve b Small	50	1/30 2/30 3/121 (5 wkts, 40 overs)	157
N. J. Falkner run out	10	4/128 5/150	

S. J. S. Kimber, M. P. Speight, A. R. Clarke and A. M. Babington did not bat.

Bowling: Merrick 8–1–28–1; Munton 8–2–8–1; Reeve 8–0–40–1; P. A. Smith 8–0–38–0; Small 8–0–29–1.

Warwickshire

*T. A. Lloyd run out	1	G. C. Small c Imran b Pigott	8
P. A. Smith b Imran	1	†P. C. L. Holloway not out	7
Asif Din b Clarke	34	B 1, l-b 8, w 4	13
D. A. Banks b Kimber	29		
D. A. Thorne not out	33	1/2 2/3 3/71 (7 wkts, 40 overs)	149
N. M. K. Smith lbw b Clarke	0	4/73 5/78	
D. A. Reeve c C. M. Wells b Imran	23	6/111 7/129	

T. A. Merrick and T. A. Munton did not bat.

Bowling: Imran 8–3–21–2; C. M. Wells 8–1–11–0; Pigott 8–0–44–1; Kimber 7–0–31–1; Babington 2–0–11–0; Clarke 7–2–22–2.

Umpires: B. J. Meyer and P. B. Wight.

At Northampton, July 24. SUSSEX lost to NORTHAMPTONSHIRE by five wickets.

SUSSEX v GLAMORGAN

At Eastbourne, July 31. Tied. Toss: Sussex.

Glamorgan

J. A. Hopkins c and b Clarke	33	J. Derrick run out	0
*H. Morris c Moores b C. M. Wells	8	†C. P. Metson not out	7
M. P. Maynard not out	92		
G. C. Holmes b Clarke	15	L-b 4, w 1	5
R. J. Shastri c Speight b Pigott	31		
A. R. Butcher c Babington b Clarke	0	1/11 2/75 3/99 (8 wkts, 40 overs)	194
R. C. Ontong b Clarke	2	4/163 5/164 6/172	
J. G. Thomas b Pigott	1	7/175 8/176	

S. R. Barwick did not bat.

Bowling: C. M. Wells 8–0–23–1; Babington 8–0–48–0; Kimber 8–1–50–0; Pigott 8–0–45–2; Clarke 8–1–24–4.

Sussex

N. J. Lenham c Morris b Ontong	18	A. C. S. Pigott not out	20
A. P. Wells lbw b Derrick	31	L-b 11, w 8, n-b 3	22
C. M. Wells run out	2		
*P. W. G. Parker c Morris b Barwick	42	1/57 2/57 3/72 (4 wkts, 40 overs)	194
I. J. Gould not out	59	4/158	

†P. Moores, M. P. Speight, S. J. S. Kimber, A. R. Clarke and A. M. Babington did not bat.

Bowling: Barwick 8–0–31–1; Thomas 7–0–33–0; Ontong 8–1–23–1; Derrick 8–0–41–1; Shastri 5–0–31–0; Holmes 4–0–24–0.

Umpires: D. G. L. Evans and D. O. Oslear.

At Worcester, August 7. SUSSEX lost to WORCESTERSHIRE by eight wickets.

SUSSEX v LANCASHIRE

At Hove, August 14. Lancashire won by five wickets. Toss: Sussex.

Sussex

*P. W. G. Parker c Fowler b Watkinson 4
M. P. Speight b Wasim 37
C. M. Wells c and b Watkinson 85
A. P. Wells run out 51
I. J. Gould c Simmons b Wasim 8
A. C. S. Pigott not out 12
N. J. Lenham not out 4
L-b 10, w 3, n-b 4 17

1/24 2/65 3/191 4/192 5/203 (5 wkts, 40 overs) 218

†P. Moores, S. J. S. Kimber, A. R. Clarke and A. M. Babington did not bat.

Bowling: Watkinson 8–1–41–2; Allott 7–0–26–0; Austin 8–0–46–0; Wasim 8–0–39–2; Simmons 7–0–38–0; Hayhurst 2–0–18–0.

Lancashire

G. D. Mendis c Gould b Kimber 51
G. Fowler c Babington b Clarke 34
N. H. Fairbrother c A. P. Wells b Kimber 3
A. N. Hayhurst run out 27
M. Watkinson c Parker b Pigott 58
Wasim Akram not out 20
*D. P. Hughes not out 16
L-b 7, w 3 10

1/74 2/93 3/94 4/177 5/184 (5 wkts, 39.4 overs) 219

I. D. Austin, P. J. W. Allott, J. Simmons and †W. K. Hegg did not bat.

Bowling: Pigott 8–0–51–1; C. M. Wells 8–2–28–0; Babington 8–0–51–0; Clarke 7.4–1–32–1; Kimber 8–0–50–2.

Umpires: B. Leadbeater and B. J. Meyer.

At Maidstone, August 28. SUSSEX lost to KENT by four wickets.

WARWICKSHIRE

At Manchester, May 1. WARWICKSHIRE lost to LANCASHIRE by one wicket.

WARWICKSHIRE v YORKSHIRE

At Birmingham, May 8. Yorkshire won by 27 runs. Toss: Warwickshire.

Yorkshire

M. D. Moxon c Moles b Gifford 41
A. A. Metcalfe c and b Reeve 27
J. D. Love c Small b Reeve 43
†D. L. Bairstow c Humpage b Small 4
P. E. Robinson b Merrick 30
S. N. Hartley b Smith 20
*P. Carrick b Merrick 3
P. J. Hartley not out 21
L-b 14, w 5 19

1/62 2/98 3/103 4/152 5/166 6/174 7/208 (7 wkts, 40 overs) 208

S. D. Fletcher, P. W. Jarvis and C. Shaw did not bat.

Bowling: Merrick 8–1–32–2; Parsons 6–1–23–0; Reeve 8–0–42–2; Small 8–1–25–1; Gifford 8–0–51–1; Smith 2–0–21–1.

Warwickshire

*T. A. Lloyd c Bairstow b Shaw 17
†G. W. Humpage b Jarvis 4
A. I. Kallicharran c Moxon b Carrick . 32
A. J. Moles c Jarvis b P. J. Hartley ... 79
P. A. Smith b Fletcher 13
Asif Din b Fletcher 5
D. A. Reeve run out 21
T. A. Merrick b Jarvis 2
G. J. Parsons not out 4
G. C. Small not out 1
L-b 3 3

1/9 2/38 3/66 4/97 5/121 6/166 7/174 8/178 (8 wkts, 40 overs) 181

N. Gifford did not bat.

Bowling: Jarvis 8–0–41–2; Fletcher 8–0–36–2; P. J. Hartley 8–0–52–1; Shaw 8–1–17–1; Carrick 8–0–32–1.

Umpires: K. J. Lyons and D. R. Shepherd.

WARWICKSHIRE v GLAMORGAN

At Birmingham, May 15. Glamorgan won by ten wickets. Toss: Glamorgan. This was Glamorgan's first win by ten wickets in the Sunday League and took the number of ten-wicket wins in the competition to twenty.

Warwickshire

*T. A. Lloyd c Maynard b Barwick ... 15
†G. W. Humpage b Thomas 19
A. I. Kallicharran st Metson b Ontong . 10
A. J. Moles c Metson b Derrick 27
P. A. Smith c Morris b Ontong 0
Asif Din c Metson b Shastri 12
T. A. Merrick c Ontong b Holmes 19
D. A. Reeve c Metson b Derrick 4
G. J. Parsons not out 16
G. C. Small run out 1
A. R. K. Pierson not out 5
L-b 9, w 4, n-b 1 14

1/30 2/41 3/51 4/51 5/76 6/109 7/113 8/122 9/127 (9 wkts, 40 overs) 142

Bowling: Thomas 8–1–20–1; Barwick 8–0–32–1; Ontong 8–1–22–2; Derrick 8–0–23–2; Shastri 5–0–26–1; Holmes 3–0–10–1.

Glamorgan

J. A. Hopkins not out 55
*H. Morris not out 72
B 2, l-b 5, w 6, n-b 3 16

(no wkt, 36 overs) 143

M. P. Maynard, A. R. Butcher, R. J. Shastri, G. C. Holmes, R. C. Ontong, J. G. Thomas, †C. P. Metson, S. R. Barwick and J. Derrick did not bat.

Bowling: Merrick 8–0–24–0; Small 8–1–23–0; Smith 2–0–15–0; Reeve 8–0–37–0; Pierson 8–0–25–0; Parsons 2–0–12–0.

Umpires: J. C. Balderstone and K. E. Palmer.

WARWICKSHIRE v ESSEX

At Birmingham, May 22. Warwickshire won by six wickets. Toss: Essex.

Essex

P. J. Prichard lbw b Merrick 7
B. R. Hardie c Pierson b Reeve 10
A. R. Border b Munton 9
A. W. Lilley lbw b Reeve 14
*K. W. R. Fletcher run out 1
G. Miller b Gifford 20
†D. E. East c Humpage b Reeve 1
N. A. Foster c Munton b Reeve 40
I. L. Pont b Reeve 12
T. D. Topley not out 9
J. K. Lever b Merrick 1
L-b 4, w 2 6

1/8 2/20 3/23 4/34 5/47 6/49 7/76 8/117 9/129 (36.2 overs) 130

Bowling: Merrick 6.2–2–16–2; Munton 8–2–17–1; Smith 6–2–20–0; Reeve 7–1–23–5; Gifford 7–1–29–1; Pierson 2–0–21–0.

Warwickshire

*T. A. Lloyd c Border b Miller 21
A. J. Moles c and b Border 21
Asif Din st East b Miller 8
A. J. Kallicharran not out 31
†G. W. Humpage run out 26
P. A. Smith not out 14
L-b 3, w 3, n-b 6 12

1/39 2/51 3/62 4/107 (4 wkts, 35.5 overs) 133

D. A. Reeve, T. A. Merrick, A. R. K. Pierson, T. A. Munton and N. Gifford did not bat.

Bowling: Pont 5.5–0–29–0; Lever 6–0–31–0; Miller 8–0–12–2; Foster 7–0–26–0; Topley 5–2–16–0; Border 4–0–16–1.

Umpires: J. Birkenshaw and B. Dudleston.

At Bristol, May 29. GLOUCESTERSHIRE v WARWICKSHIRE. No result.

WARWICKSHIRE v NOTTINGHAMSHIRE

At Birmingham, June 5. Warwickshire won by 29 runs. Toss: Nottinghamshire.

Warwickshire

*T. A. Lloyd b Evans 30
A. J. Moles lbw b Bore 15
Asif Din c Scott b Evans 10
P. A. Smith c Hemmings b Birch 32
†G. W. Humpage run out 0
D. A. Reeve c Cairns b Fraser-Darling 69
N. M. K. Smith c Pollard b Birch 3
T. A. Merrick c Hemmings b Birch 4
G. C. Small c Bore b Fraser-Darling 4
N. Gifford not out 2
T. A. Munton not out (
B 1, l-b 9, w 4, n-b 1 15

1/51 2/57 3/61 4/62 5/123 6/134 7/153 8/180 9/182 (9 wkts, 40 overs) 184

Bowling: Cairns 5–1–30–0; Bore 8–0–30–1; Evans 8–0–25–2; Hemmings 8–0–29–0; Fraser Darling 8–0–34–2; Birch 3–0–26–3.

Nottinghamshire

D. W. Randall b Gifford 35
*R. T. Robinson lbw b Munton 22
P. Pollard b Gifford 17
C. D. Fraser-Darling c Reeve b Gifford 9
J. D. Birch run out 18
M. Newell b Reeve 23
C. L. Cairns b Merrick 4
K. P. Evans not out 4
E. E. Hemmings not out
B 1, l-b 16, w 4, n-b 2 2

1/38 2/88 3/91 4/108 5/140 6/147 7/155 (7 wkts, 40 overs) 15

†C. W. Scott and M. K. Bore did not bat.

Bowling: Merrick 8–0–30–1; Munton 8–2–10–1; Reeve 8–0–37–1; Gifford 8–1–23–3; Smal 8–0–38–0.

Umpires: M. J. Kitchen and A. G. T. Whitehead.

At Bath, June 12. WARWICKSHIRE beat SOMERSET by 32 runs.

WARWICKSHIRE v KENT

At Birmingham, June 19. Kent won by four wickets. Toss: Warwickshire. The sixth-wicket stand of 100 between C. S. and G. R. Cowdrey was a record for Kent in the Sunday League.

Warwickshire

*T. A. Lloyd run out	66
†G. W. Humpage c Pienaar b G. R. Cowdrey	53
P. A. Smith b G. R. Cowdrey	8
T. A. Merrick c and b Davis	3
A. J. Moles c Taylor b Davis	5
Asif Din c Ellison b Penn	7
S. J. Green not out	10
D. A. Thorne not out	11
L-b 10, w 7	17
1/90 2/109 3/125 4/137 5/153 6/160 (6 wkts, 40 overs)	180

N. M. K. Smith, T. A. Munton and N. Gifford did not bat.

Bowling: Ellison 8–0–35–0; Penn 7–0–30–1; Pienaar 5–0–29–0; C. S. Cowdrey 4–0–17–0; G. R. Cowdrey 8–0–32–2; Davis 8–0–27–2.

Kent

M. R. Benson b Merrick	0
N. R. Taylor c Thorne b P. A. Smith	13
C. J. Tavaré b Munton	10
S. G. Hinks c Lloyd b P. A. Smith	23
*C. S. Cowdrey not out	63
R. F. Pienaar c Humpage b Gifford	3
G. R. Cowdrey b Merrick	53
R. M. Ellison not out	7
B 2, l-b 9, w 2	13
1/0 2/13 3/45 4/50 5/62 6/162 (6 wkts, 39 overs)	185

†S. A. Marsh, C. Penn and R. P. Davis did not bat.

Bowling: Merrick 8–2–32–2; Munton 7–3–17–1; P. A. Smith 8–0–43–2; N. M. K. Smith 4–0–19–0; Gifford 8–0–31–1; Moles 4–0–32–0.

Umpires: J. W. Holder and N. T. Plews.

At The Oval, July 3. SURREY v WARWICKSHIRE. No result.

At Hove, July 10. WARWICKSHIRE lost to SUSSEX by 8 runs.

WARWICKSHIRE v HAMPSHIRE

At Birmingham, July 17. Warwickshire won by 111 runs. Toss: Hampshire.

Warwickshire

T. A. Lloyd b Jefferies	13
G. W. Humpage lbw b Cowley	56
Asif Din b Jefferies	29
D. A. Banks c and b Tremlett	27
D. A. Thorne c Cowley b Jefferies	2
D. A. Reeve not out	36
P. A. Smith c Nicholas b Tremlett	9
G. C. Small not out	1
B 3, l-b 21, w 7, n-b 3	34
1/26 2/124 3/126 4/132 5/187 6/199 (6 wkts, 39 overs)	207

T. A. Merrick, T. A. Munton and A. R. K. Pierson did not bat.

Bowling: Jefferies 8–0–36–3; Connor 8–1–28–0; Ayling 7–0–35–0; Tremlett 8–0–46–2; Cowley 8–1–38–1.

Hampshire

V. P. Terry b Merrick	0	T. M. Tremlett b Small	8
*M. C. J. Nicholas b Munton	7	N. G. Cowley b Small	0
R. A. Smith b Smith	22	C. A. Connor not out	5
D. R. Turner c Humpage b Munton	16	B 3, l-b 12, w 3, n-b 1	19
C. L. Smith c Asif Din b Reeve	1		—
J. R. Ayling lbw b Smith	3	1/1 2/11 3/56 (32.3 overs)	96
S. T. Jefferies b Smith	0	4/56 5/61 6/61	
†R. J. Parks c Reeve b Small	15	7/62 8/87 9/89	

Bowling: Merrick 5–1–8–1; Munton 8–1–22–2; Smith 8–1–26–3; Reeve 3–0–6–1; Pierson 5–0–13–0; Small 3.3–1–6–3.

Umpires: B. Dudleston and B. J. Meyer.

At Lord's, July 24. WARWICKSHIRE lost to MIDDLESEX by six wickets.

At Derby, July 31. WARWICKSHIRE beat DERBYSHIRE by 8 runs.

WARWICKSHIRE v NORTHAMPTONSHIRE

At Birmingham, August 7. Northamptonshire won by five wickets. Toss: Northamptonshire.

Warwickshire

*T. A. Lloyd b Lillee	0	G. C. Small b Walker	5
†G. W. Humpage c G. Cook b Lillee	18	A. R. K. Pierson not out	2
Asif Din not out	93		
D. A. Thorne b Brown	20	L-b 4, w 2, n-b 1	7
D. A. Reeve b Wild	1		—
S. J. Green c Larkins b Wild	1	1/1 2/26 3/59 (8 wkts, 40 overs)	184
S. D. Myles run out	32	4/61 5/69 6/129	
G. J. Parsons b Lillee	5	7/150 8/171	

T. A. Munton did not bat.

Bowling: Walker 8–1–35–1; Lillee 8–0–38–3; Brown 8–0–46–1; N. G. B. Cook 8–0–20–0; Wild 8–1–41–2.

Northamptonshire

A. Fordham lbw b Small	30	†D. Ripley not out	24
W. Larkins c Lloyd b Munton	11		
N. A. Stanley c Munton b Reeve	18	L-b 10, w 5	15
D. J. Wild not out	74		—
*G. Cook c Humpage b Small	8	1/18 2/51 3/74 (5 wkts, 39.5 overs)	186
M. R. Gouldstone run out	6	4/93 5/113	

S. J. Brown, D. K. Lillee, N. G. B. Cook and A. Walker did not bat.

Bowling: Parsons 8–0–38–0; Munton 8–0–38–1; Pierson 8–0–22–0; Reeve 7.5–0–38–1; Small 8–0–40–2.

Umpires: J. W. Holder and A. A. Jones.

WARWICKSHIRE v LEICESTERSHIRE

At Birmingham, August 14. Warwickshire won by seven wickets in a match reduced by rain to 36 overs a side. Toss: Warwickshire.

Leicestershire

L. Potter c Pierson b Munton 0
N. E. Briers c Humpage b Merrick 8
P. N. Hepworth c Tedstone b Reeve .. 15
J. J. Whitaker b Munton 13
*D. I. Gower st Tedstone b Pierson ... 30
P. Willey lbw b Reeve 7
P. A. J. DeFreitas c and b Reeve 1
†P. Whitticase c Tedstone b Reeve 0
J. P. Agnew st Tedstone b Pierson 9
L. Tennant c and b Pierson 5
L. B. Taylor not out 2
L-b 9, w 10 19

1/5 2/15 3/39 4/60 5/80 6/87 7/88 8/88 9/105 (35.2 overs) 109

Bowling: Merrick 8–2–21–1; Munton 8–1–17–2; Small 6–0–24–0; Reeve 6–1–17–4; Pierson 7.2–2–21–3.

Warwickshire

*T. A. Lloyd b Tennant 16
G. W. Humpage c Whitticase b Taylor . 28
Asif Din b Agnew 0
D. A. Thorne not out 35
D. A. Reeve not out 24
L-b 5, w 2 7

1/32 2/39 3/66 (3 wkts, 31.1 overs) 110

S. D. Myles, †G. A. Tedstone, G. C. Small, T. A. Merrick, T. A. Munton and A. R. K. Pierson did not bat.

Bowling: DeFreitas 6–0–22–0; Tennant 8–2–18–1; Agnew 7.1–1–29–1; Willey 6–1–16–0; Taylor 4–0–20–1.

Umpires: R. Julian and R. Palmer.

At Worcester, August 28. WARWICKSHIRE lost to WORCESTERSHIRE by ten wickets.

WORCESTERSHIRE

At Manchester, April 24. WORCESTERSHIRE lost to LANCASHIRE by seven wickets.

WORCESTERSHIRE v NOTTINGHAMSHIRE

At Worcester, May 1. Nottinghamshire won by five wickets, having been set a revised target of 157 off 25 overs. Rain, which caused several interruptions, had earlier restricted Worcestershire's innings to 27 overs. Toss: Nottinghamshire.

Worcestershire

T. S. Curtis c and b Hemmings 45
*I. T. Botham c Birch b Cooper 22
G. A. Hick c Birch b Pick 19
D. B. D'Oliveira not out 54
S. J. O'Shaughnessy b Hemmings 6
M. J. Weston b Stephenson 9
N. V. Radford c Johnson b Stephenson 1
P. J. Newport c Pick b Cooper 1
†S. J. Rhodes not out 2
L-b 7, w 3 10

1/52 2/87 3/119 4/139 5/160 6/162 7/164 (7 wkts, 27 overs) 169

G. R. Dilley and A. P. Pridgeon did not bat.

Bowling: Pick 6–0–58–1; Cooper 7–1–32–2; Stephenson 8–0–35–2; Hemmings 6–0–37–2.

Nottinghamshire

B. C. Broad c Radford b Pridgeon	35	†B. N. French not out	17
*R. T. Robinson c Rhodes b Pridgeon	20		
P. Johnson c Radford b Botham	3	B 2, l-b 9, n-b 2	13
D. W. Randall c Weston b Radford	20		—
J. D. Birch not out	41	1/53 2/61 3/75 (5 wkts, 24.4 overs)	157
F. D. Stephenson b Radford	8	4/113 5/123	

K. P. Evans, R. A. Pick, K. E. Cooper and E. E. Hemmings did not bat.

Bowling: Dilley 5–0–26–0; Pridgeon 8–0–44–2; Botham 7.4–0–50–1; Radford 4–0–26–2.

Umpires: D. R. Shepherd and D. S. Thompsett.

At Taunton, May 8. WORCESTERSHIRE beat SOMERSET by seven wickets.

WORCESTERSHIRE v YORKSHIRE

At Worcester, May 15. Worcestershire won by five wickets. Toss: Worcestershire. Hick passed 1,000 runs in all cricket in his thirteenth innings of the season. He reached 100 off 91 balls, his second fifty taking just 22, and in all he hit four sixes and six fours.

Yorkshire

M. D. Moxon c Hick b Newport	79	S. N. Hartley not out	38
A. A. Metcalfe c Neale b Pridgeon	23		
K. Sharp b Hick	11	L-b 13, w 3, n-b 1	17
J. D. Love c Rhodes b Newport	5		—
P. E. Robinson not out	45	1/46 2/92 3/109 (5 wkts, 40 overs)	223
†D. L. Bairstow c Rhodes b Newport	5	4/130 5/153	

*P. Carrick, S. D. Fletcher, A. Sidebottom and C. Shaw did not bat.

Bowling: Dilley 8–0–52–0; Pridgeon 8–0–19–1; Radford 8–0–39–0; Botham 5–0–39–0; Newport 8–0–31–3; Hick 3–0–30–1.

Worcestershire

T. S. Curtis lbw b Carrick	53	S. J. O'Shaughnessy not out	1
I. T. Botham c Bairstow b Sidebottom	9		
G. A. Hick c and b Sidebottom	111	L-b 9, w 2	11
D. B. D'Oliveira c Moxon b Shaw	24		—
*P. A. Neale not out	14	1/21 2/108 3/205 (5 wkts, 39.1 overs)	224
†S. J. Rhodes c Robinson b Shaw	1	4/209 5/212	

P. J. Newport, N. V. Radford, G. R. Dilley and A. P. Pridgeon did not bat.

Bowling: Sidebottom 8–0–36–2; Shaw 7.1–0–27–2; Fletcher 8–0–58–0; Carrick 8–0–34–1; Moxon 8–0–60–0.

Umpires: J. D. Bond and B. Dudleston.

At Leicester, May 22. WORCESTERSHIRE beat LEICESTERSHIRE by four wickets.

At Lord's, June 5. WORCESTERSHIRE lost to MIDDLESEX by 45 runs.

WORCESTERSHIRE v HAMPSHIRE

At Worcester, June 12. Worcestershire won by 151 runs. Toss: Hampshire.

Worcestershire

T. S. Curtis lbw b Connor 88
†S. J. Rhodes c Parks b Bakker 10
G. A. Hick c Turner b James 11
D. B. D'Oliveira b Connor 29
*P. A. Neale c Parks b James 15
M. J. Weston b Connor 28
N. V. Radford not out 12
P. J. Newport run out 1
R. K. Illingworth not out 0
L-b 2 2

1/25 2/50 3/96 4/126 5/176 6/187 7/188 (7 wkts, 40 overs) 196

G. R. Dilley and A. P. Pridgeon did not bat.

Bowling: Bakker 8–0–39–1; Connor 8–0–44–3; James 8–0–33–2; Ayling 8–0–37–0; Cowley 8–0–41–0.

Hampshire

V. P. Terry c Rhodes b Pridgeon 20
C. L. Smith c Radford b Weston 1
R. A. Smith b Weston 0
D. R. Turner c Dilley b Weston 3
*M. C. J. Nicholas lbw b Dilley 0
J. R. Ayling c Pridgeon b Weston 0
K. D. James run out 5
†R. J. Parks c Rhodes b Radford 0
N. G. Cowley retired hurt 3
C. A. Connor b Pridgeon 5
P. J. Bakker not out 6
W 1, n-b 1 2

1/2 2/2 3/9 4/11 5/16 6/26 7/27 8/35 9/45 (23.4 overs) 45

Bowling: Dilley 6–2–8–1; Weston 8–2–11–4; Radford 6–0–22–1; Pridgeon 3.4–1–4–2.

Umpires: D. J. Constant and J. W. Holder.

At Knypersley, June 19. WORCESTERSHIRE beat DERBYSHIRE by 69 runs.

WORCESTERSHIRE v GLOUCESTERSHIRE

At Hereford, July 3. No result.

At The Oval, July 10. WORCESTERSHIRE beat SURREY by 39 runs.

At Folkestone, July 24. WORCESTERSHIRE beat KENT by seven wickets.

WORCESTERSHIRE v NORTHAMPTONSHIRE

At Worcester, July 31. Worcestershire won by six wickets. Toss: Worcestershire.

Northamptonshire

R. J. Bailey c Rhodes b Weston 5
W. Larkins c Illingworth b Weston 9
D. J. Capel c Rhodes b Newport 25
R. G. Williams c Rhodes b Pridgeon . . 16
*G. Cook b Radford 21
D. J. Wild c Rhodes b Pridgeon 7
N. A. Stanley not out 14
†W. Noon not out 9
L-b 10, w 6, n-b 1 17

1/8 2/25 3/54 4/77 5/89 6/105 (6 wkts, 29 overs) 123

S. J. Brown, D. K. Lillee and A. Walker did not bat.

Bowling: Weston 6–1–10–2; Newport 6–0–19–1; Radford 6–0–29–1; Pridgeon 6–0–27–2; O'Shaughnessy 5–0–28–0.

Worcestershire

T. S. Curtis c Noon b Walker	8	M. J. Weston not out	9
S. J. O'Shaughnessy b Capel	33	L-b 8, w 5, n-b 1	14
G. A. Hick c Noon b Brown	23		—
D. A. Leatherdale b Brown	0	1/9 2/47 3/47 (4 wkts, 28 overs)	124
*P. A. Neale not out	37	4/95	

†S. J. Rhodes, P. J. Newport, R. K. Illingworth, N. V. Radford and A. P. Pridgeon did not bat.

Bowling: Lillee 6–0–21–0; Walker 6–0–21–1; Brown 5–0–25–2; Capel 6–0–30–1; Wild 5–0–19–0.

Umpires: J. D. Bond and J. H. Harris.

WORCESTERSHIRE v SUSSEX

At Worcester, August 7. Worcestershire won by eight wickets. Toss: Worcestershire. Parker became the first Sussex player to score 4,000 runs in the Sunday League.

Sussex

M. P. Speight c Bent b Newport	7	†P. Moores st Rhodes b Hick	1
*P. W. G. Parker not out	74	S. J. S. Kimber run out	5
C. M. Wells c Rhodes b Newport	8		
A. P. Wells c Bent b Illingworth	14	L-b 12, w 6	18
I. J. Gould c Neale b Hick	7		—
M. W. Pringle b Hick	11	1/13 2/27 3/70 (9 wkts, 40 overs)	165
A. C. S. Pigott c Weston b Hick	20	4/88 5/100 6/139	
A. R. Clarke b Radford	0	7/140 8/150 9/165	

A. M. Babington did not bat.

Bowling: Weston 8–0–23–0; Newport 5–0–12–2; Illingworth 8–0–24–1; Pridgeon 5–0–22–0; Hick 7–0–42–4; Radford 7–0–30–1.

Worcestershire

P. Bent c and b Clarke	36	D. A. Leatherdale not out	51
S. J. O'Shaughnessy c Parker b C. M. Wells	15	L-b 9, w 3	12
			—
G. A. Hick not out	52	1/46 2/65 (2 wkts, 32.4 overs)	166

*P. A. Neale, M. J. Weston, †S. J. Rhodes, P. J. Newport, R. K. Illingworth, N. V. Radford and A. P. Pridgeon did not bat.

Bowling: Babington 8–0–37–0; C. M. Wells 8–1–21–1; Kimber 7–0–31–0; Clarke 5–0–36–1; Pigott 3–0–23–0; Pringle 1.4–0–9–0.

Umpires: D. J. Constant and J. H. Hampshire.

At Swansea, August 14. WORCESTERSHIRE beat GLAMORGAN by seven wickets.

WORCESTERSHIRE v ESSEX

At Worcester, August 21. Worcestershire won by 18 runs in a match reduced to 36 overs a side after rain had delayed the start. Toss: Essex.

Worcestershire

T. S. Curtis c East b Childs	21	M. J. Weston not out	10
S. J. O'Shaughnessy c Gooch b Pringle	2	L-b 14, n-b 1	15
G. A. Hick c Childs b Stephenson	59		
D. B. D'Oliveira b Gooch	18	1/7 2/50 3/101 (4 wkts, 36 overs)	179
*P. A. Neale not out	54	4/123	

†S. J. Rhodes, P. J. Newport, R. K. Illingworth, N. V. Radford and A. P. Pridgeon did not bat.

Bowling: Pringle 7–0–34–1; Topley 7–0–37–0; Waugh 5–1–28–0; Childs 8–1–29–1; Gooch 7–0–26–1; Stephenson 2–0–11–1.

Essex

*G. A. Gooch c and b Illingworth	32	J. P. Stephenson not out	22
B. R. Hardie c Illingworth b Pridgeon	47	T. D. Topley run out	1
M. E. Waugh lbw b Radford	12	J. H. Childs b Illingworth	1
D. R. Pringle st Rhodes b Pridgeon	8	B 2, l-b 13, w 2, n-b 1	18
P. J. Prichard b Pridgeon	14		
A. W. Lilley b Radford	4	1/59 2/95 3/112 (34.3 overs)	161
N. Hussain c O'Shaughnessy b Pridgeon	0	4/126 5/131 6/133	
†D. E. East b Radford	2	7/136 8/154 9/158	

Bowling: Weston 7–0–21–0; Newport 5–0–20–0; Hick 5–0–23–0; Illingworth 3.3–0–17–2; Pridgeon 7–0–36–4; Radford 7–0–29–3.

Umpires: D. R. Shepherd and P. B. Wight.

WORCESTERSHIRE v WARWICKSHIRE

At Worcester, August 28. Worcestershire won by ten wickets, in a match reduced by rain to 36 overs, to retain the Refuge Assurance League title. Toss: Worcestershire.

Warwickshire

*T. A. Lloyd c Rhodes b Dilley	2	A. A. Donald b Pridgeon	7
P. A. Smith c O'Shaughnessy b Weston	11	A. R. K. Pierson run out	6
Asif Din lbw b Radford	16	T. A. Munton not out	6
A. I. Kallicharran c Neale b Radford	0	B 2, l-b 7, w 3, n-b 1	13
D. A. Thorne st Rhodes b Weston	2		
D. A. Banks c Rhodes b Radford	6	1/4 2/20 3/25 (36 overs)	82
†P. C. L. Holloway c Rhodes b Pridgeon	13	4/34 5/34 6/45	
G. C. Small c Rhodes b Radford	0	7/45 8/68 9/73	

Bowling: Weston 8–1–22–2; Dilley 7–2–10–1; Radford 7–2–14–4; Illingworth 7–1–12–0; Pridgeon 7–1–15–2.

Worcestershire

T. S. Curtis not out	35
S. J. O'Shaughnessy not out	43
L-b 4, w 1	5
(no wkt, 27.1 overs)	83

G. A. Hick, D. B. D'Oliveira, *P. A. Neale, M. J. Weston, †S. J. Rhodes, R. K. Illingworth, N. V. Radford, G. R. Dilley and A. P. Pridgeon did not bat.

Bowling: Small 5–1–5–0; Donald 5–0–21–0; Smith 4.1–1–14–0; Pierson 8–0–30–0; Munton 5–0–9–0.

Umpires: J. H. Harris and M. J. Kitchen.

YORKSHIRE

YORKSHIRE v DERBYSHIRE

At Leeds, May 1. No result. Rain, which had already caused the match to be reduced to 31 overs a side, returned before Yorkshire had faced the statutory twenty overs. Toss: Yorkshire.

Derbyshire

*K. J. Barnett c Love b Fletcher 26	P. G. Newman not out 27
P. D. Bowler lbw b Sidebottom 4	F. A. Griffith run out 8
B. Roberts lbw b S. N. Hartley 18	O. H. Mortensen run out 0
J. E. Morris c Robinson b Sidebottom . 16	
S. C. Goldsmith c Fletcher b P. J. Hartley . 40	L-b 9, w 2, n-b 1 12
M. A. Holding run out 1	1/25 2/56 3/62 (31 overs) 157
†B. J. M. Maher b Fletcher 5	4/81 5/96 6/109
A. E. Warner lbw b Fletcher 0	7/109 8/138 9/156

Bowling: Shaw 6–0–25–0; Sidebottom 7–0–33–2; S. N. Hartley 5–0–29–1; Fletcher 6–1–18–3; Moxon 1–0–4–0; P. J. Hartley 6–0–39–1.

Yorkshire

M. D. Moxon b Newman 1	P. E. Robinson not out 11
R. J. Blakey not out 12	L-b 1 1
J. D. Love c Maher b Mortensen 9	
*†D. L. Bairstow c Roberts b Mortensen 2	1/2 2/17 3/19 (3 wkts, 12 overs) 36

A. A. Metcalfe, S. N. Hartley, A. Sidebottom, P. J. Hartley, S. D. Fletcher and C. Shaw did not bat.

Bowling: Newman 3–0–6–1; Mortensen 6–1–14–2; Griffith 3–0–15–0.

Umpires: J. D. Bond and B. Leadbeater.

At Birmingham, May 8. YORKSHIRE beat WARWICKSHIRE by 27 runs.

At Worcester, May 15. YORKSHIRE lost to WORCESTERSHIRE by five wickets.

At Canterbury, May 22. YORKSHIRE beat KENT by 43 runs.

YORKSHIRE v HAMPSHIRE

At Middlesbrough, May 29. Hampshire won by seven wickets, having been set a revised target of 90 off twenty overs. Toss: Hampshire.

Yorkshire

M. D. Moxon c Parks b Jefferies 44	†D. L. Bairstow not out 22
A. A. Metcalfe c R. A. Smith b Cowley 19	L-b 2, w 2 4
K. Sharp c Parks b Jefferies 17	
P. E. Robinson not out 35	1/50 2/81 3/87 (3 wkts, 31.3 overs) 141

P. J. Hartley, *P. Carrick, A. Sidebottom, S. D. Fletcher, P. W. Jarvis and C. Shaw did not bat.

Bowling: Connor 5.3–1–15–0; Jefferies 6–0–30–2; Ayling 6–1–33–0; Andrew 6–0–26–0; Cowley 8–0–35–1.

Hampshire

R. A. Smith c Sidebottom b Jarvis	15
V. P. Terry c Robinson b Jarvis	14
D. R. Turner not out	27
*M. C. J. Nicholas c Bairstow b Jarvis	19
C. L. Smith not out	8
B 2, l-b 4, n-b 1	7
1/25 2/34 3/63 (3 wkts, 19 overs)	90

J. R. Ayling, N. G. Cowley, S. T. Jefferies, †R. J. Parks, C. A. Connor and S. J. W. Andrew did not bat.

Bowling: Jarvis 8–0–36–3; Sidebottom 8–1–32–0; Fletcher 2–0–11–0; Shaw 1–0–5–0.

Umpires: B. J. Meyer and R. A. White.

YORKSHIRE v SURREY

At Leeds, June 5. Yorkshire won by four wickets. Toss: Yorkshire.

Surrey

†C. J. Richards b Carrick	18
D. M. Smith b Hartley	33
A. J. Stewart c Shaw b Hartley	60
M. A. Lynch c Robinson b Hartley	4
D. M. Ward b Shaw	22
*I. A. Greig c Byas b Shaw	9
Zahid Sadiq c Robinson b Sidebottom	23
C. K. Bullen not out	21
M. A. Feltham b Fletcher	11
S. T. Clarke not out	0
L-b 6, w 1, n-b 4	11
1/42 2/88 3/106 4/122 5/144 6/160 7/188 8/211 (8 wkts, 40 overs)	212

M. P. Bicknell did not bat.

Bowling: Sidebottom 8–0–49–1; Shaw 8–0–35–2; Carrick 4–1–23–1; Fletcher 8–0–40–1; Moxon 4–0–20–0; Hartley 8–0–39–3.

Yorkshire

M. D. Moxon c Stewart b Bicknell	3
A. A. Metcalfe c Lynch b Bullen	79
K. Sharp b Bullen	18
P. E. Robinson c Stewart b Bullen	20
D. Byas not out	69
S. N. Hartley c Greig b Feltham	8
†R. J. Blakey b Clarke	2
*P. Carrick not out	4
L-b 10, w 3	13
1/10 2/106 3/107 4/154 5/177 6/182 (6 wkts, 37.3 overs)	216

A. Sidebottom, S. D. Fletcher, and C. Shaw did not bat.

Bowling: Bicknell 8–0–28–1; Greig 6.3–0–44–0; Feltham 8–0–60–1; Clarke 7–0–17–1; Bullen 8–0–57–3.

Umpires: K. J. Lyons and D. O. Oslear.

YORKSHIRE v ESSEX

At Sheffield, June 19. Yorkshire won by four wickets. Toss: Yorkshire.

Essex

B. R. Hardie b Fletcher	59
J. P. Stephenson c Bairstow b Shaw	2
*A. R. Border c Bairstow b Shaw	0
P. J. Prichard b Fletcher	9
A. W. Lilley lbw b P. J. Hartley	6
N. Hussain c Bairstow b Fletcher	4
G. Miller c Robinson b P. J. Hartley	29
I. L. Pont c Fletcher b Shaw	36
T. D. Topley lbw b Fletcher	0
J. K. Lever not out	5
†A. D. Brown not out	1
L-b 16, w 6, n-b 1	23
1/8 2/10 3/26 4/40 5/50 6/98 7/167 8/167 9/169 (9 wkts, 40 overs)	174

Bowling: Shaw 8–0–39–3; Sidebottom 8–1–13–0; Fletcher 8–0–28–4; P. J. Hartley 8–2–34–2; Carrick 4–0–17–0; S. N. Hartley 4–0–27–0.

Yorkshire

K. Sharp c Border b Miller 52	*P. Carrick run out 0
A. A. Metcalfe c Stephenson b Topley . 79	P. J. Hartley not out 4
P. E. Robinson b Pont 19	L-b 4, w 2, n-b 1 7
D. Byas c Brown b Topley 2	
S. N. Hartley not out 15	1/126 2/139 3/142 (6 wkts, 39 overs) 178
†D. L. Bairstow c Stephenson b Pont . . 0	4/172 5/172 6/173

A. Sidebottom, S. D. Fletcher and C. Shaw did not bat.

Bowling: Lever 8–0–28–0; Pont 7–0–33–2; Stephenson 8–1–35–0; Topley 8–0–41–2; Miller 8–1–37–1.

Umpires: J. Birkenshaw and B. Hassan.

At Hove, June 26. YORKSHIRE lost to SUSSEX by seven wickets.

YORKSHIRE v LEICESTERSHIRE

At Hull, July 3. Yorkshire won by six wickets. Toss: Leicestershire.

Leicestershire

L. Potter not out 66	C. C. Lewis not out 28
*N. E. Briers b Shaw 22	L-b 13, w 8 21
P. Willey c Love b Carrick 23	
J. J. Whitaker b Fletcher 12	1/46 2/98 3/128 (3 wkts, 40 overs) 172

P. N. Hepworth, J. D. R. Benson, †P. Whitticase, J. P. Agnew, G. J. F. Ferris and L. B. Taylor did not bat.

Bowling: Sidebottom 8–0–35–0; Fletcher 8–2–33–1; Hartley 7–0–28–0; Shaw 8–0–23–1; Carrick 8–0–26–1; Love 1–0–14–0.

Yorkshire

K. Sharp b Taylor 56	J. D. Love not out 2
A. A. Metcalfe b Taylor 20	L-b 15, w 2, n-b 1 18
P. E. Robinson run out 47	
D. Byas not out 21	1/53 2/133 3/140 (4 wkts, 37.4 overs) 173
S. N. Hartley b Agnew 9	4/163

†D. L. Bairstow, *P. Carrick, A. Sidebottom, C. Shaw and S. D. Fletcher did not bat.

Bowling: Agnew 6–1–21–1; Ferris 7.4–1–28–0; Taylor 8–0–30–2; Lewis 5–0–29–0; Willey 8–0–28–0; Potter 3–0–22–0.

Umpires: H. D. Bird and P. J. Eele.

At Northampton, July 10. NORTHAMPTONSHIRE v YORKSHIRE. No result.

At Nottingham, July 17. YORKSHIRE beat NOTTINGHAMSHIRE by seven wickets.

At Cardiff, July 24. YORKSHIRE lost to GLAMORGAN by 15 runs.

YORKSHIRE v LANCASHIRE

At Scarborough, July 31. Lancashire won by two wickets. Toss: Lancashire.

Yorkshire

A. A. Metcalfe c Hayhurst b Simmons . 69
D. Byas c Fairbrother b Austin 41
J. D. Love b Hayhurst 5
P. E. Robinson b Austin 7
S. N. Hartley c and b Simmons 14
†D. L. Bairstow b Austin 0
*P. Carrick not out 38
A. Sidebottom b Wasim 10
P. J. Hartley b Wasim 0
S. D. Fletcher not out 4
L-b 15, w 4, n-b 1 20

1/83 2/104 3/124 4/136 5/136 6/149 7/180 8/191 (8 wkts, 40 overs) 208

C. Shaw did not bat.

Bowling: Watkinson 8–0–57–0; Hayhurst 8–1–36–1; Wasim 8–1–30–2; Austin 8–0–35–3; Simmons 8–1–35–2.

Lancashire

G. D. Mendis c S. N. Hartley b Shaw . 9
G. Fowler c and b Carrick 24
T. E. Jesty lbw b P. J. Hartley 7
N. H. Fairbrother c Metcalfe b Carrick 46
M. Watkinson c Metcalfe b Carrick ... 19
*D. P. Hughes c Metcalfe b Carrick ... 34
Wasim Akram c Bairstow b P. J. Hartley 29
A. N. Hayhurst b Sidebottom 20
I. D. Austin not out 10
J. Simmons not out 0
L-b 8, w 3 11

1/17 2/32 3/53 4/78 5/138 6/152 7/196 8/198 (8 wkts, 39 overs) 209

†W. K. Hegg did not bat.

Bowling: Sidebottom 8–0–45–1; Shaw 8–0–29–1; P. J. Hartley 7–0–45–2; Fletcher 8–0–42–0; Carrick 8–0–40–4.

Umpires: J. W. Holder and R. Palmer.

At Cheltenham, August 7. YORKSHIRE lost to GLOUCESTERSHIRE by three wickets.

YORKSHIRE v SOMERSET

At Scarborough, August 14. Somerset won by 2 runs. Toss: Somerset.

Somerset

J. J. E. Hardy c Blakey b Fletcher 30
G. D. Rose b Shaw 10
J. G. Wyatt run out 89
S. R. Waugh run out 38
R. J. Bartlett b Fletcher 23
*V. J. Marks not out 11
†N. D. Burns run out 22
N. A. Mallender not out 5
B 2, l-b 3, w 1, n-b 1 7

1/25 2/61 3/135 4/194 5/195 6/226 (6 wkts, 40 overs) 235

M. W. Cleal, A. N. Jones and C. H. Dredge did not bat.

Bowling: Sidebottom 8–0–45–0; Shaw 8–1–40–1; Fletcher 8–0–37–2; Hartley 5–0–40–0; Moxon 3–0–18–0; Carrick 8–0–50–0.

Yorkshire

K. Sharp c Burns b Rose 29
A. A. Metcalfe lbw b Dredge 2
P. E. Robinson c and b Marks 51
D. Byas lbw b Jones 0
M. D. Moxon c Dredge b Jones 68
†R. J. Blakey lbw b Marks 25
*P. Carrick c Wyatt b Dredge 21
P. J. Hartley b Mallender 11
A. Sidebottom b Jones 1
C. Shaw not out 13
S. D. Fletcher not out 2
L-b 8, w 2 10

1/10 2/61 3/66 4/92 5/143 6/182 7/200 8/209 9/224 (9 wkts, 40 overs) 233

Bowling: Dredge 8–0–40–2; Mallender 8–2–30–1; Rose 7–0–42–1; Jones 8–0–46–3; Marks 7–0–50–2; Cleal 2–0–17–0.

Umpires: J. H. Hampshire and N. T. Plews.

YORKSHIRE v MIDDLESEX

At Leeds, August 28. Yorkshire won by four wickets when they achieved a revised target of 143 off 38 overs. Toss: Middlesex. Rain twice interrupted play during Yorkshire's innings.

Middlesex

W. N. Slack c Blakey b Pickles 15
J. D. Carr c Fletcher b Shaw 0
A. Needham c Fletcher b Pickles 7
*M. W. Gatting b Fletcher 11
M. A. Roseberry c Moxon b Fletcher .. 10
M. R. Ramprakash c Shaw b Fletcher . 51
†K. R. Brown b Carrick 5
J. F. Sykes b Fletcher 21
S. P. Hughes not out 12
A. R. C. Fraser c Shaw b Hartley 2
N. G. Cowans not out 0
L-b 12, w 4 16

1/2 2/23 3/24 4/47 5/57 6/86 7/130 8/140 9/147 (9 wkts, 40 overs) 150

Bowling: Pickles 8–2–19–2; Shaw 8–3–13–1; Fletcher 8–0–37–4; Hartley 8–0–29–1; Carrick 5–0–20–1; Moxon 3–0–20–0.

Yorkshire

M. D. Moxon c Sykes b Needham 21
A. A. Metcalfe b Fraser 10
D. Byas c Sykes b Hughes 43
P. E. Robinson c Gatting b Hughes ... 25
J. D. Love c Brown b Carr 5
†R. J. Blakey not out 13
*P. Carrick b Hughes 8
C. S. Pickles not out 7
B 1, l-b 6, w 2, n-b 2 11

1/20 2/53 3/105 4/112 5/121 6/131 (6 wkts, 34.5 overs) 143

C. Shaw, P. J. Hartley and S. D. Fletcher did not bat.

Bowling: Cowans 8–1–24–0; Fraser 8–1–19–1; Needham 7–0–33–1; Carr 5–0–23–1 Hughes 6.5–0–37–3.

Umpires: J. Birkenshaw and K. J. Lyons.

SUNDAY LEAGUE RECORDS

Batting

Highest score: 176 – G. A. Gooch, Essex v Glamorgan (Southend), 1983.

Most hundreds: 11 – C. G. Greenidge; 9 – K. S. McEwan and B. A. Richards. 305 hundreds have been scored in the League.

Most runs: D. L. Amiss 7,040; C. T. Radley 6,650; D. R. Turner 6,429; C. G. Greenidge 6,348; C. E. B. Rice 6,265; G. M. Turner 6,144; P. Willey 5,975; Younis Ahmed 5,897.

Most runs in a season: 814 – C. E. B. Rice (Nottinghamshire), 1977.

Most sixes in an innings: 13 – I. T. Botham, Somerset v Northamptonshire (Wellingborough School), 1986.

Most sixes by a team in an innings: 18 – Derbyshire v Worcestershire (Knypersley), 1985.

Most sixes in a season: 26 – I. V. A. Richards (Somerset), 1977.

Highest total: 310 for five – Essex v Glamorgan (Southend), 1983.

Highest total – batting second: 301 for six – Warwickshire v Essex (Colchester), 1982.

Highest match aggregate: 604 – Surrey (304) v Warwickshire (300 for nine) (The Oval), 1985.

Lowest total: 23 – Middlesex v Yorkshire (Leeds), 1974.

Shortest completed innings: 16 overs – Northamptonshire 59 v Middlesex (Tring), 1974.

Shortest match: 2 hr 13 min (40.3 overs) – Essex v Northamptonshire (Ilford), 1971.

Biggest victories: 190 runs, Kent beat Northamptonshire (Brackley), 1973.

There have been 21 instances of victory by ten wickets – by Derbyshire, Essex (twice), Glamorgan, Hampshire, Leicestershire (twice), Middlesex (twice), Northamptonshire, Nottinghamshire, Somerset (twice), Surrey (twice), Warwickshire, Worcestershire (twice) and Yorkshire (three times). This does not include those matches in which the side batting second was set a reduced target.

Ties (28): Nottinghamshire v Kent (Nottingham), 1969, in a match reduced to twenty overs.

Gloucestershire v Hampshire (Bristol), 1972; Gloucestershire v Northamptonshire (Bristol), 1972.

Surrey v Worcestershire (Byfleet), 1973.

Middlesex v Lancashire (Lord's), 1974; Sussex v Leicestershire (Hove), 1974.

Lancashire v Worcestershire (Manchester), 1975; Somerset v Glamorgan (Taunton), 1975.

Warwickshire v Kent (Birmingham), 1980.

Kent v Lancashire (Maidstone), 1981.

Yorkshire v Nottinghamshire (Hull), 1982; Hampshire v Lancashire (Southampton), 1982; Surrey v Hampshire (The Oval), 1982.

Worcestershire v Nottinghamshire (Hereford), 1983; Lancashire v Worcestershire (Manchester), 1983, in a match reduced to nineteen overs; Warwickshire v Worcestershire (Birmingham), 1983, Warwickshire's innings having been reduced to ten overs.

Middlesex v Essex (Lord's), 1984.

Essex v Leicestershire (Chelmsford), 1985; Northamptonshire v Lancashire (Northampton), 1985; Lancashire v Glamorgan (Manchester), 1985.

Kent v Surrey (Canterbury), 1986; Middlesex v Warwickshire (Lord's), 1986; Yorkshire v Warwickshire (Leeds), 1986.

Hampshire v Gloucestershire (Southampton), 1987; Hampshire v Derbyshire (Southampton), 1987.

Essex v Sussex (Ilford), 1988; Surrey v Derbyshire (The Oval), 1988; Sussex v Glamorgan (Eastbourne), 1988.

Record partnerships for each wicket

239 for 1st	G. A. Gooch and B. R. Hardie, Essex v Nottinghamshire at Nottingham	1985
273 for 2nd	G. A. Gooch and K. S. McEwan, Essex v Nottinghamshire at Nottingham	1983
215 for 3rd	W. Larkins and R. G. Williams, Northamptonshire v Worcestershire at Luton	1982
219 for 4th	C. G. Greenidge and C. L. Smith, Hampshire v Surrey at Southampton	1987
185 for 5th	B. M. McMillan and Asif Din, Warwickshire v Essex at Chelmsford	1986
121 for 6th	C. P. Wilkins and A. J. Borrington, Derbyshire v Warwickshire at Chesterfield	1972
132 for 7th	K. R. Brown and N. F. Williams, Middlesex v Somerset at Lord's	1988
95* for 8th	D. Breakwell and K. F. Jennings, Somerset v Nottinghamshire at Nottingham	1976
105 for 9th	D. G. Moir and R. W. Taylor, Derbyshire v Kent at Derby	1984
57 for 10th	D. A. Graveney and J. B. Mortimore, Gloucestershire v Lancashire at Tewkesbury	1973

Bowling

Best analyses: eight for 26, K. D. Boyce, Essex v Lancashire (Manchester), 1971; seven for 15, R. A. Hutton, Yorkshire v Worcestershire (Leeds), 1969; seven for 39, A. Hodgson, Northamptonshire v Somerset (Northampton), 1976; seven for 41, A. N. Jones, Sussex v Nottinghamshire (Nottingham), 1986; six for 6, R. W. Hooker, Middlesex v Surrey (Lord's), 1969; six for 7, M. Hendrick, Derbyshire v Nottinghamshire (Nottingham), 1972.

Four wickets in four balls: A. Ward, Derbyshire v Sussex (Derby), 1970.

Hat-tricks (18): A. Ward, Derbyshire v Sussex (Derby), 1970; R. Palmer, Somerset v Gloucestershire (Bristol), 1970; K. D. Boyce, Essex v Somerset (Westcliff), 1971; G. D. McKenzie, Leicestershire v Essex (Leicester), 1972; R. G. D. Willis, Warwickshire v Yorkshire (Birmingham), 1973; W. Blenkiron, Warwickshire v Derbyshire (Buxton), 1974; A. Buss, Sussex v Worcestershire (Hastings), 1974; J. M. Rice, Hampshire v Northamptonshire (Southampton), 1975; M. A. Nash, Glamorgan v Worcestershire (Worcester), 1975; A. Hodgson, Northamptonshire v Somerset (Northampton), 1976; A. E. Cordle, Glamorgan v Hampshire (Portsmouth), 1979; C. J. Tunnicliffe, Derbyshire v Worcestershire (Derby), 1979; M. D. Marshall, Hampshire v Surrey (Southampton), 1981; I. V. A. Richards, Somerset v Essex (Chelmsford), 1982; P. W. Jarvis, Yorkshire v Derbyshire (Derby), 1982; R. M. Ellison, Kent v Hampshire (Canterbury), 1983; G. C. Holmes, Glamorgan v Nottinghamshire (Ebbw Vale), 1987; K. Saxelby, Nottinghamshire v Worcestershire (Nottingham), 1987.

Most economical analysis: 8–8–0–0, B. A. Langford, Somerset v Essex (Yeovil), 1969.

Most expensive analyses: 8–0–88–1, E. E. Hemmings, Nottinghamshire v Somerset (Nottingham), 1983; 7.5–0–89–3, G. Miller, Derbyshire v Gloucestershire (Gloucester), 1984.

Most wickets in a season: 34 – R. J. Clapp (Somerset), 1974 and C. E. B. Rice (Nottinghamshire), 1986.

Most wickets: J. K. Lever 365; D. L. Underwood 346; S. Turner 303; J. Simmons 290; N. Gifford 284; J. N. Shepherd 267; T. E. Jesty 248; R. D. Jackman 234.

Wicket-keeping and Fielding

Most dismissals: D. L. Bairstow 243 (222 ct, 21 st); R. W. Taylor 236 (187 ct, 49 st); E. W. Jones 223 (184 ct, 39 st).

Most dismissals in a season: 29 (26 ct, 3 st) – S. J. Rhodes (Worcestershire), 1988.

Most dismissals in an innings: 7 (6 ct, 1 st) – R. W. Taylor, Derbyshire v Lancashire (Manchester), 1975.

Most catches in an innings: 6 – K. Goodwin, Lancashire v Worcestershire (Worcester), 1969, and R. W. Taylor, Derbyshire v Lancashire (Manchester), 1975.

Most stumpings in an innings: 4 – S. J. Rhodes, Worcestershire v Warwickshire (Birmingham), 1986.

Most catches by a fielder: (not a wicket-keeper): J. F. Steele 101; G. Cook 90; C. T. Radley 90.

Most catches in a season: 16 – J. M. Rice (Hampshire), 1978.

Most catches in an innings: 5 – J. M. Rice, Hampshire v Warwickshire (Southampton), 1978.

CHAMPIONS: 1969-88

1969	Lancashire	1979	Somerset
1970	Lancashire	1980	Warwickshire
1971	Worcestershire	1981	Essex
1972	Kent	1982	Sussex
1973	Kent	1983	Yorkshire
1974	Leicestershire	1984	Essex
1975	Hampshire	1985	Essex
1976	Kent	1986	Hampshire
1977	Leicestershire	1987	Worcestershire
1978	Hampshire	1988	Worcestershire

REFUGE ASSURANCE CUP, 1988

.ancashire became the first holders of the Refuge Assurance Cup, beating he Refuge Assurance League champions, Worcestershire, by 52 runs in the vell-attended final at Edgbaston on the last Sunday of the season. Qualification for the Cup competition was via the League, with the first four n the Sunday table going forward to the mid-week semi-finals. The hampions and runners-up gained the home ties, with the champions playing he fourth-placed county and the runners-up meeting the third-placed team. 'he matches were of 40 overs per side and played using an orange ball – an xperiment that did not meet with universal approval. In addition to winning he Refuge Assurance Cup, Lancashire received £5,000 in prizemoney and Vorcestershire £2,500. Gloucestershire and Middlesex, the losing semi-nalists, each received £1,250. Mike Watkinson, Man of the Match in the nal, received £300, and the Man of the Match in each of the semi-finals 150.

SEMI-FINALS

GLOUCESTERSHIRE v LANCASHIRE

t Bristol, September 7. Lancashire won by three wickets. Toss: Lancashire. Allott, whose owling had done much to contain Gloucestershire, hit the fifth ball of the final over for four take Lancashire into the final. At the other end of the match, he had bowled Athey with his st ball, and had Stovold, when 10 and 11, not been reprieved in consecutive overs from

Allott, Lancashire's target might have been less than 100. On a slow pitch, and with the orange ball moving considerably in the air, batting was not easy, as Gloucestershire learnt to their cost when they tried to accelerate against Simmons's off-spin. Lancashire found Graveney's slow left-arm spin similarly economical. The dismissal of Fairbrother, Jesty and Hayhurst in the space of seven balls, followed three overs later by that of Austin, brought Gloucestershire back into the game, but Watkinson and Allott made sure this was only a temporary setback.

Man of the Match: P. J. W. Allott.

Gloucestershire

A. W. Stovold b Simmons 40
C. W. J. Athey b Allott 0
P. Bainbridge c Hegg b Allott 4
K. M. Curran c Watkinson b Hayhurst. 9
P. W. Romaines c Jesty b Simmons . . . 15
A. J. Wright lbw b Simmons 10
†R. C. Russell c Watkinson b Austin . . 1
M. W. Alleyne b Watkinson 15
V. S. Greene run out 2
*D. A. Graveney not out 3
K. B. S. Jarvis not out 4
L-b 6, w 8 14

1/1 2/14 3/43 4/74 5/75 6/79 7/95 8/104 9/111 (9 wkts, 40 overs) 117

Bowling: Watkinson 8–0–29–1; Allott 8–4–14–2; Hayhurst 8–0–24–1; Austin 8–0–30–1 Simmons 8–1–14–3.

Lancashire

G. D. Mendis c Alleyne b Jarvis 1
G. Fowler c Russell b Curran 19
A. N. Hayhurst st Russell b Graveney . 26
N. H. Fairbrother run out 18
M. Watkinson not out 18
T. E. Jesty lbw b Greene 0
I. D. Austin lbw b Greene 3
*D. P. Hughes run out . . . .
P. J. W. Allott not out 1
L-b 5, w 9, n-b 2 1

1/8 2/38 3/77 4/77 5/77 6/86 7/99 (7 wkts, 39.5 overs) 12

J. Simmons and †W. K. Hegg did not bat.

Bowling: Greene 8–3–16–2; Jarvis 8–1–17–1; Curran 4–0–15–1; Bainbridge 7.5–0–33–0 Graveney 8–1–18–1; Alleyne 4–0–17–0.

Umpires: J. W. Holder and N. T. Plews.

WORCESTERSHIRE v MIDDLESEX

At Worcester, September 7. Worcestershire won by seven wickets. Toss: Worcestershire. A dry pitch of uncertain bounce also encouraged the quick bowlers with generous movement o the seam and made batting a struggle. Not even Hick, the game's top-scorer, was able dominate the bowling, and although needing to score at less than 4 runs an over, Worceste shire won with only eight balls remaining. Leatherdale batted well, as he had in the Lord final the previous Saturday, and outscored Hick quite handsomely in their partnership of for the third wicket. Only a spirited last-wicket stand of 36 between Downton and Cowar had given the Middlesex bowlers a total to defend.

Man of the Match: G. A. Hick.

Middlesex

W. N. Slack c Rhodes b Weston 7
J. D. Carr run out 17
*M. W. Gatting c Pridgeon b Radford . 9
R. O. Butcher b Illingworth 14
M. R. Ramprakash c Leatherdale b Radford . 11
J. E. Emburey b Radford 6
†P. R. Downton not out 30
A. Needham c Neale b Radford 2
S. P. Hughes lbw b Illingworth . . . .
A. R. C. Fraser b Illingworth . . . .
N. G. Cowans not out . . . .
L-b 14, w 6, n-b 2 . . . .

1/17 2/42 3/53 4/75 5/75 6/82 7/92 8/110 9/110 (9 wkts, 40 overs) 1

Bowling: Weston 8–0–28–1; Dilley 8–0–29–0; Pridgeon 8–2–23–0; Radford 8–1–23- Illingworth 8–0–29–3.

Worcestershire

T. S. Curtis c Gatting b Emburey 17
†S. J. Rhodes b Cowans 1
G. A. Hick not out 74
D. A. Leatherdale b Hughes 41

*P. A. Neale not out 1
L-b 4, w 8, n-b 1 13

1/7 2/75 3/141 (3 wkts, 38.4 overs) 147

D. B. D'Oliveira, M. J. Weston, R. K. Illingworth, N. V. Radford, G. R. Dilley and A. P. Pridgeon did not bat.

Bowling: Cowans 8–2–18–1; Fraser 7.4–2–26–0; Carr 8–2–22–0; Emburey 8–1–37–1; Hughes 7–1–40–1.

Umpires: B. Dudleston and J. H. Hampshire.

FINAL

LANCASHIRE v WORCESTERSHIRE

At Birmingham, September 18. Lancashire won by 52 runs. Toss: Worcestershire. Worcestershire, winners of the Refuge Assurance League and the Britannic Assurance Championship, were denied a unique treble when Lancashire won the first Refuge Assurance Cup final. The victory was unexpectedly comfortable and against the odds, although Lancashire were doing nothing more than repeating the first Sunday match of the season in April when they beat the same opponents by seven wickets with 3.4 overs to spare at Old Trafford. And it was all the more satisfying because they had to overcome the loss of two wickets for 4 runs after being put in to bat. The recovery was started by Fowler and Fairbrother and continued by Jesty, who played beautifully, and Watkinson, who batted belligerently, in a partnership of 81 in nine overs. The target was well within Worcestershire's range but they, too, made a poor start, lacked the powers of a real recovery and, having lost their last five wickets in three overs, were all out with 4.1 overs remaining. Watkinson was a popular Man of the Match, following his unbeaten 42 with the important wicket of Hick and the catch that removed the growing threat of Neale. An attendance of 14,616, producing receipts of £106,000, was testimony to the popularity of the new competition and of a cup final at a venue other than Lord's.

Lancashire

G. D. Mendis b Weston 0
G. Fowler c Neale b Pridgeon 26
A. N. Hayhurst st Rhodes b Weston ... 1
N. H. Fairbrother c Radford b Newport 38
T. E. Jesty b Radford 59
M. Watkinson not out 42

I. D. Austin not out 6
B 4, l-b 12, w 13 29

1/1 2/4 3/69 4/113 5/194 (5 wkts, 40 overs) 201

D. P. Hughes, P. J. W. Allott, J. Simmons and †W. K. Hegg did not bat.

Bowling: Weston 8–0–19–2; Newport 8–0–40–1; Radford 8–0–44–1; Pridgeon 8–1–48–1; Illingworth 8–0–34–0.

Worcestershire

T. S. Curtis c Hegg b Hayhurst 32
T. J. O'Shaughnessy c Mendis b Allott . 4
G. A. Hick b Watkinson 2
D. A. Leatherdale b Simmons 30
*P. A. Neale c Watkinson b Austin ... 42
M. J. Weston c Hegg b Hayhurst 1
†S. J. Rhodes c Hughes b Hayhurst ... 20
P. J. Newport c Hegg b Austin 2

N. V. Radford c Hegg b Hayhurst 0
R. K. Illingworth c Hegg b Austin 0
A. P. Pridgeon not out 2
L-b 10, w 4 14

1/19 2/24 3/75 4/79 5/90 6/134 7/145 8/145 9/146 (35.5 overs) 149

Bowling: Watkinson 6–2–10–1; Allott 6–2–10–1; Austin 7.5–0–51–3; Simmons 8–0–22–1; Hayhurst 8–0–46–4.

Umpires: J. Birkenshaw and J. W. Holder.

THE AUSTRALIAN ABORIGINAL TEAM IN ENGLAND, 1988

By MURRAY HEDGCOCK

The 1988 Qantas Australian Aboriginal Cricket Team fell short of its objective of winning 90 per cent of its 28 one-day matches in Britain. The tally was sixteen wins, ten defeats, one abandoned and one drawn through rain, this last sadly being the showcase final appearance against MCC at Lord's. But the team succeeded on two major counts. It played with consistent good sportsmanship, making a favourable impression on and off the field. And the tour confirmed a future for Aboriginal cricket, with the prospect of a new structure for the game in Australia, aimed at getting Aborigines into the Test team.

The tour was arranged at short notice, although the idea had been planted some years earlier by Aborigines interested in expanding sporting opportunities for their race. Lacking the TCCB network for match and travel arrangements, the Aborigines depended heavily on their British liaison officer, David Burt of Interaction Associates, who proved invaluable. The locally recruited coach driver and baggage man, Doug Herbert, also played his full, cheery share. There was some confusion about tour links with the Australian Bicentenary celebrations, activists arguing that the native people of Australia had nothing to celebrate over the "white invasion" of 1788. It was claimed by some that the tourists were "Uncle Toms", going along with whites in return for handouts – in this case, an overseas trip. But most Aborigines' reaction was favourable, and no more than one or two possible tour candidates declined on political grounds. In the end, no official Bicentenary money was accepted; the tour was achieved through business and sports authority sponsorship. In this respect, it commemorated more truly the historic 1868 visit to Britain by the first Aboriginal team, indeed the first sports side of any kind to leave Australia, which pre-dated the pioneer white cricket team to England by a decade.

The man largely responsible for getting the 1988 tour off the ground, and then ensuring its success, was Mark Ella, Australia's former rugby union captain. It needed Ella's high profile to gain business support and the endorsement of politicians, led by Prime Minister Bob Hawke, a great cricket enthusiast, to make the tour possible. It also required Mr Hawke's direct appeal to MCC to have the match at Lord's switched from the Nursery to the main square after the choice of the original venue was seen as a much resented snub. Ella's reputation was essential to guarantee the team proper attention, and to ensure a balanced itinerary. As chairman of the fledgling Aboriginal Cricket Association, he led from the front and pledged that he would continue to direct the organisation until it built a firm base. Ella played a couple of times and showed his fielding to be first-class.

The team was pitchforked into its opening match at The Oval within 4 hours of arriving, and the players wilted in unexpected heat. "We were practically going to sleep in the field from jet-lag", said Mike Mainhardt, a one-time Queensland fast bowler and the only player with first-class experience. The match was played so early because of work, fixture and travel complications. It was the first of six games against strengthened county Second XIs – Surrey, Kent, Sussex, Hampshire, Glamorgan and Lancashire all of which were lost. The tourists were given a rough introduction to both the single-minded pursuit of individual success and the professional skills of young county players. They also discovered quickly how tight and tough is the English approach at all levels to the limited-overs game. Captained by the Seconds' coach, Chris Waller, Surrey dismissed the tourists for 171 and knocked off the runs for the loss of one wicket. This was the only match when politics intruded; an Aboriginal lands-right demonstration was defused when the tour management persuaded the Surrey authorities to let the protesters inside on a guarantee (which was kept) of no disruption of play.

At Canterbury 48 hours later, a twenty-over thrash, after rain wrecked the scheduled game, again saw the one-day skills of young professionals administer a sharp lesson. The first game against a club team, at the historic Old Deer Park home of Richmond CC, brought the tourists up against five players with first-class backgrounds, plus a couple of experienced young Australians. As the Aboriginals' captain, John McGuire, later commented wrily: "We came to play cricket against Englishmen, and we seemed to play against more Australians than anyone else." By the time the Aboriginals met Australia House at the BBC ground at Motspur Park, they were not surprised to face the former New South Wales and Test fast bowler, Dave Gilbert, in a side captained by Ian Maddocks, the former Victoria wicket-keeper.

This was to be a pattern throughout the tour: the Aboriginal team had ironically received too much advance publicity for its own good – or at least for its chances of continuous success. Newspaper stories and television coverage, showing the team beating sides in Australia which included former Test players, had given match organisers in Britain an exaggerated idea of the tourists' strength. Most sides they met seemed to be reinforced with guests: the Gentlemen of Middlesex, for instance, were reinforced by the New Zealand fast bowler, Danny Morrison. It was much to the credit of the players, and especially to the team's leaders – Ella, McGuire and the coach, Ian King, a former Queensland Sheffield Shield fast bowler – that they stuck to their task and began to win. By the tour's end, they had vastly improved not only individual skills but also the team effort. The fielding was sounder; running between wickets, chaotic early, was much improved; the batting was resourceful right to No. 11.

Some of the tourists hope to return to club or league cricket in England. The tour came too late for older players to accept such opportunity, but there was a promising nucleus of youngsters who should develop. Sean Appoo, a tall, straight-backed all-rounder, not unreasonably compared with Greg Chappell in his classic front-of-the-wicket style, was one such: at 21 he played some fine innings, although erratic. Teenager Joey Marsh, a determined left-handed bat, improved after a shaky start, scored an unbeaten hundred against Combined Services towards the end of the tour, and headed the averages. McGuire, a left-handed opener who had been in the Western Australia squad, played some pleasing innings, especially when able to get on the front foot. He had the satisfaction of hitting the team's first century, 110 against Farnham, and scored 659 runs with an average of almost 33. Bert Pearce, a lanky off-spinner from Sydney's Manly club, was never afraid to toss the ball up, learnt much, and led the bowling averages with 21 wickets. Mainhardt's experience was invaluable; he moved the ball, knew the virtues of attacking the wicket from a full length, and was the bowling backbone with 26 dismissals. The vice-captain, Neil Bulger, a punishing left-handed bat, thoughtful left-arm bowler, tireless field and reserve wicket-keeper, was the workhorse of the side. The pity was that the tour came too late for him to use it as a step to first-class cricket.

The Aboriginal Cricket Association is confident that it has laid the foundation for a genuine contribution to cricket in Australia, as well as enhancing the status and prospects of the Aboriginal people. The team was met with warmth and enthusiasm; only one match saw any hint of racial prejudice, which was refreshingly absent elsewhere. Perhaps England expected the Aborigines to look more like the dark-skinned introverted bushmen of the 1868 team. In fact, several of the party were more European in feature than Aboriginal, while their number included civil servants, a teacher and a lecturer studying for his doctorate. On their side, the team hugely enjoyed their visit. They had few health problems, thanks to sensible management, but found English club cricket a tough game. For players brought up in the Australian pattern of two-day matches, Saturday to Saturday, they met problems in pacing an innings and exerting the necessary miserly control of bowling and fielding. They also wished for more time to see England, rather than being whisked day by day from hotel to hotel for the next match. But they did have the honour of meeting The Queen at Buckingham Palace, and they took home a wider, welcome knowledge of Britain as well as of cricket.

The tour party comprised the following: Mark Ella (*manager*), Ian King (*coach*), John McGuire (*captain*), Sean Appoo, Paul Bagshaw, Dwayne Breckenridge, Neil Bulger, Norman Fry, Donald Gardner, Eddie Graham-Vanderbyl, Pius Gregory, Greg James, Michael Mainhardt, Laurie Marks, Joe Marsh, Dennis Monaghan, Bert Pearce, Darrin Thompson and Michael Williams.

COUNTY BENEFITS AWARDED FOR 1989

Derbyshire	Club funds.
Essex	J. K. Lever (Testimonial).
Glamorgan	R. C. Ontong.
Gloucestershire	P. Bainbridge.
Hampshire	M. N. S. Taylor (Testimonial).
Kent	C. S. Cowdrey.
Lancashire	Old Trafford Pavilion Fund.
Leicestershire	L. B. Taylor.
Middlesex	R. O. Butcher.
Northamptonshire	R. G. Williams.
Nottinghamshire	J. D. Birch.
Somerset	D. Breakwell/ T. Gard.
Surrey	G. S. Clinton.
Sussex	Club – 150th Anniversary Fund.
Worcestershire	A. P. Pridgeon.
Yorkshire	J. D. Love.

MINOR COUNTIES CHAMPIONSHIP, 1988

By MICHAEL BERRY and ROBERT BROOKE

In one way or another, the 1988 Minor Counties season was almost exclusively the preserve of Cheshire and Dorset. Cheshire won the Championship for the third time, having earlier made national headlines with their one-wicket victory over Northamptonshire in the first round of the NatWest Bank Trophy. Dorset claimed their first major honour by winning the Holt Trophy one-day competition. But if Cheshire and Dorset shared the winners' rostrum, Cambridgeshire finished in the shadows for the second successive season. The misfortune of losing both finals in 1987 was repeated as they again reached the Championship and one-day deciders, only to be runners-up in both once more.

The first leg of Cambridgeshire's unfortunate double was at Weymouth, where they were beaten by Dorset in the final of the Holt Trophy. At different stages they appeared well poised to win this tense, low-scoring match, but ultimately they were beaten by two wickets. The Reverend Andrew Wingfield Digby was thus able to celebrate his first term as captain of **Dorset** by receiving the county's first ever trophy.

Just over a week later, Wingfield Digby was back in the news as a result of Dorset's 18-run victory over Cheshire at Sherborne School. Nationwide interest met Wingfield Digby's decision to present Cheshire with 56 extras in one over in a bid to prevent the match drifting to a tame draw. Cheshire, 92 for six with eleven overs left and needing 201 to win, watched Graeme Calway bowl fourteen consecutive wides that were allowed to run to the boundary. A further 4 runs came off the bat to leave Calway with an over costing 60 runs and Cheshire elevated to 152 for six. Taking up the challenge, they were dismissed for 182 in the penultimate over. The Test and County Cricket Board, while accepting that no Law had been broken, suggested that such tactics went against the spirit of the game, but the Dorset captain was unrepentant. Like Frank Collyer's similar tactics for Hertfordshire against Suffolk in 1984, Wingfield Digby's move was boldly enterprising while at the same time worryingly extreme. For good measure, Dorset went on to win two of their next three games off the last ball.

For **Cheshire**, that defeat by Dorset was little more than an academic setback. They took the Western Division title with five wins from their nine regional games and again looked the best side by some distance. Their depth of batting was without equal, and if their bowling was made up largely of spinners, four of them – John O'Brien, Simon Dyson, Mark Boocock and Geoff Blackburn – shared 110 Championship wickets. Dyson, whose 23 wickets in three Western Division games won him the Frank Edwards Trophy for bowling, and Boocock were both leg-spinners. O'Brien, slow left-arm, was their leading wicket-taker with 36 Championship wickets, in addition to a hat-trick against Derbyshire in the second round of the NatWest Bank Trophy. It was the first hat-trick by a Minor Counties player in the competition.

Berkshire just pipped Dorset for second place in the West. The miserly off-spin of Peter Lewington helped them win three matches, with Jefferson Jones and Mark Stear providing the seam back-up. Towards the end of the season, Phil Heseltine, a new recruit, showed promise as a middle-order batsman. **Oxfordshire** had three up-and-coming cricketers who shone in 1988. Tim Lester scored 679 runs, Geoff Ford hit hundreds in both innings against Wiltshire, and David Hale had match figures of eleven for 69 against Wales in the opening game. Although Hale never quite lived up to that start, the 22-year-old fast bowler showed sufficient potential to gain a place in the Minor Counties side against the touring Sri Lankans in August.

Wiltshire and Shropshire made up the NatWest Bank Trophy qualifiers from the Western Division. **Wiltshire** slipped into the frame with wins over Buckinghamshire and Shropshire late in the season. The bowling of newcomer Jeremy Thompson was a major bonus in a summer which saw them suffer from problems of availability. Chris Trembath took a hat-trick in the win over **Shropshire**, who had to be content with a solitary victory over Cornwall. Tony Parton, a stylish left-hander, was one of the discoveries of the season, while Geoff Edmunds was one of many slow left-armers around the Minor Counties circuit to excel during the season.

Devon, apart from Kevin Rice topping 500 runs for the first time, had only a single win over Buckinghamshire to cheer them. At one time it even seemed likely that 1988 might have seen the end of Doug Yeabsley's career at this level, with injury forcing the retirement of the 47-year-old opening bowler who made his début for Devon in 1959. **Buckinghamshire**, the 1987 champions, avoided what would have been an alarming fall from grace to bottom place by winning their final match, against Oxfordshire. Colin Tungate distinguished himself by taking seven catches behind the wicket off the bowling of Chris Booden in the first innings against Wales at Bletchley.

Wales never found it easy to adapt to the format of two-day cricket, but their début year was not without its moments. Nigel Roberts, a hard-hitting, gutsy left-hander, accumulated 617 runs and Gerwyn Edwards took twenty relatively cheap wickets. Although they failed to win a game in either the Championship or the one-day matches, they could none the less take heart from **Cornwall**, who celebrated their first win for three years when they beat Dorset by two wickets in the last over at Truro. Jeremy Grigg, a sixteen year old making his début, figured prominently in this victory by making 67, and during the year the county introduced several other useful newcomers, particularly Stephen Williams, whose 550 runs included two centuries.

In the Eastern Division, **Cambridgeshire** won five of their nine games and as in 1987 owed much to Stuart Turner. His 58 wickets, the most in the Championship, took his two-year tally since leaving Essex to 97. Turner's valuable work with the ball was matched by the 787 runs freely scored by Ian Lawrence. In the end, though, it was a season remembered for what they came so close to achieving, rather than what they did achieve.

Durham, in second place, leant on the experience of men like Neil Riddell, Steve Greensword and Steve Atkinson. Paul Burn maintained his progress and Gary Brown, from Middlesex, blended in well to an already formidable batting line-up. Ian Conn finished the summer with 45 wickets, by far the quick bowler's best return. **Staffordshire's** hopes of a sustained title assault were hit by the loss of Joey Benjamin and David Banks to Warwickshire, of Mark Frost to Surrey, and the unavailability of Jon Addison. Although the batting possessed plenty of style, particularly in Phil Oliver and David Cartledge, their bowling fell short of its customary standard. Oliver, who finished top of the Minor Counties averages, won the Wilfred Rhodes Award for batting. Against Norfolk at Old Hill, he hit blistering hundreds in both innings, 136 not out and 124, with 224 of those 260 runs coming in boundaries.

Chris Gladwin, previously of Essex, had an excellent first season with **Suffolk**, who were without the services of their injured captain, Simon Clements. Mark Bailey was a more than capable replacement, and Gladwin's all-round skills augmented the penetrative bowling of Russell Green. **Hertfordshire** also had to endure an injury to their captain when Peter Neal suffered a fractured jaw late in the campaign. Earlier problems had revolved round a lack of available players, although David Surridge's return after injury was a bonus. Bill Merry took a hat-trick against Cumberland early on but later became another casualty. Neil Vartan caused a stir against Lincolnshire at Stevenage when he hit a maiden hundred from 75 deliveries.

Cumberland and Northumberland filled the Eastern Division's remaining places for the 1989 NatWest Bank Trophy. Bernard Reidy and Steven Sharp scored most runs for **Cumberland** and Richard Ellwood, a slow left-arm bowler, picked up 31 wickets. Off-spinner Malcolm Woods took his second hat-trick against Durham in four seasons. **Northumberland** replaced Chris Old as their professional with Adrian Dalby, an all-rounder, who was the pick of their bowlers and chipped in with some useful batting performances.

Norfolk, who had finished bottom of the regional table in the two previous seasons, improved by two places, thanks to their first win in 32 games. They ended this barren spell by beating Northumberland at Lakenham, with David Thomas hitting the winning runs to celebrate his last-minute call-up to the representative side for the match against the Sri Lankans the next day. Steve Plumb, the captain, had a rare old season, netting 830 Championship runs (the best tally since Richard Hayward's 853 for Buckinghamshire in 1983), scoring the first double-century in the competition for 27 years – a match-saving 204 not out over six and a half hours against Cumberland at Millom – and hitting 108 off 112 balls against the Sri Lankans.

Neither Bedfordshire nor Lincolnshire managed a win. **Bedfordshire**, under the spirited guidance of Roger Knight, came close on several occasions. Kevin Gentle and Philip Hoare made useful runs but the bowling badly lacked penetration. **Lincolnshire's** captain, Harry Pougher, opted to call it a day at the age of 47 after a season that saw the county beaten four times in nine Championship matches. Paul Todd, owing to his Glamorgan commitments, and Neil Priestley were sorely missed and Lincolnshire's batting never matched the output of recent seasons. Neil French, brother of the Nottinghamshire wicket-keeper, David Marshall and Jim Griffiths were their only real successes.

MINOR COUNTIES CHAMPIONSHIP, 1988

					Drawn				
					W	*T*	*L*		
					1st	*1st*	*1st*		
Eastern Division	*P*	*W*	*T*	*L*	*Inns*	*Inns*	*Inn*	*NR*	*Pts*
Cambridgeshire[NW]	9	5	0	0	1	0	2	1	57
Durham[NW]	9	3	0	1	4	0	1	0	43
Staffordshire[NW]	9	3	0	2*	2	0	1	1	42
Suffolk[NW]	9	2	0	2*	5	0	0	0	38
Hertfordshire[NW]	9	2	0	2†	0	0	3	2	33
Cumberland[NW]	9	2	0	1*	1	1	4	0	32
Northumberland[NW]	9	1	0	3*	3	1	1	0	25
Norfolk	9	1	0	2	2	0	4	0	20
Bedfordshire	9	0	0	2†	2	0	5	0	17
Lincolnshire	9	0	0	4*	2	0	1	2	14
Western Division									
Cheshire[NW]	9	5	1	1*	1	0	1	0	62
Berkshire[NW]	9	3	0	2	4	0	0	0	42
Dorset[NW]	9	3	0	1	2	1	2	0	40
Oxfordshire[NW]	9	1	1	1*	4	1	1	0	33
Wiltshire[NW]	9	2	0	2	1	0	3	1	28
Shropshire[NW]	9	1	0	1*	3	0	4	0	26
Devon	9	1	0	1	2	1	3	1	23
Buckinghamshire	9	1	0	3*	2	0	3	0	22
Wales	9	0	0	3†	3	1	1	1	20
Cornwall	9	1	0	3	0	0	4	1	16

* *Denotes first-innings points (3) in one match lost outright.*
† *Denotes first-innings points (3) in two matches lost outright.*
NW *Denotes qualified for NatWest Bank Trophy in 1989.*
Win = 10 pts, Tie = 5 pts, First-innings win = 3 pts, First-innings tie = 2 pts, First-innings loss = 1 pt, No result = 2 pts.

CHAMPIONSHIP PLAY-OFF

CAMBRIDGESHIRE v CHESHIRE

At Worcester, September 11. Cheshire won by 13 runs. Toss: Cambridgeshire. Cheshire's total of 191 never looked totally secure from the moment the Cambridgeshire openers took 25 runs off the first three overs. Later, Benson looked in good form, but the run-outs of Adams and Turner in the 40th over swung the game in Cheshire's favour. Cambridgeshire recovered from 116 for six to reach 166 without further loss in the 51st over. Redfarn was then dismissed by Murphy, and the tailenders were left with too much to do. Earlier, Varey had top-scored for Cheshire, his diligent 67 combating a New Road wicket that offered some eccentric bounce.

Cheshire

B. Wood c Turner b Benson 24
J. J. Hitchmough run out 9
I. Cockbain b Collard 26
D. W. Varey b Turner 67
*N. T. O'Brien lbw b Benson 2
S. T. Crawley c Collard b Lethbridge .. 16
†S. Bramhall lbw b Lethbridge 9
J. S. Hitchmough c Lethbridge b Collard 19
S. Dyson c Garnham b Lethbridge 0
A. J. Murphy c Dicks b Lethbridge ... 5
J. F. M. O'Brien not out 2
L-b 4, w 5, n-b 3 12

1/13 2/54 3/78 4/81 5/123 6/135 7/176 8/183 9/187 (53.3 overs) 191

Bowling: Turner 10–2–34–1; Lethbridge 10.3–2–47–4; Benson 11–1–34–2; Collard 11–2–54–2; Stephenson 11–3–18–0.

Cambridgeshire

*N. T. Gadsby b Dyson	28	C. Lethbridge b Dyson	0
I. S. Lawrence c and b Dyson	18	D. C. Collard b Murphy	3
†M. A. Garnham c and b J. S. Hitchmough	4	M. G. Stephenson not out	1
J. D. R. Benson b J. F. M. O'Brien	30	B 4, l-b 8, w 4, n-b 2	18
P. A. Redfarn c Dyson b Murphy	37		
N. J. Adams run out	1	1/40 2/51 3/63 (54.2 overs)	178
S. Turner run out	1	4/107 5/115 6/116	
P. J. Dicks c Dyson b Murphy	37	7/166 8/168 9/171	

Bowling: Murphy 10.2–1–41–3; J. S. Hitchmough 11–2–29–1; Dyson 11–1–30–3; J. F. M. O'Brien 11–0–27–1; N. T. O'Brien 6–1–20–0; Wood 5–1–19–0.

Umpires: C. Smith and R. T. Wilson.

HOLT TROPHY KNOCKOUT FINAL

CAMBRIDGESHIRE v DORSET

At Weymouth, July 24. Dorset won by two wickets. Toss: Dorset. A tense final brought a historic triumph for Dorset, playing on a home ground at Weymouth Cricket Club. A pitch that had been awash 24 hours before the game always favoured the bowlers and Cambridgeshire, put in, struggled to 123 for nine off a reduced allocation of 50 overs. At one time they had lost half their side for just 43. Dorset's reply followed a similar course as Turner's impressive early spell accounted for Merriman, Calway and Claughton. At tea they were 47 for five off 25 overs, but Stone's good sense and sound strokeplay turned the game and Dorset won with four balls to spare.

Cambridgeshire 123 for nine (50 overs) (I. C. D. Stuart three for 32); Dorset 127 for eight (49.2 overs) (C. Stone 34; S. Turner three for 12, D. C. Collard three for 26).

*In the averages that follow, * against a score signifies not out, * against a name signifies the captain and † signifies a wicket-keeper.*

BEDFORDSHIRE

Secretary – A. J. PEARCE, 15 Dene Way, Upper Caldecote, Biggleswade SG18 9DL

Matches 9: Lost – Cumberland, Durham. Won on first innings – Cambridgeshire, Hertfordshire. Lost on first innings – Lincolnshire, Norfolk, Northumberland, Staffordshire, Suffolk.

Batting Averages

	M	*I*	*NO*	*R*	*HI*	*100s*	*Avge*
K. Gentle	8	15	0	531	80	0	35.40
P. D. B. Hoare	9	17	0	465	75	0	27.35
S. D. L. Davis	9	17	1	413	86	0	25.81
*R. D. V. Knight	8	15	0	366	61	0	24.40
T. C. Thomas	9	17	4	253	61*	0	19.46
S. J. Lines	4	8	1	127	51	0	18.14

	M	I	NO	R	HI	100s	Avge
R. D. O. Earl	6	11	3	115	38*	0	14.37
J. R. Wake	8	15	1	197	46*	0	14.07
M. E. Gear	4	7	0	88	35	0	12.57
†N. S. Randall	3	5	1	42	11	0	10.50
†V. E. Thomas	5	10	5	44	15*	0	8.80
G. A. R. Harris	9	14	5	36	11	0	4.00

Played in seven matches: P. A. Waterman 5*, 0, 5*, 7, 0*. Played in four matches: S. E. Blott 1, 4*, 0, 0*, 12*. Played in two matches: D. J. Harris 11, 2, 2, 5. Played in one match: A. Dean 17, 1*; D. C. Garratt 5, 3; A. J. Moulding 24, 16; T. C. Taylor did not bat.

Bowling Averages

	O	M	R	W	BB	Avge
S. E. Blott	111	19	327	15	4-42	21.80
R. D. O. Earl	151.4	37	420	19	5-40	22.10
J. R. Wake	175.3	36	542	20	4-19	27.10
R. D. V. Knight ...	120	22	374	12	4-53	31.16
G. A. R. Harris	188	36	643	20	3-59	32.15
P. A. Waterman ...	124.2	20	438	13	4-58	33.69

Also bowled: A. Dean 2–0–18–0; P. D. B. Hoare 80–15–290–6.

BERKSHIRE

Secretary – C. F. V. MARTIN, Paradise Cottage, Paradise Road, Henley-on-Thames, Oxon RG9 1UB

Matches 9: Won – Cornwall, Wales, Wiltshire. Lost – Dorset, Oxfordshire. Won on first innings – Buckinghamshire, Cheshire, Devon, Shropshire.

Batting Averages

	M	I	NO	R	HI	100s	Avge
G. R. J. Roope ...	6	7	5	176	48	0	88.00
G. Headley	4	6	1	232	102*	1	46.40
P. G. Heseltine ...	5	8	1	317	98*	0	45.28
D. B. Gorman	7	13	5	291	62	0	36.37
M. G. Lickley	9	17	1	520	85*	0	32.50
G. E. Loveday	9	17	2	487	85*	0	32.46
*M. L. Simmons ..	5	7	1	144	49	0	24.00
T. P. J. Dodd	7	11	1	164	55*	0	16.40
†M. E. Stevens	9	7	4	37	16	0	12.33
M. G. Stear	7	7	0	34	26	0	4.85
P. Oxley	3	6	2	16	11*	0	4.00

Played in nine matches: J. H. Jones 1*, 1*, 4*; P. J. Lewington 4, 8. Played in four matches: D. J. B. Hartley 0, 0, 5. Played in three matches: K. S. Murray 16, 38, 38, 37, 3. Played in one match: M. Amjad 7*, 3; S. Massey 9: N. Waters 10, 4.

Bowling Averages

	O	M	R	W	BB	Avge
P. J. Lewington ...	302.5	94	658	54	7-70	12.18
T. P. J. Dodd	134	39	343	18	3-13	19.05
M. G. Stear	205.2	48	534	25	6-36	21.36
J. H. Jones	205.2	38	564	26	5-37	21.69

Also bowled: M. Amjad 5.4–0–24–2; D. J. B. Hartley 36–5–116–2; G. Headley 47–12–121–6; M. G. Lickley 2–0–5–0; G. E. Loveday 1–0–2–0; S. Massey 7–4–19–0; P. Oxley 4–2–2–0; G. R. J. Roope 2–1–2–1; M. L. Simmons 5–2–5–0.

BUCKINGHAMSHIRE

Secretary – S. J. TOMLIN, Orchardleigh Cottage, Bigfrith Lane, Cookham Dean SL6 9PH

Matches 9: Won – Oxfordshire. Lost – Cheshire, Devon, Wiltshire. Won on first innings – Cornwall, Shropshire. Lost on first innings – Berkshire, Dorset, Wales.

Batting Averages

	M	*I*	*NO*	*R*	*HI*	*100s*	*Avge*
A. R. Harwood	5	10	2	434	142*	1	54.25
M. J. Roberts	4	8	1	338	155*	1	48.28
T. Butler	8	16	5	421	87	0	38.27
B. S. Percy	5	7	0	214	73	0	30.57
*N. G. Hames	9	16	2	260	57	0	18.57
S. Burrow	5	8	0	132	39	0	16.50
G. R. Black	7	12	3	134	50*	0	14.88
S. A. Sawyer	6	7	1	88	34	0	14.66
A. W. Lyon	6	7	2	67	21*	0	13.40
T. J. A. Scriven	6	7	0	80	27	0	11.42
†D. J. Goldsmith ...	8	7	3	20	10	0	5.00

Played in eight matches: C. D. Booden 0, 0, 2*, 0*, 0*, 0. Played in four matches: R. W. M. Tredwell 5, 5, 4. Played in three matches: S. M. Shearman 5, 0, 7, 2. Played in two matches: P. D. Atkins 20, 26, 20, 58; P. D. Dolphin 37, 0, 2, 32; M. Jean-Jacques 19*, 5, 16; †C. J. Tungate 15*, 4, 0*, 12. Played in one match: S. J. Edwards 2, 0*; N. W. Farrow 36*, 0; S. G. Lynch 0, 7; M. E. Milton 50, 51; C. Jackson did not bat.

Bowling Averages

	O	*M*	*R*	*W*	*BB*	*Avge*
T. J. A. Scriven ...	139	25	475	26	7-68	18.26
S. Burrow	76	28	200	10	5-45	20.00
C. D. Booden	204.1	57	514	25	7-17	20.56
G. R. Black	118.3	3	326	14	5-49	23.28

Also bowled: T. Butler 0.4–0–4–0; S. J. Edwards 16–5–40–1; N. G. Hames 3–0–39–0; A. R. Harwood 6.4–4–34–1; C. Jackson 19.1–2–65–1; M. Jean-Jacques 69–13–215–3; S. G. Lynch 2–0–12–0; A. W. Lyon 142–37–381–8; M. E. Milton 33–8–116–3; B. S. Percy 27.5–7–89–3; S. A. Sawyer 14–3–49–3; R. W. M. Tredwell 62–10–245–4.

CAMBRIDGESHIRE

Secretary – P. W. GOODEN, The Redlands, Oakington Road, Cottenham, Cambridge CB4 4TW

Matches 9: Won – Lincolnshire, Norfolk, Northumberland, Staffordshire, Suffolk. Won on first innings – Cumberland. Lost on first innings – Bedfordshire, Durham. No result – Hertfordshire.

Batting Averages

	M	I	NO	R	HI	100s	Avge
I. S. Lawrence ...	9	17	4	787	144	2	60.53
P. A. Redfarn	7	12	4	277	86*	0	34.62
N. J. Adams	7	10	2	249	66*	0	31.12
*N. T. Gadsby ...	9	17	3	425	97*	0	30.35
†M. A. Garnham .	4	7	1	155	64*	0	25.83
S. Turner	8	10	2	182	63*	0	22.75
P. J. Dicks	9	14	2	248	45	0	20.66
G. H. Masterson .	4	6	1	75	27	0	15.00
D. C. Collard	9	6	3	41	14*	0	13.66

Played in eight matches: M. G. Stephenson 0, 6, 7*, 7*, 13*. Played in seven matches: A. P. A. Wykes 17*, 3, 8*. Played in six matches: C. R. F. Green 0, 5*, 2*. Played in four matches: A. Howorth 44*, 2*, 0, 20*. Played in two matches: †C. W. A. Thornely 1; †G. G. Whitbread 0. Played in one match: R. C. Iliffe 18; C. Lethbridge 2; †M. L. Saggers and D. C. Wing did not bat.

Bowling Averages

	O	M	R	W	BB	Avge
S. Turner	346.4	98	763	58	6-38	13.15
C. R. F. Green	91	29	266	11	4-28	24.18
M. G. Stephenson ...	144	38	363	13	4-53	27.92
D. C. Collard	198.1	40	589	20	4-52	29.45

Also bowled: N. J. Adams 2–0–12–0; N. T. Gadsby 2–1–11–0; A. Howorth 61.4–12–163–6; C. Lethbridge 28–9–48–6; D. C. Wing 38–9–88–1; A. P. A. Wykes 99.3–29–301–8.

CHESHIRE

Secretary – J. B. PICKUP, 2 Castle Street, Northwich CW8 1AB

Matches 9: Won – Buckinghamshire, Cornwall, Devon, Wales, Wiltshire. Tied – Oxfordshire. Lost – Dorset. Won on first innings – Shropshire. Lost on first innings – Berkshire.

Batting Averages

	M	I	NO	R	HI	100s	Avge
I. Cockbain	8	15	4	681	119	3	61.90
*N. T. O'Brien	9	15	5	343	61	0	34.30
I. J. Tansley	8	15	2	410	110*	1	31.53
B. Wood	9	18	2	431	80	0	26.93
D. W. Varey	6	12	2	245	55	0	24.50
J. J. Hitchmough ...	7	11	0	228	72	0	20.72
†N. Smith	9	9	4	93	36	0	18.60
S. T. Crawley	8	13	1	217	40	0	18.08
G. J. Blackburn	9	12	5	87	32	0	12.42

Played in eight matches: J. F. M. O'Brien 7, 0, 1, 1*, 1*. Played in six matches: M. G. Boocock 2*, 0, 0; A. Fox 2*, 0, 9, 6. Played in three matches: S. Dyson 0*, 1*; J. S. Hitchmough 1*, 4.

Bowling Averages

	O	M	R	W	BB	Avge
S. Dyson	107.2	38	206	23	7-39	8.95
J. S. Hitchmough	97	30	212	16	6-57	13.25
M. G. Boocock	139.5	43	363	21	4-41	17.28
J. F. M. O'Brien	292.1	98	730	36	5-49	20.27
G. J. Blackburn	258	79	637	30	6-58	21.23
A. Fox	96	15	272	10	2-16	27.20

Also bowled: I. Cockbain 10.3–2–51–0; S. T. Crawley 33–7–109–1; N. T. O'Brien 63–25–112–7; B. Wood 36–13–61–1.

CORNWALL

Secretary – T. D. MENEER, Falbridge, Penvale Cross, Penryn, Cornwall

Matches 9: Won – Dorset. Lost – Berkshire, Cheshire, Shropshire. Lost on first innings – Buckinghamshire, Devon, Oxfordshire, Wiltshire. No result – Wales.

Batting Averages

	M	I	NO	R	HI	100s	Avge
S. Williams	9	17	2	550	111*	2	36.66
S. Hooper	8	15	3	429	77	0	35.75
E. Nicholson	8	14	3	352	133*	2	32.00
M. S. T. Dunstan	5	9	0	212	52	0	23.55
P. J. Stephens	7	13	0	306	77	0	23.53
†D. Aunger	8	10	4	122	48*	0	20.33
*F. T. Willetts	6	7	0	88	41	0	12.57
C. C. Lovell	8	14	4	116	26	0	11.60

Played in seven matches: D. A. Toseland 39*, 0, 24, 15*; S. Turner 3*, 3*, 0, 5*, 0*. Played in four matches: R. G. Furse 14*, 30, 10, 19, 31. Played in three matches: A. J. Buzza 11*, 0*, 7*; S. A. Hunt 28, 17, 0, 0; V. K. Meneer 54, 32, 2, 21, 62; A. Penberthy 28, 54, 43, 20, 61. Played in two matches: J. F. Grigg 67, 2*; A. H. Watts 20, 12. Played in one match: P. Berryman 0, 1; †S. Bone 2, 7; P. I. Johns 0, 0*; M. W. Pooley 0; S. Wherry 23, 0; S. Eva did not bat.

Bowling Averages

	O	M	R	W	BB	Avge
R. G. Furse	46	7	188	10	5-67	18.80
C. C. Lovell	172	26	666	23	5-40	28.95
D. A. Toseland	222.4	49	645	18	6-70	35.83
S. Turner	149	25	437	10	3-34	43.70

Also bowled: P. Berryman 8–0–47–1; S. Bone 4–1–32–0; A. J. Buzza 51–3–203–6; M. S. T. Dunstan 5–0–31–1; S. Hooper 8–0–68–2; S. A. Hunt 23.3–2–114–5; P. I. Johns 20–2–51–0; V. K. Meneer 24–4–100–1; A. Penberthy 45–7–132–2; M. W. Pooley 14–3–33–3; P. J. Stephens 10.4–1–52–0; A. H. Watts 33–5–154–4; F. T. Willetts 8.2–0–63–0; S. Williams 5–0–29–0.

CUMBERLAND

Secretary – M. BEATY, 9 Abbey Drive, Natland, Kendal, Cumbria LA9 7QN

Matches 9: Won – Bedfordshire, Lincolnshire. Lost – Hertfordshire. Won on first innings – Norfolk. Tied on first innings – Northumberland. Lost on first innings – Cambridgeshire, Durham, Staffordshire, Suffolk.

Batting Averages

	M	*I*	*NO*	*R*	*HI*	*100s*	*Avge*
K. A. Hayes	4	8	0	293	110	1	36.62
B. W. Reidy	7	13	1	430	81	0	35.83
S. Sharp	9	17	2	474	83	0	31.60
†S. M. Dutton	6	10	4	165	76*	0	27.50
D. Halliwell	5	6	3	74	21*	0	24.66
G. J. Clarke	9	16	2	323	57*	0	23.07
M. D. Woods	9	11	2	192	41	0	21.33
†C. R. Knight	6	11	1	189	57*	0	18.90
*J. R. Moyes	9	14	0	246	57	0	17.57
C. J. Stockdale ...	6	11	0	184	45	0	16.72
S. Wall	6	9	1	120	29*	0	15.00
M. G. Scothern ...	6	8	3	60	18*	0	12.00
R. Ellwood	9	8	4	24	9	0	6.00

Played in two matches: R. I. Cooper 6, 68*, 4*, 8; G. D. Hodgson 67, 52, 61. Played in one match: †W. N. Boustead 54; †M. Burns 2; S. Harvey 0*; S. James did not bat.

Bowling Averages

	O	*M*	*R*	*W*	*BB*	*Avge*
R. Ellwood	189	52	491	31	6-48	15.83
D. Halliwell ...	144.3	39	426	20	5-55	21.30
M. D. Woods ..	270.5	62	701	32	5-59	21.90
S. Wall	119.2	26	355	15	5-49	23.66
B. W. Reidy ...	152.3	39	384	13	3-26	29.53

Also bowled: G. J. Clarke 6–1–18–1; R. I. Cooper 7–5–5–0; S. Harvey 8–0–32–1; S. James 17–2–71–0; C. R. Knight 2–1–4–0; J. R. Moyes 4.2–1–19–0; M. G. Scothern 119–30–422–7.

DEVON

Secretary – G. R. EVANS, Blueberry Haven, 20 Boucher Road, Budleigh Salterton EX9 6JF

Matches 9: Won – Buckinghamshire. Lost – Cheshire. Won on first innings – Cornwall, Shropshire. Tied on first innings – Dorset. Lost on first innings – Berkshire, Oxfordshire, Wales. No result – Wiltshire.

Batting Averages

	M	*I*	*NO*	*R*	*HI*	*100s*	*Avge*
G. P. Randall-Johnson ...	6	9	2	259	75	0	37.00
K. G. Rice	9	16	1	534	100	1	35.60
N. G. Folland	5	8	1	221	83	0	31.57
N. R. Gaywood	7	10	1	273	80	0	30.33
R. P. Twose	8	14	2	358	57	0	29.83
G. Wallen	4	6	0	176	99	0	29.33
R. I. Dawson	4	7	3	88	26	0	22.00
T. W. Ward	8	10	5	106	43	0	21.20
N. A. Folland	4	6	0	114	51	0	19.00
†R. C. Turpin	8	10	4	106	38*	0	17.66
*J. H. Edwards	9	12	1	130	37	0	11.81

Played in seven matches: M. C. Woodman 1, 8, 20, 8, 1*. Played in three matches: A. W. Allin 4, 15, 0, 1; R. K. Benton 1, 0; R. G. Twose 1, 13, 51, 71; D. I. Yeabsley 11*, 8. Played in one match: D. Beckett 2*; M. A. Cottam 18, 22; T. Farkins 8*; P. K. Harding 0*; J. D. Jenkins 0*; R. Luckett 0; N. Wonnacott 0*; G. White did not bat.

Bowling Averages

	O	*M*	*R*	*W*	*BB*	*Avge*
T. W. Ward	152.3	17	570	20	5-84	28.50
M. C. Woodman ...	199.5	41	568	15	4-96	37.86

Also bowled: A. W. Allin 101–27–332–9; D. Beckett 22–2–100–2; R. K. Benton 64.2–8–281–8; M. A. Cottam 31–8–99–2; J. H. Edwards 4–0–14–0; N. A. Folland 7–0–50–2; N. G. Folland 4–0–10–0; J. D. Jenkins 16–0–92–1; G. P. Randall-Johnson 3–0–29–1; K. G. Rice 67.2–16–276–8; R. G. Twose 3–0–24–0; R. P. Twose 6–0–51–1; G. White 15–4–57–1; D. I. Yeabsley 68.3–22–174–5.

DORSET

Secretary – D. J. W. BRIDGE, Long Acre, Tinney's Lane, Sherborne DT9 3DY

Matches 9: Won – Berkshire, Cheshire, Wales. Lost – Cornwall. Won on first innings – Buckinghamshire, Wiltshire. Tied on first innings – Devon. Lost on first innings – Oxfordshire, Shropshire.

Batting Averages

	M	*I*	*NO*	*R*	*HI*	*100s*	*Avge*
J. R. Hall	5	6	3	121	44	0	40.33
C. Stone	5	7	3	158	42*	0	39.50
A. J. Foot	5	9	3	181	42	0	30.16
R. P. Merriman	8	16	1	415	112	1	27.66
J. A. Claughton	5	10	1	243	85	0	27.00
†V. B. Lewis	4	7	2	121	63	0	24.20
G. S. Calway	8	15	1	335	103	1	23.92
S. W. D. Rintoul	8	15	2	305	60	0	23.46
S. Sawney	8	14	3	195	38	0	17.72
N. R. Taylor	8	8	2	91	44	0	15.16
I. C. D. Stuart	8	14	1	197	62	0	15.15
*A. R. Wingfield Digby ...	8	10	3	58	26	0	8.28
R. V. Morgan	3	6	0	29	13	0	4.83

Played in five matches: C. M. Graham 8, 37*, 0. Played in four matches: †D. A. Ridley 1, 0, 18*, 18. Played in two matches: R. V. Lewis 14, 24*, 27, 0; M. C. Wagstaffe 0, 34, 0, 4. Played in one match: †R. J. Blitz 9, 2; P. A. Nation and S. Westlake did not bat.

Bowling Averages

	O	*M*	*R*	*W*	*BB*	*Avge*
C. Stone	125	55	226	14	6-20	16.14
N. R. Taylor	192.4	53	529	25	6-38	21.16
A. R. Wingfield Digby ...	208.2	64	557	26	4-56	21.42
I. C. D. Stuart	90	23	289	13	4-44	22.23

Also bowled: G. S. Calway 37–4–160–4; C. M. Graham 76.1–12–262–4; J. R. Hall 37–4–146–3; R. P. Merriman 51–5–173–4; P. A. Nation 16–4–43–1; S. Sawney 78.1–12–295–7; M. C. Wagstaffe 39–14–82–3.

DURHAM

Secretary – J. ILEY, Roselea, Springwell Avenue, Durham DH1 4LY

Matches 9: Won – Bedfordshire, Hertfordshire, Staffordshire. Lost – Suffolk. Won on first innings – Cambridgeshire, Cumberland, Lincolnshire, Norfolk. Lost on first innings – Northumberland.

Batting Averages

	M	*I*	*NO*	*R*	*HI*	*100s*	*Avge*
*N. A. Riddell	8	12	5	367	63	0	52.42
G. K. Brown	9	16	1	632	114	1	42.13
S. Greensword	8	13	6	260	75*	0	37.14
A. S. Patel	4	8	2	213	67	0	35.50
P. Burn	8	15	2	454	103*	1	34.92
J. D. Glendenen	5	9	2	238	80	0	34.00
S. R. Atkinson	5	10	0	325	64	0	32.50
J. Tindale	8	10	1	108	31	0	12.00
J. W. Lister	4	7	0	84	29	0	12.00
I. E. Conn	9	7	1	34	19*	0	5.66

Played in eight matches: †A. R. Fothergill 25, 1*, 12*, 4, 2. Played in six matches: J. Johnston 1, 1. Played in five matches: S. Peel 0, 7*, 3*. Played in three matches: D. Beach 1*, 0. Played in two matches: W. Johnson 38, 39, 3, 93; K. Trotter 1*, 19*. Played in one match: A. C. Day 3*; J. Dunn 8; D. C. Jackson 6, 1*; D. Playfor 9; D. G. Young did not bat.

Bowling Averages

	O	*M*	*R*	*W*	*BB*	*Avge*
I. E. Conn	272.2	57	845	45	6-37	18.77
J. Johnston	169	44	428	21	6-71	20.38
S. Greensword	135.3	38	395	18	3-17	21.94
S. Peel	84.5	20	258	11	4-29	23.45

Also bowled: D. Beach 62–19–198–5; G. K. Brown 14–3–42–0; P. Burn 6–0–14–0; A. C. Day 21.3–8–48–6; J. Dunn 3–0–5–0; J. D. Glendenen 4–0–30–0; D. C. Jackson 4–0–23–0; A. S. Patel 52–15–151–6; N. A. Riddell 7–1–42–1; J. Tindale 71–14–272–9; K. Trotter 54–15–168–7; D. G. Young 20–5–59–1.

HERTFORDSHIRE

Secretary – D. DREDGE, 38 Santers Lane, Potters Bar EN6 2BX

Matches 9: Won – Cumberland, Suffolk. Lost – Durham, Staffordshire. Lost on first innings – Bedfordshire, Northumberland, Norfolk. No result – Cambridgeshire, Lincolnshire.

Batting Averages

	M	*I*	*NO*	*R*	*HI*	*100s*	*Avge*
N. P. G. Wright	7	13	1	415	107*	1	34.58
R. N. R. Vartan	4	7	0	228	125	1	32.57
S. P. Henderson	5	8	0	181	64	0	22.62
A. J. T. Miller	5	9	0	165	61	0	18.33
B. G. Evans	3	6	0	109	44	0	18.16
†M. W. C. Olley	9	16	4	211	38	0	17.58
M. C. G. Wright	9	16	2	241	33	0	17.21
T. S. Smith	6	9	3	89	53*	0	14.83
*E. P. Neal	8	12	1	160	27	0	14.54
L. S. P. Fishpool	3	6	2	42	14	0	10.50

Played in six matches: D. Surridge 2*, 0*, 1. Played in five matches: W. G. Merry 50, 2, 0. Played in three matches: S. A. Dean 0, 0, 1, 12, 0; M. N. Forbes 1*; R. J. Hailey 4; G. Herath 10*, 26, 0, 24. Played in two matches: G. A. Buchanan 42, 26, 0, 1; N. J. C. Gandon 0, 93, 22, 17; A. R. Garofall 10, 13*, 12*, 0; M. C. Ilott 4*; N. J. Ilott 68*, 11, 50; C. Thomas 52, 22, 32; A. P. Wright 1*, 12, 8*. Played in one match: C. Cavenor 2*; N. Gilbert 17; T. C. E. Stancombe 16*, 3*.

Bowling Averages

	O	*M*	*R*	*W*	*BB*	*Avge*
A. R. Garofall . . .	56	15	132	10	4-36	13.20
D. Surridge	156.2	42	387	23	7-61	16.82
T. S. Smith	123.2	26	355	20	4-35	17.75
W. G. Merry	68.2	14	233	12	6-31	19.41

Also bowled: C. Cavenor 33–6–97–3; L. S. P. Fishpool 62–14–185–8; M. N. Forbes 67.2–14–217–3; N. J. C. Gandon 1–0–1–0; R. J. Hailey 39.3–8–151–4; G. Herath 5.2–0–24–1; M. C. Ilott 39–9–122–5; A. J. T. Miller 0.3–0–1–0; E. P. Neal 68–17–265–6; T. C. E. Stancombe 15–0–80–2; C. Thomas 17–7–51–5; A. P. Wright 6–0–44–1; N. P. G. Wright 1–1–0–0.

LINCOLNSHIRE

Secretary – D. H. WRIGHT, 18 Spencers Road, Ketton, Stamford

Matches 9: Lost – Cambridgeshire, Cumberland, Northumberland, Suffolk. Won on first innings – Bedfordshire, Norfolk. Lost on first innings – Durham. No result – Hertfordshire, Staffordshire.

Batting Averages

	M	*I*	*NO*	*R*	*HI*	*100s*	*Avge*
C. Wicks	6	11	1	234	47	0	23.40
G. J. Carsberg . . .	8	14	0	317	84	0	22.64
P. R. Butler	8	15	2	289	76*	0	22.23
†S. N. Warman . .	5	7	0	131	51	0	18.71
M. A. Fell	8	14	1	227	55	0	17.46
J. G. Franks	4	7	0	104	63	0	14.85
*H. Pougher	7	12	2	147	23	0	14.70
M. Sharp	5	8	0	106	42	0	13.25
†N. P. Dobbs . . .	5	6	3	39	16	0	13.00
N. French	7	12	2	110	55	0	11.00
D. Marshall	9	14	3	85	27*	0	7.72
B. J. Griffiths	6	7	4	20	8	0	6.66

Played in four matches: R. L. Burton 4, 10, 12, 0, 10. Played in three matches: S. C. Chamberlin 8, 35*, 5, 0, 9. Played in two matches: T. N. Bradford 50, 7, 0; R. A. Johnson 31, 0, 5, 0; T. F. Nichols 7, 9, 4*; N. Priestley 3, 5, 5, 24. Played in one match: R. L. Ashton 0, 3; T. J. Hopper 2*, 10; N. J. B. Illingworth 6; D. B. Storer 0, 4; S. Braithwaite and C. S. Knapton did not bat.

Bowling Averages

	O	*M*	*R*	*W*	*BB*	*Avge*
N. French	110.2	27	297	18	6-27	16.50
R. L. Burton	59	20	185	11	7-53	16.81
D. Marshall	206.5	53	509	30	5-45	16.96
B. J. Griffiths	157.3	40	455	23	8-64	19.78

Also bowled: R. L. Ashton 14–0–65–1; T. N. Bradford 3–0–6–0; S. Braithwaite 4–0–29–0; P. R. Butler 51.5–2–160–6; G. J. Carsberg 1–0–7–0; M. A. Fell 44–8–103–4; T. J. Hopper 8–2–13–0; N. J. B. Illingworth 12–5–56–2; R. A. Johnson 32–13–65–2; C. S. Knapton 10–3–43–1; T. F. Nichols 22–5–74–2; H. Pougher 1–1–0–0; C. Wicks 3.5–0–13–0.

NORFOLK

Secretary – S. J. SKINNER, 27 Colkett Drive, Old Catton, Norwich NR6 7ND

Matches 9: Won – Northumberland. Lost – Cambridgeshire, Staffordshire. Won on first innings – Bedfordshire, Hertfordshire. Lost on first innings – Cumberland, Durham, Lincolnshire, Suffolk.

Batting Averages

	M	*I*	*NO*	*R*	*HI*	*100s*	*Avge*
*S. G. Plumb	8	16	1	830	204*	1	55.33
P. Coote	3	6	1	248	91*	0	49.60
R. D. Huggins	9	17	5	488	86	0	40.66
F. L. Q. Handley	3	6	0	240	100	1	40.00
N. D. Cook	3	6	1	137	68*	0	27.40
D. R. Thomas	7	13	7	160	56*	0	26.66
D. M. Stamp	3	6	1	99	36*	0	19.80
J. Whitehead	5	10	1	171	31	0	19.00
R. Kingshott	9	12	2	156	31	0	15.60
D. G. Savage	7	12	0	132	45	0	11.00
E. R. Hodson	7	12	0	86	20	0	7.16

Played in seven matches: †A. N. Payne 0*, 0, 1*, 0, 0*. Played in four matches: M. T. Ellis 0, 9, 8*, 1; J. S. Tate 10*, 0*, 0, 5, 0*. Played in three matches: R. L. Bradford 1, 2, 14, 21, 63; J. C. M. Lewis 2, 1*, 39*. Played in two matches: R. J. Belmont 9, 24, 29; S. B. Dixon 35, 19, 52, 68; †D. E. Mattocks 8, 1, 0; M. J. Rayner 8, 4, 6, 0*; G. M. Roff 0; E. L. Tuck 1, 0, 0, 0. Played in one match: K. P. Cooper 6, 5*; S. N. Waymouth 17.

Bowling Averages

	O	*M*	*R*	*W*	*BB*	*Avge*
D. R. Thomas	139.3	34	419	19	4-63	22.05
R. Kingshott	248.4	67	793	28	5-30	28.32
J. S. Tate	125	39	348	10	4-39	34.80
S. G. Plumb	148.3	32	549	11	3-84	49.90

Also bowled: R. J. Belmont 21–4–70–3; M. T. Ellis 82–15–356–9; E. R. Hodson 4–0–27–1; J. C. M. Lewis 52–12–140–4; M. J. Rayner 49.4–12–131–9; G. M. Roff 23–7–94–3; D. G. Savage 66–20–218–2; E. L. Tuck 46–13–149–3; S. N. Waymouth 1–0–15–0.

NORTHUMBERLAND

Secretary – G. H. THOMPSON, Northumberland County Cricket Ground, Osborne Avenue, Jesmond, Newcastle upon Tyne NE2 1JS

Matches 9: Won – Lincolnshire. Lost – Cambridgeshire, Norfolk, Staffordshire. Won on first innings – Bedfordshire, Durham, Hertfordshire. Tied on first innings – Cumberland. Lost on first innings – Suffolk.

Batting Averages

	M	*I*	*NO*	*R*	*HI*	*100s*	*Avge*
G. R. Morris	9	18	2	520	101*	1	32.50
K. Pearson	7	14	1	394	102*	1	30.30
*M. E. Younger	9	16	3	379	75	0	29.15
M. S. Tiffin	9	15	6	259	33*	0	28.77
J. R. Purvis	9	12	6	150	57*	0	25.00
A. Dalby	7	14	1	291	52	0	22.38
P. N. S. Dutton	6	12	2	213	57	0	21.30

	M	*I*	*NO*	*R*	*HI*	*100s*	*Avge*
D. Smart	4	8	0	151	52	0	18.87
R. Dreyer	3	6	0	111	45	0	18.50
M. B. Anderson ...	5	10	1	111	36	0	12.33

Played in seven matches: C. J. Harker 2*, 4*. Played in six matches: †B. Storey 6*, 0, 0*, 2, 6*. Played in five matches: P. C. Graham 12, 2, 2, 1. Played in three matches: C. Pleasants 2*, 12. Played in two matches: †K. Corby 8*; S. G. Lishman 49, 5, 7; M. E. Richardson 9, 6, 4, 12; S. P. Scott did not bat. Played in one match: C. S. Campbell 7, 12; G. D. Halliday 0.

Bowling Averages

	O	*M*	*R*	*W*	*BB*	*Avge*
J. R. Purvis	62.1	9	253	12	2-1	21.08
P. C. Graham	130.1	42	276	12	3-23	23.00
A. Dalby	169.5	35	548	23	6-35	23.82
C. J. Harker	188	49	529	21	4-52	25.19
M. E. Younger ...	113	28	366	10	3-36	36.60

Also bowled: M. B. Anderson 2.2–0–19–0; C. S. Campbell 18.3–2–82–1; R. Dreyer 49.5–12–123–8; P. N. S. Dutton 70.3–9–271–9; G. D. Halliday 18.3–5–46–1; S. G. Lishman 31–3–116–3; G. R. Morris 1–0–5–1; C. Pleasants 51–11–168–3; S. P. Scott 29–4–81–2; M. S. Tiffin 0.1–0–0–1.

OXFORDSHIRE

Secretary – J. E. O. SMITH, 2 The Green, Horton-cum-Studley OX9 1AE

Matches 9: Won – Berkshire. Tied – Cheshire. Lost – Buckinghamshire. Won on first innings – Cornwall, Devon, Dorset, Wiltshire. Tied on first innings – Wales. Lost on first innings – Shropshire.

Batting Averages

	M	*I*	*NO*	*R*	*HI*	*100s*	*Avge*
T. A. Lester	8	16	6	679	97*	0	67.90
*P. J. Garner	9	16	3	601	94*	0	46.23
G. C. Ford	7	14	2	466	113	2	38.83
M. D. Nurton	7	14	1	334	62	0	25.69
P. J. Densham ...	3	6	0	120	54	0	20.00
G. P. Savin	7	6	3	46	20*	0	15.33
C. J. Clements ...	6	10	1	108	35	0	12.00
R. A. Evans	9	9	3	64	17	0	10.66
†A. Crossley	9	12	1	89	37	0	8.09
K. A. Arnold	8	6	2	19	10*	0	4.75

Played in nine matches: I. J. Curtis 0*, 0. Played in five matches: D. A. Hale 4, 11, 4, 11. Played in three matches: R. N. Busby 1, 11*, 2*, 22; P. M. Jobson 82*, 5, 7*, 40; S. R. Porter 18, 20*, 0. Played in two matches: S. R. Moss did not bat. Played in one match: D. A. J. Wise 3*, 41.

Bowling Averages

	O	*M*	*R*	*W*	*BB*	*Avge*
D. A. Hale	83.4	14	286	18	6-45	15.88
I. J. Curtis	293.2	72	811	34	6-81	23.85
K. A. Arnold ...	203.3	60	513	19	7-64	27.00
R. A. Evans	236	67	599	21	4-62	28.52

Also bowled: R. N. Busby 49–11–117–5; G. C. Ford 3–0–30–1; P. J. Garner 27.3–5–100–1; S. R. Moss 21–3–74–0; G. P. Savin 60–13–147–8.

SHROPSHIRE

Secretary – N. H. BIRCH, 8 Port Hill Close, Copthorne, Shrewsbury SY3 8RR

Matches 9: Won – Cornwall. Lost – Wiltshire. Won on first innings – Dorset, Oxfordshire, Wales. Lost on first innings – Berkshire, Buckinghamshire, Cheshire, Devon.

Batting Averages

	M	*I*	*NO*	*R*	*HI*	*100s*	*Avge*
J. S. Johnson ...	9	15	2	598	99	0	46.00
T. Parton	7	13	2	499	95	0	45.36
*J. Foster	9	15	3	486	133*	2	40.50
J. B. R. Jones ...	7	12	2	358	90	0	35.80
M. R. Davies ...	8	10	2	261	50*	0	32.62
P. B. Wormald ..	7	8	3	155	53	0	31.00
J. A. Smith	6	7	1	91	44*	0	15.16
†D. J. Ashley ...	9	11	0	120	20	0	10.90
A. S. Barnard ...	8	6	2	41	13	0	10.25
G. Edmunds	9	7	1	46	20	0	7.66

Played in eight matches: J. S. Roberts 0*, 10, 0. Played in two matches: J. T. Aspinal 31, 8; M. R. Cronin 5*; J. P. Dawson 1*, 14*, 9*; A. N. Johnson 27, 25, 8; J. D. Wase 7*. Played in one match: K. Humphreys 0; P. D. Sadler 4.

Bowling Averages

	O	*M*	*R*	*W*	*BB*	*Avge*
J. S. Roberts	152	33	438	20	5-39	21.90
G. Edmunds	259.5	72	640	25	5-29	25.60
P. B. Wormald ..	128.4	23	441	16	5-72	27.56
A. S. Barnard ...	209	45	601	16	3-35	37.56

Also bowled: J. T. Aspinal 7–4–10–0; M. R. Cronin 17–0–81–1; J. P. Dawson 34–5–150–3; J. B. R. Jones 5–0–21–0; J. A. Smith 66.1–7–234–3.

STAFFORDSHIRE

Secretary – W. S. BOURNE, 10 The Pavement, Brewood ST19 9BZ

Matches 9: Won – Hertfordshire, Norfolk, Northumberland. Lost – Cambridgeshire, Durham. Won on first innings – Bedfordshire, Cumberland. Lost on first innings – Suffolk. No result – Lincolnshire.

Batting Averages

	M	*I*	*NO*	*R*	*HI*	*100s*	*Avge*
P. R. Oliver	6	11	5	459	136*	2	76.50
D. Cartledge	8	15	0	627	102	1	41.80
J. A. Waterhouse ...	9	16	4	491	71*	0	40.91
H. V. Patel	8	15	3	449	120*	2	37.41
S. J. Dean	9	17	0	579	111	2	34.05
*N. J. Archer	9	13	5	203	54*	0	25.37
†A. Griffiths	9	10	2	129	46	0	16.12
D. C. Blank	9	7	2	72	37*	0	14.40

Played in nine matches: A. J. Webster 15, 4*, 11*, 4, 13*. Played in six matches: S. P. Perryman 0*, 3. Played in five matches: C. E. Dowen 0, 0*, 4. Played in three matches: R. W. Flower 6*. Played in two matches: D. A. Banks 85, 13, 7, 33*; A. J. Dutton 1; J. Potts 9. Played in one match: A. C. Hawkins 2; A. E. Lea 4*, 3; J. E. Benjamin did not bat.

Bowling Averages

	O	*M*	*R*	*W*	*BB*	*Avge*
D. C. Blank	231	49	678	28	4-20	24.21
R. W. Flower	94.3	24	322	13	4-63	24.76
S. P. Perryman	169.3	37	504	20	5-50	25.20
A. J. Webster	288.4	61	857	30	6-72	28.56

Also bowled: N. J. Archer 2.3–0–25–0; D. A. Banks 9–3–47–0; J. E. Benjamin 40–19–66–4; D. Cartledge 37.5–9–129–6; C. E. Dowen 88.2–15–343–7; A. J. Dutton 6–2–25–0; A. C. Hawkins 6–1–38–0; P. R. Oliver 2–0–17–1; J. Potts 51–9–175–4.

SUFFOLK

Secretary – R. S. BARKER, 301 Henley Road, Ipswich IP1 6TB

Matches 9: Won – Durham, Lincolnshire. Lost – Cambridgeshire, Hertfordshire. Won on first innings – Bedfordshire, Cumberland, Norfolk, Northumberland, Staffordshire.

Batting Averages

	M	*I*	*NO*	*R*	*HI*	*100s*	*Avge*
C. Gladwin	7	14	1	461	104	1	35.46
M. J. Peck	4	8	1	240	57	0	34.28
H. J. W. Wright	6	8	2	204	86	0	34.00
†S. J. Halliday	9	15	4	364	61*	0	33.09
M. S. A. McEvoy	6	11	1	322	79	0	32.20
P. J. Caley	9	17	1	443	70	0	27.68
J. W. Edrich	8	15	0	335	58	0	22.33
K. P. Offord	5	8	1	127	49*	0	18.14
P. J. Hayes	9	10	5	90	29	0	18.00
R. Heap	3	6	0	97	64	0	16.16
J. J. Zagni	7	11	3	111	45	0	13.87
R. A. Pybus	4	6	3	36	15*	0	12.00
*M. D. Bailey	9	6	2	23	14*	0	5.75

Played in seven matches: R. C. Green 5*, 0, 5, 1*. Played in two matches: A. J. King 10, 6, 6, 1*; G. Morgan 24, 6, 29. Played in one match: P. W. Harvey 0*, 0*; N. Shahid 58, 33.

Bowling Averages

	O	*M*	*R*	*W*	*BB*	*Avge*
R. C. Green	207.2	51	614	39	7-50	15.74
R. A. Pybus	83.2	6	343	16	4-49	21.43
M. D. Bailey	144	29	458	15	3-13	30.53
H. J. W. Wright	120.4	26	374	12	5-67	31.16
P. J. Hayes	164.3	46	439	14	4-25	31.35
P. J. Caley	116	14	484	13	4-103	37.23

Also bowled: C. Gladwin 81.3–11–296–9; J. W. Edrich 4.1–0–51–0; P. W. Harvey 12–1–53–3; N. Shahid 19–4–64–2; J. J. Zagni 46–4–190–0.

WALES

Secretary – BILL EDWARDS, 59a King Edward Road, Swansea SA1 4LN

Matches 9: Lost – Berkshire, Cheshire, Dorset. Won on first innings – Buckinghamshire, Devon, Wiltshire. Tied on first innings – Oxfordshire. Lost on first innings – Shropshire. No result – Cornwall.

Batting Averages

	M	I	NO	R	HI	100s	Avge
N. G. Roberts . . .	9	15	2	617	103*	1	47.46
A. L. Jones	3	6	0	236	96	0	39.33
*G. P. Ellis	8	14	0	374	105	1	26.71
B. J. Lloyd	6	7	2	130	33	0	26.00
M. Tremellen . . .	5	8	3	130	58*	0	26.00
C. M. Elward . . .	9	16	2	342	127	1	24.42
A. C. Puddle	9	15	2	259	65*	0	19.92
D. A. Francis . . .	7	10	2	151	40	0	18.87
S. G. Watkins . . .	5	6	2	39	21	0	9.75
M. A. R. Jones . .	4	7	0	66	26	0	9.42
A. R. Davies	7	7	1	45	15	0	7.50
†M. Davies	9	8	5	12	7	0	4.00

Played in four matches: H. Rogers 1*, J. Kitson 2*. Played in three matches: G. Edwards 0, 0*, 1, 15*. Played in two matches: R. Brown 1*; M. Williams 14*, 0, 8, 0. Played in one match: D. Ricketts 1*; H. Williams 17, 1; S. Williams 8.

Bowling Averages

	O	M	R	W	BB	Avge
G. Edwards	126.4	52	283	20	7-51	14.15
A. R. Davies . . .	168.4	68	391	18	5-28	21.72
G. P. Ellis	117.1	27	362	16	6-41	22.62
B. J. Lloyd	163	48	407	13	4-43	31.30

Also bowled: R. Brown 9–4–22–2; C. M. Elward 8–1–70–0; D. A. Francis 3–0–16–0; M. A. R. Jones 27–2–92–2; J. Kitson 51–11–194–4; D. Ricketts 9–0–43–1; N. G. Roberts 70–13–217–8; H. Rogers 68.4–13–219–5; M. Tremellen 5–1–21–0; S. G. Watkins 68.5–6–311–7; H. Williams 7–1–38–0; M. Williams 0.3–0–8–0.

WILTSHIRE

Secretary – C. R. SHEPPARD, 45 Ipswich Street, Swindon, Wiltshire SN2 1DB

Matches 9: Won – Buckinghamshire, Shropshire. Lost – Berkshire, Cheshire. Won on first innings – Cornwall. Lost on first innings – Dorset, Oxfordshire, Wales. No result – Devon.

Batting Averages

	M	I	NO	R	HI	100s	Avge
K. N. Foyle	5	8	2	272	111	1	45.33
D. J. Mercer	9	17	6	443	114*	1	40.27
R. J. Lanchbury	7	13	2	334	70	0	30.36
*R. C. Cooper	8	10	2	232	68*	0	29.00
B. Ponting	3	6	0	141	38	0	23.50
B. H. White	8	15	1	333	51	0	23.78
M. C. Seaman	3	6	0	119	36	0	19.83
[illegible]. Thompson	7	8	1	105	30	0	15.00
K. St J. D. Emery . . .	4	7	2	63	23	0	12.60
C. R. Trembath	4	7	1	74	30	0	12.33
†J. Cullip	5	8	1	69	20*	0	9.85
D. P. Simpkins	7	9	1	57	25	0	7.12
P. Meehan	9	7	2	29	19*	0	5.80

Played in four matches: A. J. Jones 5*, 0, 2, 0, 3*. Played in three matches: †W. Johnson 0, 1, 20; M. A. Watts 7, 2, 41, 6*. Played in two matches: C. C. Ellison 0*, 20; J. J. Newman 29, 14, 0, 3; R. R. Savage 1, 4, 3, 8*; P. H. Tucker 0, 12; A. J. Ward 9, 5.

Bowling Averages

	O	*M*	*R*	*W*	*BB*	*Avge*
J. Thompson	125.1	29	377	22	5-43	17.13
C. R. Trembath	87.4	18	305	15	5-32	20.33
P. Meehan	158.1	34	545	15	4-87	36.33

Also bowled: R. C. Cooper 38.2–4–170–7; C. C. Ellison 44–16–125–5; K. St J. D. Emery 62.4–7–294–7; K. N. Foyle 1–0–9–0; A. P. Jones 50.4–5–164–6; B. Ponting 12–1–75–0; D. P. Simpkins 153–28–524–8; A. J. Ward 42–9–132–7; M. A. Watts 44–9–120–7; B. H. White 1–0–5–0.

TOP TEN MINOR COUNTIES CHAMPIONSHIP AVERAGES, 1988

BATTING

(Qualification: 8 innings)

	M	*I*	*NO*	*R*	*HI*	*100s*	*Avge*
P. R. Oliver (*Staffordshire*)	6	11	5	459	136*	2	76.50
T. A. Lester (*Oxfordshire*)	8	16	6	679	97*	0	67.90
I. Cockbain (*Cheshire*)	8	15	4	681	119	3	61.90
I. S. Lawrence (*Cambridgeshire*)	9	17	4	787	144	2	60.53
S. G. Plumb (*Norfolk*)	8	16	1	830	204*	1	55.33
A. R. Harwood (*Buckinghamshire*)	5	10	2	434	142*	1	54.25
N. A. Riddell (*Durham*)	8	12	5	367	63	0	52.42
M. J. Roberts (*Buckinghamshire*)	4	8	1	338	155*	1	48.28
N. G. Roberts (*Wales*)	9	15	2	617	103*	1	47.46
P. J. Garner (*Oxfordshire*)	9	16	3	601	94*	0	46.23

BOWLING

(Qualification: 20 wickets)

	O	*M*	*R*	*W*	*BB*	*Avge*
S. Dyson (*Cheshire*)	107.2	38	206	23	7-39	8.95
P. J. Lewington (*Berkshire*)	302.5	94	658	54	7-70	12.18
S. Turner (*Cambridgeshire*)	346.4	98	763	58	6-38	13.15
G. Edwards (*Wales*)	126.4	52	283	20	7-51	14.15
R. C. Green (*Suffolk*)	207.2	51	614	39	7-50	15.74
R. Ellwood (*Cumberland*)	189	52	491	31	6-48	15.83
D. Surridge (*Hertfordshire*)	156.2	42	387	23	7-61	16.82
D. Marshall (*Lincolnshire*)	206.5	53	509	30	5-45	16.96
J. Thompson (*Wiltshire*)	125.1	29	377	22	5-43	17.13
M. G. Boocock (*Cheshire*)	139.5	43	363	21	4-41	17.28

THE MINOR COUNTIES CHAMPIONS

1895 Norfolk / Durham / Worcestershire
1896 Worcestershire
1897 Worcestershire
1898 Worcestershire
1899 Northamptonshire / Buckinghamshire
1900 Glamorgan / Durham / Northamptonshire
1901 Durham
1902 Wiltshire
1903 Northamptonshire
1904 Northamptonshire
1905 Norfolk
1906 Staffordshire
1907 Lancashire II
1908 Staffordshire
1909 Wiltshire
1910 Norfolk
1911 Staffordshire
1912 In abeyance
1913 Norfolk
1914 Staffordshire
1920 Staffordshire
1921 Staffordshire
1922 Buckinghamshire
1923 Buckinghamshire
1924 Berkshire
1925 Buckinghamshire
1926 Durham
1927 Staffordshire
1928 Berkshire
1929 Oxfordshire
1930 Durham
1931 Leicestershire II
1932 Buckinghamshire
1933 Undecided
1934 Lancashire II
1935 Middlesex II
1936 Hertfordshire
1937 Lancashire II
1938 Buckinghamshire
1939 Surrey II
1946 Suffolk
1947 Yorkshire
1948 Lancashire II
1949 Lancashire II
1950 Surrey II
1951 Kent II
1952 Buckinghamshire
1953 Berkshire
1954 Surrey II
1955 Surrey II
1956 Kent II
1957 Yorkshire II
1958 Yorkshire II
1959 Warwickshire II
1960 Lancashire II
1961 Somerset II
1962 Warwickshire II
1963 Cambridgeshire
1964 Lancashire II
1965 Somerset II
1966 Lincolnshire
1967 Cheshire
1968 Yorkshire II
1969 Buckinghamshire
1970 Bedfordshire
1971 Yorkshire II
1972 Bedfordshire
1973 Shropshire
1974 Oxfordshire
1975 Hertfordshire
1976 Durham
1977 Suffolk
1978 Devon
1979 Suffolk
1980 Durham
1981 Durham
1982 Oxfordshire
1983 Hertfordshire
1984 Durham
1985 Cheshire
1986 Cumberland
1987 Buckinghamshire
1988 Cheshire

LANCASHIRE CLOSE THEIR MEMBERSHIP

Because of the demand in recent years for Test match tickets at Old Trafford, and the fact that members were not able always to get the type of seating they require, Lancashire decided to close the membership of the county club from June 25, 1988. With membership at around 12,000, the club was anxious that the limited seating capacity in the membership area should not become too congested.

HONOURS' LIST

In 1988, the following were decorated for their services to cricket:

New Year's Honours: D. L. Amiss (England) MBE, J. H. Oakley (New Zealand) CBE.

Queen's Birthday Honours: D. C. Boon (Australia) MBE, Miss A. T. Collins (England WCA) OBE, C. J. Cooper (English Schools CA) MBE, R. W. Reeks (Bedfordshire) BEM, J. G. Wright (New Zealand) MBE.

In addition to the above, H. A. Pawson (Oxford University and Kent) was awarded the OBE for services to angling.

SECOND ELEVEN CHAMPIONSHIP, 1988

Again weakened by injuries to first-team players, **Derbyshire** called on 30 players during a wet season which five times saw them forfeit innings in attempts to secure results. A rise of three places to fourteenth was satisfactory in the circumstances. Chris Adams's 724 runs included 101 against Northamptonshire and Tim O'Gorman confirmed his promise with two big hundreds. But overall the batting was unimpressive and a major factor in the lack of success. Karl Krikken again kept wicket well, particularly towards the end of the season, and ended with 28 dismissals, as well as 300 runs. Dave Hallack, easily the best bowler, captured 40 wickets at 13.65, including six for 36 against Leicestershire, six for 53 against Nottinghamshire and six for 86 against Lancashire, but the other quick bowlers fell below expectations.

Essex enjoyed one of their most successful seasons, rising to fourth. Eleven hundreds were scored by nine batsmen, with John Stephenson hitting 108 and 102 not out against Hampshire at Southend and Paul Prichard an unbeaten 258 against Sussex in his one appearance. Keith Butler was the leading run-maker and Ian Redpath and Robert Pook were consistent performers. The leading bowlers were the slow left-armer, Andrew Golding, and Ian Pont, whose first-innings return of nine for 50 against Nottinghamshire at Southend was the best in the Championship. In the same match Nasser Hussain held five catches at short leg, Mark Waugh scored 124 and Michael Field-Buss took seven for 74 in the second innings. Field-Buss also took six for 67 against Hampshire while Stephenson captured five in an innings three times.

Glamorgan, with only two wins in a summer frustrated by the weather, dropped five places to twelfth. Paul Roebuck, with 139 against Leicestershire and 108 against Lancashire, topped the batting averages, while Michael Cann scored the most runs (620), including 107 against Worcestershire. Despite playing for two-thirds of the season in the first team, Steve Watkin was the leading wicket-taker, although the season's best return was Steve Monkhouse's seven for 96.

Gloucestershire, without a win, subsided to the bottom of the table. The only batsman to pass 400 runs was Malcolm Pooley, the Young England all-rounder, who won promotion to the first team in August. "Vibert" Greene and Pooley bore the brunt of the seam bowling, taking 23 and 17 wickets respectively, but the leading spinners, Courtney Ricketts and Martyn Ball, proved expensive.

First-team calls weakened **Hampshire** but three victories in the last four matches lifted them back to the top half of the table. Richard Scott, Tony Middleton, Rupert Cox and Mark O'Connor all passed 600 runs, yet the batting was generally sketchy. Scott headed both averages with 710 runs and 30 wickets, and had a particularly fine match against Sussex at Southampton, taking six for 68 and scoring 147. His other century, 102 not out, was against Gloucestershire.

Alan Ealham came out of retirement to lead the defending champions, **Kent**, who, fielding a young and inexperienced side, dropped to thirteenth. Johnny Longley and Paul Farbrace both scored 700 runs, with the latter again excelling behind the stumps (31 ct, 7 st). Farbrace hit 134 against Surrey and 100 against Somerset. Matthew Fleming, Trevor Ward, David Sabine and Vince Wells all passed 450 runs, in addition to which Wells took 31 wickets and Sabine 23 bowling medium pace. Off-spinner Mark Harman was the leading wicket-taker, his figures boosted by a match return of ten for 117 against Essex. Fleming, Mark Dobson and Mark Ealham were offered contracts for 1989.

Lancashire's captain and wicket-keeper, John Stanworth, stimulated excellent team spirit throughout the season. Graham Lloyd, son of David, the county's former captain, was the only player in the Second Eleven Championship to reach 1,000 runs. He compiled four centuries – 144 against Leicestershire, 133 against Worcestershire, 105 against Glamorgan, all at Old Trafford, and 119 against Derbyshire at Ilkeston. Seven more were hit by five other players, among them Nick Speak, who totalled 889 runs, and off-spinner Dexter Fitton, who was again the leading bowler in the Championship, with 55 wickets. Peter Martin bowled well and fast for his 46 wickets, including six for 40 against Kent, and Tony Murphy, with 40, took five in an innings three times.

Leicestershire slipped five places to fifteenth. The batting was dominated by Peter Hepworth and Justin Benson, who totalled 935 and 773 runs respectively. Glen Bruk-Jackson, a Zimbabwean who played in the Youth World Cup in Australia, was next highest with 397. Hepworth showed his liking for Worcestershire's bowlers by scoring 159 against them at Leicester and 187 when the sides met again at Kidderminster. On the first occasion Mike Garnham made 203 not out, and on the second Benson hit 129. Lloyd Tennant fulfilled his promise of the previous season with 39 wickets, including a return of six for 56 against Northamptonshire.

Although weakened by first-team calls, **Middlesex** were again unbeaten. Their strength lay in their batting and a five-pronged spin attack comprising Philip Tufnell, Alex Barnett, Paul Weekes, Jamie Sykes and Andrew Needham. Tufnell picked up 34 wickets in seven matches, while seventeen-year-old Barnett, also a left-arm spinner, created an impact in his first full season with 46 wickets. Alastair Fraser bore the brunt of the seam bowling. Of the nine batsmen who averaged more than 40, Mike Roseberry was the most prolific, his 909 runs including 215 not out against Northamptonshire. Once he overcame the barrier of reaching his maiden hundred, he increased in confidence. Ian Hutchinson followed three ducks with some brilliant innings, including 146 not out in a total of 526 for seven against Hampshire at Southampton, but he missed the last six weeks with a back injury.

Northamptonshire, often fielding an inexperienced side, played positive and exciting cricket. Three matches were won and five others decided in the final over. Neil Stanley and Anthony Penberthy played with increasing maturity, and Blair Hartland, a New Zealander in his second season of a two-year scholarship, scored more than 500 runs in the last four matches to total 857. He compiled the side's highest score, 188 against Sussex, and hit 104 against Worcestershire at Oundle School. Although injury restricted him to nine appearances, Gareth Smith took 25 wickets, including a match-winning return of seven for 47 against Worcestershire at Oundle School, the best for the side for many years. Andy Roberts, a young leg-spinner, showed considerable promise, and Wayne Noon, with 41 dismissals, looked a wicket-keeper of real potential.

Nottinghamshire coped well with the demands caused by first-team injuries to win six matches and finish third, twelve places higher than in 1987. They were greatly assisted by their two overseas scholarship players, Chris Cairns from New Zealand and the South African, David Callaghan. The latter's 934 runs included five centuries, two of which were scored against Lancashire at Manchester. Duncan Martindale's 700 runs, at an average of 77.77, included 139 against Northamptonshire and 122 not out against Leicestershire. Cairns was the leading wicket-taker with 33, Mike Bore headed the averages, and off-spinner Graham Harding was the only bowler to take six wickets in an innings, with six for 75 against Northamptonshire. David Fraser-Darling made the leading all-round contribution with 27 wickets and 348 runs, including 101 against Leicestershire, but he was not retained.

Somerset, under the captaincy of Trevor Gard, played positive cricket, yet disappointingly failed to win a match. However, close finishes against Surrey, Warwickshire and Worcestershire could have gone either way. The pick of the batsmen was Mark Douglas, on a player exchange from New Zealand, whose 640 runs included an innings of 152. The other three-figure innings were Garth Townsend's 102 against Warwickshire, Paul Bail's 113 against Lancashire, and Julian Wyatt's 151 against Gloucestershire at Taunton. Of the bowlers, Colin Dredge was the only one to emerge with any credit.

Surrey, with a young side that continued the county's policy of attacking cricket, won the Championship for the first time since 1975. Unbeaten, but needing an eighth win in their last fixture at Hove, they made sure of success in two days. Darren Bicknell totalled 883 runs, including 138 not out against Hampshire, 108 not out against Leicestershire and 99 and 105 not out against Essex at Chelmsford. Zahid Sadiq also passed 800 runs, with 120 against Essex at Banstead and 107 against Somerset, while nineteen-year-old Graham Thorpe, in his first full season, took 25 wickets and scored 706 runs, including 123 against Lancashire and 103 not out against Essex at Banstead. Mark Frost bowled with pace to take 48 wickets, including seven for 20 against Hampshire at The Oval, where Keith Medlycott took a hat-trick in the same match. Neil Kendrick bowled his slow left-arm spin superbly, Graham Brown kept wicket consistently well, and there was some excellent close-catching by Thorpe and Kendrick.

Sussex pursued a rebuilding policy by giving opportunities to 37 players, including several young, local cricketers, and were therefore encouraged to finish tenth. James Hall, Keith Greenfield, Meyrick Pringle and Simon Kimber all passed 400 runs, while Martin Speight's eight innings brought 381 runs. Pringle's best performances came against Kent: he scored 104 when the sides met at Hastings and took ten wickets in the return match at Maidstone. He and Kimber both bowled steadily, while Philip Threlfall showed tremendous pace.

Warwickshire, captained by Geoff Tedstone, maintained good team spirit throughout a season made difficult by the weather. Two bowlers enjoyed profitable first seasons: Joey Benjamin took the most wickets with 43, and the slow left-arm spinner, Robert Earl, followed with 31, including nine for 70 in Gloucestershire's first innings at Cheltenham. In addition Allan Donald produced some explosive match-winning spells and Adrian Pierson bowled his off-spin consistently. The leading run-scorer, with 876, was Jason Ratcliffe, whose father, D.P., played for the county from 1957 to 1968. He struck 157 against Somerset as Warwickshire successfully chased a target of 297 to win. The most consistent batting came from Alastair Storie, whose 708 (average 64.36) included 109 not out against Worcestershire and 164 against Gloucestershire. Eighteen-year-old Simon Green, on a Youth Training Scheme, provided excellent support with 660 runs and a century against Yorkshire.

Worcestershire were in contention for the title until the end of the season but had to settle for second place. David Leatherdale and Paul Bent were the most consistent performers in a strong batting side and both won first-team recognition. A niggling back injury prevented Stuart Lampitt from building on his earlier opportunities at this level. Wicket-taking was shared between the experienced Paul Pridgeon and the persistent Steve McEwan, but with a slow left-armer in Richard Stemp and a leg-spinner in M. P. Briers, Mark Scott could usually call on a varied attack, especially when off-spinners Damian D'Oliveira and Bent were playing. Stuart Bevins established himself as an able wicket-keeper in a competent fielding side.

Joint winners in 1987, **Yorkshire** slipped to ninth place. Thirteen centuries were scored by eight batsmen, with Simon Kellett being taken on the staff after scoring 916 runs, including 102 against Derbyshire and 129 against Surrey. Neil Nicholson also hit two hundreds in his total of 726 runs, while Kevin Sharp took a liking to Somerset's bowling at Bath, where he compiled an unbeaten 238. Off-spinner Philip Berry took the most wickets, closely followed by Paul Booth, slow left-arm.

SECOND ELEVEN CHAMPIONSHIP, 1988

					Bonus Points			
Win = 16 points	*P*	*W*	*L*	*D*	*Batting*	*Bowling*	*Pts*	*Avge*
1 – Surrey (8)	17	8	0	9	45	48	221	13.00
2 – Worcestershire (12)	15	7	2	6	38	34	184	12.27
3 – Nottinghamshire (15)	15	6	3	6	29	41	166	11.07
4 – Essex (11)	15	4	5	6	40	50	154	10.27
5 – Lancashire (3)	20	6	2	12	42	57	195	9.75
6 – Warwickshire (6)	17	5	3	9	31	47	158	9.29
7 – Hampshire (5)	14	4	2	8	24	39	127	9.07
8 – Middlesex (14)	15	4	0	11	38	32	134	8.93
9 – Yorkshire (1)	16	4	1	11	43	28	135	8.44
10 – Sussex (4)	14	2	5	7	28	52	112	8.00
11 – Northamptonshire (13)	17	3	4	10	37	41	126	7.41
12 – Glamorgan (7)	12	2	5	5	20	27	79	6.58
13 – Kent (1)	16	1	6	9	37	52	105	6.56
14 – Derbyshire (17)	14	1	5	8	16	39	71	5.07
15 – Leicestershire (10)	18	1	6	11	27	48	91	5.06
16 – Somerset (8)	15	0	5	10	36	35	71	4.73
17 – Gloucestershire (16)	14	0	4	10	19	35	54	3.86

1987 positions in brackets.

Note: The averages to determine the positions in the Championship are shown to two corrected decimal places.

The following matches were abandoned and are not included in the above table: June 8, 9, 10 – Glamorgan v Nottinghamshire at Abergavenny; August 31, September 1, 2 – Glamorgan v Warwickshire at Cardiff.

*In the averages that follow, * against a score signifies not out, * against a name signifies the captain and † signifies a wicket-keeper.*

DERBYSHIRE SECOND ELEVEN

Matches 14: Won – Northamptonshire. Lost – Lancashire (twice), Nottinghamshire (twice), Worcestershire. Drawn – Gloucestershire (twice) Leicestershire (twice), Northamptonshire, Worcestershire, Yorkshire (twice).

Batting Averages

	M	*I*	*NO*	*R*	*HI*	*100s*	*Avge*
T. J. G. O'Gorman	5	8	2	370	162	2	61.66
*A. Hill	14	13	8	194	41	0	38.80
C. J. Adams	14	21	0	724	101	1	34.47
R. Sharma	6	9	2	235	103*	1	33.57
R. J. Finney	10	16	0	424	56	0	26.50
J. R. Lumley	5	8	1	174	99*	0	24.85
A. Cooke	4	6	0	138	44	0	23.00
†K. M. Krikken	14	19	5	300	84*	0	21.42
D. Hallack	12	14	1	227	59	0	17.46
F. A. Griffith	8	9	2	108	31	0	15.42
M. Wakefield	14	16	0	226	55	0	14.12
M. Beardshall	13	15	5	102	22	0	10.20
S. J. Base	6	8	3	38	19	0	7.60
M. Jean-Jacques	9	10	1	31	15	0	3.44

Played in three matches: R. G. Watson 67, 28, 10. Played in two matches: P. E. Ellis 2, 9; P. J. Tebay 5, 47, 8. Played in one match: A. Bell 0, 10; A. M. Brown 3, 1; S. J. Foster 4, 0; T. Harris 0, 0; G. T. Headley 20; B. Roberts 11, 0; J. R. Robinson 3, 0; C. Saville 1, 9; D. Snellgrove 9, 5. D. Cork, T. Kirk, W. G. Lovell and N. R. Newman did not bat.

Bowling Averages

	O	*M*	*R*	*W*	*BB*	*Avge*
D. Hallack	208.2	43	546	40	6-36	13.65
M. Jean-Jacques	248.2	60	666	24	5-52	27.75
S. J. Base	144.2	18	416	14	4-73	29.71
R. Sharma	170	57	316	10	4-32	31.60
M. Wakefield	181.1	57	467	13	5-44	35.92
M. Beardshall	310.3	53	947	23	5-70	41.17
F. A. Griffith	123.5	27	435	10	3-47	43.50

Also bowled: C. J. Adams 2–0–18–0; A. Bell 4–0–20–1; A. Cooke 32–6–119–2; R. J. Finney 28–9–88–1; A. Hill 3–0–21–0; N. R. Newman 22–5–59–1; T. J. G. O'Gorman 1–0–7–0; B. Roberts 4–1–18–0; C. Saville 4–1–23–1; D. Snellgrove 6–4–3–0.

ESSEX SECOND ELEVEN

Matches 15: Won – Gloucestershire, Nottinghamshire (twice), Sussex. Lost – Hampshire, Kent, Northamptonshire, Surrey, Sussex. Drawn – Hampshire, Kent, Middlesex (twice), Northamptonshire, Surrey.

Batting Averages

	M	*I*	*NO*	*R*	*HI*	*100s*	*Avge*
M. E. Waugh	3	5	1	278	124	1	69.50
J. P. Stephenson	5	8	1	438	108	2	62.57
R. Leppard	2	4	1	186	93	0	62.00
N. Hussain	4	7	2	219	110	1	43.80

	M	*I*	*NO*	*R*	*HI*	*100s*	*Avge*
R. N. Pook	12	19	3	614	115*	1	38.37
I. Redpath	11	21	3	668	153*	2	37.11
K. Butler	14	22	2	728	110	1	36.40
J. D. Kenny	5	9	0	264	102	1	29.33
I. L. Pont	10	9	3	168	70	0	28.00
†A. D. Brown	12	8	4	109	36*	0	27.25
*R. E. East	11	7	3	97	50*	0	24.25
A. Seymour	11	17	4	303	79*	0	23.30
A. T. Van-Lint	4	7	1	118	44	0	19.66
A. K. Golding	13	15	1	214	62	0	15.28
T. D. Topley	2	4	0	60	23	0	15.00
T. E. Parker	3	6	2	59	28	0	14.75
P. R. Bushnell	3	5	2	40	12	0	13.33
M. G. Field-Buss	11	18	1	207	52	0	12.17
I. Binns	3	6	0	72	28	0	12.00
N. V. Knight	2	4	0	48	26	0	12.00
N. Shahid	4	4	1	20	16	0	6.66
M. C. Ilott	4	5	2	6	5	0	2.00

Played in two matches: B. J. Debenham 54, 97, 41; B. R. Hardie 12, 129, 28; J. H. Childs did not bat. Played in one match: P. S. Brown 3, 0; G. M. Charlesworth 18, 13; D. E. East 3; G. W. Ecclestone 2, 53*; S. D. Fitzgerald 6*, 5; R. Herbert 31, 12*; A. W. Lilley 40; P. J. Prichard 258*; N. M. Rose 1*, 0.

Bowling Averages

	O	*M*	*R*	*W*	*BB*	*Avge*
J. H. Childs	36.4	19	60	7	3-3	8.57
T. D. Topley	60	17	160	10	4-40	16.00
J. P. Stephenson	155.5	33	391	24	6-55	16.29
I. L. Pont	292.1	67	787	37	9-50	21.27
A. Seymour	140	33	387	17	3-61	22.76
A. T. Van-Lint	126.5	23	402	17	6-74	23.64
M. C. Ilott	102.5	24	262	11	5-39	23.81
A. K. Golding	423.3	125	968	36	4-24	26.88
T. E. Parker	85	7	335	11	3-42	30.45
M. G. Field-Buss	369.4	104	922	29	7-67	31.79
M. E. Waugh	53	7	171	4	3-53	42.75
N. Shahid	102.1	19	360	6	2-33	60.0

Also bowled: P. R. Bushnell 59.2–8–231–1; G. M. Charlesworth 25–4–73–3; R. E. East 30–11–48–3; R. Herbert 66–13–208–1; A. W. Lilley 2–0–3–0; I. Redpath 5.1–0–25–0 N. M. Rose 20–5–50–2.

GLAMORGAN SECOND ELEVEN

Matches 12: Won – Gloucestershire, Worcestershire. Lost – Lancashire, Leicestershire Nottinghamshire, Warwickshire, Worcestershire. Drawn – Gloucestershire, Lancashire, Leicestershire, Somerset (*twice*). *Abandoned – Nottinghamshire, Warwickshire.*

Batting Averages

	M	*I*	*NO*	*R*	*HI*	*100s*	*Avge*
P. G. P. Roebuck	8	13	2	474	139	2	43.0
*J. F. Steele	7	8	5	126	29	0	42.0
*M. J. Cann	10	18	1	620	107	1	36.4
P. A. Cottey	8	15	1	490	85	0	35.0
C. J. P. G. van Zyl	3	5	1	122	35	0	30.5
S. L. Watkin	6	6	3	91	39*	0	30.3

	M	*I*	*NO*	*R*	*HI*	*100s*	*Avge*
*P. A. Todd	7	13	3	295	68*	0	29.50
I. Smith	9	16	1	419	78	0	27.93
†M. L. Roberts	9	15	0	352	86	0	23.46
S. P. James	8	14	0	300	69	0	21.42
M. Davies	11	16	3	234	37	0	18.00
S. W. Maddock	4	8	0	141	47	0	17.62
A. Dale	5	8	0	131	57	0	16.37
P. D. North	7	12	3	140	29	0	15.55
R. D. B. Croft	3	5	0	74	67	0	14.80
S. J. Moorcroft	7	10	1	97	21	0	10.77
S. Monkhouse	9	6	2	29	9	0	7.25
S. Bastien	6	6	2	18	8*	0	4.50

Played in two matches: D. L. Hemp 8, 2, 3. Played in one match: †P. Mason 8*; R. Nancarrow 3, 28; T. A. Parton 24, 71. †A. Shaw did not bat.

Bowling Averages

	O	*M*	*R*	*W*	*BB*	*Avge*
S. L. Watkin	183	45	482	26	6-37	18.53
S. J. Moorcroft	84.3	13	323	15	5-42	21.53
R. D. B. Croft	94.5	19	313	12	5-83	26.08
S. Monkhouse	211	39	645	22	7-96	29.31
M. Davies	240	60	685	22	5-53	31.13
I. Smith	98.2	21	302	9	4-62	33.55
S. Bastien	120.4	33	312	7	2-39	44.57
M. J. Cann	117.1	21	374	8	2-31	46.75
P. D. North	154	67	309	5	2-50	61.80

Also bowled: A. Dale 18–8–43–3; S. W. Maddock 6–1–42–0; R. Nancarrow 3–1–10–0; P. G. P. Roebuck 2–0–21–0; P. A. Todd 2.2–0–21–0; C. J. P. G. van Zyl 59–12–153–3.

GLOUCESTERSHIRE SECOND ELEVEN

Matches 14: Lost – Essex, Glamorgan, Hampshire, Worcestershire. Drawn – Derbyshire (twice), Glamorgan, Hampshire, Kent, Somerset (twice), Warwickshire (twice), Worcestershire.

Batting Averages

	M	*I*	*NO*	*R*	*HI*	*100s*	*Avge*
. W. Lloyds	3	4	1	187	81	0	62.33
M. W. Pooley	11	18	4	517	91*	0	36.92
K. B. K. Ibadulla	6	12	2	359	71	0	35.90
M. W. Alleyne	5	8	0	255	89	0	31.87
D. A. Graham	3	6	1	159	63	0	31.80
I. P. Butcher	6	9	0	274	66	0	30.44
. J. Debenham	4	8	0	224	69	0	28.00
. C. K. Smith	10	16	3	351	88	0	27.00
. L. P. Meadows	4	6	1	127	69	0	25.40
. S. Greene	9	12	2	240	52*	0	24.00
N. M. Pritchard	6	11	0	257	60	0	23.36
A. J. Goldsmith	7	11	0	236	78	0	21.45
D. J. Thomas	8	13	2	222	98*	0	20.18
M. C. J. Ball	9	14	4	190	55	0	19.00
D. J. Adams	4	7	0	129	40	0	18.42
C. I. O. Ricketts	8	12	2	171	50	0	17.10
A. D. A. Chidgey	5	9	0	140	55	0	15.55

	M	*I*	*NO*	*R*	*HI*	*100s*	*Avge*
D. J. Chubbs	11	12	6	72	21*	0	12.00
M. A. Challenger	2	4	1	34	15	0	11.33
*†A. J. Brassington	7	9	1	65	26	0	8.12
†R. J. Williams	8	9	0	39	24	0	4.33
A. M. Smith	6	5	1	4	4	0	1.00

Played in three matches: K. B. S. Jarvis 0, 0*. Played in two matches: C. L. Horner 4, 0*, 0*; N. J. Pitts 48, 2. Played in one match: M. A. V. Bell 17*; A. M. Brown 15, 9; N. C. W. Fenton 0; J. D. Glendenning 15, 0; W. M. Smith 20, 19.

Bowling Averages

	O	*M*	*R*	*W*	*BB*	*Avge*
M. A. V. Bell	11	4	14	4	4-14	3.50
K. B. S. Jarvis	59	14	133	7	3-62	19.00
J. W. Lloyds	57	12	154	8	4-46	19.25
V. S. Greene	252.4	53	670	23	4-65	29.13
C. L. Horner	34	4	130	4	2-40	32.50
M. W. Pooley	189.4	54	555	17	5-91	32.64
D. J. Adams	127	32	374	11	5-103	34.00
A. M. Smith	94.5	13	308	8	3-32	38.50
C. I. O. Ricketts	219.4	52	624	15	5-70	41.60
M. C. J. Ball	189.2	37	639	15	3-29	42.60
D. J. Thomas	129	25	419	9	2-64	46.55

Also bowled: M. W. Alleyne 47–7–163–2; I. P. Butcher 16–8–27–3; M. A. Challenger 6.1–0–19–0; D. J. Chubbs 108.4–16–382–3; N. C. W. Fenton 13–3–49–0; K. B. K. Ibadulla 32.2–8–114–3; J. L. P. Meadows 16.2–1–61–1; N. J. Pitts 27–5–65–2; O. C. K. Smith 9–1–50–1; R. Williams 17.2–2–83–2.

HAMPSHIRE SECOND ELEVEN

Matches 14: Won – Essex, Gloucestershire, Kent, Sussex. Lost – Middlesex, Surrey. Drawn – Essex, Gloucestershire, Kent, Middlesex, Somerset (twice), Surrey, Sussex.

Batting Averages

	M	*I*	*NO*	*R*	*HI*	*100s*	*Avge*
P. J. Bakker	4	3	2	68	29*	0	68.0
J. Wood	3	5	2	149	62	0	49.6
R. J. Scott	11	20	2	710	147	2	39.4
T. C. Middleton	13	23	4	688	105*	1	36.2
R. M. F. Cox	14	25	2	676	80	0	29.3
N. G. Cowley	2	4	1	79	38*	0	26.3
M. E. O'Connor	14	25	1	628	145	1	26.1
S. J. W. Andrew	4	5	0	126	62	0	25.2
*T. M. Tremlett	9	15	6	220	38	0	24.4
P. Gover	2	3	0	68	48	0	22.6
†A. N. Aymes	14	21	3	406	101	1	22.5
K. D. James	5	8	1	153	76*	0	21.8
A. D. Mullally	13	11	2	138	74	0	15.3
I. J. Turner	13	14	4	137	33*	0	13.7
K. J. Shine	13	11	4	93	22*	0	13.2
S. D. Udal	13	17	3	166	57*	0	11.8

Played in two matches: R. J. Maru 49, 2. Played in one match: S. J. Ball 14*; C. A. Conn[illegible] 15; M. Lane 2; S. D. Lerigo 0*; R. S. Morris 4.

Bowling Averages

	O	M	R	W	BB	Avge
R. J. Scott	173.2	44	430	30	6-53	14.33
K. D. James	130.1	38	403	22	5-45	18.31
T. M. Tremlett	155	57	298	15	3-12	19.86
N. G. Cowley	52.4	14	122	6	4-72	20.33
P. J. Bakker	93.2	29	215	9	3-39	23.88
I. J. Turner	269.1	81	659	18	4-67	36.61
A. D. Mullally	349.5	74	979	26	3-25	37.65
S. D. Udal	235.5	69	609	16	3-47	38.06
K. J. Shine	262.3	52	817	20	5-69	40.85

Also bowled: S. J. W. Andrew 5–1–8–0; S. J. Ball 8–1–28–0; C. A. Connor 15–2–49–2; S. D. Lerigo 19–1–68–0; R. J. Maru 47.2–15–100–5.

KENT SECOND ELEVEN

Matches 16: Won – Essex. Lost – Hampshire, Middlesex (twice), Surrey, Sussex, Yorkshire. Drawn – Essex, Gloucestershire, Hampshire, Lancashire (twice), Somerset, Surrey, Sussex, Yorkshire.

Batting Averages

	M	I	NO	R	HI	Avge
R. F. Pienaar	2	4	1	189	100*	63.00
. G. Hinks	5	8	1	310	95	44.28
A. G. E. Ealham	14	19	12	296	72*	42.28
M. V. Fleming	9	17	3	492	86	35.14
I. Longley	14	25	0	754	143	30.16
P. Farbrace	16	27	1	783	134	30.11
. R. Ward	10	17	1	472	99	29.50
G. R. Cowdrey	3	4	0	115	81	28.75
. P. Igglesden	4	6	2	109	30	27.25
. J. Wells	12	20	1	482	76	25.36
D. J. Sabine	15	26	2	575	80	23.95
M. C. Dobson	14	22	4	388	58	21.55
M. A. Ealham	11	19	2	326	70	19.17
D. J. M. Kelleher	8	13	0	232	46	17.84
. J. Llong	7	11	3	109	27*	13.62
. L. Alleyne	11	17	2	177	43	11.80
. N. Wren	5	6	1	41	20	8.20
M. D. Harman	11	15	3	77	14	6.41

Played in two matches: D. B. M. Fox, 13 runs. Played in one match: R. P. Davis 29; M. Day 3; W. Falla 1. M. V. Patel did not bat.

Bowling Averages

	O	M	R	W	BB	Avge
. F. Pienaar	40.2	10	107	6	3-30	17.83
P. Igglesden	71	17	150	8	2-28	18.75
J. Wells	223.4	60	647	31	5-52	20.87
. D. Harman	332	101	785	36	6-66	21.80
J. M. Kelleher	178.2	55	431	19	5-17	22.68
. L. Alleyne	255.1	51	689	28	6-58	24.60
J. Sabine	235.4	53	770	23	6-49	33.47
. C. Dobson	271.4	80	845	24	5-22	35.20
. V. Fleming	126	27	356	8	3-42	44.50
N. Wren	95.3	13	369	8	5-50	46.12
A. Ealham	92.2	17	307	6	1-10	51.16
J. Llong	96	19	368	6	2-36	61.33

Also bowled: G. R. Cowdrey 28–11–59–2; R. P. Davis 20–6–68–1; D. B. M. Fox 21–4–60–3; S. G. Hinks 14.4–3–43–2; J. I. Longley 3–0–15–0; M. V. Patel 9–4–41–1; T. R. Ward 2–0–11–0.

LANCASHIRE SECOND ELEVEN

Matches 20: Won – Derbyshire (twice), Glamorgan, Northamptonshire, Nottinghamshire, Yorkshire. Lost – Surrey, Worcestershire. Drawn – Glamorgan, Kent (twice), Leicestershire (twice), Northamptonshire, Nottinghamshire, Somerset, Surrey, Warwickshire (twice), Yorkshire.

Batting Averages

	M	*I*	*NO*	*R*	*HI*	*100s*	*Avge*
A. N. Hayhurst	4	6	3	300	102*	1	100.00
M. A. Atherton	5	8	1	363	118	2	51.85
I. D. Austin	15	20	4	756	119*	2	47.25
G. D. Lloyd	20	31	1	1,108	144	4	36.93
S. P. Titchard	16	23	6	584	94	0	34.35
N. J. Speak	20	30	3	889	133	1	32.92
J. Abrahams	14	19	4	482	64*	0	32.13
C. D. Matthews	4	4	1	86	52	0	28.66
T. E. Jesty	4	7	0	197	87	0	28.14
J. D. Fitton	17	20	5	344	111	1	22.93
D. J. Makinson	18	18	3	318	55	0	21.20
G. Yates	12	14	4	195	50*	0	19.50
P. J. Martin	18	14	5	147	57*	0	16.33
M. A. Crawley	4	4	0	60	28	0	15.00
*†J. Stanworth	20	14	2	151	35	0	12.58
A. J. Murphy	17	8	5	35	18	0	11.66
S. Dearden	2	3	0	14	11	0	4.66

Played in four matches: I. Folley 22, 1. Played in one match: G. Fowler 59; P. Heaton 3 R. Irani 0; N. D. Perry 12; D. J. Rayton 2*; A. S. Williams 0.

Bowling Averages

	O	*M*	*R*	*W*	*BB*	*Avge*
I. D. Austin	189.1	66	376	21	4-7	17.9
C. D. Matthews	90	20	288	14	4-46	20.5
P. J. Martin	364	93	949	46	6-40	20.6
J. Abrahams	182.3	47	414	20	6-105	20.7
J. D. Fitton	540.4	153	1,262	55	6-109	22.9
M. A. Atherton	90.3	22	231	10	4-79	23.1
A. N. Hayhurst	54	15	148	6	2-15	24.6
A. J. Murphy	370.4	81	1,143	40	6-61	28.5
I. Folley	109.1	31	243	8	4-91	30.3
D. J. Makinson	221.5	45	701	20	4-81	35.0

Also bowled: M. A. Crawley 4–0–26–0; S. Dearden 14–8–13–2; P. Heaton 27.2–9–35–3 R. Irani 3–0–14–0; G. D. Lloyd 14–0–171–1; D. J. Rayton 14–5–25–2; N. J. Spea 11–0–110–1; G. Yates 47.4–12–162–3.

LEICESTERSHIRE SECOND ELEVEN

Matches 18: Won – Glamorgan. Lost – Northamptonshire, Nottinghamshire, Surrey (twice) Warwickshire (twice). Drawn – Derbyshire (twice), Glamorgan, Lancashire (twice), Middlesex Northamptonshire, Nottinghamshire, Sussex, Worcestershire (twice).

Batting Averages

	I	*NO*	*R*	*HI*	*100s*	*Avge*
T. J. Boon	6	1	257	69	0	51.40
P. N. Hepworth	27	2	935	187	2	37.40
J. D. R. Benson	25	0	773	129	1	30.92
F. Hussein	6	0	124	38	0	20.66
G. Bruk-Jackson	20	0	397	70	0	19.85
B. Smith	22	2	349	96*	0	17.45
†M. Bailey	24	3	332	89	0	15.80
A. Lewin	8	0	119	47	0	14.87
R. A. Cobb	14	1	191	63	0	14.69
G. Codrington	6	0	84	31	0	14.00
W. G. Lovell	13	9	56	17*	0	14.00
M. I. Gidley	19	5	173	45	0	12.35
L. Tennant	21	2	198	40	0	10.42
R. Edmunds	17	5	125	34*	0	10.41
P. M. Such	11	3	73	24	0	9.12
L. B. Taylor	7	1	24	13	0	4.00

Also batted: A. Brown 20 runs; K. Dand 2; P. A. J. DeFreitas 48 runs; E. Essop-Adam 13; G. J. F. Ferris 16 runs; N. Gamble 24 runs; M. A. Garnham 203*, 20; C. Griffiths 37 runs; P. Hemming 3 runs; C. C. Lewis 155 runs; T. M. Moody 2; P. Newton 6 runs; P. Nixon 67 runs; A. Roseberry 46 runs; J. J. Whitaker 99, 77.

Bowling Averages

	O	*M*	*R*	*W*	*BB*	*Avge*
L. B. Taylor	139.3	34	399	19	5-119	21.00
P. A. J. DeFreitas	82	22	184	8	4-56	23.00
P. M. Such	275.4	81	690	24	5-35	28.75
P. Hemming	81	16	321	9	4-115	35.66
M. I. Gidley	229.4	44	648	18	5-90	36.00
L. Tennant	460.1	95	1,442	39	6-56	36.97
G. Codrington	85	9	301	7	2-41	43.00
R. Edmunds	306.4	79	804	18	3-18	44.66
J. D. R. Benson	79	6	338	5	2-63	67.60
W. G. Lovell	175	33	549	6	3-69	91.50

Also bowled: D. C. Boon 3–1–8–0; G. Bruk-Jackson 2–0–26–1; K. Dand 5–0–27–0; G. J. F. Ferris 26–8–47–3; N. Gamble 2–0–20–0; C. Griffiths 24–3–70–0; P. N. Hepworth [illegible]–0–4–1; C. C. Lewis 28–12–55–4; T. M. Moody 14–1–34–1; P. Newton 30–5–131–4.

MIDDLESEX SECOND ELEVEN

Matches 15: Won – Hampshire, Kent (twice), Northamptonshire. Drawn – Essex (twice), Hampshire, Leicestershire, Northamptonshire, Surrey (twice), Sussex (twice), Warwickshire (twice).

Batting Averages

	M	*I*	*NO*	*R*	*HI*	*Avge*
[illegible]. O. Butcher	2	4	1	319	117	106.33
C. T. Radley	9	12	5	478	97*	68.28
M. R. Ramprakash	5	9	2	438	204*	62.57
M. A. Roseberry	11	18	3	909	215*	60.60
[illegible]. R. Brown	2	3	1	105	51*	52.50
[illegible]. Needham	7	10	0	506	146	50.60
[illegible]. C. Pooley	4	7	3	183	65	45.75
[illegible]. J. F. Hutchinson	9	12	2	440	158	44.00

	M	*I*	*NO*	*R*	*HI*	*Avge*
J. F. Sykes	7	10	0	438	127	43.80
T. A. Radford	5	8	2	205	61*	34.16
D. L. Harris	2	3	1	56	37*	28.00
†C. H. H. Pegg	3	4	1	77	27*	25.66
A. G. J. Fraser	11	8	1	163	78	23.28
D. M. Kutner	2	4	1	68	40	22.66
P. N. Weekes	12	17	2	281	66	18.73
N. R. C. MacLaurin	12	19	1	295	51	16.38
P. C. R. Tufnell	7	5	1	55	25*	13.75
†M. W. C. Olley	4	6	1	55	25	11.00
R. P. Gofton	4	5	0	54	19	10.80
P. A. Nixon	4	4	1	28	10	9.33
W. W. Daniel	3	3	1	9	5*	4.50
A. A. Barnett	14	10	3	30	9	4.28

Played in three matches: A. D. Towse 1, 8*, 13*. Played in two matches: S. P. Hughes 10, 9*. Played in one match: J. Allen 32; D. M. Bowen 8, 26; G. A. Buchanan 11; N. D. J. Cartmel 0; A. R. Caddick 0, 0; A. Habib 3; G. T. Headley 8, 63; M. Keech 13; K. R. Morris 0, 0; K. J. Piper 16, 5*; G. M. Pooley 21; M. J. Redhead 6; C. Remy 30*; R. J. Sims 0; W. N. Slack 152*; N. F. Williams 25; G. Winterbourne 7. R. M. Carter, A. R. C. Fraser, J. R. Hemstock and S. D. Welch did not bat.

Bowling Averages

	O	*M*	*R*	*W*	*BB*	*Avge*
A. Needham	85.5	39	143	13	4-34	11.00
P. C. R. Tufnell	236.2	88	465	34	7-66	13.67
S. P. Hughes	62.5	13	153	8	5-64	19.12
A. A. Barnett	449.2	133	1,111	46	5-43	24.15
J. F. Sykes	111.1	29	264	10	2-30	26.40
A. D. Towse	86	20	239	6	2-71	39.83
A. G. J. Fraser	170	20	606	14	4-27	43.28
P. N. Weekes	176	46	471	8	5-84	58.87

Also bowled: K. R. Brown 2–0–12–0; A. R. Caddick 46–14–114–5; R. M. Carte 25–2–97–3; W. W. Daniel 46–6–193–4; A. R. C. Fraser 29–8–77–2; R. P. Gofton 22.5–5–100–5; A. Habib 5–1–12–1; D. L. Harris 16–3–28–2; G. T. Headley 10–1–30–0; J. R. Hemstock 12–0–36–0; I. J. F. Hutchinson 0.5–0–3–1; D. M. Kutner 15–0–61–1; N. R. C. MacLaurin 3–0–12–0; K. R. Morris 10–0–57–0; T. A. Radford 6–0–34–2; M. R. Ramprakash 12–4–27–2; C. Remy 23.4–5–98–5; M. A. Roseberry 10–2–53–0; S. D. Welch 22–5–112–2; N. F. Williams 10–0–20–0; G. Winterbourne 14–1–55–2.

NORTHAMPTONSHIRE SECOND ELEVEN

Matches 17: Won – Essex, Leicestershire, Worcestershire. Lost – Derbyshire, Lancashire Middlesex, Nottinghamshire. Drawn – Derbyshire, Essex, Lancashire, Leicestershire, Middlesex Nottinghamshire, Sussex, Worcestershire, Yorkshire (twice).

Batting Averages

	M	*I*	*NO*	*R*	*HI*	*Avge*
D. J. Wild	3	6	3	190	84	63.3
*R. M. Carter	13	16	7	475	100*	52.7
N. A. Stanley	13	23	3	891	138*	44.5
B. R. Hartland	15	23	1	857	188	38.9
A. Fordham	8	14	0	474	96	33.8
A. Penberthy	17	27	4	703	118	30.5
M. R. Gouldstone	11	20	2	518	103	28.7

	M	*I*	*NO*	*R*	*HI*	*Avge*
†W. Noon	17	26	4	418	60*	19.00
S. J. Brown	12	14	3	207	52	18.81
D. S. Hoffman	12	11	5	107	25	17.83
M. R. Baker	13	18	3	240	48	16.00
G. Smith	9	12	6	94	30*	15.66
B. Debenham	4	7	0	99	42	14.14
A. Roberts	16	22	4	169	23	9.38

Also batted: D. Boden 14*; P. Boxford 17, 6; D. Clarke 17, 1; G. Cook 73; N. G. B. Cook 0*, 4; D. Gormley 1, 50*; C. Mellors 100*, 17, 10, 32*; D. Pollock 11, 20, 50, 5; A. Robinson 13, 2, 0; M. A. Robinson 2*, 2, 0, 8; A. Walker 0, 0; R. G. Williams 18, 6. A. Howarth and R. G. Twose played in one match but did not bat.

Bowling Averages

	O	*M*	*R*	*W*	*Avge*
R. M. Carter	36.3	0	125	7	17.85
M. R. Baker	176.5	44	515	25	20.60
A. Fordham	14	2	90	4	22.50
A. Walker	104.2	29	257	11	23.36
D. S. Hoffman	315.4	71	957	40	23.92
G. Smith	214.2	44	697	25	27.88
M. A. Robinson	145	36	370	10	37.00
A. Penberthy	214.1	42	682	17	40.11
S. J. Brown	316	49	972	24	40.50
A. Roberts	262	67	787	18	43.72

Also bowled: D. Boden 6–0–29–0; N. G. B. Cook 17–7–20–0; B. Debenham 2–0–19–0; M. R. Gouldstone 14–2–100–2; A. Howarth 31.2–8–117–1; C. Mellors 15–5–54–2; N. A. Stanley 16–0–72–0; R. G. Twose 7–0–31–0; D. J. Wild 23–4–97–0.

NOTTINGHAMSHIRE SECOND ELEVEN

Matches 15: Won – Derbyshire (twice), Glamorgan, Leicestershire, Northamptonshire, Sussex. Lost – Essex (twice), Lancashire. Drawn – Lancashire, Leicestershire, Northamptonshire, Warwickshire, Yorkshire (twice). Abandoned – Glamorgan.

Batting Averages

	M	*I*	*NO*	*R*	*HI*	*100s*	*Avge*
D. J. R. Martindale	10	14	5	700	139	2	77.77
D. J. Callaghan	14	21	4	934	127	5	54.94
P. Pollard	12	18	1	690	106	1	40.58
R. J. Evans	13	21	1	783	141	1	39.15
†B. N. French	2	4	0	143	118	1	35.75
M. Saxelby	11	12	1	317	67	0	28.81
K. P. Evans	3	4	2	56	29*	0	28.00
M. Newell	5	8	1	190	55*	0	27.14
C. D. Fraser-Darling	11	17	4	348	101	1	26.76
F. J. Cooke	7	4	3	21	14	0	21.00
J. D. Harding	8	9	4	97	28	0	19.40
G. W. Mike	11	12	2	145	48	0	14.50
C. L. Cairns	13	12	1	159	60	0	14.45
G. R. Sanders	6	9	1	90	40	0	11.25
C. M. Charlesworth	4	5	1	37	18	0	9.25
D. J. Millns	7	4	3	8	7*	0	8.00
M. K. Bore	9	6	2	26	10	0	6.50

Also batted: K. R. Blackburn 8, 4; B. C. Broad 26, 9; D. R. Laing 30 runs; C. T. McKnight *; P. Newell 16, 1; K. Saxelby 11*, 2; C. W. Scott 47 runs; K. D. Standen 4*; C. J. Stockdale 3, 4.

Bowling Averages

	O	*M*	*R*	*W*	*BB*	*Avge*
M. K. Bore	250.3	105	457	22	5-34	20.77
K. P. Evans	112.3	35	257	11	5-49	23.36
G. D. Harding	122.3	28	426	17	6-75	25.05
C. L. Cairns	266	55	852	33	4-75	25.81
C. D. Fraser-Darling	203.3	41	707	27	3-41	26.18
K. Saxelby	55	21	106	4	3-30	26.50
G. W. Mike	132	29	498	17	3-11	29.29
D. J. Millns	156.2	40	474	16	4-41	29.62
D. J. Callaghan	161.3	44	477	16	3-36	29.81
C. T. McKnight	159	49	440	11	2-22	40.00
M. Saxelby	109.2	14	356	6	2-22	59.33

Also bowled: G. M. Charlesworth 11–2–50–2; R. J. Evans 2–1–2–0; D. R. Laing 16–6–39–1; P. Newell 3–0–22–0; P. Pollard 1–0–3–0.

SOMERSET SECOND ELEVEN

Matches 15: Lost – Surrey, Warwickshire, Worcestershire, Yorkshire (twice). Drawn – Glamorgan (twice), Gloucestershire (twice), Hampshire (twice), Kent, Lancashire, Warwickshire, Worcestershire.

Batting Averages

	M	*I*	*NO*	*R*	*HI*	*Avge*
R. J. Bartlett	2	4	2	256	89	128.00
R. J. Harden	5	7	3	252	78	63.00
N. A. Felton	8	14	4	444	87	44.40
M. Douglas	11	17	2	640	152	42.66
J. C. M. Atkinson	6	8	1	282	70	40.28
N. J. Pringle	9	16	4	456	97	38.00
P. A. C. Bail	7	13	1	394	113	32.83
G. Townsend	11	19	0	564	102	29.68
T. J. A. Scriven	9	13	3	234	57	23.40
*†T. Gard	9	11	4	140	33	20.00
R. Baigent	8	14	1	233	64	17.92
M. W. Cleal	7	12	3	156	36	17.33
C. H. Dredge	9	9	4	73	38*	14.60
G. V. Palmer	12	18	2	210	33	13.12
D. J. Foster	3	4	1	34	23	11.33

Also batted: D. Adams 34*, 20; A. Goldsmith 36, 29; J. Hall 15, 4*; A. Keitch 71, 6*; J. Kerslake 31*, 1, 0; C. C. Lovell 42, 4; G. Lovell 2*, 0*; A. R. Phillips 47 runs; K. Piper 21, 13; P. J. Rendall 45 runs; A. Robinson 40, 43; P. J. Robinson 5; P. M. Roebuck 82, 4; B. C. Rose 11, 9; C. Thorne 4, 1; H. R. J. Trump 41 runs; R. G. Twose 4; R. G. Woolston 56 runs; J. G. Wyatt 176 runs.

Bowling Averages

	O	*M*	*R*	*W*	*BB*	*Avge*
P. J. Robinson	22.4	8	56	4	3-43	14.00
R. J. Harden	23	2	82	4	2-27	20.50
C. H. Dredge	319.2	88	781	31	5-26	25.19
D. J. Foster	79	11	276	9	5-43	30.66
T. J. A. Scriven	333.2	76	975	28	3-19	34.82
N. J. Pringle	117	23	359	9	3-53	39.88
M. W. Cleal	204.5	39	605	15	4-32	40.33
R. J. Woolston	177.1	47	558	13	2-31	42.92
G. V. Palmer	311.3	54	1,220	24	3-63	50.83

Also bowled: D. Adams 41–13–100–1; J. C. M. Atkinson 12–2–38–1; R. Baigent 31–9–93–1; J. Brock 33–10–77–1; N. A. Felton 1–0–8–0; J. Hall 20–9–35–2; C. C. Lovell 18–2–66–1; G. Lovell 31–4–109–1; A. R. Phillips 1.2–1–0–1; P. J. Rendall 51.4–9–178–0; P. M. Roebuck 3–0–13–0; P. Smith 17–3–51–1; C. Thorne 9–0–58–0; H. R. J. Trump 44–10–128–2; J. G. Wyatt 1–0–2–0.

SURREY SECOND ELEVEN

Matches 17: Won – Essex, Hampshire, Kent, Lancashire, Leicestershire (twice), Somerset, Sussex. Drawn – Essex, Hampshire, Kent, Lancashire, Middlesex (twice), Sussex, Yorkshire (twice).

Batting Averages

	M	*I*	*NO*	*R*	*HI*	*Avge*
D. J. Bicknell	12	21	3	883	138*	49.05
J. D. Robinson	11	16	2	541	125*	38.64
Zahid Sadiq	16	24	0	808	120	33.66
A. D. Brown	14	21	3	588	82	32.66
G. P. Thorpe	17	25	3	706	123	32.09
A. H. Gray	5	7	2	142	59	28.40
C. S. Mays	5	6	1	132	41*	26.40
*C. K. Bullen	6	9	2	165	83	23.57
J. Boiling	11	9	5	94	42*	23.50
†G. E. Brown	14	13	4	181	48	20.11
N. M. Kendrick	14	17	5	241	43	20.08

Bowling Averages

	O	*M*	*R*	*W*	*Avge*
K. T. Medlycott	36.1	15	63	9	7.00
M. P. Bicknell	69.2	23	133	12	11.08
J. D. Robinson	115	10	336	22	15.27
C. S. Mays	120.5	34	304	19	16.00
A. H. Gray	81.3	19	235	12	19.58
J. Boiling	343.4	117	691	32	21.59
M. Frost	321.4	52	1,095	48	22.81
S. D. Lerigo	69	15	204	8	25.50
N. M. Kendrick	472	153	1,204	45	26.75
N. H. Peters	102.2	24	271	10	27.10
G. P. Thorpe	282.1	70	850	25	34.00

SUSSEX SECOND ELEVEN

Matches 14: Won – Essex, Kent. Lost – Essex, Hampshire, Nottinghamshire, Surrey, Warwickshire. Drawn – Hampshire, Kent, Leicestershire, Middlesex (twice), Northamptonshire, Surrey.

Batting Averages

	M	*I*	*NO*	*R*	*HI*	*100s*	*Avge*
†M. P. Speight	4	8	0	381	114	1	47.62
A. M. Green	2	4	0	185	153	1	46.25
M. W. Pringle	9	13	1	456	104	1	38.00
S. J. S. Kimber	10	17	4	401	110*	1	30.84
N. J. Falkner	7	13	1	365	131	1	30.41
K. Greenfield	13	22	2	562	82	0	28.10
I. W. Hall	14	25	2	589	86	0	25.60
A. R. Clarke	3	4	0	100	48	0	25.00
I. C. Waring	9	13	5	188	49	0	23.50

	M	I	NO	R	HI	100s	Avge
I. Salisbury	2	4	0	90	41	0	22.50
R. I. Alikhan	5	6	0	121	58	0	20.16
P. A. W. Heseltine	10	13	3	172	39*	0	17.20
D. K. Standing	4	5	0	81	65	0	16.20
R. A. Bunting	5	5	3	27	15*	0	13.50
P. V. Boarer	8	12	2	132	36	0	13.20
A. R. Hansford	3	5	1	47	33	0	11.75
†P. Moores	5	7	0	76	28	0	10.85
D. J. Panto	5	8	0	85	35	0	10.62
R. G. Bickell	6	11	1	103	56	0	10.30
P. W. Threlfall	8	12	3	68	16	0	7.55
J. Finch	2	4	0	15	12	0	3.75
R. Learmouth	3	4	0	12	8	0	3.00

Played in one match: A. M. Babington 12; B. Donelan 7, 6; I. Cox 22, 1; C. Gladwin 31, 3; C. Gott 18, 1*; I. J. Gould 27; R. Guttridge 20*, 17*; R. Hanley 9, 0; M. J. Hastwell 1; J. A. Jameson 21, 4*; N. J. Lenham 9; P. Richardson 71, 23; D. Stevens 0, 0; D. Webb 10, 5; C. M. Wells 100, 99.

Bowling Averages

	O	M	R	W	BB	Avge
R. I. Alikhan	24	5	65	4	3-48	16.25
A. M. Babington	50	13	116	7	5-67	16.57
M. W. Pringle	201.3	48	551	31	6-34	17.77
A. R. Hansford	54	17	143	7	4-40	20.42
R. Learmouth	54	16	153	6	4-90	25.50
P. W. Threlfall	149	23	533	20	3-50	26.65
A. R. Clarke	76	20	251	9	4-97	27.88
S. J. S. Kimber	248.2	52	720	24	4-50	30.00
I. Salisbury	37	10	127	4	4-56	31.75
R. A. Bunting	125	17	452	12	3-50	37.66
P. A. W. Heseltine	326.1	90	924	23	5-59	40.17
P. V. Boarer	126.5	15	490	12	2-36	40.83

Also bowled: R. G. Bickell 30–3–152–2; J. Dean 18–8–34–3; B. Donelan 23–6–70–1; A. M. Green 24–1–116–3; R. Guttridge 4–1–7–0; N. J. Lenham 6–0–26–1; D. J. Panto 62–6–222–3; P. Richardson 3–1–7–0; D. K. Standing 10–4–22–0; C. M. Wells 13.5–0–75–2.

WARWICKSHIRE SECOND ELEVEN

Matches 17: Won – Glamorgan, Leicestershire (twice), Somerset, Sussex. Lost – Worcestershire (twice), Yorkshire. Drawn – Gloucestershire (twice), Lancashire (twice), Middlesex (twice), Nottinghamshire, Somerset, Yorkshire. Abandoned – Glamorgan.

Batting Averages

	M	I	NO	R	HI	100s	Avge
A. C. Storie	8	14	3	708	164	2	64.36
T. L. Penney	2	3	1	93	53	0	46.50
†P. C. L. Holloway	3	5	1	184	65*	0	46.00
I. G. Steer	3	4	2	92	46	0	46.00
S. J. Green	13	22	5	660	101	1	38.82
G. D. Hodgson	8	15	2	491	53*	0	37.76
J. D. Ratcliffe	15	28	0	876	157	1	31.28
*†G. A. Tedstone	11	16	2	403	100	1	28.78
†G. W. Humpage	3	5	0	135	104	1	27.00
G. P. Williamson	10	16	5	269	51	0	24.45
S. D. Myles	12	21	5	344	44	0	21.50

	M	*I*	*NO*	*R*	*HI*	*100s*	*Avge*
D. A. Thorne	9	16	3	277	103*	1	21.30
N. M. K. Smith	15	22	2	421	64	0	21.05
J. E. Benjamin	15	12	4	151	25	0	18.87
A. A. Donald	7	8	2	102	24	0	17.00
E. T. Milburn	5	5	2	49	22	0	16.33
R. D. O. Earl	10	6	3	27	12	0	9.00
A. R. K. Pierson	7	8	3	45	16	0	9.00
G. J. Parsons	5	4	0	36	20	0	9.00
R. S. Weir	9	6	3	20	9*	0	6.66
T. A. Munton	4	4	0	11	8	0	2.75

Played in four matches: O. Chagar 23*, 7. Played in one match: D. A. Banks 87; C. E. Eksteen 2; A. J. Moles 3; J. F. M. O'Brien 2; T. Parton 54, 39; †K. J. Piper 51*; D. A. Reeve 64; P. A. Smith 91, 5; R. G. Twose 18*, 10.

Bowling Averages

	O	*M*	*R*	*W*	*BB*	*Avge*
S. J. Green	25	8	68	4	2-6	17.00
A. A. Donald	209.2	53	510	28	5-41	18.21
T. A. Munton	147	52	313	16	5-58	19.56
G. J. Parsons	141.1	51	336	15	5-56	22.40
A. R. K. Pierson	232.2	70	618	27	4-27	22.88
J. E. Benjamin	415.4	101	994	43	5-42	23.11
R. D. O. Earl	282.3	91	721	31	9-70	23.25
R. S. Weir	212.5	44	614	19	4-102	32.31
N. M. K. Smith	258.1	70	733	19	3-33	38.57

Also bowled: D. A. Banks 4–1–17–0; O. Chagar 70–16–228–3; C. E. Eksteen 21–4–62–1; E. T. Milburn 55.1–6–215–2; A. J. Moles 5–2–10–1; S. D. Myles 32.5–7–109–3; J. F. M. O'Brien 34–6–145–2; T. L. Penney 2–0–13–0; J. D. Ratcliffe 1.4–0–13–0; D. A. Reeve 33–12–63–3; P. A. Smith 10–0–33–0; I. G. Steer 21–8–59–0; G. P. Williamson 11.2–2–33–0.

WORCESTERSHIRE SECOND ELEVEN

Matches 15: Won – Derbyshire, Glamorgan, Gloucestershire, Lancashire, Somerset, Warwickshire (twice). Lost – Glamorgan, Northamptonshire. Drawn – Derbyshire, Gloucestershire, Leicestershire (twice), Northamptonshire, Somerset.

Batting Averages

	M	*I*	*NO*	*R*	*HI*	*Avge*
*M. S. Scott	15	10	7	213	64*	71.00
L. P. Vorster	7	9	1	462	101	57.75
D. B. D'Oliveira	8	11	2	484	106*	53.77
D. A. Leatherdale	6	9	2	337	123*	48.14
P. Bent	13	22	2	872	90	43.60
S. R. Lampitt	14	21	3	690	100	38.33
C. M. Tolley	8	10	1	298	75	33.11
M. P. Briers	10	13	5	209	73	26.12
J. P. Wright	14	22	2	451	104*	22.55
†S. R. Bevins	13	11	4	146	55*	20.85
S. M. McEwan	12	14	4	208	29	20.80
R. M. Ellcock	10	8	3	100	29	20.00
R. D. Stemp	13	11	3	113	26*	14.12

Also batted: A. Da Costa 3, 2, 0, 73, 73; G. R. Haynes 1, 2, 0, 21, 26; R. K. Illingworth 1, 1, 0, 17, 17; G. J. Lord 4, 6, 1, 101*, 263; N. H. Podmore 1, 2, 1, 1, 1; A. P. Pridgeon 5, 3, 0, 30, 50; S. J. O'Shaughnessy 2, 2, 1, 152*, 223; M. J. Weston 3, 5, 0, 87, 141; J. R. Wood 1, 1, 0, 25, 25. D. W. Headley did not bat.

Bowling Averages

	O	*M*	*R*	*W*	*Avge*
S. J. O'Shaughnessy	41.1	9	118	7	16.85
A. P. Pridgeon	170.2	48	406	24	16.91
S. M. McEwan	283.4	52	826	34	24.29
S. R. Lampitt	120.2	29	341	13	26.23
R. M. Ellcock	212.1	47	633	23	27.52
M. J. Weston	50.1	13	112	4	28.00
D. B. D'Oliveira	94.5	21	265	9	29.44
P. Bent	55.5	14	165	5	33.00
R. D. Stemp	262.5	54	888	24	37.00
M. P. Briers	164.1	26	679	12	56.58
C. M. Tolley	141	31	460	8	57.50

Also bowled: G. R. Haynes 17–6–57–1; D. W. Headley 17–1–53–3; R. K. Illingworth 25–11–32–2; D. A. Leatherdale 67–10–198–2; G. J. Lord 21–3–85–1; N. Podmore 3–2–2–1; M. S. Scott 5–0–33–1; J. P. Wright 17–3–76–0.

YORKSHIRE SECOND ELEVEN

Matches 16: Won – Kent, Somerset (twice), Warwickshire. Lost – Lancashire. Drawn – Derbyshire (twice), Kent, Lancashire, Northamptonshire (twice), Nottinghamshire (twice), Surrey (twice), Warwickshire.

Batting Averages

	M	*I*	*NO*	*R*	*HI*	*100s*	*Avge*
J. D. Love	3	5	2	290	103*	2	96.66
K. Sharp	5	7	2	400	238*	1	80.00
I. G. Swallow	7	5	1	259	89	0	64.75
A. A. Metcalfe	3	4	1	191	112	1	63.66
†D. L. Bairstow	4	5	1	248	130*	1	62.00
†R. J. Blakey	9	15	4	599	104*	2	54.45
*S. N. Hartley	12	16	2	623	150	2	44.50
S. A. Kellett	16	24	2	916	129	2	41.63
N. G. Nicholson	15	21	3	726	139*	2	40.33
P. Grayson	6	7	0	263	92	0	37.57
M. N. Bowen	3	4	0	150	73	0	37.50
D. Byas	9	15	1	464	84	0	33.14
E. Greenwood	3	4	0	103	70	0	25.75
B. Parker	6	9	1	191	65	0	23.87
S. J. Dennis	9	8	3	108	32	0	21.60
P. J. Berry	15	13	3	190	51	0	19.00
R. J. Robinson	2	4	0	75	64	0	18.75
P. A. Booth	12	12	6	84	14	0	14.00
C. S. Pickles	5	5	0	21	16	0	4.20
P. J. Hartley	4	4	0	13	9	0	3.25
P. N. Anderson	13	8	1	9	4*	0	1.28

Played in three matches: S. D. Fletcher 18, 8*, 0; P. W. Jarvis 32*, 5, 54. Played in two matches: D. Gough 3*, 4*; D. N. Pike 6, 12*. Played in one match: M. Doidge 33; A. D. Towse 0. I. J. Houseman, C. A. Newton and P. E. Robinson did not bat.

Bowling Averages

	O	*M*	*R*	*W*	*BB*	*Avge*
S. D. Fletcher	95	27	247	14	6-42	17.64
I. G. Swallow	104.5	27	277	14	5-27	19.78
P. W. Jarvis	40	8	125	5	2-40	25.00
P. J. Berry	280	68	866	32	5-61	27.06
P. J. Hartley	105.5	14	300	11	5-72	27.27
P. A. Booth	301.4	79	825	29	5-95	28.44
S. J. Dennis	214.1	52	629	20	5-32	31.45
D. Byas	38	6	127	4	2-15	31.75
D. Gough	44.4	8	147	4	3-39	36.75
M. Doidge	52	15	147	4	4-58	36.75
C. S. Pickles	62.5	10	203	5	3-24	40.60
P. N. Anderson	223.5	27	838	17	5-98	49.29

Also bowled: M. N. Bowen 10.5–1–44–1; P. Grayson 29–10–54–1; S. N. Hartley 12–3–32–1; I. J. Houseman 35.4–7–98–3; S. A. Kellett 7–0–46–0; N. G. Nicholson 6–1–26–0; B. Parker 1–0–7–0; R. J. Robinson 15–3–39–0; A. D. Towse 22–6–61–1.

SECOND ELEVEN CHAMPIONS

1959	Gloucestershire	1970	Kent	1981	Hampshire
1960	Northamptonshire	1971	Hampshire	1982	Worcestershire
1961	Kent	1972	Nottinghamshire	1983	Leicestershire
1962	Worcestershire	1973	Essex	1984	Yorkshire
1963	Worcestershire	1974	Middlesex	1985	Nottinghamshire
1964	Lancashire	1975	Surrey	1986	Lancashire
1965	Glamorgan	1976	Kent	1987	Kent / Yorkshire
1966	Surrey	1977	Yorkshire		
1967	Hampshire	1978	Sussex	1988	Surrey
1968	Surrey	1979	Warwickshire		
1969	Kent	1980	Glamorgan		

BAIN CLARKSON TROPHY, 1988

	P	*W*	*L*	*NR*	*Pts*	*Runs/100b*
North Zone						
Yorkshire	10	7	2	1	15	59.65
Lancashire	10	6	3	1	13	63.08
Derbyshire	10	6	4	0	12	55.30
Northamptonshire	10	4	4	2	10	54.06
Nottinghamshire	10	3	7	0	6	56.16
Leicestershire	10	2	8	0	4	50.47
South-West Zone						
Worcestershire	8	6	2	0	12	70.31
Warwickshire	8	4	3	1	9	63.52
Somerset	8	3	4	1	7	66.75
Glamorgan	8	3	4	1	7	55.57
Gloucestershire	8	2	5	1	5	53.28
South-East Zone						
Kent	10	6	1	3	15	74.10
Surrey	10	7	2	1	15	58.16
Middlesex	10	5	5	0	10	65.32
Sussex	10	3	5	2	8	57.74
Hampshire	10	3	6	1	7	58.63
Essex	10	2	7	1	5	58.51

ROUND-ROBIN MATCHES

At Worcester, August 14. Kent won by 46 runs. Kent 251 for seven (M. C. Dobson 117 not out, J. I. Longley 76); Worcestershire 205 (S. R. Lampitt 94).

At Leeds, August 16. Worcestershire won by eight wickets. Yorkshire 157 for nine (S. R. Lampitt three for 36); Worcestershire 158 for two (S. R. Lampitt 67 not out, D. B. D'Oliveira 66 not out).

At Canterbury, August 21. Yorkshire won by eight wickets after achieving a revised target. Kent 93 for seven (P. N. Anderson four for 21); Yorkshire 85 for two (D. Byas 55 not out).

FINAL

YORKSHIRE v KENT

At Leeds, September 5. Yorkshire won by seven wickets. Toss: Yorkshire.
Man of the Match: R. J. Blakey.

Kent

S. G. Hinks c Grayson b Swallow 88
M. C. Dobson st Blakey b Hartley 35
T. R. Ward b Shaw 67
J. I. Longley b Anderson 30
M. V. Fleming lbw b Fletcher 16
V. J. Wells not out 12
D. J. Sabine b Shaw 0
†P. Farbrace b Fletcher 1
D. J. M. Kelleher run out 3
L-b 12, w 4, n-b 2 18

1/111 2/159 3/214 4/241 5/263 6/263 7/264 8/270 (8 wkts, 55 overs) 270

*A. G. E. Ealham and M. D. Harman did not bat.

Bowling: Fletcher 11–2–61–2; Anderson 11–1–69–1; Shaw 10–0–51–2; Booth 11–1–28–0; Swallow 5–0–19–1; Hartley 7–1–30–1.

Yorkshire

S. A. Kellett b Harman 52
D. Byas c Wells b Sabine 91
†R. J. Blakey run out 70
*S. N. Hartley not out 43
N. G. Nicholson not out 10
L-b 7, w 1 8

1/125 2/172 3/261 (3 wkts, 53 overs) 274

I. G. Swallow, P. Grayson, P. A. Booth, C. Shaw, S. D. Fletcher and P. N. Anderson did not bat.

Bowling: Kelleher 10–0–44–0; Wells 10–0–56–0; Harman 11–1–44–1; Fleming 6–2–30–0; Dobson 10–0–62–0; Sabine 6–0–31–1.

Umpires: D. O. Oslear and A. G. T. Whitehead.

WARWICK UNDER-25 COMPETITION, 1988

	P	*W*	*L*	*T*	*NR*	*Pts*
Group A						
Lancashire	3	3	0	0	0	12
Derbyshire	3	2	1	0	0	8
Yorkshire	3	1	2	0	0	4
Nottinghamshire	3	0	3	0	0	0
Group B						
Middlesex	3	2	0	0	1	10
Leicestershire	3	2	1	0	0	8
Essex	3	1	1	0	1	6
Northamptonshire	3	0	3	0	0	0

	P	*W*	*L*	*T*	*NR*	*Pts*
Group C						
Surrey	3	3	0	0	0	12
Kent	3	1	1	1	0	6
Sussex	3	0	1	2	0	4
Hampshire	3	0	2	1	0	2
Group D						
Warwickshire	4	4	0	0	0	16
Glamorgan	4	3	1	0	0	12
Worcestershire	4	2	2	0	0	8
Somerset	4	1	3	0	0	4
Gloucestershire	4	0	4	0	0	0

SEMI-FINALS

At Manchester, August 14. Lancashire won by nine wickets. Middlesex 141 for eight; Lancashire 142 for one (G. D. Lloyd 56 not out, J. D. Fitton 56 not out).

At Coventry and North Warwick CC, August 21. Warwickshire won by six wickets. Surrey 155 for nine (G. P. Thorpe 66 not out); Warwickshire 156 for four (S. J. Green 47, A. C. Storie 43).

FINAL

LANCASHIRE v WARWICKSHIRE

At Birmingham, September 4. Warwickshire won by 5 runs. Toss: Lancashire.

Warwickshire

J. D. Ratcliffe c Speak b Atherton 55
G. D. Hodgson c Crawley b Fitton 48
S. J. Green b Austin 41
D. A. Thorne b Austin 3
S. D. Myles b Austin 18
N. M. K. Smith c Fitton b Austin 4
†P. C. L. Holloway b Austin 1
A. R. K. Pierson not out 4
*T. A. Munton b Austin 7
R. D. O. Earl not out 0
B 1, l-b 16, w 1 18

1/113 2/121 3/135 4/174 5/178 6/186 7/187 8/197 (8 wkts, 40 overs) 199

R. S. Weir did not bat.

Bowling: Martin 6–2–24–0; Bolton 7–0–34–0; Austin 8–0–37–6; Crawley 3–0–17–0; Fitton 8–1–32–1; Atherton 8–1–38–1.

Lancashire

G. D. Lloyd b Munton 4
N. J. Speak b Weir 0
M. A. Atherton b Smith 56
I. D. Austin c and b Earl 20
*J. D. Fitton c Holloway b Munton ... 38
G. Yates b Smith 8
M. A. Crawley run out 23
S. P. Titchard b Pierson 21
P. J. Martin not out 5
G. Bolton not out 1
B 5, l-b 8, w 4, n-b 1 18

1/7 2/7 3/42 4/114 5/138 6/149 7/181 8/192 (8 wkts, 40 overs) 194

†S. Kennedy did not bat.

Bowling: Weir 8–1–25–1; Munton 8–0–39–2; Pierson 8–1–45–1; Earl 8–1–34–1; Smith 8–0–38–2.

Umpires: K. J. Lyons and R. A. White.

UAU CHAMPIONSHIP, 1988

By any standards it was a successful season for the UAU. Their players are now well established in the Combined Universities side and recognition of the high standards being achieved has followed from this. The UAU Championship ended on a high note with an excellent final at the Racecourse Ground, Derby, after another closely contested competition. Furthermore, the season's champions, Swansea, had emerged from the shadows to carry off the Harry McKechnie Trophy in grand style, thereby preventing Durham from winning it three times in a row.

Yet, for much of the season, it had looked as if Durham would once more carry all before them. They qualified with ease in their regional division, had a bye in the fourth round, and then visited Nottingham. Nottingham chose to bat first on a good wicket but made very slow progress, especially against the spin of James Boiling (four for 34), and were all out for 115 after 57 overs. Durham's reply was spearheaded by Martin Speight, whose cavalier 56 not out took them to victory in the nineteenth over. In their quarter-final, Durham travelled to Leeds, where the home side needed all of 60 overs to accumulate 113, with the spinners Graham Harding (five for 40) and Boiling (four for 28) confining Leeds for 45 overs. Again Speight (41 not out) led the way and Durham won comfortably by six wickets.

Now, however, Durham encountered unexpected problems. During a long and demanding cricket week against first-class opposition, they lost their vice-captain, Steve Foster, with a bad eye injury, and their leading bowler, Boiling, with a split and dislocated finger. Speight and Tim O'Gorman were also injured but able to continue. Replacements were hard to find because their successful Second XI players, still in the Junior Championship, were cup-tied and not available for selection. Durham, therefore, drafted Roger Layton, who had not played for the University since 1985, and Bob Hazell, who had never played for the University before. Both acquitted themselves admirably, but at best it was a makeshift arrangement.

These changes seemed to have little impact on Durham in their semi-final at Worksop, for their opponents, East Anglia, were not strong enough to exploit them. Put in to bat, East Anglia made a dismal start, losing their first three wickets with only 4 runs on the board. Benedict Thorne (26) and the captain, John Price (39), slowly re-established East Anglia, but when Thorne was bowled by Layton with the score 54, 27 overs had already elapsed. Layton (four for 52) led the way as East Anglia were bowled out for 135 in the 60th over. Nasser Hussain (35) and O'Gorman (58) began a brisk response by Durham and, as thundery rain threatened to cut the game short, the irrepressible Speight (38 not out) brought matters to a timely close.

The other half of the draw contained Exeter and Loughborough, and it was anticipated that at least one of these would be in contention in the final stages. It was not to be, for this was Swansea's season and they came through powerfully, qualifying for the knockout stages with comfortable victories over UWIST and Cardiff. In the next round they met Bath, for whom this was a new and welcome advance. Led by their successful bowler, Paul Hayward-Surry, they pressed Swansea to within 10 runs and, given more experience, may have won through. Swansea frittered away their early advantage, using only 49 overs to reach 178 all out. Steve James (57), Adrian Dale (38) and Alan Hughes (29) were their leading contributors, while Tim Smith (four for 41) and David Sutton (five for 60) dominated the bowling. Bath responded well and by tea Guy Houghton (44) and Guy Partridge (25) had taken them to a strong position with only two wickets down. After the interval, however, Swansea fielded tightly and, despite a fine unbeaten 47 by Simon Reed, Bath fell victim to the pressure. Julian Francis (five for 49) and Dale (three for 39) steered Swansea into the quarter-finals.

There they met Exeter in a desperately close affair. On a slow wicket, Swansea, batting first, made only 142, with their wicket-keeper, Adrian Tayler, contributing a vital 48. For Exeter their left-arm seamer, Mike Smith, although nursing an injury, took three for 28 and all-rounder Ian Stuart four for 29. At tea, Exeter were halfway to their target with only two wickets down and 35 overs left. After the break they let the match slip away from them, and yet, with one over left, should still have won: they needed only 2 runs with two wickets in hand. Off the first ball, bowled by Francis, Tim Priffti hoisted a catch to Dale at mid-off; off the second, the last pair ran themselves out and let Swansea into the last four.

Swansea's semi-final match with Manchester was played at Repton College. On a good wicket, small ground and fast outfield, Manchester were restricted to 212 for eight in their 60 overs, with Path Rasan carrying his bat for 107. In such helpful surroundings Rasan may have wished he had played a more forceful innings, for the target was well within Swansea's reach. Led by their Glamorgan player, James (73), they made an excellent start and, despite a mid-order collapse, held on to win by four wickets with three overs to spare. They had reached their first final.

FINAL

DURHAM v SWANSEA

At Derby, June 22. Swansea won by 56 runs. Toss: Durham. Hussain put Swansea in to bat on an excellent pitch with a quick outfield in the expectation that his strong batting, which included three first-class players, would cope with the target set. His tactics had not reckoned with the all-round talents of Dale, who had an outstanding day. First, with Swansea 24 in the twelfth over, he joined James in a partnership which added 154. Neither batted with great aggression, but they accumulated patiently and not until James glanced a full toss to Butler at backward square leg was any real chance given. Dale and the left-handed John Williams then put on 46 vigorously, and even when Dale left to a spectacular running catch by Hussain, there seemed little Durham could do to stem the flow of runs. Williams hit two pulled sixes in his unbeaten 40. Chasing 273, Durham found themselves 125 for five in the 30th over. Hussain and O'Gorman never got into their stride, Mark Simmons, a Freshman, was no match for the occasion, and Butler and Mark Boobbyer fell to Dale without scoring. However, Speight, who averaged more than 100 for Durham in the season, was giving another bravura performance, and he hit a six and eleven fours while scoring 84 of 111 runs added during his stay. In attempting to retain the bowling, he bunted a catch off the ubiquitous Dale, who rounded off his considerable contribution by bowling Harding soon after tea. Hazell, a nimble and athletic runner, mistakenly believed that Layton and Eddie Flanders were equally fleet-footed and despatched both of them back to the pavilion before he himself was bowled by the Swansea spinner, Iwan Rees.

Swansea

S. P. James c Butler b Harding	82
N. M. Pritchard c Harding b Flanders	14
A. Dale c Hussain b Layton	110
†A. S. Tayler c Layton b Harding	5
J. D. Williams not out	40
A. D. Hughes c Speight b Boobbyer	9
B 4, l-b 5, w 3	12
1/24 2/178 3/200 4/246 5/272 (5 wkts, 60 overs)	272

*N. B. Morgan, I. L. Rees, R. C. Wood, A. O. Uzor and J. G. Francis did not bat.

Bowling: Boobbyer 15–2–57–1; Flanders 8–2–24–1; Easterbrook 16–0–67–0; Layton 8–0–35–1; Harding 13–2–80–2.

Durham

*N. Hussain c Wood b Uzor	13
T. J. G. O'Gorman c Wood b Uzor	28
M. B. Simmons c and b Rees	12
†M. P. Speight c Wood b Dale	84
P. J. Butler b Dale	0
M. T. Boobbyer c Tayler b Dale	0
G. D. Harding b Dale	31
P. C. Hazell b Rees	29
R. Layton run out	1
E. M. Flanders run out	1
S. Easterbrook not out	0
B 3, l-b 5, w 4, n-b 5	17
1/33 2/51 3/94 4/107 5/125 6/162 7/202 8/214 9/216 (52.3 overs)	216

Bowling: Francis 10–1–36–0; Uzor 9–1–40–2; Dale 17–1–64–4; Rees 16.3–2–68–2.

THE LANCASHIRE LEAGUES, 1988

By CHRIS ASPIN

Damp pitches from July onwards spoiled a season which had promised an unusually rich harvest for batsmen in the Lancashire and the Central Lancashire Leagues. Even so, there was much good cricket, with Australian players in particular excelling with both bat and ball. Geoff Lawson took 86 League and 21 Cup wickets for Haslingden, who retained the Lancashire League championship – their fourth in six years – and reached the final of the Worsley Cup. East Lancashire were runners-up in the League and worthy winners of the Cup final at Blackburn, which was watched by more than 3,000 spectators, who paid a record £1,700 at the gates. Lawson took seven for 39 to hold the home side to 155 for eight, but Haslingden were bowled out for 110 with only Michael Ingham (52) putting up much resistance. His innings earned a £200 collection. Tom Moody, the Western Australian, signed by East Lancashire as a batsman, blossomed as a bowler and ended the season with 80 wickets as well as 780 runs. Rod Tucker, Accrington's professional from New South Wales, topped the averages with 977 runs at 57.47. Other Australians to impress were Peter Taylor (Church), until his recall for Australia's Pakistan tour, and Steve Wundke (Bacup).

Manzoor Elahi, the Pakistan Test player, made 833 runs and took 52 wickets for Lowerhouse, who re-signed him for 1989, and there were also consistently good performances from the South African, David Norman (Rawtenstall), and Bernard Reidy. The outstanding bowling performance was by Anton Ferreira, the former Warwickshire player, who took all ten Accrington wickets for 45. All the batsmen were caught, eight by the wicket-keeper, Michael Bradley, who created a League record.

Craig Smith, with 847 runs at 40.33, broke the amateur batting record at Rishton. His nearest rivals were David Usher (Bacup) with 752 (34.18), Paul Garaghty (Nelson) with 717 (35.85), and Steve Ashworth (Ramsbottom) with 695 (31.59). Three amateurs took 50 or more wickets: Colin Kuhn (Rishton) 55 at 19.41, Keith Roscoe (Rawtenstall) 54 at 19.17, and Trevor Jones (Burnley) 50 at 19.80. Pat Calderbank (Nelson) qualified for a League award when he took his 1,000th wicket after 23 years. He finished the season with 44 at 18.00.

Rishton made history by engaging fourteen different professionals. The Indian batsman, Mohammad Azharuddin, was injured in the fourth match and withdrew from his contract. There followed a succession of substitutes, including Salim Malik, who was recalled for Test duty, and Dennis Lillee, who had none for 86 in his one appearance.

June 18 will long be remembered in the Central Lancashire League. At Werneth, Rochdale amassed a record 326 for four, with professional Mike Veletta (150) and Nigel Hunter (122) adding 215 for the third wicket. Werneth replied with 306 for nine, Les Reifer, their West Indian professional, hitting 130. Never before had two sides topped 300 in the same game. The seven matches that day produced six individual centuries and a total of 3,109 runs at the remarkable average of 33.40 for each of the 93 wickets which fell. Middleton, for whom the West Indian, Kelvin Williams, was professional, won the CLL championship by seven points from the 1987 winners, Norden. The Norden professional, Manoj Prabhakar, and Ezra Moseley, of Littleborough, both completed the double of 1,000 runs and 100 wickets. Good all-round performances came from Jenson Joseph (Heywood), Aaron Daley

(Walsden), Collis King (Oldham) and Chetan Sharma (Milnrow). Veletta might have set new records had he not been recalled for Australia's tour to Pakistan; in 21 innings he scored 1,233 runs at 72.52, easily topping the averages.

Gavin Brown, an Australian who played as an amateur for Oldham, scored 1,015 runs (44.13). Tim Orrell (Werneth) made 877 (39.86), Russell Davies (Norden) 774 (40.73), and Andrew Walsh (Walsden) 756 (32.86). For once, the bowling averages were headed by an amateur, Tony Pickersgill, of Royton, whose 87 wickets cost 11.39 each. He also had the season's best return – nine for 59 against Heywood – and twice took eight wickets in an innings. Francis Daly (Radcliffe) took 61 wickets at 18.83 and Barry Holmes (Middleton) 60 at 13.31. Crompton regularly fielded six players over the age of 40 and in Cec Wright, who was 55, had surely the oldest professional in a senior league. He took 67 wickets and bowled a maximum 24 overs on eight occasions.

Oldham won the Lees Wood Cup, restricting Littleborough to 147 for seven and passing this with only one wicket down.

MATTHEW BROWN LANCASHIRE LEAGUE

	P	*W*	*L*	*D*	*Pts*	*Professional*	*Runs*	*Avge*	*Wkts*	*Avge*
Haslingden	26	16	6	4	78	G. F. Lawson	431	21.55	86	11.82
East Lancashire	26	14	6	6	72	T. M. Moody	780	43.33	80	13.68
Rishton	26	14	8	3	69*	†				
Rawtenstall	26	13	9	4	62	D. Norman	800	53.33	59	19.39
Church	26	12	10	4	57	P. L. Taylor	559	43.00	56	12.54
Ramsbottom	26	11	12	3	54	Ijaz Faqih	426	28.40	28	21.89
Lowerhouse	26	11	11	4	52	Manzoor Elahi	833	55.53	52	17.77
Bacup	26	10	10	5	50*	S. C. Wundke	784	37.33	61	17.85
Accrington	26	10	13	3	49	R. J. Tucker	977	57.47	58	22.44
Burnley	26	10	12	4	47	Mudassar Nazar	821	48.28	38	20.50
Nelson	26	9	13	4	46	A. M. Ferreira	439	23.10	62	17.40
Todmorden	26	8	12	6	42	S. R. Greaves	847	44.57	43	23.90
Enfield	26	7	13	6	39	B. W. Reidy	700	38.88	65	17.21
Colne	26	6	16	4	30	W. T. Greenidge	94	6.71	55	22.85

* *Includes two points for one tied match.*
† *Rishton called on fourteen professionals.*
Note: One point awarded for dismissing the opposition.

BROTHER CENTRAL LANCASHIRE LEAGUE

	P	*W*	*L*	*D*	*Pts*	*Professional*	*Runs*	*Avge*	*Wkts*	*Avge*
Middleton	28	18	2	7	89*	K. C. Williams	877	41.76	73	12.78
Norden	28	16	5	7	82	M. Prabhakar	1,159	57.95	102	12.34
Milnrow	28	14	6	8	74	Chetan Sharma	725	48.33	51	19.76
Littleborough	28	14	7	7	69	E. A. Moseley	1,114	55.70	111	12.27
Rochdale	28	12	9	7	63	M. R. J. Veletta	1,233	72.52	10	28.80
Oldham	28	12	8	8	61	C. L. King	766	38.30	55	20.61
Royton	28	11	10	7	59	M. E. Welwyn	630	23.33	33	20.94
Crompton	28	10	12	6	52	C. Wright	172	9.56	67	21.38
Werneth	28	10	11	7	50	E. L. Reifer	480	40.00	24	26.46
						G. Yates	402	36.55	18	20.67
Heywood	28	8	11	8	45*	J. Joseph	765	33.26	82	14.37
Stockport	28	7	14	6	43*	R. Berry	884	32.74	33	15.54
Walsden	28	8	14	6	43	A. G. Daley	864	39.27	73	18.79
Radcliffe	28	7	14	7	40	M. R. Chadwick	868	41.33	37	22.64
Hyde	28	5	17	6	30	M. J. R. Rindel	754	31.41	15	33.40
Ashton	28	4	16	7	24*	R. Patel	566	29.78	46	19.98

* *Includes two points for a tied match.*
Note: Five points awarded for an outright win; three for a limited win.

IRISH CRICKET IN 1988

By DEREK SCOTT

Ireland reduced their matches from ten in 1987 to six; three three-day matches against their usual annual opponents and three limited-overs matches against professional county sides. Although the weather was generally wet once again, the international programme escaped almost unscathed. If anything, Ireland could have done with more rain in the Scotland fixture at Dumfries, where the centenary match was lost by an innings, reversing the result of 1888.

The team was rarely at full strength in the latter part of the season and suffered from the retirement of S. C. Corlett. A period of transition was beginning; four new players appeared during the season, in stark contrast to 1987 when there were none. One of the four, R. A. McCollum, a batsman, came and went after the three matches against the county teams, a good example of unluckily coming in at the wrong time. The other three were quick bowlers; A. N. Nelson, N. E. Thompson and P. Wallace. Nelson was a find. He is tall and bowls straight and his fourteen wickets in the six games (average 24.64) topped the wickets' list. Thompson proved to be a useful all-rounder who did better with bat than ball, while Wallace came in as a replacement against Scotland to become the first capped player from St Johnston, a team in Co. Donegal. G. D. Harrison, who took twelve wickets with his off-spin, had the best average (21.66), and in general the bowling improved if average runs per wicket is the guideline.

Although the batting collapsed badly against Scotland, seven players averaged 20 or more. M. F. Cohen had four fifties (three in a row) and amassed 344 runs (average 38.22), while Harrison, in fine all-round form, scored 277 runs (average 30.77) and reached 1,000 runs for Ireland, the 25th player to do so. Warke batted steadily, and Lewis and Vincent reached 50 in an innings for the first time. The wicket-keeping of P. B. Jackson, the team's captain, was, as usual, of a high standard and he had eleven victims in five matches.

Downpatrick was at its best for the first visit there of MCC for the 74th match in a series dating back to 1858. The pitch was excellent and the sun shone for three days. Ireland wasted winning the toss by collapsing for 138, only three batsmen reaching double figures. By the close, MCC were 126 for two, but next day four Irish bowlers shared the wickets and MCC's lead was restricted to 79. Warke and Cohen put up 103 for Ireland's first wicket, with Cohen scoring his second fifty of the match, and Masood hit a marvellous 57. Ireland declared after lunch on the third day, setting MCC 267 to win in 139 minutes plus twenty overs, but although A. J. T. Miller scored 94, the visitors probably went too slowly for too long. A target of 132 from the last twenty overs, even with eight wickets in hand, proved too difficult. With the Irish spinners, Halliday and Harrison, taking four wickets in the last fourteen overs, MCC were 206 for seven at the close. When P. J. Bakker, representing MCC, was recalled by Hampshire for a Sunday League match, Ireland gave permission for MCC's twelfth man to take over.

Bristol had a sunny day for the NatWest Bank Trophy match against Gloucestershire. Ireland, electing to bat, developed a good position as Cohen (66) put on 54 with Masood for the second wicket and 80 with D. A. Lewis for the fourth. With thirteen overs to go Ireland were 142 for three but, not helped by two run-outs, they collapsed to 186 all out. Gloucestershire, led by a Stovold century, scored the runs with ease.

The Worcestershire matches in late June had a touch of the curate's egg about them. The county brought all their available stars but the pitch at Beechgrove, Derry, staging its first international for seventeen years, did not measure up to the calibre of the players. The spinners dominated, even though each side held them back too long. The result was that after O'Shaughnessy and Lord put on 91 for their first wicket, Worcestershire were all out for 200 (Halliday four for 57, Masood three for 30). For Ireland, Warke and Cohen managed 56 together before Illingworth took five for 40 in a total of 152. The pitch was better the next day at Malahide, Dublin, and O'Shaughnessy, Hick and Newport all made fifties in 286 for eight. Harrison's fine 76 gave respectability to Ireland's 171 for nine. These one-day limited-overs exhibition matches pose a problem. The visitors ought to bat first to put on a batting display, but the Irish innings can be boring and sometimes farcical if Ireland cannot match the professionals' run-rate and expertise.

The 1988 entry of Wales into the Minor Counties Championship showed favourably in the three-day match on the excellent Clontarf pitch in mid-July. As Wales played with more purpose and *élan* than hitherto in this series, 1,032 runs were scored in a match which finished with the last Welsh pair playing out the last eight balls. They were within 49 runs of victory, having made a gallant effort to score 282 in 170 minutes plus twenty overs. Ireland declared twice. First-innings runs came from Warke (83), Cohen (75) and Lewis (53 not out), his first half-century for Ireland. He added another in the second innings, when D. A. Vincent (52 not out) also got a first half-century. For Wales D. A. Francis had a splendid double of 85 and 69. A. C. Puddle joined him in a stand of 119 for the fifth wicket to save the Welsh first innings, while Elward and Ellis had 88 up in 80 minutes for the first wicket in the second innings.

The Scottish match is best left to mentions elsewhere. Dumfries was a new venue and a lovely little town which the Irish won't mind if they never see again! Suffice it to say, Ireland were outplayed in all facets of the game. To make matters worse, they presented a cup to mark the centenary, sent their hosts in, and left the new trophy in Scotland.

The Interprovincial Championship gained a new sponsor in its 23rd year when the Ulster Bank stepped in to fill a void. South Leinster won it for the third time and were unbeaten in their five matches; indeed they have lost only twice in the last five seasons, both times to their Dublin rivals, North Leinster. South Leinster's Under-19 team emulated their seniors by winning the similar interprovincial competition at this age-level. The Under-15 festival, staged in the north-west, saw the Northern Union emerge from the four competing teams as winners.

The seventh year of the National Schweppes Cup brought a second win by Lurgan, the first team to achieve this. Graham Hunter, son of W.R. of cricket and rugby fame, scored a brilliant century against North Down to win the match and the Man of the Match Award. In the North and North-West, doubles were achieved by Waringstown and Donemana respectively. The former won the John Player Cup for the fifteenth time in 24 years and the Lombard & Ulster Bank League for the fourteenth time in the same period. Although it was Waringstown's first double since 1979, in only three years of the last 24 have they failed to win one of the competitions. Donemana won their fourth successive League title in the North-West and threw in the Cup for good measure. It is interesting that neither Waringstown nor Donemana engages a professional player, of whom there are many in the two northern unions.

In Leinster (Dublin) the three titles were shared. Carlisle won the Belvedere Bond League, their first senior title of any sort; Clontarf won the Wiggins Teape League, a 50-overs competition played in August; and the Sportsgear Cup went to YMCA, who thus achieved a hat-trick of wins in this competition. In Munster, Limerick brought off a Cup-League double, probably the first time this has happened.

SCOTTISH CRICKET IN 1988

By WATSON BLAIR

Apart from the glorious month of June, adverse weather played havoc with cricket throughout Scotland. July and August were particularly dismal, with countless abandonments prevailing; with both overhead and under-foot conditions appalling, weeks sometimes passed without a ball being bowled. Not even the acquisition of Clive Rice for the national limited-overs competitions could do much to lighten the gloom, although the Scottish Cricket Union is confident that his inspiring leadership, coupled with his excellent coaching, will pay dividends in 1989. Certainly the SCU needs a fillip in 1989, for last season produced a record loss of £14,937, following a loss of £8,208 in 1987.

With the group matches of the Benson and Hedges Cup coming so soon in the season, few of Scotland's players had an opportunity for much match practice. The squad, as in previous years, played two limited-overs matches at Worcester in mid-April which the full-strength county side won comfortably on fast, bouncy pitches. Two further warm-ups, with Rice in action for the first, were played in dismal weather at Stenhousemuir. Then came the campaign serious. Derbyshire won the opening match, at Hamilton Crescent, Glasgow, by seven wickets, but two points were obtained when Leicestershire made a fruitless trip to Titwood, Glasgow. This was the second time in the competition that Scotland and Leicestershire had shared the points because of rain. Scores of more than 300 by Warwickshire at Edgbaston and Lancashire at Old Trafford proved too much for the Scots, who sustained defeats by 123 and 154 runs respectively. Half-centuries by Ian Philip and Rice at Birmingham and a sterling not out 60 from Richard Swan at Manchester were the Scottish highlights.

The NatWest Bank Trophy match was similarly disappointing. Myreside, Edinburgh, attracted a large attendance, and the overhead conditions were ideal. Unfortunately the pitch, slow, soft and damp, was well below par and came in for a lot of criticism. Glamorgan struggled, but with crucial chances behind the wicket being missed, they managed to reach 179. Rice's allotted spell produced four wickets for 29 runs, while Clarence Parfitt, one of the season's new caps, troubled the county batsmen with his accurate slow bowling. However, Ravi Shastri, with a Glamorgan NatWest/Gillette record of five for 13, sent the Scots stumbling to 94.

In the five national one-day matches, no Scotland batsman achieved 100 runs. Rice's three innings realised 94 runs, and Swan's four, one of them not out, accumulated 83 runs. The leading wicket-taker was also Rice, with seven for 177 runs.

The MCC match at Lord's in July was ruined by rain. But it was a quite different story the following month when the centenary match between Scotland and Ireland, at Nunholm, Dumfries, resulted in a home victory by an innings and 43 runs. Scotland's batting was of the highest order. Bruce Patterson scored exactly 100 on his first-class début, and Gordon McGurk, another new cap, David Haggo and Mike Smith all batted well to set the Irish a formidable task. Scotland's bowling was spearheaded by Jim Govan, whose nine wickets in Ireland's two innings were mainly responsible for the modest response. It was also good to see Willie Morton, formerly of Warwickshire, back in action for his native country. Scotland became the first winners of the new trophy, presented by the Irish Cricket Union, for annual competition between the two countries.

Three Scotland B matches were played, all away from home, against Durham University and the Second XIs of Lancashire and Leicestershire. That against Leicestershire was spoilt by rain, while the other two were lost. Originally these three fixtures were scheduled as two-day matches, but they were rearranged as limited-overs games, at which the university side and the counties were more experienced. At under-19 level, the Scottish Young Cricketers drew a rain-affected three-day match with the Welsh Schools and later achieved a creditable draw, over two days, against the English Schools at Edgbaston. Keith Sheridan and Craig McKnight, both of Poloc, with match figures of ten for 90 and five for 118 and the support of superb fielding, restricted the opposition to under 200 in both innings. In the corresponding matches at under-16, Scotland beat the Welsh Schools at Glasgow and came close to repeating that success against the English Schools at Edgbaston. Set to score 270 to win, the English boys were forced on to the defensive and finished with 223 for eight.

On the domestic front, the new Municipal General Insurance Area Championship saw Edinburgh pip Strathclyde West and Strathclyde East by virtue of a better striking-rate to emerge as Scotland's representatives in the NCA County Associations Championship. Victories over Yorkshire CA and Lancashire CA took them into the final, where at Canterbury they went down to Kent CA by 62 runs. Ironically, in a play-off for the MGI Trophy, Edinburgh were beaten by Strathclyde West. The Jean and Henry Thow Rosebowl for the Under-23 Championship was again won by North District, their third success in four years.

Clydesdale Bank became the fourth sponsors of the Scottish Cup. The league sections were completed before the really bad weather set in, but the knockout stages were seriously hit. After two attempts to play the final at Hamilton Crescent, the match was moved to Lochside Park, Forfar. Three days before the third attempt, a thunderstorm turned a firm pitch into an extremely difficult one and the more experienced Clydesdale beat Aberdeen GSFP to not only retain the trophy but record their third success in four years and their sixth in all. The 1989 Scottish Cup will consist of 32 clubs, playing in eight sections, with the section winners qualifying for the quarter-finals.

Lochside Park was also the venue for the W. M. Mann & Co (Investments) Ltd Small Clubs final, in which Dyce defeated Crieff with two wickets and an over to spare. The pre-season Indoor Sixes, sponsored by Maclays of

Alloa, were won by Watsonians, who triumphed over Aberdeenshire, the holders, in an exciting final at Meadowbank Stadium, Edinburgh. For the first time in twenty years West of Scotland won the D. M. Hall & Son Western Union Championship, while on the other side of the country Carlton, in their 125th year, carried off the Ryden & Partners East League for the first time. Carlton completed the double by winning the Masterton Trophy. The Stoddard Carpets Scottish Counties Championship was retained by Aberdeenshire, while the Challenge Cup in the same league, and sponsored by the same company, was won by Ayrshire for the first time.

The Famous Grouse Awards for the Team of the Month went to Woodham (May), Penicuik (June), Clydesdale (July) and Carlton (August). The last-named were also recipients of the Team of the Year award. New awards to the year's batsman, bowler, all-rounder and wicket-keeper were won respectively by Bruce Patterson (Ayr), George Innes (Carlton), Jim Govan (Carlton) and David Haggo (Ayrshire).

The winners of the other league and cup competitions were – *Edinburgh Woollen Mill Border League:* Kelso, for the fifth successive year. *Border League Cup:* Kelso, for the third successive year. *Strathmore Union:* Arbroath United, for the fourth time in five years. *Three Counties Cup:* Brechin. *Two Counties Cup:* Lowside, for the first time. *Abbey Life Glasgow and District League:* Irvine, for the third successive year. *Glasgow Evening Cricket Association:* Queen's Park. *Glasgow and District Knockout Cup:* Glasgow HSFP/KA. *Macallan North of Scotland League:* Huntly. *North of Scotland Senior Knockout Cup:* Northern Counties. *Intersport Forth Cricket Union:* Stirling County (Williamfield XI). *3D Sports Perthshire Cricket League:* Mayfield. *Shetland CA Outdoor League:* Knab. *West League Cup:* Ayr. *Rowan Charity Cup:* Clydesdale. *National Club Championship* (Scottish Region): Clydesdale. *Western Cup:* Greenock. *Sealink South-West League:* Stranraer. *Edinburgh Parks Trophy:* Corstorphine. *Scottish New Towns Development Corporations Trophy:* Glenrothes. *Strathclyde Cricket League:* Clydesdale.

At the Annual General Meeting of the Scottish Cricket Union at Glasgow in mid-December 1988, Neil Bowman, a former Forfarshire player, was elected president of the Union. He is the third representative from the county to occupy the presidency. To cope with the deficits of 1987 and 1988, the SCU has been forced to reduce its very successful senior weekend coaching courses, increase club membership fees, reduce the number of Scotland B fixtures and restrict warm-up and other representative matches. An appeal for an increase in honorary membership and other sponsorship, both direct and indirect, was made by the president and the treasurer.

ESSO/NAYC UNDER-19 COUNTY FESTIVAL, 1988

By JOHN MINSHULL-FOGG

Warwickshire beat Surrey by 7 runs at the Christ Church College ground, Oxford, to become champions of the third Esso/National Association of Young Cricketers Under-19 Festival, in which 30 counties participated. From August 8 to 13, they played at venues at Oxford and Cambridge in a series of round-robin matches before the winners of each section met in the final. Surrey won the Cambridge section and Warwickshire the Oxford one. In the region finals, Surrey (236 for six) beat Essex (235 for eight) by four wickets, and Warwickshire (94 for five) beat Hampshire (93) by five wickets.

The competition, won by Lancashire in 1986 and Yorkshire in 1987, fills a vital gap in the young cricketer's progression from school and club to county standards. Its lack of reliance on the artificial playing conditions of limited-overs cricket is praiseworthy. Each match is of 54 overs a side, but there is neither limit to the number of overs one bowler is allowed nor restriction on field placings. This gives young captains an excellent training in the many aspects of the game and allows the spinners to bowl to the field-settings which suit their methods. It has value, too, in making batsmen appreciate the skills of run-making to different types of fields, especially the need for the quickly taken first run. In fact, the games are played as cricket was not so many years ago.

It is hoped that in 1989, the fourth year of sponsorship by Esso Youth Sport, the number of competing counties will be increased to 32 to allow 16 at each university centre. Possibly there will also be some changes to the format. In its recent form, twelve points have been awarded for a win, with bowling bonus points earned for the number of wickets taken. There have not been batting bonus points.

FINAL

SURREY v WARWICKSHIRE

At Christ Church College, Oxford, August 13. Warwickshire won by 7 runs. Toss: Surrey. Put in on a damp pitch and slow outfield, Warwickshire did not find runs easy to come by. Only a partnership of 48 for the sixth wicket between Steer and Waqar Mohamed gave the innings any real substance. Cowell, the Surrey slow left-armer, found the conditions more to his liking and was the pick of the bowlers. Apart from MacMillan, who scored 82 of 139 before being eighth out, the Surrey batting was undistinguished, and with their last pair at the wicket, they required 8 to win from the last over. Off the first ball, Cowell, backing up, was sent back by Hollioake and Chagar, the bowler, ball in hand, beat him in the race to the non-striker's end.

Warwickshire

Wasim Khan c and b Watkinson	2
Shahid Mubarik c Hodgson b Cowell	20
A. Hunt b Watkinson	0
*G. P. Williamson c Wight b Watkinson	13
I. G. Steer c Lewis b Cowell	48
D. Ostler c Smith b Cowell	7
Waqar Mohamed run out	24
O. Chagar c MacMillan b Wight	14
†W. K. Badger run out	21
Parvaz Mirza c Hodgson b Hollioake	4
A. Stevenson not out	0
L-b 5, w 2, n-b 2	9
1/6 2/6 3/30 4/44 5/58 6/106 7/130 8/144 9/157 (54 overs)	162

Bowling: Watkinson 12–1–55–3; Hollioake 7–1–21–1; Wight 20–8–38–1; Cowell 15–3–43–3.

Surrey

G. I. MacMillan lbw b Steer	82	S. Watkinson c Badger b Chagar	0
M. Wight c Williamson b Chagar	7	C. Cowell run out	8
†J. Hodgson c Ostler b Stevenson	17	A. Hollioake not out	5
*A. Smith b Stevenson	8	L-b 6, w 3	9
R. Kahloon run out	14		—
D. Lewis b Stevenson	0	1/27 2/58 3/69 4/114 (53.1 overs)	155
A. Armstrong lbw b Steer	0	5/126 6/127 7/138	
J. Cox c Chagar b Stevenson	5	8/139 9/149	

Bowling: Chagar 20.1–4–43–2; Mirza 3–0–10–0; Stevenson 22–3–65–4; Waqar Mohamed 3–0–14–0; Steer 5–0–17–2.

Umpires: M. Johnson and J. Weston.

I ZINGARI RESULTS, 1988

Matches – 25: Won 9, Lost 1, Drawn 13, Abandoned 2.

April 23	Charterhouse	Lost by eight wickets
May 7	Honourable Artillery Company	Won by six wickets
May 8	Sandhurst Wanderers	Drawn
May 15	Staff College	Won by 161 runs
May 21	Eton Ramblers	Drawn
May 21	Winchester College	Won by 42 runs
May 28	Eton College	Drawn
June 2	Harrow School	Drawn
June 4	Hurlingham CC	Abandoned
June 5	Earl of Carnarvon's XI	Won by four wickets
June 18	Guards CC	Won by 78 runs
June 26	Lavinia, Duchess of Norfolk's XI	Won by eight wickets
July 2	IZ of Australia	Drawn
July 3	Hagley CC	Abandoned
July 9	Green Jackets Club	Drawn
July 9	Bradfield Waifs	Drawn
July 10	Rickling Green CC	Won by eight wickets
July 16	Leicester Gentlemen	Drawn
July 17	Sir John Starkey's XI	Drawn
July 24	Royal Armoured Corps	Drawn
July 30	Band of Brothers	Won by 45 runs
July 31	R. Leigh-Pemberton's XI	Drawn
August 13, 14	South Wales Hunts XI	Drawn
August 20	Hampshire Hogs	Won by seven wickets
September 4	Captain R. H. Hawkins' XI	Drawn

SCHOOLS CRICKET IN 1988

Eight of the players selected for the English Schools Under-19 side in 1987 were available again in 1988, owing to younger players having been selected in place of those involved in the 1987 International Youth Tournament in Ireland. Of the internationals, only that against Irish Schools resulted in an outright win, although those against Welsh Schools and Scottish CU Colts might well have been won had the middle-order batting been positive enough to allow earlier declarations.

Including the two matches at Lord's, played under the appellation of MCC Schools, sixteen players appeared for the senior Schools side. They were: N. V. Knight (*captain*), M. C. J. Ball, N. A. Derbyshire, B. C. A. Ellison, D. A. Graham, N. J. Gregory, A. Habib, D. W. Headley, I. J. Houseman, M. C. Ilott, M. J. Kellaway, J. J. Lewis, M. Patel, P. J. Rendall, N. Shahid and R. W. Sladdin. Their schools may be found in the scorecards of matches played at the MCC Festival, Oxford. Players eligible for the Under-17 matches against the Sri Lankan Schools were not considered for the games against Irish Schools and Scottish CU Colts.

The strength of the team lay in its top-order batsmen and spin bowlers, with a major factor in its success being the captaincy of Knight, the winner of the Gray-Nicolls Trophy, who was quietly efficient and astute in his bowling changes. He was also in fine form with the bat, scoring 369 runs in eight innings, and with his opening partner, Lewis, he always provided a positive start. If not quite reaching the heights of the previous season, Graham gave sound support, while Habib showed much flair and promise for the future. Shahid's best batting form eluded him, but his leg-spin always commanded respect and brought him seventeen wickets. He shared the majority of the 66 wickets taken with Ball, the off-spinner, who was the leading wicket-taker with nineteen, bowling an excellent line either over or round the wicket. Another thirteen were shared between two slow left-armers, Sladdin and Patel, although the latter played in only one match, owing to a school tour. With the efficient Kellaway setting an example behind the stumps, the catching and ground fielding were good.

A feature of the year was the number of schools players who appeared in first-class cricket. M. R. Ramprakash, although still eligible, was not considered for English Schools in view of his commitments with Middlesex. Ball played for Gloucestershire, P. C. L. Holloway, who was withdrawn from the MCC Schools Festival to stand by for Warwickshire, later played for the county, and Ilott was released from the games against Irish Schools and Scottish CU Colts to make his Championship début for Essex.

Against Welsh Schools at Usk on July 24, 25, English Schools won the toss and elected to bat, as they did in all three home internationals. Well placed at 162 for four, they finally scored only 191 for eight from their 60 overs, the middle order having failed to build on their good start. The Welsh captain, R. D. B. Croft, bowled his off-spin intelligently to take six for 63. In reply, Welsh Schools managed 167 for six, thanks mainly to an innings of 67 from D. L. Hemp. The spinners, Shahid, Ball and Patel, bowled 48 of the 60 overs. England's second innings followed a similar pattern to the first; from 160 for three the required acceleration did not materialise, the declaration was delayed, and Welsh Schools were eventually set 226 in 100 minutes and twenty overs. They lost Hemp for 38, Patel took four wickets in four overs, and the tenth-wicket pair had to survive the last five balls to save the match at 101 for nine. Patel finished with four for 13 and Ball three for 17.

The side then went to Dublin for the first time in four years to play Irish Schools at Leinster CC on August 2, 3. Lewis (40), Knight (73) and Graham (48) again gave the innings substance, taking them towards 235 for five in 55 overs. When Irish Schools replied, Headley took the first two wickets, but the brunt of the bowling was borne by Shahid (four for 46) and Ball. At 129 for nine, Irish Schools were in danger of being asked to follow on, but after five tense overs this was averted and they were dismissed for 155. Led by Knight's 72, English Schools declared after 28 overs at 153 for three, a lead of 233. Following a hostile opening spell from Houseman (three for 32), Irish Schools again lost wickets to Shahid (three for 15) and Ball. Despite a brave 55 in 174 minutes from Dunn, the home side could manage only 104, leaving English Schools winners by 129 runs.

The final game, against Scottish CU Colts, was played at Edgbaston on August 4, 5. Knight (54) and Lewis (36) put on 111 for the first wicket, but apart from Shahid (46) the others made little of the slow left-arm duo of McKnight (two for 48) and Sheridan (five for 49). In reply to England's 197 for nine in 60 overs, the Scottish batsmen fared little better against the slow left-arm bowling of Sladdin (five for 23) and were dismissed for 149 in 59.1 overs. After an opening partnership of 78, Knight 35, Lewis 61, English Schools struggled to 172 for eight before declaring, again unable to cope with Sheridan (five for 41) and McKnight (three for 70). Set 221 to win, Scottish CU Colts were given an ideal start of 95 for the first wicket, but as wickets fell to Headley and Ball (four for 14), they settled for a draw at 141 for eight.

The first tour of England by an Under-17 Schools team saw Sri Lanka play two-day games against two different ESCA XIs, three one-day games and two three-day games against English Schools Under-17. The two-day games at Guildford and Molesey CC were both drawn. The Sri Lankans won the first one-day match, played at Uxbridge, by 123 runs after English Schools had collapsed from 61 for one to 92 all out. However, at Chelmsford the following day the Sri Lankans were dismissed for 161 in reply to England's 220 for four (A. Williams 112 not out, K. Jahangir 53). The deciding match at The Oval was abandoned without a ball bowled. Rain intervened again in the first three-day match, at Taunton, in which the Sri Lankans declared at 305 for seven and finished at 79 for one after English Schools, helped by an unbeaten century from Holloway, had in turn declared at 313 for five. The second three-day match, at Canterbury, was also drawn. The Sri Lankans made 174 from 92 overs (J. C. Hallett five for 35) and had English Schools 36 for four before T. Radford, with an unbeaten half-century, led a recovery to 187. Faring much better second time around, the visitors declared at 303 for six to set a target of 291 at 5 runs an over. A double-century partnership between Radford (107) and R. Warren (99) put them on course, but the later batsmen could not sustain the momentum and English Schools were 247 for six when bad light intervened.

Rain, which spoiled most of the Welsh Schools' international season, did not prevent their being outclassed by the Sri Lankan side at Pontarddulais. That they scored as many as 227 in reply to the Sri Lankans' 320 for two declared was due to a five-hour 112 from the captain, G. D. Lucas, who added 81 for the ninth wicket with G. Isaac. The match ended in a draw, with the Sri Lankans 183 for two in their second innings.

The Under-19 side, captained by the Glamorgan Colt, R. D. B. Croft, drew their matches against Irish Schools and Scotland Under-19, in addition to that against English Schools. Lucas again provided the only major score with 70.

The MCC Schools Festival at Oxford was again fortunate to lose only a small amount of time to the rain, mainly on the second of the four days. It did, however, cause the HMC game to be transferred hastily to the Lincoln College Ground from Magdalen College School.

HMC SOUTHERN SCHOOLS v THE REST

At Lincoln College, July 16, 17. Drawn. A wet wicket on the first day had all the batsmen struggling, with the notable exception of Knight. Not until Ellison came in with The Rest 80 for six was the initiative temporarily wrested from the bowlers. Long, slow left-arm, bowled with great accuracy on a wicket giving some help to take seven for 16. Southern Schools fared little better, and had Knight not been dropped early on, they would have been dismissed very cheaply by some tight seam bowling from Headley, Derbyshire and Ellison. Conditions were easier on the second day. Williams and Timm gave The Rest a sound start, Knight having declared 41 behind, and when Southern Schools were set a target of 200 in 48 overs, Shahid and Ecclestone put on 102 for the first wicket, the latter blossoming after a slow start. The loss of three wickets for 13 runs arrested their progress and with Headley and Ellison giving nothing away, the target was looking unattainable when rain ended play with eleven overs remaining. The wicket-keeping on both sides was sound; the fielding of Knight and Headley outstanding.

The Rest

First innings		Second innings	
A. S. Williams (*Bury GS*) c Turner b Long	10	c Kutner b Shahid	43
D. M. J. Timm (*William Hulme's GS*) c Turner b Usher	18	run out	25
C. G. Stanton (*Warwick*) c Turner b Long	24	b Long	0
†J. P. Crawley (*Manchester GS*) b Long	2	not out	41
J. R. C. Dakin (*Sedbergh*) c and b Long	16	run out	24
*N. J. Gregory (*Ipswich*) c Knight b Long	21	c Knight b Jahangir	19
D. W. Headley (*Royal GS, Worcester*) b Long	1	not out	2
B. C. A. Ellison (*Rugby*) c Usher b Long	37		
C. P. Goodier (*King's, Chester*) not out	4		
S. J. White (*King's, Macclesfield*) not out	0		
Extras	16	Extras	4
1/28 2/36 3/44 4/69 5/74 6/80 7/140 8/140 (8 wkts dec.)	149	1/41 2/51 3/78 4/121 5/151 (5 wkts dec.)	158

N. A. Derbyshire (*Ampleforth*) did not bat.

Bowling: *First Innings*—Jahangir 10–4–21–0; Usher 12–3–32–1; Holdsworth 13–3–29–0; Long 21–14–16–7; Shahid 13–4–45–0. *Second Innings*—Usher 6–1–15–0; Jahangir 7–0–24–1; Holdsworth 5–1–22–0; Long 9–2–32–1; Kutner 9–2–27–0; Shahid 6–1–35–1.

HMC Southern Schools

First innings		Second innings	
T. C. Nicholson (*Eastbourne*) c Crawley b Headley	5	(3) c and b Ellison	4
*N. V. Knight (*Felsted*) not out	67		
M. J. Hastwell (*Hurstpierpoint*) c Crawley b Headley	4	(4) c Stanton b Ellison	1
S. C. Ecclestone (*Bryanston*) c Crawley b Headley	0	(1) run out	38
D. M. Kutner (*City of London*) c and b Derbyshire	5	not out	0
N. Shahid (*Ipswich*) c and b Ellison	4	(2) not out	66
K. Jahangir (*Aldenham*) c Crawley b Ellison	5		
†I. D. Turner (*St George's, Weybridge*) not out	4		
Extras	14	Extras	7
1/27 2/38 3/38 4/60 5/100 6/103 (6 wkts dec.)	108	1/102 2/111 3/115 (3 wkts)	116

B. C. Usher (*Malvern*), C. M. Long (*Brighton*) and R. J. W. Holdsworth (*Clifton*) did not bat.

Bowling: *First Innings*—Derbyshire 10–2–32–1; Headley 10–2–27–3; Goodier 7–2–8–0; Ellison 7–1–27–2. *Second Innings*—Headley 12–4–25–0; Derbyshire 4–2–6–0; White 9–2–37–0; Goodier 7–1–31–0; Ellison 5–0–11–2.

ESCA NORTH v ESCA SOUTH

At Keble College, Oxford, July 16, 17. ESCA North won by 4 runs. With only Goldthorp and Irani able to master the left-arm seam-spin combination of Ilott and Patel, the North were restricted to 158 in their 60 overs. Rain limited the South's reply to 37 overs on the first day, with Habib unbeaten on 53, scored in 62 minutes with nine fours. Further rain next morning delayed the start until after lunch, whereupon the South, having declared 21 behind at their overnight score, bowled out the North for 84. The spinners, Ball and Patel, shared the wickets on a helpful pitch. A target of 114 with ample time looked well within the South's grasp until four wickets fell for 1 run and at 66 for eight the balance had swung to the North. However, Ball and Kellaway added 19, and Ilott joined Kellaway to add another 24 before, with nine balls remaining, Houseman bowled Kellaway to bring his side an exciting victory.

ESCA North

Batsman	First innings		Second innings	
*G. Wells (*King George V, Southport*)	lbw b Ilott	0	(2) c Habib b Patel	28
D. Weston (*Holy Trinity, Halifax*)	b Ball	19	(1) b Ball	4
J. R. Goldthorp (*Leeds GS*)	c Rendall b Patel	52	(11) b Patel	15
T. Bradford (*Branston, Lincoln*)	c Phillips b Patel	21	(3) c Kellaway b Ball	0
J. Gunn (*Baysgarth, Hull*)	c Kellaway b Ilott	2	(4) b Patel	13
J. Hughes (*St Christopher Hatton, Northampton*)	b Ilott	4	(5) c and b Ball	2
R. Irani (*Smithhills HS, Bolton*)	c Habib b Patel	41	(6) b Ball	2
†A. Johnson (*Royal GS, Colchester*)	c Phillips b Patel	1	(7) lbw b Ball	1
R. W. Sladdin (*Sowerby Bridge HS*)	not out	4	(8) c Ball b Patel	1
C. Hawkes (*Loughborough GS*)	not out	1	(9) not out	15
I. J. Houseman (*Harrogate GS*)	(did not bat)	–	(10) lbw b Ball	0
	B 5, l-b 3, w 4, n-b 1	13	L-b 2, n-b 1	3
	1/0 2/59 3/97 4/104 5/104 6/123 7/132 8/155 (8 wkts)	158	1/18 2/18 3/47 4/47 5/50 6/51 7/52 8/57 9/61	84

Bowling: *First Innings*—Ilott 21–7–42–3; Rendall 7–3–13–0; Laudat 9–2–28–0; Ball 9–2–21–1; Patel 14–1–46–4. *Second Innings*—Ilott 7–2–9–0; Rendall 9–3–15–0; Ball 19–10–17–6; Patel 17–3–41–4.

ESCA South

Batsman	First innings		Second innings	
D. Parsons (*Eastleigh C of E*)	c Johnson b Hughes	29	b Houseman	2
P. J. Rendall (*Broadoak, Weston-super-Mare*)	run out	7	(5) c Weston b Hawkes	8
*D. A. Graham (*Chipping Campden*)	b Irani	12	b Sladdin	27
A. Habib (*Taunton*)	not out	53	(7) c Bradford b Hawkes	1
A. Phillips (*Aston Tech. Coll.*)	c Weston b Irani	0	(4) c Johnson b Hawkes	1
S. Laudat (*Oxford School*)	not out	10	c Gunn b Sladdin	8
J. J. Lewis (*King Edward VI, Chelmsford*)	(did not bat)	–	(2) run out	10
M. C. J. Ball (*Bath C of E*)	(did not bat)	–	b Houseman	13
M. Patel (*Dartford GS*)	(did not bat)	–	lbw b Hawkes	0
†M. J. Kellaway (*Eastleigh C of E*)	(did not bat)	–	b Houseman	19
M. C. Ilott (*Francis Combe, Watford*)	(did not bat)	–	not out	4
	L-b 6, w 1, n-b 11	18	B 11, l-b 3, w 1, n-b 1	16
	1/34 2/61 3/61 4/61 (4 wkts dec.)	129	1/4 2/19 3/25 4/45 5/65 6/65 7/66 8/66 9/85	109

Bowling: *First Innings*—Houseman 9–1–27–0; Hughes 9–0–32–1; Irani 9–0–42–2; Sladdin 6–1–18–0; Hawkes 4–3–4–0. *Second Innings*—Houseman 13.3–2–15–3; Irani 11–5–25–0; Sladdin 14–3–37–2; Hawkes 12–7–18–4.

At Keble College, Oxford, July 18. N. V. Knight's XI won by eight wickets. G. Wells's XI 99 (B. C. A. Ellison five for 28); N. V. Knight's XI 103 for two (N. V. Knight 41 not out).

At Wadham College, July 18. Drawn. N. J. Gregory's XI 230 for three dec. (D. M. J. Timm 53, A. Habib 100 not out [sixteen fours], N. J. Gregory 43 not out); D. A. Graham's XI 191 for six (J. J. Lewis 62).

At Christ Church College, July 19. MCC Schools East won by six wickets in a twelve-a-side match. MCC Schools West 115 (A. Habib 41 not out; B. C. A. Ellison five for 32); MCC Schools East 116 for five (N. V. Knight 33 not out; N. A. Derbyshire three for 29).

The match at Lord's between MCC and MCC Schools may be found in the MCC section, and that at Lord's between MCC Schools and the National Association of Young Cricketers may be found in Other Matches at Lord's, 1988.

Reports from the Schools

Despite the loss of many fixtures to the weather, five batsmen from the schools reviewed here passed 1,000 runs: N. A. Hunt of Nottingham HS (1,108), J. W. S. Porter of Dauntsey's (1,104), T. C. Nicholson of Eastbourne (1,056), S. Smyth of Foyle and Londonderry College (1,026) and N. V. Knight of Felsted (1,013). Porter's runs came in just thirteen innings at an average of 110.40, while Knight averaged 101.30. Four bowlers took 60 wickets or more: R. Cousins of Wellingborough (72), S. M. Aga of Arnold (69), N. Shahid of Ipswich (67) and C. G. Oswald of Warwick (62). Shahid was the leading all-rounder with 937 runs in addition to his 67 wickets, while others of note were A. J. Clarke of Victoria College, Jersey (947 runs, 42 wickets), P. J. Le Cornu from the same school (920 runs, 43 wickets) and P. D. Chrispin of King Edward VI, Southampton (712 runs, 48 wickets). Of the thirteen other bowlers who took 50 wickets, A. G. Webster of Bradford GS scored 618 runs, G. A. H. Awudu of Bedford Modern 599, and B. C. A. Ellison of Rugby 514. The only hat-trick reported was performed by P. McGowan of Brentwood.

At **Aldenham**, K. Jahangir headed the averages with 508 runs and 49 wickets and went on to play for English Schools Under-17 v Sri Lanka Schools. For **Alleyn's**, a young side, J. Papanastasiou (right-arm fast) and A. C. Winter (right-arm fast-medium) played a major part in their four victories, especially those v Highgate and Wilson's. But the batting relied too heavily on the HMC Under-15 player, P. C. Berglund. An encouraging feature in a disappointing season for **Allhallows** was the promise shown by P. Holland, a fifth former, who opened both the batting and bowling. **Ampleforth** opened with three wins in April, yet won only once more in the next eleven matches. Under the captaincy of J. R. Elliot, they were a happy side, and in D. H. Churton and W. H. Crichton-Stuart they had two spinners who bowled well in harness together. The absence through injury of R. Booth, a talented wicket-keeper, and the unavailability for academic reasons of another key player were handicaps not easily overcome. It is a matter of concern to learn that the English Schools opening bowler, N. A. Derbyshire, seemingly lacked motivation or commitment during the term, to the extent that the school did not put his name forward for the Oxford trials.

In **Arnold's** season of rebuilding, S. M. Aga's left-arm spin bowling brought him a school record of 69 wickets, including nine for 61 v Silcoates, and S. Taylor's leg-spin captured 23 wickets, including six for 38 v William Hulme's GS. The captain, A. D. Jones, scored 100 not out v Queen Elizabeth's GS, Wakefield, while B. S. Little had innings of 100 not out v Hutton GS and 107 v Bangor GS. A young **Ashville College** side did well, beating the XL Club, Mount St Mary's, Giggleswick, Batley GS, Scarborough College, Old Ashvillians, Harrogate GS, Dame Allan's and Queen Elizabeth GS, Wakefield. Their four defeats were at the hands of MCC, Pocklington, Bradford GS and Royal GS, Newcastle.

Another successful season for **Ballymena Academy GS** culminated in their winning the Ulster Schools Cup and being undefeated on a tour to Edinburgh. The team was built on a nucleus of experienced players under the captaincy of the all-rounder, J. T. Glass. P. S. Rainey (medium) led the attack with 51 wickets, and there was an encouraging return of 35 wickets for the young leg-spinner, C. B. Williams. Glass, Rainey and J. M. Kennedy, the school's most prolific batsman with 677 runs, were selected for Ulster Schools. A young **Bancroft's** side matured as the season progressed, showing commitment and enthusiasm under the captaincy of A. C. H. Knight and laying a foundation for future seasons. Knight's unbeaten 106 v the Royal Anglian Regiment was a highlight. G. P. Brown bore the brunt of the bowling, opening with genuine fire but suffering from some weak close-catching, R. Patel was an effective stock seamer, and P. Brown developed as an off-spinner, obtaining turn and flighting the ball intelligently. G. J. Maynard was a reliable opening bat but tended to lose his wicket once he looked set.

Bangor GS recovered from a mediocre start to record seven wins, including that v hitherto unbeaten King's Macclesfield. They were hampered by injuries to bowlers N. S. Taylor and R. G. Scott, as well as to the captain, S. C. McKenna, who none the less headed the batting averages. That **Barnard Castle** enjoyed a much better season than was expected resulted mainly from the consistent bowling of C. M. Fairey and J. G. H. Murphy. The latter also dominated the batting. **Bedford**, although without any old colours, were unbeaten by schools and had the better of most drawn games. Haileybury were beaten by 111 runs. Sensibly led by M. J. Simms, whose seam bowling improved with every match, the XI was characterised by an unselfish and enthusiastic attitude throughout. The Australian all-rounder, R. E. Sims, lent some welcome aggression to the side's performances.

Bedford Modern School enjoyed wins v Kimbolton, Stamford, Nottingham HS, Royal GS Colchester, Wolverhampton GS and the Gentlemen of Bedfordshire, the last-mentioned by one wicket in the penultimate over. G. A. H. Awudu, a right-hand batsman and fast bowler, virtually beat Stamford single-handed, scoring 109 and taking six for 54. Among other match-winning returns was seven for 37 v Royal GS, Colchester. N. R. Ali backed him well with the new ball and there was good support from M. T. Cavanagh, a leg-spinner, and the captain, G. C. Black (left-arm fast-medium). P. A. Simmonds, one of five batsmen to pass 300 runs, scored 77 in 50 minutes v Nottingham HS and 111 v Gentlemen of Bedfordshire. **Beechen Cliff**, beaten only in their last match, recorded six victories, the highlight being that by five wickets over a strong Bath CC side, achieving a target of 214. As many as 23 players appeared for the XI, which D. J. Adams led by example, ensuring that enjoyment remained a priority. The bowling honours were again shared by the spinners, S. M. Priscott (slow left-arm) and J. D. Colbourne (leg-spin).

Berkhamsted began promisingly with two draws and a win v Brentwood, only to suffer three successive defeats and endure three more draws before beating a strong Old Boys side and, in their last match, Kimbolton. A failure to score runs fast enough, and the bowlers' inability to contain consistently, were weaknesses in a season that nevertheless had its moments. A record of no wins does scant justice to an inexperienced **Bishop's Stortford** XI which improved markedly as the term progressed. In three of their drawn games, their opponents survived with nine wickets down. R. N. McIntyre and R. D. F. Wright were useful all-rounders, with the latter scoring the side's only hundred, v Framlingham. The bowling generally lacked penetration, and the spin attack was disappointing, but dropped slip catches merely compounded the problem.

Blundell's, who lost to Taunton, Sherborne, MCC, Clifton and the Devon Dumplings, also went without a win, although rain cost them a likely victory v King's, Taunton. The most consistent batsman was N. A. MacIver, who, with C. D. Bending, passed 300 runs, while R. S. Castle (left-arm medium) was the leading bowler. **Bradfield**, with an experienced XI, enjoyed one of their most successful seasons, beating Charterhouse, Westminster, Winchester and Wellington plus five club sides. R. W. F. Perry, an opening batsmen scored 599 runs including 109 not out v Radley, as well as heading the bowling averages. J. D. Pearce was the leading wicket-taker, his slow left-arm spin claiming 34 wickets, and the team's accurate bowling and outstanding fielding were features of the season. Bradfield took part in the Sir Garfield Sobers Schools Festival in Barbados in August, as did **Bradford GS**, whose first overseas tour it was. Consequently, 1988 was the longest and fullest season in Bradford's history, with 34 matches, of which they won eighteen. Schools beaten included Royal GS Lancaster, Bolton and William Hulme's GS, and in the Barbados tournament Sherborne, Tonbridge and Presentation College, Trinidad. A strong bowling attack dismissed its opponents 22 times, and although the batting averages were dented by some poor pitches in the Caribbean, the year saw a number of fine innings played.

Brentwood's cricket was dominated by their captain M. D. Wilkins, a left-hand bat and off-spin bowler. Even on slow pitches his power enabled him to pierce the field or hit over the top; his unbeaten 115 v Berkhamsted, for example, included six sixes. Fourteen-year-old G. K. Fletcher, a left-handed opening batsman, scored an excellent 50 against an attack that included the former Essex off-spinner, D. L. Acfield. Against Framlingham, P. McGowan, a leg-spinner, had a hat-trick in his return of seven for 59. For **Brighton College**, J. P. Gibson and the captain, C. P. Sweet, scored 701 and 601 runs respectively. C. M. Long's 53 wickets included seven for 17 v Hurstpierpoint. Their nine victories improved their record to 99 wins in the last nine years.

A young **Canford** side did better than expected, defeating the XL Club, King Edward VI Southampton, Bryanston, Sherborne and MCC. Their leading batsmen were J. A. Perry and the captain and wicket-keeper, J. P. Blissard-Barnes, while T. R. Murray-Walker (medium) headed the bowling. **Caterham**, showing excellent team spirit under the able captaincy of R. L. M. Mauger, compensated for any lack of remarkable individual performances by every member of the side contributing at some stage. Of the batsmen N. B. Driscoll, S. J. Dawes and D. N. Podbur were exciting to watch, but the bowling depended too heavily on the fast-medium opener, D. J. Paisey. **Cheltenham College** enjoyed some good wins, notably those v Shrewsbury and Dean Close. **Chigwell's** record of only one win – over Buckhurst Hill CC – did not reflect the overall standard of their cricket. Good bowling saw them dismiss many of their opponents, but not quickly enough for the batsmen to capitalise. The captain, D. Clark, hit eight sixes in his 126 v Woodford Wells CC; the season's best bowling return was A. Brandon's six for 14 v Forest.

Christ College, Brecon, were particularly badly hit by the weather with eight matches abandoned without a ball bowled. Of their four wins, the most exciting was at home v Royal GS, Worcester. Put in, the College struggled to 141 all out and in reply Royal GS cruised to 61 for one. However, R. T. W. Horne, having conceded 18 runs from his first two overs, found line, lift and movement to bowl out the visitors for 81 and finish with seven for 28. The side batted in depth, and a predominantly seam attack was well supported by splendid catching and ground fielding. **Christ's Hospital**, another generally strong fielding side, managed only two wins, but the introduction of several promising Colts during the season provided optimism for the future. The strength of the XI was their bowling, with T. K. W. Welch and T. A. Fooks, the openers, performing consistently.

A young, exciting **Clayesmore** side enjoyed their best season for many years, winning eight games and losing only to Sherborne. The captain, G. Owton, opening batsman and wicket-keeper, increased to nine his centuries for the XI, hitting five in 1988 – 113 v Canford, 132 v Fosters, 116 v Hardye's, 100 not out v Millfield and 106 v MCC. Fifteen-year-old J. C. Latimer (né Rumball) scored his maiden hundred, 112 not out v Bearwood College, having converted to opening batsman when a disc injury restricted his promising pace bowling. J. Dike's in-swing bowling brought him 50 wickets, including seven for 28 v Victoria College, Jersey, and five in an innings another four times. **Clifton College**, also a young side, began well by beating Cheltenham, Blundell's and Colston's, just failed to beat Marlborough in an exciting draw, and lost by 1 run to Rugby. Highlights were returns of nine for 37 by C. M. Spiro v Taunton and nine for 52 from R. J. W. Holdsworth, the captain, v Colston's, both bowlers swinging the ball at fast-medium. Hundreds were scored by four batsmen, of whom R. J. R. Clark was the most accomplished. J. R. A. Williams captained Wales Under-15 and M. G. N. Windows represented HMC Under-15.

Given the side's youth and inexperience, **Colfe's** had a successful season. Much depended on R. Harmer, the captain and an accomplished left-handed opening bat, but injuries to the opening bowler, M. Wainman, and to P. Whiteland, a right-hand bat and leg-spin bowler, restricted the side's prospects in the later part of the season. **Colston's**, too, were hampered in the second half of the season by an injury to a key bowler, J. C. Reice's accurate medium pace being much missed. They had begun well with wins over Bristol Cathedral School, Queen Elizabeth's Hospital, Wycliffe College and Kingswood. **Coventry School – Bablake** retained the Birmingham and Warwickshire Under-19 Cup for the third year in succession and the eighth time in ten years. Most of their six wins came in that competition. The two defeats were by Royal GS Worcester and King Henry VIII, Coventry, and some drawn games could have gone either way. The captain, D. J. Barr, a left-handed batsman, played for Warwickshire Under-19 and M. G. H. Sutton, slow left-arm, for Warwickshire Under-15.

Cranbrook could not live up to the high standards of the previous two XIs, but the young side were ably captained by R. P. T. Lisle and showed promise for 1989. S. P. France was the quickest bowler on their school fixture list, while K. Wookey looked to have the potential to develop into an excellent all-rounder. If suffering a lean season in terms of matches won, **Cranleigh** none the less played some exciting cricket. In the draw v King's, Canterbury, there was a century by each side (R. A. J. Grove 105) and Cranleigh, chasing 263, were 5 runs short with nine wickets down at the end. The Lancing match finished with the scores level. T. C. Crouch (slow left-arm) and N. C. Radbourne (off-spin) bore the brunt of the bowling and benefited from generally enthusiastic fielding. The season culminated in an enjoyable two-week tour of Canada.

Outstanding for **Dauntsey's** was the captain, J. W. S. Porter, who in thirteen innings scored 1,104 runs, nearly four times more than the next batsman and 230 more than his own school record of the previous year. His speed of scoring led to several victories when a target had been set, and there were memorable wins v MCC, beaten in the final over, and King Edward's, Bath, when the winning four was hit off the last ball. N. L. Jephson advanced both with the bat and behind the stumps, while the medium-pace bowling of A. R. Gilmour became more accurate and hostile as the season progressed. **Dean Close** enjoyed an increasingly successful season in which four matches were won and one tied. T. A. Edginton, the captain and leading batsman, included 101 not out v Monmouth among several high scores, and bowled his left-arm spin well at times. T. M. Churchill, another slow left-armer saw the results of his dedication and application when he finished with the most wickets. In a season of rebuilding, with only three returning from the previous XI, **Denstone** recorded notable victories over Bromsgrove and Abbot Beyne. Against the latter, the medium-pace all-rounder, J. Snape, returned eight for 46 and went on to head both averages and to captain English Schools Under-15. Although **Dover College** were unable to overcome the handicap of a weak attack, the batting was sound, with twelve fifties being hit in addition to the two hundreds from J. D. Rowse, a Kent Schools Under-16 representative. The captain, S. P. Howkins, ended his four years in the XI with a total of 1,757 runs and 105 wickets, the second-best record since the war.

Downside put out one of their best XIs for many years. A varied, well-balanced attack provided the captain, D. P. Morris, with many options and bowled out the opposition in eigh[t] of their thirteen matches. Dismissed themselves only twice, the side batted in depth, with si[x] batsmen scoring fifties and G. C. J. Barrington making 107 not out in 25 overs v Strathallan. **The Duke of York's Royal Military School** likewise enjoyed their most successful season o[f] late, playing well as a unit and working enthusiastically in the field. A. P. Glasby, the captain batted soundly and correctly and recorded the side's only hundred, while A. G. Wilkinson an[d] S. Gale both bowled well. On tour they beat Abingdon by one wicket, and at Royal GS, High Wycombe, were beaten by 1 run off the last ball. An excellent season brought **Dulwich Colleg[e]** seven wins, with Whitgift, Mill Hill, Ampleforth, Strathallan and Royal GS, Lancaster amon[g] the teams beaten. In a drawn game, St Paul's, with whom they tied in 1987, finished just 1 run behind Dulwich's 206 for seven declared, while in the Founder's Day match v Merchan[t] Taylors', Dulwich scored 303 in 54 overs for the loss of five wickets. The captain, T. D. J. Ufton (son of the former Kent player, D. G. Ufton), made 132 not out in two hours. N. K. M. Talonpoika, a Colt, scored two centuries and topped both averages. Although the bowlin[g] could not match the batting, the fielding was outstanding. D. V. Trivedi claimed 21 dismissal[s] behind the stumps (19 ct, 2 st), and J. P. Howland held nine catches.

At **Durham**, fourteen-year-old W. P. C. Weston, a left-handed opening batsman and left-arm fast bowler, showed much promise, scoring 458 runs and topping the bowling average with 31 wickets. The captain, A. G. Clayton, returned six for 52 in the tie v Pocklington an[d] finished with 33 wickets. The School won the Barclays Under-17 Cup, beating Millfield o[n] run-rate in a rain-affected final.

On **Eastbourne College's** tour of New Zealand at Easter, the left-handed T. C. Nicholso[n] scored 420 runs at 52.50 and then amassed a further 1,056 at 55.57, a College record, in th[e] school term. He scored centuries v MCC, Cranleigh, Ardingly and Hurstpierpoint – agains[t] whom he and A. J. T. Halliday put on 174 for the first wicket. Fast bowler E. S. H. Giddir[ns] took 56 wickets, including nine for 14 (all bowled) against an Indian Schools XI and eight f[or] 32 v Brighton College. F. A. Ali's 34 wickets included seven for 41 against a South Africa[n] Schoolboys XI. Two early wins by **The Edinburgh Academy** were followed by two losses and series of draws, a general brittleness in the batting and a temporary loss of form by two bowlers contributing to the malaise. However, on the damp wickets of July, opponents were bowled out for under 120 in six successive innings, and a run of five consecutive victories brought the season to a pleasing conclusion. **Elizabeth College, Guernsey**, were unbeaten for the second time in three years in a season which saw them undertake a five-match tour of the mainland, followed by a four-school festival in Guernsey. Their better performances were achieved mostly when batting first. S. B. R. Mackay and D. J. Marshall formed the basis of the batting, well supported by the captain and left-hander, N. E. G. Garrett. Mackay's 121 v King Edward VI, Southampton, was the side's only century, and notable performances with the ball were P. J. A. Moody's five for 9 v Victoria College, Jersey, and Garrett's six for 36 v Tiffin. In an enthralling game which either school could have won, Millfield finished with 168 for nine, chasing 177 to win.

The season at **Ellesmere College** provided handsome pickings for the Marvell brothers, both of whom scored 400 runs. D. J., a sound wicket-keeper, hit 101 not out v Rydal School, sharing a stand of 181 with his younger brother, M. J., whose left-arm spin bowling claimed 45 wickets and was instrumental in most of the team's six victories. A moderate **Eltham College** side made a poor start to the season, losing six of their first seven matches. The second half saw a revival, led by the captain, S. J. Goodfellow, whose fast-medium bowling and aggressive batting confirmed him as a useful all-rounder. **Emanuel**, who won eight matches, were runners-up in the Surrey Cup and semi-finalists in the London Cup. M. D. Coe was an outstanding all-rounder with 42 wickets and 848 runs, while the captain, S. J. Legg, also totalled 800 runs and hit the side's only hundred. The bowling of **Enfield GS** was weak, but by the end of the season, their batting had become both attractive and effective. The last two matches were won when chasing runs against the clock. Three centuries were scored in consecutive matches, D. Bowen successively hitting 135 v Merchant Taylors' and the first hundred for the School v MCC, and O. White hitting 109 v Queen Elizabeth's, Barnet.

A successful **Epsom College** XI was built on a trio of medium-pace bowlers – P. J. Vickars, W. E. J. Crawford and D. A. George – who set up the situations which resulted in most of the six wins. KCS Wimbledon, Dulwich, Christ's Hospital and St John's, Leatherhead were the schools beaten; Lancing and King's, Canterbury inflicted the only defeats. Vickars took seven for 38 v Christ's Hospital and six for 41 v Dulwich. D. R. Bance and G. D. Saunders-Griffiths both played three-figure innings, but the batting rarely inspired long-term confidence. **Eton**, a relatively inexperienced side, benefited from their winter tour of Hong Kong and Australia to achieve five wins – Bradfield by seven wickets, Charterhouse by nine wickets, the touring King's School, Parramatta by six wickets, the Butterflies and MCC. They did, however, suffer their first defeats in two years – to Radley, by three wickets off the last ball, and to Eton Ramblers. J. K. Erith (fast-medium) and T. P. M. Fleming (slow left-arm) were again the pick of the bowlers, while the batting was characterised by consistency rather than great deeds. Against Bradfield the left-handed H. R. E. Petre, an exciting batsman, helped Eton score 29 from the last eleven balls to win the match. **Exeter School's** young side managed more wins than in recent years but were possibly fortunate to escape with just the one defeat, by Simon Langton GS. The left-handed C. L. Bawden, again the leading batsman, shared in an opening partnership of 161 v Wellington School with R. P. Corney, the captain. The bowling was average, the fielding commendable.

Felsted's unbeaten record, with nine victories, owed much to the outstanding all-round feats of their captain, N. V. Knight. He also captained the English Schools and played for Essex II. A left-handed opening batsman, he hit five hundreds to top 1,000 runs for the second successive season, averaging 101.30; this took his total for the XI in four seasons to more than 3,000 runs, including ten centuries. Two of his hundreds and 280 runs came in his last three matches. He made a brilliant unbeaten 168 v Winchester, scoring 109 of the last 112 runs and breaking the School record for an individual innings – 158 not out by his brother, A. V. Knight, in 1986. In addition, mixing right-arm seam and wrist-spin, he took the most wickets, including a match-winning spell of five for 8 from ten overs in the 2-run victory over Uppingham. A highlight for **Fettes College** was the return of seven for 30 v Loretto by J. R. S. Lloyd. **Forest's** captain, A. C. Richards, led his side by example, and whether batting or bowling his off-spin he had another fine season. His 104 in the win over the XL Club was the XI's only hundred. There were important contributions from P. I. O'Neill at No. 4, B. J. Barnett, a left-hander who was also an outstanding fielder, and A. R. Heyes, the wicket-keeper. P. Butler and L. Adenaike, the opening bowlers, had tremendous stamina, and it was a hostile spell of six for 32 from Adenaike that helped beat Brentwood.

A strong, all-round **Foyle and Londonderry College** XI gained thirteen wins, capturing the Gordon McCullough Memorial Cup and reaching the final of the Northern Bank Schools Cup. The batting was dominated by S. Smyth, the captain, whose 1,026 runs included five centuries. He also captained Ulster Schools, for whom the bowlers, M. Simpson and S. Baldrick, were likewise selected, although injury prevented Baldrick from playing. **Framlingham** reported an encouraging season, with their young side enjoying a run of four consecutive wins against schools. In the eight-wicket victory v Bishop's Stortford, 201 was added for the second wicket by S. E. Iliffe (106 not out) and S. C. Giller (92). Giller, as well as heading the batting averages, was the leading wicket-taker.

Giggleswick, beaten in all five games on a three-city pre-season tour of Australia, began well at home by defeating Oakwood and the XL Club. However, lacking consistency, especially in their batting, they managed only one more win. The captain, M. P. Kaye, a left-handed batsman and spin bowler, enjoyed another good all-round season. **Glenalmond**, beaten only by Merchiston Castle, had schools wins v Fettes, Kelvinside, The Edinburgh Academy and Strathallan. Though out for seven weeks owing to injury, the captain, J. P. Brown, scored the most runs, including the side's only hundred. The bowling was impressive in its depth and variety, reflecting perhaps the amount of cricket played at the school. While a young side struggled to score runs on the North Lawn, **Gordonstoun's** bowlers were a dominant factor in a season which saw the XI win seven of their eleven matches. At **Grenville College** the wicket-keeper, G. S. Dermody, dominated the batting, C. P. Ely took the most wickets, and S. Wait, a fifteen-year-old who represented Devon in that age group, opened the bowling to good effect in his first season. **Gresham's**, beaten only by Ipswich in schools matches, were indebted to their seam bowling and the batting of T. Allison, H. E. M. Spence and S. Mussellwhite, a strong captain.

A winter tour of the Far East provided **Haberdashers' Aske's** with valuable experience and engendered a good team spirit which stood them in good stead for the 1988 season. They played entertaining cricket and were unbeaten, the most exciting of their eleven wins being v Queen Elizabeth's, Barnet, when they scored 124 in 12.3 overs. In a strong batting line-up A. V. Spencer, the captain, and D. I. Chippeck batted superbly to score more than 600 runs apiece, Chippeck's including 120 v Enfield GS. The penetrative attack had three good seamers in D. A. Jordan, D. G. Musgrave and B. V. Arumugam, with D. B. Quinn (leg-spin) and M. I. Yeabsley (off-spin) lending contrast. **Haileybury** also benefited from a winter tour, the experience gained in Australia being a factor in their nine victories. Fine leg-spin bowling brought M. C. Goodson 45 wickets, with his return of six for 37 instrumental in the defeat of Harrow. He also scored 431 runs. D. C. L. Beynon, in his first year as captain, showed much promise and scored 619 runs.

Hampton enjoyed a successful, satisfying season with ten wins, only one loss, and a memorable draw v MCC in which they finished 1 run short of victory. The bowling, generally penetrative, was built around the left-arm spin of S. J. Patel, well supported by seamers S. A. H. Cochrane and R. A. F. Hall, each in his first season. J. P. Diprose scored two centuries and C. R. Westaway one, but the batting proved more solid when setting rather than chasing a target. A. J. B. Sales combined captaincy with wicket-keeping to good effect. **Highgate's** four wins included one by ten wickets v the XL Club and another by nine wickets v Westminster. D. N. Amato, the captain, was a consistent all-rounder, with 40 wickets and 45[illegible] runs, including four consecutive fifties. Also noteworthy was the match-winning bowling of R. N. A. Davenport, who took seven for 23 when Abingdon were bowled out for 59 – the only time they were dismissed by another school. Fielding an experienced side, **Hipperholme GS** had hoped for better results than one win and eight defeats, though three of these were by the narrowest of margins. On the bright side, there were some good bowling performances, particularly J. Hemingway's six for 39 v Habergham and J. F. Holt's six for 20 v Read. **Hurstpierpoint** could not repeat their success of 1987, although their Colts did win the Lord's Taverners' Trophy final in which M. Semmence took five for 9 v Oundle. M. J. Hastwell, who headed the XI's batting averages, played for Sussex II.

Ipswich had an outstanding season, winning eleven of their sixteen matches and losing only to the Old Boys in the last over after a declaration. N. Shahid was again their key player, scoring 937 runs and taking 67 wickets with his leg-spin. In all schools and representative games, he took 103 wickets. Shahid and the captain, N. J. Gregory, shared three century opening partnerships, two of which ensured ten-wicket wins v Gresham's and the Gentlemen of Suffolk, and both represented English Schools. Shahid also played for Essex II. T. Young's eleven catches and nineteen stumpings were another fine effort. **Kelly College** lost only one schools match, beat Wellington School in a close finish, and had the better of draws v Allhallows and Plymouth College. A. Adebayo, the captain and left-hand bat, hit a hundred and three fifties, while J. R. Wigley, another left-hander, usually gave the innings a good start. Adebayo, L. R. Shapcott and D. B. Broughton, all medium-pacers, were the pick of the bowlers but had to work for their wickets on the hard, flat pitches of May and June. A relatively young **Kent College** XI provided the school's most successful season for more than a decade, winning six games and losing only once. A strong batting side, they were captained by J. Barker, who opened the batting with S. Warley, the leading run-scorer, and kept wicket. In a balanced attack, G. Jenkins and R. Grove (both fast-medium) combined with fourteen-year-old E. McCabe (slow left-arm) to take most wickets.

King Edward VI College, Stourbridge, missed out on potential wins because of bad weather and unfavourable declarations. S. Mees and the captain, G. R. Haynes, who broke his own College record with an innings of 155 not out, scored consistently and quickly but lacked support. J. I. Hill (slow left-arm) took the most wickets in an attack which struggled at times on good pitches. The positive captaincy of M. Treherne, if sometimes costing matches by his declarations, brought **King Edward VI, Southampton** eleven wins. The mainstay of the team was P. D. Chrispin, left-hand bat and opening bowler, who collected 48 wickets and 712 runs. M. L. Tidby bowled his off-spin tenaciously and J. D. Stanley, opening the batting, scored 709 runs. **King Edward's, Birmingham**, lost only to MCC. The captain, P. N. J. Inglis, scored 116 v Camp Hill, M. J. Goodall's leg-breaks reaped six for 54 v Warwick, and M. M. Dean (fast-medium) took seven for 24 v Royal GS, Worcester. **King Henry VIII, Coventry**, enjoyed their best season for many years. Fine fielding supported an attack in which J. N. Plevin (fast-medium) was outstanding. His return of eight for 14 was the significant contribution in the six-wicket defeat of Coventry School, Bablake, the Warwickshire Under-19 champions. K. P. Street scored a maiden century v J. B. Vent's XI, and Colts P. H. Harrison, M. D. Scott and G. Gascoyne all made promising contributions.

King William's College, Isle of Man, reported cricket varying from excellent to dreadful. The former resulted in victories v Solihull, Aldenham, MCC and Queen Elizabeth GS, Wakefield. The captain, A. P. Woodward, bowled at a useful pace for long spells to take 43 wickets, as well as making a considerable contribution with the bat. M. L. Craine, an opening batsman, headed the averages in his first full season. **King's College, Taunton**, beat Canford, Monmouth and the XL Club, and with all except the captain expected to return, hopes are high for 1989. N. K. L. Coulson led his young side well and had an excellent year personally with 577 runs and 30 wickets. The left-arm spinner, D. J. G. Dowsett looked a good prospect, as did A. F. Lacy-Smith, an opening bowler, and M. F. D. Robinson, a batsman who bowled tidily. Indifferent results for **King's College School, Wimbledon**, stemmed from some inconsistent and diffident batting, even from experienced players. The steadiest batting came from the fifteen-year-old J. Parrish, and D. W. Talbot turned in consistently good all-round performances.

King's School, Bruton, reported a much more rewarding season than in 1987, with victories over Compton House, Allhallows, the Old Boys, Sexeys School, Bristol GS and – in the final over – King's, Taunton. Leading the side maturely and with some vision, J. Petrie had a good term with bat and ball, while wicket-keeper-batsman N. Allison produced an array of scoring strokes to head the batting averages. Unbeaten in schools matches, **King's, Canterbury**, defeated Epsom, Highgate, Eastbourne and St Lawrence College. They batted first in every match, winning the toss only once, and might have won more games with another strike bowler to support J. R. Davies. His 48 wickets included a return of seven for 54 which nearly brought victory v Sutton Valence, the only school to bowl them out. Runs were plentiful, with four century opening partnerships. The left-handed opening batsman, N. V. Daley, scored 145 not out in King's 262 for two declared v Cranleigh (258 for nine). **King's, Chester**, recorded six wins and only one loss, but their July was frustrating with seven fixtures completely rained off and three washed out soon after starting. If anything, the XI missed a depth in bowling to support the powerful batting line-up and the off-spin of the captain, C. P. Goodier.

An inexperienced side, **King's, Ely**, worked well together to produce a series of excellent wins, many in close finishes. The batting was dominated by the captain, T. D. Gallop, and C. J. Claxton, a left-hander who opened for Cambridgeshire Under-19, while D. Hindle, who captained Cambridgeshire Under-17, took 44 wickets bowling his left-arm slows. **King's, Macclesfield**, having drawn their first match, then set a school record by winning eight in succession before their fortunes changed and they won only one of the last ten. Schools beaten were Cheadle Hulme, William Hulme's GS, Arnold, Bolton, Stockport GS, Birkenhead, Rossall and Abbot Beyne. Their strong point was the leg-spin bowling of S. J. White, who took 50 wickets for the second successive season, and played for The Rest at Oxford, while there was positive batting from the captain and wicket-keeper, S. R. Swindells. After a predictably shaky start, the young **King's, Rochester**, XI played well and were unlucky not to win many of their drawn games. M. J. Walker, a fourteen-year-old left-handed opening batsman, was an outstanding prospect whose 818 runs included 124 v Chatham House. A possible weakness was the lack of penetrative bowling to support the captain, I. J. Nightingale, who captured 58 wickets.

Another school fielding an inexperienced side, **King's, Worcester**, struggled to score enough runs for a useful attack to bowl at. Some valuable all-round performances came from D. A. W. Hughes, whose century against a Jersey Schools XI ended the season on a high note. **Kingston GS** only once scored more than 150. With the senior players falling below expectations, the junior players took a long time to find their feet, although E. S. Gratton and M. E. Bendel hinted at better times ahead. **Kingswood**, with a stronger batting side than for many years, were dismissed only once. On the other hand, only one school side, Dauntsey's, was bowled out; set 194, they collapsed to 37 all out as J. M. Thompson took seven for 14. The captain, R. W. Lewis, increased his career aggregate to a new school record.

Lancing's single defeat was by Tonbridge in the first match of the season; thereafter they won ten and drew five games in probably the College's longest unbeaten sequence. They beat Brighton College, Hurstpierpoint and Eastbourne to win the Langdale Cup, and in other fixtures defeated Sussex Schools, Free Foresters, Ardingly, Epsom, Sussex Martlets, Hurstpierpoint and Charterhouse. A tight, accurate attack was spearheaded by A. S. Puddephatt (fast), with R. H. D. Spink (medium) and A. R. Hewitt (off-spin) supporting admirably. Bowling first and chasing low scores left few opportunities for heavy scoring, but five batsmen scored 300 runs. Of these, the captain, A. A. Gosden, with 374 runs, achieved Lancing's highest recorded average, 93.50. For **Leeds GS** T. C. Walton had an outstanding season, scoring 632 runs at 126.40 and taking 41 wickets at medium pace, which culminated in his selection for England Schools Under-15. Equally significant were the all-round contributions of J. R. Goldthorp (leg-spin and googlies) and G. O. J. Hill (medium), who put on four century opening stands, including 216 in the win v Bradford GS and 195 in the defeat by Nottingham HS. Both played for Yorkshire Senior Schools and Goldthorp for ESCA North. Other schools beaten were Ermysled's GS, Hipperholme GS, Hymer's College, Bradford GS and Woodhouse Grove.

Leighton Park went without a win, although twice they were close to victory. They lacked bowlers to support the medium-paced openers, P. Wall and I. Dhajoo, and a batsman to complement the run-scoring of the captain, J. Thomas, who represented Berkshire Schools Under-19. **The Leys** fielded their strongest batting side for some years. The wicket-keeper, D. O. Solomon, scored 124 v Felsted, and notable contributions came from the captain, C. W. Barker, P. R. Searle and N. R. Lankester. However, Searle (fast-medium) and Lankester (leg-breaks) were the only bowlers to take ten wickets, and at least four likely victories eluded the side because they failed to prise out the last batsmen. The Leys participated in the schools festival in Barbados. **Liverpool College**, with a young side, managed only one victory, but it was an impressive one, achieving a target of 225 to beat Manchester GS. The batting was grittier than in 1987, but the bowlers, suffering from inexperience and often lacking control failed to dismiss any school side. **Lord Wandsworth College** had five wins over schools. Their strength lay in the batsmen's ability to chase a target, with eleven fifties coming from the top four. The stylish batting of M. J. Critchley was a delight to watch. Although lacking penetration, the attack was sufficiently containing.

Lord Williams's School, Thame, failed to live up to their pre-season promise, especially with the bat. With the captain, T. Jordan, not striking form until well into the season, much depended on the all-rounders, M. Bateman and G. Stanbury. In schools matches they beat Aylesbury GS by six wickets and drew close games v Magdalen College School (the scores were level) and Wellingborough School. Against **Loretto's** economical attack, only Glenalmond passed 150. The captain, M. C. Eglinton, took the most wickets, while S. S. Hodgson's slow-medium in-swingers brought him returns of four for 6 v Dollar Academy and five for 1 v Kelvinside Academy. The batting was at times brittle, too much depending on

Hodgson, who opened the innings. A right-arm bowler, he batted left-handed. They were unbeaten at the St Peter's, York, festival and finished with a good win v Cranleigh. **Loughborough GS** reported another successful season; their one defeat by Uppingham was the first by a school for some years. They bowled better than they batted, but there was a fine unbeaten 111 v Union HS by the captain, I. Bell, who also captained Midlands Schools. The slow left-armer, C. J. Hawkes, took 34 wickets and went on to play for English Schools v Sri Lanka Under-17; S. Pickering took eight for 36 v King Henry VIII, Coventry.

It was a season of rebuilding for **Magdalen College School**, but they had many exciting finishes, including one tied match. Although several inexperienced players developed well, the batting understandably lacked the depth to back up the captain, J. A. Turner, and M. B. Bixby, an outstanding Colt. The leading wicket-taker was again S. N. Webb (slow left-arm). J. R. Wileman, the **Malvern College** captain, was pre-eminent, with 31 wickets bowling medium-fast and 783 runs, including 106 not out in his first match of the season and 133 not out v Marlborough. Against Clifton, he and B. C. Usher reached three figures off consecutive balls and he also took five for 36. **Manchester GS** did better before half-term, when good team performances resulted in wins v Bolton, Stockport GS, Shrewsbury and Birkenhead. Later, doubts over the quality of the bowling were realised and only two more matches were won – v Newcastle-under-Lyme and King Edward VII, Lytham. The batting was excellent, with J. P. Crawley, opener and also wicket-keeper, scoring 900 runs, including 152 not out v Royal GS, Lancaster, and 160 not out v Liverpool College in successive matches. His opening partner, the left-handed D. J. Worsley, while more circumspect, hit a delightful unbeaten 124 v Arnold and M. J. P. Ward, striking a rich vein late in the season, hit an unbeaten 100 v Bury. C. F. Sinton, a thirteen-year-old leg-spinner brought in to balance the attack, was the discovery of the season and finished with the most wickets, including six for 55 v Bradford GS.

Marlborough College were undefeated; but unable to bowl sides out on good pitches, and rarely set a realistic target because of their strong batting line-up, they managed only four wins. Opposing captains invariably recalled their 296 in 55 overs v Free Foresters. J. S. Kerr, a positive captain, was the most prolific batsman, D. M. A. Bevan (medium) the most consistent wicket-taker, and M. A. Foulds was outstanding in the field. T. C. Marcon showed promise behind the stumps. **Merchant Taylors', Crosby**, overcame the absence through injury for much of the season of their captain and wicket-keeper-batsman, R. W. Glynne-Jones. They lost just the once and had a ten-wicket win v King William's College, Isle of Man, as one of two victories. I. G. Sutcliffe, opening bat and off-spinner, impressed in his first full season, scoring 109 v Leeds GS, and I. K. Wright, the acting-captain, batted with patience and application. **Merchant Taylors', Northwood**, batted vigorously to beat St Albans, Enfield GS, University College School, Westminster, Mill Hill and Bryanston in schools matches and lost only to Highgate. With 867 runs, including 140 not out v Westminster, A. J. Brand scored more than anyone since the legendary Raphael and Dennis in 1901. Bowling off-spin, he also took 35 wickets, six of them for 20 v Highgate. With the seam bowling disappointing, much depended on Brand and the fifteen-year-old slow left-arm spinner, R. A. Hawkey, who took 52 wickets.

Merchiston Castle won their first five schools matches, and after defeats by Ballymena Academy GS and The Edinburgh Academy, they finished by beating Denstone and Nottingham HS on a tour of the Midlands. S. J. Elworthy, 32 wickets at 8.03 apiece, and S. D. L. Francis (left-arm) comprised an effective seam bowling partnership that gave little away and was supported by admirable fielding. The side batted all the way down the order. The season was made memorable by D. M. Streek's innings of 242 in a two-day match v Fettes College. He hit his first hundred in 80 minutes before lunch and batted in all for three and a quarter hours, hitting 37 fours and one six. With A. H. W. Boyle he added 237 for the fourth wicket and Merchiston Castle declared at 379 for six. It is believed that Streek's innings, the total and the partnership are all records for Scottish schoolboy cricket. **Millfield**, unbeaten by schools for the third successive season, were a powerful batting side who recorded six centuries. D. L. Hemp hit three of them. With the England Under-17 strike bowler, J. C. Hallett, frequently unavailable because of injury, the bowling was steady rather than penetrative. G. D. Lucas captained Welsh Schools Under 17 and along with Hemp played for the Under-19 side. [*Note:* In the Millfield report in the 1988 *Wisden* it states incorrectly that G. D. Lucas batted with P. C. L. Holloway in an unbroken opening partnership of 252. The stand, worth 250, was between Holloway (103 not out) and D. Luckes (132 not out).]

Mill Hill had a disappointing season; they beat MCC but lost seven schools matches. **Milton Abbey's** young side enjoyed an exciting season, with strong batting and good fielding to support their spinners, H. E. Panter (slow left-arm) and H. G. H. Groves (off-breaks). R. S. Padmore, 121 not out v Allhallows, and S. J. E. Courage, the captain and wicket-keeper, with 121 v King's, Bruton, played the outstanding innings. **Monkton Combe's** season was their most successful for some years. They won seven matches – five against schools – and lost only to MCC. The opening partnership of R. S. Deacock and R. J. Payne, well supported by the captain, M. P. Davis, underpinned the batting; the bowling was spearheaded by N. F. Robb, who took 36 wickets at medium pace.

Newcastle-under-Lyme School found that batting could be an embarrassingly difficult business. Only M. H. Colclough, a third-former and Staffordshire Under-17 representative, demonstrated an ability to build an innings. Consequently, the hostile bowling of D. J. Brock was often wasted. A young **Norwich School** side acquitted themselves well, achieving good wins v Holbrook RHS, St Joseph's and King Edward VI, King's Lynn, and coming close in other encounters. The pace bowling of N. R. Temperley brought him 32 wickets, while the batting potential shown by A. J. Rushmer, R. F. Blackburn, A. J. R. Williamson and S. E. Jessup, augurs well for 1989. Although disappointing in terms of results, the season of **Nottingham HS** was memorable for the batting of the captain, N. A. Hunt, whose 1,108 runs included five centuries, three of them in consecutive games.

As expected, **The Oratory's** experienced XI excelled, going through the season unbeaten. Nine wins included those v Douai by 193 runs, St Edmund's College, Pangbourne College and Shiplake College, all by four wickets, and MCC by five wickets. Few sides could cope with the all-round attack, spearheaded by S. R. Wright, who bowled fast and well for his 42 wickets at 8.64, including six for 31 v Leighton Park. The batting, headed by P. J. Coverdale, the captain, was strong, with fifteen-year-old J. Clarke an outstanding prospect. **Oundle** were rewarded for playing positive cricket. In schools matches they lost only to Stowe, following a declaration, and beat Mill Hill, The Leys, Uppingham, Oakham and St Edward's. Batting through the order, they were able to achieve targets, often against the clock. The captain, R. Jenkins (fast-medium) bowled exceptionally well for his 52 wickets, including six for 58 v Rugby, and took his total in three years to 133. **Oakham** looked a useful side in the field, with I. Forsyth a particularly effective medium-pace bowler, but the batting was weak. An exception was the opening batsman, U. Malhotra, an exchange student from Delhi, who scored 500 runs.

The Perse beat Culford, Chigwell and a Cambridgeshire County Club XI, and went close in a number of drawn games. Despite the presence of several attacking batsmen, and expectations aroused by the captain, N. M. Law's 100 not out in the first match v Framlingham, the batting disappointed in the latter part of the season. Off-spinner D. L. Young, the leading bowler, took seven for 81 v Old Perseans, and there were sustained spells of hostile fast bowling by R. M. C. Scott. An enjoyable and successful season for **Plymouth College** culminated in a tour to Denmark, where the Danish Under-18 side inflicted their only defeat of the summer. The attack was well led by C. Vinson, whose return of seven for 12 in nine overs v Warwick was a highlight. The first six batsmen did all that was expected of them, usually at a brisk rate, and there were hundreds from S. Summers and A. Kerr, the wicket-keeper, whose 25 dismissals included six stumpings.

Pocklington won ten of their first fourteen matches before rain affected six. The outstanding game was a tie v Durham. The opening partnership of A. T. Pettinger and M. J. Wood, who scored 1,406 runs between them, provided a strong base from which to set a target or chase one. Wood was also the leading bowler, his leg-spin accounting for 51 batsmen. **Prior Park College** had a mixed season. Although batting collapses led to two of their defeats, the team's real weakness was an inability to bowl sides out and capitalise on winning positions. M. Woodhouse topped the batting averages for the third year, to finish his career with 1,600 runs for the XI, and G. Lee, an off-spinning all-rounder, is expected to be the mainstay in 1989.

In a season which saw a return to home matches, **Queen Elizabeth GS, Wakefield**, were hampered both by injuries and by a negative attitude on the part of some players. Too often heads were allowed to drop under pressure. Notable exceptions were the captain, P. Maynard, G. Millman and G. Littlewood. With no one batsman capable of holding the innings together it required three or four to make moderate scores to give the bowlers a chance and this did not always eventuate. Victories were achieved over Hipperholme GS, William Hulme's GS, Oakwood, Batley GS and Old Savilians. Despite their lack of a penetrative attack. **Queen's College, Taunton**, reported a satisfactory season, in which they lost only to Wesley College from Perth, Australia. The captain, B. C. Wixey, headed the averages, and M. Knight and M. E. Gibson played valuable supporting innings. A more penetrative attack might have led to fewer draws.

Unbeaten by schools, **Radley** owed much to their captain, M. J. Lowrey, whose 686 runs included an innings of 144 v Winchester. **Ratcliffe College**, lacking any depth of batting, were carried by their captain, R. J. Adcock, who scored the side's only hundred – v Robert Smyth – and was the most penetrative bowler with his left-arm swing. **Reading's** young side was built around O. D. Beckett and T. J. C. Dance – left-hand opening bat and right-arm opening bowler – who scored nearly 1,000 runs between them. Beckett hit 119 not out v Royal GS, Colchester, and 102 not out v Reading Blue Coat; Dance scored 111 v his old school, Lord Wandsworth College, and took six for 36 v Reading Blue Coat and seven for 22 v Leighton Park. Dismissing Pangbourne College for 25, Dance took six for 12 and B. D. Hall, a leg-spinner, four for 11. The failure of the senior batsmen in the **Reed's** XI to score consistently placed a heavy burden on two promising all-rounders, J. R. Dharmasena and J. R. Ovenden. Five of the sixteen fixtures were won. A talented **Reigate GS** side developed a frustrating tendency to squander winning positions, although there were eight good victories, including those by eight wickets v Emanuel and Caterham. The captain, C. S. Bates, J. P. Jackson and M. M. G. Wright led the way with the bat, and J. S. Hudson made 100 v Hampton. The main back-up for the XI's outstanding left-arm seam bowler, D. F. Rowlinson, whose 49 wickets were the best return in recent times, came from the left-arm spin of D. M. Gregory.

Under the captaincy of J. Fellows, **Rendcomb** played some fine cricket to win six matches, losing just one. The attack was well-balanced with pace from C. Huck, seam support from C. Bannister and N. Suffolk, and contrasting spin from A. Jones (left-arm) and H. Le Fleming (off-breaks). Early in the season, runs were not scored quickly enough, but the rate improved later. **Repton** beat Rugby, Oakham, Malvern, Wrekin and the Repton Pilgrims, losing only to MCC and Royal GS, Worcester. They had the upper hand in many of their nine draws, but struggled to bowl out the opposition. There were some notable batting performances, with three-figure innings from the captain, C. E. Wall, R. F. Williamson, R. A. C. Jerman and A. E. Jordan. **Rossall's** bowlers similarly lacked the ability to force a win, which resulted in eleven draws and just three wins – v Merchant Taylors' Crosby, the XL Club and Old Rossallians. The captain, D. M. Indo, led the batting by example, becoming the first Rossall player for several years to top 500 runs, while fourteen-year-old J. Elliott did well to head the batting averages in his first season.

Royal GS, Guildford, frequently bowling sides out cheaply, won ten of their last thirteen matches. P. Challinor, who also scored the side's only century, and M. Gore provided the edge to an incisive attack. **Royal GS, Worcester**, followed an Easter tour of Zimbabwe with an excellent domestic season. D. W. Headley was often too quick for schoolboy batsmen, and the leg-spin of the captain, J. S. Waters, gave contrasting support. G. T. G. Burrow and M. J. N. Taylor, who made two hundreds, provided a solid start to the batting, and M. J. Walker invariably made runs when it mattered. Headley represented English Schools, as did the **Rugby** captain, B. C. A. Ellison, who had an outstanding all-round season for his school. Against Marlborough he scored 104 not out and took six for 93; in the 1-run victory over Clifton, his figures were nine for 81. Another highlight was the opening partnership of 128 v Stowe between R. R. Montgomerie and G. A. D. Whittaker. Rugby's Under-15s were runners-up in the Lord's Taverners' Trophy, which augurs well for the future. **Rydal** put behind them an early defeat by Birkenhead to develop into a useful side, beaten thereafter only by MCC. The high point was a first win v William Hulme's GS, in which the captain, A. G. Moore, scored a fine century. The bowling revolved around P. J. Acheson (leg-spin) and the opener, R. L. Stewart, who returned six for 5 v Ruthin.

St Albans began a run of six consecutive wins with the stuff of schoolboy fiction. H. E. Sherman, having had his nose broken during fielding practice beforehand, took six for 5 in his first match in the XI to help defeat local rivals, St Columba's. The sequence ended with victory over the Old Boys for the first time in 25 years. The batting had depth and wickets were easier to come by than in recent years. In their centenary year, **St Dunstan's** enjoyed their second successive season unbeaten by schools. They lost only to a strong Old Boys side. The opening batsman, M. J. Dowse, scored consistently, but the outstanding batting came from G. R. S. Scovell, who hit three hundreds in the last five matches: 104 not out v Royal GS, Guildford, 100 not out v the XL Club, and 100 v Barnard Castle. The last two were scored in successive matches, with the second fifties coming from eleven and thirteen balls respectively. Bowling leg-breaks and googlies, Scovell was also the leading wicket-taker. A tour of Australis was planned for December. **St Edmund's, Canterbury**, had an enjoyable season of positive cricket played under the intelligent and selfless captaincy of M. J. E. Horton. J. D. Bowden, a fourteen-year-old left-hander, came within 40 runs of the school record and hit 162 v the XL Club. Another highlight was the ten-wicket win v the Old Boys.

The results of **St Edward's, Oxford**, failed to do justice to their potential. There were particularly good performances v Abingdon, Eton and MCC. Although generally lacking the penetration to achieve positive results, the bowlers stuck to their task well and particular improvement was shown by J. M. E. Lawes (off-spin) and M. S. Ghalib (leg-break/googly). The batting was always explosive, if occasionally irresponsible, but A. C. Dobson was a dependable opening bat. T. H. C. Hancock's all-round contribution revealed him as a player of considerable promise. **St George's, Weybridge**, beaten only by MCC, defeated Kingston GS, St Benedict's, Tiffin and St John's, Leatherhead. I. D. Turner, who scored the most runs and captured 28 wickets with his off-breaks, took six for 46 v St John's, Leatherhead – and later kept wicket for HMC Southern Schools at Oxford. J. Sayers's 101 not out v Tiffin was the side's only hundred, and the left-arm spinner, T. Clark's 34 wickets included six in an innings v St Benedict's.

St John's, Leatherhead, beat the XL Club, KCS Wimbledon and Whitgift to win more matches than in 1987, but defeats still outnumbered victories. Nor could they take comfort from any outstanding individual performances. The young players of **St Joseph's, Ipswich**, made pleasing progress, and could have won more games with greater experience in the middle-order batting. At **St Lawrence College** much depended on L. M. Willsmer, right-hand bat and medium-pace swing bowler, but R. J. Elliott looked a fine prospect. Their three wins came v Dover College, Framlingham and Old Lawrentians. **St Paul's**, for whom seven batsmen passed 150 runs, reported an unremarkable season in which they were unbeaten by schools. Following their tied match v Dulwich by 1987, they finished the 1988 fixture on 205 for seven in reply to Dulwich's 206 for seven declared. **St Peter's, York**, drew twelve of their eighteen matches. In a batting line-up boasting depth and ability, W. J. Robinson played some fine, aggressive innings, including 125 not out v Pocklington. P. F. Wand bowled his slow left-arm spin impressively and N. P. Durham kept to a consistently high standard. At the end of term, St Peter's hosted a successful six-school festival.

Sedbergh's season did not quite live up to the expectations inspired by a successful tour of Trinidad at Christmas. No batsman scored heavily, and only S. D. Gawthorpe with any consistency. A well-balanced attack proved too strong for most opposition, but too many sides were content to settle for a draw from an early stage. Highlights for **Sevenoaks** were innings of 100 not out v Brentwood by J. D. Fry and 100 v Ardingly by D. E. Neil-Dwyer. **Sherborne**, ably captained by T. R. Ashworth, beat Bradfield, Clifton, Blundell's and Haileybury, and in schools matches lost only to Canford. There were fine innings by P. Hodges and S. J. Leeke, particularly their unbroken fifth-wicket partnership of 150 v Millfield, and M. C. Evans. The bowling, built on the pace of R. P. O. Springfield and the off-spin of Hodges, was backed up proficiently in the field and by the excellent wicket-keeping of J. de la Hey. **Shrewsbury's** relatively inexperienced XI recorded encouraging wins v Malvern, Uppingham and Ellesmere, thanks mainly to the batting and astute captaincy of J. M. Jones. The runs (435) and wickets (40) of D. J. Bowett proved valuable, as did the bowling of his left-arm opening partner, D. M. W. Roberts, whose 27 wickets included six for 22 v Malvern.

In a highly successful season, **Simon Langton GS** won ten times, losing only to Exmouth CC. The batting was strong, founded on the first three – N. S. Cox (left-hand), D. G. Newton and N. R. Henn. P. C. Relf captained the XI efficiently and bowled his off-breaks with considerable success, often in tandem with A. D. Judge (slow left-arm). **Solihull's** early-season pattern was rather like the weather's – scattered showers and sunny intervals. They lost three times through poor batting and then produced an opening stand of 160 v King's, Worcester, with a century from E. J. M. Jones. A tour of the Isle of Man heralded an improvement with victory by 193 runs over an island Under-19 XI, P. Wheeler scoring an unbeaten 100 in a total of 273 for two. Subsequently, Bromsgrove, Old Sils, University College School and Barnard

Castle were also beaten. An unbroken seventh-wicket partnership of 119 between D. C. Pritchard (93) and M. Bevins (44) carried Solihull to victory when Barnard Castle's 228 for nine looked out of reach.

Stamford, who beat only Nottingham HS, were disappointed not to do better. The batsmen too often failed to build on a start of 20 or 30, while in turn the bowlers struggled to maintain a consistent line and length. A tie v the Old Boys, resulting from enterprising batting by the school, was one of the season's few highlights. Although winning only three matches, **Stockport GS** enjoyed their cricket. The captain, I. Millner (left-hand), several times held the innings together and won selection for Cheshire Under-19. R. Patel, when he recovered from injury, was the most reliable bowler, and his seven for 53 v William Hulme's GS was a major factor in Stockport's most convincing victory. P. Duckworth, slow left-arm bowler and left-handed batsman, contributed a number of valuable all-round performances.

Stonyhurst remained unbeaten by a school for the second successive season, although Sedbergh came close to upsetting their record. While the lack of penetrative bowling was a handicap, the splendid example set by the captain, G. O'Driscoll, with the bat made the school difficult to beat. His two impressive unbeaten centuries, the highest 146 v Royal GS, Lancaster, were the best innings by a Stonyhurst cricketer for some time. **Strathallan**, a weak side on paper, performed better than expected and won five times. Their success owed much to the consistent batting of the opener, R. B. Moffat, and the effective strike bowling of R. A. Hatfield and R. G. Brown. A highlight for **Sutton Valence**, who won nine matches, was J. Barr's return of seven for 23 v the XL Club.

For **Taunton**, with eight wins and only one defeat, two players were outstanding. P. C. L. Holloway, the captain and wicket-keeper, who had joined the school from Millfield, scored 568 runs, including 152 not out v Fettes. In addition, he was called up by his county, Warwickshire, to make his first-class début and represented English Schools Under-17. A Habib, who headed the batting averages, represented English Schools Under-17 and Under-19, having been the leading run-scorer at the MCC Schools Festival. Had **Tiffin's** ability to score runs been matched by a similar ability to take wickets, they would have had a wonderful season. N. J. B. Howell, opening bat and captain, amassed 902 runs, with two hundreds and seven fifties, and J. Matthews, a forcing middle-order left-hander, also hit two hundreds. Both played for Surrey Young Cricketers. With D. K. Jones, Howell put on a record-breaking opening partnership of 250 v St Benedict's, each reaching three figures. Their five victories were all against school sides. **Trent College**, a young side, played attractive, attacking cricket and an encouraging season resulted. T. C. White's three hundreds equalled the school record, and I. R. Birch's 32 wickets indicated that there is still a place in the game for the leg-spinner.

Trinity beat eight sides, among them Eltham College, King's Rochester, Caterham, Emanuel and KCS Wimbledon, but with a fixture list of 21 games they had hoped for more wins. The bowling, if somewhat disappointing, possessed an effective medium-pacer in J. D. Good, who took 50 wickets; J. D. Morley was the leading batsman with more than 700 runs. The season was rounded off with a tour of Holland. A highlight for **University College School** was an innings of 103 not out v Westminster by fourteen-year-old R. J. Ayre. The only other player to reach three figures was A. J. Stewart, who headed the batting. Missing key players through injuries, **Uppingham** could manage wins only v Bishop's Stortford, Trent and Loughborough GS. The major innings was an excellent unbeaten 104 by J. H. Renison v Repton. **Victoria College, Jersey**, were dominated by two outstanding all-rounders: A. J. Clarke (947 runs, 42 wickets) and the captain, P. J. Le Cornu (920 runs, 43 wickets). Le Cornu finished five seasons in the XI with an aggregate of 3,105 runs, beating W. Jenner's record by 77, while Clarke's 111 v Elizabeth College, Jersey, was only the third post-war century for Victoria against their Channel Islands rival.

Prompted by the attacking captaincy of C. G. Stanton, **Warwick School** were involved in some close finishes, with four matches being decided off the last ball. Stanton scored centuries v the XL Club and Royal GS, Worcester, but the most successful player was the all-rounder, C. G. Oswald, whose well-controlled off-spin brought him 62 wickets, seven more than the school record set by G. J. Lord in 1979. **Watford GS**, while competently captained by M. Kendall, had a lean season, beating only Tiffin and drawing eleven games. Often, victory was but a few runs or wickets away when stumps were drawn. A. Griffin set a school record of 613 runs, 532 of them coming before the end of May.

Wellingborough beat Wisbech GS, Watford GS, Alleyn's, Trent College, Kimbolton and Ratcliffe in an excellent season; their only defeat was by Millfield at a festival in Guernsey. R. Cousins had an outstanding season, bowling with genuine pace at times to finish with 72 wickets, while J. M. Attfield confirmed his promise with 608 runs and 35 wickets, bowling off-breaks. **Wellington College** beat Winchester, lost to Bradfield and MCC, and drew the other twelve matches played. M. C. K. Hodgson, a left-hander, hit a hundred v Stowe and was the mainstay of the batting. But the middle order was fragile. The bowling, steady if unspectacular, was not helped by vital catches being dropped, although the ground fielding was keen. **Wellington School**, too, suffered from the dropping of critical catches. They lacked the batting and bowling to achieve many positive results, but a young side gained valuable experience.

Despite hopes of something better following a winter tour of India, **Westminster's** performances were maddeningly uneven, four victories being interspersed with overwhelming defeats. The captain, J. Hyam's failure to score runs haunted others, and without the aggressive contribution of D. J. Cogan, who scored 104 not out v Lords and Commons, the record would have been dire. The bowling was similarly nondescript, with A. Lancaster, the most promising bowler, missing much of the season through injury. **Whitgift** won four matches, including those v Trinity and Christ's Hospital, but in other schools matches lost to Brighton, Dulwich, KCS Wimbledon and St John's, Leatherhead. The batting tended to be unreliable, with the exception of N. S. Auer, who passed 600 runs for the second season. **William Hulme's GS** maintained their reputation for positive cricket, with only one match drawn, apart from the three curtailed by rain. The win at Birkenhead, chasing 215, was a highlight, and an innings of 144 not out from the opening batsman and captain, D. M. J. Timm, resulted in a splendid victory v King Edward's, Lytham. On tour, their out-cricket was of the highest standard and ensured wins v Pocklington, Hymers and Bolton Abbey CC. However, A. D. Cleary's six wickets were just not enough to prevent Bradford GS from winning off the last ball.

Woodhouse Grove, with a relatively inexperienced side, played positive cricket and were rewarded with wins v Bootham, Bradford GS, Hymers and Queen Elizabeth GS, Wakefield. Their only defeat was at the hands of Leeds GS. J. L. Gomersall's sound technique stood him in good stead at the start of the innings and, a more forceful batsman than in 1987, he was selected for Yorkshire Senior Schools. S. N. Lee, who played for Yorkshire Schools Under-15, took 28 wickets with well-controlled, well-flighted leg-spin and googlies, including seven for 58 v Bootham and six for 48 v Bradford GS. **Worksop's** young side improved as the season progressed. The batting relied on fourteen-year-old R. A. Kettleborough, although others, especially J. D. Goode, played useful innings. The bowling was steady but often lacked the penetration to force a win. **Wrekin College**, also with a young side, achieved some excellent results, including wins v MCC, Wellington CC, Shropshire Gentlemen and Liverpool College. S. R. Jackson led by example with both bat and ball, and C. C. P. Davies, a junior Colt, revealed some good stroke-play when scoring 116 runs in his two appearances.

Wycliffe College reported a generally disappointing season, not least because of the weather, but their young players did gain valuable experience. J. F. P. Tovey and G. M. Collins opened the batting with some consistency, M. H. Workman and R. M. Clements provided fleeting moments of class, and the captain, S. G. Cady, put together some hard-hitting innings towards the end of the season. J. M. Thomas deserved more wickets from his canny medium pace, but the one bowler capable of working his way through a side was Cady with his left-arm quicks. **Wyggeston and Queen Elizabeth I Sixth Form College** were unbeaten, winning five of their seven matches. Another five were abandoned. The captain, J. L. Green (fast-medium), had figures of seven for 30 and nine for 11 in the defeats of King Edward's, Stourbridge and Lawrence Sheriff respectively. They won the Leicestershire Under-19 Cup for the third consecutive year, beating John Cleveland College in the final as they had in 1987.

THE SCHOOLS

(Qualification: Batting 100 runs; Bowling: 10 wickets)

* *On name indicates captain.* * *On figures indicates not out.*

Note: The line for batting reads Innings–Not Outs–Runs–Highest Innings–Average; that for bowling reads Overs–Maidens–Runs–Wickets–Average.

ABINGDON SCHOOL

Played 16: Won 3, Lost 5, Drawn 8

Master i/c: T. O'Mahony

Batting—*P. D. Lunn 9–0–396–110–44.00; G. R. Peddy 16–3–384–65–29.53; N. D. Franklin 14–1–320–93–24.61; J. S. Greenland 13–0–293–79–22.53; M. Snow 14–1–289–44–22.23; R. J. Tilley 12–1–241–76–21.90; R. J. Winsley 12–5–143–43–20.42; E. J. Tilley 13–2–149–36–13.54.

Bowling—P. D. Lunn 177–44–441–38–11.60; E. J. Tilley 79–22–234–12–19.50; R. E. Clark 150–37–420–21–20.00; M. J. Herd 111–22–328–10–32.80.

ALDENHAM SCHOOL

Played 13: Won 3, Lost 3, Drawn 7. Abandoned 1

Master i/c: P. K. Smith

Batting—K. Jahangir 13–1–508–103*–42.33; M. A. Knopp 13–1–377–104*–31.41; *G. E. Peel 11–0–251–67–22.81; W. Pethybridge 9–1–180–48–22.50; P. M. O. Pennick 11–3–138–70–17.25; T. G. Munyard 9–1–108–34–13.50; J. M. B. Clemow 10–2–100–65–12.50.

Bowling—K. Jahangir 197–82–401–49–8.18; P. M. O. Pennick 94.6–19–328–18–18.22; G. E. Peel 89–8–359–13–27.61.

ALLEYN'S SCHOOL

Played 16: Won 4, Lost 4, Drawn 7, Tied 1. Abandoned 1

Master i/c: S. E. Smith

Batting—P. C. Berglund 18–3–385–87*–25.66; D. S. Herridge 15–2–283–77*–21.76; G. R. Harrison 15–2–279–58*–21.46; *S. J. Clare 18–1–293–45–17.23; J. Papanastasiou 13–4–129–32–14.33; V. B. Jeffery 13–3–108–31*–10.80; J. Naish 17–3–147–47*–10.50; A. C. Winter 15–0–138–47–9.20.

Bowling—J. Papanastasiou 192–36–529–44–12.02; A. C. Winter 228–62–613–33–18.57; N. E. Humber 73–15–268–13–20.61; G. I. Wharton 97–22–278–13–21.38; P. C. Berglund 153–34–428–17–25.17.

ALLHALLOWS SCHOOL

Played 12: Won 1, Lost 6, Drawn 5

Master i/c: P. L. Petherbridge

Batting—P. Holland 12–1–325–81–29.54; T. Elmhirst 9–1–162–60*–20.25; C. Cuff 10–0–189–55–18.90; *R. Enticott 11–1–137–41*–13.70.

Bowling—R. Enticott 68–15–223–10–22.30; P. Holland 85.2–7–330–13–25.38.

AMPLEFORTH COLLEGE

Played 14: Won 4, Lost 5, Drawn 5. Abandoned 3

Master i/c: J. G. Willcox

Batting—*J. R. Elliot 14–2–387–72*–32.25; P. T. Lucas 13–2–348–64–31.63; B. Stones 11–3–199–58*–24.87; P. Bingham 7–1–148–38–24.66; N. A. Derbyshire 11–4–136–44*–19.42; J. Thompson 14–1–250–62*–19.23; B. Dow 12–1–181–31*–16.45; G. Easterby 14–0–223–60–15.92.

Bowling—D. H. Churton 195.4–57–509–36–14.13; J. Thompson 46.4–8–150–10–15.00; N. A. Derbyshire 135–22–458–22–20.81; W. H. Crichton-Stuart 152.4–55–421–19–22.15; B. Dow 95.5–25–256–10–25.60.

ARDINGLY COLLEGE

Played 18: Won 2, Lost 7, Drawn 9. Abandoned 1

Master i/c: T. J. Brooker

Batting—M. T. E. Peirce 8–2–203–96*–33.83; P. A. Bradford 17–6–348–65*–31.63; *T. W. Butterworth 18–1–520–82*–30.58; J. A. Newman 14–3–310–65*–28.18; M. Newcomb 8–1–182–79–26.00; P. R. Spencer 18–0–405–65–22.50; N. P. Mather 18–0–286–58–15.88; T. D. James 10–3–104–29*–14.85; J. St G. L. Jessop 14–1–161–64–12.38.

Bowling—T. D. James 240–53–861–36–23.91; R. C. P. Maynard 120.5–14–513–16–32.06; J. A. K. Maynard 93–15–387–12–32.25; P. R. Spencer 109–25–388–11–35.27; T. W. Butterworth 190–44–659–15–43.93.

ARNOLD SCHOOL

Played 20: Won 6, Lost 6, Drawn 8

Master i/c: S. Burnage

Batting—*A. D. Jones 20–2–580–100*–32.22; B. S. Little 18–1–516–107–30.35; P. M. Aga 18–5–274–63*–21.07; M. Clinning 18–1–326–61–19.17; A. Flynn 14–0–153–26–10.92; S. Birtwistle 16–4–127–28*–10.58; S. M. Aga 16–4–125–30–10.41; C. Leather 13–0–108–25–8.30.

Bowling—B. S. Little 33.4–7–104–12–8.66; S. M. Aga 362.2–98–978–69–14.17; S. Taylor 120.5–18–418–23–18.17; A. D. Jones 96.3–16–347–12–28.91.

ASHVILLE COLLEGE, HARROGATE

Played 17: Won 9, Lost 4, Drawn 4. Abandoned 3

Master i/c: J. M. Bromley — Cricket professional: P. J. Kippax

Batting—A. W. Alexander 17–2–557–86–37.13; T. C. Drummond 17–2–387–71*–25.80; S. J. Walmsley 16–0–304–61–19.00; R. D. Gunning 11–3–134–64–16.75; B. J. Drummond 15–1–222–43*–15.85; A. J. B. Casey 16–1–134–38*–8.93.

Bowling—B. J. Drummond 112–35–281–21–13.38; S. B. Henderson 157–39–500–35–14.28; A. W. Alexander 110–11–346–20–17.30; S. J. Walmsley 122–23–350–20–17.50; R. D. Gunning 108–26–371–20–18.55.

BALLYMENA ACADEMY GRAMMAR SCHOOL

Played 27: Won 19, Lost 3, Drawn 5. Abandoned 1

Master i/c: E. C. B. Jackson

Batting—*J. T. Glass 22–8–476–73*–34.00; J. M. Kennedy 25–5–677–58–33.85; J. J. S. McBurney 21–5–414–86–25.87; P. S. Rainey 22–6–324–45–20.25; R. H. Bill 12–4–109–23*–13.62; M. G. Glass 17–0–193–40–11.35; S. J. Surgeoner 22–0–183–31–8.31.

Bowling—P. S. Rainey 190–50–415–51–8.13; J. M. Kennedy 38–4–130–13–10.00; C. B. Williams 104–10–394–35–11.25; J. T. Glass 145–20–502–42–11.95; M. G. Glass 125–24–371–26–14.26; J. J. S. McBurney 158–31–376–26–14.46; R. D. Barclay 62–9–173–10–17.30.

BANCROFT'S SCHOOL

Played 20: Won 6, Lost 6, Drawn 8. Abandoned 1

Master i/c: J. G. Bromfield

Batting—*A. C. H. Knight 21–3–476–106*–26.44; D. J. Clark 5–0–113–69–22.60; G. P. Brown 21–1–407–72–20.35; G. J. Maynard 19–0–360–88–18.94; T. W. Clark 19–5–229–42*–16.35; G. A. Fisher 19–2–225–73–13.23; J. P. Manning 16–4–146–27–12.16; P. Brown 17–1–171–32*–10.68.

Bowling—D. J. Clark 37.4–4–120–13–9.23; A. Azad 38–6–110–10–11.00; P. Brown 137.5–21–465–37–12.56; G. P. Brown 195.4–52–586–35–16.74; R. Patel 158–35–463–27–17.14.

BANGOR GRAMMAR SCHOOL

Played 19: Won 7, Lost 6, Drawn 5, Tied 1. Abandoned 1

Master i/c: C. C. J. Harte

Batting—*S. C. McKenna 8–1–200–65–28.57; S. L. Mann 15–2–342–94*–26.30; D. W. Rothwell 12–2–227–84*–22.70; N. S. Taylor 15–2–255–58*–19.61; R. G. Scott 18–4–235–39–16.78; M. D. McLellan 11–1–149–29–14.90; S. R. McIlroy 10–1–131–41–14.55; P. A. McIlwane 15–3–162–28*–13.50.

Bowling—M. W. R. McCord 162.2–24–500–38–13.15; R. G. Scott 120.5–24–350–24–14.58; M. W. Orr 80–23–192–11–17.45; S. L. Mann 90–8–328–14–23.42; N. S. Taylor 91.2–15–313–12–26.08.

BARNARD CASTLE SCHOOL

Played 21: Won 8, Lost 2, Drawn 11. Abandoned 2

Master i/c: C. P. Johnson

Batting—J. G. H. Murphy 21–5–588–66*–36.75; D. M. Parr 15–7–232–54*–29.00; M. E. Jobling 18–3–389–61*–25.93; R. D. Whittaker 20–2–384–47–21.33; G. H. Douglas-Hiley 13–3–178–75*–17.80; J. Simon 13–4–149–36*–16.55; *R. E. W. Shield 19–1–256–59–14.22.

Bowling—J. M. W. B. Ward 69–13–217–15–14.46; J. G. H. Murphy 277–72–753–47–16.02; R. E. W. Shield 91.3–12–300–17–17.64; G. H. Douglas-Hiley 102.2–19–342–19–18.00; C. M. Fairey 302.2–76–851–47–18.10.

BEDFORD SCHOOL

Played 15: Won 4, Lost 2, Drawn 9. Abandoned 4

Master i/c: D. W. Jarrett Cricket professional: R. G. Caple

Batting—R. E. Sims 17–2–479–61–31.93; G. L. Machin 15–3–332–65*–27.66; M. W. J. Heslett 16–3–337–50–25.92; B. W. Bardner 12–7–120–38–24.00; M. J. Slack 16–1–300–93–20.00; R. W. H. Smith 17–0–286–41–16.82; R. G. O. Spencer 12–2–160–44–16.00; A. A. J. Woodford 9–2–107–43–15.28; D. R. Bolgar 13–2–139–40–12.63.

Bowling—R. W. H. Smith 128–33–339–29–11.68; *M. J. Simms 116.5–31–352–24–14.66; B. W. Bardner 160–39–459–30–15.30; G. L. Machin 75–16–170–10–17.00; R. E. Sims 107–21–287–14–20.50; R. A. Jones 177–41–463–19–24.36.

BEDFORD MODERN SCHOOL

Played 18: Won 6, Lost 2, Drawn 10. Abandoned 3

Master i/c: N. J. Chinneck

Batting—G. A. H. Awudu 18–2–599–109–37.43; *G. C. Black 17–3–383–63–27.35; P. A. Simmonds 14–1–352–111–27.07; A. C. Mackenzie 16–2–326–42–23.28; D. J. Outtrim 18–0–390–66–21.66; E. J. Seymour 12–1–177–48–16.09; E. R. Osborn 16–2–186–33*–13.28.

Bowling—N. R. Ali 128–38–273–21–13.00; G. A. H. Awudu 273.2–59–750–54–13.88; G. C. Black 136.5–39–317–21–15.09; M. T. Cavanagh 160.5–28–520–24–21.66.

BEECHEN CLIFF SCHOOL, BATH

Played 9: Won 6, Lost 1, Drawn 2. Abandoned 2

Master i/c: K. J. L. Mabe Cricket professional: P. J. Colbourne

Batting—S. M. Priscott 4–3–126–41*–126.00; G. Brown 3–1–115–67–57.50; *D. J. Adams 8–4–170–61–42.50; D. W. Benton 6–1–189–89–37.80; P. C. McCoy 6–2–142–53*–35.50.

Bowling—S. M. Priscott 87.4–25–241–19–12.68; J. D. Colbourne 62.5–12–248–17–14.58.

BERKHAMSTED SCHOOL

Played 11: Won 3, Lost 3, Drawn 5. Abandoned 4

Master i/c: F. J. Davis Cricket professional: M. Herring

Batting—*C. D. Collett 11–2–262–92*–29.11; D. T. Hodges 11–1–262–43–26.20; E. P. Shek 11–0–230–111–20.90; J. P. Crowther 7–1–109–40*–18.16; A. P. Spooner 9–0–152–40–16.88.

Bowling—T. McA. Prentice 131–22–399–21–19.00; C. M. Lovegrove 181–46–449–23–19.52; R. D. Collett 78–8–231–10–23.10; D. T. Hodges 212–53–558–23–24.26.

BISHOP'S STORTFORD COLLEGE

Played 12: Won 0, Lost 6, Drawn 6. Abandoned 6

Master i/c: D. A. Hopper Cricket professional: E. G. Witherden

Batting—R. D. F. Wright 10–1–280–101–31.11; R. N. McIntyre 12–2–284–52–28.40; W. A. J. Pugh 5–0–107–53–21.40; *P. E. B. Armitage 11–0–225–50–20.45; D. N. Child 12–0–150–49–12.50; J. R. Torrance 12–0–107–19–8.91.

Bowling—R. D. F. Wright 96.3–17–309–18–17.16; R. N. McIntyre 148.5–33–445–18–24.72; J. R. Torrance 184–44–541–20–27.05.

BLOXHAM SCHOOL

Played 15: Won 4, Lost 5, Drawn 6. Abandoned 1

Master i/c: I. K. George

Batting—D. Hill 13–5–371–62*–46.37; *N. Baig 15–1–590–81–42.14; M. Day 15–1–268–38–19.14; E. Hockey 11–1–185–44*–18.50; A. Russell 11–0–155–54–14.09.

Bowling—M. Day 181–32–558–28–19.92; E. Hockey 133–32–417–20–20.85; M. Thompson 145.2–32–405–19–21.31; N. Baig 200–36–606–25–24.24.

BLUNDELL'S SCHOOL

Played 14: Won 0, Lost 5, Drawn 9. Abandoned 3

Master i/c: E. R. Crowe Cricket professional: E. Steele

Batting—A. S. J. Horton 13–4–243–47–27.00; N. A. MacIver 13–0–330–67–25.38; C. D. Bending 14–1–322–88–24.76; M. R. N. Hunt 7–0–126–56–18.00; A. J. Rew 13–1–185–47–15.41; D. J. Jewell 12–1–153–41*–13.90; *P. G. Wilson 10–0–130–28–13.00; P. D. Rogers 11–0–127–48–11.54; C. E. Bayly 13–1–125–35–10.41.

Bowling—R. S. Castle 215–64–588–32–18.37; A. J. Cartwright 101–19–432–21–20.57; P. G. Wilson 140.4–33–503–16–31.43; C. D. Bending 102–10–407–11–37.00.

BRADFIELD COLLEGE

Played 17: Won 9, Lost 4, Drawn 4

Master i/c: F. R. Dethridge Cricket professional: J. F. Harvey

Batting—R. W. F. Perry 17–2–599–109*–39.93; J. C. Adams 16–1–399–72–26.60; *W. A. Oscroft 16–1–354–64–23.60; W. D. Cairns 15–2–198–33–15.23; T. Findjan 16–2–209–33–14.92; D. J. Wiggins 16–0–174–27–10.87.

Bowling—R. W. F. Perry 137–39–304–25–12.16; W. A. Oscroft 177–47–421–33–12.75; J. D. Pearce 226–76–492–34–14.47; E. G. Browning 176–38–451–29–15.55.

BRADFORD GRAMMAR SCHOOL

Played 34: Won 18, Lost 11, Drawn 5. Abandoned 3

Master i/c: A. G. Smith

Batting—D. R. Chadwick 31–5–759–127–29.19; A. G. Webster 28–4–618–95–25.75; S. Henry 16–0–329–67–20.56; A. G. Stott 17–0–319–61–18.76; *P. R. Miles 28–4–445–45–18.54; J. P. Collen 32–4–511–64–18.25; D. C. Whitfield 24–4–362–58–18.10; N. H. W. Marshall 23–2–240–33–11.42; R. A. F. Kitchen 23–6–169–41*–9.94; R. A. Midgley 17–3–103–24–7.35.

Bowling—A. G. Webster 231.3–46–592–55–10.76; R. A. Midgley 112.5–15–376–27–13.92; R. A. F. Kitchen 239.5–49–683–48–14.22; P. R. Miles 213–51–771–53–14.54; D. Priestley 50.2–15–174–10–17.40; A. G. Stott 45–3–199–11–18.09; P. R. Booth 159–30–466–22–21.18; J. D. Morton 73.4–9–321–15–21.40.

BRENTWOOD SCHOOL

Played 13: Won 2, Lost 3, Drawn 8. Abandoned 2

Master i/c: P. J. Whitcombe Cricket professional: K. C. Preston

Batting—*M. D. Wilkins 13–1–349–115*–29.08; J. G. Northwood 13–2–290–50*–26.36; C. J. Wilkins 12–2–263–50*–26.30; R. T. Goodey 10–0–159–52–15.90; G. K. Fletcher 9–0–112–50–12.44; P. McGowan 11–2–102–43–11.33; M. A. Spackman 11–0–122–28–11.09.

Bowling—M. D. Wilkins 192–52–494–27–18.29; P. McGowan 158–17–544–24–22.66; I. F. Stronach 155–41–407–16–25.43; A. Majumdar 100–20–310–11–28.18; A. A. Witney 116–22–296–10–29.60.

BRIGHTON COLLEGE

Played 19: Won 9, Lost 3, Drawn 7. Abandoned 1

Master i/c: J. Spencer Cricket professional: J. D. Morley

Batting—J. P. Gibson 19–0–701–157–36.89; *C. P. Sweet 18–1–601–98–35.35; R. B. Holt 16–4–412–91–34.33; C. N. Gates 19–2–422–65–24.82; R. Oliphant-Callum 17–1–381–73–23.81; C. P. Hart 14–6–176–56*–22.00; P. E. Chettleburgh 12–2–200–43–20.00; N. D. Grey 9–4–100–38*–20.00; D. Clout 12–2–102–21*–10.20.

Bowling—C. M. Long 311–128–717–53–13.52; C. P. Sweet 217.3–52–556–39–14.25; C. P. Hart 224.2–57–611–33–18.51.

BROMSGROVE SCHOOL

Played 16: Won 5, Lost 5, Drawn 6. Abandoned 2

Master i/c: D. Langlands

Batting—*P. C. Duffy 14–6–762–111*–95.25; J. C. Reed-Daunter 11–2–289–63–32.11; A. Burton 7–0–156–44–22.28; W. Guck 13–3–174–31–17.40; H. W. Humphries 11–3–103–31–12.87; R. H. M. Beddall 11–1–128–42–12.80.

Bowling—P. C. Duffy 122.3–9–429–31–13.83; A. Wylie 145.2–37–328–23–14.26; J. C. Reed-Daunter 92–12–299–11–27.18.

BRYANSTON SCHOOL

Played 15: Won 3, Lost 5, Drawn 7. Abandoned 1

Master i/c: M. C. Wagstaffe

Batting—S. C. Ecclestone 12–3–751–126–83.44; R. G. Lee 14–1–412–117–31.69; T. Clarke 10–3–108–33*–15.42; J. Singleton 11–3–106–27–13.25; T. J. Millard 11–0–125–37–11.36.

Bowling—R. G. Lee 186.4–29–558–31–18.00; S. C. Ecclestone 139.3–31–438–17–25.76.

CANFORD SCHOOL

Played 16: Won 5, Lost 6, Drawn 5

Master i/c: H. A. Jarvis   Cricket professionals: D. Shackleton and P. Knowles

Batting—J. A. Perry 16–1–433–70–28.86; *J. P. Blissard-Barnes 16–1–422–73–28.13; N. M. Roussel 12–5–168–49*–24.00; R. E. M. Robinson 13–1–263–75–21.91; D. J. C. Allom 14–3–231–54*–21.00; M. L. Harris 8–2–115–34–19.16; J. G. E. Bartholomew 14–0–226–43–16.14; M. W. Forward 12–0–120–25–10.00.

Bowling—T. R. Murray-Walker 187–25–547–35–15.62; J. R. Murray-Walker 118–22–327–15–21.80; A. G. Easton 150.3–24–491–20–24.55; N. M. Roussel 167.1–37–522–19–27.47.

CATERHAM SCHOOL

Played 16: Won 2, Lost 4, Drawn 10. Abandoned 1

Master i/c: A. G. Simon

Batting—N. B. Driscoll 15–2–406–67–31.23; S. J. Dawes 13–0–293–67–22.53; K. A. Amaning 14–2–260–77–21.66; D. N. Podbur 15–1–302–97–21.57; *R. L. M. Mauger 15–1–256–51–18.28; D. J. Mear 12–2–150–33–15.00; M. W. Shackel 15–2–167–31–12.84.

Bowling—D. J. Paisey 220–48–576–37–15.56; N. B. Driscoll 123.3–27–385–24–16.04; S. A. Ghyas 97.1–17–332–16–20.75; R. L. M. Mauger 47.5–2–232–11–21.09.

CHARTERHOUSE

Played 15: Won 5, Lost 6, Drawn 4. Abandoned 2

Master i/c: J. M. Knight   Cricket professional: R. V. Lewis

Batting—G. I. MacMillan 15–3–549–116*–45.75; C. E. L. Simson 16–2–589–112–42.07; *A. E. Ivermee 16–3–286–82*–22.00; G. R. Brooke 13–2–208–76–18.90; J. N. B. Bovill 11–0–195–46–17.72; P. Gorman 12–2–162–55–16.20; A. T. Grundy 11–1–145–58–14.50; S. Wilkinson 12–1–136–50–12.36.

Bowling—J. N. B. Bovill 198.5–61–493–43–11.46; C. W. Oatley 167–56–392–21–18.66; G. I. MacMillan 105–21–307–15–20.46; A. E. Ivermee 121–23–373–17–21.94; P. Gorman 128.5–26–425–17–25.00.

CHELTENHAM COLLEGE

Played 16: Won 6, Lost 4, Drawn 6. Abandoned 2

Master i/c: W. J. Wesson   Cricket professional: M. W. Stovold

Batting—*G. F. Hill 16–2–432–89–30.85; T. N. Wyatt-Gunning 12–0–314–57–26.16; J. R. Boddington 14–0–366–81–26.14; I. O. Kirkland 15–2–330–98–25.38; E. G. Boyd 15–4–249–46–22.63; R. W. Harris 13–7–102–43*–17.00; M. A. Crowther 12–0–106–38–8.83.

Bowling—M. A. Crowther 128.3–19–513–28–18.32; T. N. Wyatt-Gunning 193.5–28–656–32–20.50; A. R. Whitten 157–31–536–26–20.61; G. F. Hill 86.3–17–314–11–28.54; J. R. Davison 94–19–306–10–30.60.

CHIGWELL SCHOOL

Played 13: Won 1, Lost 6, Drawn 6. Abandoned 2

Master i/c: D. N. Morrison

Batting—*D. Clark 12–0–367–126–30.58; J. Carpenter 13–1–360–72–30.00; T. Tarring 13–1–199–52*–16.58; M. Flack 12–1–117–37–10.63.

Bowling—G. Haysom 78–18–203–12–16.91; I. Maskey 68–8–246–12–20.50; D. Clark 96.2–19–309–14–22.07; J. Carpenter 115.2–27–302–13–23.23; X. Ferguson 108.3–22–338–13–26.00.

CHRIST COLLEGE, BRECON

Played 12: Won 4, Lost 1, Drawn 7. Abandoned 8

Master i/c: C. W. Kleiser

Batting—E. P. M. Holland 9–4–152–55*–30.40; *M. Yendle 12–2–273–87–27.30; K. R. W. Lumby 9–2–188–54*–26.85; K. L. Miller 10–2–178–52–22.25; R. T. W. Horne 12–3–190–63–21.11; M. J. Williams 8–2–113–30–18.83; S. D. Hooper 7–0–101–80–14.42; N. D. Powell 11–0–111–28–10.09.

Bowling—E. P. M. Holland 104.3–32–231–22–10.50; R. T. W. Horne 71.1–12–214–19–11.26; M. Yendle 63.3–10–179–11–16.27; K. L. Miller 105–32–227–10–22.70.

CHRIST'S HOSPITAL

Played 16: Won 2, Lost 6, Drawn 8

Master i/c: R. H. Sutcliffe Cricket professional: A. Karim

Batting—S. J. Hitch 12–1–221–50–20.09; *J. R. Atkinson 11–1–192–64–19.20; R. A. Dawson 7–0–118–39–16.85; J. M. Sillett 14–1–206–67*–15.84; J. H. Newsum 11–1–156–59–15.60; J. D. English 15–0–220–69–14.66; P. M. Emerson 13–0–186–38–14.30; J. P. Saunders 11–0–142–34–12.90.

Bowling—T. K. W. Welch 178–37–392–30–13.06; T. A. Fooks 182–33–519–32–16.21; J. D. English 114–18–384–22–17.45; J. R. Atkinson 98–12–419–15–27.93.

CLAYESMORE SCHOOL

Played 15: Won 8, Lost 1, Drawn 6. Abandoned 2

Master i/c: R. P. Merriman

Batting—*G. Owton 15–3–782–132–65.16; J. C. Latimer 11–4–316–112*–45.14; J. Dike 13–3–214–65*–21.40; R. Greene 13–2–178–69–16.18.

Bowling—J. C. Latimer 36–9–85–10–8.50; J. Dike 182–48–462–50–9.24; C. Eitzen 57.2–6–188–16–11.75; T. Bradbury 108.3–27–260–20–13.00; P. Griffiths 59–14–184–13–14.15.

CLIFTON COLLEGE

Played 19: Won 3, Lost 6, Drawn 10. Abandoned 1

Master i/c: C. M. E. Colquhoun Cricket professional: F. J. Andrew

Batting—R. J. R. Clark 19–1–740–116–41.11; J. R. A. Williams 15–1–535–108–38.21; T. C. Henderson 15–5–358–114*–35.80; J. A. R. Niven 16–3–446–107*–34.30; M. G. N. Windows 14–5–275–45–30.55; J. P. Parish 12–2–182–38–18.20; J. C. Leek 9–0–123–33–13.66; *R. J. W. Holdsworth 12–4–105–35*–13.12.

Bowling—C. M. Spiro 282.1–41–994–39–25.48; R. J. W. Holdsworth 322.5–71–1,053–38–27.71; J. A. R. Niven 197.2–41–673–17–39.58.

COLFE'S SCHOOL

Played 15: Won 5, Lost 4, Drawn 6

Master i/c: P. Hollingum

Batting—*R. Harmer 15–3–562–102*–46.83; J. Carr 14–5–225–48*–25.00; M. Horder 11–2–149–45–16.55; C. Webb 9–0–140–47–15.55; M. Brierley 14–1–197–34–15.15; G. Davies 13–0–137–25–10.53; P. Mears 14–0–133–39–9.50.

Bowling—M. Wainman 106–19–282–17–16.58; R. Harmer 74–10–261–15–17.40; R. Reynolds 110–21–418–19–22.00; M. Horder 79–9–267–12–22.25; A. Wooff 83–19–245–10–24.50; J. Carr 143.1–28–430–12–35.83.

COLSTON'S SCHOOL

Played 18: Won 4, Lost 5, Drawn 9. Abandoned 2

Master i/c: M. P. B. Tayler

Batting—J. A. Franklin 17–6–561–92*–51.00; *R. L. Rees Jones 17–2–468–102–31.20; S. J. Harwood 13–5–211–45*–26.37; J. E. Vickery 17–1–408–69–25.50; D. J. Hobbs 8–1–146–59*–20.85; M. J. Brittain 10–2–139–52–17.37; M. N. Winrow 16–0–254–94–15.87.

Bowling—J. C. Reice 139.3–25–436–28–15.57; S. J. Davey 147–20–485–17–28.52; J. E. Vickery 120.3–13–548–18–30.44; R. L. Rees Jones 147–18–581–18–32.27; M. J. Brittain 80.2–7–434–10–43.40.

COVENTRY SCHOOL – BABLAKE

Played 17: Won 6, Lost 2, Drawn 9

Master i/c: B. J. Sutton

Batting—*D. J. Barr 16–3–595–92–45.76; D. Ormerod 17–5–375–63–31.25; D. Hopkins 17–0–412–122–24.23; D. Kingham 16–1–303–47–20.20; S. Jervis 15–3–232–47*–19.33; M. Enever 9–2–114–32*–16.28; D. Haywood 12–4–107–26–13.37.

Bowling—B. Parham 149.5–35–413–29–14.24; Azhar Khan 97.3–17–295–16–18.43; D. Hopkins 103.1–21–371–18–20.61; M. G. H. Sutton 110–28–302–14–21.57; D. Haywood 75–19–262–11–23.81.

CRANBROOK SCHOOL

Played 10: Won 1, Lost 4, Drawn 5. Abandoned 1

Master i/c: D. Firminger

Batting—*R. P. T. Lisle 11–1–246–43–24.60; S. P. France 8–3–106–34*–21.20; J. C. Honey 11–2–177–41–19.66; A. P. N. Secker 10–2–151–44*–18.87; K. Wookey 8–1–127–35–18.14.

Bowling—K. Wookey 78.9–13–227–16–14.18; S. P. France 104.8–19–337–20–16.85.

CRANLEIGH SCHOOL

Played 18: Won 2, Lost 5, Drawn 11

Master i/c: C. J. Lush

Batting—P. J. Humphreys 4–1–114–62–38.00; R. A. J. Grove 18–1–576–105–33.88; *N. C. Radbourne 17–1–426–58*–26.62; B. Gurung 18–0–451–71–25.05; I. J. F. Wyness 16–3–267–40–20.53; S. L. McGuire 9–2–111–21–15.85; J. A. Letts 14–3–170–28–15.45; W. R. Stephens 15–4–149–43–13.54.

Bowling—N. C. Radbourne 196–39–618–28–22.07; T. C. Crouch 208–48–655–28–23.39; J. A. Letts 72–14–248–10–24.80; T. G. Robinson 67–12–248–10–24.80; I. J. F. Wyness 128–16–527–13–40.53.

DAUNTSEY'S SCHOOL

Played 14: Won 6, Lost 2, Drawn 6

Master i/c: M. K. F. Johnson Cricket professional: P. Rutledge

Batting—*J. W. S. Porter 13–3–1,104–146*–110.40; R. P. M. Smith 12–3–257–72*–28.55; N. L. Jephson 12–1–293–63–26.63; R. Pollach 10–3–132–46–18.85; N. M. Harvey 9–3–103–16–17.16; K. D. Tadhunter 13–1–176–42–14.66.

Bowling—R. Pollach 109.1–19–339–23–14.73; E. J. Rayner 114–15–398–20–19.90; A. R. Gilmour 144.1–27–491–23–21.34; J. W. S. Porter 126–13–443–19–23.31.

DEAN CLOSE SCHOOL

Played 12: Won 4, Lost 4, Drawn 3, Tied 1. Abandoned 3

Master i/c: C. M. Kenyon Cricket professional: C. Gabbitas

Batting—*T. A. Edginton 11–1–448–101*–44.80; G. G. Hunton 7–0–176–80–25.14; D. A. Breese 8–0–176–50–22.00; S. K. Organ 12–1–174–37–15.81; C. J. Townsend 11–1–158–65–15.80; T. M. Churchill 10–0–116–51–11.60; R. J. Husband 12–0–128–40–10.66.

Bowling—T. M. Churchill 119.3–25–400–36–11.11; T. A. Edginton 144–28–483–28–17.25; C. N. C. Hodges 84–20–250–11–22.72; S. K. Organ 96.1–24–351–10–35.10.

DENSTONE COLLEGE

Played 11: Won 2, Lost 4, Drawn 5. Abandoned 3

Master i/c: A. N. James

Batting—J. Snape 10–3–305–74–43.57; *P. R. Dennis-Jones 9–3–156–47*–26.00; A. J. Gagie 10–3–151–61*–21.57; A. S. H. Oyston 10–1–171–96–19.00.

Bowling—J. Snape 112.4–34–303–16–18.93; J. Broughton 52–5–196–10–19.60; R. J. Harris 89–19–267–11–24.27.

DOUAI SCHOOL

Played 8: Won 0, Lost 4, Drawn 4. Abandoned 3

Master i/c: J. Shaw

Batting—J. Adcock 6–3–119–46–39.66; M. Allen 6–1–126–55–25.20.

Bowling—*R. Lumb 120–18–394–11–35.81; T. Padgham 104–9–514–11–46.72.

DOVER COLLEGE

Played 16: Won 1, Lost 13, Drawn 2. Abandoned 1

Master i/c: D. C. Butler

Batting—J. D. Rouse 14–1–560–104–43.07; *S. P. Howkins 16–1–417–83–27.80; D. M. Rouse 16–1–360–60–24.00; D. J. Winwood 16–1–262–48–17.46; S. J. Schilder 14–0–240–58–17.14.

Bowling—S. P. Howkins 303.1–48–1,051–46–22.84; J. D. Rouse 141.5–18–555–12–46.25.

DOWNSIDE SCHOOL

Played 13: Won 6, Lost 2, Drawn 5. Abandoned 2

Master i/c: K. J. M. Burke

Batting—A. C. Ratcliffe 12–5–354–78*–50.57; G. C. J. Barrington 12–2–321–107*–32.10; S. M. J. Roberts 13–4–279–59*–31.00; *D. P. Morris 9–3–180–54–30.00; T. S. Pascal 11–0–240–81–21.81; N. C. R. Holmes 12–0–223–53–18.58; J. M. R. Higgins 11–0–191–47–17.36.

Bowling—C. E. Crossland 140.5–53–365–28–13.05; R. C. Thesiger 96–18–279–16–17.43; N. C. R. Holmes 49–5–175–10–17.50; J. M. Thesiger 92–23–223–12–18.58; G. C. J. Barrington 150.1–40–405–16–25.31.

DUKE OF YORK'S ROYAL MILITARY SCHOOL

Played 16: Won 4, Lost 4, Drawn 8

Master i/c: S. Salisbury — Cricket professional: P. R. Bradbury

Batting—*A. P. Glasby 16–2–425–102*–30.35; C. N. Conway 11–2–258–80–28.66; S. Gale 13–0–263–57–20.23; M. I. Ive 14–3–196–42–17.81; R. A. Saunders 15–0–253–63–16.86; S. R. Fowler 15–3–177–40–14.75; D. J. Belcher 14–0–188–54–13.42; S. J. G. Lile 12–1–116–27–10.54; M. A. Hulme 15–1–137–36*–9.78.

Bowling—A. G. Wilkinson 162–33–505–34–14.85; S. J. G. Lile 145–29–400–25–16.00; S. Gale 150–36–491–25–19.64; A. P. Glasby 100–13–385–16–24.06; S. R. Fowler 120–29–425–15–28.33.

DULWICH COLLEGE

Played 15: Won 7, Lost 3, Drawn 5

Master i/c: N. D. Cousins — Cricket professionals: A. R. Ranson and W. A. Smith

Batting—N. K. M. Talonpoika 15–1–538–106–38.42; *T. D. J. Ufton 15–1–465–132*–33.21; M. E. Peffers 14–0–249–51–17.78; J. P. Howland 15–0–252–52–16.80; R. C. Tulsiani 11–1–152–33–15.20; A. P. Agar 14–4–145–43–14.50; R. F. Hollis 12–3–101–31*–11.22.

Bowling—N. K. M. Talonpoika 92.2–5–365–22–16.59; R. W. Penry-Jones 157–31–498–18–27.66; R. F. Hollis 148.1–35–478–17–28.11; R. C. Tulsiani 97–14–311–11–28.27.

DURHAM SCHOOL

Played 15: Won 9, Lost 1, Drawn 4, Tied 1. Abandoned 1

Master i/c: N. J. Willings — Cricket professional: M. Hirsch

Batting—A. Roseberry 11–2–490–68–54.44; N. S. Whitfield 13–4–424–93–47.11; W. P. C. Weston 14–1–458–92*–35.23; C. J. Lally 8–3–119–45*–23.80; S. N. Monk 13–3–200–58–20.00; A. C. Bloore 11–2–126–32–14.00; *A. G. Clayton 12–0–108–42–9.00.

Bowling—W. P. C. Weston 189–50–453–31–14.61; A. Roseberry 104–29–300–19–15.78; A. G. Clayton 228.1–59–543–33–16.45; N. S. Whitfield 161.2–45–398–24–16.58.

EASTBOURNE COLLEGE

Played 22: Won 10, Lost 6, Drawn 6

Master i/c: N. L. Wheeler — Cricket professional: A. E. James

Batting—T. C. Nicholson 21–2–1,056–139–55.57; E. S. H. Giddins 11–5–190–92–31.66; *G. E. Thwaites 21–2–573–77–30.15; A. J. T. Halliday 20–2–538–85*–29.88; T. J. Duffill 22–7–384–75*–25.60; P. J. Buckland 11–3–156–60–19.50; P. D. Horscroft 16–1–289–63–19.26; J. F. C. Toomer 16–3–206–53*–15.84; F. A. Ali 12–2–106–27–10.60.

Bowling—E. S. H. Giddins 261–75–741–56–13.23; H. A. Skinner 54–6–225–12–18.75; F. A. Ali 275–72–743–34–21.85; G. E. Thwaites 128–27–454–16–28.37; P. J. Buckland 191–38–688–23–29.91.

THE EDINBURGH ACADEMY

Played 18: Won 10, Lost 3, Drawn 5

Master i/c: A. R. Dyer Cricket professional: G. Reifer

Batting—C. J. Stirling 11–4–195–52–27.85; M. K. Wilkinson 16–2–337–53*–24.07; *M. T. Innes 20–3–390–60–22.94; K. F. Dyer 20–3–386–88*–22.70; N. R. Dyer 16–4–258–50*–21.50; A. R. J. Monaghan 18–2–300–46–18.75.

Bowling—C. J. S. Cairns 206.1–61–493–41–12.02; A. R. J. Monaghan 74.1–7–254–21–12.09; M. M. A. Simpson 193.1–48–513–33–15.54; N. R. Dyer 268.4–75–629–32–19.65; J. J. Edmond 118.3–38–258–10–25.80.

ELIZABETH COLLEGE, GUERNSEY

Played 24: Won 7, Lost 0, Drawn 17

Master i/c: M. E. Kinder

Batting—S. B. R. Mackay 20–3–653–121–38.41; D. J. Marshall 20–1–540–69*–28.42; *N. E. G. Garrett 19–6–244–35–18.76; P. K. Philp 17–3–235–37–16.78; M. L. Jefferies 15–1–221–52–15.78; O. Chadwick 18–5–194–36–14.92; M. Daley 12–5–104–61*–14.85.

Bowling—D. J. Marshall 105–21–298–26–11.46; W. M. Walden 113.4–27–310–22–14.09; S. B. R. Mackay 132–33–360–25–14.40; N. E. G. Garrett 159.4–30–457–31–14.74; R. J. B. Turville 146.2–40–380–24–15.83; P. J. A. Moody 150.3–40–407–23–17.69.

ELLESMERE COLLEGE

Played 15: Won 6, Lost 3, Drawn 6. Abandoned 2

Master i/c: E. Marsh Cricket professional: R. K. Sethi

Batting—M. J. Marvell 15–6–432–92–48.00; D. J. Marvell 15–3–448–101*–37.33; *C. M. Reed 13–4–278–56–30.88; M. R. Winn 13–0–258–58–19.84; J. S. Marsh 12–0–219–44–18.25; T. A. R. Elston 16–1–250–65–16.66; N. J. B. Allan 12–4–128–28–16.00; W. J. Hart 12–2–150–32–15.00.

Bowling—M. J. Marvell 283–99–597–45–13.26; J. G. Slater 138–22–260–13–20.00; C. M. Reed 203–52–528–22–24.00.

ELTHAM COLLEGE

Played 13: Won 2, Lost 7, Drawn 4. Abandoned 3

Masters i/c: P. McCartney and B. M. Withecombe Cricket professional: R. Winup

Batting—L. W. Neil-Dwyer 11–3–337–61*–42.12; *S. J. Goodfellow 10–1–232–73*–25.77; R. A. Morgan 11–1–250–102*–25.00; J. J. Guthrie 11–2–211–103*–23.44; N. S. White 8–1–120–41–17.14.

Bowling—S. P. Allen 79.3–16–294–19–15.47; S. J. Goodfellow 159.1–27–493–28–17.60; S. G. Hughes 97–12–288–12–24.00; N. A. O'Leary 89.5–17–344–13–26.46.

EMANUEL SCHOOL

Played 21: Won 8, Lost 7, Drawn 6. Abandoned 1

Master i/c: R. M. Woodall

Batting—M. D. Coe 18–2–848–83–53.00; *S. J. Legg 21–1–826–107–41.30; A. Din 17–0–437–40–25.70; A. Riley 13–5–189–54*–23.62; I. Tournès 16–3–222–71*–17.07; P. Ratna 19–0–302–61–15.89; J. D. Cole 16–3–157–37*–12.07.

Bowling—M. D. Coe 242–73–647–42–15.40; J. D. Cole 201–51–511–27–18.92; D. Shore 177–47–469–22–21.31; D. Kohli 109–14–327–15–21.80.

ENFIELD GRAMMAR SCHOOL

Played 18: Won 5, Lost 7, Drawn 6. Abandoned 2

Master i/c: J. J. Conroy

Batting—D. Bowen 16–0–643–135–40.18; J. King 16–4–401–90*–33.41; O. White 17–1–502–109*–31.37; S. Chandler 6–1–134–40*–26.80; T. Holmes 9–3–156–27–26.00; S. Ewins 11–0–131–32–11.90; A. Griggs 15–0–172–46–11.46; P. Cully 11–0–122–31–11.09.

Bowling—P. Nicholls 169.5–24–611–28–21.82; N. Lutwyche 133.2–15–504–20–25.20; S. Graham 74.3–11–293–11–26.63; J. Gillespie 88.2–12–432–11–39.27; C. Browne 116–24–400–10–40.00.

EPSOM COLLEGE

Played 12: Won 6, Lost 2, Drawn 4

Master i/c: M. D. Hobbs

Batting—G. D. Saunders-Griffiths 8–0–205–117–25.62; D. R. Bance 13–1–302–104*–25.16; D. A. George 9–4–109–29–21.80; G. K. Cohen 12–1–228–45–20.72; *G. A. Coles 13–2–219–66*–19.90; M. J. Merrington 13–0–227–65–17.46; P. J. Vickars 10–2–124–37*–15.50; J. C. A. Collier 12–0–105–25–8.75.

Bowling—P. J. Vickars 180.5–43–465–34–13.67; W. E. J. Crawford 88–20–275–20–13.75; D. A. George 110.2–22–293–18–16.27; N. A. Morris 135.5–17–493–15–32.86.

ETON COLLEGE

Played 14: Won 5, Lost 2, Drawn 7. Abandoned 1

Master i/c: J. A. Claughton — Cricket professional: J. M. Rice

Batting—H. R. E. Petre 13–5–386–71*–48.25; C. H. G. St George 14–3–389–84*–35.36; A. G. Bignell 14–1–367–68–28.23; J. E. Carr 12–1–281–83–25.54; S. R. B. Martin 14–0–261–50–18.64; J. C. Prichard 11–4–126–43*–18.00; J. T. Trusted 9–3–103–42*–17.16.

Bowling—*J. K. Erith 172.2–39–494–30–16.46; E. B. J. Johnson 197.4–40–586–34–17.23; T. P. M. Fleming 244.1–53–556–27–20.59.

EXETER SCHOOL

Played 13: Won 4, Lost 1, Drawn 8. Abandoned 2

Master i/c: M. C. Wilcock

Batting—C. L. Bawden 13–2–344–82–31.27; J. P. L. Hottot 11–1–229–54–22.90; *R. P. Corney 13–1–250–76–20.83; C. Q. Taylor 10–0–198–54–19.80; M. J. Stevenson 8–0–103–30–12.87.

Bowling—M. J. Stevenson 141.4–25–387–21–18.42; P. R. Taverner 170.1–38–467–24–19.45.

FELSTED SCHOOL

Played 17: Won 9, Lost 0, Drawn 8

Master i/c: M. Surridge Cricket professional: G. O. Barker

Batting—*N. V. Knight 16–6–1,013–168*–101.30; R. J. Bentley 10–3–333–55–47.57; T. F. C. Cooper 16–2–509–82–36.35; S. J. Keys 12–2–342–73–34.20; J. D. Collard 17–0–379–59–22.29; R. J. Slater 8–3–104–33–20.80; S. E. Carson 15–2–234–61–18.00.

Bowling—R. J. Slater 66–14–176–16–11.00; T. F. C. Cooper 101–20–312–21–14.85; R. F. Kirby 89–23–236–14–16.85; G. R. Hussey 101–24–288–15–19.20; N. V. Knight 121–29–423–22–19.22; C. S. G. Staveley 159–49–457–17–26.88; I. F. Morgan 151–38–411–15–27.40.

FETTES COLLEGE

Played 11: Won 2, Lost 4, Drawn 5. Abandoned 4

Master i/c: M. C. G. Peel Cricket professional: J. van Geloven

Batting—*J. L. MacLean 11–2–313–111*–34.77; J. A. Cardwell Moore 11–2–235–68*–26.11; N. H. Turner 7–2–105–22*–21.00; A. F. Rhodes 8–1–103–44–14.71; C. F. Hendry 9–1–100–27*–12.50.

Bowling—J. L. MacLean 178.1–33–437–30–14.56; J. R. S. Lloyd 189–37–536–30–17.86; P. de Bernier 96–16–316–16–19.75.

FOREST SCHOOL

Played 16: Won 6, Lost 5, Drawn 5

Master i/c: S. Turner

Batting—*A. C. Richards 16–2–696–104–49.71; P. I. O'Neill 15–2–503–76–38.69; B. J. Barnett 13–5–273–62*–34.12; A. R. Heyes 13–0–212–53–16.30; P. Butler 16–2–187–37–13.35.

Bowling—A. C. Richards 172–62–438–34–12.88; P. Butler 184–36–522–33–15.81; L. Adenaike 241–53–681–30–22.70.

FOYLE AND LONDONDERRY COLLEGE

Played 22: Won 13, Lost 4, Drawn 5

Masters i/c: G. R. McCarter and I. McKracken

Batting—*S. Smyth 19–1–1,026–165–57.00; T. Dougherty 7–2–159–79*–31.80; M. Simpson 18–3–421–66*–28.06; G. Watson 15–2–263–46–20.23; D. Deans 20–1–326–41–17.15; S. Baldrick 17–2–246–79*–16.40; R. Curry 21–1–298–89–14.90; B. Smyth 18–4–191–39–14.50.

Bowling—M. Simpson 206–75–360–42–8.57; S. Baldrick 139–42–310–34–9.11; D. Deans 155.2–38–382–34–11.23; G. Watson 84–9–369–25–14.76; A. Cooke 89.2–11–368–14–26.28.

FRAMLINGHAM COLLEGE

Played 14: Won 5, Lost 3, Drawn 6. Abandoned 1

Master i/c: P. J. Hayes Cricket professional: C. Rutterford

Batting—S. C. Giller 14–4–437–92–43.70; S. E. Iliffe 14–1–361–106*–27.76; R. Gemmill 12–2–212–45–21.20; *P. C. E. Gubbins 11–2–174–62–19.33; K. H. Ip 11–1–154–55*–15.40; N. I. Barker 12–0–118–38–9.83.

Bowling—S. C. Giller 184.3–63–422–32–13.18; M. J. Rutterford 85.1–27–192–14–13.71; M. J. Anstes 153.1–41–428–24–17.83.

GIGGLESWICK SCHOOL

Played 14: Won 3, Lost 4, Drawn 7. Abandoned 2

Master i/c: R. C. Green Cricket professional: T. M. Moody

Batting—*M. P. Kaye 14–1–375–73–28.84; A. G. Holmes 13–0–258–60–19.84; G. B. Callan 13–2–211–63*–19.18; D. A. V. Caton 14–0–261–50–18.64; D. M. Keoghan 14–3–168–35–15.27.

Bowling—M. P. Kaye 133–17–473–30–15.76; T. I. Bentley 59–8–207–12–17.25; D. A. V. Caton 64–7–223–10–22.30; J. R. Jackson 122–15–436–19–22.94.

THE GLASGOW ACADEMY

Played 12: Won 2, Lost 9, Drawn 1

Master i/c: S. W. McAslan Cricket professional: P. A. Cooper

Batting—R. K. S. Fleming 11–0–146–63–13.27; L. S. Sandberg 11–2–103–36*–11.44; K. Matthews 12–0–128–58–10.66; A. S. Campbell 12–2–104–23–10.40.

Bowling—R. K. S. Fleming 82.4–12–261–17–15.35; A. S. Campbell 101.5–15–285–15–19.00; D. W. Hutton 108.3–12–337–14–24.07.

GLENALMOND

Played 13: Won 6, Lost 1, Drawn 6. Abandoned 2

Master i/c: A. J. N. James Cricket professional: W. J. Dennis

Batting—*J. P. Brown 6–1–321–100*–64.20; I. M. S. Wilson 11–1–269–80–26.90; B. Hastie 13–4–175–33–19.44; N. H. Brown 10–2–122–44–15.25; D. R. Oswald 14–1–178–55–13.69; W. G. Sutton 14–0–174–49–12.42; R. M. Jebb 12–3–103–35–11.44.

Bowling—J. C. Caldwell 46.3–12–122–12–10.16; I. M. S. Wilson 131.1–48–309–30–10.30; B. Hastie 132.3–32–348–21–16.57; M. W. J. Crow 110.3–15–326–19–17.15; R. M. Jebb 107.5–23–335–17–19.70.

GORDONSTOUN SCHOOL

Played 11: Won 7, Lost 3, Drawn 1

Master i/c: C. J. Barton

Batting—S. Thompson 9–2–281–63–40.14; A. Alireza 10–0–192–43–19.20; T. Larkman 11–1–158–42–15.80.

Bowling—P. Wivell 52–11–166–14–11.85; T. Larkman 103–30–260–14–18.57; H. Cliffe-Thomson 71–6–205–10–20.50.

GRENVILLE COLLEGE

Played 16: Won 6, Lost 9, Drawn 1

Master i/c: R. J. Davis

Batting—G. S. Dermody 15–1–375–65–26.78; T. B. Rex 6–0–142–47–23.66; *V. A. Evans 10–1–191–58–21.22; D. J. Grigg 8–1–110–30–15.71; D. Puddepha 10–1–133–43–14.77.

Bowling—J. Dodd 27–2–137–11–12.45; V. A. Evans 40–0–177–12–14.75; C. P. Ely 66–3–283–19–14.89; S. Wait 88–10–312–17–18.35.

GRESHAM'S SCHOOL

Played 14: Won 5, Lost 3, Drawn 6. Abandoned 4

Master i/c: A. M. Ponder

Batting—T. Allison 13–2–449–130*–40.81; H. E. M. Spence 12–2–356–73–35.60; *S. Mussellwhite 14–1–302–59*–23.23; D. J. Newton 9–2–128–34–18.28; I. D. Barnett 11–2–155–41–17.22.

Bowling—C. Jackson 125.2–39–289–25–11.56; N. J. Roper 118–31–295–22–13.40; T. Allison 74.1–15–228–13–17.53; I. D. Barnett 118–23–342–19–18.00.

HABERDASHERS' ASKE'S SCHOOL, ELSTREE

Played 20: Won 11, Lost 0, Drawn 9

Master i/c: D. I. Yeabsley

Batting—D. I. Chippeck 20–6–602–120–43.00; *A. V. Spencer 20–3–635–94–37.35; S. T. Arumugam 10–1–281–51*–31.22; R. W. Thacker 9–3–119–34*–19.83; B. V. Arumugam 15–5–194–43*–19.40; B. B. Moore 16–3–179–41–13.76.

Bowling—D. A. Jordan 58–24–86–14–6.14; M. I. Yeabsley 127.2–29–380–30–12.66; D. G. Musgrave 215–60–498–29–17.17; D. B. Quinn 173.2–26–632–32–19.75; B. V. Arumugam 115.1–23–301–14–21.50.

HAILEYBURY

Played 19: Won 9, Lost 2, Drawn 8. Abandoned 1

Master i/c: M. S. Seymour — Cricket professional: P. M. Ellis

Batting—*D. C. L. Beynon 19–4–619–114*–41.26; L. Conroy 5–1–155–65–38.75; M. C. Goodson 17–4–431–73*–33.15; I. E. Simmons 16–1–330–96–22.00; J. B. Jouning 19–0–394–101–20.73; E. G. Stapley 15–5–206–59*–20.60.

Bowling—D. C. L. Beynon 61–22–128–12–10.66; M. C. Goodson 323–100–541–45–12.02; E. G. Stapley 82–20–220–16–13.75; E. G. Erith 253–60–668–37–18.05; G. A. Ritchie 69–18–185–10–18.50.

HAMPTON SCHOOL

Played 17: Won 10, Lost 1, Drawn 6. Abandoned 2

Master i/c: G. R. Cocksworth

Batting—J. P. Diprose 13–1–484–111–40.33; C. R. Westaway 17–3–408–107*–29.14; D. W. Rixon 15–0–415–89–27.66; A. J. Maclenan 9–2–180–53*–25.71; *A. J. B. Sales 16–1–319–51–21.26; A. A. J. Bingham 14–3–229–38*–20.81; S. A. H. Cochrane 11–3–129–36–16.12.

Bowling—R. A. F. Hall 180–20–459–37–12.40; S. J. Patel 226–25–626–47–13.31; S. A. H. Cochrane 133–20–345–24–14.37; J. G. J. Alexander 106–18–262–18–14.55; A. J. Maclenan 97–12–410–21–19.52.

HARROW SCHOOL

Played 17: Won 5, Lost 4, Drawn 8

Master i/c: W. Snowden — Cricket professional: P. Davis

Batting—*C. Keey 18–2–703–119–43.93; J. K. Bourne 18–4–460–101–32.85; C. Raper 16–6–299–44–29.90; M. Boralessa 14–1–383–76–29.46; C. A. Abraham 14–6–233–59–29.12; M. B. T. de Souza-Girao 17–0–263–40–15.47.

Bowling—C. Raper 196–49–335–29–11.55; J. E. Oppenheimer 181–27–406–29–14.00; R. D. Nelson 123–29–260–17–15.29; G. R. C. Bucknall 79–14–266–17–15.64; J. A. R. Hill 276–48–534–24–22.25.

HEREFORD CATHEDRAL SCHOOL

Played 15: Won 5, Lost 0, Drawn 9, Tied 1

Master i/c: A. H. Connop

Batting—*N. Denny 14–6–481–76*–60.12; G. Powell 12–1–364–61–33.09; R. Binnersley 11–2–267–73–29.66; A. Mills 14–1–294–56*–22.61; S. Price 11–5–120–26*–20.00; A. Glinos 8–2–114–36–19.00; R. King 13–1–169–43–14.08.

Bowling—S. Price 84–23–216–16–13.50; G. Powell 148–39–435–29–15.00; M. Previté 59.5–6–261–16–16.31; S. Partridge 141.5–36–462–22–21.00.

HIGHGATE SCHOOL

Played 15: Won 4, Lost 5, Drawn 6. Abandoned 2

Master i/c: C. J. Davies Cricket professional: R. E. Jones

Batting—*D. N. Amato 15–2–451–72*–34.69; E. A. Wass 13–0–326–90–25.07; F. E. J. Wawn 15–3–205–42–17.08; J. R. L. Reed 9–1–130–49–16.25; D. E. Luka 12–1–168–28*–15.27.

Bowling—J. E. Stoecker 109–21–290–20–14.50; R. N. A. Davenport 191–48–548–37–14.81; D. N. Amato 260.2–68–652–40–16.30.

HIPPERHOLME GRAMMAR SCHOOL

Played 10: Won 1, Lost 8, Drawn 1. Abandoned 3

Master i/c: I. Hugill

Batting—L. Senior 9–4–161–82*–32.20; *J. F. Holt 7–1–111–31–18.50; J. Hemingway 9–0–129–38–14.33; R. Sandford 8–0–101–48–12.62.

Bowling—J. F. Holt 106–28–261–23–11.34; D. Revill 27–1–121–10–12.10; J. Hemingway 93.1–13–286–19–15.05.

HURSTPIERPOINT COLLEGE

Played 15: Won 5, Lost 4, Drawn 6

Master i/c: M. E. Allbrook Cricket professional: D. J. Semmence

Batting—M. J. Hastwell 14–3–594–114*–54.00; W. J. Pike 17–4–370–86*–28.46; P. N. Juniper 15–1–341–90–24.35; D. P. B. McGovern 13–0–228–62–17.53; E. W. Welch 13–0–219–46–16.84; H. I. Cordan 10–3–115–34*–16.42.

Bowling—S. C. Twine 145.4–47–378–28–13.50; H. I. Cordan 107–29–293–17–17.23; M. J. Hastwell 114.4–32–324–17–19.05; C. D. J. Humphries 80.2–9–376–11–34.18.

IPSWICH SCHOOL

Played 16: Won 11, Lost 1, Drawn 4

Master i/c: P. M. Rees Cricket professional: R. E. East

Batting—N. Shahid 16–5–937–180*–85.18; A. Douglas 15–4–464–117*–42.18; *N. J. Gregory 16–5–448–64*–40.72; A. Cloke 10–3–185–63*–26.42; C. Jermyn 11–2–198–80–22.00.

Bowling—N. Shahid 350–107–703–67–10.49; C. Mallam 138–32–394–20–19.70; J. Ledden 175.3–35–528–19–27.78; J. Paul 112–20–349–10–34.90.

KELLY COLLEGE

Played 14: Won 5, Lost 3, Drawn 6. Abandoned 3

Master i/c: G. C. L. Cooper Cricket professional: N. Wonnacott

Batting—*A. Adebayo 12–2–498–106–49.80; J. R. Wigley 14–3–255–61*–23.18; S. J. Goaman 9–1–181–41–22.62; J. N. Edwards 8–3–107–38–21.40; K. R. Burgess 12–1–183–57–16.63.

Bowling—R. I. Loraine 67–14–212–13–16.30; A. Adebayo 108–21–306–18–17.00; L. R. Shapcott 91.1–20–291–17–17.11; D. B. Broughton 85–23–279–12–23.25; K. R. Burgess 62–13–247–10–24.70.

KENT COLLEGE

Played 12: Won 6, Lost 1, Drawn 5

Master i/c: G. D. Opie

Batting—S. Warley 12–2–454–95*–45.40; D. Moon 7–2–158–53–31.60; G. Jenkins 12–1–266–99–24.18; *J. Barker 11–1–237–94–23.70; K. Bullen 8–2–142–54*–23.66; J. Hooker 11–2–203–54–22.55; J. Venton 9–1–117–36–14.62.

Bowling—G. Jenkins 106.4–18–311–20–15.55; R. Grove 105–26–290–17–17.05; E. McCabe 74–9–275–16–17.18.

KIMBOLTON SCHOOL

Played 13: Won 3, Lost 4, Drawn 6. Abandoned 6

Master i/c: T. J. Williams

Batting—*A. W. T. Ramply 13–0–388–81–29.84; R. J. T. Ramply 13–2–281–53*–25.54; S. D. Godden 12–0–240–59–20.00; A. D. Moffat 10–2–127–35*–15.87.

Bowling—I. R. A. Prideaux 130.2–37–271–17–15.94; S. D. Godden 122.5–34–294–18–16.33; G. S. Littlewood 47.3–10–187–11–17.00; A. W. T. Ramply 113.3–27–322–17–18.94; R. J. T. Ramply 92–22–238–11–21.63.

KING EDWARD VI COLLEGE, STOURBRIDGE

Played 13: Won 4, Lost 3, Drawn 6. Abandoned 5

Master i/c: M. L. Ryan

Batting—*G. R. Haynes 6–2–325–155*–81.25; S. Mees 12–1–370–93–33.63; J. I. Hill 7–3–117–46–29.25; R. C. K. Simmonds 8–2–143–36–23.83; J. M. Davies 9–3–138–56*–23.00; G. O'Hanlon 11–2–149–50–16.55; A. D. Hadley 11–2–133–29–14.77.

Bowling—G. R. Haynes 58–17–99–15–6.60; A. J. R. Hingley 66–15–170–13–13.07; J. I. Hill 145–44–355–24–14.79; A. D. Hadley 93.5–21–254–16–15.87.

KING EDWARD VI SCHOOL, SOUTHAMPTON

Played 24: Won 11, Lost 5, Drawn 8. Abandoned 1

Master i/c: R. J. Putt

Batting—P. D. Chrispin 21–3–712–112*–39.55; J. D. Stanley 22–0–709–123–32.22; J. A. Heywood 15–2–356–84*–27.38; A. S. Wright 18–4–295–70*–21.07; J. A. Shepherd 21–3–369–55*–20.50; R. P. Knights 9–2–133–33*–19.00; C. B. Blishen 19–2–242–63*–14.23.

Bowling—P. D. Chrispin 207–48–533–48–11.10; P. R. Cook 73–17–236–19–12.42; M. L. Tidby 154–24–538–31–17.35; B. Quantrill 74–21–260–14–18.57; R. M. Salter 61–9–256–10–25.60.

KING EDWARD VII SCHOOL, LYTHAM

Played 18: Won 2, Lost 5, Drawn 11

Master i/c: S. T. Godfrey

Batting—E. J. McKnight 13–1–412–83*–34.33; G. A. Roberts 18–3–496–62*–33.06; *J. A. Greenslade 17–2–420–108*–28.00; R. W. Grime 10–2–129–30–16.12; P. J. MacAuley 12–2–152–25–15.20; C. D. Thompson 17–2–164–32–10.93; P. D. Shipston 13–2–114–26*–10.36.

Bowling—P. C. Beverley 116.4–30–327–21–15.57; P. D. Shipston 135–24–473–17–27.82.

KING EDWARD'S SCHOOL, BIRMINGHAM

Played 16: Won 4, Lost 1, Drawn 11. Abandoned 6

Master i/c: M. D. Stead Cricket professional: P. J. Knowles

Batting—*P. N. J. Inglis 14–1–598–116–46.00; A. P. Hitchins 15–2–428–95–32.92; M. M. Dean 13–3–264–65*–26.40; J. B. Pritchard 13–0–307–66–23.61; M. J. Goodall 12–4–187–57*–23.37.

Bowling—M. J. Goodall 174.5–51–505–30–16.83; M. M. Dean 181.4–54–485–28–17.32; J. B. Pritchard 69.1–8–255–11–23.18; J. P. Coates 171–23–641–22–29.13.

KING HENRY VIII SCHOOL, COVENTRY

Played 15: Won 8, Lost 3, Drawn 4. Abandoned 1

Master i/c: G. P. C. Courtois

Batting—R. J. Field 15–5–366–50*–36.60; K. P. Street 15–2–418–100*–32.15; P. H. Harrison 14–4–315–68*–31.50; M. D. Scott 12–4–127–34*–15.87; G. Gascoyne 15–0–231–35–15.40.

Bowling—J. N. Plevin 196.3–68–360–42–8.57; M. D. Scott 89–14–280–15–18.66; P. J. Cobb 127–22–361–17–21.23; J. P. Pearson 92.1–20–287–12–23.91.

KING WILLIAM'S COLLEGE, ISLE OF MAN

Played 11: Won 4, Lost 4, Drawn 3. Abandoned 2

Master i/c: T. M. Manning Cricket professional: D. Mark

Batting—M. L. Craine 11–1–369–72*–36.90; *A. P. Woodward 11–1–357–91–35.70; C. J. McGowan 7–1–110–36–18.33; G. A. R. Grenville-Wood 9–1–146–34–18.25; R. S. McAleer 10–1–125–40–13.88.

Bowling—A. P. Woodward 207.4–39–608–43–14.13; G. A. R. Grenville-Wood 82.3–18–326–15–21.73.

KING'S COLLEGE, TAUNTON

Played 14: Won 3, Lost 4, Drawn 7

Master i/c: R. J. R. Yeates Cricket professional: R. E. Marshall

Batting—*N. K. L. Coulson 13–1–577–117–48.08; G. P. Singh 10–0–296–78–29.60; M. F. D. Robinson 13–2–268–52–24.36; W. J. K. Greswell 13–3–187–40–18.70; G. E. D. Davies 13–0–207–46–15.92; A. D. Bagshaw 12–1–165–68–15.00; P. N. Miller 13–0–194–50–14.92.

Bowling—N. K. L. Coulson 213.2–45–554–30–18.46; A. F. Lacy-Smith 58.5–6–256–13–19.69; D. J. G. Dowsett 181–34–530–26–20.38.

KING'S COLLEGE SCHOOL, WIMBLEDON

Played 14: Won 3, Lost 5, Drawn 6

Master i/c: A. G. P. Lang Cricket professional: L. J. Moody

Batting—J. Parrish 14–5–314–73*–34.88; D. W. Talbot 11–1–278–92*–27.80; *J. Q. Cooper 11–0–215–38–19.54; N. Ash 13–4–154–52*–17.11; B. J. D. Cook 11–1–142–51–14.20; R. J. Nightingale 10–1–102–32–11.33.

Bowling—F. Hasan 78.5–22–218–15–14.53; D. W. Talbot 194.4–57–520–29–17.93; N. J. Stafford 90.5–23–262–14–18.71; T. A. Preston 137.3–34–452–20–22.60; J. Q. Cooper 141.1–40–444–13–34.15.

KING'S SCHOOL, BRUTON

Played 13: Won 6, Lost 3, Drawn 4. Abandoned 1

Master i/c: D. C. Elstone

Batting—N. Allison 9–1–235–69–29.37; C. Squire 14–2–340–81–28.33; R. Ashfield 11–3–189–39–23.62; T. Mornement 13–3–223–79–22.30; *J. Petrie 13–1–246–66–20.50; A. Lewis 10–1–132–63*–14.66; J. Holland 13–0–175–33–13.46.

Bowling—J. Petrie 89.3–16–292–20–14.60; R. Ashfield 55.4–7–203–13–15.61; N. Gammon 151.1–22–426–24–17.75.

THE KING'S SCHOOL, CANTERBURY

Played 14: Won 4, Lost 1, Drawn 9. Abandoned 1

Master i/c: A. W. Dyer Cricket professional: D. V. P. Wright

Batting—N. V. Daley 14–2–542–145*–45.16; M. G. le Huray 14–4–407–89–40.70; *S. R. Turner 13–1–442–79–36.83; M. I. Holden 11–5–145–54*–24.16; J. R. Davies 13–2–243–50–22.09; A. J. H. Brown 13–1–238–50–19.83.

Bowling—J. R. Davies 231–61–561–48–11.68; T. A. F. Epps 86–21–237–19–12.47; T. J. Ward 152.3–40–430–20–21.50.

THE KING'S SCHOOL, CHESTER

Played 17: Won 6, Lost 1, Drawn 10. Abandoned 7

Master i/c: K. H. Mellor

Batting—G. W. Jones 13–1–573–88–47.75; A. R. H. Mais 17–5–401–65–33.41; J. A. Sowerby 13–3–276–56*–27.60; *C. P. Goodier 15–5–267–83*–26.70; J. Casey 14–1–336–67–25.84.

Bowling—C. P. Goodier 210.4–51–555–43–12.90; S. Williams 147–43–373–28–13.32; J. Casey 82–11–267–16–16.68; I. D. Kamaly-Asl 76–15–241–10–24.10.

THE KING'S SCHOOL, ELY

Played 16: Won 8, Lost 2, Drawn 6. Abandoned 1

Master i/c: R. M. Parsons Cricket professional: T. Morley

Batting—R. J. Claxton 14–4–473–84–47.30; *T. D. Gallop 12–2–429–101–42.90; B. Bowens 14–3–235–49–21.36; M. C. Doggett 15–3–242–57–20.16.

Bowling—J. S. Wheeler 147–48–365–30–12.16; D. Hindle 204–50–623–44–14.15; R. J. Claxton 166–27–548–31–17.67.

THE KING'S SCHOOL, MACCLESFIELD

Played 19: Won 9, Lost 6, Drawn 4. Abandoned 3

Master i/c: D. M. Harbord

Batting—*S. R. Swindells 19–5–552–90–39.42; A. Jerman 13–2–276–78–25.09; D. Jenkins 19–1–388–93–21.55; A. Wilson 18–2–323–67–20.18; M. R. Palmer 8–0–106–42–13.25; P. Hammond 11–1–122–25*–12.20; S. J. White 13–3–117–26–11.70.

Bowling—S. J. White 266–85–641–54–11.87; A. Jerman 99–23–215–16–13.43; M. R. Palmer 185–40–518–27–19.18; P. Hammond 170–25–521–26–20.03.

KING'S SCHOOL, ROCHESTER

Played 18: Won 2, Lost 3, Drawn 13. Abandoned 1

Master i/c: J. S. Irvine

Batting—M. J. Walker 16–1–818–124–54.53; N. D. Twiddy 18–1–551–95–32.41; J. J. Hogben 14–1–306–67–23.53; R. B. Lister 14–3–162–55–14.72; A. C. Mackenzie 16–4–114–21*–9.50; *I. J. Nightingale 15–2–122–48–9.38.

Bowling—I. J. Nightingale 326–75–814–58–14.03; N. D. Twiddy 116–20–296–21–14.09; J. A. Beslee 100–18–270–17–15.88; M. G. Tutton 99.5–15–351–17–20.64; M. J. Walker 98.5–13–295–12–24.58.

THE KING'S SCHOOL, WORCESTER

Played 17: Won 2, Lost 6, Drawn 8, Tied 1

Master i/c: D. P. Iddon

Batting—D. A. W. Hughes 18–0–465–109–25.83; R. G. Tomlinson 18–0–316–37–17.55; A. W. Underwood 17–2–257–76*–17.13; R. P. Dow 18–0–265–48–14.72; A. P. Thompson 18–4–193–35–13.78; A. A. Robinson 16–2–141–36–10.07; R. E. Bishop 15–1–100–28–7.14.

Bowling—A. T. Crabbe 58–9–179–11–16.27; D. A. W. Hughes 154.5–23–597–29–20.58; J. M. Malins 108.2–8–462–20–23.10; M. J. Jelfs 89–13–330–13–25.38.

KINGSTON GRAMMAR SCHOOL

Played 17: Won 2, Lost 11, Drawn 4. Abandoned 2

Master i/c: R. J. Sturgeon

Batting—J. Snelling 17–1–268–51–16.75; E. S. Gratton 15–1–226–79*–16.14; R. A. Chandler 16–1–241–85*–16.06; R. A. Iley 13–0–157–29–12.07; M. Avoth 17–0–196–36–11.52; *R. J. Paler 17–0–186–91–10.94; M. E. Bendel 14–1–139–28–10.69; S. J. Sherman 13–1–107–25–8.91.

Bowling—L. Chester 109.4–20–361–16–22.56; E. S. Gratton 140.2–22–503–20–25.15; S. J. Dowle 117.2–10–455–15–30.33; R. A. Chandler 106–5–520–17–30.58; M. E. Bendel 173.2–26–638–19–33.57.

KINGSWOOD SCHOOL

Played 12: Won 4, Lost 3, Drawn 5

Master i/c: R. J. Lewis

Batting—A. J. Sutherland 10–4–248–67*–41.33; *R. W. Lewis 11–2–318–83*–35.33; J. H. Darby 10–3–206–75*–29.42; P. E. Mills 11–0–290–66–26.36; H. R. Roper 11–0–267–49–24.27; R. M. Francis 9–0–199–44–22.11.

Bowling—R. W. Lewis 44.5–8–169–12–14.08; M. D. Beresford-Smith 101.5–23–316–19–16.63; D. J. Coleman 46.1–5–167–10–16.70; J. M. Thompson 95.1–16–373–19–19.63.

LANCING COLLEGE

Played 16: Won 10, Lost 1, Drawn 5. Abandoned 1

Master i/c: E. A. Evans-Jones Cricket professional: R. G. Davies

Batting—*A. A. Gosden 10–6–374–71*–93.50; C. D. A. R. Hand 4–2–117–40–58.50 J. A. Martin 13–5–312–80*–39.00; A. K. Rimmer 15–6–324–84*–36.00; P. M. Alcock 15–2–333–53–25.61; R. J. Cotton 15–1–351–55–25.07.

Bowling—A. S. Puddephatt 178.3–57–425–39–10.89; R. H. D. Spink 127–27–327–25–13.08 A. R. Hewitt 167–50–433–29–14.93; A. A. Gosden 93.2–24–289–18–16.05; B. W. Watson 91–13–320–11–29.09.

LEEDS GRAMMAR SCHOOL

Played 19: Won 7, Lost 3, Drawn 9. Abandoned 1

Master i/c: I. R. Briars

Batting—T. C. Walton 14–9–632–122*–126.40; G. O. J. Hill 19–7–855–112*–71.25; J. R. Goldthorp 17–3–792–139–56.57; J. D. Flint 14–1–327–57–25.15; R. G. Bourne 10–3–126–34–18.00; D. P. Hyde 9–2–110–52–15.71.

Bowling—T. C. Walton 220.2–50–589–41–14.36; G. O. J. Hill 86–16–233–16–14.56; J. M. Shaw 52.3–12–199–10–19.90; J. R. Goldthorp 167.4–25–572–27–21.18; A. J. Hodgson 148.2–42–432–20–21.60.

LEIGHTON PARK SCHOOL

Played 14: Won 0, Lost 4, Drawn 10. Abandoned 1

Master i/c: R. C. Boyd

Batting—*J. Thomas 12–0–460–75–38.33; D. Park 6–0–178–88–29.66; J. Allen 13–0–181–29–13.92; I. Dhajoo 11–1–115–24*–11.50.

Bowling—D. Park 39–8–155–10–15.50; P. Wall 92–14–224–11–20.36; J. Allen 117–16–406–13–31.23; I. Dhajoo 106–9–423–13–32.53.

THE LEYS SCHOOL

Played 15: Won 3, Lost 3, Drawn 9. Abandoned 3

Master i/c: P. R. Chamberlain Cricket professional: D. Gibson

Batting—D. O. Solomon 14–1–529–124–40.69; *C. W. Barker 14–0–441–107–31.50; P. R. Searle 15–3–378–74*–31.50; C. R. D. Bullen 10–6–121–39–30.25; N. R. Lankester 4–0–392–79*–28.00; J. S. Lewis 10–2–159–39–19.87; J. P. S. Tipple 9–0–148–38–16.44; [illegible]. D. Spencer 12–2–145–48*–14.50.

Bowling—P. R. Searle 205.3–56–481–29–16.58; N. R. Lankester 169.4–18–532–26–20.46.

LIVERPOOL COLLEGE

Played 11: Won 1, Lost 6, Drawn 4

Master i/c: Rev. J. R. Macauley

Batting—*A. J. Pye 10–0–237–82–23.70; G. Locke 9–1–157–41*–19.62; B. Owen –1–125–38–17.85; J. A. Harrington 11–1–167–39–16.70.

Bowling—J. A. Harrington 126–21–410–20–20.50; B. Owen 90–8–319–11–29.00.

LLANDOVERY COLLEGE

Played 12: Won 4, Lost 5, Drawn 3. Abandoned 4

Master i/c: T. G. Marks

Batting—D. M. I. Simcock 12–2–263–74–26.30; R. C. Jones 12–2–238–89*–23.80; *K. J. Whiskerd 10–2–137–39–17.12; S. W. Comley 9–3–101–37*–16.83; D. W. Thompson-Smith 12–0–136–35–11.33.

Bowling—S. O. H. Thomas 79–5–415–23–18.04; M. J. A. B. Lewis 53–9–191–10–19.10; M. Patel 91–14–347–11–31.54.

LORD WANDSWORTH COLLEGE

Played 15: Won 6, Lost 3, Drawn 6

Master i/c: G. R. Smith

Batting—M. J. Critchley 14–4–412–59*–41.20; M. Culley 13–2–386–76–35.09; *D. Carrington 13–1–365–64–30.41; E. J. Kearney 9–3–150–57–25.00; D. A. Berry 14–0–273–58–19.50.

Bowling—G. P. Hunter 110–24–333–17–19.58; D. L. C. Berry 93–16–302–14–21.57; D. A. Berry 134–11–598–27–22.14; D. J. Robinson 69–6–318–12–26.50; J. Bryce 73–12–386–14–27.57.

LORD WILLIAMS'S SCHOOL, THAME

Played 12: Won 3, Lost 4, Drawn 5. Abandoned 2

Master i/c: A. M. Brannan

Batting—G. Stanbury 11–3–204–51–25.50; M. Bateman 11–2–210–35–23.33; M. Khan 12–2–194–60*–19.40; *T. Jordan 12–0–219–43–18.25; G. Morris 10–1–117–44–13.00; T. Fairn 12–2–122–27–12.20.

Bowling—M. Bateman 90.3–35–126–22–5.72; G. Stanbury 122.1–24–367–32–11.46; S. Blackwell 34.2–5–142–10–14.20; R. Stanley 78–16–203–11–18.45.

LORETTO SCHOOL

Played 17: Won 4, Lost 3, Drawn 10. Abandoned 1

Master i/c: R. G. Selley

Batting—S. S. Hodgson 14–1–418–95–32.15; S. A. L. Rutherford 16–2–302–72*–21.57; *M. C. Eglinton 17–3–254–58–18.14.

Bowling—S. S. Hodgson 42–15–110–17–6.47; A. C. N. Smith 141–33–330–23–14.34; M. C. Eglinton 220–62–556–38–14.63; A. C. F. Mason 132–42–287–19–15.10; J. A. G. Gran 121–24–335–17–19.70.

LOUGHBOROUGH GRAMMAR SCHOOL

Played 15: Won 7, Lost 1, Drawn 7. Abandoned 1

Master i/c: E. Thorpe

Batting—*I. Bell 13–3–420–111*–42.00; C. Jones 15–2–380–85–29.23; W. Dessau 12–2–277–60*–27.70; G. Leeson 14–1–248–44–19.07; S. Pickering 14–2–196–39*–16.33.

Bowling—C. J. Hawkes 169–53–433–34–12.73; W. Dessaur 97.5–26–276–15–18.40; R. Fothergill 121–33–270–14–19.28; S. Pickering 113.4–23–333–16–20.81; C. Jones 142.3–28–462–22–21.00.

MAGDALEN COLLEGE SCHOOL

Played 13: Won 3, Lost 3, Drawn 6, Tied 1. Abandoned 5

Master i/c: N. A. Rollings

Batting—*J. A. Turner 12–3–343–100*–38.11; M. B. Bixby 12–1–348–60*–31.63; S. N. Web 10–4–127–31*–21.16; T. H. Boyles 12–0–232–48–19.33; J. C. Bobby 10–0–133–38–13.30; M. W. Suckling 11–0–133–39–12.09.

Bowling—D. Briggs 31–2–136–10–13.60; S. D. Stinchcombe 71–8–235–12–19.58; D. M. A Andrews 55–5–198–10–19.80; J. A. Brady 110.4–27–288–13–22.15; S. N. Web 178.3–39–589–25–23.56.

MALVERN COLLEGE

Played 16: Won 4, Lost 6, Drawn 6. Abandoned 4

Master i/c: A. J. Murtagh Cricket professional: R. W. Tolchard

Batting—*J. R. Wileman 15-4-783-133*-71.18; I. K. Timberlake 4-1-125-60*-41.66; B. C. Usher 16-3-482-100-37.07; T. W. B. Read 9-2-144-43*-20.57; A. J. Hardwicke 12-1-175-68-15.90; A. C. Hiscock 14-0-195-28-13.92.

Bowling—J. R. Wileman 162.1-36-522-31-16.83; A. D. Noon 71.1-8-326-13-25.07; B. C. Usher 191-42-545-21-25.95; J. F. Phillips 114-16-405-12-33.75.

MANCHESTER GRAMMAR SCHOOL

Played 16: Won 6, Lost 2, Drawn 8. Abandoned 1

Master i/c: D. Moss

Batting—J. P. Crawley 14-6-900-160*-112.50; M. J. P. Ward 14-7-411-100*-58.71; D. J. Worsley 12-2-408-124*-40.80; D. N. Dada 7-0-188-75-26.85; S. E. Maggi -2-126-29-21.00; I. R. Cross 10-1-141-46-15.66.

Bowling—C. F. Sinton 173.5-30-518-32-16.18; M. C. Jones 124.3-37-273-16-17.06; R. B. Hennis 131.1-21-405-20-20.25; D. J. Worsley 136-35-364-16-22.75.

MARLBOROUGH COLLEGE

Played 17: Won 4, Lost 0, Drawn 13

Master i/c: R. B. Pick Cricket professional: R. M. Ratcliffe

Batting—S. C. G. Thomson 15-3-498-96-41.50; G. W. Barker 17-5-492-77*-41.00; *J. S. Kerr 16-3-531-123*-40.84; E. A. M. Longfield 10-7-122-33*-40.66; T. C. Marcon 0-5-158-36*-31.60; D. M. A. Bevan 12-0-336-88-28.00; M. A. Foulds 13-0-308-71-23.69; . J. Robinson 17-2-348-54-23.20.

Bowling—D. M. A. Bevan 150-32-440-31-14.19; J. S. Kerr 129-22-415-22-18.86; J. J. Hey 08-28-278-12-23.16; G. F. J. Riding 102.3-23-360-13-27.69; E. A. M. Longfield 48-41-421-13-32.38; N. J. E. Cook 182-29-677-20-33.85.

MERCHANT TAYLORS' SCHOOL, CROSBY

Played 15: Won 2, Lost 1, Drawn 12. Abandoned 3

Master i/c: Rev. D. A. Smith Cricket professional: G. E. Trim

Batting—I. G. Sutcliffe 13-2-418-109-38.00; D. L. Clift 12-2-202-59-20.20; I. K. Wright 10-3-133-31*-19.00; A. E. Antrobus 11-2-165-37-18.33; R. M. R. Williams 10-1-146-44-16.22; T. J. Ryan 13-2-177-54-16.09; G. S. Glynne-Jones 0-1-108-53*-12.00.

Bowling—T. J. Ryan 95.5-15-360-21-17.14; I. K. Wright 125.4-31-368-20-18.40; . R. McGee 138-32-408-16-25.50; I. G. Sutcliffe 134.4-24-424-14-30.28.

MERCHANT TAYLORS' SCHOOL, NORTHWOOD

Played 23: Won 8, Lost 1, Drawn 14. Abandoned 1

Master i/c: W. M. B. Ritchie

Batting—A. J. Brand 22-6-867-140*-54.18; K. J. Clifford 22-2-644-109*-32.20; . R. Harrison 20-3-426-93-25.05; J. L. Atkins 16-2-330-89-23.57; R. A. Hawkey -7-219-40*-18.25; *A. P. Solomons 16-2-184-35*-13.14.

Bowling—A. T. S. Nicholson 56.5-21-100-14-7.14; R. A. Hawkey 287.1-62-966-52-18.57; . J. Brand 308-94-728-35-20.80; S. W. Faulks 224.2-60-664-24-27.66; N. W. Bransdon 72.3-38-452-16-28.25.

MERCHISTON CASTLE SCHOOL

Played 17: Won 9, Lost 4, Drawn 4

Master i/c: C. W. Swan Cricket professional: I. Philip

Batting—D. M. Streek 18–1–639–242–37.58; P. W. R. Martin 16–2–369–57*–26.35; A. J. K. Wilson 16–0–295–55–18.43; S. A. Hailstone 15–5–166–36*–16.60; A. H. W. Boyle 16–2–220–65–15.71.

Bowling—S. J. Elworthy 120–46–257–32–8.03; S. D. L. Francis 201–64–450–34–13.23; D. M. Streek 181–43–474–32–14.81.

MILLFIELD SCHOOL

Played 18: Won 6, Lost 1, Drawn 11

Master i/c: A. D. Curtis Cricket professional: G. C. Wilson

Batting—G. W. White 2–1–123–84*–123.00; D. L. Hemp 13–7–691–114*–115.16; J. A. Brimacombe 6–4–165–63*–82.50; I. Fletcher 15–4–668–113–60.72; R. I. Dawson 5–0–240–104–48.00; J. G. Humphrey 5–1–174–82–43.50; G. W. Hart 11–3–233–45–29.12; *G. D. Lucas 10–4–163–43–27.16; J. C. Hallett 8–2–133–59*–22.16.

Bowling—J. C. Hallett 143.1–37–337–26–12.96; G. W. White 55.4–11–195–13–15.00; S. D. Sutcliffe 65.2–11–222–12–18.50; J. R. Holliday 102–28–280–15–18.66; J. M. Box 178.5–44–508–23–22.08; N. F. Gibbs 136.2–34–457–16–28.56.

MILL HILL SCHOOL

Played 14: Won 1, Lost 8, Drawn 5. Abandoned 1

Master i/c: R. J. Denning Cricket professional: G. A. R. Lock

Batting—A. B. Dell 13–1–439–78–36.58; A. J. McKelvie 7–2–114–43–22.80; M. R. Jacobson 9–3–116–49*–19.33; J. H. Bohn 14–0–226–54–16.14; C. B. Forde 12–1–172–52–15.63; *P. Achan 14–0–215–74–15.35; N. C. Propper 14–2–180–59–15.00.

Bowling—J. Handforth 75–19–166–11–15.09; G. E. S. Brock 123–23–396–20–19.80; C. B. Forde 143–33–397–20–19.85; P. Achan 73–15–235–10–23.50; E. M. Latte 157–31–534–21–25.42.

MILTON ABBEY SCHOOL

Played 13: Won 6, Lost 4, Drawn 3

Master i/c: P. W. Wood

Batting—J. F. A. Baring 11–3–357–55–44.62; *S. J. E. Courage 13–1–454–121–37.83; R. S. Padmore 12–2–376–121*–37.60; A. J. Butler 10–5–157–35*–31.40; C. P. Coo 12–2–207–67–20.70.

Bowling—H. E. Panter 105.2–34–300–30–10.00; R. G. Curran 101.1–27–274–21–13.04; H. G. H. Groves 138.1–37–432–28–15.42; M. C. Freegard 114–17–339–19–17.84.

MONKTON COMBE SCHOOL

Played 12: Won 7, Lost 1, Drawn 4

Master i/c: P. C. Sibley Cricket professional: N. D. Botto

Batting—R. S. Deacock 11–1–399–88–39.90; R. J. Payne 10–0–368–77–36.80; *M. P. Davi 9–1–261–76–32.62; T. Simmons 11–3–196–41–24.50; R. A. Johns 9–1–168–60–21.00; M. J. Wheeldon 8–2–111–50–18.50.

Bowling—S. J. Kandavanam 86–20–228–17–13.41; N. F. Robb 184.3–38–504–36–14.00; S. J. Waters 34–4–169–10–16.90; W. B. Taylar 60.4–6–276–16–17.25.

NEWCASTLE-UNDER-LYME SCHOOL

Played 14: Won 5, Lost 5, Drawn 4. Abandoned 2

Master i/c: R. K. Martindale

Batting—M. H. Colclough 11–2–257–45*–28.55; D. J. Brock 10–1–202–72–22.44; *R. W. Johnson 11–0–216–47–19.63; N. R. Hood 10–1–174–55–19.33; J. C. Mayo 13–0–240–57–18.46; J. N. Snape 12–1–147–23–13.36; J. I. Sheridan 12–1–140–24–12.72; J. N. Britton 12–2–126–38*–12.60.

Bowling—D. J. Brock 127–28–297–27–14.70; M. H. Colclough 75.5–20–251–14–17.92; R. G. Mawby 92–22–291–15–19.40; M. Pate 89.3–12–318–16–19.87.

NORWICH SCHOOL

Played 18: Won 3, Lost 5, Drawn 10

Master i/c: P. M. Evans

Batting—A. J. Rushmer 13–5–252–58*–31.50; R. F. Blackburn 17–0–338–101–19.88; A. J. R. Williamson 17–1–305–78–19.06; S. E. Jessup 17–3–240–43–17.14; S. M. Hall 13–4–137–42–15.22; N. A. Colman 11–1–138–41*–13.80; W. P. Hems 11–0–104–27–9.45.

Bowling—N. R. Temperley 180–38–485–32–15.15; A. J. R. Williamson 70–6–268–14–19.14; A. J. Rushmer 92–12–328–13–25.23; P. B. Allen 157.1–40–425–15–28.33.

NOTTINGHAM HIGH SCHOOL

Played 18: Won 5, Lost 7, Drawn 6. Abandoned 2

Master i/c: P. G. Morris Cricket professional: H. Latchman

Batting—*N. A. Hunt 19–4–1,108–144–73.86; S. A. O'Brien 18–3–365–72–24.33; M. J. Bonsall 8–3–111–51*–22.20; T. R. Leman 18–0–275–54–15.27; R. I. Howarth 1–2–131–26*–14.55; N. P. Carr 14–1–166–67–12.76.

Bowling—J. Kennedy 115.1–24–317–20–15.85; R. I. Howarth 179.1–35–567–31–18.29; R. W. Dixon 81.4–16–248–13–19.07; T. R. Leman 137.4–31–411–21–19.57; S. A. O'Brien 109.5–15–349–17–20.52; A. S. Chisholm 151–43–433–14–30.92.

THE ORATORY SCHOOL

Played 13: Won 9, Lost 0, Drawn 4. Abandoned 3

Master i/c: P. L. Tomlinson

Batting—*P. J. Coverdale 10–4–321–76*–53.50; J. Clarke 5–1–179–84*–44.75; D. J. Sillence –1–247–63–35.28; C. Chaundler 3–0–102–45–34.00; J. N. Wallis 12–0–248–57–20.66; M. Sillence 8–2–112–48–18.66; S. R. Wright 9–2–112–28*–16.00; R. D. Unwin 2–0–153–46–12.75; K. O'Flynn 10–0–111–43–11.10.

Bowling—S. R. Wright 167–48–363–42–8.64; J. N. Wallis 40–10–146–15–9.73; B. G. Welsh 5–8–110–11–10.00; M. Sillence 43–4–170–15–11.33; R. D. Unwin 122.3–29–336–25–13.44.

OUNDLE SCHOOL

Played 19: Won 8, Lost 4, Drawn 7. Abandoned 3

Master i/c: V. G. B. Cushing Cricket professional: T. Howorth

Batting—J. McAlpine 16–4–435–74–36.25; R. Sharp 14–2–332–84–27.66; *R. Jenkins 6–3–346–63–26.61; A. Chadwick 18–3–373–65–24.86; J. Arnold 15–4–236–43–21.45; . Allerton 8–2–124–25–20.66; N. Williamson 15–4–213–35–19.36; T. Harrison 9–0–353–45–18.57; G. Spragg 8–0–105–28–13.12; W. Cartledge 13–3–111–20–11.10.

Bowling—S. Smale 139–47–422–25–16.88; R. Jenkins 309–64–943–52–18.13; J. Arnold 3–12–350–15–23.33; J. McAlpine 304–59–891–38–23.44.

OAKHAM SCHOOL

Played 15: Won 3, Lost 2, Drawn 10. Abandoned 5

Master i/c: J. Wills

Batting—U. Malhotra 14–1–524–97*–40.30; A. Pike 14–1–324–68–24.92; *S. Gilliver 13–1–243–50–20.25; C. Howard 13–3–163–44–16.30; D. Ross 13–1–181–41–15.08; N. Kingham 13–2–105–28–9.54.

Bowling—I. Forsyth 192–61–451–28–16.10; D. Ross 154.3–42–420–24–17.50; J. Boughey 145.4–26–475–22–21.59.

THE PERSE SCHOOL

Played 17: Won 3, Lost 4, Drawn 10.

Master i/c: A. W. Billinghurst Cricket professional: D. C. Collard

Batting—B. J. G. Edgar 12–3–294–60*–32.66; *N. M. Law 14–2–369–100*–30.75; R. J. Doel 16–0–462–78–28.87; D. L. Young 14–4–216–46–21.60; P. J. Doel 14–0–249–56–17.78; J. G. S. Agar 14–0–201–47–14.35; W. R. T. Chalk 12–1–129–45–11.72.

Bowling—D. L. Young 208.4–37–582–35–16.62; N. M. Law 106.4–16–302–17–17.76; R. M. C. Scott 153.5–41–388–18–21.55; J. A. Standley 100–25–300–13–23.07.

PLYMOUTH COLLEGE

Played 21: Won 10, Lost 1, Drawn 10

Master i/c: T. J. Stevens

Batting—R. Colegate 17–6–714–83–64.90; S. Summers 19–3–672–107–42.00; A. Kerr 18–6–442–102*–36.83; P. Stewart 14–4–274–63*–27.40; R. Barker 20–4–365–67–22.81; M. Ellyatt 13–5–124–35–15.50; C. Vinson 13–3–129–40–12.90.

Bowling—S. Nicholson 106–30–346–28–12.35; C. Vinson 193–48–519–37–14.02; S. Howell 120.3–24–395–20–19.75; S. Macartney 104.5–14–419–21–19.95; *B. Fox 113–18–529–23–23.00.

POCKLINGTON SCHOOL

Played 21: Won 13, Lost 3, Drawn 4, Tied 1. Abandoned 2

Master i/c: D. Nuttall

Batting—A. T. Pettinger 22–4–768–114–42.66; M. J. Wood 21–3–638–111–35.44; A. J. Inns 20–3–577–59–33.94; R. S. Hunter 14–3–250–51*–22.72; J. D. Burnet 11–3–103–25–12.87; *R. M. Ineson 17–4–166–45–12.76; C. M. Haynes 16–1–159–27–10.60.

Bowling—M. J. Wood 245.5–61–680–51–13.33; R. S. Hunter 198.2–59–491–35–14.02; R. J. Cox 216.5–52–493–33–14.93; S. K. Wilson 119–38–294–19–15.47; J. A. Webster 136.2–19–539–24–22.45.

PRIOR PARK COLLEGE

Played 14: Won 3, Lost 5, Drawn 6. Abandoned 3

Master i/c: P. B. Fisher Cricket professional: E. Russell

Batting—M. Woodhouse 14–0–631–116–45.07; G. Lee 13–3–339–53*–33.90; M. Polledri 12–2–229–94*–22.90; G. Adekoya 10–0–145–42–14.50; A. McKeon 10–0–116–34–11.60.

Bowling—G. Lee 153–25–480–27–17.77; *J. Powell 135–39–369–20–18.45; M. Woodhouse 53–10–194–10–19.40.

QUEEN ELIZABETH GRAMMAR SCHOOL, WAKEFIELD

Played 14: Won 5, Lost 4, Drawn 5. Abandoned 2

Master i/c: T. Barker

Batting—S. Bailey 7–1–145–74–24.16; *P. Maynard 12–3–178–37*–19.77; P. Dickinson 14–0–268–52–19.14; G. Littlewood 12–1–184–37–16.72; H. Gledhill 9–1–118–34*–14.75; G. Hunt 11–1–108–34–10.80.

Bowling—R. Bramley 76–19–198–13–15.23; S. Bailey 66–18–172–11–15.63; J. Smith 64–10–217–10–21.70; R. Bhagobati 102–15–365–15–24.33; G. Millman 100–17–320–11–29.09.

QUEEN'S COLLEGE, TAUNTON

Played 15: Won 4, Lost 1, Drawn 10

Master i/c: J. W. Davies

Batting—*B. C. Wixey 11–1–355–80–35.50; M. E. Gibson 11–1–246–56–24.60; K. Griffith 11–5–144–52–24.00; C. Amor 6–1–110–37–22.00; M. Knight 10–0–195–73–19.50; S. Burt 11–0–179–59–16.27.

Bowling—B. C. Wixey 91–19–263–23–11.43; S. Mirghavamedin 80–16–286–17–16.82; C. Amor 83–26–188–10–18.80; M. E. Irish 104–25–302–13–23.23; N. Jenner 91–22–301–11–27.36.

RADLEY COLLEGE

Played 14: Won 6, Lost 1, Drawn 7. Abandoned 1

Master i/c: G. de W. Waller Cricket professionals: A. G. Robinson and A. R. Wagner

Batting—*M. J. Lowrey 15–2–686–144–52.76; H. C. L. Sinclair 4–1–136–65–45.33; R. J. A. Wates 9–6–109–53*–36.33; B. R. A. Lamb 14–5–206–68–22.88; J. T. M. Samuda 15–1–320–62–22.85; R. A. Jardine-Brown 13–1–252–67–21.00; R. G. Fuller 14–0–237–81–16.92; R. B. Waller 10–2–120–44*–15.00.

Bowling—J. R. Pearce-Smith 114–28–253–17–14.88; G. D. L. Powell 260–107–515–33–15.60; M. J. Lowrey 181–48–443–23–19.26; R. B. Waller 147–44–376–19–19.78.

RATCLIFFE COLLEGE

Played 14: Won 3, Lost 8, Drawn 3. Abandoned 1

Master i/c: R. M. Hughes

Batting—*R. J. Adcock 13–2–320–104–29.09; M. Meredith 14–1–209–39–16.07; M. Hilton 14–2–118–22–9.83.

Bowling—R. J. Adcock 105.2–25–323–22–14.68; J. Astill 107.4–26–350–12–29.16.

READING SCHOOL

Played 13: Won 5, Lost 2, Drawn 6. Abandoned 3

Master i/c: R. G. Owen Cricket professional: A. Dindar

Batting—O. D. Beckett 12–6–533–119*–88.83; T. J. C. Dance 12–3–459–111–51.00; I. C. Orpwood 13–3–243–58–24.30; J. M. Cole 8–0–139–66–17.37; G. J. Orpwood 9–0–155–31–17.22.

Bowling—T. J. C. Dance 127–26–346–30–11.53; B. D. Hall 144–29–457–21–21.76.

REED'S SCHOOL

Played 16: Won 5, Lost 4, Drawn 7

Master i/c: G. R. Martin

Batting—S. M. Shiells 16–2–355–100*–25.35; J. R. Ovenden 13–3–246–54*–24.60; *O. W. Pendered 15–2–238–49–18.30; J. R. Dharmasena 14–2–217–34–18.08; J. A. Lyne 14–2–214–86–17.83; A. R. W. Balls 14–2–198–50–16.50.

Bowling—J. R. Dharmasena 237.4–69–627–42–14.92; J. R. Ovenden 143.1–31–487–27–18.03; S. M. Shiells 100.5–20–425–19–22.36.

REIGATE GRAMMAR SCHOOL

Played 23: Won 8, Lost 3, Drawn 12. Abandoned 2

Master i/c: D. C. R. Jones Cricket professional: H. Newton

Batting—*C. S. Bates 18–4–551–79*–39.35; J. R. Chapman 6–2–142–56–35.50; J. P. Jackson 23–2–658–92–31.33; M. M. G. Wright 21–0–547–90–26.04; P. A. Radford 21–3–429–75–23.83; J. S. Hudson 15–0–326–100–21.73; D. M. Gregory 23–4–398–64–20.94; G. J. Lawson 13–5–158–39*–19.75.

Bowling—D. F. Rowlinson 279.3–56–791–49–16.14; M. P. Lander 198.5–41–563–32–17.59; D. N. Abbott 199.2–41–541–28–19.32; D. M. Gregory 268.1–69–775–40–19.37; G. J. Lawson 84.5–17–305–15–20.33.

RENDCOMB COLLEGE

Played 12: Won 6, Lost 1, Drawn 5. Abandoned 1

Master i/c: P. Sykes Cricket professional: D. Essenhigh

Batting—W. Sherwood 11–5–253–49–42.16; J. Carroll 12–3–301–50*–33.44; R. Tate 7–2–121–48*–24.20; *J. Fellows 13–1–286–64–23.83; K. Holmes 9–4–102–26–20.40.

Bowling—A. Jones 109–24–309–33–9.36; H. Le Fleming 43.4–12–152–15–10.13; C. Bannister 83.4–21–240–17–14.11; N. Suffolk 85.1–19–267–16–16.68; C. Huck 99–18–285–14–20.35.

REPTON SCHOOL

Played 16: Won 5, Lost 2, Drawn 9. Abandoned 2

Master i/c: M. Stones Cricket professional: M. K. Kettle

Batting—R. F. Williamson 14–4–640–128*–64.00; *C. E. Wall 15–2–634–142*–48.76; R. A. C. Jerman 10–2–256–100*–32.00; R. N. Wall 12–3–273–89*–30.33; A. E. Jordan 17–1–447–110*–27.93; D. R. Hand 12–2–276–85*–27.60; H. B. Dytham 7–2–118–54–23.60; M. J. Hunter 11–1–129–42–12.90.

Bowling—A. Schumann 62–16–197–12–16.41; D. R. Hand 129–32–437–20–21.85; N. Moxon 132–40–409–17–24.05; R. N. Wall 82–19–268–10–26.80; C. E. Wall 132–34–409–14–29.21.

ROSSALL SCHOOL

Played 17: Won 3, Lost 3, Drawn 11. Abandoned 1

Master i/c: R. J. Clapp

Batting—J. Elliott 16–3–442–78–34.00; *D. M. Indo 18–1–518–71–30.47; T. J. Stephenson 14–2–313–63–26.08; W. E. Hayes 17–1–383–57–23.93; N. H. Crust 13–5–154–41*–19.25; C. M. Cocker 17–2–167–59–11.13.

Bowling—J. M. G. Woods 51–10–180–10–18.00; S. D. Holmes 187–40–531–22–24.13; W. E. Hayes 194–41–645–24–26.87; N. H. Crust 108–17–385–13–29.61; T. J. Stephenson 88–12–325–10–32.50.

ROYAL GRAMMAR SCHOOL, GUILDFORD

Played 17: Won 10, Lost 2, Drawn 5. Abandoned 2

Master i/c: S. B. R. Shore

Batting—A. Stedman 13–2–405–61*–36.81; A. P. Challinor 13–3–366–112*–36.60; *M. Gore 13–4–280–47–31.11; B. Ray 14–1–296–92–22.76; L. Jones 17–0–342–66–20.11; A. Job 10–2–135–28–16.87; D. Goodchild 11–3–123–35–15.37; N. Thomson 13–2–133–31–12.09.

Bowling—A. P. Challinor 166.1–46–399–46–8.67; M. Hoyle 69–19–174–13–13.38; A. Stedman 84.5–16–221–16–13.81; M. Gore 222.3–57–551–36–15.30; N. Thomson 166–36–399–25–15.96.

ROYAL GRAMMAR SCHOOL, NEWCASTLE

Played 16: Won 7, Lost 2, Drawn 7. Abandoned 2

Master i/c: D. W. Smith Cricket professional: J. N. Graham

Batting—*S. W. Johnson 14–3–547–107–49.72; O. Youll 15–2–398–81*–30.61; C. Barnes 12–4–218–67*–27.25; M. Hackett 11–2–229–89*–25.44; J. R. Barton 14–1–308–71*–23.69; P. Venn 13–3–208–62*–20.80; J. R. Tyson 8–2–108–23*–18.00; A. Markham 10–2–111–29–13.87.

Bowling—A. Markham 73.5–22–185–15–12.33; C. Graham 155.3–38–363–29–12.51; M. Skinner 43–8–178–12–14.83; P. Venn 165.1–32–486–29–16.75; S. W. Johnson 135.2–32–345–20–17.25.

ROYAL GRAMMAR SCHOOL, WORCESTER

Played 19: Won 11, Lost 1, Drawn 7. Abandoned 5

Master i/c: B. M. Rees Cricket professional: M. J. Horton

Batting—M. J. Walker 19–5–681–109*–48.64; M. J. N. Taylor 18–3–622–104*–41.46; G. T. G. Burrow 19–0–604–83–31.78; *J. S. Waters 13–4–168–58*–18.66; P. C. Fearnley 17–3–236–60–16.85; D. W. Headley 11–4–117–32–16.71.

Bowling—D. W. Headley 191.5–57–461–46–10.02; J. S. Waters 230.5–73–519–37–14.02; S. D. C. Haynes 184–56–380–26–14.61; A. D. Baker 128–37–311–20–15.55.

RUGBY SCHOOL

Played 14: Won 4, Lost 1, Drawn 9. Abandoned 3

Master i/c: K. Siviter Cricket professional: W. J. Stewart

Batting—M. G. Semmens 9–5–148–44*–37.00; *B. C. A. Ellison 15–1–514–104*–36.71; S. P. Corkill 14–4–297–75*–29.70; R. R. Montgomerie 15–1–405–83–28.92; G. A. D. Whittaker 15–0–423–96–28.20; G. W. Jepson 12–3–221–61*–24.55; G. W. Roberts 11–3–136–32*–17.00; S. D. A. Drewett 11–1–148–36–14.80.

Bowling—B. C. A. Ellison 230.2–59–631–51–12.37; M. G. Semmens 87.1–15–326–23–14.17; A. L. C. Winchester 171.2–44–491–24–20.45.

RYDAL SCHOOL

Played 12: Won 6, Lost 2, Drawn 4

Master i/c: M. H. Stevenson Cricket professional: R. W. C. Pitman

Batting—J. R. Hogg 12–2–411–66*–41.10; *A. G. Moore 11–1–409–109–40.90; R. L. Stewart 10–3–135–45–19.28; H. S. L. Bradley 12–2–162–63–16.20; M. J. Anwyl 10–0–113–31–11.30.

Bowling—A. G. Moore 81–25–190–17–11.17; R. L. Stewart 168.5–40–388–32–12.12; P. J. Acheson 148.3–21–481–27–17.81.

ST ALBANS SCHOOL

Played 17: Won 7, Lost 3, Drawn 7. Abandoned 1

Master i/c: N. A. Woodsmith Cricket professional: G. Cooper

Batting—A. L. Dalwood 17–4–541–82*–41.61; *T. E. Preest 15–2–405–82–31.15; M. Henchley 12–1–240–62–21.81; G. J. Dill 17–2–227–43–15.13; E. B. Le Fleming 12–2–150–28–15.00; K. D. Black 11–2–109–36–12.11; E. J. Foster 10–0–102–16–10.20.

Bowling—H. E. Sherman 60–12–200–13–15.38; E. J. Foster 167–40–565–33–17.12; E. B. Le Fleming 113–19–310–18–17.22; G. J. Dill 121–25–406–23–17.65; W. Wilkins 65–12–188–10–18.80.

ST DUNSTAN'S COLLEGE

Played 16: Won 7, Lost 1, Drawn 8. Abandoned 3

Master i/c: C. Matten

Batting—G. R. S. Scovell 13–2–538–104*–48.90; M. J. Dowse 16–2–579–105*–41.35; H. Davies 15–1–348–58–24.85; L. Tyler 10–3–166–56*–23.71; *J. J. Platford 14–1–213–56–16.38.

Bowling—S. Cooper 35–5–102–12–8.50; G. R. S. Scovell 142–38–367–29–12.65; T. Evans-Argent 142–31–382–25–15.28; N. Middleton 100–18–260–17–15.29; H. Davies 124–29–338–17–19.88; J. Andrews 121–17–423–18–23.50.

ST EDMUND'S SCHOOL, CANTERBURY

Played 13: Won 2, Lost 3, Drawn 8. Abandoned 1

Master i/c: D. E. Knight Cricket professional: D. V. P. Wright

Batting—J. D. Bowden 13–2–594–162–54.00; *M. J. E. Horton 12–2–286–57–28.60; N. C. Kennett 11–0–309–53–28.09; P. J. Mitchell 12–1–217–88–19.72; D. K. Stewart 13–1–187–65–15.58.

Bowling—G. P. Semadeni 50.3–9–153–11–13.90; N. C. Kennett 94–21–292–16–18.25; R. Hayes 61–6–220–10–22.00; P. J. Mitchell 115.4–17–399–17–23.47; D. K. Stewart 89–5–455–14–32.50.

ST EDWARD'S SCHOOL, OXFORD

Played 12: Won 3, Lost 3, Drawn 5, Tied 1

Master i/c: P. G. Badger Cricket professional: S. N. V. Waterton

Batting—T. H. C. Hancock 6–1–296–70*–59.20; A. E. R. Craven-Smith 11–2–285–65*–31.66; *M. J. J. Wethey 11–1–313–77*–31.30; A. C. Dobson 12–1–319–86*–29.00; J. M. E. Lawes 10–1–236–81–26.22; R. J. C. Hawkins 10–2–200–65–25.00.

Bowling—T. H. C. Hancock 63–14–156–11–14.18; J. M. E. Lawes 149–40–408–15–27.20; G. A. Wright 120.2–27–395–11–35.90; M. S. Ghalib 81–13–376–10–37.60.

ST GEORGE'S COLLEGE, WEYBRIDGE

Played 13: Won 4, Lost 1, Drawn 8. Abandoned 5

Master i/c: B. V. O'Gorman

Batting—I. D. Turner 13–0–481–94–37.00; J. Sayers 13–2–343–101*–31.18; M. Church 9–4–137–46–27.40; A. Hollioake 9–2–188–62–26.85; C. Bennett 13–0–339–124–26.07; T. Clark 7–1–110–29–18.33; T. Segal 11–0–169–39–15.36; B. Williams 12–0–172–52–14.33; P. Smyth 12–3–111–43–12.33.

Bowling—T. Clark 203.4–50–544–34–16.00; A. Hollioake 111–24–310–18–17.22; I. D. Turner 164–26–513–28–18.32; R. Aspinall 115–34–311–15–20.73.

ST JOHN'S SCHOOL, LEATHERHEAD

Played 12: Won 3, Lost 6, Drawn 3. Abandoned 1

Master i/c: A. B. Gale Cricket professional: E. Shepperd

Batting—T. S. S. Walton 6–2–135–82*–33.75; *I. B. George 11–1–272–76*–27.20; T. P. Fairclough 8–1–143–33–20.42; M. E. Randall 11–1–192–55–19.20; M. N. Cooper 12–2–120–26–12.00.

Bowling—A. C. Hill 103.2–30–251–15–16.73; R. E. Smart 142–35–403–23–17.52; G. J. Parkinson 69–20–185–10–18.50.

ST JOSEPH'S COLLEGE, IPSWICH

Played 14: Won 1, Lost 2, Drawn 11

Master i/c: A. C. Rutherford Cricket professional: J. Pugh

Batting—B. Chilcott 13–2–372–106*–33.81; J. McLoughlin 13–3–211–54*–21.10; D. White 9–2–130–49–18.57; D. Hamer 13–0–226–56–17.38; J. Newland 10–1–125–73–13.88.

Bowling—J. McLoughlin 84–11–282–19–14.84; J. Cockburn 89.3–18–271–18–15.05; W. Webb 125–19–399–22–18.13; A. Dupont 112–16–355–18–19.72.

ST LAWRENCE COLLEGE

Played 11: Won 3, Lost 2, Drawn 6. Abandoned 2

Master i/c: N. O. S. Jones Cricket professional: L. A. C. D'Arcy

Batting—R. J. Elliott 8–2–235–73*–39.16; L. M. Willsmer 8–1–232–64*–33.14; R. S. Chhabra 10–1–208–42–23.11; P. N. Unachukwu 10–1–184–65*–20.44; G. P. Carson 10–1–111–44–12.33.

Bowling—L. M. Willsmer 188–56–478–33–14.48; *A. Bird 121–18–348–12–29.00; C. P. Burr 119.3–32–375–10–37.50.

ST PAUL'S SCHOOL

Played 15: Won 2, Lost 3, Drawn 10. Abandoned 3

Master i/c: G. Hughes Cricket professional: E. W. Whitfield

Batting—N. E. Gomm 8–5–110–50–36.66; D. J. Gordon-Smith 13–7–198–43*–33.00; D. H. L. Edwards 8–1–180–51–25.71; J. M. York 13–0–332–70–25.53; S. C. Klein 9–1–169–44–21.12; J. M. Porteus 8–2–117–29*–19.50; I. C. Colak-Antic 13–0–211–56–16.23; P. W. T. Neate 13–0–211–43–16.23; T. L. Morris 12–0–193–38–16.08.

Bowling—D. J. Gordon-Smith 179.3–28–527–27–19.51; N. E. Gomm 116–31–338–15–22.53; S. A. Vogt 150–28–472–18–26.22; J. M. Porteus 72.3–13–272–10–27.20.

ST PETER'S SCHOOL, YORK

Played 18: Won 4, Lost 2, Drawn 12. Abandoned 2

Master i/c: D. Kirby Cricket professional: K. J. Mohan

Batting—W. J. Robinson 16–3–638–125*–49.07; R. Hutchinson 16–2–424–84*–30.28; *N. D. Muirhead 16–2–409–64–29.21; T. E. J. Cooper 17–1–464–74*–29.00; J. N. Renshaw 13–3–196–39*–19.60; M. D. Donoghue 11–1–177–41–17.70.

Bowling—P. F. Wand 232.3–87–530–33–16.06; M. D. Donoghue 213.5–47–674–32–21.06; N. D. Muirhead 205.2–31–712–27–26.37.

SEDBERGH SCHOOL

Played 13: Won 3, Lost 2, Drawn 8. Abandoned 1

Master i/c: M. J. Morris

Batting—S. D. Gawthorpe 15–2–388–73–29.84; A. J. Meadows 10–4–175–90–29.16; J. R. C. Dakin 13–1–320–59*–26.66; C. St J. S. Peppiatt 11–2–227–115*–25.22; J. N. Ayton 10–1–178–47–19.77; *R. A. E. Scott 13–2–193–58–17.54.

Bowling—J. R. C. Dakin 100.4–32–222–21–10.57; J. N. Gundill 147–39–328–25–13.12; A. M. Skinner 221.3–69–494–32–15.43; M. S. Wrigley 150.4–30–430–23–18.69.

SEVENOAKS SCHOOL

Played 17: Won 3, Lost 3, Drawn 11. Abandoned 1

Master i/c: I. J. B. Walker

Batting—T. R. Payton 11–8–106–30*–35.33; D. E. Neil-Dwyer 14–1–386–100–29.69; O. Iqbal 16–0–470–77–29.37; J. D. Fry 15–2–365–100*–28.07; J. M. Perrott 16–2–313–89–22.35; J. N. Gould 13–4–190–39–21.11; *B. C. Shah 17–0–352–71–20.70; N. P. Stirk 7–1–119–42–19.83; S. M. Popham 16–3–180–40–13.84; G. M. Siddle 11–2–112–40–12.44.

Bowling—S. T. S. Smith 123.5–27–415–22–18.86; J. D. Fry 230.2–52–692–30–23.06.

SHERBORNE SCHOOL

Played 17: Won 6, Lost 3, Drawn 8. Abandoned 1

Master i/c: G. C. Allen Cricket professional: C. Stone

Batting—P. Hodges 10–3–253–84–36.14; *T. R. Ashworth 13–3–273–66–27.30; S. J. Leeke 12–3–237–88*–26.33; B. D. Atwell 14–1–316–71–24.30; T. A. Batchelar 15–0–355–70–23.66; M. C. Evans 7–2–117–84*–23.40; J. E. Pratt 12–3–182–64–20.22.

Bowling—R. P. O. Springfield 165–51–389–31–12.54; T. R. Ashworth 81.4–16–229–17–13.47; P. Hodges 156.2–47–376–26–14.46.

SHIPLAKE COLLEGE

Played 12: Won 3, Lost 4, Drawn 5

Master i/c: P. M. Davey

Batting—D. S. Simmons 12–1–367–69–33.36; E. J. Rydon 10–2–201–59–25.12; D. E. Hyman 11–2–225–52–25.00; J. L. Edgar 11–3–148–42–18.50; M. H. Nunn 9–0–138–69–15.33.

Bowling—M. H. Nunn 103–31–264–22–12.00; *T. J. Wilson 103–17–354–23–15.39; D. S. Simmons 47–9–150–12–12.50; S. J. Clark 58–5–253–10–25.30.

SHREWSBURY SCHOOL

Played 17: Won 7, Lost 2, Drawn 8. Abandoned 2

Master i/c: J. M. Williams Cricket professionals: P. H. Bromley and Y. Manack

Batting—*J. M. Jones 16–1–504–93–33.60; D. J. Bowett 16–3–435–99–33.46; E. J. W. Maxwell 10–0–229–69–22.90; P. J. Heyworth 10–0–223–87–22.30; D. P. Lightning 14–2–231–53–19.25; A. D. Browne 17–1–267–69*–16.68.

Bowling—D. J. Bowett 194.3–48–497–40–12.42; D. M. W. Roberts 144.3–28–400–27–14.81; J. L. Wagstaff 122–27–330–18–18.33; P. S. Bullock 113.1–25–369–20–18.45.

SIMON LANGTON GRAMMAR SCHOOL

Played 16: Won 10, Lost 1, Drawn 5. Abandoned 5

Master i/c: R. F. Harriott

Batting—D. G. Newton 15–1–618–95*–44.14; L. J. Scales 3–0–112–68–37.33; N. S. Cox 14–2–427–103*–35.58; *P. C. Relf 13–2–375–105–34.09; N. R. Henn 14–2–397–65–33.08.

Bowling—A. D. Judge 139.4–37–351–29–12.10; P. C. Relf 127–25–435–31–14.03; M. D. Bentley 54.1–8–163–11–14.81; A. R. Danes 75.2–9–231–15–15.40; T. J. Stevens 89–14–239–12–19.91; R. C. Stevens 83–16–245–11–22.27.

SIR ROGER MANWOOD'S SCHOOL

Played 8: Won 4, Lost 2, Drawn 2. Abandoned 1

Master i/c: P. Firminger

Batting—*A. Crofts 5–3–160–54*–80.00; M. May 7–1–298–95*–49.66; S. Wellard 6–3–122–54*–40.66; L. Marsh 8–1–239–70*–34.14; D. Deadman 7–2–118–32*–23.60.

Bowling—T. Squire 73.2–11–222–12–18.50; D. Hill 104.1–21–317–17–18.64.

SOLIHULL SCHOOL

Played 15: Won 5, Lost 5, Drawn 5

Master i/c: M. R. Brough Cricket professional: G. Briant

Batting—D. C. Pritchard 14–3–402–93*–36.54; P. Wheeler 8–1–247–100*–35.28; J. M. A. Inglis 10–2–227–48*–28.37; D. J. Kelly 15–2–281–61–21.61; E. J. M. Jones 14–1–225–103–17.30; R. E. Hatcliffe 11–1–166–57–16.60; P. Goodson 11–0–148–39–13.45.

Bowling—R. E. Hatcliffe 78–13–280–21–13.33; J. M. A. Inglis 69.2–12–216–15–14.40; S. K. Bushell 71.1–24–211–11–19.18; D. C. Pritchard 117–13–492–24–20.50; S. A. Randall 79–13–272–13–20.92; N. Heath 108–16–351–15–23.40.

STAMFORD SCHOOL

Played 13: Won 1, Lost 6, Drawn 5, Tied 1. Abandoned 2

Master i/c: S. N. Webster

Batting—*D. M. Aldridge 14–1–346–60–26.61; D. Richardson 14–2–271–75*–22.58; M. S. Lock 10–2–177–33–22.12; R. D. Simpson 6–0–103–41–17.16; J. J. Mackie 9–1–127–34–15.87; B. G. Martin 12–1–157–34–14.27; A. T. Forster 13–0–180–48–13.84.

Bowling—D. Richardson 111–27–341–20–17.05; B. G. Martin 159–30–457–21–21.76; D. M. Aldridge 158–38–540–17–31.76; T. Atkinson 115–24–415–11–37.72.

STOCKPORT GRAMMAR SCHOOL

Played 14: Won 3, Lost 6, Drawn 5

Master i/c: C. Dunkerley

Batting—*I. Millner 14–4–398–85–39.80; P. Duckworth 13–3–224–44–22.40; H. Grayson 13–1–290–44–24.16; M. Baulkwill 12–0–170–33–14.16; R. Patel 11–2–111–24–12.33; J. Healey 12–0–120–29–10.00.

Bowling—R. Patel 154.5–30–416–32–13.00; P. Duckworth 91–8–338–21–16.09; B. Anderson 139–25–481–24–20.04.

STONYHURST COLLEGE

Played 8: Won 2, Lost 1, Drawn 5. Abandoned 1

Master i/c: J. M. Fairburn

Batting—*G. O'Driscoll 9–2–536–146*–76.57; P. Flood 8–1–190–45*–27.14; B. Hammond 9–1–177–54–22.12.

Bowling—P. Keown 44.3–12–117–12–9.75; L. O'Doherty 87.3–24–235–14–16.78; J. Wareing 72–16–224–12–18.66; B. Hammond 131–31–338–12–28.16.

STOWE SCHOOL

Played 14: Won 2, Lost 3, Drawn 9. Abandoned 5

Master i/c: G. A. Cottrell Cricket professional: M. J. Harris

Batting—*W. J. P. Atkinson 11–0–477–98–43.36; R. B. Pumfrey 11–0–383–66–34.81; H. P. V. Scott-Gall 10–3–236–70–33.71; G. J. Amdor 12–3–194–53*–21.55; D. T. H. Rotheroe 10–1–152–68*–16.88.

Bowling—H. P. V. Scott-Gall 114–26–376–18–20.88; R. B. Pumfrey 136–9–399–18–22.16; B. I. DeWynter 106.2–24–361–11–32.81; M. J. T. Jefferson 148–7–495–10–49.50.

STRATHALLAN SCHOOL

Played 15: Won 5, Lost 4, Drawn 6. Abandoned 1

Master i/c: R. J. W. Proctor

Batting—R. B. Moffat 12–2–352–63–35.20; R. G. Eason 12–1–314–60*–28.54; J. A. Jacobsen 14–2–256–56*–21.33; *G. M. Adam 10–1–185–64–20.55; G. D. Wallace 10–3–103–22*–14.71; S. Neish 9–0–119–49–13.22.

Bowling—R. A. Hatfield 152.4–39–384–22–17.45; R. G. Brown 200–42–568–30–18.93; G. M. Adam 95–13–288–15–19.20; J. C. M. van Beusekom 81–23–264–13–20.30; G. N. Reid 121.3–35–350–15–23.33; D. G. Thorburn 67–11–248–10–24.80.

SUTTON VALENCE SCHOOL

Played 17: Won 9, Lost 2, Drawn 6

Master i/c: D. Pickard

Batting—J. Cowell 8–3–204–49*–40.80; J. Barr 16–1–449–55–29.93; A. Barr 16–2–412–62–29.42; Y. Patel 15–4–208–53–18.90; M. Chambers 13–1–198–37–16.50; P. Heine 15–0–192–39–12.80.

Bowling—C. Dennison 32–6–72–10–7.20; J. Barr 168.1–37–471–39–12.07; A. Barr 78–20–191–15–12.73; D. Patel 190.2–44–483–34–14.20; Y. Patel 157.1–33–376–26–14.46; R. Girling 181.5–43–502–27–18.59.

TAUNTON SCHOOL

Played 12: Won 8, Lost 1, Drawn 3. Abandoned 4

Master i/c: R. P. Smith

Batting—*P. C. L. Holloway 12–2–568–152*–56.80; A. Habib 11–4–394–84*–56.28; M. J. Amor 11–3–263–52–32.87; A. Maynard 9–4–124–44–24.80; B. Scofield 12–0–215–49–17.91; N. A. Blake 10–1–135–28–15.00.

Bowling—G. Bennett 132.5–40–275–24–11.45; J. Seward 112.4–25–280–21–13.33; B. Scofield 109.4–24–298–20–14.90; T. Joy 80.1–23–162–10–16.20; J. Neale 102.5–30–254–12–21.16.

TIFFIN SCHOOL

Played 21: Won 5, Lost 3, Drawn 12, Tied 1. Abandoned 1

Master i/c: M. J. Williams

Batting—*N. J. B. Howell 21–2–902–124*–47.47; J. Matthews 20–1–722–113–38.00; R. D. Nash 21–2–501–77–26.36; D. K. Jones 16–2–320–113–22.85; A. N. Hones 12–6–113–26–18.83; T. C. M. Phillips 19–5–254–62*–18.14; A. W. Kennis 20–1–296–47–15.57; M. J. Watts 11–1–123–29–12.30.

Bowling—R. H. Beeching 56–14–154–11–14.00; T. C. M. Phillips 194.1–39–671–32–20.96; A. N. Hones 386.2–93–1,047–46–22.76; R. M. Evans 150–41–443–19–23.31; R. D. Nash 133.2–31–449–16–28.06.

TONBRIDGE SCHOOL

Played 19: Won 6, Lost 4, Drawn 9

Master i/c: S. J. G. Doggart Cricket professional: H. Mutton

Batting—D. R. Penfold 20–5–799–101*–53.26; C. J. Hollins 18–1–654–107–38.47; R. D. Gill 18–0–622–146–34.55; C. J. M. Bates 13–3–326–59–32.60; J. A. Richardson 10–3–200–46*–28.57; M. S. Nolan 18–2–403–55–25.18; M. C. Cook 8–3–115–37–23.00; R. Nayar 10–2–124–35–15.50; J. P. Arscott 13–2–123–34*–11.18.

Bowling—J. S. Durling 241–76–568–30–18.93; C. J. Hollins 92–28–291–13–22.38; A. G. Hunn 234.4–48–721–31–23.25; J. R. Honeyfield 141–27–469–20–23.45; R. Nayar 151–30–553–22–25.13; P. Beaumont 91–12–336–11–30.54.

TRENT COLLEGE

Played 16: Won 7, Lost 2, Drawn 7

Master i/c: T. P. Woods

Batting—T. C. White 14–2–565–135*–47.08; I. R. Birch 10–3–319–71–45.57; T. A. Ellis 12–4–313–83–39.12; A. W. Bocking 15–2–296–68*–22.76; J. D. Evans 11–0–234–45–21.27.

Bowling—M. A. Slade 131.3–46–243–18–13.50; C. G. Pye 82.4–20–208–15–13.86; A. W. Bocking 37.5–9–158–11–14.36; I. R. Birch 167.2–34–460–32–14.37; T. A. Ellis 141.2–35–414–28–14.78.

TRINITY SCHOOL

Played 21: Won 8, Lost 2, Drawn 11. Abandoned 2

Masters i/c: A. Gist and B. Widger

Batting—J. D. Morley 19–0–759–132–39.94; *P. A. Gardner 15–6–248–51*–27.55; M. A. Butcher 7–1–150–55*–25.00; A. J. Budge 20–0–471–74–23.55; J. D. Good 14–7–148–25*–21.14; A. P. Hubbard 20–1–367–110*–19.31; D. M. P. Turner 20–1–331–86–17.42; J. B. Orpin 19–0–285–62–15.00; C. Stokes 20–4–204–40–12.75.

Bowling—J. D. Good 286.3–76–685–50–13.70; P. A. Gardner 186–59–381–26–14.65; D. M. P. Turner 102.1–12–343–23–14.91; M. A. Butcher 66–12–192–12–16.00; P. B. Wren 128–34–374–14–26.71.

TRURO SCHOOL

Played 10: Won 1, Lost 8, Drawn 1

Master i/c: A. J. D. Aldwinckle

Batting—*J. A. Johnston 9–0–186–55–20.66; R. J. Smart 9–1–164–44–20.50.

Bowling—J. A. Johnston 68.5–6–260–16–16.25; D. J. B. Johns 111.5–18–348–19–18.31.

UNIVERSITY COLLEGE SCHOOL

Played 15: Won 2, Lost 8, Drawn 5. Abandoned 3

Master i/c: S. M. Bloomfield   Cricket professional: W. E. Jones

Batting—A. J. Stewart 13–1–502–132–41.83; R. J. Ayre 12–1–270–103*–25.54; S. K. Cattermole 12–0–261–67–21.75; *A. G. B. Bloch 12–0–227–94–18.91; J. E. Freeson 10–2–131–40*–16.37.

Bowling—S. Rush 140.5–25–468–24–19.50; K. Schofield 114.3–24–382–16–23.87; S. K. Cattermole 125–20–401–14–28.64; D. Sibson 151.2–28–448–14–32.00.

UPPINGHAM SCHOOL

Played 15: Won 3, Lost 5, Drawn 7. Abandoned 4

Master i/c: I. E. W. Sanders   Cricket professional: M. R. Hallam

Batting—J. H. Renison 12–2–284–104*–28.40; R. J. Howe 15–1–381–47–27.21; N. M. Leppington 13–4–213–41*–23.66; *M. C. Renison 11–1–209–58–20.90; E. R. Fowler 14–0–232–74–16.57; W. A. J. Wauchope 8–0–115–50–14.37; P. J. E. Spencer 10–2–115–30–14.37; M. R. Dodson 10–0–106–58–10.60.

Bowling—P. J. E. Spencer 190–51–489–32–15.28; G. M. Leather 136.3–28–429–22–19.50; E. R. Fowler 73–14–201–10–20.10; J. E. R. Scott 173.1–47–451–18–25.05; N. M. Leppington 93–10–352–14–25.14.

VICTORIA COLLEGE, JERSEY

Played 25: Won 8, Lost 3, Drawn 14

Master i/c: D. A. R. Ferguson   Cricket professional: R. A. Pearce

Batting—*P. J. Le Cornu 22–3–920–126*–48.42; A. J. Clarke 25–4–947–111–45.09; D. J. Pearce 23–3–482–71*–24.10; G. C. Ferguson 17–4–283–56–21.76; N. F. Le Feuvre 15–2–246–46–18.92; S. L. J. Weithley 20–5–209–40–13.93; S. F. Thomas 16–1–140–27–9.33; S. A. A. Gothard 18–2–138–29*–8.62; B. M. Vowden 20–1–145–34–7.63.

Bowling—S. L. J. Weithley 91–23–280–20–14.00; A. J. Clarke 232–49–711–42–16.92; D. K. Bower 81.3–34–367–21–17.47; P. J. Le Cornu 274–69–797–43–18.53; S. A. A. Gothard 216.2–40–753–30–25.10; B. M. Vowden 101–12–453–18–25.16.

WARWICK SCHOOL

Played 18: Won 5, Lost 4, Drawn 8, Tied 1. Abandoned 1

Master i/c: S. P. Sutcliffe   Cricket professional: N. Horner

Batting—*C. G. Stanton 17–1–543–119–33.93; C. G. Oswald 17–5–336–84*–28.00; G. Rawstorne 14–5–237–80–26.33; J. D. Moffatt 15–0–307–60–20.46; C. J. French 17–0–301–69–17.70; A. J. Bolton 9–1–129–31–16.12; B. Dalby 17–0–217–39–12.76.

Bowling—C. G. Oswald 329–86–959–62–15.46; J. R. Quinn 246–55–662–34–19.47; J. Ward 78–20–220–10–22.00; N. J. Corstorphine 139–28–434–19–22.84.

WATFORD GRAMMAR SCHOOL

Played 15: Won 1, Lost 3, Drawn 11

Master i/c: P. G. Lidington

Batting—A. Griffin 15–5–613–115*–61.30; P. Windmill 15–0–367–87–24.46; B. Watson 15–0–357–78–23.80; S. Easterbrook 12–3–211–39–23.44; C. Funnell 9–0–190–46–21.11; G. Warren 14–3–127–25–11.54.

Bowling—N. Walker 132.3–29–477–32–14.90; S. Easterbrook 185.4–43–527–30–17.56; R. Harradine 112–23–379–18–21.05; J. Dunstone 118–30–361–15–24.06.

WELLINGBOROUGH SCHOOL

Played 21: Won 8, Lost 1, Drawn 12. Abandoned 3

Master i/c: C. J. Ford Cricket professional: J. C. J. Dye

Batting—J. M. Attfield 20–9–608–80*–55.27; *M. Ingram 15–4–586–93–53.27; S. McMillan 19–4–281–56–18.73; N. Haste 15–5–175–38*–17.50; M. Chacksfield 15–3–202–59*–16.83; A. Woodward 12–2–142–34–14.20.

Bowling—R. Cousins 329.5–98–693–72–9.62; J. M. Attfield 241.2–75–615–35–17.57; J. J. Attfield 125–23–420–19–22.10; N. Haste 182–44–478–20–23.90.

WELLINGTON COLLEGE

Played 15: Won 1, Lost 2, Drawn 12. Abandoned 2

Masters i/c: K. M. Hopkins and C. M. St G. Potter Cricket professional: P. J. Lewington

Batting—M. C. K. Hodgson 16–2–568–111*–40.57; H. C. E. Green 11–0–240–50–21.81; D. R. Blomfield 16–2–301–48–21.50; E. V. Quibell 13–2–194–53–17.63; A. P. D. Wyke 14–4–143–46–14.30; S. M. Chew 10–1–100–20–11.11; C. J. G. Yeldham 12–1–115–40–10.45; *R. W. A. Sleigh 13–0–130–27–10.00; J. D. C. Carr-Smith 13–0–119–28–9.15.

Bowling—J. D. C. Carr-Smith 86–14–277–16–17.31; E. V. Quibell 179–49–482–22–21.90; T. A. Marden 161.3–19–558–25–22.32; R. J. H. Brett 196.4–38–575–21–27.38.

WELLINGTON SCHOOL, SOMERSET

Played 13: Won 4, Lost 3, Drawn 6. Abandoned 2

Master i/c: P. M. Pearce

Batting—*J. Govier 13–0–346–72–26.61; S. Comins 12–2–248–46–24.80; J. Austin 12–3–210–45*–23.33; J. Smith 13–0–269–61–20.69; C. Vellacott 13–0–265–96–20.38; N. Loudon 13–5–159–33–19.87.

Bowling—N. Hutchins 67–20–187–12–15.58; J. Govier 108.5–17–425–26–16.34; N. Loudon 146.2–34–486–27–18.00.

WESTMINSTER SCHOOL

Played 13: Won 4, Lost 3, Drawn 6

Master i/c: J. Cogan Cricket professional: R. Gilson

Batting—D. J. Cogan 13–1–425–104*–35.41; A. Breach 12–0–240–78–20.00; A. Coles 12–0–179–45–14.91; *J. Hyam 13–1–158–50*–13.16; J. M. Cogan 13–1–134–35*–11.16

Bowling—W. Brooks 68–9–266–13–20.46; D. Earle 86.3–15–328–12–27.33.

WHITGIFT SCHOOL

Played 19: Won 4, Lost 8, Drawn 7. Abandoned 1

Master i/c: P. C. Fladgate Cricket professional: F. Angles

Batting—N. S. Auer 20–3–631–100*–37.11; A. R. Biswas 20–1–376–83*–19.78; D. J. Fredrickson 12–0–188–49–15.66; J. S. Harford 12–1–166–38*–15.09; T. G. A. Griffiths 16–0–233–49–14.56; A. J. Bustard 12–0–163–54–13.58; C. E. Bruin 18–4–188–42–13.42; *S. J. Hill 18–2–193–50–12.06; G. M. Ward 14–5–102–26–11.33.

Bowling—C. E. Bruin 174.3–29–391–25–15.64; N. S. Auer 169–46–422–25–16.88; R. J. Targett 183.4–41–496–29–17.10; S. J. Hill 302.1–69–798–27–29.55; A. J. S. Baxter 90–10–390–12–32.50.

WILLIAM HULME'S GRAMMAR SCHOOL

Played 20: Won 8, Lost 8, Drawn 4. Abandoned 2

Master i/c: I. J. Shaw

Batting—*D. M. J. Timm 17–4–791–144*–60.84; N. J. Ridings 15–1–461–88*–32.92; N. J. Partington 8–1–166–47–23.71; I. R. Jordan 12–3–171–61*–19.00; I. D. Butler 14–3–207–49–18.81; A. W. Kloss 11–0–184–38–16.72; D. Loveland 10–2–119–27–14.87.

Bowling—D. Loveland 65–10–220–13–16.92; I. R. Jordan 122–31–348–19–18.31; A. D. Cleary 85–19–241–13–18.53; S. V. Kapadia 161–37–458–24–19.08; A. S. Partington 155–31–445–21–21.19; D. M. J. Timm 136–28–462–19–24.31; A. K. Hollingworth 76–8–258–10–25.80.

WINCHESTER COLLEGE

Played 15: Won 2, Lost 8, Drawn 5. Abandoned 1

Master i/c: P. J. Metcalfe Cricket professional: K. N. Foyle

Batting—D. A. de Lanoy Meijer 15–2–507–88–39.00; J. Collett 6–1–144–42–28.80; D. O. D. Williams 10–2–161–50–20.12; B. T. H. G. Pollard 14–1–256–51–19.69; *R. J. E. Hall 15–0–294–87–19.60; J. P. Maclay 14–1–241–54–18.53; M. A. Raison 14–0–187–53–13.35; R. A. Sanders 15–0–186–31–12.40.

Bowling—J. P. Maclay 99–13–375–15–25.00; A. R. B. Large 179–34–636–23–27.65; D. A. de Lanoy Meijer 119–10–493–16–30.81; G. Baker 98–14–424–12–35.33.

WOODBRIDGE SCHOOL

Played 10: Won 2, Lost 1, Drawn 7

Master i/c: M. Lubbock

Batting—B. Sindell 10–0–298–74–29.80; *J. Harper 10–1–260–61–28.88; J. Carpenter 9–1–182–51–22.75; S. Dunn 10–0–114–34–11.40.

Bowling—J. Harper 131–46–366–22–16.63; P. Donnison 125–33–309–15–20.60; R. Hallam 115–30–265–11–24.09.

WOODHOUSE GROVE SCHOOL

Played 11: Won 4, Lost 1, Drawn 6. Abandoned 3

Master i/c: E. R. Howard Cricket professional: R. Dani

Batting—J. L. Gomersall 11–3–370–87*–46.25; M. A. Beever 6–3–136–73*–45.33; *C. A. Miller 10–3–261–101*–37.28; J. C. M. Dobbs 9–2–171–51*–24.42; D. M. Lawson 11–0–243–62–22.09; S. J. P. Amos 8–2–107–36*–17.83.

Bowling—B. D. Cadman 61–16–178–14–12.71; S. N. Lee 107.2–18–404–28–14.42; M. W. Richardson 101.4–20–314–16–19.62.

WORKSOP COLLEGE

Played 13: Won 2, Lost 3, Drawn 8. Abandoned 1

Master i/c: N. S. Broadbent Cricket professional: A. Kettleborough

Batting—R. A. Kettleborough 12–3–546–95–60.66; J. D. Goode 12–3–271–100*–30.11; M. D. Holden 9–2–199–51*–28.42; C. R. G. Oldfield 6–0–111–32–18.50; D. H. Ellis 8–2–106–41*–17.66; J. D. Beardsley 10–1–158–35*–17.55; P. K. R. Patel 11–0–137–34–12.45.

Bowling—D. H. Ellis 95–20–304–13–23.38; J. D. Goode 117–21–359–13–27.61; J. Theobald 122–23–340–12–28.33; R. A. Kettleborough 126–38–347–10–34.70.

WREKIN COLLEGE

Played 15: Won 7, Lost 2, Drawn 6. Abandoned 4

Master i/c: R. Yates-Ward Cricket professional: T. J. Harrison

Batting—C. C. P. Davies 2-0-116-74-58.00; *S. R. Jackson 14-3-435-69-39.54; J. A. D. Mallinson 15-1-244-50-17.42; A. L. Tilsley 11-5-101-26*-16.83; M. R. Savage 14-2-189-42-15.75; S. R. D. H. Lander 9-0-125-40-13.88; G. R. Shafto 10-1-122-37-13.55; P. J. Garvey 11-1-127-40-12.70; J. B. Dixon 10-0-125-28-12.50.

Bowling—A. L. Tilsley 81.2-14-252-16-15.75; S. R. Jackson 216.4-47-686-36-19.05; G. R. Shafto 55.2-4-216-11-19.63.

WYCLIFFE COLLEGE

Played 18: Won 3, Lost 5, Drawn 10. Abandoned 1

Master i/c: P. Woolley Cricket professional: K. Biddulph

Batting—*S. G. Cady 9-1-229-64-28.62; J. F. P. Tovey 13-1-265-62-22.08; G. A. McDade 8-1-154-59-22.00; G. M. Collins 13-0-278-58-21.38; M. H. Workman 8-1-132-33*-18.85; R. M. Clements 12-2-167-49-16.70.

Bowling—S. G. Cady 137-14-392-23-17.04; J. M. Thomas 106-9-310-17-18.23; J. F. P. Tovey 85-8-334-14-23.85.

WYGGESTON & QUEEN ELIZABETH I SIXTH FORM COLLEGE

Played 7: Won 5, Lost 0, Drawn 2. Abandoned 5

Master i/c: G. G. Wells

Batting—*J. L. Green 5-0-177-77-35.40; L. R. F. Ewen 4-0-104-68-26.00

Bowling—J. L. Green 60.3-20-126-23-5.47; M. Bulsara 33-1-114-12-9.50.

CRICKET ASSOCIATIONS AND SOCIETIES

AUCKLAND CRICKET SOCIETY: *Secretary* J. H. Palmer, Eden Park, PO Box 2860, Auckland 1, New Zealand.

AUSTRALIAN CRICKET SOCIETY: Chris Harte, GPO Box 696, Adelaide, 5001, South Australia.

BLACKLEY CRICKET SOCIETY: *Secretary* D. N. Butterfield, 7 Bayswater Terrace, Halifax, West Yorkshire, HX3 0NB.

CAMBRIDGE UNIVERSITY CRICKET SOCIETY: *Secretary* R. Wheal, St John's College, Cambridge.

CHELTENHAM CRICKET SOCIETY: *Secretary* N. Cooke, Wickets, 10 Welland Lodge Road, Cheltenham, Gloucestershire GL52 3EZ.

CHESTERFIELD CRICKET SOCIETY: *Secretary* J. S. Cook, 44 Morris Avenue, Newbold, Chesterfield, Derbyshire S41 7BA.

COUNCIL OF CRICKET SOCIETIES, THE: *Secretary* J. Featherstone, 205 Hyde Park Road, Leeds, Yorkshire LS6 1AH.

CRICKET MEMORABILIA SOCIETY: *Secretary* A. Sheldon, 29 Highclere Road, Crumpsall, Manchester M8 6WS.

CRICKET SOCIETY, THE: *Secretary* E. B. Budd, 180 Grove End Gardens, London NW8 9LS.

CRICKET SOCIETY, THE (Midland Branch): *Secretary* Dr A. A. Walker, "Sarnia", Hernes Nest, Bewdley, Worcestershire DY12 2ET.

CRICKET STATISTICIANS, ASSOCIATION OF: *Secretary* P. Wynne-Thomas, 3 Radcliffe Road, West Bridgford, Nottingham NG2 5FF.

CRICKET STATISTICIANS AND SCORERS OF INDIA, ASSOCIATION OF: *Secretary* Dr Vasant Naik, 102 B. Madhav Wadi, M.M.G. Road, Dadar, Bombay 400 014, India.

DUKINFIELD AND DISTRICT CRICKET LOVERS' SOCIETY: *Secretary* A. Ollerenshaw, 16 Crescent Close, Dukinfield, Greater Manchester.

EAST RIDING CRICKET SOCIETY: *Secretary* R. P. Thompson, 151 Park Avenue, Hull HU5 3EX.

ESSEX CRICKET SOCIETY: *Secretary* P. Roberts, 5 Longacres, Hanover Square, Feering, Colchester, Essex CO5 9QP.

FYLDE COAST CRICKET SOCIETY: *Secretary* W. J. Thompson, 26 Roseacre, Blackpool, Lancashire FY4 2PN.

HAMPSHIRE CRICKET SOCIETY: *Secretary* F. Bailey, 7 Lightfoot Grove, Basingstoke, Hampshire.

HEAVY WOOLLEN CRICKET SOCIETY: *Secretary* G. S. Cooper, 27 Milford Grove, Gomersal, Cleckheaton, West Yorkshire.

INDIA, THE CRICKET SOCIETY OF: *Secretary* Sandeep Singh Nakai, G-58, East of Kailash, New Delhi 110 065 India.

LANCASHIRE AND CHESHIRE CRICKET SOCIETY: *Secretary* H. W. Pardoe, "Crantock", 117a Barlow Moor Road, Didsbury, Manchester M20 8TS.

LINCOLNSHIRE CRICKET LOVERS' SOCIETY: *Secretary* C. Kennedy, 26 Eastwood Avenue, Great Grimsby, South Humberside DN34 5BE.

MERSEYSIDE CRICKET SOCIETY: *Secretary* W. T. Robins, 11 Yew Tree Road, Hunts Cross, Liverpool L25 9QN.

NORFOLK CRICKET SOCIETY: *Secretary* S. J. Skinner, 27 Colkett Drive, Old Catton, Norwich NR6 7ND.

NORTHERN CRICKET SOCIETY: *Secretary* K. Harvey, 1 Old Park Road, Roundhay, Leeds, Yorkshire LS8 1JT.

NOTTINGHAM CRICKET LOVERS' SOCIETY: *Secretary* G. Blagdurn, 2 Inham Circus, Chilwell, Beeston, Nottingham NG9 4FN.

OXFORD UNIVERSITY CRICKET SOCIETY: *Secretary* F. Wilson, Keble College, Oxford.

PAKISTAN ASSOCIATION OF CRICKET STATISTICIANS: *Secretary* Abid Ali Kazi, 5-A, 11/1 Sunset Lane, Phase 11, Defence Housing Society, Karachi, Pakistan.

ROTHERHAM CRICKET SOCIETY: *Secretary* J. A. R. Atkin, 15 Gallow Tree Road, Rotherham, South Yorkshire S65 3FE.

SCOTLAND, CRICKET SOCIETY OF: *Secretary* A. J. Robertson, 5 Riverside Road, Eaglesham, Glasgow G76 0DQ.

SOMERSET WYVERNS: *Secretary* G. Evison, 61 Welbeck Avenue, Bedgrove, Aylesbury, Buckinghamshire HP21 7BJ.

SOUTH AFRICA, CRICKET SOCIETY OF: *Secretary* J. Landau, PO Box 78040, Sandton, Transvaal 2146, South Africa.

STOURBRIDGE AND DISTRICT CRICKET SOCIETY: *Secretary* R. Barber, 6 Carlton Avenue, Pedmore, Stourbridge, West Midlands DY9 9ED.

SUSSEX CRICKET SOCIETY: *Secretary* B. Rowe, "Crofton", Woodlands, Hove BN3 6TJ.

WEST LANCASHIRE CRICKET SOCIETY: *Secretary* G. O. Shipton, 9 Breeze Road, Southport, Lancashire PR8 2HG.

WOMBWELL CRICKET LOVERS' SOCIETY: *Secretary* J. Sokell, 42 Woodstock Road, Barnsley, South Yorkshire S75 1DX.

ZIMBABWE, CRICKET SOCIETY OF: *Secretary* L. G. Morgenrood, 10 Elsworth Avenue, Belgravia, Harare, Zimbabwe.

OVERSEAS CRICKET, 1987-88

Note: Throughout this section, matches not first-class are denoted by the use of a dagger.

ENGLAND IN PAKISTAN, 1987-88

By MARTIN JOHNSON

England's sixth tour to Pakistan was ill-conceived from the outset, coming immediately after the World Cup, when both public and player interest were never going to be high, and following so closely on the five-Test series in England in the summer of 1987. The Pakistanis' visit to England had not been without acrimony, but not even the most hardened pessimist would have forecast that England's tour several months later would lead to some of the most shameful scenes witnessed in any sport, never mind one traditionally associated with fair play, courtesy, and high moral values.

At one point, amidst allegations and counter-allegations of cheating, verbal abuse, crisis telephone calls to and from the Test and County Cricket Board at Lord's, and a threat of strike action by the visiting players, it looked as if the tour might be abandoned in mid-series. However, after the England captain, Mike Gatting, had been ordered to write an unconditional apology to umpire Shakoor Rana, to which his team-mates reacted by producing an outspoken, contract-breaching statement, protesting at the Board's instruction, the Second Test in Faisalabad was eventually completed. So, too, was the tour, which will go down as one of the more squalid in international cricket's history. Just about the only worthy memory of it was the bowling of the leg-spinner, Abdul Qadir, who in becoming only the fourth player to take 30 or more wickets in a three-Test series condemned England to their eighth defeat in eleven series and their third defeat in their last three series against Pakistan.

The seeds of discontent had been blowing in the wind ever since the first meeting between the two countries in Pakistan, on E. R. Dexter's 1961-62 tour. England won the first Test of that series. But they had not won another there, and a succession of visiting teams had returned home thinking that they had not been allowed to. At best they had come to regard the home umpires as incompetent; at worst, cheats. On Pakistan's 1982 tour to England, however, resentment went the other way. In a tight, three-Test series, the teams were level at one apiece before the deciding game at Headingley. There, umpire David Constant gave a decision which had a significant bearing on England squeezing home by three wickets. Afterwards Imran Khan, the Pakistan captain, was critical of the umpiring and blamed it for Pakistan's defeat.

Pakistan, who had been campaigning for neutral umpires since 1980, were further incensed before the start of their 1987 tour of England when the TCCB overruled their objections to umpires Constant and Ken Palmer. Both men stood in two Tests, and at Lord's and again at The Oval, umpire Constant was involved in incidents which aroused controversy. Pakistan's outwardly genial but outspoken manager, Haseeb Ahsan, described Constant as a "disgraceful person" – and when England embarked on their own tour, it was felt by some that Haseeb would orchestrate swift retribution. It was an unhealthy attitude, but one made understandable by suspicions that the pressure on Pakistan to win the Test series, after a nation-numbing defeat in the World Cup semi-finals, and again in the following one-day international series, almost guaranteed some use of shady tactics. In addition, following the retirement of Imran Khan, the captaincy had passed to Javed Miandad, a volatile character and one viewed with grave misgivings by the England players.

It was in this disagreeable climate that the First Test began in Lahore, and there the long-smouldering bonfire at last caught alight. England's refusal to entertain Pakistan's objections to umpires Constant and Palmer rebounded on them when their own protest about the appointment of the controversial Shakeel Khan was ignored. The English players claimed afterwards that no fewer than nine incorrect decisions had been given in favour of Pakistan's bowlers, while during the match their disgust and disillusion had boiled over in an extraordinary incident involving Chris Broad. Given out, caught at the wicket, by Shakeel, Broad refused to accept the decision, and almost a minute elapsed before he was at last persuaded by his partner, Graham Gooch, to depart the crease.

Pakistan demanded that Broad be sent home as punishment, but the tour manager, Peter Lush, took the view that a "stern reprimand" would suffice. This was a mistake. Regardless of the provocation to which Mr Lush undoubtedly considered Broad and all the team had been subjected, a heavy fine should have been imposed for such a flagrant breach of discipline. Nor was this the right time for the manager to criticise openly the umpiring, as he did, and call for neutral umpires in Test matches. His statement more or less gave Gatting *carte-blanche* to inflame the row publicly after the match, which Pakistan won easily by an innings. Qadir had figures of nine for 56 in the first innings and four for 45 in the second. Gatting, not to put too fine a point on it, accused the umpires of cheating when he said: "We knew roughly what to expect but never imagined it would be quite so blatant. They were desperate to win a Test match, but if I was them I wouldn't be very happy about the way they did it."

And so, in embittered mood – and with many of the players privately considering that Broad had done cricket a service by highlighting what they saw as years of injustice to visiting teams – the touring party moved on to the Montgomery Biscuit Factory at Sahiwal, where there was a three-day match against the Punjab Chief Minister's XI. Absent, however, were the manager and captain. They, along with Gooch and Neil Foster, remained in Lahore for three days before the team travelled to Faisalabad for the Second Test.

There, despite the England management's complaint that their request to be informed of the umpiring appointments in private and in advance had not been met in Lahore, they again learnt only through the local press of the two officials for the match. And they were less than delighted to discover that Shakoor Rana was one of them. The umpire's reputation for upsetting visiting teams, notably when the New Zealand captain, J. V. Coney, led his team off the field in protest during the Karachi Test in 1984-85, was already known to them.

On the second day of the Faisalabad Test match, there had already been one unsavoury incident, following Shakoor's rejection of a bat-pad appeal from Bill Athey, when, three deliveries from the end of play, an extraordinary sequence of events was set in motion by a furious on-the-field row between Gatting and the umpire. Shakoor accused Gatting of sharp practice in allegedly moving a fielder without informing the batsman (which Gatting denied). Within seconds the two were locked in a toe-to-toe, finger-wagging exchange – scenes that were to arouse mixed reactions from TV viewers in Britain. Shakoor accused the England captain of heaping abuse on him; Gatting claimed that he was sworn at first and also called a cheat.

It was not until the following morning that the full magnitude of the row became clear. Shakoor refused to take the field until he received an apology from Gatting, and Gatting declined to apologise unless the umpire reciprocated. The third day's play was lost while officials of both camps strove for an acceptable solution. At one stage a settlement looked forthcoming, but Shakoor (prompted, it is thought, by the Pakistan captain, Javed Miandad) dug his heels in again after initially agreeing to a joint apology.

Negotiations continued through the night and into the rest day, with Shakoor confined to a hotel room. But Mr Lush's exhaustive attempts to resolve the impasse were frequently frustrated by the elusiveness of Pakistani officials. On the afternoon of the abortive third day, Ijaz Butt, secretary of the BCCP, left Faisalabad for Lahore; when Mr Lush undertook the two-and-a-half-hour drive there himself, in the hope of discussing the situation with the BCCP president, Lt-General Safdar Butt, he was told that the general was out to dinner. He was thus forced to stay overnight in Lahore so that he could meet the two Butts next day, along with Haseeb, who was both a BCCP member and chairman of Pakistan's selectors.

Throughout, the England management were in contact with Lord's. By coincidence, the TCCB's Winter Meeting was being held on the day that was the rest day in Faisalabad, and it was there that the private decision was taken to instruct Gatting to apologise if no compromise could be reached. Both the manager and the captain were furious at the order, but they had little option but to comply. Consequently, on the morning of the fourth day Gatting handed the umpire the following, hand-written note. "Dear Shakoor Rana, I apologise for the bad language used during the 2nd day of the Test match at Fisalabad (*sic*). Mike Gatting, 11th Dec 1987."

In London, the TCCB issued a statement which read:

> It was unanimously agreed that the current Test match in Faisalabad should restart today after the rest day. The Board manager in Pakistan, Peter Lush, was advised of this decision immediately and asked to take whatever action was necessary to implement it. In reaching their decision the members of the Board recognised the extremely difficult circumstances of the tour and the inevitable frustration for the players arising from those circumstances, but they believe it to be in the long-term interests of the game as a whole for the match to be completed. The Board will be issuing a statement on the tour when it is finished, but in the meantime the chairman and chief executive will be going to Karachi for the final Test next week.

In Faisalabad, Mr Lush issued a statement which read:

> The Test and County Cricket Board has instructed me as manager of the England team to do everything possible to ensure that this Test match continues today and that we honour our obligations to complete the tour of Pakistan. We have tried to resolve amicably the differences between Mike Gatting and umpire Shakoor Rana following their heated exchange of

> words which took place on the second day. We all hoped this could have been achieved in private and with a handshake. Umpire Shakoor Rana has stated he would continue to officiate in this match if he received a written apology from Mike Gatting. The umpire has made it clear he will not apologise for the remarks he made to the England captain. In the wider interests of the game Mike Gatting has been instructed by the Board to write an apology to Shakoor Rana, and this he has now done.

The players themselves had already agreed to refuse to play on if their captain received such an instruction, but when it came, they eventually decided to continue under protest. This they made public in the form of a fiercely worded statement voicing their unequivocal support for the captain and their disgust with the Board.

> The England players deplore the fact that it was not possible to effect a compromise solution between Mike Gatting and umpire Shakoor Rana. We would have expected the governing bodies of both countries to use their influence and authority to resolve the problem.
>
> What is beyond dispute is that the umpire was the first to use foul and abusive language to the England captain. This was clearly heard by England players close to the incident. Mike Gatting was ready to apologise two days ago for his response, provided the umpire would do the same.
>
> We also wish to register a unanimous protest that the TCCB should consider it necessary to issue instructions through our manager, Peter Lush, to order the captain to make an unconditional apology to the umpire. By doing so, the captain, in the "wider interests of the game", felt he was forced to act against his own free will.
>
> An earlier statement from the TCCB said that the problem had been left in the hands of the England management to resolve as they thought fit. The instructions issued to the manager last night left him virtually no room for manoeuvre.
>
> The TCCB exerted pressure on Mike Gatting and on the rest of us and we are unanimous in the view that the same "wider interests of the game" referred to by our Board had been completely ignored by the BCCP, who did not exert similar pressure on the umpire.
>
> The incident was sad for cricket but the solution forced upon us is even sadder.

There was suspicion in the England camp that the TCCB had bowed to both political and financial pressures, regardless of their "wider interest" claims. This the Board denied, although it was later conceded that a senior Foreign Office official had voiced government concern, and also that a substantial slice of the tour guarantee money had yet to be paid by Pakistan. Such was the strength of feeling conveyed back to Lord's that when Mr A. C. Smith, the Board's chief executive, and its chairman, Mr Raman Subba Row, flew out to Karachi, they were in a conciliatory rather than a punitive mood.

Gatting, who had been contemplating resignation, was placated by Mr Subba Row's announcement of the Board's full backing for him, plus the concession that the Board was at fault – not only for not appreciating the full extent of the team's problems, but also in not sending representatives to Lahore when the first hint of serious unrest surfaced. Furthermore, Mr Subba Row accepted the players' claim that Shakoor had initiated the swearing episode and also had called the England captain a cheat. This, said the Board chairman, had been "totally unjustified". However, he was less successful in his attempts to secure a belated apology from the umpire, although after the tour it was learnt that Gatting had received a letter from Shakoor Rana. It was not made public by the England captain at the time (during the Third Test) because it was an expression of regret rather than an apology.

It was odd, none the less, that Gatting declined to mention at the time that he had received a communication, however unsatisfactory he personally felt it to be. Even odder, though, was the decision to try to keep secret the award of £1,000 to each player by way of a "hardship bonus". When, as it inevitably did, it came into the open, the Board was badly placed to fend off allegations that the money had been awarded either by way of a "bribe" to save the tour or as "conscience money" for its poor handling of the affair. Mr Subba Row was later reprimanded for acting unilaterally, and it is highly unlikely that the Board would have agreed to the payment. Whatever England's grievances, they had received extra financial reward for having performed poorly, both as cricketers and as ambassadors for their country.

Even allowing for the umpiring, England's batsmen made little of Qadir, who said afterwards that he had never bowled better than in the First Test. Emburey's unorthodox methods proved more successful than other more conventional ones, and he topped the Test averages, scoring only 18 runs fewer than Gooch. In Karachi, Capel confirmed his growing reputation as a batsman, but his bowling was disappointing on unresponsive pitches. Nor was he handled well by his captain. England's seven main bowlers took fewer wickets between them (29) than Qadir on his own. All in all, the disgraceful events at Lahore and Faisalabad tended to deflect from the fact that the team performed poorly. Sadder still was the thought that cricket may never again recapture its reputation as a bastion for old-style values.

ENGLAND TOUR RESULTS

Test matches – Played 3: Lost 1, Drawn 2.
First-class matches – Played 5: Lost 1, Drawn 4.
Loss – Pakistan.
Draws – Pakistan (2), President's XI, Punjab Chief Minister's XI.
One-day internationals – Played 3: Won 3.

TEST MATCH AVERAGES

PAKISTAN – BATTING

	T	*I*	*NO*	*R*	*HI*	*100s*	*Avge*
Salim Malik	3	4	1	143	60	0	47.66
Abdul Qadir	3	3	0	137	61	0	45.66
Wasim Akram	2	2	0	77	40	0	38.50
Ramiz Raja	3	4	1	110	50	0	36.66
Mudassar Nazar	3	4	0	131	120	1	32.75
Javed Miandad	3	3	0	88	65	0	29.33
Ijaz Ahmed	3	3	0	55	44	0	18.33
Iqbal Qasim	3	3	0	36	24	0	12.00
Ashraf Ali	3	3	0	23	12	0	7.66

Played in two Tests: Aamer Malik 5, 98*; Tauseef Ahmed 5*, 5*. Played in one Test: Asif Mujtaba 7; Saleem Jaffer 0; Shoaib Mohammad 0.

* *Signifies not out.*

BOWLING

	O	M	R	W	BB	Avge
Abdul Qadir	234.4	68	437	30	9-56	14.56
Tauseef Ahmed ...	71.2	25	128	5	3-28	25.60
Iqbal Qasim	114.2	33	268	10	5-83	26.80
Saleem Jaffer	65.5	15	153	5	3-79	30.60

Also bowled: Aamer Malik 10–0–46–0; Mudassar Nazar 26–8–56–2; Salim Malik 12–4–23–1; Shoaib Mohammad 1–1–0–0; Wasim Akram 40.1–7–102–2.

ENGLAND – BATTING

	T	I	NO	R	HI	100s	Avge
J. E. Emburey	3	6	3	207	74*	0	69.00
G. A. Gooch	3	6	0	225	93	0	37.50
B. C. Broad	3	6	0	204	116	1	34.00
M. W. Gatting	3	6	0	128	79	0	21.33
D. J. Capel	3	6	0	125	98	0	20.83
B. N. French	3	5	1	80	38*	0	20.00
C. W. J. Athey	3	6	0	92	27	0	15.33
N. A. Foster	2	4	0	40	39	0	10.00
P. A. J. DeFreitas ...	2	4	0	38	15	0	9.50
N. G. B. Cook	3	5	0	33	14	0	6.60
R. T. Robinson	2	4	1	16	7*	0	5.33

Played in one Test: G. R. Dilley 0*, 0*; N. H. Fairbrother 3, 1; E. E. Hemmings 1*.

* *Signifies not out.*

BOWLING

	O	M	R	W	BB	Avge
N. A. Foster	44	10	104	6	4-42	17.33
N. G. B. Cook	93.3	35	195	7	3-87	27.85
P. A. J. DeFreitas ...	52.5	10	170	6	5-86	28.33
J. E. Emburey	124	48	251	7	3-49	35.85

Also bowled: B. C. Broad 1–0–4–0; D. J. Capel 13–1–59–1; G. R. Dilley 21–2–102–1; G. A. Gooch 2–1–4–0; E. E. Hemmings 25–8–51–1.

ENGLAND AVERAGES – FIRST-CLASS MATCHES

BATTING

	M	I	NO	R	HI	100s	Avge
J. E. Emburey	4	7	3	216	74*	0	54.00
R. T. Robinson	4	7	1	261	118	1	43.50
G. A. Gooch	3	6	0	225	93	0	37.50
C. W. J. Athey	5	9	1	256	101*	1	32.00
B. N. French	4	7	2	147	45	0	29.40
B. C. Broad	5	9	0	251	116	1	27.88
D. J. Capel	5	8	0	207	98	0	25.87
M. W. Gatting	4	7	0	141	79	0	20.14
E. E. Hemmings	3	3	1	35	34	0	17.50
N. H. Fairbrother ...	3	5	0	76	66	0	15.20
P. A. J. DeFreitas ...	3	6	0	79	25	0	13.16
N. G. B. Cook	5	7	1	72	32	0	12.00
N. A. Foster	2	4	0	40	39	0	10.00
G. R. Dilley	3	4	3	6	4*	0	6.00

Played in one match: P. W. Jarvis 8; R. C. Russell 4.

* *Signifies not out.*

BOWLING

	O	M	R	W	BB	Avge
N. A. Foster	44	10	104	6	4-42	17.33
P. A. J. DeFreitas	64.1	14	195	9	5-86	21.66
N. G. B. Cook	129.2	47	277	10	3-37	27.70
E. E. Hemmings	61.3	17	170	6	4-70	28.33
J. E. Emburey	134	50	278	8	3-49	34.75
D. J. Capel	45	7	172	4	2-66	43.00
G. R. Dilley	50	7	206	4	2-8	51.50

Also bowled: B. C. Broad 1–0–4–0; M. W. Gatting 7–2–21–0; G. A. Gooch 2–1–4–0; P. W. Jarvis 17–2–51–1.

FIELDING

11 – B. N. French (10 ct, 1 st); 3 – G. A. Gooch; 2 – N. H. Fairbrother, substitutes (B. N. French, G. A. Gooch); 1 – B. C. Broad, M. W. Gatting, P. W. Jarvis, R. T. Robinson.

PRESIDENT'S XI v ENGLAND XI

At Rawalpindi, November 14, 15, 16. Drawn. Toss: England XI. A yawn of a match, played on a slow pitch of low bounce, saw neither side show the remotest interest in winning. The home team's captain, Abdul Qadir, spent long periods off the field, and all told bowled only three overs after coming on, as sixth change, when England were 218 for one. Understandably enough, he did not want England to face too much of his bowling before the Test series, and the centuries from Robinson (192 balls, 264 minutes, nineteen fours) and Athey (246 balls, 268 minutes, fifteen fours) were made against an undemanding attack. Asif Mujtaba's 157 for the President's XI, his highest first-class score, occupied 356 minutes, included 27 fours and earned him a belated call-up for Pakistan's one-day international squad.

Close of play: First day, England XI 274-3 (C. W. J. Athey 96*, D. J. Capel 12*); Second day, President's XI 92-1 (Asif Mohammad 37*, Asif Mujtaba 39*).

England XI

B. C. Broad b Sajjad	30
R. T. Robinson st Zulqarnain b Zahid	118
C. W. J. Athey retired hurt	101
N. H. Fairbrother lbw b Sajjad	1
D. J. Capel lbw b Sabih	67
*M. W. Gatting c Zulqarnain b Mohsin	13
†R. C. Russell c Salim Raza b Mohsin	4
N. G. B. Cook not out	7
E. E. Hemmings c Sajjad b Sabih	0
G. R. Dilley b Sabih	2
P. W. Jarvis b Sajjad	8
B 13, l-b 9, n-b 12	34
1/70 2/224 3/239 4/334 5/338 6/366 7/366 8/372 9/385	385

C. W. J. Athey retired hurt at 307.

Bowling: Mohsin 19–3–83–2; Waheed 23–1–88–0; Sabih 26–8–72–3; Sajjad 36.4–16–56–3; Zahid 16–6–33–1; Mujtaba 3–0–7–0; Aamer 5–1–17–0; Qadir 3–1–7–0.

President's XI

Asif Mohammad lbw b Hemmings	56
Salim Raza lbw b Jarvis	4
Asif Mujtaba c sub b Capel	157
Aamer Malik lbw b Dilley	10
Zahid Ahmad b Hemmings	36
†Zulqarnain c sub b Hemmings	14
Sabih Azhar lbw b Capel	1
Sajjad Akbar not out	12
*Abdul Qadir c Jarvis b Hemmings	12
B 1, l-b 3, w 1, n-b 11	16
1/14 2/148 3/205 4/279 5/279 6/285 7/302 8/318	(8 wkts) 318

Mohsin Kamal and Waheed Niazi did not bat.

Bowling: Dilley 18–3–61–1; Jarvis 17–2–51–1; Cook 17–5–45–0; Capel 21–5–66–2; Hemmings 23.3–7–70–4; Gatting 7–2–21–0.

Umpires: Amanullah Khan and Javed Akhtar.

†PAKISTAN v ENGLAND

First One-day International

At Lahore, November 18. England won by two wickets. Toss: Pakistan. England got themselves bogged down chasing an apparently comfortable target, with Athey scoring only 20 in 21 overs. At one stage they were 140 for eight with only three of their 45 overs remaining. However, DeFreitas won the match in the final over with a six over long-off off Qadir, who was captaining the side in the absence of Miandad, who had flu. Pakistan had earlier struggled on a slow, turning pitch, especially against Emburey, and suffered a further setback when Salim Yousuf dislocated his thumb in England's first over. Salim Malik took over as wicket-keeper from the third over.

Man of the Match: J. E. Emburey.

Pakistan

Ramiz Raja c Gatting b Capel	38
Shoaib Mohammad c French b Foster	11
Salim Malik run out	30
Ijaz Ahmed c Gooch b Hemmings	17
Mudassar Nazar c Fairbrother b Foster	10
†Salim Yousuf c French b Hemmings	22
Manzoor Elahi b Emburey	14
Wasim Akram b Emburey	5
*Abdul Qadir run out	7
Zahid Ahmad c and b Emburey	0
Saleem Jaffer not out	2
B 1, l-b 5, w 2, n-b 2	10
1/25 (2) 2/62 (1) 3/96 (4) 4/102 (3) 5/132 (5) 6/138 (6) 7/154 (7) 8/163 (9) 9/163 (10) 10/166 (8) (41.3 overs)	166

Bowling: DeFreitas 7–1–19–0; Foster 8–1–37–2; Capel 9–0–43–1; Emburey 8.3–2–17–3; Hemmings 9–0–44–2.

England

G. A. Gooch b Qadir	43
B. C. Broad c Manzoor b Wasim	1
*M. W. Gatting lbw b Qadir	16
C. W. J. Athey lbw b Wasim	20
D. J. Capel run out	8
N. J. Fairbrother b Zahid	25
J. E. Emburey c Ijaz b Zahid	4
P. A. J. DeFreitas not out	14
N. A. Foster lbw b Wasim	0
†B. N. French not out	7
B 13, l-b 10, w 4, n-b 2	29
1/5 (2) 2/61 (1) 3/74 (3) 4/89 (5) 5/120 (4) 6/127 (7) 7/138 (6) 8/140 (9) (8 wkts, 44.3 overs)	167

E. E. Hemmings did not bat.

Bowling: Wasim 9–0–25–3; Saleem Jaffer 3–0–18–0; Mudassar 9–1–19–0; Manzoor 2–0–12–0; Qadir 8.3–2–32–2; Zahid 9–1–24–2; Shoaib 4–0–14–0.

Umpires: Shakeel Khan and Shakoor Rana.

†PAKISTAN v ENGLAND

Second One-day International

At Karachi, November 20. England won by 23 runs. Toss: England. Gooch's 142 off 134 balls, with fourteen fours, was the second-highest score by an England player in a one-day international, the highest being D. I. Gower's 158 against New Zealand at Brisbane in 1982-83. Capel's 50, from 37 balls, included three successive sixes off Shoaib Mohammad. Defending an impressive total, England bowled and fielded poorly, allowing another weakened Pakistan side to get within 23 runs. Ramiz Raja completed a hat-trick of unusual dismissals against England in 1987. Incorrectly given run out when walking for a catch off a no-ball in Perth, and run out without facing at The Oval in the Texaco Trophy, he was here given out obstructing the field when looking for a second run off the final delivery to reach his hundred. It was the first such dismissal in a one-day international.

Man of the Match: G. A. Gooch.

England

G. A. Gooch st Zulqarnain b Qadir	142	N. A. Foster not out	5
B. C. Broad c Manzoor b Qadir	22		
*M. W. Gatting run out	21	B 3, l-b 9, w 6, n-b 2	20
N. H. Fairbrother b Zahid	2		—
D. J. Capel not out	50	1/70 (2) 2/135 (3) (6 wkts, 44 overs)	263
J. E. Emburey c Manzoor b Qadir	1	3/140 (4) 4/249 (1)	
P. A. J. DeFreitas b Mohsin	0	5/251 (6) 6/251 (7)	

C. W. J. Athey, †B. N. French and E. E. Hemmings did not bat.

Bowling: Wasim 4–1–9–0; Mohsin 9–0–57–1; Manzoor 3–0–19–0; Zahid 7–0–37–1; Asif 3–0–25–0; Qadir 8–0–30–3; Salim Malik 5–0–32–0; Shoaib 5–0–42–0.

Pakistan

Ramiz Raja obstructing the field	99	Zahid Ahmad not out	3
Shoaib Mohammad run out	37		
Salim Malik c Fairbrother b Foster	35	L-b 7, w 7	14
Manzoor Elahi run out	17		—
*Abdul Qadir c Broad b Foster	0	1/77 (2) 2/138 (3) (8 wkts, 44 overs)	240
Ijaz Ahmed c Athey b Emburey	26	3/172 (4) 4/172 (5)	
Wasim Akram c Foster b Emburey	9	5/214 (6) 6/228 (7)	
Asif Mujtaba b Capel	0	7/230 (8) 8/240 (1)	

†Zulqarnain and Mohsin Kamal did not bat.

Bowling: DeFreitas 9–1–35–0; Foster 9–0–47–2; Capel 8–1–41–1; Hemmings 9–0–45–0; Emburey 9–0–65–2.

Umpires: Khizar Hayat and Mahboob Shah.

†PAKISTAN v ENGLAND

Third One-day International

At Peshawar, November 22. England won by 98 runs. Toss: England. Still without Javed Miandad and further weakened by Wasim Akram's absence because of a groin strain, Pakistan were beaten comfortably with 79 balls to spare. Only Salim Malik (78 balls, one four) offered any resistance. Shoaib was ruled out for the First Test when, with Pakistan 11 for one, he missed an attempted hook off DeFreitas, was struck and needed four stitches to his left eyebrow. England's innings had been built around half-centuries from Gooch (78 balls), Broad (110 balls) and Gatting (51 balls).

Man of the Match: N. A. Foster.

England

G. A. Gooch c Zulqarnain b Mudassar	57	N. A. Foster not out	2
B. C. Broad b Shakil	66	†R. C. Russell not out	2
*M. W. Gatting c Manzoor b Qadir	53	B 1, l-b 7, w 5, n-b 5	18
D. J. Capel st Zulqarnain b Tauseef	25		—
J. E. Emburey run out	3	1/101 (1) 2/168 (2) (8 wkts, 45 overs)	236
P. A. J. DeFreitas c Shoaib b Qadir	3	3/214 (4) 4/221 (5)	
C. W. J. Athey st Zulqarnain b Qadir	6	5/221 (3) 6/231 (6)	
N. H. Fairbrother run out	1	7/232 (7) 8/234 (8)	

N. G. B. Cook did not bat.

Bowling: Mohsin 9–0–37–0; Shakil 9–0–50–1; Mudassar 9–0–33–1; Tauseef 9–0–59–1; Qadir 9–0–49–3.

Pakistan

Ramiz Raja lbw b Foster	5	Tauseef Ahmed not out	0
Shoaib Mohammad retired hurt	6	Shakil Khan b Foster	0
Salim Malik b Cook	52		
Ijaz Ahmed c Russell b Cook	15	L-b 3, w 3, n-b 6	12
Mudassar Nazar b Capel	1		—
Manzoor Elahi c Gooch b Emburey	21	1/11 (1) 2/34 (4) 3/43 (5) (31.5 overs)	138
*Abdul Qadir c Russell b DeFreitas	21	4/78 (6) 5/122 (7)	
†Zulqarnain c Russell b DeFreitas	0	6/126 (8) 7/138 (3)	
Mohsin Kamal b Foster	5	8/138 (9) 9/138 (11)	

Bowling: DeFreitas 7–0–31–2; Foster 6.5–0–20–3; Cook 6–1–18–2; Capel 9–0–44–1; Emburey 3–0–22–1.

Umpires: Amanullah Khan and Javed Akhtar.

PAKISTAN v ENGLAND

First Test Match

At Lahore, November 25, 26, 27, 28. Pakistan won by an innings and 87 runs with a day to spare. A number of controversial decisions, Broad's refusal to walk when given out, and Gatting's post-match allegations of unfair umpiring all overshadowed a magnificent bowling performance by Abdul Qadir. The Pakistan leg-spinner returned match figures of thirteen for 101, having also taken ten wickets against England at The Oval three months earlier. His first-innings analysis of nine for 56 was the best in Test cricket by a Pakistani. Indeed, it was the best by any bowler against England; only H. J. Tayfield and A. A. Mailey had previously taken nine wickets in an England innings.

England's decision to bat first was an obvious one in view of the pitch having been under-prepared to favour the three spin bowlers included by Pakistan. England opted for two, Emburey and Cook, and with Capel subsequently bowling only three overs, the decision to omit Hemmings looked even more curious as the match progressed than it had before the start.

But for Broad's 192-minute vigilance for 41, and stout resistance from Foster, French and Cook at the end of the innings, England would not have reached three figures. Foster's 39 was his highest in Tests. Qadir had come on after just ten overs to determine England's fate, yet when Pakistan batted, Emburey and Cook were disappointing. Mudassar's ninth Test hundred on the sub-continent, and his tenth in all, took him 323 minutes and included eighteen fours. His 50-over partnership of 142 with Miandad took Pakistan to a commanding lead of more than 200, although when 24 Miandad was given a life by French off Cook, a miss England could ill afford in the circumstances. The England wicket-keeper did not give one of his tidiest displays, and next day he seemed fortunate to be awarded the stumping that dismissed Qadir. Certainly the volatile Qadir could not believe the decision by Shakeel Khan, and he exchanged words with the umpire and the England captain before leaving.

England had already been upset at several umpiring decisions in the first innings, notably from Shakeel Khan, but worse was to follow. When this same official adjudged Broad caught behind off the left-arm spinner, Iqbal Qasim, on the third afternoon, Broad stood his ground. Almost a minute elapsed before Gooch persuaded him to go. A number of other decisions also angered England, who were eventually dismissed for 130 half an hour after lunch on the fourth day. This equalled their previous lowest total against Pakistan, made at The Oval in 1954.

Broad was later "severely reprimanded" by the tour manager, and many observers considered him fortunate to escape a heavy fine. Mr Lush criticised the umpiring at the same time, and after the game Gatting was even more severe in his comments. Mr Stewart, the team manager, was also upset. However, although England undoubtedly received a raw deal, not one of the three appeared to acknowledge that the batting had been woefully sub-standard. The attendance throughout the match was even more abject, as indeed it was to be for the entire series. When the first ball was bowled, fewer than 200 spectators were at the ground to see it.

Man of the Match: Abdul Qadir.

Close of play: First day, Pakistan 13-0 (Mudassar Nazar 11*, Ramiz Raja 0*); Second day, Pakistan 277-4 (Ijaz Ahmed 27*, Asif Mujtaba 2*); Third day, England 47-4 (M. W. Gatting 6*, B. N. French 4*).

England

G. A. Gooch b Qadir	12	– c Ashraf b Iqbal	15
B. C. Broad c Asif b Qadir	41	– c Ashraf b Iqbal	13
R. T. Robinson c Ashraf b Qadir	6	– lbw b Qadir	1
*M. W. Gatting lbw b Qadir	0	– lbw b Qadir	23
C. W. J. Athey lbw b Qadir	5	– c Ashraf b Tauseef	2
D. J. Capel c Asif b Tauseef	0	– (7) c Miandad b Qadir	0
P. A. J. DeFreitas lbw b Qadir	5	– (8) c Tauseef b Iqbal	15
J. E. Emburey b Qadir	0	– (9) not out	38
N. A. Foster lbw b Qadir	39	– (10) c sub (Akram Raza) b Tauseef	1
†B. N. French not out	38	– (6) lbw b Qadir	9
N. G. B. Cook c Miandad b Qadir	10	– b Tauseef	5
B 4, l-b 14, n-b 1	19	B 4, l-b 4	8
1/22 (1) 2/36 (3) 3/36 (4) 4/44 (5) 5/55 (6) 6/70 (7) 7/81 (8) 8/94 (2) 9/151 (9) 10/175 (11)	175	1/23 (2) 2/24 (3) 3/38 (1) 4/43 (5) 5/66 (6) 6/70 (7) 7/73 (4) 8/105 (8) 9/116 (10) 10/130 (11)	130

Bowling: *First Innings*—Wasim 14–4–32–0; Mudassar 5–3–9–0; Qadir 37–13–56–9; Tauseef 23–9–38–1; Iqbal 4–0–22–0. *Second Innings*—Wasim 2–0–6–0; Mudassar 1–0–4–0; Qadir 36–14–45–4; Tauseef 20.2–7–28–3; Iqbal 20–10–39–3.

Pakistan

Mudassar Nazar lbw b Foster	120
Ramiz Raja b Emburey	35
Salim Malik b Emburey	0
*Javed Miandad c Gooch b Cook	65
Ijaz Ahmed b DeFreitas	44
Asif Mujtaba b Foster	7
†Ashraf Ali b Emburey	7
Wasim Akram c Broad b Cook	40
Abdul Qadir st French b Cook	38
Iqbal Qasim run out	1
Tauseef Ahmed not out	5
B 18, l-b 8, n-b 4	30
1/71 (2) 2/71 (3) 3/213 (4) 4/272 (1) 5/290 (6) 6/301 (5) 7/328 (7) 8/360 (8) 9/370 (10) 10/392 (9)	392

Bowling: DeFreitas 29–7–84–1; Foster 23–6–58–2; Emburey 48–16–109–3; Cook 31–10–87–3; Capel 3–0–28–0.

Umpires: Amanullah Khan and Shakeel Khan.

PUNJAB CHIEF MINISTER'S XI v ENGLAND XI

At Sahiwal, December 2, 3, 4. Drawn. Toss: England XI. With the bowling of Abdul Qadir fresh in the memory, England were bowled out by a seventeen-year-old leg-spinner, Mushtaq Ahmed, whose six for 81 included a spell of five for 28 from 75 balls. Zahoor Elahi, with 62 off 56 balls, and Salim Malik gave the home team a sound start before Dilley, despite problems with overstepping, found some life in the pitch and forced Malik to retire hurt with a bruised thumb. England batted well in their second innings, but because of the possibility of Mushtaq having to replace Qadir in the Test side, they faced only seven overs of his leg-spin. In the event, Qadir recovered from a heel injury in time to play at Faisalabad.

Close of play: First day, England XI 279; Second day, England XI 9-0 (B. C. Broad 2*, R. T. Robinson 7*).

England XI

B. C. Broad c Anil b Saleem Jaffer	0	– c Anil b Zakir	17
R. T. Robinson b Mushtaq	51	– c Zakir b Akram	76
N. H. Fairbrother c Mansoor b Saleem Jaffer	5	– c sub b Zulfiqar	66
C. W. J. Athey c and b Mushtaq	43	– lbw b Akram	20
D. J. Capel c Zahoor b Mushtaq	15		
P. A. J. DeFreitas c Aamer Sohail b Mushtaq	25	– (5) c Zahoor b Anwar	16
*J. E. Emburey c Aamer Sohail b Mushtaq	9		
†B. N. French c Anwar b Akram	45	– (6) not out	22
E. E. Hemmings c Salim Malik b Zulfiqar	34		
N. G. B. Cook c Anwar b Mushtaq	32		
G. R. Dilley not out	4		
B 4, l-b 10, w 1, n-b 1	16	B 1, l-b 4	5
1/0 2/49 3/112 4/119 5/132 6/154 7/171 8/228 9/275	279	1/45 2/126 3/160 4/185 5/222	(5 wkts dec.) 222

Bowling: *First Innings*—Saleem Jaffer 16–4–31–2; Zakir 5–3–20–0; Zulfiqar 24–5–69–1; Mushtaq 36.1–11–81–6; Akram 15–2–44–1; Aamer Sohail 4–1–20–0. *Second Innings*—Saleem Jaffer 11–3–31–0; Zakir 15–4–29–1; Mushtaq 7–0–32–0; Akram 21–4–58–2; Zulfiqar 7.4–1–25–1; Anwar 15–1–42–1.

Punjab Chief Minister's XI

Aamer Sohail c Fairbrother b Capel	0	– not out	12
Zahoor Elahi b Emburey	62	– b Dilley	0
*Salim Malik retired hurt	27		
Mansoor Rana c French b DeFreitas	42		
Anwar Miandad lbw b Hemmings	12	– (3) b DeFreitas	3
Akram Raza c Fairbrother b Cook	37	– (4) c French b Dilley	0
†Anil Dalpat run out	1	– (5) not out	0
Zakir Khan lbw b DeFreitas	4		
Saleem Jaffer not out	7		
Mushtaq Ahmed b Cook	0		
Zulfiqar Butt c French b Cook	3		
B 1, l-b 7, n-b 12	20	N-b 6	6
1/16 2/100 3/157 4/159 5/160 6/175 7/209 8/211 9/215	215	1/12 2/16 3/17	(3 wkts) 21

In the first innings Salim Malik retired hurt at 106.

Bowling: *First Innings*—Dilley 8–2–35–0; Capel 11–1–47–1; Hemmings 13–2–49–1 DeFreitas 8.2–4–12–2; Cook 18.5–7–37–3; Emburey 10–2–27–1. *Second Innings*—Dille 3–0–8–2; DeFreitas 3–0–13–1.

Umpires: Iftikar Malik and Masroor Ali.

PAKISTAN v ENGLAND

Second Test Match

At Faisalabad, December 7, 8, 9, 11, 12. Drawn. One of the most acrimonious Test matches i history almost brought about the cancellation of the tour, while the bitter rows that led to th loss of a whole day's play, and half an hour from another, might have cost England thei chance of levelling the series.

Gatting won another good toss on a pitch which had again been prepared for the spinners, and this time England also included three slow bowlers. Broad's 421-minute hundred, his first of any kind since his 112 in Melbourne almost a year earlier, was the cornerstone of an England total well above par for the conditions. He shared half-century partnerships with Gooch and Athey, and put on 117 with his captain before reaching his century in the penultimate over of the day. Attacking the spinners, Gatting himself made 79 off only 81 deliveries, including fourteen fours, a masterly innings apparently sparked by anger at what he considered to be another display of abject umpiring.

The official who most upset him during England's innings was Shakoor Rana. And three deliveries from the end of what had been an absorbing second day, with Pakistan struggling at 106 for five, the two of them became embroiled in an exchange which produced a situation provoking headlines in countries with only the vaguest interest in cricket. The incident occurred when Gatting moved Capel up from deep square leg to prevent a single. He had, he said later, told the batsman, Salim Malik, what he was doing. However, as Hemmings came in to bowl, Gatting signalled to Capel that he had come close enough, whereupon Shakoor Rana, standing at square leg, stopped play to inform Malik of Capel's position. Shakoor claimed that Gatting had been unfairly moving the fielder behind the batsman's back; Gatting informed the umpire that he was, in his opinion, overstepping his bounds. The language employed throughout the discourse was basic.

Shakoor's refusal to play on until he received an apology from Gatting was suspected by some of having more than a little to do with Pakistan's parlous position, and by the time Gatting's enforced apology had restored an uneasy truce, six hours of playing time had been lost. Ironically, a further three and a half hours were then lost to rain and bad light on the fourth day.

Having bowled Pakistan out for 191 by the close, England began the final day with a lead of 101. By lunch (106 for two), they had increased this to 207, Gooch giving them a good start with 65 from 74 balls. But Pakistan bowled just 24 overs in the morning session, and when four wickets fell in half an hour in the afternoon, England had little hope of victory. Realistically, their chance had evaporated once Pakistan refused to make up for the lost third day. Gatting's declaration left his bowlers 100 minutes in which to bowl out Pakistan, and they did not even get that long. In keeping with the conduct of everything to do with the match, Miandad called his batsmen in when the last twenty overs were due to start. That the Laws make no provision for such an early closure did not prevent the umpires from drawing stumps immediately.

Man of the Match: B. C. Broad.

Close of play: First day, England 254-4 (B. C. Broad 101*, N. G. B. Cook 1*); Second day, Pakistan 106-5 (Salim Malik 54*, Aamer Malik 1*); Third day, No play; Fourth day, Pakistan 191.

England

G. A. Gooch c Aamer Malik b Iqbal	28	– lbw b Qadir	65
B. C. Broad b Tauseef	116	– st Ashraf b Qadir	14
C. W. J. Athey c Aamer Malik b Qadir	27	– b Mudassar	20
*M. W. Gatting b Qadir	79	– c Qadir b Iqbal	8
R. T. Robinson c Ashraf b Qadir	2	– (8) not out	7
N. G. B. Cook c Ashraf b Iqbal	2		
D. J. Capel c Aamer Malik b Qadir	1	– lbw b Iqbal	2
J. E. Emburey st Ashraf b Iqbal	15	– (5) not out	10
N. A. Foster c Aamer Malik b Iqbal	0	– (6) c Miandad b Qadir	0
†B. N. French st Ashraf b Iqbal	2		
E. E. Hemmings not out	1		
B 10, l-b 5, w 1, n-b 3	19	B 1, l-b 9, n-b 1	11
1/73 (1) 2/124 (3) 3/241 (4) 4/249 (5) 5/258 (6) 6/259 (7) 7/288 (8) 8/288 (9) 9/288 (2) 10/292 (10)	292	1/47 (2) 2/102 (3) 3/107 (1) 4/115 (4) 5/115 (6) 6/120 (7) (6 wkts dec.)	137

Bowling: *First Innings*—Aamer Malik 5–0–19–0; Mudassar 3–0–8–0; Qadir 42–7–105–4; Tauseef 28–9–62–1; Iqbal 35.2–7–83–5; Shoaib 1–1–0–0. *Second Innings*—Mudassar 12–1–33–1; Aamer Malik 3–0–20–0; Qadir 15–3–45–3; Iqbal 10–2–29–2.

Pakistan

Mudassar Nazar c French b Foster	1	– b Cook	4
Ramiz Raja c Gooch b Foster	12	– not out	13
Salim Malik b Cook	60	– not out	28
*Javed Miandad b Emburey	19		
Ijaz Ahmed c Robinson b Emburey	11		
Shoaib Mohammad b Emburey	0		
Aamer Malik c French b Foster	5		
†Ashraf Ali c French b Foster	4		
Abdul Qadir c Gooch b Cook	38		
Iqbal Qasim lbw b Hemmings	24		
Tauseef Ahmed not out	5		
L-b 5, n-b 7	12	B 4, l-b 1, n-b 1	6
1/11 (1) 2/22 (2) 3/58 (4) 4/77 (5) 5/77 (6) 6/115 (7) 7/122 (3) 8/123 (8) 9/175 (10) 10/191 (9)	191	1/15 (1)	(1 wkt) 51

Bowling: *First Innings*—Foster 18–4–42–4; Capel 7–1–23–0; Hemmings 18–5–35–1; Emburey 21–8–49–3; Cook 20.3–10–37–2. *Second Innings*—Foster 3–0–4–0; Gooch 2–1–4–0; Emburey 2–0–3–0; Cook 9–3–15–1; Hemmings 7–3–16–0; Broad 1–0–4–0.

Umpires: Khizar Hayat and Shakoor Rana.

PAKISTAN v ENGLAND

Third Test Match

At Karachi, December 16, 17, 18, 20, 21. Drawn. There was yet another hiatus before the final Test when the Pakistan authorities appointed the controversial First Test umpire, Shakeel Khan, to stand again. It was a decision lacking in sensitivity, and following protests by the England management, he was withdrawn. After abortive – and probably none too serious – attempts to secure neutral officials from India, his place was taken by Mahboob Shah, one of Pakistan's three World Cup umpires. Another, Khizar Hayat, had already been chosen for this match.

Following Pakistan's escape at Faisalabad, this time a flat pitch had been prepared. None the less England, after winning the toss for the seventh time in eight tour matches, attempted to abuse it by slumping to 85 for six in their first innings. Pakistan had strengthened their pace attack by including Wasim Akram and Saleem Jaffer, while England brought in DeFreitas and Dilley for Hemmings and the injured Foster. Fairbrother replaced Robinson.

Emburey and Capel rebuilt the innings with a stand of 114 in 41 overs and were parted only by the second new ball, which Emburey carved straight to Qadir on the third-man boundary. French then supported Capel, who was only 2 runs short of a maiden Test century when he was last out, beaten by Qadir's googly, having batted for 372 minutes.

Pakistan also got themselves into trouble, losing Ramiz, Miandad and Ijaz in eight balls after being 105 for one from only 27 overs. However, from 146 for six Aamer, Wasim (despite suffering from a strained groin) and Qadir pulled them round to a handy first-innings lead. Qadir's Test-best 61 included four big sixes off Emburey and six fours, while Aamer, like Capel, missed by 2 runs his maiden Test hundred. He had batted for almost seven hours and had faced 329 balls when he ran out of partners, DeFreitas finishing off the tail to return his first five-wicket figures in a Test innings.

England again lost wickets cheaply, slipping to 115 for five, and despite Gooch's fine 93 (375 minutes, eight fours), his dismissal on the final morning allowed Pakistan to entertain real hopes of victory. Emburey again batted well, however, keeping Pakistan at bay for more than five and a half hours, and Cook survived for two hours eleven minutes before providing Qadir with his second ten-wicket return of the series. The captains' agreement during the tea interval to settle then and there for a draw left Emburey 1 run short of his highest score for England. It was an unusual way to finish a Test match, but with no other result possible, both sides were keen to end what had been a squalid and joyless series.

Man of the Match: Abdul Qadir.

Close of play: First day, England 222-7 (D. J. Capel 53*, B. N. French 10*); Second day, Pakistan 122-4 (Salim Malik 55*, Aamer Malik 1*); Third day, Pakistan 345-8 (Aamer Malik 91*, Iqbal Qasim 10*); Fourth day, England 150-5 (G. A. Gooch 79*, J. E. Emburey 9*).

England

G. A. Gooch c Ashraf b Wasim	12	– b Mudassar	93
B. C. Broad lbw b Wasim	7	– lbw b Qadir	13
C. W. J. Athey b Qadir	26	– c Ashraf b Saleem Jaffer	12
*M. W. Gatting b Qadir	18	– lbw b Saleem Jaffer	0
N. H. Fairbrother c sub (Asif Mujtaba) b Saleem Jaffer	3	– c sub (Asif Mujtaba) b Qadir	1
D. J. Capel b Qadir	98	– c Iqbal b Qadir	24
P. A. J. DeFreitas b Qadir	12	– (9) lbw b Qadir	6
J. E. Emburey c Qadir b Saleem Jaffer	70	– (7) not out	74
†B. N. French c Miandad b Salim Malik	31	– (8) lbw b Saleem Jaffer	0
N. G. B. Cook lbw b Qadir	2	– b Qadir	14
G. R. Dilley not out	0	– not out	0
L-b 8, w 1, n-b 6	15	B 9, l-b 5, w 1, n-b 6	21
1/20 (1) 2/41 (2) 3/55 (3) 4/72 (4) 5/72 (5) 6/85 (7) 7/199 (8) 8/274 (9) 9/291 (10) 10/294 (6)	294	1/34 (2) 2/54 (3) 3/54 (4) 4/61 (5) 5/115 (6) 6/175 (1) 7/176 (8) 8/187 (9) 9/246 (10)	(9 wkts) 258

Bowling: *First Innings*—Wasim 24.1–3–64–2; Saleem Jaffer 23.5–6–74–2; Qadir 49.4–15–88–5; Iqbal 18–4–51–0; Mudassar 1–1–0–0; Salim Malik 5–2–9–1. *Second Innings*—Saleem Jaffer 42–9–79–3; Aamer Malik 2–0–7–0; Qadir 55–16–98–5; Iqbal 27–10–44–0; Salim Malik 7–2–14–0; Mudassar 4–3–2–1.

Pakistan

Mudassar Nazar lbw b DeFreitas	6
Ramiz Raja c French b Cook	50
Salim Malik c Gatting b DeFreitas	55
*Javed Miandad lbw b Emburey	4
Ijaz Ahmed run out	0
Aamer Malik not out	98
†Ashraf Ali c French b Dilley	12
Wasim Akram c French b DeFreitas	37
Abdul Qadir b Capel	61
Iqbal Qasim c French b DeFreitas	11
Saleem Jaffer lbw b DeFreitas	0
L-b 11, n-b 8	19
1/18 (1) 2/105 (2) 3/110 (4) 4/110 (5) 5/122 (3) 6/146 (7) 7/222 (8) 8/316 (9) 9/349 (10) 10/353 (11)	353

Bowling: Dilley 21–2–102–1; DeFreitas 23.5–3–86–5; Emburey 53–24–90–1; Cook 3–12–56–1; Capel 3–0–8–1.

Umpires: Khizar Hayat and Mahboob Shah.

ENGLAND IN NEW ZEALAND AND AUSTRALIA, 1987-88

By ALAN LEE

Some tours live in the memory for many years. This one was gratefully forgotten, by those who played and those who watched, soon after the last ball was bowled.

After the explosive events on the pre-Christmas tour of Pakistan, peace might well have been the first priority. It was not, however, worthily achieved, for amid the relentless drudgery of slow and undistinguished cricket, England's players again allowed their on-field behaviour to plunge to unacceptable levels. Chris Broad and Graham Dilley were fined for tawdry incidents during Test matches; certain others might have been considered fortunate to escape sanction. The most alarming aspect of all was that the players themselves, and even their team manager, Mr Micky Stewart, seemed unwilling to acknowledge the poor impression which was being created by such conduct. Their oft-repeated reasoning was that other Test teams behaved similarly. True or not, this was no justification. England teams have prided themselves on maintaining certain standards; should this principle be sacrificed, the game would be on a course inevitably ending in the gutter.

Broad's indiscretion occurred during the Australian Bicentennial Test match in Sydney, a glittering event attended by good crowds and played in a fine spirit. Having batted for more than seven hours, scoring 139, Broad petulantly smashed the stumps with his bat after playing on to Waugh. His action was the mark of a man who finds it difficult to accept dismissal, whatever his score at the time. It was nothing new to see him look disbelieving when out, as those who saw the Pakistan tour would agree; but unless he curtails such behaviour, his very capable batting will be undermined and a promising Test career could be cut short. On this occasion the England management acted promptly to fine the player £500.

Dilley's fine, of £250, for loudly swearing when appeals for a catch were rejected during the First Test against New Zealand in Christchurch, was accompanied by a managerial smokescreen which sought to excuse his outburst. The decision to punish had plainly not met with the agreement of the captain, Mike Gatting, whose attitude to overseas umpires appeared not to have altered. Although Gatting indulged in nothing as overtly appalling as his row with Shakoor Rana in Pakistan, his expressions and gestures regularly spoke volumes. There were too many times when he appeared to be leading English dissent against decisions, rather than calming it. It was impossible to pretend that the series was well umpired, but that is hardly the point.

Gatting probably began this tour with an ambivalent attitude to a job he had kept against the wishes of certain high-ranking officials. There was a part of him challenging the authorities to strip him of power; another part of him, well aware of the overwhelming support he could command within the dressing-room, wanted nothing more than to leave the unpleasantness behind and prove himself above it all. The latter emotion finally won through. By the end of the tour he was speaking much more positively of the future, while there were signs of an increasing tactical awareness and a burgeoning confidence in all he did on the field. Whatever one's opinion of his temper, he was the best man available to captain the side and he finished the tour carrying the goodwill of those inside and outside the team environs.

In the absence of Gooch, Gower and Botham, none of whom was available, Gatting was the only England batsman capable of playing the type of innings likely to dominate an attack and influence a Test match. That he failed to do so, in the limited opportunities available to him, contributed to the lack of purpose apparent in much of England's cricket. So many of the others, both batsmen and bowlers, were at a stage of their Test careers when a poor tour can be held as proof of inadequacy; consequently, caution was paramount in their play. In New Zealand, this led to stalemate because the home team, deprived early on of their champion, Richard Hadlee, and their new batting star, Andrew Jones, had neither the resources nor the courage to attack. The series thus became an unending round of shadow-boxing.

All four Tests on the tour were drawn, although England called the tune for much of the one game in Australia, and for virtually all of the opening Test in New Zealand, played on a Christchurch wicket extravagantly helpful to seam bowlers. Had England been able to call on Neil Foster, in support of Dilley, they might have won in Christchurch and so provoked more aggressive cricket in the next two Tests. Sadly, however, Foster was already back in England for surgery on the knee he had injured in Australia.

Dilley responded well to the challenge of being the undisputed senior bowler. He took eight wickets in Christchurch and seven in Auckland, bowling with the consistent control of a high-quality performer. All of his victims in the first innings at Christchurch, where his return of six for 38 was a career best, were caught close to the wicket, a testimony to his line. Unfortunately, he failed once again to complete a series without injury, breaking down on the first day of the final Test in Wellington and taking no part in the one-day series which followed.

Paul Jarvis, 22 years old, was the pick of the other bowlers and was unlucky to be left out in Wellington after doing little wrong in the first two Tests. He appeared able to adapt from five-day to one-day cricket rather better than either Phillip DeFreitas or Neal Radford, neither of whom enhanced his reputation. John Emburey's work with the ball was again largely unrewarding. Although he had emerged as an increasingly prolific, if unorthodox, batsman and was a customarily good catcher – though not in New Zealand – it was an indictment of the spin bowling available in England that he had retained his Test place without challenge while taking so few wickets. He bowled a defensive trajectory, immensely good in one-day cricket, to a field setting which would have made the slow bowlers of old cringe, and he seldom looked like bowling out a Test team. Eddie Hemmings, the second spinner, out-bowled Emburey in Sydney, where Australia were obliged to follow on, but he played in only one subsequent Test – on the unresponsive Wellington pitch. At 39, however, he was not the long-term answer.

Among the batsmen, there were features to admire in the play of Broad, Martyn Moxon and Tim Robinson. Broad's two Test centuries, followed by another in the one-day international in Napier, were made with the diligence of an opener whose outlook was not dissimilar to Boycott's in its intensity. Moxon improved with every week of the tour and ended it looking a decent deputy for Gooch. Robinson, meanwhile, discarded his old inhibitions and batted with far more freedom to very good effect.

Neil Fairbrother and Bill Athey had disappointing tours, but David Capel, by his dedicated attitude and consistent results, indicated that he had a future in the all-rounder's role if he could knock the rough edges off his bowling. Bruce French's wicket-keeping, previously so undemonstratively good, at times looked scruffy on tour. With his stand-in, Jack Richards, also failing to impress in his few openings, most judges were left with the feeling that a change was necessary.

The most disappointing aspect of the cricket in New Zealand was the pitches. At Christchurch, the bowlers were given too much help; at Auckland and Wellington, they were given none at all, the bounce being low and the pace drearily slow. Unless more pace and life can be injected into the Test surfaces in this country, there is the prospect of more series like this one. A final thought was that the winter's cricket was too long. The England team was away from home, in all, for five and a half months, playing seven Tests and sixteen one-day internationals in four countries. Those who stayed the course were undoubtedly glad when it was over, and that is not the way to be. It seemed apparent that an administrative re-think was required lest more players opt out of England sides because they cannot face the grind of touring.

ENGLAND TOUR RESULTS

Test matches – Played 4: Drawn 4.
First-class matches – Played 8: Won 2, Lost 1, Drawn 5.
Wins – Northern Districts, President's XI.
Loss – Shell XI.
Draws – Australia, New Zealand (3), Wellington.
One-day internationals – Played 5: Won 2, Lost 3. *Wins* – New Zealand (2). *Losses* – Australia, New Zealand (2).

TEST MATCH AVERAGES – NEW ZEALAND v ENGLAND

NEW ZEALAND – BATTING

	T	*I*	*NO*	*R*	*HI*	*100s*	*Avge*
M. J. Greatbatch	2	3	1	186	107*	1	93.00
K. R. Rutherford	2	3	1	138	107*	1	69.00
I. D. S. Smith	3	4	2	92	33*	0	46.00
J. G. Wright	3	5	0	221	103	1	44.20
M. D. Crowe	3	5	0	216	143	1	43.20
J. G. Bracewell	3	5	1	152	54	0	38.00
T. J. Franklin	3	5	0	125	62	0	25.00
M. C. Snedden	2	3	0	34	20	0	11.33
J. J. Crowe	2	4	0	40	28	0	10.00

Played in three Tests: E. J. Chatfield 0*, 10; D. K. Morrison 0, 14*. Played in one Test: R. J. Hadlee 37; A. H. Jones 8, 54*; R. H. Vance 47; S. L. Boock did not bat.

* *Signifies not out.*

BOWLING

	O	M	R	W	BB	Avge
E. J. Chatfield	126.1	51	198	13	4-36	15.23
D. K. Morrison ...	80.2	14	269	8	5-69	33.62
M. C. Snedden	90	31	202	6	4-45	33.66
J. G. Bracewell	68	18	148	3	3-88	49.33

Also bowled: S. L. Boock 26–9–53–1; R. J. Hadlee 18–3–50–0; K. R. Rutherford 6–1–9–0.

ENGLAND – BATTING

	T	I	NO	R	HI	100s	Avge
M. D. Moxon	3	4	1	208	99	0	69.33
B. C. Broad	3	4	0	204	114	1	51.00
J. E. Emburey	3	3	0	106	45	0	35.33
M. W. Gatting	3	4	1	106	42	0	35.33
R. T. Robinson	3	4	0	126	70	0	31.50
G. R. Dilley	3	3	2	17	8*	0	17.00
P. W. Jarvis	2	3	1	34	14	0	17.00
P. A. J. DeFreitas ...	2	2	0	20	16	0	10.00
B. N. French	3	3	0	23	13	0	7.66
D. J. Capel	3	3	0	16	11	0	5.33

Played in two Tests: N. H. Fairbrother 1. Played in one Test: C. W. J. Athey 22, 19; N. V. Radford 8; E. E. Hemmings did not bat.

* *Signifies not out.*

BOWLING

	O	M	R	W	BB	Avge
G. R. Dilley	104.5	33	210	15	6-38	14.00
P. W. Jarvis	98	31	201	6	2-43	33.50
P. A. J. DeFreitas ...	91.1	33	175	4	2-39	43.75
D. J. Capel	109.2	22	274	5	2-57	54.80
J. E. Emburey	133.5	48	236	3	1-28	78.66

Also bowled: N. H. Fairbrother 2–0–9–0; M. W. Gatting 23–5–61–2; E. E. Hemmings 45–15–107–0; M. D. Moxon 2–0–3–0; N. V. Radford 50–8–132–1.

ENGLAND AVERAGES – FIRST-CLASS MATCHES

Note: The following averages include England v Australia, the Bicentennial Test match, in Sydney.

BATTING

	M	I	NO	R	HI	100s	Avge
B. C. Broad	7	9	1	537	139	3	67.12
M. W. Gatting	7	9	3	364	97*	0	60.66
M. D. Moxon	8	10	2	482	117*	1	60.25
R. T. Robinson	7	11	1	489	166	1	48.90
P. W. Jarvis	5	5	3	85	36*	0	42.50

	M	*I*	*NO*	*R*	*HI*	*100s*	*Avge*
J. E. Emburey	6	6	1	193	45	0	38.60
N. H. Fairbrother	5	6	2	126	46	0	31.50
C. W. J. Athey	6	9	0	200	60	0	22.22
B. N. French	6	5	1	88	47	0	22.00
G. R. Dilley	7	5	3	30	13	0	15.00
C. J. Richards	2	3	1	30	20*	0	15.00
D. J. Capel	7	7	1	88	21	0	14.66
P. A. J. DeFreitas	4	5	0	64	41	0	12.80

Played in four matches: E. E. Hemmings 8*; N. V. Radford 8, 23. Played in three matches: N. A. Foster 27*, 19.

* *Signifies not out.*

BOWLING

	O	*M*	*R*	*W*	*BB*	*Avge*
G. R. Dilley	201.1	48	506	23	6-38	22.00
D. J. Capel	196.2	45	476	15	3-50	31.73
N. V. Radford	134	32	351	11	4-24	31.90
P. W. Jarvis	159	43	410	12	4-24	34.16
N. A. Foster	86	23	226	6	2-23	37.66
P. A. J. DeFreitas	150.1	40	383	8	2-27	47.87
J. E. Emburey	239.2	73	505	7	1-10	72.14
E. E. Hemmings	164.4	43	409	5	3-53	81.80

Also bowled: C. W. J. Athey 4–0–25–0; N. H. Fairbrother 2–0–9–0; M. W. Gatting 29.2–6–78–3; M. D. Moxon 4–0–8–0.

FIELDING

16 – B. N. French; 7 – M. D. Moxon; 6 – C. W. J. Athey; 5 – J. E. Emburey; 4 – D. J. Capel, C. J. Richards; 3 – N. H. Fairbrother, N. A. Foster, N. V. Radford; 2 – P. A. J. DeFreitas, R. T. Robinson; 1 – B. C. Broad, G. R. Dilley, M. W. Gatting.

WELLINGTON v ENGLAND XI

At Wellington, January 18, 19, 20. Drawn. Toss: Wellington. Although their opening match was rendered meaningless when rain washed out the second day, England were not entirely frustrated. There was encouragement, on the first day, from the lively seam bowling of Dilley and Foster; then, after an obliging declaration by Wellington permitted the tourists a day's batting practice, three of the leading players impressed. Broad and Moxon, surviving an early alarm or two, put on 171 for the first wicket, and the former completed a fluent century before retiring with a slight groin strain. Gatting batted less than two hours and struck thirteen fours in his 82. A one-day match was hastily arranged for the blank day following the first-class fixture, and England again performed with professional competence to win by eight wickets. However, an Achilles' tendon injury to DeFreitas, after he had bowled seven overs, provided some cause for concern.

Close of play: First day, Wellington 188-6 (G. P. Burnett 87*, G. N. Cederwall 8*); Second day, No play.

Wellington

B. A. Edgar c Emburey b Dilley	10
G. P. Burnett not out	87
G. R. Larsen c French b Foster	11
T. D. Ritchie c Radford b Foster	0
A. J. Rohrs b Radford	4
*†E. B. McSweeney c Foster b Emburey	10
I. W. Ormiston c Gatting b Capel	47
G. N. Cederwall not out	8
B 3, l-b 2, n-b 6	11
	—
1/16 2/56 3/60 4/65 5/101 6/172 (6 wkts dec.)	188

S. J. Maguiness, B. R. Williams and J. P. Millmow did not bat.

Bowling: Dilley 11–2–25–1; Foster 16–7–23–2; Capel 19–2–55–1; Radford 22–6–44–1; Emburey 16–5–35–1; Moxon 1–0–1–0.

England XI

B. C. Broad retired hurt	100
M. D. Moxon c Cederwall b Williams	62
C. W. J. Athey c and b Williams	14
*M. W. Gatting b Millmow	82
N. H. Fairbrother not out	22
D. J. Capel not out	19
L-b 5, w 1, n-b 5	11
	—
1/171 2/191 3/281 (3 wkts)	310

J. E. Emburey, †B. N. French, N. A. Foster, N. V. Radford and G. R. Dilley did not bat.

B. C. Broad retired hurt at 171.

Bowling: Millmow 16–3–41–1; Cederwall 16–2–65–0; Maguiness 14–4–38–0; Larsen 8–2–37–0; Ormiston 20–1–74–0; Williams 21–8–41–2; Rohrs 2–0–9–0.

Umpires: F. R. Goodall and S. J. Woodward.

†At Wellington, January 21. England XI won by eight wickets. Toss: Wellington. Wellington 202 (49.5 overs) (G. P. Burnett 63, G. R. Larsen 31, T. D. Ritchie 32; D. J. Capel four for 47); England XI 203 for two (45.5 overs) (M. D. Moxon 59, R. T. Robinson 45, C. W. J. Athey 50 not out, J. E. Emburey 41 not out).

NORTHERN DISTRICTS v ENGLAND XI

At Hamilton, January 23, 24, 25. England XI won by seven wickets. Toss: England XI. Responding to a generous declaration on an excellent batting pitch, England were carried to victory, with 15.3 overs in hand, by a remarkable innings from Robinson. Normally thought of as an introspective accumulator, Robinson shed all inhibitions and struck ten sixes and thirteen fours in scoring 166 from 158 balls. Such was his dominant mood that Athey, his opening partner, contributed only 60 to a stand of 208. England, having been set 294 in a minimum 77 overs, maintained the cavalier spirit to the end, Foster finishing the game with a six. Only thirteen wickets fell during the three days, yet there was again a penetrative new-ball spell from Dilley on the opening morning. Cooper, with a forthright century, then set the pattern of batting control for the remainder of the game. A second successive century opening stand by Broad and Moxon for England was followed by another half-century for Gatting. Hick made amends for his first-innings failure with an innings of ever-accelerating momentum which included seven sixes. Little did anyone imagine that he would be upstaged, as a big hitter, by Robinson.

Close of play: First day, England XI 53-0 (B. C. Broad 32*, M. D. Moxon 18*); Second day, Northern Districts 162-2 (D. J. White 55*, G. A. Hick 82*).

Northern Districts

G. E. Bradburn c Athey b Dilley	0	– lbw b Capel	11
L. M. Crocker c Athey b Dilley	11	– c Moxon b Foster	7
D. J. White c Athey b Hemmings	64	– lbw b Foster	80
G. A. Hick c Foster b Capel	19	– c Capel b Hemmings	146
B. G. Cooper not out	116		
*C. M. Kuggeleijn not out	27		
†B. A. Young (did not bat)		– (5) not out	3
B 1, l-b 1, n-b 3	5	B 4, l-b 1, n-b 2	7
1/0 2/23 3/60 4/164	(4 wkts dec.) 242	1/16 2/24 3/212 4/254	(4 wkts dec.) 254

S. A. Thomson, M. R. McKinnon, K. Treiber and B. J. Barrett did not bat.

Bowling: *First Innings*—Dilley 16–2–49–2; Foster 19–2–73–0; Jarvis 11–1–51–0; Capel 6–2–13–1; Hemmings 17–2–54–1. *Second Innings*—Dilley 11–2–37–0; Foster 17–2–76–2; Capel 8–3–14–1; Hemmings 9.4–1–54–1; Jarvis 6–0–39–0; Athey 4–0–25–0; Moxon 1–0–4–0.

England XI

B. C. Broad run out	75		
M. D. Moxon c White b McKinnon	46		
R. T. Robinson not out	19	– (2) c Cooper b Treiber	166
*M. W. Gatting not out	54		
C. W. J. Athey (did not bat)		– (1) c Crocker b Kuggeleijn	60
D. J. Capel (did not bat)		– (3) b Kuggeleijn	13
†B. N. French (did not bat)		– (4) not out	18
N. A. Foster (did not bat)		– (5) not out	27
B 1, l-b 4, w 2, n-b 2	9	L-b 8, w 1, n-b 6	15
1/107 2/134	(2 wkts dec.) 203	1/208 2/254 3/256	(3 wkts) 299

E. E. Hemmings, P. W. Jarvis and G. R. Dilley did not bat.

Bowling: *First Innings*—Treiber 14–1–54–0; Thomson 9–0–31–0; Barrett 16–3–48–0; McKinnon 22–8–60–1; Bradburn 2–1–5–0. *Second Innings*—Treiber 19–3–83–1; Thomson 6–2–11–0; McKinnon 21–3–77–0; Barrett 6–0–36–0; Bradburn 5–0–55–0; Kuggeleijn 8–2–18–2; Crocker 1–0–5–0; Cooper 0.3–0–6–0.

Umpires: B. L. Aldridge and G. C. Morris.

AUSTRALIA v ENGLAND

Bicentennial Test Match

At Sydney, January 29, 30, 31, February 1, 2. Drawn. This would not have qualified as a memorable Test match under any circumstances; but for it to be dismissed as tedious, because it paled in contrast to other events in Australia's colourful bicentennial celebrations, was unfair. It was destined to be an attritional affair once England had amassed 425 and inflicted the follow-on. Australia's pride was then salvaged by an innings from Boon, rich in discipline and defiance, spanning more than eight hours. For the connoisseur, the cricket was absorbing until midway through the final day, when the draw became inevitable. But it must be said that it was not a match of great distinction or quality play; nor, considering the two sides, was it likely to be. Australia's loudly heralded renaissance was largely based on the evidence of limited-overs competitions and they remained some way short of being a powerful five-day side. England, despite controlling this match for much of its duration, were currently a team of no great flair, and the shortcomings of their bowling were exposed when the game was there to be won.

Recent traditions dictated that the toss would be crucial, but as it transpired, the pitch was not as helpful to spin as had been anticipated. Gatting was right to bat first, having omitted DeFreitas from the England twelve. Australia, who preferred Dodemaide to Hughes, were unfortunate to go unrewarded through the first session, in which three catches were missed and the bat was beaten on numerous occasions. McDermott was especially unlucky. Sleep, the leg-spinner, broke the opening stand, but Robinson then played with refreshing authority for almost two and a half hours. Broad was past 100 by the close; his fourth hundred, on separate grounds, in only six Tests in Australia. Only one other Englishman, J. H. Edrich, had made Test centuries on four Australian grounds.

Broad achieved rightful acclaim for his feat, yet sacrificed it early on the second day by reacting to his dismissal in a childish manner. Bowled, off his body, by Waugh, he flattened the leg stump with a violently swung bat. It was a petulant gesture quite without logic, for he had been fortunate to survive several torrid periods on the opening day and, in 434 minutes at the crease, had never played with complete conviction. Mr Lush, the tour manager, instantly applied the maximum available fine, £500, and Broad was warned that any future transgression would result in sterner punishment.

This incident detracted from another good day for England, who progressed to their formidable total through useful contributions right down the order. Six wickets fell to the Australian spinners, which was more than England's pair of slow bowlers achieved in the subsequent three days. Australia lost Boon, Marsh and Border early on the third day, Capel taking two wickets with indifferent balls, and they were reduced to a defensive operation from then on. The pre-lunch session on the fourth day was the tensest of the game as Australia crept to within 12 runs of avoiding the follow-on before a marvellously acrobatic catch by Foster at mid-on denied them. With a little more than five sessions left, England should have expected to win. The pitch, however, was becoming slower and less cooperative by the hour. Australia seemed suddenly to remember they were playing Test and not one-day cricket, and, to frustrate England further, the weather again deteriorated.

Almost two hours had been lost to bad light on the third evening; another 90 minutes were sacrificed on the fourth when Gatting, unintelligently, recalled Dilley in failing light. With Boon and Marsh resuming in the same immovable mood, England's chance quickly disappeared on the final day. Boon, unrecognisable from the loose, diffident player who had failed so often against England a year earlier, hit his highest Test score, his sixth hundred for Australia, and remained unbeaten to the end, having faced 431 balls and hit fourteen fours. England ended disappointed and, with both their strike bowlers, Foster and Dilley, off the field injured, in some disarray. The match was watched by an aggregate crowd of 103,831, well below official forecasts.

Man of the Match: D. C. Boon.

Close of play: First day, England 221-2 (B. C. Broad 116*, M. W. Gatting 3*); Second day, Australia 14-0 (D. C. Boon 12*, G. R. Marsh 1*); Third day, Australia 164-7 (P. R. Sleep 20*, P. L. Taylor 7*); Fourth day, Australia 101-0 (G. R. Marsh 41*, D. C. Boon 54*).

England

B. C. Broad b Waugh	139
M. D. Moxon b Sleep	40
R. T. Robinson c Veletta b Dodemaide	43
*M. W. Gatting c Dyer b Waugh	13
C. W. J. Athey c and b Taylor	37
D. J. Capel c Sleep b Taylor	21
J. E. Emburey st Dyer b Sleep	23
†B. N. French st Dyer b Taylor	47
N. A. Foster c Border b Taylor	19
E. E. Hemmings not out	8
G. R. Dilley b Waugh	13
B 4, l-b 9, w 1, n-b 8	22
1/93 (2) 2/192 (3) 3/245 (4) 4/262 (1) 5/313 (5) 6/314 (6) 7/346 (7) 8/387 (9) 9/410 (8) 10/425 (11)	425

Bowling: McDermott 35–8–65–0; Dodemaide 36–10–98–1; Taylor 34–10–84–4; Waugh 22.5–5–51–3; Sleep 45–8–114–2.

Australia

D. C. Boon c French b Foster	12	(2) not out 184
G. R. Marsh c French b Capel	5	(1) c Athey b Emburey 56
D. M. Jones c Emburey b Hemmings	56	c Moxon b Capel 24
*A. R. Border c Broad b Capel	2	not out 48
M. R. J. Veletta c Emburey b Hemmings	22	
S. R. Waugh c French b Dilley	27	
P. R. Sleep c Athey b Foster	41	
†G. C. Dyer lbw b Dilley	0	
P. L. Taylor c French b Hemmings	20	
A. I. C. Dodemaide not out	12	
C. J. McDermott c Foster b Dilley	1	
L-b 10, w 1, n-b 5	16	B 3, l-b 7, n-b 6 16
1/18 (1) 2/25 (2) 3/34 (4) 4/82 (5) 5/116 (3) 6/147 (6) 7/153 (8) 8/183 (9) 9/209 (7) 10/214 (11)	214	1/162 (1) 2/218 (3) (2 wkts) 328

Bowling: *First Innings*—Dilley 19.1–4–54–3; Foster 19–6–27–2; Emburey 30–10–57–0; Capel 6–3–13–2; Hemmings 22–3–53–3. *Second Innings*—Foster 15–6–27–0; Capel 17–4–38–1; Dilley 13–1–48–0; Hemmings 52–15–107–0; Emburey 38–5–98–1.

Umpires: A. R. Crafter and P. J. McConnell.

†AUSTRALIA v ENGLAND

Bicentennial One-day International

At Melbourne, February 4. Australia won by 22 runs. Toss: Australia. Apart from the fifteen-over period at the start of England's innings, when Broad and Robinson were in confident concert, Australia's ninth consecutive victory in one-day internationals always seemed likely. England had made no secret of their view that this game was a chore rather than an occasion, and their cricket reflected the mood. They were, in fact, losers in every sense, because their failure to bowl more than 48 of the scheduled 50 overs in three and a half hours cost them a fine which accounted for all their appearance money. The slow over-rate was partly due to their conceding eighteen no-balls and wides, of which Radford was responsible for ten. Australia batted with conviction, whereas England, Jarvis apart, bowled poorly. England's batting was no better, a sequence of careless shots ruining the solid start, and although Gatting, defying a fever to play, briefly ignited hopes, Australia always had too much in hand.

Man of the Match: G. R. Marsh. *Attendance:* 54,159.

Australia

D. C. Boon c and b Capel 33
G. R. Marsh run out 87
D. M. Jones c sub (M. D. Moxon) b Emburey . 30
M. R. J. Veletta c Capel b Emburey . . . 13
S. R. Waugh run out 27
*A. R. Border c Gatting b DeFreitas . . 19
A. I. C. Dodemaide not out 7
P. L. Taylor not out 1
L-b 6, w 5, n-b 7 18

1/70 (1) 2/133 (3) 3/169 (4) 4/184 (2) 5/222 (5) 6/233 (6) (6 wkts, 48 overs) 235

†G. C. Dyer, S. P. Davis and M. R. Whitney did not bat.

Bowling: DeFreitas 10–1–43–1; Radford 10–0–61–0; Capel 8–1–30–1; Jarvis 10–0–42–0; Emburey 10–0–53–2.

England

B. C. Broad c Dyer b Waugh 25
R. T. Robinson c Dodemaide b Whitney 35
P. A. J. DeFreitas run out 21
C. W. J. Athey c Border b Davis 4
N. H. Fairbrother st Dyer b Taylor . . . 22
*M. W. Gatting c Border b Whitney . . 37
D. J. Capel c Taylor b Davis 18
J. E. Emburey b Dodemaide 26
†C. J. Richards not out 14
N. V. Radford not out 0
L-b 9, w 1, n-b 1 11

1/58 (2) 2/65 (1) 3/82 (4) 4/96 (3) 5/123 (5) 6/172 (7) 7/175 (6) 8/213 (8) (8 wkts, 48 overs) 213

P. W. Jarvis did not bat.

Bowling: Whitney 10–1–37–2; Dodemaide 10–1–35–1; Davis 10–0–55–2; Waugh 10–0–42–1; Taylor 8–0–35–1.

Umpires: R. C. Bailhache and A. R. Crafter.

SHELL XI v ENGLAND XI

At New Plymouth, February 7, 8, 9. Shell XI won by five wickets. Toss: Shell XI. England's batting failed abjectly in both innings on a pitch aiding the seamers for two days, and although Dilley and Jarvis performed well, their bowlers were guilty of too much that was short, too much that was wide and, again, too many no-balls, Radford (19) and DeFreitas (17) being the chief culprits. The undisciplined cricket on show was a cause of concern. Robinson batted impeccably in the first innings on a damp surface, and although almost half the opening day was lost to rain, Emburey was able to declare overnight. The second day, sunny and warm, saw one of the world's most beautiful grounds in its full glory and England, having dismissed the invitation team cheaply, seemed bound for a victory. Instead, they contrived to lose eight wickets in two and a half hours, and not even a ninth-wicket stand of 67 between Emburey and Jarvis could put the game out of the Shell team's reach on an easier third-day pitch. Jones played well for his 72 as the Shell XI won with eleven balls to spare, although he was twice reprieved. Emburey recalled him, owing to doubt whether a catch had carried to Richards, when he was given out for 1, and Fairbrother dropped him on 15.

Close of play: First day, England XI 243-6 (J. E. Emburey 32*, C. J. Richards 20*); Second day, England XI 104-8 (J. E. Emburey 8*, P. W. Jarvis 1*).

England XI

First innings		Second innings	
B. C. Broad c Greatbatch b Watson	3	c Horne b Barrett	16
M. D. Moxon c Greatbatch b Millmow	4	c McSweeney b Kuggeleijn	5
R. T. Robinson c sub b Brown	74	(6) lbw b Kuggeleijn	4
C. W. J. Athey c McSweeney b Barrett	17	c Jones b Millmow	24
N. H. Fairbrother c McSweeney b Kuggeleijn	46	(3) b Barrett	15
P. A. J. DeFreitas lbw b Barrett	41	(8) c McSweeney b Millmow	0
*J. E. Emburey not out	32	(9) b Millmow b Brown	32
†C. J. Richards not out	20	(7) c McSweeney b Millmow	3
N. V. Radford (did not bat)		(5) b Kuggeleijn	23
P. W. Jarvis (did not bat)		not out	36
G. R. Dilley (did not bat)		not out	0
L-b 2, n-b 4	6	L-b 2, n-b 5	7
1/3 2/7 3/44 4/112 5/181 6/201 (6 wkts dec.)	243	1/6 2/33 3/38 4/79 5/83 6/91 7/91 8/97 9/164 (9 wkts dec.)	165

Bowling: *First Innings*—Millmow 14–3–48–1; Watson 7–4–15–1; Barrett 11–0–68–2; Kuggeleijn 10–1–55–1; Brown 17–2–55–1. *Second Innings*—Millmow 15–2–49–3; Kuggeleijn 19–5–47–3; Barrett 12–2–66–2; Brown 2–1–1–1.

Shell XI

First innings		Second innings	
P. A. Horne c Richards b DeFreitas	0	c and b DeFreitas	25
*R. H. Vance lbw b Radford	12	lbw b Radford	34
A. H. Jones b DeFreitas	12	c and b Emburey	72
M. J. Greatbatch b Dilley	12	run out	28
C. M. Kuggeleijn b Jarvis	21	c Richards b Jarvis	46
T. E. Blain c Emburey b Dilley	5	not out	44
†E. B. McSweeney c Robinson b Emburey	38	not out	5
V. R. Brown c Dilley b Jarvis	4		
J. P. Millmow c Richards b Jarvis	5		
B. J. Barrett lbw b Jarvis	0		
W. Watson not out	3		
L-b 6, n-b 21	27	B 1, l-b 4, w 1, n-b 11	17
1/0 2/21 3/38 4/56 5/64 6/98 7/107 8/123 9/123	139	1/59 2/66 3/112 4/206 5/260 (5 wkts)	271

Bowling: *First Innings*—DeFreitas 9–2–27–2; Radford 12–2–51–1; Jarvis 13–4–24–4; Dilley 9–2–21–2; Emburey 3.3–1–10–1. *Second Innings*—Dilley 17.1–2–62–0; DeFreitas 14–1–50–1; Emburey 18–4–69–1; Jarvis 12–3–36–1; Radford 15–3–49–1.

Umpires: G. I. J. Cowan and R. L. McHarg.

NEW ZEALAND v ENGLAND

First Test Match

At Christchurch, February 12, 13, 14, 16, 17. Drawn. This match began amid excitement and expectation. The mood did not last. That it ended in stalemate was largely the fault of the weather, which accounted for five hours of playing time. That it ended in local disappointment was due to an injury which foiled Hadlee's attempt, on his home-town ground, to take the one wicket he needed to overtake I. T. Botham and set a new world Test record. Hadlee strained a calf muscle on the first afternoon, having bowled eighteen profitless overs, and took no further part in the game, or the series, a grievous blow to New Zealand. It was the first time in his 74 Tests that Hadlee had broken down and, without him, New Zealand's attack was modest, with the skilful exception of Chatfield.

As had become customary at Lancaster Park, the pitch had too great a say in the course of the game. It began green and moist, the bounce was never consistent, and, for three days at least, there was exaggerated help for the seamers. Both captains felt it was not an ideal Test pitch, and in Gatting's case frustration overcame criticism. Having left themselves all of the final day to dismiss New Zealand a second time, England were mortified to find that a combination of the heavy roller and the rare appearance of the sun had drained the pitch of its spite.

New Zealand won the toss and chose to bowl. Moxon went early, an ominous sign, but thereafter Broad and Robinson played with character and considerable good fortune against the moving ball. They put on 168 in 223 minutes before the erratic Morrison picked up two wickets with long-hops. Broad, however, went on to complete his third century in four Tests, and his sixth in only ten Tests overseas. It was yet another testimony to his appetite for runs and his fine, five-day temperament; it was not, however, a memorable innings, with just eleven fours coming in 5 hours 41 minutes. Emburey held together the lower order and, critically, saw the score past 300, giving New Zealand a very tough order.

At 40 for four on the second evening, New Zealand were desperate. All four wickets fell to Dilley, who kept a disciplined off-stump line and troubled everyone. Jeff Crowe and Bracewell delayed England, and Hadlee, hobbling badly and batting for three hours with a runner, made the highest score before becoming Dilley's sixth victim in his best Test analysis.

England's second innings was messy; they were 55 for two at the close of the third day but could not resume, owing to rain, until four o'clock on the fourth. The mission then was to score another 100 runs in the remainder of the day and this was virtually achieved, although they were all out in the attempt. The final day was mercifully dry (50 minutes were lost to bad light) but New Zealand, intent only on survival, achieved their aim comfortably. Dilley, who took two further wickets, was involved in an unsavoury incident in mid-afternoon, releasing a shouted series of swear-words when an appeal was rejected. He was fined £250 by an apparently divided tour committee and the Test ended with a sense of resentment invading the England dressing-room once again.

Close of play: First day, England 235-4 (C. W. J. Athey 18*, D. J. Capel 10*); Second day, New Zealand 83-4 (J. J. Crowe 15*, J. G. Bracewell 22*); Third day, England 55-2 (M. D. Moxon 27*, M. W. Gatting 3*); Fourth day, England 152.

England

First innings		Second innings	
B. C. Broad c Smith b Snedden	114	c sub (M. J. Greatbatch) b Chatfield	20
M. D. Moxon c Jones b Morrison	1	c Jones b Chatfield	27
R. T. Robinson c Smith b Morrison	70	c Wright b Chatfield	2
*M. W. Gatting c sub (M. J. Greatbatch) b Morrison	8	b Snedden	23
C. W. J. Athey c sub (M. J. Greatbatch) b Morrison	22	c Smith b Snedden	19
D. J. Capel c Bracewell b Chatfield	11	c M. D. Crowe b Chatfield	0
J. E. Emburey c Jones b Morrison	42	run out	19
†B. N. French c Smith b Chatfield	7	c J. J. Crowe b Snedden	3
P. A. J. DeFreitas c Morrison b Chatfield	4	lbw b Snedden	16
P. W. Jarvis c Smith b Chatfield	14	not out	10
G. R. Dilley not out	7	c Jones b Morrison	2
L-b 11, w 1, n-b 7	19	L-b 7, n-b 4	11
1/7 (2) 2/175 (3) 3/187 (4) 4/219 (1) 5/237 (6) 6/241 (5) 7/248 (8) 8/260 (9) 9/285 (10) 10/319 (7)	319	1/32 (1) 2/38 (3) 3/55 (2) 4/95 (5) 5/96 (6) 6/99 (4) 7/118 (8) 8/125 (7) 9/147 (9) 10/152 (11)	152

Bowling: *First Innings*—Hadlee 18–3–50–0; Morrison 21.1–3–69–5; Chatfield 42–13–87–4; Snedden 33–9–86–1; Bracewell 6–1–16–0. *Second Innings*—Morrison 21.1–4–64–1; Chatfield 30–13–36–4; Snedden 23–8–45–4.

New Zealand

First innings		Second innings	
J. G. Wright c Moxon b Dilley	10	lbw b Dilley	23
T. J. Franklin c Athey b Dilley	10	lbw b Dilley	12
A. H. Jones c French b Dilley	8	not out	54
M. D. Crowe c Moxon b Dilley	5	c French b Jarvis	6
*J. J. Crowe c French b DeFreitas	28	lbw b DeFreitas	0
J. G. Bracewell c French b Dilley	31	not out	20
R. J. Hadlee c French b Dilley	37		
†I. D. S. Smith c Capel b Jarvis	13		
M. C. Snedden lbw b DeFreitas	0		
D. K. Morrison b Jarvis	0		
E. J. Chatfield not out	0		
B 2, l-b 12, n-b 12	26	B 6, l-b 4, n-b 5	15
1/20 (1) 2/25 (2) 3/32 (3) 4/40 (4) 5/96 (6) 6/131 (5) 7/151 (8) 8/155 (9) 9/156 (10) 10/168 (7)	168	1/37 (2) 2/43 (1) 3/61 (4) 4/78 (5)	(4 wkts) 130

Bowling: *First Innings*—DeFreitas 22–6–39–2; Dilley 24.5–9–38–6; Capel 10–2–32–0; Jarvis 21–8–43–2; Emburey 4–3–2–0. *Second Innings*—Dilley 18–5–32–2; DeFreitas 19–6–26–1; Jarvis 17–7–30–1; Emburey 10–4–16–0; Capel 13–5–16–0.

Umpires: B. L. Aldridge and S. J. Woodward.

PRESIDENT'S XI v ENGLAND XI

At Dunedin, February 19, 20, 21. England XI won by eight wickets. Toss: England XI. A match which had been played at a slow pace, in chilly weather and with barely any spectators, came illogically to life in its final session when a declaration by White, the President's XI captain, asked England to score 160 in 33 overs. Whether White had miscalculated, or had simply tired of the direction the game had taken, Gatting was particularly grateful. He chose to open the innings himself and, having been dropped at slip first ball, struck an unbeaten 97 off 98 balls, winning the game with his fourteenth four from the first ball of the final over. It had hitherto been an unrewarding game for the touring team, although Moxon, his Test place under some pressure, scored a painstaking century in almost six hours and Radford bowled well for match figures of seven for 75. On the debit side, the bowling of DeFreitas indicated a temporary loss of confidence, and England's slip fielders put down five chances. For the President's team, Rutherford played attractively and earned a recall to the New Zealand side for the Second Test.

Close of play: First day, England 11-0 (M. D. Moxon 8*, R. T. Robinson 3*); Second day, President's XI 5-1 (D. J. White 1*, T. J. Wilson 2*).

President's XI

K. J. Burns lbw b Radford	28	– lbw b Radford	2
*D. J. White c Richards b Radford	0	– lbw b Jarvis	38
D. N. Patel c Fairbrother b Radford	0	– (4) b Radford	8
K. R. Rutherford c Robinson b DeFreitas	57	– (5) lbw b Capel	41
R. T. Latham b Radford	13	– (6) not out	58
D. J. Walker c Radford b Capel	0	– (7) c Radford b Capel	43
E. J. Gray not out	19	– (8) lbw b Capel	2
†B. A. Young c Moxon b Gatting	48	– (9) not out	3
T. J. Wilson (did not bat)		– (3) lbw b Radford	5
L-b 5, n-b 11	16	B 2, l-b 3, w 1, n-b 8	14
1/0 2/2 3/81 4/104 5/109 6/109 7/181 (7 wkts dec.)	181	1/2 2/13 3/39 4/102 5/119 6/197 7/205 (7 wkts dec.)	214

J. P. Millmow and R. P. de Groen did not bat.

Bowling: *First Innings*—DeFreitas 22–3–68–1; Radford 19–9–24–4; Jarvis 12–4–25–0; Hemmings 13–5–23–0; Capel 12–3–19–1; Gatting 6.2–1–17–1. *Second Innings*—Radford 16–4–51–3; Capel 19–6–50–3; DeFreitas 14–1–63–0; Hemmings 6–2–11–0; Jarvis 7–0–34–1.

England XI

M. D. Moxon not out	117		
R. T. Robinson c Young b de Groen	19	– lbw b Latham	38
*M. W. Gatting b Wilson	12	– (1) not out	97
N. H. Fairbrother b Latham	26	– not out	16
C. W. J. Athey c Walker b Millmow	3	– (3) c Wilson b Latham	4
D. J. Capel c sub b Latham	19		
†C. J. Richards b Latham	7		
P. A. J. DeFreitas c Walker b Wilson	3		
P. W. Jarvis not out	15		
B 4, l-b 7, w 1, n-b 3	15	B 1, l-b 6, n-b 1	8
1/42 2/74 3/78 4/131 5/148 6/200 7/203 (7 wkts dec.)	236	1/107 2/127 (2 wkts)	163

N. V. Radford and E. E. Hemmings did not bat.

In the first innings N. H. Fairbrother, when 0, retired at 74 and resumed at 148.

Bowling: *First Innings*—Millmow 19–3–49–1; de Groen 22–8–36–1; Wilson 23–6–67–2; Latham 17–3–43–3; Gray 8–0–30–0. *Second Innings*—Millmow 4–0–24–0; de Groen 8–0–46–0; Wilson 12.1–0–61–0; Latham 8–2–25–2.

Umpires: R. S. Dunne and J. A. Holland.

NEW ZEALAND v ENGLAND

Second Test Match

At Auckland, February 25, 26, 27, 28, 29. Drawn. One of the most soulless Test matches of recent history came to life only briefly, the final session of the penultimate day hinting mischievously at the chance of an England victory. Greatbatch, a stocky, combative left-hander who was making his début for New Zealand, scorned such a prospect by batting throughout the last day for an admirable, unbeaten century. A match marked by three individual innings of intense stamina, by poor crowds, contentious umpiring and a bland pitch, ended with the New Zealand captain, Jeff Crowe, losing his job after a run of low scores. Wright was promoted for the final Test at Wellington.

England made two changes from the side that played in the first Test, Athey and DeFreitas giving way to Fairbrother and Radford. With Jones and, crucially, Hadlee unfit, New Zealand brought in Greatbatch and Rutherford, two young batsmen. Their decision to play only four specialist bowlers revealed premeditated negative thinking, but as it transpired, neither side's attack was equipped to overcome the somnolent pitch. Dilley, for England, and Chatfield, for New Zealand, bowled tirelessly and to great effect.

At the end of a slow opening day, New Zealand had mustered only 186 for three after being put in by an optimistic Gatting. Wright, having edged the first ball of the match between wicket-keeper and first slip at catchable height, was 101 not out; Dilley's figures were one for 34 from sixteen overs. Much was to alter early the following day. Wright was out in the second over and no-one else threatened a long stay. Dilley took four for 26 in a splendid spell and New Zealand were all out in mid-afternoon.

England navigated to the close for the loss of Broad, who once again showed displeasure at an umpiring decision. On the third day they needed to score quickly against New Zealand's weak attack to maintain hope of victory. But after a promising morning they fell away badly against the persevering Chatfield, who bowled a remarkable spell of 8–7–2–2 with the second new ball. Moxon, overcoming early problems, was caught at slip 1 run short of a well-merited first Test century, having batted for just over five and threequarter hours, and England closed at 302 for eight with the game in no-man's-land. Their eventual lead of 22 was easily seen off by the New Zealand openers, who profited from dropped catches to put on 117. A draw seemed inevitable now, but England suddenly initiated a collapse. Three wickets went for 2 runs, and when Martin Crowe, to a dubious lbw decision, and Rutherford also fell, New Zealand at stumps were only 132 ahead with five wickets in hand.

Next day, Greatbatch suffocated the fleeting excitement with an innings of great application. All three of his partners played significant roles, and the game ended with England fielding three substitutes for footsore bowlers while Fairbrother and Moxon completed the formalities. Fewer than 25,000 people watched the match, an indication of the fading interest in the tour.

Close of play: First day, New Zealand, 186-3 (J. G. Wright 101*, M. J. Greatbatch 5*); Second day, England 97-1 (M. D. Moxon 42*, R. T. Robinson 37*); Third day, England 302-8 (J. E. Emburey 40*, N. V. Radford 5*); Fourth day, New Zealand 154-5 (M. J. Greatbatch 6*, M. C. Snedden 0*).

New Zealand

J. G. Wright c French b Dilley	103	– (2) c French b Radford	49
T. J. Franklin b Jarvis	27	– (1) b Dilley	62
*J. J. Crowe c Capel b Dilley	11	– lbw b Dilley	1
M. D. Crowe c Capel b Emburey	36	– lbw b Jarvis	26
M. J. Greatbatch c French b Dilley	11	– not out	107
K. R. Rutherford b Capel	29	– b Emburey	2
J. G. Bracewell c Moxon b Dilley	9	– (8) lbw b Gatting	38
†I. D. S. Smith c French b Jarvis	23	– (9) not out	23
M. C. Snedden c Moxon b Dilley	14	– (7) c French b Capel	20
D. K. Morrison not out	14		
E. J. Chatfield c French b Capel	10		
B 1, l-b 2, w 2, n-b 9	14	B 8, l-b 8, n-b 6	22
1/77 (2) 2/98 (3) 3/169 (4) 4/191 (1) 5/207 (5) 6/219 (7) 7/254 (6) 8/262 (8) 9/279 (9) 10/301 (11)	301	1/117 (1) 2/119 (2) 3/119 (3) 4/150 (4) 5/153 (6) 6/232 (7) 7/296 (8)	(7 wkts) 350

Bowling: *First Innings*—Dilley 28–9–60–5; Jarvis 33–9–74–2; Radford 30–4–79–0; Capel 26.2–4–57–2; Emburey 17–7–28–1. *Second Innings*—Dilley 23–9–44–2; Jarvis 27–7–54–1; Radford 20–4–53–1; Emburey 57–24–91–1; Capel 21–4–40–1; Gatting 17–4–40–1; Fairbrother 2–0–9–0; Moxon 2–0–3–0.

England

B. C. Broad c M. D. Crowe b Bracewell 9	P. W. Jarvis c Smith b Snedden 10
M. D. Moxon c J. J. Crowe b Chatfield 99	N. V. Radford b Chatfield 8
R. T. Robinson c Morrison b Bracewell 54	G. R. Dilley not out 8
*M. W. Gatting c Smith b Morrison .. 42	B 12, l-b 12, n-b 5 29
N. H. Fairbrother c Smith b Chatfield . 1	—
D. J. Capel c Bracewell b Morrison ... 5	1/27 (1) 2/135 (3) 3/211 (2) 4/220 (4) 323
J. E. Emburey c Smith b Chatfield 45	5/222 (5) 6/234 (6) 7/267 (8)
†B. N. French c Franklin b Bracewell . 13	8/282 (9) 9/308 (10) 10/323 (7)

Bowling: Morrison 32–7–95–2; Chatfield 31.1–15–37–4; Bracewell 39–8–88–3; Snedden 34–14–71–1; Rutherford 5–1–8–0.

Umpires: F. R. Goodall and R. L. McHarg.

NEW ZEALAND v ENGLAND

Third Test Match

At Wellington, March 3, 4, 5, 6, 7. Drawn. When rain washed out the last two days of this match, it was in most eyes a fitting end to a series which had failed to capture the imagination. The draw extended England's sorry sequence to thirteen Tests without a victory, equalling their record. Once New Zealand had won the toss and entrenched themselves on a pitch bare of grass – and almost bare of hope for the bowlers – there was never a chance that they would end the run here. Dilley, England's most effective bowler in this series, broke down on the first day, a knee injury ruling him out for the remainder of the match. If this was not enough of a handicap, England added some self-inflicted wounds by dropping crucial catches. Crowe, missed on 6, went on to score 143 from 333 balls, including fourteen fours; Rutherford, dropped on 1, made an unbeaten 107 from 181 balls; and Bracewell, put down when 5 and 23, added insult to injury with 54. Even England's ground-fielding, one of their consistently strong suits, deserted them.

There were certain extenuating circumstances. Dilley's injury left them with only two specialist seamers, of whom DeFreitas, surprisingly recalled in place of Jarvis, justified selection by conceding only 110 runs in 50.1 overs, delivered without a single lapse into the over-stepping which had plagued him. And as the Second and Third Tests were played back to back, with only two days between, England found themselves fielding for four consecutive match days.

On the first day, New Zealand's scoring-rate rarely exceeded 2 runs per over. Wright batted 44 overs for his 36 and, although Vance played a perky innings in his first Test, Crowe was in no mood to sacrifice his last chance to make a mark on the series. He gathered pace only as his century approached, shortly before lunch on the second day. When he reached it, with a pull for four against Hemmings, he had made a hundred in each of his last six Test series. His only regret, a rueful one, was in getting out to Gatting, who put himself on as a last resort and struck second ball. The fourth-wicket stand of 155 between Crowe and Greatbatch was a New Zealand record against England. After both were out in the afternoon session, the most fluent batting of the series was launched on a glorious evening in the most attractive of New Zealand's Test grounds. Rutherford, hitherto a frustration to New Zealand's selectors, played a sumptuous array of off-side shots in scoring 66 runs in the session. He closed on 91 and passed his maiden Test century early on the third morning with a typically delicate late-cut. His partnership of 134 with Bracewell for the sixth wicket was another New Zealand record against England.

Wright's declaration left New Zealand just 39 short of their record Test score against England. It also left England with no ambition other than survival. Broad and Moxon, with an opening stand of 129 in almost three hours, ensured that the critical early period was overcome, and in truth New Zealand's flimsy attack was never likely to dismiss any Test line-up twice. Moxon played another innings of admirable resolution and had made 81, in a little short of five hours, by the end of the third day. Sadly, the weather deprived him of the opportunity to complete his first Test century.

Close of play: First day, New Zealand 192-3 (M. D. Crowe 57*, M. J. Greatbatch 34*); Second day, New Zealand 451-5 (K. R. Rutherford 91*, J. G. Bracewell 43*); Third day, England 183-2, (M. D. Moxon 81*, M. W. Gatting 33*); Fourth day, No play.

New Zealand

*J. G. Wright c Fairbrother b Capel	36	J. G. Bracewell c Fairbrother b Capel	54
T. J. Franklin lbw b DeFreitas	14	†I. D. S. Smith not out	33
R. H. Vance run out	47	L-b 10	10
M. D. Crowe lbw b Gatting	143		
M. J. Greatbatch c DeFreitas b Emburey	68	1/33 (2) 2/79 (1) 3/132 (3) (6 wkts dec.)	512
K. R. Rutherford not out	107	4/287 (5) 5/336 (4) 6/470 (7)	

D. K. Morrison, S. L. Boock and E. J. Chatfield did not bat.

Bowling: Dilley 11–1–36–0; DeFreitas 50.1–21–110–1; Capel 39–7–129–2; Emburey 45.5–10–99–1; Hemmings 45–15–107–0; Gatting 6–1–21–1.

England

B. C. Broad b Boock	61
M. D. Moxon not out	81
R. T. Robinson c Smith b Chatfield	0
*M. W. Gatting not out	33
L-b 6, n-b 2	8
1/129 (1) 2/132 (3) (2 wkts)	183

N. H. Fairbrother, D. J. Capel, J. E. Emburey, †B. N. French, P. A. J. DeFreitas, E. E. Hemmings and G. R. Dilley did not bat.

Bowling: Morrison 6–0–41–0; Chatfield 23–10–38–1; Bracewell 23–9–44–0; Boock 26–9–53–1; Rutherford 1–0–1–0.

Umpires: B. L. Aldridge and S. J. Woodward.

†NEW ZEALAND v ENGLAND

First One-day International

At Dunedin, March 9. England won by five wickets. Toss: New Zealand. Although it took them until the final over to complete their victory, England always looked likely winners after restricting New Zealand to 204 by taking their last five wickets for 16 runs. Emburey, having taken only three wickets during the Test series, now captured four, but New Zealand badly lost their way after Wright had given them a splendid start with a fluent 70 from 91 balls. Needing to score at a shade better than 4 runs an over, England began well enough. But crisis loomed when Broad, having looked capable of a match-winning innings, was thrown out by Crowe to leave them 68 for three in the 21st over. Gatting scored at a run a ball to restore command, and 78 in nineteen overs from Fairbrother and Capel made victory all but certain. Capel's fine 48 ended with England 13 short and two overs left, but Fairbrother won the match with a flurry of fours. Chatfield's remarkably economical bowling was to no avail.

Man of the Match: J. G. Wright.

New Zealand

R. B. Reid c Broad b DeFreitas	8	W. Watson not out	0
*J. G. Wright c Moxon b Radford	70	E. J. Chatfield st French b Emburey	0
M. D. Crowe b Jarvis	18		
M. J. Greatbatch c Capel b Emburey	28	L-b 13, w 5, n-b 1	19
K. R. Rutherford c French b Capel	13		
C. M. Kuggeleijn c Gatting b DeFreitas	34	1/24 (1) 2/50 (3) 3/127 (4) (49.4 overs)	204
J. G. Bracewell run out	7	4/140 (2) 5/157 (5) 6/188 (7)	
†I. D. S. Smith b Emburey	0	7/190 (8) 8/204 (6) 9/204 (9)	
M. C. Snedden b Emburey	7	10/204 (11)	

Bowling: DeFreitas 10–1–26–2; Radford 10–0–47–1; Capel 10–1–45–1; Jarvis 10–2–34–1; Emburey 9.4–0–39–4.

England

B. C. Broad run out	33	J. E. Emburey not out	2
M. D. Moxon c Smith b Chatfield	6		
R. T. Robinson lbw b Snedden	17	L-b 6, w 2, n-b 1	9
*M. W. Gatting c Kuggeleijn b Rutherford	42	1/28 (2) 2/53 (3) (5 wkts, 49.2 overs)	207
N. H. Fairbrother not out	50	3/68 (1) 4/114 (4)	
D. J. Capel c Smith b Chatfield	48	5/192 (6)	

P. A. J. DeFreitas, †B. N. French, P. W. Jarvis and N. V. Radford did not bat.

Bowling: Watson 10–2–46–0; Chatfield 10–2–15–2; Kuggeleijn 7–0–31–0; Snedden 10–1–46–1; Bracewell 7.2–0–42–0; Rutherford 5–0–21–1.

Umpires: R. L. McHarg and G. C. Morris.

†NEW ZEALAND v ENGLAND

Second One-day International

At Christchurch, March 12. England won by six wickets. Toss: England. An undistinguished match was won with ease by England, who took a 2-0 lead in the four-match series. Overnight rain delayed the start, reducing the overs to 45 per side, and Gatting chose to field first. Wright again batted combatively with little top-order support, and at 86 for five a humble total looked likely. Kuggeleijn and Bracewell put on 63 in fourteen overs to give the final score substance, but New Zealand wasted any chance they had by dropping both Broad and Moxon in single figures. Broad, in all, was missed three times in an eccentric innings, and there was some appalling cricket from both sides before England won with thirteen balls to spare.

Man of the Match: B. C. Broad.

New Zealand

R. B. Reid c Broad b Capel	8	M. C. Snedden not out	1
*J. G. Wright c DeFreitas b Emburey	43	W. Watson not out	2
M. D. Crowe c French b DeFreitas	2	L-b 5, w 3	8
M. J. Greatbatch run out	15		
K. R. Rutherford run out	5	1/24 (1) 2/26 (3) (8 wkts, 45 overs)	186
C. M. Kuggeleijn b Emburey	40	3/53 (4) 4/68 (5)	
J. G. Bracewell run out	43	5/86 (2) 6/149 (6)	
†I. D. S. Smith c Fairbrother b Emburey	19	7/183 (7) 8/183 (8)	

E. J. Chatfield did not bat.

Bowling: DeFreitas 9–0–53–1; Capel 9–3–27–1; Jarvis 9–0–33–0; Radford 9–0–30–0; Emburey 9–1–38–3.

England

B. C. Broad c Rutherford b Snedden	56	D. J. Capel not out	6
M. D. Moxon c Kuggeleijn b Watson	17	L-b 4, w 3	7
R. T. Robinson c Chatfield b Rutherford	44		
*M. W. Gatting b Watson	33	1/37 (2) 2/112 (1) (4 wkts, 42.5 overs)	188
N. H. Fairbrother not out	25	3/151 (3) 4/167 (4)	

J. E. Emburey, P. A. J. DeFreitas, †B. N. French, P. W. Jarvis and N. V. Radford did not bat.

Bowling: Watson 9–1–31–2; Chatfield 7–0–32–0; Bracewell 5–0–28–0; Snedden 9–0–33–1; Kuggeleijn 6–0–31–0; Rutherford 6.5–0–29–1.

Umpires: B. L. Aldridge and G. C. Morris.

†NEW ZEALAND v ENGLAND

Third One-day International

At Napier, March 16. New Zealand won by seven wickets. Toss: New Zealand. Complacency and carelessness may have had much to do with this extraordinary about-turn. After twice outplaying New Zealand, once embarrassingly so, England simply did not make sufficient runs on a fine batting pitch. They then let themselves down with fielding of a deplorable standard. Broad, playing more responsibly than of late, dominated England's innings, his 106 coming from 139 balls, but from 137 for three, with 23 overs left, the innings fell away alarmingly. When New Zealand batted, Wright increased his tally for the series to 214 in three games and was mobbed, somewhat roughly, by elements of the 12,000 crowd when he became the first New Zealander for four years to hit a limited-overs century. Greatbatch and Rutherford finished the job, putting on 51 in nine carefree overs.

Man of the Match: J. G. Wright.

England

B. C. Broad b Snedden	106
C. W. J. Athey run out	0
R. T. Robinson c Smith b Snedden	36
P. A. J. DeFreitas c Kuggeleijn b Rutherford	23
*M. W. Gatting b Rutherford	6
N. H. Fairbrother c and b Kuggeleijn	1
D. J. Capel c Morrison b Kuggeleijn	14
J. E. Emburey c and b Snedden	15
P. W. Jarvis not out	5
†B. N. French b Chatfield	0
N. V. Radford c Rutherford b Snedden	0
L-b 10, w 2, n-b 1	13
1/1 (2) 2/80 (3) 3/114 (4) 4/137 (5) 5/142 (6) 6/186 (7) 7/205 (1) 8/216 (8) 9/218 (10) 10/219 (11) (47.3 overs)	219

Bowling: Morrison 7–0–32–0; Watson 5–0–24–0; Chatfield 9–0–40–1; Snedden 8.3–0–34–4; Rutherford 10–0–39–2; Kuggeleijn 8–0–40–2.

New Zealand

*J. G. Wright c Robinson b Emburey	101
R. H. Vance b DeFreitas	5
A. H. Jones b Jarvis	16
M. J. Greatbatch not out	64
K. R. Rutherford not out	27
L-b 6, w 4	10
1/24 (2) 2/62 (3) 3/172 (1) (3 wkts, 46.3 overs)	223

C. M. Kuggeleijn, †I. D. S. Smith, M. C. Snedden, D. K. Morrison, W. Watson and E. J. Chatfield did not bat.

Bowling: DeFreitas 10–2–30–1; Capel 9–0–50–0; Jarvis 9.3–1–45–1; Radford 8–0–31–0; Emburey 7–0–47–1; Gatting 3–0–14–0.

Umpires: F. R. Goodall and S. J. Woodward.

†NEW ZEALAND v ENGLAND

Fourth One-day International

At Auckland, March 19. New Zealand won by four wickets. Toss: New Zealand. Fielding their strongest team for the first time since the First Test, New Zealand won an exciting, fluctuating match with four balls to spare. Jones and Hadlee, returning after injury, were the architects of a win which squared the series 2-2, and the difference their full-time presence might have made to the Tests and internationals is incalculable. England, put in to bat, made a poor start, Watson rather than Hadlee causing their distress. Solid contributions from

Gatting, Fairbrother and Capel took them past 200, with 60 coming from the last ten overs. The best crowd of the tour, around 20,000, saw Wright and Jones set up the win with 86 from 24 overs, but tight bowling from Jarvis and Radford changed the picture. When Hadlee joined Jones, 71 were required from twelve overs with five wickets standing. Jones, lucky not to be run out when 49, reprieved in the deep when 71, and dropped again at 82, fell for 90 in the 48th over, leaving Hadlee, roared on by the excited crowd, to ensure victory with a straight six off Emburey.

Man of the Match: A. H. Jones.

England

B. C. Broad b Snedden	12	P. W. Jarvis run out	0
M. D. Moxon b Watson	19	†B. N. French c Greatbatch b Chatfield	2
P. A. J. DeFreitas c Crowe b Watson	6	N. V. Radford not out	0
R. T. Robinson c Kuggeleijn b Rutherford	13	L-b 12, w 5, n-b 1	18
*M. W. Gatting c Wright b Watson	48	1/33 (2) 2/33 (1) 3/41 (3) (50 overs)	208
N. H. Fairbrother b Kuggeleijn	54	4/71 (4) 5/146 (5) 6/179 (6)	
D. J. Capel b Chatfield	25	7/197 (8) 8/197 (9)	
J. E. Emburey b Chatfield	11	9/208 (10) 10/208 (7)	

Bowling: Hadlee 10–0–43–0; Watson 10–0–36–3; Snedden 10–2–30–1; Chatfield 10–2–31–3; Rutherford 5–0–28–1; Kuggeleijn 5–0–28–1.

New Zealand

*J. G. Wright b Radford	47	†I. D. S. Smith not out	1
A. H. Jones c Radford b Jarvis	90		
M. D. Crowe c French b Jarvis	13	B 3, l-b 12, w 5	20
M. J. Greatbatch c Radford b Jarvis	5		
K. R. Rutherford lbw b Jarvis	0	1/86 (1) 2/115 (3) (6 wkts, 49.2 overs)	211
C. M. Kuggeleijn b Capel	2	3/129 (4) 4/129 (5)	
R. J. Hadlee not out	33	5/138 (6) 6/199 (2)	

M. C. Snedden, W. Watson and E. J. Chatfield did not bat.

Bowling: DeFreitas 10–0–45–0; Capel 10–0–42–1; Jarvis 9.2–1–33–4; Radford 10–2–32–1; Emburey 10–0–44–0.

Umpires: R. L. McHarg and S. J. Woodward.

THE WEST INDIANS IN INDIA, 1987-88

By DICKY RUTNAGUR

The interests of cricket were not best served by either the timing of this tour or the cavalier fashion in which the Board of Control for Cricket in India, influenced by financial considerations and driven by internal politics, chopped and changed the itinerary even after the tour had started. The World Cup tournament, which was so vigorously promoted and which had only just ended, left the country with no appetite for any form of international cricket except the overs-limit variety. The Test matches, regrettably, were received as enthusiastically as sandwiches filled with the leftovers of the Christmas turkey. The thrilling First Test, at Delhi, was played before very thin crowds and on no day of the series was any ground completely full.

In such an atmosphere, the first-class games outside the Tests also suffered from lack of support. Member associations of the Indian Board were reluctant to host these fixtures, yet all clamoured to stage one-day internationals. To meet this demand, the Board went to the extent of cancelling, at the eleventh hour, the Second Test match at Nagpur and substituting it with two one-day internationals in addition to the five originally scheduled. Nagpur had initially been allotted this Test match when Kanpur was unable to stage it. Mr Jackie Hendriks, the West Indians' manager, was unhappy at the shortening of the Test series, which he considered to be the main business on the agenda, and he accepted the rearrangement most reluctantly. He was told by Board officials that Nagpur had backed out of staging the Test match, but officials of the local association denied the allegation. Instead of the Test match, Nagpur was given a one-day international and the other went to Calcutta, whence the pressure for the revision of the programme originated.

The granting of a one-day international to Calcutta created further complications and controversy over the status of the one-day international in Ahmedabad, which figured in the original itinerary and the proceeds of which were to go to the Cricketers' Benevolent Fund. The Board declared that the Ahmedabad match would be one of the series – "official", as they called it. However, the West Indians were not agreeable to this, although they were prepared to play the match. A great amount of pressure was brought to bear on their manager, but Mr Hendriks would not yield. In the event, neither the public nor the Indian team was told of the Board's enforced change of stance; the first that Ravi Shastri, the Indian captain, heard about it was from his opposite number, Viv Richards, as they were walking out to toss. West Indies won the Charminar Challenge one-day series 6-1, as well as the match at Ahmedabad, and most of their victories were gained decisively. Yet, crowds flocked to them. The low attendances at the Test matches, however, left the host associations incurring heavy losses.

The 1-1 result of the four-match Test series was not a true index of the strength of the teams. While West Indies were not the side they once were, they were distinctly superior. A more appropriate result would have been 2-1 in their favour, although even then it would not have been a just one. The Indian victory in the final Test was gained on a Madras pitch that made a mockery of Test cricket.

Except for the Third, in which an abysmally slow pitch at Eden Gardens rendered the contest between bat and ball completely uneven, the Test matches were absorbing. The opening Test was enlivened as much by the conditions on the first day as by the inept batting of both sides, who were each dismissed for their lowest totals against each other. The captains attributed the collapses to the problem of making an immediate transition from one-day cricket to Test matches. West Indies had had only one intervening match in which to adjust, while the Indians had played no first-class cricket since before the World Cup. The balance in this match was swayed by a solid, responsible innings from Richards which yielded his only century of the rubber.

All four fast bowlers played by West Indies in this match excelled themselves for accuracy. The Second Test, which seemed to be petering out after the weather had intervened, was brought to life by bowling of fierce pace from Patrick Patterson. But after sustaining an injury, he never bowled again with the same hostility, and it was Courtney Walsh, putting in a tremendous amount of work, who emerged as the outstanding bowler with 26 wickets in the series at under 17 runs each.

Four hundreds and six other scores of 50 or more were made in the dreary Third Test, of which the highlight was a maiden Test century from Hooper. The quality of his batting stamped him as a player of class. The Fourth Test was dominated by the nineteen-year-old leg-spinner, Narendra Hirwani, who on his début took sixteen wickets, but India's comfortable win was owed, to no small extent, to a magnificent century by Kapil Dev.

Playing their first series since the retirement of Sunil Gavaskar, India missed him less than might have been expected. His replacement as opening batsman, Arun Lal, twice passed 50 and averaged 32.42. The mainstay of the Indian batting was Dilip Vengsarkar, the captain, with a three-figure average, and it was ironic that the Test India won was the one he missed through injury. India's bowling, except for flashes of brilliance from Kapil Dev, looked quite ordinary and incapable of bowling out West Indies twice until the sensational advent in the last Test of Hirwani. He was aided, it must be stressed, by a deplorably under-prepared pitch.

WEST INDIAN TOUR RESULTS

Test matches – Played 4: Won 1, Lost 1, Drawn 2.
First-class matches – Played 7: Won 2, Lost 1, Drawn 4. Abandoned 1.
Wins – India, BCCI President's XI.
Loss – India.
Draws – India (2), Indian Under-25 XI, North Zone.
Abandoned – Hyderabad.
One-day internationals – Played 8: Won 7, Lost 1.

TEST MATCH AVERAGES

INDIA – BATTING

	T	*I*	*NO*	*R*	*HI*	*100s*	*Avge*
D. B. Vengsarkar	3	5	2	305	102*	2	101.66
M. Azharuddin	3	5	0	185	60	0	37.00
Arun Lal	4	7	0	227	93	0	32.42
Kapil Dev	4	7	0	221	109	1	31.57
K. Srikkanth	4	7	0	204	71	0	29.14

	T	*I*	*NO*	*R*	*HI*	*100s*	*Avge*
Arshad Ayub	4	7	2	133	57	0	26.60
K. S. More	4	7	1	131	49	0	21.83
Chetan Sharma	3	5	1	73	27	0	18.25
R. J. Shastri	4	7	1	105	47	0	17.50
M. Amarnath	3	5	0	56	43	0	11.20
Maninder Singh	3	5	2	3	2*	0	1.00

Played in one Test: N. D. Hirwani 1; R. Lamba 1, 0; S. V. Manjrekar 5, 10*; W. V. Raman 9, 83; Ajay Sharma 30, 23.

* *Signifies not out.*

BOWLING

	O	*M*	*R*	*W*	*BB*	*Avge*
N. D. Hirwani	33.5	6	136	16	8-61	8.50
Chetan Sharma	57.2	4	268	10	5-55	26.80
R. J. Shastri	87.3	24	228	8	4-71	28.50
Kapil Dev	113	35	309	8	3-41	38.62
Arshad Ayub	156	34	400	6	4-72	66.66
Maninder Singh	96.5	19	310	2	1-68	155.00

Also bowled: M. Amarnath 12.5–0–42–0; Arun Lal 1.3–1–1–0; W. V. Raman 1–0–7–1; Ajay Sharma 4–0–9–0; K. Srikkanth 3–0–7–0.

WEST INDIES – BATTING

	T	*I*	*NO*	*R*	*HI*	*100s*	*Avge*
I. V. A. Richards	4	6	1	295	109*	1	59.00
C. L. Hooper	3	4	1	147	100*	1	49.00
C. G. Greenidge	3	6	0	260	141	1	43.33
A. L. Logie	4	7	1	250	101	1	41.66
R. B. Richardson	4	8	2	226	89	0	37.66
D. L. Haynes	4	8	1	201	58	0	28.71
P. J. L. Dujon	4	6	2	97	40*	0	24.25
C. G. Butts	3	3	0	56	38	0	18.66
W. W. Davis	4	5	0	45	30	0	9.00
C. A. Walsh	4	4	0	29	16	0	7.25

Played in four Tests: B. P. Patterson 5*, 21*, 0*, 0*. Played in one Test: W. K. M. Benjamin 19; R. A. Harper 4; P. V. Simmons 8, 14.

* *Signifies not out.*

BOWLING

	O	*M*	*R*	*W*	*BB*	*Avge*
C. A. Walsh	137.1	24	437	26	5-54	16.80
B. P. Patterson	117.1	14	456	17	5-24	26.82
W. W. Davis	112.1	10	390	13	4-76	30.00
I. V. A. Richards	50	11	103	3	1-28	34.33

Also bowled: W. K. M. Benjamin 30–3–93–2; C. G. Butts 114–24–305–2; R. A. Harper 12–3–13–0; C. L. Hooper 38–9–102–2.

WEST INDIAN AVERAGES – FIRST-CLASS MATCHES

BATTING

	M	*I*	*NO*	*R*	*HI*	*100s*	*Avge*
E. A. E. Baptiste	2	2	1	97	75*	0	97.00
I. V. A. Richards	6	8	2	439	138*	2	73.16
W. K. M. Benjamin	3	3	2	63	37*	0	63.00
C. G. Greenidge	5	9	0	529	174	2	58.77
R. B. Richardson	7	12	2	456	147	1	45.60
P. J. L. Dujon	6	9	3	269	123	1	44.83
A. L. Logie	6	10	1	375	101	1	41.66
C. L. Hooper	5	6	1	189	100*	1	37.80
D. L. Haynes	5	9	1	271	70	0	33.87
R. A. Harper	3	4	0	112	82	0	28.00
P. V. Simmons	4	6	0	151	72	0	25.16
D. Williams	2	2	0	43	33	0	21.50
C. G. Butts	6	6	0	121	47	0	20.16
C. A. Walsh	5	5	0	79	50	0	15.80
W. W. Davis	7	8	1	89	30	0	12.71

Played in five matches: B. P. Patterson 5*, 21*, 0*, 0*, 11*.

* *Signifies not out.*

BOWLING

	O	*M*	*R*	*W*	*BB*	*Avge*
E. A. E. Baptiste	60.2	13	172	12	7-70	14.33
C. A. Walsh	147.1	24	472	29	5-54	16.27
I. V. A. Richards	59	16	131	5	1-8	26.20
B. P. Patterson	135.1	21	505	19	5-24	26.57
W. W. Davis	161.1	18	563	18	4-76	31.27
R. A. Harper	47	12	126	4	2-48	31.50
W. K. M. Benjamin	75	14	223	6	2-29	37.16
C. L. Hooper	58	12	175	3	2-42	58.33
C. G. Butts	174.1	27	528	4	2-59	132.00

FIELDING

13 – P. J. L. Dujon (12 ct, 1 st); 10 – R. B. Richardson; 8 – R. A. Harper; 6 – C. L. Hooper; 5 – I. V. A. Richards; 4 – W. W. Davis, C. G. Greenidge, P. V. Simmons; 3 – C. G. Butts, A. L. Logie; 2 – W. K. M. Benjamin, D. Williams; 1 – D. L. Haynes.

RANJI TROPHY CHAMPIONS (HYDERABAD) v WEST INDIANS

At Hyderabad, November 14, 15, 16. Abandoned. A cyclone on the eve of the match made the ground unplayable.

INDIAN UNDER-25 XI v WEST INDIANS

At Chandigarh, November 20, 21, 22. Drawn. The West Indians, who led by 322 runs on the first innings, forfeited their right to enforce the follow-on and took batting practice instead. Their colossal score, coming after Richards had chosen to bat, was based on a third-wicket partnership of 303 between Greenidge, whose 174, scored off 212 balls, included twenty fours and six sixes, and Richards, who struck eighteen fours and two sixes in 138 off 160 balls. The only substantial scores in the Under-25's reply, on a still-impeccable pitch, came from Sanjeev Sharma, an all-rounder, and the opening bowler, Jaspal Singh, who added 135 for the eighth wicket. The feature of the final day's play, when the ball sometimes kept low, was the bowling of Hirwani who, remarkably accurate for a leg-spinner, took all the wickets to fall in the West Indians' second innings.

Close of play: First day, West Indians 428-5 (A. L. Logie 52*, C. G. Butts 10*); Second day, Indian Under-25 XI 228.

West Indians

C. G. Greenidge retired, out	174	– (3) c and b Hirwani	37
P. V. Simmons c and b Kasliwal	8	– (1) b Hirwani	72
R. B. Richardson c Manjrekar b Jaspal	3	– (2) b Hirwani	37
*I. V. A. Richards retired hurt	138		
†P. J. L. Dujon run out	7	– (5) not out	42
A. L. Logie lbw b S. Sharma	52	– (7) c Saldanha b Hirwani	19
R. A. Harper c Pandit b Jaspal	24	– (4) c Pandit b Hirwani	2
C. G. Butts c Jaspal b Hirwani	47	– (6) b Hirwani	15
W. W. Davis b Hirwani	21	– (8) not out	0
C. A. Walsh c Saldanha b Azim Khan	50		
B. P. Patterson not out	11		
B 1, l-b 8, w 2, n-b 4	15	L-b 13	13
1/25 2/28 3/331 4/340 5/394 6/428 7/479 8/494 9/550	550	1/71 2/154 3/155 4/165 5/195 6/215	(6 wkts dec.) 237

Bowling: *First Innings*—Kasliwal 16–1–54–1; Jaspal 21–2–122–2; S. Sharma 21–0–107–1; Azim Khan 25.5–3–132–1; Hirwani 30–3–126–2. *Second Innings*—Kasliwal 7–1–29–0; S. Sharma 5–1–22–0; Hirwani 30–7–100–6; Azim Khan 27–9–73–0; Saldanha 1–1–0–0.

Indian Under-25 XI

C. Saldanha c Simmons b Walsh	6	– b Patterson	4
M. Nayyar c Harper b Patterson	4	– not out	16
K. Bhaskar Pillai c and b Davis	22		
S. V. Manjrekar lbw b Walsh	0	– (3) not out	17
*C. S. Pandit c Logie b Walsh	4		
†S. K. Kulkarni b Davis	12		
Azim Khan c Dujon b Davis	13		
Sanjeev Sharma b Harper	76		
Jaspal Singh c Simmons b Richards	70		
N. D. Hirwani b Harper	0		
P. Kasliwal not out	0		
B 4, l-b 5, w 1, n-b 11	21	B 4	4
1/11 2/13 3/14 4/19 5/37 6/72 7/73 8/208 9/208	228	1/7	(1 wkt) 41

Bowling: *First Innings*—Patterson 13–5–37–1; Davis 13–1–46–3; Walsh 8–0–25–3; Harper 9–2–48–2; Butts 4–0–43–0; Richards 1–0–20–1. *Second Innings*—Patterson 5–2–12–1; Davis 5–3–13–0; Harper 3–1–2–0; Walsh 2–0–10–0.

Umpires: S. K. Ghosh and P. G. Pandit.

INDIA v WEST INDIES

First Test Match

At Delhi, November 25, 26, 28, 29. West Indies won by five wickets. Taken unawares by conditions uncharacteristic of the Feroz Shah Kotla ground – notorious for tall scores and dull draws – both sides were dismissed in the first innings for their lowest totals against each other.

Vengsarkar, in his first Test as captain, won the toss and, despite evidence of moisture in the pitch, elected to bat. He foresaw some help in the fourth innings for the spinners, of whom India had three, including a new cap in Arshad Ayub, an off-spinner. On the opening day, however, seventeen of the eighteen wickets that fell were credited to the fast bowlers. India were bowled out in only 145 minutes for 75, their lowest score in a home Test. The ball swung readily for Davis, who had a big hand in initiating the collapse, and the bounce, too, was much livelier than is usual at this ground. Although the Indian batting did betray dreadful shortcomings, all four West Indies' fast bowlers deserved commendation for keeping a consistent line on or around off stump. This required the batsmen to play at the ball, and resulted in eight of them being caught in the arc between wicket-keeper and gully; the other two were bowled. The catching was of outstanding quality.

Undermined by a splendid opening spell from Kapil Dev, West Indies at one stage looked unlikely to match India's score, for they were 29 for six after ten overs. However, Haynes, who had not scored then, became the mainstay of the innings, and aided by plucky knocks from Davis, Benjamin and Walsh he put West Indies 52 ahead. For the third time in his 66 Tests, Haynes batted through the innings and was last out, rarely appearing uncomfortable in his stay of three and a half hours. He hit eleven fours. Kapil Dev and Chetan Sharma collaborated in the destruction of the innings, which may have ended sooner had India possessed a third seamer.

India made another disastrous start in their second innings and, despite a solid 40 by Arun Lal, were only 30 runs ahead when Shastri was fourth out. The early damage this time was done by Patterson, who claimed eight wickets in the match, and India's plight would have been worse had Vengsarkar, consistently in trouble outside his off stump, not been dropped by Dujon when he was 21 and the score 71 for three. India's recovery after Shastri's dismissal was interrupted when Manjrekar, who had batted soundly for 78 minutes and seen the score to 105, was struck over the left eye by a ball from Benjamin that got up quickly from just short of a length.

However, a flamboyant 44, off only 41 balls, by Kapil Dev turned India's fortunes. His partnership of 73 with Vengsarkar was succeeded by one of 96 for the sixth wicket between Vengsarkar and More, who took care of the second new ball on the third morning. Vengsarkar batted for 405 minutes for his sixteenth Test century, during which he scored his 6,000th run in Test cricket, and when he and More were out in quick succession, the tail wagged productively. West Indies were left to score 276 runs on a pitch which had now stopped helping the pace bowlers, but had become dry enough to offer hope to the spinners. Indeed, Ayub, the newcomer, took four wickets, but Maninder Singh bowled poorly. After an opening stand of 62, West Indies declined to 111 for four, but the issue was settled by a brilliant 109 not out off 102 balls from Richards. With Logie and Dujon proving staunch allies, he batted with great responsibility, and yet not without flair. There were thirteen fours in his 21st Test hundred, his seventh against India.

Close of play: First day, West Indies 118-8 (D. L. Haynes 45*, C. A. Walsh 12*); Second day, India 210-5 (D. B. Vengsarkar 74*, K. S. More 18*); Third day, West Indies 80-2 (R. B. Richardson 15*, W. W. Davis 1*).

India

First innings		Second innings	
K. Srikkanth c Dujon b Patterson	0	– c Harper b Patterson	5
Arun Lal c Greenidge b Davis	20	– c Benjamin b Walsh	40
R. Lamba b Davis	1	– b Patterson	0
*D. B. Vengsarkar c Harper b Davis	10	– c Greenidge b Walsh	102
R. J. Shastri c Richardson b Benjamin	6	– c Harper b Patterson	4
S. V. Manjrekar c Harper b Patterson	5	– retired hurt	10
Kapil Dev c Dujon b Walsh	7	– lbw b Benjamin	44
†K. S. More not out	12	– c Dujon b Walsh	49
Arshad Ayub c Harper b Patterson	7	– lbw b Walsh	17
Chetan Sharma c Richardson b Patterson	0	– b Walsh	24
Maninder Singh b Patterson	0	– not out	2
L-b 1, w 3, n-b 3	7	B 17, l-b 7, w 5, n-b 1	30
1/0 2/7 3/32 4/42 5/42 6/52 7/58 8/75 9/75	75	1/6 2/6 3/66 4/82 5/178 6/274 7/277 8/318 9/327	327

Bowling: *First Innings*—Patterson 8.5–1–24–5; Davis 11–2–20–3; Benjamin 7–0–17–1; Walsh 4–0–13–1. *Second Innings*—Patterson 29–6–100–3; Davis 20–3–60–0; Benjamin 23–3–76–1; Walsh 29.3–9–54–5; Harper 12–3–13–0.

West Indies

C. G. Greenidge lbw b Kapil Dev	0	– lbw b Ayub 33
D. L. Haynes c Lamba b C. Sharma	45	– hit wkt b Ayub 27
R. B. Richardson lbw b Kapil Dev	4	– c Lamba b Kapil Dev 31
*I. V. A. Richards c More b C. Sharma	9	– (5) not out 109
A. L. Logie lbw b C. Sharma	4	– (6) lbw b Ayub 46
†P. J. L. Dujon c Lamba b Kapil Dev	5	– (7) not out 12
R. A. Harper run out	4	
W. W. Davis c and b C. Sharma	6	– (4) c sub (C. S. Pandit) b Ayub 1
W. K. M. Benjamin b Ayub	19	
C. A. Walsh c Lamba b C. Sharma	16	
B. P. Patterson not out	5	
B 3, l-b 1, w 1, n-b 5	10	B 1, l-b 9, n-b 7 17
1/0 2/4 3/13 4/17 5/25 6/29 7/49 8/102 9/122	127	1/62 2/69 3/91 4/111 5/203 (5 wkts) 276

Bowling: *First Innings*—Kapil Dev 18–8–41–3; C. Sharma 13.1–2–55–5; Maninder 7–3–13–0; Ayub 9–4–14–1. *Second Innings*—Kapil Dev 20–8–44–1; C. Sharma 11–1–44–0; Maninder 20–4–75–0; Ayub 25–4–72–4; Shastri 9–2–30–0; Arun Lal 0.3–0–1–0.

Umpires: D. N. Dotiwala and V. K. Ramaswamy.

DULEEP TROPHY CHAMPIONS (NORTH ZONE) v WEST INDIANS

At Pune, December 3, 4, 5. Drawn. The pitch was so good for batting that not even the first innings was completed. North Zone, most of whose Test players were rested, fielded a scratch side. The West Indians, having won the toss, put up a towering score based on Richardson's 147, off 181 balls and including 24 fours and two sixes. There were also sizeable contributions, attractively made, from Greenidge, Haynes, Hooper, Harper and Baptiste. With the touring team batting until lunch on the second day, North Zone had nothing to play for but a draw and they too piled up runs remorselessly. Lamba, a disappointment in the First Test, made an unconvincing hundred, but Amarnath, with 71, convinced the selectors that he remained worthy of a Test place.

Close of play: First day, West Indians 374-5 (R. A. Harper 31*, E. A. E. Baptiste 11*); Second day, North Zone 167-1 (R. Lamba 64*, M. Amarnath 51*).

West Indians

C. G. Greenidge st Vinayak b M. I. Singh	58
D. L. Haynes c and b A. Sharma	70
R. B. Richardson b Prabhakar	147
P. V. Simmons c and b M. I. Singh	2
C. L. Hooper c sub b A. Sharma	41
*R. A. Harper b A. Sharma	82
E. A. E. Baptiste not out	75
†D. Williams c Vinayak b A. Sharma	33
W. K. M. Benjamin not out	7
L-b 5, n-b 16	21
1/108 2/193 3/196 4/313 5/354 6/472 7/524 (7 wkts dec.)	536

W. W. Davis and C. G. Butts did not bat.

Bowling: Prabhakar 18–1–104–1; Ghai 17–1–133–0; Amarnath 9–2–14–0; M. I. Singh 46–7–175–2; A. Sharma 26–4–105–4.

North Zone

S. C. Khanna lbw b Baptiste 25
R. Lamba c Hooper b Harper 101
*M. Amarnath c Simmons b Harper . . . 71
K. Bhaskar Pillai c Harper b Benjamin. 12
Gursharan Singh c Harper b Butts 65
Ajay Sharma c and b Hooper 99
K. P. Amarjeet not out 33
M. Prabhakar not out 17
B 17, l-b 17, n-b 11 45

1/57 2/231 3/231 4/257 5/374 6/437 (6 wkts) 468

†R. Vinayak, R. S. Ghai and M. I. Singh did not bat.

Bowling: Davis 19–3–58–0; Benjamin 24–7–67–1; Baptiste 25–4–75–1; Butts 33–3–98–1; Hooper 20–3–73–1; Harper 23–6–63–2.

Umpires: S. B. Kulkarni and R. V. Ramani.

†INDIA v WEST INDIES

First One-day International

At Nagpur, December 8. West Indies won by 10 runs. A match of fluctuating fortunes was marred by a controversial umpiring decision which brought about the dismissal of Vengsarkar. Umpire Mehra first turned down an appeal for a slip catch by Richards, whereupon the West Indies captain appealed to the square-leg umpire. When he indicated that he was unsighted and could not give a ruling, Richards's tantrum virtually coerced Mr Mehra into reversing his decision. West Indies, winning the toss, were given a good start by Greenidge and Haynes, but the latter's run-out triggered a collapse which reduced West Indies to 128 for seven. They were rescued by an aggressive partnership of 65 in nine overs between Hooper and Benjamin, whose 31 off 33 balls included three sixes. Undermined by Patterson, who took three wickets in each of his spells, India at 31 for five looked out of contention. They were revived by a heroic 87, off 64 balls, by Kapil Dev and his partnership of 113 with Shastri. Another collapse ensued, but a last-wicket stand between the fluent More and a determined Maninder Singh kept the game alive.

Man of the Match: B. P. Patterson.

West Indies

D. L. Haynes run out 20
C. G. Greenidge b Maninder 36
R. B. Richardson c Gaekwad b Maninder . 11
*I. V. A. Richards st More b Maninder 1
A. L. Logie lbw b Shastri 13
C. L. Hooper not out 57
†P. J. L. Dujon c Vengsarkar b Shastri . 4
R. A. Harper st More b Gaekwad 7
W. K. M. Benjamin b Kapil Dev 31
C. A. Walsh not out 3
L-b 12, w 2, n-b 6 20

1/51 2/71 3/73 4/81 5/101 6/107 7/128 8/193 (8 wkts, 50 overs) 203

B. P. Patterson did not bat.

Bowling: Kapil Dev 7–0–13–1; C. Sharma 7–0–49–0; Maninder 8–0–40–3; Ayub 10–0–26–0; Shastri 10–1–24–2; Gaekwad 8–0–39–1.

India

K. Srikkanth c Richards b Patterson . . 5
Arun Lal b Patterson 7
A. D. Gaekwad lbw b Patterson 0
*D. B. Vengsarkar c Richards b Benjamin . 8
C. S. Pandit lbw b Richards 6
R. J. Shastri b Patterson 20
Kapil Dev c Haynes b Patterson 87
†K. S. More c Haynes b Patterson 33
Arshad Ayub b Hooper 4
Chetan Sharma lbw b Walsh 2
Maninder Singh not out 4
B 2, l-b 7, w 3, n-b 5 17

1/13 2/13 3/18 4/31 5/31 6/144 7/145 8/150 9/155 (44.4 overs) 193

Bowling: Patterson 9.4–0–29–6; Walsh 9–0–21–1; Richards 9–1–39–1; Benjamin 10–1–53–1; Hooper 7–0–42–1.

Umpires: R. Mehra and V. Vikramraju.

INDIA v WEST INDIES

Second Test Match

At Bombay, December 11, 12, 13, 15, 16. Drawn. But for the loss through rain of 613 minutes (156 overs) on the first three days, the second being totally blank, West Indies would surely have won. Although they led by only 56 runs on the first innings, they dismissed India in the second for just 173, leaving them needing 118 for victory. However, they had only eleven overs in which to force home their advantage in the series and gave up the attempt after two overs.

West Indies made two changes to the side that won the First Test. Harper had incurred a long-term injury in the previous match and was replaced by the team's other off-spinner, Butts, while to reinforce the batting, which had looked vulnerable at Delhi, they included the uncapped Hooper. That meant leaving out Benjamin and weakening the pace attack. India's batting proved no more reliable, despite the inclusion of Amarnath and Azharuddin, who missed the First Test through indisposition. Winning the toss again, they batted unevenly, and although West Indies did not bowl particularly well, they scored no more than 281. Of the first 85, Srikkanth made 71 in his usual breezy fashion, hitting eleven fours and a six. Vengsarkar batted doggedly for 51 in 140 minutes, but it took the tail to give the total a semblance of respectability. Early in the innings, only Walsh of the three fast bowlers kept a good line, and Butts justified his inclusion by taking the crucial wickets of Vengsarkar and Kapil Dev in mid-innings.

West Indies, beginning their reply with fifteen overs left on the third day, ran into trouble on the fourth. The pitch, dry and brown at the start, was now affording some spin and West Indies were 146 for four when Logie was run out. With the previous ball, Maninder Singh had bowled Richards, who was trying to overpower the bowling without being on terms with his timing. He succumbed to a beautiful delivery which pitched middle and leg and hit his off stump. The faltering innings was sustained by Richardson who, without being quite at ease, made a staunch 89 spread over 229 minutes and 186 balls. India paid dearly for Amarnath's failure to take a difficult chance at long leg which Richardson offered when 20.

West Indies were still behind when their specialist batsmen were dismissed, but the tail was defiant. During a last-wicket stand between Butts and Patterson, Chetan Sharma, using the second new ball, bowled frequent bumpers at Patterson, a lack of tact India were to regret when they began their second innings early on the final day. West Indies retaliated in full measure and the Indians proved vulnerable. Srikkanth, revelling in the short stuff, made 65 from 78 balls, hitting ten fours, but thereafter only Vengsarkar and Ayub achieved double figures. Their partnership, formed at 132 for seven and lasting 64 minutes, saved India from a crisis caused by Patterson, who took four of his five wickets in a spell of eleven overs between lunch and tea.

Close of play: First day, India 99-3 (D. B. Vengsarkar 7*, M. Azharuddin 6*); Second day, No play; Third day, West Indies 49-0 (C. G. Greenidge 11*, D. L. Haynes 36*); Fourth day, West Indies 327-9 (C. G. Butts 17*, B. P. Patterson 12*).

India

First innings		Second innings	
K. Srikkanth b Walsh	71	– b Patterson	65
Arun Lal c Richardson b Walsh	3	– c Greenidge b Patterson	1
M. Amarnath c Butts b Walsh	1	– c Richards b Walsh	8
*D. B. Vengsarkar st Dujon b Butts	51	– not out	40
M. Azharuddin run out	34	– c Davis b Patterson	5
R. J. Shastri c Richards b Davis	0	– c Butts b Davis	5
Kapil Dev c Greenidge b Butts	47	– c Dujon b Patterson	5
†K. S. More c Dujon b Patterson	9	– c Richards b Patterson	0
Arshad Ayub c Richardson b Walsh	8	– b Walsh	18
Chetan Sharma not out	22	– b Walsh	0
Maninder Singh c Richards b Walsh	0	– c Richardson b Walsh	0
B 4, l-b 15, n-b 16	35	B 1, l-b 5, w 8, n-b 12	26
1/60 2/74 3/85 4/157 5/162 6/222 7/241 8/247 9/271	281	1/16 2/58 3/105 4/112 5/126 6/132 7/132 8/173 9/173	173

Bowling: *First Innings*—Patterson 17–3–78–1; Davis 15–0–71–1; Walsh 17.4–2–54–5; Butts 18–5–59–2. *Second Innings*—Patterson 16–1–68–5; Davis 15–2–59–1; Walsh 14–2–40–4; Butts 1–1–0–0.

West Indies

C. G. Greenidge c Arun Lal b Shastri	15	– c Kapil Dev b C. Sharma	2
D. L. Haynes c sub (C. S. Pandit) b Shastri	58	– not out	0
R. B. Richardson lbw b C. Sharma	89	– not out	0
*I. V. A. Richards b Maninder	37		
A. L. Logie run out	0		
C. L. Hooper lbw b Kapil Dev	37		
†P. J. L. Dujon c and b Shastri	14		
C. G. Butts c More b Shastri	18		
W. W. Davis c and b C. Sharma	30		
C. A. Walsh c Srikkanth b C. Sharma	5		
B. P. Patterson not out	21		
L-b 8, w 1, n-b 4	13	L-b 1, n-b 1	2
1/55 2/99 3/146 4/146 5/210 6/258 7/258 8/300 9/308	337	1/3	(1 wkt) 4

Bowling: *First Innings*—Kapil Dev 25–8–72–1; C. Sharma 13–1–64–3; Ayub 20–1–54–0; Maninder 17–5–68–1; Shastri 28.3–9–71–4. *Second Innings*—Kapil Dev 1–0–2–0; C. Sharma 1–0–1–1.

Umpires: R. B. Gupta and P. D. Reporter.

BCCI PRESIDENT'S XI v WEST INDIANS

At Visakhapatnam, December 18, 19, 20. West Indians won by an innings and 83 runs. Toss: West Indians. Intended as a trial for Indian cricketers on the verge of international selection, the match was played on a pitch that was worse than poor, in that it posed the threat of injury, while the outfield was hopelessly uneven. The big West Indian total belied the nature of the pitch but was a true commentary on the home side's bowling. Dujon brought a splendid technique to bear upon his innings of 123, which included eight fours and two sixes. With the pitch getting progressively worse, the hapless President's XI batsmen never knew whether the ball would lift to their heads or shoot along the ground. Manjrekar, who was hit over the eye in the First Test, suffered another blow on the face during a brave innings when his side followed on, but a face protector under the helmet prevented serious injury.

Close of play: First day, West Indians 347-9 (W. W. Davis 20*); Second day, BCCI President's XI 97-4 (S. V. Manjrekar 31*, S. Viswanath 0*).

West Indians

R. B. Richardson c Gaekwad b G. Sharma	43
P. V. Simmons b Raman	47
P. J. L. Dujon c Rajput b G. Sharma	123
A. L. Logie c A. Sharma b G. Sharma	54
C. L. Hooper c and b G. Sharma	1
E. A. E. Baptiste c and b Raman	22
*I. V. A. Richards c Patel b Raman	6
†D. Williams c Gaekwad b G. Sharma	10
C. G. Butts lbw b G. Sharma	3
W. W. Davis c sub b Raman	23
W. K. M. Benjamin not out	37
B 11, l-b 9, n-b 5	25
1/80 2/100 3/202 4/204 5/241 6/249 7/263 8/273 9/347	394

Bowling: Randhir 6–0–31–0; Patel 7–1–30–0; Raman 32.1–4–94–4; G. Sharma 39–5–136–6; Gudge 17–2–59–0; Gaekwad 2–0–9–0; A. Sharma 2–0–15–0.

BCCI President's XI

A. D. Gaekwad b Baptiste	33	– c Hooper b Benjamin	25
. S. Rajput c Williams b Benjamin	1	– c Richardson b Baptiste	4
K. A. Qayyum b Davis	0	– lbw b Baptiste	4
S. V. Manjrekar c Hooper b Benjamin	4	– c Dujon b Baptiste	47
Ajay Sharma c Hooper b Baptiste	27	– c Simmons b Richards	27
S. Viswanath b Baptiste	0	– c Williams b Davis	5
W. V. Raman b Baptiste	7	– lbw b Baptiste	51
Gopal Sharma c Benjamin b Butts	7	– c Butts b Baptiste	17
S. C. Gudge run out	8	– b Baptiste	8
Randhir Singh run out	2	– c Hooper b Baptiste	13
R. Patel not out	0	– not out	6
N-b 4	4	B 4, l-b 1, n-b 6	11
/9 2/10 3/28 4/54 5/54 /72 7/81 8/87 9/92	93	1/18 2/39 3/43 4/97 5/120 6/120 7/145 8/165 9/193	218

Bowling: *First Innings*—Davis 7–1–26–1; Benjamin 13–3–29–2; Baptiste 9–1–27–4; Butts .1–0–11–1. *Second Innings*—Baptiste 26.2–8–70–7; Benjamin 8–1–34–1; Butts 21–0–71–0; Richards 8–5–8–1; Davis 5–0–30–1.

Umpires: B. Nagaraja Rao and D. V. Pathak.

†INDIA v WEST INDIES

Second One-day International

At Gauhati, December 23. West Indies won by 52 runs. Because of the early fall of darkness n the region, the match was shortened to 45 overs a side. West Indies, without Greenidge, who was indisposed, brought in Simmons, while the Indians made no fewer than three changes. Amarnath, Azharuddin and Prabhakar replaced Arun Lal, Pandit and Chetan Sharma. A slow pitch, tailor-made for India, restricted West Indian strokeplay, but then India themselves made heavy weather of batting on it and collapsed as they sought to accelerate following a partnership of 58 between Amarnath and Vengsarkar. Kapil Dev batted bravely for 22 off 29 balls but ran out of partners. For West Indies, Simmons, Richards (52 balls) and Logie rose above the limitations imposed by the pitch to keep the score moving without resort to extravagant strokes.

Man of the Match: I. V. A. Richards.

West Indies

D. L. Haynes b Maninder	17
P. V. Simmons c Srikkanth b Amarnath	34
R. B. Richardson c More b Amarnath	10
I. V. A. Richards st More b Shastri	41
A. L. Logie lbw b Kapil Dev	34
C. L. Hooper c Kapil Dev b Shastri	2
R. A. Harper not out	18
W. K. M. Benjamin st More b Shastri	4
†P. J. L. Dujon not out	13
L-b 12, w 2	14
1/40 2/62 3/74 4/143 5/145 6/163 7/170 (7 wkts, 45 overs)	187

. A. Walsh and B. P. Patterson did not bat.

Bowling: Kapil Dev 9–1–47–1; Prabhakar 4–0–22–0; Maninder 9–3–19–1; Amarnath -1–21–2; Shastri 9–0–30–3; Ayub 5–0–36–0.

India

. Srikkanth b Walsh	1
. D. Gaekwad b Benjamin	12
M. Amarnath c Richardson b Hooper	33
D. B. Vengsarkar c Harper b Richards	24
M. Azharuddin c and b Hooper	3
Kapil Dev not out	22
. J. Shastri b Walsh	12
K. S. More c Dujon b Patterson	1
M. Prabhakar lbw b Walsh	1
Arshad Ayub run out	6
Maninder Singh b Walsh	0
B 8, l-b 8, w 4	20
1/9 2/25 3/83 4/89 5/89 6/117 7/118 8/122 9/134 (41.3 overs)	135

Bowling: Patterson 8–2–20–1; Walsh 7.3–2–16–4; Benjamin 5–1–15–1; Harper 9–0–21–0
Richards 8–0–37–1; Hooper 4–1–10–2.

Umpires: S. K. Ghosh and R. V. Ramani.

INDIA v WEST INDIES

Third Test Match

At Calcutta, December 26, 27, 28, 30, 31. Drawn. A plumb pitch, hard and sparsely grassec made for little excitement and produced the seventh draw in the last eight Test matches playe at Eden Gardens. An aggregate of 1,252 runs in the match included four hundreds and si other scores over 50. On the other hand, only sixteen wickets fell.

West Indies, who won the toss for the first time in the series, batted for all but 25 minutes c the first two days, generally with little enterprise. Greenidge, who made 141, went to his firs 50 off only 62 balls, but needed 176 to reach his fourteenth Test hundred. He faced 265 balls i all and hit five sixes and fourteen fours. Richardson and Richards, who were associated wit him in century partnerships for successive wickets, took 130 and 134 balls making 51 and 6 respectively. Logie was more lively, needing only 134 balls for his hundred and hitting fiftee fours. Hooper, playing in only his second Test, batted with enough authority to suggest h could have scored more rapidly if required to do so, but his approach was attuned to the polic of steady accumulation. His maiden Test hundred, on the completion of which Richard declared, included seven fours and three sixes, the last of which was a magnificent drive ove extra-cover off Maninder Singh. The Indian out-cricket on the opening day was poo Significant lapses were Maninder's dropping of Richardson, off his own bowling, when h was 16, and Amarnath's wide throw from mid-on when there was a good chance of runnin out Greenidge, then 97.

What little pace and bounce there was in the pitch had gone by the time India batted. Aru Lal, whose 93 included thirteen fours, and Amarnath gave the innings a foundation with second-wicket partnership of 96, and then Vengsarkar hit his second hundred of the series; hi seventeenth in Tests and sixth against West Indies. No sooner had he completed it, howeve in 332 minutes, with eleven fours, than he was struck on the hand by Davis and had to reti with a fracture. A fourth-wicket stand of 104 between Vengsarkar and Azharuddin, whic negotiated the second new ball, had ensured the saving of the follow-on. Azharuddin, whe 21, survived an appeal for a catch at second slip, taken low down by Richardson off Walsh and its rejection led to an altercation between a furious Richards and umpire Reporter.

The Indians, far from being overawed by the size of the West Indies total, treated th bowling on its merit, and only Vengsarkar's innings could be described as staid. Despite th lack of encouragement from the pitch, Walsh bowled with great spirit and stamina for his fo wickets. And just when West Indies' attack seemed to be running aground, Davis, during steady spell delivered off a short run, struck twice in close succession.

Close of play: First day, West Indies 263-2 (C. G. Greenidge 133*, I. V. A. Richards 55* Second day, India 20-0 (K. Srikkanth 7*, Arun Lal 11*); Third day, India 304-3 (D. I Vengsarkar 53*, M. Azharuddin 60*); Fourth day, India 521-7 (Arshad Ayub 43*, Cheta Sharma 5*).

West Indies

C. G Greenidge c More b Kapil Dev ....141 – c sub (Sanjeev Sharma) b Shastri. 6
D. L. Haynes c Srikkanth b Kapil Dev .... 5 – c and b Shastri 4
R. B. Richardson c Azharuddin b Shastri...... 51 – not out ....
*I. V. A. Richards c Kapil Dev b C. Sharma .. 68
A. L. Logie c and b Maninder...............101 – (4) not out 2
C. L. Hooper not out 100
†P. J. L. Dujon not out..................... 40
B 2, l-b 12, n-b 10 .... 24 B 4, l-b 2, n-b 7 1

1/13 2/160 3/284 4/288 5/457 (5 wkts dec.) 530 1/114 2/129 (2 wkts) 15

C. A. Walsh, B. P. Patterson, C. G. Butts and W. W. Davis did not bat.

Bowling: *First Innings*—Kapil Dev 28-6-103-2; C. Sharma 15.1-0-80-1; Maninder 6.5-5-111-1; Ayub 46-5-146-0; Shastri 22-4-60-1; Amarnath 3.5-0-16-0. *Second Innings*—Kapil Dev 10-2-19-0; C. Sharma 4-0-24-0; Maninder 16-2-43-0; Ayub 14-5-34-0; Amarnath 4-0-11-0; Shastri 10-3-13-2; Srikkanth 3-0-7-0; Arun Lal 1-1-0-0.

India

K. Srikkanth c Dujon b Walsh 23
Arun Lal lbw b Walsh 93
M. Amarnath b Davis 43
D. B. Vengsarkar retired hurt 102
M. Azharuddin c Logie b Walsh 60
R. J. Shastri b Davis 47
Kapil Dev lbw b Davis 4
†K. S. More c Richardson b Richards . 44
Arshad Ayub c Richardson b Patterson. 57
Chetan Sharma b Walsh 27
Maninder Singh not out 1
B 12, l-b 25, n-b 27 64

1/56 2/152 3/201 4/305 5/403 6/410 7/505 8/553 9/565 565

Bowling: Patterson 22.2-0-107-1; Walsh 29-3-136-4; Davis 27-3-84-3; Butts 30-13-122-0; Richards 24-6-39-1; Hooper 20-5-40-0.

Umpires: R. B. Gupta and P. D. Reporter.

†INDIA v WEST INDIES

Third One-day International

At Calcutta, January 2. India won by 56 runs. Led for the first time by Shastri, and with a side containing three untried players, India ended a run of eight consecutive defeats by West Indies in one-day cricket. Taking into account that West Indies had batted second on all three occasions when India had beaten them, Shastri opted to bat on winning the toss. India confronted their opponents with a score of 222 founded on a second-wicket stand of 128 in 24 overs between Arun Lal, who made 51, and Amarnath, who batted with much authority for 70 off 83 balls, hitting nine fours. The loss of two quick wickets after their separation slowed India down, but the innings was given further substance by Azharuddin and Shastri. Except for Richardson, who was run out in an unfortunate manner, West Indies found runs hard to get on a pitch that had lost the little pace it had. Maninder Singh, who put the heaviest restraint on them, took his 50th one-day international wicket when he accounted for Greenidge.

Man of the Match: M. Amarnath.

India

K. Srikkanth c Dujon b Walsh 1
Arun Lal c Greenidge b Hooper 51
M. Amarnath run out 70
Sanjeev Sharma c Richardson b Richards . 0
M. Azharuddin run out 44
Kapil Dev c Benjamin b Richards 1
*R. J. Shastri lbw b Patterson 25
W. V. Raman not out 8
†K. S. More not out 9
L-b 10, w 2, n-b 1 13

1/2 2/130 3/131 4/138 5/140 6/194 7/210 (7 wkts, 45 overs) 222

Ajay Sharma and Maninder Singh did not bat.

Bowling: Patterson 9-0-36-1; Walsh 9-2-26-1; Baptiste 5-0-23-0; Benjamin 5-0-29-0; Richards 9-0-48-2; Hooper 8-0-50-1.

West Indies

C. G. Greenidge c Amarnath b Maninder . 44
D. L. Haynes lbw b Kapil Dev 3
R. B. Richardson run out 28
*I. V. A. Richards c Arun Lal b Maninder . 3
A. L. Logie c Azharuddin b Shastri ... 38
C. L. Hooper lbw b Kapil Dev 27
W. K. M. Benjamin c and b Shastri ... 1
†P. J. L. Dujon run out 2
E. A. E. Baptiste lbw b Amarnath 6
C. A. Walsh c sub b S. Sharma 2
B. P. Patterson not out 3
L-b 6, w 2, n-b 1 9

1/12 2/53 3/65 4/92 5/152 6/153 7/153 8/158 9/162 (41.5 overs) 166

Bowling: Kapil Dev 7–1–20–2; S. Sharma 5.5–0–29–1; Amarnath 9–0–46–1; Maninde 9–0–19–2; Shastri 9–1–31–2; A. Sharma 2–0–15–0.

Umpires: R. B. Gupta and P. D. Reporter.

†INDIA v WEST INDIES

Fourth One-day International

At Rajkot, January 5. West Indies won by six wickets. India were weakened by the absenc through injury of the two players chiefly instrumental in their winning the previous match Amarnath and Maninder Singh. West Indies, too, had their handicaps, illness keeping ou Dujon, and Greenidge and Haynes incurring injuries in the field. However, Richards playe one of his truly great innings to settle the issue, having already taken three wickets after Indi elected to bat. His 110, off only 77 balls, featured seven fours and seven sixes, three of whic were hit off consecutive balls from Shastri. His last 60 came from only 28 balls. West Indie would have had fewer runs to chase had they not allowed as many as five "lives" to Ramar whose 95 off 123 balls included six fours. They were fined Rs15,000 for failing to bowl th scheduled 46 overs.

Man of the Match: I. V. A. Richards.

India

K. Srikkanth c Williams b Benjamin . . 32
Arun Lal c Greenidge b Patterson 10
W. V. Raman c Baptiste b Patterson . . 95
M. Azharuddin c and b Richards 24
Kapil Dev c Logie b Richards 22
*R. J. Shastri c and b Hooper 7
†S. Viswanath c Baptiste b Richards . . 1
S. V. Manjrekar not out 1
Ajay Sharma not out . . . .
L-b 8, n-b 1 . . . .

1/34 2/69 3/119 4/151 5/173 6/176 7/214 (7 wkts, 43 overs) 22

Sanjeev Sharma and Arshad Ayub did not bat.

Bowling: Patterson 8–1–49–2; Walsh 8–0–39–0; Benjamin 9–0–35–1; Baptiste 9–1–40–(Richards 8–0–42–3; Hooper 1–0–8–1.

West Indies

D. L. Haynes b Raman 49
R. B. Richardson c Kapil Dev b S. Sharma . 27
A. L. Logie c Viswanath b Ayub 12
*I. V. A. Richards not out 110
C. L. Hooper c Manjrekar b Kapil Dev 12
E. A. E. Baptiste not out . . . .
L-b 7, w 1 . . . .

1/38 2/77 3/147 4/191 (4 wkts, 40.1 overs) 22

W. K. M. Benjamin, †D. Williams, C. G. Greenidge, C. A. Walsh and B. P. Patterson d not bat.

Bowling: Kapil Dev 8–1–22–1; S. Sharma 6–0–31–1; A. Sharma 3–0–12–0; Ayu 10–1–55–1; Shastri 9–1–50–0; Raman 4–0–44–1; Srikkanth 0.1–0–4–0.

Umpires: D. N. Dotiwala and S. B. Kulkarni.

†INDIA v WEST INDIES

Charity One-day International

At Ahmedabad, January 7. West Indies won by 2 runs. Toss: India. At the time it was playe a certain amount of confusion surrounded the status of this match. The Indian authorities ha wanted to include it as part of the Charminar Challenge series, but West Indies would n accede to this. The match was, however, designated an official one-day international.

Man of the Match: K. Srikkanth.

West Indies

R. B. Richardson b C. Sharma	4	D. Williams run out	1
P. V. Simmons lbw b Kapil Dev	20	W. W. Davis b Kapil Dev	10
P. J. L. Dujon c and b C. Sharma	11	B. P. Patterson not out	13
I. V. A. Richards b Amarnath	17	B 7, l-b 10, w 1, n-b 3	21
A. L. Logie c Srikkanth b Ayub	30		—
C. L. Hooper c Arun Lal b Srikkanth	33	1/6 2/28 3/55 (48.3 overs)	196
. A. E. Baptiste run out	31	4/65 5/111 6/163	
W. K. M. Benjamin b Ayub	5	7/166 8/168 9/173	

Bowling: C. Sharma 7–0–31–2; S. Sharma 5–1–24–0; Amarnath 10–1–28–1; Kapil Dev .3–0–21–2; Ayub 10–1–37–2; Shastri 3–0–23–0; Srikkanth 5–1–15–1.

India

K. Srikkanth c Baptiste b Richards	53	Chetan Sharma not out	16
Arun Lal c Williams b Patterson	16	Arshad Ayub c Simmons b Patterson	14
M. Amarnath c Simmons b Baptiste	21	Sanjeev Sharma not out	1
W. V. Raman c Williams b Benjamin	14	B 1, l-b 8, w 3	12
Kapil Dev run out	21		—
. V. Manjrekar c Richards b Benjamin	0	1/26 2/69 3/98 (9 wkts, 50 overs)	194
R. J. Shastri b Davis	19	4/127 5/127 6/136	
S. Viswanath b Patterson	7	7/160 8/162 9/191	

Bowling: Patterson 9–2–26–3; Davis 10–2–35–1; Benjamin 10–0–30–2; Baptiste 10–0–49–1; Richards 10–1–43–1; Hooper 1–0–2–0.

Umpires: P. G. Pandit and R. V. Ramani.

INDIA v WEST INDIES

Fourth Test Match

At Madras, January 11, 12, 14, 15. India won by 255 runs, with a day to spare, the most ecisive of their six victories against West Indies. Its main author was a new cap in Hirwani, bespectacled, nineteen-year-old leg-spinner, who had the assistance of an under-prepared itch which afforded turn from the opening day. In the circumstances, the scales were tipped eavily in India's favour when Shastri, captaining for the first time in a Test match, won the oss. Hirwani captured eight wickets in each innings to equal the Australian R. A. L. Massie's eat of taking sixteen wickets on his début, against England at Lord's in 1972. If Hirwani was ble to give the ball air, as he did, and challenge the batsmen to counter-attack, it was because f India's first-innings total of 382, which was owed principally to a dashing 109 by Kapil Dev, scored off only 119 balls and including seventeen fours.

Although the ball turned extravagantly, the seven other spinners in the match, while owling 154 overs between them, could not take more than seven wickets. The collapse of the West Indians for scores of 184 and 160, the second time in 156 minutes, not only was ndicative of their mistrust of the pitch, but also underlined the vulnerability of the new eneration of their batsmen to leg-spin. Certainly, in conditions which put a premium on xperience, they missed Greenidge, who was kept out by an injured thumb. He was replaced y Simmons, hitherto uncapped. Besides Hirwani, India included two newcomers in the all-unders, Raman and Ajay Sharma, and they too played vital roles in shaping India's victory, heir first over West Indies since 1978-79.

In India's first innings, Ajay Sharma batted for two hours and assisted a rampant Kapil Dev in adding 113 for the sixth wicket. It was an essential partnership, for despite a confident 9 from Arul Lal, India were in the shadows at 156 for five when Kapil Dev came to the icket. The recovery was sustained and India totalled 382. Although conditions were of no elp to pace bowlers, Walsh again bowled superbly. The only significant contributions in West Indies' reply came from Richardson, who stayed for two hours, Richards, whose 68 ncluded eight fours, and Dujon. Richards, taking all manner of chances, produced some stounding strokes but needed generous measures of luck to play in that vein and survive. Hirwani bowled him on the third morning, when in seven overs and three balls he took all five emaining wickets at a cost of 26 runs as West Indies just sneaked past the follow-on figure.

With almost three days available in which to force home their advantage, India took their time to increase their lead. Added caution was compelled by the loss of three wickets for 37, two of them to Walsh, who again distinguished himself. The mainstay of the innings was Raman, the débutant, who showed immense maturity in making 83 spread over 257 minutes, although while he was batting with Azharuddin, their 87 came in almost even time. West Indies, in their second innings, batted as if resigned to their lot. Except for Haynes, all of them flung their bats in desperate fashion; only Logie, whose 67 off 62 balls was quite spectacular and Butts attacked with any measure of success, adding 59 in 43 minutes. The pitch, if a nightmare for the batsmen, made equally high demands on the wicket-keepers, and More deserved much credit for stumping six batsmen in the match, five of them in the second innings. Both figures were a record for stumpings in a Test.

Close of play: First day, India 308-6 (Kapil Dev 104*, R. J. Shastri 5*); Second day, West Indies 147-5 (I. V. A. Richards 62*, P. J. L. Dujon 4*); Third day, India 181-4 (W. V. Raman 82*, Ajay Sharma 22*).

India

K. Srikkanth c Davis b Walsh	23	– lbw b Davis	17
Arun Lal c Logie b Hooper	69	– lbw b Walsh	1
M. Amarnath c Dujon b Walsh	3	– (4) c Richardson b Walsh	1
W. V. Raman c Dujon b Davis	9	– (3) c Dujon b Walsh	83
M. Azharuddin c Haynes b Hooper	47	– c Davis b Richards	39
Ajay Sharma lbw b Richards	30	– lbw b Patterson	23
Kapil Dev c Richards b Walsh	109	– lbw b Patterson	5
*R. J. Shastri b Davis	23	– not out	20
†K. S. More b Davis	17	– c Dujon b Walsh	0
Arshad Ayub not out	23	– not out	3
N. D. Hirwani c Richardson b Davis	1		
B 15, l-b 4, n-b 9	28	B 8, l-b 7, n-b 10	25
	——		——
1/30 2/38 3/64 4/153 5/156 6/269 7/313 8/342 9/369	382	1/3 2/36 3/37 (8 wkts dec.) 4/124 5/185 6/185 7/190 8/194	217

Bowling: *First Innings*—Patterson 15–1–62–0; Walsh 27–3–85–3; Davis 18.1–0–76–4; Butts 24–4–62–0; Richards 8–1–36–1; Hooper 12–3–42–2. *Second Innings*—Patterson 9–2–17–2; Walsh 16–5–55–4; Davis 6–0–20–1; Butts 21–1–62–0; Hooper 6–1–20–0; Richards 18–4–28–1.

West Indies

D. L. Haynes c Kapil Dev b Shastri	13	– lbw b Hirwani	6
P. V. Simmons c and b Kapil Dev	8	– c Amarnath b Hirwani	14
R. B. Richardson c Azharuddin b Hirwani	36	– c Amarnath b Ayub	7
*I. V. A. Richards b Hirwani	68	– c Kapil Dev b Hirwani	4
A. L. Logie c Azharuddin b Hirwani	12	– st More b Hirwani	67
C. L. Hooper lbw b Hirwani	2	– st More b Hirwani	8
†P. J. L. Dujon st More b Hirwani	24	– st More b Hirwani	2
C. G. Butts c Raman b Hirwani	0	– c A. Sharma b Hirwani	38
W. W. Davis lbw b Hirwani	1	– st More b Hirwani	7
C. A. Walsh c More b Hirwani	8	– st More b Raman	0
B. P. Patterson not out	0	– not out	0
B 8, l-b 2, n-b 2	12	B 4, l-b 1, n-b 2	7
	——		——
1/17 2/47 3/98 4/128 5/132 6/163 7/175 8/175 9/183	184	1/22 2/24 3/33 4/41 5/61 6/79 7/138 8/153 9/160	160

Bowling: *First Innings*—Kapil Dev 7–0–20–1; Amarnath 3–0–8–0; Shastri 13–6–29–1; Ayub 28–10–47–0; Hirwani 18.3–3–61–8; A. Sharma 4–0–9–0. *Second Innings*—Kapil Dev 4–3–8–0; Amarnath 2–0–7–0; Shastri 5–0–25–0; Ayub 14–5–33–1; Hirwani 15.2–3–75–8; Raman 1–0–7–1.

Umpires: R. B. Gupta and P. D. Reporter.

†INDIA v WEST INDIES

Fifth One-day International

ıt Faridabad, January 19. West Indies won by four wickets. Toss: India. India's highest score ı the series to date, which included Amarnath's first hundred in a one-day international, put ɔ strain on the West Indians. Amarnath's sturdy hundred included five fours and a six, but ıe only other worthwhile contribution to the Indian total was 45, off 44 balls, by Kapil Dev. 'ollowing a second-wicket stand of 108 between Simmons and Richardson, West Indies lost ıeir way against an unlikely bowler in Srikkanth, but Logie and Hooper put them back n course.

Man of the Match: M. Amarnath.

ndia

. Srikkanth b Baptiste	28
ırun Lal c Dujon b Walsh	0
1. Amarnath not out	100
V. V. Raman b Benjamin	13
1. Azharuddin b Baptiste	2
.apil Dev c Hooper b Benjamin	45
*R. J. Shastri c Baptiste b Davis	28
†K. S. More not out	9
L-b 4, n-b 1	5
1/3 2/50 3/73 4/76 5/142 6/213 (6 wkts, 50 overs)	230

'hetan Sharma, Maninder Singh and Arshad Ayub did not bat.

Bowling: Walsh 10–1–42–1; Davis 10–0–69–1; Benjamin 10–2–38–2; Baptiste 10–2–41–2; .ichards 8–1–31–0; Hooper 2–0–5–0.

Vest Indies

. L. Haynes b Kapil Dev	12
. V. Simmons c and b Srikkanth	67
. B. Richardson lbw b Srikkanth	49
1. V. A. Richards c Arun Lal b Srikkanth	9
. L. Logie run out	29
. L. Hooper not out	39
†P. J. L. Dujon st More b Shastri	9
E. A. E. Baptiste not out	3
B 1, l-b 13	14
1/18 2/126 3/144 4/155 5/192 6/223 (6 wkts, 49.1 overs)	231

. A. Walsh, W. W. Davis and W. K. M. Benjamin did not bat.

Bowling: Kapil Dev 9–1–37–1; C. Sharma 5–0–25–0; Amarnath 6–0–14–0; Maninder 1–0–55–0; Ayub 10–0–37–0; Shastri 4–0–24–1; Srikkanth 6–0–25–3.

Umpires: S. D. Ghosh and V. K. Ramaswamy.

†INDIA v WEST INDIES

Sixth One-day International

t Gwalior, January 22. West Indies won by 73 runs. India's inclusion of Hirwani, the leg-inning hero of the Fourth Test, made no impact on West Indies. Although they started oderately, losing four wickets in making 103 after Shastri put them in, their fortunes were nt soaring by a superb maiden one-day international hundred from Hooper, who batted with quiet charm initially and then became so aggressive that he struck 58 of the last 67 runs off ıly 33 balls. He hit twelve fours and two sixes in his unbeaten 113, and with Logie added 108 r the fifth wicket. With Patterson striking thrice in a lively opening spell, India had no undation on which to build a reply. They were spared humiliation by a handsome 52 from apil Dev and 73 scored in rather desperate fashion by Shastri.

Man of the Match: C. L. Hooper.

West Indies

D. L. Haynes b S. Sharma 5
P. V. Simmons lbw b Ayub 21
R. B. Richardson c Ayub b Shastri 30
*I. V. A. Richards c S. Sharma b Amarnath . 33
A. L. Logie c S. Sharma b Ayub 54
C. L. Hooper not out 113
E. A. E. Baptiste run out . . . .
W. K. M. Benjamin not out . . . .
B 2, l-b 14, w 2 1

1/8 2/55 3/65 4/103 5/211 6/268 (6 wkts, 50 overs) 27

†P. J. L. Dujon, C. A. Walsh and B. P. Patterson did not bat.

Bowling: S. Sharma 6–0–42–1; Amarnath 10–0–43–1; Ayub 9–1–36–2; Shastri 9–0–48–1 Hirwani 10–0–34–0; Raman 3–0–23–0; Kapil Dev 3–0–36–0.

India

K. Srikkanth c Baptiste b Patterson . . . 9
Arun Lal b Patterson 0
M. Amarnath c Dujon b Patterson 3
W. V. Raman c Dujon b Walsh 1
M. Azharuddin c Dujon b Benjamin . . . 23
Kapil Dev b Baptiste 52
*R. J. Shastri not out 73
†K. S. More run out 10
Arshad Ayub st Dujon b Richards 1
Sanjeev Sharma c Haynes b Richards .
N. D. Hirwani b Patterson . . . .
B 4, l-b 8, w 4, n-b 3 1

1/1 2/14 3/14 4/15 5/88 6/94 7/117 8/134 9/152 (41 overs) 20

Bowling: Patterson 8–0–29–4; Walsh 6–1–23–1; Benjamin 10–1–34–1; Baptiste 5–0–37–1 Richards 9–0–34–2; Hooper 2–0–27–0; Simmons 1–0–9–0.

Umpires: D. N. Dotiwala and S. B. Kulkarni.

†INDIA v WEST INDIES

Seventh One-day International

At Trivandrum, January 25. West Indies won by nine wickets. Toss: West Indies. Despite flamboyant 101 off 105 balls by Srikkanth, who was dropped in the slips in the first over of th match, India could not extend West Indies. Even on a good batting pitch, their batting faile to achieve consistency. Srikkanth, who struck ten fours and three sixes, was supported only b Amarnath (84 balls) and Azharuddin. Requiring 240 to win, West Indies were taken to withi 76 runs of their target by an opening partnership between Greenidge, who seemed none th worse for a three-week break from the game, and Simmons, who put on 164 in 28 overs Greenidge's 84 was made off 75 balls, with four fours and five sixes, while Simmons, althoug more sedate (129 balls), hit four fours and four sixes in his first hundred at this level.

Man of the Match: P. V. Simmons. *Man of the Series:* I. V. A. Richards.

India

K. Srikkanth b Baptiste 101
R. Lamba lbw b Patterson 8
M. Amarnath b Patterson 56
Kapil Dev lbw b Richards 1
*R. J. Shastri st Williams b Richards . . 3
M. Azharuddin c Baptiste b Davis 36
†K. S. More c Richards b Patterson . . . 3
S. V. Manjrekar not out 14
Sanjeev Sharma run out . . . .
Maninder Singh not out . . . .
B 2, l-b 7, w 1, n-b 4 1

1/33 2/160 3/161 4/167 5/200 6/203 7/231 8/234 (8 wkts, 45 overs) 23

N. D. Hirwani did not bat.

Bowling: Patterson 9–0–34–3; Davis 9–0–59–1; Benjamin 9–0–41–0; Baptiste 9–0–51–1 Richards 8–0–40–2; Hooper 1–0–5–0.

West Indies

C. G. Greenidge st More b Maninder . 84
P. V. Simmons not out 104
R. B. Richardson not out 37
B 1, l-b 12, w 1, n-b 2 16

1/164 (1 wkt, 43.5 overs) 241

*I. V. A. Richards, †D. Williams, B. P. Patterson, W. W. Davis, W. K. M. Benjamin, E. A. E. Baptiste, C. L. Hooper and A. L. Logie did not bat.

Bowling: Kapil Dev 4–0–28–0; S. Sharma 7.5–0–47–0; Amarnath 5–0–21–0; Maninder 9–0–42–1; Hirwani 9–0–40–0; Shastri 2–0–24–0; Srikkanth 7–0–26–0.

Umpires: P. G. Pandit and V. Vikramraju.

THE DELOITTE RATINGS

Initiated by the former England captain, E. R. Dexter, in 1987, the Deloitte Ratings rank Test cricketers on a scale from 0 to 1,000 according to their performances in Test matches since 1981. The ratings are calculated by computer and take into account playing conditions, the quality of the opposition and the results of the matches. The value of a player's performance is assessed in relation to the Deloitte Ratings of the opposing players and it also reflects his ability to score match-winning runs or take match-winning wickets. Updated after every Test match, with a player's most recent performances carrying more weight than his earlier ones, the Deloitte Ratings endeavour to provide a current assessment of a Test cricketer's form and his place among his peers. The Rating for a new Test cricketer is delayed until he has played sufficient matches to establish himself, usually two or three appearances, although in the following list N. D. Hirwani and P. J. Newport have been included after just one Test match.

The leading 30 batsmen and bowlers in the Ratings after the 1988 series between England and West Indies and the match between England and Sri Lanka were:

	Batsmen	*Rating*	*Bowlers*	*Rating*
1.	D. B. Vengsarkar (*India*)	911	M. D. Marshall (*WI*)	902
2.	A. R. Border (*Aust.*)	826	R. J. Hadlee (*NZ*)	882
3.	I. V. A. Richards (*WI*)	804	Imran Khan (*Pak.*)	851
4.	M. D. Crowe (*NZ*)	750	W. K. M. Benjamin (*WI*)	709
5.	Javed Miandad (*Pak.*)	739	N. D. Hirwani (*India*)	670
6.	C. G. Greenidge (*WI*)	678	Wasim Akram (*Pak.*)	665
7.	A. Ranatunga (*SL*)	678	E. J. Chatfield (*NZ*)	652
8.	D. M. Jones (*Aust.*)	671	Chetan Sharma (*India*)	641
9.	P. J. L. Dujon (*WI*)	663	S. R. Waugh (*Aust.*)	636
10.	G. A. Gooch (*Eng.*)	649	B. A. Reid (*Aust.*)	621
11.	D. C. Boon (*Aust.*)	646	G. R. Dilley (*Eng.*)	616
12.	D. L. Haynes (*WI*)	628	Kapil Dev (*India*)	586
13.	A. L. Logie (*WI*)	620	C. A. Walsh (*WI*)	584
14.	R. B. Richardson (*WI*)	609	J. R. Ratnayeke (*SL*)	580
15.	M. Azharuddin (*India*)	590	N. A. Foster (*Eng.*)	573
16.	Salim Malik (*Pak.*)	589	Abdul Qadir (*Pak.*)	571
17.	D. I. Gower (*Eng.*)	580	C. J. McDermott (*Aust.*)	569
18.	J. G. Wright (*NZ*)	574	Tauseef Ahmed (*Pak.*)	535
19.	A. H. Jones (*NZ*)	570	R. J. Shastri (*India*)	524
20.	Salim Yousuf (*Pak.*)	567	A. I. C. Dodemaide (*Aust.*)	508
21.	B. C. Broad (*Eng.*)	556	C. E. L. Ambrose (*WI*)	497
22.	Imran Khan (*Pak.*)	555	S. L. Boock (*NZ*)	494
23.	Kapil Dev (*India*)	542	P. L. Taylor (*Aust.*)	493
24.	R. J. Hadlee (*NZ*)	539	Mudassar Nazar (*Pak.*)	486
25.	Mudassar Nazar (*Pak.*)	526	R. A. Harper (*WI*)	484
26.	G. R. Marsh (*Aust.*)	519	Iqbal Qasim (*Pak.*)	480
27.	M. W. Gatting (*Eng.*)	519	Maninder Singh (*India*)	474
28.	D. S. B. P. Kuruppu (*SL*)	508	J. G. Bracewell (*NZ*)	470
29.	A. J. Lamb (*Eng.*)	498	W. W. Davis (*WI*)	460
30.	Ramiz Raja (*Pak.*)	497	B. P. Patterson (*WI*)	451

THE NEW ZEALANDERS IN AUSTRALIA, 1987-88

By CHRIS HARTE

The seventeenth New Zealand team to visit Australia – although only the fourth for a Test series – arrived in Perth fewer than three weeks after competing in the World Cup in India. From the start the side looked jaded, and with the captain, Jeff Crowe, sadly out of form, the tourists leant heavily on their two star players, Martin Crowe and Richard Hadlee. Moreover, the hectic itinerary, comprising three Tests and the same number of other first-class fixtures, was top heavy with one-day matches. It was a weary Kiwi team that returned home in late January.

With the Australian public appearing to lose interest in the played-for-television one-day international series, the gripping hours of the season came on the final day of the Third Test in Melbourne on the penultimate day of 1987. As Australia, chasing 247 for victory and a 2-0 series win, collapsed to 227 for nine, the tail-end batsmen, Craig McDermott and Michael Whitney, survived 4.5 overs to deprive New Zealand of a drawn rubber. Hadlee, who bowled the final over to Whitney, also lost his chance to claim the Test bowling record. However, it was the New Zealand all-rounder's sportsmanship in defeat which subsequently dominated the Australian media.

The New Zealanders began their tour with a day/night victory in Perth over Western Australia, then thrashed the Sheffield Shield champions by an innings and 96 runs in two and a half days. Hadlee took five wickets in each innings, and Martin Crowe and Dipak Patel scored centuries with ease. An easily won match in Renmark against a South Australian Country XI was followed by a defeat in Adelaide by three wickets after Jeff Crowe's declaration on the third afternoon. Off-spinner John Bracewell claimed ten wickets in the match, at one time bowling 31 consecutive overs.

The First Test in Brisbane was won by Australia on the fourth afternoon. New Zealand were on the back foot from the start, when Ken Rutherford fell to the fourth delivery of the match, and when Australia batted David Boon's 143, his highest in Tests, held their innings together. The New Zealanders had only themselves to blame for a nine wickets defeat, for there was not really that much difference between the sides. The Adelaide Test was played in exceptionally hot conditions, which gave even more kudos to the 150 scored by Andrew Jones in only his third Test. The Australian captain, Allan Border, with a career-highest score of 205, passed Sir Donald Bradman and Greg Chappell to become his country's leading Test run-getter, while the match ended in a tame draw.

After a drawn match in Devonport against Tasmania, where Philip Horne's 125 earned him a Test place at Melbourne, and victory over the Prime Minister's XI in a 50-overs match on the lush Manuka Oval in Canberra, the tourists made a determined bid to square the series. Certainly, the final Test, in front of 127,184 spectators, was an enthralling match and a credit to cricket, played in a hard but fair manner. The ebbs and flows over five days made for an absorbing contest.

For the final three weeks of their tour, the New Zealanders took part in the three-way World Series Cup competition, along with Australia and Sri Lanka. As expected they qualified for the finals where Australia won the first two matches in a manner befitting the World Cup holders.

NEW ZEALAND TOUR RESULTS

Test matches – Played 3: Lost 1, Drawn 2.
First-class matches – Played 6: Won 1, Lost 2, Drawn 3.
Win – Western Australia.
Losses – Australia, South Australia.
Draws – Australia (2), Tasmania.
One-day internationals – Played 10: Won 4, Lost 6. *Wins* – Australia, Sri Lanka (3). *Losses* – Australia (5), Sri Lanka.
Other non first-class matches – Played 3: Won 3. *Wins* – Western Australia, South Australian Country XI, Prime Minister's XI.

TEST MATCH AVERAGES

AUSTRALIA – BATTING

	T	*I*	*NO*	*R*	*HI*	*100s*	*Avge*
A. R. Border	3	4	0	288	205	1	72.00
P. R. Sleep	3	4	0	211	90	0	52.75
D. C. Boon	3	5	0	237	143	1	47.40
S. R. Waugh	3	4	0	147	61	0	36.75
G. R. Marsh	3	5	1	122	31*	0	30.50
C. J. McDermott	3	4	1	83	33	0	27.66
G. C. Dyer	3	4	0	93	60	0	23.25
M. R. J. Veletta	3	4	0	84	39	0	21.00
D. M. Jones	3	5	1	52	38*	0	13.00

Played in two Tests: B. A. Reid 8*, 5. Played in one Test: A. I. C. Dodemaide 50, 3; M. G. Hughes 5; T. B. A. May 14*; M. R. Whitney 0*, 2*.

* *Signifies not out.*

BOWLING

	O	*M*	*R*	*W*	*BB*	*Avge*
A. I. C. Dodemaide	48.3	14	106	7	6-58	15.14
B. A. Reid	57	16	114	7	4-53	16.28
M. G. Hughes	35	12	97	5	3-40	19.40
C. J. McDermott	144.1	30	426	17	5-97	25.05
P. R. Sleep	124	31	342	7	3-61	48.86

Also bowled: D. M. Jones 14–6–29–1; T. B. A. May 84–23–202–4; S. R. Waugh 75–26–169–2; M. R. Whitney 53.3–11–137–4.

NEW ZEALAND – BATTING

	T	*I*	*NO*	*R*	*HI*	*100s*	*Avge*
M. D. Crowe	3	6	0	396	137	1	66.00
A. H. Jones	3	6	0	323	150	1	53.83
J. G. Wright	3	6	0	248	99	0	41.33
D. N. Patel	3	6	0	192	62	0	32.00
R. J. Hadlee	3	6	1	111	36	0	22.20
I. D. S. Smith	3	6	1	80	44	0	16.00
J. J. Crowe	3	6	0	78	25	0	13.00
J. G. Bracewell	3	5	0	53	32	0	10.60

Played in three Tests: D. K. Morrison 0, 2, 0, 0. Played in two Tests: E. J. Chatfield 0*, 1*, 6*, 1*. Played in one Test: E. J. Gray 23, 14; P. A. Horne 7, 27; K. R. Rutherford 0, 2; M. C. Snedden 0, 8*.

* *Signifies not out.*

BOWLING

	O	*M*	*R*	*W*	*BB*	*Avge*
R. J. Hadlee	156	44	353	18	5-67	19.61
J. G. Bracewell ...	141.5	27	339	8	2-58	42.37
D. K. Morrison ...	101.4	14	354	8	4-86	44.25

Also bowled: E. J. Chatfield 85–27–154–2; E. J. Gray 44–10–102–0; D. N. Patel 22.1–9–52–0; M. C. Snedden 32–6–89–1.

NEW ZEALAND AVERAGES – FIRST-CLASS MATCHES

BATTING

	M	*I*	*NO*	*R*	*HI*	*100s*	*Avge*
M. D. Crowe	5	9	1	715	144	3	89.37
P. A. Horne	3	5	0	218	125	1	43.60
A. H. Jones	6	11	0	439	150	1	39.90
J. G. Wright	5	10	0	383	99	0	38.30
D. N. Patel	6	11	0	374	105	1	34.00
R. J. Hadlee	5	8	3	151	36	0	30.20
E. J. Gray	3	5	1	89	26	0	22.25
I. D. S. Smith	6	11	2	193	62	0	21.44
K. R. Rutherford ...	4	7	0	133	36	0	19.00
J. G. Bracewell	4	7	1	106	41*	0	17.66
J. J. Crowe	6	11	0	158	36	0	14.36

Played in five matches: D. K. Morrison 0, 2, 0, 0, 5*, 1. Played in four matches: E. J. Chatfield 0*, 1*, 4*, 6*, 1*. Played in two matches: M. C. Snedden 0, 8*; W. Watson 0, 27*, 0.

* *Signifies not out.*

BOWLING

	O	*M*	*R*	*W*	*BB*	*Avge*
R. J. Hadlee	237.4	63	564	29	5-30	19.44
W. Watson	69.2	13	201	8	4-42	25.12
J. G. Bracewell ...	207.5	39	553	18	7-98	30.72
D. K. Morrison ...	158.3	25	555	16	4-86	34.68
E. J. Gray	83	21	193	5	3-60	38.60
E. J. Chatfield	180	55	352	8	3-52	44.00

Also bowled: D. N. Patel 72.4–16–212–3; M. C. Snedden 64–10–171–3.

FIELDING

14 – I. D. S. Smith (13 ct, 1 st); 6 – J. J. Crowe; 5 – A. H. Jones; 4 – J. G. Bracewell; M. D. Crowe, E. J. Gray, K. R. Rutherford; 3 – D. N. Patel, J. G. Wright; 2 – P. A. Horne, substitutes (K. R. Rutherford 2); 1 – E. J. Chatfield, R. J. Hadlee, D. K. Morrison.

†At Perth, November 18 (day/night). New Zealanders won by four wickets. Toss: Western Australia. Western Australia 192 (45.2 overs) (G. M. Wood 38, W. S. Andrews 48; M. C. Snedden three for 20); New Zealanders 193 for six (48.5 overs) (K. R. Rutherford 54, A. H. Jones 84 not out; P. A. Capes three for 25).

WESTERN AUSTRALIA v NEW ZEALANDERS

At Perth, November 20, 21, 22. New Zealanders won by an innings and 96 runs with a day to spare. Put in to bat, Western Australia crumbled before the touring side's Hadlee-inspired fast bowling and lasted for just two sessions on a good pitch. Martin Crowe and Patel added 164 in even time for the fifth wicket for the New Zealanders, and before the declaration Veletta became the tenth Australian to take five or more fielding catches in an innings. Hadlee again captured five wickets – for the 93rd time in his career – as Western Australia in their second innings found no answer to his bowling and were dismissed before tea on the third day.

Close of play: First day, New Zealanders 66-1 (P. A. Horne 23*, I. D. S. Smith 0*); Second day, Western Australia 13-1 (G. R. Marsh 9*, T. M. Moody 2*).

Western Australia

G. R. Marsh c Jones b Watson	7	– (2) c Rutherford b Hadlee	9
M. R. J. Veletta b Morrison	11	– (1) c J. J. Crowe b Hadlee	0
T. M. Moody b Morrison	10	– c Rutherford b Watson	43
*G. M. Wood b Hadlee	25	– lbw b Hadlee	11
W. S. Andrews lbw b Hadlee	32	– c Patel b Watson	1
K. H. MacLeay c Smith b Hadlee	20	– lbw b Hadlee	0
†T. J. Zoehrer hit wkt b Morrison	7	– c Gray b Hadlee	8
C. D. Matthews c M. D. Crowe b Patel	8	– c Horne b Watson	19
P. A. Capes not out	1	– c Jones b Watson	5
B. A. Reid c Gray b Hadlee	5	– c Horne b Morrison	9
S. J. Milosz b Hadlee	0	– not out	0
N-b 5	5	L-b 4, n-b 8	12
1/13 2/30 3/31 4/82 5/93 6/101 7/125 8/125 9/131	131	1/0 2/13 3/42 4/47 5/50 6/69 7/99 8/103 9/113	117

Bowling: *First Innings*—Hadlee 16.2–7–37–5; Morrison 13–5–33–3; Watson 17–5–41–1; Patel 8–1–17–1; Gray 2–0–3–0. *Second Innings*—Hadlee 17–3–30–5; Morrison 12–3–41–1; Watson 16.2–4–42–4.

New Zealanders

P. A. Horne c Veletta b Capes	24
K. R. Rutherford c Veletta b Milosz	36
†I. D. S. Smith lbw b MacLeay	2
A. H. Jones c Marsh b Matthews	7
M. D. Crowe c Zoehrer b MacLeay	119
D. N. Patel c Veletta b Reid	105
*J. J. Crowe lbw b MacLeay	0
E. J. Gray c Veletta b MacLeay	2
R. J. Hadlee not out	30
W. Watson c Veletta b Reid	0
L-b 2, n-b 17	19
1/65 2/68 3/70 4/99 5/263 6/265 7/277 8/336 9/344 (9 wkts dec.)	344

D. K. Morrison did not bat.

Bowling: Capes 23–2–85–1; MacLeay 25–9–75–4; Reid 23–4–61–2; Milosz 17–6–53–1; Matthews 18–2–62–1; Andrews 2–0–6–0.

Umpires: G. J. Bibby and P. J. McConnell.

†At Renmark, November 25. New Zealanders won by 85 runs. Toss: New Zealanders. New Zealanders 197 for eight (50 overs) (K. R. Rutherford 33, A. H. Jones 46, R. J. Hadlee 34 not out; G. Stephenson three for 37); South Australian Country XI 112 (45.2 overs) (W. Watson three for 15, E. J. Gray three for 24).

SOUTH AUSTRALIA v NEW ZEALANDERS

At Adelaide, November 27, 28, 29, 30. South Australia won by three wickets. Put in to bat, the New Zealanders made the most of an unusually green Adelaide pitch, Martin Crowe scoring his second successive century in 196 minutes with two sixes and twenty fours. The ease and confidence of his batting appeared to relax his team-mates, who were still winding down from their recent World Cup travels. Hookes hit a three-hour 128 on the second day as the touring side gained a 118-run lead, which had been extended to 385 by the time Jeff Crowe declared on the third afternoon. Bracewell, who had taken seven wickets in the first innings, increased his tally for the match to ten as he tried to stem South Australia's relentless grind towards victory. Bishop, a hard-hitting opener, held the top order together, Phillips organised the rest, and the win came with just four balls remaining.

Close of play: First day, New Zealanders 360-7 (R. J. Hadlee 10*, I. D. S. Smith 21*); Second day, New Zealanders 33-0 (K. R. Rutherford 19*, J. G. Wright 13*); Third day, South Australia 65-1 (G. A. Bishop 46*, M. D. Haysman 3*).

New Zealanders

K. R. Rutherford c and b George	36	– lbw b Smart	22
J. G. Wright c George b May	34	– lbw b Gladigau	39
A. H. Jones run out	65	– lbw b Gladigau	26
M. D. Crowe c O'Connor b May	144	– (8) not out	56
D. N. Patel c Hilditch b May	13	– c Gladigau b May	35
*J. J. Crowe c Hookes b May	13	– (4) c Hilditch b Sleep	21
J. G. Bracewell c O'Connor b Sleep	12	– (6) not out	41
R. J. Hadlee not out	10		
†I. D. S. Smith not out	21	– (7) c Gladigau b May	18
L-b 5, w 1, n-b 6	12	B 3, l-b 2, n-b 4	9
1/65 2/85 3/243 4/301 5/306 6/327 7/329 (7 wkts dec.)	360	1/36 2/84 3/95 4/148 5/153 6/178 (6 wkts dec.)	267

M. C. Snedden and E. J. Chatfield did not bat.

Bowling: *First Innings*—Gladigau 12–4–33–0; Smart 16–1–69–0; George 12–0–65–1; May 27–3–92–4; Sleep 31–12–96–1. *Second Innings*—Gladigau 12–6–26–2; Smart 7–1–29–1; George 16–1–66–0; May 26–5–85–2; Sleep 20–8–30–1; Haysman 6–1–26–0.

South Australia

G. A. Bishop c M. D. Crowe b Chatfield	3	– (2) c Chatfield b Bracewell	123
A. M. J. Hilditch c Hadlee b Bracewell	34	– (1) run out	10
M. D. Haysman c and b Bracewell	43	– lbw b Snedden	43
*D. W. Hookes c J. J. Crowe b Bracewell	128	– (7) b Bracewell	7
†W. B. Phillips lbw b Bracewell	0	– b Snedden	75
P. R. Sleep b Bracewell	6	– c Rutherford b Bracewell	25
D. F. G. O'Connor b Bracewell	13	– (4) lbw b Hadlee	42
T. B. A. May run out	1	– not out	42
P. W. Gladigau b Patel	10	– not out	2
H. W. G. Smart c J. J. Crowe b Bracewell	1		
S. P. George not out	0		
W 1, n-b 2	3	B 7, l-b 7, n-b 3	17
1/10 2/71 3/103 4/103 5/131 6/201 7/216 8/232 9/242	242	1/46 2/164 3/192 4/299 5/313 6/324 7/382 (7 wkts)	386

Bowling: *First Innings*—Hadlee 14–3–42–0; Chatfield 15–6–24–1; Snedden 13–2–42–0; Bracewell 31–4–98–7; Patel 14.3–4–36–1. *Second Innings*—Hadlee 34.2–6–102–1; Chatfield 21–5–62–0; Snedden 19–2–40–2; Bracewell 35–8–116–3; Patel 11–0–52–0.

Umpires: A. R. Crafter and D. J. Harper.

AUSTRALIA v NEW ZEALAND

First Test Match

At Brisbane, December 4, 5, 6, 7. Australia won by nine wickets with a day to spare. Border, playing on his home ground, had no hesitation in fielding when he won the toss. On a pitch slightly under-prepared owing to torrential rain, the New Zealanders lost Rutherford to the fourth ball of the match, Veletta marking his début with a catch at forward short leg from his first touch of the ball. They crawled to 48 for two by lunch, and only Martin Crowe, with 67 from 163 balls, held an end up as all crashed around him. The innings finished a quarter of an hour into the second morning, whereupon Boon took his first chance in what was to be a golden season for him. As Australia totalled 305, he made 143 in 342 minutes from 255 deliveries, hitting fifteen fours. The New Zealand fast bowler, Morrison, a product of D. K. Lillee's personal coaching scheme and the game's other Test newcomer, returned a respectable four for 86 from 28 overs, while Hadlee moved ahead of Lillee as the second-highest wicket-taker in Test cricket when he dismissed Marsh. In reply, New Zealand had only a sparkling cameo innings by Patel to save them from a worse defeat. Jones batted for two hours twenty minutes for 45, but Patel's ninth-wicket partnership of 52 in an hour with Morrison gave the crowd a modicum of fun on the fourth day. Requiring less than 100 for victory, Australia won with ease at 3.47 p.m. to claim two Test wins in succession for the first time in four years and avenge the innings defeat by New Zealand at Brisbane two years earlier. The attendance of 28,153 for the four days was nearly double that at the corresponding match in 1985.

Man of the Match: D. C. Boon.

Close of play: First day, New Zealand 181-9 (J. G. Bracewell 6*); Second day, Australia 219-6 (P. R. Sleep 0*); Third day, New Zealand 131-5 (D. N. Patel 8*, R. J. Hadlee 17*).

New Zealand

First innings		Second innings	
K. R. Rutherford c Veletta b Reid	0	(2) c Dyer b McDermott	2
J. G. Wright c Dyer b Hughes	38	(1) lbw b Reid	15
A. H. Jones b McDermott	4	c Border b Reid	45
M. D. Crowe c Waugh b Hughes	67	c Jones b Hughes	23
*J. J. Crowe lbw b Waugh	16	lbw b Reid	12
D. N. Patel c Dyer b McDermott	17	c Dyer b Hughes	62
R. J. Hadlee c Boon b Hughes	8	c Marsh b McDermott	24
J. G. Bracewell c Veletta b McDermott	11	c Dyer b McDermott	0
†I. D. S. Smith lbw b Reid	2	c Veletta b Reid	9
D. K. Morrison c Waugh b McDermott	0	c Dyer b Waugh	2
E. J. Chatfield not out	0	not out	1
B 1, l-b 7, w 4, n-b 11	23	B 6, l-b 1, w 1, n-b 9	17
1/0 2/28 3/80 4/133 5/143 6/153 7/175 8/180 9/181	186	1/18 2/20 3/66 4/103 5/104 6/142 7/142 8/152 9/204	212

Bowling: *First Innings*—Reid 25–10–40–2; McDermott 22.2–6–43–4; Hughes 18–5–40–3; Waugh 22–9–35–1; Sleep 6–1–20–0. *Second Innings*—Reid 25–6–53–4; McDermott 21–2–79–3; Hughes 17–7–57–2; Sleep 14–5–14–0; Waugh 2–1–2–1.

Australia

First innings		Second innings	
G. R. Marsh c Bracewell b Hadlee	25	(2) not out	31
D. C. Boon run out	143	(1) lbw b Bracewell	24
D. M. Jones b Hadlee	2	not out	38
*A. R. Border lbw b Morrison	9		
M. R. J. Veletta c Rutherford b Bracewell	4		
S. R. Waugh c Jones b Morrison	21		
P. R. Sleep c and b Bracewell	39		
†G. C. Dyer lbw b Hadlee	8		
C. J. McDermott c Wright b Morrison	22		
M. G. Hughes c Smith b Morrison	5		
B. A. Reid not out	8		
B 3, l-b 5, w 2, n-b 9	19	L-b 1, w 1, n-b 2	4
1/65 2/72 3/110 4/131 5/219 6/219 7/250 8/286 9/291	305	1/37	(1 wkt) 97

Bowling: *First Innings*—Hadlee 31–5–95–3; Morrison 28–7–86–4; Chatfield 34–11–58–0; Bracewell 24.5–3–58–2. *Second Innings*—Hadlee 8–3–14–0; Morrison 8–0–32–0; Bracewell 13–3–32–1; Patel 3.1–0–18–0.

Umpires: A. R. Crafter and M. W. Johnson.

AUSTRALIA v NEW ZEALAND

Second Test Match

At Adelaide, December 11, 12, 13, 14, 15. Drawn. A lifeless pitch ensured that any other result would be virtually impossible, and in intense heat, watched by 30,083 spectators, one of the dullest Test matches seen in Australia was played out. In an attempt to regain his form, the New Zealand captain, Jeff Crowe, chose to open the innings. But, having won the toss, he lasted just three balls before looping a delivery from Reid to Veletta at forward short leg. Wright and Jones added 128, after which Martin Crowe and Jones took the score to 268 at stumps on the first day with Jones, in his third Test, having hit his maiden Test century. Next morning Crowe became his country's leading century-maker in Tests when he reached his eighth from 130 balls. Their third-wicket partnership of 213 in 234 minutes was broken threequarters of an hour before lunch when Crowe fell to a catch at extra-cover, having made 137 from 184 balls with seventeen fours and a six. Jones ground his way on to become only the nineteenth New Zealander to reach 150 in Tests. Having been in for almost seven and a half hours he was run out by a superb throw from McDermott, whose figures of four for 135 from 45.5 overs of fast bowling do not tell the full story of his effort in century-plus temperatures. Australia had lost Reid early in the match, the left-arm swing bowler going off with a back injury, and McDermott had to carry the attack.

The third day saw an incident which will remain indelibly in the memory as an example of sportsmanship of the highest level. Jeff Crowe, taking the ball low down at wide mid-on from Patel's bowling, signalled "no catch" to what appeared to have been Border's dismissal for 66. Only Crowe knew if it was a catch or not, for not even the prying eyes of the nine television cameras were able to pass judgement. It was unfortunate that the opposite would happen during the next Test. After his let-off Border, who might also have been stumped when 57, reached his 22nd century for Australia in his 91st Test, and in doing so he passed the Test aggregates of Sir Leonard Hutton (6,971) and Sir Donald Bradman (6,996). Next day he overtook G. S. Chappell's 7,110 runs to claim the Australian record and become the seventh-highest run-maker in Test cricket. His 205 in ten hours, from 485 balls and containing twenty boundaries, was a career-best score. Later Border said: "To pass Sir Donald's total is a great achievement, but you have to get it in its true perspective. It's taken me nearly twice as long as the little fellow. It's just mind-boggling as to how good he must have been."

With Waugh, Sleep and Dyer all hitting half-centuries, the Australians amassed 496 – an 11-run lead – before Hadlee dismissed Reid on the final morning to finish with five or more wickets in a Test innings for the 30th time. New Zealand used the rest of the day in match practice and the local spin attack of May and Sleep took three wickets each.

Man of the Match: A. R. Border.

Close of play: First day, New Zealand 268-2 (A. H. Jones 128*, M. D. Crowe 88*); Second day, Australia 17-0 (G. R. Marsh 5*, D. C. Boon 6*); Third day, Australia 225-4 (A. R. Border 105*, P. R. Sleep 6*); Fourth day, Australia 496-9 (T. B. A. May 14*, B. A. Reid 5*).

New Zealand

First innings		Second innings	
*J. J. Crowe c Veletta b Reid	0	– c Boon b May	19
J. G. Wright c Waugh b May	45	– b McDermott	8
A. H. Jones run out	150	– c Border b Sleep	64
M. D. Crowe c sub (M. G. Hughes) b Sleep	137	– c Border b Sleep	8
D. N. Patel c Marsh b McDermott	35	– c Boon b May	40
E. J. Gray c Boon b McDermott	23	– c Border b May	14
R. J. Hadlee c and b Jones	36	– (9) not out	3
J. G. Bracewell c Sleep b McDermott	32		
†I. D. S. Smith not out	8	– (8) c Dyer b Sleep	5
M. C. Snedden c Veletta b McDermott	0	– (7) not out	8
B 3, l-b 7, w 1, n-b 8	19	B 2, l-b 4, n-b 7	13
1/0 2/128 3/341 4/346 5/398 6/405 7/473 8/481 9/485	(9 wkts dec.) 485	1/16 2/57 3/77 4/139 5/153 6/170 7/179	(7 wkts) 182

D. K. Morrison did not bat.

Bowling: *First Innings*—Reid 7–0–21–1; McDermott 45.5–10–135–4; Waugh 31–11–71–0; May 54–13–134–1; Sleep 34–5–109–1; Jones 3–1–5–1. *Second Innings*—McDermott 10–3–29–1; Waugh 10–4–17–0; Sleep 32–14–61–3; May 30–10–68–3; Jones 3–2–1–0.

Australia

G. R. Marsh c Gray b Hadlee	30
D. C. Boon b Hadlee	6
D. M. Jones c Smith b Hadlee	0
*A. R. Border st Smith b Bracewell	205
S. R. Waugh lbw b Snedden	61
P. R. Sleep c Smith b Morrison	62
M. R. J. Veletta c sub (K. R. Rutherford) b Bracewell	10
†G. C. Dyer run out	60
C. J. McDermott lbw b Hadlee	18
T. B. A. May not out	14
B. A. Reid c Smith b Hadlee	5
B 2, l-b 13, w 1, n-b 9	25
1/29 2/29 3/85 4/201 5/355 6/380 7/417 8/451 9/489	496

Bowling: Hadlee 42–16–68–5; Morrison 22–0–89–1; Bracewell 48–8–122–2; Snedden 32–6–89–1; Gray 44–10–102–0; Patel 7–3–11–0.

Umpires: R. C. Bailhache and S. G. Randell.

TASMANIA v NEW ZEALANDERS

At Devonport, December 18, 19, 20, 21. Drawn. Toss: New Zealanders. On one of the best surfaces in Australia, Horne, an opening batsman and a New Zealand international badminton player, compiled a determined 125 against a weak Tasmanian attack. His sixteen boundaries, in just under five hours at the crease, formed an innings which won him his third Test cap a week later. A defiant 85 by Taylor in exactly three hours helped the home team finish 105 runs in arrears, and the young Tasmanians then shocked their visitors by dismissing them for 143 to set up the opportunity of an unlikely victory. However, the target of 249 in 79 overs proved beyond them and New Zealand were closer to winning at the end, defied by Boon who reached his hundred in the final over. The Tasmanian wicket-keeper Soule's nine dismissals in the match were a state record, passing the seven of G. Henty in 1927-28 and R. D. Woolley in 1982-83.

Close of play: First day, New Zealanders 327-6 (E. J. Gray 9*, I. D. S. Smith 30*); Second day, Tasmania 170-4 (M. D. Taylor 55*, B. A. Cruse 32*); Third day, New Zealanders 108-6 (E. J. Gray 3*, I. D. S. Smith 4*).

New Zealanders

J. G. Wright c Cooley b Faulkner	32	– b Bower	30
P. A. Horne c Soule b Faulkner	125	– c Soule b Cooley	35
A. H. Jones c Soule b Faulkner	14	– (5) lbw b Faulkner	4
K. R. Rutherford st Soule b Cruse	34	– c Faulkner b Cooley	3
*J. J. Crowe run out	36	– (3) c Soule b Faulkner	10
D. N. Patel c Soule b Hughes	29	– c Soule b Faulkner	0
E. J. Gray not out	24	– c Soule b Cooley	26
†I. D. S. Smith b Bower	62	– c Boon b Bower	10
D. K. Morrison retired hurt	5	– (10) run out	1
W. Watson not out	27	– (9) c Soule b Faulkner	0
E. J. Chatfield (did not bat)		– not out	4
L-b 12, n-b 10	22	B 5, l-b 10, w 1, n-b 4	20
1/61 2/79 3/170 4/248 5/269 6/293 7/370 (7 wkts dec.)	410	1/42 2/83 3/91 4/97 5/97 6/101 7/116 8/117 9/137	143

Bowling: *First Innings*—Cooley 26–4–96–0; Bower 31–4–98–1; Faulkner 33–11–77–3; Cruse 17–1–68–1; Hughes 14–2–59–1. *Second Innings*—Cooley 16.5–2–47–3; Bower 15–2–44–2; Faulkner 24–11–37–4.

Tasmania

D. C. Boon lbw b Gray	44	– (2) not out	101
N. Jelich c Wright b Chatfield	0	– (1) lbw b Morrison	3
G. A. Hughes c Wright b Watson	27	– b Chatfield	26
M. D. Taylor c Smith b Chatfield	85	– lbw b Chatfield	1
D. J. Buckingham b Gray	5	– c Smith b Chatfield	13
B. A. Cruse c Jones b Patel	32	– (8) c and b Gray	4
P. I. Faulkner c Smith b Morrison	46	– c Morrison b Gray	10
†R. E. Soule c Smith b Watson	17	– (9) b Gray	6
*B. F. Davison not out	30	– (6) c J. J. Crowe b Watson	23
T. J. Cooley c Smith b Morrison	4	– not out	7
T. D. Bower c J. J. Crowe b Morrison	2		
L-b 5, n-b 8	13	L-b 8, n-b 6	14
1/8 2/65 3/84 4/98 5/170 6/217 7/258 8/285 9/289	305	1/4 2/68 3/70 4/94 (8 wkts) 5/134 6/167 7/174 8/186	208

Bowling: *First Innings*—Morrison 19.5–1–85–3; Chatfield 30–10–60–2; Watson 20–2–72–2; Gray 15–7–28–2; Patel 17–2–55–1. *Second Innings*—Morrison 12–2–42–1; Chatfield 29–7–52–3; Watson 16–2–46–1; Gray 22–4–60–3.

Umpires: S. G. Randell and D. R. Close.

†At Canberra, December 23. New Zealanders won by 37 runs. Toss: New Zealanders. New Zealanders 201 (49.5 overs) (K. R. Rutherford 63, J. G. Bracewell 39; G. Irvine five for 42); Prime Minister's XI 164 (46.2 overs) (M. A. Taylor 32, G. R. J. Matthews 34, M. E. Waugh 35; J. G. Bracewell four for 40).

AUSTRALIA v NEW ZEALAND

Third Test Match

At Melbourne, December 26, 27, 28, 29, 30. Drawn. The 24th Test between these two countries contained all the ingredients of a classic match, including not just exciting performances but also controversy and a heroic finish. The 127,184 spectators could not have wished for more. Put in to bat, the New Zealanders had reached 119 for one when, half an hour before tea, Jones edged a delivery from McDermott and watched as the Australian wicket-keeper, Dyer, rolled over then showed the ball in his raised right hand, indicating a clean catch. Umpire Crafter, sensing something was amiss, delayed his decision until umpire French at square leg indicated that the ball had carried. But television replays showed the ball bouncing out of Dyer's gloves and on to the ground, with the wicket-keeper scooping the ball back into his gloves before appealing. Wright, the New Zealand vice-captain, batted for 310 minutes before flashing outside off-stump, having hit ten fours in his 99. He thus became the third New Zealander to fall 1 run short of a Test hundred, following J. E. F. Beck (v South Africa, 1953-54) and R. J. Hadlee (v England 1983-84).

Continuing from their overnight 242 for five, the tourists soon lost Martin Crowe for 82, from 147 deliveries, and needed Smith's 44 to see them to 317. Then it was the turn of Hadlee to show his skills. He took four for 62 in three spells which left Australia precariously placed at 170 for five at the end of the second day. Waugh fell without addition on the third morning; but Sleep with 90 in 310 minutes (256 balls) and Dodemaide, who was to follow his début half-century with six wickets, put on a record 61 for the ninth wicket to give Australia a first-innings lead of 40 runs. New Zealand's openers remained unbeaten for almost two hours; but once Dodemaide had effected a breakthrough, only Martin Crowe, with a fine 79 in just under two hours, including twelve fours, seemed able to guide his country's batting. When he reached 34, he became only the seventh player, and the first since L. Hutton in 1948, to score 4,000 first-class runs in a calendar year, while the catch that ended his innings was Border's 100th in Tests.

By dismissing New Zealand for 286 from the third ball of the final day, Australia had allowed themselves a minimum of 92 overs to score 247 for victory. At 176 for four, with Waugh and Veletta looking confident, they needed only 71 to win with 28 overs left. But at 5.17 p.m., when the score was 199 for five, Hadlee was brought back into the attack. Until the finish at 6.49 p.m. he gave his all for his country as 23,859 spectators watched in suspense. Elsewhere Australians were glued to their television sets; even the high-rating quiz shows were cancelled for the evening.

The wickets fell: Sleep at 209, Veletta at 209, Dyer at 216, and Dodemaide at 227. Hadlee had taken ten wickets in a Test match for a record eighth time, passing S. F. Barnes, C. V. Grimmett and D. K. Lillee, all with seven, and needed just one more wicket to pass I. T. Botham's record of 373 wickets in Tests. However, the last Australian pair, McDermott and Whitney, held out for 4.5 overs to claim a draw and give Australia the Trans-Tasman Trophy for the first time. When Whitney, playing in his first Test since 1981, dug out Hadlee's final ball of the match, the New Zealand fast bowler walked down the pitch to the exuberant batsman, put an arm around his shoulder and shook his hand. It was a sporting gesture of the highest order, and Hadlee's nomination as both Man of the Match and Man of the Series was greeted with spontaneous applause from an emotionally drained crowd.

Close of play: First day, New Zealand 242-5 (M. D. Crowe 76*, J. G. Bracewell 4*); Second day, Australia 170-5 (S. R. Waugh 55*, P. R. Sleep 16*); Third day, New Zealand 0-0 (P. A. Horne 0*, J. G. Wright 0*); Fourth day, New Zealand 285-9 (I. D. S. Smith 12*, E. J. Chatfield 0*).

New Zealand

First innings		Second innings	
P. A. Horne c Dyer b Dodemaide	7	c Boon b Dodemaide	27
J. G. Wright c Dyer b McDermott	99	b Sleep	43
A. H. Jones c Dyer b McDermott	40	run out	20
M. D. Crowe c Veletta b McDermott	82	c Border b Dodemaide	79
*J. J. Crowe lbw b McDermott	6	c Boon b Sleep	25
D. N. Patel b McDermott	0	c Dyer b Dodemaide	38
J. G. Bracewell c Dyer b Whitney	9	(8) c Veletta b Dodemaide	1
R. J. Hadlee c Dodemaide b Whitney	11	(7) lbw b Sleep	29
†I. D. S. Smith c Jones b Whitney	44	c Dyer b Dodemaide	12
D. K. Morrison c Border b Whitney	0	b Dodemaide	0
E. J. Chatfield not out	6	not out	1
B 1, l-b 4, n-b 8	13	B 2, l-b 8, n-b 1	11
1/32 2/119 3/187 4/221 5/223 6/254 7/254 8/280 9/294	317	1/73 2/76 3/158 4/178 5/220 6/272 7/272 8/281 9/285	286

Bowling: *First Innings*—McDermott 35–8–97–5; Whitney 33.3–6–92–4; Dodemaide 20–4–48–1; Waugh 10–1–44–0; Sleep 12–1–31–0. *Second Innings*—McDermott 10–1–43–0; Whitney 20–5–45–0; Dodemaide 28.3–10–58–6; Sleep 26–5–107–3; Jones 8–3–23–0.

Australia

First innings		Second innings	
D. C. Boon lbw b Hadlee	10	(2) c M. D. Crowe b Morrison	54
G. R. Marsh c sub (K. R. Rutherford) b Hadlee	13	(1) c Bracewell b Hadlee	23
D. M. Jones c Smith b Hadlee	4	c M. D. Crowe b Chatfield	8
*A. R. Border c J. J. Crowe b Bracewell	31	lbw b Hadlee	43
M. R. J. Veletta lbw b Hadlee	31	c Patel b Bracewell	39
S. R. Waugh c Jones b Bracewell	55	c Patel b Chatfield	10
P. R. Sleep lbw b Hadlee	90	lbw b Hadlee	20
†G. C. Dyer run out	21	c Smith b Hadlee	4
A. I. C. Dodemaide c Smith b Morrison	50	lbw b Hadlee	3
C. J. McDermott b Morrison	33	not out	10
M. R. Whitney not out	0	not out	2
L-b 8, n-b 11	19	B 1, l-b 9, n-b 4	14
1/24 2/30 3/31 4/78 5/121 6/170 7/213 8/293 9/354	357	1/45 2/59 3/103 4/147 5/176 6/209 7/209 8/216 9/227	(9 wkts) 230

Bowling: *First Innings*—Hadlee 44–11–109–5; Morrison 27.4–5–93–2; Chatfield 30–10–55–0; Bracewell 32–8–69–2; Patel 12–6–23–0. *Second Innings*—Hadlee 31–9–67–5; Morrison 16–2–54–1; Chatfield 21–6–41–2; Bracewell 24–5–58–1.

Umpires: A. R. Crafter and R. A. French.

New Zealand's matches v Australia and Sri Lanka in the Benson and Hedges World Series Cup (January 3–January 24) may be found in that section.

THE SRI LANKANS IN AUSTRALIA, 1987-88

By CHRIS HARTE

A new-look Sri Lankan team, containing only eight of the players who had represented their country in the recent World Cup, arrived in Perth two days before Christmas to participate in the triangular World Series Cup tournament and then play their first Test match in Australia. Notable among the absentees were Duleep Mendis, who had led his country in nineteen Tests and 60 one-day internationals and was, along with Sidath Wettimuny, its most-capped player; Roy Dias, who with twenty caps had played in three Tests fewer than these two; Vinothen John and Rumesh Ratnayake. The 35-year-old Mendis had declared himself unavailable for business reasons and to devote more time to his family. His successor as captain was 28-year-old Ranjan Madugalle, who had played in nineteen Test matches, including Sri Lanka's inaugural Test against England in February 1982.

Undertaking an itinerary to which little thought had been given, the Sri Lankans started with a one-day win over Western Australia. But their only other noteworthy success was a World Series Cup victory over New Zealand on Hobart's new Bellerive Oval. Their two first-class matches up to the Test were drawn, with Tasmania holding the slight advantage in Hobart and the Sri Lankans considerably on top against Victoria in Melbourne.

The Test match, in Perth, attracted so little interest that only the first session of play each day was televised nationally. The daily attendance figures of 3,761, 3,566, 3,030 and 250 – a total of 10,607 – amounted to the lowest attendance at a Test in Australia since 1887-88 and was the fourth lowest on record. As the Australian captain, Allan Border, was prompted to remark, his state team, Queensland, attracted more spectators to a single day's play than turned up for four in Perth. Just an hour and a quarter of the fourth day was all Australia required to complete a convincing victory by an innings and 108 runs.

SRI LANKAN TOUR RESULTS

Test match – Played 1: Lost 1.
First-class matches – Played 3: Lost 1, Drawn 2.
Loss – Australia.
Draws – Tasmania, Victoria.
One-day internationals – Played 8: Won 1, Lost 7. *Win* – New Zealand. *Losses* – Australia (4), New Zealand (3).
Other non first-class matches – Played 7: Won 5, Lost 1, Drawn 1. *Wins* – Western Australia, Western Australian Country XI, Australian Country XI, Northern Territory Invitation XI, Victorian Country XI. *Loss* – South Australia. *Draw* – Western Australia.

SRI LANKAN AVERAGES – FIRST-CLASS MATCHES

BATTING

	M	*I*	*NO*	*R*	*HI*	*100s*	*Avge*
A. P. Gurusinha	2	3	0	164	118	1	54.66
J. R. Ratnayeke	2	4	1	130	39*	0	43.33
A. Ranatunga	3	5	0	191	68	0	38.20

	M	*I*	*NO*	*R*	*HI*	*100s*	*Avge*
R. S. Mahanama	3	5	0	158	51	0	31.60
R. S. Madugalle	3	5	0	123	56	0	24.60
P. A. de Silva	3	5	0	92	69	0	18.40
R. G. de Alwis	2	4	1	40	30*	0	13.33
D. S. B. P. Kuruppu	3	5	0	65	22	0	13.00
G. F. Labrooy	3	4	0	43	25	0	10.75
S. M. S. Kaluperuma ...	2	3	0	32	26	0	10.66
C. P. H. Ramanayake ...	3	4	0	33	15	0	8.25

Played in two matches: S. Jeganathan 2*, 3*. Played in one match: K. N. Amalean 7*, 0*; M. A. R. Samarasekera 4.

* *Signifies not out.*

BOWLING

	O	*M*	*R*	*W*	*BB*	*Avge*
G. F. Labrooy	89.5	21	236	10	7-71	23.60
K. N. Amalean	22.2	1	97	4	4-97	24.25
A. Ranatunga	38	6	106	4	3-66	26.50
J. R. Ratnayeke	66	11	177	5	4-98	35.40
C. P. H. Ramanayake .	70	9	253	5	3-99	50.60

Also bowled: P. A. de Silva 22–1–81–1; S. Jeganathan 34.1–2–124–2; S. M. S. Kaluperuma 26–3–108–0; M. A. R. Samarasekera 5.5–1–11–0.

FIELDING

4 – R. G. de Alwis; 2 – P. A. de Silva, G. F. Labrooy; 1 – K. N. Amalean, A. P. Gurusinha, D. S. B. P. Kuruppu, R. S. Mahanama, C. P. H. Ramanayake, A. Ranatunga.

†At Perth, December 26 (day/night). Sri Lankans won by 61 runs. Toss: Western Australia. Sri Lankans 291 for five (49 overs) (R. S. Mahanama 64, P. A. de Silva 112, A. Ranatunga 51); Western Australia 230 for nine (49 overs) (T. M. Moody 45, G. Shipperd 49, T. J. Zoehrer 39; P. A. de Silva three for 49).

†At Perth, December 28, 29. Drawn. Toss: Western Australia. Western Australia 484 for eight dec. (G. Shipperd 64, M. W. McPhee 131, T. M. Moody 57, W. S. Andrews 70. K. J. Hughes 46, T. G. Breman 71 not out; P. A. de Silva four for 109); Sri Lankans 382 for seven (A. P. Gurusinha 202, D. S. B. P. Kuruppu 40, P. A. de Silva 52, M. A. R. Samarasekera 55).

†At Mandurah, December 31. Sri Lankans won by 143 runs. Toss: Western Australian Country XI. Sri Lankans 245 for five (45 overs) (A. Ranatunga 106 not out, D. S. B. P. Kuruppu 51); Western Australian Country XI 102 (42.2 overs) (G. Lang 31; S. Jeganathan three for 20, S. M. S. Kaluperuma four for 15).

Sri Lanka's matches v Australia and New Zealand in the Benson and Hedges World Series Cup (January 2–January 19) may be found in that section.

TASMANIA v SRI LANKANS

At Hobart, January 23, 24, 25. Drawn. Rain and bad light spoilt the first encounter between the teams. Having chosen to field first, the tourists lost Samarasekera on the first morning when he was carried from the ground after falling heavily and injuring his right ankle while bowling on the slippery pitch. Tasmania's declaration at five o'clock on the second day left the

Sri Lankans time for batting practice only, and after an uncertain start they used it effectively. The left-handed Gurusinha scored his country's initial first-class hundred in Australia, his 118 in 323 minutes (232 balls) including eight fours. His sixth-wicket partnership of 131 in 162 minutes with the captain, Madugalle, saw the Sri Lankans out of trouble.

Close of play: First day, Tasmania 85-1 (E. J. Harris 39*, N. C. P. Courtney 0*); Second day, Sri Lankans 32-2 (A. P. Gurusinha 9*, S. M. S. Kaluperuma 0*).

Tasmania

E. J. Harris lbw b Labrooy 56
G. A. Hughes b Ramanayake 39
N. C. P. Courtney c Labrooy b Jeganathan . 38
M. D. Taylor lbw b Ramanayake 5
D. J. Buckingham c Kuruppu b Ramanayake . 71
R. D. Woolley c de Silva b Jeganathan . 21
*P. I. Faulkner not out 69
†R. E. Soule not out 15
L-b 16, w 2, n-b 7 25

1/80 2/126 3/131 4/173 5/203 6/277 (6 wkts dec.) 339

T. J. Cooley, D. K. Lillee and C. M. Young did not bat.

Bowling: Labrooy 31–12–57–1; Ramanayake 31–6–99–3; Samarasekera 5.5–1–11–0; Jeganathan 25.1–2–83–2; Ranatunga 4–0–18–0; Kaluperuma 13–3–46–0; de Silva 3–0–9–0.

Sri Lankans

R. S. Mahanama c Harris b Cooley ... 5
†D. S. B. P. Kuruppu c Lillee b Cooley. 11
A. P. Gurusinha b Hughes 118
S. M. S. Kaluperuma lbw b Young 26
P. A. de Silva lbw b Young 0
A. Ranatunga c Hughes b Lillee 14
*R. S. Madugalle lbw b Faulkner 56
M. A. R. Samarasekera c Cooley b Hughes . 4
G. F. Labrooy c Harris b Cooley 25
C. P. H. Ramanayake c Faulkner b Cooley . 15
S. Jeganathan not out 2
L-b 7, w 6, n-b 14 27

1/10 2/32 3/79 4/85 5/112 6/243 7/252 8/257 9/297 303

Bowling: Lillee 24–9–58–1; Cooley 22.1–1–95–4; Faulkner 19–3–55–1; Young 12–4–42–2; Harris 5–0–26–0; Hughes 10–5–20–2.

Umpires: M. G. Gandy and D. R. Gregg.

†At Canberra, January 27. Sri Lankans won by 14 runs. Toss: Australian Country XI. Sri Lankans 238 for six (49 overs) (A. Ranatunga 78, A. P. Gurusinha 95; G. Irvine four for 49); Australian Country XI 224 for nine (49 overs) (G. Phillips 39, M. Curry 37, T. Waldron 44; G. F. Labrooy three for 53).

†At Alice Springs, January 30. Sri Lankans won by 115 runs. Toss: Northern Territory Invitation XI. Sri Lankans 251 for five (50 overs) (D. S. B. P. Kuruppu 34, P. A. de Silva 70, A. Ranatunga 84); Northern Territory Invitation XI 136 (43.3 overs) (C. P. H. Ramanayake four for 12).

†At Alice Springs, January 31. South Australia won by six wickets. Toss: Sri Lankans. Sri Lankans 131 (39.3 overs) (Extras 30); South Australia 132 for four (39.1 overs) (A. M. J. Hilditch 53 not out, D. F. G. O'Connor 39; P. A. de Silva three for 38).

†At Bendigo, February 3. Sri Lankans won by 110 runs. Toss: Victorian Country XI. Sri Lankans 262 for five (50 overs) (D. S. B. P. Kuruppu 33, R. S. Mahanama 61, A. P. Gurusinha 116 not out); Victorian Country XI 152 (47.5 overs) (R. Schultz 44, B. Tippett 30, R. Bott 30 not out; G. F. Labrooy four for 26).

VICTORIA v SRI LANKANS

At Melbourne, February 6, 7, 8, 9. Drawn. The Victorian public showed little interest in the match, with only 2,360 attending over the four days. Put in on a damp pitch, which delayed he start, the Sri Lankans were dismissed from what became the final ball of the first day. On he second day, Labrooy claimed seven wickets in only his fourth first-class match as Victoria failed by 11 runs to match the visitors' total. However, a poisoned toe prevented the young Sri Lankan swing bowler from bowling in the second innings when Victoria set out to score 374 from 73 overs. Watts and Siddons, the latter getting off the mark with a six over long-on, added 198 in 165 minutes for the third wicket, but with only four and a half hours provided for on the last day the eventual draw had always seemed the likeliest result.

Close of play: First day, Sri Lankans 157; Second day, Sri Lankans 79-1 (R. S. Mahanama 0*, A. P. Gurusinha 12*); Third day, Sri Lankans 362-6 (J. R. Ratnayeke 39*, R. G. de Alwis 30*).

Sri Lankans

R. S. Mahanama c Dodemaide b Davis	33	– lbw b Reiffel	51
D. S. B. P. Kuruppu c Dimattina b Reiffel	10	– c Young b Davis	22
A. P. Gurusinha c Dimattina b Davis	11	– c Whatmore b Davis	35
P. A. de Silva c Siddons b Reiffel	10	– c and b Davis	69
A. Ranatunga c Dimattina b Davis	9	– c Reiffel b Hughes	68
*R. S. Madugalle b Davis	20	– b Dodemaide	34
J. R. Ratnayeke c Dimattina b Hughes	29	– not out	39
†R. G. de Alwis run out	2	– not out	30
C. P. H. Ramanayake c Whatmore b Davis	9		
G. F. Labrooy c Dimattina b Dodemaide	10		
S. Jeganathan not out	3		
L-b 4, w 4, n-b 3	11	L-b 8, w 1, n-b 5	14
1/26 2/40 3/67 4/78 5/87 6/119 7/122 8/136 9/145	157	1/53 2/101 3/170 4/191 5/288 6/292	(6 wkts dec.) 362

Bowling: *First Innings*—Hughes 19–3–56–1; Reiffel 15–4–30–2; Dodemaide 11.5–5–17–1; Davis 20–8–50–5. *Second Innings*—Hughes 27–3–83–1; Reiffel 24–3–94–1; Dodemaide 22–9–48–1; Davis 24–6–57–3; Jackson 9–1–44–0; Young 6–1–13–0; Watts 6–0–15–0.

Victoria

D. F. Whatmore c de Alwis b Labrooy	5	– lbw b Ramanayake	0
G. M. Watts b Ranatunga	30	– b Ranatunga	122
D. M. Jones b Labrooy	6	– b Ranatunga	35
J. D. Siddons lbw b Labrooy	4	– c Mahanama b Ranatunga	103
*. W. Young c Gurusinha b Labrooy	0	– (6) not out	9
A. I. C. Dodemaide lbw b Ramanayake	32	– (7) not out	14
†M. G. D. Dimattina c Ranatunga b Labrooy	22		
. W. Jackson lbw b Ratnayeke	1		
M. G. Hughes c de Alwis b Labrooy	15	– (5) lbw b de Silva	0
P. R. Reiffel not out	6		
S. P. Davis c de Silva b Labrooy	3		
L-b 8, w 2, n-b 12	22	L-b 8, w 1, n-b 5	14
1/5 2/28 3/32 4/32 5/58 6/99 7/115 8/117 9/138	146	1/2 2/69 3/267 4/269 5/275	(5 wkts) 297

Bowling: *First Innings*—Ratnayeke 13–4–19–1; Labrooy 22.5–4–71–7; Ramanayake 2–1–44–1; Ranatunga 6–3–4–1. *Second Innings*—Ratnayeke 13–1–60–0; Ramanayake 0–0–52–1; Ranatunga 20–1–66–3; Jeganathan 9–0–41–0; de Silva 18–1–70–1.

Umpires: R. Guy and D. E. Holden.

AUSTRALIA v SRI LANKA

Test Match

At Perth, February 12, 13, 14, 15. Australia won by an innings and 108 runs. A one-sided match, written off by the media as "a waste of time", lived up to all the forecasts. Sri Lanka were hopelessly outplayed, and had Border, captaining his country for the 31st consecutive time, put greater pressure on his team, the winning margin would have been greater. Despite the ease of the win, he later criticised his players for their lack of application; the Australians put down several catches in the two Sri Lankan innings.

Border chose to bat on winning the toss, whereupon Boon and Marsh put together their fifth century opening stand in Tests. The highlight of the day was the partnership for the third wicket between Jones and Border, who added 156 in 151 minutes. Border missed out on the century that was there for the taking, but Jones recorded his third Test hundred in the last over of the day. Dropped at mid-wicket when 98, he ran 2 from the shot to reach three figures.

An improved bowling effort by the Sri Lankans, who used seven bowlers in the innings, restricted the Australians to only 122 runs on the second day and dismissed them midway through the afternoon. However, only Mahanama of their early batsmen looked comfortable against the pace, movement and bounce of McDermott and Hughes, and next day the match was settled in the strange atmosphere of a practically deserted ground. Ranatunga resisted for just over two and threequarter hours for his half-century but Ratnayeke, with a blast of boundaries, was the only other batsman to score significantly before the innings ended and Sri Lanka were asked to follow on. By the close they had lost four more wickets, and next morning it took just 75 minutes for the Australians to wrap up the innings. Hughes claimed four of the wickets to finish with his first five-wicket return in a Test innings.

Man of the Match: D. M. Jones.

Close of play: First day, Australia 333-3 (D. M. Jones 100*, M. R. J. Veletta 10*); Second day, Sri Lanka 85-3 (R. S. Mahanama 37*, A. Ranatunga 11*); Third day, Sri Lanka 78-4 (A. Ranatunga 24*, R. S. Madugalle 5*).

Australia

G. R. Marsh b Labrooy	53
D. C. Boon b Ratnayeke	64
D. M. Jones lbw b Labrooy	102
*A. R. Border b Ratnayeke	88
M. R. J. Veletta c de Alwis b Ratnayeke	21
S. R. Waugh c Labrooy b Amalean	20
†G. C. Dyer c Ramanayake b Amalean	38
P. L. Taylor c Amalean b Ratnayeke	18
A. I. C. Dodemaide not out	16
C. J. McDermott c de Alwis b Amalean	4
M. G. Hughes b Amalean	8
L-b 12, w 5, n-b 6	23
1/120 2/133 3/289 4/346 5/346 6/380 7/418 8/434 9/443	455

Bowling: Ratnayeke 40–6–98–4; Labrooy 36–5–108–2; Ramanayake 17–2–58–0; Amalean 22.2–1–97–4; Kaluperuma 13–0–62–0; Ranatunga 8–2–18–0; de Silva 1–0–2–0.

Sri Lanka

R. S. Mahanama c Dyer b Dodemaide	41	run out	28
D. S. B. P. Kuruppu c Marsh b McDermott	19	c Dyer b Dodemaide	3
S. M. S. Kaluperuma lbw b McDermott	0	c and b Hughes	6
P. A. de Silva lbw b Waugh	6	lbw b Dodemaide	7
A. Ranatunga c and b Waugh	55	lbw b Dodemaide	45
*R. S. Madugalle c Border b Dodemaide	6	c Veletta b Hughes	7
J. R. Ratnayeke c Marsh b McDermott	24	c Dyer b Dodemaide	38
†R. G. de Alwis c Dyer b Waugh	0	c Waugh b Hughes	8
C. P. H. Ramanayake c Dyer b Waugh	9	c Veletta b Hughes	0
G. F. Labrooy c Dyer b Dodemaide	4	b Hughes	4
K. N. Amalean not out	7	not out	0
B 1, l-b 6, w 2, n-b 14	23	L-b 6, n-b 1	7
1/51 2/51 3/60 4/93 5/107 6/147 7/148 8/181 9/182	194	1/36 2/42 3/42 4/66 5/83 6/111 7/130 8/131 9/153	153

Bowling: *First Innings*—McDermott 20–3–50–3; Hughes 18–2–61–0; Dodemaide 22.3–6–40–3; Waugh 20–7–33–4; Taylor 2–1–3–0. *Second Innings*—McDermott 4–2–8–0; Hughes 21–7–67–5; Waugh 8–4–14–0; Dodemaide 19.1–7–58–4.

Umpires: R. C. Bailhache and P. J. McConnell.

THE PAKISTANIS IN THE WEST INDIES, 1987-88

By QAMAR AHMED

Pakistan's third tour of the West Indies produced an entertaining and absorbing series. Pakistan won the First Test, the Second was drawn, and West Indies won the Third to preserve their unbeaten record at home since 1972-73. It was a result that Pakistan could reflect on with pride, for not since the drawn 1973-74 rubber with England had West Indies failed to win a home series.

Yet there had been a time when Pakistan looked towards the tour with apprehension. Imran Khan, their captain and inspirational all-rounder, was in retirement, Wasim Akram was suffering from groin and hernia injuries which would require surgery before the tour, and Abdul Qadir's recurring kidney ailment was again troubling him. However, in mid-January Imran yielded to immense public pressure and a personal request from the President of Pakistan, General Zia-ul-Haq, to come out of retirement and lead the touring team. It was a decision which no-one regretted, for the Test series that followed was an epic one.

The early indications were not promising. While Imran, Wasim and Qadir were still regaining match fitness, Pakistan lost the one-day international series 5-0. Worse, Tauseef Ahmed, the economical off-spinner, returned home after only two games because of injury. Ijaz Faqih, an off-spinning all-rounder who had scored a hundred against India a year earlier, joined the team as a replacement. But once the Test matches began, Pakistan bounced back admirably. West Indies, without Vivian Richards, their captain, and Malcolm Marshall, were beaten in four days at Georgetown, with Imran producing a morale-boosting match return of eleven for 121. The four-day match against a West Indies Under-23 XI was won by 211 runs, and in the Second Test, at Port-of-Spain, Pakistan chased a target of 372 with much verve before Qadir played out the final five deliveries to secure the draw in a nail-biting finish. At Barbados, an unbroken ninth-wicket stand of 61 between Jeffrey Dujon and Winston Benjamin squared the series in a match of fluctuating fortunes and high drama.

Unfortunately, the tension at Kensington Oval overflowed into an unsavoury incident on the boundary on the last morning. Qadir, after having appeals against Dujon and Benjamin turned down by umpire Archer, became involved with a 21-year-old spectator, Albert Auguste. Infuriated at an insulting remark, he turned and threw a punch at the heckler, hitting him on the arm. Qadir later received a summons from the police, but with the matter being decided out of court for a settlement of $US1,000, Auguste did not press charges against the Pakistan leg-spinner.

That Pakistan became the first country to beat West Indies in a home Test since Australia in 1977-78 was due mainly to Imran's spirited performances with the ball and the masterly batting of Javed Miandad. Imran went on to finish the series with 23 wickets, the most by a bowler on either side, while Miandad, who had previously not scored a hundred against West Indies, followed his 114 in the First Test with 102 in the Second and was the leading run-getter in the series. These two, along with Mudassar Nazar and the manager, Intikhab Alam, had been on Pakistan's previous tour of the

Caribbean, in 1976-77. Then, twelve first-class matches were played, including five Tests. This time, the tour was not as well balanced.

After a single four-day game, Pakistan were pitched in against West Indies in the one-day international series. Another four-day game separated the fourth and fifth one-day internationals, and then came the First Test. It was not the ideal preparation for a team containing so many players without experience of the conditions. Moreover, in addition to the recently capped Aamer Malik, three players were making their first tours with the senior side: Moin-ul-Atiq, an opening batsman, and Naved Anjum and Haafiz Shahid, both fast-medium bowlers. Salim Yousuf, as against England on Pakistan's previous tour, showed the effectiveness of his cavalier batting under pressure, and Shoaib Mohammad, with a double-hundred against the Board XI at Georgetown and two half-centuries in the last Test, hinted that he might be justifying the faith placed in him. Qadir bowled well, but in patches, while Wasim, except for the final Test, was never fully fit.

Although Pakistan managed to make regular inroads into the West Indian batting, they invariably recovered (as did Pakistan) through their middle and lower order. The success of Dujon, Gus Logie and Carl Hooper at different times showed that West Indies were rebuilding solidly. Marshall and Benjamin were their leading wicket-takers, supported by Curtly Ambrose who, after an unimpressive Test début, improved as the series progressed.

The umpiring of the series, except for a few debatable decisions, was good; yet at the end of the series Imran, an admirer of West Indian umpiring, had become disenchanted. "Umpiring had been outstanding throughout the series", he said immediately after West Indies had levelled the rubber. "Unfortunately, during the second innings of the Bridgetown Test we were disappointed. Three vital mistakes went against us."

PAKISTANI TOUR RESULTS

Test matches – Played 3: Won 1, Lost 1, Drawn 1.
First-class matches – Played 6: Won 2, Lost 1, Drawn 3.
Wins – West Indies, West Indies Under-23 XI.
Loss – West Indies.
Draws – West Indies, WICBC President's XI, West Indies Board XI.
One-day internationals – Played 5: Lost 5.

TEST MATCH AVERAGES

WEST INDIES – BATTING

	T	*I*	*NO*	*R*	*HI*	*100s*	*Avge*
I. V. A. Richards	2	4	0	278	123	1	69.50
P. J. L. Dujon	3	6	2	185	106*	1	46.25
R. B. Richardson	3	6	0	240	75	0	40.00
C. L. Hooper	3	6	0	156	54	0	26.00
M. D. Marshall	2	4	1	75	48	0	25.00
C. G. Greenidge	3	6	0	135	43	0	22.50
A. L. Logie	3	6	0	126	80	0	21.00
W. K. M. Benjamin	3	6	1	89	40*	0	17.80
C. A. Walsh	3	5	1	52	14*	0	13.00
D. L. Haynes	3	6	0	75	48	0	12.50
C. E. L. Ambrose	3	6	2	47	25*	0	11.75

Played in one Test: B. P. Patterson 10, 0; P. V. Simmons 16, 11.

* *Signifies not out.*

BOWLING

	O	*M*	*R*	*W*	*BB*	*Avge*
I. V. A. Richards	17	4	44	3	2-17	14.66
M. D. Marshall	91.4	14	284	15	5-65	18.93
W. K. M. Benjamin	100	16	293	12	3-32	24.41
B. P. Patterson	26	1	101	4	3-82	25.25
C. E. L. Ambrose	114.2	18	365	7	2-64	52.14
C. L. Hooper	47.1	6	164	3	1-35	54.66
C. A. Walsh	86	15	230	4	3-80	57.50

PAKISTAN – BATTING

	T	*I*	*NO*	*R*	*HI*	*100s*	*Avge*
Javed Miandad	3	5	0	282	114	2	56.40
Salim Yousuf	3	5	1	196	62	0	49.00
Shoaib Mohammad	3	6	1	189	64	0	37.80
Salim Malik	3	5	0	147	66	0	29.40
Ijaz Ahmed	2	3	0	77	43	0	25.66
Ramiz Raja	3	6	1	126	54	0	25.20
Imran Khan	3	5	1	90	43*	0	22.50
Mudassar Nazar	3	6	0	115	41	0	19.16
Abdul Qadir	3	5	2	55	19	0	18.33
Wasim Akram	3	5	1	49	38	0	12.25
Ijaz Faqih	2	3	1	15	10*	0	7.50

Played in one Test: Aamer Malik 32, 2; Saleem Jaffer 1*, 4.

* *Signifies not out.*

BOWLING

	O	*M*	*R*	*W*	*BB*	*Avge*
Imran Khan	129.5	16	416	23	7-80	18.08
Wasim Akram	117	22	319	11	4-73	29.00
Abdul Qadir	162.4	21	538	14	4-83	38.42

Also bowled: Ijaz Faqih 36–4–133–2; Mudassar Nazar 16–6–36–2; Saleem Jaffer 12–1–60–1; Salim Malik 1–0–6–0; Shoaib Mohammad 8–1–22–2.

PAKISTANI AVERAGES – FIRST-CLASS MATCHES

BATTING

	M	*I*	*NO*	*R*	*HI*	*100s*	*Avge*
Javed Miandad	4	7	0	456	114	3	65.14
Shoaib Mohammad	5	10	2	461	208*	1	57.62
Naved Anjum	2	3	1	81	48	0	40.50
Ramiz Raja	5	10	1	338	82	0	37.55
Salim Yousuf	5	8	1	254	62	0	36.28
Salim Malik	6	11	1	334	86	0	33.40
Ijaz Ahmed	5	9	1	236	84	0	29.50
Mudassar Nazar	6	11	1	272	72	0	27.20
Aamer Malik	4	8	0	200	51	0	25.00
Wasim Akram	4	7	2	121	56*	0	24.20
Imran Khan	5	8	1	167	44	0	23.85
Ijaz Faqih	3	5	1	76	51	0	19.00
Haafiz Shahid	2	3	0	47	37	0	15.66
Abdul Qadir	5	8	2	72	19	0	12.00
Saleem Jaffer	2	4	3	9	4	0	9.00

Played in one match: Moin-ul-Atiq 38, 22; Tauseef Ahmed 2, 2; Zakir Khan 0, 11*.

* *Signifies not out.*

BOWLING

	O	*M*	*R*	*W*	*BB*	*Avge*
Zakir Khan	18.1	2	52	5	3-24	10.40
Saleem Jaffer	34.2	2	141	7	6-67	20.14
Imran Khan	180.5	22	589	29	7-80	20.31
Abdul Qadir	214.3	36	703	26	6-42	27.03
Mudassar Nazar	30	7	87	3	2-24	29.00
Wasim Akram	127	23	350	12	4-73	29.16
Salim Malik	34.4	1	169	5	4-101	33.80
Ijaz Faqih	60	13	187	5	3-54	37.40
Haafiz Shahid	29	3	114	3	2-54	38.00

Also bowled: Aamer Malik 5–2–15–1; Moin-ul-Atiq 3–0–6–0; Naved Anjum 34–3–99–2; Shoaib Mohammad 16.4–2–43–2; Tauseef Ahmed 35–11–69–0.

FIELDING

11 – Aamer Malik (6 ct, 5 st); 10 – Salim Yousuf (9 ct, 1 st); 8 – Salim Malik; 5 – Javed Miandad; 4 – Ijaz Ahmed; 2 – Abdul Qadir, Imran Khan, Mudassar Nazar, Shoaib Mohammad; 1 – Ramiz Raja, Saleem Jaffer, substitute (Naved Anjum), Wasim Akram.

WICBC PRESIDENT'S XI v PAKISTANIS

At Kingston, March 6, 7, 8, 9. Drawn. Toss: Pakistanis. With a first-innings lead of just 21, the touring team faced the prospect of an embarrassing first-match defeat when they lost four wickets for 20 after tea on the third day. However, Imran and Miandad added 78 for the fifth wicket, and Miandad batted on until after tea on the fourth day, when he was eighth out, having compiled a determined century that contained only four boundaries. The low bounce did not make strokeplay easy, but the President's XI spinners, Harper and Hooper, never exploited the conditions fully. On the opening day, Mudassar Nazar had been forced to retire hurt, concussed after being hit on the helmet by a bouncer from Bishop. It was the spinners who caused the collapse after tea from 214 for two to 279 for seven. When the home side batted, Imran took two wickets in three balls, but the honours went to Saleem Jaffer, who finished with six for 67.

Close of play: First day, Pakistanis 279-7 (Naved Anjum 0*, Tauseef Ahmed 0*); Second day, WICBC President's XI 208-4 (K. L. T. Arthurton 25*, A. H. Gray 0*); Third day, Pakistanis 106-4 (Javed Miandad 20*, Imran Khan 13*).

Pakistanis

Mudassar Nazar retired hurt	1	– absent injured	
Ramiz Raja c Williams b Harper	25	– (1) c Best b Harper	40
Salim Malik c and b Harper	86	– c Harper b Benjamin	5
Javed Miandad c Best b Hooper	63	– run out	111
Aamer Malik c Bishop b Hooper	42	– (2) c Harper b Benjamin	21
Ijaz Ahmed c Hooper b Benjamin	29	– (5) lbw b Harper	0
*Imran Khan c Simmons b Hooper	4	– (6) c sub b Hooper	44
†Salim Yousuf lbw b Bishop	8	– (7) b Harper	20
Naved Anjum c and b Hooper	48	– (8) lbw b Gray	13
Tauseef Ahmed c Williams b Benjamin	2	– (9) lbw b Arthurton	2
Saleem Jaffer not out	3	– (10) not out	1
B 6, l-b 4, w 3, n-b 8	21	B 1, l-b 5, n-b 8	14
1/47 2/179 3/216 4/249 5/253 6/279 7/279 8/295 9/332	332	1/56 2/62 3/76 4/76 5/154 6/199 7/241 8/268 9/271	271

In the first innings, Mudassar Nazar retired hurt at 1.

Bowling: *First Innings*—Gray 16–1–53–0; Bishop 17–3–68–1; Harper 24–7–61–2; Benjamin 22–6–68–2; Hooper 24.2–5–72–4. *Second Innings*—Gray 18–2–32–1; Bishop 17–2–40–0; Benjamin 12–5–30–2; Harper 28–4–60–3; Hooper 33–2–89–1; Arthurton 2.3–0–6–1; Best 2–0–8–0.

WICBC President's XI

P. V. Simmons b Naved	39	
W. W. Lewis c Salim Malik b Saleem Jaffer	47	– (1) not out 29
C. A. Best c Miandad b Saleem Jaffer	13	– not out 10
K. L. T. Arthurton lbw b Imran	41	
C. L. Hooper lbw b Naved	67	
A. H. Gray lbw b Saleem Jaffer	20	
T. R. O. Payne c Salim Yousuf b Imran	0	– (2) c Salim Yousuf b Aamer 4
*R. A. Harper b Saleem Jaffer	30	
†D. Williams lbw b Saleem Jaffer	6	
W. K. M. Benjamin b Saleem Jaffer	18	
I. R. Bishop not out	0	
B 5, l-b 15, n-b 10	30	B 4, l-b 1, n-b 2 7
1/74 2/100 3/114 4/208 5/232 6/232 7/260 8/278 9/308	311	1/22 (1 wkt) 50

Bowling: *First Innings*—Imran 20–1–64–2; Saleem Jaffer 18.2–0–67–6; Naved 15–1–53–2; Tauseef 30–9–60–0; Salim Malik 7–0–47–0. *Second Innings*—Saleem Jaffer 4–1–14–0; Naved 4–0–7–0; Aamer 5–2–15–1; Tauseef 5–2–9–0.

Umpires: S. Buckner and A. J. Gaynor.

†WEST INDIES v PAKISTAN

First One-day International

At Kingston, March 12. West Indies won by 47 runs. Toss: Pakistan. An unbeaten century by Logie, his first in a one-day international, enabled West Indies to put on a daunting 241 for four after Imran, on his return to international cricket, had sent back Haynes with his second ball and dismissed Simmons in his third over. Logie and Richardson added 187 in 36 overs before Richardson played on to Jaffer for 84 from 124 balls. Dropped by Anjum when 68, Logie reached his hundred off 113 balls in the 43rd over. Pakistan suffered an immediate setback when Ambrose, in his first match for West Indies, took wickets with his third and ninth deliveries. Ramiz dragged an attempted hook on to his stumps and Shoaib was bowled. Miandad and Ijaz put on 76 in fourteen overs for the fourth wicket, but Ambrose, recalled for a second spell, had Miandad caught and then yorked Imran. When Ijaz was sixth out in the 34th over, the result was as good as settled.

Man of the Match: A. L. Logie.

West Indies

D. L. Haynes b Imran	0	C. L. Hooper not out 1
P. V. Simmons c Ramiz b Imran	15	B 3, l-b 10, w 1, n-b 3 17
R. B. Richardson b Saleem Jaffer	84	
A. L. Logie not out	109	1/0 2/25 3/212 (4 wkts, 46 overs) 241
*I. V. A. Richards b Imran	15	4/236

†P. J. L. Dujon, W. K. M. Benjamin, C. E. L. Ambrose, C. A. Walsh and B. P. Patterson did not bat.

Bowling: Imran 8–1–36–3; Saleem Jaffer 10–1–55–1; Naved 10–1–37–0; Zakir 10–0–54–0; Tauseef 5–0–28–0; Shoaib 3–0–18–0.

Pakistan

Ramiz Raja b Ambrose	5	†Salim Yousuf c Logie b Patterson 10
Shoaib Mohammad b Ambrose	3	Zakir Khan not out 11
Salim Malik b Walsh	20	
Javed Miandad c Richards b Ambrose	47	B 10, l-b 12, w 9, n-b 4 35
Ijaz Ahmed run out	39	
*Imran Khan b Ambrose	7	1/7 2/8 3/55 4/131 (7 wkts, 46 overs) 194
Naved Anjum not out	17	5/145 6/146 7/163

Tauseef Ahmed and Saleem Jaffer did not bat.

Bowling: Patterson 10–2–21–1; Ambrose 10–1–39–4; Walsh 10–1–37–1; Benjamin 10–1–34–0; Richards 5–1–30–0; Hooper 1–0–11–0.

Umpires: J. R. Gayle and D. Sang Hue.

†WEST INDIES v PAKISTAN

Second One-day International

At St John's, March 15. West Indies won by five wickets. Toss: West Indies. Pakistan never recovered after losing wickets in the fifth, sixth and eighth overs. Patterson had Ramiz caught at mid-wicket by Hooper; Ambrose had Salim Malik taken in the slips, low down, by Greenidge, having hit him on the boot first ball, and 1 run later, he yorked Mudassar. Imran batted superbly for his 53, and Yousuf and Wasim hit out effectively, but a total of 166 was not enough. The target was made to look easy by Greenidge and Simmons as they put on 88 for the first wicket in eighteen overs. Simmons hit nine fours in his 54; Greenidge, who after missing the first game was leading West Indies for the first time, lasted another four overs for his 35. Imran and Mudassar picked up three more wickets, but West Indies won comfortably with 8.5 overs to spare. Haynes, after twisting his ankle during practice, was replaced by Best.

Man of the Match: W. K. M. Benjamin.

Pakistan

Mudassar Nazar b Ambrose	4	Wasim Akram c Simmons b Ambrose	18
Ramiz Raja c Hooper b Patterson	14	Haafiz Shahid not out	7
Salim Malik c Greenidge b Ambrose	0	Saleem Jaffer not out	2
Javed Miandad c Dujon b Benjamin	24	L-b 2, w 7, n-b 3	12
Ijaz Ahmed c Simmons b Benjamin	6		
*Imran Khan c and b Ambrose	53	1/20 2/23 3/24 (9 wkts, 46 overs)	166
Naved Anjum b Benjamin	2	4/40 5/72 6/78	
†Salim Yousuf run out	24	7/118 8/156 9/163	

Bowling: Patterson 8–0–37–1; Ambrose 10–2–35–4; Benjamin 10–1–27–3; Walsh 10–1–25–0; Hooper 8–0–40–0.

West Indies

*C. G. Greenidge c Imran b Haafiz	35	†P. J. L. Dujon not not	11
P. V. Simmons b Mudassar	54		
R. B. Richardson c Miandad b Mudassar	12	L-b 2, w 2, n-b 4	8
C. A. Best lbw b Imran	17		
A. L. Logie c Ijaz b Imran	9	1/88 2/104 3/106 (5 wkts, 37.1 overs)	167
C. L. Hooper not out	21	4/123 5/144	

W. K. M. Benjamin, C. E. L. Ambrose, C. A. Walsh and B. P. Patterson did not bat.

Bowling: Imran 7–1–38–2; Wasim 6–1–22–0; Saleem Jaffer 8.1–0–36–0; Haafiz 9–0–39–1; Mudassar 7–1–30–2.

Umpires: L. H. Barker and P. C. White.

†WEST INDIES v PAKISTAN

Third One-day International

At Port-of-Spain, March 18. West Indies won by 50 runs, so winning the series with two matches remaining. Toss: Pakistan. West Indies, put in, compiled their highest score against Pakistan in one-day internationals. Haynes, back in the side, led the way with his tenth hundred at this level, his 142 not out coming from 132 balls and including thirteen fours and a six. He added 152 with Richardson (76 balls, twelve fours) for the second wicket in just 24 overs. When 85, Haynes was adjudged lbw to Jaffer in the 34th over, only for Imran to withdraw the appeal when the batsman, as he walked away, indicated that he had hit the ball. Pakistan made a spirited reply. Ramiz (53 balls) and Mudassar put on 70 in fourteen overs, and Salim Malik kept the match alive with 85 off 55 balls, hitting ten fours and a six. However, Ambrose came back to dismiss him with a low return catch, Hooper caught Imran in the following over, and the next three wickets could manage only 17. A crowd of some 26,000 witnessed 58 fours and two sixes in the feast of batting.

Man of the Match: D. L. Haynes.

West Indies

D. L. Haynes not out 142	C. L. Hooper not out 27
P. V. Simmons c Salim Malik b Naved 12	B 4, l-b 12, w 4 20
R. B. Richardson c Qadir b Saleem Jaffer 78	—
*C. G. Greenidge c and b Salim Malik 27	1/28 2/180 3/236 (4 wkts, 47 overs) 315
A. L. Logie c Salim Yousuf b Imran ... 9	4/270

†P. J. L. Dujon, W. K. M. Benjamin, C. E. L. Ambrose, C. A. Walsh and B. P. Patterson did not bat.

Bowling: Imran 8–0–48–1; Naved 9–0–56–1; Saleem Jaffer 9–0–58–1; Qadir 10–0–64–0; Mudassar 4–0–32–0; Salim Malik 7–0–41–1.

Pakistan

Ramiz Raja b Benjamin 47	Naved Anjum c Walsh b Patterson 7
Mudassar Nazar c Dujon b Benjamin .. 33	Abdul Qadir c Dujon b Ambrose 2
†Salim Yousuf c Ambrose b Walsh 8	Saleem Jaffer not out 2
Aamer Malik run out 12	
Javed Miandad c Ambrose b Hooper .. 17	B 4, l-b 5, w 11, n-b 3 23
Salim Malik c and b Ambrose 85	—
*Imran Khan c Hooper b Patterson ... 20	1/70 2/80 3/106 (43.3 overs) 265
Ijaz Ahmed c sub (A. H. Gray)	4/111 5/188 6/242
b Patterson . 9	7/248 8/260 9/260

Bowling: Patterson 10–0–78–3; Ambrose 8.3–0–29–2; Walsh 8–1–43–1; Benjamin 10–0–65–2; Hooper 7–0–41–1.

Umpires: C. E. Cumberbatch and Mohammed Hosein.

†WEST INDIES v PAKISTAN

Fourth One-day International

At Port-of-Spain, March 20. West Indies won by seven wickets. Toss: Pakistan. Pakistan chose to bat first this time on the same wicket that was used for the previous game and recorded their highest total against West Indies. But their bowling let them down. Moin-ul-Atiq and Ramiz Raja put on Pakistan's first three-figure opening stand against West Indies in one-day games before Ramiz (72 balls, one six, ten fours) was caught in the seventeenth over. Imran, having sportingly allowed the substitute, Williams, to keep wicket when Dujon was injured, ironically was caught by him. The last five overs brought 56 runs as Miandad hit three sixes over square leg off Patterson in his 59 from 49 balls. Patterson's last three overs cost 39 runs. Moin, on his début, made a fine 46 from 56 balls. Greenidge (51 balls, three sixes, seven fours) and Simmons spurred West Indies into the chase, putting on 112 for the first wicket by the fourteenth over. One of Greenidge's two sixes off Imran landed in the third tier of the Constantine stand at long-on. The last eight overs brought 65 runs as Richardson (87 balls) and Best raced to the target. The match contained eleven sixes and 42 fours.

Man of the Match: C. G. Greenidge.

Pakistan

Ramiz Raja c Greenidge b Patterson .. 71	†Salim Yousuf not out 8
Moin-ul-Atiq c Greenidge b Gray 46	Haafiz Shahid not out 2
Salim Malik b Gray 26	
Javed Miandad c Richardson b Patterson 59	B 3, l-b 15, w 1, n-b 5 24
*Imran Khan c sub (D. Williams)	—
b Benjamin . 16	1/109 2/139 3/160 (6 wkts, 43 overs) 271
Ijaz Ahmed c Gray b Patterson 19	4/194 5/256 6/256

Shoaib Mohammad, Abdul Qadir and Zakir Khan did not bat.

Bowling: Patterson 9–0–77–3; Walsh 9–0–43–0; Gray 10–0–45–2; Benjamin 8–0–58–1; Hooper 7–0–30–0.

West Indies

*C. G. Greenidge b Haafiz	66	C. A. Best not out	32
P. V. Simmons c Salim Yousuf b Haafiz	49	B 4, l-b 7, w 3, n-b 3	17
R. B. Richardson not out	79		—
A. L. Logie c and b Salim Malik	29	1/112 2/149 3/207 (3 wkts, 40.1 overs)	272

C. L. Hooper, †P. J. L. Dujon, W. K. M. Benjamin, A. H. Gray, C. A. Walsh and B. P. Patterson did not bat.

Bowling: Imran 8–0–76–0; Zakir 6–0–49–0; Qadir 10–0–42–0; Haafiz 9.1–1–56–2; Salim Malik 4–0–23–1; Shoaib 3–0–15–0.

Umpires: G. T. Browne and C. E. Cumberbatch.

WEST INDIES BOARD XI v PAKISTANIS

At Georgetown, March 24, 25, 26, 27. Drawn. Toss: Pakistanis. A chanceless, unbeaten 208 (25 fours) by Shoaib Mohammad, his first double-hundred and the first by a Pakistani in the West Indies since his father, Hanif, scored 337 in the Bridgetown Test of 1957-58, put the tourists in an impregnable position. After the openers had put on 91, Shoaib and Aamer Malik (174 balls) added 146 for the third wicket. Shoaib's hundred, reached before the close, contained thirteen fours; his double-hundred came in 490 minutes with 24 fours. Twenty minutes later, at tea, the Pakistanis declared. Earlier in the day, Bishop and Gray had shown that the pitch was quickening, with some deliveries bouncing awkwardly, and Imran used the conditions well to hint at a follow-on. Arthurton, a left-hander from Nevis, precluded this possibility by batting for five hours, his 132 including fifteen boundaries. Had Qadir not pulled a leg muscle in his first over, the outcome might have been different, as he illustrated in the second innings when he took three wickets in his first four overs. But by then, with the Pakistanis having batted on until tea, a draw was the expected result. Aamer Malik kept wicket in both innings after Salim Yousuf also suffered an injury.

Close of play: First day, Pakistanis 269-3 (Shoaib Mohammad 101*, Haafiz Shahid 8*); Second day, West Indies Board XI 82-3 (K. L. T. Arthurton 7*, R. Seeram 17*); Third day, Pakistanis 42-1 (Mudassar Nazar 13*, Shoaib Mohammad 1*).

Pakistanis

Mudassar Nazar c Seeram b Harper	47	– b Butts	72
Moin-ul-Atiq b Butts	38	– c Seeram b Gray	22
Shoaib Mohammad not out	208	– c Dhaniram b Harper	43
Aamer Malik lbw b Bishop	51	– (5) c Lambert b Butts	9
Haafiz Shahid b Bishop	10		
Salim Malik c Simmons b Gray	1	– (4) not out	40
Ijaz Ahmed c Gray b Bishop	19	– (6) not out	22
*Imran Khan c Collymore b Harper	29		
†Salim Yousuf lbw b Collymore	30		
Abdul Qadir run out	10		
Naved Anjum not out	20		
B 1, l-b 9, w 1, n-b 21	32	B 5, l-b 13, n-b 4	22
	—		—
1/91 2/103 3/249 4/273 5/274 6/311 7/382 8/435 9/462 (9 wkts dec.)	495	1/41 2/145 3/165 4/176 (4 wkts dec.)	230

Bowling: *First Innings*—Gray 26–5–85–1; Bishop 25–1–100–3; Collymore 21–4–63–1; Butts 41–7–107–1; Harper 39–3–117–2; Dhaniram 5–1–13–0. *Second Innings*—Gray 13–3–38–1; Bishop 10–1–40–0; Collymore 3–0–10–0; Butts 26–6–66–2; Harper 18–2–42–1; Dhaniram 2–0–9–0; Arthurton 2–0–7–0.

Vest Indies Board XI

:. B. Lambert b Imran . . . . 28 – c Aamer b Qadir 15
. Dhaniram b Imran . . . . 1 – st Aamer b Qadir 7
. V. Simmons b Haafiz . . . . 20 – not out 41
:. L. T. Arthurton c Aamer b Salim Malik . . . .132 – c Imran b Qadir 4
:. Seeram b Imran . . . . 25 – st Aamer b Salim Malik 6
R. A. Harper lbw b Imran . . . . 0 – not out 10
). J. Collymore c and b Salim Malik 25
D. Williams c and b Salim Malik 10
:. G. Butts c Aamer b Mudassar 48
.. H. Gray st Aamer b Salim Malik 15
R. Bishop not out 6
B 8, l-b 16, w 1, n-b 6 . . . . 31 B 5, l-b 2 7

'9 2/50 3/56 4/101 5/101 341 1/26 2/27 3/39 4/74 (4 wkts) 90
'181 7/200 8/314 9/321

Bowling: *First Innings*—Imran 21–4–75–4; Haafiz 7–0–27–1; Naved 13–2–28–0; Qadir 2–0–8–0; Shoaib 8.4–1–21–0; Mudassar 14–1–51–1; Salim Malik 20.4–0–101–4; Ioin-ul-Atiq 3–0–6–0. *Second Innings*—Imran 10–1–34–0; Naved 2–0–11–0; Qadir 9–3–27–3; alim Malik 2–0–11–1.

Umpires: M. N. Baksh and R. C. Haynes.

†WEST INDIES v PAKISTAN

Fifth One-day International

.t Georgetown, March 30. West Indies won by seven wickets. Toss: West Indies. Marshall turned to the West Indian team for his first match of the series and a more than capacity rowd of 20,000 saw him dismiss Shoaib in his second over. Ramiz (88 balls, twelve fours) and Iiandad got the innings going with 52 in eleven overs before Gray removed Ramiz and Salim Ialik with successive balls. Miandad, who when 34 survived an appeal for hit wicket, went n to score his first hundred against West Indies off the last ball of the innings – the 99th he eceived. His sixth one-day international hundred, it was also the first for Pakistan against Vest Indies in one-day games and contained ten fours. Simmons (73 balls, two sixes, one five, even fours) and Richardson (98 balls, ten fours) added 157 in 26 overs for West Indies' econd wicket, and when Imran dismissed them both, Dujon and Greenidge took West Indies their clean sweep of the series.

Man of the Match: Javed Miandad.

'akistan

.amiz Raja b Gray 67
'hoaib Mohammad c Dujon b Marshall 0
Aamer Malik run out 6
aved Miandad not out 100
alim Malik c Benjamin b Gray 0
Imran Khan run out 17
az Ahmed b Walsh 10
Wasim Akram c Haynes b Gray 0
Ijaz Faqih not out 6
B 3, l-b 6, n-b 6 15

1/1 2/42 3/94 4/94 5/160 6/183 7/184 (7 wkts, 43 overs) 221

.bdul Qadir and Saleem Jaffer did not bat.

Bowling: Marshall 10–2–42–1; Walsh 10–2–50–1; Gray 10–0–44–3; Benjamin 7–0–31–0; Iooper 6–0–45–0.

West Indies

D. L. Haynes c Salim Malik b Wasim . 9
P. V. Simmons b Imran 79
R. B. Richardson c Ijaz Ahmed b Imran 68
†P. J. L. Dujon not out 18
*C. G. Greenidge not out ....
B 9, l-b 13, w 1, n-b 2 ....
1/15 2/172 3/182 (3 wkts, 37 overs) 2

A. L. Logie, C. L. Hooper, M. D. Marshall, W. K. M. Benjamin, A. H. Gray and C. A. Wal did not bat.

Bowling: Imran 8–0–59–2; Wasim 10–0–62–1; Qadir 7–1–23–0; Saleem Jaffer 5–1–31– Ijaz Faqih 7–0–28–0.

Umpires: D. M. Archer and C. Duncan.

WEST INDIES v PAKISTAN

First Test Match

At Georgetown, April 2, 3, 4, 6. Pakistan won by nine wickets. Toss: West Indies. Contrary expectations, Pakistan won the First Test convincingly, inflicting on West Indies their fi home defeat since April 1978, when Australia beat them, also at Georgetown. Pakistar success was due principally to inspired spells of fast bowling by Imran Khan, who finish with match figures of eleven for 121 in his first Test since being coaxed from retirement.

With Richards recovering from an operation for haemorrhoids and Marshall out with knee injury, Greenidge led West Indies and chose to bat first on a newly laid pitch. They we soon in trouble when Imran dismissed Haynes and off-spinner Ijaz Faqih bowled Simmo with his first delivery. However, Greenidge and Richardson added 54, and Richardson, Log and Hooper, with sensible batting, took the score to 219 for four by tea. Logie's dismissal af the resumption brought on a slump, and only a last-wicket stand of 34 between Ambrose a Patterson saw West Indies to 292. Imran took the last five wickets, including a spell of four f 9 in three overs.

Pakistan lost Ramiz early on the second morning, but Mudassar batted defiantly befo Ambrose yorked him for his first Test wicket, whereupon Shoaib and Miandad added 70 f the third wicket. Miandad and Malik then put on 90 in two and threequarter hours, Ma when 7 reaching 2,000 Test runs. Miandad, caught off a no-ball when 27 and dropped Dujon when 87, was 96 at the end of a day which had seen Benjamin warned by ump Barker for intimidatory bowling. Next morning, having been on 99 for 38 minutes, he reach his sixteenth Test hundred and his first against West Indies. When fifth out for 114, he h batted for six and threequarter hours, faced 234 balls and hit twelve fours. A dedicat innings of 62 by Salim Yousuf gave a final boost to a total also swelled by 71 extr This exceeded by 3 the previous highest in a Test innings, also conceded against Pakista at Bridgetown in 1976-77; including those from which runs were scored, there were no-balls.

An infected toe prevented Imran from bowling more than two overs in the final session, b helped by the rest day which followed and treatment with antibiotics, he was able to resu on the fourth morning. Qadir removed Simmons and Richardson early on, and af Greenidge and Logie had added 65 in even time, Imran dismissed them both, Yousuf catchi Logie one-handed and well to his right. After lunch, Imran's introduction of Shoai occasional off-breaks brought two wickets with successive balls, Qadir had Hooper caug and finally Walsh and Patterson were deceived by Imran in successive balls. Pakistan need 30 runs for victory and by tea the match was over.

Man of the Match: Imran Khan.

Close of play: First day, West Indies 292; Second day, Pakistan 249-4 (Javed Miandad 96 Ijaz Ahmed 10*); Third day, West Indies 25-1 (P. V. Simmons 11*, R. B. Richardson 6*

Vest Indies

). L. Haynes c Salim Yousuf b Imran	1	– b Ijaz Faqih	5
'. V. Simmons b Ijaz Faqih	16	– b Qadir	11
R. B. Richardson c Shoaib b Imran	75	– c Salim Yousuf b Qadir	16
C. G. Greenidge c Salim Malik b Wasim	17	– b Imran	43
A. L. Logie lbw b Qadir	80	– c Salim Yousuf b Imran	24
C. L. Hooper c Wasim b Imran	33	– c Salim Malik b Qadir	30
†P. J. L. Dujon lbw b Imran	15	– c Imran b Shoaib	11
W. K. M. Benjamin lbw b Imran	2	– c Miandad b Shoaib	0
C. A. Walsh b Imran	7	– c Salim Yousuf b Imran	14
C. E. L. Ambrose not out	25	– not out	1
B. P. Patterson b Imran	10	– b Imran	0
B 2, l-b 3, n-b 6	11	B 4, l-b 8, n-b 5	17
/7 2/41 3/95 4/144 5/220 /244 7/248 8/249 9/258	292	1/18 2/34 3/44 4/109 5/120 6/145 7/145 8/166 9/172	172

Bowling: *First Innings*—Imran 22.4–2–80–7; Wasim 14–5–41–1; Ijaz Faqih 14–0–60–1; Qadir 24–2–91–1; Mudassar 5–2–9–0; Salim Malik 1–0–6–0. *Second Innings*—Wasim –1–7–0; Imran 14.4–0–41–4; Ijaz Faqih 15–4–38–1; Qadir 25–5–66–3; Shoaib 2–0–8–2.

'akistan

Mudassar Nazar b Ambrose	29	– lbw b Patterson	0
Ramiz Raja c Haynes b Patterson	5	– not out	18
hoaib Mohammad c Greenidge b Walsh	46	– not out	13
aved Miandad b Patterson	114		
alim Malik c Greenidge b Patterson	27		
jaz Ahmed c Haynes b Ambrose	31		
Imran Khan c Simmons b Benjamin	24		
Salim Yousuf lbw b Walsh	62		
jaz Faqih b Hooper	5		
Abdul Qadir b Walsh	19		
Wasim Akram not out	2		
B 21, l-b 8, w 4, n-b 38	71	N-b 1	1
/20 2/57 3/127 4/217 5/297 /300 7/364 8/383 9/423	435	1/0	(1 wkt) 32

Bowling: *First Innings*—Patterson 24–1–82–3; Ambrose 28–5–108–2; Walsh 27–4–80–3; Benjamin 31–3–99–1; Hooper 12–0–37–1. *Second Innings*—Patterson 2–0–19–1; Ambrose .3–0–13–0.

Umpires: D. M. Archer and L. H. Barker.

WEST INDIES UNDER-23 XI v PAKISTANIS

At Castries, April 9, 10, 11, 12. Pakistanis won by 211 runs. Toss: Pakistanis. Five Pakistani atsmen put up half-centuries against an inexperienced attack. Ijaz Ahmed hit a six and ten ours in a stay of 2 hours 38 minutes, and when he was out Wasim Akram struck four sixes nd four fours in his punishing 56 not out. For the second match in succession, Arthurton aved his side with a century against the tourists, batting delightfully for 219 minutes and itting a six and 24 fours. With Adams, who also batted more than three hours, he added 120 or the fifth wicket. Bounce and swing accounted for the Pakistanis in the second innings. Only Ramiz, shrugging off a blow on the helmet by Bishop, batted with sufficient application, lthough on the final morning the last-wicket pair remained for another 70 minutes before eing parted. The Under-23s had four and a half hours in which to score 371 or, as seemed nore likely, achieve a draw. Instead, beginning with the dismissal of Morgan at 99 and upported by Zakir Khan's accurate swing bowling, Qadir ran through his repertoire and the nnings. Within an hour after tea, the Pakistanis had won a handsome victory.

Close of play: First day, Pakistanis 317-5 (Ijaz Ahmed 59*, Ijaz Faqih 12*); Second day, West Indies Under-23 XI 160-4 (K. L. T. Arthurton 92*, J. C. Adams 20*); Third day, akistanis 138-9 (Haafiz Shahid 16*, Zakir Khan 4*).

Pakistanis

*Mudassar Nazar b Perry	30	– (9) lbw b Perry	7
Ramiz Raja c Arthurton b Perry	82	– (1) lbw b Perry	65
Shoaib Mohammad b Perry	17	– (2) b Bishop	4
Salim Malik c Murray b Adams	53	– (3) lbw b Bishop	2
†Aamer Malik c Lara b Browne	43	– (4) lbw b Browne	0
Ijaz Ahmed c Adams b Dhanraj	84	– (5) c Murray b Browne	5
Ijaz Faqih b Arthurton	51	– (6) b Bishop	10
Wasim Akram not out	56	– (7) c Browne b Dhanraj	16
Abdul Qadir st Murray b Arthurton	3	– (8) c Lara b Dhanraj	4
Haafiz Shahid c Murray b Arthurton	0	– c Bishop b Perry	37
Zakir Khan b Bishop	0	– not out	11
B 4, l-b 4, n-b 20	28	B 1, l-b 8, n-b 3	12
1/87 2/133 3/162 4/211 5/295 6/355 7/434 8/446 9/446	447	1/5 2/11 3/12 4/30 5/49 6/92 7/103 8/113 9/134	173

Bowling: *First Innings*—Bishop 24.4–4–101–1; Browne 29–1–97–1; Dhanraj 27–4–98–1; Perry 40–8–119–3; Adams 5–0–10–1; Arthurton 5–0–14–3. *Second Innings*—Bishop 18–5–52–3; Browne 13–1–39–2; Perry 15.5–3–51–3; Dhanraj 12–2–18–2; Arthurton 3–2–4–0

West Indies Under 23 XI

D. S. Morgan c Mudassar b Haafiz	9	– b Qadir	45
S. Dhaniram lbw b Zakir	0	– b Wasim	15
*B. C. Lara b Haafiz	6	– (5) lbw b Zakir	11
K. L. T. Arthurton c Salim Malik b Qadir	124	– c Ramiz b Qadir	4
R. I. C. Holder c Salim Malik b Ijaz Faqih	10	– (3) c and b Qadir	25
J. C. Adams not out	51	– b Qadir	5
†J. R. Murray st Aamer b Qadir	2	– lbw b Zakir	0
N. O. Perry b Ijaz Faqih	3	– lbw b Qadir	0
I. R. Bishop b Qadir	0	– not out	0
B. St A. Browne c Ijaz Ahmed b Ijaz Faqih	0	– (11) lbw b Qadir	19
R. Dhanraj lbw b Zakir	6	– (10) lbw b Zakir	0
B 14, l-b 8, n-b 17	39	B 10, l-b 19, w 2, n-b 4	35
1/7 2/11 3/38 4/84 5/204 6/206 7/211 8/214 9/215	250	1/45 2/99 3/105 4/114 5/137 6/138 7/138 8/138 9/138	159

Bowling: *First Innings*—Zakir 7.1–1–28–2; Haafiz 16–3–54–2; Qadir 27–7–88–3; Ijaz Faqih 23–8–54–3; Salim Malik 4–1–4–0. *Second Innings*—Wasim 10–1–31–1; Haafiz 6–0–33–0; Zakir 11–1–24–3; Qadir 15.3–5–42–6; Ijaz Faqih 1–1–0–0.

Umpires: G. T. Browne and M. A. Hippolyte.

WEST INDIES v PAKISTAN

Second Test Match

At Port-of-Spain, April 14, 15, 16, 17, 19. Drawn. Toss: Pakistan. In a nail-biting finish to a dramatic final day which had seen each side achieve a match-winning position, Abdul Qadir, the No. 11 batsman, survived the last five balls from Richards to maintain Pakistan's lead in the series. Requiring 372 to win, Pakistan were 31 runs short of victory after Javed Miandad had drawn them nearer and nearer the target with a flawless 102 compiled over seven hours seven minutes. His seventeenth Test hundred, it came from 240 balls and contained seven fours and a five. On his dismissal, in the over before the last twenty overs began, 84 were still needed; but when Marshall dismissed the hard-hitting Wasim Akram at 311, the odds favoured West Indies. Salim Yousuf and Ijaz Faqih defended tenaciously until the last over, when Yousuf's dismissal, lbw to the first ball, brought in Qadir to play out the last tense scene.

Pakistan were unchanged from the First Test, but West Indies were able to bring back Richards and Marshall, and Benjamin retained his place because Patterson was unfit. Put in, West Indies lost Greenidge to the last ball of Imran's first over and Haynes with only 25 on the board. Richardson and Logie added 55, and a stand of 58 in thirteen overs between Richards and Dujon improved the situation. Richards struck 49 in 43 balls with eight fours, and when he was seventh out, Imran and Qadir quickly wrapped up the innings, each finishing with four wickets. Imran, in bowling Walsh, became the fourth-highest wicket-taker in Tests.

Pakistan's jubilation was soon dashed as between tea and stumps they lost five wickets for 55. Two more wickets fell on the second morning for the addition of only 13 runs, but Malik and Yousuf, dropped when 3 by Dujon, put on 94 valuable runs, a record for Pakistan's eighth wicket against West Indies. Malik batted 171 minutes for his 66. By the close, West Indies were 58 ahead with Haynes, Greenidge and Logie all out to Imran. The third day's play was dominated by Richards, who reached his 22nd Test century in 232 minutes off 134 balls. He soon lost Richardson, who the previous afternoon had passed 2,000 Test runs, but found support from Hooper and Dujon in stands that yielded 94 and 97 runs respectively. Early in the day, when he was 25, Richards became embroiled in a dispute with the Pakistan fielders, threateningly waving his bat at Yousuf after an appeal for lbw off Imran's bowling had been rejected by umpire Cumberbatch. Imran protested to the umpire about Richards's behaviour, and the situation was soon defused. In the later stages of his innings, Richards was suffering from cramp and nausea.

By the close of the third day, Qadir had taken his 200th Test wicket, that of Marshall, but Dujon was still there, and next morning he added 90 runs for the last two wickets with Benjamin and Walsh. He also completed his fifth Test hundred, having batted for five and a quarter hours and hit thirteen fours. Imran and Qadir again took the major share of the wickets. By lunch Pakistan had begun their second innings. Ramiz provided them with an attacking start, but when he was the third wicket to fall in the space of 7 runs, Miandad and Salim Malik withdrew to a defensive position. It was only after the rest day that Miandad, adding 113 for the sixth wicket with the nineteen-year-old Ijaz Ahmed, raised the prospect of victory. With their dismissals, first of Ijaz and then Miandad, Pakistan's most realistic chance disappeared.

Man of the Match: I. V. A. Richards.

Close of play: First day, Pakistan 55-5 (Salim Malik 5*, Ijaz Ahmed 1*); Second day, West Indies 78-3 (R. B. Richardson 39*, I. V. A. Richards 7*); Third day, West Indies 329-8 (P. J. L. Dujon 70*, W. K. M. Benjamin 4*); Fourth day, Pakistan 107-3 (Javed Miandad 9*, Salim Malik 17*).

West Indies

C. G. Greenidge c Ijaz Ahmed b Imran	1	– c sub (Naved Anjum) b Imran . . 29
D. L. Haynes lbw b Wasim	17	– c Ijaz Ahmed b Imran . . . 0
R. B. Richardson c Qadir b Wasim	42	– c Salim Yousuf b Imran . . . 40
A. L. Logie c Miandad b Qadir	18	– b Imran . . . 1
I. V. A. Richards c Miandad b Qadir	49	– lbw b Wasim . . . 123
C. L. Hooper c Salim Yousuf b Qadir	0	– c Ijaz Ahmed b Imran . . . 26
†P. J. L. Dujon c Salim Yousuf b Imran	24	– not out . . . 106
M. D. Marshall not out	10	– b Qadir . . . 2
C. E. L. Ambrose lbw b Imran	4	– lbw b Qadir . . . 9
W. K. M. Benjamin b Qadir	0	– lbw b Qadir . . . 16
C. A. Walsh b Imran	5	– st Salim Yousuf b Qadir . . . 12
L-b 2, n-b 2	4	B 9, l-b 14, n-b 4 . . . 27
1/2 2/25 3/80 4/89 5/89 6/147 7/157 8/166 9/167	174	1/1 2/55 3/66 4/81 5/175 6/272 7/284 8/301 9/357 . . . 391

Bowling: *First Innings*—Imran 16.3–2–38–4; Wasim 14–4–35–2; Ijaz Faqih 3–0–13–0; Mudassar 1–0–3–0; Qadir 19–2–83–4. *Second Innings*—Imran 45–9–115–5; Wasim 25–4–75–1; Qadir 47.4–6–148–4; Ijaz Faqih 4–0–22–0; Shoaib 3–0–8–0.

Pakistan

Mudassar Nazar c Haynes b Marshall	14	– c Dujon b Benjamin 1
Ramiz Raja c Richardson b Marshall	1	– c Richards b Marshall 4
Shoaib Mohammad c Richards b Ambrose	12	– b Benjamin . . . .
Javed Miandad b Benjamin	18	– c Richards b Ambrose 10
Ijaz Faqih c Richards b Benjamin	0	– (10) not out 1
Salim Malik c Logie b Hooper	66	– (5) lbw b Walsh 3
Ijaz Ahmed c Logie b Benjamin	3	– st Dujon b Richards 4
*Imran Khan c Logie b Marshall	4	– (6) c Dujon b Benjamin . . . .
†Salim Yousuf c Dujon b Marshall	39	– (8) lbw b Richards 3
Wasim Akram run out	7	– (9) c Hooper b Marshall . . . .
Abdul Qadir not out	17	– not out . . . .
B 1, l-b 4, n-b 8	13	B 17, l-b 17, w 2, n-b 25 . 6
1/3 2/25 3/46 4/49 5/50 6/62 7/68 8/162 9/170	194	1/60 2/62 3/67 4/153 5/169 6/282 7/288 8/311 9/341 (9 wkts) 341

Bowling: *First Innings*—Marshall 20–4–55–4; Ambrose 14–3–44–1; Walsh 8–1–23–0 Benjamin 8–0–32–3; Hooper 9.1–1–35–1. *Second Innings*—Marshall 30–4–85–2; Ambros 30–7–62–1; Benjamin 32–9–73–3; Walsh 29–8–52–1; Hooper 4–1–18–0; Richards 4–1–17–2

Umpires: L. H. Barker and C. E. Cumberbatch.

WEST INDIES v PAKISTAN

Third Test Match

At Bridgetown, April 22, 23, 24, 26, 27. West Indies won by two wickets. Toss: West Indies Pakistan's hope of becoming the first team from their country to win a series in the Wes Indies was dashed at the last by a match-winning stand of 61 between Dujon and Benjamin who came together at 207 for eight with West Indies needing another 59 to win and defeat in sight. Their unbeaten ninth-wicket stand enabled West Indies to square the series half an hou after lunch on the final day.

West Indies went into the match unchanged; Pakistan brought in Aamer Malik and Saleem Jaffer for Ijaz Ahmed and Ijaz Faqih. Put in, the Pakistanis batted at times well, at time carelessly, and they needed the scintillating eighth-wicket partnership of 67 between Salim Yousuf and Wasim Akram to ensure that earlier good work by Ramiz, Shoaib and Aamer wa not wasted. They put on 50 in five overs, but in attempting to hook Marshall, Yousu managed only to deflect the ball on to his face, breaking his nose in two places. Marshal followed up with two wickets to end the innings, Qadir becoming his 250th Test wicket. With Yousuf injured, Aamer Malik kept wicket in both innings for Pakistan.

West Indies made a poor start on the second morning, but Hooper played well for 54 Haynes grafted for 286 minutes for his 48, and Richards blasted a dynamic 67 from 80 balls his fifty coming from 51 balls. When 61, he became the third West Indian to score 7,000 run in Tests. However, a close-of-play score of 226 for eight reflected a position lost: West Indie had been 198 for three until Mudassar sent back Haynes and Logie with successive balls Marshall and Benjamin pulled their side back with a ninth-wicket partnership of 58 at almos a run a minute, Marshall's 48 from 62 balls containing a six and six fours. West Indies finishe just 3 runs adrift, and when Pakistan slumped to 177 for six by the close, they appeared t have gained the upper hand. Shoaib and Mudassar had put on 94 for the second wicket Shoaib compiling his second fifty of the match, but in the final hour Pakistan had lost wicket quickly. Miandad was caught at the wicket, Aamer was brilliantly taken by Logie at forwar short-leg, and Salim Malik fell to Benjamin after being softened up by Marshall.

On the fourth morning, Imran and the injured Yousuf added 52 for the eighth wicket, wit Yousuf, dropped first ball by Richards and having to bat some of the time with a runne because of dizziness, making a brave 28. Imran finished unbeaten with 43, having see another 85 runs added that day. By the close, honours were about even, with Haynes Greenidge, Richardson, Hooper and Logie out and a further 112 needed. But when Ambrose the night-watchman, and Richards fell in the first 35 minutes next morning, and Marshall wa lbw to Wasim, victory was in Pakistan's grasp. Instead, Benjamin and Dujon snatched it away from them, Benjamin finally hitting the winning boundary off Qadir.

It had not been a happy day for the Pakistani leg-spinner. Denied two confident appeals for w and a catch off Dujon, he had allowed himself to get involved with a heckler on the oundary. A punch was thrown, the heckler was hit, and $US1,000 were paid to the offended arty in an out-of-court settlement so that Qadir would not have to remain in Barbados to ce charges.

Man of the Match: M. D. Marshall. *Man of the Series:* Imran Khan.

Close of play: First day, Pakistan 309; Second day, West Indies 226-8 (M. D. Marshall 15*, '. K. M. Benjamin 0*); Third day, Pakistan 177-6 (Imran Khan 6*, Wasim Akram 0*); ourth day, West Indies 154-5 (I. V. A. Richards 26*, C. E. L. Ambrose 0*).

'akistan

ludassar Nazar b Ambrose	18	– c Greenidge b Hooper	41
.amiz Raja c Greenidge b Benjamin	54	– c Logie b Marshall	4
hoaib Mohammad c Greenidge b Ambrose	54	– c and b Richards	64
aved Miandad c Richardson b Marshall	14	– c Dujon b Marshall	34
alim Malik b Marshall	15	– lbw b Benjamin	9
amer Malik c Hooper b Benjamin	32	– c Logie b Marshall	2
Imran Khan c Dujon b Benjamin	18	– not out	43
Salim Yousuf retired hurt	32	– (9) c Richards b Benjamin	28
Vasim Akram c Benjamin b Marshall	38	– (8) lbw b Marshall	0
.bdul Qadir c Walsh b Marshall	17	– c Greenidge b Marshall	2
aleem Jaffer not out	1	– b Ambrose	4
L-b 7, n-b 9	16	B 3, l-b 14, n-b 14	31
'46 2/99 3/128 4/155 5/186 '215 7/218 8/297 9/309	309	1/6 2/100 3/153 4/165 5/167 6/169 7/182 8/234 9/245	262

n the first innings, Salim Yousuf retired hurt at 285.

Bowling: *First Innings*—Marshall 18.4–3–79–4; Ambrose 14–0–64–2; Benjamin 14–3–52–3; Valsh 10–1–53–0; Richards 6–0–19–0; Hooper 12–3–35–0. *Second Innings*—Marshall 3–3–65–5; Ambrose 26.5–3–74–1; Walsh 12–1–22–0; Benjamin 15–1–37–2; Hooper 0–1–39–1; Richards 7–3–8–1.

Vest Indies

. G. Greenidge lbw b Imran	10	– c Shoaib b Saleem Jaffer	35
. L. Haynes c Aamer b Mudassar	48	– c Salim Malik b Wasim	4
. B. Richardson c Aamer b Wasim	3	– st Aamer b Qadir	64
. L. Hooper b Wasim	54	– run out	13
I. V. A. Richards c Mudassar b Wasim	67	– b Wasim	39
. L. Logie c Miandad b Mudassar	0	– b Qadir	3
P. J. L. Dujon run out	0	– (8) not out	29
. D. Marshall c Aamer b Imran	48	– (9) lbw b Wasim	15
. E. L. Ambrose lbw b Imran	7	– (7) c Saleem Jaffer b Wasim	1
. K. M. Benjamin run out	31	– not out	40
. A. Walsh not out	14		
B 5, l-b 11, n-b 8	24	B 9, l-b 6, n-b 10	25
'18 2/21 3/100 4/198 5/198 '199 7/201 8/225 9/283	306	1/21 2/78 3/118 4/128 5/150 6/159 7/180 8/207	(8 wkts) 268

Bowling: *First Innings*—Imran 25–3–108–3; Wasim 27–1–88–3; Qadir 15–1–35–0; Saleem affer 7–1–35–0; Mudassar 10–4–24–2. *Second Innings*—Wasim 31–7–73–4; Imran 6–0–34–0; adir 32–5–115–2; Saleem Jaffer 5–0–25–1; Shoaib 3–1–6–0.

Umpires: D. M. Archer and L. H. Barker.

BENSON AND HEDGES WORLD SERIES CUP, 1987-88

†AUSTRALIA v SRI LANKA

At Perth, January 2. Australia won by 81 runs. Put in to bat on a near perfect pitch, Australi got away to a flying start with Boon dominating. His 56 from 81 balls gave confidence to th later batsmen, who struck out freely. With Sri Lanka needing exactly 5 runs an over fc victory, their top order fell to Dodemaide and Waugh. De Alwis (41 balls) and Labroo enlivened the later stages with 50 for the ninth wicket in 29 minutes before Dodemaid picked up the last two wickets to become the second player after U. S. H. Karnain (Sri Lank v New Zealand, 1983-84) to take five wickets in his first one-day international.

Man of the Match: S. R. Waugh. *Attendance:* 9,036.

Australia

D. C. Boon c and b de Silva 56
G. R. Marsh c de Alwis b Ramanayake . 14
D. M. Jones c Gurusinha b de Silva . . . 55
*A. R. Border c Mahanama b de Silva . 31
M. R. J. Veletta run out 27
S. R. Waugh not out 35
†G. C. Dyer run out 9
A. I. C. Dodemaide c Mahanama b Ratnayeke .
C. J. McDermott not out . . . .
B 4, l-b 7, w 4, n-b 3 1

1/57 2/84 3/143 4/189 5/199 6/224 7/238 (7 wkts, 50 overs) 24

T. B. A. May and M. R. Whitney did not bat.

Bowling: Ratnayeke 9–0–35–1; Labrooy 9–0–38–0; Amalean 6–1–27–0; Ramanayak 7–1–33–1; de Silva 10–0–58–3; Ranatunga 9–0–47–0.

Sri Lanka

R. S. Mahanama c Dodemaide b Waugh 19
A. P. Gurusinha c Dyer b Dodemaide . 0
P. A. de Silva b Dodemaide 11
A. Ranatunga c Border b Dodemaide . . 7
*R. S. Madugalle c Border b Waugh . . . 7
H. P. Tillekeratne c Dyer b May 9
J. R. Ratnayeke b Whitney 19
†R. G. de Alwis c Marsh b Dodemaide 44
C. P. H. Ramanayake c Jones b Waugh.
G. F. Labrooy lbw b Dodemaide 3
K. N. Amalean not out . . . .
B 4, l-b 3, w 2, n-b 4 1

1/2 2/20 3/33 4/49 5/50 6/78 7/82 8/118 9/168 (44.2 overs) 16

Bowling: Dodemaide 7.2–0–21–5; McDermott 5–1–15–0; Whitney 10–0–26–1; Waug 10–2–34–3; May 10–3–49–1; Jones 2–0–16–0.

Umpires: P. J. McConnell and T. A. Price.

†AUSTRALIA v NEW ZEALAND

At Perth, January 3 (day/night). New Zealand won by 1 run. What was to prove the mos exciting match of the series saw Australia suffer their only defeat of the season. Ne Zealand's gamble of batting first paid off when Jones scored a well-compiled 87 from 10 balls. His second-wicket stand of 106 with Martin Crowe came in 78 minutes off 117 ball Australia's Jones (92 from 91 balls) was their stalwart as all except Boon fell cheaply. Whe Jones was ninth out, Australia needed 12 runs for victory from ten balls, but with just 2 run required Whitney lofted the fourth ball of the final over to wide mid-off.

Man of the Match: A. H. Jones. *Attendance:* 24,200.

New Zealand

J. G. Wright c and b McDermott 13
A. H. Jones c Boon b Waugh 87
M. D. Crowe c Dyer b Taylor 45
*J. J. Crowe c Taylor b Whitney 0
D. N. Patel c Dyer b Taylor 3
†T. E. Blain c Border b McDermott . . . 16
R. J. Hadlee c Taylor b Dodemaide . . . 23
J. G. Bracewell run out 4
M. C. Snedden not out 11
S. R. Gillespie run out 6
E. J. Chatfield not out 1
L-b 16, w 5, n-b 2 23

1/27 2/133 3/134 (9 wkts, 50 overs) 232
4/145 5/177 6/189
7/203 8/219 9/228

Bowling: Dodemaide 10–1–43–1; McDermott 10–0–37–2; Waugh 10–0–49–1; Whitney 10–0–46–1; Taylor 10–0–41–2.

Australia

G. R. Marsh c sub (P. A. Horne) b Bracewell . 24
D. C. Boon c Patel b Bracewell 44
D. M. Jones run out 92
*A. R. Border lbw b Hadlee 3
M. R. J. Veletta b Hadlee 7
S. R. Waugh c Blain b Hadlee 0
†G. C. Dyer c sub (P. A. Horne) b Snedden . 4
P. L. Taylor c J. J. Crowe b Chatfield . 16
C. J. McDermott c Patel b Chatfield . . 7
A. I. C. Dodemaide not out 9
M. R. Whitney c Bracewell b Snedden . 3
L-b 11, w 6, n-b 5 22

1/78 2/81 3/84 (49.4 overs) 231
4/102 5/105 6/132
7/183 8/198 9/221

Bowling: Chatfield 10–1–39–2; Hadlee 10–0–35–3; Gillespie 7–1–48–0; Snedden 9.4–0–51–2; Bracewell 10–1–27–2; Patel 3–0–20–0.

Umpires: R. C. Bailhache and P. J. McConnell.

†NEW ZEALAND v SRI LANKA

At Sydney, January 5 (day/night). New Zealand won by six wickets. Toss: Sri Lanka. An ordinary match will be remembered for the high degree of sportsmanship shown by the New Zealand team and, in particular, their captain, Jeff Crowe. In Sri Lanka's 45th over, a drive from Ratnayeke struck the non-striker, Asoka de Silva, deflected on to umpire Crafter's leg, and then bounced back to the bowler, Chatfield, who broke the stumps with de Silva out of his ground. The batsman walked, only to be chased by Crowe, who told him there had been no appeal as the dismissal had been considered unfair. De Silva accordingly returned to the crease. Ratnayeke eventually top-scored for Sri Lanka, but to no avail as New Zealand, pacing themselves well, ran out easy winners.

Man of the Match: E. J. Chatfield. *Attendance*: 8,063.

Sri Lanka

R. S. Mahanama b Morrison 0
A. P. Gurusinha run out 23
P. A. de Silva c Blain b Chatfield 5
A. Ranatunga c Blain b Snedden 35
*R. S. Madugalle c M. D. Crowe b Morrison . 13
H. P. Tillekeratne lbw b Snedden 0
†R. G. de Alwis c Patel b Bracewell . . . 32
J. R. Ratnayeke c Wright b Chatfield . . 41
G. F. Labrooy c Patel b Chatfield 3
E. A. R. de Silva b Chatfield 6
C. P. H. Ramanayake not out 11
L-b 3, w 2 5

1/0 2/14 3/40 (48.2 overs) 174
4/76 5/76 6/82
7/134 8/147 9/159

Bowling: Morrison 10–2–43–2; Hadlee 9–4–12–0; Chatfield 9.2–1–32–4; Bracewell 10–0–41–1; Snedden 10–1–43–2.

New Zealand

J. G. Wright c Mahanama b Ramanayake . 41
A. H. Jones c and b Ramanayake 34
M. D. Crowe c P. A. de Silva b Labrooy 52
D. N. Patel c de Alwis b Ratnayeke . . . 29
†T. E. Blain not out 5
*J. J. Crowe not out 6
B 1, l-b 6, w 4 11

1/80 2/82 3/167 4/167 (4 wkts, 48.4 overs) 178

R. J. Hadlee, J. G. Bracewell, M. C. Snedden, D. K. Morrison and E. J. Chatfield did not bat.

Bowling: Ratnayeke 9.4–0–40–1; Labrooy 10–1–37–1; Ramanayake 10–2–28–2; E. A. R. de Silva 10–1–17–0; Ranatunga 5–0–27–0; P. A. de Silva 4–0–22–0.

Umpires: A. R. Crafter and R. A. French.

†AUSTRALIA v NEW ZEALAND

At Melbourne, January 7 (day/night). Australia won by 6 runs. Toss: Australia. A match-saving 68 by Waugh in heat which exceeded 40°C saw Australia reach a respectable total after an early collapse in which Gillespie claimed the wickets of Marsh and Border with his first two balls. Jones and Waugh added 88 for the fifth wicket from 113 balls with intense concentration needed and unofficial drinks supplied every other over. Dodemaide was the pick of the Australian bowlers, and his dismissal of Martin Crowe when the score was 168 removed the will of the New Zealand lower order.

Man of the Match: S. R. Waugh. *Attendance:* 61,316.

Australia

D. C. Boon b Chatfield 9
G. R. Marsh c Patel b Gillespie 12
D. M. Jones b Snedden 48
*A. R. Border c Wright b Gillespie . . . 0
M. R. J. Veletta c Blain b Snedden . . . 4
S. R. Waugh b Snedden 68
†G. C. Dyer c Jones b Chatfield 38
P. L. Taylor run out 2
A. I. C. Dodemaide c Gillespie b Hadlee 8
C. J. McDermott c M. D. Crowe b Chatfield . 9
M. R. Whitney not out 2
L-b 12, n-b 4 16

1/17 2/31 3/31 4/39 5/127 6/192 7/195 8/197 9/211 (49.4 overs) 216

Bowling: Chatfield 10–2–31–3; Hadlee 8.4–1–42–1; Snedden 10–1–36–3; Gillespie 9–0–41–2; Bracewell 8–0–32–0; Patel 4–0–22–0.

New Zealand

J. G. Wright run out 20
A. H. Jones c Dodemaide b McDermott 59
D. N. Patel b Whitney 12
M. D. Crowe b Dodemaide 37
*J. J. Crowe c and b Taylor 9
†T. E. Blain b Dodemaide 7
R. J. Hadlee c Taylor b Waugh 23
J. G. Bracewell c Boon b McDermott . . 9
M. C. Snedden c Waugh b McDermott . 3
S. R. Gillespie not out 8
E. J. Chatfield not out 0
B 4, l-b 10, w 6, n-b 3 23

1/47 2/79 3/121 4/138 5/157 6/168 7/180 8/188 9/209 (9 wkts, 50 overs) 210

Bowling: Dodemaide 10–1–25–2; McDermott 10–0–50–3; Whitney 10–0–46–1; Waugh 10–0–41–1; Taylor 10–0–34–1.

Umpires: R. C. Bailhache and P. J. McConnell.

†NEW ZEALAND v SRI LANKA

At Adelaide, January 9. New Zealand won by four wickets. Toss: Sri Lanka. Giving one of their best displays of the tour, the Sri Lankans lost to New Zealand mainly because of inexperience, which revealed itself in the final overs. Jeff Crowe, the New Zealand captain, omitted himself from the team on account of his poor form, and watched nervously –

occasionally while substitute fielder – as four of the top Sri Lankan batsmen hammered the New Zealand bowling. Mahanama (51 from 85 balls) and Aravinda de Silva (51 from 56) provided attacking cricket for the small crowd. Acting-captain Wright and Jones added 102 for New Zealand's second wicket in 22 overs, but after a stutter 6 runs were required from the final three balls. Blain hit a two and then a boundary to claim victory with a ball to spare.

Man of the Match: R. J. Hadlee. *Attendance:* 4,023.

Sri Lanka

R. S. Mahanama c Blain b Snedden ... 51
†D. S. B. P. Kuruppu c Hadlee b Morrison . 23
A. P. Gurusinha c and b Gillespie 7
P. A. de Silva c Jones b Chatfield 51
A. Ranatunga c Gillespie b Hadlee 42
*R. S. Madugalle c Crowe b Gillespie . 3
M. A. R. Samarasekera b Gillespie 3
J. R. Ratnayeke c Rutherford b Hadlee 23
G. F. Labrooy b Hadlee 0
E. A. R. de Silva c Chatfield b Morrison 15
C. P. H. Ramanayake not out 3
L-b 12, w 2, n-b 6 20

1/35 2/66 3/121 4/160 5/187 6/192 7/206 8/207 9/234 (49.5 overs) 241

Bowling: Morrison 5.5–1–39–2; Hadlee 10–1–35–3; Chatfield 10–1–43–1; Gillespie 10–0–40–3; Snedden 10–0–47–1; Patel 4–0–25–0.

New Zealand

K. R. Rutherford c Kuruppu b Ratnayeke . 1
*J. G. Wright run out 61
A. H. Jones b Ramanayake 63
M. D. Crowe c Gurusinha b Ramanayake . 39
D. N. Patel st Kuruppu b P. A. de Silva 9
R. J. Hadlee c Gurusinha b Ratnayeke . 25
†T. E. Blain not out 25
M. C. Snedden not out 0
B 2, l-b 3, w 6, n-b 8 19

1/1 2/103 3/164 4/180 5/204 6/236 (6 wkts, 49.5 overs) 242

S. R. Gillespie, D. K. Morrison and E. J. Chatfield did not bat.

Bowling: Labrooy 10–2–39–0; Ratnayeke 9.5–0–44–2; Ramanayake 7–0–47–2; E. A. R. de Silva 10–2–40–0; P. A. de Silva 9–0–41–1; Samarasekera 4–0–26–0.

Umpires: L. J. King and P. J. McConnell.

†AUSTRALIA v SRI LANKA

At Adelaide, January 10. Australia won by 81 runs. Toss: Australia. A splendid, courageous century by Boon set up an easy victory for Australia. After reaching his second century in one-day internationals, Boon, who was suffering from dehydration, was unwell at the crease, but continued after treatment. His 122 from 131 balls contained fifteen boundaries. McDermott, promoted in the batting order, struck one of the longest straight sixes seen at the ground, carrying the Cathedral end mound. The Australian bowlers, of whom Dodemaide once again was the pick, went through the motions in the heat, dismissing Sri Lankan batsmen at regular intervals. Mahanama's entertaining half-century came from 78 deliveries.

Man of the Match: D. C. Boon. *Attendance:* 14,826.

Australia

G. R. Marsh run out 37
D. C. Boon c Madugalle b P. A. de Silva .122
D. M. Jones c Gurusinha b Labrooy ... 69
*A. R. Border c E. A. R. de Silva b Ratnayeke . 13
M. R. J. Veletta run out 5
S. R. Waugh not out 8
C. J. McDermott run out 8
†G. C. Dyer not out 3
B 4, l-b 16, w 4 24

1/115 2/199 3/244 4/268 5/274 6/282 (6 wkts, 50 overs) 289

P. L. Taylor, A. I. C. Dodemaide and M. R. Whitney did not bat.

Bowling: Ratnayeke 10–0–49–1; Labrooy 10–0–44–1; Ramanayake 8–0–46–0; E. A. R. de Silva 4–0–27–0; Ranatunga 8–0–50–0; P. A. de Silva 10–0–53–1.

Sri Lanka

R. S. Mahanama c Veletta b Whitney . 50
D. S. B. P. Kuruppu b McDermott 5
A. P. Gurusinha run out 43
P. A. de Silva run out 43
A. Ranatunga c Veletta b Dodemaide . . 23
*R. S. Madugalle lbw b Dodemaide . . . 7
J. R. Ratnayeke b Dodemaide 1
†R. G. de Alwis not out 11
E. A. R. de Silva c Veletta b McDermott 3
G. F. Labrooy not out 3
B 1, l-b 11, w 6, n-b 1 19

1/9 2/106 3/132 (8 wkts, 50 overs) 208
4/172 5/187 6/189
7/190 8/197

C. P. H. Ramanayake did not bat.

Bowling: Dodemaide 10–1–27–3; McDermott 10–0–31–2; Whitney 10–0–53–1; Waugh 10–0–37–0; Taylor 10–1–48–0.

Umpires: A. R. Crafter and M. W. Johnson.

†NEW ZEALAND v SRI LANKA

At Hobart, January 12. Sri Lanka won by four wickets. In the first major match played at Bellerive Oval, the new headquarters of the Tasmanian Cricket Association, Sri Lanka defeated New Zealand with some ease to record their first one-day international victory since beating India at Kanpur in December 1986. So ended a run of fourteen consecutive losses. Put in, New Zealand lost five wickets for 70 before Blain and Hadlee (52 from 68 balls) saved the innings with 95 in 77 minutes. Mahanama and Aravinda de Silva were the architects of Sri Lanka's victory, both scoring half-centuries in front of a very supportive crowd. Australian and New Zealand records, which include the match between the two countries at Sydney in March 1983 for the Bushfire Appeal Fund, showed this to be Hadlee's 100th one-day international. Unhappily, it was marked by the start of the crowd abuse towards him which became worse as the series progressed.

Man of the Match: R. S. Mahanama. *Attendance:* 6,180.

New Zealand

K. R. Rutherford b Ranatunga 24
J. G. Wright c Madugalle b Ratnayeke . 8
*J. J. Crowe run out 0
M. D. Crowe c de Alwis b Ramanayake 25
D. N. Patel c P. A. de Silva b Ranatunga 0
T. E. Blain not out 49
R. J. Hadlee c sub (H. P. Tillekeratne) b Ratnayeke . 52
†I. D. S. Smith c Mahanama b Ratnayeke . 9
S. R. Gillespie not out 9
L-b 9, w 11, n-b 3 23

1/29 2/32 3/67 (7 wkts, 50 overs) 199
4/67 5/70
6/165 7/178

D. K. Morrison and E. J. Chatfield did not bat.

Bowling: Ratnayeke 9–1–33–3; Labrooy 10–0–43–0; Ranatunga 10–1–34–2; Ramanayake 10–2–30–1; Gurusinha 2–0–15–0; E. A. R. de Silva 5–1–16–0; P. A. de Silva 4–0–19–0.

Sri Lanka

R. S. Mahanama run out 58
D. S. B. P. Kuruppu c M. D. Crowe b Morrison . 12
A. P. Gurusinha c Smith b Hadlee 5
P. A. de Silva c Chatfield b Gillespie . . 55
A. Ranatunga c Morrison b Hadlee . . . 11
*R. S. Madugalle c Wright b Rutherford 10
J. R. Ratnayeke not out 21
†R. G. de Alwis not out 7
B 1, l-b 10, w 5, n-b 5 21

1/24 2/33 3/136 (6 wkts, 46.3 overs) 200
4/151 5/167 6/185

G. F. Labrooy, E. A. R. de Silva and C. P. H. Ramanayake did not bat.

Bowling: Chatfield 10–1–30–0; Hadlee 10–1–22–2; Morrison 8.3–1–36–1; Gillespie 10–0–51–1; Patel 3–0–25–0; Rutherford 5–0–25–1.

Umpires: M. W. Johnson and S. G. Randell.

†AUSTRALIA v SRI LANKA

At Melbourne, January 14 (day/night). Australia won by 38 runs. Toss: Australia. Australia's all-round superiority showed through as Sri Lanka were comfortably beaten by them for the third time in the tournament. Veletta (46 from 68 balls) and Border (61 from 60) gave the innings the impetus it needed, and Taylor, following an unbeaten 27 with four for 38, showed his value in this type of cricket. Ranatunga (67 from 86 balls) and Madugalle added 97 for the fifth wicket, but after the latter's dismissal the Sri Lankan innings fell apart.

Man of the Match: P. L. Taylor. *Attendance:* 28,818.

Australia

D. C. Boon c Ranatunga b Ratnayeke	1
G. R. Marsh c de Alwis b Labrooy	0
D. M. Jones c Mahanama b Ranatunga	31
M. R. J. Veletta b Jeganathan	46
S. R. Waugh c de Alwis b Labrooy	27
*A. R. Border c Labrooy b de Silva	61
†G. C. Dyer c Madugalle b Labrooy	4
P. L. Taylor not out	27
C. J. McDermott c Gurusinha b Labrooy	19
A. I. C. Dodemaide not out	10
L-b 11, w 6	17
1/2 2/6 3/66 4/90 5/158 6/172 7/190 8/220 (8 wkts, 50 overs)	243

T. B. A. May did not bat.

Bowling: Ratnayeke 8–0–24–1; Labrooy 10–1–39–4; Ramanayake 5–0–32–0; Ranatunga 10–0–47–1; Jeganathan 7–0–36–1; de Silva 10–0–54–1.

Sri Lanka

R. S. Mahanama b Dodemaide	7
D. S. B. P. Kuruppu lbw b Waugh	22
A. P. Gurusinha c Border b McDermott	7
P. A. de Silva c Boon b McDermott	10
A. Ranatunga run out	67
*R. S. Madugalle c and b Taylor	44
†R. G. de Alwis c Veletta b Taylor	0
J. R. Ratnayeke c Dyer b Dodemaide	16
G. F. Labrooy c McDermott b Taylor	13
S. Jeganathan c Border b Taylor	1
C. P. H. Ramanayake not out	6
L-b 8, w 3, n-b 1	12
1/14 2/27 3/38 4/66 5/163 6/163 7/164 8/183 9/189 (44.5 overs)	205

Bowling: Dodemaide 7.5–2–36–2; McDermott 10–2–42–2; Waugh 7–0–33–1; May 10–0–48–0; Taylor 10–1–38–4.

Umpires: R. C. Bailhache and R. A. French.

†NEW ZEALAND v SRI LANKA

At Brisbane, January 16. New Zealand won by four wickets. Toss: New Zealand. Rain before the start of play reduced the match to 43 overs, which became 39 when New Zealand bowled their overs too slowly. They were subsequently fined $A1,600. Only Kuruppu overcame the problem of a slow outfield with a hard-hitting 47, sharing in partnerships of 52 in 99 balls with Mahanama and 43 in 41 with de Silva. Accurate bowling by Chatfield, conceding only 3 runs per over, made Sri Lanka's task even more difficult. Crowe took control while he was at the crease, seeing 96 runs added before he was splendidly run out by the combined effort of Ramanayake and Labrooy. It was left to Hadlee, striking a lofted on-drive, to win the match with eleven balls to spare.

Man of the Match: M. D. Crowe. *Attendance:* 5,546.

Sri Lanka

R. S. Mahanama c Blain b Chatfield	12
D. S. B. P. Kuruppu c Patel b Morrison	47
A. P. Gurusinha run out	0
P. A. de Silva run out	25
A. Ranatunga run out	25
*R. S. Madugalle c Blain b Morrison	5
M. A. R. Samarasekera c Snedden b Chatfield	8
J. R. Ratnayeke not out	15
†R. G. de Alwis c Rutherford b Chatfield	2
G. F. Labrooy not out	2
L-b 9, w 12, n-b 2	23
1/52 2/54 3/97 4/103 5/111 6/139 7/142 8/145 (8 wkts, 39 overs)	164

C. P. H. Ramanayake did not bat.

Bowling: Hadlee 9–1–25–0; Morrison 6–0–39–2; Chatfield 9–2–27–3; Gillespie 8–0–39–0; Snedden 7–0–25–0.

New Zealand

K. R. Rutherford b Labrooy	1
*J. G. Wright c Ranatunga b Ramanayake	22
A. H. Jones c de Alwis b Ranatunga	29
M. D. Crowe run out	43
D. N. Patel c Ranatunga b Ramanayake	1
†T. E. Blain b Ranatunga	17
R. J. Hadlee not out	21
M. C. Snedden not out	15
B 2, l-b 5, w 10, n-b 1	18
1/1 2/43 3/78 4/90 5/122 6/139 (6 wkts, 37.1 overs)	167

S. R. Gillespie, D. K. Morrison and E. J. Chatfield did not bat.

Bowling: Ratnayeke 7.1–0–40–0; Labrooy 8–1–32–1; Ramanayake 8–2–28–2; Samarasekera 3–0–18–0; Ranatunga 8–0–35–2; de Silva 3–1–7–0.

Umpires: R. C. Bailhache and C. D. Timmins.

†AUSTRALIA v NEW ZEALAND

At Brisbane, January 17. Australia won by five wickets. Toss: Australia. Quick thinking by the 'Gabba's curator, Kevin Mitchell, saved the match from being a washout. With New Zealand 137 for three after 40.3 overs, and Jones dominating the innings, Mitchell ran on to the pitch, his groundstaff and tractor following, and removed the stumps to the astonishment of umpires Crafter and Johnson. Within seconds a rain squall hit the ground, but the covers were on and the pitch was saved from becoming a quagmire. The curator's intervention meant that only 37 minutes of play were lost, although the match was reduced to 44 overs a side. Chatfield took wickets with successive balls in his first over, after which Boon (48 from 47 balls) slipped the Australians' reply into top gear. He and Jones put on 77 off 82 deliveries for the third wicket, and when both were out Veletta and Waugh (45 from 38 balls) added 64 from 72 deliveries. Border, playing in his 100th WSC match, out of 101, saw his side to victory with 10.4 overs to spare.

Man of the Match: S. R. Waugh. *Attendance:* 21,690.

New Zealand

J. G. Wright c Dyer b Waugh	19
A. H. Jones b Waugh	65
*J. J. Crowe c McDermott b Taylor	41
M. D. Crowe c Davis b Taylor	1
R. J. Hadlee not out	9
V. R. Brown c Dyer b McDermott	10
†T. E. Blain not out	8
L-b 13, w 8, n-b 2	23
1/42 2/128 3/131 4/156 5/168 (5 wkts, 44 overs)	176

K. R. Rutherford, M. C. Snedden, S. R. Gillespie and E. J. Chatfield did not bat.

Bowling: Dodemaide 9–1–26–0; McDermott 10–0–49–1; Davis 10–0–33–0; Waugh 8–1–23–2; Taylor 7–0–32–2.

Australia

G. R. Marsh c Blain b Chatfield	1	*A. R. Border not out	9
D. C. Boon lbw b Snedden	48		
C. J. McDermott c Blain b Chatfield	0	L-b 8, w 2, n-b 1	11
D. M. Jones c Brown b Snedden	31		
M. R. J. Veletta not out	32	1/2 2/2 3/79 (5 wkts, 33.2 overs)	177
S. R. Waugh c Blain b Snedden	45	4/90 5/154	

†G. C. Dyer, P. L. Taylor, A. I. C. Dodemaide and S. P. Davis did not bat.

Bowling: Chatfield 5–2–19–2; Hadlee 7–0–28–0; Snedden 8–2–40–3; Gillespie 6.2–0–31–0; Brown 7–0–51–0.

Umpires: A. R. Crafter and M. W. Johnson.

†AUSTRALIA v SRI LANKA

At Sydney, January 19 (day/night). Australia won by three wickets. Toss: Sri Lanka. A face-saving innings of 79 from 100 balls by de Silva, just when Australia's bowlers seemed ready to inflict a crushing defeat, saw Sri Lanka reach 188. Both Whitney and Waugh recorded their best bowling figures in a one-day international. However, the Sri Lankan batsmen's struggle was put into better perspective as Australia made hard work of reaching their target and won with only three balls to spare. Veletta, in recording his best score in the competition, batted from the fall of the second wicket until the end, his stand of 73 with Dodemaide in three-quarters of an hour saving his team from embarrassment.

Man of the Match: M. R. J. Veletta. *Attendance:* 18,716.

Sri Lanka

R. S. Mahanama c Border b Whitney	12	†R. G. de Alwis c Marsh b Dodemaide	4
D. S. B. P. Kuruppu b Whitney	2	G. F. Labrooy not out	6
A. P. Gurusinha c Jones b Whitney	37	C. P. H. Ramanayake not out	5
S. M. S. Kaluperuma b Waugh	4	B 2, l-b 16, w 3, n-b 1	22
P. A. de Silva c Dyer b Waugh	79		
A. Ranatunga c Marsh b Waugh	16	1/16 2/27 3/39 (9 wkts, 50 overs)	188
*R. S. Madugalle lbw b Waugh	0	4/113 5/140 6/148	
J. R. Ratnayeke c Boon b Whitney	1	7/162 8/172 9/179	

Bowling: Whitney 10–2–34–4; Dodemaide 10–1–34–1; Waugh 10–0–33–4; May 10–0–22–0; Taylor 10–1–47–0.

Australia

D. C. Boon c Mahanama b Ratnayeke	15	A. I. C. Dodemaide c Kaluperuma b Labrooy	30
G. R. Marsh c Gurusinha b Ramanayake	8	P. L. Taylor not out	10
D. M. Jones c de Alwis b Ramanayake	9		
M. R. J. Veletta not out	68	L-b 10, w 3, n-b 4	17
S. R. Waugh c Mahanama b Ramanayake	16	1/25 2/30 3/49 (7 wkts, 49.3 overs)	189
*A. R. Border c and b de Silva	12	4/72 5/91	
†G. C. Dyer b Ranatunga	4	6/100 7/173	

T. B. A. May and M. R. Whitney did not bat.

Bowling: Ratnayeke 10–1–32–1; Labrooy 9.3–1–43–1; Ramanayake 10–0–35–3; Ranatunga 9–0–35–1; de Silva 10–0–31–1; Kaluperuma 1–0–3–0.

Umpires: T. A. Prue and S. G. Randell.

†AUSTRALIA v NEW ZEALAND

At Sydney, January 20 (day/night). Australia won by 78 runs. Toss: Australia. In front of an all-ticket, sell-out crowd New Zealand, who were without Hadlee, Wright and Martin Crowe, put up only token resistance in the last of the twelve qualifying matches. Marsh, who had had an ordinary series up to this game, scored his fifth century in one-day internationals (101 from 148 balls with five fours and a five) before falling in the 50th over. When New Zealand batted, Davis took three of the first five wickets, and after Brown was dismissed the lengthy tail collapsed. The final five wickets fell for the addition of only 24 runs.

Man of the Match: G. R. Marsh. *Attendance:* 41,813.

Australia

G. R. Marsh c Brown b Chatfield 101
D. C. Boon c Blain b Snedden 8
D. M. Jones c Bracewell b Gillespie ... 15
M. R. J. Veletta c Gillespie b Bracewell 19
S. R. Waugh c Crowe b Watson 0
*A. R. Border run out 22
†G. C. Dyer c Crowe b Brown 11
C. J. McDermott c Jones b Chatfield .. 18
A. I. C. Dodemaide not out 11
P. L. Taylor not out 3
B 2, l-b 6, w 4, n-b 1 13

1/17 2/50 3/88 4/88 5/145 6/162 7/194 8/217 (8 wkts, 50 overs) 221

S. P. Davis did not bat.

Bowling: Snedden 10–1–36–1; Chatfield 10–3–26–2; Watson 10–1–49–1; Gillespie 6–0–31–1; Bracewell 10–1–47–1; Brown 4–0–24–1.

New Zealand

†T. E. Blain c Jones b McDermott 1
A. H. Jones c Dyer b Davis 19
*J. J. Crowe c Veletta b Dodemaide ... 6
K. R. Rutherford c McDermott b Davis 10
D. N. Patel b Davis 13
V. R. Brown st Dyer b Taylor 32
J. G. Bracewell b Waugh 38
M. C. Snedden c Veletta b Taylor 6
S. R. Gillespie lbw b Taylor 2
W. Watson c Boon b Waugh 1
E. J. Chatfield not out 1
L-b 7, w 5, n-b 2 14

1/3 2/30 3/34 4/48 5/73 6/119 7/131 8/138 9/141 (44.5 overs) 143

Bowling: Dodemaide 9–1–21–1; McDermott 8–1–31–1; Davis 10–1–27–3; Waugh 7.5–0–33–2; Taylor 10–2–24–3.

Umpires: A. R. Crafter and L. J. King.

QUALIFYING TABLE

	P	*W*	*L*	*Pts*	*Run-rate*
Australia	8	7	1	14	4.74
New Zealand	8	4	4	8	4.08
Sri Lanka	8	1	7	2	4.02

†AUSTRALIA v NEW ZEALAND

First Final Match

At Melbourne, January 22 (day/night). Australia won by eight wickets. Toss: New Zealand. Australia won the first match of the finals in convincing fashion after their thoroughly professional bowling and fielding display had restricted New Zealand to 177 on a good Melbourne pitch. The Crowe brothers put on 44 from 66 deliveries for the third New Zealand wicket and looked set for a large partnership until Martin Crowe (48 from 72 balls) top-edged a ball from Dodemaide in the 29th over. His brother was brilliantly run out by his opposite number, Border, from mid-wicket, after which Hadlee (34 off 48 balls) faced an uphill struggle. In reply, Boon dominated, and when he went with the score 73, Jones and Veletta shared an unbeaten stand of 107 from 131 balls to ensure victory.

Attendance: 48,802.

New Zealand

J. G. Wright c Dyer b Davis	16
A. H. Jones c Dyer b Dodemaide	4
M. D. Crowe c Dyer b Dodemaide	48
*J. J. Crowe run out	33
R. J. Hadlee c Boon b McDermott	34
†T. E. Blain run out	1
V. R. Brown c Waugh b Davis	2
J. G. Bracewell c Border b Waugh	17
M. C. Snedden c Taylor b McDermott	15
W. Watson c Border b Waugh	1
E. J. Chatfield not out	3
L-b 2, w 1	3
1/11 2/47 3/91 4/126 5/129 6/132 7/143 8/161 9/169 (49.5 overs)	177

Bowling: Dodemaide 10–2–29–2; McDermott 9.5–0–37–2; Davis 10–1–27–2; Waugh 10–0–47–2; Taylor 10–0–35–0.

Australia

D. C. Boon c Bracewell b Watson	47
G. R. Marsh b Watson	9
D. M. Jones not out	58
M. R. J. Veletta not out	57
B 2, l-b 3, w 2, n-b 2	9
1/33 2/73 (2 wkts, 44.5 overs)	180

*A. R. Border, S. R. Waugh, †G. C. Dyer, A. I. C. Dodemaide, C. J. McDermott, P. L. Taylor and S. P. Davis did not bat.

Bowling: Chatfield 7.5–2–19–0; Hadlee 9–0–36–0; Snedden 10–3–39–0; Watson 10–3–36–2; Bracewell 8–0–45–0.

Umpires: R. C. Bailhache and P. J. McConnell.

†AUSTRALIA v NEW ZEALAND

Second Final Match

At Sydney, January 24. Australia won by six wickets. Toss: Australia. In a match reduced by rain to 38 overs, and played under lights for a brief time because of the overcast conditions, the Australian superiority over New Zealand in the one-day series was shown yet again. Tight, accurate bowling by Dodemaide, McDermott, Davis and Taylor, against a visiting team showing signs of world-weariness, was the dominant factor. In the New Zealand innings, Jones remained unbeaten with 56 from 82 balls, and his stand of 60 with Jeff Crowe (42 from 40 balls) was the one highlight. When Australia replied, Hadlee bowled with his usual accuracy before retiring with a knee injury, and there was a fifth WSC half-century, from 70 balls, for Jones as the New Zealanders went through the motions. The World Series Cup was once again presented on television rather than on the field, much to the disappointment of the players who earned it and the spectators who took the trouble to turn up.

Man of the Finals: D. M. Jones. *Attendance:* 29,356.

New Zealand

†T. E. Blain c Veletta b McDermott	9
J. G. Wright c Waugh b Dodemaide	8
M. D. Crowe b Davis	8
A. H. Jones not out	56
R. J. Hadlee c Border b Waugh	19
*J. J. Crowe c Jones b McDermott	42
D. N. Patel not out	11
L-b 11, w 4	15
1/20 2/21 3/31 4/79 5/139 (5 wkts, 38 overs)	168

J. G. Bracewell, M. C. Snedden, W. Watson and E. J. Chatfield did not bat.

Bowling: Dodemaide 8–0–27–1; McDermott 8–0–29–2; Davis 8–1–23–1; Taylor 7–0–27–0; Waugh 7–0–51–1.

Australia

G. R. Marsh c Wright b Hadlee 5
D. C. Boon c Snedden b Watson 43
C. J. McDermott c M. D. Crowe b Snedden . 24
D. M. Jones not out 53
M. R. J. Veletta c sub (K. R. Rutherford) b Snedden . 30
*A. R. Border not out 11
L-b 3 3

1/12 2/48 3/91 4/145 (4 wkts, 34.1 overs) 169

S. R. Waugh, †G. C. Dyer, A. I. C. Dodemaide, P. L. Taylor and S. P. Davis did not bat.

Bowling: Hadlee 8–2–22–1; Chatfield 6–2–34–0; Snedden 8–0–45–2; Bracewell 7–0–37–0; Watson 5.1–0–28–1.

Umpires: A. R. Crafter and P. J. McConnell.

SHARJAH CUP, 1987-88

India, led by Ravi Shastri in the absence of Dilip Vengsarkar, who was serving a six-month ban imposed by the Indian Board of Control, convincingly won the Sharjah Cup and the first prize of $US30,000. New Zealand and Sri Lanka made up the three-nation tournament, which offered $US150,000 in prizemoney, awards and benefits. The major beneficiary was the former Indian captain and all-rounder, Lala Amarnath, while his son, Mohinder, who was playing in the tournament, was the minor beneficiary. Richard Hadlee of New Zealand was the recipient of a special award. There was considerable interest in the appearance of the new Indian leg-spinner, Narendra Hirwani. He did not disappoint his country's thousands of supporters who work in the Arab Emirates, twice taking four wickets against New Zealand and winning the Man of the Series award.

†INDIA v SRI LANKA

At Sharjah, March 25. India won by 18 runs. Toss: Sri Lanka. Sri Lanka bowled and fielded magnificently to restrict India to 219 on a good batting pitch. But nerves and inexperience told against them in the end. With victory seemingly in their grasp, they lost eight wickets for 50 runs – three of them to run-outs. Shastri, in his 99th one-day international, took his 100th wicket when More stumped Madugalle.

Man of the Match: P. A. de Silva.

India

K. Srikkanth c Mahanama b Ramanayake . 32
N. S. Sidhu b Ratnayeke 17
M. Amarnath run out 1
W. V. Raman c Madugalle b de Silva . 21
M. Azharuddin b Ramanayake 7
Kapil Dev c Madugalle b de Silva 48
*R. J. Shastri c Mahanama b Ratnayeke 26
†K. S. More run out 9
Arshad Ayub not out 31
Chetan Sharma not out 12
B 1, l-b 7, w 2, n-b 5 15

1/31 2/32 3/63 4/71 5/125 6/140 7/152 8/198 (8 wkts, 50 overs) 219

N. D. Hirwani did not bat.

Bowling: Ratnayeke 10–0–34–2; Labrooy 9–0–41–0; Ramanayake 7–0–37–2; Anurasiri 10–0–44–0; de Silva 9–2–28–2; Ranatunga 5–0–27–0.

Sri Lanka

R. S. Mahanama b Hirwani 51
D. S. B. P. Kuruppu c Shastri b C. Sharma . 6
A. P. Gurusinha run out 0
P. A. de Silva b Hirwani 88
A. Ranatunga c Azharuddin b Shastri . 8
*R. S. Madugalle st More b Shastri . . . 11
†R. G. de Alwis c Srikkanth b Kapil Dev 2
J. R. Ratnayeke run out 4
G. F. Labrooy run out 0
C. P. H. Ramanayake run out 11
S. D. Anurasiri not out 3
B 3, l-b 10, w 3, n-b 1 17

1/14 2/14 3/151 4/158 5/177 6/180 7/181 8/182 9/190 (49.2 overs) 201

Bowling: Kapil Dev 9.2–2–26–1; C. Sharma 6–3–19–1; Amarnath 6–0–26–0; Shastri 8–0–40–2; Hirwani 10–1–40–2; Ayub 10–0–37–0.

Umpires: Khizar Hayat and Mahboob Shah.

†INDIA v NEW ZEALAND

At Sharjah, March 27. India won by 73 runs. Toss: New Zealand. India's total, built around a partnership of 158 between Amarnath and Sidhu, was the highest by any country in Sharjah, while Amarnath's hundred was only the third scored there. New Zealand looked out of sorts in the field, dropping four catches, missing several possible run-outs, and rarely putting India under pressure.

Man of the Match: M. Amarnath.

India

K. Srikkanth b Watson	1
N. S. Sidhu c Rutherford b Watson	88
W. V. Raman c Greatbatch b Hadlee	1
M. Amarnath not out	102
Kapil Dev c Kuggeleijn b Hadlee	5
M. Azharuddin run out	29
*R. J. Shastri c Smith b Hadlee	29
†K. S. More not out	3
L-b 4, w 4, n-b 1	9
1/1 2/4 3/162 4/167 5/212 6/260 (6 wkts, 50 overs)	267

Chetan Sharma, Arshad Ayub and N. D. Hirwani did not bat.

Bowling: Hadlee 10–0–54–3; Watson 10–2–36–2; Morrison 10–0–45–0; Chatfield 10–0–57–0; Rutherford 5–0–38–0; Kuggeleijn 5–0–33–0.

New Zealand

*J. G. Wright c More b Kapil Dev	19
R. H. Vance c More b Ayub	42
A. H. Jones c and b Azharuddin	6
M. J. Greatbatch c More b Hirwani	45
K. R. Rutherford c sub b Hirwani	3
†I. D. S. Smith b Hirwani	17
C. M. Kuggeleijn st More b Hirwani	3
R. J. Hadlee not out	35
D. K. Morrison st More b Ayub	6
W. Watson not out	4
B 1, l-b 6, w 6, n-b 1	14
1/32 2/46 3/118 4/120 5/124 6/139 7/144 8/175 (8 wkts, 50 overs)	194

E. J. Chatfield did not bat.

Bowling: Kapil Dev 10–2–30–1; C. Sharma 7–0–28–0; Azharuddin 4–0–15–1; Shastri 8–1–29–0; Hirwani 10–0–43–4; Ayub 10–1–41–2; Raman 1–0–1–0.

Umpires: Khizar Hayat and Mahboob Shah.

†NEW ZEALAND v SRI LANKA

At Sharjah, March 29. New Zealand won by 99 runs. Toss: Sri Lanka. New Zealand, putting behind them their previous performance, came within 9 runs of equalling India's record score, made against them two days earlier. Vance and Jones put on 94 for the second wicket, after which Jones (98 balls) and Rutherford (58 balls, eight fours) added 103. Sri Lanka looked a shadow of the team that had threatened India in the opening match.

Man of the Match: A. H. Jones.

New Zealand

*J. G. Wright c Kuruppu b Ratnayeke	0
R. H. Vance run out	45
A. H. Jones run out	85
K. R. Rutherford st Kuruppu b E. A. R. de Silva	65
D. N. Patel run out	27
M. J. Greatbatch c Kaluperuma b Ratnayeke	15
†T. E. Blain run out	6
C. M. Kuggeleijn not out	7
D. K. Morrison run out	0
W. Watson not out	2
L-b 4, w 2	6
1/0 2/94 3/197 4/201 5/223 6/248 7/248 8/249 (8 wkts, 50 overs)	258

E. J. Chatfield did not bat.

Bowling: Ratnayeke 10–0–33–2; Labrooy 7–0–41–0; Anurasiri 10–0–49–0; E. A. R. de Silva 10–0–42–1; Ranatunga 8–0–44–0; P. A. de Silva 4–0–31–0; Amalean 1–0–14–0.

Sri Lanka

†D. S. B. P. Kuruppu run out 46	G. F. Labrooy b Morrison 5
A. P. Gurusinha c Vance b Watson . . . 27	S. D. Anurasiri not out 5
*R. S. Madugalle c Jones b Kuggeleijn . 15	K. N. Amalean run out 6
P. A. de Silva c Blain b Rutherford . . . 1	L-b 3, w 8, n-b 1 12
A. Ranatunga b Kuggeleijn 6	——
J. R. Ratnayeke c Blain b Patel 25	1/50 2/93 3/96 (42.5 overs) 159
S. M. S. Kaluperuma lbw b Patel 7	4/96 5/111 6/124
E. A. R. de Silva c Jones b Patel 4	7/140 8/142 9/150

Bowling: Morrison 8–0–36–1; Chatfield 8–0–24–0; Watson 5–0–19–1; Kuggeleijn 10–2–32–2; Rutherford 5–0–23–1; Patel 6.5–0–22–3.

Umpires: Khizar Hayat and Mahboob Shah.

SEMI-FINAL

†NEW ZEALAND v SRI LANKA

At Sharjah, March 31. New Zealand won by 43 runs. Toss: New Zealand. New Zealand and Sri Lanka met for the second time in three days for a place in the final against India. Wright and Vance began confidently, raising 50 in 12.1 overs, and Vance, improving on his highest score from the previous match, narrowly missed his first one-day international hundred. Sri Lanka made a better fist of their reply but lost the initiative when four wickets fell for 25.

Man of the Match: R. H. Vance.

New Zealand

R. H. Vance run out 96	D. N. Patel lbw b E. A. R. de Silva . . . 0
*J. G. Wright st de Alwis b P. A. de Silva . 45	C. M. Kuggeleijn not out 24
A. H. Jones b Ranatunga 33	†T. E. Blain not out 6
M. J. Greatbatch run out 12	B 1, l-b 5, w 4 10
K. R. Rutherford c Gurusinha b E. A. R. de Silva . 9	——
	1/76 2/146 3/180 (7 wkts, 50 overs) 249
R. J. Hadlee c Ratnayeke b E. A. R. de Silva . 14	4/199 5/204
	6/204 7/230

W. Watson and E. J. Chatfield did not bat.

Bowling: Ratnayeke 8–0–27–0; Labrooy 10–0–65–0; P. A. de Silva 10–1–41–1; Ranatunga 10–0–43–1; Anurasiri 4–0–29–0; E. A. R. de Silva 8–0–38–3.

Sri Lanka

R. S. Mahanama c Rutherford b Patel . 43	E. A. R. de Silva b Chatfield 10
D. S. B. P. Kuruppu c Vance b Watson 0	G. F. Labrooy b Watson 1
A. P. Gurusinha lbw b Hadlee 60	S. D. Anurasiri not out 3
P. A. de Silva c and b Kuggeleijn 1	L-b 12, w 1, n-b 1 14
A. Ranatunga b Patel 2	——
*R. S. Madugalle run out 25	1/0 2/90 3/92 (9 wkts, 50 overs) 206
J. R. Ratnayeke c Greatbatch b Watson 31	4/95 5/115 6/158
†R. G. de Alwis not out 16	7/174 8/192 9/196

Bowling: Hadlee 10–1–25–1; Watson 9–1–37–3; Chatfield 10–0–48–1; Kuggeleijn 10–0–37–1; Patel 10–0–45–2; Jones 1–0–2–0.

Umpires: Khizar Hayat and Mahboob Shah.

FINAL

†INDIA v NEW ZEALAND

At Sharjah, April 1. India won by 52 runs. Toss: India. An analysis of Chatfield's bowling figures summed up India's innings. His first five overs cost 6 runs; his last, the 50th, cost 18. India, having taken 32 overs to reach 100, added 150 in the next eighteen, with 50 coming from the last 21 balls. Partnerships of 72 between Amarnath (71 balls) and Shastri, who began with a first-ball six, and 73 between Shastri and Kapil Dev (26 balls) provided the momentum. Shastri hit three fours and three sixes in his 68-ball 72 which took him past 2,000 runs in one-day internationals. Wright played fluently until running himself out, but Greatbatch, dropped at 5 and 23, was less convincing. The leg-spin of Hirwani stifled the New Zealand middle order. Smith hit 40 from 33 balls to leave 56 needed from the last ten overs, but his dismissal signalled the end for New Zealand.

Man of the Match: R. J. Shastri.

India

K. Srikkanth b Chatfield	14
N. S. Sidhu c Hadlee b Patel	33
W. V. Raman b Kuggeleijn	7
M. Amarnath c Greatbatch b Morrison	58
M. Azharuddin run out	6
*R. J. Shastri b Hadlee	72
Kapil Dev not out	49
†K. S. More c Morrison b Chatfield	5
Arshad Ayub not out	0
B 1, l-b 3, w 2	6
1/28 2/49 3/70 4/82 5/154 6/227 7/232 (7 wkts, 50 overs)	250

Sanjeev Sharma and N. D. Hirwani did not bat.

Bowling: Hadlee 10–0–49–1; Watson 7–2–37–0; Chatfield 10–0–57–2; Kuggeleijn 10–0–38–1; Patel 9–0–32–1; Morrison 4–0–33–1.

New Zealand

R. H. Vance c More b S. Sharma	3
*J. G. Wright run out	55
A. H. Jones lbw b Amarnath	15
M. J. Greatbatch c Kapil Dev b Hirwani	47
D. N. Patel c Shastri b Hirwani	1
R. J. Hadlee c Ayub b Hirwani	3
C. M. Kuggeleijn c Srikkanth b Hirwani	7
†I. D. S. Smith c S. Sharma b Raman	40
D. K. Morrison b Kapil Dev	7
W. Watson b Shastri	10
E. J. Chatfield not out	1
L-b 7, w 2	9
1/15 2/60 3/92 4/94 5/94 6/113 7/160 8/182 9/196 (45.3 overs)	198

Bowling: Kapil Dev 7.3–2–14–1; S. Sharma 6–0–21–1; Shastri 9–0–25–1; Amarnath 2–0–14–1; Hirwani 10–0–46–4; Ayub 9–0–48–0; Raman 2–0–23–1.

Umpires: Khizar Hayat and Mahboob Shah.

McDONALD'S BICENTENNIAL YOUTH WORLD CUP, 1987-88

By KENNETH R. BULLOCK

Arranged by the Australian Cricket Board as part of the country's Bicentennial celebrations, the first Youth World Cup attracted to Australia young cricketers from thirteen countries. In addition to teams from the seven ICC full-member countries, there was an ICC Associates team comprising players drawn from six associate-member countries. This unique team was captained by a Zimbabwean, managed by a Canadian and coached by an Australian.

The tournament was played as a series of round-robin preliminary matches in the Riverland and Sunraysia regions on the South Australia, Victoria and New South Wales borders, followed by the semi-finals and final at the Adelaide Oval. The playing conditions were those used for Australia's World Series Cup competition, with matches limited to 50 overs a side, a fielding circle, and only two fielders allowed outside it for the first fifteen overs. It was a form of cricket not familiar to some of the players, all of whom had to be under twenty on January 1, 1988.

As became apparent as the tournament progressed, the host country were a powerful, well-balanced combination, coached by the former Victorian batsman, Jack Potter. They lost only once in the round-robin matches, to Pakistan, and by then they were already assured of their top-of-the-table ranking. In their semi-final they accounted for England with some ease and then scored a decisive victory over Pakistan in the final to emulate the World Cup-winning achievement of their seniors. Pakistan had reached the final by beating West Indies. If England, nine of whose players had first-class experience with their counties, were disappointed at failing to reach the final, they had nevertheless already been beaten by Australia, India and Sri Lanka in the round-robin. Sri Lanka, fifth in the final table, had good reason to return home pleased, but India, who included the Test-match leg-spinner, Hirwani, and New Zealand probably felt they should have done better. The ICC Associates lost all seven matches but went close to victories over England and Sri Lanka.

The Australian Cricket Board is to be congratulated for its enterprise and for the professional manner in which the tournament was arranged. Once the visiting teams were in Australia, most of their expenses were covered by sponsorship, with the players being billeted in pairs with local families. The cricket was top class, and it would come as no surprise if the event were repeated in four years' time.

The teams, comprising fourteen players each, were as follows:

Australia: G. R. Parker (*captain*), H. Armstrong, D. Berry, T. D. Bower, M. Collins, L. Ferguson, W. Holdsworth, S. G. Law, B. McFadyen, A. D. Mullally, D. Playle, J. C. Scuderi, A. E. Tucker, B. D. Williams.

England: M. A. Atherton (*captain*), M. W. Alleyne, M. P. Bicknell, J. Boiling, S. J. Brown, W. K. Hegg, N. Hussain, C. C. Lewis, P. J. Martin, M. W. Pooley, M. R. Ramprakash, N. A. Stanley, H. R. J. Trump, T. R. Ward.

ICC Associates: T. Penney (Zimbabwe) (*captain*), G. Bruk-Jackson (Zimbabwe), J. Christiansen (Denmark), E. Dube and E. Essop-Adam (Zimbabwe), N. Ifill (Canada), Amin-ul-Islam (Bangladesh), M. Houben (Netherlands), N. Kirmani (Canada), T. de Leede (Netherlands), K. Lightbourn and D. Minors (Bermuda), Harun-or-Rashid (Bangladesh), S. Sorensen (Denmark).

India: M. Senthilnathan (*captain*), P. Amre, S. Bannerjee, R. Biswal, M. Chaturvedi, A. Deshpande, N. D. Hirwani, A. Kripal Singh, N. Mongia, J. Ramdas, G. Shyam Sunder, Sukhvinder Singh, S. L. Venkatapathi Raju, K. Virdi.

New Zealand: L. K. Germon (*captain*), A. Caddick, C. L. Cairns, G. de Joux, P. Dobbs, M. Douglas, A. Gale, M. Hastings, H. Kember, M. Kimber, S. Peterson, C. Pringle, S. Roberts, S. A. Thomson.

Pakistan: Zahoor Elahi (*captain*), Aaqib Javed, Basit Ali, Imzamamul Haq, Muhammad Nawaz, Mushtaq Ahmed, Rehan Kahloon, Riffaqat Ali, Shahid Anwar, Shahid Nawaz, Shakil Khan, Wasim Ali, Zulfiqar Ali, Zulfiqar Butt.

Sri Lanka: R. Weerakkody (*captain*), A. Allirajah, R. Amunugama, C. Fernando, U. C. Hathurusinghe, S. Jayasuriya, R. Kaluwitharna, Chaminda Mendis, D. C. M. Perera, K. G. Priyantha, S. Ranatunga, J. Samarasekera, C. Unantenne, C. D. U. S. Weerasinghe.

West Indies: B. C. Lara (*captain*), J. C. Adams, K. N. Browne, R. Dhanraj, H. Gangapersad, S. Halden, R. I. C. Holder, R. D. Jacobs, N. O. Perry, R. Samuels, T. Samuels, S. Skeete, D. T. Telemaque, D. Thomas.

Results

At Mildura, February 28. Australia won by 73 runs. Australia 238 for five (50 overs) (B. D. Williams 112, D. Playle 52, G. R. Parker 33 not out); West Indies 165 (39.5 overs) (R. D. Jacobs 36, J. C. Adams 32; A. E. Tucker four for 42).

At Berri, February 28. New Zealand won by 12 runs. New Zealand 178 for nine (50 overs) (P. Dobbs 40, S. A. Thomson 37, M. Douglas 30; S. Jayasuriya three for 34); Sri Lanka 166 (47.4 overs) (C. Mendis 43, S. Ranatunga 32; A. Gale three for 30).

At Renmark, February 28. India won by two wickets. England 172 for eight (50 overs) (M. A. Atherton 80, M. R. Ramprakash 46; Sukhvinder Singh three for 29); India 173 for eight (49.4 overs) (M. Senthilnathan 47).

At Merbein, February 28. Pakistan won by five wickets. ICC Associates 163 (49.2 overs) (Harun-or-Rashid 38; Shakil Khan four for 26, Mushtaq Ahmed three for 30); Pakistan 166 for five (35.2 overs) (Shahid Nawaz 47, Imzamamul Haq 33).

At Wentworth, February 29. West Indies won by 34 runs. West Indies 236 for nine (50 overs) (B. C. Lara 64, Extras 40); New Zealand 202 for nine (50 overs) (S. A. Thomson 44, M. Douglas 44).

At Barmera, February 29. Pakistan won by seven wickets. Sri Lanka 151 (48.3 overs) (C. Mendis 74); Pakistan 152 for three (39.2 overs) (Zahoor Elahi 71, Shahid Anwar 31).

At Mildura, February 29. England won by 30 runs. England 205 for eight (50 overs) (N. Hussain 68, M. W. Alleyne 40, M. A. Atherton 34; K. Lightbourn three for 45); ICC Associates 175 (48.3 overs) (T. Penney 55, T. de Leede 45, G. Bruk-Jackson 33; M. A. Atherton four for 25).

At Berri, February 29. Australia won by seven wickets. India 132 (45.3 overs) (N. Mongia 46; B. McFadyen four for 20); Australia 136 for three (39.2 overs) (S. G. Law 72 not out, L. Ferguson 32 not out).

At Wentworth, March 2. Pakistan won by 68 runs. Pakistan 194 for seven (50 overs) (Shahid Anwar 43, Imzamamul Haq 39); India 126 (39.3 overs) (A. Kripal Singh 30; Zahoor Elahi four for 15).

At Loxton, March 2. New Zealand won by four wickets. ICC Associates 131 (41.2 overs) (G. Bruk-Jackson 40; C. L. Cairns four for 18, S. Peterson three for 18); New Zealand 132 for six (37.3 overs) (S. Peterson 32).

At Merbein, March 2. Australia won by 24 runs. Australia 249 (48.4 overs) (B. D. Williams 75, L. Ferguson 39, S. G. Law 30; C. Mendis four for 35); Sri Lanka 225 (47.4 overs) (C. Mendis 63, U. C. Hathurusinghe 53; A. E. Tucker three for 50).

At Renmark, March 2. England won by 63 runs. England 174 for seven (50 overs) (N. Hussain 50, M. W. Alleyne 31); West Indies 111 (43.2 overs) (J. Boiling three for 26).

At Barmera, March 3. Sri Lanka won by four wickets. England 102 (41.1 overs) (N. Hussain 35; U. C. Hathurusinghe three for 36, C. Fernando three for 29); Sri Lanka 103 for six (35.5 overs) (A. Allirajah 32).

At Mildura, March 3. West Indies won by 20 runs. West Indies 121 (49 overs) (Mushtaq Ahmed three for 28); Pakistan 101 (43.4 overs) (S. Skeete three for 25).

At Wentworth, March 3. Australia won by 177 runs. Australia 303 for eight (50 overs) (G. R. Parker 103, J. C. Scuderi 66, H. Armstrong 46; J. Christiansen three for 44); ICC Associates 126 (44.2 overs) (B. McFadyen four for 26, A. E. Tucker three for 17).

At Loxton, March 3. India won by 44 runs. India 164 (46.3 overs) (M. Senthilnathan 52, J. Ramdas 32; A. Gale three for 30); New Zealand 120 (45.5 overs) (S. Roberts 36, S. A. Thomson 32; J. Ramdas three for 24, N. D. Hirwani three for 26).

At Loxton, March 6. Pakistan won by seven wickets. New Zealand 198 for seven (50 overs) (S. A. Thomson 56, C. L. Cairns 34; Mushtaq Ahmed three for 42); Pakistan 199 for three (46 overs) (Shahid Anwar 51, Basit Ali 47, Shahid Nawaz 43 not out, Imzamamul Haq 45 not out).

At Merbein, March 6. West Indies won by 70 runs. West Indies 193 for six (50 overs) (R. D. Jacobs 76, J. C. Adams 32 not out); India 123 (46 overs) (N. Mongia 36).

At Renmark, March 6. Australia won by 60 runs. Australia 206 for seven (50 overs) (S. G. Law 89, G. R. Parker 48); England 146 (49 overs) (C. C. Lewis 66, H. R. J. Trump 36 not out; J. C. Scuderi five for 27).

At Mildura, March 6. Sri Lanka won by 47 runs. Sri Lanka 231 for seven (50 overs) (A. Allirajah 54, S. Ranatunga 61; T. de Leede three for 41, E. Essop-Adam three for 41); ICC Associates 184 for seven (50 overs) (T. de Leede 49, T. Penney 42, E. Essop-Adam 40; C. Fernando three for 29).

At Berri, March 7. India won by seven wickets. ICC Associates 111 (45 overs) (E. Essop-Adam 40; S. L. Venkatapathi Raju three for 19); India 112 for three (29 overs).

At Wentworth, March 7. Australia won by 48 runs. Australia 254 (49.3 overs) (B. D. Williams 58, S. G. Law 67; C. L. Cairns four for 43); New Zealand 206 for eight (50 overs) (S. Roberts 56, L. K. Germon 53 not out; W. Holdsworth four for 36).

At Merbein, March 7. England won by 56 runs. England 126 (46.3 overs) (M. R. Ramprakash 53, N. Hussain 48; Mushtaq Ahmed three for 34, Zulfiqar Butt three for 13); Pakistan 70 (24.1 overs) (Zahoor Elahi 35; C. C. Lewis five for 39, J. Boiling three for 7).

At Barmera, March 7. West Indies won by 100 runs. West Indies 201 for eight (50 overs) (R. I. C. Holder 63, B. C. Lara 38; K. G. Priyantha three for 32, D. C. M. Perera three for 30); Sri Lanka 101 (39.4 overs) (S. Skeete four for 20).

At Renmark, March 8. England won by 39 runs. England 193 for six (50 overs) (M. A. Atherton 51, N. Hussain 61, C. C. Lewis 36 not out); New Zealand 154 (44.3 overs) (M. Douglas 36, S. Peterson 32; C. C. Lewis four for 35).

At Berri, March 8. Sri Lanka won by 50 runs. Sri Lanka 190 for nine (50 overs) (S. Jayasuriya 53, J. Samarasekera 42, C. Fernando 30; S. Bannerjee three for 19, N. D. Hirwani three for 47); India 140 (28.2 overs).

At Wentworth, March 8. West Indies won by 123 runs. West Indies 272 for six (50 overs) (D. T. Telemaque 35 retired hurt, J. C. Adams 65, B. C. Lara 45, H. Gangapersad 33 not out); ICC Associates 149 for seven (50 overs) (T. Penney 74 not out, E. Essop-Adam 35).

At Mildura, March 8. Pakistan won by 32 runs. Pakistan 199 (49.4 overs) (Shahid Anwar 49, Wasim Ali 32; W. Holdsworth four for 36); Australia 167 (47.2 overs) (L. Ferguson 32; Shahid Anwar four for 45, Mushtaq Ahmed three for 42).

FINAL TABLE

	P	W	L	Pts	Run-rate
Australia	7	6	1	12	4.58
West Indies	7	5	2	10	3.71
Pakistan	7	5	2	10	3.36
England	7	4	3	8	3.19
Sri Lanka	7	3	4	6	3.47
India	7	3	4	6	2.95
New Zealand	7	2	5	4	3.52
ICC Associates	7	0	7	0	2.97

SEMI-FINALS

At Adelaide, March 10. Pakistan won by two wickets. West Indies 203 for eight (50 overs) (J. C. Adams 65, B. C. Lara 42); Pakistan 204 for eight (47.5 overs) (Shahid Anwar 76, Zahoor Elahi 43).

At Adelaide, March 11. Australia won by seven wickets. England 194 (50 overs) (M. W. Alleyne 56, N. Hussain 58); Australia 196 for three (45.2 overs) (B. D. Williams 57, D. Playle 36, L. Ferguson 40 not out, G. R. Parker 39 not out).

FINAL

AUSTRALIA v PAKISTAN

At Adelaide, March 13. Australia won by five wickets. Toss: Australia. A dynamic hundred from Williams, an opening batsman from New South Wales, was the basis of Australia's victory. Pakistan, put in, had batted steadily but never commandingly against an attack in which the Sydney leg-spinner, Tucker, was the most economical. However, a total of 201 did not look sufficient to tax Australia's batting depth and so it proved as Williams and Law, a Queenslander, added 97 for the second wicket. Williams gave a chance at 92, and when he was eventually caught at short mid-on in the 44th over, Australia were just 10 runs away from completing a cricketing World Cup double in their Bicentennial Year.

Man of the Match: B. D. Williams.

Pakistan

Shahid Anwar c Playle b Mullally 8
Basit Ali lbw b Parker 23
*Zahoor Elahi c Holdsworth b Mullally 35
Shahid Nawaz c Berry b Parker 35
Imzamamul Haq c Ferguson b Holdsworth . 37
Muhammad Nawaz c Mullally b Parker 14
Zulfiqar Butt b Holdsworth 19
†Riffaqat Ali c Berry b Holdsworth . . . 4
Mushtaq Ahmed run out 3
Zulfiqar Ali run out 5
Shakil Khan not out 8
L-b 4, w 5, n-b 1 10

1/10 2/59 3/88 4/125 5/149 6/171 7/183 8/186 9/186 (49.3 overs) 201

Bowling: Holdsworth 9.3–1–38–3; Mullally 10–1–53–2; Scuderi 10–0–38–0; Parker 10–0–36–3; Tucker 10–0–32–0.

Australia

B. D. Williams c Mushtaq b Zulfiqar Butt .108
D. Playle c Riffaqat b Imzamamul 12
S. G. Law c Zahoor b Anwar 44
L. Ferguson b Mushtaq 9
*G. R. Parker c and b Mushtaq 10
H. Armstrong not out 7
J. C. Scuderi not out 3
L-b 1, w 7, n-b 1 9

1/34 2/131 3/167 4/192 5/192 (5 wkts, 45.5 overs) 202

A. E. Tucker, †D. Berry, A. D. Mullally and W. Holdsworth did not bat.

Bowling: Shakil 6–0–21–0; Zulfiqar Ali 3–0–19–0; Imzamamul 6.5–0–28–1; Anwar 10–0–41–1; Mushtaq 10–0–59–2; Zulfiqar Butt 10–1–33–1.

Umpires: A. R. Crafter and R. J. Evans.

LEADING RUN-SCORERS

	M	*I*	*NO*	*R*	*HI*	*Avge*
B. D. Williams (*Aust.*) ..	9	9	0	471	112	52.33
S. G. Law (*Aust.*)	8	8	1	352	89	50.28
N. Hussain (*Eng.*)	8	8	0	330	68	41.25
Shahid Anwar (*Pak.*) ...	9	9	0	300	76	33.33
J. C. Adams (*WI*)	8	8	3	272	65	54.40
G. R. Parker (*Aust.*)	9	8	2	245	103	40.83
C. Mendis (*SL*)	7	7	0	240	74	34.28
Zahoor Elahi (*Pak.*)	9	9	0	235	71	26.11
S. A. Thomson (*NZ*)	7	7	1	234	56	39.00
T. Penney (*ICC*)	7	7	1	233	74*	38.83
B. C. Lara (*WI*)	8	8	0	222	64	27.75
Imzamamul Haq (*Pak.*) .	9	8	2	220	45*	36.66
R. D. Jacobs (*WI*)	8	8	0	218	76	27.25

LEADING WICKET-TAKERS

	O	*M*	*R*	*W*	*Avge*	*Runs/ over*
W. Holdsworth (*Aust.*) ...	72.2	10	238	19	12.52	3.29
Mushtaq Ahmed (*Pak.*) ..	83	4	308	19	16.21	3.71
C. C. Lewis (*Eng.*)	69.5	6	235	16	14.68	3.36
C. L. Cairns (*NZ*)	59	5	249	15	16.60	4.22
S. Skeete (*WI*)	70	9	240	13	18.46	3.43
J. Boiling (*Eng.*)	74.1	8	208	12	17.33	2.80
J. C. Scuderi (*Aust.*)	75	10	230	12	19.16	3.07
A. E. Tucker (*Aust.*)	79.5	8	263	12	21.91	3.29
Zulfiqar Butt (*Pak.*)	80.3	9	234	11	21.27	2.91
Shakil Khan (*Pak.*)	54.4	5	164	11	14.90	3.00
R. Dhanraj (*WI*)	67.4	3	208	11	18.90	3.07
N. D. Hirwani (*Ind.*)	65.2	4	213	10	21.30	3.26

CRICKET IN AUSTRALIA, 1987-88

By JOHN MACKINNON

For the second year running, Western Australia won the Sheffield Shield, defending their title decisively in Perth with a five-wicket victory over Queensland. They were nigh invincible on their home ground, winning four matches there in addition to the final. And victories in Hobart and Adelaide ensured a healthy points total, only two fewer than the previous year.

The domestic season in Australia began in an atmosphere of anticipation. Not only were the so-called "rebels", those Australians who had toured South Africa, eligible for state selection, but Queensland had signed Ian Botham in their bid to win the Shield for the first time. Initially, Queensland looked to be on a winner. Botham batted, bowled and fielded successfully, and the crowds flocked in, further encouraged by the Queensland Cricket Association's imaginative move to charge one dollar for admission. The mood spread across the country, and in Newcastle, Adelaide and Perth, state players found themselves performing before large and appreciative audiences.

Outright decisions were achieved in 20 of the 30 games, mostly without resort to declarations. The strange points system, introduced in 1986-87, whereby the two points for a first-innings win were forfeited in the event of outright defeat, remained in force, much to the chagrin of David Hookes, generally the most daring of the captains, who gambled and lost in Melbourne.

Graeme Wood deserved every accolade for taking Western Australia to their eleventh title. Injury deprived him of Bruce Reid's services early in the season, and Peter Capes, another left-arm fast bowler, also succumbed. But these losses brought out the best in Chris Matthews, Terry Alderman and Ken MacLeay. Matthews took 57 first-class wickets, as in the previous season, and was a constant threat to all batsmen. He swung the bat effectively, too, which was as well as the side often needed runs from the tail. After their successes of the previous year, the loss of form of Geoff Marsh, Mike Veletta and Tom Moody was a worry. Moody was finally left out. Wood, however, was irrepressible. His form got better and better, and a match-winning hundred in the final convinced the selectors that he should be recalled to the Australian team for the tour of Pakistan early in 1988-89. Kim Hughes earned his place on merit, but he never really settled, was dropped and then was brought back again for the final. Wayne Andrews swung his bat heartily, and Jamie Brayshaw, the twenty-year-old son of Ian, looked a good prospect. Western Australia paid only lip service to spin bowling. Steve Milosz, a leg-spinner, arrived from Tasmania, ran into Botham's assault in Brisbane, and later lost his place. Tom Hogan took some wickets in Tasmania, but with such depth in seam bowling, spin was apparently deemed a luxury.

Queensland's fortunes deteriorated as the season progressed, reaching their nadir at Perth in March. Botham's appearance looked to be just the fillip the side needed; their batting sparkled, their bowlers devastated, they won their matches. Then the wheels fell off. Humiliation in Brisbane in the McDonald's Cup by New South Wales, two losses to Tasmania – one in the McDonald's Cup – and defeat by Victoria led up to the infamous flight to Perth for the final. There, Queensland looked a beaten side before they took the field. That they pushed the champions as hard as they did was a tribute to the determination of such players as Dirk Tazelaar and Carl Rackemann.

Tazelaar had a splendid season. His fast-medium left-arm bowling gave the Queensland attack an incisive edge, and with Craig McDermott battling a knee injury, he took on the responsibility of spearhead with great gusto. Deservedly, he was equal first in the umpires' voting for Player of the Year. Rackemann's return to Shield cricket was delayed by injury, but he found his rhythm and was ultimately bowling as fast and aggressively as ever. McDermott began the season brilliantly. Reverting to his long run, he looked set for a great year, but he fell foul of injury and was only half-fit for the final. Botham's all-round contribution – 29 wickets and 646 runs, including seven fifties – speaks for itself. However, he failed to score a century and never took more than three wickets in an innings, which, while indicating consistency, reveals also that the match-winning efforts hoped for never eventuated. The batting was dependent on Allan Border, and the Australian captain, although looking tired by the season's end, rarely failed to provide runs. Robbie Kerr lacked a regular opening partner and only rarely lived up to his promise, Glenn Trimble could destroy any attack but only occasionally did, and Greg Ritchie should have contributed more. Ian Healy took over as wicket-keeper for the last four matches, Peter Anderson having broken his thumb, and in that short time he satisfied the national selectors that he was the best in the country.

New South Wales lost the services of their captain before a ball was bowled when Dirk Wellham announced his retirement. Greg Dyer inherited the captaincy, but after his involvement in "the catch that wasn't" in the Melbourne Test, his game was subjected to the severest scrutiny by the media and not surprisingly suffered as a consequence. It was New South Wales' batting that generally failed to measure up. Mark Waugh was a glorious exception. He shared the Player of the Year award with Tazelaar and entranced spectators all over the country with his uninhibited strokeplay and brilliant fielding. His twin brother, Stephen, played one innings of consequence for the state – against Victoria – but if his batting disappointed, his bowling improved in variety and control. Geoff Lawson, restored to fitness, was the leading bowler in the national averages, but would have learned that selection for his country depended as much on attitude as on performance. Greg Matthews, a much-improved bowler, had the best figures of any spinner, but his batting fell away badly. Peter Taylor, although bowling only 200 first-class overs, again found favour with the national selectors, especially after some excellent performances in one-day cricket; and Mike Whitney also achieved national recognition. However, Whitney's inability to bowl an in-swinger was a handicap. It was expected that the return of John Dyson and Steve Smith might be a boon to the side. yet in spite of the poor form of Mark Taylor, Steve Small and Mark O'Neill, the "rebels" earned selection only as an afterthought, and in no time they were out again. The future may now lie in the hands of younger players such as Scott Hookey, Graham Smith and Trevor Bayliss.

Victoria's strength was in batting. Dav Whatmore had a splendid year and hit a career-highest score in Perth. His opening partner, Gary Watts, came back to the side for the second half of the season and struck three centuries. Dean Jones, the captain, treated all bowlers with such disdain that, although playing a number of exciting innings, he still did not fully realise his potential. Jamie Siddons, a real dasher, was the player to catch the eye. His achievements were as spectacular as his methods – a thousand runs, four hundreds and selection for the Pakistan tour. Paul Young, in spite of averaging 60, could not retain his place among such talent. The bowlers had a tough time, especially at the MCG. Merv Hughes was all fire and brimstone as usual, but had still to convince in the Test arena, while Denis Hickey, so promising and quick two years earlier, disappointed. Simon Davis was stand-in captain one moment and out of the side the next. With Simon O'Donnell unavailable while undergoing chemotherapy treatment for lymphoma, Tony Dodemaide took up the mantle as his state's (and country's) leading all-rounder. His ability to bowl the out-swinger made him a more complete medium-pace bowler, and a return of 45 wickets was a fair reward for his efforts.

South Australia could field enough individual brilliance to give hope for the future, but the old problem of not taking wickets was harshly evident. Peter Gladigau, a much-improved player, led the fast bowling but often lacked support. Andrew Zesers, a star of the previous year, was largely ineffective and Tim May spent so much of the season as Australia's twelfth man that he had every reason to be dispirited. Peter Sleep bowled a lot of overs, but it was his batting that kept him in the Test team. Shane George, at seventeen, had his moments, but as a fast bowler he still had much to learn. Chris Killen, a burly import from New South Wales, may be an asset. The batting was dominated by Hookes, who overcame a tiresome wrist injury, from falling off his bicycle, and managed to combine his usual flair with a strong sense of responsibility. He was helped to a great extent by the excellence of his opening batsmen. Andrew Hilditch, eschewing the hook, grafted in his own methodical way, while Glenn Bishop, a powerful, upright batsman, never shirked from playing his strokes and gave his team its early impetus. Wayne Phillips was the best of the others, a reluctant wicket-keeper who expressed the desire to concentrate on his batting in order to make better use of his batting talents.

Tasmania had another depressing year. Brian Davison returned as captain, but at 41 he found runs hard to come by. Not so his predecessor, David Boon, who had a vintage season. Gone was the hesitant, shuffling footwork of previous times. Buoyed by a successful World Cup, Boon's confidence soared as he plundered the bowlers in Shield and Test matches alike. Mick Taylor, after a slow start, was almost as prolific. He was especially partial to the South Australian bowling, scoring 382 runs in two successive innings. Glenn Hughes and Danny Buckingham made their runs at a good rate and Peter Faulkner was handy in the middle order. But the Tasmanian attack came in for a terrible hammering. Although the recruiting of Dennis Lillee, coming out of retirement at 38, lent some credibility at one end, there were usually some easy pickings at the other. Tasmania's win over Queensland ended a barren run of 44 matches without victory, and was achieved without Lillee, injured, in the crucial fourth innings. But the Queensland batsmen contributed significantly to their own demise as they sought valuable points in reckless fashion.

It was a pity that a season which had many worthy aspects should end in acrimony. The Queensland/Botham affair, concluding with the termination of Botham's contract, heralded some public soul-searching by the team's major sponsor, who questioned the need for 22 delegates to man an administration which had failed to achieve its principal goal – winning the Shield. Western Australia parted company with the curator at the WACA,

John Maley, who had worked wonders in re-surfacing the ground and relocating the pitch area. He had lost his battle to prevent football being played there, and his fears were borne out in the latter part of the season when pitches developed big cracks and deteriorated quite noticeably. Preparation of the Sydney wicket seemed often to be thwarted by the weather, and no doubt by the rigours of the football season. In Melbourne, bat dominated ball so emphatically that the Victorian captain, inevitably, complained; and even in Adelaide, the curator came in for his share of criticism as he strove to find a fair balance. All the double-centuries were scored there. The Test match and South Australia-Tasmania game especially were dreadful contests, so dominant was the batting, yet when a little grass was left on top and wickets tumbled, cries of alarm and indignation were soon evident.

An agreeable move by the Australian Board was to appoint the former Victorian batsman, Jack Potter, to head the Australian Institute of Sport's Youth Squad; sixteen of Australia's best young cricketers brought together in Adelaide for special training, seminars and coaching. Potter, a fine captain and a born leader, has no time for the histrionics that often pervade the modern game. It is to be hoped that the venture is a success, and that Potter's message is heeded not just by his squad but by others making their way in the sport.

FIRST-CLASS AVERAGES, 1987-88

BATTING

(Qualification: 500 runs)

	M	*I*	*NO*	*R*	*HI*	*100s*	*Avge*
G. M. Wood (*WA*)	12	18	3	1,050	186*	3	70.00
D. C. Boon (*Tas.*)	12	21	2	1,287	184*	5	67.73
J. D. Siddons (*Vic.*)	11	18	2	1,077	241*	4	67.31
M. E. Waugh (*NSW*)	10	16	3	833	116	4	64.07
A. R. Border (*Qld*)	13	22	3	1,164	205	4	61.26
D. W. Hookes (*SA*)	11	20	1	1,149	132	4	60.47
P. W. Young (*Vic.*)	9	14	5	543	164*	1	60.33
G. M. Watts (*Vic.*)	5	10	0	563	176	3	56.30
D. F. Whatmore (*Vic.*)	11	19	1	912	170	2	50.66
A. M. J. Hilditch (*SA*)	11	20	1	922	185	2	48.52
M. D. Taylor (*Tas.*)	12	22	0	1,003	216	2	45.59
G. A. Bishop (*SA*)	11	20	1	833	123	3	43.84
D. M. Jones (*Vic.*)	12	19	1	751	191	3	41.72
P. R. Sleep (*SA*)	14	22	3	775	104*	1	40.78
R. B. Kerr (*Qld*)	11	21	1	793	107	2	39.65
G. M. Ritchie (*Qld*)	10	18	1	638	100*	1	37.52
W. B. Phillips (*SA*)	11	19	1	669	126	1	37.16
S. R. Waugh (*NSW*)	10	15	1	517	170	1	36.92
G. S. Trimble (*Qld*)	11	20	2	660	138*	2	36.66
G. A. Hughes (*Tas.*)	12	22	1	754	147	1	35.90
D. J. Buckingham (*Tas.*)	11	20	1	668	126	3	35.15
W. S. Andrews (*WA*)	11	19	2	594	72	0	34.94
P. I. Faulkner (*Tas.*)	10	18	3	512	78*	0	34.13
I. T. Botham (*Qld*)	11	19	0	646	70	0	34.00
G. R. Marsh (*WA*)	13	23	2	671	120*	1	31.95
T. M. Moody (*WA*)	11	19	0	568	144	1	29.89
M. R. J. Veletta (*WA*)	13	21	1	552	106	1	27.60
B. F. Davison (*Tas.*)	11	21	1	530	73	0	26.50

* *Signifies not out.*

BOWLING

(Qualification: 20 wickets)

	O	*M*	*R*	*W*	*BB*	*Avge*
G. F. Lawson (*NSW*)	336.3	102	792	42	6-31	18.85
S. R. Waugh (*NSW*)	218.3	59	499	23	5-50	21.69
C. D. Matthews (*WA*)	443.3	83	1,277	57	8-101	22.40
D. Tazelaar (*Qld*)	375	92	1,036	46	6-52	22.52
G. R. J. Matthews (*NSW*)	335.4	103	746	32	6-97	23.31
C. G. Rackemann (*Qld*)	280.1	68	733	31	5-69	23.64
M. R. Whitney (*NSW*)	290.2	63	762	32	5-33	23.81
T. M. Alderman (*WA*)	394	114	944	39	6-91	24.20
K. H. MacLeay (*WA*)	271.3	78	690	28	5-99	24.64
A. I. C. Dodemaide (*Vic.*)	420.4	103	1,125	45	6-58	25.00
C. J. McDermott (*Qld*)	376.1	75	1,087	41	7-54	26.51
P. A. Capes (*WA*)	325.1	69	887	32	4-87	27.71
I. T. Botham (*Qld*)	311.5	82	805	29	3-12	27.75
P. W. Gladigau (*SA*)	349.3	76	1,104	38	7-85	29.05
M. G. Hughes (*Vic.*)	319.5	74	930	32	5-67	29.06
J. N. Maguire (*Qld*)	293	64	810	25	5-60	32.40
T. V. Hohns (*Qld*)	270.4	64	743	22	5-100	33.77
S. P. George (*SA*)	206.1	21	778	23	6-51	33.82
A. K. Zesers (*SA*)	423.2	141	983	29	4-86	33.89
P. W. Jackson (*Vic.*)	371.1	116	947	26	3-55	36.42
T. B. A. May (*SA*)	309	73	812	22	4-55	36.90
S. P. Davis (*Vic.*)	312	65	814	21	5-50	38.76
P. I. Faulkner (*Tas.*)	348.4	102	896	21	4-37	42.66
P. R. Sleep (*SA*)	512	123	1,479	32	4-91	46.21
D. J. Hickey (*Vic.*)	239	27	942	20	4-90	47.10
T. J. Cooley (*Tas.*)	308	28	1,275	20	4-95	63.75

SHEFFIELD SHIELD, 1987-88

	Played	*Won*	*Lost*	*Drawn*	*1st Inns Pts*	*Pts*	*Penalty Pts Deducted*	*Total*
Western Australia	10	6	2	2	2	38	0	38
Queensland	10	5	3	2	2	32	0	32
New South Wales	10	4	4	2	0	24	0	24
Victoria	10	2	1	7	10	22	0	22
South Australia	10	2	4	4	4	16	0	16
Tasmania	10	1	6	3	0	6	0.2	5.8

Outright win = 6 pts; lead on first innings in a drawn game = 2 pts.

NEW SOUTH WALES v SOUTH AUSTRALIA

At Sydney, November 14, 15, 16. New South Wales won by six wickets. New South Wales 6 pts. Toss: New South Wales. Torrential rain in the week leading up to the match prevented any sort of preparation to a pitch which made batting a lottery. Although Hilditch resisted stoutly for nearly four hours, Lawson and Whitney duly disposed of the South Australian batting with a series of kickers and shooters. Gladigau returned the compliment, dismissing the New South Wales openers before stumps, but next day the night-watchman, Peter Taylor batted positively for nearly three hours. Gladigau's figures were his best in Shield cricket, as were Lawson's in South Australia's second innings. Appearing fully recovered from his back injuries, Lawson was unplayable and left New South Wales a reasonable task for victory Steve Waugh batted aggressively and his brother again showed good form.

South Australia

. A. Bishop c Matthews b Lawson	13	– lbw b Lawson	0
.. M. J. Hilditch c P. L. Taylor b Whitney	57	– c O'Neill b Whitney	16
1. D. Haysman b Lawson	0	– c Matthews b Whitney	33
D. W. Hookes c O'Neill b Lawson	11	– (5) c S. R. Waugh b Matthews	14
W. B. Phillips c Matthews b Gilbert	23	– (6) c S. R. Waugh b Gilbert	5
. R. Sleep b S. R. Waugh	16	– (7) b Lawson	28
. F. G. O'Connor lbw b Whitney	3	– (8) c and b Lawson	9
. B. A. May c Lawson b Whitney	11	– (4) c Dyer b Lawson	13
. K. Zesers c Dyer b Whitney	11	– b Lawson	0
. W. Gladigau c Small b Whitney	1	– c sub b Lawson	0
R. Carmichael not out	1	– not out	5
B 4, l-b 13, n-b 7	24	L-b 5, n-b 3	8
'26 2/26 3/40 4/99 5/129 '136 7/147 8/158 9/163	171	1/0 2/38 3/60 4/77 5/86 6/87 7/102 8/104 9/106	131

Bowling: *First Innings*—Lawson 12–7–18–3; Gilbert 12–2–34–1; Whitney 14.4–3–33–5; . L. Taylor 7–1–32–0; S. R. Waugh 12–5–16–1; Matthews 7–0–21–0. *Second Innings*—awson 18.2–9–31–6; Gilbert 13–3–28–1; Whitney 15–4–29–2; P. L. Taylor 3–1–6–0; S. R. /augh 5–0–14–0; Matthews 10–4–18–1.

New South Wales

M. Small lbw b Gladigau	6	– c O'Connor b Gladigau	4
1. A. Taylor c Phillips b Gladigau	3	– lbw b Zesers	8
. L. Taylor c Haysman b Sleep	78		
. R. Gilbert lbw b Zesers	13		
1. E. Waugh lbw b Gladigau	28	– (3) b Zesers	25
R. Waugh c Phillips b Sleep	6	– (4) c Hilditch b Zesers	36
1. D. O'Neill lbw b Gladigau	1	– (5) not out	16
. R. J. Matthews c Haysman b Gladigau	36	– (6) not out	6
†G. C. Dyer c Haysman b May	16		
. F. Lawson lbw b Zesers	11		
1. R. Whitney not out	0		
B 3, l-b 2, w 2, n-b 1	8	L-b 1, w 1, n-b 1	3
'11 2/12 3/46 4/130 5/134 '135 7/141 8/178 9/204	206	1/6 2/28 3/54 4/89	(4 wkts) 98

Bowling: *First Innings*—Gladigau 21–6–48–5; Zesers 15.5–9–17–2; Carmichael 7–2–19–0; 1ay 17–3–47–1; Sleep 19–3–70–2. *Second Innings*—Gladigau 10.4–1–35–1; Zesers 15–5–28–3; 1ay 1–0–1–0; Sleep 9–4–33–0.

Umpires: R. A. Emerson and R. A. French.

QUEENSLAND v VICTORIA

t Brisbane, November 14, 15, 16, 17. Queensland won by five wickets. Queensland 6 pts. oss: Queensland. McDermott, well supported by Botham's slip catching, had all the batsmen trouble on the opening day, which closed with Hickey having Courtice caught by /hatmore following Jones's declaration. Nearly 11,500 spectators enjoyed the second day's re. Queensland were in trouble early at 35 for four, but Trimble and Border batted superbly, dding 231 in 224 minutes. Trimble hit eleven fours and two sixes before being caught at mid-, whereupon Botham joined Border and hit 58 in 42 minutes, clubbing four sixes and seven urs. Border batted for 351 minutes and hit twenty fours and three sixes. Victoria's batsmen ayed better in the second innings, but Queensland had an easy task, even though their early atting again failed. It was left to Border, coming in at No. 7, to steer his side to victory.

Victoria

M. B. Quinn c Anderson b Tazelaar	5	– (2) lbw b Henschell
D. F. Whatmore lbw b McDermott	51	– (1) lbw b McDermott
*D. M. Jones c Anderson b McDermott	31	– c Kerr b Tazelaar
J. D. Siddons c Maguire b Tazelaar	28	– c Anderson b Henschell
P. W. Young c Botham b McDermott	30	– lbw b Henschell
A. I. C. Dodemaide c Botham b McDermott	45	– c Botham b McDermott
D. A. Emerson c Botham b McDermott	0	– b Botham
†M. G. D. Dimattina c Botham b Henschell	11	– c Anderson b Tazelaar
R. J. Bright lbw b Botham	8	– b Tazelaar
D. J. Hickey not out	3	– c Trimble b Botham
S. P. Davis (did not bat)		– not out
L-b 4, n-b 10	14	L-b 11, n-b 18
1/22 2/78 3/119 4/129 5/170 6/170 7/196 8/215 9/226 (9 wkts dec.)	226	1/25 2/124 3/153 4/197 5/218 6/234 7/268 8/286 9/293

Bowling: *First Innings*—McDermott 20–3–65–5; Botham 19–6–35–1; Tazelaar 16–4–33– Maguire 12–3–25–0; Henschell 20–4–64–1. *Second Innings*—McDermott 26–2–78–2; Botha 18–4–42–2; Tazelaar 28.2–8–70–3; Maguire 13–8–17–0; Henschell 29–11–71–3; Bord 1–0–4–0.

Queensland

R. B. Kerr c Jones b Hickey	2	– (2) c Whatmore b Davis
B. A. Courtice c Whatmore b Hickey	1	– (1) b Hickey
†P. W. Anderson c Jones b Davis	1	– (5) lbw b Davis
G. M. Ritchie lbw b Davis	19	– (3) c Jones b Hickey
*A. R. Border b Dodemaide	168	– (7) not out
G. S. Trimble c Young b Dodemaide	112	– c Bright b Dodemaide
I. T. Botham b Dodemaide	58	
A. B. Henschell lbw b Dodemaide	0	– (4) not out
C. J. McDermott c Davis b Hickey	12	
D. Tazelaar not out	16	
J. N. Maguire not out	2	
B 1, l-b 6, w 1, n-b 6	14	L-b 1
1/5 2/6 3/10 4/35 5/266 6/354 7/354 8/375 9/391 (9 wkts dec.)	405	1/4 2/36 3/38 4/38 5/71 (5 wkts) 1

Bowling: *First Innings*—Hickey 27–4–94–3; Davis 22–2–65–2; Dodemaide 30–6–89– Bright 11–0–62–0; Emerson 10–0–76–0; Jones 2–0–12–0. *Second Innings*—Hickey 9–2–41– Davis 15–4–36–2; Dodemaide 6–1–22–1; Emerson 3–0–13–0; Jones 1.4–1–2–0.

Umpires: M. W. Johnson and C. D. Timmins.

WESTERN AUSTRALIA v TASMANIA

At Perth, November 14, 15, 16, 17. Western Australia won by an innings and 137 ru Western Australia 6 pts. Toss: Western Australia. Except for Reid, the Western Australi bowlers had an excellent game, none more so than the former Tasmanian leg-spinner, Milo Western Australia's batsmen made short work of some moderate Tasmanian bowling. Moo was in his most punishing form, batting for almost five hours and hitting a six and fourte fours, while Veletta was equally enterprising with a six and nine fours during a stay of fo and a quarter hours. The left-handers, Wood and Andrews, continued the onslaught in a sta of 127, and before long Wood's declaration gave his bowlers time to gain the easiest victories. It was a depressing start to the season for Tasmania and especially for Davisc returning to the side as captain.

'asmania

. C. Boon c Zoehrer b MacLeay .... 22 – (2) c MacLeay b Capes 69
. Jelich c Marsh b Capes .... 12 – (1) run out 8
. A. Hughes c Veletta b MacLeay .... 0 – b Milosz 55
I. D. Taylor c Zoehrer b Capes .... 4 – lbw b Matthews 24
. J. Buckingham lbw b Milosz .... 20 – (6) c Matthews b Capes 5
3. F. Davison c Zoehrer b Capes .... 8 – (7) c Wood b Milosz 7
I. Faulkner c Wood b Matthews .... 9 – (8) not out 0
R. E. Soule not out .... 39 – (9) c Zoehrer b Capes 0
. J. Cooley c Marsh b Milosz .... 3 – absent injured
. L. Broadby lbw b Milosz .... 4 – (5) c Andrews b Milosz 5
. D. Bower c Zoehrer b MacLeay .... 1 – (10) lbw b Milosz 1
B 2, l-b 4, n-b 7 .... 13 L-b 9, w 1, n-b 5 15

32 2/36 3/36 4/41 5/52 135 1/46 2/110 3/156 4/172 5/176 189
79 7/96 8/113 9/121 6/184 7/188 8/188 9/189

Bowling: *First Innings*—Reid 16–5–38–0; MacLeay 19–7–25–3; Capes 21–8–32–3; latthews 9–2–21–1; Milosz 13–6–13–3. *Second Innings*—Reid 11–3–47–0; MacLeay 6–2–8–0; apes 13–4–23–3; Matthews 19–4–49–1; Milosz 26.3–7–53–4.

Vestern Australia

. R. Marsh c Soule b Cooley 5
I. R. J. Veletta c Buckingham b Bower .106
. M. Moody b Bower 144
G. M. Wood c Buckingham b Faulkner 83
'. S. Andrews b Boon 72
. H. MacLeay not out 22
C. D. Matthews b Hughes 6
P. A. Capes not out 5
L-b 11, w 2, n-b 5 18

1/16 2/250 3/285 4/412 5/428 6/453 (6 wkts dec.) 461

T. J. Zoehrer, S. J. Milosz and B. A. Reid did not bat.

Bowling: Cooley 27–3–115–1; Bower 32–4–103–2; Faulkner 30–3–88–1; Broadby –1–81–0; Hughes 9–0–43–1; Boon 3–0–20–1.

Umpires: P. J. McConnell and T. A. Prue.

SOUTH AUSTRALIA v QUEENSLAND

t Adelaide, November 20, 21, 22, 23. Drawn. South Australia 2 pts. Toss: South Australia. his game attracted an aggregate attendance of nearly 18,000, the best for a Shield match at e Adelaide Oval for many years, but as a contest it was a stop-start affair. On the second y, after some slow batting by South Australia, Kerr and Ritchie scored only 48 in the two urs between tea and stumps. The best batting came from Hookes, whose 89 in 166 minutes cluded a six and ten fours; he looked set for a century until he pulled a Botham long-hop to ep square leg. Botham batted responsibly but was unable to coax the Queensland tail into a st-innings lead as May and Sleep, the home spinners, bowled well. In the flurry for outright ints on the final day, some generous Queensland bowling enabled South Australia to set a rget of 279 in 69 overs, but Queensland never quite came to terms with the task. In the end ey were thankful to hold out for a draw. George, aged 17 years and 30 days, showed a fine mperament on his début and fully deserved his two wickets.

outh Australia

. M. J. Hilditch c McDermott b Maguire .... 56 – (2) not out 91
. A. Bishop c Trimble b Botham .... 22 – (1) c Courtice b Henschell 37
. D. Haysman c Courtice b Botham 60
). W. Hookes c Courtice b Botham .... 89 – (3) c Trimble b Henschell 67
V. B. Phillips b Tazelaar .... 13 – (4) c Maguire b Henschell 5

P. R. Sleep c Trimble b Maguire .... 70 – (5) not out ....
D. F. G. O'Connor st Anderson b Henschell ... 22
T. B. A. May b Maguire 1
A. K. Zesers c Ritchie b Maguire 4
P. W. Gladigau c Anderson b Maguire 25
S. P. George not out 4
L-b 6, n-b 15 .... 21 L-b 1, n-b 2 ....

1/42 2/112 3/192 4/221 5/266 387 1/55 2/175 3/193 (3 wkts dec.) 20
6/319 7/322 8/334 9/375

Bowling: *First Innings*—McDermott 29–5–107–0; Tazelaar 28–5–79–1; Bothar 28–10–57–3; Maguire 24.5–1–60–5; Henschell 35–12–78–1. *Second Innings*—McDermo 1–0–3–0; Tazelaar 2–1–6–0; Maguire 2–0–11–0; Henschell 20–1–84–3; Border 8–0–60–(Ritchie 8–0–44–0.

Queensland

B. A. Courtice lbw b George .... 13 – (2) b Zesers ....
R. B. Kerr c Haysman b George .... 91 – (1) c Hilditch b Gladigau 6
G. M. Ritchie c Hookes b Sleep .... 30 – c Gladigau b May 5
*A. R. Border b Gladigau .... 34 – c Gladigau b Sleep 2
G. S. Trimble c Haysman b May .... 32 – st Phillips b May 2
I. T. Botham c Phillips b Sleep .... 66 – c Haysman b Sleep 1
A. B. Henschell b May .... 11 – c Bishop b May ....
†P. W. Anderson lbw b May .... 16 – lbw b Sleep ....
C. J. McDermott lbw b May .... 4 – not out ....
D. Tazelaar not out .... 0 – not out ....
J. N. Maguire st Phillips b Sleep 1
B 1, l-b 7, w 1, n-b 11 .... 20 B 1, l-b 5, w 1, n-b 1 ....

1/27 2/89 3/160 4/183 5/257 318 1/21 2/122 3/140 4/179 (8 wkts) 21
6/279 7/301 8/310 9/317 5/183 6/194 7/200 8/209

Bowling: *First Innings*—Gladigau 21–9–50–1; George 20–2–62–2; Zesers 24–16–33–0; Slee 45.5–9–110–3; May 32–15–55–4. *Second Innings*—Gladigau 15–0–57–1; George 3–0–24–(Zesers 13–3–24–1; Sleep 19–3–53–3; May 21–4–46–3.

Umpires: A. R. Crafter and M. G. O'Connell.

VICTORIA v TASMANIA

At Melbourne, November 20, 21, 22, 23. Drawn. Victoria 2 pts. Toss: Victoria. A docile pitc initially a source of pleasure to Victoria's batsmen, ultimately frustrated their bowlers an enabled Tasmania to hold out for a draw. For Victoria, Jones and Young made runs at w against the inexperienced Tasmanians and then, thanks to a belated spell of swing bowling b Dodemaide, Jones was able to enforce the follow-on with more than a day left. Hughes hel the Tasmanian batting together with two gritty efforts, surviving a couple of blows to the hea from his Victorian namesake in the first innings before going on to his first Shield hundred. I the second innings, he looked good for another before lofting a drive to cover.

Victoria

M. B. Quinn run out 36
D. F. Whatmore c and b Broadby 24
*D. M. Jones c Taylor b Broadby 191
J. D. Siddons c Soule b Cooley 5
P. W. Young not out 164
M. G. Hughes c Buckingham b Cooley 20
A. I. C. Dodemaide not out 3
L-b 4, w 5, n-b 15 2

1/42 2/97 3/110 4/335 5/389 (5 wkts dec.) 50

D. A. Emerson, †M. G. D. Dimattina, D. J. Hickey and S. P. Davis did not bat.

Bowling: Cooley 26–1–105–2; Bower 30–4–108–0; Broadby 38–4–147–2; de Winter 8–4–94–0; Hughes 16–3–43–0.

Tasmania

. Cox b Hughes	1	– (2) c Dimattina b Hughes 35
). C. Boon c Dimattina b Hughes	24	– (1) c Siddons b Davis 22
;. A. Hughes c Dimattina b Dodemaide	147	– c Quinn b Emerson 95
1. D. Taylor c Dimattina b Hickey	10	– b Hickey 59
). J. Buckingham run out	35	– c Quinn b Hickey 11
B. F. Davison c Young b Dodemaide	40	– run out 20
. J. de Winter c Jones b Dodemaide	2	– b Quinn 51
R. E. Soule c Dimattina b Hickey	22	– c Hickey b Emerson 16
. J. Cooley c Jones b Dodemaide	10	– lbw b Hickey 0
:. L. Broadby not out	12	– not out 23
. D. Bower c Siddons b Dodemaide	4	– not out 0
L-b 10, w 4, n-b 3	17	B 4, l-b 9, w 6, n-b 3 22
/8 2/31 3/65 4/141 5/226 /232 7/276 8/307 9/310	324	1/50 2/89 3/183 4/214 5/256 6/259 7/285 8/285 9/354 (9 wkts) 354

Bowling: *First Innings*—Hughes 20–6–43–2; Hickey 24–3–88–2; Davis 12–3–27–0; Emerson 4–3–90–0; Jones 14–6–23–0; Dodemaide 19.4–2–43–5. *Second Innings*—Hughes 21–5–68–1; Iickey 20–2–72–3; Davis 23–6–48–1; Emerson 22–5–47–2; Jones 7–1–19–0; Dodemaide 1–5–79–0; Siddons 2–0–5–0; Quinn 1–0–3–1.

Umpires: R. C. Bailhache and D. W. Holt.

NEW SOUTH WALES v QUEENSLAND

.t Newcastle, November 27, 28, 29. Queensland won by 333 runs. Queensland 6 pts. Toss: ueensland. After enjoying the better fortune on the first day, New South Wales subsided ;nominiously, Queensland winning on the third afternoon. Queensland's pace bowlers made 1ort work of their opponents' batting in both innings, and McDermott, with Tazelaar's ccuracy providing an excellent foil, made better use of the lively pitch than the New South /ales fast men. His seven for 54 in the second innings was his best Shield performance. The atting of Kerr and Border in Queensland's second innings, when they shared a partnership of)6, was a consequence of splendid application and selective strokeplay. A consolation for lew South Wales was the support given by the Newcastle public, 18,000 watching the three 1ys of cricket.

Queensland

. A. Courtice c M. A. Taylor b Gilbert	0	– (2) b Whitney 9
. B. Kerr c Dyer b Lawson	0	– (1) c M. A. Taylor b Matthews 107
. M. Ritchie c Dyer b S. R. Waugh	64	– b Whitney 0
A. R. Border b Whitney	21	– st Dyer b P. L. Taylor 101
. S. Trimble lbw b Lawson	1	– not out 68
T. Botham b Gilbert	25	– c Dyer b P. L. Taylor 20
. B. Henschell b S. R. Waugh	5	– c Matthews b P. L. Taylor 0
P. W. Anderson c S. R. Waugh b Lawson	36	– not out 18
. J. McDermott c Small b S. R. Waugh	18	
. Tazelaar not out	24	
N. Maguire lbw b Lawson	3	
B 1, l-b 6, n-b 6	13	B 1, l-b 21 22
2 2/7 3/77 4/78 5/114 122 7/140 8/166 9/194	210	1/26 2/26 3/232 4/232 5/267 6/267 (6 wkts dec.) 345

Bowling: *First Innings*—Lawson 18–5–41–4; Gilbert 14–2–47–2; Whitney 15–1–58–1; S. R. Waugh 14–4–38–3; P. L. Taylor 4–0–19–0. *Second Innings*—Lawson 13–2–39–0; Gilbe 14–3–40–0; Whitney 13–4–51–2; S. R. Waugh 12–0–45–0; P. L. Taylor 23–4–89–3; Matthev 17–4–49–1; O'Neill 1–0–2–0; M. E. Waugh 2–0–8–0.

New South Wales

S. M. Small c Courtice b Maguire .... 27 – c Anderson b McDermott ......
M. A. Taylor lbw b Botham .... 9 – c Botham b McDermott ....
P. L. Taylor b McDermott .... 9 – (8) not out 2
M. E. Waugh lbw b McDermott .... 0 – (3) c Courtice b Tazelaar ......
S. R. Waugh c Kerr b McDermott .... 9 – (4) b McDermott 1
M. D. O'Neill lbw b Tazelaar .... 15 – (5) b Tazelaar ....
G. R. J. Matthews not out .... 47 – (6) lbw b McDermott ....
*†G. C. Dyer c Anderson b Botham .... 0 – (7) c Anderson b McDermott ...
G. F. Lawson c Courtice b Botham .... 0 – c Anderson b McDermott ......
D. R. Gilbert c Henschell b Tazelaar .... 9 – b Tazelaar ....
M. R. Whitney c Trimble b Tazelaar .... 1 – b McDermott ....
L-b 4, n-b 9 .... 13 L-b 7, n-b 3 1

1/35 2/43 3/46 4/49 5/61 6/90 7/92 8/97 9/127 — 139 — 1/13 2/20 3/34 4/34 5/41 6/46 7/59 8/59 9/72 — 8

Bowling: *First Innings*—McDermott 21–7–56–3; Tazelaar 16.3–3–37–3; Magui 16–5–30–1; Botham 6–2–12–3. *Second Innings*—McDermott 11–1–54–7; Tazelaar 10–2–22–

Umpires: R. A. French and R. G. Harris.

VICTORIA v WESTERN AUSTRALIA

At Melbourne, November 27, 28, 29, 30. Drawn. Victoria 2 pts. Toss: Victoria. A game whic seemed destined to be a draw from the start finished as a practice session which Mars exploited in a 330-minute innings on the last day. Victoria deserved first-innings points an could thank their left-arm spinner, Jackson, in his first game of the season, who bowle superbly. Whatmore and Quinn gave the Victorian innings its best start for fourteen year and Young continued his good form, only to be deprived of a second consecutive century b Jones's declaration.

Western Australia

G. R. Marsh c Young b Dodemaide .... 16 – (2) not out 12
M. R. J. Veletta b Davis .... 25 – (1) st Dimattina b Jackson 5
T. M. Moody c Dimattina b Hughes .... 47 – c Young b Jones 4
*G. M. Wood c Jackson b Hughes 74
W. S. Andrews c Dimattina b Hughes .... 4 – (4) st Dimattina b Jackson .....
†T. J. Zoehrer c Quinn b Jackson .... 28 – (5) not out ....
K. H. MacLeay c Dimattina b Hickey 28
C. D. Matthews b Hickey 36
P. A. Capes c Davis b Jackson 12
B. A. Reid b Jackson 1
S. J. Milosz not out 7
L-b 11, w 2 .... 13 B 7, l-b 2 ....

1/42 2/46 3/105 4/113 5/184 6/210 7/262 8/281 9/283 — 291 — 1/87 2/204 3/207 (3 wkts) 23

Bowling: *First Innings*—Hughes 28–6–55–3; Hickey 27–3–100–2; Davis 16–5–35– Dodemaide 11–3–26–1; Jackson 34.3–12–55–3; Jones 5–0–9–0. *Second Innings*—Hugh 13–5–30–0; Hickey 9–2–29–0; Davis 11–4–22–0; Dodemaide 11–2–45–0; Jacksc 33–10–74–2; Jones 13–3–28–1; Young 1–1–0–0.

/ictoria

1. B. Quinn c Zoehrer b Capes 81
). F. Whatmore c Milosz b Matthews .127
D. M. Jones c Wood b Capes 29
. D. Siddons c Zoehrer b MacLeay . . . 0
. W. Young not out 93
A. I. C. Dodemaide not out 71
B 2, l-b 9, n-b 19 30

1/197 2/258 3/259 4/261 (4 wkts dec.) 431

'. W. Jackson, †M. G. D. Dimattina, M. G. Hughes, D. J. Hickey and S. P. Davis did not bat.

Bowling: Capes 18–1–60–2; MacLeay 25–6–77–1; Matthews 23–3–72–1; Reid 36–12–87–0; 1ilosz 36–9–83–0; Andrews 20–2–41–0.

Umpires: R. C. Bailhache and L. J. King.

TASMANIA v NEW SOUTH WALES

.t Devonport, December 4, 5, 6, 7. New South Wales won by an innings and 38 runs. New ɔuth Wales 6 pts. Toss: Tasmania. Apart from a gallant rearguard action on the last day, the asmanians had little to offer. Their bowlers could take only four wickets in the match; their atsmen were unable to combat either pace or spin. The match marked the return to the New ɔuth Wales side of Smith and Rixon, with the former finding few terrors in the Tasmanian ɔwling as he went to 84 in 114 minutes, and Rixon keeping as well as ever. O'Neill and /augh both made effortless centuries, Waugh's first in Shield cricket taking two and a half ɔurs. Lawson maintained his excellent bowling form and celebrated his 30th birthday on the ɔurth day with his twentieth five-wicket return. Tasmania's dwindling reputation was arginally restored in their second innings by a determined effort from Buckingham, who atted for five and a half hours with a sprained ankle, using a runner throughout.

'asmania

Cox b Whitney . . . . 6 – (2) b Lawson 6
'. Jelich c Rixon b Lawson . . . . 7 – (1) b Whitney 24
'. A. Hughes lbw b Lawson . . . . 18 – c Lawson b Bennett 7
1. D. Taylor b Whitney . . . . 0 – c Rixon b Whitney 19
. J. Buckingham c Waugh b Lawson . . . . 31 – c Matthews b Lawson 112
B. F. Davison c Matthews b P. L. Taylor . . . . 41 – c Smith b Lawson 25
. J. de Winter c Matthews b P. L. Taylor . . . . 14 – b Waugh 2
R. E. Soule c Whitney b Matthews . . . . 2 – c O'Neill b Lawson 45
'. L. Broadby b P. L. Taylor . . . . 2 – c Waugh b Lawson 7
. J. Cooley c Bayliss b Matthews . . . . 0 – not out 17
. D. Bower not out . . . . 0 – c Waugh b Bennett 8
L-b 5, n-b 8 . . . . 13 B 1, l-b 8, n-b 14 23

'13 2/13 3/17 4/71 5/77 '121 7/132 8/132 9/134 134 1/24 2/39 3/58 4/77 5/134 6/139 7/239 8/268 9/269 295

Bowling: *First Innings*—Lawson 16–4–22–3; Whitney 16–4–31–2; Waugh 10–2–28–0; P. L. aylor 15–8–19–3; Bennett 4–0–19–0; Matthews 9.1–5–10–2. *Second Innings*—Lawson 5–12–72–5; Whitney 27–3–89–2; Waugh 7–4–5–1; P. L. Taylor 16–2–41–0; Bennett 2–5–49–2; Matthews 19–10–29–0; O'Neill 1–0–1–0.

lew South Wales

B. Smith c Soule b de Winter 84
1. A. Taylor c Soule b de Winter 72
. H. Bayliss c de Winter b Cooley . . . 38
1. D. O'Neill not out 130
. R. J. Matthews c de Winter b Broadby . 24
M. E. Waugh not out 101
B 4, l-b 6, w 1, n-b 7 18

1/113 2/188 3/240 4/280 (4 wkts dec.) 467

S. J. Rixon, *M. J. Bennett, P. L. Taylor, G. F. Lawson and M. R. Whitney did not bat.

Bowling: Cooley 24–3–112–1; Bower 19–1–81–0; Broadby 36.5–5–128–1; de Wint
28–6–80–2; Hughes 14–0–56–0.

Umpires: D. R. Close and S. G. Randell.

VICTORIA v SOUTH AUSTRALIA

At Melbourne, December 11, 12, 13, 14. Victoria won by six wickets. Victoria 6 pts. Tos South Australia. South Australia battled over three days to earn two first-innings points, onl to forfeit them on the last day in the helter-skelter for an outright result. Batsmen we generally in command on the easy-paced pitch, and there were some exhilarating strokes fro Bishop, Hookes and Phillips in South Australia's first-day 352 for five. Victoria, at 283 f eight, looked in danger of following on, but Whiteside took charge, scoring his runs in thr hours. On the last morning, Bishop and Hookes plundered the Victorian bowling to set up declaration at lunch which left Victoria 68 overs in which to make 282. The splendid hitting Siddons decided the match, for in reaching his highest score, he took the Victorians to the target with 3.5 overs to spare.

South Australia

A. M. J. Hilditch c Dimattina b Davis	34	– c Dimattina b Hickey
G. A. Bishop c Dimattina b Dodemaide	79	– not out 8
M. D. Haysman c Young b Jackson	0	– c Young b Jackson 2
*D. W. Hookes c Whatmore b Dodemaide	93	– not out 4
†W. B. Phillips c Whatmore b Dodemaide	126	
D. S. Lehmann c Frazer b Jackson	10	
H. B. Jolly lbw b Davis	65	
N. R. Plummer c Young b Davis	23	
A. K. Zesers c Dimattina b Jackson	6	
P. W. Gladigau c Siddons b Davis	11	
S. P. George not out	0	
L-b 15, w 3, n-b 3	21	B 1, l-b 4
1/77 2/82 3/162 4/243 5/268 6/397 7/439 8/452 9/468	468	1/0 2/65 (2 wkts dec.) 15

Bowling: *First Innings*—Hickey 24–2–104–0; Davis 28–5–70–4; Dodemaide 37–7–112–
Jackson 40–8–137–3; Whiteside 10–1–30–0. *Second Innings*—Hickey 11–0–45–1; Dav
9–1–36–0; Dodemaide 7–0–36–0; Jackson 9–2–36–1.

Victoria

M. B. Quinn lbw b Gladigau	13	
D. F. Whatmore lbw b George	69	– (1) c Hookes b Plummer 4
I. D. Frazer c Jolly b Haysman	76	– (2) c and b Gladigau 1
J. D. Siddons c Phillips b George	64	– not out 12
P. W. Young lbw b Gladigau	9	– (3) run out 6
A. I. C. Dodemaide lbw b George	2	– not out
W. G. Whiteside not out	84	– (5) run out 1
†M. G. D. Dimattina c Phillips b Zesers	8	
P. W. Jackson lbw b George	1	
D. J. Hickey not out	10	
L-b 7, w 1, n-b 1	9	B 6, l-b 8, w 1 1
1/42 2/154 3/171 4/213 5/225 6/249 7/270 8/283	(8 wkts dec.) 345	1/43 2/73 3/174 4/228 (4 wkts) 28

*S. P. Davis did not bat.

Bowling: *First Innings*—Gladigau 30–9–57–2; George 28–4–81–4; Zesers 48–20–85–
Plummer 28–9–69–0; Jolly 3–0–10–0; Haysman 12–2–36–1. *Second Innings*—Gladiga
12–0–47–1; George 10–1–48–0; Zesers 22.1–0–121–0; Plummer 20–1–55–1.

Umpires: D. E. Holden and L. J. King.

WESTERN AUSTRALIA v NEW SOUTH WALES

At Perth, December 11, 12, 13. Western Australia won by an innings and 10 runs. Western Australia 6 pts. Toss: New South Wales. New South Wales plunged to new depths of ineptitude as Western Australia completed the easiest of wins in just over two days. Western Australia welcomed back their South African tourists, Alderman, Hughes and Shipperd, and Alderman and Hughes had first-innings points safely secured by the first evening – Alderman with an inspired piece of swing bowling and Hughes with a measured innings that occupied four hours. Chris Matthews destroyed the New South Wales second innings with his sustained hostility, only Greg Matthews showing any form with a fighting innings to follow his splendid spin bowling, which had most of the Western Australian batsmen struggling. It was the third time in four matches that the New South Welshmen had been party to a result achieved with more than a day to spare.

New South Wales

S. B. Smith c Alderman b Matthews	17	– (2) b Capes	0
M. A. Taylor c Zoehrer b Capes	12	– (1) lbw b Capes	8
T. H. Bayliss c Andrews b MacLeay	7	– c Hughes b Matthews	24
M. D. O'Neill c Andrews b Alderman	20	– lbw b Alderman	0
G. R. J. Matthews c Zoehrer b Matthews	5	– c Zoehrer b Matthews	53
M. E. Waugh c Andrews b Alderman	5	– c MacLeay b Matthews	6
†S. J. Rixon c MacLeay b Alderman	11	– c Alderman b Matthews	0
*M. J. Bennett c Zoehrer b Matthews	6	– c Alderman b Matthews	2
D. R. Gilbert b Alderman	10	– lbw b Alderman	10
G. F. Lawson b Alderman	13	– c Wood b Matthews	12
M. R. Whitney not out	2	– not out	2
L-b 3, w 1, n-b 3	7	B 4, l-b 6, n-b 4	14
1/29 2/40 3/40 4/45 5/64 6/79 7/88 8/90 9/102	115	1/1 2/24 3/29 4/55 5/81 6/81 7/95 8/115 9/120	131

Bowling: *First Innings*—Capes 7–2–20–1; MacLeay 8–3–18–1; Matthews 15–4–39–3; Alderman 13.5–1–35–5. *Second Innings*—Capes 11–3–23–2; MacLeay 4–1–10–0; Matthews 16.4–2–56–6; Alderman 22–6–31–2; Milosz 1–0–1–0.

Western Australia

K. J. Hughes st Rixon b Matthews	76
G. Shipperd c Taylor b Lawson	9
T. M. Moody c Taylor b Lawson	38
C. D. Matthews c Taylor b Whitney	4
*G. M. Wood c Taylor b Matthews	40
W. S. Andrews lbw b Gilbert	9
†T. J. Zoehrer c Rixon b Bennett	18
K. H. MacLeay b Matthews	2
P. A. Capes lbw b Matthews	23
T. M. Alderman c Waugh b Matthews	11
S. J. Milosz not out	0
L-b 8, n-b 18	26
1/32 2/107 3/126 4/154 5/169 6/220 7/220 8/224 9/251	256

Bowling: Lawson 23–6–60–2; Whitney 18–3–40–1; Gilbert 14–2–55–1; Waugh 2–0–11–0; Matthews 26.5–6–49–5; Bennett 14–6–33–1.

Umpires: R. J. Evans and T. A. Prue.

NEW SOUTH WALES v VICTORIA

At Sydney, December 18, 19, 20, 21. Drawn. Toss: New South Wales. The home state's pressure came to nought when rain and bad light reduced play to three and a half hours on the third day and to only five overs on the fourth. The Waugh twins dominated the first two days, Steve showing hitherto unrealised powers of concentration for seven hours in reaching his highest score. Mark needed only three hours for his runs as he took toll of the tiring bowlers and unleashed some brilliant strokes. Victoria's batsmen could not cope with a hostile spell of bowling by Whitney, who was well supported by the two off-spinners, Matthews and Peter Taylor, but a stubborn last-wicket stand between Dimattina and Davis, lasting over an hour, foiled New South Wales' bid for first-innings points. Dyer, their captain, received an official reprimand from the Australian Cricket Board for describing the umpires' decision to stop play for bad light as "a stupid bloody thing".

New South Wales

S. B. Smith c Dimattina b Hughes 0
M. A. Taylor b Jackson 35
S. R. Waugh c Dimattina b Dodemaide .170
M. D. O'Neill c Jones b Dodemaide ... 36
G. R. J. Matthews c Jones b Jackson .. 27
M. E. Waugh not out 114
*†G. C. Dyer c Dimattina b Dodemaide 0
P. L. Taylor c Dimattina b Dodemaide . 1
M. J. Bennett lbw b Jackson 7
G. F. Lawson c Young b Dodemaide .. 28
M. R. Whitney not out 5
B 1, l-b 7, w 3, n-b 4 15

1/1 2/107 3/182 4/259 (9 wkts dec.) 438
5/285 6/287 7/289 8/314 9/419

Bowling: Hughes 10–3–22–1; Davis 35–5–121–0; Dodemaide 45–9–114–5; Jackson 53–14–128–3; Jones 12–2–26–0; Whiteside 4–0–19–0.

Victoria

D. F. Whatmore c Matthews b Whitney 31
W. G. Whiteside c Dyer b Whitney ... 23
*D. M. Jones c Dyer b Whitney 1
J. D. Siddons c S. R. Waugh b Whitney 27
P. W. Young b Matthews 10
I. D. Frazer c M. E. Waugh b Whitney 12
A. I. C. Dodemaide lbw b Matthews .. 22
†M. G. D. Dimattina not out 46
P. W. Jackson b P. L. Taylor 8
M. G. Hughes c sub b P. L. Taylor ... 0
S. P. Davis not out 2
B 4, l-b 9 13

1/35 2/36 3/62 4/76 5/88 (9 wkts) 195
6/120 7/139 8/168 9/172

Bowling: Lawson 18–5–44–0; Whitney 25–5–68–5; Matthews 20–8–40–2; Bennett 8–4–13–0; P. L. Taylor 16–9–17–2.

Umpires: R. A. Emerson and I. S. Thomas.

QUEENSLAND v WESTERN AUSTRALIA

At Brisbane, December 18, 19, 20. Queensland won by ten wickets. Queensland 6 pts. Toss: Queensland. Western Australia never recovered from the fast bowling of Tazelaar and McDermott on the first day, and when Wood had a finger broken by a lifting ball from Botham, their batting was in disarray. Moody and Matthews resisted bravely, adding 84 in 91 minutes, but they could not stop Tazelaar, who finished with career-best figures. Queensland's reply was carefully guided by a five-hour century from Kerr, but the tempo increased dramatically when Botham arrived. He hit the leg-spinner, Milosz, for three sixes in one over, and Tazelaar also struck out effectively. Western Australia's second innings began badly against some inspired bowling, and although the middle order battled hard, Queensland's victory was complete on the third evening.

Western Australia

G. R. Marsh c Anderson b McDermott .... 4 – (2) c Kerr b Tazelaar 8
M. R. J. Veletta c Border b Tazelaar .... 4 – (1) c Trimble b Botham 4
T. M. Moody run out .... 89 – c Ritchie b Botham 3
*G. M. Wood not out .... 9 – absent injured
K. J. Hughes b McDermott .... 22 – (4) lbw b McDermott 3
†T. J. Zoehrer c Ritchie b Tazelaar .... 4 – (5) c Anderson b Tazelaar 51
T. G. Breman c Anderson b Tazelaar .... 6 – (6) lbw b Henschell 36
C. D. Matthews b Tazelaar .... 45 – (7) c Kerr b Maguire 33
P. A. Capes c Barsby b Botham .... 13 – (8) c Kerr b Henschell 15
T. M. Alderman lbw b Tazelaar .... 2 – (9) b Maguire 18
S. J. Milosz b Tazelaar .... 2 – (10) not out 1
L-b 5, n-b 12 .... 17 B 6, l-b 7, n-b 7 20

1/4 2/11 3/73 4/90 5/98 217 1/17 2/21 3/21 4/38 5/119 192
6/182 7/206 8/214 9/214 6/121 7/154 8/182 9/192

G. M. Wood retired hurt at 34 and resumed at 214-9.

Bowling: *First Innings*—McDermott 20–2–53–2; Tazelaar 18.5–5–52–6; Botham 15–2–52–1; Maguire 12–4–25–0; Henschell 15–5–30–0. *Second Innings*—McDermott 14–7–21–1; Tazelaar 15–2–47–2; Botham 12–3–32–2; Maguire 11.4–2–41–2; Henschell 16–6–38–2.

Queensland

R. B. Kerr c Alderman b Milosz	102	– (2) not out	31
T. J. Barsby c Veletta b Alderman	2	– (1) not out	50
†P. W. Anderson c Capes b Matthews	35		
G. M. Ritchie lbw b Capes	2		
*A. R. Border c Zoehrer b Matthews	18		
G. S. Trimble c Alderman b Breman	15		
I. T. Botham c Matthews b Breman	53		
A. B. Henschell b Matthews	11		
C. J. McDermott lbw b Alderman	0		
D. Tazelaar not out	43		
J. N. Maguire c Milosz b Alderman	10		
L-b 6, w 4, n-b 17	27	B 4, l-b 1, n-b 6	11
1/4 2/95 3/99 4/147 5/187 6/219 7/251 8/251 9/271	318	(no wkt)	92

Bowling: *First Innings*—Capes 13–3–30–1; Alderman 31–6–70–3; Matthews 25–3–69–3; Breman 17–0–83–2; Milosz 16–4–60–1. *Second Innings*—Capes 6–1–21–0; Alderman 3–1–18–0; Matthews 6–0–19–0; Breman 4–1–12–0; Milosz 5–0–17–0.

Umpires: M. W. Johnson and C. D. Timmins.

QUEENSLAND v NEW SOUTH WALES

At Brisbane, January 1, 2, 3, 4. Queensland won by 52 runs. Queensland 6 pts. Toss: New South Wales. Hohns and Rackemann marked their return to the Queensland side with significant contributions. Put in on a green wicket, Queensland generally struggled until Hohns and Tazelaar added 114 in two hours for the eighth wicket against some moderate bowling. Another dismal batting performance saw New South Wales avoid the follow-on by just 1 run, but their bowlers struck back, reducing the Queensland second innings to 61 for six. Ritchie, helped by Anderson in a partnership of 126 in 200 minutes, effected the recovery, and New South Wales' task of scoring 353 looked insurmountable. However, a hard-hitting innings by O'Neill inspired his colleagues, although his effort lost some impact when a fiery spell by Rackemann caused three wickets to fall for 2 runs. It was an exciting climax to Sunday's play for a crowd of 12,500. On the fourth day Waugh played brilliantly, scoring freely off Botham, but the English all-rounder had the final say, catching Waugh and then disposing of the tail with the new ball.

Queensland

*R. B. Kerr c Waugh b Gilbert	7	– (2) c Waugh b Gilbert	0
T. J. Barsby c Rixon b Lawson	8	– (1) c Rixon b Lawson	0
G. M. Ritchie c Taylor b Waugh	4	– not out	100
G. S. Trimble c Lawson b Waugh	67	– c Rixon b Jones	18
A. B. Henschell run out	21	– lbw b Lawson	4
I. T. Botham c Jones b Waugh	19	– c Rixon b Waugh	11
T. V. Hohns c Taylor b Gilbert	55	– b Waugh	0
†P. W. Anderson lbw b Matthews	17	– c O'Neill b Matthews	54
D. Tazelaar b Gilbert	56	– b Bennett	0
J. N. Maguire not out	0	– c and b Matthews	3
C. G. Rackemann b Gilbert	0	– b Matthews	0
B 2, l-b 5, w 1, n-b 16	24	B 5, l-b 1, n-b 7	13
1/11 2/15 3/36 4/89 5/134 6/141 7/163 8/277 9/278	278	1/0 2/0 3/41 4/46 5/61 6/61 7/187 8/194 9/203	203

Bowling: *First Innings*—Lawson 22–8–45–1; Gilbert 23–6–61–4; Waugh 10–0–49–3; Jones 16–2–49–0; Matthews 15–4–49–1; Bennett 8–2–18–0. *Second Innings*—Lawson 20–4–45–2; Gilbert 13–3–40–1; Waugh 10–1–33–2; Jones 13–3–31–1; Matthews 16.3–4–41–3; Bennett 5–1–7–1.

New South Wales

First innings		Second innings	
M. A. Taylor lbw b Maguire	22	(2) c Anderson b Hohns	71
S. B. Smith lbw b Botham	15	(1) c Kerr b Botham	4
J. Dyson lbw b Tazelaar	3	c Anderson b Tazelaar	10
M. D. O'Neill c Trimble b Tazelaar	9	c Barsby b Rackemann	70
G. R. J. Matthews b Maguire	21	(6) c Trimble b Rackemann	0
M. E. Waugh c Anderson b Tazelaar	4	(7) c Botham b Tazelaar	88
†S. J. Rixon c Tazelaar b Rackemann	12	(8) c Anderson b Botham	28
*M. J. Bennett c Trimble b Rackemann	5	(9) lbw b Botham	8
G. F. Lawson c Ritchie b Maguire	2	(10) c Anderson b Rackemann	2
D. R. Gilbert not out	17	(5) c Ritchie b Rackemann	0
R. A. Jones run out	8	not out	6
L-b 2, w 1, n-b 8	11	B 1, l-b 7, n-b 5	13
1/25 2/45 3/45 4/65 5/73 6/89 7/100 8/102 9/104	129	1/7 2/20 3/131 4/133 5/133 6/238 7/271 8/285 9/292	300

Bowling: *First Innings*—Tazelaar 15.1–3–33–3; Botham 11–7–12–1; Rackemann 15–4–26–2; Maguire 19–2–56–3. *Second Innings*—Tazelaar 23–6–64–2; Botham 17.2–4–61–3; Rackemann 20–4–54–4; Maguire 11–2–44–0; Hohns 20–4–57–1; Henschell 4–1–12–0.

Umpires: P. D. Parker and C. D. Timmins.

SOUTH AUSTRALIA v WESTERN AUSTRALIA

At Adelaide, January 1, 2, 3, 4. Western Australia won by three wickets. Western Australia 6 pts. Toss: Western Australia. The match was virtually decided on the first day, when South Australia collapsed and were all out for 158. Alderman, and to a lesser extent Matthews and Capes, moved the ball around disconcertingly. Western Australia also struggled but achieved a 79-run lead thanks to some cavalier batting from Andrews and disciplined defence by Wood. A crowd of more than 7,000 on the third day enjoyed some absorbing cricket as Hilditch inspired a South Australian recovery, mixing sound defence with enterprising strokes in an innings of almost seven hours. On the last day Western Australia were required to make 250 off a minimum of 88 overs, and through some splendid batting by Wood and Hughes they won with ten balls to spare.

South Australia

First innings		Second innings	
A. M. J. Hilditch c Zoehrer b Matthews	35	(2) b Alderman	166
G. A. Bishop b Matthews	19	(1) c Hughes b Capes	2
M. D. Haysman c Zoehrer b Capes	16	lbw b Alderman	6
*D. W. Hookes c Zoehrer b Capes	4	c Shipperd b Matthews	29
†W. B. Phillips b Matthews	3	c Moody b Capes	25
P. R. Sleep st Zoehrer b Milosz	38	run out	15
H. B. Jolly c Capes b Alderman	9	c Zoehrer b Alderman	28
A. K. Zesers c Zoehrer b Alderman	2	c Zoehrer b Alderman	8
P. W. Gladigau run out	13	b Matthews	3
S. P. George c Zoehrer b Matthews	2	c Zoehrer b Matthews	10
S. D. H. Parkinson not out	0	not out	17
L-b 10, w 2, n-b 5	17	B 3, l-b 13, w 1, n-b 2	19
1/56 2/68 3/87 4/91 5/93 6/112 7/118 8/142 9/158	158	1/6 2/17 3/74 4/138 5/178 6/262 7/284 8/291 9/293	328

Bowling: *First Innings*—Capes 19–4–46–2; Alderman 27–11–57–2; Matthews 21–4–41–4; Milosz 4–2–4–1. *Second Innings*—Capes 34–4–86–2; Alderman 29–10–67–4; Matthews 26.4–2–79–3; Milosz 20–1–61–0; Moody 5–2–19–0.

Western Australia

G. Shipperd c Hookes b Gladigau . . . . 10 – (2) run out 14
M. W. McPhee c Gladigau b Sleep . . . . 28 – (1) b Gladigau 1
T. M. Moody c Hookes b Parkinson . . . . 7 – c Phillips b Gladigau 13
*G. M. Wood c Hookes b Gladigau . . . . 42 – lbw b Zesers 82
K. J. Hughes c Sleep b George . . . . 21 – run out 62
W. S. Andrews b Sleep . . . . 55 – c Gladigau b Sleep 19
†T. J. Zoehrer c Haysman b Sleep . . . . 0 – not out 28
C. D. Matthews c Sleep b Gladigau . . . . 24 – lbw b Sleep 15
P. A. Capes c Hilditch b Zesers . . . . 17 – not out 1
T. M. Alderman c Phillips b Zesers 11
S. J. Milosz not out 0
B 4, l-b 12, w 2, n-b 4 . . . . 22 B 9, l-b 5, w 1 15

1/38 2/48 3/53 4/85 5/166 237 1/7 2/23 3/58 4/169 (7 wkts) 250
6/168 7/196 8/213 9/234 5/189 6/213 7/245

Bowling: *First Innings*—Gladigau 22–8–43–3; Parkinson 18–3–61–1; George 9–0–28–1; Sleep 24–11–50–3; Zesers 18.3–7–27–2; Haysman 6–3–12–0. *Second Innings*—Gladigau 10.2–2–36–2; Parkinson 8–3–18–0; George 7–1–25–0; Sleep 24–5–64–2; Zesers 22–5–54–1; Haysman 8–1–22–0; Hookes 7–1–17–0.

Umpires: D. J. Harper and M. G. O'Connell.

QUEENSLAND v TASMANIA

At Brisbane, January 8, 9, 10. Queensland won by an innings and 4 runs. Queensland 6 pts. Toss: Tasmania. Davison having chosen to field, Tasmania enjoyed some short-lived success as Queensland lost three wickets for 53. However, their lack of an experienced pace bowler allowed Kerr and Henschell to add 102 in two hours, with Henschell, who had two lives, hitting ten fours in his three-and-a-half-hour innings. Anderson and Tazelaar put on 75 in 68 minutes for the eighth wicket to complete the recovery. Tasmania's batsmen had no answer to Queensland's fast bowlers, and when Tazelaar completed a fine all-round performance by destroying Tasmania's second innings, the match was over before tea on the third day.

Queensland

*R. B. Kerr c Faulkner b Harris 64
T. J. Barsby c de Winter b Cooley 10
G. M. Ritchie run out 22
G. S. Trimble b Faulkner 1
A. B. Henschell c Cruse b Faulkner . . . 89
I. T. Botham c Davison b Harris 27
T. V. Hohns c Cruse b Faulkner 14
†P. W. Anderson c Cruse b Cooley 55
D. Tazelaar c and b Cooley 25
J. N. Maguire not out 0
C. G. Rackemann c Soule b de Winter . 0
B 3, l-b 4, w 3, n-b 7 17

1/12 2/51 3/53 4/155 5/193 324
6/231 7/245 8/320 9/324

Bowling: Cooley 27–3–112–3; de Winter 29.5–6–77–1; Faulkner 24–10–66–3; Harris 18–7–32–2; Cruse 11–3–30–0.

Tasmania

S. L. Saunders lbw b Botham . . . . 0 – (6) c Kerr b Tazelaar 20
G. A. Hughes c Barsby b Rackemann . . . . 37 – (3) c Anderson b Rackemann . . . 32
D. J. Buckingham c Anderson b Tazelaar . . . . . 4 – (4) c Anderson b Botham 8
M. D. Taylor lbw b Maguire . . . . 35 – (5) c Anderson b Maguire 28
E. J. Harris lbw b Tazelaar . . . . 15 – (1) c Trimble b Tazelaar 11
B. A. Cruse c Botham b Tazelaar . . . . 31 – (7) c Botham b Tazelaar 11
P. I. Faulkner c Ritchie b Rackemann . . . . 6 – (8) c Trimble b Tazelaar 4
*B. F. Davison c Trimble b Rackemann . . . . . . 13 – (9) b Hohns 4
†R. E. Soule c Botham b Hohns . . . . 0 – (10) not out 16
A. J. de Winter c Maguire b Rackemann . . . . . 17 – (2) lbw b Botham 2
T. J. Cooley not out . . . . 0 – c Anderson b Tazelaar 1
L-b 9, n-b 6 . . . . 15 L-b 3, n-b 7 10

1/3 2/24 3/77 4/90 5/135 173 1/6 2/16 3/33 4/76 5/85 147
6/136 7/155 8/156 9/156 6/107 7/124 8/125 9/137

Bowling: *First Innings*—Tazelaar 14–6–32–3; Botham 15–5–32–1; Rackemann 14.5–3–51–4; Maguire 11–3–37–1; Hohns 12–5–12–1. *Second Innings*—Tazelaar 16.5–2–54–5; Botham 9–2–23–2; Rackemann 11–0–37–1; Maguire 7–2–10–1; Hohns 11–6–20–1.

Umpires: C. A. Bertwistle and C. D. Timmins.

WESTERN AUSTRALIA v VICTORIA

At Perth, January 8, 9, 10, 11. Drawn. Western Australia 2 pts. Toss: Western Australia. Victoria's first innings, which lasted more than eight hours, revolved around a seven-hour vigil by Whatmore. Dropped four times – three of the chances coming off consecutive balls by Milosz when he was 125 and 127 – he went on to his highest score and hit 25 fours. Hughes was in a hostile mood as he dismissed Western Australia's first three batsmen before stumps and caused McPhee to retire hurt with a badly gashed eye, but on the third day Wood and Zoehrer added 165 in three and a half hours to gain first-innings points. Zoehrer was in dashing form, hitting fifteen fours to all parts of the ground, while Wood batted circumspectly for almost seven and a quarter hours, overcoming a painful hand injury and hitting a six and fifteen boundaries in his unbeaten 150. The fourth day was meaningless with Victoria batting throughout.

Victoria

M. B. Quinn c Zoehrer b Matthews	8	– (2) b Capes	4
D. F. Whatmore b Capes	170	– (1) c Milosz b Capes	51
I. D. Frazer c Alderman b Matthews	12	– c sub b Matthews	33
J. D. Siddons lbw b Matthews	26	– b Capes	52
P. W. Young c Zoehrer b Alderman	7	– not out	66
W. G. Whiteside st Zoehrer b Milosz	20	– run out	23
†M. G. D. Dimattina c Zoehrer b Alderman	26	– not out	10
P. W. Jackson b Capes	31		
M. G. Hughes c Zoehrer b Matthews	11		
D. J. Hickey run out	11		
*S. P. Davis not out	2		
L-b 5, n-b 4	9	B 5, l-b 12	17
1/38 2/73 3/117 4/143 5/203 6/277 7/277 8/292 9/322	333	1/9 2/81 3/146 4/155 5/198	(5 wkts) 256

Bowling: *First Innings*—Capes 34.1–16–61–2; Alderman 38–11–93–2; Matthews 31–4–107–4; Milosz 27–9–67–1. *Second Innings*—Capes 22–5–56–3; Alderman 19–8–40–0; Matthews 16–3–60–1; Milosz 28–10–74–0; Andrews 7–4–9–0.

Western Australia

G. Shipperd c Young b Hughes	17
M. W. McPhee retired hurt	20
T. M. Moody c Whiteside b Hughes	17
*G. M. Wood not out	150
K. J. Hughes lbw b Hughes	7
W. S. Andrews c Dimattina b Hickey	50
P. A. Capes run out	2
†T. J. Zoehrer c Hickey b Jackson	109
C. D. Matthews lbw b Whiteside	20
T. M. Alderman b Whiteside	9
S. J. Milosz not out	0
L-b 5, w 4, n-b 17	26
1/19 2/81 3/96 4/176 5/182 6/347 7/406 8/426	(8 wkts dec.) 427

Bowling: Hughes 31–5–103–3; Davis 21–3–40–0; Hickey 23–0–103–1; Whiteside 26–7–78–2; Jackson 35.1–11–98–1.

Umpires: R. J. Evans and T. A. Prue.

TASMANIA v SOUTH AUSTRALIA

At Devonport, January 15, 16, 17, 18. South Australia won by an innings and 69 runs. South Australia 6 pts. Toss: South Australia. Lillee's return to first-class cricket at the age of 38 was the major point of interest before the match, but it was the seventeen-year-old George who first captured the limelight, taking four for 15 in his first seven overs when Tasmania were put in on a rain-affected pitch. Lillee's reply was dramatic, accounting for Hilditch with his first ball, and he was treated with respect by all the batsmen. Hookes (two sixes, sixteen fours) and Phillips took control on the second day, adding 187 for the third wicket to follow their unbeaten, record stand of 462 when the teams met the previous season. South Australia declared at lunch on the third day with a lead of 352, whereupon George dismissed both Tasmanian openers in his first two overs and was unlucky not to have Taylor as well, caught behind. Next day he had his revenge, but not before Taylor had batted well for four and a half hours, hitting nineteen fours in his 166. Pyke, in his first game after a football injury, showed good all-round form, being especially effective with the second new ball to end the match.

Tasmania

E. J. Harris c Jolly b Hookes	17	– (2) lbw b George	0
R. J. Bennett c Phillips b George	3	– (1) c Bishop b George	0
G. A. Hughes c Zesers b George	0	– run out	21
M. D. Taylor c Phillips b George	1	– b George	166
R. D. Woolley b George	1	– c and b Pyke	10
*B. F. Davison lbw b George	20	– lbw b Zesers	6
P. I. Faulkner c Hookes b Zesers	19	– c George b Pyke	57
A. I. de Winter b Pyke	21	– c Sleep b Pyke	7
†R. E. Soule c Hookes b George	11	– lbw b Pyke	0
T. J. Cooley c Phillips b Zesers	2	– b Pyke	0
D. K. Lillee not out	0	– not out	2
B 1, l-b 1, w 4, n-b 10	16	L-b 3, w 1, n-b 10	14
1/10 2/11 3/16 4/18 5/37 6/56 7/83 8/106 9/109	111	1/0 2/3 3/29 4/58 5/71 6/259 7/270 8/270 9/274	283

Bowling: *First Innings*—George 21–2–51–6; Pyke 11–3–15–1; Zesers 17.1–4–32–2; Hookes 8–3–11–1. *Second Innings*—George 22.1–2–71–3; Pyke 18–4–47–5; Zesers 22–4–75–1; Hookes 1–0–1–0; Sleep 29–12–63–0; Plummer 6–2–14–0; Jolly 2–0–9–0.

South Australia

A. M. J. Hilditch c Soule b Lillee	0
G. A. Bishop c Davison b Cooley	22
†W. B. Phillips c Lillee b Harris	85
*D. W. Hookes c Cooley b Harris	132
M. D. Haysman c Soule b Lillee	47
P. R. Sleep c Taylor b Lillee	1
H. B. Jolly c Faulkner b Lillee	19
J. K. Pyke c Woolley b Harris	64
N. R. Plummer c Bennett b Harris	39
A. K. Zesers not out	8
S. P. George not out	5
B 8, l-b 13, w 2, n-b 18	41
1/0 2/34 3/221 4/293 5/294 6/324 7/341 8/450 9/451	(9 wkts dec.) 463

Bowling: Lillee 45–10–99–4; Faulkner 46.3–20–105–0; de Winter 5.3–1–25–0; Cooley 25–1–128–1; Hughes 4–1–28–0; Harris 21–2–57–4.

Umpires: D. R. Close and P. Howard.

WESTERN AUSTRALIA v QUEENSLAND

At Perth, January 15, 16, 17, 18. Western Australia won by three wickets. Western Australia 6 pts. Toss: Western Australia. Even without their Test players, the two strongest teams in the competition staged a memorable match which drew a crowd of 12,121 on the third day and 29,194 in all, the second-highest Shield attendance at Perth. Put in, Queensland battled for their runs against a persistent seam attack, Kerr taking three and threequarter hours over 59.

Western Australia's batsmen also had to fight hard, and the big Sunday crowd saw an enthralling contest for first-innings points, resolved when MacLeay guided Capes and Alderman through two important partnerships to set up a lead of 45. With the wicket deteriorating, Queensland struggled in their second innings, and it was thanks to Botham (58 in 80 minutes) that they could set Western Australia a target. At 153 for three, the home side looked certain winners, but a run-out and Rackemann effected a collapse to put the game in the balance. Brayshaw, aged twenty and in his first match, prevented any further decline and took his side to victory with nine overs to spare. Injuries to Alderman (strained hamstring) and Tazelaar (elbow) handicapped both teams, but Botham responded for Queensland by bowling unchanged for 26 overs.

Queensland

*R. B. Kerr c Capes b Alderman	59	– lbw b MacLeay	25
T. J. Barsby b Capes	5	– lbw b MacLeay	22
G. M. Ritchie c MacLeay b Alderman	76	– lbw b Matthews	19
G. S. Trimble c Zoehrer b Matthews	2	– c Andrews b Capes	30
A. B. Henschell lbw b Alderman	9	– c Zoehrer b Matthews	4
I. T. Botham c Alderman b Capes	70	– c Zoehrer b Capes	58
T. V. Hohns lbw b Alderman	32	– lbw b MacLeay	23
†P. W. Anderson c Zoehrer b Capes	0	– c Brayshaw b MacLeay	14
D. Tazelaar lbw b Capes	17	– b MacLeay	20
J. N. Maguire c Wood b MacLeay	10	– c Zoehrer b Capes	4
C. G. Rackemann not out	2	– not out	10
L-b 14, n-b 7	21	L-b 4, w 1, n-b 4	9
1/20 2/141 3/150 4/151 5/171 6/256 7/259 8/276 9/295	303	1/45 2/64 3/79 4/87 5/131 6/179 7/202 8/205 9/220	238

Bowling: *First Innings*—Capes 35–3–87–4; MacLeay 22.5–5–48–1; Alderman 32.3–7–87–4; Matthews 21–2–67–1. *Second Innings*—Capes 18–3–68–3; MacLeay 24.3–4–99–5; Matthews 13–1–43–2; Moody 6–0–24–0.

Western Australia

T. M. Moody b Botham	33	– b Rackemann	14
M. W. McPhee c Anderson b Maguire	44	– b Botham	28
J. A. Brayshaw c Anderson b Rackemann	36	– not out	60
*G. M. Wood c Anderson b Maguire	61	– c Barsby b Botham	15
K. J. Hughes b Rackemann	0	– (6) c Maguire b Rackemann	0
W. S. Andrews lbw b Botham	66	– (5) run out	39
†T. J. Zoehrer c Botham b Hohns	16	– hit wkt b Rackemann	0
C. D. Matthews c Kerr b Rackemann	16	– c Botham b Rackemann	9
K. H. MacLeay c Anderson b Maguire	38	– not out	9
P. A. Capes c and b Rackemann	13		
T. M. Alderman not out	7		
B 1, l-b 8, w 1, n-b 8	18	B 10, l-b 9, w 1	20
1/60 2/85 3/179 4/182 5/193 6/259 7/284 8/284 9/304	348	1/41 2/57 3/95 4/153 5/159 6/159 7/169	(7 wkts) 194

Bowling: *First Innings*—Tazelaar 7.3–1–31–0; Botham 27.3–3–89–2; Rackemann 28–6–56–4; Maguire 17.4–4–70–3; Henschell 7–2–26–0; Hohns 21–2–67–1. *Second Innings*—Botham 28–8–51–2; Rackemann 30.2–5–65–4; Hohns 10–3–19–0; Maguire 13–2–40–0.

Umpires: R. J. Evans and P. J. McConnell.

SOUTH AUSTRALIA v NEW SOUTH WALES

At Adelaide, January 22, 23, 24, 25. South Australia won by 63 runs. South Australia 6 pts. Toss: South Australia. Having gambled and lost in Melbourne in December, Hookes achieved victory after a daring declaration that left New South Wales a whole day in which to make 283. However, his tantrum after being run out for 9 on the third evening was unworthy of him.

Rain washed out play on the second day with South Australia 280 for seven, Hookes having batted superbly for two hours, hitting a six and twelve fours; but on the third morning he allowed the innings to meander for another 70 minutes, during which only 39 runs were added. New South Wales responded aggressively with Smith and Dyson in splendid form, and Bennett's declaration, 169 behind, set up the eventual run-chase. As it happened, the New South Wales batsmen were not up to the task. Smith again batted well, but thereafter only Waugh's marvellous hitting in a stay of 109 minutes held up the steady South Australian attack. He struck four sixes, all off Sleep, as well as seven fours.

South Australia

First innings		Second innings	
G. A. Bishop c Smith b Jones	67	(2) b Lawson	26
A. M. J. Hilditch c Emery b Gilbert	4	(1) c Taylor b Jones	14
†W. B. Phillips c Dyson b Jones	5	not out	49
*D. W. Hookes c Matthews b Gilbert	82	run out	9
M. D. Haysman b Matthews	0	not out	10
P. R. Sleep c Smith b O'Neill	58		
H. B. Jolly lbw b Gilbert	41		
J. K. Pyke c Emery b Gilbert	9		
A. K. Zesers not out	21		
P. W. Gladigau b Gilbert	0		
S. P. George c Waugh b Lawson	2		
B 5, l-b 9, n-b 16	30	L-b 2, n-b 3	5
1/10 2/26 3/142 4/143 5/192 6/258 7/279 8/311 9/311	319	1/38 2/44 3/53 (3 wkts dec.)	113

Bowling: *First Innings*—Lawson 30.1–12–53–1; Gilbert 31–6–94–5; Jones 11–0–49–2; Waugh 2–0–11–0; Bennett 10–0–35–0; Matthews 25–7–55–1; O'Neill 4–2–8–1. *Second Innings*—Lawson 10–3–29–1; Gilbert 10–0–40–0; Jones 6–1–21–1; Matthews 6–1–21–0.

New South Wales

First innings		Second innings	
M. A. Taylor b Gladigau	15	(2) run out	3
S. B. Smith c Sleep b George	49	(1) st Phillips b Sleep	51
J. Dyson not out	60	c Hookes b Pyke	28
M. D. O'Neill not out	18	lbw b Gladigau	8
M. E. Waugh (did not bat)		b Zesers	72
G. R. J. Matthews (did not bat)		lbw b Gladigau	10
†P. A. Emery (did not bat)		c Pyke b Zesers	18
*M. J. Bennett (did not bat)		lbw b Sleep	5
D. R. Gilbert (did not bat)		lbw b Sleep	13
G. F. Lawson (did not bat)		b Zesers	5
R. A. Jones (did not bat)		not out	1
L-b 2, n-b 6	8	L-b 3, n-b 2	5
1/22 2/97 (2 wkts dec.)	150	1/13 2/85 3/85 4/116 5/127 6/184 7/193 8/213 9/218	219

Bowling: *First Innings*—Gladigau 7–1–36–1; George 10–0–50–1; Pyke 15–5–37–0; Zesers 7–2–13–0; Sleep 3–0–12–0. *Second Innings*—Gladigau 15–2–39–2; George 7–1–25–0; Pyke 8–1–32–1; Zesers 25.5–12–42–3; Sleep 25–5–78–3.

Umpires: P. M. Cronin and M. G. O'Connell.

TASMANIA v VICTORIA

At Launceston, January 29, 30, 31, February 1. Drawn. Victoria 2 pts. Toss: Victoria. Tasmania's last pair, Young and Cooley, held out for five overs to thwart Victoria's bid for victory. Set to score 258 runs in 71 overs, Tasmania lost five wickets for 15 before the final rearguard action saved them. For Victoria, Watts hit his first hundred after a break of four seasons from Shield cricket, having recorded a "pair" against New South Wales in his last

Hohns and Henschell then finished off the tail, South Australia losing their last five wickets for 10 runs. Queensland's second innings teetered unsteadily, and but for Border's 52nd hundred they would have lost their grip. Given lives at 18 and 87, he batted for five hours and hit fifteen fours. South Australia's target was 293 in a minimum of 53 overs, but after a dashing opening stand, in which 50 came up in nine overs, wickets fell at critical times. It was left to Jolly and Zesers to negotiate the final five and a half overs.

Queensland

R. B. Kerr c Hookes b George	4	– lbw b Gladigau	3
T. J. Barsby run out	102	– b George	12
G. S. Trimble c O'Connor b Sleep	57	– st Phillips b May	27
*A. R. Border b Gladigau	37	– not out	118
A. B. Henschell run out	46	– b Zesers	0
I. T. Botham c Phillips b Sleep	60	– c O'Connor b Zesers	37
T. V. Hohns c Hookes b Zesers	0	– c Hookes b May	0
†I. A. Healy c Hilditch b Sleep	23	– c Jolly b Sleep	30
D. Tazelaar c O'Connor b Sleep	25	– run out	19
J. N. Maguire b Zesers	3	– lbw b Gladigau	2
C. G. Rackemann not out	4	– b Gladigau	4
B 3, l-b 7, w 3, n-b 11	24	B 5, l-b 8, n-b 6	19
1/10 2/173 3/178 4/241 5/295 6/295 7/329 8/373 9/377	385	1/13 2/35 3/63 4/64 5/154 6/155 7/212 8/259 9/261	271

Bowling: *First Innings*—Gladigau 24–5–99–1; George 13–1–78–1; Zesers 32–12–62–2; May 12–1–44–0; Sleep 28.1–5–91–4; Hookes 2–1–1–0. *Second Innings*—Gladigau 10.3–1–31–3; George 5–0–30–1; May 37–9–78–2; Zesers 27–9–69–2; Sleep 14–2–44–1; Jolly 1–0–6–0.

South Australia

G. A. Bishop c Tazelaar b Hohns	100	– (2) c Trimble b Hohns	34
A. M. J. Hilditch c Botham b Rackemann	49	– (1) c Tazelaar b Henschell	21
†W. B. Phillips b Hohns	36	– run out	53
*D. W. Hookes c Maguire b Henschell	112	– st Healy b Hohns	26
T. B. A. May c Henschell b Hohns	0	– (9) b Henschell	5
P. R. Sleep c Botham b Hohns	4	– c Botham b Henschell	52
D. F. G. O'Connor not out	35	– c Maguire b Hohns	21
H. B. Jolly lbw b Hohns	0	– not out	13
A. K. Zesers c Healy b Henschell	0	– (10) not out	0
S. P. George c Healy b Henschell	0		
P. W. Gladigau run out	3	– (5) c Tazelaar b Henschell	15
L-b 11, w 2, n-b 12	25	B 5, l-b 1, n-b 1	7
1/157 2/169 3/228 4/228 5/242 6/354 7/354 8/357 9/357	364	1/56 2/56 3/101 4/130 5/192 6/224 7/231 8/243	(8 wkts) 247

Bowling: *First Innings*—Tazelaar 18–3–51–0; Botham 13–3–47–0; Rackemann 20–4–58–1; Maguire 13–2–41–0; Hohns 45–13–100–5; Henschell 27.2–10–56–3. *Second Innings*—Rackemann 4–0–15–0; Tazelaar 3–0–23–0; Henschell 27–7–101–4; Hohns 26–2–102–3.

Umpires: M. W. Johnson and C. D. Timmins.

VICTORIA v NEW SOUTH WALES

At Melbourne, February 12, 13, 14, 15. Drawn. Victoria 2 pts. Toss: Victoria. Victoria's batsmen made the most of some erratic bowling by the New South Wales pacemen, and only some steady off-spinning by Matthews kept the score within reasonable bounds. In contrast, Hickey's pace soon had New South Wales struggling, and Victoria ultimately enjoyed a healthy first-innings lead. Second time round, Siddons batted enterprisingly to score his runs from 169 balls. He took especially heavy toll of the New South Wales spinners, hitting Robertson for four fours in one over. Davis declared before lunch on the fourth day, and although the early New South Wales batsmen failed again, Waugh's class saved his side from defeat. His hundred, his third of the season, came from 170 balls and contained fourteen fours.

Victoria

First innings		Second innings	
D. F. Whatmore c Emery b Lawson	55	(2) lbw b Lawson	4
G. M. Watts c Waugh b Lawson	66	(1) lbw b Lawson	0
W. G. Ayres c Waugh b Matthews	6	c Dyson b Matthews	28
J. D. Siddons c Gilbert b Matthews	71	c Emery b Lawson	130
P. W. Young c Taylor b Matthews	10	(6) not out	28
W. G. Whiteside c Taylor b Matthews	80		
†M. G. D. Dimattina run out	60	(5) b Robertson	15
P. W. Jackson run out	6		
P. R. Reiffel c Waugh b Matthews	22		
D. J. Hickey c and b Matthews	1		
*S. P. Davis not out	1		
L-b 13, n-b 12	25	B 6, n-b 1	7
1/90 2/111 3/211 4/218 5/249 6/353 7/373 8/385 9/394	403	1/0 2/11 3/94 4/145 5/212 (5 wkts dec.)	212

Bowling: *First Innings*—Lawson 25–3–79–2; Whitney 24–5–71–0; Gilbert 23–4–91–0; Matthews 49.1–19–97–6; Robertson 17–6–37–0; O'Neill 5–0–15–0. *Second Innings*—Lawson 9–4–20–3; Whitney 9–3–23–0; Matthews 18–3–52–1; Gilbert 3.4–0–11–0; Robertson 14.3–3–62–1; O'Neill 11–1–38–0.

New South Wales

First innings		Second innings	
M. A. Taylor c Watts b Hickey	29	c Young b Reiffel	0
S. B. Smith c Watts b Hickey	0	(3) c Siddons b Hickey	32
J. Dyson b Hickey	17	(2) lbw b Davis	19
M. E. Waugh c Young b Jackson	69	not out	100
M. D. O'Neill run out	18	c Whatmore b Jackson	16
G. R. J. Matthews c Dimattina b Whiteside	62	c Young b Jackson	4
†P. A. Emery c Whatmore b Reiffel	11	not out	28
G. R. Robertson c Davis b Reiffel	38		
D. R. Gilbert c Young b Hickey	8		
*G. F. Lawson c Young b Jackson	5		
M. R. Whitney not out	5		
L-b 10, n-b 7	17	L-b 4, n-b 3	7
1/5 2/39 3/55 4/80 5/178 6/211 7/219 8/238 9/247	279	1/3 2/51 3/59 4/96 5/102 (5 wkts)	206

Bowling: *First Innings*—Hickey 27–5–90–4; Reiffel 25.3–6–57–2; Davis 15–3–44–0; Jackson 30–11–68–2; Young 2–0–6–0; Whiteside 1–0–4–1. *Second Innings*—Hickey 13–2–43–1; Reiffel 7.5–1–32–1; Jackson 23–10–55–2; Davis 14–2–35–1; Whiteside 7–2–18–0; Whatmore 1–0–1–0; Siddons 3–0–18–0.

Umpires: B. Guy and L. J. King.

SOUTH AUSTRALIA v TASMANIA

At Adelaide, February 18, 19, 20, 21. Drawn. South Australia 2 pts, Tasmania −0.2 pt. Toss: Tasmania. Tasmania took advantage of perfect conditions to bat until tea on the second day and amass their highest total in Shield cricket. Taylor batted for seven and a half hours for his 216, Buckingham four hours for his 126, and their fourth-wicket stand of 258 in better than even time was the highest for any Tasmanian wicket against South Australia. Bishop and Hilditch gave South Australia a perfect start with an effortless stand lasting three and three-quarter hours, but O'Connor's arrival slowed the run-rate to a crawl. He spent five and a half hours over 75, although Hilditch pressed on efficiently until he was caught in the gully after batting for nearly seven hours. Hookes, benefiting from three lives, sustained his team's effort with 112 from 215 balls and received good support from Phillips and Sleep. For Tasmania, Lillee demonstrated his fitness with a marathon stint of hostile bowling, but his over-zealous tongue cost him a fine of $A300. Tasmania's failure to win first-innings points was compounded by their being docked 0.2 of a point for a slow over-rate on the final day.

Tasmania

G. A. Hughes b George 32
D. C. Boon lbw b Gladigau 18
N. C. P. Courtney b Zesers 14
M. D. Taylor b George 216
D. J. Buckingham c May b Zesers 126
*B. F. Davison c Hilditch b Gladigau . 55
P. I. Faulkner c Phillips b Hookes 46
†R. E. Soule c O'Connor b George 18
T. J. Cooley c Zesers b May 30
T. D. Bower not out 10
D. K. Lillee c Sleep b Hookes 12
L-b 9, w 1, n-b 5 15

1/30 2/47 3/80 4/338 5/449 6/489 7/515 8/568 9/570 — 592

Bowling: Gladigau 35–3–139–2; George 23–6–74–3; Zesers 35–5–109–2; May 51–10–158–1; Sleep 18–1–81–0; Hookes 5–0–22–2.

South Australia

G. A. Bishop c sub b Hughes 101
A. M. J. Hilditch c Taylor b Lillee 185
D. F. G. O'Connor c Soule b Cooley .. 75
*D. W. Hookes c Cooley b Lillee 112
†W. B. Phillips c Taylor b Lillee 67
P. R. Sleep not out 57
H. B. Jolly c Davison b Cooley 13
T. B. A. May c Soule b Lillee 3
A. K. Zesers b Courtney 5
P. W. Gladigau c Davison b Courtney . 25
S. P. George lbw b Boon 1
B 8, l-b 7, w 2, n-b 12 29

1/199 2/335 3/429 4/545 5/564 6/579 7/591 8/607 9/660 — 673

Bowling: Lillee 55–7–165–4; Bower 6–0–26–0; Faulkner 51–15–136–0; Cooley 38–2–137–2; Hughes 41–11–100–1; Boon 10.4–4–25–1; Courtney 7–0–44–2; Taylor 3–0–15–0; Davison 3–0–10–0.

Umpires: A. R. Crafter and D. J. Harper.

NEW SOUTH WALES v WESTERN AUSTRALIA

At Sydney, February 24, 25, 26, 27. New South Wales won by 131 runs. New South Wales 6 pts. Toss: New South Wales. An ill-timed and inappropriate criticism of Dyer's declaration on the third evening by the Western Australian captain, Wood, could not disguise his team's failure to overcome the inconsistent New South Welshmen. Mark Waugh's innings on the first day was quite outstanding, and his fourth-wicket partnership with O'Neill, 155 in three hours, was crucial on a wicket helping the seam bowlers and also allowing some slow turn. Dyer's invitation for Western Australia to score 333 in more than a day seemed fair, but only Marsh showed the determination and technique necessary. Steve Waugh's bowling was the telling factor, ending a stubborn partnership between Marsh and Moody and destroying the Western Australian middle order in a spell of three for 8 in 36 balls.

New South Wales

First innings		Second innings	
M. A. Taylor lbw b Capes	18	c Veletta b MacLeay	2
J. Dyson c Hogan b MacLeay	1	c Marsh b Matthews	3
S. R. Waugh b Alderman	9	c Zoehrer b Matthews	14
M. D. O'Neill lbw b MacLeay	68	st Zoehrer b MacLeay	11
M. E. Waugh c Wood b Capes	95	b Alderman	1
G. R. J. Matthews lbw b Matthews	17	c Veletta b Hogan	41
T. H. Bayliss c Matthews b Alderman	5	c and b Andrews	68
*†G. C. Dyer lbw b Alderman	9	(9) c Marsh b Hogan	7
P. L. Taylor not out	46	(8) not out	42
G. F. Lawson c Zoehrer b Matthews	6	not out	21
M. R. Whitney b MacLeay	5		
B 2, l-b 5, w 9	16	L-b 3	3
1/5 2/23 3/33 4/188 5/200 6/217 7/217 8/247 9/263	295	1/7 2/7 3/25 4/26 5/38 6/117 7/161 8/174	(8 wkts dec.) 213

Bowling: *First Innings*—Capes 24–7–66–2; MacLeay 20.5–3–47–3; Alderman 33–11–67–3; Matthews 21–5–71–2; Hogan 10–1–37–0. *Second Innings*—Matthews 13–3–35–2; MacLeay 19–8–35–2; Alderman 16–8–22–1; Hogan 21–5–73–2; Andrews 12–0–45–1.

Western Australia

First innings		Second innings	
G. R. Marsh c M. A. Taylor b Whitney	4	lbw b Matthews	82
M. R. J. Veletta c Matthews b Whitney	16	lbw b Lawson	5
T. M. Moody c Dyer b Matthews	9	(4) c M. E. Waugh b S. R. Waugh	21
*G. M. Wood c sub b Matthews	28	(5) c and b S. R. Waugh	0
W. S. Andrews c S. R. Waugh b Matthews	46	(6) c sub b S. R. Waugh	7
†T. J. Zoehrer c M. E. Waugh b S. R. Waugh	23	(7) c Dyer b Lawson	5
K. H. MacLeay run out	14	(8) lbw b Lawson	2
C. D. Matthews c M. E. Waugh b Matthews	27	(9) c sub b S. R. Waugh	40
T. G. Hogan c M. E. Waugh b P. L. Taylor	0	(10) not out	15
P. A. Capes not out	0	(3) c M. A. Taylor b P. L. Taylor	0
T. M. Alderman b P. L. Taylor	0	c Dyer b Whitney	4
B 6, l-b 3	9	B 5, l-b 9, w 4, n-b 2	20
1/5 2/32 3/36 4/84 5/132 6/134 7/174 8/174 9/176	176	1/14 2/18 3/97 4/97 5/123 6/135 7/141 8/141 9/192	201

Bowling: *First Innings*—Lawson 12–4–29–0; Whitney 16–2–46–2; Matthews 29–9–58–4; P. L. Taylor 11.2–6–15–2; S. R. Waugh 8–1–19–1. *Second Innings*—Lawson 18–6–41–3; Whitney 13.1–4–22–1; Matthews 26–9–50–1; P. L. Taylor 22–7–44–1; S. R. Waugh 3–5–30–4.

Umpires: R. A. French and A. G. Marshall.

TASMANIA v QUEENSLAND

At Launceston, February 24, 25, 26, 27. Tasmania won by 94 runs. Tasmania 6 pts. Toss: Tasmania. Not even the most fervent Tasmanian supporter dared contemplate this win over the Shield front-runners. The expectation was even more remote when injuries to Lillee and Faulkner reduced their bowling strength virtually to Young and Broadby in the second innings. The Tasmanian batting, however, excelled. Boon, dropped by Border at third slip off the first ball of the match, never looked back, sharing century opening stands in each innings with the aggressive Hughes, the first time such a feat had been achieved for Tasmania. He scored two superb hundreds. Whereas his first-innings 108 required 203 balls, his 143 on the third afternoon came off 165 balls and included a six and 23 fours. In a desperate effort to take vital outright points, Border declared the Queensland first innings 118 runs in arrears, a brave decision as Trimble was going well, his 138 having taken only three hours. Tasmania's declaration left Queensland 89 overs from which to score 409. Kerr and Ritchie struck 150 in under even time, taking heavy toll of Young, but he fought back impressively, claiming five more wickets and running out Ritchie as Queensland lost nine wickets in the final session. It was Tasmania's first win in 45 first-class matches.

Tasmania

First innings		Second innings	
D. C. Boon b Hohns	108	c Kerr b Hohns	143
G. A. Hughes c Kerr b Rackemann	71	c Healy b Maguire	56
N. C. P. Courtney c Kerr b Maguire	14	lbw b Maguire	1
M. D. Taylor c Kerr b Botham	89	c Border b Hohns	18
D. J. Buckingham c Barsby b Rackemann	7	lbw b Botham	13
*B. F. Davison c Hohns b Tazelaar	73	b Botham	7
P. I. Faulkner not out	78	(9) c Kerr b Tazelaar	1
†R. E. Soule b Hohns	1	(7) lbw b Botham	0
C. L. Broadby c Healy b Hohns	9	(8) not out	42
D. K. Lillee b Hohns	18		
C. M. Young st Healy b Hohns	0		
L-b 6, w 1, n-b 6	13	B 1, l-b 5, n-b 3	9
1/126 2/157 3/223 4/254 5/321 6/403 7/404 8/441 9/475	481	1/124 2/147 3/215 4/236 5/238 6/238 7/263 8/290	(8 wkts dec.) 290

Bowling: *First Innings*—Rackemann 33–4–121–2; Tazelaar 19–1–94–1; Botham 23–8–67–1; Hohns 39.5–6–115–5; Maguire 28–3–78–1. *Second Innings*—Rackemann 4–0–33–0; Tazelaar 6.1–0–22–1; Maguire 22–4–81–2; Hohns 33–7–107–2; Botham 13–3–41–3.

Queensland

R. B. Kerr c Buckingham b Broadby	62 – st Soule b Broadby	96
T. J. Barsby c Soule b Lillee	34 – c sub b Young	23
G. M. Ritchie c Soule b Young	6 – run out	85
*A. R. Border c Boon b Young	47 – c Broadby b Young	17
G. S. Trimble not out	138 – b Broadby	6
I. T. Botham lbw b Faulkner	3 – b Young	10
†I. A. Healy not out	58 – (8) not out	22
T. V. Hohns (did not bat)	– (7) b Young	16
D. Tazelaar (did not bat)	– run out	4
J. N. Maguire (did not bat)	– c Boon b Young	2
C. G. Rackemann (did not bat)	– b Young	0
B 4, l-b 3, w 2, n-b 6	15 L-b 11, w 2, n-b 20	33
1/49 2/59 3/125 4/180 5/195 (5 wkts dec.)	363 1/71 2/221 3/229 4/236 5/256 6/262 7/307 8/311 9/314	314

Bowling: *First Innings*—Lillee 6.2–0–27–1; Young 17.4–1–114–2; Faulkner 23–10–51–1; Broadby 34–6–112–1; Hughes 8–0–29–0; Courtney 4–0–23–0. *Second Innings*—Davison 9–3–18–0; Young 23.5–0–120–6; Buckingham 7–1–16–0; Broadby 30–4–117–2; Courtney 8–0–32–0.

Umpires: M. G. Gandy and S. G. Randell.

SOUTH AUSTRALIA v VICTORIA

At Adelaide, February 24, 25, 26, 27. Drawn. Victoria 2 pts. Toss: Victoria. When seventeen wickets fell on the first day, it seemed unlikely that the game would run its course. Gladigau took full advantage of a wicket offering the faster bowlers assistance to return career-best figures, but after May had sustained a broken bone in his hand from a ball by Hughes on the second morning, the batsmen held sway. Enjoying the easier conditions, Jones and Siddons added 172 in 182 minutes in Victoria's second innings, and Siddons batted for seven hours, hitting a six and 30 fours, before Jones declared on the third afternoon. Requiring 473 for victory, South Australia by stumps had made a spirited response with 142 for two, Hilditch and Hookes having put on 100 for the third wicket. Hilditch was caught down the leg side from the first ball of the fourth day, and when Hookes and Phillips were out soon after, a Victorian victory looked a formality. However, Sleep and Jolly dropped anchor and batted throughout the afternoon session. When the umpires ended the game thirteen minutes early after Hughes had unleashed a bouncer in the fading light, Sleep's dedicated innings had occupied five hours and 269 balls.

Victoria

D. F. Whatmore c Jolly b Gladigau	8 – b Pyke	22
G. M. Watts lbw b Gladigau	25 – c Jolly b Gladigau	3
*D. M. Jones c Phillips b Pyke	15 – c Hookes b Gladigau	101
J. D. Siddons c Phillips b Gladigau	58 – not out	241
W. G. Whiteside c Phillips b Gladigau	0 – (6) c Hookes b Zesers	25
A. I. C. Dodemaide c Phillips b Gladigau	3 – (5) c Hookes b Zesers	3
†M. G. D. Dimattina c Hookes b Gladigau	8 – not out	43
P. W. Jackson c Zesers b Gladigau	5	
D. J. Hickey b Zesers	20	
M. G. Hughes c Pyke b May	24	
S. P. Davis not out	5	
L-b 5, w 1, n-b 1	7 L-b 11, w 3, n-b 3	17
1/11 2/51 3/53 4/53 5/61 6/123 7/124 8/141 9/165	178 1/13 2/43 3/215 4/249 5/353 (5 wkts dec.)	455

Bowling: *First Innings*—Gladigau 24–7–85–7; Pyke 15–6–43–1; Zesers 16–5–41–1; May 1–0–4–1. *Second Innings*—Gladigau 37–4–143–2; Pyke 35–3–136–1; Sleep 20–2–89–0; Zesers 30–10–65–2; Hookes 4–0–11–0.

South Australia

A. M. J. Hilditch c Siddons b Hickey	11	– (2) c Dimattina b Hughes	67
G. A. Bishop c Whatmore b Dodemaide	19	– (1) c Siddons b Dodemaide	8
†W. B. Phillips lbw b Hughes	3	– (5) b Jackson	24
*D. W. Hookes c Jones b Davis	60	– c sub b Dodemaide	65
P. R. Sleep run out	0	– (6) not out	104
D. F. G. O'Connor c Whiteside b Dodemaide	0	– (3) b Hughes	13
H. B. Jolly c Dimattina b Dodemaide	16	– c Dimattina b Hughes	53
J. K. Pyke b Dodemaide	4	– not out	31
T. B. A. May retired hurt	2		
A. K. Zesers not out	15		
P. W. Gladigau c Whatmore b Jackson	17		
B 4, l-b 2, w 1, n-b 7	14	B 4, l-b 8, w 1, n-b 7	20
1/16 2/28 3/52 4/68 5/76 6/116 7/116 8/125 9/161	161	1/13 2/42 3/142 4/172 5/197 6/313	(6 wkts) 385

Bowling: *First Innings*—Hughes 15–4–52–1; Hickey 8–0–43–1; Dodemaide 19–7–37–4; Davis 6–2–19–1; Jackson 1–0–4–1. *Second Innings*—Hughes 31.2–5–91–3; Dodemaide 33–7–75–2; Hickey 17–2–90–0; Davis 10–0–37–0; Jackson 32–15–53–1; Jones 8–3–16–0; Whiteside 5–0–11–0.

Umpires: P. M. Cronin and M. G. O'Connell.

NEW SOUTH WALES v TASMANIA

At Sydney, March 2, 3, 4, 5. New South Wales won by eight wickets. New South Wales 6 pts. Toss: Tasmania. While Boon and Taylor were adding 166 in 193 minutes, Tasmania were in control on the first day. But then Steve Waugh dismissed them both in a spell of three for 3 in sixteen balls, and next morning he went on to record career-best figures. Mark Waugh continued his brilliant batting form, making light of the conditions which caused others to struggle as he moved to his century off 165 balls, and Mark Taylor, whose lack of runs had made his selection surprising, scored a sturdy hundred, batting for five and a half hours. Dyer showed enterprise in Tasmania's second innings by opening the bowling with his spinners, Matthews and Peter Taylor, and the former obliged by dismissing Boon and Hughes in the gathering gloom. On the last day, Lawson capped a successful season with another hostile spell to make New South Wales' final task a simple one.

Tasmania

D. C. Boon c M. A. Taylor b S. R. Waugh	93	– c M. A. Taylor b Matthews	4
G. A. Hughes b Whitney	7	– c Dyson b Matthews	16
K. Bradshaw c P. L. Taylor b S. R. Waugh	4	– c M. E. Waugh b Lawson	7
M. D. Taylor c Dyer b S. R. Waugh	81	– c P. L. Taylor b Lawson	86
D. J. Buckingham c Dyer b S. R. Waugh	2	– c Bayliss b Lawson	36
*B. F. Davison c Bayliss b Whitney	48	– c M. E. Waugh b Lawson	2
P. I. Faulkner c M. A. Taylor b Whitney	26	– st Dyer b Matthews	20
A. J. de Winter c M. E. Waugh b Whitney	26	– lbw b Lawson	22
†R. E. Soule c Dyer b Whitney	0	– lbw b Lawson	2
C. L. Broadby not out	10	– not out	0
T. J. Cooley c Dyer b S. R. Waugh	13	– c Bayliss b Matthews	4
B 7, l-b 6, n-b 4	17	L-b 4, n-b 1	5
1/18 2/29 3/195 4/196 5/201 6/271 7/284 8/288 9/301	327	1/6 2/21 3/66 4/149 5/151 6/158 7/192 8/200 9/200	204

Bowling: *First Innings*—Lawson 20–4–84–0; Whitney 26–10–54–5; S. R. Waugh 23.4–2–50–5; P. L. Taylor 21–3–60–0; Matthews 23–6–53–0; M. E. Waugh 3–0–13–0. *Second Innings*—Matthews 19–4–54–4; P. L. Taylor 25–5–76–0; Lawson 16–4–40–6; Whitney 5–1–10–0; S. R. Waugh 5–0–20–0.

New South Wales

S. G. Hookey b Broadby	16	– c Davison b Hughes	44
M. A. Taylor c Taylor b de Winter	144	– c Buckingham b Broadby	3
J. Dyson c Soule b de Winter	5	– not out	11
S. R. Waugh st Soule b Broadby	55	– not out	9
M. E. Waugh run out	116		
G. R. J. Matthews run out	1		
T. H. Bayliss c Boon b Faulkner	37		
P. L. Taylor c Boon b Hughes	31		
*†G. C. Dyer c Hughes b de Winter	25		
G. F. Lawson not out	14		
M. R. Whitney run out	1		
L-b 11, w 4	15	B 4, l-b 1	5
1/32 2/39 3/167 4/309 5/310 6/374 7/397 8/423 9/456	460	1/18 2/52	(2 wkts) 72

Bowling: *First Innings*—Cooley 24–1–95–0; de Winter 29–4–92–3; Broadby 49.1–8–147–2; Hughes 12–2–38–1; Faulkner 26–5–57–1; Bradshaw 6–1–20–0. *Second Innings*—Faulkner 4–0–17–0; Broadby 15–8–21–1; Hughes 11.5–3–29–1.

Umpires: R. A. French and G. E. Reed.

VICTORIA v QUEENSLAND

At Melbourne, March 2, 3, 4, 5. Victoria won by 207 runs. Victoria 6 pts. Toss: Queensland. Needing outright points to finish top of the table, and so have home advantage in the final, Queensland made a vain attempt to score 376 off 64 overs and ended up losing their second successive match. Their cause was further upset by a back injury to Botham which impeded his batting and had prevented him from bowling in Victoria's second innings. Botham's verbal extravagance towards some spectators on the first day cost him a $A500 fine for breaching the players' code of behaviour. The destiny of the game swung strongly towards Victoria when Siddons and Watts enjoyed a lively third-wicket partnership of 136 on the third day. Siddons was severe on the leg-spin of Hohns, and Watts batted for 322 minutes in a watchful innings. At stumps Victoria were 300 ahead with six wickets in hand, and Jones's refusal to declare on the last day effectively ended Queensland's hopes of victory. Nevertheless, they began with a blaze of runs, taking 83 from the first eleven overs as Ritchie struck 48 off 31 balls.

Victoria

D. F. Whatmore c Barsby b Hohns	85	– run out	30
G. M. Watts c Healy b Tazelaar	17	– c Healy b Rackemann	116
*D. M. Jones c Botham b Rackemann	13	– lbw b Maguire	20
J. D. Siddons c Trimble b Botham	9	– c Barsby b Rackemann	76
W. G. Ayres c Healy b Maguire	46	– c Healy b Maguire	21
W. G. Whiteside lbw b Tazelaar	16	– (7) c Healy b Tazelaar	15
A. I. C. Dodemaide c Botham b Rackemann	20	– (8) c Border b Maguire	0
†M. G. D. Dimattina lbw b Tazelaar	16	– (6) c Healy b Tazelaar	25
P. W. Jackson not out	6	– c Trimble b Maguire	0
P. R. Reiffel c Healy b Tazelaar	1	– not out	1
M. G. Hughes b Tazelaar	4	– c Healy b Maguire	8
B 1, l-b 10, w 3, n-b 9	23	L-b 12, n-b 4	16
1/52 2/82 3/115 4/150 5/171 6/204 7/243 8/245 9/248	256	1/66 2/111 3/247 4/249 5/291 6/307 7/308 8/318 9/322	328

Bowling: *First Innings*—Rackemann 25–12–47–2; Botham 17–2–53–1; Maguire 20–7–55–1; Tazelaar 31–13–55–5; Hohns 13–5–35–1. *Second Innings*—Rackemann 31–15–72–2; Tazelaar 32–10–87–2; Maguire 39.5–10–89–5; Hohns 16–3–68–0.

Queensland

Batsman	First Innings		Second Innings	
R. B. Kerr	c Whatmore b Hughes	4	c Siddons b Reiffel	4
†I. A. Healy	b Reiffel	17	(7) c Dimattina b Hughes	12
G. M. Ritchie	c Siddons b Reiffel	29	c Whatmore b Dodemaide	48
*A. R. Border	c Jones b Dodemaide	33	b Dodemaide	12
G. S. Trimble	c Dimattina b Hughes	18	c Jones b Reiffel	0
I. T. Botham	c Hughes b Reiffel	35	c Whatmore b Jackson	21
T. J. Barsby	run out	28	(2) c Jones b Hughes	47
T. V. Hohns	c Ayres b Reiffel	22	not out	17
D. Tazelaar	c Siddons b Hughes	13	c Jones b Jackson	0
J. N. Maguire	c Dimattina b Hughes	2	c Dodemaide b Reiffel	4
C. G. Rackemann	not out	0	run out	0
	L-b 2, w 6	8	L-b 2, w 1	3
	1/8 2/25 3/84 4/106 5/110 6/169 7/175 8/207 9/207	209	1/10 2/83 3/105 4/114 5/114 6/142 7/148 8/149 9/162	168

Bowling: *First Innings*—Hughes 16.3–4–43–4; Reiffel 22–3–80–4; Dodemaide 16–3–59–1; Jackson 10–3–25–0. *Second Innings*—Hughes 14–4–59–2; Reiffel 12–3–62–3; Dodemaide 5–0–21–2; Jackson 8.3–2–24–2.

Umpires: R. C. Bailhache and D. W. Holt.

WESTERN AUSTRALIA v SOUTH AUSTRALIA

At Perth, March 2, 3, 4, 5. Western Australia won by seven wickets. Western Australia 6 pts. Toss: Western Australia. Reid, playing in his first match for three months, made a dramatic return on a seaming wicket to take five for 15 in a nine-over spell. In turn, the South Australian bowlers reduced Western Australia to 95 for six by the close, with Killen in his first game proving especially hostile. Wood, suffering from headaches, had dropped himself down the order and on the second day he played a masterly innings. He batted in all for more than six hours, hit 27 fours, and with MacLeay added 160, a Western Australian record for the eighth wicket. His own score of 186 was a personal best. South Australia made a much better fist of their second innings but lost their last four wickets for 11 runs against some persistent bowling by Alderman and Matthews at the end of the third day. With their early batsmen again failing, Western Australia made heavy weather of scoring 36 for victory on the final morning.

South Australia

Batsman	First Innings		Second Innings	
A. M. J. Hilditch	c Andrews b MacLeay	13	(2) c and b Matthews	59
G. A. Bishop	c Veletta b Alderman	21	(1) b MacLeay	55
D. F. G. O'Connor	c Andrews b Matthews	8	lbw b MacLeay	20
*D. W. Hookes	c Zoehrer b Alderman	2	c Zoehrer b Matthews	65
†W. B. Phillips	c Veletta b Reid	13	c Moody b Brayshaw	59
P. R. Sleep	c Zoehrer b Reid	34	lbw b Alderman	9
H. B. Jolly	not out	18	lbw b Alderman	5
J. K. Pyke	c Zoehrer b Reid	0	c Zoehrer b Matthews	41
C. M. Killen	b Reid	0	lbw b Matthews	0
A. K. Zesers	b Reid	7	not out	0
P. W. Gladigau	c Brayshaw b Matthews	15	b Alderman	5
	B 1, l-b 4, w 2	7	B 3, l-b 4, w 1, n-b 5	13
	1/25 2/44 3/46 4/46 5/89 6/104 7/104 8/108 9/116	138	1/114 2/122 3/166 4/208 5/217 6/223 7/320 8/324 9/326	331

Bowling: *First Innings*—Reid 14–6–34–5; MacLeay 9–4–21–1; Matthews 10.2–2–34–2; Alderman 15–2–44–2. *Second Innings*—Reid 21–5–48–0; MacLeay 22–3–88–2; Alderman 23.4–5–80–3; Matthews 31–11–79–4; Brayshaw 5–2–13–1; Andrews 5–1–16–0.

Western Australia

G. R. Marsh c Phillips b Killen	1	– c Phillips b Killen	0
T. M. Moody c Hookes b Gladigau	0	– c Pyke b Killen	9
J. A. Brayshaw lbw b Killen	20	– lbw b Gladigau	0
M. R. J. Veletta c Hookes b Zesers	5	– not out	13
W. S. Andrews c Hilditch b Zesers	8	– not out	13
*G. M. Wood not out	186		
†T. J. Zoehrer c Jolly b Zesers	20		
C. D. Matthews c Bishop b Pyke	64		
K. H. MacLeay b Pyke	67		
T. M. Alderman c Zesers b Pyke	17		
B. A. Reid b Zesers	25		
L-b 13, w 1, n-b 7	21	L-b 1	1
1/1 2/3 3/22 4/37 5/37 6/88 7/184 8/344 9/390	434	1/1 2/2 3/10	(3 wkts) 36

Bowling: *First Innings*—Gladigau 24–6–80–1; Killen 26–8–98–2; Zesers 32.5–12–86–4; Sleep 14–3–59–0; Pyke 26–3–98–3. *Second Innings*—Gladigau 7–2–20–1; Killen 6.5–3–15–2.

Umpires: P. J. McConnell and T. A. Prue.

FINAL

WESTERN AUSTRALIA v QUEENSLAND

At Perth, March 18, 19, 20, 21, 22. Western Australia won by five wickets. Toss: Western Australia. Needing only a draw to retain the Sheffield Shield, Western Australia won the final shortly after lunch on the fifth day. Wood gained the early initiative by winning the toss, but inviting Queensland to bat was a brave move considering that Western Australia had their left-arm strike bowlers, Reid and Capes, out with injury. A teenage left-armer, Mullally, had been brought in for his first match. The bowlers responded well with Matthews taking eight wickets and also having had Border dropped at slip before scoring. Western Australia replied shakily as Rackemann, almost single-handedly, upset their early batting by taking three wickets and running out Hughes. At 186 for five on the third morning, with the match in the balance, Andrews joined his captain and together they added 136 in 138 minutes. The two left-handers swung hard at anything loose and ensured a useful first-innings lead, but Andrews's dismissal heralded a collapse with the last five wickets falling for 22. Wood was last out after 6 hours 39 minutes of wonderful concentration and admirable stroke selection. Queensland's second innings fell foul of Alderman's precision seam bowling. Between tea and stumps on the third day they lost four wickets for 58, and although Botham and Hohns prevented a rout, the innings was over at tea next day. Marsh and Veletta scored nearly half of the 162 required for victory in a careful opening partnership before the persistent Tazelaar picked up four wickets. Andrews despatched him for six over square leg to win the match, which was attended by a total of 31,905 and played in unseasonably hot temperatures (37.7°C to 41.7°C) on the first four days.

Queensland

R. B. Kerr c Marsh b Matthews	46	– c Andrews b Alderman	2
T. J. Barsby c Zoehrer b Matthews	48	– b MacLeay	21
G. M. Ritchie c MacLeay b Matthews	33	– lbw b Alderman	34
*A. R. Border c Andrews b MacLeay	66	– c Veletta b Matthews	6
G. S. Trimble c Zoehrer b Mullally	15	– lbw b Alderman	3
I. T. Botham c MacLeay b Matthews	9	– c MacLeay b Alderman	54
D. Tazelaar c Zoehrer b Matthews	6	– (10) c Wood b Alderman	5
T. V. Hohns lbw b Matthews	14	– (7) not out	59
†I. A. Healy lbw b Matthews	14	– (8) c Zoehrer b Alderman	0
C. J. McDermott not out	8	– (9) c Andrews b Mullally	1
C. G. Rackemann b Matthews	0	– b MacLeay	8
B 9, l-b 9, w 8, n-b 4	30	B 9, l-b 7, n-b 7	23
1/63 2/115 3/161 4/200 5/234 6/235 7/253 8/266 9/289	289	1/9 2/38 3/46 4/49 5/88 6/162 7/164 8/169 9/194	216

Bowling: *First Innings*—Mullally 17–2–55–1; MacLeay 27–10–53–1; Alderman 26–10–62–0; Matthews 32.5–7–101–8. *Second Innings*—Alderman 28–4–91–6; MacLeay 17.2–6–40–2; Matthews 27–9–52–1; Mullally 12–6–17–1.

Western Australia

G. R. Marsh c Healy b Rackemann	41	– b Tazelaar	39
M. R. J. Veletta c Barsby b Rackemann	23	– lbw b Tazelaar	59
J. A. Brayshaw c Border b Rackemann	24	– c Botham b Tazelaar	4
*G. M. Wood run out	141	– c Healy b Tazelaar	0
K. J. Hughes run out	11	– c sub b Botham	21
K. H. MacLeay lbw b McDermott	2		
W. S. Andrews lbw b Rackemann	71	– (6) not out	20
†T. J. Zoehrer c Healy b Rackemann	0	– (7) not out	10
C. D. Matthews c Barsby b Hohns	2		
T. M. Alderman lbw b Hohns	0		
A. D. Mullally not out	2		
L-b 15, n-b 12	27	L-b 8, n-b 1	9
1/61 2/75 3/140 4/153 5/186 6/322 7/326 8/335 9/335	344	1/78 2/82 3/82 4/125 5/133	(5 wkts) 162

Bowling: *First Innings*—McDermott 24–4–80–1; Tazelaar 32–10–79–0; Rackemann 30–7–69–5; Botham 24–7–66–0; Hohns 19.5–7–35–2. *Second Innings*—Botham 16–3–33–1; Rackemann 14–4–29–0; McDermott 7–1–21–0; Tazelaar 22.4–7–65–4; Hohns 4–1–6–0.

Umpires: A. R. Crafter and P. J. McConnell.

SHEFFIELD SHIELD WINNERS

1892-93	Victoria	1920-21	New South Wales
1893-94	South Australia	1921-22	Victoria
1894-95	Victoria	1922-23	New South Wales
1895-96	New South Wales	1923-24	Victoria
1896-97	New South Wales	1924-25	Victoria
1897-98	Victoria	1925-26	New South Wales
1898-99	Victoria	1926-27	South Australia
1899-1900	New South Wales	1927-28	Victoria
1900-01	Victoria	1928-29	New South Wales
1901-02	New South Wales	1929-30	Victoria
1902-03	New South Wales	1930-31	Victoria
1903-04	New South Wales	1931-32	New South Wales
1904-05	New South Wales	1932-33	New South Wales
1905-06	New South Wales	1933-34	Victoria
1906-07	New South Wales	1934-35	Victoria
1907-08	Victoria	1935-36	South Australia
1908-09	New South Wales	1936-37	Victoria
1909-10	South Australia	1937-38	New South Wales
1910-11	New South Wales	1938-39	South Australia
1911-12	New South Wales	1939-40	New South Wales
1912-13	South Australia	1940-46	No competition
1913-14	New South Wales	1946-47	Victoria
1914-15	Victoria	1947-48	Western Australia
1915-19	No competition	1948-49	New South Wales
1919-20	New South Wales	1949-50	New South Wales

1950-51	Victoria	1969-70	Victoria
1951-52	New South Wales	1970-71	South Australia
1952-53	South Australia	1971-72	Western Australia
1953-54	New South Wales	1972-73	Western Australia
1954-55	New South Wales	1973-74	Victoria
1955-56	New South Wales	1974-75	Western Australia
1956-57	New South Wales	1975-76	South Australia
1957-58	New South Wales	1976-77	Western Australia
1958-59	New South Wales	1977-78	Western Australia
1959-60	New South Wales	1978-79	Victoria
1960-61	New South Wales	1979-80	Victoria
1961-62	New South Wales	1980-81	Western Australia
1962-63	Victoria	1981-82	South Australia
1963-64	South Australia	1982-83	New South Wales
1964-65	New South Wales	1983-84	Western Australia
1965-66	New South Wales	1984-85	New South Wales
1966-67	Victoria	1985-86	New South Wales
1967-68	Western Australia	1986-87	Western Australia
1968-69	South Australia	1987-88	Western Australia

New South Wales have won the Shield 39 times, Victoria 24, South Australia 12, Western Australia 11, Queensland 0, Tasmania 0.

†McDONALD'S CUP, 1987-88

At Perth, February 19. Western Australia won by 2 runs. Western Australia 170 (49.5 overs); Victoria 168 (49.5 overs) (D. M. Jones 54).

At Brisbane, February 21. New South Wales won by 153 runs. New South Wales 287 for seven (50 overs) (J. Dyson 79, S. G. Hookey 77, S. R. Waugh 56); Queensland 134 (34.4 overs).

At Launceston, February 28. Tasmania won by five wickets. Queensland 150 for eight (50 overs) (A. B. Henschell 47 not out; R. J. Tucker four for 31); Tasmania 151 for five (40.4 overs) (D. C. Boon 73).

At Adelaide, February 28. Victoria won by 6 runs. Victoria 232 (49.5 overs) (G. M. Watts 81; C. M. Killen four for 33, P. W. Gladigau four for 46); South Australia 226 for six (50 overs) (J. K. Pyke 76 not out; P. W. Jackson four for 26).

At Sydney, March 6. New South Wales won by four wickets, having been set a revised target of 120 runs off 39 overs. Tasmania 154 (47.4 overs); New South Wales 123 for six (38.5 overs).

At Perth, March 6. South Australia won by four wickets. Western Australia 225 for seven (50 overs) (G. R. Marsh 105); South Australia 229 for six (49.1 overs) (G. A. Bishop 119 not out).

Semi-finals

At Adelaide, March 12. South Australia won by seven wickets, having been set a revised target of 194 off 44 overs. Tasmania 220 for eight (50 overs) (D. C. Boon 62); South Australia 194 for three (41.1 overs) (D. B. Scott 46, D. W. Hookes 57 not out).

At Sydney, March 13. New South Wales won by five wickets. Victoria 180 for seven (50 overs); New South Wales 184 for five (43 overs) (G. L. Smith 58 not out).

FINAL

†NEW SOUTH WALES v SOUTH AUSTRALIA

At Sydney, March 27. New South Wales won by 23 runs. Toss: New South Wales.
Man of the Match: G. L. Smith.

New South Wales

S. G. Hookey c Hookes b Zesers	8	P. L. Taylor not out	9
M. A. Taylor c Phillips b Johnston	30	*†G. C. Dyer not out	2
S. R. Waugh c Hookes b Scott	23	B 2, l-b 7, w 2, n-b 1	12
M. E. Waugh c Bishop b Scott	38		
T. H. Bayliss b Gladigau	44	1/40 2/40 3/98 (7 wkts, 50 overs)	219
G. R. J. Matthews c Johnston b Scott	11	4/107 5/155	
G. L. Smith c Zesers b May	42	6/174 7/217	

G. F. Lawson and M. R. Whitney did not bat.

Bowling: Gladigau 10–0–41–1; Johnston 10–0–27–1; Zesers 10–1–32–1; Scott 10–0–41–3; Pyke 2–0–28–0; May 8–0–41–1.

South Australia

G. A. Bishop c P. L. Taylor b S. R. Waugh	26	J. K. Pyke b S. R. Waugh	38
A. M. J. Hilditch b P. L. Taylor	28	D. A. H. Johnston not out	2
D. B. Scott c Hookey b Matthews	15	L-b 4, w 1, n-b 3	8
*D. W. Hookes run out	31		
†W. B. Phillips run out	0	1/55 2/57 3/99 (6 wkts, 50 overs)	196
P. R. Sleep not out	48	4/100 5/105 6/193	

A. K. Zesers, T. B. A. May and P. W. Gladigau did not bat.

Bowling: Lawson 10–1–55–0; Whitney 10–0–42–0; S. R. Waugh 10–2–37–2; P. L. Taylor 10–0–29–1; Matthews 10–1–29–1.

Umpires: R. A. French and I. S. Thomas.

CRICKET IN SOUTH AFRICA, 1987-88

By PETER SICHEL

There was a feeling, early in the 1987-88 season, that Transvaal would relinquish their domination of the Castle Currie Cup, which they had won four times in the previous five seasons. They began it in moderate fashion, narrowly beating Border in a Nissan Shield match, losing to the Impalas in a Benson and Hedges encounter, and finally being knocked out of the Nissan tournament by their traditional rivals, Western Province. Without Graeme Pollock and Alan Kourie, who had retired, and then losing Neal Radford to an England tour of New Zealand, they were in a process of rebuilding; moreover, Kevin McKenzie had torn ligaments in his leg, necessitating surgery, and was out for the season.

However, by personal example and astute captaincy, Clive Rice ensured that Transvaal would again be in contention at the season's end. In the process, some promising juniors became successful seniors by correct application and hard work. Rice's example was an inspiration to his players, all of whom responded with enthusiasm. Rod Estwick proved a wonderful acquisition in the absence of Radford and Hugh Page, and his 36 wickets at a little over 16 runs apiece demonstrated his value. Bruce Roberts and Louis Vorster, two young players, gave notice of the immense talent available in the province, both batting with skill and determination throughout the season. The experience of Jimmy Cook, Rice and Henry Fotheringham, despite the last-mentioned's loss of form, was a source of inspiration to a side in a transitional stage, and to come from behind to clinch a 28th premier title smacks of expert leadership together with courage and grit. Transvaal deserved their success, and will almost certainly remain the side to beat in the coming years.

Natal were something of an enigma. They were a good side, but could, with application, have been a better one. Too often their batsmen got themselves out when seemingly well set. Natal enjoyed a purple patch in mid-season, winning four matches on the trot, but fell at the last, losing to Transvaal by ten wickets at Kingsmead. This cost them a place in the final, which went instead to Orange Free State.

Orange Free State benefited immensely from the presence of Allan Lamb and Sylvester Clarke, but perhaps too much was expected of them. When they failed, which in Lamb's case was not often, the contributions of the remainder of the side were disappointing. Their resounding victory over Eastern Province at Bloemfontein was a fine effort, but it was almost entirely due to a record-breaking 294 by Lamb, who was helped in a South African fifth-wicket record partnership of 355 by his captain, Joubert Strydom. Thereafter, except for two other hundreds and three fifties from Lamb, little in the batting department was achieved. This was underlined when Lamb went back to England two-thirds of the way through the season. He did return for the final, at the Wanderers in March, but it was asking a lot to expect him to produce again the form necessary to guide a young but willing Free State team to their first Currie Cup triumph.

Eastern Province were unlucky to lose their Australian import, Rod McCurdy, early in the season, for his absence revealed a distinct lack of penetration in the bowling. Greg Thomas, the Glamorgan fast bowler, was isappointing, being particularly expensive at times, and the other seamers ere no more than steady. There was a fine array of spinners, but apart from t St George's Park they seldom had a turning wicket on which to display ieir skills. Undoubtedly, Eastern Province's strength lay in their batting. heir first five were as good as, if not better than, any in the country. Mark ushmere had a great season, hitting three hundreds in the Currie Cup, and as ably assisted by Phillip Amm, Kepler Wessels and Ken McEwan. But it as Dave Callaghan who really caught the eye. Here was a fine prospect who njoyed nothing more than going on to the attack. Much will be heard of him the future.

Northern Transvaal were the only side not to register a victory. After the nfortunate loss of probably their most talented batsman, Roy Pienaar, early n the season with a broken hand, much responsibility rested with the more enior players, who responded admirably. Among the bowlers, Fanie de 'illiers impressed with his seamers, while Gerbrand Grobler developed oticeably. Willie Morris bowled his left-arm spinners with guile and ntelligence and was rewarded with 24 wickets at a little over 25 each. It as hoped that a vote of confidence would be given to this side, because ney would surely respond with match-winning performances in future easons.

Western Province were an unpredictable side. Their batting let them down t vital stages, and yet they had some of the finest batsmen in the country. eter Kirsten failed to make a hundred, and Darryl Cullinan, apart from one r two instances, again failed to stamp his authority on an innings. His aiden Currie Cup hundred continued to elude him. His class was evident uring a match-saving 95 not out at Bloemfontein, where heavy rain ended lay an hour ahead of schedule and almost certainly cost him his hundred. Of ne bowlers, Garth le Roux, Stephen Jefferies and Eric Simons performed eroically, with Jefferies's ten for 59 in Orange Free State's second innings at ape Town as fine an exhibition of seam bowling as one could wish to see. wo fine young players emerged in Craig Matthews, a medium-pacer and ower-order batsman, and David Rundle, an off-spinner of promise and ower-order batsman. At Durban, Rundle's control and variation were nmaculate, and he obtained sufficient turn to defeat the best Natal could ffer.

Throughout, a good season was enjoyed by bigger crowds than before. Vhether or not the format adopted for the Castle Currie Cup was an nprovement on the old system, whereby each province played all the others n a home and away basis, was open to debate. Under the new arrangement, ne competition was played in two sections, with the three teams in each ection playing each other at home and away and also playing the teams in ne other section once. A review, taking into account the thoughts of the layers and the spectators, was considered likely.

FIRST-CLASS AVERAGES, 1987-88

BATTING

(Qualification: 8 innings, average 35.00)

	M	*I*	*NO*	*R*	*HI*	*100s*	*Av*
A. J. Lamb (*OFS*)	8	12	2	878	294	3	87.
A. J. Moles (*Griqualand W.*)	6	12	2	657	200*	3	65.
G. Kirsten (*W. Province B*)	6	11	4	424	163*	1	60.
C. E. B. Rice (*Transvaal*)	8	10	2	459	150*	2	57.
M. W. Rushmere (*E. Province*)	8	14	3	576	140	3	52.
P. J. A. Visagie (*N. Transvaal/N. Transvaal B*)	8	13	2	543	164	2	49.
S. A. Jones (*Boland*)	7	12	2	487	209*	1	48.
B. Roberts (*Transvaal/Transvaal B*)	10	13	1	568	174	2	47.
K. S. McEwan (*E. Province*)	8	11	1	468	104	1	46.
M. S. Venter (*Transvaal B*)	7	13	1	557	131	1	46.
K. C. Wessels (*E. Province*)	8	12	1	504	130	2	45.
V. G. Cresswell (*N. Transvaal B*)	6	9	1	363	102	1	45.
A. C. Hudson (*Natal/Natal B*)	9	17	2	649	148	2	43.
M. H. Austen (*W. Province/W. Province B*)	9	16	1	642	202*	2	42.
G. M. Walsh (*Natal B*)	6	10	2	339	138*	2	42.
M. J. R. Rindel (*N. Transvaal/N. Transvaal B*)	7	13	2	463	157*	1	42.
P. G. Amm (*E. Province*)	9	15	1	571	129	1	40.
E. N. Trotman (*Border*)	6	12	2	402	101*	1	40.
D. J. Callaghan (*E. Province/E. Province B*)	9	13	0	520	148	1	40.
I. L. Howell (*Border*)	6	10	4	240	55*	0	40.
P. N. Kirsten (*W. Province*)	7	12	2	398	82	0	39.
A. L. Wilmot (*Border*)	6	12	1	435	135	2	39.
S. J. Cook (*Transvaal*)	8	16	5	422	159	1	38.
K. J. Barnett (*Boland*)	6	11	1	383	73	0	38.
K. G. Bauermeister (*Border*)	6	9	2	265	74	0	37.
T. N. Lazard (*W. Province*)	7	11	0	416	90	0	37.
B. M. Osborne (*Border*)	6	12	2	376	86	0	37.
C. S. Stirk (*Natal B*)	6	11	1	371	154	1	37.
L. P. Vorster (*Transvaal*)	8	11	1	368	174	1	36.
J. M. Arthur (*Griqualand W.*)	6	12	1	400	123	1	36.
D. H. Howell (*Transvaal B*)	5	8	0	286	151	1	35.
V. F. du Preez (*N. Transvaal*)	7	13	1	423	92*	0	35.

* *Signifies not out.*

BOWLING

(Qualification: 20 wickets)

	O	*M*	*R*	*W*	*BB*	*Av*
N. V. Radford (*Transvaal*)	109.5	20	313	24	6-38	13.
S. J. Base (*Boland*)	224	58	541	35	6-28	15.
S. T. Clarke (*OFS*)	231.4	58	504	32	7-48	15.
R. O. Estwick (*Transvaal*)	235.4	79	591	36	5-17	16.
C. E. B. Rice (*Transvaal*)	218.3	75	498	30	5-14	16.
M. James (*Transvaal/Transvaal B*)	227.3	76	519	29	7-45	17.
A. P. Igglesden (*W. Province B*)	191.2	36	565	31	5-52	18.
C. J. P. G. van Zyl (*OFS*)	203	49	472	25	4-40	18.
P. J. Newport (*Boland*)	170.2	31	448	23	4-32	19.
O. Henry (*Boland*)	258.4	71	713	36	6-57	19.
C. D. Mitchley (*Transvaal B*)	181.1	42	513	25	5-108	20.
P. B. Clift (*Natal*)	208.4	58	474	23	5-53	20.

	O	*M*	*R*	*W*	*BB*	*Avge*
. L. S. Armitage (*E. Province/E. Province B*)	266.1	89	560	27	6-64	20.74
. D. Topley (*Griqualand W.*)	221.2	56	652	29	5-50	22.48
T. Jefferies (*W. Province*)	289.2	72	793	35	10-59	22.65
1. R. Hobson (*Natal B*)	147.5	16	501	22	4-25	22.77
'. B. Rundle (*W. Province*)	270.1	76	628	27	6-37	23.25
. L. Symcox (*N. Transvaal B*)	279.1	77	703	30	7-93	23.43
. S. de Villiers (*N. Transvaal*)	207.3	48	594	25	4-29	23.76
. S. le Roux (*W. Province*)	201.1	38	505	21	4-60	24.04
L. Howell (*Border*)	247.5	81	510	21	6-89	24.28
. O. Simons (*W. Province/W. Province B*)	203.3	41	591	24	4-35	24.62
. J. Packer (*Natal*)	219.3	30	825	33	6-38	25.00
/. F. Morris (*N. Transvaal*)	208.4	48	609	24	6-59	25.37
. K. McGlashan (*Natal/Natal B*)	222	46	636	25	8-122	25.44
1. W. Pringle (*E. Province/E. Province B*)	164	20	515	20	6-33	25.75
. Grobler (*N. Transvaal/N. Transvaal B*)	253.1	47	818	28	4-47	29.21
G. Thomas (*E. Province*)	222.4	40	678	23	4-92	29.47
. E. Smith (*Transvaal B*)	215.2	49	621	21	4-54	29.57
. A. Donald (*OFS*)	263.1	53	755	25	4-39	30.20
. G. Shaw (*E. Province*)	406.4	146	835	27	6-112	30.92

CASTLE CURRIE CUP, 1987-88

	Played	*Won*	*Lost*	*Drawn*	*Bonus Points Batting*	*Bonus Points Bowling*	*Total Pts*
orthern Section							
ransvaal	7	5	0	2	11	33	119
atal	7	4	2	1	10	30	100
orthern Transvaal	7	0	5	2	9	30	39
outhern Section							
range Free State	7	2	3	2	15	27	72
'estern Province	7	2	2	3	9	28	67
astern Province	7	1	2	4	16	22	53

inal: *Transvaal beat Orange Free State by ten wickets.*

*the following scores, * by the name of a team indicates that they won the toss.*

t Bloemfontein, December 17, 18, 19. Orange Free State won by six wickets. Eastern rovince* 268 for seven dec. (K. C. Wessels 101, D. J. Callaghan 70; B. T. Player three for 73) nd 280 (P. G. Amm 60, K. C. Wessels 130; C. J. P. G. van Zyl three for 47); Orange Free ate 517 for eight dec. (A. I. Kallicharran 37, A. J. Lamb 294, J. J. Strydom 107; R. J. IcCurdy four for 109) and 33 for four. *Orange Free State 23 pts, Eastern Province 5 pts.*

At Durban, December 19, 20, 21. Drawn. Natal 266 (A. C. Hudson 72, N. P. Daniels 41, . K. McGlashan 30 not out; D. B. Rundle five for 59) and 208 (M. B. Logan 47, T. R. Iadsen 50; D. B. Rundle six for 37); Western Province* 396 for eight dec. (T. N. Lazard 90, . Seeff 125, G. S. le Roux 47 not out; C. M. Lister-James three for 65) and 71 for five. *'estern Province 7 pts, Natal 4 pts.*

At Johannesburg, December 19, 20, 21. Transvaal won by two wickets. Northern ransvaal* 206 (L. J. Barnard 50, K. D. Verdoorn 39, M. J. R. Rindel 38; B. M. McMillan ve for 39) and 251 (L. J. Barnard 46, A. M. Ferreira 72; N. V. Radford four for 80); ransvaal 192 (C. E. B. Rice 34, B. Roberts 38; P. S. de Villiers three for 52, R. F. Pienaar ur for 40) and 269 for eight (L. P. Vorster 45, C. E. B. Rice 73, B. Roberts 43 not out, N. V. adford 31 not out; W. F. Morris three for 60). *Transvaal 21 pts, Northern Transvaal 7 pts.*

At Port Elizabeth, December 26, 27, 28. Drawn. Northern Transvaal* 204 (K. D. Verdoor 57, R. C. Ontong 56; J. G. Thomas three for 25, T. G. Shaw three for 81, R. L. S. Armitag four for 70) and 312 for five dec. (V. F. du Preez 79, L. J. Barnard 102, N. T. Day 56 not ou R. C. Ontong 33 not out; T. G. Shaw three for 69); Eastern Province 277 (M. W. Rushme 136 not out; P. S. de Villiers three for 49, W. F. Morris three for 89) and 205 for eight (P. C Amm 75, D. J. Callaghan 35; P. S. de Villiers three for 48, W. F. Morris three for 79). *Easte Province 6 pts, Northern Transvaal 5 pts.*

At Johannesburg, December 26, 27, 28. Transvaal won by nine wickets. Natal* 176 (R. M Bentley 45, M. B. Logan 52; N. V. Radford five for 42, B. M. McMillan four for 35) and 8 (T. R. Madsen 33; N. V. Radford six for 38, R. O. Estwick three for 19); Transvaal 193 (M Yachad 50, L. P. Vorster 64; P. B. Clift four for 46, R. M. Bentley three for 10) and 67 for or (S. J. Cook 35 not out). *Transvaal 21 pts, Natal 6 pts.*

At Cape Town, December 26, 27, 28. Western Province won by an innings and 76 run Orange Free State* 134 (D. B. Rundle five for 33) and 113 (A. J. Lamb 30 not out; S. T Jefferies ten for 59); Western Province 323 (T. N. Lazard 69, L. Seeff 50, P. N. Kirsten 5 A. P. Kuiper 50, G. S. le Roux 30; S. T. Clarke three for 82, C. J. P. G. van Zyl three for 45 *Western Province 22 pts, Orange Free State 4 pts.*

At Cape Town, January 1, 2, 3. Transvaal won by eight wickets. Western Province* 15 (J. J. E. Hardy 43, A. P. Kuiper 40; N. V. Radford three for 38, R. O. Estwick three for 2 B. M. McMillan three for 38) and 246 (T. N. Lazard 40, P. N. Kirsten 57, D. J. Cullinan 5 N. V. Radford four for 68); Transvaal 370 for six dec. (L. P. Vorster 174, B. Roberts 10 C. E. B. Rice 44 not out; G. S. le Roux three for 58) and 37 for two. *Transvaal 22 pts, Wester Province 3 pts.*

At Durban, January 1, 2, 3. Natal won by ten wickets. Northern Transvaal 243 (V. F. d Preez 92 not out, R. C. Ontong 41; T. J. Packer six for 67) and 170 (N. T. Day 57, P. J. A Visagie 31; T. J. Packer three for 49); Natal* 312 (P. H. Rayner 60, N. P. Daniels 47, C. M Lister-James 45, P. B. Clift 35; R. C. Ontong six for 70) and 102 for no wkt (B. J. Whitfie 31 not out, A. C. Hudson 70 not out). *Natal 22 pts, Northern Transvaal 6 pts.*

At Port Elizabeth, January 1, 2, 3. Drawn. Orange Free State* 297 (P. J. R. Steyn 49, L. J Wilkinson 70, A. J. Lamb 88, J. W. Lloyds 38; J. G. Thomas three for 66, A. L. Hobson thre for 80) and 232 for four (L. J. Wilkinson 31, A. C. Storie 53, A. J. Lamb 56 not out, L. Pott 44); Eastern Province 433 (P. G. Amm 129, M. W. Rushmere 140, K. S. McEwan 58, D. J Richardson 65 not out; M. J. Procter three for 144, J. W. Lloyds three for 115). *Easte Province 6 pts, Orange Free State 4 pts.*

At Verwoerdburg, January 8, 9, 10. Drawn. Transvaal* 587 for six dec. (S. J. Cook 159, B Roberts 174, C. E. B. Rice 150 not out, R. V. Jennings 42) and 1 for no wkt; Norther Transvaal 411 (V. F. du Preez 70, P. J. A. Visagie 164, W. F. Morris 58, G. Grobler 3 C. E. B. Rice four for 66). *Transvaal 7 pts, Northern Transvaal 5 pts.*

At Bloemfontein, January 8, 9, 11. Drawn. Orange Free State 248 (L. J. Wilkinson 33, A. J Lamb 39, J. W. Lloyds 38; G. S. le Roux four for 60) and 226 for nine dec. (A. J. Lamb 10 R. J. East 58 not out; S. T. Jefferies three for 66, E. O. Simons three for 33); Wester Province* 130 (S. T. Clarke four for 49, A. A. Donald three for 46, C. J. P. G. van Zyl thre for 27) and 205 for four (P. N. Kirsten 82, D. J. Cullinan 95 not out). *Orange Free State 7 p Western Province 5 pts.*

At Pietermaritzburg, January 9, 10, 11. Natal won by four wickets. Eastern Province 3 for eight dec. (K. S. McEwan 34, D. J. Callaghan 148, D. J. Richardson 45; T. J. Packer thre for 86, P. B. Clift three for 45) and 98 for no wkt dec. (P. G. Amm 62 not out); Natal* 154 f seven dec. (R. M. Bentley 51; P. A. Rayment three for 59) and 257 for six (A. C. Hudson 5 M. B. Logan 48, P. H. Rayner 51, N. P. Daniels 31 not out). *Natal 19 pts, Eastern Provin 5 pts.*

At Cape Town, January 15, 16. Western Province won by six wickets. Northern Transva 195 (N. T. Day 60, G. Grobler 42; G. S. le Roux three for 43, S. T. Jefferies four for 55) an 96 (A. M. Ferreira 34; S. T. Jefferies five for 48, A. P. Kuiper four for 12); Western Province 120 (S. T. Jefferies 30; P. S. de Villiers four for 29, T. Bosch four for 38) and 173 for fo (M. H. Austen 83, P. N. Kirsten 48 not out). *Western Province 20 pts, Northern Transvaal 6 pt*

At Port Elizabeth, January 15, 16, 17. Drawn. Transvaal* 225 (S. J. Cook 47, M. Yachad 7, R. V. Jennings 65 not out; A. L. Hobson four for 86) and 236 for eight dec. (H. R. 'otheringham 150 not out, B. Roberts 34; P. A. Rayment three for 53, A. L. Hobson three for 7); Eastern Province 257 (K. C. Wessels 46, D. J. Callaghan 42, D. J. Richardson 72; R. O. :stwick four for 47) and 23 for one. *Eastern Province 7 pts, Transvaal 6 pts.*

At Bloemfontein, January 15, 16, 18. Natal won by three wickets. Orange Free State* 301 A. J. Lamb 133, J. W. Lloyds 31, S. T. Clarke 60; T. J. Packer three for 95) and 252 (A. J. .amb 59, J. W. Lloyds 40, R. J. East 43; T. J. Packer three for 51, P. B. Clift three for 53, :. M. Bentley three for 75); Natal 333 (B. J. Whitfield 113, R. M. Bentley 67, N. P. Daniels 7; C. J. P. G. van Zyl four for 40) and 222 for seven (B. J. Whitfield 59, T. R. Madsen 36, :. M. Lister-James 41 not out; S. T. Clarke three for 19). *Natal 22 pts, Orange Free State 7 pts.*

At Verwoerdburg, January 22, 23, 24. Natal won by six wickets. Northern Transvaal* 197 V. F. du Preez 57, A. M. Ferreira 51; T. J. Packer six for 38) and 289 (N. T. Day 47, M. J. R. :indel 83 not out; C. M. Lister-James four for 53); Natal 329 (B. J. Whitfield 33, M. B. Logan 7, R. M. Bentley 42, T. R. Madsen 33, N. P. Daniels 43, P. B. Clift 37; G. Grobler four for 3) and 158 for four (R. M. Bentley 36, P. H. Rayner 33, A. C. Hudson 47; P. S. de Villiers hree for 32). *Natal 22 pts, Northern Transvaal 5 pts.*

At Johannesburg, January 22, 23, 24. Transvaal won by nine wickets. Orange Free State 63 (R. J. East 58; R. O. Estwick four for 45, C. E. B. Rice four for 48) and 51 (R. O. Estwick ve for 17, C. E. B. Rice three for 9); Transvaal* 130 (G. E. McMillan 34 not out; S. T. :larke seven for 48, A. A. Donald three for 48) and 85 for one (S. J. Cook 56 not out). *'ransvaal 20 pts, Orange Free State 6 pts.*

At Port Elizabeth, January 22, 23, 24. Eastern Province won by an innings and 27 runs. Vestern Province* 274 (T. N. Lazard 66, L. Seeff 48, P. N. Kirsten 42, A. P. Kuiper 51; T. G. haw six for 112) and 91 (T. N. Lazard 38; T. G. Shaw three for 17, A. L. Hobson three for 9); Eastern Province 392 for nine dec. (P. G. Amm 61, M. W. Rushmere 136, K. S. McEwan 8; S. T. Jefferies three for 91, D. B. Rundle four for 96). *Eastern Province 19 pts, Western 'rovince 2 pts.*

At Cape Town, January 29, 30, 31. Drawn. Western Province 454 for nine dec. (T. N. .azard 76, M. H. Austen 202 not out, P. N. Kirsten 43; J. G. Thomas four for 122); Eastern 'rovince* 292 (M. W. Rushmere 37, K. C. Wessels 41, K. S. McEwan 97; G. S. le Roux four or 72, C. R. Matthews three for 56) and 217 for four (M. W. Rushmere 43, K. C. Wessels 34, :. S. McEwan 53 not out, D. J. Callaghan 72). *Western Province 8 pts, Eastern Province 5 pts.*

At Verwoerdburg, January 29, 30, 31. Orange Free State won by 24 runs. Orange Free tate* 186 (P. J. R. Steyn 43, J. J. Strydom 37, S. T. Clarke 39; W. F. Morris four for 37) and 04 (C. J. van Heerden 30, R. J. East 56; G. Grobler three for 55, W. F. Morris six for 59); Iorthern Transvaal 124 (S. T. Clarke four for 47, A. A. Donald four for 39) and 242 (V. F. du 'reez 32, L. J. Barnard 56, N. T. Day 45; S. T. Clarke five for 48, C. J. P. G. van Zyl four for 1). *Orange Free State 21 pts, Northern Transvaal 5 pts.*

At Durban, January 30, 31, February 1. Transvaal won by ten wickets. Natal* 97 (P. H. :ayner 45; C. E. B. Rice five for 14) and 168 (M. B. Logan 32, P. H. Rayner 36; C. E. B. Rice our for 21, M. James five for 55); Transvaal 254 (B. M. McMillan 35, G. E. McMillan 39, :. E. B. Rice 101; C. M. Lister-James three for 35, P. B. Clift five for 53) and 14 for no wkt. *'ransvaal 22 pts, Natal 5 pts.*

'inal

\t Johannesburg, February 11, 12, 13, 14. Transvaal won by ten wickets. Orange Free State 44 (L. J. Wilkinson 30, C. J. P. G. van Zyl 31; R. O. Estwick four for 41, B. M. McMillan hree for 18) and 166 (A. J. Lamb 33, R. J. East 50 not out; R. O. Estwick four for 63, B. M. AcMillan three for 7); Transvaal* 279 (L. P. Vorster 36, B. Roberts 64, C. E. B. Rice 38, :. V. Jennings 43, R. O. Estwick 43 not out; A. A. Donald four for 83, C. J. P. G. van Zyl our for 71) and 34 for no wkt.

CURRIE CUP WINNERS

1889-90	Transvaal	1954-55	Natal
1890-91	Griqualand West	1955-56	Western Province
1892-93	Western Province	1958-59	Transvaal
1893-94	Western Province	1959-60	Natal
1894-95	Transvaal	1960-61	Natal
1896-97	Western Province	1962-63	Natal
1897-98	Western Province	1963-64	Natal
1902-03	Transvaal	1965-66	Natal/Transvaal (Tied)
1903-04	Transvaal	1966-67	Natal
1904-05	Transvaal	1967-68	Natal
1906-07	Transvaal	1968-69	Transvaal
1908-09	Western Province	1969-70	Transvaal/W. Province (Tied)
1910-11	Natal	1970-71	Transvaal
1912-13	Natal	1971-72	Transvaal
1920-21	Western Province	1972-73	Transvaal
1921-22	Transvaal/Natal/W. Prov. (Tied)	1973-74	Natal
1923-24	Transvaal	1974-75	Western Province
1925-26	Transvaal	1975-76	Natal
1926-27	Transvaal	1976-77	Natal
1929-30	Transvaal	1977-78	Western Province
1931-32	Western Province	1978-79	Transvaal
1933-34	Natal	1979-80	Transvaal
1934-35	Transvaal	1980-81	Natal
1936-37	Natal	1981-82	Western Province
1937-38	Natal/Transvaal (Tied)	1982-83	Transvaal
1946-47	Natal	1983-84	Transvaal
1947-48	Natal	1984-85	Transvaal
1950-51	Transvaal	1985-86	Western Province
1951-52	Natal	1986-87	Transvaal
1952-53	Western Province	1987-88	Transvaal

SAB BOWL, 1987-88

	Played	Won	Lost	Drawn	Bonus Points Batting	Bonus Points Bowling	Total Pts
Northern Section							
Transvaal B	6	2	2	2	13	26	69
Northern Transvaal B	6	1	1	4	16	27	58
Natal B	6	1	2	3	13	22	50
Griqualand West	6	1	1	4	9	24	48
Southern Section							
Boland	6	3	2	1	9	23	77
Western Province B	6	2	1	3	10	25	65
Eastern Province B	6	1	3	2	5	26	46
Border	6	1	1	4	11	18	44

Final: *Boland beat Transvaal B by 259 runs.*

At Pietermaritzburg, October 30, 31, November 1. Natal B won by 39 runs. Natal B* 258 fo[r] nine dec. (M. D. Mellor 55, M. A. W. Bowman 30, M. J. Pearse 69, C. A. Lowe 49; G. W Symmonds four for 37, T. D. Topley three for 97) and 187 for two dec. (C. S. Stirk 41, P. H Rayner 100 not out, G. M. Walsh 35 not out); Griqualand West 193 (A. J. Moles 50, A. D Methven 57; M. R. Hobson four for 62, R. K. McGlashan three for 23) and 213 (D. R Hewson 50, I. Human 54, P. McLaren 30 not out; M. R. Hobson four for 25). *Natal B 23 pts Griqualand West 6 pts.*

At Port Elizabeth, November 6, 7, 8. Eastern Province B won by three wickets. Border 211 :. N. Trotman 68, G. L. Hayes 38; M. W. Pringle three for 45, R. L. S. Armitage three for 2) and 246 (A. L. Wilmot 135, B. M. Osborne 44; C. Wulfsohn four for 69, B. E. van der yver five for 82); Eastern Province B* 142 (R. L. S. Armitage 34; W. K. Watson five for 36, . G. Bauermeister three for 60) and 319 for seven (J. W. Furstenburg 57, A. V. Birrell 78, M. lichau 48, M. W. Pringle 50 not out; W. K. Watson three for 85). *Eastern Province B 20 pts, order 7 pts.*

At Kimberley, November 13, 14, 15. Griqualand West won by 57 runs. Griqualand West*)2 (A. J. Moles 114; M. James six for 62) and 116 (C. D. Mitchley three for 21); Transvaal B 10 (C. E. Eksteen 31; P. McLaren four for 19, T. D. Topley five for 50) and 151 (B. Roberts 3; G. W. Symmonds four for 47, T. D. Topley five for 81). *Griqualand West 21 pts, Transvaal 5 pts.*

At Stellenbosch, November 13, 14, 16. Boland won by 44 runs. Boland* 195 (S. A. Jones 79; . P. Igglesden five for 52) and 198 (K. J. Barnett 45, S. A. Jones 41; A. P. Igglesden five for); Western Province B 199 (J. B. Commins 51, M. B. Minnaar 40 not out; S. J. Base three r 44, P. J. Newport four for 32) and 150 (M. H. Austen 38; S. J. Base three for 23, P. Anker ree for 42, O. Henry three for 57). *Boland 21 pts, Western Province B 6 pts.*

At Uitenhage, November 20, 21, 23. Boland won by an innings and 15 runs. Boland* 312 V. S. Truter 107, O. Henry 91, P. Anker 36 not out); Eastern Province B 136 (M. Michau 30, . Wulfsohn 31 not out; P. J. Newport four for 36) and 161 (A. V. Birrell 67, B. E. van der yver 49; O. Henry five for 41). *Boland 22 pts, Eastern Province B 3 pts.*

At Verwoerdburg, November 20, 21, 22. Northern Transvaal B won by seven wickets. orthern Transvaal B* 309 for eight dec. (P. J. A. Visagie 146 not out, V. G. Cresswell 30, . L. Symcox 35; M. D. Clare three for 54) and 40 for three; Natal B 104 (C. A. Lowe 33; . Grobler three for 37) and 244 (G. M. Walsh 113; P. L. Symcox six for 72). *Northern ransvaal B 23 pts, Natal B 4 pts.*

At Durban, November 26, 27, 28. Drawn. Natal B* 301 for eight dec. (P. H. Rayner 57, . A. Scott 75, M. J. Pearse 41, C. A. Lowe 42; G. E. McMillan three for 23) and 41 for one; ransvaal B 387 (D. H. Howell 151, M. S. Venter 57, M. J. Mitchley 48, G. E. McMillan 31; . K. McGlashan four for 60). *Transvaal B 6 pts, Natal B 4 pts.*

At Cape Town, November 26, 27, 28. Drawn. Western Province B* 353 for seven dec. (G. irsten 163 not out, E. O. Simons 68, M. B. Minnaar 31) and 195 for four dec. (K. J. Bridgens), F. B. Touzel 75 not out); Border 278 for seven dec. (B. M. Osborne 68, A. L. Wilmot 31, L. Howell 55 not out, K. G. Bauermeister 74; E. O. Simons three for 70) and 221 for seven . L. Howell 49, K. G. Bauermeister 72 not out). *Western Province B 4 pts, Border 4 pts.*

At Verwoerdburg, December 4, 5, 6. Drawn. Griqualand West 278 (A. J. Moles 111, J. M. rthur 37; G. Grobler four for 47, A. Geringer three for 58) and 109 for no wkt (A. J. Moles not out, J. M. Arthur 42 not out); Northern Transvaal B* 302 for five dec. (A. Da Costa 80, . Geringer 113, P. J. A. Visagie 34 not out). *Northern Transvaal B 9 pts, Griqualand West pts.*

At Cape Town, December 11, 12, 13. Drawn. Eastern Province B 179 (A. van N. Snyman 3; A. P. Igglesden three for 46, E. O. Simons three for 55) and 242 (A. van N. Snyman 43, . E. van der Vyver 54, C. Wulfsohn 36; A. P. Igglesden three for 84, E. O. Simons three for); Western Province B* 227 for six dec. (M. H. Austen 35, A. P. Plantema 37, G. Kirsten) not out) and 131 for six (M. H. Austen 33; M. W. Pringle six for 33). *Western Province B pts, Eastern Province B 4 pts.*

At Stellenbosch, December 11, 12. Border won by eight wickets. Boland* 71 (J. A. Carse ur for 16) and 97 (K. J. Barnett 36; I. L. Howell three for 30, G. L. Hayes four for 30); order 124 (E. N. Trotman 34, G. L. Hayes 35; S. J. Base six for 28, O. Henry four for 39) and 5 for two. *Border 20 pts, Boland 5 pts.*

At Kimberley, December 11, 12, 13. Drawn. Griqualand West* 359 (J. M. Arthur 123, . D. Methven 63, T. D. Topley 47, I. Human 33; C. S. Stirk four for 73, M. D. Mellor three r 20) and 117 for four (A. J. Moles 44; R. K. McGlashan three for 33); Natal B 510 for four ec. (A. C. Hudson 148, M. D. Tramontino 59, G. M. Walsh 138 not out, C. S. Stirk 44, D. A. cott 86 not out). *Natal B 6 pts, Griqualand West 3 pts.*

At Verwoerdburg, December 19, 20, 21. Transvaal B won by 88 runs. Transvaal B* 20 (M. S. Venter 57, B. McBride 68; G. L. Ackermann five for 36) and 260 for nine dec. (W Kirsh 109, M. S. Venter 62; P. L. Symcox seven for 93); Northern Transvaal B 210 (V. C Cresswell 102, P. J. A. Visagie 54; M. James five for 68) and 167 (V. G. Cresswell 66; J. Hooper three for 50, M. James seven for 45). *Transvaal B 22 pts, Northern Transvaal B 6 pt*

At East London, December 26, 27, 28. Drawn. Border* 325 for nine dec. (M. J. P. Ford 6 E. N. Trotman 54, A. L. Wilmot 105; A. J. McClement four for 77) and 246 for five (M. J. Ford 41, B. W. Lones 57, B. M. Osborne 41, E. N. Trotman 101 not out); Western Province 400 (M. H. Austen 121, F. B. Touzel 38, G. Kirsten 56, K. J. Bridgens 79, J. During 41 n out; H. Lindenberg three for 100, I. L. Howell six for 89). *Western Province B 8 pts, Bord 5 pts.*

At East London, January 1, 2, 3. Drawn. Border* 226 (B. M. Osborne 52, E. N. Trotma 37, K. G. Bauermeister 48; M. K. van Vuuren three for 60, P. A. Rayment four for 55, D. Ferrant three for 70) and 337 for four dec. (M. J. P. Ford 73, B. W. Lones 74, B. M. Osborn 86, A. L. Wilmot 50, I. L. Howell 40 not out); Eastern Province B 283 (A. van N. Snyman 4 P. I. Barclay 34, M. Michau 51, A. V. Birrell 41, P. A. Amm 36; J. A. Carse three for 56) an 176 for nine (P. I. Barclay 59, M. Michau 38; I. L. Howell four for 52). *Eastern Province 7 pts, Border 4 pts.*

At Johannesburg, January 8, 9, 10. Drawn. Transvaal B 219 (W. Kirsh 34, N. E. Wright 9 M. J. Mitchley 41; P. Botha three for 30, P. L. Symcox four for 39) and 247 for five dec. (M. Venter 80, N. E. Wright 32, D. H. Howell 34, M. J. Mitchley 64 not out); Northern Transva B* 290 for six dec. (G. J. Turner 58, A. Geringer 73, M. J. R. Rindel 46) and 22 for no wk *Transvaal B 5 pts, Northern Transvaal B 8 pts.*

At Cape Town, January 8, 9, 11. Western Province B won by 68 runs. Western Province 289 for six dec. (A. P. Plantema 66, J. J. E. Hardy 75, J. B. Commins 63, G. Kirsten 38 n out; P. J. Newport three for 81) and 186 for nine dec. (A. J. McClement 33 not out; S. J. Ba three for 84, P. J. Newport three for 36, J. D. du Toit three for 42); Boland* 273 (K. J. Barne 44, G. P. Thomas 47, S. Nackerdien 60, J. D. du Toit 36, P. J. Newport 32; A. P. Igglesde four for 73) and 134 (K. J. Barnett 33; A. P. Igglesden four for 57, J. During three for 30 *Western Province B 22 pts, Boland 4 pts.*

At Durban, January 15, 16, 17. Drawn. Natal B 303 for nine dec. (M. J. Pearse 4 M. A. W. Bowman 31, D. Norman 97) and 297 for seven dec. (C. S. Stirk 154, D. A. Scott 3 M. J. Pearse 53); Northern Transvaal B* 321 for eight dec. (A. Da Costa 49, G. J. Turner 3 M. J. R. Rindel 157 not out, P. L. Symcox 36; R. P. Snell three for 71) and 199 for eig (V. G. Cresswell 53, G. J. Turner 30, A. Geringer 48; M. D. Mellor four for 88). *Norther Transvaal B 8 pts, Natal B 7 pts.*

At Stellenbosch, January 15, 16, 18. Boland won by seven wickets. Eastern Province B* 18 (A. V. Birrell 45; S. J. Base three for 46, O. Henry four for 69) and 133 (M. Michau 76 not ou S. J. Base three for 39, O. Henry six for 57); Boland 245 (K. J. Barnett 73, J. D. du Toit 4 R. L. S. Armitage six for 68) and 78 for three (K. J. Barnett 51 not out; R. L. S. Armitag three for 31). *Boland 21 pts, Eastern Province B 6 pts.*

At Johannesburg, January 15, 16, 17. Drawn. Griqualand West 121 (W. C. Wilson 3 C. D. Mitchley four for 41, S. Jacobs three for 26) and 259 (A. J. Moles 40, J. M. Arthur 7 I. F. Mellett 54; P. E. Smith three for 57, P. C. Botha three for 33); Transvaal B* 257 (M. Venter 131, N. E. Wright 56; P. McLaren three for 45, T. D. Topley three for 78, D. G. Mil four for 34) and 53 for three. *Transvaal B 8 pts, Griqualand West 5 pts.*

At Port Elizabeth, January 29, 30, 31. Western Province B won by 60 runs. Wester Province B 150 (A. P. Plantema 69; M. K. van Vuuren three for 47, G. A. Katz three for 2 and 263 (A. P. Plantema 49, J. J. E. Hardy 71, M. B. Minnaar 36 not out; R. L. S. Armitag six for 64); Eastern Province B* 268 (P. I. Barclay 82, P. A. Amm 40, M. K. van Vuuren 3 not out; A. P. Igglesden four for 60) and 85 (E. O. Simons four for 35, A. J. McClement thre for 14). *Western Province B 18 pts, Eastern Province B 6 pts.*

At Kimberley, January 29, 30, 31. Drawn. Griqualand West 338 for four dec. (A. J. Mol 200 not out, J. M. Arthur 51, I. F. Mellett 30, M. N. Kellow 38) and 177 for six dec. (I. F Mellett 52, P. McLaren 38 not out; P. L. Symcox four for 43); Northern Transvaal B* 24 (V. G. Cresswell 44, P. J. A. Visagie 55, B. L. van Onselen 42, M. Ferreira 31; P. McLare three for 61, T. D. Topley four for 62) and 184 for nine (B. L. van Onselen 35; T. D. Tople five for 51). *Griqualand West 8 pts, Northern Transvaal B 4 pts.*

At East London, January 29, 30, February 1. Drawn. Boland* 502 for six dec. (P. J. Newport 46, S. A. Jones 209 not out, O. Henry 125, N. M. Lambrechts 42); Border 310 (M. J. P. Ford 64, B. W. Lones 139, B. M. Osborne 38; S. J. Base five for 68, P. Anker three for 40) and 259 for six (B. W. Lones 30, E. N. Trotman 51, A. L. Wilmot 48, I. L. Howell 50 not out, K. G. Bauermeister 35 not out; P. Anker three for 40). *Boland 4 pts, Border 4 pts.*

At Johannesburg, January 29, 30, 31. Transvaal B won by ten wickets. Natal B* 199 (M. D. Tramontino 55, R. J. Varner 33; P. E. Smith four for 54, C. D. Mitchley three for 46, S. Elworthy three for 45) and 162 (M. D. Mellor 70; S. Elworthy four for 56); Transvaal B 333 (M. S. Venter 62, N. E. Wright 46, D. H. Howell 49, B. McBride 55, K. J. Kerr 53; M. D. Clare three for 57, M. R. Hobson four for 43) and 29 for no wkt. *Transvaal B 23 pts, Natal B 5 pts.*

Final

At Stellenbosch, February 5, 6, 7, 8. Boland won by 259 runs. Boland* 367 (W. S. Truter 42, P. J. Newport 86, J. D. du Toit 89, C. F. Spilhaus 44 not out; C. D. Mitchley five for 108, S. Elworthy three for 86) and 257 for five dec. (K. J. Barnett 41, S. Nackerdien 70, S. A. Jones 54; C. D. Mitchley three for 84); Transvaal B 168 (N. E. Wright 36, K. J. Rule 36; P. J. Newport three for 20, P. Anker three for 48, O. Henry three for 40) and 197 (K. J. Rule 33, B. McBride 30, K. J. Kerr 49 not out; P. Anker three for 19, O. Henry three for 71).

OTHER FIRST-CLASS MATCHES

At Durban, October 27, 28, 29. Natal won by two wickets. SA Defence Force* 186 for five dec. (R. F. Pienaar 38, P. G. Amm 48; R. K. McGlashan three for 53) and 265 (R. F. Pienaar 32, P. G. Amm 54, E. J. Venter 41, M. J. R. Rindel 36, M. B. Billson 40, A. J. Forde 30; R. K. McGlashan eight for 122); Natal 197 for five dec. (B. J. Whitfield 50, A. C. Hudson 40, M. B. Logan 39, T. R. Madsen 34) and 255 for eight (A. C. Hudson 115 not out, T. R. Madsen 61; R. F. Pienaar five for 95).

At Port Elizabeth, December 5, 7, 8. Eastern Province won by an innings and 51 runs. SA Universities* 122 (P. A. Tullis 36; R. J. McCurdy six for 11) and 267 (M. H. Austen 32, J. B. Commins 70, D. B. Rundle 45, P. A. Tullis 34; J. G. Thomas four for 92, T. G. Shaw four for 58); Eastern Province 440 (A. van N. Snyman 43, K. C. Wessels 69, K. S. McEwan 104, D. J. Callaghan 58, D. J. Richardson 50; M. R. Hobson four for 97).

†NISSAN SHIELD, 1987-88

(50 overs per side)

At Stellenbosch, October 3. Boland won by five wickets. Griqualand West 186 for six (J. M. Arthur 32, M. N. Kellow 88; K. J. Barnett three for 27); Boland 187 for five (G. P. Thomas 43, S. Nackerdien 35; T. D. Topley three for 44).

At Kimberley, October 17. Boland won by 68 runs. Boland 265 for eight (K. J. Barnett 70, S. Nackerdien 78, C. F. Spilhaus 50; P. McLaren four for 59); Griqualand West 197 for nine (A. J. Moles 50, J. M. Arthur 32, I. F. Mellett 38; S. J. Base three for 28).

At Bloemfontein, October 21. Orange Free State won by two wickets. Western Province 211 for nine (P. N. Kirsten 52, S. T. Jefferies 46 not out; A. I. Kallicharran three for 43); Orange Free State 212 for eight (P. J. R. Steyn 57, L. J. Wilkinson 65; C. R. Matthews three for 38).

At Stellenbosch, October 24. Eastern Province won by 7 runs. Eastern Province 195 for eight (P. G. Amm 44, M. W. Rushmere 39, K. C. Wessels 51; S. J. Base three for 21, O. Henry three for 39); Boland 188 (S. A. Jones 51, J. D. du Toit 58; R. J. McCurdy four for 15).

At Verwoerdburg, October 31. Northern Transvaal won by four wickets. Natal 251 for six (M. B. Logan 36, A. C. Hudson 43, R. M. Bentley 33, C. L. King 52 not out, C. M. Lister-James 43 not out); Northern Transvaal 252 for six (V. F. du Preez 45, K. D. Verdoorn 102, N. T. Day 51).

At East London, October 31. Transvaal won by 3 runs. Transvaal 262 for five (S. J. Cook 115, K. A. McKenzie 42, R. V. Jennings 41 not out; I. L. Howell three for 40); Border 259 for seven (W. V. Rippon 40, G. L. Hayes 62, B. M. Osborne 36, I. L. Howell 64 not out).

At Johannesburg, November 7. Transvaal won by 27 runs. Transvaal 277 for four (S. J. Cook 126, M. Yachad 106); Orange Free State 250 for nine (L. J. Wilkinson 40, A. C. Storie 97, S. T. Clarke 32; N. V. Radford three for 35, B. M. McMillan three for 30).

At Stellenbosch, November 7. Natal won by 198 runs. Natal 291 for six (M. B. Logan 48, R. M. Bentley 60, D. Bestall 44, T. R. Madsen 51, C. L. King 31 not out); Boland 93 (S. A. Jones 31; H. L. Alleyne three for 6).

At Cape Town, November 14. Western Province won by 168 runs. Western Province 282 for six (L. Seeff 100, P. N. Kirsten 62, D. J. Cullinan 33); Border 114 (G. L. Hayes 33; S. T. Jefferies four for 15).

At Port Elizabeth, November 14. Eastern Province won by 6 runs. Eastern Province 232 for six (M. W. Rushmere 106, K. S. McEwan 39; P. S. de Villiers three for 31); Northern Transvaal 226 for nine (R. F. Pienaar 77, L. J. Barnard 106; R. J. McCurdy four for 42).

At Bloemfontein, November 21. Orange Free State won by 141 runs. Orange Free State 259 for seven (A. I. Kallicharran 40, J. J. Strydom 70, A. C. Storie 54 not out); Border 118 (S. T. Clarke three for 12, C. J. van Heerden three for 26).

At Durban, November 21. Eastern Province won by five wickets. Natal 259 for eight (R. M. Bentley 112, D. Bestall 71; R. J. McCurdy three for 44); Eastern Province 263 for five (K. C. Wessels 98, D. J. Richardson 94).

At Verwoerdburg, November 28. Northern Transvaal won by four wickets. Boland 176 (O. Henry 32, P. J. Newport 57; T. Bosch four for 20, W. F. Morris three for 36); Northern Transvaal 177 for six (N. T. Day 72 not out, R. C. Ontong 44 not out).

At Johannesburg, November 28. Western Province won by five wickets. Transvaal 176 (L. P. Vorster 32, B. M. McMillan 43, B. McBride 32; A. P. Kuiper three for 32); Western Province 177 for five (L. Seeff 41, P. N. Kirsten 72, D. J. Cullinan 43).

Semi-finals

First leg: At Verwoerdburg, February 20. Northern Transvaal won by 109 runs. Northern Transvaal 239 for nine (V. F. du Preez 91, N. T. Day 82; S. T. Clarke six for 31); Orange Free State 130 (A. J. Lamb 31).

First leg: At Cape Town, February 20. Eastern Province won by one wicket. Western Province 174 (J. J. E. Hardy 31, S. T. Jefferies 30; J. G. Thomas three for 32, D. J. Callaghan three for 23); Eastern Province 178 for nine (K. C. Wessels 38, D. J. Richardson 49, T. G. Shaw 30; G. S. le Roux three for 22, C. R. Matthews three for 19).

Second leg: At Port Elizabeth, February 27. Eastern Province won by four wickets. Western Province 244 for five (L. Seeff 35, D. J. Cullinan 57, A. P. Kuiper 37 not out, E. O. Simons 51 not out; T. G. Shaw three for 21); Eastern Province 248 for six (P. G. Amm 80, M. W. Rushmere 81, K. C. Wessels 44).

Second leg: At Virginia, February 27. Orange Free State won by 14 runs. Orange Free State 216 for nine (A. J. Lamb 71, R. J. East 47 not out, S. T. Clarke 33; A. M. Ferreira three for 33); Northern Transvaal 202 (R. F. Pienaar 69, N. T. Day 35; S. T. Clarke three for 32, A. A. Donald three for 26).

Third leg: At Virginia, February 28. Northern Transvaal won by 9 runs. Northern Transvaal 170 for five (V. F. du Preez 38, R. F. Pienaar 68); Orange Free State 161 for nine (A. J. Lamb 43; W. F. Morris three for 17).

Final

At Verwoerdburg, March 13. Eastern Province won by seven wickets. Northern Transvaal 216 for seven (R. F. Pienaar 62, L. J. Barnard 48, M. J. R. Rindel 37); Eastern Province 218 for three (K. S. McEwan 90 not out, D. J. Callaghan 92 not out).

†BENSON AND HEDGES TROPHY, 1987-88

(*Day/night matches of 45 overs per side*)

At Stellenbosch, October 14. Eastern Province won by 9 runs. Eastern Province 214 for five (P. G. Amm 34, M. W. Rushmere 110); Impalas 205 for nine (S. A. Jones 38 not out, J. D. du Toit 51).

At Stellenbosch, October 21. Impalas won by 29 runs. Impalas 251 for seven (K. J. Barnett 31, J. M. Arthur 38, A. D. Methven 47, S. A. Jones 47; N. V. Radford three for 31); Transvaal 222 (M. Yachad 49, B. M. McMillan 43, N. V. Radford 31; S. J. Base three for 24).

At Verwoerdburg, October 21. No result. Eastern Province 244 for six (P. G. Amm 30, M. W. Rushmere 55, K. C. Wessels 51, K. S. McEwan 62); Northern Transvaal 17 for two.

At Virginia, October 28. Impalas won by 5 runs. Impalas 192 (S. Nackerdien 38, S. A. Jones 41, K. G. Bauermeister 37; A. A. Donald three for 21, L. J. Wilkinson four for 48); Orange Free State 187 (P. J. R. Steyn 52, L. J. Wilkinson 70).

At Johannesburg, November 4. Eastern Province won by 44 runs. Eastern Province 207 for four (M. W. Rushmere 37, K. C. Wessels 81 not out); Transvaal 163 (B. M. McMillan 75, R. V. Jennings 37; R. J. McCurdy three for 28, P. A. Rayment three for 23).

At Bloemfontein, November 4. Orange Free State won by seven wickets after being set a revised target of 170 in 33 overs. Northern Transvaal 201 for six (V. F. du Preez 41, L. J. Barnard 30, M. J. R. Rindel 56 not out; B. T. Player three for 25); Orange Free State 170 for three (P. J. R. Steyn 48, L. J. Wilkinson 54).

At Verwoerdburg, October 16. Northern Transvaal won by 9 runs. Northern Transvaal 229 for five (R. F. Pienaar 83, L. J. Barnard 86); Western Province 220 (P. N. Kirsten 65; A. M. Ferreira five for 44).

At Stellenbosch, November 18. Western Province won by 71 runs. Western Province 272 for seven (T. N. Lazard 40, L. Seeff 50, D. J. Cullinan 74, J. J. E. Hardy 40); Impalas 201 (E. N. Trotman 66; C. R. Matthews four for 65).

At Cape Town, November 25. Western Province won by seven wickets. Natal 209 for seven (M. B. Logan 110, N. P. Daniels 36; C. R. Matthews three for 29); Western Province 210 for three (T. N. Lazard 88 not out, P. N. Kirsten 55, D. J. Cullinan 41).

At Port Elizabeth, November 27. Eastern Province won by 73 runs. Eastern Province 238 for four (P. G. Amm 48, M. W. Rushmere 121, K. C. Wessels 38); Orange Free State 165 (A. I. Kallicharran 38; T. G. Shaw three for 37).

At Johannesburg, December 4. Northern Transvaal won by five wickets. Transvaal 249 for two (S. J. Cook 116, H. R. Fotheringham 52, L. P. Vorster 53 not out); Northern Transvaal 253 for five (R. F. Pienaar 48, L. J. Barnard 71, R. C. Ontong 57 not out; C. E. B. Rice three for 44).

At Johannesburg, December 9. Transvaal won by one wicket. Natal 160 (N. P. Daniels 63, T. J. Packer 30 not out; B. M. McMillan four for 46); Transvaal 163 for nine (B. Roberts 30, L. P. Vorster 42; H. L. Alleyne four for 25).

At Durban, December 11. Natal won by five wickets. Northern Transvaal 126 (T. J. Packer three for 29, H. L. Alleyne three for 30, C. M. Lister-James three for 11); Natal 129 for five (R. M. Bentley 33, T. R. Madsen 49 not out; P. S. de Villiers three for 28).

At Port Elizabeth, December 12. Western Province won by 11 runs. Western Province 145 (G. S. le Roux 33; R. J. McCurdy four for 13); Eastern Province 134 (M. W. Rushmere 35).

At Cape Town, December 15. Transvaal won by 101 runs. Transvaal 224 for eight (S. J. Cook 38, M. Yachad 72, L. P. Vorster 32, B. M. McMillan 36; G. S. le Roux four for 25); Western Province 123 for nine (G. S. le Roux 39; N. V. Radford three for 15, K. J. Kerr three for 41).

At Verwoerdburg, February 17. Impalas won by virtue of having lost fewer wickets with the scores level. Impalas 208 for seven (A. J. Moles 47; P. S. de Villiers three for 52); Northern Transvaal 208 for nine (V. F. du Preez 62; P. McLaren three for 24, O. Henry three for 37).

At Cape Town, February 24. Western Province won by 91 runs. Western Province 244 for four (M. H. Austen 54, L. Seeff 82, A. P. Kuiper 48 not out); Orange Free State 153 for nine (J. J. Strydom 55 not out; E. O. Simons three for 25).

At Port Elizabeth, February 24. Eastern Province won by 49 runs. Eastern Province 174 for eight (K. C. Wessels 45, K. S. McEwan 31; T. J. Packer four for 28); Natal 125 (M. W. Pringle three for 16, M. K. van Vuuren four for 23).

At Virginia, March 9. Transvaal won by eight wickets. Orange Free State 121 (D. P. le Roux 32; C. D. Mitchley three for 27); Transvaal 122 for two (S. J. Cook 31, H. R. Fotheringham 69 not out).

At Durban, March 11. Natal won by seven wickets after being set a revised target of 95 in 28 overs. Orange Free State 118 (C. J. van Heerden 32 not out; H. L. Alleyne four for 35); Natal 95 for three.

Semi-finals

First leg: At Johannesburg, March 15. Transvaal won by eight wickets. Eastern Province 171 (M. W. Rushmere 34, D. J. Callaghan 80; R. O. Estwick four for 23); Transvaal 172 for two (S. J. Cook 85 not out, L. P. Vorster 34 not out).

First leg: At Stellenbosch, March 16. Western Province won by 143 runs. Western Province 257 for six (P. N. Kirsten 93, J. J. E. Hardy 75 not out; S. J. Base three for 45); Impalas 114 (K. G. Bauermeister 48; G. S. le Roux three for 28, S. T. Jefferies three for 16).

Second leg: At Cape Town, March 18. Western Province won by 48 runs. Western Province 185 for nine (A. P. Kuiper 76; S. J. Base four for 37); Impalas 137 (S. Nackerdien 47, S. A. Jones 37; E. O. Simons three for 34).

Second leg: At Port Elizabeth, March 18. Eastern Province won by 44 runs. Eastern Province 235 for four (P. G. Amm 54, M. W. Rushmere 70, K. S. McEwan 47, D. J. Callaghan 39 not out); Transvaal 191 (H. R. Fotheringham 33, R. V. Jennings 41 not out; D. J. Callaghan three for 27).

Third leg: At Port Elizabeth, March 19. Transvaal won by five wickets. Eastern Province 208 for seven (M. W. Rushmere 41, D. J. Callaghan 75 not out, D. J. Richardson 32); Transvaal 209 for five (S. J. Cook 94, M. Yachad 37, L. P. Vorster 56; P. A. Rayment three for 35).

Final

At Johannesburg, March 25. Western Province won by five wickets. Transvaal 189 (L. P. Vorster 41, B. Roberts 31; A. P. Kuiper four for 28); Western Province 190 for five (L. Seeff 42, P. N. Kirsten 64).

CRICKET IN THE WEST INDIES, 1987-88

By TONY COZIER

In a season when sponsorship of the annual first-class championship changed after 22 years, Jamaica ended a prolonged wait by winning the inaugural Red Stripe Cup, the replacement for the Shell Shield. Jamaica had won the Shield only once in its 21 seasons, as far back as 1968-69, and the triumph was not only overdue but appropriate. The new sponsors are brewers of Jamaica's best-known beer. Having secured the Red Stripe Cup, the Jamaicans were within one wicket and one ball of capturing the double. They lost the limited-overs Geddes Grant-Harrison Line Trophy final to Barbados when two dropped catches by a substitute allowed the Barbados last-wicket pair to sneak home with 2 runs off the last delivery.

The West Indies Cricket Board of Control (WICBC) took the decision on a change of sponsor because the new agreement guaranteed an unabridged championship for at least five years. In 1986-87, because of heavy financial losses, the Shell Shield had to be divided in half, with two zones of three teams each leading to a final. The Shield was the first regular competition to be staged in the West Indies and was possible only through the monetary commitment of the Shell Oil Company, which was fittingly thanked by the Board for its undeniable contribution to the advance of West Indies cricket.

The first Red Stripe Cup was a great success for several reasons. The new sponsors engaged in lively promotion, the race for the title was keen throughout, with four teams still in contention when the last round of matches started, and the Test players were all available for the final three rounds. There was a noticeable increase in public interest and crowds, especially at Kingston's Sabina Park, which recorded its largest attendances since its modernisation in 1983. Jamaica, making their bid for the Cup, played their final three matches there.

Home advantage, aided by the return of Jeffrey Dujon, Patrick Patterson and Courtney Walsh from India and of Michael Holding from a professional engagement in New Zealand, clinched the Cup for Jamaica. They beat Windward Islands by an innings and then Barbados by 53 runs in a close, tense, top-of-the-standings match. This left them requiring only a draw in their final match, against Trinidad & Tobago, which they comfortably achieved. Jamaica played solid, all-round cricket throughout. A vital ingredient was the team spirit encouraged by the leadership of Marlon Tucker, a West Indies youth team captain of 1980 who was leading the island for the first time at senior level. Even on the return of Holding, captain for the two previous seasons, and Dujon, another former captain, Tucker was retained in the position. He seemed to get the best out of his players and he himself made an important contribution with his off-spin, taking twenty wickets, including eleven in the important match against Barbados.

Leeward Islands fielded the strongest and best-balanced team once Vivian Richards, Richie Richardson, Winston Benjamin and Eldine Baptiste returned from India. In the fast bowler, Curtly Ambrose, they possessed the Player of the Season, a tall and imposing personality whose 35 wickets in his first full season eclipsed Winston Davis's 33 of 1982-83 as the tournament record. With such considerable depth, the Leewards won their final three matches by massive margins – 305 runs over Jamaica, an innings and 36 runs over Guyana, and ten wickets over Barbados. They were only four points behind Jamaica at the end. A narrow defeat by Trinidad & Tobago and a draw against bottom-placed Windward Islands in their first two matches were setbacks for which they could not ultimately compensate.

Trinidad & Tobago, in spite of the fact that not one of their batsmen scored a century in the five matches, played steadily throughout to finish third ahead of Barbados, whose effort foundered with successive defeats by Jamaica and the Leewards in their final two matches. Guyana, hard-hit by injuries that limited Roger Harper to one match and prevented Carl Hooper from playing at all, and Windward Islands, three of whose most experienced players had retired, filled the last two positions and were well back.

In spite of generally slow pitches, the subject of much adverse comment, the fast bowlers were dominant. There were only five totals over 400; eleven outright results were recorded in the fifteen matches. No-one was more dominant than Ambrose. Six feet, seven inches tall and with a beanpole physique, he was a virtual unknown prior to the season, having played just one first-class match – against Guyana in 1985-86. He endured being no-balled for throwing by the Test umpire, Clyde Cumberbatch, in his first match against Trinidad & Tobago but never lost his pace, his accuracy, or his thirst for wickets. His yorker was his most destructive ball, particularly in his match analysis of twelve for 133 against Guyana. Nine of his victims were bowled. He became an automatic choice for the West Indies team for the series against Pakistan that followed; yet another of the increasing number of Antiguans to advance to Test cricket.

Malcolm Marshall returned as captain of Barbados after his self-imposed rest from the World Cup and the tour of India. Although he did not appear fully fit, and expressed his frustration at the nature of the pitches, even taking to bowling a few overs of leg-spin at one stage (and capturing three wickets with it), he nevertheless finished with 27 wickets at 17.25. Joel Garner, having retired from Test cricket a few months earlier, took 23 wickets alongside Marshall for Barbados, but the most encouraging performance came from Ian Bishop, a twenty-year-old Trinidadian, whose nineteen wickets at under 14 runs apiece emphasised his immense promise and earned him a place in the team to tour England.

Apart from Tucker, there were two other spinners with twenty or more wickets in the five matches. One was his fellow-Jamaican, Robert Haynes, whose bouncy leg-spin gained him 22 wickets to add to the 236 runs he scored as a powerful and forthright left-handed batsman. The other was Ranjie Nanan, the veteran Trinidad & Tobago off-spinner who, with twenty wickets in his sixteenth season, became the first bowler to pass 200 wickets in inter-territorial cricket in the West Indies.

One batsman, Clayton Lambert, totalled more than 500 runs, heading both the aggregates (549) and the averages at 78.42. A sequence of consistent scores, among them two centuries, carried him past Roy Fredericks's previous Guyana record of 545 for the number of runs in a season. Like Fredericks, Lambert is a left-handed opening batsman with a belligerent approach to fast bowling. He and the stylish right-hander, Ravindranauth Seeram, shared three century partnerships during the season, among them 221 for the second wicket against the Windwards. Seeram was one of three other batsmen with more than 400 runs. His 424 were at an average of 60.57. Wayne Lewis, Jamaica's right-handed opener, adopted attack as his creed to total 428 at 61.14, and Thelston Payne, Barbados's middle-order left-hander and a former deputy West Indies wicket-keeper, enjoyed his best season since 1983 with 461 at 51.22. His 127 against the Windwards was his first century in five years. The highest individual innings was Richardson's 176 in the Leewards' emphatic, first-ever victory over Barbados.

An otherwise happy season was spoiled by unbecoming squabbles over the umpiring by captains, managers and senior players. Marshall was fined $US250 for accusing the umpires of cheating in Barbados's match against Jamaica, and Desmond Haynes, the Test opener, was fined for knocking over his stumps after being given out lbw in the same match. There were frequent displays of dissent on the field and critical comments off it. Hesketh Benjamin, the Leewards' manager, made the claim that umpire Cumberbatch, a Trinidadian, had called Ambrose for throwing in order to protect the place in the West Indies team of Tony Gray, a Trinidadian. It was an attitude that accentuated the continuing insular tendency in West Indies cricket.

Trinidad & Tobago retained the annual Northern Telecom youth championship in Jamaica in July, 1987, but the 1988 tournament, staged in Barbados in July, was won by the home team. In both, the left-handed batting of the Trinidad & Tobago captain, Brian Lara, and the leg-spin bowling of his team-mate, Rajindra Dhanraj, were the main features. Lara, captain of the West Indies team to the first Youth World Cup in Australia in February, scored two hundreds in each tournament, while Dhanraj had a combined tally of 79 wickets in the ten matches.

As they did in 1987, Lancashire toured Jamaica and Hampshire visited Barbados as part of their preparation for their 1988 county programme. Having lost badly in 1987, Lancashire now had the better of a drawn three-day match against Jamaica, while Hampshire won one and lost one of two limited-overs matches against Barbados.

The presidency of the WICBC changed at its meeting in Kingston in May when Clyde Walcott, the former Test batsman, selector and team manager, was elected to succeed Allan Rae. Walcott's contemporary in the Test team in the 1950s, Rae stepped down after seven years in the post. Walcott, aged 62, scored 3,798 runs (average 56.68) in 44 Tests between 1948 and 1960. The headquarters of the Board moved from Kingston to Bridgetown as a consequence of his appointment.

RED STRIPE CUP AVERAGES, 1987-88

BATTING

(Qualification: 200 runs)

	M	*I*	*NO*	*R*	*HI*	*100s*	*Avge*
C. B. Lambert (*Guyana*)	5	9	2	549	162	2	78.42
K. L. T. Arthurton (*Leeward I.*)	5	8	2	380	121	1	63.33
W. W. Lewis (*Jamaica*)	5	8	1	428	132	1	61.14
R. Seeram (*Guyana*)	5	9	2	424	119	1	60.57
P. J. L. Dujon (*Jamaica*)	3	4	0	241	108	1	60.25
T. R. O. Payne (*Barbados*)	5	9	0	461	127	1	51.22
C. G. Greenidge (*Barbados*)	3	6	1	215	70	0	43.00
D. S. Morgan (*Jamaica*)	4	6	1	205	101*	1	41.00
M. D. Marshall (*Barbados*)	5	9	1	298	77	0	37.25
R. M. Otto (*Leeward I.*)	5	8	2	221	74*	0	36.83

	M	I	NO	R	HI	100s	Avge
C. A. Best (*Barbados*)	5	9	0	328	98	0	36.44
L. L. Harris (*Leeward I.*)	5	6	0	204	63	0	34.00
R. C. Haynes (*Jamaica*)	5	8	1	236	87	0	33.71
M. C. Neita (*Jamaica*)	5	7	0	231	58	0	33.00
D. J. Collymore (*Windward I.*)	5	10	2	262	87*	0	32.75
C. B. Burnett (*Guyana*)	5	7	0	228	63	0	32.57
D. A. Joseph (*Windward I.*)	5	10	0	308	109	1	30.80
L. C. Sebastien (*Windward I.*)	5	10	0	302	116	1	30.20
A. L. Grant (*Barbados*)	5	9	1	223	75	0	27.87

* *Signifies not out.*

BOWLING

(Qualification: 10 wickets)

	O	M	R	W	BB	Avge
I. R. Bishop (*T & T*)	96	13	260	19	4-42	13.68
M. A. Tucker (*Jamaica*)	143.1	46	298	20	6-38	14.90
R. Nanan (*T & T*)	196	72	305	20	5-31	15.25
C. E. L. Ambrose (*Leeward I.*)	189.2	34	543	35	7-66	15.51
W. K. M. Benjamin (*Leeward I.*)	83.4	21	239	14	5-50	17.07
M. D. Marshall (*Barbados*)	159.5	35	466	27	5-24	17.25
J. Garner (*Barbados*)	148.5	26	450	23	4-39	19.56
C. A. Walsh (*Jamaica*)	93	19	286	14	5-45	20.42
E. T. Willett (*Leeward I.*)	102	26	248	12	3-42	20.66
A. H. Gray (*T & T*)	108	15	349	14	4-54	24.92
R. C. Haynes (*Jamaica*)	231	62	564	22	6-53	25.63
D. J. Collymore (*Windward I.*)	146	20	423	16	4-72	26.43
B. P. Patterson (*Jamaica*)	80.3	16	282	10	3-43	28.20
G. E. Charles (*Guyana*)	166.2	14	430	14	5-48	30.71
H. W. D. Springer (*Barbados*)	125	20	353	11	4-63	32.09
J. T. Etienne (*Windward I.*)	165	33	484	15	3-31	32.26
T. Z. Kentish (*Windward I.*)	170	29	406	10	3-57	40.60

RED STRIPE CUP, 1987-88

	Played	Won	Lost	Drawn	1st-inns lead in drawn match	Points
Jamaica	5	3	1	1	1	56
Leeward Islands	5	3	1	1	0	52
Trinidad & Tobago	5	2	0	3	1	48
Barbados	5	2	2	1	0	36
Guyana	5	1	3	1	0	20
Windward Islands	5	0	4	1	1	8

Win = 16 pts; draw = 4 pts; 1st-innings lead in drawn match = 4 pts.

*In the following scores, * by the name of the team indicates that they won the toss.*

At Pointe-á-Pierre, January 22, 23, 24, 25. Trinidad & Tobago won by two wickets. Leeward Islands 147 (L. L. Harris 49; I. R. Bishop four for 23, R. Nanan three for 24) and 195 (K. L. T. Arthurton 69; I. R. Bishop four for 42, R. Nanan four for 32); Trinidad & Tobago* 171 (R. Nanan 48; C. E. L. Ambrose three for 37) and 172 for eight (A. Rajah 31, H. A. Gomes 33; C. E. L. Ambrose three for 43). *Trinidad & Tobago 16 pts.*

At Albion, Guyana, January, 29, 30, 31, February 1. Jamaica won by nine wickets. Guyana 260 (C. B. Lambert 39, S. Dhaniram 30, A. F. D. Jackman 32, R. Seeram 31, C. B. Burnett 50; R. C. Haynes three for 56, M. A. Tucker three for 42) and 242 (S. Dhaniram 45, C. B. Burnett 52; R. C. Haynes four for 51); Jamaica* 358 (W. W. Lewis 85, R. C. Haynes 87, J. C. Adams 34, M. A. Tucker 43; C. V. Solomon three for 67, S. Matthews three for 100) and 147 for one (W. W. Lewis 72 not out, D. S. Morgan 56). *Jamaica 16 pts.*

At St John's, January 29, 30, 31, February 1. Drawn. Windward Islands 244 (D. A. Joseph 70; T. A. Merrick three for 59, E. T. Willett three for 50) and 233 for eight dec. (D. T. Telemaque 71, D. A. Joseph 30, D. J. Collymore 35; E. T. Willett three for 42); Leeward Islands* 238 (R. M. Otto 59, L. L. Harris 52, T. A. Merrick 33 not out; J. T. Etienne three for 57) and 95 for two (K. L. T. Arthurton 35 not out, R. M. Otto 38 not out). *Windward Islands 8 pts, Leeward Islands 4 pts.*

At Port-of-Spain, January 29, 30, 31, February 1. Drawn. Barbados* 250 (R. I. C. Holder 33, T. R. O. Payne 31, M. D. Marshall 71; I. R. Bishop three for 48, R. Dhanraj four for 67) and 204 for nine (C. A. Best 77, A. L. Grant 32 not out; A. H. Gray four for 54); Trinidad & Tobago 292 (B. C. Lara 92, H. A. Gomes 36, R. Nanan 46 not out; J. Garner three for 71, W. E. Reid three for 42). *Trinidad & Tobago 8 pts, Barbados 4 pts.*

At St George's, February 4, 5, 6, 7. Barbados won by 144 runs. Barbados* 279 (T. R. O. Payne 127, A. L. Grant 75; W. W. Davis three for 85, D. J. Collymore four for 72) and 241 for seven dec. (T. R. O. Payne 53, M. D. Marshall 55 not out, W. E. Reid 31; D. J. Collymore three for 47, J. T. Etienne three for 64); Windward Islands 154 (D. J. Collymore 52 not out; J. Garner three for 39, M. D. Marshall five for 55) and 222 (L. D. John 30, J. D. Charles 40, L. C. Sebastien 55; M. D. Marshall four for 54, J. Garner four for 59). *Barbados 16 pts.*

At Hampton Court, Guyana, February 5, 6, 7, 8. Drawn after rain had prevented play on the first three days. Guyana 178 for two dec. (C. B. Lambert 102 not out, R. Seeram 58 not out) v Trinidad & Tobago*. *Guyana 4 pts, Trinidad & Tobago 4 pts.*

At Basseterre, February 5, 6, 7, 8. Leeward Islands won by 305 runs. Leeward Islands* 186 (A. C. H. Walsh 41, V. A. Eddy 38 not out; R. C. Haynes six for 85) and 401 for three dec. (A. L. Kelly 79, A. C. H. Walsh 37, E. A. E. Baptiste 99, K. L. T. Arthurton 77 not out, R. M. Otto 74 not out); Jamaica 96 (W. K. M. Benjamin five for 50, C. E. L. Ambrose five for 40) and 186 (M. C. Neita 34, A. G. Daley 32; C. E. L. Ambrose four for 52). *Leeward Islands 16 pts.*

At Kingston, February 13, 14, 15, 16. Jamaica won by an innings and 36 runs. Windward Islands* 236 (D. A. Joseph 109, D. J. Collymore 44; B. P. Patterson three for 43, C. A. Walsh five for 45) and 233 (D. A. Joseph 32, L. C. Sebastien 48, J. R. Murray 31 not out; B. P. Patterson three for 59, M. A. Holding three for 32, M. A. Tucker three for 26); Jamaica 505 for five dec. (W. W. Lewis 132, D. S. Morgan 101 not out, P. J. L. Dujon 108, M. C. Neita 58, R. C. Haynes 36; J. T. Etienne three for 105). *Jamaica 16 pts.*

At Bridgetown, February 13, 14, 15, 16. Barbados won by ten wickets. Guyana 233 (C. B. Lambert 39, S. Dhaniram 31, R. Seeram 39, C. B. Burnett 38; M. D. Marshall three for 67, H. W. D. Springer four for 63) and 309 (C. B. Lambert 59, R. Seeram 87, C. B. Burnett 63; M. D. Marshall three for 67, J. Garner four for 64); Barbados* 474 for eight dec. (C. G. Greenidge 41, D. L. Haynes 64, C. A. Best 98, T. R. O. Payne 92, M. D. Marshall 77, J. Garner 61; C. G. Butts three for 121) and 71 for no wkt (C. G. Greenidge 36 not out, D. L. Haynes 33 not out). *Barbados 16 pts.*

At Roseau, February 19, 20, 21, 22. Trinidad & Tobago won by 74 runs. Trinidad & Tobago 201 (P. V. Simmons 64, K. A. Williams 33, D. Williams 44 not out; W. W. Davis three for 49, T. Z. Kentish three for 57) and 146 (P. V. Simmons 45, D. Williams 36; J. T. Etienne three for 31); Windward Islands* 172 (D. J. Collymore 87 not out; A. H. Gray four for 56, I. R. Bishop three for 23) and 101 (L. D. John 53; R. Nanan five for 31, G. Mahabir four for 30). *Trinidad & Tobago 16 pts.*

At St John's, February 19, 20, 21, 22. Leeward Islands won by an innings and 36 runs. Guyana 140 (C. B. Lambert 40; C. E. L. Ambrose seven for 66) and 232 (C. B. Lambert 43, J. I. Simpson 51, R. Seeram 40, I. D. Harper 51 not out; C. E. L. Ambrose five for 67); Leeward Islands* 408 (K. L. T. Arthurton 121, I. V. A. Richards 119, L. L. Harris 63; B. St A. Browne three for 95, G. E. Charles five for 97). *Leeward Islands 16 pts.*

At Kingston, February 20, 21, 22, 23. Jamaica won by 53 runs. Jamaica* 263 (W. W. Lewis 49, P. J. L. Dujon 37, R. C. Haynes 30; J. Garner four for 39) and 198 (M. C. Neita 55; M. D. Marshall five for 24); Barbados 181 (T. R. O. Payne 82, A. L. Grant 43; M. A. Tucker six for 38) and 227 (C. G. Greenidge 70, C. A. Best 54; M. A. Tucker five for 66). *Jamaica 16 pts.*

At Bridgetown, February 26, 27, 28, 29. Leeward Islands won by ten wickets. Barbados 243 (D. L. Haynes 39, C. A. Best 53, M. D. Marshall 56; C. E. L. Ambrose three for 66) and 208 (C. G. Greenidge 46, D. L. Haynes 35, T. R. O. Payne 37; W. K. M. Benjamin four for 53, N. C. Guishard three for 39); Leeward Islands* 406 (R. B. Richardson 176, E. A. E. Baptiste 58, K. L. T. Arthurton 46, I. V. A. Richards 70; J. Garner three for 95, M. D. Marshall four for 80) and 47 for no wkt (A. L. Kelly 30 not out). *Leeward Islands 16 pts.*

At Albion, Guyana, February 26, 27, 28, 29. Guyana won by nine wickets. Windward Islands* 177 (L. D. John 46, J. R. Murray 47; G. E. Charles five for 48) and 297 (L. C. Sebastien 116); Guyana 395 (C. B. Lambert 162, R. Seeram 119, S. Mohamed 47; D. J. Collymore three for 88) and 85 for one (C. B. Lambert 38 not out, R. Seeram 36 not out). *Guyana 16 pts.*

At Kingston, February 26, 27, 28, 29. Drawn. Trinidad & Tobago* 228 (K. A. Williams 77, A. L. Logie 46; R. C. Haynes six for 53) and 300 for nine (K. A. Williams 43, A. L. Logie 45, H. A. Gomes 66, A. H. Gray 47; C. A. Walsh three for 61, A. G. Daley three for 66); Jamaica 378 (W. W. Lewis 44, P. J. L. Dujon 80, M. C. Neita 45, C. A. Davidson 55; R. Nanan three for 99). *Jamaica 8 pts, Trinidad and Tobago 4 pts.*

SHELL SHIELD AND RED STRIPE CUP WINNERS

The Shell Shield was replaced by the Red Stripe Cup after the 1986-87 season.

1965-66	Barbados	1977-78	Barbados
1966-67	Barbados	1978-79	Barbados
1968-69	Jamaica	1979-80	Barbados
1969-70	Trinidad	1980-81	Combined Islands
1970-71	Trinidad	1981-82	Barbados
1971-72	Barbados	1982-83	Guyana
1972-73	Guyana	1983-84	Barbados
1973-74	Barbados	1984-85	Trinidad & Tobago
1974-75	Guyana	1985-86	Barbados
1975-76	Trinidad / Barbados	1986-87	Guyana
1976-77	Barbados	1987-88	Jamaica

GUYSTAC TROPHY, 1987-88

At Camp Ayangana Ground, Georgetown, October 30, 31, November 1, 2. Drawn. Demerara 284 (M. A. Harper 85, R. Seeram 45, I. D. Harper 70, C. G. Butts 32; C. V. Solomon three for 71, R. Doodnauth five for 83) and 77 for four; Berbice 216 (S. Dhaniram 72, H. Evans 47; C. G. Butts five for 56).

JAMAICA v LANCASHIRE

At Kingston, April 5, 6, 7. Drawn. Jamaica 271 (W. W. Lewis 71, C. St G. O'Connor 36, L. A. Cunningham 46, P. A. Francis 36, A. G. Daley 30; M. Watkinson three for 50, I. Folley four for 73) and 103 for seven (L. A. Cunningham 35; M. Watkinson three for 18, J. Simmons three for 34); Lancashire 390 (G. Fowler 33, G. D. Mendis 71, N. H. Fairbrother 106, A. N. Hayhurst 83; A. G. Daley six for 103, E. L. Wilson three for 89).

†GEDDES GRANT-HARRISON LINE TROPHY, 1987-88

Zone A

At Port-of-Spain, January 27. Barbados won by eight wickets after achieving a revised target of 116 in 35 overs. Trinidad and Tobago 132 for six (40 overs) (H. A. Gomes 38 not out); Barbados 119 for two (31.4 overs) (C. A. Best 53 not out, P. J. C. Alleyne 30).

At Hampton Court, Guyana, February 3. Guyana won by three wickets. Trinidad & Tobago 184 for eight (45 overs) (A. Rajah 56); Guyana 187 for seven (44 overs) (R. Seeram 58; I. R. Bishop three for 35).

At Bridgetown, February 11. Barbados won by eight wickets. Guyana 161 (48 overs) (C. L. Hooper 58; J. Garner four for 22); Barbados 164 for two (C. G. Greenidge 63, C. A. Best 78 not out).

Zone B

At Plymouth, Montserrat, January 27. Leeward Islands won by five wickets. Windward Islands 117 for nine (50 overs) (G. J. F. Ferris three for 38); Leeward Islands 118 for five (48.3 overs) (K. L. T. Arthurton 33).

At Charlestown, Nevis, February 3. Jamaica won by 38 runs. Jamaica 162 for six (37 overs) (W. W. Lewis 46, M. C. Neita 32; E. T. Willett three for 37); Leeward Islands 124 (31.2 overs) (R. M. Otto 43, V. A. Eddy 39; A. G. Daley three for 39, R. C. Haynes four for 26).

At Kingston, February 11. Jamaica won by four wickets. Windward Islands 206 for six (50 overs) (L. C. Sebastien 54, S. L. Mahon 38, D. J. Collymore 36; R. C. Haynes three for 36); Jamaica 207 for six (46.2 overs) (W. W. Lewis 60, P. J. L. Dujon 50, M. A. Tucker 33 not out).

Final

At Kingston, March 3. Barbados won by one wicket. Jamaica 218 for eight (46 overs) (R. C. Haynes 83, C. A. Davidson 43 not out); Barbados 219 for nine (46 overs) (D. L. Haynes 58, T. R. O. Payne 44, A. L. Grant 40; B. P. Patterson three for 45, C. A. Walsh three for 46).

Man of the Match: R. C. Haynes.

CRICKET IN NEW ZEALAND, 1987-88

By C. R. BUTTERY

The Shell Trophy series ended on a controversial note with the joint leaders, Otago and Auckland, each thinking they had won the competition. Auckland, after drawing their final match with Northern Districts, finished equal on 52 points with Otago, who defeated Wellington outright. The winner was to be the team with the higher runs-per-wicket differential over the series. Unfortunately for Auckland, when earlier computing how many runs they needed and how many wickets they could lose against Northern Districts, they had based their calculations on an incorrect newspaper score which showed that Otago took nine wickets in an innings against Wellington when in fact all ten fell. The difference was enough to give Otago a margin of 0.272 over Auckland and bring them the trophy for the second time in three years.

Nevertheless, credit must be given to Auckland for their efforts. They lost no fewer than nine players at various times on international duty, and for the first half of the season they languished in last place. With the return of the New Zealand side from Australia in January, Auckland were able to field a full-strength side for the first time, and the results were immediately apparent. Two outright wins in the next two matches saw them rise to the top of the table by the end of the seventh round, and with a little more luck they could have won the trophy. Their opening batsman, Trevor Franklin, deserves special mention. In 1986, as the New Zealand team were about to leave England, he suffered multiple fractures to his leg when hit by a runaway trolley at Gatwick Airport. At one stage amputation of the leg was a distinct possibility, and at the very least it was thought that his first-class cricketing days were over. Since then, Franklin doggedly fought his way back to health, and the start of the season saw him resume his place in the Auckland side. He scored a century in the first match, three more during the season, and was selected for all three Tests against the visiting England side. It was a remarkable comeback.

Otago's success was due in no small measure to the shrewd leadership of Warren Lees. Lees, the most experienced captain in the competition, led his side with considerable skill. This was demonstrated by his two declarations in the last match with Wellington which enabled Otago to win outright and take the sixteen points needed to move into first place. Otago were also well served by their batsmen, which was particularly satisfying as the batting had let them down in previous years. Richard Hoskin and Kevin Burns each scored more than 500 runs in the season for the province, while Ken Rutherford, when available, batted with distinction.

Great things were expected from Northern Districts, who had the services of Worcestershire's Graeme Hick for the season. Hick, one of the most exciting young batsmen in the game, lived up to expectations, scoring 827 runs with an average of 63.61. He was largely responsible for lifting Northern Districts to third place after they had finished last the previous year. Only four points separated Northern Districts from the competition winners; had they been able to gain first-innings points from any of the three matches they won outright, they may have won the competition.

Wellington, rather surprisingly, finished in only fourth place. The batting was strong, with Robert Vance and Bruce Edgar by far the best pair of opening batsmen in the country. Vance hit three hundreds and was rewarded with his Test début against England at the relatively advanced age of 32. Against Central Districts, at Levin, Gavin Larsen and Ervin McSweeney led a recovery from 79 for four with a New Zealand fifth-wicket record of 341. The unavailability of Ewen Chatfield, because of his absence with the New Zealand team, considerably weakened the bowling. However, Jonathan Millmow, a young medium-pace bowler, showed promise in taking 31 wickets and could be Chatfield's successor in due course. The veteran Australian leg-spinner, 41-year-old Bob Holland, also took 31 wickets.

The absence of Martin Crowe severely restricted Central Districts' performances. In 1986-87 Crowe practically won the competition for Central Districts on his own, and without him the side looked ordinary. Crowe was available for only one match, in which he scored an unbeaten century. However, Mark Greatbatch continued to provide strength to the batting and was another to gain Test selection against England, making an unbeaten century in his first appearance for New Zealand.

Canterbury once again showed that without Richard Hadlee and John Wright there was little depth to the side. Rod Latham was the only batsman to show any real form, scoring 679 runs at an average of 52.23. Michael Holding, the former West Indian international fast bowler, proved his worth, collecting 29 wickets at a low cost, and at times bowled with considerable fire.

The Shell Cup limited-overs competition was also won by Otago, who thus made a clean sweep of the Shell Series. They won four of their five games, while Northern Districts finished runners-up with three victories after being narrowly defeated by Otago in the final round. Two retired international cricketers, Edgar and Lance Cairns, headed the batting and bowling averages respectively. Edgar scored 220 runs at an average of 55.00 and Cairns took fourteen wickets at a cost of 9.64 runs apiece.

Probably too much cricket was available to the public during the summer. Several of the Shell Series games had to compete firstly with live telecasts of the New Zealand team's matches in Australia, and later with the visiting England side's matches. This, together with the absence of top players, caused attendances to fall and each of the six major associations suffered a financial loss for the season.

FIRST-CLASS AVERAGES, 1987-88

BATTING

(Qualification: 5 completed innings, average 25)

	M	*I*	*NO*	*R*	*HI*	*100s*	*Avge*
R. H. Vance (*Wellington*)	9	14	3	731	121	3	66.45
G. A. Hick (*N. Districts*)	9	14	1	827	146	4	63.61
M. D. Crowe (*C. Districts*)	4	7	1	349	143	2	58.16
K. R. Rutherford (*Otago*)	7	12	1	629	182	2	57.18
B. A. Young (*N. Districts*)	10	14	7	384	94	0	54.85
W. K. Lees (*Otago*)	7	10	4	319	112	1	53.16

	M	I	NO	R	HI	100s	Avge
J. G. Bracewell (*Auckland*)	5	7	1	315	104	1	52.50
R. T. Latham (*Canterbury*)	9	16	3	679	141*	2	52.23
B. A. Edgar (*Wellington*)	9	15	2	676	103*	1	52.00
R. N. Hoskin (*Otago*)	8	14	2	599	157	3	49.91
D. J. Walker (*Otago*)	9	16	5	536	77	0	48.72
E. B. McSweeney (*Wellington*)	9	12	2	459	205*	1	45.90
M. R. Pringle (*Auckland*)	6	7	1	271	77	0	45.16
M. J. Greatbatch (*C. Districts*)	10	19	1	795	149	2	44.16
J. G. Wright (*Canterbury*)	4	7	0	291	103	1	41.57
T. J. Franklin (*Auckland*)	10	16	0	664	120	4	41.50
G. R. Larsen (*Wellington*)	9	13	2	451	161	1	41.00
C. J. Smith (*C. Districts*)	8	15	2	530	122*	1	40.76
C. M. Kuggeleijn (*N. Districts*)	9	13	2	429	87	0	39.00
B. G. Cooper (*N. Districts*)	9	12	1	415	116*	1	37.72
D. J. White (*N. Districts*)	10	16	1	522	80	0	34.80
S. A. Thomson (*N. Districts*)	6	6	1	174	84	0	34.80
K. J. Burns (*Otago*)	9	16	0	550	136	2	34.37
S. W. Duff (*C. Districts*)	7	11	4	238	70*	0	34.00
P. A. Horne (*Auckland*)	5	8	0	270	66	0	33.75
L. M. Crocker (*N. Districts*)	9	14	0	470	99	0	33.57
E. J. Gray (*Wellington*)	9	12	3	293	66*	0	32.55
C. W. Flanagan (*Canterbury*)	3	5	0	158	50	0	31.60
B. R. Blair (*Otago*)	8	14	0	413	86	0	29.50
R. J. Harden (*C. Districts*)	8	14	0	409	82	0	29.21
P. E. McEwan (*Canterbury*)	8	15	1	400	118	1	28.57
J. J. Crowe (*Auckland*)	5	7	1	165	125	1	27.50
S. P. Robertson (*C. Districts*)	8	15	0	404	94	0	26.93
D. A. Dempsey (*Canterbury*)	8	16	1	393	121	1	26.20
W. P. Fowler (*Auckland*)	8	12	1	285	56	0	25.90
D. J. Boyle (*Canterbury*)	6	10	0	255	60	0	25.50
I. R. Snook (*C. Districts*)	7	11	3	201	100*	1	25.12

* *Signifies not out.*

BOWLING

(Qualification: 15 wickets)

	O	M	R	W	BB	Avge
M. A. Holding (*Canterbury*)	258.5	90	488	29	7-52	16.82
E. J. Chatfield (*Wellington*)	175.1	59	320	16	4-36	20.00
W. Watson (*Auckland*)	181.2	50	468	23	6-55	20.34
M. C. Snedden (*Auckland*)	191	63	404	18	5-31	22.44
S. L. Boock (*Otago*)	421.2	150	948	42	6-110	22.57
W. P. Fowler (*Auckland*)	132.1	36	364	16	6-41	22.75
R. G. Holland (*Wellington*)	249.2	76	738	31	7-69	23.80
J. P. Millmow (*Wellington*)	264.5	67	776	31	4-19	25.03
M. W. Priest (*Canterbury*)	260.2	68	732	28	5-63	26.14
G. K. Robertson (*C. Districts*)	223.4	53	635	23	5-34	27.60
N. A. Mallender (*Otago*)	185.4	45	477	17	4-64	28.05
K. Treiber (*N. Districts*)	308.4	82	812	25	6-96	32.48
B. J. Barrett (*N. Districts*)	248.2	43	817	25	4-41	32.68
C. W. H. Lawrence (*Canterbury*)	212.5	41	684	20	4-43	34.20
D. K. Morrison (*Auckland*)	161	31	520	15	5-69	34.66
T. J. Wilson (*Otago*)	293.3	57	957	27	5-82	35.44
R. P. de Groen (*Auckland*)	169.3	35	551	15	4-71	36.73
E. J. Gray (*Wellington*)	289	88	663	17	4-63	39.00
M. R. McKinnon (*N. Districts*)	266.4	70	612	15	4-27	40.80

SHELL TROPHY, 1987-88

	Played	*Won*	*Lost*	*Drawn*	*1st Inns Pts*	*Total Pts*
Otago	8	3	1	4	16	52
Auckland	8	3	2	3	16	52†
Northern Districts	8	3	1	4	12	48†
Wellington	8	2	2	4	18	42*
Central Districts	8	2	3	3	14	38*
Canterbury	8	1	5	2	20	32

Outright win = 12 pts; lead on first innings = 4 pts.

* *First-innings points shared in one match.*

† *First-innings points shared in two matches.*

*In the following scores, * by the name of a team indicates that they won the toss.*

At Lancaster Park, Christchurch, January 5, 6, 7. Canterbury won by nine wickets. Canterbury 309 for eight dec. (P. E. McEwan 35, D. J. Boyle 56, R. T. Latham 101, L. K. Germon 37 not out; W. Watson three for 86) and 34 for one; Auckland* 102 (A. T. R. Hellaby 36 not out; M. A. Holding five for 29) and 240 (T. J. Franklin 106, W. P. Fowler 55; M. A. Holding three for 63, A. J. Hintz three for 56). *Canterbury 16 pts.*

At Pukekura Park, New Plymouth, January 5, 6, 7. Otago won by six wickets. Central Districts* 266 for eight dec. (C. J. Smith 31, M. J. Greatbatch 93, S. W. Duff 70 not out; T. J. Wilson five for 82) and 283 for six dec. (C. J. Smith 71, M. J. Greatbatch 53, R. J. Harden 82; T. J. Wilson four for 93); Otago 240 (K. J. Burns 48, B. R. Blair 34, R. N. Hoskin 46; D. A. Stirling three for 58, K. W. Martin four for 60) and 310 for four (K. B. K. Ibadulla 107, K. J. Burns 72, R. N. Hoskin 38 not out). *Otago 12 pts, Central Districts 4 pts.*

At Seddon Park, Hamilton, January 5, 6, 7. Northern Districts won by five wickets. Wellington* 325 for six dec. (B. A. Edgar 39, R. H. Vance 85, T. D. Ritchie 102 not out, E. B. McSweeney 48; D. A. Beard three for 52) and 193 for three dec. (R. H. Vance 117 not out); Northern Districts 217 (D. J. White 58, C. M. Kuggeleijn 60, B. A. Young 69 not out; J. P. Millmow three for 27, R. G. Holland three for 83) and 302 for five (L. M. Crocker 99, G. E. Bradburn 58, G. A. Hick 64, C. M. Kuggeleijn 30 not out; G. R. Larsen three for 46). *Northern Districts 12 pts, Wellington 4 pts.*

At Lancaster Park, Christchurch, January 9, 10, 11. Northern Districts won by 122 runs. Northern Districts* 229 (B. G. Cooper 50, C. M. Kuggeleijn 87; A. J. Hintz three for 51, C. W. H. Lawrence three for 50) and 276 for two dec. (G. E. Bradburn 52, L. M. Crocker 66, D. J. White 33 not out, G. A. Hick 113 not out); Canterbury 254 for eight dec. (J. G. Boyle 50, P. E. McEwan 37, M. C. Bremner 35) and 129 (D. A. Dempsey 35; B. J. Barrett four for 56, C. M. Kuggeleijn three for eight). *Northern Districts 12 pts, Canterbury 4 pts.*

At Carisbrook, Dunedin, January 9, 10, 11. Otago won by four wickets. Auckland* 286 (T. J. Franklin 120, S. W. Brown 69, A. T. R. Hellaby 32; N. A. Mallender three for 55, S. L. Boock four for 85) and 137 (V. R. Brown 33, W. P. Fowler 43; S. L. Boock four for 31, T. J. Wilson four for 48); Otago 288 for seven dec. (S. J. McCullum 42, R. N. Hoskin 101, W. K. Lees 53 not out; R. P. de Groen three for 83) and 136 for six (K. J. Burns 34, D. J. Walker 47; W. Watson four for 49). *Otago 16 pts.*

At Basin Reserve, Wellington, January 9, 10, 11. Drawn. Wellington* 293 for seven dec. (B. A. Edgar 92, E. J. Gray 66 not out, E. B. McSweeney 72) and 219 for no wkt dec. (R. H. Vance 107 not out, B. A. Edgar 103 not out); Central Districts 237 for nine dec. (S. P. Robertson 31, C. J. Smith 42, S. W. Duff 50; E. J. Gray three for 53, R. G. Holland four for 53) and 195 for seven (M. J. Greatbatch 34, R. J. Harden 41, S. J. Gill 53; R. G. Holland four for 84). *Wellington 4 pts.*

At Eden Park, Auckland, January 13, 14, 15. Drawn. Auckland* 253 for eight dec. (R. B. Reid 87, V. R. Brown 60, P. J. Kelly 32 not out; J. P. Millmow four for 63) and 224 (S. W. Brown 61, M. R. Pringle 76; R. G. Holland seven for 69); Wellington 225 (R. H. Vance 98, G. N. Cederwall 30; R. P. de Groen four for 71, I. D. Fisher three for 58) and 217 for eight (G. R. Larsen 35, E. J. Gray 62, S. J. Maguiness 43; I. D. Fisher four for 37). *Auckland 4 pts.*

At Horton Park, Blenheim, January 13, 14, 15. Central Districts won by 149 runs. Central Districts* 294 for three dec. (S. P. Robertson 36, C. J. Smith 122 not out, D. J. Guthardt 82 not out; M. W. Priest three for 95) and 246 for eight dec. (M. J. Greatbatch 149; M. W. Priest three for 107, A. J. Nuttall three for 65); Canterbury 234 for nine dec. (D. A. Dempsey 39, R. T. Latham 98; S. W. Duff three for 25) and 157 (D. J. Boyle 31; G. K. Robertson three for 37, S. W. Duff three for 30). *Central Districts 16 pts.*

At Molyneux Park, Alexandra, January 13, 14, 15. Northern Districts won by 50 runs. Northern Districts 118 (B. A. Young 34; N. A. Mallender three for 25, S. L. Boock four for 53) and 275 for eight dec. (D. J. White 68, G. A. Hick 90, B. A. Young 38 not out; S. L. Boock three for 77); Otago* 125 (D. J. Walker 49; K. Treiber five for 35) and 218 (K. J. Burns 44, D. J. Walker 54 not out, J. K. Lindsay 41; K. Treiber four for 60, M. R. McKinnon four for 27). *Northern Districts 12 pts, Otago 4 pts.*

At Lancaster Park, Christchurch, January 17, 18, 19. Drawn. Canterbury* 264 (P. E. McEwan 73, M. W. Priest 50, C. W. Flanagan 31, L. K. Germon 32 not out; N. A. Mallender four for 64, T. J. Wilson three for 83) and 54 for no wkt (D. A. Dempsey 38 not out); Otago 221 (D. J. Walker 77, N. A. Mallender 41 not out; M. A. Holding seven for 52, C. W. Flanagan three for 51). *Canterbury 4 pts.*

At Albert Park, Te Awamutu, January 17, 18, 19. Drawn. Central Districts* 135 (M. J. Greatbatch 40; B. J. Barrett four for 41) and 175 for five (S. P. Robertson 69, M. J. Greatbatch 37); Northern Districts 259 (L. M. Crocker 65, B. A. Young 94, T. McKenna four for 52). *Northern Districts 4 pts.*

At Eden Park, Auckland, January 25, 26, 27. Auckland won by 60 runs. Auckland* 204 (P. A. Horne 30, W. P. Fowler 56, M. J. Bradley 37 not out; C. W. H. Lawrence three for 33, D. J. Hartshorn three for 56) and 329 for nine dec. (T. J. Franklin 116, M. R. Pringle 77; M. A. Holding six for 77); Canterbury 336 (P. E. McEwan 118, P. G. Kennedy 59, A. J. Hintz 62, C. W. H. Lawrence 33; D. K. Morrison three for 84, W. P. Fowler three for 54) and 137 (M. A. Holding 31; W. P. Fowler six for 41). *Auckland 12 pts, Canterbury 4 pts.*

At Levin Park Domain, Levin, January 25, 26, 27. Wellington won by an innings and 82 runs. Central Districts 131 (S. P. Robertson 30; G. N. Cederwall three for 46) and 222 (M. J. Greatbatch 47; J. P. Millmow four for 48, E. J. Gray four for 63); Wellington* 435 for five dec. (G. R. Larsen 161, E. B. McSweeney 205 not out; G. K. Robertson three for 86). *Wellington 16 pts.*

At Eden Park, Auckland, January 29, 30, 31. Auckland won by 58 runs. Auckland 400 for seven dec. (P. A. Horne 31, S. W. Brown 40, J. J. Crowe 125, W. P. Fowler 30, J. G. Bracewell 104; T. McKenna three for 84) and 174 for three dec. (T. J. Franklin 100, P. A. Horne 43); Central Districts 269* (S. P. Robertson 36, C. J. Smith 32, T. E. Blain 75, G. K. Robertson 44; W. Watson six for 55) and 247 (M. J. Greatbatch 56, R. J. Harden 42, T. E. Blain 62; J. G. Bracewell three for 73). *Auckland 16 pts.*

At Seddon Park, Hamilton, January 29, 30, 31. Drawn. Northern Districts* 520 for eight dec. (L. M. Crocker 53, D. J. White 31, G. A. Hick 122, B. G. Cooper 88, C. M. Kuggeleijn 87, S. A. Thomson 84; S. L. Boock three for 158); Otago 457 (K. J. Burns 136, K. R. Rutherford 44, R. N. Hoskin 157; K. Treiber six for 96). *Northern Districts 4 pts.*

At Basin Reserve, Wellington, January 29, 30, 31. Wellington won by nine wickets. Canterbury* 220 (R. T. Latham 91, D. J. Hartshorn 38; J. P. Millmow three for 50, G. N. Cederwall four for 49, F. Beyeler three for 52) and 84 (R. T. Latham 35; J. P. Millmow four for 19); Wellington 248 for seven dec. (B. A. Edgar 98, G. R. Larsen 55; M. W. Priest three for 21) and 57 for one (B. A. Edgar 33 not out). *Wellington 16 pts.*

At Eden Park, Auckland, February 2, 3, 4. Auckland won by an innings and 25 runs. Northern Districts 64 (M. C. Snedden five for 31, W. Watson four for 14) and 233 (B. G. Cooper 37, S. A. Thomson 75; M. C. Snedden four for 42, J. G. Bracewell three for 64); Auckland* 322 (P. A. Horne 66, T. J. Franklin 50, D. N. Patel 93, J. G. Bracewell 59; S. A. Thomson three for 59, B. J. Barrett three for 53, M. R. McKinnon three for 58). *Auckland 16 pts.*

At Lancaster Park, Christchurch, February 2, 3, 4. Central Districts won by eight wickets. Canterbury 100 (G. K. Robertson five for 34, G. R. Logan three for 24) and 218 (J. G. Wright 70, C. W. Flanagan 32; G. K. Robertson three for 38, K. W. Martin three for 81); Central Districts* 138 for nine dec. (R. J. Harden 31; C. W. H. Lawrence four for 43) and 182 for two (C. J. Smith 46 not out, M. D. Crowe 119 not out). *Central Districts 16 pts.*

At Centennial Park, Oamaru, February 2, 3, 4. Drawn. Otago 342 for four dec. (K. J. Burns 112, K. R. Rutherford 182) and 258 for seven dec. (D. J. Walker 43, W. K. Lees 112); Wellington* 327 (B. A. Edgar 96, T. D. Ritchie 30, E. B. McSweeney 35, E. J. Gray 37, F. Beyeler 43 not out; S. L. Boock six for 110) and 76 for one (R. H. Vance 42 not out). *Otago 4 pts.*

At Fitzherbert Park, Palmerston North, February 6, 7, 8. Drawn. Central Districts* 359 for five dec. (S. P. Robertson 94, C. J. Smith 63, I. R. Snook 100 not out, R. J. Harden 42); Northern Districts 194 for eight (L. M. Crocker 65, G. A. Hick 62, B. A. Young 41 not out; K. W. Martin five for 76). *Central Districts 2 pts, Northern Districts 2 pts.*

At Carisbrook, Dunedin, February 6, 7, 8. Drawn. Canterbury* 420 for six dec. (D. A. Dempsey 121, D. J. Boyle 60, R. T. Latham 141 not out; K. Johnson three for 117) and 191 for seven dec. (D. A. Dempsey 44, C. W. Flanagan 50; S. L. Boock four for 65); Otago 292 (K. R. Rutherford 68, B. R. Blair 86; M. W. Priest five for 63) and 271 for nine (K. R. Rutherford 56, B. R. Blair 55, D. J. Walker 65 not out; M. W. Priest five for 100). *Canterbury 4 pts.*

At Basin Reserve, Wellington, February 6, 7, 8. Drawn. Wellington* 181 for one (B. A. Edgar 53, G. P. Burnett 82 not out, G. R. Larsen 35 not out); Auckland did not bat. *Wellington 2 pts, Auckland 2 pts.*

At Seddon Park, Hamilton, February 10, 11, 12. Drawn. Northern Districts* 432 for six dec. (L. M. Crocker 60, B. T. Spragg 47, G. A. Hick 141, D. J. White 77, B. G. Cooper 43, C. M. Kuggeleijn 41); Auckland 313 for four (P. A. Horne 61, J. F. Reid 112, D. N. Patel 44, M. R. Pringle 51 not out). *Auckland 2 pts, Northern Districts 2 pts.*

At Basin Reserve, Wellington, February 10, 11, 12. Otago won by 146 runs. Otago* 310 for eight dec. (S. J. McCullum 46, R. N. Hoskin 61, D. J. Walker 60, W. K. Lees 68 not out; R. G. Holland five for 81) and 273 for eight dec. (B. R. Blair 64, R. N. Hoskin 105; R. G. Holland three for 105); Wellington 293 for nine dec. (R. H. Vance 121, G. R. Larsen 74, E. J. Gray 38; S. L. Boock three for 61, J. K. Lindsay five for 110) and 144 (B. A. Edgar 35; S. L. Boock four for 32, J. K. Lindsay five for 48). *Otago 16 pts.*

PLUNKET SHIELD AND SHELL TROPHY WINNERS

The Plunket Shield was replaced by the Shell Trophy after the 1974-75 season.

1921-22 Auckland
1922-23 Canterbury
1923-24 Wellington
1924-25 Otago
1925-26 Wellington
1926-27 Auckland
1927-28 Wellington
1928-29 Auckland
1929-30 Wellington
1930-31 Canterbury
1931-32 Wellington
1932-33 Otago
1933-34 Auckland
1934-35 Canterbury
1935-36 Wellington
1936-37 Auckland
1937-38 Auckland
1938-39 Auckland
1939-40 Auckland
1940-45 No competition
1945-46 Canterbury
1946-47 Auckland
1947-48 Otago
1948-49 Canterbury
1949-50 Wellington
1950-51 Otago

CRICKET IN INDIA, 1987-88

By P. N. SUNDARESAN

The month-long tension and excitement generated by the Reliance World Cup in October and early November appeared to leave the Indian cricket enthusiast too drained to evince any interest in the country's domestic programme. Even the tour by the West Indians, in the past an assured draw, proved a flop with the public, and only the final Test at Madras made a small profit, the prospect of an Indian victory having attracted the fans for the second half of the match.

Public response was even worse to the Ranji Trophy knockout rounds, as epitomised by the presence of only a handful of spectators, mainly officials, to witness and applaud Tamil Nadu's victory over Railways on the last morning of the final. In addition, there was widespread criticism of certain aspects of the competition, including the casual interest shown by some senior players, and there were calls for the regeneration of the national championship. However, the response of the Indian Board, who suggested a one-day international tournament involving India and the two countries scheduled to tour in 1988-89, New Zealand and England, did not seem the appropriate solution to the problem.

Tamil Nadu, formerly Madras state, won the Ranji Trophy championship after a lapse of 33 years, having won it for the first time in 1954-55. They had reached the final on four other occasions, only to be beaten by Bombay (1935-36, 1967-68, 1972-73) and Maharashtra (1940-41), and there was a close resemblance between their progress in the season under discussion and that in 1972-73. Each time, all their knockout matches were played at the Chidambaram Stadium in Madras; each time they won the toss in the quarter- and semi-final matches and lost the toss in the final. As the Tamil Nadu batsmen utilised the advantage of batting first to register large scores, moving from one record figure to another, it was hard to credit that this was the same ground where the nineteen-year-old leg-spinner, Narendra Hirwani, had established an Indian bowling record of sixteen for 136 to help defeat West Indies and so draw the series. Little more than a month later, a pitch which had been a spinner's paradise had changed colour and Tamil Nadu's batsmen were running up more than a thousand runs in their Ranji Trophy quarter-final against Uttar Pradesh. Against Punjab in the semi-final they scored a record for Tamil Nadu in a Ranji Trophy innings, 601, and bettered it in the final with 709 in their only innings against Railways, who were beaten by an innings and 144 runs.

Following the retirement of two batting stalwarts in Abdul Jabbar and Venkatraman Sivaramakrishnan, plus the frequent absence of Srikkanth because of international commitments, Tamil Nadu's success contained an element of surprise. Moreover, the task of rebuilding the side had fallen to a new captain, the right-hand batsman and left-arm spinner, S. Vasudevan. With his simple, straightforward approach, he was able to get the best out of his young players, and his bowlers, especially, rose to the challenge admirably. Margasagayam Venkatramana, an off-spinner from the districts, showed fine control over the basics of spin bowling and, with 35 wickets in his first season, was the discovery of the Ranji Trophy championship. The outstanding batsman was the left-hander, Robin Singh, an immigrant from the West Indies who scored four of the ten hundreds registered by Tamil Nadu in the Ranji Trophy. Another three came from Laxman Sivaramakrishnan, whose batting compensated for his indifferent form with the ball, and such was the depth of batting available to him that Vasudevan, normally a middle-order batsman, had to demote himself to No. 10. Nevertheless, the state selectors showed much wisdom in persuading Venkatraman Sivaramakrishnan to come out of retirement for the knockout rounds, for the veteran played vital innings in the semi-final and final.

The other finalists, Railways, in a determined bid to improve their performance in the championship, had recruited players who had made their mark in recent seasons, among them Yusuf Ali Khan, K. B. Kala, wicket-keeper Pradeep Bhatnagar and Sunil Valson. Thus strengthened, they won the Central Zone league and eventually qualified for the final for the first time. However, they were fortunate to get past Delhi in their semi-final tie. Rain in Delhi washed out the first two days, and on the remaining two days Delhi scored 230 for five declared, to which Railways replied with 140 for three. As no decision could be reached on first innings, the quotient rule was applied (runs scored divided by wickets lost) and Railways went through by 0.66.

The highest individual score in the Ranji Trophy was K. S. Chavan's 247 for Baroda against Bombay in a West Zone match. B. P. Patel, the Karnataka veteran, was again in good touch to amass 596 runs, and so become the leading run-scorer in the Ranji Trophy, while his team-mate, A. R. Bhat, was the leading bowler in the championship, his incisive left-arm spinners bringing him 36 wickets at an average of 23.20. He also returned the best figures for an innings (eight for 43) and match (fifteen for 84) in Karnataka's 67-run victory over Tamil Nadu in the South Zone division. Sourajit Mohapatra of Orissa enjoyed a thrilling début in the championship, taking six for 23, including a hat-trick, and seven for 40 against Tripura.

The Duleep Trophy matches were played at the same time as the World Cup matches and brought into focus the contrasting approach of batsmen to their task in the two types of cricket. A. D. Gaekwad and S. V. Manjrekar of West Zone and R. Lamba of North Zone in particular indulged in heavy scoring as they built their innings pragmatically. Gaekwad scored 195 against Central Zone and 216 against North Zone in the final, while Manjrekar hit 278 against Central Zone, adding 288 with Gaekwad for the second wicket. Lamba hit a career-best 320 against West Zone, the first triple-century in the competition, which set him handsomely on his way towards 1,000 runs for the first-class season. He batted for approximately twelve hours, faced 471 balls, and hit six sixes and 30 fours. Boosted by this great effort, North Zone scored 368 in reply to West Zone's 444, and with West Zone holding out in their second innings (284 for six), North Zone won the trophy by virtue of their first-innings lead.

After the World Cup, Sunil Gavaskar announced his desire to bid farewell to first-class cricket, and during the season Gundappa Viswanath also announced his retirement. Although Viswanath had been out of the international limelight for five years, he had continued to assist Karnataka; in 93 matches in the Ranji Trophy he scored 5,653 runs (average 45.95). Gavaskar played 66 times for Bombay in the Ranji Trophy for an aggregate of 5,335 runs (average 70.19). Each in his own way enriched the game; Gavaskar building his scores with a shrewd assessment of circumstances and situations, Viswanath taking each ball as it came and playing with a spontaneity and freshness that was always a delight.

This review cannot pass without mention of the ban imposed on Dilip Vengsarkar who, having been elevated to the captaincy of the Indian team for the series against West Indies, broke his contract with the Indian Board by writing comments on the matches for newspapers. He was suspended from first-class cricket for six months and so missed the Ranji Trophy knockout matches. He was also omitted from the Indian team for the Sharjah Cup tournament in March, as were Manoj Prabhakar and Maninder Singh following their unseemly clash during the Steel Trophy tournament in Delhi. Maninder, playing for the Steel Authority Club, and Prabhakar, of the Banking Sports Club, came to blows after an exchange of words on the field of play. The Delhi and District Association, to whom both owed allegiance, severely reprimanded them, and the Indian selectors supported the association's action.

FIRST-CLASS AVERAGES, 1987-88

BATTING

(Qualification: 500 runs)

	I	*NO*	*R*	*HI*	*100s*	*Avge*
R. Lamba (*Delhi*)	13	0	1,097	320	5	84.38
Gursharan Singh (*Punjab*)	8	1	529	132*	3	75.57
B. P. Patel (*Karnataka*)	10	2	596	144	3	74.50
A. D. Gaekwad (*Baroda*)	11	2	625	216	2	69.44
Robin Singh (*Tamil Nadu*)	10	2	555	152	4	69.37
S. V. Manjrekar (*Bombay*)	14	4	678	278	1	67.80
L. S. Rajput (*Bombay*)	15	1	928	275	4	66.28
M. Nayyar (*Delhi*)	12	2	653	184	2	65.30
K. B. Kala (*Railways*)	9	1	522	203*	2	65.25
Arun Lal (*Bengal*)	12	0	777	205	2	64.75
R. S. Ghai (*Punjab*)	10	2	517	99	0	64.62
L. Sivaramakrishnan (*Tamil Nadu*)	11	2	531	124	3	59.00
K. Bhaskar Pillai (*Delhi*)	12	3	530	129	2	58.00
W. V. Raman (*Tamil Nadu*)	13	1	637	182	1	53.08
V. B. Chandrasekhar (*Tamil Nadu*)	13	1	551	160	1	45.91
C. Saldanha (*Karnataka*)	13	0	531	144	1	40.84

* *Signifies not out.*

BOWLING

(Qualification: 20 wickets)

	O	*M*	*R*	*W*	*Avge*
L. Venkatapathy Raju (*Hyderabad*)	121.3	38	276	20	13.80
D. Chopra (*Punjab*)	275.3	87	546	32	17.06
M. Venkatramana (*Tamil Nadu*)	239.1	55	716	35	20.45
S. Vasudevan (*Tamil Nadu*)	265.4	78	600	27	22.22
A. R. Bhat (*Karnataka*)	286.4	64	780	35	22.28
N. Konwar (*Assam*)	177	19	592	25	23.68
Deepak Sharma (*Haryana*)	238.3	42	628	26	24.15
N. D. Hirwani (*Madhya Pradesh*)	267.1	31	923	38	24.28
K. Jayakumar (*Kerala*)	146.5	24	618	24	25.75
B. S. Mangesh (*Andhra*)	194	47	541	21	25.76

	O	*M*	*R*	*W*	*Avge*
N. S. Yadav (*Hyderabad*)	286.4	65	727	28	25.96
Arshad Ayub (*Hyderabad*)	279.4	61	712	27	26.37
B. Arun (*Tamil Nadu*)	155	28	609	23	26.47
V. Venkatram (*Bihar*)	191	27	538	20	26.90
Madan Lal (*Delhi*)	216.2	35	656	23	28.52
. Talwar (*Haryana*)	300.2	55	856	30	28.53
R. P. Singh (*Uttar Pradesh*)	190.2	21	728	24	30.33
M. I. Singh (*Punjab*)	344	82	833	27	30.85
K. K. Sharma (*Uttar Pradesh*)	182.1	19	721	23	31.34

RANJI TROPHY, 1987-88

*In the following scores, (M) indicates that the match was played on coir matting, (T) that it was played on turf, and * by the name of a team indicates that they won the toss.*

Central Zone

At Moradabad (M), November 14, 15, 16. Drawn. Uttar Pradesh 238 (S. S. Khandkar 32, P. N. S. Rana 67, Gopal Sharma 42; S. Takle four for 31, S. Jugade four for 48) and 268 for eight dec. (V. S. Yadav 39, S. S. Khandkar 64, K. K. Sharma 53, R. Sapru 49; S. Jugade six for 84); Vidarbha* 283 (P. Hingnikar 92, S. Gujar 63; R. P. Singh three for 48, K. K. Sharma four for 65) and 91 for five (R. Pankule 32). *Uttar Pradesh 11 pts, Vidarbha 14 pts.*

At Bhilwara (M), November 20, 21, 22. Rajasthan won by eight wickets. Vidarbha 285 (P. Shetty 32, S. Gujar 36, S. Phadkar 53, A. Sahastrabudhe 31 not out; S. Mishra three for 78, Ratan Singh five for 114) and 191 (S. Takle 55 not out; R. Rathore four for 33, S. Mishra three for 61); Rajasthan* 311 (A. Mudkavi 38, S. Mudkavi 41, A. Asawa 128, D. Jain 51 not out; S. Jugade five for 91) and 170 for two (Dalbir Singh 91 not out, S. Mudkavi 36 not out). *Rajasthan 20 pts, Vidarbha 8 pts.*

At Bhilai (T), November 20, 21, 22. Drawn. Madhya Pradesh 223 (A. Vijayvargiya 43; K. K. Sharma four for 105, R. P. Singh three for 57) and 254 (A. Vijayvargiya 115, R. Talwar 55; Gopal Sharma five for 62, M. A. Ansari three for 66); Uttar Pradesh* 265 (V. S. Yadav 100, S. S. Khandkar 39, R. Sapru 58; S. Lahore six for 83) and 128 for five (S. S. Khandkar 56). *Uttar Pradesh 13 pts, Madhya Pradesh 9 pts.*

At Bhopal (T), November 27, 28, 29. Railways won by an innings and 15 runs. Railways* 408 for six dec. (R. D. Khanwilkar 30, P. Amre 186 not out, K. B. Kala 74, Durga Prasad 59; N. D. Hirwani three for 92); Madhya Pradesh 198 (S. Ansari 63, C. P. Singh 30; S. Valson seven for 59) and 195 (A. Vijayvargiya 64, R. Talwar 39; H. Joshi three for 51, Durga Prasad five for 63). *Railways 20 pts, Madhya Pradesh 2 pts.*

At Birsingpur (T), December 4, 5, 6. Drawn. Uttar Pradesh* 493 (V. S. Yadav 93, S. S. Khandkar 34, S. Chaturvedi 64, R. Sapru 50, P. N. S. Rana 42, R. P. Singh 51, Gopal Sharma 36, K. K. Sharma 33; Ajay Sharma three for 106, K. Bharatan three for 119) and 24 for two dec.; Railways 452 (K. B. Kala 203 not out, P. Bhatnagar 105, K. Bharatan 65; R. P. Singh five for 83) and 11 for no wkt. *Uttar Pradesh 11 pts, Railways 10 pts.*

At Birsingpur (T), December 4, 5, 6. Drawn. Uttar Pradesh* 493 (V. S. Yadav 93, S. S. Khandkar 34, S. Chaturvedi 64, R. Sapru 50, P. N. S. Rana 42, R. P. Singh 51, Gopal Sharma 36, K. K. Sharma 33; Ajay Sharma three for 106, K. Bharatan three for 119) and 24 for two dec.; Railways 452 (K. B. Kala 203 not out, P. Bhatnagar 105, K. Bharatan 65; R. P. Singh five for 83) and 11 for no wkt. *Uttar Pradesh 11 pts, Railways 10 pts.*

At Kota (M), December 4, 5, 6. Drawn. Madhya Pradesh* 234 (S. Ansari 43, R. Talwar 54, C. P. Singh 41, M. Satokar 36 not out; P. Sunderam seven for 75) and 318 (R. Talwar 48, C. P. Singh 69, S. Lahore 89, R. Patel 30; P. Sunderam six for 99); Rajasthan 316 (A. Mudkavi 63, Padam Shastri 80, S. Mudkavi 73; N. D. Hirwani five for 95) and 136 for five (Padam Shastri 32). *Rajasthan 16 pts, Madhya Pradesh 11 pts.*

At Agra (T), December 11, 12, 13. Abandoned without a ball bowled owing to rain. *Railways 4 pts, Rajasthan 4 pts.*

At Nagpur (T), December 11, 12, 13. Drawn. Madhya Pradesh 493 for eight dec. (S. Ansari 37, A. Vijayvargiya 84, R. Talwar 199, C. P. Singh 44, M. Sahni 47, M. Satokar 51; S. Takle three for 110, V. Gawate three for 150); Vidarbha* 306 (P. Hingnikar 48, S. Phadkar 79,

H. Wasu 31 not out; R. Patel three for 91, J. Vegud six for 138) and 202 for two (U. Fa 102 not out, P. Hingnikar 54). *Madhya Pradesh 14 pts, Vidarbha 8 pts.*

At Nagpur (T), December 18, 19, 20. Railways won by 31 runs. Railways* 270 (N. Chu 56, K. B. Kala 43, K. Bharatan 53, Hyder Ali 36; H. Wasu four for 84) and 240 for eight de (P. Bhatnagar 58, N. Churi 32, Durga Prasad 55; H. Wasu four for 71); Vidarbha 149 and 33 (S. Gujar 101, S. Phadkar 72, V. Gawate 34; Durga Prasad three for 62, H. Joshi four for 76 *Railways 19 pts, Vidarbha 8 pts.*

At Obera (T), December 18, 19, 20. Drawn. Uttar Pradesh 357 (Indrapal Singh 76, S. Khandkar 45, R. Sapru 48, P. N. S. Rana 71 not out; S. Vyas six for 82) and 64 for no wk Rajasthan* 219 (Padam Shastri 30, S. Mudkavi 60 not out, R. Rathore 32; K. K. Sharm three for 58, R. P. Singh four for 48) and 174 for nine dec. (Dalbir Singh 52, S. Mudkavi 4(M. Ali five for 48, R. P. Singh three for 42). *Uttar Pradesh 16 pts, Rajasthan 7 pts.*

Railways 53 pts, Uttar Pradesh 51 pts, Rajasthan 47 pts, Vidarbha 38 pts, Madhya Prades 36 pts. Railways and Uttar Pradesh qualified for the knockout stage.

East Zone

At Hazaribagh (T), January 5, 6, 7. Bihar won by an innings and 144 runs. Bihar* 349 (H Gidwani 116, A. Hussain 81, Ujjal Das 41, Satish Singh 31; A. Das four for 146); Tripur 60 (K. V. P. Rao four for 6, V. Venkatram three for 7) and 145 (S. Paul 44, Subra Chowdhary 36; K. V. P. Rao three for 24, S. Ranjan five for 39). *Bihar 23 pts, Tripura 3 pts*

At Jamshedpur (T), January 10, 11, 12. Bihar won by 189 runs. Bihar* 170 (P. Khanna 3 H. Gidwani 49; N. Konwar four for 68, S. G. Chakraborthy four for 42) and 217 for two de (P. Khanna 31, A. Dayal 47, H. Gidwani 101 not out, S. S. Karim 33 not out); Assam 72 (V Venkatram four for 29) and 126 (M. Kakoti 46; K. V. P. Rao four for 31, V. Venkatram thre for 40, S. Ranjan three for 27). *Bihar 15 pts, Assam 4 pts.*

At Cuttack (T), January 11, 12, 13. Orissa won by an innings and 151 runs. Orissa 369 fo eight dec. (Soumitra Chowdhary 31, R. Biswal 57, S. Mitra 69, A. Khatua 84, P. Bose 5 Subrata Chowdhary three for 91); Tripura* 134 (S. Paul 45, S. S. Ray 47; H. Praharaj thre for 43, S. Mohapatra six for 23 including a hat-trick) and 84 (S. Mohapatra seven for 40 *Orissa 24 pts, Tripura 2 pts.*

At Sambalpur (T), January 15, 16, 17. Orissa won by 156 runs. Orissa* 236 (D. Mahanty 8 S. Mohapatra 36; N. Konwar six for 84) and 216 for nine dec. (S. Mitra 54, A. Khatua 5 H. Praharaj 40 not out; N. Konwar four for 71); Assam 160 (R. Bora 80; M. Saudagar eigh for 64) and 136 (R. Bora 35; M. Saudagar four for 47, R. Biswal three for 10). *Orissa 17 pt Assam 7 pts.*

At Calcutta (T), January 15, 16, 17. Bengal won by an innings and 206 runs. Tripura* 8 (J. Singh four for 34, D. Mukherjee five for 17) and 94 (S. Paul 37; S. Singh five for 3 D. Mukherjee five for 28); Bengal 384 for five dec. (I. B. Roy 50, K. Dubey 139, J. Mukherje 49, A. Malhotra 93; A. Saha three for 116). *Bengal 23 pts, Tripura 1 pt.*

At Sambalpur (T), January 22, 23, 24. Drawn. Bihar 277 (S. S. Karim 106, Avinash Kuma 36; S. Mohapatra four for 80) and 182 for four dec. (P. Khanna 69, H. Gidwani 57 not out Orissa* 226 (S. Mitra 43, H. Praharaj 31; Randhir Singh three for 55) and 137 for six (A. Ro 59 not out). *Bihar 16 pts, Orissa 10 pts.*

At Calcutta (T), January 22, 23, 24. Drawn. Bengal* 443 (I. B. Roy 110, S. Ganguly 10 A. Malhotra 48, J. Mukherjee 62; N. Konwar three for 116) and 260 for four (I. B. Roy 4 K. Dubey 108, A. Malhotra 84); Assam 254 (R. Das 49, M. Kakoti 33, S. G. Chakraborth 43 not out; A. Bhattacharjee five for 62). *Bengal 16 pts, Assam 7 pts.*

At Ranchi (T), January 27, 28, 29. Drawn. Bihar* 557 for eight dec. (P. Khanna 8 A. Dayal 121, H. Gidwani 65, A. Hussain 46, R. Arora 110 not out, V. Venkatram 79 A. Bhattacharjee three for 134); Bengal 309 for seven (K. Dubey 120, I. B. Roy 62, P. Roy 42 V. Venkatram six for 109). *Bihar 11 pts, Bengal 7 pts.*

At Gauhati (T), February 10, 11, 12. Assam won by an innings and 104 runs. Tripura 13 (M. Kakoti eight for 63) and 189 (S. Paul 71, Subrata Chowdhary 49, C. R. Paul 33 not ou N. Konwar five for 45, S. Uzir three for 48); Assam* 425 for six dec. (R. Das 170, R. Bor 126, P. Dutta 95). *Assam 24 pts, Tripura 3 pts.*

At Cuttack (T), February 16, 17, 18. Drawn. Bengal* 348 for six dec. (I. B. Roy 71, Arun al 74, A. Malhotra 44, J. Mukherjee 79, A. Bhattacharjee 33) and 313 for nine dec. (Arun al 75, J. Mukherjee 45, A. Bhattacharjee 32, S. Banerjee 53 not out; P. Agarwal five for 111, 1. Saudagar three for 48); Orissa 134 (D. Mahanty 51, A. Bhattacharjee three for 14, . Sensharma three for 55) and 43 for three. *Bengal 14 pts, Orissa 7 pts.*

Bihar 65 pts, Bengal 60 pts, Orissa 58 pts, Assam 42 pts, Tripura 9 pts. Bihar and Bengal ualified for the knockout stage.

lorth Zone

.t Srinagar (T), October 6, 7, 8. Jammu and Kashmir won by an innings and 74 runs. Iimachal Pradesh 118 (V. Sen 33; A. Pirzada three for 28) and 239 (Inderjit Singh 66, V. Sen 3; R. K. Gupta six for 38); Jammu and Kashmir* 431 for seven dec. (A. Aijaz 56, Vidya haskar 125, A. Gupta 50, S. Pervez 103, S. Chowdhary 44; Om Prakash four for 65). *Jammu nd Kashmir 21 pts, Himachal Pradesh 2 pts.*

At Delhi (T), November 14, 15, 16. Drawn. Jammu and Kashmir* 373 (Vidya Bhaskar 71, Iirmal Singh 88, S. Pervez 92, I. Gandru 62; R. K. Verma four for 97) and 248 for seven (R. andit 33, Vidya Bhaskar 52 not out, S. Pervez 84; S. Rai three for 24); Services 370 (A. S. ajwa 92, Gauri Shankar 93, B. Ghosh 85, A. K. Seth 44; I. Gandru five for 48, Ravi Kant ıree for 93). *Services 13 pts, Jammu and Kashmir 13 pts.*

At Amritsar (T), November 14, 15, 16. Punjab won by an innings and 156 runs. Punjab 451 ɔr six dec. (D. Pandove 94, S. Chopra 70, Gursharan Singh 42, R. Puri 61 not out, R. S. Ghai 7); Himachal Pradesh* 142 (Inderjit Singh 33; R. S. Ghai three for 48, D. Chopra three for 3) and 153 (Raj Kumar 48, D. Berki 31; D. Chopra five for 37). *Punjab 22 pts, Himachal radesh 2 pts.*

At Mohan Nagar (T), November 18, 19, 20. Delhi won by an innings and 58 runs. Jammu nd Kashmir 204 (A. Aijaz 32, Vidya Bhaskar 46, A. Gupta 61; Maninder Singh seven for 62) nd 196 (R. Pandit 71; M. Prabhakar four for 52, A. Wason three for 19); Delhi* 458 for eight ec. (S. C. Khanna 143, Ajay Sharma 53, K. Azad 96, M. Prabhakar 32, Madan Lal 49; Iarender Sharma five for 145). *Delhi 21 pts, Jammu and Kashmir 4 pts.*

At Gurgaon (T), November 19, 20. Haryana won by an innings and 117 runs. Himachal radesh 116 (Kapil Dev four for 38, Chetan Sharma three for 50) and 178 (Inderjit Singh 48, . Sen 38, Ravinder Kumar 30; Kapil Dev five for 61); Haryana* 411 for eight dec. (K. P. merjeet 79, Kapil Dev 87, R. Chadda 53, R. Jolly 73, Chetan Sharma 55; Shakti Singh five r 123). *Haryana 24 pts, Himachal Pradesh 4 pts.*

At Rohtak (T), November 23, 24, 25. Drawn. Jammu and Kashmir* 231 (A. Aijaz 52, R. andit 30, S. Chowdhary 67; Deepak Sharma six for 76, Balkishan three for 47) and 302 for ght (R. Pandit 119, Nirmal Singh 57, Zahoor Bhat 42 not out; Deepak Sharma five for 101); aryana 489 for eight dec. (K. P. Amarjeet 126, Yashpal Sharma 78, R. Chadda 123, R. Jolly) not out). *Haryana 12 pts, Jammu and Kashmir 7 pts.*

At Delhi (T), November 23, 24. Delhi won by an innings and 187 runs. Himachal Pradesh 28 (V. Sen 74; Madan Lal four for 37, M. Prabhakar four for 47) and 166 (R. Nayyar 78; A. /ason three for 42); Delhi* 481 for one dec. (M. Nayyar 184, S. C. Khanna 220 not out, . Bhaskar Pillai 62 not out). *Delhi 23 pts.*

At Delhi (T), November 27, 28, 29. Services won by an innings and 11 runs. Himachal radesh 169 (Inderjit Singh 41, Raj Kumar 49; B. Ghosh three for 28, R. H. Khan four for 48) ıd 247 (Inderjit Singh 38, R. Nayyar 63; S. Sadangi five for 71, B. Ghosh three for 37); ervices* 427 for five dec. (A. S. Bajwa 64, K. M. Roshan 50, B. Ghosh 95, A. K. Seth 120, auri Shankar 38 not out; Shakti Singh three for 68). *Services 21 pts, Himachal Pradesh 1 pt.*

At Ludhiana (T), November 28, 29, 30. Punjab won by an innings and 80 runs. Punjab 300). Chopra 35, R. S. Ghai 99, M. I. Singh 34; R. Pandit four for 42); Jammu and Kashmir* (D. Chopra four for 22, M. I. Singh six for 34) and 139 (Z. Bhatt 50; D. Chopra six for 29). *unjab 21 pts, Jammu and Kashmir 3 pts.*

At Delhi (T), December 1, 2, 3. Delhi won by ten wickets. Services 171 (A. S. Bajwa 34, hinmoy Sharma 46; P. Jain six for 36) and 187 (Sudhakar Rao 44, Chinmoy Sharma 63 not ıt; P. Jain three for 61, S. Srivastava three for 61, K. Azad three for 41); Delhi* 356 for eight ec. (M. Nayyar 52, S. Bharadwaj 77, A. Mohindra 54, Madan Lal 80, Bantoo Singh 39; B. hosh three for 114) and 3 for no wkt. *Delhi 17 pts, Services 2 pts.*

At Delhi (T), December 5, 6, 7. Drawn. Haryana* 333 (N. Goel 94, Yashpal Sharma 35, I Chadda 61, Aman Kumar 53 not out; S. S. Saini four for 73) and 164 for eight dec. (Deepa Sharma 59 not out, R. Chadda 30, Aman Kumar 30; S. S. Saini five for 60); Delhi 419 f seven dec. (M. Nayyar 178, K. Azad 100, Bantoo Singh 39; Yashpal Sharma five for 106 *Delhi 15 pts, Haryana 8 pts.*

At Jullundur (M), December 6, 7, 8. Drawn. Punjab 485 for six dec. (R. Kalsi 59, S. Chop 72, Gursharan Singh 121, A. Kapoor 170); Services* 269 (A. S. Bajwa 60, Chinmoy Sharn 101, S. Rai 47; D. Chopra four for 55, M. I. Singh three for 56) and 157 for four (A. K. Se 102 not out). *Punjab 15 pts, Services 5 pts.*

At Amritsar (T), December 10, 11, 12. Drawn. Punjab* 207 (R. Kalsi 41, S. Chopra 4 Madan Lal four for 49, P. Jain three for 73, Ajay Sharma three for 28); Delhi 164 for fo (M. Prabhakar 51 not out, Ajay Sharma 35 not out; D. Chopra three for 46). *Delhi 7 p Punjab 5 pts.*

At Faridabad (T), December 11, 12, 13. Haryana won by 86 runs. Haryana* 237 (N. Go 30, Deepak Sharma 50, R. Chadda 78; S. Sadangi three for 64, Srinivasan six for 39) and 1 (S. Sadangi three for 48, Srinivasan five for 32); Services 182 (B. Ghosh 35, Gauri Shankar 5 S. Talwar three for 46) and 88 (Deepak Sharma five for 32, S. Talwar four for 24). *Harya 17 pts, Services 9 pts.*

At Faridabad (T), December 15, 16, 17. Drawn. Punjab* 579 (R. Kalsi 41, A. Kapoor 7 Gursharan Singh 100, R. S. Ghai 83, Bhupinder Singh 56, D. Chopra 74, Arun Sharma 80 n out; S. Talwar five for 180, Deepak Sharma five for 259); Haryana 139 for three (Deepa Sharma 36, N. Goel 40, K. P. Amerjeet 37 not out). *Punjab 6 pts, Haryana 3 pts.*

In Punjab's innings Deepak Sharma bowled 97 overs, just one over fewer than S. Ramadhi record of 98, West Indies v England at Birmingham 1957.

Delhi 83 pts, Punjab 69 pts, Haryana 64 pts, Services 50 pts, Jammu and Kashmir 48 p Himachal Pradesh 9 pts. Delhi and Punjab qualified for the knockout stage.

South Zone

At Margao (T), November 8, 9, 10. Drawn. Goa 183 (S. Mahadevan 31, H. Angley 54 not ou N. S. Yadav five for 54, Arshad Ayub four for 51) and 299 (R. Pednekar 30, S. Dhuri 88, Revankar 73, H. Angley 46 not out; M. V. Narasimha Rao five for 66); Hyderabad* 2 (Jyothi Shetty 50, M. V. Ramanamurthy 42, Ehtesham-ud-Din Ali 47, R. Yadav 34 not out; Kamat five for 47) and 84 for seven (V. Korgaonkar three for 29). *Hyderabad 13 pts, G 11 pts.*

At Panaji (T), November 12, 13, 14. Drawn. Goa* 148 (S. Pednekar 30 not out; K. Jayakumar five for 65, V. Hariharan four for 33) and 277 (R. Pednekar 38, S. Kangralkar 5 H. Angley 77 not out; K. G. Jayakumar three for 73, V. Hariharan three for 68); Kerala 2 (Narayanan Kutty 31, T. P. Ajitkumar 38, S. Ramesh 48; S. Pednekar four for 51) and 35 f no wkt. *Kerala 12 pts, Goa 7 pts.*

At Gulbarga (T), November 22, 23, 24. Karnataka won by an innings and 47 runs. Goa 1 (A. R. Bhat three for 55, Sanath Kumar five for 37) and 314 (S. Kangralkar 108, Mahadevan 83; A. R. Bhat three for 96, Sanath Kumar seven for 81); Karnataka* 525 for s dec. (S. M. H. Kirmani 106, P. Ramesh Rao 36, B. P. Patel 144, R. M. H. Binny 101 not o K. Jeswant 71 not out). *Karnataka 22 pts, Goa 3 pts.*

At Hyderabad (T), December 5, 6, 7. Drawn. Andhra 416 (M. F. Rehman 39, A. R. Kh 91, V. Chamundeswarnath 54, J. K. Ghiya 91; R. Yadav three for 101) and 219 for sev (A. R. Khan 35, G. A. Pratapkumar 74; K. A. Qayyum three for 17); Hyderabad* 445 for s dec. (A. Azeem 32, M. Azharuddin 61, K. A. Qayyum 76, V. Jaisimha 42, M. V. Narasim Rao 64, Ehtesham-ud-Din Ali 106 not out, Jyothi Shetty 33 not out). *Hyderabad 14 pts, Andh 9 pts.*

At Raichur (T), December 5, 6, 7. Drawn. Karnataka 445 for nine dec. (M. Srinivasaprasad 31, G. R. Viswanath 35, B. P. Patel 124, R. M. H. Binny 78, K. Jeswant not out) and 263 for six dec. (C. Saldanha 60, S. M. H. Kirmani 33 not out, B. P. Patel 46 n out, S. Viswanath 48); Kerala* 340 (S. Santosh 52, S. Rajesh 70, S. Ramesh 69; A. R. Bh five for 126) and 6 for no wkt. *Karnataka 15 pts, Kerala 11 pts.*

At Salem (M), December 12, 13, 14. Tamil Nadu won by seven wickets. Kerala 170 (Robin ıgh five for 44) and 113 (T. C. Sudeesh 42 not out; Robin Singh six for 28); Tamil Nadu* 5 (P. C. Prakash 36, L. Sivaramakrishnan 30; K. G. Jayakumar five for 62) and 101 for ·ee (V. B. Chandrasekhar 45 not out; V. Hariharan three for 44). *Tamil Nadu 17 pts, rala 6 pts.*

At Visakhapatnam (M), December 12, 13, 14. Drawn. Goa 303 (S. Shinde 57, S. Dhuri 57, Bangera 37, S. Pednekar 44; B. S. Mangesh five for 72) and 214 for nine dec. (D. Bangera not out; S. Krishnamohan six for 80); Andhra* 326 for nine dec. (M. F. Rehman 86, V. S. D. Kamaraju 61, J. K. Ghiya 58; S. Pednekar four for 77) and 34 for no wkt. *Andhra pts, Goa 11 pts.*

At Secunderabad (T), December 12, 13, 14. Drawn. Hyderabad* 417 (A. Azeem 33, Arun ul 71, K. A. Qayyum 76, V. Jaisimha 59, M. V. Narasimha Rao 81; A. R. Bhat four for 3, K. Jeswant five for 92); Karnataka 158 (S. M. H. Kirmani 47, G. R. Viswanath 41; N. S. dav four for 32, L. Venkatapathy Raju four for 34) and 204 for seven (M. R. nivasaprasad 32, C. Saldanha 31, B. P. Patel 43, S. Viswanath 46 not out; N. S. Yadav ·ee for 55, L. Venkatapathy Raju three for 33). *Hyderabad 15 pts, Karnataka 6 pts.*

At Guntur (M), December 19, 20, 21. Tamil Nadu won by an innings and 82 runs. Andhra 5 (K. V. S. D. Kamaraju 41; B. Arun four for 62, S. Vasudevan four for 11) and 159 (K. B. mamurthy 39 not out; L. Sivaramakrishnan three for 43, M. Venkatramana three for 14); mil Nadu* 357 (V. B. Chandrasekhar 48, U. R. Radhakrishnan 64, P. C. Prakash 47 not :, R. Madhavan 30, D. Girish 87; B. S. Mangesh five for 129, J. K. Ghiya four for 110). *mil Nadu 23 pts, Andhra 3 pts.*

At Erode (M), December 27, 28, 29. Tamil Nadu won by an innings and 91 runs. Tamil ıdu 458 for eight dec. (U. R. Radhakrishnan 40, W. V. Raman 86, L. Sivaramakrishnan 4, Robin Singh 107 not out; N. Vernekar three for 80); Goa* 144 (C. Ashok 47; K. unkumar three for 41) and 223 (D. Bangera 36, C. Ashok 46, H. Angle 46 not out; M. nkatramana three for 44, L. Sivaramakrishnan three for 68). *Tamil Nadu 23 pts, Goa 2 pts.*

At Kottayam (M), January 2, 3, 4. Drawn. Kerala 191 (T. C. Sudeesh 70, K. Jayaraman 37; S. Mangesh four for 69, J. K. Ghiya three for 73) and 327 for eight (Narayanan Kutty 102, C. Sudeesh 31, T. P. Ajitkumar 58, S. Ramesh 53; B. S. Mangesh three for 75); Andhra* 4 (L. K. Adiseshu 46, M. F. Rehman 115, V. Chamundeswarnath 80 not out; S. Santosh ır for 87). *Andhra 13 pts, Kerala 7 pts.*

At Madras (T), January 2, 3, 4. Drawn. Tamil Nadu* 411 (V. B. Chandrasekhar 83, U. R. dhakrishnan 37, P. C. Prakash 42, L. Sivaramakrishnan 44, Robin Singh 101 not out, D. rish 54; L. Venkatapathy Raju five for 93) and 64 for one (V. B. Chandrasekhar 33, C. S. ·eshkumar 30 not out); Hyderabad 429 for four dec. (Jyothi Shetty 113. A. Azeem 93, K. A. yyum 30, V. Jaisimha 83 not out, M. V. Narasimha Rao 40 not out; B. Arun three for 105). *derabad 11 pts, Tamil Nadu 7 pts.*

At Kottayam (M), January 7, 8, 9. Hyderabad won by nine wickets. Kerala 161 (T. Mathew V. Hariharan 35 not out; L. Venkatapathy Raju six for 52) and 230 (T. Mathew 80, S. mesh 34; N. S. Yadav five for 73, M. V. Narasimha Rao three for 75); Hyderabad* 309 (A. eem 71, Arun Paul 79, K. A. Qayyum 50, L. Venkatapathy Raju 33; K. G. Jayakumar four 102, S. Santosh three for 97) and 85 for one (A. Azeem 58 not out). *Hyderabad 16 pts, rala 5 pts.*

At Bangalore (T), January 8, 9, 10. Karnataka won by 67 runs. Karnataka* 253 (C. danha 38, G. R. Viswanath 37, K. Jeswant 45 not out; M. Venkatramana six for 107) and (S. M. H. Kirmani 30; S. Vasudevan six for 30); Tamil Nadu 156 (B. Arun 36; A. R. Bhat ht for 43) and 124 (U. R. Radhakrishnan 36; A. R. Bhat seven for 41). *Karnataka 19 pts, mil Nadu 9 pts.*

At Kurnool (M), January 17, 18, 19. Drawn. Karnataka 413 for nine dec. (C. Saldanha 92, mesh Rao 43, R. M. H. Binny 67, B. P. Patel 100 not out, K. Jeswant 58; J. K. Ghiya four 95) and 267 for seven dec. (C. Saldanha 45, S. Viswanath 83); Andhra* 290 (L. K. iseshu 75, V. Chamundeswarnath 76; H. Surendra three for 69) and 42 for one (L. K. iseshu 34 not out). *Karnataka 16 pts, Andhra 11 pts.*

mil Nadu 79 pts, Karnataka 78 pts, Hyderabad 69 pts, Andhra 53 pts, Kerala 41 pts, Goa pts. Tamil Nadu and Karnataka qualified for the knockout stage.

West Zone

At Rajkot (T), November 22, 23, 24. Baroda won by ten wickets. Saurashtra* 272 (I Chauhan 52, B. Jadeja 39, A. Pandya 34, B. Radia 36; R. Patel three for 70, A. Petiwale fi for 36) and 92 (R. Patel five for 33, D. V. Pardeshi three for 16); Baroda 364 (R. Parikh 1: K. S. Chavan 96, V. S. Wadkar 34, T. B. Arothe 38; B. Radia six for 106) and 1 for no wk *Baroda 18 pts, Saurashtra 4 pts.*

At Narmadanagar (Broach) (T), November 22, 23, 24. Drawn. Gujarat 326 (P. Bhatt 62, Mistry 59, B. K. Patel 61, D. Patel 63; V. V. Oak four for 70, S. C. Gudge three for 72) and (S. V. Ranjane three for 19, S. J. Jadhav five for 18); Maharashtra* 241 (S. Kalyani 98, M. I Gunjal 56; D. Patel three for 66, N. Patel three for 45) and 60 for three (R. Poonawala 31 n out). *Gujarat 12 pts, Maharashtra 11 pts.*

At Baroda (T), December 19, 20, 21. Drawn. Baroda 536 for six dec. (R. Parikh 137, K. Chavan 247, T. B. Arothe 35, M. Narula 50; S. V. Nayak four for 155); Bombay* 451 for fo (S. S. Hattangadi 115, A. Sippy 81, C. S. Pandit 80, Iqbal Khan 95 not out, J. Thakre 44 n out; A. Palkar four for 104). *Baroda 7 pts, Bombay 6 pts.*

At Pune (T), December 19, 20, 21. Drawn. Saurashtra* 356 (K. Chauhan 35, B. Jadeja 3 S. Keshwala 130, B. Radia 42 not out, C. Mankad 37; Azim Khan four for 71, S. J. Jadh three for 79) and 80 for one dec. (S. Tanna 33 not out); Maharashtra 262 (P. R. Pradhan 5 M. D. Gunjal 49, S. Sugwekar 61; S. Keshwala four for 32, A. K. Patel three for 34) and 44 f two. *Saurashtra 12 pts, Maharashtra 8 pts.*

At Baroda (T), December 25, 26, 27. Drawn. Baroda 305 (R. Parikh 57, M. Narula 1(V. S. Wadkar 31, A. H. Palkar 33 not out; D. Patel three for 102, J. Saigal three for 34) a 263 for three dec. (R. Parikh 74 not out, S. R. Gaekwad 65, A. D. Gaekwad 45 not out, N Narula 34); Gujarat* 325 (S. Talati 79, B. Mistry 69, J. Zinto 62 not out; A. D. Gaekwad fo for 73) and 94 for two (S. Talati 46 not out, P. Bhatt 45). *Baroda 16 pts, Gujarat 13 pts.*

At Bombay (T), December 25, 26, 27. Drawn. Saurashtra* 139 (A. K. Patel 50; R. Kulkarni three for 25) and 416 for six (B. Jadeja 43, A. Pandya 198 not out, S. Keshwala 5 A. K. Patel 59); Bombay 472 for four dec. (L. S. Rajput 150, S. S. Hattangadi 186, A. Sippy not out, R. R. Kulkarni 33 not out; V. Gohil four for 127). *Bombay 14 pts, Saurashtra 4 p*

At Bulsar (T), January 2, 3, 4. Bombay won by 82 runs. Bombay* 293 (A. Sippy 111 not o C. S. Pandit 61; J. Zinto five for 102) and 202 for two dec. (L. S. Rajput 112 not out, S. Kulkarni 68); Gujarat 169 (S. Talati 44, P. Bhatt 40; S. V. Nayak three for 55, K. D. Mokas three for 47, L. S. Rajput three for four) and 244 (P. Bhatt 41, P. Desai 47, B. K. Patel 69, Patel 43; K. D. Mokashi five for 39, L. S. Rajput four for 64). *Bombay 18 pts, Gujarat 5 pt*

At Pune (T), January 2, 3, 4. Drawn. Maharashtra* 392 for seven dec. (R. Poonawala 14 S. Kalyani 62, S. Sugwekar 100 not out) and 203 for seven dec. (P. R. Pradhan 47, S. Kalya 30, M. D. Gunjal 43, Azim Khan 32); Baroda 254 (R. Parikh 37, T. B. Arothe 33, M. Naru 36, V. S. Wadkar 59; S. J. Jadhav five for 83, S. C. Gudge three for 34) and 223 for four (T. Arothe 102 not out, A. D. Gaekwad 69 not out). *Maharashtra 17 pts, Baroda 12 pts.*

At Bombay (T), January 9, 10, 11. Drawn. Bombay* 467 (L. S. Rajput 86, S. S. Hattanga 118, S. K. Kulkarni 42, C. S. Pandit 38, Iqbal Khan 49, R. R. Kulkarni 50; S. J. Jadhav fo for 103, S. C. Gudge three for 127) and 11 for one; Maharashtra 471 for eight dec. (S. Kalya 59, M. D. Gunjal 120, S. Sugwekar 50, N. Fadnis 70 not out, S. J. Jadhav 71). *Maharasht 9 pts, Bombay 8 pts.*

At Rajkot (T), January 10, 11, 12. Drawn. Saurashtra* 445 (S. Tanna 89, B. Jadeja 117, Keshwala 58, A. K. Patel 59, B. Pujara 39 not out; J. Zinto four for 120) and 15 for no wk Gujarat 327 (S. Talati 86, P. Bhatt 42, M. Parmar 34; B. Radia three for 61, A. K. Patel thr for 76). *Saurashtra 10 pts, Gujarat 7 pts.*

Baroda 53 pts, Bombay 46 pts, Maharashtra 45 pts, Gujarat 37 pts, Saurashtra 30 pts. Baro and Bombay qualified for the knockout stage.

re-quarter-finals

: Varanasi (T), February 12, 13, 14, 15. Uttar Pradesh were declared the winners on the toss a coin. Owing to the loss of 904 minutes' play, because of rain and bad light, Baroda were able to complete their first innings, and as they had lost no wickets it was not considered ssible to apply the quotient rule. Baroda's appeal against this decision was rejected by the CCI. Uttar Pradesh* 301 (V. S. Yadav 95, S. Chaturvedi 57, K. K. Sharma 40); Baroda 7 for wkt.

At Bombay (T), February 12, 13, 14, 15. Drawn. Bombay were declared winners by virtue their first-innings lead. Bombay* 408 (L. S. Rajput 139, S. V. Manjrekar 80, S. V. Nayak ; A. R. Bhat three for 158, K. Jeswant five for 60) and 137 for four (S. V. Manjrekar 50 not t); Karnataka 396 (C. Saldanha 144, B. P. Patel 91, K. Jeswant 45; A. Kher three for 68, . D. Mokashi four for 71).

uarter-finals

: Delhi (T), February 27, 28, 29, March 1. Drawn. Railways were declared winners by virtue their first-innings lead. Railways* 483 for four dec. (P. Karkera 110, Yusuf Ali Khan 68, N. iuri 49, D. Arora 113, K. B. Kala 119 not out) and 49 for no wkt (P. Bhatnagar 30 not out); har 320 (A. Dayal 36, S. S. Karim 114; K. Bharatan three for 30).

At Chandigarh (T), February 27, 28, 29, March 1. Drawn. Punjab were declared winners by rtue of their quotient of 97.75 compared with Bengal's quotient of 69.00. Bengal* 414 for six c. (I. B. Roy 54, Arun Lal 205, A. Malhotra 48, J. Mukherjee 42 not out, S. Banerjee 45); injab 391 for four (A. Kapoor 73, N. S. Sidhu 66, Gursharan Singh 132 not out, D. Chopra).

At Madras (T), February 29, March 1, 2, 3. Drawn. Tamil Nadu were declared winners by rtue of their first-innings lead. Tamil Nadu* 578 (V. B. Chandrasekhar 160, W. V. Raman , P. C. Prakash 45, L. Sivaramakrishnan 124, D. Girish 40; K. K. Sharma three for 114, P. Singh three for 158) and 493 for eight dec. (K. Srikkanth 58, W. V. Raman 182, P. C. akash 45, V. Sivaramakrishnan 68, M. Venkatramana 48; K. L. Tajwani three for 167, . A. Ansari four for 171); Uttar Pradesh 190 (Indrapal Singh 41; M. Venkatramana five for) and 31 for no wkt.

At Delhi (T), February 27, 28, 29, March 1. Drawn. Delhi were declared winners by virtue their first-innings lead. Bombay 329 (S. V. Manjrekar 49, S. V. Nayak 42, R. J. Shastri 94; njeev Sharma five for 81) and 203 for five (S. K. Kulkarni 49, S. V. Manjrekar 31 not out, bal Khan 34); Delhi* 508 (R. Lamba 242, K. Azad 51, M. Amarnath 32, Ajay Sharma 43, Vinayak 45, Sanjeev Sharma 33; R. S. Lele six for 130).

emi-finals

: Madras (T), March 11, 12, 13, 14. Drawn. Tamil Nadu were declared winners by virtue of eir first-innings lead. Tamil Nadu* 601 (K. Srikkanth 35, W. V. Raman 30, P. C. Prakash , V. Sivaramakrishnan 122, Robin Singh 152, B. Arun 62; Bhupinder Singh four for 117, D. iopra four for 160) and 157 for six (L. Sivaramakrishnan 52, B. Arun 37); Punjab 416 (A. apoor 81, N. S. Sidhu 146, Gursharan Singh 33, R. S. Ghai 88; S. Vasudevan three for 138, . Venkatramana four for 172).

At Delhi (T), March 11, 12, 13, 14. Drawn. Railways were declared winners by virtue of eir quotient of 46.66 compared with Delhi's quotient of 46.00. Delhi 230 for five dec. (M. ayyar 42, K. Bhaskar Pillai 74 not out, M. Prabhakar 33); Railways* 140 for three (Yusuf i Khan 44).

inal

: Madras (T), March 25, 26, 27, 29, 30. Tamil Nadu won by an innings and 144 runs. ailways* 317 (Yusuf Ali Khan 87, N. Churi 112; M. Venkatramana seven for 94) and 248 . Karkera 48, N. Churi 34, K. B. Kala 38; S. Vasudevan seven for 59); Tamil Nadu 709 J. R. Radhakrishnan 30, V. B. Chandrasekhar 89, P. C. Prakash 50, V. Sivaramakrishnan , Robin Singh 131, L. Sivaramakrishnan 101, B. Arun 39, D. Girish 55, S. Vasudevan 30; yder Ali three for 139).

RANJI TROPHY WINNERS

1934-35	Bombay	1961-62	Bombay
1935-36	Bombay	1962-63	Bombay
1936-37	Nawanagar	1963-64	Bombay
1937-38	Hyderabad	1964-65	Bombay
1938-39	Bengal	1965-66	Bombay
1939-40	Maharashtra	1966-67	Bombay
1940-41	Maharashtra	1967-68	Bombay
1941-42	Bombay	1968-69	Bombay
1942-43	Baroda	1969-70	Bombay
1943-44	Western India	1970-71	Bombay
1944-45	Bombay	1971-72	Bombay
1945-46	Holkar	1972-73	Bombay
1946-47	Baroda	1973-74	Karnataka
1947-48	Holkar	1974-75	Bombay
1948-49	Bombay	1975-76	Bombay
1949-50	Baroda	1976-77	Bombay
1950-51	Holkar	1977-78	Karnataka
1951-52	Bombay	1978-79	Delhi
1952-53	Holkar	1979-80	Delhi
1953-54	Bombay	1980-81	Bombay
1954-55	Madras	1981-82	Delhi
1955-56	Bombay	1982-83	Karnataka
1956-57	Bombay	1983-84	Bombay
1957-58	Baroda	1984-85	Bombay
1958-59	Bombay	1985-86	Delhi
1959-60	Bombay	1986-87	Hyderabad
1960-61	Bombay	1987-88	Tamil Nadu

IRANI CUP, 1987-88

Ranji Trophy Champions (Hyderabad) v Rest of India

At Hyderabad (T), October 30, 31, November 1, 3, 4. Drawn. Hyderabad were declar winners by virtue of their first-innings lead. Hyderabad* 405 (V. Mohanraj 47, V. Manoh 31, K. A. Qayyum 106, M. V. Narasimha Rao 65, Ehtesham-ud-Din Ali 30, N. S. Yadav 3 R. S. Ghai five for 117) and 256 for six (V. Mohanraj 30, V. Jaisimha 92 not out, Ehtesha ud-Din Ali 35); Rest of India 378 (R. Lamba 53, Arun Lal 53, S. V. Manjrekar 59, Yashp Sharma 37, Sanjeev Sharma 50, M. I. Singh 39; Arshad Ayub six for 105).

DULEEP TROPHY, 1987-88

At Jodhpur (T), October 8, 9, 10, 11. Drawn. North Zone were declared winners by virtue their first-innings lead. North Zone* 536 (R. Lamba 197, M. Nayyar 67, M. Amarnath 30, Bhaskar Pillai 129; Randhir Singh three for 139, Avinash Kumar three for 101, Bhattacharjee three for 114) and 216 for three (K. Bhaskar Pillai 103 not out, Ajay Sharr 60); East Zone 241 (Arun Lal 143; Sanjeev Sharma three for 69).

Semi-finals

At Nagpur (T), October 15, 16, 17, 18. Drawn. West Zone were declared winners by virtue their first-innings lead. West Zone 676 for eight dec. (A. D. Gaekwad 195, S. V. Manjrek 278, S. Keshwala 49, A. K. Patel 43 not out, Azim Khan 32 not out; K. K. Sharma three f 113) and 445 for three (L. S. Rajput 275, M. D. Gunjal 63 not out, S. K. Kulkarni 80); Cent Zone* 360 (Yusuf Ali Khan 35, S. Ansari 53, R. P. Singh 79, Padam Shastri 118; A. K. Pa three for 96, Azim Khan three for 61, A. D. Gaekwad three for 39).

At Kanpur (T), October 15, 16, 17, 18. North Zone won by 149 runs. North Zone* 334 (R. amba 114, M. Amarnath 40, Ajay Sharma 35; Arshad Ayub eight for 65) and 283 (K. Azad :, R. Vinayak 88, Sanjeev Sharma 45; B. Arun four for 68, Arshad Ayub three for 62); South one 177 (C. Saldanha 48, K. A. Qayyum 32, Arshad Ayub 33; K. Azad three for 28) and 291 :. Saldanha 36, W. V. Raman 60, B. Arun 89; Ajay Sharma three for 43).

inal

t Bhilai (T), October 21, 22, 23, 25, 26. Drawn. North Zone were declared winners by virtue ' their first-innings lead. West Zone* 444 (A. D. Gaekwad 216, S. Keshwala 60, S. K. ulkarni 42; Ajay Sharma three for 30) and 284 for six (L. S. Rajput 83, S. V. Manjrekar 40, K. Kulkarni 66; S. Talwar five for 91); North Zone 868 (M. Nayyar 66, R. Lamba 320, M. marnath 32, K. Bhaskar Pillai 64, Madan Lal 107, R. S. Ghai 79, Sanjeev Sharma 52 not it; R. Patel three for 86).

INDIA v NEW ZEALAND, 1988-89

ıdia took the series 2-1 with a convincing ten-wicket win in the Third Test, in which New ealand recorded their lowest total in India. The home side also won at Bangalore, where ost of the New Zealand side were affected by illness, but lost at Bombay, where R. J. Hadlee ok ten wickets in a Test match for the ninth time. When Hadlee had Arun Lal caught by . M. Kuggeleijn in the first innings at Bangalore, he became the leading wicket-taker in ests, passing the previous record of 373, which he had shared with I. T. Botham since ecember 30, 1987. He finished the series with 391 Test wickets, having taken five in a Test ınings for the 33rd and 34th times.

irst Test: At Bangalore, November 12, 13, 14, 16, 17. India won by 172 runs. India 384 for ne dec. (N. S. Siddhu 116, D. B. Vengsarkar 75, M. Azharuddin 42, R. J. Shastri 54, K. S. lore 46; R. J. Hadlee five for 65) and 141 for one dec. (K. Srikkanth 58 not out, Arun Lal 33, . S. Siddhu 43 not out); New Zealand 189 (A. H. Jones 45, I. D. S. Smith 30; Kapil Dev ıree for 24, Arshad Ayub four for 51) and 164 (J. G. Wright 58; Arshad Ayub four for 53, . D. Hirwani six for 59).

econd Test: At Bombay, November 24, 25, 26, 27, 29. New Zealand won by 136 runs. New ealand 236 (J. G. Wright 33, M. J. Greatbatch 46, J. G. Bracewell 52; N. D. Hirwani three ır 82, R. J. Shastri four for 45) and 279 (J. G. Wright 36, A. H. Jones 78, M. J. Greatbatch l, I. D. S. Smith 54, J. G. Bracewell 32; Arshad Ayub five for 50, N. D. Hirwani four for 93); ıdia 234 (K. Srikkanth 94, R. J. Shastri 32; R. J. Hadlee six for 49) and 145 (Arun Lal 47, apil Dev 36; R. J. Hadlee four for 39, J. G. Bracewell six for 51).

hird Test: At Hyderabad, December 2, 3, 4, 6. India won by ten wickets with more than a ay and a half to spare. New Zealand 254 (M. J. Greatbatch 90 not out, I. D. S. Smith 79; anjeev Sharma three for 37, Arshad Ayub four for 55) and 124 (J. G. Wright 62, R. J. Hadlee l; Kapil Dev three for 21, N. D. Hirwani three for 43, Arshad Ayub three for 36); India 358 K. Srikkanth 69, D. B. Vengsarkar 32, R. J. Shastri 42, M. Azharuddin 81, Kapil Dev 40; . J. Hadlee three for 99, E. J. Chatfield three for 82, M. C. Snedden four for 69) and 22 for o wkt.

CRICKET IN PAKISTAN, 1987-88

By ABID ALI KAZI

The 1987-88 season in Pakistan started with cricket experiencing a euphori never before known in the country. Pakistan, along with India, was co-host o the fourth World Cup, and the major cricket-playing nations were coming t take part in one of the richest spectacles staged for the game. Ultimatel there was disappointment for both host nations when neither could progres beyond the semi-final stage. Imran Khan, who had said he would retire at th end of the competition, had to take his bow prematurely – after the semi-fina against Australia at Gaddafi Stadium instead of the final, which Pakista had been expected to reach and win. Later, on the insistence of the Pakista people and after a special appeal from the President of Pakistan, Genera Mohammad Zia-ul-Haq, Imran came out of retirement to captain Pakistan i the West Indies in April.

The Test series between Pakistan and England, which began little mor than two weeks after the World Cup ended, was one of the most poorl attended in Pakistan's history. There had been, simply, too much cricket, an the series was further destroyed by the disputes which surrounded umpirin decisions. These began during the Lahore Test and matured in th Faisalabad Test, when a day's play was lost following the slanging matc between the England captain, Mike Gatting, and umpire Shakoor Rana. Thi situation had no precedent in Test history. There was talk of the series bein called off, but fortunately it continued and the English players left Pakista with the promise of being awarded an extra £1,000 each for the "hardship suffered in Pakistan.

Owing to the World Cup and the tour by England, the domestic season i Pakistan was pushed into the background. It had started in early Septembe with the Wills Cup One-day Tournament, which was played according t World Cup rules as part of the preparations for the forthcoming competition

The 1987-88 first-class season was a short one compared with the previou year's, when a record number of first-class matches (126) was played. Only 5 first-class matches were played in 1987-88, comprising the last round of th Patron's Trophy, a shortened Quaid-e-Azam Trophy, and the five matches o the England tour. As during the previous season, it was decided that th group matches of the BCCP Patron's Trophy would not be first-class, suc status being accorded only to matches played in the pre-quarter-finals quarter-finals, semi-finals and final. A total of 37 teams took part and wer divided into eight groups. The first four groups included only departmenta sides, while the other four were made up of city and divisional teams. Tw teams from each of the departmental groups and one from each of the othe groups qualified for the first-class rounds. Habib Bank, with all thei international players present, won the trophy after a lapse of ten years beating United Bank in the final by six wickets.

The Quaid-e-Azam Trophy was originally to be contested by the twelv teams which reached the final first-class rounds of the Patron's Trophy, eac playing the others once on a league basis. However, the number wa increased to thirteen when the BCCP decided to include Railways, who ha failed to qualify, and this meant that on a single league basis 78 matche would have had to be played. To save time, the teams were divided into two groups and so the final number of matches was reduced to 39, including the semi-finals and final. PIA, by defeating United Bank by 309 runs, became the national champions for only the third time in the competition's history and for the first time since 1979-80. United Bank maintained their record of being constant runners-up; beaten into second place in the four major competitions in 1986-87, they also lost all three major finals in the season under review. With the Quaid-e-Azam Trophy not finishing until early April, there was no time left to play the BCCP President's Cup and the PACO Cup.

In the shortened season, no batsman scored 1,000 runs, as opposed to six who did so a year earlier. The highest aggregate was 840 (average 60.00) by Asif Mujtaba of PIA. Others who passed 750 runs were Rawalpindi's Nadeem Abbasi (769), PIA's Zahid Ahmad (767) and Habib Bank's Aamer Sohail (763). The batting averages were headed by United Bank's Moin-ul-Atiq, with 528 runs at 75.42. The season's highest individual score was 179 by PIA's Zahid Ahmad, against ADBP in the semi-final of the Quaid-e-Azam Trophy.

Only four bowlers captured 50 or more wickets, as against as many as seventeen the previous season. The leading wicket-taker was United Bank's Masood Anwar, with 67 at an average of 20.04; the others to reach the half-century mark were Habib Bank's Nadeem Ghauri with 65 (average 16.87), ADBP's Khatib Rizwan with 50 (average 20.08), and Raja Sarfraz of Rawalpindi with 50 (average 24.92). Mohammad Nazir, the Railways captain, took 27 wickets in just three matches at 12.18 apiece to top the bowling averages. The season's best innings return was Abdul Qadir's nine for 56 against England in the First Test at Lahore, while the best match figures were fifteen for 122 by Sajjad Akbar of PNSC. Against Karachi, in a Quaid-e-Azam Trophy match, he took nine for 59 and six for 63, in addition to which he hit a half-century in PNSC's second innings.

United Bank's Ashraf Ali, who set a national record with 70 dismissals in 1986-87, was again the leading wicket-keeper with 40. Others with 25 or more dismissals were Habib Bank's Tahir Rasheed with 34 and Anil Dalpat of PIA with 28. The leading fielder was Ghaffar Kazmi of ADBP, whose fifteen catches included four held while keeping wicket.

Major changes were made at the Board of Control for Cricket in Pakistan (BCCP) following the England tour. Lt-Gen. Ghulam Safdar Butt, the president, Ijaz Butt, the secretary, and the World Cup Directorate officials, Yawar Saeed and Tahir Memon, made way for new office-bearers after having staged a successful World Cup competition. Lt-Gen. (retd) Zahid Ali Akbar took over the presidency; the new secretary, Arif Abbasi, had served in the same capacity under the former president of the Board, Air Marshal Nur Khan, several years previously. Haseeb Ahsan's place as the chief of the selectors was taken by Intikhab Alam, the other two selectors being Salah-ud-Din and Iftikhar Mohammad.

FIRST-CLASS AVERAGES, 1987-88

BATTING

(Qualification: 350 runs, average 25)

	M	*I*	*NO*	*R*	*HI*	*100s*	*Avge*
Moin-ul-Atiq (*United Bank*)	4	8	1	528	157	3	75.42
Azhar Khan (*Habib Bank*)	6	9	3	425	73*	0	70.83
Asif Mujtaba (*PIA*)	10	17	3	840	157	3	60.00
Javed Miandad (*Habib Bank*)	6	8	2	358	144*	1	59.66
Nadeem Abbasi (*Rawalpindi*)	8	15	1	769	120*	2	54.92
Zahid Ahmad (*PIA*)	9	15	1	767	179	2	54.78
Shaukat Mirza (*Habib Bank*)	7	11	3	424	108*	2	53.00
Nasir Wasti (*PNSC*)	6	11	3	417	108	1	52.12
Aamer Sohail (*Habib Bank*)	10	17	2	763	125	4	50.86
Rizwan-uz-Zaman (*PIA*)	7	14	1	661	133*	2	50.84
Ijaz Ahmed (*Habib Bank*)	7	10	0	493	125	1	49.30
Salim Malik (*Habib Bank*)	7	10	2	381	95	0	47.62
Mansoor Akhtar (*United Bank*)	10	18	3	649	132	2	43.26
Shafiq Ahmed (*United Bank*)	10	17	1	690	155*	1	43.12
Agha Zahid (*Habib Bank*)	9	16	0	679	162	2	42.43
Sajid Ali (*National Bank*)	6	12	1	457	100	1	41.54
Atif Rauf (*ADBP*)	9	12	1	449	99	0	40.81
Rizwan Qazi (*Lahore City/Lahore*)	6	10	1	364	68	0	40.44
Abdullah Khan (*PNSC*)	7	14	1	520	155*	1	40.00
Nasir Shah (*Karachi*)	5	10	0	382	118	2	38.20
Ghaffar Kazmi (*ADBP*)	9	13	1	455	98	0	37.91
Sajid Khan (*Karachi*)	7	14	1	489	131	2	37.61
Anwar-ul-Haq (*MCB*)	7	14	1	487	102*	1	37.46
Arshad Pervez (*Habib Bank*)	8	13	2	403	118*	1	36.63
Zafar Ahmed (*Karachi*)	7	12	2	364	103	1	36.40
Masood Anwar (*ADBP*)	9	13	1	435	144	1	36.25
Mujahid Hameed (*Rawalpindi*)	7	12	2	356	81	0	35.60
Saifullah (*United Bank*)	11	20	1	673	175*	1	35.42
Qaiser Rasheed (*PNSC*)	7	14	1	445	99	0	34.23
Salah-ud-Din (*MCB*)	7	13	2	372	103*	1	33.81
Anwar Miandad (*Habib Bank*)	11	16	4	402	101*	1	33.50
Manzoor Elahi (*ADBP*)	9	12	0	394	103	1	32.83
Raees Ahmed (*Karachi*)	6	12	0	390	97	0	32.50
Ali Zia (*United Bank*)	10	17	1	513	112	2	32.06
Mansoor Rana (*ADBP*)	9	12	0	371	58	0	30.91
Ashraf Ali (*United Bank*)	13	17	2	417	80*	0	27.80
Jamal Siddiqi (*Rawalpindi*)	8	15	1	373	99*	0	26.64
Asad Mahmood (*MCB*)	7	14	0	358	88	0	25.57

* *Signifies not out.*

BOWLING

(Qualification: 20 wickets)

	O	*M*	*R*	*W*	*BB*	*Avge*
Mohammad Nazir (*Railways*)	162.1	39	329	27	8-99	12.18
Nadeem Ghauri (*Habib Bank*)	492	166	1,097	65	7-100	16.87
Abdul Qadir (*Habib Bank*)	293.1	81	648	36	9-56	18.00
Iqbal Qasim (*National Bank*)	312.5	79	769	39	6-40	19.71
Masood Anwar (*United Bank*)	522.3	130	1,343	67	7-53	20.04

	O	*M*	*R*	*W*	*BB*	*Avge*
Khatib Rizwan (*ADBP*)	389	89	1,004	50	7-52	20.08
Iqbal Sikandar (*PIA*)	227	33	615	30	6-50	20.50
Kazim Mehdi (*HBFC*)	179.2	36	580	28	5-48	20.71
Sajjad Akbar (*PNSC*)	425.2	121	958	46	9-59	20.82
Raees Ahmed (*Karachi*)	210.4	39	626	26	6-51	24.07
Wasim Haider (*PIA*)	137.3	10	537	22	5-66	24.40
Raja Afaq (*ADBP*)	374.2	87	980	40	7-62	24.50
Kamal Merchant (*United Bank*)	222.4	58	540	22	4-41	24.54
Raja Sarfraz (*Rawalpindi*)	430.2	83	1,246	50	6-29	24.92
Farrukh Zaman (*MCB*)	277	44	809	31	6-78	26.09
Waheed Niazi (*Habib Bank*)	314.4	47	1,080	40	6-57	27.00
Sikander Bakht (*United Bank*)	184.2	26	743	27	5-88	27.51
Ali Ahmed (*HBFC*)	225	40	712	25	5-49	28.48
Nadeem Khan (*Karachi*)	256.5	42	715	24	5-58	29.79
Azeem Hafeez (*PNSC*)	192	36	634	21	4-50	30.19
Akram Raza (*Habib Bank*)	438	126	970	29	3-60	33.44
Amin Lakhani (*PNSC*)	270.1	55	760	21	7-94	36.19
Shakeel Ahmed (*Rawalpindi*)	315.3	51	993	23	5-102	43.17

*In the following scores, * by the name of a team indicates that they won the toss.*

BCCP PATRON'S TROPHY, 1987-88

Note: First innings closed at 65 overs in the pre-quarter-finals and quarter-finals, and at 85 overs in the semi-finals and final.

Pre-Quarter-finals

At National Stadium, Karachi, January 24, 25, 26. PNSC won by 74 runs. PNSC* 221 (Sajjad Akbar 72, Azeem Hafeez 69; Zulfiqar Ali three for 61) and 263 for six dec. (Ramiz Raja 102, Qaiser Rasheed 44, Farrukh Bari 38 not out, Mohsin Kamal 30; Zulfiqar Ali three for 85); PIA 237 for five (Rizwan-uz-Zaman 38, Asif Mujtaba 98 not out, Zahid Ahmad 49; Azeem Hafeez three for 62) and 173 (Asif Mohammad 52; Sajjad Akbar five for 59).

At Bakhtiari Youth Centre Ground, Karachi, January 24, 25, 26. Karachi Blues won by seven wickets. Multan* 200 (Zakir Hussain 100, Inzamam-ul-Haq 34; Naved-ul-Haq three for 57, Nadeem Khan three for 55) and 239 for nine dec. (Inzamam-ul-Haq 106, Dildar Malik 31); Karachi Blues 223 for six (Sajid Khan 48, Zafar Ali 53, Shujaat Ali 42; Abubakar Siddiq three for 41) and 217 for three (Sajid Khan 52 not out, Raees Ahmed 97).

At LCCA Ground, Lahore, January 24, 25, 26. Rawalpindi won by nine wickets. Lahore City A 214 (Hammad Khan 35, Rizwan Qazi 52, Haider Jahangir 31, Jabbar Rahim 33; Raja Sarfraz five for 73) and 257 for seven dec. (Babar Zaman 38, Rizwan Qazi 51, Wasim Ali 106; Raja Sarfraz three for 88); Rawalpindi* 227 for four (Nadeem Abbasi 55, Jamal Siddiqi 74, Shahid Javed 38) and 248 for one (Nadeem Abbasi 120 not out, Jamal Siddiqi 99 not out).

At Jinnah Stadium, Sialkot, January 24, 25, 26. Drawn. Habib Bank qualified for the quarter-finals by virtue of their first-innings lead. Habib Bank 278 for five (Agha Zahid 45, Arshad Pervez 40, Aamer Sohail 46, Ijaz Ahmed 59, Anwar Miandad 37 not out, Naved Anjum 31 not out) and 259 (Akram Raza 112, Ijaz Ahmed 41, Anwar Miandad 45; Shahzad Ilyas three for 37, Kazim Mehdi four for 86, Sohail Khan three for 73); HBFC* 190 (Munir-ul-Haq 33, Tariq Alam 49; Waheed Niazi four for 67, Nadeem Ghauri three for 57) and 70 for five.

Quarter-finals

At National Stadium, Karachi, January 28, 29, 30. Drawn. Muslim Commercial Bank qualified for the semi-finals by virtue of their first-innings lead. Muslim Commercial Bank* 263 for seven (Babar Basharat 115, Salah-ud-Din 72; Shakeel Sajjad three for 64) and 323 (Asad Mahmood 39, Saleemullah 34, Babar Basharat 61, Salah-ud-Din 32, Ilyas Khan 61; Raees Ahmed five for 96); Karachi Blues 206 (Raees Ahmed 64; Mohiuddin Khan six for 79) and 172 for four (Zafar Ahmed 62 not out, Sohail Shajani 48 not out; Nadeem Yousuf three for 40).

At LCCA Ground, Lahore, January 28, 29, 30. Drawn. United Bank qualified for the semi-finals by virtue of their first-innings lead. Rawalpindi 240 for eight (Jamal Siddiqi 37, Mujahid Hameed 56, Mohammad Arif, sen. 43; Sikander Bakht three for 33) and 278 for eight dec. (Mujahid Hameed 81, Mohammad Arif, sen. 37, Zafar Abbasi 50, Raja Sarfraz 34 not out; Sikander Bakht four for 71); United Bank* 243 for nine (Moin-ul-Atiq 66, Ashraf Ali 55; Raja Sarfraz four for 91) and 175 for one (Saifullah 36, Moin-ul-Atiq 102 not out).

At Gaddafi Stadium, Lahore, January 28, 29, 30. ADBP won by 39 runs. ADBP 203 (Raja Afaq 65, Qasim Shera 44; Mohsin Kamal four for 101, Abdullah Khan four for 49) and 361 (Masood Anwar 46, Bilal Ahmed 44, Mansoor Rana 42, Atif Rauf 99, Ghaffar Kazmi 63; Mohsin Kamal five for 117, Abdullah Khan three for 59); PNSC* 193 (Ramiz Raja 46, Sajjad Akbar 44 not out; Zakir Khan three for 85, Qasim Shera four for 32) and 332 (Ramiz Raja 47, Abdullah Khan 43, Farrukh Bari 86, Mahmood Hamid 75; Raja Afaq three for 77).

At Jinnah Stadium, Sialkot, January 28, 29, 30. Habib Bank won by default when National Bank conceded the match before the start of play on the final day. National Bank 135 for eight (Sajid Ali 41; Nadeem Ghauri six for 39) and 83 for one (Sajid Ali 65); Habib Bank* 288 for eight (Aamer Sohail 125, Javed Miandad 47; Barkatullah three for 45).

Semi-finals

At National Stadium, Karachi, February 2, 3, 4, 5. Drawn. Habib Bank qualified for the final by virtue of their first-innings lead. Habib Bank* 378 for six (Agha Zahid 162, Ijaz Ahmed 125, Salim Malik 40; Farrukh Zaman three for 138) and 568 (Agha Zahid 108, Ijaz Ahmed 93, Aamer Sohail 112, Salim Malik 40, Naved Anjum 52, Tahir Rasheed 86 not out; Mohiuddin Khan three for 137, Farrukh Zaman three for 75); Muslim Commercial Bank 180 (Ijaz Faqih 38; Naved Anjum four for 56, Nadeem Ghauri three for 47) and 244 for two (Anwar-ul-Haq 102 not out, Asif Ali 102 not out).

At LCCA Ground, Lahore, February 2, 3, 4, 5. United Bank won by 348 runs. United Bank 314 (Mansoor Akhtar 132, Ashraf Ali 35; Manzoor Elahi three for 32) and 421 (Saifullah 32, Moin-ul-Atiq 157, Mansoor Akhtar 39, Shafiq Ahmed 88; Raja Afaq three for 127, Khatib Rizwan four for 109); ADBP* 186 (Mansoor Rana 48, Atif Rauf 44, Ghaffar Kazmi 37; Tauseef Ahmed three for 56) and 201 (Najeeb Wahid 31, Atif Rauf 31, Raja Afaq 36, Qasim Shera 33; Masood Anwar four for 41).

Final

At Gaddafi Stadium, Lahore, February 8, 9, 10, 11. Habib Bank won by six wickets. United Bank 230 (Saifullah 34, Tauseef Ahmed 34, Masood Anwar 34, Sikander Bakht 36; Waheed Niazi three for 56, Naved Anjum five for 74) and 336 (Moin-ul-Atiq 134, Mansoor Akhtar 34, Shafiq Ahmed 51, Ali Zia 32; Waheed Niazi three for 80, Abdul Qadir four for 121); Habib Bank* 320 for eight (Ijaz Ahmed 62, Salim Malik 32, Javed Miandad 144 not out; Kamal Merchant three for 55) and 250 for four (Agha Zahid 32, Ijaz Ahmed 35, Salim Malik 95, Javed Miandad 48 not out; Tauseef Ahmed four for 112).

QUAID-E-AZAM TROPHY, 1987-88

Note: First innings closed at 85 overs.

Group A

At Bahawal Stadium, Bahawalpur, February 15, 16, 17. PIA won by seven wickets. PIA* 297 (Rizwan-uz-Zaman 53, Feroze Mehdi 40, Asif Mujtaba 51, Extras 33; Farrukh Zaman four for 120, Ilyas Khan four for 42) and 81 for three (Rizwan-uz-Zaman 31, Feroze Mehdi 30); Muslim Commercial Bank 104 (Tanvir Ali four for 33, Asif Mujtaba six for 25) and 272 (Anwar-ul-Haq 51, Asad Mahmood 88, Salah-ud-Din 59; Zahid Ahmad three for 52). *PIA 18 pts, Muslim Commercial Bank 4 pts.*

At National Stadium, Karachi, February 15, 16, 17, 18. Drawn. Habib Bank 277 for six (Arshad Pervez 48, Anwar Miandad 48, Shaukat Mirza 44, Azhar Khan 73 not out, Tahir Rasheed 32 not out; Sajjad Akbar five for 84) and 298 for three dec. (Agha Zahid 69, Anwar Miandad 32, Shaukat Mirza 100 not out, Azhar Khan 67 not out); PNSC* 144 (Waheed Niazi five for 53) and 314 for nine (Qaiser Rasheed 99, Abdullah Khan 49, Mahmood Hamid 113 not out; Nadeem Ghauri seven for 100). *Habib Bank 10 pts, PNSC 3 pts.*

At Montgomery Biscuit Factory Ground, Sahiwal, February 15, 16, 17, 18. Karachi won by 312 runs. Karachi 276 for nine (Nasir Shah 100, Zafar Ahmed 76; Nadeem Iqbal three for 46) and 313 for six dec. (Sajid Khan 100, Zafar Ali 74, Raees Ahmed 38, Shujaat Ali 48); Multan* 167 (Zakir Hussain 41, Amjad Abbas 33; Raees Ahmed six for 51) and 110 (Amjad Abbas 43; Zahid Ahmed four for 36, Raees Ahmed four for 53). *Karachi 18 pts, Multan 5 pts.*

At Bahawal Stadium, Bahawalpur, February 20, 21, 22. Muslim Commercial Bank won by 13 runs. Muslim Commercial Bank* 187 (Altaf Sheikh 42, Mohiuddin Khan 33, Ilyas Khan 63; Azeem Hafeez four for 50, Sajjad Akbar four for 53) and 161 (Salah-ud-Din 32, Saleemullah Khan 33; Abdullah Khan three for 18, Sajjad Akbar three for 49, Amin Lakhani three for 42); PNSC 154 (Qaiser Rasheed 46, Nasir Wasti 31; Farrukh Zaman six for 78, Ilyas Khan four for 44) and 181 (Nasir Wasti 81 not out, Mahmood Hamid 37; Salah-ud-Din five for 47). *Muslim Commercial Bank 16 pts, PNSC 5 pts.*

At Montgomery Biscuit Factory Ground, Sahiwal, February 20, 21, 22. PIA won by an innings and 11 runs. PIA* 351 for seven (Feroze Mehdi 163, Hammad Butt 39, Zahid Ahmad 80); Multan 126 (Sajid Waheed 40; Iqbal Sikandar four for 36) and 214 (Mohammad Zahid 110; Iqbal Sikandar three for 50). *PIA 18 pts, Multan 4 pts.*

At National Stadium, Karachi, February 20, 21, 22, 23. Habib Bank won by seven wickets. Karachi* 162 (Nasir Shah 75, Nadeem Khan 40 not out; Waheed Niazi six for 57) and 336 (Sajid Khan 131, Zafar Ahmed 103; Nadeem Ghauri six for 113); Habib Bank 250 for nine (Agha Zahid 46, Azhar Khan 49, Anwar Miandad 30, Tahir Rasheed 31; Irfan Habib four for 57) and 252 for three (Arshad Pervez 58, Aamer Sohail 90, Shaukat Mirza 66 not out). *Habib Bank 18 pts, Karachi 5 pts.*

At Bahawal Stadium, Bahawalpur, February 25, 26, 27. Habib Bank won by ten wickets. Muslim Commercial Bank* 155 (Anwar-ul-Haq 33, Asad Mahmood 44; Nadeem Ghauri five for 56, Akram Raza three for 60) and 171 (Altaf Sheikh 92 not out; Nadeem Ghauri five for 61); Habib Bank 322 for six (Azhar Khan 57, Anwar Miandad 101 not out, Tehsin Javed 44) and 5 for no wkt. *Habib Bank 18 pts, Muslim Commercial Bank 4 pts.*

At National Stadium, Karachi, February 25, 26, 27, 28. PIA won by 145 runs. PIA* 305 for seven (Feroze Mehdi 48, Asif Mujtaba 47, Zahid Ahmad 49, Hammad Butt 38, Anil Dalpat 51, Wasim Haider 41 not out; Raees Ahmed three for 109) and 312 for eight dec. (Rizwan-uz-Zaman 113, Asif Mujtaba 102 not out, Zahid Ahmad 58; Akhtar Munir four for 96); Karachi 181 (Sajid Khan 40, Zafar Ali 51, Nadeem Khan 34; Zahid Ahmed three for 26, Iqbal Sikandar three for 58) and 291 (Nasir Shah 118, Zafar Ahmed 59, Shakeel Sajjad 37; Rashid Khan three for 55, Iqbal Sikandar six for 118). *PIA 18 pts, Karachi 6 pts.*

At Montgomery Biscuit Factory Ground, Sahiwal, February 25, 26, 27, 28. PNSC won by seven wickets. Multan* 204 (Sajid Waheed 76; Azeem Hafeez three for 69, Sajjad Akbar three for 40) and 257 (Mohammad Zahid 36, Zakir Hussain 31, Sajid Waheed 45, Waqar Younus 46 not out, Mohammad Afzal 39; Sajjad Akbar three for 94, Amin Lakhani seven for 94); PNSC 325 for four (Abdullah Khan 155 not out, Farrukh Bari 71, Nasir Wasti 56 not out) and 138 for three (Farrukh Bari 54, Nasir Wasti 53 not out). *PNSC 18 pts, Multan 5 pts.*

At National Stadium, Karachi, March 1, 2, 3, 4. PIA won by three wickets. PNSC* 254 (Qaiser Rasheed 78, Abdullah Khan 61, Amin Lakhani 38; Iqbal Sikandar six for 50) and 335 (Qaiser Rasheed 42, Abdullah Khan 57, Nasir Wasti 108, Mahmood Hamid 45, Azeem Hafeez 34; Zahid Ahmad three for 44, Iqbal Sikandar six for 114); PIA 301 for five (Rizwan-uz-Zaman 133 not out, Shahid Mohammad 31, Zahid Ahmad 46, Wasim Haider 57; Amin Lakhani four for 155) and 289 for seven (Rizwan-uz-Zaman 81, Zahid Ahmad 68, Wasim Haider 52 not out, Anil Dalpat 32, Extras 35; Azeem Hafeez three for 44). *PIA 18 pts, PNSC 7 pts.*

At Bakhtiari Youth Centre Ground, Karachi, March 2, 3, 4. Muslim Commercial Bank won by 105 runs. Muslim Commercial Bank* 254 for six (Anwar-ul-Haq 85, Altaf Sheikh 37, Ijaz Faqih 55) and 126 (Anwar-ul-Haq 41; Nadeem Khan five for 62, Akhtar Munir four for 27); Karachi 155 (Raees Ahmed 79; Ijaz Faqih six for 72, Ilyas Khan three for 22) and 120 (Ijaz Faqih five for 47, Farrukh Zaman five for 62). *Muslim Commercial Bank 18 pts, Karachi 4 pts.*

At Montgomery Biscuit Factory Ground, Sahiwal, March 2, 3, 4. Habib Bank won by nine wickets. Multan* 185 (Tariq Chishty 50, Mohammad Afzal 37; Waheed Niazi four for 53, Nadeem Ghauri five for 47) and 273 (Mohammad Zahid 86, Saleem Sajjad 66; Nadeem Ghauri six for 85); Habib Bank 365 for six (Agha Zahid 32, Aamer Sohail 110, Shaukat Mirza 48, Azhar Khan 65, Tahir Rasheed 34 not out) and 95 for one (Arshad Pervez 37 not out). *Habib Bank 18 pts, Multan 5 pts.*

At Aga Khan Gymkhana Ground, Karachi, March 6, 7, 8, 9. PNSC won by 64 runs. PNSC* 254 for eight (Qaiser Rasheed 82, Abdullah Khan 48, Azhar Sultan 35 not out; Raees Ahmed four for 99) and 170 (Azhar Sultan 38, Sajjad Akbar 51; Nadeem Khan five for 58, Zafar Ahmed three for 13); Karachi 174 (Sajid Khan 46, Raees Ahmed 30; Sajjad Akbar nine for 59) and 186 (Nasir Shah 31, Raees Ahmed 41, Ishtiaq Ahmed 43, Shakeel Sajjad 33; Sajjad Akbar six for 63). *PNSC 18 pts, Karachi 5 pts.*

At National Stadium, Karachi, March 7, 8, 9, 10. Drawn. PIA 245 for nine (Rizwan-uz-Zaman 35, Asif Mujtaba 57, Hammad Butt 63 not out; Nadeem Ghauri four for 94, Akram Raza three for 60) and 280 for seven dec. (Rizwan-uz-Zaman 57, Zahid Ahmad 116 not out; Nadeem Ghauri three for 60); Habib Bank* 317 for four (Aamer Sohail 114, Shaukat Mirza 108 not out, Azhar Khan 31). *Habib Bank 10 pts, PIA 5 pts.*

At Montgomery Biscuit Factory Ground, Sahiwal, March 7, 8, 9, 10. Drawn. Muslim Commercial Bank* 306 (Anwar-ul-Haq 39, Asad Mahmood 30, Salah-ud-Din 103 not out; Nadeem Iqbal three for 69, Mohammad Afzal three for 32) and 212 for five (Asad Mahmood 50, Tariq Khan 34, Salah-ud-Din 42 not out, Nasir-ud-Din 41 not out); Multan 251 (Mohammad Zahid 34, Tariq Mahboob 57, Tariq Chishty 58 not out, Sajid Waheed 45; Mohiuddin Khan three for 72, Farrukh Zaman four for 74). *Muslim Commercial Bank 10 pts, Multan 8 pts.*

PIA 77 pts, Habib Bank 74 pts, Muslim Commercial Bank 52 pts, PNSC 51 pts, Karachi 38 pts, Multan 27 pts. PIA and Habib Bank qualified for the semi-finals.

Group B

At Iqbal Stadium, Faisalabad, February 15, 16, 17. ADBP won by an innings and 46 runs. ADBP 375 for six (Masood Anwar 144, Sabih Azhar 59, Manzoor Elahi 103); HBFC* 210 (Saadat Ali 30, Tariq Alam 37, Rafat Alam 37; Raja Afaq seven for 62, Khatib Rizwan three for 54) and 119 (Rafat Alam 32; Raja Afaq five for 47, Khatib Rizwan four for 44). *ADBP 18 pts, HBFC 6 pts.*

At Pindi Club Ground, Rawalpindi, February 15, 16, 17, 18. United Bank won by 291 runs. United Bank* 279 for nine (Saifullah 38, Mansoor Akhtar 40, Ashraf Ali 80 not out, Kamal Merchant 34; Raja Sarfraz three for 121, Shakeel Ahmed five for 102) and 354 for three dec. (Saifullah 175 not out, Moin-ul-Atiq 44, Shafiq Ahmed 58, Mansoor Akhtar 60 not out); Rawalpindi 127 (Shakeel Ahmed 35 not out; Masood Anwar seven for 53) and 215 (Nadeem Abbasi 88; Shahid Butt three for 64, Masood Anwar seven for 77). *United Bank 18 pts, Rawalpindi 4 pts.*

At Bagh-e-Jinnah Ground, Lahore, February 15, 16, 17, 18. Abandoned without a ball bowled. *Lahore 5 pts, National Bank 5 pts.*

At Municipal Stadium, Gujranwala, February 20, 21, 22, 23. Drawn. National Bank* 200 (Shahid Tanvir 32; Khatib Rizwan four for 50) and 205 for six (Mohammad Jamil 45, Ameer Akbar 36, Asad Rauf 33, Shahid Tanvir 37; Raja Afaq three for 55); ADBP 230 (Atif Rauf 59, Ghaffar Kazmi 49; Afzaal Butt three for 17, Tahir Shah three for 47, Iqbal Qasim three for 74). *ADBP 9 pts, National Bank 7 pts.*

At Bagh-e-Jinnah Ground, Lahore, February 20, 21, 22, 23. United Bank won by an innings and 92 runs. United Bank 306 for six (Mahmood Rasheed 104, Shafiq Ahmed 34, Ali Zia 55, Ashraf Ali 42 not out); Lahore* 95 (Masood Anwar six for 29) and 119 (Bari Raza 38; Sajid Bashir three for 43, Masood Anwar five for 39). *United Bank 18 pts, Lahore 3 pts.*

At Pindi Club Ground, Rawalpindi, February 20, 21, 22, 23. Drawn. HBFC* 261 for six (Munir-ul-Haq 42, Tariq Alam 93, Sagheer Abbas 52, Rafat Alam 31 not out) and 22 for two; Rawalpindi 192 (Nadeem Abbasi 36, Mohammad Arif, sen. 33; Ali Ahmed three for 65, Kazim Mehdi five for 59). *HBFC 10 pts, Rawalpindi 5 pts.*

At Pindi Club Ground, Rawalpindi, February 25, 26. National Bank won by ten wickets. Railways* 146 (Pervez Shah 31 not out; Iqbal Qasim five for 56, Hafeez-ur-Rehman five for 57) and 134 (Barkatullah three for 46, Hafeez-ur-Rehman four for 35); National Bank 257 (Sajid Ali 63, Saeed Azad 96; Mohammad Nazir eight for 99) and 24 for no wicket. *National Bank 18 pts, Railways 4 pts.*

At Municipal Stadium, Gujranwala, February 25, 26, 27, 28. Drawn. Lahore* 250 for nine (Salman Ahmed 32, Saleem Raza 30, Hammad Khan 88 not out, Rizwan Qazi 34; Raja Afaq three for 79) and 229 for eight (Saleem Raza 71, Salman Ahmed 39; Raja Afaq three for 93, Qasim Shera four for 19); ADBP 360 (Masood Anwar 33, Atif Rauf 86, Manzoor Elahi 87, Raja Afaq 35; Babar Zaman six for 119). *ADBP 10 pts, Lahore 8 pts.*

At Iqbal Stadium, Faisalabad, February 25, 26, 27, 28. United Bank won by 214 runs. United Bank* 293 (Mansoor Akhtar 116, Sajid Bashir 50; Kazim Mehdi five for 79) and 231 for nine dec. (Mansoor Akhtar 31, Saifullah 61, Shafiq Ahmed 54, Ali Zia 36; Mohinder Kumar three for 47, Kazim Mehdi three for 75); HBFC 150 (Saadat Ali 36, Shahid Saeed 30; Masood Anwar three for 31) and 160 (Shahid Saeed 30, Munir-ul-Haq 46; Masood Anwar three for 72). *United Bank 18 pts, HBFC 5 pts.*

At Iqbal Stadium, Faisalabad, March 2, 3, 4. HBFC won by 30 runs. HBFC* 231 (Saleem Taj 81, Tariq Alam 48; Mohammad Nazir seven for 66) and 82 (Mohammad Nazir six for 24, Sajid Bokhari three for 19); Railways 180 (Abid Sarwar 33, Shakeel Ahmed 43; Ali Ahmed four for 69; Kazim Mehdi four for 44) and 103 (Abid Sarwar 39; Kazim Mehdi five for 48, Sohail Khan four for 13). *HBFC 17 pts, Railways 6 pts.*

At Gaddafi Stadium, Lahore, March 2, 3, 4, 5. Drawn. National Bank 293 (Sajid Ali 100, Ameer Akbar 53, Extras 40; Masood Anwar five for 121, Kamal Merchant four for 74) and 296 for nine dec. (Sajid Ali 53, Ameer Akbar 36, Shahid Tanvir 67; Ali Zia three for 59, Masood Anwar three for 86); United Bank* 299 for nine (Saifullah 58, Shafiq Ahmed 75, Saeed Anwar 37, Kamal Merchant 50 not out; Iqbal Qasim three for 51) and 154 for five (Saifullah 38, Shafiq Ahmed 40, Saeed Anwar 34 not out). *United Bank 10 pts, National Bank 8 pts.*

At Pindi Club Ground, Rawalpindi, March 2, 3, 4, 5. ADBP won by 145 runs. ADBP* 276 (Masood Anwar 38, Najeeb Wahid 36, Mansoor Rana 50, Ghaffar Kazmi 67; Raja Sarfraz five for 92) and 214 (Raja Afaq 60 not out; Raja Sarfraz five for 68); Rawalpindi 133 (Nadeem Abbasi 44, Raja Sarfraz 30; Khatib Rizwan seven for 52) and 212 (Shiraz Khan 46; Raja Afaq four for 70, Khatib Rizwan four for 63). *ADBP 18 pts, Rawalpindi 4 pts.*

At Gaddafi Stadium, Lahore, March 8, 9, 10, 11. Drawn. ADBP 288 for eight (Bilal Ahmed 65, Atif Rauf 69, Mansoor Rana 37; Masood Anwar five for 86); United Bank* 122 for four (Mansoor Akhtar 43 not out, Ali Zia 30 not out; Manzoor Elahi three for 53). *ADBP 6 pts, United Bank 4 pts.*

At Iqbal Stadium, Faisalabad, March 8, 9, 10, 11. Drawn. National Bank* 199 (Sajid Ali 31, Shahid Tanvir 34, Hafeez-ur-Rehman 33 not out; Ali Ahmed five for 77) and 69 for three (Shahid Tanvir 47; Mohinder Kumar three for 29); HBFC 254 for nine (Shahid Saeed 38, Rafat Alam 30, Sagheer Abbas 82 not out; Barkatullah three for 85). *HBFC 10 pts, National Bank 6 pts.*

At Bagh-e-Jinnah Ground, Lahore, March 8, 9, 10, 11. Drawn. Lahore 56 for one (Saleem Raza 37); Railways* did not bat. *No points were awarded.*

At Bagh-e-Jinnah Ground, Lahore, March 14, 15, 16. HBFC won by an innings and 34 runs. Lahore 112 (Mohinder Kumar four for 50, Shahzad Ilyas four for 30) and 155 (Rizwan Qazi 37, Haroon Rashid 51; Ali Ahmed five for 49); HBFC* 301 for five (Pervez Akhtar 45, Saleem Taj 120, Sagheer Abbas 51 not out). *HBFC 18 pts, Lahore 3 pts.*

At Gaddafi Stadium, Lahore, March 14, 15, 16. ADBP won by nine wickets. Railways 134 (Shakeel Ahmed 58; Manzoor Elahi three for 41, Asif Faridi three for 34, Khatib Rizwan four for 30) and 295 (Musleh-ud-Din 56, Abid Sarwar 110; Khatib Rizwan five for 103, Raja Afaq three for 85); ADBP* 264 (Ghaffar Kazmi 98, Manzoor Elahi 64; Musleh-ud-Din three for 73, Kifayat Hussain four for 82, Pervez Shah three for 72) and 166 for one (Masood Anwar 79 not out, Ghaffar Kazmi 71 not out). *ADBP 18 pts, Railways 4 pts.*

At Pindi Club Ground, Rawalpindi, March 14, 15, 16, 17. Drawn. National Bank* 159 (Tahir Shah 81; Raja Sarfraz five for 68, Mohammad Arif, sen. four for 43) and 216 for four dec. (Saleem Pervez 72, Sajid Ali 37, Ameer Akbar 49); Rawalpindi 113 (Shahid Javed 33 not out; Iqbal Qasim six for 40) and 255 for nine (Nadeem Abbasi 64, Sajjad Ahmed 49, Mohammad Arif, sen. 49; Iqbal Qasim four for 100). *National Bank 7 pts, Rawalpindi 4 pts.*

At Gaddafi Stadium, Lahore, March 20, 21, 22, 23. United Bank won by 31 runs. United Bank 370 for seven (Shafiq Ahmed 155 not out, Ali Zia 112; Musleh-ud-Din four for 76) and 262 for three dec. (Saifullah 42, Mahmood Rasheed 84 not out, Ali Zia 103); Railways* 230 for nine (Musleh-ud-Din 32, Pervez Shah 44 not out, Kifayat Hussain 36; Ali Zia three for 41) and 371 (Wasif Butt 50, Pervez Shah 136, Babar Altaf 43, Extras 36; Kamal Merchant four for 41, Mushtaq Ahmed three for 100). *United Bank 18 pts, Railways 7 pts.*

At Pindi Club Ground, Rawalpindi, March 20, 21, 22, 23. Drawn. Lahore* 314 (Babar Zaman 54, Shahid Nawaz 100, Kamran Khan 30, Rizwan Qazi 63; Raja Sarfraz four for 119, Shakeel Ahmed four for 118) and 435 for eight dec. (Saleem Raza 42, Kamran Khan 61, Hammad Khan 111, Rizwan Qazi 68, Nawaz Malik 32, Extras 31; Raja Sarfraz three for 141); Rawalpindi 309 for eight (Nadeem Abbasi 70, Mujahid Hameed 79, Shiraz Khan 37, Raja Sarfraz 30, Sajjad Ahmed 55 not out) and 224 for three (Nadeem Abbasi 103, Shahid Javed 101 not out). *Lahore 10 pts, Rawalpindi 8 pts.*

At Pindi Club Ground, Rawalpindi, March 26, 27, 28, 29. Drawn. Rawalpindi 204 for seven (Nadeem Abbasi 63, Jamal Siddiqi 62; Mohammad Nazir three for 76, Sajid Bokhari four for 96) and 208 for six dec. (Nadeem Abbasi 55, Shahid Javed 55, Mujahid Hameed 32; Mohammad Nazir three for 64, Abdul Sami three for 46); Railways* 144 (Babar Altaf 31; Raja Sarfraz six for 29) and 88 for one (Wasif Butt 39 not out). *Rawalpindi 9 pts, Railways 4 pts.*

United Bank 86 pts, ADBP 79 pts, HBFC 66 pts, National Bank 51 pts, Rawalpindi 34 pts, Lahore 29 pts, Railways 25 pts. United Bank and ADBP qualified for the semi-finals.

Semi-finals

At Aga Khan Gymkhana Ground, Karachi, April 1, 2, 3, 4. Drawn. PIA qualified for the final by virtue of their first-innings lead. PIA* 238 (Nasir Khan 62, Asif Mujtaba 54, Asif Mohammad 34; Khatib Rizwan seven for 84) and 554 for seven (Rizwan-uz-Zaman 44, Nasir Khan 64, Hammad Butt 36, Asif Mujtaba 53, Zahid Ahmad 179, Iqbal Sikandar 107 not out, Extras 35; Asif Faridi three for 77); ADBP 183 (Atif Rauf 33, Mansoor Rana 58, Maqsood Kundi 34 not out; Zulfiqar Ali four for 32, Wasim Haider five for 74).

At Gaddafi Stadium, Lahore, April 1, 2, 3, 4. United Bank won by 62 runs. United Bank 250 (Saifullah 55, Kamal Merchant 80; Nadeem Ghauri four for 71) and 284 (Saifullah 56, Shafiq Ahmed 39, Ali Zia 55, Ashraf Ali 30, Masood Anwar 42 not out; Agha Zahid three for 55); Habib Bank* 265 for six (Arshad Pervez 118 not out, Aamer Sohail 31, Tahir Rasheed 31; Masood Anwar four for 152) and 207 (Agha Zahid 32, Azhar Khan 64; Masood Anwar six for 54, Mushtaq Ahmed three for 85).

Final

At Gaddafi Stadium, Lahore, April 7, 8, 9. PIA won by 309 runs. PIA 369 for eight (Hammad Butt 112, Asif Mujtaba 122 not out, Zahid Ahmad 32, Wasim Haider 38; Sikander Bakht five for 107) and 212 (Nasir Khan 37, Wasim Haider 45 not out; Sikander Bakht five for 88, Masood Anwar three for 27); United Bank* 97 (Rashid Khan three for 39, Zulfiqar Ali five for 52) and 175 (Mansoor Akhtar 67; Rashid Khan three for 63, Wasim Haider five for 66).

QUAID-E-AZAM TROPHY WINNERS

1953-54	Bahawalpur	1973-74	Railways
1954-55	Karachi	1974-75	Punjab A
1956-57	Punjab	1975-76	National Bank
1957-58	Bahawalpur	1976-77	United Bank
1958-59	Karachi	1977-78	Habib Bank
1959-60	Karachi	1978-79	National Bank
1961-62	Karachi Blues	1979-80	PIA
1962-63	Karachi A	1980-81	United Bank
1963-64	Karachi Blues	1981-82	National Bank
1964-65	Karachi Blues	1982-83	United Bank
1966-67	Karachi	1983-84	National Bank
1968-69	Lahore	1984-85	United Bank
1969-70	PIA	1985-86	Karachi
1970-71	Karachi Blues	1986-87	National Bank
1972-73	Railways	1987-88	PIA

†WILLS CUP, 1987-88

Semi-finals

At National Stadium, Karachi, September 18. United Bank won by 59 runs. United Bank* 208 for seven (50 overs) (Mansoor Akhtar 54, Ali Zia 66, Ashraf Ali 36 not out); ADBP 149 (47.5 overs) (Masood Anwar 32, Manzoor Elahi 38; Saeed Anwar three for 28).

At Shahi Bagh Stadium, Peshawar, September 18. PIA won by four wickets. Habib Bank 222 for seven (50 overs) (Javed Miandad 48, Aamer Sohail 67 not out); PIA* 224 for six (47.3 overs) (Shoaib Mohammad 67, Asif Mohammad 65, Wasim Akram 42).

Final

At Gaddafi Stadium, Lahore, September 25. PIA won by two wickets. United Bank 206 for eight (49 overs) (Mansoor Akhtar 45, Ali Zia 64, Saeed Anwar 51); PIA* 212 for eight (47.4 overs) (Zahid Ahmad 46, Aamer Malik 67).

PAKISTAN v AUSTRALIA, 1988-89

Pakistan, with their innings victory in the First Test at Karachi, won the series 1-0. The Second and Third Tests were drawn. In the First Test, Javed Miandad completed his fifth Test double-century, each having been made against different countries. Border's 23rd Test century, in the Second Test, took him to fifth place in the list of Test century-makers behind S. M. Gavaskar, D. G. Bradman, G. S. Sobers and G. S. Chappell, and in the Third Test Javed Miandad passed 7,000 runs in Tests.

First Test: At Karachi, September 15, 16, 17, 19, 20. Pakistan won by an innings and 188 runs. Pakistan 469 for nine dec. (Shoaib Mohammad 94, Javed Miandad 211, Tauseef Ahmed 35, Salim Malik 45, Extras 33; B. A. Reid four for 109, T. B. A. May four for 97); Australia 165 (P. L. Taylor 54 not out; Iqbal Qasim five for 35) and 116 (Iqbal Qasim four for 49, Abdul Qadir three for 33).

Second Test: At Faisalabad, September 23, 24, 25, 27, 28. Drawn. Pakistan 316 (Javed Miandad 43, Ijaz Ahmed 122, Salim Yousuf 62, Tauseef Ahmed 35 not out; B. A. Reid three for 92, A. I. C. Dodemaide four for 87) and 378 for nine dec. (Ramiz Raja 32, Shoaib Mohammad 74, Javed Miandad 107, Salim Yousuf 66 not out; B. A. Reid four for 100, T. B. A. May three for 126); Australia 321 (G. R. Marsh 51, G. M. Wood 32, A. R. Border 113 not out; Tauseef Ahmed three for 73) and 67 for three.

Third Test: At Lahore, October 7, 8, 9, 10, 11. Drawn. Australia 340 (D. C. Boon 43, G. R. Marsh 64, A. R. Border 75, S. R. Waugh 59; Abdul Qadir three for 88, Tauseef Ahmed three for 86) and 161 for three dec. (G. R. Marsh 84 not out); Pakistan 233 (Ramiz Raja 64; B. A. Reid three for 53, A. I. C. Dodemaide three for 56, T. B. A. May three for 73) and 153 for eight (Mudassar Nazar 49; T. B. A. May three for 39, P. L. Taylor four for 78).

CRICKET IN SRI LANKA, 1987-88

By GERRY VAIDYASEKERA

Throughout the season in review, cricket attracted much attention and publicity in Sri Lanka. Even cricket in the schools drew large crowds, with interest being generated by the selection of a Sri Lanka Schools Cricket Association side to tour England at the same time as the national team. Given such enthusiasm for the game, Australia's decision not to tour the island in April, because of fears for the safety of their players, was especially disappointing. Furthermore, it left a vacuum as the Sri Lankan cricketers prepared for their tour of England later in the year. To fill this, the Board of Control promoted an invitation tournament, with prizemoney of Rs125,000. Six teams participated, with Sinhalese Sports Club emerging as the winners.

The Lakspray Trophy, the island's premier competition, was won by the 125-year-old Colombo Cricket Club, at one time a predominant European club, who enjoyed a handsome victory over Galle Cricket Club in the final. In Division Two, Sinhalese Sports Club and Kalutara Physical Culture Circle shared the Delmege Forsyth Trophy. On their way to the final, Kalutara won all their matches. Old Anandians, comprised mostly of schoolboys, won the Division Three Trophy from the more experienced Wattala CC, who were contesting the final for the third successive year.

Colombo B, by virtue of their first-innings lead over Colombo A in the four-day final, were champions of the fifth National Cricket Tournament for the President's Trophy. The Robert Senanayake Trophy was shared by the defending champions, Nationalised Services CA, and the Mercantile CA when the weather ruined play for the second successive day of their three-day final. The Brown's Trophy tournament, played to a 50 overs' format for the first time instead of 45 overs, was contested by twenty teams in two groups. Nondescripts won it for the fourth time, bringing them closer to Sinhalese SC, who have won it six times since the tournament was inaugurated in 1970. Nondescripts, captained by Sridharan Jeganathan, also won the BRC Challenge Trophy for 1987.

The Bristol Trophy competition was also altered, with the age limit being lowered to under-23 from the previous under-25 level. The 33 competing teams initially played in four groups on a league basis, which provided the qualifiers for a knockout round. In the final, Colombo CC beat Tamil Union. Ranjith Madurasinghe, the Kurunegala Youth captain and off-spinner, captured six wickets for 7 runs in ten overs in one match; in another match, for Wattala, Priyantha Munasinghe performed a hat-trick and P. G. S. Chandrasiri took five catches and made two stumpings.

In the junior (under-15 and under-17) tournaments, 238 teams played under the auspices of the Sri Lanka Schools Cricket Association. Plans are afoot to form a pool of 30 cricketers from these age-groups, from the provinces, for special training through the Sri Lanka Cricket Foundation. Ananda College, led by the Sri Lankan youth international, Sanjeeva Ranatunga, won the Coca-Cola Bottlers' Trophy, the schools limited-overs tournament, beating St Peter's College in the final.

For the second time, a woman filled the post of president of the Ratnapura District Cricket Association. Mrs Kamala Punchinilame was unanimously lected. Elsewhere on the island, news was made when the inmates of the Mahara and Bogambara prisons played a cricket match for the first time on the open Mahara prison ground. Previously this fixture had taken place within the confines of the prisons.

CRICKET IN ZIMBABWE, 1987-88

Prior to Zimbabwe's participation in the 1987 Reliance World Cup in Pakistan and India, New South Wales arrived in Zimbabwe for a three-week tour during which they played the national side in six limited-overs matches and two three-day, first-class fixtures. The visitors, captained by Dirk Wellham, triumphed in the one-day series by five matches to one, although the games were not all as one-sided as the final result might indicate. Ali Shah, with scores of 50 and 98, and David Houghton were Zimbabwe's best batsmen in the one-day matches, but apart from them only young Wayne James, making his début for the country, averaged in excess of 35. John Traicos and Peter Rawson were the most successful bowlers for Zimbabwe, but unfortunately Rawson sustained an injury at the end of the series which affected his performances in the subsequent World Cup tournament.

The two first-class matches, both at Harare, were drawn. They were evenly contested, but clearly three days were not long enough to obtain a result on the placid pitches on which the games were played. Andy Pycroft played an outstanding innings of 104 from 162 balls for Zimbabwe in the first of these matches, while the second marked the return of Kevin Curran to the Zimbabwe side.

At the World Cup, Zimbabwe lost all six of their matches. None the less, they competed effectively against the three Test-playing countries in their group, in particular in both matches against New Zealand. In Zimbabwe's first game of the tournament, New Zealand scored 242 for seven in their 50 overs and Zimbabwe failed by just 3 runs to reach that total, being dismissed in the last over of the match. Houghton's 141 from 138 balls in Zimbabwe's total of 239 was reckoned to be one of the outstanding innings of the competition. It was generally thought that Zimbabwe were the best fielding team there, and as in the 1983 World Cup, John Traicos emphasised his ranking among the leading spinners in limited-overs cricket. But generally speaking the lack of consistent cricket at this level prevented some good performances being translated into more regular challenges for victory.

In March 1988, a Sri Lanka B team, captained by Roy Dias and containing six others who had played either Test cricket or official one-day internationals, visited Zimbabwe. An enthralling, five-match one-day series ended with the tourists winning the deciding game by 5 runs after the series had been square at two-all. The opening match had set the tone for an exciting series with both sides scoring 145 in 50 overs and the Sri Lankans, nine wickets down, being adjudged the winners as a result of losing one less wicket. The three first-class games played on the tour were all drawn. The outstanding player in the series on both sides was Sri Lanka's Athula Samarasekera. For Zimbabwe, Eddo Brandes revealed the extent to which he had developed as an all-rounder with some excellent, hostile fast bowling and some scintillating, hard-hitting innings.

Encouragingly, during the tour three young players emerged to wi national honours and help shape a new Zimbabwe side. Trevor Penney, middle-order batsman and leg-spinner, had captained and batted successfull for the ICC Associate Members team in the Youth World Cup, played a fev weeks earlier in Australia, and Glen Bruk-Jackson, a top-order batsman wh had scored a double-hundred in the National League the previous season, wa also a member of that team. Darrell Goodwin, a dashing opening batsman made an unpromising start by being dismissed in his first over against the Sr Lankans, but by the end of the tour he had scored two half-centuries agains them. Two other young Zimbabweans, Ebrahim Essop-Adam and Etha Dube, were selected for the ICC Associate Members team for the Yout World Cup, while at home Andrew Flower, Douglas Rogers and Christophe James made substantial progress.

In preparation for the Sri Lankan tour, the Zimbabwe Cricket Unio employed the services of Barry Dudleston, the former Leicestershire an Gloucestershire player, now a first-class umpire, as coach to the Zimbabw side. His expert guidance was seen to bear fruit, if not so immediatel at the time, when a Young New Zealand team toured Zimbabwe for a serie of one-day and first-class matches in September and October 1988. Alwyn Pichanick.

FIRST-CLASS MATCHES, 1987-88

New South Wales in Zimbabwe

At Harare, September 8, 9, 10. Drawn. Toss: Zimbabwe. Zimbabwe 325 (R. D. Brown 46 A. J. Pycroft 104, G. A. Paterson 59; M. R. Whitney three for 67, D. R. Gilbert three for 68 and 106 for five (P. L. Taylor three for 44); New South Wales 404 (M. E. Waugh 61, M. D O'Neill 45, D. M. Wellham 36, G. C. Dyer 35, G. R. J. Matthews 72, P. L. Taylor 105 not out E. A. Brandes four for 143, A. P. C. Lock three for 88).

At Harare, September 19, 21, 22. Drawn. Toss: New South Wales. New South Wales 23 for four dec. (S. M. Small 78, M. A. Taylor 44, M. E. Waugh 42, M. D. O'Neill 38) and 238 fo five dec. (G. R. J. Matthews 41, G. C. Dyer 49, P. L. Taylor 71; A. J. Traicos four for 77) Zimbabwe 169 for four dec. (A. J. Pycroft 57 not out, D. L. Houghton 54) and 161 for fiv (A. J. Pycroft 44, A. C. Waller 39 not out; G. R. J. Matthews three for 61).

Sri Lanka B in Zimbabwe

At Harare, March 22, 23, 24. Sri Lanka B won by an innings and 4 runs. Toss: Zimbabwe B Zimbabwe B 108 (D. G. Goodwin 33, T. L. Penney 47 not out; K. I. W. Wijegunewarden three for 20, R. G. C. E. Wijesuriya three for 10) and 244 (D. G. Goodwin 40, D. L. Houghto 126, D. B. Lake 30; M. V. Deshapriya four for 60); Sri Lanka B 356 for five dec. (D. C Wikremasinghe 69, A. M. de Silva 76, B. R. Jurangpathy 60, R. L. Dias 34, H. P. Tillekeratn 61 not out; L. L. de Grandhomme three for 117).

At Harare, April 1, 2, 4. Drawn. Toss: Sri Lanka B. Sri Lanka B 262 (M. A. R Samarasekera 77, R. L. Dias 39, B. R. Jurangpathy 46, U. S. H. Karnain 35; E. A. Brande five for 76) and 138 for six (A. M. de Silva 31, H. P. Tillekeratne 38 not out); Zimbabwe 22 for eight dec. (D. G. Goodwin 66, P. W. E. Rawson 72 not out; R. G. C. E. Wijesuriya si for 102).

At Harare, April 6, 7, 8. Drawn. Toss: Sri Lanka B. Zimbabwe 231 (K. J. Arnott 64, D. L Houghton 40, P. W. E. Rawson 34; N. L. K. Ratnayake three for 44, R. G. C. E. Wijesuriy four for 83) and 164 for three (K. J. Arnott 40 not out, G. K. Bruk-Jackson 33, T. L. Penne 67 not out); Sri Lanka B 380 for five dec. (M. A. R. Samarasekera 79, H. P. Tillekeratne 12 not out, A. G. D. Wikremasinghe 103 not out; A. J. Traicos three for 76).

CRICKET IN DENMARK, 1988

Of all the achievements by Danish cricketers in 1988, that by Ole Mortensen of topping the English county first-class bowling averages must rank as the most meritorious. In a season restricted by injury, the Derbyshire seam bowler took 34 wickets at 13.64 runs apiece. This apart, fine efforts were turned in by Søren Mikkelsen for the national team in Canada, although a first-ever loss was suffered there to the home country. Reinstated as an amateur, 23-year-old Søren Henriksen, after two seasons with Lancashire, fully justified his selection as captain of the national side.

On the domestic scene, the Svanholm club regained the national title, with Glostrup finishing strongly to take second place and the 1987 champions, Esbjerg, third. Three clubs, AB, Chang and Herning, were equal fourth, leaving Skanderborg and Køge, after one season, to be relegated. For 1989, KB and Kerteminde come up into the first division, the latter for the first time. Svanholm also won the knockout cup competition and took the Junior title with ease. Their young batsman, Jesper Christiansen, who was in the ICC Associate Members team at the Youth World Cup in Australia earlier in the year, was in excellent form. In the Boys', under-15, division the Pakistani club, Nørrebro, were convincing winners, but in the Lilleput, under-13, division Esbjerg proved too strong for another Copenhagen Pakistani club, Albertlund.

In women's cricket, AB regained the title they lost in 1987, beating Esbjerg convincingly. In The Netherlands, the Danish national women's team went through a tournament unbeaten, although the Dutch national side were not pitted against the Danes. A quadrangular women's tournament in Jutland in 1989, involving Holland, Denmark, Ireland and an English side, will give a better indication of how the countries stand.

The Forty Clubs' triangular tournament at Herning, in conjunction with the local club, Dansk XL CC's 25th anniversary, was won by Holland's SGS CC, although they went down rather badly to the VBB side from West Berlin. Herning will host the cricket section of the Masters' Games in 1989. Other prominent visitors to Denmark included a strong Pakistan B team, which contained several Test players, and Bancroft's School, on a fourth visit, as part of their 250 years' jubilee celebrations. – Peter S. Hargreaves.

CRICKET IN THE NETHERLANDS, 1988

For cricketers in The Netherlands, the high point of the 1988 season came not on the Dutch cricket fields but in the committee rooms at Lord's, where, at the ICC meeting in July, The Netherlands won the vote to host the 1990 ICC Trophy, the Associate Members' world championship. The fourth time the tournament will be staged, it will be the first time that it has been held outside England. There will be no better opportunity for the Dutch to avenge their defeat by Zimbabwe in the 1986 final at Lord's.

On the field, the Dutch national team continued to impress. A four-week tour of New Zealand in March produced six wins from eleven matches, including one in an afternoon/evening match against a strong Martin Crowe Invitation XI. At home, Holland entertained two English county sides. At

Nijmegen in May, Hampshire were beaten by 4 runs in the first of two one-day matches but won the second by seven wickets. At The Hague in June Leicestershire beat the Dutch by eight wickets. The Hague CC also witnessed the greatest spectacle of the summer when, on July 9, the Dutch team, strengthened by among others John Emburey, beat an Allan Lamb XI containing such international cricketers as Allan Border, David Gower, Jeffrey Dujon, Sylvester Clarke and Greg Thomas. The star of the show, however, was Dutchman Robert Lifmann, from VOC Rotterdam, who scored a brilliant 121 not out. The match was part of Lamb's benefit programme. Also in July, The Netherlands, under the captaincy of Steven Lubbers, recorded a historic victory over MCC at Lord's. An unbeaten 117 by Cees Ruskamp, of Royal UD Deventer, was the basis of an emphatic nine-wicket victory.

Kampong, from Utrecht, took the Premier League championship away from the provinces of North and South Holland for the first time in its long history, winning fourteen of their eighteen matches. Key roles were played by their Australian professional, Peter Cantrell, who scored more than 1,000 runs, and the Dutch internationals, Ronnie Elferink and Floris Jansen. HBS of The Hague won the 40-over knockout trophy, contested for the first time since the 1970s, by beating Royal UD Deventer in the final. Huib Visee, another Dutch international player, scored 103. Once again, a number of junior teams – in three age groups – toured England with great success, and the Dutch Ladies team travelled to Australia to take part in their World Cup tournament in December. Off the field, Dutch cricket continued to show all the characteristics of maturity, and 1988 saw the opening of a splendid new administrative centre in Amstelveen, as well as indoor cricket schools in Amsterdam and The Hague. – David Hardy.

CRICKET IN CANADA, 1988

The major senior event of 1988 was the ten-day tour by Denmark in July, the Danes' second visit to Canada. Their itinerary comprised six matches in Ontario, of which they won three and lost two. They lost their first match by three wickets to a strong Toronto and District Cricket League side, but followed this setback with three comfortable wins against Ontario, Southern Ontario Cricket Association and the Hamilton and District League. When the first match against Canada at Ross Lord Park, Toronto, was abandoned midway through after a heavy downpour, the second match provided a fitting climax to a fine week of cricket by the Danish side.

Denmark in their 60 overs scored 215, being all out. P. Jensen (25), A. F. Hansen (48) and S. Mikkelsen (94) were the only players to score in double figures. T. Forde (three for 37) and P. Jacobs (two for 31) were Canada's leading bowlers. In Canada's reply, a third-wicket partnership of 73 between P. Prashad (55) and M. Prashad (73), followed by 100 for the fourth wicket by M. Prashad and P. Jayasekera (66), saw Canada advance to 205. However, as wickets began to fall and the overs to run out, the closing stages were tense. Off the penultimate ball of the match, bowled by the Danish captain, S. Henriksen, Canada reached 216 to win by three wickets. It was the first time Canada had beaten Denmark in limited-overs cricket, having lost to them previously in 1979 in the ICC Trophy. In allowing them to meet outside the four-yearly Associate Members competition, the brief tour was a distinct success for the two countries.

Cricket continued to thrive in British Columbia, Alberta, Manitoba and Ontario, and in Saskatchewan there was an upsurge in both senior and junior cricket. In the Maritimes, however, Nova Scotia were without a ground for the whole season and so no league cricket was possible. New Brunswick hosted a festival weekend in Saint John, with teams from Quebec and Nova Scotia attending.

For the first time in many years, the Eastern Canada and Western Canada champions met in a national final when Brockton Point CC of Vancouver beat Guelph CC of Ontario to win the John Ross Trophy club competition. A senior select event, enabling the top 52 players in Canada to gain experience in a training camp, was held in Ontario immediately following the Denmark-Canada match, and a similar event was also held in Vancouver. At junior level, an under-18 national training camp was organised in Winnipeg, with 65 young cricketers participating. Ontario won the Canada/UK 40 Trophy and British Columbia were runners-up.

During the year, coaching and certification clinics were held in numerous centres across Canada. In April, two Test match umpires from the West Indies conducted a national umpiring clinic in Toronto, while the coaching development scheme, centred in Regina, Saskatchewan, had a successful year. Looking forward, in 1989 Canada will send a national under-19 team to England to participate in the eighth International Youth Tournament, to be held at Radley College in July, and as part of the preparations for the 1990 ICC Trophy tournament in The Netherlands, plans have been made to send the senior side to Jamaica and Barbados. – Kenneth R. Bullock.

WORLD RECORD PARTNERSHIP

A world record partnership of 664 runs unbroken for the third wicket was compiled by two schoolboys during the Harris Shield tournament for Bombay schools. Vinod Kambli, a sixteen-year-old left-hander, and fourteen-year-old Sachin Tendulkar were playing for Sharadashram Vidyamandir (English) against St Xavier's High School at the Sassanian Ground (Azad Maidan) in Bombay on February 23, 24, 25, 1988. Kambli hit three sixes and 49 fours in his innings of 349 not out and followed it by taking six wickets for 37, bowling off-breaks, as St Xavier's were dismissed for 145, leaving Sharadashram Vidyamandir (English) the winners by 603 runs. Tendulkar's 326 not out contained one six and 48 fours. Details of the innings are as follows.

Sharadashram Vidyamandir (English)

A. Ranade c N. Dias b Sanghani	42
†R. Mulye c Bahutule b Sanghani	18
V. Kambli not out	349
*S. Tendulkar not out	326
B 5, l-b 3, w 5	13
1/29 2/84 (2 wkts dec.)	748

A. Muzumdar, P. Bhiwandkar, M. Phadke, S. Sinha, S. Jadhav, R. Bashte and S. Ambapkar did not bat.

Bowling: A. Sanghani 22–1–98–2; S. Sasnur 14–0–79–0; M. Walawalkar 22–0–161–0; J. Kothari 7–0–38–0; S. Bahutule 27–0–182–0; S. Saherwala 2–0–31–0; K. Apte 26–0–149–0.

WOMEN'S CRICKET, 1988

By CAROL SALMON

At a time when the cricketing fraternity seemed to be grasping for positive thoughts on the future of the game, the Women's Cricket Association was shaking some of the cobwebs from its administration. The introduction of a national league gave club cricketers more than the popular knockout competition to look forward to. In all, 27 clubs joined the first league, which had elimination rounds played on a regional basis. For those wishing to progress to a higher level came the first county championship to be held in tournament form, and territorial matches were re-introduced after a lapse of ten years. Ruth Prideaux, a former international, became England's first official coach, and she devised a programme which included, for the first time, lectures on sports psychology.

The season, therefore, produced many landmarks, but controversy seemed constantly to be bubbling beneath the surface. It began with the surprise withdrawal of Carole Hodges as England captain, and ended in unprecedented criticism of the selection of the teams for the final England trial in preparation for the World Cup in Australia in November and December.

Following the disappointments against Australia in 1987, an England winter training squad was announced with many of the old familiar faces missing. Among these was the spinner, Gill McConway, a successful performer against Australia in 1985 and 1987. Then came the resignation of Hodges, after a début series against India in 1986 and a traumatic one against Australia. Debate continued throughout the summer over Hodges's successor, and finally the selectors put their faith in Yorkshire's Jane Powell. She had demonstrated her motivational ability when she took her county to the championship, and the North through an unbeaten run in the territorial tournament. But the naming of eight of the successful Yorkshire team for the final England trial in Birmingham on September 11 proved the last straw for a section of the WCA membership. They demanded an extraordinary general meeting to discuss the competency of the England selection panel: Pam Crain (East Anglia), Gail Donnison (East Midlands), Sue Hilliam (Yorkshire), Sheila Keen (Surrey) and Chris Watmough (Surrey). This was ruled out of order by the Executive Committee of the WCA, but the chairman, Cathy Mowat, led an investigation into the complaints. Lack of communication between selectors and players was high on the list of grievances.

In the event, four of those Yorkshire players found their way into the World Cup party, while the selection of seventeen-year-old Debbie Maybury and nineteen-year-old Suzie Kitson underlined a trend that began to emerge in 1987. England selectors now appear prepared to throw youngsters in at the deep end, much as New Zealand and Australia have been doing – perhaps through necessity – for years. It remains to be seen whether some of England's lost international ground can be regained. However, there was no questioning the attitude and appetite of the squad, which had an average age of just under 25. They tackled an intensive preparatory programme with vigour – and mainly at their own expense.

The dedication of women cricketers cannot be ignored. Despite the loss of the customary Sports Council grant for overseas tours – which meant a minimum of £750 from each player towards World Cup costs alone – there was no shortage of applicants for the final fourteen. Lack of finance and the distance players have to travel for fixtures remain the biggest problems confronting the WCA. Of late, questions have been asked of the membership's ability to continue to meet the cost of running an office in London and funding a professional administrator.

But, as it was for all cricketers in England, the abysmal weather was probably the biggest single talking-point in a busy season. The elements relented sufficiently in late July for players and supporters to appreciate fully the wickets and facilities available in Cambridge at the five-day county championship. Only the West Midlands were absent. Yorkshire and Surrey emerged as pool winners, overcoming the anticipated challenges of East Midlands and Middlesex. The loss of their captain, Karen Hicken, with a dislocated shoulder cut short East Midlands' aspirations. Rain gave Surrey a glorious chance of taking the county title in the final at Chigwell, Essex, ten days later. Its interference left them with 20 runs needed from six overs with five wickets in hand, but Yorkshire's all-round strength prevailed. Spectators could be forgiven if above all else they savoured the thrilling performance of Surrey's Janette Brittin, who batted, bowled and particularly fielded on a quite different plane.

The North won convincingly the territorial tournament at Oxford over the August Bank Holiday weekend. Yorkshire all-rounder Janet Aspinall continued one of her best domestic seasons, and on the one occasion when the North looked vulnerable – against the South – newcomers Maybury and Clare Taylor had the confidence to wrest back the initiative and further impress the England selectors. The England Possibles v Probables match in Birmingham was something of a disappointment as nerves played a big part. An innings of 88 off 115 deliveries from Hodges proved the winning of the match for the Possibles.

The England World Cup party was: Jane Powell (*captain*), Janet Aspinall, Debbie Maybury and Clare Taylor (Yorkshire); Janette Brittin (*vice-captain*), Caroline Barrs and Patsy Lovell (Surrey); Jo Chamberlain, Karen Hicken and Wendy Watson (East Midlands); Carole Hodges (Lancashire & Cheshire); Suzie Kitson (East Anglia); Lisa Nye and Gill Smith (Middlesex). The manager was Norma Izard and the coach, Ruth Prideaux.

As anticipated, the annual cricket week in Colwall was affected by its close proximity to the county championship and the territorial tournament. However, eight teams took part in a thoroughly entertaining August week, and the WCA moved swiftly in an attempt to continue the week's attraction by putting more space between the events in the 1989 calendar. Wolverhampton proved popular first-time winners of the national club knockout competition, but disappointingly torrential rain washed out the semi-finals and final of the national league, leaving Somerset Wanderers and Redoubtables to share the first such award.

The wind of change was not all felt on the playing field, for the WCA's Constitutional Reform Committee made far-reaching recommendations on changes of membership and administrative structure. These go before the annual general meeting. The appointment of a Domestic Review Committee will lead to a specially prepared programme to take England through to staging the 1993 World Cup. This will mark the twentieth anniversary of the first World Cup for women, also held in England. The 1989 season sees the first European Cup, with teams from Ireland, England and The Netherlands travelling to play Denmark. England will stage the second European Cup in the East Midlands in 1990.

During May, the death occurred of one of the WCA's founder members, Kathleen May Doman, who was 93. In the Queen's Birthday Honours' List, the WCA president, Audrey Collins, received the OBE.

OVERS BOWLED AND RUNS SCORED IN THE BRITANNIC ASSURANCE CHAMPIONSHIP, 1988

	Over-rate per hour			*Run-rate per 100 balls*		
	1st half	*2nd half*	*Total*	*1st half*	*2nd half*	*Total*
Derbyshire (14)	18.6586	18.5407	18.6006	48.5648	49.0438	48.8132
Essex (3)	18.8134	19.0005	18.9124	52.2925	55.3593	53.8355
Glamorgan (17)	18.6890	19.3054	18.9977	47.4294	48.4779	47.9530
Gloucestershire (10)	17.4212‡	19.1512	18.2336	54.0897	51.6205	52.7641
Hampshire (15)	18.5840	18.8874	18.7359	47.8611	46.3806	47.1346
Kent (2)	19.1351	18.2223*	18.6703	47.6545	53.5184	50.5406
Lancashire (9)	18.7034	18.6491	18.6771	47.7243	48.4642	48.0762
Leicestershire (8)	18.1950*	17.7513†	17.9815	46.2731	49.8134	48.0569
Middlesex (7)	17.8361†	19.2848	18.5495	51.3080	54.7010	52.9732
Northamptonshire (12)	17.8560†	18.5917	18.2383	48.5730	47.0265	47.7751
Nottinghamshire (5)	18.5664	18.6976	18.6298	44.7865	55.5669	49.6199
Somerset (11)	18.1999*	18.5834	18.3799	50.0845	47.8762	48.9330
Surrey (4)	18.1034*	18.5464	18.3017	54.6571	50.2872	52.3254
Sussex (16)	18.6278	18.7233	18.6786	45.8931	49.0251	47.5193
Warwickshire (6)	18.2901*	18.6316	18.4735	46.3334	48.3600	47.3553
Worcestershire (1)	18.5119	18.5865	18.5531	47.6446	53.8713	50.7459
Yorkshire (13)	18.0816*	18.6824	18.3806	44.7744	52.9337	49.3438

1988	average rate	18.9202		43.9340
1987	average rate	18.64		51.79
1986	average rate	18.49		52.22
1985	average rate	18.43		52.61
1984	average rate	16.88		51.82
1983	average rate	18.96		50.68
1982	average rate	19.06		51.38
1981	average rate	18.62		50.86
1980	average rate	18.95		50.47
1979	average rate	19.36		48.37
1978	average rate	19.45		47.53

1988 Championship positions are shown in brackets.
* £2,000 fine. † £3,000 fine. ‡ £4,000 fine. § £5,000 fine. ‖ £6,000 fine.

Note: In 1984, no financial penalty was incurred for failure to achieve a required over-rate, and the figures for that year do not make any allowance for the fall of wickets, which the figures for other years do.

BIRTHS AND DEATHS OF CRICKETERS

The qualifications are as follows:

1. All players who have appeared in a Test match or a one-day international for a Test-match playing country.

2. English county players who have appeared in 50 or more first-class matches during their careers and, if dead, were still living ten years ago.

3. Players who appeared in fifteen or more first-class matches in the 1988 English season.

4. English county captains, county caps and captains of Oxford and Cambridge Universities who, if dead, were still living ten years ago.

5. All players chosen as *Wisden* Cricketers of the Year, including the Public Schoolboys chosen for the 1918 and 1919 Almanacks. Cricketers of the Year are identified by the italic notation *CY* and year of appearance.

6. Players or personalities not otherwise qualified who are thought to be of sufficient interest to merit inclusion.

Key to abbreviations and symbols

CUCC – Cambridge University, OUCC – Oxford University.

Australian states: NSW – New South Wales, Qld – Queensland, S. Aust. – South Australia, Tas. – Tasmania, Vic. – Victoria, W. Aust. – Western Australia.

Indian teams: Guj. – Gujarat, H'bad – Hyderabad, Ind. Rlwys – Indian Railways, Ind. Serv. – Indian Services, J/K – Jammu and Kashmir, Karn. – Karnataka (Mysore to 1972-73), M. Pradesh – Madhya Pradesh (Central India [C. Ind.] to 1939-40, Holkar to 1954-55, Madhya Bharat to 1956-57), M'tra – Maharashtra, Naw. – Nawanagar, Raja. – Rajasthan, S'tra – Saurashtra (West India [W. Ind.] to 1945-46, Kathiawar to 1949-50), S. Punjab – Southern Punjab (Patiala to 1958-59, Punjab since 1968-69), TC – Travancore-Colchin (Kerala since 1956-57), TN – Tamil Nadu (Madras to 1959-60), U. Pradesh – Uttar Pradesh (United Provinces [U. Prov.] to 1948-49), Vidarbha (CP & Berar to 1949-50, Madhya Pradesh to 1956-57).

New Zealand provinces: Auck. – Auckland, Cant. – Canterbury, C. Dist. – Central Districts, N. Dist. – Northern Districts, Wgtn – Wellington.

Pakistani teams: ADBP – Agricultural Development Bank of Pakistan, B'pur – Bahawalpur, HBL – Habib Bank Ltd, HBFC – House Building Finance Corporation, IDBP – Industrial Development Bank of Pakistan, Kar. – Karachi, MCB – Muslim Commercial Bank, NBP – National Bank of Pakistan, NWFP – North-West Frontier Province, PACO – Pakistan Automobile Corporation, PIA – Pakistan International Airlines, PNSC – Pakistan National Shipping Corporation, Pak. Us – Pakistan Universities, Pak. Rlwys – Pakistan Railways, PWD – Public Works Department, R'pindi – Rawalpindi, UBL – United Bank Ltd, WAPDA – Water and Power Development Authority.

South African provinces: E. Prov. – Eastern Province, Griq. W. – Griqualand West, N. Tvl – Northern Transvaal, NE Tvl – North-Eastern Transvaal, OFS – Orange Free State, Rhod. – Rhodesia, Tvl – Transvaal, W. Prov. – Western Province.

West Indies islands: B'dos – Barbados, BG – British Guiana (Guyana since 1966), Jam. – Jamaica, T/T – Trinidad and Tobago, Comb. Is. – Combined Islands.

* *Denotes Test player.* ** *Denotes appeared for two countries. There is a list of Test players country by country from page 85.*
† *Denotes also played for team under its previous name.*

Aamer Hameed (Pak. Us, Lahore, Punjab & OUCC) b Oct. 18, 1954
*Aamer Malik (ADBP) b Jan. 3, 1963
Abberley, R. N. (Warwicks.) b April 22, 1944
*A'Beckett, E. L. (Vic.) b Aug. 11, 1907
*Abdul Kadir (Kar. & NBP) b May 10, 1944
*Abdul Qadir (HBL, Lahore & Punjab) b Sept. 15, 1955
*Abel, R. (Surrey; *CY 1890*) b Nov. 30, 1857, d Dec. 10, 1936
Abell, Sir G. E. B. (OUCC, Worcs. & N. Ind.) b June 22, 1904
Aberdare, 3rd Lord (*see* Bruce, Hon. C. N.)
*Abid Ali, S. (H'bad) b Sept. 9, 1941
Abrahams, J. (Lancs.) b July 21, 1952
*Absolom, C. A. (CUCC & Kent) b June 7, 1846, d July 30, 1889
Acfield D. L. (CUCC & Essex) b July 24, 1947
*Achong, E. (T/T) b Feb. 16, 1904, d Aug. 29, 1986
Ackerman, H. M. (Border, NE Tvl, Northants, Natal & W. Prov.) b April 28, 1947
A'Court, D. G. (Glos.) b July 27, 1937
Adam, Sir Ronald, 2nd Bt (Pres. MCC 1946-47) b Oct. 30, 1885, d Dec. 26, 1982
Adams, P. W. (Cheltenham & Sussex; *CY 1919*) b 1900, d Feb. 28, 1962
*Adcock, N. A. T. (Tvl & Natal; *CY 1961*) b March 8, 1931
*Adhikari, H. R. (Guj., Baroda & Ind. Serv.) b July 31, 1919
*Afaq Hussain (Kar., Pak. Us, PIA & PWD) b Dec. 31, 1939
Afford, J. A. (Notts.) b May 12, 1964
*Aftab Baloch (PWD, Kar., Sind, NBP & PIA) b April 1, 1953
*Aftab Gul (Punjab U., Pak. Us & Lahore) b March 31, 1946
*Agha Saadat Ali (Pak. Us, Punjab, B'pur & Lahore) b June 21, 1929
*Agha Zahid (Pak. Us, Punjab, Lahore & HBL) b Jan. 7, 1953
*Agnew, J. P. (Leics; *CY 1988*) b April 4, 1960
*Ahangama, F. S. (SL) b Sept. 14, 1959
Ainsworth, Lt-Cdr M. L. Y. (Worcs.) b May 13, 1922, d Aug. 28, 1978
Aird, R. (CUCC & Hants; Sec. MCC 1953-62, Pres. MCC 1968-69) b May 4, 1902, d Aug. 16, 1986
Aitchison, Rev. J. K. (Scotland) b May 26, 1920
Alabaster, G. D. (Cant., N. Dist. & Otago) b Dec. 10, 1933
*Alabaster, J. C. (Otago) b July 11, 1930
Alcock, C. W. (Sec. Surrey CCC 1872-1907, Editor *Cricket* 1882-1907) b Dec. 2, 1842, d Feb. 26, 1907
Alderman, A. E. (Derbys.) b Oct. 30, 1907
*Alderman, T. M. (W. Aust., Kent & Glos.; *CY 1982*) b June 12, 1956
Aldridge, K. J. (Worcs & Tas.) b March 13, 1935
Alexander of Tunis, 1st Lord (Pres. MCC 1955-56) b Dec. 10, 1891, d June 16, 1969
*Alexander, F. C. M. (CUCC & Jam.) b Nov. 2, 1928
*Alexander, G. (Vic.) b April 22, 1851, d Nov. 6, 1930
*Alexander, H. H. (Vic.) b June 9, 1905
Alikhan, R. I. (Sussex & PIA) b Dec. 28, 1962
*Alim-ud-Din (Rajputna, Guj., Sind, B'pur, Kar. & PWD) b Dec. 15, 1930
*Allan, D. W. (B'dos) b Nov. 5, 1937
*Allan, F. E. (Vic.) b Dec. 2, 1849, d Feb. 9, 1917
Allan, J. M. (OUCC, Kent, Warwicks. & Scotland) b April 2, 1932
*Allan, P. J. (Qld) b Dec. 31, 1935
*Allcott, C. F. W. (Auck.) b Oct. 7, 1896, d Nov. 21, 1973
Allen, A. W. (CUCC & Northants) b Dec. 22, 1912
Allen, B. O. (CUCC & Glos.) b Oct. 13, 1911, d May 1, 1981
*Allen, D. A. (Glos.) b Oct. 29, 1935
*Allen, Sir G. O. (CUCC & Middx; Pres. MCC 1963-64; *special portrait 1987*) b July 31, 1902
Allen, M. H. J. (Northants & Derbys.) b Jan. 7, 1933
*Allen, R. C. (NSW) b July 2, 1858, d May 2, 1952
Alletson, E. B. (Notts.) b March 6, 1884, d July 5, 1963
Alley, W. E. (NSW & Som.; *CY 1962*) b Feb. 3, 1919
Alleyne, H. L. (B'dos, Worcs., Natal & Kent) b Feb. 28, 1957
*Allom, M. J. C. (CUCC & Surrey; Pres. MCC 1969-70) b March 23, 1906
*Allott, P. J. W. (Lancs. & Wgtn) b Sept. 14, 1956
Altham, H. S. (OUCC, Surrey & Hants; Pres. MCC 1959-60) b Nov. 30, 1888, d March 11, 1965
*Amalean, K. N. (SL) b April 7, 1965
*Amarnath, Lala (N. Ind., S. Punjab, Guj., Patiala, U. Pradesh & Ind. Rlwys) b Sept. 11, 1911
*Amarnath, M. (Punjab & Delhi; *CY 1984*) b Sept. 24, 1950
*Amarnath, S. (Punjab & Delhi) b Dec. 30, 1948
*Amar Singh, L. (Patiala, W. Ind. & Naw.) b Dec. 4, 1910, d May 20, 1940
*Ambrose, C. E. L. (Leewards) b Sept. 21, 1963
*Amerasinghe, A. M. J. G. (SL) b Feb. 2, 1954

*Ames, L. E. G. (Kent; *CY 1929*) b Dec. 3, 1905
**Amir Elahi (Baroda, N. Ind., S. Punjab & B'pur) b Sept. 1, 1908, d Dec. 28, 1980
*Amiss, D. L. (Warwicks.; *CY 1975*) b April 7, 1943
Anderson, I. S. (Derbys. & Boland) b April 24, 1960
*Anderson, J. H. (W. Prov.) b April 26, 1874, d March 11, 1926
*Anderson, R. W. (Cant., N. Dist., Otago & C. Dist.) b Oct. 2, 1948
*Anderson, W. McD. (Otago, C. Dist. & Cant.) b Oct. 8, 1919, d Dec. 21, 1979
Andrew, C. R. (CUCC) b Feb. 18, 1963
*Andrew, K. V. (Northants) b Dec. 15, 1929
Andrew, S. J. W. (Hants) b Jan. 27, 1966
*Andrews, B. (Cant., C. Dist. & Otago) b April 4, 1945
*Andrews, T. J. E. (NSW) b Aug. 26, 1890, d Jan. 28, 1970
Andrews, W. H. R. (Som.) b April 14, 1908
Angell, F. L. (Som.) b June 29, 1922
*Anil Dalpat (Kar. & PIA) b Sept. 20, 1963
*Anurasiri, S. D. (SL) b Feb. 25, 1966
*Anwar Hussain (N. Ind., Bombay, Sind & Kar.) b July 16, 1920
*Anwar Khan (Kar., Sind & NBP) b Dec. 24, 1955
*Appleyard, R. (Yorks.; *CY 1952*) b June 27, 1924
*Apte, A. L. (Ind. Us, Bombay & Raja.) b Oct. 24, 1934
*Apte, M. L. (Bombay & Bengal) b Oct. 5, 1932
*Archer, A. G. (Worcs.) b Dec. 6, 1871, d July 15, 1935
*Archer, K. A. (Qld) b Jan. 17, 1928
*Archer, R. G. (Qld) b Oct. 25, 1933
*Arif Butt (Lahore & Pak. Rlwys) b May 17, 1944
Arlott, John, (Writer & Broadcaster) b Feb. 25, 1914
*Armitage, T. (Yorks.) b April 25, 1848, d Sept. 21, 1922
Armstrong, N. F. (Leics.) b Dec. 22, 1892
Armstrong, T. R. (Derbys.) b Oct. 13, 1909
*Armstrong, W. W. (Vic.; *CY 1903*) b May 22, 1879, d July 13, 1947
*Arnold, E. G. (Worcs.) b Nov. 7, 1876, d Oct. 25, 1942
*Arnold, G. G. (Surrey & Sussex; *CY 1972*) b Sept. 3, 1944
*Arnold, J. (Hants) b Nov. 30, 1907, d April 4, 1984
Arnold, P. (Cant. & Northants) b Oct. 16, 1926
*Arshad Ayub (H'bad) b Aug. 2, 1958
Arshad Pervez (Sargodha, Lahore, Pak. Us, Servis Ind., HBL & Punjab) b Oct. 1, 1952
*Arthurton, K. L. T. (Leewards) b Feb. 21, 1965
*Arun, B. (TN) b Dec. 14, 1962
*Arun Lal, J. (Delhi & Bengal) b Aug. 1, 1955
*Asgarali, N. (T/T) b Dec. 28, 1920
Ashdown, W. H. (Kent) b Dec. 27, 1898, d Sept. 15, 1979
*Ashley, W. H. (W. Prov.) b Feb. 10, 1862, d July 14, 1930
*Ashraf Ali (Lahore, Income Tax, Pak Us, Pak Rlwys & UBL) b April 22, 1958
Ashton, C. T. (CUCC & Essex) b Feb. 19, 1901, d Oct. 31, 1942
Ashton, G. (CUCC & Worcs.) b Sept. 27, 1896, d Feb. 6, 1981
Ashton, Sir H. (CUCC & Essex; *CY 1922*; Pres. MCC 1960-61) b Feb. 13, 1898, d June 17,1979
Asif Din, M. (Warwicks.) b Sept. 21, 1960
*Asif Iqbal (H'bad, Kar., Kent, PIA & NBP; *CY 1968*) b June 6, 1943
*Asif Masood (Lahore, Punjab U. & PIA) b Jan. 23, 1946
*Asif Mujtaba (Kar. & PIA) b Nov. 4, 1967
Aslett, D. G. (Kent) b Feb. 12, 1958
Aspinall, R. (Yorks.) b Nov. 27, 1918
*Astill, W. E. (Leics.; *CY 1933*) b March 1, 1888, d Feb. 10, 1948
Atherton, M. A. (CUCC & Lancs.) b March 23, 1968
*Athey, C. W. J. (Yorks. & Glos.) b Sept. 27, 1957
Atkinson, C. R. M. (Som.) b July 23, 1931
*Atkinson, D. St E. (B'dos & T/T) b Aug. 9, 1926
*Atkinson, E. St E. (B'dos) b Nov. 6, 1927
Atkinson, G. (Som. & Lancs.) b March 29, 1938
Atkinson, T. (Notts.) b Sept. 27, 1930
Attenborough, G. R. (S. Aust.) b Jan. 17, 1951
*Attewell, W. (Notts.; *CY 1892*) b June 12, 1861, d June 11, 1927
Austin, Sir H. B. G. (B'dos) b July 15, 1877, d July 27, 1943
*Austin, R. A. (Jam.) b Sept. 5, 1954
Avery, A. V. (Essex) b Dec. 19, 1914
Aworth, C. J. (CUCC & Surrey) b Feb. 19, 1953
Ayling, J. R. (Hants) b June 13, 1967
Aylward, J. (Hants & All-England) b 1741, d Dec. 27, 1827
*Azad, K. (Delhi) b Jan. 2, 1959
*Azeem Hafeez (Kar., Allied Bank & PIA) b July 29, 1963
*Azhar Khan (Lahore, Punjab, Pak. Us., PIA & HBL) b Sept. 7, 1955
*Azharuddin, M. (H'bad) b Feb. 8, 1963
*Azmat Rana (B'pur, PIA, Punjab, Lahore & MCB) b Nov. 3, 1951

Babington, A. M. (Sussex) b July 22, 1963
*Bacchus, S. F. A. F. (Guyana, W. Prov. & Border) b Jan. 31, 1954
*Bacher, Dr A. (Tvl) b May 24, 1942
*Badcock, C. L. (Tas. & S. Aust.) b April 10, 1914, d Dec. 13, 1982
*Badcock, F. T. (Wgtn & Otago) b Aug. 9, 1895, d Sept. 19, 1982
*Baichan, L. (Guyana) b May 12, 1946
*Baig, A. A. (H'bad, OUCC & Som.) b March 19, 1939
Bailey, Sir D. T. L. (Glos.) b Aug. 5, 1918
Bailey, J. (Hants) b April 6, 1908, d Feb. 9, 1988
Bailey, J. A. (Essex & OUCC; Sec. MCC 1974-87) b June 22, 1930
*Bailey, R. J. (Northants) b Oct. 28, 1963
*Bailey, T. E. (Essex & CUCC; *CY 1950*) b Dec. 3, 1923
Baillie, A. W. (Sec. MCC 1858-63) b June 22, 1830, d May 10, 1867
Bainbridge, P. (Glos.; *CY 1986*) b April 16, 1958
*Bairstow, D. L. (Yorks. & Griq. W.) b Sept. 1, 1951
Baker, R. P. (Surrey) b April 9, 1954
*Bakewell, A. H. (Northants; *CY 1934*) b Nov. 2, 1908, d Jan. 23, 1983
*Balaskas, X. C. (Griq. W., Border, W. Prov., Tvl & NE Tvl) b Oct. 15, 1910
*Balderstone, J. C. (Yorks. & Leics.) b Nov. 16, 1940
Baldry, D. O. (Middx & Hants) b Dec. 26, 1931
Baldwin, H. G. (Surrey; Umpire) b March 16, 1893, d March 7, 1969
*Banerjee, S. A. (Bengal & Bihar) b Nov. 1, 1919
*Banerjee, S. N. (Bengal, Naw., Bihar & M. Pradesh) b Oct. 3, 1911, d Oct. 14, 1980
*Bannerman, A. C. (NSW) b March 21, 1854, d Sept. 19, 1924
*Bannerman, Charles (NSW) b July 23, 1851, d Aug. 20, 1930
Bannister, J. D. (Warwicks.) b Aug. 23, 1930
*Baptiste, E. A. E. (Kent & Leewards) b March 12, 1960
*Baqa Jilani, M. (N. Ind.) b July 20, 1911, d July 2, 1941
Barber, A. T. (OUCC & Yorks.) b June 17, 1905, d March 10, 1985
*Barber, R. T. (Wgtn & C. Dist.) b June 23, 1925
*Barber, R. W. (Lancs., CUCC & Warwicks; *CY 1967*) b Sept. 26, 1935
*Barber, W. (Yorks.) b April 18, 1901, d Sept. 10, 1968
Barclay, J. R. T. (Sussex & OFS) b Jan. 22, 1954
*Bardsley, W. (NSW; *CY 1910*) b Dec. 7, 1882, d Jan. 20, 1954
Baring, A. E. G. (Hants) b Jan. 21, 1910, d Aug. 29, 1986
Barker, G. (Essex) b July 6, 1931
Barling, T. H. (Surrey) b Sept. 1, 1906
Barlow, A. (Lancs.) b Aug. 31, 1915, d May 9, 1983
Barlow, E. A. (OUCC & Lancs.) b Feb. 24, 1912, d June 27, 1980
*Barlow, E. J. (Tvl, E. Prov., W. Prov., Derbys. & Boland) b Aug. 12, 1940
*Barlow, G. D. (Middx) b March 26, 1950
*Barlow, R. G. (Lancs.) b May 28, 1851, d July 31, 1919
Barnard, H. M. (Hants) b July 18, 1933
Barnes, A. R. (Sec. Aust. Cricket Board 1960-81) b Sept. 12, 1916
*Barnes, S. F. (Warwicks. & Lancs.; *CY 1910*) b April 19, 1873, d Dec. 26, 1967
*Barnes, S. G. (NSW) b June 5, 1916, d Dec. 16, 1973
*Barnes, W. (Notts.; *CY 1890*) b May 27, 1852, d March 24, 1899
*Barnett, B. A. (Vic.) b March 23, 1908, d June 29, 1979
*Barnett, C. J. (Glos.; *CY 1937*) b July 3, 1910
*Barnett, K. J. (Derbys. & Boland; *CY 1989*) b July 17, 1960
Barnwell, C. J. P. (Som.) b June 23, 1914
Baroda, Maharaja of (Manager, Ind. in Eng., 1959) b April 2, 1930, d Sept. 1, 1988
*Barratt, F. (Notts.) b April 12, 1894, d Jan. 29, 1947
Barratt, R. J. (Leics.) b May 3, 1942
*Barrett, A. G. (Jam.) b April 5, 1942
Barrett, B. J. (Auck., C. Dist., Worcs. & N. Dist.) b Nov. 16, 1966
*Barrett, J. E. (Vic.) b Oct. 15, 1866, d Feb. 9, 1916
Barrick, D. W. (Northants) b April 28, 1926
*Barrington, K. F. (Surrey; *CY 1960*) b Nov. 24, 1930, d March 14, 1981
Barron, W. (Lancs. & Northants) b Oct. 26, 1917
*Barrow, I. (Jam.) b Jan. 6, 1911, d April 2, 1979
*Bartlett, E. L. (B'dos) b March 18, 1906, d Dec. 21, 1976
*Bartlett, G. A. (C. Dist. & Cant.) b Feb. 3, 1941
Bartlett, H. T. (CUCC, Surrey & Sussex; *CY 1939*) b Oct. 7, 1914, d June 26, 1988
Bartlett, R. J. (Som.) b Oct. 8, 1966
Bartley, T. J. (Umpire) b March 19, 1908, d April 2, 1964
Barton, M. R. (OUCC & Surrey) b Oct. 14, 1914
*Barton, P. T. (Wgtn) b Oct. 9, 1935
*Barton, V. A. (Kent & Hants) b Oct. 6, 1867, d March 23, 1906

Barwick, S. R. (Glam.) b Sept. 6, 1960
Bates, D. L. (Sussex) b May 10, 1933
*Bates, W. (Yorks.) b Nov. 19, 1855, d Jan. 8, 1900
*Baumgartner, H. V. (OFS & Tvl) b Nov. 17, 1883, d April 8, 1938
Baxter, A. D. (Devon, Lancs., Middx & Scotland) b Jan. 20, 1910, d Jan. 28, 1986
*Bean, G. (Notts & Sussex) b March 7, 1864, d March 16, 1923
Bear, M. J. (Essex & Cant.) b Feb. 23, 1934
*Beard, D. D. (C. Dist. & N. Dist.) b Jan. 14, 1920, d July 15, 1982
*Beard, G. R. (NSW) b Aug. 19, 1950
Beauclerk, Lord Frederick (Middx, Surrey & MCC) b May 8, 1773, d April 22, 1850
Beaufort, 10th Duke of (Pres. MCC 1952-53) b April 4, 1900, d Feb. 5, 1984
*Beaumont, R. (Tvl) b Feb. 4, 1884, d May 25, 1958
*Beck, J. E. F. (Wgtn) b Aug. 1, 1934
Becker, G. C. (W. Aust.) b March 13, 1936
*Bedi, B. S. (N. Punjab, Delhi & Northants) b Sept. 25, 1946
*Bedser, A. V. (Surrey; *CY 1947*) b July 4, 1918
Bedser, E. A. (Surrey) b July 4, 1918
Beet, G. (Derbys.; Umpire) b April 24, 1886, d Dec. 13, 1946
*Begbie, D. W. (Tvl) b Dec. 12, 1914
Beldham, W. (Hambledon & Surrey) b Feb. 5, 1766, d Feb. 20, 1862
*Bell, A. J. (W. Prov. & Rhod.) b April 15, 1906, d Aug. 2, 1985
Bell, R. V. (Middx & Sussex) b Jan. 7, 1931
*Bell, W. (Cant.) b Sept. 5, 1931
Bellamy, B. W. (Northants) b April 22, 1891, d Dec. 20, 1985
*Benaud, J. (NSW) b May 11, 1944
*Benaud, R. (NSW; *CY 1962*) b Oct. 6, 1930
*Benjamin, W. K. M. (Leewards & Leics.) b Dec. 31, 1964
Bennett, C. T. (CUCC, Surrey & Middx) b Aug. 10, 1902, d Feb. 3, 1978
Bennett, D. (Middx) b Dec. 18, 1933
Bennett, G. M. (Som.) b Dec. 17, 1909, d July 26, 1982
*Bennett, M. J. (NSW) b Oct. 16, 1956
Bennett, N. H. (Surrey) b Sept. 23, 1912
Bennett, R. (Lancs.) b June 16, 1940
*Benson, M. R. (Kent) b July 6, 1958
Bernard, J. R. (CUCC & Glos.) b Dec. 7, 1938
Berry, L. G. (Leics.) b April 28, 1906, d Feb. 5, 1985
*Berry, R. (Lancs., Worcs. & Derbys.) b Jan. 29, 1926
Bessant, J. G. (Glos.) b Nov. 11, 1892, d Jan. 18, 1982
*Best, C. A. (B'dos) b May 14, 1959
*Betancourt, N. (T/T) b June 4, 1887, d Oct. 12, 1947
Bhalekar, R. B. (M'tra) b Feb. 17, 1952
*Bhandari, P. (Delhi & Bengal) b Nov. 27, 1935
*Bhat, R. (Karn.) b April 16, 1958
Bick, D. A. (Middx) b Feb. 22, 1936
Bickmore, A. F. (OUCC & Kent) b May 19, 1899, d March 18, 1979
Bicknell, M. P. (Surrey) b Jan. 14, 1969
Biddulph, K. D. (Som.) b May 29, 1932
Biggs, A. L. (E. Prov.) b April 26, 1946
*Bilby, G. P. (Wgtn) b May 7, 1941
*Binks, J. G. (Yorks.; *CY 1969*) b Oct. 5, 1935
*Binny, R. M. H. (Karn.) b July 19, 1955
*Binns, A. P. (Jam.) b July 24, 1929
Birch, J. D. (Notts.) b June 18, 1955
Bird, H. D. (Yorks. & Leics.; Umpire) b April 19, 1933
*Bird, M. C. (Lancs. & Surrey) b March 25, 1888, d Dec. 9, 1933
Bird, R. E. (Worcs.) b April 4, 1915, d Feb. 20, 1985
*Birkenshaw, J. (Yorks., Leics. & Worcs.) b Nov. 13, 1940
*Birkett, L. S. (B'dos, BG & T/T) b April 14, 1904
Birrell, H. B. (E. Prov., Rhod. & OUCC) b Dec. 1, 1927
Bishop, G. A. (S. Aust.) b Feb. 25, 1960
Bishop, I. R. (T/T) b Oct. 24, 1967
*Bisset, Sir Murray (W. Prov.) b April 14, 1876, d Oct. 24, 1931
*Bissett, G. F. (Griq. W., W. Prov. & Tvl) b Nov. 5, 1905, d Nov. 14, 1965
Bissex, M. (Glos.) b Sept. 28, 1944
*Blackham, J. McC. (Vic.; *CY 1891*) b May 11, 1854, d Dec. 28, 1932
*Blackie, D. D. (Vic.) b April 5, 1882, d April 18, 1955
Blackledge, J. F. (Lancs.) b April 15, 1928
*Blain, T. E. (C. Dist.) b Feb. 17, 1962
Blair, B. R. (Otago) b Dec. 27, 1957
*Blair, R. W. (Wgtn & C. Dist.) b June 23, 1932
Blake, D. E. (Hants) b April 27, 1925
Blake, Rev. P. D. S. (OUCC & Sussex) b May 23, 1927
Blakey, R. J. (Yorks.) b Jan. 15, 1967
*Blanckenberg, J. M. (W. Prov. & Natal) b Dec. 31, 1893, 'presumed dead'
*Bland, K. C. (Rhod., E. Prov. & OFS; *CY 1966*) b April 5, 1938
Blenkiron, W. (Warwicks.) b July 21, 1942
Bligh, Hon. Ivo (*see* 8th Earl of Darnley)
Block, S. A. (CUCC & Surrey) b July 15, 1908, d Oct. 7, 1979
Blofeld, H. C. (CUCC) b Sept. 23, 1939
Blundell, Sir E. D. (CUCC & NZ) b May 29, 1907, d Sept. 24, 1984
*Blunt, R. C. (Cant. & Otago; *CY 1928*) b Nov. 3, 1900, d June 22, 1966
*Blythe, C. (Kent; *CY 1904*) b May 30, 1879, d Nov. 8, 1917

*Board, J. H. (Glos.) b Feb. 23, 1867, d April 16, 1924
*Bock, E. G. (Griq. W., Tvl & W. Prov.) b Sept. 17, 1908, d Sept. 5, 1961
Bodkin, P. E. (CUCC) b Sept. 15, 1924
*Bolton, B. A. (Cant. & Wgtn) b May 31, 1935
*Bolus, J. B. (Yorks., Notts. & Derbys.) b Jan. 31, 1934
*Bond, G. E. (W. Prov.) b April 5, 1909, d Aug. 27, 1965
Bond, J. D. (Lancs. & Notts.; *CY 1971*) b May 6, 1932
*Bonnor, G. J. (Vic. & NSW) b Feb. 25, 1855, d June 27, 1912
*Boock, S. L. (Otago & Cant.) b Sept. 20, 1951
*Boon, D. C. (Tas.) b Dec. 29, 1960
Boon, T. J. (Leics.) b Nov. 1, 1961
*Booth, B. C. (NSW) b Oct. 19, 1933
Booth, B. J. (Lancs. & Leics.) b Dec. 3, 1935
Booth, F. S. (Lancs.) b Feb. 12, 1907, d Jan. 21, 1980
*Booth, M. W. (Yorks.; *CY 1914*) b Dec. 10, 1886, d July 1, 1916
Booth, P. (Leics.) b Nov. 2, 1952
Booth, R. (Yorks. & Worcs.) b Oct. 1, 1926
*Borde, C. G. (Baroda & M'tra) b July 21, 1934
*Border, A. R. (NSW, Glos, Qld & Essex; *CY 1982*) b July 27, 1955
Bore, M. K. (Yorks. & Notts.) b June 2, 1947
Borrington, A. J. (Derbys.) b Dec. 8, 1948
*Bosanquet, B. J. T. (OUCC & Middx; *CY 1905*) b Oct. 13, 1877, d Oct. 12, 1936
Bose, G. (Bengal) b May 20, 1947
Boshier, B. S. (Leics.) b March 6, 1932
*Botham, I. T. (Som. & Worcs.; *CY 1978*) b Nov. 24, 1955
*Botten, J. T. (NE Tvl & N. Tvl) b June 21, 1938
Boucher, J. C. (Ireland) b Dec. 22, 1910
Bourne, W. A. (B'dos & Warwicks.) b Nov. 15, 1952
*Bowden, M. P. (Surrey & Tvl) b Nov. 1, 1865, d Feb. 19, 1892
*Bowes, W. E. (Yorks.; *CY 1932*) b July 25, 1908, d Sept. 5, 1987
Bowler, P. D. (Leics., Tas. & Derbys.) b July 30, 1963
*Bowley, E. H. (Sussex & Auck.; *CY 1930*) b June 6, 1890, d July 9, 1974
Bowley, F. L. (Worcs.) b Nov. 9, 1873, d May 31, 1943
Bowman, R. (OUCC & Lancs.) b Jan. 26, 1934
Box, T. (Sussex) b Feb. 7, 1808, d July 12, 1876
*Boyce, K. D. (B'dos & Essex; *CY 1974*) b Oct. 11, 1943
*Boycott, G. (Yorks. & N. Tvl; *CY 1965*) b Oct. 21, 1940
Boyd-Moss, R. J. (CUCC & Northants) b Dec. 16, 1959
Boyes, G. S. (Hants) b March 31, 1899, d Feb. 11, 1973
*Boyle, H. F. (Vic.) b Dec. 10, 1847, d Nov. 21, 1907
*Bracewell, B. P. (C. Dist., Otago & N. Dist.) b Sept. 14, 1959
*Bracewell, J. G. (Otago & Auck.) b April 15, 1958
*Bradburn, W. P. (N. Dist.) b Nov. 24, 193
*Bradley, W. M. (Kent) b Jan. 2, 1875, d June 19, 1944
*Bradman, Sir D. G. (NSW & S. Aust.; *CY 1931*) b Aug. 27, 1908
Bradshaw, J. C. (Leics.) b Jan. 25, 1902, d Nov. 8, 1984
Brain, B. M. (Worcs. & Glos.) b Sept. 13, 1940
Bramall, Field-Marshal The Lord (Pres. MCC 1988-89) b Dec. 18, 1923
*Brann, W. H. (E. Prov.) b April 4, 1899, d Sept. 22, 1953
Brassington, A. J. (Glos.) b Aug. 9, 1954
*Braund, L. C. (Surrey & Som.; *CY 1902*) b Oct. 18, 1875, d Dec. 22, 1955
Bray, C. (Essex) b April 6, 1898
Brayshaw, I. J. (W. Aust.) b Jan. 14, 194
Brazier, A. F. (Surrey & Kent) b Dec. 7, 1924
Breakwell, D. (Northants & Som.) b July 2 1948
*Brearley, J. M. (CUCC & Middx; *CY 1977*) b April 28, 1942
*Brearley, W. (Lancs.; *CY 1909*) b March 11, 1876, d Jan. 30, 1937
*Brennan, D. V. (Yorks.) b Feb. 10, 1920, d Jan. 9, 1985
Bridge, W. B. (Warwicks.) b May 29, 193
Bridger, Rev. J. R. (Hants) b April 8, 1920, d July 14, 1986
Brierley, T. L. (Glam. & Lancs.) b June 15, 1910
Briers, N. E. (Leics.) b Jan. 15, 1955
*Briggs, John (Lancs.; *CY 1889*) b Oct. 3, 1862, d Jan. 11, 1902
*Bright, R. J. (Vic.) b July 13, 1954
*Briscoe, A. W. (Tvl) b Feb. 6, 1911, d April 22, 1941
*Broad, B. C. (Glos. & Notts.) b Sept. 29, 1957
Broadbent, R. G. (Worcs.) b June 21, 192
Brocklehurst, B. G. (Som.) b Feb. 18, 192
*Brockwell, W. (Kimberley & Surrey; *CY 1895*) b Jan. 21, 1865, d July 1, 1935
Broderick, V. (Northants) b Aug. 17, 192
Brodhurst, A. H. (CUCC & Glos.) b July 21, 1916
*Bromfield, H. D. (W. Prov.) b June 26, 1932

Bromley, E. H. (W. Aust. & Vic.) b Sept. 2, 1912, d Feb. 1, 1967

Bromley-Davenport, H. R. (CUCC, Bombay Eur. & Middx) b Aug. 18, 1870, d May 23, 1954

Brookes, D. (Northants; *CY 1957*) b Oct. 29, 1915

Brookes, W. H. (Editor of *Wisden* 1936-39) b Dec. 5, 1894, d May 28, 1955

Brooks, R. A. (OUCC & Som.) b June 14, 1943

Brown, A. (Kent) b Oct. 17, 1935

Brown, A. S. (Glos.) b June 24, 1936

Brown, D. J. (Warwicks.) b Jan. 30, 1942

Brown, D. W. J. (Glos.) b Feb. 26, 1942

Brown, E. (Warwicks.) b Nov. 27, 1911, d April 14, 1978

Brown, F. R. (CUCC, Surrey & Northants; *CY 1933*; Pres. MCC 1971-72) b Dec. 16, 1910

Brown, G. (Hants) b Oct. 6, 1887, d Dec. 3, 1964

Brown, J. (Scotland) b Sept. 24, 1931

Brown, J. T. (Yorks.; *CY 1895*) b Aug. 20, 1869, d Nov. 4, 1904

Brown, K. R. (Middx) b March 18, 1963

Brown, L. S. (Tvl, NE Tvl & Rhod.) b Nov. 24, 1910, d Sept. 1, 1983

Brown, R. D. (Zimb.) b March 11, 1951

Brown, S. M. (Middx) b Dec. 8, 1917, d Dec. 28, 1987

Brown, V. R. (Cant.) b Nov. 3, 1959

Brown, W. A. (NSW & Qld; *CY 1939*) b July 31, 1912

Brown, W. C. (Northants) b Nov. 13, 1900, d Jan. 20, 1986

Browne, C. R. (B'dos & BG) b Oct. 8, 1890, d Jan. 12, 1964

Bruce, Hon. C. N. (3rd Lord Aberdare) (OUCC & Middx) b Aug. 2, 1885, d Oct. 4, 1957

Bruce, S. D. (W. Prov. & OFS) b Jan. 11, 1954

Bruce, W. (Vic.) b May 22, 1864, d Aug. 3, 1925

Bruyns, A. (W. Prov. & Natal) b Sept. 19, 1946

Bryan, G. J. (Kent) b Dec. 29, 1902

Bryan, J. L. (CUCC & Kent; *CY 1922*) b May 26, 1896, d April 23, 1985

Bryan, R. T. (Kent) b July 30, 1898, d July 27, 1970

Buckenham, C. P. (Essex) b Jan. 16, 1876, d Feb. 23, 1937

Buckingham, J. (Warwicks.) b Jan. 21, 1903, d Jan. 25, 1987

Budd, E. H. (Middx & All-England) b Feb. 23, 1785, d March 29, 1875

Budd, W. L. (Hants) b Oct. 25, 1913, d Aug. 23, 1986

Bull, F. G. (Essex; *CY 1898*) b April 2, 1875, d Sept. 16, 1910

Buller, J. S. (Yorks. & Worcs.) b Aug. 23, 1909, d Aug. 7, 1970

Bunting, R. A. (Sussex) b April 25, 1965

Burden, M. D. (Hants) b Oct. 4, 1930, d Nov. 9, 1987

*Burge, P. J. (Qld; *CY 1965*) b May 17, 1932

*Burger, C. G. de V. (Natal) b July 12, 1935

Burgess, G. I. (Som.) b May 5, 1943

*Burgess, M. G. (Auck.) b July 17, 1944

*Burke, C. (Auck.) b March 22, 1914

*Burke, J. W. (NSW; *CY 1957*) b June 12, 1930, d Feb. 2, 1979

*Burke, S. F. (NE Tvl & OFS) b March 11, 1934

*Burki, Javed (Pak. Us, OUCC, Punjab, Lahore, Kar., R'pindi & NWFP) b May 8, 1938

*Burn, E. J. K. (K. E.) (Tas.) b Sept. 17, 1862, d July 20, 1956

Burnet, J. R. (Yorks.) b Oct. 11, 1918

Burns, N. D. (Essex, W. Prov. & Som.) b Sept. 19, 1965

Burnup, C. J. (CUCC & Kent; *CY 1903*) b Nov. 21, 1875, d April 5, 1960

Burrough, H. D. (Som.) b Feb. 6, 1909

Burton, D. C. F. (CUCC & Yorks.) b Sept. 13, 1887, d Sept. 24, 1971

*Burton, F. J. (Vic. & NSW) b 1866, d Aug. 25, 1929

*Burtt, T. B. (Cant.) b Jan. 22, 1915, d May 24, 1988

Buse, H. T. F. (Som.) b Aug. 5, 1910

Bushby, M. H. (CUCC) b July 29, 1931

Buss, A. (Sussex) b Sept. 1, 1939

Buss, M. A. (Sussex & OFS) b Jan. 24, 1944

Buswell, J. E. (Northants) b July 3, 1909

*Butcher, A. R. (Surrey & Glam.) b Jan. 7, 1954

*Butcher, B. F. (Guyana; *CY 1970*) b Sept. 3, 1933

Butcher, I. P. (Leics. & Glos.) b July 1, 1962

*Butcher, R. O. (Middx, B'dos & Tas.) b Oct. 14, 1953

*Butler, H. J. (Notts.) b March 12, 1913

*Butler, L. S. (T/T) b Feb. 9, 1929

*Butt, H. R. (Sussex) b Dec. 27, 1865, d Dec. 21, 1928

*Butts, C. G. (Guyana) b July 8, 1957

Buxton, I. R. (Derbys.) b April 17, 1938

*Buys, I. D. (W. Prov.) b Feb. 3, 1895, dead

*Bynoe, M. R. (B'dos) b Feb. 23, 1941

Caccia, Lord (Pres. MCC 1973-74) b Dec. 21, 1905

Caesar, Julius (Surrey & All-England) b March 25, 1830, d March 6, 1878

Caffyn, W. (Surrey & NSW) b Feb. 2, 1828, d Aug. 28, 1919

Caine, C. Stewart (Editor of *Wisden* 1926-33) b Oct. 28, 1861, d April 15, 1933

*Cairns, B. L. (C. Dist., Otago & N. Dist.) b Oct. 10, 1949
Calder, H. L. (Cranleigh; *CY 1918*) b 1900
*Callaway, S. T. (NSW & Cant.) b Feb. 6, 1868, d Nov. 25, 1923
*Callen, I. W. (Vic. & Boland) b May 2, 1955
*Calthorpe, Hon. F. S. Gough- (CUCC, Sussex & Warwicks.) b May 27, 1892, d Nov. 19, 1935
*Camacho, G. S. (Guyana) b Oct. 15, 1945
*Cameron, F. J. (Jam.) b June 22, 1923
*Cameron, F. J. (Otago) b June 1, 1932
*Cameron, H. B. (Tvl, E. Prov. & W. Prov.; *CY 1936*) b July 5, 1905, d Nov. 2, 1935
*Cameron, J. H. (CUCC, Jam. & Som.) b April 8, 1914
*Campbell, T. (Tvl) b Feb. 9, 1882, d Oct. 5, 1924
Cannings, V. H. D. (Warwicks. & Hants) b April 3, 1919
*Capel, D. J. (Northants & E. Prov.) b Feb. 6, 1963
Caple, R. G. (Middx & Hants) b Dec. 8, 1939
Cardus, Sir Neville (Cricket Writer) b April 3, 1888, d Feb. 27, 1975
*Carew, G. McD. (B'dos) b June 4, 1910, d Dec. 9, 1974
*Carew, M. C. (T/T) b Sept. 15, 1937
*Carkeek, W. (Vic.) b Oct. 17, 1878, d Feb. 20, 1937
*Carlson, P. H. (Qld) b Aug. 8, 1951
*Carlstein, P. R. (OFS, Tvl, Natal & Rhod.) b Oct. 28, 1938
Carmody, D. K. (NSW & W. Aust.) b Feb. 16, 1919, d Oct. 21, 1977
Carpenter, D. (Glos.) b Sept. 12, 1935
Carpenter, R. (Cambs. & Utd England XI) b Nov. 18, 1830, d July 13, 1901
*Carr, A. W. (Notts.; *CY 1923*) b May 21, 1893, d Feb. 7, 1963
*Carr, D. B. (OUCC & Derbys.; *CY 1960*; Sec. TCCB 1974-86) b Dec. 28, 1926
*Carr, D. W. (Kent; *CY 1910*) b March 17, 1872, d March 23, 1950
Carr, J. D. (OUCC & Middx) b June 15, 1963
Carrick, P. (Yorks. & E. Prov.) b July 16, 1952
Carrigan, A. H. (Qld) b Aug. 26, 1917
Carrington, E. (Derbys.) b March 25, 1914
Carse, J. A. (Rhod., W. Prov., E. Prov. & Northants) b Dec. 13, 1958
*Carter, C. P. (Natal & Tvl) b April 23, 1881, d Nov. 8, 1952
*Carter, H. (NSW) b Halifax, Yorks. March 15, 1878, d June 8, 1948
Carter, R. G. (Warwicks.) b April 14, 1933
Carter, R. G. M. (Worcs.) b July 11, 1937
Carter, R. M. (Northants & Cant.) b May 25, 1960

Cartwright, H. (Derbys.) b May 12, 1951
*Cartwright, T. W. (Warwicks., Som. Glam.) b July 22, 1935
Carty, R. A. (Hants) b July 28, 1922, March 31, 1984
Cass, G. R. (Essex, Worcs. & Tas.) b Apr 23, 1940
Castell, A. T. (Hants) b Aug. 6, 1943
Castle, F. (Som.) b April 9, 1909
Catt, A. W. (Kent & W. Prov.) b Oct. 1933
*Catterall, R. H. (Tvl, Rhod., Natal & OFS *CY 1925*) b July 10, 1900, d Jan. 2, 196
*Cave, H. B. (Wgtn & C. Dist.) b Oct. 1 1922
Chalk, F. G. H. (OUCC & Kent) b Sept. 1910, d Feb. 20, 1943
*Challenor, G. (B'dos) b June 28, 1888, July 30, 1947
*Chandrasekhar, B. S. (†Karn.; *CY 1972*) May 17, 1945
*Chang, H. S. (Jam.) b July 22, 1952
*Chapman, A. P. F. (Uppingham, OUCC Kent; *CY 1919*) b Sept. 3, 1900, d Sep 16, 1961
*Chapman, H. W. (Natal) b June 30, 1890, Dec. 1, 1941
Chapman, T. A. (Leics. & Rhod.) b Ma 14, 1919, d Feb. 19, 1979
*Chappell, G. S. (S. Aust., Som. & Qld; *C 1973*) b Aug. 7, 1948
*Chappell, I. M. (S. Aust. & Lancs.; *C 1976*) b Sept. 26, 1943
*Chappell, T. M. (S. Aust., W. Aust. NSW) b Oct. 21, 1952
*Chapple, M. E. (Cant. & C. Dist.) b Ju 25, 1930, d July 31, 1985
*Charlton, P. C. (NSW) b April 9, 1867, Sept. 30, 1954
*Charlwood, H. R. J. (Sussex) b Dec. 1 1846, d June 6, 1888
*Chatfield, E. J. (Wgtn) b July 3, 1950
*Chatterton, W. (Derbys.) b Dec. 27, 1861, March 19, 1913
*Chauhan, C. P. S. (M'tra & Delhi) b Ju 21, 1947
Cheatle, R. G. L. (Sussex & Surrey) b Ju 31, 1953
*Cheetham, J. E. (W. Prov.) b May 26, 192 d Aug. 21, 1980
Chester, F. (Worcs.; Umpire) b Jan. 2 1895, d April 8, 1957
Chesterton, G. H. (OUCC & Worcs.) July 15, 1922
*Chevalier, G. A. (W. Prov.) b March 1937
*Childs, J. H. (Glos. & Essex; *CY 1987*) Aug. 15, 1951
Childs-Clarke, A. W. (Middx & Northant b May 13, 1905, d Feb. 19, 1980
*Chipperfield, A. G. (NSW) b Nov. 1 1905, d July 29, 1987

hisholm, R. H. E. (Scotland) b May 22, 1927
howdhury, N. R. (Bihar & Bengal) b May 23, 1923, d Dec. 14, 1979
hristiani, C. M. (BG) b Oct. 28, 1913, d April 4, 1938
hristiani, R. J. (BG) b July 19, 1920
hristopherson, S. (Kent; Pres. MCC 1939-45) b Nov. 11, 1861, d April 6, 1949
hristy, J. A. J. (Tvl & Qld) b Dec. 12, 1904, d Feb. 1, 1971
hubb, G. W. A. (Border & Tvl) b April 12, 1911, d Aug. 28, 1982
lark, D. G. (Kent; Pres. MCC 1977-78) b Jan. 27, 1919
lark, E. A. (Middx) b April 15, 1937
lark, E. W. (Northants) b Aug. 9, 1902, d April 28, 1982
lark, L. S. (Essex) b March 6, 1914
lark, T. H. (Surrey) b Oct. 4, 1924, d June 15, 1981
lark, W. M. (W. Aust.) b Sept. 19, 1953
larke, A. R. (Sussex) b Dec. 23, 1961
larke, Dr C. B. (B'dos, Northants & Essex) b April 7, 1918
larke, R. W. (Northants) b April 22, 1924, d Aug. 3, 1981
larke, S. T. (B'dos, Surrey & Tvl) b Dec. 11, 1954
larke, William (Notts.; founded All-England XI & Trent Bridge ground) b Dec. 24, 1798, d Aug. 25, 1856
larkson, A. (Yorks. & Som.) b Sept. 5, 1939
laughton, J. A. (OUCC & Warwicks.) b Sept. 17, 1956
lay, J. C. (Glam.) b March 18, 1898, d Aug. 12, 1973
lay, J. D. (Notts.) b Oct. 15, 1924
layton, G. (Lancs. & Som.) b Feb. 3, 1938
lements, S. M. (OUCC) b April 19, 1956
leverley, D. C. (Auck.) b Dec. 23, 1909
lift, Patrick B. (Rhod., Leics. & Natal) b July 14, 1953
lift, Philip B. (Glam.) b Sept. 3, 1918
linton, G. S. (Kent, Surrey & Zimb.-Rhod.) b May 5, 1953
lose, D. B. (Yorks. & Som.; _CY 1964_) b Feb. 24, 1931
obb, R. A. (Leics.) b May 18, 1961
obham, 9th Visct (Worcs.) b Oct. 23, 1881, d July 31, 1949
obham, 10th Visct (Hon. C. J. Lyttelton) (Worcs.; Pres. MCC 1954) b Aug. 8, 1909, d March 20, 1977
ochrane, J. A. K. (Tvl & Griq. W.) b July 15, 1909, d June 15, 1987
oen, S. K. (OFS, W. Prov., Tvl & Border) b Oct. 14, 1902, d Jan. 28, 1967
olah, S. M. H. (Bombay, W. Ind. & Naw.) b Sept. 22, 1902, d Sept. 11, 1950

Colchin, Robert ("Long Robin") (Kent & All-England) b Nov. 1713, d April 1750
*Coldwell, L. J. (Worcs.) b Jan. 10, 1933
Coleman, C. A. R. (Leics.) b July 7, 1906, d June 14, 1978
*Colley, D. J. (NSW) b March 15, 1947
Collin, T. (Warwicks.) b April 7, 1911
*Collinge, R. O. (C. Dist., Wgtn & N. Dist.) b April 2, 1946
*Collins, H. L. (NSW) b Jan. 21, 1889, d May 28, 1959
Collins, R. (Lancs.) b March 10, 1934
*Colquhoun, I. A. (C. Dist.) b June 8, 1924
Coman, P. G. (Cant.) b April 13, 1943
*Commaille, J. M. M. (W. Prov., Natal, OFS & Griq. W.) b Feb. 21, 1883, d July 27, 1956
*Compton, D. C. S. (Middx & Holkar; _CY 1939_) b May 23, 1918
Compton, L. H. (Middx) b Sept. 12, 1912, d Dec. 27, 1984
*Coney, J. V. (Wgtn; _CY 1984_) b June 21, 1952
*Congdon, B. E. (C. Dist., Wgtn, Otago & Cant.; _CY 1974_) b Feb. 11, 1938
*Coningham, A. (NSW & Qld) b July 14, 1863, d June 13, 1939
*Connolly, A. N. (Vic. & Middx) b June 29, 1939
Connor, C. A. (Hants) b March 24, 1961
Constable, B. (Surrey) b Feb. 19, 1921
Constant, D. J. (Kent & Leics.; Umpire) b Nov. 9, 1941
*Constantine, Lord L. N. (T/T & B'dos; _CY 1940_) b Sept. 21, 1902, d July 1, 1971
Constantine, L. S. (T/T) b May 25, 1874, d Jan. 5, 1942
*Contractor, N. J. (Guj. & Ind. Rlwys) b March 7, 1934
*Conyngham, D. P. (Natal, Tvl & W. Prov.) b May 10, 1897, d July 7, 1979
*Cook, C. (Glos.) b Aug. 23, 1921
*Cook, F. J. (E. Prov.) b 1870, dead
*Cook, G. (Northants & E. Prov.) b Oct. 9, 1951
*Cook, N. G. B. (Leics. & Northants) b June 17, 1956
Cook, S. J. (Tvl) b July 31, 1953
Cook, T. E. (Sussex) b Feb. 5, 1901, d Jan. 15, 1950
*Cooper, A. H. C. (Tvl) b Sept 2, 1893, d July 18, 1963
*Cooper, B. B. (Middx, Kent & Vic.) b March 15, 1844, d Aug. 7, 1914
Cooper, F. S. Ashley- (Cricket Historian) b March 17, 1877, d Jan. 31, 1932
Cooper, G. C. (Sussex) b Sept. 2, 1936
Cooper, H. P. (Yorks. & N. Tvl) b April 17, 1949
Cooper, K. E. (Notts.) b Dec. 27, 1957
*Cooper, W. H. (Vic.) b Sept. 11, 1849, d April 5, 1939

*Cope, G. A. (Yorks.) b Feb. 23, 1947
*Copson, W. H. (Derbys.; *CY 1937*) b April 27, 1908, d Sept. 14, 1971
Cordle, A. E. (Glam.) b Sept. 21, 1940
*Corling, G. E. (NSW) b July 13, 1941
Cornford, J. H. (Sussex) b Dec. 9, 1911, d June 17, 1985
*Cornford, W. L. (Sussex) b Dec. 25, 1900, d Feb. 6, 1964
Cornwallis, Capt. Hon. W. S. (2nd Lord Cornwallis) (Kent) b March 14, 1892, d Jan. 4, 1982
Corrall, P. (Leics.) b July 16, 1906
Corran, A. J. (OUCC & Notts.) b Nov. 25, 1936
*Cosier, G. J. (Vic., S. Aust. & Qld) b April 25,1953
*Cottam, J. T. (NSW) b Sept. 5, 1867, d Jan. 30, 1897
*Cottam, R. M. H. (Hants & Northants) b Oct. 16, 1944
*Cotter, A. (NSW) b Dec. 3, 1884, d Oct. 31, 1917
Cotton, J. (Notts. & Leics.) b Nov. 7, 1940
Cottrell, G. A. (CUCC) b March 23, 1945
Coulson, S. S. (Leics.) b Oct. 17, 1898, d Oct. 3, 1981
*Coulthard, G. (Vic.) b Aug. 1, 1856, d Oct. 22, 1883
*Coventry, Hon. C. J. (Worcs.) b Feb. 26, 1867, d June 2, 1929
Coverdale, S. P. (CUCC, Yorks., & Northants) b Nov. 20, 1954
Cowan, M. J. (Yorks.) b June 10, 1933
*Cowans, N. G. (Middx) b April 17, 1961
*Cowdrey, C. S. (Kent) b Oct. 20, 1957
Cowdrey, G. R. (Kent) b June 27, 1964
*Cowdrey, M. C. (OUCC & Kent; *CY 1956*; Pres. MCC 1986-87) b Dec. 24, 1932
*Cowie, J. (Auck.) b March 30, 1912
Cowley, N. G. (Hants) b March 1, 1953
*Cowper, R. M. (Vic. & W. Aust.) b Oct. 5, 1940
Cox, A. L. (Northants) b July 22, 1907, d Nov. 1986
Cox, G., jun. (Sussex) b Aug. 23, 1911, d March 30, 1985
Cox, G. R. (Sussex) b Nov. 29, 1873, d March 24, 1949
*Cox, J. L. (Natal) b June 28, 1886, d July 4, 1971
*Coxon, A. (Yorks.) b Jan. 18, 1916
Crabtree, H. P. (Essex) b April 30, 1906, d May 28, 1982
Craig, E. J. (CUCC & Lancs.) b March 26, 1942
*Craig, I. D. (NSW) b June 12, 1935
Cranfield, L. M. (Glos.) b Aug. 29, 1909
Cranmer, P. (Warwicks.) b Sept. 10, 1914
*Cranston, J. (Glos.) b Jan. 9, 1859, d Dec. 10, 1904
*Cranston, K. (Lancs.) b Oct. 20, 1917

*Crapp, J. F. (Glos.) b Oct. 14, 1912, d F[illegible] 15, 1981
*Crawford, J. N. (Surrey, S. Aust., Wgtn [illegible] Otago; *CY 1907*) b Dec. 1, 1886, d M[illegible] 2, 1963
*Crawford, P. (NSW) b Aug. 3, 1933
Crawley, A. M. (OUCC & Kent; Pr[illegible] MCC 1972-73) b April 10, 1908
Crawley, L. G. (CUCC, Worcs. & Essex[illegible] July 26, 1903, d July 9, 1981
Cray, S. J. (Essex) b May 29, 1921
*Cresswell, G. F. (Wgtn & C. Dist.) [illegible] March 22, 1915, d Jan. 10, 1966
*Cripps, G. (W. Prov.) b Oct. 19, 1865, [illegible] July 27, 1943
*Crisp, R. J. (Rhod., W. Prov. & Worcs.[illegible] May 28, 1911
*Croft, C. E. H. (Guyana & Lancs.) b Mar[illegible] 15, 1953
*Cromb, I. B. (Cant.) b June 25, 1905, [illegible] March 6, 1984
Crookes, N. S. (Natal) b Nov. 15, 1935
Cross, G. F. (Leics.) b Nov. 15, 1943
*Crowe, J. J. (S. Aust. & Auck.) b Sept. [illegible] 1958
*Crowe, M. D. (Auck., C. Dist. & Som.; [illegible] *1985*) b Sept. 22, 1962
Crump, B. S. (Northants) b April 25, 19[illegible]
Crush, E. (Kent) b April 25, 1917
Cumbes, J. (Lancs., Surrey, Worcs. [illegible] Warwicks.) b May 4, 1944
*Cunis, R. S. (Auck. & N. Dist.) b Jan. [illegible] 1941
*Curnow, S. H. (Tvl) b Dec. 16, 1907, d J[illegible] 28, 1986
Curran, K. M. (Glos. & Zimb.) b Sept. [illegible] 1959
*Curtis, T. S. (Worcs. & CUCC) b Jan. [illegible] 1960
Cuthbertson, G. B. (Middx, Sussex [illegible] Northants) b March 28, 1901
Cutmore, J. A. (Essex) b Dec. 28, 1898, [illegible] Nov. 30, 1985
*Cuttell, W. R. (Lancs.; *CY 1898*) b Sept. [illegible] 1864, d Dec. 9, 1929

*Da Costa, O. C. (Jam.) b Sept. 11, 1907, [illegible] Oct. 1, 1936
Dacre, C. C. (Auck. & Glos.) b May [illegible] 1899, d Nov. 2, 1975
Daer, A. G. (Essex) b Nov. 22, 1906, d J[illegible] 16, 1980
Daft, Richard (Notts. & All-England) [illegible] Nov. 2, 1835, d July 18, 1900
Dakin, G. F. (E. Prov.) b Aug. 13, 193[illegible]
Dalmeny, Lord (6th Earl of Rosebe[illegible] (Middx & Surrey) b Jan. 8, 1882, d M[illegible] 30, 1974
*Dalton, E. L. (Natal) b Dec. 2, 1906, d Ju[illegible] 3, 1981
*Dani, H. T. (M'tra & Ind. Serv.) b May [illegible] 1933

*aniel, W. W. (B'dos, Middx & W. Aust.) b Jan. 16, 1956
*'Arcy, J. W. (Cant., Wgtn & Otago) b April 23, 1936
*are, R. (Hants) b Nov. 26, 1921
*arling, J. (S. Aust.; *CY 1900*) b Nov. 21, 1870, d Jan. 2, 1946
*arling, L. S. (Vic.) b Aug. 14, 1909
*arling, W. M. (S. Aust.) b May 1, 1957
*arnley, 8th Earl of (Hon. Ivo Bligh) (CUCC & Kent; Pres. MCC 1900) b March 13, 1859, d April 10, 1927
*avey, J. (Glos.) b Sept. 4, 1944
*avidson, A. K. (NSW; *CY 1962*) b June 14, 1929
*avies, Dai (Glam.) b Aug. 26, 1896, d July 16, 1976
*avies, Emrys (Glam.) b June 27, 1904, d Nov. 10, 1975
*avies, E. Q. (E. Prov., Tvl & NE Tvl) b Aug. 26, 1909, d Nov. 11, 1976
*avies, H. D. (Glam.) b July 23, 1932
*avies, H. G. (Glam.) b April 23, 1913
*avies, J. G. W. (CUCC & Kent; Pres. MCC 1985-86) b Sept. 10, 1911
*avies, T. (Glam.) b Oct. 25, 1960
*avis, B. A. (T/T & Glam.) b May 2, 1940
*avis, C. A. (T/T) b Jan. 1, 1944
*avis, E. (Northants) b March 8, 1922
*avis, I. C. (NSW & Qld) b June 25, 1953
*avis, M. R. (Som.) b Feb. 26, 1962
*avis, P. C. (Northants) b May 24, 1915
*avis, R. C. (Glam.) b Jan. 1, 1946
*avis, R. P. (Kent) b March 18, 1966
*avis, S. P. (Vic.) b Nov. 8, 1959
*avis, W. W. (Windwards, Glam., Tas. & Northants) b Sept. 18, 1958
*avison, B. F. (Rhod., Leics, Tas. & Glos.) b Dec. 21, 1946
*avison, I. (Notts.) b Oct. 4, 1937
*awkes, G. O. (Leics. & Derbys.) b July 19, 1920
*awson, E. W. (CUCC & Leics.) b Feb. 13, 1904, d June 4, 1979
*awson, O. C. (Natal & Border) b Sept. 1, 1919
*ay, A. P. (Kent; *CY 1910*) b April 10, 1885, d Jan. 22, 1969
e Alwis, R. G. (SL) b Feb. 15, 1959
*ean, H. (Lancs.) b Aug. 13, 1884, d March 12, 1957
*eane, H. G. (Natal & Tvl) b July 21, 1895, d Oct. 21, 1939
*e Caires, F. I. (BG) b May 12, 1909, d Feb. 2, 1959
*e Courcy, J. H. (NSW) b April 18, 1927
*eed, J. A. (Kent) b Sept. 12, 1901, d Oct. 19, 1980
*eFreitas, P. A. J. (Leics.) b Feb. 18, 1966
*elisle, G. P. S. (Middx & OUCC) b Dec. 25, 1934
*ell, A. R. (Qld) b Aug. 6, 1947
*de Mel, A. L. F. (SL) b May 9, 1959
*Dempster, C. S. (Wgtn, Leics., Scotland & Warwicks.; *CY 1932*) b Nov. 15, 1903, d Feb. 14, 1974
*Dempster, E. W. (Wgtn) b Jan. 25, 1925
*Denness, M. H. (Scotland, Kent & Essex; *CY 1975*) b Dec. 1, 1940
Dennett, E. G. (Glos.) b April 27, 1880, d Sept. 14, 1937
Denning, P. W. (Som.) b Dec. 16, 1949
Dennis, F. (Yorks.) b June 11, 1907
Dennis, S. J. (Yorks. & OFS) b Oct. 18, 1960
*Denton, D. (Yorks.; *CY 1906*) b July 4, 1874, d Feb. 16, 1950
Denton, W. H. (Northants) b Nov. 2, 1890, d April 23, 1979
Deodhar, D. B. (M'tra; oldest living Ranji Trophy player) b Jan. 14, 1892
*Depeiza, C. C. (B'dos) b Oct. 10, 1927
Derrick, J. (Glam.) b Jan. 15, 1963
*Desai, R. B. (Bombay) b June 20, 1939
De Saram, F. C. (OUCC & Ceylon) b Sept. 5, 1912, d April 11, 1983
de Silva, A. M. (SL) b Dec. 3, 1963
de Silva, D. L. S. (SL) b Nov. 17, 1956, d April 12, 1980
*de Silva, D. S. (SL) b June 11, 1942
*de Silva, E. A. R. (SL) b March 28, 1956
de Silva, G. N. (SL) b March 12, 1955
*de Silva, G. R. A. (SL) b Dec. 12, 1952
*de Silva, P. A. (SL) b Oct. 17, 1965
de Smidt, R. (W. Prov.) b Nov. 24, 1883, d Aug. 3, 1986
Devereux, L. N. (Middx, Worcs. & Glam.) b Oct. 20, 1931
*Dewdney, C. T. (Jam.) b Oct. 23, 1933
*Dewes, J. G. (CUCC & Middx) b Oct. 11, 1926
Dews, G. (Worcs.) b June 5, 1921
*Dexter, E. R. (CUCC & Sussex; *CY 1961*) b May 15, 1935
*Dias, R. L. (SL) b Oct. 18, 1952
Dibbs, A. H. A. (Pres. MCC 1983-84) b Dec. 9, 1918, d Nov. 28, 1985
*Dick, A. E. (Otago & Wgtn) b Oct. 10, 1936
*Dickinson, G. R. (Otago) b March 11, 1903, d March 17, 1978
*Dilley, G. R. (Kent, Natal & Worcs.) b May 18, 1959
Diment, R. A. (Glos. & Leics.) b Feb. 9, 1927
*Dipper, A. E. (Glos.) b Nov. 9, 1885, d Nov. 7, 1945
*Divecha, R. V. (Bombay, OUCC, Northants, Vidarbha & S'tra) b Oct. 18, 1927
Diver, A. J. D. (Cambs., Middx, Notts. & All-England) b June 6, 1824, d March 25, 1876
Dixon, A. L. (Kent) b Nov. 27, 1933

*Dixon, C. D. (Tvl) b Feb. 12, 1891, d Sept. 9, 1969
Dodds, T. C. (Essex) b May 29, 1919
*Dodemaide, A. I. C. (Vic.) b Oct. 5, 1963
Doggart, A. G. (CUCC, Durham & Middx) b June 2, 1897, d June 7, 1963
*Doggart, G. H. G. (CUCC & Sussex; Pres. MCC 1981-82) b July 18, 1925
*D'Oliveira, B. L. (Worcs.; *CY 1967*) b Oct. 4, 1931
D'Oliveira, D. B. (Worcs.) b Oct. 19, 1960
*Dollery, H. E. (Warwicks. & Wgtn; *CY 1952*) b Oct. 14, 1914, d Jan. 20, 1987
Dollery, K. R. (Qld, Auck., Tas. & Warwicks.) b Dec. 9, 1924
*Dolphin, A. (Yorks.) b Dec. 24, 1885, d Oct. 23, 1942
*Donnan, H. (NSW) b Nov. 12, 1864, d Aug. 13, 1956
*Donnelly, M. P. (Wgtn, Cant., Middx, Warwicks. & OUCC; *CY 1948*) b Oct. 17, 1917
*Dooland, B. (S. Aust. & Notts.; *CY 1955*) b Nov. 1, 1923, d Sept. 8, 1980
Dorrinton, W. (Kent & All-England) b April 29, 1809, d Nov. 8, 1848
Dorset, 3rd Duke of (Kent) b March 24, 1745, d July 19, 1799
*Doshi, D. R. (Bengal, Notts., Warwicks. & S'tra) b Dec. 22, 1947
*Douglas, J. W. H. T. (Essex; *CY 1915*) b Sept. 3, 1882, d Dec. 19, 1930
Dowding, A. L. (OUCC) b April 4, 1929
*Dowe, U. G. (Jam.) b March 29, 1949
*Dower, R. R. (E. Prov.) b June 4, 1876, d Sept. 15, 1964
*Dowling, G. T. (Cant.) b March 4, 1937
*Downton, P. R. (Kent & Middx) b April 4, 1957
Draper, E. J. (E. Prov. & Griq. W.) b Sept. 27, 1934
*Draper, R. G. (E. Prov. & Griq. W.) b Dec. 24, 1926
Dredge, C. H. (Som.) b Aug. 4, 1954
*Druce, N. F. (CUCC & Surrey; *CY 1898*) b Jan. 1, 1875, d Oct. 27, 1954
Drybrough, C. D. (OUCC & Middx) b Aug. 31, 1938
*D'Souza, A. (Kar., Peshawar & PIA) b Jan. 17, 1939
*Ducat, A. (Surrey; *CY 1920*) b Feb. 16, 1886, d July 23, 1942
*Duckworth, C. A. R. (Natal & Rhod.) b March 22, 1933
*Duckworth, G. (Lancs.; *CY 1929*) b May 9, 1901, d Jan. 5, 1966
Dudleston, B. (Leics., Glos. & Rhod.) b July 16, 1945
*Duff, R. A. (NSW) b Aug. 17, 1878, d Dec. 13, 1911
*Dujon, P. J. L. (Jam.; *CY 1989*) b May 28, 1956

*Duleepsinhji, K. S. (CUCC & Sussex; C *1930*) b June 13, 1905, d Dec. 5, 1959
*Dumbrill, R. (Natal & Tvl) b Nov. 19, 19
*Duminy, J. P. (OUCC, W. Prov. & Tvl) Dec. 16, 1897, d Jan. 31, 1980
*Duncan, J. R. F. (Qld & Vic.) b March 2 1944
*Dunell, O. R. (E. Prov.) b July 15, 1856, Oct. 21, 1929
*Dunning, J. A. (Otago & OUCC) b Feb. 1903, d June 24, 1971
*Du Preez, J. H. (Rhod. & Zimb.) b No 14, 1942
*Durani, S. A. (S'tra, Guj. & Raja.) b De 11, 1934
Durose, A. J. (Northants) b Oct. 10, 194
*Durston, F. J. (Middx) b July 11, 1893, April 8, 1965
*Du Toit, J. F. (SA) b April 5, 1868, d Ju 10, 1909
Dye, J. C. J. (Kent, Northants & E. Prov b July 24, 1942
Dyer, D. D. (Natal & Tvl) b Dec. 3, 194
*Dyer, D. V. (Natal) b May 2, 1914
*Dyer, G. C. (NSW) b March 16, 1959
Dyer, R. I. H. B. (Warwicks.) b Dec. 2 1958
*Dymock, G. (Qld) b July 21, 1945
Dyson, A. H. (Glam.) b July 10, 1905, June 7, 1978
Dyson, J. (Lancs.) b July 8, 1934
*Dyson, John (NSW) b June 11, 1954

*Eady, C. J. (Tas.) b Oct. 29, 1870, d De 20, 1945
Eagar, E. D. R. (OUCC, Glos. & Hants) Dec. 8, 1917, d Sept. 13, 1977
Eagar, M. A. (OUCC & Glos.) b March 2 1934
Eaglestone, J. T. (Middx & Glam.) b Ju 24, 1923
Ealham, A. G. E. (Kent) b Aug. 30, 194
East, D. E. (Essex) b July 27, 1959
East, R. E. (Essex) b June 20, 1947
Eastman, G. F. (Essex) b April 7, 1903
Eastman, L. C. (Essex & Otago) b June 1897, d April 17, 1941
*Eastwood, K. H. (Vic.) b Nov. 23, 1935
*Ebeling, H. I. (Vic.) b Jan. 1, 1905, d Ja 12, 1980
Eckersley, P. T. (Lancs.) b July 2, 1904, Aug. 13, 1940
*Edgar, B. A. (Wgtn) b Nov. 23, 1956
Edinburgh, HRH Duke of (Pres. MC 1948-49, 1974-75) b June 10, 1921
Edmeades, B. E. A. (Essex) b Sept. 17, 194
*Edmonds, P. H. (CUCC, Middx & Prov.) b March 8, 1951
Edmonds, R. B. (Warwicks.) b March 1941
Edrich, B. R. (Kent & Glam.) b Aug. 1 1922

Edrich, E. H. (Lancs.) b March 27, 1914
Edrich, G. A. (Lancs.) b July 13, 1918
Edrich, J. H. (Surrey; *CY 1966*) b June 21, 1937
Edrich, W. J. (Middx; *CY 1940*) b March 26, 1916, d April 23, 1986
Edwards, G. N. (C. Dist.) b May 27, 1955
Edwards, J. D. (Vic.) b June 12, 1862, d July 31, 1911
Edwards, M. J. (CUCC & Surrey) b March 1, 1940
Edwards, R. (W. Aust. & NSW) b Dec. 1, 1942
Edwards, R. M. (B'dos) b June 3, 1940
Edwards, W. J. (W. Aust.) b Dec. 23, 1949
Eele, P. J. (Som.) b Jan. 27, 1935
Eggar, J. D. (OUCC, Hants & Derbys.) b Dec. 1, 1916, d May 3, 1983
Ehtesham-ud-Din (Lahore, Punjab, PIA, NBP & UBL) b Sept. 4, 1950
Elgie, M. K. (Natal) b March 6, 1933
Elliott, C. S. (Derbys.) b April 24, 1912
Elliott, H. (Derbys.) b Nov. 2, 1891, d Feb. 2, 1976
Elliott, Harold (Lancs.; Umpire) b June 15, 1904, d April 15, 1969
Ellis, G. P. (Glam.) b May 24, 1950
Ellis, J. L. (Vic.) b May 9, 1890, d July 26, 1974
Ellis, R. G. P. (OUCC & Middx) b Oct. 20 1960
Ellison, R. M. (Kent & Tas.; *CY 1986*) b Sept. 21, 1959
Elms, R. B. (Kent & Hants) b April 5, 1949
Emburey, J. E. (Middx & W. Prov.; *CY 1984*) b Aug. 20, 1952
Emery, R. W. G. (Auck. & Cant.) b March 28, 1915, d Dec. 18, 1982
Emery, S. H. (NSW) b Oct. 16, 1885, d Jan. 7, 1967
Emmett, G. M. (Glos.) b Dec. 2, 1912, d Dec. 18, 1976
Emmett, T. (Yorks.) b Sept. 3, 1841, d June 30, 1904
Endean, W. R. (Tvl) b May 31, 1924
Engineer, F. M. (Bombay & Lancs.) b Feb. 25, 1938
Enthoven, H. J. (CUCC & Middx) b June 4, 1903, d June 29, 1975
Evans, A. J. (OUCC, Hants & Kent) b May 1, 1889, d Sept. 18, 1960
Evans, D. G. L. (Glam.; Umpire) b July 27, 1933
Evans, E. (NSW) b March 6, 1849, d July 2, 1921
Evans, G. (OUCC, Glam. & Leics.) b Aug. 13, 1915
Evans, J. B. (Glam.) b Nov. 9, 1936
Evans, T. G. (Kent; *CY 1951*) b Aug. 18, 1920
Every, T. (Glam.) b Dec. 19, 1909
Eyre, T. J. P. (Derbys.) b Oct. 17, 1939

Faber, M. J. J. (OUCC & Sussex) b Aug. 15, 1950
*Fagg, A. E. (Kent) b June 18, 1915, d Sept. 13, 1977
Fairbairn, A. (Middx) b Jan. 25, 1923
*Fairbrother, N. H. (Lancs.) b Sept. 9, 1963
*Fairfax, A. G. (NSW) b June 16, 1906, d May 17, 1955
Fairservice, C. (Kent & Middx) b Aug. 21, 1909
Fairservice, W. J. (Kent) b May 16, 1881, d June 26, 1971
Falcon, M. (CUCC) b July 21, 1888, d Feb. 27, 1976
Fallows, J. A. (Lancs.) b July 25, 1907, d Jan. 20, 1974
*Fane, F. L. (OUCC & Essex) b April 27, 1875, d Nov. 27, 1960
Fantham, W. E. (Warwicks.) b May 14, 1918
*Farnes, K. (CUCC & Essex; *CY 1939*) b July 8, 1911, d Oct. 20, 1941
*Farooq Hamid (Lahore & PIA) b March 3, 1945
*Farrer, W. S. (Border) b Dec. 8, 1936
*Farrimond, W. (Lancs.) b May 23, 1903, d Nov. 14, 1979
*Farrukh Zaman (Peshawar, NWFP, Punjab & MCB) b April 2, 1956
*Faulkner, G. A. (Tvl) b Dec. 17, 1881, d Sept. 10, 1930
*Favell, L. E. (S. Aust.) b Oct. 6, 1929, d June 14, 1987
*Fazal Mahmood (N. Ind., Punjab & Lahore; *CY 1955*) b Feb. 18, 1927
Fearnley, C. D. (Worcs.) b April 12, 1940
Featherstone, N. G. (Tvl, N. Tvl, Middx & Glam.) b Aug. 20, 1949
'Felix', N. (Wanostrocht) (Kent, Surrey & All-England) b Oct. 4, 1804, d Sept. 3, 1876
*Fellows-Smith, J. P. (OUCC, Tvl & Northants) b Feb. 3, 1932
Feltham, M. A. (Surrey) b June 26, 1963
Felton, N. A. (Som.) b Oct. 24, 1960
*Fender, P. G. H. (Sussex & Surrey; *CY 1915*) b Aug. 22, 1892, d June 15, 1985
*Ferguson, W. (T/T) b Dec. 14, 1917, d Feb. 23, 1961
*Fernandes, M. P. (BG) b Aug. 12, 1897, d May 8, 1981
Fernando, E. R. (SL) b Feb. 22, 1944
*Fernando, E. R. N. S. (SL) b Dec. 19, 1955
Ferreira, A. M. (N. Tvl & Warwicks.) b April 13, 1955
Ferris, G. J. F. (Leics. & Leewards) b Oct. 18, 1964
**Ferris, J. J. (NSW, Glos. & S. Aust.; *CY 1889*) b May 21, 1867, d Nov. 21, 1900
*Fichardt, C. G. (OFS) b March 20, 1870, d May 30, 1923

Fiddling, K. (Yorks. & Northants) b Oct. 13, 1917
*Fielder, A. (Kent; *CY 1907*) b July 19, 1877, d Aug. 30, 1949
*Findlay, T. M. (Comb. Is. & Windwards) b Oct. 19, 1943
Findlay, W. (OUCC & Lancs.; Sec. Surrey CCC, Sec. MCC 1926-36) b June 22, 1880, d June 19, 1953
*Fingleton, J. H. (NSW) b April 28, 1908, d Nov. 22, 1981
*Finlason, C. E. (Tvl & Griq. W.) b Feb. 19, 1860, d July 31, 1917
Finney, R. J. (Derbys.) b Aug. 2, 1960
Firth, J. (Yorks. & Leics.) b June 27, 1918, d Sept. 6, 1981
Firth, Rev. Canon J. D'E. E. (Winchester, OUCC & Notts.; *CY 1918*) b Jan. 21, 1900, d Sept. 21, 1957
*Fisher, F. E. (Wgtn & C. Dist.) b July 28, 1924
Fisher, P. B. (OUCC, Middx & Worcs.) b Dec. 19, 1954
*Fishlock, L. B. (Surrey; *CY 1947*) b Jan. 2, 1907, d June 26, 1986
Fitzgerald, R. A. (CUCC & Middx; Sec. MCC 1863-76) b Oct. 1, 1834, d Oct. 28, 1881
*Flavell, J. A. (Worcs.; *CY 1965*) b May 15, 1929
*Fleetwood-Smith, L. O'B. (Vic.) b March 30, 1910, d March 16, 1971
Fletcher, D. A. G. (Rhod. & Zimb.) b Sept. 27, 1948
Fletcher, D. G. W. (Surrey) b July 6, 1924
*Fletcher, K. W. R. (Essex; *CY 1974*) b May 20, 1944
Fletcher, S. D. (Yorks.) b June 8, 1964
*Floquet, C. E. (Tvl) b Nov. 3, 1884, d Nov. 22, 1963
*Flowers, W. (Notts.) b Dec. 7, 1856, d Nov. 1, 1926
Foat, J. C. (Glos.) b Nov. 21, 1952
*Foley, H. (Wgtn) b Jan. 28, 1906, d Oct. 16, 1948
Folley, I. (Lancs.) b Jan. 9, 1963
Foord, C. W. (Yorks.) b June 11, 1924
Forbes, C. (Notts.) b Aug. 9, 1936
*Ford, F. G. J. (CUCC & Middx) b Dec. 14, 1866, d Feb. 7, 1940
Ford, N. M. (OUCC, Derbys. & Middx) b Nov. 18, 1906
Ford, R. G. (Glos.) b March 3, 1907, d Oct. 1981
Foreman, D. J. (W. Prov. & Sussex) b Feb. 1, 1933
Fosh, M. K. (CUCC & Essex) b Sept. 26, 1957
Foster, D. G. (Warwicks.) b March 19, 1907, d Oct. 13, 1980
*Foster, F. R. (Warwicks.; *CY 1912*) b Jan. 31, 1889, d May 3, 1958

Foster, G. N. (OUCC, Worcs. & Kent) Oct. 16, 1884, d Aug. 11, 1971
Foster, H. K. (OUCC & Worcs.; *CY 191* b Oct. 30, 1873, d June 23, 1950
Foster, M. K. (Worcs.) b Jan. 1, 1889, Dec. 3, 1940
*Foster, M. L. C. (Jam.) b May 9, 1943
*Foster, N. A. (Essex; *CY 1988*) b May 1962
Foster, P. G. (Kent) b Oct. 9, 1916
*Foster, R. E. (OUCC & Worcs.; *CY 190* b April 16, 1878, d May 13, 1914
*Fothergill, A. J. (Som.) b Aug. 26, 1854, Aug. 1, 1932
Fotheringham, H. R. (Natal & Tvl) b Apr 4, 1953
*Fowler, G. (Lancs.) b April 20, 1957
Fowler, W. P. (Derbys., N. Dist. & Auck b March 13, 1959
*Francis, B. C. (NSW & Essex) b Feb. 1 1948
Francis, D. A. (Glam.) b Nov. 29, 1953
*Francis, G. N. (B'dos) b Dec. 7, 1897, Jan. 12, 1942
*Francis, H. H. (Glos. & W. Prov.) b Ma 26, 1868, d Jan. 7, 1936
Francke, F. M. (SL & Qld) b March 2 1941
*Francois, C. M. (Griq. W.) b June 20, 189 d May 26, 1944
*Frank, C. N. (Tvl) b Jan. 27, 1891, d De 26, 1961
*Frank, W. H. B. (SA) b Nov. 23, 1872, Feb. 16, 1945
Franklin, H. W. F. (OUCC, Surrey Essex) b June 30, 1901, d May 25, 198
*Franklin, T. J. (Auck.) b March 18, 1962
Fraser, A. R. C. (Middx) b Aug. 8, 1965
*Frederick, M. C. (B'dos, Derbys. & Jam.) May 6, 1927
*Fredericks, R. C. (†Guyana & Glam.; *C 1974*) b Nov. 11, 1942
*Freeman, A. P. (Kent; *CY 1923*) b May 1 1888, d Jan. 28, 1965
*Freeman, D. L. (Wgtn) b Sept. 8, 1914
*Freeman, E. W. (S. Aust.) b July 13, 194
*Freer, F. W. (Vic.) b Dec. 4, 1915
*French, B. N. (Notts.) b Aug. 13, 1959
Frost, G. (Notts.) b Jan. 15, 1947
Fry, C. A. (OUCC, Hants & Northants) Jan. 14, 1940
*Fry, C. B. (OUCC, Sussex & Hants; *C 1895*) b April 25, 1872, d Sept. 7, 1956
*Fuller, E. R. H. (W. Prov.) b Aug. 2, 193
*Fuller, R. L. (Jam.) b Jan. 30, 1913, d Ma 3, 1987
*Fullerton, G. M. (Tvl) b Dec. 8, 1922
Funston, G. K. (NE Tvl & Griq. W.) Nov. 21, 1948
*Funston, K. J. (NE Tvl, OFS & Tvl) b De 3, 1925
*Furlonge, H. A. (T/T) b June 19, 1934

*Gadkari, C. V. (M'tra & Ind. Serv.) b Feb. 3, 1928
*Gaekwad, A. D. (Baroda) b Sept. 23, 1952
*Gaekwad, D. K. (Baroda) b Oct. 27, 1928
*Gaekwad, H. G. (†M. Pradesh) b Aug. 29, 1923
*Gale, R. A. (Middx) b Dec. 10, 1933
*Gallichan, N. (Wgtn) b June 3, 1906, d March 25, 1969
*Gamsy, D. (Natal) b Feb. 17, 1940
*Gandotra, A. (Delhi & Bengal) b Nov. 24, 1948
*Gannon, J. B. (W. Aust.) b Feb. 8, 1947
*Ganteaume, A. G. (T/T) b Jan. 22, 1921
Gard, T. (Som.) b June 2, 1957
Gardner, F. C. (Warwicks.) b June 4, 1922, d Jan. 13, 1979
Gardner, L. R. (Leics.) b Feb. 23, 1934
Garland-Wells, H. M. (OUCC & Surrey) b Nov. 14, 1907
Garlick, R. G. (Lancs. & Northants) b April 11, 1917, d May 16, 1988
*Garner, J. (B'dos, Som. & S. Aust.; *CY 1980*) b Dec. 16, 1952
Garnham, M. A. (Glos. & Leics.) b Aug. 20, 1960
*Garrett, T. W. (NSW) b July 26, 1858, d Aug. 6, 1943
*Gaskin, B. B. MacG. (BG) b March 21, 1908, d May 1, 1979
*Gatting, M. W. (Middx; *CY 1984*) b June 6, 1957
*Gaunt, R. A. (W. Aust. & Vic.) b Feb. 26, 1934
*Gavaskar, S. M. (Bombay & Som.; *CY 1980*) b July 10, 1949
*Gay, L. H. (CUCC, Hants & Som.) b March 24, 1871, d Nov. 1, 1949
Geary, A. C. T. (Surrey) b Sept. 11, 1900
*Geary, G. (Leics.; *CY 1927*) b July 9, 1893, d March 6, 1981
*Gedye, S. G. (Auck.) b May 2, 1929
*Gehrs, D. R. A. (S. Aust.) b Nov. 29, 1880, d June 25, 1953
Ghai, R. S. (Punjab) b June 12, 1960
*Ghavri, K. D. (S'tra & Bombay) b Feb. 28, 1951
*Ghazali, M. E. Z. (M'tra & Pak. Serv.) b June 15, 1924
*Ghorpade, J. M. (Baroda) b Oct. 2, 1930, d March 29, 1978
*Ghulam Abbas (Kar., NBP & PIA) b May 1, 1947
*Ghulam Ahmed (H'bad) b July 4, 1922
*Gibb, P. A. (OUCC, Scotland, Yorks. & Essex) b July 11, 1913, d Dec. 7, 1977
Gibbons, H. H. (Worcs.) b Oct. 10, 1904, d Feb. 16, 1973
*Gibbs, G. L. (BG) b Dec. 27, 1925, d Feb. 21, 1979
*Gibbs, L. R. (†Guyana, S. Aust. & Warwicks.; *CY 1972*) b Sept. 29, 1934
Gibbs, P. J. K. (OUCC & Derbys.) b Aug. 17, 1944
Gibson, C. H. (Eton, CUCC & Sussex; *CY 1918*) b Aug. 23, 1900, d Dec. 31, 1976
Gibson, D. (Surrey) b May 1, 1936
*Giffen, G. (S. Aust.; *CY 1894*) b March 27, 1859, d Nov. 29, 1927
*Giffen, W. F. (S. Aust.) b Sept. 20, 1861, d June 29, 1949
*Gifford, N. (Worcs. & Warwicks.; *CY 1975*) b March 30, 1940
*Gilbert, D. R. (NSW) b Dec. 29, 1960
*Gilchrist, R. (Jam. & H'bad) b June 28, 1934
Giles, R. J. (Notts.) b Oct. 17, 1919
Gill, A. (Notts.) b Aug. 4, 1940
Gilhouley, K. (Yorks. & Notts.) b Aug. 8, 1934
*Gillespie, S. R. (Auck.) b March 2, 1957
Gilliat, R. M. C. (OUCC & Hants) b May 20, 1944
*Gilligan, A. E. R. (CUCC, Surrey & Sussex; *CY 1924*; Pres. MCC 1967-68) b Dec. 23, 1894, d Sept. 5, 1976
*Gilligan, A. H. H. (Sussex) b June 29, 1896, d May 5, 1978
Gilligan, F. W. (OUCC & Essex) b Sept. 20, 1893, d May 4, 1960
*Gilmour, G. J. (NSW) b June 26, 1951
*Gimblett, H. (Som.; *CY 1953*) b Oct. 19, 1914, d March 30, 1978
Gladstone, G. (*see* Marais, G. G.)
Gladwin, Chris (Essex) b May 10, 1962
*Gladwin, Cliff (Derbys.) b April 3, 1916, d April 10, 1988
*Gleeson, J. W. (NSW & E. Prov.) b March 14, 1938
*Gleeson, R. A. (E. Prov.) b Dec. 6, 1873, d Sept. 27, 1919
*Glover, G. K. (Kimberley & Griq. W.) b May 13, 1870, d Nov. 15, 1938
Glover, T. R. (OUCC) b Nov. 26, 1951
Goddard, G. F. (Scotland) b May 19, 1938
*Goddard, J. D. C. (B'dos) b April 21, 1919, d Aug. 26, 1987
*Goddard, T. L. (Natal & NE Tvl) b Aug. 1, 1931
*Goddard, T. W. (Glos.; *CY 1938*) b Oct. 1, 1900, d May 22, 1966
Goel, R. (Patiala & Haryana) b Sept. 29, 1942
Goldsmith, S. C. (Kent & Derbys.) b Dec. 19, 1964
Goldstein, F. S. (OUCC, Northants, Tvl & W. Prov.) b Oct. 14, 1944
*Gomes, H. A. (T/T & Middx; *CY 1985*) b July 13, 1953
Gomes, S. A. (T/T) b Oct. 18, 1950
*Gomez, G. E. (T/T) b Oct. 10, 1919
*Gooch, G. A. (Essex & W. Prov.; *CY 1980*) b July 23, 1953

Goodway, C. C. (Warwicks.) b July 10, 1909
Goodwin, K. (Lancs.) b June 25, 1938
Goodwin, T. J. (Leics.) b Jan. 22, 1929
Goonatillake, F. R. M. de S. (SL) b. Aug. 15, 1951
*Goonatillake, H. M. (SL) b Aug. 16, 1952
Goonesena, G. (Ceylon, Notts., CUCC & NSW) b Feb. 16, 1931
*Gopalan, M. J. (Madras) b June 6, 1909
*Gopinath, C. D. (Madras) b March 1, 1930
*Gordon, N. (Tvl) b Aug. 6, 1911
Gore, A. C. (Eton & Army; *CY 1919*) b May 14, 1900
Gothard, E. J. (Derbys.) b Oct. 1, 1904, d Jan. 17, 1979
Gould, I. J. (Middx, Auck. & Sussex) b Aug. 19, 1957
*Gover, A. R. (Surrey; *CY 1937*) b Feb. 29, 1908
*Gower, D. I. (Leics.; *CY 1979*) b April 1, 1957
Gower, G. M. (Border) b July 10, 1952
Gowrie, 1st Lord (Pres. MCC 1948-49) b July 6, 1872, d May 2, 1955
Grace, Dr Alfred b May 17, 1840, d May 24, 1916
Grace, Dr Alfred H. (Glos.) b March 10, 1866, d Sept. 16, 1929
Grace, C. B. (Clifton) b March 1882, d June 6, 1938
*Grace, Dr E. M. (Glos.) b Nov. 28, 1841, d May 20, 1911
Grace, Dr Edgar M. (MCC) (son of E. M. Grace) b Oct. 6, 1886, d Nov. 24, 1974
*Grace, G. F. (Glos.) b Dec. 13, 1850, d Sept. 22, 1880
Grace, Dr Henry (Glos.) b Jan. 31, 1833, d Nov. 15, 1895
Grace, Dr H. M. (father of W. G., E. M. and G. F.) b Feb. 21, 1808, d Dec. 23, 1871
Grace, Mrs H. M. (mother of W. G., E. M. and G. F.) b July 18, 1812, d July 25, 1884
*Grace, Dr W. G. (Glos.; *CY 1896*) b July 18, 1848, d Oct. 23, 1915
Grace, W. G., jun. (CUCC & Glos.) b July 6, 1874, d March 2, 1905
Graf, S. F. (Vic., W. Aust. & Hants) b May 19, 1957
*Graham, H. (Vic. & Otago) b Nov. 22, 1870, d Feb. 7, 1911
Graham, J. N. (Kent) b May 8, 1943
*Graham, R. (W. Prov.) b Sept. 16, 1877, d April 21, 1946
*Grant, G. C. (CUCC, T/T & Rhod.) b May 9, 1907, d Oct. 26, 1978
*Grant, R. S. (CUCC & T/T) b Dec. 15, 1909, d Oct. 18, 1977
Graveney, D. A. (Glos.) b Jan. 21, 1953
Graveney, J. K. (Glos.) b Dec. 16, 1924
*Graveney, T. W. (Glos., Worcs. & Qld; *C 1953*) b June 16, 1927
Graves, P. J. (Sussex & OFS) b May 19 1946
*Gray, A. H. (T/T & Surrey) b May 23, 196
*Gray, E. J. (Wgtn) b Nov. 18, 1954
Gray, J. R. (Hants) b May 19, 1926
Gray, L. H. (Middx) b Dec. 16, 1915, d Jan 3, 1983
Greasley, D. G. (Northants) b Jan. 20, 192
*Greatbatch, M. J. (C. Dist.) b Dec. 11 1963
Green, A. M. (Sussex & OFS) b May 28 1960
Green, D. J. (Derbys. & CUCC) b Dec. 18 1935
Green, D. M. (OUCC, Lancs. & Glos.; *C 1969*) b Nov. 10, 1939
Green, Brig. M. A. (Glos. & Essex) b Oct 3, 1891, d Dec. 28, 1971
*Greenhough, T. (Lancs.) b Nov. 9, 1931
*Greenidge, A. E. (B'dos) b Aug. 20, 1956
*Greenidge, C. G. (Hants & B'dos; *C 1977*) b May 1, 1951
*Greenidge, G. A. (B'dos & Sussex) b Ma 26, 1948
Greensmith, W. T. (Essex) b Aug. 16, 193
*Greenwood, A. (Yorks.) b Aug. 20, 1847, Feb. 12, 1889
Greenwood, H. W. (Sussex & Northants) Sept. 4, 1909, d March 24, 1979
Greenwood, P. (Lancs.) b Sept. 11, 1924
Greetham, C. (Som.) b Aug. 28, 1936
*Gregory, David W. (NSW; first Australia captain) b April 15, 1845, d Aug. 4, 191
*Gregory, E. J. (NSW) b May 29, 1839, April 22, 1899
*Gregory, J. M. (NSW; *CY 1922*) b Aug. 14 1895, d Aug. 7, 1973
*Gregory, R. G. (Vic.) b Feb. 26, 1916, June 10, 1942
*Gregory, S. E. (NSW; *CY 1897*) b April 14 1870, d August 1, 1929
*Greig, A. W. (Border, E. Prov. & Sussex *CY 1975*) b Oct. 6, 1946
*Greig, I. A. (CUCC, Border, Sussex & Surrey) b Dec. 8, 1955
*Grell, M. G. (T/T) b Dec. 18, 1899, d Jan 11, 1976
*Grieve, B. A. F. (Eng.) b May 28, 1864, Nov. 19, 1917
Grieves, K. J. (NSW & Lancs.) b Aug. 27 1925
*Grieveson, R. E. (Tvl) b Aug. 24, 1909
*Griffin, G. M. (Natal & Rhod.) b June 12 1939
*Griffith, C. C. (B'dos; *CY 1964*) b Dec. 14 1938
Griffith, G. ("Ben") (Surrey & Ut England XI) b Dec. 20, 1833, d May 3 1879

Griffith, H. C. (B'dos) b Dec. 1, 1893, d March 18, 1980
Griffith, K. (Worcs.) b Jan. 17, 1950
Griffith, M. G. (CUCC & Sussex) b Nov. 25, 1943
Griffith, S. C. (CUCC, Surrey & Sussex; Sec. MCC 1962-74; Pres. MCC 1979-80) b June 16, 1914
Griffiths, B. J. (Northants) b June 13, 1949
Griffiths, Sir W. H. (CUCC & Glam.) b Sept. 26, 1923
Grimmett, C. V. (Wgtn, Vic. & S. Aust.; *CY 1931*) b Dec. 25, 1891, d May 2, 1980
Grimshaw, N. (Northants) b May 5, 1911
Groube, T. U. (Vic.) b Sept. 2, 1857, d Aug. 5, 1927
Grout, A. T. W. (Qld) b March 30, 1927, d Nov. 9, 1968
Grove, C. W. (Warwicks. & Worcs.) b Dec. 16, 1912, d Feb. 15, 1982
Grover, J. N. (OUCC) b Oct. 15, 1915
Groves, M. G. M. (OUCC, Som. & W. Prov.) b Jan. 14, 1943
Grundy, J. (Notts. & Utd England XI) b March 5, 1824, d Nov. 24, 1873
Guard, G. M. (Bombay & Guj.) b Dec. 12, 1925, d March 13, 1978
Guest, C. E. J. (Vic. & W. Aust.) b Oct. 7, 1937
Guha, S. (Bengal) b Jan. 31, 1946
*Guillen, S. C. (T/T & Cant.) b Sept. 24, 1924
Guise, J. L. (OUCC & Middx) b Nov. 25, 1903
Gunasekera, Y. (SL) b Nov. 8, 1957
*Gul Mahomed (N. Ind., Baroda, H'bad, Punjab & Lahore) b Oct. 15, 1921
Guneratne, R. P. W. (SL) b Jan. 26, 1962
Gunn, G. (Notts.; *CY 1914*) b June 13, 1879, d June 28, 1958
Gunn, G. V. (Notts.) b June 21, 1905, d Oct. 14, 1957
Gunn, J. (Notts.; *CY 1904*) b July 19, 1876, d Aug. 21, 1963
Gunn, T. (Sussex) b Sept. 27, 1935
Gunn, William (Notts.; *CY 1890*) b Dec. 4, 1858, d Jan. 29, 1921
Gupte, B. P. (Bombay, Bengal & Ind. Rlwys) b Aug. 30, 1934
Gupte, S. P. (Bombay, Bengal, Raja. & T/T) b Dec. 11, 1929
Gurusinha, A. P. (SL) b Sept. 16, 1966
Gurr, D. R. (OUCC & Som.) b March 27, 1956
Guy, J. W. (C. Dist., Wgtn, Northants, Cant., Otago & N. Dist.) b Aug. 29, 1934

Haafiz Shahid (WAPDA) b May 10, 1963
Hacker, P. J. (Notts., Derbys. & OFS) b July 16, 1952
Hadlee, B. G. (Cant.) b Dec. 14, 1941
Hadlee, D. R. (Cant.) b Jan. 6, 1948
*Hadlee, R. J. (Cant., Notts. & Tas.; *CY 1982*) b July 3, 1951
*Hadlee, W. A. (Cant. & Otago) b June 4, 1915
Hafeez, A. (*see* Kardar)
*Haig, N. E. (Middx) b Dec. 12, 1887, d Oct. 27, 1966
*Haigh, S. (Yorks.; *CY 1901*) b March 19, 1871, d Feb. 27, 1921
Halfyard, D. J. (Kent & Notts.) b April 3, 1931
*Hall, A. E. (Tvl & Lancs.) b Jan. 23, 1896, d Jan. 1, 1964
*Hall, G. G. (NE Tvl & E. Prov.) b May 24, 1938, d June 26, 1987
Hall, I. W. (Derbys.) b Dec. 27, 1939
Hall, Louis (Yorks.; *CY 1890*) b Nov. 1, 1852, d Nov. 19, 1915
Hall, T. A. (Derbys. & Som.) b Aug. 19, 1930, d April 21, 1984
*Hall, W. W. (B'dos, T/T & Qld) b Sept. 12, 1937
Hallam, A. W. (Lancs. & Notts.; *CY 1908*) b Nov. 12, 1869, d July 24, 1940
Hallam, M. R. (Leics.) b Sept. 10, 1931
*Halliwell, E. A. (Tvl & Middx; *CY 1905*) b Sept. 7, 1864, d Oct. 2, 1919
*Hallows, C. (Lancs.; *CY 1928*) b April 4, 1895, d Nov. 10, 1972
Hallows, J. (Lancs.; *CY 1905*) b Nov. 14, 1873, d May 20, 1910
*Halse, C. G. (Natal) b Feb. 28, 1935
*Hamence, R. A. (S. Aust.) b Nov. 25, 1915
Hamer, A. (Yorks. & Derbys.) b Dec. 8, 1916
Hammond, H. E. (Sussex) b Nov. 7, 1907, d June 16, 1985
*Hammond, J. R. (S. Aust.) b April 19, 1950
*Hammond, W. R. (Glos.; *CY 1928*) b June 19, 1903, d July 1, 1965
*Hampshire, J. H. (Yorks., Derbys. & Tas.) b Feb. 10, 1941
*Hands, P. A. M. (W. Prov.) b March 18, 1890, d April 27, 1951
*Hands, R. H. M. (W. Prov.) b July 26, 1888, d April 20, 1918
*Hanif Mohammad (B'pur, Kar. & PIA; *CY 1968*) b Dec. 21, 1934
*Hanley, M. A. (Border & W. Prov.) b Nov. 10, 1918
Hanley, R. W. (E. Prov., OFS, Tvl & Northants) b Jan. 29, 1952
*Hanumant Singh (M. Pradesh & Raja.) b March 29, 1939
Harden, R. J. (Som. & C. Dist.) b Aug. 16, 1965
Hardie, B. R. (Scotland & Essex) b Jan. 14, 1950
*Hardikar, M. S. (Bombay) b Feb. 8, 1936
*Hardinge, H. T. W. (Kent; *CY 1915*) b Feb. 25, 1886, d May 8, 1965

*Hardstaff, J. (Notts.) b Nov. 9, 1882, d April 2, 1947
*Hardstaff, J., jun. (Notts. & Auck.; *CY 1938*) b July 3, 1911
Hardy, J. J. E. (Hants, Som. & W. Prov.) b Oct. 10, 1960
Harfield, L. (Hants) b Aug. 16, 1905, d Nov. 19, 1985
*Harford, N. S. (C. Dist. & Auck.) b Aug. 30, 1930, d March 30, 1981
*Harford, R. I. (Auck.) b May 30, 1936
Harman, R. (Surrey) b Dec. 28, 1941
*Haroon Rashid (Kar., Sind, NBP, PIA & UBL) b March 25, 1953
*Harper, R. A. (Guyana & Northants) b March 17, 1963
*Harris, 4th Lord (OUCC & Kent; Pres. MCC 1895) b Feb. 3, 1851, d March 24, 1932
Harris, David (Hants & All-England) b 1755, d May 19, 1803
Harris, M. J. (Middx, Notts., E. Prov. & Wgtn) b May 25, 1944
*Harris, P. G. Z. (Cant.) b July 18, 1927
*Harris, R. M. (Auck.) b July 27, 1933
*Harris, T. A. (Griq. W. & Tvl) b Aug. 27, 1916
Harrison, L. (Hants) b June 8, 1922
*Harry, J. (Vic.) b Aug. 1, 1857, d Oct. 27, 1919
Hart, G. E. (Middx) b Jan. 13, 1902, d April 11, 1987
Hart, R. T. (C. Dist.) b Nov. 7, 1961
*Hartigan, G. P. D. (Border) b Dec. 30, 1884, d Jan. 7, 1955
*Hartigan, R. J. (NSW & Qld) b Dec. 12, 1879, d June 7, 1958
*Hartkopf, A. E. V. (Vic.) b Dec. 28, 1889, d May 20, 1968
Hartley, A. (Lancs.; *CY 1911*) b April 11, 1879, d Oct. 1918
*Hartley, J. C. (OUCC & Sussex) b Nov. 15, 1874, d March 8, 1963
Hartley, P. J. (Warwicks. & Yorks.) b April 18, 1960
Hartley, S. N. (Yorks. & OFS) b March 18, 1956
Harvey, J. F. (Derbys.) b Sept. 27, 1939
*Harvey, M. R. (Vic.) b April 29, 1918
Harvey, P. F. (Notts.) b Jan. 15, 1923
*Harvey, R. L. (Natal) b Sept. 14, 1911
*Harvey, R. N. (Vic. & NSW; *CY 1954*) b Oct. 8, 1928
Harvey-Walker, A. J. (Derbys.) b July 21, 1944
Hasan Jamil (Kalat, Kar., Pak. Us & PIA) b July 25, 1952
*Haseeb Ahsan (Peshawar, Pak. Us, Kar. & PIA) b July 15, 1939
Hassan, B. (Notts.) b March 24, 1944
*Hassett, A. L. (Vic.; *CY 1949*) b Aug. 28, 1913

*Hastings, B. F. (Wgtn, C. Dist. & Cant.) b March 23, 1940
*Hathorn, C. M. H. (Tvl) b April 7, 1878, d May 17, 1920
*Hawke, 7th Lord (CUCC & Yorks.; *CY 1909*; Pres. MCC 1914-18) b Aug. 16, 1860, d Oct. 10, 1938
*Hawke, N. J. N. (W. Aust., S. Aust. & Tas.) b June 27, 1939
Hawker, Sir Cyril (Essex; Pres. MCC 1970-71) b July 21, 1900
Hawkins, D. G. (Glos.) b May 18, 1935
*Hayes, E. G. (Surrey & Leics.; *CY 1907*) b Nov. 6, 1876, d Dec. 2, 1953
*Hayes, F. C. (Lancs.) b Dec. 6, 1946
*Hayes, J. A. (Auck. & Cant.) b Jan. 11, 1927
Hayes, K. A. (OUCC & Lancs.) b Sept. 26, 1962
Haygarth, A. (Sussex; Historian) b Aug. 4, 1825, d May 1, 1903
*Haynes, D. L. (B'dos) b Feb. 15, 1956
Haysman, M. D. (S. Aust. & Leics.) b April 22, 1961
Hayward, T. (Cambs. & All-England) b March 21, 1835, d July 21, 1876
*Hayward, T. W. (Surrey; *CY 1895*) b March 29, 1871, d July 19, 1939
Haywood, P. R. (Leics.) b March 30, 1947
*Hazare, V. S. (M'tra, C. Ind. & Baroda) b March 11, 1915
Hazell, H. L. (Som.) b Sept. 30, 1909
Hazlerigg, Lord, formerly Hon. A. G. (CUCC & Leics.) b Feb. 24, 1910
*Hazlitt, G. R. (Vic. & NSW) b Sept. 4, 1888, d Oct. 30, 1915
*Headley, G. A. (Jam.; *CY 1934*) b May 30, 1909, d Nov. 30, 1983
*Headley, R. G. A. (Worcs. & Jam.) b June 29, 1939
Hearn, P. (Kent) b Nov. 18, 1925
*Hearne, Alec (Kent; *CY 1894*) b July 22, 1863, d May 16, 1952
**Hearne, Frank (Kent & W. Prov.) b Nov. 23, 1858, d July 14, 1949
*Hearne, G. A. L. (W. Prov.) b March 27, 1888, d Nov. 13, 1978
*Hearne, George G. (Kent) b July 7, 1856, d Feb. 13, 1932
*Hearne, J. T. (Middx; *CY 1892*) b May 3, 1867, d April 17, 1944
*Hearne, J. W. (Middx; *CY 1912*) b Feb. 11, 1891, d Sept. 13, 1965
Hearne, Thos. (Middx) b Sept. 4, 1826, d May 13, 1900
Hearne, Thos., jun. (Lord's Ground Superintendent) b Dec. 29, 1849, d Jan. 29, 1910
Heath, G. E. M. (Hants) b Feb. 20, 1913
Heath, M. (Hants) b March 9, 1934
Hedges, B. (Glam.) b Nov. 10, 1927

Hedges, L. P. (Tonbridge, OUCC, Kent & Glos.; *CY 1919*) b July 13, 1900, d Jan. 12, 1933
Hegg, W. K. (Lancs.) b Feb. 23, 1968
Heine, P. S. (NE Tvl, OFS & Tvl) b June 28, 1928
Hemmings, E. E. (Warwicks. & Notts.) b Feb. 20, 1949
Hemsley, E. J. O. (Worcs.) b Sept. 1, 1943
Henderson, M. (Wgtn) b Aug. 2, 1895, d June 17, 1970
Henderson, R. (Surrey; *CY 1890*) b March 30, 1865, d Jan. 29, 1931
Henderson, S. P. (CUCC, Worcs. & Glam.) b Sept. 24, 1958
Hendren, E. H. (Middx; *CY 1920*) b Feb. 5, 1889, d Oct. 4, 1962
Hendrick, M. (Derbys. & Notts.; *CY 1978*) b Oct. 22, 1948
Hendriks, J. L. (Jam.) b Dec. 21, 1933
Hendry, H. L. (NSW & Vic.) b May 24, 1895, d Dec. 16, 1988
Henry, O. (W. Prov., Boland & Scotland) b Jan. 23, 1952
Herman, O. W. (Hants) b Sept. 18, 1907, d June 24, 1987
Herman, R. S. (Middx, Border, Griq. W. & Hants) b Nov. 30, 1946
Heron, J. G. (Zimb.) b Nov. 8, 1948
*Heseltine, C. (Hants) b Nov. 26, 1869, d June 13, 1944
Hever, N. G. (Middx & Glam.) b Dec. 17, 1924, d Sept. 11, 1987
Hewetson, E. P. (OUCC & Warwicks.) b May 27, 1902, d Dec. 26, 1977
Hewett, H. T. (OUCC & Som.; *CY 1893*) b May 25, 1864, d March 4, 1921
Heyn, P. D. (SL) b June 26, 1945
*Hibbert, P. A. (Vic.) b July 23, 1952
Hick, G. A. (Worcs., Zimb. & N. Dist.; *CY 1987*) b May 23, 1966
Higgins, H. L. (Worcs.) b Feb. 24, 1894, d Sept. 15, 1979
*Higgs, J. D. (Vic.) b July 11, 1950
*Higgs, K. (Lancs. & Leics.; *CY 1968*) b Jan. 14, 1937
Hignell, A. J. (CUCC & Glos.) b Sept. 4, 1955
*Hilditch, A. M. J. (NSW & S. Aust.) b May 20, 1956
Hill, Alan (Derbys. & OFS) b June 29, 1950
*Hill, Allen (Yorks.) b Nov. 14, 1843, d Aug. 29, 1910
*Hill, A. J. L. (CUCC & Hants) b July 26, 1871, d Sept. 6, 1950
*Hill, C. (S. Aust.; *CY 1900*) b March 18, 1877, d Sept. 5, 1945
Hill, E. (Som.) b July 9, 1923
Hill, G. (Hants) b April 15, 1913
*Hill, J. C. (Vic.) b June 25, 1923, d Aug. 11, 1974
Hill, L. W. (Glam.) b April 14, 1942
Hill, M. (Notts., Derbys & Som.) b Sept. 14, 1935
Hill, N. W. (Notts.) b Aug. 22, 1935
Hill, W. A. (Warwicks.) b April 27, 1910
Hills, J. J. (Glam.; Umpire) b Oct. 14, 1897, d Oct. 1969
Hills, R. W. (Kent) b Jan. 8, 1951
Hill-Wood, C. K. (OUCC & Derbys.) b June 5, 1907, d Sept. 21, 1988
Hill-Wood, Sir W. W. (CUCC & Derbys.) b Sept. 8, 1901, d Oct. 10, 1980
Hilton, C. (Lancs. & Essex) b Sept. 26, 1937
Hilton, J. (Lancs. & Som.) b Dec. 29, 1930
*Hilton, M. J. (Lancs.; *CY 1957*) b Aug. 2, 1928
*Hime, C. F. W. (Natal) b Oct. 24, 1869, d Dec. 6, 1940
*Hindlekar, D. D. (Bombay) b Jan. 1, 1909, d March 30, 1949
Hinks, S. G. (Kent) b Oct. 12, 1960
*Hirst, G. H. (Yorks.; *CY 1901*) b Sept. 7, 1871, d May 10, 1954
*Hirwani, N. D. (M. Pradesh) b Oct. 18, 1968
*Hitch, J. W. (Surrey; *CY 1914*) b May 7, 1886, d July 7, 1965
Hitchcock, R. E. (Cant. & Warwicks.) b Nov. 28, 1929
*Hoad, E. L. G. (B'dos) b Jan. 29, 1896, d March 5, 1986
*Hoare, D. E. (W. Aust.) b Oct. 19, 1934
*Hobbs, Sir J. B. (Surrey; *CY 1909, special portrait 1926*) b Dec. 16, 1882, d Dec. 21, 1963
*Hobbs, R. N. S. (Essex & Glam.) b May 8, 1942
Hobson, D. L. (E. Prov. & W. Prov.) b Sept. 3, 1951
*Hodges, J. H. (Vic.) b July 31, 1856, d Jan. 17, 1933
Hodgkinson, G. F. (Derbys.) b Feb. 19, 1914, d Jan. 7, 1987
Hodgson, A. (Northants) b Oct. 27, 1951
Hofmeyr, M. B. (OUCC & NE Tvl) b Dec. 9, 1925
*Hogan, T. G. (W. Aust.) b Sept. 23, 1956
*Hogg, R. M. (S. Aust.) b March 5, 1951
Hogg, W. (Lancs. & Warwicks.) b July 12, 1955
*Holder, V. A. (B'dos, Worcs. & OFS) b Oct. 8, 1945
*Holding, M. A. (Jam., Lancs., Derbys., Tas. & Cant.; *CY 1977*) b Feb. 16, 1954
*Hole, G. B. (NSW & S. Aust.) b Jan. 6, 1931
*Holford, D. A. J. (B'dos & T/T) b April 16, 1940
*Holland, R. G. (NSW & Wgtn) b Oct. 19, 1946
*Hollies, W. E. (Warwicks.; *CY 1955*) b June 5, 1912, d April 16, 1981
Hollingdale, R. A. (Sussex) b March 6, 1906

Holmes, Gp Capt. A. J. (Sussex) b June 30, 1899, d May 21, 1950
*Holmes, E. R. T. (OUCC & Surrey; *CY 1936*) b Aug. 21, 1905, d Aug. 16, 1960
Holmes, G. C. (Glam.) b Sept. 16, 1958
*Holmes, P. (Yorks.; *CY 1920*) b Nov. 25, 1886, d Sept. 3, 1971
Holt, A. G. (Hants) b April 8, 1911
*Holt, J. K., jun. (Jam.) b Aug. 12, 1923
Home of the Hirsel, Lord (Middx; Pres. MCC 1966-67) b July 2, 1903
Hone, Sir B. W. (S. Aust. & OUCC) b July 1, 1907, d May 28, 1978
*Hone, L. (MCC) b Jan. 30, 1853, d Dec. 31, 1896
Hooker, J. E. H. (NSW) b March 6, 1898, d Feb. 12, 1982
Hooker, R. W. (Middx) b Feb. 22, 1935
*Hookes, D. W. (S. Aust.) b May 3, 1955
*Hooper, C. L. (Guyana) b Dec. 15, 1966
*Hopkins, A. J. Y. (NSW) b May 3, 1874, d April 25, 1931
Hopkins, J. A. (Glam. & E. Prov.) b June 16, 1953
Hopkins, V. (Glos.) b Jan. 21, 1911, d Aug. 6, 1984
*Hopwood, J. L. (Lancs.) b Oct. 30, 1903, d June 15, 1985
*Horan, T. P. (Vic.) b March 8, 1854, d April 16, 1916
*Hordern, H. V. (NSW & Philadelphians) b Feb. 10, 1883, d June 17, 1938
*Hornby, A. N. (Lancs.) b Feb. 10, 1847, d Dec. 17, 1925
*Horne, P. A. (Auck.) b Jan. 21, 1960
Horner, N. F. (Yorks. & Warwicks.) b May 10, 1926
*Hornibrook, P. M. (Qld) b July 27, 1899, d Aug. 25, 1976
Horsfall, R. (Essex & Glam.) b June 26, 1920, d Aug. 25, 1981
Horton, H. (Worcs. & Hants) b April 18, 1923
Horton, J. (Worcs.) b Aug. 12, 1916
*Horton, M. J. (Worcs. & N. Dist.) b April 21, 1934
Hossell, J. J. (Warwicks.) b May 25, 1914
*Hough, K. W. (Auck.) b Oct. 24, 1928
*Howard, A. B. (B'dos) b Aug. 27, 1946
Howard, A. H. (Glam.) b Dec. 11, 1910
Howard, B. J. (Lancs.) b May 21, 1926
Howard, K. (Lancs.) b June 29, 1941
*Howard, N. D. (Lancs.) b May 18, 1925, d May 31, 1979
Howard, Major R. (Lancs.; MCC Team Manager) b April 17, 1890, d Sept. 10, 1967
*Howarth, G. P. (Auck., Surrey & N. Dist.) b March 29, 1951
*Howarth, H. J. (Auck.) b Dec. 25, 1943
*Howell, H. (Warwicks.) b Nov. 29, 1890, d July 9, 1932
*Howell, W. P. (NSW) b Dec. 29, 1869, d July 14, 1940
Howland, C. B. (CUCC, Sussex & Kent) b Feb. 6, 1936
*Howorth, R. (Worcs.) b April 26, 1909, d April 2, 1980
Hughes, D. P. (Lancs. & Tas.; *CY 1988*) b May 13, 1947
*Hughes, K. J. (W. Aust.; *CY 1981*) b Jan. 26, 1954
*Hughes, M. G. (Vic. & Essex) b Nov. 23, 1961
Hughes, S. P. (Middx & N. Tvl) b Dec. 20, 1959
Huish, F. H. (Kent) b Nov. 15, 1869, d March 16, 1957
Hulme, J. H. A. (Middx) b Aug. 26, 1904
Human, J. H. (CUCC & Middx) b Jan. 13, 1912
Humpage, G. W. (Warwicks. & OFS; *CY 1985*) b April 24, 1954
Humphries, D. J. (Leics. & Worcs.) b Aug. 6, 1953
*Humphries, J. (Derbys.) b May 19, 1876, d May 8, 1946
Hunt, A. V. (Scotland & Bermuda) b Oct. 1, 1910
*Hunt, W. A. (NSW) b Aug. 26, 1908, d Dec. 31, 1983
*Hunte, C. C. (B'dos; *CY 1964*) b May 9, 1932
*Hunte, E. A. C. (T/T) b Oct. 3, 1905, d June 26, 1967
Hunter, David (Yorks.) b Feb. 23, 1860, d Jan. 11, 1927
*Hunter, Joseph (Yorks.) b Aug. 3, 1855, d Jan. 4, 1891
Hurd, A. (CUCC & Essex) b Sept. 7, 1937
*Hurst, A. G. (Vic.) b July 15, 1950
Hurst, R. J. (Middx) b Dec. 29, 1933
*Hurwood, A. (Qld) b June 17, 1902, d Sept. 26, 1982
*Hussain, M. Dilawar (C. Ind. & U. Prov.) b March 19, 1907, d Aug. 26, 1967
*Hutchings, K. L. (Kent; *CY 1907*) b Dec. 7, 1882, d Sept. 3, 1916
Hutchinson, J. M. (Derbys.) b Nov. 29, 1896
*Hutchinson, P. (SA) b Jan. 26, 1862, d Sept. 30, 1925
*Hutton, Sir Leonard (Yorks.; *CY 1938*) b June 23, 1916
*Hutton, R. A. (CUCC, Yorks. & Tvl) b Sept. 6, 1942
*Hylton, L. G. (Jam.) b March 29, 1905, d May 17, 1955

*Ibadulla, K. (Punjab, Warwicks., Tas. & Otago) b Dec. 20, 1935
*Ibrahim, K. C. (Bombay) b Jan. 26, 1919
*Iddon, J. (Lancs.) b Jan. 8, 1902, d April 17, 1946

Igglesden, A. P. (Kent & W. Prov.) b Oct. 8, 1964
*Ijaz Ahmed (Gujranwala, PACO & HBL) b Sept. 20, 1968
*Ijaz Butt (Pak. Us, Punjab, Lahore, R'pindi & Multan) b March 10, 1938
*Ijaz Faqih (Kar., Sind, PWD & MCB) b March 24, 1956
*Ikin, J. T. (Lancs.) b March 7, 1918, d Sept. 15, 1984
*Illingworth, R. (Yorks. & Leics.; *CY 1960*) b June 8, 1932
Illingworth, R. K. (Worcs.) b Aug. 23, 1963
*Imran Khan (Lahore, Dawood, Worcs., OUCC, PIA, Sussex & NSW; *CY 1983*) b Nov. 25, 1952
*Imtiaz Ahmed (N. Ind., Comb. Us, NWFP, Pak. Serv., Peshawar & PAF) b Jan. 5, 1928
*Imtiaz Ali (T/T) b July 28, 1954
Inchmore, J. D. (Worcs. & N. Tvl) b Feb. 22, 1949
*Indrajitsinhji, K. S. (S'tra & Delhi) b June 15, 1937
Ingle, R. A. (Som.) b Nov. 5, 1903
Ingleby-Mackenzie, A. C. D. (Hants) b Sept. 15, 1933
Inman C. C. (Ceylon & Leics.) b Jan. 29, 1936
Innes, G. A. S. (W. Prov. & Tvl) b Nov. 16, 1931, d July 19, 1982
*Inshan Ali (T/T) b Sept. 25, 1949
*Insole, D. J. (CUCC & Essex; *CY 1956*) b April 18, 1926
*Intikhab Alam (Kar., PIA, Surrey, PWD, Sind & Punjab) b Dec. 28, 1941
*Inverarity, R. J. (W. Aust. & S. Aust.) b Jan. 31, 1944
*Iqbal Qasim (Kar., Sind & NBP) b Aug. 6, 1953
*Irani, J. K. (Sind) b Aug. 18, 1923, d Feb. 25, 1982
*Iredale, F. A. (NSW) b June 19, 1867, d April 15, 1926
Iremonger, J. (Notts.; *CY 1903*) b March 5, 1876, d March 25, 1956
*Ironmonger, H. (Qld & Vic.) b April 7, 1882, d June 1, 1971
*Ironside, D. E. J. (Tvl) b May 2, 1925
*Irvine, B. L. (W. Prov., Natal, Essex & Tvl) b March 9, 1944
*Israr Ali (S. Punjab, B'pur & Multan) b May 1, 1927
*Iverson, J. B. (Vic.) b July 27, 1915, d Oct. 24, 1973

*Jackman, R. D. (Surrey, W. Prov. & Rhod.; *CY 1981*) b Aug. 13, 1945
*Jackson, A. A. (NSW) b Sept. 5, 1909, d Feb. 16, 1933
Jackson, A. B. (Derbys.) b Aug. 21, 1933
Jackson, Sir A. H. M. (Derbys.) b Nov. 9, 1899, d Oct. 11, 1983
*Jackson, Rt Hon. Sir F. S. (CUCC & Yorks.; *CY 1894*; Pres. MCC 1921) b Nov. 21, 1870, d March 9, 1947
Jackson, G. R. (Derbys.) b June 23, 1896, d Feb. 21, 1966
*Jackson, H. L. (Derbys.; *CY 1959*) b April 5, 1921
Jackson, John (Notts. & All-England) b May 21, 1833, d Nov. 4, 1901
Jackson, P. F. (Worcs.) b May 11, 1911
Jacques, T. A. (Yorks.) b Feb. 19, 1905
*Jahangir Khan (N. Ind. & CUCC) b Feb. 1, 1910, d July 23, 1988
*Jai, L. P. (Bombay) b April 1, 1902, d Jan. 29, 1968
*Jaisimha, M. L. (H'bad) b March 3, 1939
Jakeman, F. (Yorks. & Northants) b Jan. 10, 1920, d May 18, 1986
*Jalal-ud-Din (PWD, Kar., IDBP & Allied Bank) b June 12, 1959
James, A. E. (Sussex) b Aug. 7, 1924
*James, K. C. (Wgtn & Northants) b March 12, 1904, d Aug. 21, 1976
James, K. D. (Middx, Hants & Wgtn) b March 18, 1961
James, R. M. (CUCC & Wgtn) b Oct. 2, 1934
*Jameson, J. A. (Warwicks.) b June 30, 1941
*Jamshedji, R. J. D. (Bombay) b Nov. 18, 1892, d April 5, 1976
*Jardine, D. R. (OUCC & Surrey; *CY 1928*) b Oct. 23, 1900, d June 18, 1958
Jardine, M. R. (OUCC & Middx) b June 8, 1869, d Jan. 16, 1947
*Jarman, B. N. (S. Aust.) b Feb. 17, 1936
Jarrett, D. W. (OUCC & CUCC) b April 19, 1952
*Jarvis, A. H. (S. Aust.) b Oct. 19, 1860, d Nov. 15, 1933
Jarvis, K. B. S. (Kent & Glos.) b April 23, 1953
*Jarvis, P. W. (Yorks.) b June 29, 1965
*Jarvis, T. W. (Auck. & Cant.) b July 29, 1944
*Javed Akhtar (R'pindi & Pak. Serv.) b Nov. 21, 1940
*Javed Miandad (Kar., Sind, Sussex, HBL & Glam.; *CY 1982*) b June 12, 1957
*Jayantilal, K. (H'bad) b Jan. 13, 1948
*Jayasekera, R. S. A. (SL) b Dec. 7, 1957
Jayasinghe, S. (Ceylon & Leics.) b Jan. 19, 1931
Jayasinghe, S. A. (SL) b July 15, 1955
Jefferies, S. T. (W. Prov., Derbys., Lancs. & Hants) b Dec. 8, 1959
Jefferson, R. I. (CUCC & Surrey) b Aug. 15, 1941
*Jeganathan, S. (SL) b July 11, 1951
*Jenkins, R. O. (Worcs.; *CY 1950*) b Nov. 24, 1918

Jenkins, V. G. J. (OUCC & Glam.) b Nov. 2, 1911
*Jenner, T. J. (W. Aust. & S. Aust.) b Sept. 8, 1944
*Jennings, C. B. (S. Aust.) b June 5, 1884, d June 20, 1950
Jennings, K. F. (Som.) b Oct. 5, 1953
Jennings, R. V. (Tvl) b Aug. 9, 1954
Jepson, A. (Notts.) b July 12, 1915
*Jessop, G. L. (CUCC & Glos.; *CY 1898*) b May 19, 1874, d May 11, 1955
Jesty, T. E. (Hants., Border, Griq. W., Cant., Surrey & Lancs.; *CY 1983*) b June 2, 1948
Jewell, Major M. F. S. (Sussex & Worcs.) b Sept. 15, 1885, d May 28, 1978
*John, V. B. (SL) b May 27, 1960
Johnson, C. (Yorks.) b Sept. 5, 1947
*Johnson, C. L. (Tvl) b 1871, d May 31, 1908
Johnson, G. W. (Kent & Tvl) b Nov. 8, 1946
*Johnson, H. H. H. (Jam.) b July 17, 1910, d June 24, 1987
Johnson, H. L. (Derbys.) b Nov. 8, 1927
*Johnson, I. W. (Vic.) b Dec. 8, 1918
Johnson, L. A. (Northants) b Aug. 12, 1936
*Johnson, L. J. (Qld) b March 18, 1919, d April 20, 1977
Johnson, P. (Notts.) b April 24, 1965
Johnson, P. D. (CUCC & Notts.) b Nov. 12, 1949
*Johnson, T. F. (T/T) b Jan. 10, 1917, d April 5, 1985
Johnston, B. A. (Broadcaster) b June 24, 1912
*Johnston, W. A. (Vic.; *CY 1949*) b Feb. 26, 1922
Jones, A. (Glam., W. Aust., N. Tvl & Natal; *CY 1978*) b Nov. 4, 1938
Jones, A. A. (Sussex, Som., Middx, Glam., N. Tvl & OFS) b Dec. 9, 1947
*Jones, A. H. (Wgtn) b May 9, 1959
Jones, A. L. (Glam.) b June 1, 1957
Jones, A. N. (Sussex, Border & Som.) b July 22, 1961
*Jones, A. O. (Notts. & CUCC; *CY 1900*) b Aug. 16, 1872, d Dec. 21, 1914
Jones, B. J. R. (Worcs.) b Nov. 2, 1955
*Jones, C. M. (C. E. L.) (BG) b Nov. 3, 1902, d Dec. 10, 1959
*Jones, D. M. (Vic.) b March 24, 1961
*Jones, Ernest (S. Aust. & W. Aust.) b Sept. 30, 1869, d Nov. 23, 1943
Jones, E. C. (Glam.) b Dec. 14, 1912
Jones, E. W. (Glam.) b June 25, 1942
*Jones, I. J. (Glam.) b Dec. 10, 1941
Jones, K. V. (Middx) b March 28, 1942
*Jones, P. E. (T/T) b June 6, 1917
Jones, P. H. (Kent) b June 19, 1935
*Jones, S. P. (NSW, Qld & Auck.) b Aug. 1, 1861, d July 14, 1951
Jones, W. E. (Glam.) b Oct. 31, 1916
Jordan, J. M. (Lancs.) b Feb. 7, 1932
Jorden, A. M. (CUCC & Essex) b Jan. 28, 1947
Jordon, R. C. (Vic.) b Feb. 17, 1937
*Joshi, P. G. (M'tra) b Oct. 27, 1926, d Jan. 8, 1987
Joshi, U. C. (S'tra, Ind. Rlwys, Guj. & Sussex) b Dec. 23, 1944
*Joslin, L. R. (Vic.) b Dec. 13, 1947
Jowett, D. C. P. R. (OUCC) b Jan. 24, 1931
Judd, A. K. (CUCC & Hants) b Jan. 1, 1904, d Feb. 15, 1988
Judge, P. F. (Middx, Glam. & Bengal) b May 23, 1916
Julian, R. (Leics.) b Aug. 23, 1936
*Julien, B. D. (T/T & Kent) b March 13, 1950
*Jumadeen, R. R. (T/T) b April 12, 1948
*Jupp, H. (Surrey) b Nov. 19, 1841, d April 8, 1889
*Jupp, V. W. C. (Sussex & Northants; *CY 1928*) b March 27, 1891, d July 9, 1960
*Jurangpathy, B. R. (SL) b June 25, 1967

*Kallicharran, A. I. (Guyana, Warwicks., Qld, Tvl & OFS; *CY 1983*) b March 21, 1949
*Kaluperuma, L. W. (SL) b May 25, 1949
*Kaluperuma, S. M. S. (SL) b Oct. 22, 1961
*Kanhai, R. B. (†Guyana, T/T, W. Aust., Warwicks. & Tas.; *CY 1964*) b Dec. 26, 1935
*Kanitkar, H. S. (M'tra) b Dec. 8, 1942
*Kapil Dev (Haryana, Northants & Worcs.; *CY 1983*) b Jan. 6, 1959
**Kardar, A. H. (formerly Abdul Hafeez) (N. Ind., OUCC, Warwicks. & Pak. Serv.) b Jan. 17, 1925
Karnain, U. S. H. (SL) b Aug. 11, 1962
*Keeton, W. W. (Notts.; *CY 1940*) b April 30, 1905, d Oct. 10, 1980
Keighley, W. G. (OUCC & Yorks.) b Jan. 10, 1925
*Keith, H. J. (Natal) b Oct. 25, 1927
Kelleher, H. R. A. (Surrey & Northants) b March 3, 1929
*Kelleway, C. (NSW) b April 25, 1886, d Nov. 16, 1944
Kelly, J. (Notts.) b Sept. 15, 1930
*Kelly, J. J. (NSW; *CY 1903*) b May 10, 1867, d Aug. 14, 1938
Kelly, J. M. (Lancs. & Derbys.) b March 19, 1922, d Nov. 13, 1979
*Kelly, T. J. D. (Vic.) b May 3, 1844, d July 20, 1893
*Kempis, G. A. (Natal) b Aug. 4, 1865, d May 19, 1890
*Kendall, T. (Vic. & Tas.) b Aug. 24, 1851, d Aug. 17, 1924
Kennedy, A. (Lancs.) b Nov. 4, 1949
*Kennedy, A. S. (Hants; *CY 1933*) b Jan. 24, 1891, d Nov. 15, 1959

*Kenny, R. B. (Bombay & Bengal) b Sept. 29, 1930, d Nov. 21, 1985
*Kent, M. F. (Qld) b Nov. 23, 1953
*Kentish, E. S. M. (Jam. & OUCC) b Nov. 21, 1916
*Kenyon, D. (Worcs.; *CY 1963*) b May 15, 1924
*Kerr, R. B. (Qld) b June 16, 1961
*Kerr, J. L. (Cant.) b Dec. 28, 1910
Kerr, K. J. (Tvl & Warwicks.) b Sept. 11, 1961
Kerslake, R. C. (CUCC & Som.) b Dec. 26, 1942
Kettle, M. K. (Northants) b March 18, 1944
*Khalid Hassan (Punjab & Lahore) b July 14, 1937
*Khalid Wazir (Pak.) b April 27, 1936
*Khan Mohammad (N. Ind., Pak. Us, Som., B'pur, Sind, Kar. & Lahore) b Jan. 1, 1928
Khanna, S. C. (Delhi) b June 3, 1956
Kidd, E. L. (CUCC & Middx) b Oct. 18, 1889, d July 2, 1984
Kilborn, M. J. (OUCC) b Sept. 20, 1962
*Killick, Rev. E. T. (CUCC & Middx) b May 9, 1907, d May 18, 1953
Kilner, Norman (Yorks. & Warwicks.) b July 21, 1895, d April 28, 1979
*Kilner, Roy (Yorks.; *CY 1924*) b Oct. 17, 1890, d April 5, 1928
Kimpton, R. C. M. (OUCC & Worcs.) b Sept. 21, 1916
*King, C. L. (B'dos, Glam., Worcs. & Natal) b June 11, 1951
*King, F. McD. (B'dos) b Dec. 14, 1926
King, I. M. (Warwicks. & Essex) b Nov. 10, 1931
King, J. B. (Philadelphia) b Oct. 19, 1873, d Oct. 17, 1965
*King, J. H. (Leics.) b April 16, 1871, d Nov. 18, 1946
*King, L. A. (Jam. & Bengal) b Feb. 27, 1939
Kingsley, Sir P. G. T. (OUCC) b May 26, 1908
*Kinneir, S. P. (Warwicks.; *CY 1912*) b May 13, 1871, d Oct. 16, 1928
*Kippax, A. F. (NSW) b May 25, 1897, d Sept. 4, 1972
Kirby, D. (CUCC & Leics.) b Jan. 18, 1939
*Kirmani, S. M. H. (†Karn.) b Dec. 29, 1949
Kirsten, P. N. (W. Prov., Sussex & Derbys.) b May 14, 1955
*Kischenchand, G. (W. Ind., Guj. & Baroda) b April 14, 1925
Kitchen, M. J. (Som.) b Aug. 1, 1940
*Kline, L. F. (Vic.) b Sept. 29, 1934
*Knight, A. E. (Leics.; *CY 1904*) b Oct. 8, 1872, d April 25, 1946
*Knight, B. R. (Essex & Leics.) b Feb. 18, 1938
*Knight, D. J. (OUCC & Surrey; *CY 1915*) b May 12, 1894, d Jan. 5, 1960
Knight, R. D. V. (CUCC, Surrey, Glos. & Sussex) b Sept. 6, 1946
Knight, W. H. (Editor of *Wisden* 1870-79) b Nov. 29, 1812, d Aug. 16, 1879
*Knott, A. P. E. (Kent & Tas.; *CY 1970*) b April 9, 1946
Knott, C. H. (OUCC & Kent) b March 20, 1901, d June 18, 1988
Knott, C. J. (Hants) b Nov. 26, 1914
Knowles, J. (Notts.) b March 25, 1910
Knox, G. K. (Lancs.) b April 22, 1937
*Knox, N. A. (Surrey; *CY 1907*) b Oct. 10, 1884, d March 3, 1935
Kortright, C. J. (Essex) b Jan. 9, 1871, d Dec. 12, 1952
*Kotze, J. J. (Tvl & W. Prov.) b Aug. 7, 1879, d July 7, 1931
Kourie, A. J. (Tvl) b July 30, 1951
*Kripal Singh, A. G. (Madras & H'bad) b Aug. 6, 1933, d July 23, 1987
*Krishnamurthy, P. (H'bad) b July 12, 1947
Kuggeleijn, C. M. (N. Dist.) b May 10, 1956
Kuiper, A. P. (W. Prov.) b Aug. 24, 1959
*Kulkarni, R. R. (Bombay) b Sept. 25, 1962
*Kulkarni, U. N. (Bombay) b March 7, 1942
*Kumar, V. V. (†TN) b June 22, 1935
*Kunderan, B. K. (Ind. Rlwys & Mysore) b Oct. 2, 1939
*Kuruppu, D. S. B. P. (SL) b Jan. 5, 1962
*Kuruppuarachchi, A. K. (SL) b Nov. 1, 1964
*Kuys, F. (W. Prov.) b March 21, 1870, d Sept. 12, 1953
Kynaston, R. (Middx; Sec. MCC 1846-58) b Nov. 5, 1805, d June 21, 1874

*Labrooy, G. F. (SL) b June 7, 1964
Lacey, Sir F. E. (CUCC & Hants; Sec MCC 1898-1926) b Oct. 19, 1859, d May 26, 1946
*Laird, B. M. (W. Aust.) b Nov. 21, 1950
*Laker, J. C. (Surrey, Auck. & Essex; *CY 1952*) b Feb. 9, 1922, d April 23, 1986
*Lall Singh (S. Punjab) b Dec. 16, 1909, d Nov. 19, 1985
*Lamb, A. J. (W. Prov., Northants & OFS; *CY 1981*) b June 20, 1954
Lamb, T. M. (OUCC, Middx & Northants) b March 24, 1953
*Lamba, R. (Delhi) b Jan. 2, 1958
Lambert, G. E. (Glos. & Som.) b May 11, 1919
Lambert, R. H. (Ireland) b July 18, 1874, d March 24, 1956
Lambert, Wm (Surrey) b 1779, d April 19, 1851
Lampard, A. W. (Vic. & AIF) b July 3, 1885, d Jan. 11, 1984
*Lance, H. R. (NE Tvl & Tvl) b June 6, 1940

Langdale, G. R. (Derbys. & Som.) b March 11, 1916
Langford, B. A. (Som.) b Dec. 17, 1935
*Langley, G. R. (S. Aust.; *CY 1957*) b Sept. 14, 1919
*Langridge, James (Sussex; *CY 1932*) b July 10, 1906, d Sept. 10, 1966
Langridge, J. G. (John) (Sussex; *CY 1950*) b Feb. 10, 1910
Langridge, R. J. (Sussex) b April 13, 1939
*Langton, A. B. C. (Tvl) b March 2, 1912, d Nov. 27, 1942
*Larkins, W. (Northants & E. Prov.) b Nov. 22, 1953
*Larter, J. D. F. (Northants) b April 24, 1940
*Larwood, H. (Notts.; *CY 1927*) b Nov. 14, 1904
*Lashley, P. D. (B'dos) b Feb. 11, 1937
Latchman, A. H. (Middx & Notts.) b July 26, 1943
*Laughlin, T. J. (Vic.) b Jan. 30, 1951
*Laver, F. (Vic.) b Dec. 7, 1869, d Sept. 24, 1919
*Lawrence, D. V. (Glos.) b Jan. 28, 1964
*Lawrence, G. B. (Rhod. & Natal) b March 31, 1932
Lawrence, J. (Som.) b March 29, 1914
*Lawry, W. M. (Vic.; *CY 1962*) b Feb. 11, 1937
*Lawson, G. F. (NSW & Lancs.) b Dec. 7, 1957
Leadbeater, B. (Yorks.) b Aug. 14, 1943
*Leadbeater, E. (Yorks. & Warwicks.) b Aug. 15, 1927
Leary, S. E. (Kent) b April 30, 1933, d Aug. 21, 1988
Lee, C. (Yorks. & Derbys.) b March 17, 1924
Lee, F. S. (Middx & Som.) b July 24, 1905, d March 30, 1982
Lee, G. M. (Notts. & Derbys.) b June 7, 1887, d Feb. 29, 1976
*Lee, H. W. (Middx) b Oct. 26, 1890, d April 21, 1981
Lee, J. W. (Middx & Som.) b Feb. 1, 1904, d June 20, 1944
Lee, P. G. (Northants & Lancs.; *CY 1976*) b Aug. 27, 1945
*Lee, P. K. (S. Aust.) b Sept. 14, 1904, d Aug. 9, 1980
*Lees, W. K. (Otago) b March 19, 1952
*Lees, W. S. (Surrey; *CY 1906*) b Dec. 25, 1875, d Sept. 10, 1924
Leese, Sir Oliver, Bt (Pres. MCC 1965-66) b Oct. 27, 1894, d Jan. 20, 1978
*Legall, R. A. (B'dos & T/T) b Dec. 1, 1925
Legard, E. (Warwicks.) b Aug. 23, 1935
*Leggat, I. B. (C. Dist.) b June 7, 1930
*Leggat, J. G. (Cant.) b May 27, 1926, d March 8, 1973
*Legge, G. B. (OUCC & Kent) b Jan. 26, 1903, d Nov. 21, 1940
Lenham, L. J. (Sussex) b May 24, 1936
Lenham, N. J. (Sussex) b Dec. 17, 1965
*le Roux, F. L. (Tvl & E. Prov.) b Feb. 5, 1882, d Sept. 22, 1963
le Roux, G. S. (W. Prov. & Sussex) b Sept. 4, 1955
*Leslie, C. F. H. (OUCC & Middx) b Dec. 8, 1861, d Feb. 12, 1921
Lester, E. (Yorks.) b Feb. 18, 1923
Lester, G. (Leics.) b Dec. 27, 1915
Lester, Dr J. A. (Philadelphia) b Aug. 1, 1871, d Sept. 3, 1969
Lethbridge, C. (Warwicks.) b June 23, 1961
*Lever, J. K. (Essex & Natal; *CY 1979*) b Feb. 24, 1949
*Lever, P. (Lancs. & Tas.) b Sept. 17, 1940
*Leveson Gower, Sir H. D. G. (OUCC & Surrey) b May 8, 1873, d Feb. 1, 1954
*Levett, W. H. V. (Kent) b Jan. 25, 1908
Lewington, P. J. (Warwicks.) b Jan. 30, 1950
*Lewis, A. R. (CUCC & Glam.) b July 6, 1938
Lewis, C. (Kent) b July 27, 1908
Lewis, C. C. (Leics.) b Feb. 14, 1968
Lewis, D. J. (OUCC & Rhod.) b July 27, 1927
*Lewis, D. M. (Jam.) b Feb. 21, 1946
Lewis, E. B. (Warwicks.) b Jan. 5, 1918, d Oct. 19, 1983
Lewis, E. J. (Glam. & Sussex) b Jan. 31, 1942
*Lewis, P. T. (W. Prov.) b Oct. 2, 1884, d Jan. 30, 1976
Lewis, R. V. (Hants) b Aug. 6, 1947
*Leyland, M. (Yorks.; *CY 1929*) b July 20, 1900, d Jan. 1, 1967
*Liaqat Ali (Kar., Sind, HBL & PIA) b May 21, 1955
Liddicutt, A. E. (Vic.) b Oct. 17, 1891, d April 8, 1983
Lightfoot, A. (Northants) b Jan. 8, 1936
Lill, J. C. (S. Aust.) b Dec. 7, 1933
*Lillee, D. K. (W. Aust., Tas. & Northants; *CY 1973*) b July 18, 1949
*Lilley, A. A. (Warwicks.; *CY 1897*) b Nov. 28, 1866, d Nov. 17, 1929
Lilley, A. W. (Essex) b May 8, 1959
Lilley, B. (Notts.) b Feb. 11, 1895, d Aug. 4, 1950
Lillywhite, Fred (Sussex; Editor of *Lillywhite's Guide to Cricketers*) b July 23, 1829, d Sept. 15, 1866
Lillywhite, F. W. ("William") (Sussex) b June 13, 1792, d Aug. 21, 1854
*Lillywhite, James, jun. (Sussex) b Feb. 23, 1842, d Oct. 25, 1929
*Lindsay, D. T. (NE Tvl, N. Tvl & Tvl) b Sept 4, 1939
*Lindsay, J. D. (Tvl & NE Tvl) b Sept. 8, 1909

*Lindsay, N. V. (Tvl & OFS) b July 30, 1886, d Feb. 2, 1976
*Lindwall, R. R. (NSW & Qld; *CY 1949*) b Oct. 3, 1921
*Ling, W. V. S. (Griq. W. & E. Prov.) b Oct. 3, 1891, d Sept. 26, 1960
*Lissette, A. F. (Auck. & N. Dist.) b Nov. 6, 1919, d Jan. 24, 1973
Lister, J. (Yorks. & Worcs.) b May 14, 1930
Lister, W. H. L. (Lancs.) b Oct. 7, 1911
Livingston, L. (NSW & Northants) b May 3, 1920
Livingstone, D. A. (Hants) b Sept. 21, 1933, d Sept. 8, 1988
Livsey, W. H. (Hants) b Sept. 23, 1893, d Sept. 12, 1978
*Llewellyn, C. B. (Natal & Hants; *CY 1911*) b Sept. 26, 1876, d June 7, 1964
Llewellyn, M. J. (Glam.) b Nov. 27, 1953
Lloyd, B. J. (Glam.) b Sept. 6, 1953
*Lloyd, C. H. (†Guyana & Lancs.; *CY 1971*) b Aug. 31, 1944
*Lloyd, D. (Lancs.) b March 18, 1947
*Lloyd, T. A. (Warwicks. & OFS) b Nov. 5, 1956
Lloyds, J. W. (Som., OFS & Glos.) b Nov. 17, 1954
*Loader, P. J. (Surrey and W. Aust.; *CY 1958*) b Oct. 25, 1929
Lobb, B. (Warwicks. & Som.) b Jan. 11, 1931
*Lock, G. A. R. (Surrey, Leics. & W. Aust.; *CY 1954*) b July 5, 1929
Lock, H. C. (Surrey) b May 8, 1903, d May 18, 1978
Lockwood, Ephraim (Yorks.) b April 4, 1845, d Dec. 19, 1921
*Lockwood, W. H. (Notts. & Surrey; *CY 1899*) b March 25, 1868, d April 26, 1932
Lockyer, T. (Surrey & All-England) b Nov. 1, 1826, d Dec. 22, 1869
*Logan, J. D. (SA) b June 24, 1880, d Jan. 3, 1960
*Logie, A. L. (T/T) b Sept. 28, 1960
*Lohmann, G. A. (Surrey, W. Prov. & Tvl; *CY 1889*) b June 2, 1865, d Dec. 1, 1901
Lomax, J. G. (Lancs. & Som.) b May 5, 1925
Long, A. (Surrey & Sussex) b Dec. 18, 1940
Longfield, T. C. (CUCC & Kent) b May 12, 1906, d Dec. 21, 1981
Lord, G. J. (Warwicks. & Worcs.) b April 25, 1961
Lord, Thomas (Middx; founder of Lord's) b Nov. 23, 1755, d Jan. 13, 1832
*Love, H. S. B. (NSW & Vic.) b Aug. 10, 1895, d July 22, 1969
Love, J. D. (Yorks.) b April 22, 1955
Lowndes, W. G. L. F. (OUCC & Hants) b Jan. 24, 1898, d May 23, 1982
*Lowry, T. C. (Wgtn, CUCC & Som.) b Feb. 17, 1898, d July 20, 1976
*Lowson, F. A. (Yorks.) b July 1, 1925, d Sept. 8, 1984
*Loxton, S. J. E. (Vic.) b March 29, 1921
*Lucas, A. P. (CUCC, Surrey, Middx & Essex) b Feb. 20, 1857, d Oct. 12, 1923
Luckes, W. T. (Som.) b Jan. 1, 1901, d Oct. 27, 1982
*Luckhurst, B. W. (Kent; *CY 1971*) b Feb. 5, 1939
Lumb, R. G. (Yorks.) b Feb. 27, 1950
*Lundie, E. B. (E. Prov., W. Prov. & Tvl) b March 15, 1888, d Sept. 12, 1917
Lynch, M. A. (Surrey & Guyana) b May 21, 1958
Lyon, B. H. (OUCC & Glos.; *CY 1931*) b Jan. 19, 1902, d June 22, 1970
Lyon, J. (Lancs.) b May 17, 1951
Lyon, M. D. (CUCC & Som.) b April 22, 1898, d Feb. 17, 1964
*Lyons, J. J. (S. Aust.) b May 21, 1863, d July 21, 1927
Lyons, K. J. (Glam.) b Dec. 18, 1946
*Lyttelton, Rt Hon. Alfred (CUCC & Middx; Pres. MCC 1898) b Feb. 7, 1857, d July 5, 1913
Lyttelton, Rt Rev. Hon. A. T. (MCC) b Jan. 7, 1852, d Feb. 19, 1903
Lyttelton, Rev. Hon. C. F. (CUCC & Worcs.) b Jan. 26, 1887, d Oct. 3, 1931
Lyttelton, Hon. C. G. (CUCC) b Oct. 27, 1842, d June 9, 1922
Lyttelton, Hon. C. J. (*see* 10th Visct Cobham)
Lyttelton, Rev. Hon. E. (CUCC & Middx) b July 23, 1855, d Jan. 26, 1942
Lyttelton, Hon. G. W. S. (CUCC) b June 12, 1847, d Dec. 5, 1913
Lyttelton, Hon. R. H. (MCC) b Jan. 18, 1854, d Nov. 7, 1939

*McAlister, P. A. (Vic.) b July 11, 1869, d May 10, 1938
*Macartney, C. G. (NSW & Otago; *CY 1922*) b June 27, 1886, d Sept. 9, 1958
*Macaulay, G. G. (Yorks.; *CY 1924*) b Dec. 7, 1897, d Dec. 14, 1940
*Macaulay, M. J. (Tvl, W. Prov., OFS, NE Tvl & E. Prov.) b April 19, 1939
*MacBryan, J. C. W. (CUCC & Som.; *CY 1925*) b July 22, 1892, d July 15, 1983
*McCabe, S. J. (NSW; *CY 1935*) b July 16, 1910, d Aug. 25, 1968
McCanlis, M. A. (OUCC, Surrey & Glos.) b June 17, 1906
*McCarthy, C. N. (Natal & CUCC) b March 24, 1929
*McConnon, J. E. (Glam.) b June 21, 1922
*McCool, C. L. (NSW, Qld & Som.) b Dec. 9, 1915, d April 5, 1986
McCorkell, N. T. (Hants) b March 23, 1912
*McCormick, E. L. (Vic.) b May 16, 1906

*McCosker, R. B. (NSW; *CY 1976*) b Dec. 11, 1946
McCurdy, R. J. (Vic., Derbys., S. Aust. & E. Prov.) b Dec. 30, 1959
*McDermott, C. J. (Qld; *CY 1986*) b April 14, 1965
*McDonald, C. C. (Vic.) b Nov. 17, 1928
*McDonald, E. A. (Tas., Vic. & Lancs.; *CY 1922*) b Jan. 6, 1891, d July 22, 1937
*McDonnell, P. S. (Vic., NSW & Qld) b Nov. 13, 1858, d Sept. 24, 1896
McEvoy, M. S. A. (Essex & Worcs.) b Jan. 25, 1956
McEwan, K. S. (E. Prov., W. Prov., Essex & W. Aust; *CY 1978*) b July 16, 1952
*McEwan, P. E. (Cant.) b Dec. 19, 1953
McFarlane, L. L. (Northants, Lancs. & Glam.) b Aug. 19, 1952
*McGahey, C. P. (Essex; *CY 1902*) b Feb. 12, 1871, d Jan. 10, 1935
*MacGibbon, A. R. (Cant.) b Aug. 28, 1924
*McGirr, H. M. (Wgtn) b Nov. 5, 1891, d April 14, 1964
*McGlew, D. J. (Natal; *CY 1956*) b March 11, 1929
*MacGregor, G. (CUCC & Middx; *CY 1891*) b Aug. 31, 1869, d Aug. 20, 1919
*McGregor, S. N. (Otago) b Dec. 18, 1931
McHugh, F. P. (Yorks. & Glos.) b Nov. 15, 1925
*McIlwraith, J. (Vic.) b Sept. 7, 1857, d July 5, 1938
Macindoe, D. H. (OUCC) b Sept. 1, 1917, d March 3, 1986
*McIntyre, A. J. (Surrey; *CY 1958*) b May 14, 1918
McIntyre, J. M. (Auck. & Cant.) b July 4, 1944
*Mackay, K. D. (Qld) b Oct. 24, 1925, d June 13, 1982
McKay-Coghill, D. (Tvl) b Nov. 4, 1941
McKechnie, B. J. (Otago) b Nov. 6, 1953
*McKenzie, G. D. (W. Aust. & Leics.; *CY 1965*) b June 24, 1941
McKenzie, K. A. (NE Tvl & Tvl) b July 16, 1948
*McKibbin, T. R. (NSW) b Dec. 10, 1870, d Dec. 15, 1939
*McKinnon, A. H. (E. Prov. & Tvl) b Aug. 20, 1932, d Dec. 2, 1983
*MacKinnon, F. A. (CUCC & Kent) b April 9, 1848, d Feb. 27, 1947
McLachlan, I. M. (CUCC & S. Aust.) b Oct. 2, 1936
*MacLaren, A. C. (Lancs.; *CY 1895*) b Dec. 1, 1871, d Nov. 17, 1944
*McLaren, J. W. (Qld) b Dec. 24, 1887, d Nov. 17, 1921
*Maclean, J. A. (Qld) b April 27, 1946
Maclean, J. F. (Worcs. & Glos.) b March 1, 1901, d March 9, 1986
*McLean, R. A. (Natal; *CY 1961*) b July 9, 1930
MacLeay, K. H. (W. Aust.) b April 2, 1959
*McLeod, C. E. (Vic.) b Oct. 24, 1869, d Nov. 26, 1918
*McLeod, E. G. (Auck. & Wgtn; oldest surviving Test player) b Oct. 14, 1900
*McLeod, R. W. (Vic.) b Jan. 19, 1868, d June 14, 1907
McMahon, J. W. (Surrey & Som.) b Dec. 28, 1919
*McMahon, T. G. (Wgtn) b Nov. 8, 1929
*McMaster, J. E. P. (Eng.) b March 16, 1861, d June 7, 1929
McMillan, B. M. (Tvl & Warwicks.) b Dec. 22, 1963
*McMillan, Q. (Tvl) b June 23, 1904, d July 3, 1948
*McMorris, E. D. A. (Jam.) b April 4, 1935
*McRae, D. A. N. (Cant.) b Dec. 25, 1912
*McShane, P. G. (Vic.) b 1857, d Dec. 11, 1903
McSweeney, E. B. (C. Dist. & Wgtn) b March 8, 1957
McVicker, N. M. (Warwicks. & Leics.) b Nov. 4, 1940
*McWatt, C. A. (BG) b Feb. 1, 1922
*Madan Lal (Punjab & Delhi) b March 20, 1951
*Maddocks, L. V. (Vic. & Tas.) b May 24, 1926
*Madray, I. S. (BG) b July 2, 1934
*Madugalle, R. S. (SL) b April 22, 1959
*Madurasinghe, A. W. R. (SL) b Jan. 30, 1961
*Maguire, J. N. (Qld) b Sept. 15, 1956
*Mahanama, R. S. (SL) b May 31, 1966
Maher, B. J. M. (Derbys.) b Feb. 11, 1958
*Mahmood Hussain (Pak. Us, Punjab, Kar., E. Pak. & NTB) b April 2, 1932
*Mailey, A. A. (NSW) b Jan. 3, 1886, d Dec. 31, 1967
*Majid Khan (Lahore, Pak. Us, CUCC, Glam., PIA, Qld & Punjab; *CY 1970*) b Sept. 28, 1946
*Maka, E. S. (Bombay) b March 5, 1922
*Makepeace, H. (Lancs.) b Aug. 22, 1881, d Dec. 19, 1952
Malcolm, D. E. (Derbys.) b Feb. 22, 1963
*Malhotra, A. (Haryana) b Jan. 26, 1957
Mallender, N. A. (Northants, Otago & Som.) b Aug. 13, 1961
*Mallett, A. A. (S. Aust.) b July 13, 1945
Mallett, A. W. H. (OUCC & Kent) b Aug. 29, 1924
*Malone, M. F. (W. Aust. & Lancs.) b Oct. 9, 1950
Malone, S. J. (Essex, Hants & Glam.) b Oct. 19, 1953
*Maninder Singh (Delhi) b June 13, 1965
*Manjrekhar, S. V. (Bombay) b July 12, 1965

*Manjrekar, V. L. (Bombay, Bengal, Andhra, U. Pradesh, Raja. & M'tra) b Sept. 26, 1931, d Oct. 18, 1983
*Mankad, A. V. (Bombay) b Oct. 12, 1946
*Mankad, V. (M. H.) (W. Ind., Naw., M'tra, Guj., Bengal, Bombay & Raja.; *CY 1947*) b April 12, 1917, d Aug. 21, 1978
*Mann, A. L. (W. Aust.) b Nov. 8, 1945
*Mann, F. G. (CUCC & Middx; Pres. MCC 1984-85) b Sept. 6, 1917
*Mann, F. T. (CUCC & Middx) b March 3, 1888, d Oct. 6, 1964
Mann, J. P. (Middx) b June 13, 1919
*Mann, N. B. F. (Natal & E. Prov.) b Dec. 28, 1920, d July 31, 1952
Manning, J. S. (S. Aust. & Northants) b June 11, 1924, d May 5, 1988
*Mansell, P. N. F. (Rhod.) b March 16, 1920
*Mansoor Akhtar (Kar., UBL & Sind) b Dec. 25, 1956
*Mantri, M. K. (Bombay & M'tra) b Sept. 1, 1921
*Manzoor Elahi (Multan, Pak. Rlwys & IDBP) b April 15, 1963
*Maqsood Ahmed (S. Punjab, R'pindi & Kar.) b March 26, 1925
*Marais, G. G. ("G. Gladstone") (Jam.) b Jan. 14, 1901, d May 19, 1978
Marie, G. V. (OUCC) b Feb. 17, 1945
*Markham, L. A. (Natal) b Sept. 12, 1924
*Marks, V. J. (OUCC, Som. & W. Aust.) b June 25, 1955
Marlar, R. G. (CUCC & Sussex) b Jan. 2, 1931
Marner, P. T. (Lancs. & Leics.) b March 31, 1936
*Marr, A. P. (NSW) b March 28, 1862, d March 15, 1940
*Marriott, C. S. (CUCC, Lancs. & Kent) b Sept. 14, 1895, d Oct. 13, 1966
Marsden, Tom (Eng.) b 1805, d Feb. 27, 1843
Marsh, F. E. (Derbys.) b July 7, 1920
*Marsh, G. R. (W. Aust.) b Dec. 31, 1958
*Marsh, R. W. (W. Aust.; *CY 1982*) b Nov. 11, 1947
Marsh, S. A. (Kent) b Jan. 27, 1961
Marshal, Alan (Qld & Surrey; *CY 1909*) b June 12, 1883, d July 23, 1915
Marshall, J. M. A. (Warwicks.) b Oct. 26, 1916
*Marshall, M. D. (B'dos & Hants; *CY 1983*) b April 18, 1958
*Marshall, N. E. (B'dos & T/T) b Feb. 27, 1924
*Marshall, R. E. (B'dos & Hants; *CY 1959*) b April 25, 1930
Martin, E. J. (Notts.) b Aug. 17, 1925
*Martin, F. (Kent; *CY 1892*) b Oct. 12, 1861, d Dec. 13, 1921
*Martin, F. R. (Jam.) b Oct. 12, 1893, d Nov. 23, 1967
Martin, J. D. (OUCC & Som.) b Dec. 23, 1941
*Martin, J. W. (NSW & S. Aust.) b July 28, 1931
*Martin, J. W. (Kent) b Feb. 16, 1917, d Jan. 4, 1987
Martin, S. H. (Worcs., Natal & Rhod.) b Jan. 11, 1909
*Martindale, E. A. (B'dos) b Nov. 25, 1909, d March 17, 1972
Maru, R. J. (Middx & Hants) b Oct. 28, 1962
*Marx, W. F. E. (Tvl) b July 4, 1895, d June 2, 1974
*Mason, J. R. (Kent; *CY 1898*) b March 26, 1874, d Oct. 15, 1958
Masood Iqbal (Lahore, Punjab U., Pak. Us & HBL) b April 17, 1952
*Massie, H. H. (NSW) b April 11, 1854, d Oct. 12, 1938
*Massie, R. A. L. (W. Aust.; *CY 1973*) b April 14, 1947
*Matheson, A. M. (Auck.) b Feb. 27, 1906, d Dec. 31, 1985
*Mathias, Wallis (Sind, Kar. & NBP) b Feb. 4, 1935
*Matthews, A. D. G. (Northants & Glam.) b May 3, 1904, d July 29, 1977
*Matthews, C. D. (W. Aust.) b Sept. 22, 1962
Matthews, C. S. (Notts.) b Oct. 17, 1929
*Matthews, G. R. J. (NSW) b Dec. 15, 1959
*Matthews, T. J. (Vic.) b April 3, 1884, d Oct. 14, 1943
*Mattis, E. H. (Jam.) b April 11, 1957
Maudsley, R. H. (OUCC & Warwicks.) b April 8, 1918, d Sept. 29, 1981
*May, P. B. H. (CUCC & Surrey; *CY 1952*; Pres. MCC 1980-81) b Dec. 31, 1929
*May, T. B. A. (S. Aust.) b Jan. 26, 1962
Mayer, J. H. (Warwicks.) b March 2, 1902, d Sept. 6, 1981
Mayes, R. (Kent) b Oct. 7, 1921
Maynard, C. (Warwicks. & Lancs.) b April 8, 1958
*Maynard, M. P. (Glam.) b March 21, 1966
*Mayne, E. R. (S. Aust. & Vic.) b July 2, 1882, d Oct. 26, 1961
*Mayne, L. C. (W. Aust.) b Jan. 23, 1942
*Mead, C. P. (Hants; *CY 1912*) b March 9, 1887, d March 26, 1958
*Mead, W. (Essex; *CY 1904*) b March 25, 1868, d March 18, 1954
Meads, E. A. (Notts.) b Aug. 17, 1916
*Meale, T. (Wgtn) b Nov. 11, 1928
*Meckiff, I. (Vic.) b Jan. 6, 1935
Medlycott, K. T. (Surrey) b May 12, 1965
*Meher-Homji, K. R. (W. Ind. & Bombay) b Aug. 9, 1911, d Feb. 10, 1982
*Mehra, V. L. (E. Punjab, Ind. Rlwys & Delhi) b March 12, 1938

*Meintjes, D. J. (Tvl) b June 9, 1890, d July 17, 1979
*Melle, M. G. (Tvl & W. Prov.) b June 3, 1930
Melluish, M. E. L. (CUCC & Middx) b June 13, 1932
*Melville, A. (OUCC, Sussex, Natal & Tvl; *CY 1948*) b May 19, 1910, d April 18, 1983
Mence, M. D. (Warwicks. & Glos.) b April 13, 1944
Mendis, G. D. (Sussex & Lancs.) b April 20, 1955
*Mendis, L. R. D. (SL) b Aug. 25, 1952
*Mendonca, I. L. (BG) b July 13, 1934
Mercer, J. (Sussex, Glam. & Northants; *CY 1927*) b April 22, 1895, d Aug. 31, 1987
*Merchant, V. M. (Bombay; *CY 1937*) b Oct. 12, 1911, d Oct. 27, 1987
Merrick, T. A. (Leewards & Warwicks.) b June 10, 1963
*Merritt, W. E. (Cant. & Northants) b Aug. 18, 1908, d June 9, 1977
*Merry, C. A. (T/T) b Jan. 20, 1911, d April 19, 1964
Metcalfe, A. A. (Yorks.) b Dec. 25, 1963
Metson, C. P. (Middx & Glam.) b July 2, 1963
*Meuleman, K. D. (Vic. & W. Aust.) b Sept. 5, 1923
*Meuli, E. M. (C. Dist.) b Feb. 20, 1926
Meyer, B. J. (Glos.) b Aug. 21, 1932
Meyer, R. J. O. (CUCC, Som. & W. Ind.) b March 15, 1905
Mian Mohammad Saaed (N. Ind. Patiala & S. Punjab; Pak.'s first captain) b Aug. 31, 1910, d Aug. 23, 1979
*Middleton, J. (W. Prov.) b Sept. 30, 1865, d Dec. 23, 1913
**Midwinter, W. E. (Vic. & Glos.) b June 19, 1851, d Dec. 3, 1890
*Milburn, B. D. (Otago) b Nov. 24, 1943
*Milburn, C. (Northants & W. Aust.; *CY 1967*) b Oct. 23, 1941
*Milkha Singh, A. G. (Madras) b Dec. 31, 1941
Miller, A. J. T. (OUCC & Middx) b May 30, 1963
*Miller, A. M. (Eng.) b Oct. 19, 1869, d June 26, 1959
*Miller, G. (Derbys., Natal & Essex) b Sept. 8, 1952
*Miller, K. R. (Vic., NSW & Notts.; *CY 1954*) b Nov. 28, 1919
*Miller, L. S. M. (C. Dist. & Wgtn) b March 31, 1923
Miller, R. (Warwicks.) b Jan. 6, 1941
*Miller, R. C. (Jam.) b Dec. 24, 1924
*Milligan, F. W. (Yorks.) b March 19, 1870, d March 31, 1900
*Millman, G. (Notts.) b Oct. 2, 1934
*Mills, C. H. (Surrey, Kimberley & W. Prov.) b Nov. 26, 1867, d July 26, 1948
*Mills, J. E. (Auck.) b Sept. 3, 1905, d Dec. 11, 1972
Mills, J. M. (CUCC & Warwicks.) b July 27, 1921
Mills, J. P. C. (CUCC & Northants) b Dec. 6, 1958
Milner, J. (Essex) b Aug. 22, 1937
*Milton, C. A. (Glos.; *CY 1959*) b March 10, 1928
*Milton, W. H. (W. Prov.) b Dec. 3, 1854, d March 6, 1930
*Minnett, R. B. (NSW) b June 13, 1888, d Oct. 21, 1955
"Minshull", John (scorer of first recorded century) b *circa* 1741, d Oct. 1793
*Miran Bux, (Pak. Serv., Punjab & R'pindi) b April 20, 1907
*Misson, F. M. (NSW) b Nov. 19, 1938
*Mitchell, A. (Yorks.) b Sept. 13, 1902, d Dec. 25, 1976
*Mitchell, B. (Tvl; *CY 1936*) b Jan. 8, 1909
Mitchell, C. G. (Som.) b Jan. 27, 1929
**Mitchell, F. (CUCC, Yorks. & Tvl; *CY 1902*) b Aug. 13, 1872, d Oct. 11, 1935
*Mitchell, T. B. (Derbys.) b Sept. 4, 1902
*Mitchell-Innes, N. S. (OUCC & Som.) b Sept. 7, 1914
Mobey, G. S. (Surrey) b March 5, 1904
*Modi, R. S. (Bombay) b Nov. 11, 1924
*Mohammad Aslam (N. Ind. & Pak. Rlwys) b Jan. 5, 1920
*Mohammad Farooq (Kar.) b April 8, 1938
*Mohammad Ilyas (Lahore & PIA) b March 19, 1946
*Mohammad Munaf (Sind, E. Pak., Kar. & PIA) b Nov. 2, 1935
*Mohammad Nazir (Pak. Rlwys) b March 8, 1946
*Mohsin Kamal (Lahore, Allied Bank & PNSC) b June 16, 1963
*Mohsin Khan (Pak. Rlwys, Kar., Sind., Pak. Us & HBL) b March 15, 1955
Moin-ul-Atiq (UBL) b Aug. 5, 1964
*Moir, A. McK. (Otago) b July 17, 1919
Moir, D. G. (Derbys. & Scotland) b April 13, 1957
*Mold, A. W. (Lancs.; *CY 1892*) b May 27, 1863, d April 29, 1921
Moles, A. J. (Warwicks. & Griq. W.) b Feb. 12, 1961
*Moloney, D. A. R. (Wgtn, Otago & Cant.) b Aug. 11, 1910, d July 15, 1942
Monckton of Brenchley, 1st Lord (Pres. MCC 1956-57) b Jan. 17, 1891, d Jan. 9, 1965
Monkhouse, G. (Surrey) b April 26, 1954
*Moodie, G. H. (Jam.) b Nov. 25, 1915
Moody, T. M. (W. Aust.) b Oct. 2, 1965
*Moon, L. J. (CUCC & Middx) b Feb. 9, 1878, d Nov. 23, 1916
*Mooney, F. L. H. (Wgtn) b May 26, 1921

Moore, D. N. (OUCC & Glos.) b Sept. 26, 1910
Moore, H. I. (Notts.) b Feb. 28, 1941
Moore, R. H. (Hants) b Nov. 14, 1913
*More, K. S. (Baroda) b Sept. 4, 1962
Morgan, D. C. (Derbys.) b Feb. 26, 1929
Morgan, J. T. (CUCC & Glam.) b May 7, 1907, d Dec. 18, 1976
Morgan, M. (Notts.) b May 21, 1936
*Morgan, R. W. (Auck.) b Feb. 12, 1941
*Morkel, D. P. B. (W. Prov.) b Jan. 25, 1906, d Oct. 6, 1980
*Morley, F. (Notts.) b Dec. 16, 1850, d Sept. 28, 1884
Morley, J. D. (Sussex) b Oct. 20, 1950
*Moroney, J. (NSW) b July 24, 1917
*Morris, A. R. (NSW; *CY 1949*) b Jan. 19, 1922
Morris, H. (Glam.) b Oct. 5, 1963
Morris, H. M. (CUCC & Essex) b April 16, 1898, d Nov. 18, 1984
Morris, J. E. (Derbys.) b April 1, 1964
*Morris, S. (Vic.) b June 22, 1855, d Sept. 20, 1931
*Morrison, B. D. (Wgtn) b Dec. 17, 1933
*Morrison, D. K. (Auck.) b Feb. 3, 1966
*Morrison, J. F. M. (C. Dist. & Wgtn) b Aug. 27, 1947
Mortensen, O. H. (Denmark & Derbys.) b Jan. 29, 1958
*Mortimore, J. B. (Glos.) b May 14, 1933
Mortlock, W. (Surrey & Utd Eng. XI) b July 18, 1832, d Jan. 23, 1884
Moseley, E. A. (B'dos, Glam. & E. Prov.) b Jan. 5, 1958
Moseley, H. R. (B'dos & Som.) b May 28, 1948
*Moses, H. (NSW) b Feb. 13, 1858, d Dec. 7, 1938
*Moss, A. E. (Middx) b Nov. 14, 1930
*Moss, J. K. (Vic.) b June 29, 1947
*Motz, R. C. (Cant.; *CY 1966*) b Jan. 12, 1940
Moulding, R. P. (OUCC & Middx) b Jan. 3, 1958
*Moule, W. H. (Vic.) b Jan. 31, 1858, d Aug. 24, 1939
*Moxon, M. D. (Yorks. & Griq. W.) b May 4, 1960
*Mudassar Nazar (Lahore, Punjab, Pak. Us, HBL, PIA & UBL) b April 6, 1956
*Muddiah, V. M. (Mysore & Ind. Serv.) b June 8, 1929
*Mufasir-ul-Haq (Kar., Dacca, PWD, E. Pak. & NBP) b Aug. 16, 1944, d July 27, 1983
Muncer, B. L. (Middx & Glam.) b Oct. 23, 1913, d Jan. 18, 1982
Munden, V. S. (Leics.) b Jan. 2, 1928
*Munir Malik (Punjab, R'pindi, Pak. Serv. & Kar.) b July 10, 1934
Munton, T. A. (Warwicks.) b July 30, 1965
**Murdoch, W. L. (NSW & Sussex) b Oct. 18, 1854, d Feb. 18, 1911
*Murray, A. R. A. (E. Prov.) b April 30, 1922
*Murray, B. A. G. (Wgtn) b Sept. 18, 1940
*Murray, D. A. (B'dos) b Sept. 29, 1950
*Murray, D. L. (T/T, CUCC, Notts. & Warwicks.) b May 20, 1943
*Murray, J. T. (Middx; *CY 1967*) b April 1, 1935
Murray-Willis, P. E. (Worcs. & Northants) b July 14, 1910
Murrell, H. R. (Kent & Middx) b Nov. 19, 1879, d Aug. 15, 1952
Murrills, T. J. (CUCC) b Dec. 22, 1953
*Musgrove, H. (Vic.) b Nov. 27, 1860, d Nov. 2, 1931
*Mushtaq Ali, S. (C. Ind., Guj., †M. Pradesh & U. Pradesh) b Dec. 17, 1914
*Mushtaq Mohammad (Kar., Northants & PIA; *CY 1963*) b Nov. 22, 1943
Mynn, Alfred (Kent & All-Eng.) b Jan. 19, 1807, d Oct. 31, 1861

*Nadkarni, R. G. (M'tra & Bombay) b April 4, 1932
Naeem Ahmed (Kar., Pak. Us, NBP, UBL & PIA) b Sept. 20, 1952
*Nagel, L. E. (Vic.) b March 6, 1905, d Nov. 23, 1971
*Naik, S. S. (Bombay) b Feb. 21, 1945
*Nanan, R. (T/T) b May 29, 1953
*Naoomal Jaoomal, M. (N. Ind. & Sind) b April 17, 1904, d July 18, 1980
*Narasimha Rao, M. V. (H'bad) b Aug. 11, 1954
Naseer Malik (Khairpair & NBP) b Feb. 1, 1950
Nash, J. E. (S. Aust.) b April 16, 1950
*Nash, L. J. (Tas. & Vic.) b May 2, 1910, d July 24, 1986
Nash, M. A. (Glam.) b May 9, 1945
*Nasim-ul-Ghani (Kar., Pak. Us, Dacca, E. Pak., PWD & NBP) b May 14, 1941
*Naushad Ali (Kar., E. Pak., R'pindi, Peshawar, NWFP, Punjab & Pak. Serv.) b Oct. 1, 1943
Naved Anjum (Lahore, UBL & HBL) b July 27, 1963
*Navle, J. G. (Rajputna, C. Ind., Holkar & Gwalior) b Dec. 7, 1902, d Sept. 7, 1979
*Nayak, S. V. (Bombay) b Oct. 20, 1954
*Nayudu, Col. C. K. (C. Ind., Andhra, U. Pradesh & Holkar; *CY 1933*) b Oct. 31, 1895, d Nov. 14, 1967
*Nayudu, C. S. (C. Ind., Holkar, Baroda, Bengal, Andhra & U. Pradesh) b April 18, 1914
*Nazar Mohammad (N. Ind. & Punjab) b March 5, 1921
*Nazir Ali, S. (S. Punjab & Sussex) b June 8, 1906, d Feb. 18, 1975

Neale, P. A. (Worcs.; *CY 1989*) b June 5, 1954
*Neblett, J. M. (B'dos & BG) b Nov. 13, 1901, d March 28, 1959
Needham, A. (Surrey & Middx) b March 23, 1957
*Nel, J. D. (W. Prov.) b July 10, 1928
Nevell, W. T. (Middx, Surrey & Northants) b June 13, 1916
*Newberry, C. (Tvl) b 1889, d Aug. 1, 1916
Newell, M. (Notts.) b Feb. 25, 1965
*Newham, W. (Sussex) b Dec 12, 1860, d June 26, 1944
Newland, Richard (Sussex) b *circa* 1718, d May 29, 1791
Newman, G. C. (OUCC & Middx) b April 26, 1904, d Oct. 13, 1982
*Newman, Sir J. (Wgtn & Cant.) b July 3, 1902
Newman, J. A. (Hants & Cant.) b Nov. 12, 1884, d Dec. 21, 1973
Newman, P. G. (Derbys.) b Jan. 10, 1959
*Newport, P. J. (Worcs. & Boland) b Oct. 11, 1962
*Newson, E. S. (Tvl & Rhod.) b Dec. 2, 1910, d April 24, 1988
Newstead, J. T. (Yorks.; *CY 1909*) b Sept. 8, 1877, d March 25, 1952
*Niaz Ahmed (Dacca, PWD, E. Pak. & Pak. Rlwys) b Nov. 11, 1945
Nicholas, M. C. J. (Hants) b Sept. 29, 1957
Nicholls, D. (Kent) b Dec. 8, 1943
Nicholls, R. B. (Glos.) b Dec. 4, 1933
*Nichols, M. S. (Essex; *CY 1934*) b Oct. 6, 1900, d Jan. 26, 1961
Nicholson, A. G. (Yorks.) b June 25, 1938, d Nov. 4, 1985
*Nicholson, F. (OFS) b Sept. 17, 1909, d July 30, 1982
*Nicolson, J. F. W. (Natal & OUCC) b July 19, 1899, d Dec. 13, 1935
*Nissar, Mahomed (Patiala, S. Punjab & U. Pradesh) b Aug. 1, 1910, d March 11, 1963
*Nitschke, H. C. (S. Aust.) b April 14, 1905, d Sept. 29, 1982
*Noble, M. A. (NSW; *CY 1900*) b Jan. 28, 1873, d June 22, 1940
*Noblet, G. (S. Aust.) b Sept. 14, 1916
*Noreiga, J. M. (T/T) b April 15, 1936
Norfolk, 16th Duke of (Pres. MCC 1957-58) b May 30, 1908, d Jan. 31, 1975
Norman, M. E. J. C. (Northants & Leics.) b Jan. 19, 1933
*Norton, N. O. (W. Prov. & Border) b May 11, 1881, d June 27, 1968
*Nothling, O. E. (NSW & Qld) b Aug. 1, 1900, d Sept. 26, 1965
*Nourse, A. D. ("Dudley") (Natal; *CY 1948*) b Nov. 12, 1910, d Aug. 14, 1981
*Nourse, A. W. ("Dave") (Natal, Tvl & W. Prov.) b Jan. 26, 1878, d July 8, 1948
Nugent, 1st Lord (Pres. MCC 1962-63) b Aug. 11, 1895, d April 27, 1973
*Nunes, R. K. (Jam.) b June 7, 1894, d July 22, 1958
*Nupen, E. P. (Tvl) b Jan. 1, 1902, d Jan. 29, 1977
*Nurse, S. M. (B'dos; *CY 1967*) b Nov. 10, 1933
Nutter, A. E. (Lancs. & Northants) b June 28, 1913
*Nyalchand, S. (W. Ind., Kathiawar, Guj. & S'tra) b Sept. 14, 1919
Nye, J. K. (Sussex) b May 23, 1914
Nyren, John (Hants) b Dec. 15, 1764, d June 28, 1837
Nyren, Richard (Hants & Sussex) b 1734, d April 25, 1797

Oakes, C. (Sussex) b Aug. 10, 1912
Oakes, J. (Sussex) b March 3, 1916
*Oakman, A. S. M. (Sussex) b April 20, 1930
Oates, T. W. (Notts.) b Aug. 9, 1875, d June 18, 1949
Oates, W. F. (Yorks. & Derbys.) b June 11, 1929
O'Brien, F. P. (Cant. & Northants) b Feb. 11, 1911
*O'Brien, L. P. (Vic.) b July 2, 1907
*O'Brien, Sir T. C. (OUCC & Middx) b Nov. 5, 1861, d Dec. 9, 1948
*Ochse, A. E. (Tvl) b March 11, 1870, d April 11, 1918
*Ochse, A. L. (E. Prov.) b Oct. 11, 1899, d May 6, 1949
*O'Connor, J. (Essex) b Nov. 6, 1897, d Feb. 22, 1977
*O'Connor, J. D. A. (NSW & S. Aust.) b Sept. 9, 1875, d Aug. 23, 1941
Odendaal, A. (CUCC & Boland) b May 4, 1954
*O'Donnell, S. P. (Vic.) b Jan. 26, 1963
*Ogilvie, A. D. (Qld) b June 3, 1951
*O'Keeffe, K. J. (NSW & Som.) b Nov. 25, 1949
*Old, C. M. (Yorks., Warwicks. & N. Tvl; *CY 1979*) b Dec. 22, 1948
*Oldfield, N. (Lancs. & Northants) b May 5, 1911
*Oldfield, W. A. (NSW; *CY 1927*) b Sept. 9, 1894, d Aug. 10, 1976
Oldham, S. (Yorks. & Derbys.) b July 26, 1948
Oldroyd, E. (Yorks.) b Oct. 1, 1888, d Dec. 27, 1964
*O'Linn, S. (Kent, W. Prov. & Tvl) b May 5, 1927
Oliver, P. R. (Warwicks.) b May 9, 1956
O'Neill, M. D. (NSW) b March 5, 1959
*O'Neill, N. C. (NSW; *CY 1962*) b Feb. 19, 1937
Ontong, R. C. (Border, Tvl, N. Tvl & Glam.) b Sept. 9, 1955

Opatha, A. R. M. (SL) b Aug. 5, 1947
Ord, J. S. (Warwicks.) b July 12, 1912
*O'Reilly, W. J. (NSW; *CY 1935*) b Dec. 20, 1905
O'Riordan, A. J. (Ireland) b July 20, 1940
Ormrod, J. A. (Worcs. & Lancs.) b Dec. 22, 1942
O'Shaughnessy, S. J. (Lancs. & Worcs.) b Sept. 9, 1961
Oslear, D. O. (Umpire) b March 3, 1929
*O'Sullivan, D. R. (C. Dist. & Hants) b Nov. 16, 1944
Outschoorn, L. (Worcs.) b Sept. 26, 1918
*Overton, G. W. F. (Otago) b June 8, 1919
*Owen-Smith, H. G. O. (W. Prov., OUCC & Middx; *CY 1930*) b Feb. 18, 1909
Owen-Thomas, D. R. (CUCC & Surrey) b Sept. 20, 1948
*Oxenham, R. K. (Qld) b July 28, 1891, d Aug. 16, 1939

Packe, M. St J. (Leics.) b Aug. 21, 1916, d Dec. 20, 1978
*Padgett, D. E. V. (Yorks.) b July 20, 1934
*Padmore, A. L. (B'dos) b Dec. 17, 1946
Page, H. A. (Tvl & Essex) b July 3, 1962
Page, J. C. T. (Kent) b May 20, 1930
Page, M. H. (Derbys.) b June 17, 1941
*Page, M. L. (Cant.) b May 8, 1902, d Feb. 13, 1987
*Pai, A. M. (Bombay) b April 28, 1945
*Paine, G. A. E. (Middx & Warwicks.; *CY 1935*) b June 11, 1908, d March 30, 1978
*Pairaudeau, B. H. (BG & N. Dist.) b April 14, 1931
*Palairet, L. C. H. (OUCC & Som.; *CY 1893*) b May 27, 1870, d March 27, 1933
Palairet, R. C. N. (OUCC & Som.; Joint-Manager MCC in Australia 1932-33) b June 25, 1871, d Feb. 11, 1955
Palia, P. E. (Madras, U. Prov., Bombay, Mysore & Bengal) b Sept. 5, 1910, d Sept. 9, 1981
*Palm, A. W. (W. Prov.) b June 8, 1901, d Aug. 17, 1966
*Palmer, C. H. (Worcs. & Leics.; Pres. MCC 1978-79) b May 15, 1919
*Palmer, G. E. (Vic. & Tas.) b Feb. 22, 1860, d Aug. 22, 1910
Palmer, G. V. (Som.) b Nov. 1, 1965
*Palmer, K. E. (Som.) b April 22, 1937
Palmer, R. (Som.) b July 12, 1942
*Pandit, C. S. (Bombay) b Sept. 30, 1961
Pardon, Charles Frederick (Editor of *Wisden* 1887-90) b March 28, 1850, d April 18, 1890
Pardon, Sydney H. (Editor of *Wisden* 1891-1925) b Sept. 23, 1855, d Nov. 20, 1925
*Parfitt, P. H. (Middx; *CY 1963*) b Dec. 8, 1936
Paris, C. G. A. (Hants; Pres. MCC 1975-76) b Aug. 20, 1911
Parish, R. J. (Aust. Administrator) b May 7, 1916
*Park, R. L. (Vic.) b July 30, 1892, d Jan. 23, 1947
*Parkar, G. A. (Bombay) b Oct. 24, 1955
*Parkar, R. D. (Bombay) b Oct. 31, 1946
Parkar, Z. (Bombay) b Nov. 22, 1957
*Parker, C. W. L. (Glos.; *CY 1923*) b Oct. 14, 1882, d July 11, 1959
*Parker, G. M. (SA) b May 27, 1899, d May 1, 1969
Parker, G. W. (CUCC & Glos.) b Feb. 11, 1912
Parker, J. F. (Surrey) b April 23, 1913, d Jan. 27, 1983
*Parker, J. M. (N. Dist. & Worcs.) b Feb. 21, 1951
Parker, J. P. (Hants) b Nov. 29, 1902, d Aug. 9, 1984
*Parker, N. M. (Otago & Cant.) b Aug. 28, 1948
*Parker, P. W. G. (CUCC, Sussex & Natal) b Jan. 15, 1956
*Parkhouse, W. G. A. (Glam.) b Oct. 12, 1925
*Parkin, C. H. (Yorks. & Lancs.; *CY 1924*) b Feb. 18, 1886, d June 15, 1943
*Parkin, D. C. (E. Prov., Tvl & Griq. W.) b Feb. 18, 1870, d March 20, 1936
Parks, H. W. (Sussex) b July 18, 1906, d May 7, 1984
*Parks, J. H. (Sussex & Cant.; *CY 1938*) b May 12, 1903, d Nov. 21, 1980
*Parks, J. M. (Sussex & Som.; *CY 1968*) b Oct. 21, 1931
Parks, R. J. (Hants) b June 15, 1959
Parr, F. D. (Lancs.) b June 1, 1928
Parr, George (Notts. & All-England) b May 22, 1826, d June 23, 1891
*Parry, D. R. (Comb. Is. & Leewards) b Dec. 22, 1954
*Parsana, D. D. (S'tra, Ind. Rlwys & Guj.) b Dec. 2, 1947
Parsons, A. B. D. (CUCC & Surrey) b Sept. 20, 1933
Parsons, A. E. W. (Auck. & Sussex) b Jan. 9, 1949
Parsons, G. J. (Leics., Warwicks., Boland & Griq. W.) b Oct. 17, 1959
Parsons, Canon J. H. (Warwicks.) b May 30, 1890, d Feb. 2, 1981
*Partridge, J. T. (Rhod.) b Dec. 9, 1932, d June 7, 1988
Partridge, N. E. (Malvern, CUCC & Warwicks.; *CY 1919*) b Aug. 10, 1900, d March 10, 1982
Partridge, R. J. (Northants) b Feb. 11, 1912
*Pascoe, L. S. (NSW) b Feb. 13, 1950
Pasqual, S. P. (SL) b Oct. 15, 1961
*Passailaigue, C. C. (Jam.) b Aug. 1902, d Jan. 7, 1972
*Patankar, C. T. (Bombay) b Nov. 24, 1930

**Pataudi, Iftikhar Ali, Nawab of (OUCC, Worcs., Patiala, N. Ind. & S. Punjab; *CY 1932*) b March 16, 1910, d Jan. 5, 1952
*Pataudi, Mansur Ali, Nawab of (Sussex, OUCC, Delhi & H'bad; *CY 1968*) b Jan. 5, 1941
Patel, A. (S'tra) b March 6, 1957
*Patel, B. P. (Karn.) b Nov. 24, 1952
*Patel, D. N. (Worcs. & Auck.) b Oct. 25, 1958
*Patel, J. M. (Guj.) b Nov. 26, 1924
Paterson, R. F. T. (Essex) b Sept. 8, 1916, d May 29, 1980
Pathmanathan, G. (OUCC, CUCC & SL) b Jan. 23, 1954
*Patiala, Maharaja of (N. Ind., Patiala & S. Punjab) b Jan. 17, 1913, d June 17, 1974
*Patil, S. M. (Bombay) b Aug. 18, 1956
*Patil, S. R. (M'tra) b Oct. 10, 1933
*Patterson, B. P. (Jam., Tas. & Lancs.) b Sept. 15, 1961
Pauline, D. B. (Surrey & Glam.) b Dec. 15, 1960
Pawson, A. G. (OUCC & Worcs.) b May 30, 1888, d Feb. 25, 1986
Pawson, H. A. (OUCC & Kent) b Aug. 22, 1921
Payn, L. W. (Natal) b May 6, 1915
*Payne, T. R. O. (B'dos) b Feb. 13, 1957
*Paynter, E. (Lancs.; *CY 1938*) b Nov. 5, 1901, d Feb. 5, 1979
Payton, W. R. D. (Notts.) b Feb. 13, 1882, d May 2, 1943
Pearce, G. (Sussex) b Oct. 27, 1908, d June 16, 1986
Pearce, T. A. (Kent) b Dec. 18, 1910, d Aug. 11, 1982
Pearce, T. N. (Essex) b Nov. 3, 1905
*Pearse, C. O. C. (Natal) b Oct. 10, 1884, d May 7, 1953
Pearson, D. B. (Worcs.) b March 29, 1937
*Peate, E. (Yorks.) b March 2, 1856, d March 11, 1900
Peck, I. G. (CUCC & Northants) b Oct. 18, 1957
*Peebles, I. A. R. (OUCC, Middx & Scotland; *CY 1931*) b Jan. 20, 1908, d Feb. 28, 1980
*Peel, R. (Yorks.; *CY 1889*) b Feb. 12, 1857, d Aug. 12, 1941
*Pegler, S. J. (Tvl) b July 28, 1888, d Sept. 10, 1972
*Pellew, C. E. (S. Aust.) b Sept. 21, 1893, d May 9, 1981
Penn, C. (Kent) b June 19, 1963
*Penn, F. (Kent) b March 7, 1851, d Dec. 26, 1916
Pepper, C. G. (NSW and Aust. Serv.; Umpire) b Sept. 15, 1918
Perera, K. G. (SL) b May 22, 1964
Perkins, C. G. (Northants) b June 4, 1911
Perkins, H. (CUCC & Cambs.; Sec. MCC 1876-97) b Dec. 10, 1832, d May 6, 1916
*Perks, R. T. D. (Worcs.) b Oct. 4, 1911, d Nov. 22, 1977
Perrin, P. A. (Essex; *CY 1905*) b May 26, 1876, d Nov. 20, 1945
Perryman, S. P. (Warwicks. & Worcs.) b Oct. 22, 1955
*Pervez Sajjad (Lahore, PIA & Kar.) b Aug. 30, 1942
*Petherick, P. J. (Otago & Wgtn) b Sept. 25, 1942
*Petrie, E. C. (Auck. & N. Dist.) b May 22, 1927
*Phadkar, D. G. (M'tra, Bombay, Bengal & Ind. Rlwys) b Dec. 10, 1925, d March 17, 1985
Phebey, A. H. (Kent) b Oct. 1, 1924
Phelan, P. J. (Essex) b Feb. 9, 1938
*Philipson, H. (OUCC & Middx) b June 8, 1866, d Dec. 4, 1935
*Phillip, N. (Comb. Is., Windwards & Essex) b June 12, 1948
Phillipps, J. H. (NZ Manager) b Jan. 1, 1898, d June 8, 1977
Phillips, R. B. (NSW & Qld) b May 23, 1954
*Phillips, W. B. (S. Aust.) b March 1, 1958
Phillipson, C. P. (Sussex) b Feb. 10, 1952
Phillipson, W. E. (Lancs.) b Dec. 3, 1910
*Philpott, P. I. (NSW) b Nov. 21, 1934
Piachaud, J. D. (OUCC, Hants & Ceylon) b March 1, 1937
Pick, R. A. (Notts.) b Nov. 19, 1963
Pickles, L. (Som.) b Sept. 17, 1932
Pienaar, R. F. (Tvl, W. Prov., N. Tvl & Kent) b July 17, 1961
Pieris, H. S. M. (SL) b Feb. 16, 1946
*Pierre, L. R. (T/T) b June 5, 1921
*Pigott, A. C. S. (Sussex & Wgtn) b June 4, 1958
Pilch, Fuller (Norfolk & Kent) b March 17, 1804, d May 1, 1870
Pilling, H. (Lancs.) b Feb. 23, 1943
*Pilling, R. (Lancs.; *CY 1891*) b July 5, 1855, d March 28, 1891
*Pithey, A. J. (Rhod. & W. Prov.) b July 17, 1933
*Pithey, D. B. (Rhod., OUCC, Northants, W. Prov., Natal & Tvl) b Oct. 4, 1936
Pitman, R. W. C. (Hants) b Feb. 21, 1933
*Place, W. (Lancs.) b Dec 7, 1914
Platt, R. K. (Yorks. & Northants) b Dec. 21, 1932
*Playle, W. R. (Auck. & W. Aust.) b Dec. 1, 1938
Pleass, J. E. (Glam.) b May 21, 1923
*Plimsoll, J. B. (W. Prov. & Natal) b Oct. 27, 1917
Pocock, N. E. J. (Hants) b Dec. 15, 1951
*Pocock, P. I. (Surrey & N. Tvl) b Sept. 24, 1946

Pointer, G. A. (CUCC) b May 2, 1967
*Pollard, R. (Lancs.) b June 19, 1912, d Dec. 16, 1985
*Pollard, V. (C. Dist. & Cant.) b Burnley Sept. 7, 1945
Pollock, A. J. (CUCC) b April 19, 1962
Pollock, P. M. (E. Prov.; *CY 1966*) b June 30, 1941
Pollock, R. G. (E. Prov. & Tvl; *CY 1966*) b Feb. 27, 1944
Ponsford, W. H. (Vic.; *CY 1935*) b Oct. 19, 1900
Pont, K. R. (Essex) b Jan. 16, 1953
Poole, C. J. (Notts.) b March 13, 1921
Pooley, E. (Surrey & first England tour) b Feb. 13, 1838, d July 18, 1907
*Poore, M. B. (Cant.) b June 1, 1930
Poore, Brig-Gen. R. M. (Hants & SA; *CY 1900*) b March 20, 1866, d July 14, 1938
Pope, A. V. (Derbys.) b Aug. 15, 1909
Pope, G. H. (Derbys.) b Jan. 27, 1911
*Pope, R. J. (NSW) b Feb. 18, 1864, d July 27, 1952
Popplewell, N. F. M. (CUCC & Som.) b Aug. 8, 1957
Portal of Hungerford, 1st Lord (Pres. MCC 1958-59) b May 21, 1893, d April 22, 1971
Porter, A. (Glam.) b March 25, 1914
Porter, G. D. (W. Aust.) b March 18, 1955
Pothecary, E. A. (Hants) b March 1, 1906
*Pothecary, J. E. (W. Prov.) b Dec. 6, 1933
Potter, G. (Sussex) b Oct. 26, 1931
Potter, J. (Vic.) b April 13, 1938
Potter, L. (Kent, Griq. W., Leics. & OFS) b Nov. 7, 1962
*Pougher, A. D. (Leics.) b April 19, 1865, d May 20, 1926
Pountain, F. R. (Sussex) b April 23, 1941
Powell, A. G. (CUCC & Essex) b Aug. 17, 1912, d June 7, 1982
*Powell, A. W. (Griq. W.) b July 18, 1873, d Sept. 11, 1948
*Prabhakar, M. (Delhi) b April 15, 1963
*Prasanna, E. A. S. (†Karn.) b May 22, 1940
Pratt, R. C. E. (Surrey) b May 5, 1928, d June 7, 1977
Pratt, R. L. (Leics.) b Nov. 15, 1938
Prentice, F. T. (Leics.) b April 22, 1912, d July 10, 1978
Pressdee, J. S. (Glam. & NE Tvl) b June 19, 1933
Preston, Hubert (Editor of *Wisden* 1944-51) b Dec. 16, 1868, d Aug. 6, 1960
Preston, K. C. (Essex) b Aug. 22, 1925
Preston, Norman (Editor of *Wisden* 1951-80) b March 18, 1903, d March 6, 1980
Pretlove, J. F. (CUCC & Kent) b Nov. 23, 1932
Price, D. G. (CUCC) b Feb. 7, 1965
Price, E. J. (Lancs. & Essex) b Oct. 27, 1918
*Price, J. S. E. (Middx) b July 22, 1937
*Price, W. F. (Middx) b April 25, 1902, d Jan. 13, 1969
Prichard, P. J. (Essex) b Jan. 7, 1965
*Prideaux, R. M. (CUCC, Kent, Northants, Sussex & OFS) b July 13, 1939
Pridgeon, A. P. (Worcs.) b Feb. 22, 1954
*Prince, C. F. H. (W. Prov., Border & E. Prov.) b Sept. 11, 1874, d March 5, 1948
*Pringle, D. R. (CUCC & Essex) b Sept. 18, 1958
Pritchard, T. L. (Wgtn, Warwicks. & Kent) b March 10, 1917
*Procter, M. J. (Glos., Natal, W. Prov., Rhod. & OFS; *CY 1970*) b Sept. 15, 1946
Prodger, J. M. (Kent) b Sept. 1, 1935
*Promnitz, H. L. E. (Border, Griq. W. & OFS) b Feb. 23, 1904, d Sept. 7, 1983
Prouton, R. O. (Hants) b March 1, 1926
Puckett, C. W. (W. Aust.) b Feb. 21, 1911
Pugh, C. T. M. (Glos.) b March 13, 1937
Pullan, D. A. (Notts.) b May 1, 1944
*Pullar, G. (Lancs. & Glos.; *CY 1960*) b Aug. 1, 1935
Pullinger, G. R. (Essex) b March 14, 1920, d Aug. 4, 1982
*Puna, N. (N. Dist.) b Oct. 28, 1929
*Punjabi, P. H. (Sind & Guj.) b Sept. 20, 1921
Pycroft, A. J. (Zimb.) b June 6, 1956
Pydanna, M. (Guyana) b Jan. 27, 1950

*Qasim Omar (Kar. & MCB) b Feb. 9, 1957
Quaife, B. W. (Warwicks. & Worcs.) b Nov. 24, 1899, d Nov. 28, 1984
*Quaife, William (W. G.) (Warwicks. & Griq. W.; *CY 1902*) b March 17, 1872, d Oct. 13, 1951
Quick, I. W. (Vic.) b Nov. 5, 1933
*Quinn, N. A. (Griq. W. & Tvl) b Feb. 21, 1908, d Aug. 5, 1934

*Rabone, G. O. (Wgtn & Auck.) b Nov. 6, 1921
*Rackemann, C. G. (Qld) b June 3, 1960
*Radford, N. V. (Lancs., Tvl & Worcs.; *CY 1986*) b June 7, 1957
*Radley, C. T. (Middx; *CY 1979*) b May 13, 1944
*Rae, A. F. (Jam.) b Sept. 30, 1922
Raees Mohammad (Kar.) b Dec. 24, 1932
*Rai Singh, K. (S. Punjab & Ind. Serv.) b Feb. 24, 1922
Rait Kerr, Col. R. S. (Sec. MCC 1936-52) b April 13, 1891, d April 2, 1961
Rajadurai, B. E. A. (SL) b Aug. 24, 1965
*Rajindernath, V. (N. Ind., U. Prov., S. Punjab, Bihar & E. Punjab) b Jan. 7, 1928
*Rajinder Pal (Delhi, S. Punjab & Punjab) b Nov. 18, 1937
*Rajput, L. S. (Bombay) b Dec. 18, 1961
Ralph, L. H. R. (Essex) b May 22, 1920

*Ramadhin, S. (T/T & Lancs.; *CY 1951*) b May 1, 1929
*Raman, W. V. (TN) b March 23, 1965
*Ramanayake, C. P. H. (SL) b Jan. 8, 1965
*Ramaswami, C. (Madras) b June 18, 1896, 'presumed dead'
*Ramchand, G. S. (Sind, Bombay & Raja.) b July 26, 1927
*Ramiz Raja (Lahore, Allied Bank & PNSC) b July 14, 1962
*Ramji, L. (W. Ind.) b 1900, d Dec. 20, 1948
Ramsamooj, D. (T/T & Northants) b July 5, 1932
*Ranasinghe, A. N. (SL) b Oct. 13, 1956
*Ranatunga, A. (SL) b Dec. 1, 1963
*Randall, D. W. (Notts.; *CY 1980*) b Feb. 24, 1951
Randhir Singh (Orissa & Bihar) b Aug. 16, 1957
*Rangachari, C. R. (Madras) b April 14, 1916
*Rangnekar, K. M. (M'tra, Bombay & †M. Pradesh) b June 27, 1917, d Oct. 11, 1984
*Ranjane, V. B. (M'tra & Ind. Rlwys) b July 22, 1937
*Ranjitsinhji, K. S., afterwards H. H. the Jam Saheb of Nawanagar (CUCC & Sussex; *CY 1897*) b Sept. 10, 1872, d April 2, 1933
*Ransford, V. S. (Vic.; *CY 1910*) b March 20, 1885, d March 19, 1958
Ransom, V. J. (Hants & Surrey) b March 17, 1918
*Rashid Khan (PWD, Kar. & PIA) b Dec. 15, 1959
Ratcliffe, R. M. (Lancs.) b Nov. 29, 1951
*Ratnayake, R. J. (SL) b Jan. 2, 1964
*Ratnayeke, J. R. (SL) b May 2, 1960
Rayment, A. W. H. (Hants) b May 29, 1928
Raymer, V. N. (Qld) b May 4, 1918
*Read, H. D. (Surrey & Essex) b Jan. 28, 1910
*Read, J. M. (Surrey; *CY 1890*) b Feb. 9, 1859, d Feb. 17, 1929
*Read, W. W. (Surrey; *CY 1893*) b Nov. 23, 1855, d Jan. 6, 1907
Reddick, T. B. (Middx, Notts. & W. Prov.) b Feb. 17, 1912, d June 1, 1982
*Reddy, B. (TN) b Nov. 12, 1954
Redman, J. (Som.) b March 1, 1926, d Sept. 19, 1981
*Redmond, R. E. (Wgtn & Auck.) b Dec. 29, 1944
*Redpath, I. R. (Vic.) b May 11, 1941
Reed, B. L. (Hants) b Sept. 17, 1937
*Reedman, J. C. (S. Aust.) b Oct. 9, 1865, d March 25, 1924
Rees, A. (Glam.) b Feb. 17, 1938
Reeve, D. A. (Sussex & Warwicks.) b April 2, 1963
Reeves, W. (Essex; Umpire) b Jan. 22, 1875, d March 22, 1944
*Rege, M. R. (M'tra) b March 18, 1924
*Rehman, S. F. (Punjab, Pak. Us & Lahore) b June 11, 1935
*Reid, B. A. (W. Aust.) b March 14, 1963
*Reid, J. F. (Auck.) b March 3, 1956
*Reid, J. R. (Wgtn & Otago; *CY 1959*) b June 3, 1928
Reid, K. P. (E. Prov. & Northants) b July 24, 1951
*Reid, N. (W. Prov.) b Dec 26, 1890, d June 10, 1947
Reid, R. B. (Wgtn & Auck.) b Dec. 3, 1958
Reidy, B. W. (Lancs.) b Sept. 18, 1953
*Relf, A. E. (Sussex & Auck.; *CY 1914*) b June 26, 1874, d March 26, 1937
*Renneburg, D. A. (NSW) b Sept. 23, 1942
Revill, A. C. (Derbys. & Leics.) b March 27, 1923
Reynolds, B. L. (Northants) b June 10, 1932
Rhodes, A. E. G. (Derbys.) b Oct. 10, 1916, d Oct. 18, 1983
*Rhodes, H. J. (Derbys.) b July 22, 1936
Rhodes, S. D. (Notts.) b March 24, 1910
Rhodes, S. J. (Yorks. & Worcs.) b June 17, 1964
*Rhodes, W. (Yorks.; *CY 1899*) b Oct. 29, 1877, d July 8, 1973
Rice, C. E. B. (Tvl & Notts.; *CY 1981*) b July 23, 1949
Rice, J. M. (Hants) b Oct. 23, 1949
*Richards, A. R. (W. Prov.) b 1868, d Jan. 9, 1904
*Richards, B. A. (Natal, Glos., Hants & S. Aust.; *CY 1969*) b July 21, 1945
*Richards, C. J. (Surrey & OFS) b Aug. 10, 1958
Richards, G. (Glam.) b Nov. 29, 1951
*Richards, I. V. A. (Comb. Is., Leewards, Som. & Qld; *CY 1977*) b March 7, 1952
*Richards, W. H. M. (SA) b Aug. 1862, d Jan. 4, 1903
*Richardson, A. J. (S. Aust.) b July 24, 1888, d Dec. 23, 1973
Richardson, A. W. (Derbys.) b March 4, 1907, d July 29, 1983
Richardson, D. J. (E. Prov. & N. Tvl) b Sept. 16, 1959
*Richardson, D. W. (Worcs.) b Nov. 3, 1934
Richardson, G. W. (Derbys.) b April 26, 1938
*Richardson, P. E. (Worcs. & Kent; *CY 1957*) b July 4, 1931
*Richardson, R. B. (Leewards) b Jan. 12, 1962
*Richardson, T. (Surrey & Som.; *CY 1897*) b Aug. 11, 1870, d July 2, 1912
*Richardson, V. Y. (S. Aust.) b Sept. 7, 1894, d Oct. 29, 1969
*Richmond, T. L. (Notts.) b June 23, 1890, d Dec. 29, 1957

*Rickards, K. R. (Jam. & Essex) b Aug. 23, 1923
Riddington, A. (Leics.) b Dec. 22, 1911
*Ridgway, F. (Kent) b Aug. 10, 1923
Ridings, P. L. (S. Aust.) b Oct. 2, 1917
*Rigg, K. E. (Vic.) b May 21, 1906
Riley, H. (Leics.) b Oct. 3, 1902
*Ring, D. T. (Vic.) b Oct. 14, 1918
Ripley, D. (Northants) b Sept. 13, 1966
Rist, F. H. (Essex) b March 30, 1914
*Ritchie, G. M. (Qld) b Jan. 23, 1960
*Rixon, S. J. (NSW) b Feb. 25, 1954
*Rizwan-uz-Zaman (Kar. & PIA) b Sept. 4, 1962
*Roach, C. A. (T/T) b March 13, 1904, d April 16, 1988
*Roberts, A. D. G. (N. Dist.) b May 6, 1947
*Roberts, A. M. E. (Comb. Is., Leewards, Hants, NSW & Leics.; *CY 1975*) b Jan. 29, 1951
*Roberts, A. T. (Windwards) b Sept. 18, 1937
*Roberts, A. W. (Cant. & Otago) b Aug. 20, 1909, d May 13, 1978
Roberts, B. (Tvl & Derbys.) b May 30, 1962
Roberts, Pascal (T/T) b Dec 15, 1937
Roberts, W. B. (Lancs. & Victory Tests) b Sept. 27, 1914, d Aug. 24, 1951
*Robertson, G. K. (C. Dist.) b July 15, 1960
*Robertson, J. B. (W. Prov.) b June 5, 1906, d July 5, 1985
*Robertson, J. D. (Middx; *CY 1948*) b Feb. 22, 1917
*Robertson, W. R. (Vic.) b Oct. 6, 1861, d June 24, 1938
Robertson-Glasgow, R. C. (OUCC & Som.) b July 15, 1901, d March 4, 1965
Robins, D. H. (Warwicks.) b June 26, 1914
Robins, R. V. C. (Middx) b March 13, 1935
*Robins, R. W. V. (CUCC & Middx; *CY 1930*) b June 3, 1906, d Dec. 12, 1968
Robinson, A. L. (Yorks.) b Aug. 17, 1946
Robinson, Emmott (Yorks.) b Nov. 16, 1883, d Nov. 17, 1969
Robinson, Ellis P. (Yorks. & Som.) b Aug. 10, 1911
Robinson, H. B. (OUCC & Canada) b March 3, 1919
Robinson, M. (Glam., Warwicks., H'bad & Madras) b July 16, 1921
Robinson, P. E. (Yorks.) b Aug. 3, 1963
Robinson, P. J. (Worcs. & Som.) b Feb. 9, 1943
Robinson, Ray (Writer) b July 8, 1908, d July 6, 1982
*Robinson, R. D. (Vic.) b June 8, 1946
*Robinson, R. H. (NSW, S. Aust. & Otago) b March 26, 1914, d Aug. 10, 1965
*Robinson, R. T. (Notts.; *CY 1986*) b Nov. 21, 1958
Robson, E. (Som.) b May 1, 1870, d May 23, 1924
Rochford, P. (Glos.) b Aug. 27, 1928
*Rodriguez, W. V. (T/T) b June 25, 1934
Roe, B. (Som.) b Jan. 27, 1939
Roebuck, P. M. (CUCC & Som.; *CY 1988*) b March 6, 1956
Rogers, N. H. (Hants) b March 9, 1918
Rogers, R. E. (Qld) b Aug. 24, 1916
Romaines, P. W. (Northants, Glos. & Griq. W.) b Dec. 25, 1955
*Roope, G. R. J. (Surrey & Griq. W.) b July 12, 1946
*Root, C. F. (Derbys. & Worcs.) b April 16, 1890, d Jan. 20, 1954
*Rorke, G. F. (NSW) b June 27, 1938
*Rose, B. C. (Som.; *CY 1980*) b June 4, 1950
Rose, G. D. (Middx & Som.) b April 12, 1964
Rosebery, 6th Earl of (*see* Dalmeny, Lord)
*Rose-Innes, A. (Kimberley & Tvl) b Feb. 16, 1868, d Nov. 22, 1946
Ross, C. J. (Wgtn & OUCC) b June 24, 1954
Rotherham, G. A. (Rugby, CUCC, Warwicks. & Wgtn; *CY 1918*) b May 28, 1899, d Jan. 31, 1985
Rouse, S. J. (Warwicks.) b Jan. 20, 1949
Routledge, R. (Middx) b July 7, 1920
*Routledge, T. W. (W. Prov. & Tvl) b April 18, 1867, d May 9, 1927
*Rowan, A. M. B. (Tvl) b Feb. 7, 1921
*Rowan, E. A. B. (Tvl; *CY 1952*) b July 20, 1909
*Rowe, C. G. (Wgtn & C. Dist.) b June 30, 1915
Rowe, C. J. C. (Kent & Glam.) b May 5, 1953
Rowe, E. J. (Notts.) b July 21, 1920
*Rowe, G. A. (W. Prov.) b June 15, 1874, d Jan. 8, 1950
*Rowe, L. G. (Jam. & Derbys.) b Jan. 8, 1949
*Roy, A. (Bengal) b June 5, 1945
*Roy, Pankaj (Bengal) b May 31, 1928
*Roy, Pranab (Bengal) b Feb. 10, 1957
*Royle, Rev. V. P. F. A. (OUCC & Lancs.) b Jan. 29, 1854, d May 21, 1929
*Rumsey, F. E. (Worcs., Som. & Derbys.) b Dec. 4, 1935
*Russell, A. C. [C. A. G.] (Essex; *CY 1923*) b Oct. 7, 1887, d March 23, 1961
Russell, P. E. (Derbys.) b May 9, 1944
*Russell, R. C. (Glos.) b Aug. 15, 1963
Russell, S. E. (Middx & Glos.) b Oct. 4, 1937
*Russell, W. E. (Middx) b July 3, 1936
Russom, N. (CUCC & Som.) b Dec. 3, 1958
Rutherford, I. A. (Worcs. & Otago) b June 30, 1957
*Rutherford, J. W. (W. Aust.) b Sept. 25, 1929
*Rutherford, K. R. (Otago) b Oct. 26, 1965

Ryan, M. (Yorks.) b June 23, 1933
*Ryder, J. (Vic.) b Aug. 8, 1889, d April 3, 1977

Saadat Ali (Lahore, UBL & HBFC) b Feb. 6, 1955
*Sadiq Mohammad (Kar., PIA, Tas., Essex, Glos. & UBP) b May 3, 1945
Sadler, W. C. H. (Surrey) b Sept. 24, 1896, d Feb. 12, 1981
*Saeed Ahmed (Punjab, Pak. Us, Lahore, PIA, Kar., PWD & Sind) b Oct. 1, 1937
*Saggers, R. A. (NSW) b May 15, 1917, d March 1987
Sainsbury, G. E. (Essex & Glos.) b Jan. 17, 1958
Sainsbury, P. J. (Hants; *CY 1974*) b June 13, 1934
*St Hill, E. L. (T/T) b March 9, 1904, d May 21, 1957
*St Hill, W. H. (T/T) b July 6, 1893, d 1957
Sajid Ali (Kar. & NBP) b July 1, 1963
*Salah-ud-Din (Kar., PIA & Pak. Us) b Feb. 14, 1947
Sale, R., jun. (OUCC, Warwicks. & Derbys.) b Oct. 4, 1919, d Feb. 3, 1987
*Saleem Altaf (Lahore & PIA) b April 19, 1944
*Saleem Jaffer (Kar. & UBL) b Nov. 19, 1962
*Salim Malik (Lahore & HBL; *CY 1988*) b April 16, 1963
*Salim Yousuf (Sind, Kar., IDBP, Allied Bank & Customs) b Dec. 7, 1959
*Samaranayake, A. D. A. (SL) b Feb. 25, 1962
Samarasekera, M. A. R. (SL) b Aug. 4, 1961
Sampson, H. (Yorks. & All-England) b March 13, 1813, d March 29, 1885
*Samuelson, S. V. (Natal) b Nov. 21, 1883, d Nov. 18, 1958
*Sandham, A. (Surrey; *CY 1923*) b July 6, 1890, d April 20, 1982
*Sandhu, B. S. (Bombay) b Aug. 3, 1956
*Sardesai, D. N. (Bombay) b Aug. 8, 1940
*Sarfraz Nawaz (Lahore, Punjab, Northants, Pak. Rlwys & UBL) b Dec. 1, 1948
*Sarwate, C. T. (CP & B, M'tra, Bombay & †M. Pradesh) b June 22, 1920
*Saunders, J. V. (Vic. & Wgtn) b Feb. 3, 1876, d Dec. 21, 1927
Savage, J. S. (Leics. & Lancs.) b March 3, 1929
Savage, R. Le Q. (OUCC & Warwicks.) b Dec. 10, 1955
Savill, L. A. (Essex) b June 30, 1935
Saville, G. J. (Essex) b Feb. 5, 1944
Saxelby, K. (Notts.) b Feb. 23, 1959
*Saxena, R. C. (Delhi & Bihar) b Sept. 20, 1944

Sayer, D. M. (OUCC & Kent) b Sept. 1 1936
*Scarlett, R. O. (Jam.) b Aug. 15, 1934
Schofield, R. M. (C. Dist.) b Nov. 6, 193
*Schultz, S. S. (CUCC & Lancs.) b Aug. 2 1857, d Dec. 18, 1937
*Schwarz, R. O. (Middx & Natal; *CY 190* b May 4, 1875, d Nov. 18, 1918
*Scott, A. P. H. (Jam.) b July 29, 1934
Scott, Christopher J. (Lancs.) b Sept. 1 1959
Scott, Colin J. (Glos.) b May 1, 1919
Scott, C. W. (Notts.) b Jan. 23, 1964
*Scott, H. J. H. (Vic.) b Dec. 26, 1858, Sept. 23, 1910
Scott, M. E. (Northants) b May 8, 1936
*Scott, O. C. (Jam.) b Aug. 25, 1893, d Jun 16, 1961
*Scott, R. H. (Cant.) b March 6, 1917
Scott, S. W. (Middx; *CY 1893*) b March 24 1854, d Dec. 8, 1933
*Scott, V. J. (Auck.) b July 31, 1916, d Aug 2, 1980
*Scotton, W. H. (Notts.) b Jan. 15, 1856, July 9, 1893
Seabrook, F. J. (CUCC & Glos.) b Jan. 9 1899, d Aug. 7, 1979
*Sealey, B. J. (T/T) b Aug. 12, 1899, d Sept 12, 1963
*Sealy, J. E. D. (B'dos & T/T) b Sept. 11 1912, d Jan. 3, 1982
Seamer, J. W. (Som. & OUCC) b June 23 1913
*Seccull, A. W. (Kimberley, W. Prov. & Tvl b Sept. 14, 1868, d July 20, 1945
Seeff, L. J. (W. Prov.) b May 1, 1959
*Sekar, T. A. P. (TN) b March 28, 1955
*Selby, J. (Notts.) b July 1, 1849, d March 11, 1894
Sellers, A. B. (Yorks.; *CY 1940*) b March 5 1907, d Feb. 20, 1981
*Sellers, R. H. D. (S. Aust.) b Aug. 20, 194
*Selvey, M. W. W. (CUCC, Surrey, Middx Glam. & OFS) b April 25, 1948
*Sen, P. (Bengal) b May 31, 1926, d Jan. 27 1970
*Sen Gupta, A. K. (Ind. Serv.) b Aug. 3 1939
*Serjeant, C. S. (W. Aust.) b Nov. 1, 1951
Seymour, James (Kent) b Oct. 25, 1879, d Sept. 30, 1930
*Seymour, M. A. (W. Prov.) b June 5, 193
*Shackleton, D. (Hants.; *CY 1959*) b Aug 12, 1924
*Shafiq Ahmed (Lahore, Punjab, NBP & UBL) b March 28, 1949
*Shafqat Rana (Lahore & PIA) b Aug. 10 1943
*Shahid Israr (Kar. & Sind) b March 1, 1950
*Shahid Mahmoud (Kar., Pak. Us & PWD) b March 17, 1939
Shakil Khan (WAPDA) b May 28, 1968

Shalders, W. A. (Griq. W. & Tvl) b Feb. 12, 1880, d March 18, 1917
*Sharma, Ajay (Delhi) b April 3, 1964
*Sharma, Chetan (Haryana) b Jan. 3, 1966
*Sharma, Gopal (U. Pradesh) b Aug. 3, 1960
*Sharma, P. (Raja.) b Jan. 5, 1948
Sharma, Sanjeev (Delhi) b Aug. 25, 1965
Sharp, G. (Northants) b March 12, 1950
Sharp, H. P. (Middx) b Oct. 6, 1917
*Sharp, J. (Lancs.) b Feb. 15, 1878, d Jan. 28, 1938
Sharp, K. (Yorks. & Griq. W.) b April 6, 1959
*Sharpe, D. (Punjab, Pak. Rlwys, Lahore & S. Aust.) b Aug. 3, 1937
*Sharpe, J. W. (Surrey & Notts.; *CY 1892*) b Dec. 9, 1866, d June 19, 1936
*Sharpe, P. J. (Yorks. & Derbys.; *CY 1963*) b Dec. 27, 1936
*Shastri, R. J. (Bombay & Glam.) b May 27, 1962
*Shaw, Alfred (Notts. & Sussex) b Aug. 29, 1842, d Jan. 16, 1907
Shaw, C. (Yorks.) b Feb. 17, 1964
*Sheahan, A. P. (Vic.) b Sept. 30, 1946
Sheffield, J. R. (Essex & Wgtn) b Nov. 19, 1906
*Shepherd, B. K. (W. Aust.) b April 23, 1937
Shepherd, D. J. (Glam.; *CY 1970*) b Aug. 12, 1927
Shepherd, D. R. (Glos.) b Dec. 27, 1940
*Shepherd, J. N. (B'dos, Kent, Rhod. & Glos.; *CY 1979*) b Nov. 9, 1943
Shepherd, T. F. (Surrey) b Dec. 5, 1889, d Feb. 13, 1957
*Sheppard, Rt Rev. D. S. (Bishop of Liverpool) (CUCC & Sussex; *CY 1953*) b March 6, 1929
*Shepstone, G. H. (Tvl) b April 8, 1876, d July 3, 1940
*Sherwell, P. W. (Tvl) b Aug. 17, 1880, d April 17, 1948
*Sherwin, M. (Notts.; *CY 1891*) b Feb. 26, 1851, d July 3, 1910
*Shillingford, G. C. (Comb. Is. & Windwards) b Sept. 25, 1944
*Shillingford, I. T. (Comb. Is. & Windwards) b April 18, 1944
*Shinde, S. G. (Baroda, M'tra & Bombay) b Aug. 18, 1923, d June 22, 1955
Shipman, A. W. (Leics.) b March 7, 1901, d Dec. 12, 1979
Shirreff, A. C. (CUCC, Hants, Kent & Som.) b Feb. 12, 1919
*Shivnarine, S. (Guyana) b May 13, 1952
*Shoaib Mohammad (Kar. & PIA) b Jan. 8, 1962
*Shodhan, R. H. (Guj. & Baroda) b Oct. 18, 1928
Short, A. M. (Natal) b Sept. 27, 1947
*Shrewsbury, Arthur (Notts.; *CY 1890*) b April 11, 1856, d May 19, 1903
*Shrimpton, M. J. F. (C. Dist. & N. Dist.) b June 23, 1940
*Shuja-ud-Din, Col. (N. Ind., Pak. Us, Pak. Serv., B'pur & R'pindi) b April 10, 1930
*Shukla, R. C. (Bihar & Delhi) b Feb. 4, 1948
*Shuter, J. (Kent & Surrey) b Feb. 9, 1855, d July 5, 1920
*Shuttleworth, K. (Lancs. & Leics.) b Nov. 13, 1944
*Sidebottom, A. (Yorks. & OFS) b April 1, 1954
*Sidhu, N. S. (Punjab) b Oct. 20, 1963
*Siedle, I. J. (Natal) b Jan. 11, 1903, d Aug. 24, 1982
*Sievers, M. W. (Vic.) b April 13, 1912, d May 10, 1968
*Sikander Bakht (PWD, PIA, Sind, Kar. & UBL) b Aug. 25, 1957
Silk, D. R. W. (CUCC & Som.) b Oct. 8, 1931
*Silva, S. A. R. (SL) b Dec. 12, 1960
Sime, W. A. (Notts.) b Feb. 8, 1909, d May 5, 1982
Simmons, J. (Lancs. & Tas.; *CY 1985*) b March 28, 1941
*Simmons, P. V. (T/T) b April 18, 1963
*Simpson, R. B. (NSW & W. Aust.; *CY 1965*) b Feb. 3, 1936
*Simpson, R. T. (Notts. & Sind; *CY 1950*) b Feb. 27, 1920
*Simpson-Hayward, G. H. (Worcs.) b June 7, 1875, d Oct. 2, 1936
Sims, Sir Arthur (Cant.) b July 22, 1877, d April 27, 1969
*Sims, J. M. (Middx) b May 13, 1903, d April 27, 1973
*Sinclair, B. W. (Wgtn) b Oct. 23, 1936
*Sinclair, I. McK. (Cant.) b June 1, 1933
*Sinclair, J. H. (Tvl) b Oct. 16, 1876, d Feb. 23, 1913
*Sincock, D. J. (S. Aust.) b Feb. 1, 1942
*Sinfield, R. A. (Glos.) b Dec. 24, 1900, d March 17, 1988
*Singh, Charan K. (T/T) b 1938
Singh, R. P. (U. Pradesh) b Jan. 6, 1963
Singh, Swaranjit (CUCC, Warwicks., E. Punjab & Bengal) b July 18, 1931
Singleton, A. P. (OUCC, Worcs. & Rhod.) b Aug. 5, 1914
*Sivaramakrishnan, L. (TN) b Dec. 31, 1965
Skeet, C. H. L. (OUCC & Middx) b Aug. 17, 1895, d April 20, 1978
Skelding, Alec (Leics.) b Sept. 5, 1886, d April 17, 1960
Skinner, A. F. (Derbys. & Northants) b April 22, 1913, d Feb. 28, 1982
Skinner, D. A. (Derbys.) b March 22, 1920
Skinner, L. E. (Surrey & Guyana) b Sept. 7, 1950
*Slack, W. N. (Middx & Windwards) b Dec. 12, 1954

Slade, D. N. F. (Worcs.) b Aug. 24, 1940
Slade, W. D. (Glam.) b Sept. 27, 1941
*Slater, K. N. (W. Aust.) b March 12, 1935
*Sleep, P. R. (S. Aust.) b May 4, 1957
*Slight, J. (Vic.) b Oct. 20, 1855, d Dec. 9, 1930
Slocombe, P. A. (Som.) b Sept. 6, 1954
*Smailes, T. F. (Yorks.) b March 27, 1910, d Dec. 1, 1970
Smales, K. (Yorks. & Notts.) b Sept. 15, 1927
*Small, G. C. (Warwicks. & S. Aust.) b Oct. 18, 1961
Small, John, sen. (Hants & All-England) b April 19, 1737, d Dec. 31, 1826
*Small, J. A. (T/T) b Nov. 3, 1892, d April 26, 1958
*Small, M. A. (B'dos) b Feb. 12, 1964
Smart, J. A. (Warwicks.) b April 12, 1891, d Oct. 3, 1979
Smedley, M. J. (Notts.) b Oct. 28, 1941
*Smith, A. C. (OUCC & Warwicks.; Chief Exec. TCCB 1987-) b Oct. 25, 1936
*Smith, Sir C. Aubrey (CUCC, Sussex & Tvl) b July 21, 1863, d Dec. 20, 1948
*Smith, C. I. J. (Middx; *CY 1935*) b Aug. 25, 1906, d Feb. 9, 1979
*Smith, C. J. E. (Tvl) b Dec. 25, 1872, d March 27, 1947
*Smith, C. L. (Natal, Glam. & Hants; *CY 1984*) b Oct. 15, 1958
Smith, C. S. (CUCC & Lancs.) b Oct. 1, 1932
*Smith, C. W. (B'dos) b July 29, 1933
*Smith, Denis (Derbys.; *CY 1936*) b Jan. 24, 1907, d Sept. 12, 1979
*Smith, D. B. M. (Vic.) b Sept. 14, 1884, d July 29, 1963
Smith, D. H. K. (Derbys. & OFS) b June 29, 1940
*Smith, D. M. (Surrey & Worcs.) b Jan. 9, 1956
*Smith, D. R. (Glos.) b Oct. 5, 1934
*Smith, D. V. (Sussex) b June 14, 1923
Smith, Edwin (Derbys.) b Jan. 2, 1934
*Smith, E. J. (Warwicks.) b Feb. 6, 1886, d Aug. 31, 1979
*Smith, F. B. (Cant.) b March 13, 1922
*Smith, F. W. (Tvl) No details of birth or death known
Smith, G. (Kent) b Nov. 30, 1925
Smith, G. J. (Essex) b April 2, 1935
*Smith, Harry (Glos.) b May 21, 1890, d Nov. 12, 1937
*Smith, H. D. (Otago & Cant.) b Jan. 8, 1913, d Jan. 25, 1986
*Smith, I. D. S. (C. Dist.) b Feb. 28, 1957
Smith, K. D. (Warwicks.) b July 9, 1956
Smith, L. D. (Otago) b Dec. 23, 1914, d Nov. 1, 1978
Smith, M. J. (Middx) b Jan. 4, 1942
*Smith, M. J. K. (OUCC, Leics. & Warwicks.; *CY 1960*) b June 30, 1933
Smith, N. (Yorks. & Essex) b April 1, 194
*Smith, O. G. (Jam.; *CY 1958*) b May 1933, d Sept. 9, 1959
Smith, P. A. (Warwicks.) b April 5, 1964
Smith, Ray (Essex) b Aug. 10, 1914
Smith, Roy (Som.) b April 14, 1930
*Smith, R. A. (Natal & Hants) b Sept. 1 1963
Smith, R. C. (Leics.) b Aug. 3, 1935
*Smith, S. B. (NSW) b Oct. 18, 1961
Smith, S. G. (T/T, Northants & Auck.; *C 1915*) b Jan. 15, 1881, d Oct. 25, 1963
*Smith, T. P. B. (Essex; *CY 1947*) b Oct. 30 1908, d Aug. 4, 1967
*Smith, V. I. (Natal) b Feb. 23, 1925
Smith, W. A. (Surrey) b Sept. 15, 1937
Smith, W. C. (Surrey; *CY 1911*) b Oct. 4 1877, d July 16, 1946
*Smithson, G. A. (Yorks. & Leics.) b Nov 1, 1926, d Sept. 6, 1970
*Snedden, C. A. (Auck.) b Jan. 7, 1918
*Snedden, M. C. (Auck.) b Nov. 23, 1958
Snellgrove, K. L. (Lancs.) b Nov. 12, 194
*Snooke, S. D. (W. Prov. & Tvl) b Nov. 11 1878, d April 4, 1959
*Snooke, S. J. (Border, W. Prov. & Tvl) Feb. 1, 1881, d Aug. 14, 1966
*Snow, J. A. (Sussex; *CY 1973*) b Oct. 13 1941
Snowden, A. W. (Northants) b Aug. 15 1913, d May 7, 1981
Snowden, W. (CUCC) b Sept. 27, 1952
*Sobers, Sir G. S. (B'dos, S. Aust. & Notts. *CY 1964*) b July 28, 1936
*Sohoni, S. W. (M'tra, Baroda & Bombay) March 5, 1918
Solanky, J. W. (E. Africa & Glam.) b June 30, 1942
*Solkar, E. D. (Bombay & Sussex) b March 18, 1948
*Solomon, J. S. (BG) b Aug. 26, 1930
*Solomon, W. R. T. (Tvl & E. Prov.) b April 23, 1872, d July 12, 1964
*Sood, M. M. (Delhi) b July 6, 1939
Southern, J. W. (Hants) b Sept. 2, 1952
*Southerton, James (Surrey, Hants & Sussex b Nov. 16, 1827, d June 16, 1880
Southerton, S. J. (Editor of *Wisden* 1934-35 b July 7, 1874, d March 12, 1935
*Sparling, J. T. (Auck.) b July 24, 1938
Spencer, C. T. (Leics.) b Aug. 18, 1931
Spencer, J. (CUCC & Sussex) b Oct. 6 1949
Spencer, T. W. (Kent) b March 22, 1914
Sperry, J. (Leics.) b March 19, 1910
*Spofforth, F. R. (NSW & Vic.) b Sept. 9 1853, d June 4, 1926
*Spooner, R. H. (Lancs.; *CY 1905*) b Oct. 21, 1880, d Oct. 2, 1961
*Spooner, R. T. (Warwicks.) b Dec. 30, 1919

Springall, J. D. (Notts.) b Sept. 19, 1932
Srikkanth, K. (TN) b Dec. 21, 1959
Srinivasan, T. E. (TN) b Oct. 26, 1950
Stackpole, K. R. (Vic.; *CY 1973*) b July 10, 1940
Standen, J. A. (Worcs.) b May 30, 1935
Standing, D. K. (Sussex) b Oct. 21, 1963
Stanyforth, Lt-Col. R. T. (Yorks.) b May 30, 1892, d Feb. 20, 1964
Staples, S. J. (Notts.; *CY 1929*) b Sept. 18, 1892, d June 4, 1950
Starkie, S. (Northants) b April 4, 1926
Statham, J. B. (Lancs.; *CY 1955*) b June 17, 1930
Stayers, S. C. (†Guyana & Bombay) b June 9, 1937
Stead, B. (Yorks., Essex, Notts. & N. Tvl) b June 21, 1939, d April 15, 1980
Steel, A. G. (CUCC & Lancs.; Pres. MCC 1902) b Sept. 24, 1858, d June 15, 1914
Steele, D. S. (Northants & Derbys.; *CY 1976*) b Sept. 29, 1941
Steele, J. F. (Leics., Natal & Glam.) b July 23, 1946
Stephens, E. J. (Glos.) b March 23, 1910
Stephenson, F. D. (B'dos, Glos., Tas. & Notts.; *CY 1989*) b April 8, 1959
Stephenson, G. R. (Derbys. & Hants) b Nov. 19, 1942
Stephenson, H. H. (Surrey & All-England) b May 3, 1832, d Dec. 17, 1896
Stephenson, H. W. (Som.) b July 18, 1920
Stephenson, J. P. (Essex) b March 14, 1965
Stephenson, Lt-Col. J. R. (Sec. MCC 1987-) b Feb. 25, 1931
Stephenson, Lt-Col. J. W. A. (Essex & Worcs.) b Aug. 1, 1907, d May 20, 1982
Stevens, Edward ("Lumpy") (Hants) b *circa* 1735, d Sept. 7, 1819
*Stevens, G. B. (S. Aust.) b Feb. 29, 1932
*Stevens, G. T. S. (UCS, OUCC & Middx; *CY 1918*) b Jan. 7, 1901, d Sept. 19, 1970
*Stevenson, G. B. (Yorks. & Northants) b Dec. 16, 1955
Stevenson, K. (Derbys. & Hants) b Oct. 6, 1950
Stevenson, M. H. (CUCC & Derbys.) b June 13, 1927
Stewart, A. J. (Surrey) b April 8, 1963
*Stewart, M. J. (Surrey; *CY 1958*) b Sept. 16, 1932
*Stewart, R. B. (SA) b Sept. 3, 1856, d Sept. 12, 1913
Stewart, R. W. (Glos. & Middx) b Feb. 28, 1945
Stewart, W. J. (Warwicks. & Northants) b Aug. 31, 1934
*Stirling, D. A. (C. Dist.) b Oct. 5, 1961
Stocks, F. W. (Notts.) b Nov. 6, 1917
*Stoddart, A. E. (Middx; *CY 1893*) b March 11, 1863, d April 4, 1915
*Stollmeyer, J. B. (T/T) b April 11, 1921
*Stollmeyer, V. H. (T/T) b Jan. 24, 1916
*Storer, W. (Derbys.; *CY 1899*) b Jan. 25, 1867, d Feb. 28, 1912
Storey, S. J. (Surrey & Sussex) b Jan. 6, 1941
Stott, L. W. (Auck.) b Dec. 8, 1946
Stott, W. B. (Yorks.) b July 18, 1934
Stovold, A. W. (Glos. & OFS) b March 19, 1953
*Street, G. B. (Sussex) b Dec. 6, 1889, d April 24, 1924
*Stricker, L. A. (Tvl) b May 26, 1884, d Feb. 5, 1960
Stringer, P. M. (Yorks. & Leics.) b Feb. 23, 1943
*Strudwick, H. (Surrey; *CY 1912*) b Jan. 28, 1880, d Feb. 14, 1970
Strydom, W. T. (OFS) b March 21, 1942
*Studd, C. T. (CUCC & Middx) b Dec. 2, 1860, d July 16, 1931
*Studd, G. B. (CUCC & Middx) b Oct. 20, 1859, d Feb. 13, 1945
Studd, Sir Peter M. (CUCC) b Sept. 15, 1916
Sturt, M. O. C. (Middx) b Sept. 12, 1940
*Subba Row, R. (CUCC, Surrey & Northants; *CY 1961*) b Jan. 29, 1932
*Subramanya, V. (Mysore) b July 16, 1936
Such, P. M. (Notts. & Leics.) b June 12, 1964
Sudhakar Rao, R. (Karn.) b Aug. 8, 1952
Sueter, T. (Hants & Surrey) b *circa* 1749, d Feb. 17, 1827
*Sugg, F. H. (Yorks., Derbys. & Lancs.; *CY 1890*) b Jan. 11, 1862, d May 29, 1933
Sullivan, J. (Lancs.) b Feb. 5, 1945
Sully, H. (Som. & Northants) b Nov. 1, 1939
*Sunderram, G. R. (Bombay & Raja.) b March 29, 1930
Sunnucks, P. R. (Kent) b June 22, 1916
*Surendranath, R. (Ind. Serv.) b Jan. 4, 1937
Surridge, W. S. (Surrey; *CY 1953*) b Sept. 3, 1917
*Surti, R. F. (Guj., Raja. & Qld) b May 25, 1936
*Susskind, M. J. (CUCC, Middx & Tvl) b June 8, 1891, d July 9, 1957
*Sutcliffe, B. (Auck., Otago & N. Dist.; *CY 1950*) b Nov. 17, 1923
*Sutcliffe, H. (Yorks.; *CY 1920*) b Nov. 24, 1894, d Jan. 22, 1978
Sutcliffe, S. P. (OUCC & Warwicks.) b May 22, 1960
Sutcliffe, W. H. H. (Yorks.) b Oct. 10, 1926
Suttle, K. G. (Sussex) b Aug. 25, 1928
*Swamy, V. N. (Ind. Serv.) b May 23, 1924, d May 1, 1983
Swanton, E. W. (Middx; Writer) b Feb. 11, 1907
Swarbrook, F. W. (Derbys., Griq. W. & OFS) b Dec. 17, 1950

Swart, P. D. (Rhod., W. Prov., Glam. & Boland) b April 27, 1946
*Swetman, R. (Surrey, Notts & Glos.) b Oct. 25, 1933
Sydenham, D. A. D. (Surrey) b April 6, 1934
Symington, S. J. (Leics.) b Sept. 16, 1926

*Taber, H. B. (NSW) b April 29, 1940
*Taberer, H. M. (OUCC & Natal) b Oct. 7, 1870, d June 5, 1932
*Tahir Naqqash (Servis Ind., MCB, Punjab & Lahore) b July 6, 1959
Tait, A. (Northants & Glos.) b Dec. 27, 1953
*Talat Ali (Lahore, PIA & UBL) b May 29, 1950
Talbot, R. O. (Cant. & Otago) b Nov. 26, 1903, d Jan. 5, 1983
*Tallon, D. (Qld; *CY 1949*) b Feb. 17, 1916, d Sept. 7, 1984
*Tamhane, N. S. (Bombay) b Aug. 4, 1931
*Tancred, A. B. (Kimberley, Griq. W. & Tvl) b Aug. 20, 1865, d Nov. 23, 1911
*Tancred, L. J. (Tvl) b Oct. 7, 1876, d July 28, 1934
*Tancred, V. M. (Tvl) b 1875, d June 3, 1904
Tang Choon, R. P. (T/T) b 1914, d Sept. 5, 1985
*Tapscott, G. L. (Griq. W.) b Nov. 7, 1889, d Dec. 13, 1940
*Tapscott, L. E. (Griq. W.) b March 18, 1894, d July 7, 1934
*Tarapore, K. K. (Bombay) b Dec. 17, 1910, d June 15, 1986
Tarbox, C. V. (Worcs.) b July 2, 1891, d June 15, 1978
Tarrant, F. A. (Vic., Middx & Patiala; *CY 1908*) b Dec. 11, 1880, d Jan. 29, 1951
Tarrant, George F. (Cambs. & All-England) b Dec. 7, 1838, d July 2, 1870
*Taslim Arif (Kar., Sind & NBP) b May 1, 1954
*Tate, F. W. (Sussex) b July 24, 1867, d Feb. 24, 1943
*Tate, M. W. (Sussex; *CY 1924*) b May 30, 1895, d May 18, 1956
*Tattersall, R. (Lancs.) b Aug. 17, 1922
*Tauseef Ahmed (PWD, UBL & Kar.) b May 10, 1958
*Tavaré, C. J. (OUCC & Kent) b Oct. 27, 1954
Tayfield, A. (Natal, Tvl & NE Tvl) b June 21, 1931
*Tayfield, H. J. (Natal, Rhod. & Tvl; *CY 1956*) b Jan. 30, 1929
*Taylor, A. I. (Tvl) b July 25, 1925
Taylor, B. (Essex; *CY 1972*) b June 19, 1932
*Taylor, B. R. (Cant. & Wgtn) b July 12, 1943
*Taylor, Daniel (Natal) b Jan. 9, 1887, d Jan. 24, 1957
*Taylor, D. D. (Auck. & Warwicks.) March 2, 1923, d Dec. 5, 1980
Taylor, D. J. S. (Surrey, Som. & Griq. W b Nov. 12, 1942
Taylor, G. R. (Hants) b Nov. 25, 1909, Oct. 31, 1986
*Taylor, H. W. (Natal, Tvl & W. Prov. *CY 1925*) b May 5, 1889, d Feb. 8, 197
*Taylor, J. M. (NSW) b Oct. 10, 1895, May 12, 1971
*Taylor, J. O. (T/T) b Jan. 3, 1932
*Taylor, K. (Yorks. & Auck.) b Aug. 2 1935
Taylor, K. A. (Warwicks.) b Sept. 29, 191
*Taylor, L. B. (Leics. & Natal) b Oct. 2 1953
Taylor, M. L. (Lancs.) b July 16, 1904, March 14, 1978
Taylor, M. N. S. (Notts. & Hants) b Nov 12, 1942
Taylor, N. R. (Kent) b July 21, 1959
*Taylor, P. L. (NSW) b Aug. 22, 1956
Taylor, R. M. (Essex) b Nov. 30, 1909, Jan. 1984
*Taylor, R. W. (Derbys.; *CY 1977*) b Jul 17, 1941
Taylor, T. L. (CUCC & Yorks.; *CY 1901*) May 25, 1878, d March 16, 1960
Taylor, W. (Notts.) b Jan. 24, 1947
Tennekoon, A. P. B. (SL) b Oct. 29, 1946
*Tennyson, 3rd Lord (Hon. L. H.) (Hants *CY 1914*) b Nov. 7, 1889, d June 6, 195
*Terry, V. P. (Hants) b Jan. 14, 1959
*Theunissen, N. H. (W. Prov.) b May 4 1867, d Nov. 9, 1929
Thomas, D. J. (Surrey, N. Tvl & Glos.) June 30, 1959
*Thomas, G. (NSW) b March 21, 1938
*Thomas, J. G. (Glam., Border & E. Prov. b Aug. 12, 1960
Thompson, A. W. (Middx) b April 17, 191
*Thompson, G. J. (Northants; *CY 1906*) Oct. 27, 1877, d March 3, 1943
Thompson, J. R. (CUCC & Warwicks.) May 10, 1918
*Thompson, Nathaniel (NSW) b April 21 1838, d Sept. 2, 1896
Thompson, R. G. (Warwicks.) b Sept. 26 1932
*Thoms, G. R. (Vic.) b March 22, 1927
*Thomson, A. L. (Vic.) b Dec. 2, 1945
*Thomson, J. R. (NSW, Qld & Middx) Aug. 16, 1950
*Thomson, K. (Cant.) b Feb. 26, 1941
*Thomson, N. I. (Sussex) b Jan. 23, 1929
Thorne, D. A. (Warwicks & OUCC) b Dec 12, 1964
Thornton, C. I. (CUCC, Kent & Middx) March 20, 1850, d Dec. 10, 1929
*Thornton, P. G. (Yorks., Middx & SA) Dec. 24, 1867, d Jan. 31, 1939

Thurlow, H. M. (Qld) b Jan. 10, 1903, d Dec. 3, 1975
Tillekeratne, H. P. (SL) b July 14, 1967
Tilly, H. W. (Middx) b May 25, 1932
Timms, B. S. V. (Hants & Warwicks.) b Dec. 17, 1940
Timms, J. E. (Northants) b Nov. 3, 1906, d May 18, 1980
Timms, W. W. (Northants) b Sept. 28, 1902, d Sept. 30, 1986
Tindall, M. (CUCC & Middx) b March 31, 1914
Tindall, R. A. E. (Surrey) b Sept. 23, 1935
Tindill, E. W. T. (Wgtn) b Dec. 18, 1910
Tissera, M. H. (SL) b March 23, 1939
Titmus, F. J. (Middx, Surrey & OFS; *CY 1963*) b Nov. 24, 1932
Todd, L. J. (Kent) b June 19, 1907, d Aug. 20, 1967
Todd, P. A. (Notts. & Glam.) b March 12, 1953
Tolchard, J. G. (Leics.) b March 17, 1944
Tolchard, R. W. (Leics.) b June 15, 1946
Tomlins, K. P. (Middx & Glos.) b Oct. 23, 1957
Tomlinson, D. S. (Rhod. & Border) b Sept. 4, 1910
Tompkin, M. (Leics.) b Feb. 17, 1919, d Sept. 27, 1956
Toogood, G. J. (OUCC) b Nov. 19, 1961
Toohey, P. M. (NSW) b April 20, 1954
Tooley, C. D. M. (OUCC) b April 19, 1964
Topley, T. D. (Surrey, Essex & Griq. W.) b Feb. 25, 1964
Tordoff, G. G. (CUCC & Som.) b Dec. 6, 1929
Toshack, E. R. H. (NSW) b Dec. 15, 1914
Townsend, A. (Warwicks.) b Aug. 26, 1921
Townsend, A. F. (Derbys.) b March 29, 1912
Townsend, C. L. (Glos.; *CY 1899*) b Nov. 7, 1876, d Oct. 17, 1958
Townsend, D. C. H. (OUCC) b April 20, 1912
Townsend, L. F. (Derbys. & Auck.; *CY 1934*) b June 8, 1903
Traicos, A. J. (Rhod. & Zimb.) b May 17, 1947
Travers, J. P. F. (S. Aust.) b Jan. 10, 1871, d Sept. 15, 1942
Tremlett, M. F. (Som. & C. Dist.) b July 5, 1923, d July 30, 1984
Tremlett, T. M. (Hants) b July 26, 1956
Tribe, G. E. (Vic. & Northants; *CY 1955*) b Oct. 4, 1920
Trim, J. (BG) b Jan. 24, 1915, d Nov. 12, 1960
Trimble, G. S. (Qld) b Jan. 1, 1963
Trimble, S. C. (Qld) b Aug. 16, 1934
Trimborn, P. H. J. (Natal) b May 18, 1940
**Trott, A. E. (Vic., Middx & Hawkes Bay; *CY 1899*) b Feb. 6, 1873, d July 30, 1914
*Trott, G. H. S. (Vic.; *CY 1894*) b Aug. 5, 1866, d Nov. 10, 1917
*Troup, G. B. (Auck.) b Oct. 3, 1952
*Trueman, F. S. (Yorks.; *CY 1953*) b Feb. 6, 1931
*Trumble, H. (Vic.; *CY 1897*) b May 12, 1867, d Aug. 14, 1938
*Trumble, J. W. (Vic.) b Sept. 16, 1863, d Aug. 17, 1944
*Trumper, V. T. (NSW; *CY 1903*) b Nov. 2, 1877, d June 28, 1915
*Truscott, P. B. (Wgtn) b Aug. 14, 1941
*Tuckett, L. (OFS) b Feb. 6, 1919
*Tuckett, L. R. (Natal & OFS) b April 19, 1885, d April 8, 1963
*Tufnell, N. C. (CUCC & Surrey) b June 13, 1887, d Aug. 3, 1951
Tuke, Sir Anthony (Pres. MCC 1982-83) b Aug. 22, 1920
Tunnicliffe, C. J. (Derbys.) b Aug. 11, 1951
Tunnicliffe, H. T. (Notts.) b March 4, 1950
Tunnicliffe, J. (Yorks.; *CY 1901*) b Aug. 26, 1866, d July 11, 1948
*Turnbull, M. J. (CUCC & Glam.; *CY 1931*) b March 16, 1906, d Aug. 5, 1944
*Turner, A. (NSW) b July 23, 1950
Turner, C. (Yorks.) b Jan. 11, 1902, d Nov. 19, 1968
*Turner, C. T. B. (NSW; *CY 1889*) b Nov. 16, 1862, d Jan. 1, 1944
Turner, D. R. (Hants & W. Prov.) b Feb. 5, 1949
Turner, F. M. (Leics.) b Aug. 8, 1934
*Turner, G. M. (Otago, N. Dist. & Worcs.; *CY 1971*) b May 26, 1947
Turner, S. (Essex & Natal) b July 18, 1943
*Twentyman-Jones, P. S. (W. Prov.) b Sept. 13, 1876, d March 8, 1954
Twining, R. H. (OUCC & Middx; Pres. MCC 1964-65) b Nov. 3, 1889, d Jan. 3, 1979
*Tyldesley, E. (Lancs.; *CY 1920*) b Feb. 5, 1889, d May 5, 1962
*Tyldesley, J. T. (Lancs.; *CY 1902*) b Nov. 22, 1873, d Nov. 27, 1930
*Tyldesley, R. K. (Lancs.; *CY 1925*) b March 11, 1897, d Sept. 17, 1943
*Tylecote, E. F. S. (OUCC & Kent) b June 23, 1849, d March 15, 1938
*Tyler, E. J. (Som.) b Oct. 13, 1864, d Jan. 21, 1917
*Tyson, F. H. (Northants; *CY 1956*) b June 6, 1930

Ufton, D. G. (Kent) b May 31, 1928
*Ulyett, G. (Yorks.) b Oct. 21, 1851, d June 18, 1898
*Umrigar, P. R. (Bombay & Guj.) b March 28, 1926
*Underwood, D. L. (Kent; *CY 1969*) b June 8, 1945
Unwin, F. St G. (Essex) b April 23, 1911

*Valentine, A. L. (Jam.; *CY 1951*) b April 29, 1930
*Valentine, B. H. (CUCC & Kent) b Jan. 17, 1908, d Feb. 2, 1983
*Valentine, V. A. (Jam.) b April 4, 1908, d July 6, 1972
*Vance, R. H. (Wgtn) b March 31, 1955
*van der Bijl, P. G. (W. Prov. & OUCC) b Oct. 21, 1907, d Feb. 16, 1973
van der Bijl, V. A. P. (Natal, Middx & Tvl; *CY 1981*) b March 19, 1948
Van der Gucht, P. I. (Glos. & Bengal) b Nov. 2, 1911
*Van der Merwe, E. A. (Tvl) b Nov. 9, 1904, d Feb. 28, 1971
*Van der Merwe, P. L. (W. Prov. & E. Prov.) b March 14, 1937
van Geloven, J. (Yorks. & Leics.) b Jan. 4, 1934
*Van Ryneveld, C. B. (W. Prov. & OUCC) b March 19, 1928
van Zyl, C. J. P. G. (OFS & Glam.) b Oct. 1, 1961
Varachia, R. (First Pres. SA Cricket Union) b Oct. 12, 1915, d Dec. 11, 1981
Varey, D. W. (CUCC & Lancs.) b Oct. 15, 1961
*Varnals, G. D. (E. Prov., Tvl & Natal) b July 24, 1935
Vaulkhard, P. (Notts. & Derbys.) b Sept. 15, 1911
*Vengsarkar, D. B. (Bombay; *CY 1987*) b April 6, 1956
*Veivers, T. R. (Qld) b April 6, 1937
*Veletta, M. R. J. (W. Aust.) b Oct. 30, 1963
*Venkataraghavan, S. (†TN & Derbys.) b April 21, 1946
*Verity, H. (Yorks.; *CY 1932*) b May 18, 1905, d July 31, 1943
*Vernon, G. F. (Middx) b June 20, 1856, d Aug. 10, 1902
Vernon, M. T. (W. Aust.) b Feb. 9, 1937
Vigar, F. H. (Essex) b July 7, 1917
*Viljoen, K. G. (Griq. W., OFS & Tvl) b May 14, 1910, d Jan. 21, 1974
*Vincent, C. L. (Tvl) b Feb. 16, 1902, d Aug. 24, 1968
*Vine, J. (Sussex; *CY 1906*) b May 15, 1875, d April 25, 1946
*Vintcent, C. H. (Tvl & Griq. W.) b Sept. 2, 1866, d Sept. 28, 1943
Virgin, R. T. (Som., Northants & W. Prov.; *CY 1971*) b Aug. 26, 1939
*Viswanath, G. R. (†Karn.) b Feb. 12, 1949
*Viswanath, S. (Karn.) b Nov. 29, 1962
*Vivian, G. E. (Auck.) b Feb. 28, 1946
*Vivian, H. G. (Auck.) b Nov. 4, 1912, d Aug. 12, 1983
*Voce, W. (Notts.; *CY 1933*) b Aug. 8, 1909, d June 6, 1984
*Vogler, A. E. E. (Middx, Natal, Tvl & E. Prov.; *CY 1908*) b Nov. 28, 1876, d Aug. 9, 1946
*Vizianagram, Maharaj Kumar Sir Vijaya o (U. Prov.) b Dec. 28, 1905, d Dec. 2, 196
Vonhagt, D. M. (SL) b March 31, 1965

*Waddington, A. (Yorks.) b Feb. 4, 1893, Oct. 28, 1959
Waddington, J. E. (Griq. W.) b Dec. 30 1918, d Nov. 24, 1985
*Wade, H. F. (Natal) b Sept. 14, 1905, Nov. 22, 1980
Wade, T. H. (Essex) b Nov. 24, 1910, d Jul 25, 1987
*Wade, W. W. (Natal) b June 18, 1914
*Wadekar, A. L. (Bombay) b April 1, 1941
*Wadsworth, K. J. (C. Dist. & Cant.) Nov. 30, 1946, d Aug. 19, 1976
*Wainwright, E. (Yorks.; *CY 1894*) b Apri 8, 1865, d Oct. 28, 1919
*Waite, J. H. B. (E. Prov. & Tvl) b Jan. 19 1930
*Waite, M. G. (S. Aust.) b Jan. 7, 1911, Dec. 16, 1985
*Walcott, C. L. (B'dos & BG; *CY 1958*) Jan. 17, 1926
*Walcott, L. A. (B'dos) b Jan. 18, 1894, Feb. 27, 1984
Walden, F. I. (Northants; Umpire) March 1, 1888, d May 3, 1949
Walford, M. M. (OUCC & Som.) b Nov 27, 1915
Walker, A. (Northants) b July 7, 1962
Walker, A. K. (NSW & Notts.) b Oct. 4 1925
Walker, C. (Yorks. & Hants) b June 27 1920
Walker, C. W. (S. Aust.) b Feb. 19, 1909, Dec. 21, 1942
Walker, I. D. (Middx) b Jan. 8, 1844, d July 6, 1898
*Walker, M. H. N. (Vic.) b Sept. 12, 1948
*Walker, P. M. (Glam., Tvl & W. Prov.) Feb. 17, 1936
Walker, W. (Notts.; oldest living County Champ. player) b Nov. 24, 1892
*Wall, T. W. (S. Aust.) b May 13, 1904, d March 25, 1981
*Wallace, W. M. (Auck.) b Dec. 19, 1916
Waller, C. E. (Surrey & Sussex) b Oct. 3, 1948
*Walsh, C. A. (Jam. & Glos.; *CY 1987*) Oct. 30, 1962
Walsh, J. E. (NSW & Leics.) b Dec. 4, 1912, d May 20, 1980
*Walter, K. A. (Tvl) b Nov. 5, 1939
*Walters, C. F. (Glam. & Worcs.; *CY 1934*) b Aug. 28, 1905
*Walters, F. H. (Vic. & NSW) b Feb. 9, 1860, d June 1, 1922
Walters, J. (Derbys.) b Aug. 7, 1949
*Walters, K. D. (NSW) b Dec. 21, 1945
Walton, A. C. (OUCC & Middx) b Sept. 26, 1933

Waqar Hassan (Pak. Us, Punjab, Pak. Serv. & Kar.) b Sept. 12, 1932
Ward, Alan (Derbys., Leics. & Border) b Aug. 10, 1947
*Ward, Albert (Yorks. & Lancs.; *CY 1890*) b Nov. 21, 1865, d Jan. 6, 1939
Ward, B. (Essex) b Feb. 28, 1944
Ward, D. (Glam.) b Aug. 30, 1934
Ward, D. M. (Surrey) b Feb. 10, 1961
*Ward, F. A. (S. Aust.) b Feb. 23, 1909, d March 25, 1974
*Ward, J. T. (Cant.) b March 11, 1937
*Ward, T. A. (Tvl) b Aug. 2, 1887, d Feb. 16, 1936
Ward, William (MCC & Hants) b July 24, 1787, d June 30, 1849
*Wardle, J. H. (Yorks.; *CY 1954*) b Jan. 8, 1923, d July 23, 1985
*Warnapura, B. (SL) b March 1, 1953
*Warnaweera, K. P. J. (SL) b Nov. 23, 1960
Warne, F. B. (Worcs., Vic. & Tvl) b Oct. 3, 1906
Warner, A. E. (Worcs. & Derbys.) b May 12, 1959
*Warner, Sir Pelham (OUCC & Middx; *CY 1904, special portrait 1921*; Pres. MCC 1950-51) b Oct. 2, 1873, d Jan. 30, 1963
*Warr, J. J. (CUCC & Middx; Pres. MCC 1987-88) b July 16, 1927
*Warren, A. R. (Derbys.) b April 2, 1875, d Sept. 3, 1951
*Washbrook, C. (Lancs.; *CY 1947*) b Dec. 6, 1914
*Wasim Akram (Lahore, PACO, PNSC & Lancs.) b June 3, 1966
*Wasim Bari (Kar., PIA & Sind) b March 23, 1948
*Wasim Raja (Lahore, Sargodha, Pak. Us, PIA, Punjab & NBP) b July 3, 1952
Wass, T. G. (Notts.; *CY 1908*) b Dec. 26, 1873, d Oct. 27, 1953
Wassell, A. (Hants) b April 15, 1940
Watkin, S. L. (Glam.) b Sept. 15, 1964
*Watkins, A. J. (Glam.) b April 21, 1922
*Watkins, J. C. (Natal) b April 10, 1923
*Watkins, J. R. (NSW) b April 16, 1943
Watkinson, M. (Lancs.) b Aug. 1, 1961
*Watson, C. (Jam. & Delhi) b July 1, 1938
Watson, F. B. (Lancs.) b Sept. 17, 1898, d Feb. 1, 1976
*Watson, G. D. (Vic., W. Aust. & NSW) b March 8, 1945
Watson, G. G. (NSW, W. Aust. & Worcs.) b Jan. 29, 1955
*Watson, W. (Yorks. & Leics.; *CY 1954*) b March 7, 1920
*Watson, W. (Auck.) b Aug. 31, 1965
*Watson, W. J. (NSW) b Jan. 31, 1931
Watson, W. K. (Border, N. Tvl, E. Prov. & Notts.) b May 21, 1955
*Watt, L. (Otago) b Sept. 17, 1924
Watts, E. A. (Surrey) b Aug. 1, 1911, d May 2, 1982
Watts, H. E. (CUCC & Som.) b March 4, 1922
Watts, P. D. (Northants & Notts.) b March 31, 1938
Watts, P. J. (Northants) b June 16, 1940
*Waugh, S. R. (NSW & Som.; *CY 1989*) b June 2, 1965
*Wazir Ali, S. (C. Ind., S. Punjab & Patiala) b Sept. 15, 1903, d June 17, 1950
*Wazir Mohammad (B'pur & Kar.) b Dec. 22, 1929
Weale, S. D. (OUCC) b Sept. 16, 1967
*Webb, M. G. (Otago & Cant.) b June 22, 1947
*Webb, P. N. (Auck.) b July 14, 1957
Webb, R. J. (Otago) b Sept. 15, 1952
Webb, R. T. (Sussex) b July 11, 1922
Webb, S. G. (Manager Australians in England 1961) b Jan. 31, 1900, d Aug. 5, 1976
*Webbe, A. J. (OUCC & Middx) b Jan. 16, 1855, d Feb. 19, 1941
Webster, J. (CUCC & Northants) b Oct. 28, 1917
Webster, Dr R. V. (Warwicks. & Otago) b June 10, 1939
Webster, W. H. (CUCC & Middx; Pres. MCC 1976-77) b Feb. 22, 1910, d June 19, 1986
*Weekes, E. D. (B'dos; *CY 1951*) b Feb. 26, 1925
*Weekes, K. H. (Jam.) b Jan. 24, 1912
Weeks, R. T. (Warwicks.) b April 30, 1930
*Weerasinghe, C. D. U. S. (SL) b March 1, 1968
*Weir, G. L. (Auck.) b June 2, 1908
*Wellard, A. W. (Som.; *CY 1936*) b April 8, 1902, d Dec. 31, 1980
*Wellham, D. M. (NSW) b March 13, 1959
Wellings, E. M. (OUCC & Surrey) b April 6, 1909
Wells, A. P. (Sussex) b Oct. 2, 1961
Wells, B. D. (Glos. & Notts.) b July 27, 1930
Wells, C. M. (Sussex, Border & W. Prov.) b March 3, 1960
Wenman, E. G. (Kent & England) b Aug. 18, 1803, d Dec. 31, 1879
Wensley, A. F. (Sussex) b May 23, 1898, d June 17, 1970
*Wesley, C. (Natal) b Sept. 5, 1937
*Wessels, K. C. (OFS, W. Prov., N. Tvl, Sussex, Qld & E. Prov.) b Sept. 14, 1957
West, G. H. (Editor of *Wisden* 1880-86) b 1851, d Oct. 6, 1896
*Westcott, R. J. (W. Prov.) b Sept. 19, 1927
Weston, M. J. (Worcs.) b April 8, 1959
*Wettimuny, M. D. (SL) b June 11, 1951
*Wettimuny, S. (SL; *CY 1985*) b Aug. 12, 1956

Wettimuny, S. R. de S. (SL) b Aug. 12, 1956
*Wharton, A. (Lancs. & Leics.) b April 30, 1923
*Whatmore, D. F. (Vic.) b March 16, 1954
Wheatley, K. J. (Hants) b Jan. 20, 1946
Wheatley, O. S. (CUCC, Warwicks. & Glam.; *CY 1969*) b May 28, 1935
Whitaker, Haddon (Editor of *Wisden* 1940-43) b Aug. 30, 1908, d Jan. 5, 1982
*Whitaker, J. J. (Leics.; *CY 1987*) b May 5, 1962
Whitcombe, P. A. (OUCC & Middx) b April 23, 1923
White, A. F. T. (CUCC, Warwicks. & Worcs.) b Sept. 5, 1915
*White, D. W. (Hants & Glam.) b Dec. 14, 1935
White, E. C. S. (NSW) b July 14, 1913
*White, G. C. (Tvl) b Feb. 5, 1882, d Oct. 17, 1918
*White, J. C. (Som.; *CY 1929*) b Feb. 19, 1891, d May 2, 1961
White, Hon. L. R. (5th Lord Annaly) (Middx & Victory Test) b March 15, 1927
White, R. A. (Middx & Notts.) b Oct. 6, 1936
White, R. C. (CUCC, Glos. & Tvl) b Jan. 29, 1941
*White, W. A. (B'dos) b Nov. 20, 1938
Whitehead, J. P. (Yorks. & Worcs.) b Sept. 3, 1925
Whitehouse, J. (Warwicks.) b April 8, 1949
*Whitelaw, P. E. (Auck.) b Feb. 10, 1910, d Aug. 28, 1988
Whitfield, B. J. (Natal) b March 14, 1959
Whitfield, E. W. (Surrey & Northants) b May 31, 1911
Whiting, N. H. (Worcs.) b Oct. 2, 1920
Whitington, R. S. (S. Aust. & Victory Tests; Writer) b June 30, 1912, d March 13, 1984
*Whitney, M. R. (NSW & Glos.) b Feb. 24, 1959
Whittaker, G. J. (Surrey) b May 29, 1916
Whitticase, P. (Leics.) b March 15, 1965
Whittingham, N. B. (Notts.) b Oct. 22, 1940
*Whitty, W. J. (S. Aust.) b Aug. 15, 1886, d Jan. 30, 1974
*Whysall, W. W. (Notts.; *CY 1925*) b Oct. 31, 1887, d Nov. 11, 1930
*Wiener, J. M. (Vic.) b May 1, 1955
*Wight, C. V. (BG) b July 28, 1902, d Oct. 4, 1969
*Wight, G. L. (BG) b May 28, 1929
Wight, P. B. (BG, Som., & Cant.) b June 25, 1930
*Wijesuriya, R. G. C. E. (SL) b Feb. 18, 1960
Wilcox, D. R. (CUCC & Essex) b June 4, 1910, d Feb. 6, 1953

Wild, D. J. (Northants) b Nov. 28, 1962
*Wiles, C. A. (B'dos & T/T) b Aug. 11, 1892 d Nov. 4, 1957
Wilkins, A. H. (Glam., Glos. & N. Tvl) b Aug. 22, 1953
Wilkins, C. P. (Derbys., Border, E. Prov. & Natal) b July 31, 1944
*Wilkinson, L. L. (Lancs.) b Nov. 5, 1916
Wilkinson, P. A. (Notts.) b Aug. 23, 1951
Wilkinson, Col. W. A. C. (OUCC) b Dec 6, 1892, d Sept. 19, 1983
Willatt, G. L. (CUCC, Notts. & Derbys.) b May 7, 1918
*Willett, E. T. (Comb. Is. & Leewards) b May 1, 1953
Willett, M. D. (Surrey) b April 21, 1933
*Willey, P. (Northants, E. Prov. & Leics.) b Dec. 6, 1949
*Williams, A. B. (Jam.) b Nov. 21, 1949
Williams, C. B. (B'dos) b March 8, 1926
Williams, Lord C. C. P. (OUCC & Essex) b Feb. 9, 1933
Williams, D. (T/T) b Nov. 4, 1963
Williams, D. L. (Glam.) b Nov. 20, 1946
*Williams, E. A. V. (B'dos) b April 10, 1914
Williams, N. F. (Middx, Windwards & Tas.) b July 2, 1962
Williams, R. G. (Northants) b Aug. 10, 1957
*Williams, R. J. (Natal) b April 12, 1912, d May 14, 1984
Williamson, J. G. (Northants) b April 4, 1936
*Willis, R. G. D. (Surrey, Warwicks. & N. Tvl; *CY 1978*) b May 30, 1949
*Willoughby, J. T. (SA) b Nov. 7, 1874, d *circa* 1955
Willsher, E. (Kent & All-England) b Nov. 22, 1828, d Oct. 7, 1885
Wilmot, K. (Warwicks.) b April 3, 1911
Wilson, A. (Lancs.) b April 24, 1921
Wilson, A. E. (Middx & Glos.) b May 18, 1910
*Wilson, Rev. C. E. M. (CUCC & Yorks.) b May 15, 1875, d Feb. 8, 1944
*Wilson, D. (Yorks. & MCC) b Aug. 7, 1937
Wilson, E. F. (Surrey) b June 24, 1907, d March 3, 1981
*Wilson, E. R. (CUCC & Yorks.) b March 25, 1879 d July 21, 1957
Wilson, J. V. (Yorks.; *CY 1961*) b Jan. 17, 1921
*Wilson, J. W. (Vic. & S. Aust.) b Aug. 20, 1921, d Oct. 13, 1985
Wilson, P. H. L. (Surrey, Som. & N. Tvl) b Aug. 17, 1958
Wilson, R. C. (Kent) b Feb. 18, 1928
*Wimble, C. S. (Tvl) b Jan. 9, 1864, d Jan. 28, 1930
Windows, A. R. (Glos. & CUCC) b Sept. 25, 1942
Winfield, H. M. (Notts.) b June 13, 1933

Wingfield Digby, Rev. A. R. (OUCC) b July 25, 1950
Winn, C. E. (OUCC & Sussex) b Nov. 13, 1926
Winslow, P. L. (Sussex, Tvl & Rhod.) b May 21, 1929
Wisden, John (Sussex; founder John Wisden and Co. and *Wisden's Cricketers' Almanack*) b Sept. 5, 1826, d April 5, 1884
Wishart, K. L. (BG) b Nov. 28, 1908, d Oct. 18, 1972
Wolton, A. V. G. (Warwicks.) b June 12, 1919
Wood, A. (Yorks.; *CY 1939*) b Aug. 25, 1898, d April 1, 1973
Wood, B. (Yorks., Lancs., Derbys. & E. Prov.) b Dec. 26, 1942
Wood, C. J. B. (Leics.) b Nov. 21, 1875, d June 5, 1960
Wood, D. J. (Sussex) b May 19, 1914
Wood, G. E. C. (CUCC & Kent) b Aug. 22, 1893, d March 18, 1971
Wood, G. M. (W. Aust.) b Nov. 6, 1956
Wood, H. (Kent & Surrey; *CY 1891*) b Dec. 14, 1854, d April 30, 1919
Wood, R. (Lancs. & Vic.) b March 7, 1860, d Jan. 6, 1915
Woodcock, A. J. (S. Aust.) b Feb. 27, 1948
Woodcock, John C. (Editor of *Wisden* 1980-86) b Aug. 7, 1926
Woodfull, W. M. (Vic.; *CY 1927*) b Aug. 22, 1897, d Aug. 11, 1965
Woodhead, F. G. (Notts.) b Oct. 30, 1912
Woodhouse, G. E. S. (Som.) b Feb. 15, 1924, d Jan. 19, 1988
*Woods, S. M. J. (CUCC & Som.; *CY 1889*) b April 14, 1867, d April 30, 1931
Wookey, S. M. (CUCC & OUCC) b Sept. 2, 1954
Wooler, C. R. D. (Leics. & Rhod.) b June 30, 1930
Wooller, W. (CUCC & Glam.) b Nov. 20, 1912
Woolley, C. N. (Glos. & Northants) b May 5, 1886, d Nov. 3, 1962
*Woolley, F. E. (Kent; *CY 1911*) b May 27, 1887, d Oct. 18, 1978
*Woolley, R. D. (Tas.) b Sept. 16, 1954
*Woolmer, R. A. (Kent, Natal & W. Prov.; *CY 1976*) b May 14, 1948
*Worrall, J. (Vic.) b May 12, 1863, d Nov. 17, 1937
*Worrell, Sir F. M. M. (B'dos & Jam.; *CY 1951*) b Aug. 1, 1924, d March 13, 1967
Worsley, D. R. (OUCC & Lancs.) b July 18, 1941
Worsley, Sir W. A. 4th Bt (Yorks.; Pres. MCC 1961-62) b April 5, 1890, d Dec. 4, 1973
*Worthington, T. S. (Derbys.; *CY 1937*) b Aug. 21, 1905, d Aug. 31, 1973
Wright, A. (Warwicks.) b Aug. 25, 1941
Wright, A. J. (Glos.) b July 27, 1962
*Wright, C. W. (CUCC & Notts.) b May 27, 1863, d Jan. 10, 1936
*Wright, D. V. P. (Kent; *CY 1940*) b Aug. 21, 1914
*Wright, J. G. (N. Dist., Derbys. & Cant.) b July 5, 1954
*Wright, K. J. (W. Aust. & S. Aust.) b Dec. 27, 1953
Wright, L. G. (Derbys.; *CY 1906*) b June 15, 1862, d Jan. 11, 1953
Wyatt, J. G. (Som.) b June 19, 1963
*Wyatt, R. E. S. (Warwicks. & Worcs.; *CY 1930*) b May 2, 1901
*Wynne, O. E. (Tvl & W. Prov.) b June 1, 1919, d July 13, 1975
*Wynyard, E. G. (Hants) b April 1, 1861, d Oct. 30, 1936

Yachad, M. (N. Tvl & Tvl) b Nov. 17, 1960
*Yadav, N. S. (H'bad) b Jan. 26, 1957
*Yajurvindra Singh (M'tra & S'tra) b Aug. 1, 1952
*Yallop, G. N. (Vic.) b Oct. 7, 1952
*Yardley, B. (W. Aust.) b Sept. 5, 1947
*Yardley, N. W. D. (CUCC & Yorks.; *CY 1948*) b March 19, 1915
Yardley, T. J. (Worcs. & Northants) b Oct. 27, 1946
Yarnold, H. (Worcs.) b July 6, 1917, d Aug. 13, 1974
*Yashpal Sharma (Punjab) b Aug. 11, 1954
Yawar Saeed (Som. & Punjab) b Jan. 22, 1935
*Yograj Singh (Haryana & Punjab) b March 25, 1958
Young, D. M. (Worcs. & Glos.) b April 15, 1924
*Young, H. I. (Essex) b Feb. 5, 1876, d Dec. 12, 1964
*Young, J. A. (Middx) b Oct. 14, 1912
*Young, R. A. (CUCC & Sussex) b Sept. 16, 1885, d July 1, 1968
*Younis Ahmed (Lahore, Kar., Surrey, PIA, S. Aust., Worcs. & Glam.) b Oct. 20, 1947
*Yuile, B. W. (C. Dist.) b Oct. 29, 1941

*Zaheer Abbas (Kar., Glos., PWD, Dawood Indust., Sind & PIA; *CY 1972*) b July 24, 1947
Zahid Ahmed (PIA) b Nov. 15, 1961
*Zakir Khan (Sind, Peshawar & ADBP) b April 3, 1963
Zesers, A. K. (S. Aust.) b March 11, 1967
*Zoehrer, T. J. (W. Aust.) b Sept. 25, 1961
*Zulch, J. W. (Tvl) b Jan. 2, 1886, d May 19, 1924
*Zulfiqar Ahmed (B'pur & PIA) b Nov. 22, 1926
*Zulqarnain (Pak. Rlwys & Lahore) b May 25, 1962

OBITUARIES

ADAMS, AIR COMMODORE CYRIL DOUGLAS, OBE, who died in 1988 aged 90, played five times for the RAF in inter-services matches between 192 and 1932. A right-hand middle-order bat and right-arm fast-medium bowler, h scored 173 runs with an average of 19.22 and a highest innings of 46 not ou against the Army, and took eleven wickets at 33.90. He played some count cricket for his native Dorset.

ALDERSON, RALPH, who died on April 4, 1988, aged 67, was a competen right-handed batsman and good enough to be chosen twice for Lancashire in 194 and 1949. On his second appearance he was deputising for Cyril Washbrook, wh was on Test match duty, and made 55 against Kent at Old Trafford. In the sam season he made 800 runs at an average of 30 for Lancashire Second XI, thu making a major contribution to their ultimate success in the Minor Countie Championship. After his retirement Alderson umpired at second-class level fron 1964 to 1968 and remained a member of the coaching staff at Old Trafford fo several years.

ANGUS, THOMAS, died suddenly, aged 53, at Englefield Green, Surrey, o May 14, 1988, during a match, having retired ill after opening the batting for hi club side. A right-arm medium-fast bowler, when he joined the groundstaff a Lord's he was one of a crop of young players to whom Middlesex were looking fo success in the mid-fifties. Angus played in seven matches for the county, but dic not make the grade in spite of good-looking figures; his 23 wickets cost him 15.3 runs apiece. A projected trial for Somerset never took place, and he later playe for Durham County and as a much respected professional in league cricket in th north-east.

ARROWSMITH, ROBERT LANGFORD (BOB), who died on October 22 1988, at the age of 82, made a significant contribution to *Wisden Cricketers Almanack* as its principal obituary writer from the 1976 edition until the 198 edition. For at least ten years before that he was a regular contributor, and h wrote also for various journals and books. His knowledge of cricket wa encyclopaedic and catholic; he was not simply a writer who could use hi references. Rather, he understood how cricket was played, how it should b played, and those who played it. In some instances he had played alongside thos of whom he was writing, not in first-class cricket but for one of a number of clubs among them MCC, I Zingari, Free Foresters, Band of Brothers, Butterflies, Cryptics and Grasshoppers. A tall, left-handed bat, he was in the Charterhouse X in 1925 and played for his college, Oriel, in his four years at Oxford. He had a great love of Kent cricket and wrote a history of the county club as well a histories of I Zingari (with B. J. W. Hill) and the Butterflies. His writing wa marked by his language, his wit and a sense of fun; no-one reading him, o meeting him, could describe him as dull. He was, moreover, concerned about the accuracy of what he wrote, not because he was a pedant about accuracy bu because he desired it as a virtue. He taught Classics at Lancing from 1929 to 193 and then until 1965 at Charterhouse, where he was a housemaster from 1950.

BAILEY, JAMES (JIM), died in Southampton on February 9, 1988, aged 79. He played his first match for Hampshire in 1927 and his last in 1952, but in those twenty seasons there were only eight in which he played any considerable part. It is perhaps easiest to consider him separately as a bat and as a bowler. As a bowler, he had a highly eccentric career. His batting presents no special problems. It was not until 1931 that he achieved much and then, given a place in the hope of strengthening the batting, he made 922 runs with an average of 19.61. He normally went in first with Arnold, and five times they put up more than 100 together. Arnold was a brilliant right-hander and it might seem that Bailey, an essentially defensive left-hander, was an ideal partner. But, with Mead to follow, the tax on the patience of spectators must have been intolerable. Mead, however slowly he scored, was a great player, a genius, but there was no trace of greatness about Bailey, though one might admire his determination. His one century that season, against Nottinghamshire at Bournemouth, took five hours. In 1932, when he blossomed out as a bowler, his batting average fell to 16.88, but in 1933, when his bowling was a failure, it rose again to 23.66. His highest score then was 106 in three hours against Leicestershire.

At this point he left Hampshire and joined the Lord's staff to qualify for Middlesex. Two years at Lord's showed that he had little prospect there and in 1936 and 1937 he played for Accrington in the Lancashire League. But in 1938, when Mead had retired, Hampshire recalled Bailey to lend solidity to their batting and, playing in a few matches, he was useful without doing anything sensational. In 1939, with 1,329 runs and an average of 32.41, he at least fulfilled expectations as a batsman, and in the first four seasons after the war, in an inexperienced side, his soundness was invaluable. In three of these seasons he made more than 1,000 runs and in 1948 took over a hundred wickets as well, being the first Hampshire player to do the double since 1930; none has done it since.

His slow left-arm bowling first attracted attention in May 1932, when he took seven for 7 against Nottinghamshire at Trent Bridge, and for a few weeks it was so deadly that he was top of the first-class averages. On the hard wickets in June and July he fell away so much that he lost his place in the side, but in August he took seven for 83 against Yorkshire at Bournemouth and finished the season with 76 wickets at 21.93. After this, his complete failure as a bowler in 1933 seems inexplicable. By his next full season in 1939, the county already had two slow left-handers in Boyes and Creese but desperately needed an opener, and Bailey was often employed in this role; after all, Blythe for years regularly opened for Kent. However, not unnaturally, Bailey proved expensive, his 44 wickets costing 31.68 runs each. In 1946 he was hampered by a bad leg and could bowl very little; in 1947 he did his full share, but was still expensive. In 1948 he met with astonishing success and was by some considered the best bowler of his type in England. He took 121 wickets at 18.13 apiece, besides making 1,399 runs, and against Leicestershire at Southampton he made 62 and 77 and took eleven for 70. In 1949, though he took 86 wickets, they cost 30.95 runs each. The mystery of his one great bowling season remains unexplained.

Bailey retired at the end of 1949, but reappeared for one match in 1952 without success. In all first-class cricket he scored 9,500 runs with an average of 24.93: he made five hundreds. His 473 wickets cost 27.24 each. In later years he was a very active member of the county committee.

BARTLETT, HUGH TRYON, collapsed and died on June 26, 1988, aged 73, while watching his old county, Sussex, playing in a Refuge Assurance League match, a form of the game in which he would surely have excelled had he been born several generations later. He was arguably the hardest-hitting left-hander to play first-class cricket with appreciable success. His record as a schoolboy was phenomenal. He was in the XI at Dulwich College for a full five years, during which he amassed 2,783 runs at an overall average of 50.60, and he finished his third year as captain in 1933 by making double-centuries against Mill Hill and Bedford. Such feats naturally brought him recognition in a wider field. In 1932 he made 45 and 22 for the Public Schools against the Army on the losing side and in the following year played the decisive innings of 87 in the same match, which after an unpromising start the boys won by 45 runs.

At Cambridge, even though he scored nearly 2,000 runs for the University, averaging just short of 36, he was never quite the dominating figure his admirers hoped he would be. He had always put attack before defence, and at first-class level flaws in his technique were exposed. In his three matches against Oxford, scores of 12 in a total of 400 in 1934, 0 and 24 the following year, and finally 0 as captain in 1936, when he was able to declare at 432 for nine, were a bitter disappointment. These personal failures with the bat, almost certainly to be accounted for by his nervousness and uncertainty as a starter, were to some extent offset by his leadership at Lord's against Oxford, which was rewarded by an eight-wicket victory.

Bartlett had made a few appearances for Surrey before throwing in his lot with Sussex in 1937. Throughout the winter of 1937-38 he worked hard at improving his defence and in cutting out loose shots, and in 1938 he emerged as a much sounder player without any diminution of his attacking powers. In a season of many memorable innings, in which he hit forty sixes, his undefeated 175 at Lord's for the Gentlemen and 157 for Sussex against the Australians at Hove were outstanding. At Lord's his remarkable display, which included four sixes and 24 fours, dwarfed everything else in the match and gained victory for his side by 133 runs. His onslaught on the Australians earned him the Lawrence Trophy for the fastest hundred of the season in 57 minutes. He had made only 4 runs in his first fourteen minutes at the crease before accelerating to his 100. Selection for the MCC tour of South Africa in 1938-39 was richly deserved, but with England so strong in batting Bartlett did not play in any of the five Test matches. He must have chafed at the bit as he watched the funereal proceedings throughout much of that series. In the last pre-war season his Championship average of 33 was some 18 points lower than in the previous year, but 60 for the Gentlemen in their second innings at Lord's was enough to remind the selectors of his ability. He was chosen for the MCC tour of India in the winter of 1939-40, which was cancelled owing to the outbreak of war.

After the war, during which he was awarded the DFC, he played four full seasons for Sussex, succeeding S. C. Griffith as captain in 1947. He largely failed to recapture his best pre-war form, though he did have a Championship aggregate of 1,430 runs in 1947, a year rich in plenty for batsmen, and his powers of leadership were fully tested by the weakness of Sussex during this period, especially in bowling. He remained popular with the players, but was unable to produce anything above mediocre results. It was not the happiest period of his career and he resigned the captaincy at the end of the 1949 season, never to play for the county again. Happy relations were restored when he was elected president in 1976.

Bartlett's early development was greatly influenced by Frank Woolley, who appropriately enough, as captain of the Players, was an admiring spectator of his great innings at Lord's; and at school C. S. Marriott gave him much help and advice. Their combined influences produced a player good enough to stand comparison with A. P. F. Chapman as a forcing left-hander in the inter-war years; but whether Bartlett's temperament would have proved a handicap at the highest level is a question he was never given an opportunity to answer. In a first-class career of 217 matches, he made 10,098 runs, including 7,074 for Sussex, at an average of 31.95 with sixteen hundreds. By far his best season was 1938 when he finished fifth in the general averages with 57.33 in 31 innings and an aggregate of 1,548 runs.

BEAN, LESLIE HUGH, who died on January 13, 1988, aged 81, played in three first-class matches for Somerset in 1929 as an amateur. He was something of an all-rounder but did not achieve anything of note. He enjoyed greater success with Dorset.

BILL, OSCAR WENDELL, died at Sydney in May 1988, aged 78. A right-hand batsman, in 1929-30 at the age of nineteen he scored 115 for New South Wales against Tasmania at Sydney on his first-class début. This was the first of six hundreds in a career which embraced 23 appearances for New South Wales to 1934-35 and concluded in 1935-36 with the Maharajah of Patiala's private Australian team in India and Ceylon, when he scored 740 runs. In 1930-31 he hit 153 against Queensland at the Exhibition Ground in Brisbane, his highest score, and at Sydney helped Bradman add 234 in 135 minutes for the fifth wicket against Victoria. His score was exactly 100; Bradman's 220 was his third double-hundred of the season. He had, when MCC played New South Wales at Sydney in 1929-30, appeared as substitute first for the touring team and then for the state side, spending almost four days in the field. In 35 first-class matches, he scored 1,931 runs with an average of 37.86.

BISHOP, LEONARD GEORGE, who died in June 1988, aged 80, was an exceptional batsman in south-east London club cricket in the years before the Second World War. He scored as many as 116 centuries, figures good enough to suggest that he might have been successful in the first-class game. He would have enjoyed dining out on the story that he joined the groundstaff at Lord's in 1934 on the same day as Denis Compton, with whose emerging genius, not to mention the expertise of the young Bill Edrich and Jack Robertson, he felt unable to compete. He gave up the unequal struggle after two years.

BOON, MALCOLM KITTSON (MICK), died in Christchurch on July 12, 1988, at the age of 85. A wicket-keeper of considerable skill and a useful right-handed batsman, he appeared eleven times for Canterbury and once for New Zealand, against New South Wales at Lancaster Park in 1923-24. He was bowled by Macartney for 0 and Mailey for 1; his single victim, Hendry, already had 110 in the book when he was caught. When he withdrew from the side for the second match, the young Wellington wicket-keeper, K. C. James, made the first of 61 representative appearances for New Zealand. In 1962, Boon represented New Zealand at bowls at the Commonwealth Games in Perth.

BRAND, JAMES SAMSON, died on January 8, 1988, at the age of 74. He played for Scotland against Ireland in Dublin in his one first-class match in 1939. He had some success behind the stumps, but with just 12 runs in his two innings he made little contribution with the bat to his side's victory by 162 runs. In Scotland's second innings, when they were pressing for runs, he was one of J. C. Boucher's seven victims.

BROWN, SYDNEY MAURICE, who died on December 28, 1987, aged 70, was an attacking opening batsman of considerable flair. He was born within the boundaries of Kent, but crossed the river to play for Middlesex, where his successful start in the Second XI in 1937 was noted with enthusiasm; the county had not had a settled opening pair for some years. In 1938 he made his maiden century, 114 against Lancashire at Old Trafford, finished not far short of 1,000 runs for the season, and was capped. Disappointing form in 1939 was followed by the six-year interruption of his developing career. However, he made his mark in 1946 with two centuries and more than 1,300 runs in the Championship, foreshadowing his greatest year, 1947, when he and Jack Robertson, in pursuance of Walter Robins's aggressive tactics, blazed the trail for Compton and Edrich to follow. This famous quartet made more than 8,000 runs between them in the Championship, which Middlesex won decisively, having been runners-up for the five previous seasons. These were heady days at Lord's and large crowds were in regular attendance. Brown, with 2,078 runs in all matches, was by no means overshadowed in the continual quest for rapid runs as the platform for success. H shared nine partnerships with Robertson of more than 100, four of which call fo special mention. Their 310 together in three and a half hours against Nottin hamshire beat a long-established Middlesex record for the first wicket, and the followed it immediately with 222 against Yorkshire at Lord's. Later the Esse bowlers were scattered to the winds to the tune of 169 in a mere 78 minutes, an their 147 against Northamptonshire helped to clinch the Championship with victory by the margin of 355 runs.

This sort of thing could hardly be repeated, but the rest of Brown's career wa studded with exceptional performances which redeemed periods of comparativ failure. The majority of his hundreds were large ones and had a decisive influenc on the run of play. His undefeated 150 against Glamorgan at Cardiff in 1948 was masterly achievement and technically correct, bringing victory by two wicke after five and a quarter hours at the crease. The following season he chos Canterbury as the venue for his first double-century; his 200 was "a thorough good display" spread over five hours and ten minutes and contained 21 fours. I 1951 he enjoyed his second-best season, scoring nearly 1,700 runs with 232 not ou against Somerset at Lord's the centrepiece. Brown's successes and Robertson heavy scoring meant that the Middlesex batting was firing on all four cylinder again. But by 1955 the end was near. He was 37, and although he reached hi thousand runs for the ninth time, his season's average was down to 22.57. Perhap he was right to retire there and then.

Thus ended a period of gallantry and enterprise for Middlesex in which Brow played a full part, often employing a wide range of strokes when at the crease. H preferred to score off the back foot and could hit with considerable power, a when he nearly deposited the unfortunate Buse of Somerset over the Grand Stan at Lord's in the course of his highest innings. His fielding in the deep was out standing, and he contributed greatly to the entertainment at headquarters, wher he remained a popular figure. He enjoyed a sunlit and lucrative benefit matc against Sussex in 1953 to which he contributed two fine innings. He made 15,75 runs in his first-class career at an average of 29.17 with 22 hundreds; he hel 152 catches and also made two stumpings.

BURTT, THOMAS BROWNING (TOM), who died at Christchurch on Ma 24, 1988, aged 73, made only one New Zealand tour overseas but it was a triump for him. In England in 1949, in a hot and dry summer when the pitches generall favoured the batsmen, his accurate slow left-arm bowling brought him 128 wicket at an average of 22.88 from 1,231 overs. The next-best harvest was 62 b Cresswell, whose 692 overs were also the most by any other tourist. Twice Burt took eleven wickets in a match, and he took five or more wickets in an inning eleven times, including seven for 102 (eleven for 182 in the match) at Worcester ir the second fixture of the tour. In the four drawn Tests he was the leading wicket taker with seventeen at 33.41, including his best-ever Test return of six for 15 from 45 overs in sweltering heat at Manchester.

New Zealand's bowling in this series was not their strongest suit, but they played their hand cannily, bowling accurately and giving nothing away in the field. Burtt, stockily built and bustling in his style, served this stratagem admirably, conceding less than 3 runs an over, bowling a tight off-stump line to a packed off-side field. While specialising in a perfect length, he varied his fligh skilfully to make batsmen think carefully before advancing down the wicket tc him. Unusually, he imparted spin by flicking the ball with his second finger rathe than his forefinger and he was also known to offer some wrist-spin – but "only when I'm pushed".

In his ten Test matches between 1946-47, against Hammond's Englishmen, and the South Africans of 1952-53 he took 33 wickets at 35.45; in 84 first-class matches rom 1943-44 he took 408 wickets at 22.19, a New Zealand record until Richard Hadlee passed it. His best figures were eight for 35 for Canterbury against Otago t Dunedin in 1953-54. He also scored 1,644 runs, with 68 not out at Derby in 1949 his best, while in Tests he obtained 252 runs at 21.00, usually low in the order. However, after reaching his highest score, 42, against England at Christchurch in 950-51, he opened New Zealand's second innings in an emergency at Wellington nd scored 31. He batted as he bowled, left-handed, and generally in a manner ery much in keeping with his vast good humour. He certainly enjoyed taking 4 runs off Johnny Wardle in the last over he faced in first-class cricket, for Canterbury against MCC in 1954-55. In 1937 and 1938 he had represented New Zealand at hockey.

CAESAR, WILLIAM CECIL, who died on April 5, 1988, at the age of 88, made four appearances in first-class cricket as an amateur, the first being for Surrey in 1922, when he was a distinctly quick right-arm bowler. His next three were not until 1946 and all for Somerset. This gap of 24 years between appearances has only once been exceeded. Caesar's best performance with the ball was four for 59 against Leicestershire at Melton Mowbray in his first match for Somerset, and in all he took ten wickets at 25.20 apiece. As a tailender he was unable to make more than a negligible contribution. Caesar was a very fine soccer player, an amateur international, who at one time or another turned out for Darlington, Fulham, Walsall and Brentford.

CARLESS, ERNEST FRANCIS, who died on September 26, 1987, aged 75, played three matches for Glamorgan between 1934 and 1946. He was a useful right-handed batsman, wicket-keeper and an occasional purveyor of off-spin. His highest score of 25 was made in his début against Surrey at Cardiff, but thereafter he had few chances to make his mark. He played for Devon, but became well known in South Wales as a long-serving professional for Barry. A fine soccer player, he appeared for Plymouth Argyle and Cardiff City, for whom he played against Moscow Dynamo on their celebrated tour in the autumn of 1945.

CASTLEDINE, STAFFORD WILLIAM THOMAS, died in Nottingham in June 1988, aged 76. He was a useful right-hand bat and slow left-arm bowler, who played as a professional for Nottinghamshire in five matches in 1933 and 1934. He met with little success in either department.

COOMARASWAMY, SATYENDRA, who died on January 15, 1988, at the age of 68, was the oldest surviving captain of Ceylon. He was an honorary member of MCC. A middle-order batsman and leg-spinner, first for Royal College and later for Tamil Union, he made his début for Ceylon against the 1948 Australians, dismissing Harvey and Hamence with consecutive balls and finishing with four wickets. In 1948-49, against Goddard's West Indians, he scored 6 and 35 in Ceylon's first match and 57 and 41 not out in the second, but his single wicket in the West Indians' two innings cost 164 runs. When Coomaraswamy led his country against the Commonwealth XI, led by Bill Alley, in 1949-50, he had the rare distinction of captaining his country before his club, although later in 1950 he was to lead Tamil Union to the club championship. He had been Ceylon's champion at 100 yards.

COPE, SIDNEY ALFRED, who died at Gravesend on April 14, 1986, at the age of 81, made a single appearance for Kent in 1924. He belonged to that rare breed of fast left-arm bowlers, but failed to make an impression with one wicket for 27 runs in seven overs. He was later given a trial by Warwickshire, whose authorities unfortunately pronounced him to be temperamentally unsuited to a cricket career.

CORNELIUS, BERNARD WILLIAM, who died on October 7, 1987, aged 6 made one Championship appearance for Northamptonshire in 1947, being chose as a batsman against Leicestershire at Leicester. Northamptonshire won a notab victory by six wickets, their first over Leicestershire for twenty years and one only two secured during a typically lean season. Cornelius, who was associate with the Northampton Vallence club, saw Dennis Brookes make a fine 210 an was at the wicket when the winning run was made, being 9 not out.

CRAWFORD, CYRIL GORE, who died in Christchurch on June 17, 198 aged 86, played twelve times for Canterbury between 1923-24 and 1931-32, h best innings for the province being 61 against New South Wales in 1923-24 and 7 against Victoria in 1924-25. A stylish right-hand batsman, noted for his footwor he went to Australia in 1925-26 with W. R. Patrick's New Zealand side, his be score being 121 in the tourists' 681 in a two-day match against Northern Distric at Maitland, New South Wales. His two first-class appearances, however, pr duced only 31 runs after an inauspicious beginning against Victoria, hit wicke bowled Hendry for 0. In the Victorian innings, Hendry hit an unbeaten 325 in 32 minutes, at the time the highest score against a New Zealand representative sid Crawford later played a major part in cricket administration and was a li member of the Canterbury Cricket Association. He was also a representativ rugby referee.

DARASHAH, SAFI, died at Bangalore on April 2, 1988, at the age of 85. vibrant, always meticulously dressed man who radiated cheer on and off the fiel he had considerable influence in moulding cricketers in Mysore state. H captained Mysore (now Karnataka) in ten matches and took them to the final c the Ranji Trophy in 1941-42. In 1939-40, he played for the Parsees in the Bomba Pentangular Tournament. A middle-order batsman and bowler of medium-pac off-cutters, to deliver which he literally danced the few steps to the crease, h scored 1,353 runs and took 59 wickets, average 22.93, in the Ranji Trophy.

ELLIS, STANLEY, who died on February 14, 1987, at Blackburn, was a lef handed batsman and an off-spinner. He was given five games in the Champior ship in 1923 by Lancashire, one of the most formidable teams of those days, and a the end of the season headed their bowling averages with eleven wickets from 36. overs at an average of 8.09. Against Gloucestershire at Old Trafford he had matc figures of six for 38. In the following season, in a further three matches, he wa much less successful and failed to establish himself. However, between 1929 an 1937 he made a considerable reputation for himself in the north-east, taking 29 wickets for Durham County in 68 matches. At the time of his death, at the age c 90, Ellis, whose father and brother, Walker, had both played for the county, wa the oldest surviving Lancashire player.

ETHERIDGE, ROBERT JAMES (BOBBY), died suddenly at Gloucester o April 4, 1988, aged 54. An excellent natural wicket-keeper and an aggressiv middle-order batsman, he made 39 appearances for Gloucestershire between 195 and 1966, failing to gain a regular place in the county side only because of th consistency of Barrie Meyer. Etheridge was also a professional footballer c distinction who played more than 300 times for Bristol City, and had he no accepted a football engagement at the beginning of the 1957 season, he might we have made the No. 1 wicket-keeping spot his own. He was to regret this decisio and always hankered after regular first-class cricket. However, he found som consolation in many feats of heavy scoring for Gloucester City at club level. Goo enough to be chosen occasionally as a batsman, he made 796 first-class runs at a average of 15.92 with 48 against Essex at Bristol in 1964 as his highest score. H also made 33 catches and eight stumpings.

FAIRBAIRN, SIR ROBERT DUNCAN, who died on March 26, 1988, aged 77, was a good enough batsman to represent Scotland against Yorkshire in 1938. He also appeared for the Europeans against the Parsees in the Bombay Pentangular tournament of 1944-45. He was a notable footballer, playing as an amateur for St Johnstone, Partick Thistle, Queen's Park and the Corinthian-Casuals. Chairman of the Clydesdale Bank from 1975 to 1985, he was knighted in 1985.

FERNANDO, DR C. D. L., who died in Kandy in September 1987, was a great benefactor of sports in Sri Lanka. A good opening fast bowler, he represented Colombo University and the Kandy District Cricket Association, playing with some success for the latter against visiting teams. He was part-time manager of the Sri Lankan Test team in 1983-84 when the New Zealanders were on the island.

FLEMING, IAN DOUGLAS KEITH, died on July 4, 1988, aged 79. A forcing right-hand bat, he formed a fine opening partnership with P. G. T. Kingsley in the Winchester XIs of 1926 and 1927. In 1926 they opened the batting for the Public Schools XV against Woodfull's Australians. Fleming scored 11. His greatest triumphs were in 1927, when Winchester were unbeaten and he hit 109 against Charterhouse, 210 in 200 minutes against Eton and a more circumspect 110 in 3 hours 40 minutes for the Schools against the Army at Lord's, before going on to score more than 1,000 runs in good club cricket after term. A player who watched the ball come on to the bat, he drove and hooked powerfully and there were 22 fours and a six in his double-hundred, the highest score in this match since J. L. Guise's 278 for Winchester in 1921. Instead of going up to university he began his career and was not seen in first-class cricket until 1934 when, taking some holiday, he appeared three times for Kent. The first of these games was against Essex at Brentwood at the end of May. He did not get in until Kent were 707 for four, Ashdown having scored his record 332 and Woolley 172, but Ames was still there, and while scoring an unbeaten 42 himself Fleming saw him reach his double-hundred. At this point, Chapman declared at 803 for four, the county's record score. He met with little success in his next two games but later that season scored 66 for Leveson Gower's XI against Oxford at Reigate. He played in the same match the following season, and while this was the sum of his first-class cricket, he continued to score a lot of runs in club cricket, making a valuable contribution to the Band of Brothers. In his five first-class matches he scored 183 runs with an average of 30.50.

FORDHAM, CYRIL BERNARD, who died on April 22, 1988, aged 81, played in five first-class matches for representative Minor Counties XIs in the years from 1931 to 1937. In 1933 he distinguished himself with a century in each innings against Oxford University, his scores being 140 and 100 not out. This exceptional feat was largely responsible for his first-class average of 51.75 from a total of 414 runs. Fordham played regularly for Hertfordshire in the Minor Counties Championship from 1925 until the outbreak of war, enjoying great success with the bat and scoring almost 6,000 runs with an average not far short of 33. His off-spinners brought him nearly 230 wickets at 17 apiece. Like C. H. Titchmarsh and P. G. T. Kingsley, two other Hertfordshire stalwarts in the inter-war years, he was a good enough player to have made his mark in the first-class game.

FULLWOOD, WALTER, who died in January 1988 at the age of 80, kept wicket for Derbyshire in six matches in 1946 before giving way in mid-season to Denis Smith, the county's leading batsman. Fullwood was perhaps being too severely tested by Copson, Gladwin and the leg-spinner, Rhodes, to make the job his own. However, he took five catches and made one stumping as well as scoring 41 runs for an average of 4.55. He later played as a professional for Highgate.

GAEKWAD, LT-COLONEL FATESINGRAO, who died in Bombay on September 1, 1988, at the age of 58, was as the Maharajah of Baroda a popular manager of the Indian touring team to England in 1959. Later he managed the Indian teams to Pakistan in 1978-79 and 1982-83, by which time the Indian royal families had lost their titles by government edict. A right-hand batsman of some style, and there was considerable style in all "Jackie" Baroda did, he first appeared as a sixteen year old for Baroda in the Ranji Trophy in 1946-47 and continued in the side until 1957-58, for four years as captain, scoring 624 runs at an average of 22.28. His highest innings, 99, came in his début season and helped Baroda defeat Hyderabad in the semi-final of the Ranji Trophy. They went on to win the final, thanks to the world record partnership of 577 between Gul Mahomed and V. S. Hazare for the fourth wicket. He was president of the Board of Control for Cricket in India from 1963-64 to 1965-66 and an honorary life member of MCC. A man of wit, humour and great personal wealth, he was a member of parliament in India from 1962 to 1967 and did much for the World Wildlife Fund. Radio listeners in Britain and beyond came to know him as a member of the BBC commentary team.

GARLICK, RICHARD GORDON, who died at Blackpool on May 16, 1988, aged 71, made an impact for the first time at Old Trafford in 1938. His off-breaks at not much below medium pace produced 41 wickets for the Second XI and thirteen for the senior team. Aggressive lower-order batting and sharp fielding added to his value as a promising young professional at a time when Lancashire were very much in the shadow of their rivals across the Pennines. He maintained his progress in 1939 before the war interrupted his career for six years. The return of first-class cricket in 1946 found Garlick not completely assured of a place in the Championship side, but with 52 wickets at under 20 apiece he had not lost ground. However, in 1947 he did not make the most of his opportunities and that winter he was released from Old Trafford in company with Albert Nutter and Norman Oldfield to join the struggling Northamptonshire side. The three new recruits were unable to lift the morale of the Midland county. Years of continuous failure had left their mark. Of the three, Garlick was the least successful, but salvation was not far below the horizon in the form of the redoubtable F. R. Brown, who was offered and accepted the captaincy for 1949. Brown's positive approach and dynamic leadership were a tonic to all concerned and Garlick's reaction to the new atmosphere of confidence and self-belief was a revelation. Feeling that his efforts were appreciated, he responded with a haul of 73 wickets in the Championship, his off-breaks nicely complementing his captain's leg-spinners. In the course of Northamptonshire's best season since 1913, Garlick had several splendid matches, earning praise for his "clever spin bowling". The following year he did even better with 84 Championship wickets at a reasonable cost and seemed to be on the verge of great things for his new county, when he decided to move into league cricket. His loss was greatly regretted by supporters of the club, appreciative of the contribution he had made towards such a spectacular revival. In a total of 121 first-class matches (44 for Lancashire and 77 for Northamptonshire) he took 332 wickets for an average of 26.11, with six for 27 against Derbyshire at Buxton in 1946 his best effort. His forthright methods with the bat brought him 1,664 runs for the useful average of 13.86.

GEMMILL, WILLIAM NEILSON (WILLIE), who died on September 18, 1987, aged 87, was one of that determined group of amateur cricketers who saw Glamorgan attain first-class status in 1921. When MCC were beaten by ten wickets at Swansea in 1920, as Glamorgan were establishing their credentials, the second-innings runs were scored by Colonel Arthur O'Bree, who was born at Poona, India, and Gemmill, who was born on the South-West Pacific island of

Iew Caledonia and later educated at King's School, Taunton. A right-hand atsman, somewhat inconsistent perhaps, Gemmill scored 1,243 runs at 14.28 in is 48 first-class matches for the county, with a highest score of 77 against Sussex t Hove in 1922.

GLADWIN, CLIFFORD, who died in Chesterfield on April 10, 1988, aged 72, layed in one match for Derbyshire in 1939. After the war, in thirteen consecutive easons until his retirement in 1958, he proved to be among the most consistent of owlers, a medium-fast in-swinger, who with his friend, Leslie Jackson, made p the best opening attack possessed by any of the counties in the decade after 947. Gladwin, whose father had appeared in a few games for Derbyshire, was letermined not to allow the interruption of the war to interfere with his de- elopment. He joined the ranks of the Bradford League, whose policy was to ttract the best players from all parts of the country, and by 1945 he had taken lenty of wickets in the League's main competition. An analysis of eight for 41 gainst Yorkshire in a two-day match at Chesterfield was further evidence of his rogress, and 1946 found him better prepared than most for a full Championship eason. His return of 109 wickets for an average of 18.36 soon attracted the ttention of the selectors, and his chance came in the Third Test of 1947 against outh Africa at Old Trafford, where he had to contend with much obdurate and lefensive batting. In the tourists' first innings he conceded a mere 58 runs in 50 vers, a considerable feat of stamina in a high wind which was strong enough to verturn one of the sightscreens. He was picked for the final Test at The Oval, a natch played in scorching weather and in front of large crowds sitting round the ing in "the lightest permissible summer attire". In these unfamiliar surroundings, he big man from the Peak District obliged with 51 not out in England's first nnings, but in 32 overs he did not take a wicket. Doubts were cast about his ability o break through at the highest level. In the meantime, he helped to reduce the Gentlemen to 25 for five in their second innings at Lord's in conditions much nore to his liking.

Such bowlers as Pollard and Coxon were preferred to him in the 1948 series igainst Australia, but his good form in the Championship won him a place on MCC's winter tour of South Africa under F. G. Mann. By Christmas he had become a national hero, but not for his bowling. In the First Test at Durban, in he tightest of finishes, he had negotiated the leg-bye which gave England a one- wicket victory off the last ball. Eye-witnesses recall that he and his partner, Bedser, indulged in a jubilation one-step as they left the field. The tour was made, but Gladwin could manage only thirteen wickets in the five Tests at an average of 31.45. His last Test was against New Zealand at Lord's in 1949, when he came up igainst Martin Donnelly at his brilliant best.

No longer distracted by the calls of Test cricket, Gladwin settled down to building his county career. For a time he flirted with batsmanship, narrowly missing the double in 1949 and scoring his only century, an unbeaten 124 against Nottinghamshire at Trent Bridge; but more and more he concentrated on developing a mean and miserly approach to his bowling, which he quickly brought to a fine art. The away match with Derbyshire was an experience which few opposing batsmen would contemplate with relish. On a green wicket, in a poor light and amid the paraphernalia of sawdust and towels, they would find themselves hemmed in by a ring of short legs, facing sharpish in-swing pitched just short of a length and on a testing line. Gladwin was apparently able to maintain his almost metronomic consistency by virtue of a short run-up, a lightness of step and a general economy in his action. He attacked from the full width of the crease and could make the occasional ball hold its line as a variant. He always gave of his best and he demanded the best from his fielders, whose occasional lapses led to a degree of intolerance which was understood and forgiven because he was such a trier.

HEWAN, GETHYN ELLIOT, who died on July 1, 1988, at the age of 71, was headmaster of Cranbrook School, Sydney from 1951 to 1963 and, on returning to England, head of Allhallows School, Rousdon from 1965 to 1974 after teaching for a few terms at Winchester. A very talented all-round games player, he won a double Blue at Cambridge for hockey and cricket, being captain of hockey in 1938, the year of his only appearance in the University cricket match at Lord's.

He learnt much of his cricket at Marlborough, where he was a member of the XI from 1933 to 1935 and captain in the last two years. In 1935, by when he had become a dominating and aggressive opener and a much improved bowler of slow off-breaks, his scores of 205 against the Free Foresters, 178 against Wellington and finally 176 and 98 against Rugby at Lord's were of Bradmanesque proportions. His aggregate of 274 in the big match is generally considered to be one of the finest schoolboy batting achievements of the inter-war years. All seemed set fair for a Blue as a Freshman, but Hewan was to suffer two years of frustration and disappointment, ironically being awarded a Blue for his bowling in a year when Cambridge were exceptionally weak in this department. His analysis of 36.5–7–91–6 in Oxford's first innings suggests he was treated perhaps with exaggerated respect, for when the chance to win the match for Cambridge came his way during the last afternoon, he was unable to produce bowling of sufficient penetration. A lively innings of 35 at No. 8 helped to give his side the initiative in a match which was eventually spoilt by the weather.

Hewan served in the 3rd Regiment Royal Horse artillery during the war and was mentioned in dispatches. By this time his golf had taken over from his cricket and he was Danish Amateur Champion in 1950. In 1965, after his return from Australia, he reached the final of the President's Putter, an exceptional achievement for a man of 48 in January in a field bristling with undergraduates. Many of his pupils will recall with delight his skill as a conjuror and his prowess at billiards. In his one short season of first-class cricket, he made 187 runs for Cambridge at an average of 20.77 with a highest score of 88 against Hampshire at Southampton. He took 20 wickets at 36.25 apiece.

HILL-WOOD, CHARLES KERRISON HILL, who died on September 21, 1988, aged 81, was the last survivor of the four brothers who played for Eton and Derbyshire and variously at Oxford or Cambridge, although only three of them won Blues. Their father, as S. H. Wood, captained Derbyshire at the turn of the century. After two years in the Eton XI, Charles Hill-Wood did little in the Freshmen's match in 1927 to displace any of the previous year's bowlers still in residence, but in 1928 he was bowling with appreciable pace and went into the University Match having taken 38 wickets. Left-arm and fast-medium, he bowled with a quite individual action, almost coming off the wrong foot, it seemed, and he made the ball swing into the right-hander. However, he could also cut it away to the slips, and when supported by his field he took a number of wickets this way. At Lord's, he opened the bowling against Cambridge and his brother, Denis, opened the batting; but while his six wickets for 79 in the first innings gave Oxford the chance to keep on equal terms on the first two days, it was his defiant batting on the third evening which saved the match for his side. An hour and threequarter's play remained and Cambridge were seeking the last three Oxford wickets when Hill-Wood, out first ball in the first innings, joined H. M. Garland-Wells. There was still half an hour to go when the last man, Benson, came in, and at seven minutes to seven Hill-Wood, who throughout had played only those balls he had to, survived a high chance to short leg. A few minutes later, the match was safely drawn.

Going on to play for Derbyshire, he took 21 Championship wickets at 32 each, and in 1929 he looked a much better bowler. Though he disappointed against Cambridge, when his two wickets cost 174 runs, he took 51 wickets at 25.33 for

Oxford, including a career-best performance against Northamptonshire at Kettering. After the University had scored 380, with Aidan Crawley hitting 204, he and E. M. Wellings bowled out the county for 76 in less than 22 overs, Hill-Wood taking six for 24 in his eleven overs. When Northamptonshire followed on, he took seven for 68 in 22.5 overs and Oxford won by an innings and 121 runs. In his eight games for Derbyshire that season he scored 206 runs, proving useful as a lower-order right-hand bat, and took twelve wickets at 34.33. His 37 wickets for Oxford in 1930 cost 33.54, and at Lord's he suffered from poor catching in the Cambridge second innings after his three wickets and then 47 runs had secured for Oxford a small first-innings lead. In their second innings, Oxford were bowled out for 101, leaving Cambridge the winners by 205 runs, an amazing volte-face and recompense perhaps for being thwarted by Hill-Wood two years earlier. He played no regular first-class cricket after this. In his 58 first-class matches, the last of which was for the Europeans against the Muslims in the Bombay Quadrangular Tournament of 1935-36, he took 185 wickets at 29.98 and scored 1,256 runs at 19.62.

HODGKINS, JOHN SEYMOUR, died on August 16, 1988, at the age of 72. An attacking right-hand bat and right-arm fast bowler in club cricket in Nottingham, in 1938 he was called up by the county when Jepson was injured to play against Lancashire at Trent Bridge. He took one wicket, that of Oldfield, for 62 runs and scored 1 and 0. He was more fortunate when invited to play against Yorkshire in Jepson's benefit match in 1951. Coming to the wicket immediately upon Trueman's hat-trick, and Nottinghamshire having lost their first six wickets for 18, he scored 34 before becoming the seventh of Trueman's eight wickets. In the second innings he scored 27, having conceded 107 runs for one wicket in a Yorkshire innings of 377 for five declared; Hutton 194 not out. In his only other first-class match, against Surrey at Trent Bridge in 1946, he scored 44. Precluded by a hearing difficulty from military service, he had played regularly for the county in wartime cricket and taken hat-tricks against Kent and RAF XIs.

HOLLINGS, ALFRED MAURICE, who died in Wellington on March 5, 1988, aged 81, played seven times for the province as an all-rounder between 1926-27 and 1930-31. He scored 330 runs at 30.00, in two successive innings scoring 65 not out, his best score, and took five wickets for 45.00.

HORSLEY, RUPERT HARRY, who died on March 5, 1988, was a member of the Winchester XI before going up to Oxford in 1924, winning his colours as a right-hand middle-order batsman and wicket-keeper. He did not play in the Freshmen's match, but made 57 not out as a Senior in 1926 in a good innings in which he drove finely. In the following year he played in three matches for the University, substituting for G. E. B. Abell, a wicket-keeper of exceptional ability, whom he had no real chance of replacing in the team for Lord's. However, he made a good impression with nine catches and one stumping, and with a top score of 25 he totalled 78 runs for an average of 19.50. Horsley, whose father played for Durham and W. G. Grace's London County team, was 82 at the time of his death.

JACKMAN, CHARLES KEITH QUENTIN, who died in Auckland on February 23, 1988, aged 82, was a talented wicket-keeper for Canterbury and Auckland who in sixteen first-class matches claimed 48 dismissals. In 1935-36, playing for Canterbury against Wellington, he set a New Zealand record with four stumpings in an innings and seven in the match, six coming off the bowling of the Test leg-spinner, Bill Merritt. His season's tally of thirteen stumpings included the third-over dismissal of Jim Parks off the medium-pace bowling of E. D. Blundell in the second of two appearances for a New Zealand side against E. R. T. Holmes's MCC tourists.

JAHANGIR KHAN, DR MOHAMMAD, who died in Lahore on July 23, 1988, aged 78, played four Test matches for India in the 1930s and, after Partition, made an important contribution as a player, administrator and selector to the development of cricket in Pakistan. His son, Majid, captained Pakistan, as did his nephews, Javed Burki and Imran Khan. All three emulated him in gaining Blues; Majid like his father at Cambridge, his cousins at Oxford. An elder son, Asad, won his Blues at Oxford.

A medium-fast bowler and attacking right-hand bat, Jahangir Khan made a spectacular entry into first-class cricket at Lawrence Gardens, Lahore in March 1929, scoring 108 and then taking two for 25 and seven for 42 as the Muslims beat the Hindus by an innings and 88 runs. In his second game, also in that Lahore Tournament, opening the bowling against the Europeans he took ten wickets (six for 49 and four for 48) as the Muslims won by an innings and 74 runs. He was not called on to bat. His début in Test cricket, if not as dramatic, did not pass unnoticed. At Lord's in 1932, in India's inaugural Test, he dismissed Holmes, Woolley, Hammond and Paynter in the second innings while conceding just 60 runs from 30 overs. He had not taken a wicket in the first innings. In the first-class matches on the tour, he scored 448 runs at 19.47 and took 53 wickets at 29.05, bowling from an economical approach with a side-on action and somewhat slinging delivery which allowed him to vary his pace and at times produce an unexpected quicker ball. He was then 22, and it goes without saying that he was a great asset to Cambridge in his four years after going up that autumn. He played at Lord's against Oxford from 1933 to 1936 and was prominent in the convincing Cambridge wins of his last two years, capturing six wickets in 1935 and again in 1936. Equally important, his accuracy and stamina enabled him to tie down the opposing batsmen for long periods. Later in 1936 he joined up with the Indian touring side and played in all three Tests but with little influence on their fortunes. He did not take a wicket and two innings of 13 at Lord's were his best with the bat. Outside the Tests he took 40 wickets at 21.90 and scored 276 runs at 17.25.

It was in 1936 also that there occurred the "sparrow incident" with which his name has become associated. Playing for Cambridge against MCC at Lord's, he was bowling to T. N. Pearce, who had just played a defensive push when it was noticed that the bails had been dislodged. It was then that a dead sparrow was found beside the stumps. The unfortunate bird was stuffed and subsequently displayed in the Memorial Gallery at Lord's; but while legend has it that the sparrow was struck by the ball in flight, it is thought no-one actually saw this happen.

While at Cambridge, Jahangir was invited in 1933 and 1934 to represent the Gentlemen against the Players at Folkestone and he also appeared for MCC. From 1940-41 to 1945-46 he played for Northern India, as captain in the first two seasons, and after Partition for Punjab from 1951-52 to 1955-56, by when he was 46. In 111 first-class matches he scored 3,319 runs with an average of 22.12 and four hundreds, took 326 wickets at 25.06 and held 79 catches. His highest score was 133 for Cambridge against Nottinghamshire at Fenner's in 1936 and his best bowling eight for 33 for the Muslims against the Europeans at Lahore in 1929-30.

JUDD, ARTHUR KENNETH (PETER), who died on February 15, 1988, aged 84, gained a Blue at Cambridge in 1927 without having achieved anything of note as a boy at St Paul's and played for Hampshire between 1925 and 1935, when he accepted a posting in Nigeria. In 1926, having played twice for Hampshire the previous season, he made 119 against Warwickshire at Portsmouth, the first of his two first-class hundreds, and other useful performances gave him an aggregate of 341 runs at an average of just over 20, figures which were certain to bring him into the reckoning for an extended trial at Cambridge in 1927. He had played in the Freshmen's match without success as a batsman, going in late, but achieved an analysis of 20–7–55–4 with his slow leg-breaks. Innings of 23 and 87 (run out) in the Seniors' match in 1927 set him on course for his Blue, but he would probably have been the first to admit to his personal good fortune being linked to the illness of K. S. Duleepsinhji, who was unable to play again that season after starting with a superb 254 not out against Middlesex. Judd made 47 against Sussex and then 73 and 62 not out against a full Nottinghamshire side which included Larwood. Thereafter he was a model of consistency at No. 4, his driving calling for special comment on a number of occasions, and against Oxford at Lord's he played a major hand in Cambridge's 116-run victory with 124 in the second innings. It was an innings very much of two parts, the second being greatly superior to the first, and a boisterous partnership with R. W. V. Robins in 55 minutes gave Cambridge a position of strength which they never looked like surrendering. In all, he made [illegible]67 runs for the University at an average of 39.23.

He batted lower down the order when playing for Hampshire in subsequent seasons, but made the occasional useful knock at No. 9 or No. 10. Two analyses in 1928 in the Championship probably surprised him as much as his opponents. On a helpful wicket he returned six for 65 against Somerset at Weston, a stumping and three catches behind the wicket testifying to the teasing nature of his slow spinners; and in the following match, in conditions which favoured the batting side at Leicester, he took four wickets for 111. Before the start of the 1928 season he had played in Jamaica as a member of the side taken there by his county captain, Lionel Tennyson. He made 75 against All Jamaica in the final match of the tour. In 84 first-class matches, Judd scored 2,624 runs in 141 innings for an average of 21.33. His 30 wickets cost 34.53.

KHANVILKAR, RANJIT, died on July 8, 1988, at the age of 27 when the train from Bangalore, where he was resident, to Trivandrum in the south left the rails and seven of the carriages were submerged in a lake; 111 people died in the tragedy. A tall, right-hand middle-order batsman and medium-pace bowler, he made his début for Karnataka in the Ranji Trophy in 1980-81 and in the following season's final scored 113 in their total of 705 against Delhi, who went 1 run better to win on the first innings. His 32 at No. 9 in the 1982-83 final was essential to Karnataka's successful attempt to overhaul Bombay's 534 and so win the Ranji Trophy for the third time in ten years. In 24 matches for Karnataka to 1985-86 he scored 1,025 runs and took 26 wickets. On joining the railway service he then played for them in the championship. In 1984-85 he scored 156 for South Zone against West Zone at Bombay.

KNOTT, CHARLES HAROLD (JOHN), who died on June 18, 1988, at the age of 87, was the oldest living Kent cricketer as well as the oldest living Blue, having played for Oxford in the University Matches of 1922, 1923 and 1924. In all he played in 136 first-class matches in a career which extended from 1921 till 1939. With nine centuries to his credit, he scored 5,633 runs in 206 innings at an average of 31.46; he also took 24 wickets and held 66 catches. A fierce striker of the ball, he was much feared as a middle-order batsman by opponents, even in his schoolboy days, and he was a cover-point of the highest class. These qualities more or less guaranteed him a place in the Kent side in August after the summer term at Tonbridge, where he was a master for the whole of his working life.

Going as a boy to Tonbridge, he followed in the footsteps of his elder brother, Freddy, who had made a hundred for Kent when still at the school. In 1919 he really made his mark with a sensational innings of 220 against Lancing, adding 290 in partnership with L. P. Hedges, the last 230 of which came in an hour. This innings and another century earned him selection for the Lord's Schools against The Rest. The following year he took 44 wickets with his leg-breaks, and so it was with something of the reputation of an all-rounder that he went up to Oxford.

However, he failed to gain a Blue as a Freshman and in 1922 only came into th reckoning on tour with an innings of 109 not out at Leicester, No success attende his efforts at Lord's against Cambridge; he was twice clean bowled by Gubb Allen, who had a great match. Next season, when he was secretary, he enjoyed th most consistent spell of his whole career. In the last three matches before th meeting with Cambridge he played innings of 66, 48 not out, 65, 105 not out, 1 and 70; at Lord's, his contribution to a riot of big hitting was 42 as Oxford won b an innings and 227 runs. He was captain of a moderate side in 1924 and gave splendid lead with innings of 83 and 74 in The Parks against Middlesex whe everyone was short of practice. *Wisden* said of him that he was "hardly a clas batsman, but a very effective one". This was his busiest year in first-class crick and for Oxford and Kent he totalled 938 runs at an average of 28.42.

In later years he generally made between 400 and 500 runs for Kent. In 1927 when in the absence of A. P. F. Chapman, A. J. Evans and G. B. Legge he wa called upon to lead the county against the reigning champions, Lancashire, at Ol Trafford, he made 96 in two and a quarter hours; with his dashing methods he no only confounded his dour, professional opponents but startled the spectators a well. But it was in August 1928, the summer of 414 centuries, that he played hi most celebrated innings, not for Kent, for whom he was short of runs, but for th Harlequins against the touring West Indians at Eastbourne. In a remarkabl display of aggression, he amassed 261 not out in six hours; with A. J. Evans he pu on 160 runs in under the hour. His chief hits included five sixes, a five and 2 fours. The tourists were defeated by an innings and 105 runs. Not content wit this savage treatment, he greeted the next West Indian tourists in 1933 with 15 not out, another powerful knock which paved the way for a Kent victory by a innings and 93. Two other innings shine out from those inter-war years. In 192 he took part in that memorable match between Kent and Sussex at Hastings in which 1,451 runs were made and Duleepsinhji made 115 and 246. Knott' contribution was an unbeaten 140 in Kent's first innings, made in two and a quarter hours. And in 1934, against Northamptonshire at Dover, he hit 118 in a manner which was scarcely overshadowed by Woolley's 103 in 63 minutes whic made him the first winner of the Lawrence Trophy.

Knott's great strength evidently lay in his driving. Colin Cowdrey, in a tribut written for the *Cricketer*, says: "He was superbly built, immensely strong in th wrist and forearm." He played the game naturally and without fuss; along wit many an amateur of his generation he did not believe in coaching and made n bones about it as master-in-charge of cricket at Tonbridge, a position he held fo some 30 years. Again we must turn to Cowdrey, by far his most distinguishe product at Tonbridge, to complete the picture: "He presented an awesom figure . . . a real martinet with regard to punctuality, dress and the old world courtesies. A man of few words, he was particularly hard on the talented player who wasted it. He believed that to be part of a good fielding side was the greatest fun of all and he revelled in conducting the daily fielding practice, where his humour and sense of fun was infectious."

LAWRIE, PERCY EDWARD, died in Teignmouth Hospital, on February 6, 1988, aged 85. A member of the Eton XI in 1920 and 1921, he made in his second year 545 runs with an average of 42.15 and at Lord's played two invaluable innings of 53 and 67 not out, which had much to do with a narrow victory for his side and showed that he had a splendid temperament for the big occasion. In August he played for Hampshire against Glamorgan at Southampton and made 49, helping Newman to add 150 for the second wicket in two hours. After this, his failure to get a Blue in his three years at Oxford must have been a great disappointment. In 1922 he failed in the Freshmen's match, but an innings of 56 for Hampshire against the University secured him a trial. However, Oxford batting was strong and neither in that year nor in the two following ones could he keep his place. Meanwhile in 1923 he played regularly for Hampshire in the vacation, scoring 520 runs with an average of 23.63 and making 107 at Leicester in under two hours to help avert threatening defeat. He played little for the county later, though his last appearance was not until 1928. In all first-class cricket he made 1,084 runs with an average of 21.25. He was a particularly fine off-driver.

LAXMAN SINGH died on July 19, 1988, aged 40, following a fall at his home at Gandhinagar in Gujarat. A consistent scorer, he opened the batting for Rajasthan from 1966-67 to 1977-78, having made his début while still a schoolboy. As a member of Indian schools teams he toured England in 1967, scoring 973 runs at 74.84, and Australia in 1967-68, when his average was 46.37 from 891 runs. His aggregate of 1,758 runs at 32.55 in the Ranji Trophy championship included three centuries, the highest of which was his unbeaten 231 in 1974-75 against Madhya Pradesh at Indore, when he and Parthasarthy Sharma (161) added 289 for the second wicket. Laxman Singh scored a further 517 runs, average 25.85, in the Duleep Trophy for Central Zone, with 124 against South Zone in 1975-76 his only century.

LEARY, STUART EDWARD, was found dead on Table Mountain, Cape Town on August 23, 1988 and is thought to have died two days earlier. He was 55. He had played for Kent from 1951 to 1971, and in all first-class games he scored 16,517 runs with an average of 31.10 and took 146 wickets at 33.80 as a right-hand middle-order batsman and leg-break bowler. Quite outstanding as a schoolboy cricketer – he was Sea Point High's first South African Schools cap – rugby fly-half and soccer forward in Cape Town, he came to Britain in 1949 at the age of sixteen to join Charlton Athletic as a professional soccer player. He made his first-team début two years later and was soon established as a centre-forward of skill and perception. Towards the end of this career he played for Queen's Park Rangers.

It was in 1951 also that he first played for Kent, having the previous year been offered professional terms by the Durham League club, Whitburn, home town of the Charlton manager, Jimmy Seed. His début was at Ilford, and he confirmed the promise that was noted there by scoring 74 against Minor Counties at Canterbury a few days later. Another of Charlton's South Africans, Syd O'Linn, made his Kent début that season and in eight innings topped the county's Championship averages. For the next few years, soccer and National Service in the RAF occupied Leary's attention, and it was not until 1957 that he managed more than an occasional appearance. Then, in his first full season, he passed a thousand runs for the first of nine times and his aggregate of 1,231 included his first three hundreds. As well as hitting his maiden century against Cambridge, 102 not out in 140 minutes, he took five wickets for 34 in the University's second innings to spin Kent to victory. He could turn the ball a long way, and he also bowled a useful googly. His best performance was five for 22 at Swansea in 1961, when Glamorgan were bowled out for 73, having made 319 in their first innings. Leary's figures in that were four for 58 in nineteen overs.

That summer was also his best with the bat; his 1,440 runs were scored at an average of 38.91 and he hit three hundreds. He was not a dashing batsman; his method was to work the ball rather than stroke it elegantly. Still, there were 23 boundaries in the highest of his eighteen centuries, 158 in four and a half hours against Northamptonshire at Kettering in 1963. He and R. C. Wilson put on 283 together, just 38 short of Kent's record for the third wicket. But if his batting did not mirror his style on the soccer pitch, his fielding was its equal, especially at short leg where his anticipation and reflexes set him apart. He took 362 catches, and his six in an innings against Cambridge in 1958 equalled the record for Kent.

Another Kent record was his benefit of £9,100 in 1967, the county's best season for 38 years; they won the Gillette Cup and were runners-up in the Championship. Leary scored 1,042 runs, achieving his thousand for the last time, but when Kent won the Championship in 1970, their centenary season, he could not hold his place in the three-day side. However, he played a leading role in their filling second place in the John Player League, and his seventeen sixes were the most in the competition that season. The next year, 1971, was his last. He was soon to return to South Africa, where he gave much back to the game as a coach, encouraging children of all races. He became Director of Coaching for the Western Province Cricket Union and was manager of the side which won both the Currie Cup and Datsun Shield in 1981-82.

LITHGOW, BRIGADIER ANTHONY ONSLOW LAWRENCE, who died in July 1988, aged 67, will always have a place in the annals of Eton v Harrow matches. He not only captained Harrow in 1939, when they won for the first time since 1908, but was the central figure at the moment of triumph. Obedient to Patsy Hendren's advice to attack the bowling in the fourth innings, he finished the match with three successive boundaries to the pavilion rails. His undefeated 67 was the outstanding innings in the eight-wicket victory, and amid scenes of tremendous enthusiasm a crowd of young bloods irrupted on to the field and hoisted Lithgow and his partner shoulder-high back to the pavilion. A fight of top-hats ensued but the authorities, embarrassed by a mêlée of carnations and umbrellas, made no official protest. They were not to find themselves similarly under siege until the sixties, when they were confronted with the vulgarities of a new age in the form of limited-overs finals. Lithgow would have succeeded at first-class level, but the war changed his life. The qualities of leadership he displayed at Lord's were amply fulfilled in Korea, where he commanded a battalion of the Black Watch with courage and distinction.

LIVINGSTONE, DAINTES ABBIA (DANNY), who died in his native Antigua on September 8, 1988, aged 54, was as an attacking left-hand batsman a member of the Hampshire side when the county won the Championship in 1961 for the first time. He had initially qualified for Warwickshire, but more than 500 runs for their Second XI in 1957 was not enough to interest them. Hampshire gave him a trial and in 1959 he scored more than 850 runs for the second team and averaged over 100 in Club and Ground matches; he also made his first-class début, scoring 37 and 14 against Oxford at Bournemouth. He did not win a regular place in 1960, but in 1961 he established himself with 1,643 runs at 28.32, including an unbeaten 102 against Northamptonshire at Southampton, his maiden first-class hundred. In Hampshire's penultimate match, when they beat Derbyshire to make certain of the Championship, his was the catch in the deep which dismissed Bob Taylor, who had been organising a stubborn resistance on the last evening, and brought the match to a close.

While 1961 was understandably Livingstone's most memorable season, 1962 was his best. Batting with a new maturity, he scored 1,817 runs at 37.08 and, against Surrey at Southampton, made his career-highest score of 200. Dropped first ball, he batted for nearly five hours, hit three sixes and 22 fours, and with nineteen-year-old Alan Castell (76) turned round a position of 128 for eight by adding 230, a county record for the ninth wicket. That season he also made an untroubled 101 not out against the touring Pakistanis, and in 1963 his brilliant 151 against the West Indians set up an enthralling match which finished with the tourists' last pair at the wicket and ten fielders clustered around the bat. By now he had become a thoroughly reliable batsman, and in 1964, when he scored 117 and 105 not out in the match against Kent at Canterbury, he assumed the mantle of leading run-scorer, the position for so long held by Roy Marshall. But the ollowing year his batting fell away badly, and although he reached his thousand uns for the fifth time in 1967 and again in 1970, his consistency had deserted him. he last of his sixteen hundreds came at the beginning of the 1970 season, 103 gainst Middlesex at Lord's where he and Marshall (189 not out) added 263 for the ourth wicket, another Hampshire record. He had two more seasons and then, in 973, returned to Antigua to take up a post as Director of Sports with the ntiguan government, going on to do much for the development of cricket and occer on the island. He captained Antigua and also managed the Leewards and ombined Islands sides.

In 301 first-class matches, he scored 12,722 runs with an average of 27.89. An xcellent fielder, he held 243 catches and also made two stumpings.

MACDONALD-WATSON, SURGEON-CAPTAIN ALISTAIR, OBE, who ied on November 19, 1987, aged 78, played in four matches for Somerset in 1932 nd 1933. A fast right-arm bowler, he took five for 27 in his second match against erbyshire at Ilkeston and was the main instrument in their downfall for a total of 1. No such distinction attended his efforts as a batsman for he managed just 2 uns in six innings. In all he took eight wickets for 219 runs at a cost of 27.37 per icket.

McINTOSH, ROBERT IAN FANSHAWE, who died on March 21, 1988, at udleigh Salterton, aged 80, played for Oxford University from 1927 to 1929, inning his Blue in 1927 and 1928. He was, at least in his first year in residence, a nore than useful medium-pace opening bowler. For three years in the Uppingham I, he was the mainstay of their attack, and in 1925, his second year, he was hosen for The Rest against the Lord's Schools. A breakdown in health prevented im from playing, and it seems that his constitution was far from strong at that tage of his life; it may well have been a major factor in his loss of form in his last ear at Oxford. In 1926, as captain at Uppingham, he took 45 wickets at a mere 1.24 each, and he was one of the few boys who did himself any sort of justice gainst the Army for the Public Schools, returning an analysis of 17.3–4–64–4.

His chances of gaining a Blue as a Freshman were increased by the illness of V. N. McBride, who was expected to bear the brunt of the opening bowling for xford. McIntosh stepped into the breach with a series of consistent perfor-nances, culminating in eight wickets in the big match at Lord's. In Cambridge's econd innings he took the important wicket of R. W. V. Robins, thus giving xford a sporting chance of winning the match. His overall record for the year as 26 wickets at 23.15 apiece in 220.5 overs. In 1928 he was made to work wice as hard by his captain, M. A. McCanlis, and occasionally suffered heavy unishment, especially at the hands of Kent and Gloucestershire. His 34 wickets ost him more than 38 runs each and by the time of the University Match he had robably shot his bolt. Possibly not in the best of health and discouraged by aving to bowl on so many over-prepared wickets the previous summer, he was ever in serious contention for a Blue in 1929. Thereafter he vanishes from the cene, only to reappear again in February 1934 for Madras against Jardine's trong MCC team. Along with the other bowlers he took a hammering, the ouring team's total of 603 being at that time a record for the ground. In all, he ook 69 wickets in 24 first-class matches at an average of 32.94; a batting average f 11.50 from 161 runs owed more to a high percentage of not outs than to any rowess as a batsman.

MANNING, JOHN STEPHEN (JACK), who died in Adelaide on May 5, 988, aged 63, played for three seasons for his native South Australia in the heffield Shield from 1951-52 to 1953-54 before deciding to try his luck in England vith his orthodox left-arm spin. Two successful seasons with Colne in the

Lancashire League persuaded Northamptonshire to sign him. They saw him as the ideal foil for George Tribe, whose left-arm wrist-spin had done so much to boost their new-found success. This turned out to be an inspired move, and in four full Championship seasons from 1956 to 1959 Manning captured 415 wickets for an average of 20.56.

In his formative years Manning cultivated sharp spin from leg as his chief weapon. Few had developed this method of taking wickets in Australia before his time, and in successive MCC tours before the war, Verity and Jack White had been able to contain rather than destroy; in 1946-47 James Langridge was not a force to be reckoned with. Manning, then, was something of a novelty when he broke into the small, tight circle of Shield players, and in his three seasons at the top in Australia he took 66 wickets for an average of 29.95. In 1952-53 his 2[illegible] wickets made him a vital component in Paul Ridings's winning South Australian side. In England, where conditions favoured his methods, he obtained over 100 wickets for Northamptonshire in 1956, and with yet another left-arm spinner M. H. J. Allen from Bedford, also on hand, the county were employing a unique combination. In 1957, the trio took as many as 305 Championship wickets between them. There were other factors in the county's success in finishing second to Surrey, such as the speed of Tyson and the shrewd captaincy of Dennis Brookes, but the three left-arm spinners must take the chief word of praise. In this and in his other three seasons, Manning's outstanding performances were so numerous as to be almost commonplace. As well as his eight for 43 against Gloucestershire at Peterborough in 1959, match figures of eleven for 80 against Nottinghamshire at Northampton in the same season are worthy of recall. Only in 1958 did he fail to take 100 wickets.

After a few unsuccessful matches in 1960 Manning, victim of some ruthless rebuilding at Northampton, was relegated to the Second XI, which promptly won the Championship. Released from his contract, he returned to Australia to play and coach around Adelaide. Although he had never had any great pretensions with the bat, he was capable of a useful innings at No. 8 or No. 9 in the order. Certainly he would have retained clearer memories of his only century in first-class cricket than of his many achievements with the ball. His 132 against Yorkshire at Harrogate in 1957 led to a major recovery after his side had slipped to 105 for five. In a total of 146 first-class matches in Australia and England Manning made 2,766 runs for an average of 15.71. His 513 wickets cost as little as 22.73 apiece.

NEWSON, EDWARD SURRURIER (BOB), OBE, who died in Durban on April 24, 1988, aged 77, opened the bowling in his three Test matches for South Africa, against England at Johannesburg in 1930-31 and eight years later in the last two Tests against Hammond's side. Yet he might easily have missed his début, for he had not received notification of his selection and arrived at work as usual on the morning of the match. His father brought his kit to the Old Wanderers ground by tram as his son, recently turned twenty, lined up for the team photograph in borrowed clothes. Newson did not take a wicket but, joining Quintin McMillan with South Africa 81 for nine in the first innings, he helped add a further 45 before Tate bowled him for 10. As South Africa won by 28 runs, and the next four Tests in the series were all drawn, it was a vital contribution. He took a wicket in each innings at Johannesburg in 1938-39 and another two (for 58) in the first innings of the "timeless Test" at Durban, where he was South Africa's most economical bowler in terms of runs per over. His four Test wickets averaged 66.25 each.

Newson made his Currie Cup début for Transvaal in 1929-30, but studies and career restricted him to just four games between 1931 and 1938. After the war he moved to Rhodesia, playing for them until 1949-50 and in 1946-47, against Griqualand West at Kimberley, reaching his only first-class century in 65 minutes.

n 24 first-class matches, he took 60 wickets at 26.03 and scored 553 runs at 17.83 ith a highest score of 114. His best bowling figures were five for 54 for Rhodesia gainst MCC at Bulawayo in 1948-49. An overnight storm had penetrated the overs and he took all five wickets for 13 runs in his first seven overs on the second norning.

PAGE, GEORGE SCOTT, who died on March 20, 1988, a few months short of is 89th birthday, was almost certainly the last surviving cricketer to have played oth against Warwick Armstrong's 1921 Australians and the Australian Imperial orces team in 1919. A cavalier batsman and outstanding fielder for Durham ounty between 1919 and 1926, against the AIF at West Hartlepool he became ne of Jack Gregory's 131 victims on the tour, being beaten and bowled by sheer ace. In 1921 at Sunderland he managed to see off Ted McDonald in each innings, nly to hole out in the deep to Armstrong and Arthur Mailey respectively for cores of 24 and 29. Page was a rugby player of skill and flair who represented urham 22 times as a centre-threequarter.

PARKER, FREDERICK ANTHONY VIVIAN, who died on May 26, 1988, ged 75, was a more than useful right-handed batsman for the Army and ombined Services who in 1946 appeared for Hampshire against the Indian ouring team and Kent but with little success. Between these two matches, owever, he registered a first-class century when, with an innings of 116 for the ervices against Northamptonshire at Kettering, he turned about a first-innings osition of 28 for four and set his side on the way to victory by eight wickets. In is five first-class matches, he totalled 147 runs with an average of 16.33.

PARTHASARATHY, T. V. died at Madras on December 5, 1988, aged 72. A uent opening batsman and wicket-keeper, he played in one unofficial "Test" gainst the Australian Services team at Calcutta in 1945-46. His Ranji Trophy ppearances were few but varied; in seven matches he represented Karnataka, Madras and Bengal, scoring 350 runs at 26.92 and claiming nine catches and a tumping.

PARTRIDGE, JOSEPH TITUS (JOE), who died in tragic circumstances at his ative Bulawayo on June 7, 1988, aged 55, made a major contribution to the uccess of T. L. Goddard's South African side in Australia in 1963-64. He and eter Pollock, opening the bowling, took 25 wickets each in the five Tests, the nost for either country in a series drawn 1-1; but whereas Pollock's wickets came rimarily from his pace, Partridge, right-arm medium-fast, relied more on ccuracy, stamina and swing. His stock ball was the in-swinger, which he could traighten off the pitch and occasionally cut away to the slips, but months of ractice had also given him an out-swinger. Bespectacled and strongly built, he vas a willing competitor, even on the hottest days, and in fourteen first-class natches in Australia and New Zealand that season he took 63 wickets at 26.30. igures of four for 108 on a well-grassed pitch in the Melbourne Test showed what e could achieve and he followed this with four for 88 and five for 123 at Sydney, vhere before the Test series he had taken five for 75 and four for 42 in the state ame. At Adelaide, where South Africa won by ten wickets to level the series, he nanaged only one wicket, as he had on his début at Brisbane, but back at Sydney e relished the heavy atmosphere and took seven for 91 from 31.1 eight-ball overs n Australia's first innings of the final Test. Four for 51 at Dunedin and six for 86 n 40 overs at Auckland were his significant performances in the three Tests in New Zealand.

Partridge first played for Rhodesia in the Currie Cup as a nineteen year old in 951-52, and in subsequent seasons he steadily established himself. Figures of six or 26 against a visiting Surrey side and an analysis of 12.5–8–9–7 against Border at Bulawayo, contributing to 32 wickets at 20.03 in 1959-60, could not persua South Africa's selectors to send him to England in 1960, where the conditio would have encouraged his method. But there could be no ignoring his 53 wicke at 13.98 in 1961-62 and 64 at 16.62 in 1962-63. The Australasian tour followed, b his triumph was short-lived. Against England in 1964-65 his six wickets in thr Tests cost 293 runs, and omission from the Fifth Test brought his brief inte national career to an end. In eleven Test matches he had taken 44 wickets 31.20. He was now 33. Two more seasons with Rhodesia took his aggregate in t Currie Cup to 195 wickets at 18.80 and his record in 77 first-class matches to 3 at 20.80. His best return was eight for 69, followed by six for 32 in the secor innings, at Salisbury in 1961-62 when Rhodesia beat Natal for the first time. limited batsman, he scored 523 runs at 9.17 and held 21 catches.

PATEL, K. R., who died at Bangalore on April 12, 1988, played as an a rounder in the Ranji Trophy for Mysore from 1949 to 1951 and in 1958-59 and f Hyderabad from 1951 to 1955, scoring 283 runs and taking eight wickets at 55. each. He was an uncle of B. P. Patel, the Indian Test cricketer.

PORRITT, B. W. E. (BILL), a former All-Ceylon cricketer, died in Austral where he had been living for some years. He was one of the first schoolboys win a Ceylon cap when, while a pupil at Royal College, he played again Woodfull's 1934 team to England and bowled Bill Brown. That same year he to fifteen for 66 for Royal College against Trinity. Porritt bowled both right- and le arm in club cricket and was the leading bowler in the Kalutara Town club whic won the Daily News Trophy in 1939. In 1940-41 he toured India as vice-captain the All-Ceylon side and met with some success.

RAISON, MAX, who died on July 25, 1988, aged 86, was one of a number amateur cricketers who helped out Essex in the years between the wars. A righ hand bat and right-arm medium-pace bowler, he scored 451 runs at 18.04 and too fourteen wickets at 41.07 in seventeen appearances from 1928 to 1930. Among h five wickets for 104 against Gloucestershire at Chelmsford in 1928 was that Hammond, bowled for 244.

RECORDON, LIONEL WALTHER, who died on October 6, 1988, aged 8 played eleven times for Kent in four years in the second half of the 192 principally as a right-hand batsman although in his three years in the XI Brighton College he had attracted some attention by his leg-spin bowling. He w captain of the school XI in 1925. For Kent, he scored 242 runs with an average 18.61 but did not take a wicket.

ROACH, CLIFFORD ARCHIBALD, who died on April 16, 1988, at the a of 84, was the last surviving member of the side which, under R. K. Nunes, playe in West Indies' first Test match, at Lord's in 1928. In that match, batting in th middle order, he scored 0 (run out) and 16, but it was in his customary position an attacking opening batsman that, against England at Barbados in the First Te of 1929-30, he became the first West Indian to score a Test century. His 12 containing twenty fours, was also his maiden first-class hundred, and he followe it with 77 in the second innings. To this distinction he added West Indies' fir Test double-hundred two Tests later at Georgetown, having in the inter recorded a pair at his home ground, Port-of-Spain, and suggested subsequently the selectors that he stand down. The wise men decided otherwise and, led b Roach's 209, a hundred in each innings from Headley and nine wickets b Constantine, West Indies won by 289 runs their first Test victory. Roach, who h three sixes and 23 fours, put on 144 for the first wicket with Hunte and then 19 with Headley as he raced to his second hundred in 74 minutes. In the second innings he was stumped by Ames for 22.

He made his début for Trinidad in 1923-24, having played his early cricket on the island's matting wickets. A confirmed strokemaker, equally fluent off front and back foot, he came to terms sufficiently with the conditions in England in 1928, although it is significant perhaps that his tour aggregate of 1,222 runs at 26.56 did not include a century. However, he gave much pleasure to spectators, not least with his brilliant fielding, particularly in the covers. In the other two Tests played that summer, he top-scored for West Indies with 50 at Old Trafford and 53 at The Oval, where he and Challenor got the match under way with 91 in 70 minutes. With C. G. Grant's side in Australia in 1930-31 he scored 637 runs at 24.50 in the first-class matches, but after beginning with 56 at Adelaide he endured a lean run in the Tests until scoring 31 and 34 in the Fifth Test at Sydney, where West Indies gained their first victory over Australia.

In England in 1933 he again began unhappily in the Tests with a pair at Lord's, caught first ball when West Indies followed on, only to recover with 13 and 64 at Old Trafford and 8 and 56 at The Oval, reaching his half-century in just 33 minutes. Against Surrey, earlier in the tour, he had scored 128 before lunch there and gone on to 180 in 170 minutes, his highest innings in a tour aggregate of 1,286 at 25.72. His final Test match was at Barbados against England in 1934-35, when on a pitch drying after rain he scored 9 and 10 not out to take his total runs from sixteen matches to 952 with an average of 30.70. He had also taken two wickets. In 98 first-class matches he scored 4,851 runs at 28.04 with his double-hundred at Georgetown the highest of his five centuries. His five wickets cost 105.20 apiece.

ROHRS, ANTHONY JOHN, who died in a car accident on June 24, 1988, aged 26, had played twice for Wellington in the previous season, making his first-class début against Mike Gatting's visiting England team and scoring 4 in his only innings. He was selected for the Shell Trophy match against Auckland at the Basin Reserve but the weather allowed only three hours' play and he did not bat.

SEABROOK, WALTER GEORGE, died on June 13, 1988, aged 84. The younger brother of F. J. Seabrook, a successful schoolmaster cricketer who appeared regularly for Gloucestershire in August, he played in just one match for the same county against Kent in 1928 without any success. His useful left-handed batting and left-arm medium-pace bowling had gained him his colours at Haileybury.

SELVADURAI, A. J. D. N., who died in September 1988, was a well-known supporter of cricket, athletics, tennis and hockey in Sri Lanka. A thoughtful seam bowler, useful batsman and a fielder with a strong arm, he played for Ceylon in December 1945 against Lindsay Hassett's Australian Services side in the last three-day match of their Indian tour. In Ceylon's second innings of 159, the Oxford Blue, F. C. de Saram, and Selvadurai each scored 23, the highest for their side but insufficient to prevent an innings defeat.

SHUCKBURGH, SIR CHARLES GERALD STEWKLEY, died on April 5, 1988, at the age of 77. He was a right-handed batsman, considered good enough by the Warwickshire selectors to fill a place in the county side in a Championship match against Nottinghamshire at Edgbaston in 1930, in spite of an unsuccessful Freshmen's match at Oxford earlier that season. The story goes that Norman Kilner and Sam Staples between them arranged for the young sprig of nobility to be allowed to get off the mark; but when the chance came he was too petrified to move from the crease to respond to this act of courtesy. Whether he went through similar anguish before making his one catch has not been recorded. Sir Charles

against Surrey at The Oval. While his bowling proved to be accurate enough, perhaps lacked sufficient subtlety to trouble first-class opponents, and h seventeen wickets cost more than 50 runs each, a far cry from his schoolb figures. In 1929, when it was hoped he would move ahead, he tended to mark tin and he dropped out of the side to meet Cambridge at Lord's. In his last year residence, he was allowed only one chance to re-establish himself; in a rai affected game he had one innings and did not get a bowl. Only the four Sedbergian to win a Blue up to that time, he scored 644 runs in first-class match average 25.76, and took 26 wickets at 47.30.

SOUTHBY, SIR ARCHIBALD RICHARD CHARLES, who died on April 1988, at the age of 77, performed well enough at Eton to be chosen for t Freshmen's match at Oxford in 1930, but he achieved little of note and did n play in a first-class match in England until 1939, when he opened for the Arn against Cambridge at Fenner's. His other six first-class appearances were in Ind between 1935 and 1937 for Madras in the Ranji Trophy and for the Europeans. H never looked like fulfilling the promise of his schooldays, managing 158 runs twelve innings with a highest score of 33.

SPENCE, LESLIE MAGNUS (LES), who died on September 23, 1988, ag 81, did much towards the rebuilding of the Glamorgan club after the Seco World War, initially as one of the triumvirate of assistant secretaries wh supported J. C. Clay and subsequently as honorary secretary, a post he filled un shortly before his death.

THOMPSON, WILFRID SYDENHAM, who died on December 17, 198 aged 76, was one of the last survivors of the team which served Norfolk so well the decade before the Second World War. A charismatic, commanding figure wh during war-time service with the Coldstream Guards rose to the rank of major, was a bowler of explosive pace and a hitter of numerous sixes of quite prodigio carry. In the Uppingham XI in 1930, he made his début for Norfolk two yea later and was captain from 1947 to 1950. He subsequently served for many yea on the committee and was president in 1975-76. He played also for MCC, Fr Foresters and the Musketeers, but mostly his club cricket was for West Norfolk. scratch golfer, Thompson also represented his county at that sport and at rugb

TOON, JAMES HARRY CECIL, who died on October 26, 1987, aged 7 played in one match for Northamptonshire in 1946 against the Combined Servic at Kettering. An all-rounder of medium pace, he had more luck with the ball th with the bat and in the Services' two innings took four wickets for 126 runs.

TYLER, BERNARD, died in November 1987, aged 85. He was a great serva of Liverpool CC for nearly 40 years, eight as senior professional and the rest head groundsman. A fast-medium right-arm bowler who batted down the ord he played in nine matches for Northamptonshire in 1923 and 1924 and five f Leicestershire from 1926 to 1928, scoring 135 runs (average 7.10) and taki eleven wickets at 50.27 apiece.

WALTER, CYRIL VINCENT, who died in Christchurch on March 23, ag 75, played twice for Canterbury in 1945-46, scoring 29 runs for an average of 7.7 Better known as a hockey coach, he was the father of the Television New Zeala cricket producer, Ian Walter, whose obituary appeared in the 1988 *Wisden*.

WANKHEDE, SESHRAO KRISHNARAO, who died in Bombay on Janua 30, 1988, aged 73, was president of the Board of Control for Cricket in India fro

1980-81 to 1982-83. But it was as president of the Bombay Cricket Association from 1963-64 that he played his most far-reaching role in Indian cricket affairs. For more than 30 years the Association had been dissatisfied with a situation which saw them beholden to the Cricket Club of India for the distribution of profits from Test and first-class cricket at the Brabourne Stadium, which the CCI owned, and for the allocation of seats for Test matches there. When in 1971, with England due to tour India in 1972-73, the CCI would not agree to provide more seats for the Association's member clubs, the BCA at Wankhede's instigation decided to build its own stadium and so vacate its tenancy of the Brabourne Stadium, leaving this famous, splendid ground with little more than its history. Since 1973-74 virtually all international and first-class cricket in Bombay has been played at the stadium which bears Wankhede's name.

WHITE, CYRIL DE LACEY, died at East London on December 2, 1987, aged 78. Playing for Border at Queenstown in 1946-47, he caught three Griqualand West batsmen off successive balls while fielding at forward short leg to Ray Beesly, a left-arm medium-fast bowler. Only one other fielder had achieved such a hat-trick, G. J. Thompson of Northamptonshire in 1914; G. O. Dawkes of Derbyshire, who subsequently performed the feat in 1958, was a wicket-keeper. A solid left-hand opening bat, whose brother Clive also represented Border, White made the first of 38 first-class appearances for Border in 1929-30 and the last in 1949-50, having scored 1,454 runs at 21.33, taken 32 catches and become the first batsman to score 1,000 runs for the province, for whom he also played Currie Cup rugby. His highest innings was 189 against Natal in 1934-35.

WHITELAW, PAUL ERSKINE, died at Auckland on August 28, 1988, aged 78. A right-hand batsman with a fine technique, he was called up to open the batting for New Zealand against England in 1932-33 when his fellow Aucklander, Mills, withdrew. In the two Tests he scored 30, 17 not out, 12 and 5 not out. It was in these matches, on MCC's homeward journey from the bodyline series, that Hammond hit 227 and 336 not out. These were Whitelaw's only Test matches, although he represented his country twice against E. R. T. Holmes's MCC side in 1935-36 and against Sir Julien Cahn's XI in 1938-39. His outstanding success came in 1936-37 when, for Auckland against Otago at Dunedin, he and Bill Carson, a twenty-year-old left-hander, added 445 in 268 minutes, which stood as a world record for the third wicket until 1976-77. Coming together when Auckland were 25 for two, they put on 100 in 85 minutes, 200 in 156 minutes, 300 in 190 minutes and 400 in 247 minutes. Carson hit 38 fours in his 290. Whitelaw, who batted for 331 minutes, hit a six and 21 fours in his 195, the highest of his five first-class hundreds. He played 43 times for Auckland between 1928 and 1947 and in all first-class matches scored 2,739 runs for an average of 37.52. In 1960, he donated an almost complete set of *Wisdens* to the Auckland Cricket Association.

WINLAW, ASHLEY WILLIAM EDGELL, who died on February 13, 1988, aged 74, captained Winchester against Eton in 1933 in the 100th match between the two schools. A right-handed batsman and wicket-keeper, he subsequently played in one first-class match for the Minor Counties against the Indian tourists in 1936, making 13 and 0, and appeared for Bedfordshire.

WOODHOUSE, GEORGE EDWARD SEALY, who died suddenly on January 19, 1988, aged 63, was in 1949 Somerset's youngest captain, having shared the leadership in the previous year with N. S. Mitchell-Innes and J. W. Seamer. In the Marlborough XI from 1940 to 1942, he made steady progress as an all-rounder, with a century to his credit in 1941 against Wellington, sharing in a first-wicket stand of 184, a school record. By 1942 he was captain and the mainstay of the batting – his 72 against Rugby at Lord's was a match-saving innings – and the following year he won a war-time Blue at Cambridge, having averaged more than 60 in home matches at Fenner's.

Born and bred in the West Country, he made his début for Somerset against Middlesex at Taunton in 1946. Erratic and unpredictable as ever, Somerset in this match made 523 for nine declared, the centre-piece of which was a partnership of 200 for the fourth wicket between Woodhouse and Harold Gimblett, to which Woodhouse contributed 70, but after so promising a start he found time to play in only a limited number of matches in 1947 and 1948. His one century was made against Leicestershire at Leicester in 1947 and helped Somerset to a six-wicket victory. Assuming the captaincy in 1949, he usually relegated himself to the middle order in an effort to add substance to an unreliable batting side in what was a season of remarkable changes of fortune. Ten matches were lost in a row, but the arrival of the two schoolmasters, M. M. Walford and Hugh Watts, in August ushered in some weeks of stability and success. Woodhouse's batting method was based on orthodox lines, but he never really fulfilled his youthful promise, scoring 2,048 runs in 65 first-class matches for an average of 19.69. He represented Dorset & Wilts at rugby and identified with life in Dorset after giving up active sport.

WRIGLEY, OSCAR LLEWELLYN, who died in Wellington on December 26, 1987, played four first-class matches for Wellington and the New Zealand Air Force between 1939-40 and 1942-43. Though scoring only 81 in his four innings, he did have the satisfaction of a half-century, 52, for the Air Force against the Army in his last first-class innings. Later he contributed to the game as a selector of age-group representative teams.

In the 1988 Almanack, there was an obituary notice for J. W. Brook. We regret that this should not have appeared, and any distress caused by its publication is sincerely regretted. Additionally, the obituary notice of Herbert Trenholm, MBE was incorrectly recorded as Herbert Trentham. We apologise for both these errors.

THE LAWS OF CRICKET

(1980 CODE)

INDEX TO THE LAWS

Law 1. The Players ... 1182
Law 2. Substitutes and Runners: Batsman or Fieldsman Leaving the Field: Batsman Retiring: Batsman Commencing Innings ... 1182
Law 3. The Umpires ... 1183
Law 4. The Scorers ... 1185
Law 5. The Ball ... 1186
Law 6. The Bat ... 1186
Law 7. The Pitch ... 1186
Law 8. The Wickets ... 1187
Law 9. The Bowling, Popping and Return Creases ... 1187
Law 10. Rolling, Sweeping, Mowing, Watering the Pitch and Re-marking of Creases ... 1188
Law 11. Covering the Pitch ... 1189
Law 12. Innings ... 1189
Law 13. The Follow-on ... 1190
Law 14. Declarations ... 1190
Law 15. Start of Play ... 1190
Law 16. Intervals ... 1191
Law 17. Cessation of Play ... 1192
Law 18. Scoring ... 1193
Law 19. Boundaries ... 1194
Law 20. Lost Ball ... 1195
Law 21. The Result ... 1195
Law 22. The Over ... 1196
Law 23. Dead Ball ... 1197
Law 24. No-ball ... 1198
Law 25. Wide-ball ... 1199
Law 26. Bye and Leg-bye ... 1200
Law 27. Appeals ... 1200
Law 28. The Wicket is Down ... 1201
Law 29. Batsman Out of His Ground ... 1201
Law 30. Bowled ... 1201
Law 31. Timed Out ... 1202
Law 32. Caught ... 1202
Law 33. Handled the Ball ... 1203
Law 34. Hit the Ball Twice ... 1203
Law 35. Hit Wicket ... 1203
Law 36. Leg Before Wicket ... 1204
Law 37. Obstructing the Field ... 1204
Law 38. Run Out ... 1205
Law 39. Stumped ... 1205
Law 40. The Wicket-keeper ... 1205
Law 41. The Fieldsman ... 1206
Law 42. Unfair Play ... 1206
42.1. Responsibilities of Captains ... 1206
42.2. Responsibilities of Umpires ... 1206
42.3. Intervention by the Umpire ... 1206
42.4. Lifting the Seam ... 1207
42.5. Changing the Condition of the Ball ... 1207
42.6. Incommoding the Striker ... 1207

42.7. Obstruction of a Batsman in Running 1207
42.8. The Bowling of Fast Short-pitched Balls 1207
42.9. The Bowling of Fast High Full Pitches 1207
42.10. Time Wasting 1208
42.11. Players Damaging the Pitch 1208
42.12. Batsman Unfairly Stealing a Run 1208
42.13. Player's Conduct 1208

LAW 1. THE PLAYERS

1. Number of Players and Captain

A match is played between two sides each of eleven players, one of whom shall be captain. In the event of the captain not being available at any time, a deputy shall act for him.

2. Nomination of Players

Before the toss for innings, the captain shall nominate his players, who may not thereafter be changed without the consent of the opposing captain.

Note

(a) More or Less than Eleven Players a Side
A match may be played by agreement between sides of more or less than eleven players, but not more than eleven players may field.

LAW 2. SUBSTITUTES AND RUNNERS: BATSMAN OR FIELDSMAN LEAVING THE FIELD: BATSMAN RETIRING: BATSMAN COMMENCING INNINGS

1. Substitutes

In normal circumstances, a substitute shall be allowed to field only for a player who satisfies the umpire that he has become injured or become ill during the match. However, in very exceptional circumstances, the umpires may use their discretion to allow a substitute for a player who has to leave the field or does not take the field for other wholly acceptable reasons, subject to consent being given by the opposing captain. If a player wishes to change his shirt, boots, etc., he may leave the field to do so (no changing on the field), but no substitute will be allowed.

2. Objection to Substitutes

The opposing captain shall have no right of objection to any player acting as substitute in the field, nor as to where he shall field, although he may object to the substitute acting as wicket-keeper.

Experimental Law: The opposing captain shall have no right of objection to any player acting as substitute on the field, nor as to where he shall field; however no substitute shall act as wicket-keeper. (It has been recommended that this Experimental Law should apply in all levels of cricket from April 1, 1989).

3. Substitute not to Bat or Bowl

A substitute shall not be allowed to bat or bowl.

4. A Player for whom a Substitute has Acted

A player may bat, bowl or field even though a substitute has acted for him.

5. Runner

A runner shall be allowed for a batsman who, during the match, is incapacitated by illness or injury. The person acting as runner shall be a member of the batting side and shall, if possible, have already batted in that innings.

6. Runner's Equipment

ıe player acting as runner for an injured batsman shall wear the same external protective uipment as the injured batsman.

7. Transgression of the Laws by an Injured Batsman or Runner

n injured batsman may be out should his runner break any one of Laws 33 (Handled the Ball), (Obstructing the Field) or 38 (Run Out). As striker he remains himself subject to the Laws. ırthermore, should he be out of his ground for any purpose and the wicket at the wicket-eper's end be put down he shall be out under Law 38 (Run Out) or Law 39 (Stumped), espective of the position of the other batsman or the runner, and no runs shall be scored.

When not the striker, the injured batsman is out of the game and shall stand where he does not terfere with the play. Should he bring himself into the game in any way, then he shall suffer the nalties that any transgression of the Laws demands.

8. Fieldsman Leaving the Field

o fieldsman shall leave the field or return during a session of play without the consent of the npire at the bowler's end. The umpire's consent is also necessary if a substitute is required for a ıldsman, when his side returns to the field after an interval. If a member of the fielding side aves the field or fails to return after an interval and is absent from the field for longer than teen minutes, he shall not be permitted to bowl after his return until he has been on the field r at least that length of playing time for which he was absent. This restriction shall not apply at e start of a new day's play.

9. Batsman Leaving the Field or Retiring

batsman may leave the field or retire at any time owing to illness, injury or other unavoidable use, having previously notified the umpire at the bowler's end. He may resume his innings at e fall of a wicket, which for the purposes of this Law shall include the retirement of another tsman.

If he leaves the field or retires for any other reason he may resume his innings only with the nsent of the opposing captain.

When a batsman has left the field or retired and is unable to return owing to illness, injury or her unavoidable cause, his innings is to be recorded as "retired, not out". Otherwise it is to be corded as "retired, out".

0. Commencement of a Batsman's Innings

batsman shall be considered to have commenced his innings once he has stepped on to the eld of play.

ote

(a) Substitutes and Runners

For the purpose of these Laws, allowable illnesses or injuries are those which occur at any time after the nomination by the captains of their teams.

LAW 3. THE UMPIRES

1. Appointment

efore the toss for innings, two umpires shall be appointed, one for each end, to control the ame with absolute impartiality as required by the Laws.

2. Change of Umpires

o umpire shall be changed during a match without the consent of both captains.

3. Special Conditions

Before the toss for innings, the umpires shall agree with both captains on any special conditio affecting the conduct of the match.

4. The Wickets

The umpires shall satisfy themselves before the start of the match that the wickets are prope pitched.

5. Clock or Watch

The umpires shall agree between themselves and inform both captains before the start of t match on the watch or clock to be followed during the match.

6. Conduct and Implements

Before and during a match the umpires shall ensure that the conduct of the game and t implements used are strictly in accordance with the Laws.

7. Fair and Unfair Play

The umpires shall be the sole judges of fair and unfair play.

•

8. Fitness of Ground, Weather and Light

(a) The umpires shall be the sole judges of the fitness of the ground, weather and light fo play.

(i) However, before deciding to suspend play, or not to start play, or not to resum play after an interval or stoppage, the umpires shall establish whether bo captains (the batsmen at the wicket may deputise for their captain) wish commence or to continue in the prevailing conditions; if so, their wishes shall b met.

(ii) In addition, if during play the umpires decide that the light is unfit, only th batting side shall have the option of continuing play. After agreeing to continue play in unfit light conditions, the captain of the batting side (or a batsman at th wicket) may appeal against the light to the umpires, who shall uphold the appe only if, in their opinion, the light has deteriorated since the agreement to continu was made.

(b) After any suspension of play, the umpires, unaccompanied by any of the players c officials, shall, on their own initiative, carry out an inspection immediately the conditior improve and shall continue to inspect at intervals. Immediately the umpires decide tha play is possible they shall call upon the players to resume the game.

9. Exceptional Circumstances

In exceptional circumstances, other than those of weather, ground or light, the umpires ma decide to suspend or abandon play. Before making such a decision the umpires shall establish, the circumstances allow, whether both captains (the batsmen at the wicket may deputise fc their captain) wish to continue in the prevailing conditions; if so, their wishes shall be me

10. Position of Umpires

The umpires shall stand where they can best see any act upon which their decision may b required.

Subject to this over-riding consideration, the umpire at the bowler's end shall stand where h does not interfere with either the bowler's run-up or the striker's view.

The umpire at the striker's end may elect to stand on the off instead of the leg side of th pitch, provided he informs the captain of the fielding side and the striker of his intention to d so.

11. Umpires Changing Ends

The umpires shall change ends after each side has had one innings.

12. Disputes

All disputes shall be determined by the umpires, and if they disagree the actual state of things shall continue.

13. Signals

The following code of signals shall be used by umpires who will wait until a signal has been answered by a scorer before allowing the game to proceed.

Boundary	– by waving the arm from side to side.
Boundary 6	– by raising both arms above the head.
Bye	– by raising an open hand above the head.
Dead Ball	– by crossing and re-crossing the wrists below the waist.
Leg-bye	– by touching a raised knee with the hand.
No-ball	– by extending one arm horizontally.
Out	– by raising the index finger above the head. If not out, the umpire shall call "not out".
Short run	– by bending the arm upwards and by touching the nearer shoulder with the tips of the fingers.
Wide	– by extending both arms horizontally.

14. Correctness of Scores

The umpires shall be responsible for satisfying themselves on the correctness of the scores throughout and at the conclusion of the match. See Law 21.6 (Correctness of Result).

Notes

(a) Attendance of Umpires
The umpires should be present on the ground and report to the ground executive or the equivalent at least thirty minutes before the start of a day's play.

(b) Consultation between Umpires and Scorers
Consultation between umpires and scorers over doubtful points is essential.

(c) Fitness of Ground
The umpires shall consider the ground as unfit for play when it is so wet or slippery as to deprive the bowlers of a reasonable foothold, the fieldsmen, other than the deep-fielders, of the power of free movement, or the batsmen of the ability to play their strokes or to run between the wickets. Play should not be suspended merely because the grass and the ball are wet and slippery.

(d) Fitness of Weather and Light
The umpires should suspend play only when they consider that the conditions are so bad that it is unreasonable or dangerous to continue.

LAW 4. THE SCORERS

1. Recording Runs

All runs scored shall be recorded by scorers appointed for the purpose. Where there are two scorers they shall frequently check to ensure that the score sheets agree.

2. Acknowledging Signals

The scorers shall accept and immediately acknowledge all instructions and signals given to them by the umpires.

LAW 5. THE BALL

1. Weight and Size

The ball, when new, shall weigh not less than $5\frac{1}{2}$ ounces/155.9g, nor more than $5\frac{3}{4}$ ounces/163g and shall measure not less than $8\frac{13}{16}$ inches/22.4cm, nor more than 9 inches/22.9cm in circumference.

2. Approval of Balls

All balls used in matches shall be approved by the umpires and captains before the start of the match.

3. New Ball

Subject to agreement to the contrary, having been made before the toss, either captain may demand a new ball at the start of each innings.

4. New Ball in Match of Three or More Days' Duration

In a match of three or more days' duration, the captain of the fielding side may demand a new ball after the prescribed number of overs has been bowled with the old one. The governing body for cricket in the country concerned shall decide the number of overs applicable in that country which shall be not less than 75 six-ball overs (55 eight-ball overs).

5. Ball Lost or Becoming Unfit for Play

In the event of a ball during play being lost or, in the opinion of the umpires, becoming unfit for play, the umpires shall allow it to be replaced by one that in their opinion has had a similar amount of wear. If a ball is to be replaced, the umpires shall inform the batsman.

Note

(a) Specifications

The specifications, as described in 1 above, shall apply to top-grade balls only. The following degrees of tolerance will be acceptable for other grades of ball.

(i) *Men's Grades 2–4*
Weight: $5\frac{5}{16}$ ounces/150g to $5\frac{13}{16}$ ounces/165g.
Size: $8\frac{11}{16}$ inches/22.0cm to $9\frac{1}{16}$ inches/23.0cm.

(ii) *Women's*
Weight: $4\frac{15}{16}$ ounces/140g to $5\frac{5}{16}$ ounces/150g.
Size: $8\frac{1}{4}$ inches/21.0cm to $8\frac{7}{8}$ inches/22.5cm.

(iii) *Junior*
Weight: $4\frac{5}{16}$ ounces/133g to $5\frac{1}{16}$ ounces/143g.
Size: $8\frac{1}{16}$ inches/20.5cm to $8\frac{11}{16}$ inches/22.0cm.

LAW 6. THE BAT

1. Width and Length

The bat overall shall not be more than 38 inches/96.5cm in length; the blade of the bat shall be made of wood and shall not exceed $4\frac{1}{4}$ inches/10.8cm at the widest part.

Note

(a) The blade of the bat may be covered with material for protection, strengthening or repair. Such material shall not exceed $\frac{1}{16}$ inch/1.56mm in thickness.

LAW 7. THE PITCH

1. Area of Pitch

The pitch is the area between the bowling creases – see Law 9 (The Bowling and Popping Creases). It shall measure 5ft/1.52m in width on either side of a line joining the centre of the middle stumps of the wickets – see Law 8 (The Wickets).

2. Selection and Preparation

Before the toss for innings, the executive of the ground shall be responsible for the selection and preparation of the pitch; thereafter the umpires shall control its use and maintenance.

3. Changing Pitch

The pitch shall not be changed during a match unless it becomes unfit for play, and then only with the consent of both captains.

4. Non-Turf Pitches

In the event of a non-turf pitch being used, the following shall apply:

(a) Length: That of the playing surface to a minimum of 58ft/17.68m.

(b) Width: That of the playing surface to a minimum of 6ft/1.83m.

See Law 10 (Rolling, Sweeping, Mowing, Watering the Pitch and Re-marking of Creases) Note (a).

LAW 8. THE WICKETS

1. Width and Pitching

Two sets of wickets, each 9 inches/22.86cm wide, and consisting of three wooden stumps with two wooden bails upon the top, shall be pitched opposite and parallel to each other at a distance of 22 yards/20.12m between the centres of the two middle stumps.

2. Size of Stumps

The stumps shall be of equal and sufficient size to prevent the ball from passing between them. Their tops shall be 28 inches/71.1cm above the ground, and shall be dome-shaped except for the bail grooves.

3. Size of Bails

The bails shall be each $4\frac{3}{8}$ inches/11.1cm in length and when in position on the top of the stumps shall not project more than $\frac{1}{2}$ inch/1.3cm above them.

Notes

(a) Dispensing with Bails
In a high wind the umpires may decide to dispense with the use of bails.

(b) Junior Cricket
For junior cricket, as defined by the local governing body, the following measurements for the wickets shall apply:

Width – 8 inches/20.32cm.
Pitched – 21 yards/19.20m.
Height – 27 inches/68.58cm.
Bails – each $3\frac{7}{8}$ inches/9.84cm in length and should not project more than $\frac{1}{2}$ inch/1.3cm above the stumps.

LAW 9. THE BOWLING, POPPING AND RETURN CREASES

1. The Bowling Crease

The bowling crease shall be marked in line with the stumps at each end and shall be 8 feet 8 inches/2.64m in length, with the stumps in the centre.

2. The Popping Crease

The popping crease, which is the back edge of the crease marking, shall be in front of and parallel with the bowling crease. It shall have the back edge of the crease marking 4 feet/1.22m from the centre of the stumps and shall extend to a minimum of 6 feet/1.83m on either side of the line of the wicket.

The popping crease shall be considered to be unlimited in length.

3. The Return Crease

The return crease marking, of which the inside edge is the crease, shall be at each end of th bowling crease and at right angles to it. The return crease shall be marked to a minimum of feet/1.22m behind the wicket and shall be considered to be unlimited in length. A forwar extension shall be marked to the popping crease.

LAW 10. ROLLING, SWEEPING, MOWING, WATERING TH PITCH AND RE-MARKING OF CREASES

1. Rolling

During the match the pitch may be rolled at the request of the captain of the batting side, for period of not more than seven minutes before the start of each innings, other than the firs innings of the match, and before the start of each day's play. In addition, if, after the toss an before the first innings of the match, the start is delayed, the captain of the batting side sha have the right to have the pitch rolled for not more than seven minutes.

The pitch shall not otherwise be rolled during the match.

The seven minutes' rolling permitted before the start of a day's play shall take place not earlie than half an hour before the start of play and the captain of the batting side may delay suc rolling until ten minutes before the start of play should he so desire.

If a captain declares an innings closed less than fifteen minutes before the resumption of play and the other captain is thereby prevented from exercising his option of seven minutes' rollin or if he is so prevented for any other reason, the time for rolling shall be taken out of the norma playing time.

2. Sweeping

Such sweeping of the pitch as is necessary during the match shall be done so that the seve minutes allowed for rolling the pitch, provided for in 1 above, is not affected.

3. Mowing

(a) Responsibilities of Ground Authority and of Umpires

All mowings which are carried out before the toss for innings shall be the responsibility o the ground authority; thereafter they shall be carried out under the supervision of th umpires. See Law 7.2 (Selection and Preparation).

(b) Initial Mowing

The pitch shall be mown before play begins on the day the match is scheduled to start, o in the case of a delayed start on the day the match is expected to start. See 3(a) above (Responsibilities of Ground Authority and of Umpires).

(c) Subsequent Mowings in a Match of Two or More Days' Duration

In a match of two or more days' duration, the pitch shall be mown daily before play begins Should this mowing not take place because of weather conditions, rest days or othe reasons, the pitch shall be mown on the first day on which the match is resumed.

(d) Mowing of the Outfield in a Match of Two or More Days' Duration

In order to ensure that conditions are as similar as possible for both sides, the outfield shal normally be mown before the commencement of play on each day of the match, if grounc and weather conditions allow. See Note (b) to this Law.

4. Watering

The pitch shall not be watered during a match.

5. Re-marking Creases

Whenever possible the creases shall be re-marked.

6. Maintenance of Foot-holes

In wet weather, the umpires shall ensure that the holes made by the bowlers and batsmen are cleaned out and dried whenever necessary to facilitate play. In matches of two or more days' uration, the umpires shall allow, if necessary, the re-turfing of foot-holes made by the bowler in is delivery stride, or the use of quick-setting fillings for the same purpose, before the start of ach day's play.

7. Securing of Footholds and Maintenance of Pitch

During play, the umpires shall allow either batsman to beat the pitch with his bat and players to ecure their footholds by the use of sawdust, provided that no damage to the pitch is so caused, nd Law 42 (Unfair Play) is not contravened.

Notes

(a) Non-turf Pitches

The above Law 10 applies to turf pitches.

The game is played on non-turf pitches in many countries at various levels. Whilst the conduct of the game on these surfaces should always be in accordance with the Laws of Cricket, it is recognised that it may sometimes be necessary for governing bodies to lay down special playing conditions to suit the type of non-turf pitch used in their country.

In matches played against touring teams, any special playing conditions should be agreed in advance by both parties.

(b) Mowing of the Outfield in a Match of Two or More Days' Duration

If, for reasons other than ground and weather conditions, daily and complete mowing is not possible, the ground authority shall notify the captains and umpires, before the toss for innings, of the procedure to be adopted for such mowing during the match.

(c) Choice of Roller

If there is more than one roller available, the captain of the batting side shall have a choice.

LAW 11. COVERING THE PITCH

1. Before the Start of a Match

Before the start of a match, complete covering of the pitch shall be allowed.

2. During a Match

The pitch shall not be completely covered during a match unless prior arrangement or regulations so provide.

3. Covering Bowlers' Run-up

Whenever possible, the bowlers' run-up shall be covered, but the covers so used shall not extend further than 4 feet/1.22m in front of the popping crease.

Note

(a) Removal of Covers

The covers should be removed as promptly as possible whenever the weather permits.

LAW 12. INNINGS

1. Number of Innings

A match shall be of one or two innings of each side according to agreement reached before the start of play.

2. Alternate Innings

In a two-innings match each side shall take their innings alternately except in the case provided for in Law 13 (The Follow-on).

3. The Toss

The captains shall toss for the choice of innings on the field of play not later than fifteen minutes before the time scheduled for the match to start, or before the time agreed upon for play to start.

4. Choice of Innings

The winner of the toss shall notify his decision to bat or to field to the opposing captain not later than ten minutes before the time scheduled for the match to start, or before the time agreed upon for play to start. The decision shall not thereafter be altered.

5. Continuation after One Innings of Each Side

Despite the terms of 1 above, in a one-innings match, when a result has been reached on the first innings, the captains may agree to the continuation of play if, in their opinion, there is a prospect of carrying the game to a further issue in the time left. See Law 21 (Result).

Notes

(a) Limited Innings – One-innings Match
In a one-innings match, each innings may, by agreement, be limited by a number of overs or by a period of time.

(b) Limited Innings – Two-innings Match
In a two-innings match, the first innings of each side may, by agreement, be limited to a number of overs or by a period of time.

LAW 13. THE FOLLOW-ON

1. Lead on First Innings

In a two-innings match the side which bats first and leads by 200 runs in a match of five days or more, by 150 runs in a three-day or four-day match, by 100 runs in a two-day match, or by 75 runs in a one-day match, shall have the option of requiring the other side to follow their innings.

2. Day's Play Lost

If no play takes place on the first day of a match of two or more days' duration, 1 above shall apply in accordance with the number of days' play remaining from the actual start of the match.

LAW 14. DECLARATIONS

1. Time of Declaration

The captain of the batting side may declare an innings closed at any time during a match, irrespective of its duration.

2. Forfeiture of Second Innings

A captain may forfeit his second innings, provided his decision to do so is notified to the opposing captain and umpires in sufficient time to allow seven minutes' rolling of the pitch. See Law 10 (Rolling, Sweeping, Mowing, Watering the Pitch and Re-marking of Creases). The normal ten-minute interval between innings shall be applied.

LAW 15. START OF PLAY

1. Call of Play

At the start of each innings and of each day's play, and on the resumption of play after any interval or interruption, the umpire at the bowler's end shall call "play".

2. Practice on the Field

At no time on any day of the match shall there be any bowling or batting practice on the pitch.

No practice may take place on the field if, in the opinion of the umpires, it could result in a waste of time.

3. Trial Run-up

No bowler shall have a trial run-up after "play" has been called in any session of play, except at the fall of a wicket when an umpire may allow such a trial run-up if he is satisfied that it will not cause any waste of time.

LAW 16. INTERVALS

1. Length

The umpire shall allow such intervals as have been agreed upon for meals, and ten minutes between each innings.

2. Luncheon Interval – Innings Ending or Stoppage within Ten Minutes of Interval

If an innings ends or there is a stoppage caused by weather or bad light within ten minutes of the agreed time for the luncheon interval, the interval shall be taken immediately.

The time remaining in the session of play shall be added to the agreed length of the interval but no extra allowance shall be made for the ten-minute interval between innings.

3. Tea Interval – Innings Ending or Stoppage within Thirty Minutes of Interval

If an innings ends or there is a stoppage caused by weather or bad light within thirty minutes of the agreed time for the tea interval, the interval shall be taken immediately.

The interval shall be of the agreed length and, if applicable, shall include the ten-minute interval between innings.

4. Tea Interval – Continuation of Play

If, at the agreed time for the tea interval, nine wickets are down, play shall continue for a period not exceeding thirty minutes or until the innings is concluded.

5. Tea Interval – Agreement to Forgo

At any time during the match, the captains may agree to forgo a tea interval.

6. Intervals for Drinks

If both captains agree before the start of a match that intervals for drinks may be taken, the option to take such intervals shall be available to either side. These intervals shall be restricted to one per session, shall be kept as short as possible, shall not be taken in the last hour of the match, and in any case shall not exceed five minutes.

The agreed times for these intervals shall be strictly adhered to, except that if a wicket falls within five minutes of the agreed time then drinks shall be taken out immediately.

If an innings ends or there is a stoppage caused by weather or bad light within thirty minutes of the agreed time for a drinks interval, there will be no interval for drinks in that session.

At any time during the match the captains may agree to forgo any such drinks interval.

Notes

(a) Tea Interval – One-day Match

In a one-day match, a specific time for the tea interval need not necessarily be arranged, and it may be agreed to take this interval between the innings of a one-innings match.

(b) Changing the Agreed Time of Intervals

In the event of the ground, weather or light conditions causing a suspension of play, the umpires, after consultation with the captains, may decide in the interests of time-saving to bring forward the time of the luncheon or tea interval.

LAW 17. CESSATION OF PLAY

1. Call of Time

The umpire at the bowler's end shall call "time" on the cessation of play before any interval or interruption of play, at the end of each day's play, and at the conclusion of the match. See Law 27 (Appeals).

2. Removal of Bails

After the call of "time", the umpires shall remove the bails from both wickets.

3. Starting a Last Over

The last over before an interval or the close of play shall be started provided the umpire, after walking at his normal pace, has arrived at his position behind the stumps at the bowler's end before time has been reached.

4. Completion of the Last Over of a Session

The last over before an interval or the close of play shall be completed unless a batsman is out or retires during that over within two minutes of the interval or the close of play or unless the players have occasion to leave the field.

5. Completion of the Last Over of a Match

An over in progress at the close of play on the final day of a match shall be completed at the request of either captain, even if a wicket falls after time has been reached.

If, during the last over, the players have occasion to leave the field, the umpires shall call "time" and there shall be no resumption of play and the match shall be at an end.

6. Last Hour of Match – Number of Overs

The umpires shall indicate when one hour of playing time of the match remains according to the agreed hours of play. The next over after that moment shall be the first of a minimum of 20 six-ball overs (15 eight-ball overs), provided a result is not reached earlier or there is no interval or interruption of play.

7. Last Hour of Match – Intervals between Innings and Interruptions of Play

If, at the commencement of the last hour of the match, an interval or interruption of play is in progress or if, during the last hour, there is an interval between innings or an interruption of play, the minimum number of overs to be bowled on the resumption of play shall be reduced in proportion to the duration, within the last hour of the match, of any such interval or interruption.

The minimum number of overs to be bowled after the resumption of play shall be calculated as follows:

(a) In the case of an interval or interruption of play being in progress at the commencement of the last hour of the match, or in the case of a first interval or interruption, a deduction shall be made from the minimum of 20 six-ball overs (or 15 eight-ball overs).

(b) If there is a later interval or interruption, a further deduction shall be made from the minimum number of overs which should have been bowled following the last resumption of play.

(c) These deductions shall be based on the following factors:

(i) The number of overs already bowled in the last hour of the match or, in the case of a later interval or interruption, in the last session of play.

(ii) The number of overs lost as a result of the interval or interruption allowing one six-ball over for every full three minutes (or one eight-ball over for every full four minutes) of interval or interruption.

(iii) Any over left uncompleted at the end of an innings to be excluded from these calculations.

(iv) Any over left uncompleted at the start of an interruption of play to be completed when play is resumed and to count as one over bowled.

(v) An interval to start with the end of an innings and to end ten minutes later; an interruption to start on the call of "time" and to end on the call of "play".

(d) In the event of an innings being completed and a new innings commencing during the last hour of the match, the number of overs to be bowled in the new innings shall be calculated on the basis of one six-ball over for every three minutes or part thereof remaining for play (or one eight-ball over for every four minutes or part thereof remaining for play); or alternatively on the basis that sufficient overs be bowled to enable the full minimum quota of overs to be completed under circumstances governed by (a), (b) and (c) above. In all such cases the alternative which allows the greater number of overs shall be employed.

8. Bowler Unable to Complete an Over during Last Hour of the Match

If, for any reason, a bowler is unable to complete an over during the period of play referred to in 6 above, Law 22.7 (Bowler Incapacitated or Suspended during an Over) shall apply.

LAW 18. SCORING

1. A Run

The score shall be reckoned by runs. A run is scored:

(a) So often as the batsmen, after a hit or at any time while the ball is in play, shall have crossed and made good their ground from end to end.

(b) When a boundary is scored. See Law 19 (Boundaries).

(c) When penalty runs are awarded. See 6 below.

2. Short Runs

(a) If either batsman runs a short run, the umpire shall call and signal "one short" as soon as the ball becomes dead and that run shall not be scored. A run is short if a batsman fails to make good his ground on turning for a further run.

(b) Although a short run shortens the succeeding one, the latter, if completed, shall count.

(c) If either or both batsmen deliberately run short the umpire shall, as soon as he sees that the fielding side have no chance of dismissing either batsman, call and signal "dead ball" and disallow any runs attempted or previously scored. The batsmen shall return to their original ends.

(d) If both batsmen run short in one and the same run, only one run shall be deducted.

(e) Only if 3 or more runs are attempted can more than one be short and then, subject to (c) and (d) above, all runs so called shall be disallowed. If there has been more than one short run the umpires shall instruct the scorers as to the number of runs disallowed.

3. Striker Caught

If the striker is caught, no run shall be scored.

4. Batsman Run Out

If a batsman is run out, only that run which was being attempted shall not be scored. If, however, an injured striker himself is run out, no runs shall be scored. See Law 2.7 (Transgression of the Laws by an Injured Batsman or Runner).

5. Batsman Obstructing the Field

If a batsman is out Obstructing the Field, any runs completed before the obstruction occurs shall be scored unless such obstruction prevents a catch being made, in which case no runs shall be scored.

6. Runs Scored for Penalties

Runs shall be scored for penalties under Laws 20 (Lost Ball), 24 (No-ball), 25 (Wide-ball), 41.1 (Fielding the Ball) and for boundary allowances under Law 19 (Boundaries).

7. Batsman Returning to Wicket he has Left

If, while the ball is in play, the batsmen have crossed in running, neither shall return to the wicket he has left, even though a short run has been called or no run has been scored as in the case of a catch. Batsmen, however, shall return to the wickets they originally left in the cases of a boundary and of any disallowance of runs and of an injured batsman being, himself, run out. See Law 2.7 (Transgression by an Injured Batsman or Runner).

Note

(a) Short Run
A striker taking stance in front of his popping crease may run from that point without penalty.

LAW 19. BOUNDARIES

1. The Boundary of the Playing Area

Before the toss for innings, the umpires shall agree with both captains on the boundary of the playing area. The boundary shall, if possible, be marked by a white line, a rope laid on the ground, or a fence. If flags or posts only are used to mark a boundary, the imaginary line joining such points shall be regarded as the boundary. An obstacle, or person, within the playing area shall not be regarded as a boundary unless so decided by the umpires before the toss for innings. Sightscreens within, or partially within, the playing area shall be regarded as the boundary and when the ball strikes or passes within or under or directly over any part of the screen, a boundary shall be scored.

2. Runs Scored for Boundaries

Before the toss for innings, the umpires shall agree with both captains the runs to be allowed for boundaries, and in deciding the allowance for them, the umpires and captains shall be guided by the prevailing custom of the ground. The allowance for a boundary shall normally be 4 runs, and 6 runs for all hits pitching over and clear of the boundary line or fence, even though the ball has been previously touched by a fieldsman. 6 runs shall also be scored if a fieldsman, after catching a ball, carries it over the boundary. See Law 32 (Caught) Note (a). 6 runs shall not be scored when a ball struck by the striker hits a sightscreen full pitch if the screen is within, or partially within, the playing area, but if the ball is struck directly over a sightscreen so situated, 6 runs shall be scored.

3. A Boundary

A boundary shall be scored and signalled by the umpire at the bowler's end whenever, in his opinion:

(a) A ball in play touches or crosses the boundary, however marked.

(b) A fieldsman with ball in hand touches or grounds any part of his person on or over a boundary line.

(c) A fieldsman with ball in hand grounds any part of his person over a boundary fence or board. This allows the fieldsman to touch or lean on or over a boundary fence or board in preventing a boundary.

4. Runs Exceeding Boundary Allowance

The runs completed at the instant the ball reaches the boundary shall count if they exceed the boundary allowance.

5. Overthrows or Wilful Act of a Fieldsman

If the boundary results from an overthrow or from the wilful act of a fieldsman, any runs already completed and the allowance shall be added to the score. The run in progress shall count provided that the batsmen have crossed at the instant of the throw or act.

Note

(a) Position of Sightscreens
Sightscreens should, if possible, be positioned wholly outside the playing area, as near as possible to the boundary line.

LAW 20. LOST BALL

1. Runs Scored

If a ball in play cannot be found or recovered, any fieldsman may call "lost ball" when 6 runs shall be added to the score; but if more than 6 have been run before "lost ball" is called, as many runs as have been completed shall be scored. The run in progress shall count provided that the batsmen have crossed at the instant of the call of "lost ball".

2. How Scored

The runs shall be added to the score of the striker if the ball has been struck, but otherwise to the score of byes, leg-byes, no-balls or wides as the case may be.

LAW 21. THE RESULT

1. A Win – Two-innings Matches

The side which has scored a total of runs in excess of that scored by the opposing side in its two completed innings shall be the winners.

2. A Win–One-innings Matches

(a) One-innings matches, unless played out as in 1 above, shall be decided on the first innings, but see Law 12.5 (Continuation after One Innings of Each Side).

(b) If the captains agree to continue play after the completion of one innings of each side in accordance with Law 12.5 (Continuation after One Innings of Each Side) and a result is not achieved on the second innings, the first innings result shall stand.

3. Umpires Awarding a Match

(a) A match shall be lost by a side which, during the match, (i) refuses to play, or (ii) concedes defeat, and the umpires shall award the match to the other side.

(b) Should both batsmen at the wickets or the fielding side leave the field at any time without the agreement of the umpires, this shall constitute a refusal to play and, on appeal, the umpires shall award the match to the other side in accordance with (a) above.

4. A Tie

The result of a match shall be a tie when the scores are equal at the conclusion of play, but only if the side batting last has completed its innings.

If the scores of the completed first innings of a one-day match are equal, it shall be a tie but only if the match has not been played out to a further conclusion.

5. A Draw

A match not determined in any of the ways as in 1, 2, 3 and 4 above shall count as a draw.

6. Correctness of Result

Any decision as to the correctness of the scores shall be the responsibility of the umpires. See Law 3.14 (Correctness of Scores).

If, after the umpires and players have left the field in the belief that the match has been concluded, the umpires decide that a mistake in scoring has occurred, which affects the result, and provided time has not been reached, they shall order play to resume and to continue until the agreed finishing time unless a result is reached earlier.

If the umpires decide that a mistake has occurred and time has been reached, the umpires shall immediately inform both captains of the necessary corrections to the scores and, if applicable, to the result.

LAW 26. BYE AND LEG-BYE

1. Byes

If the ball, not having been called "wide" or "no-ball", passes the striker without touching his bat or person, and any runs are obtained, the umpire shall signal "bye" and the run or runs shall be credited as such to the batting side.

2. Leg-byes

If the ball, not having been called "wide" or "no-ball", is unintentionally deflected by the striker's dress or person, except a hand holding the bat, and any runs are obtained the umpire shall signal "leg-bye" and the run or runs so scored shall be credited as such to the batting side.

Such leg-byes shall be scored only if, in the opinion of the umpire, the striker has:

(a) Attempted to play the ball with his bat; or

(b) Tried to avoid being hit by the ball.

3. Disallowance of Leg-byes

In the case of a deflection by the striker's person, other than in 2(a) and (b) above, the umpire shall call and signal "dead ball" as soon as 1 run has been completed or when it is clear that a run is not being attempted, or the ball has reached the boundary.

On the call and signal of "dead ball" the batsmen shall return to their original ends and no runs shall be allowed.

LAW 27. APPEALS

1. Time of Appeals

The umpires shall not give a batsman out unless appealed to by the other side which shall be done prior to the bowler beginning his run-up or bowling action to deliver the next ball. Under Law 23.1 (f) (The Ball Becomes Dead), the ball is dead on "over" being called; this does not, however, invalidate an appeal made prior to the first ball of the following over provided "time" has not been called–see Law 17.1 (Call of Time).

2. An Appeal "How's That?"

An appeal "How's That?" shall cover all ways of being out.

3. Answering Appeals

The umpire at the bowler's wicket shall answer appeals before the other umpire in all cases except those arising out of Law 35 (Hit Wicket) or Law 39 (Stumped) or Law 38 (Run Out) when this occurs at the striker's wicket.

When either umpire has given a batsman not out, the other umpire shall, within his jurisdiction, answer the appeal or a further appeal, provided it is made in time in accordance with 1 above (Time of Appeals).

4. Consultation by Umpires

An umpire may consult with the other umpire on a point of fact which the latter may have been in a better position to see and shall then give his decision. If, after consultation, there is still doubt remaining the decision shall be in favour of the batsman.

5. Batsman Leaving his Wicket under a Misapprehension

The umpires shall intervene if satisfied that a batsman, not having been given out, has left his wicket under a misapprehension that he has been dismissed.

6. Umpire's Decision

The umpire's decision is final. He may alter his decision, provided that such alteration is made promptly.

7. Withdrawal of an Appeal

In exceptional circumstances the captain of the fielding side may seek permission of the umpire to withdraw an appeal provided the outgoing batsman has not left the playing area. If this is allowed, the umpire shall cancel his decision.

LAW 28. THE WICKET IS DOWN

1. Wicket Down

The wicket is down if:

(a) Either the ball or the striker's bat or person completely removes either bail from the top of the stumps. A disturbance of a bail, whether temporary or not, shall not constitute a complete removal, but the wicket is down if a bail in falling lodges between two of the stumps.

(b) Any player completely removes with his hand or arm a bail from the top of the stumps, provided that the ball is held in that hand or in the hand of the arm so used.

(c) When both bails are off, a stump is struck out of the ground by the ball, or a player strikes or pulls a stump out of the ground, provided that the ball is held in the hand(s) or in the hand of the arm so used.

2. One Bail Off

If one bail is off, it shall be sufficient for the purpose of putting the wicket down to remove the remaining bail, or to strike or pull any of the three stumps out of the ground in any of the ways stated in 1 above.

3. All the Stumps Out of the Ground

If all the stumps are out of the ground, the fielding side shall be allowed to put back one or more stumps in order to have an opportunity of putting the wicket down.

4. Dispensing with Bails

If owing to the strength of the wind, it has been agreed to dispense with the bails in accordance with Law 8, Note (a) (Dispensing with Bails), the decision as to when the wicket is down is one for the umpires to decide on the facts before them. In such circumstances and if the umpires so decide, the wicket shall be held to be down even though a stump has not been struck out of the ground.

Note

(a) Remaking the Wicket

If the wicket is broken while the ball is in play, it is not the umpire's duty to remake the wicket until the ball has become dead–see Law 23 (Dead Ball). A member of the fielding side, however, may remake the wicket in such circumstances.

LAW 29. BATSMAN OUT OF HIS GROUND

1. When out of his Ground

A batsman shall be considered to be out of his ground unless some part of his bat in his hand or of his person is grounded behind the line of the popping crease.

LAW 30. BOWLED

1. Out Bowled

The striker shall be out *Bowled* if:

(a) His wicket is bowled down, even if the ball first touches his bat or person.

(b) He breaks his wicket by hitting or kicking the ball on to it before the completion of a stroke, or as a result of attempting to guard his wicket. See Law 34.1 (Out Hit the Ball Twice).

Note

(a) Out Bowled–Not lbw

The striker is out bowled if the ball is deflected on to his wicket even though a decision against him would be justified under Law 36 (lbw).

LAW 31. TIMED OUT

1. Out Timed Out

An incoming batsman shall be out *Timed Out* if he wilfully takes more than two minutes to come in–the two minutes being timed from the moment a wicket falls until the new batsman steps on to the field of play.

If this is not complied with and if the umpire is satisfied that the delay was wilful and if an appeal is made, the new batsman shall be given out by the umpire at the bowler's end.

2. Time to be Added

The time taken by the umpires to investigate the cause of the delay shall be added at the normal close of play.

Notes

(a) Entry in Scorebook

The correct entry in the scorebook when a batsman is given out under this Law is "timed out", and the bowler does not get credit for the wicket.

(b) Batsmen Crossing on the Field of Play

It is an essential duty of the captains to ensure that the in-going batsman passes the out-going one before the latter leaves the field of play.

LAW 32. CAUGHT

1. Out Caught

The striker shall be out *Caught* if the ball touches his bat or if it touches below the wrist his hand or glove, holding the bat, and is subsequently held by a fieldsman before it touches the ground.

2. A Fair Catch

A catch shall be considered to have been fairly made if:

(a) The fieldsman is within the field of play throughout the act of making the catch.

(i) The act of making the catch shall start from the time when the fieldsman first handles the ball and shall end when he both retains complete control over the further disposal of the ball and remains within the field of play.

(ii) In order to be within the field of play, the fieldsman may not touch or ground any part of his person on or over a boundary line. When the boundary is marked by a fence or board the fieldsman may not ground any part of his person over the boundary fence or board, but may touch or lean over the boundary fence or board in completing the catch.

(b) The ball is hugged to the body of the catcher or accidentally lodges in his dress or, in the case of the wicket-keeper, in his pads. However, a striker may not be caught if a ball lodges in a protective helmet worn by a fieldsman, in which case the umpire shall call and signal "dead ball". See Law 23 (Dead Ball).

(c) The ball does not touch the ground even though a hand holding it does so in effecting the catch.

(d) A fieldsman catches the ball, after it has been lawfully played a second time by the striker, but only if the ball has not touched the ground since being first struck.

(e) A fieldsman catches the ball after it has touched an umpire, another fieldsman or the other batsman. However, a striker may not be caught if a ball has touched a protective helmet worn by a fieldsman.

(f) The ball is caught off an obstruction within the boundary provided it has not previously been agreed to regard the obstruction as a boundary.

3. Scoring of Runs

If a striker is caught, no run shall be scored.

Notes

(a) Scoring from an Attempted Catch
When a fieldsman carrying the ball touches or grounds any part of his person on or over a boundary marked by a line, 6 runs shall be scored.

(b) Ball Still in Play
If a fieldsman releases the ball before he crosses the boundary, the ball will be considered to be still in play and it may be caught by another fieldsman. However, if the original fieldsman returns to the field of play and handles the ball, a catch may not be made.

LAW 33. HANDLED THE BALL

1. Out Handled the Ball

Either batsman on appeal shall be out *Handled the Ball* if he wilfully touches the ball while in play with the hand not holding the bat unless he does so with the consent of the opposite side.

Note

(a) Entry in Scorebook
The correct entry in the scorebook when a batsman is given out under this Law is "handled the ball', and the bowler does not get credit for the wicket.

LAW 34. HIT THE BALL TWICE

1. Out Hit the Ball Twice

The striker, on appeal, shall be out *Hit the Ball Twice* if, after the ball is struck or is stopped by any part of his person, he wilfully strikes it again with his bat or person except for the sole purpose of guarding his wicket: this he may do with his bat or any part of his person other than his hands, but see Law 37.2 (Obstructing a Ball From Being Caught).

For the purpose of this Law, a hand holding the bat shall be regarded as part of the bat.

2. Returning the Ball to a Fieldsman

The striker, on appeal, shall be out under this Law if, without the consent of the opposite side, he uses his bat or person to return the ball to any of the fielding side.

3. Runs from Ball Lawfully Struck Twice

No runs except those which result from an overthrow or penalty – see Law 41 (The Fieldsman) – shall be scored from a ball lawfully struck twice.

Notes

(a) Entry in Scorebook
The correct entry in the scorebook when the striker is given out under this Law is "hit the ball twice", and the bowler does not get credit for the wicket.

(b) Runs Credited to the Batsman
Any runs awarded under 3 above as a result of an overthrow or penalty shall be credited to the striker, provided the ball in the first instance has touched the bat, or, if otherwise, as extras.

LAW 35. HIT WICKET

1. Out Hit Wicket

The striker shall be out *Hit Wicket* if, while the ball is in play:

(a) His wicket is broken with any part of his person, dress, or equipment as a result of any action taken by him in preparing to receive or in receiving a delivery, or in setting off for his first run, immediately after playing, or playing at, the ball.

10. Time Wasting

Any form of time wasting is unfair.

(a) In the event of the captain of the fielding side wasting time or allowing any member of his side to waste time, the umpire at the bowler's end shall adopt the following procedure:

(i) In the first instance he shall caution the captain of the fielding side and inform the other umpire of what has occurred.

(ii) If this caution is ineffective he shall repeat the above procedure and indicate to the captain that this is a final warning.

(iii) The umpire shall report the occurrence to the captain of the batting side as soon as the players leave the field for an interval.

(iv) Should the above procedure prove ineffective the umpire shall report the occurrence to the executive of the fielding side and to any governing body responsible for that match, who shall take appropriate action against the captain and the players concerned.

(b) In the event of a bowler taking unnecessarily long to bowl an over the umpire at the bowler's end shall adopt the procedures, other than the calling of "no-ball", of caution, final warning, action against the bowler and reporting.

(c) In the event of a batsman wasting time (See Note (f)) other than in the manner described in Law 31 (Timed Out), the umpire at the bowler's end shall adopt the following procedure:

(i) In the first instance he shall caution the batsman and inform the other umpire at once, and the captain of the batting side, as soon as the players leave the field for an interval, of what has occurred.

(ii) If this proves ineffective, he shall repeat the caution, indicate to the batsman that this is a final warning and inform the other umpire.

(iii) The umpire shall report the occurrence to both captains as soon as the players leave the field for an interval.

(iv) Should the above procedure prove ineffective, the umpire shall report the occurrence to the executive of the batting side and to any governing body responsible for that match, who shall take appropriate action against the player concerned.

11. Players Damaging the Pitch

The umpires shall intervene and prevent players from causing damage to the pitch which may assist the bowlers of either side. See Note (c).

(a) In the event of any member of the fielding side damaging the pitch, the umpire shall follow the procedure of caution, final warning, and reporting as set out in 10(a) above.

(b) In the event of a bowler contravening this Law by running down the pitch after delivering the ball, the umpire at the bowler's end shall first caution the bowler. If this caution is ineffective the umpire shall adopt the procedures, as set out in 8 above other than the calling and signalling of "no-ball".

(c) In the event of a batsman damaging the pitch the umpire at the bowler's end shall follow the procedures of caution, final warning and reporting as set out in 10(c) above.

12. Batsman Unfairly Stealing a Run

Any attempt by the batsman to steal a run during the bowler's run-up is unfair. Unless the bowler attempts to run out either batsman – see Law 24.4 (Bowler Throwing at Striker's Wicket before Delivery) and Law 24.5 (Bowler Attempting to Run Out Non-striker before Delivery) – the umpire shall call and signal "dead ball" as soon as the batsmen cross in any such attempt to run. The batsmen shall then return to their original wickets.

13. Player's Conduct

In the event of a player failing to comply with the instructions of an umpire, criticising his decisions by word or action, or showing dissent, or generally behaving in a manner which might ring the game into disrepute, the umpire concerned shall, in the first place, report the matter to e other umpire and to the player's captain requesting the latter to take action. If this proves effective, the umpire shall report the incident as soon as possible to the executive of the layer's team and to any governing body responsible for the match, who shall take any further ction which is considered appropriate against the player or players concerned.

otes

(a) The Condition of the Ball
Umpires shall make frequent and irregular inspections of the condition of the ball.

(b) Drying of a Wet Ball
A wet ball may be dried on a towel or with sawdust.

(c) Danger Area
The danger area on the pitch, which must be protected from damage by a bowler, shall be regarded by the umpires as the area contained by an imaginary line 4 feet/1.22m from the popping crease, and parallel to it, and within two imaginary and parallel lines drawn down the pitch from points on that line 1 foot/30.48cm on either side of the middle stump.

(d) Fast Short-pitched Balls
As a guide, a fast short-pitched ball is one which pitches short and passes, or would have passed, above the shoulder height of the striker standing in a normal batting stance at the crease.

(e) The Bowling of Fast Full Pitches
The bowling of one fast, high full pitch shall be considered to be unfair if, in the opinion of the umpire, it is deliberate, bowled at the striker, and if it passes or would have passed above the shoulder height of the striker when standing in a normal batting stance at the crease.

(f) Time Wasting by Batsmen
Other than in exceptional circumstances, the batsman should always be ready to take strike when the bowler is ready to start his run-up.

INTERNATIONAL CRICKET CONFERENCE

On June 15, 1909, representatives of cricket in England, Australia and South Africa met Lord's and founded the Imperial Cricket Conference. Membership was confined to th governing bodies of cricket in countries within the British Commonwealth where Test crick was played. India, New Zealand and West Indies were elected as members on May 31, 192 Pakistan on July 21, 1953, and Sri Lanka on July 21, 1981. South Africa ceased to be a memb of the ICC on leaving the British Commonwealth in May, 1961.

On July 15, 1965, the Conference was renamed the International Cricket Conference and ne rules were adopted to permit the election of countries from outside the British Commonwealt

CONSTITUTION

Chairman: The President of MCC for the time being or his nominee.
Secretary: The Secretary of MCC.
Foundation members: United Kingdom and Australia.
Full members: India, New Zealand, West Indies, Pakistan and Sri Lanka.
Associate members*: Argentina (1974), Bangladesh (1977), Bermuda (1966), Canada (1968 Denmark (1966), East Africa (1966), Fiji (1965), Gibraltar (1969), Hong Kong (1969), Isra (1974), Kenya (1981), Malaysia (1967), Netherlands (1966), Papua New Guinea (1973 Singapore (1974), USA (1965), West Africa (1976) and Zimbabwe (1981).
Affiliate members*: Bahamas (1987), France (1987), Italy (1984), Nepal (1988), Switzerlan (1985).

* *Year of election shown in parentheses.*

MEMBERSHIP

The following governing bodies for cricket shall be eligible for election.

Foundation Members: The governing bodies for cricket in the United Kingdom and Australi are known as Foundation Members, and while being Full Members of the Conference suc governing bodies have certain additional rights as set out in the rules of the Conference.

Full Members: The governing body for cricket recognised by the Conference of a country, o countries associated for cricket purposes, of which the representative teams are accepted a qualified to play official Test matches.

Associate Members: The governing body for cricket recognised by the Conference of country, or countries associated for cricket purposes, not qualifying as Full Members but wher cricket is firmly established and organised.

Chairman: J. Buzaglo (*Gibraltar*). *Deputy Chairman:* K. R. Bullock (*Canada*). *Hon. Treasurer* G. Davis (Israel).

TEST MATCHES

1. Duration of Test Matches

Within a maximum of 30 hours' playing time, the duration of Test matches shall be a matter fo negotiation and agreement between the two countries in any particular series of Test matches

When agreeing the Playing Conditions prior to the commencement of a Test series, th participating countries may:

(a) Extend the playing hours of the last Test beyond the limit of 30 hours, in a series i which, at the conclusion of the penultimate match, one side does not hold a lead of mor than one match.

(b) Allow an extension of play by one hour on any of the first four days of a Test match, i the event of play being suspended for one hour or more on that day, owing to weathe interference.

(c) Play on the rest day, conditions and circumstances permitting, should a full day's play be lost on either the second or third scheduled days of play.

(d) Make up time lost in excess of five minutes in each day's play owing to circumstances outside the game, other than acts of God.

ote. The umpires shall determine when such time shall be made up. This could, if conditions nd circumstances permit, include the following day.

2. Qualification Rules

cricketer is qualified to play in a Test match or one-day international either by birth or sidence.

(a) Qualification by birth. A cricketer, unless debarred by the Conference, is always eligible to play for the country of his birth.

(b) Qualification by residence. A cricketer, unless debarred by the Conference, shall be eligible to play for any country in which he is residing and has been residing during the four immediately preceding years, provided that he has not played for the country of his birth during that period.

'otes

(a) Notwithstanding anything hereinbefore contained, any player who has once played in a Test match or one-day international for any country shall not afterwards be eligible to play in a Test match or one-day international against that country, without the consent of its governing body.

(b) The ICC in conjunction with the governing body of any country may impose more stringent qualification rules for that country.

FIRST-CLASS MATCHES

1. Definitions

(a) A match of three or more days' duration between two sides of eleven players officially adjudged first-class shall be regarded as a first-class fixture.

(b) In the following Rules the term "governing body" is restricted to Foundation Members, Full Members and Associate Members of the Conference.

2. Rules

(a) Foundation and Full Members of the ICC shall decide the status of matches of three or more days' duration played in their countries.

(b) In matches of three or more days' duration played in countries which are not Foundation Members or Full Members of the ICC:

- (i) If the visiting team comes from a country which is a Foundation or Full Member of the ICC, that country shall decide the status of matches.
- (ii) If the visiting team does not come from a country which is a Foundation or Full Member of the ICC, or is a Commonwealth team composed of players from different countries, the ICC shall decide the status of matches.

Notes

(a) Governing bodies agree that the interest of first-class cricket will be served by ensuring that first-class status is *not* accorded to any match in which one or other of the teams taking part cannot on a strict interpretation of the definition be adjudged first-class.

(b) In case of any disputes arising from these Rules, the Secretary of the ICC shall refer the matter for decision to the Conference, failing unanimous agreement by postal communication being reached.

The Bowling of Fast, Short-pitched Balls

A bowler shall be limited to one fast, short-pitched ball per over. If he bowls a second, th umpire shall call and signal "No ball". If the bowler is no-balled a second time in the innings fo the same offence, the bowler shall be warned, and after a further offence he shall be taken o and not allowed to bowl again in the innings.

RULES COMMON TO THE BENSON AND HEDGES CUP AND THE NATWEST BANK TROPHY

The Result

1. *A Tie*

In the event of a tie, the following shall apply:

(i) The side taking the greater number of wickets shall be the winner.

(ii) If both sides are all out, the side with the higher overall scoring-rate shall be th winner.

(iii) If the result cannot be decided by either of the first two methods, the winner sha be the side with the higher rate after 30 overs or, if still equal, after twenty or, if sti equal, after ten.

2. *Unfinished Match*

If a match remains unfinished after the allocated number of days, the winner shall be the sid which has scored the faster in runs per over throughout the innings, provided that at least twent overs have been bowled at the side batting second. If the scoring-rate is the same, the side losin fewer wickets in the first twenty overs of each innings shall be the winner.

If, however, at any time on the last day the umpires are satisfied that there is insufficient tim remaining to achieve a definite result or, where applicable, for the side batting second t complete its maximum number of overs, provided it has not already received twenty or mor overs, they shall order a new match to be started, allowing an equal number of overs per sid (minimum ten overs per side) bearing in mind the time remaining for play until scheduled clos of play. In this event, team selection for the new match will be restricted to the eleven player and twelfth man originally chosen, unless authorised otherwise in advance by the Chie Executive of the Board. If, however, the team batting second has received twenty overs or mor when the umpires decide that there is insufficient time remaining to achieve a definite result the match shall not be resumed nor shall a new match be started.

In the event of no result being obtained within this rule, the captains should agree, i circumstances (outdoors or indoors) permit, to a bowling contest to achieve a result, fiv cricketers from each team to bowl overarm, two deliveries each, at three stumps at a distance o 22 yards. The team scoring the greater number of hits shall be the winner. If the scores are equal the same cricketers will bowl one ball each alternately to achieve a result on a "sudden death' basis. If circumstances make this form of contest impossible, the match shall be decided by th toss of a coin, except in a Benson and Hedges zonal match which shall be declared to have "Nc Result".

RULES AND PLAYING CONDITIONS APPLYING ONLY TO THE BENSON AND HEDGES CUP

Duration and Hours of Play

The matches, of 55 overs per side, will be completed in one day, if possible, but two days will be allocated for zonal league matches and three days for knockout matches in case of weather interference. Matches started on Saturday but not completed may only be continued on Sunday with the approval of the Board.

Normal hours will be 11 a.m. to 7.30 p.m.

Over-rates

The allotted playing-time for completing 55 overs is 3 hours, 25 minutes.

Qualification of Players

The Combined Universities qualification will take precedence in respect of those players who are also qualified for county clubs and no cricketer may play for more than one team in the same year's competition.

Scoring System

In the zonal league matches the winning team scores two points. In a "no result" match each side scores one point.

If two or more teams in any zone finish with an equal number of points, their position in the table shall be based on the faster run-rate in all zonal league matches in which the side batting second is scheduled at the start of their innings to bat for 30 overs or more. This is calculated by balls bowled divided by runs scored multiplied by 100. In the event of any side being *all out* in less than its full quota of overs, the average run-rate shall be based on the full quota of overs to which it was entitled and not the number of overs in which it was dismissed.

RULES AND PLAYING CONDITIONS APPLYING ONLY TO THE NATWEST BANK TROPHY

Duration and Hours of Play

The matches, of 60 overs per side, will be completed in one day, if possible, but three days will be allocated in case of weather interference.

Cup Final only: If the match starts not less than half an hour late, owing to weather or the state of the ground, and not more than one and a half hours late, each innings shall be limited to 50 overs. If, however, the start is delayed for more than one and a half hours, the 60-over limit shall apply.

Normal hours will be 10.30 a.m. to 7.30 p.m.

The captains of the teams in the final shall be warned that heavy shadows may move across the pitch towards the end of the day and that no appeal against the light will be considered in such circumstances.

Over-rates

The allotted playing-time for completing 60 overs is 3 hours, 45 minutes.

RULES AND PLAYING CONDITIONS APPLYING ONLY TO THE REFUGE ASSURANCE LEAGUE

Hours of Play

Normal hours of play shall be 2.00-7.00 p.m. (1.30-6.30 for televised matches) with a tea interval of twenty minutes at the end of the over in progress at 4.20 p.m. (3.50 for televised matches), or between innings, whichever is the earlier. The duration and time of the tea interval can be varied in the case of an interrupted match. Close of play shall normally be at 7.00 p.m. (6.30 for televised matches) but play may continue after that time if, in the opinion of the umpires, the overs remaining can be completed by 7.10 p.m. (6.40 p.m.)

Length of Innings

(i) In an uninterrupted match:

(a) Each side shall bat for 40 overs unless all out earlier.

(b) If the side fielding first fails to bowl 40 overs by 4.20 p.m. (3.50 for televised matches), the over shall be completed and the side batting second shall receive the same number of overs as their opponents.

(c) If the team batting first is all out within two minutes of the scheduled time for the tea interval, the innings of the side batting second shall be limited to the same number of overs as their opponents have received, the over in which the last wicket falls to count as a complete over.

(ii) In matches where the start is delayed or play is suspended:

(a) The object shall be to rearrange the number of overs so that both teams may receive the same number of overs (minimum ten each). The calculation of the overs to be bowled shall be based on an average rate of one over per $3\frac{1}{2}$ minutes or part thereof in the time remaining before 7.00 p.m. (6.30 p.m. for televised matches).

(b) If the start is delayed by not more than an hour and the match is thereby reduced to no fewer than 31 overs a side, the time of the close of the first innings shall be fixed allowing $3\frac{1}{2}$ minutes for each over. If the team fielding first fails to bowl the revised number of overs by the agreed time, the principles set out in (i) b and c shall apply.

(c) Where play is suspended after the match has started on the basis of each team batting for more than twenty overs, the number of overs should be rearranged so that both teams may bat for the same number of overs (minimum of 20 each); the calculation as above.

(d) If, owing to a suspension of play during or immediately prior to the start of the innings of the team batting second, it is not possible for that team to have the opportunity of batting for the same number of overs (minimum 20 overs) as their opponents, they will bat for a number of overs to be calculated as above. The team batting second shall not bat for a greater number of overs than their opponents unless the latter have been all out in fewer than the agreed number of overs.

(e) If there is insufficient time to provide for a match as above (20 overs minimum), that match shall be void and, conditions permitting, a new match of ten overs each side shall be played provided play begins no later than 5.40 p.m. (5.10 for televised matches). If there is any suspension of play during the ten-overs match, it will be abandoned as a "No result".

(f) In the event of play being suspended in a match which began on the basis of each team batting for less than 20 overs (ten overs minimum), that match shall be void and, conditions permitting, a new match of ten overs per side shall be played as described in (e) above.

Over-rates

The allotted playing-time for completing 40 overs is 2 hours 20 minutes.

Limitation of the Bowler's Run-up

The bowler's run-up, including his preliminary approach, shall be limited to 15 yards, to be measured from the wicket.

The Result

(i) Where both sides have had the opportunity to bat for the same number of overs and the scores are level, the result is a tie, no account being taken of the number of wickets which have fallen.

(ii) If, owing to suspension of play, the number of overs in the innings of the side batting second has to be revised, their target score, which they must exceed to win the match, shall be calculated by multiplying the revised number of overs by the average runs per over scored by the side batting first. If the target score involves a fraction, the final scores cannot be equal and the result cannot be a tie.

(iii) If a match is abandoned before the side batting second has received its allotted number of overs, the result shall be decided on the average run-rate throughout both innings, provided the team batting second has received not less than twenty overs.

(iv) If a result cannot be achieved as above, the match shall be declared "No result".

(v) If the team batting first has been all out without using its full quota of overs, the calculation of the run-rate shall be based on the full quota of overs to which it was entitled.

Scoring of Points

(i) The team winning a match to score four points.

(ii) In a "tie" each team to score two points.

(iii) In a "No Result" match each team to score two points.

(iv) If two or more teams finish with an equal number of points for any of the first four places, their final positions will be decided by:

(a) The most wins or, if still equal

(b) The most away wins or, if still equal

(c) The higher run-rate throughout the season.

RULES AND PLAYING CONDITIONS APPLYING ONLY TO THE REFUGE ASSURANCE CUP

Duration and Hours of Play

The matches, of 40 overs per side, will be completed in one day, if possible, but two days will be allocated in case of weather interference. Normal hours will be 1.00 p.m. to 6.00 p.m., but the umpires may order extra time if, in their opinion, a finish can be obtained on that day.

Over-rates

The allocated playing-time for completing 40 overs is 2 hours 20 minutes.

Limitation of the Bowler's Run-up

The bowler's run-up, including his preliminary approach, shall be limited to 15 yards, to be measured from the wicket.

The Result

1. *A Tie*

The rules are those as for the Benson and Hedges Cup and NatWest Bank Trophy, except that in the instance of 1.(iii), after ten overs a result can be decided in a graduation of single overs; i.e. nine, eight, seven overs, etc.

2. *Unfinished Match*

The rules are those as for the Benson and Hedges Cup and NatWest Bank Trophy, except that the first paragraph shall read:

If a match remains unfinished after two days, the winner shall be the team which has scored the faster in runs per over throughout the innings, provided that at least twenty overs have been bowled at the side batting second. If the side batting first has been all out in fewer than its full quota of overs, the calculation of its average scoring rate will be based on the full quota of overs to which it would have been entitled, and not on the number of overs in which it was dismissed. If the scoring rate is the same, the winner shall be the side with the higher score after twenty overs or, if still equal, after ten overs and, if still equal, in single overs thereafter; i.e. nine, eight, seven overs, etc.

ADDRESSES OF REPRESENTATIVE BODIES

INTERNATIONAL CRICKET CONFERENCE: Lt-Col. J. R. Stephenson, OBE, Lord's Ground, London NW8 8QN.

ENGLAND: Cricket Council, A. C. Smith, Lord's Ground, London NW8 8QN.

AUSTRALIA: Australian Cricket Board, D. L. Richards, 70 Jolimont Street, Jolimont, Victoria 3002.

WEST INDIES: West Indies Cricket Board of Control, G. S. Camacho, Kensington Oval, Fontabelle, St Michael, Barbados.

INDIA: Board of Control for Cricket in India, R. S. Mahendra, Vijay Nagar Colony, Bhiwani 125 021, Haryana.

NEW ZEALAND: New Zealand Cricket Council, G. T. Dowling, OBE, PO Box 958, Christchurch.

PAKISTAN: Board of Control for Cricket in Pakistan, A. A. K. Abbasi, Gaddafi Stadium, Lahore.

SRI LANKA: Board of Control for Cricket in Sri Lanka, Nuski Mohamed, 35 Maitland Place, Colombo 7.

SOUTH AFRICA: South African Cricket Union, Dr A. Bacher, PO Box 55009, Northlands 2116, Transvaal.
South African Cricket Board, A. I. Mangera, PO Box 54059, Vrededorp 2141, Transvaal.

ARGENTINA: Argentine Cricket Association, R. H. Gooding, c/o The English Club, 25 de Mayo 586, 1002 Buenos Aires.

BANGLADESH: Bangladesh Cricket Control Board, T. M. Islam, The Stadium, Dacca.

BERMUDA: Bermuda Cricket Board of Control, C. W. Butterfield, PO Box 992, Hamilton.

CANADA: Canadian Cricket Association, K. R. Bullock, PO Box 1364, Brockville, Ontario, K6V 5Y6.

DENMARK: Danish Cricket Association, J. Holmen, Idraettens Hus, Brøndby, D-K 2605.

EAST AFRICA: East and Central African Cricket Conference, S. Patel, PO Box 71712, Ndola, Zambia.

FIJI: Fiji Cricket Association, P. I. Knight, PO Box 300, Suva.

GIBRALTAR: Gibraltar Cricket Association, T. J. Finlayson, 21 Sandpits House, Withams Road.

HONG KONG: Hong Kong Cricket Association, S. K. Sipahimalani, Centre for Media Resources, University of Hong Kong, Knowles Bldg, Pokfulam Road.

ISRAEL: Israel Cricket Association, N. Davidson, PO Box 93, Ben-Gurion Airport 70100.

KENYA: Kenya Cricket Association, B. Mauladad, PO Box 40462, Nairobi.

MALAYSIA: Malaysian Cricket Association, K. Sivanesan, D/A Unit Kemajuan, Jabatan Kemajuan, Shah Alam, (Tkt 2) Knmpinks PKNS, 50505 Shah Alam, Selangor.

NETHERLANDS: Royal Netherlands Cricket Board, Hon. Secretary, Neuiwe Kalfjeslaan 21-B, 1182 AA Amstelveen.

PAPUA NEW GUINEA: Papua New Guinea Cricket Board of Control, A. Lowther, PO Box 6022, Boroko.

SINGAPORE: Singapore Cricket Association, R. Sivasubramaniam, 5000-D Marine Parade Road 22-16, Laguna Park, Singapore 1544.

USA: United States of America Cricket Association, Naseeruddin Khan, 2361 Hickory Road, Plymouth Meeting, Pennsylvania 19462.

WEST AFRICA: West Africa Cricket Conference, C. Enahoro, National Sports Commission, National Stadium, PO Box 145 – Surulere, Lagos.

ZIMBABWE: Zimbabwe Cricket Union, A. L. A. Pichanick, PO Box 452, Harare.

BRITISH UNIVERSITIES SPORTS FEDERATION: 28 Woburn Square, London WC1.

CLUB CRICKET CONFERENCE: A. E. F. Stevens, 353 West Barnes Lane, New Malden, Surrey, KT3 6JF.

ENGLAND SCHOOLS' CRICKET ASSOCIATION: C. J. Cooper, 68 Hatherley Road, Winchester, Hampshire SO22 6RR.

IRISH CRICKET UNION: D. Scott, 45 Foxrock Park, Foxrock, Dublin 18, Ireland.

MINOR COUNTIES CRICKET ASSOCIATION: D. J. M. Armstrong, Thorpe Cottage, Mill Common, Ridlington, North Walsham, NR28 9TY.

NATIONAL CRICKET ASSOCIATION. B. J. Aspital, Lord's Ground, London NW8 8QN.

SCARBOROUGH CRICKET FESTIVAL: Colin T. Adamson, Cricket Ground, North Marine Road, Scarborough, North Yorkshire, YO12 7TJ.

SCOTTISH CRICKET UNION: R. W. Barclay, Admin. Office, 18 Ainslie Place, Edinburgh, EH3 6AU.

COMBINED SERVICES: Lt-Col. K. Hitchcock, c/o Army Sport Control Board, Clayton Barracks, Aldershot, Hampshire GU11 2BG.

THE SPORTS COUNCIL: Director-General, 16 Upper Woburn Place, London WC1 0QP.

ASSOCIATION OF CRICKET UMPIRES: L. J. Cheeseman, 16 Ruden Way, Epsom Downs, Surrey, KT17 3LN.

WOMEN'S CRICKET ASSOCIATION: 16 Upper Woburn Place, London WC1 0QP.

The addresses of MCC, the First-Class Counties, and Minor Counties are given at the head of each separate section.

MEETINGS IN 1988

TCCB SPRING MEETING

Concern about dissent and indiscipline on the field of play was expressed at the Spring Meeting of the TCCB, held at Lord's on March 3. The Board, having considered the findings of its Cricket Committee, Executive Committee and a Special Meeting following the winter's troubled tour of Pakistan, emphasised that it was essential that dissent and indiscipline be kept out of the game at all levels. With the England team being the focus of public attention, the England selectors, who remained unchanged from 1987, would be directed to note a player's behaviour as well as his form. "If you don't behave, you don't play" would be the message to the players. Talks would be held with the Cricketers' Association to ensure the players were aware of the need to preserve the game's image, and following the pre-season meetings of the umpires and the county captains there would be a meeting attended by representatives of both parties.

The Board noted with interest the changes that had occurred in the top level of cricket administration in Pakistan and it hoped soon to start rebuilding relations with the BCCP. The format of future tours would be examined by the Tours Committee, but awareness was expressed that any reduction of cricket played overseas could affect the number of tours to and Test matches played in England. The Board decided to bid to stage the fifth World Cup in 1991 or 1992.

It was agreed that a first-class umpire should stand in Second XI matches so that young cricketers would learn how a first-class umpire interprets the Laws and conducts the game generally. Following the recommendation of a working party of groundsmen, who considered that the frequent use of the heavy roller deadened pitches, it was decided that in the County Championship only light hand rollers of 5cwt maximum would be available to captains for the duration of a match. During the coming season, the preparation of pitches would be monitored by D. B. Carr, chairman of the Pitches Committee, and T. M. Lamb, the TCCB's cricket secretary.

TCCB SUMMER MEETING

At its Summer Meeting, held at Lord's on August 12, the TCCB took action to improve England's recent record at Test match level by asking its Cricket Committee to produce special recommendations. The fixture list, the quality of pitches and the influence of overseas players were itemised for particular attention. Additionally, it was decided that counties would be sent another copy of the Palmer Report for their consideration. The Board agreed to increase the minimum number of fixtures in the Second XI Championship to sixteen and to end the 40-over Warwick Under-25 Competition.

INTERNATIONAL CRICKET CONFERENCE

At the Annual Meeting of the International Cricket Conference, held at Lord's on July 5, 6, the decision on the future position of cricketers who have contacts with South Africa was postponed until a Special Meeting in January 1989. Two further resolutions had been added to that proposed by West Indies, and seconded by India, at the Special Meeting on June 26, 1987. Both, while recognising the right of a member country to select its team without interference from another member, acknowledged the right of governments to refuse entry to their country. West Indies had proposed and Sri Lanka had seconded a resolution that, in any instance of entry being refused, the player *shall* be replaced. Australia proposed and Pakistan seconded a resolution that, in such an instance, the player *may* be replaced. The Special Meeting in January would also consider details of a new constitution for the ICC.

Among other subjects under discussion at the Annual Meeting was that of Test match umpires. It was agreed that a sub-committee would study the feasibility of an international panel of umpires. While the matter of short-pitched bowling was raised, no action was taken. Similarly, a suggestion to limit the weight of bats, including the rubber grip, to 2lb 12oz met a recommendation from a sub-committee that no action should be taken. A sub-committee was set up to examine proposals to tighten the rules governing the qualification of players for Test matches. It was decided that a register of players breaching an international code of conduct would be held by the ICC, that the 1990 ICC Trophy would be held in June in The Netherlands, and that Nepal would become an Affiliate Member.

TCCB WINTER MEETING

At its Winter Meeting, held at Lord's on December 7, 8, the TCCB voted 13-5, with o abstention, not to alter the regulations for qualification for England. It had been proposed th the period of qualification for cricketers originating from ICC Associate Member countries t reduced to four years. The Board expressed its determination that as far as possible Englis county and Test cricket should be played by Englishmen, and to this end it was agreed principle that, for county cricket, only one overseas registration per county should be allowe as soon as practicable. There was concern that a change of the qualification rules might le to an increase in the number of players from Associate Member countries, and if it we thought that places in the England team were being taken by newly qualified players, th could be a disincentive to young English cricketers and a discouragement to aspirations play for their country. The Board heard that a Special Meeting of the TCCB would be held c January 19, 1989 to consider the resolutions being put to the ICC Special Meeting on th position of cricketers maintaining sporting links with South Africa.

On pitches, which had given cause for concern in 1988, the Board agreed to support th recommendation of the Pitches Committee that a penalty of 25 points be deducted from th home county for pitches that were clearly unsuitable and for which there were no extenuatir circumstances. It was intended to ask the Australian touring team in 1989 to agree to pay fine for failing to achieve fifteen overs an hour in the Test matches. The Australians woul also be asked to allow an extra half-hour or eight overs, whichever was greater, at the end of day's play in a Test match, except for the fifth day, if one side believed that a finish could b achieved.

A modification was made to the Playing Conditions preventing the use of a substitute fo five overs in domestic competitions. The umpires would henceforth be allowed to arbitrat and permit a substitute immediately in the event of an obvious and serious injury. In th Refuge Assurance League and Cup, the limitation of the bowler's run-up was extended fror 15 to 22 yards, with an addition of ten minutes' playing-time per innings. In the Benson an Hedges Cup, the tea interval was set for 4.30 p.m. or after 25 overs (previously 35), whicheve was later.

TCCB DISCIPLINE COMMITTEE MEETINGS

At a meeting of the Discipline Committee, held at Lord's on August 3, M. W. Gatting wa fined £5,000 for publishing without the TCCB's consent a chapter in his autobiography *Leading from the Front*, dealing with his confrontation with the Pakistani umpire, Shakoo Rana, at Faisalabad in December 1987. Gatting, who was legally represented at the six-hou hearing, was cleared of a second charge of breach of contract relating to extracts of th chapter which appeared by way of preview in the *Sunday Times* of June 12.

At a meeting of the Discipline Committee, held at Lord's on December 14, C. S. Cowdre was fined £500 for making without the TCCB's consent a statement, published in the *Sun* o September 2, which was critical of the England selectors. Of his not being retained a England's captain, following his recovery from the injury which caused him to miss the Tes match at The Oval, he said: "I am deeply hurt no-one has bothered to tell me where I wen wrong and why I am no longer the right man to captain England."

DATES IN CRICKET HISTORY

344(*c*)	Club-ball, an early form of single-wicket cricket, played; believed to have started in the thirteenth century.
550(*c*)	Cricket played at "The Free School", Guildford.
595	G. Florio's Italian-English Dictionary mentioned cricket.
610	Reference to "Cricketing" between Weald and Upland near Chevening, Kent.
611	Reference to cricket in John Bullokar's "England Expositor".
622	Six parishioners at Boxgrove, Sussex, prosecuted for playing cricket in the churchyard on a Sunday.
636(*c*)	Reference to cricket at East Horsley, Surrey.
646	First recorded cricket match, at Coxheath, Kent.
647	Probable reference to cricket being played by Winchester scholars on St Catherine's Hill in a latin poem by Robert Matthew.
670(*c*)	John Churchill, later Duke of Marlborough, played cricket at St Paul's School.
676	First reference to the game abroad, played by English residents at Aleppo, Syria.
677	The Earl of Sussex went to a "crekitt" match at ye Dicker in Sussex.
694	2s. 6d. paid for a Wagger [*sic*] about a cricket match at Lewis [*sic*].
706	First full description of a cricket match: in a latin poem by William Goldwin, of Eton and King's, Cambridge.
709	First "County Match": Kent v London.
	William Byrd of Westover, Virginia, played cricket with his friends.
710	First reference to University cricket, Cambridge.
721	Cricket played by mariners of the East India Company at Cambay, India.
727	Articles of Agreement governed conduct of matches between teams of the Duke of Richmond and Mr Brodrick of Peperharow.
	First mention of cricket at Oxford University.
729	Date of the earliest surviving bat, inscribed "J.C." (John Chitty) 1729, now in the pavilion at Kennington Oval.
730	First recorded game on the Artillery Ground, Finsbury: London v Surrey. Has remained the HAC (Honourable Artillery Company) ground ever since.
736	Crews of HM ships played cricket in Lisbon.
744	June 18, first great match of which the full score is preserved, Kent beating All England by one wicket on the HAC ground.
	Laws of Cricket, revision of an earlier code, made by the London Club, of which Frederick Louis, Prince of Wales, father of George III, was President.
	First recorded admission charge, 2d. at the HAC ground.
751	Old Etonians played Gentlemen of England.
	Cricket mentioned as far north as Durham and Yorkshire.
	First recording of the score at the fall of each wicket.
	A match between New York and London played in USA, "according to the London method".
763	First mention of cricket in Wales; in Pembroke.
767(*c*)	Formation of the Hambledon Club playing first on Broadhalfpenny and then Windmill Down. They often defeated All England and their great days lasted until 1796. Their great players, immortalised by Nyren, evolved a new and much improved technique.
769	The first recorded century, Minshull's 107 for the Duke of Dorset's XI v Wrotham.
771	Sheffield played Nottingham.
774	"Batts" advertised for sale by a maker, William Staples of Sevenoaks.
776	Earliest known scorecards, printed by Pratt, scorer to the Vine Club, Sevenoaks.
777	First record of a bowler being credited for catches off his bowling.
780	Dukes, of Penshurst, (established 1760) made the first six-seamed ball and presented it to the Prince of Wales, afterwards George IV. Farington's diary of 1811 stated the Duke family had been making cricket balls for 250 years.
785	Canadians playing in Montreal.
787	First match, Middlesex v Essex, on Thomas Lord's first ground (Dorset Square).
	MCC formed by members of White Conduit Club.
	First mention of a county club: Oxfordshire.
788	June 27, MCC played their first match at Lord's.
	First revision of the Laws by MCC, dated May 30.

1791 Publication of the first record of match scores by Samuel Britcher: these subsequentl covered the chief matches until 1805.

1792 In India, the Calcutta CC formed.

1794 First recorded school match: Charterhouse v Westminster at Lord's.

1800 Publication of the first book on technique, by Thomas Boxall.

1803 William Pitt referred to cricket when introducing his Defence Act.

Cricket regularly played in Sydney, Australia.

1805 Eton beat Harrow at Lord's by an innings. The poet, Lord Byron, was in the Harrow side.

1806 First Gentlemen v Players match at Lord's.

Cricket played in Argentina.

A meeting held of St Anne's CC in Barbados.

1807 First mention of "straight-armed" (round-arm) bowling, by John Willes of Kent.

1808 A match advertised in Cape Town between officers of the Artillery Mess and officers of the Colony "for 1,000 dollars a side".

1809 Lord opened his second ground at "North Bank".

1810 Lowest-ever recorded score in an important match: 6 by "The Bs" v England at Lord's.

1814 Lord's third ground opened on its present site, the original turf of the first ground being transplanted at each move.

1815 A match played on June 12 by officers of the Brigade of Guards near Brussels, visited by the Duke of Wellington.

1817 William Lambert became the first batsman to score two centuries in a match: 107 and 157 for Sussex v Epsom.

1820 First recorded score over 200: 278 by William Ward for MCC v Norfolk at Lord's, a ground record for 105 years.

1821 First century in Gentlemen v Players at Lord's: 113 not out by Thomas Beagley (Players).

1822 John Willes, Kent v MCC at Lord's, no-balled for throwing; i.e. round-arm bowling.

1826 First recorded century in a school match: 146 not out by W. Meyrick for Winchester v Harrow.

1827 First University match; drawn.

Three experimental matches, Sussex v England, played to test round-arm bowling as developed by William Lillywhite and James Broadbridge.

1828 MCC authorised round-arm bowling, allowing the bowler to raise his hand level with the elbow.

1832 First reference to cricket in New Zealand, in the diary of Archdeacon Williams.

1833 John Nyren's *Young Cricketer's Tutor* and *The Cricketers of my Time*, the authority for late eighteenth century cricket and its personalities, were published.

1835 A revised code of the Laws adopted by MCC.

1836 First North v South match, long recognised as the season's greatest match.

1838 Trent Bridge ground, Nottingham, opened by William Clarke, who eight years later formed the All-England XI to play matches against odds throughout the country.

Melbourne CC formed in Australia.

Mexican CC in existence.

1839 First recorded century in Australia: 120 by F. A. Paulett in Melbourne.

1841 The Duke of Wellington ordered a cricket ground to be made as an adjunct to every military barracks.

1842 The Canterbury Week started and "The Old Stagers" formed.

1843 Port Elizabeth CC formed in South Africa.

1844 The first match between Canada and the USA.

1845 The Surrey Club formed and the first match played at Kennington Oval.

I Zingari formed, based on Canterbury.

1846 Fenner's ground at Cambridge opened, leased in 1873 by the CUCC who bought the freehold in 1892.

Telegraph scoreboard introduced at Lord's.

1848 W. G. Grace born.

Edmund Hinkly (Kent) took all ten wickets v England at Lord's.

1849 First Yorkshire v Lancashire match.

1850 J. Wisden bowled all ten batsmen in one innings, North v South at Lord's.

1851 First Australian Inter-Colonial match: Tasmania v Victoria at Launceston.

1852 The United All-England XI formed to rival the All-England XI, with Wisden and Dean as secretaries.

1853 First mention of a "champion" county, Nottinghamshire.

1855 About this time mowing machines were first used on grounds, though sheep continued to crop Lord's for many years.
W. Clarke took 476 wickets in all cricket during the season.

1857 The Cricketers Fund Friendly Society instituted. For ten years the great match, AEE v UAEE, was played in its support. From 1884 until his death in 1932 Lord Harris was its President.

1858 Birth of the "hat-trick", when a hat was awarded to a bowler who had taken wickets with three successive balls.

1859 George Parr's team, the first to tour abroad, visited USA and Canada. The matches drew great crowds and, together with general tour experiences, were well described by the team's scorer, Fred Lillywhite, pioneer author of tour books.

1860 First Inter-Provincial match in New Zealand: Wellington v Auckland.

1862 Edgar Willsher, playing for England v Surrey at Kennington Oval, was no-balled by John Lillywhite for having his hand above the shoulder. Play, suspended for the day, was resumed next morning with another umpire replacing Lillywhite. This led to overarm bowling being legalised two years later.
H. H. Stephenson's team, the first to visit Australia, was sponsored by Spiers and Ponds who cleared over £11,000. All matches were against odds. Charles Lawrence remained as a coach in Sydney.

1864 June 10, "Overhand bowling" authorised.
W. G. Grace's first appearance in big cricket two days before his sixteenth birthday. He scored 170 and 56 not out for South Wales Club v Gentlemen of Sussex.
Surrey became the first champion county of the regular series.
First issue of *John Wisden's Cricketers' Almanack* published.
The second English team (Parr's) in Australia, again against odds, was also the first side to visit New Zealand. William Caffyn (Surrey) stayed behind as a coach in Melbourne.

1865 Practice nets were first used at Lord's.

1866 Cricket played in Denmark, and the Christiana CC formed in Oslo, Norway.

1867 A long period of ill-feeling between professionals of North and South and of the two All-England XIs culminated in the end of the two great matches involving those sides.
MCC sent a team to Paris.

1868 A team of Australian Aborigines, managed by Charles Lawrence, toured England.

1870 A heavy roller first used at Lord's, heralding a great improvement in pitches.

1871 W. G. Grace's greatest year: the first batsman to reach 2,000 runs in a first-class season (2,739, average 78.25), a feat unequalled except by Grace himself until A. E. Stoddart and William Gunn exceeded 2,000 in 1893. In benefit matches played for Willsher, Stephenson and John Lillywhite, and depending much on his success, he scored 189 not out, 268 and 217.

1872 First experiment at Lord's of covering the pitch before the start of a match.

1876 W. G. Grace established two records: (1) The first score of 300 in first-class cricket (344 for MCC v Kent at Canterbury); his next two scores for Gloucestershire were 127 v Nottinghamshire and 318 v Yorkshire. (2) 400 not out for All-England XI v XXII of Grimsby.

1877 The first Test match: England v Australia at Melbourne, won by Australia by 45 runs. With 165, Charles Bannerman of Australia scored the first Test hundred.

1878 First tour of England by an official Australian team, led by D. W. Gregory. Their sensational defeat of a very strong MCC side, by nine wickets in a single day, established Australia's status.
First tour of Australia by a New Zealand team, Canterbury.

1880 The first Test match in England at Kennington Oval, England beating Australia by five wickets, W. G. Grace 152, W. L. Murdoch 153 not out.

1882 First Australian Test win in England, by 7 runs at Kennington Oval. A spectator died from excitement. The tradition of "The Ashes" established by an "obituary notice" to English cricket in the *Sporting Times*.

1884 A completely revised Code of Laws adopted by MCC, omitting the laws for settling bets.
First use of the title "Test Match" in the *Melbourne Argus*, September 16.
First Gentlemen of Philadelphia team visited England.

1884-85 First series of five Tests in Australia, England winning three.

1888-89 Present Lord's pavilion built.
First English team, led by C. Aubrey Smith, toured South Africa and won the first Test match played between the two countries.

1889 Currie Cup tournament in South Africa established.

1889-90 First English team visited India.

1890 South African Cricket Association formed.

1891 First West Indies Triangular Tournament between Barbados, Trinidad and Demerara.

1892-93 Sheffield Shield competition started in Australia.
Visit of first Dutch team to England.

1894 First South African tour of England.
New Zealand Cricket Council formed.

1895 1,000 runs were scored in May for the first time: in 22 days by W. G. Grace, aged 47, who also made his 100th hundred.
First English tour of West Indies.

1898 Board of Control set up to administer Tests in England.

1899 First five-Test series in England: Australia won the only finished match by ten wickets at Lord's. For the first time a Selection Committee chose the England sides, formerly chosen by ground authorities.
V. T. Trumper's 300 not out v Sussex was the first score of 300 by a visiting Australian.
Record individual score, 628 not out, made by A. E. J. Collins for Clark's v North Town in a junior House match at Clifton College.

1900 First West Indies team toured England.

1901 C. B. Fry scored six centuries in successive innings, a feat since equalled by D. G. Bradman (1938-39) and M. J. Procter (1970-71).

1902 Easter classes for boys instituted at Lord's.

1903 Abortive agitation for a wider wicket and timeless Tests in England.

1905 Australian Board of Control set up.
If necessary to decide a rubber, the last Test in England to be played to a finish. The first necessity for this occurred in 1912, England winning in four days at Kennington Oval.
First MCC team, captained by P. F. Warner, toured South Africa, whose cricket repute was firmly established by their winning four Tests, a triumph for googly-type bowlers on matting pitches.

1909 Imperial Cricket Conference (ICC) formed with MCC, Australia and South Africa as members.

1911 Warwickshire became the first county to win the Championship outside those who originated the event.
First MCC team visited West Indies.
First All-Indian team visited England.

1912 First and only Triangular Tournament in England, preceded by Test Trials for the first time.

1913-14 S. F. Barnes took 49 wickets in four Tests in South Africa, a series record for all Tests.

1919 Two-day County Championship matches with very long playing hours proved a failure.

1922 MCC visited Denmark for the first time.

1925 J. B. Hobbs equalled and passed W. G. Grace's record of 126 centuries with two in the same match for Surrey v Somerset.

1926 India, New Zealand and West Indies admitted to the Imperial Cricket Conference.
Women's Cricket Association formed.
Victoria scored a record 1,107 (W. H. Ponsford 352) v New South Wales in Melbourne.

1926-27 First MCC team visited India.

1927 First New Zealand team toured England.

1928 A. P. Freeman (Kent) exceeded 300 wickets in season with 304.

1930 Tests v Australia in England lengthened from three to four days. D. G. Bradman scored record 974 in a series, average 139.14, including 309 in a single day at Leeds.

1932 P. Holmes and H. Sutcliffe made 555 for Yorkshire's first wicket v Essex, surpassing 554 by their fellow Yorkshiremen J. T. Brown and J. Tunnicliffe v Derbyshire in 1898.

1932-33 "Bodyline" controversy during the MCC tour of Australia.

1935 MCC condemned direct attack (intimidatory bowling) and issued instructions to umpires against its future practice.
South Africa, under H. F. Wade, gained their first Test win in England.

1937 Sir Pelham Warner became the first cricketer to be knighted.

1938 The Test match v Australia at Lord's the first to be partly televised.
L. Hutton made 364 in England's Test record score of 903 for seven declared at Kennington Oval.

1947 Major revision of the Laws of Cricket by MCC.
D. C. S. Compton (3,816) and W. J. Edrich (3,539) surpassed T. Hayward's record aggregate for an English season of 3,518 in 1906. Compton also made eighteen centuries, exceeding Hobbs's 1925 previous record by two.

1948 First five-day Tests played in England. Australians hit 721 in day v Essex at Southend.
West Indies first country to visit Pakistan: no Test was played.

1949 Election of the first 26 professional cricketers to Honorary Life Membership of MCC.

1950 West Indies gained their first Test victory in England.

1951-52 India gained their first Test victory against England.

1952 Pakistan admitted to ICC membership.
Surrey began a run of seven consecutive County Championships.

1953 Imperial Cricket Memorial Gallery at Lord's opened by HRH The Duke of Edinburgh.
Association of Cricket Umpires formed.

1954 Pakistan became the first country to win a Test on its first visit to England.

1955 First Australian tour of West Indies. They became the first visiting team to win a rubber there.

1956 New Zealand gained their first Test victory, against West Indies in Auckland.
J. C. Laker took nineteen wickets in a match, England v Australia at Manchester.

1958 G. S. Sobers, 365 not out v Pakistan, beat L. Hutton's record individual Test score.

1960 The first tie in Tests: Australia v West Indies in Brisbane; West Indies 453 and 284, Australia 505 and 232.

1961 South Africa ceased membership of ICC on leaving the Commonwealth.

1963 The distinction between amateur and professional abolished in English first-class cricket.
One-day limited-overs county competitions began with the Gillette Cup.

1964 F. S. Trueman became the first bowler to exceed 300 Test wickets.

1965 ICC changed its title from Imperial to International Cricket Conference, and Ceylon, Fiji and USA became Associate Members.

1965-66 First Shell Shield tournament in West Indies.

1966 Bermuda, Denmark, East Africa and the Netherlands became ICC Associate Members.

1967 Cricketers' Association formed.
Malaysia became an ICC Associate Member.

1968 Canada became an ICC Associate Member.
Cricket Council formed; the Test and County Cricket Board (TCCB) replaced the Board of Control for Test matches at home and the Advisory County Cricket Committee.
Scheduled MCC tour of South Africa cancelled upon the non-acceptance of B. L. D'Oliveira by the South African Government.

1969 John Player League for Sunday cricket inaugurated.
Gibraltar and Hong Kong became ICC Associate Members.

1969-70 South Africa at home played their last Test series to date, beating Australia 4-1.

1970 Proposed South African tour of England cancelled at the request of the British Government after anti-Apartheid protests.

1971 India gained their first Test victory in England.

1972 Benson and Hedges Cup inaugurated.

1973 Bookmakers in operation at Trent Bridge, Lord's, Kennington Oval and Leeds, a reversion to the nineteenth century practice.
Papua-New Guinea became an ICC Associate Member.

1974 Argentina, Israel and Singapore became ICC Associate Members.

1975 First Prudential World Cup, a single-innings tournament involving eight countries, won by West Indies, who beat Australia in the final at Lord's.

1976 In the Golden Jubilee year of the Women's Cricket Association, women played for the first time at Lord's, England beating Australia in a 60-over match.
West Africa became an ICC Associate Member.

1977 Formation of the multi-racial South African Cricket Union.
Bangladesh became an ICC Associate Member.

1977 An Australian, Kerry Packer, signed 51 of the world's best players in opposition to the ICC. In a High Court action that followed, Packer won on all counts and ICC member countries had to pay £250,000 in legal costs. There followed two Australian seasons of rebel cricket (World Series Cricket) competing with the official game.
County Championship sponsored for the first time (by Schweppes).
1979 Packer's TV Channel 9 granted exclusive rights for Test and other "official" matches in Australia.
Sri Lanka won the first ICC Trophy competition for Associate Members.
MCC ceded control of overseas tours to the TCCB.
1980 Laws of Cricket rewritten.
World Series Cricket disbanded, participants not penalised.
1981 Sri Lanka admitted to full ICC Membership.
Kenya and Zimbabwe became ICC Associate Members.
1982 Sri Lanka played their first Test, losing to England in Colombo.
R. W. Marsh (Australia) became the first wicket-keeper with 300 Test victims.
A team of English cricketers, led by G. A. Gooch, played a series of matches in South Africa. Though admitted by TCCB to have broken no rule of that body, all were barred from Test cricket for three years.
A compulsory minimum of 96 overs a day, weather permitting, introduced in a Test series in England.
1983 India won a surprising victory over West Indies in the final of the Prudential World Cup.
New Zealand gained their first Test victory in England.
1983-84 New Zealand won a rubber against England for the first time, in New Zealand.
Pakistan beat England in Pakistan for the first time.
First visit by an official England team to Fiji.
1984 West Indies became the first side to gain a clean sweep in a five-Test series against England in England.
Counties obliged to bowl 117 overs a day, weather permitting, in the Championship.
1985 Four-day matches against some counties included in the Australian tour of England as an experiment.
1985-86 Proposed England B tours of Bangladesh and Zimbabwe cancelled when visas refused to England players who had played in South Africa.
Sri Lanka won their first Test match, beating India in Colombo.
1986 New Zealand won a series in England for the first time.
1986-87 The second tie in Tests: India v Australia at Madras; Australia 574 for seven dec. and 170 for five dec., India 397 and 347.
1987 ICC introduced as an experimental rule a compulsory minimum of fifteen overs an hour, weather permitting, in Test cricket.
Period of qualification for England reduced from ten years to seven.
1987-88 World Cup held outside England for the first time; played in India and Pakistan. Australia beat England in the final at Calcutta.
1988 Four-day matches played in the County Championship for the first time.
1988-89 England tour of India cancelled when the Indian government refused visas to eight England players with South African links.

EVOLUTION OF THE LAWS

THE PITCH. The length of 22 yards, laid down in 1744 and identical with the length of the agricultural chain, has never varied. The 46 inches between creases was increased to 48 in 1819. In 1744 the length of the bowling crease was set at 3 feet on each side of the wicket; this was increased to 4 feet in 1902, and became 3ft 11½ inches in 1939 when the width of the wicket was increased from 8 to 9 inches. Until the 1830s, when whitewash was introduced, creases were cut in the turf. Originally the pitch went untouched during a match, but in 1788 by mutual consent it could, in the course of it, be rolled, watered, covered and mown. In the same year the use of sawdust was authorised. In 1849 the pitch could be swept and rolled between innings at the request of either side, but in 1860 the rolling decision was solely in the hands of the side batting next. In 1883 rolling before play each day was permitted for ten minutes, but in 1931 the period for all rolling was reduced to seven minutes. Covering the bowler's footholds and the batsman's standing ground was authorised in 1910.

HE WICKET. About 1700 the wicket consisted of two stumps covering 6 inches in breadth id 22 inches in height with one bail. About 1776 a third stump was introduced, the easurements remaining unchanged. In 1785 one or two bails could be used, and in 1798 the eight was increased to 24 inches and the width to 7 inches. The height was increased by 2 ches, the width by 1 inch and two bails became compulsory about 1819; another inch was lded to both height and width some four years later, and the wicket then remained unchanged r more than 100 years. In 1931 the height became 28 inches and the width was set at not less ıan 8 and not more than 9 inches. The latter became statutory in 1947.

HE BAT. No dimensions laid down for the original long, curved bat. First ruling, 1771, limited e width to $4\frac{1}{2}$ inches, and in 1835 the length was limited to 38 inches. A year later Dark's bats ere being sold by Sadd of Cambridge for 8s. 6d. each. In 1853-54 cane handles were troduced, and rubber handle covers in 1880. (Early bats were very heavy. William Ward made s 278 in 1820 with one of 4lb 2oz.)

HE BALL. Between 5 and 6 ounces in 1744, it was changed 30 years later to between $5\frac{1}{2}$ and $5\frac{3}{4}$ unces. In 1838 the circumference was set at between 9 and $9\frac{1}{4}$ inches, reduced in 1927 to etween $8\frac{13}{16}$ and 9 inches. In 1907 a new ball could be taken after 200 runs. That practice ıanged after the Second World War, when a series of experiments culminated in the current rovision for a new ball after 85 six-ball overs.

HE OVER. In 1744, four balls were customary, but six in rural games. Five or six balls were galised for one-day games, and six balls were first used in Australian first-class cricket in 1884. year later six were also in vogue in Philadelphia. In 1889 a five-ball over was introduced for vo- and three-day games, with eight or ten permitted in Philadelphia a year later, the eight-ball ver being used there in competitions until the 1920s. Six balls for two- and three-day games ere introduced in 1900, and in 1918 Australia's eight-ball over was authorised. This was tried English county cricket in 1939 but rated a failure. In 1947 it was ruled that the final over must e completed, even though full time may have been reached.

O-BALL. In the early nineteenth century no-balls were called only for over-stepping the rease. In 1816 legislation that the bowler's hand must be below the elbow at the moment of elivery was the first move against throwing, and in 1835 it was stipulated that the hand must ot be above the shoulder. Overarm bowling was authorised in 1864. Twenty years later it was ipulated that umpires must be "absolutely satisfied" that the ball was bowled, not thrown or rked. In 1899 *either* umpire was allowed to call a no-ball. In 1947 it was decreed that the back ot, at the moment of delivery, need not be grounded though it must be behind the bowling rease. Judging no-balls on the front foot in relation to the batting crease was introduced, at first xperimentally, in 1963.

ECLARATIONS. These were first authorised in 1889, but only on the third day or in one-day atches. This was extended to after lunch on the second day in 1900 and was allowed on the first ay of a two-day match, but not later than 100 minutes before the time fixed for drawing stumps. n 1957 declarations could be lawfully made at any time.

OLLOW-ON. The first recorded instance was in 1787, no size of lead then being stipulated. he follow-on was made compulsory after a deficit of 100 runs in 1835. This was temporarily educed (1854-94) to a deficit of 80 runs and raised to 120 in the latter year. In 1900 it was made ptional when 150 behind, and in 1922 the figure was set at 200 in Australian first-class cricket. ubsequently this became general for five-day Tests. The declaration was in abeyance in the ounty Championship in 1961 and 1962.

OSS. The toss conferred choice of innings and pitch in 1744. In 1774 the visiting side was iven choice of both, and about 1809 the toss decided the choice of innings while umpires chose he pitch.

BW. In 1774 a batsman was out if, *with design*, he used his leg to prevent the ball hitting the icket. The design clause was omitted in 1788, but it was stipulated that the ball must be pitched straight". About 1821 this was amended to "delivered straight", though there followed reversion to the 1788 version in 1839. The first recorded lbw dismissal came in 1795. A strong move in 1901 to have "pitched straight" abolished failed to get the necessary two-thirds majori at an MCC meeting. In 1935 the Law was first widened to embrace balls pitched outside the o stump, though the ball had to strike the batsman in line between wicket and wicket. First mov towards the current Law, penalising a batsman making no attempt to meet ball with bat ar struck on his person outside the off stump, were made in 1970.

STUMPED. First recorded instance in 1744.

SCORING. The score at the fall of each wicket was first recorded in 1751; the first know stroke-by-stroke record of a match followed in 1769. In 1777 the bowler was first credited wi catches off his bowling. Wides were first recorded as such in 1827, no-balls in 1830 and leg-by in 1848. In 1836 it was decided that the bowler should be credited by name with wickets batsmen caught and stumped off him. In 1844 wides could be "run for".

BOUNDARIES. In 1884 boundaries were first mentioned in the Laws, but they had been operation, with varying allowances, long before. Not until 1910 were hits over the bounda credited with 6 runs. Previously only hits out of the ground were so rewarded.

CRICKET DRESS

EIGHTEENTH CENTURY. Three-cornered or jockey hats, often with silver or gold lace shirts, generally frilled; nankeen breeches; silk stockings; buckled shoes. The Hambledon Clu wore sky-blue coats with buttons engraved "C.C." The first MCC uniform was in azure blue

1800-1850. Trousers gradually replaced breeches, and tall "beaver" hats in black or whi became general. Shirts were no longer frilled but were worn with rather high collars an spreading bow ties. Singlets instead of shirts were not uncommon. Wide braces were often wor and belts with metal clasps round the waist. Black "Oxford" shoes were usually worn. Late i the period the tall hat gave way to a full flannel cap, white or chequered, or, less commonly, straw hat, often of a haymaker's shape. Short white flannel jackets appeared as forerunners c the blazer. T. Lockyer (Surrey) was reputedly the first to wear "a cricket coat".

1850-1880. I Zingari started a vogue for club cricket colours, often as ribbons round whit bowler hats, which were becoming the popular headgear. Club caps – sometimes of pillbo shape – date from the middle of the century, but Eton may have sported their light blue caps a early as 1831 and the Rugby XI theirs in 1843. Winchester wore their blue caps in 1851 an Harrow their striped ones a year later. The Cambridge blue cap seems to date from 1861 an Oxford's certainly from 1863. Coloured shirts became common as uniform; e.g. a pattern c coloured spots, stripes or checks on white. The All-England XI wore white shirts with pin spots.

1880 ONWARDS. Coloured shirts disappeared, except that Rugby School still retained thei blue ones for the First XI. White shirts, at first starched, were the rule, and ties began t disappear. White buckskin boots arrived in the early 1880s, gradually edging out the brown an brown-and-white type. By the end of the Golden Age, cricketers appeared as they hav continued to until the present day, except that some still kept up their trousers with rolle coloured scarves, some even doing so after the First World War.

PROTECTIVE GEAR. About 1800 a player named Robinson experimented with board strapped to his legs. He was greeted with mirth, but in the middle 1830s the first pads wer produced and became larger and more protective with time. Tubular batting gloves had already appeared in the previous decade, and wicket-keeping gloves, which also gained in strength with the years, first appeared in the middle of the nineteenth century. Thigh pads, seldom used unti after the Second World War, came later. After that chest pads followed, and in 1978 batsmer began wearing helmets, often with vizors. Finally, with an increase in fast, short-pitched bowling, forearm guards were regularly seen.

CRICKET BOOKS, 1988

By JOHN ARLOTT

he 86 books of this year's review include several of significance, one unique olume of history, one volume monumental in size, several quite original tudies, and overall they maintain a high level.

A History of Cricket (Barrie & Jenkins; £15.95), by Benny Green, is quite nlike any of the other histories of the game. Mr Green has studied his ubject extremely closely and his decision has been to write a history at once actual and entertaining. It is a story-teller's book, built around characters nd anecdotes, but the characters are real and the stories are true. It has bviously been written with pleasure and is immensely readable, without xaggeration or omission. Behind all the obvious enjoyment and the humour s a considerable wealth of knowledge and study. What other cricket history, or instance, contains such a quotation as this one from Carr's *Dictionary of Extraordinary English Cricketers*, concerning the Reverend Elisha Fawcett c 1817) "who devoted his life to teaching the natives of the Admiralty slands the Commandments of God and the Laws of Cricket. Too poor to urchase a monument to this good man, his parishioners erected his wooden eg upon his grave. In that fertile clime it miraculously took root, and for many years provided a bountiful harvest of bats." This is an unfailing fount f the diverting and unexpected. The characters are lively, many of the tories fresh, and the illustrations, many in colour, vary between the classic nd the surprising. It will be read with considerable enjoyment.

In *The Illustrated History of the Test Match* (Sidgwick & Jackson; £15.95), hose diligent authors, Peter Arnold and Peter Wynne-Thomas, have approached their task most intelligently. Their purpose was to produce a omplete review of the 110 years (1877 to 1987) of cricket between all the Test-playing countries. They have described every series and, while they have not slavishly given complete scorecards, except of historic matches, they ummarise scores, note outstanding performances and provide full averages or every series. There are also perceptive biographical sketches of the most mportant players, a complete register of all Test cricketers, outstanding ecords, and most thoughtfully selected illustrations. It is a highly efficient ompilation.

The Players (Heinemann/Kingswood; £14.95), by Ric Sissons, is a rare and mportant work. Sub-titled "A Social History of the Professional Cricketer", t is precisely that, putting human flesh on to the statistics of the game. The uthor grew up in Nottinghamshire and Derbyshire before studying at the Universities of Sussex and London: he now works in Sydney as a managing director of a publishing house and as a cricket historian. Thus the danger of English or Australian bias is obviated. This is a scholarly study by a man who has gone to original sources for his material; what he has written is authentic. He has clear-mindedly dealt with the many so-called amateurs who were, in fact, professionals. The student of cricket history will be more fully informed for reading this penetrating analysis of the game at its truly human level.

A major book of cricket history has been produced by Michael Manley, who was for some years Prime Minister of Jamaica and is now Leader of the Opposition there. It is *A History of West Indies Cricket* (André Deutsch; £17.95), and it is a very solid work indeed – 576 pages. The author has a background as an historian and describes himself as "a devoted follower c the sport and a visceral supporter of the West Indies". He is valuably able t see the immense social importance of cricket in West Indian developmer and unity, which is probably greater than in any other country. The author' own experience of the game began when, at the age of ten, he watche George Headley make 270 not out against the English team of 1934-35: an he saw Learie Constantine. In those days, of course, West Indies were not, i terms of results, a major power, but he can continue his story to the point a which they became the most powerful all-round side in the world. He himse has played a part in West Indies' cricket history; he was effective in th matter of "The Packer Affair", which he believes was vital in their cricket ing progress. Indeed, he sees cricket, as Clive Lloyd expresses it in th introduction, as "The instrument of Caribbean cohesion". This is likely t remain basically the standard work on the subject for many years to come

The Diamond Jubilee (1928-1988) of West Indian cricket has also bee marked by *100 Great West Indian Cricketers from Challenor to Richard* (Hansib Publishing; £14.95), by Bridgette Lawrence, a British-born studen of the game there, and Reg Scarlett, the former Jamaican player. While nc of the weight of the previous volume, it is biographically sound and readable with each player's career record complementing the biographical studies. Th illustration is lively and the whole is informed by a genuine enthusiasm.

Professor G. Derek West, an historian at McMaster University, Ontario, i the author of *The Elevens of England* (Darf; £9.95). This is a study of th wandering elevens of the mid-nineteenth century, an important basic facto in the spread of cricket through England. Starting with William Clarke an his All-England XI and continuing through to the United North of Englan XI and Yorkshire United, he shows their growth and their character. H produces, too, such anecdotes as that of John Thewlis, the Yorkshirema who, refusing to take off his jacket while batting on a warm day, explained "Ah warn't going to show 'em t'oles in me shirt". Professor West ha produced an absorbing historical study with genuine period feeling Readable, and revealing, it belongs on the bookshelf of cricket history.

Those touring elevens were, in effect, the creators of the first-class game ir England and, hence, in the world. In *Cricket's Silver Lining 1864-1914* (Collin Willow; £15), David Rayvern Allen has selected with rare acumen the bes writing of those 50 years before broadcasting, film and television took awa what he has perceptively called "the mystique of the legendary characters o the game". This was the period of the outward spread from the County Championship to tours in and from America, Canada, Australia, South Africa and India; visits from the Aborigines, Australians, Parsees and Philadelphians, culminating with historical nicety in the first and only Triangular Tournament – that between Australia, South Africa and England in England in 1912. Mr Allen has good taste and a lively capacity fo research. In its way this is more profound than many so-called histories o the subject, in that it rouses the imagination and goes back to some of the earliest and, in its fashion, the most illuminating writing on the game.

The 1988 tour of England by an Aboriginal team was most happily marked by the publication of a second and enlarged edition of *Cricket Walkabout* (Macmillan, in association with the Department of Aboriginal Affairs; £10.95), an account of the original Aboriginal tours of 1867-68, by John Mulvaney and Rex Harcourt. Mr Mulvaney was Professor of Pre-History at the Australian National University and later a member of the Council of the

Institute of Aboriginal Studies; Mr Harcourt is Research Librarian of the Melbourne Cricket Club. This enlarged edition of their study was made possible by two "supportive barrackers" – Bill O'Reilly, himself an eminent modern player, who gave the accounts ledger of the original tour to the Melbourne Club; and a descendant of Charles Lawrence, the 1868 captain, who gave the authors access to family papers. Thus they have been able to put together an intriguing, historically valuable account of that early visit by "square, broad-shouldered fellows, with their burly, black faces and their beaming eyes, dashing about the field with their lithe suppleness". The standing of the two authors guarantees the quality of their work; it is full of illuminating facts and data, providing a unique view of an almost unique aspect of the game of cricket.

Homes of Cricket (Macdonald/Queen Anne Press; £14.95), by George Plumptre, with E. W. Swanton as Consultant Editor, contains descriptions of the 55 grounds where county matches were played during the 1987 season. For those with long memories, Patrick Eagar's admirable photographs – some of them in colour – are both striking and nostalgic. Cricket certainly has changed in modern years, but so, most emphatically, have the grounds on which it is played. The method adopted takes a tour from Lord's through the Home Counties, the West, North and down through the major University grounds. While topography is obviously the main emphasis, no book of cricket history can ignore the game's great players and they are dealt with sympathetically by an enthusiast who obviously enjoyed his journey. The saddest note of the volume deals with the plan to abolish the town-centre ground at Hastings. Apparently this was described by a local councillor as "a major step forward". It is a minor local tragedy, but that should not detract from a most attractive book.

The Crisis of Captaincy: Servant and Master in English Cricket (Christopher Helm; £12.95), by David Lemmon, is a thought-provoking book. The relationship between captain and player used, of old, to be generally social. It has latterly become much more positively a question of success, the latest example of which is the Gloucestershire cricket committee's decision to dismiss David Graveney. There have, however, as Mr Lemmon points out, been many other recent significant issues such as Brearley–Botham and Mike Gatting's troubles. Other interesting chapters are "The Age of Bradman", "The Twilight of the Amateur", "The Age of the Professional" and, appropriately finally, "Winning – the Cause for Concern". It is a book to stimulate thought and argument.

Peter Wynne-Thomas, the county's curator and librarian, and secretary of the Association of Cricket Statisticians, is the author of *Nottinghamshire, Cricket's Double Champions 1987* (Heinemann/Kingswood; £10.95). It is not only an account of that much relished double success – the County Championship and the NatWest Bank Trophy, both narrowly achieved – but also the facts of an anxiety about the departure of the county's two outstanding overseas players, Clive Rice and Richard Hadlee. Those two men, though, are not alone in the author's attention or the reader's interest. Well-liked locals such as Derek Randall come into the story, as do manager Ken Taylor and Ron Allsopp, the Trent Bridge groundsman for 35 years. The final narrative stages concern the county's attempt to win three titles in 1987: they missed the treble but the double, clearly, left them extremely happy.

The year in review has seen the launch of a series of county cricket histories, each consisting of two separate sections – a personal view from someone closely concerned with the county and, second, the strict history. So far, the first four volumes have appeared. *The History of Glamorgan County Cricket Club* (Christopher Helm; £15.95), by Andrew Hignell, has a personal view by Tony Lewis. In a way this is, and will remain, unique among the county histories in that it is, at heart, national – in other words, the story of Welsh cricket. It may not have the trappings of antiquity to be found about some other counties, though W. G. Grace played for the South Wales club from which Glamorgan sprang. In fact, 1988 was the centenary of the county club. Much of the history's material is concerned with recent events, not all of them happy. On the other hand, there are stirring, and very Welsh, appreciations of the two Championship wins and defeats of the Australians. Tony Lewis remarks at one point, "The history of Glamorgan makes *Pilgrim's Progress* sound like a day in the life of Peter Rabbit". It is much personalised around such people as Johnnie Clay, Maurice Turnbull, Wilfred Wooller, Ossie Wheatley and Lewis, most substantially documented, with a wealth of statistics, and intelligently illustrated.

The History of Hampshire County Cricket Club (Christopher Helm; £12.95) is by Peter Wynne-Thomas, historian and librarian of Trent Bridge. He has a long story to tell – from a somewhat obscure reference of 1729, through Hambledon to the present day. The early years in the Championship, and even such outstanding performers as Philip Mead and Lord Tennyson, could not bring the county the success it enjoyed, to some people's surprise, in 1961. It has been a county full of characters as diverse as Colin Ingleby-Mackenzie and Derek Shackleton and a whole clutch of highly talented performers, not the least of them introduced from overseas, but it has assimilated them all. The last chapter heading is "The West Indian Influence", but without doubt a fresh phase will soon be established. Famous matches are recorded in full, there are biographical details of outstanding players, results of all inter-county matches 1864-1987, results in the limited-overs competitions, an analysis of grounds on which matches have been played, major team and individual records, and a late page, historically, gives a list of the main Hambledon players. [The personal view in this volume is provided by John Arlott.]

The History of Kent County Cricket Club (Christopher Helm; £13.95), by Dudley Moore, is ushered in by a personal view from Derek Underwood. The main story runs from 1776 and a triple killing through some happier and less bloodthirsty events to the first Championship win in 1906 – and on to the rich successes of the 1970s. It holds such great names as Colin Blythe, Frank Fielder, "Tich" Freeman, Doug Wright, Derek Underwood, J. R. Mason, K. L. Hutchings, Frank Woolley, Colin Cowdrey, Percy Chapman, Bryan Valentine and – Kent's particular strength – the wicket-keepers; Les Ames, Godfrey Evans, Jack Hubble, Fred Huish, Alan Knott and "Hopper" Levett. The story is a rich and often picturesque one, full of ripe characters and great performances, and, in the fashion of the series, the illustrations are pleasing and relevant. The statistics are similar to those of the Hampshire volume.

In *The History of Middlesex County Cricket Club* (Christopher Helm; £14.95), by David Lemmon, the personal view is given by Denis Compton. Once again, the pattern of great scorecards, sharp illustrations, statistics of all the county's players, match results and personal records is maintained. The story is an absorbing one, never more absorbing for the modern reader – nor, surely, for one of any age – than during the period of the great triumphs of Compton and Bill Edrich. A series of captains has left a deeper imprint on

THE PAVILION LIBRARY

New for 1989, to be published on 15 May

CRICKET ALL HIS LIFE

The Cricket Writings of E.V. Lucas
Assembled by Sir Rupert Hart-Davis

In 1950 Sir Rupert Hart-Davis collected the cream of Lucas's popular cricket writings in this masterly anthology. This new edition also has an introduction by John Arlott.

224 pages 216 x 138mm

THE CRICKET CAPTAINS OF ENGLAND

Alan Gibson

The dramatic story of the group of men who have led England to victory and defeat on the cricket field has the priceless asset of a magnificent cast that includes William Clark, W.G. Grace, Jackson and Fry, Douglas, Jardine, Cowdrey, Illingworth, Botham and Gooch.

256 pages 8pp b/w
216 x 138mm

DOUBLE CENTURY

Cricket in the Times Volume One: 1785-1935
Edited by Marcus Williams

Volume One of the monumental *Times* cricket anthology, first published on the paper's 200th birthday, brings together the best cricket writing in 'The Thunderer' from the eighteenth century to the 1930s.

312 pages 216 x 138mm

SORT OF A CRICKET PERSON

E. W. Swanton
With a new introduction by the author

By general agreement E.W. Swanton has been one of the most influential and authoritative commentators on cricket since the war. This is his personal story of his life in cricket up till shortly before his retirement.

328 pages 8pp b/w
216 x 138mm

Editorial address: Pavilion Books,
196 Shaftesbury Avenue,
London WC2 8JL

All available in paperback at £7.99, in bookshops.

Middlesex than on most counties. The select bibliography, as in the case of Kent, is impressive; it would weigh down a shelf with history and perception.

Don Mosey, the author of *We Don't Play it for Fun* (Methuen; £10.95), describes his book as "quite simply, a sentimental outpouring of the love and reverence [he has] nurtured for Yorkshire cricket for more than 50 years". Thus he effectively gives the lie to the impression of Yorkshiremen as "hard" cricketers. Certainly they can be, and are shown to be, highly competitive, but the author's use of the word "sentimental" is not inappropriate. In telling the story he has, of course, to start with the record books of years before he was born, but he continues through the hero-worship of boyhood and comes on finally to players with whom he has personal acquaintance. The chapter on "Archetypal Yorkies" was to be expected, as were those on Sutcliffe and Leyland, Sir Leonard Hutton, Verity and Bowes, and "Fiery Fred". In many ways no passages of the book are more revealing than those on Geoffrey Boycott, who is clearly not now the author's favourite cricketer. All in all, this is a compelling read, full of the writer's most genuine feelings and prejudices.

Glamorgan Cricketers 1888-1987 (Association of Cricket Statisticians; £2.50; currently free to members) continues that series of player-records, giving their births, deaths (where appropriate) and statistics within a workmanlike 30 pages.

Cricket Grounds of Hampshire (Association of Cricket Statisticians; currently free to members) is a 28-page booklet with all the relevant information of the county's first-class grounds and others used by the Second XI. This is a worthy little series, soon to outgrow the adjective "little" and, with completion, to become an authoritative reference.

Guildford's Jubilee 1938-1988 (Guildford Cricket Club, Guildford, Surrey; £2), edited by the club's president, David Frith, was produced to celebrate 50 years of county cricket on the town's local ground. It is a 44-page quarto, most generously illustrated and with a thorough historical coverage of first-class cricket there.

A nostalgic and, in some ways, a moving cricket history is *Before and After Bramall Lane* (Sheffield United CC; £4.95; or from the author, 205 High Greave, Sheffield S5 9GS, plus 75p p. & p.), by Keith Farnsworth. Sub-titled "Sheffield United CC and Yorkshire Cricket in Sheffield", it relates the story of the county game at Bramall Lane from 1854 until it was pressured out by the soccer club after the 1973 season. County cricket is still played in the Sheffield district, but now at Abbeydale. Over those 120 years at Bramall Lane, all the great Yorkshire players appeared there, and Mr Farnsworth has gathered together accounts of outstanding performances, some amusing anecdotes, and even an evocative piece of verse. Primarily a local book, it now becomes something of a souvenir, easy to read and, especially for the Yorkshireman, an essential local document.

The Cricket Clubs of Christchurch: A History (Southern Evening Echo and Christchurch Cricket Club, Dorset; £5), by Tom Kelly, deals with the clubs in that small Hampshire/Dorset area. From the famous painting of 1850 which hangs in the Long Room at Lord's until the present day, it discusses several clubs – Mudeford, Highcliffe, Bramsgore, West Hants Water Company, Somerford, Christchurch, Hurn – the Colemore and De Zoete Cups, and sorties into the area, especially for benefit matches, by sides composed largely or entirely of county players. It is a friendly, essentially local book with plenty of photographic illustrations and period quotations.

Not to be confused with the foregoing, *Christ Church Institute Cricket Club, Beckenham Centenary 1887-1987* (from the Centenary sub-committee, 11 Rectory Green, Hayne Road, Beckenham, Kent BR3 4HX; no price given) is a single club history dating from 1887. "No ordinary year, it witnessed Queen Victoria's Golden Jubilee and the centenary of MCC." There are some pleasing period photographs, none better than that of the side setting off to a pre-First World War away game in a coach and pair.

First in the Field is a history of the Birmingham and District Cricket League (KAF Brewing Books, Studley, Warwickshire; £7.95), which claims to be the oldest cricket league. It was formed in December 1888, and this account of its doings is a substantial, 232-page account with a list of its players. It has a foreword by Charles Palmer and a year-by-year history in fair detail. There are, of course, famous names in it, especially some of the professionals; among them Bill Merritt, S. F. Barnes, Eric Hollies and George Headley. There are, too, generous illustrations over those 100 years.

South Loughton Cricket Club 50 Years 1938-1988 (from Andrew Shields, 48 Davies Lane, Leytonstone, London E11 3DR; £2.50) is an octavo of records, stories, officers and photographs of the club over its half-century of existence.

Peter Pan and Cricket (Constable; £12.95), by David Rayvern Allen, is a collection of mainly autobiographical writing by James Barrie. It is as whimsical, as gentle, as appreciative, and as gently humorous as one would expect. Barrie was, he explained, "Not *Wisden* material", but from time to time, particularly in his correspondence, one comes upon such passages as: "Augustine Birrell once hit so hard that he smashed the bat of Anon, which had been kindly lent to him, and instead of grieving he called out gloriously, 'Fetch me some more bats'." Barrie founded his own cricket club, called the Allahakbarries, and while they may not have been of genuinely outstanding playing ability, nevertheless Charles Macartney and Arthur Mailey were persuaded to play for them. Perhaps that team, like its creator, was not *Wisden* material, but that major work of cricket reference devoted four and a half lines to an obituary of Barrie. This is a successful attempt to link the gentle charm of Barrie's writing to his love for cricket.

The Boundary Book Second Innings (Pelham Books; £14.95), compiled and edited by Leslie Frewin, with a preface by HRH Prince Philip, is an impressive collection. Successor to *The Boundary Book* of 1962, it is a weighty, 384-page collection ranging widely in time and type of material – prose, verse, interviews, cartoons and photographs. It also goes outside the normal field of cricket writers. Contributions from Lord Olivier, Sir John Mills, Sir Arthur Conan Doyle, Sir John Betjeman and Leslie Thomas are among the many that make up a highly pleasurable piece of reading. All the fees and royalties are donated to the Lord's Taverners' charities to aid disabled children and youth cricket.

The NatWest Boundary Book (Macmillan; £16.95), a Lord's Taverners Australia miscellany of cricket, is also compiled and edited by Leslie Frewin, with a preface by HRH Prince Philip and an introduction by Sir Donald Bradman. Like the other *Boundary Book*, it ranges widely, but its themes and the majority of its contributors are Australian. It has attractive illustrations, and there are some surprises in store – such as a message from the Honorary Taverner, His Serene Highness Prince Rainier of Monaco. Its humour is often acute and extremely Australian, and altogether it is another good read. Its publication coincided with Australia's Bicentennial Year, and the profits

are to be channelled through the Lord's Taverners Australia to aid disadvantaged Australian children.

Cricket's Lighter Side: A Cricketer Collection (Simon & Schuster; £8.95) is a collection edited by Christopher Martin-Jenkins. As editor of *The Cricketer* he writes in his introduction: "One of the editorial decisions taken when *The Cricketer's* office moved to Redhill in 1981 was to try to include in every issue of the magazine at least one article which would make people smile, if not laugh." That has been achieved, as this collection shows, in essays, anecdotes, drawings, full-page cartoons and some rather surprising advertisements. It is easy to read and a most friendly bedside book.

More Cricket on the Air: A Further Selection from BBC Broadcasts (BBC Books; £12.95) has been made by David Rayvern Allen. It is extremely revealing and especially impressive for its interviews with famous cricketers who never, or rarely, broke into print themselves. Much of the material is original from its broadcast days. The section entitled "Feminine Form" is fresh and refreshing. There are two extracts of actual commentary, and some relishable humour, but it is the interviews that really compel attention.

From Brisbane to Karachi with the Test Match Special Team (Macdonald/Queen Anne Press; £10.95), edited by Peter Baxter, is fronted by a coloured caricature of the broadcasters who contribute to the volume. After a foreword by Willie Rushton, they deal with England in Australia 1986-87, England v Pakistan 1987, with separate accounts of the Tests, the MCC Bicentenary match, the World Cup and England in Pakistan. There are also sundry essays by Don Mosey, Trevor Bailey, Peter Baxter, Henry Blofeld and Brian Johnston. It is a cheerful, informal, but also informative, account, and it is most amusingly illustrated.

The Illustrated Wisden Anthology 1864-1988 (St Michael; £12.99) is edited by Benny Green, who is moving on familiar ground, for he has searched and researched the long shelves of *Wisden* before. This, however, is a single-volume collection and, while *Wisden* has been only sparingly illustrated, the pictures chosen here from a wide field do reflect the copy and its periods. Mr Green has chosen well and arranged cleverly. There is an emphasis on match accounts, as there was not in Mr Green's previous selections, but it is by no means the worse for that. Indeed, to the follower of cricket, it is immensely readable and the illustrations are most happily and evocatively employed.

The British Academy of Cricket Manual for Gentlemen and Players (Pavilion Books; £12.95) is written and designed by Martin Ward and Paul Oldman. Much may be gathered from its sub-title: "A MENTOR and GUIDE on all matters relating to Cricket with notes on PROPER SPORTING BEHAVIOUR, the whole being an AUTHORISED DIGEST of Legislation expressed in simple Lessons and Strict REGULATIONS." Most handsomely printed and produced, it seems to be intended as an elaborate and generously illustrated 240-page joke. However, it will not necessarily make all its readers laugh.

How to Win at Cricket: or The Skipper's Guide (Hodder & Stoughton; £12.95), by E. M. Rose, is a thoughtful guide to cricket captaincy. Mr Rose was captain of Rugby School, a Cambridge Blue, and for many years played for, and captained, the Limpsfield club in Surrey. He is, too, a National Cricket Association coach, a member of MCC, and an industrialist whose hobbies are cricket, golf and painting in oils. He has written a perceptive and thought-provoking study of captaincy which is expressed most cogently and is, above all, full of good, sound common sense. As Trevor Bailey points out

in his preface, "A glance at seven of the finest post-war internation captains reveals that there is no standard model". To state the obvious, the is only one captain in a cricket eleven and many are inclined to envy and criticise him. Although he has not been a professional captain – and indee he is not necessarily the worse for that – Mr Rose has written a genuine workmanlike study. He obviously much admires Mike Brearley, and h writing is completely independent.

The Basic Principles of Cricket (Warwickshire County Cricket Supporter Association; £1.50), by Neal Abberley, is a 32-page booklet of good, sour advice for the young from an experienced player, county coach, and you organiser for the Warwickshire club. There is no extravagance, just som helpful drawings and soundly made points.

West Indian Summer: the Test Series of 1988 (Hodder & Stoughton; £12.9 consists of photographs and montages by Patrick Eagar and textual accoun by Alan Ross. These two clearly work well together. Mr Ross is concerne mainly with lucid captions and a commentary to what are probably the fine cricket photographs Mr Eagar has yet collected into a single book. Th combination of the two is both generous and entertaining.

Cricket Odyssey (Pavilion Books; £14.95) is an account, by Scyld Berry, c England on tour in 1987-88. That most considerable journey took in th World Cup in India and Pakistan, the Bicentennial Test in Sydney, and th Test series in Pakistan and New Zealand. It had many of the usual curren but also some disturbing undercurrents. For the captain, Mike Gatting, th Test series in Pakistan in particular was unhappy. Mr Berry has taken balanced look at the whole touring business, its background and the setting c the matches. It is a highly stimulating and satisfying account, and the photo graphs by Graham Morris accompany it well.

The "rebel" Australian tours in South Africa, 1985-86 and 1986-87, gav rise to three publications by Chris Harte. These tours were quite unlike th average cricket tour to which the reader is normally accustomed and must b accepted in that light. The first was *Cricket Safari*, sub-titled "A Pictoria View of the Australian Team in South Africa, 1985-87" (Sports Marketing North Adelaide, South Australia; limited edition 2,000 copies; $A4.95 inc p. & p. seamail), an eighteen-page octavo with photo illustrations an averages. The second volume, produced, we are informed, because th demand for *Cricket Safari* was "quite incredible", is titled *Seven Tests* (Sport Marketing, North Adelaide, South Australia; $A5). It is concerned, almos solely, with the scores and relevant illustrations in a 40-page booklet whic summarises events in matches and the other matters thrown up by such tours

The third volume, *Two Tours and Pollock* (Sports Marketing, Nort Adelaide, South Australia; $A19.95; available in the UK from Martin Wood 2 St John's Road, Sevenoaks, Kent; £8.95), again by Chris Harte, is a altogether more substantial volume. A 320-page octavo with many phot illustrations, scores and averages, it completes Mr Harte's study of the tw tours. He is at pains to let the "rebel" captain, Kim Hughes, speak fo himself, and he records, in many instances revealingly – even, in thei implications, movingly – the feelings of the players concerned. As well as th busy text, there are ample, and some unusual, illustrations in this story of a often disturbing series of matches in which politics frequently overwhelme cricket. These are not entirely happy books but they do throw light on unfamiliar cricket events and, as such, form an essential part of the history o the game.

Queensland versus South Australia: A Statistical Survey (available in the UK om Appleby's Books, 5 St John's Street, Keswick, Cumbria; £5.50; or from oger Page, 55 Tarcoola Drive, Yallambie, Victoria, Australia; $A12.50 plus ɔstage), by John King, is the seventh of that author's Australian state-match ıstories. In the now familiar format, it runs to 46 cyclostyled foolscap pages very complete statistics and records.

Cricket's Statistics Year by Year 1946-1987 (Stanley Paul; £14.95), by Fred rueman and Don Mosey, covers those 41 years in the form of a dialogue etween the two, footnoted with statistics by Wendy Wimbush. For each year ıey give England's Test performances, home or away, and leading averages, ıe Championship table, main first-class averages, winners of the minor ɔmpetitions, and the results of one-day internationals. They discuss the chief vents and the main personalities in easy, lucid and sometimes humorous ıshion. The illustrations are wide-ranging.

The McDonald's Bicentennial Youth World Cup (Australian Cricket Board of ontrol; $A5.95), edited by Chris Harte, is a 96-page souvenir programme of ıat tournament in Australia in February and March 1988. It provides all the elevant information of planning and fixtures, plus biographical notes on the layers of the eight competing teams.

Qantas Aboriginal Cricket Tour of England 1988 (Qantas Airways) is a 6-page quarto souvenir. It begins with a message from Her Majesty The ueen, continues with notes on the first – 1868 – Aboriginal tour of England, nd goes on to up-to-date player profiles, history and a short essay setting ustralian cricket in perspective.

Western Creek Cricket Club Tour of England 1988 (Western Creek Cricket lub, PO Box 47, Western Creek, ACT 2611, Australia) is a 40-page octavo ouvenir with relevant feature articles, fixtures, biographical notes and ortraits of the players.

Dumbleton Day (from the author, The Coach House, Ponsonby, Seascale, umbria CA20 1BX; £1.25) is Nico Craven's annual contribution, concerned hiefly this time with a match between Eton Ramblers and Dumbleton. It is a ompanionable 12-page octavo.

The Five Seasons (Oak Press, 9 Oak Lane, Bradford BO9 4PU; £2.30) is a 2-page octavo, by Colin Shakespeare, issued in a limited edition of 500 opies, 26 of which have been lettered A to Z and signed by the author. It is he poet's third book and the first six poems are on the theme of cricket. The emainder are on more generally poetic themes.

First Wicket Down (W. H. Allen; £10.95), by John Parker, is a murder ıystery story. The author is a former Sports Editor of ITN who is known for is Tillingfold stories. Still an active club cricketer, he is the father of Paul arker of Sussex and England. He writes easily, and the plot holds his reader ırough to the end.

The Test Within (Stanley Paul; £10.95), by Frank Tyson, is sub-titled Talent and Temperament in 22 Cricketers". Mr Tyson writes from first-and experience of playing against or watching his 22 subjects. He has not nly observed them closely but uses his literary and perceptive skills to luminate their characters. It is one of the most thoughtful books written by ny cricketer, and the subjects themselves – from Len Hutton to Kapil Dev y way of Fred Trueman and Ian Botham – will undoubtedly read it bsorbedly.

The Ten Greatest Test Teams (Sidgwick & Jackson; £12.95), by Tom Graveney with Norman Giller, puts between covers, and in 176 pages, a phase of that absorbing game which cricket enthusiasts have played for yea – picking great teams; in this instance, only for the post-war period. They a teams that did actually take the field and they run from Don Bradman's 194 Australia to Clive Lloyd's West Indies of 1984. There is an account of th matches of each series and there are biographical sketches of the playe concerned. Tom Graveney was a happy choice as author. He played first-cla cricket for Gloucestershire, Worcestershire and Queensland between 194 and 1972 and in 79 Tests; in recent years he has been a much respecte television commentator. He was always an observant player and one wh tended to see the best in anyone else, batsman or bowler, so this book giv much scope for discussion as well as argument. The final assessment and th computer verdict can be left for the reader's diversion.

A major event in cricket publishing is *The Bradman Albums* (Macdonal Queen Anne Press, 2 volumes; £50) which run to 800 pages and have regula introductory notes by Sir Donald Bradman himself. It consists, as the tit page declares, of selections from Sir Donald's official collection. That wa started by Sir Donald's mother, then added to by her, his wife, relations, brother-in-law, his literary agent, and even some strangers. Hedley Brideso chief librarian of the State Library of South Australia, eventually persuade Sir Donald to put his scrapbooks into the custody of that library, from whic the staff compiled 52 volumes, bound in leather and permanently housed i the Mortlock Library on North Terrace, Adelaide, where they may b consulted by the public. Rigby Publishers, in Australia, conceived the idea o condensing the material into two volumes for publication. They cover mos of the major events of Sir Donald's first-class career from 1927 to 194 generally by means of reproduction of reports, scores, correspondence an articles. It is, indeed, a weighty publication, ending with the great batsman last appearance on Sydney Cricket Ground. That was in the Oldfield–Kippa testimonial when, unfortunately, Sir Donald was unable to finish the matc owing to a fall in the field. It has been most intelligently done and the genera standard of reproduction is of striking period quality, recalling the events o Sir Donald's cricketing life as they occurred. Monumental is the term for it

Bradman v Gavaskar (Lucknow Publishing House, Lucknow, India; Rs3 is a statistical comparison, running to 82 pages, of the performances of thos two record-breaking batsmen and includes some other world cricket records

Henry Blofeld has titled his opinions and anecdotes of cricket from 1984 t 1988 *My Dear Old Thing* (Stanley Paul; £10.95) and sub-titled it "Talkin Cricket". He ranges the world, on and off the field, observing players exchanging ideas, making humorous and profound comment, and generall enjoying himself and entertaining his reader. His experience of the game watching and reporting it, is wide, and his sense of humour all but unfailing The illustrations, too, are pertinent and the comments on them interesting

Botham: A Biography (Dent; £12.95), by Patrick Murphy, is an interestin and quite convincing biography of one of the most remarkable players th game has known. Mr Murphy has, and voices, his own opinions but h includes also those of Botham and his fellow players. It is an extremel human book, a readable one, and the story ends substantially with th comment of John Emburey. "An amazing bloke and, as all-rounders go, w will be lucky to see one like Ian Botham in the next fifty years."

Swings and Roundabouts (Pelham Books; £12.95), by Graham Dilley an Graham Otway, tells the story, from the age of twenty to date, of the Kent Worcestershire and England fast bowler who came back after losing almost

year to major surgery on a back injury. Graham Otway, who was large responsible for writing it, was cricket correspondent of the Press Associatic until he joined *Today*. He has covered every major England tour since 198 Here he skilfully gets inside the story of a most interesting cricketer. Th illustrations, too, are pleasing.

Fox on the Run (Viking; £12.95), by Graeme Fowler with Peter Hall, is review of the career of the Lancashire and England batsman whose caree has proved erratic. Within a few months of his scoring a double-century in Test in India, injury and loss of form reduced him to the Lancashire Secon XI. The story is absorbing and the opinions, many of them quite refreshing pertinent, are very much Fowler's own.

'Big Bird' Flying High (Arthur Barker; £9.95) is the autobiography of Joe Garner, the impressively tall Barbadian fast bowler who made the ball rear s high off a length that many of the best batsmen in the world found hir uniquely difficult to play. His experiences in Barbados, in the Lancashir League, with Somerset and, above all, in Test matches for West Indies, ar the theme of his book; and the final chapter consists of a conversatio between Joel Garner and 'Big Bird' on the subject of his leaving Somerset. " had not really wanted to talk about the more disenchanting aspects of my sta with Somerset", he remarks.

Leading from the Front (Macdonald/Queen Anne Press; £12.95), th autobiography of Mike Gatting with Angela Patmore, is the book tha brought the Middlesex and England captain into some controversy. Angel Patmore has written other studies on sport and is the author of one o pressure in top-class sport. It is intriguing to compare this book and its effect with those of cricketers of only a few years ago. The difference is never mor strikingly reflected than in one of the illustrations, captioned "Bangalor 1982: Sunil Gavaskar's 100 sparks fanatical reactions".

The Test Match Career of Sir Jack Hobbs (Spellmount; £12.95), by Cliv Porter, is a characteristically meticulous study of that great batsman whon his fellows called "The Master". Mr Porter is the most painstakingly accurat of cricket writers. He has clearly researched his subject to the last degree an should, it is understood, not be blamed for the misprints in the book. Thi account follows not only Sir Jack's Test career but his major cricket fo Surrey and the Players.

All Round View (Chatto & Windus; £12.95), by Imran Khan, emphasise not only that player's cricketing ability and knowledge but also his capacit for setting out ideas. As current press readers will appreciate, he is ar extremely literate man and here he mixes opinions with his account of events The former are firmly conveyed; in his own words, "I was never the boot licking type". Sound in his ideas about other players, he is also extremel illuminating about himself. One of a family of eight first-class cricketers, he has standards to apply and he applies them most relevantly. It is difficult no to believe that he has a career to come solely as a writer if he wishes to take it

Lancashire's Clive Lloyd (John Sherratt, 78 Park Road, Timperley Cheshire; £6), by Tony Derlien, with a foreword by Clive Lloyd himself, is a soft-bound 109-page octavo. The author explains in his preface: "This book tells only half of a story. There are two elements in Clive Lloyd's career; his West Indian cricket and his Lancashire cricket." He goes on, "I am a Manchester man". Hence he has written about Lloyd's career with his county, which is striking enough, in all conscience, and which, of course, spills over into the international game.

V. M. Merchant (Association of Cricket Statisticians; £2.25) is Numbe Three in the Association's Famous Cricketers series. It traces Merchant career and figures with the Association's characteristic concentration an accuracy over 28 octavo pages.

Cricket Master Class (Macdonald/Queen Anne Press; £13.95), by Vi Richards with Patrick Murphy, is, on the face of it, an instructional boo However, in his advice "Intended for the reasonably experienced playe whether school, college or club standard", Richards writes from first-han experience. Thus it is also a technical autobiography which, along the wa passes opinions on bowlers – and some batsmen – of all nations against whor Richards has played. The illustrations are illuminating about the methods c great players as are, with due modesty, Richards's own opinion of them.

Sobers: Twenty Years at the Top (Macmillan; £11.95), by Sir Garfiel Sobers with Brian Scovell, is a backward look by one of the greatest al rounders. The man who never wore a helmet, nor even a thigh pad, agains fast bowling makes Roy Gilchrist the fastest of his time. Above all, this is book of opinion on players – batsmen, bowlers, captains, the author himsel and the cricket of his time. It is astute about cricket and cricketers, warr about human beings and eminently readable.

Glenn Turner, captain and opening batsman of both Worcestershire an New Zealand, has called his autobiography, written with the help of hi brother, Brian, *Opening Up* (Hodder & Stoughton; £12.95). His career wa not completely smooth; at one point the New Zealand Cricket Counci announced his suspension, even though he was at the time their first full time professional captain. His cricket took him all over the world and hi opinions of other players are not only perceptive but extremely generous: an his views of the game are sound and rounded.

Johnny Wardle: Cricket Conjuror (David & Charles; £9.95) is a life story by Alan Hill, of a man who wrested both laughter and bitterness from th game. Wardle's was a strange story: he could be a humorist and, almos immediately, an aggressive man; his dismissal by Yorkshire in 1958 was tragedy for him and for cricket. After that he gained great affection wit Nelson and Rishton in the Lancashire League, and for Cambridgeshire h played a considerable part in the winning of the Minor Counties Champion ship in 1963. Before his death at 62 he was reconciled with Yorkshire, wh made him an Honorary Life Member; he was about to be appointed by th county as a bowling consultant when he died of a tumour of the brain. Ala Hill is Yorkshire-born and he feels for Wardle in both humour and tragedy It is an affectionate study in which the author does not close his eyes t his subject's flaws, yet in the end he brings him out with sympathy.

The weighty *Benson and Hedges Cricket Year* (Pelham Books; £16.95) edited by David Lemmon, is the seventh edition. It deals with all first-clas cricket, and much of the one-day play, everywhere in the world, fron September 1987 to the end of the English season in September 1988. Runnin to 479 quarto pages, replete with scores and averages from all those theatre of the game, it is a quite admirable work of reference which is finding permanently important place in the records of the game. The production i attractive and the illustration, in both black and white and colour, i generous.

Playfair Cricket Annual 1988 (Macdonald/Queen Anne Press; £1.75), editec by Bill Frindall, has now reached the seniority of 41 years and editions It is an ideal pocket reference to the game. It consists of 256 pages, with biographical notes on players and generous statistics – Test career records for all nations and first-class career records for English county players. It covers the one-day competitions and the Universities and provides notes on the first-class umpires.

ACS International Cricket Year Book 1988 (Association of Cricket Statisticians; no price given), compiled by a wide, representative and authoritative range of members of the Association, is an impressively exhaustive statistical record. It covers every cricketer who appeared in a first-class match or an important one-day limited-overs match in the 1987 English season or in the 1986-87 season in Australia, India, New Zealand, Pakistan, Sharjah, South Africa, Sri Lanka, West Indies or Zimbabwe. It thus includes every current major cricketer in the world. It runs to 96 octavo pages and is compiled with the Association's detailed accuracy.

Minor Counties Cricket Annual and Official Handbook 1988 (Association of Cricket Statisticians; £2.75), compiled by David Armstrong, Kenneth S. C. Trushell and Robert W. Brooke, is a review of the Minor Counties season of 1987 and a list of fixtures for 1988. It provides biographical and statistical records of all the Minor Counties players of 1987.

Allan's Australian Cricket Annual 1987-88 (from the editor, 219 St George's Terrace, Perth WA 6000, Australia; $A7, incl. p. & p. seamail) is a most ambitious compilation, edited by Allan Miller, with records by Ross Dundas and assistance from correspondents in other countries. It consists of 120 foolscap cyclostyled pages and gives details of all matches played by first-class teams, whether the matches themselves were judged first-class or not, in Australia in 1987-88 and on three tours by Australian state teams overseas. There is most commendable attention to detail, and it is as thorough a review of this particular field as can be obtained or has been available for many years.

Benson & Hedges West Indies Cricket Annual 1988 (Caribbean Communications, 116 Queens Road, Hersham, Walton-on-Thames, Surrey KT12 5LL; no price given) continues under the editorship of Tony Cozier, giving ample statistical coverage of all West Indian cricket and of domestic fixtures, even in minor competitions. A Who's Who of West Indian cricket completes this most generously produced and illustrated 88-page quarto.

Heartaches Cricketers Almanack for 1988 (Heartaches Ltd, Romeyns Court, Great Milton, Oxon., limited edition of 100; £12.50 incl. p. & p.) is the fourteenth of such annuals from Tim Rice. It consists of 104 pages and is full of facts, jokes, drawings and ideas about the club's matches, players, opponents; there is even, on one page, how to find the musical, *Chess*, in New York. Averages are included, but they are not necessarily the fun of the book.

The Cricket Diary 1988 (Long-handle Press, 14b Claverton Buildings, Bath BA2 4LD; £3.95) is again edited and published by John Dixon, the former Gloucestershire bowler. A companionable cricket diary, it has many relevant and useful facts, some amusing illustrations, and diverting anniversaries. The edition for 1989 is priced at £4.50.

The Cricketers' Who's Who 1988 (Collins Willow; £8.95), compiled and edited by Ian Sproat, is a bulky, 512-page reference book which goes into considerable detail. The year's tourists and University players are included, and every man is listed who played at least once for his county in 1987 in the County Championship or one of the one-day competitions. The statistics are

all but complete, but some could not be included for reasons of time. No other reference book gives such intimate family details of its subjects.

The Carphone Gallery of Cricketers (Macdonald/Queen Anne Press; £3.95), by Bill Frindall, is a pictorial autograph album. Running from county to county, it has an action photograph and a head-and-shoulders portrait of every county captain, and a head-and-shoulders portrait of every player on the county circuit. There are potted biographies of each player, details of the teams' performances in 1987, and a photograph of a major ground of every county. Below each portrait is space for a signature.

The following county yearbooks include each county's matches – first and second team – of the preceding season, as well as the indicated feature articles.

Essex County Cricket Club 1988 Handbook (Essex County Cricket Club; £3.50) is edited by Peter Edwards. It has a foreword by the president, Tom Pearce, and features by Sir Donald Bradman – 40 years after his Australians scored 721 runs in a day against Essex at Southend – Alec Bedser, Bert Sutcliffe, Keith Fletcher, Doug Insole, David Acfield, David East, David Lloyd, Ralph Dellor, Stuart Turner, David Lemmon, Mike Marshall, Sandy Wilmot and Bernard Webber. It is most generously set out and illustrated, and runs to more than 240 pages.

Hampshire Handbook 1988 (Hampshire County Cricket Club; £3.25) is edited by Tony Mitchener. It has features by Cecil Paris, John Hughes (interviewing the late Jim Bailey) and Peter Marshall, verse by Imogen Grosberg and statistics by Vic Isaacs.

Kent County Cricket Annual 1988 (Kent County Cricket Club; £2.50) has an annual report signed by D. G. Denne, a Who's Who of current Kent players, and features by Derek Carlaw, Derek Ufton, John F. Griffiths, Les Ames and R. J. Evans.

Middlesex County Cricket Club Review 1987/88 (Middlesex County Cricket Club; £4) has a most thorough report by F. G. Mann and M. P. Murray, and features by Matthew Engel, Charles Robins, Terry Cooper and David Lemmon.

Irish Cricket Union Yearbook 1988 (Irish Cricket Union, Able Press, 22 St Catherine's Court, Newgrove Avenue, Dublin 4; £1, plus 50p p. & p.) is edited by Francis Xavier Carty. It contains features on the retirement of Simon Corlett, and studies of Ireland's eight Test cricketers. There are full reports of all Ireland's games in 1987, and averages, and of the Schweppes All-Ireland Cup and provincial games. There is also a review of 100 years of matches between Ireland and Scotland.

The Cricketer Quarterly (29 Cavendish Road, Redhill, Surrey RH1 4AH; £1.65), edited by Richard Lockwood, reached its sixteenth volume in 1988. It continues to provide details of major cricket in England, particularly, and throughout the world, and it now includes the highly revealing Deloitte Ratings. The printing remains of a high order.

The Cricketer International (29 Cavendish Road, Redhill, Surrey RH1 4AH; £1.10) continues monthly under the editorship of Christopher Martin-Jenkins. Among the contributors are Peter Roebuck, Gerald Howat, E. W. Swanton, Alan Lee, Peter Perchard, Alf Gover, Michael Owen-Smith, John Woodcock and the editor.

Wisden Cricket Monthly (6 Beech Lane, Guildown, Guildford, Surrey GU2 5ES; £1.10) continues under the editorship of David Frith, with Steven Lynch as his deputy. Among the fairly regular contributors are Jack

Bannister, Neil Hallam, Doug Ibbotson, Jonathan Rice, David Foot, Ted Corbett, E. M. Wellings, David Gower, the editor and deputy editor.

Cricketer (Newspress, 250 Spencer Street, Melbourne 3000, Australia; $A2.75), published from October to April, is edited by Ken Piesse. Leading contributors are Ian Brayshaw, Richard Cashman, Jack Pollard, Phil Wilkins and Doug Ackerly; the chief photographer is Patrick Eagar. Illustration is generous, with some of it in colour.

New Zealand Cricket (RPL Sporting Publications, 12 Heather Street, Parnell, Auckland, New Zealand; $NZ2.75), monthly from October to March, has Bob Howitt as its managing editor. Among its correspondents are Dick Brittenden, Peter Lampp, Paul Lewis, Andy Quick, Brent Edwards, John Morrison and Dean McLachan.

Australian Cricket Journal (details of subscription from GPO Box 696, Adelaide 5001, South Australia) is edited by Chris Harte. A quarterly which in 1988 went into its fourth year, it is one of the most scholarly of cricket publications; well produced, intelligently and enlighteningly written. Among recent contributors have been Keith Sanderford, George Kirsch, Peter Wynne-Thomas, Dave Crowe, Mike Spurrier and the editor.

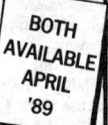

ERRATA

WISDEN, 1984

Page 1102 In the Auckland second innings, B. Abernethy's bowling figures were 19.5–4–72–0; not as stated. Abernethy was substitute for R. J. Webb, who during the match was called up by the New Zealand selectors to strengthen the New Zealand side playing in Australia.

WISDEN, 1986

Page 991 Kapil Dev captained India v Pakistan; not S. M. Gavaskar.

Page 1027 In Victoria's second innings v Tasmania, M. D. Taylor batted No. 4 and was bowled by Brown for 5. P. W. Young did not bat in this innings.

WISDEN, 1988

Page 135 K. C. Wessels's 135 and 105* at Port Elizabeth were for Australian XI v South Africa; not as stated.

Page 156 The most recent instances of hat-tricks omit the following:
J. During Western Province B v Eastern Province B at Cape Town, 1986-87.

Page 612 In the Nottinghamshire first innings, P. Johnson was lbw b Radford.

Page 773 In the Nottinghamshire v Somerset fixture, a match of eighteen overs a side commenced at 4.45 p.m. but further rain after ten minutes led to play being abandoned. The scorecard is as follows:

Nottinghamshire

R. J. Hadlee c Pringle b Palmer	5
P. Johnson not out	4
*C. E. B. Rice not out	0
1/9 (1 wkt, 2.3 overs)	9

P. Pollard, M. Newell, D. J. R. Martindale, J. D. Birch, †C. W. Scott, E. E. Hemmings, R. A. Pick and K. Saxelby did not bat.

Bowling: Rose 1.3–0–5–0; Palmer 1–0–4–1.

Somerset

*P. M. Roebuck, J. J. E. Hardy, N. A. Felton, R. J. Harden, N. J. Pringle, V. J. Marks, †N. D. Burns, G. V. Palmer, G. D. Rose, A. N. Jones and D. J. Foster.

Umpires: B. Leadbeater and K. J. Lyons.

Page 863 The unbroken partnership for Millfield was for 250 runs between P. C. L. Holloway (103*) and D. Luckes (132*); not Holloway and G. Lucas as stated.

Page 1215 For Trentham, Herbert, read Trenholm, Herbert.

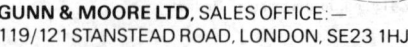

FIXTURES, 1989

** Indicates Sunday play.* *† Not first-class.*

4d = Play over 4 days; where not indicated, first-class matches are of 3 days' duration.

Saturday, April 15

Lord's* (4d) MCC v Worcs.
Cambridge* Cambridge U. v Glam.
Oxford Oxford U. v Northants

Wednesday, April 19

Cambridge Cambridge U. v Glos.
Oxford Oxford U. v Surrey

Thursday, April 20

Derby (4d) Derbys. v Northants
Southampton (4d) Hants v Somerset
Canterbury (4d) Kent v Essex
Leicester (4d) Leics. v Glam.
Lord's (4d) Middx v Yorks.
Nottingham (4d) Notts. v Worcs.
Birmingham (4d) Warwicks. v Lancs.

Tuesday, April 25

†**Benson and Hedges Cup** (1 day)

Cambridge Combined Universities v Surrey
Derby Derbys. v Somerset
Cardiff Glam. v Kent
Manchester Lancs. v Leics.
Lord's Middx v Worcs.
Jesmond Minor Counties v Yorks.
Hove Sussex v Essex
Birmingham Warwicks. v Northants

Thursday, April 27

Chelmsford (4d) Essex v Middx
Bristol (4d) Glos. v Northants
Manchester (4d) Lancs. v Notts.
The Oval (4d) Surrey v Hants
Hove (4d) Sussex v Kent
Birmingham* (4d) Warwicks. v Worcs.
Cambridge Cambridge U. v Leics.
Oxford Oxford U. v Derbys.

Friday, April 28

Taunton* (4d) Somerset v Glam.

Tuesday, May 2

†**Benson and Hedges Cup** (1 day)

Chelmsford Essex v Hants
Bristol Glos. v Middx
Canterbury Kent v Sussex
Leicester Leics. v Warwicks.
Nottingham Notts. v Derbys.
Perth (North Inch) Scotland v Lancs.
Taunton Somerset v Minor Counties
The Oval Surrey v Worcs.

Wednesday, May 3

Lord's †MCC v MCC Young Cricketers (1 day)

Thursday, May 4

Chelmsford (4d) Essex v Derbys.
Cardiff (4d) Glam. v Glos.
Southampton (4d) Hants v Kent
Lord's (4d) Middx v Surrey
Northampton (4d) Northants v Leics.
Taunton (4d) Somerset v Sussex
Worcester (4d) Worcs. v Lancs.
Leeds (4d) Yorks. v Notts.
Cambridge Cambridge U. v Warwicks.

Friday, May 5

West Bromwich Dartmouth †League Cricket Conference v Australians (1 day)

Sunday, May 7

Arundel †Lavinia, Duchess of Norfolk's XI v Australians (1 day)

Tuesday, May 9

Hove †Sussex v Australians (1 day)

†Benson and Hedges Cup (1 day)

Oxford	Combined Universities v Middx
Southampton	Hants v Glam.
Canterbury	Kent v Essex
Leicester	Leics. v Scotland
Oxton (Birkenhead)	Minor Counties v Notts.
Northampton	Northants v Lancs.
Worcester	Worcs. v Glos.
Leeds	Yorks. v Somerset

Thursday, May 11

Lord's	†MCC v Australians (1 day)

†Benson and Hedges Cup (1 day)

Derby	Derbys. v Minor Counties
Chelmsford	Essex v Glam.
Northampton	Northants v Leics.
Nottingham	Notts. v Yorks.
The Oval	Surrey v Glos.
Hove	Sussex v Hants
Birmingham	Warwicks. v Scotland
Worcester	Worcs. v Combined Universities

Saturday, May 13

Worcester*	Worcs. v Australians

†Benson and Hedges Cup (1 day)

Swansea	Glam. v Sussex
Bristol	Glos. v Combined Universities
Southampton	Hants v Kent
Manchester	Lancs. v Warwicks.
Lord's	Middx v Surrey
Glasgow (Hamilton Cres.)	Scotland v Northants
Taunton	Somerset v Notts.
Leeds	Yorks. v Derbys.

Tuesday, May 16

Northampton (4d)	Northants v Yorks.

Wednesday, May 17

Taunton	Somerset v Australians
Chesterfield	Derbys. v Leics.
Manchester	Lancs. v Warwicks.
Lord's	Middx v Hants
Hove	Sussex v Surrey
Cambridge	Cambridge U. v Kent
Oxford	Oxford U. v Notts.

Saturday, May 20

Lord's*	Middx v Australians
Swansea	Glam. v Northants
Bristol	Glos. v Essex
Dartford*	Kent v Derbys.
Nottingham*	Notts. v Hants
Taunton	Somerset v Lancs.
Birmingham	Warwicks. v Surrey

Tuesday, May 23

Leeds	†Yorks. v Australians (1 day)

Wednesday, May 24

Leicester	Leics. v Kent
The Oval	Surrey v Lancs.
Worcester	Worcs. v Notts.
Leeds	Yorks. v Derbys.
Cambridge	Cambridge U. v Essex
Oxford	Oxford U. v Middx

Thursday, May 25

Manchester	†ENGLAND v AUSTRALIA (1st 1-day Texaco Trophy)

Saturday, May 27

Nottingham	†ENGLAND v AUSTRALIA (2nd 1-day Texaco Trophy)
Chelmsford	Essex v Somerset
Cardiff	Glam. v Notts.
Bristol	Glos. v Worcs.
Bournemouth	Hants v Leics.
Liverpool	Lancs. v Sussex
The Oval	Surrey v Yorks.
Birmingham	Warwicks. v Middx

Monday, May 29

Lord's	†ENGLAND v AUSTRALIA (3rd 1-day Texaco Trophy)

Wednesday, May 31

†Benson and Hedges Cup – Quarter-Finals (1 day)

Manchester or Birmingham	Lancs. or Warwicks. v Australians

Saturday, June 3

erby*	Derbys. v Australians
ınbridge Wells	Kent v Hants
orthampton	Northants v Surrey
ottingham	Notts. v Yorks.
rmingham	Warwicks. v Sussex
orcester	Worcs. v Glam.

Wednesday, June 7

ardiff	Glam. v Somerset
asingstoke	Hants v Surrey
ınbridge Wells	Kent v Sussex
eicester	Leics. v Yorks.
ord's	Middx v Notts.
orthampton	Northants v Glos.
uneaton (Griff & Coton)	Warwicks. v Derbys.
xford	Oxford. U. v Lancs.

Thursday, June 8

eeds	ENGLAND v AUSTRALIA (1st Cornhill Test, 5 days)

Saturday, June 10

bergavenny	Glam. v Middx
eicester	Leics. v Glos.
ottingham	Notts. v Kent
aunton	Somerset v Yorks.
he Oval	Surrey v Essex
ove	Sussex v Northants
Vorcester	Worcs. v Derbys.
xford	Oxford U. v Hants
ord's	†Eton v Harrow (1 day)

Wednesday, June 14

†Benson and Hedges Cup – Semi-Finals (1 day)

irmingham or Manchester	Warwicks. or Lancs. v Australians
arrogate	†Tilcon Trophy (3 days)

Saturday, June 17

Northampton*	Northants v Australians
erby	Derbys. v Sussex
helmsford	Essex v Leics.
Manchester	Lancs. v Glam.
ath	Somerset v Kent
he Oval	Surrey v Middx
arrogate	Yorks. v Glos.
ambridge*	Cambridge U. v Notts.

Wednesday, June 21

Ilford	Essex v Hants
Southport	Lancs. v Northants
Bath	Somerset v Glos.
Birmingham	Warwicks. v Glam.
Sheffield	Yorks. v Worcs.
Hove	Sussex v Camb. U.

Thursday, June 22

Lord's	ENGLAND v AUSTRALIA (2nd Cornhill Test, 5 days)

Saturday, June 24

Ilford	Essex v Warwicks.
Southampton	Hants v Sussex
Manchester	Lancs. v Kent
Leicester	Leics. v Notts.
Luton	Northants v Somerset
The Oval	Surrey v Glos.
Worcester	Worcs. v Middx
Leeds	Yorks. v Glam.

Wednesday, June 28

Oxford	†Oxford & Camb. Univs v Australians (1 day)

†NatWest Bank Trophy – First Round (1 day)

March	Cambs. v Worcs.
Chester (Boughton Hall)	Cheshire v Hants
Carlisle	Cumb. v Lancs.
Derby	Derbys. v Ireland
Darlington	Durham v Middx
Cardiff	Glam. v Staffs.
Hitchin	Herts. v Notts.
Canterbury	Kent v Dorset
Jesmond	Northumb. v Surrey
Oxford (Christ Church)	Oxon. v Glos.
Telford (St George's)	Salop. v Leics.
Taunton	Somerset v Essex
Bury St Edmunds	Suffolk v Northants
Hove	Sussex v Berks.
Birmingham	Warwicks. v Wilts.
Leeds	Yorks. v Scotland

Saturday, July 1

Neath*	Glamorgan v Australians
Derby	Derbys. v Somerset
Gloucester	Glos. v Notts.
Southampton	Hants v Yorks.
Hinckley	Leics. v Warwicks.
Lord's	Middx v Lancs.
Northampton	Northants v Worcs.
Horsham	Sussex v Essex

Wednesday, July 5

Derby	Derbys. v Essex
Gloucester	Glos. v Sussex
Maidstone	Kent v Northants
Leicester	Leics. v Lancs.
Guildford	Surrey v Notts.
Worcester	Worcs. v Warwicks.
Lord's	Oxford U. v Cambridge U.

Thursday, July 6

Birmingham	ENGLAND v AUSTRALIA (3rd Cornhill Test, 5 days)

Saturday, July 8

Swansea	Glam. v Essex
Maidstone	Kent v Glos.
Lord's	Middx v Derbys.
Northampton	Northants v Hants
Nottingham	Notts. v Warwicks.
Guildford	Surrey v Somerset
Kidderminster	Worcs. v Leics.
Middlesbrough	Yorks. v Sussex
Dublin (Clontarf)*	Ireland v Scotland

Wednesday, July 12

†NatWest Bank Trophy – Second Round (1 day)

March or Worcester	Cambs. or Worcs. v Derbys. or Ireland
Darlington or Uxbridge	Durham or Middx v Herts. or Notts.
Cardiff or Burton (Ind Coope)	Glam. or Staffs. v Cheshire or Hants
Canterbury or Bournemouth (Dean Park)	Kent or Dorset v Warwicks. or Wilts.
Jesmond or The Oval	Northumb. or Surrey v Yorks. or Scotland
Oxford (Christ Church) or Bristol	Oxon. or Glos. v Cumb. or Lancs.
Taunton or Chelmsford	Somerset or Essex v Suffolk or Northants
Hove or Finchampstead	Sussex or Berks. v Salop. or Leics.

Saturday, July 15

Lord's	†BENSON AND HEDGES CUP FINAL (1 day)
Glasgow (Hamilton Cres.)	†Scotland v Australians (1 day)

Monday, July 17

Trowbridge	†Minor Counties v Australians (1 day)

Wednesday, July 19

Southampton	Hants v Australians
Southend	Essex v Kent
Bristol	Glos. v Glam.
Manchester	Lancs. v Worcs.
Leicester	Leics. v Northants
Nottingham	Notts. v Somerset
Leeds	Yorks. v Middx
Lord's	†MCC v MCC Schools (1 day)

Thursday, July 20

Lord's	†MCC Schools v NAYC (1 day)

Friday, July 21

Lord's	†NCA Young Cricketers v Combined Services (1 day)

Saturday, July 22

Bristol*	Glos. v Australians
Derby	Derbys. v Glam.
Southend	Essex v Yorks.
Portsmouth	Hants v Lancs.
Uxbridge	Middx v Kent
Northampton	Northants v Notts.
Taunton	Somerset v Leics.
Hove	Sussex v Worcs.

Wednesday, July 26

Cardiff	Glam. v Leics.
Portsmouth	Hants v Glos.
Uxbridge	Middx v Essex
Northampton	Northants v Derbys.
Worksop	Notts. v Lancs.
Hove	Sussex v Somerset
Birmingham	Warwicks v Yorks.
Worcester	Worcs. v Surrey

Thursday, July 27

Manchester	ENGLAND v AUSTRALIA (4th Cornhill Test, 5 days)

Saturday, July 29

Derby	Derbys. v Surrey
Cardiff	Glam. v Hants
Lord's	Middx v Leics.
Nottingham	Notts. v Essex
Birmingham	Warwicks. v Glos.
Worcester	Worcs. v Kent

Wednesday, August 2

†NatWest Bank Trophy – Quarter-Finals (1 day)

ɔttingham or The Oval	Notts. or Surrey v Australians

Thursday, August 3

ɪsmond	†England XI v Rest of the World XI (1 day)

Friday, August 4

ɪsmond	†England XI v Rest of the World XI (1 day)

Saturday, August 5

ːicester*	Leics. v Australians
ɛrby	Derbys. v Hants
olchester	Essex v Worcs.
heltenham	Glos. v Lancs.
anterbury	Kent v Warwicks.
'eston-super-Mare	Somerset v Middx
he Oval	Surrey v Glam.
astbourne	Sussex v Notts.
heffield	Yorks. v Northants
'rmingham	†England Young Cricketers v New Zealand Young Cricketers (1st 1-day "International")

Sunday, August 6

'orthampton	†England Young Cricketers v New Zealand Young Cricketers (2nd 1-day "International")

Tuesday, August 8

ord's	†England Young Cricketers v New Zealand Young Cricketers (3rd 1-day "International")

Wednesday, August 9

:hesterfield	Derbys. v Lancs.
:olchester	Essex v Northants
:heltenham	Glos. v Middx
ɜournemouth	Hants v Warwicks.
:anterbury	Kent v Surrey
Veston-super-Mare	Somerset v Worcs.
:astbourne	Sussex v Leics.

Thursday, August 10

Nottingham	ENGLAND v AUSTRALIA (5th Cornhill Test, 5 days)

Saturday, August 12

Swansea	Glam. v Sussex
Cheltenham	Glos. v Derbys.
Bournemouth	Hants v Worcs.
Lytham	Lancs. v Essex
Lord's	Middx v Northants
Birmingham	Warwicks. v Somerset
Scarborough	Yorks. v Kent

Monday, August 14

†Bain Clarkson Trophy (1st semi-final, 1 day)

Tuesday, August 15

†Bain Clarkson Trophy (2nd semi-final, 1 day)

Wednesday, August 16

†NatWest Bank Trophy – Semi-Finals (1 day)

Canterbury or Hove	Kent or Sussex v Australians

Saturday, August 19

Chelmsford*	Essex v Australians
Canterbury	Kent v Glam.
Manchester	Lancs. v Yorks.
Leicester	Leics. v Surrey
Northampton	Northants v Warwicks.
Nottingham	Notts. v Derbys.
Taunton	Somerset v Hants
Hastings	Sussex v Middx
Lord's	†Minor Counties Knockout Competition Final (1 day)

Sunday, August 20

Scarborough	†England Young Cricketers v New Zealand Young Cricketers (1st "Test", 4 days)

Wednesday, August 23

Lord's	†MCC v Ireland (2 days)

Thursday, August 24

The Oval	ENGLAND v AUSTRALIA (6th Cornhill Test, 5 days)
Chesterfield (4d)	Derbys. v Yorks.
Swansea (4d)	Glam. v Warwicks.
Folkestone (4d)	Kent v Leics.
Manchester (4d)	Lancs. v Surrey
Northampton (4d)	Northants v Essex
Nottingham (4d)	Notts. v Middx
Hove (4d)	Sussex v Glos.
Worcester* (4d)	Worcs. v Somerset

Friday, August 25

Lord's	†National Club Championship Final (1 day)

Saturday, August 26

Lord's	†Hydro Village Championship Final (1 day)

Tuesday, August 29

Chelmsford (4d)	Essex v Surrey
Leicester (4d)	Leics. v Derbys.
Hove (4d)	Sussex v Hants
Worcester (4d)	Worcs. v Glos.
Leeds (4d)	Yorks. v Warwicks.
Canterbury	†England Young Cricketers v New Zealand Young Cricketers (2nd "Test", 4 days)

Wednesday, August 30

Scarborough	Michael Parkinson International XI match

Saturday, September 2

Lord's	†NATWEST BANK TROPHY FINAL (1 day)
Scarborough	†Michael Parkinson International XI match (1 day)

Sunday, September 3

Scarborough	†Four Counties Knockout Competition (3 day
Hove	†Seeboard Trophy (3 days)

Monday, September 4

†Bain Clarkson Trophy Final (1 day)

Wednesday, September 6

†**Refuge Assurance Cup – Semi-Finals** (1 da

Thursday, September 7

Scarborough	†Yorkshire v The Yorkshiremen (1 day)

Friday, September 8

Derby* (4d)	Derbys. v Notts.
Bristol* (4d)	Glos. v Somerset
Southampton* (4d)	Hants v Glam.
Leicester* (4d)	Leics. v Essex
Lord's* (4d)	Middx v Sussex
The Oval* (4d)	Surrey v Kent
Birmingham* (4d)	Warwicks. v Northants
Scarborough* (4d)	Yorks. v Lancs.
Manchester*	†England Young Cricketers v New Zealand Young Cricketers (3rd "Test", 4 days)

Sunday, September 10

Worcester	†Minor Counties Championship Play off (1 day)

Wednesday, September 13

Pontypridd (4d)	Glam. v Worcs.
Bristol (4d)	Glos. v Hants
Canterbury (4d)	Kent v Middx
Manchester (4d)	Lancs. v Derbys.
Nottingham (4d)	Notts. v Leics.
Taunton (4d)	Somerset v Warwicks.
The Oval (4d)	Surrey v Sussex

Sunday, September 17

Birmingham	†REFUGE ASSURANCE CUI FINAL (1 day)

AUSTRALIAN TOUR, 1989

MAY

5	West Bromwich Dartmouth	†v League Cricket Conference (1 day)
7	Arundel	†v Lavinia, Duchess of Norfolk's XI (1 day)
9	Hove	†v Sussex (1 day)
1	Lord's	†v MCC (1 day)
3	Worcester*	v Worcs.
7	Taunton	v Somerset
0	Lord's*	v Middx
3	Leeds	†v Yorks. (1 day)
5	Manchester	†v ENGLAND (1st 1-day Texaco Trophy)
7	Nottingham	†v ENGLAND (2nd 1-day Texaco Trophy)
9	Lord's	†v ENGLAND (3rd 1-day Texaco Trophy)
1	Manchester or Birmingham	v Lancs. or Warwicks.

JUNE

3	Derby*	v Derbys.
8	Leeds	v ENGLAND (1st Cornhill Test, 5 days)
4	Birmingham or Manchester	v Warwicks. or Lancs.
7	Northampton*	v Northants
2	Lord's	v ENGLAND (2nd Cornhill Test, 5 days)
28	Oxford	†v Oxford & Camb. Univs. (1 day)

JULY

1	Neath*	v Glam.
6	Birmingham	v ENGLAND (3rd Cornhill Test, 5 days)
15	Glasgow (Hamilton Crescent)	†v Scotland (1 day)
17	Trowbridge	†v Minor Counties (1 day)
19	Southampton	v Hants
22	Bristol*	v Glos.
27	Manchester	v ENGLAND (4th Cornhill Test, 5 days)

AUGUST

2	Nottingham or The Oval	v Notts. or Surrey
5	Leicester*	v Leics.
10	Nottingham	v ENGLAND (5th Cornhill Test, 5 days)
16	Canterbury or Hove	v Kent or Sussex
19	Chelmsford*	v Essex
24	The Oval	v ENGLAND (6th Cornhill Test, 5 days)

†REFUGE ASSURANCE LEAGUE, 1989

APRIL

23–Derbys. v Northants (Derby); Hants v Somerset (Southampton); Kent v Essex (Canterbury); Leics. v Glam. (Leicester); Middx v Yorks. (Lord's); Notts. v Worcs. (Nottingham); Surrey v Glos. (The Oval); Warwicks. v Lancs. (Birmingham).

30–Essex v Middx (Chelmsford); Lancs. v Notts. (Manchester); Leics. v Derbys. (Leicester); Surrey v Hants (The Oval); Sussex v Kent (Hove).

MAY

7–Essex v Derbys. (Chelmsford); Glam. v Glos. (Newport); Hants v Kent (Southampton); Middx v Surrey (Lord's); Northants v Warwicks. (Northampton); Somerset v Sussex (Taunton); Worcs. v Lancs. (Worcester); Yorks. v Notts. (Leeds).

14–Derbys. v Lancs. (Leek); Essex v Hants (Chelmsford); Glos. v Middx (Bristol); Kent v Surrey (Canterbury); Leics. v Yorks. (Leicester).

21–Glam. v Northants (Cardiff); Glos. v Essex (Bristol); Somerset v Lancs. (Taunton); Sussex v Leics. (Hove); Worcs. v Surrey (Worcester); Yorks. v Warwicks. (Leeds).

28–Essex v Somerset (Chelmsford); Glam. v Notts. (Llanelli); Glos. v Worcs. (Bristol); Hants v Leics. (Bournemouth); Kent v Northants (Canterbury); Lancs. v Sussex (Manchester); Surrey v Yorks. (The Oval); Warwicks. v Middx (Birmingham).

JUNE

4–Leics. v Lancs. (Leicester); Middx v Hants (Lord's); Northants v Surrey (Northampton); Notts. v Somerset (Nottingham); Warwicks. v Sussex (Birmingham); Worcs. v Glam. (Worcester).

11–Glam. v Middx (Merthyr Tydfil); Hants v Warwicks. (Basingstoke); Leics. v Glos. (Leicester); Notts. v Kent (Nottingham); Somerset v Yorks. (Taunton); Surrey v Essex (The Oval); Sussex v Northants (Hove); Worcs. v Derbys. (Worcester).

18–Derbys. v Sussex (Derby); Essex v Leics. (Chelmsford); Lancs. v Glam. (Blackpool); Somerset v Kent (Bath); Warwicks. v Worcs. (Birmingham); Yorks. v Glos. (Leeds).

25–Essex v Warwicks. (Ilford); Hants v Sussex (Southampton); Lancs. v Kent (Manchester); Northants v Leics. (Luton); Notts. v Derbys. (Nottingham); Somerset v Glos. (Bath); Worcs. v Middx (Worcester); Yorks. v Glam. (Hull).

JULY

2–Derbys. v Somerset (Derby); Glos. v Notts. (Gloucester); Hants v Yorks. (Southampton); Leics. v Warwicks. (Leicester); Middx v Lancs. (Lord's); Northants v Worcs. (Tring); Sussex v Essex (Horsham).

9–Glam. v Essex (Neath); Kent v Glos. (Maidstone); Middx v Derbys. (Lord's); Northants v Hants (Northampton); Notts. v Warwicks. (Nottingham); Surrey v Somerset (The Oval); Worcs. v Leics. (Worcester); Yorks. v Sussex (Middlesbrough).

16–Glos. v Hants (Bristol); Kent v Derby (Canterbury); Lancs. v Northants (Ma chester); Leics. v Notts. (Leicester Somerset v Glam. (Taunton); Surrey Sussex (The Oval); Yorks. v Worc (Scarborough).

23–Derbys. v Glam. (Heanor); Ess v Yorks. (Southend); Hants Lancs. (Portsmouth); Middx v Ke (Lord's); Northants v Notts. (Finedon Somerset v Leics. (Taunton); Sussex Worcs. (Hove); Warwicks. v Surre (Birmingham).

30–Derbys. v Surrey (Derby); Glam. v Han (Swansea); Middx v Leics. (Lord's Northants v Somerset (Northampton Notts. v Essex (Nottingham); Warwick v Glos. (Birmingham); Worcs. v Ker (Worcester).

AUGUST

6–Derbys. v Hants (Derby); Essex Worcs. (Colchester); Glos. v Lancs (Cheltenham); Kent v Warwicks (Canterbury); Somerset v Midd (Weston-super-Mare); Surrey v Glam (The Oval); Sussex v Notts. (East bourne); Yorks. v Northants (Sheffield)

13–Glam. v Sussex (Ebbw Vale); Glos v Derbys. (Cheltenham); Hants Worcs. (Bournemouth); Lancs. v Esse (Manchester); Middx v Northant (Lord's); Surrey v Notts. (The Oval) Warwicks. v Somerset (Birmingham) Yorks. v Kent (Scarborough).

20–Glos. v Northants (Moreton-in-Marsh) Kent v Glam. (Canterbury); Lancs v Yorks. (Manchester); Leics. v Surrey (Leicester); Notts. v Hants (Nottingham); Sussex v Middx (Hastings); Warwicks. v Derbys (Birmingham); Worcs. v Somerset (Worcester).

27–Derbys. v Yorks. (Chesterfield); Glam. v Warwicks. (Aberystwyth); Kent v Leics. (Folkestone); Lancs. v Surrey (Manchester); Northants v Essex (Northampton); Notts. v Middx (Nottingham); Sussex v Glos. (Hove).

†MINOR COUNTIES CHAMPIONSHIP, 1989

All matches are of two days' duration.

MAY

–Lincs. v Herts. (Sleaford); Northumb. v Beds. (Jesmond); Wales v Oxon. (Colwyn Bay).

–Dorset v Bucks. (Sherborne School).

–Cumb. v Beds. (Netherfield, Kendal); Durham v Herts. (Sunderland).

–Suffolk v Cambs. (Framlingham).

JUNE

–Wales v Bucks. (Ammanford).

1–Beds. v Staffs. (Henlow); Berks. v Wilts. (Kidmore End); Herts. v Cumb. (Tring); Northumb. v Norfolk (Jesmond).

2–Cheshire v Cornwall (Stalybridge).

3–Durham v Norfolk (Stockton on Tees); Lincs. v Cumb. (Bourne); Wilts. v Wales (Trowbridge).

4–Salop. v Cornwall (Shifnal).

1–Cambs. v Lincs. (Wisbech); Cheshire v Wales (Neston).

5–Cornwall v Devon (Truro); Herts. v Staffs. (Potter's Bar); Northumb. v Lincs. (Jesmond); Oxon. v Bucks. (Pressed Steel Fisher).

JULY

2–*Bucks. v Berks. (Beaconsfield); *Herts. v Northumb. (Bishop's Stortford); *Lincs. v Norfolk (Burghley Park).

3–Dorset v Wales (Dorchester).

4–Suffolk v Northumb. (Ransomes, Ipswich).

5–Staffs. v Cambs. (Ind Coope, Burton upon Trent).

6–Devon v Dorset (Sidmouth).

9–Durham v Northumb. (Gateshead Fell); Herts. v Beds. (Hitchin); Oxon. v Berks. (Christ Church, Oxford); Salop. v Cheshire (Shrewsbury).

12–Berks. v Dorset (Finchampstead).

16–Beds. v Durham (Luton); Cornwall v Bucks. (Falmouth); Oxon. v Cheshire (Banbury XX Club); Staffs. v Lincs. (Bignall End).

17–Norfolk v Cumb. (North Runcton).

18–Cambs. v Durham (Fenner's, Cambridge); Devon v Bucks. (Exmouth); Salop. v Wales (Bridgnorth); Wilts. v Cheshire (BR, Swindon).

19–Suffolk v Cumb. (Ipswich School).

23–Cornwall v Berks. (St Austell); Northumb. v Cambs. (Jesmond); Oxon. v Salop. (Morris Motors, Oxford).

25–Cumb. v Cambs. (Barrow); Devon v Berks. (Bovey Tracey); Staffs. v Durham (Leek); Wilts. v Salop. (Chippenham).

30–Beds. v Suffolk (Southill Park); Cheshire v Dorset (Warrington); Lincs. v Durham (Grimsby Town); Norfolk v Herts. (Lakenham); Staffs. v Northumb. (Stone).

AUGUST

1–Salop. v Dorset (Newport).

2–Norfolk v Beds. (Lakenham); Suffolk v Herts. (Mildenhall); Wales v Berks. (Ebbw Vale).

4–Norfolk v Suffolk (Lakenham).

6–Beds. v Lincs. (Bedford Town); Bucks. v Cheshire (Slough); Cumb. v Durham (Carlisle); Herts. v Cambs. (Hertford); Wilts. v Dorset (Marlborough).

7–Cornwall v Oxon. (Wadebridge); Norfolk v Staffs. (Lakenham).

8–Berks. v Cheshire (Reading CC).

9–Devon v Oxon. (Torquay); Suffolk v Staffs. (Bury St Edmunds).

13–Berks. v Salop. (Falkland CC); Lincs. v Suffolk (Lincoln Lindum); Northumb. v Cumb. (Jesmond); Wilts. v Oxon. (Devizes).

14–Wales v Cornwall (Usk).

15–Bucks. v Salop. (Marlow); Durham v Suffolk (Hartlepool).

16–Cambs. v Norfolk (March); Cumb. v Staffs. (Millom); Dorset v Cornwall (Weymouth).

21–Wales v Devon (Swansea).

22–Cornwall v Wilts. (Helston).

23–Dorset v Oxon (Weymouth).

24–Devon v Wilts. (Torquay).

27–Bucks. v Wilts. (Amersham).

28–Salop. v Devon (Wellington).

29–Cambs. v Beds. (Fenner's, Cambridge).

30–Cheshire v Devon (Toft).

SEPTEMBER

10–Play-off (Worcester).

* *Unless either of the sides is in the Knockout Competition semi-finals.*

†MINOR COUNTIES KNOCKOUT COMPETITION, 1989

All matches are of one day's duration.

Qualifying Round

May 21 Bucks. v Herts. (Beaconsfield); Norfolk v Beds. (Swardeston); Oxon. v Berks. (Christ Church, Oxford); Suffolk v Cambs. (Framlingham).

First Round

June 4 Bucks. or Herts. v Oxon. or Berks. (Aylesbury or Stevenage); Dorset v Cornwall (Sherborne School); Durham v Cumb. (Durham City); Lincs. v Northumb. (Ros Grimsby); Norfolk or Beds. v Suffo or Cambs. (To be arranged); Salop. Wales (Perkins, Shrewsbury); Staf v Cheshire (Old Hill); Wilts. v Devc (Trowbridge).

Quarter-finals to be played on June 18.

Semi-finals to be played on July 2.

Final to be played on August 19 at Lord's

Note: Second XI fixtures not available at time of going to press.

LORDS AND COMMONS RESULTS, 1988

Played 14: Won 4, Lost 5, Drawn 5. Cancelled 2.

April 27. Drawn. Lords and Commons 95 for four v ACAS.
May 4. Drawn. v St Paul's. Abandoned after two overs.
May 10. Westminster School won by 161 runs. Westminster School 252 for eight dec.; Lords an Commons 91.
May 18. Drawn. Lords and Commons 130 for eight dec.; Diplomatic Service 117 for eight
June 1. Commonwealth Secretariat won by six wickets. Lords and Commons 125 for six dec. Commonwealth Secretariat 131 for four.
June 8. Lords and Commons won by five wickets. Mandarins 133 for nine dec.; Lords an Commons 134 for five.
June 14. Lords and Commons won by two wickets. Conservative Agents 164 for eight dec. Lords and Commons 168 for eight.
June 28. Lords and Commons won by 28 runs. Lords and Commons 218 for eight dec.; Guard 190.
July 1. Dutch Parliament won by 14 runs. Dutch Parliament 144; Lords and Commons 130
July 2. Drawn. Dutch Parliament 182 for seven; Lords and Commons 43 for five.
July 7. Drawn. MCC 260 for one dec.; Lords and Commons 161 for seven.
July 21. Old Westminsters won by nine wickets. Lords and Commons 108; Old Westminster 109 for one.
August 24. Lords and Commons won by five wickets. Law Society 123; Lords and Common 124 for five.
September 9. Harrow Wanderers won by 47 runs. Harrow Wanderers 224 for six (50 overs); Lords and Commons 177.

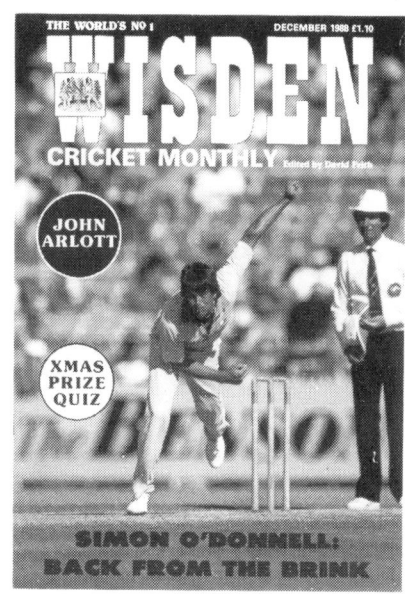